2020-202tion

Federa Incomax

Code and ulations
Selected Sens

As of June 1, 20

Edited by

ROBERT J. PERC
Fondren FoundatCentennial Chair for Faculty Excellence
and Professor of I
University of Texchool of Law

Editorial Staff

Production . . . . r Schencker

ISBN 978-0-8080-5461-0

2700 Lake Cook Road
Riverwoods, IL 60015
800 344 3734
CCHCPELink.com

Do not send returns to the above address. If for any reason yare not satisfied with your book purchase, it can easily be returned within 3ys of shipment. Please go to *support.cch.com/returns* to initiate your return. If 1 require further assistance with your return, please call: (800) 344-3734 M-F, 8 a. – 6 p.m CT.

Printed in Canada

Editorial Board

Preface

This volume provides a selection of the Internal Revenue Code and Treasury Regulations provisions relating to the income tax. The selection reflects the collective judgment of the seven tax teachers who constitute the Editorial Board.

This edition is current through June 1, 2020. It reflects all changes in the Code and Regulations through that date.

The CPI-adjusted dollar amounts for 2020 are provided beginning at page ix, and a caution note precedes each Code section affected by CPI adjustment. The most commonly used depreciation schedules are provided as well.

Caution notes precede many sections of the Regulations that do not reflect later changes in the Code. For example, the note preceding Reg. § 1.331-1 explains that Reg. § 1.331-1 does not reflect the 1982 amendments to Section 331 that deleted references to partial liquidations. No effort has been made to flag all such inconsistencies. Proposed regulations are included in numeric order with final and temporary regulations.

The volume provides thorough coverage of the provisions most commonly addressed in income tax courses relating to individuals and business enterprises, together with limited coverage of many provisions of less general interest. Space limitations, however, have required exclusion of narrow provisions, such as those affecting only specialized businesses, *e.g.*, insurance. Virtually all provisions relating to foreign income and foreign taxpayers have been omitted; they are provided in a separate volume published by Wolters Kluwer. Many provisions have been edited to remove obsolete items and material of marginal importance. Ellipsis marks are provided wherever material is omitted within a Code or Regulation section. Many Regulations that merely restate the corresponding Code provision have been omitted. The volume is intended only for instructional use, and practitioners will of course need to consult the full, current text of the law.

The contents of this work are available in electronic form at download.cchcpelink.com/FITSCR20-21.pdf. The electronic version is available only to purchasers of this volume, and access is subject to the License Agreement set forth on the following page.

The popularity of this volume is a tribute to the hard work of the editorial staff at Wolters Kluwer, whose diligence continues to assure a volume that is both current and correct. Thanks to Karen Notaro for her leadership, and to Mary Ellen Guth and Jennifer Schencker for the meticulous care and attention they have devoted to this volume over many years. It has been a pleasure and privilege to work with them.

We want this book to meet the needs of as many tax teachers as possible, and we appreciate all suggestions toward that end. Communications and suggestions regarding future editions should be sent to Professor Robert J. Peroni, University of Texas School of Law, 727 East Dean Keeton Street, Austin, TX 78705, or rperoni@law.utexas.edu.

We dedicate this volume to the memory of our dear friend and colleague, Martin B. Dickinson, who was the outstanding coordinating editor of this volume for many years. We will greatly miss him.

Robert J. Peroni

June 2020

LICENSE AGREEMENT FOR ELECTRONIC FILES TO ACCOMPANY

Federal Income Tax Code & Regulations Selected Sections

download.cchcpelink.com/FITSCR20-21.pdf

Your password for opening this file is: F3d3r@l

PLEASE READ THE TERMS AND CONDITIONS OF THIS LICENSE AGREEMENT CAREFULLY.

THE ELECTRONIC FILES ACCESSIBLE THROUGH THE ONLINE MATERIAL ARE COPYRIGHTED AND LICENSED. BY OPENING THE ELECTRONIC FILES YOU ARE ACCEPTING AND AGREEING TO THE TERMS OF THIS LICENSE AGREEMENT. IF YOU ARE NOT WILLING TO BE BOUND BY THE TERMS OF THIS LICENSE AGREEMENT, YOU SHOULD NOT ACCESS THE ELECTRONIC FILES.

1. License Grant. Licensor hereby grants to you, and you accept, a nonexclusive license to use the files, and any computer programs contained therein. You agree that you will not assign, sublease, transfer, pledge, lease, rent, post, or share your rights under the License Agreement.

2. Licensor's Rights. You acknowledge and agree that the online materials and all files therein are proprietary products of Licensor protected under U.S. copyright law. You further acknowledge and agree that all right, title, and interest in and to the files and content including associated intellectual property rights, is and shall remain with Licensor. This License Agreement does not convey to you an interest in or to the files accessed through the online materials or other platform. This License Agreement does not convey to you an interest in the files but only a limited right of use revocable in accordance with the terms of this License Agreement.

3. Term. This License Agreement is effective upon your accessing the files and shall continue until terminated. You may terminate this License Agreement by not accessing the files on this site. Licensor may terminate this License Agreement upon the breach by you of any term hereof. Upon such termination by Licensor you agree to refrain from accessing the website.

4. Limitation of Liability. Licensor's cumulative liability to you or any other party for any loss or damages resulting from any claims, demands, or actions arising out of or relating to this Agreement shall not exceed the license fee paid to Licensor for the use of the Files. IN NO EVENT SHALL LICENSOR BE LIABLE FOR ANY INDIRECT, INCIDENTAL, CONSEQUENTIAL, SPECIAL, OR EXEMPLARY DAMAGES (INCLUDING, BUT NOT LIMITED TO, LOSS OF DATA, BUSINESS INTERRUPTION, OR LOST PROFITS) EVEN IF LICENSOR HAS BEEN ADVISED OF THE POSSIBILITY OF SUCH DAMAGES.

5. Miscellaneous. The License Agreement shall be construed and governed in accordance with the laws of the State of Delaware. Should any term of this License Agreement be declared void or unenforceable by any court of competent jurisdiction, such declaration shall have no effect on the remaining terms hereof. The failure of either party to enforce any rights granted hereunder or to take action against the other party in the event of any breach hereunder shall not be deemed a waiver by that party as to subsequent enforcement of rights or subsequent actions in the event of future breaches.

Contents

CONSUMER PRICE INDEX ADJUSTMENTS FOR 2020

Certain dollar amounts stated in the Internal Revenue Code are adjusted for inflation each year, based on changes in the Chained Consumer Price Index for All Urban Consumers (CPI), published by the United States Department of Labor.

A caution note precedes each Code section that is subject to CPI adjustment.

The adjusted amounts applicable to taxable years beginning in 2020 are set forth in certain IRS pronouncements, relevant portions of which are reproduced below. Each adjusted dollar amount is to be substituted for the amount stated in the Code for all purposes relating to taxable years beginning in 2020.

Tax Rate Tables and Other Provisions

Revenue Procedure 2019-44, 2019-47 I.R.B. 1093

* * *

SECTION 3. 2020 ADJUSTED ITEMS

.01 *Tax Rate Tables.* For taxable years beginning in 2020, the tax rate tables under § 1 are as follows:

TABLE 1—Section 1(j)(2)(A).—MARRIED INDIVIDUALS FILING JOINT RETURNS AND SURVIVING SPOUSES

If Taxable Income Is:	*The Tax Is:*
Not over $19,750	10% of the taxable income
Over $19,750 but not over $80,250	$1,975 plus 12% of the excess over $19,750
Over $80,250 but not over $171,050	$9,235 plus 22% of the excess over $80,250
Over $171,050 but not over $326,600	$29,211 plus 24% of the excess over $171,050
Over $326,600 but not over $414,700	$66,543 plus 32% of the excess over $326,600
Over $414,700 but not over $622,050	$94,735 plus 35% of the excess over $414,700
Over $622,050	$167,307.50 plus 37% of the excess over $622,050

TABLE 2—Section 1(j)(2)(B).—HEADS OF HOUSEHOLDS

If Taxable Income Is:	*The Tax Is:*
Not over $14,100	10% of the taxable income
Over $14,100 but not over $53,700	$1,410 plus 12% of the excess over $14,100
Over $53,700 but not over $85,500	$6,162 plus 22% of the excess over $53,700
Over $85,500 but not over $163,300	$13,158 plus 24% of the excess over $85,500
Over $163,300 but not over $207,350	$31,830 plus 32% of the excess over $163,300
Over $207,350 but not over $518,400	$45,926 plus 35% of the excess over $207,350
Over $518,400	$154,793.50 plus 37% of the excess over $518,400

TABLE 3—Section 1(j)(2)(C).—UNMARRIED INDIVIDUALS (OTHER THAN SURVIVING SPOUSES AND HEADS OF HOUSEHOLDS)

If Taxable Income Is:	*The Tax Is:*
Not over $9,875	10% of the taxable income
Over $9,875 but not over $40,125	$987.50 plus 12% of the excess over $9,875
Over $40,125 but not over $85,525	$4,617.50 plus 22% of the excess over $40,125
Over $85,525 but not over $163,300	$14,605.50 plus 24% of the excess over $85,525
Over $163,300 but not over $207,350	$33,271.50 plus 32% of the excess over $163,300
Over $207,350 but not over $518,400	$47,367.50 plus 35% of the excess over $207,350
Over $518,400	$156,235.50 plus 37% of the excess over $518,400

TABLE 4—Section 1(j)(2)(D).—MARRIED INDIVIDUALS FILING SEPARATE RETURNS

If Taxable Income Is:	*The Tax Is:*
Not over $9,875	10% of the taxable income
Over $9,875 but not over $40,125	$987.50 plus 12% of the excess over $9,875
Over $40,125 but not over $85,525	$4,617.50 plus 22% of the excess over $40,125
Over $85,525 but not over $163,300	$14,605.50 plus 24% of the excess over $85,525
Over $163,300 but not over $207,350	$33,271.50 plus 32% of the excess over $163,300
Over $207,350 but not over $311,025	$47,367.50 plus 35% of the excess over $207,350
Over $311,025	$83,653.75 plus 37% of the excess over $311,025

TABLE 5—Section 1(j)(2)(E).—ESTATES AND TRUSTS

If Taxable Income Is:	*The Tax Is:*
Not over $2,600	10% of the taxable income
Over $2,600 but not over $9,450	$260 plus 24% of the excess over $2,600
Over $9,450 but not over $12,950	$1,904 plus 35% of the excess over $9,450
Over $12,950	$3,129 plus 37% of the excess over $12,950

.02 *Unearned Income of Minor Children (the "Kiddie Tax")*. For taxable years beginning in 2020, the amount in § 1(g)(4)(A)(ii)(I), which is used to reduce the net unearned income reported on the child's return that is subject to the "kiddie tax," is $1,100. This $1,100 amount is the same as the amount provided in § 63(c)(5)(A), as adjusted for inflation. The same $1,100 amount is used for purposes of § 1(g)(7) (that is, to determine whether a parent may elect to include a child's gross income in the parent's gross income and to calculate the "kiddie tax"). For example, one of the requirements for the parental election is that a child's gross income is more than the amount referenced in § 1(g)(4)(A)(ii)(I) but less than 10 times that amount; thus, a child's gross income for 2020 must be more than $1,100 but less than $11,000.

.03 *Maximum Capital Gains Rate*. For taxable years beginning in 2020, the Maximum Zero Rate Amount under § 1(h)(1)(B)(i) is $80,000 in the case of a joint return or surviving spouse ($40,000 in the case of a married individual filing a separate return), $53,600 in the case of an individual who is a head of household (§ 2(b)), $40,000 in the case of any other individual (other than an estate or trust), and $2,650 in the case of an estate or trust. The Maximum 15-percent Rate Amount under § 1(h)(1)(C)(ii)(I) is $496,600 in the case of a joint return or surviving spouse ($248,300 in the case of a married individual filing a separate return), $469,050 in the case of an individual who is the head of a household (§ 2(b)), $441,450 in the case of any other individual (other than an estate or trust), and $13,150 in the case of an estate or trust.

.04 *Adoption Credit*. For taxable years beginning in 2020, under § 23(a)(3) the credit allowed for an adoption of a child with special needs is $14,300. For taxable years beginning in 2020, under § 23(b)(1) the maximum credit allowed for other adoptions is the amount of qualified adoption expenses up to $14,300. The available adoption credit begins to phase out under § 23(b)(2)(A) for taxpayers with modified adjusted gross income in excess of $214,520 and is completely phased out for taxpayers with modified adjusted gross income of $254,520 or more. (See section 3.20 for the adjusted items relating to adoption assistance programs.)

.05 *Child Tax Credit*. For taxable years beginning in 2020, the value used in § 24(d)(1)(A) to determine the amount of credit under § 24 that may be refundable is $1,400.

.06 *Lifetime Learning Credit.* For taxable years beginning in 2020, a taxpayer's modified adjusted gross income in excess of $59,000 ($118,000 for a joint return) is used to determine the reduction under § 25A(d)(2) in the amount of the Lifetime Learning Credit otherwise allowable under § 25A(a)(2).

.07 *Earned Income Credit.*

(1) *In general.* For taxable years beginning in 2020, the following amounts are used to determine the earned income credit under § 32(b). The "earned income amount" is the amount of earned income at or above which the maximum amount of the earned income credit is allowed. The "threshold phaseout amount" is the amount of adjusted gross income (or, if greater, earned income) above which the maximum amount of the credit begins to phase out. The "completed phaseout amount" is the amount of adjusted gross income (or, if greater, earned income) at or above which no credit is allowed. The threshold phaseout amounts and the completed phaseout amounts shown in the table below for married taxpayers filing a joint return include the increase provided in § 32(b)(2)(B), as adjusted for inflation for taxable years beginning in 2020.

Item	*Number of Qualifying Children* One	Two	Three or More	None
Earned Income Amount	$10,540	$14,800	$14,800	$7,030
Maximum Amount of Credit	$3,584	$5,920	$6,660	$538
Threshold Phaseout Amount (Single, Surviving Spouse, or Head of Household)	$19,330	$19,330	$19,330	$8,790
Completed Phaseout Amount (Single, Surviving Spouse, or Head of Household)	$41,756	$47,440	$50,954	$15,820
Threshold Phaseout Amount (Married Filing Jointly)	$25,220	$25,220	$25,220	$14,680
Completed Phaseout Amount (Married Filing Jointly)	$47,646	$53,330	$56,844	$21,710

The instructions for the Form 1040 series provide tables showing the amount of the earned income credit for each type of taxpayer.

(2) *Excessive Investment Income.* For taxable years beginning in 2020, the earned income tax credit is not allowed under § 32(i)(1) if the aggregate amount of certain investment income exceeds $3,650.

* * *

.12 *Exemption Amounts for Alternative Minimum Tax.* For taxable years beginning in 2020, the exemption amounts under § 55(d)(1) are:

Joint Returns or Surviving Spouses	$113,400
Unmarried Individuals (other than Surviving Spouses)	$72,900
Married Individuals Filing Separate Returns	$56,700
Estates and Trusts	$25,400

For taxable years beginning in 2020, under § 55(b)(1), the excess taxable income above which the 28 percent tax rate applies is:

Married Individuals Filing Separate Returns	$98,950
Joint Returns, Unmarried Individuals (other than surviving spouses), and Estates and Trusts	$197,900

For taxable years beginning in 2020, the amounts used under § 55(d)(2) to determine the phaseout of the exemption amounts are:

Joint Returns or Surviving Spouses	$1,036,800
Unmarried Individuals (other than Surviving Spouses)	$518,400
Married Individuals Filing Separate Returns	$518,400
Estates and Trusts	$84,800

.13 *Alternative Minimum Tax Exemption for a Child Subject to the "Kiddie Tax."* For taxable years beginning in 2020, for a child to whom the § 1(g) "kiddie tax" applies, the exemption amount under

§§55(d) and 59(j) for purposes of the alternative minimum tax under §55 may not exceed the sum of (1) the child's earned income for the taxable year, plus (2) $7,900.

.14 *Certain Expenses of Elementary and Secondary School Teachers.* For taxable years beginning in 2020, under §62(a)(2)(D) the amount of the deduction allowed under §162 that consists of expenses paid or incurred by an eligible educator in connection with books, supplies (other than nonathletic supplies for courses of instruction in health or physical education), computer equipment (including related software and services) and other equipment, and supplementary materials used by the eligible educator in the classroom is $250.

* * *

.16 *Standard Deduction.*

(1) *In general.* For taxable years beginning in 2020, the standard deduction amounts under §63(c)(2) are as follows:

Filing Status	*Standard Deduction*
Married Individuals Filing Joint Returns and Surviving Spouses (§1(j)(2)(A))	$24,800
Heads of Households (§1(j)(2)(B))	$18,650
Unmarried Individuals (other than Surviving Spouses and Heads of Households) (§1(j)(2)(C))	$12,400
Married Individuals Filing Separate Returns (§1(j)(2)(D))	$12,400

(2) *Dependent.* For taxable years beginning in 2020, the standard deduction amount under §63(c)(5) for an individual who may be claimed as a dependent by another taxpayer cannot exceed the greater of (1) $1,100, or (2) the sum of $350 and the individual's earned income.

(3) *Aged or blind.* For taxable years beginning in 2020, the additional standard deduction amount under §63(f) for the aged or the blind is $1,300. The additional standard deduction amount is increased to $1,650 if the individual is also unmarried and not a surviving spouse.

.17 *Cafeteria Plans.* For taxable years beginning in 2020, the dollar limitation under §125(i) on voluntary employee salary reductions for contributions to health flexible spending arrangements is $2,750.

.18 *Qualified Transportation Fringe Benefit.* For taxable years beginning in 2020, the monthly limitation under §132(f)(2)(A) regarding the aggregate fringe benefit exclusion amount for transportation in a commuter highway vehicle and any transit pass is $270. The monthly limitation under §132(f)(2)(B) regarding the fringe benefit exclusion amount for qualified parking is $270.

.19 *Income from United States Savings Bonds for Taxpayers Who Pay Qualified Higher Education Expenses.* For taxable years beginning in 2020, the exclusion under §135, regarding income from United States savings bonds for taxpayers who pay qualified higher education expenses, begins to phase out for modified adjusted gross income above $123,550 for joint returns and $82,350 for all other returns. The exclusion is completely phased out for modified adjusted gross income of $153,550 or more for joint returns and $97,350 or more for all other returns.

* * *

.25 *Gross Income Limitation for a Qualifying Relative.* For taxable years beginning in 2020, the exemption amount referenced in §152(d)(1)(B) is $4,300.

.26 *Election to Expense Certain Depreciable Assets.* For taxable years beginning in 2020, under §179(b)(1), the aggregate cost of any §179 property that a taxpayer elects to treat as an expense cannot exceed $1,040,000 and under §179(b)(5)(A), the cost of any sport utility vehicle that may be taken into account under §179 cannot exceed $25,900. Under §179(b)(2), the $2,590,000 limitation is reduced (but not below zero) by the amount the cost of §179 property placed in service during the 2020 taxable year exceeds $2,590,000.

.27 *Qualified Business Income.* For taxable years beginning in 2020, the threshold amount under §199A(e)(2) is $326,600 for married filing joint returns, $163,300 for married filing separate returns, and $163,300 for all other returns.

.28 *Eligible Long-Term Care Premiums.* For taxable years beginning in 2020, the limitations under §213(d)(10), regarding eligible long-term care premiums includible in the term "medical care," are as follows:

Attained Age Before the Close of the Taxable Year	Limitation on Premiums
40 or less	$430
More than 40 but not more than 50	$810
More than 50 but not more than 60	$1,630
More than 60 but not more than 70	$4,350
More than 70	$5,430

* * *

.30 *Interest on Education Loans.* For taxable years beginning in 2020, the $2,500 maximum deduction for interest paid on qualified education loans under § 221 begins to phase out under § 221(b)(2)(B) for taxpayers with modified adjusted gross income in excess of $70,000 ($140,000 for joint returns), and is completely phased out for taxpayers with modified adjusted gross income of $85,000 or more ($170,000 or more for joint returns).

.31 *Limitation on Use of Cash Method of Accounting.* For taxable years beginning in 2020, a corporation or partnership meets the gross receipts test of § 448(c) for any taxable year if the average annual gross receipts of such entity for the 3-taxable-year period ending with the taxable year which precedes such taxable year does not exceed $26,000,000.

.32 *Threshold for Excess Business Loss.* For taxable years beginning in 2020, in determining a taxpayer's excess business loss, the amount under § 461(l)(3)(A)(ii)(II) is $259,000 ($518,000 for joint returns).

* * *

.35 *Special Rules for Credits and Deductions.* For taxable years beginning in 2020, the amount of the deduction under § 642(b)(2)(C)(i) is $4,300.

* * *

.40 *Debt Instruments Arising Out of Sales or Exchanges.* For calendar year 2020, a qualified debt instrument under § 1274A(b) has stated principal that does not exceed $6,039,100, and a cash method debt instrument under § 1274A(c)(2) has stated principal that does not exceed $4,313,600.

* * *

.49 *Property Exempt from Levy.* For calendar year 2020, the value of property exempt from levy under § 6334(a)(2) (fuel, provisions, furniture, and other household personal effects, as well as arms for personal use, livestock, and poultry) cannot exceed $9,690. The value of property exempt from levy under § 6334(a)(3) (books and tools necessary for the trade, business, or profession of the taxpayer) cannot exceed $4,850.

.50 *Exempt Amount of Wages, Salary, or Other Income.* For taxable years beginning in 2020, the dollar amount used to calculate the amount determined under § 6334(d)(4)(B) is $4,300.

* * *

.52 *Failure to File Tax Return.* In the case of any return required to be filed in 2021, the amount of the addition to tax under § 6651(a) for failure to file a tax return within 60 days of the due date of such return (determined with regard to any extensions of time for filing) shall not be less than the lesser of $330 or 100 percent of the amount required to be shown as tax on such returns.

* * *

.60 *Attorney Fee Awards.* For fees incurred in calendar year 2020, the attorney fee award limitation under § 7430(c)(1)(B)(iii) is $210 per hour.

* * *

Elective Deferrals and IRA Contributions: Sections 25B, 219, and 408A

Notice 2019-59, 2019-47 I.R.B. 1091

* * *

The Code also provides that several retirement-related amounts are to be adjusted using the cost-of-living adjustment under § 1(f)(3). After taking the applicable rounding rules into account, the amounts for 2020 are as follows:

The adjusted gross income limitation under § 25B(b)(1)(A) for determining the retirement savings contributions credit for married taxpayers filing a joint return is increased from $38,500 to $39,000; the limitation under § 25B(b)(1)(B) is increased from $41,500 to $42,500; and the limitation under § § 25B(b)(1)(C) and 25B(b)(1)(D) is increased from $64,000 to $65,000.

The adjusted gross income limitation under § 25B(b)(1)(A) for determining the retirement savings contributions credit for taxpayers filing as head of household is increased from $28,875 to $29,250; the limitation under § 25B(b)(1)(B) is increased from $31,125 to $31,875; and the limitation under § § 25B(b)(1)(C) and 25B(b)(1)(D) is increased from $48,000 to $48,750.

The adjusted gross income limitation under § 25B(b)(1)(A) for determining the retirement savings contributions credit for all other taxpayers is increased from $19,250 to $19,500; the limitation under § 25B(b)(1)(B) is increased from $20,750 to $21,250; and the limitation under § § 25B(b)(1)(C) and 25B(b)(1)(D) is increased from $32,000 to $32,500.

The deductible amount under § 219(b)(5)(A) for an individual making qualified retirement contributions remains unchanged at $6,000.

The applicable dollar amount under § 219(g)(3)(B)(i) for determining the deductible amount of an IRA contribution for taxpayers who are active participants filing a joint return or as a qualifying widow(er) is increased from $103,000 to $104,000. The applicable dollar amount under § 219(g)(3)(B)(ii) for all other taxpayers who are active participants (other than married taxpayers filing separate returns) is increased from $64,000 to $65,000. If an individual or the individual's spouse is an active participant, the applicable dollar amount under § 219(g)(3)(B)(iii) for a married individual filing a separate return is not subject to an annual cost-of-living adjustment and remains $0. The applicable dollar amount under § 219(g)(7)(A) for a taxpayer who is not an active participant but whose spouse is an active participant is increased from $193,000 to $196,000.

Accordingly, under § 219(g)(2)(A), the deduction for taxpayers making contributions to a traditional IRA is phased out for single individuals and heads of household who are active participants in a qualified plan (or another retirement plan specified in § 219(g)(5)) and have adjusted gross incomes (as defined in § 219(g)(3)(A)) between $65,000 and $75,000, increased from between $64,000 and $74,000. For married couples filing jointly, if the spouse who makes the IRA contribution is an active participant, the income phase-out range is between $104,000 and $124,000, increased from between $103,000 and $123,000. For an IRA contributor who is not an active participant and is married to someone who is an active participant, the deduction is phased out if the couple's income is between $196,000 and $206,000, increased from between $193,000 and $203,000. For a married individual filing a separate return who is an active participant, the phase-out range is not subject to an annual cost-of-living adjustment and remains $0 to $10,000.

The adjusted gross income limitation under § 408A(c)(3)(B)(ii)(I) for determining the maximum Roth IRA contribution for married taxpayers filing a joint return or for taxpayers filing as a qualifying widow(er) is increased from $193,000 to $196,000. The adjusted gross income limitation under § 408A(c)(3)(B)(ii)(II) for all other taxpayers (other than married taxpayers filing separate returns) is increased from $122,000 to $124,000. The applicable dollar amount under § 408A(c)(3)(B)(ii)(III) for a married individual filing a separate return is not subject to an annual cost-of-living adjustment and remains $0.

Accordingly, under § 408A(c)(3)(A), the adjusted gross income phase-out range for taxpayers making contributions to a Roth IRA is $196,000 to $206,000 for married couples filing jointly, increased from $193,000 to $203,000. For singles and heads of household, the income phase-out range is $124,000 to $139,000, increased from $122,000 to $137,000. For a married individual filing a separate return, the phase-out range is not subject to an annual cost-of-living adjustment and remains $0 to $10,000.

* * *

DEPRECIATION TABLES

The Commissioner of Internal Revenue has promulgated tables that may, at the election of the taxpayer, be used in implementing the Accelerated Cost Recovery System of depreciation provided by Section 168. The most frequently used tables are reproduced below. Table 1 covers most personal property, and Table 6 covers residential rental property. Both are from Rev. Proc. 87-57, 1987-2 CB 687. Table A-7a, taken from IRS Publication 946, covers nonresidential real property placed in service on or after May 13, 1993. Tables for other circumstances, including the mid-quarter convention and the Section 168(g) alternative depreciation system, may be found in Rev. Proc. 87-57 and IRS Publication 946.

In the case of Table 1, the depreciation percentages reflect the 200 percent declining balance method, switching to straight line method, for property with applicable recovery periods of 3, 5, 7, or 10 years and the 150 percent declining balance method, switching to straight line method, for property with applicable recovery periods of 15 or 20 years.

The tables below set forth the percentages to be applied against the basis of the asset, after reducing the basis to reflect any deductions available under Sections 168(k) and 179. The percentages set forth in the table are applied each year to the basis remaining after application of Section 179, without any reduction for prior depreciation deductions under Section 168(a). For example, assume that the taxpayer purchases an asset subject to a 5-year recovery period, and that after reducing the basis to reflect any deduction available under Section 179, the remaining basis is $100,000. Under Table 1 below, the first-year depreciation is $20,000, the second-year depreciation is $32,000, the third-year depreciation is $19,200, and so on.

Note: Sections 168(k)(6)(A)(i) and (B)(i), enacted as part of the Tax Cuts and Jobs Act, provide for immediate deduction of the entire cost of qualifying property placed in service after September 27, 2017, and before January 1, 2023. In the case of such property no basis will remain to support depreciation deductions under Section 168(a).

Table 1. General Depreciation System
Applicable Depreciation Method: 200 or 150 Percent Declining Balance Switching to Straight Line
Applicable Recovery Periods: 3, 5, 7, 10, 15, 20 years
Applicable Convention: Half-year

			and the Recovery Period is:			
If the Recovery Year is:	*3-year*	*5-year*	*7-year*	*10-year*	*15-year*	*20-year*
			the Depreciation Rate is:			
1	33.33	20.00	14.29	10.00	5.00	3.750
2	44.45	32.00	24.49	18.00	9.50	7.219
3	14.81	19.20	17.49	14.40	8.55	6.677
4	7.41	11.52	12.49	11.52	7.70	6.177
5		11.52	8.93	9.22	6.93	5.713
6		5.76	8.92	7.37	6.23	5.285
7			8.93	6.55	5.90	4.888
8			4.46	6.55	5.90	4.522
9				6.56	5.91	4.462
10				6.55	5.90	4.461
11				3.28	5.91	4.462
12					5.90	4.461
13					5.91	4.462
14					5.90	4.461
15					5.91	4.462
16					2.95	4.461
17						4.462
18						4.461
19						4.462
20						4.461
21						2.231

Table 6. General Depreciation System
Applicable Depreciation Method: Straight Line
Applicable Recovery Period: 27.5 years
Applicable Convention: Mid-month

If the Recovery Year is:	*And the Month in the First Recovery Year the Property is Placed in Service is:*											
	1	*2*	*3*	*4*	*5*	*6*	*7*	*8*	*9*	*10*	*11*	*12*
	the Depreciation Rate is:											
1	3.485	3.182	2.879	2.576	2.273	1.970	1.667	1.364	1.061	0.758	0.455	0.152
2	3.636	3.636	3.636	3.636	3.636	3.636	3.636	3.636	3.636	3.636	3.636	3.636
3	3.636	3.636	3.636	3.636	3.636	3.636	3.636	3.636	3.636	3.636	3.636	3.636
4	3.636	3.636	3.636	3.636	3.636	3.636	3.636	3.636	3.636	3.636	3.636	3.636
5	3.636	3.636	3.636	3.636	3.636	3.636	3.636	3.636	3.636	3.636	3.636	3.636
6	3.636	3.636	3.636	3.636	3.636	3.636	3.636	3.636	3.636	3.636	3.636	3.636
7	3.636	3.636	3.636	3.636	3.636	3.636	3.636	3.636	3.636	3.636	3.636	3.636
8	3.636	3.636	3.636	3.636	3.636	3.636	3.636	3.636	3.636	3.636	3.636	3.636
9	3.636	3.636	3.636	3.636	3.636	3.636	3.636	3.636	3.636	3.636	3.636	3.636
10	3.637	3.637	3.637	3.637	3.637	3.637	3.636	3.636	3.636	3.636	3.636	3.636
11	3.636	3.636	3.636	3.636	3.636	3.636	3.637	3.637	3.637	3.637	3.637	3.637
12	3.637	3.637	3.637	3.637	3.637	3.637	3.636	3.636	3.636	3.636	3.636	3.636
13	3.636	3.636	3.636	3.636	3.636	3.636	3.637	3.637	3.637	3.637	3.637	3.637
14	3.637	3.637	3.637	3.637	3.637	3.637	3.636	3.636	3.636	3.636	3.636	3.636
15	3.636	3.636	3.636	3.636	3.636	3.636	3.637	3.637	3.637	3.637	3.637	3.637
16	3.637	3.637	3.637	3.637	3.637	3.637	3.636	3.636	3.636	3.636	3.636	3.636
17	3.636	3.636	3.636	3.636	3.636	3.636	3.637	3.637	3.637	3.637	3.637	3.637
18	3.637	3.637	3.637	3.637	3.637	3.637	3.636	3.636	3.636	3.636	3.636	3.636
19	3.636	3.636	3.636	3.636	3.636	3.636	3.637	3.637	3.637	3.637	3.637	3.637
20	3.637	3.637	3.637	3.637	3.637	3.637	3.636	3.636	3.636	3.636	3.636	3.636
21	3.636	3.636	3.636	3.636	3.636	3.636	3.637	3.637	3.637	3.637	3.637	3.637
22	3.637	3.637	3.637	3.637	3.637	3.637	3.636	3.636	3.636	3.636	3.636	3.636
23	3.636	3.636	3.636	3.636	3.636	3.636	3.637	3.637	3.637	3.637	3.637	3.637
24	3.637	3.637	3.637	3.637	3.637	3.637	3.636	3.636	3.636	3.636	3.636	3.636
25	3.636	3.636	3.636	3.636	3.636	3.636	3.637	3.637	3.637	3.637	3.637	3.637
26	3.637	3.637	3.637	3.637	3.637	3.637	3.636	3.636	3.636	3.636	3.636	3.636
27	3.636	3.636	3.636	3.636	3.636	3.636	3.637	3.637	3.637	3.637	3.637	3.637
28	1.970	2.273	2.576	2.879	3.182	3.485	3.636	3.636	3.636	3.636	3.636	3.636
29	0.000	0.000	0.000	0.000	0.000	0.000	0.152	0.455	0.758	1.061	1.364	1.667

Table A-7a. Nonresidential Real Property
Applicable Depreciation Method: Straight Line
Applicable Recovery Period: 39 years
Applicable Convention: Mid-month

If the Recovery Year is:	*And the Month in the First Recovery Year the Property is Placed in Service is:*											
	1	*2*	*3*	*4*	*5*	*6*	*7*	*8*	*9*	*10*	*11*	*12*
	the Depreciation Rate is:											
1	2.461	2.247	2.033	1.819	1.605	1.391	1.177	0.963	0.749	0.535	0.321	0.107
2—39	2.564	2.564	2.564	2.564	2.564	2.564	2.564	2.564	2.564	2.564	2.564	2.564
40	0.107	0.321	0.535	0.749	0.963	1.177	1.391	1.605	1.819	2.033	2.247	2.461

Table of Code and Regulations Sections

UNITED STATES CODE

TITLE 26—INTERNAL REVENUE CODE

SUBTITLE A—INCOME TAXES

CHAPTER 1—NORMAL TAXES AND SURTAXES

SUBCHAPTER A—DETERMINATION OF TAX LIABILITY

* Code provision or regulation not reproduced.

* Code provision or regulation not reproduced.

* Code provision or regulation not reproduced.

* Code provision or regulation not reproduced.

* Code provision or regulation not reproduced.

* Code provision or regulation not reproduced.

* Code provision or regulation not reproduced.

* Code provision or regulation not reproduced.

* Code provision or regulation not reproduced.

* Code provision or regulation not reproduced.

* Code provision or regulation not reproduced.

* Code provision or regulation not reproduced.

* Code provision or regulation not reproduced.

* Code provision or regulation not reproduced.

* Code provision or regulation not reproduced.

* Code provision or regulation not reproduced.

* Code provision or regulation not reproduced.

* Code provision or regulation not reproduced.

* Code provision or regulation not reproduced.

* Code provision or regulation not reproduced.

* Code provision or regulation not reproduced.

* Code provision or regulation not reproduced.

* Code provision or regulation not reproduced.

* Code provision or regulation not reproduced.

* Code provision or regulation not reproduced.

Internal Revenue Code

UNITED STATES CODE

TITLE 26—INTERNAL REVENUE CODE OF 1986

SUBTITLE A—INCOME TAXES

CHAPTER 1—NORMAL TAXES AND SURTAXES

SUBCHAPTER A—DETERMINATION OF TAX LIABILITY

PART I—TAX ON INDIVIDUALS

»»→ Caution: Pursuant to Section 1(j)(1)(B), for taxable years beginning after December 31, 2017, and before January 1, 2026, the tax rates set forth in Section 1(a) through (e) are supplanted by the rates set forth in Section 1(j)(2) through (6).

»»→ Caution: As provided in Sections 1(f) and (j)(3), the income brackets set forth in Section 1(j)(2) are adjusted for taxable years beginning after 2018 to reflect increases in the Chained Consumer Price Index. As provided in Section 1(j)(5)(C), the dollar amounts set forth in Section 1(j)(5)(B) are adjusted for taxable years after 2018 to reflect increases in the Chained Consumer Price Index. The adjusted amounts applicable to taxable years beginning in 2020 are provided in the material beginning at page ix.

[Sec. 1]

SECTION 1. TAX IMPOSED.

[Sec. 1(a)]

(a) MARRIED INDIVIDUALS FILING JOINT RETURNS AND SURVIVING SPOUSES.—There is hereby imposed on the taxable income of—

(1) every married individual (as defined in section 7703) who makes a single return jointly with his spouse under section 6013, and

(2) every surviving spouse (as defined in section 2(a)),

a tax determined in accordance with the following table:

If taxable income is:	The tax is:
Not over $36,900	15% of taxable income.
Over $36,900 but not over $89,150	$5,535, plus 28% of the excess over $36,900.
Over $89,150 but not over $140,000	$20,165, plus 31% of the excess over $89,150.
Over $140,000 but not over $250,000	$35,928.50, plus 36% of the excess over $140,000.
Over $250,000	$75,528.50, plus 39.6% of the excess over $250,000.

[Sec. 1(b)]

(b) HEADS OF HOUSEHOLDS.—There is hereby imposed on the taxable income of every head of a household (as defined in section 2(b)) a tax determined in accordance with the following table:

If taxable income is:	The tax is:
Not over $29,600	15% of taxable income.
Over $29,600 but not over $76,400	$4,440, plus 28% of the excess over $29,600.
Over $76,400 but not over $127,500	$17,544, plus 31% of the excess over $76,400.
Over $127,500 but not over $250,000	$33,385, plus 36% of the excess over $127,500.
Over $250,000	$77,485, plus 39.6% of the excess over $250,000.

[Sec. 1(c)]

(c) UNMARRIED INDIVIDUALS (OTHER THAN SURVIVING SPOUSES AND HEADS OF HOUSEHOLDS).—There is hereby imposed on the taxable income of every individual (other than a surviving spouse as defined in section 2(a) or the head of a household as defined in section 2(b)) who is not a married individual (as defined in section 7703) a tax determined in accordance with the following table:

If taxable income is:	The tax is:
Not over $22,100	15% of taxable income.
Over $22,100 but not over $53,500	$3,315, plus 28% of the excess over $22,100.
Over $53,500 but not over $115,000	$12,107, plus 31% of the excess over $53,500.
Over $115,000 but not over $250,000	$31,172, plus 36% of the excess over $115,000.
Over $250,000	$79,772, plus 39.6% of the excess over $250,000.

[Sec. 1(d)]

(d) MARRIED INDIVIDUALS FILING SEPARATE RETURNS.—There is hereby imposed on the taxable income of every married individual (as defined in section 7703) who does not make a single return jointly with his spouse under section 6013, a tax determined in accordance with the following table:

If taxable income is:	The tax is:
Not over $18,450	15% of taxable income.
Over $18,450 but not over $44,575	$2,767.50, plus 28% of the excess over $18,450.
Over $44,575 but not over $70,000	$10,082.50, plus 31% of the excess over $44,575.
Over $70,000 but not over $125,000	$17,964.25, plus 36% of the excess over $70,000.
Over $125,000	$37,764.25, plus 39.6% of the excess over $125,000.

[Sec. 1(e)]

(e) ESTATES AND TRUSTS.—There is hereby imposed on the taxable income of—

(1) every estate, and

(2) every trust,

taxable under this subsection a tax determined in accordance with the following table:

If taxable income is:	The tax is:
Not over $1,500	15% of taxable income.
Over $1,500 but not over $3,500	$225, plus 28% of the excess over $1,500.
Over $3,500 but not over $5,500	$785, plus 31% of the excess over $3,500.
Over $5,500 but not over $7,500	$1,405, plus 36% of the excess over $5,500.
Over $7,500	$2,125, plus 39.6% of the excess over $7,500.

[Sec. 1(f)]

(f) PHASEOUT OF MARRIAGE PENALTY IN 15-PERCENT BRACKET; ADJUSTMENTS IN TAX TABLES SO THAT INFLATION WILL NOT RESULT IN TAX INCREASES.—

(1) IN GENERAL.—Not later than December 15 of 1993, and each subsequent calendar year, the Secretary shall prescribe tables which shall apply in lieu of the tables contained in subsections (a), (b), (c), (d), and (e) with respect to taxable years beginning in the succeeding calendar year.

(2) METHOD OF PRESCRIBING TABLES.—The table which under paragraph (1) is to apply in lieu of the table contained in subsection (a), (b), (c), (d), or (e), as the case may be, with respect to taxable years beginning in any calendar year shall be prescribed—

(A) except as provided in paragraph (8), by increasing the minimum and maximum dollar amounts for each bracket for which a tax is imposed under such table by the cost-of-living adjustment for such calendar year, determined—

(i) except as provided in clause (ii), by substituting "1992" for "2016" in paragraph (3)(A)(ii), and

(ii) in the case of adjustments to the dollar amounts at which the 36 percent rate bracket begins or at which the 39.6 percent rate bracket begins, by substituting "1993" for "2016" in paragraph (3)(A)(ii),

(B) by not changing the rate applicable to any rate bracket as adjusted under subparagraph (A), and

(C) by adjusting the amounts setting forth the tax to the extent necessary to reflect the adjustments in the rate brackets.

(3) COST-OF-LIVING ADJUSTMENT.—For purposes of this subsection—

(A) IN GENERAL.—The cost-of-living adjustment for any calendar year is the percentage (if any) by which—

(i) the C-CPI-U for the preceding calendar year, exceeds

(ii) the CPI for calendar year 2016, multiplied by the amount determined under subparagraph (B).

(B) AMOUNT DETERMINED.—The amount determined under this clause is the amount obtained by dividing—

(i) the C-CPI-U for calendar year 2016, by

(ii) the CPI for calendar year 2016.

(C) SPECIAL RULE FOR ADJUSTMENTS WITH A BASE YEAR AFTER 2016.—For purposes of any provision of this title which provides for the substitution of a year after 2016 for "2016" in subparagraph (A)(ii), subparagraph (A) shall be applied by substituting "the C-CPI-U for calendar year 2016" for "the CPI for calendar year 2016" and all that follows in clause (ii) thereof.

(4) CPI FOR ANY CALENDAR YEAR.—For purposes of paragraph (3), the CPI for any calendar year is the average of the Consumer Price Index as of the close of the 12-month period ending on August 31 of such calendar year.

(5) CONSUMER PRICE INDEX.—For purposes of paragraph (4), the term "Consumer Price Index" means the last Consumer Price Index for all-urban consumers published by the Department of Labor. For purposes of the preceding sentence, the revision of the Consumer Price Index which is most consistent with the Consumer Price Index for calendar year 1986 shall be used.

(6) C-CPI-U.—For purposes of this subsection—

(A) IN GENERAL.—The term "C-CPI-U" means the Chained Consumer Price Index for All Urban Consumers (as published by the Bureau of Labor Statistics of the Department of Labor). The values of the Chained Consumer Price Index for All Urban Consumers taken into account for purposes of determining the cost-of-living adjustment for any calendar year under this subsection shall be the latest values so published as of the date on which such Bureau publishes the initial value of the Chained Consumer Price Index for All Urban Consumers for the month of August for the preceding calendar year.

(B) DETERMINATION FOR CALENDAR YEAR.—The C-CPI-U for any calendar year is the average of the C-CPI-U as of the close of the 12-month period ending on August 31 of such calendar year.

(7) ROUNDING.—

(A) IN GENERAL.—If any increase determined under paragraph (2)(A), section 63(c)(4), section 68(b)(2) or section 151(d)(4) is not a multiple of $50, such increase shall be rounded to the next lowest multiple of $50.

(B) TABLE FOR MARRIED INDIVIDUALS FILING SEPARATELY.—In the case of a married individual filing a separate return, subparagraph (A) (other than with respect to sections 63(c)(4) and 151(d)(4)(A)) shall be applied by substituting "$25" for "$50" each place it appears.

* * *

[Sec. 1(g)]

(g) CERTAIN UNEARNED INCOME OF CHILDREN TAXED AS IF PARENT'S INCOME.—

(1) IN GENERAL.—In the case of any child to whom this subsection applies, the tax imposed by this section shall be equal to the greater of—

(A) the tax imposed by this section without regard to this subsection, or

(B) the sum of—

(i) the tax which would be imposed by this section if the taxable income of such child for the taxable year were reduced by the net unearned income of such child, plus

(ii) such child's share of the allocable parental tax.

(2) CHILD TO WHOM SUBSECTION APPLIES.—This subsection shall apply to any child for any taxable year if—

(A) such child—

(i) has not attained age 18 before the close of the taxable year, or

(ii) (I) has attained age 18 before the close of the taxable year and meets the age requirements of section 152(c)(3) (determined without regard to subparagraph (B) thereof), and

(II) whose earned income (as defined in section 911(d)(2)) for such taxable year does not exceed one-half of the amount of the individual's support (within the meaning of section 152(c)(1)(D) after the application of section 152(f)(5) (without regard to subparagraph (A) thereof)) for such taxable year,

(B) either parent of such child is alive at the close of the taxable year, and

(C) such child does not file a joint return for the taxable year.

(3) ALLOCABLE PARENTAL TAX.—For purposes of this subsection—

(A) IN GENERAL.—The term "allocable parental tax" means the excess of—

(i) the tax which would be imposed by this section on the parent's taxable income if such income included the net unearned income of all children of the parent to whom this subsection applies, over

(ii) the tax imposed by this section on the parent without regard to this subsection.

For purposes of clause (i), net unearned income of all children of the parent shall not be taken into account in computing any exclusion, deduction, or credit of the parent.

(B) CHILD'S SHARE.—A child's share of any allocable parental tax of a parent shall be equal to an amount which bears the same ratio to the total allocable parental tax as the child's net unearned income bears to the aggregate net unearned income of all children of such parent to whom this subsection applies.

(C) SPECIAL RULE WHERE PARENT HAS DIFFERENT TAXABLE YEAR.—Except as provided in regulations, if the parent does not have the same taxable year as the child, the allocable parental tax shall be determined on the basis of the taxable year of the parent ending in the child's taxable year.

(4) NET UNEARNED INCOME.—For purposes of this subsection—

(A) IN GENERAL.—The term "net unearned income" means the excess of—

(i) the portion of the adjusted gross income for the taxable year which is not attributable to earned income (as defined in section 911(d)(2)), over

(ii) the sum of—

(I) the amount in effect for the taxable year under section 63(c)(5)(A) (relating to limitation on standard deduction in the case of certain dependents), plus

(II) The greater of the amount described in subclause (I) or, if the child itemizes his deductions for the taxable year, the amount of the itemized deductions allowed by this chapter for the taxable year which are directly connected with the production of the portion of adjusted gross income referred to in clause (i).

(B) LIMITATION BASED ON TAXABLE INCOME.—The amount of the net unearned income for any taxable year shall not exceed the individual's taxable income for such taxable year.

(C) TREATMENT OF DISTRIBUTIONS FROM QUALIFIED DISABILITY TRUSTS.—For purposes of this subsection, in the case of any child who is a beneficiary of a qualified disability trust (as defined in section 642(b)(2)(C)(ii)), any amount included in the income of such child under sections 652 and 662 during a taxable year shall be considered earned income of such child for such taxable year.

(5) SPECIAL RULES FOR DETERMINING PARENT TO WHOM SUBSECTION APPLIES.—For purposes of this subsection, the parent whose taxable income shall be taken into account shall be—

(A) in the case of parents who are not married (within the meaning of section 7703), the custodial parent (within the meaning of section 152(e)) of the child, and

(B) in the case of married individuals filing separately, the individual with the greater taxable income.

(6) PROVIDING OF PARENT'S TIN.—The parent of any child to whom this subsection applies for any taxable year shall provide the TIN of such parent to such child and such child shall include such TIN on the child's return of tax imposed by this section for such taxable year.

(7) ELECTION TO CLAIM CERTAIN UNEARNED INCOME OF CHILD ON PARENT'S RETURN.—

(A) IN GENERAL.—If—

(i) any child to whom this subsection applies has gross income for the taxable year only from interest and dividends (including Alaska Permanent Fund dividends),

(ii) such gross income is more than the amount described in paragraph (4)(A)(ii)(I) and less than 10 times the amount so described,

(iii) no estimated tax payments for such year are made in the name and TIN of such child, and no amount has been deducted and withheld under section 3406, and

(iv) the parent of such child (as determined under paragraph (5)) elects the application of subparagraph (B),

such child shall be treated (other than [for] purposes of this paragraph) as having no gross income for such year and shall not be required to file a return under section 6012.

(B) INCOME INCLUDED ON PARENT'S RETURN.—In the case of a parent making the election under this paragraph—

(i) the gross income of each child to whom such election applies (to the extent the gross income of such child exceeds twice the amount described in paragraph (4)(A)(ii)(I)) shall be included in such parent's gross income for the taxable year,

(ii) the tax imposed by this section for such year with respect to such parent shall be the amount equal to the sum of—

(I) the amount determined under this section after the application of clause (i), plus

(II) for each such child, 10 percent of the lesser of the amount described in paragraph (4)(A)(ii)(I) or the excess of the gross income of such child over the amount so described, and

(iii) any interest which is an item of tax preference under section 57(a)(5) of the child shall be treated as an item of tax preference of such parent (and not of such child).

(C) REGULATIONS.—The Secretary shall prescribe such regulations as may be necessary or appropriate to carry out the purposes of this paragraph.

[Sec. 1(h)]

(h) MAXIMUM CAPITAL GAINS RATE.—

(1) IN GENERAL.—If a taxpayer has a net capital gain for any taxable year, the tax imposed by this section for such taxable year shall not exceed the sum of—

(A) a tax computed at the rates and in the same manner as if this subsection had not been enacted on the greater of—

(i) taxable income reduced by the net capital gain, or

(ii) the lesser of—

(I) the amount of taxable income taxed at a rate below 25 percent; or

(II) taxable income reduced by the adjusted net capital gain;

(B) 0 percent of so much of the adjusted net capital gain (or, if less, taxable income) as does not exceed the excess (if any) of—

(i) the amount of taxable income which would (without regard to this paragraph) be taxed at a rate below 25 percent, over

(ii) the taxable income reduced by the adjusted net capital gain;

(C) 15 percent of the lesser of—

(i) so much of the adjusted net capital gain (or, if less, taxable income) as exceeds the amount on which a tax is determined under subparagraph (B), or

(ii) the excess of—

(I) the amount of taxable income which would (without regard to this paragraph) be taxed at a rate below 39.6 percent, over

(II) the sum of the amounts on which a tax is determined under subparagraphs (A) and (B),

(D) 20 percent of the adjusted net capital gain (or, if less, taxable income) in excess of the sum of the amounts on which tax is determined under subparagraphs (B) and (C),

(E) 25 percent of the excess (if any) of—

(i) the unrecaptured section 1250 gain (or, if less, the net capital gain (determined without regard to paragraph (11))), over

(ii) the excess (if any) of—

(I) the sum of the amount on which tax is determined under subparagraph (A) plus the net capital gain, over

(II) taxable income; and

(F) 28 percent of the amount of taxable income in excess of the sum of the amounts on which tax is determined under the preceding subparagraphs of this paragraph.

(2) NET CAPITAL GAIN TAKEN INTO ACCOUNT AS INVESTMENT INCOME.—For purposes of this subsection, the net capital gain for any taxable year shall be reduced (but not below zero) by the amount which the taxpayer takes into account as investment income under section 163(d)(4)(B)(iii).

(3) ADJUSTED NET CAPITAL GAIN.—For purposes of this subsection, the term "adjusted net capital gain" means the sum of—

(A) net capital gain (determined without regard to paragraph (11)) reduced (but not below zero) by the sum of—

(i) unrecaptured section 1250 gain, and

(ii) 28-percent rate gain, plus

(B) qualified dividend income (as defined in paragraph (11)).

(4) 28-PERCENT RATE GAIN.—For purposes of this subsection, the term "28-percent rate gain" means the excess (if any) of—

(A) the sum of—

(i) collectibles gain; and

(ii) section 1202 gain, over

(B) the sum of—

(i) collectibles loss;

(ii) the net short-term capital loss, and

(iii) the amount of long-term capital loss carried under section 1212(b)(1)(B) to the taxable year.

(5) COLLECTIBLES GAIN AND LOSS.—For purposes of this subsection—

(A) IN GENERAL.—The terms "collectibles gain" and "collectibles loss" mean gain or loss (respectively) from the sale or exchange of a collectible (as defined in section 408(m) without regard to paragraph (3) thereof) which is a capital asset held for more than 1 year but only to the extent such gain is taken into account in computing gross income and such loss is taken into account in computing taxable income.

(B) PARTNERSHIPS, ETC.—For purposes of subparagraph (A), any gain from the sale of an interest in a partnership, S corporation, or trust which is attributable to unrealized appreciation in the value of collectibles shall be treated as gain from the sale or exchange of a collectible. Rules similar to the rules of section 751 shall apply for purposes of the preceding sentence.

(6) UNRECAPTURED SECTION 1250 GAIN.—For purposes of this subsection—

(A) IN GENERAL.—The term "unrecaptured section 1250 gain" means the excess (if any) of—

(i) the amount of long-term capital gain (not otherwise treated as ordinary income) which would be treated as ordinary income if section 1250(b)(1) included all depreciation and the applicable percentage under section 1250(a) were 100 percent, over

(ii) the excess (if any) of—

(I) the amount described in paragraph (4)(B); over

(II) the amount described in paragraph (4)(A).

(B) LIMITATION WITH RESPECT TO SECTION 1231 PROPERTY.—The amount described in subparagraph (A)(i) from sales, exchanges, and conversions described in section 1231(a)(3)(A) for any taxable year shall not exceed the net section 1231 gain (as defined in section 1231(c)(3)) for such year.

(7) SECTION 1202 GAIN.—For purposes of this subsection, the term "section 1202 gain" means the excess of—

(A) the gain which would be excluded from gross income under section 1202 but for the percentage limitation in section 1202(a), over

(B) the gain excluded from gross income under section 1202.

(8) COORDINATION WITH RECAPTURE OF NET ORDINARY LOSSES UNDER SECTION 1231.—If any amount is treated as ordinary income under section 1231(c), such amount shall be allocated among the separate categories of net section 1231 gain (as defined in section 1231(c)(3)) in such manner as the Secretary may by forms or regulations prescribe.

(9) REGULATIONS.—The Secretary may prescribe such regulations as are appropriate (including regulations requiring reporting) to apply this subsection in the case of sales and exchanges by pass-thru entities and of interests in such entities.

(10) PASS-THRU ENTITY DEFINED.—For purposes of this subsection, the term "pass-thru entity" means—

(A) a regulated investment company;

(B) a real estate investment trust;

(C) an S corporation;

(D) a partnership;

(E) an estate or trust;

(F) a common trust fund; and

(G) a qualified electing fund (as defined in section 1295).

(11) DIVIDENDS TAXED AS NET CAPITAL GAIN.—

(A) IN GENERAL.—For purposes of this subsection, the term "net capital gain" means net capital gain (determined without regard to this paragraph) increased by qualified dividend income.

(B) QUALIFIED DIVIDEND INCOME.—For purposes of this paragraph—

(i) IN GENERAL.—The term "qualified dividend income" means dividends received during the taxable year from—

(I) domestic corporations, and

(II) qualified foreign corporations.

(ii) CERTAIN DIVIDENDS EXCLUDED.—Such term shall not include—

(I) any dividend from a corporation which for the taxable year of the corporation in which the distribution is made, or the preceding taxable year, is a corporation exempt from tax under section 501 or 521,

(II) any amount allowed as a deduction under section 591 (relating to deduction for dividends paid by mutual savings banks, etc.), and

(III) any dividend described in section 404(k).

(iii) COORDINATION WITH SECTION 246(c).—Such term shall not include any dividend on any share of stock—

(I) with respect to which the holding period requirements of section 246(c) are not met (determined by substituting in section 246(c) "60 days" for "45 days" each place it appears and by substituting "121-day period" for "91-day period"), or

(II) to the extent that the taxpayer is under an obligation (whether pursuant to a short sale or otherwise) to make related payments with respect to positions in substantially similar or related property.

(C) QUALIFIED FOREIGN CORPORATIONS.—

(i) IN GENERAL.—Except as otherwise provided in this paragraph, the term "qualified foreign corporation" means any foreign corporation if—

(I) such corporation is incorporated in a possession of the United States, or

(II) such corporation is eligible for benefits of a comprehensive income tax treaty with the United States which the Secretary determines is satisfactory for purposes of this paragraph and which includes an exchange of information program.

(ii) DIVIDENDS ON STOCK READILY TRADABLE ON UNITED STATES SECURITIES MARKET.—A foreign corporation not otherwise treated as a qualified foreign corporation under clause (i) shall be so treated with respect to any dividend paid by such corporation if the stock with respect to which such dividend is paid is readily tradable on an established securities market in the United States.

(iii) EXCLUSION OF DIVIDENDS OF CERTAIN FOREIGN CORPORATIONS.—Such term shall not include—

(I) any foreign corporation which for the taxable year of the corporation in which the dividend was paid, or the preceding taxable year, is a passive foreign investment company (as defined in section 1297), and

(II) any corporation which first becomes a surrogate foreign corporation (as defined in section 7874(a)(2)(B)) after the date of the enactment of this subclause, other than a foreign corporation which is treated as a domestic corporation under section 7874(b).

(iv) COORDINATION WITH FOREIGN TAX CREDIT LIMITATION.—Rules similar to the rules of section 904(b)(2)(B) shall apply with respect to the dividend rate differential under this paragraph.

(D) SPECIAL RULES.—

(i) AMOUNTS TAKEN INTO ACCOUNT AS INVESTMENT INCOME.—Qualified dividend income shall not include any amount which the taxpayer takes into account as investment income under section 163(d)(4)(B).

(ii) EXTRAORDINARY DIVIDENDS.—If a taxpayer to whom this section applies receives, with respect to any share of stock, qualified dividend income from 1 or more dividends which are extraordinary dividends (within the meaning of section 1059(c)), any loss on the sale or exchange of such share shall, to the extent of such dividends, be treated as long-term capital loss.

(iii) TREATMENT OF DIVIDENDS FROM REGULATED INVESTMENT COMPANIES AND REAL ESTATE INVESTMENT TRUSTS.—A dividend received from a regulated investment company or a real estate investment trust shall be subject to the limitations prescribed in sections 854 and 857.

* * *

[Sec. 1(j)]

(j) MODIFICATIONS FOR TAXABLE YEARS 2018 THROUGH 2025.—

(1) IN GENERAL.—In the case of a taxable year beginning after December 31, 2017, and before January 1, 2026—

(A) subsection (i) shall not apply, and

(B) this section (other than subsection (i)) shall be applied as provided in paragraphs (2) through (6).

(2) RATE TABLES.—

(A) MARRIED INDIVIDUALS FILING JOINT RETURNS AND SURVIVING SPOUSES.—The following table shall be applied in lieu of the table contained in subsection (a):

If taxable income is:	The tax is:
Not over $19,050	10% of taxable income.
Over $19,050 but not over $77,400	$1,905, plus 12% of the excess over $19,050.
Over $77,400 but not over $165,000	$8,907, plus 22% of the excess over $77,400.
Over $165,000 but not over $315,000	$28,179, plus 24% of the excess over $165,000.
Over $315,000 but not over $400,000	$64,179, plus 32% of the excess over $315,000.
Over $400,000 but not over $600,000	$91,379, plus 35% of the excess over $400,000.
Over $600,000	$161,379 plus 37% of the excess over $600,000.

(B) HEADS OF HOUSEHOLDS.—The following table shall be applied in lieu of the table contained in subsection (b):

If taxable income is:	The tax is:
Not over $13,600	10% of taxable income.
Over $13,600 but not over $51,800	$1,360, plus 12% of the excess over $13,600.
Over $51,800 but not over $82,500	$5,944, plus 22% of the excess over $51,800.
Over $82,500 but not over $157,500	$12,698, plus 24% of the excess over $82,500.
Over $157,500 but not over $200,000	$30,698, plus 32% of the excess over $157,500.
Over $200,000 but not over $500,000	$44,298, plus 35% of the excess over $200,000.
Over $500,000	$149,298, plus 37% of the excess over $500,000.

(C) UNMARRIED INDIVIDUALS OTHER THAN SURVIVING SPOUSES AND HEADS OF HOUSEHOLDS.—The following table shall be applied in lieu of the table contained in subsection (c):

If taxable income is:	The tax is:
Not over $9,525	10% of taxable income.
Over $9,525 but not over $38,700	$952.50, plus 12% of the excess over $9,525.
Over $38,700 but not over $82,500	$4,453.50, plus 22% of the excess over $38,700.
Over $82,500 but not over $157,500	$14,089.50, plus 24% of the excess over $82,500.
Over $157,500 but not over $200,000	$32,089.50, plus 32% of the excess over $157,500.
Over $200,000 but not over $500,000	$45,689.50, plus 35% of the excess over $200,000.
Over $500,000	$150,689.50, plus 37% of the excess over $500,000.

(D) MARRIED INDIVIDUALS FILING SEPARATE RETURNS.—The following table shall be applied in lieu of the table contained in subsection (d):

If taxable income is:	The tax is:
Not over $9,525	10% of taxable income.
Over $9,525 but not over $38,700	$952.50, plus 12% of the excess over $9,525.
Over $38,700 but not over $82,500	$4,453.50, plus 22% of the excess over $38,700.
Over $82,500 but not over $157,500	$14,089.50, plus 24% of the excess over $82,500.
Over $157,500 but not over $200,000	$32,089.50, plus 32% of the excess over $157,500.

If taxable income is:	The tax is:
Over $200,000 but not over $300,000	$45,689.50, plus 35% of the excess over $200,000.
Over $300,000	$80,689.50, plus 37% of the excess over $300,000.

(E) ESTATES AND TRUSTS.—The following table shall be applied in lieu of the table contained in subsection (e):

If taxable income is:	The tax is:
Not over $2,550	10% of taxable income.
Over $2,550 but not over $9,150	$255, plus 24% of the excess over $2,550.
Over $9,150 but not over $12,500	$1,839, plus 35% of the excess over $9,150.
Over $12,500	$3,011.50, plus 37% of the excess over $12,500.

(F) REFERENCES TO RATE TABLES.—Any reference in this title to a rate of tax under subsection (c) shall be treated as a reference to the corresponding rate bracket under subparagraph (C) of this paragraph, except that the reference in section 3402(q)(1) to the third lowest rate of tax applicable under subsection (c) shall be treated as a reference to the fourth lowest rate of tax under subparagraph (C).

(3) ADJUSTMENTS.—

(A) NO ADJUSTMENT IN 2018.—The tables contained in paragraph (2) shall apply without adjustment for taxable years beginning after December 31, 2017, and before January 1, 2019.

(B) SUBSEQUENT YEARS.—For taxable years beginning after December 31, 2018, the Secretary shall prescribe tables which shall apply in lieu of the tables contained in paragraph (2) in the same manner as under paragraphs (1) and (2) of subsection (f) (applied without regard to clauses (i) and (ii) of subsection (f)(2)(A)), except that in prescribing such tables—

(i) subsection (f)(3) shall be applied by substituting "calendar year 2017" for "calendar year 2016" in subparagraph (A)(ii) thereof,

(ii) subsection (f)(7)(B) shall apply to any unmarried individual other than a surviving spouse or head of household, and

(iii) subsection (f)(8) shall not apply.

(4) [Stricken]

(5) APPLICATION OF CURRENT INCOME TAX BRACKETS TO CAPITAL GAINS BRACKETS.—

(A) IN GENERAL.—Section 1(h)(1) shall be applied—

(i) by substituting "below the maximum zero rate amount" for "which would (without regard to this paragraph) be taxed at a rate below 25 percent" in subparagraph (B)(i), and

(ii) by substituting "below the maximum 15-percent rate amount" for "which would (without regard to this paragraph) be taxed at a rate below 39.6 percent" in subparagraph (C)(ii)(I).

(B) MAXIMUM AMOUNTS DEFINED.—For purposes of applying section 1(h) with the modifications described in subparagraph (A)—

(i) MAXIMUM ZERO RATE AMOUNT.—The maximum zero rate amount shall be—

(I) in the case of a joint return or surviving spouse, $77,200,

(II) in the case of an individual who is a head of household (as defined in section 2(b)), $51,700,

(III) in the case of any other individual (other than an estate or trust), an amount equal to ½ of the amount in effect for the taxable year under subclause (I), and

(IV) in the case of an estate or trust, $2,600.

(ii) MAXIMUM 15-PERCENT RATE AMOUNT.—The maximum 15-percent rate amount shall be—

(I) in the case of a joint return or surviving spouse, $479,000 (½ such amount in the case of a married individual filing a separate return),

(II) in the case of an individual who is the head of a household (as defined in section 2(b)), $452,400,

(III) in the case of any other individual (other than an estate or trust), $425,800, and

(IV) in the case of an estate or trust, $12,700.

(C) INFLATION ADJUSTMENT.—In the case of any taxable year beginning after 2018, each of the dollar amounts in clauses (i) and (ii) of subparagraph (B) shall be increased by an amount equal to—

(i) such dollar amount, multiplied by

(ii) the cost-of-living adjustment determined under subsection (f)(3) for the calendar year in which the taxable year begins, determined by substituting "calendar year 2017" for "calendar year 2016" in subparagraph (A)(ii) thereof.

If any increase under this subparagraph is not a multiple of $50, such increase shall be rounded to the next lowest multiple of $50.

* * *

[Sec. 2]

SEC. 2. DEFINITIONS AND SPECIAL RULES.

[Sec. 2(a)]

(a) DEFINITION OF SURVIVING SPOUSE.—

(1) IN GENERAL.—For purposes of section 1, the term "surviving spouse" means a taxpayer—

(A) whose spouse died during either of his two taxable years immediately preceding the taxable year, and

(B) who maintains as his home a household which constitutes for the taxable year the principal place of abode (as a member of such household) of a dependent (i) who (within the meaning of section 152, determined without regard to subsections (b)(1), (b)(2), and (d)(1)(B) thereof) is a son, stepson, daughter, or stepdaughter of the taxpayer, and (ii) with respect to whom the taxpayer is entitled to a deduction for the taxable year under section 151.

For purposes of this paragraph, an individual shall be considered as maintaining a household only if over half of the cost of maintaining the household during the taxable year is furnished by such individual.

(2) LIMITATIONS.—Notwithstanding paragraph (1), for purposes of section 1 a taxpayer shall not be considered to be a surviving spouse—

(A) if the taxpayer has remarried at any time before the close of the taxable year, or

(B) unless, for the taxpayer's taxable year during which his spouse died, a joint return could have been made under the provisions of section 6013 (without regard to subsection (a)(3) thereof).

* * *

[Sec. 2(b)]

(b) DEFINITION OF HEAD OF HOUSEHOLD.—

(1) IN GENERAL.—For purposes of this subtitle, an individual shall be considered a head of a household if, and only if, such individual is not married at the close of his taxable year, is not a surviving spouse (as defined in subsection (a)), and either—

(A) maintains as his home a household which constitutes for more than one-half of such taxable year the principal place of abode, as a member of such household, of—

(i) a qualifying child of the individual (as defined in section 152(c), determined without regard to section 152(e)), but not if such child—

(I) is married at the close of the taxpayer's taxable year, and

(II) is not a dependent of such individual by reason of section 152(b)(2) or 152(b)(3), or both, or

(ii) any other person who is a dependent of the taxpayer, if the taxpayer is entitled to a deduction for the taxable year for such person under section 151, or

(B) maintains a household which constitutes for such taxable year the principal place of abode of the father or mother of the taxpayer, if the taxpayer is entitled to a deduction for the taxable year for such father or mother under section 151.

For purposes of this paragraph, an individual shall be considered as maintaining a household only if over half of the cost of maintaining the household during the taxable year is furnished by such individual.

(2) DETERMINATION OF STATUS.—For purposes of this subsection—

(A) an individual who is legally separated from his spouse under a decree of divorce or of separate maintenance shall not be considered as married;

(B) a taxpayer shall be considered as not married at the close of his taxable year if at any time during the taxable year his spouse is a nonresident alien; and

(C) a taxpayer shall be considered as married at the close of his taxable year if his spouse (other than a spouse described in subparagraph (B)) died during the taxable year.

(3) LIMITATIONS.—Notwithstanding paragraph (1), for purposes of this subtitle a taxpayer shall not be considered to be a head of a household—

(A) if at any time during the taxable year he is a nonresident alien; or

(B) by reason of an individual who would not be a dependent for the taxable year but for—

(i) subparagraph (H) of section 152(d)(2), or

(ii) paragraph (3) of section 152(d).

[Sec. 2(c)]

(c) CERTAIN MARRIED INDIVIDUALS LIVING APART.—For purposes of this part, an individual shall be treated as not married at the close of the taxable year if such individual is so treated under the provisions of section 7703(b).

* * *

[Sec. 3]

SEC. 3. TAX TABLES FOR INDIVIDUALS.

[Sec. 3(a)]

(a) IMPOSITION OF TAX TABLE TAX.—

(1) IN GENERAL.—In lieu of the tax imposed by section 1, there is hereby imposed for each taxable year on the taxable income of every individual—

(A) who does not itemize his deductions for the taxable year, and

(B) whose taxable income for such taxable year does not exceed the ceiling amount,

a tax determined under tables, applicable to such taxable year, which shall be prescribed by the Secretary and which shall be in such form as he determines appropriate. In the table so prescribed, the amounts of the tax shall be computed on the basis of the rates prescribed by section 1.

(2) CEILING AMOUNT DEFINED.—For purposes of paragraph (1), the term "ceiling amount" means, with respect to any taxpayer, the amount (not less than $20,000) determined by the Secretary for the tax rate category in which such taxpayer falls.

(3) AUTHORITY TO PRESCRIBE TABLES FOR TAXPAYERS WHO ITEMIZE DEDUCTIONS.—The Secretary may provide that this section shall apply also for any taxable year to individuals who itemize their deductions. Any tables prescribed under the preceding sentence shall be on the basis of taxable income.

[Sec. 3(b)]

(b) SECTION INAPPLICABLE TO CERTAIN INDIVIDUALS.—This section shall not apply to—

(1) an individual making a return under section 443(a)(1) for a period of less than 12 months on account of a change in annual accounting period, and

(2) an estate or trust.

* * *

PART II—TAX ON CORPORATIONS

[Sec. 11]

SEC. 11. TAX IMPOSED.

[Sec. 11(a)]

(a) CORPORATIONS IN GENERAL.—A tax is hereby imposed for each taxable year on the taxable income of every corporation.

[Sec. 11(b)]

(b) AMOUNT OF TAX.—The amount of the tax imposed by subsection (a) shall be 21 percent of taxable income.

[Sec. 11(c)]

(c) EXCEPTIONS.—Subsection (a) shall not apply to a corporation subject to a tax imposed by—

(1) section 594 (relating to mutual savings banks conducting life insurance business),

(2) subchapter L (sec. 801 and following, relating to insurance companies), or

(3) subchapter M (sec. 851 and following, relating to regulated investment companies and real estate investment trusts).

* * *

PART IV—CREDITS AGAINST TAX

Subpart A—Nonrefundable Personal Credits

[Sec. 21]

SEC. 21. EXPENSES FOR HOUSEHOLD AND DEPENDENT CARE SERVICES NECESSARY FOR GAINFUL EMPLOYMENT.

[Sec. 21(a)]

(a) ALLOWANCE OF CREDIT.—

(1) IN GENERAL.—In the case of an individual for which there are 1 or more qualifying individuals (as defined in subsection (b)(1)) with respect to such individual, there shall be allowed as a credit against the tax imposed by this chapter for the taxable year an amount equal to the applicable percentage of the employment-related expenses (as defined in subsection (b)(2)) paid by such individual during the taxable year.

(2) APPLICABLE PERCENTAGE DEFINED.—For purposes of paragraph (1), the term "applicable percentage" means 35 percent reduced (but not below 20 percent) by 1 percentage point for each $2,000 (or fraction thereof) by which the taxpayer's adjusted gross income for the taxable year exceeds $15,000.

[Sec. 21(b)]

(b) DEFINITIONS OF QUALIFYING INDIVIDUAL AND EMPLOYMENT-RELATED EXPENSES.—For purposes of this section—

(1) QUALIFYING INDIVIDUAL.—The term "qualifying individual" means—

(A) a dependent of the taxpayer (as defined in section 152(a)(1)) who has not attained age 13,

(B) a dependent of the taxpayer (as defined in section 152, determined without regard to subsections (b)(1), (b)(2), and (d)(1)(B)) who is physically or mentally incapable of caring for himself or herself and who has the same principal place of abode as the taxpayer for more than one-half of such taxable year, or

(C) the spouse of the taxpayer, if the spouse is physically or mentally incapable of caring for himself or herself and who has the same principal place of abode as the taxpayer for more than one-half of such taxable year.

(2) EMPLOYMENT-RELATED EXPENSES.—

(A) IN GENERAL.—The term "employment-related expenses" means amounts paid for the following expenses, but only if such expenses are incurred to enable the taxpayer to be gainfully employed for any period for which there are 1 or more qualifying individuals with respect to the taxpayer:

(i) expenses for household services, and

(ii) expenses for the care of a qualifying individual.

Such term shall not include any amount paid for services outside the taxpayer's household at a camp where the qualifying individual stays overnight.

(B) EXCEPTION.—Employment-related expenses described in subparagraph (A) which are incurred for services outside the taxpayer's household shall be taken into account only if incurred for the care of—

(i) a qualifying individual described in paragraph (1)(A), or

(ii) a qualifying individual (not described in paragraph (1)(A)) who regularly spends at least 8 hours each day in the taxpayer's household.

(C) DEPENDENT CARE CENTERS.—Employment-related expenses described in subparagraph (A) which are incurred for services provided outside the taxpayer's household by a dependent care center (as defined in subparagraph (D)) shall be taken into account only if—

(i) such center complies with all applicable laws and regulations of a State or unit of local government, and

(ii) the requirements of subparagraph (B) are met.

(D) DEPENDENT CARE CENTER DEFINED.—For purposes of this paragraph, the term "dependent care center" means any facility which—

(i) provides care for more than six individuals (other than individuals who reside at the facility), and

(ii) receives a fee, payment, or grant for providing services for any of the individuals (regardless of whether such facility is operated for profit).

[Sec. 21(c)]

(c) DOLLAR LIMIT ON AMOUNT CREDITABLE.—The amount of the employment-related expenses incurred during any taxable year which may be taken into account under subsection (a) shall not exceed—

(1) $3,000 if there is 1 qualifying individual with respect to the taxpayer for such taxable year, or

(2) $6,000 if there are 2 or more qualifying individuals with respect to the taxpayer for such taxable year.

The amount determined under paragraph (1) or (2) (whichever is applicable) shall be reduced by the aggregate amount excludable from gross income under section 129 for the taxable year.

[Sec. 21(d)]

(d) EARNED INCOME LIMITATION.—

(1) IN GENERAL.—Except as otherwise provided in this subsection, the amount of the employment-related expenses incurred during any taxable year which may be taken into account under subsection (a) shall not exceed—

(A) in the case of an individual who is not married at the close of such year, such individual's earned income for such year, or

(B) in the case of an individual who is married at the close of such year, the lesser of such individual's earned income or the earned income of his spouse for such year.

(2) SPECIAL RULE FOR SPOUSE WHO IS A STUDENT OR INCAPABLE OF CARING FOR HIMSELF.—In the case of a spouse who is a student or a qualified individual described in subsection (b)(1)(C), for purposes of paragraph (1), such spouse shall be deemed for each month during which such spouse is a full-time student at an educational institution, or is such a qualifying individual, to be gainfully employed and to have earned income of not less than—

(A) $250 if subsection (c)(1) applies for the taxable year, or

(B) $500 if subsection (c)(2) applies for the taxable year.

In the case of any husband and wife, this paragraph shall apply with respect to only one spouse for any one month.

[Sec. 21(e)]

(e) SPECIAL RULES.—For purposes of this section—

(1) PLACE OF ABODE.—An individual shall not be treated as having the same principal place of abode of the taxpayer if at any time during the taxable year of the taxpayer the relationship between the individual and the taxpayer is in violation of local law.

(2) MARRIED COUPLES MUST FILE JOINT RETURN.—If the taxpayer is married at the close of the taxable year, the credit shall be allowed under subsection (a) only if the taxpayer and his spouse file a joint return for the taxable year.

(3) MARITAL STATUS.—An individual legally separated from his spouse under a decree of divorce or of separate maintenance shall not be considered as married.

(4) CERTAIN MARRIED INDIVIDUALS LIVING APART.—If—

(A) an individual who is married and who files a separate return—

(i) maintains as his home a household which constitutes for more than one-half of the taxable year the principal place of abode of a qualifying individual, and

(ii) furnishes over half of the cost of maintaining such household during the taxable year, and

(B) during the last 6 months of such taxable year such individual's spouse is not a member of such household,

such individual shall not be considered as married.

(5) SPECIAL DEPENDENCY TEST IN CASE OF DIVORCED PARENTS, ETC.—If—

(A) section 152(e) applies to any child with respect to any calendar year, and

(B) such child is under the age of 13 or is physically or mentally incapable of caring for himself,

in the case of any taxable year beginning in such calendar year, such child shall be treated as a qualifying individual described in subparagraph (A) or (B) of subsection (b)(1) (whichever is appropriate) with respect to the custodial parent (as defined in section 152(e)(4)(A)), and shall not be treated as a qualifying individual with respect to the noncustodial parent.

(6) PAYMENTS TO RELATED INDIVIDUALS.—No credit shall be allowed under subsection (a) for any amount paid by the taxpayer to an individual—

(A) with respect to whom, for the taxable year, a deduction under section 151(c) (relating to deduction for personal exemptions for dependents) is allowable either to the taxpayer or his spouse, or

(B) who is a child of the taxpayer (within the meaning of section 152(f)(1)) who has not attained the age of 19 at the close of the taxable year.

For purposes of this paragraph, the term "taxable year" means the taxable year of the taxpayer in which the service is performed.

(7) STUDENT.—The term "student" means an individual who during each of 5 calendar months during the taxable year is a full-time student at an educational organization.

(8) EDUCATIONAL ORGANIZATION.—The term "educational organization" means an educational organization described in section 170(b)(1)(A)(ii).

(9) IDENTIFYING INFORMATION REQUIRED WITH RESPECT TO SERVICE PROVIDER.—No credit shall be allowed under subsection (a) for any amount paid to any person unless—

(A) the name, address, and taxpayer identification number of such person are included on the return claiming the credit, or

(B) if such person is an organization described in section 501(c)(3) and exempt from tax under section 501(a), the name and address of such person are included on the return claiming the credit.

In the case of a failure to provide the information required under the preceding sentence, the preceding sentence shall not apply if it is shown that the taxpayer exercised due diligence in attempting to provide the information so required.

(10) IDENTIFYING INFORMATION REQUIRED WITH RESPECT TO QUALIFYING INDIVIDUALS.—No credit shall be allowed under this section with respect to any qualifying individual unless the TIN of such individual is included on the return claiming the credit.

[Sec. 21(f)]

(f) REGULATIONS.—The Secretary shall prescribe such regulations as may be necessary to carry out the purposes of this section.

»»→ Caution: As provided in Section 23(h), the dollar amounts set forth in Section (a)(3), (b)(1), and (b)(2)(A)(i) are adjusted for taxable years beginning after 2002 to reflect increases in the Chained Consumer Price Index. The adjusted amounts applicable to taxable years beginning in 2020 are provided in the material beginning at page ix.

[Sec. 23]

SEC. 23. ADOPTION EXPENSES.

[Sec. 23(a)]

(a) ALLOWANCE OF CREDIT.—

(1) IN GENERAL.—In the case of an individual, there shall be allowed as a credit against the tax imposed by this chapter the amount of the qualified adoption expenses paid or incurred by the taxpayer.

(2) YEAR CREDIT ALLOWED.—The credit under paragraph (1) with respect to any expense shall be allowed—

(A) in the case of any expense paid or incurred before the taxable year in which such adoption becomes final, for the taxable year following the taxable year during which such expense is paid or incurred, and

(B) in the case of an expense paid or incurred during or after the taxable year in which such adoption becomes final, for the taxable year in which such expense is paid or incurred.

(3) $10,000 CREDIT FOR ADOPTION OF CHILD WITH SPECIAL NEEDS REGARDLESS OF EXPENSES.—In the case of an adoption of a child with special needs which becomes final during a taxable year, the taxpayer shall be treated as having paid during such year qualified adoption expenses with respect to such adoption in an amount equal to the excess (if any) of $10,000 over the aggregate qualified adoption expenses actually paid or incurred by the taxpayer with respect to such adoption during such taxable year and all prior taxable years.

[Sec. 23(b)]

(b) LIMITATIONS.—

(1) DOLLAR LIMITATION.—The aggregate amount of qualified adoption expenses which may be taken into account under subsection (a) for all taxable years with respect to the adoption of a child by the taxpayer shall not exceed $10,000.

(2) INCOME LIMITATION.—

(A) IN GENERAL.—The amount allowable as a credit under subsection (a) for any taxable year (determined without regard to subsection (c)) shall be reduced (but not below zero) by an amount which bears the same ratio to the amount so allowable (determined without regard to this paragraph but with regard to paragraph (1)) as—

(i) the amount (if any) by which the taxpayer's adjusted gross income exceeds $150,000, bears to

(ii) $40,000.

(B) DETERMINATION OF ADJUSTED GROSS INCOME.—For purposes of subparagraph (A), adjusted gross income shall be determined without regard to sections 911, 931, and 933.

(3) DENIAL OF DOUBLE BENEFIT.—

(A) IN GENERAL.—No credit shall be allowed under subsection (a) for any expense for which a deduction or credit is allowed under any other provision of this chapter.

(B) GRANTS.—No credit shall be allowed under subsection (a) for any expense to the extent that funds for such expense are received under any Federal, State, or local program.

[Sec. 23(c)]

(c) CARRYFORWARDS OF UNUSED CREDIT.—

(1) IN GENERAL.—If the credit allowable under subsection (a) for any taxable year exceeds the limitation imposed by section 26(a) for such taxable year reduced by the sum of the credits allowable under this subpart (other than this section and section 25D), such excess shall be carried to the succeeding taxable year and added to the credit allowable under subsection (a) for such taxable year.

(2) LIMITATION.—No credit may be carried forward under this subsection to any taxable year following the fifth taxable year after the taxable year in which the credit arose. For purposes of the preceding sentence, credits shall be treated as used on a first-in first-out basis.

[Sec. 23(d)]

(d) DEFINITIONS.—For purposes of this section—

(1) QUALIFIED ADOPTION EXPENSES.—The term "qualified adoption expenses" means reasonable and necessary adoption fees, court costs, attorney fees, and other expenses—

(A) which are directly related to, and the principal purpose of which is for, the legal adoption of an eligible child by the taxpayer,

(B) which are not incurred in violation of State or Federal law or in carrying out any surrogate parenting arrangement,

(C) which are not expenses in connection with the adoption by an individual of a child who is the child of such individual's spouse, and

(D) which are not reimbursed under an employer program or otherwise.

(2) ELIGIBLE CHILD.—The term "eligible child" means any individual who—

(A) has not attained age 18, or

(B) is physically or mentally incapable of caring for himself.

(3) CHILD WITH SPECIAL NEEDS.—The term "child with special needs" means any child if—

(A) a State has determined that the child cannot or should not be returned to the home of his parents,

(B) such State has determined that there exists with respect to the child a specific factor or condition (such as his ethnic background, age, or membership in a minority or sibling group, or the presence of factors such as medical conditions or physical, mental, or emotional handicaps) because of which it is reasonable to conclude that such child cannot be placed with adoptive parents without providing adoption assistance, and

(C) such child is a citizen or resident of the United States (as defined in section 217(h)(3)).

[Sec. 23(e)]

(e) SPECIAL RULES FOR FOREIGN ADOPTIONS.—In the case of an adoption of a child who is not a citizen or resident of the United States (as defined in section 217(h)(3))—

(1) subsection (a) shall not apply to any qualified adoption expense with respect to such adoption unless such adoption becomes final, and

(2) any such expense which is paid or incurred before the taxable year in which such adoption becomes final shall be taken into account under this section as if such expense were paid or incurred during such year.

[Sec. 23(f)]

(f) FILING REQUIREMENTS.—

(1) MARRIED COUPLES MUST FILE JOINT RETURNS.—Rules similar to the rules of paragraphs (2), (3), and (4) of section 21(e) shall apply for purposes of this section.

(2) TAXPAYER MUST INCLUDE TIN.—

(A) IN GENERAL.—No credit shall be allowed under this section with respect to any eligible child unless the taxpayer includes (if known) the name, age, and TIN of such child on the return of tax for the taxable year.

(B) OTHER METHODS.—The Secretary may, in lieu of the information referred to in subparagraph (A), require other information meeting the purposes of subparagraph (A), including identification of an agent assisting with the adoption.

[Sec. 23(g)]

(g) BASIS ADJUSTMENTS.—For purposes of this subtitle, if a credit is allowed under this section for any expenditure with respect to any property, the increase in the basis of such property which would (but for this subsection) result from such expenditure shall be reduced by the amount of the credit so allowed.

[Sec. 23(h)]

(h) ADJUSTMENTS FOR INFLATION.—In the case of a taxable year beginning after December 31, 2002, each of the dollar amounts in subsection (a)(3) and paragraphs (1) and (2)(A)(i) of subsection (b) shall be increased by an amount equal to—

(1) such dollar amount, multiplied by

(2) the cost-of-living adjustment determined under section 1(f)(3) for the calendar year in which the taxable year begins, determined by substituting "calendar year 2001" for "calendar year 2016" in subparagraph (A) thereof.

If any amount as increased under the preceding sentence is not a multiple of $10, such amount shall be rounded to the nearest multiple of $10.

[Sec. 23(i)]

(i) REGULATIONS.—The Secretary shall prescribe such regulations as may be appropriate to carry out this section and section 137, including regulations which treat unmarried individuals who pay or incur qualified adoption expenses with respect to the same child as 1 taxpayer for purposes of applying the dollar amounts in subsections (a)(3) and (b)(1) of this section and in section 137(b)(1).

»»→ Caution: As provided in Section 24(h)(5)(B), the dollar amount set forth in Section 24(h)(5)(A) is adjusted for taxable years beginning after 2018 to reflect increases in the Chained Consumer Price Index. The adjusted amount applicable to taxable years beginning in 2020 is provided in the material beginning at page ix.

[Sec. 24]

SEC. 24. CHILD TAX CREDIT.

[Sec. 24(a)]

(a) ALLOWANCE OF CREDIT.—There shall be allowed as a credit against the tax imposed by this chapter for the taxable year with respect to each qualifying child of the taxpayer for which the taxpayer is allowed a deduction under section 151 an amount equal to $1,000.

[Sec. 24(b)]

(b) LIMITATIONS.—

(1) LIMITATION BASED ON ADJUSTED GROSS INCOME.—The amount of the credit allowable under subsection (a) shall be reduced (but not below zero) by $50 for each $1,000 (or fraction thereof) by which the taxpayer's modified adjusted gross income exceeds the threshold amount. For purposes of the preceding sentence, the term "modified adjusted gross income" means adjusted gross income increased by any amount excluded from gross income under section 911, 931, or 933.

(2) THRESHOLD AMOUNT.—For purposes of paragraph (1), the term "threshold amount" means—

(A) $110,000 in the case of a joint return,

(B) $75,000 in the case of an individual who is not married, and

(C) $55,000 in the case of a married individual filing a separate return.

For purposes of this paragraph, marital status shall be determined under section 7703.

[Sec. 24(c)]

(c) QUALIFYING CHILD.—For purposes of this section—

(1) IN GENERAL.—The term "qualifying child" means a qualifying child of the taxpayer (as defined in section 152(c)) who has not attained age 17.

(2) EXCEPTION FOR CERTAIN NONCITIZENS.—The term "qualifying child" shall not include any individual who would not be a dependent if subparagraph (A) of section 152(b)(3) were applied without regard to all that follows "resident of the United States".

[Sec. 24(d)]

(d) PORTION OF CREDIT REFUNDABLE.—

(1) IN GENERAL.—The aggregate credits allowed to a taxpayer under subpart C shall be increased by the lesser of—

(A) the credit which would be allowed under this section without regard to this subsection and the limitation under section 26(a) or

(B) the amount by which the aggregate amount of credits allowed by this subpart (determined without regard to this subsection) would increase if the limitation imposed by section 26(a) were increased by the greater of—

(i) 15 percent of so much of the taxpayer's earned income (within the meaning of section 32) which is taken into account in computing taxable income for the taxable year as exceeds $3,000, or

(ii) in the case of a taxpayer with 3 or more qualifying children, the excess (if any) of—

(I) the taxpayer's social security taxes for the taxable year, over

(II) the credit allowed under section 32 for the taxable year.

The amount of the credit allowed under this subsection shall not be treated as a credit allowed under this subpart and shall reduce the amount of credit otherwise allowable under subsection (a) without regard to section 26(a). For purposes of subparagraph (B), any amount excluded from gross income by reason of section 112 shall be treated as earned income which is taken into account in computing taxable income for the taxable year.

(2) SOCIAL SECURITY TAXES.—For purposes of paragraph (1)—

(A) IN GENERAL.—The term "social security taxes" means, with respect to any taxpayer for any taxable year—

(i) the amount of the taxes imposed by sections 3101 and 3201(a) on amounts received by the taxpayer during the calendar year in which the taxable year begins,

(ii) 50 percent of the taxes imposed by section 1401 on the self-employment income of the taxpayer for the taxable year, and

(iii) 50 percent of the taxes imposed by section 3211(a) on amounts received by the taxpayer during the calendar year in which the taxable year begins.

(B) COORDINATION WITH SPECIAL REFUND OF SOCIAL SECURITY TAXES.—The term "social security taxes" shall not include any taxes to the extent the taxpayer is entitled to a special refund of such taxes under section 6413(c).

(C) SPECIAL RULE.—Any amounts paid pursuant to an agreement under section 3121(l) (relating to agreements entered into by American employers with respect to foreign affiliates) which are equivalent to the taxes referred to in subparagraph (A)(i) shall be treated as taxes referred to in such subparagraph.

(3) EXCEPTION FOR TAXPAYERS EXCLUDING FOREIGN EARNED INCOME.—Paragraph (1) shall not apply to any taxpayer for any taxable year if such taxpayer elects to exclude any amount from gross income under section 911 for such taxable year.

[Sec. 24(e)]

(e) IDENTIFICATION REQUIREMENTS.—

(1) QUALIFYING CHILD IDENTIFICATION REQUIREMENT.—No credit shall be allowed under this section to a taxpayer with respect to any qualifying child unless the taxpayer includes the name and taxpayer identification number of such qualifying child on the return of tax for the taxable year and such taxpayer identification number was issued on or before the due date for filing such return.

(2) TAXPAYER IDENTIFICATION REQUIREMENT.—No credit shall be allowed under this section if the taxpayer identification number of the taxpayer was issued after the due date for filing the return for the taxable year.

[Sec. 24(f)]

(f) TAXABLE YEAR MUST BE FULL TAXABLE YEAR.—Except in the case of a taxable year closed by reason of the death of the taxpayer, no credit shall be allowable under this section in the case of a taxable year covering a period of less than 12 months.

[Sec. 24(g)]

(g) RESTRICTIONS ON TAXPAYERS WHO IMPROPERLY CLAIMED CREDIT IN PRIOR YEAR.—

(1) TAXPAYERS MAKING PRIOR FRAUDULENT OR RECKLESS CLAIMS.—

(A) IN GENERAL.—No credit shall be allowed under this section for any taxable year in the disallowance period.

(B) DISALLOWANCE PERIOD.—For purposes of subparagraph (A), the disallowance period is—

(i) the period of 10 taxable years after the most recent taxable year for which there was a final determination that the taxpayer's claim of credit under this section was due to fraud, and

(ii) the period of 2 taxable years after the most recent taxable year for which there was a final determination that the taxpayer's claim of credit under this section was due to reckless or intentional disregard of rules and regulations (but not due to fraud).

(2) TAXPAYERS MAKING IMPROPER PRIOR CLAIMS.—In the case of a taxpayer who is denied credit under this section for any taxable year as a result of the deficiency procedures under subchapter B of chapter 63, no credit shall be allowed under this section for any subsequent taxable year unless the taxpayer provides such information as the Secretary may require to demonstrate eligibility for such credit.

[Sec. 24(h)]

(h) SPECIAL RULES FOR TAXABLE YEARS 2018 THROUGH 2025.—

(1) IN GENERAL.—In the case of a taxable year beginning after December 31, 2017, and before January 1, 2026, this section shall be applied as provided in paragraphs (2) through (7).

(2) CREDIT AMOUNT.—Subsection (a) shall be applied by substituting "$2,000" for "$1,000".

(3) LIMITATION.—In lieu of the amount determined under subsection (b)(2), the threshold amount shall be $400,000 in the case of a joint return ($200,000 in any other case).

(4) PARTIAL CREDIT ALLOWED FOR CERTAIN OTHER DEPENDENTS.—

(A) IN GENERAL.—The credit determined under subsection (a) (after the application of paragraph (2)) shall be increased by $500 for each dependent of the taxpayer (as defined in section 152) other than a qualifying child described in subsection (c).

(B) EXCEPTION FOR CERTAIN NONCITIZENS.—Subparagraph (A) shall not apply with respect to any individual who would not be a dependent if subparagraph (A) of section 152(b)(3) were applied without regard to all that follows "resident of the United States".

(C) CERTAIN QUALIFYING CHILDREN.—In the case of any qualifying child with respect to whom a credit is not allowed under this section by reason of paragraph (7), such child shall be treated as a dependent to whom subparagraph (A) applies.

(5) MAXIMUM AMOUNT OF REFUNDABLE CREDIT.—

(A) IN GENERAL.—The amount determined under subsection (d)(1)(A) with respect to any qualifying child shall not exceed $1,400, and such subsection shall be applied without regard to paragraph (4) of this subsection.

(B) ADJUSTMENT FOR INFLATION.—In the case of a taxable year beginning after 2018, the $1,400 amount in subparagraph (A) shall be increased by an amount equal to—

(i) such dollar amount, multiplied by

(ii) the cost-of-living adjustment determined under section 1(f)(3) for the calendar year in which the taxable year begins, determined by substituting "2017" for "2016" in subparagraph (A)(ii) thereof.

If any increase under this clause is not a multiple of $100, such increase shall be rounded to the next lowest multiple of $100.

(6) EARNED INCOME THRESHOLD FOR REFUNDABLE CREDIT.—Subsection (d)(1)(B)(i) shall be applied by substituting "$2,500" for "$3,000".

(7) SOCIAL SECURITY NUMBER REQUIRED.—No credit shall be allowed under this section to a taxpayer with respect to any qualifying child unless the taxpayer includes the social security number of such child on the return of tax for the taxable year. For purposes of the preceding sentence, the term "social security number" means a social security number issued to an individual by the Social Security Administration, but only if the social security number is issued—

(A) to a citizen of the United States or pursuant to subclause (I) (or that portion of subclause (III) that relates to subclause (I)) of section 205(c)(2)(B)(i) of the Social Security Act, and

(B) before the due date for such return.

Caution: As provided in Section 25A(h), the amounts provided in Section 25A(d)(2) are adjusted for taxable years after 2001 to reflect increases in the Chained Consumer Price Index. The adjusted amounts applicable to taxable years beginning in 2020 are provided in the material beginning at page ix.

[Sec. 25A]

SEC. 25A. AMERICAN OPPORTUNITY AND LIFETIME LEARNING CREDITS.

[Sec. 25A(a)]

(a) ALLOWANCE OF CREDIT.—In the case of an individual, there shall be allowed as a credit against the tax imposed by this chapter for the taxable year the amount equal to the sum of—

(1) the American Opportunity Tax Credit, plus

(2) the Lifetime Learning Credit.

[Sec. 25A(b)]

(b) AMERICAN OPPORTUNITY TAX CREDIT.—

(1) PER STUDENT CREDIT.—In the case of any eligible student for whom an election is in effect under this section for any taxable year, the American Opportunity Tax Credit is an amount equal to the sum of—

(A) 100 percent of so much of the qualified tuition and related expenses paid by the taxpayer during the taxable year (for education furnished to the eligible student during any academic period beginning in such taxable year) as does not exceed $2,000, plus

(B) 25 percent of such expenses so paid as exceeds $2,000 but does not exceed $4,000.

(2) LIMITATIONS APPLICABLE TO AMERICAN OPPORTUNITY TAX CREDIT.—

(A) CREDIT ALLOWED ONLY FOR 4 TAXABLE YEARS.—An election to have this section apply with respect to any eligible student for purposes of the American Opportunity Tax Credit under subsection (a)(1) may not be made for any taxable year if such an election (by the taxpayer or any other individual) is in effect with respect to such student for any 4 prior taxable years.

(B) CREDIT ALLOWED FOR YEAR ONLY IF INDIVIDUAL IS AT LEAST ½ TIME STUDENT FOR PORTION OF YEAR.—The American Opportunity Tax Credit under subsection (a)(1) shall not be allowed for a taxable year with respect to the qualified tuition and related expenses of an individual unless such individual is an eligible student for at least one academic period which begins during such year.

(C) CREDIT ALLOWED ONLY FOR FIRST 4 YEARS OF POSTSECONDARY EDUCATION.—The American Opportunity Tax Credit under subsection (a)(1) shall not be allowed for a taxable year with respect to the qualified tuition and related expenses of an eligible student if the student has completed (before the beginning of such taxable year) the first 4 years of postsecondary education at an eligible educational institution.

(D) DENIAL OF CREDIT IF STUDENT CONVICTED OF A FELONY DRUG OFFENSE.—The American Opportunity Tax Credit under subsection (a)(1) shall not be allowed for qualified tuition and related expenses for the enrollment or attendance of a student for any academic period if such student has been convicted of a Federal or State felony offense consisting of the possession or distribution of a controlled substance before the end of the taxable year with or within which such period ends.

(3) ELIGIBLE STUDENT.—For purposes of this subsection, the term "eligible student" means, with respect to any academic period, a student who—

(A) meets the requirements of section 484(a)(1) of the Higher Education Act of 1965 (20 U.S.C. 1091(a)(1)), as in effect on the date of the enactment of this section, and

(B) is carrying at least ½ the normal full-time work load for the course of study the student is pursuing.

(4) RESTRICTIONS ON TAXPAYERS WHO IMPROPERLY CLAIMED AMERICAN OPPORTUNITY TAX CREDIT IN PRIOR YEARS.—

(A) TAXPAYERS MAKING PRIOR FRAUDULENT OR RECKLESS CLAIMS.—

(i) IN GENERAL.—No American Opportunity Tax Credit shall be allowed under this section for any taxable year in the disallowance period.

(ii) DISALLOWANCE PERIOD.—For purposes of subparagraph (A), the disallowance period is—

(I) the period of 10 taxable years after the most recent taxable year for which there was a final determination that the taxpayer's claim of the American Opportunity Tax Credit under this section was due to fraud, and

(II) the period of 2 taxable years after the most recent taxable year for which there was a final determination that the taxpayer's claim of the American Opportunity Tax Credit under this section was due to reckless or intentional disregard of rules and regulations (but not due to fraud).

(B) TAXPAYERS MAKING IMPROPER PRIOR CLAIMS.—In the case of a taxpayer who is denied the American Opportunity Tax Credit under this section for any taxable year as a result of the deficiency procedures under subchapter B of chapter 63, no American Opportunity Tax Credit shall be allowed under this section for any subsequent taxable year unless the taxpayer provides such information as the Secretary may require to demonstrate eligibility for such credit.

[Sec. 25A(c)]

(c) LIFETIME LEARNING CREDIT.—

(1) PER TAXPAYER CREDIT.—The Lifetime Learning Credit for any taxpayer for any taxable year is an amount equal to 20 percent of so much of the qualified tuition and related expenses paid by the taxpayer during the taxable year (for education furnished during any academic period beginning in such taxable year) as does not exceed $10,000.

(2) SPECIAL RULES FOR DETERMINING EXPENSES.—

(A) COORDINATION WITH AMERICAN OPPORTUNITY TAX CREDIT.—The qualified tuition and related expenses with respect to an individual who is an eligible student for whom a American Opportunity Tax Credit under subsection (a)(1) is allowed for the taxable year shall not be taken into account under this subsection.

(B) EXPENSES ELIGIBLE FOR LIFETIME LEARNING CREDIT.—For purposes of paragraph (1), qualified tuition and related expenses shall include expenses described in subsection (f)(1) with respect to any course of instruction at an eligible educational institution to acquire or improve job skills of the individual.

[Sec. 25A(d)]

(d) LIMITATIONS BASED ON MODIFIED ADJUSTED GROSS INCOME.—

(1) AMERICAN OPPORTUNITY TAX CREDIT.—The American Opportunity Tax Credit (determined without regard to this paragraph) shall be reduced (but not below zero) by the amount which bears the same ratio to such credit (as so determined) as—

(A) the excess of—

(i) the taxpayer's modified adjusted gross income for such taxable year, over

(ii) $80,000 ($160,000 in the case of a joint return), bears to

(B) $10,000 ($20,000 in the case of a joint return).

(2) LIFETIME LEARNING CREDIT.—The Lifetime Learning Credit (determined without regard to this paragraph) shall be reduced (but not below zero) by the amount which bears the same ratio to such credit (as so determined) as—

(A) the excess of—

(i) the taxpayer's modified adjusted gross income for such taxable year, over

(ii) $40,000 ($80,000 in the case of a joint return), bears to

(B) $10,000 ($20,000 in the case of a joint return).

(3) MODIFIED ADJUSTED GROSS INCOME.—For purposes of this subsection, the term "modified adjusted gross income" means the adjusted gross income of the taxpayer for the taxable year increased by any amount excluded from gross income under section 911, 931, or 933.

[Sec. 25A(e)]

(e) ELECTION NOT TO HAVE SECTION APPLY.—A taxpayer may elect not to have this section apply with respect to the qualified tuition and related expenses of an individual for any taxable year.

[Sec. 25A(f)]

(f) DEFINITIONS.—For purposes of this section—

(1) QUALIFIED TUITION AND RELATED EXPENSES.—

(A) IN GENERAL.—The term "qualified tuition and related expenses" means tuition and fees required for the enrollment or attendance of—

(i) the taxpayer,

(ii) the taxpayer's spouse, or

(iii) any dependent of the taxpayer with respect to whom the taxpayer is allowed a deduction under section 151,

at an eligible educational institution for courses of instruction of such individual at such institution.

(B) EXCEPTION FOR EDUCATION INVOLVING SPORTS, ETC.—Such term does not include expenses with respect to any course or other education involving sports, games, or hobbies, unless such course or other education is part of the individual's degree program.

(C) EXCEPTION FOR NONACADEMIC FEES.—Such term does not include student activity fees, athletic fees, insurance expenses, or other expenses unrelated to an individual's academic course of instruction.

(D) REQUIRED COURSE MATERIALS TAKEN INTO ACCOUNT FOR AMERICAN OPPORTUNITY TAX CREDIT.—For purposes of determining the American Opportunity Tax Credit, subparagraph (A) shall be applied by substituting "tuition, fees, and course materials" for "tuition and fees".

(2) ELIGIBLE EDUCATIONAL INSTITUTION.—The term "eligible educational institution" means an institution—

(A) which is described in section 481 of the Higher Education Act of 1965 (20 U.S.C. 1088), as in effect on the date of the enactment of this section, and

(B) which is eligible to participate in a program under title IV of such Act.

[Sec. 25A(g)]

(g) SPECIAL RULES.—

(1) IDENTIFICATION REQUIREMENT.—

(A) IN GENERAL.—No credit shall be allowed under subsection (a) to a taxpayer with respect to the qualified tuition and related expenses of an individual unless the taxpayer includes the name and taxpayer identification number of such individual on the return of tax for the taxable year.

(B) ADDITIONAL IDENTIFICATION REQUIREMENTS WITH RESPECT TO AMERICAN OPPORTUNITY TAX CREDIT.—

(i) STUDENT.—The requirements of subparagraph (A) shall not be treated as met with respect to the American Opportunity Tax Credit unless the individual's taxpayer identification number was issued on or before the due date for filing the return of tax for the taxable year.

(ii) TAXPAYER.—No American Opportunity Tax Credit shall be allowed under this section if the taxpayer identification number of the taxpayer was issued after the due date for filing the return for the taxable year.

(iii) INSTITUTION.—No American Opportunity Tax Credit shall be allowed under this section unless the taxpayer includes the employer identification number of any institution to which qualified tuition and related expenses were paid with respect to the individual.

(2) ADJUSTMENT FOR CERTAIN SCHOLARSHIPS, ETC.—The amount of qualified tuition and related expenses otherwise taken into account under subsection (a) with respect to an individual for an academic period shall be reduced (before the application of subsections (b), (c), and (d)) by the sum of any amounts paid for the benefit of such individual which are allocable to such period as—

(A) a qualified scholarship which is excludable from gross income under section 117,

(B) an educational assistance allowance under chapter 30, 31, 32, 34, or 35 of title 38, United States Code, or under chapter 1606 of title 10, United States Code, and

(C) a payment (other than a gift, bequest, devise, or inheritance within the meaning of section 102(a)) for such individual's educational expenses, or attributable to such individual's enrollment at an eligible educational institution, which is excludable from gross income under any law of the United States.

(3) TREATMENT OF EXPENSES PAID BY DEPENDENT.—If a deduction under section 151 with respect to an individual is allowed to another taxpayer for a taxable year beginning in the calendar year in which such individual's taxable year begins—

(A) no credit shall be allowed under subsection (a) to such individual for such individual's taxable year,

(B) qualified tuition and related expenses paid by such individual during such individual's taxable year shall be treated for purposes of this section as paid by such other taxpayer, and

(C) a statement described in paragraph (8) and received by such individual shall be treated as received by the taxpayer.

(4) TREATMENT OF CERTAIN PREPAYMENTS.—If qualified tuition and related expenses are paid by the taxpayer during a taxable year for an academic period which begins during the first 3 months following such taxable year, such academic period shall be treated for purposes of this section as beginning during such taxable year.

(5) DENIAL OF DOUBLE BENEFIT.—No credit shall be allowed under this section for any expense for which a deduction is allowed under any other provision of this chapter.

(6) NO CREDIT FOR MARRIED INDIVIDUALS FILING SEPARATE RETURNS.—If the taxpayer is a married individual (within the meaning of section 7703), this section shall apply only if the taxpayer and the taxpayer's spouse file a joint return for the taxable year.

(7) NONRESIDENT ALIENS.—If the taxpayer is a nonresident alien individual for any portion of the taxable year, this section shall apply only if such individual is treated as a resident alien of the United States for purposes of this chapter by reason of an election under subsection (g) or (h) of section 6013.

(8) PAYEE STATEMENT REQUIREMENT.—Except as otherwise provided by the Secretary, no credit shall be allowed under this section unless the taxpayer receives a statement furnished under section 6050S(d) which contains all of the information required by paragraph (2) thereof.

[Sec. 25A(h)]

(h) INFLATION ADJUSTMENT.—

(1) IN GENERAL.—In the case of a taxable year beginning after 2001, the $40,000 and $80,000 amounts in subsection (d)(2) shall each be increased by an amount equal to—

(A) such dollar amount, multiplied by

(B) the cost-of-living adjustment determined under section 1(f)(3) for the calendar year in which the taxable year begins, determined by substituting "calendar year 2000" for "calendar year 2016" in subparagraph (A)(ii) thereof.

(2) ROUNDING.—If any amount as adjusted under paragraph (1) is not a multiple of $1,000, such amount shall be rounded to the next lowest multiple of $1,000.

[Sec. 25A(i)]

(i) PORTION OF AMERICAN OPPORTUNITY TAX CREDIT MADE REFUNDABLE.—Forty percent of so much of the credit allowed under subsection (a) as is attributable to the American Opportunity Tax Credit (determined after application of subsection (d) and without regard to this paragraph and section 26(a)) shall be treated as a credit allowable under subpart C (and not allowed under subsection (a)). The preceding sentence shall not apply to any taxpayer for any taxable year if such taxpayer is a child to whom subsection (g) of section 1 applies for such taxable year.

[Sec. 25A(j)]

(j) REGULATIONS.—The Secretary may prescribe such regulations as may be necessary or appropriate to carry out this section, including regulations providing for a recapture of the credit allowed under this section in cases where there is a refund in a subsequent taxable year of any amount which was taken into account in determining the amount of such credit.

»»→ Caution: As provided in Section 25B(b)(3), the dollar amounts set forth in Section 25B(b)(1) are adjusted for taxable years after 2006 to reflect increases in the Chained Consumer Price Index. The amounts applicable to taxable years beginning in 2020 are provided in the material beginning at page xiv.

[Sec. 25B]

SEC. 25B. ELECTIVE DEFERRALS AND IRA CONTRIBUTIONS BY CERTAIN INDIVIDUALS.

[Sec. 25B(a)]

(a) ALLOWANCE OF CREDIT.—In the case of an eligible individual, there shall be allowed as a credit against the tax imposed by this subtitle for the taxable year an amount equal to the applicable percentage of so much of the qualified retirement savings contributions of the eligible individual for the taxable year as do not exceed $2,000.

[Sec. 25B(b)]

(b) APPLICABLE PERCENTAGE.—For purposes of this section—

(1) JOINT RETURNS.—In the case of a joint return, the applicable percentage is—

(A) if the adjusted gross income of the taxpayer is not over $30,000, 50 percent,

(B) if the adjusted gross income of the taxpayer is over $30,000 but not over $32,500, 20 percent,

(C) if the adjusted gross income of the taxpayer is over $32,500 but not over $50,000, 10 percent, and

(D) if the adjusted gross income of the taxpayer is over $50,000, zero percent.

(2) OTHER RETURNS.—In the case of—

(A) a head of household, the applicable percentage shall be determined under paragraph (1) except that such paragraph shall be applied by substituting for each dollar amount therein (as adjusted under paragraph (3)) a dollar amount equal to 75 percent of such dollar amount, and

(B) any taxpayer not described in paragraph (1) or subparagraph (A), the applicable percentage shall be determined under paragraph (1) except that such paragraph shall be applied by substituting for each dollar amount therein (as adjusted under paragraph (3)) a dollar amount equal to 50 percent of such dollar amount.

(3) INFLATION ADJUSTMENT.—In the case of any taxable year beginning in a calendar year after 2006, each of the dollar amount[s] in paragraph (1) shall be increased by an amount equal to—

(A) such dollar amount, multiplied by

(B) the cost-of-living adjustment determined under section 1(f)(3) for the calendar year in which the taxable year begins, determined by substituting "calendar year 2005" for "calendar year 2016" in subparagraph (A)(ii) thereof.

Any increase determined under the preceding sentence shall be rounded to the nearest multiple of $500.

[Sec. 25B(c)]

(c) ELIGIBLE INDIVIDUAL.—For purposes of this section—

(1) IN GENERAL.—The term "eligible individual" means any individual if such individual has attained the age of 18 as of the close of the taxable year.

(2) DEPENDENTS AND FULL-TIME STUDENTS NOT ELIGIBLE.—The term "eligible individual" shall not include—

(A) any individual with respect to whom a deduction under section 151 is allowed to another taxpayer for a taxable year beginning in the calendar year in which such individual's taxable year begins, and

(B) any individual who is a student (as defined in section 152(f)(2)).

[Sec. 25B(d)]

(d) QUALIFIED RETIREMENT SAVINGS CONTRIBUTIONS.—For purposes of this section—

(1) IN GENERAL.—The term "qualified retirement savings contributions" means, with respect to any taxable year, the sum of—

(A) the amount of the qualified retirement contributions (as defined in section 219(e)) made by the eligible individual,

(B) the amount of—

(i) any elective deferrals (as defined in section 402(g)(3)) of such individual, and

(ii) any elective deferral of compensation by such individual under an eligible deferred compensation plan (as defined in section 457(b)) of an eligible employer described in section 457(e)(1)(A),

(C) the amount of voluntary employee contributions by such individual to any qualified retirement plan (as defined in section 4974(c)), and

(D) the amount of contributions made before January 1, 2026, by such individual to the ABLE account (within the meaning of section 529A) of which such individual is the designated beneficiary.

(2) REDUCTION FOR CERTAIN DISTRIBUTIONS.—

(A) IN GENERAL.—The qualified retirement savings contributions determined under paragraph (1) shall be reduced (but not below zero) by the aggregate distributions received by the individual during the testing period from any entity of a type to which contributions under paragraph (1) may be made. The preceding sentence shall not apply to the portion of any distribution which is not includible in gross income by reason of a trustee-to-trustee transfer or a rollover distribution.

(B) TESTING PERIOD.—For purposes of subparagraph (A), the testing period, with respect to a taxable year, is the period which includes—

(i) such taxable year,

(ii) the 2 preceding taxable years, and

(iii) the period after such taxable year and before the due date (including extensions) for filing the return of tax for such taxable year.

(C) EXCEPTED DISTRIBUTIONS.—There shall not be taken into account under subparagraph (A)—

(i) any distribution referred to in section 72(p), 401(k)(8), 401(m)(6), 402(g)(2), 404(k), or 408(d)(4), and

(ii) any distribution to which section 408A(d)(3) applies.

(D) TREATMENT OF DISTRIBUTIONS RECEIVED BY SPOUSE OF INDIVIDUAL.—For purposes of determining distributions received by an individual under subparagraph (A) for any taxable year, any distribution received by the spouse of such individual shall be treated as received by such individual if such individual and spouse file a joint return for such taxable year and for the taxable year during which the spouse receives the distribution.

[Sec. 25B(e)]

(e) ADJUSTED GROSS INCOME.—For purposes of this section, adjusted gross income shall be determined without regard to sections 911, 931, and 933.

[Sec. 25B(f)]

(f) INVESTMENT IN THE CONTRACT.—Notwithstanding any other provision of law, a qualified retirement savings contribution shall not fail to be included in determining the investment in the contract for purposes of section 72 by reason of the credit under this section.

[Sec. 25B(g)—Stricken]

[Sec. 25B(h)—Stricken]

[Sec. 26]

SEC. 26. LIMITATION BASED ON TAX LIABILITY; DEFINITION OF TAX LIABILITY.

[Sec. 26(a)]

(a) LIMITATION BASED ON AMOUNT OF TAX.—The aggregate amount of credits allowed by this subpart for the taxable year shall not exceed the sum of—

(1) the taxpayer's regular tax liability for the taxable year reduced by the foreign tax credit allowable under section 27, and

(2) the tax imposed by section 55(a) for the taxable year.

[Sec. 26(b)]

(b) REGULAR TAX LIABILITY.—For purposes of this part—

(1) IN GENERAL.—The term "regular tax liability" means the tax imposed by this chapter for the taxable year.

(2) EXCEPTION FOR CERTAIN TAXES.—For purposes of paragraph (1), any tax imposed by any of the following provisions shall not be treated as tax imposed by this chapter:

(A) section 55 (relating to minimum tax),

(B) [Stricken.]

(C) subsection (m)(5)(B), (q), (t), or (v) of section 72 (relating to additional taxes on certain distributions),

* * *

(E) section 530(d)(4) (relating to additional tax on certain distributions from Coverdell education savings accounts),

(F) section 531 (relating to accumulated earnings tax),

(G) section 541 (relating to personal holding company tax),

* * *

(I) section 1374 (relating to tax on certain certain built-in gains of S corporations),

(J) section 1375 (relating to tax imposed when passive investment income of corporation having subchapter C earnings and profits exceeds 25 percent of gross receipts),

* * *

(O) sections 453(l)(3) and 453A(c) (relating to interest on certain deferred tax liabilities),

* * *

(S) sections 106(e)(3)(A)(ii), 223(b)(8)(B)(i)(II), and 408(d)(9)(D)(i)(II) (relating to certain failures to maintain high deductible health plan coverage),

(T) section 170(o)(3)(B) (relating to recapture of certain deductions for fractional gifts),

(U) section 223(f)(4) (relating to additional tax on health savings account distributions not used for qualified medical expenses),

(V) subsections (a)(1)(B)(i) and (b)(4)(A) of section 409A (relating to interest and additional tax with respect to certain deferred compensation),

(W) section 36(f) (relating to recapture of homebuyer credit),

(X) section 457A(c)(1)(B) (relating to determinability of amounts of compensation), and

(Y) section 529A(c)(3)(A) (relating to additional tax on ABLE account distributions not used for qualified disability expenses).

[Sec. 26(c)]

(c) TENTATIVE MINIMUM TAX.—For purposes of this part, the term "tentative minimum tax" means the amount determined under section 55(b)(1).

Subpart C—Refundable Credits

[Sec. 31]

SEC. 31. TAX WITHHELD ON WAGES.

[Sec. 31(a)]

(a) WAGE WITHHOLDING FOR INCOME TAX PURPOSES.—

(1) IN GENERAL.—The amount withheld as tax under chapter 24 shall be allowed to the recipient of the income as a credit against the tax imposed by this subtitle.

(2) YEAR OF CREDIT.—The amount so withheld during any calendar year shall be allowed as a credit for the taxable year beginning in such calendar year. If more than one taxable year begins in a calendar year, such amount shall be allowed as a credit for the last taxable year so beginning.

* * *

»→ Caution: As provided in Section 32(j), the dollar amounts set forth in Sections 32(b)(2) and 32(i)(1) are adjusted for taxable years after 1996 to reflect increases in the Chained Consumer Price Index. As provided in Section 32(b)(2)(B)(ii), the dollar amount set forth in Section 32(b)(2)(B)(i) is adjusted for taxable years after 2015 to reflect increases in the Chained Consumer Price Index. The Section 32(b) and 32(i)(1) amounts applicable to taxable years beginning in 2020 are set forth in the material beginning at page ix.

[Sec. 32]

SEC. 32. EARNED INCOME.

[Sec. 32(a)]

(a) ALLOWANCE OF CREDIT.—

(1) IN GENERAL.—In the case of an eligible individual, there shall be allowed as a credit against the tax imposed by this subtitle for the taxable year an amount equal to the credit percentage of so much of the taxpayer's earned income for the taxable year as does not exceed the earned income amount.

(2) LIMITATION.—The amount of the credit allowable to a taxpayer under paragraph (1) for any taxable year shall not exceed the excess (if any) of—

(A) the credit percentage of the earned income amount, over

(B) the phaseout percentage of so much of the adjusted gross income (or, if greater, the earned income) of the taxpayer for the taxable year as exceeds the phaseout amount.

[Sec. 32(b)]

(b) PERCENTAGES AND AMOUNTS.—For purposes of subsection (a)—

(1) PERCENTAGES.—The credit percentage and the phaseout percentage shall be determined as follows:

In the case of an eligible individual with:	*The credit percentage is:*	*The phaseout percentage is:*
1 qualifying child	34	15.98
2 qualifying children	40	21.06
3 or more qualifying children	45	21.06
No qualifying children	7.65	7.65

(2) AMOUNTS.—

(A) IN GENERAL.—Subject to subparagraph (B), the earned income amount and the phaseout amount shall be determined as follows:

In the case of an eligible individual with:	*The earned income amount is:*	*The phaseout amount is:*
1 qualifying child	$6,330	$11,610
2 or more qualifying children	$8,890	$11,610
No qualifying children	$4,220	$ 5,280

(B) JOINT RETURNS.—In the case of a joint return filed by an eligible individual and such individual's spouse, the phaseout amount determined under subparagraph (A) shall be increased by $5,000.

[Sec. 32(c)]

(c) DEFINITIONS AND SPECIAL RULES.—For purposes of this section—

(1) ELIGIBLE INDIVIDUAL.—

(A) IN GENERAL.—The term "eligible individual" means—

(i) any individual who has a qualifying child for the taxable year, or

(ii) any other individual who does not have a qualifying child for the taxable year, if—

(I) such individual's principal place of abode is in the United States for more than one-half of such taxable year,

(II) such individual (or, if the individual is married, either the individual or the individual's spouse) has attained age 25 but not attained age 65 before the close of the taxable year, and

(III) such individual is not a dependent for whom a deduction is allowable under section 151 to another taxpayer for any taxable year beginning in the same calendar year as such taxable year.

For purposes of preceding sentence, marital status shall be determined under section 7703.

(B) QUALIFYING CHILD INELIGIBLE.—If an individual is the qualifying child of a taxpayer for any taxable year of such taxpayer beginning in a calendar year, such individual shall not be treated as an eligible individual for any taxable year of such individual beginning in such calendar year.

(C) EXCEPTION FOR INDIVIDUAL CLAIMING BENEFITS UNDER SECTION 911 .—The term "eligible individual" does not include any individual who claims the benefits of section 911 (relating to citizens or residents living abroad) for the taxable year.

(D) LIMITATION ON ELIGIBILITY OF NONRESIDENT ALIENS.—The term "eligible individual" shall not include any individual who is a nonresident alien individual for any portion of the taxable year unless such individual is treated for such taxable year as a resident of the United States for purposes of this chapter by reason of an election under subsection (g) or (h) of section 6013.

(E) IDENTIFICATION NUMBER REQUIREMENT.—No credit shall be allowed under this section to an eligible individual who does not include on the return of tax for the taxable year—

(i) such individual's taxpayer identification number, and

(ii) if the individual is married (within the meaning of section 7703), the taxpayer identification number of such individual's spouse.

(F) INDIVIDUALS WHO DO NOT INCLUDE TIN, ETC., OF ANY QUALIFYING CHILD.—No credit shall be allowed under this section to any eligible individual who has one or more qualifying children if no qualifying child of such individual is taken into account under subsection (b) by reason of paragraph (3)(D).

(2) EARNED INCOME.—

(A) The term "earned income" means—

(i) wages, salaries, tips, and other employee compensation, but only if such amounts are includible in gross income for the taxable year, plus

(ii) the amount of the taxpayer's net earnings from self-employment for the taxable year (within the meaning of section 1402(a)), but such net earnings shall be determined with regard to the deduction allowed to the taxpayer by section 164(f).

(B) For purposes of subparagraph (A)—

(i) the earned income of an individual shall be computed without regard to any community property laws,

(ii) no amount received as a pension or annuity shall be taken into account,

(iii) no amount to which section 871(a) applies (relating to income of nonresident alien individuals not connected with United States business) shall be taken into account,

(iv) no amount received for services provided by an individual while the individual is an inmate at a penal institution shall be taken into account,

(v) no amount described in subparagraph (A) received for service performed in work activities as defined in paragraph (4) or (7) of section 407(d) of the Social Security Act to which the taxpayer is assigned under any State program under part A of title IV of such Act shall be taken into account, but only to the extent such amount is subsidized under such State program, and

(vi) a taxpayer may elect to treat amounts excluded from gross income by reason of section 112 as earned income.

(3) QUALIFYING CHILD.—

(A) IN GENERAL.—The term "qualifying child" means a qualifying child of the taxpayer (as defined in section 152(c), determined without regard to paragraph (1)(D) thereof and section 152(e)).

(B) MARRIED INDIVIDUAL.—The term "qualifying child" shall not include an individual who is married as of the close of the taxpayer's taxable year unless the taxpayer is entitled to a deduction under section 151 for such taxable year with respect to such individual (or would be so entitled but for section 152(e)).

(C) PLACE OF ABODE.—For purposes of subparagraph (A), the requirements of section 152(c)(1)(B) shall be met only if the principal place of abode is in the United States.

(D) IDENTIFICATION REQUIREMENTS.—

(i) IN GENERAL.—A qualifying child shall not be taken into account under subsection (b) unless the taxpayer includes the name, age, and TIN of the qualifying child on the return of tax for the taxable year.

(ii) OTHER METHODS.—The Secretary may prescribe other methods for providing the information described in clause (i).

(4) TREATMENT OF MILITARY PERSONNEL STATIONED OUTSIDE THE UNITED STATES.—For purposes of paragraphs (1)(A)(ii)(I) and (3)(C), the principal place of abode of a member of the Armed Forces of the United States shall be treated as in the United States during any period

during which such member is stationed outside the United States while serving on extended active duty with the Armed Forces of the United States. For purposes of the preceding sentence, the term "extended active duty" means any period of active duty pursuant to a call or order to such duty for a period in excess of 90 days or for an indefinite period.

[Sec. 32(d)]

(d) MARRIED INDIVIDUALS.—In the case of an individual who is married (within the meaning of section 7703), this section shall apply only if a joint return is filed for the taxable year under section 6013.

[Sec. 32(e)]

(e) TAXABLE YEAR MUST BE FULL TAXABLE YEAR.—Except in the case of a taxable year closed by reason of the death of the taxpayer, no credit shall be allowable under this section in the case of a taxable year covering a period of less than 12 months.

[Sec. 32(f)]

(f) AMOUNT OF CREDIT TO BE DETERMINED UNDER TABLES.—

(1) IN GENERAL.—The amount of the credit allowed by this section shall be determined under tables prescribed by the Secretary.

(2) REQUIREMENTS FOR TABLES.—The tables prescribed under paragraph (1) shall reflect the provisions of subsections (a) and (b) and shall have income brackets of not greater than $50 each—

(A) for earned income between $0 and the amount of earned income at which the credit is phased out under subsection (b), and

(B) for adjusted gross income between the dollar amount at which the phaseout begins under subsection (b) and the amount of adjusted gross income at which the credit is phased out under subsection (b).

[Sec. 32(g)—Repealed]

[Sec. 32(h)—Repealed]

[Sec. 32(i)]

(i) DENIAL OF CREDIT FOR INDIVIDUALS HAVING EXCESSIVE INVESTMENT INCOME.—

(1) IN GENERAL.—No credit shall be allowed under subsection (a) for the taxable year if the aggregate amount of disqualified income of the taxpayer for the taxable year exceeds $2,200.

(2) DISQUALIFIED INCOME.—For purposes of paragraph (1), the term "disqualified income" means—

(A) interest or dividends to the extent includible in gross income for the taxable year,

(B) interest received or accrued during the taxable year which is exempt from tax imposed by this chapter,

(C) the excess (if any) of—

(i) gross income from rents or royalties not derived in the ordinary course of a trade or business, over

(ii) the sum of—

(I) the deductions (other than interest) which are clearly and directly allocable to such gross income, plus

(II) interest deductions properly allocable to such gross income,

(D) the capital gain net income (as defined in section 1222) of the taxpayer for such taxable year, and

(E) the excess (if any) of—

(i) the aggregate income from all passive activities for the taxable year (determined without regard to any amount included in earned income under subsection (c)(2) or described in a preceding subparagraph), over

(ii) the aggregate losses from all passive activities for the taxable year (as so determined).

For purposes of subparagraph (E), the term "passive activity" has the meaning given such term by section 469.

[Sec. 32(j)]

(j) INFLATION ADJUSTMENTS.—

(1) IN GENERAL.—In the case of any taxable year beginning after 2015, each of the dollar amounts in subsections (b)(2) and (i)(1) shall be increased by an amount equal to—

(A) such dollar amount, multiplied by

(B) the cost-of-living adjustment determined under section 1(f)(3) for the calendar year in which the taxable year begins, determined by substituting in subparagraph (A)(ii) thereof—

(i) in the case of amounts in subsections (b)(2)(A) and (i)(1), "calendar year 1995" for "calendar year 2016", and

(ii) in the case of the $5,000 amount in subsection (b)(2)(B), "calendar year 2008" for "calendar year 2016".

(2) ROUNDING.—

(A) IN GENERAL.—If any dollar amount in subsection (b)(2)(A) (after being increased under subparagraph (B) thereof), after being increased under paragraph (1), is not a multiple of $10, such dollar amount shall be rounded to the nearest multiple of $10.

(B) DISQUALIFIED INCOME THRESHOLD AMOUNT.—If the dollar amount in subsection (i)(1), after being increased under paragraph (1), is not a multiple of $50, such amount shall be rounded to the next lowest multiple of $50.

* * *

Subpart D—Business Related Credits

[Sec. 45D]

SEC. 45D. NEW MARKETS TAX CREDIT.

* * *

[Sec. 45D(e)]

(e) LOW-INCOME COMMUNITY.—For purposes of this section—

(1) IN GENERAL.—The term "low-income community" means any population census tract if—

(A) the poverty rate for such tract is at least 20 percent, or

(B)(i) in the case of a tract not located within a metropolitan area, the median family income for such tract does not exceed 80 percent of statewide median family income, or

(ii) in the case of a tract located within a metropolitan area, the median family income for such tract does not exceed 80 percent of the greater of statewide median family income or the metropolitan area median family income.

Subparagraph (B) shall be applied using possessionwide median family income in the case of census tracts located within a possession of the United States.

(2) TARGETED POPULATIONS.—The Secretary shall prescribe regulations under which 1 or more targeted populations (within the meaning of section 103(20) of the Riegle Community Development and Regulatory Improvement Act of 1994 (12 U.S.C. 4702(20))) may be treated as low-income communities. Such regulations shall include procedures for determining which entities are qualified active low-income community businesses with respect to such populations.

(3) AREAS NOT WITHIN CENSUS TRACTS.—In the case of an area which is not tracted for population census tracts, the equivalent county divisions (as defined by the Bureau of the Census for purposes of defining poverty areas) shall be used for purposes of determining poverty rates and median family income.

(4) TRACTS WITH LOW POPULATION.—A population census tract with a population of less than 2,000 shall be treated as a low-income community for purposes of this section if such tract—

(A) is within an empowerment zone the designation of which is in effect under section 1391, and

(B) is contiguous to 1 or more low-income communities (determined without regard to this paragraph).

(5) MODIFICATION OF INCOME REQUIREMENT FOR CENSUS TRACTS WITHIN HIGH MIGRATION RURAL COUNTIES.—

(A) IN GENERAL.—In the case of a population census tract located within a high migration rural county, paragraph (1)(B)(i) shall be applied by substituting "85 percent" for "80 percent".

(B) HIGH MIGRATION RURAL COUNTY.—For purposes of this paragraph, the term "high migration rural county" means any county which, during the 20-year period ending with the year in which the most recent census was conducted, has a net out-migration of inhabitants from the county of at least 10 percent of the population of the county at the beginning of such period.

* * *

Subpart E—Rules for Computing Investment Credit

[Sec. 49]

SEC. 49. AT-RISK RULES.

[Sec. 49(a)]

(a) GENERAL RULE.—

(1) CERTAIN NONRECOURSE FINANCING EXCLUDED FROM CREDIT BASE.—

* * *

(C) CREDIT BASE DEFINED.—For purposes of this paragraph, the term "credit base" means—

* * *

(iii) the basis of any property which is part of a qualifying advanced coal project under section 48A,

(iv) the basis of any property which is part of a qualifying gasification project under section 48B, and

(v) the basis of any property which is part of a qualifying advanced energy project under section 48C.

(D) NONQUALIFIED NONRECOURSE FINANCING.—

* * *

(iv) QUALIFIED PERSON.—For purposes of this paragraph, the term "qualified person" means any person which is actively and regularly engaged in the business of lending money and which is not—

(I) a related person with respect to the taxpayer,

(II) a person from which the taxpayer acquired the property (or a related person to such person), or

(III) a person who receives a fee with respect to the taxpayer's investment in the property (or a related person to such person).

(v) RELATED PERSON.—For purposes of this subparagraph, the term "related person" has the meaning given such term by section 465(b)(3)(C). Except as otherwise provided in regulations prescribed by the Secretary, the determination of whether a person is a related person shall be made as of the close of the taxable year in which the property is placed in service.

* * *

Subpart G—Credit Against Regular Tax for Prior Year Minimum Tax Liability

[Sec. 53]

SEC. 53. CREDIT FOR PRIOR YEAR MINIMUM TAX LIABILITY.

[Sec. 53(a)]

(a) ALLOWANCE OF CREDIT.—There shall be allowed as a credit against the tax imposed by this chapter for any taxable year an amount equal to the minimum tax credit for such taxable year.

[Sec. 53(b)]

(b) MINIMUM TAX CREDIT.—For purposes of subsection (a), the minimum tax credit for any taxable year is the excess (if any) of—

(1) the adjusted net minimum tax imposed for all prior taxable years beginning after 1986, over

(2) the amount allowable as a credit under subsection (a) for such prior taxable years.

[Sec. 53(c)]

(c) LIMITATION.—The credit allowable under subsection (a) for any taxable year shall not exceed the excess (if any) of—

(1) The regular tax liability of the taxpayer for such taxable year reduced by the sum of the credits allowable under subparts A, B, D, E, and F of this part, over

(2) the tentative minimum tax for the taxable year.

[Sec. 53(d)]

(d) DEFINITIONS.—For purposes of this section—

(1) Net minimum tax.—

(A) IN GENERAL.—The term "net minimum tax" means the tax imposed by section 55.

(B) CREDIT NOT ALLOWED FOR EXCLUSION PREFERENCES.—

(i) ADJUSTED NET MINIMUM TAX.—The adjusted net minimum tax for any taxable year is—

(I) the amount of the net minimum tax for such taxable year, reduced by

(II) the amount which would be the net minimum tax for such taxable year if the only adjustments and items of tax preference taken into account were those specified in clause (ii).

(ii) SPECIFIED ITEMS.—The following are specified in this clause—

(I) the adjustments provided for in subsection (b)(1) of section 56, and

(II) the items of tax preference described in paragraphs (1), (5), and (7) of section 57(a).

(iii) CREDIT ALLOWABLE FOR EXCLUSION PREFERENCES OF CORPORATIONS.—In the case of a corporation—

(I) the preceding provisions of this subparagraph shall not apply, and

(II) the adjusted net minimum tax for any taxable year is the amount of the net minimum tax for such year.

(2) TENTATIVE MINIMUM TAX.—The term "tentative minimum tax" has the meaning given to such term by section 55(b), except that in the case of a corporation, the tentative minimum tax shall be treated as zero.

(3) AMT TERM REFERENCES.—In the case of a corporation, any references in this subsection to section 55, 56, or 57 shall be treated as a reference to such section as in effect before the amendments made by Tax Cuts and Jobs Act.

[Sec. 53(e)]

(e) PORTION OF CREDIT TREATED AS REFUNDABLE.—

(1) IN GENERAL.—In the case of any taxable year of a corporation beginning in 2018 or 2019, the limitation under subsection (c) shall be increased by the AMT refundable credit amount for such year.

(2) AMT REFUNDABLE CREDIT AMOUNT.—For purposes of paragraph (1), the AMT refundable credit amount is an amount equal to 50 percent (100 percent in the case of a taxable year beginning in 2021) of the excess (if any) of—

(A) the minimum tax credit determined under subsection (b) for the taxable year, over

(B) the minimum tax credit allowed under subsection (a) for such year (before the application of this subsection for such year).

(3) CREDIT REFUNDABLE.—For purposes of this title (other than this section), the credit allowed by reason of this subsection shall be treated as a credit allowed under subpart C (and not this subpart).

(4) SHORT TAXABLE YEARS.—In the case of any taxable year of less than 365 days, the AMT refundable credit amount determined under paragraph (2) with respect to such taxable year shall be the amount which bears the same ratio to such amount determined without regard to this paragraph as the number of days in such taxable year bears to 365.

(5) SPECIAL RULE.—In the case of a corporation making an election under this paragraph—

(A) paragraph (1) shall not apply, and

(B) subsection (c) shall not apply to the first taxable year of such corporation beginning in 2018.

[Sec. 53(f)—Stricken]

PART VI—ALTERNATIVE MINIMUM TAX

»»→ Caution: As provided in Section 55(d)(4)(B), certain dollar amounts set forth in Section 55(d)(4)(A) are adjusted for taxable years after 2018 to reflect increases in the Chained Consumer Price Index. The dollar amounts applicable to taxable years beginning in 2020 are provided in the material beginning at page ix.

[Sec. 55]

SEC. 55. ALTERNATIVE MINIMUM TAX IMPOSED.

[Sec. 55(a)]

(a) GENERAL RULE.—In the case of a taxpayer other than a corporation, there is hereby imposed (in addition to any other tax imposed by this subtitle) a tax equal to the excess (if any) of—

(1) the tentative minimum tax for the taxable year, over

(2) the regular tax for the taxable year.

[Sec. 55(b)]

(b) TENTATIVE MINIMUM TAX.—For purposes of this part—

(1) AMOUNT OF TENTATIVE TAX.—

(A) IN GENERAL.—The tentative minimum tax for the taxable year is the sum of—

(i) 26 percent of so much of the taxable excess as does not exceed $175,000, plus

(ii) 28 percent of so much of the taxable excess as exceeds $175,000.

The amount determined under the preceding sentence shall be reduced by the alternative minimum tax foreign tax credit for the taxable year.

(B) TAXABLE EXCESS.—For purposes of this subsection, the term "taxable excess" means so much of the alternative minimum taxable income for the taxable year as exceeds the exemption amount.

(C) MARRIED INDIVIDUAL FILING SEPARATE RETURN.—In the case of a married individual filing a separate return, subparagraph (A) shall be applied by substituting 50 percent of the dollar amount otherwise applicable under clause (i) and clause (ii) thereof. For purposes of the preceding sentence, marital status shall be determined under section 7703.

(2) ALTERNATIVE MINIMUM TAXABLE INCOME.—The term "alternative minimum taxable income" means the taxable income of the taxpayer for the taxable year—

(A) determined with the adjustments provided in section 56 and section 58, and

(B) increased by the amount of the items of tax preference described in section 57.

If a taxpayer is subject to the regular tax, such taxpayer shall be subject to the tax imposed by this section (and, if the regular tax is determined by reference to an amount other than taxable income, such amount shall be treated as the taxable income of such taxpayer for purposes of the preceding sentence).

(3) MAXIMUM RATE OF TAX ON NET CAPITAL GAIN OF NONCORPORATE TAXPAYERS.—The amount determined under the first sentence of paragraph (1)(A) shall not exceed the sum of—

(A) the amount determined under such first sentence computed at the rates and in the same manner as if this paragraph had not been enacted on the taxable excess reduced by the lesser of—

(i) the net capital gain; or

(ii) the sum of—

(I) the adjusted net capital gain, plus

(II) the unrecaptured section 1250 gain, plus

(B) 0 percent of so much of the adjusted net capital gain (or, if less, taxable excess) as does not exceed an amount equal to the excess described in section 1(h)(1)(B), plus

(C) 15 percent of the lesser of—

(i) so much of the adjusted net capital gain (or, if less, taxable excess) as exceeds the amount on which tax is determined under subparagraph (B), or

(ii) the excess described in section 1(h)(1)(C)(ii), plus

(D) 20 percent of the adjusted net capital gain (or, if less, taxable excess) in excess of the sum of the amounts on which tax is determined under subparagraphs (B) and (C), plus

(E) 25 percent of the amount of taxable excess in excess of the sum of the amounts on which tax is determined under the preceding subparagraphs of this paragraph.

Terms used in this paragraph which are also used in section 1(h) shall have the respective meanings given such terms by section 1(h) but computed with the adjustments under this part.

[Sec. 55(c)]

(c) REGULAR TAX.—

(1) IN GENERAL.—For purposes of this section, the term "regular tax" means the regular tax liability for the taxable year (as defined in section 26(b)) reduced by the foreign tax credit allowable under section 27(a). Such term shall not include any increase in tax under section 45(e)(11)(C), 49(b) or 50(a) or subsection (j) or (k) of section 42.

(2) COORDINATION WITH INCOME AVERAGING FOR FARMERS AND FISHERMEN.—Solely for purposes of this section, section 1301 (relating to averaging of farm and fishing income) shall not apply in computing the regular tax liability.

(3) CROSS REFERENCES.—

For provisions providing that certain credits are not allowable against the tax imposed by this section, see 30C(d)(2), and 38(c).

[Sec. 55(d)]

(d) EXEMPTION AMOUNT.—For purposes of this section—

(1) EXEMPTION AMOUNT FOR TAXPAYERS OTHER THAN CORPORATIONS.—In the case of a taxpayer other than a corporation, the term "exemption amount" means—

(A) $78,750 in the case of—

(i) a joint return, or

(ii) a surviving spouse,

(B) $50,600 in the case of an individual who—

(i) is not a married individual, and

(ii) is not a surviving spouse,

(C) 50 percent of the dollar amount applicable under subparagraph (A) in the case of a married individual who files a separate return, and

(D) $22,500 in the case of an estate or trust.

For purposes of this paragraph, the term "surviving spouse" has the meaning given to such term by section 2(a), and marital status shall be determined under section 7703.

(2) PHASE-OUT OF EXEMPTION AMOUNT.—The exemption amount of any taxpayers shall be reduced (but not below zero) by an amount equal to 25 percent of the amount by which the alternative minimum taxable income of the taxpayer exceeds—

(A) $150,000 in the case of a taxpayer described in paragraph (1)(A),

(B) $112,500 in the case of a taxpayer described in paragraph (1)(B), and

(C) 50 percent of the dollar amount applicable under subparagraph (A) in the case of a taxpayer described in subparagraph (C) or (D) of paragraph (1).

In the case of a taxpayer described in paragraph (1)(C), alternative minimum taxable income shall be increased by the lesser of (i) 25 percent of the excess of alternative minimum taxable income (determined without regard to this sentence) over the minimum amount of such income (as so determined) for which the exemption amount under paragraph (1)(C) is zero, or (ii) such exemption amount (determined without regard to this paragraph).

(3) INFLATION ADJUSTMENT.—

(A) IN GENERAL.—In the case of any taxable year beginning in a calendar year after 2012, the amounts described in subparagraph (B) shall each be increased by an amount equal to—

(i) such dollar amount, multiplied by

(ii) the cost-of-living adjustment determined under section 1(f)(3) for the calendar year in which the taxable year begins, determined by substituting "calendar year 2011" for "calendar year 2016" in subparagraph (A)(ii) thereof.

(B) AMOUNTS DESCRIBED.—The amounts described in this subparagraph are—

(i) each of the dollar amounts contained in subsection (b)(1)(A),

(ii) each of the dollar amounts contained in subparagraphs (A), (B), and (D) of paragraph (1), and

(iii) each of the dollar amounts in subparagraphs (A) and (B) of paragraph (2).

(C) ROUNDING.—Any increased amount determined under subparagraph (A) shall be rounded to the nearest multiple of $100.

(4) SPECIAL RULE FOR TAXABLE YEARS BEGINNING AFTER 2017 AND BEFORE 2026.—

(A) IN GENERAL.—In the case of any taxable year beginning after December 31, 2017, and before January 1, 2026—

(i) paragraph (1) shall be applied—

(I) by substituting "$109,400" for "$78,750" in subparagraph (A), and

(II) by substituting "$70,300" for "$50,600" in subparagraph (B),

(ii) paragraph (2) shall be applied—

(I) by substituting "$1,000,000" for "$150,000" in subparagraph (A),

(II) by substituting "50 percent of the dollar amount applicable under subparagraph (A)" for "$112,500" in subparagraph (B), and

(III) in the case of a taxpayer described in paragraph (1)(D), without regard to the substitution under subclause (I), and

(iii) subsection (j) of section 59 shall not apply.

(B) INFLATION ADJUSTMENT.—

(i) IN GENERAL.—In the case of any taxable year beginning in a calendar year after 2018, the amounts described in clause (ii) shall each be increased by an amount equal to—

(I) such dollar amount, multiplied by

(II) the cost-of-living adjustment determined under section 1(f)(3) for the calendar year in which the taxable year begins, determined by substituting "calendar year 2017" for "calendar year 2016" in subparagraph (A)(ii) thereof.

(ii) AMOUNTS DESCRIBED.—The amounts described in this clause are the $109,400 amount in subparagraph (A)(i)(I), the $70,300 amount in subparagraph (A)(i)(II), and the $1,000,000 amount in subparagraph (A)(ii)(I).

(iii) ROUNDING.—Any increased amount determined under clause (i) shall be rounded to the nearest multiple of $100.

(iv) COORDINATION WITH CURRENT ADJUSTMENTS.—In the case of any taxable year to which subparagraph (A) applies, no adjustment shall be made under paragraph (3) to any of the numbers which are substituted under subparagraph (A) and adjusted under this subparagraph.

[Sec. 55(e)]—Stricken

[Sec. 56]

SEC. 56. ADJUSTMENTS IN COMPUTING ALTERNATIVE MINIMUM TAXABLE INCOME.

[Sec. 56(a)]

(a) ADJUSTMENTS APPLICABLE TO ALL TAXPAYERS.—In determining the amount of the alternative minimum taxable income for any taxable year the following treatment shall apply (in lieu of the treatment applicable for purposes of computing the regular tax):

(1) DEPRECIATION.—

(A) IN GENERAL.—

(i) PROPERTY OTHER THAN CERTAIN PERSONAL PROPERTY.—Except as provided in clause (ii), the depreciation deduction allowable under section 167 with respect to any tangible property placed in service after December 31, 1986, shall be determined under the alternative system of section 168(g). In the case of property placed in service after December 31, 1998, the preceding sentence shall not apply but clause (ii) shall continue to apply.

(ii) 150-PERCENT DECLINING BALANCE METHOD FOR CERTAIN PROPERTY.—The method of depreciation used shall be—

(I) the 150 percent declining balance method,

(II) switching to the straight line method for the 1st taxable year for which using the straight line method with respect to the adjusted basis as of the beginning of the year will yield a higher allowance.

The preceding sentence shall not apply to any section 1250 property (as defined in section 1250(c)) (and the straight line method shall be used for such section 1250 property) or to any other property if the depreciation deduction determined under section 168 with respect to such other property for purposes of the regular tax is determined by using the straight line method.

(B) EXCEPTION FOR CERTAIN PROPERTY.—This paragraph shall not apply to property described in paragraph (1), (2), (3), or (4) of section 168(f), or in section 168(e)(3)(C)(iv).

* * *

(D) NORMALIZATION RULES.—With respect to public utility property described in section 168(i)(10), the Secretary shall prescribe the requirements of a normalization method of accounting for this section.

(2) MINING EXPLORATION AND DEVELOPMENT COSTS.—

(A) IN GENERAL.—With respect to each mine or other natural deposit (other than an oil, gas, or geothermal well) of the taxpayer, the amount allowable as a deduction under section 616(a) or 617(a) (determined without regard to section 291(b)) in computing the regular tax for costs paid or incurred after December 31, 1986, shall be capitalized and amortized ratably over the 10-year period beginning with the taxable year in which the expenditures were made.

(B) LOSS ALLOWED.—If a loss is sustained with respect to any property described in subparagraph (A), a deduction shall be allowed for the expenditures described in subparagraph (A) for the taxable year in which such loss is sustained in an amount equal to the lesser of—

(i) the amount allowable under section 165(a) for the expenditures if they had remained capitalized, or

(ii) the amount of such expenditures which have not previously been amortized under subparagraph (A).

(3) TREATMENT OF CERTAIN LONG-TERM CONTRACTS.—In the case of any long-term contract entered into by the taxpayer on or after March 1, 1986, the taxable income from such contract shall be determined under the percentage of completion method of accounting (as modified by section 460(b)). For purposes of the preceding sentence, in the case of a contract described in section 460(e)(1), the percentage of the contract completed shall be determined under section 460(b)(1) by using the simplified procedures for allocation of costs prescribed under section 460(b)(3). The first sentence of this paragraph shall not apply to any home construction contract (as defined in section 460(e)(6)).

(4) ALTERNATIVE TAX NET OPERATING LOSS DEDUCTION.—The alternative tax net operating loss dedution shall be allowed in lieu of the net operating loss deduction allowed under section 172.

(5) POLLUTION CONTROL FACILITIES.—In the case of any certified pollution control facility placed in service after December 31, 1986, the deduction allowable under section 169 (without regard to section 291) shall be determined under the alternative system of section 168(g). In the case of such a facility placed in service after December 31, 1998, such deduction shall be determined under section 168 using the straight line method.

(6) ADJUSTED BASIS.—The adjusted basis of any property to which paragraph (1) or (5) applies (or with respect to which there are any expenditures to which paragraph (2) or subsection (b)(2) applies) shall be determined on the basis of the treatment prescribed in paragraph (1), (2), or (5), or subsection (b)(2), whichever applies.

(7) SECTION 87 NOT APPLICABLE.—Section 87 (relating to alcohol fuel credit) shall not apply.

[Sec. 56(b)]

(b) ADJUSTMENTS APPLICABLE TO INDIVIDUALS.—In determining the amount of the alternative minimum taxable income of any taxpayer (other than a corporation), the following treatment shall apply (in lieu of the treatment applicable for purposes of computing the regular tax):

(1) LIMITATION ON DEDUCTIONS.—

(A) IN GENERAL.—No deduction shall be allowed—

(i) for any miscellaneous itemized deduction (as defined in section 67(b)), or

(ii) for any taxes described in paragraph (1), (2), or (3) of section 164(a) or clause (ii) of section 164(b)(5)(A).

Clause (ii) shall not apply to any amount allowable in computing adjusted gross income.

(B) INTEREST.—In determining the amount allowable as a deduction for interest, subsections (d) and (h) of section 163 shall apply, except that—

(i) in lieu of the exception under section 163(h)(2)(D), the term "personal interest" shall not include any qualified housing interest (as defined in subsection (e)),

(ii) interest on any specified private activity bond (and any amount treated as interest on a specified private activity bond under section 57(a)(5)(B)) and any deduction referred to in section 57(a)(5)(A), shall be treated as includible in gross income (or as deductible) for purposes of applying section 163(d),

(iii) in lieu of the exception under section 163(d)(3)(B)(i), the term "investment interest" shall not include any qualified housing interest (as defined in subsection (e)), and

(iv) the adjustments of this section and sections 57 and 58 shall apply in determining net investment income under section 163(d).

(C) TREATMENT OF CERTAIN RECOVERIES.—No recovery of any tax to which subparagraph (A)(ii) applied shall be included in gross income for purposes of determining alternative minimum taxable income.

(D) STANDARD DEDUCTION AND DEDUCTION FOR PERSONAL EXEMPTIONS NOT ALLOWED.—The standard deduction under section 63(c), the deduction for personal exemptions under section 151, and the deduction under section 642(b) shall not be allowed.

(E) SECTION 68 NOT APPLICABLE.—Section 68 shall not apply.

(2) CIRCULATION AND RESEARCH AND EXPERIMENTAL EXPENDITURES.—

(A) IN GENERAL.—The amount allowable as a deduction under section 173 or 174(a) in computing the regular tax for amounts paid or incurred after December 31, 1986, shall be capitalized and—

(i) in the case of circulation expenditures described in section 173, shall be amortized ratably over the 3-year period beginning with the taxable year in which the expenditures were made, or

(ii) in the case of research and experimental expenditures described in section 174(a), shall be amortized ratably over the 10-year period beginning with the taxable year in which the expenditures were made.

(B) LOSS ALLOWED.—If a loss is sustained with respect to any property described in subparagraph (A), a deduction shall be allowed for the expenditures described in subparagraph (A) for the taxable year in which such loss is sustained in an amount equal to the lesser of—

(i) the amount allowable under section 165(a) for the expenditures if they had remained capitalized, or

(ii) the amount of such expenditures which have not previously been amortized under subparagraph (A).

(C) EXCEPTION FOR CERTAIN RESEARCH AND EXPERIMENTAL EXPENDITURES.—If the taxpayer materially participates (within the meaning of section 469(h)) in an activity, this paragraph shall not apply to any amount allowable as deduction under section 174(a) for expenditures paid or incurred in connection with such activity.

(3) TREATMENT OF INCENTIVE STOCK OPTIONS.—Section 421 shall not apply to the transfer of stock acquired pursuant to the exercise of an incentive stock option (as defined in section 422). Section 422(c)(2) shall apply in any case where the disposition and the inclusion for purposes of this part are within the same taxable year and such section shall not apply in any other case. The adjusted basis of any stock so acquired shall be determined on the basis of the treatment prescribed by this paragraph.

[Sec. 56(c)—Stricken]

[Sec. 56(d)]

(d) ALTERNATIVE TAX NET OPERATING LOSS DEDUCTION DEFINED.—

(1) IN GENERAL.—For purposes of subsection (a)(4), the term "alternative tax net operating loss deduction" means the net operating loss deduction allowable for the taxable year under section 172, except that—

(A) the amount of such deduction shall not exceed the sum of—

(i) the lesser of—

(I) the amount of such deduction attributable to net operating losses (other than the deduction described in clause (ii)(I)), or

(II) 90 percent of alternative minimum taxable income determined without regard to such deduction and the deduction under section 199, plus

(ii) the lesser of—

(I) the amount of such deduction attributable to an applicable net operating loss with respect to which an election is made under section 172(b)(1)(H) (as in effect before its repeal by the Tax Increase Prevention Act of 2014), or

(II) alternative minimum taxable income determined without regard to such deduction and the deduction under section 199 reduced by the amount determined under clause (i), and

(B) in determining the amount of such deduction—

(i) the net operating loss (within the meaning of section 172(c)) for any loss year shall be adjusted as provided in paragraph (2), and

(ii) appropriate adjustments in the application of section 172(b)(2) shall be made to take into account the limitation of subparagraph (A).

(2) ADJUSTMENTS TO NET OPERATING LOSS COMPUTATION.—

(A) POST-1986 LOSS YEARS.—In the case of a loss year beginning after December 31, 1986, the net operating loss for such year under section 172(c) shall—

(i) be determined with the adustments provided in this section and section 58, and

(ii) be reduced by the items of tax preference determined under section 57 for such year.

An item of tax preference shall be taken into account under clause (ii) only to the extent such item increased the amount of the net operating loss for the taxable year under section 172(c).

(B) PRE-1987 YEARS.—In the case of loss years beginning before January 1, 1987, the amount of the net operating loss which may be carried over to taxable years beginning after December 31, 1986, for purposes of paragraph (2), shall be equal to the amount which may be carried from the loss year to the first taxable year of the taxpayer beginning after December 31, 1986.

[Sec. 56(e)]

(e) QUALIFIED HOUSING INTEREST.—For purposes of this part—

(1) IN GENERAL.—The term "qualified housing interest" means interest which is qualified residence interest (as defined in section 163(h)(3)) and is paid or accrued during the taxable year on indebtedness which is incurred in acquiring, constructing, or substantially improving any property which—

(A) is the principal residence (within the meaning of section 121) of the taxpayer at the time such interest accrues, or

(B) is a qualified dwelling which is a qualified residence (within the meaning of section 163(h)(4)).

Such term also includes interest on any indebtedness resulting from the refinancing of indebtedness meeting the requirements of the preceding sentence; but only to the extent that the amount of the indebtedness resulting from such refinancing does not exceed the amount of the refinanced indebtedness immediately before the refinancing.

(2) QUALIFIED DWELLING.—The term "qualified dwelling" means any—

(A) house,

(B) apartment,

(C) condominium, or

(D) mobile home not used on a transient basis (within the meaning of section 7701(a)(19)(C)(v)),

including all structures or other property appurtenant thereto.

* * *

[Sec. 56(f)—Repealed]

[Sec. 56(g)—Stricken]

[Sec. 57]

SEC. 57. ITEMS OF TAX PREFERENCE.

[Sec. 57(a)]

(a) GENERAL RULE.—For purposes of this part, the items of tax preference determined under this section are—

(1) DEPLETION.—With respect to each property (as defined in section 614), the excess of the deduction for depletion allowable under section 611 for the taxable year over the adjusted basis of the property at the end of the taxable year (determined without regard to the depletion deduction for the taxable year). This paragraph shall not apply to any deduction for depletion computed in accordance with section 613A(c).

(2) INTANGIBLE DRILLING COSTS.—

(A) IN GENERAL.—With respect to all oil, gas, and geothermal properties of the taxpayer, the amount (if any) by which the amount of the excess intangible drilling costs arising in the taxable year is greater than 65 percent of the net income of the taxpayer from oil, gas, and geothermal properties for the taxable year.

(B) EXCESS INTANGIBLE DRILLING COSTS.—For purposes of subparagraph (A), the amount of the excess intangible drilling costs arising in the taxable year is the excess of—

(i) the intangible drilling and development costs paid or incurred in connection with oil, gas, and geothermal wells (other than costs incurred in drilling a non-productive well) allowable under section 263(c) or 291(b) for the taxable year, over

(ii) the amount which would have been allowable for the taxable year if such costs had been capitalized and straight line recovery of intangibles (as defined in subsection (b)) had been used with respect to such costs.

(C) NET INCOME FROM OIL, GAS, AND GEOTHERMAL PROPERTIES.—For purposes of subparagraph (A), the amount of the net income of the taxpayer from oil, gas, and geothermal properties for the taxable year is the excess of—

(i) the aggregate amount of gross income (within the meaning of section 613(a)) from all oil, gas, and geothermal properties of the taxpayer received or accrued by the taxpayer during the taxable year, over

(ii) the amount of any deductions allocable to such properties reduced by the excess described in subparagraph (B) for such taxable year.

(D) PARAGRAPH APPLIED SEPARATELY WITH RESPECT TO GEOTHERMAL PROPERTIES AND OIL AND GAS PROPERTIES.—This paragraph shall be applied separately with respect to—

(i) all oil and gas properties which are not described in clause (ii), and

(ii) all properties which are geothermal deposits (as defined in section 613(e)(2)).

(E) EXCEPTION FOR INDEPENDENT PRODUCERS.—In the case of any oil or gas well—

(i) IN GENERAL.—This paragraph shall not apply to any taxpayer which is not an integrated oil company (as defined in section 291(b)(4)).

(ii) LIMITATION ON BENEFIT.—The reduction in alternative minimum taxable income by reason of clause (i) for any taxable year shall not exceed 40 percent of the alternative minimum taxable income for such year determined without regard to clause (i) and the alternative tax net operating loss deduction under section 56(a)(4).

(3) [Repealed.]

(4) [Stricken.]

(5) TAX-EXEMPT INTEREST.—

(A) IN GENERAL.—Interest on specified private activity bonds reduced by any deduction (not allowable in computing the regular tax) which would have been allowable if such interest were includible in gross income.

(B) TREATMENT OF EXEMPT-INTEREST DIVIDENDS.—Under regulations prescribed by the Secretary, any exempt-interest dividend (as defined in section 852(b)(5)(A)) shall be treated as interest on a specified private activity bond to the extent of its proportionate share of the interest on such bonds received by the company paying such dividend.

(C) SPECIFIED PRIVATE ACTIVITY BONDS.—

(i) IN GENERAL.—For purposes of this part, the term "specified private activity bond" means any private activity bond (as defined in section 141) which is issued after August 7, 1986, and the interest on which is not includible in gross income under section 103.

(ii) EXCEPTION FOR QUALIFIED 501(c)(3) BONDS.—For purposes of clause (i), the term "private activity bond" shall not include any qualified 501(c)(3) bond (as defined in section 145).

(iii) EXCEPTION FOR CERTAIN HOUSING BONDS.—For purposes of clause (i), the term "private activity bond" shall not include any bond issued after the date of the enactment of this clause if such bond is—

(I) an exempt facility bond issued as part of an issue 95 percent or more of the net proceeds of which are to be used to provide qualified residential rental projects (as defined in section 142(d)),

(II) a qualified mortgage bond (as defined in section 143(a)), or

(III) a qualified veterans' mortgage bond (as defined in section 143(b)).

The preceding sentence shall not apply to any refunding bond unless such preceding sentence applied to the refunded bond (or in the case of a series of refundings, the original bond).

(iv) EXCEPTION FOR REFUNDINGS.—For purposes of clause (i), the term "private activity bond" shall not include any refunding bond (whether a current or advance refunding) if the refunded bond (or in the case of a series of refundings, the original bond) was issued before August 8, 1986.

(v) CERTAIN BONDS ISSUED BEFORE SEPTEMBER 1, 1986.—For purposes of this subparagraph, a bond issued before September 1, 1986, shall be treated as issued before August 8, 1986, unless such bond would be a private activity bond if—

(I) paragraphs (1) and (2) of section 141(b) were applied by substituting "25 percent" for "10 percent" each place it appears,

(II) paragraphs (3), (4), and (5) of section 141(b) did not apply, and

(III) subparagraph (B) of section 141(c)(1) did not apply.

(vi) EXCEPTION FOR BONDS ISSUED IN 2009 AND 2010.—

(I) IN GENERAL.—For purposes of clause (i), the term "private activity bond" shall not include any bond issued after December 31, 2008, and before January 1, 2011.

(II) TREATMENT OF REFUNDING BONDS.—For purposes of subclause (I), a refunding bond (whether a current or advance refunding) shall be treated as issued on the date of the issuance of the refunded bond (or in the case of a series of refundings, the original bond).

(III) EXCEPTION FOR CERTAIN REFUNDING BONDS.—Subclause (II) shall not apply to any refunding bond which is issued to refund any bond which was issued after December 31, 2003, and before January 1, 2009.

(6) ACCELERATED DEPRECIATION OR AMORTIZATION ON CERTAIN PROPERTY PLACED IN SERVICE BEFORE JANUARY 1, 1987.—The amounts which would be treated as items of tax preference with respect to the taxpayer under paragraphs (2), (3), (4), and (12) of this subsection (as in effect on the day before the date of the enactment of the Tax Reform Act of 1986). The preceding sentence shall not apply to any property to which section 56(a)(1) or (5) applies.

(7) EXCLUSION FOR GAINS ON SALE OF CERTAIN SMALL BUSINESS STOCK.—An amount equal to 7 percent of the amount excluded from gross income for the taxable year under section 1202.

[Sec. 57(b)]

(b) STRAIGHT LINE RECOVERY OF INTANGIBLES DEFINED.—For purposes of paragraph (2) of subsection (a)—

(1) IN GENERAL.—The term "straight line recovery of intangibles", when used with respect to intangible drilling and development costs for any well, means (except in the case of an election under paragraph (2)) ratable amortization of such costs over the 120-month period beginning with the month in which production from such well begins.

(2) ELECTION.—If the taxpayer elects with respect to the intangible drilling and development costs for any well, the term "straight line recovery of intangibles" means any method which would be permitted for purposes of determining cost depletion with respect to such well and which is selected by the taxpayer for purposes of subsection (a)(2).

[Sec. 58]

SEC. 58. DENIAL OF CERTAIN LOSSES.

[Sec. 58(a)]

(a) DENIAL OF FARM LOSS.—

(1) IN GENERAL.—For purposes of computing the amount of the alternative minimum taxable income for any taxable year of a taxpayer other than a corporation—

(A) DISALLOWANCE OF FARM LOSS.—No loss of the taxpayer for such taxable year from any tax shelter farm activity shall be allowed.

(B) DEDUCTION IN SUCCEEDING TAXABLE YEAR.—Any loss from a tax shelter farm activity disallowed under subparagraph (A) shall be treated as a deduction allocable to such activity in the 1st succeeding taxable year.

(2) TAX SHELTER FARM ACTIVITY.—For purposes of this subsection, the term "tax shelter farm activity" means—

(A) any farming syndicate as defined in section 461(k) and

(B) any other activity consisting of farming which is a passive activity (within the meaning of section 469(c)).

(3) DETERMINATION OF LOSS.—In determining the amount of the loss from any tax shelter farm activity, the adjustments of sections 56 and 57 shall apply.

[Sec. 58(b)]

(b) DISALLOWANCE OF PASSIVE ACTIVITY LOSS.—In computing the alternative minimum taxable income of the taxpayer for any taxable year, section 469 shall apply, except that in applying section 469—

(1) the adjustments of sections 56 and 57 shall apply, and

(2) in lieu of applying section 469(j)(7), the passive activity loss of a taxpayer shall be computed without regard to qualified housing interest (as defined in section 56(e)).

[Sec. 58(c)]

(c) SPECIAL RULES.—For purposes of this section—

(1) SPECIAL RULE FOR INSOLVENT TAXPAYERS.—

(A) IN GENERAL.—The amount of losses to which subsection (a) or (b) applies shall be reduced by the amount (if any) by which the taxpayer is insolvent as of the close of the taxable year.

(B) INSOLVENT.—For purposes of this paragraph, the term "insolvent" means the excess of liabilities over the fair market value of assets.

(2) LOSS ALLOWED FOR YEAR OF DISPOSITION OF FARM SHELTER ACTIVITY.—If the taxpayer disposes of his entire interest in any tax shelter farm activity during any taxable year, the amount of the loss attributable to such activity (determined after carryovers under subsection (a)(1)(B)) shall (to the extent otherwise allowable) be allowed for such taxable year in computing alternative minimum taxable income and not treated as a loss from a tax shelter farm activity.

Caution: As provided in Section 59(j)(2), the dollar amount set forth in Section 59(j)(1)(B) is adjusted for taxable years after 1998 to reflect increases in the Chained Consumer Price Index. The adjusted amount for taxable years beginning in 2020 is provided in the material beginning at page ix.

[Sec. 59]

SEC. 59. OTHER DEFINITIONS AND SPECIAL RULES.

* * *

[Sec. 59(c)]

(c) TREATMENT OF ESTATES AND TRUSTS.—In the case of any estate or trust, the alternative minimum taxable income of such estate or trust and any beneficiary thereof shall be determined by applying part I of subchapter J with the adjustments provided in this part.

* * *

[Sec. 59(e)]

(e) OPTIONAL 10-YEAR WRITEOFF OF CERTAIN TAX PREFERENCES.—

(1) IN GENERAL.—For purposes of this title, any qualified expenditure to which an election under this paragraph applies shall be allowed as a deduction ratably over the 10-year period (3-year period in the case of circulation expenditures described in section 173) beginning with the taxable year in which such expenditure was made (or, in the case of a qualified expenditure described in paragraph (2)(C), over the 60-month period beginning with the month in which such expenditure was paid or incurred).

(2) QUALIFIED EXPENDITURE.—For purposes of this subsection, the term "qualified expenditure" means any amount which, but for an election under this subsection, would have been allowable as a deduction (determined without regard to section 291) for the taxable year in which paid or incurred under,

(A) section 173 (relating to circulation expenditures),

(B) section 174(a) (relating to research and experimental expenditures),

(C) section 263(c) (relating to intangible drilling and development expenditures),

(D) section 616(a) (relating to development expenditures), or

(E) section 617(a) (relating to mining exploration expenditures).

(3) OTHER SECTIONS NOT APPLICABLE.—Except as provided in this subsection, no deduction shall be allowed under any other section for any qualified expenditure to which an election under this subsection applies.

(4) ELECTION.—

(A) IN GENERAL.—An election may be made under paragraph (1) with respect to any portion of any qualified expenditure.

(B) REVOCABLE ONLY WITH CONSENT.—Any election under this subsection may be revoked only with the consent of the Secretary.

(C) PARTNERS AND SHAREHOLDERS OF S CORPORATIONS.—In the case of a partnership, any election under paragraph (1) shall be made separately by each partner with respect to the partner's allocable share of any qualified expenditure. A similar rule shall apply in the case of an S corporation and its shareholders.

(5) DISPOSITIONS.—

(A) APPLICATION OF SECTION 1254.—In the case of any disposition of property to which section 1254 applies (determined without regard to this section), any deduction under paragraph (1) with respect to amounts which are allocable to such property shall, for purposes of section 1254, be treated as a deduction allowable under section 263(c), 616(a), or 617(a), whichever is appropriate.

(B) APPLICATION OF SECTION 617(d).—In the case of any disposition of mining property to which section 617(d) applies (determined without regard to this subsection), any deduction under paragraph (1) with respect to amounts which are allocable to such property shall, for purposes of section 617(d), be treated as a deduction allowable under section 617(a).

(6) AMOUNTS TO WHICH ELECTION APPLY NOT TREATED AS TAX PREFERENCE.—Any portion of any qualified expenditure to which an election under paragraph (1) applies shall not be treated as an item of tax preference under section 57(a) and section 56 shall not apply to such expenditure.

[Sec. 59(f)—Stricken]

[Sec. 59(g)]

(g) TAX BENEFIT RULE.—The Secretary may prescribe regulations under which differently treated items shall be properly adjusted where the tax treatment giving rise to such items will not result in the reduction of the taxpayer's regular tax for the taxable year for which item is taken into account or for any other taxable year.

[Sec. 59(h)]

(h) COORDINATION WITH CERTAIN LIMITATIONS.—The limitations of sections 704(d), 465, and 1366(d) (and such other provisions as may be specified in regulations) shall be applied for purposes of computing the alternative minimum taxable income of the taxpayer for the taxable year with the adjustments of sections 56, 57, and 58.

[Sec. 59(i)]

(i) SPECIAL RULE FOR AMOUNTS TREATED AS TAX PREFERENCE.—For purposes of this subtitle (other than this part), any amount shall not fail to be treated as wholly exempt from tax imposed by this subtitle solely by reason of being included in alternative minimum taxable income.

[Sec. 59(j)]

(j) TREATMENT OF UNEARNED INCOME OF MINOR CHILDREN.—

(1) IN GENERAL.—In the case of a child to whom section 1(g) applies, the exemption amount for purposes of section 55 shall not exceed the sum of—

(A) such child's earned income (as defined in section 911(d)(2)) for the taxable year, plus

(B) $5,000.

(2) INFLATION ADJUSTMENT.—In the case of any taxable year beginning in a calendar year after 1998, the dollar amount in paragraph (1)(B) shall be increased by an amount equal to the product of—

(A) such dollar amount, and

(B) the cost-of-living adjustment determined under section 1(f)(3) for the calendar year in which the taxable year begins, determined by substituting "1997" for "2016" in subparagraph (A)(ii) thereof.

ıı any increase determined under the preceding sentence is not a multiple of $50, such increase shall be rounded to the nearest multiple of $50.

SUBCHAPTER B—COMPUTATION OF TAXABLE INCOME

PART I—DEFINITION OF GROSS INCOME, ADJUSTED GROSS INCOME, TAXABLE INCOME, ETC.

[Sec. 61]

SEC. 61. GROSS INCOME DEFINED.

[Sec. 61(a)]

(a) GENERAL DEFINITION.—Except as otherwise provided in this subtitle, gross income means all income from whatever source derived, including (but not limited to) the following items:

(1) Compensation for services, including fees, commissions, fringe benefits, and similar items;

(2) Gross income derived from business;

(3) Gains derived from dealings in property;

(4) Interest;

(5) Rents;

(6) Royalties;

(7) Dividends;

»»→ Caution: Code Sec. 61(a)(8), below, was stricken by P.L. 115-97, generally applicable to any divorce or separation instrument executed after December 31, 2018.

(8) Alimony and separate maintenance payments;

»»→ Caution: Former Code Sec. 61(a)(9)-(15) were redesignated by P.L. 115-97 as Code Sec. 61(a)(8)-(14), below, generally applicable to any divorce or separation instrument executed after December 31, 2018.

(8) Annuities;

(9) Income from life insurance and endowment contracts;

(10) Pensions;

(11) Income from discharge of indebtedness;

(12) Distributive share of partnership gross income;

(13) Income in respect of a decedent; and

(14) Income from an interest in an estate or trust.

[Sec. 61(b)]

(b) CROSS REFERENCES.—

For items specifically included in gross income, see part II (sec. 71 and following). For items specifically excluded from gross income, see part III (sec. 101 and following).

»»→ Caution: As provided in Section 62(d)(3), the dollar amount stated in Section 62(a)(2)(D) is adjusted for taxable years after 2015 to reflect increases in the Chained Consumer Price Index. The Section 62(a)(2)(D) dollar amount applicable to taxable years beginning in 2020 is set forth in the material beginning at page ix.

[Sec. 62]

SEC. 62. ADJUSTED GROSS INCOME DEFINED.

[Sec. 62(a)]

(a) GENERAL RULE.—For purposes of this subtitle, the term "adjusted gross income" means, in the case of an individual, gross income minus the following deductions:

(1) TRADE AND BUSINESS DEDUCTIONS.—The deductions allowed by this chapter (other than by part VII of this subchapter) which are attributable to a trade or business carried on by the taxpayer, if such trade or business does not consist of the performance of services by the taxpayer as an employee.

(2) CERTAIN TRADE AND BUSINESS DEDUCTIONS OF EMPLOYEES.—

(A) REIMBURSED EXPENSES OF EMPLOYEES.—The deductions allowed by part VI (section 161 and following) which consist of expenses paid or incurred by the taxpayer, in connection with the performance by him of services as an employee, under a reimbursement or other expense allowance arrangement with his employer. The fact that the reimbursement may be provided by a third party shall not be determinative of whether or not the preceding sentence applies.

(B) CERTAIN EXPENSES OF PERFORMING ARTISTS.—The deductions allowed by section 162 which consist of expenses paid or incurred by a qualified performing artist in connection with the performances by him of services in the performing arts as an employee.

(C) CERTAIN EXPENSES OF OFFICIALS.—The deductions allowed by section 162 which consist of expenses paid or incurred with respect to services performed by an official as an employee of a State or a political subdivision thereof in a position compensated in whole or in part on a fee basis.

(D) CERTAIN EXPENSES OF ELEMENTARY AND SECONDARY SCHOOL TEACHERS.—The deductions allowed by section 162 which consist of expenses, not in excess of $250, paid or incurred by an eligible educator—

(i) by reason of the participation of the educator in professional development courses related to the curriculum in which the educator provides instruction or to the students for which the educator provides instruction, and

(ii) in connection with books, supplies (other than nonathletic supplies for courses of instruction in health or physical education), computer equipment (including related software and services) and other equipment, and supplementary materials used by the eligible educator in the classroom.

(E) CERTAIN EXPENSES OF MEMBERS OF RESERVE COMPONENTS OF THE ARMED FORCES OF THE UNITED STATES.—The deductions allowed by section 162 which consist of expenses, determined at a rate not in excess of the rates for travel expenses (including per diem in lieu of subsistence) authorized for employees of agencies under subchapter I of chapter 57 of title 5, United States Code, paid or incurred by the taxpayer in connection with the performance of services by such taxpayer as a member of a reserve component of the Armed Forces of the United States for any period during which such individual is more than 100 miles away from home in connection with such services.

(3) LOSSES FROM SALE OR EXCHANGE OF PROPERTY.—The deductions allowed by part VI (sec. 161 and following) as losses from the sale or exchange of property.

(4) DEDUCTIONS ATTRIBUTABLE TO RENTS AND ROYALTIES.—The deductions allowed by part VI (sec. 161 and following), by section 212 (relating to expenses for production of income), and by section 611 (relating to depletion) which are attributable to property held for the production of rents or royalties.

(5) CERTAIN DEDUCTIONS OF LIFE TENANTS AND INCOME BENEFICIARIES OF PROPERTY.—In the case of a life tenant of property, or an income beneficiary of property held in trust, or an heir, legatee, or devisee of an estate, the deduction for depreciation allowed by section 167 and the deduction allowed by section 611.

(6) PENSION, PROFIT-SHARING AND ANNUITY PLANS OF SELF-EMPLOYED INDIVIDUALS.—In the case of an individual who is an employee within the meaning of section 401(c)(1), the deduction allowed by section 404.

(7) RETIREMENT SAVINGS.—The deduction allowed by section 219 (relating to deduction for certain retirement savings).

(8) [Repealed.]

(9) PENALTIES FORFEITED BECAUSE OF PREMATURE WITHDRAWAL OF FUNDS FROM TIME SAVINGS ACCOUNTS OR DEPOSITS.—The deductions allowed by section 165 for losses incurred in any transaction entered into for profit, though not connected with a trade or business to the extent that such losses include amounts forfeited to a bank, mutual savings bank, savings and loan association, building and loan association, cooperative bank or homestead association as

a penalty for premature withdrawal of funds from a time savings account, certificate of deposit, or similar class of deposit.

»»→ Caution: Code Sec. 62(a)(10), below, was stricken by P.L. 115-97, generally applicable to any divorce or separation instrument executed after December 31, 2018.

(10) ALIMONY.—The deduction allowed by section 215.

* * *

(12) CERTAIN REQUIRED REPAYMENTS OF SUPPLEMENTAL UNEMPLOYMENT COMPENSATION BENEFITS.—The deduction allowed by section 165 for the repayment to a trust described in paragraph (9) or (17) of section 501(c) of supplemental unemployment compensation benefits received from such trust if such repayment is required because of the receipt of trade readjustment allowances under section 231 or 232 of the Trade Act of 1974 (19 U.S.C. 2291 and 2292).

(13) JURY DUTY PAY REMITTED TO EMPLOYER.—Any deduction allowable under this chapter by reason of an individual remitting any portion of any jury pay to such individual's employer in exchange for payment by the employer of compensation for the period such individual was performing jury duty. For purposes of the preceding sentence, the term "jury pay" means any payment received by the individual for the discharge of jury duty.

* * *

(15) MOVING EXPENSES.—The deduction allowed by section 217.

* * *

(17) INTEREST ON EDUCATION LOANS.—The deduction allowed by section 221.

(18) HIGHER EDUCATION EXPENSES.—The deduction allowed by section 222.

(19) HEALTH SAVINGS ACCOUNTS.—The deduction allowed by section 223.

(20) COSTS INVOLVING DISCRIMINATION SUITS, ETC.—Any deduction allowable under this chapter for attorney fees and court costs paid by, or on behalf of, the taxpayer in connection with any action involving a claim of unlawful discrimination (as defined in subsection (e)) or a claim of a violation of subchapter III of chapter 37 of title 31, United States Code, or a claim made under section 1862(b)(3)(A) of the Social Security Act (42 U.S.C. 1395y(b)(3)(A)). The preceding sentence shall not apply to any deduction in excess of the amount includible in the taxpayer's gross income for the taxable year on account of a judgment or settlement (whether by suit or agreement and whether as lump sum or periodic payments) resulting from such claim.

(21) ATTORNEYS' FEES RELATING TO AWARDS TO WHISTLEBLOWERS.—

(A) IN GENERAL.—Any deduction allowable under this chapter for attorney fees and court costs paid by, or on behalf of, the taxpayer in connection with any award under—

(i) section 7623(b), or

(ii) in the case of taxable years beginning after December 31, 2017, any action brought under—

(I) section 21F of the Securities Exchange Act of 1934 (15 U.S.C. 78u-6),

(II) a State false claims act, including a State false claims act with qui tam provisions, or

(III) section 23 of the Commodity Exchange Act (7 U.S.C. 26).

(B) MAY NOT EXCEED AWARD.—Subparagraph (A) shall not apply to any deduction in excess of the amount includible in the taxpayer's gross income for the taxable year on account of such award.

(22) CHARITABLE CONTRIBUTIONS.—In the case of taxable years beginning in 2020, the amount (not to exceed $300) of qualified charitable contributions made by an eligible individual during the taxable year.

Nothing in this section shall permit the same item to be deducted more than once. Any deduction allowed by section 199A shall not be treated as a deduction described in any of the preceding paragraphs of this subsection.

[Sec. 62(b)]

(b) QUALIFIED PERFORMING ARTIST.—

(1) IN GENERAL.—For purposes of subsection (a)(2)(B), the term "qualified performing artist" means, with respect to any taxable year, any individual if—

(A) such individual performed services in the performing arts as an employee during the taxable year for at least 2 employers,

(B) the aggregate amount allowable as a deduction under section 162 in connection with the performance of such services exceeds 10 percent of such individual's gross income attributable to the performance of such services, and

(C) the adjusted gross income of such individual for the taxable year (determined without regard to subsection (a)(2)(B)) does not exceed $16,000.

(2) NOMINAL EMPLOYER NOT TAKEN INTO ACCOUNT.—An individual shall not be treated as performing services in the performing arts as an employee for any employer during any taxable year unless the amount received by such individual from such employer for the performance of such services during the taxable year equals or exceeds $200.

(3) SPECIAL RULES FOR MARRIED COUPLES.—

(A) IN GENERAL.—Except in the case of a husband and wife who lived apart at all times during the taxable year, if the taxpayer is married at the close of the taxable year, subsection (a)(2)(B) shall apply only if the taxpayer and his spouse file a joint return for the taxable year.

(B) APPLICATION OF PARAGRAPH (1).—In the case of a joint return—

(i) paragraph (1) (other than subparagraph (C) thereof) shall be applied separately with respect to each spouse, but

(ii) paragraph (1)(C) shall be applied with respect to their combined adjusted gross income.

(C) DETERMINATION OF MARITAL STATUS.—For purposes of this subsection, marital status shall be determined under section 7703(a).

(D) JOINT RETURN.—For purposes of this subsection, the term "joint return" means the joint return of a husband and wife made under section 6013.

[Sec. 62(c)]

(c) CERTAIN ARRANGEMENTS NOT TREATED AS REIMBURSEMENT ARRANGEMENTS.—For purposes of subsection (a)(2)(A), an arrangement shall in no event be treated as a reimbursement or other expense allowance arrangement if—

(1) such arrangement does not require the employee to substantiate the expenses covered by the arrangement to the person providing the reimbursement, or

(2) such arrangement provides the employee the right to retain any amount in excess of the substantiated expenses covered under the arrangement.

The substantiation requirements of the preceding sentence shall not apply to any expense to the extent that substantiation is not required under section 274(d) for such expense by reason of the regulations prescribed under the 2nd sentence thereof.

[Sec. 62(d)]

(d) DEFINITION; SPECIAL RULES.—

(1) ELIGIBLE EDUCATOR.—

(A) IN GENERAL.—For purposes of subsection (a)(2)(D), the term "eligible educator" means, with respect to any taxable year, an individual who is a kindergarten through grade 12 teacher, instructor, counselor, principal, or aide in a school for at least 900 hours during a school year.

(B) SCHOOL.—The term "school" means any school which provides elementary education or secondary education (kindergarten through grade 12), as determined under State law.

(2) COORDINATION WITH EXCLUSIONS.—A deduction shall be allowed under subsection (a)(2)(D) for expenses only to the extent the amount of such expenses exceeds the amount excludable under section 135, 529(c)(1), or 530(d)(2) for the taxable year.

(3) INFLATION ADJUSTMENT.—In the case of any taxable year beginning after 2015, the $250 amount in subsection (a)(2)(D) shall be increased by an amount equal to—

(A) such dollar amount, multiplied by

(B) the cost-of-living adjustment determined under section 1(f)(3) for the calendar year in which the taxable year begins, determined by substituting "calendar year 2014" for "calendar year 2016" in subparagraph (A)(ii) thereof.

Any increase determined under the preceding sentence shall be rounded to the nearest multiple of $50.

[Sec. 62(e)]

(e) UNLAWFUL DISCRIMINATION DEFINED.—For purposes of subsection (a)(20), the term "unlawful discrimination" means an act that is unlawful under any of the following:

(1) Section 302 of the Civil Rights Act of 1991 (42 U.S.C. 2000e-16b).

(2) Section 201, 202, 203, 204, 205, 206, 207, or 208 of the Congressional Accountability Act of 1995 (2 U.S.C. 1311, 1312, 1313, 1314, 1315, 1316, or 1317).

(3) The National Labor Relations Act (29 U.S.C. 151 et seq.).

(4) The Fair Labor Standards Act of 1938 (29 U.S.C. 201 et seq.).

(5) Section 4 or 15 of the Age Discrimination in Employment Act of 1967 (29 U.S.C. 623 or 633a).

(6) Section 501 or 504 of the Rehabilitation Act of 1973 (29 U.S.C. 791 or 794).

(7) Section 510 of the Employee Retirement Income Security Act of 1974 (29 U.S.C. 1140).

(8) Title IX of the Education Amendments of 1972 (20 U.S.C. 1681 et seq.).

(9) The Employee Polygraph Protection Act of 1988 (29 U.S.C. 2001 et seq.).

(10) The Worker Adjustment and Retraining Notification Act (29 U.S.C. 2102 et seq.).

(11) Section 105 of the Family and Medical Leave Act of 1993 (29 U.S.C. 2615).

(12) Chapter 43 of title 38, United States Code (relating to employment and reemployment rights of members of the uniformed services).

(13) Section 1977, 1979, or 1980 of the Revised Statutes (42 U.S.C. 1981, 1983, or 1985).

(14) Section 703, 704, or 717 of the Civil Rights Act of 1964 (42 U.S.C. 2000e-2, 2000e-3, or 2000e-16).

(15) Section 804, 805, 806, 808, or 818 of the Fair Housing Act (42 U.S.C. 3604, 3605, 3606, 3608, or 3617).

(16) Section 102, 202, 302, or 503 of the Americans with Disabilities Act of 1990 (42 U.S.C. 12112, 12132, 12182, or 12203).

(17) Any provision of Federal law (popularly known as whistleblower protection provisions) prohibiting the discharge of an employee, the discrimination against an employee, or any other form of retaliation or reprisal against an employee for asserting rights or taking other actions permitted under Federal law.

(18) Any provision of Federal, State, or local law, or common law claims permitted under Federal, State, or local law—

(i) providing for the enforcement of civil rights, or

(ii) regulating any aspect of the employment relationship, including claims for wages, compensation, or benefits, or prohibiting the discharge of an employee, the discrimination against an employee, or any other form of retaliation or reprisal against an employee for asserting rights or taking other actions permitted by law.

[Sec. 62(f)]

(f) DEFINITIONS RELATING TO QUALIFIED CHARITABLE CONTRIBUTIONS.—For purposes of subsection (a)(22)—

(1) ELIGIBLE INDIVIDUAL.—The term "eligible individual" means any individual who does not elect to itemize deductions.

(2) QUALIFIED CHARITABLE CONTRIBUTIONS.—The term "qualified charitable contribution" means a charitable contribution (as defined in section 170(c))—

(A) which is made in cash,

(B) for which a deduction is allowable under section 170 (determined without regard to subsection (b) thereof), and

(C) which is—

(i) made to an organization described in section 170(b)(1)(A), and

(ii) not—

(I) to an organization described in section 509(a)(3), or

(II) for the establishment of a new, or maintenance of an existing, donor advised fund (as defined in section 4966(d)(2)).

Such term shall not include any amount which is treated as a charitable contribution made in such taxable year by reason of subsection (b)(1)(G)(ii) or (d)(1) of section 170.

»→ Caution: As provided in Section 63(c)(7)(B), the dollar amounts set forth in Section 63(c)(7)(A) are adjusted for taxable years after 2018 to reflect increases in the Chained Consumer Price Index. The dollar amounts applicable to taxable years beginning in 2020 are provided in the material beginning at page ix.

[Sec. 63]

SEC. 63. TAXABLE INCOME DEFINED.

[Sec. 63(a)]

(a) IN GENERAL.—Except as provided in subsection (b), for purposes of this subtitle, the term "taxable income" means gross income minus the deductions allowed by this chapter (other than the standard deduction).

[Sec. 63(b)]

(b) INDIVIDUALS WHO DO NOT ITEMIZE THEIR DEDUCTIONS.—In the case of an individual who does not elect to itemize his deductions for the taxable year, for purposes of this subtitle, the term "taxable income" means adjusted gross income, minus—

(1) the standard deduction,

(2) the deduction for personal exemptions provided in section 151, and

(3) any deduction provided in section 199A.

[Sec. 63(c)]

(c) STANDARD DEDUCTION.—For purposes of this subtitle—

(1) IN GENERAL.—Except as otherwise provided in this subsection, the term "standard deduction" means the sum of—

(A) the basic standard deduction, and

(B) the additional standard deduction.

(2) BASIC STANDARD DEDUCTION.—For purposes of paragraph (1), the basic standard deduction is—

(A) 200 percent of the dollar amount in effect under subparagraph (C) for the taxable year in the case of—

(i) a joint return, or

(ii) a surviving spouse (as defined in section 2(a)),

(B) $4,400 in the case of a head of household (as defined in section 2(b)), or

(C) $3,000 in any other case.

(3) ADDITIONAL STANDARD DEDUCTION FOR AGED AND BLIND.—For purposes of paragraph (1), the additional standard deduction is the sum of each additional amount to which the taxpayer is entitled under subsection (f).

(4) Adjustments for inflation.—In the case of any taxable year beginning in a calendar year after 1988, each dollar amount contained in paragraph (2)(B), (2)(C), or (5) or subsection (f) shall be increased by an amount equal to—

(A) such dollar amount, multiplied by

(B) the cost-of-living adjustment determined under section 1(f)(3) for the calendar year in which the taxable year begins, by substituting for "calendar year 2016" in subparagraph (A)(ii) thereof—

(i) "calendar year 1987" in the case of the dollar amounts contained in paragraph (2)(B), (2)(C), or (5)(A) or subsection (f), and

(ii) "calendar year 1997" in the case of the dollar amount contained in paragraph (5)(B).

(5) Limitation on basic standard deduction in the case of certain dependents.—In the case of an individual with respect to whom a deduction under section 151 is allowable to another taxpayer for a taxable year beginning in the calendar year in which the individual's taxable year begins, the basic standard deduction applicable to such individual for such individual's taxable year shall not exceed the greater of—

(A) $500, or

(B) the sum of $250 and such individual's earned income.

(6) Certain individuals, etc., not eligible for standard deduction.—In the case of—

(A) a married individual filing a separate return where either spouse itemizes deductions,

(B) a nonresident alien individual,

(C) an individual making a return under section 443(a)(1) for a period of less than 12 months on account of a change in his annual accounting period, or

(D) an estate or trust, common trust fund, or partnership,

the standard deduction shall be zero.

(7) Special rules for taxable years 2018 through 2025.—In the case of a taxable year beginning after December 31, 2017, and before January 1, 2026—

(A) Increase in standard deduction.—Paragraph (2) shall be applied—

(i) by substituting "$18,000" for "$4,400" in subparagraph (B), and

(ii) by substituting "$12,000" for "$3,000" in subparagraph (C).

(B) Adjustment for inflation.—

(i) In general.—Paragraph (4) shall not apply to the dollar amounts contained in paragraphs (2)(B) and (2)(C).

(ii) Adjustment of increased amounts.—In the case of a taxable year beginning after 2018, the $18,000 and $12,000 amounts in subparagraph (A) shall each be increased by an amount equal to—

(I) such dollar amount, multiplied by

(II) the cost-of-living adjustment determined under section 1(f)(3) for the calendar year in which the taxable year begins, determined by substituting "2017" for "2016" in subparagraph (A)(ii) thereof.

If any increase under this subparagraph is not a multiple of $50, such increase shall be rounded to the next lowest multiple of $50.

[Sec. 63(d)]

(d) Itemized Deductions.—For purposes of this subtitle, the term "itemized deductions" means the deductions allowable under this chapter other than—

(1) the deductions allowable in arriving at adjusted gross income,

(2) the deduction for personal exemptions provided by section 151, and

(3) any deduction provided in section 199A.

[Sec. 63(e)]

(e) ELECTION TO ITEMIZE.—

(1) IN GENERAL.—Unless an individual makes an election under this subsection for the taxable year, no itemized deduction shall be allowed for the taxable year. For purposes of this subtitle, the determination of whether a deduction is allowable under this chapter shall be made without regard to the preceding sentence.

(2) TIME AND MANNER OF ELECTION.—Any election under this subsection shall be made on the taxpayer's return, and the Secretary shall prescribe the manner of signifying such election on the return.

(3) CHANGE OF ELECTION.—Under regulations prescribed by the Secretary, a change of election with respect to itemized deductions for any taxable year may be made after the filing of the return for such year. If the spouse of the taxpayer filed a separate return for any taxable year corresponding to the taxable year of the taxpayer, the change shall not be allowed unless, in accordance with such regulations—

(A) the spouse makes a change of election with respect to itemized deductions, for the taxable year covered in such separate return, consistent with the change of treatment sought by the taxpayer, and

(B) the taxpayer and his spouse consent in writing to the assessment (within such period as may be agreed on with the Secretary) of any deficiency, to the extent attributable to such change of election, even though at the time of the filing of such consent the assessment of such deficiency would otherwise be prevented by the operation of any law or rule of law.

This paragraph shall not apply if the tax liability of the taxpayer's spouse for the taxable year corresponding to the taxable year of the taxpayer has been compromised under section 7122.

[Sec. 63(f)]

(f) AGED OR BLIND ADDITIONAL AMOUNTS.—

(1) ADDITIONAL AMOUNTS FOR THE AGED.—The taxpayer shall be entitled to an additional amount of $600—

(A) for himself if he has attained age 65 before the close of his taxable year, and

(B) for the spouse of the taxpayer if the spouse has attained age 65 before the close of the taxable year and an additional exemption is allowable to the taxpayer for such spouse under section 151(b).

(2) ADDITIONAL AMOUNT FOR BLIND.—The taxpayer shall be entitled to an additional amount of $600—

(A) for himself if he is blind at the close of the taxable year, and

(B) for the spouse of the taxpayer if the spouse is blind as of the close of the taxable year and an additional exemption is allowable to the taxpayer for such spouse under section 151(b).

For purposes of subparagraph (B), if the spouse dies during the taxable year the determination of whether such spouse is blind shall be made as of the time of such death.

(3) HIGHER AMOUNT FOR CERTAIN UNMARRIED INDIVIDUALS.—In the case of an individual who is not married and is not a surviving spouse, paragraphs (1) and (2) shall be applied by substituting "$750" for "$600".

(4) BLINDNESS DEFINED.—For purposes of this subsection, an individual is blind only if his central visual acuity does not exceed 20/200 in the better eye with correcting lenses, or if his visual acuity is greater than 20/200 but is accompanied by a limitation in the fields of vision such that the widest diameter of the visual field subtends an angle no greater than 20 degrees.

[Sec. 63(g)]

(g) MARITAL STATUS.—For purposes of this section, marital status shall be determined under section 7703.

[Sec. 64]

SEC. 64. ORDINARY INCOME DEFINED.

For purposes of this subtitle, the term "ordinary income" includes any gain from the sale or exchange of property which is neither a capital asset nor property described in section 1231(b). Any gain from the sale or exchange of property which is treated or considered, under other provisions of this subtitle, as "ordinary income" shall be treated as gain from the sale or exchange of property which is neither a capital asset nor property described in section 1231(b).

[Sec. 65]

SEC. 65. ORDINARY LOSS DEFINED.

For purposes of this subtitle, the term "ordinary loss" includes any loss from the sale or exchange of property which is not a capital asset. Any loss from the sale or exchange of property which is treated or considered, under other provisions of this subtitle, as "ordinary loss" shall be treated as loss from the sale or exchange of property which is not a capital asset.

[Sec. 66]

SEC. 66. TREATMENT OF COMMUNITY INCOME.

[Sec. 66(a)]

(a) TREATMENT OF COMMUNITY INCOME WHERE SPOUSES LIVE APART.—If—

(1) 2 individuals are married to each other at any time during a calendar year;

(2) such individuals—

(A) live apart at all times during the calendar year, and

(B) do not file a joint return under section 6013 with each other for a taxable year beginning or ending in the calendar year;

(3) one or both of such individuals have earned income for the calendar year which is community income; and

(4) no portion of such earned income is transferred (directly or indirectly) between such individuals before the close of the calendar year,

then, for purposes of this title, any community income of such individuals for the calendar year shall be treated in accordance with the rules provided by section 879(a).

[Sec. 66(b)]

(b) SECRETARY MAY DISREGARD COMMUNITY PROPERTY LAWS WHERE SPOUSE NOT NOTIFIED OF COMMUNITY INCOME.—The Secretary may disallow the benefits of any community property law to any taxpayer with respect to any income if such taxpayer acted as if solely entitled to such income and failed to notify the taxpayer's spouse before the due date (including extensions) for filing the return for the taxable year in which the income was derived of the nature and amount of such income.

[Sec. 66(c)]

(c) SPOUSE RELIEVED OF LIABILITY IN CERTAIN OTHER CASES.—Under regulations prescribed by the Secretary, if—

(1) an individual does not file a joint return for any taxable year,

(2) such individual does not include in gross income for such taxable year an item of community income properly includible therein which, in accordance with the rules contained in section 879(a), would be treated as the income of the other spouse,

(3) the individual establishes that he or she did not know of, and had no reason to know of, such item of community income, and

(4) taking into account all facts and circumstances, it is inequitable to include such item of community income in such individual's gross income,

then, for purposes of this title, such item of community income shall be included in the gross income of the other spouse (and not in the gross income of the individual). Under procedures prescribed by the Secretary, if, taking into account all the facts and circumstances, it is inequitable to hold the individual liable for any unpaid tax or any deficiency (or any portion of either) attributable to any item for which relief is not available under the preceding sentence, the Secretary may relieve such individual of such liability.

[Sec. 66(d)]

(d) DEFINITIONS.—For purposes of this section—

(1) EARNED INCOME.—The term "earned income" has the meaning given to such term by section 911(d)(2).

(2) COMMUNITY INCOME.—The term "community income" means income which, under applicable community property laws, is treated as community income.

(3) COMMUNITY PROPERTY LAWS.—The term "community property laws" means the community property laws of a State, a foreign country, or a possession of the United States.

[Sec. 67]

SEC. 67. 2-PERCENT FLOOR ON MISCELLANEOUS ITEMIZED DEDUCTIONS.

[Sec. 67(a)]

(a) GENERAL RULE.—In the case of an individual, the miscellaneous itemized deductions for any taxable year shall be allowed only to the extent that the aggregate of such deductions exceeds 2 percent of adjusted gross income.

[Sec. 67(b)]

(b) MISCELLANEOUS ITEMIZED DEDUCTIONS.—For purposes of this section, the term "miscellaneous itemized deductions" means the itemized deductions other than—

(1) the deduction under section 163 (relating to interest),

(2) the deduction under section 164 (relating to taxes),

(3) the deduction under section 165(a) for casualty or theft losses described in paragraph (2) or (3) of section 165(c) or for losses described in section 165(d),

(4) the deductions under section 170 (relating to charitable, etc., contributions and gifts) and section 642(c) (relating to deduction for amounts paid or permanently set aside for a charitable purpose),

(5) the deduction under section 213 (relating to medical, dental, etc., expenses),

(6) any deduction allowable for impairment-related work expenses,

(7) the deduction under section 691(c) (relating to deduction for estate tax in case of income in respect of the decedent),

(8) any deduction allowable in connection with personal property used in a short sale,

(9) the deduction under section 1341 (relating to computation of tax where taxpayer restores substantial amount held under claim of right),

(10) the deduction under section 72(b)(3) (relating to deduction where annuity payments cease before investment recovered),

(11) the deduction under section 171 (relating to deduction for amortizable bond premium), and

(12) the deduction under section 216 (relating to deductions in connection with cooperative housing corporations).

* * *

[Sec. 67(d)]

(d) IMPAIRMENT-RELATED WORK EXPENSES.—For purposes of this section, the term "impairment-related work expenses" means expenses—

(1) of a handicapped individual (as defined in section 190(b)(3)) for attendant care services at the individual's place of employment and other expenses in connection with such place of employment which are necessary for such individual to be able to work, and

(2) with respect to which a deduction is allowable under section 162 (determined without regard to this section).

[Sec. 67(e)]

(e) DETERMINATION OF ADJUSTED GROSS INCOME IN CASE OF ESTATES AND TRUSTS.—For purposes of this section, the adjusted gross income of an estate or trust shall be computed in the same manner as in the case of an individual, except that—

(1) the deductions for costs which are paid or incurred in connection with the administration of the estate or trust and which would not have been incurred if the property were not held in such trust or estate, and

(2) the deductions allowable under sections 642(b), 651, and 661,

shall be treated as allowable in arriving at adjusted gross income. Under regulations, appropriate adjustments shall be made in the application of part I of subchapter J of this chapter to take into account the provisions of this section.

[Sec. 67(f)]

(f) COORDINATION WITH OTHER LIMITATION.—This section shall be applied before the application of the dollar limitation of the second sentence of section 162(a) (relating to trade or business expenses).

[Sec. 67(g)]

(g) SUSPENSION FOR TAXABLE YEARS 2018 THROUGH 2025.—Notwithstanding subsection (a), no miscellaneous itemized deduction shall be allowed for any taxable year beginning after December 31, 2017, and before January 1, 2026.

PART II—ITEMS SPECIFICALLY INCLUDED IN GROSS INCOME

»»→ Caution: Section 71 does not apply to alimony or separate maintenance payments made pursuant to a divorce or separation instrument executed after December 31, 2018.

[Sec. 71]

SEC. 71. ALIMONY AND SEPARATE MAINTENANCE PAYMENTS.

[Sec. 71(a)]

(a) GENERAL RULE.—Gross income includes amounts received as alimony or separate maintenance payments.

[Sec. 71(b)]

(b) ALIMONY OR SEPARATE MAINTENANCE PAYMENTS DEFINED.—For purposes of this section—

(1) IN GENERAL.—The term "alimony or separate maintenance payment" means any payment in cash if—

(A) such payment is received by (or on behalf of) a spouse under a divorce or separation instrument,

(B) the divorce or separation instrument does not designate such payment as a payment which is not includible in gross income under this section and not allowable as a deduction under section 215,

(C) in the case of an individual legally separated from his spouse under a decree of divorce or of separate maintenance, the payee spouse and the payor spouse are not members of the same household at the time such payment is made, and

(D) there is no liability to make any such payment for any period after the death of the payee spouse and there is no liability to make any payment (in cash or property) as a substitute for such payments after the death of the payee spouse.

(2) DIVORCE OR SEPARATION INSTRUMENT.—The term "divorce or separation instrument" means—

(A) a decree of divorce or separate maintenance or a written instrument incident to such a decree,

(B) a written separation agreement, or

(C) a decree (not described in subparagraph (A)) requiring a spouse to make payments for the support or maintenance of the other spouse.

[Sec. 71(c)]

(c) PAYMENTS TO SUPPORT CHILDREN.—

(1) IN GENERAL.—Subsection (a) shall not apply to that part of any payment which the terms of the divorce or separation instrument fix (in terms of an amount of money or a part of the payment) as a sum which is payable for the support of children of the payor spouse.

(2) TREATMENT OF CERTAIN REDUCTIONS RELATED TO CONTINGENCIES INVOLVING CHILD.—For purposes of paragraph (1), if any amount specified in the instrument will be reduced—

(A) on the happening of a contingency specified in the instrument relating to a child (such as attaining a specified age, marrying, dying, leaving school, or a similar contingency), or

(B) at a time which can clearly be associated with a contingency of a kind specified in subparagraph (A),

an amount equal to the amount of such reduction will be treated as an amount fixed as payable for the support of children of the payor spouse.

(3) SPECIAL RULE WHERE PAYMENT IS LESS THAN AMOUNT SPECIFIED IN INSTRUMENT.—For purposes of this subsection, if any payment is less than the amount specified in the instrument, then so much of such payment as does not exceed the sum payable for support shall be considered a payment for such support.

[Sec. 71(d)]

(d) SPOUSE.—For purposes of this section, the term "spouse" includes a former spouse.

[Sec. 71(e)]

(e) EXCEPTION FOR JOINT RETURNS.—This section and section 215 shall not apply if the spouses make a joint return with each other.

[Sec. 71(f)]

(f) RECOMPUTATION WHERE EXCESS FRONT-LOADING OF ALIMONY PAYMENTS.—

(1) IN GENERAL.—If there are excess alimony payments—

(A) the payor spouse shall include the amount of such excess payments in gross income for the payor spouse's taxable year beginning in the 3rd post-separation year, and

(B) the payee spouse shall be allowed a deduction in computing adjusted gross income for the amount of such excess payments for the payee's taxable year beginning in the 3rd post-separation year.

(2) EXCESS ALIMONY PAYMENTS.—For purposes of this subsection, the term "excess alimony payments" mean the sum of—

(A) the excess payments for the 1st post-separation year, and

(B) the excess payments for the 2nd post-separation year.

(3) EXCESS PAYMENTS FOR 1ST POST-SEPARATION YEAR.—For purposes of this subsection, the amount of the excess payments for the 1st post-separation year is the excess (if any) of—

(A) the amount of the alimony or separate maintenance payments paid by the payor spouse during the 1st post-separation year, over

(B) the sum of—

(i) the average of—

(I) the alimony or separate maintenance payments paid by the payor spouse during the 2nd post-separation year, reduced by the excess payments for the 2nd post-separation year, and

(II) the alimony or separate maintenance payments paid by the payor spouse during the 3rd post-separation year, plus

(ii) $15,000.

(4) EXCESS PAYMENTS FOR 2ND POST-SEPARATION YEAR.—For purposes of this subsection, the amount of the excess payments for the 2nd post-separation year is the excess (if any) of—

(A) the amount of the alimony or separate maintenance payments paid by the payor spouse during the 2nd post-separation year, over

(B) the sum of—

(i) the amount of the alimony or separate maintenance payments paid by the payor spouse during the 3rd post-separation year, plus

(ii) $15,000.

(5) EXCEPTIONS.—

(A) WHERE PAYMENT CEASES BY REASON OF DEATH OR REMARRIAGE.—Paragraph (1) shall not apply if—

(i) either spouse dies before the close of the 3rd post-separation year, or the payee spouse remarries before the close of the 3rd post-separation year, and

(ii) the alimony or separate maintenance payments cease by reason of such death or remarriage.

(B) SUPPORT PAYMENTS.—For purposes of this subsection, the term "alimony or separate maintenance payment" shall not include any payment received under a decree described in subsection (b) (2) (C).

(C) FLUCTUATING PAYMENTS NOT WITHIN CONTROL OF PAYOR SPOUSE.—For purposes of this subsection, the term "alimony or separate maintenance payment" shall not include any payment to the extent it is made pursuant to a continuing liability (over a period of not less than 3 years) to pay a fixed portion or portions of the income from a business or property or from compensation for employment or self-employment.

(6) POST-SEPARATION YEARS.—For purposes of this subsection, the term "1st post-separation years" means the 1st calendar year in which the payor spouse paid to the payee spouse alimony or separate maintenance payments to which this section applies. The 2nd and 3rd post-separation years shall be the 1st and 2nd succeeding calendar years, respectively.

[Sec. 71(g)]

(g) CROSS REFERENCES.—

(1) For deduction of alimony or separate maintenance payments, see section 215.

(2) For taxable status of income of an estate or trust in the case of divorce, etc., see section 682.

[Sec. 72]

SEC. 72. ANNUITIES; CERTAIN PROCEEDS OF ENDOWMENT AND LIFE INSURANCE CONTRACTS.

[Sec. 72(a)]

(a) GENERAL RULE FOR ANNUITIES.—

(1) INCOME INCLUSION.—Except as otherwise provided in this chapter, gross income includes any amount received as an annuity (whether for a period certain or during one or more lives) under an annuity, endowment, or life insurance contract.

(2) PARTIAL ANNUITIZATION.—If any amount is received as an annuity for a period of 10 years or more or during one or more lives under any portion of an annuity, endowment, or life insurance contract—

(A) such portion shall be treated as a separate contract for purposes of this section,

(B) for purposes of applying subsections (b), (c), and (e), the investment in the contract shall be allocated pro rata between each portion of the contract from which amounts are received as an annuity and the portion of the contract from which amounts are not received as an annuity, and

(C) a separate annuity starting date under subsection (c) (4) shall be determined with respect to each portion of the contract from which amounts are received as an annuity.

[Sec. 72(b)]

(b) EXCLUSION RATIO.—

(1) IN GENERAL.—Gross income does not include that part of any amount received as an annuity under an annuity, endowment, or life insurance contract which bears the same ratio to such amount as the investment in the contract (as of the annuity starting date) bears to the expected return under the contract (as of such date).

(2) EXCLUSION LIMITED TO INVESTMENT.—The portion of any amount received as an annuity which is excluded from gross income under paragraph (1) shall not exceed the unrecovered investment in the contract immediately before the receipt of such amount.

(3) DEDUCTION WHERE ANNUITY PAYMENTS CEASE BEFORE ENTIRE INVESTMENT RECOVERED.—

(A) IN GENERAL.—If—

(i) after the annuity starting date, payments as an annuity under the contract cease by reason of the death of an annuitant, and

(ii) as of the date of such cessation, there is unrecovered investment in the contract,

the amount of such unrecovered investment (in excess of any amount specified in subsection (e)(5) which was not included in gross income) shall be allowed as a deduction to the annuitant for his last taxable year.

(B) PAYMENTS TO OTHER PERSONS.—In the case of any contract which provides for payments meeting the requirements of subparagraphs (B) and (C) of subsection (c)(2), the deduction under subparagraph (A) shall be allowed to the person entitled to such payments for the taxable year in which such payments are received.

(C) NET OPERATING LOSS DEDUCTIONS PROVIDED.—For purposes of section 172, a deduction allowed under this paragraph shall be treated as if it were attributable to a trade or business of the taxpayer.

(4) UNRECOVERED INVESTMENT.—For purposes of this subsection, the unrecovered investment in the contract as of any date is—

(A) the investment in the contract (determined without regard to subsection (c)(2)) as of the annuity starting date, reduced by

(B) the aggregate amount received under the contract on or after such annuity starting date and before the date as of which the determination is being made, to the extent such amount was excludable from gross income under this subtitle.

[Sec. 72(c)]

(c) DEFINITIONS.—

(1) INVESTMENT IN THE CONTRACT.—For purposes of subsection (b), the investment in the contract as of the annuity starting date is—

(A) the aggregate amount of premiums or other consideration paid for the contract, minus

(B) the aggregate amount received under the contract before such date, to the extent that such amount was excludable from gross income under this subtitle or prior income tax laws.

(2) ADJUSTMENT IN INVESTMENT WHERE THERE IS REFUND FEATURE.—If—

(A) the expected return under the contract depends in whole or in part on the life expectancy of one or more individuals;

(B) the contract provides for payments to be made to a beneficiary (or to the estate of an annuitant) on or after the death of the annuitant or annuitants; and

(C) such payments are in the nature of a refund of the consideration paid,

then the value (computed without discount for interest) of such payments on the annuity starting date shall be subtracted from the amount determined under paragraph (1). Such value shall be computed in accordance with actuarial tables prescribed by the Secretary. For purposes of this paragraph and of subsection (e) (2) (A), the term "refund of the consideration paid" includes amounts payable after the death of an annuitant by reason of a provision in the contract for a life annuity with minimum period of payments certain, but (if part of the consideration was contributed by an employer) does not include that part of any payment to a beneficiary (or to the estate of the annuitant) which is not attributable to the consideration paid by the employee for the contract as determined under paragraph (1) (A).

(3) EXPECTED RETURN.—For purposes of subsection (b), the expected return under the contract shall be determined as follows:

(A) LIFE EXPECTANCY.—If the expected return under the contract, for the period on and after the annuity starting date, depends in whole or in part on the life expectancy of one or more individuals, the expected return shall be computed with reference to actuarial tables prescribed by the Secretary.

(B) INSTALLMENT PAYMENTS.—If subparagraph (A) does not apply, the expected return is the aggregate of the amounts receivable under the contract as an annuity.

(4) ANNUITY STARTING DATE.—For purposes of this section, the annuity starting date in the case of any contract is the first day of the first period for which an amount is received as an annuity under the contract.

[Sec. 72(d)]

(d) SPECIAL RULES FOR QUALIFIED EMPLOYER RETIREMENT PLANS.—

(1) SIMPLIFIED METHOD OF TAXING ANNUITY PAYMENTS.—

(A) IN GENERAL.—In the case of any amount received as an annuity under a qualified employer retirement plan—

(i) subsection (b) shall not apply, and

(ii) the investment in the contract shall be recovered as provided in this paragraph.

(B) METHOD OF RECOVERING INVESTMENT IN CONTRACT.—

(i) IN GENERAL.—Gross income shall not include so much of any monthly annuity payment under a qualified employer retirement plan as does not exceed the amount obtained by dividing—

(I) the investment in the contract (as of the annuity starting date), by

(II) the number of anticipated payments determined under the table contained in clause (iii) (or, in the case of a contract to which subsection (c)(3)(B) applies, the number of monthly annuity payments under such contract).

(ii) CERTAIN RULES MADE APPLICABLE.—Rules similar to the rules of paragraphs (2) and (3) of subsection (b) shall apply for purposes of this paragraph.

(iii) NUMBER OF ANTICIPATED PAYMENTS.—If the annuity is payable over the life of a single individual, the number of anticipated payments shall be determined as follows:

If the age of the annuitant on the annuity starting date is:	*The number of anticipated payments is:*
Not more than 55	360
More than 55 but not more than 60	310
More than 60 but not more than 65	260
More than 65 but not more than 70	210
More than 70	160

(iv) NUMBER OF ANTICIPATED PAYMENTS WHERE MORE THAN ONE LIFE.—If the annuity is payable over the lives of more than 1 individual, the number of anticipated payments shall be determined as follows:

If the combined ages of annuitants are:	*The number is:*
Not more than 110	410
More than 110 but not more than 120	360
More than 120 but not more than 130	310
More than 130 but not more than 140	260
More than 140	210

(C) ADJUSTMENT FOR REFUND FEATURE NOT APPLICABLE.—For purposes of this paragraph, investment in the contract shall be determined under subsection (c)(1) without regard to subsection (c)(2).

(D) SPECIAL RULE WHERE LUMP SUM PAID IN CONNECTION WITH COMMENCEMENT OF ANNUITY PAYMENTS.—If, in connection with the commencement of annuity payments under any qualified employer retirement plan, the taxpayer receives a lump-sum payment—

(i) such payment shall be taxable under subsection (e) as if received before the annuity starting date, and

(ii) the investment in the contract for purposes of this paragraph shall be determined as if such payment had been so received.

(E) EXCEPTION.—This paragraph shall not apply in any case where the primary annuitant has attained age 75 on the annuity starting date unless there are fewer than 5 years of guaranteed payments under the annuity.

(F) ADJUSTMENT WHERE ANNUITY PAYMENTS NOT ON MONTHLY BASIS.—In any case where the annuity payments are not made on a monthly basis, appropriate adjustments in the application of this paragraph shall be made to take into account the period on the basis of which such payments are made.

(G) QUALIFIED EMPLOYER RETIREMENT PLAN.—For purposes of this paragraph, the term "qualified employer retirement plan" means any plan or contract described in paragraph (1), (2), or (3) of section 4974(c).

(2) TREATMENT OF EMPLOYEE CONTRIBUTIONS UNDER DEFINED CONTRIBUTION PLANS.—For purposes of this section, employee contributions (and any income allocable thereto) under a defined contribution plan may be treated as a separate contract.

[Sec. 72(e)]

(e) AMOUNTS NOT RECEIVED AS ANNUITIES.—

(1) APPLICATION OF SUBSECTION.—

(A) IN GENERAL.—This subsection shall apply to any amount which—

(i) is received under an annuity, endowment, or life insurance contract, and

(ii) is not received as an annuity, if no provision of this subtitle (other than this subsection) applies with respect to such amount.

(B) DIVIDENDS.—For purposes of this section, any amount received which is in the nature of a dividend or similar distribution shall be treated as an amount not received as an annuity.

(2) GENERAL RULE.—Any amount to which this subsection applies—

(A) if received on or after the annuity starting date, shall be included in gross income, or

(B) if received before the annuity starting date—

(i) shall be included in gross income to the extent allocable to income on the contract, and

(ii) shall not be included in gross income to the extent allocable to the investment in the contract.

(3) ALLOCATION OF AMOUNTS TO INCOME AND INVESTMENT.—For purposes of paragraph (2)(B)—

(A) ALLOCATION TO INCOME.—Any amount to which this subsection applies shall be treated as allocable to income on the contract to the extent that such amount does not exceed the excess (if any) of—

(i) the cash value of the contract (determined without regard to any surrender charge) immediately before the amount is received, over

(ii) the investment in the contract at such time.

(B) ALLOCATION TO INVESTMENT.—Any amount to which this subsection applies shall be treated as allocable to investment in the contract to the extent that such amount is not allocated to income under subparagraph (A).

(4) SPECIAL RULES FOR APPLICATION OF PARAGRAPH (2)(B).—For purposes of paragraph (2)(B)—

(A) LOANS TREATED AS DISTRIBUTIONS.—If, during any taxable year, an individual—

(i) receives (directly or indirectly) any amount as a loan under any contract to which this subsection applies, or

(ii) assigns or pledges (or agrees to assign or pledge) any portion of the value of any such contract,

such amount or portion shall be treated as received under the contract as an amount not received as an annuity. The preceding sentence shall not apply for purposes of determining investment in the contract, except that the investment in the contract shall be increased by any amount included in gross income by reason of the amount treated as received under the preceding sentence.

(B) TREATMENT OF POLICYHOLDER DIVIDENDS.—Any amount described in paragraph (1)(B) shall not be included in gross income under paragraph (2)(B)(i) to the extent such amount is retained by the insurer as a premium or other consideration paid for the contract.

(C) TREATMENT OF TRANSFERS WITHOUT ADEQUATE CONSIDERATION.—

(i) IN GENERAL.—If an individual who holds an annuity contract transfers it without full and adequate consideration, such individual shall be treated as receiving an amount equal to the excess of—

(I) the cash surrender value of such contract at the time of transfer, over

(II) the investment in such contract at such time,

under the contract as an amount not received as an annuity.

(ii) EXCEPTION FOR CERTAIN TRANSFERS BETWEEN SPOUSES OR FORMER SPOUSES.—Clause (i) shall not apply to any transfer to which section 1041(a) (relating to transfers of property between spouses or incident to divorce) applies.

(iii) ADJUSTMENT TO INVESTMENT IN CONTRACT OF TRANSFEREE.—If under clause (i) an amount is included in the gross income of the transferor of an annuity contract, the investment in the contract of the transferee in such contract shall be increased by the amount so included.

(5) RETENTION OF EXISTING RULES IN CERTAIN CASES.—

(A) IN GENERAL.—In any case to which this paragraph applies—

(i) paragraphs (2)(B) and (4)(A) shall not apply, and

(ii) if paragraph (2)(A) does not apply,

the amount shall be included in gross income, but only to the extent it exceeds the investment in the contract.

(B) EXISTING CONTRACTS.—This paragraph shall apply to contracts entered into before August 14, 1982. Any amount allocable to investment in the contract after August 13, 1982, shall be treated as from a contract entered into after such date.

(C) CERTAIN LIFE INSURANCE AND ENDOWMENT CONTRACTS.—Except as provided in paragraph (10) and except to the extent prescribed by the Secretary by regulations, this paragraph shall apply to any amount not received as an annuity which is received under a life insurance or endowment contract.

(D) CONTRACTS UNDER QUALIFIED PLANS.—Except as provided in paragraph (8), this paragraph shall apply to any amount received—

(i) from a trust described in section 401(a) which is exempt from tax under section 501(a),

(ii) from a contract—

(I) purchased by a trust described in clause (i),

(II) purchased as part of a plan described in section 403(a),

(III) described in section 403(b), or

(IV) provided for employees of a life insurance company under a plan described in section 818(a)(3), or

(iii) from an individual retirement account or an individual retirement annuity.

Any dividend described in section 404(k) which is received by a participant or beneficiary shall, for purposes of this subparagraph, be treated as paid under a separate contract to which clause (ii)(I) applies.

(E) FULL REFUNDS, SURRENDERS, REDEMPTIONS, AND MATURITIES.—This paragraph shall apply to—

(i) any amount received, whether in a single sum or otherwise, under a contract in full discharge of the obligation under the contract which is in the nature of a refund of the consideration paid for the contract, and

(ii) any amount received under a contract on its complete surrender, redemption, or maturity.

In the case of any amount to which the preceding sentence applies, the rule of paragraph (2)(A) shall not apply.

(6) INVESTMENT IN THE CONTRACT.—For purposes of this subsection, the investment in the contract as of any date is—

(A) the aggregate amount of premiums or other consideration paid for the contract before such date, minus

(B) the aggregate amount received under the contract before such date, to the extent that such amount was excludable from gross income under this subtitle or prior income tax laws.

* * *

(12) ANTI-ABUSE RULES.—

(A) IN GENERAL.—For purposes of determining the amount includible in gross income under this subsection—

(i) all modified endowment contracts issued by the same company to the same policyholder during any calendar year shall be treated as 1 modified endowment contract, and

(ii) all annuity contracts issued by the same company to the same policyholder during any calendar year shall be treated as 1 annuity contract.

The preceding sentence shall not apply to any contract described in paragraph (5)(D).

(B) REGULATORY AUTHORITY.—The Secretary may by regulations prescribe such additional rules as may be necessary or appropriate to prevent avoidance of the purposes of this subsection through serial purchases of contracts or otherwise.

[Sec. 72(f)]

(f) SPECIAL RULES FOR COMPUTING EMPLOYEES' CONTRIBUTIONS.—In computing, for purposes of subsection (c)(1)(A), the aggregate amount of premiums or other consideration paid for the contract, and for purposes of subsection (e)(6), the aggregate premiums or other consideration paid, amounts contributed by the employer shall be included, but only to the extent that—

(1) such amounts were includible in the gross income of the employee under this subtitle or prior income tax laws; or

(2) if such amounts had been paid directly to the employee at the time they were contributed, they would not have been includible in the gross income of the employee under the law applicable at the time of such contribution.

Paragraph (2) shall not apply to amounts which were contributed by the employer after December 31, 1962, and which would not have been includible in the gross income of the employee by reason of the application of section 911 if such amounts had been paid directly to the employee at the time of contribution. The preceding sentence shall not apply to amounts which were contributed by the employer, as determined under regulations prescribed by the Secretary, to provide pension or annuity credits, to the extent such credits are attributable to services performed before January 1, 1963, and are provided pursuant to pension or annuity plan provisions in existence on March 12, 1962, and on that date applicable to such services, or to the extent such credits are attributable to services performed as a foreign missionary (within the meaning of section 403(b)(2)(D)(iii), as in effect before the enactment of the Economic Growth and Tax Relief Reconciliation Act of 2001).

[Sec. 72(g)]

(g) RULES FOR TRANSFEREE WHERE TRANSFER WAS FOR VALUE.—Where any contract (or any interest therein) is transferred (by assignment or otherwise) for a valuable consideration, to the extent that the contract (or interest therein) does not, in the hands of the transferee, have a basis which is determined by reference to the basis in the hands of the transferor, then—

(1) for purposes of this section, only the actual value of such consideration, plus the amount of the premiums and other consideration paid by the transferee after the transfer, shall be taken into account in computing the aggregate amount of the premiums or other consideration paid for the contract;

(2) for purposes of subsection (c) (1) (B), there shall be taken into account only the aggregate amount received under the contract by the transferee before the annuity starting date, to the extent that such amount was excludable from gross income under this subtitle or prior income tax laws; and

(3) the annuity starting date is the first day of the first period for which the transferee received an amount under the contract as an annuity.

For purposes of this subsection, the term "transferee" includes a beneficiary of, or the estate of, the transferee.

[Sec. 72(h)]

(h) OPTION TO RECEIVE ANNUITY IN LIEU OF LUMP SUM.—If—

(1) a contract provides for payment of a lump sum in full discharge of an obligation under the contract, subject to an option to receive an annuity in lieu of such lump sum;

(2) the option is exercised within 60 days after the day on which such lump sum first became payable; and

(3) part or all of such lump sum would (but for this subsection) be includible in gross income by reason of subsection (e) (1),

then, for purposes of this subtitle, no part of such lump sum shall be considered as includible in gross income at the time such lump sum first became payable.

[Sec. 72(j)]

(j) INTEREST.—Notwithstanding any other provision of this section, if any amount is held under an agreement to pay interest thereon, the interest payments shall be included in gross income.

* * *

[Sec. 72(q)]

(q) 10-PERCENT PENALTY FOR PREMATURE DISTRIBUTIONS FROM ANNUITY CONTRACTS.—

(1) IMPOSITION OF PENALTY.—If any taxpayer receives any amount under an annuity contract, the taxpayer's tax under this chapter for the taxable year in which such amount is received shall be increased by an amount equal to 10 percent of the portion of such amount which is includible in gross income.

(2) SUBSECTION NOT TO APPLY TO CERTAIN DISTRIBUTIONS.—Paragraph (1) shall not apply to any distribution—

(A) made on or after the date on which the taxpayer attains age 59½,

(B) made on or after the death of the holder (or, where the holder is not an individual, the death of the primary annuitant (as defined in subsection (s)(6)(B))),

(C) attributable to the taxpayer's becoming disabled within the meaning of subsection (m) (7),

(D) which is a part of a series of substantially equal periodic payments (not less frequently than annually) made for the life (or life expectancy) of the taxpayer or the joint lives (or joint life expectancies) of such taxpayer and his designated beneficiary,

(E) from a plan, contract, account, trust, or annuity described in subsection (e) (5) (D),

(F) allocable to investment in the contract before August 14, 1982,

(G) under a qualified funding asset (within the meaning of section 130(d), but without regard to whether there is a qualified assignment,

(H) to which subsection (t) applies (without regard to paragraph (2) thereof),

(I) under an immediate annuity contract (within the meaning of section 72(u) (4)), or

(J) which is purchased by an employer upon the termination of a plan described in section 401(a) or 403(a) and which is held by the employer until such time as the employee separates from service.

(3) CHANGE IN SUBSTANTIALLY EQUAL PAYMENTS.—If—

(A) paragraph (1) does not apply to a distribution by reason of paragraph (2) (D), and

(B) the series of payments under such paragraph are subsequently modified (other than by reason of death or disability—

(i) before the close of the 5-year period beginning on the date of the first payment and after the taxpayer attains age 59½, or

(ii) before the taxpayer attains age 59½,

the taxpayer's tax for the 1st taxable year in which such modification occurs shall be increased by an amount, determined under regulations, equal to the tax which (but for paragraph (2) (D)) would have been imposed, plus interest for the deferral period (within the meaning of subsection (t) (4) (B)).

* * *

[Sec. 72(t)]

(t) 10-PERCENT ADDITIONAL TAX ON EARLY DISTRIBUTIONS FROM QUALIFIED RETIREMENT PLANS.—

(1) IMPOSITION OF ADDITIONAL TAX.—If any taxpayer receives any amount from a qualified retirement plan (as defined in section 4974(c)), the taxpayer's tax under this chapter for the taxable year in which such amount is received shall be increased by an amount equal to 10 percent of the portion of such amount which is includible in gross income.

(2) SUBSECTION NOT TO APPLY TO CERTAIN DISTRIBUTIONS.—Except as provided in paragraphs (3) and (4), paragraph (1) shall not apply to any of the following distributions:

(A) IN GENERAL.—Distributions which are—

(i) made on or after the date on which the employee attains age 59½,

(ii) made to a beneficiary (or to the estate of the employee) on or after the death of the employee,

(iii) attributable to the employee's being disabled within the meaning of subsection (m) (7),

(iv) part of a series of substantially equal periodic payments (not less frequently than annually) made for the life (or life expectancy) of the employee or the joint lives (or joint life expectancies) of such employee and his designated beneficiary,

(v) made to an employee after separation from service after attainment of age 55,

(vi) dividends paid with respect to stock of a corporation which are described in section 404(k),

(vii) made on account of a levy under section 6331 on the qualified retirement plan, or

(viii) payments under a phased retirement annuity under section 8366a(a)(5) or 8412a(a)(5) of title 5, United States Code, or a composite retirement annuity under section 8366a(a)(1) or 8412a(a)(1) of such title.

(B) MEDICAL EXPENSES.—Distributions made to the employee (other than distributions described in subparagraph (A), (C) or (D)) to the extent such distributions do not exceed the amount allowable as a deduction under section 213 to the employee for amounts paid during the taxable year for medical care (determined without regard to whether the employee itemizes deductions for such taxable year).

(C) PAYMENTS TO ALTERNATE PAYEES PURSUANT TO QUALIFIED DOMESTIC RELATIONS ORDERS.—Any distribution to an alternate payee pursuant to a qualified domestic relations order (within the meaning of section 414(p)(1)).

(D) DISTRIBUTIONS TO UNEMPLOYED INDIVIDUALS FOR HEALTH INSURANCE PREMIUMS.—

(i) IN GENERAL.—Distributions from an individual retirement plan to an individual after separation from employment—

(I) if such individual has received unemployment compensation for 12 consecutive weeks under any Federal or State unemployment compensation law by reason of such separation,

(II) if such distributions are made during any taxable year during which such unemployment compensation is paid or the succeeding taxable year, and

(III) to the extent such distributions do not exceed the amount paid during the taxable year for insurance described in section 213(d)(1)(D) with respect to the individual and the individual's spouse and dependents (as defined in section 152, determined without regard to subsections (b)(1), (b)(2), and (d)(1)(B) thereof).

(ii) DISTRIBUTIONS AFTER REEMPLOYMENT.—Clause (i) shall not apply to any distribution made after the individual has been employed for at least 60 days after the separation from employment to which clause (i) applies.

(iii) SELF-EMPLOYED INDIVIDUALS.—To the extent provided in regulations, a self-employed individual shall be treated as meeting the requirements of clause (i)(I) if, under Federal or State law, the individual would have received unemployment compensation but for the fact the individual was self-employed.

(E) DISTRIBUTIONS FROM INDIVIDUAL RETIREMENT PLANS FOR HIGHER EDUCATION EXPENSES.—Distributions to an individual from an individual retirement plan to the extent such distributions do not exceed the qualified higher education expenses (as defined in paragraph (7)) of the taxpayer for the taxable year. Distributions shall not be taken into account under the preceding sentence if such distributions are described in subparagraph (A), (C), or (D) or to the extent paragraph (1) does not apply to such distributions by reason of subparagraph (B).

(F) DISTRIBUTIONS FROM CERTAIN PLANS FOR FIRST HOME PURCHASES.—Distributions to an individual from an individual retirement plan which are qualified first-time homebuyer distributions (as defined in paragraph (8)). Distributions shall not be taken into account under the preceding sentence if such distributions are described in subparagraph (A), (C), (D), or (E) or to the extent paragraph (1) does not apply to such distributions by reason of subparagraph (B).

(G) DISTRIBUTIONS FROM RETIREMENT PLANS TO INDIVIDUALS CALLED TO ACTIVE DUTY.—

(i) IN GENERAL.—Any qualified reservist distribution.

(ii) AMOUNT DISTRIBUTED MAY BE REPAID.—Any individual who receives a qualified reservist distribution may, at any time during the 2-year period beginning on the day after the end of the active duty period, make one or more contributions to an individual retirement plan of such individual in an aggregate amount not to exceed the amount of such distribution. The dollar limitations otherwise applicable to contributions to individual retirement plans shall not apply to any contribution made pursuant to the preceding sentence. No deduction shall be allowed for any contribution pursuant to this clause.

(iii) QUALIFIED RESERVIST DISTRIBUTION.—For purposes of this subparagraph, the term "qualified reservist distribution" means any distribution to an individual if—

(I) such distribution is from an individual retirement plan, or from amounts attributable to employer contributions made pursuant to elective deferrals described in subparagraph (A) or (C) of section 402(g)(3) or section 501(c)(18)(D)(iii),

(II) such individual was (by reason of being a member of a reserve component (as defined in section 101 of title 37, United States Code)) ordered or called to active duty for a period in excess of 179 days or for an indefinite period, and

(III) such distribution is made during the period beginning on the date of such order or call and ending at the close of the active duty period.

(iv) APPLICATION OF SUBPARAGRAPH.—This subparagraph applies to individuals ordered or called to active duty after September 11, 2001. In no event shall the 2-year period referred to in clause (ii) end before the date which is 2 years after the date of the enactment of this subparagraph.

(H) DISTRIBUTIONS FROM RETIREMENT PLANS IN CASE OF BIRTH OF CHILD OR ADOPTION.—

(i) IN GENERAL.—Any qualified birth or adoption distribution.

(ii) LIMITATION.—The aggregate amount which may be treated as qualified birth or adoption distributions by any individual with respect to any birth or adoption shall not exceed $5,000.

(iii) QUALIFIED BIRTH OR ADOPTION DISTRIBUTION.—For purposes of this subparagraph—

(I) IN GENERAL.—The term "qualified birth or adoption distribution" means any distribution from an applicable eligible retirement plan to an individual if made during the 1-year period beginning on the date on which a child of the individual is born or on which the legal adoption by the individual of an eligible adoptee is finalized.

(II) ELIGIBLE ADOPTEE.—The term "eligible adoptee" means any individual (other than a child of the taxpayer's spouse) who has not attained age 18 or is physically or mentally incapable of self-support.

(iv) TREATMENT OF PLAN DISTRIBUTIONS.—

(I) IN GENERAL.—If a distribution to an individual would (without regard to clause (ii)) be a qualified birth or adoption distribution, a plan shall not be treated as failing to meet any requirement of this title merely because the plan treats the distribution as a qualified birth or adoption distribution, unless the aggregate amount of such distributions from all plans maintained by the employer (and any member of any controlled group which includes the employer) to such individual exceeds $5,000.

(II) CONTROLLED GROUP.—For purposes of subclause (I), the term "controlled group" means any group treated as a single employer under subsection (b), (c), (m), or (o) of section 414.

(v) AMOUNT DISTRIBUTED MAY BE REPAID.—

(I) IN GENERAL.—Any individual who receives a qualified birth or adoption distribution may make one or more contributions in an aggregate amount not to exceed the amount of such distribution to an applicable eligible retirement plan of which such individual is a beneficiary and to which a rollover contribution of such distribution could be made under section 402(c), 403(a)(4), 403(b)(8), 408(d)(3), or 457(e)(16), as the case may be.

(II) LIMITATION ON CONTRIBUTIONS TO APPLICABLE ELIGIBLE RETIREMENT PLANS OTHER THAN IRAS.—The aggregate amount of contributions made by an individual under subclause (I) to any applicable eligible retirement plan which is not an individual retirement plan shall not exceed the aggregate amount of qualified birth or adoption distributions which are made from such plan to such individual. Subclause (I) shall not apply to contributions to any applicable eligible retirement plan which is not an individual retirement plan unless the individual is eligible to make contributions (other than those described in subclause (I)) to such applicable eligible retirement plan.

(III) TREATMENT OF REPAYMENTS OF DISTRIBUTIONS FROM APPLICABLE ELIGIBLE RETIREMENT PLANS OTHER THAN IRAS.—If a contribution is made under subclause (I) with respect to a qualified birth or adoption distribution from an applicable eligible retirement plan other than an individual retirement plan, then the taxpayer shall, to the extent of the amount of the contribution, be treated as having received such distribution in an eligible rollover distribution (as defined in section 402(c)(4)) and as having transferred the amount to the applicable eligible retirement plan in a direct trustee to trustee transfer within 60 days of the distribution.

(IV) TREATMENT OF REPAYMENTS FOR DISTRIBUTIONS FROM IRAS.—If a contribution is made under subclause (I) with respect to a qualified birth or adoption distribution from an individual retirement plan, then, to the extent of the amount of the contribution, such distribution shall be treated as a distribution described in section 408(d)(3) and as having been transferred to the applicable eligible retirement plan in a direct trustee to trustee transfer within 60 days of the distribution.

(vi) DEFINITION AND SPECIAL RULES.—For purposes of this subparagraph—

(I) APPLICABLE ELIGIBLE RETIREMENT PLAN.—The term "applicable eligible retirement plan" means an eligible retirement plan (as defined in section 402(c)(8)(B)) other than a defined benefit plan.

(II) EXEMPTION OF DISTRIBUTIONS FROM TRUSTEE TO TRUSTEE TRANSFER AND WITHHOLDING RULES.—For purposes of sections 401(a)(31), 402(f), and 3405, a qualified birth or adoption distribution shall not be treated as an eligible rollover distribution.

(III) TAXPAYER MUST INCLUDE TIN.—A distribution shall not be treated as a qualified birth or adoption distribution with respect to any child or eligible adoptee unless the taxpayer includes the name, age, and TIN of such child or eligible adoptee on the taxpayer's return of tax for the taxable year.

(IV) DISTRIBUTIONS TREATED AS MEETING PLAN DISTRIBUTION REQUIREMENTS.—Any qualified birth or adoption distribution shall be treated as meeting the requirements of sections 401(k)(2)(B)(i), 403(b)(7)(A)(ii), 403(b)(11), and 457(d)(1)(A).

(3) LIMITATIONS.—

(A) CERTAIN EXCEPTIONS NOT TO APPLY TO INDIVIDUAL RETIREMENT PLANS.—Subparagraphs (A)(v) and (C) of paragraph (2) shall not apply to distributions from an individual retirement plan.

(B) PERIODIC PAYMENTS UNDER QUALIFIED PLANS MUST BEGIN AFTER SEPARATION.—Paragraph (2)(A)(iv) shall not apply to any amount paid from a trust described in section 401(a) which is exempt from tax under section 501(a) or from a contract described in section 72(e)(5)(D)(ii) unless the series of payments begins after the employee separates from service.

(4) CHANGE IN SUBSTANTIALLY EQUAL PAYMENTS.—

(A) IN GENERAL.—If—

(i) paragraph (1) does not apply to a distribution by reason of paragraph (2)(A)(iv), and

(ii) the series of payments under such paragraph are subsequently modified (other than by reason of death or disability or a distribution to which paragraph (10) applies)—

(I) before the close of the 5-year period beginning with the date of the first payment and after the employee attains age 59½, or

(II) before the employee attains age 59½,

the taxpayer's tax for the 1st taxable year in which such modification occurs shall be increased by an amount, determined under regulations, equal to the tax which (but for paragraph (2)(A)(iv)) would have been imposed, plus interest for the deferral period.

(B) DEFERRAL PERIOD.—For purposes of this paragraph, the term "deferral period" means the period beginning with the taxable year in which (without regard to paragraph (2)(A)(iv)) the distribution would have been includible in gross income and ending with the taxable year in which the modification described in subparagraph (A) occurs.

(5) EMPLOYEE.—For purposes of this subsection, the term "employee" includes any participant, and in the case of an individual retirement plan, the individual for whose benefit such plan was established.

(6) SPECIAL RULES FOR SIMPLE RETIREMENT ACCOUNTS.—In the case of any amount received from a simple retirement account (within the meaning of section 408(p)) during the 2-year period beginning on the date such individual first participated in any qualified salary reduction arrangement maintained by the individual's employer under section 408(p)(2), paragraph (1) shall be applied by substituting "25 percent" for "10 percent".

(7) QUALIFIED HIGHER EDUCATION EXPENSES.—For purposes of paragraph (2)(E)—

(A) IN GENERAL.—The term "qualified higher education expenses" means qualified higher education expenses (as defined in section 529(e)(3)) for education furnished to—

(i) the taxpayer,

(ii) the taxpayer's spouse, or

(iii) any child (as defined in section 152(f)(1)) or grandchild of the taxpayer or the taxpayer's spouse, at an eligible educational institution (as defined in section 529(e)(5)).

(B) COORDINATION WITH OTHER BENEFITS.—The amount of qualified higher education expenses for any taxable year shall be reduced as provided in section 25A(g)(2).

(8) QUALIFIED FIRST-TIME HOMEBUYER DISTRIBUTIONS.—For purposes of paragraph (2)(F)—

(A) IN GENERAL.—The term "qualified first-time homebuyer distribution" means any payment or distribution received by an individual to the extent such payment or distribution is used by the individual before the close of the 120th day after the day on which such payment or distribution is received to pay qualified acquisition costs with respect to a principal residence of a first-time homebuyer who is such individual, the spouse of such individual, or any child, grandchild, or ancestor of such individual or the individual's spouse.

(B) LIFETIME DOLLAR LIMITATION.—The aggregate amount of payments or distributions received by an individual which may be treated as qualified first-time homebuyer distributions for any taxable year shall not exceed the excess (if any) of—

(i) $10,000, over

(ii) the aggregate amounts treated as qualified first-time homebuyer distributions with respect to such individual for all prior taxable years.

(C) QUALIFIED ACQUISITION COSTS.—For purposes of this paragraph, the term "qualified acquisition costs" means the costs of acquiring, constructing, or reconstructing a residence. Such term includes any usual or reasonable settlement, financing, or other closing costs.

(D) FIRST-TIME HOMEBUYER; OTHER DEFINITIONS.—For purposes of this paragraph—

(i) FIRST-TIME HOMEBUYER.—The term "first-time homebuyer" means any individual if—

(I) such individual (and if married, such individual's spouse) had no present ownership interest in a principal residence during the 2-year period ending on the date of acquisition of the principal residence to which this paragraph applies, and

(II) subsection (h) or (k) of section 1034 (as in effect on the day before the date of the enactment of this paragraph) did not suspend the running of any period of time specified in section 1034 (as so in effect) with respect to such individual on the day before the date the distribution is applied pursuant to subparagraph (A).

(ii) PRINCIPAL RESIDENCE.—The term "principal residence" has the same meaning as when used in section 121.

(iii) DATE OF ACQUISITION.—The term "date of acquisition" means the date—

(I) on which a binding contract to acquire the principal residence to which subparagraph (A) applies is entered into, or

(II) on which construction or reconstruction of such a principal residence is commenced.

(E) SPECIAL RULE WHERE DELAY IN ACQUISITION.—If any distribution from any individual retirement plan fails to meet the requirements of subparagraph (A) solely by reason of a delay or cancellation of the purchase or construction of the residence, the amount of the distribution may be contributed to an individual retirement plan as provided in section 408(d)(3)(A)(i) (determined by substituting "120th day" for "60th day" in such section), except that—

(i) section 408(d)(3)(B) shall not be applied to such contribution, and

(ii) such amount shall not be taken into account in determining whether section 408(d)(3)(B) applies to any other amount.

* * *

[Sec. 73]

SEC. 73. SERVICES OF CHILD.

[Sec. 73(a)]

(a) TREATMENT OF AMOUNTS RECEIVED.—Amounts received in respect of the services of a child shall be included in his gross income and not in the gross income of the parent, even though such amounts are not received by the child.

[Sec. 73(b)]

(b) TREATMENT OF EXPENDITURES.—All expenditures by the parent or the child attributable to amounts which are includible in the gross income of the child (and not of the parent) solely by reason of subsection (a) shall be treated as paid or incurred by the child.

[Sec. 73(c)]

(c) PARENT DEFINED.—For purposes of this section, the term "parent" includes an individual who is entitled to the services of a child by reason of having parental rights and duties in respect of the child.

* * *

[Sec. 74]

SEC. 74. PRIZES AND AWARDS.

[Sec. 74(a)]

(a) GENERAL RULE.—Except as otherwise provided in this section or in section 117 (relating to qualified scholarships), gross income includes amounts received as prizes and awards.

[Sec. 74(b)]

(b) EXCEPTION FOR CERTAIN PRIZES AND AWARDS TRANSFERRED TO CHARITIES.—Gross income does not include amounts received as prizes and awards made primarily in recognition of religious, charitable, scientific, educational, artistic, literary, or civic achievement, but only if—

(1) the recipient was selected without any action on his part to enter the contest or proceeding;

(2) the recipient is not required to render substantial future services as a condition to receiving the prize or award; and

(3) the prize or award is transferred by the payor to a governmental unit or organization described in paragraph (1) or (2) of section 170(c) pursuant to a designation made by the recipient.

[Sec. 74(c)]

(c) EXCEPTIONS FOR CERTAIN EMPLOYEE ACHIEVEMENT AWARDS.—

(1) IN GENERAL.—Gross income shall not include the value of an employee achievement award (as defined in section 274(j)) received by the taxpayer if the cost to the employer of the employee achievement award does not exceed the amount allowable as a deduction to the employer for the cost of the employee achievement award.

(2) EXCESS DEDUCTION AWARD.—If the cost to the employer of the employee achievement award received by the taxpayer exceeds the amount allowable as a deduction to the employer, then gross income includes the greater of—

(A) an amount equal to the portion of the cost to the employer of the award that is not allowable as a deduction to the employer (but not in excess of the value of the award), or

(B) the amount by which the value of the award exceeds the amount allowable as a deduction to the employer.

The remaining portion of the value of such award shall not be included in the gross income of the recipient.

(3) TREATMENT OF TAX-EXEMPT EMPLOYERS.—In the case of an employer exempt from taxation under this subtitle, any reference in this subsection to the amount allowable as a deduction to the employer shall be treated as a reference to the amount which would be allowable as a deduction to the employer if the employer were not exempt from taxation under this subtitle.

(4) CROSS REFERENCE.—

For provisions excluding certain de minimis fringes from gross income, see section 132(e).

[Sec. 74(d)]

(d) EXCEPTION FOR OLYMPIC AND PARALYMPIC MEDALS AND PRIZES.—

(1) IN GENERAL.—Gross income shall not include the value of any medal awarded in, or any prize money received from the United States Olympic Committee on account of, competition in the Olympic Games or Paralympic Games.

(2) LIMITATION BASED ON ADJUSTED GROSS INCOME.—

(A) IN GENERAL.—Paragraph (1) shall not apply to any taxpayer for any taxable year if the adjusted gross income (determined without regard to this subsection) of such taxpayer for such taxable year exceeds $1,000,000 (half of such amount in the case of a married individual filing a separate return).

(B) COORDINATION WITH OTHER LIMITATIONS.—For purposes of sections 86, 135, 137, 219, 221, 222, and 469, adjusted gross income shall be determined after the application of paragraph (1) and before the application of subparagraph (A).

[Sec. 79]

SEC. 79. GROUP-TERM LIFE INSURANCE PURCHASED FOR EMPLOYEES.

[Sec. 79(a)]

(a) GENERAL RULE.—There shall be included in the gross income of an employee for the taxable year an amount equal to the cost of group-term life insurance on his life provided for part or all of such year under a policy (or policies) carried directly or indirectly by his employer (or employers); but only to the extent that such cost exceeds the sum of—

(1) the cost of $50,000 of such insurance, and

(2) the amount (if any) paid by the employee toward the purchase of such insurance.

[Sec. 79(b)]

(b) EXCEPTIONS.—Subsection (a) shall not apply to—

(1) the cost of group-term life insurance on the life of an individual which is provided under a policy carried directly or indirectly by an employer after such individual has terminated his employment with such employer and is disabled (within the meaning of section 72(m)(7)),

(2) the cost of any portion of the group-term life insurance on the life of an employee provided during part or all of the taxable year of the employee under which—

(A) the employer is directly or indirectly the beneficiary, or

(B) a person described in section 170(c) is the sole beneficiary,

for the entire period during such taxable year for which the employee receives such insurance, and

(3) the cost of any group-term life insurance which is provided under a contract to which section 72(m)(3) applies.

[Sec. 79(c)]

(c) DETERMINATION OF COST OF INSURANCE.—For purposes of this section and section 6052, the cost of group-term insurance on the life of an employee provided during any period shall be determined on the basis of uniform premiums (computed on the basis of 5-year age brackets) prescribed by regulations by the Secretary.

[Sec. 79(d)]

(d) NONDISCRIMINATION REQUIREMENTS.—

(1) IN GENERAL.—In the case of a discriminatory group-term life insurance plan—

(A) subsection (a)(1) shall not apply with respect to any key employee, and

(B) the cost of group-term life insurance on the life of any key employee shall be the greater of—

(i) such cost determined without regard to subsection (c), or

(ii) such cost determined with regard to subsection (c).

(2) DISCRIMINATORY GROUP-TERM LIFE INSURANCE PLAN.—For purposes of this subsection, the term "discriminatory group-term life insurance plan" means any plan of an employer for providing group-term life insurance unless—

(A) the plan does not discriminate in favor of key employees as to eligibility to participate, and

(B) the type and amount of benefits available under the plan do not discriminate in favor of participants who are key employees.

(3) NONDISCRIMINATORY ELIGIBILITY CLASSIFICATION.—

(A) IN GENERAL.—A plan does not meet requirements of subparagraph (A) of paragraph (2) unless—

(i) such plan benefits 70 percent or more of all employees of the employer,

(ii) at least 85 percent of all employees who are participants under the plan are not key employees,

(iii) such plan benefits such employees as qualify under a classification set up by the employer and found by the Secretary not to be discriminatory in favor of key employees, or

(iv) in the case of a plan which is part of a cafeteria plan, the requirements of section 125 are met.

(B) EXCLUSION OF CERTAIN EMPLOYEES.—For purposes of subparagraph (A), there may be excluded from consideration—

(i) employees who have not completed 3 years of service;

(ii) part-time or seasonal employees;

(iii) employees not included in the plan who are included in a unit of employees covered by an agreement between employee representatives and one or more employers which the Secretary finds to be a collective bargaining agreement, if the benefits provided under the plan were the subject of good faith bargaining between such employee representatives and such employer or employers; and

(iv) employees who are nonresident aliens and who receive no earned income (within the meaning of section 911(d)(2)) from the employer which constitutes income from sources within the United States (within the meaning of section 861(a)(3)).

(4) NONDISCRIMINATORY BENEFITS.—A plan does not meet the requirements of paragraph (2)(B) unless all benefits available to participants who are key employees are available to all other participants.

(5) SPECIAL RULE.—A plan shall not fail to meet the requirements of paragraph (2)(B) merely because the amount of life insurance on behalf of the employees under the plan bears a uniform relationship to the total compensation or the basic or regular rate of compensation of such employees.

(6) KEY EMPLOYEE DEFINED.—For purposes of this subsection, the term "key employee" has the meaning given to such term by paragraph (1) of section 416(i). Such term also includes any former employee if such employee when he retired or separated from service was a key employee.

* * *

(8) TREATMENT OF FORMER EMPLOYEES.—To the extent provided in regulations, this subsection shall be applied separately with respect to former employees.

[Sec. 79(e)]

(e) EMPLOYEE INCLUDES FORMER EMPLOYEE.—For purposes of this section, the term "employee" includes a former employee.

* * *

[Sec. 82]

SEC. 82. REIMBURSEMENT FOR MOVING EXPENSES.

Except as provided in section 132(a)(6), there shall be included in gross income (as compensation for services) any amount received or accrued, directly or indirectly, by an individual as a payment for or reimbursement of expenses of moving from one residence to another residence which is attributable to employment or self-employment.

[Sec. 83]

SEC. 83. PROPERTY TRANSFERRED IN CONNECTION WITH PERFORMANCE OF SERVICES.

[Sec. 83(a)]

(a) GENERAL RULE.—If, in connection with the performance of services, property is transferred to any person other than the person for whom such services are performed, the excess of—

(1) the fair market value of such property (determined without regard to any restriction other than a restriction which by its terms will never lapse) at the first time the rights of the person having the beneficial interest in such property are transferable or are not subject to a substantial risk of forfeiture, whichever occurs earlier, over

(2) the amount (if any) paid for such property,

shall be included in the gross income of the person who performed such services in the first taxable year in which the rights of the person having the beneficial interest in such property are transferable or are not subject to a substantial risk of forfeiture, whichever is applicable. The preceding sentence shall not apply if such person sells or otherwise disposes of such property in an arm's length transaction before his rights in such property become transferable or not subject to a substantial risk of forfeiture.

[Sec. 83(b)]

(b) ELECTION TO INCLUDE IN GROSS INCOME IN YEAR OF TRANSFER.—

(1) IN GENERAL.—Any person who performs services in connection with which property is transferred to any person may elect to include in his gross income, for the taxable year in which such property is transferred, the excess of—

(A) the fair market value of such property at the time of transfer (determined without regard to any restriction other than a restriction which by its terms will never lapse), over

(B) the amount (if any) paid for such property.

If such election is made, subsection (a) shall not apply with respect to the transfer of such property, and if such property is subsequently forfeited, no deduction shall be allowed in respect of such forfeiture.

(2) ELECTION.—An election under paragraph (1) with respect to any transfer of property shall be made in such manner as the Secretary prescribes and shall be made not later than 30 days after the date of such transfer. Such election may not be revoked except with the consent of the Secretary.

[Sec. 83(c)]

(c) SPECIAL RULES.—For purposes of this section—

(1) SUBSTANTIAL RISK OF FORFEITURE.—The rights of a person in property are subject to a substantial risk of forfeiture if such person's rights to full enjoyment of such property are conditioned upon the future performance of substantial services by any individual.

(2) TRANSFERABILITY OF PROPERTY.—The rights of a person in property are transferable only if the rights in such property of any transferee are not subject to a substantial risk of forfeiture.

(3) SALES WHICH MAY GIVE RISE TO SUIT UNDER SECTION 16(B) OF THE SECURITIES EXCHANGE ACT OF 1934.—So long as the sale of property at a profit could subject a person to suit under section 16(b) of the Securities Exchange Act of 1934, such person's rights in such property are—

(A) subject to a substantial risk of forfeiture, and

(B) not transferable.

(4) For purposes of determining an individual's basis in property transferred in connection with the performance of services, rules similar to the rules of section 72(w) shall apply.

[Sec. 83(d)]

(d) CERTAIN RESTRICTIONS WHICH WILL NEVER LAPSE.—

(1) VALUATION.—In the case of property subject to a restriction which by its terms will never lapse, and which allows the transferee to sell such property only at a price determined under a formula, the price so determined shall be deemed to be the fair market value of the property unless established to the contrary by the Secretary, and the burden of proof shall be on the Secretary with respect to such value.

(2) CANCELLATION.—If, in the case of property subject to a restriction which by its terms will never lapse, the restriction is cancelled, then, unless the taxpayer establishes—

(A) that such cancellation was not compensatory, and

(B) that the person, if any, who would be allowed a deduction if the cancellation were treated as compensatory, will treat the transaction as not compensatory, as evidenced in such manner as the Secretary shall prescribe by regulations,

the excess of the fair market value of the property (computed without regard to the restrictions) at the time of cancellation over the sum of—

(C) the fair market value of such property (computed by taking the restriction into account) immediately before the cancellation, and

(D) the amount, if any, paid for the cancellation,

shall be treated as compensation for the taxable year in which such cancellation occurs.

[Sec. 83(e)]

(e) APPLICABILITY OF SECTION.—This section shall not apply to—

(1) a transaction to which section 421 applies,

(2) a transfer to or from a trust described in section 401(a) or a transfer under an annuity plan which meets the requirements of section 404(a)(2),

(3) the transfer of an option without a readily ascertainable fair market value,

(4) the transfer of property pursuant to the exercise of an option with a readily ascertainable fair market value at the date of grant, or

(5) group-term life insurance to which section 79 applies.

[Sec. 83(f)]

(f) HOLDING PERIOD.—In determining the period for which the taxpayer has held property to which subsection (a) applies, there shall be included only the period beginning at the first time his rights in such property are transferable or are not subject to a substantial risk of forfeiture, whichever occurs earlier.

[Sec. 83(g)]

(g) CERTAIN EXCHANGES.—If property to which subsection (a) applies is exchanged for property subject to restrictions and conditions substantially similar to those to which the property given in such exchange was subject, and if section 354, 355, 356, or 1036 (or so much of section 1031 as relates to section 1036) applied to such exchange, or if such exchange was pursuant to the exercise of a conversion privilege—

(1) such exchange shall be disregarded for purposes of subsection (a), and

(2) the property received shall be treated as property to which subsection (a) applies.

[Sec. 83(h)]

(h) DEDUCTION BY EMPLOYER.—In the case of a transfer of property to which this section applies or a cancellation of a restriction described in subsection (d), there shall be allowed as a deduction under section 162, to the person for whom were performed the services in connection with which such property was transferred, an amount equal to the amount included under subsection (a), (b), or (d)(2) in the gross income of the person who performed such services. Such deduction shall be allowed for the taxable year of such person in which or with which ends the taxable year in which such amount is included in the gross income of the person who performed such services.

[Sec. 83(i)]

(i) QUALIFIED EQUITY GRANTS.—

(1) IN GENERAL.—For purposes of this subtitle—

(A) TIMING OF INCLUSION.—If qualified stock is transferred to a qualified employee who makes an election with respect to such stock under this subsection, subsection (a) shall be applied by including the amount determined under such subsection with respect to such stock in income of the employee in the taxable year determined under subparagraph (B) in lieu of the taxable year described in subsection (a).

(B) TAXABLE YEAR DETERMINED.—The taxable year determined under this subparagraph is the taxable year of the employee which includes the earliest of—

(i) the first date such qualified stock becomes transferable (including, solely for purposes of this clause, becoming transferable to the employer),

(ii) the date the employee first becomes an excluded employee,

(iii) the first date on which any stock of the corporation which issued the qualified stock becomes readily tradable on an established securities market (as determined by the Secretary, but not including any market unless such market is recognized as an established securities market by the Secretary for purposes of a provision of this title other than this subsection),

(iv) the date that is 5 years after the first date the rights of the employee in such stock are transferable or are not subject to a substantial risk of forfeiture, whichever occurs earlier, or

(v) the date on which the employee revokes (at such time and in such manner as the Secretary provides) the election under this subsection with respect to such stock.

(2) QUALIFIED STOCK.—

(A) IN GENERAL.—For purposes of this subsection, the term "qualified stock" means, with respect to any qualified employee, any stock in a corporation which is the employer of such employee, if—

(i) such stock is received—

(I) in connection with the exercise of an option, or

(II) in settlement of a restricted stock unit, and

(ii) such option or restricted stock unit was granted by the corporation—

(I) in connection with the performance of services as an employee, and

(II) during a calendar year in which such corporation was an eligible corporation.

(B) LIMITATION.—The term "qualified stock" shall not include any stock if the employee may sell such stock to, or otherwise receive cash in lieu of stock from, the corporation at the time that the rights of the employee in such stock first become transferable or not subject to a substantial risk of forfeiture.

(C) ELIGIBLE CORPORATION.—For purposes of subparagraph (A) (ii) (II)—

(i) IN GENERAL.—The term "eligible corporation" means, with respect to any calendar year, any corporation if—

(I) no stock of such corporation (or any predecessor of such corporation) is readily tradable on an established securities market (as determined under paragraph (1) (B) (iii)) during any preceding calendar year, and

(II) such corporation has a written plan under which, in such calendar year, not less than 80 percent of all employees who provide services to such corporation in the United States (or any possession of the United States) are granted stock options, or are granted restricted stock units, with the same rights and privileges to receive qualified stock.

(ii) SAME RIGHTS AND PRIVILEGES.—For purposes of clause (i) (II)—

(I) except as provided in subclauses (II) and (III), the determination of rights and privileges with respect to stock shall be made in a similar manner as under section 423(b) (5),

(II) employees shall not fail to be treated as having the same rights and privileges to receive qualified stock solely because the number of shares available to all employees is not equal in amount, so long as the number of shares available to each employee is more than a de minimis amount, and

(III) rights and privileges with respect to the exercise of an option shall not be treated as the same as rights and privileges with respect to the settlement of a restricted stock unit.

(iii) EMPLOYEE.—For purposes of clause (i) (II), the term "employee" shall not include any employee described in section 4980E (d) (4) or any excluded employee.

(iv) SPECIAL RULE FOR CALENDAR YEARS BEFORE 2018.—In the case of any calendar year beginning before January 1, 2018, clause (i) (II) shall be applied without regard to whether the rights and privileges with respect to the qualified stock are the same.

(3) QUALIFIED EMPLOYEE; EXCLUDED EMPLOYEE.—For purposes of this subsection—

(A) IN GENERAL.—The term "qualified employee" means any individual who—

(i) is not an excluded employee, and

(ii) agrees in the election made under this subsection to meet such requirements as are determined by the Secretary to be necessary to ensure that the withholding requirements of the corporation under chapter 24 with respect to the qualified stock are met.

(B) EXCLUDED EMPLOYEE.—The term "excluded employee" means, with respect to any corporation, any individual—

(i) who is a 1-percent owner (within the meaning of section 416(i)(1)(B)(ii)) at any time during the calendar year or who was such a 1 percent owner at any time during the 10 preceding calendar years,

(ii) who is or has been at any prior time—

(I) the chief executive officer of such corporation or an individual acting in such a capacity, or

(II) the chief financial officer of such corporation or an individual acting in such a capacity,

(iii) who bears a relationship described in section 318(a)(1) to any individual described in subclause (I) or (II) of clause (ii), or

(iv) who is one of the 4 highest compensated officers of such corporation for the taxable year, or was one of the 4 highest compensated officers of such corporation for any of the 10 preceding taxable years, determined with respect to each such taxable year on the basis of the shareholder disclosure rules for compensation under the Securities Exchange Act of 1934 (as if such rules applied to such corporation).

(4) ELECTION.—

(A) TIME FOR MAKING ELECTION.—An election with respect to qualified stock shall be made under this subsection no later than 30 days after the first date the rights of the employee in such stock are transferable or are not subject to a substantial risk of forfeiture, whichever occurs earlier, and shall be made in a manner similar to the manner in which an election is made under subsection (b).

(B) LIMITATIONS.—No election may be made under this section with respect to any qualified stock if—

(i) the qualified employee has made an election under subsection (b) with respect to such qualified stock,

(ii) any stock of the corporation which issued the qualified stock is readily tradable on an established securities market (as determined under paragraph (1)(B)(iii)) at any time before the election is made, or

(iii) such corporation purchased any of its outstanding stock in the calendar year preceding the calendar year which includes the first date the rights of the employee in such stock are transferable or are not subject to a substantial risk of forfeiture, unless—

(I) not less than 25 percent of the total dollar amount of the stock so purchased is deferral stock, and

(II) the determination of which individuals from whom deferral stock is purchased is made on a reasonable basis.

(C) DEFINITIONS AND SPECIAL RULES RELATED TO LIMITATION ON STOCK REDEMPTIONS.—

(i) DEFERRAL STOCK.—For purposes of this paragraph, the term "deferral stock" means stock with respect to which an election is in effect under this subsection.

(ii) DEFERRAL STOCK WITH RESPECT TO ANY INDIVIDUAL NOT TAKEN INTO ACCOUNT IF INDIVIDUAL HOLDS DEFERRAL STOCK WITH LONGER DEFERRAL PERIOD.—Stock purchased by a corporation from any individual shall not be treated as deferral stock for purposes of subparagraph (B)(iii) if such individual (immediately after such purchase) holds any deferral stock with respect to which an election has been in effect under this subsection for a longer period than the election with respect to the stock so purchased.

(iii) PURCHASE OF ALL OUTSTANDING DEFERRAL STOCK.—The requirements of subclauses (I) and (II) of subparagraph (B)(iii) shall be treated as met if the stock so purchased includes all of the corporation's outstanding deferral stock.

(iv) REPORTING.—Any corporation which has outstanding deferral stock as of the beginning of any calendar year and which purchases any of its outstanding stock during such calendar year shall include on its return of tax for the taxable year in which, or with which, such calendar year ends the total dollar amount of its outstanding stock so purchased during such calendar year and such other information as the Secretary requires for purposes of administering this paragraph.

(5) CONTROLLED GROUPS.—For purposes of this subsection, all persons treated as a single employer under section 414(b) shall be treated as 1 corporation.

(6) NOTICE REQUIREMENT.—Any corporation which transfers qualified stock to a qualified employee shall, at the time that (or a reasonable period before) an amount attributable to such stock would (but for this subsection) first be includible in the gross income of such employee—

(A) certify to such employee that such stock is qualified stock, and

(B) notify such employee—

(i) that the employee may be eligible to elect to defer income on such stock under this subsection, and

(ii) that, if the employee makes such an election—

(I) the amount of income recognized at the end of the deferral period will be based on the value of the stock at the time at which the rights of the employee in such stock first become transferable or not subject to substantial risk of forfeiture, notwithstanding whether the value of the stock has declined during the deferral period,

(II) the amount of such income recognized at the end of the deferral period will be subject to withholding under section 3401(i) at the rate determined under section 3402(t), and

(III) the responsibilities of the employee (as determined by the Secretary under paragraph (3)(A)(ii)) with respect to such withholding.

(7) RESTRICTED STOCK UNITS.—This section (other than this subsection), including any election under subsection (b), shall not apply to restricted stock units.

[Sec. 85]

SEC. 85. UNEMPLOYMENT COMPENSATION.

[Sec. 85(a)]

(a) GENERAL RULE.—In the case of an individual, gross income includes unemployment compensation.

[Sec. 85(b)]

(b) UNEMPLOYMENT COMPENSATION DEFINED.—For purposes of this section, the term "unemployment compensation" means any amount received under a law of the United States or of a State which is in the nature of unemployment compensation.

[Sec. 86]

SEC. 86. SOCIAL SECURITY AND TIER 1 RAILROAD RETIREMENT BENEFITS.

[Sec. 86(a)]

(a) IN GENERAL.—

(1) IN GENERAL.—Except as provided in paragraph (2), gross income for the taxable year of any taxpayer described in subsection (b) (notwithstanding section 207 of the Social Security Act) includes social security benefits in an amount equal to the lesser of—

(A) one-half of the social security benefits received during the taxable year, or

(B) one-half of the excess described in subsection (b)(1).

(2) ADDITIONAL AMOUNT.—In the case of a taxpayer with respect to whom the amount determined under subsection (b)(1)(A) exceeds the adjusted base amount, the amount included in gross income under this section shall be equal to the lesser of—

(A) the sum of—

(i) 85 percent of such excess, plus

(ii) the lesser of the amount determined under paragraph (1) or an amount equal to one-half of the difference between the adjusted base amount and the base amount of the taxpayer, or

(B) 85 percent of the social security benefits received during the taxable year.

[Sec. 86(b)]

(b) TAXPAYERS TO WHOM SUBSECTION (a) APPLIES.—

(1) IN GENERAL.—A taxpayer is described in this subsection if—

(A) the sum of—

(i) the modified adjusted gross income of the taxpayer for the taxable year, plus

(ii) one-half of the social security benefits received during the taxable year, exceeds

(B) the base amount.

(2) MODIFIED ADJUSTED GROSS INCOME.—For purposes of this subsection, the term "modified adjusted gross income" means adjusted gross income—

(A) determined without regard to this section and sections 135, 137, 221, 222, 911, 931, and 933, and

(B) increased by the amount of interest received or accrued by the taxpayer during the taxable year which is exempt from tax.

[Sec. 86(c)]

(c) BASE AMOUNT AND ADJUSTED BASE AMOUNT.—For purposes of this section—

(1) BASE AMOUNT.—The term "base amount" means—

(A) except as otherwise provided in this paragraph, $25,000,

(B) $32,000 in the case of a joint return, and

(C) zero in the case of a taxpayer who—

(i) is married as of the close of the taxable year (within the meaning of section 7703) but does not file a joint return for such year, and

(ii) does not live apart from his spouse at all times during the taxable year.

(2) ADJUSTED BASE AMOUNT.—The term "adjusted base amount" means—

(A) except as otherwise provided in this paragraph, $34,000,

(B) $44,000 in the case of a joint return, and

(C) zero in the case of a taxpayer described in paragraph (1)(C).

[Sec. 86(d)]

(d) SOCIAL SECURITY BENEFIT.—

(1) IN GENERAL.—For purposes of this section, the term "social security benefit" means any amount received by the taxpayer by reason of entitlement to—

(A) a monthly benefit under title II of the Social Security Act, or

(B) a tier 1 railroad retirement benefit.

(2) ADJUSTMENT FOR REPAYMENTS DURING YEAR.—

(A) IN GENERAL.—For purposes of this section, the amount of social security benefits received during any taxable year shall be reduced by any repayment made by the taxpayer during the taxable year of a social security benefit previously received by the taxpayer (whether or not such benefit was received during the taxable year).

(B) DENIAL OF DEDUCTION.—If (but for this subparagraph) any portion of the repayments referred to in subparagraph (A) would have been allowable as a deduction for the taxable year under section 165, such portion shall be allowable as a deduction only to the extent it exceeds the social security benefits received by the taxpayer during the taxable year (and not repaid during such taxable year).

(3) WORKMEN'S COMPENSATION BENEFITS SUBSTITUTED FOR SOCIAL SECURITY BENEFITS.—For purposes of this section, if, by reason of section 224 of the Social Security Act (or by reason of section 3(a)(1) of the Railroad Retirement Act of 1974), any social security benefit is reduced by reason of the receipt of a benefit under a workmen's compensation act, the term "social security benefit" includes that portion of such benefit received under the workmen's compensation act which equals such reduction.

(4) TIER 1 RAILROAD RETIREMENT BENEFIT.—For purposes of paragraph (1), the term "tier 1 railroad retirement benefit" means—

(A) the amount of the annuity under the Railroad Retirement Act of 1974 equal to the amount of the benefit to which the taxpayer would have been entitled under the Social Security Act if all of the service after December 31, 1936, of the employee (on whose employment record the annuity is being paid) had been included in the term "employment" as defined in the Social Security Act, and

(B) a monthly annuity amount under section 3(f)(3) of the Railroad Retirement Act of 1974.

(5) EFFECT OF EARLY DELIVERY OF BENEFIT CHECKS.—For purposes of subsection (a), in any case where section 708 of the Social Security Act causes social security benefit checks to be delivered before the end of the calendar month for which they are issued, the benefits involved shall be deemed to have been received in the succeeding calendar month.

* * *

PART III—ITEMS SPECIFICALLY EXCLUDED FROM GROSS INCOME

[Sec. 101]

SEC. 101. CERTAIN DEATH BENEFITS.

[Sec. 101(a)]

(a) PROCEEDS OF LIFE INSURANCE CONTRACTS PAYABLE BY REASON OF DEATH.—

(1) GENERAL RULE.—Except as otherwise provided in paragraphs (2) and (3), subsection (d), subsection (f), and subsection (j), gross income does not include amounts received (whether in a single sum or otherwise) under a life insurance contract, if such amounts are paid by reason of the death of the insured.

(2) TRANSFER FOR VALUABLE CONSIDERATION.—In the case of a transfer for a valuable consideration, by assignment or otherwise, of a life insurance contract or any interest therein, the amount excluded from gross income by paragraph (1) shall not exceed an amount equal to the sum of the actual value of such consideration and the premiums and other amounts subsequently paid by the transferee. The preceding sentence shall not apply in the case of such a transfer—

(A) if such contract or interest therein has a basis for determining gain or loss in the hands of a transferee determined in whole or in part by reference to such basis of such contract or interest therein in the hands of the transferor, or

(B) if such transfer is to the insured, to a partner of the insured, to a partnership in which the insured is a partner, or to a corporation in which the insured is a shareholder or officer.

The term "other amounts" in the first sentence of this paragraph includes interest paid or accrued by the transferee on indebtedness with respect to such contract or any interest therein if such interest paid or accrued is not allowable as a deduction by reason of section 264(a)(4).

(3) EXCEPTION TO VALUABLE CONSIDERATION RULES FOR COMMERCIAL TRANSFERS.—

(A) IN GENERAL.—The second sentence of paragraph (2) shall not apply in the case of a transfer of a life insurance contract, or any interest therein, which is a reportable policy sale.

(B) REPORTABLE POLICY SALE.—For purposes of this paragraph, the term "reportable policy sale" means the acquisition of an interest in a life insurance contract, directly or indirectly, if the acquirer has no substantial family, business, or financial relationship with the insured apart from the acquirer's interest in such life insurance contract. For purposes of the preceding sentence, the term "indirectly" applies to the acquisition of an interest in a partnership, trust, or other entity that holds an interest in the life insurance contract.

[Sec. 101(b)—Repealed]

[Sec. 101(c)]

(c) INTEREST.—If any amount excluded from gross income by subsection (a) is held under an agreement to pay interest thereon, the interest payments shall be included in gross income.

[Sec. 101(d)]

(d) PAYMENT OF LIFE INSURANCE PROCEEDS AT A DATE LATER THAN DEATH.—

(1) GENERAL RULE.—The amounts held by an insurer with respect to any beneficiary shall be prorated (in accordance with such regulations as may be prescribed by the Secretary) over the period or periods with respect to which such payments are to be made. There shall be excluded from the gross income of such beneficiary in the taxable year received any amount determined by such proration.

Gross income includes, to the extent not excluded by the preceding sentence, amounts received under agreements to which this subsection applies.

(2) AMOUNT HELD BY AN INSURER.—An amount held by an insurer with respect to any beneficiary shall mean an amount to which subsection (a) applies which is—

(A) held by any insurer under an agreement provided for in the life insurance contract, whether as an option or otherwise, to pay such amount on a date or dates later than the death of the insured, and

(B) is equal to the value of such agreement to such beneficiary

(i) as of the date of death of the insured (as if any option exercised under the life insurance contract were exercised at such time), and

(ii) as discounted on the basis of the interest rate used by the insurer in calculating payments under the agreement and mortality tables prescribed by the Secretary.

(3) APPLICATION OF SUBSECTION.—This subsection shall not apply to any amount to which subsection (c) is applicable.

* * *

[Sec. 101(g)]

(g) TREATMENT OF CERTAIN ACCELERATED DEATH BENEFITS.—

(1) IN GENERAL.—For purposes of this section, the following amounts shall be treated as an amount paid by reason of the death of an insured:

(A) Any amount received under a life insurance contract on the life of an insured who is a terminally ill individual.

(B) Any amount received under a life insurance contract on the life of an insured who is a chronically ill individual.

(2) TREATMENT OF VIATICAL SETTLEMENTS.—

(A) IN GENERAL.—If any portion of the death benefit under a life insurance contract on the life of an insured described in paragraph (1) is sold or assigned to a viatical settlement provider, the amount paid for the sale or assignment of such portion shall be treated as an amount paid under the life insurance contract by reason of the death of such insured.

(B) VIATICAL SETTLEMENT PROVIDER.—

(i) IN GENERAL.—The term "viatical settlement provider" means any person regularly engaged in the trade or business of purchasing, or taking assignments of, life insurance contracts on the lives of insureds described in paragraph (1) if—

(I) such person is licensed for such purposes (with respect to insureds described in the same subparagraph of paragraph (1) as the insured) in the State in which the insured resides, or

(II) in the case of an insured who resides in a State not requiring the licensing of such persons for such purposes with respect to such insured, such person meets the requirements of clause (ii) or (iii), whichever applies to such insured.

(ii) TERMINALLY ILL INSUREDS.—A person meets the requirements of this clause with respect to an insured who is a terminally ill individual if such person—

(I) meets the requirements of sections 8 and 9 of the Viatical Settlements Model Act of the National Association of Insurance Commissioners, and

(II) meets the requirements of the Model Regulations of the National Association of Insurance Commissioners (relating to standards for evaluation of reasonable payments) in determining amounts paid by such person in connection with such purchases or assignments.

(iii) CHRONICALLY ILL INSUREDS.—A person meets the requirements of this clause with respect to an insured who is a chronically ill individual if such person—

(I) meets requirements similar to the requirements referred to in clause (ii)(I), and

(II) meets the standards (if any) of the National Association of Insurance Commissioners for evaluating the reasonableness of amounts paid by such person in connection with such purchases or assignments with respect to chronically ill individuals.

(3) SPECIAL RULES FOR CHRONICALLY ILL INSUREDS.—In the case of an insured who is a chronically ill individual—

(A) IN GENERAL.—Paragraphs (1) and (2) shall not apply to any payment received for any period unless—

(i) such payment is for costs incurred by the payee (not compensated for by insurance or otherwise) for qualified long-term care services provided for the insured for such period, and

(ii) the terms of the contract giving rise to such payment satisfy—

(I) the requirements of section 7702B(b)(1)(B), and

(II) the requirements (if any) applicable under subparagraph (B).

For purposes of the preceding sentence, the rule of section 7702B(b)(2)(B) shall apply.

(B) OTHER REQUIREMENTS.—The requirements applicable under this subparagraph are—

(i) those requirements of section 7702B(g) and section 4980C which the Secretary specifies as applying to such a purchase, assignment, or other arrangement,

(ii) standards adopted by the National Association of Insurance Commissioners which specifically apply to chronically ill individuals (and, if such standards are adopted, the analogous requirements specified under clause (i) shall cease to apply), and

(iii) standards adopted by the State in which the policyholder resides (and if such standards are adopted, the analogous requirements specified under clause (i) and (subject to section 4980C(f)) standards under clause (ii), shall cease to apply).

(C) PER DIEM PAYMENTS.—A payment shall not fail to be described in subparagraph (A) by reason of being made on a per diem or other periodic basis without regard to the expenses incurred during the period to which the payment relates.

(D) LIMITATION ON EXCLUSION FOR PERIODIC PAYMENTS.—For limitation on amount of periodic payments which are treated as described in paragraph (1), see section 7702B(d).

(4) DEFINITIONS.—For purposes of this subsection—

(A) TERMINALLY ILL INDIVIDUAL.—The term "terminally ill individual" means an individual who has been certified by a physician as having an illness or physical condition which can reasonably be expected to result in death in 24 months or less after the date of the certification.

(B) CHRONICALLY ILL INDIVIDUAL.—The term "chronically ill individual" has the meaning given such term by section 7702B(c)(2); except that such term shall not include a terminally ill individual.

(C) QUALIFIED LONG-TERM CARE SERVICES.—The term "qualified long-term care services" has the meaning given such term by section 7702B(c).

(D) PHYSICIAN.—The term "physician" has the meaning given to such term by section 1861(r)(1) of the Social Security Act (42 U.S.C. 1395x(r)(1)).

(5) EXCEPTION FOR BUSINESS-RELATED POLICIES.—This subsection shall not apply in the case of any amount paid to any taxpayer other than the insured if such taxpayer has an insurable interest with respect to the life of the insured by reason of the insured being a director, officer, or employee of the taxpayer or by reason of the insured being financially interested in any trade or business carried on by the taxpayer.

* * *

[Sec. 101(j)]

(j) TREATMENT OF CERTAIN EMPLOYER-OWNED LIFE INSURANCE CONTRACTS.—

(1) GENERAL RULE.—In the case of an employer-owned life insurance contract, the amount excluded from gross income of an applicable policyholder by reason of paragraph (1) of subsection (a) shall not exceed an amount equal to the sum of the premiums and other amounts paid by the policyholder for the contract.

(2) EXCEPTIONS.—In the case of an employer-owned life insurance contract with respect to which the notice and consent requirements of paragraph (4) are met, paragraph (1) shall not apply to any of the following:

(A) EXCEPTIONS BASED ON INSURED'S STATUS.—Any amount received by reason of the death of an insured who, with respect to an applicable policyholder—

(i) was an employee at any time during the 12-month period before the insured's death, or

(ii) is, at the time the contract is issued—

(I) a director,

(II) a highly compensated employee within the meaning of section 414(q) (without regard to paragraph (1)(B)(ii) thereof), or

(III) a highly compensated individual within the meaning of section 105(h)(5), except that "35 percent" shall be substituted for "25 percent" in subparagraph (C) thereof.

(B) EXCEPTION FOR AMOUNTS PAID TO INSURED'S HEIRS.—Any amount received by reason of the death of an insured to the extent—

(i) the amount is paid to a member of the family (within the meaning of section 267(c)(4)) of the insured, any individual who is the designated beneficiary of the insured under the contract (other than the applicable policyholder), a trust established for the benefit of any such member of the family or designated beneficiary, or the estate of the insured, or

(ii) the amount is used to purchase an equity (or capital or profits) interest in the applicable policyholder from any person described in clause (i).

(3) EMPLOYER-OWNED LIFE INSURANCE CONTRACT.—

(A) IN GENERAL.—For purposes of this subsection, the term "employer-owned life insurance contract" means a life insurance contract which—

(i) is owned by a person engaged in a trade or business and under which such person (or a related person described in subparagraph (B)(ii)) is directly or indirectly a beneficiary under the contract, and

(ii) covers the life of an insured who is an employee with respect to the trade or business of the applicable policyholder on the date the contract is issued.

For purposes of the preceding sentence, if coverage for each insured under a master contract is treated as a separate contract for purposes of sections 817(h), 7702, and 7702A, coverage for each such insured shall be treated as a separate contract.

(B) APPLICABLE POLICYHOLDER.—For purposes of this subsection—

(i) IN GENERAL.—The term "applicable policyholder" means, with respect to any employer-owned life insurance contract, the person described in subparagraph (A)(i) which owns the contract.

(ii) RELATED PERSONS.—The term "applicable policyholder" includes any person which—

(I) bears a relationship to the person described in clause (i) which is specified in section 267(b) or 707(b)(1), or

(II) is engaged in trades or businesses with such person which are under common control (within the meaning of subsection (a) or (b) of section 52).

(4) NOTICE AND CONSENT REQUIREMENTS.—The notice and consent requirements of this paragraph are met if, before the issuance of the contract, the employee—

(A) is notified in writing that the applicable policyholder intends to insure the employee's life and the maximum face amount for which the employee could be insured at the time the contract was issued,

(B) provides written consent to being insured under the contract and that such coverage may continue after the insured terminates employment, and

(C) is informed in writing that an applicable policyholder will be a beneficiary of any proceeds payable upon the death of the employee.

(5) DEFINITIONS.—For purposes of this subsection—

(A) EMPLOYEE.—The term "employee" includes an officer, director, and highly compensated employee (within the meaning of section 414(q)).

(B) INSURED.—The term "insured" means, with respect to an employer-owned life insurance contract, an individual covered by the contract who is a United States citizen or resident. In the case of a contract covering the joint lives of 2 individuals, references to an insured include both of the individuals.

[Sec. 102]

SEC. 102. GIFTS AND INHERITANCES.

[Sec. 102(a)]

(a) GENERAL RULE.—Gross income does not include the value of property acquired by gift, bequest, devise, or inheritance.

[Sec. 102(b)]

(b) INCOME.—Subsection (a) shall not exclude from gross income—

(1) the income from any property referred to in subsection (a); or

(2) where the gift, bequest, devise, or inheritance is of income from property, the amount of such income.

Where, under the terms of the gift, bequest, devise, or inheritance, the payment, crediting, or distribution thereof is to be made at intervals, then, to the extent that it is paid or credited or to be distributed out of income from property, it shall be treated for purposes of paragraph (2) as a gift, bequest, devise, or inheritance of income from property. Any amount included in the gross income of a beneficiary under subchapter J shall be treated for purposes of paragraph (2) as a gift, bequest, devise, or inheritance of income from property.

[Sec. 102(c)]

(c) EMPLOYEE GIFTS.—

(1) IN GENERAL.—Subsection (a) shall not exclude from gross income any amount transferred by or for an employer to, or for the benefit of, an employee.

(2) CROSS REFERENCES.—

For provisions excluding certain employee achievement awards from gross income, see section 74(c).

For provisions excluding certain de minimis fringes from gross income, see section 132(e).

[Sec. 103]

SEC. 103. INTEREST ON STATE AND LOCAL BONDS.

[Sec. 103(a)]

(a) EXCLUSION.—Except as provided in subsection (b), gross income does not include interest on any State or local bond.

[Sec. 103(b)]

(b) EXCEPTIONS.—Subsection (a) shall not apply to—

(1) PRIVATE ACTIVITY BOND WHICH IS NOT A QUALIFIED BOND.—Any private activity bond which is not a qualified bond (within the meaning of section 141).

(2) ARBITRAGE BOND.—Any arbitrage bond (within the meaning of section 148).

(3) BOND NOT IN REGISTERED FORM, ETC.—Any bond unless such bond meets the applicable requirements of section 149.

[Sec. 103(c)]

(c) DEFINITIONS.—For purposes of this section and part IV—

(1) STATE OR LOCAL BOND.—The term "State or local bond" means an obligation of a state or political subdivision thereof.

(2) STATE.—The term "State" includes the District of Columbia and any possession of the United States.

[Sec. 104]

SEC. 104. COMPENSATION FOR INJURIES OR SICKNESS.

[Sec. 104(a)]

(a) IN GENERAL.—Except in the case of amounts attributable to (and not in excess of) deductions allowed under section 213 (relating to medical, etc., expenses) for any prior taxable year, gross income does not include—

(1) amounts received under workmen's compensation acts as compensation for personal injuries or sickness;

(2) the amount of any damages (other than punitive damages) received (whether by suit or agreement and whether as lump sums or as periodic payments) on account of personal physical injuries or physical sickness;

(3) amounts received through accident or health insurance (or through an arrangement having the effect of accident or health insurance) for personal injuries or sickness (other than amounts received by an employee, to the extent such amounts (A) are attributable to contributions by the employer which were not includible in the gross income of the employee, or (B) are paid by the employer);

(4) amounts received as a pension, annuity, or similar allowance for personal injuries or sickness resulting from active service in the armed forces of any country or in the Coast and Geodetic Survey or the Public Health Service, or as a disability annuity payable under the provisions of section 808 of the Foreign Service Act of 1980;

(5) amounts received by an individual as disability income attributable to injuries incurred as a direct result of a terroristic or military action (as defined in section 692(c)(2)); and

(6) amounts received pursuant to—

(A) section 1201 of the Omnibus Crime Control and Safe Streets Act of 1968 (42 U.S.C. 3796); or

(B) a program established under the laws of any State which provides monetary compensation for surviving dependents of a public safety officer who has died as the direct and proximate result of a personal injury sustained in the line of duty,

except that subparagraph (B) shall not apply to any amounts that would have been payable if death of the public safety officer had occurred other than as the direct and proximate result of a personal injury sustained in the line of duty.

For purposes of paragraph (3), in the case of an individual who is, or has been, an employee within the meaning of section 401(c)(1) (relating to self-employed individuals), contributions made on behalf of such individual while he was such an employee to a trust described in section 401(a) which is exempt from tax under section 501(a), or under a plan described in section 403(a), shall, to the extent allowed as deductions under section 404, be treated as contributions by the employer which were not includible in the gross income of the employee. For purposes of paragraph (2), emotional distress shall not be treated as a physical injury or physical sickness. The preceding sentence shall not apply to an amount of damages not in excess of the amount paid for medical care (described in subparagraph (A) or (B) of section 213(d)(1)) attributable to emotional distress.

* * *

[Sec. 104(d)]

(d) CROSS REFERENCES.—

(1) For exclusion from employee's gross income of employer contributions to accident and health plans, see section 106.

(2) For exclusion of part of disability retirement pay from the application of subsection (a)(4) of this section, see section 1403 of title 10, United States Code (relating to career compensation laws).

[Sec. 105]

SEC. 105. AMOUNTS RECEIVED UNDER ACCIDENT AND HEALTH PLANS.

[Sec. 105(a)]

(a) AMOUNTS ATTRIBUTABLE TO EMPLOYER CONTRIBUTIONS.—Except as otherwise provided in this section, amounts received by an employee through accident or health insurance for personal injuries or sickness shall be included in gross income to the extent such amounts (1) are attributable to contributions by the employer which were not includible in the gross income of the employee, or (2) are paid by the employer.

[Sec. 105(b)]

(b) AMOUNTS EXPENDED FOR MEDICAL CARE.—Except in the case of amounts attributable to (and not in excess of) deductions allowed under section 213 (relating to medical, etc., expenses) for any prior taxable year, gross income does not include amounts referred to in subsection (a) if such amounts are paid, directly or indirectly, to the taxpayer to reimburse the taxpayer for expenses incurred by him for the medical care (as defined in section 213(d)) of the taxpayer, his spouse, his dependents (as defined in section 152, determined without regard to subsections (b)(1), (b)(2), and (d)(1)(B) thereof), and any child (as defined in section 152(f)(1)) of the taxpayer who as of the end of the taxable year has not attained age 27. Any child to whom section 152(e) applies shall be treated as a dependent of both parents for purposes of this subsection.

[Sec. 105(c)]

(c) PAYMENTS UNRELATED TO ABSENCE FROM WORK.—Gross income does not include amounts referred to in subsection (a) to the extent such amounts—

(1) constitute payment for the permanent loss or loss of use of a member or function of the body, or the permanent disfigurement, of the taxpayer, his spouse, or a dependent (as

defined in section 152, determined without regard to subsections (b)(1), (b)(2), and (d)(1)(B) thereof), and

(2) are computed with reference to the nature of the injury without regard to the period the employee is absent from work.

[Sec. 105(d)—Repealed]

[Sec. 105(e)]

(e) ACCIDENT AND HEALTH PLANS.—For purposes of this section and section 104—

(1) amounts received under an accident or health plan for employees, and

(2) amounts received from a sickness and disability fund for employees maintained under the law of a State, or the District of Columbia,

shall be treated as amounts received through accident or health insurance.

[Sec. 105(f)]

(f) RULES FOR APPLICATION OF SECTION 213.—For purposes of section 213 (a) (relating to medical, dental, etc., expenses) amounts excluded from gross income under subsection (c) shall not be considered as compensation (by insurance or otherwise) for expenses paid for medical care.

[Sec. 105(g)]

(g) SELF-EMPLOYED INDIVIDUAL NOT CONSIDERED AN EMPLOYEE.—For purposes of this section, the term "employee" does not include an individual who is an employee within the meaning of section 401(c)(1) (relating to self-employed individuals).

[Sec. 105(h)]

(h) AMOUNT PAID TO HIGHLY COMPENSATED INDIVIDUALS UNDER A DISCRIMINATORY SELF-INSURED MEDICAL EXPENSE REIMBURSEMENT PLAN.—

(1) IN GENERAL.—In the case of amounts paid to a highly compensated individual under a self-insured medical reimbursement plan which does not satisfy the requirements of paragraph (2) for a plan year, subsection (b) shall not apply to such amounts to the extent they constitute an excess reimbursement of such highly compensated individual.

(2) PROHIBITION OF DISCRIMINATION.—A self-insured medical reimbursement plan satisfies the requirements of this paragraph only if—

(A) the plan does not discriminate in favor of highly compensated individuals as to eligibility to participate; and

(B) the benefits provided under the plan do not discriminate in favor of participants who are highly compensated individuals.

(3) NONDISCRIMINATORY ELIGIBILITY CLASSIFICATIONS.—

(A) IN GENERAL.—A self-insured medical reimbursement plan does not satisfy the requirements of subparagraph (A) of paragraph (2) unless such plan benefits—

(i) 70 percent or more of all employees, or 80 percent or more of all the employees who are eligible to benefit under the plan if 70 percent or more of all employees are eligible to benefit under the plan; or

(ii) such employees as qualify under a classification set up by the employer and found by the Secretary not to be discriminatory in favor of highly compensated individuals.

(B) EXCLUSION OF CERTAIN EMPLOYEES.—For purposes of subparagraph (A), there may be excluded from consideration—

(i) employees who have not completed 3 years of service;

(ii) employees who have not attained age 25;

(iii) part-time or seasonal employees;

(iv) employees not included in the plan who are included in a unit of employees covered by an agreement between employee representatives and one or more employers which the Secretary finds to be a collective bargaining agreement, if accident and health benefits were the subject of good faith bargaining between such employee representatives and such employer or employers; and

(v) employees who are nonresident aliens and who receive no earned income (within the meaning of section 911(d)(2)) from the employer which constitutes income from sources within the United States (within the meaning of section 861(a)(3)).

(4) NONDISCRIMINATORY BENEFITS.—A self-insured medical reimbursement plan does not meet the requirements of subparagraph (B) of paragraph (2) unless all benefits provided for participants who are highly compensated individuals are provided for all other participants.

(5) HIGHLY COMPENSATED INDIVIDUAL DEFINED.—For purposes of this subsection, the term "highly compensated individual" means an individual who is—

(A) one of the 5 highest paid officers,

(B) a shareholder who owns (with the application of section 318) more than 10 percent in value of the stock of the employer, or

(C) among the highest paid 25 percent of all employees (other than employees described in paragraph (3)(B) who are not participants).

(6) SELF-INSURED MEDICAL REIMBURSEMENT PLAN.—The term "self-insured medical reimbursement plan" means a plan of an employer to reimburse employees for expenses referred to in subsection (b) for which reimbursement is not provided under a policy of accident and health insurance.

(7) EXCESS REIMBURSEMENT OF HIGHLY COMPENSATED INDIVIDUAL.—For purposes of this section, the excess reimbursement of a highly compensated individual which is attributable to a self-insured medical reimbursement plan is—

(A) in the case of a benefit available to highly compensated individuals but not to all other participants (or which otherwise fails to satisfy the requirements of paragraph (2)(B)), the amount reimbursed under the plan to the employee with respect to such benefit, and

(B) in the case of benefits (other than benefits described in subparagraph (A)) paid to a highly compensated individual by a plan which fails to satisfy the requirements of paragraph (2), the total amount reimbursed to the highly compensated individual for the plan year multiplied by a fraction—

(i) the numerator of which is the total amount reimbursed to all participants who are highly compensated individuals under the plan for the plan year, and

(ii) the denominator of which is the total amount reimbursed to all employees under the plan for such plan year.

In determining the fraction under subparagraph (B), there shall not be taken into account any reimbursement which is attributable to a benefit described in subparagraph (A).

(8) CERTAIN CONTROLLED GROUPS, ETC.—All employees who are treated as employed by a single employer under subsection (b), (c), or (m) of section 414 shall be treated as employed by a single employer for purposes of this section.

(9) REGULATIONS.—The Secretary shall prescribe such regulations as may be necessary to carry out the provisions of this section.

(10) TIME OF INCLUSION.—Any amount paid for a plan year that is included in income by reason of this subsection shall be treated as received or accrued in the taxable year of the participant in which the plan year ends.

* * *

[Sec. 106]

SEC. 106. CONTRIBUTIONS BY EMPLOYER TO ACCIDENT AND HEALTH PLANS.

[Sec. 106(a)]

(a) GENERAL RULE.—Except as otherwise provided in this section, gross income of an employee does not include employer-provided coverage under an accident or health plan.

* * *

[Sec. 106(d)]

(d) CONTRIBUTIONS TO HEALTH SAVINGS ACCOUNTS.—

(1) IN GENERAL.—In the case of an employee who is an eligible individual (as defined in section 223(c)(1)), amounts contributed by such employee's employer to any health savings account (as defined in section 223(d)) of such employee shall be treated as employer-provided coverage for medical expenses under an accident or health plan to the extent such amounts do not exceed the limitation under section 223(b) (determined without regard to this subsection) which is applicable to such employee for such taxable year.

* * *

[Sec. 106(f)]

(f) REIMBURSEMENTS FOR MENSTRUAL CARE PRODUCTS.—For purposes of this section and section 105, expenses incurred for menstrual care products (as defined in section 223(d)(2)(D)) shall be treated as incurred for medical care.

[Sec. 106(g)]

(g) QUALIFIED SMALL EMPLOYER HEALTH REIMBURSEMENT ARRANGEMENT.—For purposes of this section and section 105, payments or reimbursements from a qualified small employer health reimbursement arrangement (as defined in section 9831(d)) of an individual for medical care (as defined in section 213(d)) shall not be treated as paid or reimbursed under employer-provided coverage for medical expenses under an accident or health plan if for the month in which such medical care is provided the individual does not have minimum essential coverage (within the meaning of section 5000A(f)).

[Sec. 107]

SEC. 107. RENTAL VALUE OF PARSONAGES.

In the case of a minister of the gospel, gross income does not include—

(1) the rental value of a home furnished to him as part of his compensation; or

(2) the rental allowance paid to him as part of his compensation, to the extent used by him to rent or provide a home and to the extent such allowance does not exceed the fair rental value of the home, including furnishings and appurtenances such as a garage, plus the cost of utilities.

[Sec. 108]

SEC. 108. INCOME FROM DISCHARGE OF INDEBTEDNESS.

[Sec. 108(a)]

(a) EXCLUSION FROM GROSS INCOME.—

(1) IN GENERAL.—Gross income does not include any amount which (but for this subsection) would be includible in gross income by reason of the discharge (in whole or in part) of indebtedness of the taxpayer if—

(A) the discharge occurs in a title 11 case,

(B) the discharge occurs when the taxpayer is insolvent,

(C) the indebtedness discharged is qualified farm indebtedness,

(D) in the case of a taxpayer other than a C corporation, the indebtedness discharged is qualified real property business indebtedness, or

(E) the indebtedness discharged is qualified principal residence indebtedness which is discharged—

(i) before January 1, 2021, or

(ii) subject to an arrangement that is entered into and evidenced in writing before January 1, 2021.

(2) COORDINATION OF EXCLUSIONS.—

(A) TITLE 11 EXCLUSION TAKES PRECEDENCE.—Subparagraphs (B), (C), (D), and (E) of paragraph (1) shall not apply to a discharge which occurs in a title 11 case.

(B) INSOLVENCY EXCLUSION TAKES PRECEDENCE OVER QUALIFIED FARM EXCLUSION AND QUALIFIED REAL PROPERTY BUSINESS EXCLUSION.—Subparagraphs (C) and (D) of paragraph (1) shall not apply to a discharge to the extent the taxpayer is insolvent.

(C) PRINCIPAL RESIDENCE EXCLUSION TAKES PRECEDENCE OVER INSOLVENCY EXCLUSION UNLESS ELECTED OTHERWISE.—Paragraph (1)(B) shall not apply to a discharge to which paragraph (1)(E) applies unless the taxpayer elects to apply paragraph (1)(B) in lieu of paragraph (1)(E).

(3) INSOLVENCY EXCLUSION LIMITED TO AMOUNT OF INSOLVENCY.—In the case of a discharge to which paragraph (1)(B) applies, the amount excluded under paragraph (1)(B) shall not exceed the amount by which the taxpayer is insolvent.

[Sec. 108(b)]

(b) REDUCTION OF TAX ATTRIBUTES.—

(1) IN GENERAL.—The amount excluded from gross income under subparagraph (A), (B), or (C) of subsection (a)(1) shall be applied to reduce the tax attributes of the taxpayer as provided in paragraph (2).

(2) TAX ATTRIBUTES AFFECTED; ORDER OF REDUCTION.—Except as provided in paragraph (5), the reduction referred to in paragraph (1) shall be made in the following tax attributes in the following order:

(A) NOL.—Any net operating loss for the taxable year of the discharge, and any net operating loss carryover to such taxable year.

(B) GENERAL BUSINESS CREDIT.—Any carryover to or from the taxable year of a discharge of an amount for purposes for determining the amount allowable as a credit under section 38 (relating to general business credit).

(C) MINIMUM TAX CREDIT.—The amount of the minimum tax credit available under section 53(b) as of the beginning of the taxable year immediately following the taxable year of the discharge.

(D) CAPITAL LOSS CARRYOVERS.—Any net capital loss for the taxable year of the discharge, and any capital loss carryover to such taxable year under section 1212.

(E) BASIS REDUCTION.—

(i) IN GENERAL.—The basis of the property of the taxpayer.

(ii) CROSS REFERENCE.—

For provisions for making the reduction described in clause (i), see section 1017.

(F) PASSIVE ACTIVITY LOSS AND CREDIT CARRYOVERS.—Any passive activity loss or credit carryover of the taxpayer under section 469(b) from the taxable year of the discharge.

(G) FOREIGN TAX CREDIT CARRYOVERS.—Any carryover to or from the taxable year of the discharge for purposes of determining the amount of the credit allowable under section 27.

(3) AMOUNT OF REDUCTION.—

(A) IN GENERAL.—Except as provided in subparagraph (B), the reductions described in paragraph (2) shall be one dollar for each dollar excluded by subsection (a).

(B) CREDIT CARRYOVER REDUCTION.—The reductions described in subparagraphs (B), (C), and (G) shall be 33⅓ cents for each dollar excluded by subsection (a). The reduction described in subparagraph (F) in any passive activity credit carryover shall be 33⅓ cents for each dollar excluded by subsection (a).

(4) ORDERING RULES.—

(A) REDUCTIONS MADE AFTER DETERMINATION OF TAX FOR YEAR.—The reductions described in paragraph (2) shall be made after the determination of the tax imposed by this chapter for the taxable year of the discharge.

(B) REDUCTIONS UNDER SUBPARAGRAPH (A) OR (D) OF PARAGRAPH (2).—The reductions described in subparagraph (A) or (D) of paragraph (2) (as the case may be) shall be made first in the loss for the taxable year of the discharge and then in the carryovers to such taxable year in the order of the taxable years from which each such carryover arose.

(C) REDUCTIONS UNDER SUBPARAGRAPHS (B) AND (G) OF PARAGRAPH (2).—The reductions described in subparagraphs (B) and (G) of paragraph (2) shall be made in the order in which carryovers are taken into account under this chapter for the taxable year of the discharge.

(5) ELECTION TO APPLY REDUCTION FIRST AGAINST DEPRECIABLE PROPERTY.—

(A) IN GENERAL.—The taxpayer may elect to apply any portion of the reduction referred to in paragraph (1) to the reduction under section 1017 of the basis of the depreciable property of the taxpayer.

(B) LIMITATION.—The amount to which an election under subparagraph (A) applies shall not exceed the aggregate adjusted bases of the depreciable property held by the taxpayer as of the beginning of the taxable year following the taxable year in which the discharge occurs.

(C) OTHER TAX ATTRIBUTES NOT REDUCED.—Paragraph (2) shall not apply to any amount to which an election under this paragraph applies.

[Sec. 108(c)]

(c) TREATMENT OF DISCHARGE OF QUALIFIED REAL PROPERTY BUSINESS INDEBTEDNESS.—

(1) BASIS REDUCTION.—

(A) IN GENERAL.—The amount excluded from gross income under subparagraph (D) of subsection (a)(1) shall be applied to reduce the basis of the depreciable real property of the taxpayer.

(B) CROSS REFERENCE.—For provisions making the reduction described in subparagraph (A), see section 1017.

(2) LIMITATIONS.—

(A) INDEBTEDNESS IN EXCESS OF VALUE.—The amount excluded under subparagraph (D) of subsection (a)(1) with respect to any qualified real property business indebtedness shall not exceed the excess (if any) of—

(i) the outstanding principal amount of such indebtedness (immediately before the discharge), over

(ii) the fair market value of the real property described in paragraph (3)(A) (as of such time), reduced by the outstanding principal amount of any other qualified real property business indebtedness secured by such property (as of such time).

(B) OVERALL LIMITATION.—The amount excluded under subparagraph (D) of subsection (a)(1) shall not exceed the aggregate adjusted bases of depreciable real property (determined after any reductions under subsections (b) and (g)) held by the taxpayer immediately before the discharge (other than depreciable real property acquired in contemplation of such discharge).

(3) QUALIFIED REAL PROPERTY BUSINESS INDEBTEDNESS.—The term "qualified real property business indebtedness" means indebtedness which—

(A) was incurred or assumed by the taxpayer in connection with real property used in a trade or business and is secured by such real property,

(B) was incurred or assumed before January 1, 1993, or if incurred or assumed on or after such date, is qualified acquisition indebtedness, and

(C) with respect to which such taxpayer makes an election to have this paragraph apply.

Such term shall not include qualified farm indebtedness. Indebtedness under subparagraph (B) shall include indebtedness resulting from the refinancing of indebtedness under subparagraph (B) (or this sentence), but only to the extent it does not exceed the amount of the indebtedness being refinanced.

(4) QUALIFIED ACQUISITION INDEBTEDNESS.—For purposes of paragraph (3)(B), the term "qualified acquisition indebtedness" means, with respect to any real property described in paragraph (3)(A), indebtedness incurred or assumed to acquire, construct, reconstruct, or substantially improve such property.

(5) REGULATIONS.—The Secretary shall issue such regulations as are necessary to carry out this subsection, including regulations preventing the abuse of this subsection through cross-collateralization or other means.

[Sec. 108(d)]

(d) MEANING OF TERMS; SPECIAL RULES RELATING TO CERTAIN PROVISIONS.—

(1) INDEBTEDNESS OF TAXPAYER.—For purposes of this section, the term "indebtedness of the taxpayer" means any indebtedness—

(A) for which the taxpayer is liable, or

(B) subject to which the taxpayer holds property.

(2) TITLE 11 CASE.—For purposes of this section, the term "title 11 case" means a case under title 11 of the United States Code (relating to bankruptcy), but only if the taxpayer is under the jurisdiction of the court in such case and the discharge of indebtedness is granted by the court or is pursuant to a plan approved by the court.

(3) INSOLVENT.—For purposes of this section, the term "insolvent" means the excess of liabilities over the fair market value of assets. With respect to any discharge, whether or not the taxpayer is insolvent, and the amount by which the taxpayer is insolvent, shall be determined on the basis of the taxpayer's assets and liabilities immediately before the discharge.

(4) [Stricken.]

(5) DEPRECIABLE PROPERTY.—The term "depreciable property" has the same meaning as when used in section 1017.

(6) CERTAIN PROVISIONS TO BE APPLIED AT PARTNER LEVEL.—In the case of a partnership, subsections (a), (b), (c), and (g) shall be applied at the partner level.

(7) SPECIAL RULES FOR S CORPORATION.—

(A) CERTAIN PROVISIONS TO BE APPLIED AT CORPORATE LEVEL.—In the case of an S corporation, subsections (a), (b), (c), and (g) shall be applied at the corporate level, including by not taking into account under section 1366(a) any amount excluded under subsection (a) of this section.

(B) REDUCTION IN CARRYOVER OF DISALLOWED LOSSES AND DEDUCTIONS.—In the case of an S corporation, for purposes of subparagraph (A) of subsection (b)(2), any loss or deduction which is disallowed for the taxable year of the discharge under section 1366(d)(1) shall be treated as a net operating loss for such taxable year. The preceding sentence shall not apply to any discharge to the extent that subsection (a)(1)(D) applies to such discharge.

(C) COORDINATION WITH BASIS ADJUSTMENTS UNDER SECTION 1367(b)(2).—For purposes of subsection (e)(6), a shareholder's adjusted basis in indebtedness of an S corporation shall be determined without regard to any adjustments made under section 1367(b)(2).

(8) REDUCTIONS OF TAX ATTRIBUTES IN TITLE 11 CASES OF INDIVIDUALS TO BE MADE BY ESTATE.—In any case under chapter 7 or 11 of title 11 of the United States Code to which section 1398 applies, for purposes of paragraphs (1) and (5) of subsection (b) the estate (and not the individual) shall be treated as the taxpayer. The preceding sentence shall not apply for purposes of applying section 1017 to property transferred by the estate to the individual.

(9) TIME FOR MAKING ELECTION, ETC.—

(A) TIME.—An election under paragraph (5) of subsection (b) or under paragraph (3)(C) of subsection (c) shall be made on the taxpayer's return for the taxable year in which the discharge occurs or at such other time as may be permitted in regulations prescribed by the Secretary.

(B) REVOCATION ONLY WITH CONSENT.—An election referred to in subparagraph (A), once made, may be revoked only with the consent of the Secretary.

(C) MANNER.—An election referred to in subparagraph (A) shall be made in such manner as the Secretary may by regulations prescribe.

(10) CROSS REFERENCE.—

For provision that no reduction is to be made in the basis of exempt property of an individual debtor, see section 1017(c)(1).

[Sec. 108(e)]

(e) GENERAL RULES FOR DISCHARGE OF INDEBTEDNESS (INCLUDING DISCHARGES NOT IN TITLE 11 CASES OR INSOLVENCY).—For purposes of this title—

(1) NO OTHER INSOLVENCY EXCEPTION.—Except as otherwise provided in this section, there shall be no insolvency exception from the general rule that gross income includes income from the discharge of indebtedness.

(2) INCOME NOT REALIZED TO EXTENT OF LOST DEDUCTIONS.—No income shall be realized from the discharge of indebtedness to the extent that payment of the liability would have given rise to a deduction.

(3) ADJUSTMENTS FOR UNAMORTIZED PREMIUM AND DISCOUNT.—The amount taken into account with respect to any discharge shall be properly adjusted for unamortized premium and unamortized discount with respect to the indebtedness discharged.

(4) ACQUISITION OF INDEBTEDNESS BY PERSON RELATED TO DEBTOR.—

(A) TREATED AS ACQUISITION BY DEBTOR.—For purposes of determining income of the debtor from discharge of indebtedness, to the extent provided in regulations prescribed by the Secretary, the acquisition of outstanding indebtedness by a person bearing a relationship to the debtor specified in section 267(b) or 707(b)(1) from a person who does not bear such a relationship to the debtor shall be treated as the acquisition of such indebtedness by the debtor. Such regulations shall provide for such adjustments in the treatment of any subsequent transactions involving the indebtedness as may be appropriate by reason of the application of the preceding sentence.

(B) MEMBERS OF FAMILY.—For purposes of this paragraph, sections 267(b) and 707(b)(1) shall be applied as if section 267(c)(4) provided that the family of an individual consists of the individual's spouse, the individual's children, grandchildren, and parents, and any spouse of the individual's children or grandchildren.

(C) ENTITIES UNDER COMMON CONTROL TREATED AS RELATED.—For purposes of this paragraph, two entities which are treated as a single employer under subsection (b) or (c) of section 414 shall be treated as bearing a relationship to each other which is described in section 267(b).

(5) PURCHASE-MONEY DEBT REDUCTION FOR SOLVENT DEBTOR TREATED AS PRICE REDUCTION.—If—

(A) the debt of a purchaser of property to the seller of such property which arose out of the purchase of such property is reduced,

(B) such reduction does not occur—

(i) in a title 11 case, or

(ii) when the purchaser is insolvent, and

(C) but for this paragraph, such reduction would be treated as income to the purchaser from the discharge of indebtedness,

then such reduction shall be treated as a purchase price adjustment.

(6) INDEBTEDNESS CONTRIBUTED TO CAPITAL.—Except as provided in regulations, for purposes of determining income of the debtor from discharge of indebtedness, if a debtor corporation acquires its indebtedness from a shareholder as a contribution to capital—

(A) section 118 shall not apply, but

(B) such corporation shall be treated as having satisfied the indebtedness with an amount of money equal to the shareholder's adjusted basis in the indebtedness.

(7) RECAPTURE OF GAIN ON SUBSEQUENT SALE OF STOCK.—

(A) IN GENERAL.—If a creditor acquires stock of a debtor corporation in satisfaction of such corporation's indebtedness, for purposes of section 1245—

(i) such stock (and any other property the basis of which is determined in whole or in part by reference to the adjusted basis of such stock) shall be treated as section 1245 property,

(ii) the aggregate amount allowed to the creditor—

(I) as deductions under subsection (a) or (b) of section 166 (by reason of the worthlessness or partial worthlessness of the indebtedness), or

(II) as an ordinary loss on the exchange,

shall be treated as an amount allowed as a deduction for depreciation, and

(iii) an exchange of such stock qualifying under section 354(a), 355(a), or 356(a) shall be treated as an exchange to which section 1245(b)(3) applies.

The amount determined under clause (ii) shall be reduced by the amount (if any) included in the creditor's gross income on the exchange.

(B) SPECIAL RULE FOR CASH BASIS TAXPAYERS.—In the case of any creditor who computes his taxable income under the cash receipts and disbursements method, proper adjustment shall be made in the amount taken into account under clause (ii) of subparagraph (A) for any amount which was not included in the creditor's gross income but which would have been included in such gross income if such indebtedness had been satisfied in full.

(C) STOCK OF PARENT CORPORATION.—For purposes of this paragraph, stock of a corporation in control (within the meaning of section 368(c)) of the debtor corporation shall be treated as stock of the debtor corporation.

(D) TREATMENT OF SUCCESSOR CORPORATION.—For purposes of this paragraph, the term "debtor corporation" includes a successor corporation.

(E) PARTNERSHIP RULE.—Under regulations prescribed by the Secretary, rules similar to the rules of the foregoing subparagraphs of this paragraph shall apply with respect to the indebtedness of a partnership.

(8) INDEBTEDNESS SATISFIED BY CORPORATE STOCK OR PARTNERSHIP INTEREST.—For purposes of determining income of a debtor from discharge of indebtedness, if—

(A) a debtor corporation transfers stock, or

(B) a debtor partnership transfers a capital or profits interest in such partnership,

to a creditor in satisfaction of its recourse or nonrecourse indebtedness, such corporation or partnership shall be treated as having satisfied the indebtedness with an amount of money equal to the fair market value of the stock or interest. In the case of any partnership, any discharge of indebtedness income recognized under this paragraph shall be included in the distributive shares of taxpayers which were the partners in the partnership immediately before such discharge.

(9) DISCHARGE OF INDEBTEDNESS INCOME NOT TAKEN INTO ACCOUNT IN DETERMINING WHETHER ENTITY MEETS REIT QUALIFICATIONS.—Any amount included in gross income by reason of the discharge of indebtedness shall not be taken into account for purposes of paragraphs (2) and (3) of section 856(c).

(10) INDEBTEDNESS SATISFIED BY ISSUANCE OF DEBT INSTRUMENT.—

(A) IN GENERAL.—For purposes of determining income of a debtor from discharge of indebtedness, if a debtor issues a debt instrument in satisfaction of indebtedness, such debtor shall be treated as having satisfied the indebtedness with an amount of money equal to the issue price of such debt instrument.

(B) ISSUE PRICE.—For purposes of subparagraph (A), the issue price of any debt instrument shall be determined under sections 1273 and 1274. For purposes of the preceding sentence, section 1273(b)(4) shall be applied by reducing the stated redemption price of any instrument by the portion of such stated redemption price which is treated as interest for purposes of this chapter.

[Sec. 108(f)]

(f) STUDENT LOANS.—

(1) IN GENERAL.—In the case of an individual, gross income does not include any amount which (but for this subsection) would be includible in gross income by reason of the discharge (in whole or in part) of any student loan if such discharge was pursuant to a provision of such loan under which all or part of the indebtedness of the individual would be discharged if the individual worked for a certain period of time in certain professions for any of a broad class of employers.

(2) STUDENT LOAN.—For purposes of this subsection, the term "student loan" means any loan to an individual to assist the individual in attending an educational organization described in section 170(b)(1)(A)(ii) made by—

(A) the United States, or an instrumentality or agency thereof,

(B) a State, territory, or possession of the United States, or the District of Columbia, or any political subdivision thereof,

(C) a public benefit corporation—

(i) which is exempt from taxation under section 501(c)(3),

(ii) which has assumed control over a State, county, or municipal hospital, and

(iii) whose employees have been deemed to be public employees under State law, or

(D) any educational organization described in section 170(b)(1)(A)(ii) if such loan is made—

(i) pursuant to an agreement with any entity described in subparagraph (A), (B), or (C) under which the funds from which the loan was made were provided to such educational organization, or

(ii) pursuant to a program of such educational organization which is designed to encourage its students to serve in occupations with unmet needs or in areas with unmet needs and under which the services provided by the students (or former students) are for or under the direction of a governmental unit or an organization described in section 501(c)(3) and exempt from tax under section 501(a).

The term "student loan" includes any loan made by an educational organization described in section 170(b)(1)(A)(ii) or by an organization exempt from tax under section 501(a) to refinance a loan to an individual to assist the individual in attending any such educational organization but only if the refinancing loan is pursuant to a program of the refinancing organization which is designed as described in subparagraph (D)(ii).

(3) EXCEPTION FOR DISCHARGES ON ACCOUNT OF SERVICES PERFORMED FOR CERTAIN LENDERS.—Paragraph (1) shall not apply to the discharge of a loan made by an organization described in paragraph (2)(D) if the discharge is on account of services performed for either such organization.

(4) PAYMENTS UNDER NATIONAL HEALTH SERVICE CORPS LOAN REPAYMENT PROGRAM AND CERTAIN STATE LOAN REPAYMENT PROGRAMS.—In the case of an individual, gross income shall not include any amount received under section 338B(g) of the Public Health Service Act, under a State program described in section 338I of such Act, or under any other State loan repayment or loan forgiveness program that is intended to provide for the increased availability of health care services in underserved or health professional shortage areas (as determined by such State).

(5) DISCHARGES ON ACCOUNT OF DEATH OR DISABILITY.—

(A) IN GENERAL.—In the case of an individual, gross income does not include any amount which (but for this subsection) would be includible in gross income for such taxable year by reasons of the discharge (in whole or in part) of any loan described in subparagraph (B) after December 31, 2017, and before January 1, 2026, if such discharge was—

(i) pursuant to subsection (a) or (d) of section 437 of the Higher Education Act of 1965 or the parallel benefit under part D of title IV of such Act (relating to the repayment of loan liability),

(ii) pursuant to section 464(c)(1)(F) of such Act, or

(iii) otherwise discharged on account of the death or total and permanent disability of the student.

(B) LOANS DESCRIBED.—A loan is described in this subparagraph if such loan is—

(i) a student loan (as defined in paragraph (2)), or

(ii) a private education loan (as defined in section 140(7) of the Consumer Credit Protection Act (15 U.S.C. 1650(7))).

[Sec. 108(g)]

(g) SPECIAL RULES FOR DISCHARGE OF QUALIFIED FARM INDEBTEDNESS.—

(1) DISCHARGE MUST BE BY QUALIFIED PERSON.—

(A) IN GENERAL.—Subparagraph (C) of subsection (a)(1) shall apply only if the discharge is by a qualified person.

(B) QUALIFIED PERSON.—For purposes of subparagraph (A), the term "qualified person" has the meaning given to such term by section 49(a)(1)(D)(iv); except that such term shall include any Federal, State, or local government or agency or instrumentality thereof.

(2) QUALIFIED FARM INDEBTEDNESS.—For purposes of this section, indebtedness of a taxpayer shall be treated as qualified farm indebtedness if—

(A) such indebtedness was incurred directly in connection with the operation by the taxpayer of the trade or business of farming, and

(B) 50 percent or more of the aggregate gross receipts of the taxpayer for the 3 taxable years preceding the taxable year in which the discharge of such indebtedness occurs is attributable to the trade or business of farming.

(3) AMOUNT EXCLUDED CANNOT EXCEED SUM OF TAX ATTRIBUTES AND BUSINESS AND INVESTMENT ASSETS.—

(A) IN GENERAL.—The amount excluded under subparagraph (C) of subsection (a)(1) shall not exceed the sum of—

(i) the adjusted tax attributes of the taxpayer, and

(ii) the aggregate adjusted bases of qualified property held by the taxpayer as of the beginning of the taxable year following the taxable year in which the discharge occurs.

(B) ADJUSTED TAX ATTRIBUTES.—For purposes of subparagraph (A), the term "adjusted tax attributes" means the sum of the tax attributes described in subparagraphs (A), (B), (C), (D), (F), and (G) of subsection (b)(2) determined by taking into account $3 for each $1 of the attributes described in subparagraphs (B), (C), and (G) of subsection (b)(2) and the attribute described in subparagraph (F) of subsection (b)(2) to the extent attributable to any passive activity credit carryover.

(C) QUALIFIED PROPERTY.—For purposes of this paragraph, the term "qualified property" means any property which is used or is held for use in a trade or business or for the production of income.

(D) COORDINATION WITH INSOLVENCY EXCLUSION.—For purposes of this paragraph, the adjusted basis of any qualified property and the amount of the adjusted tax attributes shall be determined after any reduction under subsection (b) by reason of amounts excluded from gross income under subsection (a)(1)(B).

[Sec. 108(h)]

(h) SPECIAL RULES RELATING TO QUALIFIED PRINCIPAL RESIDENCE INDEBTEDNESS.—

(1) BASIS REDUCTION.—The amount excluded from gross income by reason of subsection (a) (1) (E) shall be applied to reduce (but not below zero) the basis of the principal residence of the taxpayer.

(2) QUALIFIED PRINCIPAL RESIDENCE INDEBTEDNESS.—For purposes of this section, the term "qualified principal residence indebtedness" means acquisition indebtedness (within the meaning of section 163(h)(3)(B), applied by substituting "$2,000,000 ($1,000,000" for "$1,000,000 ($500,000" in clause (ii) thereof and determined without regard to the substitution described in section 163(h)(3)(F)(i)(II)) with respect to the principal residence of the taxpayer.

(3) EXCEPTION FOR CERTAIN DISCHARGES NOT RELATED TO TAXPAYER'S FINANCIAL CONDITION.—Subsection (a)(1)(E) shall not apply to the discharge of a loan if the discharge is on account of services performed for the lender or any other factor not directly related to a decline in the value of the residence or to the financial condition of the taxpayer.

(4) ORDERING RULE.—If any loan is discharged, in whole or in part, and only a portion of such loan is qualified principal residence indebtedness, subsection (a)(1)(E) shall apply only to so much of the amount discharged as exceeds the amount of the loan (as determined immediately before such discharge) which is not qualified principal residence indebtedness.

(5) PRINCIPAL RESIDENCE.—For purposes of this subsection, the term "principal residence" has the same meaning as when used in section 121.

* * *

[Sec. 109]

SEC. 109. IMPROVEMENTS BY LESSEE ON LESSOR'S PROPERTY.

Gross income does not include income (other than rent) derived by a lessor of real property on the termination of a lease, representing the value of such property attributable to buildings erected or other improvements made by the lessee.

[Sec. 111]

SEC. 111. RECOVERY OF TAX BENEFIT ITEMS.

[Sec. 111(a)]

(a) DEDUCTIONS.—Gross income does not include income attributable to the recovery during the taxable year of any amount deducted in any prior taxable year to the extent such amount did not reduce the amount of tax imposed by this chapter.

[Sec. 111(b)]

(b) CREDITS.—

(1) IN GENERAL.—If—

(A) a credit was allowable with respect to any amount for any prior taxable year, and

(B) during the taxable year there is a downward price adjustment or similar adjustment,

the tax imposed by this chapter for the taxable year shall be increased by the amount of the credit attributable to the adjustment.

(2) EXCEPTION WHERE CREDIT DID NOT REDUCE TAX.—Paragraph (1) shall not apply to the extent that the credit allowable for the recovered amount did not reduce the amount of tax imposed by this chapter.

(3) EXCEPTION FOR INVESTMENT TAX CREDIT AND FOREIGN TAX CREDIT.—This subsection shall not apply with respect to the credit determined under section 46 and the foreign tax credit.

[Sec. 111(c)]

(c) TREATMENT OF CARRYOVERS.—For purposes of this section, an increase in a carryover which has not expired before the beginning of the taxable year in which the recovery or adjustment takes place shall be treated as reducing tax imposed by this chapter.

[Sec. 111(d)]

(d) SPECIAL RULES FOR ACCUMULATED EARNINGS TAX AND FOR PERSONAL HOLDING COMPANY TAX.—In applying subsection (a) for the purpose of determining the accumulated earnings tax under section 531 or the tax under section 541 (relating to personal holding companies)—

(1) any excluded amount under subsection (a) allowed for the purposes of this subtitle (other than section 531 or section 541) shall be allowed whether or not such amount resulted in a reduction of the tax under section 531 or the tax under section 541 for the prior taxable year; and

(2) where any excluded amount under subsection (a) was not allowable as a deduction for the prior taxable year for purposes of this subtitle other than of section 531 or section 541 but was allowable for the same taxable year under section 531 or section 541, then such excluded amount shall be allowable if it did not result in a reduction of the tax under section 531 or the tax under section 541.

[Sec. 112]

SEC. 112. CERTAIN COMBAT ZONE COMPENSATION OF MEMBERS OF THE ARMED FORCES.

[Sec. 112(a)]

(a) ENLISTED PERSONNEL.—Gross income does not include compensation received for active service as a member below the grade of commissioned officer in the Armed Forces of the United States for any month during any part of which such member—

(1) served in a combat zone, or

(2) was hospitalized as a result of wounds, disease, or injury incurred while serving in a combat zone; but this paragraph shall not apply for any month beginning more than 2 years after the date of the termination of combatant activities in such zone.

With respect to service in the combat zone designated for purposes of the Vietnam conflict, paragraph (2) shall not apply to any month after January 1978.

[Sec. 112(b)]

(b) COMMISSIONED OFFICERS.—Gross income does not include so much of the compensation as does not exceed the maximum enlisted amount received for active service as a commissioned officer in the Armed Forces of the United States for any month during any part of which such officer—

(1) served in a combat zone, or

(2) was hospitalized as a result of wounds, disease, or injury incurred while serving in a combat zone; but this paragraph shall not apply for any month beginning more than 2 years after the date of the termination of combatant activities in such zone.

With respect to service in the combat zone designated for purposes of the Vietnam conflict, paragraph (2) shall not apply to any month after January 1978.

[Sec. 112(c)]

(c) DEFINITIONS.—For purposes of this section—

(1) The term "commissioned officer" does not include a commissioned warrant officer.

(2) The term "combat zone" means any area which the President of the United States by Executive Order designates, for purposes of this section or corresponding provisions of prior income tax laws, as an area in which Armed Forces of the United States are or have engaged in combat.

(3) Service is performed in a combat zone only if performed on or after the date designated by the President by Executive Order as the date of the commencing of combatant activities in such zone.

(4) The term "compensation" does not include pensions and retirement pay.

(5) The term "maximum enlisted amount" means, for any month, the sum of—

(A) the highest rate of basic pay payable for such month to any enlisted member of the Armed Forces of the United States at the highest pay grade applicable to enlisted members, and

(B) in the case of an officer entitled to special pay under section 310, or paragraph (1) or (3) of section 351(a), of title 37, United States Code, for such month, the amount of such special pay payable to such officer for such month.

[Sec. 112(d)]

(d) PRISONERS OF WAR, ETC.—

(1) MEMBERS OF THE ARMED FORCES.—Gross income does not include compensation received for active service as a member of the Armed Forces of the United States for any month during any part of which such member is in a missing status (as defined in section 551(2) of title 37, United States Code) during the Vietnam conflict as a result of such conflict, other than a period with respect to which it is officially determined under section 552(c) of such title 37 that he is officially absent from his post of duty without authority.

(2) CIVILIAN EMPLOYEES.—Gross income does not include compensation received for active service as an employee for any month during any part of which such employee is in a missing status during the Vietnam conflict as a result of such conflict. For purposes of this paragraph, the terms "active service", "employee", and "missing status" have the respective meanings given to such terms by section 5561 of title 5 of the United States Code.

(3) PERIOD OF CONFLICT.—For purposes of this subsection, the Vietnam conflict began February 28, 1961, and ends on the date designated by the President by Executive order as the date of the termination of combatant activities in Vietnam. For purposes of this subsection, an individual is in a missing status as a result of the Vietnam conflict if immediately before such status began he was performing service in Vietnam or was performing service in Southeast Asia in direct support of military operations in Vietnam.

[Sec. 115]

SEC. 115. INCOME OF STATES, MUNICIPALITIES, ETC.

Gross income does not include—

(1) income derived from any public utility or the exercise of any essential governmental function and accruing to a State or any political subdivision thereof, or the District of Columbia; or

(2) income accruing to the government of any possession of the United States, or any political subdivision thereof.

[Sec. 117]

SEC. 117. QUALIFIED SCHOLARSHIPS.

[Sec. 117(a)]

(a) GENERAL RULE.—Gross income does not include any amount received as a qualified scholarship by an individual who is a candidate for a degree at an educational organization described in section 170(b)(1)(A)(ii).

[Sec. 117(b)]

(b) QUALIFIED SCHOLARSHIP.—For purposes of this section—

(1) IN GENERAL.—The term "qualified scholarship" means any amount received by an individual as a scholarship or fellowship grant to the extent the individual establishes that, in accordance with the conditions of the grant, such amount was used for qualified tuition and related expenses.

(2) QUALIFIED TUITION AND RELATED EXPENSES.—For purposes of paragraph (1), the term "qualified tuition and related expenses" means—

(A) tuition and fees required for the enrollment or attendance of a student at an educational organization described in section 170(b)(1)(A)(ii), and

(B) fees, books, supplies, and equipment required for courses of instruction at such an educational organization.

[Sec. 117(c)]

(c) LIMITATION.—

(1) IN GENERAL.—Except as provided in paragraph (2), subsections (a) and (d) shall not apply to that portion of any amount received which represents payment for teaching, research, or other services by the student required as a condition for receiving the qualified scholarship or qualified tuition reduction.

(2) EXCEPTIONS.—Paragraph (1) shall not apply to any amount received by an individual under—

(A) the National Health Service Corps Scholarship Program under section 338A(g)(1)(A) of the Public Health Service Act,

(B) the Armed Forces Health Professions Scholarship and Financial Assistance program under subchapter I of chapter 105 of title 10, United States Code, or

(C) a comprehensive student work-learning-service program (as defined in section 448(e) of the Higher Education Act of 1965) operated by a work college (as defined in such section).

[Sec. 117(d)]

(d) QUALIFIED TUITION REDUCTION.—

(1) IN GENERAL.—Gross income shall not include any qualified tuition reduction.

(2) QUALIFIED TUITION REDUCTION.—For purposes of this subsection, the term "qualified tuition reduction" means the amount of any reduction in tuition provided to an employee of an organization described in section 170(b)(1)(A)(ii) for the education (below the graduate level) at such organization (or another organization described in section 170(b)(1)(A)(ii)) of—

(A) such employee, or

(B) any person treated as an employee (or whose use is treated as an employee use) under the rules of section 132(h).

(3) REDUCTION MUST NOT DISCRIMINATE IN FAVOR OF HIGHLY COMPENSATED, ETC.—Paragraph (1) shall apply with respect to any qualified tuition reduction provided with respect to any highly compensated employee only if such reduction is available on substantially the same terms to each member of a group of employees which is defined under a reasonable classification set up by the employer which does not discriminate in favor of highly compensated employees (within the meaning of section 414(q)). For purposes of this paragraph, the term "highly compensated employee" has the meaning given such term by section 414(q).

(5) [4] SPECIAL RULES FOR TEACHING AND RESEARCH ASSISTANTS.—In the case of the education of an individual who is a graduate student at an educational organization described in section 170(b)(1)(A)(ii) and who is engaged in teaching or research activities for such organization, paragraph (2) shall be applied as if it did not contain the phrase "(below the graduate level)".

[Sec. 118]

SEC. 118. CONTRIBUTIONS TO THE CAPITAL OF A CORPORATION.

[Sec. 118(a)]

(a) GENERAL RULE.—In the case of a corporation, gross income does not include any contribution to the capital of the taxpayer.

[Sec. 118(b)]

(b) EXCEPTIONS.—For purposes of subsection (a), the term "contribution to the capital of the taxpayer" does not include—

(1) any contribution in aid of construction or any other contribution as a customer or potential customer, and

(2) any contribution by any governmental entity or civic group (other than a contribution made by a shareholder as such).

[Sec. 118(c)]

(c) REGULATIONS.—The Secretary shall issue such regulations or other guidance as may be necessary or appropriate to carry out this section, including regulations or other guidance for determining whether any contribution constitutes a contribution in aid of construction.

[Sec. 118(d)]

(d) CROSS REFERENCES.—

(1) For basis of property acquired by a corporation through a contribution to its capital, see section 362.

(2) For special rules in the case of contributions of indebtedness, see section 108(e)(6).

[Sec. 119]

SEC. 119. MEALS OR LODGING FURNISHED FOR THE CONVENIENCE OF THE EMPLOYER.

[Sec. 119(a)]

(a) MEALS AND LODGING FURNISHED TO EMPLOYEE, HIS SPOUSE, AND HIS DEPENDENTS, PURSUANT TO EMPLOYMENT.—There shall be excluded from gross income of an employee the value of any meals or lodging furnished to him, his spouse, or any of his dependents by or on behalf of his employer for the convenience of the employer, but only if—

(1) in the case of meals, the meals are furnished on the business premises of the employer, or

(2) in the case of lodging, the employee is required to accept such lodging on the business premises of his employer as a condition of his employment.

[Sec. 119(b)]

(b) SPECIAL RULES.—For purposes of subsection (a)—

(1) PROVISIONS OF EMPLOYMENT CONTRACT OR STATE STATUTE NOT TO BE DETERMINATIVE.—In determining whether meals or lodging are furnished for the convenience of the employer, the provisions of an employment contract or of a State statute fixing terms of employment shall not be determinative of whether the meals or lodging are intended as compensation.

(2) CERTAIN FACTORS NOT TAKEN INTO ACCOUNT WITH RESPECT TO MEALS.—In determining whether meals are furnished for the convenience of the employer, the fact that a charge is made for such meals, and the fact that the employee may accept or decline such meals, shall not be taken into account.

(3) CERTAIN FIXED CHARGES FOR MEALS.—

(A) IN GENERAL.—If—

(i) an employee is required to pay on a periodic basis a fixed charge for his meals, and

(ii) such meals are furnished by the employer for the convenience of the employer, there shall be excluded from the employee's gross income an amount equal to such fixed charge.

(B) APPLICATION OF SUBPARAGRAPH (A).—Subparagraph (A) shall apply—

(i) whether the employee pays the fixed charge out of his stated compensation or out of his own funds, and

(ii) only if the employee is required to make the payment whether he accepts or declines the meals.

(4) MEALS FURNISHED TO EMPLOYEES ON BUSINESS PREMISES WHERE MEALS OF MOST EMPLOYEES ARE OTHERWISE EXCLUDABLE.—All meals furnished on the business premises of an employer to such employer's employees shall be treated as furnished for the convenience of the employer if, without regard to this paragraph, more than half of the employees to whom such meals are furnished on such premises are furnished such meals for the convenience of the employer.

* * *

[Sec. 119(d)]

(d) LODGING FURNISHED BY CERTAIN EDUCATIONAL INSTITUTIONS TO EMPLOYEES.—

(1) IN GENERAL.—In the case of an employee of an educational institution, gross income shall not include the value of qualified campus lodging furnished to such employee during the taxable year.

(2) EXCEPTION IN CASES OF INADEQUATE RENT.—Paragraph (1) shall not apply to the extent of the excess of—

(A) the lesser of—

(i) 5 percent of the appraised value of the qualified campus lodging, or

(ii) the average of the rentals paid by individuals (other than employees or students of the educational institution) during such calendar year for lodging provided by the educational institution which is comparable to the qualified campus lodging provided to the employee, over

(B) the rent paid by the employee for the qualified campus lodging during such calendar year.

The appraised value under subparagraph (A)(i) shall be determined as of the close of the calendar year in which the taxable year begins, or, in the case of a rental period not greater than 1 year, at any time during the calendar year in which such period begins.

(3) QUALIFIED CAMPUS LODGING.—For purposes of this subsection, the term "qualified campus lodging" means lodging to which subsection (a) does not apply and which is—

(A) located on, or in the proximity of, a campus of the educational institution, and

(B) furnished to the employee, his spouse, and any of his dependents by or on behalf of such institution for use as a residence.

(4) EDUCATIONAL INSTITUTION, ETC.—For purposes of this subsection—

(A) IN GENERAL.—The term "educational institution" means—

(i) an institution described in section 170(b)(1)(A)(ii) (or an entity organized under State law and composed of public institutions so described), or

(ii) an academic health center.

(B) ACADEMIC HEALTH CENTER.—For purposes of subparagraph (A), the term "academic health center" means an entity—

(i) which is described in section 170(b)(1)(A)(iii),

(ii) which receives (during the calendar year in which the taxable year of the taxpayer begins) payments under subsection (d)(5)(B) or (h) of section 1886 of the Social Security Act (relating to graduate medical education), and

(iii) which has as one of its principal purposes or functions the providing and teaching of basic and clinical medical science and research with the entity's own faculty.

[Sec. 121]

SEC. 121. EXCLUSION OF GAIN FROM SALE OF PRINCIPAL RESIDENCE.

[Sec. 121(a)]

(a) EXCLUSION.—Gross income shall not include gain from the sale or exchange of property if, during the 5-year period ending on the date of the sale or exchange, such property has been owned and used by the taxpayer as the taxpayer's principal residence for periods aggregating 2 years or more.

[Sec. 121(b)]

(b) LIMITATIONS.—

(1) IN GENERAL.—The amount of gain excluded from gross income under subsection (a) with respect to any sale or exchange shall not exceed $250,000.

(2) SPECIAL RULES FOR JOINT RETURNS.—In the case of a husband and wife who make a joint return for the taxable year of the sale or exchange of the property—

(A) $500,000 LIMITATION FOR CERTAIN JOINT RETURNS.—Paragraph (1) shall be applied by substituting "$500,000" for "$250,000" if—

(i) either spouse meets the ownership requirements of subsection (a) with respect to such property;

(ii) both spouses meet the use requirements of subsection (a) with respect to such property; and

(iii) neither spouse is ineligible for the benefits of subsection (a) with respect to such property by reason of paragraph (3).

(B) OTHER JOINT RETURNS.—If such spouses do not meet the requirements of subparagraph (A), the limitation under paragraph (1) shall be the sum of the limitations under paragraph (1) to which each spouse would be entitled if such spouses had not been married. For purposes of the preceding sentence, each spouse shall be treated as owning the property during the period that either spouse owned the property.

(3) APPLICATION TO ONLY 1 SALE OR EXCHANGE EVERY 2 YEARS.—Subsection (a) shall not apply to any sale or exchange by the taxpayer if, during the 2-year period ending on the date of such sale or exchange, there was any other sale or exchange by the taxpayer to which subsection (a) applied.

(4) SPECIAL RULE FOR CERTAIN SALES BY SURVIVING SPOUSES.—In the case of a sale or exchange of property by an unmarried individual whose spouse is deceased on the date of such sale, paragraph (1) shall be applied by substituting "$500,000" for "$250,000" if such sale occurs not later than 2 years after the date of death of such spouse and the requirements of paragraph (2)(A) were met immediately before such date of death.

(5) EXCLUSION OF GAIN ALLOCATED TO NONQUALIFIED USE.—

(A) IN GENERAL.—Subsection (a) shall not apply to so much of the gain from the sale or exchange of property as is allocated to periods of nonqualified use.

(B) GAIN ALLOCATED TO PERIODS OF NONQUALIFIED USE.—For purposes of subparagraph (A), gain shall be allocated to periods of nonqualified use based on the ratio which—

(i) the aggregate periods of nonqualified use during the period such property was owned by the taxpayer, bears to

(ii) the period such property was owned by the taxpayer.

(C) PERIOD OF NONQUALIFIED USE.—For purposes of this paragraph—

(i) IN GENERAL.—The term "period of nonqualified use" means any period (other than the portion of any period preceding January 1, 2009) during which the property is not used as the principal residence of the taxpayer or the taxpayer's spouse or former spouse.

(ii) EXCEPTIONS.—The term "period of nonqualified use" does not include—

(I) any portion of the 5-year period described in subsection (a) which is after the last date that such property is used as the principal residence of the taxpayer or the taxpayer's spouse,

(II) any period (not to exceed an aggregate period of 10 years) during which the taxpayer or the taxpayer's spouse is serving on qualified official extended duty (as defined in subsection (d)(9)(C)) described in clause (i), (ii), or (iii) of subsection (d)(9)(A), and

(III) any other period of temporary absence (not to exceed an aggregate period of 2 years) due to change of employment, health conditions, or such other unforeseen circumstances as may be specified by the Secretary.

(D) COORDINATION WITH RECOGNITION OF GAIN ATTRIBUTABLE TO DEPRECIATION.—For purposes of this paragraph—

(i) subparagraph (A) shall be applied after the application of subsection (d)(6), and

(ii) subparagraph (B) shall be applied without regard to any gain to which subsection (d)(6) applies.

[Sec. 121(c)]

(c) EXCLUSION FOR TAXPAYERS FAILING TO MEET CERTAIN REQUIREMENTS.—

(1) IN GENERAL.—In the case of a sale or exchange to which this subsection applies, the ownership and use requirements of subsection (a), and subsection (b)(3), shall not apply; but the dollar limitation under paragraph (1) or (2) of subsection (b), whichever is applicable, shall be equal to—

(A) the amount which bears the same ratio to such limitation (determined without regard to this paragraph) as

(B)(i) the shorter of—

(I) the aggregate periods, during the 5-year period ending on the date of such sale or exchange, such property has been owned and used by the taxpayer as the taxpayer's principal residence; or

(II) the period after the date of the most recent prior sale or exchange by the taxpayer to which subsection (a) applied and before the date of such sale or exchange, bears to

(ii) 2 years.

(2) SALES AND EXCHANGES TO WHICH SUBSECTION APPLIES.—This subsection shall apply to any sale or exchange if—

(A) subsection (a) would not (but for this subsection) apply to such sale or exchange by reason of—

(i) a failure to meet the ownership and use requirements of subsection (a), or

(ii) subsection (b)(3), and

(B) such sale or exchange is by reason of a change in place of employment, health, or, to the extent provided in regulations, unforeseen circumstances.

[Sec. 121(d)]

(d) SPECIAL RULES.—

(1) JOINT RETURNS.—If a husband and wife make a joint return for the taxable year of the sale or exchange of the property, subsections (a) and (c) shall apply if either spouse meets the ownership and use requirements of subsection (a) with respect to such property.

(2) PROPERTY OF DECEASED SPOUSE.—For purposes of this section, in the case of an unmarried individual whose spouse is deceased on the date of the sale or exchange of property, the period such unmarried individual owned and used such property shall include the period such deceased spouse owned and used such property before death.

(3) PROPERTY OWNED BY SPOUSE OR FORMER SPOUSE.—For purposes of this section—

(A) PROPERTY TRANSFERRED TO INDIVIDUAL FROM SPOUSE OR FORMER SPOUSE.—In the case of an individual holding property transferred to such individual in a transaction described in section 1041(a), the period such individual owns such property shall include the period the transferor owned the property.

»»→ Caution: Code Sec. 121(d)(3)(B), below, prior to amendment by P.L. 115-97, applies generally to any divorce or separation instrument executed on or before December 31, 2018.

(B) PROPERTY USED BY FORMER SPOUSE PURSUANT TO DIVORCE DECREE, ETC.—Solely for purposes of this section, an individual shall be treated as using property as such individual's principal residence during any period of ownership while such individual's spouse or former spouse is granted use of the property under a divorce or separation instrument (as defined in section 71(b)(2)).

»»→ Caution: Code Sec. 121(d)(3)(B), below, as amended by P.L. 115-97, applies generally to any divorce or separation instrument executed after December 31, 2018.

(B) PROPERTY USED BY FORMER SPOUSE PURSUANT TO DIVORCE DECREE, ETC.—Solely for purposes of this section, an individual shall be treated as using property as such individual's principal residence during any period of ownership while such individual's spouse or former spouse is granted use of the property under a divorce or separation instrument.

»»→ Caution: Code Sec. 121(d)(3)(C), below, as added by P.L. 115-97, applies generally to any divorce or separation instrument executed after December 31, 2018.

(C) DIVORCE OR SEPARATION INSTRUMENT.—For purposes of this paragraph, the term "divorce or separation instrument" means—

(i) a decree of divorce or separate maintenance or a written instrument incident to such a decree,

(ii) a written separation agreement, or

(iii) a decree (not described in clause (i)) requiring a spouse to make payments for the support or maintenance of the other spouse.

(4) TENANT-STOCKHOLDER IN COOPERATIVE HOUSING CORPORATION.—For purposes of this section, if the taxpayer holds stock as a tenant-stockholder (as defined in section 216) in a cooperative housing corporation (as defined in such section), then—

(A) the holding requirements of subsection (a) shall be applied to the holding of such stock, and

(B) the use requirements of subsection (a) shall be applied to the house or apartment which the taxpayer was entitled to occupy as such stockholder.

(5) INVOLUNTARY CONVERSIONS.—

(A) IN GENERAL.—For purposes of this section, the destruction, theft, seizure, requisition, or condemnation of property shall be treated as the sale of such property.

(B) APPLICATION OF SECTION 1033.—In applying section 1033 (relating to involuntary conversions), the amount realized from the sale or exchange of property shall be treated as being the amount determined without regard to this section, reduced by the amount of gain not included in gross income pursuant to this section.

(C) PROPERTY ACQUIRED AFTER INVOLUNTARY CONVERSION.—If the basis of the property sold or exchanged is determined (in whole or in part) under section 1033(b) (relating to basis of property acquired through involuntary conversion), then the holding and use by the taxpayer of the converted property shall be treated as holding and use by the taxpayer of the property sold or exchanged.

(6) RECOGNITION OF GAIN ATTRIBUTABLE TO DEPRECIATION.—Subsection (a) shall not apply to so much of the gain from the sale of any property as does not exceed the portion of the depreciation adjustments (as defined in section 1250(b)(3)) attributable to periods after May 6, 1997, in respect of such property.

(7) DETERMINATION OF USE DURING PERIODS OF OUT-OF-RESIDENCE CARE.—In the case of a taxpayer who—

(A) becomes physically or mentally incapable of self-care, and

(B) owns property and uses such property as the taxpayer's principal residence during the 5-year period described in subsection (a) for periods aggregating at least 1 year, then the taxpayer shall be treated as using such property as the taxpayer's principal residence during any time during such 5-year period in which the taxpayer owns the property and resides in any facility (including a nursing home) licensed by a State or political subdivision to care for an individual in the taxpayer's condition.

(8) SALES OF REMAINDER INTERESTS.—For purposes of this section—

(A) IN GENERAL.—At the election of the taxpayer, this section shall not fail to apply to the sale or exchange of an interest in a principal residence by reason of such interest being a remainder interest in such residence, but this section shall not apply to any other interest in such residence which is sold or exchanged separately.

(B) EXCEPTION FOR SALES TO RELATED PARTIES.—Subparagraph (A) shall not apply to any sale to, or exchange with, any person who bears a relationship to the taxpayer which is described in section 267(b) or 707(b).

(9) UNIFORMED SERVICES, FOREIGN SERVICE, AND INTELLIGENCE COMMUNITY.—

(A) IN GENERAL.—At the election of an individual with respect to a property, the running of the 5-year period described in subsections (a) and (c)(1)(B) and paragraph (7) of this subsection with respect to such property shall be suspended during any period that such individual or such individual's spouse is serving on qualified official extended duty—

(i) as a member of the uniformed services,

(ii) as a member of the Foreign Service of the United States, or

(iii) as an employee of the intelligence community.

(B) MAXIMUM PERIOD OF SUSPENSION.—The 5-year period described in subsection (a) shall not be extended more than 10 years by reason of subparagraph (A).

(C) QUALIFIED OFFICIAL EXTENDED DUTY.—For purposes of this paragraph—

(i) IN GENERAL.—The term "qualified official extended duty" means any extended duty while serving at a duty station which is at least 50 miles from such property or while residing under Government orders in Government quarters.

(ii) UNIFORMED SERVICES.—The term "uniformed services" has the meaning given such term by section 101(a)(5) of title 10, United States Code, as in effect on the date of the enactment of this paragraph.

(iii) FOREIGN SERVICE OF THE UNITED STATES.—The term "member of the Foreign Service of the United States" has the meaning given the term "member of the Service" by paragraph (1), (2), (3), (4), or (5) of section 103 of the Foreign Service Act of 1980, as in effect on the date of the enactment of this paragraph.

(iv) EMPLOYEE OF INTELLIGENCE COMMUNITY.—The term "employee of the intelligence community" means an employee (as defined by section 2105 of title 5, United States Code) of—

(I) the Office of the Director of National Intelligence,

(II) the Central Intelligence Agency,

(III) the National Security Agency,

(IV) the Defense Intelligence Agency,

(V) the National Geospatial-Intelligence Agency,

(VI) the National Reconnaissance Office,

(VII) any other office within the Department of Defense for the collection of specialized national intelligence through reconnaissance programs,

(VIII) any of the intelligence elements of the Army, the Navy, the Air Force, the Marine Corps, the Federal Bureau of Investigation, the Department of Treasury, the Department of Energy, and the Coast Guard,

(IX) the Bureau of Intelligence and Research of the Department of State, or

(X) any of the elements of the Department of Homeland Security concerned with the analyses of foreign intelligence information.

(v) EXTENDED DUTY.—The term "extended duty" means any period of active duty pursuant to a call or order to such duty for a period in excess of 90 days or for an indefinite period.

(D) SPECIAL RULES RELATING TO ELECTION.—

(i) ELECTION LIMITED TO 1 PROPERTY AT A TIME.—An election under subparagraph (A) with respect to any property may not be made if such an election is in effect with respect to any other property.

(ii) REVOCATION OF ELECTION.—An election under subparagraph (A) may be revoked at any time.

(10) PROPERTY ACQUIRED IN LIKE-KIND EXCHANGE.—If a taxpayer acquires property in an exchange with respect to which gain is not recognized (in whole or in part) to the taxpayer under subsection (a) or (b) of section 1031, subsection (a) shall not apply to the sale or exchange of such property by such taxpayer (or by any person whose basis in such property is determined, in whole or in part, by reference to the basis in the hands of such taxpayer) during the 5-year period beginning with the date of such acquisition.

(11) [Repealed.]

(12) PEACE CORPS.—

(A) IN GENERAL.—At the election of an individual with respect to a property, the running of the 5-year period described in subsections (a) and (c)(1)(B) and paragraph (7) of this subsection with respect to such property shall be suspended during any period that such individual or such individual's spouse is serving outside the United States—

(i) on qualified official extended duty (as defined in paragraph (9)(C)) as an employee of the Peace Corps, or

(ii) as an enrolled volunteer or volunteer leader under section 5 or 6 (as the case may be) of the Peace Corps Act (22 U.S.C. 2504, 2505).

(B) APPLICABLE RULES.—For purposes of subparagraph (A), rules similar to the rules of subparagraphs (B) and (D) of paragraph (9) shall apply.

[Sec. 121(f)]

(f) ELECTION TO HAVE SECTION NOT APPLY.—This section shall not apply to any sale or exchange with respect to which the taxpayer elects not to have this section apply.

* * *

Caution: Pursuant to Section 125(i)(2), the dollar amount set forth in Section 125(i)(1) is adjusted for taxable years beginning after 2013 to reflect increases in the Chained Consumer Price Index. The amount applicable to taxable years beginning in 2020 is provided in the material beginning at page ix.

[Sec. 125]

SEC. 125. CAFETERIA PLANS.

[Sec. 125(a)]

(a) IN GENERAL.—Except as provided in subsection (b), no amount shall be included in the gross income of a participant in a cafeteria plan solely because, under the plan, the participant may choose among the benefits of the plan.

[Sec. 125(b)]

(b) EXCEPTION FOR HIGHLY COMPENSATED PARTICIPANTS AND KEY EMPLOYEES.—

(1) HIGHLY COMPENSATED PARTICIPANTS.—In the case of a highly compensated participant, subsection (a) shall not apply to any benefit attributable to a plan year for which the plan discriminates in favor of—

(A) highly compensated individuals as to eligibility to participate, or

(B) highly compensated participants as to contributions and benefits.

(2) KEY EMPLOYEES.—In the case of a key employee (within the meaning of section 416(i)(1)), subsection (a) shall not apply to any benefit attributable to a plan [year] for which the qualified benefits provided to key employees exceed 25 percent of the aggregate of such benefits provided for all employees under the plan. For purposes of the preceding sentence, qualified benefits shall be determined without regard to the second sentence of subsection (f).

(3) YEAR OF INCLUSION.—For purposes of determining the taxable year of inclusion, any benefit described in paragraph (1) or (2) shall be treated as received or accrued in the taxable year of the participant or key employee in which the plan year ends.

[Sec. 125(c)]

(c) DISCRIMINATION AS TO BENEFITS OR CONTRIBUTIONS.—For purposes of subparagraph (B) of subsection (b)(1), a cafeteria plan does not discriminate where qualified benefits and total benefits (or employer contributions allocable to statutory nontaxable benefits and employer contributions for total benefits) do not discriminate in favor of highly compensated participants.

[Sec. 125(d)]

(d) CAFETERIA PLAN DEFINED.—For purposes of this section—

(1) IN GENERAL.—The term "cafeteria plan" means a written plan under which—

(A) all participants are employees, and

(B) the participants may choose among 2 or more benefits consisting of cash and qualified benefits.

(2) DEFERRED COMPENSATION PLANS EXCLUDED.—

(A) IN GENERAL.—The term "cafeteria plan" does not include any plan which provides for deferred compensation.

(B) EXCEPTION FOR CASH AND DEFERRED ARRANGEMENTS.—Subparagraph (A) shall not apply to a profit-sharing or stock bonus plan or rural cooperative plan (within the meaning of section 401(k)(7)) which includes a qualified cash or deferred arrangement (as defined in section 401(k)(2)) to the extent of amounts which a covered employee may elect to have the employer pay as contributions to a trust under such plan on behalf of the employee.

(C) EXCEPTION FOR CERTAIN PLANS MAINTAINED BY EDUCATIONAL INSTITUTIONS.—Subparagraph (A) shall not apply to a plan maintained by an educational organization described in section 170(b)(1)(A)(ii) to the extent of amounts which a covered employee may elect to have the employer pay as contributions for post-retirement group life insurance if—

(i) all contributions for such insurance must be made before retirement, and

(ii) such life insurance does not have a cash surrender value at any time.

For purposes of section 79, any life insurance described in the preceding sentence shall be treated as group-term life insurance.

(D) EXCEPTION FOR HEALTH SAVINGS ACCOUNTS.—Subparagraph (A) shall not apply to a plan to the extent of amounts which a covered employee may elect to have the employer pay as contributions to a health savings account established on behalf of the employee.

[Sec. 125(e)]

(e) HIGHLY COMPENSATED PARTICIPANT AND INDIVIDUAL DEFINED.—For purposes of this section—

(1) HIGHLY COMPENSATED PARTICIPANT.—The term "highly compensated participant" means a participant who is—

(A) an officer,

(B) a shareholder owning more than 5 percent of the voting power or value of all classes of stock of the employer,

(C) highly compensated, or

(D) a spouse or dependent (within the meaning of section 152, determined without regard to subsections (b)(1), (b)(2), and (d)(1)(B) thereof) of an individual described in subparagraph (A), (B), or (C).

(2) HIGHLY COMPENSATED INDIVIDUAL.—The term "highly compensated individual" means an individual who is described in subparagraph (A), (B), (C), or (D) of paragraph (1).

[Sec. 125(f)]

(f) QUALIFIED BENEFITS DEFINED.—For purposes of this section, the term "qualified benefit" means any benefit which, with the application of subsection (a), is not includible in the gross income of the employee by reason of an express provision of this chapter (other than section 106(b), 117, 127, or 132). Such term includes any group term life insurance which is includible in gross income only because it exceeds the dollar limitation of section 79 and such term includes any other benefit permitted under regulations. Such term shall not include any product which is advertised, marketed, or offered as long-term care insurance.

[Sec. 125(g)]

(g) SPECIAL RULES.—

(1) COLLECTIVELY BARGAINED PLAN NOT CONSIDERED DISCRIMINATORY.—For purposes of this section, a plan shall not be treated as discriminatory if the plan is maintained under an agreement which the Secretary finds to be a collective bargaining agreement between employee representatives and one or more employers.

(2) HEALTH BENEFITS.—For purposes of subparagraph (B) of subsection (b)(1), a cafeteria plan which provides health benefits shall not be treated as discriminatory if—

(A) contributions under the plan on behalf of each participant include an amount which—

(i) equals 100 percent of the cost of the health benefit coverage under the plan of the majority of the highly compensated participants similarly situated, or

(ii) equals or exceeds 75 percent of the cost of the health benefit coverage of the participant (similarly situated) having the highest cost health benefit coverage under the plan, and

(B) contributions or benefits under the plan in excess of those described in subparagraph (A) bear a uniform relationship to compensation.

(3) CERTAIN PARTICIPATION ELIGIBILITY RULES NOT TREATED AS DISCRIMINATORY.—For purposes of subparagraph (A) of subsection (b)(1), a classification shall not be treated as discriminatory if the plan—

(A) benefits a group of employees described in section 410(b)(2)(A)(i), and

(B) meets the requirements of clauses (i) and (ii):

(i) No employee is required to complete more than 3 years of employment with the employer or employers maintaining the plan as a condition of participation in the plan, and the employment requirement for each employee is the same.

(ii) Any employee who has satisfied the employment requirement of clause (i) and who is otherwise entitled to participate in the plan commences participation no later than the first day of the first plan year beginning after the date the employment requirement was satisfied unless the employee was separated from service before the first day of that plan year.

(4) CERTAIN CONTROLLED GROUPS, ETC.—All employees who are treated as employed by a single employer under subsection (b), (c), or (m) of section 414 shall be treated as employed by a single employer for purposes of this section.

* * *

[Sec. 125(i)]

(i) LIMITATION ON HEALTH FLEXIBLE SPENDING ARRANGEMENTS.—

(1) IN GENERAL.—For purposes of this section, if a benefit is provided under a cafeteria plan through employer contributions to a health flexible spending arrangement, such benefit shall not be treated as a qualified benefit unless the cafeteria plan provides that an employee may not elect for any taxable year to have salary reduction contributions in excess of $2,500 made to such arrangement.

(2) ADJUSTMENT FOR INFLATION.—In the case of any taxable year beginning after December 31, 2013, the dollar amount in paragraph (1) shall be increased by an amount equal to—

(A) such amount, multiplied by

(B) the cost-of-living adjustment determined under section 1(f)(3) for the calendar year in which such taxable year begins by substituting "calendar year 2012" for "calendar year 2016" in subparagraph (A)(ii) thereof.

If any increase determined under this paragraph is not a multiple of $50, such increase shall be rounded to the next lowest multiple of $50.

[Sec. 125(j)]

(j) SIMPLE CAFETERIA PLANS FOR SMALL BUSINESSES.—

(1) IN GENERAL.—An eligible employer maintaining a simple cafeteria plan with respect to which the requirements of this subsection are met for any year shall be treated as meeting any applicable nondiscrimination requirement during such year.

(2) SIMPLE CAFETERIA PLAN.—For purposes of this subsection, the term "simple cafeteria plan" means a cafeteria plan—

(A) which is established and maintained by an eligible employer, and

(B) with respect to which the contribution requirements of paragraph (3), and the eligibility and participation requirements of paragraph (4), are met.

(3) CONTRIBUTION REQUIREMENTS.—

(A) IN GENERAL.—The requirements of this paragraph are met if, under the plan the employer is required, without regard to whether a qualified employee makes any salary reduction contribution, to make a contribution to provide qualified benefits under the plan on behalf of each qualified employee in an amount equal to—

(i) a uniform percentage (not less than 2 percent) of the employee's compensation for the plan year, or

(ii) an amount which is not less than the lesser of—

(I) 6 percent of the employee's compensation for the plan year, or

(II) twice the amount of the salary reduction contributions of each qualified employee.

(B) MATCHING CONTRIBUTIONS ON BEHALF OF HIGHLY COMPENSATED AND KEY EMPLOYEES.—The requirements of subparagraph (A)(ii) shall not be treated as met if, under the plan, the rate of contributions with respect to any salary reduction contribution of a highly compensated or key employee at any rate of contribution is greater than that with respect to an employee who is not a highly compensated or key employee.

(C) ADDITIONAL CONTRIBUTIONS.—Subject to subparagraph (B), nothing in this paragraph shall be treated as prohibiting an employer from making contributions to provide qualified benefits under the plan in addition to contributions required under subparagraph (A).

(D) DEFINITIONS.—For purposes of this paragraph—

(i) SALARY REDUCTION CONTRIBUTION.—The term "salary reduction contribution" means, with respect to a cafeteria plan, any amount which is contributed to the plan at the election of the employee and which is not includible in gross income by reason of this section.

(ii) QUALIFIED EMPLOYEE.—The term "qualified employee" means, with respect to a cafeteria plan, any employee who is not a highly compensated or key employee and who is eligible to participate in the plan.

(iii) HIGHLY COMPENSATED EMPLOYEE.—The term "highly compensated employee" has the meaning given such term by section 414(q).

(iv) KEY EMPLOYEE.—The term "key employee" has the meaning given such term by section 416(i).

(4) MINIMUM ELIGIBILITY AND PARTICIPATION REQUIREMENTS.—

(A) IN GENERAL.—The requirements of this paragraph shall be treated as met with respect to any year if, under the plan—

(i) all employees who had at least 1,000 hours of service for the preceding plan year are eligible to participate, and

(ii) each employee eligible to participate in the plan may, subject to terms and conditions applicable to all participants, elect any benefit available under the plan.

(B) CERTAIN EMPLOYEES MAY BE EXCLUDED.—For purposes of subparagraph (A)(i), an employer may elect to exclude under the plan employees—

(i) who have not attained the age of 21 before the close of a plan year,

(ii) who have less than 1 year of service with the employer as of any day during the plan year,

(iii) who are covered under an agreement which the Secretary of Labor finds to be a collective bargaining agreement if there is evidence that the benefits covered under the cafeteria plan were the subject of good faith bargaining between employee representatives and the employer, or

(iv) who are described in section 410(b)(3)(C) (relating to nonresident aliens working outside the United States).

A plan may provide a shorter period of service or younger age for purposes of clause (i) or (ii).

(5) ELIGIBLE EMPLOYER.—For purposes of this subsection—

(A) IN GENERAL.—The term "eligible employer" means, with respect to any year, any employer if such employer employed an average of 100 or fewer employees on business days during either of the 2 preceding years. For purposes of this subparagraph, a year may only be taken into account if the employer was in existence throughout the year.

(B) EMPLOYERS NOT IN EXISTENCE DURING PRECEDING YEAR.—If an employer was not in existence throughout the preceding year, the determination under subparagraph (A) shall be based on the average number of employees that it is reasonably expected such employer will employ on business days in the current year.

(C) GROWING EMPLOYERS RETAIN TREATMENT AS SMALL EMPLOYER.—

(i) IN GENERAL.—If—

(I) an employer was an eligible employer for any year (a "qualified year"), and

(II) such employer establishes a simple cafeteria plan for its employees for such year,

then, notwithstanding the fact the employer fails to meet the requirements of subparagraph (A) for any subsequent year, such employer shall be treated as an eligible employer for such subsequent year with respect to employees (whether or not employees during a qualified year) of any trade or business which was covered by the plan during any qualified year.

(ii) EXCEPTION.—This subparagraph shall cease to apply if the employer employs an average of 200 or more employees on business days during any year preceding any such subsequent year.

(D) SPECIAL RULES.—

(i) PREDECESSORS.—Any reference in this paragraph to an employer shall include a reference to any predecessor of such employer.

(ii) AGGREGATION RULES.—All persons treated as a single employer under subsection (a) or (b) of section 52, or subsection (n) or (o) of section 414, shall be treated as one person.

(6) APPLICABLE NONDISCRIMINATION REQUIREMENT.—For purposes of this subsection, the term "applicable nondiscrimination requirement" means any requirement under subsection (b) of this section, section 79(d), section 105(h), or paragraph (2), (3), (4), or (8) of section 129(d).

(7) COMPENSATION.—The term "compensation" has the meaning given such term by section 414(s).

* * *

[Sec. 125(l)]

(l) REGULATIONS.—The Secretary shall prescribe such regulations as may be necessary to carry out the provisions of this section.

[Sec. 127]

SEC. 127. EDUCATIONAL ASSISTANCE PROGRAMS.

[Sec. 127(a)]

(a) EXCLUSION FROM GROSS INCOME.—

(1) IN GENERAL.—Gross income of an employee does not include amounts paid or expenses incurred by the employer for educational assistance to the employee if the assistance is furnished pursuant to a program which is described in subsection (b).

(2) $5,250 MAXIMUM EXCLUSION.—If, but for this paragraph, this section would exclude from gross income more than $5,250 of educational assistance furnished to an individual during a calendar year, this section shall apply only to the first $5,250 of such assistance so furnished.

[Sec. 127(b)]

(b) EDUCATIONAL ASSISTANCE PROGRAM.—

(1) IN GENERAL.—For purposes of this section, an educational assistance program is a separate written plan of an employer for the exclusive benefit of his employees to provide such employees with educational assistance. The program must meet the requirements of paragraphs (2) through (6) of this subsection.

(2) ELIGIBILITY.—The program shall benefit employees who qualify under a classification set up by the employer and found by the Secretary not to be discriminatory in favor of employees who are highly compensated employees (within the meaning of section 414(q)) or their dependents. For purposes of this paragraph, there shall be excluded from consideration employees not included in the program who are included in a unit of employees covered by an agreement which the Secretary of Labor finds to be a collective bargaining agreement between employee representatives and one or more employers, if there is evidence that educational assistance benefits were the subject of good faith bargaining between such employee representatives and such employer or employers.

(3) PRINCIPAL SHAREHOLDERS OR OWNERS.—Not more than 5 percent of the amounts paid or incurred by the employer for educational assistance during the year may be provided for the class of individuals who are shareholders or owners (or their spouses or dependents), each of whom (on any day of the year) owns more than 5 percent of the stock or of the capital or profits interest in the employer.

(4) OTHER BENEFITS AS AN ALTERNATIVE.—A program must not provide eligible employees with a choice between educational assistance and other remuneration includible in gross income. For purposes of this section, the business practices of the employer (as well as the written program) will be taken into account.

(5) NO FUNDING REQUIRED.—A program referred to in paragraph (1) is not required to be funded.

(6) NOTIFICATION OF EMPLOYEES.—Reasonable notification of the availability and terms of the program must be provided to eligible employees.

[Sec. 127(c)]

(c) DEFINITIONS; SPECIAL RULES.—For purposes of this section—

(1) EDUCATIONAL ASSISTANCE.—The term "educational assistance" means—

(A) the payment, by an employer, of expenses incurred by or on behalf of an employee for education of the employee (including, but not limited to, tuition, fees, and similar payments, books, supplies, and equipment),

(B) in the case of payments made before January 1, 2021, the payment by an employer, whether paid to the employee or to a lender, of principal or interest on any qualified education loan (as defined in section 221(d)(1)) incurred by the employee for education of the employee, and

(C) the provision, by an employer, of courses of instruction for such employee (including books, supplies, and equipment),

but does not include payment for, or the provision of, tools or supplies which may be retained by the employee after completion of a course of instruction, or meals, lodging, or transportation. The term "educational assistance" also does not include any payment for, or the provision of any benefits with respect to, any course or other education involving sports, games, or hobbies.

(2) EMPLOYEE.—The term "employee" includes, for any year, an individual who is an employee within the meaning of section 401(c)(1) (relating to self-employed individuals).

(3) EMPLOYER.—An individual who owns the entire interest in an unincorporated trade or business shall be treated as his own employer. A partnership shall be treated as the employer of each partner who is an employee within the meaning of paragraph (2).

(4) ATTRIBUTION RULES.—

(A) OWNERSHIP OF STOCK.—Ownership of stock in a corporation shall be determined in accordance with the rules provided under subsections (d) and (e) of section 1563 (without regard to section 1563(e)(3)(C)).

(B) INTEREST IN UNINCORPORATED TRADE OR BUSINESS.—The interest of an employee in a trade or business which is not incorporated shall be determined in accordance with regulations prescribed by the Secretary, which shall be based on principles similar to the principles which apply in the case of subparagraph (A).

(5) CERTAIN TESTS NOT APPLICABLE.—An educational assistance program shall not be held or considered to fail to meet any requirements of subsection (b) merely because—

(A) of utilization rates for the different types of educational assistance made available under the program; or

(B) successful completion, or attaining a particular course grade, is required for or considered in determining reimbursement under the program.

(6) RELATIONSHIP TO CURRENT LAW.—This section shall not be construed to affect the deduction or inclusion in income of amounts (not within the exclusion under this section) which are paid or incurred, or received as reimbursement, for educational expenses under section 117, 162 or 212.

(7) DISALLOWANCE OF EXCLUDED AMOUNTS AS CREDIT OR DEDUCTION.—No deduction or credit shall be allowed to the employee under any other section of this chapter for any amount excluded from income by reason of this section.

* * *

[Sec. 129]

SEC. 129. DEPENDENT CARE ASSISTANCE PROGRAMS.

[Sec. 129(a)]

(a) EXCLUSION.—

(1) IN GENERAL.—Gross income of an employee does not include amounts paid or incurred by the employer for dependent care assistance provided to such employee if the assistance is furnished pursuant to a program which is described in subsection (d).

(2) LIMITATION OF EXCLUSION.—

(A) IN GENERAL.—The amount which may be excluded under paragraph (1) for dependent care assistance with respect to dependent care services provided during a taxable year shall not exceed $5,000 ($2,500 in the case of a separate return by a married individual).

(B) YEAR OF INCLUSION.—The amount of any excess under subparagraph (A) shall be included in gross income in the taxable year in which the dependent care services were provided (even if payment of dependent care assistance for such services occurs in a subsequent taxable year).

(C) MARITAL STATUS.—For purposes of this paragraph, marital status shall be determined under the rules of paragraphs (3) and (4) of section 21(e).

[Sec. 129(b)]

(b) EARNED INCOME LIMITATION.—

(1) IN GENERAL.—The amount excluded from the income of an employee under subsection (a) for any taxable year shall not exceed—

(A) in the case of an employee who is not married at the close of such taxable year, the earned income of such employee for such taxable year, or

(B) in the case of an employee who is married at the close of such taxable year, the lesser of—

(i) the earned income of such employee for such taxable year, or

(ii) the earned income of the spouse of such employee for such taxable year.

(2) SPECIAL RULE FOR CERTAIN SPOUSES.—For purposes of paragraph (1), the provisions of section 21(d)(2) shall apply in determining the earned income of a spouse who is a student or incapable of caring for himself.

[Sec. 129(c)]

(c) PAYMENTS TO RELATED INDIVIDUALS.—No amount paid or incurred during the taxable year of an employee by an employer in providing dependent care assistance to such employee shall be excluded under subsection (a) if such amount was paid or incurred to an individual—

(1) with respect to whom, for such taxable year, a deduction is allowable under section 151(c) (relating to personal exemptions for dependents) to such employee or the spouse of such employee, or

(2) who is a child of such employee (within the meaning of section 152(f)(1)) under the age of 19 at the close of such taxable year.

[Sec. 129(d)]

(d) DEPENDENT CARE ASSISTANCE PROGRAM.—

(1) IN GENERAL.—For purposes of this section a dependent care assistance program is a separate written plan of an employer for the exclusive benefit of his employees to provide such employees with dependent care assistance which meets the requirements of paragraphs (2) through (8) of this subsection. If any plan would qualify as a dependent care assistance program but for a failure to meet the requirements of this subsection, then, notwithstanding such failure, such plan shall be treated as a dependent care assistance program in the case of employees who are not highly compensated employees.

(2) DISCRIMINATION.—The contributions or benefits provided under the plan shall not discriminate in favor of employees who are highly compensated employees (within the meaning of section 414(q)) or their dependents.

(3) ELIGIBILITY.—The program shall benefit employees who qualify under a classification set up by the employer and found by the Secretary not to be discriminatory in favor of employees described in paragraph (2), or their dependents.

(4) PRINCIPAL SHAREHOLDERS OR OWNERS.—Not more than 25 percent of the amounts paid or incurred by the employer for dependent care assistance during the year may be provided for the class of individuals who are shareholders or owners (or their spouses or dependents), each of whom (on any day of the year) owns more than 5 percent of the stock or of the capital or profits interest in the employer.

(5) NO FUNDING REQUIRED.—A program referred to in paragraph (1) is not required to be funded.

(6) NOTIFICATION OF ELIGIBLE EMPLOYEES.—Reasonable notification of the availability and terms of the program shall be provided to eligible employees.

(7) STATEMENT OF EXPENSES.—The plan shall furnish to an employee, on or before January 31, a written statement showing the amounts paid or expenses incurred by the employer in providing dependent care assistance to such employee during the previous calendar year.

(8) BENEFITS.—

(A) IN GENERAL.—A plan meets the requirements of this paragraph if the average benefits provided to employees who are not highly compensated employees under all plans of the employer is at least 55 percent of the average benefits provided to highly compensated employees under all plans of the employer.

(B) SALARY REDUCTION AGREEMENTS.—For purposes of subparagraph (A), in the case of any benefits provided through a salary reduction agreement, a plan may disregard any employees whose compensation is less than $25,000. For purposes of this subparagraph, the term "compensation" has the meaning given such term by section 414(q)(4), except that, under rules prescribed by the Secretary, an employer may elect to determine compensation on any other basis which does not discriminate in favor of highly compensated employees.

(9) EXCLUDED EMPLOYEES.—For purposes of paragraphs (3) and (8), there shall be excluded from consideration—

(A) subject to rules similar to the rules of section 410(b)(4), employees who have not attained the age of 21 and completed 1 year of service (as defined in section 410(a)(3)), and

(B) employees not included in a dependent care assistance program who are included in a unit of employees covered by an agreement which the Secretary finds to be a collective bargaining agreement between employee representatives and 1 or more employees, if there is evidence that dependent care benefits were the subject of good faith bargaining between such employee representatives and such employer or employers.

[Sec. 129(e)]

(e) DEFINITIONS AND SPECIAL RULES.—For purposes of this section—

(1) DEPENDENT CARE ASSISTANCE.—The term "dependent care assistance" means the payment of, or provision of, those services which if paid for by the employee would be considered employment-related expenses under section 21(b)(2) (relating to expenses for household and dependent care services necessary for gainful employment).

(2) EARNED INCOME.—The term "earned income" shall have the meaning given such term in section 32(c)(2), but such term shall not include any amounts paid or incurred by an employer for dependent care assistance to an employee.

(3) EMPLOYEE.—The term "employee" includes, for any year, an individual who is an employee within the meaning of section 401(c)(1) (relating to self-employed individuals).

(4) EMPLOYER.—An individual who owns the entire interest in an unincorporated trade or business shall be treated as his own employer. A partnership shall be treated as the employer of each partner who is an employee within the meaning of paragraph (3).

(5) ATTRIBUTION RULES.—

(A) OWNERSHIP OF STOCK.—Ownership of stock in a corporation shall be determined in accordance with the rules provided under subsections (d) and (e) of section 1563 (without regard to section 1563(e)(3)(C)).

(B) INTEREST IN UNINCORPORATED TRADE OR BUSINESS.—The interest of an employee in a trade or business which is not incorporated shall be determined in accordance with regulations prescribed by the Secretary, which shall be based on principles similar to the principles which apply in the case of subparagraph (A).

(6) UTILIZATION TEST NOT APPLICABLE.—A dependent care assistance program shall not be held or considered to fail to meet any requirements of subsection (d) (other than paragraphs

(4) and (8) thereof) merely because of utilization rates for the different types of assistance made available under the program.

(7) DISALLOWANCE OF EXCLUDED AMOUNTS AS CREDIT OR DEDUCTION.—No deduction or credit shall be allowed to the employee under any other section of this chapter for any amount excluded from the gross income of the employee by reason of this section.

(8) TREATMENT OF ONSITE FACILITIES.—In the case of an onsite facility maintained by an employer, except to the extent provided in regulations, the amount of dependent care assistance provided to an employee excluded with respect to any dependent shall be based on—

(A) utilization of the facility by a dependent of the employee, and

(B) the value of the services provided with respect to such dependent.

* * *

[Sec. 130]

SEC. 130. CERTAIN PERSONAL INJURY LIABILITY ASSIGNMENTS.

[Sec. 130(a)]

(a) IN GENERAL.—Any amount received for agreeing to a qualified assignment shall not be included in gross income to the extent that such amount does not exceed the aggregate cost of any qualified funding assets.

[Sec. 130(b)]

(b) TREATMENT OF QUALIFIED FUNDING ASSET.—In the case of any qualified funding asset—

(1) the basis of such asset shall be reduced by the amount excluded from gross income under subsection (a) by reason of the purchase of such asset, and

(2) any gain recognized on a disposition of such asset shall be treated as ordinary income.

[Sec. 130(c)]

(c) QUALIFIED ASSIGNMENT.—For purposes of this section, the term "qualified assignment" means any assignment of a liability to make periodic payments as damages (whether by suit or agreement), or as compensation under any workmen's compensation act, on account of personal injury or sickness (in a case involving physical injury or physical sickness)—

(1) if the assignee assumes such liability from a person who is a party to the suit or agreement, or the workmen's compensation claim, and

(2) if—

(A) such periodic payments are fixed and determinable as to amount and time of payment,

(B) such periodic payments cannot be accelerated, deferred, increased, or decreased by the recipient of such payments,

(C) the assignee's obligation on account of the personal injuries or sickness is no greater than the obligation of the person who assigned the liability, and

(D) such periodic payments are excludable from the gross income of the recipient under paragraph (1) or (2) of section 104(a).

The determination for purposes of this chapter of when the recipient is treated as having received any payment with respect to which there has been a qualified assignment shall be made without regard to any provision of such assignment which grants the recipient rights as a creditor greater than those of a general creditor.

[Sec. 130(d)]

(d) QUALIFIED FUNDING ASSET.—For purposes of this section, the term "qualified funding asset" means any annuity contract issued by a company licensed to do business as an insurance company under the laws of any State, or any obligation of the United States, if—

(1) such annuity contract or obligation is used by the assignee to fund periodic payments under any qualified assignment,

(2) the periods of the payments under the annuity contract or obligation are reasonably related to the periodic payments under the qualified assignment, and the amount of any such payment under the contract or obligation does not exceed the periodic payment to which it relates,

(3) such annuity contract or obligation is designated by the taxpayer (in such manner as the Secretary shall by regulations prescribe) as being taken into account under this section with respect to such qualified assignment, and

(4) such annuity contract or obligation is purchased by the taxpayer not more than 60 days before the date of the qualified assignment and not later than 60 days after the date of such assignment.

»»→ Caution: Pursuant to Section 132(f)(6), the limitation amounts set forth in Section 132(f)(2) are adjusted for taxable years beginning after 1993 to reflect increases in the Chained Consumer Price Index. The adjusted amounts applicable to taxable years beginning in 2020 are provided in the material beginning at page ix.

[Sec. 132]

SEC. 132. CERTAIN FRINGE BENEFITS.

[Sec. 132(a)]

(a) EXCLUSION FROM GROSS INCOME.—Gross income shall not include any fringe benefit which qualifies as a—

(1) no-additional-cost service,

(2) qualified employee discount,

(3) working condition fringe,

(4) de minimis fringe[,]

(5) qualified transportation fringe,

(6) qualified moving expense reimbursement,

(7) qualified retirement planning services, or

* * *

[Sec. 132(b)]

(b) NO-ADDITIONAL-COST SERVICE DEFINED.—For purposes of this section, the term "no-additional-cost service" means any service provided by an employer to an employee for use by such employee if—

(1) such service is offered for sale to customers in the ordinary course of the line of business of the employer in which the employee is performing services, and

(2) the employer incurs no substantial additional cost (including forgone revenue) in providing such service to the employee (determined without regard to any amount paid by the employee for such service).

[Sec. 132(c)]

(c) QUALIFIED EMPLOYEE DISCOUNT DEFINED.—For purposes of this section—

(1) QUALIFIED EMPLOYEE DISCOUNT.—The term "qualified employee discount" means any employee discount with respect to qualified property or services to the extent such discount does not exceed—

(A) in the case of property, the gross profit percentage of the price at which the property is being offered by the employer to customers, or

(B) in the case of services, 20 percent of the price at which the services are being offered by the employer to customers.

(2) GROSS PROFIT PERCENTAGE.—

(A) IN GENERAL.—The term "gross profit percentage" means the percent which—

(i) the excess of the aggregate sales price of property sold by the employer to customers over the aggregate cost of such property to the employer, is of

(ii) the aggregate sale price of such property.

(B) DETERMINATION OF GROSS PROFIT PERCENTAGE.—Gross profit percentage shall be determined on the basis of—

(i) all property offered to customers in the ordinary course of the line of business of the employer in which the employee is performing services (or a reasonable classification of property selected by the employer), and

(ii) the employer's experience during a representative period.

(3) EMPLOYEE DISCOUNT DEFINED.—The term "employee discount" means the amount by which—

(A) the price at which the property or services are provided by the employer to an employee for use by such employee, is less than

(B) the price at which such property or services are being offered by the employer to customers.

(4) QUALIFIED PROPERTY OR SERVICES.—The term "qualified property or services" means any property (other than real property and other than personal property of a kind held for investment) or services which are offered for sale to customers in the ordinary course of the line of business of the employer in which the employee is performing services.

[Sec. 132(d)]

(d) WORKING CONDITION FRINGE DEFINED.—For purposes of this section, the term "working condition fringe" means any property or services provided to an employee of the employer to the extent that, if the employee paid for such property or services, such payment would be allowable as a deduction under section 162 or 167.

[Sec. 132(e)]

(e) DE MINIMIS FRINGE DEFINED.—For purposes of this section—

(1) IN GENERAL.—The term "de minimis fringe" means any property or service the value of which is (after taking into account the frequency with which similar fringes are provided by the employer to the employer's employees) so small as to make accounting for it unreasonable or administratively impracticable.

(2) TREATMENT OF CERTAIN EATING FACILITIES.—The operation by an employer of any eating facility for employees shall be treated as a de minimis fringe if—

(A) such facility is located on or near the business premises of the employer, and

(B) revenue derived from such facility normally equals or exceeds the direct operating costs of such facility.

The preceding sentence shall apply with respect to any highly compensated employee only if access to the facility is available on substantially the same terms to each member of a group of employees which is defined under a reasonable classification set up by the employer which does not discriminate in favor of highly compensated employees. For purposes of subparagraph (B), an employee entitled under section 119 to exclude the value of a meal provided at such facility shall be treated as having paid an amount for such meal equal to the direct operating costs of the facility attributable to such meal.

[Sec. 132(f)]

(f) QUALIFIED TRANSPORTATION FRINGE.—

(1) IN GENERAL.— For purposes of this section, the term "qualified transportation fringe" means any of the following provided by an employer to an employee:

(A) Transportation in a commuter highway vehicle if such transportation is in connection with travel between the employee's residence and place of employment.

(B) Any transit pass.

(C) Qualified parking.

* * *

(2) LIMITATION ON EXCLUSION.— The amount of the fringe benefits which are provided by an employer to any employee and which may be excluded from gross income under subsection (a)(5) shall not exceed—

(A) $175 per month in the case of the aggregate of the benefits described in subparagraphs (A) and (B) of paragraph (1),

(B) $175 per month in the case of qualified parking, and

(C) the applicable annual limitation in the case of any qualified bicycle commuting reimbursement.

(3) CASH REIMBURSEMENTS.— For purposes of this subsection, the term "qualified transportation fringe" includes a cash reimbursement by an employer to an employee for a benefit described in paragraph (1). The preceding sentence shall apply to a cash reimbursement for any transit pass only if a voucher or similar item which may be exchanged only for a transit pass is not readily available for direct distribution by the employer to the employee.

(4) NO CONSTRUCTIVE RECEIPT.— No amount shall be included in the gross income of an employee solely because the employee may choose between any qualified transportation fringe (other than a qualified bicycle commuting reimbursement) and compensation which would otherwise be includible in gross income of such employee.

(5) DEFINITIONS.— For purposes of this subsection—

(A) TRANSIT PASS.— The term "transit pass" means any pass, token, farecard, voucher, or similar item entitling a person to transportation (or transportation at a reduced price) if such transportation is—

(i) on mass transit facilities (whether or not publicly owned), or

(ii) provided by any person in the business of transporting persons for compensation or hire if such transportation is provided in a vehicle meeting the requirements of subparagraph (B)(i).

(B) COMMUTER HIGHWAY VEHICLE.— The term "commuter highway vehicle" means any highway vehicle—

(i) the seating capacity of which is at least 6 adults (not including the driver), and

(ii) at least 80 percent of the mileage use of which can reasonably be expected to be—

(I) for purposes of transporting employees in connection with travel between their residences and their place of employment, and

(II) on trips during which the number of employees transported for such purposes is at least ½ of the adult seating capacity of such vehicle (not including the driver).

(C) QUALIFIED PARKING.— The term "qualified parking" means parking provided to an employee on or near the business premises of the employer or on or near a location from which the employee commutes to work by transportation described in subparagraph (A), in a commuter highway vehicle, or by carpool. Such term shall not include any parking on or near property used by the employee for residential purposes.

(D) TRANSPORTATION PROVIDED BY EMPLOYER.— Transportation referred to in paragraph (1)(A) shall be considered to be provided by an employer if such transportation is furnished in a commuter highway vehicle operated by or for the employer.

(E) EMPLOYEE.— For purposes of this subsection, the term "employee" does not include an individual who is an employee within the meaning of section 401(c)(1).

* * *

(6) INFLATION ADJUSTMENT.—

(A) IN GENERAL.— In the case of any taxable year beginning in a calendar year after 1999, the dollar amounts contained in subparagraphs (A) and (B) of paragraph (2) shall be increased by an amount equal to—

(i) such dollar amount, multiplied by

(ii) the cost-of-living adjustment determined under section 1(f)(3) for the calendar year in which the taxable year begins, by substituting "calendar year 1998" for "calendar year 1992".

(B) ROUNDING.— If any increase determined under subparagraph (A) is not a multiple of $5, such increase shall be rounded to the next lowest multiple of $5.

(7) COORDINATION WITH OTHER PROVISIONS.— For purposes of this section, the terms "working condition fringe" and "de minimis fringe" shall not include any qualified transportation fringe (determined without regard to paragraph (2)).

* * *

[Sec. 132(g)]

(g) QUALIFIED MOVING EXPENSE REIMBURSEMENT.—For purposes of this section—

(1) IN GENERAL.—The term "qualified moving expense reimbursement" means any amount received (directly or indirectly) by an individual from an employer as a payment for (or a reimbursement of) expenses which would be deductible as moving expenses under section 217 if directly paid or incurred by the individual. Such term shall not include any payment for (or reimbursement of) an expense actually deducted by the individual in a prior taxable year.

(2) SUSPENSION FOR TAXABLE YEARS 2018 THROUGH 2025.—Except in the case of a member of the Armed Forces of the United States on active duty who moves pursuant to a military order and incident to a permanent change of station, subsection (a)(6) shall not apply to any taxable year beginning after December 31, 2017, and before January 1, 2026.

[Sec. 132(h)]

(h) CERTAIN INDIVIDUALS TREATED AS EMPLOYEES FOR PURPOSES OF SUBSECTIONS (a)(1) AND (2).— For purposes of paragraphs (1) and (2) of subsection (a)—

(1) RETIRED AND DISABLED EMPLOYEES AND SURVIVING SPOUSE OF EMPLOYEE TREATED AS EMPLOYEE.—With respect to a line of business of an employer, the term "employee" includes—

(A) any individual who was formerly employed by such employer in such line of business and who separated from service with such employer in such line of business by reason of retirement or disability, and

(B) any widow or widower of any individual who died while employed by such employer in such line of business or while an employee within the meaning of subparagraph (A).

(2) SPOUSE AND DEPENDENT CHILDREN.—

(A) IN GENERAL.—Any use by the spouse or a dependent child of the employee shall be treated as use by the employee.

(B) DEPENDENT CHILD.—For purposes of subparagraph (A), the term "dependent child" means any child (as defined in section 152(f)(1)) of the employee—

(i) who is a dependent of the employee, or

(ii) both of whose parents are deceased and who has not attained age 25.

For purposes of the preceding sentence, any child to whom section 152(e) applies shall be treated as the dependent of both parents.

(3) SPECIAL RULE FOR PARENTS IN THE CASE OF AIR TRANSPORTATION.—Any use of air transportation by a parent of an employee (determined without regard to paragraph (1)(B)) shall be treated as use by the employee.

[Sec. 132(i)]

(i) RECIPROCAL AGREEMENTS.—For purposes of paragraph (1) of subsection (a), any service provided by an employer to an employee of another employer shall be treated as provided by the employer of such employee if—

(1) such service is provided pursuant to a written agreement between such employers, and

(2) neither of such employers incurs any substantial additional costs (including foregone revenue) in providing such service or pursuant to such agreement.

[Sec. 132(j)]

(j) SPECIAL RULES.—

(1) EXCLUSIONS UNDER SUBSECTION (a)(1) AND (2) APPLY TO HIGHLY COMPENSATED EMPLOYEES ONLY IF NO DISCRIMINATION.—Paragraphs (1) and (2) of subsection (a) shall apply with respect to any fringe benefit described therein provided with respect to any highly compensated employee only if such fringe benefit is available on substantially the same terms to each member of a group of employees which is defined under a reasonable classification set up by the employer which does not discriminate in favor of highly compensated employees.

* * *

(4) ON-PREMISES GYMS AND OTHER ATHLETIC FACILITIES.—

(A) IN GENERAL.—Gross income shall not include the value of any on-premises athletic facility provided by an employer to his employees.

(B) ON-PREMISES ATHLETIC FACILITY.—For purposes of this paragraph, the term "on-premises athletic facility" means any gym or other athletic facility—

(i) which is located on the premises of the employer,

(ii) which is operated by the employer, and

(iii) substantially all the use of which is by employees of the employer, their spouses, and their dependent children (within the meaning of subsection (h)).

* * *

(6) HIGHLY COMPENSATED EMPLOYEE.—For purposes of this section, the term "highly compensated employee" has the meaning given such term by section 414(q).

(7) AIR CARGO.—For purposes of subsection (b), the transportation of cargo by air and the transportation of passengers by air shall be treated as the same service.

(8) APPLICATION OF SECTION TO OTHERWISE TAXABLE EDUCATIONAL OR TRAINING BENEFITS.—Amounts paid or expenses incurred by the employer for education or training provided to the employee which are not excludable from gross income under section 127 shall be excluded from gross income under this section if (and only if) such amounts or expenses are a working condition fringe.

[Sec. 132(k)]

(k) CUSTOMERS NOT TO INCLUDE EMPLOYEES.—For purposes of this section (other than subsection (c)(2)), the term "customers" shall only include customers who are not employees.

[Sec. 132(l)]

(l) SECTION NOT TO APPLY TO FRINGE BENEFITS EXPRESSLY PROVIDED FOR ELSEWHERE.—This section (other than subsections (e) and (g)) shall not apply to any fringe benefits of a type the tax treatment of which is expressly provided for in any other section of this chapter.

[Sec. 132(m)]

(m) QUALIFIED RETIREMENT PLANNING SERVICES.—

(1) IN GENERAL.—For purposes of this section, the term "qualified retirement planning services" means any retirement planning advice or information provided to an employee and his spouse by an employer maintaining a qualified employer plan.

(2) NONDISCRIMINATION RULE.—Subsection (a)(7) shall apply in the case of highly compensated employees only if such services are available on substantially the same terms to each member of the group of employees normally provided education and information regarding the employer's qualified employer plan.

(3) QUALIFIED EMPLOYER PLAN.—For purposes of this subsection, the term "qualified employer plan" means a plan, contract, pension, or account described in section 219(g)(5).

* * *

[Sec. 132(o)]

(o) REGULATIONS.—The Secretary shall prescribe such regulations as may be necessary or appropriate to carry out the purposes of this section.

»»→ Caution: Pursuant to Section 135(b)(2)(B), the modified adjusted gross income amounts stated in Section 135(b)(2)(A) are adjusted for taxable years beginning after 1990 to reflect increases in the Chained Consumer Price Index. The adjusted amounts applicable to taxable years beginning in 2020 are provided in the material beginning at page ix.

[Sec. 135]

SEC. 135. INCOME FROM UNITED STATES SAVINGS BONDS USED TO PAY HIGHER EDUCATION TUITION AND FEES.

[Sec. 135(a)]

(a) GENERAL RULE.—In the case of an individual who pays qualified higher education expenses during the taxable year, no amount shall be includible in gross income by reason of the redemption during such year of any qualified United States savings bond.

[Sec. 135(b)]

(b) LIMITATIONS.—

(1) LIMITATION WHERE REDEMPTION PROCEEDS EXCEED HIGHER EDUCATION EXPENSES.—

(A) IN GENERAL.—If—

(i) the aggregate proceeds of qualified United States savings bonds redeemed by the taxpayer during the taxable year exceed

(ii) the qualified higher education expenses paid by the taxpayer during such taxable year,

the amount excludable from gross income under subsection (a) shall not exceed the applicable fraction of the amount excludable from gross income under subsection (a) without regard to this subsection.

(B) APPLICABLE FRACTION.—For purposes of subparagraph (A), the term "applicable fraction" means the fraction the numerator of which is the amount described in subparagraph (A)(ii) and the denominator of which is the amount described in subparagraph (A)(i).

(2) LIMITATION BASED ON MODIFIED ADJUSTED GROSS INCOME.—

(A) IN GENERAL.—If the modified adjusted gross income of the taxpayer for the taxable year exceeds $40,000 ($60,000 in the case of a joint return), the amount which would (but for this paragraph) be excludable from gross income under subsection (a) shall be reduced (but not below zero) by the amount which bears the same ratio to the amount which would be so excludable as such excess bears to $15,000 ($30,000 in the case of a joint return).

(B) INFLATION ADJUSTMENT.—In the case of any taxable year beginning in a calendar year after 1990, the $40,000 and $60,000 amounts contained in subparagraph (A) shall be increased by an amount equal to—

(i) such dollar amount, multiplied by

(ii) the cost-of-living adjustment under section 1(f)(3) for the calendar year in which the taxable year begins, determined by substituting "calendar year 1989" for "calendar year 2016" in subparagraph (A)(ii) thereof.

(C) Rounding.—If any amount as adjusted under subparagraph (B) is not a multiple of $50, such amount shall be rounded to the nearest multiple of $50 (or if such amount is a multiple of $25, such amount shall be rounded to the next highest multiple of $50).

[Sec. 135(c)]

(c) Definitions.—For purposes of this section—

(1) Qualified united states savings bond.—The term "qualified United States savings bond" means any United States savings bond issued—

(A) after December 31, 1989,

(B) to an individual who has attained age 24 before the date of issuance, and

(C) at discount under section 3105 of title 31, United States Code.

(2) Qualified higher education expenses.—

(A) In general.—The term "qualified higher education expenses" means tuition and fees required for the enrollment or attendance of—

(i) the taxpayer,

(ii) the taxpayer's spouse, or

(iii) any dependent of the taxpayer with respect to whom the taxpayer is allowed a deduction under section 151,

at an eligible educational institution.

(B) Exception for education involving sports, etc.—Such term shall not include expenses with respect to any course or other education involving sports, games, or hobbies other than as part of a degree program.

(C) Contributions to qualified tuition program and Coverdell education savings accounts.—Such term shall include any contribution to a qualified tuition program (as defined in section 529) on behalf of a designated beneficiary (as defined in such section), or to a Coverdell education savings account (as defined in section 530) on behalf of an account beneficiary, who is an individual described in subparagraph (A); but there shall be no increase in the investment in the contract for purposes of applying section 72 by reason of any portion of such contribution which is not includible in gross income by reason of this subparagraph.

(3) Eligible educational institution.—The term "eligible educational institution" has the meaning given such term by section 529(e)(5).

(4) Modified adjusted gross income.—The term "modified adjusted gross income" means the adjusted gross income of the taxpayer for the taxable year determined—

(A) without regard to this section and sections 137, 221, 222, 911, 931, and 933, and

(B) after the application of sections 86, 469, and 219.

[Sec. 135(d)]

(d) Special Rules.—

(1) Adjustment for certain scholarships and veterans benefits.—The amount of qualified higher education expenses otherwise taken into account under subsection (a) with respect to the education of an individual shall be reduced (before the application of subsection (b)) by the sum of the amounts received with respect to such individual for the taxable year as—

(A) a qualified scholarship which under section 117 is not includable in gross income,

(B) an educational assistance allowance under chapter 30, 31, 32, 34, or 35 of title 38, United States Code,

(C) a payment (other than a gift, bequest, devise, or inheritance within the meaning of section 102(a)) for educational expenses, or attributable to attendance at an eligible educational institution, which is exempt from income taxation by any law of the United States, or

(D) a payment, waiver, or reimbursement of qualified higher education expenses under a qualified tuition program (within the meaning of section 529(b)).

(2) COORDINATION WITH OTHER HIGHER EDUCATION BENEFITS.—The amount of the qualified higher education expenses otherwise taken into account under subsection (a) with respect to the education of an individual shall be reduced (before the application of subsection (b)) by—

(A) the amount of such expenses which are taken into account in determining the credit allowed to the taxpayer or any other person under section 25A with respect to such expenses; and

(B) the amount of such expenses which are taken into account in determining the exclusions under sections 529(c)(3)(B) and 530(d)(2).

(3) NO EXCLUSION FOR MARRIED INDIVIDUALS FILING SEPARATE RETURNS.—If the taxpayer is a married individual (within the meaning of section 7703), this section shall apply only if the taxpayer and his spouse file a joint return for the taxable year.

(4) REGULATIONS.—The Secretary may prescribe such regulations as may be necessary or appropriate to carry out this section, including regulations requiring record keeping and information reporting.

PART IV—TAX EXEMPTION REQUIREMENTS FOR STATE AND LOCAL BONDS

Subpart A—Private Activity Bonds

[Sec. 141]

SEC. 141. PRIVATE ACTIVITY BOND; QUALIFIED BOND.

[Sec. 141(a)]

(a) PRIVATE ACTIVITY BOND.—For purposes of this title, the term "private activity bond" means any bond issued as part of an issue—

(1) which meets—

(A) the private business use test of paragraph (1) of subsection (b), and

(B) the private security or payment test of paragraph (2) of subsection (b), or

(2) which meets the private loan financing test of subsection (c).

[Sec. 141(b)]

(b) PRIVATE BUSINESS TESTS.—

(1) PRIVATE BUSINESS USE TEST.—Except as otherwise provided in this subsection, an issue meets the test of this paragraph if more than 10 percent of the proceeds of the issue are to be used for any private business use.

(2) PRIVATE SECURITY OR PAYMENT TEST.—Except as otherwise provided in this subsection, an issue meets the test of this paragraph if the payment of the principal of, or the interest on, more than 10 percent of the proceeds of such issue is (under the terms of such issue or any underlying arrangement) directly or indirectly—

(A) secured by any interest in—

(i) property used or to be used for a private business use, or

(ii) payments in respect of such property, or

(B) to be derived from payments (whether or not to the issuer) in respect of property, or borrowed money, used or to be used for a private business use.

(3) 5 PERCENT TEST FOR PRIVATE BUSINESS USE NOT RELATED OR DISPROPORTIONATE TO GOVERNMENT USE FINANCED BY THE ISSUE.—

(A) IN GENERAL.—An issue shall be treated as meeting the tests of paragraphs (1) and (2) if such tests would be met if such paragraphs were applied—

(i) by substituting "5 percent" for "10 percent" each place it appears, and

(ii) by taking into account only—

(I) the proceeds of the issue which are to be used for any private business use which is not related to any government use of such proceeds,

(II) the disproportionate related business use proceeds of the issue, and

(III) payments, property, and borrowed money with respect to any use of proceeds described in subclause (I) or (II).

(B) DISPROPORTIONATE RELATED BUSINESS USE PROCEEDS.—For purposes of subparagraph (A), the disproportionate related business use proceeds of an issue is an amount equal to the aggregate of the excesses (determined under the following sentence) for each private business use of the proceeds of an issue which is related to a government use of such proceeds. The excess determined under this sentence is the excess of—

(i) the proceeds of the issue which are to be used for the private business use, over

(ii) the proceeds of the issue which are to be used for the government use to which such private business use relates.

(4) LOWER LIMITATION FOR CERTAIN OUTPUT FACILITIES.—An issue 5 percent or more of the proceeds of which are to be used with respect to any output facility (other than a facility for the furnishing of water) shall be treated as meeting the tests of paragraphs (1) and (2) if the nonqualified amount with respect to such issue exceeds the excess of—

(A) $15,000,000, over

(B) the aggregate nonqualified amounts with respect to all prior tax-exempt issues 5 percent or more of the proceeds of which are or will be used with respect to such facility (or any other facility which is part of the same project).

There shall not be taken into account under subparagraph (B) any bond which is not outstanding at the time of the later issue or which is to be redeemed (other than in an advance refunding) from the net proceeds of the later issue.

(5) COORDINATION WITH VOLUME CAP WHERE NONQUALIFIED AMOUNT EXCEEDS $15,000,000.—If the nonqualified amount with respect to an issue—

(A) exceeds $15,000,000, but

(B) does not exceed the amount which would cause a bond which is part of such issue to be treated as a private activity bond without regard to this paragraph,

such bond shall nonetheless be treated as a private activity bond unless the issuer allocates a portion of its volume cap under section 146 to such issue in an amount equal to the excess of such nonqualified amount over $15,000,000.

(6) PRIVATE BUSINESS USE DEFINED.—

(A) IN GENERAL.—For purposes of this subsection, the term "private business use" means use (directly or indirectly) in a trade or business carried on by any person other than a governmental unit. For purposes of the preceding sentence, use as a member of the general public shall not be taken into account.

(B) CLARIFICATION OF TRADE OR BUSINESS.—For purposes of the 1st sentence of subparagraph (A), any activity carried on by a person other than a natural person shall be treated as a trade or business.

(7) GOVERNMENT USE.—The term "government use" means any use other than a private business use.

(8) NONQUALIFIED AMOUNT.—For purposes of this subsection, the term "nonqualified amount" means, with respect to an issue, the lesser of—

(A) the proceeds of such issue which are to be used for any private business use, or

(B) the proceeds of such issue with respect to which there are payments (or property or borrowed money) described in paragraph (2).

(9) EXCEPTION FOR QUALIFIED 501(c)(3) BONDS.—There shall not be taken into account under this subsection or subsection (c) the portion of the proceeds of an issue which (if issued as a separate issue) would be treated as a qualified 501(c)(3) bond if the issuer elects to treat such portion as a qualified 501(c)(3) bond.

[Sec. 141(c)]

(c) PRIVATE LOAN FINANCING TEST.—

(1) IN GENERAL.—An issue meets the test of this subsection if the amount of the proceeds of the issue which are to be used (directly or indirectly) to make or finance loans (other than loans described in paragraph (2)) to persons other than governmental units exceeds the lesser of—

(A) 5 percent of such proceeds, or

(B) $5,000,000.

(2) EXCEPTION FOR TAX ASSESSMENT, ETC., LOANS.—For purposes of paragraph (1), a loan is described in this paragraph if such loan—

(A) enables the borrower to finance any governmental tax or assessment of general application for a specific essential governmental function,

(B) is a nonpurpose investment (within the meaning of section 148(f)(6)(A)), or

(C) is a qualified natural gas supply contract (as defined in section 148(b)(4)).

* * *

[Sec. 141(e)]

(e) QUALIFIED BOND.—For purposes of this part, the term "qualified bond" means any private activity bond if—

(1) IN GENERAL.—Such bond is—

(A) an exempt facility bond,

(B) a qualified mortgage bond,

(C) a qualified veterans' mortgage bond,

(D) a qualified small issue bond,

(E) a qualified student loan bond,

(F) a qualified redevelopment bond, or

(G) a qualified 501(c)(3) bond.

(2) VOLUME CAP.—Such bond is issued as part of an issue which meets the applicable requirements of section 146, and

(3) OTHER REQUIREMENTS.—Such bond meets the applicable requirements of each subsection of section 147.

[Sec. 142]

SEC. 142. EXEMPT FACILITY BOND.

[Sec. 142(a)]

(a) GENERAL RULE.—For purposes of this part, the term "exempt facility bond" means any bond issued as part of an issue 95 percent or more of the net proceeds of which are to be used to provide—

(1) airports,

(2) docks and wharves,

(3) mass commuting facilities,

(4) facilities for the furnishing of water,

(5) sewage facilities,

(6) solid waste disposal facilities,

(7) qualified residential rental projects,

(8) facilities for the local furnishing of electric energy or gas,

(9) local district heating or cooling facilities,

(10) qualified hazardous waste facilities,

(11) high-speed intercity rail facilities,

(12) environmental enhancements of hydroelectric generating facilities,

(13) qualified public educational facilities,

(14) qualified green building and sustainable design projects, or

(15) qualified highway or surface freight transfer facilities.

[Sec. 142(b)]

(b) SPECIAL EXEMPT FACILITY BOND RULES.—For purposes of subsection (a)—

(1) CERTAIN FACILITIES MUST BE GOVERNMENTALLY OWNED.—

(A) IN GENERAL.—A facility shall be treated as described in paragraph (1), (2), (3), or (12) of subsection (a) only if all of the property to be financed by the net proceeds of the issue is to be owned by a governmental unit.

(B) SAFE HARBOR FOR LEASES AND MANAGEMENT CONTRACTS.—For purposes of subparagraph (A), property leased by a governmental unit shall be treated as owned by such governmental unit if—

(i) the lessee makes an irrevocable election (binding on the lessee and all successors in interest under the lease) not to claim depreciation or an investment credit with respect to such property,

(ii) the lease term (as defined in section 168(i)(3)) is not more than 80 percent of the reasonably expected economic life of the property (as determined under section 147(b)), and

(iii) the lessee has no option to purchase the property other than at fair market value (as of the time such option is exercised).

Rules similar to the rules of the preceding sentence shall apply to management contracts and similar types of operating agreements.

(2) LIMITATION ON OFFICE SPACE.—An office shall not be treated as described in a paragraph of subsection (a) unless—

(A) the office is located on the premises of a facility described in such a paragraph, and

(B) not more than a de minimis amount of the functions to be performed at such office is not directly related to the day-to-day operations at such facility.

[Sec. 142(c)]

(c) AIRPORTS, DOCKS AND WHARVES, MASS COMMUTING FACILITIES AND HIGH-SPEED INTERCITY RAIL FACILITIES.—For purposes of subsection (a)—

(1) STORAGE AND TRAINING FACILITIES.—Storage or training facilities directly related to a facility described in paragraph (1), (2), (3) or (11) of subsection (a) shall be treated as described in the paragraph in which such facility is described.

(2) EXCEPTION FOR CERTAIN PRIVATE FACILITIES.—Property shall not be treated as described in paragraph (1), (2), (3) or (11) of subsection (a) if such property is described in any of the following subparagraphs and is to be used for any private business use (as defined in section 141(b)(6)).

(A) Any lodging facility.

(B) Any retail facility (including food and beverage facilities) in excess of a size necessary to serve passengers and employees at the exempt facility.

(C) Any retail facility (other than parking) for passengers or the general public located outside the exempt facility terminal.

(D) Any office building for individuals who are not employees of a governmental unit or of the operating authority for the exempt facility.

(E) Any industrial park or manufacturing facility.

[Sec. 142(d)]

(d) QUALIFIED RESIDENTIAL RENTAL PROJECT.—For purposes of this section—

(1) IN GENERAL.—The term "qualified residential rental project" means any project for residential rental property if, at all times during the qualified project period, such project

meets the requirements of subparagraph (A) or (B), whichever is elected by the issuer at the time of the issuance of the issue with respect to such project:

(A) 20-50 TEST.—The project meets the requirements of this subparagraph if 20 percent or more of the residential units in such project are occupied by individuals whose income is 50 percent or less of area median gross income.

(B) 40-60 TEST.—The project meets the requirements of this subparagraph if 40 percent or more of the residential units in such project are occupied by individuals whose income is 60 percent or less of area median gross income.

For purposes of this paragraph, any property shall not be treated as failing to be residential rental property merely because part of the building in which such property is located is used for purposes other than residential rental purposes.

* * *

[Sec. 142(k)]

(k) QUALIFIED PUBLIC EDUCATIONAL FACILITIES.—

(1) IN GENERAL.—For purposes of subsection (a)(13), the term "qualified public educational facility" means any school facility which is—

(A) part of a public elementary school or a public secondary school, and

(B) owned by a private, for-profit corporation pursuant to a public-private partnership agreement with a State or local educational agency described in paragraph (2).

(2) PUBLIC-PRIVATE PARTNERSHIP AGREEMENT DESCRIBED.—A public-private partnership agreement is described in this paragraph if it is an agreement—

(A) under which the corporation agrees—

(i) to do 1 or more of the following: construct, rehabilitate, refurbish, or equip a school facility, and

(ii) at the end of the term of the agreement, to transfer the school facility to such agency for no additional consideration, and

(B) the term of which does not exceed the term of the issue to be used to provide the school facility.

(3) SCHOOL FACILITY.—For purposes of this subsection, the term "school facility" means—

(A) any school building,

(B) any functionally related and subordinate facility and land with respect to such building, including any stadium or other facility primarily used for school events, and

(C) any property, to which section 168 applies (or would apply but for section 179), for use in a facility described in subparagraph (A) or (B).

(4) PUBLIC SCHOOLS.—For purposes of this subsection, the terms "elementary school" and "secondary school" have the meanings given such terms by section 14101 of the Elementary and Secondary Education Act of 1965 (20 U.S.C. 8801), as in effect on the date of the enactment of this subsection.

(5) ANNUAL AGGREGATE FACE AMOUNT OF TAX-EXEMPT FINANCING.—

(A) IN GENERAL.—An issue shall not be treated as an issue described in subsection (a)(13) if the aggregate face amount of bonds issued by the State pursuant thereto (when added to the aggregate face amount of bonds previously so issued during the calendar year) exceeds an amount equal to the greater of—

(i) $10 multiplied by the State population, or

(ii) $5,000,000.

(B) ALLOCATION RULES.—

(i) IN GENERAL.—Except as otherwise provided in this subparagraph, the State may allocate the amount described in subparagraph (A) for any calendar year in such manner as the State determines appropriate.

(ii) RULES FOR CARRYFORWARD OF UNUSED LIMITATION.—A State may elect to carry forward an unused limitation for any calendar year for 3 calendar years following the calendar year in which the unused limitation arose under rules similar to the rules of section 146(f), except that the only purpose for which the carryforward may be elected is the issuance of exempt facility bonds described in subsection (a)(13).

* * *

[Sec. 144]

SEC. 144. QUALIFIED SMALL ISSUE BOND; QUALIFIED STUDENT LOAN BOND; QUALIFIED REDEVELOPMENT BOND.

[Sec. 144(a)]

(a) QUALIFIED SMALL ISSUE BOND.—

(1) IN GENERAL.—For purposes of this part, the term "qualified small issue bond" means any bond issued as part of an issue the aggregate authorized face amount of which is $1,000,000 or less and 95 percent or more of the net proceeds of which are to be used—

(A) for the acquisition, construction, reconstruction, or improvement of land or property of a character subject to the allowance for depreciation, or

(B) to redeem part or all of a prior issue which was issued for purposes described in subparagraph (A) or this subparagraph.

(2) CERTAIN PRIOR ISSUES TAKEN INTO ACCOUNT.—If—

(A) the proceeds of 2 or more issues of bonds (whether or not the issuer of each such issue is the same) are or will be used primarily with respect to facilities located in the same incorporated municipality or located in the same county (but not in any incorporated municipality),

(B) the principal user of such facilities is or will be the same person or 2 or more related persons, and

(C) but for this paragraph, paragraph (1) (or the corresponding provision of prior law) would apply to each such issue,

then, for purposes of paragraph (1), in determining the aggregate face amount of any later issue there shall be taken into account the aggregate face amount of tax-exempt bonds issued under all prior such issues and outstanding at the time of such later issue (not including as outstanding any bond which is to be redeemed (other than in an advance refunding) from the net proceeds of the later issue).

(3) RELATED PERSONS.—For purposes of this subsection, a person is a related person to another person if—

(A) the relationship between such persons would result in a disallowance of losses under section 267 or 707(b), or

(B) such persons are members of the same controlled group of corporations (as defined in section 1563(a), except that "more than 50 percent" shall be substituted for "at least 80 percent" each place it appears therein).

(4) $10,000,000 LIMIT IN CERTAIN CASES.—

(A) IN GENERAL.—At the election of the issuer with respect to any issue, this subsection shall be applied—

(i) by substituting "$10,000,000" for "$1,000,000" in paragraph (1), and

(ii) in determining the aggregate face amount of such issue, by taking into account not only the amount described in paragraph (2), but also the aggregate amount of capital expenditures with respect to facilities described in subparagraph (B) paid or incurred during the 6-year period beginning 3 years before the date of such issue and ending 3 years after such date (and financed otherwise than out of the proceeds of outstanding tax-exempt issues to which paragraph (1) (or the corresponding provision of prior law) applied), as if the aggregate amount of such capital expenditures constituted the face amount of a prior outstanding issue described in paragraph (2).

(B) FACILITIES TAKEN INTO ACCOUNT.—For purposes of subparagraph (A)(ii), the facilities described in this subparagraph are facilities—

(i) located in the same incorporated municipality or located in the same county (but not in any incorporated municipality), and

(ii) the principal user of which is or will be the same person or 2 or more related persons.

For purposes of clause (i), the determination of whether or not facilities are located in the same governmental unit shall be made as of the date of issue of the issue in question.

(C) CERTAIN CAPITAL EXPENDITURES NOT TAKEN INTO ACCOUNT.—For purposes of subparagraph (A)(ii), any capital expenditure—

(i) to replace property destroyed or damaged by fire, storm, or other casualty, to the extent of the fair market value of the property replaced,

(ii) required by a change made after the date of issue of the issue in question in a Federal or State law or local ordinance of general application or required by a change made after such date in rules and regulations of general application issued under such a law or ordinance,

(iii) required by circumstances which could not be reasonably foreseen on such date of issue or arising out of a mistake of law or fact (but the aggregate amount of expenditures not taken into account under this clause with respect to any issue shall not exceed $1,000,000), or

(iv) described in clause (i) or (ii) of section 41(b)(2)(A) for which a deduction was allowed under section 174(a),

shall not be taken into account.

(D) LIMITATION ON LOSS OF TAX EXEMPTION.—In applying subparagraph (A)(ii) with respect to capital expenditures made after the date of any issue, no bond issued as a part of such issue shall cease to be treated as a qualified small issue bond by reason of any such expenditure for any period before the date on which such expenditure is paid or incurred.

(E) CERTAIN REFINANCING ISSUES.—In the case of any issue described in paragraph (1)(B), an election may be made under subparagraph (A) of this paragraph only if all of the prior issues being redeemed are issues to which paragraph (1) (or the corresponding provision of prior law) applied. In applying subparagraph (A)(ii) with respect to such a refinancing issue, capital expenditures shall be taken into account only for purposes of determining whether the prior issues being redeemed qualified (and would have continued to qualify) under paragraph (1) (or the corresponding provision of prior law).

(F) AGGREGATE AMOUNT OF CAPITAL EXPENDITURES WHERE THERE IS URBAN DEVELOPMENT ACTION GRANT.—In the case of any issue 95 percent or more of the net proceeds of which are to be used to provide facilities with respect to which an urban development action grant has been made under section 119 of the Housing and Community Development Act of 1974, capital expenditures of not to exceed $10,000,000 shall not be taken into account for purposes of applying subparagraph (A)(ii). This subparagraph shall not apply to bonds issued after December 31, 2006.

(G) ADDITIONAL CAPITAL EXPENDITURES NOT TAKEN INTO ACCOUNT.—With respect to bonds issued after December 31, 2006, in addition to any capital expenditure described in subparagraph (C), capital expenditures of not to exceed $10,000,000 shall not be taken into account for purposes of applying subparagraph (A)(ii).

(5) ISSUES FOR RESIDENTIAL PURPOSES.—This subsection shall not apply to any bond issued as part of an issue 5 percent or more of the net proceeds of which are to be used directly or indirectly to provide residential real property for family units.

(6) LIMITATIONS ON TREATMENT OF BONDS AS PART OF THE SAME ISSUE.—

(A) IN GENERAL.—For purposes of this subsection, separate lots of bonds which (but for this subparagraph) would be treated as part of the same issue shall be treated as separate issues unless the proceeds of such lots are to be used with respect to 2 or more facilities—

(i) which are located in more than 1 State, or

(ii) which have, or will have, as the same principal user the same person or related persons.

(B) FRANCHISES.—For purposes of subparagraph (A), a person (other than a governmental unit) shall be considered a principal user of a facility if such person (or a group of related persons which includes such person)—

(i) guarantees, arranges, participates in, or assists with the issuance (or pays any portion of the cost of issuance) of any bond the proceeds of which are to be used to finance or refinance such facility, and

(ii) provides any property, or any franchise, trademark, or trade name (within the meaning of section 1253), which is to be used in connection with such facility.

(7) SUBSECTION NOT TO APPLY IF BONDS ISSUED WITH CERTAIN OTHER TAX-EXEMPT BONDS.—This subsection shall not apply to any bond issued as part of an issue (other than an issue to which paragraph (4) applies) if the interest on any other bond which is part of such issue is excluded from gross income under any provision of law other than this subsection.

(8) RESTRICTIONS ON FINANCING CERTAIN FACILITIES.—This subsection shall not apply to an issue if—

(A) more than 25 percent of the net proceeds of the issue are to be used to provide a facility the primary purpose of which is one of the following: retail food and beverage services, automobile sales or service, or the provision of recreation or entertainment; or

(B) any portion of the proceeds of the issue is to be used to provide the following: any private or commercial golf course, country club, massage parlor, tennis club, skating facility (including roller skating, skateboard, and ice skating), racquet sports facility (including any handball or racquetball court), hot tub facility, suntan facility, or racetrack.

(9) AGGREGATION OF ISSUES WITH RESPECT TO SINGLE PROJECT.—For purposes of this subsection, 2 or more issues part or all of the net proceeds of which are to be used with respect to a single building, an enclosed shopping mall, or a strip of offices, stores, or warehouses using substantial common facilities shall be treated as 1 issue (and any person who is a principal user with respect to any of such issues shall be treated as a principal user with respect to the aggregated issue).

(10) AGGREGATE LIMIT PER TAXPAYER.—

(A) IN GENERAL.—This subsection shall not apply to any issue if the aggregate authorized face amount of such issue allocated to any test-period beneficiary (when increased by the outstanding tax-exempt facility-related bonds of such beneficiary) exceeds $40,000,000.

(B) OUTSTANDING TAX-EXEMPT FACILITY-RELATED BONDS.—

(i) IN GENERAL.—For purposes of applying subparagraph (A) with respect to any issue, the outstanding tax-exempt facility-related bonds of any person who is a test-period beneficiary with respect to such issue is the aggregate amount of tax-exempt bonds referred to in clause (ii)—

(I) which are allocated to such beneficiary, and

(II) which are outstanding at the time of such later issue (not including as outstanding any bond which is to be redeemed (other than in an advance refunding) from the net proceeds of the later issue).

(ii) BONDS TAKEN INTO ACCOUNT.—For purposes of clause (i), the bonds referred to in this clause are—

(I) exempt facility bonds, qualified small issue bonds, and qualified redevelopment bonds, and

(II) industrial development bonds (as defined in section 103(b)(2), as in effect on the day before the date of the enactment of the Tax Reform Act of 1986) to which section 141(a) does not apply.

(C) ALLOCATION OF FACE AMOUNT OF ISSUE.—

(i) IN GENERAL.—Except as otherwise provided in regulations, the portion of the face amount of an issue allocated to any test-period beneficiary of a facility financed by the proceeds of such issue (other than an owner of such facility) is an amount which bears the same relationship to the entire face amount of such issue as the portion of such facility used by such beneficiary bears to the entire facility.

(ii) OWNERS.—Except as otherwise provided in regulations, the portion of the face amount of an issue allocated to any test-period beneficiary who is an owner of a facility financed by the proceeds of such issue is an amount which bears the same relationship to the entire face amount of such issue as the portion of such facility owned by such beneficiary bears to the entire facility.

(D) TEST-PERIOD BENEFICIARY.—For purposes of this paragraph, except as provided in regulations, the term "test-period beneficiary" means any person who is an owner or a principal user of facilities being financed by the issue at any time during the 3-year period beginning on the later of—

(i) the date such facilities were placed in service, or

(ii) the date of issue.

(E) TREATMENT OF RELATED PERSONS.—For purposes of this paragraph, all persons who are related (within the meaning of paragraph (3)) to each other shall be treated as 1 person.

* * *

(12) TERMINATION DATES.—

(A) IN GENERAL.—This subsection shall not apply to—

(i) any bond (other than a bond described in clause (ii)) issued after December 31, 1986, or

(ii) any bond (or series of bonds) issued to refund a bond issued on or before such date unless—

(I) the average maturity date of the issue of which the refunding bond is a part is not later than the average maturity date of the bonds to be refunded by such issue,

(II) the amount of the refunding bond does not exceed the outstanding amount of the refunded bond, and

(III) the net proceeds of the refunding bond are used to redeem the refunded bond not later than 90 days after the date of the issuance of the refunding bond.

For purposes of clause (ii)(I), average maturity shall be determined in accordance with section 147(b)(2)(A).

(B) BONDS ISSUED TO FINANCE MANUFACTURING FACILITIES AND FARM PROPERTY.—Subparagraph (A) shall not apply to any bond issued as part of an issue 95 percent or more of the net proceeds of which are to be used to provide—

(i) any manufacturing facility, or

(ii) any land or property in accordance with section 147(c)(2).

(C) MANUFACTURING FACILITY.—For purposes of this paragraph—

(i) IN GENERAL.—The term "manufacturing facility" means any facility which is used in the manufacturing or production of tangible personal property (including the processing resulting in a change in the condition of such property). A rule similar to the rule of section 142(b)(2) shall apply for purposes of the preceding sentence.

(ii) CERTAIN FACILITIES INCLUDED.—Such term includes facilities which are directly related and ancillary to a manufacturing facility (determined without regard to this clause) if—

(I) such facilities are located on the same site as the manufacturing facility, and

(II) not more than 25 percent of the net proceeds of the issue are used to provide such facilities.

(iii) SPECIAL RULES FOR BONDS ISSUED IN 2009 AND 2010.—In the case of any issue made after the date of enactment of this clause and before January 1, 2011, clause (ii) shall not apply and the net proceeds from a bond shall be considered to be used to provide a manufacturing facility if such proceeds are used to provide—

(I) a facility which is used in the creation or production of intangible property which is described in section 197(d)(1)(C)(iii), or

(II) a facility which is functionally related and subordinate to a manufacturing facility (determined without regard to this subclause) if such facility is located on the same site as the manufacturing facility.

* * *

[Sec. 145]

SEC. 145. QUALIFIED 501(c)(3) BOND.

[Sec. 145(a)]

(a) IN GENERAL.—For purposes of this part, except as otherwise provided in this section, the term "qualified 501(c)(3) bond" means any private activity bond issued as part of an issue if—

(1) all property which is to be provided by the net proceeds of the issue is to be owned by a 501(c)(3) organization or a governmental unit, and

(2) such bond would not be a private activity bond if—

(A) 501(c)(3) organizations were treated as governmental units with respect to their activities which do not constitute unrelated trades or businesses, determined by applying section 513(a), and

(B) paragraphs (1) and (2) of section 141(b) were applied by substituting "5 percent" for "10 percent" each place it appears and by substituting "net proceeds" for "proceeds" each place it appears.

[Sec. 145(b)]

(b) $150,000,000 LIMITATION ON BONDS OTHER THAN HOSPITAL BONDS.—

(1) IN GENERAL.—A bond (other than a qualified hospital bond) shall not be treated as a qualified 501(c)(3) bond if the aggregate authorized face amount of the issue (of which such bond is a part) allocated to any 501(c)(3) organization which is a test-period beneficiary (when increased by the outstanding tax-exempt nonhospital bonds of such organization) exceeds $150,000,000.

* * *

Subpart B—Requirements Applicable to All State and Local Bonds

[Sec. 148]

SEC. 148. ARBITRAGE.

[Sec. 148(a)]

(a) ARBITRAGE BOND DEFINED.—For purposes of section 103, the term "arbitrage bond" means any bond issued as part of an issue any portion of the proceeds of which are reasonably expected (at the time of issuance of the bond) to be used directly or indirectly—

(1) to acquire higher yielding investments, or

(2) to replace funds which were used directly or indirectly to acquire higher yielding investments.

For purposes of this subsection, a bond shall be treated as an arbitrage bond if the issuer intentionally uses any portion of the proceeds of the issue of which such bond is a part in a manner described in paragraph (1) or (2).

[Sec. 148(b)]

(b) HIGHER YIELDING INVESTMENTS.—For purposes of this section—

(1) IN GENERAL.—The term "higher yielding investments" means any investment property which produces a yield over the term of the issue which is materially higher than the yield on the issue.

(2) INVESTMENT PROPERTY.—The term "investment property" means—

(A) any security (within the meaning of section 165(g)(2)(A) or (B)),

(B) any obligation,

(C) any annuity contract,

(D) any investment-type property, or

(E) in the case of a bond other than a private activity bond, any residential rental property for family units which is not located within the jurisdiction of the issuer and which is not acquired to implement a court ordered or approved housing desegregation plan.

* * *

[Sec. 149]

SEC. 149. BONDS MUST BE REGISTERED TO BE TAX EXEMPT; OTHER REQUIREMENTS.

* * *

[Sec. 149(d)]

(d) ADVANCE REFUNDINGS.—

(1) IN GENERAL.—Nothing in section 103(a) or in any other provision of law shall be construed to provide an exemption from Federal income tax for interest on any bond issued to advance refund another bond.

(2) ADVANCE REFUNDING.—For purposes of this part, a bond shall be treated as issued to advance refund another bond if it is issued more than 90 days before the redemption of the refunded bond.

(3) REGULATIONS.—The Secretary shall prescribe such regulations as may be necessary or appropriate to carry out the purposes of this subsection.

* * *

Subpart C—Definitions and Special Rules

[Sec. 150]

SEC. 150. DEFINITIONS AND SPECIAL RULES.

[Sec. 150(a)]

(a) GENERAL RULE.—For purposes of this part—

(1) BOND.—The term "bond" includes any obligation.

(2) GOVERNMENTAL UNIT NOT TO INCLUDE FEDERAL GOVERNNMENT.—The term "governmental unit" does not include the United States or any agency or instrumentality thereof.

(3) NET PROCEEDS.—The term "net proceeds" means, with respect to any issue, the proceeds of such issue reduced by amounts in a reasonably required reserve or replacement fund.

(4) 501(c)(3) ORGANIZATION.—The term "501(c)(3) organization" means any organization described in section 501(c)(3) and exempt from tax under section 501(a).

(5) OWNERSHIP OF PROPERTY.—Property shall be treated as owned by a governmental unit if it is owned on behalf of such unit.

(6) TAX-EXEMPT BOND.—The term "tax-exempt" means, with respect to any bond (or issue), that the interest on such bond (or on the bonds issued as part of such issue) is excluded from gross income.

* * *

PART V—DEDUCTIONS FOR PERSONAL EXEMPTIONS

[Sec. 151]

SEC. 151. ALLOWANCE OF DEDUCTIONS FOR PERSONAL EXEMPTIONS.

[Sec. 151(a)]

(a) ALLOWANCE OF DEDUCTIONS.—In the case of an individual, the exemptions provided by this section shall be allowed as deductions in computing taxable income.

[Sec. 151(b)]

(b) TAXPAYER AND SPOUSE.—An exemption of the exemption amount for the taxpayer; and an additional exemption of the exemption amount for the spouse of the taxpayer if a joint return is not made by the taxpayer and his spouse, and if the spouse, for the calendar year in which the taxable year of the taxpayer begins, has no gross income and is not the dependent of another taxpayer.

[Sec. 151(c)]

(c) ADDITIONAL EXEMPTION FOR DEPENDENTS.—An exemption of the exemption amount for each individual who is a dependent (as defined in section 152) of the taxpayer for the taxable year.

[Sec. 151(d)]

(d) EXEMPTION AMOUNT.—For purposes of this section—

(1) IN GENERAL.—Except as otherwise provided in this subsection, the term "exemption amount" means $2,000.

(2) EXEMPTION AMOUNT DISALLOWED IN CASE OF CERTAIN DEPENDENTS.—In the case of an individual with respect to whom a deduction under this section is allowable to another taxpayer for a taxable year beginning in the calendar year in which the individual's taxable year begins, the exemption amount applicable to such individual for such individual's taxable year shall be zero.

(3) PHASEOUT.—

(A) IN GENERAL.—In the case of any taxpayer whose adjusted gross income for the taxable year exceeds the applicable amount in effect under section 68(b), the exemption amount shall be reduced by the applicable percentage.

(B) APPLICABLE PERCENTAGE.—For purposes of subparagraph (A), the term "applicable percentage" means 2 percentage points for each $2,500 (or fraction thereof) by which the taxpayer's adjusted gross income for the taxable year exceeds the applicable amount in effect under section 68(b). In the case of a married individual filing a separate return, the preceding sentence shall be applied by substituting "$1,250" for "$2,500". In no event shall the applicable percentage exceed 100 percent.

(C) COORDINATION WITH OTHER PROVISIONS.—The provisions of this paragraph shall not apply for purposes of determining whether a deduction under this section with respect to any individual is allowable to another taxpayer for any taxable year.

(4) INFLATION ADJUSTMENT.—Except as provided in paragraph (5), in the case of any taxable year beginning in a calendar year after 1989, the dollar amount contained in paragraph (1) shall be increased by an amount equal to—

(A) such dollar amount, multiplied by

(B) the cost-of-living adjustment determined under section 1(f)(3) for the calendar year in which the taxable year begins, by substituting "calendar year 1988" for "calendar year 2016" in subparagraph (A)(ii) thereof.

(5) SPECIAL RULES FOR TAXABLE YEARS 2018 THROUGH 2025.—In the case of a taxable year beginning after December 31, 2017, and before January 1, 2026—

(A) EXEMPTION AMOUNT.—The term "exemption amount" means zero.

(B) REFERENCES.—For purposes of any other provision of this title, the reduction of the exemption amount to zero under subparagraph (A) shall not be taken into account in determining whether a deduction is allowed or allowable, or whether a taxpayer is entitled to a deduction, under this section.

[Sec. 151(e)]

(e) IDENTIFYING INFORMATION REQUIRED.—No exemption shall be allowed under this section with respect to any individual unless the TIN of such individual is included on the return claiming the exemption.

[Sec. 152]

SEC. 152. DEPENDENT DEFINED.

[Sec. 152(a)]

(a) IN GENERAL.—For purposes of this subtitle, the term "dependent" means—

(1) a qualifying child, or

(2) a qualifying relative.

[Sec. 152(b)]

(b) EXCEPTIONS.—For purposes of this section—

(1) DEPENDENTS INELIGIBLE.—If an individual is a dependent of a taxpayer for any taxable year of such taxpayer beginning in a calendar year, such individual shall be treated as having no dependents for any taxable year of such individual beginning in such calendar year.

(2) MARRIED DEPENDENTS.—An individual shall not be treated as a dependent of a taxpayer under subsection (a) if such individual has made a joint return with the individual's spouse under section 6013 for the taxable year beginning in the calendar year in which the taxable year of the taxpayer begins.

(3) CITIZENS OR NATIONALS OF OTHER COUNTRIES.—

(A) IN GENERAL.—The term "dependent" does not include an individual who is not a citizen or national of the United States unless such individual is a resident of the United States or a country contiguous to the United States.

(B) EXCEPTION FOR ADOPTED CHILD.—Subparagraph (A) shall not exclude any child of a taxpayer (within the meaning of subsection (f)(1)(B)) from the definition of "dependent" if—

(i) for the taxable year of the taxpayer, the child has the same principal place of abode as the taxpayer and is a member of the taxpayer's household, and

(ii) the taxpayer is a citizen or national of the United States.

[Sec. 152(c)]

(c) QUALIFYING CHILD.—For purposes of this section—

(1) IN GENERAL.—The term "qualifying child" means, with respect to any taxpayer for any taxable year, an individual—

(A) who bears a relationship to the taxpayer described in paragraph (2),

(B) who has the same principal place of abode as the taxpayer for more than one-half of such taxable year,

(C) who meets the age requirements of paragraph (3),

(D) who has not provided over one-half of such individual's own support for the calendar year in which the taxable year of the taxpayer begins, and

(E) who has not filed a joint return (other than only for a claim of refund) with the individual's spouse under section 6013 for the taxable year beginning in the calendar year in which the taxable year of the taxpayer begins.

(2) RELATIONSHIP.—For purposes of paragraph (1)(A), an individual bears a relationship to the taxpayer described in this paragraph if such individual is—

(A) a child of the taxpayer or a descendant of such a child, or

(B) a brother, sister, stepbrother, or stepsister of the taxpayer or a descendant of any such relative.

(3) AGE REQUIREMENTS.—

(A) IN GENERAL.—For purposes of paragraph (1)(C), an individual meets the requirements of this paragraph if such individual is younger than the taxpayer claiming such individual as a qualifying child and—

(i) has not attained the age of 19 as of the close of the calendar year in which the taxable year of the taxpayer begins, or

(ii) is a student who has not attained the age of 24 as of the close of such calendar year.

(B) SPECIAL RULE FOR DISABLED.—In the case of an individual who is permanently and totally disabled (as defined in section 22(e)(3)) at any time during such calendar year, the requirements of subparagraph (A) shall be treated as met with respect to such individual.

(4) SPECIAL RULE RELATING TO 2 OR MORE WHO CAN CLAIM THE SAME QUALIFYING CHILD.—

(A) IN GENERAL.—Except as provided in subparagraphs (B) and (C), if (but for this paragraph) an individual may be claimed as a qualifying child by 2 or more taxpayers for a taxable year beginning in the same calendar year, such individual shall be treated as the qualifying child of the taxpayer who is—

(i) a parent of the individual, or

(ii) if clause (i) does not apply, the taxpayer with the highest adjusted gross income for such taxable year.

(B) MORE THAN 1 PARENT CLAIMING QUALIFYING CHILD.—If the parents claiming any qualifying child do not file a joint return together, such child shall be treated as the qualifying child of—

(i) the parent with whom the child resided for the longest period of time during the taxable year, or

(ii) if the child resides with both parents for the same amount of time during such taxable year, the parent with the highest adjusted gross income.

(C) NO PARENT CLAIMING QUALIFYING CHILD.—If the parents of an individual may claim such individual as a qualifying child but no parent so claims the individual, such individual may be claimed as the qualifying child of another taxpayer but only if the adjusted gross income of such taxpayer is higher than the highest adjusted gross income of any parent of the individual.

[Sec. 152(d)]

(d) QUALIFYING RELATIVE.—For purposes of this section—

(1) IN GENERAL.—The term "qualifying relative" means, with respect to any taxpayer for any taxable year, an individual—

(A) who bears a relationship to the taxpayer described in paragraph (2),

(B) whose gross income for the calendar year in which such taxable year begins is less than the exemption amount (as defined in section 151(d)),

(C) with respect to whom the taxpayer provides over one-half of the individual's support for the calendar year in which such taxable year begins, and

(D) who is not a qualifying child of such taxpayer or of any other taxpayer for any taxable year beginning in the calendar year in which such taxable year begins.

(2) RELATIONSHIP.—For purposes of paragraph (1)(A), an individual bears a relationship to the taxpayer described in this paragraph if the individual is any of the following with respect to the taxpayer:

(A) A child or a descendant of a child.

(B) A brother, sister, stepbrother, or stepsister.

(C) The father or mother, or an ancestor of either.

(D) A stepfather or stepmother.

(E) A son or daughter of a brother or sister of the taxpayer.

(F) A brother or sister of the father or mother of the taxpayer.

(G) A son-in-law, daughter-in-law, father-in-law, mother-in-law, brother-in-law, or sister-in-law.

(H) An individual (other than an individual who at any time during the taxable year was the spouse, determined without regard to section 7703, of the taxpayer) who, for the taxable year of the taxpayer, has the same principal place of abode as the taxpayer and is a member of the taxpayer's household.

(3) SPECIAL RULE RELATING TO MULTIPLE SUPPORT AGREEMENTS.—For purposes of paragraph (1)(C), over one-half of the support of an individual for a calendar year shall be treated as received from the taxpayer if—

(A) no one person contributed over one-half of such support,

(B) over one-half of such support was received from 2 or more persons each of whom, but for the fact that any such person alone did not contribute over one-half of such support, would have been entitled to claim such individual as a dependent for a taxable year beginning in such calendar year, .

(C) the taxpayer contributed over 10 percent of such support, and

(D) each person described in subparagraph (B) (other than the taxpayer) who contributed over 10 percent of such support files a written declaration (in such manner and form as the Secretary may by regulations prescribe) that such person will not claim such individual as a dependent for any taxable year beginning in such calendar year.

(4) SPECIAL RULE RELATING TO INCOME OF HANDICAPPED DEPENDENTS.—

(A) IN GENERAL.—For purposes of paragraph (1)(B), the gross income of an individual who is permanently and totally disabled (as defined in section 22(e)(3)) at any time during the taxable year shall not include income attributable to services performed by the individual at a sheltered workshop if—

(i) the availability of medical care at such workshop is the principal reason for the individual's presence there, and

(ii) the income arises solely from activities at such workshop which are incident to such medical care.

(B) SHELTERED WORKSHOP DEFINED.—For purposes of subparagraph (A), the term "sheltered workshop" means a school—

(i) which provides special instruction or training designed to alleviate the disability of the individual, and

(ii) which is operated by an organization described in section 501(c)(3) and exempt from tax under section 501(a), or by a State, a possession of the United States, any political subdivision of any of the foregoing, the United States, or the District of Columbia.

»→ Caution: Code Sec. 152(d)(5), below, prior to amendment by P.L. 115-97, applies generally to any divorce or separation instrument executed on or before December 31, 2018.

(5) SPECIAL RULES FOR SUPPORT.—For purposes of this subsection—

(A) payments to a spouse which are includible in the gross income of such spouse under section 71 or 682 shall not be treated as a payment by the payor spouse for the support of any dependent, and

(B) in the case of the remarriage of a parent, support of a child received from the parent's spouse shall be treated as received from the parent.

»»→ ***Caution: Code Sec. 152(d)(5), below, as amended by P.L. 115-97, applies generally to any divorce or separation instrument executed after December 31, 2018.***

(5) SPECIAL RULES FOR SUPPORT.—

(A) IN GENERAL.—For purposes of this subsection—

(i) payments to a spouse of alimony or separate maintenance payments shall not be treated as a payment by the payor spouse for the support of any dependent, and

(ii) in the case of the remarriage of a parent, support of a child received from the parent's spouse shall be treated as received from the parent.

(B) ALIMONY OR SEPARATE MAINTENANCE PAYMENT.—For purposes of subparagraph (A), the term "alimony or separate maintenance payment" means any payment in cash if—

(i) such payment is received by (or on behalf of) a spouse under a divorce or separation instrument (as defined in section 121(d)(3)(C)),

(ii) in the case of an individual legally separated from the individual's spouse under a decree of divorce or of separate maintenance, the payee spouse and the payor spouse are not members of the same household at the time such payment is made, and

(iii) there is no liability to make any such payment for any period after the death of the payee spouse and there is no liability to make any payment (in cash or property) as a substitute for such payments after the death of the payee spouse.

[Sec. 152(e)]

(e) SPECIAL RULE FOR DIVORCED PARENTS, ETC.—

(1) IN GENERAL.—Notwithstanding subsection (c)(1)(B), (c)(4), or (d)(1)(C), if—

(A) a child receives over one-half of the child's support during the calendar year from the child's parents—

(i) who are divorced or legally separated under a decree of divorce or separate maintenance,

(ii) who are separated under a written separation agreement, or

(iii) who live apart at all times during the last 6 months of the calendar year, and—

(B) such child is in the custody of 1 or both of the child's parents for more than one-half of the calendar year, such child shall be treated as being the qualifying child or qualifying relative of the noncustodial parent for a calendar year if the requirements described in paragraph (2) or (3) are met.

(2) EXCEPTION WHERE CUSTODIAL PARENT RELEASES CLAIM TO EXEMPTION FOR THE YEAR.—For purposes of paragraph (1), the requirements described in this paragraph are met with respect to any calendar year if—

(A) the custodial parent signs a written declaration (in such manner and form as the Secretary may by regulations prescribe) that such custodial parent will not claim such child as a dependent for any taxable year beginning in such calendar year, and

(B) the noncustodial parent attaches such written declaration to the noncustodial parent's return for the taxable year beginning during such calendar year.

* * *

(4) CUSTODIAL PARENT AND NONCUSTODIAL PARENT.—For purposes of this subsection—

(A) CUSTODIAL PARENT.—The term "custodial parent" means the parent having custody for the greater portion of the calendar year.

(B) NONCUSTODIAL PARENT.—The term "noncustodial parent" means the parent who is not the custodial parent.

(5) EXCEPTION FOR MULTIPLE-SUPPORT AGREEMENT.—This subsection shall not apply in any case where over one-half of the support of the child is treated as having been received from a taxpayer under the provision of subsection (d)(3).

(6) SPECIAL RULE FOR SUPPORT RECEIVED FROM NEW SPOUSE OF PARENT.—For purposes of this subsection, in the case of the remarriage of a parent, support of a child received from the parent's spouse shall be treated as received from the parent.

[Sec. 152(f)]

(f) OTHER DEFINITIONS AND RULES.—For purposes of this section—

(1) CHILD DEFINED.—

(A) IN GENERAL.—The term "child" means an individual who is—

(i) a son, daughter, stepson, or stepdaughter of the taxpayer, or

(ii) an eligible foster child of the taxpayer.

(B) ADOPTED CHILD.—In determining whether any of the relationships specified in subparagraph (A)(i) or paragraph (4) exists, a legally adopted individual of the taxpayer, or an individual who is lawfully placed with the taxpayer for legal adoption by the taxpayer, shall be treated as a child of such individual by blood.

(C) ELIGIBLE FOSTER CHILD.—For purposes of subparagraph (A)(ii), the term "eligible foster child" means an individual who is placed with the taxpayer by an authorized placement agency or by judgment, decree, or other order of any court of competent jurisdiction.

(2) STUDENT DEFINED.—The term "student" means an individual who during each of 5 calendar months during the calendar year in which the taxable year of the taxpayer begins—

(A) is a full-time student at an educational organization described in section 170(b)(1)(A)(ii), or

(B) is pursuing a full-time course of institutional on-farm training under the supervision of an accredited agent of an educational organization described in section 170(b)(1)(A)(ii) or of a State or political subdivision of a State.

(3) DETERMINATION OF HOUSEHOLD STATUS.—An individual shall not be treated as a member of the taxpayer's household if at any time during the taxable year of the taxpayer the relationship between such individual and the taxpayer is in violation of local law.

(4) BROTHER AND SISTER.—The terms "brother" and "sister" include a brother or sister by the half blood.

(5) SPECIAL SUPPORT TEST IN CASE OF STUDENTS.—For purposes of subsections (c)(1)(D) and (d)(1)(C), in the case of an individual who is—

(A) a child of the taxpayer, and

(B) a student,

amounts received as scholarships for study at an educational organization described in section 170(b)(1)(A)(ii) shall not be taken into account.

(6) TREATMENT OF MISSING CHILDREN.—

(A) IN GENERAL.—Solely for the purposes referred to in subparagraph (B), a child of the taxpayer—

(i) who is presumed by law enforcement authorities to have been kidnapped by someone who is not a member of the family of such child or the taxpayer, and

(ii) who had, for the taxable year in which the kidnapping occurred, the same principal place of abode as the taxpayer for more than one-half of the portion of such year before the date of the kidnapping,

shall be treated as meeting the requirement of subsection (c)(1)(B) with respect to a taxpayer for all taxable years ending during the period that the child is kidnapped.

(B) PURPOSES.—Subparagraph (A) shall apply solely for purposes of determining—

(i) the deduction under section 151(c),

(ii) the credit under section 24 (relating to child tax credit),

(iii) whether an individual is a surviving spouse or a head of a household (as such terms are defined in section 2), and

(iv) the earned income credit under section 32.

(C) COMPARABLE TREATMENT OF CERTAIN QUALIFYING RELATIVES.—For purposes of this section, a child of the taxpayer—

(i) who is presumed by law enforcement authorities to have been kidnapped by someone who is not a member of the family of such child or the taxpayer, and

(ii) who was (without regard to this paragraph) a qualifying relative of the taxpayer for the portion of the taxable year before the date of the kidnapping,

shall be treated as a qualifying relative of the taxpayer for all taxable years ending during the period that the child is kidnapped.

(D) TERMINATION OF TREATMENT.—Subparagraphs (A) and (C) shall cease to apply as of the first taxable year of the taxpayer beginning after the calendar year in which there is a determination that the child is dead (or, if earlier, in which the child would have attained age 18).

(7) CROSS REFERENCES.—

For provision treating child as dependent of both parents for purposes of certain provisions, see sections 105(b), 132(h)(2)(B), and 213(d)(5).

PART VI—ITEMIZED DEDUCTIONS FOR INDIVIDUALS AND CORPORATIONS

[Sec. 161]

SEC. 161. ALLOWANCE OF DEDUCTIONS.

In computing taxable income under section 63, there shall be allowed as deductions the items specified in this part, subject to the exceptions provided in part IX (sec. 261 and following, relating to items not deductible).

[Sec. 162]

SEC. 162. TRADE OR BUSINESS EXPENSES.

[Sec. 162(a)]

(a) IN GENERAL.—There shall be allowed as a deduction all the ordinary and necessary expenses paid or incurred during the taxable year in carrying on any trade or business, including—

(1) a reasonable allowance for salaries or other compensation for personal services actually rendered;

(2) traveling expenses (including amounts expended for meals and lodging other than amounts which are lavish or extravagant under the circumstances) while away from home in the pursuit of a trade or business; and

(3) rentals or other payments required to be made as a condition to the continued use or possession, for purposes of the trade or business, of property to which the taxpayer has not taken or is not taking title or in which he has no equity.

For purposes of the preceding sentence, the place of residence of a Member of Congress (including any Delegate and Resident Commissioner) within the State, congressional district, or possession which he represents in Congress shall be considered his home, but amounts expended by such Members within each taxable year for living expenses shall not be deductible for income tax purposes. For purposes of paragraph (2), the taxpayer shall not be treated as being temporarily away from home during any period of employment if such period exceeds 1 year. The preceding sentence shall not apply to any Federal employee during any period for which such employee is certified by the Attorney General (or the designee thereof) as traveling on behalf of the United States in temporary duty status to investigate or prosecute, or provide support services for the investigation or prosecution of, a Federal crime.

[Sec. 162(b)]

(b) CHARITABLE CONTRIBUTIONS AND GIFTS EXCEPTED.—No deduction shall be allowed under subsection (a) for any contribution or gift which would be allowable as a deduction under section 170 were it not for the percentage limitations, the dollar limitations, or the requirements as to the time of payment, set forth in such section.

[Sec. 162(c)]

(c) ILLEGAL BRIBES, KICKBACKS, AND OTHER PAYMENTS.—

(1) ILLEGAL PAYMENTS TO GOVERNMENT OFFICIALS OR EMPLOYEES.—No deduction shall be allowed under subsection (a) for any payment made, directly or indirectly, to an official or employee of any government, or of any agency or instrumentality of any government, if the payment constitutes an illegal bribe or kickback or, if the payment is to an official or employee of a foreign government, the payment is unlawful under the Foreign Corrupt Practices Act of 1977. The burden of proof in respect of the issue, for the purposes of this paragraph, as to whether a payment constitutes an illegal bribe or kickback (or is unlawful under the Foreign Corrupt Practices Act of 1977) shall be upon the Secretary to the same extent as he bears the burden of proof under section 7454 (concerning the burden of proof when the issue relates to fraud).

(2) OTHER ILLEGAL PAYMENTS.—No deduction shall be allowed under subsection (a) for any payment (other than a payment described in paragraph (1)) made, directly or indirectly, to any person, if the payment constitutes an illegal bribe, illegal kickback, or other illegal payment under any law of the United States, or under any law of a State (but only if such State law is generally enforced), which subjects the payor to a criminal penalty or the loss of license or privilege to engage in a trade or business. For purposes of this paragraph, a kickback includes a payment in consideration of the referral of a client, patient, or customer. The burden of proof in respect of the issue, for purposes of this paragraph, as to whether a payment constitutes an illegal bribe, illegal kickback, or other illegal payment shall be upon the Secretary to the same extent as he bears the burden of proof under section 7454 (concerning the burden of proof when the issue relates to fraud).

(3) KICKBACKS, REBATES, AND BRIBES UNDER MEDICARE AND MEDICAID.—No deduction shall be allowed under subsection (a) for any kickback, rebate, or bribe made by any provider of services, supplier, physician, or other person who furnishes items or services for which payment is or may be made under the Social Security Act, or in whole or in part out of Federal funds under a State plan approved under such Act, if such kickback, rebate, or bribe is made in connection with the furnishing of such items or services or the making or receipt of such payments. For purposes of this paragraph, a kickback includes a payment in consideration of the referral of a client, patient, or customer.

* * *

[Sec. 162(e)]

(e) DENIAL OF DEDUCTION FOR CERTAIN LOBBYING AND POLITICAL EXPENDITURES.—

(1) IN GENERAL.—No deduction shall be allowed under subsection (a) for any amount paid or incurred in connection with—

(A) influencing legislation,

(B) participation in, or intervention in, any political campaign on behalf of (or in opposition to) any candidate for public office,

(C) any attempt to influence the general public, or segments thereof, with respect to elections, legislative matters, or referendums, or

(D) any direct communication with a covered executive branch official in an attempt to influence the official actions or positions of such official.

(2) APPLICATION TO DUES OF TAX-EXEMPT ORGANIZATIONS.—No deduction shall be allowed under subsection (a) for the portion of dues or other similar amounts paid by the taxpayer to an organization which is exempt from tax under this subtitle which the organization notifies the taxpayer under section 6033(e)(1)(A)(ii) is allocable to expenditures to which paragraph (1) applies.

(3) INFLUENCING LEGISLATION.—For purposes of this subsection—

(A) IN GENERAL.—The term "influencing legislation" means any attempt to influence any legislation through communication with any member or employee of a legislative body, or with any government official or employee who may participate in the formulation of legislation.

(B) LEGISLATION.—The term "legislation" has the meaning given such term by section 4911(e)(2).

(4) OTHER SPECIAL RULES.—

(A) EXCEPTION FOR CERTAIN TAXPAYERS.—In the case of any taxpayer engaged in the trade or business of conducting activities described in paragraph (1), paragraph (1) shall not apply to expenditures of the taxpayer in conducting such activities directly on behalf of another person (but shall apply to payments by such other person to the taxpayer for conducting such activities).

(B) DE MINIMIS EXCEPTION.—

(i) IN GENERAL.—Paragraph (1) shall not apply to any in-house expenditures for any taxable year if such expenditures do not exceed $2,000. In determining whether a taxpayer exceeds the $2,000 limit under this clause, there shall not be taken into account overhead costs otherwise allocable to activities described in paragraphs (1)(A) and (D).

(ii) IN-HOUSE EXPENDITURES.—For purposes of clause (i), the term "in-house expenditures" means expenditures described in paragraphs (1)(A) and (D) other than—

(I) payments by the taxpayer to a person engaged in the trade or business of conducting activities described in paragraph (1) for the conduct of such activities on behalf of the taxpayer, or

(II) dues or other similar amounts paid or incurred by the taxpayer which are allocable to activities described in paragraph (1).

(C) EXPENSES INCURRED IN CONNECTION WITH LOBBYING AND POLITICAL ACTIVITIES.—Any amount paid or incurred for research for, or preparation, planning, or coordination of, any activity described in paragraph (1) shall be treated as paid or incurred in connection with such activity.

(5) COVERED EXECUTIVE BRANCH OFFICIAL.—For purposes of this subsection, the term "covered executive branch official" means—

(A) the President,

(B) the Vice President,

(C) any officer or employee of the White House Office of the Executive Office of the President, and the 2 most senior level officers of each of the other agencies in such Executive Office, and

(D)(i) any individual serving in a position in level I of the Executive Schedule under section 5312 of title 5, United States Code, (ii) any other individual designated by the President as having Cabinet level status, and (iii) any immediate deputy of an individual described in clause (i) or (ii).

(6) CROSS REFERENCE.—

For reporting requirements and alternative taxes related to this subsection, see section 6033(e).

[Sec. 162(f)]

(f) FINES, PENALTIES, AND OTHER AMOUNTS.—

(1) IN GENERAL.—Except as provided in the following paragraphs of this subsection, no deduction otherwise allowable shall be allowed under this chapter for any amount paid or incurred (whether by suit, agreement, or otherwise) to, or at the direction of, a government or governmental entity in relation to the violation of any law or the investigation or inquiry by such government or entity into the potential violation of any law.

(2) EXCEPTION FOR AMOUNTS CONSTITUTING RESTITUTION OR PAID TO COME INTO COMPLIANCE WITH LAW.—

(A) IN GENERAL.—Paragraph (1) shall not apply to any amount that—

(i) the taxpayer establishes.—

(I) constitutes restitution (including remediation of property) for damage or harm which was or may be caused by the violation of any law or the potential violation of any law, or

(II) is paid to come into compliance with any law which was violated or otherwise involved in the investigation or inquiry described in paragraph (1),

(ii) is identified as restitution or as an amount paid to come into compliance with such law, as the case may be, in the court order or settlement agreement, and

(iii) in the case of any amount of restitution for failure to pay any tax imposed under this title in the same manner as if such amount were such tax, would have been allowed as a deduction under this chapter if it had been timely paid.

The identification under clause (ii) alone shall not be sufficient to make the establishment required under clause (i).

(B) LIMITATION.—Subparagraph (A) shall not apply to any amount paid or incurred as reimbursement to the government or entity for the costs of any investigation or litigation.

(3) EXCEPTION FOR AMOUNTS PAID OR INCURRED AS THE RESULT OF CERTAIN COURT ORDERS.—Paragraph (1) shall not apply to any amount paid or incurred by reason of any order of a court in a suit in which no government or governmental entity is a party.

(4) EXCEPTION FOR TAXES DUE.—Paragraph (1) shall not apply to any amount paid or incurred as taxes due.

(5) TREATMENT OF CERTAIN NONGOVERNMENTAL REGULATORY ENTITIES.—For purposes of this subsection, the following nongovernmental entities shall be treated as governmental entities:

(A) Any nongovernmental entity which exercises self-regulatory powers (including imposing sanctions) in connection with a qualified board or exchange (as defined in section 1256(g)(7)).

(B) To the extent provided in regulations, any nongovernmental entity which exercises self-regulatory powers (including imposing sanctions) as part of performing an essential governmental function.

[Sec. 162(g)]

(g) TREBLE DAMAGE PAYMENTS UNDER THE ANTITRUST LAWS.—If in a criminal proceeding a taxpayer is convicted of a violation of the antitrust laws, or his plea of guilty or nolo contendere to an indictment or information charging such a violation is entered or accepted in such a proceeding, no deduction shall be allowed under subsection (a) for two-thirds of any amount paid or incurred—

(1) on any judgment for damages entered against the taxpayer under section 4 of the Act entitled "An Act to supplement existing laws against unlawful restraints and monopolies, and for other purposes", approved October 15, 1914 (commonly known as the Clayton Act), on account of such violation or any related violation of the antitrust laws which occurred prior to the date of the final judgment of such conviction, or

(2) in settlement of any action brought under such section 4 on account of such violation or related violation.

* * *

[Sec. 162(k)]

(k) STOCK REACQUISITION EXPENSES.—

(1) IN GENERAL.—Except as provided in paragraph (2), no deduction otherwise allowable shall be allowed under this chapter for any amount paid or incurred by a corporation in connection with the reacquisition of its stock or of the stock of any related person (as defined in section 465(b)(3)(C)).

(2) EXCEPTIONS.—Paragraph (1) shall not apply to—

(A) CERTAIN SPECIFIC DEDUCTIONS.—Any—

(i) deduction allowable under section 163 (relating to interest),

(ii) deduction for amounts which are properly allocable to indebtedness and amortized over the term of such indebtedness, or

(iii) deduction for dividends paid (within the meaning of section 561).

(B) STOCK OF CERTAIN REGULATED INVESTMENT COMPANIES.—Any amount paid or incurred in connection with the redemption of any stock in a regulated investment company which issues only stock which is redeemable upon the demand of the shareholder.

[Sec. 162(l)]

(l) SPECIAL RULES FOR HEALTH INSURANCE COSTS OF SELF-EMPLOYED INDIVIDUALS.—

(1) ALLOWANCE OF DEDUCTION.—In the case of a taxpayer who is an employee within the meaning of section 401(c)(1), there shall be allowed as a deduction under this section an amount equal to the amount paid during the taxable year for insurance which constitutes medical care for—

(A) the taxpayer,

(B) the taxpayer's spouse,

(C) the taxpayer's dependents, and

(D) any child (as defined in section 152(f)(1)) of the taxpayer who as of the end of the taxable year has not attained age 27.

(2) LIMITATIONS.—

(A) DOLLAR AMOUNT.—No deduction shall be allowed under paragraph (1) to the extent that the amount of such deduction exceeds the taxpayer's earned income (within the meaning of section 401(c)) derived by the taxpayer from the trade or business with respect to which the plan providing the medical care coverage is established.

(B) OTHER COVERAGE.—Paragraph (1) shall not apply to any taxpayer for any calendar month for which the taxpayer is eligible to participate in any subsidized health plan maintained by any employer of the taxpayer or of the spouse of, or any dependent, or individual described in subparagraph (D) of paragraph (1) with respect to, the taxpayer. The preceding sentence shall be applied separately with respect to—

(i) plans which include coverage for qualified long-term care services (as defined in section 7702B(c)) or are qualified long-term care insurance contracts (as defined in section 7702B(b)), and

(ii) plans which do not include such coverage and are not such contracts.

(C) LONG-TERM CARE PREMIUMS.—In the case of a qualified long-term care insurance contract (as defined in section 7702B(b)), only eligible long-term care premiums (as defined in section 213(d)(10)) shall be taken into account under paragraph (1).

(3) COORDINATION WITH MEDICAL DEDUCTION.—Any amount paid by a taxpayer for insurance to which paragraph (1) applies shall not be taken into account in computing the amount allowable to the taxpayer as a deduction under section 213(a).

* * *

(5) TREATMENT OF CERTAIN S CORPORATION SHAREHOLDERS.—This subsection shall apply in the case of any individual treated as a partner under section 1372(a), except that—

(A) for purposes of this subsection, such individual's wages (as defined in section 3121) from the S corporation shall be treated as such individual's earned income (within the meaning of section 401(c)(1)), and

(B) there shall be such adjustments in the application of this subsection as the Secretary may by regulations prescribe.

[Sec. 162(m)]

(m) CERTAIN EXCESSIVE EMPLOYEE REMUNERATION.—

(1) IN GENERAL.—In the case of any publicly held corporation, no deduction shall be allowed under this chapter for applicable employee remuneration with respect to any covered

employee to the extent that the amount of such remuneration for the taxable year with respect to such employee exceeds $1,000,000.

(2) PUBLICLY HELD CORPORATION.—For purposes of this subsection, the term "publicly held corporation" means any corporation which is an issuer (as defined in section 3 of the Securities Exchange Act of 1934 (15 U.S.C. 78c))—

(A) the securities of which are required to be registered under section 12 of such Act (15 U.S.C. 78l), or

(B) that is required to file reports under section 15(d) of such Act (15 U.S.C. 78o(d)).

(3) COVERED EMPLOYEE.—For purposes of this subsection, the term "covered employee" means any employee of the taxpayer if—

(A) such employee is the principal executive officer or principal financial officer of the taxpayer at any time during the taxable year, or was an individual acting in such a capacity,

(B) the total compensation of such employee for the taxable year is required to be reported to shareholders under the Securities Exchange Act of 1934 by reason of such employee being among the 3 highest compensated officers for the taxable year (other than any individual described in subparagraph (A)), or

(C) was a covered employee of the taxpayer (or any predecessor) for any preceding taxable year beginning after December 31, 2016.

Such term shall include any employee who would be described in subparagraph (B) if the reporting described in such subparagraph were required as so described.

(4) APPLICABLE EMPLOYEE REMUNERATION.—For purposes of this subsection—

(A) IN GENERAL.—Except as otherwise provided in this paragraph, the term "applicable employee remuneration" means, with respect to any covered employee for any taxable year, the aggregate amount allowable as a deduction under this chapter for such taxable year (determined without regard to this subsection) for remuneration for services performed by such employee (whether or not during the taxable year).

(B) EXCEPTION FOR EXISTING BINDING CONTRACTS.—The term "applicable employee remuneration" shall not include any remuneration payable under a written binding contract which was in effect on February 17, 1993, and which was not modified thereafter in any material respect before such remuneration is paid.

(C) REMUNERATION.—For purposes of this paragraph, the term "remuneration" includes any remuneration (including benefits) in any medium other than cash, but shall not include—

(i) any payment referred to in so much of section 3121(a)(5) as precedes subparagraph (E) thereof, and

(ii) any benefit provided to or on behalf of an employee if at the time such benefit is provided it is reasonable to believe that the employee will be able to exclude such benefit from gross income under this chapter.

For purposes of clause (i), section 3121(a)(5) shall be applied without regard to section 3121(v)(1).

(D) COORDINATION WITH DISALLOWED GOLDEN PARACHUTE PAYMENTS.—The dollar limitation contained in paragraph (1) shall be reduced (but not below zero) by the amount (if any) which would have been included in the applicable employee remuneration of the covered employee for the taxable year but for being disallowed under section 280G.

(E) COORDINATION WITH EXCISE TAX ON SPECIFIED STOCK COMPENSATION.—The dollar limitation contained in paragraph (1) with respect to any covered employee shall be reduced (but not below zero) by the amount of any payment (with respect to such employee) of the tax imposed by section 4985 directly or indirectly by the expatriated corporation (as defined in such section) or by any member of the expanded affiliated group (as defined in such section) which includes such corporation.

(F) SPECIAL RULE FOR REMUNERATION PAID TO BENEFICIARIES, ETC.—Remuneration shall not fail to be applicable employee remuneration merely because it is includible in the income of, or paid to, a person other than the covered employee, including after the death of the covered employee.

* * *

[Sec. 162(p)]

(p) TREATMENT OF EXPENSES OF MEMBERS OF RESERVE COMPONENT OF ARMED FORCES OF THE UNITED STATES.—For purposes of subsection (a)(2), in the case of an individual who performs services as a member of a reserve component of the Armed Forces of the United States at any time during the taxable year, such individual shall be deemed to be away from home in the pursuit of a trade or business for any period during which such individual is away from home in connection with such service.

[Sec. 162(q)]

(q) PAYMENTS RELATED TO SEXUAL HARASSMENT AND SEXUAL ABUSE.—No deduction shall be allowed under this chapter for—

(1) any settlement or payment related to sexual harassment or sexual abuse if such settlement or payment is subject to a nondisclosure agreement, or

(2) attorney's fees related to such a settlement or payment.

* * *

[Sec. 163]

SEC. 163. INTEREST.

[Sec. 163(a)]

(a) GENERAL RULE.—There shall be allowed as a deduction all interest paid or accrued within the taxable year on indebtedness.

[Sec. 163(b)]

(b) INSTALLMENT PURCHASES WHERE INTEREST CHARGE IS NOT SEPARATELY STATED.—

(1) GENERAL RULE.—If personal property or educational services are purchased under a contract—

(A) which provides that payment of part or all of the purchase price is to be made in installments, and

(B) in which carrying charges are separately stated but the interest charge cannot be ascertained,

then the payments made during the taxable year under the contract shall be treated for purposes of this section as if they included interest equal to 6 percent of the average unpaid balance under the contract during the taxable year. For purposes of the preceding sentence, the average unpaid balance is the sum of the unpaid balance outstanding on the first day of each month beginning during the taxable year, divided by 12. For purposes of this paragraph, the term "educational services" means any service (including lodging) which is purchased from an educational organization described in section 170(b)(1)(A)(ii) and which is provided for a student of such organization.

(2) LIMITATION.—In the case of any contract to which paragraph (1) applies, the amount treated as interest for any taxable year shall not exceed the aggregate carrying charges which are properly attributable to such taxable year.

[Sec. 163(c)]

(c) REDEEMABLE GROUND RENTS.—For purposes of this subtitle, any annual or periodic rental under a redeemable ground rent (excluding amounts in redemption thereof) shall be treated as interest on an indebtedness secured by a mortgage.

[Sec. 163(d)]

(d) LIMITATION ON INVESTMENT INTEREST.—

(1) IN GENERAL.—In the case of a taxpayer other than a corporation, the amount allowed as a deduction under this chapter for investment interest for any taxable year shall not exceed the net investment income of the taxpayer for the taxable year.

(2) CARRYFORWARD OF DISALLOWED INTEREST.—The amount not allowed as a deduction for any taxable year by reason of paragraph (1) shall be treated as investment interest paid or accrued by the taxpayer in the succeeding taxable year.

(3) INVESTMENT INTEREST.—For purposes of this subsection—

(A) IN GENERAL.—The term "investment interest" means any interest allowable as a deduction under this chapter (determined without regard to paragraph (1)) which is paid or accrued on indebtedness properly allocable to property held for investment.

(B) EXCEPTIONS.—The term "investment interest" shall not include—

(i) any qualified residence interest (as defined in subsection (h)(3)), or

(ii) any interest which is taken into account under section 469 in computing income or loss from a passive activity of the taxpayer.

(C) PERSONAL PROPERTY USED IN SHORT SALE.—For purposes of this paragraph, the term "interest" includes any amount allowable as a deduction in connection with personal property used in a short sale.

(4) NET INVESTMENT INCOME.—For purposes of this subsection—

(A) IN GENERAL.—The term "net investment income" means the excess of—

(i) investment income, over

(ii) investment expenses.

(B) INVESTMENT INCOME.—The term "investment income" means the sum of—

(i) gross income from property held for investment (other than any gain taken into account under clause (ii)(I)),

(ii) the excess (if any) of—

(I) the net gain attributable to the disposition of property held for investment, over

(II) the net capital gain determined by only taking into account gains and losses from dispositions of property held for investment, plus

(iii) so much of the net capital gain referred to in clause (ii)(II) (or, if lesser, the net gain referred to in clause (ii)(I)) as the taxpayer elects to take into account under this clause.

Such term shall include qualified dividend income (as defined in section 1(h)(11)(B)) only to the extent the taxpayer elects to treat such income as investment income for purposes of this subsection.

(C) INVESTMENT EXPENSES.—The term "investment expenses" means the deductions allowed under this chapter (other than for interest) which are directly connected with the production of investment income.

(D) INCOME AND EXPENSES FROM PASSIVE ACTIVITIES.—Investment income and investment expenses shall not include any income or expenses taken into account under section 469 in computing income or loss from a passive activity.

(5) PROPERTY HELD FOR INVESTMENT.—For purposes of this subsection—

(A) IN GENERAL.—The term "property held for investment" shall include—

(i) any property which produces income of a type described in section 469(e)(1), and

(ii) any interest held by a taxpayer in an activity involving the conduct of a trade or business—

(I) which is not a passive activity, and

(II) with respect to which the taxpayer does not materially participate.

(B) INVESTMENT EXPENSES.—In the case of property described in subparagraph (A)(i), expenses shall be allocated to such property in the same manner as under section 469.

(C) TERMS.—For purposes of this paragraph, the terms "activity", "passive activity", and "materially participate" have the meanings given such terms by section 469.

[Sec. 163(e)]

(e) ORIGINAL ISSUE DISCOUNT.—

(1) IN GENERAL.—The portion of the original issue discount with respect to any debt instrument which is allowable as a deduction to the issuer for any taxable year shall be equal to the aggregate daily portions of the original issue discount for days during such taxable year.

(2) DEFINITIONS AND SPECIAL RULES.—For purposes of this subsection—

(A) DEBT INSTRUMENT.—The term "debt instrument" has the meaning given such term by section 1275(a)(1).

(B) DAILY PORTIONS.—The daily portion of the original issue discount for any day shall be determined under section 1272(a) (without regard to paragraph (7) thereof and without regard to section 1273(a)(3)).

(C) SHORT-TERM OBLIGATIONS.—In the case of an obligor of a short-term obligation (as defined in section 1283(a)(1)(A)) who uses the cash receipts and disbursements method of accounting, the original issue discount (and any other interest payable) on such obligation shall be deductible only when paid.

* * *

(5) SPECIAL RULES FOR ORIGINAL ISSUE DISCOUNT ON CERTAIN HIGH YIELD OBLIGATIONS.—

(A) IN GENERAL.—In the case of an applicable high yield discount obligation issued by a corporation—

(i) no deduction shall be allowed under this chapter for the disqualified portion of the original issue discount on such obligation, and

(ii) the remainder of such original issue discount shall not be allowable as a deduction until paid.

For purposes of this paragraph, rules similar to the rules of subsection (i)(3)(B) shall apply in determining the amount of the original issue discount and when the original issue discount is paid.

(B) DISQUALIFIED PORTION TREATED AS STOCK DISTRIBUTION FOR PURPOSES OF DIVIDEND RECEIVED DEDUCTION.—

(i) IN GENERAL.—Solely for purposes of sections 243, 245, 246, and 246A, the dividend equivalent portion of any amount includible in gross income of a corporation under section 1272(a) in respect of an applicable high yield discount obligation shall be treated as a dividend received by such corporation from the corporation issuing such obligation.

(ii) DIVIDEND EQUIVALENT PORTION.—For purposes of clause (i), the dividend equivalent portion of any amount includible in gross income under section 1272(a) in respect of an applicable high yield discount obligation is the portion of the amount so includible—

(I) which is attributable to the disqualified portion of the original issue discount on such obligation, and

(II) which would have been treated as a dividend if it had been a distribution made by the issuing corporation with respect to stock in such corporation.

(C) DISQUALIFIED PORTION.—

(i) IN GENERAL.—For purposes of this paragraph, the disqualified portion of the original issue discount on any applicable high yield discount obligation is the lesser of—

(I) the amount of such original issue discount, or

(II) the portion of the total return on such obligation which bears the same ratio to such total return as the disqualified yield on such obligation bears to the yield to maturity on such obligation.

(ii) DEFINITIONS.—For purposes of clause (i), the term "disqualified yield" means the excess of the yield to maturity on the obligation over the sum referred to in subsection (i)(1)(B) plus 1 percentage point, and the term "total return" is the amount which would have been the original issue discount on the obligation if interest described in the parenthetical in section 1273(a)(2) were included in the stated redemption price at maturity.

(D) EXCEPTION FOR S CORPORATIONS.—This paragraph shall not apply to any obligation issued by any corporation for any period for which such corporation is an S corporation.

(E) EFFECT ON EARNINGS AND PROFITS.—This paragraph shall not apply for purposes of determining earnings and profits; except that, for purposes of determining the dividend equivalent portion of any amount includible in gross income under section 1272(a) in respect of an applicable high yield discount obligation, no reduction shall be made for any amount attributable to the disqualified portion of any original issue discount on such obligation.

(F) SUSPENSION OF APPLICATION OF PARAGRAPH.—

(i) TEMPORARY SUSPENSION.—This paragraph shall not apply to any applicable high yield discount obligation issued during the period beginning on September 1, 2008, and ending on December 31, 2009, in exchange (including an exchange resulting from a modification of the debt instrument) for an obligation which is not an applicable high yield discount obligation and the issuer (or obligor) of which is the same as the issuer (or obligor) of such applicable high yield discount obligation. The preceding sentence shall not apply to any obligation the interest on which is interest described in section 871(h)(4) (without regard to subparagraph (D) thereof) or to any obligation issued to a related person (within the meaning of section 108(e)(4)).

(ii) SUCCESSIVE APPLICATION.—Any obligation to which clause (i) applies shall not be treated as an applicable high yield discount obligation for purposes of applying this subparagraph to any other obligation issued in exchange for such obligation.

(iii) SECRETARIAL AUTHORITY TO SUSPEND APPLICATION.—The Secretary may apply this paragraph with respect to debt instruments issued in periods following the period described in clause (i) if the Secretary determines that such application is appropriate in light of distressed conditions in the debt capital markets.

(G) CROSS REFERENCE.—

For definition of applicable high yield discount obligation, see subsection (i).

(6) CROSS REFERENCES.—

For provision relating to deduction of original issue discount on tax-exempt obligation, see section 1288.

For special rules in the case of the borrower under certain loans for personal use, see section 1275(b).

* * *

[Sec. 163(h)]

(h) DISALLOWANCE OF DEDUCTION FOR PERSONAL INTEREST.—

(1) IN GENERAL.—In the case of a taxpayer other than a corporation, no deduction shall be allowed under this chapter for personal interest paid or accrued during the taxable year.

(2) PERSONAL INTEREST.—For purposes of this subsection, the term "personal interest" means any interest allowable as a deduction under this chapter other than—

(A) interest paid or accrued on indebtedness properly allocable to a trade or business (other than the trade or business of performing services as an employee),

(B) any investment interest (within the meaning of subsection (d)),

(C) any interest which is taken into account under section 469 in computing income or loss from a passive activity of the taxpayer,

(D) any qualified residence interest (within the meaning of paragraph (3)),

(E) any interest payable under section 6601 on any unpaid portion of the tax imposed by section 2001 for the period during which an extension of time for payment of such tax is in effect under section 6163, and

(F) any interest allowable as a deduction under section 221 (relating to interest on educational loans).

(3) QUALIFIED RESIDENCE INTEREST.—For purposes of this subsection—

(A) IN GENERAL.—The term "qualified residence interest" means any interest which is paid or accrued during the taxable year on—

(i) acquisition indebtedness with respect to any qualified residence of the taxpayer, or

(ii) home equity indebtedness with respect to any qualified residence of the taxpayer.

For purposes of the preceding sentence, the determination of whether any property is a qualified residence of the taxpayer shall be made as of the time the interest is accrued.

(B) ACQUISITION INDEBTEDNESS.—

(i) IN GENERAL.—The term "acquisition indebtedness" means any indebtedness which—

(I) is incurred in acquiring, constructing, or substantially improving any qualified residence of the taxpayer, and

(II) is secured by such residence.

Such term also includes any indebtedness secured by such residence resulting from the refinancing of indebtedness meeting the requirements of the preceding sentence (or this sentence); but only to the extent the amount of the indebtedness resulting from such refinancing does not exceed the amount of the refinanced indebtedness.

(ii) $1,000,000 LIMITATION.—The aggregate amount treated as acquisition indebtedness for any period shall not exceed $1,000,000 ($500,000 in the case of a married individual filing a separate return).

(C) HOME EQUITY INDEBTEDNESS.—

(i) IN GENERAL.—The term "home equity indebtedness" means any indebtedness (other than acquisition indebtedness) secured by a qualified residence to the extent the aggregate amount of such indebtedness does not exceed—

(I) the fair market value of such qualified residence, reduced by

(II) the amount of acquisition indebtedness with respect to such residence.

(ii) LIMITATION.—The aggregate amount treated as home equity indebtedness for any period shall not exceed $100,000 ($50,000 in the case of a separate return by a married individual).

* * *

(F) SPECIAL RULES FOR TAXABLE YEARS 2018 THROUGH 2025.—

(i) IN GENERAL.—In the case of taxable years beginning after December 31, 2017, and before January 1, 2026—

(I) DISALLOWANCE OF HOME EQUITY INDEBTEDNESS INTEREST.—Subparagraph (A)(ii) shall not apply.

(II) LIMITATION ON ACQUISITION INDEBTEDNESS.—Subparagraph (B)(ii) shall be applied by substituting "$750,000 ($375,000[)]" for "$1,000,000 ($500,000[)]".

(III) TREATMENT OF INDEBTEDNESS INCURRED ON OR BEFORE DECEMBER 15, 2017.—Subclause (II) shall not apply to any indebtedness incurred on or before December 15, 2017, and, in applying such subclause to any indebtedness incurred after such date, the limitation under such subclause shall be reduced (but not below zero) by the amount of any indebtedness incurred on or before December 15, 2017, which is treated as acquisition indebtedness for purposes of this subsection for the taxable year.

(IV) BINDING CONTRACT EXCEPTION.—In the case of a taxpayer who enters into a written binding contract before December 15, 2017, to close on the purchase of a principal residence before January 1, 2018, and who purchases such residence before April 1, 2018, subclause (III) shall be applied by substituting "April 1, 2018" for "December 15, 2017".

(ii) TREATMENT OF LIMITATION IN TAXABLE YEARS AFTER DECEMBER 31, 2025.—In the case of taxable years beginning after December 31, 2025, the limitation under subparagraph (B)(ii) shall be applied to the aggregate amount of indebtedness of the taxpayer described in subparagraph (B)(i) without regard to the taxable year in which the indebtedness was incurred.

(iii) TREATMENT OF REFINANCINGS OF INDEBTEDNESS.—

(I) IN GENERAL.—In the case of any indebtedness which is incurred to refinance indebtedness, such refinanced indebtedness shall be treated for purposes of clause (i)(III) as incurred on the date that the original indebtedness was incurred to the extent the amount of the indebtedness resulting from such refinancing does not exceed the amount of the refinanced indebtedness.

(II) LIMITATION ON PERIOD OF REFINANCING.—Subclause (I) shall not apply to any indebtedness after the expiration of the term of the original indebtedness or, if the principal of such original indebtedness is not amortized over its term, the expiration of the term of the 1st refinancing of such indebtedness (or if earlier, the date which is 30 years after the date of such 1st refinancing).

(iv) COORDINATION WITH EXCLUSION OF INCOME FROM DISCHARGE OF INDEBTEDNESS.—Section 108(h)(2) shall be applied without regard to this subparagraph.

(4) OTHER DEFINITIONS AND SPECIAL RULES.—For purposes of this subsection—

(A) QUALIFIED RESIDENCE.—

(i) IN GENERAL.—The term "qualified residence" means—

(I) the principal residence (within the meaning of section 121) of the taxpayer, and

(II) 1 other residence of the taxpayer which is selected by the taxpayer for purposes of this subsection for the taxable year and which is used by the taxpayer as a residence (within the meaning of section 280A(d)(1)).

(ii) MARRIED INDIVIDUALS FILING SEPARATE RETURNS.—If a married couple does not file a joint return for the taxable year—

(I) such couple shall be treated as 1 taxpayer for purposes of clause (i), and

(II) each individual shall be entitled to take into account 1 residence unless both individuals consent in writing to 1 individual taking into account the principal residence and 1 other residence.

(iii) RESIDENCE NOT RENTED.—For purposes of clause (i)(II), notwithstanding section 280A(d)(1), if the taxpayer does not rent a dwelling unit at any time during a taxable year, such unit may be treated as a residence for such taxable year.

(B) SPECIAL RULE FOR COOPERATIVE HOUSING CORPORATIONS.—Any indebtedness secured by stock held by the taxpayer as a tenant-stockholder (as defined in section 216) in a cooperative housing corporation (as so defined) shall be treated as secured by the house or apartment which the taxpayer is entitled to occupy as such a tenant-stockholder. If stock described in the preceding sentence may not be used to secure indebtedness, indebtedness shall be treated as so secured if the taxpayer establishes to the satisfaction of the Secretary that such indebtedness was incurred to acquire such stock.

(C) UNENFORCEABLE SECURITY INTERESTS.—Indebtedness shall not fail to be treated as secured by any property solely because, under any applicable State or local homestead or other debtor protection law in effect on August 16, 1986, the security interest is ineffective or the enforceability of the security interest is restricted.

(D) SPECIAL RULES FOR ESTATES AND TRUSTS.—For purposes of determining whether any interest paid or accrued by an estate or trust is qualified residence interest, any residence held by such estate or trust shall be treated as a qualified residence of such estate or trust if such estate or trust establishes that such residence is a qualified residence of a beneficiary who has a present interest in such estate or trust or an interest in the residuary of such estate or trust.

(E) QUALIFIED MORTGAGE INSURANCE.—The term "qualified mortgage insurance" means—

(i) mortgage insurance provided by the Department of Veterans Affairs, the Federal Housing Administration, or the Rural Housing Service, and

(ii) private mortgage insurance (as defined by section 2 of the Homeowners Protection Act of 1998 (12 U.S.C. 4901), as in effect on the date of the enactment of this subparagraph).

(F) SPECIAL RULES FOR PREPAID QUALIFIED MORTGAGE INSURANCE.—Any amount paid by the taxpayer for qualified mortgage insurance that is properly allocable to any mortgage the payment of which extends to periods that are after the close of the taxable year in which such amount is paid shall be chargeable to capital account and shall be treated as paid in such periods to which so allocated. No deduction shall be allowed for the unamortized balance of such account if such mortgage is satisfied before the end of its term. The preceding sentences shall not apply to amounts paid for qualified mortgage insurance provided by the Department of Veterans Affairs or the Rural Housing Service.

[Sec. 163(j)]

(j) LIMITATION ON BUSINESS INTEREST.—

(1) IN GENERAL.—The amount allowed as a deduction under this chapter for any taxable year for business interest shall not exceed the sum of—

(A) the business interest income of such taxpayer for such taxable year,

(B) 30 percent of the adjusted taxable income of such taxpayer for such taxable year, plus

(C) the floor plan financing interest of such taxpayer for such taxable year.

The amount determined under subparagraph (B) shall not be less than zero.

(2) CARRYFORWARD OF DISALLOWED BUSINESS INTEREST.—The amount of any business interest not allowed as a deduction for any taxable year by reason of paragraph (1) shall be treated as business interest paid or accrued in the succeeding taxable year.

(3) EXEMPTION FOR CERTAIN SMALL BUSINESSES.—In the case of any taxpayer (other than a tax shelter prohibited from using the cash receipts and disbursements method of accounting under section 448(a)(3)) which meets the gross receipts test of section 448(c) for any taxable year, paragraph (1) shall not apply to such taxpayer for such taxable year. In the case of any taxpayer which is not a corporation or a partnership, the gross receipts test of section 448(c) shall be applied in the same manner as if such taxpayer were a corporation or partnership.

(4) APPLICATION TO PARTNERSHIPS, ETC.—

(A) IN GENERAL.—In the case of any partnership—

(i) this subsection shall be applied at the partnership level and any deduction for business interest shall be taken into account in determining the non-separately stated taxable income or loss of the partnership, and

(ii) the adjusted taxable income of each partner of such partnership—

(I) shall be determined without regard to such partner's distributive share of any items of income, gain, deduction, or loss of such partnership, and

(II) shall be increased by such partner's distributive share of such partnership's excess taxable income.

For purposes of clause (ii)(II), a partner's distributive share of partnership excess taxable income shall be determined in the same manner as the partner's distributive share of nonseparately stated taxable income or loss of the partnership.

(B) SPECIAL RULES FOR CARRYFORWARDS.—

(i) IN GENERAL.—The amount of any business interest not allowed as a deduction to a partnership for any taxable year by reason of paragraph (1) for any taxable year—

(I) shall not be treated under paragraph (2) as business interest paid or accrued by the partnership in the succeeding taxable year, and

(II) shall, subject to clause (ii), be treated as excess business interest which is allocated to each partner in the same manner as the non-separately stated taxable income or loss of the partnership.

(ii) TREATMENT OF EXCESS BUSINESS INTEREST ALLOCATED TO PARTNERS.—If a partner is allocated any excess business interest from a partnership under clause (i) for any taxable year—

(I) such excess business interest shall be treated as business interest paid or accrued by the partner in the next succeeding taxable year in which the partner is allocated excess taxable income from such partnership, but only to the extent of such excess taxable income, and

(II) any portion of such excess business interest remaining after the application of subclause (I) shall, subject to the limitations of subclause (I), be treated as business interest paid or accrued in succeeding taxable years.

For purposes of applying this paragraph, excess taxable income allocated to a partner from a partnership for any taxable year shall not be taken into account under paragraph (1)(A) with respect to any business interest other than excess business interest from the partnership until all such excess business interest for such taxable year and all preceding taxable years has been treated as paid or accrued under clause (ii).

(iii) BASIS ADJUSTMENTS.—

(I) IN GENERAL.—The adjusted basis of a partner in a partnership interest shall be reduced (but not below zero) by the amount of excess business interest allocated to the partner under clause (i)(II).

(II) SPECIAL RULE FOR DISPOSITIONS.—If a partner disposes of a partnership interest, the adjusted basis of the partner in the partnership interest shall be increased immediately before the disposition by the amount of the excess (if any) of the amount of the basis reduction under subclause (I) over the portion of any excess business interest allocated to the partner under clause (i)(II) which has previously been treated under clause (ii) as business interest paid or accrued by the partner. The preceding sentence shall also apply to transfers of the partnership interest (including by reason of death) in a transaction in which gain is not recognized in whole or in part. No deduction shall be allowed to the transferor or transferee under this chapter for any excess business interest resulting in a basis increase under this subclause.

(C) EXCESS TAXABLE INCOME.—The term "excess taxable income" means, with respect to any partnership, the amount which bears the same ratio to the partnership's adjusted taxable income as—

(i) the excess (if any) of—

(I) the amount determined for the partnership under paragraph (1)(B), over

(II) the amount (if any) by which the business interest of the partnership, reduced by the floor plan financing interest, exceeds the business interest income of the partnership, bears to

(ii) the amount determined for the partnership under paragraph (1)(B).

(D) APPLICATION TO S CORPORATIONS.—Rules similar to the rules of subparagraphs (A) and (C) shall apply with respect to any S corporation and its shareholders.

(5) BUSINESS INTEREST.—For purposes of this subsection, the term "business interest" means any interest paid or accrued on indebtedness properly allocable to a trade or business. Such term shall not include investment interest (within the meaning of subsection (d)).

(6) BUSINESS INTEREST INCOME.—For purposes of this subsection, the term "business interest income" means the amount of interest includible in the gross income of the taxpayer for the taxable year which is properly allocable to a trade or business. Such term shall not include investment income (within the meaning of subsection (d)).

(7) TRADE OR BUSINESS.—For purposes of this subsection—

(A) IN GENERAL.—The term "trade or business" shall not include—

(i) the trade or business of performing services as an employee,

(ii) any electing real property trade or business,

(iii) any electing farming business, or

(iv) the trade or business of the furnishing or sale of—

(I) electrical energy, water, or sewage disposal services,

(II) gas or steam through a local distribution system, or

(III) transportation of gas or steam by pipeline,

if the rates for such furnishing or sale, as the case may be, have been established or approved by a State or political subdivision thereof, by any agency or instrumentality of the United States, by a public service or public utility commission or other similar body of any State or political subdivision thereof, or by the governing or ratemaking body of an electric cooperative.

(B) ELECTING REAL PROPERTY TRADE OR BUSINESS.—For purposes of this paragraph, the term "electing real property trade or business" means any trade or business which is described in section 469(c)(7)(C) and which makes an election under this subparagraph. Any such election shall be made at such time and in such manner as the Secretary shall prescribe, and, once made, shall be irrevocable.

(C) ELECTING FARMING BUSINESS.—For purposes of this paragraph, the term "electing farming business" means—

(i) a farming business (as defined in section 263A(e)(4)) which makes an election under this subparagraph, or

(ii) any trade or business of a specified agricultural or horticultural cooperative (as defined in section 199A(g)(2)) with respect to which the cooperative makes an election under this subparagraph.

Any such election shall be made at such time and in such manner as the Secretary shall prescribe, and, once made, shall be irrevocable.

(8) ADJUSTED TAXABLE INCOME.—For purposes of this subsection, the term "adjusted taxable income" means the taxable income of the taxpayer—

(A) computed without regard to—

(i) any item of income, gain, deduction, or loss which is not properly allocable to a trade or business,

(ii) any business interest or business interest income,

(iii) the amount of any net operating loss deduction under section 172,

(iv) the amount of any deduction allowed under section 199A, and

(v) in the case of taxable years beginning before January 1, 2022, any deduction allowable for depreciation, amortization, or depletion, and

(B) computed with such other adjustments as provided by the Secretary.

(9) FLOOR PLAN FINANCING INTEREST DEFINED.—For purposes of this subsection—

(A) IN GENERAL.—The term "floor plan financing interest" means interest paid or accrued on floor plan financing indebtedness.

(B) FLOOR PLAN FINANCING INDEBTEDNESS.—The term "floor plan financing indebtedness" means indebtedness—

(i) used to finance the acquisition of motor vehicles held for sale or lease, and

(ii) secured by the inventory so acquired.

(C) MOTOR VEHICLE.—The term "motor vehicle" means a motor vehicle that is any of the following:

(i) Any self-propelled vehicle designed for transporting persons or property on a public street, highway, or road.

(ii) A boat.

(iii) Farm machinery or equipment.

(10) SPECIAL RULE FOR TAXABLE YEARS BEGINNING IN 2019 AND 2020.—

(A) IN GENERAL.—

(i) IN GENERAL.—Except as provided in clause (ii) or (iii), in the case of any taxable year beginning in 2019 or 2020, paragraph (1)(B) shall be applied by substituting "50 percent" for "30 percent".

(ii) SPECIAL RULE FOR PARTNERSHIPS.—In the case of a partnership—

(I) clause (i) shall not apply to any taxable year beginning in 2019, but

(II) unless a partner elects not to have this subclause apply, in the case of any excess business interest of the partnership for any taxable year beginning in 2019 which is allocated to the partner under paragraph (4)(B)(i)(II)—

(aa) 50 percent of such excess business interest shall be treated as business interest which, notwithstanding paragraph (4)(B)(ii), is paid or accrued by the partner in the partner's first taxable year beginning in 2020 and which is not subject to the limits of paragraph (1), and

(bb) 50 percent of such excess business interest shall be subject to the limitations of paragraph (4)(B)(ii) in the same manner as any other excess business interest so allocated.

(iii) ELECTION OUT.—A taxpayer may elect, at such time and in such manner as the Secretary may prescribe, not to have clause (i) apply to any taxable year. Such an election, once made, may be revoked only with the consent of the Secretary. In the case of a partnership, any such election shall be made by the partnership and may be made only for taxable years beginning in 2020.

(B) ELECTION TO USE 2019 ADJUSTED TAXABLE INCOME FOR TAXABLE YEARS BEGINNING IN 2020.—

(i) IN GENERAL.—Subject to clause (ii), in the case of any taxable year beginning in 2020, the taxpayer may elect to apply this subsection by substituting the adjusted taxable income of the taxpayer for the last taxable year beginning in 2019 for the adjusted taxable income for such taxable year. In the case of a partnership, any such election shall be made by the partnership.

(ii) SPECIAL RULE FOR SHORT TAXABLE YEARS.—If an election is made under clause (i) for a taxable year which is a short taxable year, the adjusted taxable income for the taxpayer's last taxable year beginning in 2019 which is substituted under clause (i) shall be equal to the amount which bears the same ratio to such adjusted taxable income determined without regard to this clause as the number of months in the short taxable year bears to 12.

(11) CROSS REFERENCES.—

(A) For requirement that an electing real property trade or business use the alternative depreciation system, see section 168(g)(1)(F).

(B) For requirement that an electing farming business use the alternative depreciation system, see section 168(g)(1)(G).

* * *

[Sec. 163(l)]

(l) DISALLOWANCE OF DEDUCTION ON CERTAIN DEBT INSTRUMENTS OF CORPORATIONS.—

(1) IN GENERAL.—No deduction shall be allowed under this chapter for any interest paid or accrued on a disqualified debt instrument.

(2) DISQUALIFIED DEBT INSTRUMENT.—For purposes of this subsection, the term "disqualified debt instrument" means any indebtedness of a corporation which is payable in equity of the issuer or a related party or equity held by the issuer (or any related party) in any other person.

(3) SPECIAL RULES FOR AMOUNTS PAYABLE IN EQUITY.—For purposes of paragraph (2), indebtedness shall be treated as payable in equity of the issuer or any other person only if—

(A) a substantial amount of the principal or interest is required to be paid or converted, or at the option of the issuer or a related party is payable in, or convertible into, such equity,

(B) a substantial amount of the principal or interest is required to be determined, or at the option of the issuer or a related party is determined, by reference to the value of such equity, or

(C) the indebtedness is part of an arrangement which is reasonably expected to result in a transaction described in subparagraph (A) or (B).

For purposes of this paragraph, principal or interest shall be treated as required to be so paid, converted, or determined if it may be required at the option of the holder or a related party and there is a substantial certainty the option will be exercised.

(4) CAPITALIZATION ALLOWED WITH RESPECT TO EQUITY OF PERSONS OTHER THAN ISSUER AND RELATED PARTIES.—If the disqualified debt instrument of a corporation is payable in equity held by the issuer (or any related party) in any other person (other than a related party), the basis of such equity shall be increased by the amount not allowed as a deduction by reason of paragraph (1) with respect to the instrument.

(5) EXCEPTION FOR CERTAIN INSTRUMENTS ISSUED BY DEALERS IN SECURITIES.—For purposes of this subsection, the term "disqualified debt instrument" does not include indebtedness issued by a dealer in securities (or a related party) which is payable in, or by reference to, equity (other than equity of the issuer or a related party) held by such dealer in its capacity as a dealer in securities. For purposes of this paragraph, the term "dealer in securities" has the meaning given such term by section 475.

(6) RELATED PARTY.—For purposes of this subsection, a person is a related party with respect to another person if such person bears a relationship to such other person described in section 267(b) or 707(b).

(7) REGULATIONS.—The Secretary shall prescribe such regulations as may be necessary or appropriate to carry out the purposes of this subsection, including regulations preventing avoidance of this subsection through the use of an issuer other than a corporation.

* * *

[Sec. 164]

SEC. 164. TAXES.

[Sec. 164(a)]

(a) GENERAL RULE.—Except as otherwise provided in this section, the following taxes shall be allowed as a deduction for the taxable year within which paid or accrued:

(1) State and local, and foreign, real property taxes.

(2) State and local personal property taxes.

(3) State and local, and foreign, income, war profits, and excess profits taxes.

(4) The GST tax imposed on income distributions.

In addition, there shall be allowed as a deduction State and local, and foreign, taxes not described in the preceding sentence which are paid or accrued within the taxable year in carrying on a trade or business or an activity described in section 212 (relating to expenses for production of income). Notwithstanding the preceding sentence, any tax (not described in the first sentence of this subsection) which is paid or accrued by the taxpayer in connection with an acquisition or disposition of property shall be treated as part of the cost of the acquired property or, in the case of a disposition, as a reduction in the amount realized on the disposition.

[Sec. 164(b)]

(b) DEFINITIONS AND SPECIAL RULES.—For purposes of this section—

(1) PERSONAL PROPERTY TAXES.—The term "personal property tax" means an ad valorem tax which is imposed on an annual basis in respect of personal property.

(2) STATE OR LOCAL TAXES.—A State or local tax includes only a tax imposed by a State, a possession of the United States, or a political subdivision of any of the foregoing, or by the District of Columbia.

(3) FOREIGN TAXES.—A foreign tax includes only a tax imposed by the authority of a foreign country.

(4) SPECIAL RULES FOR GST TAX.—

(A) IN GENERAL.—The GST tax imposed on income distributions is—

(i) the tax imposed by section 2601, and

(ii) any State tax described in section 2604 (as in effect before its repeal),

but only to the extent such tax is imposed on a transfer which is included in the gross income of the distributee and to which section 666 does not apply.

(B) SPECIAL RULE FOR TAX PAID BEFORE DUE DATE.—Any tax referred to in subparagraph (A) imposed with respect to a transfer occurring during the taxable year of the distributee (or, in the case of a taxable termination, the trust) which is paid not later than the time prescribed by law (including extensions) for filing the return with respect to such transfer shall be treated as having been paid on the last day of the taxable year in which the transfer was made.

(5) GENERAL SALES TAXES.—For purposes of subsection (a)—

(A) ELECTION TO DEDUCT STATE AND LOCAL SALES TAXES IN LIEU OF STATE AND LOCAL INCOME TAXES.—At the election of the taxpayer for the taxable year, subsection (a) shall be applied—

(i) without regard to the reference to State and local income taxes, and

(ii) as if State and local general sales taxes were referred to in a paragraph thereof.

(B) DEFINITION OF GENERAL SALES TAX.—The term "general sales tax" means a tax imposed at one rate with respect to the sale at retail of a broad range of classes of items.

(C) SPECIAL RULES FOR FOOD, ETC.—In the case of items of food, clothing, medical supplies, and motor vehicles—

(i) the fact that the tax does not apply with respect to some or all of such items shall not be taken into account in determining whether the tax applies with respect to a broad range of classes of items, and

(ii) the fact that the rate of tax applicable with respect to some or all of such items is lower than the general rate of tax shall not be taken into account in determining whether the tax is imposed at one rate.

(D) ITEMS TAXED AT DIFFERENT RATES.—Except in the case of a lower rate of tax applicable with respect to an item described in subparagraph (C), no deduction shall be allowed under this paragraph for any general sales tax imposed with respect to an item at a rate other than the general rate of tax.

(E) COMPENSATING USE TAXES.—A compensating use tax with respect to an item shall be treated as a general sales tax. For purposes of the preceding sentence, the term "compensating use tax" means, with respect to any item, a tax which—

(i) is imposed on the use, storage, or consumption of such item, and

(ii) is complementary to a general sales tax, but only if a deduction is allowable under this paragraph with respect to items sold at retail in the taxing jurisdiction which are similar to such item.

(F) SPECIAL RULE FOR MOTOR VEHICLES.—In the case of motor vehicles, if the rate of tax exceeds the general rate, such excess shall be disregarded and the general rate shall be treated as the rate of tax.

(G) SEPARATELY STATED GENERAL SALES TAXES.—If the amount of any general sales tax is separately stated, then, to the extent that the amount so stated is paid by the consumer (other than in connection with the consumer's trade or business) to the seller, such amount shall be treated as a tax imposed on, and paid by, such consumer.

(H) AMOUNT OF DEDUCTION MAY BE DETERMINED UNDER TABLES.—

(i) IN GENERAL.—At the election of the taxpayer for the taxable year, the amount of the deduction allowed under this paragraph for such year shall be—

(I) the amount determined under this paragraph (without regard to this subparagraph) with respect to motor vehicles, boats, and other items specified by the Secretary, and

(II) the amount determined under tables prescribed by the Secretary with respect to items to which subclause (I) does not apply.

(ii) REQUIREMENTS FOR TABLES.—The tables prescribed under clause (i)—

(I) shall reflect the provisions of this paragraph,

(II) shall be based on the average consumption by taxpayers on a State-by-State basis (as determined by the Secretary) of items to which clause (i)(I) does not apply, taking into account filing status, number of dependents, adjusted gross income, and rates of State and local general sales taxation, and

(III) need only be determined with respect to adjusted gross incomes up to the applicable amount (as determined under section 68(b)).

(6) LIMITATION ON INDIVIDUAL DEDUCTIONS FOR TAXABLE YEARS 2018 THROUGH 2025.—In the case of an individual and a taxable year beginning after December 31, 2017, and before January 1, 2026—

(A) foreign real property taxes shall not be taken into account under subsection (a)(1), and

(B) the aggregate amount of taxes taken into account under paragraphs (1), (2), and (3) of subsection (a) and paragraph (5) of this subsection for any taxable year shall not exceed $10,000 ($5,000 in the case of a married individual filing a separate return).

The preceding sentence shall not apply to any foreign taxes described in subsection (a)(3) or to any taxes described in paragraph (1) and (2) of subsection (a) which are paid or accrued in carrying on a trade or business or an activity described in section 212. For purposes of subparagraph (B), an amount paid in a taxable year beginning before January 1, 2018, with respect to a State or local income tax imposed for a taxable year beginning after December 31, 2017, shall be treated as paid on the last day of the taxable year for which such tax is so imposed.

[Sec. 164(c)]

(c) DEDUCTION DENIED IN CASE OF CERTAIN TAXES.—No deduction shall be allowed for the following taxes:

(1) Taxes assessed against local benefits of a kind tending to increase the value of the property assessed; but this paragraph shall not prevent the deduction of so much of such taxes as is properly allocable to maintenance or interest charges.

(2) Taxes on real property, to the extent that subsection (d) requires such taxes to be treated as imposed on another taxpayer.

[Sec. 164(d)]

(d) APPORTIONMENT OF TAXES ON REAL PROPERTY BETWEEN SELLER AND PURCHASER.—

(1) GENERAL RULE.—For purposes of subsection (a), if real property is sold during any real property tax year, then—

(A) so much of the real property tax as is properly allocable to that part of such year which ends on the day before the date of the sale shall be treated as a tax imposed on the seller, and

(B) so much of such tax as is properly allocable to that part of such year which begins on the date of the sale shall be treated as a tax imposed on the purchaser.

(2) SPECIAL RULES.—

(A) In the case of any sale of real property, if—

(i) a taxpayer may not, by reason of his method of accounting, deduct any amount for taxes unless paid, and

(ii) the other party to the sale is (under the law imposing the real property tax) liable for the real property tax for the real property tax year,

then for purposes of subsection (a) the taxpayer shall be treated as having paid, on the date of the sale, so much of such tax as, under paragraph (1) of this subsection, is treated as imposed on the taxpayer. For purposes of the preceding sentence, if neither party is liable for the tax, then the party holding the property at the time the tax becomes a lien on the property shall be considered liable for the real property tax for the real property tax year.

(B) In the case of any sale of real property, if the taxpayer's taxable income for the taxable year during which the sale occurs is computed under an accrual method of accounting, and if no election under section 461 (c) (relating to the accrual of real property taxes) applies, then, for purposes of subsection (a), that portion of such tax which—

(i) is treated, under paragraph (1) of this subsection, as imposed on the taxpayer, and

(ii) may not, by reason of the taxpayer's method of accounting, be deducted by the taxpayer for any taxable year,

shall be treated as having accrued on the date of the sale.

[Sec. 164(e)]

(e) TAXES OF SHAREHOLDER PAID BY CORPORATION.—Where a corporation pays a tax imposed on a shareholder on his interest as a shareholder, and where the shareholder does not reimburse the corporation, then—

(1) the deduction allowed by subsection (a) shall be allowed to the corporation; and

(2) no deduction shall be allowed the shareholder for such tax.

[Sec. 164(f)]

(f) DEDUCTION FOR ONE-HALF OF SELF-EMPLOYMENT TAXES.—

(1) IN GENERAL.—In the case of an individual, in addition to the taxes described in subsection (a), there shall be allowed as a deduction for the taxable year an amount equal to one-half of the taxes imposed by section 1401 (other than the taxes imposed by section 1401(b)(2)) for such taxable year.

(2) DEDUCTION TREATED AS ATTRIBUTABLE TO TRADE OR BUSINESS.—For purposes of this chapter, the deduction allowed by paragraph (1) shall be treated as attributable to a trade or business carried on by the taxpayer which does not consist of the performance of services by the taxpayer as an employee.

* * *

[Sec. 165]

SEC. 165. LOSSES.

[Sec. 165(a)]

(a) GENERAL RULE.—There shall be allowed as a deduction any loss sustained during the taxable year and not compensated for by insurance or otherwise.

[Sec. 165(b)]

(b) AMOUNT OF DEDUCTION.—For purposes of subsection (a), the basis for determining the amount of the deduction for any loss shall be the adjusted basis provided in section 1011 for determining the loss from the sale or other disposition of property.

[Sec. 165(c)]

(c) LIMITATION ON LOSSES OF INDIVIDUALS.—In the case of an individual, the deduction under subsection (a) shall be limited to—

(1) losses incurred in a trade or business;

(2) losses incurred in any transaction entered into for profit, though not connected with a trade or business; and

(3) except as provided in subsection (h), losses of property not connected with a trade or business or a transaction entered into for profit, if such losses arise from fire, storm, shipwreck, or other casualty, or from theft.

[Sec. 165(d)]

(d) WAGERING LOSSES.—Losses from wagering transactions shall be allowed only to the extent of the gains from such transactions. For purposes of the preceding sentence, in the case of taxable years beginning after December 31, 2017, and before January 1, 2026, the term "losses from wagering transactions" includes any deduction otherwise allowable under this chapter incurred in carrying on any wagering transaction.

[Sec. 165(e)]

(e) THEFT LOSSES.—For purposes of subsection (a), any loss arising from theft shall be treated as sustained during the taxable year in which the taxpayer discovers such loss.

[Sec. 165(f)]

(f) CAPITAL LOSSES.—Losses from sales or exchanges of capital assets shall be allowed only to the extent allowed in sections 1211 and 1212.

[Sec. 165(g)]

(g) WORTHLESS SECURITIES.—

(1) GENERAL RULE.—If any security which is a capital asset becomes worthless during the taxable year, the loss resulting therefrom shall, for purposes of this subtitle, be treated as a loss from the sale or exchange, on the last day of the taxable year, of a capital asset.

(2) SECURITY DEFINED.—For purposes of this subsection, the term "security" means—

(A) a share of stock in a corporation;

(B) a right to subscribe for, or to receive, a share of stock in a corporation; or

(C) a bond, debenture, note, or certificate, or other evidence of indebtedness, issued by a corporation or by a government or political subdivision thereof, with interest coupons or in registered form.

(3) SECURITIES IN AFFILIATED CORPORATION.—For purposes of paragraph (1), any security in a corporation affiliated with a taxpayer which is a domestic corporation shall not be treated as a capital asset. For purposes of the preceding sentence, a corporation shall be treated as affiliated with the taxpayer only if—

(A) the taxpayer owns directly stock in such corporation meeting the requirements of section 1504(a)(2), and

(B) more than 90 percent of the aggregate of its gross receipts for all taxable years has been from sources other than royalties, rents (except rents derived from rental of properties to employees of the corporation in the ordinary course of its operating business), dividends, interest (except interest received on deferred purchase price of operating assets sold), annuities, and gains from sales or exchanges of stocks and securities.

In computing gross receipts for purposes of the preceding sentence, gross receipts from sales or exchanges of stocks and securities shall be taken into account only to the extent of gains therefrom.

[Sec. 165(h)]

(h) TREATMENT OF CASUALTY GAINS AND LOSSES.—

(1) DOLLAR LIMITATION PER CASUALTY.—Any loss of an individual described in subsection (c)(3) shall be allowed only to the extent that the amount of the loss to such individual arising from each casualty, or from each theft, exceeds $500 ($100 for taxable years beginning after December 31, 2009).

(2) NET CASUALTY LOSS ALLOWED ONLY TO THE EXTENT IT EXCEEDS 10 PERCENT OF ADJUSTED GROSS INCOME.—

(A) IN GENERAL.—If the personal casualty losses for any taxable year exceed the personal casualty gains for such taxable year, such losses shall be allowed for the taxable year only to the extent of the sum of—

(i) the amount of the personal casualty gains for the taxable year, plus

(ii) so much of such excess as exceeds 10 percent of the adjusted gross income of the individual.

(B) SPECIAL RULE WHERE PERSONAL CASUALTY GAINS EXCEED PERSONAL CASUALTY LOSSES.—If the personal casualty gains for any taxable year exceed the personal casualty losses for such taxable year—

(i) all such gains shall be treated as gains from sales or exchanges of capital assets, and

(ii) all such losses shall be treated as losses from sales or exchanges of capital assets.

(3) DEFINITIONS OF PERSONAL CASUALTY GAIN AND PERSONAL CASUALTY LOSS.—For purposes of this subsection—

(A) PERSONAL CASUALTY GAIN.—The term "personal casualty gain" means the recognized gain from any involuntary conversion of property, which is described in subsection (c)(3) arising from fire, storm, shipwreck, or other casualty, or from theft.

(B) PERSONAL CASUALTY LOSS.—The term "personal casualty loss" means any loss described in subsection (c)(3). For purposes of paragraph (2), the amount of any personal casualty loss shall be determined after the application of paragraph (1).

(4) SPECIAL RULES.—

(A) PERSONAL CASUALTY LOSSES ALLOWABLE IN COMPUTING ADJUSTED GROSS INCOME TO THE EXTENT OF PERSONAL CASUALTY GAINS.—In any case to which paragraph (2)(A) applies, the deduction for personal casualty losses for any taxable year shall be treated as a deduction allowable in computing adjusted gross income to the extent such losses do not exceed the personal casualty gains for the taxable year.

(B) JOINT RETURNS.—For purposes of this subsection, a husband and wife making a joint return for the taxable year shall be treated as 1 individual.

(C) DETERMINATION OF ADJUSTED GROSS INCOME IN CASE OF ESTATES AND TRUSTS.—For purposes of paragraph (2), the adjusted gross income of an estate or trust shall be computed in the same manner as in the case of an individual, except that the deductions for costs paid or incurred in connection with the administration of the estate or trust shall be treated as allowable in arriving at adjusted gross income.

(D) COORDINATION WITH ESTATE TAX.—No loss described in subsection (c)(3) shall be allowed if, at the time of filing the return, such loss has been claimed for estate tax purposes in the estate tax return.

(E) CLAIM REQUIRED TO BE FILED IN CERTAIN CASES.—Any loss of an individual described in subsection (c)(3) to the extent covered by insurance shall be taken into account under this section only if the individual files a timely insurance claim with respect to such loss.

(5) LIMITATION FOR TAXABLE YEARS 2018 THROUGH 2025.—

(A) IN GENERAL.—In the case of an individual, except as provided in subparagraph (B), any personal casualty loss which (but for this paragraph) would be deductible in a taxable year beginning after December 31, 2017, and before January 1, 2026, shall be allowed as a deduction under subsection (a) only to the extent it is attributable to a Federally declared disaster (as defined in subsection (i)(5)).

(B) EXCEPTION RELATED TO PERSONAL CASUALTY GAINS.—If a taxpayer has personal casualty gains for any taxable year to which subparagraph (A) applies—

(i) subparagraph (A) shall not apply to the portion of the personal casualty loss not attributable to a Federally declared disaster (as so defined) to the extent such loss does not exceed such gains, and

(ii) in applying paragraph (2) for purposes of subparagraph (A) to the portion of personal casualty loss which is so attributable to such a disaster, the amount of personal casualty gains taken into account under paragraph (2)(A) shall be reduced by the portion of such gains taken into account under clause (i).

[Sec. 165(i)]

(i) DISASTER LOSSES.—

(1) ELECTION TO TAKE DEDUCTION FOR PRECEDING YEAR.—Notwithstanding the provisions of subsection (a), any loss occurring in a disaster area and attributable to a federally declared disaster may, at the election of the taxpayer, be taken into account for the taxable year immediately preceding the taxable year in which the disaster occurred.

(2) YEAR OF LOSS.—If an election is made under this subsection, the casualty resulting in the loss shall be treated for purposes of this title as having occurred in the taxable year for which the deduction is claimed.

(3) AMOUNT OF LOSS.—The amount of the loss taken into account in the preceding taxable year by reason of paragraph (1) shall not exceed the uncompensated amount determined on the basis of the facts existing at the date the taxpayer claims the loss.

(4) USE OF DISASTER LOAN APPRAISALS TO ESTABLISH AMOUNT OF LOSS.—Nothing in this title shall be construed to prohibit the Secretary from prescribing regulations or other guidance under which an appraisal for the purpose of obtaining a loan of Federal funds or a loan guarantee from the Federal Government as a result of a federally declared disaster may be used to establish the amount of any loss described in paragraph (1) or (2).

(5) FEDERALLY DECLARED DISASTERS.—For purposes of this subsection—

(A) IN GENERAL.—The term "Federally declared disaster" means any disaster subsequently determined by the President of the United States to warrant assistance by the Federal Government under the Robert T. Stafford Disaster Relief and Emergency Assistance Act.

(B) DISASTER AREA.—The term "disaster area" means the area so determined to warrant such assistance.

[Sec. 166]

SEC. 166. BAD DEBTS.

[Sec. 166(a)]

(a) GENERAL RULE.—

(1) WHOLLY WORTHLESS DEBTS.—There shall be allowed as a deduction any debt which becomes worthless within the taxable year.

(2) PARTIALLY WORTHLESS DEBTS.—When satisfied that a debt is recoverable only in part, the Secretary may allow such debt, in an amount not in excess of the part charged off within the taxable year, as a deduction.

[Sec. 166(b)]

(b) AMOUNT OF DEDUCTION.—For purposes of subsection (a), the basis for determining the amount of the deduction for any bad debt shall be the adjusted basis provided in section 1011 for determining the loss from the sale or other disposition of property.

[Sec. 166(c)—Repealed]

[Sec. 166(d)]

(d) NONBUSINESS DEBTS.—

(1) GENERAL RULE.—In the case of a taxpayer other than a corporation—

(A) subsection (a) shall not apply to any nonbusiness debt; and

(B) where any nonbusiness debt becomes worthless within the taxable year, the loss resulting therefrom shall be considered a loss from the sale or exchange, during the taxable year, of a capital asset held for not more than 1 year.

(2) NONBUSINESS DEBT DEFINED.—For purposes of paragraph (1), the term "nonbusiness debt" means a debt other than—

(A) a debt created or acquired (as the case may be) in connection with a trade or business of the taxpayer; or

(B) a debt the loss from the worthlessness of which is incurred in the taxpayer's trade or business.

[Sec. 166(e)]

(e) WORTHLESS SECURITIES.—This section shall not apply to a debt which is evidenced by a security as defined in section 165(g) (2) (C).

* * *

[Sec. 167]

SEC. 167. DEPRECIATION.

[Sec. 167(a)]

(a) GENERAL RULE.—There shall be allowed as a depreciation deduction a reasonable allowance for the exhaustion, wear and tear (including a reasonable allowance for obsolescence)—

(1) of property used in the trade or business, or

(2) of property held for the production of income.

[Sec. 167(b)]

(b) CROSS REFERENCE.—

For determination of depreciation deduction in case of property to which section 168 applies, see section 168.

[Sec. 167(c)]

(c) BASIS FOR DEPRECIATION.—

(1) IN GENERAL.—The basis on which exhaustion, wear and tear, and obsolescence are to be allowed in respect of any property shall be the adjusted basis provided in section 1011, for the purpose of determining the gain on the sale or other disposition of such property.

(2) SPECIAL RULE FOR PROPERTY SUBJECT TO LEASE.—If any property is acquired subject to a lease—

(A) no portion of the adjusted basis shall be allocated to the leasehold interest, and

(B) the entire adjusted basis shall be taken into account in determining the depreciation deduction (if any) with respect to the property subject to the lease.

[Sec. 167(d)]

(d) LIFE TENANTS AND BENEFICIARIES OF TRUSTS AND ESTATES.—In the case of property held by one person for life with remainder to another person, the deduction shall be computed as if the life tenant were the absolute owner of the property and shall be allowed to the life tenant. In the case of property held in trust, the allowable deduction shall be apportioned between the income beneficiaries and the trustee in accordance with the pertinent provisions of the instrument creating the trust, or, in the absence of such provisions, on the basis of the trust income allocable to each. In the case of an estate, the allowable deduction shall be apportioned between the estate and the heirs, legatees, and devisees on the basis of the income of the estate allocable to each.

[Sec. 167(e)]

(e) CERTAIN TERM INTERESTS NOT DEPRECIABLE.—

(1) IN GENERAL.—No depreciation deduction shall be allowed under this section (and no depreciation or amortization deduction shall be allowed under any other provision of this subtitle) to the taxpayer for any term interest in property for any period during which the remainder interest in such property is held (directly or indirectly) by a related person.

(2) COORDINATION WITH OTHER PROVISIONS.—

(A) SECTION 273.—This subsection shall not apply to any term interest to which section 273 applies.

(B) SECTION 305(e).—This subsection shall not apply to the holder of the dividend rights which were separated from any stripped preferred stock to which section 305(e)(1) applies.

(3) BASIS ADJUSTMENTS.—If, but for this subsection, a depreciation or amortization deduction would be allowable to the taxpayer with respect to any term interest in property—

(A) the taxpayer's basis in such property shall be reduced by any depreciation or amortization deductions disallowed under this subsection, and

(B) the basis of the remainder interest in such property shall be increased by the amount of such disallowed deductions (properly adjusted for any depreciation deductions allowable under subsection (d) to the taxpayer).

(4) SPECIAL RULES.—

(A) DENIAL OF INCREASE IN BASIS OF REMAINDERMAN.—No increase in the basis of the remainder interest shall be made under paragraph (3)(B) for any disallowed deductions attributable to periods during which the term interest was held—

(i) by an organization exempt from tax under this subtitle, or

(ii) by a nonresident alien individual or foreign corporation but only if income from the term interest is not effectively connected with the conduct of a trade or business in the United States.

(B) COORDINATION WITH SUBSECTION (d).—If, but for this subsection, a depreciation or amortization deduction would be allowable to any person with respect to any term interest in property, the principles of subsection (d) shall apply to such person with respect to such term interest.

(5) DEFINITIONS.—For purposes of this subsection—

(A) TERM INTEREST IN PROPERTY.—The term "term interest in property" has the meaning given such term by section 1001(e)(2).

(B) RELATED PERSON.—The term "related person" means any person bearing a relationship to the taxpayer described in subsection (b) or (e) of section 267.

(6) REGULATIONS.—The Secretary shall prescribe such regulations as may be necessary to carry out the purposes of this subsection, including regulations preventing avoidance of this subsection through cross-ownership arrangements or otherwise.

[Sec. 167(f)]

(f) TREATMENT OF CERTAIN PROPERTY EXCLUDED FROM SECTION 197.—

(1) COMPUTER SOFTWARE.—

(A) IN GENERAL.—If a depreciation deduction is allowable under subsection (a) with respect to any computer software, such deduction shall be computed by using the straight line method and a useful life of 36 months.

(B) COMPUTER SOFTWARE.—For purposes of this section, the term "computer software" has the meaning given to such term by section 197(e)(3)(B); except that such term shall not include any such software which is an amortizable section 197 intangible.

(C) TAX-EXEMPT USE PROPERTY SUBJECT TO LEASE.—In the case of computer software which would be tax-exempt use property as defined in subsection (h) of section 168 if such section applied to computer software, the useful life under subparagraph (A) shall not be less than 125 percent of the lease term (within the meaning of section 168(i)(3)).

(2) CERTAIN INTERESTS OR RIGHTS ACQUIRED SEPARATELY.—If a depreciation deduction is allowable under subsection (a) with respect to any property described in subparagraph (B), (C), or (D) of section 197(e)(4), such deduction shall be computed in accordance with regulations prescribed by the Secretary. If such property would be tax-exempt use property as defined in subsection (h) of section 168 if such section applied to such property, the useful life under such regulations shall not be less than 125 percent of the lease term (within the meaning of section 168(i)(3)).

(3) MORTGAGE SERVICING RIGHTS.—If a depreciation deduction is allowable under subsection (a) with respect to any right described in section 197(e)(6), such deduction shall be computed by using the straight line method and a useful life of 108 months.

* * *

[Sec. 167(i)]

(i) CROSS REFERENCES.—

(1) For additional rule applicable to depreciation of improvements in the case of mines, oil and gas wells, other natural deposits, and timber, see section 611.

(2) For amortization of goodwill and certain other intangibles, see section 197.

»»→ Caution: Note: The Commissioner of Internal Revenue has promulgated optional tables for use by taxpayers in implementing the provisions of Section 168. The most important of the tables are reproduced beginning at page xv.

[Sec. 168]

SEC. 168. ACCELERATED COST RECOVERY SYSTEM.

[Sec. 168(a)]

(a) GENERAL RULE.—Except as otherwise provided in this section, the depreciation deduction provided by section 167(a) for any tangible property shall be determined by using—

(1) the applicable depreciation method,

(2) the applicable recovery period, and

(3) the applicable convention.

[Sec. 168(b)]

(b) APPLICABLE DEPRECIATION METHOD.—For purposes of this section—

(1) IN GENERAL.—Except as provided in paragraphs (2) and (3), the applicable depreciation method is—

(A) the 200 percent declining balance method,

(B) switching to the straight line method for the 1st taxable year for which using the straight line method with respect to the adjusted basis as of the beginning of such year will yield a larger allowance.

(2) 150 PERCENT DECLINING BALANCE METHOD IN CERTAIN CASES.—Paragraph (1) shall be applied by substituting "150 percent" for "200 percent" in the case of—

(A) any 15-year or 20-year property not referred to in paragraph (3),

(B) any property (other than property described in paragraph (3)) which is a qualified smart electric meter or qualified smart electric grid system, or

(C) any property (other than property described in paragraph (3)) with respect to which the taxpayer elects under paragraph (5) to have the provisions of this paragraph apply.

(3) PROPERTY TO WHICH STRAIGHT LINE METHOD APPLIES.—The applicable depreciation method shall be the straight line method in the case of the following property:

(A) Nonresidential real property.

(B) Residential rental property.

(C) Any railroad grading or tunnel bore.

(D) Property with respect to which the taxpayer elects under paragraph (5) to have the provisions of this paragraph apply.

(E) Property described in subsection (e) (3) (D) (ii).

(F) Water utility property described in subsection (e) (5).

(G) Qualified improvement property described in subsection (e) (6).

(4) SALVAGE VALUE TREATED AS ZERO.—Salvage value shall be treated as zero.

(5) ELECTION.—An election under paragraph (2) (D) or (3) (D) may be made with respect to 1 or more classes of property for any taxable year and once made with respect to any class shall apply to all property in such class placed in service during such taxable year. Such an election, once made, shall be irrevocable.

[Sec. 168(c)]

(c) APPLICABLE RECOVERY PERIOD.—For purposes of this section, the applicable recovery period shall be determined in accordance with the following table:

In the case of:	*The applicable recovery period is:*
3-year property	3 years
5-year property	5 years
7-year property	7 years
10-year property	10 years
15-year property	15 years
20-year property	20 years
Water utility property	25 years
Residential rental property	27.5 years
Nonresidential real property	39 years
Any railroad grading or tunnel bore	50 years

[Sec. 168(d)]

(d) APPLICABLE CONVENTION.—For purposes of this section—

(1) IN GENERAL.—Except as otherwise provided in this subsection, the applicable convention is the half-year convention.

(2) REAL PROPERTY.—In the case of—

(A) nonresidential real property,

(B) residential rental property, and

(C) any railroad grading or tunnel bore,

the applicable convention is the mid-month convention.

(3) SPECIAL RULE WHERE SUBSTANTIAL PROPERTY PLACED IN SERVICE DURING LAST 3 MONTHS OF TAXABLE YEAR.—

(A) IN GENERAL.—Except as provided in regulations, if during any taxable year—

(i) the aggregate bases of property to which this section applies placed in service during the last 3 months of the taxable year, exceed

(ii) 40 percent of the aggregate bases of property to which this section applies placed in service during such taxable year,

the applicable convention for all property to which this section applies placed in service during such taxable year shall be the mid-quarter convention.

(B) CERTAIN PROPERTY NOT TAKEN INTO ACCOUNT.—For purposes of subparagraph (A), there shall not be taken into account—

(i) any nonresidential real property, and residential rental property and railroad grading or tunnel bore, and

(ii) any other property placed in service and disposed of during the same taxable year.

(4) DEFINITIONS.—

(A) HALF-YEAR CONVENTION.—The half-year convention is a convention which treats all property placed in service during any taxable year (or disposed of during any taxable year) as placed in service (or disposed of) on the mid-point of such taxable year.

(B) MID-MONTH CONVENTION.—The mid-month convention is a convention which treats all property placed in service during any month (or disposed of during any month) as placed in service (or disposed of) on the mid-point of such month.

(C) MID-QUARTER CONVENTION.—The mid-quarter convention is a convention which treats all property placed in service during any quarter of a taxable year (or disposed of during any quarter of a taxable year) as placed in service (or disposed of) on the mid-point of such quarter.

[Sec. 168(e)]

(e) CLASSIFICATION OF PROPERTY.—For purposes of this section—

(1) IN GENERAL.—Except as otherwise provided in this subsection, property shall be classified under the following table:

Property shall be treated as:	*If such property has a class life (in years) of:*
3-year property	4 or less
5-year property	More than 4 but less than 10
7-year property	10 or more but less than 16
10-year property	16 or more but less than 20
15-year property	20 or more but less than 25
20-year property	25 or more.

(2) RESIDENTIAL RENTAL OR NONRESIDENTIAL REAL PROPERTY.—

(A) RESIDENTIAL RENTAL PROPERTY.—

(i) RESIDENTIAL RENTAL PROPERTY.—The term "residential rental property" means any building or structure if 80 percent or more of the gross rental income from such building or structure for the taxable year is rental income from dwelling units.

(ii) DEFINITIONS.—For purposes of clause (i)—

(I) the term "dwelling unit" means a house or apartment used to provide living accommodations in a building or structure, but does not include a unit in a hotel, motel, or other establishment more than one-half of the units in which are used on a transient basis, and

(II) if any portion of the building or structure is occupied by the taxpayer, the gross rental income from such building or structure shall include the rental value of the portion so occupied.

(B) NONRESIDENTIAL REAL PROPERTY.—The term "nonresidential real property" means section 1250 property which is not—

(i) residential rental property, or

(ii) property with a class life of less than 27.5 years.

(3) CLASSIFICATION OF CERTAIN PROPERTY.—

(A) 3-YEAR PROPERTY.—The term "3-year property" includes—

(i) any race horse—

(I) which is placed in service before January 1, 2021, and

(II) which is placed in service after December 31, 2020, and which is more than 2 years old at the time such horse is placed in service by such purchaser,

(ii) any horse other than a race horse which is more than 12 years old at the time it is placed in service, and

(iii) any qualified rent-to-own property.

(B) 5-YEAR PROPERTY.—The term "5-year property" includes—

(i) any automobile or light general purpose truck,

(ii) any semi-conductor manufacturing equipment,

(iii) any computer-based telephone central office switching equipment,

(iv) any qualified technological equipment,

(v) any section 1245 property used in connection with research and experimentation,

(vi) any property which—

(I) is described in subparagraph (A) of section 48(a)(3) (or would be so described if "solar or wind energy" were substituted for "solar energy" in clause (i) thereof and the last sentence of such section did not apply to such subparagraph),

(II) is described in paragraph (15) of section 48(l) (as in effect on the day before the date of the enactment of the Revenue Reconciliation Act of 1990) and has a power production capacity of not greater than 80 megawatts, or

(III) is described in section 48(l)(3)(A)(ix) (as in effect on the day before the date of the enactment of the Revenue Reconciliation Act of 1990), and

(vii) any machinery or equipment (other than any grain bin, cotton ginning asset, fence, or other land improvement) which is used in a farming business (as defined in section 263A(e)(4)), the original use of which commences with the taxpayer after December 31, 2017.

Nothing in any provision of law shall be construed to treat property as not being described in subclause (I) or (II) of clause (vi) by reason of being public utility property.

(C) 7-YEAR PROPERTY.—The term "7-year property" includes—

(i) any railroad track,

(ii) any motorsports entertainment complex,

(iii) any Alaska natural gas pipeline,

(iv) any natural gas gathering line the original use of which commences with the taxpayer after April 11, 2005, and

(v) any property which—

(I) does not have a class life, and

(II) is not otherwise classified under paragraph (2) or this paragraph.

(D) 10-YEAR PROPERTY.—The term "10-year property" includes—

(i) any single purpose agricultural or horticultural structure (within the meaning of subsection (i)(13)),

(ii) any tree or vine bearing fruit or nuts,

(iii) any qualified smart electric meter, and

(iv) any qualified smart electric grid system.

(E) 15-YEAR PROPERTY.—The term "15-year property" includes—

(i) any municipal wastewater treatment plant,

(ii) any telephone distribution plant and comparable equipment used for 2-way exchange of voice and data communications,

(iii) any section 1250 property which is a retail motor fuels outlet (whether or not food or other convenience items are sold at the outlet),

(iv) initial clearing and grading land improvements with respect to gas utility property,

(v) any section 1245 property (as defined in section 1245(a)(3)) used in the transmission at 69 or more kilovolts of electricity for sale and the original use of which commences with the taxpayer after April 11, 2005,

(vi) any natural gas distribution line the original use of which commences with the taxpayer after April 11, 2005, and which is placed in service before January 1, 2011, and

(vii) any qualified improvement property.

(F) 20-YEAR PROPERTY.—The term "20-year property" means initial clearing and grading land improvements with respect to any electric utility transmission and distribution plant.

(4) RAILROAD GRADING OR TUNNEL BORE.—The term "railroad grading or tunnel bore" means all improvements resulting from excavations (including tunneling), construction of embankments, clearings, diversions of roads and streams, sodding of slopes, and from similar work necessary to provide, construct, reconstruct, alter, protect, improve, replace, or restore a roadbed or right-of-way for railroad track.

(5) WATER UTILITY PROPERTY.—The term "water utility property" means property—

(A) which is an integral part of the gathering, treatment, or commercial distribution of water, and which, without regard to this paragraph, would be 20-year property, and

(B) any municipal sewer.

(6) QUALIFIED IMPROVEMENT PROPERTY.—

(A) IN GENERAL.—The term "qualified improvement property" means any improvement made by the taxpayer to an interior portion of a building which is nonresidential real property if such improvement is placed in service after the date such building was first placed in service.

(B) CERTAIN IMPROVEMENTS NOT INCLUDED.—Such term shall not include any improvement for which the expenditure is attributable to—

(i) the enlargement of the building,

(ii) any elevator or escalator, or

(iii) the internal structural framework of the building.

[Sec. 168(f)]

(f) PROPERTY TO WHICH SECTION DOES NOT APPLY.—This section shall not apply to—

(1) CERTAIN METHODS OF DEPRECIATION.—Any property if—

(A) the taxpayer elects to exclude such property from the application of this section, and

(B) for the 1st taxable year for which a depreciation deduction would be allowable with respect to such property in the hands of the taxpayer, the property is properly depreciated under the unit-of-production method or any method of depreciation not expressed in a term of years (other than the retirement-replacement-betterment method or similar method).

(2) CERTAIN PUBLIC UTILITY PROPERTY.—Any public utility property (within the meaning of subsection (i)(10)) if the taxpayer does not use a normalization method of accounting.

(3) FILMS AND VIDEO TAPE.—Any motion picture film or video tape.

(4) SOUND RECORDINGS.—Any works which result from the fixation of a series of musical, spoken, or other sounds, regardless of the nature of the material (such as discs, tapes, or other phonorecordings) in which such sounds are embodied.

* * *

[Sec. 168(g)]

(g) ALTERNATIVE DEPRECIATION SYSTEM FOR CERTAIN PROPERTY.—

(1) IN GENERAL.—In the case of—

(A) any tangible property which during the taxable year is used predominantly outside the United States,

(B) any tax-exempt use property,

(C) any tax-exempt bond financed property,

(D) any imported property covered by an Executive order under paragraph (6),

(E) any property to which an election under paragraph (7) applies,

(F) any property described in paragraph (8), and

(G) any property with a recovery period of 10 years or more which is held by an electing farming business (as defined in section 163(j)(7)(C)),

the depreciation deduction provided by section 167(a) shall be determined under the alternative depreciation system.

(2) ALTERNATIVE DEPRECIATION SYSTEM.—For purposes of paragraph (1), the alternative depreciation system is depreciation determined by using—

(A) the straight line method (without regard to salvage value),

(B) the applicable convention determined under subsection (d), and

(C) a recovery period determined under the following table:

In the case of:	*The recovery period shall be:*
(i) Property not described in clause (ii) or (iii)	The class life.
(ii) Personal property with no class life	12 years.
(iii) Residential rental property	30 years
(iv) Nonresidential real property	40 years
(v) Any railroad grading or tunnel bore or water utility property	50 years

(3) SPECIAL RULES FOR DETERMINING CLASS LIFE.—

(A) TAX-EXEMPT USE PROPERTY SUBJECT TO LEASE.—In the case of any tax-exempt use property subject to a lease, the recovery period used for purposes of paragraph (2) shall (notwithstanding any other subparagraph of this paragraph) in no event be less than 125 percent of the lease term.

(B) SPECIAL RULE FOR CERTAIN PROPERTY ASSIGNED TO CLASSES.—For purposes of paragraph (2), in the case of property described in any of the following subparagraphs of subsection (e)(3), the class life shall be determined as follows:

If property is described in subparagraph:	*The class life is:*
(A) (iii)	4
(B) (ii)	5
(B) (iii)	9.5
(B) (vii)	10
(C) (i)	10
(C) (iii)	22
(C) (iv)	14
(D) (i)	15
(D) (ii)	20
(E) (i)	24
(E) (ii)	24
(E) (iii)	20
(E) (iv)	20
(E) (v)	30
(E) (vi)	35
(E) (vii)	20
(F)	25

(C) QUALIFIED TECHNOLOGICAL EQUIPMENT.—In the case of any qualified technological equipment, the recovery period used for purposes of paragraph (2) shall be 5 years.

(D) AUTOMOBILES, ETC.—In the case of any automobile or light general purpose truck, the recovery period used for purposes of paragraph (2) shall be 5 years.

(E) CERTAIN REAL PROPERTY.—In the case of any section 1245 property which is real property with no class life, the recovery period used for purposes of paragraph (2) shall be 40 years.

(4) EXCEPTION FOR CERTAIN PROPERTY USED OUTSIDE UNITED STATES.—Subparagraph (A) of paragraph (1) shall not apply to—

(A) any aircraft which is registered by the Administrator of the Federal Aviation Agency and which is operated to and from the United States or is operated under contract with the United States;

(B) rolling stock which is used within and without the United States and which is—

(i) of a rail carrier subject to part A of subtitle IV of title 49, or

(ii) of a United States person (other than a corporation described in clause (i)) but only if the rolling stock is not leased to one or more foreign persons for periods aggregating more than 12 months in any 24-month period;

(C) any vessel documented under the laws of the United States which is operated in the foreign or domestic commerce of the United States;

(D) any motor vehicle of a United States person (as defined in section 7701(a)(30)) which is operated to and from the United States;

(E) any container of a United States person which is used in the transportation of property to and from the United States;

(F) any property (other than a vessel or an aircraft of a United States person which is used for the purpose of exploring for, developing, removing, or transporting resources from the outer Continental Shelf (within the meaning of section 2 of the Outer Continental Shelf Lands Act, as amended and supplemented; (43 U.S.C. 1331));

(G) any property which is owned by a domestic corporation or by a United States citizen (other than a citizen entitled to the benefits of section 931 or 933) and which is used predominantly in a possession of the United States by such a corporation or such a citizen, or by a corporation created or organized in, or under the law of, a possession of the United States;

(H) any communications satellite (as defined in section 103(3) of the Communications Satellite Act of 1962, 47 U.S.C. 702(3)), or any interest therein, of a United States person;

(I) any cable, or any interest therein, of a domestic corporation engaged in furnishing telephone service to which section 168(i)(10)(C) applies (or of a wholly owned domestic subsidiary of such a corporation), if such cable is part of a submarine cable system which constitutes part of a communication link exclusively between the United States and one or more foreign countries;

(J) any property (other than a vessel or an aircraft) of a United States person which is used in international or territorial waters within the northern portion of the Western Hemisphere for the purpose of exploring for, developing, removing, or transporting resources from ocean waters or deposits under such waters;

(K) any property described in section 48(l)(3)(A)(ix) (as in effect on the day before the date of the enactment of the Revenue Reconciliation Act of 1990) which is owned by a United States person and which is used in international or territorial waters to generate energy for use in the United States; and

(L) any satellite (not described in subparagraph (H)) or other spacecraft (or any interest therein) held by a United States person if such satellite or other spacecraft was launched from within the United States.

For purposes of subparagraph (J), the term "northern portion of the Western Hemisphere" means the area lying west of the 30th meridian west of Greenwich, east of the international dateline, and north of the Equator, but not including any foreign country which is a country of South America.

(5) TAX-EXEMPT BOND FINANCED PROPERTY.—For purposes of this subsection—

(A) IN GENERAL.—Except as otherwise provided in this paragraph, the term "tax-exempt bond financed property" means any property to the extent such property is financed (directly or indirectly) by an obligation the interest on which is exempt from tax under section 103(a).

(B) ALLOCATION OF BOND PROCEEDS.—For purposes of subparagraph (A), the proceeds of any obligation shall be treated as used to finance property acquired in connection with the issuance of such obligation in the order in which such property is placed in service.

(C) QUALIFIED RESIDENTIAL RENTAL PROJECTS.—The term "tax-exempt bond financed property" shall not include any qualified residential rental project (within the meaning of section 142(a)(7)).

* * *

(7) ELECTION TO USE ALTERNATIVE DEPRECIATION SYSTEM.—

(A) IN GENERAL.—If the taxpayer makes an election under this paragraph with respect to any class of property for any taxable year, the alternative depreciation system under this subsection shall apply to all property in such class placed in service during such taxable year. Notwithstanding the preceding sentence, in the case of nonresidential real property or residential rental property, such election may be made separately with respect to each property.

(B) ELECTION IRREVOCABLE.—An election under subparagraph (A), once made, shall be irrevocable.

(8) ELECTING REAL PROPERTY TRADE OR BUSINESS.—The property described in this paragraph shall consist of any nonresidential real property, residential rental property, and qualified improvement property held by an electing real property trade or business (as defined in 163(j)(7)(B)).

* * *

[Sec. 168(i)]

(i) DEFINITIONS AND SPECIAL RULES.—For purposes of this section—

(1) CLASS LIFE.—Except as provided in this section, the term "class life" means the class life (if any) which would be applicable with respect to any property as of January 1, 1986, under subsection (m) of section 167 (determined without regard to paragraph (4) and as if the taxpayer had made an election under such subsection). The Secretary, through an office established in the Treasury, shall monitor and analyze actual experience with respect to all depreciable assets. The reference in this paragraph to subsection (m) of section 167 shall be

treated as a reference to such subsection as in effect on the day before the date of the enactment of the Revenue Reconciliation Act of 1990.

(2) QUALIFIED TECHNOLOGICAL EQUIPMENT.—

(A) IN GENERAL.—The term "qualified technological equipment" means—

(i) any computer or peripheral equipment,

(ii) any high technology telephone station equipment installed on the customer's premises, and

(iii) any high technology medical equipment.

(B) COMPUTER OR PERIPHERAL EQUIPMENT DEFINED.—For purposes of this paragraph—

(i) IN GENERAL.—The term "computer or peripheral equipment" means—

(I) any computer, and

(II) any related peripheral equipment.

(ii) COMPUTER.—The term "computer" means a programmable electronically activated device which—

(I) is capable of accepting information, applying prescribed processes to the information, and supplying the results of these processes with or without human intervention, and

(II) consists of a central processing unit containing extensive storage, logic, arithmetic, and control capabilities.

(iii) RELATED PERIPHERAL EQUIPMENT.—The term "related peripheral equipment" means any auxiliary machine (whether on-line or off-line) which is designed to be placed under the control of the central processing unit of a computer.

(iv) EXCEPTIONS.—The term "computer or peripheral equipment" shall not include—

(I) any equipment which is an integral part of other property which is not a computer,

(II) typewriters, calculators, adding and accounting machines, copiers, duplicating equipment, and similar equipment, and

(III) equipment of a kind used primarily for amusement or entertainment of the user.

(C) HIGH TECHNOLOGY MEDICAL EQUIPMENT.—For purposes of this paragraph, the term "high technology medical equipment" means any electronic, electromechanical, or computer-based high technology equipment used in the screening, monitoring, observation, diagnosis, or treatment of patients in a laboratory, medical, or hospital environment.

(3) LEASE TERM.—

(A) IN GENERAL.—In determining a lease term—

(i) there shall be taken into account options to renew,

(ii) the term of a lease shall include the term of any service contract or similar arrangement (whether or not treated as a lease under section 7701(e))—

(I) which is part of the same transaction (or series of related transactions) which includes the lease, and

(II) which is with respect to the property subject to the lease or substantially similar property,

(iii) 2 or more successive leases which are part of the same transaction (or a series of related transactions) with respect to the same or substantially similar property shall be treated as 1 lease.

(B) SPECIAL RULE FOR FAIR RENTAL OPTIONS ON NONRESIDENTIAL REAL PROPERTY OR RESIDENTIAL RENTAL PROPERTY.—For purposes of clause (i) of subparagraph (A), in the case of nonresidential real property or residential rental property, there shall not be taken into account any option to renew at fair market value, determined at the time of renewal.

(4) GENERAL ASSET ACCOUNTS.—Under regulations, a taxpayer may maintain 1 or more general asset accounts for any property to which this section applies. Except as provided in regulations, all proceeds realized on any disposition of property in a general asset account shall be included in income as ordinary income.

(5) CHANGES IN USE.—The Secretary shall, by regulations, provide for the method of determining the deduction allowable under section 167(a) with respect to any tangible property for any taxable year (and the succeeding taxable years) during which such property changes status under this section but continues to be held by the same person.

(6) TREATMENTS OF ADDITIONS OR IMPROVEMENTS TO PROPERTY.—In the case of any addition to (or improvement of) any property—

(A) any deduction under subsection (a) for such addition or improvement shall be computed in the same manner as the deduction of such property would be computed if such property had been placed in service at the same time as such addition or improvement, and

(B) the applicable recovery period for such addition or improvement shall begin on the later of—

(i) the date on which such addition (or improvement) is placed in service, or

(ii) the date on which the property with respect to which such addition (or improvement) was made is placed in service.

(7) TREATMENT OF CERTAIN TRANSFEREES.—

(A) IN GENERAL.—In the case of any property transferred in a transaction described in subparagraph (B), the transferee shall be treated as the transferor for purposes of computing the depreciation deduction determined under this section with respect to so much of the basis in the hands of the transferee as does not exceed the adjusted basis in the hands of the transferor. In any case where this section as in effect before the amendments made by section 201 of the Tax Reform Act of 1986 applied to the property in the hands of the transferor, the reference in the preceding sentence to this section shall be treated as a reference to this section as so in effect.

(B) TRANSACTIONS COVERED.—The transactions described in this subparagraph are—

(i) any transaction described in section 332, 351, 361, 721, or 731, and

(ii) any transaction between members of the same affiliated group during any taxable year for which a consolidated return is made by such group.

(C) PROPERTY REACQUIRED BY THE TAXPAYER.—Under regulations, property which is disposed of and then reaquired by the taxpayer shall be treated for purposes of computing the deduction allowable under subsection (a) as if such property had not been disposed of.

(D) [Repealed.]

(8) TREATMENT OF LEASEHOLD IMPROVEMENTS.—

(A) IN GENERAL.—In the case of any building erected (or improvements made) on leased property, if such building or improvement is property to which this section applies, the depreciation deduction shall be determined under the provisions of this section.

(B) TREATMENT OF LESSOR IMPROVEMENTS WHICH ARE ABANDONED AT TERMINATION OF LEASE.—An improvement—

(i) which is made by the lessor of leased property for the lessee of such property, and

(ii) which is irrevocably disposed of or abandoned by the lessor at the termination of the lease by such lessee,

shall be treated for purposes of determining gain or loss under this title as disposed of by the lessor when so disposed of or abandoned.

(C) CROSS REFERENCE.—

For treatment of qualified long-term real property constructed or improved in connection with cash or rent reduction from lessor to lessee, see section 110(b).

* * *

(11) RESEARCH AND EXPERIMENTATION.—The term "research and experimentation" has the same meaning as the term research and experimental has under section 174.

(12) SECTION 1245 AND 1250 PROPERTY.—The terms "section 1245 property" and "section 1250 property" have the meanings given such terms by sections 1245(a)(3) and 1250(c), respectively.

(13) SINGLE PURPOSE AGRICULTURAL OR HORTICULTURAL STRUCTURE.—

(A) IN GENERAL.—The term "single purpose agricultural or horticultural structure" means—

(i) a single purpose livestock structure, and

(ii) a single purpose horticultural structure.

(B) DEFINITIONS.—For purposes of this paragraph—

(i) SINGLE PURPOSE LIVESTOCK STRUCTURE.—The term "single purpose livestock structure" means any enclosure or structure specifically designed, constructed, and used—

(I) for housing, raising, and feeding a particular type of livestock and their produce, and

(II) for housing the equipment (including any replacements) necessary for the housing, raising, and feeding referred to in subclause (I).

(ii) SINGLE PURPOSE HORTICULTURAL STRUCTURE.—The term "single purpose horticultural structure" means—

(I) a greenhouse specifically designed, constructed, and used for the commercial production of plants, and

(II) a structure specifically designed, constructed, and used for the commercial production of mushrooms.

(iii) STRUCTURES WHICH INCLUDE WORK SPACE.—An enclosure or structure which provides work space shall be treated as a single purpose agricultural or horticultural structure only if such work space is solely for—

(I) the stocking, caring for, or collecting of livestock or plants (as the case may be) or their produce,

(II) the maintenance of the enclosure or structure, and

(III) the maintenance or replacement of the equipment or stock enclosed or housed therein.

(iv) LIVESTOCK.—The term "livestock" includes poultry.

* * *

[Sec. 168(k)]

(k) SPECIAL ALLOWANCE FOR CERTAIN PROPERTY.—

(1) ADDITIONAL ALLOWANCE.—In the case of any qualified property—

(A) the depreciation deduction provided by section 167(a) for the taxable year in which such property is placed in service shall include an allowance equal to the applicable percentage of the adjusted basis of the qualified property, and

(B) the adjusted basis of the qualified property shall be reduced by the amount of such deduction before computing the amount otherwise allowable as a depreciation deduction under this chapter for such taxable year and any subsequent taxable year.

(2) QUALIFIED PROPERTY.—For purposes of this subsection—

(A) IN GENERAL.—The term "qualified property" means property—

(i)(I) to which this section applies which has a recovery period of 20 years or less,

(II) which is computer software (as defined in section 167(f)(1)(B)) for which a deduction is allowable under section 167(a) without regard to this subsection,

(III) which is water utility property, or

(IV) which is a qualified film or television production (as defined in subsection (d) of section 181) for which a deduction would have been allowable under section 181 without regard to subsections (a)(2) and (g) of such section or this subsection, or

(V) which is a qualified live theatrical production (as defined in subsection (e) of section 181) for which a deduction would have been allowable under section 181 without regard to subsections (a)(2) and (g) of such section or this subsection,

(ii) the original use of which begins with the taxpayer or the acquisition of which by the taxpayer meets the requirements of clause (ii) of subparagraph (E), and

(iii) which is placed in service by the taxpayer before January 1, 2027.

(B) CERTAIN PROPERTY HAVING LONGER PRODUCTION PERIODS TREATED AS QUALIFIED PROPERTY.—

(i) IN GENERAL.—The term "qualified property" includes any property if such property—

(I) meets the requirements of clauses (i) and (ii) of subparagraph (A),

(II) is placed in service by the taxpayer before January 1, 2028,

(III) is acquired by the taxpayer (or acquired pursuant to a written binding contract entered into) before January 1, 2027,

(IV) has a recovery period of at least 10 years or is transportation property,

(V) is subject to section 263A, and

(VI) meets the requirements of clause (iii) of section 263A(f)(1)(B) (determined as if such clause also applies to property which has a long useful life (within the meaning of section 263A(f))).

(ii) ONLY PRE-JANUARY 1, 2027 BASIS ELIGIBLE FOR ADDITIONAL ALLOWANCE.—In the case of property which is qualified property solely by reason of clause (i), paragraph (1) shall apply only to the extent of the adjusted basis thereof attributable to manufacture, construction, or production before January 1, 2027.

(iii) TRANSPORTATION PROPERTY.—For purposes of this subparagraph, the term "transportation property" means tangible personal property used in the trade or business of transporting persons or property.

(iv) APPLICATION OF SUBPARAGRAPH.—This subparagraph shall not apply to any property which is described in subparagraph (C).

(C) CERTAIN AIRCRAFT.—The term "qualified property" includes property—

(i) which meets the requirements of subparagraph (A)(ii) and subclauses (II) and (III) of subparagraph (B)(i),

(ii) which is an aircraft which is not a transportation property (as defined in subparagraph (B)(iii)) other than for agricultural or firefighting purposes,

(iii) which is purchased and on which such purchaser, at the time of the contract for purchase, has made a nonrefundable deposit of the lesser of—

(I) 10 percent of the cost, or

(II) $100,000, and

(iv) which has—

(I) an estimated production period exceeding 4 months, and

(II) a cost exceeding $200,000.

(D) EXCEPTION FOR ALTERNATIVE DEPRECIATION PROPERTY.—The term "qualified property" shall not include any property to which the alternative depreciation system under subsection (g) applies, determined—

(i) without regard to paragraph (7) of subsection (g) (relating to election to have system apply), and

(ii) after application of section 280F(b) (relating to listed property with limited business use).

(E) SPECIAL RULES.—

(i) SELF-CONSTRUCTED PROPERTY.—In the case of a taxpayer manufacturing, constructing, or producing property for the taxpayer's own use, the requirements of subclause (III) of subparagraph (B)(i) shall be treated as met if the taxpayer begins manufacturing, constructing, or producing the property before January 1, 2027.

(ii) ACQUISITION REQUIREMENTS.—An acquisition of property meets the requirements of this clause if—

(I) such property was not used by the taxpayer at any time prior to such acquisition, and

(II) the acquisition of such property meets the requirements of paragraphs (2)(A), (2)(B), (2)(C), and (3) of section 179(d).

(iii) SYNDICATION.—For purposes of subparagraph (A)(ii), if—

(I) property is used by a lessor of such property and such use is the lessor's first use of such property,

(II) such property is sold by such lessor or any subsequent purchaser within 3 months after the date such property was originally placed in service (or, in the case of multiple units of property subject to the same lease, within 3 months after the date the final unit is placed in service, so long as the period between the time the first unit is placed in service and the time the last unit is placed in service does not exceed 12 months), and

(III) the user of such property after the last sale during such 3-month period remains the same as when such property was originally placed in service,

such property shall be treated as originally placed in service not earlier than the date of such last sale.

* * *

(3) [Stricken.]

* * *

(6) APPLICABLE PERCENTAGE.—For purposes of this subsection—

(A) IN GENERAL.—Except as otherwise provided in this paragraph, the term "applicable percentage" means—

(i) in the case of property placed in service after September 27, 2017, and before January 1, 2023, 100 percent,

(ii) in the case of property placed in service after December 31, 2022, and before January 1, 2024, 80 percent,

(iii) in the case of property placed in service after December 31, 2023, and before January 1, 2025, 60 percent,

(iv) in the case of property placed in service after December 31, 2024, and before January 1, 2026, 40 percent, and

(v) in the case of property placed in service after December 31, 2025, and before January 1, 2027, 20 percent.

(B) RULE FOR PROPERTY WITH LONGER PRODUCTION PERIODS.—In the case of property described in subparagraph (B) or (C) of paragraph (2), the term "applicable percentage" means—

(i) in the case of property placed in service after September 27, 2017, and before January 1, 2024, 100 percent,

(ii) in the case of property placed in service after December 31, 2023, and before January 1, 2025, 80 percent,

(iii) in the case of property placed in service after December 31, 2024, and before January 1, 2026, 60 percent,

(iv) in the case of property placed in service after December 31, 2025, and before January 1, 2027, 40 percent, and

(v) in the case of property placed in service after December 31, 2026, and before January 1, 2028, 20 percent.

(C) RULE FOR PLANTS BEARING FRUITS AND NUTS.—In the case of a specified plant described in paragraph (5), the term "applicable percentage" means—

(i) in the case of a plant which is planted or grafted after September 27, 2017, and before January 1, 2023, 100 percent,

(ii) in the case of a plant which is planted or grafted after December 31, 2022, and before January 1, 2024, 80 percent,

(iii) in the case of a plant which is planted or grafted after December 31, 2023, and before January 1, 2025, 60 percent,

(iv) in the case of a plant which is planted or grafted after December 31, 2024, and before January 1, 2026, 40 percent, and

(v) in the case of a plant which is planted or grafted after December 31, 2025, and before January 1, 2027, 20 percent.

(7) ELECTION OUT.—If a taxpayer makes an election under this paragraph with respect to any class of property for any taxable year, paragraphs (1) and (2)(F) shall not apply to any qualified property in such class placed in service during such taxable year. An election under this paragraph may be revoked only with the consent of the Secretary.

* * *

[Sec. 169]

SEC. 169. AMORTIZATION OF POLLUTION CONTROL FACILITIES.

[Sec. 169(a)]

(a) ALLOWANCE OF DEDUCTION.—Every person, at his election, shall be entitled to a deduction with respect to the amortization of the amortizable basis of any certified pollution control facility (as defined in subsection (d)), based on a period of 60 months. Such amortization deduction shall be an amount, with respect to each month of such period within the taxable year, equal to the amortizable basis of the pollution control facility at the end of such month divided by the number of months (including the month for which the deduction is computed) remaining in the period. Such amortizable basis at the end of the month shall be computed without regard to the amortization deduction for such month. The amortization deduction provided by this section with respect to any month shall be in lieu of the depreciation deduction with respect to such pollution control facility for such month provided by section 167. The 60-month period shall begin, as to any pollution control facility, at the election of the taxpayer, with the month following the month in which such facility was completed or acquired, or with the succeeding taxable year.

[Sec. 169(b)]

(b) ELECTION OF AMORTIZATION.—The election of the taxpayer to take the amortization deduction and to begin the 60-month period with the month following the month in which the facility is completed or acquired, or with the taxable year succeeding the taxable year in which such facility is completed or acquired, shall be made by filing with the Secretary, in such manner, in such form, and within such time, as the Secretary may by regulations prescribe, a statement of such election.

[Sec. 169(c)]

(c) TERMINATION OF AMORTIZATION DEDUCTION.—A taxpayer which has elected under subsection (b) to take the amortization deduction provided in subsection (a) may, at any time after making such election, discontinue the amortization deduction with respect to the remainder of the amortization period, such discontinuance to begin as of the beginning of any month specified by the taxpayer in a notice in writing filed with the Secretary before the beginning of such month. The depreciation deduction provided under section 167 shall be allowed, beginning with the first month as to which the amortization deduction does not apply, and the taxpayer shall not be entitled to any further amortization deduction under this section with respect to such pollution control facility.

[Sec. 169(d)]

(d) DEFINITIONS AND SPECIAL RULES.—For purposes of this section—

(1) CERTIFIED POLLUTION CONTROL FACILITY.—The term "certified pollution control facility" means a new identifiable treatment facility which is used, in connection with a plant or other property in operation before January 1, 1976, to abate or control water or atmospheric pollution or contamination by removing, altering, disposing, storing, or preventing the creation or emission of pollutants, contaminants, wastes, or heat and which—

(A) the State certifying authority having jurisdiction with respect to such facility has certified to the Federal certifying authority as having been constructed, reconstructed, erected, or acquired in conformity with the State program or requirements for abatement or control of water or atmospheric pollution or contamination;

(B) the Federal certifying authority has certified to the Secretary (i) as being in compliance with the applicable regulations of Federal agencies and (ii) as being in furtherance of the general policy of the United States for cooperation with the States in the prevention and abatement of water pollution under the Federal Water Pollution Control Act, as amended (33 U. S. C. 466 et seq.), or in the prevention and abatement of atmospheric pollution and contamination under the Clean Air Act, as amended (42 U.S.C. 1857 et seq.); and

(C) does not significantly—

(i) increase the output or capacity, extend the useful life, or reduce the total operating costs of such plant or other property (or any unit thereof), or

(ii) alter the nature of the manufacturing or production process or facility.

(2) STATE CERTIFYING AUTHORITY.—The term "State certifying authority" means, in the case of water pollution, the State water pollution control agency as defined in section 13(a) of the Federal Water Pollution Control Act and, in the case of air pollution, the air pollution control agency as defined in section 302(b) of the Clean Air Act. The term "State certifying authority" includes any interstate agency authorized to act in place of a certifying authority of the State.

(3) FEDERAL CERTIFYING AUTHORITY.—The term "Federal certifying authority" means, in the case of water pollution, the Secretary of the Interior and, in the case of air pollution, the Secretary of Health and Human Services.

(4) NEW IDENTIFIABLE TREATMENT FACILITY.—

(A) IN GENERAL.—For purposes of paragraph (1), the term "new identifiable treatment facility" includes only tangible property (not including a building and its structural components, other than a building which is exclusively a treatment facility) which is of a character subject to the allowance for depreciation provided in section 167, which is identifiable as a treatment facility, and which is property—

(i) the construction, reconstruction, or erection of which is completed by the taxpayer after December 31, 1968, or

(ii) acquired after December 31, 1968, if the original use of the property commences with the taxpayer and commences after such date.

In applying this section in the case of property described in clause (i) there shall be taken into account only that portion of the basis which is properly attributable to construction, reconstruction, or erection after December 31, 1968.

(B) CERTAIN FACILITIES PLACED IN OPERATION AFTER APRIL 11, 2005.—In the case of any facility described in paragraph (1) solely by reason of paragraph (5), subparagraph (A) shall be applied by substituting "April 11, 2005" for "December 31, 1968" each place it appears therein.

(5) SPECIAL RULE RELATING TO CERTAIN ATMOSPHERIC POLLUTION CONTROL FACILITIES.—In the case of any atmospheric pollution control facility which is placed in service after April 11, 2005, and used in connection with an electric generation plant or other property which is primarily coal fired—

(A) paragraph (1) shall be applied without regard to the phrase "in operation before January 1, 1976", and

(B) in the case of a facility placed in service in connection with a plant or other property placed in operation after December 31, 1975, this section shall be applied by substituting "84" for "60" each place it appears in subsections (a) and (b).

[Sec. 169(e)]

(e) PROFITMAKING ABATEMENT WORKS, ETC.—The Federal certifying authority shall not certify any property under subsection (d)(1)(B) to the extent it appears that by reason of profits derived through the recovery of wastes or otherwise in the operation of such property, its costs will be recovered over its actual useful life.

[Sec. 169(f)]

(f) AMORTIZABLE BASIS.—

(1) DEFINED.—For purposes of this section, the term "amortizable basis" means that portion of the adjusted basis (for determining gain) of a certified pollution control facility which may be amortized under this section.

(2) SPECIAL RULES.—

(A) If a certified pollution control facility has a useful life (determined as of the first day of the first month for which a deduction is allowable under this section) in excess of 15 years, the amortizable basis of such facility shall be equal to an amount which bears the same ratio to the portion of the adjusted basis of such facility, which would be eligible for amortization but for the application of this subparagraph, as 15 bears to the number of years of useful life of such facility.

(B) The amortizable basis of a certified pollution control facility with respect to which an election under this section is in effect shall not be increased, for purposes of this section, for additions or improvements after the amortization period has begun.

[Sec. 169(g)]

(g) DEPRECIATION DEDUCTION.—The depreciation deduction provided by section 167 shall, despite the provisions of subsection (a), be allowed with respect to the portion of the adjusted basis which is not the amortizable basis.

[Sec. 169(i)]

(i) LIFE TENANT AND REMAINDERMAN.—In the case of property held by one person for life with remainder to another person, the deduction under this section shall be computed as if the life tenant were the absolute owner of the property and shall be allowable to the life tenant.

[Sec. 169(j)]

(j) CROSS REFERENCE.—For special rule with respect to certain gain derived from the disposition of property the adjusted basis of which is determined with regard to this section, see section 1245.

[Sec. 170]

SEC. 170. CHARITABLE, ETC., CONTRIBUTIONS AND GIFTS.

[Sec. 170(a)]

(a) ALLOWANCE OF DEDUCTION.—

(1) GENERAL RULE.—There shall be allowed as a deduction any charitable contribution (as defined in subsection (c)) payment of which is made within the taxable year. A charitable contribution shall be allowable as a deduction only if verified under regulations prescribed by the Secretary.

(2) CORPORATIONS ON ACCRUAL BASIS.—In the case of a corporation reporting its taxable income on the accrual basis, if—

(A) the board of directors authorizes a charitable contribution during any taxable year, and

(B) payment of such contribution is made after the close of such taxable year and on or before the 15th day of the fourth month following the close of such taxable year,

then the taxpayer may elect to treat such contribution as paid during such taxable year. The election may be made only at the time of the filing of the return for such taxable year, and shall be signified in such manner as the Secretary shall by regulations prescribe.

(3) FUTURE INTERESTS IN TANGIBLE PERSONAL PROPERTY.—For purposes of this section, payment of a charitable contribution which consists of a future interest in tangible personal property shall be treated as made only when all intervening interests in, and rights to the actual possession or enjoyment of, the property have expired or are held by persons other than the taxpayer or those standing in a relationship to the taxpayer described in section 267(b) or 707(b). For purposes of the preceding sentence, a fixture which is intended to be severed from the real property shall be treated as tangible personal property.

[Sec. 170(b)]

(b) PERCENTAGE LIMITATIONS.—

(1) INDIVIDUALS.—In the case of an individual, the deduction provided in subsection (a) shall be limited as provided in the succeeding subparagraphs.

(A) GENERAL RULE.—Any charitable contribution to—

(i) a church or a convention or association of churches,

(ii) an educational organization which normally maintains a regular faculty and curriculum and normally has a regularly enrolled body of pupils or students in attendance at the place where its educational activities are regularly carried on,

(iii) an organization the principal purpose or functions of which are the providing of medical or hospital care or medical education or medical research, if the organization is a hospital, or if the organization is a medical research organization directly engaged in the continuous active conduct of medical research in conjunction with a hospital, and during the calendar year in which the contribution is made such organization is committed to spend such contributions for such research before January 1 of the fifth calendar year which begins after the date such contribution is made,

(iv) an organization which normally receives a substantial part of its support (exclusive of income received in the exercise or performance by such organization of its charitable, educational, or other purpose or function constituting the basis for its exemption under section 501(a)) from the United States or any State or political subdivision thereof or from direct or indirect contributions from the general public, and which is organized and operated exclusively to receive, hold, invest, and administer property and to make expenditures to or for the benefit of a college or university which is an organization referred to in clause (ii) of this subparagraph and which is an agency or instrumentality of a State or political subdivision thereof, or which is owned or operated by a State or political subdivision thereof or by an agency or instrumentality of one or more States or political subdivisions,

(v) a governmental unit referred to in subsection (c)(1),

(vi) an organization referred to in subsection (c)(2) which normally receives a substantial part of its support (exclusive of income received in the exercise or performance by such organization of its charitable, educational, or other purpose or function constituting the basis for its exemption under section 501(a)) from a governmental unit referred to in subsection (c)(1) or from direct or indirect contributions from the general public,

(vii) a private foundation described in subparagraph (F),

(viii) an organization described in section 509(a)(2) or (3), or

(ix) an agricultural research organization directly engaged in the continuous active conduct of agricultural research (as defined in section 1404 of the National Agricultural Research, Extension, and Teaching Policy Act of 1977) in conjunction with a land-grant college or university (as defined in such section) or a non-land grant college of agriculture (as defined in such section), and during the calendar year in which the contribution is made such organization is committed to spend such contribution for such research before January 1 of the fifth calendar year which begins after the date such contribution is made,

shall be allowed to the extent that the aggregate of such contributions does not exceed 50 percent of the taxpayer's contribution base for the taxable year.

(B) OTHER CONTRIBUTIONS.—Any charitable contribution other than a charitable contribution to which subparagraph (A) applies shall be allowed to the extent that the aggregate of such contributions does not exceed the lesser of—

(i) 30 percent of the taxpayer's contribution base for the taxable year, or

(ii) the excess of 50 percent of the taxpayer's contribution base for the taxable year over the amount of charitable contributions allowable under subparagraph (A) (determined without regard to subparagraph (C)).

If the aggregate of such contributions exceeds the limitation of the preceding sentence, such excess shall be treated (in a manner consistent with the rules of subsection (d)(1)) as a charitable contribution (to which subparagraph (A) does not apply) in each of the 5 succeeding taxable years in order of time.

(C) SPECIAL LIMITATION WITH RESPECT TO CONTRIBUTIONS DESCRIBED IN SUBPARAGRAPH (a) OF CERTAIN CAPITAL GAIN PROPERTY.—

(i) In the case of charitable contributions described in subparagraph (A) of capital gain property to which subsection (e)(1)(B) does not apply, the total amount of contributions of such property which may be taken into account under subsection (a) for any taxable year shall not exceed 30 percent of the taxpayer's contribution base for such year. For purposes of this subsection, contributions of capital gain property to which this subparagraph applies shall be taken into account after all other charitable contributions (other than charitable contributions to which subparagraph (D) applies).

(ii) If charitable contributions described in subparagraph (A) of capital gain property to which clause (i) applies exceeds 30 percent of the taxpayer's contribution base for any taxable year, such excess shall be treated, in a manner consistent with the rules of subsection (d)(1), as a charitable contribution of capital gain property to which clause (i) applies in each of the 5 succeeding taxable years in order of time.

(iii) At the election of the taxpayer (made at such time and in such manner as the Secretary prescribes by regulations), subsection (e)(1) shall apply to all contributions of capital gain property (to which subsection (e)(1)(B) does not otherwise apply) made by the taxpayer during the taxable year. If such an election is made, clauses (i) and (ii) shall not apply to contributions of capital gain property made during the taxable year, and, in applying subsection (d)(1) for such taxable year with respect to contributions of capital gain property made in any prior contribution year for which an election was not made under this clause, such contributions shall be reduced as if subsection (e)(1) had applied to such contributions in the year in which made.

(iv) For purposes of this paragraph, the term "capital gain property" means, with respect to any contribution, any capital asset the sale of which at its fair market value at the time of the contribution would have resulted in gain which would have been long-term capital gain. For purposes of the preceding sentence, any property which is property used in the trade or business (as defined in section 1231(b)) shall be treated as a capital asset.

(D) SPECIAL LIMITATION WITH RESPECT TO CONTRIBUTIONS OF CAPITAL GAIN PROPERTY TO ORGANIZATIONS NOT DESCRIBED IN SUBPARAGRAPH (A).—

(i) IN GENERAL.—In the case of charitable contributions (other than charitable contributions to which subparagraph (A) applies) of capital gain property, the total amount of such contributions of such property taken into account under subsection (a) for any taxable year shall not exceed the lesser of—

(I) 20 percent of the taxpayer's contribution base for the taxable year, or

(II) the excess of 30 percent of the taxpayer's contribution base for the taxable year over the amount of the contributions of capital gain property to which subparagraph (C) applies.

For purposes of this subsection, contributions of capital gain property to which this subparagraph applies shall be taken into account after all other charitable contributions.

(ii) CARRYOVER.—If the aggregate amount of contributions described in clause (i) exceeds the limitation of clause (i), such excess shall be treated (in a manner consistent with the rules of subsection (d)(1)) as a charitable contribution of capital gain property to which clause (i) applies in each of the 5 succeeding taxable years in order of time.

(E) CONTRIBUTIONS OF QUALIFIED CONSERVATION CONTRIBUTIONS.—

(i) IN GENERAL.—Any qualified conservation contribution (as defined in subsection (h)(1)) shall be allowed to the extent the aggregate of such contributions does not exceed the excess of 50 percent of the taxpayer's contribution base over the amount of all other charitable contributions allowable under this paragraph.

(ii) CARRYOVER.—If the aggregate amount of contributions described in clause (i) exceeds the limitation of clause (i), such excess shall be treated (in a manner consistent with the rules of subsection (d)(1)) as a charitable contribution to which clause (i) applies in each of the 15 succeeding years in order of time.

(iii) COORDINATION WITH OTHER SUBPARAGRAPHS.—For purposes of applying this subsection and subsection (d)(1), contributions described in clause (i) shall not be treated as described in subparagraph (A), (B), (C), or (D) and such subparagraphs shall apply without regard to such contributions.

(iv) SPECIAL RULE FOR CONTRIBUTION OF PROPERTY USED IN AGRICULTURE OR LIVESTOCK PRODUCTION.—

(I) IN GENERAL.—If the individual is a qualified farmer or rancher for the taxable year for which the contribution is made, clause (i) shall be applied by substituting "100 percent" for "50 percent".

(II) EXCEPTION.—Subclause (I) shall not apply to any contribution of property made after the date of the enactment of this subparagraph which is used in agriculture or livestock production (or available for such production) unless such contribution is subject to a restriction that such property remain available for such production. This subparagraph shall be applied separately with respect to property to which subclause (I) does not apply by reason of the preceding sentence prior to its application to property to which subclause (I) does apply.

(v) DEFINITION.—For purposes of clause (iv), the term "qualified farmer or rancher" means a taxpayer whose gross income from the trade or business of farming (within the meaning of section 2032A(e)(5)) is greater than 50 percent of the taxpayer's gross income for the taxable year.

(F) CERTAIN PRIVATE FOUNDATIONS.—The private foundations referred to in subparagraph (A)(vii) and subsection (e)(1)(B) are—

(i) a private operating foundation (as defined in section 4942(j)(3)),

(ii) any other private foundation (as defined in section 509(a)) which, not later than the 15th day of the third month after the close of the foundation's taxable year in which contributions are received, makes qualifying distributions (as defined in section 4942(g), without regard to paragraph (3) thereof), which are treated, after the application of section 4942(g)(3), as distributions out of corpus (in accordance with section 4942(h)) in an amount equal to 100 percent of such contributions, and with respect to which the taxpayer obtains adequate records or other sufficient evidence from the foundation showing that the foundation made such qualifying distributions, and

(iii) a private foundation all of the contributions to which are pooled in a common fund and which would be described in section 509(a)(3) but for the right of any substantial contributor (hereafter in this clause called "donor") or his spouse to designate annually the recipients, from among organizations described in paragraph (1) of section 509(a), of the income attributable to the donor's contribution to the fund and to direct (by deed or by will) the payment, to an organization described in such paragraph (1), of the corpus in the common fund attributable to the donor's contribution; but this clause shall apply only if all of the income of the common fund is required to be (and is) distributed to one or more organizations described in such paragraph (1) not later than the 15th day of the third month after the close of the taxable year in which the income is realized by the fund and only if all of the corpus attributable to any donor's contribution to the fund is required to be (and is) distributed to one or more of such organizations not later than one year after his death or after the death of his surviving spouse if she has the right to designate the recipients of such corpus.

(G) INCREASED LIMITATION FOR CASH CONTRIBUTIONS.—

(i) IN GENERAL.—In the case of any contribution of cash to an organization described in subparagraph (A), the total amount of such contributions which may be taken into account under subsection (a) for any taxable year beginning after December 31, 2017, and before January 1, 2026, shall not exceed 60 percent of the taxpayer's contribution base for such year.

(ii) CARRYOVER.—If the aggregate amount of contributions described in clause (i) exceeds the applicable limitation under clause (i) for any taxable year described in such clause, such excess shall be treated (in a manner consistent with the rules of subsection (d)(1)) as a charitable contribution to which clause (i) applies in each of the 5 succeeding years in order of time.

(iii) COORDINATION WITH SUBPARAGRAPHS (A) AND (B).—

(I) IN GENERAL.—Contributions taken into account under this subparagraph shall not be taken into account under subparagraph (A).

(II) LIMITATION REDUCTION.—For each taxable year described in clause (i), and each taxable year to which any contribution under this subparagraph is carried over under clause (ii), subparagraph (A) shall be applied by reducing (but not below zero) the contribution limitation allowed for the taxable year under such subparagraph by the aggregate contributions allowed under this subparagraph for such taxable year, and subparagraph (B) shall be applied by treating any reference to subparagraph (A) as a reference to both subparagraph (A) and this subparagraph.

(H) CONTRIBUTION BASE DEFINED.—For purposes of this section, the term "contribution base" means adjusted gross income (computed without regard to any net operating loss carryback to the taxable year under section 172).

(2) CORPORATIONS.—In the case of a corporation—

(A) IN GENERAL.—The total deductions under subsection (a) for any taxable year (other than for contributions to which subparagraph (B) or (C) applies) shall not exceed 10 percent of the taxpayer's taxable income.

(B) QUALIFIED CONSERVATION CONTRIBUTIONS BY CERTAIN CORPORATE FARMERS AND RANCHERS.—

(i) IN GENERAL.—Any qualified conservation contribution (as defined in subsection (h)(1))—

(I) which is made by a corporation which, for the taxable year during which the contribution is made, is a qualified farmer or rancher (as defined in paragraph (1)(E)(v)) and the stock of which is not readily tradable on an established securities market at any time during such year, and

(II) which, in the case of contributions made after the date of the enactment of this subparagraph, is a contribution of property which is used in agriculture or livestock production (or available for such production) and which is subject to a restriction that such property remain available for such production,

shall be allowed to the extent the aggregate of such contributions does not exceed the excess of the taxpayer's taxable income over the amount of charitable contributions allowable under subparagraph (A).

(ii) CARRYOVER.—If the aggregate amount of contributions described in clause (i) exceeds the limitation of clause (i), such excess shall be treated (in a manner consistent with the rules of subsection (d)(2)) as a charitable contribution to which clause (i) applies in each of the 15 succeeding taxable years in order of time.

(C) QUALIFIED CONSERVATION CONTRIBUTIONS BY CERTAIN NATIVE CORPORATIONS.—

(i) IN GENERAL.—Any qualified conservation contribution (as defined in subsection (h)(1)) which—

(I) is made by a Native Corporation, and

(II) is a contribution of property which was land conveyed under the Alaska Native Claims Settlement Act,

shall be allowed to the extent that the aggregate amount of such contributions does not exceed the excess of the taxpayer's taxable income over the amount of charitable contributions allowable under subparagraph (A).

(ii) CARRYOVER.—If the aggregate amount of contributions described in clause (i) exceeds the limitation of clause (i), such excess shall be treated (in a manner consistent with the rules of subsection (d)(2)) as a charitable contribution to which clause (i) applies in each of the 15 succeeding taxable years in order of time.

(iii) NATIVE CORPORATION.—For purposes of this subparagraph, the term "Native Corporation" has the meaning given such term by section 3(m) of the Alaska Native Claims Settlement Act.

(D) TAXABLE INCOME.—For purposes of this paragraph, taxable income shall be computed without regard to—

(i) this section,

(ii) part VIII (except section 248),

(iii) any net operating loss carryback to the taxable year under section 172,

(iv) any capital loss carryback to the taxable year under section 1212(a)(1)

(v) section 199A(g).

[Sec. 170(c)]

(c) CHARITABLE CONTRIBUTION DEFINED.—For purposes of this section, the term "charitable contribution" means a contribution or gift to or for the use of—

(1) A State, a possession of the United States, or any political subdivision of any of the foregoing, or the United States or the District of Columbia, but only if the contribution or gift is made for exclusively public purposes.

(2) A corporation, trust, or community chest, fund, or foundation—

(A) created or organized in the United States or in any possession thereof, or under the law of the United States, any State, the District of Columbia, or any possession of the United States;

(B) organized and operated exclusively for religious, charitable, scientific, literary, or educational purposes, or to foster national or international amateur sports competition (but only if no part of its activities involve the provision of athletic facilities or equipment), or for the prevention of cruelty to children or animals;

(C) no part of the net earnings of which inures to the benefit of any private shareholder or individual; and

(D) which is not disqualified for tax exemption under section 501(c)(3) by reason of attempting to influence legislation, and which does not participate in, or intervene in (including the publishing or distributing of statements), any political campaign on behalf of (or in opposition to) any candidate for public office.

A contribution or gift by a corporation to a trust, chest, fund, or foundation shall be deductible by reason of this paragraph only if it is to be used within the United States or any of its possessions exclusively for purposes specified in subparagraph (B). Rules similar to the rules of section 501(j) shall apply for purposes of this paragraph.

(3) A post or organization of war veterans, or an auxiliary unit or society of, or trust or foundation for, any such post or organization—

(A) organized in the United States or any of its possessions, and

(B) no part of the net earnings of which inures to the benefit of any private shareholder or individual.

(4) In the case of a contribution or gift by an individual, a domestic fraternal society, order, or association, operating under the lodge system, but only if such contribution or gift is to be used exclusively for religious, charitable, scientific, literary, or educational purposes, or for the prevention of cruelty to children or animals.

(5) A cemetery company owned and operated exclusively for the benefit of its members, or any corporation chartered solely for burial purposes as a cemetery corporation and not permitted by its charter to engage in any business not necessarily incident to that purpose, if such company or corporation is not operated for profit and no part of the net earnings of such company or corporation inures to the benefit of any private shareholder or individual.

For purposes of this section, the term "charitable contribution" also means an amount treated under subsection (g) as paid for the use of an organization described in paragraph (2), (3), or (4).

[Sec. 170(d)]

(d) CARRYOVERS OF EXCESS CONTRIBUTIONS.—

(1) INDIVIDUALS.—

(A) IN GENERAL.—In the case of an individual, if the amount of charitable contributions described in subsection (b)(1)(A) payment of which is made within a taxable year (hereinafter in this paragraph referred to as the "contribution year") exceeds 50 percent of the taxpayer's contribution base for such year, such excess shall be treated as a charitable contribution described in subsection (b)(1)(A) paid in each of the 5 succeeding taxable years in order of time, but, with respect to any such succeeding taxable year, only to the extent of the lesser of the two following amounts:

(i) the amount by which 50 percent of the taxpayer's contribution base for such succeeding taxable year exceeds the sum of the charitable contributions described in subsection (b)(1)(A) payment of which is made by the taxpayer within such succeeding taxable year (determined without regard to this subparagraph) and the charitable contributions described in subsection (b)(1)(A) payment of which was made in taxable years before the contribution year which are treated under this subparagraph as having been paid in such succeeding taxable year; or

(ii) in the case of the first succeeding taxable year, the amount of such excess, and in the case of the second, third, fourth, or fifth succeeding taxable year, the portion of such excess not treated under this subparagraph as a charitable contribution described in subsection (b)(1)(A) paid in any taxable year intervening between the contribution year and such succeeding taxable year.

(B) SPECIAL RULE FOR NET OPERATING LOSS CARRYOVERS.—In applying subparagraph (A), the excess determined under subparagraph (A) for the contribution year shall be reduced to the extent that such excess reduces taxable income (as computed for purposes of the second sentence of section 172(b)(2)) and increases the net operating loss deduction for a taxable year succeeding the contribution year.

(2) CORPORATIONS.—

(A) IN GENERAL.—Any contribution made by a corporation in a taxable year (hereinafter in this paragraph referred to as the "contribution year") in excess of the amount deductible for such year under subsection (b)(2)(A) shall be deductible for each of the 5 succeeding taxable years in order of time, but only to the extent of the lesser of the two following amounts: (i) the excess of the maximum amount deductible for such succeeding taxable year under subsection (b)(2)(A) over the sum of the contributions made in such year plus the aggregate of the excess contributions which were made in taxable years before the contribution year and which are deductible under this subparagraph for such succeeding taxable year; or (ii) in the case of the first succeeding taxable year, the amount of such excess contribution, and in the case of the second, third, fourth, or fifth succeeding taxable year, the portion of such excess contribution not deductible under this subparagraph for any taxable year intervening between the contribution year and such succeeding taxable year.

(B) SPECIAL RULE FOR NET OPERATING LOSS CARRYOVERS.—For purposes of subparagraph (A), the excess of—

(i) the contributions made by a corporation in a taxable year to which this section applies, over

(ii) the amount deductible in such year under the limitation in subsection (b)(2)(A),

shall be reduced to the extent that such excess reduces taxable income (as computed for purposes of the second sentence of section 172(b)(2)) and increases a net operating loss carryover under section 172 to a succeeding taxable year.

[Sec. 170(e)]

(e) CERTAIN CONTRIBUTIONS OF ORDINARY INCOME AND CAPITAL GAIN PROPERTY.—

(1) GENERAL RULE.—The amount of any charitable contribution of property otherwise taken into account under this section shall be reduced by the sum of—

(A) the amount of gain which would not have been long-term capital gain (determined without regard to section 1221(b)(3)) if the property contributed had been sold by the taxpayer at its fair market value (determined at the time of such contribution), and

(B) in the case of a charitable contribution—

(i) of tangible personal property—

(I) if the use by the donee is unrelated to the purpose or function constituting the basis for its exemption under section 501 (or, in the case of a governmental unit, to any purpose or function described in subsection (c)), or

(II) which is applicable property (as defined in paragraph (7)(C), but without regard to clause (ii) thereof) which is sold, exchanged, or otherwise disposed of by the donee before the last day of the taxable year in which the contribution was made and with respect to which the donee has not made a certification in accordance with paragraph (7)(D),

(ii) to or for the use of a private foundation (as defined in section 509(a)), other than a private foundation described in subsection (b)(1)(F),

(iii) of any patent, copyright (other than a copyright described in section 1221(a)(3) or 1231(b)(1)(C)), trademark, trade name, trade secret, know-how, software (other than software described in section 197(e)(3)(A)(i)), or similar property, or applications or registrations of such property, or

(iv) of any taxidermy property which is contributed by the person who prepared, stuffed, or mounted the property or by any person who paid or incurred the cost of such preparation, stuffing, or mounting,

the amount of gain which would have been long-term capital gain if the property contributed had been sold by the taxpayer at its fair market value (determined at the time of such contribution).

For purposes of applying this paragraph (other than in the case of gain to which section 617(d)(1), 1245(a), 1250(a), 1252(a), or 1254(a) applies), property which is property used in the trade or business (as defined in section 1231(b)) shall be treated as a capital asset. For purposes of applying this paragraph in the case of a charitable contribution of stock in an S corporation, rules similar to the rules of section 751 shall apply in determining whether gain on such stock would have been long-term capital gain if such stock were sold by the taxpayer.

(2) ALLOCATION OF BASIS.—For purposes of paragraph (1), in the case of a charitable contribution of less than the taxpayer's entire interest in the property contributed, the taxpayer's adjusted basis in such property shall be allocated between the interest contributed and any interest not contributed in accordance with regulations prescribed by the Secretary.

(3) SPECIAL RULE FOR CERTAIN CONTRIBUTIONS OF INVENTORY AND OTHER PROPERTY.—

(A) QUALIFIED CONTRIBUTIONS.—For purposes of this paragraph, a qualified contribution shall mean a charitable contribution of property described in paragraph (1) or (2) of section 1221(a), by a corporation (other than a corporation which is an S corporation) to an organization which is described in section 501(c)(3) and is exempt under section 501(a) (other than a private foundation, as defined in section 509(a), which is not an operating foundation, as defined in section 4942(j)(3)), but only if—

(i) the use of the property by the donee is related to the purpose or function constituting the basis for its exemption under section 501 and the property is to be used by the donee solely for the care of the ill, the needy, or infants;

(ii) the property is not transferred by the donee in exchange for money, other property, or services;

(iii) the taxpayer receives from the donee a written statement representing that its use and disposition of the property will be in accordance with the provisions of clauses (i) and (ii); and

(iv) in the case where the property is subject to regulation under the Federal Food, Drug, and Cosmetic Act, as amended, such property must fully satisfy the applicable requirements of such Act and regulations promulgated thereunder on the date of transfer and for one hundred and eighty days prior thereto.

(B) AMOUNT OF REDUCTION.—The reduction under paragraph (1)(A) for any qualified contribution (as defined in subparagraph (A)) shall be no greater than the sum of—

(i) one-half of the amount computed under paragraph (1)(A) (computed without regard to this paragraph), and

(ii) the amount (if any) by which the charitable contribution deduction under this section for any qualified contribution (computed by taking into account the amount determined in clause (i), but without regard to this clause) exceeds twice the basis of such property.

* * *

(E) This paragraph shall not apply to so much of the amount of the gain described in paragraph (1)(A) which would be long-term capital gain but for the application of sections 617, 1245, 1250, or 1252.

* * *

(5) SPECIAL RULE FOR CONTRIBUTIONS OF STOCK FOR WHICH MARKET QUOTATIONS ARE READILY AVAILABLE.—

(A) IN GENERAL.—Subparagraph (B)(ii) of paragraph (1) shall not apply to any contribution of qualified appreciated stock.

(B) QUALIFIED APPRECIATED STOCK.—Except as provided in subparagraph (C), for purposes of this paragraph, the term "qualified appreciated stock" means any stock of a corporation—

(i) for which (as of the date of the contribution) market quotations are readily available on an established securities market, and

(ii) which is capital gain property (as defined in subsection (b)(1)(C)(iv)).

(C) DONOR MAY NOT CONTRIBUTE MORE THAN 10 PERCENT OF STOCK OF CORPORATION.—

(i) IN GENERAL.—In the case of any donor, the term "qualified appreciated stock" shall not include any stock of a corporation contributed by the donor in a contribution to which paragraph (1)(B)(ii) applies (determined without regard to this paragraph) to the extent that the amount of the stock so contributed (when increased by the aggregate amount of all prior such contributions by the donor of stock in such corporation) exceeds 10 percent (in value) of all of the outstanding stock of such corporation.

(ii) SPECIAL RULE.—For purposes of clause (i), an individual shall be treated as making all contributions made by any member of his family (as defined in section 267(c)(4)).

* * *

(7) RECAPTURE OF DEDUCTION ON CERTAIN DISPOSITIONS OF EXEMPT USE PROPERTY.—

(A) IN GENERAL.—In the case of an applicable disposition of applicable property, there shall be included in the income of the donor of such property for the taxable year of such donor in which the applicable disposition occurs an amount equal to the excess (if any) of—

(i) the amount of the deduction allowed to the donor under this section with respect to such property, over

(ii) the donor's basis in such property at the time such property was contributed.

(B) APPLICABLE DISPOSITION.—For purposes of this paragraph, the term "applicable disposition" means any sale, exchange, or other disposition by the donee of applicable property—

(i) after the last day of the taxable year of the donor in which such property was contributed, and

(ii) before the last day of the 3-year period beginning on the date of the contribution of such property,

unless the donee makes a certification in accordance with subparagraph (D).

(C) APPLICABLE PROPERTY.—For purposes of this paragraph, the term "applicable property" means charitable deduction property (as defined in section 6050L(a) (2) (A))—

(i) which is tangible personal property the use of which is identified by the donee as related to the purpose or function constituting the basis of the donee's exemption under section 501, and

(ii) for which a deduction in excess of the donor's basis is allowed.

(D) CERTIFICATION.—A certification meets the requirements of this subparagraph if it is a written statement which is signed under penalty of perjury by an officer of the donee organization and—

(i) which—

(I) certifies that the use of the property by the donee was substantial and related to the purpose or function constituting the basis for the donee's exemption under section 501, and

(II) describes how the property was used and how such use furthered such purpose or function, or

(ii) which—

(I) states the intended use of the property by the donee at the time of the contribution, and

(II) certifies that such intended use has become impossible or infeasible to implement.

[Sec. 170(f)]

(f) DISALLOWANCE OF DEDUCTION IN CERTAIN CASES AND SPECIAL RULES.—

(1) IN GENERAL.—No deduction shall be allowed under this section for a contribution to or for the use of an organization or trust described in section 508(d) or 4948(c) (4) subject to the conditions specified in such sections.

(2) CONTRIBUTIONS OF PROPERTY PLACED IN TRUST.—

(A) REMAINDER INTEREST.—In the case of property transferred in trust, no deduction shall be allowed under this section for the value of a contribution of a remainder interest unless the trust is a charitable remainder annuity trust or a charitable remainder unitrust (described in section 664), or a pooled income fund (described in section 642(c) (5)).

(B) INCOME INTERESTS, ETC.—No deduction shall be allowed under this section for the value of any interest in property (other than a remainder interest) transferred in trust unless the interest is in the form of a guaranteed annuity or the trust instrument specifies that the interest is a fixed percentage distributed yearly of the fair market value of the trust property (to be determined yearly) and the grantor is treated as the owner of such interest for purposes of applying section 671. If the donor ceases to be treated as the owner of such an interest for purposes of applying section 671, at the time the donor ceases to be so treated, the donor shall for purposes of this chapter be considered as having received an amount of income equal to the amount of any deduction he received under this section for the contribution reduced by the discounted value of all amounts of income earned by the trust and taxable to him before the time at which he ceases to be treated as the owner of the interest. Such amounts of income shall be discounted to the date of the contribution. The Secretary shall prescribe such regulations as may be necessary to carry out the purposes of this subparagraph.

(C) DENIAL OF DEDUCTION IN CASE OF PAYMENTS BY CERTAIN TRUSTS.—In any case in which a deduction is allowed under this section for the value of an interest in property described in subparagraph (B), transferred in trust, no deduction shall be allowed under this section to the grantor or any other person for the amount of any contribution made by the trust with respect to such interest.

(D) EXCEPTION.—This paragraph shall not apply in a case in which the value of all interests in property transferred in trust are deductible under subsection (a).

(3) DENIAL OF DEDUCTION IN CASE OF CERTAIN CONTRIBUTIONS OF PARTIAL INTERESTS IN PROPERTY.—

(A) IN GENERAL.—In the case of a contribution (not made by a transfer in trust) of an interest in property which consists of less than the taxpayer's entire interest in such property, a deduction shall be allowed under this section only to the extent that the value of the interest contributed would be allowable as a deduction under this section if such interest had been transferred in trust. For purposes of this subparagraph, a contribution by a taxpayer of the right to use property shall be treated as a contribution of less than the taxpayer's entire interest in such property.

(B) EXCEPTIONS.—Subparagraph (A) shall not apply to—

(i) a contribution of a remainder interest in a personal residence or farm,

(ii) a contribution of an undivided portion of the taxpayer's entire interest in property, and

(iii) a qualified conservation contribution.

(4) VALUATION OF REMAINDER INTEREST IN REAL PROPERTY.—For purposes of this section, in determining the value of a remainder interest in real property, depreciation (computed on the straight line method) and depletion of such property shall be taken into account, and such value shall be discounted at a rate of 6 percent per annum, except that the Secretary may prescribe a different rate.

(5) REDUCTION FOR CERTAIN INTEREST.—If, in connection with any charitable contribution, a liability is assumed by the recipient or by any other person, or if a charitable contribution is of property which is subject to a liability, then, to the extent necessary to avoid the duplication of amounts, the amount taken into account for purposes of this section as the amount of the charitable contribution—

(A) shall be reduced for interest (i) which has been paid (or is to be paid) by the taxpayer, (ii) which is attributable to the liability, and (iii) which is attributable to any period after the making of the contribution, and

(B) in the case of a bond, shall be further reduced for interest (i) which has been paid (or is to be paid) by the taxpayer on indebtedness incurred or continued to purchase or carry such bond, and (ii) which is attributable to any period before the making of the contribution.

The reduction pursuant to subparagraph (B) shall not exceed the interest (including interest equivalent) on the bond which is attributable to any period before the making of the contribution and which is not (under the taxpayer's method of accounting) includible in the gross income of the taxpayer for any taxable year. For purposes of this paragraph, the term "bond" means any bond, debenture, note, or certificate or other evidence of indebtedness.

(6) DEDUCTIONS FOR OUT-OF-POCKET EXPENDITURES.—No deduction shall be allowed under this section for an out-of-pocket expenditure made by any person on behalf of an organization described in subsection (c) (other than an organization described in section 501(h)(5) (relating to churches, etc.)) if the expenditure is made for the purpose of influencing legislation (within the meaning of section 501(c)(3)).

(7) REFORMATIONS TO COMPLY WITH PARAGRAPH (2).—

(A) IN GENERAL.—A deduction shall be allowed under subsection (a) in respect of any qualified reformation (within the meaning of section 2055(e)(3)(B)).

(B) RULES SIMILAR TO SECTION 2055 (e) (3) TO APPLY.—For purposes of this paragraph, rules similar to the rules of section 2055(e) (3) shall apply.

(8) SUBSTANTIATION REQUIREMENT FOR CERTAIN CONTRIBUTIONS.—

(A) GENERAL RULE.—No deduction shall be allowed under subsection (a) for any contribution of $250 or more unless the taxpayer substantiates the contribution by a contemporaneous written acknowledgment of the contribution by the donee organization that meets the requirements of subparagraph (B).

(B) CONTENT OF ACKNOWLEDGEMENT.—An acknowledgement meets the requirements of this subparagraph if it includes the following information:

(i) The amount of cash and a description (but not value) of any property other than cash contributed.

(ii) Whether the donee organization provided any goods or services in consideration, in whole or in part, for any property described in clause (i).

(iii) A description and good faith estimate of the value of any goods or services referred to in clause (ii) or, if such goods or services consist solely of intangible religious benefits, a statement to that effect.

For purposes of this subparagraph, the term "intangible religious benefit" means any intangible religious benefit which is provided by an organization organized exclusively for religious purposes and which generally is not sold in a commercial transaction outside the donative context.

(C) CONTEMPORANEOUS.—For purposes of subparagraph (A), an acknowledgment shall be considered to be contemporaneous if the taxpayer obtains the acknowledgment on or before the earlier of—

(i) the date on which the taxpayer files a return for the taxable year in which the contribution was made, or

(ii) the due date (including extensions) for filing such return.

(D) REGULATIONS.—The Secretary shall prescribe such regulations as may be necessary or appropriate to carry out the purposes of this paragraph, including regulations that may provide that some or all of the requirements of this paragraph do not apply in appropriate cases.

(9) DENIAL OF DEDUCTION WHERE CONTRIBUTION FOR LOBBYING ACTIVITIES.—No deduction shall be allowed under this section for a contribution to an organization which conducts activities to which section 162(e) (1) applies on matters of direct financial interest to the donor's trade or business, if a principal purpose of the contribution was to avoid Federal income tax by securing a deduction for such activities under this section which would be disallowed by reason of section 162(e) if the donor had conducted such activities directly. No deduction shall be allowed under section 162(a) for any amount for which a deduction is disallowed under the preceding sentence.

* * *

(11) QUALIFIED APPRAISAL AND OTHER DOCUMENTATION FOR CERTAIN CONTRIBUTIONS.—

(A) IN GENERAL.—

(i) DENIAL OF DEDUCTION.—In the case of an individual, partnership, or corporation, no deduction shall be allowed under subsection (a) for any contribution of property for which a deduction of more than $500 is claimed unless such person meets the requirements of subparagraphs (B), (C), and (D), as the case may be, with respect to such contribution.

(ii) EXCEPTIONS.—

(I) READILY VALUED PROPERTY.—Subparagraphs (C) and (D) shall not apply to cash, property described in subsection (e) (1) (B) (iii) or section 1221(a) (1), publicly traded securities (as defined in section 6050L(a) (2) (B)), and any qualified vehicle described in paragraph (12) (A) (ii) for which an acknowledgement under paragraph (12) (B) (iii) is provided.

(II) Reasonable cause.—Clause (i) shall not apply if it is shown that the failure to meet such requirements is due to reasonable cause and not to willful neglect.

(B) Property description for contributions of more than $500.—In the case of contributions of property for which a deduction of more than $500 is claimed, the requirements of this subparagraph are met if the individual, partnership or corporation includes with the return for the taxable year in which the contribution is made a description of such property and such other information as the Secretary may require. The requirements of this subparagraph shall not apply to a C corporation which is not a personal service corporation or a closely held C corporation.

(C) Qualified appraisal for contributions of more than $5,000.—In the case of contributions of property for which a deduction of more than $5,000 is claimed, the requirements of this subparagraph are met if the individual, partnership, or corporation obtains a qualified appraisal of such property and attaches to the return for the taxable year in which such contribution is made such information regarding such property and such appraisal as the Secretary may require.

(D) Substantiation for contributions of more than $500,000.—In the case of contributions of property for which a deduction of more than $500,000 is claimed, the requirements of this subparagraph are met if the individual, partnership, or corporation attaches to the return for the taxable year a qualified appraisal of such property.

(E) Qualified appraisal and appraiser.—For purposes of this paragraph—

(i) Qualified appraisal.—The term "qualified appraisal" means, with respect to any property, an appraisal of such property which—

(I) is treated for purposes of this paragraph as a qualified appraisal under regulations or other guidance prescribed by the Secretary, and

(II) is conducted by a qualified appraiser in accordance with generally accepted appraisal standards and any regulations or other guidance prescribed under subclause (I).

(ii) Qualified appraiser.—Except as provided in clause (iii), the term 'qualified appraiser' means an individual who—

(I) has earned an appraisal designation from a recognized professional appraiser organization or has otherwise met minimum education and experience requirements set forth in regulations prescribed by the Secretary,

(II) regularly performs appraisals for which the individual receives compensation, and

(III) meets such other requirements as may be prescribed by the Secretary in regulations or other guidance.

(iii) Specific appraisals.—An individual shall not be treated as a qualified appraiser with respect to any specific appraisal unless—

(I) the individual demonstrates verifiable education and experience in valuing the type of property subject to the appraisal, and

(II) the individual has not been prohibited from practicing before the Internal Revenue Service by the Secretary under section 330(c) of title 31, United States Code, at any time during the 3-year period ending on the date of the appraisal.

(F) Aggregation of similar items of property.—For purposes of determining thresholds under this paragraph, property and all similar items of property donated to 1 or more donees shall be treated as 1 property.

(G) Special rule for pass-thru entities.—In the case of a partnership or S corporation, this paragraph shall be applied at the entity level, except that the deduction shall be denied at the partner or shareholder level.

(H) Regulations.—The Secretary may prescribe such regulations as may be necessary or appropriate to carry out the purposes of this paragraph, including regulations that may provide that some or all of the requirements of this paragraph do not apply in appropriate cases.

(12) CONTRIBUTIONS OF USED MOTOR VEHICLES, BOATS, AND AIRPLANES.—

(A) IN GENERAL.—In the case of a contribution of a qualified vehicle the claimed value of which exceeds $500—

(i) paragraph (8) shall not apply and no deduction shall be allowed under subsection (a) for such contribution unless the taxpayer substantiates the contribution by a contemporaneous written acknowledgement of the contribution by the donee organization that meets the requirements of subparagraph (B) and includes the acknowledgement with the taxpayer's return of tax which includes the deduction, and

(ii) if the organization sells the vehicle without any significant intervening use or material improvement of such vehicle by the organization, the amount of the deduction allowed under subsection (a) shall not exceed the gross proceeds received from such sale.

(B) CONTENT OF ACKNOWLEDGEMENT.—An acknowledgement meets the requirements of this subparagraph if it includes the following information:

(i) The name and taxpayer identification number of the donor.

(ii) The vehicle identification number or similar number.

(iii) In the case of a qualified vehicle to which subparagraph (A)(ii) applies—

(I) a certification that the vehicle was sold in an arm's length transaction between unrelated parties,

(II) the gross proceeds from the sale, and

(III) a statement that the deductible amount may not exceed the amount of such gross proceeds.

(iv) In the case of a qualified vehicle to which subparagraph (A)(ii) does not apply—

(I) a certification of the intended use or material improvement of the vehicle and the intended duration of such use, and

(II) a certification that the vehicle would not be transferred in exchange for money, other property, or services before completion of such use or improvement.

(v) Whether the donee organization provided any goods or services in consideration, in whole or in part, for the qualified vehicle.

(vi) A description and good faith estimate of the value of any goods or services referred to in clause (v) or, if such goods or services consist solely of intangible religious benefits (as defined in paragraph (8)(B)), a statement to that effect.

(C) CONTEMPORANEOUS.—For purposes of subparagraph (A), an acknowledgement shall be considered to be contemporaneous if the donee organization provides it within 30 days of—

(i) the sale of the qualified vehicle, or

(ii) in the case of an acknowledgement including a certification described in subparagraph (B)(iv), the contribution of the qualified vehicle.

(D) INFORMATION TO SECRETARY.—A donee organization required to provide an acknowledgement under this paragraph shall provide to the Secretary the information contained in the acknowledgement. Such information shall be provided at such time and in such manner as the Secretary may prescribe.

(E) QUALIFIED VEHICLE.—For purposes of this paragraph, the term "qualified vehicle" means any—

(i) motor vehicle manufactured primarily for use on public streets, roads, and highways,

(ii) boat, or

(iii) airplane.

Such term shall not include any property which is described in section 1221(a)(1).

(F) Regulations or other guidance.—The Secretary shall prescribe such regulations or other guidance as may be necessary to carry out the purposes of this paragraph. The Secretary may prescribe regulations or other guidance which exempts sales by the donee organization which are in direct furtherance of such organization's charitable purpose from the requirements of subparagraphs (A)(ii) and (B)(iv)(II).

* * *

(16) Contributions of clothing and household items.—

(A) In general.—In the case of an individual, partnership, or corporation, no deduction shall be allowed under subsection (a) for any contribution of clothing or a household item unless such clothing or household item is in good used condition or better.

(B) Items of minimal value.—Notwithstanding subparagraph (A), the Secretary may by regulation deny a deduction under subsection (a) for any contribution of clothing or a household item which has minimal monetary value.

(C) Exception for certain property.—Subparagraphs (A) and (B) shall not apply to any contribution of a single item of clothing or a household item for which a deduction of more than $500 is claimed if the taxpayer includes with the taxpayer's return a qualified appraisal with respect to the property.

(D) Household items.—For purposes of this paragraph—

(i) In general.—The term "household items" includes furniture, furnishings, electronics, appliances, linens, and other similar items.

(ii) Excluded items.—Such term does not include—

(I) food,

(II) paintings, antiques, and other objects of art,

(III) jewelry and gems, and

(IV) collections.

(E) Special rule for pass-thru entities.—In the case of a partnership or S corporation, this paragraph shall be applied at the entity level, except that the deduction shall be denied at the partner or shareholder level.

(17) Recordkeeping.—No deduction shall be allowed under subsection (a) for any contribution of a cash, check, or other monetary gift unless the donor maintains as a record of such contribution a bank record or a written communication from the donee showing the name of the donee organization, the date of the contribution, and the amount of the contribution.

(18) Contributions to donor advised funds.—A deduction otherwise allowed under subsection (a) for any contribution to a donor advised fund (as defined in section 4966(d)(2)) shall only be allowed if—

(A) the sponsoring organization (as defined in section 4966(d)(1)) with respect to such donor advised fund is not—

(i) described in paragraph (3), (4), or (5) of subsection (c), or

(ii) a type III supporting organization (as defined in section 4943(f)(5)(A)) which is not a functionally integrated type III supporting organization (as defined in section 4943(f)(5)(B)), and

(B) the taxpayer obtains a contemporaneous written acknowledgment (determined under rules similar to the rules of paragraph (8)(C)) from the sponsoring organization (as so defined) of such donor advised fund that such organization has exclusive legal control over the assets contributed.

[Sec. 170(g)]

(g) Amounts Paid To Maintain Certain Students as Members of Taxpayer's Household.—

(1) In general.—Subject to the limitations provided by paragraph (2), amounts paid by the taxpayer to maintain an individual (other than a dependent, as defined in section 152

(determined without regard to subsections (b)(1), (b)(2), and (d)(1)(B) thereof), or a relative of the taxpayer) as a member of his household during the period that such individual is—

(A) a member of the taxpayer's household under a written agreement between the taxpayer and an organization described in paragraph (2), (3), or (4) of subsection (c) to implement a program of the organization to provide educational opportunities for pupils or students in private homes, and

(B) a full-time pupil or student in the twelfth or any lower grade at an educational organization described in section 170(b)(1)(A)(ii) located in the United States,

shall be treated as amounts paid for the use of the organization.

(2) LIMITATIONS.—

(A) AMOUNT.—Paragraph (1) shall apply to amounts paid within the taxable year only to the extent that such amounts do not exceed $50 multiplied by the number of full calendar months during the taxable year which fall within the period described in paragraph (1). For purposes of the preceding sentence, if 15 or more days of a calendar month fall within such period such month shall be considered as a full calendar month.

(B) COMPENSATION OR REIMBURSEMENT.—Paragraph (1) shall not apply to any amount paid by the taxpayer within the taxable year if the taxpayer receives any money or other property as compensation or reimbursement for maintaining the individual in his household during the period described in paragraph (1).

(3) RELATIVE DEFINED.—For purposes of paragraph (1), the term "relative of the taxpayer" means an individual who, with respect to the taxpayer, bears any of the relationships described in subparagraphs (A) through (G) of section 152(d)(2).

(4) NO OTHER AMOUNT ALLOWED AS DEDUCTION.—No deduction shall be allowed under subsection (a) for any amount paid by a taxpayer to maintain an individual as a member of his household under a program described in paragraph (1)(A) except as provided in this subsection.

[Sec. 170(h)]

(h) QUALIFIED CONSERVATION CONTRIBUTION.—

(1) IN GENERAL.—For purposes of subsection (f)(3)(B)(iii), the term "qualified conservation contribution" means a contribution—

(A) of a qualified real property interest,

(B) to a qualified organization,

(C) exclusively for conservation purposes.

(2) QUALIFIED REAL PROPERTY INTEREST.—For purposes of this subsection, the term "qualified real property interest" means any of the following interests in real property:

(A) the entire interest of the donor other than a qualified mineral interest,

(B) a remainder interest, and

(C) a restriction (granted in perpetuity) on the use which may be made of the real property.

(3) QUALIFIED ORGANIZATION.—For purposes of paragraph (1), the term "qualified organization" means an organization which—

(A) is described in clause (v) or (vi) of subsection (b)(1)(A), or

(B) is described in section 501(c)(3) and—

(i) meets the requirements of section 509(a)(2), or

(ii) meets the requirements of section 509(a)(3) and is controlled by an organization described in subparagraph (A) or in clause (i) of this subparagraph.

(4) CONSERVATION PURPOSE DEFINED.—

(A) IN GENERAL.—For purposes of this subsection, the term "conservation purpose" means—

(i) the preservation of land areas for outdoor recreation by, or the education of, the general public,

(ii) the protection of a relatively natural habitat of fish, wildlife, or plants, or similar ecosystem,

(iii) the preservation of open space (including farmland and forest land) where such preservation is—

(I) for the scenic enjoyment of the general public, or

(II) pursuant to a clearly delineated Federal, State, or local governmental conservation policy,

and will yield a significant public benefit, or

(iv) the preservation of an historically important land area or a certified historic structure.

(B) SPECIAL RULES WITH RESPECT TO BUILDINGS IN REGISTERED HISTORIC DISTRICTS.—In the case of any contribution of a qualified real property interest which is a restriction with respect to the exterior of a building described in subparagraph (C)(ii), such contribution shall not be considered to be exclusively for conservation purposes unless—

(i) such interest—

(I) includes a restriction which preserves the entire exterior of the building (including the front, sides, rear, and height of the building), and

(II) prohibits any change in the exterior of the building which is inconsistent with the historical character of such exterior,

(ii) the donor and donee enter into a written agreement certifying, under penalty of perjury, that the donee—

(I) is a qualified organization (as defined in paragraph (3)) with a purpose of environmental protection, land conservation, open space preservation, or historic preservation, and

(II) has the resources to manage and enforce the restriction and a commitment to do so, and

(iii) in the case of any contribution made in a taxable year beginning after the date of the enactment of this subparagraph, the taxpayer includes with the taxpayer's return for the taxable year of the contribution—

(I) a qualified appraisal (within the meaning of subsection (f)(11)(E)) of the qualified property interest,

(II) photographs of the entire exterior of the building, and

(III) a description of all restrictions on the development of the building.

(C) CERTIFIED HISTORIC STRUCTURE.—For purposes of subparagraph (A)(iv), the term "certified historic structure" means—

(i) any building, structure, or land area which is listed in the National Register, or

(ii) any building which is located in a registered historic district (as defined in section 47(c)(3)(B)) and is certified by the Secretary of the Interior to the Secretary as being of historic significance to the district.

A building, structure, or land area satisfies the preceding sentence if it satisfies such sentence either at the time of the transfer or on the due date (including extensions) for filing the transferor's return under this chapter for the taxable year in which the transfer is made.

(5) EXCLUSIVELY FOR CONSERVATION PURPOSES.—For purposes of this subsection—

(A) CONSERVATION PURPOSE MUST BE PROTECTED.—A contribution shall not be treated as exclusively for conservation purposes unless the conservation purpose is protected in perpetuity.

(B) NO SURFACE MINING PERMITTED.—

(i) IN GENERAL.—Except as provided in clause (ii), in the case of a contribution of any interest where there is a retention of a qualified mineral interest, subparagraph (A) shall not be treated as met if at any time there may be extraction or removal of minerals by any surface mining method.

(ii) SPECIAL RULE.—With respect to any contribution of property in which the ownership of the surface estate and mineral interests has been and remains separated, subparagraph (A) shall be treated as met if the probability of surface mining occurring on such property is so remote as to be negligible.

(6) QUALIFIED MINERAL INTEREST.—For purposes of this subsection, the term "qualified mineral interest" means—

(A) subsurface oil, gas or other minerals, and

(B) the right to access to such minerals.

[Sec. 170(i)]

(i) STANDARD MILEAGE RATE FOR USE OF PASSENGER AUTOMOBILE.—For purposes of computing the deduction under this section for use of a passenger automobile, the standard mileage rate shall be 14 cents per mile.

[Sec. 170(j)]

(j) DENIAL OF DEDUCTION FOR CERTAIN TRAVEL EXPENSES.—No deduction shall be allowed under this section for traveling expenses (including amounts expended for meals and lodging) while away from home, whether paid directly or by reimbursement, unless there is no significant element of personal pleasure, recreation, or vacation in such travel.

[Sec. 170(k)—Stricken]

[Sec. 170(l)]

(k) (l) TREATMENT OF CERTAIN AMOUNTS PAID TO OR FOR THE BENEFIT OF INSTITUTIONS OF HIGHER EDUCATION.—

(1) IN GENERAL.—No deduction shall be allowed under this section for any amount described in paragraph (2).

(2) AMOUNT DESCRIBED.—For purposes of paragraph (1), an amount is described in this paragraph if—

(A) the amount is paid by the taxpayer to or for the benefit of an educational organization—

(i) which is described in subsection (b) (1) (A) (ii), and

(ii) which is an institution of higher education (as defined in section 3304(f)), and

(B) the taxpayer receives (directly or indirectly) as a result of paying such amount the right to purchase tickets for seating at an athletic event in an athletic stadium of such institution.

If any portion of a payment is for the purchase of such tickets, such portion and the remaining portion (if any) of such payment shall be treated as separate amounts for purposes of this subsection.

* * *

[Sec. 170(o)]

(o) SPECIAL RULES FOR FRACTIONAL GIFTS.—

(1) DENIAL OF DEDUCTION IN CERTAIN CASES.—

(A) IN GENERAL.—No deduction shall be allowed for a contribution of an undivided portion of a taxpayer's entire interest in tangible personal property unless all interests in the property are held immediately before such contribution by—

(i) the taxpayer, or

(ii) the taxpayer and the donee.

(B) EXCEPTIONS.—The Secretary may, by regulation, provide for exceptions to subparagraph (A) in cases where all persons who hold an interest in the property make proportional contributions of an undivided portion of the entire interest held by such persons.

(2) VALUATION OF SUBSEQUENT GIFTS.—In the case of any additional contribution, the fair market value of such contribution shall be determined by using the lesser of—

(A) the fair market value of the property at the time of the initial fractional contribution, or

(B) the fair market value of the property at the time of the additional contribution.

(3) RECAPTURE OF DEDUCTION IN CERTAIN CASES; ADDITION TO TAX.—

(A) RECAPTURE.—The Secretary shall provide for the recapture of the amount of any deduction allowed under this section (plus interest) with respect to any contribution of an undivided portion of a taxpayer's entire interest in tangible personal property—

(i) in any case in which the donor does not contribute all of the remaining interests in such property to the donee (or, if such donee is no longer in existence, to any person described in section 170(c)) on or before the earlier of—

(I) the date that is 10 years after the date of the initial fractional contribution, or

(II) the date of the death of the donor, and

(ii) in any case in which the donee has not, during the period beginning on the date of the initial fractional contribution and ending on the date described in clause (i)—

(I) had substantial physical possession of the property, and

(II) used the property in a use which is related to a purpose or function constituting the basis for the organizations' exemption under section 501.

(B) ADDITION TO TAX.—The tax imposed under this chapter for any taxable year for which there is a recapture under subparagraph (A) shall be increased by 10 percent of the amount so recaptured.

(4) DEFINITIONS.—For purposes of this subsection—

(A) ADDITIONAL CONTRIBUTION.—The term "additional contribution" means any charitable contribution by the taxpayer of any interest in property with respect to which the taxpayer has previously made an initial fractional contribution.

(B) INITIAL FRACTIONAL CONTRIBUTION.—The term "initial fractional contribution" means, with respect to any taxpayer, the first charitable contribution of an undivided portion of the taxpayer's entire interest in any tangible personal property.

* * *

[Sec. 171]

SEC. 171. AMORTIZABLE BOND PREMIUM.

[Sec. 171(a)]

(a) GENERAL RULE.—In the case of any bond, as defined in subsection (d), the following rules shall apply to the amortizable bond premium (determined under subsection (b)) on the bond:

(1) TAXABLE BONDS.—In the case of a bond (other than a bond the interest on which is excludable from gross income), the amount of the amortizable bond premium for the taxable year shall be allowed as a deduction.

(2) TAX-EXEMPT BONDS.—In the case of any bond the interest on which is excludable from gross income, no deduction shall be allowed for the amortizable bond premium for the taxable year.

(3) CROSS REFERENCE.—

For adjustment to basis on account of amortizable bond premium, see section 1016 (a) (5).

(b) AMORTIZABLE BOND PREMIUM.—

(1) AMOUNT OF BOND PREMIUM.—For purposes of paragraph (2), the amount of bond premium, in the case of the holder of any bond, shall be determined—

(A) with reference to the amount of the basis (for determining loss on sale or exchange) of such bond,

(B) (i) with reference to the amount payable on maturity (or if it results in a smaller amortizable bond premium attributable to the period before the call date, with reference to the amount payable on the earlier call date), in the case of a bond described in subsection (a) (1), and

(ii) with reference to the amount payable on maturity or on an earlier call date, in the case of a bond described in subsection (a) (2).

(C) with adjustments proper to reflect unamortized bond premium, with respect to the bond, for the period before the date as of which subsection (a) becomes applicable with respect to the taxpayer with respect to such bond.

In no case shall the amount of bond premium on a convertible bond include any amount attributable to the conversion features of the bond.

(2) AMOUNT AMORTIZABLE.—The amortizable bond premium of the taxable year shall be the amount of the bond premium attributable to such year. In the case of a bond to which paragraph (1) (B) (i) applies and which has a call date, the amount of bond premium attributable to the taxable year in which the bond is called shall include an amount equal to the excess of the amount of the adjusted basis (for determining loss on sale or exchange) of such bond as of the beginning of the taxable year over the amount received on redemption of the bond or (if greater) the amount payable on maturity.

(3) METHOD OF DETERMINATION.—

(A) IN GENERAL.—Except as provided in regulations prescribed by the Secretary, the determinations required under paragraphs (1) and (2) shall be made on the basis of the taxpayer's yield to maturity determined by—

(i) using the taxpayer's basis (for purposes of determining loss on sale or exchange) of the obligation, and

(ii) compounding at the close of each accrual period (as defined in section 1272(a) (5)).

(B) SPECIAL RULE WHERE EARLIER CALL DATE IS USED.—For purposes of subparagraph (A), if the amount payable on an earlier call date is used under paragraph (1) (B) (i) in determining the amortizable bond premium attributable to the period before the earlier call date, such bond shall be treated as maturing on such date for the amount so payable and then reissued on such date for the amount so payable.

(4) TREATMENT OF CERTAIN BONDS ACQUIRED IN EXCHANGE FOR OTHER PROPERTY.—

(A) IN GENERAL.—If—

(i) a bond is acquired by any person in exchange for other property, and

(ii) the basis of such bond is determined (in whole or in part) by reference to the basis of such other property,

for purposes of applying this subsection to such bond while held by such person, the basis of such bond shall not exceed its fair market value immediately after the exchange. A similar rule shall apply in the case of such bond while held by any other person whose basis is determined (in whole or in part) by reference to the basis in the hands of the person referred to in clause (i).

(B) SPECIAL RULE WHERE BOND EXCHANGED IN REORGANIZATION.—Subparagraph (A) shall not apply to an exchange by the taxpayer of a bond for another bond if such exchange is a part of a reorganization (as defined in section 368). If any portion of the basis of the taxpayer in a bond transferred in such an exchange is not taken into account in determining bond premium by reason of this paragraph, such portion shall not be taken into account in determining the amount of bond premium on any bond received in the exchange.

[Sec. 171(c)]

(c) ELECTION AS TO TAXABLE BONDS.—

(1) ELIGIBILITY TO ELECT; BONDS WITH RESPECT TO WHICH ELECTION PERMITTED.—In the case of bonds the interest on which is not excludable from gross income, this section shall apply only if the taxpayer has so elected.

(2) MANNER AND EFFECT OF ELECTION.—The election authorized under this subsection shall be made in accordance with such regulations as the Secretary shall prescribe. If such election is made with respect to any bond (described in paragraph (1)) of the taxpayer, it shall also apply to all such bonds held by the taxpayer at the beginning of the first taxable year to which the election applies and to all such bonds thereafter acquired by him and shall be binding for all subsequent taxable years with respect to all such bonds of the taxpayer, unless, on application by the taxpayer, the Secretary permits him, subject to such conditions as the Secretary deems necessary, to revoke such election. In the case of bonds held by a common trust fund, as defined in section 584(a), the election authorized under this subsection shall be exercisable with respect to such bonds only by the common trust fund. In case of bonds held by an estate or trust, the election authorized under this subsection shall be exercisable with respect to such bonds only by the fiduciary.

[Sec. 171(d)]

(d) BOND DEFINED.—For purposes of this section, the term "bond" means any bond, debenture, note, or certificate or other evidence of indebtedness, but does not include any such obligation which constitutes stock in trade of the taxpayer or any such obligation of a kind which would properly be included in the inventory of the taxpayer if on hand at the close of the taxable year, or any such obligation held by the taxpayer primarily for sale to customers in the ordinary course of his trade or business.

[Sec. 171(e)]

(e) TREATMENT AS OFFSET TO INTEREST PAYMENTS.—Except as provided in regulations, in the case of any taxable bond—

(1) the amount of any bond premium shall be allocated among the interest payments on the bond under rules similar to the rules of subsection (b)(3), and

(2) in lieu of any deduction under subsection (a), the amount of any premium so allocated to any interest payment shall be applied against (and operate to reduce) the amount of such interest payment.

For purposes of the preceding sentence, the term "taxable bond" means any bond the interest of which is not excludable from gross income.

* * *

[Sec. 172]

SEC. 172. NET OPERATING LOSS DEDUCTION.

[Sec. 172(a)]

(a) DEDUCTION ALLOWED.—There shall be allowed as a deduction for the taxable year an amount equal to—

(1) in the case of a taxable year beginning before January 1, 2021, the aggregate of the net operating loss carryovers to such year, plus the net operating loss carrybacks to such year, and

(2) in the case of a taxable year beginning after December 31, 2020, the sum of—

(A) the aggregate amount of net operating losses arising in taxable years beginning before January 1, 2018, carried to such taxable year, plus

(B) the lesser of—

(i) the aggregate amount of net operating losses arising in taxable years beginning after December 31, 2017, carried to such taxable year, or

(ii) 80 percent of the excess (if any) of—

(I) taxable income computed without regard to the deductions under this section and sections 199A and 250, over

(II) the amount determined under subparagraph (A).

[Sec. 172(b)]

(b) NET OPERATING LOSS CARRYBACKS AND CARRYOVERS.—

(1) YEARS TO WHICH LOSS MAY BE CARRIED.—

(A) GENERAL RULE.—A net operating loss for any taxable year—

(i) shall be a net operating loss carryback to the extent provided in subparagraphs (B), (C) (i), and (D), and

(ii) except as provided in subparagraph (C) (ii), shall be a net operating loss carryover—

(I) in the case of a net operating loss arising in a taxable year beginning before January 1, 2018, to each of the 20 taxable years following the taxable year of the loss, and

(II) in the case of a net operating loss arising in a taxable year beginning after December 31, 2017, to each taxable year following the taxable year of the loss.

(B) FARMING LOSSES.—

(i) IN GENERAL.—In the case of any portion of a net operating loss for the taxable year which is a farming loss with respect to the taxpayer, such loss shall be a net operating loss carryback to each of the 2 taxable years preceding the taxable year of such loss.

(ii) FARMING LOSS.—For purposes of this section, the term "farming loss" means the lesser of—

(I) the amount which would be the net operating loss for the taxable year if only income and deductions attributable to farming businesses (as defined in section 263A(e) (4)) are taken into account, or

(II) the amount of the net operating loss for such taxable year.

(iii) COORDINATION WITH PARAGRAPH (2).—For purposes of applying paragraph (2), a farming loss for any taxable year shall be treated as a separate net operating loss for such taxable year to be taken into account after the remaining portion of the net operating loss for such taxable year.

(iv) ELECTION.—Any taxpayer entitled to a 2-year carryback under clause (i) from any loss year may elect not to have such clause apply to such loss year. Such election shall be made in such manner as prescribed by the Secretary and shall be made by the due date (including extensions of time) for filing the taxpayer's return for the taxable year of the net operating loss. Such election, once made for any taxable year, shall be irrevocable for such taxable year.

(C) INSURANCE COMPANIES.—In the case of an insurance company (as defined in section 816(a)) other than a life insurance company, the net operating loss for any taxable year—

(i) shall be a net operating loss carryback to each of the 2 taxable years preceding the taxable year of such loss, and

(ii) shall be a net operating loss carryover to each of the 20 taxable years following the taxable year of the loss.

(D) SPECIAL RULE FOR LOSSES ARISING IN 2018, 2019, AND 2020.—

(i) IN GENERAL.—In the case of any net operating loss arising in a taxable year beginning after December 31, 2017, and before January 1, 2021—

(I) such loss shall be a net operating loss carryback to each of the 5 taxable years preceding the taxable year of such loss, and

(II) subparagraphs (B) and (C) (i) shall not apply.

(ii) SPECIAL RULES FOR REITS.—For purposes of this subparagraph—

(I) IN GENERAL.—A net operating loss for a REIT year shall not be a net operating loss carryback to any taxable year preceding the taxable year of such loss.

(II) SPECIAL RULE.—In the case of any net operating loss for a taxable year which is not a REIT year, such loss shall not be carried to any preceding taxable year which is a REIT year.

(III) REIT YEAR.—For purposes of this subparagraph, the term "REIT year" means any taxable year for which the provisions of part II of subchapter M (relating to real estate investment trusts) apply to the taxpayer.

(iii) SPECIAL RULE FOR LIFE INSURANCE COMPANIES.—In the case of a life insurance company, if a net operating loss is carried pursuant to clause (i) (I) to a life insurance company taxable year beginning before January 1, 2018, such net operating loss carryback shall be treated in the same manner as an operations loss carryback (within the meaning of section 810 as in effect before its repeal) of such company to such taxable year.

* * *

(2) AMOUNT OF CARRYBACKS AND CARRYOVERS.—The entire amount of the net operating loss for any taxable year (hereinafter in this section referred to as the "loss year") shall be carried to the earliest of the taxable years to which (by reason of paragraph (1)) such loss may be carried. The portion of such loss which shall be carried to each of the other taxable years shall be the excess, if any, of the amount of such loss over the sum of the taxable income for each of the prior taxable years to which such loss may be carried. For purposes of the preceding sentence, the taxable income for any such prior taxable year shall—

(A) be computed with the modifications specified in subsection (d) other than paragraphs (1), (4), and (5) thereof, and by determining the amount of the net operating loss deduction without regard to the net operating loss for the loss year or for any taxable year thereafter,

(B) not be considered to be less than zero, and

(C) for taxable years beginning after December 31, 2020, be reduced by 20 percent of the excess (if any) described in subsection (a) (2) (B) (ii) for such taxable year.

(3) ELECTION TO WAIVE CARRYBACK.—Any taxpayer entitled to a carryback period under paragraph (1) may elect to relinquish the entire carryback period with respect to a net operating loss for any taxable year. Such election shall be made in such manner as may be prescribed by the Secretary, and shall be made by the due date (including extensions of time) for filing the taxpayer's return for the taxable year of the net operating loss for which the election is to be in effect. Such election, once made for any taxable year, shall be irrevocable for such taxable year.

[Sec. 172(c)]

(c) NET OPERATING LOSS DEFINED.—For purposes of this section, the term "net operating loss" means the excess of the deductions allowed by this chapter over the gross income. Such excess shall be computed with the modifications specified in subsection (d).

[Sec. 172(d)]

(d) MODIFICATIONS.—The modifications referred to in this section are as follows:

(1) NET OPERATING LOSS DEDUCTION.—No net operating loss deduction shall be allowed.

(2) CAPITAL GAINS AND LOSSES OF TAXPAYERS OTHER THAN CORPORATONS.—In the case of a taxpayer other than a corporation—

(A) the amount deductible on account of losses from sales or exchanges of capital assets shall not exceed the amount includable on account of gains from sales or exchanges of capital assets; and

(B) the exclusion provided by section 1202 shall not be allowed.

(3) DEDUCTION FOR PERSONAL EXEMPTIONS.—No deduction shall be allowed under section 151 (relating to personal exemptions). No deduction in lieu of any such deduction shall be allowed.

(4) NONBUSINESS DEDUCTIONS OF TAXPAYERS OTHER THAN CORPORATIONS.—In the case of a taxpayer other than a corporation, the deductions allowable by this chapter which are not attributable to a taxpayer's trade or business shall be allowed only to the extent of the amount of the gross income not derived from such trade or business. For purposes of the preceding sentence—

(A) any gain or loss from the sale or other disposition of—

(i) property, used in the trade or business, of a character which is subject to the allowance for depreciation provided in section 167, or

(ii) real property used in the trade or business,

shall be treated as attributable to the trade or business;

(B) the modifications specified in paragraphs (1), (2)(B), and (3) shall be taken into account;

(C) any deduction for casualty or theft losses allowable under paragraph (2) or (3) of section 165(c) shall be treated as attributable to the trade or business; and

(D) any deduction allowed under section 404 to the extent attributable to contributions which are made on behalf of an individual who is an employee within the meaning of section 401(c)(1) shall not be treated as attributable to the trade or business of such individual.

(5) COMPUTATION OF DEDUCTION FOR DIVIDENDS RECEIVED.—The deductions allowed by sections 243 (relating to dividends received by corporations) and 245 (relating to dividends received from certain foreign corporations) shall be computed without regard to section 246(b) (relating to limitation on aggregate amount of deductions).

(6) MODIFICATIONS RELATED TO REAL ESTATE INVESTMENT TRUSTS.—In the case of any taxable year for which part II of subchapter M (relating to real estate investment trusts) applies to the taxpayer—

(A) the net operating loss for such taxable year shall be computed by taking into account the adjustments described in section 857(b)(2) (other than the deduction for dividends paid described in section 857(b)(2)(B));

(B) where such taxable year is a "prior taxable year" referred to in paragraph (2) of subsection (b), the term "taxable income" in such paragraph shall mean "real estate investment trust taxable income" (as defined in section 857(b)(2)); and

(C) subsection (a)(2)(B)(ii)(I) shall be applied by substituting "real estate investment trust taxable income (as defined in section 857(b)(2) but without regard to the deduction for dividends paid (as defined in section 561))" for "taxable income".

(7) [Stricken]

(8) QUALIFIED BUSINESS INCOME DEDUCTION.—Any deduction under section 199A shall not be allowed.

(9) DEDUCTION FOR FOREIGN-DERIVED INTANGIBLE INCOME.—The deduction under section 250 shall not be allowed.

[Sec. 172(e)]

(e) LAW APPLICABLE TO COMPUTATIONS.—In determining the amount of any net operating loss carryback or carryover to any taxable year, the necessary computations involving any other taxable year shall be made under the law applicable to such other taxable year.

* * *

[Sec. 172(g)—Stricken]

[Sec. 172(i)]

(i) CROSS REFERENCES.—

(1) For treatment of net operating loss carryovers in certain corporate acquisitions, see section 381.

(2) For special limitation on net operating loss carryovers in case of a corporate change of ownership, see section 382.

* * *

[Sec. 174]

SEC. 174. AMORTIZATION OF RESEARCH AND EXPERIMENTAL EXPENDITURES.

[Sec. 174(a)]

(a) TREATMENT AS EXPENSES.—

(1) IN GENERAL.—A taxpayer may treat research or experimental expenditures which are paid or incurred by him during the taxable year in connection with his trade or business as expenses which are not chargeable to capital account. The expenditures so treated shall be allowed as a deduction.

(2) WHEN METHOD MAY BE ADOPTED.—

(A) WITHOUT CONSENT.—A taxpayer may, without the consent of the Secretary, adopt the method provided in this subsection for his first taxable year for which expenditures described in paragraph (1) are paid or incurred.

(B) WITH CONSENT.—A taxpayer may, with the consent of the Secretary, adopt at any time the method provided in this subsection.

(3) SCOPE.—The method adopted under this subsection shall apply to all expenditures described in paragraph (1). The method adopted shall be adhered to in computing taxable income for the taxable year and for all subsequent taxable years unless, with the approval of the Secretary, a change to a different method is authorized with respect to part or all of such expenditures.

[Sec. 174(b)]

(b) AMORTIZATION OF CERTAIN RESEARCH AND EXPERIMENTAL EXPENDITURES.—

(1) IN GENERAL.—At the election of the taxpayer, made in accordance with regulations prescribed by the Secretary, research or experimental expenditures which are—

(A) paid or incurred by the taxpayer in connection with his trade or business,

(B) not treated as expenses under subsection (a), and

(C) chargeable to capital account but not chargeable to property of a character which is subject to the allowance under section 167 (relating to allowance for depreciation, etc.) or section 611 (relating to allowance for depletion),

may be treated as deferred expenses. In computing taxable income, such deferred expenses shall be allowed as a deduction ratably over such period of not less than 60 months as may be selected by the taxpayer (beginning with the month in which the taxpayer first realizes benefits from such expenditures). Such deferred expenses are expenditures properly chargeable to capital account for purposes of section 1016 (a) (1) (relating to adjustments to basis of property).

(2) TIME FOR AND SCOPE OF ELECTION.—The election provided by paragraph (1) may be made for any taxable year, but only if made not later than the time prescribed by law for filing the return for such taxable year (including extensions thereof). The method so elected, and the period selected by the taxpayer, shall be adhered to in computing taxable income for the taxable year for which the election is made and for all subsequent taxable years unless, with the approval of the Secretary, a change to a different method (or to a different period) is authorized with respect to part or all of such expenditures. The election shall not apply to any expenditure paid or incurred during any taxable year before the taxable year for which the taxpayer makes the election.

[Sec. 174(c)]

(c) LAND AND OTHER PROPERTY.—This section shall not apply to any expenditure for the acquisition or improvement of land, or for the acquisition or improvement of property to be used in connection with the research or experimentation and of a character which is subject to the allowance under section 167 (relating to allowance for depreciation, etc.) or section 611 (relating to allowance for depletion); but for purposes of this section allowances under section 167, and allowances under section 611, shall be considered as expenditures.

[Sec. 174(d)]

(d) EXPLORATION EXPENDITURES.—This section shall not apply to any expenditure paid or incurred for the purpose of ascertaining the existence, location, extent, or quality of any deposit of ore or other mineral (including oil and gas).

[Sec. 174(e)]

(e) ONLY REASONABLE RESEARCH EXPENDITURES ELIGIBLE.—This section shall apply to a research or experimental expenditure only to the extent that the amount thereof is reasonable under the circumstances.

[Sec. 174(f)]

(f) CROSS REFERENCES.—

(1) For adjustments to basis of property for amounts allowed as deductions as deferred expenses under subsection (b), see section 1016 (a) (14).

(2) For election of 10-year amortization of expenditures allowable as a deduction under subsection (a), see section 59(e).

[Sec. 178]

SEC. 178. AMORTIZATION OF COST OF ACQUIRING A LEASE.

[Sec. 178(a)]

(a) GENERAL RULE.—In determining the amount of the deduction allowable to a lessee for exhaustion, wear and tear, obsolescence, or amortization in respect of any cost of acquiring the lease, the term of the lease shall be treated as including all renewal options (and any other period for which the parties reasonably expect the lease to be renewed) if less than 75 percent of such cost is attributable to the period of the term of the lease remaining on the date of its acquisition.

[Sec. 178(b)]

(b) CERTAIN PERIODS EXCLUDED.—For purposes of subsection (a), in determining the period of the term of the lease remaining on the date of acquisition, there shall not be taken into account any period for which the lease may subsequently be renewed, extended, or continued pursuant to an option exercisable by the lessee.

»» Caution: As provided in Section 179(b)(6), the dollar amounts set forth in Sections 179(b)(1) and (2) are adjusted for taxable years after 2015 to reflect increases in the Chained Consumer Price Index. The adjusted amounts applicable to taxable years beginning in 2020 are provided in the material beginning at page ix.

[Sec. 179]

SEC. 179. ELECTION TO EXPENSE CERTAIN DEPRECIABLE BUSINESS ASSETS.

[Sec. 179(a)]

(a) TREATMENT AS EXPENSES.—A taxpayer may elect to treat the cost of any section 179 property as an expense which is not chargeable to capital account. Any cost so treated shall be allowed as a deduction for the taxable year in which the section 179 property is placed in service.

[Sec. 179(b)]

(b) LIMITATIONS.—

(1) DOLLAR LIMITATION.—The aggregate cost which may be taken into account under subsection (a) for any taxable year shall not exceed $1,000,000.

(2) REDUCTION IN LIMITATION.—The limitation under paragraph (1) for any taxable year shall be reduced (but not below zero) by the amount by which the cost of section 179 property placed in service during such taxable year exceeds $2,500,000.

(3) LIMITATION BASED ON INCOME FROM TRADE OR BUSINESS.—

(A) IN GENERAL.—The amount allowed as a deduction under subsection (a) for any taxable year (determined after the application of paragraphs (1) and (2)) shall not exceed the aggregate amount of taxable income of the taxpayer for such taxable year which is derived from the active conduct by the taxpayer of any trade or business during such taxable year.

(B) CARRYOVER OF DISALLOWED DEDUCTION.—The amount allowable as a deduction under subsection (a) for any taxable year shall be increased by the lesser of—

(i) the aggregate amount disallowed under subparagraph (A) for all prior taxable years (to the extent not previously allowed as a deduction by reason of this subparagraph), or

(ii) the excess (if any) of—

(I) the limitation of paragraphs (1) and (2) (or if lesser, the aggregate amount of taxable income referred to in subparagraph (A)), over

(II) the amount allowable as a deduction under subsection (a) for such taxable year without regard to this subparagraph.

(C) COMPUTATION OF TAXABLE INCOME.—For purposes of this paragraph, taxable income derived from the conduct of a trade or business shall be computed without regard to the deduction allowable under this section.

(4) MARRIED INDIVIDUALS FILING SEPARATELY.—In the case of a husband and wife filing separate returns for the taxable year—

(A) such individuals shall be treated as 1 taxpayer for purposes of paragraphs (1) and (2), and

(B) unless such individuals elect otherwise, 50 percent of the cost which may be taken into account under subsection (a) for such taxable year (before application of paragraph (3)) shall be allocated to each such individual.

(5) LIMITATION ON COST TAKEN INTO ACCOUNT FOR CERTAIN PASSENGER VEHICLES.—

(A) IN GENERAL.—The cost of any sport utility vehicle for any taxable year which may be taken into account under this section shall not exceed $25,000.

(B) SPORT UTILITY VEHICLE.—For purposes of subparagraph (A)—

(i) IN GENERAL.—The term "sport utility vehicle" means any 4-wheeled vehicle—

(I) which is primarily designed or which can be used to carry passengers over public streets, roads, or highways (except any vehicle operated exclusively on a rail or rails),

(II) which is not subject to section 280F, and

(III) which is rated at not more than 14,000 pounds gross vehicle weight.

(ii) CERTAIN VEHICLES EXCLUDED.—Such term does not include any vehicle which—

(I) is designed to have a seating capacity of more than 9 persons behind the driver's seat,

(II) is equipped with a cargo area of at least 6 feet in interior length which is an open area or is designed for use as an open area but is enclosed by a cap and is not readily accessible directly from the passenger compartment, or

(III) has an integral enclosure, fully enclosing the driver compartment and load carrying device, does not have seating rearward of the driver's seat, and has no body section protruding more than 30 inches ahead of the leading edge of the windshield.

(6) INFLATION ADJUSTMENT.—

(A) IN GENERAL.—In the case of any taxable year beginning after 2018, the dollar amounts in paragraphs (1), (2), and (5)(A) shall each be increased by an amount equal to—

(i) such dollar amount, multiplied by

(ii) the cost-of-living adjustment determined under section 1(f)(3) for the calendar year in which the taxable year begins, determined by substituting "calendar year 2017" for "calendar year 2016" in subparagraph (A)(ii) thereof.

(B) ROUNDING.—The amount of any increase under subparagraph (A) shall be rounded to the nearest multiple of $10,000 ($100 in the case of any increase in the amount under paragraph (5)(A)).

[Sec. 179(c)]

(c) ELECTION.—

(1) IN GENERAL.—An election under this section for any taxable year shall—

(A) specify the items of section 179 property to which the election applies and the portion of the cost of each of such items which is to be taken into account under subsection (a), and

(B) be made on the taxpayer's return of the tax imposed by this chapter for the taxable year.

Such election shall be made in such manner as the Secretary may by regulations prescribe.

(2) ELECTION.—Any election made under this section, and any specification contained in any such election, may be revoked by the taxpayer with respect to any property, and such revocation, once made, shall be irrevocable.

[Sec. 179(d)]

(d) DEFINITIONS AND SPECIAL RULES.—

(1) SECTION 179 PROPERTY.—For purposes of this section, the term "section 179 property" means property—

(A) which is—

(i) tangible property (to which section 168 applies), or

(ii) computer software (as defined in section 197(e)(3)(B)) which is described in section 197(e)(3)(A)(i) and to which section 167 applies,

(B) which is—

(i) section 1245 property (as defined in section 1245(a)(3)), or

(ii) at the election of the taxpayer, qualified real property (as defined in subsection (e)), and

(C) which is acquired by purchase for use in the active conduct of a trade or business.

Such term shall not include any property described in section 50(b) (other than paragraph (2) thereof).

(2) PURCHASE DEFINED.—For purposes of paragraph (1), the term "purchase" means any acquisition of property, but only if—

(A) the property is not acquired from a person whose relationship to the person acquiring it would result in the disallowance of losses under section 267 or 707(b) (but, in applying section 267(b) and (c) for purposes of this section, paragraph (4) of section 267(c) shall be treated as providing that the family of an individual shall include only his spouse, ancestors, and lineal descendants),

(B) the property is not acquired by one component member of a controlled group from another component member of the same controlled group, and

(C) the basis of the property in the hands of the person acquiring it is not determined—

(i) in whole or in part by reference to the adjusted basis of such property in the hands of the person from whom acquired, or

(ii) under section 1014(a) (relating to property acquired from a decedent).

(3) COST.—For purposes of this section, the cost of property does not include so much of the basis of such property as is determined by reference to the basis of other property held at any time by the person acquiring such property.

(4) SECTION NOT TO APPLY TO ESTATES AND TRUSTS.—This section shall not apply to estates and trusts.

(5) SECTION NOT TO APPLY TO CERTAIN NONCORPORATE LESSORS.—This section shall not apply to any section 179 property which is purchased by a person who is not a corporation and with respect to which such person is the lessor unless—

(A) the property subject to the lease has been manufactured or produced by the lessor, or

(B) the term of the lease (taking into account options to renew) is less than 50 percent of the class life of the property (as defined in section 168(i)(1)), and for the period consisting of the first 12 months after the date on which the property is transferred to the lessee the sum of the deductions with respect to such property which are allowable to the lessor solely by reason of section 162 (other than rents and reimbursed amounts with respect to such property) exceeds 15 percent of the rental income produced by such property.

(6) DOLLAR LIMITATION OF CONTROLLED GROUP.—For purposes of subsection (b) of this section—

(A) all component members of a controlled group shall be treated as one taxpayer, and

(B) the Secretary shall apportion the dollar limitation contained in subsection (b)(1) among the component members of such controlled group in such manner as he shall by regulations prescribe.

(7) CONTROLLED GROUP DEFINED.—For purposes of paragraphs (2) and (6), the term "controlled group" has the meaning assigned to it by section 1563(a), except that, for such purposes, the phrase "more than 50 percent" shall be substituted for the phrase "at least 80 percent" each place it appears in section 1563(a)(1).

(8) TREATMENT OF PARTNERSHIPS AND S CORPORATIONS.—In the case of a partnership, the limitations of subsection (b) shall apply with respect to the partnership and with respect to each partner. A similar rule shall apply in the case of an S corporation and its shareholders.

* * *

(10) RECAPTURE IN CERTAIN CASES.—The Secretary shall, by regulations, provide for recapturing the benefit under any deduction allowable under subsection (a) with respect to any property which is not used predominantly in a trade or business at any time.

[Sec. 179(e)]

(e) QUALIFIED REAL PROPERTY.—For purposes of this section, the term "qualified real property" means—

(1) any qualified improvement property described in section 168(e)(6), and

(2) any of the following improvements to nonresidential real property placed in service after the date such property was first placed in service:

(A) Roofs.

(B) Heating, ventilation, and air-conditioning property.

(C) Fire protection and alarm systems.

(D) Security systems.

[Sec. 183]

SEC. 183. ACTIVITIES NOT ENGAGED IN FOR PROFIT.

[Sec. 183(a)]

(a) GENERAL RULE.—In the case of an activity engaged in by an individual or an S corporation, if such activity is not engaged in for profit, no deduction attributable to such activity shall be allowed under this chapter except as provided in this section.

[Sec. 183(b)]

(b) DEDUCTIONS ALLOWABLE.—In the case of an activity not engaged in for profit to which subsection (a) applies, there shall be allowed—

(1) the deductions which would be allowable under this chapter for the taxable year without regard to whether or not such activity is engaged in for profit, and

(2) a deduction equal to the amount of the deductions which would be allowable under this chapter for the taxable year only if such activity were engaged in for profit, but only to the extent that the gross income derived from such activity for the taxable year exceeds the deductions allowable by reason of paragraph (1).

[Sec. 183(c)]

(c) ACTIVITY NOT ENGAGED IN FOR PROFIT DEFINED.—For purposes of this section, the term "activity not engaged in for profit" means any activity other than one with respect to which deductions are allowable for the taxable year under section 162 or under paragraph (1) or (2) of section 212.

[Sec. 183(d)]

(d) PRESUMPTION.—If the gross income derived from an activity for 3 or more of the taxable years in the period of 5 consecutive taxable years which ends with the taxable year exceeds the deductions attributable to such activity (determined without regard to whether or not such activity is engaged in for profit), then, unless the Secretary establishes to the contrary, such activity shall be presumed for purposes of this chapter for such taxable year to be an activity engaged in for profit. In the case of an activity which consists in major part of the breeding, training, showing, or racing of horses, the preceding sentence shall be applied by substituting "2" for "3" and "7" for "5".

[Sec. 183(e)]

(e) SPECIAL RULE.—

(1) IN GENERAL.—A determination as to whether the presumption provided by subsection (d) applies with respect to any activity shall, if the taxpayer so elects, not be made before the close of the fourth taxable year (sixth taxable year, in the case of an activity described in the last sentence of such subsection) following the taxable year in which the taxpayer first engages in the activity.

(2) INITIAL PERIOD.—If the taxpayer makes an election under paragraph (1), the presumption provided by subsection (d) shall apply to each taxable year in the 5-taxable year (or 7-taxable year) period beginning with the taxable year in which the taxpayer first engages in the activity, if the gross income derived from the activity for 3 (or 2 if applicable) or more of the taxable years in such period exceeds the deductions attributable to the activity (determined without regard to whether or not the activity is engaged in for profit).

(3) ELECTION.—An election under paragraph (1) shall be made at such time and manner, and subject to such terms and conditions, as the Secretary may prescribe.

(4) TIME FOR ASSESSING DEFICIENCY ATTRIBUTABLE TO ACTIVITY.—If a taxpayer makes an election under paragraph (1) with respect to an activity, the statutory period for the assessment of any deficiency attributable to such activity shall not expire before the expiration of 2 years after the date prescribed by law (determined without extensions) for filing the return of tax under chapter 1 for the last taxable year in the period of 5 taxable years (or 7 taxable years) to which the election relates. Such deficiency may be assessed notwithstanding the provisions of any law or rule of law which would otherwise prevent such an assessment.

[Sec. 186]

SEC. 186. RECOVERIES OF DAMAGES FOR ANTITRUST VIOLATIONS, ETC.

[Sec. 186(a)]

(a) ALLOWANCE OF DEDUCTION.—If a compensatory amount which is included in gross income is received or accrued during the taxable year for a compensable injury, there shall be allowed as a deduction for the taxable year an amount equal to the lesser of—

(1) the amount of such compensatory amount, or

(2) the amount of the unrecovered losses sustained as a result of such compensable injury.

[Sec. 186(b)]

(b) COMPENSABLE INJURY.—For purposes of this section, the term "compensable injury" means—

(1) injuries sustained as a result of an infringement of a patent issued by the United States,

(2) injuries sustained as a result of a breach of contract or a breach of fiduciary duty or relationship, or

(3) injuries sustained in business, or to property, by reason of any conduct forbidden in the antitrust laws for which a civil action may be brought under section 4 of the Act entitled "An Act to supplement existing laws against unlawful restraints and monopolies, and for other purposes", approved October 15, 1914 (commonly known as the Clayton Act).

[Sec. 186(c)]

(c) COMPENSATORY AMOUNT.—For purposes of this section, the term "compensatory amount" means the amount received or accrued during the taxable year as damages as a result of an award in, or in settlement of, a civil action for recovery for a compensable injury, reduced by any amounts paid or incurred in the taxable year in securing such award or settlement.

[Sec. 186(d)]

(d) UNRECOVERED LOSSES.—

(1) IN GENERAL.—For purposes of this section, the amount of any unrecovered loss sustained as a result of any compensable injury is—

(A) the sum of the amount of the net operating losses (as determined under section 172) for each taxable year in whole or in part within the injury period, to the extent that such net operating losses are attributable to such compensable injury, reduced by

(B) the sum of—

(i) the amount of the net operating losses described in subparagraph (A) which were allowed for any prior taxable year as a deduction under section 172 as a net operating loss carryback or carryover to such taxable year, and

(ii) the amounts allowed as a deduction under subsection (a) for any prior taxable year for prior recoveries of compensatory amounts for such compensable injury.

(2) INJURY PERIOD.—For purposes of paragraph (1), the injury period is—

(A) with respect to any infringement of a patent, the period in which such infringement occurred,

(B) with respect to a breach of contract or breach of fiduciary duty or relationship, the period during which amounts would have been received or accrued but for the breach of contract or breach of fiduciary duty or relationship, and

(C) with respect to injuries sustained by reason of any conduct forbidden in the antitrust laws, the period in which such injuries were sustained.

(3) NET OPERATING LOSSES ATTRIBUTABLE TO COMPENSABLE INJURIES.—For purposes of paragraph (1)—

(A) a net operating loss for any taxable year shall be treated as attributable to a compensable injury to the extent of the compensable injury sustained during such taxable year, and

(B) if only a portion of a net operating loss for any taxable year is attributable to a compensable injury, such portion shall (in applying section 172 for purposes of this section) be considered to be a separate net operating loss for such year to be applied after the other portion of such net operating loss.

[Sec. 186(e)]

(e) EFFECT ON NET OPERATING LOSS CARRYOVERS.—If for the taxable year in which a compensatory amount is received or accrued any portion of a net operating loss carryover to such year is attributable to the compensable injury for which such amount is received or accrued, such portion of such net operating loss carryover shall be reduced by an amount equal to—

(1) the deduction allowed under subsection (a) with respect to such compensatory amount, reduced by

(2) any portion of the unrecovered losses sustained as a result of the compensable injury with respect to which the period for carryover under section 172 has expired.

[Sec. 195]

SEC. 195. START-UP EXPENDITURES.

[Sec. 195(a)]

(a) CAPITALIZATION OF EXPENDITURES.—Except as otherwise provided in this section, no deduction shall be allowed for start-up expenditures.

[Sec. 195(b)]

(b) ELECTION TO DEDUCT.—

(1) ALLOWANCE OF DEDUCTION.—If a taxpayer elects the application of this subsection with respect to any start-up expenditures—

(A) the taxpayer shall be allowed a deduction for the taxable year in which the active trade or business begins in an amount equal to the lesser of—

(i) the amount of start-up expenditures with respect to the active trade or business, or

(ii) $5,000, reduced (but not below zero) by the amount by which such start-up expenditures exceed $50,000, and

(B) the remainder of such start-up expenditures shall be allowed as a deduction ratably over the 180-month period beginning with the month in which the active trade or business begins.

(2) DISPOSITIONS BEFORE CLOSE OF AMORTIZATION PERIOD.—In any case in which a trade or business is completely disposed of by the taxpayer before the end of the period to which paragraph (1) applies, any deferred expenses attributable to such trade or business which were not allowed as a deduction by reason of this section may be deducted to the extent allowable under section 165.

* * *

[Sec. 195(c)]

(c) DEFINITIONS.—For purposes of this section—

(1) START-UP EXPENDITURES.—The term "start-up expenditure" means any amount—

(A) paid or incurred in connection with—

(i) investigating the creation or acquisition of an active trade or business, or

(ii) creating an active trade or business, or

(iii) any activity engaged in for profit and for the production of income before the day on which the active trade or business begins, in anticipation of such activity becoming an active trade or business, and

(B) which, if paid or incurred in connection with the operation of an existing active trade or business (in the same field as the trade or business referred to in subparagraph (A)), would be allowable as a deduction for the taxable year in which paid or incurred.

The term "start-up expenditure" does not include any amount with respect to which a deduction is allowable under section 163(a), 164, or 174.

(2) BEGINNING OF TRADE OR BUSINESS.—

(A) IN GENERAL.—Except as provided in subparagraph (B), the determination of when an active trade or business begins shall be made in accordance with such regulations as the Secretary may prescribe.

(B) ACQUIRED TRADE OR BUSINESS.—An acquired active trade or business shall be treated as beginning when the taxpayer acquires it.

[Sec. 195(d)]

(d) ELECTION.—

(1) TIME FOR MAKING ELECTION.—An election under subsection (b) shall be made not later than the time prescribed by law for filing the return for the taxable year in which the trade or business begins (including extensions thereof).

(2) SCOPE OF ELECTION.—The period selected under subsection (b) shall be adhered to in computing taxable income for the taxable year for which the election is made and all subsequent taxable years.

[Sec. 197]

SEC. 197. AMORTIZATION OF GOODWILL AND CERTAIN OTHER INTANGIBLES.

[Sec. 197(a)]

(a) GENERAL RULE.—A taxpayer shall be entitled to an amortization deduction with respect to any amortizable section 197 intangible. The amount of such deduction shall be determined by amortizing the adjusted basis (for purposes of determining gain) of such intangible ratably over the 15-year period beginning with the month in which such intangible was acquired.

[Sec. 197(b)]

(b) NO OTHER DEPRECIATION OR AMORTIZATION DEDUCTION ALLOWABLE.—Except as provided in subsection (a), no depreciation or amortization deduction shall be allowable with respect to any amortizable section 197 intangible.

[Sec. 197(c)]

(c) AMORTIZABLE SECTION 197 INTANGIBLE.—For purposes of this section—

(1) IN GENERAL.—Except as otherwise provided in this section, the term "amortizable section 197 intangible" means any section 197 intangible—

(A) which is acquired by the taxpayer after the date of the enactment [August 10, 1993] of this section, and

(B) which is held in connection with the conduct of a trade or business or an activity described in section 212.

(2) EXCLUSION OF SELF-CREATED INTANGIBLES, ETC.—The term "amortizable section 197 intangible" shall not include any section 197 intangible—

(A) which is not described in subparagraph (D), (E), or (F) of subsection (d)(1), and

(B) which is created by the taxpayer.

This paragraph shall not apply if the intangible is created in connection with a transaction (or series of related transactions) involving the acquisition of assets constituting a trade or business or substantial portion thereof.

(3) ANTI-CHURNING RULES.—

For exclusion of intangibles acquired in certain transactions, see subsection (f)(9).

[Sec. 197(d)]

(d) SECTION 197 INTANGIBLE.—For purposes of this section—

(1) IN GENERAL.—Except as otherwise provided in this section, the term "section 197 intangible" means—

(A) goodwill,

(B) going concern value,

(C) any of the following intangible items:

(i) workforce in place including its composition and terms and conditions (contractual or otherwise) of its employment,

(ii) business books and records, operating systems, or any other information base (including lists or other information with respect to current or prospective customers),

(iii) any patent, copyright, formula, process, design, pattern, knowhow, format, or other similar item,

(iv) any customer-based intangible,

(v) any supplier-based intangible, and

(vi) any other similar item,

(D) any license, permit, or other right granted by a governmental unit or an agency or instrumentality thereof,

(E) any covenant not to compete (or other arrangement to the extent such arrangement has substantially the same effect as a covenant not to compete) entered into in connection with an acquisition (directly or indirectly) of an interest in a trade or business or substantial portion thereof, and

(F) any franchise, trademark, or trade name.

(2) CUSTOMER-BASED INTANGIBLE.—

(A) IN GENERAL.—The term "customer-based intangible" means—

(i) composition of market,

(ii) market share, and

(iii) any other value resulting from future provision of goods or services pursuant to relationships (contractual or otherwise) in the ordinary course of business with customers.

(B) SPECIAL RULE FOR FINANCIAL INSTITUTIONS.—In the case of a financial institution, the term "customer-based intangible" includes deposit base and similar items.

(3) SUPPLIER-BASED INTANGIBLE.—The term "supplier-based intangible" means any value resulting from future acquisitions of goods or services pursuant to relationships (contractual or otherwise) in the ordinary course of business with suppliers of goods or services to be used or sold by the taxpayer.

[Sec. 197(e)]

(e) EXCEPTIONS.—For purposes of this section, the term "section 197 intangible" shall not include any of the following:

(1) FINANCIAL INTERESTS.—Any interest—

(A) in a corporation, partnership, trust, or estate, or

(B) under an existing futures contract, foreign currency contract, notional principal contract, or other similar financial contract.

(2) LAND.—Any interest in land.

(3) COMPUTER SOFTWARE.—

(A) IN GENERAL.—Any—

(i) computer software which is readily available for purchase by the general public, is subject to a nonexclusive license, and has not been substantially modified, and

(ii) other computer software which is not acquired in a transaction (or series of related transactions) involving the acquisition of assets constituting a trade or business or substantial portion thereof.

(B) COMPUTER SOFTWARE DEFINED.—For purposes of subparagraph (A), the term "computer software" means any program designed to cause a computer to perform a desired function. Such term shall not include any data base or similar item unless the data base or item is in the public domain and is incidental to the operation of otherwise qualifying computer software.

(4) CERTAIN INTERESTS OR RIGHTS ACQUIRED SEPARATELY.—Any of the following not acquired in a transaction (or series of related transactions) involving the acquisition of assets constituting a trade business or substantial portion thereof:

(A) Any interest in a film, sound recording, video tape, book, or similar property.

(B) Any right to receive tangible property or services under a contract or granted by a governmental unit or agency or instrumentality thereof.

(C) Any interest in a patent or copyright.

(D) To the extent provided in regulations, any right under a contract (or granted by a governmental unit or an agency or instrumentality thereof) if such right—

(i) has a fixed duration of less than 15 years, or

(ii) is fixed as to amount and, without regard to this section, would be recoverable under a method similar to the unit-of-production method.

(5) INTERESTS UNDER LEASES AND DEBT INSTRUMENTS.—Any interest under—

(A) an existing lease of tangible property, or

(B) except as provided in subsection (d) (2) (B), any existing indebtedness.

(6) MORTGAGE SERVICING.—Any right to service indebtedness which is secured by residential real property unless such right is acquired in a transaction (or series of related transactions) involving the acquisition of assets (other than rights described in this paragraph) constituting a trade or business or substantial portion thereof.

(7) CERTAIN TRANSACTION COSTS .—Any fees for professional services, and any transaction costs, incurred by parties to a transaction with respect to which any portion of the gain or loss is not recognized under part III of subchapter C.

[Sec. 197(f)]

(f) SPECIAL RULES.—

(1) TREATMENT OF CERTAIN DISPOSITIONS, ETC.—

(A) IN GENERAL.—If there is a disposition of any amortizable section 197 intangible acquired in a transaction or series of related transactions (or any such intangible becomes worthless) and one or more other amortizable section 197 intangibles acquired in such transaction or series of related transactions are retained—

(i) no loss shall be recognized by reason of such disposition (or such worthlessness), and

(ii) appropriate adjustments to the adjusted bases of such retained intangibles shall be made for any loss not recognized under clause (i).

(B) SPECIAL RULE FOR COVENANTS NOT TO COMPETE.—In the case of any section 197 intangible which is a covenant not to compete (or other arrangement) described in subsection (d) (1) (E), in no event shall such covenant or other arrangement be treated as disposed of (or becoming worthless) before the disposition of the entire interest described in such subsection in connection with which such covenant (or other arrangement) was entered into.

(C) SPECIAL RULE.—All persons treated as a single taxpayer under section 41 (f) (1) shall be so treated for purposes of this paragraph.

(2) TREATMENT OF CERTAIN TRANSFERS.—

(A) IN GENERAL.—In the case of any section 197 intangible transferred in a transaction described in subparagraph (B), the transferee shall be treated as the transferor for purposes of applying this section with respect to so much of the adjusted basis in the hands of the transferee as does not exceed the adjusted basis in the hands of the transferor.

(B) TRANSACTIONS COVERED.—The transactions described in this subparagraph are—

(i) any transaction described in section 332, 351, 361, 721, 731, 1031, or 1033, and

(ii) any transaction between members of the same affiliated group during any taxable year for which a consolidated return is made by such group.

(3) TREATMENT OF AMOUNTS PAID PURSUANT TO COVENANTS NOT TO COMPETE, ETC.—Any amount paid or incurred pursuant to a covenant or arrangement referred to in subsection (d)(1)(E) shall be treated as an amount chargeable to capital account.

(4) TREATMENT OF FRANCHISES, ETC.—

(A) FRANCHISE.—The term "franchise" has the meaning given to such term by section 1253(b)(1).

(B) TREATMENT OF RENEWALS.—Any renewal of a franchise, trademark, or trade name (or of a license, a permit, or other right referred to in subsection (d)(1)(D)) shall be treated as an acquisition. The preceding sentence shall only apply with respect to costs incurred in connection with such renewal.

(C) CERTAIN AMOUNTS NOT TAKEN INTO ACCOUNT.—Any amount to which section 1253(d)(1) applies shall not be taken into account under this section.

(5) TREATMENT OF CERTAIN REINSURANCE TRANSACTIONS.—In the case of any amortizable section 197 intangible resulting from an assumption reinsurance transaction, the amount taken into account as the adjusted basis of such intangible under this section shall be the excess of—

(A) the amount paid or incurred by the acquirer under the assumption reinsurance transaction, over

(B) the amount required to be capitalized under section 848 in connection with such transaction.

Subsection (b) shall not apply to any amount required to be capitalized under section 848.

(6) TREATMENT OF CERTAIN SUBLEASES.—For purposes of this section, a sublease shall be treated in the same manner as a lease of the underlying property involved.

(7) TREATMENT AS DEPRECIABLE.—For purposes of this chapter, any amortizable section 197 intangible shall be treated as property which is of a character subject to the allowance for depreciation provided in section 167.

(8) TREATMENT OF CERTAIN INCREMENTS IN VALUE.—This section shall not apply to any increment in value if, without regard to this section, such increment is properly taken into account in determining the cost of property which is not a section 197 intangible.

(9) ANTI-CHURNING RULES.—For purposes of this section—

(A) IN GENERAL.—The term "amortizable section 197 intangible" shall not include any section 197 intangible which is described in subparagraph (A) or (B) of subsection (d)(1) (or for which depreciation or amortization would not have been allowable but for this section) and which is acquired by the taxpayer after the date of the enactment of this section, if—

(i) the intangible was held or used at any time on or after July 25, 1991, and on or before such date of enactment by the taxpayer or a related person,

(ii) the intangible was acquired from a person who held such intangible at any time on or after July 25, 1991, and on or before such date of enactment, and, as part of the transaction, the user of such intangible does not change, or

(iii) the taxpayer grants the right to use such intangible to a person (or a person related to such person) who held or used such intangible at any time on or after July 25, 1991, and on or before such date of enactment.

For purposes of this subparagraph, the determination of whether the user of property changes as part of a transaction shall be determined in accordance with regulations prescribed by the Secretary. For purposes of this subparagraph, deductions allowable under section 1253(d) shall be treated as deductions allowable for amortization.

(B) EXCEPTION WHERE GAIN RECOGNIZED.—If—

(i) subparagraph (A) would not apply to an intangible acquired by the taxpayer but for the last sentence of subparagraph (C)(i), and

(ii) the person from whom the taxpayer acquired the intangible elects, notwithstanding any other provision of this title—

(I) to recognize gain on the disposition of the intangible, and

(II) to pay a tax on such gain which, when added to any other income tax on such gain under this title, equals such gain multiplied by the highest rate of income tax applicable to such person under this title,

then subparagraph (A) shall apply to the intangible only to the extent that the taxpayer's adjusted basis in the intangible exceeds the gain recognized under clause (ii)(I).

(C) RELATED PERSON DEFINED.—For purposes of this paragraph—

(i) RELATED PERSON.—A person (hereinafter in this paragraph referred to as the "related person") is related to any person if—

(I) the related person bears a relationship to such person specified in section 267(b) or section 707(b)(1), or

(II) the related person and such person are engaged in trades or businesses under common control (within the meaning of subparagraphs (A) and (B) of section 41(f)(1)).

For purposes of subclause (I), in applying section 267(b) or 707(b)(1), "20 percent" shall be substituted for "50 percent".

(ii) TIME FOR MAKING DETERMINATION.—A person shall be treated as related to another person if such relationship exists immediately before or immediately after the acquisition of the intangible involved.

(D) ACQUISITIONS BY REASON OF DEATH.—Subparagraph (A) shall not apply to the acquisition of any property by the taxpayer if the basis of the property in the hands of the taxpayer is determined under section 1014(a).

(E) SPECIAL RULE FOR PARTNERSHIPS.—With respect to any increase in the basis of partnership property under section 732, 734, or 743, determinations under this paragraph shall be made at the partner level and each partner shall be treated as having owned and used such partner's proportionate share of the partnership assets.

(F) ANTI-ABUSE RULES.—The term "amortizable section 197 intangible" does not include any section 197 intangible acquired in a transaction, one of the principal purposes of which is to avoid the requirement of subsection (c)(1) that the intangible be acquired after the date of the enactment of this section or to avoid the provisions of subparagraph (A).

[Sec. 197(g)]

(g) REGULATIONS.—The Secretary shall prescribe such regulations as may be appropriate to carry out the purposes of this section, including such regulations as may be appropriate to prevent avoidance of the purposes of this section through related persons or otherwise.

»»→ Caution: Pursuant to Section 199A(e)(2)(B), the dollar amount stated in Section 199A(e)(2)(A) is adjusted for taxable years beginning after 2018 to reflect increases in the Chained Consumer Price Index. The dollar amount applicable to taxable years beginning in 2020 is provided in the material beginning at page ix.

[Sec. 199A]

SEC. 199A. QUALIFIED BUSINESS INCOME.

[Sec. 199A(a)]

(a) ALLOWANCE OF DEDUCTION.—In the case of a taxpayer other than a corporation, there shall be allowed as a deduction for any taxable year an amount equal to the lesser of—

(1) the combined qualified business income amount of the taxpayer, or

(2) an amount equal to 20 percent of the excess (if any) of—

(A) the taxable income of the taxpayer for the taxable year, over

(B) the net capital gain (as defined in section 1(h)) of the taxpayer for such taxable year.

[Sec. 199A(b)]

(b) COMBINED QUALIFIED BUSINESS INCOME AMOUNT.—For purposes of this section—

(1) IN GENERAL.—The term "combined qualified business income amount" means, with respect to any taxable year, an amount equal to—

(A) the sum of the amounts determined under paragraph (2) for each qualified trade or business carried on by the taxpayer, plus

(B) 20 percent of the aggregate amount of the qualified REIT dividends and qualified publicly traded partnership income of the taxpayer for the taxable year.

(2) DETERMINATION OF DEDUCTIBLE AMOUNT FOR EACH TRADE OR BUSINESS.—The amount determined under this paragraph with respect to any qualified trade or business is the lesser of—

(A) 20 percent of the taxpayer's qualified business income with respect to the qualified trade or business, or

(B) the greater of—

(i) 50 percent of the W–2 wages with respect to the qualified trade or business, or

(ii) the sum of 25 percent of the W–2 wages with respect to the qualified trade or business, plus 2.5 percent of the unadjusted basis immediately after acquisition of all qualified property.

(3) MODIFICATIONS TO LIMIT BASED ON TAXABLE INCOME.—

(A) EXCEPTION FROM LIMIT.—In the case of any taxpayer whose taxable income for the taxable year does not exceed the threshold amount, paragraph (2) shall be applied without regard to subparagraph (B).

(B) PHASE-IN OF LIMIT FOR CERTAIN TAXPAYERS.—

(i) IN GENERAL.—If—

(I) the taxable income of a taxpayer for any taxable year exceeds the threshold amount, but does not exceed the sum of the threshold amount plus $50,000 ($100,000 in the case of a joint return), and

(II) the amount determined under paragraph (2)(B) (determined without regard to this subparagraph) with respect to any qualified trade or business carried on by the taxpayer is less than the amount determined under paragraph (2)(A) with respect [to] such trade or business,

then paragraph (2) shall be applied with respect to such trade or business without regard to subparagraph (B) thereof and by reducing the amount determined under subparagraph (A) thereof by the amount determined under clause (ii).

(ii) AMOUNT OF REDUCTION.—The amount determined under this subparagraph is the amount which bears the same ratio to the excess amount as—

(I) the amount by which the taxpayer's taxable income for the taxable year exceeds the threshold amount, bears to

(II) $50,000 ($100,000 in the case of a joint return).

(iii) EXCESS AMOUNT.—For purposes of clause (ii), the excess amount is the excess of—

(I) the amount determined under paragraph (2)(A) (determined without regard to this paragraph), over

(II) the amount determined under paragraph (2)(B) (determined without regard to this paragraph).

(4) WAGES, ETC.—

(A) IN GENERAL.—The term "W–2 wages" means, with respect to any person for any taxable year of such person, the amounts described in paragraphs (3) and (8) of section

6051(a) paid by such person with respect to employment of employees by such person during the calendar year ending during such taxable year.

(B) LIMITATION TO WAGES ATTRIBUTABLE TO QUALIFIED BUSINESS INCOME.—Such term shall not include any amount which is not properly allocable to qualified business income for purposes of subsection (c)(1).

(C) RETURN REQUIREMENT.—Such term shall not include any amount which is not properly included in a return filed with the Social Security Administration on or before the 60th day after the due date (including extensions) for such return.

(5) ACQUISITIONS, DISPOSITIONS, AND SHORT TAXABLE YEARS.—The Secretary shall provide for the application of this subsection in cases of a short taxable year or where the taxpayer acquires, or disposes of, the major portion of a trade or business or the major portion of a separate unit of a trade or business during the taxable year.

(6) QUALIFIED PROPERTY.—For purposes of this section:

(A) IN GENERAL.—The term "qualified property" means, with respect to any qualified trade or business for a taxable year, tangible property of a character subject to the allowance for depreciation under section 167—

(i) which is held by, and available for use in, the qualified trade or business at the close of the taxable year,

(ii) which is used at any point during the taxable year in the production of qualified business income, and

(iii) the depreciable period for which has not ended before the close of the taxable year.

(B) DEPRECIABLE PERIOD.—The term "depreciable period" means, with respect to qualified property of a taxpayer, the period beginning on the date the property was first placed in service by the taxpayer and ending on the later of—

(i) the date that is 10 years after such date, or

(ii) the last day of the last full year in the applicable recovery period that would apply to the property under section 168 (determined without regard to subsection (g) thereof).

(7) SPECIAL RULE WITH RESPECT TO INCOME RECEIVED FROM COOPERATIVES.—In the case of any qualified trade or business of a patron of a specified agricultural or horticultural cooperative, the amount determined under paragraph (2) with respect to such trade or business shall be reduced by the lesser of—

(A) 9 percent of so much of the qualified business income with respect to such trade or business as is properly allocable to qualified payments received from such cooperative, or

(B) 50 percent of so much of the W-2 wages with respect to such trade or business as are so allocable.

[Sec. 199A(c)]

(c) QUALIFIED BUSINESS INCOME.—For purposes of this section—

(1) IN GENERAL.—The term "qualified business income" means, for any taxable year, the net amount of qualified items of income, gain, deduction, and loss with respect to any qualified trade or business of the taxpayer. Such term shall not include any qualified REIT dividends or qualified publicly traded partnership income.

(2) CARRYOVER OF LOSSES.—If the net amount of qualified income, gain, deduction, and loss with respect to qualified trades or businesses of the taxpayer for any taxable year is less than zero, such amount shall be treated as a loss from a qualified trade or business in the succeeding taxable year.

(3) QUALIFIED ITEMS OF INCOME, GAIN, DEDUCTION, AND LOSS.—For purposes of this subsection—

(A) IN GENERAL.—The term "qualified items of income, gain, deduction, and loss" means items of income, gain, deduction, and loss to the extent such items are—

(i) effectively connected with the conduct of a trade or business within the United States (within the meaning of section 864(c), determined by substituting "qualified trade or business (within the meaning of section 199A)" for "nonresident alien individual or a foreign corporation" or for "a foreign corporation" each place it appears), and

(ii) included or allowed in determining taxable income for the taxable year.

(B) EXCEPTIONS.—The following items shall not be taken into account as a qualified item of income, gain, deduction, or loss:

(i) Any item of short-term capital gain, short-term capital loss, long-term capital gain, or long-term capital loss.

(ii) Any dividend, income equivalent to a dividend, or payment in lieu of dividends described in section 954(c)(1)(G). Any amount described in section 1385(a)(1) shall not be treated as described in this clause.

(iii) Any interest income other than interest income which is properly allocable to a trade or business.

(iv) Any item of gain or loss described in subparagraph (C) or (D) of section 954(c)(1) (applied by substituting "qualified trade or business" for "controlled foreign corporation").

(v) Any item of income, gain, deduction, or loss taken into account under section 954(c)(1)(F) (determined without regard to clause (ii) thereof and other than items attributable to notional principal contracts entered into in transactions qualifying under section 1221(a)(7)).

(vi) Any amount received from an annuity which is not received in connection with the trade or business.

(vii) Any item of deduction or loss properly allocable to an amount described in any of the preceding clauses.

(4) TREATMENT OF REASONABLE COMPENSATION AND GUARANTEED PAYMENTS.—Qualified business income shall not include—

(A) reasonable compensation paid to the taxpayer by any qualified trade or business of the taxpayer for services rendered with respect to the trade or business,

(B) any guaranteed payment described in section 707(c) paid to a partner for services rendered with respect to the trade or business, and

(C) to the extent provided in regulations, any payment described in section 707(a) to a partner for services rendered with respect to the trade or business.

[Sec. 199A(d)]

(d) QUALIFIED TRADE OR BUSINESS.—For purposes of this section—

(1) IN GENERAL.—The term "qualified trade or business" means any trade or business other than—

(A) a specified service trade or business, or

(B) the trade or business of performing services as an employee.

(2) SPECIFIED SERVICE TRADE OR BUSINESS.—The term "specified service trade or business" means any trade or business—

(A) which is described in section 1202(e)(3)(A) (applied without regard to the words "engineering, architecture,") or which would be so described if the term "employees or owners" were substituted for "employees" therein, or

(B) which involves the performance of services that consist of investing and investment management, trading, or dealing in securities (as defined in section 475(c)(2)), partnership interests, or commodities (as defined in section 475(e)(2)).

(3) EXCEPTION FOR SPECIFIED SERVICE BUSINESSES BASED ON TAXPAYER'S INCOME.—

(A) IN GENERAL.—If, for any taxable year, the taxable income of any taxpayer is less than the sum of the threshold amount plus $50,000 ($100,000 in the case of a joint return), then—

(i) any specified service trade or business of the taxpayer shall not fail to be treated as a qualified trade or business due to paragraph (1)(A), but

(ii) only the applicable percentage of qualified items of income, gain, deduction, or loss, and the W–2 wages and the unadjusted basis immediately after acquisition of qualified property, of the taxpayer allocable to such specified service trade or business shall be taken into account in computing the qualified business income, W–2 wages, and the unadjusted basis immediately after acquisition of qualified property of the taxpayer for the taxable year for purposes of applying this section.

(B) APPLICABLE PERCENTAGE.—For purposes of subparagraph (A), the term "applicable percentage" means, with respect to any taxable year, 100 percent reduced (not below zero) by the percentage equal to the ratio of—

(i) the taxable income of the taxpayer for the taxable year in excess of the threshold amount, bears to

(ii) $50,000 ($100,000 in the case of a joint return).

[Sec. 199A(e)]

(e) OTHER DEFINITIONS.—For purposes of this section—

(1) TAXABLE INCOME.—Except as otherwise provided in subsection (g)(2)(B), taxable income shall be computed without regard to any deduction allowable under this section.

(2) THRESHOLD AMOUNT.—

(A) IN GENERAL.—The term "threshold amount" means $157,500 (200 percent of such amount in the case of a joint return).

(B) INFLATION ADJUSTMENT.—In the case of any taxable year beginning after 2018, the dollar amount in subparagraph (A) shall be increased by an amount equal to—

(i) such dollar amount, multiplied by

(ii) the cost-of-living adjustment determined under section 1(f)(3) for the calendar year in which the taxable year begins, determined by substituting "calendar year 2017" for "calendar year 2016" in subparagraph (A)(ii) thereof.

The amount of any increase under the preceding sentence shall be rounded as provided in section 1(f)(7).

(3) QUALIFIED REIT DIVIDEND.—The term "qualified REIT dividend" means any dividend from a real estate investment trust received during the taxable year which—

(A) is not a capital gain dividend, as defined in section 857(b)(3), and

(B) is not qualified dividend income, as defined in section 1(h)(11).

(4) QUALIFIED PUBLICLY TRADED PARTNERSHIP INCOME.—The term "qualified publicly traded partnership income" means, with respect to any qualified trade or business of a taxpayer, the sum of—

(A) the net amount of such taxpayer's allocable share of each qualified item of income, gain, deduction, and loss (as defined in subsection (c)(3) and determined after the application of subsection (c)(4)) from a publicly traded partnership (as defined in section 7704(a)) which is not treated as a corporation under section 7704(c), plus

(B) any gain recognized by such taxpayer upon disposition of its interest in such partnership to the extent such gain is treated as an amount realized from the sale or exchange of property other than a capital asset under section 751(a).

[Sec. 199A(f)]

(f) SPECIAL RULES.—

(1) APPLICATION TO PARTNERSHIPS AND S CORPORATIONS.—

(A) IN GENERAL.—In the case of a partnership or S corporation—

(i) this section shall be applied at the partner or shareholder level,

(ii) each partner or shareholder shall take into account such person's allocable share of each qualified item of income, gain, deduction, and loss, and

(iii) each partner or shareholder shall be treated for purposes of subsection (b) as having W–2 wages and unadjusted basis immediately after acquisition of qualified property for the taxable year in an amount equal to such person's allocable share of the W–2 wages and the unadjusted basis immediately after acquisition of qualified property of the partnership or S corporation for the taxable year (as determined under regulations prescribed by the Secretary).

For purposes of clause (iii), a partner's or shareholder's allocable share of W–2 wages shall be determined in the same manner as the partner's or shareholder's allocable share of wage expenses. For purposes of such clause, partner's or shareholder's allocable share of the unadjusted basis immediately after acquisition of qualified property shall be determined in the same manner as the partner's or shareholder's allocable share of depreciation. For purposes of this subparagraph, in the case of an S corporation, an allocable share shall be the shareholder's pro rata share of an item.

(B) APPLICATION TO TRUSTS AND ESTATES.—Rules similar to the rules under section 199(d)(1)(B)(i) (as in effect on December 1, 2017) for the apportionment of W–2 wages shall apply to the apportionment of W–2 wages and the apportionment of unadjusted basis immediately after acquisition of qualified property under this section.

(C) TREATMENT OF TRADES OR BUSINESS IN PUERTO RICO.—

(i) IN GENERAL.—In the case of any taxpayer with qualified business income from sources within the commonwealth of Puerto Rico, if all such income is taxable under section 1 for such taxable year, then for purposes of determining the qualified business income of such taxpayer for such taxable year, the term "United States" shall include the Commonwealth of Puerto Rico.

(ii) SPECIAL RULE FOR APPLYING LIMIT.—In the case of any taxpayer described in clause (i), the determination of W–2 wages of such taxpayer with respect to any qualified trade or business conducted in Puerto Rico shall be made without regard to any exclusion under section 3401(a)(8) for remuneration paid for services in Puerto Rico.

(2) COORDINATION WITH MINIMUM TAX.—For purposes of determining alternative minimum taxable income under section 55, qualified business income shall be determined without regard to any adjustments under sections 56 through 59.

(3) DEDUCTION LIMITED TO INCOME TAXES.—The deduction under subsection (a) shall only be allowed for purposes of this chapter.

(4) REGULATIONS.—The Secretary shall prescribe such regulations as are necessary to carry out the purposes of this section, including regulations—

(A) for requiring or restricting the allocation of items and wages under this section and such reporting requirements as the Secretary determines appropriate, and

(B) for the application of this section in the case of tiered entities.

[Sec. 199A(g)]

(g) DEDUCTION FOR INCOME ATTRIBUTABLE TO DOMESTIC PRODUCTION ACTIVITIES OF SPECIFIED AGRICULTURAL OR HORTICULTURAL COOPERATIVES.—

(1) ALLOWANCE OF DEDUCTION.—

(A) IN GENERAL.—In the case of a taxpayer which is a specified agricultural or horticultural cooperative, there shall be allowed as a deduction an amount equal to 9 percent of the lesser of—

(i) the qualified production activities income of the taxpayer for the taxable year, or

(ii) the taxable income of the taxpayer for the taxable year.

(B) LIMITATION.—

(i) IN GENERAL.—The deduction allowable under subparagraph (A) for any taxable year shall not exceed 50 percent of the W-2 wages of the taxpayer for the taxable year.

(ii) W-2 WAGES.—For purposes of this subparagraph, the W-2 wages of the taxpayer shall be determined in the same manner as under subsection (b)(4) (without regard to subparagraph (B) thereof and after application of subsection (b)(5)), except that such wages shall not include any amount which is not properly allocable to domestic production gross receipts for purposes of paragraph (3)(A).

(C) TAXABLE INCOME OF COOPERATIVES DETERMINED WITHOUT REGARD TO CERTAIN DEDUCTIONS.—For purposes of this subsection, the taxable income of a specified agricultural or horticultural cooperative shall be computed without regard to any deduction allowable under subsection (b) or (c) of section 1382 (relating to patronage dividends, per-unit retain allocations, and nonpatronage distributions).

(2) DEDUCTION ALLOWED TO PATRONS.—

(A) IN GENERAL.—In the case of any eligible taxpayer who receives a qualified payment from a specified agricultural or horticultural cooperative, there shall be allowed as a deduction for the taxable year in which such payment is received an amount equal to the portion of the deduction allowed under paragraph (1) to such cooperative which is—

(i) allowed with respect to the portion of the qualified production activities income to which such payment is attributable, and

(ii) identified by such cooperative in a written notice mailed to such taxpayer during the payment period described in section 1382(d).

(B) LIMITATION BASED ON TAXABLE INCOME.—The deduction allowed to any taxpayer under this paragraph shall not exceed the taxable income of the taxpayer determined without regard to the deduction allowed under this paragraph and after taking into account any deduction allowed to the taxpayer under subsection (a) for the taxable year.

(C) COOPERATIVE DENIED DEDUCTION FOR PORTION OF QUALIFIED PAYMENTS.—The taxable income of a specified agricultural or horticultural cooperative shall not be reduced under section 1382 by reason of that portion of any qualified payment as does not exceed the deduction allowable under subparagraph (A) with respect to such payment.

(D) ELIGIBLE TAXPAYER.—For purposes of this paragraph, the term "eligible taxpayer" means—

(i) a taxpayer other than a corporation, or

(ii) a specified agricultural or horticultural cooperative.

(E) QUALIFIED PAYMENT.—For purposes of this section, the term "qualified payment" means, with respect to any eligible taxpayer, any amount which—

(i) is described in paragraph (1) or (3) of section 1385(a),

(ii) is received by such taxpayer from a specified agricultural or horticultural cooperative, and

(iii) is attributable to qualified production activities income with respect to which a deduction is allowed to such cooperative under paragraph (1).

(3) QUALIFIED PRODUCTION ACTIVITIES INCOME.—For purposes of this subsection—

(A) IN GENERAL.—The term "qualified production activities income" for any taxable year means an amount equal to the excess (if any) of—

(i) the taxpayer's domestic production gross receipts for such taxable year, over

(ii) the sum of—

(I) the cost of goods sold that are allocable to such receipts, and

(II) other expenses, losses, or deductions (other than the deduction allowed under this subsection), which are properly allocable to such receipts.

(B) ALLOCATION METHOD.—The Secretary shall prescribe rules for the proper allocation of items described in subparagraph (A) for purposes of determining qualified production activities income. Such rules shall provide for the proper allocation of items whether or not such items are directly allocable to domestic production gross receipts.

(C) SPECIAL RULES FOR DETERMINING COSTS.—

(i) IN GENERAL.—For purposes of determining costs under subclause (I) of subparagraph (A)(ii), any item or service brought into the United States shall be treated as acquired by purchase, and its cost shall be treated as not less than its value immediately after it entered the United States. A similar rule shall apply in determining the adjusted basis of leased or rented property where the lease or rental gives rise to domestic production gross receipts.

(ii) EXPORTS FOR FURTHER MANUFACTURE.—In the case of any property described in clause (i) that had been exported by the taxpayer for further manufacture, the increase in cost or adjusted basis under clause (i) shall not exceed the difference between the value of the property when exported and the value of the property when brought back into the United States after the further manufacture.

(D) DOMESTIC PRODUCTION GROSS RECEIPTS.—

(i) IN GENERAL.—The term "domestic production gross receipts" means the gross receipts of the taxpayer which are derived from any lease, rental, license, sale, exchange, or other disposition of any agricultural or horticultural product which was manufactured, produced, grown, or extracted by the taxpayer (determined after the application of paragraph (4)(B)) in whole or significant part within the United States. Such term shall not include gross receipts of the taxpayer which are derived from the lease, rental, license, sale, exchange, or other disposition of land.

(ii) RELATED PERSONS.—

(I) IN GENERAL.—The term "domestic production gross receipts" shall not include any gross receipts of the taxpayer derived from property leased, licensed, or rented by the taxpayer for use by any related person.

(II) RELATED PERSON.—For purposes of subclause (I), a person shall be treated as related to another person if such persons are treated as a single employer under subsection (a) or (b) of section 52 or subsection (m) or (o) of section 414, except that determinations under subsections (a) and (b) of section 52 shall be made without regard to section 1563(b).

(4) SPECIFIED AGRICULTURAL OR HORTICULTURAL COOPERATIVE.—For purposes of this section—

(A) IN GENERAL.—The term "specified agricultural or horticultural cooperative" means an organization to which part I of subchapter T applies which is engaged—

(i) in the manufacturing, production, growth, or extraction in whole or significant part of any agricultural or horticultural product, or

(ii) in the marketing of agricultural or horticultural products.

(B) APPLICATION TO MARKETING COOPERATIVES.—A specified agricultural or horticultural cooperative described in subparagraph (A)(ii) shall be treated as having manufactured, produced, grown, or extracted in whole or significant part any agricultural or horticultural product marketed by the specified agricultural or horticultural cooperative which its patrons have so manufactured, produced, grown, or extracted.

(5) DEFINITIONS AND SPECIAL RULES.—

(A) SPECIAL RULE FOR AFFILIATED GROUPS.—

(i) IN GENERAL.—All members of an expanded affiliated group shall be treated as a single corporation for purposes of this subsection.

(ii) PARTNERSHIPS OWNED BY EXPANDED AFFILIATED GROUPS.—For purposes of paragraph (3)(D), if all of the interests in the capital and profits of a partnership are owned by members of a single expanded affiliated group at all times during the taxable year of such partnership, the partnership and all members of such group shall be treated as a single taxpayer during such period.

(iii) EXPANDED AFFILIATED GROUP.—For purposes of this subsection, the term "expanded affiliated group" means an affiliated group as defined in section 1504(a), determined—

(I) by substituting "more than 50 percent" for "at least 80 percent" each place it appears, and

(II) without regard to paragraphs (2) and (4) of section 1504(b).

(iv) ALLOCATION OF DEDUCTION.—Except as provided in regulations, the deduction under paragraph (1) shall be allocated among the members of the expanded affiliated group in proportion to each member's respective amount (if any) of qualified production activities income.

(B) SPECIAL RULE FOR COOPERATIVE PARTNERS.—In the case of a specified agricultural or horticultural cooperative which is a partner in a partnership, rules similar to the rules of subsection (f)(1) shall apply for purposes of this subsection.

(C) TRADE OR BUSINESS REQUIREMENT.—This subsection shall be applied by only taking into account items which are attributable to the actual conduct of a trade or business.

(D) UNRELATED BUSINESS TAXABLE INCOME.—For purposes of determining the tax imposed by section 511, this section shall be applied by substituting "unrelated business taxable income" for "taxable income" each place it appears in this section (other than this subparagraph).

(E) SPECIAL RULE FOR COOPERATIVE WITH OIL RELATED QUALIFIED PRODUCTION ACTIVITIES INCOME.—

(i) IN GENERAL.—If a specified agricultural or horticultural cooperative has oil related qualified production activities income for any taxable year, the amount otherwise allowable as a deduction under paragraph (1) shall be reduced by 3 percent of the least of—

(I) the oil related qualified production activities income of the cooperative for the taxable year,

(II) the qualified production activities income of the cooperative for the taxable year, or

(III) taxable income.

(ii) OIL RELATED QUALIFIED PRODUCTION ACTIVITIES INCOME.—For purposes of this subparagraph, the term "oil related qualified production activities income" means for any taxable year the qualified production activities income which is attributable to the production, refining, processing, transportation, or distribution of oil, gas, or any primary product thereof (within the meaning of section 927(a)(2)(C), as in effect before its repeal) during such taxable year.

(6) REGULATIONS.—The Secretary shall prescribe such regulations as are necessary to carry out the purposes of this subsection, including regulations which prevent more than 1 taxpayer from being allowed a deduction under this subsection with respect to any activity described in paragraph (3)(D)(i). Such regulations shall be based on the regulations applicable to cooperatives and their patrons under section 199 (as in effect before its repeal).

[Sec. 199A(h)]

(h) ANTI-ABUSE RULES.—The Secretary shall—

(1) apply rules similar to the rules under section 179(d)(2) in order to prevent the manipulation of the depreciable period of qualified property using transactions between related parties, and

(2) prescribe rules for determining the unadjusted basis immediately after acquisition of qualified property acquired in like-kind exchanges or involuntary conversions.

[Sec. 199A(i)]

(i) TERMINATION.—This section shall not apply to taxable years beginning after December 31, 2025.

PART VII—ADDITIONAL ITEMIZED DEDUCTIONS FOR INDIVIDUALS

[Sec. 211]

SEC. 211. ALLOWANCE OF DEDUCTIONS.

In computing taxable income under section 63, there shall be allowed as deductions the items specified in this part, subject to the exceptions provided in part IX (section 261 and following, relating to items not deductible).

»»→ Caution: Section 67(g) suspends deductions under Section 212 during the period 2018 through 2025, except for deductions described in Section 62(a).

[Sec. 212]

SEC. 212. EXPENSES FOR PRODUCTION OF INCOME.

In the case of an individual, there shall be allowed as a deduction all the ordinary and necessary expenses paid or incurred during the taxable year—

(1) for the production or collection of income;

(2) for the management, conservation, or maintenance of property held for the production of income; or

(3) in connection with the determination, collection, or refund of any tax.

»»→ Caution: Pursuant to Section 213(d)(10)(B), the dollar amounts specified in Section 213(d)(10)(A) are adjusted for taxable years beginning after 1997 to reflect increases in the Chained Consumer Price Index. The adjusted amounts applicable to taxable years beginning in 2020 are provided in the material beginning at page ix.

[Sec. 213]

SEC. 213. MEDICAL, DENTAL, ETC., EXPENSES.

[Sec. 213(a)]

(a) ALLOWANCE OF DEDUCTION.—There shall be allowed as a deduction the expenses paid during the taxable year, not compensated for by insurance or otherwise, for medical care of the taxpayer, his spouse, or a dependent (as defined in section 152, determined without regard to subsections (b)(1), (b)(2), and (d)(1)(B) thereof), to the extent that such expenses exceed 10 percent of adjusted gross income.

[Sec. 213(b)]

(b) LIMITATION WITH RESPECT TO MEDICINE AND DRUGS.—An amount paid during the taxable year for medicine or a drug shall be taken into account under subsection (a) only if such medicine or drug is a prescribed drug or is insulin.

[Sec. 213(c)]

(c) SPECIAL RULE FOR DECEDENTS.—

(1) TREATMENT OF EXPENSES PAID AFTER DEATH.—For purposes of subsection (a), expenses for the medical care of the taxpayer which are paid out of his estate during the 1-year period beginning with the day after the date of his death shall be treated as paid by the taxpayer at the time incurred.

(2) LIMITATION.—Paragraph (1) shall not apply if the amount paid is allowable under section 2053 as a deduction in computing the taxable estate of the decedent, but this paragraph shall not apply if (within the time and in the manner and form prescribed by the Secretary) there is filed—

(A) a statement that such amount has not been allowed as a deduction under section 2053, and

(B) a waiver of the right to have such amount allowed at any time as a deduction under section 2053.

[Sec. 213(d)]

(d) DEFINITIONS.—For purposes of this section—

(1) The term "medical care" means amounts paid—

(A) for the diagnosis, cure, mitigation, treatment, or prevention of disease, or for the purpose of affecting any structure or function of the body,

(B) for transportation primarily for and essential to medical care referred to in subparagraph (A),

(C) for qualified long-term care services (as defined in section 7702B(c)), or

(D) for insurance (including amounts paid as premiums under part B of title XVIII of the Social Security Act, relating to supplementary medical insurance for the aged) covering medical care referred to in subparagraphs (A) and (B) or for any qualified long-term care insurance contract (as defined in section 7702B(b)).

In the case of a qualified long-term care insurance contract (as defined in section 7702B(b)), only eligible long-term care premiums (as defined in paragraph (10)) shall be taken into account under subparagraph (D).

(2) AMOUNTS PAID FOR CERTAIN LODGING AWAY FROM HOME TREATED AS PAID FOR MEDICAL CARE.—Amounts paid for lodging (not lavish or extravagant under the circumstances) while away from home primarily for and essential to medical care referred to in paragraph (1)(A) shall be treated as amounts paid for medical care if—

(A) the medical care referred to in paragraph (1)(A) is provided by a physician in a licensed hospital (or in a medical care facility which is related to, or the equivalent of, a licensed hospital), and

(B) there is no significant element of personal pleasure, recreation, or vacation in the travel away from home.

The amount taken into account under the preceding sentence shall not exceed $50 for each night for each individual.

(3) PRESCRIBED DRUG.—The term "prescribed drug" means a drug or biological which requires a prescription of a physician for its use by an individual.

(4) PHYSICIAN.—The term "physician" has the meaning given to such term by section 1861(r) of the Social Security Act (42 U.S.C. 1395x(r)).

(5) SPECIAL RULE IN THE CASE OF CHILD OF DIVORCED PARENTS, ETC.—Any child to whom section 152(e) applies shall be treated as a dependent of both parents for purposes of this section.

(6) In the case of an insurance contract under which amounts are payable for other than medical care referred to in subparagraphs (A), (B), and (C) of paragraph (1)—

(A) no amount shall be treated as paid for insurance to which paragraph (1)(D) applies unless the charge for such insurance is either separately stated in the contract, or furnished to the policyholder by the insurance company in a separate statement,

(B) the amount taken into account as the amount paid for such insurance shall not exceed such charge, and

(C) no amount shall be treated as paid for such insurance if the amount specified in the contract (or furnished to the policyholder by the insurance company in a separate statement) as the charge for such insurance is unreasonably large in relation to the total charges under the contract.

(7) Subject to the limitations of paragraph (6) [(5) after 1984], premiums paid during the taxable year by a taxpayer before he attains the age of 65 for insurance covering medical care (within the meaning of subparagraphs (A), (B), and (C) of paragraph (1)) for the taxpayer, his spouse, or a dependent after the taxpayer attains the age of 65 shall be treated as expenses paid during the taxable year for insurance which constitutes medical care if premiums for such insurance are payable (on a level payment basis) under the contract for a period of 10 years or more or until the year in which the taxpayer attains the age of 65 (but in no case for a period of less than 5 years).

(8) The determination of whether an individual is married at any time during the taxable year shall be made in accordance with the provisions of section 6013(d) (relating to determination of status as husband and wife).

(9) COSMETIC SURGERY.—

(A) IN GENERAL.—The term "medical care" does not include cosmetic surgery or other similar procedures, unless the surgery or procedure is necessary to ameliorate a deformity arising from, or directly related to, a congenital abnormality, a personal injury resulting from an accident or trauma, or disfiguring disease.

(B) COSMETIC SURGERY DEFINED.—For purposes of this paragraph, the term "cosmetic surgery" means any procedure which is directed at improving the patient's appearance and does not meaningfully promote the proper function of the body or prevent or treat illness or disease.

(10) ELIGIBLE LONG-TERM CARE PREMIUMS.—

(A) IN GENERAL.—For purposes of this section, the term "eligible long-term care premiums" means the amount paid during a taxable year for any qualified long-term care insurance contract (as defined in section 7702B(b)) covering an individual, to the extent such amount does not exceed the limitation determined under the following table:

In the case of an individual with an attained age before the close of the taxable year of:	*The limitation is:*
40 or less	$200
More than 40 but not more than 50	375
More than 50 but not more than 60	750
More than 60 but not more than 70	2,000
More than 70	2,500

(B) INDEXING.—

(i) IN GENERAL.—In the case of any taxable year beginning in a calendar year after 1997, each dollar amount contained in subparagraph (A) shall be increased by the medical care cost adjustment of such amount for such calendar year. If any increase determined under the preceding sentence is not a multiple of $10, such increase shall be rounded to the nearest multiple of $10.

(ii) MEDICAL CARE COST ADJUSTMENT.—For purposes of clause (i), the medical care cost adjustment for any calendar year is the percentage (if any) by which—

(I) the medical care component of the C-CPI-U (as defined in section 1(f)(6)) for August of the preceding calendar year, exceeds

(II) such component of the CPI (as defined in section 1(f)(4)) for August of 1996, multiplied by the amount determined under section 1(f)(3)(B).

The Secretary shall, in consultation with the Secretary of Health and Human Services, prescribe an adjustment which the Secretary determines is more appropriate for purposes of this paragraph than the adjustment described in the preceding sentence, and the adjustment so prescribed shall apply in lieu of the adjustment described in the preceding sentence.

(11) CERTAIN PAYMENTS TO RELATIVES TREATED AS NOT PAID FOR MEDICAL CARE.—An amount paid for a qualified long-term care service (as defined in section 7702B(c)) provided to an individual shall be treated as not paid for medical care if such service is provided—

(A) by the spouse of the individual or by a relative (directly or through a partnership, corporation, or other entity) unless the service is provided by a licensed professional with respect to such service, or

(B) by a corporation or partnership which is related (within the meaning of section 267(b) or 707(b)) to the individual.

For purposes of this paragraph, the term "relative" means an individual bearing a relationship to the individual which is described in any of subparagraphs (A) through (G) of section 152(d)(2). This paragraph shall not apply for purposes of section 105(b) with respect to reimbursements through insurance.

[Sec. 213(e)]

(e) EXCLUSION OF AMOUNTS ALLOWED FOR CARE OF CERTAIN DEPENDENTS.—Any expense allowed as a credit under section 21 shall not be treated as an expense paid for medical care.

[Sec. 213(f)]

(f) TEMPORARY SPECIAL RULE.—In the case of taxable years beginning before January 1, 2021, subsection (a) shall be applied with respect to a taxpayer by substituting "7.5 percent" for "10 percent".

»» Caution: Section 215 does not apply to alimony or separate maintenance payments made pursuant to a divorce or separation instrument executed after December 31, 2018.

[Sec. 215]

SEC. 215. ALIMONY, ETC., PAYMENTS.

[Sec. 215(a)]

(a) GENERAL RULE.—In the case of an individual, there shall be allowed as a deduction an amount equal to the alimony or separate maintenance payments paid during such individual's taxable year.

[Sec. 215(b)]

(b) ALIMONY OR SEPARATE MAINTENANCE PAYMENTS DEFINED.—For purposes of this section, the term "alimony or separate maintenance payment" means any alimony or separate maintenance payment (as defined in section 71(b)) which is includible in the gross income of the recipient under section 71.

[Sec. 215(c)]

(c) REQUIREMENT OF IDENTIFICATION NUMBER.—The Secretary may prescribe regulations under which—

(1) any individual receiving alimony or separate maintenance payments is required to furnish such individual's taxpayer identification number to the individual making such payments, and

(2) the individual making such payments is required to include such taxpayer identification number on such individual's return for the taxable year in which such payments are made.

[Sec. 215(d)]

(d) COORDINATION WITH SECTION 682.—No deduction shall be allowed under this section with respect to any payment if, by reason of section 682 (relating to income of alimony trusts), the amount thereof is not includible in such individual's gross income.

[Sec. 216]

SEC. 216. DEDUCTION OF TAXES, INTEREST, AND BUSINESS DEPRECIATION BY COOPERATIVE HOUSING CORPORATION TENANT-STOCKHOLDER.

[Sec. 216(a)]

(a) ALLOWANCE OF DEDUCTION.—In the case of a tenant-stockholder (as defined in subsection (b) (2)), there shall be allowed as a deduction amounts (not otherwise deductible) paid or accrued to a cooperative housing corporation within the taxable year, but only to the extent that such amounts represent the tenant-stockholder's proportionate share of—

(1) the real estate taxes allowable as a deduction to the corporation under section 164 which are paid or incurred by the corporation on the houses or apartment building and on the land on which such houses (or building) are situated, or

(2) the interest allowable as a deduction to the corporation under section 163 which is paid or incurred by the corporation on its indebtedness contracted—

(A) in the acquisition, construction, alteration, rehabilitation, or maintenance of the houses or apartment building, or

(B) in the acquisition of the land on which the houses (or apartment building) are situated.

(b) DEFINITIONS.—For purposes of this section—

(1) COOPERATIVE HOUSING CORPORATION.—The term "cooperative housing corporation" means a corporation—

(A) having one and only one class of stock outstanding,

(B) each of the stockholders of which is entitled, solely by reason of his ownership of stock in the corporation, to occupy for dwelling purposes a house, or an apartment in a building, owned or leased by such corporation,

(C) no stockholder of which is entitled (either conditionally or unconditionally) to receive any distribution not out of earnings and profits of the corporation except on a complete or partial liquidation of the corporation, and

(D) meeting 1 or more of the following requirements for the taxable year in which the taxes and interest described in subsection (a) are paid or incurred:

(i) 80 percent or more of the corporation's gross income for such taxable year is derived from tenant-stockholders.

(ii) At all times during such taxable year, 80 percent or more of the total square footage of the corporation's property is used or available for use by the tenant-stockholders for residential purposes or purposes ancillary to such residential use.

(iii) 90 percent or more of the expenditures of the corporation paid or incurred during such taxable year are paid or incurred for the acquisition, construction, management, maintenance, or care of the corporation's property for the benefit of the tenant-stockholders.

(2) TENANT-STOCKHOLDER.—The term "tenant-stockholder" means a person who is a stockholder in a cooperative housing corporation, and whose stock is fully paid-up in an amount not less than an amount shown to the satisfaction of the Secretary as bearing a reasonable relationship to the portion of the value of the corporation's equity in the houses or apartment building and the land on which situated which is attributable to the house or apartment which such person is entitled to occupy.

(3) TENANT-STOCKHOLDER'S PROPORTIONATE SHARE.—

(A) IN GENERAL.—Except as provided in subparagraph (B), the term "tenant-stockholder's proportionate share" means that proportion which the stock of the cooperative housing corporation owned by the tenant-stockholder is of the total outstanding stock of the corporation (including any stock held by the corporation).

(B) SPECIAL RULE WHERE ALLOCATION OF TAXES OR INTEREST REFLECT COST TO CORPORATION OF STOCKHOLDER'S UNIT.—

(i) IN GENERAL.—If, for any taxable year—

(I) each dwelling unit owned or leased by a cooperative housing corporation is separately allocated a share of such corporation's real estate taxes described in subsection (a)(1) or a share of such corporation's interest described in subsection (a)(2), and

(II) such allocations reasonably reflect the cost to such corporation of such taxes, or of such interest, attributable to the tenant-stockholder's dwelling unit (and such unit's share of the common areas),

then the term "tenant-stockholder's proportionate share" means the shares determined in accordance with the allocations described in subclause (II).

(ii) ELECTION BY CORPORATION REQUIRED.—Clause (i) shall apply with respect to any cooperative housing corporation only if such corporation elects its application. Such an election, once made, may be revoked only with the consent of the Secretary.

* * *

[Sec. 216(c)]

(c) TREATMENT AS PROPERTY SUBJECT TO DEPRECIATION.—

(1) IN GENERAL.—So much of the stock of a tenant-stockholder in a cooperative housing corporation as is allocable, under regulations prescribed by the Secretary, to a proprietary lease or right of tenancy in property subject to the allowance for depreciation under section 167(a) shall, to the extent such proprietary lease or right of tenancy is used by such tenant-stockholder in a trade or business or for the production of income, be treated as property subject to the allowance for depreciation under section 167(a). The preceding sentence shall not be construed to limit or deny a deduction for depreciation under section 167(a) by a cooperative housing corporation with respect to property owned by such a corporation and leased to tenant-stockholders.

(2) DEDUCTION LIMITED TO ADJUSTED BASIS IN STOCK.—

(A) IN GENERAL.—The amount of any deduction for depreciation allowable under section 167(a) to tenant-stockholder with respect to any stock for any taxable year by reason of paragraph (1) shall not exceed the adjusted basis of such stock as of the close of the taxable year of the tenant-stockholder in which such deduction was incurred.

(B) CARRYFORWARD OF DISALLOWED AMOUNT.—The amount of any deduction which is not allowed by reason of subparagraph (A) shall, subject to the provisions of subparagraph (A), be treated as a deduction allowable under section 167(a) in the succeeding taxable year.

* * *

[Sec. 216(e)]

(e) DISTRIBUTIONS BY COOPERATIVE HOUSING CORPORATIONS.—Except as provided in regulations, no gain or loss shall be recognized on the distribution by a cooperative housing corporation of a dwelling unit to a stockholder in such cooperation if such distribution is in exchange for the stockholder's stock in such corporation and such dwelling unit is used as his principal residence (within the meaning of section 121).

→ Caution: As provided in Section 219(b)(5)(D), the dollar amount set forth in Section 219(b)(5)(A) is adjusted for taxable years after 2009 to reflect increases in the Chained Consumer Price Index. As provided in Section 219(g)(8), certain dollar amounts set forth in Section 219(g)(3) and (7) are adjusted for taxable years after 2006 to reflect increases in the Chained Consumer Price Index. The adjusted amounts applicable to taxable years beginning in 2020 are provided in the material beginning at page ix.

[Sec. 219]

SEC. 219. RETIREMENT SAVINGS.

[Sec. 219(a)]

(a) ALLOWANCE OF DEDUCTION.—In the case of an individual, there shall be allowed as a deduction an amount equal to the qualified retirement contributions of the individual for the taxable year.

[Sec. 219(b)]

(b) MAXIMUM AMOUNT OF DEDUCTION—

(1) IN GENERAL.—The amount allowable as a deduction under subsection (a) to any individual for any taxable year shall not exceed the lesser of—

(A) the deductible amount, or

(B) an amount equal to the compensation includible in the individual's gross income for such taxable year.

(2) SPECIAL RULE FOR EMPLOYER CONTRIBUTIONS UNDER SIMPLIFIED EMPLOYEE PENSIONS.—This section shall not apply with respect to an employer contribution to a simplified employee pension.

(3) PLANS UNDER SECTION 501(c)(18).—Notwithstanding paragraph (1), the amount allowable as a deduction under subsection (a) with respect to any contributions on behalf of a employee to a plan described in section 501(c)(18) shall not exceed the lesser of—

(A) $7,000 or

(B) an amount equal to 25 percent of the compensation (as defined in section 415(c)(3)) includible in the individual's gross income for such taxable year.

(4) SPECIAL RULE FOR SIMPLE RETIREMENT ACCOUNTS.—This section shall not apply with respect to any amount contributed to a simple retirement account established under section 408(p).

(5) DEDUCTIBLE AMOUNT.—For purposes of paragraph (1)(A)—

(A) IN GENERAL.—The deductible amount is $5,000.

(B) CATCH-UP CONTRIBUTIONS FOR INDIVIDUALS 50 OR OLDER.—

(i) IN GENERAL.—In the case of an individual who has attained the age of 50 before the close of the taxable year, the deductible amount for such taxable year shall be increased by the applicable amount.

(ii) APPLICABLE AMOUNT.—For purposes of clause (i), the applicable amount is $1,000.

(C) COST-OF-LIVING ADJUSTMENT.—

(i) IN GENERAL.—In the case of any taxable year beginning in a calendar year after 2008, the $5,000 amount under subparagraph (A) shall be increased by an amount equal to—

(I) such dollar amount, multiplied by

(II) the cost-of-living adjustment determined under section 1(f)(3) for the calendar year in which the taxable year begins, determined by substituting "calendar year 2007" for "calendar year 2016" in subparagraph (A)(ii) thereof.

(ii) ROUNDING RULES.—If any amount after adjustment under clause (i) is not a multiple of $500, such amount shall be rounded to the next lower multiple of $500.

[Sec. 219(c)]

(c) KAY BAILEY HUTCHINSON SPOUSAL IRA.—

(1) IN GENERAL.—In the case of an individual to whom this paragraph applies for the taxable year, the limitation of paragraph (1) of subsection (b) shall be equal to the lesser of—

(A) the dollar amount in effect under subsection (b)(1)(A) for the taxable year, or

(B) the sum of—

(i) the compensation includible in such individual's gross income for the taxable year, plus

(ii) the compensation includible in the gross income of such individual's spouse for the taxable year reduced by—

(I) the amount allowed as a deduction under subsection (a) to such spouse for such taxable year,

(II) the amount of any designated nondeductible contribution (as defined in section 408(o)) on behalf of such spouse for such taxable year, and

(III) the amount of any contribution on behalf of such spouse to a Roth IRA under section 408A for such taxable year.

(2) INDIVIDUALS TO WHOM PARAGRAPH (1) APPLIES.—Paragraph (1) shall apply to any individual if—

(A) such individual files a joint return for the taxable year, and

(B) the amount of compensation (if any) includible in such individual's gross income for the taxable year is less than the compensation includible in the gross income of such individual's spouse for the taxable year.

[Sec. 219(d)]

(d) OTHER LIMITATIONS AND RESTRICTIONS.—

(1) [Repealed.]

(2) RECONTRIBUTED AMOUNTS.—No deduction shall be allowed under this section with respect to a rollover contribution described in section 402(c), 403(a)(4), 403(b)(8), 408(d)(3), or 457(e)(16).

(3) AMOUNTS CONTRIBUTED UNDER ENDOWMENT CONTRACT.—In the case of an endowment contract described in section 408(b), no deduction shall be allowed under this section for that portion of the amounts paid under the contract for the taxable year which is properly allocable, under regulations prescribed by the Secretary, to the cost of life insurance.

(4) DENIAL OF DEDUCTION FOR AMOUNT CONTRIBUTED TO INHERITED ANNUITIES OR ACCOUNTS.—No deduction shall be allowed under this section with respect to any amount paid to an inherited individual retirement account or individual retirement annuity (within the meaning of section 408(d)(3)(C)(ii)).

[Sec. 219(e)]

(e) QUALIFIED RETIREMENT CONTRIBUTION.—For purposes of this section, the term "qualified retirement contribution" means—

(1) any amount paid in cash for the taxable year by or on behalf of an individual to an individual retirement plan for such individual's benefit, and

(2) any amount contributed on behalf of any individual to a plan described in section 501(c)(18).

[Sec. 219(f)]

(f) OTHER DEFINITIONS AND SPECIAL RULES.—

(1) COMPENSATION.—For purposes of this section, the term "compensation" includes earned income (as defined in section 401(c)(2)). The term "compensation" does not include any amount received as a pension or annuity and does not include any amount received as deferred compensation. For purposes of this paragraph, section 401(c)(2) shall be applied as if the term trade or business for purposes of section 1402 included service described in subsection (c)(6). The term "compensation" includes any differential wage payment (as defined in section 3401(h)(2)). The term "compensation" shall include any amount which is included in the individual's gross income and paid to the individual to aid the individual in the pursuit of graduate or postdoctoral study.

(2) MARRIED INDIVIDUALS.—The maximum deduction under subsection (b) shall be computed separately for each individual, and this section shall be applied without regard to any community property laws.

(3) TIME WHEN CONTRIBUTIONS DEEMED MADE.—For purposes of this section, a taxpayer shall be deemed to have made a contribution to an individual retirement plan on the last day of the preceding taxable year if the contribution is made on account of such taxable year and is made not later than the time prescribed by law for filing the return for such taxable year (not including extensions thereof).

(4) [Stricken.]

(5) EMPLOYER PAYMENTS.—For purposes of this title, any amount paid by an employer to an individual retirement plan shall be treated as payment of compensation to the employee (other than a self-employed individual who is an employee within the meaning of section 401(c)(1)) includible in his gross income in the taxable year for which the amount was contributed, whether or not a deduction for such payment is allowable under this section to the employee.

(6) EXCESS CONTRIBUTIONS TREATED AS CONTRIBUTION MADE DURING SUBSEQUENT YEAR FOR WHICH THERE IS AN UNUSED LIMITATION.—

(A) IN GENERAL.—If for the taxable year the maximum amount allowable as a deduction under this section for contributions to an individual retirement plan exceeds the amount contributed, then the taxpayer shall be treated as having made an additional contribution for the taxable year in an amount equal to the lesser of—

(i) the amount of such excess, or

(ii) the amount of the excess contributions for such taxable year (determined under section 4973(b)(2) without regard to subparagraph (C) thereof).

(B) AMOUNT CONTRIBUTED.—For purposes of this paragraph, the amount contributed—

(i) shall be determined without regard to this paragraph, and

(ii) shall not include any rollover contribution.

(C) SPECIAL RULE WHERE EXCESS DEDUCTION WAS ALLOWED FOR CLOSED YEAR.—Proper reduction shall be made in the amount allowable as a deduction by reason of this paragraph for any amount allowed as a deduction under this section for a prior taxable year for which the period for assessing deficiency has expired if the amount so allowed exceeds the amount which should have been allowed for such prior taxable year.

(7) ELECTION NOT TO DEDUCT CONTRIBUTIONS.—

For election not to deduct contributions to individual retirement plans, see section 408(o)(2)(B)(ii).

[Sec. 219(g)]

(g) LIMITATION ON DEDUCTION FOR ACTIVE PARTICIPANTS IN CERTAIN PENSION PLANS.—

(1) IN GENERAL.—If (for any part of any plan year ending with or within a taxable year) an individual or the individual's spouse is an active participant, each of the dollar limitations contained in subsections (b)(1)(A) and (c)(1)(A) for such taxable year shall be reduced (but not below zero) by the amount determined under paragraph (2).

(2) AMOUNT OF REDUCTION.—

(A) IN GENERAL.—The amount determined under this paragraph with respect to any dollar limitation shall be the amount which bears the same ratio to such limitation as—

(i) the excess of—

(I) the taxpayer's adjusted gross income for such taxable year, over

(II) the applicable dollar amount, bears to

(ii) $10,000 ($20,000 in the case of a joint return).

(B) NO REDUCTION BELOW $200 UNTIL COMPLETE PHASEOUT.—No dollar limitation shall be reduced below $200 under paragraph (1) unless (without regard to this subparagraph) such limitation is reduced to zero.

(C) ROUNDING.—Any amount determined under this paragraph which is not a multiple of $10 shall be rounded to the next lowest $10.

(3) ADJUSTED GROSS INCOME; APPLICABLE DOLLAR AMOUNT.—For purposes of this subsection—

(A) ADJUSTED GROSS INCOME.—Adjusted gross income of any taxpayer shall be determined—

(i) after application of sections 86 and 469, and

(ii) without regard to sections 135, 137, 221, 222, and 911 or the deduction allowable under this section.

(B) APPLICABLE DOLLAR AMOUNT.—The term "applicable dollar amount" means the following:

(i) In the case of a taxpayer filing a joint return, $80,000.

(ii) In the case of any other taxpayer (other than a married individual filing a separate return), $50,000.

(iii) In the case of a married individual filing a separate return, zero.

(4) SPECIAL RULE FOR MARRIED INDIVIDUALS FILING SEPARATELY AND LIVING APART.—A husband and wife who—

(A) file separate returns for any taxable year, and

(B) live apart at all times during such taxable year,

shall not be treated as married individuals for purposes of this subsection.

(5) ACTIVE PARTICIPANT.—For purposes of this subsection, the term "active participant" means, with respect to any plan year, an individual—

(A) who is an active participant in—

(i) a plan described in section 401(a) which includes a trust exempt from tax under section 501(a),

(ii) an annuity plan described in section 403(a),

(iii) a plan established for its employees by the United States, by a State or political subdivision thereof, or by an agency or instrumentality of any of the foregoing,

(iv) an annuity contract described in section 403(b),

(v) a simplified employee pension (within the meaning of section 408(k)), or

(vi) any simple retirement account (within the meaning of section 408(p)), or

(B) who makes deductible contributions to a trust described in section 501(c)(18).

The determination of whether an individual is an active participant shall be made without regard to whether or not such individual's rights under a plan, trust, or contract are nonforfeitable. An eligible deferred compensation plan (within the meaning of section 457(b)) shall not be treated as a plan described in subparagraph (A)(iii).

(6) CERTAIN INDIVIDUALS NOT TREATED AS ACTIVE PARTICIPANTS.—For purposes of this subsection, any individual described in any of the following subparagraphs shall not be treated as an active participant for any taxable year solely because of any participation so described:

(A) MEMBERS OF RESERVE COMPONENTS.—Participation in a plan described in subparagraph (A)(iii) of paragraph (5) by reason of service as a member of a reserve component of the Armed Forces (as defined in section 10101 of title 10), unless such individual has served in excess of 90 days on active duty (other than active duty for training) during the year.

(B) VOLUNTEER FIREFIGHTERS.—A volunteer firefighter—

(i) who is a participant in a plan described in subparagraph (A)(iii) of paragraph (5) based on his activity as a volunteer firefighter, and

(ii) whose accrued benefit as of the beginning of the taxable year is not more than an annual benefit of $1,800 (when expressed as a single life annuity commencing at age 65).

(7) SPECIAL RULE FOR SPOUSES WHO ARE NOT ACTIVE PARTICIPANTS.—If this subsection applies to an individual for any taxable year solely because their spouse is an active participant, then, in applying this subsection to the individual (but not their spouse)—

(A) the applicable dollar amount under paragraph (3)(B)(i) shall be $150,000; and

(B) the amount applicable under paragraph (2)(A)(ii) shall be $10,000.

(8) INFLATION ADJUSTMENT.—In the case of any taxable year beginning in a calendar year after 2006, each of the dollar amounts in paragraphs (3)(B)(i), (3)(B)(ii), and (7)(A) shall be increased by an amount equal to—

(A) such dollar amount, multiplied by

(B) the cost-of-living adjustment determined under section 1(f)(3) for the calendar year in which the taxable year begins, determined by substituting "calendar year 2005" for "calendar year 2016" in subparagraph (A)(ii) thereof.

Any increase determined under the preceding sentence shall be rounded to the nearest multiple of $1,000.

»»→ Caution: As provided in Section 221(f), certain of the amounts provided in Section 221(b)(2) are adjusted for taxable years after 2002 to reflect increases in the Chained Consumer Price Index. The adjusted amounts applicable to taxable years beginning in 2020 are provided in the material beginning at page ix.

[Sec. 221]

SEC. 221. INTEREST ON EDUCATION LOANS.

[Sec. 221(a)]

(a) ALLOWANCE OF DEDUCTION.—In the case of an individual, there shall be allowed as a deduction for the taxable year an amount equal to the interest paid by the taxpayer during the taxable year on any qualified education loan.

[Sec. 221(b)]

(b) MAXIMUM DEDUCTION.—

(1) IN GENERAL.—Except as provided in paragraph (2), the deduction allowed by subsection (a) for the taxable year shall not exceed $2,500.

(2) LIMITATION BASED ON MODIFIED ADJUSTED GROSS INCOME.—

(A) IN GENERAL.—The amount which would (but for this paragraph) be allowable as a deduction under this section shall be reduced (but not below zero) by the amount determined under subparagraph (B).

(B) AMOUNT OF REDUCTION.—The amount determined under this subparagraph is the amount which bears the same ratio to the amount which would be so taken into account as—

(i) the excess of—

(I) the taxpayer's modified adjusted gross income for such taxable year, over

(II) $50,000 ($100,000 in the case of a joint return), bears to

(ii) $15,000 ($30,000 in the case of a joint return).

(C) MODIFIED ADJUSTED GROSS INCOME.—The term "modified adjusted gross income" means adjusted gross income determined—

(i) without regard to this section and sections 222, 911, 931, and 933, and

(ii) after application of sections 86, 135, 137, 219, and 469.

[Sec. 221(c)]

(c) DEPENDENTS NOT ELIGIBLE FOR DEDUCTION.—No deduction shall be allowed by this section to an individual for the taxable year if a deduction under section 151 with respect to such individual is allowed to another taxpayer for the taxable year beginning in the calendar year in which such individual's taxable year begins.

[Sec. 221(d)]

(d) DEFINITIONS.—For purposes of this section—

(1) QUALIFIED EDUCATION LOAN.—The term "qualified education loan" means any indebtedness incurred by the taxpayer solely to pay qualified higher education expenses—

(A) which are incurred on behalf of the taxpayer, the taxpayer's spouse, or any dependent of the taxpayer as of the time the indebtedness was incurred,

(B) which are paid or incurred within a reasonable period of time before or after the indebtedness is incurred, and

(C) which are attributable to education furnished during a period during which the recipient was an eligible student.

Such term includes indebtedness used to refinance indebtedness which qualifies as a qualified education loan. The term "qualified education loan" shall not include any indebtedness owed to a person who is related (within the meaning of section 267(b) or 707(b)(1)) to the taxpayer or to any person by reason of a loan under any qualified employer plan (as defined in section 72(p)(4)) or under any contract referred to in section 72(p)(5).

(2) QUALIFIED HIGHER EDUCATION EXPENSES.—The term "qualified higher education expenses" means the cost of attendance (as defined in section 472 of the Higher Education Act of 1965, 20 U.S.C. 1087ll, as in effect on the day before the date of the enactment of the Taxpayer Relief Act of 1997) at an eligible educational institution, reduced by the sum of—

(A) the amount excluded from gross income under section 127, 135, 529, or 530 by reason of such expenses, and

(B) the amount of any scholarship, allowance, or payment described in section 25A(g)(2).

For purposes of the preceding sentence, the term "eligible educational institution" has the same meaning given such term by section 25A(f)(2), except that such term shall also include an institution conducting an internship or residency program leading to a degree or certificate awarded by an institution of higher education, a hospital, or a health care facility which offers postgraduate training.

(3) ELIGIBLE STUDENT.—The term "eligible student" has the meaning given such term by section 25A(b)(3).

(4) DEPENDENT.—The term "dependent" has the meaning given such term by section 152 (determined without regard to subsections (b)(1), (b)(2), and (d)(1)(B) thereof).

[Sec. 221(e)]

(e) SPECIAL RULES.—

(1) DENIAL OF DOUBLE BENEFIT.—No deduction shall be allowed under this section for any amount for which a deduction is allowable under any other provision of this chapter, or for which an exclusion is allowable under section 127 to the taxpayer by reason of the payment by the taxpayer's employer of any indebtedness on a qualified education loan of the taxpayer. The deduction otherwise allowable under subsection (a) (prior to the application of subsection (b)) to the taxpayer for any taxable year shall be reduced (but not below zero) by so much of the distributions treated as a qualified higher education expense under section 529(c)(9) with respect to loans of the taxpayer as would be includible in gross income under section 529(c)(3)(A) for such taxable year but for such treatment.

(2) MARRIED COUPLES MUST FILE JOINT RETURN.—If the taxpayer is married at the close of the taxable year, the deduction shall be allowed under subsection (a) only if the taxpayer and the taxpayer's spouse file a joint return for the taxable year.

(3) MARITAL STATUS.—Marital status shall be determined in accordance withsection 7703.

[Sec. 221(f)]

(f) INFLATION ADJUSTMENTS.—

(1) IN GENERAL.—In the case of a taxable year beginning after 2002, the $50,000 and $100,000 amounts in subsection (b)(2) shall each be increased by an amount equal to—

(A) such dollar amount, multiplied by

(B) the cost-of-living adjustment determined under section 1(f)(3) for the calendar year in which the taxable year begins, determined by substituting "calendar year 2001" for "calendar year 2016" in subparagraph (A)(ii) thereof.

(2) ROUNDING.—If any amount as adjusted under paragraph (1) is not a multiple of $5,000, such amount shall be rounded to the next lowest multiple of $5,000.

»»→ Caution: As provided in Section 223(g), the dollar amounts set forth in Sections 223(b)(2) and (c)(2)((A) are adjusted for taxable years after 2004 to reflect increases in the Chained Consumer Price Index.

[Sec. 223]

SEC. 223. HEALTH SAVINGS ACCOUNTS.

[Sec. 223(a)]

(a) DEDUCTION ALLOWED.—In the case of an individual who is an eligible individual for any month during the taxable year, there shall be allowed as a deduction for the taxable year an amount equal to the aggregate amount paid in cash during such taxable year by or on behalf of such individual to a health savings account of such individual.

[Sec. 223(b)]

(b) LIMITATIONS.—

(1) IN GENERAL.—The amount allowable as a deduction under subsection (a) to an individual for the taxable year shall not exceed the sum of the monthly limitations for months during such taxable year that the individual is an eligible individual.

(2) MONTHLY LIMITATION.—The monthly limitation for any month is 1/12 of—

(A) in the case of an eligible individual who has self-only coverage under a high deductible health plan as of the first day of such month, $2,250.

(B) in the case of an eligible individual who has family coverage under a high deductible health plan as of the first day of such month, $4,500.

(3) ADDITIONAL CONTRIBUTIONS FOR INDIVIDUALS 55 OR OLDER.—

(A) IN GENERAL.—In the case of an individual who has attained age 55 before the close of the taxable year, the applicable limitation under subparagraphs (A) and (B) of paragraph (2) shall be increased by the additional contribution amount.

(B) ADDITIONAL CONTRIBUTION AMOUNT.—For purposes of this section, the additional contribution amount is the amount determined in accordance with the following table:

For taxable years beginning in:	The additional contribution amount is:
2004	$500
2005	$600
2006	$700
2007	$800
2008	$900
2009 and thereafter	$1,000 .

(4) COORDINATION WITH OTHER CONTRIBUTIONS.—The limitation which would (but for this paragraph) apply under this subsection to an individual for any taxable year shall be reduced (but not below zero) by the sum of—

(A) the aggregate amount paid for such taxable year to Archer MSAs of such individual,

(B) the aggregate amount contributed to health savings accounts of such individual which is excludable from the taxpayer's gross income for such taxable year under section 106(d) (and such amount shall not be allowed as a deduction under subsection (a)), and

(C) the aggregate amount contributed to health savings accounts of such individual for such taxable year under section 408(d)(9) (and such amount shall not be allowed as a deduction under subsection (a)).

Subparagraph (A) shall not apply with respect to any individual to whom paragraph (5) applies.

(5) SPECIAL RULE FOR MARRIED INDIVIDUALS.—In the case of individuals who are married to each other, if either spouse has family coverage—

(A) both spouses shall be treated as having only such family coverage (and if such spouses each have family coverage under different plans, as having the family coverage with the lowest annual deductible), and

(B) the limitation under paragraph (1) (after the application of subparagraph (A) and without regard to any additional contribution amount under paragraph (3))—

(i) shall be reduced by the aggregate amount paid to Archer MSAs of such spouses for the taxable year, and

(ii) after such reduction, shall be divided equally between them unless they agree on a different division.

(6) DENIAL OF DEDUCTION TO DEPENDENTS.—No deduction shall be allowed under this section to any individual with respect to whom a deduction under section 151 is allowable to another taxpayer for a taxable year beginning in the calendar year in which such individual's taxable year begins.

(7) MEDICARE ELIGIBLE INDIVIDUALS.—The limitation under this subsection for any month with respect to an individual shall be zero for the first month such individual is entitled to benefits under title XVIII of the Social Security Act and for each month thereafter.

(8) INCREASE IN LIMIT FOR INDIVIDUALS BECOMING ELIGIBLE INDIVIDUALS AFTER THE BEGINNING OF THE YEAR.—

(A) IN GENERAL.—For purposes of computing the limitation under paragraph (1) for any taxable year, an individual who is an eligible individual during the last month of such taxable year shall be treated—

(i) as having been an eligible individual during each of the months in such taxable year, and

(ii) as having been enrolled, during each of the months such individual is treated as an eligible individual solely by reason of clause (i), in the same high deductible health plan in which the individual was enrolled for the last month of such taxable year.

(B) FAILURE TO MAINTAIN HIGH DEDUCTIBLE HEALTH PLAN COVERAGE.—

(i) IN GENERAL.—If, at any time during the testing period, the individual is not an eligible individual, then—

(I) gross income of the individual for the taxable year in which occurs the first month in the testing period for which such individual is not an eligible individual is increased by the aggregate amount of all contributions to the health savings account of the individual which could not have been made but for subparagraph (A), and

(II) the tax imposed by this chapter for any taxable year on the individual shall be increased by 10 percent of the amount of such increase.

(ii) EXCEPTION FOR DISABILITY OR DEATH.—Subclauses (I) and (II) of clause (i) shall not apply if the individual ceased to be an eligible individual by reason of the death of the individual or the individual becoming disabled (within the meaning of section 72(m)(7)).

(iii) TESTING PERIOD.—The term "testing period" means the period beginning with the last month of the taxable year referred to in subparagraph (A) and ending on the last day of the 12th month following such month.

[Sec. 223(c)]

(c) DEFINITIONS AND SPECIAL RULES.—For purposes of this section—

(1) ELIGIBLE INDIVIDUAL.—

(A) IN GENERAL.—The term "eligible individual" means, with respect to any month, any individual if—

(i) such individual is covered under a high deductible health plan as of the 1st day of such month, and

(ii) such individual is not, while covered under a high deductible health plan, covered under any health plan—

(I) which is not a high deductible health plan, and

(II) which provides coverage for any benefit which is covered under the high deductible health plan.

(B) CERTAIN COVERAGE DISREGARDED.—Subparagraph (A)(ii) shall be applied without regard to—

(i) coverage for any benefit provided by permitted insurance,

(ii) coverage (whether through insurance or otherwise) for accidents, disability, dental care, vision care, long-term care, or (in the case of plan years beginning on or before December 31, 2021) telehealth and other remote care, and

(iii) for taxable years beginning after December 31, 2006, coverage under a health flexible spending arrangement during any period immediately following the end of a plan year of such arrangement during which unused benefits or contributions remaining at the end of such plan year may be paid or reimbursed to plan participants for qualified benefit expenses incurred during such period if—

(I) the balance in such arrangement at the end of such plan year is zero, or

(II) the individual is making a qualified HSA distribution (as defined in section 106(e)) in an amount equal to the remaining balance in such arrangement as of the end of such plan year, in accordance with rules prescribed by the Secretary.

(C) SPECIAL RULE FOR INDIVIDUALS ELIGIBLE FOR CERTAIN VETERANS BENEFITS.—An individual shall not fail to be treated as an eligible individual for any period merely because the individual receives hospital care or medical services under any law administered by the Secretary of Veterans Affairs for a service-connected disability (within the meaning of section 101(16) of title 38, United States Code).

(2) HIGH DEDUCTIBLE HEALTH PLAN.—

(A) IN GENERAL.—The term "high deductible health plan" means a health plan—

(i) which has an annual deductible which is not less than—

(I) $1,000 for self-only coverage, and

(II) twice the dollar amount in subclause (I) for family coverage, and

(ii) the sum of the annual deductible and the other annual out-of-pocket expenses required to be paid under the plan (other than for premiums) for covered benefits does not exceed—

(I) $5,000 for self-only coverage, and

(II) twice the dollar amount in subclause (I) for family coverage.

(B) EXCLUSION OF CERTAIN PLANS.—Such term does not include a health plan if substantially all of its coverage is coverage described in paragraph (1)(B).

(C) SAFE HARBOR FOR ABSENCE OF PREVENTIVE CARE DEDUCTIBLE.—A plan shall not fail to be treated as a high deductible health plan by reason of failing to have a deductible for preventive care (within the meaning of section 1861 of the Social Security Act, except as otherwise provided by the Secretary).

(D) SPECIAL RULES FOR NETWORK PLANS.—In the case of a plan using a network of providers—

(i) ANNUAL OUT-OF-POCKET LIMITATION.—Such plan shall not fail to be treated as a high deductible health plan by reason of having an out-of-pocket limitation for services provided outside of such network which exceeds the applicable limitation under subparagraph (A)(ii).

(ii) ANNUAL DEDUCTIBLE.—Such plan's annual deductible for services provided outside of such network shall not be taken into account for purposes of subsection (b)(2).

(E) SAFE HARBOR FOR ABSENCE OF DEDUCTIBLE FOR TELEHEALTH.—In the case of plan years beginning on or before December 31, 2021, a plan shall not fail to be treated as a high deductible health plan by reason of failing to have a deductible for telehealth and other remote care services.

(3) PERMITTED INSURANCE.—The term "permitted insurance" means—

(A) insurance if substantially all of the coverage provided under such insurance relates to—

(i) liabilities incurred under workers' compensation laws,

(ii) tort liabilities,

(iii) liabilities relating to ownership or use of property, or

(iv) such other similar liabilities as the Secretary may specify by regulations,

(B) insurance for a specified disease or illness, and

(C) insurance paying a fixed amount per day (or other period) of hospitalization.

(4) FAMILY COVERAGE.—The term "family coverage" means any coverage other than self-only coverage.

(5) ARCHER MSA.—The term "Archer MSA" has the meaning given such term in section 220(d).

[Sec. 223(d)]

(d) HEALTH SAVINGS ACCOUNT.—For purposes of this section—

(1) IN GENERAL.—The term "health savings account" means a trust created or organized in the United States as a health savings account exclusively for the purpose of paying the qualified medical expenses of the account beneficiary, but only if the written governing instrument creating the trust meets the following requirements:

(A) Except in the case of a rollover contribution described in subsection (f)(5) or section 220(f)(5), no contribution will be accepted—

(i) unless it is in cash, or

(ii) to the extent such contribution, when added to previous contributions to the trust for the calendar year, exceeds the sum of—

(I) the dollar amount in effect under subsection (b)(2)(B), and

(II) the dollar amount in effect under subsection (b)(3)(B).

(B) The trustee is a bank (as defined in section 408(n)), an insurance company (as defined in section 816), or another person who demonstrates to the satisfaction of the Secretary that the manner in which such person will administer the trust will be consistent with the requirements of this section.

(C) No part of the trust assets will be invested in life insurance contracts.

(D) The assets of the trust will not be commingled with other property except in a common trust fund or common investment fund.

(E) The interest of an individual in the balance in his account is nonforfeitable.

(2) QUALIFIED MEDICAL EXPENSES.—

(A) IN GENERAL.—The term "qualified medical expenses" means, with respect to an account beneficiary, amounts paid by such beneficiary for medical care (as defined in section 213(d)) for such individual, the spouse of such individual, and any dependent (as defined in section 152, determined without regard to subsections (b)(1), (b)(2), and (d)(1)(B) thereof) of such individual, but only to the extent such amounts are not compensated for by insurance or otherwise. For purposes of this subparagraph, amounts paid for menstrual care products shall be treated as paid for medical care.

(B) HEALTH INSURANCE MAY NOT BE PURCHASED FROM ACCOUNT.—Subparagraph (A) shall not apply to any payment for insurance.

(C) EXCEPTIONS.—Subparagraph (B) shall not apply to any expense for coverage under—

(i) a health plan during any period of continuation coverage required under any Federal law,

(ii) a qualified long-term care insurance contract (as defined in section 7702B(b)),

(iii) a health plan during a period in which the individual is receiving unemployment compensation under any Federal or State law, or

(iv) in the case of an account beneficiary who has attained the age specified in section 1811 of the Social Security Act, any health insurance other than a medicare supplemental policy (as defined in section 1882 of the Social Security Act).

(D) MENSTRUAL CARE PRODUCT.—For purposes of this paragraph, the term "menstrual care product" means a tampon, pad, liner, cup, sponge, or similar product used by individuals with respect to menstruation or other genital-tract secretions.

(3) ACCOUNT BENEFICIARY.—The term "account beneficiary" means the individual on whose behalf the health savings account was established.

(4) CERTAIN RULES TO APPLY.—Rules similar to the following rules shall apply for purposes of this section:

(A) Section 219(d)(2) (relating to no deduction for rollovers).

(B) Section 219(f)(3) (relating to time when contributions deemed made).

(C) Except as provided in section 106(d), section 219(f)(5) (relating to employer payments).

(D) Section 408(g) (relating to community property laws).

(E) Section 408(h) (relating to custodial accounts).

[Sec. 223(e)]

(e) TAX TREATMENT OF ACCOUNTS.—

(1) IN GENERAL.—A health savings account is exempt from taxation under this subtitle unless such account has ceased to be a health savings account. Notwithstanding the preceding sentence, any such account is subject to the taxes imposed by section 511 (relating to imposition of tax on unrelated business income of charitable, etc. organizations).

(2) ACCOUNT TERMINATIONS.—Rules similar to the rules of paragraphs (2) and (4) of section 408(e) shall apply to health savings accounts, and any amount treated as distributed under such rules shall be treated as not used to pay qualified medical expenses.

[Sec. 223(f)]

(f) TAX TREATMENT OF DISTRIBUTIONS.—

(1) AMOUNTS USED FOR QUALIFIED MEDICAL EXPENSES.—Any amount paid or distributed out of a health savings account which is used exclusively to pay qualified medical expenses of any account beneficiary shall not be includible in gross income.

(2) INCLUSION OF AMOUNTS NOT USED FOR QUALIFIED MEDICAL EXPENSES.—Any amount paid or distributed out of a health savings account which is not used exclusively to pay the qualified medical expenses of the account beneficiary shall be included in the gross income of such beneficiary.

(3) EXCESS CONTRIBUTIONS RETURNED BEFORE DUE DATE OF RETURN.—

(A) IN GENERAL.—If any excess contribution is contributed for a taxable year to any health savings account of an individual, paragraph (2) shall not apply to distributions from the health savings accounts of such individual (to the extent such distributions do not exceed the aggregate excess contributions to all such accounts of such individual for such year) if—

(i) such distribution is received by the individual on or before the last day prescribed by law (including extensions of time) for filing such individual's return for such taxable year, and

(ii) such distribution is accompanied by the amount of net income attributable to such excess contribution.

Any net income described in clause (ii) shall be included in the gross income of the individual for the taxable year in which it is received.

(B) EXCESS CONTRIBUTION.—For purposes of subparagraph (A), the term "excess contribution" means any contribution (other than a rollover contribution described in paragraph (5) or section 220(f)(5)) which is neither excludable from gross income under section 106(d) nor deductible under this section.

(4) ADDITIONAL TAX ON DISTRIBUTIONS NOT USED FOR QUALIFIED MEDICAL EXPENSES.—

(A) IN GENERAL.—The tax imposed by this chapter on the account beneficiary for any taxable year in which there is a payment or distribution from a health savings account of such beneficiary which is includible in gross income under paragraph (2) shall be increased by 20 percent of the amount which is so includible.

(B) EXCEPTION FOR DISABILITY OR DEATH.—Subparagraph (A) shall not apply if the payment or distribution is made after the account beneficiary becomes disabled within the meaning of section 72(m)(7) or dies.

(C) EXCEPTION FOR DISTRIBUTIONS AFTER MEDICARE ELIGIBILITY.—Subparagraph (A) shall not apply to any payment or distribution after the date on which the account beneficiary attains the age specified in section 1811 of the Social Security Act.

(5) ROLLOVER CONTRIBUTION.—An amount is described in this paragraph as a rollover contribution if it meets the requirements of subparagraphs (A) and (B).

(A) IN GENERAL.—Paragraph (2) shall not apply to any amount paid or distributed from a health savings account to the account beneficiary to the extent the amount received is paid into a health savings account for the benefit of such beneficiary not later than the 60th day after the day on which the beneficiary receives the payment or distribution.

(B) LIMITATION.—This paragraph shall not apply to any amount described in subparagraph (A) received by an individual from a health savings account if, at any time during the 1-year period ending on the day of such receipt, such individual received any other amount described in subparagraph (A) from a health savings account which was not includible in the individual's gross income because of the application of this paragraph.

(6) COORDINATION WITH MEDICAL EXPENSE DEDUCTION.—For purposes of determining the amount of the deduction under section 213, any payment or distribution out of a health savings account for qualified medical expenses shall not be treated as an expense paid for medical care.

(7) TRANSFER OF ACCOUNT INCIDENT TO DIVORCE.—The transfer of an individual's interest in a health savings account to an individual's spouse or former spouse under a divorce or separation instrument described in clause (i) of section 121(d)(3)(C) shall not be considered a taxable transfer made by such individual notwithstanding any other provision of this subtitle, and such interest shall, after such transfer, be treated as a health savings account with respect to which such spouse is the account beneficiary.

(8) TREATMENT AFTER DEATH OF ACCOUNT BENEFICIARY.—

(A) TREATMENT IF DESIGNATED BENEFICIARY IS SPOUSE.—If the account beneficiary's surviving spouse acquires such beneficiary's interest in a health savings account by reason of being the designated beneficiary of such account at the death of the account beneficiary, such health savings account shall be treated as if the spouse were the account beneficiary.

(B) OTHER CASES.—

(i) IN GENERAL.— If, by reason of the death of the account beneficiary, any person acquires the account beneficiary's interest in a health savings account in a case to which subparagraph (A) does not apply—

(I) such account shall cease to be a health savings account as of the date of death, and

(II) an amount equal to the fair market value of the assets in such account on such date shall be includible if such person is not the estate of such beneficiary, in such person's gross income for the taxable year which includes such date, or if such person is the estate of such beneficiary, in such beneficiary's gross income for the last taxable year of such beneficiary.

(ii) SPECIAL RULES.—

(I) REDUCTION OF INCLUSION FOR PREDEATH EXPENSES.—The amount includible in gross income under clause (i) by any person (other than the estate) shall be reduced by the amount of qualified medical expenses which were incurred by the decedent before the date of the decedent's death and paid by such person within 1 year after such date.

(II) DEDUCTION FOR ESTATE TAXES.—An appropriate deduction shall be allowed under section 691(c) to any person (other than the decedent or the decedent's spouse) with respect to amounts included in gross income under clause (i) by such person.

[Sec. 223(g)]

(g) COST-OF-LIVING ADJUSTMENT.—

(1) IN GENERAL.—Each dollar amount in subsections (b)(2) and (c)(2)(A) shall be increased by an amount equal to—

(A) such dollar amount, multiplied by

(B) the cost-of-living adjustment determined under section 1(f)(3) for the calendar year in which such taxable year begins determined by substituting for "calendar year 2016" in subparagraph (A)(ii) thereof—

(i) except as provided in clause (ii), "calendar year 1997", and

(ii) in the case of each dollar amount in subsection (c)(2)(A), "calendar year 2003".

In the case of adjustments made for any taxable year beginning after 2007, section 1(f)(4) shall be applied for purposes of this paragraph by substituting "March 31" for "August 31", and the Secretary shall publish the adjusted amounts under subsections (b)(2) and (c)(2)(A) for taxable years beginning in any calendar year no later than June 1 of the preceding calendar year.

(2) ROUNDING.—If any increase under paragraph (1) is not a multiple of $50, such increase shall be rounded to the nearest multiple of $50.

* * *

PART VIII—SPECIAL DEDUCTIONS FOR CORPORATIONS

[Sec. 241]

SEC. 241. ALLOWANCE OF SPECIAL DEDUCTIONS.

In addition to the deductions provided in part VI (sec. 161 and following), there shall be allowed as deductions in computing taxable income the items specified in this part.

[Sec. 243]

SEC. 243. DIVIDENDS RECEIVED BY CORPORATIONS.

[Sec. 243(a)]

(a) GENERAL RULE.—In the case of a corporation, there shall be allowed as a deduction an amount equal to the following percentages of the amount received as dividends from a domestic corporation which is subject to taxation under this chapter:

(1) 50 percent, in the case of dividends other than dividends described in paragraph (2) or (3);

(2) 100 percent, in the case of dividends received by a small business investment company operating under the Small Business Investment Act of 1958 (15 U.S.C. 661 and following); and

(3) 100 percent, in the case of qualifying dividends (as defined in subsection (b)(1)).

[Sec. 243(b)]

(b) QUALIFYING DIVIDENDS.—

(1) IN GENERAL.—For purposes of this section, the term "qualifying dividend" means any dividend received by a corporation—

(A) if at the close of the day on which such dividend is received, such corporation is a member of the same affiliated group as the corporation distributing such dividend, and

(B) if such dividend is distributed out of the earnings and profits of a taxable year of the distributing corporation which ends after December 31, 1963, and on each day of which the distributing corporation and the corporation receiving the dividend were members of such affiliated group.

(2) AFFILIATED GROUP.—For purposes of this subsection:

(A) IN GENERAL.—The term "affiliated group" has the meaning given such term by section 1504(a), except that for such purposes sections 1504(b)(2), and 1504(c) shall not apply.

* * *

[Sec. 243(c)]

(c) INCREASED PERCENTAGE FOR DIVIDENDS FROM 20-PERCENT OWNED CORPORATIONS.—

(1) IN GENERAL.—In the case of any dividend received from a 20-percent owned corporation, subsection (a)(1) shall be applied by substituting "65 percent" for "50 percent".

(2) 20-PERCENT OWNED CORPORATION.—For purposes of this section, the term "20-percent owned corporation" means any corporation if 20 percent or more of the stock of such corporation (by vote and value) is owned by the taxpayer. For purposes of the preceding sentence, stock described in section 1504(a)(4) shall not be taken into account.

* * *

[Sec. 246]

SEC. 246. RULES APPLYING TO DEDUCTIONS FOR DIVIDENDS RECEIVED.

[Sec. 246(a)]

(a) DEDUCTION NOT ALLOWED FOR DIVIDENDS FROM CERTAIN CORPORATIONS.—

(1) IN GENERAL.—The deductions allowed by sections 243[,] 245, and 245A shall not apply to any dividend from a corporation which, for the taxable year of the corporation in which the distribution is made, or for the next preceding taxable year of the corporation, is a corporation exempt from tax under section 501 (relating to certain charitable, etc., organizations) or section 521 (relating to farmers' cooperative associations).

* * *

[Sec. 246(b)]

(b) LIMITATION ON AGGREGATE AMOUNT OF DEDUCTIONS.—

(1) GENERAL RULE.—Except as provided in paragraph (2), the aggregate amount of the deductions allowed by section 243(a)(1), subsection (a) and (b) of section 245, and section 250 shall not exceed the percentage determined under paragraph (3) of the taxable income computed without regard to the deductions allowed by sections 172, 199A, 243(a)(1), subsection (a) and (b) of section 245, and 250, without regard to any adjustment under section 1059, and without regard to any capital loss carryback to the taxable year under section 1212(a)(1).

(2) EFFECT OF NET OPERATING LOSS.—Paragraph (1) shall not apply for any taxable year for which there is a net operating loss (as determined under section 172).

(3) SPECIAL RULES.—The provisions of paragraph (1) shall be applied—

(A) first separately with respect to dividends from 20-percent owned corporations (as defined in section 243(c)(2)) and the percentage determined under this paragraph shall be 65 percent, and

(B) then separately with respect to dividends not from 20-percent owned corporations and the percentage determined under this paragraph shall be 50 percent and the taxable income shall be reduced by the aggregate amount of dividends from 20-percent owned corporations (as so defined).

[Sec. 246(c)]

(c) EXCLUSION OF CERTAIN DIVIDENDS.—

(1) IN GENERAL.—No deduction shall be allowed under section 243[,] 245, or 245A, in respect of any dividend on any share of stock—

(A) which is held by the taxpayer for 45 days or less during the 91-day period beginning on the date which is 45 days before the date on which such share becomes ex-dividend with respect to such dividend, or

(B) to the extent that the taxpayer is under an obligation (whether pursuant to a short sale or otherwise) to make related payments with respect to positions in substantially similar or related property.

(2) 90-DAY RULE IN THE CASE OF CERTAIN PREFERENCE DIVIDENDS.—In the case of stock having preference in dividends, if the taxpayer receives dividends with respect to such stock which are attributable to a period or periods aggregating in excess of 366 days, paragraph (1)(A) shall be applied—

(A) by substituting "90 days" for "45 days" each place it appears, and

(B) by substituting "181-day period" for "91-day period".

(3) DETERMINATION OF HOLDING PERIODS.—For purposes of this subsection, in determining the period for which the taxpayer has held any share of stock—

(A) the day of disposition, but not the day of acquisition, shall be taken into account, and

(B) paragraph (3) of section 1223 shall not apply.

(4) HOLDING PERIOD REDUCED FOR PERIODS WHERE RISK OF LOSS DIMINISHED.—The holding periods determined for purposes of this subsection shall be appropriately reduced (in the manner provided in regulations prescribed by the Secretary) for any period (during such periods) in which—

(A) the taxpayer has an option to sell, is under a contractual obligation to sell, or has made (and not closed) a short sale of, substantially identical stock or securities,

(B) the taxpayer is the grantor of an option to buy substantially identical stock or securities, or

(C) under regulations prescribed by the Secretary, a taxpayer has diminished his risk of loss by holding 1 or more other positions with respect to substantially similar or related property.

The preceding sentence shall not apply in the case of any qualified covered call (as defined in section 1092(c)(4) but without regard to the requirement that gain or loss with respect to the option not be ordinary income or loss), other than a qualified covered call option to which section 1092(f) applies.

* * *

[Sec. 246A]

SEC. 246A. DIVIDENDS RECEIVED DEDUCTION REDUCED WHERE PORTFOLIO STOCK IS DEBT FINANCED.

[Sec. 246A(a)]

(a) GENERAL RULE.—In the case of any dividend on debt-financed portfolio stock, there shall be substituted for the percentage which (but for this subsection) would be used in determining the amount of the deduction allowable under section 243 or 245(a) a percentage equal to the product of—

(1) 50 percent (65 percent in the case of any dividend from a 20-percent owned corporation as defined in section 243(c)(2)), and

(2) 100 percent minus the average indebtedness percentage.

[Sec. 246A(b)]

(b) SECTION NOT TO APPLY TO DIVIDENDS FOR WHICH 100 PERCENT DIVIDENDS RECEIVED DEDUCTION ALLOWABLE.—Subsection (a) shall not apply to—

(1) qualifying dividends (as defined in section 243(b)), and

(2) dividends received by a small business investment company operating under the Small Business Investment Act of 1958.

[Sec. 246A(c)]

(c) DEBT FINANCED PORTFOLIO STOCK.—For purposes of this section—

(1) IN GENERAL.—The term "debt financed portfolio stock" means any portfolio stock if at some time during the base period there is portfolio indebtedness with respect to such stock.

(2) PORTFOLIO STOCK.—The term "portfolio stock" means any stock of a corporation unless—

(A) as of the beginning of the ex-dividend date, the taxpayer owns stock of such corporation—

(i) possessing at least 50 percent of the total voting power of the stock of such corporation, and

(ii) having a value equal to at least 50 percent of the total value of the stock of such corporation, or

(B) as of the beginning of the ex-dividend date—

(i) the taxpayer owns stock of such corporation which would meet the requirements of subparagraph (A) if "20 percent" were substituted for "50 percent" each place it appears in such subparagraph, and

(ii) stock meeting the requirements of subparagraph (A) is owned by 5 or fewer corporate shareholders.

[Sec. 246A(d)]

(d) AVERAGE INDEBTEDNESS PERCENTAGE.—For purposes of this section—

(1) IN GENERAL.—Except as provided in paragraph (2), the term "average indebtedness percentage" means the percentage obtained by dividing—

(A) the average amount (determined under regulations prescribed by the Secretary) of the portfolio indebtedness with respect to the stock during the base period, by

(B) the average amount (determined under regulations prescribed by the Secretary) of the adjusted basis of the stock during the base period.

(2) SPECIAL RULE WHERE STOCK NOT HELD THROUGHOUT BASE PERIOD.—In the case of any stock which was not held by the taxpayer throughout the base period, paragraph (1) shall be applied as if the base period consisted only of that portion of the base period during which the stock was held by the taxpayer.

(3) PORTFOLIO INDEBTEDNESS.—

(A) IN GENERAL.—The term "portfolio indebtedness" means any indebtedness directly attributable to investment in the portfolio stock.

(B) CERTAIN AMOUNTS RECEIVED FROM SHORT SALE TREATED AS INDEBTEDNESS.—For purposes of subparagraph (A), any amount received from a short sale shall be treated as indebtedness for the period beginning on the day on which such amount is received and ending on the day the short sale is closed.

(4) BASE PERIOD.—The term "base period" means, with respect to any dividend, the shorter of—

(A) the period beginning on the ex-dividend date for the most recent previous dividend on the stock and ending on the day before the ex-dividend date for the dividend involved, or

(B) the 1-year period ending on the day before the ex-dividend date for the dividend involved.

[Sec. 246A(e)]

(e) REDUCTION IN DIVIDENDS RECEIVED DEDUCTION NOT TO EXCEED ALLOCABLE INTEREST.—Under regulations prescribed by the Secretary, any reduction under this section in the amount allowable as a deduction under section 243 or 245 with respect to any dividend shall not exceed the amount of any interest deduction (including any deductible short sale expense) allocable to such dividend.

[Sec. 246A(f)]

(f) REGULATIONS.—The regulations prescribed for purposes of this section under section 7701(f) shall include regulations providing for the disallowance of interest deductions or other appropriate treatment (in lieu of reducing the dividend received deduction) where the obligor of the indebtedness is a person other than the person receiving the dividend.

[Sec. 248]

SEC. 248. ORGANIZATIONAL EXPENDITURES.

[Sec. 248(a)]

(a) ELECTION TO DEDUCT.—If a corporation elects the application of this subsection (in accordance with regulations prescribed by the Secretary) with respect to any organizational expenditures—

(1) the corporation shall be allowed a deduction for the taxable year in which the corporation begins business in an amount equal to the lesser of—

(A) the amount of organizational expenditures with respect to the taxpayer, or

(B) $5,000, reduced (but not below zero) by the amount by which such organizational expenditures exceed $50,000, and

(2) the remainder of such organizational expenditures shall be allowed as a deduction ratably over the 180-month period beginning with the month in which the corporation begins business.

[Sec. 248(b)]

(b) ORGANIZATIONAL EXPENDITURES DEFINED.—The term “organizational expenditures” means any expenditure which—

(1) is incident to the creation of the corporation;

(2) is chargeable to capital account; and

(3) is of a character which, if expended incident to the creation of a corporation having a limited life, would be amortizable over such life.

[Sec. 248(c)]

(c) TIME FOR AND SCOPE OF ELECTION.—The election provided by subsection (a) may be made for any taxable year but only if made not later than the time prescribed by law for filing the return for such taxable year (including extensions thereof). The period so elected shall be adhered to in computing the taxable income of the corporation for the taxable year for which the election is made and all subsequent taxable years.

PART IX—ITEMS NOT DEDUCTIBLE

[Sec. 261]

SEC. 261. GENERAL RULE FOR DISALLOWANCE OF DEDUCTIONS.

In computing taxable income no deduction shall in any case be allowed in respect of the items specified in this part.

[Sec. 262]

SEC. 262. PERSONAL, LIVING, AND FAMILY EXPENSES.

[Sec. 262(a)]

(a) GENERAL RULE.—Except as otherwise expressly provided in this chapter, no deduction shall be allowed for personal, living, or family expenses.

[Sec. 262(b)]

(b) TREATMENT OF CERTAIN PHONE EXPENSES.—For purposes of subsection (a), in the case of an individual, any charge (including taxes thereon) for basic local telephone service with respect to the 1st telephone line provided to any residence of the taxpayer shall be treated as a personal expense.

[Sec. 263]

SEC. 263. CAPITAL EXPENDITURES.

[Sec. 263(a)]

(a) GENERAL RULE.—No deduction shall be allowed for—

(1) Any amount paid out for new buildings or for permanent improvements or betterments made to increase the value of any property or estate. This paragraph shall not apply to—

(A) expenditures for the development of mines or deposits deductible under section 616,

(B) research and experimental expenditures deductible under section 174,

(C) soil and water conservation expenditures deductible under section 175,

(D) expenditures by farmers for fertilizer, etc., deductible under section 180,

(E) expenditures for removal of architectural and transportation barriers to the handicapped and elderly which the taxpayer elects to deduct under section 190,

(F) expenditures for tertiary injectants with respect to which a deduction is allowed under section 193,

(G) expenditures for which a deduction is allowed under section 179,

(H) expenditures for which a deduction is allowed under section 179B,

(I) expenditures for which a deduction is allowed under section 179C,

(J) expenditures for which a deduction is allowed under section 179D, or

(K) expenditures for which a deduction is allowed under section 179E.

(2) Any amount expended in restoring property or in making good the exhaustion thereof for which an allowance is or has been made.

[Sec. 263(b)—Repealed]

[Sec. 263(c)]

(c) INTANGIBLE DRILLING AND DEVELOPMENT COSTS IN THE CASE OF OIL AND GAS WELLS AND GEOTHERMAL WELLS.—Notwithstanding subsection (a), and except as provided in subsection (i), regulations shall be prescribed by the Secretary under this subtitle corresponding to the regulations which granted the option to deduct as expenses intangible drilling and development costs in the case of oil and gas wells and which were recognized and approved by the Congress in House Concurrent Resolution 50, Seventy-ninth Congress. Such regulations shall also grant the option to deduct as expenses intangible drilling and development costs in the case of wells drilled for any geothermal deposit (as defined in section 613(e)(2)) to the same extent and in the same manner as such expenses are deductible in the case of oil and gas wells. This subsection shall not apply with respect to any costs to which any deduction is allowed under section 59(e) or 291.

* * *

[Sec. 263A]

SEC. 263A. CAPITALIZATION AND INCLUSION IN INVENTORY COSTS OF CERTAIN EXPENSES.

[Sec. 263A(a)]

(a) NONDEDUCTIBILITY OF CERTAIN DIRECT AND INDIRECT COSTS.—

(1) IN GENERAL.—In the case of any property to which this section applies, any costs described in paragraph (2)—

(A) in the case of property which is inventory in the hands of the taxpayer, shall be included in inventory costs, and

(B) in the case of any other property, shall be capitalized.

(2) ALLOCABLE COSTS.—The costs described in this paragraph with respect to any property are—

(A) the direct costs of such property, and

(B) such property's proper share of those indirect costs (including taxes) part or all of which are allocable to such property.

Any cost which (but for this subsection) could not be taken into account in computing taxable income for any taxable year shall not be treated as a cost described in this paragraph.

[Sec. 263A(b)]

(b) PROPERTY TO WHICH SECTION APPLIES.—Except as otherwise provided in this section, this section shall apply to—

(1) PROPERTY PRODUCED BY TAXPAYER.—Real or tangible personal property produced by the taxpayer.

(2) PROPERTY ACQUIRED FOR RESALE.—Real or personal property described in section 1221(a)(1) which is acquired by the taxpayer for resale.

For purposes of paragraph (1), the term "tangible personal property" shall include a film, sound recording, video tape, book, or similar property.

[Sec. 263A(c)]

(c) GENERAL EXCEPTIONS.—

(1) PERSONAL USE PROPERTY.—This section shall not apply to any property produced by the taxpayer for use by the taxpayer other than in a trade or business or an activity conducted for profit.

(2) RESEARCH AND EXPERIMENTAL EXPENDITURES.—This section shall not apply to any amount allowable as a deduction under section 174.

(3) CERTAIN DEVELOPMENT AND OTHER COSTS OF OIL AND GAS WELLS OR OTHER MINERAL PROPERTY.—This section shall not apply to any cost allowable as a deduction under section 167(h), 179B, 263(c), 263(i), 291(b)(2), 616, or 617.

(4) COORDINATION WITH LONG-TERM CONTRACT RULES.—This section shall not apply to any property produced by the taxpayer pursuant to a long-term contract.

(5) TIMBER AND CERTAIN ORNAMENTAL TREES.—This section shall not apply to—

(A) trees raised, harvested, or grown by the taxpayer other than trees described in clause (ii) of subsection (e)(4)(B) (after application of the last sentence thereof), and

(B) any real property underlying such trees.

(6) COORDINATION WITH SECTION 59(e).—Paragraphs (2) and (3) shall apply to any amount allowable as a deduction under section 59(e) for qualified expenditures described in subparagraphs (B), (C), (D), and (E) of paragraph (2) thereof.

(7) COORDINATION WITH SECTION 168(k)(5).—This section shall not apply to any amount allowed as a deduction by reason of section 168(k)(5) (relating to special rules for certain plants bearing fruits and nuts).

* * *

[Sec. 263A(f)]

(f) SPECIAL RULES FOR ALLOCATION OF INTEREST TO PROPERTY PRODUCED BY THE TAXPAYER.—

(1) INTEREST CAPITALIZED ONLY IN CERTAIN CASES.—Subsection (a) shall only apply to interest costs which are—

(A) paid or incurred during the production period, and

(B) allocable to property which is described in subsection (b)(1) and which has—

(i) a long useful life,

(ii) an estimated production period exceeding 2 years, or

(iii) an estimated production period exceeding 1 year and a cost exceeding $1,000,000.

(2) ALLOCATION RULES.—

(A) IN GENERAL.—In determining the amount of interest required to be capitalized under subsection (a) with respect to any property—

(i) interest on any indebtedness directly attributable to production expenditures with respect to such property shall be assigned to such property, and

(ii) interest on any other indebtedness shall be assigned to such property to the extent that the taxpayer's interest costs could have been reduced if production expenditures (not attributable to indebtedness described in clause (i)) had not been incurred.

(B) EXCEPTION FOR QUALIFIED RESIDENCE INTEREST.—Subparagraph (A) shall not apply to any qualified residence interest (within the meaning of section 163(h)).

(C) SPECIAL RULE FOR FLOW-THROUGH ENTITIES.—Except as provided in regulations, in the case of any flow-through entity, this paragraph shall be applied first at the entity level and then at the beneficiary level.

(3) INTEREST RELATING TO PROPERTY USED TO PRODUCE PROPERTY.—This subsection shall apply to any interest on indebtedness allocable (as determined under paragraph (2)) to and property used to produce property to which this subsection applies to the extent such interest is allocable (as so determined) to the produced property.

(4) EXEMPTION FOR AGING PROCESS OF BEER, WINE, AND DISTILLED SPIRITS.—

(A) IN GENERAL.—For purposes of this subsection, the production period shall not include the aging period for—

(i) beer (as defined in section 5052(a)),

(ii) wine (as described in section 5041(a)), or

(iii) distilled spirits (as defined in section 5002(a)(8)), except such spirits that are unfit for use for beverage purposes.

(B) TERMINATION.—This paragraph shall not apply to interest costs paid or accrued after December 31, 2020.

(5) DEFINITIONS.—For purposes of this subsection—

(A) LONG USEFUL LIFE.—Property has a long useful life if such property is—

(i) real property, or

(ii) property with a class life of 20 years or more (as determined under section 168).

(B) PRODUCTION PERIOD.—The term "production period" means, when used with respect to any property, the period—

(i) beginning on the date on which production of the property begins, and

(ii) except as provided in paragraph (4), ending on the date on which the property is ready to be placed in service or is ready to be held for sale.

(C) PRODUCTION EXPENDITURES.—The term "production expenditures" means the costs (whether or not incurred during the production period) required to be capitalized under subsection (a) with respect to the property.

[Sec. 263A(g)]

(g) PRODUCTION.—For purposes of this section—

(1) IN GENERAL.—The term "produce" includes construct, build, install, manufacture, develop, or improve.

(2) TREATMENT OF PROPERTY PRODUCED UNDER CONTRACT FOR THE TAXPAYER.—The taxpayer shall be treated as producing any property produced for the taxpayer under a contract with

the taxpayer; except that only costs paid or incurred by the taxpayer (whether under such contract or otherwise) shall be taken into account in applying subsection (a) to the taxpayer.

[Sec. 263A(h)]

(h) EXEMPTION FOR FREE LANCE AUTHORS, PHOTOGRAPHERS, AND ARTISTS.—

(1) IN GENERAL.—Nothing in this section shall require the capitalization of any qualified creative expense.

(2) QUALIFIED CREATIVE EXPENSE.—For purposes of this subsection, the term "qualified creative expense" means any expense—

(A) which is paid or incurred by an individual in the trade or business of such individual (other than as an employee) of being a writer, photographer, or artist, and

(B) which, without regard to this section, would be allowable as a deduction for the taxable year.

Such term does not include any expense related to printing, photographic plates, motion picture films, video tapes, or similar items.

(3) DEFINITIONS.—For purposes of this subsection—

(A) WRITER.—The term "writer" means any individual if the personal efforts of such individual create (or may reasonably be expected to create) a literary manuscript, musical composition (including any accompanying words), or dance score.

(B) PHOTOGRAPHER.—The term "photographer" means any individual if the personal efforts of such individual create (or may reasonably be expected to create) a photograph or photographic negative or transparency.

(C) ARTIST.—

(i) IN GENERAL.—The term "artist" means any individual if the personal efforts of such individual create (or may reasonably be expected to create) a picture, painting, sculpture, statue, etching, drawing, cartoon, graphic design, or original print edition.

(ii) CRITERIA.—In determining whether any expense is paid or incurred in the trade or business of being an artist, the following criteria shall be taken into account:

(I) The originality and uniqueness of the item created (or to be created).

(II) The predominance of aesthetic value over utilitarian value of the item created (or to be created).

(D) TREATMENT OF CERTAIN CORPORATIONS.—

(i) IN GENERAL.—If—

(I) substantially all of the stock of a corporation is owned by a qualified employee-owner and members of his family (as defined in section 267(c)(4)), and

(II) the principal activity of such corporation is performance of personal services directly related to the activities of the qualified employee-owner and such services are substantially performed by the qualified employee-owner,

this subsection shall apply to any expense of such corporation which directly relates to the activities of such employee-owner in the same manner as if such expense were incurred by such employee-owner.

(ii) QUALIFIED EMPLOYEE-OWNER.—For purposes of this subparagraph, the term "qualified employee-owner" means any individual who is an employee-owner of the corporation (as defined in section 269A(b)(2)) and who is a writer, photographer, or artist.

[Sec. 263A(i)]

(i) EXEMPTION FOR CERTAIN SMALL BUSINESSES.—

(1) IN GENERAL.—In the case of any taxpayer (other than a tax shelter prohibited from using the cash receipts and disbursements method of accounting under section 448(a)(3))

which meets the gross receipts test of section 448(c) for any taxable year, this section shall not apply with respect to such taxpayer for such taxable year.

(2) APPLICATION OF GROSS RECEIPTS TEST TO INDIVIDUALS, ETC.—In the case of any taxpayer which is not a corporation or a partnership, the gross receipts test of section 448(c) shall be applied in the same manner as if each trade or business of such taxpayer were a corporation or partnership.

(3) COORDINATION WITH SECTION 481.—Any change in method of accounting made pursuant to this subsection shall be treated for purposes of section 481 as initiated by the taxpayer and made with the consent of the Secretary.

[Sec. 263A(j)]

(j) REGULATIONS.—The Secretary shall prescribe such regulations as may be necessary or appropriate to carry out the purposes of this section, including—

(1) regulations to prevent the use of related parties, pass-thru entities, or intermediaries to avoid the application of this section, and

(2) regulations providing for simplified procedures for the application of this section in the case of property described in subsection (b) (2).

[Sec. 264]

SEC. 264. CERTAIN AMOUNTS PAID IN CONNECTION WITH INSURANCE CONTRACTS.

[Sec. 264(a)]

(a) GENERAL RULE.—No deduction shall be allowed for—

(1) Premiums on any life insurance policy, or endowment or annuity contract, if the taxpayer is directly or indirectly a beneficiary under the policy or contract.

(2) Any amount paid or accrued on indebtedness incurred or continued to purchase or carry a single premium life insurance, endowment, or annuity contract.

(3) Except as provided in subsection (d), any amount paid or accrued on indebtedness incurred or continued to purchase or carry a life insurance, endowment, or annuity contract (other than a single premium contract or a contract treated as a single premium contract) pursuant to a plan of purchase which contemplates the systematic direct or indirect borrowing of part or all of the increases in the cash value of such contract (either from the insurer or otherwise).

(4) Except as provided in subsection (e), any interest paid or accrued on any indebtedness with respect to 1 or more life insurance policies owned by the taxpayer covering the life of any individual, or any endowment or annuity contracts owned by the taxpayer covering any individual.

Paragraph (2) shall apply in respect of annuity contracts only as to contracts purchased after March 1, 1954. Paragraph (3) shall apply only in respect of contracts purchased after August 6, 1963. Paragraph (4) shall apply with respect to contracts purchased after June 20, 1986.

[Sec. 264(b)]

(b) EXCEPTIONS TO SUBSECTION (a) (1).—Subsection (a) (1) shall not apply to—

(1) any annuity contract described in section 72(s) (5), and

(2) any annuity contract to which section 72(u) applies.

[Sec. 264(c)]

(c) CONTRACTS TREATED AS SINGLE PREMIUM CONTRACTS.—For purposes of subsection (a) (2), a contract shall be treated as a single premium contract—

(1) if substantially all the premiums on the contract are paid within a period of 4 years from the date on which the contract is purchased, or

(2) if an amount is deposited after March 1, 1954, with the insurer for payment of a substantial number of future premiums on the contract.

[Sec. 264(d)]

(d) EXCEPTIONS.—Subsection (a)(3) shall not apply to any amount paid or accrued by a person during a taxable year on indebtedness incurred or continued as part of a plan referred to in subsection (a)(3)—

(1) if no part of 4 of the annual premiums due during the 7-year period (beginning with the date the first premium on the contract to which such plan relates was paid) is paid under such plan by means of indebtedness,

(2) if the total of the amounts paid or accrued by such person during such taxable year for which (without regard to this paragraph) no deduction would be allowable by reason of subsection (a)(3) does not exceed $100,

(3) if such amount was paid or accrued on indebtedness incurred because of an unforeseen substantial loss of income or unforeseen substantial increase in his financial obligations, or

(4) if such indebtedness was incurred in connection with his trade or business.

For purposes of applying paragraph (1), if there is a substantial increase in the premiums on a contract, a new 7-year period described in such paragraph with respect to such contract shall commence on the date the first such increased premium is paid.

[Sec. 264(e)]

(e) SPECIAL RULES FOR APPLICATION OF SUBSECTION (a)(4).—

(1) EXCEPTION FOR KEY PERSONS.—Subsection (a)(4) shall not apply to any interest paid or accrued on any indebtedness with respect to policies or contracts covering an individual who is a key person to the extent that the aggregate amount of such indebtedness with respect to policies and contracts covering such individual does not exceed $50,000.

* * *

(3) KEY PERSON.—For purposes of paragraph (1), the term "key person" means an officer or 20-percent owner, except that the number of individuals who may be treated as key persons with respect to any taxpayer shall not exceed the greater of—

(A) 5 individuals, or

(B) the lesser of 5 percent of the total officers and employees of the taxpayer or 20 individuals.

(4) 20-PERCENT OWNER.—For purposes of this subsection, the term "20-percent owner" means—

(A) if the taxpayer is a corporation, any person who owns directly 20 percent or more of the outstanding stock of the corporation or stock possessing 20 percent or more of the total combined voting power of all stock of the corporation, or

(B) if the taxpayer is not a corporation, any person who owns 20 percent or more of the capital or profits interest in the taxpayer.

(5) AGGREGATION RULES.—

(A) IN GENERAL.—For purposes of paragraph (4)(A) and applying the $50,000 limitation in paragraph (1)—

(i) all members of a controlled group shall be treated as 1 taxpayer, and

(ii) such limitation shall be allocated among the members of such group in such manner as the Secretary may prescribe.

(B) CONTROLLED GROUP.—For purposes of this paragraph, all persons treated as a single employer under subsection (a) or (b) of section 52 or subsection (m) or (o) of section 414 shall be treated as members of a controlled group.

* * *

[Sec. 265]

SEC. 265. EXPENSES AND INTEREST RELATING TO TAX-EXEMPT INCOME.

[Sec. 265(a)]

(a) GENERAL RULE.—No deduction shall be allowed for—

(1) EXPENSES.—Any amount otherwise allowable as a deduction which is allocable to one or more classes of income other than interest (whether or not any amount of income of that class or classes is received or accrued) wholly exempt from the taxes imposed by this subtitle, or any amount otherwise allowable under section 212 (relating to expenses for production of income) which is allocable to interest (whether or not any amount of such interest is received or accrued) wholly exempt from the taxes imposed by this subtitle.

(2) INTEREST.—Interest on indebtedness incurred or continued to purchase or carry obligations the interest on which is wholly exempt from the taxes imposed by this subtitle.

* * *

(6) SECTION NOT TO APPLY WITH RESPECT TO PARSONAGE AND MILITARY HOUSING ALLOWANCES.—No deduction shall be denied under this section for interest on a mortgage on, or real property taxes on, the home of the taxpayer by reason of the receipt of an amount as—

(A) a military housing allowance, or

(B) a parsonage allowance excludable from gross income under section 107.

* * *

[Sec. 266]

SEC. 266. CARRYING CHARGES.

No deduction shall be allowed for amounts paid or accrued for such taxes and carrying charges as, under regulations prescribed by the Secretary, are chargeable to capital account with respect to property, if the taxpayer elects, in accordance with such regulations, to treat such taxes or charges as so chargeable.

[Sec. 267]

SEC. 267. LOSSES, EXPENSES, AND INTEREST WITH RESPECT TO TRANSACTIONS BETWEEN RELATED TAXPAYERS.

[Sec. 267(a)]

(a) IN GENERAL.—

(1) DEDUCTION FOR LOSSES DISALLOWED.—No deduction shall be allowed in respect of any loss from the sale or exchange of property, directly or indirectly, between persons specified in any of the paragraphs of subsection (b). The preceding sentence shall not apply to any loss of the distributing corporation (or the distributee) in the case of a distribution in complete liquidation.

(2) MATCHING OF DEDUCTION AND PAYEE INCOME ITEM IN THE CASE OF EXPENSES AND INTEREST.—If—

(A) by reason of the method of accounting of the person to whom the payment is to be made, the amount thereof is not (unless paid) includible in the gross income of such person, and

(B) at the close of the taxable year of the taxpayer for which (but for this paragraph) the amount would be deductible under this chapter, both the taxpayer and the person to whom the payment is to be made are persons specified in any of the paragraphs of subsection (b),

then any deduction allowable under this chapter in respect of such amount shall be allowable as of the day as of which such amount is includible in the gross income of the person to whom the payment is made (or, if later, as of the day on which it would be so allowable but for this paragraph). For purposes of this paragraph, in the case of a personal service corporation (within the meaning of section 441(i)(2)), such corporation and any employee-owner (within the meaning of section 269A(b)(2), as modified by section 441(i)(2)) shall be treated as persons specified in subsection (b).

* * *

[Sec. 267(b)]

(b) RELATIONSHIPS.—The persons referred to in subsection (a) are:

(1) Members of a family, as defined in subsection (c)(4);

(2) An individual and a corporation more than 50 percent in value of the outstanding stock of which is owned, directly or indirectly, by or for such individual;

(3) Two corporations which are members of the same controlled group (as defined in subsection (f));

(4) A grantor and a fiduciary of any trust;

(5) A fiduciary of a trust and a fiduciary of another trust, if the same person is a grantor of both trusts;

(6) A fiduciary of a trust and a beneficiary of such trust;

(7) A fiduciary of a trust and a beneficiary of another trust, if the same person is a grantor of both trusts;

(8) A fiduciary of a trust and a corporation more than 50 percent in value of the outstanding stock of which is owned, directly or indirectly, by or for the trust or by or for a person who is a grantor of the trust;

(9) A person and an organization to which section 501 (relating to certain educational and charitable organizations which are exempt from tax) applies and which is controlled directly or indirectly by such person or (if such person is an individual) by members of the family of such individual;

(10) A corporation and a partnership if the same persons own—

(A) more than 50 percent in value of the outstanding stock of the corporation, and

(B) more than 50 percent of the capital interest, or the profits interest, in the partnership;

(11) An S corporation and another S corporation if the same persons own more than 50 percent in value of the outstanding stock of each corporation;

(12) An S corporation and a C corporation, if the same persons own more than 50 percent in value of the outstanding stock of each corporation; or

(13) Except in the case of a sale or exchange in satisfaction of a pecuniary bequest, an executor of an estate and a beneficiary of such estate.

[Sec. 267(c)]

(c) CONSTRUCTIVE OWNERSHIP OF STOCK.—For purposes of determining, in applying subsection (b), the ownership of stock—

(1) Stock owned, directly or indirectly, by or for a corporation, partnership, estate, or trust shall be considered as being owned proportionately by or for its shareholders, partners, or beneficiaries;

(2) An individual shall be considered as owning the stock owned, directly or indirectly, by or for his family;

(3) An individual owning (otherwise than by the application of paragraph (2)) any stock in a corporation shall be considered as owning the stock owned, directly or indirectly, by or for his partner;

(4) The family of an individual shall include only his brothers and sisters (whether by the whole or half blood), spouse, ancestors, and lineal descendants; and

(5) Stock constructively owned by a person by reason of the application of paragraph (1) shall, for the purpose of applying paragraph (1), (2), or (3), be treated as actually owned by such person, but stock constructively owned by an individual by reason of the application of paragraph (2) or (3) shall not be treated as owned by him for the purpose of again applying either of such paragraphs in order to make another the constructive owner of such stock.

[Sec. 267(d)]

(d) AMOUNT OF GAIN WHERE LOSS PREVIOUSLY DISALLOWED.—

(1) IN GENERAL.—If—

(A) in the case of a sale or exchange of property to the taxpayer a loss sustained by the transferor is not allowable to the transferor as a deduction by reason of subsection (a)(1), and

(B) the taxpayer sells or otherwise disposes of such property (or of other property the basis of which in the taxpayer's hands is determined directly or indirectly by reference to such property) at a gain,

then such gain shall be recognized only to the extent that it exceeds so much of such loss as is properly allocable to the property sold or otherwise disposed of by the taxpayer.

(2) EXCEPTION FOR WASH SALES.—Paragraph (1) shall not apply if the loss sustained by the transferor is not allowable to the transferor as a deduction by reason of section 1091 (relating to wash sales).

(3) EXCEPTION FOR TRANSFERS FROM TAX INDIFFERENT PARTIES.—Paragraph (1) shall not apply to the extent any loss sustained by the transferor (if allowed) would not be taken into account in determining a tax imposed under section 1 or 11 or a tax computed as provided by either of such sections.

[Sec. 267(e)]

(e) SPECIAL RULES FOR PASS-THRU ENTITIES.—

(1) IN GENERAL.—In the case of any amount paid or incurred by, to, or on behalf of, a pass-thru entity, for purposes of applying subsection (a)(2)—

(A) such entity,

(B) in the case of—

(i) a partnership, any person who owns (directly or indirectly) any capital interest or profits interest of such partnership, or

(ii) an S corporation, any person who owns (directly or indirectly) any of the stock of such corporation,

(C) any person who owns (directly or indirectly) any capital interests or profits interest of a partnership in which such entity owns (directly or indirectly) any capital interest or profits interest, and

(D) any person related (within the meaning of subsection (b) of this section or section 707(b)(1) to a person described in subparagraph (B) or (C),

shall be treated as persons specified in a paragraph of subsection (b). Subparagraph (C) shall apply to a transaction only if such transaction is related either to the operations of the partnership described in such subparagraph or to an interest in such partnership.

(2) PASS-THRU ENTITY.—For purposes of this section, the term "pass-thru entity" means—

(A) a partnership, and

(B) an S corporation.3

(3) CONSTRUCTIVE OWNERSHIP IN THE CASE OF PARTNERSHIPS.—For purposes of determining ownership of a capital interest or profits interest of a partnership, the principles of subsection (c) shall apply, except that—

(A) paragraph (3) of subsection (c) shall not apply, and

(B) interests owned (directly or indirectly) by or for a C corporation shall be considered as owned by or for any shareholder only if such shareholder owns (directly or indirectly) 5 percent or more in value of the stock of such corporation.

(4) SUBSECTION (a)(2) NOT TO APPLY TO CERTAIN GUARANTEED PAYMENTS OF PARTNERSHIPS.—In the case of any amount paid or incurred by a partnership, subsection (a)(2) shall not apply to the extent that section 707(c) applies to such amount.

* * *

(6) CROSS REFERENCE.—For additional rules relating to partnerships, see section 707(b).

[Sec. 267(f)]

(f) CONTROLLED GROUP DEFINED; SPECIAL RULES APPLICABLE TO CONTROLLED GROUPS.—

(1) CONTROLLED GROUP DEFINED.—For purposes of this section, the term "controlled group" has the meaning given to such term by section 1563(a), except that—

(A) "more than 50 percent" shall be substituted for "at least 80 percent" each place it appears in section 1563(a), and

(B) the determination shall be made without regard to subsections (a)(4) and (e)(3)(C) of section 1563.

(2) DEFERRAL (RATHER THAN DENIAL) OF LOSS FROM SALE OR EXCHANGE BETWEEN MEMBERS.—In the case of any loss from the sale or exchange of property which is between members of the same controlled group and to which subsection (a)(1) applies (determined without regard to this paragraph but with regard to paragraph (3))—

(A) subsections (a)(1) and (d) shall not apply to such loss, but

(B) such loss shall be deferred until the property is transferred outside such controlled group and there would be recognition of loss under consolidated return principles or until such other time as may be prescribed in regulations.

* * *

(4) DETERMINATION OF RELATIONSHIP RESULTING IN DISALLOWANCE OF LOSS, FOR PURPOSES OF OTHER PROVISIONS.—For purposes of any other section of this title which refers to a relationship which would result in a disallowance of losses under this section, deferral under paragraph (2) shall be treated as disallowance.

[Sec. 267(g)]

(g) COORDINATION WITH SECTION 1041.—Subsection (a)(1) shall not apply to any transfer described in section 1041(a) (relating to transfers of property between spouses or incident to divorce).

[Sec. 269]

SEC. 269. ACQUISITIONS MADE TO EVADE OR AVOID INCOME TAX.

[Sec. 269(a)]

(a) IN GENERAL.—If—

(1) any person or persons acquire, directly or indirectly, control of a corporation, or

(2) any corporation acquires, directly or indirectly, property of another corporation, not controlled, directly or indirectly, immediately before such acquisition, by such acquiring corporation or its stockholders, the basis of which property, in the hands of the acquiring corporation, is determined by reference to the basis in the hands of the transferor corporation,

and the principal purpose for which such acquisition was made is evasion or avoidance of Federal income tax by securing the benefit of a deduction, credit, or other allowance which such person or corporation would not otherwise enjoy, then the Secretary may disallow such deduction, credit, or other allowance. For purposes of paragraphs (1) and (2), control means the ownership of stock possessing at least 50 percent of the total combined voting power of all classes of stock entitled to vote or at least 50 percent of the total value of shares of all classes of stock of the corporation.

[Sec. 269(b)]

(b) CERTAIN LIQUIDATIONS AFTER QUALIFIED STOCK PURCHASES.—

(1) IN GENERAL.—If—

(A) there is a qualified stock purchase by a corporation of another corporation,

(B) an election is not made under section 338 with respect to such purchase,

(C) the acquired corporation is liquidated pursuant to a plan of liquidation adopted not more than 2 years after the acquisition date, and

(D) the principal purpose for such liquidation is the evasion or avoidance of Federal income tax by securing the benefit of a deduction, credit, or other allowance which the acquiring corporation would not otherwise enjoy,

then the Secretary may disallow such deduction, credit, or other allowance.

(2) MEANING OF TERMS.—For purposes of paragraph (1), the terms "qualified stock purchase" and "acquisition date" have the same respective meanings as when used in section 338.

[Sec. 269(c)]

(c) POWER OF SECRETARY TO ALLOW DEDUCTION, ETC., IN PART.—In any case to which subsection (a) or (b) applies the Secretary is authorized—

(1) to allow as a deduction, credit, or allowance any part of any amount disallowed by such subsection, if he determines that such allowance will not result in the evasion or avoidance of Federal income tax for which the acquisition was made; or

(2) to distribute, apportion, or allocate gross income, and distribute, apportion, or allocate the deductions, credits, or allowances the benefit of which was sought to be secured, between or among the corporations, or properties, or parts thereof, involved, and to allow such deductions, credits, or allowances so distributed, apportioned, or allocated, but to give effect to such allowance only to such extent as he determines will not result in the evasion or avoidance of Federal income tax for which the acquisition was made; or

(3) to exercise his powers in part under paragraph (1) and in part under paragraph (2).

[Sec. 269A]

SEC. 269A. PERSONAL SERVICE CORPORATIONS FORMED OR AVAILED OF TO AVOID OR EVADE INCOME TAX.

[Sec. 269A(a)]

(a) GENERAL RULE.—If—

(1) substantially all of the services of a personal service corporation are performed for (or on behalf of) 1 other corporation, partnership, or other entity, and

(2) the principal purpose for forming, or availing of, such personal service corporation is the avoidance or evasion of Federal income tax by reducing the income of, or securing the benefit of any expense, deduction, credit, exclusion, or other allowance for, any employee-owner which would not otherwise be available,

then the Secretary may allocate all income, deductions, credits, exclusions, and other allowances between such personal service corporation and its employee-owners, if such allocation is necessary to prevent avoidance or evasion of Federal income tax or clearly to reflect the income of the personal service corporation or any of its employee-owners.

[Sec. 269A(b)]

(b) DEFINITIONS.—For purposes of this section—

(1) PERSONAL SERVICE CORPORATION.—The term "personal service corporation" means a corporation the principal activity of which is the performance of personal services and such services are substantially performed by employee-owners.

(2) EMPLOYEE-OWNER.—The term "employee-owner" means any employee who owns, on any day during the taxable year, more than 10 percent of the outstanding stock of the personal service corporation. For purposes of the preceding sentence, section 318 shall apply, except that "5 percent" shall be substituted for "50 percent" in section 318(a)(2)(C).

(3) RELATED PERSONS.—All related persons (within the meaning of section 144(a)(3)) shall be treated as 1 entity.

[Sec. 271]

SEC. 271. DEBTS OWED BY POLITICAL PARTIES, ETC.

[Sec. 271(a)]

(a) GENERAL RULE.—In the case of a taxpayer (other than a bank as defined in section 581) no deduction shall be allowed under section 166 (relating to bad debts) or under section 165 (g) (relating to worthlessness of securities) by reason of the worthlessness of any debt owed by a political party.

[Sec. 271(b)]

(b) DEFINITIONS.—

(1) POLITICAL PARTY.—For purposes of subsection (a), the term "political party" means—

(A) a political party;

(B) a national, State, or local committee of a political party; or

(C) a committee, association, or organization which accepts contributions or makes expenditures for the purpose of influencing or attempting to influence the election of presidential or vice-presidential electors or of any individual whose name is presented for election to any Federal, State, or local elective public office, whether or not such individual is elected.

(2) CONTRIBUTIONS.—For purposes of paragraph (1) (C), the term "contributions" includes a gift, subscription, loan, advance, or deposit, of money, or anything of value, and includes a contract, promise, or agreement to make a contribution, whether or not legally enforceable.

(3) EXPENDITURES.—For purposes of paragraph (1) (C), the term "expenditures" includes a payment, distribution, loan, advance, deposit, or gift, of money, or anything of value, and includes a contract, promise, or agreement to make an expenditure, whether or not legally enforceable.

[Sec. 271(c)]

(c) EXCEPTION.—In the case of a taxpayer who uses an accrual method of accounting, subsection (a) shall not apply to a debt which accrued as a receivable on a bona fide sale of goods or services in the ordinary course of a taxpayer's trade or business if—

(1) for the taxable year in which such receivable accrued, more than 30 percent of all receivables which accrued in the ordinary course of the trades and businesses of the taxpayer were due from political parties, and

(2) the taxpayer made substantial continuing efforts to collect on the debt.

[Sec. 273]

SEC. 273. HOLDERS OF LIFE OR TERMINABLE INTEREST.

Amounts paid under the laws of a State, the District of Columbia, a possession of the United States, or a foreign country as income to the holder of a life or terminable interest acquired by gift, bequest, or inheritance shall not be reduced or diminished by any deduction for shrinkage (by whatever name called) in the value of such interest due to the lapse of time.

[Sec. 274]

SEC. 274. DISALLOWANCE OF CERTAIN ENTERTAINMENT, ETC., EXPENSES.

[Sec. 274(a)]

(a) ENTERTAINMENT, AMUSEMENT, RECREATION, OR QUALIFIED TRANSPORTATION FRINGES.—

(1) IN GENERAL.—No deduction otherwise allowable under this chapter shall be allowed for any item—

(A) ACTIVITY.—With respect to an activity which is of a type generally considered to constitute entertainment, amusement, or recreation, or

(B) FACILITY.—With respect to a facility used in connection with an activity referred to in subparagraph (A).

(2) SPECIAL RULES.—For purposes of applying paragraph (1)—

(A) Dues or fees to any social, athletic, or sporting club or organization shall be treated as items with respect to facilities.

(B) An activity described in section 212 shall be treated as a trade or business.

(3) DENIAL OF DEDUCTION FOR CLUB DUES.—Notwithstanding the preceding provisions of this subsection, no deduction shall be allowed under this chapter for amounts paid or incurred for membership in any club organized for business, pleasure, recreation, or other social purpose.

(4) QUALIFIED TRANSPORTATION FRINGES.—No deduction shall be allowed under this chapter for the expense of any qualified transportation fringe (as defined in section 132(f)) provided to an employee of the taxpayer.

[Sec. 274(b)]

(b) GIFTS.—

(1) LIMITATION.—No deduction shall be allowed under section 162 or section 212 for any expense for gifts made directly or indirectly to any individual to the extent that such expense, when added to prior expenses of the taxpayer for gifts made to such individual during the same taxable year, exceeds $25. For purposes of this section, the term "gift" means any item excludable from gross income of the recipient under section 102 which is not excludable from his gross income under any other provision of this chapter, but such term does not include—

(A) an item having a cost to the taxpayer not in excess of $4.00 on which the name of the taxpayer is clearly and permanently imprinted and which is one of a number of identical items distributed generally by the taxpayer, or

(B) a sign, display rack, or other promotional material to be used on the business premises of the recipient.

(2) SPECIAL RULES.—

(A) In the case of a gift by a partnership, the limitation contained in paragraph (1) shall apply to the partnership as well as to each member thereof.

(B) For purposes of paragraph (1), a husband and wife shall be treated as one taxpayer.

[Sec. 274(c)]

(c) CERTAIN FOREIGN TRAVEL.—

(1) IN GENERAL.—In the case of any individual who travels outside the United States away from home in pursuit of a trade or business or in pursuit of an activity described in section 212, no deduction shall be allowed under section 162 or section 212 for that portion of the expenses of such travel otherwise allowable under such section which, under regulations prescribed by the Secretary, is not allocable to such trade or business or to such activity.

(2) EXCEPTION.—Paragraph (1) shall not apply to the expenses of any travel outside the United States away from home if—

(A) such travel does not exceed one week, or

(B) the portion of the time of travel outside the United States away from home which is not attributable to the pursuit of the taxpayer's trade or business or an activity described in section 212 is less than 25 percent of the total time on such travel.

(3) DOMESTIC TRAVEL EXCLUDED.—For purposes of this subsection, travel outside the United States does not include any travel from one point in the United States to another point in the United States.

[Sec. 274(d)]

(d) SUBSTANTIATION REQUIRED.—No deduction or credit shall be allowed—

(1) under section 162 or 212 for any traveling expense (including meals and lodging while away from home),

(2) for any expense for gifts, or

(3) with respect to any listed property (as defined in section 280F(d)(4)),

unless the taxpayer substantiates by adequate records or by sufficient evidence corroborating the taxpayer's own statement (A) the amount of such expense or other item, (B) the time and place of the travel or the date and description of the gift, (C) the business purpose of the expense or other item, and (D) the business relationship to the taxpayer of the person receiving the benefit. The Secretary may by regulations provide that some or all of the requirements of the preceding sentence shall not apply in the case of an expense which does not exceed an amount prescribed pursuant to such regulations. This subsection shall not apply to any qualified nonpersonal use vehicle (as defined in subsection (i)).

[Sec. 274(e)]

(e) SPECIFIC EXCEPTIONS TO APPLICATION OF SUBSECTION (a).—Subsection (a) shall not apply to—

(1) FOOD AND BEVERAGES FOR EMPLOYEES.—Expenses for food and beverages (and facilities used in connection therewith) furnished on the business premises of the taxpayer primarily for his employees.

(2) EXPENSES TREATED AS COMPENSATION.—

(A) IN GENERAL.—Except as provided in subparagraph (B), expenses for goods, services, and facilities, to the extent that the expenses are treated by the taxpayer, with respect to the recipient of the entertainment, amusement, or recreation, as compensation to an employee on the taxpayer's return of tax under this chapter and as wages to such employee for purposes of chapter 24 (relating to withholding of income tax at source on wages).

(B) SPECIFIED INDIVIDUALS.—

(i) IN GENERAL.—In the case of a recipient who is a specified individual, subparagraph (A) and paragraph (9) shall each be applied by substituting "to the extent that the expenses do not exceed the amount of the expenses which" for "to the extent that the expenses".

(ii) SPECIFIED INDIVIDUAL.—For purposes of clause (i), the term "specified individual" means any individual who—

(I) is subject to the requirements of section 16(a) of the Securities Exchange Act of 1934 with respect to the taxpayer or a related party to the taxpayer, or

(II) would be subject to such requirements if the taxpayer (or such related party) were an issuer of equity securities referred to in such section.

For purposes of this clause, a person is a related party with respect to another person if such person bears a relationship to such other person described in section 267(b) or 707(b).

(3) REIMBURSED EXPENSES.—Expenses paid or incurred by the taxpayer, in connection with the performance by him of services for another person (whether or not such other person is his employer), under a reimbursement or other expense allowance arrangement with such other person, but this paragraph shall apply—

(A) where the services are performed for an employer, only if the employer has not treated such expenses in the manner provided in paragraph (2), or

(B) where the services are performed for a person other than an employer, only if the taxpayer accounts (to the extent provided by subsection (d)) to such person.

(4) RECREATIONAL, ETC., EXPENSES FOR EMPLOYEES.—Expenses for recreational, social, or similar activities (including facilities therefor) primarily for the benefit of employees (other than employees who are highly compensated employees (within the meaning of section 414(q))). For purposes of this paragraph, an individual owning less than a 10-percent interest in the taxpayer's trade or business shall not be considered a shareholder or other owner, and for such purposes an individual shall be treated as owning any interest owned by a member of his family (within the meaning of section 267(c)(4)). This paragraph shall not apply for purposes of subsection (a)(3).

(5) EMPLOYEE, STOCKHOLDER, ETC., BUSINESS MEETINGS.—Expenses incurred by a taxpayer which are directly related to business meetings of his employees, stockholders, agents, or directors.

(6) MEETINGS OF BUSINESS LEAGUES, ETC.—Expenses directly related and necessary to attendance at a business meeting or convention of any organization described in section 501(c)(6) (relating to business leagues, chambers of commerce, real estate boards, and boards of trade) and exempt from taxation under section 501(a).

(7) ITEMS AVAILABLE TO PUBLIC.—Expenses for goods, services, and facilities made available by the taxpayer to the general public.

(8) ENTERTAINMENT SOLD TO CUSTOMERS.—Expenses for goods or services (including the use of facilities) which are sold by the taxpayer in a bona fide transaction for an adequate and full consideration in money or money's worth.

(9) EXPENSES INCLUDIBLE IN INCOME OF PERSONS WHO ARE NOT EMPLOYEES.—Expenses paid or incurred by the taxpayer for goods, services, and facilities to the extent that the expenses are includible in the gross income of a recipient of the entertainment, amusement, or recreation who is not an employee of the taxpayer as compensation for services rendered or as a prize or award under section 74. The preceding sentence shall not apply to any amount paid or incurred by the taxpayer if such amount is required to be included (or would be so required except that the amount is less than $600) in any information return filed by such taxpayer under part III of subchapter A of chapter 61 and is not so included.

For purposes of this subsection, any item referred to in subsection (a) shall be treated as an expense.

[Sec. 274(f)]

(f) INTEREST, TAXES, CASUALTY LOSSES, ETC.—This section shall not apply to any deduction allowable to the taxpayer without regard to its connection with his trade or business (or with his income-producing activity). In the case of a taxpayer which is not an individual, the preceding sentence shall be applied as if it were an individual.

[Sec. 274(g)]

(g) TREATMENT OF ENTERTAINMENT, ETC., TYPE FACILITY.—For purposes of this chapter, if deductions are disallowed under subsection (a) with respect to any portion of a facility, such portion shall be treated as an asset which is used for personal, living, and family purposes (and not as an asset used in the trade or business).

[Sec. 274(h)]

(h) ATTENDANCE AT CONVENTIONS, ETC.—

(1) IN GENERAL.—In the case of any individual who attends a convention, seminar, or similar meeting which is held outside the North American area, no deduction shall be allowed under section 162 for expenses allocable to such meeting unless the taxpayer establishes that the meeting is directly related to the active conduct of his trade or business and that, after taking into account in the manner provided by regulations prescribed by the Secretary—

(A) the purpose of such meeting and the activities taking place at such meeting,

(B) the purposes and activities of the sponsoring organizations or groups,

(C) the residences of the active members of the sponsoring organization and the places at which other meetings of the sponsoring organization or groups have been held or will be held, and

(D) such other relevant factors as the taxpayer may present,

it is as reasonable for the meeting to be held outside the North American area as within the North American area.

(2) CONVENTIONS ON CRUISE SHIPS.—In the case of any individual who attends a convention, seminar, or other meeting which is held on any cruise ship, no deduction shall be allowed under section 162 for expenses allocable to such meeting, unless the taxpayer meets the requirements of paragraph (5) and establishes that the meeting is directly related to the active conduct of his trade or business and that—

(A) the cruise ship is a vessel registered in the United States; and

(B) all ports of call of such cruise ship are located in the United States or in possessions of the United States.

With respect to cruises beginning in any calendar year, not more than $2,000 of the expenses attributable to an individual attending one or more meetings may be taken into account under section 162 by reason of the preceding sentence.

(3) DEFINITIONS.—For purposes of this subsection—

(A) NORTH AMERICAN AREA.—The term "North American area" means the United States, its possessions, and the Trust Territory of the Pacific Islands, and Canada and Mexico.

(B) CRUISE SHIP.—The term "cruise ship" means any vessel sailing within or without the territorial waters of the United States.

(4) SUBSECTION TO APPLY TO EMPLOYER AS WELL AS TO TRAVELER.—

(A) Except as provided in subparagraph (B), this subsection shall apply to deductions otherwise allowable under section 162 to any person, whether or not such person is the individual attending the convention, seminar, or similar meeting.

(B) This subsection shall not deny a deduction to any person other than the individual attending the convention, seminar, or similar meeting with respect to any amount paid by such person to or on behalf of such individual if includible in the gross income of such individual. The preceding sentence shall not apply if the amount is required to be included in any information return filed by such person under part III of subchapter A of chapter 61 and is not so included.

(5) REPORTING REQUIREMENTS.—No deduction shall be allowed under section 162 for expenses allocable to attendance at a convention, seminar, or similar meeting on any cruise ship unless the taxpayer claiming the deduction attaches to the return of tax on which the deduction is claimed—

(A) a written statement signed by the individual attending the meeting which includes—

(i) information with respect to the total days of the trip, excluding the days of transportation to and from the cruise ship port, and the number of hours of each day of the trip which such individual devoted to scheduled business activities,

(ii) a program of the scheduled business activities of the meeting, and

(iii) such other information as may be required in regulations prescribed by the Secretary; and

(B) a written statement signed by an officer of the organization or group sponsoring the meeting which includes—

(i) a schedule of business activities of each day of the meeting,

(ii) the number of hours which the individual attending the meeting attended such scheduled business activities, and

(iii) such other information as may be required in regulations prescribed by the Secretary.

* * *

(7) SEMINARS, ETC. FOR SECTION 212 PURPOSES.—No deduction shall be allowed under section 212 for expenses allocable to a convention, seminar, or similar meeting.

[Sec. 274(i)]

(i) QUALIFIED NONPERSONAL USE VEHICLE.—For purposes of subsection (d), the term "qualified nonpersonal use vehicle" means any vehicle which, by reason of its nature, is not likely to be used more than a de minimis amount for personal purposes.

[Sec. 274(j)]

(j) EMPLOYEE ACHIEVEMENT AWARDS.—

(1) GENERAL RULE.—No deduction shall be allowed under section 162 or section 212 for the cost of an employee achievement award except to the extent that such cost does not exceed the deduction limitations of paragraph (2).

(2) DEDUCTION LIMITATIONS.—The deduction for the cost of an employee achievement award made by an employer to an employee—

(A) which is not a qualified plan award, when added to the cost to the employer for all other employee achievement awards made to such employee during the taxable year which are not qualified plan awards, shall not exceed $400, and

(B) which is a qualified plan award, when added to the cost to the employer for all other employee achievement awards made to such employee during the taxable year (including employee achievement awards which are not qualified plan awards), shall not exceed $1,600.

(3) DEFINITIONS.—For purposes of this subsection—

(A) EMPLOYEE ACHIEVEMENT AWARD.—

(i) IN GENERAL.—The term "employee achievement award" means an item of tangible personal property which is—

(I) transferred by an employer to an employee for length of service achievement or safety achievement,

(II) awarded as part of a meaningful presentation, and

(III) awarded under conditions and circumstances that do not create a significant likelihood of the payment of disguised compensation.

(ii) TANGIBLE PERSONAL PROPERTY.—For purposes of clause (i), the term "tangible personal property" shall not include—

(I) cash, cash equivalents, gift cards, gift coupons, or gift certificates (other than arrangements conferring only the right to select and receive tangible personal property from a limited array of such items pre-selected or pre-approved by the employer), or

(II) vacations, meals, lodging, tickets to theater or sporting events, stocks, bonds, other securities, and other similar items.

(B) QUALIFIED PLAN AWARD.—

(i) IN GENERAL.—The term "qualified plan award" means an employee achievement award awarded as part of an established written plan or program of the taxpayer which does not discriminate in favor of highly compensated employees (within the meaning of section 414(q)) as to eligibility or benefits.

(ii) LIMITATION.—An employee achievement award shall not be treated as a qualified plan award for any taxable year if the average cost of all employee achievement awards which are provided by the employer during the year, and which would be qualified plan awards but for this subparagraph, exceeds $400. For purposes of the preceding sentence, average cost shall be determined by including the entire cost of qualified plan awards, without taking into account employee achievement awards of nominal value.

(4) SPECIAL RULES.—For purposes of this subsection—

(A) PARTNERSHIPS.—In the case of an employee achievement award made by a partnership, the deduction limitations contained in paragraph (2) shall apply to the partnership as well as to each member thereof.

(B) LENGTH OF SERVICE AWARDS.—An item shall not be treated as having been provided for length of service achievement if the item is received during the recipient's 1st 5 years of employment or if the recipient received a length of service achievement award (other than an award excludable under section 132(e)(1)) during that year or any of the prior 4 years.

[Sec. 274(k)]

(k) BUSINESS MEALS.—

(1) IN GENERAL.—No deduction shall be allowed under this chapter for the expense of any food or beverages unless—

(A) such expense is not lavish or extravagant under the circumstances, and

(B) the taxpayer (or an employee of the taxpayer) is present at the furnishing of such food or beverages.

(2) EXCEPTIONS.—Paragraph (1) shall not apply to—

(A) any expense described in paragraph (2), (3), (4), (7), (8), or (9) of subsection (e), and

(B) any other expense to the extent provided in regulations.

[Sec. 274(l)]

(l) TRANSPORTATION AND COMMUTING BENEFITS.—

(1) IN GENERAL.—No deduction shall be allowed under this chapter for any expense incurred for providing any transportation, or any payment or reimbursement, to an employee of the taxpayer in connection with travel between the employee's residence and place of employment, except as necessary for ensuring the safety of the employee.

(2) EXCEPTION.—In the case of any qualified bicycle commuting reimbursement (as described in section 132(f)(5)(F)), this subsection shall not apply for any amounts paid or incurred after December 31, 2017, and before January 1, 2026.

[Sec. 274(m)]

(m) ADDITIONAL LIMITATIONS ON TRAVEL EXPENSES.—

(1) LUXURY WATER TRANSPORTATION.—

(A) IN GENERAL.—No deduction shall be allowed under this chapter for expenses incurred for transportation by water to the extent such expenses exceed twice the aggregate per diem amounts for days of such transportation. For purposes of the preceding sentence, the term "per diem amounts" means the highest amount generally allowable with respect to a day to employees of the executive branch of the Federal Government for per diem while away from home but serving in the United States.

(B) EXCEPTIONS.—Subparagraph (A) shall not apply to—

(i) any expense allocable to a convention, seminar, or other meeting which is held on any cruise ship, and

(ii) any expense described in paragraph (2), (3), (4), (7), (8), or (9) of subsection (e).

(2) TRAVEL AS FORM OF EDUCATION.—No deduction shall be allowed under this chapter for expenses for travel as a form of education.

(3) TRAVEL EXPENSES OF SPOUSE, DEPENDENT, OR OTHERS.—No deduction shall be allowed under this chapter (other than section 217) for travel expenses paid or incurred with respect to a spouse, dependent, or other individual accompanying the taxpayer (or an officer or employee of the taxpayer) on business travel, unless—

(A) the spouse, dependent, or other individual is an employee of the taxpayer,

(B) the travel of the spouse, dependent, or other individual is for a bona fide business purpose, and

(C) such expenses would otherwise be deductible by the spouse, dependent, or other individual.

[Sec. 274(n)]

(n) ONLY 50 PERCENT OF MEAL EXPENSES ALLOWED AS DEDUCTION.—

(1) IN GENERAL.—The amount allowable as a deduction under this chapter for any expense for food or beverages shall not exceed 50 percent of the amount of such expense which would (but for this paragraph) be allowable as a deduction under this chapter.

(2) EXCEPTIONS.—Paragraph (1) shall not apply to any expense if—

(A) such expense is described in paragraph (2), (3), (4), (7), (8), or (9) of subsection (e);

(B) in the case of an employer who pays or reimburses moving expenses of an employee, such expenses are includible in the income of the employee under section 82, or

(C) such expense is for food or beverages—

(i) required by any Federal law to be provided to crew members of a commercial vessel,

(ii) provided to crew members of a commercial vessel—

(I) which is operating on the Great Lakes, the Saint Lawrence Seaway, or any inland waterway of the United States, and

(II) which is of a kind which would be required by Federal law to provide food and beverages to crew members if it were operated at sea,

(iii) provided on an oil or gas platform or drilling rig if the platform or rig is located offshore, or

(iv) provided on an oil or gas platform or drilling rig, or at a support camp which is in proximity and integral to such platform or rig, if the platform or rig is located in the United States north of 54 degrees north latitude.

Clauses (i) and (ii) of subparagraph (C) shall not apply to vessels primarily engaged in providing luxury water transportation (determined under the principles of subsection (m)). In the case of the employee, the exception of subparagraph (A) shall not apply to expenses described in subparagraph (B).

(3) SPECIAL RULE FOR INDIVIDUALS SUBJECT TO FEDERAL HOURS OF SERVICE.—In the case of any expenses for food or beverages consumed while away from home (within the meaning of section 162(a)(2)) by an individual during, or incident to, the period of duty subject to the hours of service limitations of the Department of Transportation, paragraph (1) shall be applied by substituting "80 percent" for "50 percent".

* * *

[Sec. 275]

SEC. 275. CERTAIN TAXES.

[Sec. 275(a)]

(a) GENERAL RULE.—No deduction shall be allowed for the following taxes:

(1) Federal income taxes, including—

(A) the tax imposed by section 3101 (relating to the tax on employees under the Federal Insurance Contributions Act);

(B) the taxes imposed by sections 3201 and 3211 (relating to the taxes on railroad employees and railroad employee representatives); and

(C) the tax withheld at source on wages under section 3402.

(2) Federal war profits and excess profits taxes.

(3) Estate, inheritance, legacy, succession, and gift taxes.

(4) Income, war profits, and excess profits taxes imposed by the authority of any foreign country or possession of the United States if—

(A) the taxpayer chooses to take to any extent the benefits of section 901, or

(B) such taxes are paid or accrued with respect to foreign trade income (within the meaning of section 923(b)) of a FSC.

(5) Taxes on real property, to the extent that section 164(d) requires such taxes to be treated as imposed on another taxpayer.

(6) Taxes imposed by chapters 41, 42, 43, 44, 45, 46, and 54.

Paragraph (1) shall not apply to any taxes to the extent such taxes are allowable as a deduction under section 164(f).

[Sec. 275(b)]

(b) CROSS REFERENCE.—

For disallowance of certain other taxes, see section 164(c).

[Sec. 276]

SEC. 276. CERTAIN INDIRECT CONTRIBUTIONS TO POLITICAL PARTIES.

[Sec. 276(a)]

(a) DISALLOWANCE OF DEDUCTIONS.—No deduction otherwise allowable under this chapter shall be allowed for any amount paid or incurred for—

(1) advertising in a convention program of a political party, or in any other publication if any part of the proceeds of such publication directly or indirectly inures (or is intended to inure) to or for the use of a political party or a political candidate,

(2) admission to any dinner or program, if any part of the proceeds of such dinner or program directly or indirectly inures (or is intended to inure) to or for the use of a political party or a political candidate, or

(3) admission to an inaugural ball, inaugural gala, inaugural parade, or inaugural concert, or to any similar event which is identified with a political party or a political candidate.

[Sec. 276(b)]

(b) DEFINITIONS.—For purposes of this section—

(1) POLITICAL PARTY.—The term "political party" means—

(A) a political party;

(B) a National, State, or local committee of a political party; or

(C) a committee, association, or organization, whether incorporated or not, which directly or indirectly accepts contributions (as defined in section 271(b)(2)) or make[s] expenditures (as defined in section 271(b)(3)) for the purpose of influencing or attempting to influence the selection, nomination, or election of any individual to any Federal, State, or local elective public office, or the election of presidential and vice-presidential electors, whether or not such individual or electors are selected, nominated, or elected.

(2) PROCEEDS INURING TO OR FOR THE USE OF POLITICAL CANDIDATES.—Proceeds shall be treated as inuring to or for the use of a political candidate only if—

(A) such proceeds may be used directly or indirectly for the purpose of furthering his candidacy for selection, nomination, or election to any elective public office, and

(B) such proceeds are not received by such candidate in the ordinary course of a trade or business (other than the trade or business of holding elective public office).

[Sec. 276(c)]

(c) CROSS REFERENCE.—

For disallowance of certain entertainment, etc., expenses, see section 274.

[Sec. 279]

SEC. 279. INTEREST ON INDEBTEDNESS INCURRED BY CORPORATION TO ACQUIRE STOCK OR ASSETS OF ANOTHER CORPORATION.

[Sec. 279(a)]

(a) GENERAL RULE.—No deduction shall be allowed for any interest paid or incurred by a corporation during the taxable year with respect to its corporate acquisition indebtedness to the extent that such interest exceeds—

(1) $5,000,000, reduced by

(2) the amount of interest paid or incurred by such corporation during such year on obligations (A) issued to provide consideration for an acquisition described in paragraph (1) of subsection (b), but (B) which are not corporate acquisition indebtedness.

[Sec. 279(b)]

(b) CORPORATE ACQUISITION INDEBTEDNESS.—For purposes of this section, the term "corporate acquisition indebtedness" means any obligation evidenced by a bond, debenture, note, or certificate or other evidence of indebtedness issued by a corporation (hereinafter in this section referred to as "issuing corporation") if—

(1) such obligation is issued to provide consideration for the acquisition of—

(A) stock in another corporation (hereinafter in this section referred to as "acquired corporation"), or

(B) assets of another corporation (hereinafter in this section referred to as "acquired corporation") pursuant to a plan under which at least two-thirds (in value) of all the assets (excluding money) used in trades and businesses carried on by such corporation are acquired,

(2) such obligation is either—

(A) subordinated to the claims of trade creditors of the issuing corporation generally, or

(B) expressly subordinated in right of payment to the payment of any substantial amount of unsecured indebtedness, whether outstanding or subsequently issued, of the issuing corporation,

(3) the bond or other evidence of indebtedness is either—

(A) convertible directly or indirectly into stock of the issuing corporation, or

(B) part of an investment unit or other arrangement which includes, in addition to such bond or other evidence of indebtedness, an option to acquire, directly or indirectly, stock in the issuing corporation, and

(4) as of a day determined under subsection (c)(1), either—

(A) the ratio of debt to equity (as defined in subsection (c)(2)) of the issuing corporation exceeds 2 to 1, or

(B) the projected earnings (as defined in subsection (c)(3)) do not exceed 3 times the annual interest to be paid or incurred (determined under subsection (c)(4)).

[Sec. 279(c)]

(c) RULES FOR APPLICATION OF SUBSECTION (b)(4).—For purposes of subsection (b)(4)—

(1) TIME OF DETERMINATION.—Determinations are to be made as of the last day of any taxable year of the issuing corporation in which it issues any obligation to provide consideration for an acquisition described in subsection (b)(1) of stock in, or assets of, the acquired corporation.

(2) RATIO OF DEBT TO EQUITY.—The term "ratio of debt to equity" means the ratio which the total indebtedness of the issuing corporation bears to the sum of its money and all its other assets (in an amount equal to their adjusted basis for determining gain) less such total indebtedness.

(3) PROJECTED EARNINGS.—

(A) The term "projected earnings" means the "average annual earnings" (as defined in subparagraph (B)) of—

(i) the issuing corporation only, if clause (ii) does not apply, or

(ii) both the issuing corporation and the acquired corporation, in any case where the issuing corporation has acquired control (as defined in section 368(c)), or has acquired substantially all of the properties, of the acquired corporation.

(B) The average annual earnings referred to in subparagraph (A) is, for any corporation, the amount of its earnings and profits for any 3-year period ending with the last day of a taxable year of the issuing corporation described in paragraph (1), computed without reduction for—

(i) interest paid or incurred,

(ii) depreciation or amortization allowed under this chapter,

(iii) liability for tax under this chapter, and

(iv) distributions to which section 301(c)(1) applies (other than such distributions from the acquired to the issuing corporation),

and reduced to an annual average for such 3-year period pursuant to regulations prescribed by the Secretary. Such regulations shall include rules for cases where any corporation was not in existence for all of such 3-year period or such period includes only a portion of a taxable year of any corporation.

(4) ANNUAL INTEREST TO BE PAID OR INCURRED.—The term "annual interest to be paid or incurred" means—

(A) if subparagraph (B) does not apply, the annual interest to be paid or incurred by the issuing corporation only, determined by reference to its total indebtedness outstanding, or

(B) if projected earnings are determined under clause (ii) of paragraph (3)(A), the annual interest to be paid or incurred by both the issuing corporation and the acquired corporation, determined by reference to their combined total indebtedness outstanding.

(5) SPECIAL RULES FOR BANKS AND LENDING OR FINANCE COMPANIES.—With respect to any corporation which is a bank (as defined in section 581) or is primarily engaged in a lending or finance business—

(A) in determining under paragraph (2) the ratio of debt to equity of such corporation (or of the affiliated group of which such corporation is a member), the total indebtedness of such corporation (and the assets of such corporation) shall be reduced by an amount equal to the total indebtedness owed to such corporation which arises out of the banking business of such corporation, or out of the lending or finance business of such corporation, as the case may be;

(B) in determining under paragraph (4) the annual interest to be paid or incurred by such corporation (or by the issuing and acquired corporations referred to in paragraph (4)(B) or by the affiliated group of which such corporation is a member) the amount of such interest (determined without regard to this paragraph) shall be reduced by an amount which bears the same ratio to the amount of such interest as the amount of the reduction for the taxable year under subparagraph (A) bears to the total indebtedness of such corporation; and

(C) in determining under paragraph (3)(B) the average annual earnings, the amount of the earnings and profits for the 3-year period shall be reduced by the sum of the reductions under subparagraph (B) for such period.

For purposes of this paragraph, the term "lending or finance business" means a business of making loans or purchasing or discounting accounts receivable, notes, or installment obligations.

[Sec. 279(d)]

(d) TAXABLE YEARS TO WHICH APPLICABLE.—In applying this section—

(1) FIRST YEAR OF DISALLOWANCE.—The deduction of interest on any obligation shall not be disallowed under subsection (a) before the first taxable year of the issuing corporation as of the last day of which the application of either subparagraph (A) or subparagraph (B) of subsection (b)(4) results in such obligation being corporate acquisition indebtedness.

(2) GENERAL RULE FOR SUCCEEDING YEARS.—Except as provided in paragraphs (3), (4), and (5), if an obligation is determined to be corporate acquisition indebtedness as of the last day of any taxable year of the issuing corporation, it shall be corporate acquisition indebtedness for such taxable year and all subsequent taxable years.

(3) REDETERMINATION WHERE CONTROL, ETC., IS ACQUIRED.—If an obligation is determined to be corporate acquisition indebtedness as of the close of a taxable year of the issuing corporation in which clause (i) of subsection (c)(3)(A) applied, but would not be corporate acquisition indebtedness if the determination were made as of the close of the first taxable year of such corporation thereafter in which clause (ii) of subsection (c)(3)(A) could apply,

such obligation shall be considered not to be corporate acquisition indebtedness for such later taxable year and all taxable years thereafter.

(4) SPECIAL 3-YEAR RULE.—If an obligation which has been determined to be corporate acquisition indebtedness for any taxable year would not be such indebtedness for each of any 3 consecutive taxable years thereafter if subsection (b)(4) were applied as of the close of each of such 3 years, then such obligation shall not be corporate acquisition indebtedness for all taxable years after such 3 consecutive taxable years.

(5) 5 PERCENT STOCK RULE.—In the case of obligations issued to provide consideration for the acquisition of stock in another corporation, such obligations shall be corporate acquisition indebtedness for a taxable year only if at some time and before the close of such year the issuing corporation owns 5 percent or more of the total combined voting power of all classes of stock entitled to vote of such other corporation.

[Sec. 279(e)]

(e) CERTAIN NONTAXABLE TRANSACTIONS.—An acquisition of stock of a corporation of which the issuing corporation is in control (as defined in section 368 (c)) in a transaction in which gain or loss is not recognized shall be deemed an acquisition described in paragraph (1) of subsection (b) only if immediately before such transaction (1) the acquired corporation was in existence, and (2) the issuing corporation was not in control (as defined in section 368(c)) of such corporation.

* * *

[Sec. 279(g)]

(g) AFFILIATED GROUPS.—In any case in which the issuing corporation is a member of an affiliated group, the application of this section shall be determined, pursuant to regulations prescribed by the Secretary, by treating all of the members of the affiliated group in the aggregate as the issuing corporation, except that the ratio of debt to equity of, projected earnings of, and annual interest to be paid or incurred by any corporation (other than the issuing corporation determined without regard to this subsection) shall be included in the determinations required under subparagraphs (A) and (B) of subsection (b)(4) as of any day only if such corporation is a member of the affiliated group on such day, and, in determining projected earnings of such corporation under subsection (c)(3), there shall be taken into account only the earnings and profits of such corporation for the period during which it was a member of the affiliated group. For purposes of the preceding sentence, the term "affiliated group" has the meaning assigned to such term by section 1504(a), except that all corporations other than the acquired corporation shall be treated as includible corporations (without any exclusion under section 1504(b)) and the acquired corporation shall not be treated as an includible corporation.

[Sec. 279(h)]

(h) CHANGES IN OBLIGATION.—For purposes of this section—

(1) Any extension, renewal, or refinancing of an obligation evidencing a preexisting indebtedness shall not be deemed to be the issuance of a new obligation.

(2) Any obligation which is corporate acquisition indebtedness of the issuing corporation is also corporate acquisition indebtedness of any corporation which becomes liable for such obligation as guarantor, endorser, or indemnitor or which assumes liability for such obligation in any transaction.

* * *

[Sec. 279(i)]

(i) EFFECT ON OTHER PROVISIONS.—No inference shall be drawn from any provision in this section that any instrument designated as a bond, debenture, note, or certificate or other evidence of indebtedness by its issuer represents an obligation or indebtedness of such issuer in applying any other provision of this title.

[Sec. 280A]

SEC. 280A. DISALLOWANCE OF CERTAIN EXPENSES IN CONNECTION WITH BUSINESS USE OF HOME, RENTAL OF VACATION HOMES, ETC.

[Sec. 280A(a)]

(a) GENERAL RULE.—Except as otherwise provided in this section, in the case of a taxpayer who is an individual or an S corporation, no deduction otherwise allowable under this chapter shall be allowed with respect to the use of a dwelling unit which is used by the taxpayer during the taxable year as a residence.

[Sec. 280A(b)]

(b) EXCEPTION FOR INTEREST, TAXES, CASUALTY LOSSES, ETC.—Subsection (a) shall not apply to any deduction allowable to the taxpayer without regard to its connection with his trade or business (or with his income-producing activity).

[Sec. 280A(c)]

(c) EXCEPTIONS FOR CERTAIN BUSINESS OR RENTAL USE; LIMITATION ON DEDUCTIONS FOR SUCH USE.—

(1) CERTAIN BUSINESS USE.—Subsection (a) shall not apply to any item to the extent such item is allocable to a portion of the dwelling unit which is exclusively used on a regular basis—

(A) as the principal place of business for any trade or business of the taxpayer,

(B) as a place of business which is used by patients, clients, or customers in meeting or dealing with the taxpayer in the normal course of his trade or business, or

(C) in the case of a separate structure which is not attached to the dwelling unit, in connection with the taxpayer's trade or business.

In the case of an employee, the preceding sentence shall apply only if the exclusive use referred to in the preceding sentence is for the convenience of his employer. For purposes of subparagraph (A), the term "principal place of business" includes a place of business which is used by the taxpayer for the administrative or management activities of any trade or business of the taxpayer if there is no other fixed location of such trade or business where the taxpayer conducts substantial administrative or management activities of such trade or business.

(2) CERTAIN STORAGE USE.—Subsection (a) shall not apply to any item to the extent such item is allocable to space within the dwelling unit which is used on a regular basis as a storage unit for the inventory or product samples of the taxpayer held for use in the taxpayer's trade or business of selling products at retail or wholesale, but only if the dwelling unit is the sole fixed location of such trade or business.

(3) RENTAL USE.—Subsection (a) shall not apply to any item which is attributable to the rental of the dwelling unit or portion thereof (determined after the application of subsection (e)).

(4) USE IN PROVIDING DAY CARE SERVICES.—

(A) IN GENERAL.—Subsection (a) shall not apply to any item to the extent that such item is allocable to the use of any portion of the dwelling unit on a regular basis in the taxpayer's trade or business of providing day care for children, for individuals who have attained age 65, or for individuals who are physically or mentally incapable of caring for themselves.

(B) LICENSING, ETC., REQUIREMENT.—Subparagraph (A) shall apply to items accruing for a period only if the owner or operator of the trade or business referred to in subparagraph (A)—

(i) has applied for (and such application has not been rejected),

(ii) has been granted (and such granting has not been revoked), or

(iii) is exempt from having,

a license, certification, registration, or approval as a day care center or as a family or group day care home under the provisions of any applicable State law. This subparagraph shall apply only to items accruing in periods beginning on or after the first day of the first month which begins more than 90 days after the date of the enactment of the Tax Reduction and Simplification Act of 1977.

(C) ALLOCATION FORMULA.—If a portion of the taxpayer's dwelling unit used for the purposes described in subparagraph (A) is not used exclusively for those purposes, the amount of the expenses attributable to that portion shall not exceed an amount which bears the same ratio to the total amount of the items allocable to such portion as the number of hours the portion is used for such purposes bears to the number of hours the portion is available for use.

(5) LIMITATION ON DEDUCTIONS.—In the case of a use described in paragraph (1), (2), or (4), and in the case of a use described in paragraph (3) where the dwelling unit is used by the taxpayer during the taxable year as a residence, the deductions allowed under this chapter for the taxable year by reason of being attributed to such use shall not exceed the excess of—

(A) the gross income derived from such use for the taxable year, over

(B) the sum of—

(i) the deductions allocable to such use which are allowable under this chapter for the taxable year whether or not such unit (or portion thereof) was so used, and

(ii) the deductions allocable to the trade or business (or rental activity) in which such use occurs (but which are not allocable to such use) for such taxable year.

Any amount not allowable as a deduction under this chapter by reason of the preceding sentence shall be taken into account as a deduction (allocable to such use) under this chapter for the succeeding taxable year. Any amount taken into account for any taxable year under the preceding sentence shall be subject to the limitation of the 1st sentence of this paragraph whether or not the dwelling unit is used as a residence during such taxable year.

(6) TREATMENT OF RENTAL TO EMPLOYER.—Paragraphs (1) and (3) shall not apply to any item which is attributable to the rental of the dwelling unit (or any portion thereof) by the taxpayer to his employer during any period in which the taxpayer uses the dwelling unit (or portion) in performing services as an employee of the employer.

[Sec. 280A(d)]

(d) USE AS RESIDENCE.—

(1) IN GENERAL.—For purposes of this section, a taxpayer uses a dwelling unit during the taxable year as a residence if he uses such unit (or portion thereof) for personal purposes for a number of days which exceeds the greater of—

(A) 14 days, or

(B) 10 percent of the number of days during such year for which such unit is rented at a fair rental.

For purposes of subparagraph (B), a unit shall not be treated as rented at a fair rental for any day for which it is used for personal purposes.

(2) PERSONAL USE OF UNIT.—For purposes of this section, the taxpayer shall be deemed to have used a dwelling unit for personal purposes for a day if, for any part of such day, the unit is used—

(A) for personal purposes by the taxpayer or any other person who has an interest in such unit, or by any member of the family (as defined in section 267(c)(4)) of the taxpayer or such other person;

(B) by any individual who uses the unit under an arrangement which enables the taxpayer to use some other dwelling unit (whether or not a rental is charged for the use of such other unit); or

(C) by any individual (other than an employee with respect to whose use section 119 applies), unless for such day the dwelling unit is rented for a rental which, under the facts and circumstances, is fair rental.

The Secretary shall prescribe regulations with respect to the circumstances under which use of the unit for repairs and annual maintenance will not constitute personal use under this paragraph, except that if the taxpayer is engaged in repair and maintenance on a substantially full time basis for any day, such authority shall not allow the Secretary to treat a dwelling unit as being used for personal use by the taxpayer on such day merely because other individuals who are on the premises on such day are not so engaged.

(3) RENTAL TO FAMILY MEMBER, ETC., FOR USE AS PRINCIPAL RESIDENCE.—

(A) IN GENERAL.—A taxpayer shall not be treated as using a dwelling unit for personal purposes by reason of a rental arrangement for any period if for such period such dwelling unit is rented, at a fair rental, to any person for use as such person's principal residence.

(B) SPECIAL RULES FOR RENTAL TO PERSON HAVING INTEREST IN UNIT.—

(i) RENTAL MUST BE PURSUANT TO SHARED EQUITY FINANCING AGREEMENT.—Subparagraph (A) shall apply to a rental to a person who has an interest in the dwelling unit only if such rental is pursuant to a shared equity financing agreement.

(ii) DETERMINATION OF FAIR RENTAL.—In the case of a rental pursuant to a shared equity financing agreement, fair rental shall be determined as of the time the agreement is entered into and by taking into account the occupant's qualified ownership interest.

(C) SHARED EQUITY FINANCING AGREEMENT.—For purposes of this paragraph, the term "shared equity financing agreement" means an agreement under which—

(i) 2 or more persons acquire qualified ownership interests in a dwelling unit, and

(ii) the person (or persons) holding 1 or more of such interests—

(I) is entitled to occupy the dwelling unit for use as a principal residence, and

(II) is required to pay rent to 1 or more other persons holding qualified ownership interests in the dwelling unit.

(D) QUALIFIED OWNERSHIP INTEREST.—For purposes of this paragraph, the term "qualified ownership interest" means an undivided interest for more than 50 years in the entire dwelling unit and appurtenant land being acquired in the transaction to which the shared equity financing agreement relates.

(4) RENTAL OF PRINCIPAL RESIDENCE.—

(A) IN GENERAL.—For purposes of applying subsection (c) (5) to deductions allocable to a qualified rental period, a taxpayer shall not be considered to have used a dwelling unit for personal purposes for any day during the taxable year which occurs before or after a qualified rental period described in subparagraph (B) (i), or before a qualified rental period described in subparagraph (B) (ii), if with respect to such day such unit constitutes the principal residence (within the meaning of section 121) of the taxpayer.

(B) QUALIFIED RENTAL PERIOD.—For purposes of subparagraph (A), the term "qualified rental period" means a consecutive period of—

(i) 12 or more months which begins or ends in such taxable year, or

(ii) less than 12 months which begins in such taxable year and at the end of which such dwelling unit is sold or exchanged, and

for which such unit is rented, or is held for rental, at a fair rental.

[Sec. 280A(e)]

(e) EXPENSES ATTRIBUTABLE TO RENTAL.—

(1) IN GENERAL.—In any case where a taxpayer who is an individual or an S corporation uses a dwelling unit for personal purposes on any day during the taxable year (whether or not he is treated under this section as using such unit as a residence), the amount deductible under this chapter with respect to expenses attributable to the rental of the unit (or portion thereof) for the taxable year shall not exceed an amount which bears the same relationship to such expenses as the number of days during each year that the unit (or portion thereof) is rented at a fair rental bears to the total number of days during such year that the unit (or portion thereof) is used.

(2) EXCEPTION FOR DEDUCTIONS OTHERWISE ALLOWABLE.—This subsection shall not apply with respect to deductions which would be allowable under this chapter for the taxable year whether or not such unit (or portion thereof) was rented.

[Sec. 280A(f)]

(f) DEFINITIONS AND SPECIAL RULES.—

(1) DWELLING UNIT DEFINED.—For purposes of this section—

(A) IN GENERAL.—The term "dwelling unit" includes a house, apartment, condominium, mobile home, boat, or similar property, and all structures or other property appurtenant to such dwelling unit.

(B) EXCEPTION.—The term "dwelling unit" does not include that portion of a unit which is used exclusively as a hotel, motel, inn, or similar establishment.

(2) PERSONAL USE BY SHAREHOLDERS OF S CORPORATION.—In the case of an S corporation, subparagraphs (A) and (B) of subsection (d)(2) shall be applied by substituting "any shareholder of the S corporation" for "the taxpayer" each place it appears.

(3) COORDINATION WITH SECTION 183.—If subsection (a) applies with respect to any dwelling unit (or portion thereof) for the taxable year—

(A) section 183 (relating to activities not engaged in for profit) shall not apply to such unit (or portion thereof) for such year, but

(B) such year shall be taken into account as a taxable year for purposes of applying subsection (d) of section 183 (relating to 5-year presumption).

(4) COORDINATION WITH SECTION 162(a)(2).—Nothing in this section shall be construed to disallow any deduction allowable under section 162(a)(2) (or any deduction which meets the tests of section 162(a)(2) but is allowable under another provision of this title) by reason of the taxpayer's being away from home in the pursuit of a trade or business (other than the trade or business of renting dwelling units).

[Sec. 280A(g)]

(g) SPECIAL RULE FOR CERTAIN RENTAL USE.—Notwithstanding any other provision of this section or section 183, if a dwelling unit is used during the taxable year by the taxpayer as a residence and such dwelling unit is actually rented for less than 15 days during the taxable year, then—

(1) no deduction otherwise allowable under this chapter because of the rental use of such dwelling unit shall be allowed, and

(2) the income derived from such use for the taxable year shall not be included in the gross income of such taxpayer under section 61.

[Sec. 280E]

SEC. 280E. EXPENDITURES IN CONNECTION WITH THE ILLEGAL SALE OF DRUGS.

No deduction or credit shall be allowed for any amount paid or incurred during the taxable year in carrying on any trade or business if such trade or business (or the activities which comprise such trade or business) consists of trafficking in controlled substances (within the meaning of schedule I and II of the Controlled Substances Act) which is prohibited by Federal law or the law of any State in which such trade or business is conducted.

»»→ Caution: As provided in Section 280F(d)(7), the dollar amounts stated in Section 280F(a) applicable to passenger cars placed in service after 2018 are adjusted to reflect increases in the Chained Consumer Price Index.

[Sec. 280F]

SEC. 280F. LIMITATION ON DEPRECIATION FOR LUXURY AUTOMOBILES; LIMITATION WHERE CERTAIN PROPERTY USED FOR PERSONAL PURPOSES.

[Sec. 280F(a)]

(a) LIMITATION ON AMOUNT OF DEPRECIATION FOR LUXURY AUTOMOBILES.—

(1) DEPRECIATION.—

(A) LIMITATION.—The amount of the depreciation deduction for any taxable year for any passenger automobile shall not exceed—

(i) $10,000 for the 1st taxable year in the recovery period,

(ii) $16,000 for the 2nd taxable year in the recovery period,

(iii) $9,600 for the 3rd taxable year in the recovery period, and

(iv) $5,760 for each succeeding taxable year in the recovery period.

(B) DISALLOWED DEDUCTIONS ALLOWED FOR YEARS AFTER RECOVERY PERIOD.—

(i) IN GENERAL.—Except as provided in clause (ii), the unrecovered basis of any passenger automobile shall be treated as an expense for the 1st taxable year after the recovery period. Any excess of the unrecovered basis over the limitation of clause (ii) shall be treated as an expense in the succeeding taxable year.

(ii) $5,760 LIMITATION.—The amount treated as an expense under clause (i) for any taxable year shall not exceed $5,760.

(iii) PROPERTY MUST BE DEPRECIABLE.—No amount shall be allowable as a deduction by reason of this subparagraph with respect to any property for any taxable year unless a depreciation deduction would be allowable with respect to such property for such taxable year.

(iv) AMOUNT TREATED AS DEPRECIATION DEDUCTION.—For purposes of this subtitle, any amount allowable as a deduction by reason of this subparagraph shall be treated as a depreciation deduction allowable under section 168.

(2) COORDINATION WITH REDUCTIONS IN AMOUNT ALLOWABLE BY REASON OF PERSONAL USE, ETC.—This subsection shall be applied before—

(A) the application of subsection (b), and

(B) the application of any other reduction in the amount of any depreciation deduction allowable under section 168 by reason of any use not qualifying the property for such credit or depreciation deduction.

[Sec. 280F(b)]

(b) LIMITATION WHERE BUSINESS USE OF LISTED PROPERTY NOT GREATER THAN 50 PERCENT.—

(1) DEPRECIATION.—If any listed property is not predominantly used in a qualified business use for any taxable year, the deduction allowed under section 168 with respect to such property for such taxable year and any subsequent taxable year shall be determined under section 168(g) (relating to alternative depreciation system).

(2) RECAPTURE.—

(A) WHERE BUSINESS USE PERCENTAGE DOES NOT EXCEED 50 PERCENT.—If—

(i) property is predominantly used in a qualified business use in a taxable year in which it is placed in service, and

(ii) such property is not predominantly used in a qualified business use for any subsequent taxable year, then any excess depreciation shall be included in gross income for the taxable year referred to in clause (ii), and the depreciation deduction for the taxable year referred to in clause (ii) and any subsequent taxable years shall be determined under section 168(g) (relating to alternative depreciation system).

(B) EXCESS DEPRECIATION.—For purposes of subparagraph (A), the term "excess depreciation" means the excess (if any) of—

(i) the amount of the depreciation deductions allowable with respect to the property for taxable years before the 1st taxable year in which the property was not predominantly used in a qualified business use, over

(ii) the amount which would have been so allowable if the property had not been predominantly used in a qualified business use for the taxable year in which it was placed in service.

(3) PROPERTY PREDOMINANTLY USED IN QUALIFIED BUSINESS USE.—For purposes of this subsection, property shall be treated as predominantly used in a qualified business use for any taxable year if the business use percentage for such taxable year exceeds 50 percent.

* * *

[Sec. 280F(d)]

(d) DEFINITIONS AND SPECIAL RULES.—For purposes of this section—

(1) COORDINATION WITH SECTION 179.—Any deduction allowable under section 179 with respect to any listed property shall be subject to the limitations of subsections (a) and (b), and the limitation of paragraph (3) of this subsection, in the same manner as if it were a depreciation deduction allowable under section 168.

(2) SUBSEQUENT DEPRECIATION DEDUCTIONS REDUCED FOR DEDUCTIONS ALLOCABLE TO PERSONAL USE.—Solely for purposes of determining the amount of the depreciation deduction for subsequent taxable years, if less than 100 percent of the use of any listed property during any taxable year is used in a trade or business (including the holding for the production of income), all of the use of such property during such taxable year shall be treated as use so described.

(3) DEDUCTIONS OF EMPLOYEE.—

(A) IN GENERAL.—Any employee use of listed property shall not be treated as use in a trade or business for purposes of determining the amount of any depreciation deduction allowable to the employee (or the amount of any deduction allowable to the employee for rentals or other payments under a lease of listed property) unless such use is for the convenience of the employer and required as a condition of employment.

(B) EMPLOYEE USE.—For purposes of subparagraph (A), the term "employee use" means any use in connection with the performance of services as an employee.

(4) LISTED PROPERTY.—

(A) IN GENERAL.—Except as provided in subparagraph (B), the term "listed property" means—

(i) any passenger automobile,

(ii) any other property used as a means of transportation,

(iii) any property of a type generally used for purposes of entertainment, recreation, or amusement, and

(iv) any other property of a type specified by the Secretary by regulations.

(B) EXCEPTION FOR PROPERTY USED IN BUSINESS OF TRANSPORTING PERSONS OR PROPERTY.—Except to the extent provided in regulations, clause (ii) of subparagraph (A) shall not apply to any property substantially all of the use of which is in a trade or business of providing to unrelated persons services consisting of the transportation of persons or property for compensation or hire.

(5) PASSENGER AUTOMOBILE.—

(A) IN GENERAL.—Except as provided in subparagraph (B), the term "passenger automobile" means any 4-wheeled vehicle—

(i) which is manufactured primarily for use on public streets, roads, and highways, and

(ii) which is rated at 6,000 pounds unloaded gross vehicle weight or less.

In the case of a truck or van, clause (ii) shall be applied by substituting "gross vehicle weight" for "unloaded gross vehicle weight."

(B) EXCEPTION FOR CERTAIN VEHICLES.—The term "passenger automobile" shall not include—

(i) any ambulance, hearse, or combination ambulance-hearse used by the taxpayer directly in a trade or business,

(ii) any vehicle used by the taxpayer directly in the trade or business of transporting persons or property for compensation or hire, and

(iii) under regulations, any truck or van.

(6) BUSINESS USE PERCENTAGE.—

(A) IN GENERAL.—The term "business use percentage" means the percentage of the use of any listed property during any taxable year which is a qualified business use.

(B) QUALIFIED BUSINESS USE.—Except as provided in subparagraph (C), the term "qualified business use" means any use in a trade or business of the taxpayer.

(C) EXCEPTION FOR CERTAIN USE BY 5-PERCENT OWNERS AND RELATED PERSONS.—

(i) IN GENERAL.—The term "qualified business use" shall not include—

(I) leasing property to any 5-percent owner or related person,

(II) use of property provided as compensation for the performance of services by a 5-percent owner or related person, or

(III) use of property provided as compensation for the performance of services by any person not described in subclause (II) unless an amount is included in the gross income of such person with respect to such use, and, where required, there was withholding under chapter 24.

(ii) SPECIAL RULE FOR AIRCRAFT.—Clause (i) shall not apply with respect to any aircraft if at least 25 percent of the total use of the aircraft during the taxable year consists of qualified business use not described in clause (i).

(D) DEFINITIONS.—For purposes of this paragraph—

(i) 5-PERCENT OWNER.—The term "5-percent owner" means any person who is a 5-percent owner with respect to the taxpayer (as defined in section 416(i)(1)(B)(i)).

(ii) RELATED PERSON.—The term "related person" means any person related to the taxpayer (within the meaning of section 267(b)).

(7) AUTOMOBILE PRICE INFLATION ADJUSTMENT.—

(A) IN GENERAL.—In the case of any passenger automobile placed in service after 2018, subsection (a) shall be applied by increasing each dollar amount contained in such subsection by the automobile price inflation adjustment for the calendar year in which such automobile is placed in service. Any increase under the preceding sentence shall be rounded to the nearest multiple of $100 (or if the increase is a multiple of $50, such increase shall be increased to the next higher multiple of $100).

(B) AUTOMOBILE PRICE INFLATION ADJUSTMENT.—For purposes of this paragraph—

(i) IN GENERAL.—The automobile price inflation adjustment for any calendar year is the percentage (if any) by which—

(I) the C-CPI-U automobile component for October of the preceding calendar year, exceeds

(II) the automobile component of the CPI (as defined in section 1(f)(4)) for October of 2017, multiplied by the amount determined under 1(f)(3)(B).

(ii) C-CPI-U AUTOMOBILE COMPONENT.—The term "C-CPI-U automobile component" means the automobile component of the Chained Consumer Price Index for All Urban Consumers (as described in section 1(f)(6)).

(8) UNRECOVERED BASIS.—For purposes of subsection (a)(1), the term "unrecovered basis" means the adjusted basis of the passenger automobile determined after the application of subsection (a) and as if all use during the recovery period were use in a trade or business (including the holding of property for the production of income).

(9) ALL TAXPAYERS HOLDING INTERESTS IN PASSENGER AUTOMOBILE TREATED AS 1 TAXPAYER.—All taxpayers holding interests in any passenger automobile shall be treated as 1 taxpayer for purposes of applying subsection (a) to such automobile, and the limitations of subsection (a) shall be allocated among such taxpayers in proportion to their interests in such automobile.

(10) SPECIAL RULE FOR PROPERTY ACQUIRED IN NONRECOGNITION TRANSACTIONS.—For purposes of subsection (a)(1) any property acquired in a nonrecognition transaction shall be treated as a single property originally placed in service in the taxable year in which it was placed in service after being so acquired.

* * *

[Sec. 280G]

SEC. 280G. GOLDEN PARACHUTE PAYMENTS.

[Sec. 280G(a)]

(a) GENERAL RULE.—No deduction shall be allowed under this chapter for any excess parachute payment.

[Sec. 280G(b)]

(b) EXCESS PARACHUTE PAYMENT.—For purposes of this section—

(1) IN GENERAL.—The term "excess parachute payment" means an amount equal to the excess of any parachute payment over the portion of the base amount allocated to such payment.

(2) PARACHUTE PAYMENT DEFINED.—

(A) IN GENERAL.—The term "parachute payment" means any payment in the nature of compensation to (or for the benefit of) a disqualified individual if—

(i) such payment is contingent on a change—

(I) in the ownership or effective control of the corporation, or

(II) in the ownership of a substantial portion of the assets of the corporation, and

(ii) the aggregate present value of the payments in the nature of compensation to (or for the benefit of) such individual which are contingent on such change equals or exceeds an amount equal to 3 times the base amount.

For purposes of clause (ii), payments not treated as parachute payments under paragraph (4)(A), (5), or (6) shall not be taken into account.

(B) AGREEMENTS.—The term "parachute payment" shall also include any payment in the nature of compensation to (or for the benefit of) a disqualified individual if such payment is made pursuant to an agreement which violates any generally enforced securities laws or regulations. In any proceeding involving the issue of whether any payment made to a disqualified individual is a parachute payment on account of a violation of any generally enforced securities laws or regulations, the burden of proof with respect to establishing the occurrence of a violation of such a law or regulation shall be upon the Secretary.

(C) TREATMENT OF CERTAIN AGREEMENTS ENTERED INTO WITHIN 1 YEAR BEFORE CHANGE OF OWNERSHIP.—For purposes of subparagraph (A)(i), any payment pursuant to—

(i) an agreement entered into within 1 year before the change described in subparagraph (A) (i), or

(ii) an amendment made within such 1-year period of a previous agreement,

shall be presumed to be contingent on such change unless the contrary is established by clear and convincing evidence.

(3) BASE AMOUNT.—

(A) IN GENERAL.—The term "base amount" means the individual's annualized includible compensation for the base period.

(B) ALLOCATION.—The portion of the base amount allocated to any parachute payment shall be an amount which bears the same ratio to the base amount as—

(i) the present value of such payment, bears to

(ii) the aggregate present value of all such payments.

(4) TREATMENT OF AMOUNTS WHICH TAXPAYER ESTABLISHES AS REASONABLE COMPENSATION.—In the case of any payment described in paragraph (2) (A)—

(A) the amount treated as a parachute payment shall not include the portion of such payment which the taxpayer establishes by clear and convincing evidence is reasonable compensation for personal services to be rendered on or after the date of the change described in paragraph (2) (A) (i), and

(B) the amount treated as an excess parachute payment shall be reduced by the portion of such payment which the taxpayer establishes by clear and convincing evidence is reasonable compensation for personal services actually rendered before the date of the change described in paragraph (2) (A) (i).

For purposes of subparagraph (B), reasonable compensation for services actually rendered before the date of the change described in paragraph (2) (A) (i) shall be first offset against the base amount.

(5) EXEMPTION FOR SMALL BUSINESS CORPORATIONS, ETC.—

(A) IN GENERAL.—Notwithstanding paragraph (2), the term "parachute payment" does not include—

(i) any payment to a disqualified individual with respect to a corporation which (immediately before the change described in paragraph (2) (A) (i)) was a small business corporation (as defined in section 1361 (b) but without regard to paragraph (1) (C) thereof), and

(ii) any payment to a disqualified individual with respect to a corporation (other than a corporation described in clause (i)) if—

(I) immediately before the change described in paragraph (2) (A) (i), no stock in such corporation was readily tradeable on an established securities market or otherwise, and

(II) the shareholder approval requirements of subparagraph (B) are met with respect to such payment.

The Secretary may, by regulations, prescribe that the requirements of subclause (I) of clause (ii) are not met where a substantial portion of the assets of any entity consists (directly or indirectly) of stock in such corporation and interests in such other entity are readily tradeable on an established securities market, or otherwise. Stock described in section 1504 (a) (4) shall not be taken into account under clause (ii) (I) if the payment does not adversely affect the shareholder's redemption and liquidation rights.

(B) SHAREHOLDER APPROVAL REQUIREMENTS.—The shareholder approval requirements of this subparagraph are met with respect to any payment if—

(i) such payment was approved by a vote of the persons who owned, immediately before the change described in paragraph (2) (A) (i), more than 75 percent of the voting power of all outstanding stock of the corporation, and

(ii) there was adequate disclosure to shareholders of all material facts concerning all payments which (but for this paragraph) would be parachute payments with respect to a disqualified individual.

The regulations prescribed under subsection (e) shall include regulations providing for the application of this subparagraph in the case of shareholders which are not individuals (including the treatment of nonvoting interests in an entity which is a shareholder) and where an entity holds a de minimis amount of stock in the corporation.

(6) EXEMPTION FOR PAYMENTS UNDER QUALIFIED PLANS.—Notwithstanding paragraph (2), the term "parachute payment" shall not include any payment to or from—

(A) a plan described in section 401(a) which includes a trust exempt from tax under section 501(a),

(B) an annuity plan described in section 403(a),

(C) a simplified employee pension (as defined in section 408(k)), or

(D) a simple retirement account described in section 408(p).

[Sec. 280G(c)]

(c) DISQUALIFIED INDIVIDUALS.—For purposes of this section, the term "disqualified individual" means any individual who is—

(1) an employee, independent contractor, or other person specified in regulations by the Secretary who performs personal services for any corporation, and

(2) is an officer, shareholder, or highly-compensated individual.

For purposes of this section, a personal service corporation (or similar entity) shall be treated as an individual. For purposes of paragraph (2), the term "highly-compensated individual" only includes an individual who is (or would be if the individual were an employee) a member of the group consisting of the highest paid 1 percent of the employees of the corporation or, if less, the highest paid 250 employees of the corporation.

[Sec. 280G(d)]

(d) OTHER DEFINITIONS AND SPECIAL RULES.—For purposes of this section—

(1) ANNUALIZED INCLUDIBLE COMPENSATION FOR BASE PERIOD.—The term "annualized includible compensation for the base period" means the average annual compensation which—

(A) was payable by the corporation with respect to which the change in ownership or control described in paragraph (2)(A) of subsection (b) occurs, and

(B) was includible in the gross income of the disqualified individual for taxable years in the base period.

(2) BASE PERIOD.—The term "base period" means the period consisting of the most recent 5 taxable years ending before the date on which the change in ownership or control described in paragraph (2)(A) of subsection (b) occurs (or such portion of such period during which the disqualified individual performed personal services for the corporation).

(3) PROPERTY TRANSFERS.—Any transfer of property—

(A) shall be treated as a payment, and

(B) shall be taken into account as its fair market value.

(4) PRESENT VALUE.—Present value shall be determined by using a discount rate equal to 120 percent of the applicable Federal rate (determined under section 1274(d)), compounded semiannually.

(5) TREATMENT OF AFFILIATED GROUPS.—Except as otherwise provided in regulations, all members of the same affiliated group (as defined in section 1504, determined without regard to section 1504(b)) shall be treated as 1 corporation for purposes of this section. Any person who is an officer of any member of such group shall be treated as an officer of such 1 corporation.

* * *

PART XI—SPECIAL RULES RELATING TO CORPORATE PREFERENCE ITEMS

[Sec. 291]

SEC. 291. SPECIAL RULES RELATING TO CORPORATE PREFERENCE ITEMS.

[Sec. 291(a)]

(a) REDUCTION IN CERTAIN PREFERENCE ITEMS, ETC.—For purposes of this subtitle, in the case of a corporation—

(1) SECTION 1250 CAPITAL GAIN TREATMENT.—In the case of section 1250 property which is disposed of during the taxable year, 20 percent of the excess (if any) of—

(A) the amount which would be treated as ordinary income if such property was section 1245 property, over

(B) the amount treated as ordinary income under section 1250 (determined without regard to this paragraph),

shall be treated as gain which is ordinary income under section 1250 and shall be recognized notwithstanding any other provision of this title. Under regulations prescribed by the Secretary, the provisions of this paragraph shall not apply to the disposition of any property to the extent section 1250(a) does not apply to such disposition by reason of section 1250(d).

(2) REDUCTION IN PERCENTAGE DEPLETION.—In the case of iron ore and coal (including lignite), the amount allowable as a deduction under section 613 with respect to any property (as defined in section 614) shall be reduced by 20 percent of the amount of the excess (if any) of—

(A) the amount of the deduction allowable under section 613 for the taxable year (determined without regard to this paragraph), over

(B) the adjusted basis of the property at the close of the taxable year (determined without regard to the depletion deduction for the taxable year).

* * *

(4) AMORTIZATION OF POLLUTION CONTROL FACILITIES.—If an election is made under section 169 with respect to any certified pollution control facility, the amortizable basis of such facility for purposes of such section shall be reduced by 20 percent.

[Sec. 291(b)]

(b) SPECIAL RULES FOR TREATMENT OF INTANGIBLE DRILLING COSTS AND MINERAL EXPLORATION AND DEVELOPMENT COSTS.—For purposes of this subtitle, in the case of a corporation—

(1) IN GENERAL.—The amount allowable as a deduction for any taxable year (determined without regard to this section)—

(A) under section 263(c) in the case of an integrated oil company, or

(B) under section 616(a) or 617(a),

shall be reduced by 30 percent.

(2) AMORTIZATION OF AMOUNTS NOT ALLOWABLE AS DEDUCTIONS UNDER PARAGRAPH (1).—The amount not allowable as a deduction under section 263(c), 616(a), or 617(a) (as the case may be) for any taxable year by reason of paragraph (1) shall be allowable as a deduction ratably over the 60-month period beginning with the month in which the costs are paid or incurred.

(3) DISPOSITIONS.—For purposes of section 1254, any deduction under paragraph (2) shall be treated as a deduction allowable under section 263(c), 616(a), or 617(a) (whichever is appropriate).

(4) INTEGRATED OIL COMPANY DEFINED.—For purposes of this subsection, the term "integrated oil company" means, with respect to any taxable year, any producer of crude oil to whom subsection (c) of section 613A does not apply by reason of paragraph (2) or (4) of section 613A(d).

(5) COORDINATION WITH COST DEPLETION.—The portion of the adjusted basis of any property which is attributable to amounts to which paragraph (1) applied shall not be taken into account for purposes of determining depletion under section 611.

[Sec. 291(c)]

(c) SPECIAL RULES RELATING TO POLLUTION CONTROL FACILITIES.—For purposes of this subtitle—

(1) ACCELERATED COST RECOVERY DEDUCTION.—Section 168 shall apply with respect to that portion of the basis of any property not taken into account under section 169 by reason of subsection (a)(4).

(2) 1250 RECAPTURE.—Subsection (a)(1) shall not apply to any section 1250 property which is part of a certified pollution control facility (within the meaning of section 169(d)(1)) with respect to which an election under section 169 was made.

* * *

[Sec. 291(e)]

(e) DEFINITIONS.—For purposes of this section—

* * *

(2) SECTION 1245 AND 1250 PROPERTY.—The terms "section 1245 property" and "section 1250 property" have the meanings given such terms by sections 1245(a)(3) and 1250(c), respectively.

SUBCHAPTER C—CORPORATE DISTRIBUTIONS AND ADJUSTMENTS

PART I—DISTRIBUTIONS BY CORPORATIONS

Subpart A—Effects on Recipients

[Sec. 301]

SEC. 301. DISTRIBUTIONS OF PROPERTY.

[Sec. 301(a)]

(a) IN GENERAL.—Except as otherwise provided in this chapter, a distribution of property (as defined in section 317(a)) made by a corporation to a shareholder with respect to its stock shall be treated in the manner provided in subsection (c).

[Sec. 301(b)]

(b) AMOUNT DISTRIBUTED.—

(1) GENERAL RULE.—For purposes of this section, the amount of any distribution shall be the amount of money received, plus the fair market value of the other property received.

(2) REDUCTION FOR LIABILITIES.—The amount of any distribution determined under paragraph (1) shall be reduced (but not below zero) by—

(A) the amount of any liability of the corporation assumed by the shareholder in connection with the distribution, and

(B) the amount of any liability to which the property received by the shareholder is subject immediately before, and immediately after, the distribution.

(3) DETERMINATION OF FAIR MARKET VALUE.—For purposes of this section, fair market value shall be determined as of the date of the distribution.

[Sec. 301(c)]

(c) AMOUNT TAXABLE.—In the case of a distribution to which subsection (a) applies—

(1) AMOUNT CONSTITUTING DIVIDEND.—That portion of the distribution which is a dividend (as defined in section 316) shall be included in gross income.

(2) AMOUNT APPLIED AGAINST BASIS.—That portion of the distribution which is not a dividend shall be applied against and reduce the adjusted basis of the stock.

(3) AMOUNT IN EXCESS OF BASIS.—

(A) IN GENERAL.—Except as provided in subparagraph (B), that portion of the distribution which is not a dividend, to the extent that it exceeds the adjusted basis of the stock, shall be treated as gain from the sale or exchange of property.

(B) DISTRIBUTIONS OUT OF INCREASE IN VALUE ACCRUED BEFORE MARCH 1, 1913 .—That portion of the distribution which is not a dividend, to the extent that it exceeds the adjusted basis of the stock and to the extent that it is out of increase in value accrued before March 1, 1913, shall be exempt from tax.

[Sec. 301(d)]

(d) BASIS.—The basis of property received in a distribution to which subsection (a) applies shall be the fair market value of such property.

[Sec. 301(e)]

(e) SPECIAL RULE FOR CERTAIN DISTRIBUTIONS RECEIVED BY 20 PERCENT CORPORATE SHAREHOLDER.—

(1) IN GENERAL.—Except to the extent otherwise provided in regulations, solely for purposes of determining the taxable income of any 20 percent corporate shareholder (and its adjusted basis in the stock of the distributing corporation), section 312 shall be applied with respect to the distributing corporation as if it did not contain subsections (k) and (n) thereof.

(2) 20 PERCENT CORPORATE SHAREHOLDER.—For purposes of this subsection, the term "20 percent corporate shareholder" means, with respect to any distribution, any corporation which owns (directly or through the application of section 318)—

(A) stock in the corporation making the distribution possessing at least 20 percent of the total combined voting power of all classes of stock entitled to vote, or

(B) at least 20 percent of the total value of all stock of the distributing corporation (except nonvoting stock which is limited and preferred as to dividends),

but only if, but for this subsection, the distributee corporation would be entitled to a deduction under section 243 or 245 with respect to such distribution.

(3) APPLICATION OF SECTION 312(n)(7) NOT AFFECTED.—The reference in paragraph (1) to subsection (n) of section 312 shall be treated as not including a reference to paragraph (7) of such subsection.

(4) REGULATIONS.—The Secretary shall prescribe such regulations as may be necessary or appropriate to carry out the purposes of this subsection.

[Sec. 301(f)]

(f) SPECIAL RULES.—

(1) For distributions in redemption of stock, see section 302.

(2) For distributions in complete liquidation, see part II (sec. 331 and following).

(3) For distributions in corporate organizations and reorganizations, see part III (sec. 351 and following).

(4) For taxation of dividends received by individuals at capital gain rates, see section 1(h)(11).

[Sec. 302]

SEC. 302. DISTRIBUTIONS IN REDEMPTION OF STOCK.

[Sec. 302(a)]

(a) GENERAL RULE.—If a corporation redeems its stock (within the meaning of section 317 (b)), and if paragraph (1), (2), (3), (4), or (5) of subsection (b) applies, such redemption shall be treated as a distribution in part or full payment in exchange for the stock.

[Sec. 302(b)]

(b) REDEMPTIONS TREATED AS EXCHANGES.—

(1) REDEMPTIONS NOT EQUIVALENT TO DIVIDENDS.—Subsection (a) shall apply if the redemption is not essentially equivalent to a dividend.

(2) SUBSTANTIALLY DISPROPORTIONATE REDEMPTION OF STOCK.—

(A) IN GENERAL.—Subsection (a) shall apply if the distribution is substantially disproportionate with respect to the shareholder.

(B) LIMITATION.—This paragraph shall not apply unless immediately after the redemption the shareholder owns less than 50 percent of the total combined voting power of all classes of stock entitled to vote.

(C) DEFINITIONS.—For purposes of this paragraph, the distribution is substantially disproportionate if—

(i) the ratio which the voting stock of the corporation owned by the shareholder immediately after the redemption bears to all of the voting stock of the corporation at such time,

is less than 80 percent of—

(ii) the ratio which the voting stock of the corporation owned by the shareholder immediately before the redemption bears to all of the voting stock of the corporation at such time.

For purposes of this paragraph, no distribution shall be treated as substantially disproportionate unless the shareholder's ownership of the common stock of the corporation (whether voting or nonvoting) after and before redemption also meets the 80 percent requirement of the preceding sentence. For purposes of the preceding sentence, if there is more than one class of common stock, the determinations shall be made by reference to fair market value.

(D) SERIES OF REDEMPTIONS.—This paragraph shall not apply to any redemption made pursuant to a plan the purpose or effect of which is a series of redemptions resulting in a distribution which (in the aggregate) is not substantially disproportionate with respect to the shareholder.

(3) TERMINATION OF SHAREHOLDER'S INTEREST.—Subsection (a) shall apply if the redemption is in complete redemption of all of the stock of the corporation owned by the shareholder.

(4) REDEMPTION FROM NONCORPORATE SHAREHOLDER IN PARTIAL LIQUIDATION.—Subsection (a) shall apply to a distribution if such distribution is—

(A) in redemption of stock held by a shareholder who is not a corporation, and

(B) in partial liquidation of the distributing corporation.

(5) REDEMPTIONS BY CERTAIN REGULATED INVESTMENT COMPANIES.—Except to the extent provided in regulations prescribed by the Secretary, subsection (a) shall apply to any distribution in redemption of stock of a publicly offered regulated investment company (within the meaning of section 67(c)(2)(B)) if—

(A) such redemption is upon the demand of the stockholder, and

(B) such company issues only stock which is redeemable upon the demand of the stockholder.

(6) APPLICATION OF PARAGRAPHS.—In determining whether a redemption meets the requirements of paragraph (1), the fact that such redemption fails to meet the requirements of paragraph (2), (3), or (4) shall not be taken into account. If a redemption meets the requirements of paragraph (3) and also the requirements of paragraph (1), (2), or (4), then so much of subsection (c)(2) as would (but for this sentence) apply in respect of the acquisition of an interest in the corporation within the 10-year period beginning on the date of the distribution shall not apply.

[Sec. 302(c)]

(c) CONSTRUCTIVE OWNERSHIP OF STOCK.—

(1) IN GENERAL.—Except as provided in paragraph (2) of this subsection, section 318 (a) shall apply in determining the ownership of stock for purposes of this section.

(2) FOR DETERMINING TERMINATION OF INTEREST.—

(A) In the case of a distribution described in subsection (b) (3), section 318 (a) (1) shall not apply if—

(i) immediately after the distribution the distributee has no interest in the corporation (including an interest as officer, director, or employee), other than an interest as a creditor,

(ii) the distributee does not acquire any such interest (other than stock acquired by bequest or inheritance) within 10 years from the date of such distribution, and

(iii) the distributee, at such time and in such manner as the Secretary by regulations prescribes, files an agreement to notify the Secretary of any acquisition described in clause (ii) and to retain such records as may be necessary for the application of this paragraph.

If the distributee acquires such an interest in the corporation (other than by bequest or inheritance) within 10 years from the date of the distribution, then the periods of limitation provided in sections 6501 and 6502 on the making of an assessment and the collection by levy or a proceeding in court shall, with respect to any deficiency (including interest and additions to the tax) resulting from such acquisition, include one year immediately following the date on which the distributee (in accordance with regulations prescribed by the Secretary) notifies the Secretary of such acquisition; and such assessment and collection may be made notwithstanding any provision of law or rule of law which otherwise would prevent such assessment and collection.

(B) Subparagraph (A) of this paragraph shall not apply if—

(i) any portion of the stock redeemed was acquired, directly or indirectly, within the 10-year period ending on the date of the distribution by the distributee from a person the ownership of whose stock would (at the time of distribution) be attributable to the distributee under section 318 (a), or

(ii) any person owns (at the time of the distribution) stock the ownership of which is attributable to the distributee under section 318 (a) and such person acquired any stock in the corporation, directly or indirectly, from the distributee within the 10-year period ending on the date of the distribution, unless such stock so acquired from the distributee is redeemed in the same transaction.

The preceding sentence shall not apply if the acquisition (or, in the case of clause (ii), the disposition) by the distributee did not have as one of its principal purposes the avoidance of Federal income tax.

(C) SPECIAL RULE FOR WAIVERS BY ENTITIES.—

(i) IN GENERAL.—Subparagraph (A) shall not apply to a distribution to any entity unless—

(I) such entity and each related person meet the requirements of clauses (i), (ii), and (iii) of subparagraph (A), and

(II) each related person agrees to be jointly and severally liable for any deficiency (including interest and additions to tax) resulting from an acquisition described in clause (ii) of subparagraph (A).

In any case to which the preceding sentence applies, the second sentence of subparagraph (A) and subparagraph (B)(ii) shall be applied by substituting "distributee or any related person" for "distributee" each place it appears.

(ii) DEFINITIONS.—For purposes of this subparagraph—

(I) the term "entity" means a partnership, estate, trust, or corporation; and

(II) the term "related person" means any person to whom ownership of stock in the corporation is (at the time of the distribution) attributable under section 318(a)(1) if such stock is further attributable to the entity under section 318(a)(3).

[Sec. 302(d)]

(d) REDEMPTIONS TREATED AS DISTRIBUTIONS OF PROPERTY.—Except as otherwise provided in this subchapter, if a corporation redeems its stock (within the meaning of section 317 (b)), and if subsection (a) of this section does not apply, such redemption shall be treated as a distribution of property to which section 301 applies.

[Sec. 302(e)]

(e) PARTIAL LIQUIDATION DEFINED.—

(1) IN GENERAL.—For purposes of subsection (b)(4), a distribution shall be treated as in partial liquidation of a corporation if—

(A) the distribution is not essentially equivalent to a dividend (determined at the corporate level rather than at the shareholder level), and

(B) the distribution is pursuant to a plan and occurs within the taxable year in which the plan is adopted or within the succeeding taxable year.

(2) TERMINATION OF BUSINESS.—The distributions which meet the requirements of paragraph (1)(A) shall include (but shall not be limited to) a distribution which meets the requirements of subparagraphs (A) and (B) of this paragraph:

(A) The distribution is attributable to the distributing corporation's ceasing to conduct, or consists of the assets of, a qualified trade or business.

(B) Immediately after the distribution, the distributing corporation is actively engaged in the conduct of a qualified trade or business.

(3) QUALIFIED TRADE OR BUSINESS.—For purposes of paragraph (2), the term "qualified trade or business" means any trade or business which—

(A) was actively conducted throughout the 5-year period ending on the date of the redemption, and

(B) was not acquired by the corporation within such period in a transaction in which gain or loss was recognized in whole or in part.

(4) REDEMPTION MAY BE PRO RATA.—Whether or not a redemption meets the requirements of subparagraphs (A) and (B) of paragraph (2) shall be determined without regard to whether or not the redemption is pro rata with respect to all of the shareholders of the corporation.

(5) TREATMENT OF CERTAIN PASS-THRU ENTITIES.—For purposes of determining under subsection (b)(4) whether any stock is held by a shareholder who is not a corporation, any stock held by a partnership, estate, or trust shall be treated as if it were actually held proportionately by its partners or beneficiaries.

[Sec. 302(f)]

(f) CROSS REFERENCES.—

For special rules relating to redemption—

(1) Death Taxes.—Of stock to pay death taxes, see section 303.

(2) Section 306 Stock.—Of section 306 stock, see section 306.

(3) Liquidations.—Of stock in complete liquidation, see section 331.

[Sec. 303]

SEC. 303. DISTRIBUTIONS IN REDEMPTION OF STOCK TO PAY DEATH TAXES.

[Sec. 303(a)]

(a) IN GENERAL.—A distribution of property to a shareholder by a corporation in redemption of part or all of the stock of such corporation which (for Federal estate tax purposes) is included in determining the gross estate of a decedent, to the extent that the amount of such distribution does not exceed the sum of—

(1) the estate, inheritance, legacy, and succession taxes (including any interest collected as a part of such taxes) imposed because of such decedent's death, and

(2) the amount of funeral and administration expenses allowable as deductions to the estate under section 2053 (or under section 2106 in the case of the estate of a decedent nonresident, not a citizen of the United States),

shall be treated as a distribution in full payment in exchange for the stock so redeemed.

[Sec. 303(b)]

(b) LIMITATIONS ON APPLICATION OF SUBSECTION (a).—

(1) PERIOD FOR DISTRIBUTION.—Subsection (a) shall apply only to amounts distributed after the death of the decedent and—

(A) within the period of limitations provided in section 6501 (a) for the assessment of the Federal estate tax (determined without the application of any provision other than section 6501 (a)), or within 90 days after the expiration of such period,

(B) if a petition for redetermination of a deficiency in such estate tax has been filed with the Tax Court within the time prescribed in section 6213, at any time before the expiration of 60 days after the decision of the Tax Court becomes final, or

(C) if an election has been made under section 6166 and if the time prescribed by this subparagraph expires at a later date than the time prescribed by subparagraph (B) of this paragraph, within the time determined under section 6166 for the payment of the installments.

(2) RELATIONSHIP OF STOCK TO DECEDENT'S ESTATE.—

(A) IN GENERAL.—Subsection (a) shall apply to a distribution by a corporation only if the value (for Federal estate tax purposes) of all of the stock of such corporation which is included in determining the value of the decedent's gross estate exceeds 35 percent of the excess of—

(i) the value of the gross estate of such decedent, over

(ii) the sum of the amounts allowable as a deduction under section 2053 or 2054.

(B) SPECIAL RULE FOR STOCK IN 2 OR MORE CORPORATIONS.—For purposes of subparagraph (A), stock of 2 or more corporations, with respect to each of which there is included in determining the value of the decedent's gross estate 20 percent or more in value of the outstanding stock, shall be treated as the stock of a single corporation. For purposes of the 20-percent requirement of the preceding sentence, stock which, at the decedent's death, represents the surviving spouse's interest in property held by the decedent and the surviving spouse as community property or as joint tenants, tenants by the entirety, or tenants in common shall be treated as having been included in determining the value of the decedent's gross estate.

(3) RELATIONSHIP OF SHAREHOLDER TO ESTATE TAX.—Subsection (a) shall apply to a distribution by a corporation only to the extent that the interest of the shareholder is reduced directly (or through a binding obligation to contribute) by any payment of an amount described in paragraph (1) or (2) of subsection (a).

(4) ADDITIONAL REQUIREMENTS FOR DISTRIBUTIONS MADE MORE THAN 4 YEARS AFTER DECEDENT'S DEATH.—In the case of amounts distributed more than 4 years after the date of the decedent's death, subsection (a) shall apply to a distribution by a corporation only to the extent of the lesser of—

(A) the aggregate of the amounts referred to in paragraph (1) or (2) of subsection (a) which remained unpaid immediately before the distribution, or

(B) the aggregate of the amounts referred to in paragraph (1) or (2) of subsection (a) which are paid during the 1-year period beginning on the date of such distribution.

[Sec. 303(c)]

(c) STOCK WITH SUBSTITUTED BASIS.—If—

(1) a shareholder owns stock of a corporation (referred to in this subsection as "new stock") the basis of which is determined by reference to the basis of stock of a corporation (referred to in this subsection as "old stock"),

(2) the old stock was included (for Federal estate tax purposes) in determining the gross estate of a decedent, and

(3) subsection (a) would apply to a distribution of property to such shareholder in redemption of the old stock,

then, subject to the limitations specified in subsection (b), subsection (a) shall apply in respect of a distribution in redemption of the new stock.

[Sec. 303(d)]

(d) SPECIAL RULES FOR GENERATION-SKIPPING TRANSFERS.—Where stock in a corporation is the subject of a generation-skipping transfer (within the meaning of section 2611(a)) occurring at the same time as and as a result of the death of an individual—

(1) the stock shall be deemed to be included in the gross estate of such individual;

(2) taxes of the kind referred to in subsection (a)(1) which are imposed because of the generation-skipping transfer shall be treated as imposed because of such individual's death (and for this purpose the tax imposed by section 2601 shall be treated as an estate tax);

(3) the period of distribution shall be measured from the date of the generation-skipping transfer; and

(4) the relationship of stock to the decedent's estate shall be measured with reference solely to the amount of the generation-skipping transfer.

[Sec. 304]

SEC. 304. REDEMPTION THROUGH USE OF RELATED CORPORATIONS.

[Sec. 304(a)]

(a) TREATMENT OF CERTAIN STOCK PURCHASES.—

(1) ACQUISITION BY RELATED CORPORATION (OTHER THAN SUBSIDIARY).—For purposes of sections 302 and 303, if—

(A) one or more persons are in control of each of two corporations, and

(B) in return for property, one of the corporations acquires stock in the other corporation from the person (or persons) so in control,

then (unless paragraph (2) applies) such property shall be treated as a distribution in redemption of the stock of the corporation acquiring such stock. To the extent that such distribution is treated as a distribution to which section 301 applies, the transferor and the acquiring corporation shall be treated in the same manner as if the transferor had transferred the stock so acquired to the acquiring corporation in exchange for stock of the acquiring corporation in a transaction to which section 351(a) applies, and then the acquiring corporation had redeemed the stock it was treated as issuing in such transaction.

(2) ACQUISITION BY SUBSIDIARY.—For purposes of sections 302 and 303, if—

(A) in return for property, one corporation acquires from a shareholder of another corporation stock in such other corporation, and

(B) the issuing corporation controls the acquiring corporation,

then such property shall be treated as a distribution in redemption of the stock of the issuing corporation.

[Sec. 304(b)]

(b) SPECIAL RULES FOR APPLICATION OF SUBSECTION (a).—

(1) RULE FOR DETERMINATIONS UNDER SECTION 302(b).—In the case of any acquisition of stock to which subsection (a) of this section applies, determinations as to whether the acquisition is, by reason of section 302 (b), to be treated as a distribution in part or full payment in exchange for the stock shall be made by reference to the stock of the issuing corporation. In applying section 318(a) (relating to constructive ownership of stock) with respect to section 302(b) for purposes of this paragraph, sections 318(a)(2)(C) and 318(a)(3)(C) shall be applied without regard to the 50 percent limitation contained therein.

(2) AMOUNT CONSTITUTING DIVIDEND.—In the case of any acquisition of stock to which subsection (a) applies, the determination of the amount which is a dividend (and the source thereof) shall be made as if the property were distributed—

(A) by the acquiring corporation to the extent of its earnings and profits, and

(B) then by the issuing corporation to the extent of its earnings and profits.

(3) COORDINATION WITH SECTION 351.—

(A) PROPERTY TREATED AS RECEIVED IN REDEMPTION.—Except as otherwise provided in this paragraph, subsection (a) (and not section 351 and not so much of sections 357 and 358 as relates to section 351) shall apply to any property received in a distribution described in subsection (a).

(B) CERTAIN ASSUMPTIONS OF LIABILITY, ETC.—

(i) IN GENERAL.—In the case of an acquisition described in section 351, subsection (a) shall not apply to any liability—

(I) assumed by the acquiring corporation, or

(II) to which the stock is subject,

if such liability was incurred by the transferor to acquire the stock. For purposes of the preceding sentence, the term "stock" means stock referred to in paragraph (1)(B) or (2)(A) of subsection (a).

(ii) EXTENSION OF OBLIGATIONS, ETC.—For purposes of clause (i), an extension, renewal, or refinancing of a libility which meets the requirements of clause (i) shall be treated as meeting such requirements.

(iii) CLAUSE (i) DOES NOT APPLY TO STOCK ACQUIRED FROM RELATED PERSON EXCEPT WHERE COMPLETE TERMINATION.—Clause (i) shall apply only to stock acquired by the transferor from a person—

(I) none of whose stock is attributable to the transferor under section 318(a) (other than paragraph (4) thereof), or

(II) who satisfies rules similar to the rules of section 302(c)(2) with respect to both the acquiring and the issuing corporations (determined as if such person were a distributee of each such corporation).

* * *

(4) TREATMENT OF CERTAIN INTRAGROUP TRANSACTIONS.—

(A) IN GENERAL.—In the case of any transfer described in subsection (a) of stock from 1 member of an affiliated group to another member of such group, proper adjustments shall be made to—

(i) the adjusted basis of any intragroup stock, and

(ii) the earnings and profits of any member of such group,

to the extent necessary to carry out the purposes of this section.

(B) DEFINITIONS.—For purposes of this paragraph—

(i) AFFILIATED GROUP.—The term "affiliated group" has the meaning given such term by section 1504(a).

(ii) INTRAGROUP STOCK.—The term "intragroup stock" means any stock which—

(I) is in a corporation which is a member of an affiliated group, and

(II) is held by another member of such group.

* * *

(6) AVOIDANCE OF MULTIPLE INCLUSIONS, ETC.—In the case of any acquisition to which subsection (a) applies in which the acquiring corporation or the issuing corporation is a foreign corporation, the Secretary shall prescribe such regulations as are appropriate in order to eliminate a multiple inclusion of any item in income by reason of this subpart and to provide appropriate basis adjustments (including modifications to the application of sections 959 and 961).

[Sec. 304(c)]

(c) CONTROL.—

(1) IN GENERAL.—For purposes of this section, control means the ownership of stock possessing at least 50 percent of the total combined voting power of all classes of stock entitled to vote, or at least 50 percent of the total value of shares of all classes of stock. If a person (or persons) is in control (within the meaning of the preceding sentence) of a corporation which in turn owns at least 50 percent of the total combined voting power of all stock entitled to vote of another corporation, or owns at least 50 percent of the total value of the shares of all classes of stock of another corporation, then such person (or persons) shall be treated as in control of such other corporation.

(2) STOCK ACQUIRED IN THE TRANSACTION.—For purposes of subsection (a) (1)—

(A) GENERAL RULE.—Where 1 or more persons in control of the issuing corporation transfer stock of such corporation in exchange for stock of the acquiring corporation, the stock of the acquiring corporation received shall be taken into account in determining whether such person or persons are in control of the acquiring corporation.

(B) DEFINITION OF CONTROL GROUP.—Where 2 or more persons in control of the issuing corporation transfer stock of such corporation to acquiring corporation and, after the transfer, the transferors are in control of the acquiring corporation, the person or persons in control of each corporation shall include each of the persons who so transfer stock.

(3) CONSTRUCTIVE OWNERSHIP.—

(A) IN GENERAL.—Section 318(a) (relating to constructive ownership of stock) shall apply for purposes of determining control under this section.

(B) MODIFICATION OF 50-PERCENT LIMITATIONS IN SECTION 318.—For purposes of subparagraph (A)—

(i) paragraph (2)(C) of section 318(a) shall be applied by substituting "5 percent" for "50 percent", and

(ii) paragraph (3)(C) of section 318(a) shall be applied—

(I) by substituting "5 percent" for "50 percent", and

(II) in any case where such paragraph would not apply but for subclause (I), by considering a corporation as owning the stock (other than stock in such corporation) owned by or for any shareholder of such corporation in that proportion which the value of the stock which such shareholder owned in such corporation bears to the value of all stock in such corporation.

[Sec. 305]

SEC. 305. DISTRIBUTIONS OF STOCK AND STOCK RIGHTS.

[Sec. 305(a)]

(a) GENERAL RULE.—Except as otherwise provided in this section, gross income does not include the amount of any distribution of the stock of a corporation made by such corporation to its shareholders with respect to its stock.

[Sec. 305(b)]

(b) EXCEPTIONS.—Subsection (a) shall not apply to a distribution by a corporation of its stock, and the distribution shall be treated as a distribution of property to which section 301 applies—

(1) DISTRIBUTIONS IN LIEU OF MONEY.—If the distribution is, at the election of any of the shareholders (whether exercised before or after the declaration thereof), payable either—

(A) in its stock, or

(B) in property.

(2) DISPROPORTIONATE DISTRIBUTIONS.—If the distribution (or a series of distributions of which such distribution is one) has the result of—

(A) the receipt of property by some shareholders, and

(B) an increase in the proportionate interests of other shareholders in the assets or earnings and profits of the corporation.

(3) DISTRIBUTIONS OF COMMON AND PREFERRED STOCK.—If the distribution (or a series of distributions of which such distribution is one) has the result of—

(A) the receipt of preferred stock by some common shareholders, and

(B) the receipt of common stock by other common shareholders.

(4) DISTRIBUTIONS ON PREFERRED STOCK.—If the distribution is with respect to preferred stock, other than an increase in the conversion ratio of convertible preferred stock made solely to take account of a stock dividend or stock split with respect to the stock into which such convertible stock is convertible.

(5) DISTRIBUTIONS OF CONVERTIBLE PREFERRED STOCK.—If the distribution is of convertible preferred stock, unless it is established to the satisfaction of the Secretary that such distribution will not have the result described in paragraph (2).

[Sec. 305(c)]

(c) CERTAIN TRANSACTIONS TREATED AS DISTRIBUTIONS.—For purposes of this section and section 301, the Secretary shall prescribe regulations under which a change in conversion ratio, a change in redemption price, a difference between redemption price and issue price, a redemption which is treated as a distribution to which section 301 applies, or any transaction (including a recapitalization) having a similar effect on the interest of any shareholder shall be treated as a distribution with respect to any shareholder whose proportionate interest in the earnings and profits or assets of the corporation is increased by such change, difference, redemption, or similar transaction. Regulations prescribed under the preceding sentence shall provide that—

(1) where the issuer of stock is required to redeem the stock at a specified time or the holder of stock has the option to require the issuer to redeem the stock, a redemption premium resulting from such requirement or option shall be treated as reasonable only if the amount of such premium does not exceed the amount determined under the principles of section 1273(a)(3),

(2) a redemption of premium shall not fail to be treated as a distribution (or series of distributions) merely because the stock is callable, and

(3) in any case in which a redemption premium is treated as a distribution (or series of distributions), such premium shall be taken into account under principles similar to the principles of section 1272(a).

[Sec. 305(d)]

(d) DEFINITIONS.—

(1) RIGHTS TO ACQUIRE STOCK.—For purposes of this section, the term "stock" includes rights to acquire such stock.

(2) SHAREHOLDERS.—For purposes of subsections (b) and (c), the term "shareholder" includes a holder of rights or of convertible securities.

* * *

[Sec. 305(f)]

(f) CROSS REFERENCES.—

For special rules—

(1) Relating to the receipt of stock rights in corporate organizations and reorganizations, see part III (sec. 351 and following).

(2) In the case of a distribution which results in a gift, see section 2501 and following.

(3) In the case of a distribution which has the effect of the payment of compensation, see section 61 (a)(1).

[Sec. 306]

SEC. 306. DISPOSITIONS OF CERTAIN STOCK.

[Sec. 306(a)]

(a) GENERAL RULE.—If a shareholder sells or otherwise disposes of section 306 stock (as defined in subsection (c))—

(1) DISPOSITIONS OTHER THAN REDEMPTIONS.—If such disposition is not a redemption (within the meaning of section 317 (b))—

(A) The amount realized shall be treated as ordinary income. This subparagraph shall not apply to the extent that—

(i) the amount realized, exceeds

(ii) such stock's ratable share of the amount which would have been a dividend at the time of distribution if (in lieu of section 306 stock) the corporation had distributed money in an amount equal to the fair market value of the stock at the time of distribution.

(B) Any excess of the amount realized over the sum of—

(i) the amount treated under subparagraph (A) as ordinary income, plus

(ii) the adjusted basis of the stock,

shall be treated as gain from the sale of such stock.

(C) No loss shall be recognized.

(D) TREATMENT AS DIVIDEND.—For purposes of section 1(h)(11) and such other provisions as the Secretary may specify, any amount treated as ordinary income under this paragraph shall be treated as a dividend received from the corporation.

(2) REDEMPTION.—If the disposition is a redemption, the amount realized shall be treated as a distribution of property to which section 301 applies.

[Sec. 306(b)]

(b) EXCEPTIONS.—Subsection (a) shall not apply—

(1) TERMINATION OF SHAREHOLDER'S INTEREST, ETC.—

(A) NOT IN REDEMPTION.—If the disposition—

(i) is not a redemption;

(ii) is not, directly or indirectly, to a person the ownership of whose stock would (under section 318 (a)) be attributable to the shareholder; and

(iii) terminates the entire stock interest of the shareholder in the corporation (and for purposes of this clause, section 318 (a) shall apply).

(B) IN REDEMPTION.—If the disposition is a redemption and paragraph (3) or (4) of section 302(b) applies.

(2) LIQUIDATIONS.—If the section 306 stock is redeemed in a distribution in complete liquidation to which part II (sec. 331 and following) applies.

(3) WHERE GAIN OR LOSS IS NOT RECOGNIZED.—To the extent that, under any provision of this subtitle, gain or loss to the shareholder is not recognized with respect to the disposition of the section 306 stock.

(4) TRANSACTIONS NOT IN AVOIDANCE.—If it is established to the satisfaction of the Secretary—

(A) that the distribution, and the disposition or redemption, or

(B) in the case of a prior or simultaneous disposition (or redemption) of the stock with respect to which the section 306 stock disposed of (or redeemed) was issued, that the disposition (or redemption) of the section 306 stock,

was not in pursuance of a plan having as one of its principal purposes the avoidance of Federal income tax.

[Sec. 306(c)]

(c) SECTION 306 [STOCK] DEFINED.—

(1) IN GENERAL.—For purposes of this subchapter, the term "section 306 stock" means stock which meets the requirements of subparagraph (A), (B), or (C) of this paragraph.

(A) DISTRIBUTED TO SELLER.—Stock (other than common stock issued with respect to common stock) which was distributed to the shareholder selling or otherwise disposing of such stock if, by reason of section 305 (a), any part of such distribution was not includible in the gross income of the shareholder.

(B) RECEIVED IN A CORPORATE REORGANIZATION OR SEPARATION.—Stock which is not common stock and—

(i) which was received, by the shareholder selling or otherwise disposing of such stock, in pursuance of a plan of reorganization (within the meaning of section 368 (a)), or in a distribution or exchange to which section 355 (or so much of section 356 as relates to section 355) applied, and

(ii) with respect to the receipt of which gain or loss to the shareholder was to any extent not recognized by reason of part III, but only to the extent that either the effect of the transaction was substantially the same as the receipt of a stock dividend, or the stock was received in exchange for section 306 stock.

For purposes of this section, a receipt of stock to which the foregoing provisions of this subparagraph apply shall be treated as a distribution of stock.

(C) STOCK HAVING TRANSFERRED OR SUBSTITUTED BASIS.—Except as otherwise provided in subparagraph (B), stock the basis of which (in the hands of the shareholder selling or otherwise disposing of such stock) is determined by reference to the basis (in the hands of such shareholder or any other person) of section 306 stock.

(2) EXCEPTION WHERE NO EARNINGS AND PROFITS.—For purposes of this section, the term "section 306 stock" does not include any stock no part of the distribution of which would have been a dividend at the time of the distribution if money had been distributed in lieu of the stock.

(3) CERTAIN STOCK ACQUIRED IN SECTION 351 EXCHANGE.—The term "section 306 stock" also includes any stock which is not common stock acquired in an exchange to which section 351 applied if receipt of money (in lieu of the stock) would have been treated as a dividend to any extent. Rules similar to the rules of section 304(b)(2) shall apply—

(A) for purposes of the preceding sentence, and

(B) for purposes of determining the application of this section to any subsequent disposition of stock which is section 306 stock by reason of an exchange described in the preceding sentence.

(4) APPLICATION OF ATTRIBUTION RULES FOR CERTAIN PURPOSES.—For purposes of paragraphs (1)(B)(ii) and (3), section 318(a) shall apply. For purposes of applying the preceding sentence to paragraph (3), the rules of section 304(c)(3)(B) shall apply.

[Sec. 306(d)]

(d) STOCK RIGHTS.—For purposes of this section—

(1) stock rights shall be treated as stock, and

(2) stock acquired through the exercise of stock rights shall be treated as stock distributed at the time of the distribution of the stock rights, to the extent of the fair market value of such rights at the time of the distribution.

[Sec. 306(e)]

(e) CONVERTIBLE STOCK.—For purposes of subsection (c)—

(1) if section 306 stock was issued with respect to common stock and later such section 306 stock is exchanged for common stock in the same corporation (whether or not such exchange is pursuant to a conversion privilege contained in the section 306 stock), then (except as provided in paragraph (2)) the common stock so received shall not be treated as section 306 stock; and

(2) common stock with respect to which there is a privilege of converting into stock other than common stock (or into property), whether or not the conversion privilege is contained in such stock, shall not be treated as common stock.

* * *

[Sec. 306(g)]

(g) CHANGE IN TERMS AND CONDITIONS OF STOCK.—If a substantial change is made in the terms and conditions of any stock, then, for purposes of this section—

(1) the fair market value of such stock shall be the fair market value at the time of the distribution or at the time of such change, whichever such value is higher;

(2) such stock's ratable share of the amount which would have been a dividend if money had been distributed in lieu of stock shall be determined as of the time of distribution or as of the time of such change, whichever such ratable share is higher; and

(3) subsection (c) (2) shall not apply unless the stock meets the requirements of such subsection both at the time of such distribution and at the time of such change.

[Sec. 307]

SEC. 307. BASIS OF STOCK AND STOCK RIGHTS ACQUIRED IN DISTRIBUTIONS.

[Sec. 307(a)]

(a) GENERAL RULE.—If a shareholder in a corporation receives its stock or rights to acquire its stock (referred to in this subsection as "new stock") in a distribution to which section 305 (a) applies, then the basis of such new stock and of the stock with respect to which it is distributed (referred to in this section as "old stock"), respectively, shall, in the shareholder's hands, be determined by allocating between the old stock and the new stock the adjusted basis of the old stock. Such allocation shall be made under regulations prescribed by the Secretary.

[Sec. 307(b)]

(b) EXCEPTION FOR CERTAIN STOCK RIGHTS.—

(1) IN GENERAL.—If—

(A) a corporation distributes rights to acquire its stock to a shareholder in a distribution to which section 305 (a) applies, and

(B) the fair market value of such rights at the time of the distribution is less than 15 percent of the fair market value of the old stock at such time,

then subsection (a) shall not apply and the basis of such rights shall be zero, unless the taxpayer elects under paragraph (2) of this subsection to determine the basis of the old stock and of the stock rights under the method of allocation provided in subsection (a).

(2) ELECTION.—The election referred to in paragraph (1) shall be made in the return filed within the time prescribed by law (including extensions thereof) for the taxable year in which such rights were received. Such election shall be made in such manner as the Secretary may by regulations prescribe, and shall be irrevocable when made.

* * *

Subpart B—Effects on Corporation

[Sec. 311]

SEC. 311. TAXABILITY OF CORPORATION ON DISTRIBUTION.

[Sec. 311(a)]

(a) GENERAL RULE.—Except as provided in subsection (b), no gain or loss shall be recognized to a corporation on the distribution (not in complete liquidation) with respect to its stock of—

(1) its stock (or rights to acquire its stock), or

(2) property.

[Sec. 311(b)]

(b) DISTRIBUTIONS OF APPRECIATED PROPERTY.—

(1) IN GENERAL.—If—

(A) a corporation distributes property (other than an obligation of such corporation) to a shareholder in a distribution to which subpart A applies, and

(B) the fair market value of such property exceeds its adjusted basis (in the hands of the distributing corporation),

then gain shall be recognized to the distributing corporation as if such property were sold to the distributee at its fair market value.

(2) TREATMENT OF LIABILITIES.—Rules similar to the rules of section 336(b) shall apply for purposes of this subsection.

(3) SPECIAL RULE FOR CERTAIN DISTRIBUTIONS OF PARTNERSHIP OR TRUST INTERESTS.—If the property distributed consists of an interest in a partnership or trust, the Secretary may by regulations provide that the amount of the gain recognized under paragraph (1) shall be computed without regard to any loss attributable to property contributed to the partnership or trust for the principal purpose of recognizing such loss on the distribution.

[Sec. 312]

SEC. 312. EFFECT ON EARNINGS AND PROFITS.

[Sec. 312(a)]

(a) GENERAL RULE.—Except as otherwise provided in this section, on the distribution of property by a corporation with respect to its stock, the earnings and profits of the corporation (to the extent thereof) shall be decreased by the sum of—

(1) the amount of money,

(2) the principal amount of the obligations of such corporation (or, in the case of obligations having original issue discount, the aggregate issue price of such obligations), and

(3) the adjusted basis of the other property,

so distributed.

[Sec. 312(b)]

(b) DISTRIBUTIONS OF APPRECIATED PROPERTY.—On the distribution by a corporation, with respect to its stock, of any property (other than an obligation of such corporation) the fair market value of which exceeds the adjusted basis thereof—

(1) the earnings and profits of the corporation shall be increased by the amount of such excess, and

(2) subsection (a)(3) shall be applied by substituting "fair market value" for "adjusted basis". For purposes of this subsection and subsection (a), the adjusted basis of any property is its adjusted basis as determined for purposes of computing earnings and profits.

[Sec. 312(c)]

(c) ADJUSTMENTS FOR LIABILITIES.—In making the adjustments to the earnings and profits of a corporation under subsection (a) or (b), proper adjustment shall be made for—

(1) the amount of any liability to which the property distributed is subject, and

(2) the amount of any liability of the corporation assumed by a shareholder in connection with the distribution.

[Sec. 312(d)]

(d) CERTAIN DISTRIBUTIONS OF STOCK AND SECURITIES.—

(1) IN GENERAL.—The distribution to a distributee by or on behalf of a corporation of its stock or securities, of stock or securities in another corporation, or of property, in a distribution to which this title applies, shall not be considered a distribution of the earnings and profits of any corporation—

(A) if no gain to such distributee from the receipt of such stock or securities, or property, was recognized under this title, or

(B) if the distribution was not subject to tax in the hands of such distributee by reason of section 305 (a).

(2) STOCK OR SECURITIES.—For purposes of this subsection, the term "stock or securities" includes rights to acquire stock or securities.

[Sec. 312(e)—Repealed]

[Sec. 312(f)]

(f) EFFECT ON EARNINGS AND PROFITS OF GAIN OR LOSS AND OF RECEIPT OF TAX-FREE DISTRIBUTIONS.—

(1) EFFECT ON EARNINGS AND PROFITS OF GAIN OR LOSS.—The gain or loss realized from the sale or other disposition (after February 28, 1913) of property by a corporation—

(A) for the purpose of the computation of the earnings and profits of the corporation, shall (except as provided in subparagraph (B)) be determined by using as the adjusted basis the adjusted basis (under the law applicable to the year in which the sale or other disposition was made) for determining gain, except that no regard shall be had to the value of the property as of March 1, 1913; but

(B) for purposes of the computation of the earnings and profits of the corporation for any period beginning after February 28, 1913, shall be determined by using as the adjusted basis the adjusted basis (under the law applicable to the year in which the sale or other disposition was made) for determining gain.

Gain or loss so realized shall increase or decrease the earnings and profits to, but not beyond, the extent to which such a realized gain or loss was recognized in computing taxable income under the law applicable to the year in which such sale or disposition was made. Where, in determining the adjusted basis used in computing such realized gain or loss, the adjustment to the basis differs from the adjustment proper for the purpose of determining earnings and profits, then the latter adjustment shall be used in determining the increase or decrease above provided. For purposes of this subsection, a loss with respect to which a deduction is disallowed under section 1091 (relating to wash sales of stock or securities), or the corresponding provision of prior law, shall not be deemed to be recognized.

(2) EFFECT ON EARNINGS AND PROFITS OF RECEIPT OF TAX-FREE DISTRIBUTIONS.—Where a corporation receives (after February 28, 1913) a distribution from a second corporation which (under the law applicable to the year in which the distribution was made) was not a taxable dividend to the shareholders of the second corporation, the amount of such distribution shall not increase the earnings and profits of the first corporation in the following cases:

(A) no such increase shall be made in respect of the part of such distribution which (under such law) is directly applied in reduction of the basis of the stock in respect of which the distribution was made; and

(B) no such increase shall be made if (under such law) the distribution causes the basis of the stock in respect of which the distribution was made to be allocated between such stock and the property received (or such basis would, but for section 307 (b), be so allocated).

* * *

[Sec. 312(h)]

(h) ALLOCATION IN CERTAIN CORPORATE SEPARATIONS AND REORGANIZATIONS.—

(1) SECTION 355.—In the case of a distribution or exchange to which section 355 (or so much of section 356 as relates to section 355) applies, proper allocation with respect to the earnings and profits of the distributing corporation and the controlled corporation (or corporations) shall be made under regulations prescribed by the Secretary.

(2) SECTION 368(a)(1)(C) OR (D).—In the case of a reorganization described in subparagraph (C) or (D) of section 368(a)(1), proper allocation with respect to the earnings and profits of the acquired corporation shall, under regulations prescribed by the Secretary, be made between the acquiring corporation and the acquired corporation (or any corporation which had control of the acquired corporation before the reorganization).

* * *

[Sec. 312(k)]

(k) EFFECT OF DEPRECIATION ON EARNINGS AND PROFITS.—

(1) GENERAL RULE.—For purposes of computing the earnings and profits of a corporation for any taxable year beginning after June 30, 1972, the allowance for depreciation (and amortization, if any) shall be deemed to be the amount which would be allowable for such year if the straight line method of depreciation had been used for each taxable year beginning after June 30, 1972.

(2) EXCEPTION.—If for any taxable year a method of depreciation was used by the taxpayer which the Secretary has determined results in a reasonable allowance under section 167(a) and which is the unit-of-production method or other method not expressed in a term of years, then the adjustment to earnings and profits for depreciation for such year shall be determined under the method so used (in lieu of the straight line method).

(3) EXCEPTION FOR TANGIBLE PROPERTY.—

(A) IN GENERAL.—Except as provided in subparagraph (B), in the case of tangible property to which section 168 applies, the adjustment to earnings and profits for depreciation for any taxable year shall be determined under the alternative depreciation system (within the meaning of section 168(g)(2)).

(B) TREATMENT OF AMOUNTS DEDUCTIBLE UNDER SECTION 179, 179B, 179C, 179D, or 179E.—For purposes of computing the earnings and profits of a corporation, any amount deductible under section 179, 179B, 179C, 179D, or 179E shall be allowed as a deduction ratably over the period of 5 taxable years (beginning with the taxable year for which such amount is deductible under section 179, 179B, 179C, 179D, or 179E, as the case may be).

* * *

[Sec. 312(l)]

(l) DISCHARGE OF INDEBTEDNESS INCOME.—

(1) DOES NOT INCREASE EARNINGS AND PROFITS IF APPLIED TO REDUCE BASIS.—The earnings and profits of a corporation shall not include income from the discharge of indebtedness to the extent of the amount applied to reduce basis under section 1017.

(2) REDUCTION OF DEFICIT IN EARNINGS AND PROFITS IN CERTAIN CASES.—If—

(A) the interest of any shareholder of a corporation is terminated or extinguished in a title 11 or similar case (within the meaning of section 368(a)(3)(A)), and

(B) there is a deficit in the earnings and profits of the corporation,

then such deficit shall be reduced by an amount equal to the paid-in capital which is allocable to the interest of the shareholder which is so terminated or extinguished.

* * *

[Sec. 312(n)]

(n) ADJUSTMENTS TO EARNINGS AND PROFITS TO MORE ACCURATELY REFLECT ECONOMIC GAIN AND LOSS.—For purposes of computing the earnings and profits of a corporation, the following adjustments shall be made:

(1) CONSTRUCTION PERIOD CARRYING CHARGES.—

(A) IN GENERAL.—In the case of any amount paid or incurred for construction period carrying charges—

(i) no deduction shall be allowed with respect to such amount, and

(ii) the basis of the property with respect to which such charges are allocable shall be increased by such amount.

(B) CONSTRUCTION PERIOD CARRYING CHARGES DEFINED.—For purposes of this paragraph, the term "construction period carrying charges" means all—

(i) interest paid or accrued on indebtedness incurred or continued to acquire, construct, or carry property,

(ii) property taxes, and

(iii) similar carrying charges,

to the extent such interest, taxes, or charges are attributable to the construction period for such property and would be allowable as a deduction in determining taxable income under this chapter for the taxable year in which paid or incurred.

(C) CONSTRUCTION PERIOD.—The term "construction period" has the meaning given the term production period under section 263A(f)(4)(B).

(2) INTANGIBLE DRILLING COSTS AND MINERAL EXPLORATION AND DEVELOPMENT COSTS.—

(A) INTANGIBLE DRILLING COSTS.—Any amount allowable as a deduction under section 263(c) in determining taxable income (other than costs incurred in connection with a nonproductive well)—

(i) shall be capitalized, and

(ii) shall be allowed as a deduction ratably over the 60-month period beginning with the month in which such amount was paid or incurred.

(B) MINERAL EXPLORATION AND DEVELOPMENT COSTS.—Any amount allowable as a deduction under section 616(a) or 617 in determining taxable income—

(i) shall be capitalized, and

(ii) shall be allowed as a deduction ratably over the 120-month period beginning with the later of—

(I) the month in which production from the deposit begins, or

(II) the month in which such amount was paid or incurred.

(3) CERTAIN AMORTIZATION PROVISIONS NOT TO APPLY.—Sections 173 and 248 shall not apply.

(4) LIFO INVENTORY ADJUSTMENTS.—

(A) IN GENERAL.—Earnings and profits shall be increased or decreased by the amount of any increase or decrease in the LIFO recapture amount as of the close of each taxable year; except that any decrease below the LIFO recapture amount as of the close of the taxable year preceding the 1st taxable year to which this paragraph applies to the taxpayer shall be taken into account only to the extent provided in regulations prescribed by the Secretary.

(B) LIFO RECAPTURE AMOUNT.—For purposes of this paragraph, the term "LIFO recapture amount" means the amount (if any) by which—

(i) the inventory amount of the inventory assets under the first-in, first-out method authorized by section 471, exceeds

(ii) the inventory amount of such assets under the LIFO method.

(C) DEFINITIONS.—For purposes of this paragraph—

(i) LIFO METHOD.—The term "LIFO method" means the method authorized by section 472 (relating to last-in, first-out inventories).

(ii) INVENTORY ASSETS.—The term "inventory assets" means stock in trade of the corporation, or other property of a kind which would properly be included in the inventory of the corporation if on hand at the close of the taxable year.

(iii) INVENTORY AMOUNT.—The inventory amount of assets under the first-in, first-out method authorized by section 471 shall be determined—

(I) if the corporation uses the retail method of valuing inventories under section 472, by using such method, or

(II) if subclause (I) does not apply, by using cost or market, whichever is lower.

(5) INSTALLMENT SALES.—In the case of any installment sale, earnings and profits shall be computed as if the corporation did not use the installment method.

(6) COMPLETED CONTRACT METHOD OF ACCOUNTING.—In the case of a taxpayer who uses the completed contract method of accounting, earnings and profits shall be computed as if such taxpayer used the percentage of completion method of accounting.

(7) REDEMPTIONS.—If a corporation distributes amounts in a redemption to which section 302(a) or 303 applies, the part of such distribution which is properly chargeable to earnings and profits shall be an amount which is not in excess of the ratable share of the earnings and profits of such corporation accumulated after February 28, 1913, attributable to the stock so redeemed.

* * *

Subpart C—Definitions; Constructive Ownership of Stock

[Sec. 316]

SEC. 316. DIVIDEND DEFINED.

[Sec. 316(a)]

(a) GENERAL RULE.—For purposes of this subtitle, the term "dividend" means any distribution of property made by a corporation to its shareholders—

(1) out of its earnings and profits accumulated after February 28, 1913, or

(2) out of its earnings and profits of the taxable year (computed as of the close of the taxable year without diminution by reason of any distributions made during the taxable year), without regard to the amount of the earnings and profits at the time the distribution was made.

Except as otherwise provided in this subtitle, every distribution is made out of earnings and profits to the extent thereof, and from the most recently accumulated earnings and profits. To the extent that any distribution is, under any provision of this subchapter, treated as a distribution of property to which section 301 applies, such distribution shall be treated as a distribution of property for purposes of this subsection.

* * *

[Sec. 317]

SEC. 317. OTHER DEFINITIONS.

[Sec. 317(a)]

(a) PROPERTY.—For purposes of this part, the term "property" means money, securities, and any other property; except that such term does not include stock in the corporation making the distribution (or rights to acquire such stock).

[Sec. 317(b)]

(b) REDEMPTION OF STOCK.—For purposes of this part, stock shall be treated as redeemed by a corporation if the corporation acquires its stock from a shareholder in exchange for property, whether or not the stock so acquired is cancelled, retired, or held as treasury stock.

[Sec. 318]

SEC. 318. CONSTRUCTIVE OWNERSHIP OF STOCK.

[Sec. 318(a)]

(a) GENERAL RULE.—For purposes of those provisions of this subchapter to which the rules contained in this section are expressly made applicable—

(1) MEMBERS OF FAMILY.—

(A) IN GENERAL.—An individual shall be considered as owning the stock owned, directly or indirectly, by or for—

(i) his spouse (other than a spouse who is legally separated from the individual under a decree of divorce or separate maintenance), and

(ii) his children, grandchildren, and parents.

(B) Effect of adoption.—For purposes of subparagraph (A) (ii), a legally adopted child of an individual shall be treated as a child of such individual by blood.

(2) Attribution from partnerships, estates, trusts, and corporations.—

(A) From partnerships and estates.—Stock owned, directly or indirectly, by or for a partnership or estate shall be considered as owned proportionately by its partners or beneficiaries.

(B) From trusts.—

(i) Stock owned, directly or indirectly, by or for a trust (other than an employees' trust described in section 401(a) which is exempt from tax under section 501(a)) shall be considered as owned by its beneficiaries in proportion to the actuarial interest of such beneficiaries in such trust.

(ii) Stock owned, directly or indirectly, by or for any portion of a trust of which a person is considered the owner under subpart E of part I of subchapter J (relating to grantors and others treated as substantial owners) shall be considered as owned by such person.

(C) From corporations.—If 50 percent or more in value of the stock in a corporation is owned, directly or indirectly, by or for any person, such person shall be considered as owning the stock owned, directly or indirectly, by or for such corporation, in that proportion which the value of the stock which such person so owns bears to the value of all the stock in such corporation.

(3) Attribution to partnerships, estates, trusts, and corporations.—

(A) To partnerships and estates.—Stock owned, directly or indirectly, by or for a partner or a beneficiary of an estate shall be considered as owned by the partnership or estate.

(B) To trusts.—

(i) Stock owned, directly or indirectly, by or for a beneficiary of a trust (other than an employees' trust described in section 401(a) which is exempt from tax under section 501 (a)) shall be considered as owned by the trust, unless such beneficiary's interest in the trust is a remote contingent interest. For purposes of this clause, a contingent interest of a beneficiary in a trust shall be considered remote if, under the maximum exercise of discretion by the trustee in favor of such beneficiary, the value of such interest, computed actuarially, is 5 percent or less of the value of the trust property.

(ii) Stock owned, directly or indirectly, by or for a person who is considered the owner of any portion of a trust under subpart E of part I of subchapter J (relating to grantors and others treated as substantial owners) shall be considered as owned by the trust.

(C) To corporations.—If 50 percent or more in value of the stock in a corporation is owned, directly or indirectly, by or for any person, such corporation shall be considered as owning the stock owned, directly or indirectly, by or for such person.

(4) Options.—If any person has an option to acquire stock, such stock shall be considered as owned by such person. For purposes of this paragraph, an option to acquire such an option, and each one of a series of such options, shall be considered as an option to acquire such stock.

(5) Operating rules.—

(A) In general.—Except as provided in subparagraphs (B) and (C), stock constructively owned by a person by reason of the application of paragraph (1), (2), (3), or (4), shall, for purposes of applying paragraphs (1), (2), (3), and (4), be considered as actually owned by such person.

(B) Members of family.—Stock constructively owned by an individual by reason of the application of paragraph (1) shall not be considered as owned by him for purposes of again applying paragraph (1) in order to make another the constructive owner of such stock.

(C) PARTNERSHIPS, ESTATES, TRUSTS, AND CORPORATIONS.—Stock constructively owned by a partnership, estate, trust, or corporation by reason of the application of paragraph (3) shall not be considered as owned by it for purposes of applying paragraph (2) in order to make another the constructive owner of such stock.

(D) OPTION RULE IN LIEU OF FAMILY RULE.—For purposes of this paragraph, if stock may be considered as owned by an individual under paragraph (1) or (4), it shall be considered as owned by him under paragraph (4).

(E) S CORPORATION TREATED AS PARTNERSHIP.—For purposes of this subsection—

(i) an S corporation shall be treated as a partnership, and

(ii) any shareholder of the S corporation shall be treated as a partner of such partnership.

The preceding sentence shall not apply for purposes of determining whether stock in the S corporation is constructively owned by any person.

[Sec. 318(b)]

(b) CROSS REFERENCES.—

For provisions to which the rules contained in subsection (a) apply, see—

(1) section 302 (relating to redemption of stock);

(2) section 304 (relating to redemption by related corporations);

(3) section 306 (b) (1) (A) (relating to disposition of section 306 stock);

(4) section 338(h) (3) (defining purchase);

(5) section 382(l) (3) (relating to special limitations on net operating loss carryovers);

* * *

PART II—CORPORATE LIQUIDATIONS

Subpart A—Effects on Recipients

[Sec. 331]

SEC. 331. GAIN OR LOSS TO SHAREHOLDER IN CORPORATE LIQUIDATIONS.

[Sec. 331(a)]

(a) DISTRIBUTIONS IN COMPLETE LIQUIDATION TREATED AS EXCHANGES.—Amounts received by a shareholder in a distribution in complete liquidation of a corporation shall be treated as in full payment in exchange for the stock.

[Sec. 331(b)]

(b) NONAPPLICATION OF SECTION 301.—Section 301 (relating to effects on shareholder of distributions of property) shall not apply to any distribution of property (other than a distribution referred to in paragraph (2) (B) of section 316(b)), in complete liquidation.

* * *

[Sec. 332]

SEC. 332. COMPLETE LIQUIDATIONS OF SUBSIDIARIES.

[Sec. 332(a)]

(a) GENERAL RULE.—No gain or loss shall be recognized on the receipt by a corporation of property distributed in complete liquidation of another corporation.

[Sec. 332(b)]

(b) LIQUIDATIONS TO WHICH SECTION APPLIES.—For purposes of this section, a distribution shall be considered to be in complete liquidation only if—

(1) the corporation receiving such property was, on the date of the adoption of the plan of liquidation, and has continued to be at all times until the receipt of the property, the owner of stock (in such other corporation) meeting the requirements of section 1504(a) (2); and either

(2) the distribution is by such other corporation in complete cancellation or redemption of all its stock, and the transfer of all the property occurs within the taxable year; in such case the adoption by the shareholders of the resolution under which is authorized the distribution of all the assets of such corporation in complete cancellation or redemption of all its stock shall be considered an adoption of a plan of liquidation, even though no time for the completion of the transfer of the property is specified in such resolution; or

(3) such distribution is one of a series of distributions by such other corporation in complete cancellation or redemption of all its stock in accordance with a plan of liquidation under which the transfer of all the property under the liquidation is to be completed within 3 years from the close of the taxable year during which is made the first of the series of distributions under the plan, except that if such transfer is not completed within such period, or if the taxpayer does not continue qualified under paragraph (1) until the completion of such transfer, no distribution under the plan shall be considered a distribution in complete liquidation.

If such transfer of all the property does not occur within the taxable year, the Secretary may require of the taxpayer such bond, or waiver of the statute of limitations on assessment and collection, or both, as he may deem necessary to insure, if the transfer of the property is not completed within such 3-year period, or if the taxpayer does not continue qualified under paragraph (1) until the completion of such transfer, the assessment and collection of all income taxes then imposed by law for such taxable year or subsequent taxable years, to the extent attributable to property so received. A distribution otherwise constituting a distribution in complete liquidation within the meaning of this subsection shall not be considered as not constituting such a distribution merely because it does not constitute a distribution or liquidation within the meaning of the corporate law under which the distribution is made; and for purposes of this subsection a transfer of property of such other corporation to the taxpayer shall not be considered as not constituting a distribution (or one of a series of distributions) in complete cancellation or redemption of all the stock of such other corporation, merely because the carrying out of the plan involves (A) the transfer under the plan to the taxpayer by such other corporation of property, not attributable to shares owned by the taxpayer, on an exchange described in section 361, and (B) the complete cancellation or redemption under the plan, as a result of exchanges described in section 354, of the shares not owned by the taxpayer.

* * *

[Sec. 334]

SEC. 334. BASIS OF PROPERTY RECEIVED IN LIQUIDATIONS.

[Sec. 334(a)]

(a) GENERAL RULE.—If property is received in a distribution in complete liquidation, and if gain or loss is recognized on receipt of such property, then the basis of the property in the hands of the distributee shall be the fair market value of such property at the time of the distribution.

[Sec. 334(b)]

(b) LIQUIDATION OF SUBSIDIARY.—

(1) IN GENERAL.—If property is received by a corporate distributee in a distribution in a complete liquidation to which section 332 applies (or in a transfer described in section 337(b)(1)), the basis of such property in the hands of such distributee shall be the same as it would be in the hands of the transferor; except that, in the hands of such distributee—

(A) the basis of such property shall be the fair market value of the property at the time of the distribution in any case in which gain or loss is recognized by the liquidating corporation with respect to such property, and

(B) the basis of any property described in section 362(e)(1)(B) shall be the fair market value of the property at the time of the distribution in any case in which such distributee's aggregate adjusted basis of such property would (but for this subparagraph) exceed the fair market value of such property immediately after such liquidation.

(2) CORPORATE DISTRIBUTEE.—For purposes of this subsection, the term "corporate distributee" means only the corporation which meets the stock ownership requirements specified in section 332(b).

Subpart B—Effects on Corporation

[Sec. 336]

SEC. 336. GAIN OR LOSS RECOGNIZED ON PROPERTY DISTRIBUTED IN COMPLETE LIQUIDATION.

[Sec. 336(a)]

(a) GENERAL RULE.—Except as otherwise provided in this section or section 337, gain or loss shall be recognized to a liquidating corporation on the distribution of property in complete liquidation as if such property were sold to the distributee at its fair market value.

[Sec. 336(b)]

(b) TREATMENT OF LIABILITIES.—If any property distributed in the liquidation is subject to a liability or the shareholder assumes a liability of the liquidating corporation in connection with the distribution, for purposes of subsection (a) and section 337, the fair market value of such property shall be treated as not less than the amount of such liability.

[Sec. 336(c)]

(c) EXCEPTION FOR LIQUIDATIONS WHICH ARE PART OF A REORGANIZATION.—For provision providing that this subpart does not apply to distributions in pursuance of a plan of reorganization, see section 361(c)(4).

[Sec. 336(d)]

(d) LIMITATIONS ON RECOGNITION OF LOSS.—

(1) NO LOSS RECOGNIZED IN CERTAIN DISTRIBUTIONS TO RELATED PERSONS.—

(A) IN GENERAL.—No loss shall be recognized to a liquidating corporation on the distribution of any property to a related person (within the meaning of section 267) if—

(i) such distribution is not pro rata, or

(ii) such property is disqualified property.

(B) DISQUALIFIED PROPERTY.—For purposes of subparagraph (A), the term "disqualified property" means any property which is acquired by the liquidating corporation in a transaction to which section 351 applied, or as a contribution to capital, during the 5-year period ending on the date of the distribution. Such term includes any property if the adjusted basis of such property is determined (in whole or in part) by reference to the adjusted basis of property described in the preceding sentence.

(2) SPECIAL RULE FOR CERTAIN PROPERTY ACQUIRED IN CERTAIN CARRYOVER BASIS TRANSACTIONS.—

(A) IN GENERAL.—For purposes of determining the amount of loss recognized by any liquidating corporation on any sale, exchange, or distribution of property described in subparagraph (B), the adjusted basis of such property shall be reduced (but not below zero) by the excess (if any) of—

(i) the adjusted basis of such property immediately after its acquisition by such corporation, over

(ii) the fair market value of such property as of such time.

(B) DESCRIPTION OF PROPERTY.—

(i) IN GENERAL.—For purposes of subparagraph (A), property is described in this subparagraph if—

(I) such property is acquired by the liquidating corporation in a transaction to which section 351 applied or as a contribution to capital, and

(II) the acquisition of such property by the liquidating corporation was part of a plan a principal purpose of which was to recognize loss by the liquidating corporation with respect to such property in connection with the liquidation.

Other property shall be treated as so described if the adjusted basis of such other property is determined (in whole or in part) by reference to the adjusted basis of property described in the preceding sentence.

(ii) CERTAIN ACQUISITIONS TREATED AS PART OF PLAN.—For purposes of clause (i), any property described in clause (i)(I) acquired by the liquidated corporation after the date 2 years before the date of the adoption of the plan of complete liquidation shall, except as provided in regulations, be treated as acquired as part of a plan described in clause (i)(II).

(C) RECAPTURE IN LIEU OF DISALLOWANCE.—The Secretary may prescribe regulations under which, in lieu of disallowing a loss under subparagraph (A) for a prior taxable year, the gross income of the liquidating corporation for the taxable year in which the plan of complete liquidation is adopted shall be increased by the amount of the disallowed loss.

(3) SPECIAL RULE IN CASE OF LIQUIDATION TO WHICH SECTION 332 APPLIES.—In the case of any liquidation to which section 332 applies, no loss shall be recognized to the liquidating corporation on any distribution in such liquidation. The preceding sentence shall apply to any distribution to the 80-percent distributee only if subsection (a) or (b)(1) of section 337 applies to such distribution.

[Sec. 336(e)]

(e) CERTAIN STOCK SALES AND DISTRIBUTIONS MAY BE TREATED AS ASSET TRANSFERS.—Under regulations prescribed by the Secretary, if—

(1) a corporation owns stock in another corporation meeting the requirements of section 1504(a)(2), and

(2) such corporation sells, exchanges, or distributes all of such stock,

an election may be made to treat such sale, exchange, or distribution as a disposition of all of the assets of such other corporation, and no gain or loss shall be recognized on the sale, exchange, or distribution of such stock.

[Sec. 337]

SEC. 337. NONRECOGNITION FOR PROPERTY DISTRIBUTED TO PARENT IN COMPLETE LIQUIDATION OF SUBSIDIARY.

[Sec. 337(a)]

(a) IN GENERAL.—No gain or loss shall be recognized to the liquidating corporation on the distribution to the 80-percent distributee of any property in a complete liquidation to which section 332 applies.

[Sec. 337(b)]

(b) TREATMENT OF INDEBTEDNESS OF SUBSIDIARY, ETC.—

(1) INDEBTEDNESS OF SUBSIDIARY TO PARENT.—If—

(A) a corporation is liquidated in a liquidation to which section 332 applies, and

(B) on the date of the adoption of the plan of liquidation, such corporation was indebted to the 80-percent distributee.

for purposes of this section and section 336, any transfer of property to the 80-percent distributee in satisfaction of such indebtedness shall be treated as a distribution to such distributee in such liquidation.

* * *

[Sec. 337(c)]

(c) 80-PERCENT DISTRIBUTEE.—For purposes of this section, the term "80-percent distributee" means only the corporation which meets the 80-percent stock ownership requirements specified in section 332(b). For purposes of this section, the determination of whether any corporation is an 80-percent distributee shall be made without regard to any consolidated return regulation.

* * *

[Sec. 338]

SEC. 338. CERTAIN STOCK PURCHASES TREATED AS ASSET ACQUISITIONS.

[Sec. 338(a)]

(a) GENERAL RULE.—For purposes of this subtitle, if a purchasing corporation makes an election under this section (or is treated under subsection (e) as having made such an election), then, in the case of any qualified stock purchase, the target corporation—

(1) shall be treated as having sold all of its assets at the close of the acquisition date at fair market value in a single transaction, and

(2) shall be treated as a new corporation which purchased all of the assets referred to in paragraph (1) as of the beginning of the day after the acquisition date.

[Sec. 338(b)]

(b) BASIS OF ASSETS AFTER DEEMED PURCHASE.—

(1) IN GENERAL.—For purposes of subsection (a), the assets of the target corporation shall be treated as purchased for an amount equal to the sum of—

(A) the grossed-up basis of the purchasing corporation's recently purchased stock, and

(B) the basis of the purchasing corporation's nonrecently purchased stock.

(2) ADJUSTMENT FOR LIABILITIES AND OTHER RELEVANT ITEMS.—The amount described in paragraph (1) shall be adjusted under regulations prescribed by the Secretary for liabilities of the target corporation and other relevant items.

(3) ELECTION TO STEP-UP THE BASIS OF CERTAIN TARGET STOCK.—

(A) IN GENERAL.—Under regulations prescribed by the Secretary, the basis of the purchasing corporation's nonrecently purchased stock shall be the basis amount determined under subparagraph (B) of this paragraph if the purchasing corporation makes an election to recognize gain as if such stock were sold on the acquisition date for an amount equal to the basis amount determined under subparagraph (B).

(B) DETERMINATION OF BASIS AMOUNT.—For purposes of subparagraph (A), the basis amount determined under this subparagraph shall be an amount equal to the grossed-up basis determined under subparagraph (A) of paragraph (1) multiplied by a fraction—

(i) the numerator of which is the percentage of stock (by value) in the target corporation attributable to the purchasing corporation's nonrecently purchased stock, and

(ii) the denominator of which is 100 percent minus the percentage referred to in clause (i).

(4) GROSSED-UP BASIS.—For purposes of paragraph (1), the grossed-up basis shall be an amount equal to the basis of the corporation's recently purchased stock, multiplied by a fraction—

(A) the numerator of which is 100 percent, minus the percentage of stock (by value) in the target corporation attributable to the purchasing corporation's nonrecently purchased stock, and

(B) the denominator of which is the percentage of stock (by value) in the target corporation attributable to the purchasing corporation's recently purchased stock.

(5) ALLOCATION AMONG ASSETS.—The amount determined under paragraphs (1) and (2) shall be allocated among the assets of the target corporation under regulations prescribed by the Secretary.

(6) DEFINITIONS OF RECENTLY PURCHASED STOCK AND NONRECENTLY PURCHASED STOCK.—For purposes of this subsection—

(A) RECENTLY PURCHASED STOCK.—The term "recently purchased stock" means any stock in the target corporation which is held by the purchasing corporation on the acquisition date and which was purchased by such corporation during the 12-month acquisition period.

(B) NONRECENTLY PURCHASED STOCK.—The term "nonrecently purchased stock" means any stock in the target corporation which is held by the purchasing corporation on the acquisition date and which is not recently purchased stock.

[Sec. 338(d)]

(d) PURCHASING CORPORATION; TARGET CORPORATION; QUALIFIED STOCK PURCHASE.—For purposes of this section—

(1) PURCHASING CORPORATION.—The term "purchasing corporation" means any corporation which makes a qualified stock purchase of stock of another corporation.

(2) TARGET CORPORATION.—The term "target corporation" means any corporation the stock of which is acquired by another corporation in a qualified stock purchase.

(3) QUALIFIED STOCK PURCHASE.—The term "qualified stock purchase" means any transaction or series of transactions in which stock (meeting the requirements of section 1504(a)(2)) of 1 corporation is acquired by another corporation by purchase during the 12-month acquisition period.

[Sec. 338(e)]

(e) DEEMED ELECTION WHERE PURCHASING CORPORATION ACQUIRES ASSET OF TARGET CORPORATION.—

(1) IN GENERAL.—A purchasing corporation shall be treated as having made an election under this section with respect to any target corporation if, at any time during the consistency period, it acquires any asset of the target corporation (or a target affiliate).

(2) EXCEPTIONS.—Paragraph (1) shall not apply with respect to any acquisition by the purchasing corporation if—

(A) such acquisition is pursuant to a sale by the target corporation (or the target affiliate) in the ordinary course of its trade or business,

(B) the basis of the property acquired is determined (wholly) by reference to the adjusted basis of such property in the hands of the person from whom acquired,

(C) such acquisition was before September 1, 1982, or

(D) such acquisition is described in regulations prescribed by the Secretary and meets such conditions as such regulations may provide.

(3) ANTI-AVOIDANCE RULE.—Whenever necessary to carry out the purpose of this subsection and subsection (f), the Secretary may treat stock acquisitions which are pursuant to a plan and which meet the requirements of section 1504(a)(2) as qualified stock purchases.

[Sec. 338(f)]

(f) CONSISTENCY REQUIRED FOR ALL STOCK ACQUISITIONS FROM SAME AFFILIATED GROUP.—If a purchasing corporation makes qualified stock purchases with respect to the target corporation and 1 or more target affiliates during any consistency period, then (except as otherwise provided in subsection (e))—

(1) any election under this section with respect to the first such purchase shall apply to each other such purchase, and

(2) no election may be made under this section with respect to the second or subsequent such purchase if such an election was not made with respect to the first such purchase.

[Sec. 338(g)]

(g) ELECTION.—

(1) WHEN MADE.—Except as otherwise provided in regulations, an election under this section shall be made not later than the 15th day of the 9th month, beginning after the month in which the acquisition date occurs.

(2) MANNER.—An election by the purchasing corporation under this section shall be made in such manner as the Secretary shall by regulations prescribe.

(3) ELECTION IRREVOCABLE.—An election by a purchasing corporation under this section, once made, shall be irrevocable.

[Sec. 338(h)]

(h) DEFINITIONS AND SPECIAL RULES.—For purposes of this section—

(1) 12-MONTH ACQUISITION PERIOD.—The term "12-month acquisition period" means the 12-month period beginning with the date of the first acquisition by purchase of stock included in a qualified stock purchase (or, if any of such stock was acquired in an acquisition which is a purchase by reason of subparagraph (C) of paragraph (3), the date on which the acquiring corporation is first considered under section 318(a) (other than paragraph (4) thereof) as owning stock owned by the corporation from which such acquisition was made).

(2) ACQUISITION DATE.—The term "acquisition date" means, with respect to any corporation, the first day on which there is a qualified stock purchase with respect to the stock of such corporation.

(3) PURCHASE.—

(A) IN GENERAL.—The term "purchase" means any acquisition of stock, but only if—

(i) the basis of the stock in the hands of the purchasing corporation is not determined (I) in whole or in part by reference to the adjusted basis of such stock in the hands of the person from whom acquired, or (II) under section 1014(a) (relating to property acquired from a decedent),

(ii) the stock is not acquired in an exchange to which section 351, 354, 355, or 356 applies and is not acquired in any other transaction described in regulations in which the transferor does not recognize the entire amount of the gain or loss realized on the transaction, and

(iii) the stock is not acquired from a person the ownership of whose stock would, under section 318(a) (other than paragraph (4) thereof), be attributed to the person acquiring such stock.

(B) DEEMED PURCHASE UNDER SUBSECTION (a).—The term "purchase" includes any deemed purchase under subsection (a)(2). The acquisition date for a corporation which is deemed purchased under subsection (a)(2) shall be determined under regulations prescribed by the Secretary.

(C) CERTAIN STOCK ACQUISITIONS FROM RELATED CORPORATIONS.—

(i) IN GENERAL.—Clause (iii) of subparagraph (A) shall not apply to an acquisition of stock from a related corporation if at least 50 percent in value of the stock of such related corporation was acquired by purchase (within the meaning of subparagraphs (A) and (B)).

(ii) CERTAIN DISTRIBUTIONS.—Clause (i) of subparagraph (A) shall not apply to an acquisition of stock described in clause (i) of this subparagraph if the corporation acquiring such stock—

(I) made a qualified stock purchase of stock of the related corporation, and

(II) made an election under this section (or is treated under subsection (e) as having made such an election) with respect to such qualified stock purchase.

(iii) RELATED CORPORATION DEFINED.—For purposes of this subparagraph, a corporation is a related corporation if stock owned by such corporation is treated (under section 318(a) other than paragraph (4) thereof) as owned by the corporation acquiring the stock.

(4) CONSISTENCY PERIOD.—

(A) IN GENERAL.—Except as provided in subparagraph (B), the term "consistency period" means the period consisting of—

(i) the 1-year period before the beginning of the 12-month acquisition period for the target corporation,

(ii) such acquisition period (up to and including the acquisition date), and

(iii) the 1-year period beginning on the day after the acquisition date.

(B) EXTENSION WHERE THERE IS PLAN.—The period referred to in subparagraph (A) shall also include any period during which the Secretary determines that there was in effect a plan to make a qualified stock purchase plus 1 or more other qualified stock purchases (or asset acquisitions described in subsection (e)) with respect to the target corporation or any target affiliate.

(5) AFFILIATED GROUP.—The term "affiliated group" has the meaning given to such term by section 1504(a) (determined without regard to the exceptions contained in section 1504(b)).

(6) TARGET AFFILIATE.—

(A) IN GENERAL.—A corporation shall be treated as a target affiliate of the target corporation if each of such corporations was, at any time during so much of the consistency period as ends on the acquisition date of the target corporation, a member of an affiliated group which had the same common parent.

(B) CERTAIN FOREIGN CORPORATIONS, ETC.—Except as otherwise provided in regulations (and subject to such conditions as may be provided in regulations)—

(i) the term "target affiliate" does not include a foreign corporation or a DISC, and

(ii) stock held by a target affiliate in a foreign corporation or a domestic corporation which is a DISC or described in section 1248(e) shall be excluded from the operation of this section.

(7) [Repealed.]

(8) ACQUISITIONS BY AFFILIATED GROUP TREATED AS MADE BY 1 CORPORATION.—Except as provided in regulations prescribed by the Secretary, stock and asset acquisitions made by members of the same affiliated group shall be treated as made by 1 corporation.

(9) TARGET NOT TREATED AS MEMBER OF AFFILIATED GROUP.—Except as otherwise provided in paragraph (10) or in regulations prescribed under this paragraph, the target corporation shall not be treated as a member of an affiliated group with respect to the sale described in subsection (a)(1).

(10) ELECTIVE RECOGNITION OF GAIN OR LOSS BY TARGET CORPORATION, TOGETHER WITH NONRECOGNITION OF GAIN OR LOSS ON STOCK SOLD BY SELLING CONSOLIDATED GROUP.—

(A) IN GENERAL.—Under regulations prescribed by the Secretary, an election may be made under which if—

(i) the target corporation was, before the transaction, a member of the selling consolidated group, and

(ii) the target corporation recognizes gain or loss with respect to the transaction as if it sold all of its assets in a single transaction,

then the target corporation shall be treated as a member of the selling consolidated group with respect to such sale, and (to the extent provided in regulations) no gain or loss will be recognized on stock sold or exchanged in the transaction by members of the selling consolidated group.

(B) SELLING CONSOLIDATED GROUP.—For purposes of subparagraph (A), the term "selling consolidated group" means any group of corporations which (for the taxable period which includes the transaction)—

(i) includes the target corporation, and

(ii) files a consolidated return.

To the extent provided in regulations, such term also includes any affiliated group of corporations which includes the target corporation (whether or not such group files a consolidated return).

(C) INFORMATION REQUIRED TO BE FURNISHED TO THE SECRETARY.—Under regulations, where an election is made under subparagraph (A), the purchasing corporation and the common parent of the selling consolidated group shall, at such times and in such manner as may be provided in regulations, furnish to the Secretary the following information:

(i) The amount allocated under subsection (b)(5) to goodwill or going concern value.

(ii) Any modification of the amount described in clause (i).

(iii) Any other information as the Secretary deems necessary to carry out the provisions of this paragraph.

(11) ELECTIVE FORMULA FOR DETERMINING FAIR MARKET VALUE.—For purposes of subsection (a)(1), fair market value may be determined on the basis of a formula provided in regulations prescribed by the Secretary which takes into account liabilities and other relevant items.

(12) [Repealed.]

(13) TAX ON DEEMED SALE NOT TAKEN INTO ACCOUNT FOR ESTIMATED TAX PURPOSES.—For purposes of section 6655, tax attributable to the sale described in subsection (a)(1) shall not be taken into account. The preceding sentence shall not apply with respect to a qualified stock purchase for which an election is made under paragraph (10).

(14) [Stricken.]

(15) COMBINED DEEMED SALE RETURN.—Under regulations prescribed by the Secretary, a combined deemed sale return may be filed by all target corporations acquired by a purchasing corporation on the same acquisition date if such target corporations were members of the same selling consolidated group (as defined in subparagraph (B) of paragraph (10)).

(16) COORDINATION WITH FOREIGN TAX CREDIT PROVISIONS.—Except as provided in regulations, this section shall not apply for purposes of determining the source or character of any item for purposes of subpart A of part III of subchapter N of this chapter (relating to foreign tax credit). The preceding sentence shall not apply to any gain to the extent such gain is includible in gross income as a dividend under section 1248 (determined without regard to any deemed sale under this section by a foreign corporation).

[Sec. 338(i)]

(i) REGULATIONS.—The Secretary shall prescribe such regulations as may be necessary or appropriate to carry out the purposes of this section, including—

(1) regulations to ensure that the purpose of this section to require consistency of treatment of stock and asset sales and purchases may not be circumvented through the use of any provision of law or regulations (including the consolidated return regulations) and

(2) regulations providing for the coordination of the provisions of this section with the provision of this title relating to foreign corporations and their shareholders.

Subpart D—Definition and Special Rule

[Sec. 346]

SEC. 346. DEFINITION AND SPECIAL RULE.

[Sec. 346(a)]

(a) COMPLETE LIQUIDATION.—For purposes of this subchapter, a distribution shall be treated as in complete liquidation of a corporation if the distribution is one of a series of distributions in redemption of all of the stock of the corporation pursuant to a plan.

* * *

PART III—CORPORATE ORGANIZATIONS AND REORGANIZATIONS

Subpart A—Corporate Organizations

[Sec. 351]

SEC. 351. TRANSFER TO CORPORATION CONTROLLED BY TRANSFEROR.

[Sec. 351(a)]

(a) GENERAL RULE.—No gain or loss shall be recognized if property is transferred to a corporation by one or more persons solely in exchange for stock in such corporation and immediately after the exchange such person or persons are in control (as defined in section 368(c)) of the corporation.

[Sec. 351(b)]

(b) RECEIPT OF PROPERTY.—If subsection (a) would apply to an exchange but for the fact that there is received, in addition to the stock permitted to be received under subsection (a), other property or money, then—

(1) gain (if any) to such recipient shall be recognized, but not in excess of—

(A) the amount of money received, plus

(B) the fair market value of such other property received; and

(2) no loss to such recipient shall be recognized.

[Sec. 351(c)]

(c) SPECIAL RULES WHERE DISTRIBUTION TO SHAREHOLDERS.—

(1) IN GENERAL.—In determining control for purposes of this section, the fact that any corporate transferor distributes part or all of the stock in the corporation which it receives in the exchange to its shareholders shall not be taken into account.

(2) SPECIAL RULE FOR SECTION 355.—If the requirements of section 355 (or so much of section 356 as relates to section 355) are met with respect to a distribution described in paragraph (1), then, solely for purposes of determining the tax treatment of the transfers of property to the controlled corporation by the distributing corporation, the fact that the shareholders of the distributing corporation dispose of part or all of the distributed stock, or the fact that the corporation whose stock was distributed issues additional stock, shall not be taken into account in determining control for purposes of this section.

[Sec. 351(d)]

(d) SERVICES, CERTAIN INDEBTEDNESS, AND ACCRUED INTEREST NOT TREATED AS PROPERTY.—For purposes of this section, stock issued for—

(1) services,

(2) indebtedness of the transferee corporation which is not evidenced by a security, or

(3) interest on indebtedness of the transferee corporation which accrued on or after the beginning of the transferor's holding period for the debt,

shall not be considered as issued in return for property.

[Sec. 351(e)]

(e) EXCEPTIONS.—This section shall not apply to—

(1) TRANSFER OF PROPERTY TO AN INVESTMENT COMPANY.—A transfer of property to an investment company. For purposes of the preceding sentence, the determination of whether a company is an investment company shall be made—

(A) by taking into account all stock and securities held by the company, and

(B) by treating as stock and securities—

(i) money,

(ii) stocks and other equity interests in a corporation, evidences of indebtedness, options, forward or futures contracts, notional principal contracts and derivatives,

(iii) any foreign currency,

(iv) any interest in a real estate investment trust, a common trust fund, a regulated investment company, a publicly-traded partnership (as defined in section 7704(b)) or any other equity interest (other than in a corporation) which pursuant to its terms or any other arrangement is readily convertible into, or exchangeable for, any asset described in any preceding clause, this clause or clause (v) or (viii),

(v) except to the extent provided in regulations prescribed by the Secretary, any interest in a precious metal, unless such metal is used or held in the active conduct of a trade or business after the contribution,

(vi) except as otherwise provided in regulations prescribed by the Secretary, interests in any entity if substantially all of the assets of such entity consist (directly or indirectly) of any assets described in any preceding clause or clause (viii),

(vii) to the extent provided in regulations prescribed by the Secretary, any interest in any entity not described in clause (vi), but only to the extent of the value of such interest that is attributable to assets listed in clauses (i) through (v) or clause (viii), or

(viii) any other asset specified in regulations prescribed by the Secretary.

The Secretary may prescribe regulations that, under appropriate circumstances, treat any asset described in clauses (i) through (v) as not so listed.

(2) TITLE 11 OR SIMILAR CASE.—A transfer of property of a debtor pursuant to a plan while the debtor is under the jurisdiction of a court in a title 11 or similar case (within the meaning of section 368(a)(3)(A)), to the extent that the stock received in the exchange is used to satisfy the indebtedness of such debtor.

[Sec. 351(f)]

(f) TREATMENT OF CONTROLLED CORPORATION.—If—

(1) property is transferred to a corporation (hereinafter in this subsection referred to as the "controlled corporation") in an exchange with respect to which gain or loss is not recognized (in whole or in part) to the transferor under this section, and

(2) such exchange is not in pursuance of a plan of reorganization,

section 311 shall apply to any transfer in such exchange by the controlled corporation in the same manner as if such transfer were a distribution to which subpart A of part I applies.

[Sec. 351(g)]

(g) NONQUALIFIED PREFERRED STOCK NOT TREATED AS STOCK.—

(1) IN GENERAL.—In the case of a person who transfers property to a corporation and receives nonqualified preferred stock—

(A) subsection (a) shall not apply to such transferor, and

(B) if (and only if) the transferor receives stock other than nonqualified preferred stock—

(i) subsection (b) shall apply to such transferor; and

(ii) such nonqualified preferred stock shall be treated as other property for purposes of applying subsection (b).

(2) NONQUALIFIED PREFERRED STOCK.—For purposes of paragraph (1)—

(A) IN GENERAL.—The term "nonqualified preferred stock" means preferred stock if—

(i) the holder of such stock has the right to require the issuer or a related person to redeem or purchase the stock,

(ii) the issuer or a related person is required to redeem or purchase such stock,

(iii) the issuer or a related person has the right to redeem or purchase the stock and, as of the issue date, it is more likely than not that such right will be exercised, or

(iv) the dividend rate on such stock varies in whole or in part (directly or indirectly) with reference to interest rates, commodity prices, or other similar indices.

(B) LIMITATIONS.—Clauses (i), (ii), and (iii) of subparagraph (A) shall apply only if the right or obligation referred to therein may be exercised within the 20-year period beginning on the issue date of such stock and such right or obligation is not subject to a contingency which, as of the issue date, makes remote the likelihood of the redemption or purchase.

(C) EXCEPTIONS FOR CERTAIN RIGHTS OR OBLIGATIONS.—

(i) IN GENERAL.—A right or obligation shall not be treated as described in clause (i), (ii), or (iii) of subparagraph (A) if—

(I) it may be exercised only upon the death, disability, or mental incompetency of the holder, or

(II) in the case of a right or obligation to redeem or purchase stock transferred in connection with the performance of services for the issuer or a related person (and which represents reasonable compensation), it may be exercised only upon the holder's separation from service from the issuer or a related person.

(ii) EXCEPTION.—Clause (i)(I) shall not apply if the stock relinquished in the exchange, or the stock acquired in the exchange is in—

(I) a corporation if any class of stock in such corporation or a related party is readily tradable on an established securities market or otherwise, or

(II) any other corporation if such exchange is part of a transaction or series of transactions in which such corporation is to become a corporation described in subclause (I).

(3) DEFINITIONS.—For purposes of this subsection—

(A) PREFERRED STOCK.—The term "preferred stock" means stock which is limited and preferred as to dividends and does not participate in corporate growth to any significant extent. Stock shall not be treated as participating in corporate growth to any significant extent unless there is a real and meaningful likelihood of the shareholder actually participating in the earnings and growth of the corporation. If there is not a real and meaningful likelihood that dividends beyond any limitation or preference will actually be paid, the possibility of such payments will be disregarded in determining whether stock is limited and preferred as to dividends.

(B) RELATED PERSON.—A person shall be treated as related to another person if they bear a relationship to such other person described in section 267(b) or 707(b).

(4) REGULATIONS.—The Secretary may prescribe such regulations as may be necessary or appropriate to carry out the purposes of this subsection and sections 354(a)(2)(C), 355(a)(3)(D), and 356(e). The Secretary may also prescribe regulations, consistent with the treatment under this subsection and such sections, for the treatment of nonqualified preferred stock under other provisions of this title.

[Sec. 351(h)]

(h) CROSS REFERENCES.—

(1) For special rule where another party to the exchange assumes a liability, see section 357.

(2) For the basis of stock or property received in an exchange to which this section applies, see sections 358 and 362.

(3) For special rule in the case of an exchange described in this section but which results in a gift, see section 2501 and following.

(4) For special rule in the case of an exchange described in this section but which has the effect of the payment of compensation by the corporation or by a transferor, see section 61(a)(1).

(5) For coordination of this section with section 304, see section 304(b)(3).

Subpart B—Effects on Shareholders and Security Holders

[Sec. 354]

SEC. 354. EXCHANGES OF STOCK AND SECURITIES IN CERTAIN REORGANIZATIONS.

[Sec. 354(a)]

(a) GENERAL RULE.—

(1) IN GENERAL.—No gain or loss shall be recognized if stock or securities in a corporation a party to a reorganization are, in pursuance of the plan of reorganization, exchanged solely for stock or securities in such corporation or in another corporation a party to the reorganization.

(2) LIMITATIONS.—

(A) EXCESS PRINCIPAL AMOUNT.—Paragraph (1) shall not apply if—

(i) the principal amount of any such securities received exceeds the principal amount of any such securities surrendered, or

(ii) any such securities are received and no such securities are surrendered.

(B) PROPERTY ATTRIBUTABLE TO ACCRUED INTEREST.—Neither paragraph (1) nor so much of section 356 as relates to paragraph (1) shall apply to the extent that any stock (including nonqualified preferred stock, as defined in section 351(g)(2)), securities, or other property received is attributable to interest which has accrued on securities on or after the beginning of the holder's holding period.

(C) NONQUALIFIED PREFERRED STOCK.—

(i) IN GENERAL.—Nonqualified preferred stock (as defined in section 351(g)(2)) received in exchange for stock other than nonqualified preferred stock (as so defined) shall not be treated as stock or securities.

(ii) RECAPITALIZATIONS OF FAMILY-OWNED CORPORATIONS.—

(I) IN GENERAL.—Clause (i) shall not apply in the case of a recapitalization under section 368(a)(1)(E) of a family-owned corporation.

(II) FAMILY-OWNED CORPORATION.—For purposes of this clause, except as provided in regulations, the term "family-owned corporation" means any corporation which is described in clause (i) of section 447(d)(2)(C) throughout the 8-year period beginning on the date which is 5 years before the date of the recapitalization. For purposes of the preceding sentence, stock shall not be treated as owned by a family member during any period described in section 355(d)(6)(B).

(III) EXTENSION OF STATUTE OF LIMITATIONS.—The statutory period for the assessment of any deficiency attributable to a corporation failing to be a family-owned corporation shall not expire before the expiration of 3 years after the date the Secretary is notified by the corporation (in such manner as the Secretary may prescribe) of such failure, and such deficiency may be assessed before the expiration of such 3-year period notwithstanding the provisions of any other law or rule of law which would otherwise prevent such assessment.

(3) CROSS REFERENCES.—

(A) For treatment of the exchange if any property is received which is not permitted to be received under this subsection (including nonqualified preferred stock and an excess principal amount of securities received over securities surrendered, but not including property to which paragraph (2)(B) applies), see section 356.

(B) For treatment of accrued interest in the case of an exchange described in paragraph (2)(B), see section 61.

[Sec. 354(b)]

(b) EXCEPTION.—

(1) IN GENERAL.—Subsection (a) shall not apply to an exchange in pursuance of a plan of reorganization within the meaning of subparagraph (D) or (G) of section 368(a)(1), unless—

(A) the corporation to which the assets are transferred acquires substantially all of the assets of the transferor of such assets; and

(B) the stock, securities, and other properties received by such transferor, as well as the other properties of such transferor, are distributed in pursuance of the plan of reorganization.

(2) CROSS REFERENCE.—

For special rules for certain exchanges in pursuance of plans of reorganization within the meaning of subparagraph (D) or (G) of section 368(a)(1), see section 355.

* * *

[Sec. 355]

SEC. 355. DISTRIBUTION OF STOCK AND SECURITIES OF A CONTROLLED CORPORATION.

[Sec. 355(a)]

(a) EFFECT ON DISTRIBUTEES.—

(1) GENERAL RULE.—If—

(A) a corporation (referred to in this section as the "distributing corporation")

(i) distributes to a shareholder, with respect to its stock, or

(ii) distributes to a security holder, in exchange for its securities,

solely stock or securities of a corporation (referred to in this section as "controlled corporation") which it controls immediately before the distribution,

(B) the transaction was not used principally as a device for the distribution of the earnings and profits of the distributing corporation or the controlled corporation or both (but the mere fact that subsequent to the distribution stock or securities in one or more of such corporations are sold or exchanged by all or some of the distributees (other than pursuant to an arrangement negotiated or agreed upon prior to such distribution) shall not be construed to mean that the transaction was used principally as such a device),

(C) the requirements of subsection (b) (relating to active businesses) are satisfied, and

(D) as part of the distribution, the distributing corporation distributes—

(i) all of the stock and securities in the controlled corporation held by it immediately before the distribution, or

(ii) an amount of stock in the controlled corporation constituting control within the meaning of section 368 (c), and it is established to the satisfaction of the Secretary that the retention by the distributing corporation of stock (or stock and securities) in the controlled corporation was not in pursuance of a plan having as one of its principal purposes the avoidance of Federal income tax,

then no gain or loss shall be recognized to (and no amount shall be includible in the income of) such shareholder or security holder on the receipt of such stock or securities.

(2) NON PRO RATA DISTRIBUTIONS, ETC.—Paragraph (1) shall be applied without regard to the following:

(A) whether or not the distribution is pro rata with respect to all of the shareholders of the distributing corporation,

(B) whether or not the shareholder surrenders stock in the distributing corporation, and

(C) whether or not the distribution is in pursuance of a plan of reorganization (within the meaning of section 368 (a) (1) (D)).

(3) LIMITATIONS.—

(A) EXCESS PRINCIPAL AMOUNT.—Paragraph (1) shall not apply if—

(i) the principal amount of the securities in the controlled corporation which are received exceeds the principal amount of the securities which are surrendered in connection with such distribution, or

(ii) securities in the controlled corporation are received and no securities are surrendered in connection with such distribution.

(B) STOCK ACQUIRED IN TAXABLE TRANSACTIONS WITHIN 5 YEARS TREATED AS BOOT.—For purposes of this section (other than paragraph (1)(D) of this subsection) and so much of section 356 as relates to this section, stock of a controlled corporation acquired by the distributing corporation by reason of any transaction—

(i) which occurs within 5 years of the distribution of such stock, and

(ii) in which gain or loss was recognized in whole or in part,

shall not be treated as stock of such controlled corporation, but as other property.

(C) PROPERTY ATTRIBUTABLE TO ACCRUED INTEREST.—Neither paragraph (1) nor so much of section 356 as relates to paragraph (1) shall apply to the extent that any stock (including nonqualified preferred stock, as defined in section 351(g)(2)), securities, or other property received is attributable to interest which has accrued on securities on or after the beginning of the holder's holding period.

(D) NONQUALIFIED PREFERRED STOCK.—Nonqualified preferred stock (as defined in section 351(g)(2)) received in a distribution with respect to stock other than nonqualified preferred stock (as so defined) shall not be treated as stock or securities.

(4) CROSS REFERENCES.—

(A) For treatment of the exchange if any property is received which is not permitted to be received under this subsection (including nonqualified preferred stock and an excess principal amount of securities received over securities surrendered, but not including property to which paragraph (3)(C) applies), see section 356.

(B) For treatment of accrued interest in the case of an exchange described in paragraph (3)(C), see section 61.

[Sec. 355(b)]

(b) REQUIREMENTS AS TO ACTIVE BUSINESS.—

(1) IN GENERAL.—Subsection (a) shall apply only if either—

(A) the distributing corporation, and the controlled corporation (or, if stock of more than one controlled corporation is distributed, each of such corporations), is engaged immediately after the distribution in the active conduct of a trade or business, or

(B) immediately before the distribution, the distributing corporation had no assets other than stock or securities in the controlled corporations and each of the controlled corporations is engaged immediately after the distribution in the active conduct of a trade or business.

(2) DEFINITION.—For purposes of paragraph (1), a corporation shall be treated as engaged in the active conduct of a trade or business if and only if—

(A) it is engaged in the active conduct of a trade or business,

(B) such trade or business has been actively conducted throughout the 5-year period ending on the date of the distribution,

(C) such trade or business was not acquired within the period described in subparagraph (B) in a transaction in which gain or loss was recognized in whole or in part, and

(D) control of a corporation which (at the time of acquisition of control) was conducting such trade or business—

(i) was not acquired by any distributee corporation directly (or through 1 or more corporations, whether through the distributing corporation or otherwise) within the period described in subparagraph (B) and was not acquired by the distributing corporation directly (or through 1 or more corporations) within such period, or

(ii) was so acquired by any such corporation within such period, but, in each case in which such control was so acquired, it was so acquired, only by reason of transactions in which gain or loss was not recognized in whole or in part, or only by reason of such transactions combined with acquisitions before the beginning of such period.

For purposes of subparagraph (D), all distributee corporations which are members of the same affiliated group (as defined in section 1504(a) without regard to section 1504(b)) shall be treated as 1 distributee corporation.

(3) SPECIAL RULES FOR DETERMINING ACTIVE CONDUCT IN THE CASE OF AFFILIATED GROUPS.—

(A) IN GENERAL.—For purposes of determining whether a corporation meets the requirements of paragraph (2)(A), all members of such corporation's separate affiliated group shall be treated as one corporation.

(B) SEPARATE AFFILIATED GROUP.—For purposes of this paragraph, the term "separate affiliated group" means, with respect to any corporation, the affiliated group which would be determined under section 1504(a) if such corporation were the common parent and section 1504(b) did not apply.

(C) TREATMENT OF TRADE OR BUSINESS CONDUCTED BY ACQUIRED MEMBER.—If a corporation became a member of a separate affiliated group as a result of one or more transactions in which gain or loss was recognized in whole or in part, any trade or business conducted by such corporation (at the time that such corporation became such a member) shall be treated for purposes of paragraph (2) as acquired in a transaction in which gain or loss was recognized in whole or in part.

(D) REGULATIONS.—The Secretary shall prescribe such regulations as are necessary or appropriate to carry out the purposes of this paragraph, including regulations which provide for the proper application of subparagraphs (B), (C), and (D) of paragraph (2), and modify the application of subsection (a)(3)(B), in connection with the application of this paragraph.

[Sec. 355(c)]

(c) TAXABILITY OF CORPORATION ON DISTRIBUTION.—

(1) IN GENERAL.—Except as provided in paragraph (2), no gain or loss shall be recognized to a corporation on any distribution to which this section (or so much of section 356 as relates to this section) applies and which is not in pursuance of a plan of reorganization.

(2) DISTRIBUTION OF APPRECIATED PROPERTY.—

(A) IN GENERAL.—If—

(i) in a distribution referred to in paragraph (1), the corporation distributes property other than qualified property, and

(ii) the fair market value of such property exceeds its adjusted basis (in the hands of the distributing corporation),

then gain shall be recognized to the distributing corporation as if such property were sold to the distributee at its fair market value.

(B) QUALIFIED PROPERTY.—For purposes of subparagraph (A), the term "qualified property" means any stock or securities in the controlled corporation.

(C) TREATMENT OF LIABILITIES.—If any property distributed in the distribution referred to in paragraph (1) is subject to a liability or the shareholder assumes a liability of the distributing corporation in connection with the distribution, then, for purposes of subparagraph (A), the fair market value of such property shall be treated as not less than the amount of such liability.

(3) COORDINATION WITH SECTIONS 311 AND 336(a).—Sections 311 and 336(a) shall not apply to any distribution referred to in paragraph (1).

(d) RECOGNITION OF GAIN ON CERTAIN DISTRIBUTIONS OF STOCK OR SECURITIES IN CONTROLLED CORPORATION.—

(1) IN GENERAL.—In the case of a disqualified distribution, any stock or securities in the controlled corporation shall not be treated as qualified property for purposes of subsection (c)(2) of this section or section 361(c)(2).

(2) DISQUALIFIED DISTRIBUTION.—For purposes of this subsection, the term "disqualified distribution" means any distribution to which this section (or so much of section 356 as relates to this section) applies if, immediately after the distribution—

(A) any person holds disqualified stock in the distributing corporation which constitutes a 50-percent or greater interest in such corporation, or

(B) any person holds disqualified stock in the controlled corporation (or, if stock of more than 1 controlled corporation is distributed, in any controlled corporation) which constitutes a 50-percent or greater interest in such corporation.

(3) DISQUALIFIED STOCK.—For purposes of this subsection, the term "disqualified stock" means—

(A) any stock in the distributing corporation acquired by purchase during the 5-year period ending on the date of the distribution, and

(B) any stock in any controlled corporation—

(i) acquired by purchase during the 5-year period ending on the date of the distribution, or

(ii) received in the distribution to the extent attributable to distributions on—

(I) stock described in subparagraph (A), or

(II) any securities in the distributing corporation acquired by purchase during the 5-year period ending on the date of the distribution.

(4) 50-PERCENT OR GREATER INTEREST.—For purposes of this subsection, the term "50-percent or greater interest" means stock possessing at least 50 percent of the total combined voting power of all classes of stock entitled to vote or at least 50 percent of the total value of shares of all classes of stock.

(5) PURCHASE.—For purposes of this subsection—

(A) IN GENERAL.—Except as otherwise provided in this paragraph, the term "purchase" means any acquisition but only if—

(i) the basis of the property acquired in the hands of the acquirer is not determined (I) in whole or in part by reference to the adjusted basis of such property in the hands of the person from whom acquired, or (II) under section 1014(a), and

(ii) the property is not acquired in an exchange to which section 351, 354, 355, or 356 applies.

(B) CERTAIN SECTION 351 EXCHANGES TREATED AS PURCHASES.—The term "purchase" includes any acquisition of property in an exchange to which section 351 applies to the extent such property is acquired in exchange for—

(i) any cash or cash item,

(ii) any marketable stock or security, or

(iii) any debt of the transferor.

(C) CARRYOVER BASIS TRANSACTIONS.—If—

(i) any person acquires property from another person who acquired such property by purchase (as determined under this paragraph with regard to this subparagraph), and

(ii) the adjusted basis of such property in the hands of such acquirer is determined in whole or in part by reference to the adjusted basis of such property in the hands of such other person, such acquirer shall be treated as having acquired such property by purchase on the date it was so acquired by such other person.

(6) SPECIAL RULE WHERE SUBSTANTIAL DIMINUTION OF RISK.—

(A) IN GENERAL.—If this paragraph applies to any stock or securities for any period, the running of any 5-year period set forth in subparagraph (A) or (B) of paragraph (3) (whichever applies) shall be suspended during such period.

(B) PROPERTY TO WHICH SUSPENSION APPLIES.—This paragraph applies to any stock or securities for any period during which the holder's risk of loss with respect to such stock or securities, or with respect to any portion of the activities of the corporation, is (directly or indirectly) substantially diminished by—

(i) an option,

(ii) a short sale,

(iii) any special class of stock, or

(iv) any other device or transaction.

(7) AGGREGATION RULES.—

(A) IN GENERAL.—For purposes of this subsection, a person and all persons related to such person (within the meaning of section 267(b) or 707(b)(1)) shall be treated as one person.

(B) PERSONS ACTING PURSUANT TO PLANS OR ARRANGEMENTS.—If two or more persons act pursuant to a plan or arrangement with respect to acquisitions of stock or securities in the distributing corporation or controlled corporation, such persons shall be treated as one person for purposes of this subsection.

(8) ATTRIBUTION FROM ENTITIES.—

(A) IN GENERAL.—Paragraph (2) of section 318(a) shall apply in determining whether a person holds stock or securities in any corporation (determined by substituting "10 percent" for "50 percent" in subparagraph (C) of such paragraph (2) and by treating any reference to stock as including a reference to securities).

(B) DEEMED PURCHASE RULE.—If—

(i) any person acquires by purchase an interest in any entity, and

(ii) such person is treated under subparagraph (A) as holding any stock or securities by reason of holding such interest,

such stock or securities shall be treated as acquired by purchase by such person on the later of the date of the purchase of the interest in such entity or the date such stock or securities are acquired by purchase by such entity.

(9) REGULATIONS.—The Secretary shall prescribe such regulations as may be necessary to carry out the purposes of this subsection, including—

(A) regulations to prevent the avoidance of the purposes of this subsection through the use of related persons, intermediaries, pass-thru entities, options, or other arrangements, and

(B) regulations modifying the definition of the term "purchase".

[Sec. 355(e)]

(e) RECOGNITION OF GAIN ON CERTAIN DISTRIBUTIONS OF STOCK OR SECURITIES IN CONNECTION WITH ACQUISITIONS.—

(1) GENERAL RULE.—If there is a distribution to which this subsection applies, any stock or securities in the controlled corporation shall not be treated as qualified property for purposes of subsection (c)(2) of this section or section 361(c)(2).

(2) DISTRIBUTIONS TO WHICH SUBSECTION APPLIES.—

(A) IN GENERAL.—This subsection shall apply to any distribution—

(i) to which this section (or so much of section 356 as relates to this section) applies, and

(ii) which is part of a plan (or series of related transactions) pursuant to which 1 or more persons acquire directly or indirectly stock representing a 50-percent or greater interest in the distributing corporation or any controlled corporation.

(B) PLAN PRESUMED TO EXIST IN CERTAIN CASES.—If 1 or more persons acquire directly or indirectly stock representing a 50-percent or greater interest in the distributing corporation or any controlled corporation during the 4-year period beginning on the date which is 2 years before the date of the distribution, such acquisition shall be treated as pursuant to a plan described in subparagraph (A)(ii) unless it is established that the distribution and the acquisition are not pursuant to a plan or series of related transactions.

(C) CERTAIN PLANS DISREGARDED.—A plan (or series of related transactions) shall not be treated as described in subparagraph (A)(ii) if, immediately after the completion of such plan or transactions, the distributing corporation and all controlled corporations are members of a single affiliated group (as defined in section 1504 without regard to subsection (b) thereof).

(D) COORDINATION WITH SUBSECTION (d).—This subsection shall not apply to any distribution to which subsection (d) applies.

(3) SPECIAL RULES RELATING TO ACQUISITIONS.—

(A) CERTAIN ACQUISITIONS NOT TAKEN INTO ACCOUNT.—Except as provided in regulations, the following acquisitions shall not be taken into account in applying paragraph (2)(A)(ii):

(i) The acquisition of stock in any controlled corporation by the distributing corporation.

(ii) The acquisition by a person of stock in any controlled corporation by reason of holding stock or securities in the distributing corporation.

(iii) The acquisition by a person of stock in any successor corporation of the distributing corporation or any controlled corporation by reason of holding stock or securities in such distributing or controlled corporation.

(iv) The acquisition of stock in the distributing corporation or any controlled corporation to the extent that the percentage of stock owned directly or indirectly in such corporation by each person owning stock in such corporation immediately before the acquisition does not decrease.

This subparagraph shall not apply to any acquisition if the stock held before the acquisition was acquired pursuant to a plan (or series of related transactions) described in paragraph (2)(A)(ii).

(B) ASSET ACQUISITIONS.—Except as provided in regulations, for purposes of this subsection, if the assets of the distributing corporation or any controlled corporation are acquired by a successor corporation in a transaction described in subparagraph (A), (C), or (D) of section 368(a)(1) or any other transaction specified in regulations by the Secretary, the shareholders (immediately before the acquisition) of the corporation acquiring such assets shall be treated as acquiring stock in the corporation from which the assets were acquired.

(4) DEFINITION AND SPECIAL RULES.—For purposes of this subsection—

(A) 50-PERCENT OR GREATER INTEREST.—The term "50-percent or greater interest" has the meaning given such term by subsection (d)(4).

(B) DISTRIBUTIONS IN TITLE 11 OR SIMILAR CASE.—Paragraph (1) shall not apply to any distribution made in a title 11 or similar case (as defined in section 368(a)(3)).

(C) AGGREGATION AND ATTRIBUTION RULES.—

(i) AGGREGATION.—The rules of paragraph (7)(A) of subsection (d) shall apply.

(ii) ATTRIBUTION.— Section 318(a)(2) shall apply in determining whether a person holds stock or securities in any corporation. Except as provided in regulations, section 318(a)(2)(C) shall be applied without regard to the phrase "50 percent or more in value" for purposes of the preceding sentence.

(D) SUCCESSORS AND PREDECESSORS.—For purposes of this subsection, any reference to a controlled corporation or a distributing corporation shall include a reference to any predecessor or successor of such corporation.

(E) STATUTE OF LIMITATIONS.—If there is a distribution to which paragraph (1) applies—

(i) the statutory period for the assessment of any deficiency attributable to any part of the gain recognized under this subsection by reason of such distribution shall not expire before the expiration of 3 years from the date the Secretary is notified by the taxpayer (in such manner as the Secretary may by regulations prescribe) that such distribution occurred, and

(ii) such deficiency may be assessed before the expiration of such 3-year period notwithstanding the provisions of any other law or rule of law which would otherwise prevent such assessment.

(5) REGULATIONS.—The Secretary shall prescribe such regulations as may be necessary to carry out the purposes of this subsection, including regulations—

(A) providing for the application of this subsection where there is more than 1 controlled corporation,

(B) treating 2 or more distributions as 1 distribution where necessary to prevent the avoidance of such purposes, and

(C) providing for the application of rules similar to the rules of subsection (d)(6) where appropriate for purposes of paragraph (2)(B).

[Sec. 355(f)]

(f) SECTION NOT TO APPLY TO CERTAIN INTRAGROUP DISTRIBUTIONS.—Except as provided in regulations, this section (or so much of section 356 as relates to this section) shall not apply to the distribution of stock from 1 member of an affiliated group (as defined in section 1504(a)) to another member of such group if such distribution is part of a plan (or series of related transactions) described in subsection (e)(2)(A)(ii) (determined after the application of subsection (e)).

[Sec. 355(g)]

(g) SECTION NOT TO APPLY TO DISTRIBUTIONS INVOLVING DISQUALIFIED INVESTMENT CORPORATIONS.—

(1) IN GENERAL.—This section (and so much of section 356 as relates to this section) shall not apply to any distribution which is part of a transaction if—

(A) either the distributing corporation or controlled corporation is, immediately after the transaction, a disqualified investment corporation, and

(B) any person holds, immediately after the transaction, a 50-percent or greater interest in any disqualified investment corporation, but only if such person did not hold such an interest in such corporation immediately before the transaction.

(2) DISQUALIFIED INVESTMENT CORPORATION.—For purposes of this subsection—

(A) IN GENERAL.—The term "disqualified investment corporation" means any distributing or controlled corporation if the fair market value of the investment assets of the corporation is—

(i) in the case of distributions after the end of the 1-year period beginning on the date of the enactment of this subsection, ⅔ or more of the fair market value of all assets of the corporation, and

(ii) in the case of distributions during such 1-year period, ¾ or more of the fair market value of all assets of the corporation.

(B) INVESTMENT ASSETS.—

(i) IN GENERAL.—Except as otherwise provided in this subparagraph, the term "investment assets" means—

(I) cash,

(II) any stock or securities in a corporation,

(III) any interest in a partnership,

(IV) any debt instrument or other evidence of indebtedness,

(V) any option, forward or futures contract, notional principal contract, or derivative,

(VI) foreign currency, or

(VII) any similar asset.

(ii) EXCEPTION FOR ASSETS USED IN ACTIVE CONDUCT OF CERTAIN FINANCIAL TRADES OR BUSINESSES.—Such term shall not include any asset which is held for use in the active and regular conduct of—

(I) a lending or finance business (within the meaning of section 954(h)(4)),

(II) a banking business through a bank (as defined in section 581), a domestic building and loan association (within the meaning of section 7701(a)(19)), or any similar institution specified by the Secretary, or

(III) an insurance business if the conduct of the business is licensed, authorized, or regulated by an applicable insurance regulatory body.

This clause shall only apply with respect to any business if substantially all of the income of the business is derived from persons who are not related (within the meaning of section 267(b) or 707(b)(1)) to the person conducting the business.

(iii) EXCEPTION FOR SECURITIES MARKED TO MARKET.—Such term shall not include any security (as defined in section 475(c)(2)) which is held by a dealer in securities and to which section 475(a) applies.

(iv) STOCK OR SECURITIES IN A 20-PERCENT CONTROLLED ENTITY.—

(I) IN GENERAL.—Such term shall not include any stock and securities in, or any asset described in subclause (IV) or (V) of clause (i) issued by, a corporation which is a 20-percent controlled entity with respect to the distributing or controlled corporation.

(II) LOOK-THRU RULE.—The distributing or controlled corporation shall, for purposes of applying this subsection, be treated as owning its ratable share of the assets of any 20-percent controlled entity.

(III) 20-PERCENT CONTROLLED ENTITY.—For purposes of this clause, the term "20-percent controlled entity" means, with respect to any distributing or controlled corporation, any corporation with respect to which the distributing or controlled corporation owns directly or indirectly stock meeting the requirements of section 1504(a)(2), except that such section shall be applied by substituting "20 percent" for "80 percent" and without regard to stock described in section 1504(a)(4).

(v) INTERESTS IN CERTAIN PARTNERSHIPS.—

(I) IN GENERAL.—Such term shall not include any interest in a partnership, or any debt instrument or other evidence of indebtedness, issued by the partnership, if 1 or more of the trades or businesses of the partnership are (or, without regard to the 5-year requirement under subsection (b)(2)(B), would be) taken into account by the distributing or controlled corporation, as the case may be, in determining whether the requirements of subsection (b) are met with respect to the distribution.

(II) LOOK-THRU RULE.—The distributing or controlled corporation shall, for purposes of applying this subsection, be treated as owning its ratable share of the assets of any partnership described in subclause (I).

(3) 50-PERCENT OR GREATER INTEREST.—For purposes of this subsection—

(A) IN GENERAL.—The term "50-percent or greater interest" has the meaning given such term by subsection (d)(4).

(B) ATTRIBUTION RULES.—The rules of section 318 shall apply for purposes of determining ownership of stock for purposes of this paragraph.

(4) TRANSACTION.—For purposes of this subsection, the term "transaction" includes a series of transactions.

(5) REGULATIONS.—The Secretary shall prescribe such regulations as may be necessary to carry out, or prevent the avoidance of, the purposes of this subsection, including regulations—

(A) to carry out, or prevent the avoidance of, the purposes of this subsection in cases involving—

(i) the use of related persons, intermediaries, pass-thru entities, options, or other arrangements, and

(ii) the treatment of assets unrelated to the trade or business of a corporation as investment assets if, prior to the distribution, investment assets were used to acquire such unrelated assets,

(B) which in appropriate cases exclude from the application of this subsection a distribution which does not have the character of a redemption which would be treated as a sale or exchange under section 302, and

(C) which modify the application of the attribution rules applied for purposes of this subsection.

[Sec. 355(h)]

(h) RESTRICTION ON DISTRIBUTIONS INVOLVING REAL ESTATE INVESTMENT TRUSTS.—

(1) IN GENERAL.—This section (and so much of section 356 as relates to this section) shall not apply to any distribution if either the distributing corporation or controlled corporation is a real estate investment trust.

(2) EXCEPTIONS FOR CERTAIN DISTRIBUTIONS.—

(A) DISTRIBUTIONS OF A REAL ESTATE INVESTMENT TRUST BY ANOTHER REAL ESTATE INVESTMENT TRUST.—Paragraph (1) shall not apply to any distribution if, immediately after the distribution, the distributing corporation and the controlled corporation are both real estate investment trusts.

(B) DISTRIBUTIONS OF CERTAIN TAXABLE REIT SUBSIDIARIES.—Paragraph (1) shall not apply to any distribution if—

(i) the distributing corporation has been a real estate investment trust at all times during the 3-year period ending on the date of such distribution,

(ii) the controlled corporation has been a taxable REIT subsidiary (as defined in section 856(l)) of the distributing corporation at all times during such period, and

(iii) the distributing corporation had control (as defined in section 368(c) applied by taking into account stock owned directly or indirectly, including through one or more corporations or partnerships, by the distributing corporation) of the controlled corporation at all times during such period.

A controlled corporation will be treated as meeting the requirements of clauses (ii) and (iii) if the stock of such corporation was distributed by a taxable REIT subsidiary in a transaction to which this section (or so much of section 356 as relates to this section) applies and the assets of such corporation consist solely of the stock or assets held by one or more taxable REIT subsidiaries of the distributing corporation meeting the requirements of clauses (ii) and (iii). For purposes of clause (iii), control of a partnership means ownership of at least 80 percent of the profits interest and at least 80 percent of the capital interests.

[Sec. 356]

SEC. 356. RECEIPT OF ADDITIONAL CONSIDERATION.

[Sec. 356(a)]

(a) GAIN ON EXCHANGES.—

(1) RECOGNITION OF GAIN.—If—

(A) section 354 or 355 would apply to an exchange but for the fact that

(B) the property received in the exchange consists not only of property permitted by section 354 or 355 to be received without the recognition of gain but also of other property or money,

then the gain, if any, to the recipient shall be recognized, but in an amount not in excess of the sum of such money and the fair market value of such other property.

(2) TREATMENT AS DIVIDEND.—If an exchange is described in paragraph (1) but has the effect of the distribution of a dividend (determined with the application of section 318(a)), then there shall be treated as a dividend to each distributee such an amount of the gain recognized under paragraph (1) as is not in excess of his ratable share of the undistributed earnings and profits of the corporation accumulated after February 28, 1913. The remainder, if any, of the gain recognized under paragraph (1) shall be treated as gain from the exchange of property.

[Sec. 356(b)]

(b) ADDITIONAL CONSIDERATION RECEIVED IN CERTAIN DISTRIBUTIONS.—If—

(1) section 355 would apply to a distribution but for the fact that

(2) the property received in the distribution consists not only of property permitted by section 355 to be received without the recognition of gain, but also of other property or money,

then an amount equal to the sum of such money and the fair market value of such other property shall be treated as a distribution of property to which section 301 applies.

[Sec. 356(c)]

(c) LOSS.—If—

(1) section 354 would apply to an exchange, or section 355 would apply to an exchange or distribution, but for the fact that

(2) the property received in the exchange or distribution consists not only of property permitted by section 354 or 355 to be received without the recognition of gain or loss, but also of other property or money,

then no loss from the exchange or distribution shall be recognized.

[Sec. 356(d)]

(d) SECURITIES AS OTHER PROPERTY.—For purposes of this section—

(1) IN GENERAL.—Except as provided in paragraph (2), the term "other property" includes securities.

(2) EXCEPTIONS.—

(A) SECURITIES WITH RESPECT TO WHICH NONRECOGNITION OF GAIN WOULD BE PERMITTED.—The term "other property" does not include securities to the extent that, under section 354 or 355, such securities would be permitted to be received without the recognition of gain.

(B) GREATER PRINCIPAL AMOUNT IN SECTION 354 EXCHANGE.—If—

(i) in an exchange described in section 354 (other than subsection (c) thereof), securities of a corporation a party to the reorganization are surrendered and securities of any corporation a party to the reorganization are received, and

(ii) the principal amount of such securities received exceeds the principal amount of such securities surrendered, then, with respect to such securities received, the term "other property" means only the fair market value of such excess. For purposes of this subparagraph and subparagraph (C), if no securities are surrendered, the excess shall be the entire principal amount of the securities received.

(C) GREATER PRINCIPAL AMOUNT IN SECTION 355 TRANSACTION.—If, in an exchange or distribution described in section 355, the principal amount of the securities in the controlled corporation which are received exceeds the principal amount of the securities in the distributing corporation which are surrendered, then, with respect to such securities received, the term "other property" means only the fair market value of such excess.

[Sec. 356(e)]

(e) NONQUALIFIED PREFERRED STOCK TREATED AS OTHER PROPERTY.—For purposes of this section—

(1) IN GENERAL.—Except as provided in paragraph (2), the term "other property" includes nonqualified preferred stock (as defined in section 351(g)(2)).

(2) EXCEPTION.—The term "other property" does not include nonqualified preferred stock (as so defined) to the extent that, under section 354 or 355, such preferred stock would be permitted to be received without the recognition of gain.

[Sec. 356(f)]

(f) EXCHANGES FOR SECTION 306 STOCK.—Notwithstanding any other provision of this section, to the extent that any of the other property (or money) is received in exchange for section 306 stock, an amount equal to the fair market value of such other property (or the amount of such money) shall be treated as a distribution of property to which section 301 applies.

[Sec. 356(g)]

(g) TRANSACTIONS INVOLVING GIFT OR COMPENSATION.—

For special rules for a transaction described in section 354, 355, or this section, but which—

(1) results in a gift, see section 2501 and following, or

(2) has the effect of the payment of compensation, see section 61(a)(1).

[Sec. 357]

SEC. 357. ASSUMPTION OF LIABILITY.

[Sec. 357(a)]

(a) GENERAL RULE.—Except as provided in subsections (b) and (c), if—

(1) the taxpayer receives property which would be permitted to be received under section 351 or 361 without the recognition of gain if it were the sole consideration, and

(2) as part of the consideration, another party to the exchange assumes a liability of the taxpayer,

then such assumption shall not be treated as money or other property, and shall not prevent the exchange from being within the provisions of section 351 or 361, as the case may be.

[Sec. 357(b)]

(b) TAX AVOIDANCE PURPOSE.—

(1) IN GENERAL.—If, taking into consideration the nature of the liability and the circumstances in the light of which the arrangement for the assumption was made, it appears that the principal purpose of the taxpayer with respect to the assumption described in subsection (a)—

(A) was a purpose to avoid Federal income tax on the exchange, or

(B) if not such purpose, was not a bona fide business purpose, then such assumption (in the total amount of the liability assumed pursuant to such exchange) shall, for purposes of section 351 or 361 (as the case may be), be considered as money received by the taxpayer on the exchange.

(2) BURDEN OF PROOF.—In any suit or proceeding where the burden is on the taxpayer to prove such assumption is not to be treated as money received by the taxpayer, such burden shall not be considered as sustained unless the taxpayer sustains such burden by the clear preponderance of the evidence.

[Sec. 357(c)]

(c) LIABILITIES IN EXCESS OF BASIS.—

(1) IN GENERAL.—In the case of an exchange—

(A) to which section 351 applies, or

(B) to which section 361 applies by reason of a plan of reorganization within the meaning of section 368(a)(1)(D) with respect to which stock or securities of the corporation to which the assets are transferred are distributed in a transaction which qualifies under section 355,

if the sum of the amount of the liabilities assumed exceeds the total of the adjusted basis of the property transferred pursuant to such exchange, then such excess shall be considered as a gain from the sale or exchange of a capital asset or of property which is not a capital asset, as the case may be.

(2) EXCEPTIONS.—Paragraph (1) shall not apply to any exchange—

(A) to which subsection (b)(1) of this section applies, or

(B) which is pursuant to a plan of reorganization within the meaning of section 368(a)(1)(G) where no former shareholder of the transferor corporation receives any consideration for his stock.

(3) CERTAIN LIABILITIES EXCLUDED.—

(A) IN GENERAL.—If a taxpayer transfers, in an exchange to which section 351 applies, a liability the payment of which either—

(i) would give rise to a deduction, or

(ii) would be described in section 736(a),

then, for purposes of paragraph (1), the amount of such liability shall be excluded in determining the amount of liabilities assumed.

(B) EXCEPTION.—Subparagraph (A) shall not apply to any liability to the extent that the incurrence of the liability resulted in the creation of, or an increase in, the basis of any property.

[Sec. 357(d)]

(d) DETERMINATION OF AMOUNT OF LIABILITY ASSUMED.—

(1) IN GENERAL.—For purposes of this section, section 358(d), section 358(h), section 361(b)(3), section 362(d), section 368(a)(1)(C), and section 368(a)(2)(B), except as provided in regulations—

(A) a recourse liability (or portion thereof) shall be treated as having been assumed if, as determined on the basis of all facts and circumstances, the transferee has agreed to, and is expected to, satisfy such liability (or portion), whether or not the transferor has been relieved of such liability; and

(B) except to the extent provided in paragraph (2), a nonrecourse liability shall be treated as having been assumed by the transferee of any asset subject to such liability.

(2) EXCEPTION FOR NONRECOURSE LIABILITY.—The amount of the nonrecourse liability treated as described in paragraph (1)(B) shall be reduced by the lesser of—

(A) the amount of such liability which an owner of other assets not transferred to the transferee and also subject to such liability has agreed with the transferee to, and is expected to, satisfy, or

(B) the fair market value of such other assets (determined without regard to section 7701(g)).

(3) REGULATIONS.—The Secretary shall prescribe such regulations as may be necessary to carry out the purposes of this subsection and section 362(d). The Secretary may also prescribe regulations which provide that the manner in which a liability is treated as assumed under this subsection is applied, where appropriate, elsewhere in this title.

[Sec. 358]

SEC. 358. BASIS TO DISTRIBUTEES.

[Sec. 358(a)]

(a) GENERAL RULE.—In the case of an exchange to which section 351, 354, 355, 356, or 361 applies—

(1) NONRECOGNITION PROPERTY.—The basis of the property permitted to be received under such section without the recognition of gain or loss shall be the same as that of the property exchanged—

(A) decreased by—

(i) the fair market value of any other property (except money) received by the taxpayer,

(ii) the amount of any money received by the taxpayer, and

(iii) the amount of loss to the taxpayer which was recognized on such exchange, and

(B) increased by—

(i) the amount which was treated as a dividend, and

(ii) the amount of gain to the taxpayer which was recognized on such exchange (not including any portion of such gain which was treated as a dividend).

(2) OTHER PROPERTY.—The basis of any other property (except money) received by the taxpayer shall be its fair market value.

[Sec. 358(b)]

(b) ALLOCATION OF BASIS.—

(1) IN GENERAL.—Under regulations prescribed by the Secretary, the basis determined under subsection (a) (1) shall be allocated among the properties permitted to be received without the recognition of gain or loss.

(2) SPECIAL RULE FOR SECTION 355.—In the case of an exchange to which section 355 (or so much of section 356 as relates to section 355) applies, then in making the allocation under paragraph (1) of this subsection, there shall be taken into account not only the property so permitted to be received without the recognition of gain or loss, but also the stock or securities (if any) of the distributing corporation which are retained, and the allocation of basis shall be made among all such properties.

[Sec. 358(c)]

(c) SECTION 355 TRANSACTIONS WHICH ARE NOT EXCHANGES.—For purposes of this section, a distribution to which section 355 (or so much of section 356 as relates to section 355) applies shall be treated as an exchange, and for such purposes the stock and securities of the distributing corporation which are retained shall be treated as surrendered, and received back, in the exchange.

[Sec. 358(d)]

(d) ASSUMPTION OF LIABILITY.—

(1) IN GENERAL.—Where, as part of the consideration to the taxpayer, another party to the exchange assumed a liability of the taxpayer, such assumption shall, for purposes of this section, be treated as money received by the taxpayer on the exchange.

(2) EXCEPTION.—Paragraph (1) shall not apply to the amount of any liability excluded under section 357(c)(3).

[Sec. 358(e)]

(e) EXCEPTION.—This section shall not apply to property acquired by a corporation by the exchange of its stock or securities (or the stock or securities of a corporation which is in control of the acquiring corporation) as consideration in whole or in part for the transfer of the property to it.

[Sec. 358(f)]

(f) DEFINITION OF NONRECOGNITION PROPERTY IN CASE OF SECTION 361 EXCHANGE.—For purposes of this section, the property permitted to be received under section 361 without the recognition of gain or loss shall be treated as consisting only of stock or securities in another corporation a party to the reorganization.

[Sec. 358(g)]

(g) ADJUSTMENTS IN INTRAGROUP TRANSACTIONS INVOLVING SECTION 355.—In the case of a distribution to which section 355 (or so much of section 356 as relates to section 355) applies and which involves the distribution of stock from 1 member of an affiliated group (as defined in section 1504(a) without regard to subsection (b) thereof) to another member of such group, the Secretary may, notwithstanding any other provision of this section, provide adjustments to the adjusted basis of any stock which—

(1) is in a corporation which is a member of such group, and

(2) is held by another member of such group, to appropriately reflect the proper treatment of such distribution.

[Sec. 358(h)]

(h) SPECIAL RULES FOR ASSUMPTION OF LIABILITIES TO WHICH SUBSECTION (d) DOES NOT APPLY.—

(1) IN GENERAL.—If, after application of the other provisions of this section to an exchange or series of exchanges, the basis of property to which subsection (a)(1) applies exceeds the fair market value of such property, then such basis shall be reduced (but not below such fair market value) by the amount (determined as of the date of the exchange) of any liability—

(A) which is assumed by another person as part of the exchange, and

(B) with respect to which subsection (d)(1) does not apply to the assumption.

(2) EXCEPTIONS.—Except as provided by the Secretary, paragraph (1) shall not apply to any liability if—

(A) the trade or business with which the liability is associated is transferred to the person assuming the liability as part of the exchange, or

(B) substantially all of the assets with which the liability is associated are transferred to the person assuming the liability as part of the exchange.

(3) LIABILITY.—For purposes of this subsection, the term "liability" shall include any fixed or contingent obligation to make payment, without regard to whether the obligation is otherwise taken into account for purposes of this title.

Subpart C—Effects on Corporations

[Sec. 361]

SEC. 361. NONRECOGNITION OF GAIN OR LOSS TO CORPORATIONS; TREATMENT OF DISTRIBUTIONS.

[Sec. 361(a)]

(a) GENERAL RULE.—No gain or loss shall be recognized to a corporation if such corporation is a party to a reorganization and exchanges property, in pursuance of the plan of reorganization, solely for stock or securities in another corporation a party to the reorganization.

[Sec. 361(b)]

(b) EXCHANGES NOT SOLELY IN KIND.—

(1) GAIN.—If subsection (a) would apply to an exchange but for the fact that the property received in exchange consists not only of stock or securities permitted by subsection (a) to be received without the recognition of gain, but also of other property or money, then—

(A) PROPERTY DISTRIBUTED.—If the corporation receiving such other property or money distributes it in pursuance of the plan of reorganization, no gain to the corporation shall be recognized from the exchange, but

(B) PROPERTY NOT DISTRIBUTED.—If the corporation receiving such other property or money does not distribute it in pursuance of the plan of reorganization, the gain, if any, to the corporation shall be recognized.

The amount of gain recognized under subparagraph (B) shall not exceed the sum of the money and the fair market value of the other property so received which is not so distributed.

(2) LOSS.—If subsection (a) would apply to an exchange but for the fact that the property received in exchange consists not only of property permitted by subsection (a) to be received without the recognition of gain or loss, but also of other property or money, then no loss from the exchange shall be recognized.

(3) TREATMENT OF TRANSFERS TO CREDITORS.—For purposes of paragraph (1), any transfer of the other property or money received in the exchange by the corporation to its creditors in connection with the reorganization shall be treated as a distribution in pursuance of the plan of reorganization. The Secretary may prescribe such regulations as may be necessary to prevent avoidance of tax through abuse of the preceding sentence or subsection (c)(3). In the case of a reorganization described in section 368(a)(1)(D) with respect to which stock or securities of the corporation to which the assets are transferred are distributed in a transaction which qualifies under section 355, this paragraph shall apply only to the extent that the sum of the money and the fair market value of other property transferred to such creditors does not exceed the adjusted bases of such assets transferred (reduced by the amount of the liabilities assumed (within the meaning of section 357(c))).

[Sec. 361(c)]

(c) TREATMENT OF DISTRIBUTIONS.—

(1) IN GENERAL.—Except as provided in paragraph (2), no gain or loss shall be recognized to a corporation a party to a reorganization on the distribution to its shareholders of property in pursuance of the plan of reorganization.

(2) DISTRIBUTIONS OF APPRECIATED PROPERTY.—

(A) IN GENERAL.—If—

(i) in a distribution referred to in paragraph (1), the corporation distributes property other than qualified property, and

(ii) the fair market value of such property exceeds its adjusted basis (in the hands of the distributing corporation),

then gain shall be recognized to the distributing corporation as if such property were sold to the distributee at its fair market value.

(B) QUALIFIED PROPERTY.—For purposes of this subsection, the term "qualified property" means—

(i) any stock in (or right to acquire stock in) the distributing corporation or obligation of the distributing corporation, or

(ii) any stock in (or right to acquire stock in) another corporation which is a party to the reorganization or obligation of another corporation which is such a party if such stock (or right) or obligation is received by the distributing corporation in the exchange.

(C) TREATMENT OF LIABILITIES.—If any property distributed in the distribution referred to in paragraph (1) is subject to a liability or the shareholder assumes a liability of the distributing corporation in connection with the distribution, then, for purposes of subparagraph (A), the fair market value of such property shall be treated as not less than the amount of such liability.

(3) TREATMENT OF CERTAIN TRANSFERS TO CREDITORS.—For purposes of this subsection, any transfer of qualified property by the corporation to its creditors in connection with the reorganization shall be treated as a distribution to its shareholders pursuant to the plan of reorganization.

(4) COORDINATION WITH OTHER PROVISIONS.—Section 311 and subpart B of part II of this subchapter shall not apply to any distribution referred to in paragraph (1).

(5) CROSS REFERENCE.—

For provision providing for recognition of gain in certain distributions, see section 355(d).

[Sec. 362]

SEC. 362. BASIS TO CORPORATIONS.

[Sec. 362(a)]

(a) PROPERTY ACQUIRED BY ISSUANCE OF STOCK OR AS PAID-IN SURPLUS.—If property was acquired by a corporation—

(1) in connection with a transaction to which section 351 (relating to transfer of property to corporation controlled by transferor) applies, or

(2) as paid-in surplus or as a contribution to capital,

then the basis shall be the same as it would be in the hands of the transferor, increased in the amount of gain recognized to the transferor on such transfer.

[Sec. 362(b)]

(b) TRANSFERS TO CORPORATIONS.—If property was acquired by a corporation in connection with a reorganization to which this part applies, then the basis shall be the same as it would be in the hands of the transferor, increased in the amount of gain recognized to the transferor on such transfer. This subsection shall not apply if the property acquired consists of stock or securities in a corporation a party to the reorganization, unless acquired by the exchange of stock or securities of the transferee (or of a corporation which is in control of the transferee) as the consideration in whole or in part for the transfer.

[Sec. 362(c)]

(c) SPECIAL RULE FOR CERTAIN CONTRIBUTIONS TO CAPITAL.—

(1) PROPERTY OTHER THAN MONEY.—Notwithstanding subsection (a)(2), if property other than money—

(A) is acquired by a corporation, as a contribution to capital, and

(B) is not contributed by a shareholder as such,

then the basis of such property shall be zero.

(2) MONEY.—Notwithstanding subsection (a)(2), if money—

(A) is received by a corporation, as a contribution to capital, and

(B) is not contributed by a shareholder as such,

then the basis of any property acquired with such money during the 12-month period beginning on the day the contribution is received shall be reduced by the amount of such contribution. The excess (if any) of the amount of such contribution over the amount of the reduction under the preceding sentence shall be applied to the reduction (as of the last day of the period specified in the preceding sentence) of the basis of any other property held by the taxpayer. The particular properties to which the reductions required by this paragraph shall be allocated shall be determined under regulations prescribed by the Secretary.

(3) [Repealed.]

[Sec. 362(d)]

(d) LIMITATION ON BASIS INCREASE ATTRIBUTABLE TO ASSUMPTION OF LIABILITY.—

(1) IN GENERAL.—In no event shall the basis of any property be increased under subsection (a) or (b) above the fair market value of such property (determined without regard to section 7701(g)) by reason of any gain recognized to the transferor as a result of the assumption of a liability.

(2) TREATMENT OF GAIN NOT SUBJECT TO TAX.—Except as provided in regulations, if—

(A) gain is recognized to the transferor as a result of an assumption of a nonrecourse liability by a transferee which is also secured by assets not transferred to such transferee; and

(B) no person is subject to tax under this title on such gain,

then, for purposes of determining basis under subsections (a) and (b), the amount of gain recognized by the transferor as a result of the assumption of the liability shall be determined as if the liability assumed by the transferee equaled such transferee's ratable portion of such liability determined on the basis of the relative fair market values (determined without regard to section 7701(g)) of all of the assets subject to such liability.

[Sec. 362(e)]

(e) LIMITATIONS ON BUILT-IN LOSSES.—

(1) LIMITATION ON IMPORTATION OF BUILT-IN LOSSES.—

(A) IN GENERAL.—If in any transaction described in subsection (a) or (b) there would (but for this subsection) be an importation of a net built-in loss, the basis of each property described in subparagraph (B) which is acquired in such transaction shall (notwithstanding subsections (a) and (b)) be its fair market value immediately after such transaction.

(B) PROPERTY DESCRIBED.—For purposes of subparagraph (A), property is described in this subparagraph if—

(i) gain or loss with respect to such property is not subject to tax under this subtitle in the hands of the transferor immediately before the transfer, and

(ii) gain or loss with respect to such property is subject to such tax in the hands of the transferee immediately after such transfer.

In any case in which the transferor is a partnership, the preceding sentence shall be applied by treating each partner in such partnership as holding such partner's proportionate share of the property of such partnership.

(C) IMPORTATION OF NET BUILT-IN LOSS.—For purposes of subparagraph (A), there is an importation of a net built-in loss in a transaction if the transferee's aggregate adjusted bases of property described in subparagraph (B) which is transferred in such transaction would (but for this paragraph) exceed the fair market value of such property immediately after such transaction.

(2) LIMITATION ON TRANSFER OF BUILT-IN LOSSES IN SECTION 351 TRANSACTIONS.—

(A) IN GENERAL.—If—

(i) property is transferred by a transferor in any transaction which is described in subsection (a) and which is not described in paragraph (1) of this subsection, and

(ii) the transferee's aggregate adjusted bases of such property so transferred would (but for this paragraph) exceed the fair market value of such property immediately after such transaction,

then, notwithstanding subsection (a), the transferee's aggregate adjusted bases of the property so transferred shall not exceed the fair market value of such property immediately after such transaction.

(B) ALLOCATION OF BASIS REDUCTION.—The aggregate reduction in basis by reason of subparagraph (A) shall be allocated among the property so transferred in proportion to their respective built-in losses immediately before the transaction.

(C) ELECTION TO APPLY LIMITATION TO TRANSFEROR'S STOCK BASIS.—

(i) IN GENERAL.—If the transferor and transferee of a transaction described in subparagraph (A) both elect the application of this subparagraph—

(I) subparagraph (A) shall not apply, and

(II) the transferor's basis in the stock received for property to which subparagraph (A) does not apply by reason of the election shall not exceed its fair market value immediately after the transfer.

(ii) ELECTION.—Any election under clause (i) shall be made at such time and in such form and manner as the Secretary may prescribe, and, once made, shall be irrevocable.

Subpart D—Special Rule; Definitions

[Sec. 368]

SEC. 368. DEFINITIONS RELATING TO CORPORATE REORGANIZATIONS.

[Sec. 368(a)]

(a) REORGANIZATION.—

(1) IN GENERAL.—For purposes of parts I and II and this part, the term "reorganization" means—

(A) a statutory merger or consolidation;

(B) the acquisition by one corporation, in exchange solely for all or a part of its voting stock (or in exchange solely for all or a part of the voting stock of a corporation which is in control of the acquiring corporation), of stock of another corporation if, immediately after the acquisition, the acquiring corporation has control of such other corporation (whether or not such acquiring corporation had control immediately before the acquisition);

(C) the acquisition by one corporation, in exchange solely for all or a part of its voting stock (or in exchange solely for all or a part of the voting stock of a corporation which is in control of the acquiring corporation), of substantially all of the properties of another corporation, but in determining whether the exchange is solely for stock the assumption by the acquiring corporation of a liability of the other shall be disregarded;

(D) a transfer by a corporation of all or a part of its assets to another corporation if immediately after the transfer the transferor, or one or more of its shareholders (including persons who were shareholders immediately before the transfer), or any combination thereof, is in control of the corporation to which the assets are transferred; but only if, in pursuance of the plan, stock or securities of the corporation to which the assets are transferred are distributed in a transaction which qualifies under section 354, 355, or 356;

(E) a recapitalization;

(F) a mere change in identity, form, or place of organization of one corporation, however effected; or

(G) a transfer by a corporation of all or part of its assets to another corporation in a title 11 or similar case; but only if, in pursuance of the plan, stock or securities of the corporation to which the assets are transferred are distributed in a transaction which qualifies under section 354, 355, or 356.

(2) SPECIAL RULES RELATING TO PARAGRAPH (1).—

(A) REORGANIZATIONS DESCRIBED IN BOTH PARAGRAPH (1)(C) AND PARAGRAPH (1)(D).—If a transaction is described in both paragraph (1)(C) and paragraph (1)(D), then, for purposes of this subchapter (other than for purposes of subparagraph (C)), such transaction shall be treated as described only in paragraph (1)(D).

(B) ADDITIONAL CONSIDERATION IN CERTAIN PARAGRAPH (1)(C) CASES.—If—

(i) one corporation acquires substantially all of the properties of another corporation,

(ii) the acquisition would qualify under paragraph (1)(C) but for the fact that the acquiring corporation exchanges money or other property in addition to voting stock, and

(iii) the acquiring corporation acquires, solely for voting stock described in paragraph (1)(C), property of the other corporation having a fair market value which is at least 80 percent of the fair market value of all of the property of the other corporation,

then such acquisition shall (subject to subparagraph (A) of this paragraph) be treated as qualifying under paragraph (1)(C). Solely for the purpose of determining whether clause (iii) of the preceding sentence applies, the amount of any liability assumed by the acquiring corporation shall be treated as money paid for the property.

(C) TRANSFERS OF ASSETS OR STOCK TO SUBSIDIARIES IN CERTAIN PARAGRAPH (1)(A), (1)(B), (1)(C), AND (1)(G) CASES.—A transaction otherwise qualifying under paragraph (1)(A), (1)(B), or (1)(C) shall not be disqualified by reason of the fact that part or all of the assets or stock which were acquired in the transaction are transferred to a corporation controlled by the corporation acquiring such assets or stock. A similar rule shall apply to a transaction otherwise qualifying under paragraph (1)(G) where the requirements of subparagraphs (A) and (B) of section 354(b)(1) are met with respect to the acquisition of the assets.

(D) USE OF STOCK OF CONTROLLING CORPORATION IN PARAGRAPH (1)(A) AND (1)(G) CASES.—The acquisition by one corporation, in exchange for stock of a corporation (referred to in this subparagraph as "controlling corporation") which is in control of the acquiring corporation, of substantially all of the properties of another corporation shall not disqualify a transaction under paragraph (1)(A) or (1)(G) if—

(i) no stock of the acquiring corporation is used in the transaction, and

(ii) in the case of a transaction under paragraph (1)(A), such transaction would have qualified under paragraph (1)(A) had the merger been into the controlling corporation.

(E) STATUTORY MERGER USING VOTING STOCK OF CORPORATION CONTROLLING MERGED CORPORATION.—A transaction otherwise qualifying under paragraph (1)(A) shall not be disqualified by reason of the fact that stock of a corporation (referred to in this subparagraph as the "controlling corporation") which before the merger was in control of the merged corporation is used in the transaction, if—

(i) after the transaction, the corporation surviving the merger holds substantially all of its properties and of the properties of the merged corporation (other than stock of the controlling corporation distributed in the transaction); and

(ii) in the transaction, former shareholders of the surviving corporation exchanged, for an amount of voting stock of the controlling corporation, an amount of stock in the surviving corporation which constitutes control of such corporation.

* * *

(G) DISTRIBUTION REQUIREMENT FOR PARAGRAPH (1)(C).—

(i) IN GENERAL.—A transaction shall fail to meet the requirements of paragraph (1)(C) unless the acquired corporation distributes the stock, securities, and other properties it receives, as well as its other properties, in pursuance of the plan of reorganization. For purposes of the preceding sentence, if the acquired corporation is liquidated pursuant to the plan of reorganization, any distribution to its creditors in connection with such liquidation shall be treated as pursuant to the plan of reorganization.

(ii) EXCEPTION.—The Secretary may waive the application of clause (i) to any transaction subject to any conditions the Secretary may prescribe.

(H) SPECIAL RULES FOR DETERMINING WHETHER CERTAIN TRANSACTIONS ARE QUALIFIED UNDER PARAGRAPH (1)(D).—For purposes of determining whether a transaction qualifies under paragraph (1)(D)—

(i) in the case of a transaction with respect to which the requirements of subparagraphs (A) and (B) of section 354(b)(1) are met, the term "control" has the meaning given such term by section 304(c), and

(ii) in the case of a transaction with respect to which the requirements of section 355 (or so much of section 356 as relates to section 355) are met, the fact that the shareholders of the distributing corporation dispose of part or all of the distributed stock, or the fact that the corporation whose stock was distributed issues additional stock, shall not be taken into account.

* * *

[Sec. 368(b)]

(b) PARTY TO A REORGANIZATION.—For purposes of this part, the term "a party to a reorganization" includes—

(1) a corporation resulting from a reorganization, and

(2) both corporations, in the case of a reorganization resulting from the acquisition by one corporation of stock or properties of another.

In the case of a reorganization qualifying under paragraph (1)(B) or (1)(C) of subsection (a), if the stock exchanged for the stock or properties is stock of a corporation which is in control of the acquiring corporation, the term "a party to a reorganization" includes the corporation so controlling the acquiring corporation. In the case of a reorganization qualifying under paragraph (1)(A), (1)(B), (1)(C), or (1)(G) of subsection (a) by reason of paragraph (2)(C) of subsection (a), the term "a party to a reorganization" includes the corporation controlling the corporation to which the acquired assets or stock are transferred. In the case of a reorganization qualifying under paragraph (1)(A) or (1)(G) of subsection (a) by reason of paragraph (2)(D) of that subsection, the term "a party to a reorganization" includes the controlling corporation referred to in such paragraph (2)(D). In the case of a reorganization qualifying under subsection (a)(1)(A) by reason of subsection (a)(2)(E), the term "party to a reorganization" includes the controlling corporation referred to in subsection (a)(2)(E).

[Sec. 368(c)]

(c) CONTROL DEFINED.—For purposes of part I (other than section 304), part II, this part, and part V, the term "control" means the ownership of stock possessing at least 80 percent of the total combined voting power of all classes of stock entitled to vote and at least 80 percent of the total number of shares of all other classes of stock of the corporation.

PART V—CARRYOVERS

[Sec. 381]

SEC. 381. CARRYOVERS IN CERTAIN CORPORATE ACQUISITIONS.

[Sec. 381(a)]

(a) GENERAL RULE.—In the case of the acquisition of assets of a corporation by another corporation—

(1) in a distribution to such other corporation to which section 332 (relating to liquidations of subsidiaries) applies; or

(2) in a transfer to which section 361 (relating to nonrecognition of gain or loss to corporations) applies, but only if the transfer is in connection with a reorganization described in subparagraph (A), (C), (D), (F), or (G) of section 368(a)(1),

the acquiring corporation shall succeed to and take into account, as of the close of the day of distribution or transfer, the items described in subsection (c) of the distributor or transferor corporation, subject to the conditions and limitations specified in subsections (b) and (c). For purposes of the preceding sentence, a reorganization shall be treated as meeting the requirements of subparagraph (D) or (G) of section 368(a)(1) only if the requirements of subparagraphs (A) and (B) of section 354(b)(1) are met.

[Sec. 381(b)]

(b) OPERATING RULES.—Except in the case of an acquisition in connection with a reorganization described in subparagraph (F) of section 368 (a) (1)—

(1) The taxable year of the distributor or transferor corporation shall end on the date of distribution or transfer.

(2) For purposes of this section, the date of distribution or transfer shall be the day on which the distribution or transfer is completed; except that, under regulations prescribed by the Secretary, the date when substantially all of the property has been distributed or transferred may be used if the distributor or transferor corporation ceases all operations, other than liquidating activities, after such date.

(3) The corporation acquiring property in a distribution or transfer described in subsection (a) shall not be entitled to carry back a net operating loss or a net capital loss for a taxable year ending after the date of distribution or transfer to a taxable year of the distributor or transferor corporation.

[Sec. 381(c)]

(c) ITEMS OF THE DISTRIBUTOR OR TRANSFEROR CORPORATION.—The items referred to in subsection (a) are:

(1) NET OPERATING LOSS CARRYOVERS.—The net operating loss carryovers determined under section 172, subject to the following conditions and limitations:

(A) The taxable year of the acquiring corporation to which the net operating loss carryovers of the distributor or transferor corporation are first carried shall be the first taxable year ending after the date of distribution or transfer.

(B) In determining the net operating loss deduction, the portion of such deduction attributable to the net operating loss carryovers of the distributor or transferor corporation to the first taxable year of the acquiring corporation ending after the date of distribution or transfer shall be limited to an amount which bears the same ratio to the taxable income (determined without regard to a net operating loss deduction) of the acquiring corporation in such taxable year as the number of days in the taxable year after the date of distribution or transfer bears to the total number of days in the taxable year.

(C) For the purpose of determining the amount of the net operating loss carryovers under section 172 (b) (2), a net operating loss for a taxable year (hereinafter in this subparagraph referred to as the "loss year") of a distributor or transferor corporation which ends on or before the end of a loss year of the acquiring corporation shall be considered to be a net operating loss for a year prior to such loss year of the acquiring corporation. For the same purpose, the taxable income for a "prior taxable year" (as the term is used in section 172 (b) (2)) shall be computed as provided in such section; except that, if the date of distribution or transfer is on a day other than the last day of a taxable year of the acquiring corporation—

(i) such taxable year shall (for the purpose of this subparagraph only) be considered to be 2 taxable years (hereinafter in this subparagraph referred to as the "pre-acquisition part year" and the "post-acquisition part year");

(ii) the pre-acquisition part year shall begin on the same day as such taxable year begins and shall end on the date of distribution or transfer;

(iii) the post-acquisition part year shall begin on the day following the date of distribution or transfer and shall end on the same day as the end of such taxable year;

(iv) the taxable income for such taxable year (computed with the modifications specified in section 172 (b) (2) (A) but without a net operating loss deduction) shall be divided between the pre-acquisition part year and the post-acquisition part year in proportion to the number of days in each;

(v) the net operating loss deduction for the pre-acquisition part year shall be determined as provided in section 172 (b) (2) (B), but without regard to a net operating loss year of the distributor or transferor corporation; and

(vi) the net operating loss deduction for the post-acquisition part year shall be determined as provided in section 172 (b) (2) (B).

(2) EARNINGS AND PROFITS.—In the case of a distribution or transfer described in subsection (a)—

(A) the earnings and profits or deficit in earnings and profits, as the case may be, of the distributor or transferor corporation shall, subject to subparagraph (B), be deemed to have been received or incurred by the acquiring corporation as of the close of the date of the distribution or transfer; and

(B) a deficit in earnings and profits of the distributor, transferor, or acquiring corporation shall be used only to offset earnings and profits accumulated after the date of transfer. For this purpose, the earnings and profits for the taxable year of the acquiring corporation in which the distribution or transfer occurs shall be deemed to have been accumulated after such distribution or transfer in an amount which bears the same ratio to the undistributed earnings and profits of the acquiring corporation for such taxable year (computed without regard to any earnings and profits received from the distributor or transferor corporation, as described in subparagraph (A) of this paragraph) as the number of days in the taxable year after the date of distribution or transfer bears to the total number of days in the taxable year.

(3) CAPITAL LOSS CARRYOVER.—The capital loss carryover determined under section 1212, subject to the following conditions and limitations:

(A) The taxable year of the acquiring corporation to which the capital loss carryover of the distributor or transferor corporation is first carried shall be the first taxable year ending after the date of distribution or transfer.

(B) The capital loss carryover shall be a short-term capital loss in the taxable year determined under subparagraph (A) but shall be limited to an amount which bears the same ratio to the capital gain net income (determined without regard to a short-term capital loss attributable to capital loss carryover), if any, of the acquiring corporation in such taxable year as the number of days in the taxable year after the date of distribution or transfer bears to the total number of days in the taxable year.

(C) For purposes of determining the amount of such capital loss carryover to taxable years following the taxable year determined under subparagraph (A), the capital gain net income in the taxable year determined under subparagraph (A) shall be considered to be an amount equal to the amount determined under subparagraph (B).

(4) METHOD OF ACCOUNTING.—The acquiring corporation shall use the method of accounting used by the distributor or transferor corporation on the date of distribution or transfer unless different methods were used by several distributor or transferor corporations or by a distributor or transferor corporation and the acquiring corporation. If different methods were used, the acquiring corporation shall use the method or combination of methods of computing taxable income adopted pursuant to regulations prescribed by the Secretary.

(5) INVENTORIES.—In any case in which inventories are received by the acquiring corporation, such inventories shall be taken by such corporation (in determining its income) on the same basis on which such inventories were taken by the distributor or transferor corporation, unless different methods were used by several distributor or transferor corporations or by a distributor or transferor corporation and the acquiring corporation. If different methods were used, the acquiring corporation shall use the method or combination of methods of taking inventory adopted pursuant to regulations prescribed by the Secretary.

(6) METHOD OF COMPUTING DEPRECIATION ALLOWANCE.—The acquiring corporation shall be treated as the distributor or transferor corporation for purposes of computing the depreciation allowance under sections 167 and 168 on property acquired in a distribution or transfer with respect to so much of the basis in the hands of the acquiring corporation as does not exceed the adjusted basis in the hands of the distributor or transferor corporation.

(8) INSTALLMENT METHOD.—If the acquiring corporation acquires installment obligations (the income from which the distributor or transferor corporation reports on the installment basis under section 453) the acquiring corporation shall, for purposes of section 453, be treated as if it were the distributor or transferor corporation.

(9) AMORTIZATION OF BOND DISCOUNT OR PREMIUM.—If the acquiring corporation assumes liability for bonds of the distributor or transferor corporation issued at a discount or premium, the acquiring corporation shall be treated as the distributor or transferor corporation after the date of distribution or transfer for purposes of determining the amount of amortization allowable or includible with respect to such discount or premium.

(10) TREATMENT OF CERTAIN MINING DEVELOPMENT AND EXPLORATION EXPENSES OF DISTRIBUTOR OR TRANSFEROR CORPORATION.—The acquiring corporation shall be entitled to deduct, as if it were the distributor or transferor corporation, expenses deferred under section 616 (relating to certain development expenditures) if the distributor or transferor corporation has so elected.

(11) CONTRIBUTIONS TO PENSION PLANS, EMPLOYEES' ANNUITY PLANS, AND STOCK BONUS AND PROFIT-SHARING PLANS.—The acquiring corporation shall be considered to be the distributor or transferor corporation after the date of distribution or transfer for the purpose of determining the amounts deductible under section 404 with respect to pension plans, employees' annuity plans, and stock bonus and profit-sharing plans.

(12) RECOVERY OF TAX BENEFIT ITEMS.—If the acquiring corporation is entitled to the recovery of any amounts previously deducted by (or allowable as credits to) the distributor or transferor corporation, the acquiring corporation shall succeed to the treatment under section 111 which would apply to such amounts in the hands of the distributor or transferor corporation.

(13) INVOLUNTARY CONVERSIONS UNDER SECTION 1033.—The acquiring corporation shall be treated as the distributor or transferor corporation after the date of distribution or transfer for purposes of applying section 1033.

(14) DIVIDEND CARRYOVER TO PERSONAL HOLDING COMPANY.—The dividend carryover (described in section 564) to taxable years ending after the date of distribution or transfer.

(16) CERTAIN OBLIGATIONS OF DISTRIBUTOR OR TRANSFEROR CORPORATION.—If the acquiring corporation—

(A) assumes an obligation of the distributor or transferor corporation which, after the date of the distribution or transfer, gives rise to a liability, and

(B) such liability, if paid or accrued by the distributor or transferor corporation, would have been deductible in computing its taxable income,

the acquiring corporation shall be entitled to deduct such items when paid or accrued, as the case may be, as if such corporation were the distributor or transferor corporation. This paragraph shall not apply if such obligations are reflected in the amount of stock, securities, or property transferred by the acquiring corporation to the transferor corporation for the property of the transferor corporation.

(17) DEFICIENCY DIVIDEND OF PERSONAL HOLDING COMPANY.—If the acquiring corporation pays a deficiency dividend (as defined in section 547(d)) with respect to the distributor or transferor corporation, such distributor or transferor corporation shall, with respect to such payments, be entitled to the deficiency dividend deduction provided in section 547.

(18) PERCENTAGE DEPLETION ON EXTRACTION OF ORES OR MINERALS FROM THE WASTE OR RESIDUE OF PRIOR MINING.—The acquiring corporation shall be considered to be the distributor or transferor corporation for the purpose of determining the applicability of section 613(c)(3) (relating to extraction of ores or minerals from the ground).

(19) CHARITABLE CONTRIBUTIONS IN EXCESS OF PRIOR YEARS' LIMITATIONS.—Contributions made in the taxable year ending on the date of distribution or transfer and the 4 prior taxable years by the distributor or transferor corporation in excess of the amount deductible under section 170(b)(2) for such taxable years shall be deductible by the acquiring corporation for its taxable years which begin after the date of distribution or transfer, subject to the limitations imposed in section 170(b)(2). In applying the preceding sentence, each taxable year of the distributor or transferor corporation beginning on or before the date of distribution or transfer shall be treated as a prior taxable year with reference to the acquiring corporation's taxable years beginning after such date.

* * *

(25) CREDIT UNDER SECTION 53.—The acquiring corporation shall take into account (to the extent proper to carry out the purposes of this section 53, and under such regulations as may be prescribed by the Secretary) the items required to be taken into account for purposes of section 53 in respect of the distributor or transferor corporation.

* * *

[Sec. 382]

SEC. 382. LIMITATION ON NET OPERATING LOSS CARRYFORWARDS AND CERTAIN BUILT-IN LOSSES FOLLOWING OWNERSHIP CHANGE.

[Sec. 382(a)]

(a) GENERAL RULE.—The amount of the taxable income of any new loss corporation for any post-change year which may be offset by pre-change losses shall not exceed the section 382 limitation for such year.

[Sec. 382(b)]

(b) SECTION 382 LIMITATION.—For purposes of this section—

(1) IN GENERAL.—Except as otherwise provided in this section, the section 382 limitation for any post-change year is an amount equal to—

(A) the value of the old loss corporation, multiplied by

(B) the long-term tax-exempt rate.

(2) CARRYFORWARD OF UNUSED LIMITATION.—If the section 382 limitation for any post-change year exceeds the taxable income of the new loss corporation for such year which was offset by pre-change losses, the section 382 limitation for the next post-change year shall be increased by the amount of such excess.

(3) SPECIAL RULE FOR POST-CHANGE YEAR WHICH INCLUDES CHANGE DATE.—In the case of any post-change year which includes the change date—

(A) LIMITATION DOES NOT APPLY TO TAXABLE INCOME BEFORE CHANGE.—Subsection (a) shall not apply to the portion of the taxable income for such year which is allocable to the period in such year on or before the change date. Except as provided in subsection (h)(5) and in regulations, taxable income shall be allocated ratably to each day in the year.

(B) LIMITATION FOR PERIOD AFTER CHANGE.—For purposes of applying the limitation of subsection (a) to the remainder of the taxable income for such year, the section 382 limitation shall be an amount which bears the same ratio to such limitation (determined without regard to this paragraph) as—

(i) the number of days in such year after the change date, bears to

(ii) the total number of days in such year.

[Sec. 382(c)]

(c) CARRYFORWARDS DISALLOWED IF CONTINUITY OF BUSINESS REQUIREMENTS NOT MET.—

(1) IN GENERAL.—Except as provided in paragraph (2), if the new loss corporation does not continue the business enterprise of the old loss corporation at all times during the 2-year period beginning on the change date, the section 382 limitation for any post-change year shall be zero.

(2) EXCEPTION FOR CERTAIN GAINS.—The section 382 limitation for any post-change year shall not be less than the sum of—

(A) any increase in such limitation under—

(i) subsection (h)(1)(A) for recognized built-in gains for such year, and

(ii) subsection (h)(1)(C) for gain recognized by reason of an election under section 338, plus

(B) any increase in such limitation under subsection (b)(2) for amounts described in subparagraph (A) which are carried forward to such year.

[Sec. 382(d)]

(d) PRE-CHANGE LOSS AND POST-CHANGE YEAR.—For purposes of this section—

(1) PRE-CHANGE LOSS.—The term "pre-change loss" means—

(A) any net operating loss carryforward of the old loss corporation to the taxable year ending with the ownership change or in which the change date occurs, and

(B) the net operating loss of the old loss corporation for the taxable year in which the ownership change occurs to the extent such loss is allocable to the period in such year on or before the change date.

Except as provided in subsection (h)(5) and in regulations, the net operating loss shall, for purposes of subparagraph (B), be allocated ratably to each day in the year.

(2) POST-CHANGE YEAR.—The term "post-change year" means any taxable year ending after the change date.

(3) APPLICATION TO CARRYFORWARD OF DISALLOWED INTEREST.—The term "pre-change loss" shall include any carryover of disallowed interest described in section 163(j)(2) under rules similar to the rules of paragraph (1).

[Sec. 382(e)]

(e) VALUE OF OLD LOSS CORPORATION.—For purposes of this section—

(1) IN GENERAL.—Except as otherwise provided in this subsection, the value of the old loss corporation is the value of the stock of such corporation (including any stock described in section 1504(a)(4)) immediately before the ownership change.

(2) SPECIAL RULE IN THE CASE OF REDEMPTION OR OTHER CORPORATE CONTRACTION.—If a redemption or other corporate contraction occurs in connection with an ownership change, the value under paragraph (1) shall be determined after taking such redemption or other corporate contraction into account.

(3) TREATMENT OF FOREIGN CORPORATIONS.—Except as otherwise provided in regulations, in determining the value of any old loss corporation which is a foreign corporation, there shall be taken into account only items treated as connected with the conduct of a trade or business in the United States.

[Sec. 382(f)]

(f) LONG-TERM TAX-EXEMPT RATE.—For purposes of this section—

(1) IN GENERAL.—The long-term tax-exempt rate shall be the highest of the adjusted Federal long-term rates in effect for any month in the 3-calendar-month period ending with the calendar month in which the change date occurs.

(2) ADJUSTED FEDERAL LONG-TERM RATE.—For purposes of paragraph (1), the term "adjusted Federal long-term rate" means the Federal long-term rate determined under section 1274(d), except that—

(A) paragraphs (2) and (3) thereof shall not apply, and

(B) such rate shall be properly adjusted for differences between rates on long-term taxable and tax-exempt obligations.

[Sec. 382(g)]

(g) OWNERSHIP CHANGE.—For purposes of this section—

(1) IN GENERAL.—There is an ownership change if, immediately after any owner shift involving a 5-percent shareholder or any equity structure shift—

(A) the percentage of the stock of the loss corporation owned by 1 or more 5-percent shareholders has increased by more than 50 percentage points over

(B) the lowest percentage of stock of the loss corporation (or any predecessor corporation) owned by such shareholders at any time during the testing period.

(2) OWNER SHIFT INVOLVING 5-PERCENT SHAREHOLDER.—There is an owner shift involving a 5-percent shareholder if—

(A) there is any change in the respective ownership of stock of a corporation, and

(B) such change affects the percentage of stock of such corporation owned by any person who is a 5-percent shareholder before or after such change.

(3) EQUITY STRUCTURE SHIFT DEFINED.—

(A) IN GENERAL.—The term "equity structure shift" means any reorganization (within the meaning of section 368). Such term shall not include—

(i) any reorganization described in subparagraph (D) or (G) of section 368(a)(1) unless the requirements of section 354(b)(1) are met, and

(ii) any reorganization described in subparagraph (F) of section 368(a)(1).

(B) TAXABLE REORGANIZATION-TYPE TRANSACTIONS, ETC.—To the extent provided in regulations, the term "equity structure shift" includes taxable reorganization-type transactions, public offerings, and similar transactions.

(4) SPECIAL RULES FOR APPLICATION OF SUBSECTION.—

(A) TREATMENT OF LESS THAN 5-PERCENT SHAREHOLDERS.—Except as provided in subparagraphs (B)(i) and (C), in determining whether an ownership change has occurred, all stock owned by shareholders of a corporation who are not 5-percent shareholders of such corporation shall be treated as stock owned by 1 5-percent shareholder of such corporation.

(B) COORDINATION WITH EQUITY STRUCTURE SHIFTS.—For purposes of determining whether an equity structure shift (or subsequent transaction) is an ownership change—

(i) LESS THAN 5-PERCENT SHAREHOLDERS.—Subparagraph (A) shall be applied separately with respect to each group of shareholders (immediately before such equity structure shift) of each corporation which was a party to the reorganization involved in such equity structure shift.

(ii) ACQUISITIONS OF STOCK.—Unless a different proportion is established, acquisitions of stock after such equity structure shift shall be treated as being made proportionately from all shareholders immediately before such acquisition.

(C) COORDINATION WITH OTHER OWNER SHIFTS.—Except as provided in regulations, rules similar to the rules of subparagraph (B) shall apply in determining whether there has been an owner shift involving a 5-percent shareholder and whether such shift (or subsequent transaction) results in an ownership change.

(D) TREATMENT OF WORTHLESS STOCK.—If any stock held by a 50-percent shareholder is treated by such shareholder as becoming worthless during any taxable year of such shareholder and such stock is held by such shareholder as of the close of such taxable year, for purposes of determining whether an ownership change occurs after the close of such taxable year, such shareholder—

(i) shall be treated as having acquired such stock on the 1st day of his 1st succeeding taxable year, and

(ii) shall not be treated as having owned such stock during any prior period.

For purposes of the preceding sentence, the term "50-percent shareholder" means any person owning 50 percent or more of the stock of the corporation at any time during the 3-year period ending on the last day of the taxable year with respect to which the stock was so treated.

[Sec. 382(h)]

(h) SPECIAL RULES FOR BUILT-IN GAINS AND LOSSES AND SECTION 338 GAINS.—For purposes of this section—

(1) IN GENERAL.—

(A) NET UNREALIZED BUILT-IN GAIN.—

(i) IN GENERAL.—If the old loss corporation has a net unrealized built-in gain, the section 382 limitation for any recognition period taxable year shall be increased by the recognized built-in gains for such taxable year.

(ii) LIMITATION.—The increase under clause (i) for any recognition period taxable year shall not exceed—

(I) the net unrealized built-in gain, reduced by

(II) recognized built-in gains for prior years ending in the recognition period.

(B) NET UNREALIZED BUILT-IN LOSS.—

(i) IN GENERAL.—If the old loss corporation has a net unrealized built-in loss, the recognized built-in loss for any recognition period taxable year shall be subject to limitation under this section in the same manner as if such loss were a pre-change loss.

(ii) LIMITATION.—Clause (i) shall apply to recognized built-in losses for any recognition period taxable year only to the extent such losses do not exceed—

(I) the net unrealized built-in loss, reduced by

(II) recognized built-in losses for prior taxable years ending in the recognition period.

(C) SPECIAL RULES FOR CERTAIN SECTION 338 GAINS.—If an election under section 338 is made in connection with an ownership change and the net unrealized built-in gain is zero by reason of paragraph (3)(B), then, with respect to such change, the section 382 limitation for the post-change year in which gain is recognized by reason of such election shall be increased by the lesser of—

(i) the recognized built-in gains by reason of such election, or

(ii) the net unrealized built-in gain (determined without regard to paragraph (3)(B)).

(2) RECOGNIZED BUILT-IN GAIN AND LOSS.—

(A) RECOGNIZED BUILT-IN GAIN.—The term "recognized built-in gain" means any gain recognized during the recognition period on the disposition of any asset to the extent the new loss corporation establishes that—

(i) such asset was held by the old loss corporation immediately before the change date, and

(ii) such gain does not exceed the excess of—

(I) the fair market value of such asset on the change date, over

(II) the adjusted basis of such asset on such date.

(B) RECOGNIZED BUILT-IN LOSS.—The term "recognized built-in loss" means any loss recognized during the recognition period on the disposition of any asset except to the extent the new loss corporation establishes that—

(i) such asset was not held by the old loss corporation immediately before the change date, or

(ii) such loss exceeds the excess of—

(I) the adjusted basis of such asset on the change date, over

(II) the fair market value of such asset on such date.

Such term includes any amount allowable as depreciation, amortization, or depletion for any period within the recognition period except to the extent the new loss corporation establishes that the amount so allowable is not attributable to the excess described in clause (ii).

(3) NET UNREALIZED BUILT-IN GAIN AND LOSS DEFINED.—

(A) NET UNREALIZED BUILT-IN GAIN AND LOSS.—

(i) IN GENERAL.—The terms "net unrealized built-in gain" and "net unrealized built-in loss" mean, with respect to any old loss corporation, the amount by which—

(I) the fair market value of the assets of such corporation immediately before an ownership change is more or less, respectively, than

(II) the aggregate adjusted basis of such assets at such time.

(ii) SPECIAL RULE FOR REDEMPTIONS OR OTHER CORPORATE CONTRACTIONS.—If a redemption or other corporate contraction occurs in connection with an ownership change, to the extent provided in regulations, determinations under clause (i) shall be made after taking such redemption or other corporate contractions into account.

(B) THRESHOLD REQUIREMENT.—

(i) IN GENERAL.—If the amount of the net unrealized built-in gain or net unrealized built-in loss (determined without regard to this subparagraph) of any old loss corporation is not greater than the lesser of—

(I) 15 percent of the amount determined for purposes of subparagraph (A) (i) (I), or

(II) $10,000,000,

the net unrealized built-in gain or net unrealized built-in loss shall be zero.

(ii) CASH AND CASH ITEMS NOT TAKEN INTO ACCOUNT.—In computing any net unrealized built-in gain or unrealized built-in loss under clause (i), except as provided in regulations, there shall not be taken into account—

(I) any cash or cash item, or

(II) any marketable security which has a value which does not substantially differ from adjusted basis.

(4) DISALLOWED LOSS ALLOWED AS A CARRYFORWARD.—If a deduction for any portion of a recognized built-in loss is disallowed for any post-change year, such portion—

(A) shall be carried forward to subsequent taxable years under rules similar to the rules for the carrying forward of net operating losses (or to the extent the amount so disallowed is attributable to capital losses, under rules similar to the rules for the carrying forward of net capital losses) but

(B) shall be subject to limitation under this section in the same manner as a pre-change loss.

(5) SPECIAL RULES FOR POST-CHANGE YEAR WHICH INCLUDES CHANGE DATE.—For purposes of subsection (b) (3)—

(A) in applying subparagraph (A) thereof, taxable income shall be computed without regard to recognized built-in gains to the extent such gains increased the section 382 limitation for the year (or recognized built-in losses to the extent such losses are treated as pre-change losses), and gain described in paragraph (1) (C), for the year, and

(B) in applying subparagraph (B) thereof, the section 382 limitation shall be computed without regard to recognized built-in gains, and gain described in paragraph (1) (C), for the year.

(6) TREATMENT OF CERTAIN BUILT-IN ITEMS.—

(A) INCOME ITEMS.—Any item of income which is properly taken into account during the recognition period but which is attributable to periods before the change date shall be treated as a recognized built-in gain for the taxable year in which it is properly taken into account.

(B) DEDUCTION ITEMS.—Any amount which is allowable as a deduction during the recognition period (determined without regard to any carryover) but which is attributable to periods before the change date shall be treated as a recogized built-in loss for the taxable year for which it is allowable as a deduction.

(C) ADJUSTMENTS.—The amount of the net unrealized built-in gain or loss shall be properly adjusted for amounts which would be treated as recognized built-in gains or losses under this paragraph if such amounts were properly taken into account (or allowable as a deduction) during the recognition period.

(7) RECOGNITION PERIOD, ETC.—

(A) RECOGNITION PERIOD.—The term "recognition period" means, with respect to any ownership change, the 5-year period beginning on the change date.

(B) RECOGNITION PERIOD TAXABLE YEAR.—The term "recognition period taxable year" means any taxable year any portion of which is in the recognition period.

(8) DETERMINATION OF FAIR MARKET VALUE IN CERTAIN CASES.—If 80 percent or more in value of the stock of a corporation is acquired in 1 transaction (or in a series of related transactions during any 12-month period), for purposes of determining the net unrealized built-in loss, the fair market value of the assets of such corporation shall not exceed the grossed up amount paid for such stock properly adjusted for indebtedness of the corporation and other relevent items.

(9) TAX-FREE EXCHANGES OR TRANSFERS.—The Secretary shall prescribe such regulations as may be necessary to carry out the purposes of this subsection where property held on the change date was acquired (or is subsequently transferred) in a transaction where gain or loss is not recognized (in whole or in part).

[Sec. 382(i)]

(i) TESTING PERIOD.—For purposes of this section—

(1) 3-YEAR PERIOD.—Except as otherwise provided in this section, the testing period is the 3-year period ending on the day of any owner shift involving a 5-percent shareholder or equity structure shift.

(2) SHORTER PERIOD WHERE THERE HAS BEEN RECENT OWNERSHIP CHANGE.—If there has been an ownership change under this section, the testing period for determining whether a 2nd ownership change has occurred shall not begin before the 1st day following the change date for such earlier ownership change.

(3) SHORTER PERIOD WHERE ALL LOSSES ARISE AFTER 3-YEAR PERIOD BEGINS.—The testing period shall not begin before the earlier of the 1st day of the 1st taxable year from which there is a carryforward of a loss or of an excess credit to the 1st post-change year or the taxable year in which the transaction being tested occurs. Except as provided in regulations, this paragraph shall not apply to any loss corporation which has a net unrealized built-in loss (determined after application of subsection (h)(3)(B)).

[Sec. 382(j)]

(j) CHANGE DATE.—For purposes of this section, the change date is—

(1) in the case where the last component of an ownership change is an owner shift involving a 5-percent shareholder, the date on which such shift occurs, and

(2) in the case where the last component of an ownership change is an equity structure, shift, the date of the reorganization.

[Sec. 382(k)]

(k) DEFINITIONS AND SPECIAL RULES.—For purposes of this section—

(1) LOSS CORPORATION.—The term "loss corporation" means a corporation entitled to use a net operating loss carryover or having a net operating loss for the taxable year in which the ownership change occurs. Such term shall include any corporation entitled to use a carryforward of disallowed interest described in section 381(c)(20). Except to the extent provided in regulations, such term includes any corporation with a net unrealized built-in loss.

(2) OLD LOSS CORPORATION.—The term "old loss corporation" means any corporation—

(A) with respect to which there is an ownership change, and

(B) which (before the ownership change) was a loss corporation.

(3) NEW LOSS CORPORATION.—The term "new loss corporation" means a corporation which (after an ownership change) is a loss corporation. Nothing in this section shall be treated as implying that the same corporation may not be both the old loss corporation and the new loss corporation.

(4) TAXABLE INCOME.—Taxable income shall be computed with the modifications set forth in section 172(d).

(5) VALUE.—The term "value" means fair market value.

(6) RULES RELATING TO STOCK.—

(A) PREFERRED STOCK.—Except as provided in regulations and subsection (e), the term "stock" means stock other than stock described in section 1504(a)(4).

(B) TREATMENT OF CERTAIN RIGHTS, ETC.—The Secretary shall prescribe such regulations as may be necessary—

(i) to treat warrants, options, contracts to acquire stock, convertible debt interests, and other similar interests as stock, and

(ii) to treat stock as not stock.

(C) DETERMINATIONS ON BASIS OF VALUE.—Determinations of the percentage of stock of any corporation held by any person shall be made on the basis of value.

(7) 5-PERCENT SHAREHOLDER.—The term "5-percent shareholder" means any person holding 5 percent or more of the stock of the corporation at any time during the testing period.

[Sec. 382(l)]

(l) CERTAIN ADDITIONAL OPERATING RULES.—For purposes of this section—

(1) CERTAIN CAPITAL CONTRIBUTIONS NOT TAKEN INTO ACCOUNT.—

(A) IN GENERAL.—Any capital contribution received by an old loss corporation as part of a plan a principal purpose of which is to avoid or increase any limitation under this section shall not be taken into account for purposes of this section.

(B) CERTAIN CONTRIBUTIONS TREATED AS PART OF PLAN.—For purposes of subparagraph (A), any capital contribution made during the 2-year period ending on the change date shall, except as provided in regulations, be treated as part of a plan described in subparagraph (A).

(2) ORDERING RULES FOR APPLICATION OF SECTION.—

(A) COORDINATION WITH SECTION 172(b) CARRYOVER RULES.—In the case of any pre-change loss for any taxable year (hereinafter in this subparagraph referred to as the "loss year" subject to limitation under this section, for purposes of determining under the 2nd sentence of section 172(b)(2) the amount of such loss which may be carried to any taxable year, taxable income for any taxable year shall be treated as not greater than—

(i) the section 382 limitation for such taxable year, reduced by

(ii) the unused pre-change losses for taxable years preceding the loss year.

Similar rules shall apply in the case of any credit or loss subject to limitation under section 383.

(B) ORDERING RULE FOR LOSSES CARRIED FROM SAME TAXABLE YEAR.—In any case in which—

(i) a pre-change loss of a loss corporation for any taxable year is subject to a section 382 limitation, and

(ii) a net operating loss of such corporation from such taxable year is not subject to such limitation,

taxable income shall be treated as having been offset first by the loss subject to such limitation.

(3) OPERATING RULES RELATING TO OWNERSHIP OF STOCK.—

(A) CONSTRUCTIVE OWNERSHIP.—Section 318 (relating to constructive ownership of stock) shall apply in determining ownership of stock, except that—

(i) paragraphs (1) and (5)(B) of section 318(a) shall not apply and an individual and all members of his family described in paragraph (1) of section 318(a) shall be treated as 1 individual for purposes of applying this section,

(ii) paragraph (2) of section 318(a) shall be applied—

(I) without regard to the 50-percent limitation contained in subparagraph (C) thereof, and

(II) except as provided in regulations, by treating stock attributed thereunder as no longer being held by the entity from which attributed,

(iii) paragraph (3) of section 318(a) shall be applied only to the extent provided in regulations,

(iv) except to the extent provided in regulations, an option to acquire stock shall be treated as exercised if such exercise results in an ownership change, and

(v) in attributing stock from an entity under paragraph (2) of section 318(a), there shall not be taken into account—

(I) in the case of attribution from a corporation, stock which is not treated as stock for purposes of this section, or

(II) in the case of attribution from another entity, an interest in such entity similar to stock described in subclause (I).

A rule similar to the rule of clause (iv) shall apply in the case of any contingent purchase, warrant, convertible debt, put, stock subject to a risk of forfeiture, contract to acquire stock, or similar interests.

(B) STOCK ACQUIRED BY REASON OF DEATH, GIFT, DIVORCE, SEPARATION, ETC.—If—

(i) the basis of any stock in the hands of any person is determined—

(I) under section 1014 (relating to property acquired from a decedent),

(II) section 1015 (relating to property acquired by a gift or transfer in trust), or

(III) section 1041(b)(2) (relating to transfers of property between spouses or incident to divorce),

(ii) stock is received by any person in satisfaction of a right to receive a pecuniary bequest, or

(iii) stock is acquired by a person pursuant to any divorce or separation instrument (within the meaning of section 121(d)(3)(C)),

such person shall be treated as owning such stock during the period such stock was owned by the person from whom it was acquired.

(C) CERTAIN CHANGES IN PERCENTAGE OWNERSHIP WHICH ARE ATTRIBUTABLE TO FLUCTUATIONS IN VALUE NOT TAKEN INTO ACCOUNT.—Except as provided in regulations, any change in proportionate ownership which is attributable solely to fluctuations in the relative fair market values of different classes of stock shall not be taken into account.

(4) REDUCTION IN VALUE WHERE SUBSTANTIAL NONBUSINESS ASSETS.—

(A) IN GENERAL.—If, immediately after an ownership change, the new loss corporation has substantial nonbusiness assets, the value of the old loss corporation shall be reduced by the excess (if any) of

(i) the fair market value of the nonbusiness assets of the old loss corporation, over

(ii) the nonbusiness asset share of indebtedness for which such corporation is liable.

(B) CORPORATION HAVING SUBSTANTIAL NONBUSINESS ASSETS.—For purposes of subparagraph (A)—

(i) IN GENERAL.—The old loss corporation shall be treated as having substantial nonbusiness assets if at least ⅓ of the value of the total assets of such corporation consists of nonbusiness assets.

(ii) EXCEPTION FOR CERTAIN INVESTMENT ENTITIES.—A regulated investment company to which part I of subchapter M applies, a real estate investment trust to which part II of subchapter M applies, or a REMIC to which part IV of subchapter M applies, shall not be treated as a new loss corporation having substantial nonbusiness assets.

(C) NONBUSINESS ASSETS.—For purposes of this paragraph, the term "nonbusiness assets" means assets held for investment.

(D) NONBUSINESS ASSET SHARE.—For purposes of this paragraph, the nonbusiness asset share of the indebtedness of the corporation is an amount which bears the same ratio to such indebtedness as—

(i) the fair market value of the nonbusiness assets of the corporation, bears to

(ii) the fair market value of all assets of such corporation.

(E) TREATMENT OF SUBSIDIARIES.—For purposes of this paragraph, stock and securities in any subsidiary corporation shall be disregarded and the parent corporation shall be deemed to own its ratable share of the subsidiary's assets. For purposes of the preceding sentence, a corporation shall be treated as a subsidiary if the parent owns 50 percent or more of the combined voting power of all classes of stock entitled to vote, and 50 percent or more of the total value of shares of all classes of stock.

(5) TITLE 11 OR SIMILAR CASE.—

(A) IN GENERAL.—Subsection (a) shall not apply to any ownership change if—

(i) the old loss corporation is (immediately before such ownership change) under the jurisdiction of the court in a title 11 or similar case, and

(ii) the shareholders and creditors of the old loss corporation (determined immediately before such ownership change) own (after such ownership change and as a result of being shareholders or creditors immediately before such change) stock of the new loss corporation (or stock of a controlling corporation if also in bankruptcy) which meets the requirements of section 1504(a)(2) (determined by substituting "50 percent" for "80 percent" each place it appears).

(B) REDUCTION FOR INTEREST PAYMENTS TO CREDITORS BECOMING SHAREHOLDERS.—In any case to which subparagraph (A) applies, the pre-change losses and excess credits (within the meaning of section 383(a)(2)) which may be carried to a post-change year shall be computed as if no deduction was allowable under this chapter for the interest paid or accrued by the old loss corporation on indebtedness which was converted into stock pursuant to title 11 or similar case during—

(i) any taxable year ending during the 3-year period preceding the taxable year in which the ownership change occurs, and

(ii) the period of the taxable year in which ownership change occurs on or before the change date.

(C) COORDINATION WITH SECTION 108.—In applying section 108(e)(8) to any case to which subparagraph (A) applies, there shall not be taken into account any indebtedness for interest described in subparagraph (B).

(D) SECTION 382 LIMITATION ZERO IF ANOTHER CHANGE WITHIN 2 YEARS.—If, during the 2-year period immediately following an ownership change to which this paragraph applies, an ownership change of the new loss coproration occurs, this paragraph shall not apply and the section 382 limitation with respect to the 2nd ownership change for any post-change year ending after the change date of the 2nd ownership change shall be zero.

(E) ONLY CERTAIN STOCK TAKEN INTO ACCOUNT.—For purposes of subparagraph (A)(ii), stock transferred to a creditor shall be taken into account only to the extent such stock is transferred in satisfaction of indebtedness and only if such indebtedness—

(i) was held by the creditor at least 18 months before the date of the filing of the title 11 or similar case, or

(ii) arose in the ordinary course of the trade or business of the old loss corporation and is held by the person who at all times held the beneficial interest in such indebtedness.

(F) TITLE 11 OR SIMILAR CASE.—For purposes of this paragraph, the term "title 11 or similar case" has the meaning given such term by section 368(a)(3)(A).

(G) ELECTION NOT TO HAVE PARAGRAPH APPLY.—A new loss corporation may elect, subject to such terms and conditions as the Secretary may prescribe, not to have the provisions of this paragraph apply.

(6) SPECIAL RULE FOR INSOLVENCY TRANSACTIONS.—If paragraph (5) does not apply to any reorganization described in subparagraph (G) of section 368(a)(1) or any exchange of debt for stock in a title 11 or similar case (as defined in section 368(a)(3)(A)), the value under subsection (e) shall reflect the increase (if any) in value of the old loss corporation resulting from any surrender or cancellation of creditors' claims in the transaction.

(7) COORDINATION WITH ALTERNATIVE MINIMUM TAX.—The Secretary shall by regulation provide for the application of this section to the alternative tax net operating loss deduction under section 56(d).

(8) PREDECESSOR AND SUCCESSOR ENTITIES.—Except as provided in regulations, any entity and any predecessor or successor entities of such entity shall be treated as 1 entity.

[Sec. 382(m)]

(m) REGULATIONS.—The Secretary shall prescribe such regulations as may be necessary or appropriate to carry out the purposes of this section and section 383, including (but not limited to) regulations—

(1) providing for the application of this section and section 383 where an ownership change with respect to the old loss corporation is followed by an ownership change with respect to the new loss corporation, and

(2) providing for the application of this section and section 383 in the case of a short taxable year,

(3) providing for such adjustments to the application of this section and section 383 as is necessary to prevent the avoidance of the purposes of this section and section 383, including the avoidance of such purposes through the use of related persons, pass-thru entities, or other intermediaries,

(4) providing for the application of subsection (g)(4) where there is only 1 corporation involved, and

(5) providing, in the case of any group of corporations described in section 1563(a) (determined by substituting "50 percent" for "80 percent" each place it appears and determined without regard to paragraph (4) thereof), appropriate adjustments to value, built-in gain or loss, and other items so that items are not omitted or taken into account more than once.

[Sec. 382(n)]

(n) SPECIAL RULE FOR CERTAIN OWNERSHIP CHANGES.—

(1) IN GENERAL.—The limitation contained in subsection (a) shall not apply in the case of an ownership change which is pursuant to a restructuring plan of a taxpayer which—

(A) is required under a loan agreement or a commitment for a line of credit entered into with the Department of the Treasury under the Emergency Economic Stabilization Act of 2008, and

(B) is intended to result in a rationalization of the costs, capitalization, and capacity with respect to the manufacturing workforce of, and suppliers to, the taxpayer and its subsidiaries.

(2) SUBSEQUENT ACQUISITIONS.—Paragraph (1) shall not apply in the case of any subsequent ownership change unless such ownership change is described in such paragraph.

(3) LIMITATION BASED ON CONTROL IN CORPORATION.—

(A) IN GENERAL.—Paragraph (1) shall not apply in the case of any ownership change if, immediately after such ownership change, any person (other than a voluntary employees' beneficiary association under section 501(c)(9)) owns stock of the new loss corporation possessing 50 percent or more of the total combined voting power of all classes of stock entitled to vote, or of the total value of the stock of such corporation.

(B) TREATMENT OF RELATED PERSONS.—

(i) IN GENERAL.—Related persons shall be treated as a single person for purposes of this paragraph.

(ii) RELATED PERSONS.—For purposes of clause (i), a person shall be treated as related to another person if—

(I) such person bears a relationship to such other person described in section 267(b) or 707(b), or

(II) such persons are members of a group of persons acting in concert.

[Sec. 383]

SEC. 383. SPECIAL LIMITATIONS ON CERTAIN EXCESS CREDITS, ETC.

[SEC. 383(a)]

(a) EXCESS CREDITS.—

(1) IN GENERAL.—Under regulations, if an ownership change occurs with respect to a corporation, the amount of any excess credit for any taxable year which may be used in any post-change year shall be limited to an amount determined on the basis of the tax liability which is attributable to so much of the taxable income as does not exceed the section 382 limitation for such post-change year to the extent available after the application of section 382 and subsections (b) and (c) of this section.

(2) EXCESS CREDIT.—For purposes of paragraph (1), the term "excess credit" means—

(A) any unused general business credit of the corporation under section 39, and

(B) any unused minimum tax credit of the corporation under section 53.

[Sec. 383(b)]

(b) LIMITATION ON NET CAPITAL LOSS.—If an ownership change occurs with respect to a corporation, the amount of any net capital loss under section 1212 for any taxable year before the 1st post-change year which may be used in any post-change year shall be limited under regulations which shall be based on the principles applicable under section 382. Such regulations shall provide that any such net capital loss used in a post-change year shall reduce the section 382 limitation which is applied to pre-change losses under section 382 for such year.

* * *

[Sec. 383(d)]

(d) PRO RATION RULES FOR YEAR WHICH INCLUDES CHANGE.—For purposes of this section, rules similar to the rules of subsections (b)(3) and (d)(1)(B) of section 382 shall apply.

[Sec. 383(e)]

(e) DEFINITIONS.—Terms used in this section shall have the same respective meanings as when used in section 382, except that appropriate adjustments shall be made to take into account that the limitations of this section apply to credits and net capital losses.

[Sec. 384]

SEC. 384. LIMITATION ON USE OF PREACQUISITION LOSSES TO OFFSET BUILT-IN GAINS.

[Sec. 384(a)]

(a) GENERAL RULE.—If—

(1)(A) a corporation acquires directly (or through 1 or more other corporations) control of another corporation, or

(B) the assets of a corporation are acquired by another corporation in a reorganization described in subparagraph (A), (C), or (D) of section 368(a)(1), and

(2) either of such corporations is a gain corporation,

income for any recognition period taxable year (to the extent attributable to recognized built-in gains) shall not be offset by any preacquisition loss (other than a preacquisition loss of the gain corporation).

[Sec. 384(b)]

(b) EXCEPTION WHERE CORPORATIONS UNDER COMMON CONTROL.—

(1) IN GENERAL.—Subsection (a) shall not apply to the preacquisition loss of any corporation if such corporation and the gain corporation were members of the same controlled group at all times during the 5-year period ending on the acquisition date.

(2) CONTROLLED GROUP.—For purposes of this subsection, the term "controlled group" means a controlled group of corporations (as defined in section 1563(a)); except that—

(A) "more than 50 percent" shall be substituted for "at least 80 percent" each place it appears,

(B) the ownership requirements of section 1563(a) must be met both with respect to voting power and value, and

(C) the determination shall be made without regard to subsection (a)(4) of section 1563.

(3) SHORTER PERIOD WHERE CORPORATIONS NOT IN EXISTENCE FOR 5 YEARS.—If either of the corporations referred to in paragraph (1) was not in existence throughout the 5-year period referred to in paragraph (1), the period during which such corporation was in existence (or if both, the shorter of such periods) shall be substituted for such 5-year period.

[Sec. 384(c)]

(c) DEFINITIONS.—For purposes of this section—

(1) RECOGNIZED BUILT-IN GAIN.—

(A) IN GENERAL.—The term "recognized built-in gain" means any gain recognized during the recognition period on the disposition of any asset except to the extent the gain corporation (or, in any case described in subsection (a)(1)(B), the acquiring corporation) establishes that—

(i) such asset was not held by the gain corporation on the acquisition date, or

(ii) such gain exceeds the excess (if any) of—

(I) the fair market value of such asset on the acquisition date, over

(II) the adjusted basis of such asset on such date.

(B) TREATMENT OF CERTAIN INCOME ITEMS.—Any item of income which is properly taken into account for any recognition period taxable year but which is attributable to periods before the acquisition date shall be treated as a recognized built-in gain for the taxable year in which it is properly taken into account and shall be taken into account in determining the amount of the net unrealized built-in gain.

(C) LIMITATION.—The amount of the recognized built-in gains for any recognition period taxable year shall not exceed—

(i) the net unrealized built-in gain, reduced by

(ii) the recognized built-in gains for prior years ending in the recognition period which (but for this section) would have been offset by preacquisition losses.

(2) ACQUISITION DATE..—The term "acquisition date" means—

(A) in any case described in subsection (a)(1)(A), the date on which the acquisition of control occurs, or

(B) in any case described in subsection (a)(1)(B), the date of the transfer in the reorganization.

(3) PREACQUISITION LOSS.—

(A) IN GENERAL.—The term "preacquisition loss" means—

(i) any net operating loss carryforward to the taxable year in which the acquisition date occurs, and

(ii) any net operating loss for the taxable year in which the acquisition date occurs to the extent such loss is allocable to the period in such year on or before the acquisition date.

Except as provided in regulations, the net operating loss shall, for purposes of clause (ii), be allocated ratably to each day in the year.

(B) TREATMENT OF RECOGNIZED BUILT-IN LOSS.—In the case of a corporation with a net unrealized built-in loss, the term "preacquisition loss" includes any recognized built-in loss.

(4) GAIN CORPORATION.—The term "gain corporation" means any corporation with a net unrealized built-in gain.

(5) CONTROL.—The term "control" means ownership of stock in a corporation which meets the requirements of section 1504(a)(2).

(6) TREATMENT OF MEMBERS OF SAME GROUP.—Except as provided in regulations and except for purposes of subsection (b), all corporations which are members of the same affiliated group immediately before the acquisition date shall be treated as 1 corporation. To the extent provided in regulations, section 1504 shall be applied without regard to subsection (b) thereof for purposes of the preceding sentence.

(7) TREATMENT OF PREDECESSORS AND SUCCESSORS.—Any reference in this section to a corporation shall include a reference to any predecessor or successor thereof.

(8) OTHER DEFINITIONS.—Except as provided in regulations, the terms "net unrealized built-in gain" "net unrealized built-in loss", "recognized built-in loss", "recognition period", and "recognition period taxable year", have the same respective meanings as when used in section 382(h), except that the acquisition date shall be taken into account in lieu of the change date.

[Sec. 384(d)]

(d) LIMITATION ALSO TO APPLY TO EXCESS CREDITS OR NET CAPITAL LOSSES.—Rules similar to the rules of subsection (a) shall also apply in the case of any excess credit (as defined in section 383(a)(2)) or net capital loss.

[Sec. 384(e)]

(e) ORDERING RULES FOR NET OPERATING LOSSES, ETC.—

(1) CARRYOVER RULES.—If any preacquisition loss may not offset a recognized built-in gain by reason of this section, such gain shall not be taken into account in determining under section 172(b)(2) the amount of such loss which may be carried to other taxable years. A similar rule shall apply in the case of any excess credit or net capital loss limited by reason of subsection (d).

(2) ORDERING RULE FOR LOSSES CARRIED FROM SAME TAXABLE YEAR.—In any case in which—

(A) a preacquisition loss for any taxable year is subject to limitation under subsection (a), and

(B) a net operating loss from such taxable year is not subject to such limitation, taxable income shall be treated as having been offset 1st by the loss subject to such limitation.

[Sec. 384(f)]

(f) REGULATIONS.—The Secretary shall prescribe such regulations as may be necessary to carry out the purposes of this section, including regulations to ensure that the purposes of this section may not be circumvented through—

(1) the use of any provision of law or regulations (including subchapter K of this chapter), or

(2) contributions of property to a corporation.

PART VI—TREATMENT OF CERTAIN CORPORATE INTERESTS AS STOCK OR INDEBTEDNESS

[Sec. 385]

SEC. 385. TREATMENT OF CERTAIN INTERESTS IN CORPORATIONS AS STOCK OR INDEBTEDNESS.

[Sec. 385(a)]

(a) AUTHORITY TO PRESCRIBE REGULATIONS.—The Secretary is authorized to prescribe such regulations as may be necessary or appropriate to determine whether an interest in a corporation is to be treated for purposes of this title as stock or indebtedness (or as in part stock and in part indebtedness).

[Sec. 385(b)]

(b) FACTORS.—The regulations prescribed under this section shall set forth factors which are to be taken into account in determining with respect to a particular factual situation whether a debtor-creditor relationship exists or a corporation-shareholder relationship exists. The factors so set forth in the regulations may include among other factors:

(1) whether there is a written unconditional promise to pay on demand or on a specified date a sum certain in money in return for an adequate consideration in money or money's worth, and to pay a fixed rate of interest,

(2) whether there is subordination to or preference over any indebtedness of the corporation,

(3) the ratio of debt to equity of the corporation,

(4) whether there is convertibility into the stock of the corporation, and

(5) the relationship between holdings of stock in the corporation and holdings of the interest in question.

[Sec. 385(c)]

(c) EFFECT OF CLASSIFICATION BY ISSUER.—

(1) IN GENERAL.—The characterization (as of the time of issuance) by the issuer as to whether an interest in a corporation is stock or indebtedness shall be binding on such issuer and on all holders of such interest (but shall not be binding on the Secretary).

(2) NOTIFICATION OF INCONSISTENT TREATMENT.—Except as provided in regulations, paragraph (1) shall not apply to any holder of an interest if such holder on his return discloses that he is treating such interest in a manner inconsistent with the characterization referred to in paragraph (1).

(3) REGULATIONS.—The Secretary is authorized to require such information as the Secretary determines to be necessary to carry out the provisions of this subsection.

SUBCHAPTER D—DEFERRED COMPENSATION, ETC.

PART I—PENSION, PROFIT-SHARING, STOCK BONUS PLANS, ETC.

Subpart A—General Rule

[Sec. 401]

SEC. 401. QUALIFIED PENSION, PROFIT-SHARING, AND STOCK BONUS PLANS.

* * *

[Sec. 401(c)]

(c) DEFINITIONS AND RULES RELATING TO SELF-EMPLOYED INDIVIDUALS AND OWNER-EMPLOYEES.—For purposes of this section—

(1) SELF-EMPLOYED INDIVIDUAL TREATED AS EMPLOYEE.—

(A) IN GENERAL.—The term "employee" includes, for any taxable year, an individual who is a self-employed individual for such taxable year.

(B) SELF-EMPLOYED INDIVIDUAL.—The term "self-employed individual" means, with respect to any taxable year, an individual who has earned income (as defined in paragraph (2)) for such taxable year. To the extent provided in regulations prescribed by the Secretary, such term also includes, for any taxable year—

(i) an individual who would be a self-employed individual within the meaning of the preceding sentence but for the fact that the trade or business carried on by such individual did not have net profits for the taxable year, and

(ii) an individual who has been a self-employed individual within the meaning of the preceding sentence for any prior taxable year.

(2) EARNED INCOME.—

(A) IN GENERAL.—The term "earned income" means the net earnings from self-employment (as defined in section 1402(a)), but such net earnings shall be determined—

(i) only with respect to a trade or business in which personal services of the taxpayer are a material income-producing factor,

(ii) without regard to paragraphs (4) and (5) of section 1402(c),

(iii) in the case of any individual who is treated as an employee under subparagraph (A), (C), or (D) of section 3121(d)(3), without regard to section 1402(c)(2)

(iv) without regard to items which are not included in gross income for purposes of this chapter, and the deductions properly allocable to or chargeable against such items,

(v) with regard to the deductions allowed by section 404 to the taxpayer, and

(vi) with regard to the deduction allowed to the taxpayer by section 164(f).

For purposes of this subparagraph, section 1402, as in effect for a taxable year ending on December 31, 1962, shall be treated as having been in effect for all taxable years ending before such date. For purposes of this part only (other than sections 419 and 419A), this subparagraph shall be applied as if the term "trade or business" for purposes of section 1402 included service described in section 1402(c)(6).

(C) [B] INCOME FROM DISPOSITION OF CERTAIN PROPERTY.—For purposes of this section, the term "earned income" includes gains (other than any gain which is treated under any provision of this chapter as gain from the sale or exchange of a capital asset) and net earnings derived from the sale or other disposition of, the transfer of any interest in, or the licensing of the use of property (other than good will) by an individual whose personal efforts created such property.

* * *

[Sec. 408]

SEC. 408. INDIVIDUAL RETIREMENT ACCOUNTS.

[Sec. 408(a)]

(a) INDIVIDUAL RETIREMENT ACCOUNT.—For purposes of this section, the term "individual retirement account" means a trust created or organized in the United States for the exclusive benefit of an individual or his beneficiaries, but only if the written governing instrument creating the trust meets the following requirements:

(1) Except in the case of a rollover contribution described in subsection (d)(3) or in section 402(c), 403(a)(4), 403(b)(8), or 457(e)(16), no contribution will be accepted unless it is in cash, and contributions will not be accepted for the taxable year on behalf of any individual in excess of the amount in effect for such taxable year under section 219(b)(1)(A).

(2) The trustee is a bank (as defined in subsection (n)) or such other person who demonstrates to the satisfaction of the Secretary that the manner in which such other person will administer the trust will be consistent with the requirements of this section.

(3) No part of the trust funds will be invested in life insurance contracts.

(4) The interest of an individual in the balance of his account is nonforfeitable.

(5) The assets of the trust will not be commingled with other property except in a common trust fund or common investment fund.

(6) Under regulations prescribed by the Secretary, rules similar to the rules of section 401(a)(9) and the incidental death benefit requirements of section 401(a) shall apply to the distribution of the entire interest of an individual for whose benefit the trust is maintained.

[Sec. 408(b)]

(b) INDIVIDUAL RETIREMENT ANNUITY.—For purposes of this section, the term "individual retirement annuity" means an annuity contract, or an endowment contract (as determined under regulations prescribed by the Secretary), issued by an insurance company which meets the following requirements:

(1) The contract is not transferable by the owner.

(2) Under the contract—

(A) the premiums are not fixed,

(B) the annual premium on behalf of any individual will not exceed the dollar amount in effect under section 219(b)(1)(A), and

(C) any refund of premiums will be applied before the close of the calendar year following the year of the refund toward the payment of future premiums or the purchase of additional benefits.

(3) Under regulations prescribed by the Secretary, rules similar to the rules of section 401(a)(9) and the incidental death benefit requirements of section 401(a) shall apply to the distribution of the entire interest of the owner.

(4) The entire interest of the owner is nonforfeitable.

Such term does not include such an annuity contract for any taxable year of the owner in which it is disqualified on the application of subsection (e) or for any subsequent taxable year. For purposes of this subsection, no contract shall be treated as an endowment contract if it matures later than the taxable year in which the individual in whose name such contract is purchased attains age 72; if it is not for the exclusive benefit of the individual in whose name it is purchased or his beneficiaries; or if the aggregate annual premiums under all such contracts purchased in the name of such individual for any taxable year exceed the dollar amount in effect under section 219(b)(1)(A).

* * *

[Sec. 408(d)]

(d) TAX TREATMENT OF DISTRIBUTIONS.—

(1) IN GENERAL.—Except as otherwise provided in this subsection, any amount paid or distributed out of an individual retirement plan shall be included in gross income by the payee or distributee, as the case may be, in the manner provided under section 72.

(2) SPECIAL RULES FOR APPLYING SECTION 72.—For purposes of applying section 72 to any amount described in paragraph (1)—

(A) all individual retirement plans shall be treated as 1 contract,

(B) all distributions during any taxable year shall be treated as 1 distribution, and

(C) the value of the contract, income on the contract, and investment in the contract shall be computed as of the close of the calendar year in which the taxable year begins.

For purposes of subparagraph (C), the value of the contract shall be increased by the amount of any distributions during the calendar year.

(3) ROLLOVER CONTRIBUTION.—An amount is described in this paragraph as a rollover contribution if it meets the requirements of subparagraphs (A) and (B).

(A) IN GENERAL.—Paragraph (1) does not apply to any amount paid or distributed out of an individual retirement account or individual retirement annuity to the individual for whose benefit the account or annuity is maintained if—

(i) the entire amount received (including money and any other property) is paid into an individual retirement account or individual retirement annuity (other than an endowment contract) for the benefit of such individual not later than the 60th day after the day on which he receives the payment or distribution; or

(ii) the entire amount received (including money and any other property) is paid into an eligible retirement plan for the benefit of such individual not later than the 60th day after the date on which the payment or distribution is received, except that the maximum amount which may be paid into such plan may not exceed the portion of the amount received which is includible in gross income (determined without regard to this paragraph).

For purposes of clause (ii), the term "eligible retirement plan" means an eligible retirement plan described in clause (iii), (iv), (v), or (vi) of section 402(c)(8)(B).

(B) LIMITATION.—This paragraph does not apply to any amount described in subparagraph (A)(i) received by an individual from an individual retirement account or individual retirement annuity if at any time during the 1-year period ending on the day of such receipt such individual received any other amount described in that subparagraph from an individual retirement account or an individual retirement annuity which was not includible in his gross income because of the application of this paragraph.

(C) DENIAL OF ROLLOVER TREATMENT FOR INHERITED ACCOUNTS, ETC.—

(i) IN GENERAL.—In the case of an inherited individual retirement account or individual retirement annuity—

(I) this paragraph shall not apply to any amount received by an individual from such an account or annuity (and no amount transferred from such account or annuity to another individual retirement account or annuity shall be excluded from gross income by reason of such transfer), and

(II) such inherited account or annuity shall not be treated as an individual retirement account or annuity for purposes of determining whether any other amount is a rollover contribution.

(ii) INHERITED INDIVIDUAL RETIREMENT ACCOUNT OR ANNUITY.—An individual retirement account or individual retirement annuity shall be treated as inherited if—

(I) the individual for whose benefit the account or annuity is maintained acquired such account by reason of the death of another individual, and

(II) such individual was not the surviving spouse of such other individual.

(D) PARTIAL ROLLOVERS PERMITTED.—

(i) IN GENERAL.—If any amount paid or distributed out of an individual retirement account or individual retirement annuity would meet the requirements of subparagraph (A) but for the fact that the entire amount was not paid into an eligible plan as required by clause (i) or (ii) of subparagraph (A), such amount shall be treated as meeting the requirements of subparagraph (A) to the extent it is paid into an eligible plan referred to in such clause not later than the 60th day referred to in such clause.

(ii) ELIGIBLE PLAN.—For purposes of clause (i), the term "eligible plan" means any account, annuity, contract, or plan referred to in subparagraph (A).

(E) DENIAL OF ROLLOVER TREATMENT FOR REQUIRED DISTRIBUTIONS.—This paragraph shall not apply to any amount to the extent such amount is required to be distributed under subsection (a)(6) or (b)(3).

(F) FROZEN DEPOSITS.—For purposes of this paragraph, rules similar to the rules of section 402(c)(7) (relating to frozen deposits) shall apply.

(G) SIMPLE RETIREMENT ACCOUNTS.—In the case of any payment or distribution out of a simple retirement account (as defined in subsection (p)) to which section 72(t)(6) applies, this paragraph shall not apply unless such payment or distribution is paid into another simple retirement account.

(H) APPLICATION OF SECTION 72.—

(i) IN GENERAL.—If—

(I) a distribution is made from an individual retirement plan, and

(II) a rollover contribution is made to an eligible retirement plan described in section 402(c)(8)(B)(iii), (iv), (v), or (vi) with respect to all or part of such distribution, then, notwithstanding paragraph (2), the rules of clause (ii) shall apply for purposes of applying section 72.

(ii) APPLICABLE RULES.—In the case of a distribution described in clause (i)—

(I) section 72 shall be applied separately to such distribution,

(II) notwithstanding the pro rata allocation of income on, and investment in, the contract to distributions under section 72, the portion of such distribution rolled over to an eligible retirement plan described in clause (i) shall be treated as from income on the contract (to the extent of the aggregate income on the contract from all individual retirement plans of the distributee), and

(III) appropriate adjustments shall be made in applying section 72 to other distributions in such taxable year and subsequent taxable years.

(I) WAIVER OF 60-DAY REQUIREMENT.—The Secretary may waive the 60-day requirement under subparagraphs (A) and (D) where the failure to waive such requirement would be against equity or good conscience, including casualty, disaster, or other events beyond the reasonable control of the individual subject to such requirement.

(4) CONTRIBUTIONS RETURNED BEFORE DUE DATE OF RETURN.—Paragraph (1) does not apply to the distribution of any contribution paid during a taxable year to an individual retirement account or for an individual retirement annuity if—

(A) such distribution is received on or before the day prescribed by law (including extensions of time) for filing such individual's return for such taxable year,

(B) no deduction is allowed under section 219 with respect to such contribution, and

(C) such distribution is accompanied by the amount of net income attributable to such contribution.

In the case of such a distribution, for purposes of section 61, any net income described in subparagraph (C) shall be deemed to have been earned and receivable in the taxable year in which such contribution is made.

* * *

(6) TRANSFER OF ACCOUNT INCIDENT TO DIVORCE.—The transfer of an individual's interest in an individual retirement account or an individual retirement annuity to his spouse or former spouse under a divorce or separation instrument described in clause (i) of section 121(d)(3)(C) is not to be considered a taxable transfer made by such individual notwithstanding any other provision of this subtitle, and such interest at the time of the transfer is to be treated as an individual retirement account of such spouse, and not of such individual. Thereafter such account or annuity for purposes of this subtitle is to be treated as maintained for the benefit of such spouse.

* * *

(8) DISTRIBUTIONS FOR CHARITABLE PURPOSES.—

(A) IN GENERAL.—So much of the aggregate amount of qualified charitable distributions with respect to a taxpayer made during any taxable year which does not exceed $100,000 shall not be includible in gross income of such taxpayer for such taxable year. The amount of distributions not includible in gross income by reason of the preceding sentence for a taxable year (determined without regard to this sentence) shall be reduced (but not below zero) by an amount equal to the excess of—

(i) the aggregate amount of deductions allowed to the taxpayer under section 219 for all taxable years ending on or after the date the taxpayer attains age 70½, over

(ii) the aggregate amount of reductions under this sentence for all taxable years preceding the current taxable year.

(B) QUALIFIED CHARITABLE DISTRIBUTION.—For purposes of this paragraph, the term "qualified charitable distribution" means any distribution from an individual retirement plan (other than a plan described in subsection (k) or (p))—

(i) which is made directly by the trustee to an organization described in section 170(b)(1)(A) (other than any organization described in section 509(a)(3) or any fund or account described in section 4966(d)(2)), and

(ii) which is made on or after the date that the individual for whose benefit the plan is maintained has attained age 70½.

A distribution shall be treated as a qualified charitable distribution only to the extent that the distribution would be includible in gross income without regard to subparagraph (A).

(C) CONTRIBUTIONS MUST BE OTHERWISE DEDUCTIBLE.—For purposes of this paragraph, a distribution to an organization described in subparagraph (B)(i) shall be treated as a qualified charitable distribution only if a deduction for the entire distribution would be allowable under section 170 (determined without regard to subsection (b) thereof and this paragraph).

(D) APPLICATION OF SECTION 72.—Notwithstanding section 72, in determining the extent to which a distribution is a qualified charitable distribution, the entire amount of the distribution shall be treated as includible in gross income without regard to subparagraph (A) to the extent that such amount does not exceed the aggregate amount which would have been so includible if all amounts in all individual retirement plans of the individual were distributed during such taxable year and all such plans were treated as 1 contract for purposes of determining under section 72 the aggregate amount which would have been so includible. Proper adjustments shall be made in applying section 72 to other distributions in such taxable year and subsequent taxable years.

(E) DENIAL OF DEDUCTION.—Qualified charitable distributions which are not includible in gross income pursuant to subparagraph (A) shall not be taken into account in determining the deduction under section 170.

* * *

[Sec. 408(e)]

(e) TAX TREATMENT OF ACCOUNTS AND ANNUITIES.—

(1) EXEMPTION FROM TAX.—Any individual retirement account is exempt from taxation under this subtitle unless such account has ceased to be an individual retirement account by reason of paragraph (2) or (3). Notwithstanding the preceding sentence, any such account is subject to the taxes imposed by section 511 (relating to imposition of tax on unrelated business income of charitable, etc. organizations).

* * *

(3) EFFECT OF BORROWING ON ANNUITY CONTRACT.—If during any taxable year the owner of an individual retirement annuity borrows any money under or by use of such contract, the contract ceases to be an individual retirement annuity as of the first day of such taxable year. Such owner shall include in gross income for such year an amount equal to the fair market value of such contract as of such first day.

(4) EFFECT OF PLEDGING ACCOUNT AS SECURITY.—If, during any taxable year of the individual for whose benefit an individual retirement account is established, that individual uses the account or any portion thereof as security for a loan, the portion so used is treated as distributed to that individual.

(5) PURCHASE OF ENDOWMENT CONTRACT BY INDIVIDUAL RETIREMENT ACCOUNT.—If the assets of an individual retirement account or any part of such assets are used to purchase an endowment contract for the benefit of the individual for whose benefit the account is established—

(A) to the extent that the amount of the assets involved in the purchase are not attributable to the purchase of life insurance, the purchase is treated as a rollover contribution described in subsection (d)(3), and

(B) to the extent that the amount of the assets involved in the purchase are attributable to the purchase of life, health, accident, or other insurance such amounts are treated as distributed to that individual (but the provisions of subsection (f) do not apply).

(6) COMMINGLING INDIVIDUAL RETIREMENT ACCOUNT AMOUNTS IN CERTAIN COMMON TRUST FUNDS AND COMMON INVESTMENT FUNDS.—Any common trust fund or common investment fund of individual retirement account assets which is exempt from taxation under this subtitle does not cease to be exempt on account of the participation or inclusion of assets of a trust exempt from taxation under section 501(a) which is described in section 401(a).

* * *

[Sec. 408(m)]

(m) INVESTMENT IN COLLECTIBLES TREATED AS DISTRIBUTIONS.—

(1) IN GENERAL.—The acquisition by an individual retirement account or by an individually-directed account under a plan described in section 401(a) of any collectible shall be treated (for purposes of this section and section 402) as a distribution from such account in an amount equal to the cost to such account of such collectible.

(2) COLLECTIBLE DEFINED.—For purposes of this subsection, the term "collectible" means—

(A) any work of art,

(B) any rug or antique,

(C) any metal or gem,

(D) any stamp or coin,

(E) any alcoholic beverage, or

(F) any other tangible personal property specified by the Secretary for purposes of this subsection.

(3) EXCEPTION FOR CERTAIN COINS AND BULLION.—For purposes of this subsection, the term "collectible" shall not include—

(A) any coin which is—

(i) a gold coin described in paragraph (7), (8), (9), or (10) of section 5112(a) of title 31, United States Code,

(ii) a silver coin described in section 5112(e) of title 31, United States Code,

(iii) a platinum coin described in section 5112(k) of title 31, United States Code, or

(iv) a coin issued under the laws of any State, or

(B) any gold, silver, platinum, or palladium bullion of a fineness equal to or exceeding the minimum fineness that a contract market (as described in section 5 of the Commodity Exchange Act, 7 U.S.C. 7) requires for metals which may be delivered in satisfaction of a regulated futures contract,

if such bullion is in the physical possession of a trustee described under subsection (a) of this section.

* * *

[Sec. 408(o)]

(o) DEFINITIONS AND RULES RELATING TO NONDEDUCTIBLE CONTRIBUTIONS TO INDIVIDUAL RETIREMENT PLANS.—

(1) IN GENERAL.—Subject to the provisions of this subsection, designated nondeductible contributions may be made on behalf of an individual to an individual retirement plan.

(2) LIMITS ON AMOUNTS WHICH MAY BE CONTRIBUTED.—

(A) IN GENERAL.—The amount of the designated nondeductible contributions made on behalf of any individual for any taxable year shall not exceed the nondeductible limit for such taxable year.

(B) NONDEDUCTIBLE LIMIT.—For purposes of this paragraph—

(i) IN GENERAL.—The term "nondeductible limit" means the excess of—

(I) the amount allowable as a deduction under section 219 (determined without regard to section 219(g)), over

(II) the amount allowable as a deduction under section 219 (determined with regard to section 219(g)).

(ii) TAXPAYER MAY ELECT TO TREAT DEDUCTIBLE CONTRIBUTIONS AS NONDEDUCTIBLE.—If a taxpayer elects not to deduct an amount which (without regard to this clause) is allowable as a deduction under section 219 for any taxable year, the nondeductible limit for such taxable year shall be increased by such amount.

(C) DESIGNATED NONDEDUCTIBLE CONTRIBUTIONS.—

(i) IN GENERAL.—For purposes of this paragraph, the term "designated nondeductible contribution" means any contribution to an individual retirement plan for the taxable year which is designated (in such manner as the Secretary may prescribe) as a contribution for which a deduction is not allowable under section 219.

(ii) DESIGNATION.—Any designation under clause (i) shall be made on the return of tax imposed by chapter 1 for the taxable year.

(3) TIME WHEN CONTRIBUTIONS MADE.—In determining for which taxable year a designated nondeductible contribution is made, the rule of section 219(f)(3) shall apply.

(4) INDIVIDUAL REQUIRED TO REPORT AMOUNT OF DESIGNATED NONDEDUCTIBLE CONTRIBUTIONS.—

(A) IN GENERAL.—Any individual who—

(i) makes a designated nondeductible contribution to any individual retirement plan for any taxable year, or

(ii) receives any amount from any individual retirement plan for any taxable year,

shall include on his return of the tax imposed by chapter 1 for such taxable year and any succeeding taxable year (or on such other form as the Secretary may prescribe for any such taxable year) information described in subparagraph (B).

(B) INFORMATION REQUIRED TO BE SUPPLIED.—The following information is described in this subparagraph:

(i) The amount of designated nondeductible contributions for the taxable year.

(ii) The amount of distributions from individual retirement plans for the taxable year.

(iii) The excess (if any) of—

(I) the aggregate amount of designated nondeductible contributions for all preceding taxable years, over

(II) the aggregate amount of distributions from individual retirement plans which was excludable from gross income for such taxable years.

(iv) The aggregate balance of all individual retirement plans of the individual as of the close of the calendar year in which the taxable year begins.

(v) Such other information as the Secretary may prescribe.

(C) PENALTY FOR REPORTING CONTRIBUTIONS NOT MADE.—

For penalty where individual reports designated nondeductible contributions not made, see section 6693(b).

(5) SPECIAL RULE FOR DIFFICULTY OF CARE PAYMENTS EXCLUDED FROM GROSS INCOME.—In the case of an individual who for a taxable year excludes from gross income under section 131 a qualified foster care payment which is a difficulty of care payment, if—

(A) the deductible amount in effect for the taxable year under subsection (b), exceeds

(B) the amount of compensation includible in the individual's gross income for the taxable year,

the individual may elect to increase the nondeductible limit under paragraph (2) for the taxable year by an amount equal to the lesser of such excess or the amount so excluded.

* * *

»→ Caution: As provided in Section 408A(c)(3)(D), the amounts provided in Section 408A(c)(3)(B)(ii) are adjusted for taxable years after 2006 to reflect increases in the Chained Consumer Price Index. The adjusted amounts applicable to taxable years beginning in 2020 are provided in the material at page xiv.

[Sec. 408A]

SEC. 408A. ROTH IRAS.

[Sec. 408A(a)]

(a) GENERAL RULE.—Except as provided in this section, a Roth IRA shall be treated for purposes of this title in the same manner as an individual retirement plan.

[Sec. 408A(b)]

(b) ROTH IRA.—For purposes of this title, the term "Roth IRA" means an individual retirement plan (as defined in section 7701(a)(37)) which is designated (in such manner as the Secretary may prescribe) at the time of establishment of the plan as a Roth IRA. Such designation shall be made in such manner as the Secretary may prescribe.

[Sec. 408A(c)]

(c) TREATMENT OF CONTRIBUTIONS.—

(1) NO DEDUCTION ALLOWED.—No deduction shall be allowed under section 219 for a contribution to a Roth IRA.

(2) CONTRIBUTION LIMIT.—The aggregate amount of contributions for any taxable year to all Roth IRAs maintained for the benefit of an individual shall not exceed the excess (if any) of—

(A) the maximum amount allowable as a deduction under section 219 with respect to such individual for such taxable year (computed without regard to subsection (d)(1) or (g) of such section), over

(B) the aggregate amount of contributions for such taxable year to all other individual retirement plans (other than Roth IRAs) maintained for the benefit of the individual.

(3) LIMITS BASED ON MODIFIED ADJUSTED GROSS INCOME.—

(A) DOLLAR LIMIT.—The amount determined under paragraph (2) for any taxable year shall not exceed an amount equal to the amount determined under paragraph (2)(A) for such taxable year, reduced (but not below zero) by the amount which bears the same ratio to such amount as—

(i) the excess of—

(I) the taxpayer's adjusted gross income for such taxable year, over

(II) the applicable dollar amount, bears to

(ii) $15,000 ($10,000 in the case of a joint return or a married individual filing a separate return).

The rules of subparagraphs (B) and (C) of section 219(g)(2) shall apply to any reduction under this subparagraph.

(B) DEFINITIONS.—For purposes of this paragraph—

(i) adjusted gross income shall be determined in the same manner as under section 219(g)(3), except that any amount included in gross income under subsection (d)(3) shall not be taken into account, and

(ii) the applicable dollar amount is—

(I) in the case of a taxpayer filing a joint return, $150,000,

(II) in the case of any other taxpayer (other than a married individual filing a separate return), $95,000, and

(III) in the case of a married individual filing a separate return, zero.

(C) MARITAL STATUS.—Section 219(g)(4) shall apply for purposes of this paragraph.

(D) INFLATION ADJUSTMENT.—In the case of any taxable year beginning in a calendar year after 2006, the dollar amounts in subclauses (I) and (II) of subparagraph (B)(ii) shall each be increased by an amount equal to—

(i) such dollar amount, multiplied by

(ii) the cost-of-living adjustment determined under section 1(f)(3) for the calendar year in which the taxable year begins, determined by substituting "calendar year 2005" for "calendar year 2016" in subparagraph (A)(ii) thereof.

Any increase determined under the preceding sentence shall be rounded to the nearest multiple of $1,000.

(4) MANDATORY DISTRIBUTION RULES NOT TO APPLY BEFORE DEATH.—Notwithstanding subsections (a)(6) and (b)(3) of section 408 (relating to required distributions), the following provisions shall not apply to any Roth IRA:

(A) Section 401(a)(9)(A).

(B) The incidental death benefit requirements of section 401(a).

(5) ROLLOVER CONTRIBUTIONS.—

(A) IN GENERAL.—No rollover contribution may be made to a Roth IRA unless it is a qualified rollover contribution.

(B) COORDINATION WITH LIMIT.—A qualified rollover contribution shall not be taken into account for purposes of paragraph (2).

(6) TIME WHEN CONTRIBUTIONS MADE.—For purposes of this section, the rule of section 219(f)(3) shall apply.

[Sec. 408A(d)]

(d) DISTRIBUTION RULES.—For purposes of this title—

(1) EXCLUSION.—Any qualified distribution from a Roth IRA shall not be includible in gross income.

(2) QUALIFIED DISTRIBUTION.—For purposes of this subsection—

(A) IN GENERAL.—The term "qualified distribution" means any payment or distribution—

(i) made on or after the date on which the individual attains age 59½,

(ii) made to a beneficiary (or to the estate of the individual) on or after the death of the individual,

(iii) attributable to the individual's being disabled (within the meaning of section 72(m)(7)), or

(iv) which is a qualified special purpose distribution.

(B) DISTRIBUTIONS WITHIN NONEXCLUSION PERIOD.—A payment or distribution from a Roth IRA shall not be treated as a qualified distribution under subparagraph (A) if such payment or distribution is made within the 5-taxable year period beginning with the 1st taxable year for which the individual made a contribution to a Roth IRA (or such individual's spouse made a contribution to a Roth IRA) established for such individual.

(C) DISTRIBUTIONS OF EXCESS CONTRIBUTIONS AND EARNINGS.—The term "qualified distribution" shall not include any distribution of any contribution described in section 408(d)(4) and any net income allocable to the contribution.

(3) ROLLOVERS FROM AN ELIGIBLE RETIREMENT PLAN OTHER THAN A ROTH IRA.—

(A) IN GENERAL.—Notwithstanding sections 402(c), 403(b)(8), 408(d)(3), and 457(e)(16), in the case of any distribution to which this paragraph applies—

(i) there shall be included in gross income any amount which would be includible were it not part of a qualified rollover contribution,

(ii) section 72(t) shall not apply, and

(iii) unless the taxpayer elects not to have this clause apply, any amount required to be included in gross income for any taxable year beginning in 2010 by reason of this paragraph shall be so included ratably over the 2-taxable-year period beginning with the first taxable year beginning in 2011.

Any election under clause (iii) for any distributions during a taxable year may not be changed after the due date for such taxable year.

(B) DISTRIBUTIONS TO WHICH PARAGRAPH APPLIES.—This paragraph shall apply to a distribution from an eligible retirement plan (as defined by section 402(c)(8)(B)) maintained for the benefit of an individual which is contributed to a Roth IRA maintained for the benefit of such individual in a qualified rollover contribution. This paragraph shall not apply to a distribution which is a qualified rollover contribution from a Roth IRA or a qualified rollover contribution from a designated Roth account which is a rollover contribution described in section 402A(c)(3)(A).

(C) CONVERSIONS.—The conversion of an individual retirement plan (other than a Roth IRA) to a Roth IRA shall be treated for purposes of this paragraph as a distribution to which this paragraph applies.

(D) ADDITIONAL REPORTING REQUIREMENTS.—Trustees of Roth IRAs, trustees of individual retirement plans, persons subject to section 6047(d)(1), or all of the foregoing persons, whichever is appropriate, shall include such additional information in reports required under section 408(i) or 6047 as the Secretary may require to ensure that amounts required to be included in gross income under subparagraph (A) are so included.

(E) SPECIAL RULES FOR CONTRIBUTIONS TO WHICH 2-YEAR AVERAGING APPLIES.—In the case of a qualified rollover contribution to a Roth IRA of a distribution to which subparagraph (A)(iii) applied, the following rules shall apply:

(i) ACCELERATION OF INCLUSION.—

(I) IN GENERAL.—The amount otherwise required to be included in gross income for any taxable year beginning in 2010 or the first taxable year in the 2-year period under subparagraph (A)(iii) shall be increased by the aggregate distributions from Roth IRAs for such taxable year which are allocable under paragraph (4) to the portion of such qualified rollover contribution required to be included in gross income under subparagraph (A)(i).

(II) LIMITATION ON AGGREGATE AMOUNT INCLUDED.—The amount required to be included in gross income for any taxable year under subparagraph (A)(iii) shall not exceed the aggregate amount required to be included in gross income under subparagraph (A)(iii) for all taxable years in the 2-year period (without regard to subclause (I)) reduced by amounts included for all preceding taxable years.

(ii) DEATH OF DISTRIBUTEE.—

(I) IN GENERAL.—If the individual required to include amounts in gross income under such subparagraph dies before all of such amounts are included, all remaining amounts shall be included in gross income for the taxable year which includes the date of death.

(II) SPECIAL RULE FOR SURVIVING SPOUSE.—If the spouse of the individual described in subclause (I) acquires the individual's entire interest in any Roth IRA to which such qualified rollover contribution is properly allocable, the spouse may elect to treat the remaining amounts described in subclause (I) as includible in the spouse's gross income in the taxable years of the spouse ending with or within the taxable years of such individual in which such amounts would otherwise have been includible. Any such election may not be made or changed after the due date for the spouse's taxable year which includes the date of death.

(F) SPECIAL RULE FOR APPLYING SECTION 72.—

(i) IN GENERAL.—If—

(I) any portion of a distribution from a Roth IRA is properly allocable to a qualified rollover contribution described in this paragraph; and

(II) such distribution is made within the 5-taxable year period beginning with the taxable year in which such contribution was made,

then section 72(t) shall be applied as if such portion were includible in gross income.

(ii) LIMITATION.—Clause (i) shall apply only to the extent of the amount of the qualified rollover contribution includible in gross income under subparagraph (A)(i).

(4) AGGREGATION AND ORDERING RULES.—

(A) AGGREGATION RULES.— Section 408(d)(2) shall be applied separately with respect to Roth IRAs and other individual retirement plans.

(B) ORDERING RULES.—For purposes of applying this section and section 72 to any distribution from a Roth IRA, such distribution shall be treated as made—

(i) from contributions to the extent that the amount of such distribution, when added to all previous distributions from the Roth IRA, does not exceed the aggregate contributions to the Roth IRA; and

(ii) from such contributions in the following order:

(I) Contributions other than qualified rollover contributions to which paragraph (3) applies.

(II) Qualified rollover contributions to which paragraph (3) applies on a first-in, first-out basis.

Any distribution allocated to a qualified rollover contribution under clause (ii)(II) shall be allocated first to the portion of such contribution required to be included in gross income.

(5) QUALIFIED SPECIAL PURPOSE DISTRIBUTION.—For purposes of this section, the term "qualified special purpose distribution" means any distribution to which subparagraph (F) of section 72(t)(2) applies.

(6) TAXPAYER MAY MAKE ADJUSTMENTS BEFORE DUE DATE.—

(A) IN GENERAL.—Except as provided by the Secretary, if, on or before the due date for any taxable year, a taxpayer transfers in a trustee-to-trustee transfer any contribution to an individual retirement plan made during such taxable year from such plan to any other individual retirement plan, then, for purposes of this chapter, such contribution shall be treated as having been made to the transferee plan (and not the transferor plan).

(B) SPECIAL RULES.—

(i) TRANSFER OF EARNINGS.—Subparagraph (A) shall not apply to the transfer of any contribution unless such transfer is accompanied by any net income allocable to such contribution.

(ii) NO DEDUCTION.—Subparagraph (A) shall apply to the transfer of any contribution only to the extent no deduction was allowed with respect to the contribution to the transferor plan.

(iii) CONVERSIONS.—Subparagraph (A) shall not apply in the case of a qualified rollover contribution to which subsection (d)(3) applies (including by reason of subparagraph (C) thereof).

(7) DUE DATE.—For purposes of this subsection, the due date for any taxable year is the date prescribed by law (including extensions of time) for filing the taxpayer's return for such taxable year.

[Sec. 408A(e)]

(e) QUALIFIED ROLLOVER CONTRIBUTION.—For purposes of this section—

(1) IN GENERAL.—The term "qualified rollover contribution" means a rollover contribution—

(A) to a Roth IRA from another such account,

(B) from an eligible retirement plan, but only if—

(i) in the case of an individual retirement plan, such rollover contribution meets the requirements of section 408(d)(3), and

(ii) in the case of any eligible retirement plan (as defined in section 402(c)(8)(B) other than clauses (i) and (ii) thereof), such rollover contribution meets the requirements of section 402(c), 403(b)(8), or 457(e)(16), as applicable.

For purposes of section 408(d)(3)(B), there shall be disregarded any qualified rollover contribution from an individual retirement plan (other than a Roth IRA) to a Roth IRA.

* * *

[Sec. 408A(f)]

(f) INDIVIDUAL RETIREMENT PLAN.—For purposes of this section—

(1) a simplified employee pension or a simple retirement account may not be designated as a Roth IRA; and

(2) contributions to any such pension or account shall not be taken into account for purposes of subsection (c)(2)(B).

[Sec. 409A]

SEC. 409A. INCLUSION IN GROSS INCOME OF DEFERRED COMPENSATION UNDER NONQUALIFIED DEFERRED COMPENSATION PLANS.

[Sec. 409A(a)]

(a) RULES RELATING TO CONSTRUCTIVE RECEIPT.—

(1) PLAN FAILURES.—

(A) GROSS INCOME INCLUSION.—

(i) IN GENERAL.—If at any time during a taxable year a nonqualified deferred compensation plan—

(I) fails to meet the requirements of paragraphs (2), (3), and (4), or

(II) is not operated in accordance with such requirements,

all compensation deferred under the plan for the taxable year and all preceding taxable years shall be includible in gross income for the taxable year to the extent not subject to a substantial risk of forfeiture and not previously included in gross income.

(ii) APPLICATION ONLY TO AFFECTED PARTICIPANTS.—Clause (i) shall only apply with respect to all compensation deferred under the plan for participants with respect to whom the failure relates.

(B) INTEREST AND ADDITIONAL TAX PAYABLE WITH RESPECT TO PREVIOUSLY DEFERRED COMPENSATION.—

(i) IN GENERAL.—If compensation is required to be included in gross income under subparagraph (A) for a taxable year, the tax imposed by this chapter for the taxable year shall be increased by the sum of—

(I) the amount of interest determined under clause (ii), and

(II) an amount equal to 20 percent of the compensation which is required to be included in gross income.

(ii) INTEREST.—For purposes of clause (i), the interest determined under this clause for any taxable year is the amount of interest at the underpayment rate plus 1 percentage point on the underpayments that would have occurred had the deferred compensation been includible in gross income for the taxable year in which first deferred or, if later, the first taxable year in which such deferred compensation is not subject to a substantial risk of forfeiture.

(2) DISTRIBUTIONS.—

(A) IN GENERAL.—The requirements of this paragraph are met if the plan provides that compensation deferred under the plan may not be distributed earlier than—

(i) separation from service as determined by the Secretary (except as provided in subparagraph (B)(i)),

(ii) the date the participant becomes disabled (within the meaning of subparagraph (C)),

(iii) death,

(iv) a specified time (or pursuant to a fixed schedule) specified under the plan at the date of the deferral of such compensation,

(v) to the extent provided by the Secretary, a change in the ownership or effective control of the corporation, or in the ownership of a substantial portion of the assets of the corporation, or

(vi) the occurrence of an unforeseeable emergency.

(B) SPECIAL RULES.—

(i) SPECIFIED EMPLOYEES.—In the case of any specified employee, the requirement of subparagraph (A)(i) is met only if distributions may not be made before the date which is 6 months after the date of separation from service (or, if earlier, the date of death of the employee). For purposes of the preceding sentence, a specified employee is a key employee (as defined in section 416(i) without regard to paragraph (5) thereof) of a corporation any stock in which is publicly traded on an established securities market or otherwise.

(ii) UNFORESEEABLE EMERGENCY.—For purposes of subparagraph (A)(vi)—

(I) IN GENERAL.—The term "unforeseeable emergency" means a severe financial hardship to the participant resulting from an illness or accident of the participant, the participant's spouse, or a dependent (as defined in section 152(a)) of the participant, loss of the participant's property due to casualty, or other similar extraordinary and unforeseeable circumstances arising as a result of events beyond the control of the participant.

(II) LIMITATION ON DISTRIBUTIONS.—The requirement of subparagraph (A)(vi) is met only if, as determined under regulations of the Secretary, the amounts distributed with respect to an emergency do not exceed the amounts necessary to satisfy such emergency plus amounts necessary to pay taxes reasonably anticipated as a result of the distribution, after taking into account the extent to which such hardship is or may be relieved through reimbursement or compensation by insurance or otherwise or by liquidation of the participant's assets (to the extent the liquidation of such assets would not itself cause severe financial hardship).

(C) DISABLED.—For purposes of subparagraph (A)(ii), a participant shall be considered disabled if the participant—

(i) is unable to engage in any substantial gainful activity by reason of any medically determinable physical or mental impairment which can be expected to result in death or can be expected to last for a continuous period of not less than 12 months, or

(ii) is, by reason of any medically determinable physical or mental impairment which can be expected to result in death or can be expected to last for a continuous period of not less than 12 months, receiving income replacement benefits for a period of not less than 3 months under an accident and health plan covering employees of the participant's employer.

(3) ACCELERATION OF BENEFITS.—The requirements of this paragraph are met if the plan does not permit the acceleration of the time or schedule of any payment under the plan, except as provided in regulations by the Secretary.

(4) ELECTIONS.—

(A) IN GENERAL.—The requirements of this paragraph are met if the requirements of subparagraphs (B) and (C) are met.

(B) INITIAL DEFERRAL DECISION.—

(i) IN GENERAL.—The requirements of this subparagraph are met if the plan provides that compensation for services performed during a taxable year may be deferred at the participant's election only if the election to defer such compensation is made not later than the close of the preceding taxable year or at such other time as provided in regulations.

(ii) FIRST YEAR OF ELIGIBILITY.—In the case of the first year in which a participant becomes eligible to participate in the plan, such election may be made with respect to services to be performed subsequent to the election within 30 days after the date the participant becomes eligible to participate in such plan.

(iii) PERFORMANCE-BASED COMPENSATION.—In the case of any performance-based compensation based on services performed over a period of at least 12 months, such election may be made no later than 6 months before the end of the period.

(C) CHANGES IN TIME AND FORM OF DISTRIBUTION.—The requirements of this subparagraph are met if, in the case of a plan which permits under a subsequent election a delay in a payment or a change in the form of payment—

(i) the plan requires that such election may not take effect until at least 12 months after the date on which the election is made,

(ii) in the case of an election related to a payment not described in clause (ii), (iii), or (vi) of paragraph (2)(A), the plan requires that the payment with respect to which such election is made be deferred for a period of not less than 5 years from the date such payment would otherwise have been made, and

(iii) the plan requires that any election related to a payment described in paragraph (2)(A)(iv) may not be made less than 12 months prior to the date of the first scheduled payment under such paragraph.

[Sec. 409A(b)]

(b) RULES RELATING TO FUNDING.—

(1) OFFSHORE PROPERTY IN A TRUST.—In the case of assets set aside (directly or indirectly) in a trust (or other arrangement determined by the Secretary) for purposes of paying deferred compensation under a nonqualified deferred compensation plan, for purposes of section 83 such assets shall be treated as property transferred in connection with the performance of services whether or not such assets are available to satisfy claims of general creditors—

(A) at the time set aside if such assets (or such trust or other arrangement) are located outside of the United States, or

(B) at the time transferred if such assets (or such trust or other arrangement) are subsequently transferred outside of the United States.

This paragraph shall not apply to assets located in a foreign jurisdiction if substantially all of the services to which the nonqualified deferred compensation relates are performed in such jurisdiction.

(2) EMPLOYER'S FINANCIAL HEALTH.—In the case of compensation deferred under a nonqualified deferred compensation plan, there is a transfer of property within the meaning of section 83 with respect to such compensation as of the earlier of—

(A) the date on which the plan first provides that assets will become restricted to the provision of benefits under the plan in connection with a change in the employer's financial health, or

(B) the date on which assets are so restricted,

whether or not such assets are available to satisfy claims of general creditors.

(3) TREATMENT OF EMPLOYER'S DEFINED BENEFIT PLAN DURING RESTRICTED PERIOD.—

(A) IN GENERAL.—If-

(i) during any restricted period with respect to a single-employer defined benefit plan, assets are set aside or reserved (directly or indirectly) in a trust (or other arrangement as determined by the Secretary) or transferred to such a trust or other arrangement for purposes of paying deferred compensation of an applicable covered employee under a nonqualified deferred compensation plan of the plan sponsor or member of a controlled group which includes the plan sponsor, or

(ii) a nonqualified deferred compensation plan of the plan sponsor or member of a controlled group which includes the plan sponsor provides that assets will become restricted to the provision of benefits under the plan to an applicable covered employee in connection with such restricted period (or other similar financial measure determined by the Secretary) with respect to the defined benefit plan, or assets are so restricted,

such assets shall, for purposes of section 83, be treated as property transferred in connection with the performance of services whether or not such assets are available to satisfy claims of general creditors. Clause (i) shall not apply with respect to any assets which are so set aside before the restricted period with respect to the defined benefit plan.

(B) RESTRICTED PERIOD.—For purposes of this section, the term "restricted period" means, with respect to any plan described in subparagraph (A)—

(i) any period during which the plan is in at-risk status (as defined in section 430(i)),

(ii) any period the plan sponsor is a debtor in a case under title 11, United States Code, or similar Federal or State law, and

(iii) the 12-month period beginning on the date which is 6 months before the termination date of the plan if, as of the termination date, the plan is not sufficient for benefit liabilities (within the meaning of section 4041 of the Employee Retirement Income Security Act of 1974).

(C) SPECIAL RULE FOR PAYMENT OF TAXES ON DEFERRED COMPENSATION INCLUDED IN INCOME.—If an employer provides directly or indirectly for the payment of any Federal, State, or local income taxes with respect to any compensation required to be included in gross income by reason of this paragraph—

(i) interest shall be imposed under subsection (a)(1)(B)(i)(I) on the amount of such payment in the same manner as if such payment was part of the deferred compensation to which it relates,

(ii) such payment shall be taken into account in determining the amount of the additional tax under subsection (a)(1)(B)(i)(II) in the same manner as if such payment was part of the deferred compensation to which it relates, and

(iii) no deduction shall be allowed under this title with respect to such payment.

(D) OTHER DEFINITIONS.—For purposes of this section—

(i) APPLICABLE COVERED EMPLOYEE.—The term "applicable covered employee" means any—

(I) covered employee of a plan sponsor,

(II) covered employee of a member of a controlled group which includes the plan sponsor, and

(III) former employee who was a covered employee at the time of termination of employment with the plan sponsor or a member of a controlled group which includes the plan sponsor.

(ii) COVERED EMPLOYEE.—The term "covered employee" means an individual described in section 162(m)(3) or an individual subject to the requirements of section 16(a) of the Securities Exchange Act of 1934.

(4) INCOME INCLUSION FOR OFFSHORE TRUSTS AND EMPLOYER'S FINANCIAL HEALTH.—For each taxable year that assets treated as transferred under this subsection remain set aside in a

trust or other arrangement subject to paragraph (1), (2), or (3), any increase in value in, or earnings with respect to, such assets shall be treated as an additional transfer of property under this subsection (to the extent not previously included in income).

(5) INTEREST ON TAX LIABILITY PAYABLE WITH RESPECT TO TRANSFERRED PROPERTY.—

(A) IN GENERAL.—If amounts are required to be included in gross income by reason of paragraph (1), (2), or (3) for a taxable year, the tax imposed by this chapter for such taxable year shall be increased by the sum of—

(i) the amount of interest determined under subparagraph (B), and

(ii) an amount equal to 20 percent of the amounts required to be included in gross income.

(B) INTEREST.—For purposes of subparagraph (A), the interest determined under this subparagraph for any taxable year is the amount of interest at the underpayment rate plus 1 percentage point on the underpayments that would have occurred had the amounts so required to be included in gross income by paragraph (1), (2), or (3) been includible in gross income for the taxable year in which first deferred or, if later, the first taxable year in which such amounts are not subject to a substantial risk of forfeiture.

[Sec. 409A(c)]

(c) NO INFERENCE ON EARLIER INCOME INCLUSION OR REQUIREMENT OF LATER INCLUSION.—Nothing in this section shall be construed to prevent the inclusion of amounts in gross income under any other provision of this chapter or any other rule of law earlier than the time provided in this section. Any amount included in gross income under this section shall not be required to be included in gross income under any other provision of this chapter or any other rule of law later than the time provided in this section.

[Sec. 409A(d)]

(d) OTHER DEFINITIONS AND SPECIAL RULES.—For purposes of this section:

(1) NONQUALIFIED DEFERRED COMPENSATION PLAN.—The term "nonqualified deferred compensation plan" means any plan that provides for the deferral of compensation, other than—

(A) a qualified employer plan, and

(B) any bona fide vacation leave, sick leave, compensatory time, disability pay, or death benefit plan.

(2) QUALIFIED EMPLOYER PLAN.—The term "qualified employer plan" means—

(A) any plan, contract, pension, account, or trust described in subparagraph (A) or (B) of section 219(g)(5) (without regard to subparagraph (A)(iii)),

(B) any eligible deferred compensation plan (within the meaning of section 457(b)), and

(C) any plan described in section 415(m).

(3) PLAN INCLUDES ARRANGEMENTS, ETC.—The term "plan" includes any agreement or arrangement, including an agreement or arrangement that includes one person.

(4) SUBSTANTIAL RISK OF FORFEITURE.—The rights of a person to compensation are subject to a substantial risk of forfeiture if such person's rights to such compensation are conditioned upon the future performance of substantial services by any individual.

(5) TREATMENT OF EARNINGS.—References to deferred compensation shall be treated as including references to income (whether actual or notional) attributable to such compensation or such income.

(6) AGGREGATION RULES.—Except as provided by the Secretary, rules similar to the rules of subsections (b) and (c) of section 414 shall apply.

(7) TREATMENT OF QUALIFIED STOCK.—An arrangement under which an employee may receive qualified stock (as defined in section 83(i)(2)) shall not be treated as a nonqualified deferred compensation plan with respect to such employee solely because of such employee's election, or ability to make an election, to defer recognition of income under section 83(i).

[Sec. 409A(e)]

(e) REGULATIONS.—The Secretary shall prescribe such regulations as may be necessary or appropriate to carry out the purposes of this section, including regulations—

(1) providing for the determination of amounts of deferral in the case of a nonqualified deferred compensation plan which is a defined benefit plan,

(2) relating to changes in the ownership and control of a corporation or assets of a corporation for purposes of subsection (a)(2)(A)(v),

(3) exempting arrangements from the application of subsection (b) if such arrangements will not result in an improper deferral of United States tax and will not result in assets being effectively beyond the reach of creditors,

(4) defining financial health for purposes of subsection (b)(2), and

(5) disregarding a substantial risk of forfeiture in cases where necessary to carry out the purposes of this section.

PART II—CERTAIN STOCK OPTIONS

[Sec. 421]

SEC. 421. GENERAL RULES.

[Sec. 421(a)]

(a) EFFECT OF QUALIFYING TRANSFER.—If a share of stock is transferred to an individual in a transfer in respect of which the requirements of section 422(a) or 423(a) are met—

(1) no income shall result at the time of the transfer of such share to the individual upon his exercise of the option with respect to such share;

(2) no deduction under section 162 (relating to trade or business expenses) shall be allowable at any time to the employer corporation, a parent or subsidiary corporation of such corporation, or a corporation issuing or assuming a stock option in a transaction to which section 424(a) applies, with respect to the share so transferred; and

(3) no amount other than the price paid under the option shall be considered as received by any of such corporations for the share so transferred.

[Sec. 421(b)]

(b) EFFECT OF DISQUALIFYING DISPOSITION.—If the transfer of a share of stock to an individual pursuant to his exercise of an option would otherwise meet the requirements of section 422(a) or 423(a) except that there is a failure to meet any of the holding period requirements of section 422(a)(1) or 423(a)(1), then any increase in the income of such individual or deduction from the income of his employer corporation for the taxable year in which such exercise occurred attributable to such disposition, shall be treated as an increase in income or a deduction from income in the taxable year of such individual or of such employer corporation in which such disposition occurred. No amount shall be required to be deducted and withheld under chapter 24 with respect to any increase in income attributable to a disposition described in the preceding sentence.

[Sec. 421(c)]

(c) EXERCISE BY ESTATE.—

(1) IN GENERAL.—If an option to which this part applies is exercised after the death of the employee by the estate of the decedent, or by a person who acquired the right to exercise such option by bequest or inheritance or by reason of the death of the decedent, the provisions of subsection (a) shall apply to the same extent as if the option had been exercised by the decedent, except that—

(A) the holding period and employment requirements of sections 422(a) and 423(a) shall not apply, and

(B) any transfer by the estate of stock acquired shall be considered a disposition of such stock for purposes of section 423(c).

(2) DEDUCTION FOR ESTATE TAX.—If an amount is required to be included under section 423(c) in gross income of the estate of the deceased employee or of a person described in paragraph (1), there shall be allowed to the estate or such person a deduction with respect to

the estate tax attributable to the inclusion in the taxable estate of the deceased employee of the net value for estate tax purposes of the option. For this purpose, the deduction shall be determined under section 691(c) as if the option acquired from the deceased employee were an item of gross income in respect of the decedent under section 691 and as if the amount includible in gross income under section 423(c) were an amount included in gross income under section 691 in respect of such item of gross income.

(3) BASIS OF SHARES ACQUIRED.—In the case of a share of stock acquired by the exercise of an option to which paragraph (1) applies—

(A) the basis of such share shall include so much of the basis of the option as is attributable to such share; except that the basis of such share shall be reduced by the excess (if any) of (i) the amount which would have been includible in gross income under section 423(c) if the employee had exercised the option on the date of this death and had held the share acquired pursuant to such exercise at the time of his death, over (ii) the amount which is includible in gross income under such section; and

(B) the last sentence of section 423(c) shall apply only to the extent that the amount includible in gross income under such section exceeds so much of the basis of the option as is attributable to such share.

[Sec. 421(d)]

(d) CERTAIN SALES TO COMPLY WITH CONFLICT-OF-INTEREST REQUIREMENTS.—If—

(1) a share of stock is transferred to an eligible person (as defined in section 1043(b)(1)) pursuant to such person's exercise of an option to which this part applies, and

(2) such share is disposed of by such person pursuant to a certificate of divestiture (as defined in section 1043(b)(2)),

such disposition shall be treated as meeting the requirements of section 422(a)(1) or 423(a)(1), whichever is applicable.

[Sec. 422]

SEC. 422. INCENTIVE STOCK OPTIONS.

[Sec. 422(a)]

(a) IN GENERAL.—Section 421(a) shall apply with respect to the transfer of a share of stock to an individual pursuant to his exercise of an incentive stock option if—

(1) no disposition of such share is made by him within 2 years from the date of the granting of the option nor within 1 year after the transfer of such share to him, and

(2) at all times during the period beginning on the date of the granting of the option and ending on the day 3 months before the date of such exercise, such individual was an employee of either the corporation granting such option, a parent or subsidiary corporation of such corporation, or a corporation or a parent or subsidiary corporation of such corporation issuing or assuming a stock option in a transaction to which section 424(a) applies.

[Sec. 422(b)]

(b) INCENTIVE STOCK OPTION.—For purposes of this part, the term "incentive stock option" means an option granted to an individual for any reason connected with his employment by a corporation, if granted by the employer corporation or its parent or subsidiary corporation, to purchase stock of any of such corporations, but only if—

(1) the option is granted pursuant to a plan which includes the aggregate number of shares which may be issued under options and the employees (or class of employees) eligible to receive options, and which is approved by the stockholders of the granting corporation within 12 months before or after the date such plan is adopted;

(2) such option is granted within 10 years from the date such plan is adopted, or the date such plan is approved by the stockholders, whichever is earlier;

(3) such option by its terms is not exercisable after the expiration of 10 years from the date such option is granted;

(4) the option price is not less than the fair market value of the stock at the time such option is granted;

(5) such option by its terms is not transferable by such individual otherwise than by will or the laws of descent and distribution, and is exercisable, during his lifetime, only by him; and

(6) such individual, at the time the option is granted, does not own stock possessing more than 10 percent of the total combined voting power of all classes of stock of the employer corporation or of its parent or subsidiary corporation.

Such term shall not include any option if (as of the time the option is granted) the terms of such option provide that it will not be treated as an incentive stock option. Such term shall not include any option if an election is made under section 83(i) with respect to the stock received in connection with the exercise of such option.

[Sec. 422(c)]

(c) SPECIAL RULES.—

(1) GOOD FAITH EFFORTS TO VALUE STOCK.—If a share of stock is transferred pursuant to the exercise by an individual of an option which would fail to qualify as an incentive stock option under subsection (b) because there was a failure in an attempt, made in good faith, to meet the requirement of subsection (b)(4), the requirement of subsection (b)(4) shall be considered to have been met. To the extent provided in regulations by the Secretary, a similar rule shall apply for purposes of subsection (d).

(2) CERTAIN DISQUALIFYING DISPOSITIONS WHERE AMOUNT REALIZED IS LESS THAN VALUE AT EXERCISE.—If—

(A) an individual who has acquired a share of stock by the exercise of an incentive stock option makes a disposition of such share within either of the periods described in subsection (a)(1), and

(B) such disposition is a sale or exchange with respect to which a loss (if sustained) would be recognized to such individual,

then the amount which is includible in the gross income of such individual, and the amount which is deductible from the income of his employer corporation, as compensation attributable to the exercise of such option shall not exceed the excess (if any) of the amount realized on such sale or exchange over the adjusted basis of such share.

(3) CERTAIN TRANSFERS BY INSOLVENT INDIVIDUALS.—If an insolvent individual holds a share of stock acquired pursuant to his exercise of an incentive stock option, and if such share is transferred to a trustee, receiver, or any other similar fiduciary in any proceeding under title 11 or any other similar insolvency proceeding, neither such transfer, nor any other transfer of such share for the benefit of his creditors in such proceeding, shall constitute a disposition of such share for purposes of subsection (a)(1).

(4) PERMISSIBLE PROVISIONS.—An option which meets the requirements of subsection (b) shall be treated as an incentive stock option even if—

(A) the employee may pay for the stock with stock of the corporation granting the option,

(B) the employee has a right to receive property at the time of exercise of the option, or

(C) the option is subject to any condition not inconsistent with the provisions of subsection (b).

Subparagraph (B) shall apply to a transfer of property (other than cash) only if section 83 applies to the property so transferred.

(5) 10-PERCENT SHAREHOLDER RULE.—Subsection (b)(6) shall not apply if at the time such option is granted the option price is at least 110 percent of the fair market value of the stock subject to the option and such option by its terms is not exercisable after the expiration of 5 years from the date such option is granted.

(6) SPECIAL RULE WHEN DISABLED.—For purposes of subsection (a)(2), in the case of an employee who is disabled (within the meaning of section 22(e)(3)), the 3-month period of subsection (a)(2) shall be 1 year.

(7) FAIR MARKET VALUE.—For purposes of this section, the fair market value of stock shall be determined without regard to any restriction other than a restriction which, by its terms, will never lapse.

[Sec. 422(d)]

(d) $100,000 PER YEAR LIMITATION.—

(1) IN GENERAL.—To the extent that the aggregate fair market value of stock with respect to which incentive stock options (determined without regard to this subsection) are exercisable for the 1st time by any individual during any calendar year (under all plans of the individual's employer corporation and its parent and subsidiary corporations) exceeds $100,000, such options shall be treated as options which are not incentive stock options.

(2) ORDERING RULE.—Paragraph (1) shall be applied by taking options into account in the order in which they were granted.

(3) DETERMINATION OF FAIR MARKET VALUE.—For purposes of paragraph (1), the fair market value of any stock shall be determined as of the time the option with respect to such stock is granted.

[Sec. 423]

SEC. 423. EMPLOYEE STOCK PURCHASE PLANS.

[Sec. 423(a)]

(a) GENERAL RULE.—Section 421(a) shall apply with respect to the transfer of a share of stock to an individual pursuant to his exercise of an option granted under an employee stock purchase plan (as defined in subsection (b)) if—

(1) no disposition of such share is made by him within 2 years after the date of the granting of the option nor within 1 year after the transfer of such share to him; and

(2) at all times during the period beginning with the date of the granting of the option and ending on the day 3 months before the date of such exercise, he is an employee of the corporation granting such option, a parent or subsidiary corporation of such corporation, or a corporation or a parent or subsidiary corporation of such corporation issuing or assuming a stock option in a transaction to which section 424(a) applies.

[Sec. 423(b)]

(b) EMPLOYEE STOCK PURCHASE PLAN.—For purposes of this part, the term "employee stock purchase plan" means a plan which meets the following requirements:

(1) the plan provides that options are to be granted only to employees of the employer corporation or of its parent or subsidiary corporation to purchase stock in any such corporation;

(2) such plan is approved by the stockholders of the granting corporation within 12 months before or after the date such plan is adopted;

(3) under the terms of the plan, no employee can be granted an option if such employee, immediately after the option is granted, owns stock possessing 5 percent or more of the total combined voting power or value of all classes of stock of the employer corporation or of its parent or subsidiary corporation. For purposes of this paragraph, the rules of section 424(d) shall apply in determining the stock ownership of an individual, and stock which the employee may purchase under outstanding options shall be treated as stock owned by the employee;

(4) under the terms of the plan, options are to be granted to all employees of any corporation whose employees are granted any of such options by reason of their employment by such corporation, except that there may be excluded—

(A) employees who have been employed less than 2 years,

(B) employees whose customary employment is 20 hours or less per week,

(C) employees whose customary employment is for not more than 5 months in any calendar year, and

(D) highly compensated employees (within the meaning of section 414(q));

(5) under the terms of the plan, all employees granted such options shall have the same rights and privileges, except that the amount of stock which may be purchased by any employee under such option may bear a uniform relationship to the total compensation, or the basic or regular rate of compensation, of employees, the plan may provide that no employee may purchase more than a maximum amount of stock fixed under the plan, and the rules of section 83(i) shall apply in determining which employees have a right to make an election under such section;

(6) under the terms of the plan, the option price is not less than the lesser of—

(A) an amount equal to 85 percent of the fair market value of the stock at the time such option is granted, or

(B) an amount which under the terms of the option may not be less than 85 percent of the fair market value of the stock at the time such option is exercised;

(7) under the terms of the plan, such option cannot be exercised after the expiration of—

(A) 5 years from the date such option is granted if, under the terms of such plan, the option price is to be not less than 85 percent of the fair market value of such stock at the time of the exercise of the option, or

(B) 27 months from the date such option is granted, if the option price is not determinable in the manner described in subparagraph (A);

(8) under the terms of the plan, no employee may be granted an option which permits his rights to purchase stock under all such plans of his employer corporation and its parent and subsidiary corporations to accrue at a rate which exceeds $25,000 of fair market value of such stock (determined at the time such option is granted) for each calendar year in which such option is outstanding at any time. For purposes of this paragraph—

(A) the right to purchase stock under an option accrues when the option (or any portion thereof) first becomes exercisable during the calendar year;

(B) the right to purchase stock under an option accrues at the rate provided in the option, but in no case may such rate exceed $25,000 of fair market value of such stock (determined at the time such option is granted) for any one calendar year; and

(C) a right to purchase stock which has accrued under one option granted pursuant to the plan may not be carried over to any other option; and

(9) under the terms of the plan, such option is not transferable by such individual otherwise than by will or the laws of descent and distribution, and is exercisable, during his lifetime, only by him.

For purposes of paragraphs (3) to (9), inclusive, where additional terms are contained in an offering made under a plan, such additional terms shall, with respect to options exercised under such offering, be treated as a part of the terms of such plan.

[Sec. 423(c)]

(c) Special Rule Where Option Price Is Between 85 Percent and 100 Percent of Value of Stock.—If the option price of a share of stock acquired by an individual pursuant to a transfer to which subsection (a) applies was less than 100 percent of the fair market value of such share at the time such option was granted, then, in the event of any disposition of such share by him which meets the holding period requirements of subsection (a), or in the event of his death (whenever occurring) while owning such share, there shall be included as compensation (and not as gain upon the sale or exchange of a capital asset) in his gross income, for the taxable year in which falls the date of such disposition or for the taxable year closing with his death, whichever applies, an amount equal to the lesser of—

(1) the excess of the fair market value of the share at the time of such disposition or death over the amount paid for the share under the option, or

(2) the excess of the fair market value of the share at the time the option was granted over the option price.

If the option price is not fixed or determinable at the time the option is granted, then for purposes of this subsection, the option price shall be determined as if the option were exercised at such time. In the case of the disposition of such share by the individual, the basis of the share in his hands at the time of such disposition shall be increased by an amount equal to the amount so includible in his gross income. No amount shall be required to be deducted and withheld under chapter 24 with respect to any amount treated as compensation under this subsection.

[Sec. 423(d)]

(d) COORDINATION WITH QUALIFIED EQUITY GRANTS.—An option for which an election is made under section 83(i) with respect to the stock received in connection with its exercise shall not be considered as granted pursuant an employee stock purchase plan.

SUBCHAPTER E—ACCOUNTING PERIODS AND METHODS OF ACCOUNTING

PART I—ACCOUNTING PERIODS

[Sec. 441]

SEC. 441. PERIOD FOR COMPUTATION OF TAXABLE INCOME.

[Sec. 441(a)]

(a) COMPUTATION OF TAXABLE INCOME.—Taxable income shall be computed on the basis of the taxpayer's taxable year.

[Sec. 441(b)]

(b) TAXABLE YEAR.—For purposes of this subtitle, the term "taxable year" means—

(1) the taxpayer's annual accounting period, if it is a calendar year or a fiscal year;

(2) the calendar year, if subsection (g) applies;

(3) the period for which the return is made, if a return is made for a period of less than 12 months; or

(4) in the case of a DISC filing a return for a period of at least 12 months, the period determined under subsection (h).

[Sec. 441(c)]

(c) ANNUAL ACCOUNTING PERIOD.—For purposes of this subtitle, the term "annual accounting period" means the annual period on the basis of which the taxpayer regularly computes his income in keeping his books.

[Sec. 441(d)]

(d) CALENDAR YEAR.—For purposes of this subtitle, the term "calendar year" means a period of 12 months ending on December 31.

[Sec. 441(e)]

(e) FISCAL YEAR.—For purposes of this subtitle, the term "fiscal year" means a period of 12 months ending on the last day of any month other than December. In the case of any taxpayer who has made the election provided by subsection (f), the term means the annual period (varying from 52 to 53 weeks) so elected.

[Sec. 441(f)]

(f) ELECTION OF YEAR CONSISTING OF 52-53 WEEKS.—

(1) GENERAL RULE.—A taxpayer who, in keeping his books, regularly computes his income on the basis of an annual period which varies from 52 to 53 weeks and ends always on the same day of the week and ends always—

(A) on whatever date such same day of the week last occurs in a calendar month, or

(B) on whatever date such same day of the week falls which is nearest to the last day of a calendar month,

may (in accordance with the regulations prescribed under paragraph (3)) elect to compute his taxable income for purposes of this subtitle on the basis of such annual period. This paragraph shall apply to taxable years ending after the date of the enactment of this title.

(2) SPECIAL RULES FOR 52-53-WEEK YEAR.—

(A) EFFECTIVE DATES.—In any case in which the effective date or the applicability of any provision of this title is expressed in terms of taxable years beginning, including, or ending with reference to a specified date which is the first or last day of a month, a taxable year described in paragraph (1) shall (except for purposes of the computation under section 15) be treated—

(i) as beginning with the first day of the calendar month beginning nearest to the first day of such taxable year, or

(ii) as ending with the last day of the calendar month ending nearest to the last day of such taxable year,

as the case may be.

(B) CHANGE IN ACCOUNTING PERIOD.—In the case of a change from or to a taxable year described in paragraph (1)—

(i) if such change results in a short period (within the meaning of section 443) of 359 days or more, or of less than 7 days, section 443 (b) (relating to alternative tax computation) shall not apply;

(ii) if such change results in a short period of less than 7 days, such short period shall, for purposes of this subtitle, be added to and deemed a part of the following taxable year; and

(iii) if such change results in a short period to which subsection (b) of section 443 applies, the taxable income for such short period shall be placed on an annual basis for purposes of such subsection by multiplying the gross income for such short period (minus the deductions allowed by this chapter for the short period, but only the adjusted amount of the deductions for personal exemptions as described in section 443(c)) by 365, by dividing the result by the number of days in the short period, and the tax shall be the same part of the tax computed on the annual basis as the number of days in the short period is of 365 days.

(3) SPECIAL RULE FOR PARTNERSHIPS, S CORPORATIONS, AND PERSONAL SERVICE CORPORATIONS.—The Secretary may by regulation provide terms and conditions for the application of this subsection to a partnership, S corporation, or personal service corporation (within the meaning of section 441(i)(2)).

(4) REGULATIONS.—The Secretary shall prescribe such regulations as he deems necessary for the application of this subsection.

[Sec. 441(g)]

(g) NO BOOKS KEPT; NO ACCOUNTING PERIOD.—Except as provided in section 443 (relating to returns for periods of less than 12 months), the taxpayer's taxable year shall be the calendar year if—

(1) the taxpayer keeps no books;

(2) the taxpayer does not have an annual accounting period; or

(3) the taxpayer has an annual accounting period, but such period does not qualify as a fiscal year.

* * *

[Sec. 441(i)]

(i) TAXABLE YEAR OF PERSONAL SERVICE CORPORATIONS.—

(1) IN GENERAL.—For purposes of this subtitle, the taxable year of any personal service corporation shall be the calendar year unless the corporation establishes, to the satisfaction of the Secretary, a business purpose for having a different period for its taxable year. For purposes of this paragraph, any deferral of income to shareholders shall not be treated as a business purpose.

(2) PERSONAL SERVICE CORPORATION.—For purposes of this subsection, the term "personal service corporation" has the meaning given such term by section 269A(b)(1), except that section 269A(b)(2) shall be applied—

(A) by substituting "any" for "more than 10 percent", and

(B) by substituting "any" for "50 percent or more in value" in section 318(a)(2)(C).

A corporation shall not be treated as a personal service corporation unless more than 10 percent of the stock (by value) in such corporation is held by employee-owners (within the meaning of section 269A(b)(2), as modified by the preceding sentence). If a corporation is a member of an affiliated group filing a consolidated return, all members of such group shall be taken into account in determining whether such corporation is a personal service corporation.

[Sec. 442]

SEC. 442. CHANGE OF ANNUAL ACCOUNTING PERIOD.

If a taxpayer changes his annual accounting period, the new accounting period shall become the taxpayer's taxable year only if the change is approved by the Secretary. For purposes of this subtitle, if a taxpayer to whom section 441 (g) applies adopts an annual accounting period (as defined in section 441 (c)) other than a calendar year, the taxpayer shall be treated as having changed his annual accounting period.

[Sec. 443]

SEC. 443. RETURNS FOR A PERIOD OF LESS THAN 12 MONTHS.

[Sec. 443(a)]

(a) RETURNS FOR SHORT PERIOD.—A return for a period of less than 12 months (referred to in this section as "short period") shall be made under any of the following circumstances:

(1) CHANGE OF ANNUAL ACCOUNTING PERIOD.—When the taxpayer, with the approval of the Secretary, changes his annual accounting period. In such a case, the return shall be made for the short period beginning on the day after the close of the former taxable year and ending at the close of the day before the day designated as the first day of the new taxable year.

(2) TAXPAYER NOT IN EXISTENCE FOR ENTIRE TAXABLE YEAR.—When the taxpayer is in existence during only part of what would otherwise be his taxable year.

[Sec. 443(b)]

(b) COMPUTATION OF TAX ON CHANGE OF ANNUAL ACCOUNTING PERIOD.—

(1) GENERAL RULE.—If a return is made under paragraph (1) of subsection (a), the taxable income for the short period shall be placed on an annual basis by multiplying the modified taxable income for such short period by 12, dividing the result by the number of months in the short period. The tax shall be the same part of the tax computed on the annual basis as the number of months in the short period is of 12 months.

(2) EXCEPTION.—

(A) COMPUTATION BASED ON 12-MONTH PERIOD.—If the taxpayer applies for the benefits of this paragraph and establishes the amount of his taxable income for the 12-month period described in subparagraph (B), computed as if that period were a taxable year and under the law applicable to that year, then the tax for the short period, computed under paragraph (1), shall be reduced to the greater of the following:

(i) an amount which bears the same ratio to the tax computed on the taxable income for the 12-month period as the modified taxable income computed on the basis of the short period bears to the modified taxable income for the 12-month period; or

(ii) the tax computed on the modified taxable income for the short period.

The taxpayer (other than a taxpayer to whom subparagraph (B) (ii) applies) shall compute the tax and file his return without the application of this paragraph.

(B) 12-MONTH PERIOD.—The 12-month period referred to in subparagraph (A) shall be—

(i) the period of 12 months beginning on the first day of the short period, or

(ii) the period of 12 months ending at the close of the last day of the short period, if at the end of the 12 months referred to in clause (i) the taxpayer is not in existence or (if a corporation) has theretofore disposed of substantially all of its assets.

(C) APPLICATION FOR BENEFITS.—Application for the benefits of this paragraph shall be made in such manner and at such time as the regulations prescribed under subparagraph (D) may require; except that the time so prescribed shall not be later than the time (including extensions) for filing the return for the first taxable year which ends on or after the day which is 12 months after the first day of the short period. Such application, in case the return was filed without regard to this paragraph, shall be considered a claim for credit or refund with respect to the amount by which the tax is reduced under this paragraph.

(D) REGULATIONS.—The Secretary shall prescribe such regulations as he deems necessary for the application of this paragraph.

(3) MODIFIED TAXABLE INCOME DEFINED.—For purposes of this subsection the term "modified taxable income" means, with respect to any period, the gross income for such period minus the deductions allowed by this chapter for such period (but, in the case of a short period, only the adjusted amount of the deductions for personal exemptions).

[Sec. 443(c)]

(c) ADJUSTMENT IN DEDUCTION FOR PERSONAL EXEMPTION.—In the case of a taxpayer other than a corporation, if a return is made for a short period by reason of subsection (a) (1) and if the tax is not computed under subsection (b) (2), then the exemptions allowed as a deduction under section 151 (and any deduction in lieu thereof) shall be reduced to amounts which bear the same ratio to the full exemptions as the number of months in the short period bears to 12.

[Sec. 443(d)]

(d) ADJUSTMENT IN COMPUTING MINIMUM TAX AND TAX PREFERENCES.—If a return is made for a short period by reason of subsection (a)—

(1) the alternative minimum taxable income for the short period shall be placed on an annual basis by multiplying such amount by 12 and dividing the result by the number of months in the short period, and

(2) the amount computed under paragraph (1) of section 55(a) shall bear the same relation to the tax computed on the annual basis as the number of months in the short period bears to 12.

* * *

[Sec. 444]

SEC. 444. ELECTION OF TAXABLE YEAR OTHER THAN REQUIRED TAXABLE YEAR.

[Sec. 444(a)]

(a) GENERAL RULE.—Except as otherwise provided in this section, a partnership, S corporation, or personal service corporation may elect to have a taxable year other than the required taxable year.

[Sec. 444(b)]

(b) LIMITATIONS ON TAXABLE YEARS WHICH MAY BE ELECTED.—

(1) IN GENERAL.—Except as provided in paragraphs (2) and (3), an election may be made under subsection (a) only if the deferral period of the taxable year elected is not longer than 3 months.

(2) CHANGES IN TAXABLE YEAR.—Except as provided in paragraph (3), in the case of an entity changing a taxable year, an election may be made under subsection (a) only if the deferral period of the taxable year elected is not longer than the shorter of—

(A) 3 months, or

(B) the deferral period of the taxable year which is being changed.

(3) SPECIAL RULE FOR ENTITIES RETAINING 1986 TAXABLE YEARS.—In the case of an entity's 1st taxable year beginning after December 31, 1986, an entity may elect a taxable year under subsection (a) which is the same as the entity's last taxable year beginning in 1986.

(4) DEFERRAL PERIOD.—For purposes of this subsection, except as provided in regulations, the term "deferral period" means, with respect to any taxable year of the entity, the months between—

(A) the beginning of such year, and

(B) the close of the 1st required taxable year ending within such year.

[Sec. 444(c)]

(c) EFFECT OF ELECTION.—If an entity makes an election under subsection (a), then—

(1) in the case of a partnership or S corporation, such entity shall make the payments required by section 7519, and

(2) in the case of a personal service corporation, such corporation shall be subject to the deduction limitations of section 280H.

[Sec. 444(d)]

(d) ELECTIONS.—

(1) PERSON MAKING ELECTION.—An election under subsection (a) shall be made by the partnership, S corporation, or personal service corporation.

(2) PERIOD OF ELECTION.—

(A) IN GENERAL.—Any election under subsection (a) shall remain in effect until the partnership, S corporation, or personal service corporation changes its taxable year or otherwise terminates such election. Any change to a required taxable year may be made without the consent of the Secretary.

(B) NO FURTHER ELECTION.—If an election is terminated under subparagraph (A) or paragraph (3)(A), the partnership, S corporation, or personal service corporation may not make another election under subsection (a).

(3) TIERED STRUCTURES, ETC.—

(A) IN GENERAL.—Except as otherwise provided in this paragraph—

(i) no election may be under subsection (a) with respect to any entity which is part of a tiered structure, and

(ii) an election under subsection (a) with respect to any entity shall be terminated if such entity becomes part of a tiered structure.

(B) EXCEPTIONS FOR STRUCTURES CONSISTING OF CERTAIN ENTITIES WITH SAME TAXABLE YEAR.—Subparagraph (A) shall not apply to any tiered structure which consists only of partnerships or S corporations (or both) all of which have the same taxable year.

[Sec. 444(e)]

(e) REQUIRED TAXABLE YEAR.—For purposes of this section, the term "required taxable year" means the taxable year determined under section 706(b), 1378, or 441(i) without taking into account any taxable year which is allowable by reason of business purposes. Solely for purposes of the preceding sentence, sections 706(b), 1378, and 441(i) shall be treated as in effect for taxable years beginning before January 1, 1987.

[Sec. 444(f)]

(f) PERSONAL SERVICE CORPORATION.—For purposes of this section, the term "personal service corporation" has the meaning given to such term by section 441(i)(2).

* * *

PART II—METHODS OF ACCOUNTING

Subpart A—Methods of Accounting in General

[Sec. 446]

SEC. 446. GENERAL RULE FOR METHODS OF ACCOUNTING.

[Sec. 446(a)]

(a) GENERAL RULE.—Taxable income shall be computed under the method of accounting on the basis of which the taxpayer regularly computes his income in keeping his books.

[Sec. 446(b)]

(b) EXCEPTIONS.—If no method of accounting has been regularly used by the taxpayer, or if the method used does not clearly reflect income, the computation of taxable income shall be made under such method as, in the opinion of the Secretary, does clearly reflect income.

[Sec. 446(c)]

(c) PERMISSIBLE METHODS.—Subject to the provisions of subsections (a) and (b), a taxpayer may compute taxable income under any of the following methods of accounting—

(1) the cash receipts and disbursements method;

(2) an accrual method;

(3) any other method permitted by this chapter; or

(4) any combination of the foregoing methods permitted under regulations prescribed by the Secretary.

[Sec. 446(d)]

(d) TAXPAYER ENGAGED IN MORE THAN ONE BUSINESS.—A taxpayer engaged in more than one trade or business may, in computing taxable income, use a different method of accounting for each trade or business.

[Sec. 446(e)]

(e) REQUIREMENT RESPECTING CHANGE OF ACCOUNTING METHOD.—Except as otherwise expressly provided in this chapter, a taxpayer who changes the method of accounting on the basis of which he regularly computes his income in keeping his books shall, before computing his taxable income under the new method, secure the consent of the Secretary.

[Sec. 446(f)]

(f) FAILURE TO REQUEST CHANGE OF METHOD OF ACCOUNTING.—If the taxpayer does not file with the Secretary a request to change the method of accounting, the absence of the consent of the Secretary to a change in the method of accounting shall not be taken into account—

(1) to prevent the imposition of any penalty, or the addition of any amount to tax, under this title, or

(2) to diminish the amount of such penalty or addition to tax.

»»→ Caution: As provided in Section 448(c)(4), the dollar amount set forth in Section 448(c)(1) is adjusted for taxable years after 2018 to reflect increase in the Chained Consumer Price Index. The dollar amount applicable to taxable years beginning in 2020 is set forth in the material beginning at page ix.

[Sec. 448]

SEC. 448. LIMITATION ON USE OF CASH METHOD OF ACCOUNTING.

[Sec. 448(a)]

(a) GENERAL RULE.—Except as otherwise provided in this section, in the case of a—

(1) C corporation,

(2) partnership which has a C corporation as a partner, or

(3) tax shelter,

taxable income shall not be computed under the cash receipts and disbursements method of accounting.

[Sec. 448(b)]

(b) EXCEPTIONS.—

(1) FARMING BUSINESS.—Paragraphs (1) and (2) of subsection (a) shall not apply to any farming business.

(2) QUALIFIED PERSONAL SERVICE CORPORATIONS.—Paragraphs (1) and (2) of subsection (a) shall not apply to a qualified personal service corporation, and such a corporation shall be

treated as an individual for purposes of determining whether paragraph (2) of subsection (a) applies to any partnership.

(3) ENTITIES WHICH MEET GROSS RECEIPTS TEST.—Paragraphs (1) and (2) of subsection (a) shall not apply to any corporation or partnership for any taxable year if such entity (or any predecessor) meets the gross receipts test of subsection (c) for such taxable year.

[Sec. 448(c)]

(c) GROSS RECEIPTS TEST.—For purposes of this section—

(1) IN GENERAL.—A corporation or partnership meets the gross receipts test of this subsection for any taxable year if the average annual gross receipts of such entity for the 3-taxable-year period ending with the taxable year which precedes such taxable year does not exceed $25,000,000.

(2) AGGREGATION RULES.—All persons treated as a single employer under subsection (a) or (b) of section 52 or subsection (m) or (o) of section 414 shall be treated as one person for purposes of paragraph (1).

(3) SPECIAL RULES.—For purposes of this subsection—

(A) NOT IN EXISTENCE FOR ENTIRE 3-YEAR PERIOD.—If the entity was not in existence for the entire 3-year period referred to in paragraph (1), such paragraph shall be applied on the basis of the period during which such entity (or trade or business) was in existence.

(B) SHORT TAXABLE YEARS.—Gross receipts for any taxable year of less than 12 months shall be annualized by multiplying the gross receipts for the short period by 12 and dividing the result by the number of months in the short period.

(C) GROSS RECEIPTS.—Gross receipts for any taxable year shall be reduced by returns and allowances made during such year.

(D) TREATMENT OF PREDECESSORS.—Any reference in this subsection to an entity shall include a reference to any predecessor of such entity.

(4) ADJUSTMENT FOR INFLATION.—In the case of any taxable year beginning after December 31, 2018, the dollar amount in paragraph (1) shall be increased by an amount equal to—

(A) such dollar amount, multiplied by

(B) the cost-of-living adjustment determined under section 1(f)(3) for the calendar year in which the taxable year begins, by substituting "calendar year 2017" for "calendar year 2016" in subparagraph (A)(ii) thereof.

If any amount as increased under the preceding sentence is not a multiple of $1,000,000, such amount shall be rounded to the nearest multiple of $1,000,000.

[Sec. 448(d)]

(d) DEFINITIONS AND SPECIAL RULES.—For purposes of this section—

(1) FARMING BUSINESS.—

(A) IN GENERAL.—The term "farming business" means the trade or business of farming (within the meaning of section 263A(e)(4)).

(B) TIMBER AND ORNAMENTAL TREES.—The term "farming business" includes the raising, harvesting, or growing of trees to which section 263A(c)(5) applies.

(2) QUALIFIED PERSONAL SERVICE CORPORATION.—The term "qualified personal service corporation" means any corporation—

(A) substantially all of the activities of which involve the performance of services in the fields of health, law, engineering, architecture, accounting, actuarial science, performing arts, or consulting, and

(B) substantially all of the stock of which (by value) is held directly (or indirectly through 1 or more partnerships, S corporations, or qualified personal service corporations not described in paragraph (2) or (3) of subsection (a)) by—

(i) employees performing services for such corporation in connection with the activities involving a field referred to in subparagraph (A),

(ii) retired employees who had performed such services for such corporation,

(iii) the estate of any individual described in clause (i) or (ii), or

(iv) any other person who acquired such stock by reason of the death of an individual described in clause (i) or (ii) (but only for the 2-year period beginning on the date of the death of such individual).

To the extent provided in regulations which shall be prescribed by the Secretary, indirect holdings through a trust shall be taken into account under subparagraph (B).

(3) TAX SHELTER DEFINED.—The term "tax shelter" has the meaning given such term by section 461(i)(3) (determined after application of paragraph (4) thereof). An S corporation shall not be treated as a tax shelter for purposes of this section merely by reason of being required to file a notice of exemption from registration with a State agency described in section 461(i)(3)(A), but only if there is a requirement applicable to all corporations offering securities for sale in the State that to be exempt from such registration the corporation must file such a notice.

(4) SPECIAL RULES FOR APPLICATION OF PARAGRAPH (2).—For purposes of paragraph (2)—

(A) community property laws shall be disregarded,

(B) stock held by a plan described in section 401(a) which is exempt from tax under section 501(a) shall be treated as held by an employee described in paragraph (2)(B)(i), and

(C) at the election of the common parent of an affiliated group (within the meaning of section 1504(a)), all members of such group may be treated as 1 taxpayer for purposes of paragraph (2)(B) if 90 percent or more of the activities of such group involve the performance of services in the same field described in paragraph (2)(A).

(5) SPECIAL RULE FOR CERTAIN SERVICES.—

(A) IN GENERAL.—In the case of any person using an accrual method of accounting with respect to amounts to be received for the performance of services by such person, such person shall not be required to accrue any portion of such amounts which (on the basis of such person's experience) will not be collected if—

(i) such services are in fields referred to in paragraph (2)(A), or

(ii) such person meets the gross receipts test of subsection (c) for all prior taxable years.

(B) EXCEPTION.—This paragraph shall not apply to any amount if interest is required to be paid on such amount or there is any penalty for failure to timely pay such amount.

(C) REGULATIONS.—The Secretary shall prescribe regulations to permit taxpayers to determine amounts referred to in subparagraph (A) using computations or formulas which, based on experience, accurately reflect the amount of income that will not be collected by such person. A taxpayer may adopt, or request consent of the Secretary to change to, a computation or formula that clearly reflects the taxpayer's experience. A request under the preceding sentence shall be approved if such computation or formula clearly reflects the taxpayer's experience.

(6) TREATMENT OF CERTAIN TRUSTS SUBJECT TO TAX ON UNRELATED BUSINESS INCOME.—For purposes of this section, a trust subject to tax under section 511(b) shall be treated as a C corporation with respect to its activities constituting an unrelated trade or business.

(7) COORDINATION WITH SECTION 481.—Any change in method of accounting made pursuant to this section shall be treated for purposes of section 481 as initiated by the taxpayer and made with the consent of the Secretary.

(8) USE OF RELATED PARTIES, ETC.—The Secretary shall prescribe such regulations as may be necessary to prevent the use of related parties, pass-thru entities, or intermediaries to avoid the application of this section.

Subpart B—Taxable Year for Which Items of Gross Income Included

[Sec. 451]

SEC. 451. GENERAL RULE FOR TAXABLE YEAR OF INCLUSION.

[Sec. 451(a)]

(a) GENERAL RULE.—The amount of any item of gross income shall be included in the gross income for the taxable year in which received by the taxpayer, unless, under the method of accounting used in computing taxable income, such amount is to be properly accounted for as of a different period.

[Sec. 451(b)]

(b) INCLUSION NOT LATER THAN FOR FINANCIAL ACCOUNTING PURPOSES.—

(1) INCOME TAKEN INTO ACCOUNT IN FINANCIAL STATEMENT.—

(A) IN GENERAL.—In the case of a taxpayer the taxable income of which is computed under an accrual method of accounting, the all events test with respect to any item of gross income (or portion thereof) shall not be treated as met any later than when such item (or portion thereof) is taken into account as revenue in—

(i) an applicable financial statement of the taxpayer, or

(ii) such other financial statement as the Secretary may specify for purposes of this subsection.

(B) EXCEPTION.—This paragraph shall not apply to—

(i) a taxpayer which does not have a financial statement described in clause (i) or (ii) of subparagraph (A) for a taxable year, or

(ii) any item of gross income in connection with a mortgage servicing contract.

(C) ALL EVENTS TEST.—For purposes of this section, the all events test is met with respect to any item of gross income if all the events have occurred which fix the right to receive such income and the amount of such income can be determined with reasonable accuracy.

(2) COORDINATION WITH SPECIAL METHODS OF ACCOUNTING.—Paragraph (1) shall not apply with respect to any item of gross income for which the taxpayer uses a special method of accounting provided under any other provision of this chapter, other than any provision of part V of subchapter P (except as provided in clause (ii) of paragraph (1)(B)).

(3) APPLICABLE FINANCIAL STATEMENT.—For purposes of this subsection, the term "applicable financial statement" means—

(A) a financial statement which is certified as being prepared in accordance with generally accepted accounting principles and which is—

(i) a 10–K (or successor form), or annual statement to shareholders, required to be filed by the taxpayer with the United States Securities and Exchange Commission,

(ii) an audited financial statement of the taxpayer which is used for—

(I) credit purposes,

(II) reporting to shareholders, partners, or other proprietors, or to beneficiaries, or

(III) any other substantial nontax purpose,

but only if there is no statement of the taxpayer described in clause (i), or

(iii) filed by the taxpayer with any other Federal agency for purposes other than Federal tax purposes, but only if there is no statement of the taxpayer described in clause (i) or (ii),

(B) a financial statement which is made on the basis of international financial reporting standards and is filed by the taxpayer with an agency of a foreign government which is equivalent to the United States Securities and Exchange Commission and which has reporting standards not less stringent than the standards required by such Commission, but only if there is no statement of the taxpayer described in subparagraph (A), or

(C) a financial statement filed by the taxpayer with any other regulatory or governmental body specified by the Secretary, but only if there is no statement of the taxpayer described in subparagraph (A) or (B).

(4) ALLOCATION OF TRANSACTION PRICE.—For purposes of this subsection, in the case of a contract which contains multiple performance obligations, the allocation of the transaction price to each performance obligation shall be equal to the amount allocated to each performance obligation for purposes of including such item in revenue in the applicable financial statement of the taxpayer.

(5) GROUP OF ENTITIES.—For purposes of paragraph (1), if the financial results of a taxpayer are reported on the applicable financial statement (as defined in paragraph (3)) for a group of entities, such statement shall be treated as the applicable financial statement of the taxpayer.

[Sec. 451(c)]

(c) TREATMENT OF ADVANCE PAYMENTS.—

(1) IN GENERAL.—A taxpayer which computes taxable income under the accrual method of accounting, and receives any advance payment during the taxable year, shall—

(A) except as provided in subparagraph (B), include such advance payment in gross income for such taxable year, or

(B) if the taxpayer elects the application of this subparagraph with respect to the category of advance payments to which such advance payment belongs, the taxpayer shall—

(i) to the extent that any portion of such advance payment is required under subsection (b) to be included in gross income in the taxable year in which such payment is received, so include such portion, and

(ii) include the remaining portion of such advance payment in gross income in the taxable year following the taxable year in which such payment is received.

(2) ELECTION.—

(A) IN GENERAL.—Except as otherwise provided in this paragraph, the election under paragraph (1)(B) shall be made at such time, in such form and manner, and with respect to such categories of advance payments, as the Secretary may provide.

(B) PERIOD TO WHICH ELECTION APPLIES.—An election under paragraph (1)(B) shall be effective for the taxable year with respect to which it is first made and for all subsequent taxable years, unless the taxpayer secures the consent of the Secretary to revoke such election. For purposes of this title, the computation of taxable income under an election made under paragraph (1)(B) shall be treated as a method of accounting.

(3) TAXPAYERS CEASING TO EXIST.—Except as otherwise provided by the Secretary, the election under paragraph (1)(B) shall not apply with respect to advance payments received by the taxpayer during a taxable year if such taxpayer ceases to exist during (or with the close of) such taxable year.

(4) ADVANCE PAYMENT.—For purposes of this subsection—

(A) IN GENERAL.—The term "advance payment" means any payment—

(i) the full inclusion of which in the gross income of the taxpayer for the taxable year of receipt is a permissible method of accounting under this section (determined without regard to this subsection),

(ii) any portion of which is included in revenue by the taxpayer in a financial statement described in clause (i) or (ii) of subsection (b)(1)(A) for a subsequent taxable year, and

(iii) which is for goods, services, or such other items as may be identified by the Secretary for purposes of this clause.

(B) EXCLUSIONS.—Except as otherwise provided by the Secretary, such term shall not include—

(i) rent,

(ii) insurance premiums governed by subchapter L,

(iii) payments with respect to financial instruments,

(iv) payments with respect to warranty or guarantee contracts under which a third party is the primary obligor,

(v) payments subject to section 871(a), 881, 1441, or 1442,

(vi) payments in property to which section 83 applies, and

(vii) any other payment identified by the Secretary for purposes of this subparagraph.

(C) RECEIPT.—For purposes of this subsection, an item of gross income is received by the taxpayer if it is actually or constructively received, or if it is due and payable to the taxpayer.

(D) ALLOCATION OF TRANSACTION PRICE.—For purposes of this subsection, rules similar to subsection (b)(4) shall apply.

* * *

[Sec. 453]

SEC. 453. INSTALLMENT METHOD.

[Sec. 453(a)]

(a) GENERAL RULE.—Except as otherwise provided in this section, income from an installment sale shall be taken into account for purposes of this title under the installment method.

[Sec. 453(b)]

(b) INSTALLMENT SALE DEFINED.—For purposes of this section—

(1) IN GENERAL.—The term "installment sale" means a disposition of property where at least 1 payment is to be received after the close of the taxable year in which the disposition occurs.

(2) EXCEPTIONS.—The term "installment sale" does not include—

(A) DEALER DISPOSITIONS.—Any dealer disposition (as defined in subsection (l)).

(B) INVENTORIES OF PERSONAL PROPERTY.—A disposition of personal property of a kind which is required to be included in the inventory of the taxpayer if on hand at the close of the taxable year.

[Sec. 453(c)]

(c) INSTALLMENT METHOD DEFINED.—For purposes of this section, the term "installment method" means a method under which the income recognized for any taxable year from a disposition is that proportion of the payments received in that year which the gross profit (realized or to be realized when payment is completed) bears to the total contract price.

[Sec. 453(d)]

(d) ELECTION OUT.—

(1) IN GENERAL.—Subsection (a) shall not apply to any disposition if the taxpayer elects to have subsection (a) not apply to such disposition.

(2) TIME AND MANNER FOR MAKING ELECTION.—Except as otherwise provided by regulations, an election under paragraph (1) with respect to a disposition may be made only on or before the due date prescribed by law (including extensions) for filing the taxpayer's return of the tax imposed by this chapter for the taxable year in which the disposition occurs. Such an election shall be made in the manner prescribed by regulations.

(3) ELECTION REVOCABLE ONLY WITH CONSENT.—An election under paragraph (1) with respect to any disposition may be revoked only with the consent of the Secretary.

[Sec. 453(e)]

(e) SECOND DISPOSITIONS BY RELATED PERSONS.—

(1) IN GENERAL.—If—

(A) Any person disposes of property to a related person (hereinafter in this subsection referred to as the "first disposition"), and

(B) before the person making the first disposition receives all payments with respect to such disposition, the related person disposes of the property (hereinafter in this subsection referred to as the "second disposition"),

then, for purposes of this section, the amount realized with respect to such second disposition shall be treated as received at the time of the second disposition by the person making the first disposition.

(2) 2-YEAR CUTOFF FOR PROPERTY OTHER THAN MARKETABLE SECURITIES.—

(A) IN GENERAL.—Except in the case of marketable securities, paragraph (1) shall apply only if the date of the second disposition is not more than 2 years after the date of the first disposition.

(B) SUBSTANTIAL DIMINISHING OF RISK OF OWNERSHIP.—The running of the 2-year period set forth in subparagraph (A) shall be suspended with respect to any property for any period during which the related person's risk of loss with respect to the property is substantially diminished by—

(i) the holding of a put with respect to such property (or similar property),

(ii) the holding by another person of a right to acquire the property, or

(iii) a short sale or any other transaction.

(3) LIMITATION ON AMOUNT TREATED AS RECEIVED.—The amount treated for any taxable year as received by the person making the first disposition by reason of paragraph (1) shall not exceed the excess of—

(A) the lesser of—

(i) the total amount realized with respect to any second disposition of the property occurring before the close of the taxable year, or

(ii) the total contract price for the first disposition, over

(B) the sum of—

(i) the aggregate amount of payments received with respect to the first disposition before the close of such year, plus

(ii) the aggregate amount treated as received with respect to the first disposition for prior taxable years by reason of this subsection.

(4) FAIR MARKET VALUE WHERE DISPOSITION IS NOT SALE OR EXCHANGE.—For purposes of this subsection, if the second disposition is not a sale or exchange, an amount equal to the fair market value of the property disposed of shall be substituted for the amount realized.

(5) LATER PAYMENTS TREATED AS RECEIPT OF TAX PAID AMOUNTS.—If paragraph (1) applies for any taxable year, payments received in subsequent taxable years by the person making the first disposition shall not be treated as the receipt of payments with respect to the first disposition to the extent that the aggregate of such payments does not exceed the amount treated as received by reason of paragraph (1).

(6) EXCEPTION FOR CERTAIN DISPOSITIONS.—For purposes of this subsection—

(A) REACQUISITIONS OF STOCK BY ISSUING CORPORATION NOT TREATED AS FIRST DISPOSITIONS.—Any sale or exchange of stock to the issuing corporation shall not be treated as a first disposition.

(B) INVOLUNTARY CONVERSIONS NOT TREATED AS SECOND DISPOSITIONS.—A compulsory or involuntary conversion (within the meaning of section 1033) and any transfer thereafter shall not be treated as a second disposition if the first disposition occurred before the threat or imminence of the conversion.

(C) DISPOSITIONS AFTER DEATH.—Any transfer after the earlier of—

(i) the death of the person making the first disposition, or

(ii) the death of the person acquiring the property in the first disposition,

and any transfer thereafter shall not be treated as a second disposition.

(7) EXCEPTION WHERE TAX AVOIDANCE NOT A PRINCIPAL PURPOSE.—This subsection shall not apply to a second disposition (and any transfer thereafter) if it is established to the satisfaction of the Secretary that neither the first disposition nor the second disposition had as one of its principal purposes the avoidance of Federal income tax.

(8) EXTENSION OF STATUTE OF LIMITATIONS.—The period for assessing a deficiency with respect to a first disposition (to the extent such deficiency is attributable to the application of this subsection) shall not expire before the day which is 2 years after the date on which the person making the first disposition furnishes (in such manner as the Secretary may by regulations prescribe) a notice that there was a second disposition of the property to which this subsection may have applied. Such deficiency may be assessed notwithstanding the provisions of any law or rule of law which would otherwise prevent such assessment.

[Sec. 453(f)]

(f) DEFINITIONS AND SPECIAL RULES.—For purposes of this section—

(1) RELATED PERSON.—Except for purposes of subsections (g) and (h), the term "related person" means—

(A) a person whose stock would be attributed under section 318(a) (other than paragraph (4) thereof) to the person first disposing of the property, or

(B) a person who bears a relationship described in section 267(b) to the person first disposing of the property.

(2) MARKETABLE SECURITIES.—The term "marketable securities" means any security for which, as of the date of the disposition, there was a market on an established securities market or otherwise.

(3) PAYMENT.—Except as provided in paragraph (4), the term "payment" does not include the receipt of evidences of indebtedness of the person acquiring the property (whether or not payment of such indebtedness is guaranteed by another person).

(4) PURCHASER EVIDENCES OF INDEBTEDNESS PAYABLE ON DEMAND OR READILY TRADABLE.—Receipt of a bond or other evidence of indebtedness which—

(A) is payable on demand, or

(B) is readily tradable,

shall be treated as receipt of payment.

(5) READILY TRADABLE DEFINED.—For purposes of paragraph (4), the term "readily tradable" means a bond or other evidence of indebtedness which is issued—

(A) with interest coupons attached or in registered form (other than one in registered form which the taxpayer establishes will not be readily tradable in an established securities market), or

(B) in any other form designed to render such bond or other evidence of indebtedness readily tradable in an established securities market.

(6) LIKE-KIND EXCHANGES.—In the case of any exchange described in section 1031(b)—

(A) the total contract price shall be reduced to take into account the amount of any property permitted to be received in such exchange without recognition of gain,

(B) the gross profit from such exchange shall be reduced to take into account any amount not recognized by reason of section 1031(b), and

(C) the term "payment", when used in any provision of this section other than subsection (b)(1), shall not include any property permitted to be received in such exchange without recognition of gain.

Similar rules shall apply in the case of an exchange which is described in section 356(a) and is not treated as a dividend.

(7) DEPRECIABLE PROPERTY.—The term "depreciable property" means property of a character which (in the hands of the transferee) is subject to the allowance for depreciation provided in section 167.

(8) PAYMENTS TO BE RECEIVED DEFINED.—The term "payments to be received" includes—

(A) the aggregate amount of all payments which are not contingent as to amount, and

(B) the fair market value of any payments which are contingent as to amount.

[Sec. 453(g)]

(g) SALE OF DEPRECIABLE PROPERTY TO CONTROLLED ENTITY.—

(1) IN GENERAL.—In the case of an installment sale of depreciable property between related persons—

(A) subsection (a) shall not apply,

(B) for purposes of this title—

(i) except as provided in clause (ii), all payments to be received shall be treated as received in the year of the disposition, and

(ii) in the case of any payments which are contingent as to the amount but with respect to which the fair market value may not be reasonably ascertained, the basis shall be recovered ratably, and

(C) the purchaser may not increase the basis of any property acquired in such sale by any amount before the time such amount is includible in the gross income of the seller.

(2) EXCEPTION WHERE TAX AVOIDANCE NOT A PRINCIPAL PURPOSE.—Paragraph (1) shall not apply if it is established to the satisfaction of the Secretary that the disposition did not have as one of its principal purposes the avoidance of Federal income tax.

(3) RELATED PERSONS.—For purposes of this subsection, the term "related persons" has the meaning given to such term by section 1239(b), except that such term shall include 2 or more partnerships having a relationship to each other described in section 707(b)(1)(B).

[Sec. 453(h)]

(h) USE OF INSTALLMENT METHOD BY SHAREHOLDERS IN CERTAIN LIQUIDATIONS.—

(1) RECEIPT OF OBLIGATIONS NOT TREATED AS RECEIPT OF PAYMENT.—

(A) IN GENERAL.—If, in a liquidation to which section 331 applies, the shareholder receives (in exchange for the shareholder's stock) an installment obligation acquired in respect of a sale or exchange by the corporation during the 12-month period beginning on the date a plan of complete liquidation is adopted and the liquidation is completed during such 12-month period, then, for purposes of this section, the receipt of payments under such obligation (but not the receipt of such obligation) by the shareholder shall be treated as the receipt of payment for the stock.

(B) OBLIGATIONS ATTRIBUTABLE TO SALE OF INVENTORY MUST RESULT FROM BULK SALE.—Subparagraph (A) shall not apply to an installment obligation acquired in respect of a sale or exchange of—

(i) stock in trade of the corporation,

(ii) other property of a kind which would properly be included in the inventory of the corporation if on hand at the close of the taxable year, and

(iii) property held by the corporation primarily for sale to customers in the ordinary course of its trade or business,

unless such sale or exchange is to 1 person in 1 transaction and involves substantially all of such property attributable to a trade or business of the corporation.

(C) SPECIAL RULE WHERE OBLIGOR AND SHAREHOLDER ARE RELATED PERSONS.—If the obligor of any installment obligation and the shareholder are married to each other or are related persons (within the meaning of section 1239(b)), to the extent such installment obligation is attributable to the disposition by the corporation of depreciable property—

(i) subparagraph (A) shall not apply to such obligation, and

(ii) for purposes of this title, all payments to be received by the shareholder shall be deemed received in the year the shareholder receives the obligation.

(D) COORDINATION WITH SUBSECTION (e)(1)(A).—For purposes of subsection (e)(1)(A), dispostion of property by the corporation shall be treated also as disposition of such property by the shareholder.

(E) SALES BY LIQUIDATING SUBSIDIARIES.—For purposes of subparagraph (A), in the case of controlling corporate shareholder (within the meaning of section 368(c)) of a selling corporation, an obligation acquired in respect of a sale or exchange by the selling corporation shall be treated as so acquired by such controlling corporate shareholder. The preceding sentence shall be applied successively to each controlling corporate shareholder above such controlling corporate shareholder.

(2) DISTRIBUTIONS RECEIVED IN MORE THAN 1 TAXABLE YEAR OF SHAREHOLDER.—If—

(A) paragraph (1) applies with respect to any installment obligation received by a shareholder from a corporation, and

(B) by reason of the liquidation such shareholder receives property in more than 1 taxable year,

then, on completion of the liquidation, basis previously allocated to property so received shall be reallocated for all such taxable years so that the shareholder's basis in the stock of the corporation is properly allocated among all property received by such shareholder in such liquidation.

[Sec. 453(i)]

(i) RECOGNITION OF RECAPTURE INCOME IN YEAR OF DISPOSITION.—

(1) IN GENERAL.—In the case of any installment sale of property to which subsection (a) applies—

(A) notwithstanding subsection (a), any recapture income shall be recognized in the year of the disposition, and

(B) any gain in excess of the recapture income shall be taken into account under the installment method.

(2) RECAPTURE INCOME.—For purposes of paragraph (1), the term "recapture income" means, with respect to any installment sale, the aggregate amount which would be treated as ordinary income under section 1245 or 1250 (or so much of section 751 as relates to section 1245 or 1250) for the taxable year of the disposition if all payments to be received were received in the taxable year of disposition.

[Sec. 453(j)]

(j) REGULATIONS.—

(1) IN GENERAL.—The Secretary shall prescribe such regulations as may be necessary or appropriate to carry out the provisions of this section.

(2) SELLING PRICE NOT READILY ASCERTAINABLE.—The regulations prescribed under paragraph (1) shall include regulations providing for ratable basis recovery in transactions where the gross profit or the total contract price (or both) cannot be readily ascertained.

[Sec. 453(k)]

(k) CURRENT INCLUSION IN CASE OF REVOLVING CREDIT PLANS, ETC.—In the case of—

(1) any disposition of personal property under a revolving credit plan, or

(2) any installment obligation arising out of a sale of—

(A) stock or securities which are traded on an established securities market, or

(B) to the extent provided in regulations, property (other than stock or securities) of a kind regularly traded on an established market,

subsection (a) shall not apply, and, for purposes of this title, all payments to be received shall be treated as received in the year of disposition. The Secretary may provide for the application of this subsection in whole or in part for transactions in which the rules of this subsection otherwise would be avoided through the use of related parties, pass-thru entities, or intermediaries.

[Sec. 453(l)]

(l) DEALER DISPOSITIONS.—For purposes of subsection (b)(2)(A)—

(1) IN GENERAL.—The term "dealer disposition" means any of the following dispositions:

(A) PERSONAL PROPERTY.—Any disposition of personal property by a person who regularly sells or otherwise disposes of personal property of the same type on the installment plan.

(B) REAL PROPERTY.—Any disposition of real property which is held by the taxpayer for sale to customers in the ordinary course of the taxpayer's trade or business.

(2) EXCEPTIONS.—The term "dealer disposition" does not include—

(A) FARM PROPERTY.—The disposition on the installment plan of any property used or produced in the trade or business of farming (within the meaning of section 2032A(e)(4) or (5)).

(B) TIMESHARES AND RESIDENTIAL LOTS.—

(i) IN GENERAL.—Any dispositions described in clause (ii) on the installment plan if the taxpayer elects to have paragraph (3) apply to any installment obligations which arise from such dispositions. An election under this paragraph shall not apply with respect to an installment obligation which is guaranteed by any person other than an individual.

(ii) DISPOSITIONS TO WHICH SUBPARAGRAPH APPLIES.—A disposition is described in this clause if it is a disposition in the ordinary course of the taxpayer's trade or business to an individual of—

(I) a timeshare right to use or a timeshare ownership interest in residential real property for not more than 6 weeks per year, or a right to use specified campgrounds for recreational purposes, or

(II) any residential lot, but only if the taxpayer (or any related person) is not to make any improvements with respect to such lot.

For purposes of subclause (I), a timeshare right to use (or timeshare ownership interest in) property held by the spouse, children, grandchildren, or parents of an individual shall be treated as held by such individual.

(C) CARRYING CHARGES OR INTEREST.—Any carrying charges or interest with respect to a disposition described in subparagraph (A) or (B) which are added on the books of account of the seller to the established cash selling price of the property shall be included in the total contract price of the property and, if such charges or interest are not so included, any payments received shall be treated as applying first against such carrying charges or interest.

(3) PAYMENT OF INTEREST ON TIMESHARES AND RESIDENTIAL LOTS.—

(A) IN GENERAL.—In the case of any installment obligation to which paragraph (2)(B) applies, the tax imposed by this chapter for any taxable year for which payment is received on such obligation shall be increased by the amount of interest determined in the manner provided under subparagraph (B).

(B) COMPUTATION OF INTEREST.—

(i) IN GENERAL.—The amount of interest referred to in subparagraph (A) for any taxable year shall be determined—

(I) on the amount of the tax for such taxable year which is attributable to the payments received during such taxable year on installment obligations to which this subsection applies,

(II) for the period beginning on the date of sale, and ending on the date such payment is received, and

(III) by using the applicable Federal rate under section 1274 (without regard to subsection (d)(2) thereof) in effect at the time of the sale compounded semiannually.

(ii) INTEREST NOT TAKEN INTO ACCOUNT.—For purposes of clause (i), the portion of any tax attributable to the receipt of any payment shall be determined without regard to any interest imposed under subparagraph (A).

(iii) TAXABLE YEAR OF SALE.—No interest shall be determined for any payment received in the taxable year of the disposition from which the installment obligation arises.

(C) TREATMENT AS INTEREST.—Any amount payable under this paragraph shall be taken into account in computing the amount of any deduction allowable to the taxpayer for interest paid or accrued during such taxable year.

[Sec. 453A]

SEC. 453A. SPECIAL RULES FOR NONDEALERS.

[Sec. 453A(a)]

(a) GENERAL RULE.—In the case of an installment obligation to which this section applies—

(1) interest shall be paid on the deferred tax liability with respect to such obligation in the manner provided under subsection (c), and

(2) the pledging rules under subsection (d) shall apply.

[Sec. 453A(b)]

(b) INSTALLMENT OBLIGATIONS TO WHICH SECTION APPLIES.—

(1) IN GENERAL.—This section shall apply to any obligation which arises from the disposition of any property under the installment method, but only if the sales price of such property exceeds $150,000.

(2) SPECIAL RULE FOR INTEREST PAYMENTS.—For purposes of subsection (a)(1), this section shall apply to an obligation described in paragraph (1) arising during a taxable year only if—

(A) such obligation is outstanding as of the close of such taxable year, and

(B) the face amount of all such obligations held by the taxpayer which arose during, and are outstanding as of the close of, such taxable year exceeds $5,000,000.

Except as provided in regulations, all persons treated as a single employer under subsection (a) or (b) of section 52 shall be treated as one person for purposes of this paragraph and subsection (c)(4).

(3) EXCEPTION FOR PERSONAL USE AND FARM PROPERTY.—An installment obligation shall not be treated as described in paragraph (1) if it arises from the disposition—

(A) by an individual of personal use property (within the meaning of section 1275(b)(3)), or

(B) of any property used or produced in the trade or business of farming (within the meaning of section 2032A(e)(4) or (5)).

(4) SPECIAL RULE FOR TIMESHARES AND RESIDENTIAL LOTS.—An installment obligation shall not be treated as described in paragraph (1) if it arises from a disposition described in section 453(l)(2)(B), but the provisions of section 453(l)(3) (relating to interest payments on timeshares and residential lots) shall apply to such obligation.

(5) SALES PRICE.—For purposes of paragraph (1), all sales or exchanges which are part of the same transaction (or a series of related transactions) shall be treated as 1 sale or exchange.

[Sec. 453A(c)]

(c) INTEREST ON DEFERRED TAX LIABILITY.—

(1) IN GENERAL.—If an obligation to which this section applies is outstanding as of the close of any taxable year, the tax imposed by this chapter for such taxable year shall be increased by the amount of interest determined in the manner provided under paragraph (2).

(2) COMPUTATION OF INTEREST.—For purposes of paragraph (1), the interest for any taxable year shall be an amount equal to the product of—

(A) the applicable percentage of the deferred tax liability with respect to such obligation, multiplied by

(B) the underpayment rate in effect under section 6621(a)(2) for the month with or within which the taxable year ends.

(3) DEFERRED TAX LIABILITY.—For purposes of this section, the term "deferred tax liability" means, with respect to any taxable year, the product of—

(A) the amount of gain with respect to an obligation which has not been recognized as of the close of such taxable year, multiplied by

(B) the maximum rate of tax in effect under section 1 or 11, whichever is appropriate, for such taxable year.

For purposes of applying the preceding sentence with respect to so much of the gain which, when recognized, will be treated as long-term capital gain, the maximum rate on net capital gain under section 1(h) shall be taken into account.

(4) APPLICABLE PERCENTAGE.—For purposes of this subsection, the term "applicable percentage" means, with respect to obligations arising in any taxable year, the percentage determined by dividing—

(A) the portion of the aggregate face amount of such obligations outstanding as of the close of such taxable year in excess of $5,000,000, by

(B) the aggregate face amount of such obligations outstanding as of the close of such taxable year.

(5) TREATMENT AS INTEREST.—Any amount payable under this subsection shall be taken into account in computing the amount of any deduction allowable to the taxpayer for interest paid or accrued during the taxable year.

(6) REGULATIONS.—The Secretary shall prescribe such regulations as may be necessary to carry out the provisions of this subsection including regulations providing for the application of this subsection in the case of contingent payments, short taxable years, and pass-thru entities.

[Sec. 453A(d)]

(d) PLEDGES, ETC., OF INSTALLMENT OBLIGATIONS.—

(1) IN GENERAL.—For purposes of section 453, if any indebtedness (hereinafter in this subsection referred to as "secured indebtedness") is secured by an installment obligation to which this section applies, the net proceeds of the secured indebtedness shall be treated as a payment received on such installment obligation as of the later of—

(A) the time the indebtedness becomes secured indebtedness, or

(B) the time the proceeds of such indebtedness are received by the taxpayer.

(2) LIMITATION BASED ON TOTAL CONTRACT PRICE.—The amount treated as received under paragraph (1) by reason of any secured indebtedness shall not exceed the excess (if any) of—

(A) the total contract price, over

(B) any portion of the total contract price received under the contract before the later of the times referred to in subparagraph (A) or (B) of paragraph (1) (including amounts previously treated as received under paragraph (1) but not including amounts not taken into account by reason of paragraph (3)).

(3) LATER PAYMENTS TREATED AS RECEIPT OF TAX PAID AMOUNTS.—If any amount is treated as received under paragraph (1) with respect to any installment obligation, subsequent payments received on such obligation shall not be taken into account for purposes of section 453

to the extent that the aggregate of such subsequent payments does not exceed the aggregate amount treated as received under paragraph (1).

(4) SECURED INDEBTEDNESS.—For purposes of this subsection indebtedness is secured by an installment obligation to the extent that payment of principal or interest on such indebtedness is directly secured (under the terms of the indebtedness or any underlying arrangements) by any interest in such installment obligation. A payment shall be treated as directly secured by an interest in an installment obligation to the extent an arrangement allows the taxpayer to satisfy all or a portion of the indebtedness with the installment obligation.

[Sec. 453A(e)]

(e) REGULATIONS.—The Secretary shall prescribe such regulations as may be necessary to carry out the purposes of this section, including regulations—

(1) disallowing the use of the installment method in whole or in part for transactions in which the rules of this section otherwise would be avoided through the use of related persons, pass-thru entities, or intermediaries, and

(2) providing that the sale of an interest in a partnership or other pass-thru entity will be treated as a sale of the proportionate share of the assets of the partnership or other entity.

[Sec. 453B]

SEC. 453B. GAIN OR LOSS ON DISPOSITION OF INSTALLMENT OBLIGATIONS.

[Sec. 453B(a)]

(a) GENERAL RULE.—If an installment obligation is satisfied at other than its face value or distributed, transmitted, sold, or otherwise disposed of, gain or loss shall result to the extent of the difference between the basis of the obligation and—

(1) the amount realized, in the case of satisfaction at other than face value or a sale or exchange, or

(2) the fair market value of the obligation at the time of distribution, transmission, or disposition, in the case of the distribution, transmission, or disposition otherwise than by sale or exchange.

Any gain or loss so resulting shall be considered as resulting from the sale or exchange of the property in respect of which the installment obligation was received.

[Sec. 453B(b)]

(b) BASIS OF OBLIGATION.—The basis of an installment obligation shall be the excess of the face value of the obligation over an amount equal to the income which would be returnable were the obligation satisfied in full.

[Sec. 453B(c)]

(c) SPECIAL RULE FOR TRANSMISSION AT DEATH.—Except as provided in section 691 (relating to recipients of income in respect of decedents), this section shall not apply to the transmission of installment obligations at death.

[Sec. 453B(d)]

(d) EXCEPTION FOR DISTRIBUTIONS TO WHICH SECTION 337(a) APPLIES.—Subsection (a) shall not apply to any distribution to which section 337(a) applies.

* * *

[Sec. 453B(f)]

(f) OBLIGATION BECOMES UNENFORCEABLE.—For purposes of this section, if any installment obligation is canceled or otherwise becomes unenforceable—

(1) the obligation shall be treated as if it were disposed of in a transaction other than a sale or exchange, and

(2) if the obligor and obligee are related persons (within the meaning of section 453(f)(1)), the fair market value of the obligation shall be treated as not less than its face amount.

[Sec. 453B(g)]

(g) TRANSFERS BETWEEN SPOUSES OR INCIDENT TO DIVORCE.—In the case of any transfer described in subsection (a) of section 1041 (other than a transfer in trust)—

(1) subsection (a) of this section shall not apply, and

(2) the same tax treatment with respect to the transferred installment obligation shall apply to the transferee as would have applied to the transferor.

[Sec. 453B(h)]

(h) CERTAIN LIQUIDATING DISTRIBUTIONS BY S CORPORATIONS.—If—

(1) an installment obligation is distributed by an S corporation in a complete liquidation, and

(2) receipt of the obligation is not treated as payment for the stock by reason of section 453(h)(1),

then, except for purposes of any tax imposed by subchaper S, no gain or loss with respect to the distribution of the obligation shall be recognized by the distributing corporation. Under regulations prescribed by the Secretary, the character of the gain or loss to the shareholder shall be determined in accordance with the principles of section 1366(b).

[Sec. 454]

SEC. 454. OBLIGATIONS ISSUED AT DISCOUNT.

[Sec. 454(a)]

(a) NON-INTEREST-BEARING OBLIGATIONS ISSUED AT A DISCOUNT.—If, in the case of a taxpayer owning any non-interest-bearing obligation issued at a discount and redeemable for fixed amounts increasing at stated intervals or owning an obligation described in paragraph (2) of subsection (c), the increase in the redemption price of such obligation occurring in the taxable year does not (under the method of accounting used in computing his taxable income) constitute income to him in such year, such taxpayer may, at his election made in his return for any taxable year, treat such increase as income received in such taxable year. If any such election is made with respect to any such obligation, it shall apply also to all such obligations owned by the taxpayer at the beginning of the first taxable year to which it applies and to all such obligations thereafter acquired by him and shall be binding for all subsequent taxable years, unless on application by the taxpayer the Secretary permits him, subject to such conditions as the Secretary deems necessary, to change to a different method. In the case of any such obligations owned by the taxpayer at the beginning of the first taxable year to which his election applies, the increase in the redemption price of such obligations occurring between the date of acquisition (or, in the case of an obligation described in paragraph (2) of subsection (c), the date of acquisition of the series E bond involved) and the first day of such taxable year shall also be treated as income received in such taxable year.

[Sec. 454(b)]

(b) SHORT-TERM OBLIGATIONS ISSUED ON DISCOUNT BASIS.—In the case of any obligation—

(1) of the United States; or

(2) of a State, or a possession of the United States, or any political subdivision of any of the foregoing, or of the District of Columbia,

which is issued on a discount basis and payable without interest at a fixed maturity date not exceeding 1 year from the date of issue, the amount of discount at which such obligation is originally sold shall not be considered to accrue until the date on which such obligation is paid at maturity, sold, or otherwise disposed of.

[Sec. 454(c)]

(c) MATURED UNITED STATES SAVINGS BONDS.—In the case of a taxpayer who—

(1) holds a series E United States savings bond at the date of maturity, and

(2) pursuant to regulations prescribed under chapter 31 of title 31 (A) retains his investment in such series E bond in an obligation of the United States, other than a current income obligation, or (B) exchanges such series E bond for another nontransferable obligation of the United States in an exchange upon which gain or loss is not recognized because of section 1037 (or so much of section 1031 as relates to section 1037),

the increase in redemption value (to the extent not previously includible in gross income) in excess of the amount paid for such series E bond shall be includible in gross income in the taxable year in which the obligation is finally redeemed or in the taxable year of final maturity, whichever is earlier. This subsection shall not apply to a corporation, and shall not apply in the case of any taxable year for which the taxpayer's taxable income is computed under an accrual method of accounting or for which an election made by the taxpayer under subsection (a) applies.

[Sec. 455]

SEC. 455. PREPAID SUBSCRIPTION INCOME.

[Sec. 455(a)]

(a) YEAR IN WHICH INCLUDED.—Prepaid subscription income to which this section applies shall be included in gross income for the taxable years during which the liability described in subsection (d) (2) exists.

[Sec. 455(b)]

(b) WHERE TAXPAYER'S LIABILITY CEASES.—In the case of any prepaid subscription income to which this section applies—

(1) If the liability described in subsection (d) (2) ends, then so much of such income as was not includible in gross income under subsection (a) for preceding taxable years shall be included in gross income for the taxable year in which the liability ends.

(2) If the taxpayer dies or ceases to exist, then so much of such income as was not includible in gross income under subsection (a) for preceding taxable years shall be included in gross income for the taxable year in which such death, or such cessation of existence, occurs.

[Sec. 455(c)]

(c) PREPAID SUBSCRIPTION INCOME TO WHICH THIS SECTION APPLIES.—

(1) ELECTION OF BENEFITS.—This section shall apply to prepaid subscription income if and only if the taxpayer makes an election under this section with respect to the trade or business in connection with which such income is received. The election shall be made in such manner as the Secretary may by regulations prescribe. No election may be made with respect to a trade or business if in computing taxable income the cash receipts and disbursements method of accounting is used with respect to such trade or business.

(2) SCOPE OF ELECTION.—An election made under this section shall apply to all prepaid subscription income received in connection with the trade or business with respect to which the taxpayer has made the election; except that the taxpayer may, to the extent permitted under regulations prescribed by the Secretary, include in gross income for the taxable year of receipt the entire amount of any prepaid subscription income if the liability from which it arose is to end within 12 months after the date of receipt. An election made under this section shall not apply to any prepaid subscription income received before the first taxable year for which the election is made.

(3) WHEN ELECTION MAY BE MADE.—

(A) WITH CONSENT.—A taxpayer may, with the consent of the Secretary, make an election under this section at any time.

(B) WITHOUT CONSENT.—A taxpayer may, without the consent of the Secretary, make an election under this section for his first taxable year in which he receives prepaid subscription income in the trade or business. Such election shall be made not later than the time prescribed by law for filing the return for the taxable year (including extensions thereof) with respect to which such election is made.

(4) PERIOD TO WHICH ELECTION APPLIES.—An election under this section shall be effective for the taxable year with respect to which it is first made and for all subsequent taxable years, unless the taxpayer secures the consent of the Secretary to the revocation of such election. For purposes of this title, the computation of taxable income under an election made under this section shall be treated as a method of accounting.

[Sec. 455(d)]

(d) DEFINITIONS.—For purposes of this section—

(1) PREPAID SUBSCRIPTION INCOME.—The term "prepaid subscription income" means any amount (includible in gross income) which is received in connection with, and is directly attributable to, a liability which extends beyond the close of the taxable year in which such amount is received, and which is income from a subscription to a newspaper, magazine, or other periodical.

(2) LIABILITY.—The term "liability" means a liability to furnish or deliver a newspaper, magazine, or other periodical.

(3) RECEIPT OF PREPAID SUBSCRIPTION INCOME.—Prepaid subscription income shall be treated as received during the taxable year for which it is includible in gross income under section 451 (without regard to this section).

[Sec. 455(e)]

(e) DEFERRAL OF INCOME UNDER ESTABLISHED ACCOUNTING PROCEDURES.—Notwithstanding the provisions of this section, any taxpayer who has, for taxable years prior to the first taxable year to which this section applies, reported his income under an established and consistent method or practice of accounting for prepaid subscription income (to which this section would apply if an election were made) may continue to report his income for taxable years to which this title applies in accordance with such method or practice.

Subpart C—Taxable Year for Which Deductions Taken

»»→ Caution: As provided in Section 461(l)(3)(B), the dollar amount set forth in Section 461(l)(3)(A) is adjusted for taxable years after 2018 to reflect increases in the Chained Consumer Price Index. The dollar amount applicable to taxable years beginning in 2020 is set forth in the material beginning at page ix.

[Sec. 461]

SEC. 461. GENERAL RULE FOR TAXABLE YEAR OF DEDUCTION.

[Sec. 461(a)]

(a) GENERAL RULE.—The amount of any deduction or credit allowed by this subtitle shall be taken for the taxable year which is the proper taxable year under the method of accounting used in computing taxable income.

[Sec. 461(b)]

(b) SPECIAL RULE IN CASE OF DEATH.—In the case of the death of a taxpayer whose taxable income is computed under an accrual method of accounting, any amount accrued as a deduction or credit only by reason of the death of the taxpayer shall not be allowed in computing taxable income for the period in which falls the date of the taxpayer's death.

[Sec. 461(c)]

(c) ACCRUAL OF REAL PROPERTY TAXES.—

(1) IN GENERAL.—If the taxable income is computed under an accrual method of accounting, then, at the election of the taxpayer, any real property tax which is related to a definite period of time shall be accrued ratably over that period.

(2) WHEN ELECTION MAY BE MADE.—

(A) WITHOUT CONSENT.—A taxpayer may, without the consent of the Secretary, make an election under this subsection for his first taxable year in which he incurs real property taxes. Such an election shall be made not later than the time prescribed by law for filing the return for such year (including extensions thereof).

(B) WITH CONSENT.—A taxpayer may, with the consent of the Secretary, make an election under this subsection at any time.

[Sec. 461(d)]

(d) LIMITATION ON ACCELERATION OF ACCRUAL OF TAXES.—

(1) GENERAL RULE.—In the case of a taxpayer whose taxable income is computed under an accrual method of accounting, to the extent that the time for accruing taxes is earlier than it would be but for any action of any taxing jurisdiction taken after December 31, 1960, then, under regulations prescribed by the Secretary, such taxes shall be treated as accruing at the time they would have accrued but for such action by such taxing jurisdiction.

(2) LIMITATION.—Under regulations prescribed by the Secretary, paragraph (1) shall be inapplicable to any item of tax to the extent that its application would (but for this paragraph) prevent all persons (including successors in interest) from ever taking such item into account.

[Sec. 461(e)]

(e) DIVIDENDS OR INTEREST PAID ON CERTAIN DEPOSITS OR WITHDRAWABLE ACCOUNTS.—Except as provided in regulations prescribed by the Secretary, amounts paid to, or credited to the accounts of, depositors or holders of accounts as dividends or interest on their deposits or withdrawable accounts (if such amounts paid or credited are withdrawable on demand subject only to customary notice to withdraw) by a mutual savings bank not having capital stock represented by shares, a domestic building and loan association, or a cooperative bank shall not be allowed as a deduction for the taxable year to the extent such amounts are paid or credited for periods representing more than 12 months. Any such amount not allowed as a deduction as the result of the application of the preceding sentence shall be allowed as a deduction for such other taxable year as the Secretary determines to be consistent with the preceding sentence.

[Sec. 461(f)]

(f) CONTESTED LIABILITIES.—If—

(1) the taxpayer contests an asserted liability,

(2) the taxpayer transfers money or other property to provide for the satisfaction of the asserted liability,

(3) the contest with respect to the asserted liability exists after the time of the transfer, and

(4) but for the fact that the asserted liability is contested, a deduction would be allowed for the taxable year of the transfer (or for an earlier taxable year) determined after application of subsection (h),

then the deduction shall be allowed for the taxable year of the transfer. This subsection shall not apply in respect of the deduction for income, war profits, and excess profits taxes imposed by the authority of any foreign country or possession of the United States.

[Sec. 461(g)]

(g) PREPAID INTEREST.—

(1) IN GENERAL.—If the taxable income of the taxpayer is computed under the cash receipts and disbursements method of accounting, interest paid by the taxpayer which, under regulations prescribed by the Secretary, is properly allocable to any period—

(A) with respect to which the interest represents a charge for the use or forbearance of money, and

(B) which is after the close of the taxable year in which paid,

shall be charged to capital account and shall be treated as paid in the period to which so allocable.

(2) EXCEPTION.—This subsection shall not apply to points paid in respect of any indebtedness incurred in connection with the purchase or improvement of, and secured by, the principal residence of the taxpayer to the extent that, under regulations prescribed by the Secretary, such payment of points is an established business practice in the area in which such indebtedness is incurred, and the amount of such payment does not exceed the amount generally charged in such area.

(h) CERTAIN LIABILITIES NOT INCURRED BEFORE ECONOMIC PERFORMANCE.—

(1) IN GENERAL.—For purposes of this title, in determining whether an amount has been incurred with respect to any item during any taxable year, the all events test shall not be treated as met any earlier than when economic performance with respect to such item occurs.

(2) TIME WHEN ECONOMIC PERFORMANCE OCCURS.—Except as provided in regulations prescribed by the Secretary, the time when economic performance occurs shall be determined under the following principles:

(A) SERVICES AND PROPERTY PROVIDED TO THE TAXPAYER.—If the liability of the taxpayer arises out of—

(i) the providing of services to the taxpayer by another person, economic performance occurs as such person provides such services,

(ii) the providing of property to the taxpayer by another person, economic performance occurs as the person provides such property, or

(iii) the use of property by the taxpayer, economic performance occurs as the taxpayer uses such property.

(B) SERVICES AND PROPERTY PROVIDED BY THE TAXPAYER.—If the liability of the taxpayer requires the taxpayer to provide property or services, economic performance occurs as the taxpayer provides such property or services.

(C) WORKERS COMPENSATION AND TORT LIABILITIES OF THE TAXPAYER.—If the liability of the taxpayer requires a payment to another person and—

(i) arises under any workers compensation act, or

(ii) arises out of any tort,

economic performance occurs as the payments to such person are made. Subparagraphs (A) and (B) shall not apply to any liability described in the preceding sentence.

(D) OTHER ITEMS.—In the case of any other liability of the taxpayer, economic performance occurs at the time determined under regulations prescribed by the Secretary.

(3) EXCEPTION FOR CERTAIN RECURRING ITEMS.—

(A) IN GENERAL.—Notwithstanding paragraph (1) an item shall be treated as incurred during any taxable year if—

(i) the all events test with respect to such item is met during such taxable year (determined without regard to paragraph (1)),

(ii) economic performance with respect to such item occurs within the shorter of—

(I) a reasonable period after the close of such taxable year, or

(II) 8½ months after the close of such taxable year,

(iii) such item is recurring in nature and the taxpayer consistently treats items of such kind as incurred in the taxable year in which the requirements of clause (i) are met, and

(iv) either—

(I) such item is not a material item, or

(II) the accrual of such item in the taxable year in which the requirements of clause (i) are met results in a more proper match against income than accruing such item in the taxable year in which economic performance occurs.

(B) FINANCIAL STATEMENTS CONSIDERED UNDER SUBPARAGRAPH (A)(iv).—In making a determination under subparagraph (A)(iv), the treatment of such item on financial statements shall be taken into account.

(C) PARAGRAPH NOT TO APPLY TO WORKERS COMPENSATION AND TORT LIABILITIES.—This paragraph shall not apply to any item described in subparagraph (C) of paragraph (2).

(4) ALL EVENTS TEST.—For purposes of this subsection, the all events test is met with respect to any item if all events have occurred which determine the fact of liability and the amount of such liability can be determined with reasonable accuracy.

(5) SUBSECTION NOT TO APPLY TO CERTAIN ITEMS.—This subsection shall not apply to any item for which a deduction is allowable under a provision of this title which specifically provides for a deduction for a reserve for estimated expenses.

[Sec. 461(i)]

(i) SPECIAL RULES FOR TAX SHELTERS.—

(1) RECURRING ITEM EXCEPTION NOT TO APPLY.—In the case of a tax shelter, economic performance shall be determined without regard to paragraph (3) of subsection (h).

(2) SPECIAL RULE FOR SPUDDING OF OIL OR GAS WELLS.—

(A) IN GENERAL.—In the case of a tax shelter, economic performance with respect to amounts paid during the taxable year for drilling an oil or gas well shall be treated as having occurred within a taxable year if drilling of the well commences before the close of the 90th day after the close of the taxable year.

(B) DEDUCTION LIMITED TO CASH BASIS.—

(i) TAX SHELTER PARTNERSHIPS.—In the case of a tax shelter which is a partnership, in applying section 704(d) to a deduction or loss for any taxable year attributable to an item which is deductible by reason of subparagraph (A), the term "cash basis" shall be substituted for the term "adjusted basis".

(ii) OTHER TAX SHELTERS.—Under regulations prescribed by the Secretary, in the case of a tax shelter other than a partnership, the aggregate amount of the deductions allowable by reason of subparagraph (A) for any taxable year shall be limited in a manner similar to the limitation under clause (i).

(C) CASH BASIS DEFINED.—For purposes of subparagraph (B), a partner's cash basis in a partnership shall be equal to the adjusted basis of such partner's interest in the partnership, determined without regard to—

(i) any liability of the partnership, and

(ii) any amount borrowed by the partner with respect to such partnership which—

(I) was arranged by the partnership or by any person who participated in the organization, sale, or management of the partnership (or any person related to such person within the meaning of section 465(b)(3)(C)), or

(II) was secured by any asset of the partnership.

(3) TAX SHELTER DEFINED.—For purposes of this subsection, the term "tax shelter" means—

(A) any enterprise (other than a C corporation) if at any time interests in such enterprise have been offered for sale in any offering required to be registered with any Federal or State agency having the authority to regulate the offering of securities for sale,

(B) any syndicate (within the meaning of section 1256(e)(3)(B)), and

(C) any tax shelter (as defined in section 6662(d)(2)(C)(ii)).

(4) SPECIAL RULES FOR FARMING.—In the case of the trade or business of farming (as defined in section 464(e)), in determining whether an entity is a tax shelter, the definition of farming syndicate in subsection (k) shall be substituted for subparagraphs (A) and (B) of paragraph (3).

(5) ECONOMIC PERFORMANCE.—For purposes of this subsection, the term "economic performance" has the meaning given such term by subsection (h).

* * *

[Sec. 461(l)]

(l) LIMITATION ON EXCESS BUSINESS LOSSES OF NONCORPORATE TAXPAYERS.—

(1) LIMITATION.—In the case of a taxpayer other than a corporation—

(A) for any taxable year beginning after December 31, 2017, and before January 1, 2026, subsection (j) (relating to limitation on excess farm losses of certain taxpayers) shall not apply, and

(B) for any taxable year beginning after December 31, 2020, and before January 1, 2026, any excess business loss of the taxpayer for the taxable year shall not be allowed.

(2) DISALLOWED LOSS CARRYOVER.—Any loss which is disallowed under paragraph (1) shall be treated as a net operating loss for the taxable year for purposes of determining any net operating loss carryover under section 172(b) for subsequent taxable years.

(3) EXCESS BUSINESS LOSS.—For purposes of this subsection—

(A) IN GENERAL.—The term "excess business loss" means the excess (if any) of—

(i) the aggregate deductions of the taxpayer for the taxable year which are attributable to trades or businesses of such taxpayer (determined without regard to whether or not such deductions are disallowed for such taxable year under paragraph (1) and without regard to any deduction allowable under section 172 or 199A, over

(ii) the sum of—

(I) the aggregate gross income or gain of such taxpayer for the taxable year which is attributable to such trades or businesses, plus

(II) $250,000 (200 percent of such amount in the case of a joint return).

Such excess shall be determined without regard to any deductions, gross income, or gains attributable to any trade or business of performing services as an employee.

(B) TREATMENT OF CAPITAL GAINS AND LOSSES.—

(i) LOSSES.—Deductions for losses from sales or exchanges of capital assets shall not be taken into account under subparagraph (A)(i).

(ii) GAINS.—The amount of gains from sales or exchanges of capital assets taken into account under subparagraph (A)(ii) shall not exceed the lesser of—

(I) the capital gain net income determined by taking into account only gains and losses attributable to a trade or business, or

(II) the capital gain net income.

(C) ADJUSTMENT FOR INFLATION.—In the case of any taxable year beginning after December 31, 2018, the $250,000 amount in subparagraph (A)(ii)(II) shall be increased by an amount equal to—

(i) such dollar amount, multiplied by

(ii) the cost-of-living adjustment determined under section 1(f)(3) for the calendar year in which the taxable year begins, determined by substituting "2017" for "2016" in subparagraph (A)(ii) thereof.

If any amount as increased under the preceding sentence is not a multiple of $1,000, such amount shall be rounded to the nearest multiple of $1,000.

(4) APPLICATION OF SUBSECTION IN CASE OF PARTNERSHIPS AND S CORPORATIONS.—In the case of a partnership or S corporation—

(A) this subsection shall be applied at the partner or shareholder level, and

(B) each partner's or shareholder's allocable share of the items of income, gain, deduction, or loss of the partnership or S corporation for any taxable year from trades or businesses attributable to the partnership or S corporation shall be taken into account by the partner or shareholder in applying this subsection to the taxable year of such partner or shareholder with or within which the taxable year of the partnership or S corporation ends.

For purposes of this paragraph, in the case of an S corporation, an allocable share shall be the shareholder's pro rata share of an item.

(5) ADDITIONAL REPORTING.—The Secretary shall prescribe such additional reporting requirements as the Secretary determines necessary to carry out the purposes of this subsection.

(6) COORDINATION WITH SECTION 469.—This subsection shall be applied after the application of section 469.

[Sec. 465]

SEC. 465. DEDUCTIONS LIMITED TO AMOUNT AT RISK.

[Sec. 465(a)]

(a) LIMITATION TO AMOUNT AT RISK.—

(1) IN GENERAL.—In the case of—

(A) an individual, and

(B) a C corporation with respect to which the stock ownership requirement of paragraph (2) of section 542(a) is met,

engaged in an activity to which this section applies, any loss from such activity for the taxable year shall be allowed only to the extent of the aggregate amount with respect to which the taxpayer is at risk (within the meaning of subsection (b)) for such activity at the close of the taxable year.

(2) DEDUCTION IN SUCCEEDING YEAR.—Any loss from an activity to which this section applies not allowed under this section for the taxable year shall be treated as a deduction allocable to such activity in the first succeeding taxable year.

(3) SPECIAL RULES FOR APPLYING PARAGRAPH (1)(B).—For purposes of paragraph (1)(B)—

(A) section 544(a)(2) shall be applied as if such section did not contain the phrase "or by or for his partner"; and

(B) sections 544(a)(4)(A) and 544(b)(1) shall be applied by substituting "the corporation meet the stock ownership requirements of section 542(a)(2)" for "the corporation a personal holding company."

[Sec. 465(b)]

(b) AMOUNTS CONSIDERED AT RISK.—

(1) IN GENERAL.—For purposes of this section, a taxpayer shall be considered at risk for an activity with respect to amounts including—

(A) the amount of money and the adjusted basis of other property contributed by the taxpayer to the activity, and

(B) amounts borrowed with respect to such activity (as determined under paragraph (2)).

(2) BORROWED AMOUNTS.—For purposes of this section, a taxpayer shall be considered at risk with respect to amounts borrowed for use in an activity to the extent that he—

(A) is personally liable for the repayment of such amounts, or

(B) has pledged property, other than property used in such activity, as security for such borrowed amount (to the extent of the net fair market value of the taxpayer's interest in such property).

No property shall be taken into account as security if such property is directly or indirectly financed by indebtedness which is secured by property described in paragraph (1).

(3) CERTAIN BORROWED AMOUNTS EXCLUDED.—

(A) IN GENERAL.—Except to the extent provided in regulations, for purposes of paragraph (1)(B), amounts borrowed shall not be considered to be at risk with respect to an activity if such amounts are borrowed from any person who has an interest in such activity or from a related person to a person (other than the taxpayer) having such an interest.

(B) EXCEPTIONS.—

(i) INTEREST AS CREDITOR.—Subparagraph (A) shall not apply to an interest as a creditor in the activity.

(ii) INTEREST AS SHAREHOLDER WITH RESPECT TO AMOUNTS BORROWED BY CORPORATION.—In the case of amounts borrowed by a corporation from a shareholder, subparagraph (A) shall not apply to an interest as a shareholder.

(C) RELATED PERSON.—For purposes of this subsection, a person (herein after in this paragraph referred to as the "related person") is related to any person if—

(i) the related person bears a relationship to such person specified in section 267(b) or section 707(b)(1), or

(ii) the related person and such person are engaged in trades or business under common control (within the meaning of subsections (a) and (b) of section 52).

For purposes of clause (i), in applying section 267(b) or 707(b)(1), "10 percent" shall be substituted for "50 percent."

(4) EXCEPTION.—Notwithstanding any other provision of this section, a taxpayer shall not be considered at risk with respect to amounts protected against loss through nonrecourse financing, guarantees, stop loss agreements, or other similar arrangements.

(5) AMOUNTS AT RISK IN SUBSEQUENT YEARS.—If in any taxable year the taxpayer has a loss from an activity to which subsection (a) applies, the amount with respect to which a taxpayer is considered to be at risk (within the meaning of subsection (b)) in subsequent taxable years with respect to that activity shall be reduced by that portion of the loss which (after the application of subsection (a)) is allowable as a deduction.

(6) QUALIFIED NONRECOURSE FINANCING TREATED AS AMOUNT AT RISK.—For purposes of this section—

(A) IN GENERAL.—Notwithstanding any other provision of this subsection, in the case of an activity of holding real property, a taxpayer shall be considered at risk with respect to the taxpayer's share of any qualified nonrecourse financing which is secured by real property used in such activity.

(B) QUALIFIED NONRECOURSE FINANCING.—For purposes of this paragraph, the term "qualified nonrecourse financing" means any financing—

(i) which is borrowed by the taxpayer with respect to the activity of holding real property,

(ii) which is borrowed by the taxpayer from a qualified person or represents a loan from any Federal, State, or local government or instrumentality thereof, or is guaranteed by any Federal, State, or local government,

(iii) except to the extent provided in regulations, with respect to which no person is personally liable for repayment, and

(iv) which is not convertible debt.

(C) SPECIAL RULE FOR PARTNERSHIPS.—In the case of a partnership, a partner's share of any qualified nonrecourse financing of such partnership shall be determined on the basis of the partner's share of liabilities of such partnership incurred in connection with such financing (within the meaning of section 752).

(D) QUALIFIED PERSON DEFINED.—For purposes of this paragraph—

(i) IN GENERAL.—The term "qualified person" has the meaning given such term by section 49(a)(1)(D)(iv).

(ii) CERTAIN COMMERCIALLY REASONABLE FINANCING FROM RELATED PERSONS.—For purposes of clause (i), section 49(a)(1) D)(iv) shall be applied without regard to subclause (I) thereof (relating to financing from related persons) if the financing from the related person is commercially reasonable and on substantially the same terms as loans involving unrelated persons.

(E) ACTIVITY OF HOLDING REAL PROPERTY.—For purposes of this paragraph—

(i) INCIDENTAL PERSONAL PROPERTY AND SERVICES.—The activity of holding real property includes the holding of personal property and the providing of services which are incidental to making real property available as living accommodations.

(ii) MINERAL PROPERTY.—The activity of holding real property shall not include the holding of mineral property.

[Sec. 465(c)]

(c) ACTIVITIES TO WHICH SECTION APPLIES.—

(1) TYPES OF ACTIVITIES.—This section applies to any taxpayer engaged in the activity of—

(A) holding, producing, or distributing motion picture films or video tapes,

(B) farming (as defined in section 464(e)),

(C) leasing any section 1245 property (as defined in section 1245(a)(3)),

(D) exploring for, or exploiting, oil and gas resources, or

(E) exploring for, or exploiting, geothermal deposits (as defined in section 613(e)(2))

as a trade or business or for the production of income.

(2) SEPARATE ACTIVITIES.—For purposes of this section—

(A) IN GENERAL.—Except as provided in subparagraph (B), a taxpayer's activity with respect to each—

(i) film or video tape,

(ii) section 1245 property which is leased or held for leasing,

(iii) farm,

(iv) oil and gas property (as defined under section 614), or

(v) geothermal property (as defined under section 614),

shall be treated as a separate activity.

(B) AGGREGATION RULES.—

(i) SPECIAL RULE FOR LEASES OF SECTION 1245 PROPERTY BY PARTNERSHIPS OR S CORPORATIONS.—In the case of any partnership or S corporation, all activities with respect to section 1245 properties which—

(I) are leased or held for lease, and

(II) are placed in service in any taxable year of the partnership or S corporation,

shall be treated as a single activity.

(ii) OTHER AGGREGATION RULES.—Rules similar to the rules of subparagraphs (B) and (C) of paragraph (3) shall apply for purposes of this paragraph.

(3) EXTENSION TO OTHER ACTIVITIES.—

(A) IN GENERAL.—This section also applies to each activity—

(i) engaged in by the taxpayer in carrying on a trade or business or for the production of income, and

(ii) which is not described in paragraph (1).

(B) AGGREGATION OF ACTIVITIES WHERE TAXPAYER ACTIVELY PARTICIPATES IN MANAGEMENT OF TRADE OR BUSINESS.—Except as provided in subparagraph (C), for purposes of this section, activities described in subparagraph (A) which constitute a trade or business shall be treated as one activity if—

(i) the taxpayer actively participates in the management of such trade or business, or

(ii) such trade or business is carried on by a partnership or an S corporation and 65 percent or more of the losses for the taxable year is allocable to persons who actively participate in the management of the trade or business.

(C) AGGREGATION OR SEPARATION OF ACTIVITIES UNDER REGULATIONS.—The Secretary shall prescribe regulations under which activities described in subparagraph (A) shall be aggregated or treated as separate activities.

(D) APPLICATION OF SUBSECTION (b) (3).—In the case of an activity described in subparagraph (A), subsection (b) (3) shall apply only to the extent provided in regulations prescribed by the Secretary.

* * *

(7) EXCLUSION OF ACTIVE BUSINESSES OF QUALIFIED C CORPORATIONS.—

(A) IN GENERAL.—In the case of a taxpayer which is a qualified C corporation—

(i) each qualifying business carried on by such taxpayer shall be treated as a separate activity, and

(ii) subsection (a) shall not apply to losses from such business.

(B) QUALIFIED C CORPORATION.—For purposes of subparagraph (A), the term "qualified C corporation" means any corporation described in subparagraph (B) of subsection (a) (1) which is not—

(i) a personal holding company (as defined in section 542(a)), or

(ii) a personal service corporation (as defined in section 269A(b) but determined by substituting "5 percent" for "10 percent" in section 269A(b) (2)).

(C) QUALIFYING BUSINESS.—For purposes of this paragraph, the term "qualifying business" means any active business if—

(i) during the entire 12-month period ending on the last day of the taxable year, such corporation had at least 1 full-time employee substantially all the services of whom were in the active management of such business,

(ii) during the entire 12-month period ending on the last day of the taxable year, such corporation had at least 3 full-time, nonowner employees substantially all of the services of whom were services directly related to such business,

(iii) the amount of the deductions attributable to such business which are allowable to the taxpayer solely by reason of sections 162 and 404 for the taxable year exceeds 15 percent of the gross income from such business for such year, and

(iv) such business is not an excluded business.

(D) SPECIAL RULES FOR APPLICATION OF SUBPARAGRAPH (C).—

(i) PARTNERSHIPS IN WHICH TAXPAYER IS A QUALIFIED CORPORATE PARTNER.—In the case of an active business of a partnership, if—

(I) the taxpayer is a qualified corporate partner in the partnership, and

(II) during the entire 12-month period ending on the last day of the partnership's taxable year, there was at least 1 full-time employee of the partnership (or of a qualified corporate partner) substantially all the services of whom were in the active management of such business,

then the taxpayer's proportionate share (determined on the basis of its profits interest) of the activities of the partnership in such business shall be treated as activities of the taxpayer (and clause (i) of subparagraph (C) shall not apply in determining whether such business is a qualifying business of the taxpayer).

(ii) QUALIFIED CORPORATE PARTNER.—For purposes of clause (i), the term "qualified corporate partner" means any corporation if—

(I) such corporation is a general partner in the partnership,

(II) such corporation has an interest of 10 percent or more in the profits and losses of the partnership, and

(III) such corporation has contributed property to the partnership in an amount not less than the lesser of $500,000 or 10 percent of the net worth of the corporation.

For purposes of subclause (III), and contribution of property other than money shall be taken into account at its fair market value.

(iii) DEDUCTION FOR OWNER EMPLOYEE CONPENSATION NOT TAKEN INTO ACCOUNT.—For purposes of clause (iii) of subparagraph (C), there shall not be taken into account any deduction in respect of compensation for personal services rendered by any employee (other than a non-owner employee) of the taxpayer or any member of such employee's family (within the meaning of section 318(a)(1)).

* * *

(E) DEFINITIONS.—For purposes of this paragraph—

(i) NON-OWNER EMPLOYEE.—The term "non-owner employee" means any employee who does not own, at any time during the taxable year, more than 5 percent in value of the outstanding stock of the taxpayer. For purposes of the preceding sentence, section 318 shall apply, except that "5 percent" shall be substituted for "50 percent" in section 318(a)(2)(C).

(ii) EXCLUDED BUSINESS.—The term "excluded business" means—

(I) equipment leasing (as defined in paragraph (6)), and

(II) any business involving the use, exploitation, sale, lease, or other disposition of master sound recordings, motion picture films, video tapes, or tangible or intangible assets associated with literary, artistic, musical, or similar properties.

(iii) SPECIAL RULES RELATING TO COMMUNICATIONS INDUSTRY, ETC.—

(I) BUSINESS NOT EXCLUDED WHERE TAXPAYER NOT COMPLETELY AT RISK.—A business involving the use, exploitation, sale, lease, or other disposition of property described in subclause (II) of clause (ii) shall not constitute an excluded business by reason of such subclause if the taxpayer is at risk with respect to all amounts paid or incurred (or chargeable to capital account) in such business.

(II) CERTAIN LICENSED BUSINESSES NOT EXCLUDED.—For purposes of subclause (II) of clause (ii), the provision of radio, television, cable television, or similar services pursuant to a license or franchise granted by the Federal Communications Commission or any other Federal, State, or local authority shall not constitute an excluded business by reason of such subclause.

(F) AFFILIATED GROUP TREATED AS 1 TAXPAYER.—For purposes of this paragraph—

(i) IN GENERAL.—Except as provided in subparagraph (G), the component members of an affiliated group of corporations shall be treated as a single taxpayer.

(ii) AFFILIATED GROUP OF CORPORATIONS.—The term "affiliated group of corporations" means an affiliated group (as defined in section 1504(a)) which files or is required to file consolidated income tax returns.

(iii) COMPONENT MEMBER.—The term "component member" means an includible corporation (as defined in section 1504) which is a member of the affiliated group.

(G) LOSS OF 1 MEMBER OF AFFILIATED GROUP MAY NOT OFFSET INCOME OF PERSONAL HOLDING COMPANY OR PERSONAL SERVICE CORPORATION.—Nothing in this paragraph shall permit any loss of a member of an affiliated group to be used as an offset against the income of any other member of such group which is a personal holding company (as defined in section 542(a)) or a personal service corporation (as defined in section 269A(b) but determined by substituting "5 percent" for "10 percent" in section 269A(b)(2)).

[Sec. 465(d)]

(d) DEFINITION OF LOSS.—For purposes of this section, the term "loss" means the excess of the deductions allowable under this chapter for the taxable year (determined without regard to the first sentence of subsection (a)) and allocable to an activity to which this section applies over the income received or accrued by the taxpayer during the taxable year from such activity (determined without regard to subsection (e)(1)(A)).

[Sec. 465(e)]

(e) RECAPTURE OF LOSSES WHERE AMOUNT AT RISK IS LESS THAN ZERO.—

(1) IN GENERAL.—If zero exceeds the amount for which the taxpayer is at risk in any activity at the close of any taxable year—

(A) the taxpayer shall include in his gross income for such taxable year (as income from such activity) an amount equal to such excess, and

(B) an amount equal to the amount so included in gross income shall be treated as a deduction allocable to such activity for the first succeeding taxable year.

(2) LIMITATION.—The excess referred to in paragraph (1) shall not exceed—

(A) the aggregate amount of the reductions required by subsection (b)(5) with respect to the activity by reason of losses for all prior taxable years beginning after December 31, 1978, reduced by

(B) the amounts previously included in gross income with respect to such activity under this subsection.

[Sec. 467]

SEC. 467. CERTAIN PAYMENTS FOR THE USE OF PROPERTY OR SERVICES.

[Sec. 467(a)]

(a) ACCRUAL METHOD ON PRESENT VALUE BASIS.—In the case of the lessor or lessee under any section 467 rental agreement, there shall be taken into account for purposes of this title for any taxable year the sum of—

(1) the amount of the rent which accrues during such taxable year as determined under subsection (b), and

(2) interest for the year on the amounts which were taken into account under this subsection for prior taxable years and which are unpaid.

[Sec. 467(b)]

(b) ACCRUAL OF RENTAL PAYMENTS.—

(1) ALLOCATION FOLLOWS AGREEMENT.—Except as provided in paragraph (2), the determination of the amount of the rent under any section 467 rental agreement which accrues during any taxable year shall be made—

(A) by allocating rents in accordance with the agreement, and

(B) by taking into account any rent to be paid after the close of the period in an amount determined under regulations which shall be based on present value concepts.

(2) CONSTANT RENTAL ACCRUAL IN CASE OF CERTAIN TAX AVOIDANCE TRANSACTIONS, ETC.—In the case of any section 467 rental agreement to which this paragraph applies, the portion of the rent which accrues during any taxable year shall be that portion of the constant rental amount with respect to such agreement which is allocable to such taxable year.

(3) AGREEMENTS TO WHICH PARAGRAPH (2) APPLIES.—Paragraph (2) applies to any rental payment agreement if—

(A) such agreement is a disqualified leaseback or long-term agreement, or

(B) such agreement does not provide for the allocation referred to in paragraph (1)(A).

(4) DISQUALIFIED LEASEBACK OR LONG-TERM AGREEMENT.—For purposes of this subsection, the term "disqualified leaseback or long-term agreement" means any section 467 rental agreement if—

(A) such agreement is part of a leaseback transaction or such agreement is for a term in excess of 75 percent of the statutory recovery period for the property, and

(B) a principal purpose for providing increasing rents under the agreement is the avoidance of tax imposed by this subtitle.

(5) EXCEPTIONS TO DISQUALIFICATION IN CERTAIN CASES.—The Secretary shall prescribe regulations setting forth circumstances under which agreements will not be treated as disqualified leaseback or long-term agreements, including circumstances relating to—

(A) changes in amounts paid determined by reference to price indices,

(B) rents based on a fixed percentage of lessee receipts or similar amounts,

(C) reasonable rent holidays, or

(D) changes in amounts paid to unrelated 3rd parties.

[Sec. 467(c)]

(c) RECAPTURE OF PRIOR UNDERSTATED INCLUSIONS UNDER LEASEBACK OR LONG-TERM AGREEMENTS.—

(1) IN GENERAL.—If—

(A) the lessor under any section 467 rental agreement disposes of any property subject to such agreement during the term of such agreement, and

(B) such agreement is a leaseback or long-term agreement to which paragraph (2) of subsection (b) did not apply,

the recapture amount shall be treated as ordinary income. Such gain shall be recognized notwithstanding any other provision of this subtitle.

(2) RECAPTURE AMOUNT.—For purposes of paragraph (1), the term "recapture amount" means the lesser of—

(A) the prior understated inclusions, or

(B) the excess of the amount realized (or in the case of a disposition other than a sale, exchange, or involuntary conversion, the fair market value of the property) over the adjusted basis of such property.

The amount determined under subparagraph (B) shall be reduced by the amount of any gain treated as ordinary income on the disposition under any other provision of this subtitle.

(3) PRIOR UNDERSTATED INCLUSIONS.—For purposes of this subsection, the term "prior understated inclusion" means the excess (if any) of—

(A) the amount which would have been taken into account by the lessor under subsection (a) for periods before the disposition if subsection (b)(2) had applied to the agreement, over

(B) the amount taken into account under subsection (a) by the lessor for periods before the disposition.

(4) LEASEBACK OR LONG-TERM AGREEMENT.—For purposes of this subsection, the term "leaseback or long-term agreement" means any agreement described in subsection (b)(4)(A).

(5) SPECIAL RULES.—Under regulations prescribed by the Secretary—

(A) exceptions similar to the exceptions applicable under section 1245 or 1250 (whichever is appropriate) shall apply for purposes of this subsection,

(B) any transferee in a disposition excepted by reason of subparagraph (A) who has a transferred basis in the property shall be treated in the same manner as the transferor, and

(C) for purposes of sections 170(e) and 751(c), amounts treated as ordinary income under this section shall be treated in the same manner as amounts treated as ordinary income under section 1245 or 1250.

[Sec. 467(d)]

(d) SECTION 467 RENTAL AGREEMENTS.—

(1) IN GENERAL.—Except as otherwise provided in this subsection, the term "section 467 rental agreements" means any rental agreement for the use of tangible property under which—

(A) there is at least one amount allocable to the use of property during a calendar year which is to be paid after the close of the calendar year following the calendar year in which such use occurs, or

(B) there are increases in the amount to be paid as rent under the agreement.

(2) SECTION NOT TO APPLY TO AGREEMENTS INVOLVING PAYMENTS OF $250,000 OR LESS.—This section shall not apply to any amount to be paid for the use of property if the sum of the following amounts does not exceed $250,000—

(A) the aggregate amount of payments received as consideration for such use of property, and

(B) the aggregate value of any other consideration to be received for such use of property.

For purposes of the preceding sentence, rules similar to the rules of clauses (ii) and (iii) of section 1274(c)(4)(C) shall apply.

[Sec. 467(e)]

(e) DEFINITIONS.—For purposes of this section—

(1) CONSTANT RENTAL AMOUNT.—The term "constant rental amount" means, with respect to any section 467 rental agreement, the amount which, if paid as of the close of each lease period under the agreement, would result in an aggregate present value equal to the present value of the aggregate payments required under the agreement.

(2) LEASEBACK TRANSACTION.—A transaction is a leaseback transaction if it involves a leaseback to any person who had an interest in such property at any time within 2 years before such leaseback (or to a related person).

(3) STATUTORY RECOVERY PERIOD.—

(A) IN GENERAL.—

In the case of:	*The statutory recovery period is:*
3-year property	3 years
5-year property	5 years
7-year property	7 years
10-year property	10 years
15-year and 20-year property	15 years
Residential rental property and nonresidential real property	19 years
Any railroad grading or tunnel bore	50 years .

(B) SPECIAL RULE FOR PROPERTY NOT DEPRECIABLE UNDER SECTION 168.—In the case of property to which section 168 does not apply, subparagraph (A) shall be applied as if section 168 applies to such property.

(4) DISCOUNT AND INTEREST RATE.—For purposes of computing present value and interest under subsection (a)(2), the rate used shall be equal to 110 percent of the applicable Federal rate determined under section 1274(d) (compounded semiannually) which is in effect at the time the agreement is entered into with respect to debt instruments having a maturity equal to the term of the agreement.

(5) RELATED PERSON.—The term "related person" has the meaning given to such term by section 465(b)[3](C).

(6) CERTAIN OPTIONS OF LESSEE TO RENEW NOT TAKEN INTO ACCOUNT.—Except as provided in regulations prescribed by the Secretary, there shall not be taken into account in computing the term of any agreement for purposes of this section any extension which is solely at the option of the lessee.

[Sec. 467(f)]

(f) COMPARABLE RULES WHERE AGREEMENT FOR DECREASING PAYMENTS.—Under regulations prescribed by the Secretary, rules comparable to the rules of this section shall also apply in the case of any agreement where the amount paid under the agreement for the use of property decreases during the term of the agreement.

[Sec. 467(g)]

(g) COMPARABLE RULES FOR SERVICES.—Under regulations prescribed by the Secretary, rules comparable to the rules of subsection (a)(2) shall also apply in the case of payments for services which meet requirements comparable to the requirements of subsection (d). The preceding sentence shall not apply to any amount to which section 404 or 404A (or any other provision specified in regulations) applies.

[Sec. 467(h)]

(h) REGULATIONS.—The Secretary shall prescribe such regulations as may be appropriate to carry out the purposes of this section, including regulations providing for the application of this section in the case of contingent payments.

[Sec. 469]

SEC. 469. PASSIVE ACTIVITY LOSSES AND CREDITS LIMITED.

[Sec. 469(a)]

(a) DISALLOWANCE.—

(1) IN GENERAL.—If for any taxable year the taxpayer is described in paragraph (2), neither—

(A) the passive activity loss, nor

(B) the passive activity credit,

for the taxable year shall be allowed.

(2) PERSONS DESCRIBED.—The following are described in this paragraph:

(A) any individual, estate, or trust,

(B) any closely held C corporation, and

(C) any personal service corporation.

[Sec. 469(b)]

(b) DISALLOWED LOSS OR CREDIT CARRIED TO NEXT YEAR.—Except as otherwise provided in this section, any loss or credit from an activity which is disallowed under subsection (a) shall be treated as a deduction or credit allocable to such activity in the next taxable year.

[Sec. 469(c)]

(c) PASSIVE ACTIVITY DEFINED.—For purposes of this section—

(1) IN GENERAL.—The term "passive activity" means any activity—

(A) which involves the conduct of any trade or business, and

(B) in which the taxpayer does not materially participate.

(2) PASSIVE ACTIVITY INCLUDES ANY RENTAL ACTIVITY.—Except as provided in paragraph (7), the term "passive activity" includes any rental activity.

(3) WORKING INTERESTS IN OIL AND GAS PROPERTY.—

(A) IN GENERAL.—The term "passive activity" shall not include any working interest in any oil or gas property which the taxpayer holds directly or through an entity which does not limit the liability of the taxpayer with respect to such interest.

(B) INCOME IN SUBSEQUENT YEARS.—If any taxpayer has any loss for any taxable year from a working interest in any oil or gas property which is treated as a loss which is not from a passive activity, then any net income from such property (or any property the basis of which is determined in whole or in part by reference to the basis of such property) for any succeeding taxable year shall be treated as income of the taxpayer which is not from a passive activity. If the preceding sentence applies to the net income from any property for any taxable year, any credits allowable under subpart B (other than section 27) or D of part IV of subchapter A for such taxable year which are attributable to such property shall be treated as credits not from a passive activity to the extent the amount of such credits does not exceed the regular tax liability of the taxpayer for the taxable year which is allocable to such net income.

(4) MATERIAL PARTICIPATION NOT REQUIRED FOR PARAGRAPHS (2) AND (3).—Paragraphs (2) and (3) shall be applied without regard to whether or not the taxpayer materially participates in the activity.

(5) TRADE OR BUSINESS INCLUDES RESEARCH AND EXPERIMENTATION ACTIVITY.—For purposes of paragraph (1)(A), the term "trade or business" includes any activity involving research or experimentation (within the meaning of section 174).

(6) ACTIVITY IN CONNECTION WITH TRADE OR BUSINESS OR PRODUCTION OF INCOME.—To the extent provided in regulations, for purposes of paragraph (1)(A), the term "trade or business" includes—

(A) any activity in connection with a trade or business, or

(B) any activity with respect to which expenses are allowable as a deduction under section 212.

(7) SPECIAL RULES FOR TAXPAYERS IN REAL PROPERTY BUSINESS.—

(A) IN GENERAL.—If this paragraph applies to any taxpayer for a taxable year—

(i) paragraph (2) shall not apply to any rental real estate activity of such taxpayer for such taxable year, and

(ii) this section shall be applied as if each interest of the taxpayer in rental real estate were a separate activity.

Notwithstanding clause (ii), a taxpayer may elect to treat all interests in rental real estate as one activity. Nothing in the preceding provisions of this subparagraph shall be construed as affecting the determination of whether the taxpayer materially participates with respect to any interest in a limited partnership as a limited partner.

(B) TAXPAYERS TO WHOM PARAGRAPH APPLIES.—This paragraph shall apply to a taxpayer for a taxable year if—

(i) more than one-half of the personal services performed in trades or businesses by the taxpayer during such taxable year are performed in real property trades or businesses in which the taxpayer materially participates, and

(ii) such taxpayer performs more than 750 hours of services during the taxable year in real property trades or businesses in which the taxpayer materially participates.

In the case of a joint return, the requirements of the preceding sentence are satisfied if and only if either spouse separately satisfied such requirements. For purposes of the preceding sentence, activities in which a spouse materially participates shall be determined under subsection (h).

(C) REAL PROPERTY TRADE OR BUSINESS.—For purposes of this paragraph, the term "real property trade or business" means any real property development, redevelopment, construction, reconstruction, acquisition, conversion, rental, operation, management, leasing, or brokerage trade or business.

(D) SPECIAL RULES FOR SUBPARAGRAPH (B).—

(i) CLOSELY HELD C CORPORATIONS.—In the case of a closely held C corporation, the requirements of subparagraph (B) shall be treated as met for any taxable year if more than 50 percent of the gross receipts of such corporation for such taxable year are derived from real property trades or businesses in which the corporation materially participates.

(ii) PERSONAL SERVICES AS AN EMPLOYEE.—For purposes of subparagraph (B), personal services performed as an employee shall not be treated as performed in real property trades or businesses. The preceding sentence shall not apply if such employee is a 5-percent owner (as defined in section 416(i)(1)(B)) in the employer.

[Sec. 469(d)]

(d) PASSIVE ACTIVITY LOSS AND CREDIT DEFINED.—For purposes of this section—

(1) PASSIVE ACTIVITY LOSS.—The term "passive activity loss" means the amount (if any) by which—

(A) the aggregate losses from all passive activities for the taxable year, exceed

(B) the aggregate income from all passive activities for such year.

(2) PASSIVE ACTIVITY CREDIT.—The term "passive activity credit" means the amount (if any) by which—

(A) the sum of the credits from all passive activities allowable for the taxable year under—

(i) subpart D of part IV of subchapter A, or

(ii) subpart B (other than section 27) of such part IV, exceeds

(B) the regular tax liability of the taxpayer for the taxable year allocable to all passive activities.

[Sec. 469(e)]

(e) SPECIAL RULES FOR DETERMINING INCOME OR LOSS FROM A PASSIVE ACTIVITY.—For purposes of this section—

(1) CERTAIN INCOME NOT TREATED AS INCOME FROM PASSIVE ACTIVITY.—In determining the income or loss from any activity—

(A) IN GENERAL.—There shall not be taken into account—

(i) any—

(I) gross income from interest, dividends, annuities, or royalties not derived in the ordinary course of a trade or business,

(II) expenses (other than interest) which are clearly and directly allocable to such gross income, and

(III) interest expense properly allocable to such gross income, and

(ii) gain or loss not derived in the ordinary course of a trade or business which is attributable to the disposition of property—

(I) producing income of a type described in clause (i), or

(II) held for investment.

For purposes of clause (ii), any interest in a passive activity shall not be treated as property held for investment.

(B) RETURN ON WORKING CAPITAL.—For purposes of subparagraph (A), any income, gain, or loss which is attributable to an investment of working capital shall be treated as not derived in the ordinary course of a trade or business.

(2) PASSIVE LOSSES OF CERTAIN CLOSELY HELD CORPORATIONS MAY OFFSET ACTIVE INCOME.—

(A) IN GENERAL.—If a closely held C corporation (other than a personal service corporation) has net active income for any taxable year, the passive activity loss of such taxpayer for such taxable year (determined without regard to this paragraph)—

(i) shall be allowable as a deduction against net active income, and

(ii) shall not be taken into account under subsection (a) to the extent so allowable as a deduction.

A similar rule shall apply in the case of any passive activity credit of the taxpayer.

(B) NET ACTIVE INCOME.—For purposes of this paragraph, the term "net active income" means the taxable income of the taxpayer for the taxable year determined without regard to—

(i) any income or loss from a passive activity, and

(ii) any item of gross income, expense, gain, or loss described in paragraph (1)(A).

(3) COMPENSATION FOR PERSONAL SERVICES.—Earned income (within the meaning of section 911(d)(2)(A)) shall not be taken into account in computing the income or loss from a passive activity for any taxable year.

(4) Dividends reduced by dividends received deduction.—For purposes of paragraphs (1) and (2), income from dividends shall be reduced by the amount of any dividends received deduction under section 243 or 245.

[Sec. 469(f)]

(f) Treatment of Former Passive Activities.—For purposes of this section—

(1) In general.—If an activity is a former passive activity for any taxable year—

(A) any unused deduction allocable to such activity under subsection (b) shall be offset against the income from such activity for the taxable year,

(B) any unused credit allocable to such activity under subsection (b) shall be offset against the regular tax liability (computed after the application of paragraph (1)) allocable to such activity for the taxable year, and

(C) any such deduction or credit remaining after the application of subparagraphs (A) and (B) shall continue to be treated as arising from a passive activity.

(2) Change in status of closely held C corporation or personal corporation.—If a taxpayer ceases for any taxable year to be a closely held C corporation or personal service corporation, this section shall continue to apply to losses and credits to which this section applied for any preceding taxable year in the same manner as if such taxpayer continued to be a closely held C corporation or personal service corporation, whichever is applicable.

(3) Former passive activity.—The term "former passive activity" means any activity which, with respect to the taxpayer—

(A) is not a passive activity for the taxable year, but

(B) was a passive activity for any prior taxable year.

[Sec. 469(g)]

(g) Dispositions of Entire Interest in Passive Activity.—If during the taxable year a taxpayer disposes of his entire interest in any passive activity (or former passive activity), the following rules shall apply:

(1) Fully taxable transaction.—

(A) In general.—If all gain or loss realized on such disposition is recognized, the excess of—

(i) any loss from such activity for such taxable year (determined after the application of subsection (b)), over

(ii) any net income or gain for such taxable year from all other passive activities (determined after the application of subsection (b)),

shall be treated as a loss which is not from a passive activity.

(B) Subparagraph (A) not to apply to disposition involving related party.—If the taxpayer and the person acquiring the interest bear a relationship to each other described in section 267(b) or section 707(b)(1), then subparagraph (A) shall not apply to any loss of the taxpayer until the taxable year in which such interest is acquired (in a transaction described in subparagraph (A)) by another person who does not bear such a relationship to the taxpayer.

(C) Income from prior years.—To the extent provided in regulations, income or gain from the activity for preceding taxable years shall be taken into account under subparagraph (A)(ii) for the taxable year to the extent necessary to prevent the avoidance of this section.

(2) Disposition by death.—If an interest in the activity is transferred by reason of the death of the taxpayer—

(A) paragraph (1)(A) shall apply to losses described in paragraph (1)(A) to the extent such losses are greater than the excess (if any) of—

(i) the basis of such property in the hands of the transferee, over

(ii) the adjusted basis of such property immediately before the death of the taxpayer, and

(B) any losses to the extent of the excess described in subparagraph (A) shall not be allowed as a deduction for any taxable year.

(3) INSTALLMENT SALE OF ENTIRE INTEREST.—In the case of an installment sale of an entire interest in an activity to which section 453 applies, paragraph (1) shall apply to the portion of such losses for each taxable year which bears the same ratio to all such losses as the gain recognized on such sale during such taxable year bears to the gross profit from such sale (realized or to be realized when payment is completed).

[Sec. 469(h)]

(h) MATERIAL PARTICIPATION DEFINED.—For purposes of this section—

(1) IN GENERAL.—A taxpayer shall be treated as materially participating in an activity only if the taxpayer is involved in the operations of the activity on a basis which is—

(A) regular,

(B) continuous, and

(C) substantial.

(2) INTERESTS IN LIMITED PARTNERSHIPS.—Except as provided in regulations, no interest in a limited partnership as a limited partner shall be treated as an interest with respect to which a taxpayer materially participates.

(3) TREATMENT OF CERTAIN RETIRED INDIVIDUALS AND SURVIVING SPOUSES.—A taxpayer shall be treated as materially participating in any farming activity for a taxable year if paragraph (4) or (5) of section 2032A(b) would cause the requirements of section 2032A(b)(1)(C)(ii) to be met with respect to real property used in such activity if such taxpayer had died during the taxable year.

(4) CERTAIN CLOSELY HELD C CORPORATIONS AND PERSONAL SERVICE CORPORATIONS.—A closely held C corporation or personal service corporation shall be treated as materially participating in an activity only if—

(A) 1 or more shareholders holding stock representing more than 50 percent (by value) of the outstanding stock of such corporation materially participate in such activity, or

(B) in the case of a closely held C corporation (other than a personal service corporation), the requirements of section 465(c)(7)(C) (without regard to clause (iv)) are met with respect to such activity.

(5) PARTICIPATION BY SPOUSE.—In determining whether a taxpayer materially participates, the participation of the spouse of the taxpayer shall be taken into account.

[Sec. 469(i)]

(i) $25,000 OFFSET FOR RENTAL REAL ESTATE ACTIVITIES.—

(1) IN GENERAL.—In the case of any natural person, subsection (a) shall not apply to that portion of the passive activity loss or the deduction equivalent (within the meaning of subsection (j)(5)) of the passive activity credit for any taxable year which is attributable to all rental real estate activities with respect to which such individual actively participated in such taxable year (and if any portion of such loss or credit arose in another taxable year, in such other taxable year).

(2) DOLLAR LIMITATION.—The aggregate amount to which paragraph (1) applies for any taxable year shall not exceed $25,000.

(3) PHASE-OUT OF EXEMPTION.—

(A) IN GENERAL.—In the case of any taxpayer, the $25,000 amount under paragraph (2) shall be reduced (but not below zero) by 50 percent of the amount by which the adjusted gross income of the taxpayer for the taxable year exceeds $100,000.

(B) SPECIAL PHASE-OUT OF REHABILITATION CREDIT.—In the case of any portion of the passive activity credit for any taxable year which is attributable to the rehabilitation credit determined under section 47, subparagraph (A) shall be applied by substituting "$200,000" for "$100,000".

(C) EXCEPTION FOR LOW-INCOME HOUSING CREDIT.—Subparagraph (A) shall not apply to any portion of the passive activity credit for any taxable year which is attributable to any credit determined under section 42.

(D) ORDERING RULE.—Paragraph (1) shall be applied for any taxable year—

(i) first, to the passive activity loss,

(ii) second, to the portion of the passive activity credit to which subparagraph (B) and (C) does not apply,

(iii) third, to the portion of such credit to which subparagraph (B) applies, and

(iv) then, to the portion of such credit to which subparagraph (C) applies.

(E) ADJUSTED GROSS INCOME.—For purposes of this paragraph, adjusted gross income shall be determined without regard to—

(i) any amount includible in gross income under section 86,

(ii) the amounts excludable from gross income under sections 135 and 137,

(iii) the amounts allowable as a deduction under sections 219, 221, 222, and 250 and

(iv) any passive activity loss or any loss allowable by reason of subsection (c)(7).

(4) SPECIAL RULE FOR ESTATES.—

(A) IN GENERAL.—In the case of taxable years of an estate ending less than 2 years after the date of the death of the decedent, this subsection shall apply to all rental real estate activities with respect to which such decedent actively participated before his death.

(B) REDUCTION FOR SURVIVING SPOUSE'S EXEMPTION.—For purposes of subparagraph (A), the $25,000 amount under paragraph (2) shall be reduced by the amount of the exemption under paragraph (1) (without regard to paragraph (3)) allowable to the surviving spouse of the decedent for the taxable year ending with or within the taxable year of the estate.

(5) MARRIED INDIVIDUALS FILING SEPARATELY.—

(A) IN GENERAL.—Except as provided in subparagraph (B), in the case of any married individual filing a separate return, this subsection shall be applied by substituting—

(i) "$12,500" for "$25,000" each place it appears,

(ii) "$50,000" for "$100,000" in paragraph (3)(A), and

(iii) "$100,000" for "$200,000" in paragraph (3)(B).

(B) TAXPAYERS NOT LIVING APART.—This subsection shall not apply to a taxpayer who—

(i) is a married individual filing a separate return for any taxpayer year, and

(ii) does not live apart from his spouse at all times during such taxable year.

(6) ACTIVE PARTICIPATION.—

(A) IN GENERAL.—An individual shall not be treated as actively participating with respect to any interest in any rental real estate activity for any period if, at any time during such period, such interest (including any interest of the spouse of the individual) is less than 10 percent (by value) of all interests in such activity.

(B) NO PARTICIPATION REQUIREMENT FOR LOW-INCOME HOUSING OR REHABILITATION CREDIT.—Paragraphs (1) and (4)(A) shall be applied without regard to the active participation requirement in the case of—

(i) any credit determined under section 42 for any taxable year, or

(ii) any rehabilitation credit determined under section 47, [sic]

(C) INTEREST AS A LIMITED PARTNER.—Except as provided in regulations, no interest as a limited partner in a limited partnership shall be treated as an interest with respect to which the taxpayer actively participates.

(D) PARTICIPATION BY SPOUSE.—In determining whether a taxpayer actively participates, the participation of the spouse of the taxpayer shall be taken into account.

[Sec. 469(j)]

(j) OTHER DEFINITIONS AND SPECIAL RULES.—For purposes of this section—

(1) CLOSELY HELD C CORPORATION.—The term "closely held C corporation" means any C corporation described in section 465(a)(1)(B).

(2) PERSONAL SERVICE CORPORATION.—The term "personal service corporation" has the meaning given such term by section 269A(b)(1), except that section 269A(b)(2) shall be applied—

(A) by substituting "any" for "more than 10 percent", and

(B) by substituting "any" for "50 percent or more in value" in section 318(a)(2)(C).

A corporation shall not be treated as a personal service corporation unless more than 10 percent of the stock (by value) in such corporation is held by employee-owners (within the meaning of section 269A(b)(2), as modified by the preceding sentence).

(3) REGULAR TAX LIABILITY.—The term "regular tax liability" has the meaning given such term by section 26(b).

(4) ALLOCATION OF PASSIVE ACTIVITY LOSS AND CREDIT.—The passive activity loss and the passive activity credit (and the $25,000 amount under subsection (i)) shall be allocated to activities, and within activities, on a pro rata basis in such manner as the Secretary may prescribe.

(5) DEDUCTION EQUIVALENT.—The deduction equivalent of credits from a passive activity for any taxable year is the amount which (if allowed as a deduction) would reduce the regular tax liability for such taxable year by an amount equal to such credits.

(6) SPECIAL RULE FOR GIFTS.—In the case of a disposition of any interest in a passive activity by gift—

(A) the basis of such interest immediately before the transfer shall be increased by the amount of any passive activity losses allocable to such interest with respect to which a deduction has not been allowed by reason of subsection (a), and

(B) such losses shall not be allowable as a deduction for any taxable year.

(7) QUALIFIED RESIDENCE INTEREST.—The passive activity loss of a taxpayer shall be computed without regard to qualified residence interest (within the meaning of section 163(h)(3)).

(8) RENTAL ACTIVITY.—The term "rental activity" means any activity where payments are principally for the use of tangible property.

(9) ELECTION TO INCREASE BASIS OF PROPERTY BY AMOUNT OF DISALLOWED CREDIT.—For purposes of determining gain or loss from a disposition of any property to which subsection (g)(1) applies, the transferor may elect to increase the basis of such property immediately before the transfer by an amount equal to the portion of any unused credit allowable under this chapter which reduced the basis of such property for the taxable year in which such credit arose. If the taxpayer elects the application of this paragraph, such portion of the passive activity credit of such taxpayer shall not be allowed for any taxable year.

(10) COORDINATION WITH SECTION 280A.—If a passive activity involves the use of a dwelling unit to which section 280A(c)(5) applies for any taxable year, any income, deduction, gain, or loss allocable to such use shall not be taken into account for purposes of this section for such taxable year.

(11) AGGREGATION OF MEMBERS OF AFFILIATED GROUPS.—Except as provided in regulations, all members of an affiliated group which files a consolidated return shall be treated as 1 corporation.

(12) SPECIAL RULE FOR DISTRIBUTIONS BY ESTATES OR TRUSTS.—If any interest in a passive activity is distributed by an estate or trust—

(A) the basis of such interest immediately before such distribution shall be increased by the amount of any passive activity losses allocable to such interest, and

(B) such losses shall not be allowable as a deduction for any taxable year.

[Sec. 469(k)]

(k) SEPARATE APPLICATION OF SECTION IN CASE OF PUBLICLY TRADED PARTNERSHIPS.—

(1) IN GENERAL.—This section shall be applied separately with respect to items attributable to each publicly traded partnership (and subsection (i) shall not apply with respect to items attributable to any such partnership). The preceding sentence shall not apply to any credit determined under section 42, or any rehabilitation credit determined under section 47, attributable to a publicly traded partnership to the extent the amount of any such credits exceeds the regular tax liability attributable to income from such partnership.

(2) PUBLICLY TRADED PARTNERSHIP.—For purposes of this section, the term "publicly traded partnership" means any partnership if—

(A) interests in such partnership are traded on an established securities market, or

(B) interests in such partnership are readily tradable on a secondary market (or the substantial equivalent thereof).

(3) COORDINATION WITH SUBSECTION (g).—For purposes of subsection (g), a taxpayer shall not be treated as having disposed of his entire interest in an activity of a publicly traded partnership until he disposes of his entire interest in such partnership.

(4) APPLICATION TO REGULATED INVESTMENT COMPANIES.—For purposes of this section, a regulated investment company (as defined in section 851) holding an interest in a qualified publicly traded partnership (as defined in section 851(h)) shall be treated as a taxpayer described in subsection (a)(2) with respect to items attributable to such interest.

[Sec. 469(l)]

(l) REGULATIONS.—The Secretary shall prescribe such regulations as may be necessary or appropriate to carry out provisions of this section, including regulations—

(1) which specify what constitutes an activity, material participation, or active participation for purposes of this section,

(2) which provide that certain items of gross income will not be taken into account in determining income or loss from any activity (and the treatment of expenses allocable to such income),

(3) requiring net income or gain from a limited partnership or other passive activity to be treated as not from a passive activity,

(4) which provide for the determination of the allocation of interest expense for purposes of this section, and

(5) which deal with changes in marital status and changes between joint returns and separate returns.

* * *

Subpart D—Inventories

[Sec. 471]

SEC. 471. GENERAL RULE FOR INVENTORIES.

[Sec. 471(a)]

(a) GENERAL RULE.—Whenever in the opinion of the Secretary the use of inventories is necessary in order clearly to determine the income of any taxpayer, inventories shall be taken by such taxpayer on such basis as the Secretary may prescribe as conforming as nearly as may be to the best accounting practice in the trade or business and as most clearly reflecting the income.

[Sec. 471(b)]

(b) ESTIMATES OF INVENTORY SHRINKAGE PERMITTED.—A method of determining inventories shall not be treated as failing to clearly reflect income solely because it utilizes estimates of inventory shrinkage that are confirmed by a physical count only after the last day of the taxable year if—

(1) the taxpayer normally does a physical count of inventories at each location on a regular and consistent basis, and

(2) the taxpayer makes proper adjustments to such inventories and to its estimating methods to the extent such estimates are greater than or less than the actual shrinkage.

[Sec. 471(c)]

(c) EXEMPTION FOR CERTAIN SMALL BUSINESSES.—

(1) IN GENERAL.—In the case of any taxpayer (other than a tax shelter prohibited from using the cash receipts and disbursements method of accounting under section 448(a)(3)) which meets the gross receipts test of section 448(c) for any taxable year—

(A) subsection (a) shall not apply with respect to such taxpayer for such taxable year, and

(B) the taxpayer's method of accounting for inventory for such taxable year shall not be treated as failing to clearly reflect income if such method either—

(i) treats inventory as non-incidental materials and supplies, or

(ii) conforms to such taxpayer's method of accounting reflected in an applicable financial statement of the taxpayer with respect to such taxable year or, if the taxpayer does not have any applicable financial statement with respect to such taxable year, the books and records of the taxpayer prepared in accordance with the taxpayer's accounting procedures.

(2) APPLICABLE FINANCIAL STATEMENT.—For purposes of this subsection, the term "applicable financial statement" has the meaning given the term in section 451(b)(3).

(3) APPLICATION OF GROSS RECEIPTS TEST TO INDIVIDUALS, ETC.—In the case of any taxpayer which is not a corporation or a partnership, the gross receipts test of section 448(c) shall be applied in the same manner as if each trade or business of such taxpayer were a corporation or partnership.

(4) COORDINATION WITH SECTION 481.—Any change in method of accounting made pursuant to this subsection shall be treated for purposes of section 481 as initiated by the taxpayer and made with the consent of the Secretary.

[Sec. 471(d)]

(d) CROSS REFERENCE.—

For rules relating to capitalization of direct and indirect costs of property, see section 263A.

[Sec. 472]

SEC. 472. LAST-IN, FIRST-OUT INVENTORIES.

[Sec. 472(a)]

(a) AUTHORIZATION.—A taxpayer may use the method provided in subsection (b) (whether or not such method has been prescribed under section 471) in inventorying goods specified in an application to use such method filed at such time and in such manner as the Secretary may prescribe. The change to, and the use of, such method shall be in accordance with such regulations as the Secretary may prescribe as necessary in order that the use of such method may clearly reflect income.

[Sec. 472(b)]

(b) METHOD APPLICABLE.—In inventorying goods specified in the application described in subsection (a), the taxpayer shall:

(1) Treat those remaining on hand at the close of the taxable year as being: First, those included in the opening inventory of the taxable year (in the order of acquisition) to the extent thereof; and second, those acquired in the taxable year;

(2) Inventory them at cost; and

(3) Treat those included in the opening inventory of the taxable year in which such method is first used as having been acquired at the same time and determine their cost by the average cost method.

[Sec. 472(c)]

(c) CONDITION.—Subsection (a) shall apply only if the taxpayer establishes to the satisfaction of the Secretary that the taxpayer has used no procedure other than that specified in paragraphs (1) and (3) of subsection (b) in inventorying such goods to ascertain the income, profit, or loss of the first taxable year for which the method described in subsection (b) is to be used, for the purpose of a report or statement covering such taxable year—

(1) to shareholders, partners, or other proprietors, or to beneficiaries, or

(2) for credit purposes.

[Sec. 472(d)]

(d) 3-YEAR AVERAGING FOR INCREASES IN INVENTORY VALUE.—The beginning inventory for the first taxable year for which the method described in subsection (b) is used shall be valued at cost. Any change in the inventory amount resulting from the application of the preceding sentence shall be taken into account ratably in each of the 3 taxable years beginning with the first taxable year for which the method described in subsection (b) is first used.

[Sec. 472(e)]

(e) SUBSEQUENT INVENTORIES.—If a taxpayer, having complied with subsection (a), uses the method described in subsection (b) for any taxable year, then such method shall be used in all subsequent taxable years unless—

(1) with the approval of the Secretary a change to a different method is authorized; or,

(2) the Secretary determines that the taxpayer has used for any such subsequent taxable year some procedure other than that specified in paragraph (1) of subsection (b) in inventorying the goods specified in the application to ascertain the income, profit, or loss of such subsequent taxable year for the purpose of a report or statement covering such taxable year (A) to shareholders, partners, or other proprietors, or beneficiaries, or (B) for credit purposes; and requires a change to a method different from that prescribed in subsection (b) beginning with such subsequent taxable year or any taxable year thereafter.

If paragraph (1) or (2) of this subsection applies, the change to, and the use of, the different method shall be in accordance with such regulations as the Secretary may prescribe as necessary in order that the use of such method may clearly reflect income.

[Sec. 472(f)]

(f) USE OF GOVERNMENT PRICE INDEXES IN PRICING INVENTORY.—The Secretary shall prescribe regulations permitting the use of suitable published governmental indexes in such manner and circumstances as determined by the Secretary for purposes of the method described in subsection (b).

[Sec. 472(g)]

(g) CONFORMITY RULES APPLIED ON CONTROLLED GROUP BASIS.—

(1) IN GENERAL.—Except as otherwise provided in regulations, all members of the same group of financially related corporations shall be treated as 1 taxpayer for purposes of subsections (c) and (e)(2).

(2) GROUP OF FINANCIALLY RELATED CORPORATIONS.—For purposes of paragraph (1), the term "group of financially related corporations" means—

(A) any affiliated group as defined in section 1504 determined by substituting "50 percent" for "80 percent" each place it appears in section 1504(a) and without regard to section 1504(b), and

(B) any other group of corporations which consolidate or combine for purposes of financial statements.

[Sec. 474]

SEC. 474. SIMPLIFIED DOLLAR-VALUE LIFO METHOD FOR CERTAIN SMALL BUSINESSES.

[Sec. 474(a)]

(a) GENERAL RULE.—An eligible small business may elect to use the simplified dollar-value method of pricing inventories for purposes of the LIFO method.

[Sec. 474(b)]

(b) SIMPLIFIED DOLLAR-VALUE METHOD OF PRICING INVENTORIES.—For purposes of this section—

(1) IN GENERAL.—The simplified dollar-value method of pricing inventories is a dollar-value method of pricing inventories under which—

(A) the taxpayer maintains a separate inventory pool for items in each major category in the applicable Government price index, and

(B) the adjustment for each such separate pool is based on the change from the preceding taxable year in the component of such index for the major category.

(2) APPLICABLE GOVERNMENT PRICE INDEX.—The term "applicable Government price index" means—

(A) except as provided in subparagraph (B), the Producer Price Index published by the Bureau of Labor Statistics, or

(B) in the case of a retailer using the retail method, the Consumer Price Index published by the Bureau of Labor Statistics.

(3) MAJOR CATEGORY.—The term "major category" means—

(A) in the case of the Producer Price Index, any of the 2-digit standard industrial classifications in the Producer Prices Data Report, or

(B) in the case of the Consumer Price Index, any of the general expenditure categories in the Consumer Price Index Detailed Report.

[Sec. 474(c)]

(c) ELIGIBLE SMALL BUSINESS.—For purposes of this section, a taxpayer is an eligible small business for any taxable year if the average annual gross receipts of the taxpayer for the 3 preceding taxable years do not exceed $5,000,000. For purposes of the preceding sentence, rules similar to the rules of section 448(c)(3) shall apply.

[Sec. 474(d)]

(d) SPECIAL RULES.—For purposes of this section—

(1) CONTROLLED GROUPS.—

(A) IN GENERAL.—In the case of a taxpayer which is a member of a controlled group, all persons which are component members of such group shall be treated as 1 taxpayer for purposes of determining the gross receipts of the taxpayer.

(B) CONTROLLED GROUP DEFINED.—For purposes of subparagraph (A), persons shall be treated as being component members of a controlled group if such persons would be treated as a single employer under section 52.

(2) ELECTION.—

(A) IN GENERAL.—The election under this section may be made without the consent of the Secretary.

(B) PERIOD TO WHICH ELECTION APPLIES.—The election under this section shall apply—

(i) to the taxable year for which it is made, and

(ii) to all subsequent taxable years for which the taxpayer is an eligible small business, unless the taxpayer secures the consent of the Secretary to the revocation of such election.

(3) LIFO METHOD.—The term "LIFO method" means the method provided by section 472(b).

(4) TRANSITIONAL RULES.—

(A) IN GENERAL.—In the case of a year of change under this section—

(i) the inventory pools shall—

(I) in the case of the 1st taxable year to which such an election applies, be established in accordance with the major categories in the applicable Government price index, or

(II) in the case of the 1st taxable year after such election ceases to apply, be established in the manner provided by regulations under section 472;

(ii) the aggregate dollar amount of the taxpayer's inventory as of the beginning of the year of change shall be the same as the aggregate dollar value as of the close of the taxable year preceding the year of change, and

(iii) the year of change shall be treated as a new base year in accordance with procedures provided by regulations under section 472.

(B) YEAR OF CHANGE.—For purposes of this paragraph, the year of change under this section is—

(i) the 1st taxable year to which an election under this section applies, or

(ii) in the case of a cessation of such an election, the 1st taxable year after such election ceases to apply.

[Sec. 475]

SEC. 475. MARK TO MARKET ACCOUNTING METHOD FOR DEALERS IN SECURITIES.

[Sec. 475(a)]

(a) GENERAL RULE.—Notwithstanding any other provision of this subpart, the following rules shall apply to securities held by a dealer in securities:

(1) Any security which is inventory in the hands of the dealer shall be included in inventory at its fair market value.

(2) In the case of any security which is not inventory in the hands of the dealer and which is held at the close of any taxable year—

(A) the dealer shall recognize gain or loss as if such security were sold for its fair market value on the last business day of such taxable year, and

(B) any gain or loss shall be taken into account for such taxable year.

Proper adjustment shall be made in the amount of any gain or loss subsequently realized for gain or loss taken into account under the preceding sentence. The Secretary may provide by regulations for the application of this paragraph at times other than the times provided in this paragraph.

[Sec. 475(b)]

(b) EXCEPTIONS.—

(1) IN GENERAL.—Subsection (a) shall not apply to—

(A) any security held for investment,

(B) (i) any security described in subsection (c)(2)(C) which is acquired (including originated) by the taxpayer in the ordinary course of a trade or business of the taxpayer and which is not held for sale, and (ii) any obligation to acquire a security described in clause (i) if such obligation is entered into in the ordinary course of such trade or business and is not held for sale, and

(C) any security which is a hedge with respect to—

(i) a security to which subsection (a) does not apply, or

(ii) a position, right to income, or a liability which is not a security in the hands of the taxpayer.

To the extent provided in regulations, subparagraph (C) shall not apply to any security held by a person in its capacity as a dealer in securities.

(2) IDENTIFICATION REQUIRED.—A security shall not be treated as described in subparagraph (A), (B), or (C) of paragraph (1), as the case may be, unless such security is clearly identified in the dealer's records as being described in such subparagraph before the close of the day on which it was acquired, originated, or entered into (or such other time as the Secretary may by regulations prescribe).

(3) SECURITIES SUBSEQUENTLY NOT EXEMPT.—If a security ceases to be described in paragraph (1) at any time after it was identified as such under paragraph (2), subsection (a) shall apply to any changes in value of the security occurring after the cessation.

(4) SPECIAL RULE FOR PROPERTY HELD FOR INVESTMENT.—To the extent provided in regulations, subparagraph (A) of paragraph (1) shall not apply to any security described in subparagraph (D) or (E) of subsection (c)(2) which is held by a dealer in such securities.

[Sec. 475(c)]

(c) DEFINITIONS.—For purposes of this section—

(1) DEALER IN SECURITIES DEFINED.—The term "dealer in securities" means a taxpayer who—

(A) regularly purchases securities from or sells securities to customers in the ordinary course of a trade or business; or

(B) regularly offers to enter into, assume, offset, assign or otherwise terminate positions in securities with customers in the ordinary course of a trade or business.

(2) SECURITY DEFINED.—The term "security" means any—

(A) share of stock in a corporation;

(B) partnership or beneficial ownership interest in a widely held or publicly traded partnership or trust;

(C) note, bond, debenture, or other evidence of indebtedness;

(D) interest rate, currency, or equity notional principal contract;

(E) evidence of an interest in, or a derivative financial instrument in, any security described in subparagraph (A), (B), (C), or (D), or any currency, including any option, forward contract, short position, and any similar financial instrument in such a security or currency; and

(F) position which—

(i) is not a security described in subparagraph (A), (B), (C), (D), or (E),

(ii) is a hedge with respect to such a security, and

(iii) is clearly identified in the dealer's records as being described in this subparagraph before the close of the day on which it was acquired or entered into (or such other time as the Secretary may by regulations prescribe).

Subparagraph (E) shall not include any contract to which section 1256(a) applies.

(3) HEDGE.—The term "hedge" means any position which manages the dealer's risk of interest rate or price changes or currency fluctuations, including any position which is reasonably expected to become a hedge within 60 days after the acquisition of the position.

(4) SPECIAL RULES FOR CERTAIN RECEIVABLES.—

(A) IN GENERAL.—Paragraph (2)(C) shall not include any nonfinancial customer paper.

(B) NONFINANCIAL CUSTOMER PAPER.—For purposes of subparagraph (A), the term "nonfinancial customer paper" means any receivable which—

(i) is a note, bond, debenture, or other evidence of indebtedness;

(ii) arises out of the sale of nonfinancial goods or services by a person the principal activity of which is the selling or providing of nonfinancial goods or services; and

(iii) is held by such person (or a person who bears a relationship to such person described in section 267(b) or 707(b)) at all times since issue.

[Sec. 475(d)]

(d) SPECIAL RULES.—For purposes of this section—

(1) COORDINATION WITH CERTAIN RULES.—The rules of sections 263(g), 263A, and 1256(a) shall not apply to securities to which subsection (a) applies, and section 1091 shall not apply (and section 1092 shall apply) to any loss recognized under subsection (a).

(2) IMPROPER IDENTIFICATION.—If a taxpayer—

(A) identifies any security under subsection (b)(2) as being described in subsection (b)(1) and such security is not so described, or

(B) fails under subsection (c)(2)(F)(iii) to identify any position which is described in subsection (c)(2)(F) (without regard to clause (iii) thereof) at the time such identification is required,

the provisions of subsection (a) shall apply to such security or position, except that any loss under this section prior to the disposition of the security or position shall be recognized only to the extent of gain previously recognized under this section (and not previously taken into account under this paragraph) with respect to such security or position.

(3) CHARACTER OF GAIN OR LOSS.—

(A) IN GENERAL.—Except as provided in subparagraph (B) or section 1236(b)—

(i) IN GENERAL.—Any gain or loss with respect to a security under subsection (a)(2) shall be treated as ordinary income or loss.

(ii) SPECIAL RULE FOR DISPOSITIONS.—If—

(I) gain or loss is recognized with respect to a security before the close of the taxable year, and

(II) subsection (a)(2) would have applied if the security were held as of the close of the taxable year, such gain or loss shall be treated as ordinary income or loss.

(B) EXCEPTION.—Subparagraph (A) shall not apply to any gain or loss which is allocable to a period during which—

(i) the security is described in subsection (b)(1)(C) (without regard to subsection (b)(2)),

(ii) the security is held by a person other than in connection with its activities as a dealer in securities, or

(iii) the security is improperly identified (within the meaning of subparagraph (A) or (B) of paragraph (2)).

[Sec. 475(e)]

(e) ELECTION OF MARK TO MARKET FOR DEALERS IN COMMODITIES.—

(1) IN GENERAL.—In the case of a dealer in commodities who elects the application of this subsection, this section shall apply to commodities held by such dealer in the same manner as this section applies to securities held by a dealer in securities.

(2) COMMODITY.—For purposes of this subsection and subsection (f), the term "commodity" means—

(A) any commodity which is actively traded (within the meaning of section 1092(d)(1));

(B) any notional principal contract with respect to any commodity described in subparagraph (A);

(C) any evidence of an interest in, or a derivative instrument in, any commodity described in subparagraph (A) or (B), including any option, forward contract, futures contract, short position, and any similar instrument in such a commodity; and

(D) any position which—

(i) is not a commodity described in subparagraph (A), (B), or (C),

(ii) is a hedge with respect to such a commodity, and

(iii) is clearly identified in the taxpayer's records as being described in this subparagraph before the close of the day on which it was acquired or entered into (or such other time as the Secretary may by regulations prescribe).

(3) ELECTION.—An election under this subsection may be made without the consent of the Secretary. Such an election, once made, shall apply to the taxable year for which made and all subsequent taxable years unless revoked with the consent of the Secretary.

[Sec. 475(f)]

(f) ELECTION OF MARK TO MARKET FOR TRADERS IN SECURITIES OR COMMODITIES.—

(1) TRADERS IN SECURITIES.—

(A) IN GENERAL.—In the case of a person who is engaged in a trade or business as a trader in securities and who elects to have this paragraph apply to such trade or business—

(i) such person shall recognize gain or loss on any security held in connection with such trade or business at the close of any taxable year as if such security were sold for its fair market value on the last business day of such taxable year, and

(ii) any gain or loss shall be taken into account for such taxable year.

Proper adjustment shall be made in the amount of any gain or loss subsequently realized for gain or loss taken into account under the preceding sentence. The Secretary may provide by regulations for the application of this subparagraph at times other than the times provided in this subparagraph.

(B) EXCEPTION.—Subparagraph (A) shall not apply to any security—

(i) which is established to the satisfaction of the Secretary as having no connection to the activities of such person as a trader, and

(ii) which is clearly identified in such person's records as being described in clause (i) before the close of the day on which it was acquired, originated, or entered into (or such other time as the Secretary may by regulations prescribe).

If a security ceases to be described in clause (i) at any time after it was identified as such under clause (ii), subparagraph (A) shall apply to any changes in value of the security occurring after the cessation.

(C) COORDINATION WITH SECTION 1259.—Any security to which subparagraph (A) applies and which was acquired in the normal course of the taxpayer's activities as a trader in securities shall not be taken into account in applying section 1259 to any position to which subparagraph (A) does not apply.

(D) OTHER RULES TO APPLY.—Rules similar to the rules of subsections (b)(4) and (d) shall apply to securities held by a person in any trade or business with respect to which an election under this paragraph is in effect. Subsection (d)(3) shall not apply under the preceding sentence for purposes of applying sections 1402 and 7704.

(2) TRADERS IN COMMODITIES.—In the case of a person who is engaged in a trade or business as a trader in commodities and who elects to have this paragraph apply to such trade or business, paragraph (1) shall apply to commodities held by such trader in connection with such trade or business in the same manner as paragraph (1) applies to securities held by a trader in securities.

(3) ELECTION.—The elections under paragraphs (1) and (2) may be made separately for each trade or business and without the consent of the Secretary. Such an election, once made, shall apply to the taxable year for which made and all subsequent taxable years unless revoked with the consent of the Secretary.

[Sec. 475(g)]

(g) REGULATORY AUTHORITY.—The Secretary shall prescribe such regulations as may be necessary or appropriate to carry out the purposes of this section, including rules—

(1) to prevent the use of year-end transfers, related parties, or other arrangements to avoid the provisions of this section,

(2) to provide for the application of this section to any security which is a hedge which cannot be identified with a specific security, position, right to income, or liability, and

(3) to prevent the use by taxpayers of subsection (c)(4) to avoid the application of this section to a receivable that is inventory in the hands of the taxpayer (or a person who bears a relationship to the taxpayer described in section 267(b) or 707(b)).

PART III—ADJUSTMENTS

[Sec. 481]

SEC. 481. ADJUSTMENTS REQUIRED BY CHANGES IN METHOD OF ACCOUNTING.

[Sec. 481(a)]

(a) GENERAL RULE.—In computing the taxpayer's taxable income for any taxable year (referred to in this section as the "year of the change")—

(1) if such computation is under a method of accounting different from the method under which the taxpayer's taxable income for the preceding taxable year was computed, then

(2) there shall be taken into account those adjustments which are determined to be necessary solely by reason of the change in order to prevent amounts from being duplicated or omitted, except there shall not be taken into account any adjustment in respect of any taxable year to which this section does not apply unless the adjustment is attributable to a change in the method of accounting initiated by the taxpayer.

[Sec. 481(b)]

(b) LIMITATION ON TAX WHERE ADJUSTMENTS ARE SUBSTANTIAL.—

(1) THREE YEAR ALLOCATION.—If—

(A) the method of accounting from which the change is made was used by the taxpayer in computing his taxable income for the 2 taxable years preceding the year of the change, and

(B) the increase in taxable income for the year of the change which results solely by reason of the adjustments required by subsection (a)(2) exceeds $3,000,

then the tax under this chapter attributable to such increase in taxable income shall not be greater than the aggregate increase in the taxes under this chapter (or under the corresponding provisions of prior revenue laws) which would result if one-third of such increase in taxable income were included in taxable income for the year of the change and one-third of such increase were included for each of the 2 preceding taxable years.

(2) ALLOCATION UNDER NEW METHOD OF ACCOUNTING.—If—

(A) the increase in taxable income for the year of the change which results solely by reason of the adjustments required by subsection (a)(2) exceeds $3,000, and

(B) the taxpayer establishes his taxable income (under the new method of accounting) for one or more taxable years consecutively preceding the taxable year of the change for which the taxpayer in computing taxable income used the method of accounting from which the change is made,

then the tax under this chapter attributable to such increase in taxable income shall not be greater than the net increase in the taxes under this chapter (or under the corresponding provisions of prior revenue laws) which would result if the adjustments required by subsection (a)(2) were allocated to the taxable year or years specified in subparagraph (B) to which they are properly allocable under the new method of accounting and the balance of the adjustments required by subsection (a)(2) was allocated to the taxable year of the change.

(3) SPECIAL RULES FOR COMPUTATIONS UNDER PARAGRAPHS (1) AND (2).—For purposes of this subsection—

(A) There shall be taken into account the increase or decrease in tax for any taxable year preceding the year of the change to which no adjustment is allocated under paragraph (1) or (2) but which is affected by a net operating loss (as defined in section 172) or by a capital loss carryback or carryover (as defined in section 1212), determined with reference to taxable years with respect to which adjustments under paragraph (1) or (2) are allocated.

(B) The increase or decrease in the tax for any taxable year for which an assessment of any deficiency, or a credit or refund of any overpayment, is prevented by any law or rule of law, shall be determined by reference to the tax previously determined (within the meaning of section 1314 (a)) for such year.

[Sec. 481(c)]

(c) ADJUSTMENTS UNDER REGULATIONS.—In the case of any change described in subsection (a), the taxpayer may, in such manner and subject to such conditions as the Secretary may by regulations prescribe, take the adjustments required by subsection (a) (2) into account in computing the tax imposed by this chapter for the taxable year or years permitted under such regulations.

[Sec. 481(d)]

(d) ADJUSTMENTS ATTRIBUTABLE TO CONVERSION FROM S CORPORATION TO C CORPORATION.—

(1) IN GENERAL.—In the case of an eligible terminated S corporation, any adjustment required by subsection (a) (2) which is attributable to such corporation's revocation described in paragraph (2) (A) (ii) shall be taken into account ratably during the 6-taxable year period beginning with the year of change.

(2) ELIGIBLE TERMINATED S CORPORATION.—For purposes of this subsection, the term "eligible terminated S corporation" means any C corporation—

(A) which—

(i) was an S corporation on the day before the date of the enactment of the Tax Cuts and Jobs Act, and

(ii) during the 2-year period beginning on the date of such enactment makes a revocation of its election under section 1362 (a), and

(B) the owners of the stock of which, determined on the date such revocation is made, are the same owners (and in identical proportions) as on the date of such enactment.

[Sec. 482]

SEC. 482. ALLOCATION OF INCOME AND DEDUCTIONS AMONG TAXPAYERS.

In any case of two or more organizations, trades, or businesses (whether or not incorporated, whether or not organized in the United States, and whether or not affiliated) owned or controlled directly or indirectly by the same interests, the Secretary may distribute, apportion, or allocate gross income, deductions, credits, or allowances between or among such organizations, trades, or businesses, if he determines that such distribution, apportionment, or allocation is necessary in order to prevent evasion of taxes or clearly to reflect the income of any of such organizations, trades, or businesses. In the case of any transfer (or license) of intangible property (within the meaning of section 367 (d) (4)), the income with respect to such transfer or license shall be commensurate with the income attributable to the intangible. For purposes of this section, the Secretary shall require the valuation of transfers of intangible property (including intangible property transferred with other property or services) on an aggregate basis or the valuation of such a transfer on the basis of the realistic alternatives to such a transfer, if the Secretary determines that such basis is the most reliable means of valuation of such transfers.

[Sec. 483]

SEC. 483. INTEREST ON CERTAIN DEFERRED PAYMENTS.

[Sec. 483(a)]

(a) AMOUNT CONSTITUTING INTEREST.—For purposes of this title, in the case of any payment—

(1) under any contract for the sale or exchange of any property, and

(2) to which this section applies,

there shall be treated as interest that portion of the total unstated interest under such contract which, as determined in a manner consistent with the method of computing interest under section 1272 (a), is properly allocable to such payment.

[Sec. 483(b)]

(b) TOTAL UNSTATED INTEREST.—For purposes of this section, the term "total unstated interest" means, with respect to a contract for the sale or exchange of property, an amount equal to the excess of—

(1) the sum of the payments to which this section applies which are due under the contract, over

(2) the sum of the present values of such payments and the present values of any interest payments due under the contract.

For purposes of the preceding sentence, the present value of a payment shall be determined under the rules of section 1274(b)(2) using a discount rate equal to the applicable Federal rate determined under section 1274(d).

[Sec. 483(c)]

(c) PAYMENTS TO WHICH SUBSECTION (a) APPLIES.—

(1) IN GENERAL.—Except as provided in subsection (d), this section shall apply to any payment on account of the sale or exchange of property which constitutes part or all of the sales price and which is due more than 6 months after the date of such sale or exchange under a contract—

(A) under which some or all of the payments are due more than 1 year after the date of such sale or exchange, and

(B) under which there is total unstated interest.

(2) TREATMENT OF OTHER DEBT INSTRUMENTS.—For purposes of this section, a debt instrument of the purchaser which is given in consideration for the sale or exchange of property shall not be treated as a payment, and any payment due under such debt instrument shall be treated as due under the contract for the sale or exchange.

(3) DEBT INSTRUMENT DEFINED.—For purposes of this subsection, the term "debt instrument" has the meaning given such term by section 1275(a)(1).

[Sec. 483(d)]

(d) EXCEPTIONS AND LIMITATIONS.—

(1) COORDINATION WITH ORIGINAL ISSUE DISCOUNT RULES.—This section shall not apply to any debt instrument for which an issue price is determined under section 1273(b) (other than paragraph (4) thereof) or section 1274.

(2) SALES PRICES OF $3,000 OR LESS.—This section shall not apply to any payment on account of the sale or exchange of property if it can be determined at the time of such sale or exchange that the sales price cannot exceed $3,000.

(3) CARRYING CHARGES.—In the case of the purchaser, the tax treatment of amounts paid on account of the sale or exchange of property shall be made without regard to this section if any such amounts are treated under section 163(b) as if they included interest.

(4) CERTAIN SALES OF PATENTS.—In the case of any transfer described in section 1235(a) (relating to sale or exchange of patents), this section shall not apply to any amount contingent on the productivity, use, or disposition of the property transferred.

[Sec. 483(e)]

(e) MAXIMUM RATE OF INTEREST ON CERTAIN TRANSFERS OF LAND BETWEEN RELATED PARTIES.—

(1) IN GENERAL.—In the case of any qualified sale, the discount rate used in determining the total unstated interest rate under subsection (b) shall not exceed 6 percent, compounded semiannually.

(2) QUALIFIED SALE.—For purposes of this subsection, the term "qualified sale" means any sale or exchange of land by an individual to a member of such individual's family (within the meaning of section 267(c)(4)).

(3) $500,000 LIMITATION.—Paragraph (1) shall not apply to any qualified sale between individuals made during any calendar year to the extent that the sales price for such sale

(when added to the aggregate sale price for prior qualified sales between such individuals during the calendar year) exceeds $500,000.

(4) NONRESIDENT ALIEN INDIVIDUALS.—Paragraph (1) shall not apply to any sale or exchange if any party to such sale or exchange is a nonresident alien individual.

[Sec. 483(f)]

(f) REGULATIONS.—The Secretary shall prescribe such regulations as may be necessary or appropriate to carry out the purposes of this section including regulations providing for the application of this section in the case of—

(1) any contract for the sale or exchange of property under which the liability for, or the amount or due date of, a payment cannot be determined at the time of the sale or exchange, or

(2) any change in the liability for, or the amount or due date of, any payment (including interest) under a contract for the sale or exchange of property.

[Sec. 483(g)]

(g) CROSS REFERENCES.—

(1) For treatment of assumptions, see section 1274(c)(4).

(2) For special rules for certain transactions where stated principal amount does not exceed $2,800,000, see section 1274A.

(3) For special rules in the case of the borrower under certain loans for personal use, see section 1275(b).

SUBCHAPTER F—EXEMPT ORGANIZATIONS

PART I—GENERAL RULE

[Sec. 501]

SEC. 501. EXEMPTION FROM TAX ON CORPORATIONS, CERTAIN TRUSTS, ETC.

[Sec. 501(a)]

(a) EXEMPTION FROM TAXATION.—An organization described in subsection (c) or (d) or section 401(a) shall be exempt from taxation under this subtitle unless such exemption is denied under section 502 or 503.

[Sec. 501(b)]

(b) TAX ON UNRELATED BUSINESS INCOME AND CERTAIN OTHER ACTIVITIES.—An organization exempt from taxation under subsection (a) shall be subject to tax to the extent provided in parts II, III, and VI of this subchapter, but (notwithstanding parts II, III and VI of this subchapter) shall be considered an organization exempt from income taxes for the purpose of any law which refers to organizations exempt from income taxes.

[Sec. 501(c)]

(c) LIST OF EXEMPT ORGANIZATIONS.—The following organizations are referred to in subsection (a):

(1) Any corporation organized under Act of Congress which is an instrumentality of the United States but only if such corporation—

(A) is exempt from Federal income taxes—

(i) under such Act as amended and supplemented before July 18, 1984, or

(ii) under this title without regard to any provision of law which is not contained in this title and which is not contained in a revenue Act, or

(B) is described in subsection (l).

(2) Corporations organized for the exclusive purpose of holding title to property, collecting income therefrom, and turning over the entire amount thereof, less expenses, to an organization which itself is exempt under this section. Rules similar to the rules of subparagraph (G) of paragraph (25) shall apply for purposes of this paragraph.

(3) Corporations, and any community chest, fund, or foundation, organized and operated exclusively for religious, charitable, scientific, testing for public safety, literary, or educational purposes, or to foster national or international amateur sports competition (but only if no part of its activities involve the provision of athletic facilities or equipment), or for the prevention of cruelty to children or animals, no part of the net earnings of which inures to the benefit of any private shareholder or individual, no substantial part of the activities of which is carrying on propaganda, or otherwise attempting, to influence legislation, (except as otherwise provided in subsection (h)), and which does not participate in, or intervene in (including the publishing or distributing of statements), any political campaign on behalf of (or in opposition to) any candidate for public office.

(4)(A) Civic leagues or organizations not organized for profit but operated exclusively for the promotion of social welfare, or local associations of employees, the membership of which is limited to the employees of a designated person or persons in a particular municipality, and the net earnings of which are devoted exclusively to charitable, educational, or recreational purposes.

(B) Subparagraph (A) shall not apply to an entity unless no part of the net earnings of such entity inures to the benefit of any private shareholder or individual.

(5) Labor, agricultural, or horticultural organizations.

(6) Business leagues, chambers of commerce, real-estate boards, boards of trade, or professional football leagues (whether or not administering a pension fund for football players), not organized for profit and no part of the net earnings of which inures to the benefit of any private shareholder or individual.

(7) Clubs organized for pleasure, recreation, and other nonprofitable purposes, substantially all of the activities of which are for such purposes and no part of the net earnings of which inures to the benefit of any private shareholder.

(8) Fraternal beneficiary societies, orders, or associations—

(A) operating under the lodge system or for the exclusive benefit of the members of a fraternity itself operating under the lodge system, and

(B) providing for the payment of life, sick, accident, or other benefits to the members of such society, order, or association or their dependents.

(9) Voluntary employees' beneficiary associations providing for the payment of life, sick, accident, or other benefits to the members of such association or their dependents or designated beneficiaries, if no part of the net earnings of such association inures (other than through such payments) to the benefit of any private shareholder or individual. For purposes of providing for the payment of sick and accident benefits to members of such an association and their dependents, the term "dependent" shall include any individual who is a child (as defined in section 152(f)(1)) of a member who as of the end of the calendar year has not attained age 27.

(10) Domestic fraternal societies, orders, or associations, operating under the lodge system—

(A) the net earnings of which are devoted exclusively to religious, charitable, scientific, literary, educational, and fraternal purposes, and

(B) which do not provide for the payment of life, sick, accident, or other benefits.

(11) Teachers' retirement fund associations of a purely local character, if—

(A) no part of their net earnings inures (other than through payment of retirement benefits) to the benefit of any private shareholder or individual, and

(B) the income consists solely of amounts received from public taxation, amounts received from assessments on the teaching salaries of members, and income in respect of investments.

* * *

(13) Cemetery companies owned and operated exclusively for the benefit of their members or which are not operated for profit; and any corporation chartered solely for the purpose of the disposal of bodies by burial or cremation which is not permitted by its charter to engage in any business not necessarily incident to that purpose, no part of the net earnings of which inures to the benefit of any private shareholder or individual.

(14)(A) Credit unions without capital stock organized and operated for mutual purposes and without profit.

* * *

(19) A post or organization of past or present members of the Armed Forces of the United States, or an auxiliary unit or society of, or a trust or foundation for, any such post or organization—

(A) organized in the United States or any of its possessions,

(B) at least 75 percent of the members of which are past or present members of the Armed Forces of the United States and substantially all of the other members of which are individuals who are cadets or are spouses, widows, widowers, ancestors, or lineal descendants of past or present members of the Armed Forces of the United States or of cadets, and

(C) no part of the net earnings of which inures to the benefit of any private shareholder or individual.

(20) [Stricken.]

* * *

[Sec. 501(d)]

(d) RELIGIOUS AND APOSTOLIC ORGANIZATIONS.—The following organizations are referred to in subsection (a): Religious or apostolic associations or corporations, if such associations or corporations have a common treasury or community treasury, even if such associations or corporations engage in business for the common benefit of the members, but only if the members thereof include (at the time of filing their returns) in their gross income their entire pro rata shares, whether distributed or not, of the taxable income of the association or corporation for such year. Any amount so included in the gross income of a member shall be treated as a dividend received.

* * *

[Sec. 501(g)]

(g) DEFINITION OF AGRICULTURAL.—For purposes of subsection (c)(5), the term "agricultural" includes the art or science of cultivating land, harvesting crops or aquatic resources, or raising livestock.

[Sec. 501(h)]

(h) EXPENDITURES BY PUBLIC CHARITIES TO INFLUENCE LEGISLATION.—

(1) GENERAL RULE.—In the case of an organization to which this subsection applies, exemption from taxation under subsection (a) shall be denied because a substantial part of the activities of such organization consists of carrying on propaganda, or otherwise attempting, to influence legislation, but only if such organization normally—

(A) makes lobbying expenditures in excess of the lobbying ceiling amount for such organization for each taxable year, or

(B) makes grass roots expenditures in excess of the grass roots ceiling amount for such organization for each taxable year.

(2) DEFINITIONS.—For purposes of this subsection—

(A) LOBBYING EXPENDITURES.—The term "lobbying expenditures" means expenditures for the purpose of influencing legislation (as defined in section 4911(d)).

(B) LOBBYING CEILING AMOUNT.—The lobbying ceiling amount for any organization for any taxable year is 150 percent of the lobbying nontaxable amount for such organization for such taxable year, determined under section 4911.

(C) GRASS ROOTS EXPENDITURES.—The term "grass roots expenditures" means expenditures for the purpose of influencing legislation (as defined in section 4911(d) without regard to paragraph (1)(B) thereof).

(D) GRASS ROOTS CEILING AMOUNT.—The grass roots ceiling amount for any organization for any taxable year is 150 percent of the grass roots nontaxable amount for such organization for such taxable year, determined under section 4911.

(3) ORGANIZATIONS TO WHICH THIS SUBSECTION APPLIES.—This subsection shall apply to any organization which has elected (in such manner and at such time as the Secretary may

prescribe) to have the provisions of this subsection apply to such organization and which, for the taxable year which includes the date the election is made, is described in subsection (c)(3) and—

(A) is described in paragraph (4), and

(B) is not a disqualified organization under paragraph (5).

(4) ORGANIZATIONS PERMITTED TO ELECT TO HAVE THIS SUBSECTION APPLY.—An organization is described in this paragraph if it is described in—

(A) section 170(b)(1)(A)(ii) (relating to educational institutions),

(B) section 170(b)(1)(A)(iii) (relating to hospitals and medical research organizations),

(C) section 170(b)(1)(A)(iv) (relating to organizations supporting government schools),

(D) section 170(b)(1)(A)(vi) (relating to organizations publicly supported by charitable contributions),

(E) section 170(b)(1)(A)(ix) (relating to agricultural research organizations),

(F) section 509(a)(2) (relating to organizations publicly supported by admissions, sales, etc.), or

(G) section 509(a)(3) (relating to organizations supporting certain types of public charities) except that for purposes of this subparagraph, section 509(a)(3) shall be applied without regard to the last sentence of section 509(a).

(5) DISQUALIFIED ORGANIZATIONS.—For purposes of paragraph (3) an organization is a disqualified organization if it is—

(A) described in section 170(b)(1)(A)(i) (relating to churches),

(B) an integrated auxiliary of a church or of a convention or association of churches, or

(C) a member of an affiliated group of organizations (within the meaning of section 4911(f)(2)) if one or more members of such group is described in subparagraph (A) or (B).

(6) YEARS FOR WHICH ELECTION IS EFFECTIVE.—An election by an organization under this subsection shall be effective for all taxable years of such organization which—

(A) end after the date the election is made, and

(B) begin before the date the election is revoked by such organization (under regulations prescribed by the Secretary).

(7) NO EFFECT ON CERTAIN ORGANIZATIONS.—With respect to any organization for a taxable year for which—

(A) such organization is a disqualified organization (within the meaning of paragraph (5)), or

(B) an election under this subsection is not in effect for such organization,

nothing in this subsection or in section 4911 shall be construed to affect the interpretation of the phrase, "no substantial part of the activities of which is carrying on propaganda, or otherwise attempting, to influence legislation," under subsection (c)(3).

(8) AFFILIATED ORGANIZATIONS.—

For rules regarding affiliated organizations, see section 4911(f).

[Sec. 501(i)]

(i) PROHIBITION OF DISCRIMINATION BY CERTAIN SOCIAL CLUBS.—Notwithstanding subsection (a), an organization which is described in subsection (c)(7) shall not be exempt from taxation under subsection (a) for any taxable year if, at any time during such taxable year, the charter, bylaws, or other governing instrument, of such organization or any written policy statement of such organization contains a provision which provides for discrimination against any person on the basis of race, color, or religion. The preceding sentence to the extent it relates to discrimination on the basis of religion shall not apply to—

(1) an auxiliary of a fraternal beneficiary society if such society—

(A) is described in subsection (c)(8) and exempt from tax under subsection (a), and

(B) limits its membership to the members of a particular religion, or

(2) a club which in good faith limits its membership to the members of a particular religion in order to further the teachings or principles of that religion, and not to exclude individuals of a particular race or color.

[Sec. 501(j)]

(j) SPECIAL RULES FOR CERTAIN AMATEUR SPORTS ORGANIZATIONS.—

(1) IN GENERAL.—In the case of a qualified amateur sports organization—

(A) the requirement of subsection (c)(3) that no part of its activites involve the provision of athletic facilities or equipment shall not apply, and

(B) such organization shall not fail to meet the requirements of subsection (c)(3) merely because its membership is local or regional in nature.

(2) QUALIFIED AMATEUR SPORTS ORGANIZATION DEFINED.—For purposes of this subsection, the term "qualified amateur sports organization" means any organization organized and operated exclusively to foster national or international amateur sports competition if such organization is also organized and operated primarily to conduct national or international competition in sports or to support and develop amateur athletes for national or international competition in sports.

[Sec. 501(k)]

(k) TREATMENT OF CERTAIN ORGANIZATIONS PROVIDING CHILD CARE.—For purposes of subsection (c)(3) of this section and sections 170(c)(2), 2055(a)(2), and 2522(a)(2), the term "educational purposes" includes the providing of care of children away from their homes if—

(1) substantially all of the care provided by the organization is for purposes of enabling individuals to be gainfully employed, and

(2) the services provided by the organization are available to the general public.

* * *

[Sec. 501(s)—Stricken]

PART II—PRIVATE FOUNDATIONS

[Sec. 508]

SEC. 508. SPECIAL RULES WITH RESPECT TO SECTION 501(c)(3) ORGANIZATIONS.

[Sec. 508(a)]

(a) NEW ORGANIZATIONS MUST NOTIFY SECRETARY THAT THEY ARE APPLYING FOR RECOGNITION OF SECTION 501(c)(3) STATUS.—Except as provided in subsection (c), an organization organized after October 9, 1969, shall not be treated as an organization described in section 501(c)(3)—

(1) unless it has given notice to the Secretary, in such manner as the Secretary may by regulations prescribe, that it is applying for recognition of such status, or

(2) for any period before the giving of such notice, if such notice is given after the time prescribed by the Secretary by regulations for giving notice under this subsection.

[Sec. 508(b)]

(b) PRESUMPTION THAT ORGANIZATIONS ARE PRIVATE FOUNDATIONS.—Except as provided in subsection (c), any organization (including an organization in existence on October 9, 1969) which is described in section 501(c)(3) and which does not notify the Secretary, at such time and in such manner as the Secretary may by regulations prescribe, that it is not a private foundation shall be presumed to be a private foundation.

[Sec. 508(c)]

(c) EXCEPTIONS.—

(1) MANDATORY EXCEPTIONS.—Subsections (a) and (b) shall not apply to—

(A) churches, their integrated auxiliaries, and conventions or associations of churches, or

(B) any organization which is not a private foundation (as defined in section 509(a)) and the gross receipts of which in each taxable year are normally not more than $5,000.

(2) EXCEPTIONS BY REGULATIONS.—The Secretary may by regulations exempt (to the extent and subject to such conditions as may be prescribed in such regulations) from the provisions of subsection (a) or (b) or both—

(A) educational organizations described in section 170(b)(1)(A)(ii), and

(B) any other class of organizations with respect to which the Secretary determines that full compliance with the provisions of subsections (a) and (b) is not necessary to the efficient administration of the provisions of this title relating to private foundations.

* * *

[Sec. 509]

SEC. 509. PRIVATE FOUNDATION DEFINED.

[Sec. 509(a)]

(a) GENERAL RULE.—For purposes of this title, the term "private foundation" means a domestic or foreign organization described in section 501(c)(3) other than—

(1) an organization described in section 170(b)(1)(A) (other than in clauses (vii) and (viii));

(2) an organization which—

(A) normally receives more than one-third of its support in each taxable year from any combination of—

(i) gifts, grants, contributions, or membership fees, and

(ii) gross receipts from admissions, sales of merchandise, performance of services, or furnishing of facilities, in an activity which is not an unrelated trade or business (within the meaning of section 513), not including such receipts from any person, or from any bureau or similar agency of a governmental unit (as described in section 170(c)(1)), in any taxable year to the extent such receipts exceed the greater of $5,000 or 1 percent of the organization's support in such taxable year,

from persons other than disqualified persons (as defined in section 4946) with respect to the organization, from governmental units described in section 170(c)(1), or from organizations described in section 170(b)(1)(A) (other than in clauses (vii) and (viii)), and

(B) normally receives not more than one-third of its support in each taxable year from the sum of—

(i) gross investment income (as defined in subsection (e)) and

(ii) the excess (if any) of the amount of the unrelated business taxable income (as defined in section 512) over the amount of the tax imposed by section 511;

(3) an organization which—

(A) is organized, and at all times thereafter is operated, exclusively for the benefit of, to perform the functions of, or to carry out the purposes of one or more specified organizations described in paragraph (1) or (2),

(B) is—

(i) operated, supervised, or controlled by one or more organizations described in paragraph (1) or (2),

(ii) supervised or controlled in connection with one or more such organizations, or

(iii) operated in connection with one or more such organizations, and

(C) is not controlled directly or indirectly by one or more disqualified persons (as defined in section 4946) other than foundation managers and other than one or more organizations described in paragraph (1) or (2); and

(4) an organization which is organized and operated exclusively for testing for public safety.

For purposes of paragraph (3), an organization described in paragraph (2) shall be deemed to include an organization described in section 501(c)(4), (5), or (6) which would be described in paragraph (2) if it were an organization described in section 501(c)(3).

* * *

[Sec. 509(d)]

(d) DEFINITION OF SUPPORT.—For purposes of this part and chapter 42, the term "support" includes (but is not limited to)—

(1) gifts, grants, contributions, or membership fees,

(2) gross receipts from admissions, sales of merchandise, performance of services, or furnishing of facilities in any activity which is not an unrelated trade or business (within the meaning of section 513),

(3) net income from unrelated business activities, whether or not such activities are carried on regularly as a trade or business,

(4) gross investment income (as defined in subsection (e)),

(5) tax revenues levied for the benefit of an organization and either paid to or expended on behalf of such organization, and

(6) the value of services or facilities (exclusive of services or facilities generally furnished to the public without charge) furnished by a governmental unit referred to in section 170(c)(1) to an organization without charge.

Such term does not include any gain from the sale or other disposition of property which would be considered as gain from the sale or exchange of a capital asset, or the value of exemption from any Federal, State, or local tax or any similar benefit.

[Sec. 509(e)]

(e) DEFINITION OF GROSS INVESTMENT INCOME.—For purposes of subsection (d), the term "gross investment income" means the gross amount of income from interest, dividends, payments with respect to securities loans (as defined in section 512(a)(5)), rents, and royalties, but not including any such income to the extent included in computing the tax imposed by section 511. Such term shall also include income from sources similar to those in the preceding sentence.

* * *

PART III—TAXATION OF BUSINESS INCOME OF CERTAIN EXEMPT ORGANIZATIONS

[Sec. 511]

SEC. 511. IMPOSITION OF TAX ON UNRELATED BUSINESS INCOME OF CHARITABLE, ETC., ORGANIZATIONS.

[Sec. 511(a)]

(a) CHARITABLE, ETC., ORGANIZATIONS TAXABLE AT CORPORATION RATES.—

(1) IMPOSITION OF TAX.—There is hereby imposed for each taxable year on the unrelated business taxable income (as defined in section 512) of every organization described in paragraph (2) a tax computed as provided in section 11. In making such computation for purposes of this section, the term "taxable income" as used in section 11 shall be read as "unrelated business taxable income".

(2) ORGANIZATIONS SUBJECT TO TAX.—

(A) ORGANIZATIONS DESCRIBED IN SECTIONS 401(a) AND 501(c).—The tax imposed by paragraph (1) shall apply in the case of any organization (other than a trust described in subsection (b) or an organization described in section 501(c)(1)) which is exempt, except as provided in this part or part II (relating to private foundations), from taxation under this subtitle by reason of section 501(a).

(B) STATE COLLEGES AND UNIVERSITIES.—The tax imposed by paragraph (1) shall apply in the case of any college or university which is an agency or instrumentality of any government or any political subdivision thereof, or which is owned or operated by a government or any political subdivision thereof, or by any agency or instrumentality of one or more governments or political subdivisions. Such tax shall also apply in the case of any corporation wholly owned by one or more such colleges or universities.

[Sec. 511(b)]

(b) TAX ON CHARITABLE, ETC., TRUSTS.—

(1) IMPOSITION OF TAX.—There is hereby imposed for each taxable year on the unrelated business taxable income of every trust described in paragraph (2) a tax computed as provided in section 1(e). In making such computation for purposes of this section, the term "taxable income" as used in section 1 shall be read as "unrelated business taxable income" as defined in section 512.

(2) CHARITABLE, ETC., TRUSTS SUBJECT TO TAX.—The tax imposed by paragraph (1) shall apply in the case of any trust which is exempt, except as provided in this part or part II (relating to private foundations), from taxation under this subtitle by reason of section 501(a) and which, if it were not for such exemption, would be subject to subchapter J (sec. 641 and following, relating to estates, trusts, beneficiaries, and decedents).

[Sec. 512]

SEC. 512. UNRELATED BUSINESS TAXABLE INCOME.

[Sec. 512(a)]

(a) DEFINITION.—For purposes of this title—

(1) GENERAL RULE.—Except as otherwise provided in this subsection, the term "unrelated business taxable income" means the gross income derived by any organization from any unrelated trade or business (as defined in section 513) regularly carried on by it, less the deductions allowed by this chapter which are directly connected with the carrying on of such trade or business, both computed with the modifications provided in subsection (b).

* * *

[Sec. 512(b)]

(b) MODIFICATIONS.—The modifications referred to in subsection (a) are the following:

(1) There shall be excluded all dividends, interest, payments with respect to securities loans (as defined in subsection (a)(5)), amounts received or accrued as consideration for entering into agreements to make loans, and annuities, and all deductions directly connected with such income.

(2) There shall be excluded all royalties (including overriding royalties) whether measured by production or by gross or taxable income from the property, and all deductions directly connected with such income.

(3) In the case of rents—

(A) Except as provided in subparagraph (B), there shall be excluded—

(i) all rents from real property (including property described in section 1245(a)(3)(C)), and

(ii) all rents from personal property (including for purposes of this paragraph as personal property any property described in section 1245(a)(3)(B)) leased with such real property, if the rents attributable to such personal property are an incidental amount of the total rents received or accrued under the lease, determined at the time the personal property is placed in service.

(B) Subparagraph (A) shall not apply—

(i) if more than 50 percent of the total rent received or accrued under the lease is attributable to personal property described in Subparagraph (A)(ii), or

(ii) if the determination of the amount of such rent depends in whole or in part on the income or profits derived by any person from the property leased (other than an amount based on a fixed percentage or percentages of receipts or sales).

(C) There shall be excluded all deductions directly connected with rents excluded under subparagraph (A).

(4) Notwithstanding paragraph (1), (2), (3), or (5), in the case of debt-financed property (as defined in section 514) there shall be included, as an item of gross income derived from

an unrelated trade or business, the amount ascertained under section 514(a)(1), and there shall be allowed, as a deduction, the amount ascertained under section 514(a)(2).

(5) There shall be excluded all gains or losses from the sale, exchange, or other disposition of property other than—

(A) stock in trade or other property of a kind which would properly be includible in inventory if on hand at the close of the taxable year, or

(B) property held primarily for sale to customers in the ordinary course of the trade or business.

There shall also be excluded all gains or losses recognized, in connection with the organization's investment activities, from the lapse or termination of options to buy or sell securities (as defined in section 1236(c)) or real property and all gains or losses from the forfeiture of good-faith deposits (that are consistent with established business practice) for the purchase, sale, or lease of real property in connection with the organization's investment activities.

(6) The net operating loss deduction provided in section 172 shall be allowed, except that—

(A) the net operating loss for any taxable year, the amount of the net operating loss carryback or carryover to any taxable year, and the net operating loss deduction for any taxable year shall be determined under section 172 without taking into account any amount of income or deduction which is excluded under this part in computing the unrelated business taxable income; and

(B) the terms "preceding taxable year" and "preceding taxable years" as used in section 172 shall not include any taxable year for which the organization was not subject to the provisions of this part.

(7) There shall be excluded all income derived from research for (A) the United States, or any of its agencies or instrumentalities, or (B) any State or political subdivision thereof; and there shall be excluded all deductions directly connected with such income.

(8) In the case of a college, university, or hospital, there shall be excluded all income derived from research performed for any person, and all deductions directly connected with such income.

(9) In the case of an organization operated primarily for purposes of carrying on fundamental research the results of which are freely available to the general public, there shall be excluded all income derived from research performed for any person, and all deductions directly connected with such income.

(10) In the case of any organization described in section 511 (a), the deduction allowed by section 170 (relating to charitable etc. contributions and gifts) shall be allowed (whether or not directly connected with the carrying on of the trade or business), but shall not exceed 10 percent of the unrelated business taxable income computed without the benefit of this paragraph.

(11) In the case of any trust described in section 511 (b), the deduction allowed by section 170 (relating to charitable etc. contributions and gifts) shall be allowed (whether or not directly connected with the carrying on of the trade or business), and for such purpose a distribution made by the trust to a beneficiary described in section 170 shall be considered as a gift or contribution. The deduction allowed by this paragraph shall be allowed with the limitations prescribed in section 170 (b) (1) (A) and (B) determined with reference to the unrelated business taxable income computed without the benefit of this paragraph (in lieu of with reference to adjusted gross income).

(12) Except for purposes of computing the net operating loss under section 172 and paragraph (6), there shall be allowed a specific deduction of $1,000. In the case of a diocese, province of a religious order, or a convention or association of churches, there shall also be allowed, with respect to each parish, individual church, district, or other local unit, a specific deduction equal to the lower of—

(A) $1,000, or

(B) the gross income derived from any unrelated trade or business regularly carried on by such local unit.

(13) SPECIAL RULES FOR CERTAIN AMOUNTS RECEIVED FROM CONTROLLED ENTITIES.—

(A) IN GENERAL.—If an organization (in this paragraph referred to as the "controlling organization") receives or accrues (directly or indirectly) a specified payment from another entity which it controls (in this paragraph referred to as the "controlled entity"), notwithstanding paragraphs (1), (2), and (3), the controlling organization shall include such payment as an item of gross income derived from an unrelated trade or business to the extent such payment reduces the net unrelated income of the controlled entity (or increases any net unrelated loss of the controlled entity). There shall be allowed all deductions of the controlling organization directly connected with amounts treated as derived from an unrelated trade or business under the preceding sentence.

(B) NET UNRELATED INCOME OR LOSS.—For purposes of this paragraph—

(i) NET UNRELATED INCOME.—The term "net unrelated income" means—

(I) in the case of a controlled entity which is not exempt from tax under section 501(a), the portion of such entity's taxable income which would be unrelated business taxable income if such entity were exempt from tax under section 501(a) and had the same exempt purposes as the controlling organization, or

(II) in the case of a controlled entity which is exempt from tax under section 501(a), the amount of the unrelated business taxable income of the controlled entity.

(ii) NET UNRELATED LOSS.—The term "net unrelated loss" means the net operating loss adjusted under rules similar to the rules of clause (i).

(C) SPECIFIED PAYMENT.—For purposes of this paragraph, the term "specified payment" means any interest, annuity, royalty, or rent.

(D) DEFINITION OF CONTROL.—For purposes of this paragraph—

(i) CONTROL.—The term "control" means—

(I) in the case of a corporation, ownership (by vote or value) of more than 50 percent of the stock in such corporation,

(II) in the case of a partnership, ownership of more than 50 percent of the profits interests or capital interests in such partnership, or

(III) in any other case, ownership of more than 50 percent of the beneficial interests in the entity.

(ii) CONSTRUCTIVE OWNERSHIP.— Section 318 (relating to constructive ownership of stock) shall apply for purposes of determining ownership of stock in a corporation. Similar principles shall apply for purposes of determining ownership of interests in any other entity.

(E) PARAGRAPH TO APPLY ONLY TO CERTAIN EXCESS PAYMENTS.—

(i) IN GENERAL.—Subparagraph (A) shall apply only to the portion of a qualifying specified payment received or accrued by the controlling organization that exceeds the amount which would have been paid or accrued if such payment met the requirements prescribed under section 482.

(ii) ADDITION TO TAX FOR VALUATION MISSTATEMENTS.—The tax imposed by this chapter on the controlling organization shall be increased by an amount equal to 20 percent of the larger of—

(I) such excess determined without regard to any amendment or supplement to a return of tax, or

(II) such excess determined with regard to all such amendments and supplements.

(iii) QUALIFYING SPECIFIED PAYMENT.—The term "qualifying specified payment" means a specified payment which is made pursuant to—

(I) a binding written contract in effect on the date of the enactment of this subparagraph, or

(II) a contract which is a renewal, under substantially similar terms, of a contract described in subclause (I).

(F) RELATED PERSONS.—The Secretary shall prescribe such rules as may be necessary or appropriate to prevent avoidance of the purposes of this paragraph through the use of related persons.

(14) [Repealed.]

(15) Except as provided in paragraph (4), in the case of a trade or business—

(A) which consists of providing services under license issued by a Federal regulatory agency,

(B) which is carried on by a religious order or by an educational organization described in section 170(b)(1)(A)(ii) maintained by such religious order, and which was so carried on before May 27, 1959, and

(C) less than 10 percent of the net income of which for each taxable year is used for activities which are not related to the purpose constituting the basis for the religious order's exemption,

there shall be excluded all gross income derived from such trade or business and all deductions directly connected with the carrying on of such trade or business, so long as it is established to the satisfaction of the Secretary that the rates or other charges for such services are competitive with rates or other charges charged for similar services by persons not exempt from taxation.

* * *

[Sec. 512(c)]

(c) SPECIAL RULES FOR PARTNERSHIPS.—

(1) IN GENERAL.—If a trade or business regularly carried on by a partnership of which an organization is a member is an unrelated trade or business with respect to such organization, such organization in computing its unrelated business taxable income shall, subject to the exceptions, additions, and limitations contained in subsection (b), include its share (whether or not distributed) of the gross income of the partnership from such unrelated trade or business and its share of the partnership deductions directly connected with such gross income.

(2) SPECIAL RULE WHERE PARTNERSHIP YEAR IS DIFFERENT FROM ORGANIZATION'S YEAR.—If the taxable year of the organization is different from that of the partnership, the amounts to be included or deducted in computing the unrelated business taxable income under paragraph (1) shall be based upon the income and deductions of the partnership for any taxable year of the partnership ending within or with the taxable year of the organization.

* * *

[Sec. 512(e)]

(e) SPECIAL RULES APPLICABLE TO S CORPORATIONS.—

(1) IN GENERAL.—If an organization described in section 1361(c)(2)(A)(vi) or 1361(c)(6) holds stock in an S corporation—

(A) such interest shall be treated as an interest in an unrelated trade or business; and

(B) notwithstanding any other provision of this part—

(i) all items of income, loss, or deduction taken into account under section 1366(a), and

(ii) any gain or loss on the disposition of the stock in the S corporation

shall be taken into account in computing the unrelated business taxable income of such organization.

(2) BASIS REDUCTION.—Except as provided in regulations, for purposes of paragraph (1), the basis of any stock acquired by purchase (as defined in section 1361(e)(1)(C)) shall be reduced by the amount of any dividends received by the organization with respect to the stock.

(3) EXCEPTION FOR ESOPS.—This subsection shall not apply to employer securities (within the meaning of section 409(l)) held by an employee stock ownership plan described in section 4975(e)(7).

[Sec. 513]

SEC. 513. UNRELATED TRADE OR BUSINESS.

[Sec. 513(a)]

(a) GENERAL RULE.—The term "unrelated trade or business" means, in the case of any organization subject to the tax imposed by section 511, any trade or business the conduct of which is not substantially related (aside from the need of such organization for income or funds or the use it makes of the profits derived) to the exercise or performance by such organization of its charitable, educational, or other purpose or function constituting the basis for its exemption under section 501 (or, in the case of an organization described in section 511 (a) (2) (B), to the exercise or performance of any purpose or function described in section 501 (c) (3)), except that such term does not include any trade or business—

(1) in which substantially all the work in carrying on such trade or business is performed for the organization without compensation; or

(2) which is carried on, in the case of an organization described in section 501 (c) (3) or in the case of a college or university described in section 511 (a) (2) (B), by the organization primarily for the convenience of its members, students, patients, officers, or employees, or, in the case of a local association of employees described in section 501(c)(4) organized before May 27, 1969, which is the selling by the organization of items of work-related clothes and equipment and items normally sold through vending machines, through food dispensing facilities, or by snack bars, for the convenience of its members at their usual places of employment; or

(3) which is the selling of merchandise, substantially all of which has been received by the organization as gifts or contributions.

[Sec. 513(b)]

(b) SPECIAL RULE FOR TRUSTS.—The term "unrelated trade or business" means, in the case of—

(1) a trust computing its unrelated business taxable income under section 512 for purposes of section 681; or

(2) a trust described in section 401(a), or section 501(c)(17), which is exempt from tax under section 501(a);

any trade or business regularly carried on by such trust or by a partnership of which it is a member.

[Sec. 513(c)]

(c) ADVERTISING, ETC., ACTIVITIES.—For purposes of this section, the term "trade or business" includes any activity which is carried on for the production of income from the sale of goods or the performance of services. For purposes of the preceding sentence, an activity does not lose identity as a trade or business merely because it is carried on within a larger aggregate of similar activities or within a larger complex of other endeavors which may, or may not, be related to the exempt purposes of the organization. Where an activity carried on for profit constitutes an unrelated trade or business, no part of such trade or business shall be excluded from such classification merely because it does not result in profit.

* * *

PART VIII—HIGHER EDUCATION SAVINGS ENTITIES

[Sec. 529]

SEC. 529. QUALIFIED TUITION PROGRAMS.

[Sec. 529(a)]

(a) GENERAL RULE.—A qualified tuition program shall be exempt from taxation under this subtitle. Notwithstanding the preceding sentence, such program shall be subject to the taxes imposed by section 511 (relating to imposition of tax on unrelated business income of charitable organizations).

[Sec. 529(b)]

(b) QUALIFIED TUITION PROGRAM.—For purposes of this section—

(1) IN GENERAL.—The term "qualified tuition program" means a program established and maintained by a State or agency or instrumentality thereof or by 1 or more eligible educational institutions—

(A) under which a person—

(i) may purchase tuition credits or certificates on behalf of a designated beneficiary which entitle the beneficiary to the waiver or payment of qualified higher education expenses of the beneficiary, or

(ii) in the case of a program established and maintained by a State or agency or instrumentality thereof, may make contributions to an account which is established for the purpose of meeting the qualified higher education expenses of the designated beneficiary of the account, and

(B) which meets the other requirements of this subsection.

Except to the extent provided in regulations, a program established and maintained by 1 or more eligible educational institutions shall not be treated as a qualified tuition program unless such program provides that amounts are held in a qualified trust and such program has received a ruling or determination that such program meets the applicable requirements for a qualified tuition program. For purposes of the preceding sentence, the term "qualified trust" means a trust which is created or organized in the United States for the exclusive benefit of designated beneficiaries and with respect to which the requirements of paragraphs (2) and (5) of section 408(a) are met.

(2) CASH CONTRIBUTIONS.—A program shall not be treated as a qualified tuition program unless it provides that purchases or contributions may only be made in cash.

(3) SEPARATE ACCOUNTING.—A program shall not be treated as a qualified tuition program unless it provides separate accounting for each designated beneficiary.

(4) LIMITED INVESTMENT DIRECTION.—A program shall not be treated as a qualified tuition program unless it provides that any contributor to, or designated beneficiary under, such program may, directly or indirectly, direct the investment of any contributions to the program (or any earnings thereon) no more than 2 times in any calendar year.

(5) NO PLEDGING OF INTEREST AS SECURITY.—A program shall not be treated as a qualified tuition program if it allows any interest in the program or any portion thereof to be used as security for a loan.

(6) PROHIBITION ON EXCESS CONTRIBUTIONS.—A program shall not be treated as a qualified tuition program unless it provides adequate safeguards to prevent contributions on behalf of a designated beneficiary in excess of those necessary to provide for the qualified higher education expenses of the beneficiary.

[Sec. 529(c)]

(c) TAX TREATMENT OF DESIGNATED BENEFICIARIES AND CONTRIBUTORS.—

(1) IN GENERAL.—Except as otherwise provided in this subsection, no amount shall be includible in gross income of—

(A) a designated beneficiary under a qualified tuition program, or

(B) a contributor to such program on behalf of a designated beneficiary,

with respect to any distribution or earnings under such program.

(2) GIFT TAX TREATMENT OF CONTRIBUTIONS.—For purposes of chapters 12 and 13—

(A) IN GENERAL.—Any contribution to a qualified tuition program on behalf of any designated beneficiary—

(i) shall be treated as a completed gift to such beneficiary which is not a future interest in property, and

(ii) shall not be treated as a qualified transfer under section 2503(e).

(B) TREATMENT OF EXCESS CONTRIBUTIONS.—If the aggregate amount of contributions described in subparagraph (A) during the calendar year by a donor exceeds the limitation for such year under section 2503(b), such aggregate amount shall, at the election of the donor, be taken into account for purposes of such section ratably over the 5-year period beginning with such calendar year.

(3) DISTRIBUTIONS.—

(A) IN GENERAL.—Any distribution under a qualified tuition program shall be includible in the gross income of the distributee in the manner as provided under section 72 to the extent not excluded from gross income under any other provision of this chapter.

(B) DISTRIBUTIONS FOR QUALIFIED HIGHER EDUCATION EXPENSES.—For purposes of this paragraph—

(i) IN-KIND DISTRIBUTIONS.—No amount shall be includible in gross income under subparagraph (A) by reason of a distribution which consists of providing a benefit to the distributee which, if paid for by the distributee, would constitute payment of a qualified higher education expense.

(ii) CASH DISTRIBUTIONS.—In the case of distributions not described in clause (i), if—

(I) such distributions do not exceed the qualified higher education expenses (reduced by expenses described in clause (i)), no amount shall be includible in gross income, and

(II) in any other case, the amount otherwise includible in gross income shall be reduced by an amount which bears the same ratio to such amount as such expenses bear to such distributions.

(iii) EXCEPTION FOR INSTITUTIONAL PROGRAMS.—In the case of any taxable year beginning before January 1, 2004, clauses (i) and (ii) shall not apply with respect to any distribution during such taxable year under a qualified tuition program established and maintained by 1 or more eligible educational institutions.

(iv) TREATMENT AS DISTRIBUTIONS.—Any benefit furnished to a designated beneficiary under a qualified tuition program shall be treated as a distribution to the beneficiary for purposes of this paragraph.

(v) COORDINATION WITH AMERICAN OPPORTUNITY AND LIFETIME LEARNING CREDITS.—The total amount of qualified higher education expenses with respect to an individual for the taxable year shall be reduced—

(I) as provided in section 25A(g)(2), and

(II) by the amount of such expenses which were taken into account in determining the credit allowed to the taxpayer or any other person under section 25A.

(vi) COORDINATION WITH COVERDELL EDUCATION SAVINGS ACCOUNTS.—If, with respect to an individual for any taxable year—

(I) the aggregate distributions to which clauses (i) and (ii) and section 530(d)(2)(A) apply, exceed

(II) the total amount of qualified higher education expenses otherwise taken into account under clauses (i) and (ii) (after the application of clause (v)) for such year,

the taxpayer shall allocate such expenses among such distributions for purposes of determining the amount of the exclusion under clauses (i) and (ii) and section 530(d)(2)(A).

(C) CHANGE IN BENEFICIARIES OR PROGRAMS.—

(i) ROLLOVERS.—Subparagraph (A) shall not apply to that portion of any distribution which, within 60 days of such distribution, is transferred—

(I) to another qualified tuition program for the benefit of the designated beneficiary,

(II) to the credit of another designated beneficiary under a qualified tuition program who is a member of the family of the designated beneficiary with respect to which the distribution was made, or

(III) before January 1, 2026, to an ABLE account (as defined in section 529A(e)(6)) of the designated beneficiary or a member of the family of the designated beneficiary.

Subclause (III) shall not apply to so much of a distribution which, when added to all other contributions made to the ABLE account for the taxable year, exceeds the limitation under section 529A(b)(2)(B)(i).

(ii) CHANGE IN DESIGNATED BENEFICIARIES.—Any change in the designated beneficiary of an interest in a qualified tuition program shall not be treated as a distribution for purposes of subparagraph (A) if the new beneficiary is a member of the family of the old beneficiary.

(iii) LIMITATION ON CERTAIN ROLLOVERS.—Clause (i)(I) shall not apply to any transfer if such transfer occurs within 12 months from the date of a previous transfer to any qualified tuition program for the benefit of the designated beneficiary.

(D) SPECIAL RULE FOR CONTRIBUTIONS OF REFUNDED AMOUNTS.—In the case of a beneficiary who receives a refund of any qualified higher education expenses from an eligible educational institution, subparagraph (A) shall not apply to that portion of any distribution for the taxable year which is recontributed to a qualified tuition program of which such individual is a beneficiary, but only to the extent such recontribution is made not later than 60 days after the date of such refund and does not exceed the refunded amount.

(4) ESTATE TAX TREATMENT.—

(A) IN GENERAL.—No amount shall be includible in the gross estate of any individual for purposes of chapter 11 by reason of an interest in a qualified tuition program.

(B) AMOUNTS INCLUDIBLE IN ESTATE OF DESIGNATED BENEFICIARY IN CERTAIN CASES.—Subparagraph (A) shall not apply to amounts distributed on account of the death of a beneficiary.

(C) AMOUNTS INCLUDIBLE IN ESTATE OF DONOR MAKING EXCESS CONTRIBUTIONS.—In the case of a donor who makes the election described in paragraph (2)(B) and who dies before the close of the 5-year period referred to in such paragraph, notwithstanding subparagraph (A), the gross estate of the donor shall include the portion of such contributions properly allocable to periods after the date of death of the donor.

(5) OTHER GIFT TAX RULES.—For purposes of chapters 12 and 13—

(A) TREATMENT OF DISTRIBUTIONS.—Except as provided in subparagraph (B), in no event shall a distribution from a qualified tuition program be treated as a taxable gift.

(B) TREATMENT OF DESIGNATION OF NEW BENEFICIARY.—The taxes imposed by chapters 12 and 13 shall apply to a transfer by reason of a change in the designated beneficiary under the program (or a rollover to the account of a new beneficiary) unless the new beneficiary is—

(i) assigned to the same generation as (or a higher generation than) the old beneficiary (determined in accordance with section 2651), and

(ii) a member of the family of the old beneficiary.

(6) ADDITIONAL TAX.—The tax imposed by section 530(d)(4) shall apply to any payment or distribution from a qualified tuition program in the same manner as such tax applies to a payment or distribution from a Coverdell education savings account. This paragraph shall not apply to any payment or distribution in any taxable year beginning before January 1, 2004, which is includible in gross income but used for qualified higher education expenses of the designated beneficiary.

(7) TREATMENT OF ELEMENTARY AND SECONDARY TUITION.—Any reference in this subsection to the term "qualified higher education expense" shall include a reference to expenses for

tuition in connection with enrollment or attendance at an elementary or secondary public, private, or religious school.

(8) TREATMENT OF CERTAIN EXPENSES ASSOCIATED WITH REGISTERED APPRENTICESHIP PROGRAMS.—Any reference in this subsection to the term "qualified higher education expense" shall include a reference to expenses for fees, books, supplies, and equipment required for the participation of a designated beneficiary in an apprenticeship program registered and certified with the Secretary of Labor under section 1 of the National Apprenticeship Act (29 U.S.C. 50).

(9) TREATMENT OF QUALIFIED EDUCATION LOAN REPAYMENTS.—

(A) IN GENERAL.—Any reference in this subsection to the term "qualified higher education expense" shall include a reference to amounts paid as principal or interest on any qualified education loan (as defined in section 221(d)) of the designated beneficiary or a sibling of the designated beneficiary.

(B) LIMITATION.—The amount of distributions treated as a qualified higher education expense under this paragraph with respect to the loans of any individual shall not exceed $10,000 (reduced by the amount of distributions so treated for all prior taxable years).

(C) SPECIAL RULES FOR SIBLINGS OF THE DESIGNATED BENEFICIARY.—

(i) SEPARATE ACCOUNTING.—For purposes of subparagraph (B) and subsection (d), amounts treated as a qualified higher education expense with respect to the loans of a sibling of the designated beneficiary shall be taken into account with respect to such sibling and not with respect to such designated beneficiary.

(ii) SIBLING DEFINED.—For purposes of this paragraph, the term "sibling" means an individual who bears a relationship to the designated beneficiary which is described in section 152(d)(2)(B).

[Sec. 529(d)]

(d) REPORTS.—Each officer or employee having control of the qualified tuition program or their designee shall make such reports regarding such program to the Secretary and to designated beneficiaries with respect to contributions, distributions, and such other matters as the Secretary may require. The reports required by this subsection shall be filed at such time and in such manner and furnished to such individuals at such time and in such manner as may be required by the Secretary.

[Sec. 529(e)]

(e) OTHER DEFINITIONS AND SPECIAL RULES.—For purposes of this section—

(1) DESIGNATED BENEFICIARY.—The term "designated beneficiary" means—

(A) the individual designated at the commencement of participation in the qualified tuition program as the beneficiary of amounts paid (or to be paid) to the program,

(B) in the case of a change in beneficiaries described in subsection (c)(3)(C), the individual who is the new beneficiary, and

(C) in the case of an interest in a qualified tuition program purchased by a State or local government (or agency or instrumentality thereof) or an organization described in section 501(c)(3) and exempt from taxation under section 501(a) as part of a scholarship program operated by such government or organization, the individual receiving such interest as a scholarship.

(2) MEMBER OF FAMILY.—The term "member of the family" means, with respect to any designated beneficiary—

(A) the spouse of such beneficiary;

(B) an individual who bears a relationship to such beneficiary which is described in subparagraphs (A) through (G) of section 152(d)(2);

(C) the spouse of any individual described in subparagraph (B); and

(D) any first cousin of such beneficiary.

(3) QUALIFIED HIGHER EDUCATION EXPENSES.—

(A) IN GENERAL.—The term "qualified higher education expenses" means—

(i) tuition, fees, books, supplies, and equipment required for the enrollment or attendance of a designated beneficiary at an eligible educational institution,

(ii) expenses for special needs services in the case of a special needs beneficiary which are incurred in connection with such enrollment or attendance, and

(iii) expenses for the purchase of computer or peripheral equipment (as defined in section 168(i)(2)(B)), computer software (as defined in section 197(e)(3)(B)), or Internet access and related services, if such equipment, software, or services are to be used primarily by the beneficiary during any of the years the beneficiary is enrolled at an eligible educational institution.

Clause (iii) shall not include expenses for computer software designed for sports, games, or hobbies unless the software is predominantly educational in nature. The amount of cash distributions from all qualified tuition programs described in subsection (b)(1)(A)(ii) with respect to a beneficiary during any taxable year shall, in the aggregate, include not more than $10,000 in expenses described in subsection (c)(7) incurred during the taxable year.

(B) ROOM AND BOARD INCLUDED FOR STUDENTS WHO ARE AT LEAST HALF-TIME.—

(i) IN GENERAL.—In the case of an individual who is an eligible student (as defined in section 25A(b)(3)) for any academic period, such term shall also include reasonable costs for such period (as determined under the qualified tuition program) incurred by the designated beneficiary for room and board while attending such institution. For purposes of subsection (b)(6), a designated beneficiary shall be treated as meeting the requirements of this clause.

(ii) LIMITATION.—The amount treated as qualified higher education expenses by reason of clause (i) shall not exceed—

(I) the allowance (applicable to the student) for room and board included in the cost of attendance (as defined in section 472 of the Higher Education Act of 1965 (20 U.S.C. 1087ll), as in effect on the date of the enactment of the Economic Growth and Tax Relief Reconciliation Act of 2001) as determined by the eligible educational institution for such period, or

(II) if greater, the actual invoice amount the student residing in housing owned or operated by the eligible educational institution is charged by such institution for room and board costs for such period.

(4) APPLICATION OF SECTION 514.—An interest in a qualified tuition program shall not be treated as debt for purposes of section 514.

(5) ELIGIBLE EDUCATIONAL INSTITUTION.—The term "eligible educational institution" means an institution—

(A) which is described in section 481 of the Higher Education Act of 1965 (20 U.S.C. 1088), as in effect on the date of the enactment of this paragraph, and

(B) which is eligible to participate in a program under title IV of such Act.

* * *

[Sec. 530]

SEC. 530. COVERDELL EDUCATION SAVINGS ACCOUNTS.

[Sec. 530(a)]

(a) GENERAL RULE.—A Coverdell education savings account shall be exempt from taxation under this subtitle. Notwithstanding the preceding sentence, the Coverdell education savings account shall be subject to the taxes imposed by section 511 (relating to imposition of tax on unrelated business income of charitable organizations).

[Sec. 530(b)]

(b) DEFINITIONS AND SPECIAL RULES.—For purposes of this section—

(1) COVERDELL EDUCATION SAVINGS ACCOUNT.—The term "Coverdell education savings account" means a trust created or organized in the United States exclusively for the purpose of paying the qualified education expenses of an individual who is the designated beneficiary of the trust (and designated as a Coverdell education savings account at the time created or organized), but only if the written governing instrument creating the trust meets the following requirements:

(A) No contribution will be accepted—

(i) unless it is in cash,

(ii) after the date on which such beneficiary attains age 18, or

(iii) except in the case of rollover contributions, if such contribution would result in aggregate contributions for the taxable year exceeding $2,000.

(B) The trustee is a bank (as defined in section 408(n)) or another person who demonstrates to the satisfaction of the Secretary that the manner in which that person will administer the trust will be consistent with the requirements of this section or who has so demonstrated with respect to any individual retirement plan.

(C) No part of the trust assets will be invested in life insurance contracts.

(D) The assets of the trust shall not be commingled with other property except in a common trust fund or common investment fund.

(E) Except as provided in subsection (d)(7), any balance to the credit of the designated beneficiary on the date on which the beneficiary attains age 30 shall be distributed within 30 days after such date to the beneficiary or, if the beneficiary dies before attaining age 30, shall be distributed within 30 days after the date of death of such beneficiary.

The age limitations in subparagraphs (A)(ii) and (E), and paragraphs (5) and (6) of subsection (d), shall not apply to any designated beneficiary with special needs (as determined under regulations prescribed by the Secretary).

(2) QUALIFIED EDUCATION EXPENSES.—

(A) IN GENERAL.—The term "qualified education expenses" means—

(i) qualified higher education expenses (as defined in section 529(e)(3)), and

(ii) qualified elementary and secondary education expenses (as defined in paragraph (3)).

(B) QUALIFIED TUITION PROGRAMS.—Such term shall include any contribution to a qualified tuition program (as defined in section 529(b)) on behalf of the designated beneficiary (as defined in section 529(e)(1)); but there shall be no increase in the investment in the contract for purposes of applying section 72 by reason of any portion of such contribution which is not includible in gross income by reason of subsection (d)(2).

(3) QUALIFIED ELEMENTARY AND SECONDARY EDUCATION EXPENSES.—

(A) IN GENERAL.—The term "qualified elementary and secondary education expenses" means—

(i) expenses for tuition, fees, academic tutoring, special needs services in the case of a special needs beneficiary, books, supplies, and other equipment which are incurred in connection with the enrollment or attendance of the designated beneficiary of the trust as an elementary or secondary school student at a public, private, or religious school,

(ii) expenses for room and board, uniforms, transportation, and supplementary items and services (including extended day programs) which are required or provided by a public, private, or religious school in connection with such enrollment or attendance, and

(iii) expenses for the purchase of any computer technology or equipment or Internet access and related services, if such technology, equipment, or services are to be used by the beneficiary and the beneficiary's family during any of the years the beneficiary is in school.

Clause (iii) shall not include expenses for computer software designed for sports, games, or hobbies unless the software is predominantly educational in nature.

(B) SCHOOL.—The term "school" means any school which provides elementary education or secondary education (kindergarten through grade 12), as determined under State law.

(C) COMPUTER TECHNOLOGY OR EQUIPMENT.—The term "computer technology or equipment" means computer software (as defined by section 197(e)(3)(B)), computer or peripheral equipment (as defined by section 168(i)(2)(B)), and fiber optic cable related to computer use.

(4) TIME WHEN CONTRIBUTIONS DEEMED MADE.—An individual shall be deemed to have made a contribution to a Coverdell education savings account on the last day of the preceding taxable year if the contribution is made on account of such taxable year and is made not later than the time prescribed by law for filing the return for such taxable year (not including extensions thereof).

[Sec. 530(c)]

(c) REDUCTION IN PERMITTED CONTRIBUTIONS BASED ON ADJUSTED GROSS INCOME.—

(1) IN GENERAL.—In the case of a contributor who is an individual, the maximum amount the contributor could otherwise make to an account under this section shall be reduced by an amount which bears the same ratio to such maximum amount as—

(A) the excess of—

(i) the contributor's modified adjusted gross income for such taxable year, over

(ii) $95,000 ($190,000 in the case of a joint return), bears to

(B) $15,000 ($30,000 in the case of a joint return).

(2) MODIFIED ADJUSTED GROSS INCOME.—For purposes of paragraph (1), the term "modified adjusted gross income" means the adjusted gross income of the taxpayer for the taxable year increased by any amount excluded from gross income under section 911, 931, or 933.

[Sec. 530(d)]

(d) TAX TREATMENT OF DISTRIBUTIONS.—

(1) IN GENERAL.—Any distribution shall be includible in the gross income of the distributee in the manner as provided in section 72.

(2) DISTRIBUTIONS FOR QUALIFIED EDUCATION EXPENSES.—

(A) IN GENERAL.—No amount shall be includible in gross income under paragraph (1) if the qualified education expenses of the designated beneficiary during the taxable year are not less than the aggregate distributions during the taxable year.

(B) DISTRIBUTIONS IN EXCESS OF EXPENSES.—If such aggregate distributions exceed such expenses during the taxable year, the amount otherwise includible in gross income under paragraph (1) shall be reduced by the amount which bears the same ratio to the amount which would be includible in gross income under paragraph (1) (without regard to this subparagraph) as the qualified education expenses bear to such aggregate distributions.

(C) COORDINATION WITH AMERICAN OPPORTUNITY AND LIFETIME LEARNING CREDITS AND QUALIFIED TUITION PROGRAMS.—For purposes of subparagraph (A)—

(i) CREDIT COORDINATION.—The total amount of qualified education expenses with respect to an individual for the taxable year shall be reduced—

(I) as provided in section 25A(g)(2), and

(II) by the amount of such expenses which were taken into account in determining the credit allowed to the taxpayer or any other person under section 25A.

(ii) COORDINATION WITH QUALIFIED TUITION PROGRAMS.—If, with respect to an individual for any taxable year—

(I) the aggregate distributions during such year to which subparagraph (A) and section 529(c)(3)(B) apply, exceed

(II) the total amount of qualified education expenses (after the application of clause (i)) for such year,

the taxpayer shall allocate such expenses among such distributions for purposes of determining the amount of the exclusion under subparagraph (A) and section 529(c)(3)(B).

(D) DISALLOWANCE OF EXCLUDED AMOUNTS AS DEDUCTION, CREDIT, OR EXCLUSION.—No deduction, credit, or exclusion shall be allowed to the taxpayer under any other section of this chapter for any qualified education expenses to the extent taken into account in determining the amount of the exclusion under this paragraph.

(3) SPECIAL RULES FOR APPLYING ESTATE AND GIFT TAXES WITH RESPECT TO ACCOUNT.—Rules similar to the rules of paragraphs (2), (4), and (5) of section 529(c) shall apply for purposes of this section.

(4) ADDITIONAL TAX FOR DISTRIBUTIONS NOT USED FOR EDUCATIONAL EXPENSES.—

(A) IN GENERAL.—The tax imposed by this chapter for any taxable year on any taxpayer who receives a payment or distribution from a Coverdell education savings account which is includible in gross income shall be increased by 10 percent of the amount which is so includible.

(B) EXCEPTIONS.—Subparagraph (A) shall not apply if the payment or distribution is—

(i) made to a beneficiary (or to the estate of the designated beneficiary) on or after the death of the designated beneficiary,

(ii) attributable to the designated beneficiary's being disabled (within the meaning of section 72(m)(7)),

(iii) made on account of a scholarship, allowance, or payment described in section 25A(g)(2) received by the designated beneficiary to the extent the amount of the payment or distribution does not exceed the amount of the scholarship, allowance, or payment,

(iv) made on account of the attendance of the designated beneficiary at the United States Military Academy, the United States Naval Academy, the United States Air Force Academy, the United States Coast Guard Academy, or the United States Merchant Marine Academy, to the extent that the amount of the payment or distribution does not exceed the costs of advanced education (as defined by section 2005(e)(3) of title 10, United States Code, as in effect on the date of the enactment of this section) attributable to such attendance, or

(v) an amount which is includible in gross income solely by application of paragraph (2)(C)(i)(II) for the taxable year.

(C) CONTRIBUTIONS RETURNED BEFORE CERTAIN DATE.—Subparagraph (A) shall not apply to the distribution of any contribution made during a taxable year on behalf of the designated beneficiary if—

(i) such distribution is made before the first day of the sixth month of the taxable year following the taxable year, and

(ii) such distribution is accompanied by the amount of net income attributable to such excess contribution.

Any net income described in clause (ii) shall be included in gross income for the taxable year in which such excess contribution was made.

(5) ROLLOVER CONTRIBUTIONS.—Paragraph (1) shall not apply to any amount paid or distributed from a Coverdell education savings account to the extent that the amount received is paid, not later than the 60th day after the date of such payment or distribution, into another Coverdell education savings account for the benefit of the same beneficiary or a member of the family (within the meaning of section 529(e)(2)) of such beneficiary who has not attained age 30 as of such date. The preceding sentence shall not apply to any payment or distribution if it applied to any prior payment or distribution during the 12-month period ending on the date of the payment or distribution.

(6) CHANGE IN BENEFICIARY.—Any change in the beneficiary of a Coverdell education savings account shall not be treated as a distribution for purposes of paragraph (1) if the new

beneficiary is a member of the family (as so defined) of the old beneficiary and has not attained age 30 as of the date of such change.

(7) SPECIAL RULES FOR DEATH AND DIVORCE.—Rules similar to the rules of paragraphs (7) and (8) of section 220(f) shall apply. In applying the preceding sentence, members of the family (as so defined) of the designated beneficiary shall be treated in the same manner as the spouse under such paragraph (8).

(8) DEEMED DISTRIBUTION ON REQUIRED DISTRIBUTION DATE.—In any case in which a distribution is required under subsection (b)(1)(E), any balance to the credit of a designated beneficiary as of the close of the 30-day period referred to in such subsection for making such distribution shall be deemed distributed at the close of such period.

(9) MILITARY DEATH GRATUITY.—

(A) IN GENERAL.—For purposes of this section, the term "rollover contribution" includes a contribution to a Coverdell education savings account made before the end of the 1-year period beginning on the date on which the contributor receives an amount under section 1477 of title 10, United States Code, or section 1967 of title 38 of such Code, with respect to a person, to the extent that such contribution does not exceed—

(i) the sum of the amounts received during such period by such contributor under such sections with respect to such person, reduced by

(ii) the amounts so received which were contributed to a Roth IRA under section 408A(e)(2) or to another Coverdell education savings account.

(B) ANNUAL LIMIT ON NUMBER OF ROLLOVERS NOT TO APPLY.—The last sentence of paragraph (5) shall not apply with respect to amounts treated as a rollover by subparagraph (A).

(C) APPLICATION OF SECTION 72.—For purposes of applying section 72 in the case of a distribution which is includible in gross income under paragraph (1), the amount treated as a rollover by reason of subparagraph (A) shall be treated as [an] investment in the contract.

[Sec. 530(e)]

(e) TAX TREATMENT OF ACCOUNTS.—Rules similar to the rules of paragraphs (2) and (4) of section 408(e) shall apply to any Coverdell education savings account.

[Sec. 530(f)]

(f) COMMUNITY PROPERTY LAWS.—This section shall be applied without regard to any community property laws.

[Sec. 530(g)]

(g) CUSTODIAL ACCOUNTS.—For purposes of this section, a custodial account shall be treated as a trust if the assets of such account are held by a bank (as defined in section 408(n)) or another person who demonstrates, to the satisfaction of the Secretary, that the manner in which he will administer the account will be consistent with the requirements of this section, and if the custodial account would, except for the fact that it is not a trust, constitute an account described in subsection (b)(1). For purposes of this title, in the case of a custodial account treated as a trust by reason of the preceding sentence, the custodian of such account shall be treated as the trustee thereof.

* * *

SUBCHAPTER G—CORPORATIONS USED TO AVOID INCOME TAX ON SHAREHOLDERS

PART I—CORPORATIONS IMPROPERLY ACCUMULATING SURPLUS

[Sec. 531]

SEC. 531. IMPOSITION OF ACCUMULATED EARNINGS TAX.

In addition to other taxes imposed by this chapter, there is hereby imposed for each taxable year on the accumulated taxable income (as defined in section 535) of each corporation described in section 532, an accumulated earnings tax equal to 20 percent of the accumulated taxable income.

[Sec. 532]

SEC. 532. CORPORATIONS SUBJECT TO ACCUMULATED EARNINGS TAX.

[Sec. 532(a)]

(a) GENERAL RULE.—The accumulated earnings tax imposed by section 531 shall apply to every corporation (other than those described in subsection (b)) formed or availed of for the purpose of avoiding the income tax with respect to its shareholders or the shareholders of any other corporation, by permitting earnings and profits to accumulate instead of being divided or distributed.

[Sec. 532(b)]

(b) EXCEPTIONS.—The accumulated earnings tax imposed by section 531 shall not apply to—

(1) a personal holding company (as defined in section 542),

(2) a corporation exempt from tax under subchapter F (section 501 and following), or

(3) a passive foreign investment company (as defined in section 1297).

(c) APPLICATION DETERMINED WITHOUT REGARD TO NUMBER OF SHAREHOLDERS.—The application of this part to a corporation shall be determined without regard to the number of shareholders of such corporation.

[Sec. 533]

SEC. 533. EVIDENCE OF PURPOSE TO AVOID INCOME TAX.

[Sec. 533(a)]

(a) UNREASONABLE ACCUMULATION DETERMINATIVE OF PURPOSE.—For purposes of section 532, the fact that the earnings and profits of a corporation are permitted to accumulate beyond the reasonable needs of the business shall be determinative of the purpose to avoid the income tax with respect to shareholders, unless the corporation by the preponderance of the evidence shall prove to the contrary.

[Sec. 533(b)]

(b) HOLDING OR INVESTMENT COMPANY.—The fact that any corporation is a mere holding or investment company shall be prima facie evidence of the purpose to avoid the income tax with respect to shareholders.

[Sec. 534]

SEC. 534. BURDEN OF PROOF.

[Sec. 534(a)]

(a) GENERAL RULE.—In any proceeding before the Tax Court involving a notice of deficiency based in whole or in part on the allegation that all or any part of the earnings and profits have been permitted to accumulate beyond the reasonable needs of the business, the burden of proof with respect to such allegation shall—

(1) if notification has not been sent in accordance with subsection (b), be on the Secretary, or

(2) if the taxpayer has submitted the statement described in subsection (c), be on the Secretary with respect to the grounds set forth in such statement in accordance with the provisions of such subsection.

[Sec. 534(b)]

(b) NOTIFICATION BY SECRETARY.—Before mailing the notice of deficiency referred to in subsection (a), the Secretary may send by certified mail or registered mail a notification informing the taxpayer that the proposed notice of deficiency includes an amount with respect to the accumulated earnings tax imposed by section 531.

[Sec. 534(c)]

(c) STATEMENT BY TAXPAYER.—Within such time (but not less than 30 days) after the mailing of the notification described in subsection (b) as the Secretary may prescribe by regulations, the taxpayer may submit a statement of the grounds (together with facts sufficient to show the basis thereof) on which the taxpayer relies to establish that all or any part of the earnings and profits have not been permitted to accumulate beyond the reasonable needs of the business.

[Sec. 534(d)]

(d) JEOPARDY ASSESSMENT.—If pursuant to section 6861 (a) a jeopardy assessment is made before the mailing of the notice of deficiency referred to in subsection (a), for purposes of this section such notice of deficiency shall, to the extent that it informs the taxpayer that such deficiency includes the accumulated earnings tax imposed by section 531, constitute the notification described in subsection (b), and in that event the statement described in subsection (c) may be included in the taxpayer's petition to the Tax Court.

[Sec. 535]

SEC. 535. ACCUMULATED TAXABLE INCOME.

[Sec. 535(a)]

(a) DEFINITION.—For purposes of this subtitle, the term "accumulated taxable income" means the taxable income, adjusted in the manner provided in subsection (b), minus the sum of the dividends paid deduction (as defined in section 561) and the accumulated earnings credit (as defined in subsection (c)).

[Sec. 535(b)]

(b) ADJUSTMENTS TO TAXABLE INCOME.—For purposes of subsection (a), taxable income shall be adjusted as follows:

(1) TAXES.—There shall be allowed as a deduction Federal income and excess profits taxes and income, war profits, and excess profits taxes of foreign countries and possessions of the United States (to the extent not allowable as a deduction under section 275(a)(4)), accrued during the taxable year or deemed to be paid by a domestic corporation under section 960 for the taxable year, but not including the accumulated earnings tax imposed by section 531 or the personal holding company tax imposed by section 541.

(2) CHARITABLE CONTRIBUTIONS.—The deduction for charitable contributions provided under section 170 shall be allowed without regard to section 170(b)(2).

(3) SPECIAL DEDUCTIONS DISALLOWED.—The special deductions for corporations provided in part VIII (except section 248) of subchapter B (section 241 and following, relating to the deduction for dividends received by corporations, etc.) shall not be allowed.

(4) NET OPERATING LOSS.—The net operating loss deduction provided in section 172 shall not be allowed.

(5) CAPITAL LOSSES.—

(A) IN GENERAL.—Except as provided in subparagraph (B), there shall be allowed as a deduction an amount equal to the net capital loss for the taxable year (determined without regard to paragraph (7)(A)).

(B) RECAPTURE OF PREVIOUS DEDUCTIONS FOR CAPITAL GAINS.—The aggregate amount allowable as a deduction under subparagraph (A) for any taxable year shall be reduced by the lesser of—

(i) the nonrecaptured capital gains deductions, or

(ii) the amount of the accumulated earnings and profits of the corporation as of the close of the preceding taxable year.

(C) NONRECAPTURED CAPITAL GAINS DEDUCTIONS.—For purposes of subparagraph (B), the term "nonrecaptured capital gains deductions" means the excess of—

(i) the aggregate amount allowable as a deduction under paragraph (6) for preceding taxable years beginning after July 18, 1984, over

(ii) the aggregate of the reductions under subparagraph (B) for preceding taxable years.

(6) NET CAPITAL GAINS.—

(A) IN GENERAL.—There shall be allowed as a deduction—

(i) the net capital gain for the taxable year (determined with the application of paragraph (7)), reduced by

(ii) the taxes attributable to such net capital gain.

(B) ATTRIBUTABLE TAXES.—For purposes of subparagraph (A), the taxes attributable to the net capital gain shall be an amount equal to the difference between—

(i) the taxes imposed by this subtitle (except the tax imposed by this part) for the taxable year, and

(ii) such taxes computed for such year without including in taxable income the net capital gain for the taxable year (determined without the application of paragraph (7)).

(7) CAPITAL LOSS CARRYOVERS.—

(A) UNLIMITED CARRYFORWARD.—The net capital loss for any taxable year shall be treated as a short-term capital loss in the next taxable year.

(B) SECTION 1212 INAPPLICABLE.—No allowance shall be made for the capital loss carryback or carryforward provided in section 1212.

(8) SPECIAL RULES FOR MERE HOLDING OR INVESTMENT COMPANIES.—In the case of a mere holding or investment company—

(A) CAPITAL LOSS DEDUCTION, ETC., NOT ALLOWED.—Paragraphs (5) and (7)(A) shall not apply.

(B) DEDUCTION FOR CERTAIN OFFSETS.—There shall be allowed as a deduction the net short-term capital gain for the taxable year to the extent such gain does not exceed the amount of any capital loss carryover to such taxable year under section 1212 (determined without regard to paragraph (7)(B)).

(C) EARNINGS AND PROFITS.—For purposes of subchapter C, the accumulated earnings and profits at any time shall not be less than they would be if this subsection had applied to the computation of earnings and profits for all taxable years beginning after July 18, 1984.

(9) SPECIAL RULE FOR CAPITAL GAINS AND LOSSES OF FOREIGN CORPORATIONS.—In the case of a foreign corporation, paragraph (6) shall be applied by taking into account only gains and losses which are effectively connected with the conduct of a trade or business within the United States and are not exempt from tax under treaty.

* * *

[Sec. 535(c)]

(c) ACCUMULATED EARNINGS CREDIT.—

(1) GENERAL RULE.—For purposes of subsection (a), in the case of a corporation other than a mere holding or investment company the accumulated earnings credit is (A) an amount equal to such part of the earnings and profits for the taxable year as are retained for the reasonable needs of the business, minus (B) the deduction allowed by subsection (b)(6). For purposes of this paragraph, the amount of the earnings and profits for the taxable year which are retained is the amount by which the earnings and profits for the taxable year exceed the dividends paid deduction (as defined in section 561) for such year.

(2) MINIMUM CREDIT.—

(A) IN GENERAL.—The credit allowable under paragraph (1) shall in no case be less than the amount by which $250,000 exceeds the accumulated earnings and profits of the corporation at the close of the preceding taxable year.

(B) CERTAIN SERVICE CORPORATIONS.—In the case of a corporation the principal function of which is the performance of services in the field of health, law, engineering, architecture, accounting, actuarial science, performing arts, or consulting, subparagraph (A) shall be applied by substituting "$150,000" for "$250,000".

(3) HOLDING AND INVESTMENT COMPANIES.—In the case of a corporation which is a mere holding or investment company, the accumulated earnings credit is the amount (if any) by which $250,000 exceeds the accumulated earnings and profits of the corporation at the close of the preceding taxable year.

(4) ACCUMULATED EARNINGS AND PROFITS.—For purposes of paragraphs (2) and (3), the accumulated earnings and profits at the close of the preceding taxable year shall be reduced by the dividends which under section 563(a) (relating to dividends paid after the close of the taxable year) are considered as paid during such taxable year.

(5) CROSS REFERENCE.—For limitation on credit provided in paragraph (2) or (3) in the case of certain controlled corporations, see section 1561.

* * *

[Sec. 536]

SEC. 536. INCOME NOT PLACED ON ANNUAL BASIS.

Section 443(b) (relating to computation of tax on change of annual accounting period) shall not apply in the computation of the accumulated earnings tax imposed by section 531.

[Sec. 537]

SEC. 537. REASONABLE NEEDS OF THE BUSINESS.

[Sec. 537(a)]

(a) GENERAL RULE.—For purposes of this part, the term "reasonable needs of the business" includes—

(1) the reasonably anticipated needs of the business,

(2) the section 303 redemption needs of the business, and

(3) the excess business holdings redemption needs of the business.

[Sec. 537(b)]

(b) SPECIAL RULES.—For purposes of subsection (a)—

(1) SECTION 303 REDEMPTION NEEDS.—The term "section 303 redemption needs" means, with respect to the taxable year of the corporation in which a shareholder of the corporation died or any taxable year thereafter, the amount needed (or reasonably anticipated to be needed) to make a redemption of stock included in the gross estate of the decedent (but not in excess of the maximum amount of stock to which section 303(a) may apply).

(2) EXCESS BUSINESS HOLDINGS REDEMPTION NEEDS.—The term "excess business holdings redemption needs" means the amount needed (or reasonably anticipated to be needed) to redeem from a private foundation stock which—

(A) such foundation held on May 26, 1969 (or which was received by such foundation pursuant to a will or irrevocable trust to which section 4943(c)(5) applies), and

(B) constituted excess business holdings on May 26, 1969, or would have constituted excess business holdings as of such date if there were taken into account (i) stock received pursuant to a will or trust described in subparagraph (A), and (ii) the reduction in the total outstanding stock of the corporation which would have resulted solely from the redemption of stock held by the private foundation.

(3) OBLIGATIONS INCURRED TO MAKE REDEMPTIONS.—In applying paragraphs (1) and (2), the discharge of any obligation incurred to make a redemption described in such paragraphs shall be treated as the making of such redemption.

(4) PRODUCT LIABILITY LOSS RESERVES.—The accumulation of reasonable amounts for the payment of reasonably anticipated product liability losses (as defined in section 172(f)) (as in effect before the date of the enactment of the Tax Cuts and Jobs Act), as determined under

regulations prescribed by the Secretary, shall be treated as accumulated for the reasonably anticipated needs of the business.

(5) NO INFERENCE AS TO PRIOR TAXABLE YEARS.—The application of this part to any taxable year before the first taxable year specified in paragraph (1) shall be made without regard to the fact that distributions in redemption coming within the terms of such paragraphs were subsequently made.

PART II—PERSONAL HOLDING COMPANIES

[Sec. 541]

SEC. 541. IMPOSITION OF PERSONAL HOLDING COMPANY TAX.

In addition to other taxes imposed by this chapter, there is hereby imposed for each taxable year on the undistributed personal holding company income (as defined in section 545) of every personal holding company (as defined in section 542) a personal holding company tax equal to 20 percent of the undistributed personal holding company income.

[Sec. 542]

SEC. 542. DEFINITION OF PERSONAL HOLDING COMPANY.

[Sec. 542(a)]

(a) GENERAL RULE.—For purposes of this subtitle, the term "personal holding company" means any corporation (other than a corporation described in subsection (c)) if—

(1) ADJUSTED ORDINARY GROSS INCOME REQUIREMENT.—At least 60 percent of its adjusted ordinary gross income (as defined in section 543(b)(2)) for the taxable year is personal holding company income (as defined in section 543(a)), and

(2) STOCK OWNERSHIP REQUIREMENT.—At any time during the last half of the taxable year more than 50 percent in value of its outstanding stock is owned, directly or indirectly, by or for not more than 5 individuals. For purposes of this paragraph, an organization described in section 401(a), 501(c)(17), or 509(a) or a portion of a trust permanently set aside or to be used exclusively for the purposes described in section 642(c) or a corresponding provision of a prior income tax law shall be considered an individual.

[Sec. 542(b)]

(b) CORPORATIONS FILING CONSOLIDATED RETURNS.—

(1) GENERAL RULE.—In the case of an affiliated group of corporations filing or required to file a consolidated return under section 1501 for any taxable year, the adjusted ordinary gross income requirement of subsection (a) (1) of this section shall, except as provided in paragraphs (2) and (3), be applied for such year with respect to the consolidated adjusted ordinary gross income and the consolidated personal holding company income of the affiliated group. No member of such an affiliated group shall be considered to meet such adjusted ordinary gross income requirement unless the affiliated group meets such requirement.

(2) INELIGIBLE AFFILIATED GROUP.—Paragraph (1) shall not apply to an affiliated group of corporations if—

(A) any member of the affiliated group of corporations (including the common parent corporation) derived 10 percent or more of its adjusted ordinary gross income for the taxable year from sources outside the affiliated group, and

(B) 80 percent or more of the amount described in subparagraph (A) consists of personal holding company income (as defined in section 543).

For purposes of this paragraph, section 543 shall be applied as if the amount described in subparagraph (A) were the adjusted ordinary gross income of the corporation.

(3) EXCLUDED CORPORATIONS.—Paragraph (1) shall not apply to an affiliated group of corporations if any member of the affiliated group (including the common parent corporation) is a corporation excluded from the definition of personal holding company under subsection (c).

(4) CERTAIN DIVIDEND INCOME RECEIVED BY A COMMON PARENT.—In applying paragraph (2) (A) and (B), personal holding company income and adjusted ordinary gross income shall not include dividends received by a common parent corporation from another corporation if—

(A) the common parent corporation owns, directly or indirectly, more than 50 percent of the outstanding voting stock of such other corporation, and

(B) such other corporation is not a personal holding company for the taxable year in which the dividends are paid.

* * *

[Sec. 542(c)]

(c) EXCEPTIONS.—The term "personal holding company" as defined in subsection (a) does not include—

(1) a corporation exempt from tax under subchapter F (sec. 501 and following);

(2) a bank as defined in section 581, or a domestic building and loan association within the meaning of section 7701(a)(19);

(3) a life insurance company;

(4) a surety company;

(5) a foreign corporation;

(6) a lending or finance company if—

(A) 60 percent or more of its ordinary gross income (as defined in section 543(b)(1)) is derived directly from the active and regular conduct of a lending or finance business;

(B) the personal holding company income for the taxable year (computed without regard to income described in subsection (d)(3) and income derived directly from the active and regular conduct of a lending or finance business, and computed by including as personal holding company income the entire amount of the gross income from rents, royalties, produced film rents, and compensation for use of corporate property by shareholders) is not more than 20 percent of the ordinary gross income;

(C) the sum of the deductions which are directly allocable to the active and regular conduct of its lending or finance business equals or exceeds the sum of—

(i) 15 percent of so much of the ordinary gross income derived therefrom as does not exceed $500,000, plus

(ii) 5 percent of so much of the ordinary gross income derived therefrom as exceeds $500,000; and

(D) the loans to a person who is a shareholder in such company during the taxable year by or for whom 10 percent or more in value of its outstanding stock is owned directly or indirectly (including, in the case of an individual, stock owned by members of his family as defined in section 544(a)(2)), outstanding at any time during such year do not exceed $5,000 in principal amount;

(7) a small business investment company which is licensed by the Small Business Administration and operating under the Small Business Investment Act of 1958 (15 U.S.C. 661 and following) and which is actively engaged in the business of providing funds to small business concerns under that Act. This paragraph shall not apply if any shareholder of the small business investment company owns at any time during the taxable year directly or indirectly (including, in the case of an individual, ownership by the members of his family as defined in section 544(a)(2)) a 5 per centum or more proprietary interest in a small business concern to which funds are provided by the investment company or 5 per centum or more in value of the outstanding stock of such concern; and

(8) a corporation which is subject to the jurisdiction of the court in a title 11 or similar case (within the meaning of section 368(a)(3)(A)) unless a major purpose of instituting or continuing such case is the avoidance of the tax imposed by section 541.

* * *

[Sec. 543]

SEC. 543. PERSONAL HOLDING COMPANY INCOME.

[Sec. 543(a)]

(a) GENERAL RULE.—For purposes of this subtitle, the term "personal holding company income" means the portion of the adjusted ordinary gross income which consists of:

(1) DIVIDENDS, ETC.—Dividends, interest, royalties (other than mineral, oil, or gas royalties or copyright royalties), and annuities. This paragraph shall not apply to—

(A) interest constituting rent (as defined in subsection (b)(3)),

(B) interest on amounts set aside in a reserve fund under chapter 533 or 535 of title 46, United States Code,

(C) dividends received by a United States shareholder (as defined in section 951(b)) from a controlled foreign corporation (as defined in section 957(a)),

(D) active business computer software royalties (within the meaning of subsection (d)), and

(E) interest received by a broker or dealer (within the meaning of section 3(a)(4) or (5) of the Securities and Exchange Act of 1934) in connection with—

(i) any securities or money market instruments held as property described in section 1221(a)(1),

(ii) margin accounts, or

(iii) any financing for a customer secured by securities or money market instruments.

(2) RENTS.—The adjusted income from rents; except that such adjusted income shall not be included if—

(A) such adjusted income constitutes 50 percent or more of the adjusted ordinary gross income, and

(B) the sum of—

(i) the dividends paid during the taxable year (determined under section 562),

(ii) the dividends considered as paid on the last day of the taxable year under section 563(c) (as limited by the second sentence of section 563(b)), and

(iii) the consent dividends for the taxable year (determined under section 565),

equals or exceeds the amount, if any, by which the personal holding company income for the taxable year (computed without regard to this paragraph and paragraph (6), and computed by including as personal holding company income copyright royalties and the adjusted income from mineral, oil, and gas royalties) exceeds 10 percent of the ordinary gross income.

(3) MINERAL, OIL, AND GAS ROYALTIES.—The adjusted income from mineral, oil, and gas royalties; except that such adjusted income shall not be included if—

(A) such adjusted income constitutes 50 percent or more of the adjusted ordinary gross income,

(B) the personal holding company income for the taxable year (computed without regard to this paragraph, and computed by including as personal holding company income copyright royalties and the adjusted income from rents) is not more than 10 percent of the ordinary gross income, and

(C) the sum of the deductions which are allowable under section 162 (relating to trade or business expenses) other than—

(i) deductions for compensation for personal services rendered by the shareholders, and

(ii) deductions which are specifically allowable under sections other than section 162,

equals or exceeds 15 percent of the adjusted ordinary gross income.

(4) COPYRIGHT ROYALTIES.—Copyright royalties; except that copyright royalties shall not be included if—

(A) such royalties (exclusive of royalties received for the use of, or right to use, copyrights or interests in copyrights on works created in whole, or in part, by any shareholder) constitute 50 percent or more of the ordinary gross income,

(B) the personal holding company income for the taxable year computed—

(i) without regard to copyright royalties, other than royalties received for the use of, or right to use, copyrights or interests in copyrights in works created in whole, or in part, by any shareholder owning more than 10 percent of the total outstanding capital stock of the corporation,

(ii) without regard to dividends from any corporation in which the taxpayer owns at least 50 percent of all classes of stock entitled to vote and at least 50 percent of the total value of all classes of stock and which corporation meets the requirements of this subparagraph and subparagraphs (A) and (C), and

(iii) by including as personal holding company income the adjusted income from rents and the adjusted income from mineral, oil, and gas royalties,

is not more than 10 percent of the ordinary gross income, and

(C) the sum of the deductions which are properly allocable to such royalties and which are allowable under section 162, other than—

(i) deductions for compensation for personal services rendered by the shareholders,

(ii) deductions for royalties paid or accrued, and

(iii) deductions which are specifically allowable under sections other than section 162,

equals or exceeds 25 percent of the amount by which the ordinary gross income exceeds the sum of the royalties paid or accrued and the amounts allowable as deductions under section 167 (relating to depreciation) with respect to copyright royalties.

For purposes of this subsection, the term "copyright royalties" means compensation, however designated, for the use of, or the right to use, copyrights in works protected by copyright issued under title 17 of the United States Code and to which copyright protection is also extended by the laws of any country other than the United States of America by virtue of any international treaty, convention, or agreement, or interests in any such copyrighted works, and includes payments from any person for performing rights in any such copyrighted work and payments (other than produced film rents as defined in paragraph (5)(B)) received for the use of, or right to use, films. For purposes of this paragraph, the term "shareholder" shall include any person who owns stock within the meaning of section 544. This paragraph shall not apply to active business computer software royalties.

(5) PRODUCED FILM RENTS.—

(A) Produced film rents; except that such rents shall not be included if such rents constitute 50 percent or more of the ordinary gross income.

(B) For purposes of this section, the term "produced film rents" means payments received with respect to an interest in a film for the use of, or right to use, such film, but only to the extent that such interest was acquired before substantial completion of production of such film. In the case of a producer who actively participates in the production of the film, such term includes an interest in the proceeds or profits from the film, but only to the extent such interest is attributable to such active participation.

(6) USE OF CORPORATE PROPERTY BY SHAREHOLDER.—

(A) Amounts received as compensation (however designated and from whomever received) for the use of, or the right to use, tangible property of the corporation in any case where, at any time during the taxable year, 25 percent or more in value of the outstanding stock of the corporation is owned, directly or indirectly, by or for an individual entitled to the use of the property (whether such right is obtained directly from the corporation or by means of a sublease or other arrangement).

(B) Subparagraph (A) shall apply only to a corporation which has personal holding company income in excess of 10 percent of its ordinary gross income.

(C) For purposes of the limitation in subparagraph (B), personal holding company income shall be computed—

(i) without regard to subparagraph (A) or paragraph (2),

(ii) by excluding amounts received as compensation for the use of (or right to use) intangible property (other than mineral, oil, or gas royalties or copyright royalties) if a substantial part of the tangible property used in connection with such intangible property is owned by the corporation and all such tangible and intangible property is used in the active conduct of a trade or business by an individual or individuals described in subparagraph (A), and

(iii) by including copyright royalties and adjusted income from mineral, oil, and gas royalties.

(7) PERSONAL SERVICE CONTRACTS.—

(A) Amounts received under a contract under which the corporation is to furnish personal services; if some person other than the corporation has the right to designate (by name or by description) the individual who is to perform the services, or if the individual who is to perform the services is designated (by name or by description) in the contract; and

(B) amounts received from the sale or other disposition of such a contract.

This paragraph shall apply with respect to amounts received for services under a particular contract only if at some time during the taxable year 25 percent or more in value of the outstanding stock of the corporation is owned, directly or indirectly, by or for the individual who has performed, is to perform, or may be designated (by name or by description) as the one to perform, such services.

(8) ESTATES AND TRUSTS.—Amounts includible in computing the taxable income of the corporation under part I of subchapter J (sec. 641 and following, relating to estates, trusts, and beneficiaries).

[Sec. 543(b)]

(b) DEFINITIONS.—For purposes of this part—

(1) ORDINARY GROSS INCOME.—The term "ordinary gross income" means the gross income determined by excluding—

(A) all gains from the sale or other disposition of capital assets, and

(B) all gains (other than those referred to in subparagraph (A)) from the sale or other disposition of property described in section 1231(b).

(2) ADJUSTED ORDINARY GROSS INCOME.—The term "adjusted ordinary gross income" means the ordinary gross income adjusted as follows:

(A) RENTS.—From the gross income from rents (as defined in the second sentence of paragraph (3) of this subsection) subtract the amount allowable as deductions for—

(i) exhaustion, wear and tear, obsolescence, and amortization of property other than tangible personal property which is not customarily retained by any one lessee for more than three years,

(ii) property taxes,

(iii) interest, and

(iv) rent,

to the extent allocable, under regulations prescribed by the Secretary, to such gross income from rents. The amount subtracted under this subparagraph shall not exceed such gross income from rents.

(B) MINERAL ROYALTIES, ETC.—From the gross income from mineral, oil, and gas royalties described in paragraph (4), and from the gross income from working interests in an oil or gas well, subtract the amount allowable as deductions for—

(i) exhaustion, wear and tear, obsolescence, amortization, and depletion,

(ii) property and severance taxes,

(iii) interest, and

(iv) rent,

to the extent allocable, under regulations prescribed by the Secretary, to such gross income from royalties or such gross income from working interests in oil or gas wells. The amount subtracted under this subparagraph with respect to royalties shall not exceed the gross income from such royalties, and the amount subtracted under this subparagraph with respect to working interests shall not exceed the gross income from such working interests.

(C) INTEREST.—There shall be excluded—

(i) interest received on a direct obligation of the United States held for sale to customers in the ordinary course of trade or business by a regular dealer who is making a primary market in such obligations, and

(ii) interest on a condemnation award, a judgment, and a tax refund.

(D) CERTAIN EXCLUDED RENTS.—From the gross income consisting of compensation described in subparagraph (D) of paragraph (3) subtract the amount allowable as deductions for the items described in clauses (i), (ii), (iii), and (iv) of subparagraph (A) to the extent allocable, under regulations prescribed by the Secretary, to such gross income. The amount subtracted under this subparagraph shall not exceed such gross income.

(3) ADJUSTED INCOME FROM RENTS.—The term "adjusted income from rents" means the gross income from rents, reduced by the amount subtracted under paragraph (2)(A) of this subsection. For purposes of the preceding sentence, the term "rents" means compensation, however designated, for the use of, or right to use, property, and the interest on debts owed to the corporation, to the extent such debts represent the price for which real property held primarily for sale to customers in the ordinary course of its trade or business was sold or exchanged by the corporation; but such term does not include—

(A) amounts constituting personal holding company income under subsection (a)(6),

(B) copyright royalties (as defined in subsection (a)(4)),

(C) produced film rents (as defined in subsection (a)(5)(B)),

(D) compensation, however designated, for the use of, or the right to use, any tangible personal property manufactured or produced by the taxpayer, if during the taxable year the taxpayer is engaged in substantial manufacturing or production of tangible personal property of the same type, or

(E) active business computer software royalties (as defined in subsection (d)).

(4) ADJUSTED INCOME FROM MINERAL, OIL, AND GAS ROYALTIES.—The term "adjusted income from mineral, oil, and gas royalties" means the gross income from mineral, oil, and gas royalties (including production payments and overriding royalties), reduced by the amount subtracted under paragraph (2)(B) of this subsection in respect of such royalties.

* * *

[Sec. 544]

SEC. 544. RULES FOR DETERMINING STOCK OWNERSHIP.

[Sec. 544(a)]

(a) CONSTRUCTIVE OWNERSHIP.—For purposes of determining whether a corporation is a personal holding company, insofar as such determination is based on stock ownership under section 542(a)(2), section 543(a)(7), section 543(a)(6) or section 543(a)(4)—

(1) STOCK NOT OWNED BY INDIVIDUAL.—Stock owned, directly or indirectly, by or for a corporation, partnership, estate, or trust shall be considered as being owned proportionately by its shareholders, partners, or beneficiaries.

(2) FAMILY AND PARTNERSHIP OWNERSHIP.—An individual shall be considered as owning the stock owned, directly or indirectly, by or for his family or by or for his partner. For purposes of this paragraph, the family of an individual includes only his brothers and sisters (whether by the whole or half blood), spouse, ancestors, and lineal descendants.

(3) OPTIONS.—If any person has an option to acquire stock, such stock shall be considered as owned by such person. For purposes of this paragraph, an option to acquire such an option, and each one of a series of such options, shall be considered as an option to acquire such stock.

(4) APPLICATION OF FAMILY-PARTNERSHIP AND OPTION RULES.—Paragraphs (2) and (3) shall be applied—

(A) for purposes of the stock ownership requirement provided in section 542(a)(2), if, but only if, the effect is to make the corporation a personal holding company;

(B) for purposes of section 543(a)(7) (relating to personal service contracts), of section 543(a)(6) (relating to the use of property by shareholders), or of section 543(a)(4) (relating to copyright royalties), if, but only if, the effect is to make the amounts therein referred to includible under such paragraph as personal holding company income.

(5) CONSTRUCTIVE OWNERSHIP AS ACTUAL OWNERSHIP.—Stock constructively owned by a person by reason of the application of paragraph (1) or (3) shall, for purposes of applying paragraph (1) or (2), be treated as actually owned by such person; but stock constructively owned by an individual by reason of the application of paragraph (2) shall not be treated as owned by him for purposes of again applying such paragraph in order to make another the constructive owner of such stock.

(6) OPTION RULE IN LIEU OF FAMILY AND PARTNERSHIP RULE.—If stock may be considered as owned by an individual under either paragraph (2) or (3) it shall be considered as owned by him under paragraph (3).

[Sec. 544(b)]

(b) CONVERTIBLE SECURITIES.—Outstanding securities convertible into stock (whether or not convertible during the taxable year) shall be considered as outstanding stock—

(1) for purposes of the stock ownership requirement provided in section 542(a)(2), but only if the effect of the inclusion of all such securities is to make the corporation a personal holding company;

(2) for purposes of section 543(a)(7) (relating to personal service contracts), but only if the effect of the inclusion of all such securities is to make the amounts therein referred to includible under such paragraph as personal holding company income;

(3) for purposes of section 543(a)(6) (relating to the use of property by shareholders), but only if the effect of the inclusion of all such securities is to make the amounts therein referred to includible under such paragraph as personal holding company income; and

(4) for purposes of section 543(a)(4) (relating to copyright royalties), but only if the effect of the inclusion of all such securities is to make the amounts therein referred to includible under such paragraph as personal holding company income.

The requirement in paragraphs (1), (2), (3), and (4) that all convertible securities must be included if any are to be included shall be subject to the exception that, where some of the outstanding securities are convertible only after a later date than in the case of others, the class having the earlier conversion date may be included although the others are not included, but no convertible securities shall be included unless all outstanding securities having a prior conversion date are also included.

[Sec. 545]

SEC. 545. UNDISTRIBUTED PERSONAL HOLDING COMPANY INCOME.

[Sec. 545(a)]

(a) DEFINITION.—For purposes of this part, the term "undistributed personal holding company income" means the taxable income of a personal holding company adjusted in the manner provided in subsections (b), (c), and (d), minus the dividends paid deduction as defined in section 561. In the case of a personal holding company which is a foreign corporation, not more than 10 percent in value of the outstanding stock of which is owned (within the meaning of section 958(a)) during the last half of the taxable year by United States persons, the term "undistributed personal holding company income" means the amount determined by multiplying the undistributed personal holding company income (determined without regard to this sentence) by the percentage in value of its outstanding stock which is the greatest percentage in value of its outstanding stock so owned by United States persons on any one day during such period.

[Sec. 545(b)]

(b) ADJUSTMENTS TO TAXABLE INCOME.—For the purposes of subsection (a), the taxable income shall be adjusted as follows:

(1) TAXES.—There shall be allowed as a deduction Federal income and excess profits taxes and income, war profits and excess profits taxes of foreign countries and possessions of the United States (to the extent not allowable as a deduction under section 275(a)(4)), accrued during the taxable year or deemed to be paid by a domestic corporation under section 960 for the taxable year, but not including the accumulated earnings tax imposed by section 531 or the personal holding company tax imposed by section 541.

(2) CHARITABLE CONTRIBUTIONS.—The deduction for charitable contributions provided under section 170 shall be allowed, but in computing such deduction the limitations in section 170(b)(1)(A), (B), and (D) shall apply, and section 170(b)(2) and (d)(1) shall not apply. For purposes of this paragraph, the term "contribution base" when used in section 170(b)(1) means the taxable income computed with the adjustments (other than the 10-percent limitation) provided in section 170(b)(2) and (d)(1) and without deduction of the amount disallowed under paragraph (6) of this subsection.

(3) SPECIAL DEDUCTIONS DISALLOWED.—The special deductions for corporations provided in part VIII (except section 248) of subchapter B (section 241 and following, relating to the deduction for dividends received by corporations, etc.) shall not be allowed.

(4) NET OPERATING LOSS.—The net operating loss deduction provided in section 172 shall not be allowed, but there shall be allowed as a deduction the amount of the net operating loss (as defined in section 172 (c)) for the preceding taxable year computed without the deductions provided in part VIII (except section 248) of subchapter B.

(5) NET CAPITAL GAINS.—There shall be allowed as a deduction the net capital gain for the taxable year, minus the taxes imposed by this subtitle attributable to such excess. The taxes attributable to such net capital gain shall be an amount equal to the difference between—

(A) the taxes imposed by this subtitle (except the tax imposed by this part) for such year, and

(B) such taxes computed for such year without including such net capital gain in taxable income.

(6) EXPENSES AND DEPRECIATION APPLICABLE TO PROPERTY OF THE TAXPAYER.—The aggregate of the deductions allowed under section 162 (relating to trade or business expenses) and section 167 (relating to depreciation), which are allocable to the operation and maintenance of property owned or operated by the corporation, shall be allowed only in an amount equal to the rent or other compensation received for the use of, or the right to use, the property, unless it is established (under regulations prescribed by the Secretary) to the satisfaction of the Secretary—

(A) that the rent or other compensation received was the highest obtainable, or, if none was received, that none was obtainable;

(B) that the property was held in the course of a business carried on bona fide for profit; and

(C) either that there was reasonable expectation that the operation of the property would result in a profit, or that the property was necessary to the conduct of the business.

* * *

[Sec. 546]

SEC. 546. INCOME NOT PLACED ON ANNUAL BASIS.

Section 443 (b) (relating to computation of tax on change of annual accounting period) shall not apply in the computation of the personal holding company tax imposed by section 541.

[Sec. 547]

SEC. 547. DEDUCTION FOR DEFICIENCY DIVIDENDS.

[Sec. 547(a)]

(a) GENERAL RULE.—If a determination (as defined in subsection (c)) with respect to a taxpayer establishes liability for personal holding company tax imposed by section 541 (or by a corresponding provision of a prior income tax law) for any taxable year, a deduction shall be allowed to the taxpayer for the amount of deficiency dividends (as defined in subsection (d)) for the purpose of determining the personal holding company tax for such year, but not for the purpose of determining interest, additional amounts, or assessable penalties computed with respect to such personal holding company tax.

[Sec. 547(b)]

(b) RULES FOR APPLICATION OF SECTION.—

(1) ALLOWANCE OF DEDUCTION.—The deficiency dividend deduction shall be allowed as of the date the claim for the deficiency dividend deduction is filed.

(2) CREDIT OR REFUND.—If the allowance of a deficiency dividend deduction results in an overpayment of personal holding company tax for any taxable year, credit or refund with respect to such overpayment shall be made as if on the date of the determination 2 years remained before the expiration of the period of limitation on the filing of claim for refund for the taxable year to which the overpayment relates. No interest shall be allowed on a credit or refund arising from the application of this section.

[Sec. 547(c)]

(c) DETERMINATION.—For purposes of this section, the term “determination” means—

(1) a decision by the Tax Court or a judgment, decree, or other order by any court of competent jurisdiction, which has become final;

(2) a closing agreement made under section 7121; or

(3) under regulations prescribed by the Secretary, an agreement signed by the Secretary and by, or on behalf of, the taxpayer relating to the liability of such taxpayer for personal holding company tax.

[Sec. 547(d)]

(d) DEFICIENCY DIVIDENDS.—

(1) DEFINITION.—For purposes of this section, the term “deficiency dividends” means the amount of the dividends paid by the corporation on or after the date of the determination and before filing claim under subsection (e), which would have been includible in the computation of the deduction for dividends paid under section 561 for the taxable year with respect to which the liability for personal holding company tax exists, if distributed during such taxable year. No dividends shall be considered as deficiency dividends for purposes of subsection (a) unless distributed within 90 days after the determination.

(2) EFFECT ON DIVIDENDS PAID DEDUCTION.—

(A) FOR TAXABLE YEAR IN WHICH PAID.—Deficiency dividends paid in any taxable year (to the extent of the portion thereof taken into account under subsection (a) in determining personal holding company tax) shall not be included in the amount of dividends paid for such year for purposes of computing the dividends paid deduction for such year and succeeding years.

(B) FOR PRIOR TAXABLE YEAR.—Deficiency dividends paid in any taxable year (to the extent of the portion thereof taken into account under subsection (a) in determining personal holding company tax) shall not be allowed for purposes of section 563 (b) in the computation of the dividends paid deduction for the taxable year preceding the taxable year in which paid.

[Sec. 547(e)]

(e) CLAIM REQUIRED.—No deficiency dividend deduction shall be allowed under subsection (a) unless (under regulations prescribed by the Secretary) claim therefor is filed within 120 days after the determination.

[Sec. 547(f)]

(f) SUSPENSION OF STATUTE OF LIMITATIONS AND STAY OF COLLECTION.—

(1) SUSPENSION OF RUNNING OF STATUTE.—If the corporation files a claim, as provided in subsection (e), the running of the statute of limitations provided in section 6501 on the making of assessments, and the bringing of distraint or a proceeding in court for collection, in respect of the deficiency and all interest, additional amounts, or assessable penalties, shall be suspended for a period of 2 years after the date of the determination.

(2) STAY OF COLLECTION.—In the case of any deficiency with respect to the tax imposed by section 541 established by a determination under this section—

(A) the collection of the deficiency and all interest, additional amounts, and assessable penalties shall, except in cases of jeopardy, be stayed until the expiration of 120 days after the date of the determination, and

(B) if claim for deficiency dividend deduction is filed under subsection (e), the collection of such part of the deficiency as is not reduced by the deduction for deficiency dividends provided in subsection (a) shall be stayed until the date the claim is disallowed (in whole or in part), and if disallowed in part collection shall be made only with respect to the part disallowed.

No distraint or proceeding in court shall be begun for the collection of an amount the collection of which is stayed under subparagraph (A) or (B) during the period for which the collection of such amount is stayed.

[Sec. 547(g)]

(g) DEDUCTION DENIED IN CASE OF FRAUD, ETC.—No deficiency dividend deduction shall be allowed under subsection (a) if the determination contains a finding that any part of the deficiency is due to fraud with intent to evade tax, or to wilful failure to file an income tax return within the time prescribed by law or prescribed by the Secretary in pursuance of law.

PART IV—DEDUCTION FOR DIVIDENDS PAID

[Sec. 561]

SEC. 561. DEFINITION OF DEDUCTION FOR DIVIDENDS PAID.

[Sec. 561(a)]

(a) GENERAL RULE.—The deduction for dividends paid shall be the sum of—

(1) the dividends paid during the taxable year,

(2) the consent dividends for the taxable year (determined under section 565), and

(3) in the case of a personal holding company, the dividend carryover described in section 564.

[Sec. 561(b)]

(b) SPECIAL RULES APPLICABLE.—In determining the deduction for dividends paid, the rules provided in section 562 (relating to rules applicable in determining dividends eligible for dividends paid deduction) and section 563 (relating to dividends paid after the close of the taxable year) shall be applicable.

[Sec. 562]

SEC. 562. RULES APPLICABLE IN DETERMINING DIVIDENDS ELIGIBLE FOR DIVIDENDS PAID DEDUCTION.

[Sec. 562(a)]

(a) GENERAL RULE.—For purposes of this part, the term "dividend" shall, except as otherwise provided in this section, include only dividends described in section 316 (relating to definition of dividends for purposes of corporate distributions).

[Sec. 562(b)]

(b) DISTRIBUTIONS IN LIQUIDATION.—

(1) Except in the case of a personal holding company described in section 542—

(A) in the case of amounts distributed in liquidation, the part of such distribution which is properly chargeable to earnings and profits accumulated after February 28, 1913, shall be treated as a dividend for purposes of computing the dividends paid deduction, and

(B) in the case of a complete liquidation occurring within 24 months after the adoption of a plan of liquidation, any distribution within such period pursuant to such plan shall, to the extent of the earnings and profits (computed without regard to capital losses) of the corporation for the taxable year in which such distribution is made, be treated as a dividend for purposes of computing the dividends paid deduction.

For purposes of subparagraph (A), a liquidation includes a redemption of stock to which section 302 applies. Except to the extent provided in regulations, the preceding sentence shall not apply in the case of any mere holding or investment company which is not a regulated investment company.

(2) In the case of a complete liquidation of a personal holding company occurring within 24 months after the adoption of a plan of liquidation, the amount of any distribution within such period pursuant to such plan shall be treated as a dividend for purposes of computing the dividends paid deduction, to the extent that such amount is distributed to corporate distributees and represents such corporate distributees' allocable share of the undistributed personal holding company income for the taxable year of such distribution computed without regard to this paragraph and without regard to subparagraph (B) of section 316(b)(2).

[Sec. 562(c)]

(c) PREFERENTIAL DIVIDENDS.—

(1) IN GENERAL.—Except in the case of a publicly offered regulated investment company (as defined in section 67(c)(2)(B)) or a publicly offered REIT, the amount of any distribution shall not be considered as a dividend for purposes of computing the dividends paid deduction, unless such distribution is pro rata, with no preference to any share of stock as compared with other shares of the same class, and with no preference to one class of stock as compared with another class except to the extent that the former is entitled (without reference to waivers of their rights by shareholders) to such preference. In the case of a distribution by a regulated investment company (other than a publicly offered regulated investment company (as so defined)) to a shareholder who made an initial investment of at least $10,000,000 in such company, such distribution shall not be treated as not being pro rata or as being preferential solely by reason of an increase in the distribution by reason of reductions in administrative expenses of the company.

(2) PUBLICLY OFFERED REIT.—For purposes of this subsection, the term "publicly offered REIT" means a real estate investment trust which is required to file annual and periodic reports with the Securities and Exchange Commission under the Securities Exchange Act of 1934.

[Sec. 562(d)]

(d) DISTRIBUTIONS BY A MEMBER OF AN AFFILIATED GROUP.—In the case where a corporation which is a member of an affiliated group of corporations filing or required to file a consolidated return for a taxable year is required to file a separate personal holding company schedule for such taxable year, a distribution by such corporation to another member of the affiliated group shall be considered as a dividend for purposes of computing the dividends paid deduction if such distribution would constitute a dividend under the other provisions of this section to a recipient which is not a member of an affiliated group.

* * *

[Sec. 563]

SEC. 563. RULES RELATING TO DIVIDENDS PAID AFTER CLOSE OF TAXABLE YEAR.

[Sec. 563(a)]

(a) ACCUMULATED EARNINGS TAX.—In the determination of the dividends paid deduction for purposes of the accumulated earnings tax imposed by section 531, a dividend paid after the close of any taxable year and on or before the 15th day of the fourth month following the close of such taxable year shall be considered as paid during such taxable year.

[Sec. 563(b)]

(b) PERSONAL HOLDING COMPANY TAX.—In the determination of the dividends paid deduction for purposes of the personal holding company tax imposed by section 541, a dividend paid after the close of any taxable year and on or before the 15th day of the fourth month following the close of such taxable year shall, to the extent the taxpayer elects in its return for the taxable year, be considered as paid during such taxable year. The amount allowed as a dividend by reason of the application of this subsection with respect to any taxable year shall not exceed either—

(1) The undistributed personal holding company income of the corporation for the taxable year, computed without regard to this subsection, or

(2) 20 percent of the sum of the dividends paid during the taxable year, computed without regard to this subsection.

[Sec. 563(c)]

(c) DIVIDENDS CONSIDERED AS PAID ON LAST DAY OF TAXABLE YEAR.—For the purpose of applying section 562(a), with respect to distributions under subsection (a) or (b) of this section, a distribution made after the close of a taxable year and on or before the 15th day of the fourth month following the close of the taxable year shall be considered as made on the last day of such taxable year.

[Sec. 564]

SEC. 564. DIVIDEND CARRYOVER.

[Sec. 564(a)]

(a) GENERAL RULE.—For purposes of computing the dividends paid deduction under section 561, in the case of a personal holding company the dividend carryover for any taxable year shall be the dividend carryover to such taxable year, computed as provided in subsection (b), from the two preceding taxable years.

[Sec. 564(b)]

(b) COMPUTATION OF DIVIDEND CARRYOVER.—The dividend carryover to the taxable year shall be determined as follows:

(1) For each of the 2 preceding taxable years there shall be determined the taxable income computed with the adjustments provided in section 545 (whether or not the taxpayer was a personal holding company for either of such preceding taxable years), and there shall also be determined for each such year the deduction for dividends paid during such year as provided in section 561 (but determined without regard to the dividend carryover to such year).

(2) There shall be determined for each such taxable year whether there is an excess of such taxable income over such deduction for dividends paid or an excess of such deduction for dividends paid over such taxable income, and the amount of each such excess.

(3) If there is an excess of such deductions for dividends paid over such taxable income for the first preceding taxable year, such excess shall be allowed as a dividend carryover to the taxable year.

(4) If there is an excess of such deduction for dividends paid over such taxable income for the second preceding taxable year, such excess shall be reduced by the amount determined in paragraph (5), and the remainder of such excess shall be allowed as a dividend carryover to the taxable year.

(5) The amount of the reduction specified in paragraph (4) shall be the amount of the excess of the taxable income, if any, for the first preceding taxable year over such deduction for dividends paid, if any, for the first preceding taxable year.

[Sec. 565]

SEC. 565. CONSENT DIVIDENDS.

[Sec. 565(a)]

(a) GENERAL RULE.—If any person owns consent stock (as defined in subsection (f)(1)) in a corporation on the last day of the taxable year of such corporation, and such person agrees, in a consent filed with the return of such corporation in accordance with regulations prescribed by the Secretary, to treat as a dividend the amount specified in such consent, the amount so specified shall, except as provided in subsection (b), constitute a consent dividend for purposes of section 561 (relating to the deduction for dividends paid).

[Sec. 565(b)]

(b) LIMITATIONS.—A consent dividend shall not include—

(1) an amount specified in a consent which, if distributed in money, would constitute, or be part of, a distribution which would be disqualified for purposes of the dividends paid deduction under section 562(c) (relating to preferential dividends), or

(2) an amount specified in a consent which would not constitute a dividend (as defined in section 316) if the total amounts specified in consents filed by the corporation had been distributed in money to shareholders on the last day of the taxable year of such corporation.

[Sec. 565(c)]

(c) EFFECT OF CONSENT.—The amount of a consent dividend shall be considered, for purposes of this title—

(1) as distributed in money by the corporation to the shareholder on the last day of the taxable year of the corporation, and

(2) as contributed to the capital of the corporation by the shareholder on such day.

[Sec. 565(d)]

(d) CONSENT DIVIDENDS AND OTHER DISTRIBUTIONS.—If a distribution by a corporation consists in part of money or other property, the entire amount specified in the consents and the amount of such money or other property shall be considered together for purposes of applying this title.

* * *

[Sec. 565(f)]

(f) DEFINITIONS.—

(1) CONSENT STOCK.—Consent stock, for purposes of this section, means the class or classes of stock entitled, after the payment of preferred dividends, to a share in the distribution (other than in complete or partial liquidation) within the taxable year of all the remaining earnings and profits, which share constitutes the same proportion of such distribution regardless of the amount of such distribution.

(2) PREFERRED DIVIDENDS.—Preferred dividends, for purposes of this section, means a distribution (other than in complete or partial liquidation), limited in amount, which must be made on any class of stock before a further distribution (other than in complete or partial liquidation) of earnings and profits may be made within the taxable year.

SUBCHAPTER I—NATURAL RESOURCES

PART I—DEDUCTIONS

[Sec. 611]

SEC. 611. ALLOWANCE OF DEDUCTION FOR DEPLETION.

[Sec. 611(a)]

(a) GENERAL RULE.—In the case of mines, oil and gas wells, other natural deposits, and timber, there shall be allowed as a deduction in computing taxable income a reasonable allowance for depletion and for depreciation of improvements, according to the peculiar conditions in each case; such reasonable allowance in all cases to be made under regulations prescribed by Secretary. For purposes of this part, the term "mines" includes deposits of waste or residue, the extraction of ores or minerals from which is treated as mining under section 613(c). In any case in which it is ascertained as a result of operations or of development work that the recoverable units are greater or less than the prior estimate thereof, then such prior estimate (but not the basis for depletion) shall be revised and the allowance under this section for subsequent taxable years shall be based on such revised estimate.

[Sec. 611(b)]

(b) SPECIAL RULES.—

(1) LEASES.—In the case of a lease, the deduction under this section shall be equitably apportioned between the lessor and lessee.

(2) LIFE TENANT AND REMAINDERMAN.—In the case of property held by one person for life with remainder to another person, the deduction under this section shall be computed as if the life tenant were the absolute owner of the property and shall be allowed to the life tenant.

(3) PROPERTY HELD IN TRUST.—In the case of property held in trust, the deduction under this section shall be apportioned between the income beneficiaries and the trustee in accordance with the pertinent provisions of the instrument creating the trust, or, in the absence of such provisions, on the basis of the trust income allocable to each.

(4) PROPERTY HELD BY ESTATE.—In the case of an estate, the deduction under this section shall be apportioned between the estate and the heirs, legatees, and devisees on the basis of the income of the estate allocable to each.

[Sec. 611(c)]

(c) CROSS REFERENCE.—

For other rules applicable to depreciation of improvements, see section 167.

[Sec. 612]

SEC. 612. BASIS FOR COST DEPLETION.

Except as otherwise provided in this subchapter, the basis on which depletion is to be allowed in respect of any property shall be the adjusted basis provided in section 1011 for the purpose of determining the gain upon the sale or other disposition of such property.

[Sec. 613]

SEC. 613. PERCENTAGE DEPLETION.

[Sec. 613(a)]

(a) GENERAL RULE.—In the case of the mines, wells, and other natural deposits listed in subsection (b), the allowance for depletion under section 611 shall be the percentage, specified in subsection (b), of the gross income from the property excluding from such gross income an amount equal to any rents or royalties paid or incurred by the taxpayer in respect of the property. Such allowance shall not exceed 50 percent (100 percent in the case of oil and gas properties) of the taxpayer's taxable income from the property (computed without allowances for depletion and without the deduction under section 199). For purposes of the preceding sentence, the allowable deductions taken into account with respect to expenses of mining in computing the taxable income from the property shall be decreased by an amount equal to so much of any gain which (1) is treated under section 1245 (relating to gain from disposition of certain depreciable property) as ordinary income, and (2) is properly allocable to the property. In no case shall the allowance for depletion under section 611 be less than it would be if computed without reference to this section.

[Sec. 613(b)]

(b) PERCENTAGE DEPLETION RATES.—The mines, wells, and other natural deposits, and the percentages, referred to in subsection (a) are as follows:

(1) 22 PERCENT—

(A) sulphur and uranium; and

(B) if from deposits in the United States—anorthosite, clay, laterite, and nephelite syenite (to the extent that alumina and aluminum compounds are extracted therefrom), asbestos, bauxite, celestite, chromite, corundum, fluorspar, graphite, ilmenite, kyanite, mica, olivine, quartz crystals (radio grade), rutile, block steatite talc, and zircon, and ores of the following metals: antimony, beryllium, bismuth, cadmium, cobalt, columbium, lead, lithium, manganese, mercury, molybdenum, nickel, platinum and platinum group metals, tantalum, thorium, tin, titanium, tungsten, vanadium, and zinc.

(2) 15 PERCENT—If from deposits in the United States—

(A) gold, silver, copper, and iron ore, and

(B) oil shale (except shale described in paragraph (5)).

(3) 14 PERCENT—

(A) metal mines (if paragraph (1)(B) or (2)(A) does not apply), rock asphalt, and vermiculite; and

(B) if paragraph (1)(B), (5), or (6)(B) does not apply, ball clay, bentonite, china clay, sagger clay, and clay used or sold for use for purposes dependent on its refractory properties.

(4) 10 PERCENT—asbestos (if paragraph (1)(B) does not apply), brucite, coal, lignite, perlite, sodium chloride, and wollastonite.

(5) 7½ PERCENT—clay and shale used or sold for use in the manufacture of sewer pipe or brick, and clay, shale, and slate used or sold for use as sintered or burned lightweight aggregates.

(6) 5 PERCENT—

(A) gravel, peat, pumice, sand, scoria, shale (except shale described in paragraph (2)(B) or (5)), and stone (except stone described in paragraph (7));

(B) clay used, or sold for use, in the manufacture of drainage and roofing tile, flower pots, and kindred products; and

(C) if from brine wells—bromine, calcium chloride, and magnesium chloride.

(7) 14 PERCENT—all other minerals, including, but not limited to, aplite, barite, borax, calcium carbonates, diatomaceous earth, dolomite, feldspar, fullers earth, garnet, gilsonite, granite, limestone, magnesite, magnesium carbonates, marble, mollusk shells (including clam shells and oyster shells), phosphate rock, potash, quartzite, slate, soapstone, stone (used or sold for use by the mine owner or operator as dimension stone or ornamental stone), thenardite, tripoli, trona, and (if paragraph (1)(B) does not apply) bauxite, flake graphite, fluorspar, lepidolite, mica, spodumene, and talc (including pyrophyllite), except that, unless sold on bid in direct competition with a bona fide bid to sell a mineral listed in paragraph (3), the percentage shall be 5 percent for any such other mineral (other than slate to which paragraph (5) applies) when used, or sold for use, by the mine owner or operator as rip rap, ballast, road material, rubble, concrete aggregates, or for similar purposes. For purposes of this paragraph, the term "all other minerals" does not include—

(A) soil, sod, dirt, turf, water, or mosses;

(B) minerals from sea water, the air, or similar inexhaustible sources or

(C) oil and gas wells.

For the purposes of this subsection, minerals (other than sodium chloride) extracted from brines pumped from a saline perennial lake within the United States shall not be considered minerals from an inexhaustible source.

[Sec. 613(c)]

(c) DEFINITION OF GROSS INCOME FROM PROPERTY.—For purposes of this section—

(1) GROSS INCOME FROM THE PROPERTY.—The term "gross income from the property" means, in the case of a property other than an oil or gas well and other than a geothermal deposit, the gross income from mining.

(2) MINING.—The term "mining" includes not merely the extraction of the ores or minerals from the ground but also the treatment processes considered as mining described in paragraph (4) (and the treatment processes necessary or incidental thereto), and so much of the transportation of ores or minerals (whether or not by common carrier) from the point of extraction from the ground to the plants or mills in which such treatment processes are applied thereto as is not in excess of 50 miles unless the Secretary finds that the physical and other requirements are such that the ore or mineral must be transported a greater distance to such plants or mills.

(3) EXTRACTION OF THE ORES OR MINERALS FROM THE GROUND.—The term "extraction of the ores or minerals from the ground" includes the extraction by mine owners or operators of ores or minerals from the waste or residue of prior mining. The preceding sentence shall not apply to any such extraction of the mineral or ore by a purchaser of such waste or residue or of the rights to extract ores or minerals therefrom.

(4) TREATMENT PROCESSES CONSIDERED AS MINING.—The following treatment processes where applied by the mine owner or operator shall be considered as mining to the extent they are applied to the ore or mineral in respect of which he is entitled to a deduction for depletion under section 611:

(A) In the case of coal—cleaning, breaking, sizing, dust allaying, treating to prevent freezing, and loading for shipment;

(B) in the case of sulfur recovered by the Frasch process—cleaning, pumping to vats, cooling, breaking, and loading for shipment;

(C) in the case of iron ore, bauxite, ball and sagger clay, rock asphalt, and ores or minerals which are customarily sold in the form of a crude mineral product—sorting, concentrating, sintering, and substantially equivalent processes to bring to shipping grade and form, and loading for shipment;

(D) in the case of lead, zinc, copper, gold, silver, uranium, or fluorspar ores, potash, and ores or minerals which are not customarily sold in the form of the crude mineral product—crushing, grinding, and beneficiation by concentration (gravity, flotation, amalgamation, electrostatic, or magnetic), cyanidation, leaching, crystallization, precipitation (but not including electrolytic deposition, roasting, thermal or electric smelting, or refining), or by substantially equivalent processes or combination of processes used in the separation or extraction of the product or products from the ore or the mineral or minerals from other material from the mine or other natural deposit;

(E) the pulverization of talc, the burning of magnesite, the sintering and nodulizing of phosphate rock, the decarbonation of trona, and the furnacing of quicksilver ores;

(F) in the case of calcium carbonates and other minerals when used in making cement—all processes (other than preheating of the kiln feed) applied prior to the introduction of the kiln feed into the kiln, but not including any subsequent process;

(G) in the case of clay to which paragraph (5) or (6)(B) of subsection (b) applies—crushing, grinding, and separating the mineral from waste, but not including any subsequent process;

(H) in the case of oil shale—extraction from the ground, crushing, loading into the retort, and retorting (including in situ retorting), but not hydrogenation, refining, or any other process subsequent to retorting; and

(I) any other treatment process provided for by regulations prescribed by the Secretary which, with respect to the particular ore or mineral, is not inconsistent with the preceding provisions of this paragraph.

(5) TREATMENT PROCESSES NOT CONSIDERED AS MINING.—Unless such processes are otherwise provided for in paragraph (4) (or are necessary or incidental to processes so provided for), the following processes shall not be considered as "mining": electrolytic deposition, roasting, calcining, thermal or electric smelting, refining, polishing, fine pulverization, blending with other materials, treatment effecting a chemical change, thermal action, and molding or shaping.

[Sec. 613(d)]

(d) Denial of Percentage Depletion in Case of Oil and Gas Wells.—Except as provided in Section 613A, in the case of any oil or gas well, the allowance for depletion shall be computed without reference to this section.

[Sec. 613(e)]

(e) Percentage Depletion for Geothermal Deposits.—

(1) In general.—In the case of geothermal deposits located in the United States or in a possession of the United States, for purposes of subsection (a)—

(A) such deposits shall be treated as listed in subsection (b), and

(B) 15 percent shall be deemed to be the percentage specified in subsection (b).

(2) Geothermal deposit defined.—For purposes of paragraph (1), the term "geothermal deposit" means a geothermal reservoir consisting of natural heat which is stored in rocks or in an aqueous liquid or vapor (whether or not under pressure). Such a deposit shall in no case be treated as a gas well for purposes of this section or section 613A, and this section shall not apply to a geothermal deposit which is located outside the United States or its possessions.

(3) Percentage depletion not to include lease bonuses, etc.—In the case of any geothermal deposit, the term "gross income from the property" shall, for purposes of this section, not include any amount described in section 613A(d)(5).

[Sec. 613A]

SEC. 613A. LIMITATIONS ON PERCENTAGE DEPLETION IN CASE OF OIL AND GAS WELLS.

[Sec. 613A(a)]

(a) General Rule.—Except as otherwise provided in this section, the allowance for depletion under section 611 with respect to any oil or gas well shall be computed without regard to section 613.

[Sec. 613A(b)]

(b) Exemption for Certain Domestic Gas Wells.—

(1) In general.—The allowance for depletion under section 611 shall be computed in accordance with section 613 with respect to—

(A) regulated natural gas, and

(B) natural gas sold under a fixed contract,

and 22 percent shall be deemed to be specified in subsection (b) of section 613 for purposes of subsection (a) of that section.

(2) Natural gas from geopressured brine.—The allowance for depletion under section 611 shall be computed in accordance with section 613 with respect to any qualified natural gas from geopressured brine, and 10 percent shall be deemed to be specified in subsection (b) of section 613 for purposes of subsection (a) of such section.

(3) Definitions.—For purposes of this subsection—

(A) Natural gas sold under a fixed contract.—The term "natural gas sold under a fixed contract" means domestic natural gas sold by the producer under a contract, in effect on February 1, 1975, and at all times thereafter before such sale, under which the price for such gas cannot be adjusted to reflect to any extent the increase in liabilities of the seller for tax under this chapter by reason of the repeal of percentage depletion for gas. Price increases after February 1, 1975, shall be presumed to take increases in tax liabilities into account unless the taxpayer demonstrates to the contrary by clear and convincing evidence.

(B) REGULATED NATURAL GAS.—The term "regulated natural gas" means domestic natural gas produced and sold by the producer, before July 1, 1976, subject to the jurisdiction of the Federal Power Commission, the price for which has not been adjusted to reflect to any extent the increase in liability of the seller for tax under this chapter by reason of the repeal of percentage depletion for gas. Price increases after February 1, 1975, shall be presumed to take increases in tax liabilities into account unless the taxpayer demonstrates the contrary by clear and convincing evidence.

(C) QUALIFIED NATURAL GAS FROM GEOPRESSURED BRINE.—The term "qualified natural gas from geopressured brine" means any natural gas—

(i) which is determined in accordance with section 503 of the Natural Gas Policy Act of 1978 to be produced from geopressured brine, and

(ii) which is produced from any well the drilling of which began after September 30, 1978, and before January 1, 1984.

[Sec. 613A(c)]

(c) EXEMPTION FOR INDEPENDENT PRODUCERS AND ROYALTY OWNERS.—

(1) IN GENERAL.—Except as provided in subsection (d), the allowance for depletion under section 611 shall be computed in accordance with section 613 with respect to—

(A) so much of the taxpayer's average daily production of domestic crude oil as does not exceed the taxpayer's depletable oil quantity; and

(B) so much of the taxpayer's average daily production of domestic natural gas as does not exceed the taxpayer's depletable natural gas quantity;

and 15 percent shall be deemed to be specified in subsection (b) of section 613 for purposes of subsection (a) of that section.

(2) AVERAGE DAILY PRODUCTION.—For purposes of paragraph (1)—

(A) the taxpayer's average daily production of domestic crude oil or natural gas for any taxable year, shall be determined by dividing his aggregate production of domestic crude oil or natural gas, as the case may be, during the taxable year by the number of days in such taxable year, and

(B) in the case of a taxpayer holding a partial interest in the production from any property (including an interest held in a partnership) such taxpayer's production shall be considered to be that amount of such production determined by multiplying the total production of such property by the taxpayer's percentage participation in the revenues from such property.

(3) DEPLETABLE OIL QUANTITY.—

(A) IN GENERAL.—For purposes of paragraph (1), the taxpayer's depletable oil quantity shall be equal to—

(i) the tentative quantity determined under subparagraph (B), reduced (but not below zero) by

(ii) except in the case of a taxpayer making an election under paragraph (6)(B), the taxpayer's average daily marginal production for the taxable year.

(B) TENTATIVE QUANTITY.—For purposes of subparagraph (A), the tentative quantity is 1,000 barrels.

(4) DAILY DEPLETABLE NATURAL GAS QUANTITY.—For purposes of paragraph (1), the depletable natural gas quantity of any taxpayer for any taxable year shall be equal to 6,000 cubic feet multiplied by the number of barrels of the taxpayer's depletable oil quantity to which the taxpayer elects to have this paragraph apply. The taxpayer's depletable oil quantity for any taxable year shall be reduced by the number of barrels with respect to which an election under this paragraph applies. Such election shall be made at such time and in such manner as the Secretary shall by regulations prescribe.

(5) [Stricken.]

(6) OIL AND NATURAL GAS PRODUCED FROM MARGINAL PROPERTIES.—

(A) IN GENERAL.—Except as provided in subsection (d) and subparagraph (B), the allowance for depletion under section 611 shall be computed in accordance with section 613 with respect to—

(i) so much of the taxpayer's average daily marginal production of domestic crude oil as does not exceed the taxpayer's depletable oil quantity (determined without regard to paragraph (3)(A)(ii)), and

(ii) so much of the taxpayer's average daily marginal production of domestic natural gas as does not exceed the taxpayer's depletable natural gas quantity (determined without regard to paragraph (3)(A)(ii)),

and the applicable percentage shall be deemed to be specified in subsection (b) of section 613 for purposes of subsection (a) of that section.

(B) ELECTION TO HAVE PARAGRAPH APPLY TO PRO RATA PORTION OF MARGINAL PRODUCTION.—If the taxpayer elects to have this subparagraph apply for any taxable year, the rules of subparagraph (A) shall apply to the average daily marginal production of domestic crude oil or domestic natural gas of the taxpayer to which paragraph (1) would have applied without regard to this paragraph.

(C) APPLICABLE PERCENTAGE.—For purposes of subparagraph (A), the term "applicable percentage" means the percentage (not greater than 25 percent) equal to the sum of—

(i) 15 percent, plus

(ii) 1 percentage point for each whole dollar by which $20 exceeds the reference price for crude oil for the calendar year preceding the calendar year in which the taxable year begins.

For purposes of this paragraph, the term "reference price" means, with respect to any calendar year, the reference price determined for such calendar year under section 45K(d)(2)(C).

(D) MARGINAL PRODUCTION.—The term "marginal production" means domestic crude oil or domestic natural gas which is produced during any taxable year from a property which—

(i) is a stripper well property for the calendar year in which the taxable year begins, or

(ii) is a property substantially all of the production of which during such calendar year is heavy oil.

(E) STRIPPER WELL PROPERTY.—For purposes of this paragraph, the term "stripper well property" means, with respect to any calendar year, any property with respect to which the amount determined by dividing—

(i) the average daily production of domestic crude oil and domestic natural gas from producing wells on such property for such calendar year, by

(ii) the number of such wells, is 15 barrel equivalents or less.

(F) HEAVY OIL.—For purposes of this paragraph, the term "heavy oil" means domestic crude oil produced from any property if such crude oil had a weighted average gravity of 20 degrees API or less (corrected to 60 degrees Fahrenheit).

(G) AVERAGE DAILY MARGINAL PRODUCTION.—For purposes of this subsection—

(i) the taxpayer's average daily marginal production of domestic crude oil or natural gas for any taxable year shall be determined by dividing the taxpayer's aggregate marginal production of domestic crude oil or natural gas, as the case may be, during the taxable year by the number of days in such taxable year, and

(ii) in the case of a taxpayer holding a partial interest in the production from any property (including any interest held in any partnership), such taxpayer's production shall be considered to be that amount of such production determined by multiplying the total production of such property by the taxpayer's percentage participation in the revenues from such property.

(7) SPECIAL RULES.—

(A) PRODUCTION OF CRUDE OIL IN EXCESS OF DEPLETABLE OIL QUANTITY.—If the taxpayer's average daily production of domestic crude oil exceeds his depletable oil quantity, the allowance under paragraph (1)(A) with respect to oil produced during the taxable year from each property in the United States shall be that amount which bears the same ratio to the amount of depletion which would have been allowable under section 613(a) for all of the taxpayer's oil produced from such property during the taxable year (computed as if section 613 applied to all of such production at the rate specified in paragraph (1) or (6), as the case may be) as his depletable oil quantity bears to the aggregate number of barrels representing the average daily production of domestic crude oil of the taxpayer for such year.

(B) PRODUCTION OF NATURAL GAS IN EXCESS OF DEPLETABLE NATURAL GAS QUANTITY.—If the taxpayer's average daily production of domestic natural gas exceeds his depletable natural gas quantity, the allowance under paragraph (1)(B) with respect to natural gas produced during the taxable year from each property in the United States shall be that amount which bears the same ratio to the amount of depletion which would have been allowable under section 613(a) for all of the taxpayer's natural gas produced from such property during the taxable year (computed as if section 613 applied to all of such production at the rate specified in paragraph (1) or (6), as the case may be) as the amount of his depletable natural gas quantity in cubic feet bears to the aggregate number of cubic feet representing the average daily production of domestic natural gas of the taxpayer for such year.

(C) TAXABLE INCOME FROM THE PROPERTY.—If both oil and gas are produced from the property during the taxable year, for purposes of subparagraphs (A) and (B) the taxable income from the property, in applying the taxable income limitation in section 613(a), shall be allocated between the oil production and the gas production in proportion to the gross income during the taxable year from each.

(D) PARTNERSHIPS.—In the case of a partnership, the depletion allowance shall be computed separately by the partners and not by the partnership. The partnership shall allocate to each partner his proportionate share of the adjusted basis of each partnership oil or gas property. The allocation is to be made as of the later of the date of acquisition of the oil or gas property by the partnership, or January 1, 1975. A partner's proportionate share of the adjusted basis of partnership property shall be determined in accordance with his interest in partnership capital or income and, in the case of property contributed to the partnership by a partner, section 704(c) (relating to contributed property) shall apply in determining such share. Each partner shall separately keep records of his share of the adjusted basis in each oil and gas property of the partnership, adjust such share of the adjusted basis for any depletion taken on such property, and use such adjusted basis each year in the computation of his cost depletion or in the computation of his gain or loss on the disposition of such property by the partnership. For purposes of section 732 (relating to basis of distributed property other than money), the partnership's adjusted basis in mineral property shall be an amount equal to the sum of the partners' adjusted bases in such property as determined under this paragraph.

(8) BUSINESSES UNDER COMMON CONTROL; MEMBERS OF THE SAME FAMILY.—

(A) COMPONENT MEMBERS OF CONTROLLED GROUP TREATED AS ONE TAXPAYER.—For purposes of this subsection, persons who are members of the same controlled group of corporations shall be treated as one taxpayer.

(B) AGGREGATION OF BUSINESS ENTITIES UNDER COMMON CONTROL.—If 50 percent or more of the beneficial interest in two or more corporations, trusts, or estates is owned by the same or related persons (taking into account only persons who own at least 5 percent of such beneficial interest), the tentative quantity determined under paragraph (3)(B) shall be allocated among all such entities in proportion to the respective production of domestic crude oil during the period in question by such entities.

(C) ALLOCATION AMONG MEMBERS OF THE SAME FAMILY.—In the case of individuals who are members of the same family, the tentative quantity determined under paragraph (3)(B) shall be allocated among such individuals in proportion to the respective production of domestic crude oil during the period in question by such individuals.

(D) DEFINITION AND SPECIAL RULES.—For purposes of this paragraph—

(i) the term "controlled group of corporations" has the meaning given to such term by section 1563(a), except that section 1563(b)(2) shall not apply and except that "more than 50 percent" shall be substituted for "at least 80 percent" each place it appears in section 1563(a),

(ii) a person is a related person to another person if such persons are members of the same controlled group of corporations or if the relationship between such persons would result in a disallowance of losses under section 267 or 707(b), except that for this purpose the family of an individual includes only his spouse and minor children,

(iii) the family of an individual includes only his spouse and minor children, and

(iv) each 6,000 cubic feet of domestic natural gas shall be treated as 1 barrel of domestic crude oil.

(9) SPECIAL RULE FOR FISCAL YEAR TAXPAYERS.—In applying this subsection to a taxable year which is not a calendar year, each portion of such taxable year which occurs during a single calendar year shall be treated as if it were a short taxable year.

(10) CERTAIN PRODUCTION NOT TAKEN INTO ACCOUNT.—In applying this subsection, there shall not be taken into account the production of natural gas with respect to which subsection (b) applies.

(11) SUBCHAPTER S CORPORATIONS.—

(A) COMPUTATION OF DEPLETION ALLOWANCE AT SHAREHOLDER LEVEL.—In the case of an S corporation, the allowance for depletion with respect to any oil or gas property shall be computed separately by each shareholder.

(B) ALLOCATION OF BASIS.—The S corporation shall allocate to each shareholder his pro rata share of the adjusted basis of the S corporation in each oil or gas property held by the S corporation. The allocation shall be made as of the later of the date of acquisition of the property by the S corporation, or the first day of the first taxable year of the S corporation to which the Subchapter S Revison Act of 1982 applies. Each shareholder shall separately keep records of his share of the adjusted basis in each oil and gas property of the S corporation, adjust such share of the adjusted basis for any depletion taken on such property, and use such adjusted basis each year in the computation of his cost depletion or in the computation of his gain or loss on the disposition of such property by the S corporation. In the case of any distribution of oil or gas property to its shareholders by the S corporation, the corporation's adjusted basis in the property shall be an amount equal to the sum of the shareholders' adjusted bases in such property, as determined under this subparagraph.

[Sec. 613A(d)]

(d) LIMITATIONS ON APPLICATION OF SUBSECTION (c).—

(1) LIMITATION BASED ON TAXABLE INCOME.—The deduction for the taxable year attributable to the application of subsection (c) shall not exceed 65 percent of the taxpayer's taxable income for the year computed without regard to—

(A) any depletion on production from an oil or gas property which is subject to the provisions of subsection (c),

(B) any deduction allowable under section 199A,

(C) any net operating loss carryback to the taxable year under section 172,

(D) any capital loss carryback to the taxable year under section 1212, and

(E) in the case of a trust, any distributions to its beneficiary, except in the case of any trust where any beneficiary of such trust is a member of the family (as defined in section 267(c)(4)) of a settlor who created inter vivos and testamentary trusts for members of the family and such settlor died within the last six days of the fifth month in 1970, and the law in the jurisdiction in which such trust was created requires all or a portion of the gross or net proceeds of any royalty or other interest in oil, gas, or other mineral representing any percentage depletion allowance to be allocated to the principal of the trust.

If an amount is disallowed as a deduction for the taxable year by reason of application of the preceding sentence, the disallowed amount shall be treated as an amount allowable as a deduction under subsection (c) for the following taxable year, subject to the application of the preceding sentence to such taxable year. For purposes of basis adjustments and determining whether cost depletion exceeds percentage depletion with respect to the production from a property, any amount disallowed as a deduction on the application of this paragraph shall be allocated to the respective properties from which the oil or gas was produced in proportion to the percentage depletion otherwise allowable to such properties under subsection (c).

(2) RETAILERS EXCLUDED.—Subsection (c) shall not apply in the case of any taxpayer who directly, or through a related person, sells oil or natural gas (excluding bulk sales of such items to commercial or industrial users), or any product derived from oil or natural gas (excluding bulk sales of aviation fuels to the Department of Defense)—

(A) through any retail outlet operated by the taxpayer or a related person, or

(B) to any person—

(i) obligated under an agreement or contract with the taxpayer or a related person to use a trademark, trade name, or service mark or name owned by such taxpayer or related persons, in marketing or distributing oil or natural gas or any product derived from oil or natural gas, or

(ii) given authority, pursuant to an agreement or contract with the taxpayer or a related person, to occupy any retail outlet owned, leased, or in any way controlled by the taxpayer or a related person.

Notwithstanding the preceding sentence this paragraph shall not apply in any case where the combined gross receipts from the sale of such oil, natural gas, or any product derived therefrom, for the taxable year of all retail outlets taken into account for purposes of this paragraph do not exceed $5,000,000. For purposes of this paragraph, sales of oil, natural gas, or any product derived from oil or natural gas shall not include sales made of such items outside the United States, if no domestic production of the taxpayer or a related person is exported during the taxable year or the immediately preceding taxable year.

(3) RELATED PERSON.—For purposes of this subsection, a person is a related person with respect to the taxpayer if a significant ownership interest in either the taxpayer or such person is held by the other, or if a third person has a significant ownership interest in both the taxpayer and such person. For purposes of the preceding sentence, the term "significant ownership interest" means—

(A) with respect to any corporation, 5 percent or more in value of the outstanding stock of such corporation,

(B) with respect to a partnership, 5 percent or more interest in the profits or capital of such partnership, and

(C) with respect to an estate or trust, 5 percent or more of the beneficial interests in such estate or trust.

For purposes of determining significant ownership interest, an interest owned by or for a corporation, partnership, trust, or estate shall be considered as owned directly both by itself and proportionately by its shareholders, partners, or beneficiaries, as the case may be.

(4) CERTAIN REFINERS EXCLUDED.—If the taxpayer or one or more related persons engages in the refining of crude oil, subsection (c) shall not apply to the taxpayer for a taxable year if the average daily refinery runs of the taxpayer and such persons for the taxable year exceed 75,000 barrels. For purposes of this paragraph, the average daily refinery runs for any taxable year shall be determined by dividing the aggregate refinery runs for the taxable year by the number of days in the taxable year.

(5) PERCENTAGE DEPLETION NOT ALLOWED FOR LEASE BONUSES, ETC.—In the case of any oil or gas property to which subsection (c) applies, for purposes of section 613, the term "gross income from the property" shall not include any lease bonus, advance royalty, or other amount payable without regard to production from property.

[Sec. 613A(e)]

(e) DEFINITIONS.—For purposes of this section—

(1) CRUDE OIL.—The term "crude oil" includes a natural gas liquid recovered from a gas well in lease separators or field facilities.

(2) NATURAL GAS.—The term "natural gas" means any product (other than crude oil) of an oil or gas well if a deduction for depletion is allowable under section 611 with respect to such product.

(3) DOMESTIC.—The term "domestic" refers to production from an oil or gas well located in the United States or in a possession of the United States.

(4) BARREL.—The term "barrel" means 42 United States gallons.

[Sec. 614]

SEC. 614. DEFINITION OF PROPERTY.

[Sec. 614(a)]

(a) GENERAL RULE.—For the purpose of computing the depletion allowance in the case of mines, wells, and other natural deposits, the term "property" means each separate interest owned by the taxpayer in each mineral deposit in each separate tract or parcel of land.

* * *

[Sec. 616]

SEC. 616. DEVELOPMENT EXPENDITURES.

[Sec. 616(a)]

(a) IN GENERAL.—Except as provided in subsections (b) and (d), there shall be allowed as a deduction in computing taxable income all expenditures paid or incurred during the taxable year for the development of a mine or other natural deposit (other than an oil or gas well) if paid or incurred after the existence of ores or minerals in commercially marketable quantities has been disclosed. This section shall not apply to expenditures for the acquisition or improvement of property of a character which is subject to the allowance for depreciation provided in section 167, but allowances for depreciation shall be considered, for purposes of this section, as expenditures.

[Sec. 616(b)]

(b) ELECTION OF TAXPAYER.—At the election of the taxpayer, made in accordance with regulations prescribed by the Secretary, expenditures described in subsection (a) paid or incurred during the taxable year shall be treated as deferred expenses and shall be deductible on a ratable basis as the units of produced ores or minerals benefited by such expenditures are sold. In the case of such expenditures paid or incurred during the development stage of the mine or deposit, the election shall apply only with respect to the excess of such expenditures during the taxable year over the net receipts during the taxable year from the ores or minerals produced from such mine or deposit. The election under this subsection, if made, must be for the total amount of such expenditures, or the total amount of such excess, as the case may be, with respect to the mine or deposit, and shall be binding for such taxable year.

[Sec. 616(c)]

(c) ADJUSTED BASIS OF MINE OR DEPOSIT.—The amount of expenditures which are treated under subsection (b) as deferred expenses shall be taken into account in computing the adjusted basis of the mine or deposit, except that such amount, and the adjustments to basis provided in section 1016 (a) (9), shall be disregarded in determining the adjusted basis of the property for the purpose of computing a deduction for depletion under section 611.

* * *

[Sec. 617]

SEC. 617. DEDUCTION AND RECAPTURE OF CERTAIN MINING EXPLORATION EXPENDITURES.

[Sec. 617(a)]

(a) ALLOWANCE OF DEDUCTION.—

(1) GENERAL RULE.—At the election of the taxpayer, expenditures paid or incurred during the taxable year for the purpose of ascertaining the existence, location, extent, or quality of any deposit of ore or other mineral, and paid or incurred before the beginning of the development stage of the mine, shall be allowed as a deduction in computing taxable income. This subsection shall apply only with respect to the amount of such expenditures which, but for this subsection, would not be allowable as a deduction for the taxable year. This subsection shall not apply to expenditures for the acquisition or improvement of property of a character which is subject to the allowance for depreciation provided in section 167, but allowances for depreciation shall be considered, for purposes of this subsection, as expenditures paid or incurred. In no case shall this subsection apply with respect to amounts paid or incurred for the purpose of ascertaining the existence, location, extent, or quality of any deposit of oil or gas or of any mineral with respect to which a deduction for percentage depletion is not allowable under section 613.

(2) ELECTIONS.—

(A) METHOD.—Any election under this subsection shall be made in such manner as the Secretary may by regulations prescribe.

(B) TIME AND SCOPE.—The election provided by paragraph (1) for the taxable year may be made at any time before the expiration of the period prescribed for making a claim for credit or refund of the tax imposed by this chapter for the taxable year. Such an election for the taxable year shall apply to all expenditures described in paragraph (1) paid or incurred by the taxpayer during the taxable year or during any subsequent taxable year. Such an election may not be revoked unless the Secretary consents to such revocation.

(C) DEFICIENCIES.—The statutory period for the assessment of any deficiency for any taxable year, to the extent such deficiency is attributable to an election or revocation of an election under this subsection, shall not expire before the last day of the 2-year period beginning on the day after the date on which such election or revocation of election is made; and such deficiency may be assessed at any time before the expiration of such 2-year period, notwithstanding any law or rule of law which would otherwise prevent such assessment.

[Sec. 617(b)]

(b) RECAPTURE ON REACHING PRODUCING STAGE.—

(1) RECAPTURE.—If, in any taxable year, any mine with respect to which expenditures were deducted pursuant to subsection (a) reaches the producing stage, then—

(A) If the taxpayer so elects with respect to all such mines reaching the producing stage during the taxable year, he shall include in gross income for the taxable year an amount equal to the adjusted exploration expenditures with respect to such mines, and the amount so included in income shall be treated for purposes of this subtitle as expenditures which (i) are paid or incurred on the respective dates on which the mines reach the producing stage, and (ii) are properly chargeable to capital account.

(B) If subparagraph (A) does not apply with respect to any such mine, then the deduction for depletion under section 611 with respect to the property shall be disallowed until the amount of depletion which would be allowable but for this subparagraph equals the amount of the adjusted exploration expenditures with respect to such mine.

(2) ELECTIONS.—

(A) METHOD.—Any election under this subsection shall be made in such manner as the Secretary may by regulations prescribe.

(B) TIME AND SCOPE.—The election provided by paragraph (1) for any taxable year may be made or changed not later than the time prescribed by law for filing the return (including extensions thereof) for such taxable year.

[Sec. 617(c)]

(c) RECAPTURE IN CASE OF BONUS OR ROYALTY.—If an election has been made under subsection (a) with respect to expenditures relating to a mining property and the taxpayer receives or accrues a bonus or a royalty with respect to such property, then the deduction for depletion under section 611 with respect to the bonus or royalty shall be disallowed until the amount of depletion which would be allowable but for this subsection equals the amount of the adjusted exploration expenditures with respect to the property to which the bonus or royalty relates.

[Sec. 617(d)]

(d) GAIN FROM DISPOSITIONS OF CERTAIN MINING PROPERTY.—

(1) GENERAL RULE.—Except as otherwise provided in this subsection, if mining property is disposed of the lower of—

(A) the adjusted exploration expenditures with respect to such property, or

(B) the excess of—

(i) the amount realized (in the case of a sale, exchange, or involuntary conversion), or the fair market value (in the case of any other disposition), over

(ii) the adjusted basis of such property,

shall be treated as ordinary income. Such gain shall be recognized notwithstanding any other provision of this subtitle.

(2) DISPOSITION OF PORTION OF PROPERTY.—For purposes of paragraph (1)—

(A) In the case of the disposition of a portion of a mining property (other than an undivided interest), the entire amount of the adjusted exploration expenditures with respect to such property shall be treated as attributable to such portion to the extent of the amount of the gain to which paragraph (1) applies.

(B) In the case of the disposition of an undivided interest in a mining property (or a portion thereof), a proportionate part of the adjusted exploration expenditures with respect to such property shall be treated as attributable to such undivided interest to the extent of the amount of the gain to which paragraph (1) applies.

This paragraph shall not apply to any expenditure to the extent the taxpayer establishes to the satisfaction of the Secretary that such expenditure relates neither to the portion (or interest therein) disposed of nor to any mine, in the property held by the taxpayer before the disposition, which has reached the producing stage.

(3) EXCEPTIONS AND LIMITATIONS.—Paragraphs (1), (2), and (3) of section 1245(b) (relating to exceptions and limitations with respect to gain from disposition of certain depreciable property) shall apply in respect of this subsection in the same manner and with the same effect as if references in section 1245(b) to section 1245 or any provision thereof were references to this subsection or the corresponding provisions of this subsection and as if references to section 1245 property were references to mining property.

(4) APPLICATION OF SUBSECTION.—This subsection shall apply notwithstanding any other provision of this subtitle.

(5) COORDINATION WITH SECTION 1254.—This subsection shall not apply to any disposition to which section 1254 applies.

[Sec. 617(e)]

(e) BASIS OF PROPERTY.—

(1) BASIS.—The basis of any property shall not be reduced by the amount of any depletion which would be allowable but for the application of this section.

(2) ADJUSTMENTS.—The Secretary shall prescribe such regulations as he may deem necessary to provide for adjustments to the basis of property to reflect gain recognized under subsection (d)(1).

[Sec. 617(f)]

(f) DEFINITIONS.—For purposes of this section—

(1) ADJUSTED EXPLORATION EXPENDITURES.—The term "adjusted exploration expenditures" means, with respect to any property or mine—

(A) the amount of the expenditures allowed for the taxable year and all preceding taxable years as deductions under subsection (a) to the taxpayer or any other person which are properly chargeable to such property or mine and which (but for the election under subsection (a)) would be reflected in the adjusted basis of such property or mine, reduced by

(B) for the taxable year and for each preceding taxable year, the amount (if any) by which (i) the amount which would have been allowable for percentage depletion under section 613 but for the deduction of such expenditures, exceeds (ii) the amount allowable for depletion under section 611,

properly adjusted for any amounts included in gross income under subsection (b) or (c) and for any amounts of gain to which subsection (d) applied.

(2) MINING PROPERTY.—The term "mining property" means any property (within the meaning of section 614 after the application of subsections (c) and (e) thereof) with respect to which any expenditures allowed as a deduction under subsection (a)(1) are properly chargeable.

(3) DISPOSAL OF COAL OR DOMESTIC IRON ORE WITH A RETAINED ECONOMIC INTEREST.—A transaction which constitutes a disposal of coal or iron ore under section 631(c) shall be treated as a disposition. In such a case, the excess referred to in subsection (d)(1)(B) shall be treated as equal to the gain (if any) referred to in section 631(c).

[Sec. 617(g)]

(g) SPECIAL RULES RELATING TO PARTNERSHIP PROPERTY.—

(1) PROPERTY DISTRIBUTED TO PARTNER.—In the case of any property or mine received by the taxpayer in a distribution with respect to part or all of his interest in a partnership, the adjusted exploration expenditures with respect to such property or mine include the adjusted exploration expenditures (not otherwise included under subsection (f)(1)) with respect to such property or mine immediately prior to such distribution, but the adjusted exploration expenditures with respect to any such property or mine shall be reduced by the amount of gain to which section 751(b) applied realized by the partnership (as constituted after the distribution) on the distribution of such property or mine.

(2) PROPERTY RETAINED BY PARTNERSHIP.—In the case of any property or mine held by a partnership after a distribution to a partner to which section 751(b) applied, the adjusted exploration expenditures with respect to such property or mine shall, under regulations prescribed by the Secretary, be reduced by the amount of gain to which section 751(b) applied realized by such partner with respect to such distribution on account of such property or mine.

* * *

PART III—SALES AND EXCHANGES

[Sec. 631]

SEC. 631. GAIN OR LOSS IN THE CASE OF TIMBER, COAL, OR DOMESTIC IRON ORE.

[Sec. 631(a)]

(a) ELECTION TO CONSIDER CUTTING AS SALE OR EXCHANGE.—If the taxpayer so elects on his return for a taxable year, the cutting of timber (for sale or for use in the taxpayer's trade or business) during such year by the taxpayer who owns, or has a contract right to cut, such timber (providing he has owned such timber or has held such contract right for a period of more than 1 year) shall be considered as a sale or exchange of such timber cut during such year. If such election has been made, gain or loss to the taxpayer shall be recognized in an amount equal to the difference between the fair market value of such timber, and the adjusted basis for depletion of such timber in the hands of the taxpayer. Such fair market value shall be the fair market value as of the first day of the taxable year in which such timber is cut, and shall thereafter be considered as the cost of such cut timber to the taxpayer for all purposes for which such cost is a necessary factor. If a taxpayer makes an election under this subsection, such election shall apply with respect to all timber which is owned by the taxpayer or which the taxpayer has a contract right to cut and shall be binding on the taxpayer for the taxable year for which the election is made and for all subsequent years, unless the Secretary, on showing of undue hardship, permits the taxpayer to revoke his election; such revocation, however, shall preclude any further elections under this subsection except with the consent of the Secretary. For purposes of this subsection and subsection (b), the term "timber" includes evergreen trees which are more than 6 years old at the time severed from the roots and are sold for ornamental purposes.

[Sec. 631(b)]

(b) Disposal of Timber.—In the case of the disposal of timber held for more than 1 year before such disposal, by the owner thereof under any form or type of contract by virtue of which such owner either retains an economic interest in such timber or makes an outright sale of such timber, the difference between the amount realized from the disposal of such timber and the adjusted depletion basis thereof, shall be considered as though it were a gain or loss, as the case may be, on the sale of such timber. In determining the gross income, the adjusted gross income, or the taxable income of the lessee, the deductions allowable with respect to rents and royalties shall be determined without regard to the provisions of this subsection. In the case of disposal of timber with a retained economic interest, the date of disposal of such timber shall be deemed to be the date such timber is cut, but if payment is made to the owner under the contract before such timber is cut the owner may elect to treat the date of such payment as the date of disposal of such timber. For purposes of this subsection, the term "owner" means any person who owns an interest in such timber, including a sublessor and a holder of a contract to cut timber.

[Sec. 631(c)]

(c) Disposal of Coal or Domestic Iron Ore With a Retained Economic Interest.—In the case of the disposal of coal (including lignite), or iron ore mined in the United States, held for more than 1 year before such disposal, by the owner thereof under any form of contract by virtue of which such owner retains an economic interest in such coal or iron ore, the difference between the amount realized from the disposal of such coal or iron ore and the adjusted depletion basis thereof plus the deductions disallowed for the taxable year under section 272 shall be considered as though it were a gain or loss, as the case may be, on the sale of such coal or iron ore. If for the taxable year of such gain or loss the maximum rate of tax imposed by this chapter on any net capital gain is less than such maximum rate for ordinary income, such owner shall not be entitled to the allowance for percentage depletion provided in section 613 with respect to such coal or iron ore. This subsection shall not apply to income realized by any owner as a co-adventurer, partner, or principal in the mining of such coal or iron ore, and the word "owner" means any person who owns an economic interest in coal or iron ore in place, including a sublessor. The date of disposal of such coal or iron ore shall be deemed to be the date such coal or iron ore is mined. In determining the gross income, the adjusted gross income, or the taxable income of the lessee, the deductions allowable with respect to rents and royalties shall be determined without regard to the provisions of this subsection. This subsection shall have no application, for purposes of applying subchapter G, relating to corporations used to avoid income tax on shareholders (including the determinations of the amount of the deductions under section 535(b)(6) or section 545(b)(5)). This subsection shall not apply to any disposal of iron ore or coal—

(1) to a person whose relationship to the person disposing of such iron ore or coal would result in the disallowance of losses under section 267 or 707(b), or

(2) to a person owned or controlled directly or indirectly by the same interests which own or control the person disposing of such iron ore or coal.

PART IV—MINERAL PRODUCTION PAYMENTS

[Sec. 636]

SEC. 636. INCOME TAX TREATMENT OF MINERAL PRODUCTION PAYMENTS.

[Sec. 636(a)]

(a) CARVED-OUT PRODUCTION PAYMENT.—A production payment carved out of mineral property shall be treated, for purposes of this subtitle, as if it were a mortgage loan on the property, and shall not qualify as an economic interest in the mineral property. In the case of a production payment carved out for exploration or development of a mineral property, the preceding sentence shall apply only if and to the extent gross income from the property (for purposes of section 613) would be realized, in the absence of the application of such sentence, by the person creating the production payment.

[Sec. 636(b)]

(b) RETAINED PRODUCTION PAYMENT ON SALE OF MINERAL PROPERTY.—A production payment retained on the sale of a mineral property shall be treated, for purposes of this subtitle, as if it were a purchase money mortgage loan and shall not qualify as an economic interest in the mineral property.

[Sec. 636(c)]

(c) RETAINED PRODUCTION PAYMENT ON LEASE OF MINERAL PROPERTY.—A production payment retained in a mineral property by the lessor in a leasing transaction shall be treated, for purposes of this subtitle, insofar as the lessee (or his successors in interest) is concerned, as if it were a bonus granted by the lessee to the lessor payable in installments. The treatment of the production payment in the hands of the lessor shall be determined without regard to the provisions of this subsection.

[Sec. 636(d)]

(d) DEFINITION.—As used in this section, the term "mineral property" has the meaning assigned to the term "property" in section 614(a).

[Sec. 636(e)]

(e) REGULATIONS.—The Secretary shall prescribe such regulations as may be necessary to carry out the purposes of this section.

SUBCHAPTER J—ESTATES, TRUSTS, BENEFICIARIES, AND DECEDENTS

PART I—ESTATES, TRUSTS, AND BENEFICIARIES

Subpart A—General Rules for Taxation of Estates and Trusts

[Sec. 641]

SEC. 641. IMPOSITION OF TAX.

[Sec. 641(a)]

(a) APPLICATION OF TAX.—The tax imposed by section 1(e) shall apply to the taxable income of estates or of any kind of property held in trust, including—

(1) income accumulated in trust for the benefit of unborn or unascertained persons or persons with contingent interests, and income accumulated or held for future distribution under the terms of the will or trust;

(2) income which is to be distributed currently by the fiduciary to the beneficiaries, and income collected by a guardian of an infant which is to be held or distributed as the court may direct;

(3) income received by estates of deceased persons during the period of administration or settlement of the estate; and

(4) income which, in the discretion of the fiduciary, may be either distributed to the beneficiaries or accumulated.

[Sec. 641(b)]

(b) COMPUTATION AND PAYMENT.—The taxable income of an estate or trust shall be computed in the same manner as in the case of an individual, except as otherwise provided in this part. The tax shall be computed on such taxable income and shall be paid by the fiduciary. For purposes of this subsection, a foreign trust or foreign estate shall be treated as a nonresident alien individual who is not present in the United States at any time.

[Sec. 641(c)]

(c) SPECIAL RULES FOR TAXATION OF ELECTING SMALL BUSINESS TRUSTS.—

(1) IN GENERAL.—For purposes of this chapter—

(A) the portion of any electing small business trust which consists of stock in 1 or more S corporations shall be treated as a separate trust, and

(B) the amount of the tax imposed by this chapter on such separate trust shall be determined with the modifications of paragraph (2).

(2) MODIFICATIONS.—For purposes of paragraph (1), the modifications of this paragraph are the following:

(A) Except as provided in section 1(h), the amount of the tax imposed by section 1(e) shall be determined by using the highest rate of tax set forth in section 1(e).

(B) The exemption amount under section 55(d) shall be zero.

(C) The only items of income, loss, deduction, or credit to be taken into account are the following:

(i) The items required to be taken into account under section 1366.

(ii) Any gain or loss from the disposition of stock in an S corporation.

(iii) To the extent provided in regulations, State or local income taxes or administrative expenses to the extent allocable to items described in clauses (i) and (ii).

(iv) Any interest expense paid or accrued on indebtedness incurred to acquire stock in an S corporation.

No deduction or credit shall be allowed for any amount not described in this paragraph, and no item described in this paragraph shall be apportioned to any beneficiary.

(D) No amount shall be allowed under paragraph (1) or (2) of section 1211(b).

(E) (i) Section 642(c) shall not apply.

(ii) For purposes of section 170(b)(1)(G), adjusted gross income shall be computed in the same manner as in the case of an individual, except that the deductions for costs which are paid or incurred in connection with the administration of the trust and which would not have been incurred if the property were not held in such trust shall be treated as allowable in arriving at adjusted gross income.

(3) TREATMENT OF REMAINDER OF TRUST AND DISTRIBUTIONS.—For purposes of determining—

(A) the amount of the tax imposed by this chapter on the portion of any electing small business trust not treated as a separate trust under paragraph (1), and

(B) the distributable net income of the entire trust,

the items referred to in paragraph (2)(C) shall be excluded. Except as provided in the preceding sentence, this subsection shall not affect the taxation of any distribution from the trust.

(4) TREATMENT OF UNUSED DEDUCTIONS WHERE TERMINATION OF SEPARATE TRUST.—If a portion of an electing small business trust ceases to be treated as a separate trust under paragraph (1), any carryover or excess deduction of the separate trust which is referred to in section 642(h) shall be taken into account by the entire trust.

(5) ELECTING SMALL BUSINESS TRUST.—For purposes of this subsection, the term "electing small business trust" has the meaning given such term by section 1361(e)(1).

»→ Caution: As provided in Section 642(b)(2)(C)(iii)(II), the dollar amount stated in Section 642(b)(2)(C)(iii)(I) is adjusted for taxable years after 2018 to reflect changes in the Chained Consumer Price Index. The dollar amount applicable to taxable years beginning in 2020 is set forth in the material beginning at page ix.

[Sec. 642]

SEC. 642. SPECIAL RULES FOR CREDITS AND DEDUCTIONS.

[Sec. 642(a)]

(a) FOREIGN TAX CREDIT ALLOWED.—An estate or trust shall be allowed the credit against tax for taxes imposed by foreign countries and possessions of the United States, to the extent allowed by section 901, only in respect of so much of the taxes described in such section as is not properly allocable under such section to the beneficiaries.

[Sec. 642(b)]

(b) DEDUCTION FOR PERSONAL EXEMPTION.—

(1) ESTATES.—An estate shall be allowed a deduction of $600.

(2) TRUSTS.—

(A) IN GENERAL.—Except as otherwise provided in this paragraph, a trust shall be allowed a deduction of $100.

(B) TRUSTS DISTRIBUTING INCOME CURRENTLY.—A trust which, under its governing instrument, is required to distribute all of its income currently shall be allowed a deduction of $300.

(C) DISABILITY TRUSTS.—

(i) IN GENERAL.—A qualified disability trust shall be allowed a deduction equal to the exemption amount under section 151(d), determined—

(I) by treating such trust as an individual described in section 68(b)(1)(C), and

(II) by applying section 67(e) (without the reference to section 642(b)) for purposes of determining the adjusted gross income of the trust.

(ii) QUALIFIED DISABILITY TRUST.—For purposes of clause (i), the term "qualified disability trust" means any trust if—

(I) such trust is a disability trust described in subsection (c)(2)(B)(iv) of section 1917 of the Social Security Act (42 U.S.C. 1396p), and

(II) all of the beneficiaries of the trust as of the close of the taxable year are determined by the Commissioner of Social Security to have been disabled (within the meaning of section 1614(a)(3) of the Social Security Act, 42 U.S.C. 1382c(a)(3)) for some portion of such year.

A trust shall not fail to meet the requirements of subclause (II) merely because the corpus of the trust may revert to a person who is not so disabled after the trust ceases to have any beneficiary who is so disabled.

(iii) YEARS WHEN PERSONAL EXEMPTION AMOUNT IS ZERO.—

(I) IN GENERAL.—In the case of any taxable year in which the exemption amount under section 151(d) is zero, clause (i) shall be applied by substituting "$4,150" for "the exemption amount under section 151(d)".

(II) INFLATION ADJUSTMENT.—In the case of any taxable year beginning in a calendar year after 2018, the $4,150 amount in subparagraph (A) shall be increased in the same manner as provided in section 6334(d)(4)(C).

(3) DEDUCTIONS IN LIEU OF PERSONAL EXEMPTION.—The deductions allowed by this subsection shall be in lieu of the deductions allowed under section 151 (relating to deduction for personal exemption).

[Sec. 642(c)]

(c) DEDUCTION FOR AMOUNTS PAID OR PERMANENTLY SET ASIDE FOR A CHARITABLE PURPOSE.—

(1) GENERAL RULE.—In the case of an estate or trust (other than a trust meeting the specifications of subpart B), there shall be allowed as a deduction in computing its taxable income (in lieu of the deduction allowed by section 170(a), relating to deduction for charitable, etc., contributions and gifts) any amount of the gross income, without limitation, which pursuant to the terms of the governing instrument is, during the taxable year, paid for a purpose specified in section 170(c) (determined without regard to section 170(c)(2)(A)). If a charitable contribution is paid after the close of such taxable year and on or before the last day of the year following the close of such taxable year, then the trustee or administrator may elect to treat such contribution as paid during such taxable year. The election shall be made at such time and in such manner as the Secretary prescribes by regulations.

(2) AMOUNTS PERMANENTLY SET ASIDE.—In the case of an estate, and in the case of a trust (other than a trust meeting the specifications of subpart B) required by the terms of its governing instrument to set aside amounts which was—

(A) created on or before October 9, 1969, if—

(i) an irrevocable remainder interest is transferred to or for the use of an organization described in section 170(c), or

(ii) the grantor is at all times after October 9, 1969, under a mental disability to change the terms of the trust; or

(B) established by a will executed on or before October 9, 1969, if—

(i) the testator dies before October 9, 1972, without having republished the will after October 9, 1969, by codicil or otherwise,

(ii) the testator at no time after October 9, 1969, had the right to change the portions of the will which pertain to the trust, or

(iii) the will is not republished by codicil or otherwise before October 9, 1972, and the testator is on such date and at all times thereafter under a mental disability to republish the will by codicil or otherwise,

there shall also be allowed as a deduction in computing its taxable income any amount of the gross income, without limitation, which pursuant to the terms of the governing instrument is, during the taxable year, permanently set aside for a purpose specified in section 170(c), or is to be used exclusively for religious, charitable, scientific, literary, or educational purposes, or for the prevention of cruelty to children or animals, or for the establishment, acquisition, maintenance, or operation of a public cemetery not operated for profit. In the case of a trust, the preceding sentence shall apply only to gross income earned with respect to amounts transferred to the trust before October 9, 1969, or transferred under a will to which subparagraph (B) applies.

(3) POOLED INCOME FUNDS.—In the case of a pooled income fund (as defined in paragraph (5)), there shall also be allowed as a deduction in computing its taxable income any amount of the gross income attributable to gain from the sale of a capital asset held for more than 1 year, without limitation, which pursuant to the terms of the governing instrument is, during the taxable year, permanently set aside for a purpose specified in section 170(c).

(4) ADJUSTMENTS.—To the extent that the amount otherwise allowable as a deduction under this subsection consists of gain described in section 1202(a), proper adjustment shall be made for any exclusion allowable to the estate or trust under section 1202. In the case of a trust, the deduction allowed by this subsection shall be subject to section 681 (relating to unrelated business income).

(5) DEFINITION OF POOLED INCOME FUND.—For purposes of paragraph (3), a pooled income fund is a trust—

(A) to which each donor transfers property, contributing an irrevocable remainder interest in such property to or for the use of an organization described in section 170(b)(1)(A) (other than in clauses (vii) or (viii)), and retaining an income interest for the life of one or more beneficiaries (living at the time of such transfer),

(B) in which the property transferred by each donor is commingled with property transferred by other donors who have made or make similar transfers,

(C) which cannot have investments in securities which are exempt from taxes imposed by this subtitle,

(D) which includes only amounts received from transfers which meet the requirements of this paragraph,

(E) which is maintained by the organization to which the remainder interest is contributed and of which no donor or beneficiary of an income interest is a trustee, and

(F) from which each beneficiary of an income interest receives income, for each year for which he is entitled to receive the income interest referred to in subparagraph (A), determined by the rate of return earned by the trust for such year.

For purposes of determining the amount of any charitable contribution allowable by reason of a transfer of property to a pooled fund, the value of the income interest shall be determined on the basis of the highest rate of return earned by the fund for any of the 3 taxable years immediately preceding the taxable year of the fund in which the transfer is made. In the case of funds in existence less than 3 taxable years preceding the taxable year of the fund in which a transfer is made, the rate of return shall be deemed to be 6 percent per annum, except that the Secretary may prescribe a different rate of return.

(6) TAXABLE PRIVATE FOUNDATIONS.—In the case of a private foundation which is not exempt from taxation under section 501(a) for the taxable year, the provisions of this subsection shall not apply and the provisions of section 170 shall apply.

[Sec. 642(d)]

(d) NET OPERATING LOSS DEDUCTION.—The benefit of the deduction for net operating losses provided by section 172 shall be allowed to estates and trusts under regulations prescribed by the Secretary.

[Sec. 642(e)]

(e) DEDUCTION FOR DEPRECIATION AND DEPLETION.—An estate or trust shall be allowed the deduction for depreciation and depletion only to the extent not allowable to beneficiaries under sections 167(d) and 611(b).

[Sec. 642(f)]

(f) AMORTIZATION DEDUCTIONS.—The benefit of the deductions for amortization provided by sections 169 and 197 shall be allowed to estates and trusts in the same manner as in the case of an individual. The allowable deduction shall be apportioned between the income beneficiaries and the fiduciary under regulations prescribed by the Secretary.

[Sec. 642(g)]

(g) DISALLOWANCE OF DOUBLE DEDUCTIONS.—Amounts allowable under section 2053 or 2054 as a deduction in computing the taxable estate of a decedent shall not be allowed as a deduction (or as an offset against the sales price of property in determining gain or loss) in computing the taxable income of the estate or of any other person, unless there is filed, within the time and in the manner and form prescribed by the Secretary, a statement that the amounts have not been allowed as deductions under section 2053 or 2054 and a waiver of the right to have such amounts allowed at any time as deductions under section 2053 or 2054. Rules similar to the rules of the preceding sentence shall apply to amounts which may be taken into account under section 2621(a)(2) or 2622(b). This subsection shall not apply with respect to deductions allowed under part II (relating to income in respect of decedents).

[Sec. 642(h)]

(h) UNUSED LOSS CARRYOVERS AND EXCESS DEDUCTIONS ON TERMINATION AVAILABLE TO BENEFICIARIES.—If on the termination of an estate or trust, the estate or trust has—

(1) a net operating loss carryover under section 172 or a capital loss carryover under section 1212, or

(2) for the last taxable year of the estate or trust deductions (other than the deductions allowed under subsections (b) or (c)) in excess of gross income for such year,

then such carryover or such excess shall be allowed as a deduction, in accordance with regulations prescribed by the Secretary, to the beneficiaries succeeding to the property of the estate or trust.

* * *

[Sec. 643]

SEC. 643. DEFINITIONS APPLICABLE TO SUBPARTS A, B, C, AND D.

[Sec. 643(a)]

(a) DISTRIBUTABLE NET INCOME.—For purposes of this part, the term "distributable net income" means, with respect to any taxable year, the taxable income of the estate or trust computed with the following modifications—

(1) DEDUCTION FOR DISTRIBUTIONS.—No deduction shall be taken under sections 651 and 661 (relating to additional deductions).

(2) DEDUCTION FOR PERSONAL EXEMPTION.—No deduction shall be taken under section 642 (b) (relating to deduction for personal exemptions).

(3) CAPITAL GAINS AND LOSSES.—Gains from the sale or exchange of capital assets shall be excluded to the extent that such gains are allocated to corpus and are not (A) paid, credited, or required to be distributed to any beneficiary during the taxable year, or (B) paid, permanently set aside, or to be used for the purposes specified in section 642 (c). Losses from the sale or exchange of capital assets shall be excluded, except to the extent such losses are taken into account in determining the amount of gains from the sale or exchange of capital assets which are paid, credited, or required to be distributed to any beneficiary during the taxable year. The exclusion under section 1202 shall not be taken into account.

(4) EXTRAORDINARY DIVIDENDS AND TAXABLE STOCK DIVIDENDS.—For purposes only of subpart B (relating to trusts which distribute current income only), there shall be excluded those items of gross income constituting extraordinary dividends or taxable stock dividends which the fiduciary, acting in good faith, does not pay or credit to any beneficiary by reason of his determination that such dividends are allocable to corpus under the terms of the governing instrument and applicable local law.

(5) TAX-EXEMPT INTEREST.—There shall be included any tax-exempt interest to which section 103 applies, reduced by any amounts which would be deductible in respect of disbursements allocable to such interest but for the provisions of section 265 (relating to disallowance of certain deductions).

* * *

(7) ABUSIVE TRANSACTIONS.—The Secretary shall prescribe such regulations as may be necessary or appropriate to carry out the purposes of this part, including regulations to prevent avoidance of such purposes.

If the estate or trust is allowed a deduction under section 642 (c), the amount of the modifications specified in paragraphs (5) and (6) shall be reduced to the extent that the amount of income which is paid, permanently set aside, or to be used for the purposes specified in section 642 (c) is deemed to consist of items specified in those paragraphs. For this purpose, such amount shall (in the absence of specific provisions in the governing instrument) be deemed to consist of the same proportion of each class of items of income of the estate or trust as the total of each class bears to the total of all classes.

[Sec. 643(b)]

(b) INCOME.—For purposes of this subpart and subparts B, C, and D, the term "income", when not preceded by the words "taxable", "distributable net", "undistributed net", or "gross", means the amount of income of the estate or trust for the taxable year determined under the terms of the governing instrument and applicable local law. Items of gross income constituting extraordinary dividends or taxable stock dividends which the fiduciary, acting in good faith, determines to be allocable to corpus under the terms of the governing instrument and applicable local law shall not be considered income.

[Sec. 643(c)]

(c) BENEFICIARY.—For purposes of this part, the term "beneficiary" includes heir, legatee, devisee.

* * *

[Sec. 643(e)]

(e) TREATMENT OF PROPERTY DISTRIBUTED IN KIND.—

(1) BASIS OF BENEFICIARY.—The basis of any property received by a beneficiary in a distribution from an estate or trust shall be—

(A) the adjusted basis of such property in the hands of the estate or trust immediately before the distribution, adjusted for

(B) any gain or loss recognized to the estate or trust on the distribution.

(2) AMOUNT OF DISTRIBUTION.—In the case of any distribution of property (other than cash), the amount taken into account under sections 661(a)(2) and 662(a)(2) shall be the lesser of—

(A) the basis of such property in the hands of the beneficiary (as determined under paragraph (1)), or

(B) the fair market value of such property.

(3) ELECTION TO RECOGNIZE GAIN.—

(A) IN GENERAL.—In the case of any distribution of property (other than cash) to which an election under this paragraph applies—

(i) paragraph (2) shall not apply,

(ii) gain or loss shall be recognized by the estate or trust in the same manner as if such property had been sold to the distributee at its fair market value, and

(iii) the amount taken into account under sections 661(a)(2) and 662(a)(2) shall be the fair market value of such property.

(B) ELECTION.—Any election under this paragraph shall apply to all distributions made by the estate or trust during a taxable year and shall be made on the return of such estate or trust for such taxable year.

Any such election, once made, may be revoked only with the consent of the Secretary.

(4) EXCEPTION FOR DISTRIBUTIONS DESCRIBED IN SECTION 663(a).—This subsection shall not apply to any distribution described in section 663(a).

[Sec. 643(f)]

(f) TREATMENT OF MULTIPLE TRUSTS.—For purposes of this subchapter, under regulations prescribed by the Secretary, 2 or more trusts shall be treated as 1 trust if—

(1) such trusts have substantially the same grantor or grantors and substantially the same primary beneficiary or beneficiaries, and

(2) a principal purpose of such trusts is the avoidance of the tax imposed by this chapter.

For purposes of the preceding sentence, a husband and wife shall be treated as 1 person.

[Sec. 643(g)]

(g) CERTAIN PAYMENTS OF ESTIMATED TAX TREATED AS PAID BY BENEFICIARY.—

(1) IN GENERAL.—In the case of a trust—

(A) the trustee may elect to treat any portion of a payment of estimated tax made by such trust for any taxable year of the trust as a payment made by a beneficiary of such trust,

(B) any amount so treated shall be treated as paid or credited to the beneficiary on the last day of such taxable year, and

(C) for purposes of subtitle F, the amount so treated—

(i) shall not be treated as a payment of estimated tax made by the trust, but

(ii) shall be treated as a payment of estimated tax made by such beneficiary on January 15 following the taxable year.

(2) TIME FOR MAKING ELECTION.—An election under paragraph (1) shall be made on or before the 65th day after the close of the taxable year of the trust and in such manner as the Secretary may prescribe.

(3) EXTENSION TO LAST YEAR OF ESTATE.—In the case of a taxable year reasonably expected to be the last taxable year of an estate—

(A) any reference in this subsection to a trust shall be treated as including a reference to an estate, and

(B) the fiduciary of the estate shall be treated as the trustee.

* * *

[Sec. 644]

SEC. 644. TAXABLE YEAR OF TRUSTS.

[Sec. 644(a)]

(a) IN GENERAL.—For purposes of this subtitle, the taxable year of any trust shall be the calendar year.

[Sec. 644(b)]

(b) EXCEPTION FOR TRUSTS EXEMPT FROM TAX AND CHARITABLE TRUSTS.—Subsection (a) shall not apply to a trust exempt from taxation under section 501(a) or a trust described in section 4947(a)(1).

[Sec. 645]

SEC. 645. CERTAIN REVOCABLE TRUSTS TREATED AS PART OF ESTATE.

[Sec. 645(a)]

(a) GENERAL RULE.—For purposes of this subtitle, if both the executor (if any) of an estate and the trustee of a qualified revocable trust elect the treatment provided in this section, such trust shall be treated and taxed as part of such estate (and not as a separate trust) for all taxable years of the estate ending after the date of the decedent's death and before the applicable date.

[Sec. 645(b)]

(b) DEFINITIONS.—For purposes of subsection (a)—

(1) QUALIFIED REVOCABLE TRUST.—The term "qualified revocable trust" means any trust (or portion thereof) which was treated under section 676 as owned by the decedent of the estate referred to in subsection (a) by reason of a power in the grantor (determined without regard to section 672(e)).

(2) APPLICABLE DATE.—The term "applicable date" means—

(A) if no return of tax imposed by chapter 11 is required to be filed, the date which is 2 years after the date of the decedent's death, and

(B) if such a return is required to be filed, the date which is 6 months after the date of the final determination of the liability for tax imposed by chapter 11.

[Sec. 645(c)]

(c) ELECTION.—The election under subsection (a) shall be made not later than the time prescribed for filing the return of tax imposed by this chapter for the first taxable year of the estate (determined with regard to extensions) and, once made, shall be irrevocable.

Subpart B—Trusts Which Distribute Current Income Only

[Sec. 651]

SEC. 651. DEDUCTION FOR TRUSTS DISTRIBUTING CURRENT INCOME ONLY.

[Sec. 651(a)]

(a) DEDUCTION.—In the case of any trust the terms of which—

(1) provide that all of its income is required to be distributed currently, and

(2) do not provide that any amounts are to be paid, permanently set aside, or used for the purposes specified in section 642 (c) (relating to deduction for charitable, etc., purposes),

there shall be allowed as a deduction in computing the taxable income of the trust the amount of the income for the taxable year which is required to be distributed currently. This section shall not apply in any taxable year in which the trust distributes amounts other than amounts of income described in paragraph (1).

[Sec. 651(b)]

(b) LIMITATION ON DEDUCTION.—If the amount of income required to be distributed currently exceeds the distributable net income of the trust for the taxable year, the deduction shall be limited to the amount of the distributable net income. For this purpose, the computation of distributable net income shall not include items of income which are not included in the gross income of the trust and the deductions allocable thereto.

[Sec. 652]

SEC. 652. INCLUSION OF AMOUNTS IN GROSS INCOME OF BENEFICIARIES OF TRUSTS DISTRIBUTING CURRENT INCOME ONLY.

[Sec. 652(a)]

(a) INCLUSION.—Subject to subsection (b), the amount of income for the taxable year required to be distributed currently by a trust described in section 651 shall be included in the gross income of the beneficiaries to whom the income is required to be distributed, whether distributed or not. If such amount exceeds the distributable net income, there shall be included in the gross income of each beneficiary an amount which bears the same ratio to distributable net income as the amount of income required to be distributed to such beneficiary bears to the amount of income required to be distributed to all beneficiaries.

[Sec. 652(b)]

(b) CHARACTER OF AMOUNTS.—The amounts specified in subsection (a) shall have the same character in the hands of the beneficiary as in the hands of the trust. For this purpose, the amounts shall be treated as consisting of the same proportion of each class of items entering into the computation of distributable net income of the trust as the total of each class bears to the total distributable net income of the trust, unless the terms of the trust specifically allocate different classes of income to different beneficiaries. In the application of the preceding sentence, the items of deduction entering into the computation of distributable net income shall be allocated among the items of distributable net income in accordance with regulations prescribed by the Secretary.

[Sec. 652(c)]

(c) DIFFERENT TAXABLE YEARS.—If the taxable year of a beneficiary is different from that of the trust, the amount which the beneficiary is required to include in gross income in accordance with the provisions of this section shall be based upon the amount of income of the trust for any taxable year or years of the trust ending within or with his taxable year.

Subpart C—Estates and Trusts Which May Accumulate Income or Which Distribute Corpus

[Sec. 661]

SEC. 661. DEDUCTION FOR ESTATES AND TRUSTS ACCUMULATING INCOME OR DISTRIBUTING CORPUS.

[Sec. 661(a)]

(a) DEDUCTION.—In any taxable year there shall be allowed as a deduction in computing the taxable income of an estate or trust (other than a trust to which subpart B applies), the sum of—

(1) any amount of income for such taxable year required to be distributed currently (including any amount required to be distributed which may be paid out of income or corpus to the extent such amount is paid out of income for such taxable year); and

(2) any other amounts properly paid or credited or required to be distributed for such taxable year;

but such deduction shall not exceed the distributable net income of the estate or trust.

[Sec. 661(b)]

(b) CHARACTER OF AMOUNTS DISTRIBUTED.—The amount determined under subsection (a) shall be treated as consisting of the same proportion of each class of items entering into the computation of distributable net income of the estate or trust as the total of each class bears to the total distributable net income of the estate or trust in the absence of the allocation of different classes of income under the specific terms of the governing instrument. In the application of the preceding sentence, the items of deduction entering into the computation of distributable net income (including the deduction allowed under section 642 (c)) shall be allocated among the items of distributable net income in accordance with regulations prescribed by the Secretary.

[Sec. 661(c)]

(c) LIMITATION ON DEDUCTION.—No deduction shall be allowed under subsection (a) in respect of any portion of the amount allowed as a deduction under that subsection (without regard to this subsection) which is treated under subsection (b) as consisting of any item of distributable net income which is not included in the gross income of the estate or trust.

[Sec. 662]

SEC. 662. INCLUSION OF AMOUNTS IN GROSS INCOME OF BENEFICIARIES OF ESTATES AND TRUSTS ACCUMULATING INCOME OR DISTRIBUTING CORPUS.

[Sec. 662(a)]

(a) INCLUSION.—Subject to subsection (b), there shall be included in the gross income of a beneficiary to whom an amount specified in section 661 (a) is paid, credited, or required to be distributed (by an estate or trust described in section 661), the sum of the following amounts:

(1) AMOUNTS REQUIRED TO BE DISTRIBUTED CURRENTLY.—The amount of income for the taxable year required to be distributed currently to such beneficiary, whether distributed or not. If the amount of income required to be distributed currently to all beneficiaries exceeds the distributable net income (computed without the deduction allowed by section 642 (c), relating to deduction for charitable, etc. purposes) of the estate or trust, then, in lieu of the amount provided in the preceding sentence, there shall be included in the gross income of the beneficiary an amount which bears the same ratio to distributable net income (as so computed) as the amount of income required to be distributed currently to such beneficiary bears to the amount required to be distributed currently to all beneficiaries. For purposes of this section, the phrase "the amount of income for the taxable year required to be distributed currently" includes any amount required to be paid out of income or corpus to the extent such amount is paid out of income for such taxable year.

(2) OTHER AMOUNTS DISTRIBUTED.—All other amounts properly paid, credited, or required to be distributed to such beneficiary for the taxable year. If the sum of—

(A) the amount of income for the taxable year required to be distributed currently to all beneficiaries, and

(B) all other amounts properly paid, credited, or required to be distributed to all beneficiaries

exceeds the distributable net income of the estate or trust, then, in lieu of the amount provided in the preceding sentence, there shall be included in the gross income of the beneficiary an amount which bears the same ratio to distributable net income (reduced by the amounts specified in (A)) as the other amounts properly paid, credited or required to be distributed to the beneficiary bear to the other amounts properly paid, credited, or required to be distributed to all beneficiaries.

[Sec. 662(b)]

(b) CHARACTER OF AMOUNTS.—The amounts determined under subsection (a) shall have the same character in the hands of the beneficiary as in the hands of the estate or trust. For this purpose, the amounts shall be treated as consisting of the same proportion of each class of items entering into the computation of distributable net income as the total of each class bears to the total distributable net income of the estate or trust unless the terms of the governing instrument specifically allocate different classes of income to different beneficiaries. In the application of the preceding sentence, the items of deduction entering into the computation of distributable net income (including the deduction allowed under section 642 (c)) shall be allocated among the items of distributable net income in accordance with regulations prescribed by the Secretary. In the application of this subsection to the amount determined under paragraph (1) of subsection (a), distributable net income shall be computed without regard to any portion of the deduction under section 642 (c) which is not attributable to income of the taxable year.

[Sec. 662(c)]

(c) DIFFERENT TAXABLE YEARS.—If the taxable year of a beneficiary is different from that of the estate or trust, the amount to be included in the gross income of the beneficiary shall be based on the distributable net income of the estate or trust and the amounts properly paid, credited, or required to be distributed to the beneficiary during any taxable year or years of the estate or trust ending within or with his taxable year.

[Sec. 663]

SEC. 663. SPECIAL RULES APPLICABLE TO SECTIONS 661 AND 662.

[Sec. 663(a)]

(a) EXCLUSIONS.—There shall not be included as amounts falling within section 661(a) or 662(a)—

(1) GIFTS, BEQUESTS, ETC.—Any amount which, under the terms of the governing instrument, is properly paid or credited as a gift or bequest of a specific sum of money or of specific property and which is paid or credited all at once or in not more than 3 installments. For this purpose an amount which can be paid or credited only from the income of the estate or trust shall not be considered as a gift or bequest of a specific sum of money.

(2) CHARITABLE, ETC., DISTRIBUTIONS.—Any amount paid or permanently set aside or otherwise qualifying for the deduction provided in section 642(c) (computed without regard to sections 508(d), 681, and 4948(c)(4)).

(3) DENIAL OF DOUBLE DEDUCTION.—Any amount paid, credited, or distributed in the taxable year, if section 651 or section 661 applied to such amount for a preceding taxable year of an estate or trust because credited or required to be distributed in such preceding taxable year.

[Sec. 663(b)]

(b) DISTRIBUTIONS IN FIRST SIXTY-FIVE DAYS OF TAXABLE YEAR.—

(1) GENERAL RULE.—If within the first 65 days of any taxable year of an estate or a trust, an amount is properly paid or credited, such amount shall be considered paid or credited on the last day of the preceding taxable year.

(2) LIMITATION.—Paragraph (1) shall apply with respect to any taxable year of an estate or a trust only if the executor of such estate or the fiduciary of such trust (as the case may be) elects, in such manner and at such time as the Secretary prescribes by regulations, to have paragraph (1) apply for such taxable year.

[Sec. 663(c)]

(c) SEPARATE SHARES TREATED AS SEPARATE ESTATES OR TRUSTS.—For the sole purpose of determining the amount of distributable net income in the application of sections 661 and 662, in the case of a single trust having more than one beneficiary, substantially separate and independent shares of different beneficiaries in the trust shall be treated as separate trusts. Rules similar to the rules of the preceding provisions of this subsection shall apply to treat substantially separate and independent shares of different beneficiaries in an estate having more than 1 beneficiary as separate estates. The existence of such substantially separate and independent shares and the manner of treatment as separate trusts or estates, including the application of subpart D, shall be determined in accordance with regulations prescribed by the Secretary.

[Sec. 664]

SEC. 664. CHARITABLE REMAINDER TRUSTS.

[Sec. 664(a)]

(a) GENERAL RULE.—Notwithstanding any other provision of this subchapter, the provisions of this section shall, in accordance with regulations prescribed by the Secretary, apply in the case of a charitable remainder annuity trust and a charitable remainder unitrust.

[Sec. 664(b)]

(b) CHARACTER OF DISTRIBUTIONS.—Amounts distributed by a charitable remainder annuity trust or by a charitable remainder unitrust shall be considered as having the following characteristics in the hands of a beneficiary to whom is paid the annuity described in subsection (d)(1)(A) or the payment described in subsection (d)(2)(A):

(1) First, as amounts of income (other than gains, and amounts treated as gains, from the sale or other disposition of capital assets) includible in gross income to the extent of such income of the trust for the year and such undistributed income of the trust for prior years;

(2) Second, as a capital gain to the extent of the capital gain of the trust for the year and the undistributed capital gain of the trust for prior years;

(3) Third, as other income to the extent of such income of the trust for the year and such undistributed income of the trust for prior years; and

(4) Fourth, as a distribution of trust corpus.

For purposes of this section, the trust shall determine the amount of its undistributed capital gain on a cumulative net basis.

[Sec. 664(c)]

(c) TAXATION OF TRUSTS.—

(1) INCOME TAX.—A charitable remainder annuity trust and a charitable remainder unitrust shall, for any taxable year, not be subject to any tax imposed by this subtitle.

(2) EXCISE TAX.—

(A) IN GENERAL.—In the case of a charitable remainder annuity trust or a charitable remainder unitrust which has unrelated business taxable income (within the meaning of section 512, determined as if part III of subchapter F applied to such trust) for a taxable year, there is hereby imposed on such trust or unitrust an excise tax equal to the amount of such unrelated business taxable income.

(B) CERTAIN RULES TO APPLY.—The tax imposed by subparagraph (A) shall be treated as imposed by chapter 42 for purposes of this title other than subchapter E of chapter 42.

(C) TAX COURT PROCEEDINGS.—For purposes of this paragraph, the references in section 6212(c)(1) to section 4940 shall be deemed to include references to this paragraph.

[Sec. 664(d)]

(d) DEFINITIONS.—

(1) CHARITABLE REMAINDER ANNUITY TRUST.—For purposes of this section, a charitable remainder annuity trust is a trust—

(A) from which a sum certain (which is not less than 5 percent nor more than 50 percent of the initial net fair market value of all property placed in trust) is to be paid, not less often than annually, to one or more persons (at least one of which is not an organization described in section 170(c) and, in the case of individuals, only to an individual who is living at the time of the creation of the trust) for a term of years (not in excess of 20 years) or for the life or lives of such individual or individuals,

(B) from which no amount other than the payments described in subparagraph (A) and other than qualified gratuitous transfers described in subparagraph (C) may be paid to or for the use of any person other than an organization described in section 170(c),

(C) following the termination of the payments described in subparagraph (A), the remainder interest in the trust is to be transferred to, or for the use of, an organization described in section 170(c) or is to be retained by the trust for such a use or, to the extent the remainder interest is in qualified employer securities (as defined in subsection (g)(4)), all or part of such securities are to be transferred to an employee stock ownership plan (as defined in section 4975(e)(7)) in a qualified gratuitous transfer (as defined by subsection (g)), and

(D) the value (determined under section 7520) of such remainder interest is at least 10 percent of the initial net fair market value of all property placed in the trust.

(2) CHARITABLE REMAINDER UNITRUST.—For purposes of this section, a charitable remainder unitrust is a trust—

(A) from which a fixed percentage (which is not less than 5 percent nor more than 50 percent) of the net fair market value of its assets, valued annually, is to be paid, not less often than annually, to one or more persons (at least one of which is not an organization described in section 170(c) and, in the case of individuals, only to an individual who is living at the time of the creation of the trust) for a term of years (not in excess of 20 years) or for the life or lives of such individual or individuals,

(B) from which no amount other than the payments described in subparagraph (A) and other than qualified gratuitous transfers described in subparagraph (C) may be paid to or for the use of any person other than an organization described in section 170(c),

(C) following the termination of the payments described in subparagraph (A), the remainder interest in the trust is to be transferred to, or for the use of, an organization described in section 170(c) or is to be retained by the trust for such a use or, to the extent the remainder interest is in qualified employer securities (as defined in subsection (g)(4)), all or part of such securities are to be transferred to an employee stock ownership plan (as defined in section 4975(e)(7)) in a qualified gratuitous transfer (as defined by subsection (g)), and

(D) with respect to each contribution of property to the trust, the value (determined under section 7520) of such remainder interest in such property is at least 10 percent of the net fair market value of such property as of the date such property is contributed to the trust.

(3) EXCEPTION.—Notwithstanding the provisions of paragraphs (2)(A) and (B), the trust instrument may provide that the trustee shall pay the income beneficiary for any year—

(A) the amount of the trust income, if such amount is less than the amount required to be distributed under paragraph (2)(A), and

(B) any amount of the trust income which is in excess of the amount required to be distributed under paragraph (2)(A), to the extent that (by reason of subparagraph (A)) the aggregate of the amounts paid in prior years was less than the aggregate of such required amounts.

(4) SEVERANCE OF CERTAIN ADDITIONAL CONTRIBUTIONS.—If—

(A) any contribution is made to a trust which before the contribution is a charitable remainder unitrust, and

(B) such contribution would (but for this paragraph) result in such trust ceasing to be a charitable unitrust by reason of paragraph (2)(D),

such contribution shall be treated as a transfer to a separate trust under regulations prescribed by the Secretary.

[Sec. 664(e)]

(e) VALUATION OF INTERESTS.—For purposes of determining the amount of any charitable contribution, the remainder interest of a charitable remainder annuity trust or charitable remainder unitrust shall be computed on the basis that an amount equal to 5 percent of the net fair market value of its assets (or a greater amount, if required under the terms of the trust instrument) is to be distributed each year. In the case of the early termination of a trust which is a charitable remainder unitrust by reason of subsection (d)(3), the valuation of interests in such trust for purposes of this section shall be made under rules similar to the rules of the preceding sentence.

[Sec. 664(f)]

(f) CERTAIN CONTINGENCIES PERMITTED.—

(1) GENERAL RULE.—If a trust would, but for a qualified contingency, meet the requirements of paragraph (1)(A) or (2)(A) of subsection (d), such trust shall be treated as meeting such requirements.

(2) VALUE DETERMINED WITHOUT REGARD TO QUALIFIED CONTINGENCY.—For purposes of determining the amount of any charitable contribution (or the actuarial value of any interest), a qualified contingency shall not be taken into account.

(3) QUALIFIED CONTINGENCY.—For purposes of this subsection, the term "qualified contingency" means any provision of a trust which provides that, upon the happening of a contingency, the payments described in paragraph (1)(A) or (2)(A) of subsection (d) (as the case may be) will terminate not later than such payments would otherwise terminate under the trust.

* * *

Subpart E—Grantors and Others Treated as Substantial Owners

[Sec. 671]

SEC. 671. TRUST INCOME, DEDUCTIONS, AND CREDITS ATTRIBUTABLE TO GRANTORS AND OTHERS AS SUBSTANTIAL OWNERS.

Where it is specified in this subpart that the grantor or another person shall be treated as the owner of any portion of a trust, there shall then be included in computing the taxable income and credits of the grantor or the other person those items of income, deductions, and credits against tax of the trust which are attributable to that portion of the trust to the extent that such items would be taken into account under this chapter in computing taxable income or credits against the tax of an individual. Any remaining portion of the trust shall be subject to subparts A through D. No items of a trust shall be included in computing the taxable income and credits of the grantor or of any other person solely on the grounds of his dominion and control over the trust under section 61 (relating to definition of gross income) or any other provision of this title, except as specified in this subpart.

[Sec. 672]

SEC. 672. DEFINITIONS AND RULES.

[Sec. 672(a)]

(a) ADVERSE PARTY.—For purposes of this subpart, the term "adverse party" means any person having a substantial beneficial interest in the trust which would be adversely affected by the exercise or nonexercise of the power which he possesses respecting the trust. A person having a general power of appointment over the trust property shall be deemed to have a beneficial interest in the trust.

[Sec. 672(b)]

(b) NONADVERSE PARTY.—For purposes of this subpart, the term "nonadverse party" means any person who is not an adverse party.

[Sec. 672(c)]

(c) RELATED OR SUBORDINATE PARTY.—For purposes of this subpart, the term "related or subordinate party" means any nonadverse party who is—

(1) the grantor's spouse if living with the grantor;

(2) any one of the following: The grantor's father, mother, issue, brother or sister; an employee of the grantor; a corporation or any employee of a corporation in which the stock holdings of the grantor and the trust are significant from the viewpoint of voting control; a subordinate employee of a corporation in which the grantor is an executive.

For purposes of subsection (f) and sections 674 and 675, a related or subordinate party shall be presumed to be subservient to the grantor in respect of the exercise or nonexercise of the powers conferred on him unless such party is shown not to be subservient by a preponderance of the evidence.

[Sec. 672(d)]

(d) RULE WHERE POWER IS SUBJECT TO CONDITION PRECEDENT.—A person shall be considered to have a power described in this subpart even though the exercise of the power is subject to a precedent giving of notice or takes effect only on the expiration of a certain period after the exercise of the power.

[Sec. 672(e)]

(e) GRANTOR TREATED AS HOLDING ANY POWER OR INTEREST OF GRANTOR'S SPOUSE.—

(1) IN GENERAL.—For purposes of this subpart, a grantor shall be treated as holding any power or interest held by—

(A) any individual who was the spouse of the grantor at the time of the creation of such power or interest, or

(B) any individual who became the spouse of the grantor after the creation of such power or interest, but only with respect to periods after such individual became the spouse of the grantor.

(2) MARITAL STATUS.—For purposes of paragraph (1)(A), an individual legally separated from his spouse under a decree of divorce or of separate maintenance shall not be considered as married.

* * *

[Sec. 673]

SEC. 673. REVERSIONARY INTERESTS.

[Sec. 673(a)]

(a) GENERAL RULE.—The grantor shall be treated as the owner of any portion of a trust in which he has a reversionary interest in either the corpus or the income therefrom, if, as of the inception of that portion of the trust, the value of such interest exceeds 5 percent of the value of such portion.

[Sec. 673(b)]

(b) REVERSIONARY INTEREST TAKING EFFECT AT DEATH OF MINOR LINEAL DESCENDANT BENEFICIARY.—In the case of any beneficiary who—

(1) is a lineal descendant of the grantor, and

(2) holds all of the present interests in any portion of a trust, the grantor shall not be treated under subsection (a) as the owner of such portion solely by reason of a reversionary interest in such portion which takes effect upon the death of such beneficiary before such beneficiary attains age 21.

[Sec. 673(c)]

(c) SPECIAL RULE FOR DETERMINING VALUE OF REVERSIONARY INTEREST.—For purposes of subsection (a), the value of the grantor's reversionary interest shall be determined by assuming the maximum exercise of discretion in favor of the grantor.

[Sec. 673(d)]

(d) POSTPONEMENT OF DATE SPECIFIED FOR REACQUISITION.—Any postponement of the date specified for the reacquisition of possession or enjoyment of the reversionary interest shall be treated as a new transfer in trust commencing with the date on which the postponement is effective and terminating with the date prescribed by the postponement. However, income for any period shall not be included in the income of the grantor by reason of the preceding sentence if such income would not be so includible in the absence of such postponement.

[Sec. 674]

SEC. 674. POWER TO CONTROL BENEFICIAL ENJOYMENT.

[Sec. 674(a)]

(a) GENERAL RULE.—The grantor shall be treated as the owner of any portion of a trust in respect of which the beneficial enjoyment of the corpus or the income therefrom is subject to a power of disposition, exercisable by the grantor or a nonadverse party, or both, without the approval or consent of any adverse party.

[Sec. 674(b)]

(b) EXCEPTIONS FOR CERTAIN POWERS.—Subsection (a) shall not apply to the following powers regardless of by whom held:

(1) POWER TO APPLY INCOME TO SUPPORT OF A DEPENDENT.—A power described in section 677 (b) to the extent that the grantor would not be subject to tax under that section.

(2) POWER AFFECTING BENEFICIAL ENJOYMENT ONLY AFTER OCCURRENCE OF EVENT.—A power, the exercise of which can only affect the beneficial enjoyment of the income for a period commencing after the occurrence of an event such that a grantor would not be treated as the owner under section 673 if the power were a reversionary interest; but the grantor may be treated as the owner after the occurrence of the event unless the power is relinquished.

(3) POWER EXERCISABLE ONLY BY WILL.—A power exercisable only by will, other than a power in the grantor to appoint by will the income of the trust where the income is accumulated for such disposition by the grantor or may be so accumulated in the discretion of the grantor or a nonadverse party, or both, without the approval or consent of any adverse party.

(4) POWER TO ALLOCATE AMONG CHARITABLE BENEFICIARIES.—A power to determine the beneficial enjoyment of the corpus or the income therefrom if the corpus or income is irrevocably payable for a purpose specified in section 170(c) (relating to definition of charitable contributions) or to an employee stock ownership plan (as defined in section 4975(e)(7)) in a qualified gratuitous transfer (as defined in section 664(g)(1)).

(5) POWER TO DISTRIBUTE CORPUS.—A power to distribute corpus either—

(A) to or for a beneficiary or beneficiaries or to or for a class of beneficiaries (whether or not income beneficiaries) provided that the power is limited by a reasonably definite standard which is set forth in the trust instrument; or

(B) to or for any current income beneficiary, provided that the distribution of corpus must be chargeable against the proportionate share of corpus held in trust for the payment of income to the beneficiary as if the corpus constituted a separate trust.

A power does not fall within the powers described in this paragraph if any person has a power to add to the beneficiary or beneficiaries or to a class of beneficiaries designated to receive the income or corpus, except where such action is to provide for after-born or after-adopted children.

(6) POWER TO WITHHOLD INCOME TEMPORARILY.—A power to distribute or apply income to or for any current income beneficiary or to accumulate the income for him, provided that any accumulated income must ultimately be payable—

(A) to the beneficiary from whom distribution or application is withheld, to his estate, or to his appointees (or persons named as alternate takers in default of appointment) provided that such beneficiary possesses a power of appointment which does not exclude from the class of possible appointees any person other than the beneficiary, his estate, his creditors, or the creditors of his estate, or

(B) on termination of the trust, or in conjunction with a distribution of corpus which is augmented by such accumulated income, to the current income beneficiaries in shares which have been irrevocably specified in the trust instrument.

Accumulated income shall be considered so payable although it is provided that if any beneficiary does not survive a date of distribution which could reasonably have been expected to occur within the beneficiary's lifetime, the share of the deceased beneficiary is to be paid to his appointees or to one or more designated alternate takers (other than the grantor or the grantor's estate) whose shares have been irrevocably specified. A power does not fall within the powers described in this paragraph if any person has a power to add to the beneficiary or beneficiaries or to a class of beneficiaries designated to receive the income or corpus except where such action is to provide for after-born or after-adopted children.

(7) POWER TO WITHHOLD INCOME DURING DISABILITY OF A BENEFICIARY.—A power exercisable only during—

(A) the existence of a legal disability of any current income beneficiary, or

(B) the period during which any income beneficiary shall be under the age of 21 years,

to distribute or apply income to or for such beneficiary or to accumulate and add the income to corpus. A power does not fall within the powers described in this paragraph if any person has a power to add to the beneficiary or beneficiaries or to a class of beneficiaries designated to receive the income or corpus, except where such action is to provide for after-born or after-adopted children.

(8) POWER TO ALLOCATE BETWEEN CORPUS AND INCOME.—A power to allocate receipts and disbursements as between corpus and income, even though expressed in broad language.

[Sec. 674(c)]

(c) EXCEPTION FOR CERTAIN POWERS OF INDEPENDENT TRUSTEES.—Subsection (a) shall not apply to a power solely exercisable (without the approval or consent of any other person) by a trustee or trustees, none of whom is the grantor, and no more than half of whom are related or subordinate parties who are subservient to the wishes of the grantor—

(1) to distribute, apportion, or accumulate income to or for a beneficiary or beneficiaries, or to, for, or within a class of beneficiaries; or

(2) to pay out corpus to or for a beneficiary or beneficiaries or to or for a class of beneficiaries (whether or not income beneficiaries).

A power does not fall within the powers described in this subsection if any person has a power to add to the beneficiary or beneficiaries or to a class of beneficiaries designated to receive the income or corpus, except where such action is to provide for after-born or after-adopted children. For periods during which an individual is the spouse of the grantor (within the meaning of section 672(e)(2)), any reference in this subsection to the grantor shall be treated as including a reference to such individual.

[Sec. 674(d)]

(d) POWER TO ALLOCATE INCOME IF LIMITED BY A STANDARD.—Subsection (a) shall not apply to a power solely exercisable (without the approval or consent of any other person) by a trustee or trustees, none of whom is the grantor or spouse living with the grantor, to distribute, apportion, or accumulate income to or for a beneficiary or beneficiaries, or to, for, or within a class of beneficiaries, whether or not the conditions of paragraph (6) or (7) of subsection (b) are satisfied, if such power is limited by a reasonably definite external standard which is set forth in the trust instrument. A power does not fall within the powers described in this subsection if any person has a power to add to the beneficiary or beneficiaries or to a class of beneficiaries designated to receive the income or corpus except where such action is to provide for after-born or after-adopted children.

[Sec. 675]

SEC. 675. ADMINISTRATIVE POWERS.

The grantor shall be treated as the owner of any portion of a trust in respect of which—

(1) POWER TO DEAL FOR LESS THAN ADEQUATE AND FULL CONSIDERATION.—A power exercisable by the grantor or a nonadverse party, or both, without the approval or consent of any adverse party enables the grantor or any person to purchase, exchange, or otherwise deal with or dispose of the corpus or the income therefrom for less than an adequate consideration in money or money's worth.

(2) POWER TO BORROW WITHOUT ADEQUATE INTEREST OR SECURITY.—A power exercisable by the grantor or a nonadverse party, or both, enables the grantor to borrow the corpus or income, directly or indirectly, without adequate interest or without adequate security except

where a trustee (other than the grantor) is authorized under a general lending power to make loans to any person without regard to interest or security.

(3) BORROWING OF THE TRUST FUNDS.—The grantor has directly or indirectly borrowed the corpus or income and has not completely repaid the loan, including any interest, before the beginning of the taxable year. The preceding sentence shall not apply to a loan which provides for adequate interest and adequate security, if such loan is made by a trustee other than the grantor and other than a related or subordinate trustee subservient to the grantor. For periods during which an individual is the spouse of the grantor (within the meaning of section 672(e)(2)), any reference in this paragraph to the grantor shall be treated as including a reference to such individual.

(4) GENERAL POWERS OF ADMINISTRATION.—A power of administration is exercisable in a nonfiduciary capacity by any person without the approval or consent of any person in a fiduciary capacity. For purposes of this paragraph, the term "power of administration" means any one or more of the following powers: (A) a power to vote or direct the voting of stock or other securities of a corporation in which the holdings of the grantor and the trust are significant from the viewpoint of voting control; (B) a power to control the investment of the trust funds either by directing investments or reinvestments, or by vetoing proposed investments or reinvestments, to the extent that the trust funds consist of stocks or securities of corporations in which the holdings of the grantor and the trust are significant from the viewpoint of voting control; or (C) a power to reacquire the trust corpus by substituting other property of an equivalent value.

[Sec. 676]

SEC. 676. POWER TO REVOKE.

[Sec. 676(a)]

(a) GENERAL RULE.—The grantor shall be treated as the owner of any portion of a trust, whether or not he is treated as such owner under any other provision of this part, where at any time the power to revest in the grantor title to such portion is exercisable by the grantor or a nonadverse party, or both.

[Sec. 676(b)]

(b) POWER AFFECTING BENEFICIAL ENJOYMENT ONLY AFTER OCCURRENCE OF EVENT.—Subsection (a) shall not apply to a power the exercise of which can only affect the beneficial enjoyment of the income for a period commencing after the occurrence of an event such that a grantor would not be treated as the owner under section 673 if the power were a reversionary interest. But the grantor may be treated as the owner after the occurrence of such event unless the power is relinquished.

[Sec. 677]

SEC. 677. INCOME FOR BENEFIT OF GRANTOR.

[Sec. 677(a)]

(a) GENERAL RULE.—The grantor shall be treated as the owner of any portion of a trust, whether or not he is treated as such owner under section 674, whose income without the approval or consent of any adverse party is, or, in the discretion of the grantor or a nonadverse party, or both, may be—

(1) distributed to the grantor or the grantor's spouse;

(2) held or accumulated for future distribution to the grantor or the grantor's spouse; or

(3) applied to the payment of premiums on policies of insurance on the life of the grantor or the grantor's spouse (except policies of insurance irrevocably payable for a purpose specified in section 170(c) (relating to definition of charitable contributions)).

This subsection shall not apply to a power the exercise of which can only affect the beneficial enjoyment of the income for a period commencing after the occurrence of an event such that the grantor would not be treated as the owner under section 673 if the power were a reversionary interest; but the grantor may be treated as the owner after the occurrence of the event unless the power is relinquished.

[Sec. 677(b)]

(b) OBLIGATIONS OF SUPPORT.—Income of a trust shall not be considered taxable to the grantor under subsection (a) or any other provision of this chapter merely because such income in the discretion of another person, the trustee, or the grantor acting as trustee or co-trustee, may be applied or distributed for the support or maintenance of a beneficiary (other than the grantor's spouse) whom the grantor is legally obligated to support or maintain, except to the extent that such income is so applied or distributed. In cases where the amounts so applied or distributed are paid out of corpus or out of other than income for the taxable year, such amounts shall be considered to be an amount paid or credited within the meaning of paragraph (2) of section 661(a) and shall be taxed to the grantor under section 662.

[Sec. 678]

SEC. 678. PERSON OTHER THAN GRANTOR TREATED AS SUBSTANTIAL OWNER.

[Sec. 678(a)]

(a) GENERAL RULE.—A person other than the grantor shall be treated as the owner of any portion of a trust with respect to which:

(1) such person has a power exercisable solely by himself to vest the corpus or the income therefrom in himself, or

(2) such person has previously partially released or otherwise modified such a power and after the release or modification retains such control as would, within the principles of sections 671 to 677, inclusive, subject a grantor of a trust to treatment as the owner thereof.

[Sec. 678(b)]

(b) EXCEPTION WHERE GRANTOR IS TAXABLE.—Subsection (a) shall not apply with respect to a power over income, as originally granted or thereafter modified, if the grantor of the trust or a transferor (to whom section 679 applies) is otherwise treated as the owner under the provisions of this subpart other than this section.

[Sec. 678(c)]

(c) OBLIGATIONS OF SUPPORT.—Subsection (a) shall not apply to a power which enables such person, in the capacity of trustee or co-trustee, merely to apply the income of the trust to the support or maintenance of a person whom the holder of the power is obligated to support or maintain except to the extent that such income is so applied. In cases where the amounts so applied or distributed are paid out of corpus or out of other than income of the taxable year, such amounts shall be considered to be an amount paid or credited within the meaning of paragraph (2) of section 661 (a) and shall be taxed to the holder of the power under section 662.

[Sec. 678(d)]

(d) EFFECT OF RENUNCIATION OR DISCLAIMER.—Subsection (a) shall not apply with respect to a power which has been renounced or disclaimed within a reasonable time after the holder of the power first became aware of its existence.

[Sec. 678(e)]

(e) CROSS REFERENCE.—

For provision under which beneficiary of trust is treated as owner of the portion of the trust which consists of stock in an S corporation, see section 1361(d).

Subpart F—Miscellaneous

»»→ Caution: Section 682 does not apply to alimony or separate maintenance payments made pursuant to a divorce or separation instrument executed after December 31, 2018.

[Sec. 682]

SEC. 682. INCOME OF AN ESTATE OR TRUST IN CASE OF DIVORCE, ETC.

[Sec. 682(a)]

(a) INCLUSION IN GROSS INCOME OF WIFE.—There shall be included in the gross income of a wife who is divorced or legally separated under a decree of divorce or of separate maintenance (or who is separated from her husband under a written separation agreement) the amount of the income of any trust which such wife is entitled to receive and which, except for this section, would be includible in the gross income of her husband, and such amount shall not, despite any other provision of this subtitle, be includible in the gross income of such husband. This subsection shall not apply to that part of any such income of the trust which the terms of the decree, written separation agreement, or trust instrument fix, in terms of an amount of money or a portion of such income, as a sum which is payable for the support of minor children of such husband. In case such income is less than the amount specified in the decree, agreement, or instrument, for the purpose of applying the preceding sentence, such income, to the extent of such sum payable for such support, shall be considered a payment for such support.

[Sec. 682(b)]

(b) WIFE CONSIDERED A BENEFICIARY.—For purposes of computing the taxable income of the estate or trust and the taxable income of a wife to whom subsection (a) applies, such wife shall be considered as the beneficiary specified in this part.

[Sec. 682(c)]

(c) CROSS REFERENCE.—

For definitions of "husband" and "wife", as used in this section, see section 7701 (a) (17).

[Sec. 683]

SEC. 683. USE OF TRUST AS AN EXCHANGE FUND.

[Sec. 683(a)]

(a) GENERAL RULE.—Except as provided in subsection (b), if property is transferred to a trust in exchange for an interest in other trust property and if the trust would be an investment company (within the meaning of section 351) if it were a corporation, then gain shall be recognized to the transferor.

[Sec. 683(b)]

(b) EXCEPTION FOR POOLED INCOME FUNDS.—Subsection (a) shall not apply to any transfer to a pooled income fund (within the meaning of section 642(c)(5)).

[Sec. 684]

SEC. 684. RECOGNITION OF GAIN ON CERTAIN TRANSFERS TO CERTAIN FOREIGN TRUSTS AND ESTATES.

[Sec. 684(a)]

(a) IN GENERAL.—Except as provided in regulations, in the case of any transfer of property by a United States person to a foreign estate or trust, for purposes of this subtitle, such transfer shall be treated as a sale or exchange for an amount equal to the fair market value of the property transferred, and the transferor shall recognize as gain the excess of—

(1) the fair market value of the property so transferred, over

(2) the adjusted basis (for purposes of determining gain) of such property in the hands of the transferor.

[Sec. 684(b)]

(b) EXCEPTION.—Subsection (a) shall not apply to a transfer to a trust by a United States person to the extent that any person is treated as the owner of such trust under section 671.

[Sec. 684(c)]

(c) TREATMENT OF TRUSTS WHICH BECOME FOREIGN TRUSTS.—If a trust which is not a foreign trust becomes a foreign trust, such trust shall be treated for purposes of this section as having transferred, immediately before becoming a foreign trust, all of its assets to a foreign trust.

PART II—INCOME IN RESPECT OF DECEDENTS

[Sec. 691]

SEC. 691. RECIPIENTS OF INCOME IN RESPECT OF DECEDENTS.

[Sec. 691(a)]

(a) INCLUSION IN GROSS INCOME.—

(1) GENERAL RULE.—The amount of all items of gross income in respect of a decedent which are not properly includible in respect of the taxable period in which falls the date of his death or a prior period (including the amount of all items of gross income in respect of a prior decedent, if the right to receive such amount was acquired by reason of the death of the prior decedent or by bequest, devise, or inheritance from the prior decedent) shall be included in the gross income, for the taxable year when received, of:

(A) the estate of the decedent, if the right to receive the amount is acquired by the decedent's estate from the decedent;

(B) the person who, by reason of the death of the decedent, acquires the right to receive the amount, if the right to receive the amount is not acquired by the decedent's estate from the decedent; or

(C) the person who acquires from the decedent the right to receive the amount by bequest, devise, or inheritance, if the amount is received after a distribution by the decedent's estate of such right.

(2) INCOME IN CASE OF SALE, ETC.—If a right, described in paragraph (1), to receive an amount is transferred by the estate of the decedent or a person who received such right by reason of the death of the decedent or by bequest, devise, or inheritance from the decedent, there shall be included in the gross income of the estate or such person, as the case may be, for the taxable period in which the transfer occurs, the fair market value of such right at the time of such transfer plus the amount by which any consideration for the transfer exceeds such fair market value. For purposes of this paragraph, the term "transfer" includes sale, exchange, or other disposition, or the satisfaction of an installment obligation at other than face value, but does not include transmission at death to the estate of the decedent or a transfer to a person pursuant to the right of such person to receive such amount by reason of the death of the decedent or by bequest, devise, or inheritance from the decedent.

(3) CHARACTER OF INCOME DETERMINED BY REFERENCE TO DECEDENT.—The right, described in paragraph (1), to receive an amount shall be treated, in the hands of the estate of the decedent or any person who acquired such right by reason of the death of the decedent, or by bequest, devise, or inheritance from the decedent, as if it had been acquired by the estate or such person in the transaction in which the right to receive the income was originally derived and the amount includible in gross income under paragraph (1) or (2) shall be considered in the hands of the estate or such person to have the character which it would have had in the hands of the decedent if the decedent had lived and received such amount.

(4) INSTALLMENT OBLIGATIONS ACQUIRED FROM DECEDENT.—In the case of an installment obligation reportable by the decedent on the installment method under section 453, if such obligation is acquired by the decedent's estate from the decedent or by any person by reason of the death of the decedent or by bequest, devise, or inheritance from the decedent—

(A) an amount equal to the excess of the face amount of such obligation over the basis of the obligation in the hands of the decedent (determined under section 453B) shall, for the purpose of paragraph (1), be considered as an item of gross income in respect of the decedent; and

(B) such obligation shall, for purposes of paragraphs (2) and (3), be considered a right to receive an item of gross income in respect of the decedent, but the amount includible in gross income under paragraph (2) shall be reduced by an amount equal to the basis of the obligation in the hands of the decedent (determined under section 453B).

(5) OTHER RULES RELATING TO INSTALLMENT OBLIGATIONS.—

(A) IN GENERAL.—In the case of an installment obligation reportable by the decedent on the installment method under section 453, for purposes of paragraph (2)—

(i) the second sentence of paragraph (2) shall be applied by inserting "(other than the obligor)" after "or a transfer to a person,"

(ii) any cancellation of such an obligation shall be treated as a transfer, and

(iii) any cancellation of such an obligation occurring at the death of the decedent shall be treated as a transfer by the estate of the decedent (or, if held by a person other than the decedent before the death of the decedent, by such person).

(B) FACE AMOUNT TREATED AS FAIR MARKET VALUE IN CERTAIN CASES.—In any case to which the first sentence of paragraph (2) applies by reason of subparagraph (A), if the decedent and the obligor were related persons (within the meaning of section 453(f)(1)), the fair market value of the installment obligation shall be treated as not less than its face amount.

(C) CANCELLATION INCLUDES BECOMING UNENFORCEABLE.—For purposes of subparagraph (A), an installment obligation which becomes unenforceable shall be treated as if it were canceled.

[Sec. 691(b)]

(b) ALLOWANCE OF DEDUCTIONS AND CREDIT.—The amount of any deduction specified in section 162, 163, 164, 212, or 611 (relating to deductions for expenses, interest, taxes, and depletion) or credit specified in section 27 (relating to foreign tax credit), in respect of a decedent which is not properly allowable to the decedent in respect of the taxable period in which falls the date of his death, or a prior period, shall be allowed:

(1) EXPENSES, INTEREST, AND TAXES.—In the case of a deduction specified in section 162, 163, 164, or 212 and a credit specified in section 27, in the taxable year when paid—

(A) to the estate of the decedent; except that

(B) if the estate of the decedent is not liable to discharge the obligation to which the deduction or credit relates, to the person who, by reason of the death of the decedent of by bequest, devise, or inheritance acquires, subject to such obligation, from the decedent an interest in property of the decedent.

(2) DEPLETION.—In the case of the deduction specified in section 611, to the person described in subsection (a)(1)(A), (B), or (C) who, in the manner described therein, receives the income to which the deduction relates, in the taxable year when such income is received.

[Sec. 691(c)]

(c) DEDUCTION FOR ESTATE TAX.—

(1) ALLOWANCE OF DEDUCTION.—

(A) GENERAL RULE.—A person who includes an amount in gross income under subsection (a) shall be allowed, for the same taxable year, as a deduction an amount which bears the same ratio to the estate tax attributable to the net value for estate tax purposes of all the items described in subsection (a)(1) as the value for estate tax purposes of the items of gross income or portions thereof in respect of which such person included the amount in gross income (or the amount included in gross income, whichever is lower) bears to the value for estate tax purposes of all the items described in subsection (a)(1).

(B) ESTATES AND TRUSTS.—In the case of an estate or trust, the amount allowed as a deduction under subparagraph (A) shall be computed by excluding from the gross income of the estate or trust the portion (if any) of the items described in subsection (a)(1) which is properly paid, credited, or to be distributed to the beneficiaries during the taxable year.

(2) METHOD OF COMPUTING DEDUCTION.—For purposes of paragraph (1)—

(A) The term "estate tax" means the tax imposed on the estate of the decedent or any prior decedent under section 2001 or 2101, reduced by the credits against such tax.

(B) The net value for estate tax purposes of all the items described in subsection (a)(1) shall be the excess of the value for estate tax purposes of all the items described in subsection (a)(1) over the deductions from the gross estate in respect of claims which represent the deductions and credit described in subsection (b). Such net value shall be determined with respect to the provisions of section 421(c)(2), relating to the deduction for estate tax with respect to stock options to which part II of subchapter D applies.

(C) The estate tax attributable to such net value shall be an amount equal to the excess of the estate tax over the estate tax computed without including in the gross estate such net value.

(3) SPECIAL RULE FOR GENERATION-SKIPPING TRANSFERS.—In the case of any tax imposed by chapter 13 on a taxable termination or a direct skip occurring as a result of the death of the transferor, there shall be allowed a deduction (under principles similar to the principles of this subsection) for the portion of such tax attributable to items of gross income of the trust which were not properly includible in the gross income of the trust for periods before the date of such termination.

(4) COORDINATION WITH CAPITAL GAIN PROVISIONS.—For purposes of sections 1(h), 1202, and 1211, the amount taken into account with respect to any item described in subsection (a)(1) shall be reduced (but not below zero) by the amount of the deduction allowable under paragraph (1) of this subsection with respect to such item.

[Sec. 691(d)]

(d) AMOUNTS RECEIVED BY SURVIVING ANNUITANT UNDER JOINT AND SURVIVOR ANNUITY CONTRACT.—

(1) DEDUCTION FOR ESTATE TAX.—For purposes of computing the deduction under subsection (c)(1)(A), amounts received by a surviving annuitant—

(A) as an annuity under a joint and survivor annuity contract where the decedent annuitant died after the annuity starting date (as defined in section 72(c)(4)), and

(B) during the surviving annuitant's life expectancy period,

shall, to the extent included in gross income under section 72, be considered as amounts included in gross income under subsection (a).

(2) NET VALUE FOR ESTATE TAX PURPOSES.—In determining the net value for estate tax purposes under subsection (c)(2)(B) for purposes of this subsection, the value for estate tax purposes of the items described in paragraph (1) of this subsection shall be computed—

(A) by determining the excess of the value of the annuity at the date of the death of the deceased annuitant over the total amount excludable from the gross income of the surviving annuitant under section 72 during the surviving annuitant's life expectancy period, and

(B) by multiplying the figure so obtained by the ratio which the value of the annuity for estate tax purposes bears to the value of the annuity at the date of the death of the deceased.

(3) DEFINITIONS.—For purposes of this subsection—

(A) The term "life expectancy period" means the period beginning with the first day of the first period for which an amount is received by the surviving annuitant under the contract and ending with the close of the taxable year with or in which falls the termination of the life expectancy of the surviving annuitant. For purposes of this subparagraph, the life expectancy of the surviving annuitant shall be determined, as of the date of the death of the deceased annuitant, with reference to actuarial tables prescribed by the Secretary.

(B) The surviving annuitant's expected return under the contract shall be computed, as of the death of the deceased annuitant, with reference to actuarial tables prescribed by the Secretary.

[Sec. 691(e)]

(e) CROSS REFERENCE.—

For application of this section to income in respect of a deceased partner, see section 753.

SUBCHAPTER K—PARTNERS AND PARTNERSHIPS

PART I—DETERMINATION OF TAX LIABILITY

[Sec. 701]

SEC. 701. PARTNERS, NOT PARTNERSHIP, SUBJECT TO TAX.

A partnership as such shall not be subject to the income tax imposed by this chapter. Persons carrying on business as partners shall be liable for income tax only in their separate or individual capacities.

[Sec. 702]

SEC. 702. INCOME AND CREDITS OF PARTNER.

[Sec. 702(a)]

(a) GENERAL RULE.—In determining his income tax, each partner shall take into account separately his distributive share of the partnership's—

(1) gains and losses from sales or exchanges of capital assets held for not more than 1 year,

(2) gains and losses from sales or exchanges of capital assets held for more than 1 year,

(3) gains and losses from sales or exchanges of property described in section 1231 (relating to certain property used in a trade or business and involuntary conversions),

(4) charitable contributions (as defined in section 170 (c)),

(5) dividends with respect to which section 1(h) (11) or part VIII of subchapter B applies,

(6) taxes, described in section 901, paid or accrued to foreign countries and to possessions of the United States,

(7) other items of income, gain, loss, deduction, or credit, to the extent provided by regulations prescribed by the Secretary, and

(8) taxable income or loss, exclusive of items requiring separate computation under other paragraphs of this subsection.

[Sec. 702(b)]

(b) CHARACTER OF ITEMS CONSTITUTING DISTRIBUTIVE SHARE.—The character of any item of income, gain, loss, deduction, or credit included in a partner's distributive share under paragraphs (1) through (7) of subsection (a) shall be determined as if such item were realized directly from the source from which realized by the partnership, or incurred in the same manner as incurred by the partnership.

[Sec. 702(c)]

(c) GROSS INCOME OF A PARTNER.—In any case where it is necessary to determine the gross income of a partner for purposes of this title, such amount shall include his distributive share of the gross income of the partnership.

* * *

[Sec. 703]

SEC. 703. PARTNERSHIP COMPUTATIONS.

[Sec. 703(a)]

(a) INCOME AND DEDUCTIONS.—The taxable income of a partnership shall be computed in the same manner as in the case of an individual except that—

(1) the items described in section 702 (a) shall be separately stated, and

(2) the following deductions shall not be allowed to the partnership:

(A) the deductions for personal exemptions provided in section 151,

(B) the deduction for taxes provided in section 164 (a) with respect to taxes, described in section 901, paid or accrued to foreign countries and to possessions of the United States,

(C) the deduction for charitable contributions provided in section 170,

(D) the net operating loss deduction provided in section 172,

(E) the additional itemized deductions for individuals provided in part VII of subchapter B (sec. 211 and following), and

(F) the deduction for depletion under section 611 with respect to oil and gas wells.

[Sec. 703(b)]

(b) ELECTIONS OF THE PARTNERSHIP.—Any election affecting the computation of taxable income derived from a partnership shall be made by the partnership, except that any election under—

(1) subsection (b)(5) or (c)(3) of section 108 (relating to income from discharge of indebtedness),

(2) section 617 (relating to deduction and recapture of certain mining exploration expenditures), or

(3) section 901 (relating to taxes of foreign countries and possessions of the United States),

shall be made by each partner separately.

[Sec. 704]

SEC. 704. PARTNER'S DISTRIBUTIVE SHARE.

[Sec. 704(a)]

(a) EFFECT OF PARTNERSHIP AGREEMENT.—A partner's distributive share of income, gain, loss, deduction, or credit shall, except as otherwise provided in this chapter, be determined by the partnership agreement.

[Sec. 704(b)]

(b) DETERMINATION OF DISTRIBUTIVE SHARE.—A partner's distributive share of income, gain, loss, deduction, or credit (or item thereof) shall be determined in accordance with the partner's interest in the partnership (determined by taking into account all facts and circumstances), if—

(1) the partnership agreement does not provide as to the partner's distributive share of income, gain, loss, deduction, or credit (or item thereof), or

(2) the allocation to a partner under the agreement of income, gain, loss, deduction, or credit (or item thereof) does not have substantial economic effect.

[Sec. 704(c)]

(c) CONTRIBUTED PROPERTY.—

(1) IN GENERAL.—Under regulations prescribed by the Secretary—

(A) income, gain, loss, and deduction with respect to property contributed to the partnership by a partner shall be shared among the partners so as to take account of the variation between the basis of the property to the partnership and its fair market value at the time of contribution,

(B) if any property so contributed is distributed (directly or indirectly) by the partnership (other than to the contributing partner) within 7 years of being contributed—

(i) the contributing partner shall be treated as recognizing gain or loss (as the case may be) from the sale of such property in an amount equal to the gain or loss which would have been allocated to such partner under subparagraph (A) by reason of the variation described in subparagraph (A) if the property had been sold at its fair market value at the time of the distribution,

(ii) the character of such gain or loss shall be determined by reference to the character of the gain or loss which would have resulted if such property had been sold by the partnership to the distributee, and

(iii) appropriate adjustments shall be made to the adjusted basis of the contributing partner's interest in the partnership and to the adjusted basis of the property distributed to reflect any gain or loss recognized under this subparagraph, and

(C) if any property so contributed has a built-in loss—

(i) such built-in loss shall be taken into account only in determining the amount of items allocated to the contributing partner, and

(ii) except as provided in regulations, in determining the amount of items allocated to other partners, the basis of the contributed property in the hands of the partnership shall be treated as being equal to its fair market value at the time of contribution.

For purposes of subparagraph (C), the term "built-in loss" means the excess of the adjusted basis of the property (determined without regard to subparagraph (C)(ii)) over its fair market value at the time of contribution.

(2) SPECIAL RULE FOR DISTRIBUTIONS WHERE GAIN OR LOSS WOULD NOT BE RECOGNIZED OUTSIDE PARTNERSHIPS.—Under regulations prescribed by the Secretary, if—

(A) property contributed by a partner (hereinafter referred to as the "contributing partner") is distributed by the partnership to another partner, and

(B) other property of a like kind (within the meaning of section 1031) is distributed by the partnership to the contributing partner not later than the earlier of—

(i) the 180th day after the date of the distribution described in subparagraph (A), or

(ii) the due date (determined with regard to extensions) for the contributing partner's return of the tax imposed by this chapter for the taxable year in which the distribution described in subparagraph (A) occurs,

then to the extent of the value of the property described in subparagraph (B), paragraph (1)(B) shall be applied as if the contributing partner had contributed to the partnership the property described in subparagraph (B).

(3) OTHER RULES.—Under regulations prescribed by the Secretary, rules similar to the rules of paragraph (1) shall apply to contributions by a partner (using the cash receipts and disbursements method of accounting) of accounts payable and other accrued but unpaid items. Any reference in paragraph (1) or (2) to the contributing partner shall be treated as including a reference to any successor of such partner.

[Sec. 704(d)]

(d) LIMITATION ON ALLOWANCE OF LOSSES.—

(1) IN GENERAL.—A partner's distributive share of partnership loss (including capital loss) shall be allowed only to the extent of the adjusted basis of such partner's interest in the partnership at the end of the partnership year in which such loss occurred.

(2) CARRYOVER.—Any excess of such loss over such basis shall be allowed as a deduction at the end of the partnership year in which such excess is repaid to the partnership.

(3) SPECIAL RULES.—

(A) IN GENERAL.—In determining the amount of any loss under paragraph (1), there shall be taken into account the partner's distributive share of amounts described in paragraphs (4) and (6) of section 702(a).

(B) EXCEPTION.—In the case of a charitable contribution of property whose fair market value exceeds its adjusted basis, subparagraph (A) shall not apply to the extent of the partner's distributive share of such excess.

[Sec. 704(e)]

(e) PARTNERSHIP INTERESTS CREATED BY GIFT.—

(1) DISTRIBUTIVE SHARE OF DONEE INCLUDIBLE IN GROSS INCOME.—In the case of any partnership interest created by gift, the distributive share of the donee under the partnership agreement shall be includible in his gross income, except to the extent that such share is determined without allowance of reasonable compensation for services rendered to the partnership by the donor, and except to the extent that the portion of such share attributable to donated capital is proportionately greater than the share of the donor attributable to the donor's capital. The distributive share of a partner in the earnings of the partnership shall not be diminished because of absence due to military service.

(2) PURCHASE OF INTEREST BY MEMBER OF FAMILY.—For purposes of this subsection, an interest purchased by one member of a family from another shall be considered to be created by gift from the seller, and the fair market value of the purchased interest shall be considered to be donated capital. The "family" of any individual shall include only his spouse, ancestors, and lineal descendants, and any trusts for the primary benefit of such persons.

[Sec. 704(f)]

(f) CROSS REFERENCE.—

For rules in the case of the sale, exchange, liquidation, or reduction of a partner's interest, see section 706(c)(2).

[Sec. 705]

SEC. 705. DETERMINATION OF BASIS OF PARTNER'S INTEREST.

[Sec. 705(a)]

(a) GENERAL RULE.—The adjusted basis of a partner's interest in a partnership shall, except as provided in subsection (b), be the basis of such interest determined under section 722 (relating to contributions to a partnership) or section 742 (relating to transfers of partnership interests)—

(1) increased by the sum of his distributive share for the taxable year and prior taxable years of—

(A) taxable income of the partnership as determined under section 703 (a),

(B) income of the partnership exempt from tax under this title, and

(C) the excess of the deductions for depletion over the basis of the property subject to depletion;

(2) decreased (but not below zero) by distributions by the partnership as provided in section 733 and by the sum of his distributive share for the taxable year and prior taxable years of—

(A) losses of the partnership, and

(B) expenditures of the partnership not deductible in computing its taxable income and not properly chargeable to capital account; and

(3) decreased (but not below zero) by the amount of the partner's deduction for depletion for any partnership oil and gas property to the extent such deduction does not exceed the proportionate share of the adjusted basis of such property allocated to such partner under section 613A(c)(7)(D).

[Sec. 705(b)]

(b) ALTERNATIVE RULE.—The Secretary shall prescribe by regulations the circumstances under which the adjusted basis of a partner's interest in a partnership may be determined by reference to his proportionate share of the adjusted basis of partnership property upon a termination of the partnership.

[Sec. 706]

SEC. 706. TAXABLE YEARS OF PARTNER AND PARTNERSHIP.

[Sec. 706(a)]

(a) YEAR IN WHICH PARTNERSHIP INCOME IS INCLUDIBLE.—In computing the taxable income of a partner for a taxable year, the inclusions required by section 702 and section 707 (c) with respect to a partnership shall be based on the income, gain, loss, deduction, or credit of the partnership for any taxable year of the partnership ending within or with the taxable year of the partner.

[Sec. 706(b)]

(b) TAXABLE YEAR.—

(1) PARTNERSHIP'S TAXABLE YEAR.—

(A) PARTNERSHIP TREATED AS TAXPAYER.—The taxable year of a partnership shall be determined as though the partnership were a taxpayer.

(B) TAXABLE YEAR DETERMINED BY REFERENCE TO PARTNERS.—Except as provided in subparagraph (C), a partnership shall not have a taxable year other than—

(i) the majority interest taxable year (as defined in paragraph (4)),

(ii) if there is no taxable year described in clause (i), the taxable year of all the principal partners of the partnership, or

(iii) if there is no taxable year described in clause (i) or (ii), the calendar year unless the Secretary by regulations prescribes another period.

(C) BUSINESS PURPOSE.—A partnership may have a taxable year not described in subparagraph (B) if it establishes, to the satisfaction of the Secretary, a business purpose therefor. For purposes of this subparagraph, any deferral of income to partners shall not be treated as a business purpose.

(2) PARTNER'S TAXABLE YEAR.—A partner may not change to a taxable year other than that of a partnership in which he is a principal partner unless he establishes, to the satisfaction of the Secretary, a business purpose therefor.

(3) PRINCIPAL PARTNER.—For the purpose of this subsection, a principal partner is a partner having an interest of 5 percent or more in partnership profits or capital.

(4) MAJORITY INTEREST TAXABLE YEAR; LIMITATION ON REQUIRED CHANGES.—

(A) MAJORITY INTEREST TAXABLE YEAR DEFINED.—For purposes of paragraph (1) (B) (i)—

(i) IN GENERAL.—The term "majority interest taxable year" means the taxable year (if any) which, on each testing day, constituted the taxable year of 1 or more partners having (on such day) an aggregate interest in partnership profits and capital of more than 50 percent.

(ii) TESTING DATE.—The testing days shall be—

(I) the 1st day of the partnership taxable year (determined without regard to clause (i)), or

(II) the days during such representative period as the Secretary may prescribe.

(B) FURTHER CHANGE NOT REQUIRED FOR 3 YEARS.—Except as provided in regulations necessary to prevent the avoidance of this section, if, by reason of paragraph (1) (B) (i), the taxable year of a partnership is changed, such partnership shall not be required to change to another taxable year for either of the 2 taxable years following the year of change.

(5) APPLICATION WITH OTHER SECTIONS.—Except as provided in regulations, for purposes of determining the taxable year to which a partnership is required to change by reason of this subsection, changes in taxable years of other persons required by this subsection, section 441 (i), section 584 (i), section 644, or section 1378 (a) shall be taken into account.

[Sec. 706(c)]

(c) CLOSING OF PARTNERSHIP YEAR.—

(1) GENERAL RULE.—Except in the case of a termination of a partnership and except as provided in paragraph (2) of this subsection, the taxable year of a partnership shall not close as the result of the death of a partner, the entry of a new partner, the liquidation of a partner's interest in the partnership, or the sale or exchange of a partner's interest in the partnership.

(2) TREATMENT OF DISPOSITIONS.—

(A) DISPOSITION OF ENTIRE INTEREST.—The taxable year of a partnership shall close with respect to a partner whose entire interest in the partnership terminates (whether by reason of death, liquidation, or otherwise).

(B) DISPOSITION OF LESS THAN ENTIRE INTEREST.—The taxable year of a partnership shall not close (other than at the end of a partnership's taxable year as determined under subsection (b) (1)) with respect to a partner who sells or exchanges less than his entire interest in the partnership or with respect to a partner whose interest is reduced (whether by entry of a new partner, partial liquidation of a partner's interest, gift, or otherwise).

[Sec. 706(d)]

(d) DETERMINATION OF DISTRIBUTIVE SHARE WHEN PARTNER'S INTEREST CHANGES.—

(1) IN GENERAL.—Except as provided in paragraphs (2) and (3), if during any taxable year of the partnership there is a change in any partner's interest in the partnership, each partner's distributive share of any item of income, gain, loss, deduction, or credit of the partnership for such taxable year shall be determined by the use of any method prescribed by the Secretary by regulations which takes into account the varying interests of the partners in the partnership during such taxable year.

(2) CERTAIN CASH BASIS ITEMS PRORATED OVER PERIOD TO WHICH ATTRIBUTABLE.—

(A) IN GENERAL.—If during any taxable year of the partnership there is a change in any partner's interest in the partnership, then (except to the extent provided in regulations) each partner's distributive share of any allocable cash basis item shall be determined—

(i) by assigning the appropriate portion of such item to each day in the period to which it is attributable, and

(ii) by allocating the portion assigned to any such day among the partners in proportion to their interests in the partnership at the close of such day.

(B) ALLOCABLE CASH BASIS ITEM.—For purposes of this paragraph, the term "allocable cash basis item" means any of the following items with respect to which the partnership uses the cash receipts and disbursements method of accounting:

(i) Interest.

(ii) Taxes.

(iii) Payments for services or for the use of property.

(iv) Any other item of a kind specified in regulations prescribed by the Secretary as being an item with respect to which the application of this paragraph is appropriate to avoid significant misstatements of the income of the partners.

(C) ITEMS ATTRIBUTABLE TO PERIODS NOT WITHIN TAXABLE YEAR.—If any portion of any allocable cash basis item is attributable to—

(i) any period before the beginning of the taxable year, such portion shall be assigned under subparagraph (A)(i) to the first day of the taxable year, or

(ii) any period after the close of the taxable year, such portion shall be assigned under subparagraph (A)(i) to the last day of the taxable year.

(D) TREATMENT OF DEDUCTIBLE ITEMS ATTRIBUTABLE TO PRIOR PERIODS.—If any portion of a deductible cash basis item is assigned under subparagraph (C)(i) to the first day of any taxable year—

(i) such portion shall be allocated among persons who are partners in the partnership during the period to which such portion is attributable in accordance with their varying interests in the partnership during such period, and

(ii) any amount allocated under clause (i) to a person who is not a partner in the partnership on such first day shall be capitalized by the partnership and treated in the manner provided for in section 755.

(3) ITEMS ATTRIBUTABLE TO INTEREST IN LOWER TIER PARTNERSHIP PRORATED OVER ENTIRE TAXABLE YEAR.—If—

(A) during any taxable year of the partnership there is a change in any partner's interest in the partnership (hereinafter in this paragraph referred to as the "upper tier partnership"), and

(B) such partnership is a partner in another partnership (hereinafter in this paragraph referred to as the "lower tier partnership"),

then (except to the extent provided in regulations) each partner's distributive share of any item of the upper tier partnership attributable to the lower tier partnership shall be determined by assigning the appropriate portion (determined by applying principles similar to the principles of subparagraphs (C) and (D) of paragraph (2)) of each such item to the appropriate days during which the upper tier partnership is a partner in the lower tier partnership and by allocating the portion assigned to any such day among the partners in proportion to their interests in the upper tier partnership at the close of such day.

(4) TAXABLE YEAR DETERMINED WITHOUT REGARD TO SUBSECTION (c)(2)(A).—For purposes of this subsection, the taxable year of a partnership shall be determined without regard to subsection (c)(2)(A).

[Sec. 707]

SEC. 707. TRANSACTIONS BETWEEN PARTNER AND PARTNERSHIP.

[Sec. 707(a)]

(a) PARTNER NOT ACTING IN CAPACITY AS PARTNER.—

(1) IN GENERAL.—If a partner engages in a transaction with a partnership other than in his capacity as a member of such partnership, the transaction shall, except as otherwise provided in this section, be considered as occurring between the partnership and one who is not a partner.

(2) TREATMENT OF PAYMENTS TO PARTNERS FOR PROPERTY OR SERVICES.—Under regulations prescribed by the Secretary—

(A) TREATMENT OF CERTAIN SERVICES AND TRANSFERS OF PROPERTY.—If—

(i) a partner performs services for a partnership or transfers property to a partnership,

(ii) there is a related direct or indirect allocation and distribution to such partner, and

(iii) the performance of such services (or such transfer) and the allocation and distribution, when viewed together, are properly characterized as a transaction occurring between the partnership and a partner acting other than in his capacity as a member of the partnership,

such allocation and distribution shall be treated as a transaction described in paragraph (1).

(B) TREATMENT OF CERTAIN PROPERTY TRANSFERS.—If—

(i) there is a direct or indirect transfer of money or other property by a partner to a partnership,

(ii) there is a related direct or indirect transfer of money or other property by the partnership to such partner (or another partner), and

(iii) the transfers described in clauses (i) and (ii), when viewed together, are properly characterized as a sale or exchange of property,

such transfers shall be treated either as a transaction described in paragraph (1) or as a transaction between 2 or more partners acting other than in their capacity as members of the partnership.

[Sec. 707(b)]

(b) CERTAIN SALES OR EXCHANGES OF PROPERTY WITH RESPECT TO CONTROLLED PARTNERSHIPS.—

(1) LOSSES DISALLOWED.—No deduction shall be allowed in respect of losses from sales or exchanges of property (other than an interest in the partnership), directly or indirectly, between—

(A) a partnership and a person owning, directly or indirectly, more than 50 percent of the capital interest, or the profits interest, in such partnership, or

(B) two partnerships in which the same persons own, directly or indirectly, more than 50 percent of the capital interests or profits interests.

In the case of a subsequent sale or exchange by a transferee described in this paragraph, section 267(d) shall be applicable as if the loss were disallowed under section 267(a)(1). For purposes of section 267(a)(2), partnerships described in subparagraph (B) of this paragraph shall be treated as persons specified in section 267(b).

(2) GAINS TREATED AS ORDINARY INCOME.—In the case of a sale or exchange, directly or indirectly, of property, which, in the hands of the transferee, is property other than a capital asset as defined in section 1221—

(A) between a partnership and a person owning, directly or indirectly, more than 50 percent of the capital interest, or profits interest, in such partnership, or

(B) between two partnerships in which the same persons own, directly or indirectly, more than 50 percent of the capital interests or profits interests,

any gain recognized shall be considered as ordinary income.

(3) OWNERSHIP OF A CAPITAL OR PROFITS INTEREST.—For purposes of paragraphs (1) and (2) of this subsection, the ownership of a capital or profits interest in a partnership shall be determined in accordance with the rules for constructive ownership of stock provided in section 267 (c) other than paragraph (3) of such section.

[Sec. 707(c)]

(c) GUARANTEED PAYMENTS.—To the extent determined without regard to the income of the partnership, payments to a partner for services or the use of capital shall be considered as made to one who is not a member of the partnership, but only for the purposes of section 61 (a) (relating to gross income) and, subject to section 263, for purposes of section 162 (a) (relating to trade or business expenses).

[Sec. 708]

SEC. 708. CONTINUATION OF PARTNERSHIP.

[Sec. 708(a)]

(a) GENERAL RULE.—For purposes of this subchapter, an existing partnership shall be considered as continuing if it is not terminated.

[Sec. 708(b)]

(b) TERMINATION.—

(1) GENERAL RULE.—For purposes of subsection (a), a partnership shall be considered as terminated only if no part of any business, financial operation, or venture of the partnership continues to be carried on by any of its partners in a partnership.

(2) SPECIAL RULES.—

(A) MERGER OR CONSOLIDATION.—In the case of the merger or consolidation of two or more partnerships, the resulting partnership shall, for purposes of this section, be considered the continuation of any merging or consolidating partnership whose members own an interest of more than 50 percent in the capital and profits of the resulting partnership.

(B) DIVISION OF A PARTNERSHIP.—In the case of a division of a partnership into two or more partnerships, the resulting partnerships (other than any resulting partnership the members of which had an interest of 50 percent or less in the capital and profits of the prior partnership) shall, for purposes of this section, be considered a continuation of the prior partnership.

[Sec. 709]

SEC. 709. TREATMENT OF ORGANIZATION AND SYNDICATION FEES.

[Sec. 709(a)]

(a) GENERAL RULE.—Except as provided in subsection (b), no deduction shall be allowed under this chapter to the partnership or to any partner for any amounts paid or incurred to organize a partnership or to promote the sale of (or to sell) an interest in such partnership.

[Sec. 709(b)]

(b) DEDUCTION OF ORGANIZATION FEES.—

(1) ALLOWANCE OF DEDUCTION.—If a partnership elects the application of this subsection (in accordance with regulations prescribed by the Secretary) with respect to any organizational expenses—

(A) the partnership shall be allowed a deduction for the taxable year in which the partnership begins business in an amount equal to the lesser of—

(i) the amount of organizational expenses with respect to the partnership, or

(ii) $5,000, reduced (but not below zero) by the amount by which such organizational expenses exceed $50,000, and

(B) the remainder of such organizational expenses shall be allowed as a deduction ratably over the 180-month period beginning with the month in which the partnership begins business.

(2) DISPOSITIONS BEFORE CLOSE OF AMORTIZATION PERIOD.—In any case in which a partnership is liquidated before the end of the period to which paragraph (1)(B) applies, any deferred expenses attributable to the partnership which were not allowed as a deduction by reason of this section may be deducted to the extent allowable under section 165.

(3) ORGANIZATIONAL EXPENSES DEFINED.—The organizational expenses to which paragraph (1) applies, are expenditures which—

(A) are incident to the creation of the partnership;

(B) are chargeable to capital account; and

(C) are of a character which, if expended incident to the creation of a partnership having an ascertainable life, would be amortized over such life.

PART II—CONTRIBUTIONS, DISTRIBUTIONS, AND TRANSFERS

Subpart A—Contributions to a Partnership

[Sec. 721]

SEC. 721. NONRECOGNITION OF GAIN OR LOSS ON CONTRIBUTION.

[Sec. 721(a)]

(a) GENERAL RULE.—No gain or loss shall be recognized to a partnership or to any of its partners in the case of a contribution of property to the partnership in exchange for an interest in the partnership.

[Sec. 721(b)]

(b) SPECIAL RULE.—Subsection (a) shall not apply to gain realized on a transfer of property to a partnership which would be treated as an investment company (within the meaning of section 351) if the partnership were incorporated.

[Sec. 721(c)]

(c) REGULATIONS RELATING TO CERTAIN TRANSFERS TO PARTNERSHIPS.—The Secretary may provide by regulations that subsection (a) shall not apply to gain realized on the transfer of property to a partnership if such gain, when recognized, will be includible in the gross income of a person other than a United States person.

[Sec. 721(d)]

(d) TRANSFERS OF INTANGIBLES.—

For regulatory authority to treat intangibles transferred to a partnership as sold, see section 367(d)(3).

[Sec. 722]

SEC. 722. BASIS OF CONTRIBUTING PARTNER'S INTEREST.

The basis of an interest in a partnership acquired by a contribution of property, including money, to the partnership shall be the amount of such money and the adjusted basis of such property to the contributing partner at the time of the contribution increased by the amount (if any) of gain recognized under section 721(b) to the contributing partner at such time.

[Sec. 723]

SEC. 723. BASIS OF PROPERTY CONTRIBUTED TO PARTNERSHIP.

The basis of property contributed to a partnership by a partner shall be the adjusted basis of such property to the contributing partner at the time of the contribution increased by the amount (if any) of gain recognized under section 721(b) to the contributing partner at such time.

[Sec. 724]

SEC. 724. CHARACTER OF GAIN OR LOSS ON CONTRIBUTED UNREALIZED RECEIVABLES, INVENTORY ITEMS, AND CAPITAL LOSS PROPERTY.

[Sec. 724(a)]

(a) CONTRIBUTIONS OF UNREALIZED RECEIVABLES.—In the case of any property which—

(1) was contributed to the partnership by a partner, and

(2) was an unrealized receivable in the hands of such partner immediately before such contribution,

any gain or loss recognized by the partnership on the disposition of such property shall be treated as ordinary income or ordinary loss, as the case may be.

[Sec. 724(b)]

(b) CONTRIBUTIONS OF INVENTORY ITEMS.—In the case of any property which—

(1) was contributed to the partnership by a partner, and

(2) was an inventory item in the hands of such partner immediately before such contribution,

any gain or loss recognized by the partnership on the disposition of such property during the 5-year period beginning on the date of such contribution shall be treated as ordinary income or ordinary loss, as the case may be.

[Sec. 724(c)]

(c) CONTRIBUTIONS OF CAPITAL LOSS PROPERTY.—In the case of any property which—

(1) was contributed by a partner to the partnership, and

(2) was a capital asset in the hands of such partner immediately before such contribution,

any loss recognized by the partnership on the disposition of such property during the 5-year period beginning on the date of such contribution shall be treated as a loss from the sale of a capital asset to the extent that, immediately before such contribution, the adjusted basis of such property in the hands of the partner exceeded the fair market value of such property.

[Sec. 724(d)]

(d) DEFINITIONS.—For purposes of this section—

(1) UNREALIZED RECEIVABLE.—The term "unrealized receivable" has the meaning given such term by section 751(c) (determined by treating any reference to the partnership as referring to the partner).

(2) INVENTORY ITEM.—The term "inventory item" has the meaning given such term by section 751(d) (determined by treating any reference to the partnership as referring to the partner and by applying section 1231 without regard to any holding period therein provided).

(3) SUBSTITUTED BASIS PROPERTY.—

(A) IN GENERAL.—If any property described in subsection (a), (b), or (c) is disposed of in a nonrecognition transaction, the tax treatment which applies to such property under such subsection shall also apply to any substituted basis property resulting from such transaction. A similar rule shall also apply in the case of a series of non-recognition transactions.

(B) EXCEPTION FOR STOCK IN C CORPORATION.—Subparagraph (A) shall not apply to any stock in a C corporation received in an exchange described in section 351.

Subpart B—Distributions by a Partnership

[Sec. 731]

SEC. 731. EXTENT OF RECOGNITION OF GAIN OR LOSS ON DISTRIBUTION.

[Sec. 731(a)]

(a) PARTNERS.—In the case of a distribution by a partnership to a partner—

(1) gain shall not be recognized to such partner, except to the extent that any money distributed exceeds the adjusted basis of such partner's interest in the partnership immediately before the distribution, and

(2) loss shall not be recognized to such partner, except that upon a distribution in liquidation of a partner's interest in a partnership where no property other than that described in subparagraph (A) or (B) is distributed to such partner, loss shall be recognized to the extent of the excess of the adjusted basis of such partner's interest in the partnership over the sum of—

(A) any money distributed, and

(B) the basis to the distributee, as determined under section 732, of any unrealized receivables (as defined in section 751(c)) and inventory (as defined in section 751(d)).

Any gain or loss recognized under this subsection shall be considered as gain or loss from the sale or exchange of the partnership interest of the distributee partner.

[Sec. 731(b)]

(b) PARTNERSHIPS.—No gain or loss shall be recognized to a partnership on a distribution to a partner of property, including money.

[Sec. 731(c)]

(c) TREATMENT OF MARKETABLE SECURITIES.—

(1) IN GENERAL.—For purposes of subsection (a)(1) and section 737—

(A) the term "money" includes marketable securities, and

(B) such securities shall be taken into account at their fair market value as of the date of the distribution.

(2) MARKETABLE SECURITIES.—For purposes of this subsection:

(A) IN GENERAL.—The term "marketable securities" means financial instruments and foreign currencies which are, as of the date of the distribution, actively traded (within the meaning of section 1092(d)(1)).

(B) OTHER PROPERTY.—Such term includes—

(i) any interest in—

(I) a common trust fund, or

(II) a regulated investment company which is offering for sale or has outstanding any redeemable security (as defined in section 2(a)(32) of the Investment Company Act of 1940) of which it is the issuer,

(ii) any financial instrument which, pursuant to its terms or any other arrangement, is readily convertible into, or exchangeable for, money or marketable securities,

(iii) any financial instrument the value of which is determined substantially by reference to marketable securities,

(iv) except to the extent provided in regulations prescribed by the Secretary, any interest in a precious metal which, as of the date of the distribution, is actively traded (within the meaning of section 1092(d)(1)) unless such metal was produced, used, or held in the active conduct of a trade or business by the partnership,

(v) except as otherwise provided in regulations prescribed by the Secretary, interests in any entity if substantially all of the assets of such entity consist (directly or indirectly) of marketable securities, money, or both, and

(vi) to the extent provided in regulations prescribed by the Secretary, any interest in an entity not described in clause (v) but only to the extent of the value of such interest which is attributable to marketable securities, money, or both.

(C) FINANCIAL INSTRUMENT.—The term "financial instrument" includes stocks and other equity interests, evidences of indebtedness, options, forward or future contracts, notional principal contracts, and derivatives.

(3) EXCEPTIONS.—

(A) IN GENERAL.—Paragraph (1) shall not apply to the distribution from a partnership of a marketable security to a partner if—

(i) the security was contributed to the partnership by such partner, except to the extent that the value of the distributed security is attributable to marketable securities or money contributed (directly or indirectly) to the entity to which the distributed security relates,

(ii) to the extent provided in regulations prescribed by the Secretary, the property was not a marketable security when acquired by such partnership, or

(iii) such partnership is an investment partnership and such partner is an eligible partner thereof.

(B) LIMITATION ON GAIN RECOGNIZED.—In the case of a distribution of marketable securities to a partner, the amount taken into account under paragraph (1) shall be reduced (but not below zero) by the excess (if any) of—

(i) such partner's distributive share of the net gain which would be recognized if all of the marketable securities of the same class and issuer as the distributed securities held by the partnership were sold (immediately before the transaction to which the distribution relates) by the partnership for fair market value, over

(ii) such partner's distributive share of the net gain which is attributable to the marketable securities of the same class and issuer as the distributed securities held by the partnership immediately after the transaction, determined by using the same fair market value as used under clause (i).

Under regulations prescribed by the Secretary, all marketable securities held by the partnership may be treated as marketable securities of the same class and issuer as the distributed securities.

(C) DEFINITIONS RELATING TO INVESTMENT PARTNERSHIPS.—For purposes of subparagraph (A)(iii):

(i) INVESTMENT PARTNERSHIP.—The term "investment partnership" means any partnership which has never been engaged in a trade or business and substantially all of the assets (by value) of which have always consisted of—

(I) money,

(II) stock in a corporation,

(III) notes, bonds, debentures, or other evidences of indebtedness,

(IV) interest rate, currency, or equity notional principal contracts,

(V) foreign currencies,

(VI) interests in or derivative financial instruments (including options, forward or futures contracts, short positions, and similar financial instruments) in any asset described in any other subclause of this clause or in any commodity traded on or subject to the rules of a board of trade or commodity exchange,

(VII) other assets specified in regulations prescribed by the Secretary, or

(VIII) any combination of the foregoing.

(ii) EXCEPTION FOR CERTAIN ACTIVITIES.—A partnership shall not be treated as engaged in a trade or business by reason of—

(I) any activity undertaken as an investor, trader, or dealer in any asset described in clause (i), or

(II) any other activity specified in regulations prescribed by the Secretary.

(iii) ELIGIBLE PARTNER.—

(I) IN GENERAL.—The term "eligible partner" means any partner who, before the date of the distribution, did not contribute to the partnership any property other than assets described in clause (i).

(II) EXCEPTION FOR CERTAIN NONRECOGNITION TRANSACTIONS.—The term "eligible partner" shall not include the transferor or transferee in a nonrecognition transaction involving a transfer of any portion of an interest in a partnership with respect to which the transferor was not an eligible partner.

(iv) LOOK-THRU OF PARTNERSHIP TIERS.—Except as otherwise provided in regulations prescribed by the Secretary—

(I) a partnership shall be treated as engaged in any trade or business engaged in by, and as holding (instead of a partnership interest) a proportionate share of the assets of, any other partnership in which the partnership holds a partnership interest, and

(II) a partner who contributes to a partnership an interest in another partnership shall be treated as contributing a proportionate share of the assets of the other partnership.

If the preceding sentence does not apply under such regulations with respect to any interest held by a partnership in another partnership, the interest in such other partnership shall be treated as if it were specified in a subclause of clause (i).

(4) BASIS OF SECURITIES DISTRIBUTED.—

(A) IN GENERAL.—The basis of marketable securities with respect to which gain is recognized by reason of this subsection shall be—

(i) their basis determined under section 732, increased by

(ii) the amount of such gain.

(B) ALLOCATION OF BASIS INCREASE.—Any increase in basis attributable to the gain described in subparagraph (A)(ii) shall be allocated to marketable securities in proportion to their respective amounts of unrealized appreciation before such increase.

(5) SUBSECTION DISREGARDED IN DETERMINING BASIS OF PARTNER'S INTEREST IN PARTNERSHIP AND OF BASIS OF PARTNERSHIP PROPERTY.—Sections 733 and 734 shall be applied as if no gain were recognized, and no adjustment were made to the basis of property, under this subsection.

(6) CHARACTER OF GAIN RECOGNIZED.—In the case of a distribution of a marketable security which is an unrealized receivable (as defined in section 751(c)) or an inventory item (as defined in section 751(c)) or an inventory item (as defined in section 751(d)), any gain recognized under this subsection shall be treated as ordinary income to the extent of any increase in the basis of such security attributable to the gain described in paragraph (4)(A)(ii).

(7) REGULATIONS.—The Secretary shall prescribe such regulations as may be necessary or appropriate to carry out the purposes of this subsection, including regulations to prevent the avoidance of such purposes.

[Sec. 731(d)]

(d) EXCEPTIONS.—This section shall not apply to the extent otherwise provided by section 736 (relating to payments to a retiring partner or a deceased partner's successor in interest), section 751 (relating to unrealized receivables and inventory items), and section 737 (relating to recognition of precontribution gain in case of certain distributions).

[Sec. 732]

SEC. 732. BASIS OF DISTRIBUTED PROPERTY OTHER THAN MONEY.

[Sec. 732(a)]

(a) DISTRIBUTIONS OTHER THAN IN LIQUIDATION OF A PARTNER'S INTEREST.—

(1) GENERAL RULE.—The basis of property (other than money) distributed by a partnership to a partner other than in liquidation of the partner's interest shall, except as provided in paragraph (2), be its adjusted basis to the partnership immediately before such distribution.

(2) LIMITATION.—The basis to the distributee partner of property to which paragraph (1) is applicable shall not exceed the adjusted basis of such partner's interest in the partnership reduced by any money distributed in the same transaction.

[Sec. 732(b)]

(b) DISTRIBUTIONS IN LIQUIDATION.—The basis of property (other than money) distributed by a partnership to a partner in liquidation of the partner's interest shall be an amount equal to the adjusted basis of such partner's interest in the partnership reduced by any money distributed in the same transaction.

[Sec. 732(c)]

(c) ALLOCATION OF BASIS.—

(1) IN GENERAL.—The basis of distributed properties to which subsection (a)(2) or (b) is applicable shall be allocated—

(A)(i) first to any unrealized receivables (as defined in section 751(c)) and inventory items (as defined in section 751(d)) in an amount equal to the adjusted basis of each such property to the partnership, and

(ii) if the basis to be allocated is less than the sum of the adjusted bases of such properties to the partnership, then, to the extent any decrease is required in order to have the adjusted bases of such properties equal the basis to be allocated, in the manner provided in paragraph (3), and

(B) to the extent of any basis remaining after the allocation under subparagraph (A), to other distributed properties—

(i) first by assigning to each such other property such other property's adjusted basis to the partnership, and

(ii) then, to the extent any increase or decrease in basis is required in order to have the adjusted bases of such other distributed properties equal such remaining basis, in the manner provided in paragraph (2) or (3), whichever is appropriate.

(2) METHOD OF ALLOCATING INCREASE.—Any increase required under paragraph (1)(B) shall be allocated among the properties—

(A) first to properties with unrealized appreciation in proportion to their respective amounts of unrealized appreciation before such increase (but only to the extent of each property's unrealized appreciation), and

(B) then, to the extent such increase is not allocated under subparagraph (A), in proportion to their respective fair market values.

(3) METHOD OF ALLOCATING DECREASE.—Any decrease required under paragraph (1)(A) or (1)(B) shall be allocated—

(A) first to properties with unrealized depreciation in proportion to their respective amounts of unrealized depreciation before such decrease (but only to the extent of each property's unrealized depreciation), and

(B) then, to the extent such decrease is not allocated under subparagraph (A), in proportion to their respective adjusted bases (as adjusted under subparagraph (A)).

[Sec. 732(d)]

(d) SPECIAL PARTNERSHIP BASIS TO TRANSFEREE.—For purposes of subsections (a), (b), and (c), a partner who acquired all or part of his interest by a transfer with respect to which the election provided in section 754 is not in effect, and to whom a distribution of property (other than money) is made with respect to the transferred interest within 2 years after such transfer, may elect, under regulations prescribed by the Secretary, to treat as the adjusted partnership basis of such property the adjusted basis such property would have if the adjustment provided in section 743 (b) were in effect with respect to the partnership property. The Secretary may by regulations require the application of this subsection in the case of a distribution to a transferee partner, whether or not made within 2 years after the transfer, if at the time of the transfer the fair market value of the partnership property (other than money) exceeded 110 percent of its adjusted basis to the partnership.

[Sec. 732(e)]

(e) EXCEPTION.—This section shall not apply to the extent that a distribution is treated as a sale or exchange of property under section 751(b) (relating to unrealized receivables and inventory items).

[Sec. 732(f)]

(f) CORRESPONDING ADJUSTMENT TO BASIS OF ASSETS OF A DISTRIBUTED CORPORATION CONTROLLED BY A CORPORATE PARTNER.—

(1) IN GENERAL.—If—

(A) a corporation (hereafter in this subsection referred to as the "corporate partner") receives a distribution from a partnership of stock in another corporation (hereafter in this subsection referred to as the "distributed corporation"),

(B) the corporate partner has control of the distributed corporation immediately after the distribution or at any time thereafter, and

(C) the partnership's adjusted basis in such stock immediately before the distribution exceeded the corporate partner's adjusted basis in such stock immediately after the distribution,

then an amount equal to such excess shall be applied to reduce (in accordance with subsection (c)) the basis of property held by the distributed corporation at such time (or, if the corporate partner does not control the distributed corporation at such time, at the time the corporate partner first has such control).

(2) EXCEPTION FOR CERTAIN DISTRIBUTIONS BEFORE CONTROL ACQUIRED.—Paragraph (1) shall not apply to any distribution of stock in the distributed corporation if—

(A) the corporate partner does not have control of such corporation immediately after such distribution, and

(B) the corporate partner establishes to the satisfaction of the Secretary that such distribution was not part of a plan or arrangement to acquire control of the distributed corporation.

(3) LIMITATIONS ON BASIS REDUCTION.—

(A) IN GENERAL.—The amount of the reduction under paragraph (1) shall not exceed the amount by which the sum of the aggregate adjusted bases of the property and the amount of money of the distributed corporation exceeds the corporate partner's adjusted basis in the stock of the distributed corporation.

(B) REDUCTION NOT TO EXCEED ADJUSTED BASIS OF PROPERTY.—No reduction under paragraph (1) in the basis of any property shall exceed the adjusted basis of such property (determined without regard to such reduction).

(4) GAIN RECOGNITION WHERE REDUCTION LIMITED.—If the amount of any reduction under paragraph (1) (determined after the application of paragraph (3)(A)) exceeds the aggregate adjusted bases of the property of the distributed corporation—

(A) such excess shall be recognized by the corporate partner as long-term capital gain, and

(B) the corporate partner's adjusted basis in the stock of the distributed corporation shall be increased by such excess.

(5) CONTROL.—For purposes of this subsection, the term "control" means ownership of stock meeting the requirements of section 1504(a)(2).

(6) INDIRECT DISTRIBUTIONS.—For purposes of paragraph (1), if a corporation acquires (other than in a distribution from a partnership) stock the basis of which is determined (by reason of being distributed from a partnership) in whole or in part by reference to subsection (a)(2) or (b), the corporation shall be treated as receiving a distribution of such stock from a partnership.

(7) SPECIAL RULE FOR STOCK IN CONTROLLED CORPORATION.—If the property held by a distributed corporation is stock in a corporation which the distributed corporation controls, this subsection shall be applied to reduce the basis of the property of such controlled corporation. This subsection shall be reapplied to any property of any controlled corporation which is stock in a corporation which it controls.

(8) REGULATIONS.—The Secretary shall prescribe such regulations as may be necessary to carry out the purposes of this subsection, including regulations to avoid double counting and to prevent the abuse of such purposes.

[Sec. 733]

SEC. 733. BASIS OF DISTRIBUTEE PARTNER'S INTEREST.

In the case of a distribution by a partnership to a partner other than in liquidation of a partner's interest, the adjusted basis to such partner of his interest in the partnership shall be reduced (but not below zero) by—

(1) the amount of any money distributed to such partner, and

(2) the amount of the basis to such partner of distributed property other than money, as determined under section 732.

[Sec. 734]

SEC. 734. ADJUSTMENT TO BASIS OF UNDISTRIBUTED PARTNERSHIP PROPERTY WHERE SECTION 754 ELECTION OR SUBSTANTIAL BASIS REDUCTION.

[Sec. 734(a)]

(a) GENERAL RULE.—The basis of partnership property shall not be adjusted as the result of a distribution of property to a partner unless the election, provided in section 754 (relating to optional adjustment to basis of partnership property), is in effect with respect to such partnership or unless there is a substantial basis reduction with respect to such distribution.

[Sec. 734(b)]

(b) METHOD OF ADJUSTMENT.—In the case of a distribution of property to a partner by a partnership with respect to which the election provided in section 754 is in effect or with respect to which there is a substantial basis reduction, the partnership shall—

(1) increase the adjusted basis of partnership property by—

(A) the amount of any gain recognized to the distributee partner with respect to such distribution under section 731(a)(1), and

(B) in the case of distributed property to which section 732(a)(2) or (b) applies, the excess of the adjusted basis of the distributed property to the partnership immediately before the distribution (as adjusted by section 732(d)) over the basis of the distributed property to the distributee, as determined under section 732, or

(2) decrease the adjusted basis of partnership property by—

(A) the amount of any loss recognized to the distributee partner with respect to such distribution under section 731(a)(2), and

(B) in the case of distributed property to which section 732(b) applies, the excess of the basis of the distributed property to the distributee, as determined under section 732, over the adjusted basis of the distributed property to the partnership immediately before such distribution (as adjusted by section 732(d)).

Paragraph (1)(B) shall not apply to any distributed property which is an interest in another partnership with respect to which the election provided in section 754 is not in effect.

[Sec. 734(c)]

(c) ALLOCATION OF BASIS.—The allocation of basis among partnership properties where subsection (b) is applicable shall be made in accordance with the rules provided in section 755.

[Sec. 734(d)]

(d) SUBSTANTIAL BASIS REDUCTION.—

(1) IN GENERAL.—For purposes of this section, there is a substantial basis reduction with respect to a distribution if the sum of the amounts described in subparagraphs (A) and (B) of subsection (b)(2) exceeds $250,000.

(2) REGULATIONS.—

For regulations to carry out this subsection, see section 743(d)(2).

[Sec. 734(e)]

(e) EXCEPTION FOR SECURITIZATION PARTNERSHIPS.—For purposes of this section, a securitization partnership (as defined in section 743(f)) shall not be treated as having a substantial basis reduction with respect to any distribution of property to a partner.

[Sec. 735]

SEC. 735. CHARACTER OF GAIN OR LOSS ON DISPOSITION OF DISTRIBUTED PROPERTY.

[Sec. 735(a)]

(a) SALE OR EXCHANGE OF CERTAIN DISTRIBUTED PROPERTY.—

(1) UNREALIZED RECEIVABLES.—Gain or loss on the disposition by a distributee partner of unrealized receivables (as defined in section 751(c)) distributed by a partnership, shall be considered as ordinary income or as ordinary loss, as the case may be.

(2) INVENTORY ITEMS.—Gain or loss on the sale or exchange by a distributee partner of inventory items (as defined in section 751(d)) distributed by a partnership shall, if sold or exchanged within 5 years from the date of the distribution, be considered as ordinary income or as ordinary loss, as the case may be.

[Sec. 735(b)]

(b) HOLDING PERIOD FOR DISTRIBUTED PROPERTY.—In determining the period for which a partner has held property received in a distribution from a partnership (other than for purposes of subsection (a)(2)), there shall be included the holding period of the partnership, as determined under section 1223, with respect to such property.

[Sec. 735(c)]

(c) SPECIAL RULES.—

(1) WAIVER OF HOLDING PERIODS CONTAINED IN SECTION 1231.—For purposes of this section, section 751(d) (defining inventory item) shall be applied without regard to any holding period in section 1231(b).

(2) SUBSTITUTED BASIS PROPERTY.—

(A) IN GENERAL.—If any property described in subsection (a) is disposed of in a nonrecognition transaction, the tax treatment which applies to such property under such subsection shall also apply to any substituted basis property resulting from such transaction. A similar rule shall also apply in the case of a series of nonrecognition transactions.

(B) EXCEPTION FOR STOCK IN C CORPORATION.—Subparagraph (A) shall not apply to any stock in a C corporation received in an exchange described in section 351.

[Sec. 736]

SEC. 736. PAYMENTS TO A RETIRING PARTNER OR A DECEASED PARTNER'S SUCCESSOR IN INTEREST.

[Sec. 736(a)]

(a) PAYMENTS CONSIDERED AS DISTRIBUTIVE SHARE OR GUARANTEED PAYMENT.—Payments made in liquidation of the interest of a retiring partner or a deceased partner shall, except as provided in subsection (b), be considered—

(1) as a distributive share to the recipient of partnership income if the amount thereof is determined with regard to the income of the partnership, or

(2) as a guaranteed payment described in section 707(c) if the amount thereof is determined without regard to the income of the partnership.

[Sec. 736(b)]

(b) PAYMENTS FOR INTEREST IN PARTNERSHIP.—

(1) GENERAL RULE.—Payments made in liquidation of the interest of a retiring partner or a deceased partner shall, to the extent such payments (other than payments described in paragraph (2)) are determined, under regulations prescribed by the Secretary, to be made in exchange for the interest of such partner in partnership property, be considered as a distribution by the partnership and not as a distributive share or guaranteed payment under subsection (a).

(2) SPECIAL RULES.—For purposes of this subsection, payments in exchange for an interest in partnership property shall not include amounts paid for—

(A) unrealized receivables of the partnership (as defined in section 751(c)), or

(B) good will of the partnership, except to the extent that the partnership agreement provides for a payment with respect to good will.

(3) LIMITATION ON APPLICATION OF PARAGRAPH (2).—Paragraph (2) shall apply only if—

(A) capital is not a material income-producing factor for the partnership, and

(B) the retiring or deceased partner was a general partner in the partnership.

[Sec. 737]

SEC. 737. RECOGNITION OF PRECONTRIBUTION GAIN IN CASE OF CERTAIN DISTRIBUTIONS TO CONTRIBUTING PARTNER.

[Sec. 737(a)]

(a) GENERAL RULE.—In the case of any distribution by a partnership to a partner, such partner shall be treated as recognizing gain in an amount equal to the lesser of—

(1) the excess (if any) of (A) the fair market value of property (other than money) received in the distribution over (B) the adjusted basis of such partner's interest in the partnership immediately before the distribution reduced (but not below zero) by the amount of money received in the distribution, or

(2) the net precontribution gain of the partner.

Gain recognized under the preceding sentence shall be in addition to any gain recognized under section 731. The character of such gain shall be determined by reference to the proportionate character of the net precontribution gain.

[Sec. 737(b)]

(b) NET PRECONTRIBUTION GAIN.—For purposes of this seciton, the term "net precontribution gain" means the net gain (if any) which would have been recognized by the distributee partner under section 704(c)(1)(B) if all property which—

(1) had been contributed to the partnership by the distributee partner within 7 years of the distribution, and

(2) is held by such partnership immediately before the distribution,

had been distributed by such partnership to another partner.

[Sec. 737(c)]

(c) BASIS RULES.—

(1) PARTNER'S INTEREST.—The adjusted basis of a partner's interest in a partnership shall be increased by the amount of any gain recognized by such partner under subsection (a). For purposes of determining the basis of the distributed property (other than money) such increase shall be treated as occurring immediately before the distribution.

(2) PARTNERSHIP'S BASIS IN CONTRIBUTED PROPERTY.—Appropriate adjustments shall be made to the adjusted basis of the partnership in the contributed property referred to in subsection (b) to reflect gain recognized under subsection (a).

[Sec. 737(d)]

(d) EXCEPTIONS.—

(1) DISTRIBUTIONS OF PREVIOUSLY CONTRIBUTED PROPERTY.—If any portion of the property distributed consists of property which had been contributed by the distributee partner to the partnership, such property shall not be taken into account under subsection (a)(1) and shall not be taken into account in determining the amount of the net precontribution gain. If the property distributed consists of an interest in an entity, the preceding sentence shall not apply to the extent that the value of such interest is attributable to property contributed to such entity after such interest had been contributed to the partnership.

(2) COORDINATION WITH SECTION 751.—This section shall not apply to the extent section 751(b) applies to such distribution.

[Sec. 737(e)]

(e) MARKETABLE SECURITIES TREATED AS MONEY.—For treatment of marketable securities as money for purposes of this section, see section 731(c).

Subpart C—Transfers of Interests in a Partnership

[Sec. 741]

SEC. 741. RECOGNITION AND CHARACTER OF GAIN OR LOSS ON SALE OR EXCHANGE.

In the case of a sale or exchange of an interest in a partnership, gain or loss shall be recognized to the transferor partner. Such gain or loss shall be considered as gain or loss from the sale or exchange of a capital asset, except as otherwise provided in section 751 (relating to unrealized receivables and inventory items).

[Sec. 742]

SEC. 742. BASIS OF TRANFEREE PARTNER'S INTEREST.

The basis of an interest in a partnership acquired other than by contribution shall be determined under part II of subchapter O (sec. 1011 and following).

[Sec. 743]

SEC. 743. SPECIAL RULES WHERE SECTION 754 ELECTION OR SUBSTANTIAL BUILT-IN LOSS.

[Sec. 743(a)]

(a) GENERAL RULE.—The basis of partnership property shall not be adjusted as the result of a transfer of an interest in a partnership by sale or exchange or on the death of a partner unless the election provided by section 754 (relating to optional adjustment to basis of partnership property) is in effect with respect to such partnership or unless the partnership has a substantial built-in loss immediately after such transfer.

[Sec. 743(b)]

(b) ADJUSTMENT TO BASIS OF PARTNERSHIP PROPERTY.—In the case of a transfer of an interest in a partnership by sale or exchange or upon the death of a partner, a partnership with respect to which the election provided in section 754 is in effect or which has a substantial built-in loss immediately after such transfer shall—

(1) increase the adjusted basis of the partnership property by the excess of the basis to the transferee partner of his interest in the partnership over his proportionate share of the adjusted basis of the partnership property, or

(2) decrease the adjusted basis of the partnership property by the excess of the transferee partner's proportionate share of the adjusted basis of the partnership property over the basis of his interest in the partnership.

Under regulations prescribed by the Secretary, such increase or decrease shall constitute an adjustment to the basis of partnership property with respect to the transferee partner only. A partner's proportionate share of the adjusted basis of partnership property shall be determined in accordance with his interest in partnership capital and, in the case of property contributed to the partnership by a partner, section 704(c) (relating to contributed property) shall apply in determining such share. In the case of an adjustment under this subsection to the basis of partnership property subject to depletion, any depletion allowable shall be determined separately for the transferee partner with respect to his interest in such property.

[Sec. 743(c)]

(c) ALLOCATION OF BASIS.—The allocation of basis among partnership properties where subsection (b) is applicable shall be made in accordance with the rules provided in section 755.

[Sec. 743(d)]

(d) SUBSTANTIAL BUILT-IN LOSS.—

(1) IN GENERAL.—For purposes of this section, a partnership has a substantial built-in loss with respect to a transfer of an interest in the partnership if—

(A) the partnership's adjusted basis in the partnership property exceeds by more than $250,000 the fair market value of such property, or

(B) the transferee partner would be allocated a loss of more than $250,000 if the partnership assets were sold for cash equal to their fair market value immediately after such transfer.

(2) REGULATIONS.—The Secretary shall prescribe such regulations as may be appropriate to carry out the purposes of paragraph (1) and section 734(d), including regulations aggregating related partnerships and disregarding property acquired by the partnership in an attempt to avoid such purposes.

[Sec. 743(e)]

(e) ALTERNATIVE RULES FOR ELECTING INVESTMENT PARTNERSHIPS.—

(1) NO ADJUSTMENT OF PARTNERSHIP BASIS.—For purposes of this section, an electing investment partnership shall not be treated as having a substantial built-in loss with respect to any transfer occurring while the election under paragraph (6)(A) is in effect.

(2) LOSS DEFERRAL FOR TRANSFEREE PARTNER.—In the case of a transfer of an interest in an electing investment partnership, the transferee partner's distributive share of losses (without regard to gains) from the sale or exchange of partnership property shall not be allowed except to the extent that it is established that such losses exceed the loss (if any) recognized by the transferor (or any prior transferor to the extent not fully offset by a prior disallowance under this paragraph) on the transfer of the partnership interest.

(3) NO REDUCTION IN PARTNERSHIP BASIS.—Losses disallowed under paragraph (2) shall not decrease the transferee partner's basis in the partnership interest.

(4) CERTAIN BASIS REDUCTIONS TREATED AS LOSSES.—In the case of a transferee partner whose basis in property distributed by the partnership is reduced under section 732(a)(2), the amount of the loss recognized by the transferor on the transfer of the partnership interest which is taken into account under paragraph (2) shall be reduced by the amount of such basis reduction.

(5) ELECTING INVESTMENT PARTNERSHIP.—For purposes of this subsection, the term "electing investment partnership" means any partnership if—

(A) the partnership makes an election to have this subsection apply,

(B) the partnership would be an investment company under section 3(a)(1)(A) of the Investment Company Act of 1940 but for an exemption under paragraph (1) or (7) of section 3(c) of such Act,

(C) such partnership has never been engaged in a trade or business,

(D) substantially all of the assets of such partnership are held for investment,

(E) at least 95 percent of the assets contributed to such partnership consist of money,

(F) no assets contributed to such partnership had an adjusted basis in excess of fair market value at the time of contribution,

(G) all partnership interests of such partnership are issued by such partnership pursuant to a private offering before the date which is 24 months after the date of the first capital contribution to such partnership,

(H) the partnership agreement of such partnership has substantive restrictions on each partner's ability to cause a redemption of the partner's interest, and

(I) the partnership agreement of such partnership provides for a term that is not in excess of 15 years.

The election described in subparagraph (A), once made, shall be irrevocable except with the consent of the Secretary.

(6) REGULATIONS.—The Secretary shall prescribe such regulations as may be appropriate to carry out the purposes of this subsection, including regulations for applying this subsection to tiered partnerships.

[Sec. 743(f)]

(f) EXCEPTION FOR SECURITIZATION PARTNERSHIPS.—

(1) NO ADJUSTMENT OF PARTNERSHIP BASIS.—For purposes of this section, a securitization partnership shall not be treated as having a substantial built-in loss with respect to any transfer.

(2) SECURITIZATION PARTNERSHIP.—For purposes of paragraph (1), the term "securitization partnership" means any partnership the sole business activity of which is to issue securities which provide for a fixed principal (or similar) amount and which are primarily serviced by the cash flows of a discrete pool (either fixed or revolving) of receivables or other financial assets that by their terms convert into cash in a finite period, but only if the sponsor of the pool reasonably believes that the receivables and other financial assets comprising the pool are not acquired so as to be disposed of.

Subpart D—Provisions Common to Other Subparts

[Sec. 751]

SEC. 751. UNREALIZED RECEIVABLES AND INVENTORY ITEMS.

[Sec. 751(a)]

(a) SALE OR EXCHANGE OF INTEREST IN PARTNERSHIP.—The amount of any money, or the fair market value of any property, received by a transferor partner in exchange for all or a part of his interest in the partnership attributable to—

(1) unrealized receivables of the partnership, or

(2) inventory items of the partnership,

shall be considered as an amount realized from the sale or exchange of property other than a capital asset.

[Sec. 751(b)]

(b) CERTAIN DISTRIBUTIONS TREATED AS SALES OR EXCHANGES.—

(1) GENERAL RULE.—To the extent a partner receives in a distribution—

(A) partnership property which is—

(i) unrealized receivables, or

(ii) inventory items which have appreciated substantially in value,

in exchange for all or a part of his interest in other partnership property (including money), or

(B) partnership property (including money) other than property described in subparagraph (A)(i) or (ii) in exchange for all or a part of his interest in partnership property described in subparagraph (A)(i) or (ii),

such transactions shall, under regulations prescribed by the Secretary, be considered as a sale or exchange of such property between the distributee and the partnership (as constituted after the distribution).

(2) EXCEPTIONS.—Paragraph (1) shall not apply to—

(A) a distribution of property which the distributee contributed to the partnership, or

(B) payments, described in section 736 (a), to a retiring partner or successor in interest of a deceased partner.

(3) SUBSTANTIAL APPRECIATION.—For purposes of paragraph (1)—

(A) IN GENERAL.—Inventory items of the partnership shall be considered to have appreciated substantially in value if their fair market value exceeds 120 percent of the adjusted basis to the partnership of such property.

(B) CERTAIN PROPERTY EXCLUDED.—For purposes of subparagraph (A), there shall be excluded any inventory property if a principal purpose for acquiring such property was to avoid the provisions of this subsection relating to inventory items.

[Sec. 751(c)]

(c) UNREALIZED RECEIVABLES.—For purposes of this subchapter, the term "unrealized receivables" includes, to the extent not previously includible in income under the method of accounting used by the partnership, any rights (contractual or otherwise) to payment for—

(1) goods delivered, or to be delivered, to the extent the proceeds therefrom would be treated as amounts received from the sale or exchange of property other than a capital asset, or

(2) services rendered, or to be rendered.

For purposes of this section and sections 731, 732, and 741 (but not for purposes of section 736), such term also includes mining property (as defined in section 617(f)(2)), stock in a DISC (as described in section 992(a)), section 1245 property (as defined in section 1245(a)(3)), stock in certain foreign corporations (as described in section 1248), section 1250 property (as defined in section 1250(c)), farm land (as defined in section 1252(a)), franchises, trademarks, or trade names (referred to in section 1253(a)), and an oil, gas, or geothermal property (described in section 1254) but only to the extent of the amount which would be treated as gain to which section 617(d)(1),995(c),1245(a),1248(a), 1250(a), 1252(a), 1253(a) or 1254(a) would apply if (at the time of the transaction described in this section orsection 731, 732, or 741, as the case may be) such property had been sold by the partnership at its fair market value. For purposes of this section and sections 731, 732, and 741 (but not for purposes of section 736), such term also includes any market discount bond (as defined in section 1278) and any short-term obligation (as defined in section 1283) but only to the extent of the amount which would be treated as ordinary income if (at the time of the transaction described in this section or section 731, 732, or 741, as the case may be) such property had been sold by the partnership.

[Sec. 751(d)]

(d) INVENTORY ITEMS.—For purposes of this subchapter, the term "inventory items" means—

(1) property of the partnership of the kind described in section 1221(a)(1),

(2) any other property of the partnership which, on sale or exchange by the partnership, would be considered property other than a capital asset and other than property described in section 1231, and

(3) any other property held by the partnership which, if held by the selling or distributee partner, would be considered property of the type described in paragraph (1) or (2).

* * *

[Sec. 751(f)]

(f) SPECIAL RULES IN THE CASE OF TIERED PARTNERSHIPS, ETC.—In determining whether property of a partnership is—

(1) an unrealized receivable, or

(2) an inventory item,

such partnership shall be treated as owning its proportionate share of the property of any other partnership in which it is a partner. Under regulations, rules similar to the rules of the preceding sentence shall also apply in the case of interests in trusts.

[Sec. 752]

SEC. 752. TREATMENT OF CERTAIN LIABILITIES.

[Sec. 752(a)]

(a) INCREASE IN PARTNER'S LIABILITIES.—Any increase in a partner's share of the liabilities of a partnership, or any increase in a partner's individual liabilities by reason of the assumption by such partner of partnership liabilities, shall be considered as a contribution of money by such partner to the partnership.

[Sec. 752(b)]

(b) DECREASE IN PARTNER'S LIABILITIES.—Any decrease in a partner's share of the liabilities of a partnership, or any decrease in a partner's individual liabilities by reason of the assumption by the partnership of such individual liabilities, shall be considered as a distribution of money to the partner by the partnership.

[Sec. 752(c)]

(c) LIABILITY TO WHICH PROPERTY IS SUBJECT.—For purposes of this section, a liability to which property is subject shall, to the extent of the fair market value of such property, be considered as a liability of the owner of the property.

[Sec. 752(d)]

(d) SALE OR EXCHANGE OF AN INTEREST.—In the case of a sale or exchange of an interest in a partnership, liabilities shall be treated in the same manner as liabilities in connection with the sale or exchange of property not associated with partnerships.

[Sec. 753]

SEC. 753. PARTNER RECEIVING INCOME IN RESPECT OF DECEDENT.

The amount includible in the gross income of a successor in interest of a deceased partner under section 736 (a) shall be considered income in respect of a decedent under section 691.

[Sec. 754]

SEC. 754. MANNER OF ELECTING OPTIONAL ADJUSTMENT TO BASIS OF PARTNERSHIP PROPERTY.

If a partnership files an election, in accordance with regulations prescribed by the Secretary, the basis of partnership property shall be adjusted, in the case of a distribution of property, in the manner provided in section 734 and, in the case of a transfer of a partnership interest, in the manner provided in section 743. Such an election shall apply with respect to all distributions of property by the partnership and to all transfers of interests in the partnership during the taxable year with respect to which such election was filed and all subsequent taxable years. Such election may be revoked by the partnership, subject to such limitations as may be provided by regulations prescribed by the Secretary.

[Sec. 755]

SEC. 755. RULES FOR ALLOCATION OF BASIS.

[Sec. 755(a)]

(a) GENERAL RULE.—Any increase or decrease in the adjusted basis of partnership property under section 734 (b) (relating to the optional adjustment to the basis of undistributed partnership property) or section 743 (b) (relating to the optional adjustment to the basis of partnership property in the case of a transfer of an interest in a partnership) shall, except as provided in subsection (b), be allocated—

(1) in a manner which has the effect of reducing the difference between the fair market value and the adjusted basis of partnership properties, or

(2) in any other manner permitted by regulations prescribed by the Secretary.

[Sec. 755(b)]

(b) SPECIAL RULE.—In applying the allocation rules provided in subsection (a), increases or decreases in the adjusted basis of partnership property arising from a distribution of, or a transfer of an interest attributable to, property consisting of—

(1) capital assets and property described in section 1231 (b), or

(2) any other property of the partnership,

shall be allocated to partnership property of a like character except that the basis of any such partnership property shall not be reduced below zero. If, in the case of a distribution, the adjustment to basis of property described in paragraph (1) or (2) is prevented by the absence of such property or by insufficient adjusted basis for such property, such adjustment shall be applied to subsequently acquired property of a like character in accordance with regulations prescribed by the Secretary.

[Sec. 755(c)]

(c) NO ALLOCATION OF BASIS DECREASE TO STOCK OF CORPORATE PARTNER.—In making an allocation under subsection (a) of any decrease in the adjusted basis of partnership property under section 734(b)—

(1) no allocation may be made to stock in a corporation (or any person related (within the meaning of sections 267(b) and 707(b)(1)) to such corporation) which is a partner in the partnership, and

(2) any amount not allocable to stock by reason of paragraph (1) shall be allocated under subsection (a) to other partnership property.

Gain shall be recognized to the partnership to the extent that the amount required to be allocated under paragraph (2) to other partnership property exceeds the aggregate adjusted basis of such other property immediately before the allocation required by paragraph (2).

PART III—DEFINITIONS

[Sec. 761]

SEC. 761. TERMS DEFINED.

[Sec. 761(a)]

(a) PARTNERSHIP.—For purposes of this subtitle, the term "partnership" includes a syndicate, group, pool, joint venture or other unincorporated organization through or by means of which any business, financial operation, or venture is carried on, and which is not, within the meaning of this title [subtitle], a corporation or a trust or estate. Under regulations the Secretary may, at the election of all the members of an unincorporated organization, exclude such organization from the application of all or part of this subchapter, if it is availed of—

(1) for investment purposes only and not for the active conduct of a business,

(2) for the joint production, extraction, or use of property, but not for the purpose of selling services or property produced or extracted, or

(3) by dealers in securities for a short period for the purpose of underwriting, selling, or distributing a particular issue of securities,

if the income of the members of the organization may be adequately determined without the computation of partnership taxable income.

[Sec. 761(b)]

(b) PARTNER.—For purposes of this subtitle, the term "partner" means a member of a partnership. In the case of a capital interest in a partnership in which capital is a material income-producing factor, whether a person is a partner with respect to such interest shall be determined without regard to whether such interest was derived by gift from any other person.

[Sec. 761(c)]

(c) PARTNERSHIP AGREEMENT.—For purposes of this subchapter, a partnership agreement includes any modifications of the partnership agreement made prior to, or at, the time prescribed by law for the filing of the partnership return for the taxable year (not including extensions) which are agreed to by all the partners, or which are adopted in such other manner as may be provided by the partnership agreement.

[Sec. 761(d)]

(d) LIQUIDATION OF A PARTNER'S INTEREST.—For purposes of this subchapter, the term "liquidation of a partner's interest" means the termination of a partner's entire interest in a partnership by means of a distribution, or a series of distributions, to the partner by the partnership.

[Sec. 761(e)]

(e) DISTRIBUTIONS OF PARTNERSHIP INTERESTS TREATED AS EXCHANGES.—Except as otherwise provided in regulations, for purposes of—

(1) section 708 (relating to continuation of partnership),

(2) section 743 (relating to optional adjustment to basis of partnership property), and

(3) any other provision of this subchapter specified in regulations prescribed by the Secretary, any distribution of an interest in a partnership (not otherwise treated as an exchange) shall be treated as an exchange.

[Sec. 761(f)]

(f) QUALIFIED JOINT VENTURE.—

(1) IN GENERAL.—In the case of a qualified joint venture conducted by a husband and wife who file a joint return for the taxable year, for purposes of this title—

(A) such joint venture shall not be treated as a partnership,

(B) all items of income, gain, loss, deduction, and credit shall be divided between the spouses in accordance with their respective interests in the venture, and

(C) each spouse shall take into account such spouse's respective share of such items as if they were attributable to a trade or business conducted by such spouse as a sole proprietor.

(2) QUALIFIED JOINT VENTURE.—For purposes of paragraph (1), the term "qualified joint venture" means any joint venture involving the conduct of a trade or business if—

(A) the only members of such joint venture are a husband and wife,

(B) both spouses materially participate (within the meaning of section 469(h) without regard to paragraph (5) thereof) in such trade or business, and

(C) both spouses elect the application of this subsection.

[Sec. 761(g)]

(g) CROSS REFERENCE.—

For rules in the case of the sale, exchange, liquidation, or reduction of a partner's interest, see sections 704(b) and 706(c)(2).

SUBCHAPTER M—REGULATED INVESTMENT COMPANIES AND REAL ESTATE INVESTMENT TRUSTS

PART I—REGULATED INVESTMENT COMPANIES

[Sec. 851]

SEC. 851. DEFINITION OF REGULATED INVESTMENT COMPANY.

[Sec. 851(a)]

(a) GENERAL RULE.—For purposes of this subtitle, the term "regulated investment company" means any domestic corporation—

(1) which, at all times during the taxable year—

(A) is registered under the Investment Company Act of 1940, as amended (15 U.S.C. 80a-1 to 80b-2) as a management company or unit investment trust, or

(B) has in effect an election under such Act to be treated as a business development company, or

(2) which is a common trust fund or similar fund excluded by section 3(c)(3) of such Act (15 U.S.C. 80a-3(c)) from the definition of "investment company" and is not included in the definition of "common trust fund" by section 584(a).

* * *

SUBCHAPTER N—TAX BASED ON INCOME FROM SOURCES WITHIN OR WITHOUT THE UNITED STATES

PART III—INCOME FROM SOURCES WITHOUT THE UNITED STATES

Subpart B—Earned Income of Citizens or Residents of United States

[Sec. 911]

SEC. 911. CITIZENS OR RESIDENTS OF THE UNITED STATES LIVING ABROAD.

* * *

[Sec. 911(d)]

(d) DEFINITIONS AND SPECIAL RULES.—For purposes of this section—

* * *

(2) EARNED INCOME.—

(A) IN GENERAL.—The term "earned income" means wages, salaries, or professional fees, and other amounts received as compensation for personal services actually rendered, but does not include that part of the compensation derived by the taxpayer for personal services rendered by him to a corporation which represents a distribution of earnings or profits rather than a reasonable allowance as compensation for the personal services actually rendered.

(B) TAXPAYER ENGAGED IN TRADE OR BUSINESS.—In the case of a taxpayer engaged in a trade or business in which both personal services and capital are material income-producing factors, under regulations prescribed by the Secretary, a reasonable allowance as compensation for the personal services rendered by the taxpayer, not in excess of 30 percent of his share of the net profits of such trade or business, shall be considered as earned income.

* * *

SUBCHAPTER O—GAIN OR LOSS ON DISPOSITION OF PROPERTY

PART I—DETERMINATION OF AMOUNT OF AND RECOGNITION OF GAIN OR LOSS

[Sec. 1001]

SEC. 1001. DETERMINATION OF AMOUNT OF AND RECOGNITION OF GAIN OR LOSS.

[Sec. 1001(a)]

(a) COMPUTATION OF GAIN OR LOSS.—The gain from the sale or other disposition of property shall be the excess of the amount realized therefrom over the adjusted basis provided in section 1011 for determining gain, and the loss shall be the excess of the adjusted basis provided in such section for determining loss over the amount realized.

[Sec. 1001(b)]

(b) AMOUNT REALIZED.—The amount realized from the sale or other disposition of property shall be the sum of any money received plus the fair market value of the property (other than money) received. In determining the amount realized—

(1) there shall not be taken into account any amount received as reimbursement for real property taxes which are treated under section 164(d) as imposed on the purchaser, and

(2) there shall be taken into account amounts representing real property taxes which are treated under section 164(d) as imposed on the taxpayer if such taxes are to be paid by the purchaser.

[Sec. 1001(c)]

(c) RECOGNITION OF GAIN OR LOSS.—Except as otherwise provided in this subtitle, the entire amount of the gain or loss, determined under this section, on the sale or exchange of property shall be recognized.

[Sec. 1001(d)]

(d) INSTALLMENT SALES.—Nothing in this section shall be construed to prevent (in the case of property sold under contract providing for payment in installments) the taxation of that portion of any installment payment representing gain or profit in the year in which such payment is received.

[Sec. 1001(e)]

(e) CERTAIN TERM INTERESTS.—

(1) IN GENERAL.—In determining gain or loss from the sale or other disposition of a term interest in property, that portion of the adjusted basis of such interest which is determined pursuant to section 1014, 1015, or 1041 (to the extent that such adjusted basis is a portion of the entire adjusted basis of the property) shall be disregarded.

(2) TERM INTEREST IN PROPERTY DEFINED.—For purposes of paragraph (1), the term "term interest in property" means—

(A) a life interest in property,

(B) an interest in property for a term of years, or

(C) an income interest in a trust.

(3) EXCEPTION.—Paragraph (1) shall not apply to a sale or other disposition which is a part of a transaction in which the entire interest in property is transferred to any person or persons.

PART II—BASIS RULES OF GENERAL APPLICATION

[Sec. 1011]

SEC. 1011. ADJUSTED BASIS FOR DETERMINING GAIN OR LOSS.

[Sec. 1011(a)]

(a) GENERAL RULE.—The adjusted basis for determining the gain or loss from the sale or other disposition of property, whenever acquired, shall be the basis (determined under section 1012 or other applicable sections of this subchapter and subchapters C (relating to corporate distributions and adjustments), K (relating to partners and partnerships), and P (relating to capital gains and losses)), adjusted as provided in section 1016.

[Sec. 1011(b)]

(b) BARGAIN SALE TO A CHARITABLE ORGANIZATION.—If a deduction is allowable under section 170 (relating to charitable contributions) by reason of a sale, then the adjusted basis for determining the gain from such sale shall be that portion of the adjusted basis which bears the same ratio to the adjusted basis as the amount realized bears to the fair market value of the property.

[Sec. 1012]

SEC. 1012. BASIS OF PROPERTY—COST.

[Sec. 1012(a)]

(a) IN GENERAL.—The basis of property shall be the cost of such property, except as otherwise provided in this subchapter and subchapters C (relating to corporate distributions and adjustments), K (relating to partners and partnerships), and P (relating to capital gains and losses).

[Sec. 1012(b)]

(b) SPECIAL RULE FOR APPORTIONED REAL ESTATE TAXES.—The cost of real property shall not include any amount in respect of real property taxes which are treated under section 164(d) as imposed on the taxpayer.

[Sec. 1012(c)]

(c) DETERMINATIONS BY ACCOUNT.—

(1) IN GENERAL.—In the case of the sale, exchange, or other disposition of a specified security on or after the applicable date, the conventions prescribed by regulations under this section shall be applied on an account by account basis.

(2) APPLICATION TO CERTAIN REGULATED INVESTMENT COMPANIES.—

(A) IN GENERAL.—Except as provided in subparagraph (B), any stock for which an average basis method is permissible under this section which is acquired before January 1, 2012, shall be treated as a separate account from any such stock acquired on or after such date.

(B) ELECTION FOR TREATMENT AS SINGLE ACCOUNT.—If a regulated investment company described in subparagraph (A) elects to have this subparagraph apply with respect to one or more of its stockholders—

(i) subparagraph (A) shall not apply with respect to any stock in such regulated investment company held by such stockholders, and

(ii) all stock in such regulated investment company which is held by such stockholders shall be treated as covered securities described in section 6045(g)(3) without regard to the date of the acquisition of such stock.

A rule similar to the rule of the preceding sentence shall apply with respect to a broker holding such stock as a nominee.

(3) DEFINITIONS.—For purposes of this section, the terms "specified security" and "applicable date" shall have the meaning given such terms in section 6045(g).

[Sec. 1012(d)]

(d) AVERAGE BASIS FOR STOCK ACQUIRED PURSUANT TO A DIVIDEND REINVESTMENT PLAN.—

(1) IN GENERAL.—In the case of any stock acquired after December 31, 2011, in connection with a dividend reinvestment plan, the basis of such stock while held as part of such plan shall be determined using one of the methods which may be used for determining the basis of stock in a regulated investment company.

(2) TREATMENT AFTER TRANSFER.—In the case of the transfer to another account of stock to which paragraph (1) applies, such stock shall have a cost basis in such other account equal to its basis in the dividend reinvestment plan immediately before such transfer (properly adjusted for any fees or other charges taken into account in connection with such transfer).

(3) SEPARATE ACCOUNTS; ELECTION FOR TREATMENT AS SINGLE ACCOUNT.—

(A) IN GENERAL.—Rules similar to the rules of subsection (c)(2) shall apply for purposes of this subsection.

(B) AVERAGE BASIS METHOD.—Notwithstanding paragraph (1), in the case of an election under rules similar to the rules of subsection (c)(2)(B) with respect to stock held in connection with a dividend reinvestment plan, the average basis method is permissible with respect to all such stock without regard to the date of the acquisition of such stock.

(4) DIVIDEND REINVESTMENT PLAN.—For purposes of this subsection—

(A) IN GENERAL.—The term "dividend reinvestment plan" means any arrangement under which dividends on any stock are reinvested in stock identical to the stock with respect to which the dividends are paid.

(B) INITIAL STOCK ACQUISITION TREATED AS ACQUIRED IN CONNECTION WITH PLAN.—Stock shall be treated as acquired in connection with a dividend reinvestment plan if such stock is acquired pursuant to such plan or if the dividends paid on such stock are subject to such plan.

[Sec. 1013]

SEC. 1013. BASIS OF PROPERTY INCLUDED IN INVENTORY.

If the property should have been included in the last inventory, the basis shall be the last inventory value thereof.

[Sec. 1014]

SEC. 1014. BASIS OF PROPERTY ACQUIRED FROM A DECEDENT.

[Sec. 1014(a)]

(a) IN GENERAL.—Except as otherwise provided in this section, the basis of property in the hands of a person acquiring the property from a decedent or to whom the property passed from a decedent shall, if not sold, exchanged, or otherwise disposed of before the decedent's death by such person, be—

(1) the fair market value of the property at the date of the decedent's death,

(2) in the case of an election under section 2032, its value at the applicable valuation date prescribed by such section,

(3) in the case of an election under section 2032A, its value determined under such section, or

(4) to the extent of the applicability of the exclusion described in section 2031(c), the basis in the hands of the decedent.

[Sec. 1014(b)]

(b) PROPERTY ACQUIRED FROM THE DECEDENT.—For purposes of subsection (a), the following property shall be considered to have been acquired from or to have passed from the decedent:

(1) Property acquired by bequest, devise, or inheritance, or by the decedent's estate from the decedent;

(2) Property transferred by the decedent during his lifetime in trust to pay the income for life to or on the order or direction of the decedent, with the right reserved to the decedent at all times before his death to revoke the trust;

(3) In the case of decedents dying after December 31, 1951, property transferred by the decedent during his lifetime in trust to pay the income for life to or on the order or direction of the decedent with the right reserved to the decedent at all times before his death to make any change in the enjoyment thereof through the exercise of a power to alter, amend, or terminate the trust;

(4) Property passing without full and adequate consideration under a general power of appointment exercised by the decedent by will;

* * *

(6) In the case of decedents dying after December 31, 1947, property which represents the surviving spouse's one-half share of community property held by the decedent and the surviving spouse under the community property laws of any State, or possession of the United States or any foreign country, if at least one-half of the whole of the community interest in such property was includible in determining the value of the decedent's gross estate under chapter 11 of subtitle B (section 2001 and following, relating to estate tax) or section 811 of the Internal Revenue Code of 1939;

* * *

(9) In the case of decedents dying after December 31, 1953, property acquired from the decedent by reason of death, form of ownership, or other conditions (including property acquired through the exercise or non-exercise of a power of appointment), if by reason thereof the property is required to be included in determining the value of the decedent's

gross estate under chapter 11 of subtitle B or under the Internal Revenue Code of 1939. In such case, if the property is acquired before the death of the decedent, the basis shall be the amount determined under subsection (a) reduced by the amount allowed to the taxpayer as deductions in computing taxable income under this subtitle or prior income tax laws for exhaustion, wear and tear, obsolescence, amortization, and depletion on such property before the death of the decedent. Such basis shall be applicable to the property commencing on the death of the decedent. This paragraph shall not apply to—

(A) annuities described in section 72;

(B) property to which paragraph (5) would apply if the property had been acquired by bequest; and

(C) property described in any other paragraph of this subsection.

(10) Property includible in the gross estate of the decedent under section 2044 (relating to certain property for which marital deduction was previously allowed). In any such case, the last 3 sentences of paragraph (9) shall apply as if such property were described in the first sentence of paragraph (9).

[Sec. 1014(c)]

(c) PROPERTY REPRESENTING INCOME IN RESPECT OF A DECEDENT.—This section shall not apply to property which constitutes a right to receive an item of income in respect of a decedent under section 691.

* * *

[Sec. 1014(e)]

(e) APPRECIATED PROPERTY ACQUIRED BY DECEDENT BY GIFT WITHIN 1 YEAR OF DEATH.—

(1) IN GENERAL.—In the case of a decedent dying after December 31, 1981, if—

(A) appreciated property was acquired by the decedent by gift during the 1-year period ending on the date of the decedent's death, and

(B) such property is acquired from the decedent by (or passes from the decedent to) the donor of such property (or the spouse of such donor),

the basis of such property in the hands of such donor (or spouse) shall be the adjusted basis of such property in the hands of the decedent immediately before the death of the decedent.

(2) DEFINITIONS.—For purposes of paragraph (1)—

(A) APPRECIATED PROPERTY.—The term "appreciated property" means any property if the fair market value of such property on the day it was transferred to the decedent by gift exceeds its adjusted basis.

(B) TREATMENT OF CERTAIN PROPERTY SOLD BY ESTATE.—In the case of any appreciated property described in subparagraph (A) of paragraph (1) sold by the estate of the decedent or by a trust of which the decedent was the grantor, rules similar to the rules of paragraph (1) shall apply to the extent the donor of such property (or the spouse of such donor) is entitled to the proceeds from such sale.

[Sec. 1014(f)]

(f) BASIS MUST BE CONSISTENT WITH ESTATE TAX RETURN.—For purposes of this section—

(1) IN GENERAL.—The basis of any property to which subsection (a) applies shall not exceed—

(A) in the case of property the final value of which has been determined for purposes of the tax imposed by chapter 11 on the estate of such decedent, such value, and

(B) in the case of property not described in subparagraph (A) and with respect to which a statement has been furnished under section 6035(a) identifying the value of such property, such value.

(2) EXCEPTION.—Paragraph (1) shall only apply to any property whose inclusion in the decedent's estate increased the liability for the tax imposed by chapter 11 (reduced by credits allowable against such tax) on such estate.

(3) DETERMINATION.—For purposes of paragraph (1), the basis of property has been determined for purposes of the tax imposed by chapter 11 if—

(A) the value of such property is shown on a return under section 6018 and such value is not contested by the Secretary before the expiration of the time for assessing a tax under chapter 11,

(B) in a case not described in subparagraph (A), the value is specified by the Secretary and such value is not timely contested by the executor of the estate, or

(C) the value is determined by a court or pursuant to a settlement agreement with the Secretary.

(4) REGULATIONS.—The Secretary may by regulations provide exceptions to the application of this subsection.

[Sec. 1015]

SEC. 1015. BASIS OF PROPERTY ACQUIRED BY GIFTS AND TRANSFERS IN TRUST.

[Sec. 1015(a)]

(a) GIFTS AFTER DECEMBER 31, 1920.—If the property was acquired by gift after December 31, 1920, the basis shall be the same as it would be in the hands of the donor or the last preceding owner by whom it was not acquired by gift, except that if such basis (adjusted for the period before the date of the gift as provided in section 1016) is greater than the fair market value of the property at the time of the gift, then for the purpose of determining loss the basis shall be such fair market value. If the facts necessary to determine the basis in the hands of the donor or the last preceding owner are unknown to the donee, the Secretary shall, if possible, obtain such facts from such donor or last preceding owner, or any other person cognizant thereof. If the Secretary finds it impossible to obtain such facts, the basis in the hands of such donor or last preceding owner shall be the fair market value of such property as found by the Secretary as of the date or approximate date at which, according to the best information that the Secretary is able to obtain, such property was acquired by such donor or last preceding owner.

[Sec. 1015(b)]

(b) TRANSFER IN TRUST AFTER DECEMBER 31, 1920.—If the property was acquired after December 31, 1920, by a transfer in trust (other than by a transfer in trust by a gift, bequest, or devise), the basis shall be the same as it would be in the hands of the grantor increased in the amount of gain or decreased in the amount of loss recognized to the grantor on such transfer under the law applicable to the year in which the transfer was made.

[Sec. 1015(c)]

(c) GIFT OR TRANSFER IN TRUST BEFORE JANUARY 1, 1921.—If the property was acquired by gift or transfer in trust on or before December 31, 1920, the basis shall be the fair market value of such property at the time of such acquisition.

[Sec. 1015(d)]

(d) INCREASED BASIS FOR GIFT TAX PAID.—

(1) IN GENERAL.—If—

(A) the property is acquired by gift on or after September 2, 1958, the basis shall be the basis determined under subsection (a), increased (but not above the fair market value of the property at the time of the gift) by the amount of gift tax paid with respect to such gift, or

(B) the property was acquired by gift before September 2, 1958, and has not been sold, exchanged, or otherwise disposed of before such date, the basis of the property shall be increased on such date by the amount of gift tax paid with respect to such gift, but such increase shall not exceed an amount equal to the amount by which the fair market value of the property at the time of the gift exceeded the basis of the property in the hands of the donor at the time of the gift.

(2) AMOUNT OF TAX PAID WITH RESPECT TO GIFT.—For purposes of paragraph (1), the amount of gift tax paid with respect to any gift is an amount which bears the same ratio to the amount of gift tax paid under chapter 12 with respect to all gifts made by the donor for the

calendar year (or preceding calendar period) in which such gift is made as the amount of such gift bears to the taxable gifts (as defined in section 2503(a) but computed without the deduction allowed by section 2521) made by the donor during such calendar year or period. For purposes of the preceding sentence, the amount of any gift shall be the amount included with respect to such gift in determining (for the purposes of section 2503(a)) the total amount of gifts made during the calendar year or period, reduced by the amount of any deduction allowed with respect to such gift under section 2522 (relating to charitable deduction) or under section 2523 (relating to marital deduction).

(3) GIFTS TREATED AS MADE ONE-HALF BY EACH SPOUSE.—For purposes of paragraph (1), where the donor and his spouse elected, under section 2513 to have the gift considered as made one-half by each, the amount of gift tax paid with respect to such gift under chapter 12 shall be the sum of the amounts of tax paid with respect to each half of such gift (computed in the manner provided in paragraph (2)).

(4) TREATMENT AS ADJUSTMENT TO BASIS.—For purposes of section 1016(b), an increase in basis under paragraph (1) shall be treated as an adjustment under section 1016(a).

(5) APPLICATION TO GIFTS BEFORE 1955.—With respect to any property acquired by gift before 1955, references in this subsection to any provision of this title shall be deemed to refer to the corresponding provision of the Internal Revenue Code of 1939 or prior revenue laws which was effective for the year in which such gift was made.

(6) SPECIAL RULE FOR GIFTS MADE AFTER DECEMBER 31, 1976.—

(A) IN GENERAL.—In the case of any gift made after December 31, 1976, the increase in basis provided by this subsection with respect to any gift for the gift tax paid under chapter 12 shall be an amount (not in excess of the amount of tax so paid) which bears the same ratio to the amount of tax so paid as—

(i) the net appreciation in value of the gift, bears to

(ii) the amount of the gift.

(B) NET APPRECIATION.—For purposes of paragraph (1), the net appreciation in value of any gift is the amount by which the fair market value of the gift exceeds the donor's adjusted basis immediately before the gift.

[Sec. 1015(e)]

(e) GIFTS BETWEEN SPOUSES.—In the case of any property acquired by gift in a transfer described in section 1041(a), the basis of such property in the hands of the transferee shall be determined under section 1041(b)(2) and not this section.

[Sec. 1016]

SEC. 1016. ADJUSTMENTS TO BASIS.

[Sec. 1016(a)]

(a) GENERAL RULE.—Proper adjustment in respect of the property shall in all cases be made—

(1) for expenditures, receipts, losses, or other items, properly chargeable to capital account, but no such adjustment shall be made—

(A) for—

(i) taxes or other carrying charges described in section 266; or

(ii) expenditures described in section 173 (relating to circulation expenditures),

for which deductions have been taken by the taxpayer in determining taxable income for the taxable year or prior taxable years; or

(B) for mortality, expense, or other reasonable charges incurred under an annuity or life insurance contract;

(2) in respect of any period since February 28, 1913, for exhaustion, wear and tear, obsolescence, amortization, and depletion, to the extent of the amount—

(A) allowed as deductions in computing taxable income under this subtitle or prior income tax laws, and

(B) resulting (by reason of the deductions so allowed) in a reduction for any taxable year of the taxpayer's taxes under this subtitle (other than chapter 2, relating to tax on self-employment income), or prior income, war-profits, or excess-profits tax laws,

but not less than the amount allowable under this subtitle or prior income tax laws. Where no method has been adopted under section 167 (relating to depreciation deduction), the amount allowable shall be determined under the straight line method. Subparagraph (B) of this paragraph shall not apply in respect of any period since February 28, 1913, and before January 1, 1952, unless an election has been made under section 1020 (as in effect before the date of the enactment of the Tax Reform Act of 1976). Where for any taxable year before the taxable year 1932 the depletion allowance was based on discovery value or a percentage of income, then the adjustment for depletion for such year shall be based on the depletion which would have been allowable for such year if computed without reference to discovery value or a percentage of income;

* * *

(8) in the case of property pledged to the Commodity Credit Corporation, to the extent of the amount received as a loan from the Commodity Credit Corporation and treated by the taxpayer as income for the year in which received pursuant to section 77, and to the extent of any deficiency on such loan with respect to which the taxpayer has been relieved from liability;

(9) for amounts allowed as deductions as deferred expenses under section 616(b) (relating to certain expenditures in the development of mines) and resulting in a reduction of the taxpayer's taxes under this subtitle, but not less than the amounts allowable under such section for the taxable year and prior years;

* * *

(14) for amounts allowed as deductions as deferred expenses under section 174(b)(1) (relating to research and experimental expenditures) and resulting in a reduction of the taxpayers' taxes under this subtitle, but not less than the amounts allowable under such section for the taxable year and prior years;

* * *

(17) to the extent provided in section 1367 in the case of stock of, and indebtedness owed to, shareholders of an S corporation;

* * *

(20) for amounts allowed as deductions under section 59(e) (relating to optional 10-year writeoff of certain tax preferences);

(21) to the extent provided in section 1059 (relating to reduction in basis for extraordinary dividends);

* * *

(23) in the case of property the acquisition of which resulted under section 1043, 1045, or 1397B in the nonrecognition of any part of the gain realized on the sale of other property, to the extent provided in section 1043(c), 1045(b)(3), or 1397B(b)(4), as the case may be,

* * *

[Sec. 1016(b)]

(b) SUBSTITUTED BASIS.—Whenever it appears that the basis of property in the hands of the taxpayer is a substituted basis, then the adjustments provided in subsection (a) shall be made after first making in respect of such substituted basis proper adjustments of a similar nature in respect of the period during which the property was held by the transferor, donor, or grantor, or during which the other property was held by the person for whom the basis is to be determined. A similar rule shall be applied in the case of a series of substituted bases.

* * *

[Sec. 1017]

SEC. 1017. DISCHARGE OF INDEBTEDNESS.

[Sec. 1017(a)]

(a) GENERAL RULE.—If—

(1) an amount is excluded from gross income under subsection (a) of section 108 (relating to discharge of indebtedness), and

(2) under subsection (b)(2)(E), (b)(5), or (c)(1) of section 108, any portion of such amount is to be applied to reduce basis,

then such portion shall be applied in reduction of the basis of any property held by the taxpayer at the beginning of the taxable year following the taxable year in which the discharge occurs.

[Sec. 1017(b)]

(b) AMOUNT AND PROPERTIES DETERMINED UNDER REGULATIONS.—

(1) IN GENERAL.—The amount of reduction to be applied under subsection (a) (not in excess of the portion referred to in subsection (a)), and the particular properties the bases of which are to be reduced, shall be determined under regulations prescribed by the Secretary.

(2) LIMITATION IN TITLE 11 CASE OR INSOLVENCY.—In the case of a discharge to which subparagraph (A) or (B) of section 108(a)(1) applies, the reduction in basis under subsection (a) of this section shall not exceed the excess of—

(A) the aggregate of the bases of the property held by the taxpayer immediately after the discharge, over

(B) the aggregate of the liabilities of the taxpayer immediately after the discharge.

The preceding sentence shall not apply to any reduction in basis by reason of an election under section 108(b)(5).

(3) CERTAIN REDUCTIONS MAY ONLY BE MADE IN THE BASIS OF DEPRECIABLE PROPERTY.—

(A) IN GENERAL.—Any amount which under subsection (b)(5) or (c)(1) of section 108 is to be applied to reduce basis shall be applied only to reduce the basis of depreciable property held by the taxpayer.

(B) DEPRECIABLE PROPERTY.—For purposes of this section, the term "depreciable property" means any property of a character subject to the allowance for depreciation, but only if a basis reduction under subsection (a) will reduce the amount of depreciation or amortization which otherwise would be allowable for the period immediately following such reduction.

(C) SPECIAL RULE FOR PARTNERSHIP INTERESTS.—For purposes of this section, any interest of a partner in a partnership shall be treated as depreciable property to the extent of such partner's proportionate interest in the depreciable property held by such partnership. The preceding sentence shall apply only if there is a corresponding reduction in the partnership's basis in depreciable property with respect to such partner.

(D) SPECIAL RULE IN CASE OF AFFILIATED GROUP.—For purposes of this section, if—

(i) a corporation holds stock in another corporation (hereinafter in this subparagraph referred to as the "subsidiary"), and

(ii) such corporations are members of the same affiliated group which file a consolidated return under section 1501 for the taxable year in which the discharge occurs,

then such stock shall be treated as depreciable property to the extent that such subsidiary consents to a corresponding reduction in the basis of its depreciable property.

(E) ELECTION TO TREAT CERTAIN INVENTORY AS DEPRECIABLE PROPERTY.—

(i) IN GENERAL.—At the election of the taxpayer, for purposes of this section, the term "depreciable property" includes any real property which is described in section 1221(a)(1).

(ii) ELECTION.—An election under clause (i) shall be made on the taxpayer's return for the taxable year in which the discharge occurs or at such other time as may be permitted in regulations prescribed by the Secretary. Such an election, once made, may be revoked only with the consent of the Secretary.

(F) SPECIAL RULES FOR QUALIFIED REAL PROPERTY BUSINESS INDEBTEDNESS.—In the case of any amount which under section 108(c)(1) is to be applied to reduce basis—

(i) depreciable property shall only include depreciable real property for purposes of subparagraphs (A) and (C),

(ii) subparagraph (E) shall not apply, and

(iii) in the case of property taken into account under section 108(c)(2)(B), the reduction with respect to such property shall be made as of the time immediately before disposition if earlier than the time under subsection (a).

(4) SPECIAL RULES FOR QUALIFIED FARM INDEBTEDNESS.—

(A) IN GENERAL.—Any amount which under subsection (b)(2)(E) of section 108 is to be applied to reduce basis and which is attributable to an amount excluded under subsection (a)(1)(C) of section 108—

(i) shall be applied only to reduce the basis of qualified property held by the taxpayer, and

(ii) shall be applied to reduce the basis of qualified property in the following order:

(I) First the basis of qualified property which is depreciable property.

(II) Second the basis of qualified property which is land used or held for use in the trade or business of farming.

(III) Then the basis of other qualified property.

(B) QUALIFIED PROPERTY.—For purposes of this paragraph, the term "qualified property" has the meaning given to such term by section 108(g)(3)(C).

(C) CERTAIN RULES MADE APPLICABLE.—Rules similar to the rules of subparagraphs (C), (D), and (E) of paragraph (3) shall apply for purposes of this paragraph and section 108(g).

[Sec. 1017(c)]

(c) SPECIAL RULES.—

(1) REDUCTION NOT TO BE MADE IN EXEMPT PROPERTY.—In the case of an amount excluded from gross income under section 108(a)(1)(A), no reduction in basis shall be made under this section in the basis of property which the debtor treats as exempt property under section 522 of title 11 of the United States Code.

(2) REDUCTIONS IN BASIS NOT TREATED AS DISPOSITIONS.—For purposes of this title, a reduction in basis under this section shall not be treated as a disposition.

[Sec. 1017(d)]

(d) RECAPTURE OF REDUCTIONS.—

(1) IN GENERAL.—For purposes of sections 1245 and 1250—

(A) any property the basis of which is reduced under this section and which is neither section 1245 property nor section 1250 property shall be treated as section 1245 property, and

(B) any reduction under this section shall be treated as a deduction allowed for depreciation.

(2) SPECIAL RULE FOR SECTION 1250.—For purposes of section 1250(b), the determination of what would have been the depreciation adjustments under the straight line method shall be made as if there had been no reduction under this section.

[Sec. 1019]

SEC. 1019. PROPERTY ON WHICH LESSEE HAS MADE IMPROVEMENTS.

Neither the basis nor the adjusted basis of any portion of real property shall, in the case of the lessor of such property, be increased or diminished on account of income derived by the lessor in respect of such property and excludable from gross income under section 109 (relating to improvements by lessee on lessor's property).

PART III—COMMON NONTAXABLE EXCHANGES

[Sec. 1031]

SEC. 1031. EXCHANGE OF REAL PROPERTY HELD FOR PRODUCTIVE USE OR INVESTMENT.

[Sec. 1031(a)]

(a) NONRECOGNITION OF GAIN OR LOSS FROM EXCHANGES SOLELY IN KIND.—

(1) IN GENERAL.—No gain or loss shall be recognized on the exchange of real property held for productive use in a trade or business or for investment if such real property is exchanged solely for real property of like kind which is to be held either for productive use in a trade or business or for investment.

(2) EXCEPTION FOR REAL PROPERTY HELD FOR SALE.—This subsection shall not apply to any exchange of real property held primarily for sale.

(3) REQUIREMENT THAT PROPERTY BE IDENTIFIED AND THAT EXCHANGE BE COMPLETED NOT MORE THAN 180 DAYS AFTER TRANSFER OF EXCHANGED PROPERTY.—For purposes of this subsection, any property received by the taxpayer shall be treated as property which is not like-kind property if—

(A) such property is not identified as property to be received in the exchange on or before the day which is 45 days after the date on which the taxpayer transfers the property relinquished in the exchange, or

(B) such property is received after the earlier of—

(i) the day which is 180 days after the date on which the taxpayer transfers the property relinquished in the exchange, or

(ii) the due date (determined with regard to extension) for the transferor's return of the tax imposed by this chapter for the taxable year in which the transfer of the relinquished property occurs.

[Sec. 1031(b)]

(b) GAIN FROM EXCHANGES NOT SOLELY IN KIND.—If an exchange would be within the provisions of subsection (a), of section 1035(a), of section 1036(a), or of section 1037(a), if it were not for the fact that the property received in exchange consists not only of property permitted by such provisions to be received without the recognition of gain, but also of other property or money, then the gain, if any, to the recipient shall be recognized, but in an amount not in excess of the sum of such money and the fair market value of such other property.

[Sec. 1031(c)]

(c) LOSS FROM EXCHANGES NOT SOLELY IN KIND.—If an exchange would be within the provisions of subsection (a), of section 1035(a), of section 1036(a), or of section 1037(a), if it were not for the fact that the property received in exchange consists not only of property permitted by such provisions to be received without the recognition of gain or loss, but also of other property or money, then no loss from the exchange shall be recognized.

[Sec. 1031(d)]

(d) BASIS.—If property was acquired on an exchange described in this section, section 1035(a), section 1036(a), or section 1037(a), then the basis shall be the same as that of the property exchanged, decreased in the amount of any money received by the taxpayer and increased in the amount of gain or decreased in the amount of loss to the taxpayer that was recognized on such exchange. If the property so acquired consisted in part of the type of property permitted by this section, section 1035(a), section 1036(a), or section 1037(a), to be received without the recognition of gain or loss, and in part of other property, the basis provided in this subsection shall be allocated between the properties (other than money) received, and for the purpose of the allocation there shall be assigned to such other property an amount equivalent to its fair market value at the date of the exchange. For purposes of this section, section 1035(a), and section 1036(a), where as part of the consideration to the taxpayer another party to the exchange assumed (as determined under section 357(d)) a liability of the taxpayer, such assumption shall be considered as money received by the taxpayer on the exchange.

[Sec. 1031(e)]

(e) APPLICATION TO CERTAIN PARTNERSHIPS.—For purposes of this section, an interest in a partnership which has in effect a valid election under section 761(a) to be excluded from the application of all of subchapter K shall be treated as an interest in each of the assets of such partnership and not as an interest in a partnership.

[Sec. 1031(f)]

(f) SPECIAL RULES FOR EXCHANGES BETWEEN RELATED PERSONS.—

(1) IN GENERAL.—If—

(A) a taxpayer exchanges property with a related person,

(B) there is nonrecognition of gain or loss to the taxpayer under this section with respect to the exchange of such property (determined without regard to this subsection), and

(C) before the date 2 years after the date of the last transfer which was part of such exchange—

(i) the related person disposes of such property, or

(ii) the taxpayer disposes of the property received in the exchange from the related person which was of like kind to the property transferred by the taxpayer,

there shall be no nonrecognition of gain or loss under this section to the taxpayer with respect to such exchange; except that any gain or loss recognized by the taxpayer by reason of this subsection shall be taken into account as of the date on which the disposition referred to in subparagraph (C) occurs.

(2) CERTAIN DISPOSITIONS NOT TAKEN INTO ACCOUNT.—For purposes of paragraph (1)(C), there shall not be taken into account any disposition—

(A) after the earlier of the death of the taxpayer or the death of the related person,

(B) in a compulsory or involuntary conversion (within the meaning of section 1033) if the exchange occurred before the threat or imminence of such conversion, or

(C) with respect to which it is established to the satisfaction of the Secretary that neither the exchange nor such disposition had as one of its principal purposes the avoidance of Federal income tax.

(3) RELATED PERSON.—For purposes of this subsection, the term "related person" means any person bearing a relationship to the taxpayer described in section 267(b) or 707(b)(1).

(4) TREATMENT OF CERTAIN TRANSACTIONS.—This section shall not apply to any exchange which is part of a transaction (or series of transactions) structured to avoid the purposes of this subsection.

[Sec. 1031(g)]

(g) SPECIAL RULE WHERE SUBSTANTIAL DIMINUTION OF RISK.—

(1) IN GENERAL.—If paragraph (2) applies to any property for any period, the running of the period set forth in subsection (f)(1)(C) with respect to such property shall be suspended during such period.

(2) PROPERTY TO WHICH SUBSECTION APPLIES.—This paragraph shall apply to any property for any period during which the holder's risk of loss with respect to the property is substantially diminished by—

(A) the holding of a put with respect to such property,

(B) the holding by another person of a right to acquire such property, or

(C) a short sale or any other transaction.

* * *

[Sec. 1032]

SEC. 1032. EXCHANGE OF STOCK FOR PROPERTY.

[Sec. 1032(a)]

(a) NONRECOGNITION OF GAIN OR LOSS.—No gain or loss shall be recognized to a corporation on the receipt of money or other property in exchange for stock (including treasury stock) of such corporation. No gain or loss shall be recognized by a corporation with respect to any lapse or acquisition of an option, or with respect to a securities futures contract (as defined in section 1234B), to buy or sell its stock (including treasury stock).

[Sec. 1032(b)]

(b) BASIS.—

For basis of property acquired by a corporation in certain exchanges for its stock, see section 362.

[Sec. 1033]

SEC. 1033. INVOLUNTARY CONVERSIONS.

[Sec. 1033(a)]

(a) GENERAL RULE.—If property (as a result of its destruction in whole or in part, theft, seizure, or requisition or condemnation or threat or imminence thereof) is compulsorily or involuntarily converted—

(1) CONVERSION INTO SIMILAR PROPERTY.—Into property similar or related in service or use to the property so converted, no gain shall be recognized.

(2) CONVERSION INTO MONEY.—Into money or into property not similar or related in service or use to the converted property, the gain (if any) shall be recognized except to the extent hereinafter provided in this paragraph:

(A) NONRECOGNITION OF GAIN.—If the taxpayer during the period specified in subparagraph (B), for the purpose of replacing the property so converted, purchases other property similar or related in service or use to the property so converted, or purchases stock in the acquisition of control of a corporation owning such other property, at the election of the taxpayer the gain shall be recognized only to the extent that the amount realized upon such conversion (regardless of whether such amount is received in one or more taxable years) exceeds the cost of such other property or such stock. Such election shall be made at such time and in such manner as the Secretary may by regulations prescribe. For purposes of this paragraph—

(i) no property or stock acquired before the disposition of the converted property shall be considered to have been acquired for the purpose of replacing such converted property unless held by the taxpayer on the date of such disposition; and

(ii) the taxpayer shall be considered to have purchased property or stock only if, but for the provisions of subsection (b) of this section, the unadjusted basis of such property or stock would be its cost within the meaning of section 1012.

(B) PERIOD WITHIN WHICH PROPERTY MUST BE REPLACED.—The period referred to in subparagraph (A) shall be the period beginning with the date of the disposition of the converted property, or the earliest date of the threat or imminence of requisition or condemnation of the converted property, whichever is the earlier, and ending—

(i) 2 years after the close of the first taxable year in which any part of the gain upon the conversion is realized, or

(ii) subject to such terms and conditions as may be specified by the Secretary, at the close of such later date as the Secretary may designate on application by the taxpayer. Such application shall be made at such time and in such manner as the Secretary may by regulations prescribe.

(C) TIME FOR ASSESSMENT OF DEFICIENCY ATTRIBUTABLE TO GAIN UPON CONVERSION.—If a taxpayer has made the election provided in subparagraph (A), then—

(i) the statutory period for the assessment of any deficiency, for any taxable year in which any part of the gain on such conversion is realized, attributable to such gain shall not expire prior to the expiration of 3 years from the date the Secretary is notified by the taxpayer (in such manner as the Secretary may by regulations prescribe) of the replacement of the converted property or of an intention not to replace, and

(ii) such deficiency may be assessed before the expiration of such 3-year period notwithstanding the provisions of section 6212 (c) or the provisions of any other law or rule of law which would otherwise prevent such assessment.

(D) TIME FOR ASSESSMENT OF OTHER DEFICIENCIES ATTRIBUTABLE TO ELECTION.—If the election provided in subparagraph (A) is made by the taxpayer and such other property or such stock was purchased before the beginning of the last taxable year in which any part of the gain upon such conversion is realized, any deficiency, to the extent resulting from such election, for any taxable year ending before such last taxable year may be assessed (notwithstanding the provisions of section 6212 (c) or 6501 or the provisions of any other law or rule of law which would otherwise prevent such assessment) at any time before the expiration of the period within which a deficiency for such last taxable year may be assessed.

(E) DEFINITIONS.—For purposes of this paragraph—

(i) CONTROL.—The term "control" means the ownership of stock possessing at least 80 percent of the total combined voting power of all classes of stock entitled to vote and at least 80 percent of the total number of shares of all other classes of stock of the corporation.

(ii) DISPOSITION OF THE CONVERTED PROPERTY.—The term "disposition of the converted property" means the destruction, theft, seizure, requisition, or condemnation of the converted property, or the sale or exchange of such property under threat or imminence of requisition or condemnation.

[Sec. 1033(b)]

(b) BASIS OF PROPERTY ACQUIRED THROUGH INVOLUNTARY CONVERSION.—

(1) CONVERSIONS DESCRIBED IN SUBSECTION (a)(1).—If the property was acquired as the result of a compulsory or involuntary conversion described in subsection (a)(1), the basis shall be the same as in the case of the property so converted—

(A) decreased in the amount of any money received by the taxpayer which was not expended in accordance with the provisions of law (applicable to the year in which such conversion was made) determining the taxable status of the gain or loss upon such conversion, and

(B) increased in the amount of gain or decreased in the amount of loss to the taxpayer recognized upon such conversion under the law applicable to the year in which such conversion was made.

(2) CONVERSIONS DESCRIBED IN SUBSECTION (a)(2).—In the case of property purchased by the taxpayer in a transaction described in subsection (a)(2) which resulted in the nonrecognition of any part of the gain realized as the result of a compulsory or involuntary conversion, the basis shall be the cost of such property decreased in the amount of the gain not so recognized; and if the property purchased consists of more than 1 piece of property, the basis determined under this sentence shall be allocated to the purchased properties in proportion to their respective costs.

(3) PROPERTY HELD BY CORPORATION THE STOCK OF WHICH IS REPLACEMENT PROPERTY.—

(A) IN GENERAL.—If the basis of stock in a corporation is decreased under paragraph (2), an amount equal to such decrease shall also be applied to reduce the basis of property held by the corporation at the time the taxpayer acquired control (as defined in subsection (a)(2)(E)) of such corporation.

(B) LIMITATION.—Subparagraph (A) shall not apply to the extent that it would (but for this subparagraph) require a reduction in the aggregate adjusted bases of the property of the corporation below the taxpayer's adjusted basis of the stock in the corporation (determined immediately after such basis is decreased under paragraph (2)).

(C) ALLOCATION OF BASIS REDUCTION.—The decrease required under subparagraph (A) shall be allocated—

(i) first to property which is similar or related in service or use to the converted property,

(ii) second to depreciable property (as defined in section 1017(b)(3)(B)) not described in clause (i), and

(iii) then to other property.

(D) SPECIAL RULES.—

(i) REDUCTION NOT TO EXCEED ADJUSTED BASIS OF PROPERTY.—No reduction in the basis of any property under this paragraph shall exceed the adjusted basis of such property (determined without regard to such reduction).

(ii) ALLOCATION OF REDUCTION AMONG PROPERTIES.—If more than 1 property is described in a clause of subparagraph (C), the reduction under this paragraph shall be allocated among such property in proportion to the adjusted bases of such property (as so determined).

[Sec. 1033(c)]

(c) PROPERTY SOLD PURSUANT TO RECLAMATION LAWS.—For purposes of this subtitle, if property lying within an irrigation project is sold or otherwise disposed of in order to conform to the acreage limitation provisions of Federal reclamation laws, such sale or disposition shall be treated as an involuntary conversion to which this section applies.

* * *

[Sec. 1033(g)]

(g) CONDEMNATION OF REAL PROPERTY HELD FOR PRODUCTIVE USE IN TRADE OR BUSINESS OR FOR INVESTMENT.—

(1) SPECIAL RULE.—For purposes of subsection (a), if real property (not including stock in trade or other property held primarily for sale) held for productive use in trade or business or for investment is (as the result of its seizure, requisition, or condemnation, or threat or imminence thereof) compulsorily or involuntarily converted, property of a like kind to be held either for productive use in trade or business or for investment shall be treated as property similar or related in service or use to the property so converted.

(2) LIMITATION.—Paragraph (1) shall not apply to the purchase of stock in the acquisition of control of a corporation described in subsection (a)(2)(A).

* * *

(4) SPECIAL RULE.—In the case of a compulsory or involuntary conversion described in paragraph (1), subsection (a)(2)(B)(i) shall be applied by substituting "3 years" for "2 years".

[Sec. 1033(h)]

(h) SPECIAL RULES FOR PROPERTY DAMAGED BY FEDERALLY DECLARED DISASTERS.—

(1) PRINCIPAL RESIDENCES.—If the taxpayer's principal residence or any of its contents is located in a disaster area and is compulsorily or involuntarily converted as a result of a federally declared disaster—

(A) TREATMENT OF INSURANCE PROCEEDS.—

(i) EXCLUSION FOR UNSCHEDULED PERSONAL PROPERTY.—No gain shall be recognized by reason of the receipt of any insurance proceeds for personal property which was part of such contents and which was not scheduled property for purposes of such insurance.

(ii) OTHER PROCEEDS TREATED AS COMMON FUND.—In the case of any insurance proceeds (not described in clause (i)) for such residence or contents—

(I) such proceeds shall be treated as received for the conversion of a single item of property, and

(II) any property which is similar or related in service or use to the residence so converted (or contents thereof) shall be treated for purposes of subsection (a)(2) as property similar or related in service or use to such single item of property.

(B) EXTENSION OF REPLACEMENT PERIOD.—Subsection (a)(2)(B) shall be applied with respect to any property so converted by substituting "4 years" for "2 years".

(2) TRADE OR BUSINESS AND INVESTMENT PROPERTY.—If a taxpayer's property held for productive use in a trade or business or for investment is located in a disaster area and is compulsorily or involuntarily converted as a result of a federally declared disaster, tangible property of a type held for productive use in a trade or business shall be treated for purposes of subsection (a) as property similar or related in service or use to the property so converted.

(3) FEDERALLY DECLARED DISASTER; DISASTER AREA.—The terms "federally declared disaster" and "disaster area" shall have the respective meaning given such terms by section 165(i)(5).

(4) PRINCIPAL RESIDENCE.—For purposes of this subsection, the term "principal residence" has the same meaning as when used in section 121, except that such term shall include a residence not treated as a principal residence solely because the taxpayer does not own the residence.

[Sec. 1033(i)]

(i) REPLACEMENT PROPERTY MUST BE ACQUIRED FROM UNRELATED PERSON IN CERTAIN CASES.—

(1) IN GENERAL.—If the property which is involuntarily converted is held by a taxpayer to which this subsection applies, subsection (a) shall not apply if the replacement property or stock is acquired from a related person. The preceding sentence shall not apply to the extent that the related person acquired the replacement property or stock from an unrelated person during the period applicable under subsection (a)(2)(B).

(2) TAXPAYERS TO WHICH SUBSECTION APPLIES.—This subsection shall apply to—

(A) a C corporation,

(B) a partnership in which 1 or more C corporations own, directly or indirectly (determined in accordance with section 707(b)(3)), more than 50 percent of the capital interest, or profits interest, in such partnership at the time of the involuntary conversion, and

(C) any other taxpayer if, with respect to property which is involuntarily converted during the taxable year, the aggregate of the amount of realized gain on such property on which there is realized gain exceeds $100,000.

In the case of a partnership, subparagraph (C) shall apply with respect to the partnership and with respect to each partner. A similar rule shall apply in the case of an S corporation and its shareholders.

(3) RELATED PERSON.—For purposes of this subsection, a person is related to another person if the person bears a relationship to the other person described in section 267(b) or 707(b)(1).

* * *

[Sec. 1036]

SEC. 1036. STOCK FOR STOCK OF SAME CORPORATION.

[Sec. 1036(a)]

(a) GENERAL RULE.—No gain or loss shall be recognized if common stock in a corporation is exchanged solely for common stock in the same corporation, or if preferred stock in a corporation is exchanged solely for preferred stock in the same corporation.

[Sec. 1036(b)]

(b) NONQUALIFIED PREFERRED STOCK NOT TREATED AS STOCK.—For purposes of this section, nonqualified preferred stock (as defined in section 351(g)(2)) shall be treated as property other than stock.

[Sec. 1036(c)]

(c) CROSS REFERENCES.—

(1) For rules relating to recognition of gain or loss where an exchange is not solely in kind, see subsections (b) and (c) of section 1031.

(2) For rules relating to the basis of property acquired in an exchange described in subsection (a), see subsection (d) of section 1031.

[Sec. 1038]

SEC. 1038. CERTAIN REACQUISITIONS OF REAL PROPERTY.

[Sec. 1038(a)]

(a) GENERAL RULE.—If—

(1) a sale of real property gives rise to indebtedness to the seller which is secured by the real property sold, and

(2) the seller of such property reacquires such property in partial or full satisfaction of such indebtedness,

then, except as provided in subsections (b) and (d), no gain or loss shall result to the seller from such reacquisition, and no debt shall become worthless or partially worthless as a result of such reacquisition.

[Sec. 1038(b)]

(b) AMOUNT OF GAIN RESULTING.—

(1) IN GENERAL.—In the case of a reacquisition of real property to which subsection (a) applies, gain shall result from such reacquisition to the extent that—

(A) the amount of money and the fair market value of other property (other than obligations of the purchaser) received, prior to such reacquisition, with respect to the sale of such property, exceeds

(B) the amount of the gain on the sale of such property returned as income for periods prior to such reacquisition.

(2) LIMITATION.—The amount of gain determined under paragraph (1) resulting from a reacquisition during any taxable year beginning after the date of the enactment of this section shall not exceed the amount by which the price at which the real property was sold exceeded its adjusted basis, reduced by the sum of—

(A) the amount of the gain on the sale of such property returned as income for periods prior to the reacquisition of such property, and

(B) the amount of money and the fair market value of other property (other than obligations of the purchaser received with respect to the sale of such property) paid or transferred by the seller in connection with the reacquisition of such property.

For purposes of this paragraph, the price at which real property is sold is the gross sales price reduced by the selling commissions, legal fees, and other expenses incident to the sale of such property which are properly taken into account in determining gain or loss on such sale.

(3) GAIN RECOGNIZED.—Except as provided in this section, the gain determined under this subsection resulting from a reacquisition to which subsection (a) applies shall be recognized, notwithstanding any other provision of this subtitle.

[Sec. 1038(c)]

(c) BASIS OF REACQUIRED REAL PROPERTY.—If subsection (a) applies to the reacquisition of any real property, the basis of such property upon such reacquisition shall be the adjusted basis of the indebtedness to the seller secured by such property (determined as of the date of reacquisition), increased by the sum of—

(1) the amount of the gain determined under subsection (b) resulting from such reacquisition, and

(2) the amount described in subsection (b)(2)(B).

If any indebtedness to the seller secured by such property is not discharged upon the reacquisition of such property, the basis of such indebtedness shall be zero.

[Sec. 1038(d)]

(d) INDEBTEDNESS TREATED AS WORTHLESS PRIOR TO REACQUISITION.—If, prior to a reacquisition of real property to which subsection (a) applies, the seller has treated indebtedness secured by such property as having become worthless or partially worthless—

(1) such seller shall be considered as receiving, upon the reacquisition of such property, an amount equal to the amount of such indebtedness treated by him as having become worthless, and

(2) the adjusted basis of such indebtedness shall be increased (as of the date of reacquisition) by an amount equal to the amount so considered as received by such seller.

[Sec. 1038(e)]

(e) PRINCIPAL RESIDENCES.—If—

(1) subsection (a) applies to a reacquisition of real property with respect to the sale of which gain was not recognized under section 121 (relating to gain on sale of principal residence); and

(2) within 1 year after the date of the reacquisition of such property by the seller, such property is resold by him,

then, under regulations prescribed by the Secretary, subsections (b), (c), and (d) of this section shall not apply to the reacquisition of such property and, for purposes of applying section 121, the resale of such property shall be treated as a part of the transaction constituting the original sale of such property.

[Sec. 1038(f)—Stricken]

[Sec. 1038(g)]

(g) ACQUISITION BY ESTATE, ETC., OF SELLER.—Under regulations prescribed by the Secretary, if an installment obligation is indebtedness to the seller which is described in subsection (a), and if such obligation is, in the hands of the taxpayer, an obligation with respect to which section 691(a)(4)(B) applies, then—

(1) for purposes of subsection (a), acquisition of real property by the taxpayer shall be treated as reacquisition by the seller, and

(2) the basis of the real property acquired by the taxpayer shall be increased by an amount equal to the deduction under section 691(c) which would (but for this subsection) have been allowable to the taxpayer with respect to the gain on the exchange of the obligation for the real property.

[Sec. 1041]

SEC. 1041. TRANSFERS OF PROPERTY BETWEEN SPOUSES OR INCIDENT TO DIVORCE.

[Sec. 1041(a)]

(a) GENERAL RULE.—No gain or loss shall be recognized on a transfer of property from an individual to (or in trust for the benefit of)—

(1) a spouse, or

(2) a former spouse, but only if the transfer is incident to the divorce.

[Sec. 1041(b)]

(b) TRANSFER TREATED AS GIFT; TRANSFEREE HAS TRANSFEROR'S BASIS.—In the case of any transfer of property described in subsection (a)—

(1) for purposes of this subtitle, the property shall be treated as acquired by the transferee by gift, and

(2) the basis of the transferee in the property shall be the adjusted basis of the transferor.

[Sec. 1041(c)]

(c) INCIDENT TO DIVORCE.—For purposes of subsection (a)(2), a transfer of property is incident to the divorce if such transfer—

(1) occurs within 1 year after the date on which the marriage ceases, or

(2) is related to the cessation of the marriage.

[Sec. 1041(d)]

(d) SPECIAL RULE WHERE SPOUSE IS NONRESIDENT ALIEN.—Subsection (a) shall not apply if the spouse (or former spouse) of the individual making the transfer is a nonresident alien.

[Sec. 1041(e)]

(e) TRANSFERS IN TRUST WHERE LIABILITY EXCEEDS BASIS.—Subsection (a) shall not apply to the transfer of property in trust to the extent that—

(1) the sum of the amount of the liabilities assumed, plus the amount of the liabilities to which the property is subject, exceeds

(2) the total of the adjusted basis of the property transferred.

Proper adjustment shall be made under subsection (b) in the basis of the transferee in such property to take into account gain recognized by reason of the preceding sentence.

[Sec. 1045]

SEC. 1045. ROLLOVER OF GAIN FROM QUALIFIED SMALL BUSINESS STOCK TO ANOTHER QUALIFIED SMALL BUSINESS STOCK.

[Sec. 1045(a)]

(a) NONRECOGNITION OF GAIN.—In the case of any sale of qualified small business stock held by a taxpayer other than a corporation for more than 6 months and with respect to which such taxpayer elects the application of this section, gain from such sale shall be recognized only to the extent that the amount realized on such sale exceeds—

(1) the cost of any qualified small business stock purchased by the taxpayer during the 60-day period beginning on the date of such sale, reduced by

(2) any portion of such cost previously taken into account under this section.

This section shall not apply to any gain which is treated as ordinary income for purposes of this title.

[Sec. 1045(b)]

(b) DEFINITIONS AND SPECIAL RULES.—For purposes of this section—

(1) QUALIFIED SMALL BUSINESS STOCK.—The term "qualified small business stock" has the meaning given such term by section 1202(c).

(2) PURCHASE.—A taxpayer shall be treated as having purchased any property if, but for paragraph (3), the unadjusted basis of such property in the hands of the taxpayer would be its cost (within the meaning of section 1012).

(3) BASIS ADJUSTMENTS.—If gain from any sale is not recognized by reason of subsection (a), such gain shall be applied to reduce (in the order acquired) the basis for determining gain or loss of any qualified small business stock which is purchased by the taxpayer during the 60-day period described in subsection (a).

(4) HOLDING PERIOD.—For purposes of determining whether the nonrecognition of gain under subsection (a) applies to stock which is sold—

(A) the taxpayer's holding period for such stock and the stock referred to in subsection (a)(1) shall be determined without regard to section 1223, and

(B) only the first 6 months of the taxpayer's holding period for the stock referred to in subsection (a)(1) shall be taken into account for purposes of applying section 1202(c)(2).

(5) CERTAIN RULES TO APPLY.—Rules similar to the rules of subsections (f), (g), (h), (i), (j), and (k) of section 1202 shall apply.

PART IV—SPECIAL RULES

[Sec. 1059]

SEC. 1059. CORPORATE SHAREHOLDER'S BASIS IN STOCK REDUCED BY NONTAXED PORTION OF EXTRAORDINARY DIVIDENDS.

[Sec. 1059(a)]

(a) GENERAL RULE.—If any corporation receives any extraordinary dividend with respect to any share of stock and such corporation has not held such stock for more than 2 years before the dividend announcement date—

(1) REDUCTION IN BASIS.—The basis of such corporation in such stock shall be reduced (but not below zero) by the nontaxed portion of such dividends.

(2) AMOUNTS IN EXCESS OF BASIS.—If the nontaxed portion of such dividends exceeds such basis, such excess shall be treated as gain from the sale or exchange of such stock for the taxable year in which the extraordinary dividend is received.

[Sec. 1059(b)]

(b) NONTAXED PORTION.—For purposes of this section—

(1) IN GENERAL.—The nontaxed portion of any dividend is the excess (if any) of—

(A) the amount of such dividend, over

(B) the taxable portion of such dividend.

(2) TAXABLE PORTION.—The taxable portion of any dividend is—

(A) the portion of such dividend includible in gross income, reduced by

(B) the amount of any deduction allowable with respect to such dividend under section 243, 245, or 245.

[Sec. 1059(c)]

(c) EXTRAORDINARY DIVIDEND DEFINED.—For purposes of this section—

(1) IN GENERAL.—The term "extraordinary dividend" means any dividend with respect to a share of stock if the amount of such dividend equals or exceeds the threshold percentage of the taxpayer's adjusted basis in such share of stock.

(2) THRESHOLD PERCENTAGE.—The term "theshold percentage" means—

(A) 5 percent in the case of stock which is preferred as to dividends, and

(B) 10 percent in the case of any other stock.

(3) AGGREGATION OF DIVIDENDS.—

(A) AGGREGATION WITHIN 85-DAY PERIOD.—All dividends—

(i) which are received by the taxpayer (or a person described in subparagraph (C)) with respect to any share of stock, and

(ii) which have ex-dividend dates within the same period of 85 consecutive days,

shall be treated as 1 dividend.

(B) AGGREGATION WITHIN 1 YEAR WHERE DIVIDENDS EXCEED 20 PERCENT OF ADJUSTED BASIS.—All dividends—

(i) which are received by the taxpayer (or a person described in subparagraph (C)) with respect to any share of stock, and

(ii) which have ex-dividend dates during the same period of 365 consecutive days, shall be treated as extraordinary dividends if the aggregate of such dividends exceeds 20 percent of the taxpayer's adjusted basis in such stock (determined without regard to this section).

(C) SUBSTITUTED BASIS TRANSACTIONS.—In the case of any stock, a person is described in this subparagraph if—

(i) the basis of such stock in the hands of such person is determined in whole or in part by reference to the basis of such stock in the hands of the taxpayer, or

(ii) the basis of such stock in the hands of the taxpayer is determined in whole or in part by reference to the basis of such stock in the hands of such person.

(4) FAIR MARKET VALUE DETERMINATION.—If the taxpayer establishes to the satisfaction of the Secretary the fair market value of any share of stock as of the day before the ex-dividend date, the taxpayer may elect to apply paragraphs (1) and (3) by substituting such value for the taxpayer's adjusted basis.

[Sec. 1059(d)]

(d) SPECIAL RULES.—For purposes of this section—

(1) TIME FOR REDUCTION.—Any reduction in basis under subsection (a)(1) shall be treated as occurring at the beginning of the ex-dividend date of the extraordinary dividend to which the reduction relates.

(2) DISTRIBUTIONS IN KIND.—To the extent any dividend consists of property other than cash, the amount of such dividend shall be treated as the fair market value of such property (as of the date of the distribution) reduced as provided in section 301(b)(2).

(3) DETERMINATION OF HOLDING PERIOD.—For purposes of determining the holding period of stock under subsection (a), rules similar to the rules of paragraphs (3) and (4) of section 246(c) shall apply and there shall not be taken into account any day which is more than 2 years after the date on which such share becomes ex-dividend.

(4) EX-DIVIDEND DATE.—The term "ex-dividend date" means the date on which the share of stock becomes ex-dividend.

(5) DIVIDEND ANNOUNCEMENT DATE.—The term "dividend announcement date" means, with respect to any dividend, the date on which the corporation declares, announces, or agrees to, the amount or payment of such dividend, whichever is the earliest.

(6) EXCEPTION WHERE STOCK HELD DURING ENTIRE EXISTENCE OF CORPORATION.—

(A) IN GENERAL.—Subsection (a) shall not apply to any extraordinary dividend with respect to any share of stock of a corporation if—

(i) such stock was held by the taxpayer during the entire period such corporation was in existence, and

(ii) except as provided in regulations, no earnings and profits of such corporation were attributable to transfers of property from (or earnings and profits of) a corporation which is not a qualified corporation.

(B) QUALIFIED CORPORATION.—For purposes of subparagraph (A), the term "qualified corporation" means any corporation (including a predecessor corporation)—

(i) with respect to which the taxpayer holds directly or indirectly during the entire period of such corporation's existence at least the same ownership interest as the taxpayer holds in the corporation distributing the extraordinary dividend, and

(ii) which has no earnings and profits—

(I) which were earned by, or

(II) which are attributable to gain on property which accrued during a period the corporation holding the property was,

a corporation not described in clause (i).

(C) APPLICATION OF PARAGRAPH.—This paragraph shall not apply to any extraordinary dividend to the extent such application is inconsistent with the purposes of this section.

(e) SPECIAL RULES FOR CERTAIN DISTRIBUTIONS.—

(1) TREATMENT OF PARTIAL LIQUIDATIONS AND CERTAIN REDEMPTIONS.—Except as otherwise provided in regulations—

(A) REDEMPTIONS.—In the case of any redemption of stock—

(i) which is part of a partial liquidation (within the meaning of section 302(e)) of the redeeming corporation,

(ii) which is not pro rata as to all shareholders, or

(iii) which would not have been treated (in whole or in part) as a dividend if—

(I) any options had not been taken into account under section 318(a)(4), or

(II) section 304(a) had not applied,

any amount treated as a dividend with respect to such redemption shall be treated as an extraordinary dividend to which paragraphs (1) and (2) of subsection (a) apply without regard to the period the taxpayer held such stock. In the case of a redemption described in clause (iii), only the basis in the stock redeemed shall be taken into account under subsection (a).

(B) REORGANIZATIONS, ETC.—An exchange described in section 356 which is treated as a dividend shall be treated as a redemption of stock for purposes of applying subparagraph (A).

(2) QUALIFYING DIVIDENDS.—

(A) IN GENERAL.—Except as provided in regulations, the term "extraordinary dividend" does not include any qualifying dividend (within the meaning of section 243).

(B) EXCEPTION.—Subparagraph (A) shall not apply to any portion of a dividend which is attributable to earnings and profits which—

(i) were earned by a corporation during a period it was not a member of the affiliated group, or

(ii) are attributable to gain on property which accrued during a period the corporation holding the property was not a member of the affiliated group.

(3) QUALIFIED PREFERRED DIVIDENDS.—

(A) IN GENERAL.—In the case of 1 or more qualified preferred dividends with respect to any share of stock—

(i) this section shall not apply to such dividends if the taxpayer holds such stock for more than 5 years, and

(ii) if the taxpayer disposes of such stock before it has been held for more than 5 years, the aggregate reduction under subsection (a)(1) with respect to such dividends shall not be greater than the excess (if any) of—

(I) the qualified preferred dividends paid with respect to such stock during the period the taxpayer held such stock, over

(II) the qualified preferred dividends which would have been paid during such period on the basis of the stated rate of return.

(B) RATE OF RETURN.—For the purposes of this paragraph—

(i) ACTUAL RATE OF RETURN.—The actual rate of return shall be the rate of return for the period for which the taxpayer held the stock, determined—

(I) by only taking into account dividends during such period, and

(II) by using the lesser of the adjusted basis of the taxpayer in such stock or the liquidation preference of such stock.

(ii) STATED RATE OF RETURN.—The stated rate of return shall be the annual rate of the qualified preferred dividend payable with respect to any share of stock (expressed as a percentage of the amount described in clause (i)(II)).

(C) DEFINITIONS AND SPECIAL RULES.—For purposes of this paragraph—

(i) QUALIFIED PREFERRED DIVIDEND.—The term "qualified preferred dividend" means any fixed dividend payable with respect to any share of stock which—

(I) provides for fixed preferred dividends payable not less frequently than annually, and

(II) is not in arrears as to dividends at the time the taxpayer acquires the stock.

Such term shall not include any dividend payable with respect to any share of stock if the actual rate of return on such stock exceeds 15 percent.

(ii) HOLDING PERIOD.—In determining the holding period for purposes of subparagraph (A)(ii), subsection (d)(3) shall be applied by substituting "5 years" for "2 years".

[Sec. 1059(f)]

(f) TREATMENT OF DIVIDENDS ON CERTAIN PREFERRED STOCK.—

(1) IN GENERAL.—Any dividend with respect to disqualified preferred stock shall be treated as an extraordinary dividend to which paragraphs (1) and (2) of subsection (a) apply without regard to the period the taxpayer held the stock.

(2) DISQUALIFIED PREFERRED STOCK.—For purposes of this subsection, the term "disqualified preferred stock" means any stock which is preferred as to dividends if—

(A) when issued, such stock has a dividend rate which declines (or can reasonably be expected to decline) in the future,

(B) the issue price of such stock exceeds its liquidation rights or its stated redemption price, or

(C) such stock is otherwise structured—

(i) to avoid the other provisions of this section, and

(ii) to enable corporate shareholders to reduce tax through a combination of dividend received deductions and loss on the disposition of the stock.

[Sec. 1059(g)]

(g) REGULATIONS.—The Secretary shall prescribe such regulations as may be appropriate to carry out the purposes of this section, including regulations—

(1) providing for the application of this section in the case of stock dividends, stock splits, reorganizations, and other similar transactions, in the case of stock held by pass-thru entities, and in the case of consolidated groups, and

(2) providing that the rules of subsection (f) shall apply in the case of stock which is not preferred as to dividends in cases where stock is structured to avoid the purposes of this section.

[Sec. 1060]

SEC. 1060. SPECIAL ALLOCATION RULES FOR CERTAIN ASSET ACQUISITIONS.

[Sec. 1060(a)]

(a) GENERAL RULE.—In the case of any applicable asset acquisition, for purposes of determining both—

(1) the transferee's basis in such assets, and

(2) the gain or loss of the transferor with respect to such acquisition,

the consideration received for such assets shall be allocated among such assets acquired in such acquisition in the same manner as amounts are allocated to assets under section 338(b)(5). If in connection with an applicable asset acquisition, the transferee and transferor agree in writing as to the allocation of any consideration, or as to the fair market value of any of the assets, such agreement shall be binding on both the transferee and transferor unless the Secretary determines that such allocation (or fair market value) is not appropriate.

[Sec. 1060(b)]

(b) INFORMATION REQUIRED TO BE FURNISHED TO SECRETARY.—Under regulations, the transferor and transferee in an applicable asset acquisition shall, at such times and in such manner as may be provided in such regulations, furnish to the Secretary the following information:

(1) The amount of the consideration received for the assets which is allocated to Section 197 intangibles.

(2) Any modification of the amount described in paragraph (1).

(3) Any other information with respect to other assets transferred in such acquisition as the Secretary deems necessary to carry out the provisions of this section.

[Sec. 1060(c)]

(c) APPLICABLE ASSET ACQUISITION.—For purposes of this section, the term "applicable asset acquisition" means any transfer (whether directly or indirectly)—

(1) of assets which constitute a trade or business, and

(2) with respect to which the transferee's basis in such assets is determined wholly by reference to the consideration paid for such assets.

A transfer shall not be treated as failing to be an applicable asset acquisition merely because section 1031 applies to a portion of the assets transferred.

[Sec. 1060(d)]

(d) TREATMENT OF CERTAIN PARTNERSHIP TRANSACTIONS.—In the case of a distribution of partnership property or a transfer of an interest in a partnership—

(1) the rules of subsection (a) shall apply but only for purposes of determining the value of section 197 intangibles for purposes of applying section 755, and

(2) if section 755 applies, such distribution or transfer (as the case may be) shall be treated as an applicable asset acquisition for purposes of subsection (b).

[Sec. 1060(e)]

(e) INFORMATION REQUIRED IN CASE OF CERTAIN TRANSFERS OF INTERESTS IN ENTITIES.—

(1) IN GENERAL.—If—

(A) a person who is a 10-percent owner with respect to any entity transfers an interest in such entity, and

(B) in connection with such transfer, such owner (or a related person) enters into an employment contract, covenant not to compete, royalty or lease agreement, or other agreement with the transferee,

such owner and the transferee shall, at such time and in such manner as the Secretary may prescribe, furnish such information as the Secretary may require.

(2) 10-PERCENT OWNER.—For purposes of this subsection—

(A) IN GENERAL.—The term "10-percent owner" means, with respect to any entity, any person who holds 10 percent or more (by value) of the interests in such entity immediately before the transfer.

(B) CONSTRUCTIVE OWNERSHIP.—Section 318 shall apply in determining ownership of stock in a corporation. Similar principles shall apply in determining the ownership of interests in any other entity.

(3) RELATED PERSON.—For purposes of this subsection, the term "related person" means any person who is related (within the meaning of section 267(b) or 707(b)(1)) to the 10-percent owner.

* * *

[Sec. 1061]

SEC. 1061. PARTNERSHIP INTERESTS HELD IN CONNECTION WITH PERFORMANCE OF SERVICES.

[Sec. 1061(a)]

(a) IN GENERAL.—If one or more applicable partnership interests are held by a taxpayer at any time during the taxable year, the excess (if any) of—

(1) the taxpayer's net long-term capital gain with respect to such interests for such taxable year, over

(2) the taxpayer's net long-term capital gain with respect to such interests for such taxable year computed by applying paragraphs (3) and (4) of sections [sic] 1222 by substituting "3 years" for "1 year",

shall be treated as short-term capital gain, notwithstanding section 83 or any election in effect under section 83(b).

[Sec. 1061(b)]

(b) SPECIAL RULE.—To the extent provided by the Secretary, subsection (a) shall not apply to income or gain attributable to any asset not held for portfolio investment on behalf of third party investors.

[Sec. 1061(c)]

(c) APPLICABLE PARTNERSHIP INTEREST.—For purposes of this section—

(1) IN GENERAL.—Except as provided in this paragraph or paragraph (4), the term "applicable partnership interest" means any interest in a partnership which, directly or indirectly, is transferred to (or is held by) the taxpayer in connection with the performance of substantial services by the taxpayer, or any other related person, in any applicable trade or business. The previous sentence shall not apply to an interest held by a person who is employed by another entity that is conducting a trade or business (other than an applicable trade or business) and only provides services to such other entity.

(2) APPLICABLE TRADE OR BUSINESS.—The term "applicable trade or business" means any activity conducted on a regular, continuous, and substantial basis which, regardless of whether the activity is conducted in one or more entities, consists, in whole or in part, of—

(A) raising or returning capital, and

(B) either—

(i) investing in (or disposing of) specified assets (or identifying specified assets for such investing or disposition), or

(ii) developing specified assets.

(3) SPECIFIED ASSET.—The term "specified asset" means securities (as defined in section 475(c)(2) without regard to the last sentence thereof), commodities (as defined in section 475(e)(2)), real estate held for rental or investment, cash or cash equivalents, options or derivative contracts with respect to any of the foregoing, and an interest in a partnership to the extent of the partnership's proportionate interest in any of the foregoing.

(4) EXCEPTIONS.—The term "applicable partnership interest" shall not include—

(A) any interest in a partnership directly or indirectly held by a corporation, or

(B) any capital interest in the partnership which provides the taxpayer with a right to share in partnership capital commensurate with—

(i) the amount of capital contributed (determined at the time of receipt of such partnership interest), or

(ii) the value of such interest subject to tax under section 83 upon the receipt or vesting of such interest.

(5) THIRD PARTY INVESTOR.—The term "third party investor" means a person who—

(A) holds an interest in the partnership which does not constitute property held in connection with an applicable trade or business; and

(B) is not (and has not been) actively engaged, and is (and was) not related to a person so engaged, in (directly or indirectly) providing substantial services described in paragraph (1) for such partnership or any applicable trade or business.

[Sec. 1061(d)]

(d) TRANSFER OF APPLICABLE PARTNERSHIP INTEREST TO RELATED PERSON.—

(1) IN GENERAL.—If a taxpayer transfers any applicable partnership interest, directly or indirectly, to a person related to the taxpayer, the taxpayer shall include in gross income (as short term capital gain) the excess (if any) of—

(A) so much of the taxpayer's long-term capital gains with respect to such interest for such taxable year attributable to the sale or exchange of any asset held for not more than 3 years as is allocable to such interest, over

(B) any amount treated as short term capital gain under subsection (a) with respect to the transfer of such interest.

(2) RELATED PERSON.—For purposes of this paragraph, a person is related to the taxpayer if—

(A) the person is a member of the taxpayer's family within the meaning of section 318(a)(1), or

(B) the person performed a service within the current calendar year or the preceding three calendar years in any applicable trade or business in which or for which the taxpayer performed a service.

[Sec. 1061(e)]

(e) REPORTING.—The Secretary shall require such reporting (at the time and in the manner prescribed by the Secretary) as is necessary to carry out the purposes of this section.

[Sec. 1061(f)]

(f) REGULATIONS.—The Secretary shall issue such regulations or other guidance as is necessary or appropriate to carry out the purposes of this section.

PART VII—WASH SALES; STRADDLES

[Sec. 1091]

SEC. 1091. LOSS FROM WASH SALES OF STOCK OR SECURITIES.

[Sec. 1091(a)]

(a) DISALLOWANCE OF LOSS DEDUCTION.—In the case of any loss claimed to have been sustained from any sale or other disposition of shares of stock or securities where it appears that, within a period beginning 30 days before the date of such sale or disposition and ending 30 days after such date, the taxpayer has acquired (by purchase or by an exchange on which the entire amount of gain or loss was recognized by law), or has entered into a contract or option so to acquire, substantially identical stock or securities, then no deduction shall be allowed under section 165 unless the taxpayer is a dealer in stock or securities and the loss is sustained in a transaction made in the ordinary course of such business. For purposes of this section, the term "stock or securities" shall, except as provided in regulations, include contracts or options to acquire or sell stock or securities.

[Sec. 1091(b)]

(b) STOCK ACQUIRED LESS THAN STOCK SOLD.—If the amount of stock or securities acquired (or covered by the contract or option to acquire) is less than the amount of stock or securities sold or otherwise disposed of, then the particular shares of stock or securities the loss from the sale or other disposition of which is not deductible shall be determined under regulations prescribed by the Secretary.

[Sec. 1091(c)]

(c) STOCK ACQUIRED NOT LESS THAN STOCK SOLD.—If the amount of stock or securities acquired (or covered by the contract or option to acquire) is not less than the amount of stock or securities sold or otherwise disposed of, then the particular shares of stock or securities the acquisition of which (or the contract or option to acquire which) resulted in the nondeductibility of the loss shall be determined under regulations prescribed by the Secretary.

[Sec. 1091(d)]

(d) UNADJUSTED BASIS IN CASE OF WASH SALE OF STOCK.—If the property consists of stock or securities the acquisition of which (or the contract or option to acquire which) resulted in the nondeductibility (under this section or corresponding provisions of prior internal revenue laws) of the loss from the sale or other disposition of substantially identical stock or securities, then the basis shall be the basis of the stock or securities so sold or disposed of, increased or decreased, as the case may be, by the difference, if any, between the price at which the property was acquired and the price at which such substantially identical stock or securities were sold or otherwise disposed of.

[Sec. 1091(e)]

(e) CERTAIN SHORT SALES OF STOCK OR SECURITIES AND SECURITIES FUTURES CONTRACTS TO SELL.—Rules similar to the rules of subsection (a) shall apply to any loss realized on the closing of a short sale of (or the sale, exchange, or termination of a securities futures contract to sell) stock or securities if, within a period beginning 30 days before the date of such closing and ending 30 days after such date—

(1) substantially identical stock or securities were sold, or

(2) another short sale of (or securities futures contracts to sell) substantially identical stock or securities was entered into.

For purposes of this subsection, the term "securities futures contract" has the meaning provided by section 1234B(c).

[Sec. 1091(f)]

(f) CASH SETTLEMENT.—This section shall not fail to apply to a contract or option to acquire or sell stock or securities solely by reason of the fact that the contract or option settles in (or could be settled in) cash or property other than such stock or securities.

SUBCHAPTER P—CAPITAL GAINS AND LOSSES

PART I—TREATMENT OF CAPITAL GAINS

[Sec. 1202]

SEC. 1202. PARTIAL EXCLUSION FOR GAIN FROM CERTAIN SMALL BUSINESS STOCK.

[Sec. 1202(a)]

(a) EXCLUSION.—

(1) IN GENERAL.—In the case of a taxpayer other than a corporation, gross income shall not include 50 percent of any gain from the sale or exchange of qualified small business stock held for more than 5 years.

* * *

(3) SPECIAL RULES FOR 2009 AND CERTAIN PERIODS IN 2010.—In the case of qualified small business stock acquired after the date of the enactment of this paragraph and on or before the date of the enactment of the Creating Small Business Jobs Act of 2010—

(A) paragraph (1) shall be applied by substituting "75 percent" for "50 percent", and

(B) paragraph (2) shall not apply.

In the case of any stock which would be described in the preceding sentence (but for this sentence), the acquisition date for purposes of this subsection shall be the first day on which such stock was held by the taxpayer determined after the application of section 1223.

(4) 100 PERCENT EXCLUSION FOR STOCK ACQUIRED DURING CERTAIN PERIODS IN 2010 AND THEREAFTER.—In the case of qualified small business stock acquired after the date of the enactment of the Creating Small Business Jobs Act of 2010—

(A) paragraph (1) shall be applied by substituting "100 percent" for "50 percent",

(B) paragraph (2) shall not apply, and

(C) paragraph (7) of section 57(a) shall not apply.

In the case of any stock which would be described in the preceding sentence (but for this sentence), the acquisition date for purposes of this subsection shall be the first day on which such stock was held by the taxpayer determined after the application of section 1223.

[Sec. 1202(b)]

(b) PER-ISSUER LIMITATION ON TAXPAYER'S ELIGIBLE GAIN.—

(1) IN GENERAL.—If the taxpayer has eligible gain for the taxable year from 1 or more dispositions of stock issued by any corporation, the aggregate amount of such gain from dispositions of stock issued by such corporation which may be taken into account under subsection (a) for the taxable year shall not exceed the greater of—

(A) $10,000,000 reduced by the aggregate amount of eligible gain taken into account by the taxpayer under subsection (a) for prior taxable years attributable to dispositions of stock issued by such corporation, or

(B) 10 times the aggregate adjusted bases of qualified small business stock issued by such corporation and disposed of by the taxpayer during the taxable year.

For purposes of subparagraph (B), the adjusted basis of any stock shall be determined without regard to any addition to basis after the date on which such stock was originally issued.

(2) ELIGIBLE GAIN.—For purposes of this subsection, the term "eligible gain" means any gain from the sale or exchange of qualified small business stock held for more than 5 years.

(3) TREATMENT OF MARRIED INDIVIDUALS.—

(A) SEPARATE RETURNS.—In the case of a separate return by a married individual, paragraph (1) (A) shall be applied by substituting "$5,000,000" for "$10,000,000".

(B) ALLOCATION OF EXCLUSION.—In the case of any joint return, the amount of gain taken into account under subsection (a) shall be allocated equally between the spouses for purposes of applying this subsection to subsequent taxable years.

(C) MARITAL STATUS.—For purposes of this subsection, marital status shall be determined under section 7703.

[Sec. 1202(c)]

(c) QUALIFIED SMALL BUSINESS STOCK.—For purposes of this section—

(1) IN GENERAL.—Except as otherwise provided in this section, the term "qualified small business stock" means any stock in a C corporation which is originally issued after the date of the enactment of the Revenue Reconciliation Act of 1993, if—

(A) as of the date of issuance, such corporation is a qualified small business, and

(B) except as provided in subsections (f) and (h), such stock is acquired by the taxpayer at its original issue (directly or through an underwriter)—

(i) in exchange for money or other property (not including stock), or

(ii) as compensation for services provided to such corporation (other than services performed as an underwriter of such stock).

(2) ACTIVE BUSINESS REQUIREMENTS; ETC.—

(A) IN GENERAL.—Stock in a corporation shall not be treated as qualified small business stock unless, during substantially all of the taxpayer's holding period for such stock, such corporation meets the active business requirements of subsection (e) and such corporation is a C corporation.

(B) SPECIAL RULE FOR CERTAIN SMALL BUSINESS INVESTMENT COMPANIES.—

(i) WAIVER OF ACTIVE BUSINESS REQUIREMENT.—Notwithstanding any provision of subsection (e), a corporation shall be treated as meeting the active business requirements of such subsection for any period during which such corporation qualifies as a specialized small business investment company.

(ii) SPECIALIZED SMALL BUSINESS INVESTMENT COMPANY.—For purposes of clause (i), the term "specialized small business investment company" means any eligible corporation (as defined in subsection (e)(4)) which is licensed to operate under section 301(d) of the Small Business Investment Act of 1958 (as in effect on May 13, 1993).

(3) CERTAIN PURCHASES BY CORPORATION OF ITS OWN STOCK.—

(A) REDEMPTIONS FROM TAXPAYER OR RELATED PERSON.—Stock acquired by the taxpayer shall not be treated as qualified small busienss stock if, at any time during the 4-year period beginning on the date 2 years before the issuance of such stock, the corporation issuing such stock purchased (directly or indirectly) any of its stock from the taxpayer or from a person related (within the meaning of section 267(b) or 707(b)) to the taxpayer.

(B) SIGNIFICANT REDEMPTIONS.—Stock issued by a corporation shall not be treated as qualified business stock if, during the 2-year period beginning on the date 1 year before the issuance of such stock, such corporation made 1 or more purchases of its stock with an aggregate value (as of the time of the respective purchases) exceeding 5 percent of the aggregate value of all of its stock as of the beginning of such 2-year period.

(C) TREATMENT OF CERTAIN TRANSACTIONS.—If any transaction is treated under section 304(a) as a distribution in redemption of the stock of any corporation, for purposes of subparagraphs (A) and (B), such corporation shall be treated as purchasing an amount of its stock equal to the amount treated as such a distribution under section 304(a).

[Sec. 1202(d)]

(d) QUALIFIED SMALL BUSINESS.—For purposes of this section—

(1) IN GENERAL.—The term 'qualified small business' means any domestic corporation which is a C corporation if—

(A) the aggregate gross assets of such corporation (or any predecessor thereof) at all times on or after the date of the enactment of the Revenue Reconciliation Act of 1993 and before the issuance did not exceed $50,000,000,

(B) the aggregate gross assets of such corporation immediately after the issuance (determined by taking into account amounts received in the issuance) do not exceed $50,000,000, and

(C) such corporation agrees to submit such reports to the Secretary and to shareholders as the Secretary may require to carry out the purposes of this section.

(2) AGGREGATE GROSS ASSETS.—

(A) IN GENERAL.—For purposes of paragraph (1), the term "aggregate gross assets" means the amount of cash and the aggregate adjusted bases of other property held by the corporation.

(B) TREATMENT OF CONTRIBUTED PROPERTY.—For purposes of subparagraph (A), the adjusted basis of any property contributed to the corporation (or other property with a basis determined in whole or in part by reference to the adjusted basis of property so contributed) shall be determined as if the basis of the property contributed to the corporation (immediately after such contribution) were equal to its fair market value as of the time of such contribution.

(3) AGGREGATION RULES.—

(A) IN GENERAL.—All corporations which are members of the same parent-subsidiary controlled group shall be treated as 1 corporation for purposes of this subsection.

(B) PARENT-SUBSIDIARY CONTROLLED GROUP.—For purposes of subparagraph (A), the term "parent-subsidiary controlled group" means any controlled group of corporations as defined in section 1563(a)(1), except that—

(i) "more than 50 percent" shall be substituted for "at least 80 percent" each place it appears in section 1563(a)(1), and

(ii) section 1563(a)(4) shall not apply.

(e) ACTIVE BUSINESS REQUIREMENT.—

(1) IN GENERAL.—For purposes of subsection (c)(2), the requirements of this subsection are met by a corporation for any period if during such period—

(A) at least 80 percent (by value) of the assets of such corporation are used by such corporation in the active conduct of 1 or more qualified trades or businesses, and

(B) such corporation is an eligible corporation.

(2) SPECIAL RULE FOR CERTAIN ACTIVITIES.—For purposes of paragraph (1), if, in connection with any future qualified trade or business, a corporation is engaged in—

(A) start-up activities described in section 195(c)(1)(A),

(B) activities resulting in the payment or incurring of expenditures which may be treated as research and experimental expenditures under section 174, or

(C) activities with respect to in-house research expenses described in section 41(b)(4),

assets used in such activities shall be treated as used in the active conduct of a qualified trade or business. Any determination under this paragraph shall be made without regard to whether a corporation has any gross income from such activities at the time of the determination.

(3) QUALIFIED TRADE OR BUSINESS.—For purposes of this subsection, the term "qualified trade or business" means any trade or business other than—

(A) any trade or business involving the performance of services in the fields of health, law, engineering, architecture, accounting, actuarial science, performing arts, consulting, athletics, financial services, brokerage services, or any trade or business where the principal asset of such trade or business is the reputation or skill of 1 or more of its employees,

(B) any banking, insurance, financing, leasing, investing, or similar business,

(C) any farming business (including the business of raising or harvesting trees),

(D) any business involving the production or extraction of products of a character with respect to which a deduction is allowable under section 613 or 613A, and

(E) any business of operating a hotel, motel, restaurant, or similar business.

(4) ELIGIBLE CORPORATION.—For purposes of this subsection, the term 'eligible corporation' means any domestic corporation; except that such term shall not include—

(A) a DISC or former DISC,

(B) a regulated investment company, real estate investment trust, or REMIC, and

(C) a cooperative.

(5) STOCK IN OTHER CORPORATIONS.—

(A) LOOK-THRU IN CASE OF SUBSIDIARIES.—For purposes of this subsection, stock and debt in any subsidiary corporation shall be disregarded and the parent corporation shall be deemed to own its ratable share of the subsidiary's assets, and to conduct its ratable share of the subsidiary's activities.

(B) PORTFOLIO STOCK OR SECURITIES.—A corporation shall be treated as failing to meet the requirements of paragraph (1) for any period during which more than 10 percent of the value of its assets (in excess of liabilities) consists of stock or securities in other corporations which are not subsidiaries of such corporation (other than assets described in paragraph (6)).

(C) SUBSIDIARY.—For purposes of this paragraph, a corporation shall be considered a subsidiary if the parent owns more than 50 percent of the combined voting power of all classes of stock entitled to vote, or more than 50 percent in value of all outstanding stock, of such corporation.

(6) WORKING CAPITAL.—For purposes of paragraph (1)(A), any assets which—

(A) are held as a part of the reasonably required working capital needs of a qualified trade or business of the corporation, or

(B) are held for investment and are reasonably expected to be used within 2 years to finance research and experimentation in a qualified trade or business or increases in working capital needs of a qualified trade or business,

shall be treated as used in the active conduct of a qualified trade or business. For periods after the corporation has been in existence for at least 2 years, in no event may more than 50 percent of the assets of the corporation qualify as used in the active conduct of a qualified trade or business by reason of this paragraph.

(7) MAXIMUM REAL ESTATE HOLDINGS.—A corporation shall not be treated as meeting the requirements of paragraph (1) for any period during which more than 10 percent of the total value of its assets consists of real property which is not used in the active conduct of a qualified trade or business. For purposes of the preceding sentence, the ownership of, dealing in, or renting of real property shall not be treated as the active conduct of a qualified trade or business.

(8) COMPUTER SOFTWARE ROYALTIES.—For purposes of paragraph (1), rights to computer software which produces active business computer software royalties (within the meaning of section 543(d)(1)) shall be treated as an asset used in the active conduct of a trade or business.

[Sec. 1202(f)]

(f) STOCK ACQUIRED ON CONVERSION OF OTHER STOCK.—If any stock in a corporation is acquired solely through the conversion of other stock in such corporation which is qualified small business stock in the hands of the taxpayer—

(1) the stock so acquired shall be treated as qualified small business stock in the hands of the taxpayer, and

(2) the stock so acquired shall be treated as having been held during the period during which the converted stock was held.

[Sec. 1202(g)]

(g) TREATMENT OF PASS-THRU ENTITIES.—

(1) IN GENERAL.—If any amount included in gross income by reason of holding an interest in a pass-thru entity meets the requirements of paragraph (2)—

(A) such amount shall be treated as gain described in subsection (a), and

(B) for purposes of applying subsection (b), such amount shall be treated as gain from a disposition of stock in the corporation issuing the stock disposed of by the pass-thru entity and the taxpayer's proportionate share of the adjusted basis of the pass-thru entity in such stock shall be taken into account.

(2) REQUIREMENTS.—An amount meets the requirements of this paragraph if—

(A) such amount is attributable to gain on the sale or exchange by the pass-thru entity of stock which is qualified small business stock in the hands of such entity (determined by treating such entity as an individual) and which was held by such entity for more than 5 years, and

(B) such amount is includible in the gross income of the taxpayer by reason of the holding of an interest in such entity which was held by the taxpayer on the date on which such pass-thru entity acquired such stock and at all times thereafter before the disposition of such stock by such pass-thru entity.

(3) LIMITATION BASED ON INTEREST ORIGINALLY HELD BY TAXPAYER.—Paragraph (1) shall not apply to any amount to the extent such amount exceeds the amount to which paragraph (1) would have applied if such amount were determined by reference to the interest the taxpayer held in the pass-thru entity on the date the qualified small business stock was acquired.

(4) PASS-THRU ENTITY.—For purposes of this subsection, the term "pass-thru entity" means—

(A) any partnership,

(B) any S corporation,

(C) any regulated investment company, and

(D) any common trust fund.

[Sec. 1202(h)]

(h) CERTAIN TAX-FREE AND OTHER TRANSFERS.—For purposes of this section—

(1) IN GENERAL.—In the case of a transfer described in paragraph (2), the transferee shall be treated as—

(A) having acquired such stock in the same manner as the transferor, and

(B) having held such stock during any continuous period immediately preceding the transfer during which it was held (or treated as held under this subsection) by the transferor.

(2) DESCRIPTION OF TRANSFERS.—A transfer is described in this subsection if such transfer is—

(A) by gift,

(B) at death, or

(C) from a partnership to a partner of stock with respect to which requirements similar to the requirements of subsection (g) are met at the time of the transfer (without regard to the 5-year holding period requirement).

(3) CERTAIN RULES MADE APPLICABLE.—Rules similar to the rules of section 1244(d)(2) shall apply for purposes of this section.

(4) INCORPORATIONS AND REORGANIZATIONS INVOLVING NONQUALIFIED STOCK.—

(A) IN GENERAL.—In the case of a transaction described in section 351 or a reorganization described in section 368, if qualified small business stock is exchanged for other stock which would not qualify as qualified small business stock but for this subparagraph, such other stock shall be treated as qualified small business stock acquired on the date on which the exchanged stock was acquired.

(B) LIMITATION.—This section shall apply to gain from the sale or exchange of stock treated as qualifed small business stock by reason of subparagraph (A) only to the extent of the gain which would have been recognized at the time of the transfer described in subparagraph (A) if section 351 or 368 had not applied at such time. The preceding sentence shall not apply if the stock which is treated as qualified small business stock by reason of subparagraph (A) is issued by a corporation which (as of the time of the transfer described in subparagraph (A)) is a qualified small business.

(C) SUCCESSIVE APPLICATION.—For purposes of this paragraph, stock treated as qualified small business stock under subparagraph (A) shall be so treated for subsequent transactions or reorganizations, except that the limitation of subparagraph (B) shall be applied as of the time of the first transfer to which such limitation applied (determined after the application of the second sentence of subparagraph (B)).

(D) CONTROL TEST.—In the case of a transaction described in section 351, this paragraph shall apply only if, immediately after the transaction, the corporation issuing the stock owns directly or indirectly stock representing control (within the meaning of section 368(c)) of the corporation whose stock was exchanged.

[Sec. 1202(i)]

(i) BASIS RULES.—For purposes of this section—

(1) STOCK EXCHANGED FOR PROPERTY.—In the case where the taxpayer transfers property (other than money or stock) to a corporation in exchange for stock in such corporation—

(A) such stock shall be treated as having been acquired by the taxpayer on the date of such exchange, and

(B) the basis of such stock in the hands of the taxpayer shall in no event be less than the fair market value of the property exchanged.

(2) TREATMENT OF CONTRIBUTIONS TO CAPITAL.—If the adjusted basis of any qualified small business stock is adjusted by reason of any contribution to capital after the date on which such stock was originally issued, in determining the amount of the adjustment by reason of such contribution, the basis of the contributed property shall in no event be treated as less than its fair market value on the date of the contribution.

* * *

[Sec. 1202(k)]

(k) REGULATIONS.—The Secretary shall prescribe such regulations as may be appropriate to carry out the purposes of this section, including regulations to prevent the avoidance of the purposes of this section through split-ups, shell corporations, partnerships, or otherwise.

PART II—TREATMENT OF CAPITAL LOSSES

[Sec. 1211]

SEC. 1211. LIMITATION ON CAPITAL LOSSES.

[Sec. 1211(a)]

(a) CORPORATIONS.—In the case of a corporation, losses from sales or exchanges of capital assets shall be allowed only to the extent of gains from such sales or exchanges.

[Sec. 1211(b)]

(b) OTHER TAXPAYERS.—In the case of a taxpayer other than a corporation, losses from sales or exchanges of capital assets shall be allowed only to the extent of the gains from such sales or exchanges, plus (if such losses exceed such gains) the lower of—

(1) $3,000 ($1,500 in the case of a married individual filing a separate return), or

(2) the excess of such losses over such gains.

[Sec. 1212]

SEC. 1212. CAPITAL LOSS CARRYBACKS AND CARRYOVERS.

[Sec. 1212(a)]

(a) CORPORATIONS.—

(1) IN GENERAL.—If a corporation has a net capital loss for any taxable year (hereinafter in this paragraph referred to as the "loss year"), the amount thereof shall be—

(A) a capital loss carryback to each of the 3 taxable years preceding the loss year, but only to the extent—

(i) such loss is not attributable to a foreign expropriation capital loss, and

(ii) the carryback of such loss does not increase or produce a net operating loss (as defined in section 172(c)) for the taxable year to which it is being carried back;

(B) except as provided in subparagraph (C), a capital loss carryover to each of the 5 taxable years succeeding the loss year; and

(C) a capital loss carryover to each of the 10 taxable years succeeding the loss year, but only to the extent such loss is attributable to a foreign expropriation loss,

and shall be treated as a short-term capital loss in each such taxable year. The entire amount of the net capital loss for any taxable year shall be carried to the earliest of the taxable years to which such loss may be carried, and the portion of such loss which shall be carried to each of the other taxable years to which such loss may be carried shall be the excess, if any, of such loss over the total of the capital gain net income for each of the prior taxable years to which such loss may be carried. For purposes of the preceding sentence, the capital gain net income for any such prior taxable year shall be computed without regard to the net capital loss for the loss year or for any taxable year thereafter. In the case of any net capital loss which cannot be carried back in full to a preceding taxable year by reason of clause (ii) of subparagraph (A), the capital gain net income for such prior taxable year shall in no case be treated as greater than the amount of such loss which can be carried back to such preceding taxable year upon the application of such clause (ii).

* * *

(4) SPECIAL RULES ON CARRYBACKS.—A net capital loss of a corporation shall not be carried back under paragraph (1)(A) to a taxable year—

(A) for which it is a regulated investment company (as defined in section 851), or

(B) for which it is a real estate investment trust (as defined in section 856).

[Sec. 1212(b)]

(b) OTHER TAXPAYERS.—

(1) IN GENERAL.—If a taxpayer other than a corporation has a net capital loss for any taxable year—

(A) the excess of the net short-term capital loss over the net long-term capital gain for such year shall be a short-term capital loss in the succeeding taxable year, and

(B) the excess of the net long-term capital loss over the net short-term capital gain for such year shall be a long-term capital loss in the succeeding taxable year.

(2) TREATMENT OF AMOUNTS ALLOWED UNDER SECTION 1211(b)(1) OR (2).—

(A) IN GENERAL.—For purposes of determining the excess referred to in subparagraph (A) or (B) of paragraph (1), there shall be treated as a short-term capital gain in the taxable year an amount equal to the lesser of—

(i) the amount allowed for the taxable year under paragraph (1) or (2) of section 1211(b), or

(ii) the adjusted taxable income for such taxable year.

(B) ADJUSTED TAXABLE INCOME.—For purposes of subparagraph (A), the term "adjusted taxable income" means taxable income increased by the sum of—

(i) the amount allowed for the taxable year under paragraph (1) or (2) of section 1211(b), and

(ii) the deduction allowed for such year under section 151 or any deduction in lieu thereof.

For purposes of the preceding sentence, any excess of the deductions allowed for the taxable year over the gross income for such year shall be taken into account as negative taxable income.

[Sec. 1212(c)]

(c) CARRYBACK OF LOSSES FROM SECTION 1256 CONTRACTS TO OFFSET PRIOR GAINS FROM SUCH CONTRACTS.—

(1) IN GENERAL.—If a taxpayer (other than a corporation) has a net section 1256 contracts loss for the taxable year and elects to have this subsection apply to such taxable year, the amount of such net section 1256 contracts loss—

(A) shall be a carryback to each of the 3 taxable years preceding the loss year, and

(B) to the extent that, after the application of paragraphs (2) and (3), such loss is allowed as a carryback to any such preceding taxable year—

(i) 40 percent of the amount so allowed shall be treated as a short-term capital loss from section 1256 contracts, and

(ii) 60 percent of the amount so allowed shall be treated as a long-term capital loss from section 1256 contracts.

(2) AMOUNT CARRIED TO EACH TAXABLE YEAR.—The entire amount of the net section 1256 contracts loss for any taxable year shall be carried to the earliest of the taxable years to which such loss may be carried back under paragraph (1). The portion of such loss which shall be carried to each of the 2 other taxable years to which such loss may be carried back shall be the excess (if any) of such loss over the portion of such loss which, after the application of paragraph (3), was allowed as a carryback for any prior taxable year.

(3) AMOUNT WHICH MAY BE USED IN ANY PRIOR TAXABLE YEAR.—An amount shall be allowed as a carryback under paragraph (1) to any prior taxable year only to the extent—

(A) such amount does not exceed the net section 1256 contract gain for such year, and

(B) the allowance of such carryback does not increase or produce a net operating loss (as defined in section 172(c)) for such year.

(4) NET SECTION 1256 CONTRACTS LOSS.—For purposes of paragraph (1), the term "net section 1256 contracts loss" means the lesser of—

(A) the net capital loss for the taxable year determined by taking into account only gains and losses from section 1256 contracts, or

(B) the sum of the amounts which, but for paragraph (6)(A), would be treated as capital losses in the succeeding taxable year under subparagraphs (A) and (B) of subsection (b)(1).

(5) NET SECTION 1256 CONTRACT GAIN.—For purposes of paragraph (1)—

(A) IN GENERAL.—The term "net section 1256 contract gain" means the lesser of—

(i) the capital gain net income for the taxable year determined by taking into account only gains and losses from section 1256 contracts, or

(ii) the capital gain net income for the taxable year.

(B) SPECIAL RULE.—The net section 1256 contract gain for any taxable year before the loss year shall be computed without regard to the net section 1256 contracts loss for the loss year or for any taxable year thereafter.

(6) COORDINATION WITH CARRYFORWARD PROVISIONS OF SUBSECTION (b)(1).—

(A) CARRYFORWARD AMOUNT REDUCED BY AMOUNT USED AS CARRYBACK.—For purposes of applying subsection (b)(1), if any portion of the net section 1256 contracts loss for any taxable year is allowed as a carryback under paragraph (1) to any preceding taxable year—

(i) 40 percent of the amount allowed as a carryback shall be treated as a short-term capital gain for the loss year, and

(ii) 60 percent of the amount allowed as a carryback shall be treated as a long-term capital gain for the loss year.

(B) CARRYOVER LOSS RETAINS CHARACTER AS ATTRIBUTABLE TO SECTION 1256 CONTRACT.—Any amount carried forward as a short-term or long-term capital loss to any taxable year under subsection (b)(1) (after the application of subparagraph (A)) shall, to the extent attributable to losses from section 1256 contracts, be treated as loss from section 1256 contracts for such taxable year.

(7) OTHER DEFINITIONS AND SPECIAL RULES.—For purposes of this subsection—

(A) SECTION 1256 CONTRACT.—The term "section 1256 contract" means any section 1256 contract (as defined in section 1256(b)) to which section 1256 applies.

(B) EXCLUSION FOR ESTATES AND TRUSTS.—This subsection shall not apply to any estate or trust.

PART III—GENERAL RULES FOR DETERMINING CAPITAL GAINS AND LOSSES

[Sec. 1221]

SEC. 1221. CAPITAL ASSET DEFINED.

[Sec. 1221(a)]

(a) IN GENERAL.—For purposes of this subtitle, the term "capital asset" means property held by the taxpayer (whether or not connected with his trade or business), but does not include—

(1) stock in trade of the taxpayer or other property of a kind which would properly be included in the inventory of the taxpayer if on hand at the close of the taxable year, or property held by the taxpayer primarily for sale to customers in the ordinary course of his trade or business;

(2) property, used in his trade or business, of a character which is subject to the allowance for depreciation provided in section 167, or real property used in his trade or business;

(3) a patent, invention, model or design (whether or not patented), a secret formula or process, a copyright, a literary, musical, or artistic composition, a letter or memorandum, or similar property, held by—

(A) a taxpayer whose personal efforts created such property,

(B) in the case of a letter, memorandum, or similar property, a taxpayer for whom such property was prepared or produced, or

(C) a taxpayer in whose hands the basis of such property is determined, for purposes of determining gain from a sale or exchange, in whole or part by reference to the basis of such property in the hands of a taxpayer described in subparagraph (A) or (B);

(4) accounts or notes receivable acquired in the ordinary course of trade or business for services rendered or from the sale of property described in paragraph (1);

(5) a publication of the United States Government (including the Congressional Record) which is received from the United States Government or any agency thereof, other than by purchase at the price at which it is offered for sale to the public, and which is held by—

(A) a taxpayer who so received such publication, or

(B) a taxpayer in whose hands the basis of such publication is determined, for purposes of determining gain from a sale or exchange, in whole or in part by reference to the basis of such publication in the hands of a taxpayer described in subparagraph (A);

(6) any commodities derivative financial instrument held by a commodities derivatives dealer, unless—

(A) it is established to the satisfaction of the Secretary that such instrument has no connection to the activities of such dealer as a dealer, and

(B) such instrument is clearly identified in such dealer's records as being described in subparagraph (A) before the close of the day on which it was acquired, originated, or entered into (or such other time as the Secretary may by regulations prescribe);

(7) any hedging transaction which is clearly identified as such before the close of the day on which it was acquired, originated, or entered into (or such other time as the Secretary may by regulations prescribe); or

(8) supplies of a type regularly used or consumed by the taxpayer in the ordinary course of a trade or business of the taxpayer.

[Sec. 1221(b)]

(b) DEFINITIONS AND SPECIAL RULES.—

(1) COMMODITIES DERIVATIVE FINANCIAL INSTRUMENTS.—For purposes of subsection (a)(6)—

(A) COMMODITIES DERIVATIVES DEALER.—The term "commodities derivatives dealer" means a person which regularly offers to enter into, assume, offset, assign, or terminate positions in commodities derivative financial instruments with customers in the ordinary course of a trade or business.

(B) COMMODITIES DERIVATIVE FINANCIAL INSTRUMENT.—

(i) IN GENERAL.—The term "commodities derivative financial instrument" means any contract or financial instrument with respect to commodities (other than a share of stock in a corporation, a beneficial interest in a partnership or trust, a note, bond, debenture, or other evidence of indebtedness, or a section 1256 contract (as defined in section 1256(b))), the value or settlement price of which is calculated by or determined by reference to a specified index.

(ii) SPECIFIED INDEX.—The term "specified index" means any one or more or any combination of—

(I) a fixed rate, price, or amount, or

(II) a variable rate, price, or amount,

which is based on any current, objectively determinable financial or economic information with respect to commodities which is not within the control of any of the parties to the contract or instrument and is not unique to any of the parties' circumstances.

(2) HEDGING TRANSACTION.—

(A) IN GENERAL.—For purposes of this section, the term "hedging transaction" means any transaction entered into by the taxpayer in the normal course of the taxpayer's trade or business primarily—

(i) to manage risk of price changes or currency fluctuations with respect to ordinary property which is held or to be held by the taxpayer,

(ii) to manage risk of interest rate or price changes or currency fluctuations with respect to borrowings made or to be made, or ordinary obligations incurred or to be incurred, by the taxpayer, or

(iii) to manage such other risks as the Secretary may prescribe in regulations.

(B) TREATMENT OF NONIDENTIFICATION OR IMPROPER IDENTIFICATION OF HEDGING TRANSACTIONS.—Notwithstanding subsection (a)(7), the Secretary shall prescribe regulations to properly characterize any income, gain, expense, or loss arising from a transaction—

(i) which is a hedging transaction but which was not identified as such in accordance with subsection (a)(7), or

(ii) which was so identified but is not a hedging transaction.

(3) SALE OR EXCHANGE OF SELF-CREATED MUSICAL WORKS.—At the election of the taxpayer, paragraphs (1) and (3) of subsection (a) shall not apply to musical compositions or copyrights in musical works sold or exchanged by a taxpayer described in subsection (a)(3).

(4) REGULATIONS.—The Secretary shall prescribe such regulations as are appropriate to carry out the purposes of paragraph (6) and (7) of subsection (a) in the case of transactions involving related parties.

[Sec. 1222]

SEC. 1222. OTHER TERMS RELATING TO CAPITAL GAINS AND LOSSES.

For purposes of this subtitle—

(1) SHORT-TERM CAPITAL GAIN.—The term "short-term capital gain" means gain from the sale or exchange of a capital asset held for not more than 1 year, if and to the extent such gain is taken into account in computing gross income.

(2) SHORT-TERM CAPITAL LOSS.—The term "short-term capital loss" means loss from the sale or exchange of a capital asset held for not more than 1 year, if and to the extent that such loss is taken into account in computing taxable income.

(3) LONG-TERM CAPITAL GAIN.—The term "long-term capital gain" means gain from the sale or exchange of a capital asset held for more than 1 year, if and to the extent such gain is taken into account in computing gross income.

(4) LONG-TERM CAPITAL LOSS.—The term "long-term capital loss" means loss from the sale or exchange of a capital asset held for more than 1 year, if and to the extent that such loss is taken into account in computing taxable income.

(5) NET SHORT-TERM CAPITAL GAIN.—The term "net short-term capital gain" means the excess of short-term capital gains for the taxable year over the short-term capital losses for such year.

(6) NET SHORT-TERM CAPITAL LOSS.—The term "net short-term capital loss" means the excess of short-term capital losses for the taxable year over the short-term capital gains for such year.

(7) NET LONG-TERM CAPITAL GAIN.—The term "net long-term capital gain" means the excess of long-term capital gains for the taxable year over the long-term capital losses for such year.

(8) NET LONG-TERM CAPITAL LOSS.—The term "net long-term capital loss" means the excess of long-term capital losses for the taxable year over the long-term capital gains for such year.

(9) CAPITAL GAIN NET INCOME.—The term "capital gain net income" means the excess of the gains from sales or exchanges of capital assets over the losses from such sales or exchanges.

(10) NET CAPITAL LOSS.—The term "net capital loss" means the excess of the losses from sales or exchanges of capital assets over the sum allowed under section 1211. In the case of a corporation, for the purpose of determining losses under this paragraph, amounts which are short-term capital losses under section 1212(a)(1) shall be excluded.

(11) NET CAPITAL GAIN.—The term "net capital gain" means the excess of the net long-term capital gain for the taxable year over the net short-term capital loss for such year.

[Sec. 1223]

SEC. 1223. HOLDING PERIOD OF PROPERTY.

For purposes of this subtitle—

(1) In determining the period for which the taxpayer has held property received in an exchange, there shall be included the period for which he held the property exchanged if, under this chapter, the property has, for the purpose of determining gain or loss from a sale or exchange, the same basis in whole or in part in his hands as the property exchanged, and, in the case of such exchanges the property exchanged at the time of such exchange was a capital asset as defined in section 1221 or property described in section 1231. For purposes of this paragraph—

(A) an involuntary conversion described in section 1033 shall be considered an exchange of the property converted for the property acquired, and

(B) a distribution to which section 355 (or so much of section 356 as relates to section 355) applies shall be treated as an exchange.

(2) In determining the period for which the taxpayer has held property however acquired there shall be included the period for which such property was held by any other person, if under this chapter such property has, for the purpose of determining gain or loss from a sale or exchange, the same basis in whole or in part in his hands as it would have in the hands of such other person.

(3) In determining the period for which the taxpayer has held stock or securities the acquisition of which (or the contract or option to acquire which) resulted in the nondeductibility (under section 1091 relating to wash sales) of the loss from the sale or other disposition of substantially identical stock or securities, there shall be included the period for which he held the stock or securities the loss from the sale or other disposition of which was not deductible.

(4) In determining the period for which the taxpayer has held stock or rights to acquire stock received on a distribution, if the basis of such stock or rights is determined under section 307, there shall (under regulations prescribed by the Secretary) be included the period for which he held the stock in the distributing corporation before the receipt of such stock or rights upon such distribution.

(5) In determining the period for which the taxpayer has held stock or securities acquired from a corporation by the exercise of rights to acquire such stock or securities, there shall be included only the period beginning with the date on which the right to acquire was exercised.

* * *

(7) In determining the period for which the taxpayer has held a commodity acquired in satisfaction of a commodity futures contract (other than a commodity futures contract to which section 1256 applies) there shall be included the period for which he held the commodity futures contract if such commodity futures contract was a capital asset in his hands.

(8) [Repealed.]

(9) In the case of a person acquiring property from a decedent or to whom property passed from a decedent (within the meaning of section 1014(b)), if—

(A) the basis of such property in the hands of such person is determined under section 1014, and

(B) such property is sold or otherwise disposed of by such person within 1 year after the decedent's death, then such person shall be considered to have held such property for more than 1 year.

(10) If—

(A) property is acquired by any person in a transfer to which section 1040 applies,

(B) such property is sold or otherwise disposed of by such person within 1 year after the decedent's death, and

(C) such sale or disposition is to a person who is a qualified heir (as defined in section 2032A(e)(1)) with respect to the decedent,

then the person making such sale or other disposition shall be considered to have held such property for more than 1 year.

* * *

(15) CROSS REFERENCE.—

For special holding period provision relating to certain partnership distributions, see section 735(b).

PART IV—SPECIAL RULES FOR DETERMINING CAPITAL GAINS AND LOSSES

[Sec. 1231]

SEC. 1231. PROPERTY USED IN THE TRADE OR BUSINESS AND INVOLUNTARY CONVERSIONS.

[Sec. 1231(a)]

(a) GENERAL RULE.—

(1) GAINS EXCEED LOSSES.—If—

(A) the section 1231 gains for any taxable year, exceed

(B) the section 1231 losses for such taxable year,

such gains and losses shall be treated as long-term capital gains or long-term capital losses, as the case may be.

(2) GAINS DO NOT EXCEED LOSSES.—If—

(A) the section 1231 gains for any taxable year, do not exceed

(B) the section 1231 losses for such taxable year,

such gains and losses shall not be treated as gains and losses from sales or exchanges of capital assets.

(3) SECTION 1231 GAINS AND LOSSES.—For purposes of this subsection—

(A) SECTION 1231 GAIN.—The term "section 1231 gain" means—

(i) any recognized gain on the sale or exchange of property used in the trade or business, and

(ii) any recognized gain from the compulsory or involuntary conversion (as a result of destruction in whole or in part, theft or seizure, or an exercise of the power of requisition or condemnation or the threat or imminence thereof) into other property or money of—

(I) property used in the trade or business, or

(II) any capital asset which is held for more than 1 year and is held in connection with a trade or business or a transaction entered into for profit.

(B) SECTION 1231 LOSS.—The term "section 1231 loss" means any recognized loss from a sale or exchange or conversion described in subparagraph (A).

(4) SPECIAL RULES.—For purposes of this subsection—

(A) In determining under this subsection whether gains exceed losses—

(i) the section 1231 gains shall be included only if and to the extent taken into account in computing gross income, and

(ii) the section 1231 losses shall be included only if and to the extent taken into account in computing taxable income, except that section 1211 shall not apply.

(B) Losses (including losses not compensated for by insurance or otherwise) on the destruction, in whole or in part, theft or seizure, or requisition or condemnation of—

(i) property used in the trade or business, or

(ii) capital assets which are held for more than 1 year and are held in connection with a trade or business or a transaction entered into for profit,

shall be treated as losses from a compulsory or involuntary conversion.

(C) In the case of any involuntary conversion (subject to the provisions of this subsection but for this sentence) arising from fire, storm, shipwreck, or other casualty, or from theft, of any—

(i) property used in the trade or business, or

(ii) any capital asset which is held for more than 1 year and is held in connection with a trade or business or a transaction entered into for profit,

this subsection shall not apply to such conversion (whether resulting in gain or loss) if during the taxable year the recognized losses from such conversions exceed the recognized gains from such conversions.

[Sec. 1231(b)]

(b) DEFINITION OF PROPERTY USED IN THE TRADE OR BUSINESS.—For purposes of this section—

(1) GENERAL RULE.—The term "property used in the trade or business" means property used in the trade or business, of a character which is subject to the allowance for depreciation provided in section 167, held for more than 1 year, and real property used in the trade or business, held for more than 1 year, which is not—

(A) property of a kind which would properly be includible in the inventory of the taxpayer if on hand at the close of the taxable year,

(B) property held by the taxpayer primarily for sale to customers in the ordinary course of his trade or business,

(C) a patent, invention, model or design (whether or not patented), a secret formula or process, a copyright, a literary, musical, or artistic composition, a letter or memorandum, or similar property, held by a taxpayer described in paragraph (3) of section 1221(a), or

(D) a publication of the United States Government (including the Congressional Record) which is received from the United States Government, or any agency thereof, other than by purchase at the price at which it is offered for sale to the public, and which is held by a taxpayer described in paragraph (5) of section 1221(a).

(2) TIMBER, COAL, OR DOMESTIC IRON ORE.—Such term includes timber, coal, and iron ore with respect to which section 631 applies.

(3) LIVESTOCK.—Such term includes—

(A) cattle and horses, regardless of age, held by the taxpayer for draft, breeding, dairy, or sporting purposes, and held by him for 24 months or more from the date of acquisition, and

(B) other livestock, regardless of age, held by the taxpayer for draft, breeding, dairy, or sporting purposes, and held by him for 12 months or more from the date of acquisition.

Such term does not include poultry.

(4) UNHARVESTED CROP.—In the case of an unharvested crop on land used in the trade or business and held for more than 1 year, if the crop and the land are sold or exchanged (or compulsorily or involuntarily converted) at the same time and to the same person, the crop shall be considered as "property used in the trade or business."

[Sec. 1231(c)]

(c) RECAPTURE OF NET ORDINARY LOSSES.—

(1) IN GENERAL.—The net section 1231 gain for any taxable year shall be treated as ordinary income to the extent such gain does not exceed the non-recaptured net section 1231 losses.

(2) NON-RECAPTURED NET SECTION 1231 LOSSES.—For purposes of this subsection, the term "non-recaptured net section 1231 losses" means the excess of—

(A) the aggregate amount of the net section 1231 losses for the 5 most recent preceding taxable years, over

(B) the portion of such losses taken into account under paragraph (1) for such preceding taxable years.

(3) NET SECTION 1231 GAIN.—For purposes of this subsection, the term "net section 1231 gain" means the excess of—

(A) the section 1231 gains, over

(B) the section 1231 losses.

(4) NET SECTION 1231 LOSS.—For purposes of this subsection, the term "net section 1231 loss" means the excess of—

(A) the section 1231 losses, over

(B) the section 1231 gains.

(5) SPECIAL RULES.—For purposes of determining the amount of the net section 1231 gain or loss for any taxable year, the rules of paragraph (4) of subsection (a) shall apply.

[Sec. 1234]

SEC. 1234. OPTIONS TO BUY OR SELL.

[Sec. 1234(a)]

(a) TREATMENT OF GAIN OR LOSS IN THE CASE OF THE PURCHASER.—

(1) GENERAL RULE.—Gain or loss attributable to the sale or exchange of, or loss attributable to failure to exercise, an option to buy or sell property shall be considered gain or loss from the sale or exchange of property which has the same character as the property to which the option relates has in the hands of the taxpayer (or would have in the hands of the taxpayer if acquired by him).

(2) SPECIAL RULE FOR LOSS ATTRIBUTABLE TO FAILURE TO EXERCISE OPTION.—For purposes of paragraph (1), if loss is attributable to failure to exercise an option, the option shall be deemed to have been sold or exchanged on the day it expired.

(3) NONAPPLICATION OF SUBSECTION.—This subsection shall not apply to—

(A) an option which constitutes property described in paragraph (1) of section 1221(a);

(B) in the case of gain attributable to the sale or exchange of an option, any income derived in connection with such option which, without regard to this subsection, is treated as other than gain from the sale or exchange of a capital asset; and

(C) a loss attributable to failure to exercise an option described in section 1233(c).

[Sec. 1234(b)]

(b) TREATMENT OF GRANTOR OF OPTION IN THE CASE OF STOCK, SECURITIES, OR COMMODITIES.—

(1) GENERAL RULE.—In the case of the grantor of the option, gain or loss from any closing transaction with respect to, and gain on lapse of, an option in property shall be treated as a gain or loss from the sale or exchange of a capital asset held not more than 1 year.

(2) DEFINITIONS.—For purposes of this subsection—

(A) CLOSING TRANSACTION.—The term "closing transaction" means any termination of the taxpayer's obligation under an option in property other than through the exercise or lapse of the option.

(B) PROPERTY.—The term "property" means stocks and securities (including stocks and securities dealt with on a "when issued" basis), commodities, and commodity futures.

(3) NONAPPLICATION OF SUBSECTION.—This subsection shall not apply to any option granted in the ordinary course of the taxpayer's trade or business of granting options.

[Sec. 1234(c)]

(c) TREATMENT OF OPTIONS ON SECTION 1256 CONTRACTS AND CASH SETTLEMENT OPTIONS.—

(1) SECTION 1256 CONTRACTS.—Gain or loss shall be recognized on the exercise of an option on a section 1256 contract (within the meaning of section 1256(b)).

(2) TREATMENT OF CASH SETTLEMENT OPTIONS.—

(A) IN GENERAL.—For purposes of subsections (a) and (b), a cash settlement option shall be treated as an option to buy or sell property.

(B) CASH SETTLEMENT OPTION.—For purposes of subparagraph (A), the term "cash settlement option" means any option which on exercise settles in (or could be settled in) cash or property other than the underlying property.

[Sec. 1234A]

SEC. 1234A. GAINS OR LOSSES FROM CERTAIN TERMINATIONS.

Gain or loss attributable to the cancellation, lapse, expiration, or other termination of—

(1) a right or obligation (other than a securities contract, as defined in section 1234B) with respect to property which is (or on acquisition would be) a capital asset in the hands of the taxpayer, or

(2) a section 1256 contract (as defined in section 1256) not described in paragraph (1) which is a capital asset in the hands of the taxpayer,

shall be treated as gain or loss from the sale of a capital asset. The preceding sentence shall not apply to the retirement of any debt instrument (whether or not through a trust or other participation arrangement).

[Sec. 1234B]

SEC. 1234B. GAINS OR LOSSES FROM SECURITIES FUTURES CONTRACTS.

[Sec. 1234B(a)]

(a) TREATMENT OF GAIN OR LOSS.—

(1) IN GENERAL.—Gain or loss attributable to the sale, exchange, or termination of a securities futures contract shall be considered gain or loss from the sale or exchange of property which has the same character as the property to which the contract relates has in the hands of the taxpayer (or would have in the hands of the taxpayer if acquired by the taxpayer).

(2) NONAPPLICATION OF SUBSECTION.—This subsection shall not apply to—

(A) a contract which constitutes property described in paragraph (1) or (7) of section 1221(a), and

(B) any income derived in connection with a contract which, without regard to this subsection, is treated as other than gain from the sale or exchange of a capital asset.

[Sec. 1234B(b)]

(b) SHORT-TERM GAINS AND LOSSES.—Except as provided in the regulations under section 1092(b) or this section, or in section 1233, if gain or loss on the sale, exchange, or termination of a securities futures contract to sell property is considered as gain or loss from the sale or exchange of a capital asset, such gain or loss shall be treated as short-term capital gain or loss.

[Sec. 1234B(c)]

(c) SECURITIES FUTURES CONTRACT.—For purposes of this section, the term "securities futures contract" means any security future (as defined in section 3(a)(55)(A) of the Securities Exchange Act of 1934, as in effect on the date of the enactment of this section). The Secretary may prescribe regulations regarding the status of contracts the values of which are determined directly or indirectly by reference to any index which becomes (or ceases to be) a narrow-based security index (as defined for purposes of section 1256(g)(6)).

[Sec. 1234B(d)]

(d) CONTRACTS NOT TREATED AS COMMODITY FUTURES CONTRACTS.—For purposes of this title, a securities futures contract shall not be treated as a commodity futures contract.

[Sec. 1234B(e)]

(e) REGULATIONS.—The Secretary shall prescribe such regulations as may be appropriate to provide for the proper treatment of securities futures contracts under this title.

[Sec. 1234B(f)]

(f) CROSS REFERENCE.—

For special rules relating to dealer securities futures contracts, see section 1256.

[Sec. 1235]

SEC. 1235. SALE OR EXCHANGE OF PATENTS.

[Sec. 1235(a)]

(a) GENERAL.—A transfer (other than by gift, inheritance, or devise) of property consisting of all substantial rights to a patent, or an undivided interest therein which includes a part of all such rights, by any holder shall be considered the sale or exchange of a capital asset held for more than 1 year, regardless of whether or not payments in consideration of such transfer are—

(1) payable periodically over a period generally coterminous with the transferee's use of the patent, or

(2) contingent on the productivity, use, or disposition of the property transferred.

[Sec. 1235(b)]

(b) "HOLDER" DEFINED.—For purposes of this section, the term "holder" means—

(1) any individual whose efforts created such property, or

(2) any other individual who has acquired his interest in such property in exchange for consideration in money or money's worth paid to such creator prior to actual reduction to practice of the invention covered by the patent, if such individual is neither—

(A) the employer of such creator, nor

(B) related to such creator (within the meaning of subsection (c)).

[Sec. 1235(c)]

(c) RELATED PERSONS.—Subsection (a) shall not apply to any transfer, directly or indirectly, between persons specified within any one of the paragraphs of section 267(b) or persons described in section 707(b); except that, in applying section 267(b) and (c) and section 707(b) for purposes of this section—

(1) the phrase "25 percent or more" shall be substituted for the phrase "more than 50 percent" each place it appears in section 267(b) or 707(b), and

(2) paragraph (4) of section 267(c) shall be treated as providing that the family of an individual shall include only his spouse, ancestors, and lineal descendants.

* * *

[Sec. 1236]

SEC. 1236. DEALERS IN SECURITIES.

[Sec. 1236(a)]

(a) CAPITAL GAINS.—Gain by a dealer in securities from the sale or exchange of any security shall in no event be considered as gain from the sale or exchange of a capital asset unless—

(1) the security was, before the close of the day on which it was acquired (or such earlier time as the Secretary may prescribe by regulations), clearly identified in the dealer's records as a security held for investment; and

(2) the security was not, at any time after the close of such day (or such earlier time), held by such dealer primarily for sale to customers in the ordinary course of his trade or business.

[Sec. 1236(b)]

(b) ORDINARY LOSSES.—Loss by a dealer in securities from the sale or exchange of any security shall, except as otherwise provided in section 582 (c) (relating to bond, etc., losses of banks), in no event be considered as an ordinary loss if at any time the security was clearly identified in the dealer's records as a security held for investment.

[Sec. 1236(c)]

(c) DEFINITION OF SECURITY.—For purposes of this section, the term "security" means any share of stock in any corporation, certificate of stock or interest in any corporation, note, bond, debenture, or evidence of indebtedness, or any evidence of an interest in or right to subscribe to or purchase any of the foregoing.

* * *

[Sec. 1236(e)]

(e) SPECIAL RULE FOR OPTIONS.—For purposes of subsection (a), any security acquired by a dealer pursuant to an option held by such dealer may be treated as held for investment only if the dealer, before the close of the day on which the option was acquired, clearly identified the option on his records as held for investment. For purposes of the preceding sentence, the term "option" includes the right to subscribe to or purchase any security.

[Sec. 1237]

SEC. 1237. REAL PROPERTY SUBDIVIDED FOR SALE.

[Sec. 1237(a)]

(a) GENERAL.—Any lot or parcel which is part of a tract of real property in the hands of a taxpayer other than a C corporation shall not be deemed to be held primarily for sale to customers in the ordinary course of trade or business at the time of sale solely because of the taxpayer having subdivided such tract for purposes of sale or because of any activity incident to such subdivision or sale, if—

(1) such tract, or any lot or parcel thereof, had not previously been held by such taxpayer primarily for sale to customers in the ordinary course of trade or business (unless such tract at such previous time would have been covered by this section) and, in the same taxable year in which the sale occurs, such taxpayer does not so hold any other real property; and

(2) no substantial improvement that substantially enhances the value of the lot or parcel sold is made by the taxpayer on such tract while held by the taxpayer or is made pursuant to a contract of sale entered into between the taxpayer and the buyer. For purposes of this paragraph, an improvement shall be deemed to be made by the taxpayer if such improvement was made by—

(A) the taxpayer or members of his family (as defined in section 267(c)(4)), by a corporation controlled by the taxpayer, an S corporation which included the taxpayer as a shareholder, or by a partnership which included the taxpayer as a partner; or

(B) a lessee, but only if the improvement constitutes income to the taxpayer; or

(C) Federal, State, or local government, or political subdivision thereof, but only if the improvement constitutes an addition to basis for the taxpayer; and

(3) such lot or parcel, except in the case of real property acquired by inheritance or devise, is held by the taxpayer for a period of 5 years.

[Sec. 1237(b)]

(b) SPECIAL RULES FOR APPLICATION OF SECTION.—

(1) GAINS.—If more than 5 lots or parcels contained in the same tract of real property are sold or exchanged, gain from any sale or exchange (which occurs in or after the taxable year in which the sixth lot or parcel is sold or exchanged) of any lot or parcel which comes within the provisions of paragraphs (1), (2) and (3) of subsection (a) of this section shall be deemed to be gain from the sale of property held primarily for sale to customers in the ordinary course of the trade or business to the extent of 5 percent of the selling price.

(2) EXPENDITURES OF SALE.—For the purpose of computing gain under paragraph (1) of this subsection, expenditures incurred in connection with the sale or exchange of any lot or parcel shall neither be allowed as a deduction in computing taxable income, nor treated as reducing the amount realized on such sale or exchange; but so much of such expenditures as does not exceed the portion of gain deemed under paragraph (1) of this subsection to be gain from the sale of property held primarily for sale to customers in the ordinary course of trade or business shall be so allowed as a deduction, and the remainder, if any, shall be treated as reducing the amount realized on such sale or exchange.

(3) NECESSARY IMPROVEMENTS.—No improvement shall be deemed a substantial improvement for purposes of subsection (a) if the lot or parcel is held by the taxpayer for a period of 10 years and if—

(A) such improvement is the building or installation of water, sewer, or drainage facilities or roads (if such improvement would except for this paragraph constitute a substantial improvement);

(B) it is shown to the satisfaction of the Secretary that the lot or parcel, the value of which was substantially enhanced by such improvement, would not have been marketable at the prevailing local price for similar building sites without such improvement; and

(C) the taxpayer elects, in accordance with regulations prescribed by the Secretary, to make no adjustment to basis of the lot or parcel, or of any other property owned by the taxpayer, on account of the expenditures for such improvements. Such election shall not make any item deductible which would not otherwise be deductible.

[Sec. 1237(c)]

(c) TRACT DEFINED.—For purposes of this section, the term "tract of real property" means a single piece of real property, except that 2 or more pieces of real property shall be considered a tract if at any time they were contiguous in the hands of the taxpayer or if they would be contiguous except for the interposition of a road, street, railroad, stream, or similar property. If, following the sale or exchange of any lot or parcel from a tract of real property, no further sales or exchanges of any other lots or parcels from the remainder of such tract are made for a period of 5 years, such remainder shall be deemed a tract.

[Sec. 1239]

SEC. 1239. GAIN FROM SALE OF DEPRECIABLE PROPERTY BETWEEN CERTAIN RELATED TAXPAYERS.

[Sec. 1239(a)]

(a) TREATMENT OF GAIN AS ORDINARY INCOME.—In the case of a sale or exchange of property, directly or indirectly, between related persons, any gain recognized to the transferor shall be treated as ordinary income if such property is, in the hands of the transferee, of a character which is subject to the allowance for depreciation provided in section 167.

[Sec. 1239(b)]

(b) RELATED PERSONS.—For purposes of subsection (a), the term "related persons" means—

(1) a person and all entities which are controlled entities with respect to such person,

(2) a taxpayer and any trust in which such taxpayer (or his spouse) is a beneficiary, unless such beneficiary's interest in the trust is a remote contingent interest (within the meaning of section 318(a)(3)(B)(i)), and

(3) except in the case of a sale or exchange in satisfaction of a pecuniary bequest, an executor of an estate and a beneficiary of such estate.

[Sec. 1239(c)]

(c) CONTROLLED ENTITY DEFINED.—

(1) GENERAL RULE.—For purposes of this section, the term "controlled entity" means, with respect to any person—

(A) a corporation more than 50 percent of the value of the outstanding stock of which is owned (directly or indirectly) by or for such person,

(B) a partnership more than 50 percent of the capital interest or profits interest in which is owned (directly or indirectly) by or for such person, and

(C) any entity which is a related person to such person under paragraph (3), (10), (11), or (12) of section 267(b).

(2) CONSTRUCTIVE OWNERSHIP.—For purposes of this section, ownership shall be determined in accordance with rules similar to the rules under section 267(c) (other than paragraph (3) thereof).

[Sec. 1239(d)]

(d) EMPLOYER AND RELATED EMPLOYEE ASSOCIATION.—For purposes of subsection (a), the term "related person" also includes—

(1) an employer and any person related to the employer (within the meaning of subsection (b)), and

(2) a welfare benefit fund (within the meaning of section 419(e)) which is controlled directly or indirectly by persons referred to in paragraph (1).

[Sec. 1239(e)]

(e) PATENT APPLICATIONS TREATED AS DEPRECIABLE PROPERTY.—For purposes of this section, a patent application shall be treated as property which, in the hands of the transferee, is of a character which is subject to the allowance for depreciation provided in section 167.

[Sec. 1241]

SEC. 1241. CANCELLATION OF LEASE OR DISTRIBUTOR'S AGREEMENT.

Amounts received by a lessee for the cancellation of a lease, or by a distributor of goods for the cancellation of a distributor's agreement (if the distributor has a substantial capital investment in the distributorship), shall be considered as amounts received in exchange for such lease or agreement.

[Sec. 1244]

SEC. 1244. LOSSES ON SMALL BUSINESS STOCK.

[Sec. 1244(a)]

(a) GENERAL RULE.—In the case of an individual, a loss on section 1244 stock issued to such individual or to a partnership which would (but for this section) be treated as a loss from the sale or exchange of a capital asset shall, to the extent provided in this section, be treated as an ordinary loss.

[Sec. 1244(b)]

(b) MAXIMUM AMOUNT FOR ANY TAXABLE YEAR.—For any taxable year the aggregate amount treated by the taxpayer by reason of this section as an ordinary loss shall not exceed—

(1) $50,000, or

(2) $100,000, in the case of a husband and wife filing a joint return for such year under section 6013.

[Sec. 1244(c)]

(c) SECTION 1244 STOCK DEFINED.—

(1) IN GENERAL.—For purposes of this section, the term "section 1244 stock" means stock in a domestic corporation if—

(A) at the time such stock is issued, such corporation was a small business corporation,

(B) such stock was issued by such corporation for money or other property (other than stock and securities), and

(C) such corporation, during the period of its 5 most recent taxable years ending before the date the loss on such stock was sustained, derived more than 50 percent of its aggregate gross receipts from sources other than royalties, rents, dividends, interests, annuities, and sales or exchanges of stocks or securities.

(2) RULES FOR APPLICATION OF PARAGRAPH (1)(C).—

(A) PERIOD TAKEN INTO ACCOUNT WITH RESPECT TO NEW CORPORATIONS.—For purposes of paragraph (1)(C), if the corporation has not been in existence for 5 taxable years ending before the date the loss on the stock was sustained, there shall be substituted for such 5-year period—

(i) the period of the corporation's taxable years ending before such date, or

(ii) if the corporation has not been in existence for 1 taxable year ending before such date, the period such corporation has been in existence before such date.

(B) GROSS RECEIPTS FROM SALES OF SECURITIES.—For purposes of paragraph (1)(C), gross receipts from the sales or exchanges of stock or securities shall be taken into account only to the extent of gains therefrom.

(C) NONAPPLICATION WHERE DEDUCTIONS EXCEED GROSS INCOME.—Paragraph (1)(C) shall not apply with respect to any corporation if, for the period taken into account for purposes of paragraph (1)(C), the amount of the deductions allowed by this chapter (other than by sections 172, 243, and 245) exceeds the amount of gross income.

(3) SMALL BUSINESS CORPORATION DEFINED.—

(A) IN GENERAL.—For purposes of this section, a corporation shall be treated as a small business corporation if the aggregate amount of money and other property received by the corporation for stock, as a contribution to capital, and as paid-in surplus, does not exceed $1,000,000. The determination under the preceding sentence shall be made as of the time of the issuance of the stock in question but shall include amounts received for such stock and for all stock theretofore issued.

(B) AMOUNT TAKEN INTO ACCOUNT WITH RESPECT TO PROPERTY.—For purposes of subparagraph (A), the amount taken into account with respect to any property other than money shall be the amount equal to the adjusted basis to the corporation of such property for determining gain, reduced by any liability to which the property was subject or which was assumed by the corporation. The determination under the preceding sentence shall be made as of the time the property was received by the corporation.

[Sec. 1244(d)]

(d) SPECIAL RULES.—

(1) LIMITATIONS ON AMOUNT OF ORDINARY LOSS.—

(A) CONTRIBUTIONS OF PROPERTY HAVING BASIS IN EXCESS OF VALUE.—If—

(i) section 1244 stock was issued in exchange for property,

(ii) the basis of such stock in the hands of the taxpayer is determined by reference to the basis in his hands of such property, and

(iii) the adjusted basis (for determining loss) of such property immediately before the exchange exceeded its fair market value at such time,

then in computing the amount of the loss on such stock for purposes of this section the basis of such stock shall be reduced by an amount equal to the excess described in clause (iii).

(B) INCREASES IN BASIS.—In computing the amount of the loss on stock for purposes of this section, any increase in the basis of such stock (through contributions to the capital of the corporation, or otherwise) shall be treated as allocable to stock which is not section 1244 stock.

(2) RECAPITALIZATIONS, CHANGES IN NAME, ETC.—To the extent provided in regulations prescribed by the Secretary, stock in a corporation, the basis of which (in the hands of a taxpayer) is determined in whole or in part by reference to the basis in his hands of stock in such corporation which meets the requirements of subsection (c)(1) (other than subparagraph (C) thereof), or which is received in a reorganization described in section 368(a)(1)(F) in exchange for stock which meets such requirements, shall be treated as meeting such requirements. For purposes of paragraphs (1)(C) and (3)(A) of subsection (c), a successor corporation in a reorganization described in section 368(a)(1)(F) shall be treated as the same corporation as its predecessor.

(3) RELATIONSHIP TO NET OPERATING LOSS DEDUCTION.—For purposes of section 172 (relating to the net operating loss deduction), any amount of loss treated by reason of this section as an ordinary loss shall be treated as attributable to a trade or business of the taxpayer.

(4) INDIVIDUAL DEFINED.—For purposes of this section, the term "individual" does not include a trust or estate.

[Sec. 1244(e)]

(e) REGULATIONS.—The Secretary shall prescribe such regulations as may be necessary to carry out the purposes of this section.

[Sec. 1245]

SEC. 1245. GAIN FROM DISPOSITIONS OF CERTAIN DEPRECIABLE PROPERTY.

[Sec. 1245(a)]

(a) GENERAL RULE.—

(1) ORDINARY INCOME.—Except as otherwise provided in this section, if section 1245 property is disposed of the amount by which the lower of—

(A) the recomputed basis of the property, or

(B) (i) in the case of a sale, exchange, or involuntary conversion, the amount realized, or

(ii) in the case of any other disposition, the fair market value of such property,

exceeds the adjusted basis of such property shall be treated as ordinary income. Such gain shall be recognized notwithstanding any other provision of this subtitle.

(2) RECOMPUTED BASIS.—For purposes of this section—

(A) IN GENERAL.—The term "recomputed basis" means, with respect to any property, its adjusted basis recomputed by adding thereto all adjustments reflected in such adjusted basis on account of deductions (whether in respect of the same or other property) allowed or allowable to the taxpayer or to any other person for depreciation or amortization.

(B) TAXPAYER MAY ESTABLISH AMOUNT ALLOWED.—For purposes of subparagraph (A), if the taxpayer can establish by adequate records or other sufficient evidence that the amount allowed for depreciation or amortization for any period was less than the amount allowable, the amount added for such period shall be the amount allowed.

(C) CERTAIN DEDUCTIONS TREATED AS AMORTIZATION.—Any deduction allowable under section 179, 179B, 179C, 179D, 179E, 181, 190, 193, or 194 shall be treated as if it were a deduction allowable for amortization.

(3) SECTION 1245 PROPERTY.—For purposes of this section, the term "section 1245 property" means any property which is or has been property of a character subject to the allowance for depreciation provided in section 167 and is either—

(A) personal property,

(B) other property (not including a building or its structural components) but only if such other property is tangible and has an adjusted basis in which there are reflected adjustments described in paragraph (2) for a period in which such property (or other property)—

(i) was used as an integral part of manufacturing, production, or extraction or of furnishing transportation, communications, electrical energy, gas, water, or sewage disposal services, or

(ii) constituted a research facility used in connection with any of the activities referred to in clause (i), or

(iii) constituted a facility used in connection with any of the activities referred to in clause (i) for the bulk storage of fungible commodities (including commodities in a liquid or gaseous state),

(C) so much of any real property (other than any property described in subparagraph B)) which has an adjusted basis in which there are reflected adjustments for amortization under section 169, 179, 179B, 179C, 179D, 179E, 188 (as in effect before its repeal by the Revenue Reconciliation Act of 1990), 190, 193, or 194,

(D) a single purpose agricultural or horticultural structure (as defined in section 168(i)(13)),

(E) a storage facility (not including a building or its structural components) used in connection with the distribution of petroleum or any primary product of petroleum, or

(F) any railroad grading or tunnel bore (as defined in section 168(e)(4)).

[Sec. 1245(b)]

(b) EXCEPTIONS AND LIMITATIONS.—

(1) GIFTS.—Subsection (a) shall not apply to a disposition by gift.

(2) TRANSFERS AT DEATH.—Except as provided in section 691 (relating to income in respect of a decedent), subsection (a) shall not apply to a transfer at death.

(3) CERTAIN TAX-FREE TRANSACTIONS.—If the basis of property in the hands of a transferee is determined by reference to its basis in the hands of the transferor by reason of the application of section 332, 351, 361, 721, or 731, then the amount of gain taken into account by the transferor under subsection (a)(1) shall not exceed the amount of gain recognized to the transferor on the transfer of such property (determined without regard to this section). Except as provided in paragraph (6), this paragraph shall not apply to a disposition to an organization (other than a cooperative described in section 521) which is exempt from the tax imposed by this chapter.

(4) LIKE KIND EXCHANGES; INVOLUNTARY CONVERSIONS, ETC.—If property is disposed of and gain (determined without regard to this section) is not recognized in whole or in part under section 1031 or 1033, then the amount of gain taken into account by the transferor under subsection (a)(1) shall not exceed the sum of—

(A) the amount of gain recognized on such disposition (determined without regard to this section), plus

(B) the fair market value of property acquired which is not section 1245 property and which is not taken into account under subparagraph (A).

(5) PROPERTY DISTRIBUTED BY A PARTNERSHIP TO A PARTNER.—

(A) IN GENERAL.—For purposes of this section, the basis of section 1245 property distributed by a partnership to a partner shall be deemed to be determined by reference to the adjusted basis of such property to the partnership.

(B) ADJUSTMENTS ADDED BACK.—In the case of any property described in subparagraph (A), for purposes of computing the recomputed basis of such property the amount of the adjustments added back for periods before the distribution by the partnership shall be—

(i) the amount of the gain to which subsection (a) would have applied if such property had been sold by the partnership immediately before the distribution at its fair market value at such time, reduced by

(ii) the amount of such gain to which section 751(b) applied.

(6) TRANSFERS TO TAX-EXEMPT ORGANIZATION WHERE PROPERTY WILL BE USED IN UNRELATED BUSINESS.—

(A) IN GENERAL.—The second sentence of paragraph (3) shall not apply to a disposition of section 1245 property to an organization described in section 511(a)(2) or 511(b)(2) if, immediately after such disposition, such organization uses such property in an unrelated trade or business (as defined in section 513).

(B) LATER CHANGE IN USE.—If any property with respect to the disposition of which gain is not recognized by reason of subparagraph (A) ceases to be used in an unrelated trade or business of the organization acquiring such property, such organization shall be treated for purposes of this section as having disposed of such property on the date of such cessation.

(7) TIMBER PROPERTY.—In determining, under subsection (a)(2), the recomputed basis of property with respect to which a deduction under section 194 was allowed for any taxable year, the taxpayer shall not take into account adjustments under section 194 to the extent such adjustments are attributable to the amortizable basis of the taxpayer acquired before the 10th taxable year preceding the taxable year in which gain with respect to the property is recognized.

(8) DISPOSITION OF AMORTIZABLE SECTION 197 INTANGIBLES.—

(A) IN GENERAL.—If a taxpayer disposes of more than 1 amortizable section 197 intangible (as defined in section 197(c)) in a transaction or a series of related transactions, all such amortizable 197 intangibles shall be treated as 1 section 1245 property for purposes of this section.

(B) EXCEPTION.—Subparagraph (A) shall not apply to any amortizable section 197 intangible (as so defined) with respect to which the adjusted basis exceeds the fair market value.

[Sec. 1245(c)]

(c) ADJUSTMENTS TO BASIS.—The Secretary shall prescribe such regulations as he may deem necessary to provide for adjustments to the basis of property to reflect gain recognized under subsection (a).

[Sec. 1245(d)]

(d) APPLICATION OF SECTION.—This section shall apply notwithstanding any other provision of this subtitle.

[Sec. 1250]

SEC. 1250. GAIN FROM DISPOSITIONS OF CERTAIN DEPRECIABLE REALTY.

[Sec. 1250(a)]

(a) GENERAL RULE.—Except as otherwise provided in this section—

(1) ADDITIONAL DEPRECIATION AFTER DECEMBER 31, 1975.—

(A) IN GENERAL.—If section 1250 property is disposed of after December 31, 1975, then the applicable percentage of the lower of—

(i) that portion of the additional depreciation (as defined in subsection (b)(1) or (4)) attributable to periods after December 31, 1975, in respect of the property, or

(ii) the excess of the amount realized (in the case of a sale, exchange, or involuntary conversion), or the fair market value of such property (in the case of any other disposition), over the adjusted basis of such property,

shall be treated as gain which is ordinary income. Such gain shall be recognized notwithstanding any other provision of this subtitle.

(B) APPLICABLE PERCENTAGE.—For purposes of subparagraph (A), the term "applicable percentage" means—

(i) in the case of section 1250 property with respect to which a mortgage is insured under section 221(d)(3) or 236 of the National Housing Act, or housing financed or assisted by direct loan or tax abatement under similar provisions of State or local laws and with respect to which the owner is subject to the restrictions described in section 1039(b)(1)(B), (as in effect on the day before the date of the enactment of the Revenue Reconciliation Act of 1990), 100 percent minus 1 percentage point for each full month the property was held after the date the property was held 100 full months;

(ii) in the case of dwelling units which, on the average, were held for occupancy by families or individuals eligible to receive subsidies under section 8 of the United States Housing Act of 1937, as amended, or under the provisions of State or local law authorizing similar levels of subsidy for lower-income families, 100 percent minus 1 percentage point for each full month the property was held after the date the property was held 100 full months;

(iii) in the case of section 1250 property with respect to which a depreciation deduction for rehabilitation expenditures was allowed under section 167(k), 100 percent minus 1 percentage point for each full month in excess of 100 full months after the date on which such property was placed in service;

(iv) in the case of section 1250 property with respect to which a loan is made or insured under title V of the Housing Act of 1949, 100 percent minus 1 percentage point for each full month the property was held after the date the property was held 100 full months; and

(v) in the case of all other section 1250 property, 100 percent.

In the case of a building (or a portion of a building devoted to dwelling units), if, on the average, 85 percent or more of the dwelling units contained in such building (or portion thereof) are units described in clause (ii), such building (or portion thereof) shall be treated as property described in clause (ii). Clauses (i), (ii), and (iv) shall not apply with respect to the additional depreciation described in subsection (b)(4) which was allowed under section 167(k).

* * *

[Sec. 1250(b)]

(b) ADDITIONAL DEPRECIATION DEFINED.—For purposes of this section—

(1) IN GENERAL.—The term "additional depreciation" means, in the case of any property, the depreciation adjustments in respect of such property; except that, in the case of property held more than one year, it means such adjustments only to the extent that they exceed the amount of the depreciation adjustments which would have resulted if such adjustments had been determined for each taxable year under the straight line method of adjustment.

(2) PROPERTY HELD BY LESSEE.—In the case of a lessee, in determining the depreciation adjustments which would have resulted in respect of any building erected (or other improvement made) on the leased property, or in respect of any cost of acquiring the lease, the lease period shall be treated as including all renewal periods. For purposes of the preceding sentence—

(A) the term "renewal period" means any period for which the lease may be renewed, extended, or continued pursuant to an option exercisable by the lessee, but

(B) the inclusion of renewal periods shall not extend the period taken into account by more than ⅔ of the period on the basis of which the depreciation adjustments were allowed.

(3) DEPRECIATION ADJUSTMENTS.—The term "depreciation adjustments" means, in respect of any property, all adjustments attributable to periods after December 31, 1963, reflected in the adjusted basis of such property on account of deductions (whether in respect of the same or other property) allowed or allowable to the taxpayer or to any other person for exhaustion, wear and tear, obsolescence, or amortization (other than amortization under section 168 (as in effect before its repeal by the Tax Reform Act of 1976), 169, 185 (as in effect before its repeal by the Tax Reform Act of 1986), 188 (as in effect before its repeal by the Revenue Reconciliation Act of 1990), 190, or 193). For purposes of the preceding sentence, if the taxpayer can establish by adequate records or other sufficient evidence that the amount allowed as a deduction for any period was less than the amount allowable, the amount taken into account for such period shall be the amount allowed.

(4) ADDITIONAL DEPRECIATION ATTRIBUTABLE TO REHABILITATION EXPENDITURES.—The term "additional depreciation" also means, in the case of section 1250 property with respect to which a depreciation or amortization deduction for rehabilitation expenditures was allowed under section 167(k) (as in effect on the day before the date of the enactment of the Revenue Reconciliation Act of 1990) or 191 (as in effect before its repeal by the Economic Recovery Tax Act of 1981), the depreciation or amortization adjustments allowed under such section to the extent attributable to such property, except that, in the case of such property held for more than one year after the rehabilitation expenditures so allowed were incurred, it means such adjustments only to the extent that they exceed the amount of the depreciation adjustments which would have resulted if such adjustments had been determined under the straight line method of adjustment without regard to the useful life permitted under section

167(k) (as in effect on the day before the date of the enactment of the Revenue Reconciliation Act of 1990) or 191 (as in effect before its repeal by the Economic Recovery Tax Act of 1981).

(5) METHOD OF COMPUTING STRAIGHT LINE ADJUSTMENTS.—For purposes of paragraph (1), the depreciation adjustments which would have resulted for any taxable year under the straight line method shall be determined—

(A) in the case of property to which section 168 applies, by determining the adjustments which would have resulted for such year if the taxpayer had elected the straight line method for such year using the recovery period applicable to such property, and

(B) in the case of any property to which section 168 does not apply, if a useful life (or salvage value) was used in determining the amount allowable as a deduction for any taxable year, by using such life (or value).

[Sec. 1250(c)]

(c) SECTION 1250 PROPERTY.—For purposes of this section, the term "section 1250 property" means any real property (other than section 1245 property, as defined in section 1245(a)(3)) which is or has been property of a character subject to the allowance for depreciation provided in section 167.

[Sec. 1250(d)]

(d) EXCEPTIONS AND LIMITATIONS.—

(1) GIFTS.—Subsection (a) shall not apply to a disposition by gift.

(2) TRANSFERS AT DEATH.—Except as provided in section 691 (relating to income in respect of a decedent), subsection (a) shall not apply to a transfer at death.

(3) CERTAIN TAX-FREE TRANSACTIONS.—If the basis of property in the hands of a transferee is determined by reference to its basis in the hands of the transferor by reason of the application of section 332, 351, 361, 721, or 731, then the amount of gain taken into account by the transferor under subsection (a) shall not exceed the amount of gain recognized to the transferor on the transfer of such property (determined without regard to this section). Except as provided in paragraph (6), this paragraph shall not apply to a disposition to an organization (other than a cooperative described in section 521) which is exempt from the tax imposed by this chapter.

(4) LIKE KIND EXCHANGES; INVOLUNTARY CONVERSIONS, ETC.—

(A) RECOGNITION LIMIT.—If property is disposed of and gain (determined without regard to this section) is not recognized in whole or in part under section 1031 or 1033, then the amount of gain taken into account by the transferor under subsection (a) shall not exceed the greater of the following:

(i) the amount of gain recognized on the disposition (determined without regard to this section), increased as provided in subparagraph (B), or

(ii) the amount determined under subparagraph (C).

(B) INCREASE FOR CERTAIN STOCK.—With respect to any transaction, the increase provided by this subparagraph is the amount equal to the fair market value of any stock purchased in a corporation which (but for this paragraph) would result in nonrecognition of gain under section 1033(a)(2)(A).

(C) ADJUSTMENT WHERE INSUFFICIENT SECTION 1250 PROPERTY IS ACQUIRED.—With respect to any transaction, the amount determined under this subparagraph shall be the excess of—

(i) the amount of gain which would (but for this paragraph) be taken into account under subsection (a), over

(ii) the fair market value (or cost in the case of a transaction described in section 1033(a)(2)) of the section 1250 property acquired in the transaction.

(D) BASIS OF PROPERTY ACQUIRED.—In the case of property purchased by the taxpayer in a transaction described in section 1033(a)(2), in applying [the last sentence of] section 1033(b)(2), such sentence shall be applied—

(i) first solely to section 1250 properties and to the amount of gain not taken into account under subsection (a) by reason of this paragraph, and

(ii) then to all purchased properties to which such sentence applies and to the remaining gain not recognized on the transaction as if the cost of the section 1250 properties were the basis of such properties computed under clause (i).

In the case of property acquired in any other transaction to which this paragraph applies, rules consistent with the preceding sentence shall be applied under regulations prescribed by the Secretary.

(E) ADDITIONAL DEPRECIATION WITH RESPECT TO PROPERTY DISPOSED OF.—In the case of any transaction described in section 1031 or 1033, the additional depreciation in respect of the section 1250 property acquired which is attributable to the section 1250 property disposed of shall be an amount equal to the amount of the gain which was not taken into account under subsection (a) by reason of the application of this paragraph.

(5) PROPERTY DISTRIBUTED BY A PARTNERSHIP TO A PARTNER.—

(A) IN GENERAL.—For purposes of this section, the basis of section 1250 property distributed by a partnership to a partner shall be deemed to be determined by reference to the adjusted basis of such property to the partnership.

(B) ADDITIONAL DEPRECIATION.—In respect of any property described in subparagraph (A), the additional depreciation attributable to periods before the distribution by the partnership shall be—

(i) the amount of the gain to which subsection (a) would have applied if such property had been sold by the partnership immediately before the distribution at its fair market value at such time and the applicable percentage for the property had been 100 percent, reduced by

(ii) if section 751(b) applied to any part of such gain, the amount of such gain to which section 751(b) would have applied if the applicable percentage for the property had been 100 percent.

(6) TRANSFERS TO TAX-EXEMPT ORGANIZATION WHERE PROPERTY WILL BE USED IN UNRELATED BUSINESS.—

(A) IN GENERAL.—The second sentence of paragraph (3) shall not apply to a disposition of section 1250 property to an organization described in section 511(a)(2) or 511(b)(2) if, immediately after such disposition, such organization uses such property in an unrelated trade or business (as defined in section 513),

(B) LATER CHANGE IN USE.—If any property with respect to the disposition of which gain is not recognized by reason of subparagraph (A) ceases to be used in an unrelated trade or business of the organization acquiring such property, such organization shall be treated for purposes of this section as having disposed of such property on the date of such cessation.

(7) FORECLOSURE DISPOSITIONS.—If any section 1250 property is disposed of by the taxpayer pursuant to a bid for such property at foreclosure or by operation of an agreement or of process of law after there was a default on indebtedness which such property secured, the applicable percentage referred to in paragraph (1)(B), (2)(B), or (3)(B) of subsection (a), as the case may be, shall be determined as if the taxpayer ceased to hold such property on the date of the beginning of the proceedings pursuant to which the disposition occurred, or, in the event there are no proceedings, such percentage shall be determined as if the taxpayer ceased to hold such property on the date, determined under regulations prescribed by the Secretary, on which such operation of an agreement or process of law, pursuant to which the disposition occurred, began.

[Sec. 1250(e)]

(e) HOLDING PERIOD.—For purposes of determining the applicable percentage under this section, the provisions of section 1223 shall not apply, and the holding period of section 1250 property shall be determined under the following rules:

(1) BEGINNING OF HOLDING PERIOD.—The holding period of section 1250 property shall be deemed to begin—

(A) in the case of property acquired by the taxpayer, on the day after the date of acquisition, or

(B) in the case of property constructed, reconstructed, or erected by the taxpayer, on the first day of the month during which the property is placed in service.

(2) PROPERTY WITH TRANSFERRED BASIS.—If the basis of property acquired in a transaction described in paragraph (1), (2), or (3) of subsection (d) is determined by reference to its basis in the hands of the transferor, then the holding period of the property in the hands of the transferee shall include the holding period of the property in the hands of the transferor.

[Sec. 1250(f)]

(f) SPECIAL RULES FOR PROPERTY WHICH IS SUBSTANTIALLY IMPROVED.—

(1) AMOUNT TREATED AS ORDINARY INCOME.—If, in the case of a disposition of section 1250 property, the property is treated as consisting of more than one element by reason of paragraph (3), then the amount taken into account under subsection (a) in respect of such section 1250 property as ordinary income shall be the sum of the amounts determined under paragraph (2).

(2) ORDINARY INCOME ATTRIBUTABLE TO AN ELEMENT.—For purposes of paragraph (1), the amount taken into account for any element shall be the sum of a series of amounts determined for the periods set forth in subsection (a), with the amount for any such period being determined by multiplying—

(A) the amount which bears the same ratio to the lower of the amounts specified in clause (i) or (ii) of subsection (a)(1)(A), in clause (i) or (ii) of subsection (a)(2)(A), or in clause (i) or (ii) of subsection (a)(3)(A), as the case may be, for the section 1250 property as the additional depreciation for such element attributable to such period bears to the sum of the additional depreciation for all elements attributable to such period, by

(B) the applicable percentage for such element for such period.

For purposes of this paragraph, determinations with respect to any element shall be made as if it were a separate property.

(3) PROPERTY CONSISTING OF MORE THAN ONE ELEMENT.—In applying this subsection in the case of any section 1250 property, there shall be treated as a separate element—

(A) each separate improvement,

(B) if, before completion of section 1250 property, units thereof (as distinguished from improvements) were placed in service, each such unit of section 1250 property, and

(C) the remaining property which is not taken into account under subparagraphs (A) and (B).

(4) PROPERTY WHICH IS SUBSTANTIALLY IMPROVED.—For purposes of this subsection—

(A) IN GENERAL.—The term "separate improvement" means each improvement added during the 36-month period ending on the last day of any taxable year to the capital account for the property, but only if the sum of the amounts added to such account during such period exceeds the greatest of—

(i) 25 percent of the adjusted basis of the property,

(ii) 10 percent of the adjusted basis of the property, determined without regard to the adjustments provided in paragraphs (2) and (3) of section 1016(a), or

(iii) $5,000.

For purposes of clauses (i) and (ii), the adjusted basis of the property shall be determined as of the beginning of the first day of such 36-month period, or of the holding period of the property (within the meaning of subsection (e)), whichever is the later.

(B) EXCEPTION.—Improvements in any taxable year shall be taken into account for purposes of subparagraph (A) only if the sum of the amounts added to the capital account for the property for such taxable year exceeds the greater of—

(i) $2,000, or

(ii) one percent of the adjusted basis referred to in subparagraph (A)(ii), determined, however, as of the beginning of such taxable year.

For purposes of this section, if the amount added to the capital account for any separate improvement does not exceed the greater of clause (i) or (ii), such improvement shall be treated as placed in service on the first day, of a calendar month, which is closest to the middle of the taxable year.

(C) IMPROVEMENT.—The term "improvement" means, in the case of any section 1250 property, any addition to capital account for such property after the initial acquisition or after completion of the property.

[Sec. 1250(g)]

(g) ADJUSTMENTS TO BASIS.—The Secretary shall prescribe such regulations as he may deem necessary to provide for adjustments to the basis of property to reflect gain recognized under subsection (a).

[Sec. 1250(h)]

(h) APPLICATION OF SECTION.—This section shall apply notwithstanding any other provision of this subtitle.

[Sec. 1253]

SEC. 1253. TRANSFERS OF FRANCHISES, TRADEMARKS, AND TRADE NAMES.

[Sec. 1253(a)]

(a) GENERAL RULE.—A transfer of a franchise, trademark, or trade name shall not be treated as a sale or exchange of a capital asset if the transferor retains any significant power, right, or continuing interest with respect to the subject matter of the franchise, trademark, or trade name.

[Sec. 1253(b)]

(b) DEFINITIONS.—For purposes of this section—

(1) FRANCHISE.—The term "franchise" includes an agreement which gives one of the parties to the agreement the right to distribute, sell, or provide goods, services, or facilities, within a specified area.

(2) SIGNIFICANT POWER, RIGHT, OR CONTINUING INTEREST.—The term "significant power, right, or continuing interest" includes, but is not limited to, the following rights with respect to the interest transferred:

(A) A right to disapprove any assignment of such interest, or any part thereof.

(B) A right to terminate at will.

(C) A right to prescribe the standards of quality of products used or sold, or of services furnished, and of the equipment and facilities used to promote such products or services.

(D) A right to require that the transferee sell or advertise only products or services of the transferor.

(E) A right to require that the transferee purchase substantially all of his supplies and equipment from the transferor.

(F) A right to payments contingent on the productivity, use, or disposition of the subject matter of the interest transferred, if such payments constitute a substantial element under the transfer agreement.

(3) TRANSFER.—The term "transfer" includes the renewal of a franchise, trademark, or trade name.

[Sec. 1253(c)]

(c) TREATMENT OF CONTINGENT PAYMENTS BY TRANSFEROR.—Amounts received or accrued on account of a transfer, sale, or other disposition of a franchise, trademark, or trade name which are contingent on the productivity, use, or disposition of the franchise, trademark, or trade name transferred shall be treated as amounts received or accrued from the sale or other disposition of property which is not a capital asset.

[Sec. 1253(d)]

(d) TREATMENT OF PAYMENTS BY TRANSFEREE.—

(1) CONTINGENT SERIAL PAYMENTS.—

(A) IN GENERAL.—Any amount described in subparagraph (B) which is paid or incurred during the taxable year on account of a transfer, sale, or other disposition of a franchise, trademark, or trade name shall be allowed as a deduction under section 162(a) (relating to trade or business expenses).

(B) AMOUNTS TO WHICH PARAGRAPH APPLIES.—An amount is described in this subparagraph if it—

(i) is contingent on the productivity, use, or disposition of the franchise, trademark, or trade name, and

(ii) is paid as part of a series of payments—

(I) which are payable not less frequently than annually throughout the entire term of the transfer agreement, and

(II) which are substantially equal in amount (or payable under a fixed formula).

(2) OTHER PAYMENTS.—Any amount paid or incurred on account of a transfer, sale, or other disposition of a franchise, trademark, or trade name to which paragraph (1) does not apply shall be treated as an amount chargeable to capital account.

(3) RENEWALS, ETC.—For purposes of determining the term of a transfer agreement under this section, there shall be taken into account all renewal options (and any other period for which the parties reasonably expect the agreement to be renewed).

[Sec. 1253(e)—Stricken]

[Sec. 1254]

SEC. 1254. GAIN FROM DISPOSITION OF INTEREST IN OIL, GAS, GEOTHERMAL, OR OTHER MINERAL PROPERTIES.

[Sec. 1254(a)]

(a) GENERAL RULE.—

(1) ORDINARY INCOME.—If any section 1254 property is disposed of, the lesser of—

(A) the aggregate amount of—

(i) expenditures which have been deducted by the taxpayer or any person under section 263, 616, or 617 with respect to such property and which, but for such deduction, would have been included in the adjusted basis of such property, and

(ii) the deductions for depletion under section 611 which reduced the adjusted basis of such property, or

(B) the excess of—

(i) in the case of—

(I) a sale, exchange, or involuntary conversion, the amount realized, or

(II) in the case of any other disposition, the fair market value of such property, over

(ii) the adjusted basis of such property,

shall be treated as gain which is ordinary income. Such gain shall be recognized notwithstanding any other provision of this subtitle.

(2) DISPOSITION OF PORTION OF PROPERTY.—For purposes of paragraph (1)—

(A) In the case of the disposition of a portion of section 1254 property (other than an undivided interest), the entire amount of the aggregate expenditures or deductions described in paragraph (1)(A) with respect to such property shall be treated as allocable to such portion to the extent of the amount of the gain to which paragraph (1) applies.

(B) In the case of the disposition of an undivided interest in a section 1254 property (or a portion thereof), a proportionate part of the expenditures or deductions described in paragraph (1)(A) with respect to such property shall be treated as allocable to such undivided interest to the extent of the amount of the gain to which paragraph (1) applies.

This paragraph shall not apply to any expenditures to the extent the taxpayer establishes to the satisfaction of the Secretary that such expenditures do not relate to the portion (or interest therein) disposed of.

(3) SECTION 1254 PROPERTY.—The term "section 1254 property" means any property (within the meaning of section 614) if—

(A) any expenditures described in paragraph (1)(A) are properly chargeable to such property, or

(B) the adjusted basis of such property includes adjustments for deductions for depletion under section 611.

(4) ADJUSTMENT FOR AMOUNTS INCLUDED IN GROSS INCOME UNDER SECTION 617(b)(1)(A)..—The amount of the expenditures referred to in paragraph (1)(A)(i) shall be properly adjusted for amounts included in gross income under section 617(b)(1)(A).

* * *

[Sec. 1256]

SEC. 1256. SECTION 1256 CONTRACTS MARKED TO MARKET.

[Sec. 1256(a)]

(a) GENERAL RULE.—For purposes of this subtitle—

(1) each section 1256 contract held by the taxpayer at the close of the taxable year shall be treated as sold for its fair market value on the last business day of such taxable year (and any gain or loss shall be taken into account for the taxable year),

(2) proper adjustment shall be made in the amount of any gain or loss subsequently realized for gain or loss taken into account by reason of paragraph (1),

(3) any gain or loss with respect to a section 1256 contract shall be treated as—

(A) short-term capital gain or loss, to the extent of 40 percent of such gain or loss, and

(B) long-term capital gain or loss, to the extent of 60 percent of such gain or loss, and

(4) if all the offsetting positions making up any straddle consist of section 1256 contracts to which this section applies (and such straddle is not part of a larger straddle), sections 1092 and 263(g) shall not apply with respect to such straddle.

[Sec. 1256(b)]

(b) SECTION 1256 CONTRACT DEFINED.—

(1) IN GENERAL.—For purposes of this section, the term "section 1256 contract" means—

(A) any regulated futures contract,

(B) any foreign currency contract,

(C) any nonequity option,

(D) any dealer equity option, and

(E) any dealer securities futures contract.

(2) EXCEPTIONS.—The term "section 1256 contract" shall not include—

(A) any securities futures contract or option on such a contract unless such contract or option is a dealer securities futures contract, or

(B) any interest rate swap, currency swap, basis swap, interest rate cap, interest rate floor, commodity swap, equity swap, equity index swap, credit default swap, or similar agreement.

[Sec. 1256(c)]

(c) TERMINATIONS, ETC.—

(1) IN GENERAL.—The rules of paragraphs (1), (2), and (3) of subsection (a) shall also apply to the termination (or transfer) during the taxable year of the taxpayer's obligation (or

rights) with respect to a section 1256 contract by offsetting, by taking or making delivery, by exercise or being exercised, by assignment or being assigned, by lapse, or otherwise.

(2) SPECIAL RULE WHERE TAXPAYER TAKES DELIVERY ON OR EXERCISES PART OF STRADDLE.—If—

(A) 2 or more section 1256 contracts are part of a straddle (as defined in section 1092(c)), and

(B) the taxpayer takes delivery under or exercises any of such contracts,

then, for purposes of this section, each of the other such contracts shall be treated as terminated on the day on which the taxpayer took delivery.

(3) FAIR MARKET VALUE TAKEN INTO ACCOUNT.—For purposes of this subsection, fair market value at the time of the termination (or transfer) shall be taken into account.

[Sec. 1256(d)]

(d) ELECTIONS WITH RESPECT TO MIXED STRADDLES.—

(1) ELECTION.—The taxpayer may elect to have this section not to apply to all section 1256 contracts which are part of a mixed straddle.

(2) TIME AND MANNER.—An election under paragraph (1) shall be made at such time and in such manner as the Secretary may by regulations prescribe.

(3) ELECTION REVOCABLE ONLY WITH CONSENT.—An election under paragraph (1) shall apply to the taxpayer's taxable year for which made and to all subsequent taxable years, unless the Secretary consents to a revocation of such election.

(4) MIXED STRADDLE.—For purposes of this subsection, the term "mixed straddle" means any straddle (as defined in section 1092(c))—

(A) at least 1 (but not all) of the positions of which are section 1256 contracts, and

(B) with respect to which each position forming part of such straddle is clearly identified, before the close of the day on which the first section 1256 contract forming part of the straddle is acquired (or such earlier time as the Secretary may prescribe by regulations), as being part of such straddle.

[Sec. 1256(e)]

(e) MARK TO MARKET NOT TO APPLY TO HEDGING TRANSACTIONS.—

(1) SECTION NOT TO APPLY.—Subsection (a) shall not apply in the case of a hedging transaction.

(2) DEFINITION OF HEDGING TRANSACTION.—For purposes of this subsection, the term "hedging transaction" means any hedging transaction (as defined in section 1221(b)(2)(A)) if, before the close of the day on which such transaction was entered into (or such earlier time as the Secretary may prescribe by regulations), the taxpayer clearly identifies such transaction as being a hedging transaction.

(3) SPECIAL RULE FOR SYNDICATES.—

(A) IN GENERAL.—Notwithstanding paragraph (2), the term "hedging transaction" shall not include any transaction entered into by or for a syndicate.

(B) SYNDICATE DEFINED.—For purposes of subparagraph (A), the term "syndicate" means any partnership or other entity (other than a corporation which is not an S corporation) if more than 35 percent of the losses of such entity during the taxable year are allocable to limited partners or limited entrepreneurs (within the meaning of section 461(k)(4)).

(C) HOLDINGS ATTRIBUTABLE TO ACTIVE MANAGEMENT.—For purposes of subparagraph (B), an interest in an entity shall not be treated as held by a limited partner or a limited entrepreneur (within the meaning of section 461(k)(4))—

(i) for any period if during such period such interest is held by an individual who actively participates at all times during such period in the management of such entity,

(ii) for any period if during such period such interest is held by the spouse, children, grandchildren, and parents of an individual who actively participates at all times during such period in the management of such entity,

(iii) if such interest is held by an individual who actively participated in the management of such entity for a period of not less than 5 years,

(iv) if such interest is held by the estate of an individual who actively participated in the management of such entity or is held by the estate of an individual if with respect to such individual such interest was at any time described in clause (ii), or

(v) if the Secretary determines (by regulations or otherwise) that such interest should be treated as held by an individual who actively participates in the management of such entity, and that such entity and such interest are not used (or to be used) for tax-avoidance purposes.

For purposes of this subparagraph, a legally adopted child of an individual shall be treated as a child of such individual by blood.

(4) LIMITATION ON LOSSES FROM HEDGING TRANSACTIONS.—

(A) IN GENERAL.—

(i) LIMITATION.—Any hedging loss for a taxable year which is allocable to any limited partner or limited entrepreneur (within the meaning of paragraph (3)) shall be allowed only to the extent of the taxable income of such limited partner or entrepreneur for such taxable year attributable to the trade or business in which the hedging transactions were entered into. For purposes of the preceding sentence, taxable income shall be determined by not taking into account items attributable to hedging transactions.

(ii) CARRYOVER OF DISALLOWED LOSS.—Any hedging loss disallowed under clause (i) shall be treated as a deduction attributable to a hedging transaction allowable in the first succeeding taxable year.

(B) EXCEPTION WHERE ECONOMIC LOSS.—Subparagraph (A)(i) shall not apply to any hedging loss to the extent that such loss exceeds the aggregate unrecognized gains from hedging transactions as of the close of the taxable year attributable to the trade or business in which the hedging transactions were entered into.

(C) EXCEPTION FOR CERTAIN HEDGING TRANSACTIONS.—In the case of any hedging transaction relating to property other than stock or securities, this paragraph shall apply only in the case of a taxpayer described in section 465(a)(1).

(D) HEDGING LOSS.—The term "hedging loss" means the excess of—

(i) the deductions allowable under this chapter for the taxable year attributable to hedging transactions (determined without regard to subparagraph (A)(i)), over

(ii) income received or accrued by the taxpayer during such taxable year from such transactions.

(E) UNRECOGNIZED GAIN.—The term "unrecognized gain" has the meaning given to such term by section 1092(a)(3).

[Sec. 1256(f)]

(f) SPECIAL RULES.—

(1) DENIAL OF CAPITAL GAINS TREATMENT FOR PROPERTY IDENTIFIED AS PART OF A HEDGING TRANSACTION.—For purposes of this title, gain from any property shall in no event be considered as gain from the sale or exchange of a capital asset if such property was at any time personal property (as defined in section 1092(d)(1)) identified under subsection (e)(2) by the taxpayer as being part of a hedging transaction.

(2) SUBSECTION (a)(3) NOT TO APPLY TO ORDINARY INCOME PROPERTY.—Paragraph (3) of subsection (a) shall not apply to any gain or loss which, but for such paragraph, would be ordinary income or loss.

(3) CAPITAL GAIN TREATMENT FOR TRADERS IN SECTION 1256 CONTRACTS.—

(A) IN GENERAL.—For purposes of this title, gain or loss from trading of section 1256 contracts shall be treated as gain or loss from the sale or exchange of a capital asset.

(B) EXCEPTION FOR CERTAIN HEDGING TRANSACTIONS.—Subparagraph (A) shall not apply to any section 1256 contract to the extent such contract is held for purposes of hedging property if any loss with respect to such property in the hands of the taxpayer would be ordinary loss.

(C) TREATMENT OF UNDERLYING PROPERTY.—For purposes of determining whether gain or loss with respect to any property is ordinary income or loss, the fact that the taxpayer is actively engaged in dealing in or trading section 1256 contracts related to such property shall not be taken into account.

(4) SPECIAL RULE FOR DEALER EQUITY OPTIONS AND DEALER SECURITIES FUTURES CONTRACTS OF LIMITED PARTNERS OR LIMITED ENTREPRENEURS.—In the case of any gain or loss with respect to dealer equity options, or dealer securities futures contracts, which are allocable to limited partners or limited entrepreneurs (within the meaning of subsection (e)(3))—

(A) paragraph (3) of subsection (a) shall not apply to any such gain or loss, and

(B) all such gains or losses shall be treated as short-term capital gains or losses, as the case may be.

(5) SPECIAL RULE RELATED TO LOSSES.—Section 1091 (relating to loss from wash sales of stock or securities) shall not apply to any loss taken into account by reason of paragraph (1) of subsection (a).

[Sec. 1256(g)]

(g) DEFINITIONS.—For purposes of this section—

(1) REGULATED FUTURES CONTRACTS DEFINED.—The term "regulated futures contract" means a contract—

(A) with respect to which the amount required to be deposited and the amount which may be withdrawn depends on a system of marking to market, and

(B) which is traded on or subject to the rules of a qualified board or exchange.

(2) FOREIGN CURRENCY CONTRACT DEFINED.—

(A) FOREIGN CURRENCY CONTRACT.—The term "foreign currency contract" means a contract—

(i) which requires delivery of, or the settlement of which depends on the value of, a foreign currency which is a currency in which positions are also traded through regulated futures contracts,

(ii) which is traded in the interbank market, and

(iii) which is entered into at arm's length at a price determined by reference to the price in the interbank market.

(B) REGULATIONS.—The Secretary shall prescribe such regulations as may be necessary or appropriate to carry out the purposes of subparagraph (A), including regulations excluding from the application of subparagraph (A) any contract (or type of contract) if its application thereto would be inconsistent with such purposes.

(3) NONEQUITY OPTION.—The term "nonequity option" means any listed option which is not an equity option.

(4) DEALER EQUITY OPTION.—The term "dealer equity option" means, with respect to an options dealer, any listed option which—

(A) is an equity option,

(B) is purchased or granted by such options dealer in the normal course of his activity of dealing in options, and

(C) is listed on the qualified board or exchange on which such options dealer is registered.

(5) LISTED OPTION.—The term "listed option" means any option (other than a right to acquire stock from the issuer) which is traded on (or subject to the rules of) a qualified board or exchange.

(6) EQUITY OPTION.—The term "equity option" means any option—

(A) to buy or sell stock, or

(B) the value of which is determined directly or indirectly by reference to any stock or any narrow-based security index (as defined in section 3(a)(55) of the Securities Exchange Act of 1934, as in effect on the date of the enactment of this paragraph).

The term "equity option" includes such an option on a group of stocks only if such group meets the requirements for a narrow-based security index (as so defined). The Secretary may prescribe regulations regarding the status of options the values of which are determined directly or indirectly by reference to any index which becomes (or ceases to be) a narrow-based security index (as so defined).

(7) QUALIFIED BOARD OR EXCHANGE.—The term "qualified board or exchange" means—

(A) a national securities exchange which is registered with the Securities and Exchange Commission,

(B) a domestic board of trade designated as a contract market by the Commodity Futures Trading Commission, or

(C) any other exchange, board of trade, or other market which the Secretary determines has rules adequate to carry out the purposes of this section.

(8) OPTIONS DEALER.—

(A) IN GENERAL.—The term "options dealer" means any person registered with an appropriate national securities exchange as a market maker or specialist in listed options.

(B) PERSONS TRADING IN OTHER MARKETS.—In any case in which the Secretary makes a determination under subparagraph (C) of paragraph (7), the term "options dealer" also includes any person whom the Secretary determines performs functions similar to the persons described in subparagraph (A). Such determinations shall be made to the extent appropriate to carry out the purposes of this section.

(9) DEALER SECURITIES FUTURES CONTRACT.—

(A) IN GENERAL.—The term "dealer securities futures contract" means, with respect to any dealer, any securities futures contract, and any option on such a contract, which—

(i) is entered into by such dealer (or, in the case of an option, is purchased or granted by such dealer) in the normal course of his activity of dealing in such contracts or options, as the case may be, and

(ii) is traded on a qualified board or exchange.

(B) DEALER.—For purposes of subparagraph (A), a person shall be treated as a dealer in securities futures contracts or options on such contracts if the Secretary determines that such person performs, with respect to such contracts or options, as the case may be, functions similar to the functions performed by persons described in paragraph (8)(A). Such determination shall be made to the extent appropriate to carry out the purposes of this section.

(C) SECURITIES FUTURES CONTRACT.—The term "securities futures contract" has the meaning given to such term by section 1234B.

[Sec. 1258]

SEC. 1258. RECHARACTERIZATION OF GAIN FROM CERTAIN FINANCIAL TRANSACTIONS.

[Sec. 1258(a)]

(a) GENERAL RULE.—In the case of any gain—

(1) which (but for this section) would be treated as gain from the sale or exchange of a capital asset, and

(2) which is recognized on the disposition or other termination of any position which was held as part of a conversion transaction,

such gain (to the extent such gain does not exceed the applicable imputed income amount) shall be treated as ordinary income.

[Sec. 1258(b)]

(b) APPLICABLE IMPUTED INCOME AMOUNT.—For purposes of subsection (a), the term "applicable imputed income amount" means, with respect to any disposition or other termination referred to in subsection (a), an amount equal to—

(1) the amount of interest which would have accrued on the taxpayer's net investment in the conversion transaction for the period ending on the date of such disposition or other termination (or, if earlier, the date on which the requirements of subsection (c) ceased to be satisfied) at a rate equal to 120 percent of the applicable rate, reduced by

(2) the amount treated as ordinary income under subsection (a) with respect to any prior disposition or other termination of a position which was held as a part of such transaction.

The Secretary shall by regulations provide for such reductions in the applicable imputed income amount as may be appropriate by reason of amounts capitalized under section 263(g), ordinary income received, or otherwise.

[Sec. 1258(c)]

(c) CONVERSION TRANSACTION.—For purposes of this section, the term "conversion transaction" means any transaction—

(1) substantially all of the taxpayer's expected return from which is attributable to the time value of the taxpayer's net investment in such transaction, and

(2) which is—

(A) the holding of any property (whether or not actively traded), and the entering into a contract to sell such property (or substantially identical property) at a price determined in accordance with such contract, but only if such property was acquired and such contract was entered into on a substantially contemporaneous basis,

(B) an applicable straddle,

(C) any other transaction which is marketed or sold as producing capital gains from a transaction described in paragraph (1), or

(D) any other transaction specified in regulations prescribed by the Secretary.

[Sec. 1258(d)]

(d) DEFINITIONS AND SPECIAL RULES.—For purposes of this section—

(1) APPLICABLE STRADDLE.—The term "applicable straddle" means any straddle (within the meaning of section 1092(c)).

(2) APPLICABLE RATE.—The term "applicable rate" means—

(A) the applicable Federal rate determined under section 1274(d) (compounded semiannually) as if the conversion transaction were a debt instrument, or

(B) if the term of the conversion transaction is indefinite, the Federal short-term rates in effect under section 6621(b) during the period of the conversion transaction (compounded daily).

(3) TREATMENT OF BUILT-IN LOSSES.—

(A) IN GENERAL.—If any position with a built-in loss becomes part of a conversion transaction—

(i) for purposes of applying this subtitle to such position for periods after such position becomes part of such transaction, such position shall be taken into account at its fair market value as of the time it became part of such transaction, except that

(ii) upon the disposition or other termination of such position in a transaction in which gain or loss is recognized, such built-in loss shall be recognized and shall have a character determined without regard to this section.

(B) BUILT-IN LOSS.—For purposes of subparagraph (A), the term "built-in loss" means the loss (if any) which would have been realized if the position had been disposed of or otherwise terminated at its fair market value as of the time such position became part of the conversion transaction.

(4) POSITION TAKEN INTO ACCOUNT AT FAIR MARKET VALUE.—In determining the taxpayer's net investment in any conversion transaction, there shall be included the fair market value of any position which becomes part of such transaction (determined as of the time such position became part of such transaction).

(5) SPECIAL RULE FOR OPTIONS DEALERS AND COMMODITIES TRADERS.—

(A) IN GENERAL.—Subsection (a) shall not apply to transactions—

(i) of an options dealer in the normal course of the dealer's trade or business of dealing in options, or

(ii) of a commodities trader in the normal course of the trader's trade or business of trading section 1256 contracts.

(B) DEFINITIONS .—For purposes of this paragraph—

(i) OPTIONS DEALER.—The term "options dealer" has the meaning given such term by section 1256(g)(8).

(ii) COMMODITIES TRADER.—The term "commodities trader" means any person who is a member (or, except as otherwise provided in regulations, is entitled to trade as a member) of a domestic board of trade which is designated as a contract market by the Commodity Futures Trading Commission.

(C) LIMITED PARTNERS AND LIMITED ENTREPRENEURS.—In the case of any gain from a transaction recognized by an entity which is allocable to a limited partner or limited entrepreneur (within the meaning of section 461(k)(4)), subparagraph (A) shall not apply if—

(i) substantially all of the limited partner's (or limited entrepreneur's) expected return from the entity is attributable to the time value of the partner's (or entrepreneur's) net investment in such entity,

(ii) the transaction (or the interest in the entity) was marketed or sold as producing capital gains treatment from a transaction described in subsection (c)(1), or

(iii) the transaction (or the interest in the entity) is a transaction (or interest) specified in regulations prescribed by the Secretary.

[Sec. 1259]

SEC. 1259. CONSTRUCTIVE SALES TREATMENT FOR APPRECIATED FINANCIAL POSITIONS.

[Sec. 1259(a)]

(a) IN GENERAL.—If there is a constructive sale of an appreciated financial position—

(1) the taxpayer shall recognize gain as if such position were sold, assigned, or otherwise terminated at its fair market value on the date of such constructive sale (and any gain shall be taken into account for the taxable year which includes such date), and

(2) for purposes of applying this title for periods after the constructive sale—

(A) proper adjustment shall be made in the amount of any gain or loss subsequently realized with respect to such position for any gain taken into account by reason of paragraph (1), and

(B) the holding period of such position shall be determined as if such position were originally acquired on the date of such constructive sale.

[Sec. 1259(b)]

(b) APPRECIATED FINANCIAL POSITION.—For purposes of this section—

(1) IN GENERAL.—Except as provided in paragraph (2), the term "appreciated financial position" means any position with respect to any stock, debt instrument, or partnership

interest if there would be gain were such position sold, assigned, or otherwise terminated at its fair market value.

(2) EXCEPTIONS.—The term "appreciated financial position" shall not include—

(A) any position with respect to debt if—

(i) the position unconditionally entitles the holder to receive a specified principal amount,

(ii) the interest payments (or other similar amounts) with respect to such position meet the requirements of clause (i) of section 860G(a)(1)(B), and

(iii) such position is not convertible (directly or indirectly) into stock of the issuer or any related person,

(B) any hedge with respect to a position described in subparagraph (A), and

(C) any position which is marked to market under any provision of this title or the regulations thereunder.

(3) POSITION.—The term "position" means an interest, including a futures or forward contract, short sale, or option.

[Sec. 1259(c)]

(c) CONSTRUCTIVE SALE.—For purposes of this section—

(1) IN GENERAL.—A taxpayer shall be treated as having made a constructive sale of an appreciated financial position if the taxpayer (or a related person)—

(A) enters into a short sale of the same or substantially identical property,

(B) enters into an offsetting notional principal contract with respect to the same or substantially identical property,

(C) enters into a futures or forward contract to deliver the same or substantially identical property,

(D) in the case of an appreciated financial position that is a short sale or a contract described in subparagraph (B) or (C) with respect to any property, acquires the same or substantially identical property, or

(E) to the extent prescribed by the Secretary in regulations, enters into 1 or more other transactions (or acquires 1 or more positions) that have substantially the same effect as a transaction described in any of the preceding subparagraphs.

(2) EXCEPTION FOR SALES OF NONPUBLICLY TRADED PROPERTY.—A taxpayer shall not be treated as having made a constructive sale solely because the taxpayer enters into a contract for sale of any stock, debt instrument, or partnership interest which is not a marketable security (as defined in section 453(f)) if the contract settles within 1 year after the date such contract is entered into.

(3) EXCEPTION FOR CERTAIN CLOSED TRANSACTIONS.—

(A) IN GENERAL.—In applying this section, there shall be disregarded any transaction (which would otherwise cause a constructive sale) during the taxable year if—

(i) such transaction is closed on or before the 30th day after the close of such taxable year,

(ii) the taxpayer holds the appreciated financial position throughout the 60-day period beginning on the date such transaction is closed, and

(iii) at no time during such 60-day period is the taxpayer's risk of loss with respect to such position reduced by reason of a circumstance which would be described in section 246(c)(4) if references to stock included references to such position.

(B) TREATMENT OF CERTAIN CLOSED TRANSACTIONS WHERE RISK OF LOSS ON APPRECIATED FINANCIAL POSITION DIMINISHED.—If—

(i) a transaction, which would otherwise cause a constructive sale of an appreciated financial position, is closed during the taxable year or during the 30 days thereafter, and

(ii) another transaction is entered into during the 60-day period beginning on the date the transaction referred to in clause (i) is closed—

(I) which would (but for this subparagraph) cause the requirement of subparagraph (A)(iii) not to be met with respect to the transaction described in clause (i) of this subparagraph,

(II) which is closed on or before the 30th day after the close of the taxable year in which the transaction referred to in clause (i) occurs, and

(III) which meets the requirements of clauses (ii) and (iii) of subparagraph (A),

the transaction referred to in clause (ii) shall be disregarded for purposes of determining whether the requirements of subparagraph (A)(iii) are met with respect to the transaction described in clause (i).

(4) RELATED PERSON.—A person is related to another person with respect to a transaction if—

(A) the relationship is described in section 267(b) or 707(b), and

(B) such transaction is entered into with a view toward avoiding the purposes of this section.

[Sec. 1259(d)]

(d) OTHER DEFINITIONS.—For purposes of this section—

(1) FORWARD CONTRACT.—The term "forward contract" means a contract to deliver a substantially fixed amount of property (including cash) for a substantially fixed price.

(2) OFFSETTING NOTIONAL PRINCIPAL CONTRACT.—The term "offsetting notional principal contract" means, with respect to any property, an agreement which includes—

(A) a requirement to pay (or provide credit for) all or substantially all of the investment yield (including appreciation) on such property for a specified period, and

(B) a right to be reimbursed for (or receive credit for) all or substantially all of any decline in the value of such property.

[Sec. 1259(e)]

(e) SPECIAL RULES.—

(1) TREATMENT OF SUBSEQUENT SALE OF POSITION WHICH WAS DEEMED SOLD.—If—

(A) there is a constructive sale of any appreciated financial position,

(B) such position is subsequently disposed of, and

(C) at the time of such disposition, the transaction resulting in the constructive sale of such position is open with respect to the taxpayer or any related person,

solely for purposes of determining whether the taxpayer has entered into a constructive sale of any other appreciated financial position held by the taxpayer, the taxpayer shall be treated as entering into such transaction immediately after such disposition. For purposes of the preceding sentence, an assignment or other termination shall be treated as a disposition.

(2) CERTAIN TRUST INSTRUMENTS TREATED AS STOCK.—For purposes of this section, an interest in a trust which is actively traded (within the meaning of section 1092(d)(1)) shall be treated as stock unless substantially all (by value) of the property held by the trust is debt described in subsection (b)(2)(A).

(3) MULTIPLE POSITIONS IN PROPERTY.—If a taxpayer holds multiple positions in property, the determination of whether a specific transaction is a constructive sale and, if so, which appreciated financial position is deemed sold shall be made in the same manner as actual sales.

[Sec. 1259(f)]

(f) REGULATIONS.—The Secretary shall prescribe such regulations as may be necessary or appropriate to carry out the purposes of this section.

PART V—SPECIAL RULES FOR BONDS AND OTHER DEBT INSTRUMENTS

Subpart A—Original Issue Discount

[Sec. 1271]

SEC. 1271. TREATMENT OF AMOUNTS RECEIVED ON RETIREMENT OR SALE OR EXCHANGE OF DEBT INSTRUMENTS.

[Sec. 1271(a)]

(a) GENERAL RULE.—For purposes of this title—

(1) RETIREMENT.—Amounts received by the holder on retirement of any debt instrument shall be considered as amounts received in exchange therefor.

(2) ORDINARY INCOME ON SALE OR EXCHANGE WHERE INTENTION TO CALL BEFORE MATURITY.—

(A) IN GENERAL.—If at the time of original issue there was an intention to call a debt instrument before maturity, any gain realized on the sale or exchange thereof which does not exceed an amount equal to—

(i) the original issue discount, reduced by

(ii) the portion of original issue discount previously includible in the gross income of any holder (without regard to section 1272(a)(7) (or the corresponding provisions of prior law)),

shall be treated as ordinary income.

(B) EXCEPTIONS.—This paragraph shall not apply to—

(i) any tax-exempt obligation, or

(ii) any holder who has purchased the debt instrument at a premium.

(3) CERTAIN SHORT-TERM GOVERNMENT OBLIGATIONS.—

(A) IN GENERAL.—On the sale or exchange of any short-term Government obligation, any gain realized which does not exceed an amount equal to the ratable share of the acquisition discount shall be treated as ordinary income.

(B) SHORT-TERM GOVERNMENT OBLIGATION.—For purposes of this paragraph, the term "short-term Government obligation" means any obligation of the United States or any of its possessions, or of a State or any political subdivision thereof, or of the District of Columbia, which has a fixed maturity date not more than 1 year from the date of issue. Such term does not include any tax-exempt obligation.

(C) ACQUISITION DISCOUNT.—For purposes of this paragraph, the term "acquisition discount" means the excess of the stated redemption price at maturity over the taxpayer's basis for the obligation.

(D) RATABLE SHARE.—For purposes of this paragraph, except as provided in subparagraph (E) the ratable share of the acquisition discount is an amount which bears the same ratio to such discount as—

(i) the number of days which the taxpayer held the obligation, bears to

(ii) the number of days after the date the taxpayer acquired the obligation and up to (and including) the date of its maturity.

(E) ELECTION OF ACCRUAL ON BASIS OF CONSTANT INTEREST RATE.—At the election of the taxpayer with respect to any obligation, the ratable share of the aquisition discount is the portion of the acquisition discount accruing while the taxpayer held the obligation determined (under regulations prescribed by the Secretary) on the basis of—

(i) the taxpayer's yield to maturity based on the taxpayer's cost of acquiring the obligation, and

(ii) compounding daily.

An election under this subparagraph, once made with respect to any obligation, shall be irrevocable.

(4) CERTAIN SHORT-TERM NONGOVERNMENT OBLIGATIONS.—

(A) IN GENERAL.—On the sale or exchange of any short-term nongovernment obligation, any gain realized which does not exceed an amount equal to the ratable share of the original issue discount shall be treated as ordinary income.

(B) SHORT-TERM NONGOVERNMENT OBLIGATION.—For purposes of this paragraph, the term "short-term nongovernment obligation" means any obligation which—

(i) has a fixed maturity date not more than 1 year from the date of the issue, and

(ii) is not a short-term Government obligation (as defined in paragraph (3)(B) without regard to the last sentence thereof).

(C) RATABLE SHARE.—For purposes of this paragraph, except as provided in subparagraph (D), the ratable share of the original issue discount is an amount which bears the same ratio to such discount as—

(i) the number of days which the taxpayer held the obligation, bears to

(ii) the number of days after the date of original issue and up to (and including) the date of its maturity.

(D) ELECTION OF ACCRUAL ON BASIS OF CONSTANT INTEREST RATE.—At the election of the taxpayer with respect to any obligation, the ratable share of the original issue discount is the portion of the original issue discount accruing while the taxpayer held the obligation determined (under regulations prescribed by the Secretary) on the basis of—

(i) the yield to maturity based on the issue price of the obligation, and

(ii) compounding daily.

Any election under this subparagraph, once made with respect to any obligation, shall be irrevocable.

[Sec. 1271(b)]

(b) EXCEPTION FOR CERTAIN OBLIGATIONS.—

(1) IN GENERAL.—This section shall not apply to any obligation issued by a natural person before June 9, 1997.

(2) TERMINATION.—Paragraph (1) shall not apply to any obligation purchased (within the meaning of section 1272(d)(1)) after June 8, 1997.

[Sec. 1271(d)]

(c) DOUBLE INCLUSION IN INCOME NOT REQUIRED.—This section and sections 1272 and 1286 shall not require the inclusion of any amount previously includible in gross income.

[Sec. 1272]

SEC. 1272. CURRENT INCLUSION IN INCOME OF ORIGINAL ISSUE DISCOUNT.

[Sec. 1272(a)]

(a) ORIGINAL ISSUE DISCOUNT INCLUDED IN INCOME ON BASIS OF CONSTANT INTEREST RATE.—

(1) GENERAL RULE.—For purposes of this title, there shall be included in the gross income of the holder of any debt instrument having original issue discount an amount equal to the sum of the daily portions of the original issue discount for each day during the taxable year on which such holder held such debt instrument.

(2) EXCEPTIONS.—Paragraph (1) shall not apply to—

(A) TAX-EXEMPT OBLIGATIONS.—Any tax-exempt obligation.

(B) UNITED STATES SAVINGS BONDS.—Any United States savings bond.

(C) SHORT-TERM OBLIGATIONS.—Any debt instrument which has a fixed maturity date not more than 1 year from the date of issue.

(D) LOANS BETWEEN NATURAL PERSONS.—

(i) IN GENERAL.—Any loan made by a natural person to another natural person if—

(I) such loan is not made in the course of a trade or business of the lender, and

(II) the amount of such loan (when increased by the outstanding amount of prior loans by such natural person to such other natural person) does not exceed $10,000.

(ii) CLAUSE (i) NOT TO APPLY WHERE TAX AVOIDANCE A PRINCIPAL PURPOSE.—Clause (i) shall not apply if the loan has as 1 of its principal purposes the avoidance of any Federal tax.

(iii) TREATMENT OF HUSBAND AND WIFE.—For purposes of this subparagraph, a husband and wife shall be treated as 1 person. The preceding sentence shall not apply where the spouses lived apart at all times during the taxable year in which the loan is made.

(3) DETERMINATION OF DAILY PORTIONS.—For purposes of paragraph (1), the daily portion of the original issue discount on any debt instrument shall be determined by allocating to each day in any accrual period its ratable portion of the increase during such accrual period in the adjusted issue price of the debt instrument. For purposes of the preceding sentence, the increase in the adjusted issue price for any accrual period shall be an amount equal to the excess (if any) of—

(A) the product of—

(i) the adjusted issue price of the debt instrument at the beginning of such accrual period, and

(ii) the yield to maturity (determined on the basis of compounding at the close of each accrual period and properly adjusted for the length of the accrual period), over

(B) the sum of the amounts payable as interest on such debt instrument during such accrual period.

(4) ADJUSTED ISSUE PRICE.—For purposes of this subsection, the adjusted issue price of any debt instrument at the beginning of any accrual period is the sum of—

(A) the issue price of such debt instrument, plus

(B) the adjustments under this subsection to such issue price for all periods before the first day of such accrual period.

(5) ACCRUAL PERIOD.—Except as otherwise provided in regulations prescribed by the Secretary, the term "accrual period" means a 6-month period (or shorter period from the date of original issue of the debt instrument) which ends on a day in the calendar year corresponding to the maturity date of the debt instrument or the date 6 months before such maturity date.

(6) DETERMINATION OF DAILY PORTIONS WHERE PRINCIPAL SUBJECT TO ACCELERATION.—

(A) IN GENERAL.—In the case of any debt instrument to which this paragraph applies, the daily portion of the original issue discount shall be determined by allocating to each day in any accrual period its ratable portion of the excess (if any) of—

(i) the sum of (I) the present value determined under subparagraph (B) of all remaining payments under the debt instrument as of the close of such period, and (II) the payments during the accrual period of amounts included in the stated redemption price of the debt instrument, over

(ii) the adjusted issue price of such debt instrument at the beginning of such period.

(B) DETERMINION OF PRESENT VALUE.—For purposes of subparagraph (A), the present value shall be determined on the basis of—

(i) the original yield to maturity (determined on the basis of compounding at the close of each accrual period and properly adjusted for the length of the accrual period),

(ii) events which have occurred before the close of the accrual period, and

(iii) a prepayment assumption determined in the manner prescribed by regulations.

(C) DEBT INSTRUMENTS TO WHICH PARAGRAPH APPLIES.—This paragraph applies to—

(i) any regular interest in a REMIC or qualified mortgage held by a REMIC,

(ii) any other debt instrument if payments under such debt instrument may be accelerated by reason of prepayments of other obligations securing such debt instrument (or, to the extent provided in regulations, by reason of other events), or

(iii) any pool of debt instruments the yield on which may be affected by reason of prepayments (or to the extent provided in regulations, by reason of other events).

To the extent provided in regulations prescribed by the Secretary, in the case of a small business engaged in the trade or business of selling tangible personal property at retail, clause (iii) shall not apply to debt instruments incurred in the ordinary course of such trade or business while held by such business.

(7) REDUCTION WHERE SUBSEQUENT HOLDER PAYS ACQUISITION PREMIUM.—

(A) REDUCTION.—For purposes of this subsection, in the case of any purchase after its original issue of a debt instrument to which this subsection applies, the daily portion for any day shall be reduced by an amount equal to the amount which would be the daily portion for such day (without regard to this paragraph) multiplied by the fraction determined under subparagraph (B).

(B) DETERMINATION OF FRACTION.—For purposes of subparagraph (A), the fraction determined under this subparagraph is a fraction—

(i) the numerator of which is the excess (if any) of—

(I) the cost of such debt instrument incurred by the purchaser, over

(II) the issue price of such debt instrument, increased by the portion of original issue discount previously includible in the gross income of any holder (computed without regard to this paragraph), and

(ii) the denominator of which is the sum of the daily portions for such debt instrument for all days after the date of such purchase and ending on the stated maturity date (computed without regard to this paragraph).

[Sec. 1272(b)]

(b) EXCEPTIONS.—This section shall not apply to any holder—

(1) who has purchased the debt instrument at a premium, or

(2) which is a life insurance company to which section 811(b) applies.

[Sec. 1272(c)]

(c) DEFINITION AND SPECIAL RULE.—

(1) PURCHASE DEFINED.—For purposes of this section, the term "purchase" means—

(A) any acquisition of a debt instrument, where

(B) the basis of the debt instrument is not determined in whole or in part by reference to the adjusted basis of such debt instrument in the hands of the person from whom acquired.

(2) BASIS ADJUSTMENT.—The basis of any debt instrument in the hands of the holder thereof shall be increased by the amount included in his gross income pursuant to this section.

[Sec. 1273]

SEC. 1273. DETERMINATION OF AMOUNT OF ORIGINAL ISSUE DISCOUNT.

[Sec. 1273(a)]

(a) GENERAL RULE.—For purposes of this subpart—

(1) IN GENERAL.—The term "original issue discount" means the excess (if any) of—

(A) the stated redemption price at maturity, over

(B) the issue price.

(2) STATED REDEMPTION PRICE AT MATURITY.—The term "stated redemption price at maturity" means the amount fixed by the last modification of the purchase agreement and includes interest and other amounts payable at that time (other than any interest based on a fixed rate, and payable unconditionally at fixed periodic intervals of 1 year or less during the entire term of the debt instrument).

(3) 1/4 OF 1 PERCENT DE MINIMIS RULE.—If the original issue discount determined under paragraph (1) is less than—

(A) 1/4 of 1 percent of the stated redemption price at maturity, multiplied by

(B) the number of complete years to maturity,

then the original issue discount shall be treated as zero.

[Sec. 1273(b)]

(b) ISSUE PRICE.—For purposes of this subpart—

(1) PUBLICLY OFFERED DEBT INSTRUMENTS NOT ISSUED FOR PROPERTY.—In the case of any issue of debt instruments—

(A) publicly offered, and

(B) not issued for property,

the issue price is the initial offering price to the public (excluding bond houses and brokers) at which price a substantial amount of such debt instruments was sold.

(2) OTHER DEBT INSTRUMENTS NOT ISSUED FOR PROPERTY.—In the case of any isssue of debt instruments not issued for property and not publicly offered, the issue price of each such instrument is the price paid by the first buyer of such debt instrument.

(3) DEBT INSTRUMENTS ISSUED FOR PROPERTY WHERE THERE IS PUBLIC TRADING.—In the case of a debt instrument which is issued for property and which—

(A) is part of an issue a portion of which is traded on an established securities market, or

(B) (i) is issued for stock or securities which are traded on an established securities market, or

(ii) to the extent provided in regulations, is issued for property (other than stock or securities) of a kind regularly traded on an established market,

the issue price of such debt instrument shall be the fair market value of such property.

(4) OTHER CASES.—Except in any case—

(A) to which paragraph (1), (2), or (3) of this subsection applies, or

(B) to which section 1274 applies,

the issue price of a debt instrument which is issued for property shall be the stated redemption price at maturity.

(5) PROPERTY.—In applying this subsection, the term "property" includes services and the right to use property, but such term does not include money.

[Sec. 1273(c)]

(c) SPECIAL RULES FOR APPLYING SUBSECTION (b).—For purposes of subsection (b)—

(1) INITIAL OFFERING PRICE; PRICE PAID BY THE FIRST BUYER.—The terms "initial offering price" and "price paid by the first buyer" include the aggregate payments made by the purchaser under the purchase agreement, including modifications thereof.

(2) TREATMENT OF INVESTMENT UNITS.—In the case of any debt instrument and an option, security, or other property issued together as an investment unit—

(A) the issue price for such unit shall be determined in accordance with the rules of this subsection and subsection (b) as if it were a debt instrument,

(B) the issue price determined for such unit shall be allocated to each element of such unit on the basis of the relationship of the fair market value of such element to the fair market value of all elements in such unit, and

(C) the issue price of any debt instrument included in such unit shall be the portion of the issue price of the unit allocated to the debt instrument under subparagraph (B).

[Sec. 1274]

SEC 1274. DETERMINATION OF ISSUE PRICE IN THE CASE OF CERTAIN DEBT INSTRUMENTS ISSUED FOR PROPERTY.

[Sec. 1274(a)]

(a) IN GENERAL.—In the case of any debt instrument to which this section applies, for purposes of this subpart, the issue price shall be—

(1) where there is adequate stated interest, the stated principal amount, or

(2) in any other case, the imputed principal amount.

[Sec. 1274(b)]

(b) IMPUTED PRINCIPAL AMOUNT.—For purposes of this section—

(1) IN GENERAL.—Except as provided in paragraph (3), the imputed principal amount of any debt instrument shall be equal to the sum of the present values of all payments due under such debt instrument.

(2) DETERMINATION OF PRESENT VALUE.—For purposes of paragraph (1), the present value of a payment shall be determined in the manner provided by regulations prescribed by the Secretary—

(A) as of the date of the sale or exchange, and

(B) by using a discount rate equal to the applicable Federal rate, compounded semiannually.

(3) FAIR MARKET VALUE RULE IN POTENTIALLY ABUSIVE SITUATIONS.—

(A) IN GENERAL.—In the case of any potentially abusive situation, the imputed principal amount of any debt instrument received in exchange for property shall be the fair market value of such property adjusted to take into account other consideration involved in the transaction.

(B) POTENTIALLY ABUSIVE SITUATION DEFINED.—For purposes of subparagraph (A), the term "potentially abusive situation" means—

(i) a tax shelter (as defined in section 6662(d)(2)(C)(ii), and

(ii) any other situation which, by reason of—

(I) recent sales transactions,

(II) nonrecourse financing,

(III) financing with a term in excess of the economic life of the property, or

(IV) other circumstances,

is of a type which the Secretary specifies by regulations as having potential for tax avoidance.

[Sec. 1274(c)]

(c) DEBT INSTRUMENTS TO WHICH SECTION APPLIES.—

(1) IN GENERAL.—Except as otherwise provided in this subsection, this section shall apply to any debt instrument given in consideration for the sale or exchange of property if—

(A) the stated redemption price at maturity for such debt instrument exceeds—

(i) where there is adequate stated interest, the stated principal amount, or

(ii) in any other case, the imputed principal amount of such debt instrument determined under subsection (b), and

(B) some or all of the payments due under such debt instrument are due more than 6 months after the date of such sale or exchange.

(2) ADEQUATE STATED INTEREST.—For purposes of this section, there is adequate stated interest with respect to any debt instrument if the stated principal amount for such debt instrument is less than or equal to the imputed principal amount of such debt instrument determined under subsection (b).

(3) EXCEPTIONS.—This section shall not apply to—

(A) SALES FOR $1,000,000 OR LESS OF FARMS BY INDIVIDUALS OR SMALL BUSINESSES.—

(i) IN GENERAL.—Any debt instrument arising from the sale or exchange of a farm (within the meaning of section 6420(c)(2))—

(I) by an individual, estate, or testamentary trust,

(II) by a corporation which as of the date of the sale or exchange is a small business corporation (as defined in section 1244(c)(3)), or

(III) by a partnership which as of the date of the sale or exchange meets requirements similar to those of section 1244(c)(3).

(ii) $1,000,000 LIMITATION.—Clause (i) shall apply only if it can be determined at the time of the sale or exchange that the sales price cannot exceed $1,000,000. For purposes of the preceding sentence, all sales and exchanges which are part of the same transaction (or a series of related transactions) shall be treated as 1 sale or exchange.

(B) SALES OF PRINCIPAL RESIDENCES.—Any debt instrument arising from the sale or exchange by an individual of his principal residence (within the meaning of section 121).

(C) SALES INVOLVING TOTAL PAYMENTS OF $250,000 OR LESS.—

(i) IN GENERAL.—Any debt instrument arising from the sale or exchange of property if the sum of the following amounts does not exceed $250,000:

(I) the aggregate amount of the payments due under such debt instrument and all other debt instruments received as consideration for the sale or exchange, and

(II) the aggregate amount of any other consideration to be received for the sale or exchange.

(ii) CONSIDERATION OTHER THAN DEBT INSTRUMENT TAKEN INTO ACCOUNT AT FAIR MARKET VALUE.—For purposes of clause (i), any consideration (other than a debt instrument) shall be taken into account at its fair market value.

(iii) AGGREGATION OF TRANSACTIONS.—For purposes of this subparagraph, all sales and exchanges which are part of the same transaction (or a series of related transactions) shall be treated as 1 sale or exchange.

(D) DEBT INSTRUMENTS WHICH ARE PUBLICLY TRADED OR ISSUED FOR PUBLICLY TRADED PROPERTY.—Any debt instrument to which section 1273(b)(3) applies.

(E) CERTAIN SALES OF PATENTS.—In the case of any transfer described in section 1235(a) (relating to sale or exchange of patents), any amount contingent on the productivity, use, or disposition of the property transferred.

(F) SALES OR EXCHANGES TO WHICH SECTION 483(e) APPLIES.—Any debt instrument to the extent section 483(e) (relating to certain land transfers between related persons) applies to such instrument.

(4) EXCEPTION FOR ASSUMPTIONS.—If any person—

(A) in connection with the sale or exchange of property, assumes any debt instrument, or

(B) acquires any property subject to any debt instrument,

in determining whether this section or section 483 applies to such debt instrument, such assumption (or such acquisition) shall not be taken into account unless the terms and conditions of such debt instrument are modified (or the nature of the transaction is changed) in connection with the assumption (or acquisition).

[Sec. 1274(d)]

(d) DETERMINATION OF APPLICABLE FEDERAL RATE.—For purposes of this section—

(1) APPLICABLE FEDERAL RATE.—

(A) IN GENERAL.—

In the case of a debt instrument with a term of:	*The applicable Federal rate is:*
Not over 3 years	The Federal short-term rate.
Over 3 years but not over 9 years	The Federal mid-term rate.
Over 9 years	The Federal long-term rate.

(B) DETERMINATION OF RATES.—During each calendar month, the Secretary shall determine the Federal short-term rate, mid-term rate, and long-term rate which shall apply during the following calendar month.

(C) FEDERAL RATE FOR ANY CALENDAR MONTH.—For purposes of this paragraph—

(i) FEDERAL SHORT-TERM RATE.—The Federal short-term rate shall be the rate determined by the Secretary based on the average market yield (during any 1-month period selected by the Secretary and ending in the calendar month in which the determination is made) on outstanding marketable obligations of the United States with remaining periods to maturity of 3 years or less.

(ii) FEDERAL MID-TERM AND LONG-TERM RATES.—The Federal mid-term and long-term rate shall be determined in accordance with the principles of clause (i).

(D) LOWER RATE PERMITTED IN CERTAIN CASES.—The Secretary may by regulations permit a rate to be used with respect to any debt instrument which is lower than the applicable Federal rate if the taxpayer establishes to the satisfaction of the Secretary that such lower rate is based on the same principles as the applicable Federal rate and is appropriate for the term of such instrument.

(2) LOWEST 3-MONTH RATE APPLICABLE TO ANY SALE OR EXCHANGE.—

(A) IN GENERAL.—In the case of any sale or exchange, the applicable Federal rate shall be the lowest 3-month rate.

(B) LOWEST 3-MONTH RATE.—For purposes of subparagraph (A), the term "lowest 3-month rate" means the lowest of the applicable Federal rates in effect for any month in the 3-calendar-month period ending with the 1st calendar month in which there is a binding contract in writing for such sale or exchange.

(3) TERM OF DEBT INSTRUMENT.—In determining the term of a debt instrument for purposes of this subsection, under regulations prescribed by the Secretary, there shall be taken into account options to renew or extend.

[Sec. 1274(e)]

(e) 110 PERCENT RATE WHERE SALE-LEASEBACK INVOLVED.—

(1) IN GENERAL.—In the case of any debt instrument to which this subsection applies, the discount rate used under subsection (b)(2)(B) or section 483(b) shall be 110 percent of the applicable Federal rate, compounded semiannually.

(2) LOWER DISCOUNT RATES SHALL NOT APPLY.—Section 1274A shall not apply to any debt instrument to which this subsection applies.

(3) DEBT INSTRUMENTS TO WHICH THIS SUBSECTION APPLIES.—This subsection shall apply to any debt instrument given in consideration for the sale or exchange of any property if, pursuant to a plan, the transferor or any related person leases a portion of such property after such sale or exchange.

»»→ Caution: Pursuant to Section 1274A(d)(2), each dollar amount in Section 1274A is adjusted for taxable years beginning after 1989 to reflect increases in the Chained Consumer Price Index. The adjusted amounts applicable to taxable years beginning in 2020 are provided in the material beginning at page ix.

[Sec. 1274A]

SEC. 1274A. SPECIAL RULES FOR CERTAIN TRANSACTIONS WHERE STATED PRINCIPAL AMOUNT DOES NOT EXCEED $2,800,000.

[Sec. 1274A(a)]

(a) LOWER DISCOUNT RATE.—In the case of any qualified debt instrument, the discount rate used for purposes of sections 483 and 1274 shall not exceed 9 percent, compounded semiannually.

[Sec. 1274A(b)]

(b) QUALIFIED DEBT INSTRUMENT DEFINED.—For purposes of this section, the term "qualified debt instrument" means any debt instrument given in consideration for the sale or exchange of property (other than new section 38 property within the meaning of section 48(b), as in effect on the day before the date of enactment of the Revenue Reconciliation Act of 1990) if the stated principal amount of such instrument does not exceed $2,800,000.

[Sec. 1274A(c)]

(c) ELECTION TO USE CASH METHOD WHERE STATED PRINCIPAL AMOUNT DOES NOT EXCEED $2,000,000.—

(1) IN GENERAL.—In the case of any cash method debt instrument—

(A) section 1274 shall not apply, and

(B) interest on such debt instrument shall be taken into account by both the borrower and the lender under the cash receipts and disbursements method of accounting.

(2) CASH METHOD DEBT INSTRUMENT.—For purposes of paragraph (1), the term "cash method debt instrument" means any qualified debt instrument if—

(A) the stated principal amount does not exceed $2,000,000,

(B) the lender does not use an accrual method of accounting and is not a dealer with respect to the property sold or exchanged,

(C) section 1274 would have applied to such instrument but for an election under this subsection, and

(D) an election under this subsection is jointly made with respect to such debt instrument by the borrower and lender.

(3) SUCCESSORS BOUND BY ELECTION.—

(A) IN GENERAL.—Except as provided in subparagraph (B), paragraph (1) shall apply to any successor to the borrower or lender with respect to a cash method debt instrument.

(B) EXCEPTION WHERE LENDER TRANSFERS DEBT INSTRUMENT TO ACCRUAL METHOD TAXPAYER.—If the lender (or any successor) transfers any cash method debt instrument to a taxpayer who uses an accrual method of accounting, this paragraph shall not apply with respect to such instrument for periods after such transfer.

(4) FAIR MARKET VALUE RULE IN POTENTIALLY ABUSIVE SITUATIONS.—In the case of any cash method debt instrument, section 483 shall be applied as if it included provisions similar to the provisions of section 1274(b)(3).

[Sec. 1274A(d)]

(d) OTHER SPECIAL RULES.—

(1) AGGREGATION RULES.—For purposes of this section—

(A) all sales or exchanges which are part of the same transaction (or a series of related transactions) shall be treated as 1 sale or exchange, and

(B) all debt instruments arising from the same transaction (or a series of related transactions) shall be treated as 1 debt instrument.

(2) ADJUSTMENT FOR INFLATION.—In the case of any debt instrument arising out of a sale or exchange during any calendar year after 1989, each dollar amount contained in the preceding provisions of this section shall be increased by an amount equal to—

(A) such amount, multiplied by

(B) the cost-of-living adjustment determined under section 1(f)(3) for the calendar year in which the taxable year begins, by substituting "calendar year 1988" for "calendar year 2016" in subparagraph (A)(ii) thereof.

Any increase under the preceding sentence shall be rounded to the nearest multiple of $100 (or, if such increase is a multiple of $50, such increase shall be increased to the nearest multiple of $100).

[Sec. 1274A(e)]

(e) REGULATIONS.—The Secretary shall prescribe such regulations as may be necessary to carry out the purposes of this subsection, including—

(1) regulations coordinating the provisions of this section with other provisions of this title,

(2) regulations necessary to prevent the avoidance of tax through the abuse of the provisions of subsection (c), and

(3) regulations relating to the treatment of transfers of cash method debt instruments.

[Sec. 1275]

SEC. 1275. OTHER DEFINITIONS AND SPECIAL RULES.

[Sec. 1275(a)]

(a) DEFINITIONS.—For purposes of this subpart—

(1) DEBT INSTRUMENT.—

(A) IN GENERAL.—Except as provided in subparagraph (B), the term "debt instrument" means a bond, debenture, note, or certificate or other evidence of indebtedness.

(B) EXCEPTION FOR CERTAIN ANNUITY CONTRACTS.—The term "debt instrument" shall not include any annuity contract to which section 72 applies and which—

(i) depends (in whole or in substantial part) on the life expectancy of 1 or more individuals, or

(ii) is issued by an insurance company subject to tax under subchapter L (or by an entity described in section 501(c) and exempt from tax under section 501(a) which would be subject to tax under subchapter L were it not so exempt)—

(I) in a transaction in which there is no consideration other than cash or another annuity contract meeting the requirements of this clause,

(II) pursuant to the exercise of an election under an insurance contract by a beneficiary thereof on the death of the insured party under such contract, or

(III) in a transaction involving a qualified pension or employee benefit plan.

(2) ISSUE DATE.—

(A) PUBLICLY OFFERED DEBT INSTRUMENTS.—In the case of any debt instrument which is publicly offered, the term "date of original issue" means the date on which the issue was first issued to the public.

(B) ISSUES NOT PUBLICLY OFFERED AND NOT ISSUED FOR PROPERTY.—In the case of any debt instrument to which section 1273(b)(2) applies, the term "date of original issue" means the date on which the debt instrument was sold by the issuer.

(C) OTHER DEBT INSTRUMENTS.—In the case of any debt instrument not described in subparagraph (A) or (B), the term "date of original issue" means the date on which the debt instrument was issued in a sale or exchange.

(3) TAX-EXEMPT OBLIGATION.—The term "tax-exempt obligation" means any obligation if—

(A) the interest on such obligation is not includible in gross income under section 103, or

(B) the interest on such obligation is exempt from tax (without regard to the identity of the holder) under any other provision of law.

(4) TREATMENT OF OBLIGATIONS DISTRIBUTED BY CORPORATIONS.—Any debt obligation of a corporation distributed by such corporation with respect to its stock shall be treated as if it had been issued by such corporation for property.

[Sec. 1275(b)]

(b) TREATMENT OF BORROWER IN THE CASE OF CERTAIN LOANS FOR PERSONAL USE.—

(1) SECTIONS 1274 AND 483 NOT TO APPLY.—In the case of the obligor under any debt instrument given in consideration for the sale or exchange of property, sections 1274 and 483 shall not apply if such property is personal use property.

(2) ORIGINAL ISSUE DISCOUNT DEDUCTED ON CASH BASIS IN CERTAIN CASES.—In the case of any debt instrument, if—

(A) such instrument—

(i) is incurred in connection with the acquisition or carrying of personal use property, and

(ii) has original issue discount (determined after the application of paragraph (1)), and

(B) the obligor under such instrument uses the cash receipts and disbursements method of accounting,

notwithstanding section 163(e), the original issue discount on such instrument shall be deductible only when paid.

(3) PERSONAL USE PROPERTY.—For purposes of this subsection, the term "personal use property" means any property substantially all of the use of which by the taxpayer is not in connection with a trade or business of the taxpayer or an activity described in section 212. The determination of whether property is described in the preceding sentence shall be made as of the time of issuance of the debt instrument.

[Sec. 1275(c)]

(c) INFORMATION REQUIREMENTS.—

(1) INFORMATION REQUIRED TO BE SET FORTH ON INSTRUMENT.—

(A) IN GENERAL.—In the case of any debt instrument having original issue discount, the Secretary may by regulations require that—

(i) the amount of the original issue discount, and

(ii) the issue date,

be set forth on such instrument.

(B) SPECIAL RULE FOR INSTRUMENTS NOT PUBLICLY OFFERED.—In the case of any issue of debt instruments not publicly offered, the regulations prescribed under subparagraph (A) shall not require the information to be set forth on the debt instrument before any disposition of such instrument by the first buyer.

(2) INFORMATION REQUIRED TO BE SUBMITTED TO SECRETARY.—In the case of any issue of publicly offered debt instruments having original issue discount, the issuer shall (at such time and in such manner as the Secretary shall by regulation prescribe) furnish the Secretary the following information:

(A) The amount of the original issue discount.

(B) The issue date.

(C) Such other information with respect to the issue as the Secretary may by regulations require.

For purposes of the preceding sentence, any person who makes a public offering of stripped bonds (or stripped coupons) shall be treated as the issuer of a publicly offered debt instrument having original issue discount.

(3) EXCEPTIONS.—This subsection shall not apply to any obligation referred to in section 1272(a)(2) (relating to exceptions from current inclusion of original issue discount).

(4) CROSS REFERENCE.—

For civil penalty for failure to meet requirements of this subsection, see section 6706.

[Sec. 1275(d)]

(d) REGULATION AUTHORITY.—The Secretary may prescribe regulations providing that where, by reason of varying rates of interest, put or call options, indefinite maturities, contingent payments, assumptions of debt instruments, or other circumstances, the tax treatment under this subpart (or section 163(e)) does not carry out the purposes of this subpart (or section 163(e)), such treatment shall be modified to the extent appropriate to carry out the purposes of this subpart (or section 163(e)).

Subpart B—Market Discount on Bonds

[Sec. 1276]

SEC. 1276. DISPOSITION GAIN REPRESENTING ACCRUED MARKET DISCOUNT TREATED AS ORDINARY INCOME.

[Sec. 1276(a)]

(a) ORDINARY INCOME.—

(1) IN GENERAL.—Except as otherwise provided in this section, gain on the disposition of any market discount bond shall be treated as ordinary income to the extent it does not exceed the accrued market discount on such bond. Such gain shall be recognized notwithstanding any other provision of this subtitle.

(2) DISPOSITIONS OTHER THAN SALES, ETC.—For purposes of paragraph (1), a person disposing of any market discount bond in any transaction other than a sale, exchange, or involuntary conversion shall be treated as realizing an amount equal to the fair market value of the bond.

(3) TREATMENT OF PARTIAL PRINCIPAL PAYMENTS.—

(A) IN GENERAL.—Any partial principal payment on a market discount bond shall be included in gross income as ordinary income to the extent such payment does not exceed the accrued market discount on such bond.

(B) ADJUSTMENT.—If subparagraph (A) applies to any partial principal payment on any market discount bond, for purposes of applying this section to any disposition of (or subsequent partial principal payment on) such bond, the amount of accrued market discount shall be reduced by the amount of such partial principal payment included in gross income under subparagraph (A).

(4) GAIN TREATED AS INTEREST FOR CERTAIN PURPOSES.—Except for purposes of sections 103, 871(a), 881, 1441, 1442, and 6049 (and such other provisions as may be specified in regulations), any amount treated as ordinary income under paragraph (1) or (3) shall be treated as interest for purposes of this title.

[Sec. 1276(b)]

(b) ACCRUED MARKET DISCOUNT.—For purposes of this section—

(1) RATABLE ACCRUAL.—Except as otherwise provided in this subsection or subsection (c), the accrued market discount on any bond shall be an amount which bears the same ratio to the market discount on such bond as—

(A) the number of days which the taxpayer held the bond, bears to

(B) the number of days after the date the taxpayer acquired the bond and up to (and including) the date of its maturity.

(2) ELECTION OF ACCRUAL ON BASIS OF CONSTANT INTEREST RATE (IN LIEU OF RATABLE ACCRUAL).—

(A) IN GENERAL.—At the election of the taxpayer with respect to any bond, the accrued market discount on such bond shall be the aggregate amount which would have been includible in the gross income of the taxpayer under section 1272(a) (determined without regard to paragraph (2) thereof) with respect to such bond for all periods during which the bond was held by the taxpayer if such bond had been—

(i) originally issued on the date on which such bond was acquired by the taxpayer,

(ii) for an issue price equal to the basis of the taxpayer in such bond immediately after its acquisition.

(B) COORDINATION WHERE BOND HAS ORIGINAL ISSUE DISCOUNT.—In the case of any bond having original issue discount, for purposes of applying subparagraph (A)—

(i) the stated redemption price at maturity of such bond shall be treated as equal to its revised issue price, and

(ii) the determination of the portion of the original issue discount which would have been includible in the gross income of the taxpayer under section 1272(a) shall be made under regulations prescribed by the Secretary.

(C) ELECTION IRREVOCABLE.—An election under subparagraph (A), once made with respect to any bond, shall be irrevocable.

(3) SPECIAL RULE WHERE PARTIAL PRINCIPAL PAYMENTS.—In the case of a bond the principal of which may be paid in 2 or more payments, the amount of accrued market discount shall be determined under regulations prescribed by the Secretary.

[Sec. 1276(c)]

(c) TREATMENT OF NONRECOGNITION TRANSACTIONS.—Under regulations prescribed by the Secretary—

(1) TRANSFERRED BASIS PROPERTY.—If a market discount bond is transferred in a nonrecognition transaction and such bond is transferred basis property in the hands of the transferee, for purposes of determining the amount of the accrued market discount with respect to the transferee—

(A) the transferee shall be treated as having acquired the bond on the date on which it was acquired by the transferor for an amount equal to the basis of the transferor, and

(B) proper adjustments shall be made for gain recognized by the transferor on such transfer (and for any original issue discount or market discount included in the gross income of the transferor).

(2) EXCHANGED BASIS PROPERTY.—If any market discount bond is disposed of by the taxpayer in a nonrecognition transaction and paragraph (1) does not apply to such transaction, any accrued market discount determined with respect to the property disposed of to the extent not theretofore treated as ordinary income under subsection (a)—

(A) shall be treated as accrued market discount with respect to the exchanged basis property received by the taxpayer in such transaction if such property is a market discount bond, and

(B) shall be treated as ordinary income on the disposition of the exchanged basis property received by the taxpayer in such exchange if such property is not a market discount bond.

(3) PARAGRAPH (1) TO APPLY TO CERTAIN DISTRIBUTIONS BY CORPORATIONS OR PARTNERSHIPS.—For purposes of paragraph (1), if the basis of any market discount bond in the hands of a transferee is determined under section 732(a), or 732(b), such property shall be treated as transferred basis property in the hands of such transferee.

[Sec. 1276(d)]

(d) SPECIAL RULES.—Under regulations prescribed by the Secretary—

(1) rules similar to the rules of subsection (b) of section 1245 shall apply for purposes of this section; except that—

(A) paragraph (1) of such subsection shall not apply,

(B) an exchange qualifying under section 354(a), 355(a), or 356(a) (determined without regard to subsection (a) of this section) shall be treated as an exchange described in paragraph (3) of such subsection, and

(C) paragraph (3) of section 1245(b) shall be applied as if it did not contain a reference to section 351, and

(2) appropriate adjustments shall be made to the basis of any property to reflect gain recognized under subsection (a).

[Sec. 1277]

SEC. 1277. DEFERRAL OF INTEREST DEDUCTION ALLOCABLE TO ACCRUED MARKET DISCOUNT.

[Sec. 1277(a)]

(a) GENERAL RULE.—Except as otherwise provided in this section, the net direct interest expense with respect to any market discount bond shall be allowed as a deduction for the taxable year only to the extent that such expense exceeds the portion of the market discount allocable to the days during the taxable year on which such bond was held by the taxpayer (as determined under the rules of section 1276(b)).

[Sec. 1277(b)]

(b) DISALLOWED DEDUCTION ALLOWED FOR LATER YEARS.—

(1) ELECTION TO TAKE INTO ACCOUNT IN LATER YEAR WHERE NET INTEREST INCOME FROM BOND.—

(A) IN GENERAL.—If—

(i) there is net interest income for any taxable year with respect to any market discount bond, and

(ii) the taxpayer makes an election under this subparagraph with respect to such bond,

any disallowed interest expense with respect to such bond shall be treated as interest paid or accrued by the taxpayer during such taxable year to the extent such disallowed interest expense does not exceed the net interest income with respect to such bond.

(B) DETERMINATION OF DISALLOWED INTEREST EXPENSE.—For purposes of subparagraph (A), the amount of the disallowed interest expense—

(i) shall be determined as of the close of the preceding taxable year, and

(ii) shall not include any amount previously taken into account under subparagraph (A).

(C) NET INTEREST INCOME.—For purposes of this paragraph, the term "net interest income" means the excess of the amount determined under paragraph (2) of subsection (c) over the amount determined under paragraph (1) of subsection (c).

(2) REMAINDER OF DISALLOWED INTEREST EXPENSE ALLOWED FOR YEAR OF DISPOSITION.—

(A) IN GENERAL.—Except as otherwise provided in this paragraph, the amount of the disallowed interest expense with respect to any market discount bond shall be treated as interest paid or accrued by the taxpayer in the taxable year in which such bond is disposed of.

(B) NONRECOGNITION TRANSACTIONS.—If any market discount bond is disposed of in a nonrecognition transaction—

(i) the disallowed interest expense with respect to such bond shall be treated as interest paid or accrued in the year of disposition only to the extent of the amount of gain recognized on such disposition, and

(ii) the disallowed interest expense with respect to such property (to the extent not so treated) shall be treated as disallowed interest expense—

(I) in the case of a transaction described in section 1276(c)(1), of the transferee with respect to the transferred basis property, or

(II) in the case of a transaction described in section 1276(c)(2), with respect to the exchanged basis property.

(C) DISALLOWED INTEREST EXPENSE REDUCED FOR AMOUNTS PREVIOUSLY TAKEN INTO ACCOUNT UNDER PARAGRAPH (1).—For purposes of this paragraph, the amount of the disallowed interest expense shall not include any amount previously taken into account under paragraph (1).

(3) DISALLOWED INTEREST EXPENSE.—For purposes of this subsection, the term "disallowed interest expense" means the aggregate amount disallowed under subsection (a) with respect to the market discount bond.

[Sec. 1277(c)]

(c) NET DIRECT INTEREST EXPENSE.—For purposes of this section, the term "net direct interest expense" means, with respect to any market discount bond, the excess (if any) of—

(1) the amount of interest paid or accrued during the taxable year on indebtedness which is incurred or continued to purchase or carry such bond, over

(2) the aggregate amount of interest (including original issue discount) includible in gross income for the taxable year with respect to such bond.

In the case of any financial institution which is a bank (as defined in section 585(a)(2)), the determination of whether interest is described in paragraph (1) shall be made under principles similar to the principles of section 291(e)(1)(B)(ii). Under rules similar to the rules of section 265(a)(5), short sale expenses shall be treated as interest for purposes of determining net direct interest expense.

[Sec. 1278]

SEC. 1278. DEFINITIONS AND SPECIAL RULES.

[Sec. 1278(a)]

(a) IN GENERAL.—For purposes of this part—

(1) MARKET DISCOUNT BOND.—

(A) IN GENERAL.—Except as provided in subparagraph (B), the term "market discount bond" means any bond having market discount.

(B) EXCEPTIONS.—The term "market discount bond" shall not include—

(i) SHORT-TERM OBLIGATIONS.—Any obligation with a fixed maturity date not exceeding 1 year from the date of issue.

(ii) UNITED STATES SAVINGS BONDS.—Any United States savings bond.

(iii) INSTALLMENT OBLIGATIONS.—Any installment obligation to which section 453B applies.

(C) SECTION 1277 NOT APPLICABLE TO TAX-EXEMPT OBLIGATIONS.—For purposes of section 1277, the term "market discount bond" shall not include any tax-exempt obligation (as defined in section 1275(a)(3)).

(D) TREATMENT OF BONDS ACQUIRED AT ORIGINAL ISSUE.—

(i) IN GENERAL.—Except as otherwise provided in this subparagraph or in regulations, the term "market discount bond" shall not include any bond acquired by the taxpayer at its original issue.

(ii) TREATMENT OF BONDS ACQUIRED FOR LESS THAN ISSUE PRICE.—Clause (i) shall not apply to any bond if—

(I) the basis of the taxpayer in such bond is determined under section 1012, and

(II) such basis is less than the issue price of such bond determined under subpart A of this part.

(iii) BONDS ACQUIRED IN CERTAIN REORGANIZATIONS.—Clause (i) shall not apply to any bond issued pursuant to a plan of reorganization (within the meaning of section 368(a)(1)) in exchange for another bond having market discount. Solely for purposes of section 1276, the preceding sentence shall not apply if such other bond was issued on or before July 18, 1984 (the date of the enactment of section 1276) and if the bond issued pursuant to such plan of reorganization has the same term and the same interest rate as such other bond had.

(iv) TREATMENT OF CERTAIN TRANSFERRED BASIS PROPERTY.—For purposes of clause (i), if the adjusted basis of any bond in the hands of the taxpayer is determined by reference to the adjusted basis of such bond in the hands of a person who acquired such bond at its original issue, such bond shall be treated as acquired by the taxpayer at its original issue.

(2) MARKET DISCOUNT.—

(A) IN GENERAL.—The term "market discount" means the excess (if any) of—

(i) the stated redemption price of the bond at maturity, over

(ii) the basis of such bond immediately after its acquisition by the taxpayer.

(B) COORDINATION WHERE BOND HAS ORIGINAL ISSUE DISCOUNT.—In the case of any bond having original issue discount, for purposes of subparagraph (A), the stated redemption price of such bond at maturity shall be treated as equal to its revised issue price.

(C) DE MINIMIS RULE.—If the market discount is less than ¼ of 1 percent of the stated redemption price of the bond at maturity multiplied by the number of complete years to maturity (after the taxpayer acquired the bond), then the market discount shall be considered to be zero.

(3) BOND.—The term "bond" means any bond, debenture, note, certificate, or other evidence of indebtedness.

(4) REVISED ISSUE PRICE.—The term "revised issue price" means the sum of—

(A) the issue price of the bond, and

(B) the aggregate amount of the original issue discount includible in the gross income of all holders for periods before the acquisition of the bond by the taxpayer (determined without regard to section 1272(a)(7)) or, in the case of a tax-exempt obligation, the aggregate amount of the original issue discount which accrued in the manner provided by section 1272(a) (determined without regard to paragraph (7) thereof) during periods before the acquisition of the bond by the taxpayer.

(5) ORIGINAL ISSUE DISCOUNT, ETC.—The terms "original issue discount", "stated redemption price at maturity", and "issue price" have the respective meanings given such terms by subpart A of this part.

[Sec. 1278(b)]

(b) ELECTION TO INCLUDE MARKET DISCOUNT CURRENTLY.—

(1) IN GENERAL.—If the taxpayer makes an election under this subsection—

(A) sections 1276 and 1277 shall not apply, and

(B) market discount on any market discount bond shall be included in the gross income of the taxpayer for the taxable years to which it is attributable (as determined under the rules of subsection (b) of section 1276).

Except for purposes of sections 103, 871(a), 881, 1441, 1442, and 6049 (and such other provisions as may be specified in regulations), any amount included in gross income under subparagraph (B) shall be treated as interest for purposes of this title.

(2) SCOPE OF ELECTION.—An election under this subsection shall apply to all market discount bonds acquired by the taxpayer on or after the 1st day of the 1st taxable year to which such election applies.

(3) PERIOD TO WHICH ELECTION APPLIES.—An election under this subsection shall apply to the taxable year for which is it made and for all subsequent taxable years, unless the taxpayer secures the consent of the Secretary to the revocation of such election.

(4) BASIS ADJUSTMENT.—The basis of any bond in the hands of the taxpayer shall be increased by the amount included in gross income pursuant to this subsection.

[Sec. 1278(c)]

(c) REGULATIONS.—The Secretary shall prescribe such regulations as may be necessary to carry out the purposes of this subpart, including regulations providing proper adjustments in the case of a bond the principal of which may be paid in 2 or more payments.

Subpart C—Discount on Short-Term Obligations

[Sec. 1281]

SEC. 1281. CURRENT INCLUSION IN INCOME OF DISCOUNT ON CERTAIN SHORT-TERM OBLIGATIONS.

[Sec. 1281(a)]

(a) GENERAL RULE.—In the case of any short-term obligation to which this section applies, for purposes of this title—

(1) there shall be included in the gross income of the holder an amount equal to the sum of the daily portions of the acquisition discount for each day during the taxable year on which such holder held such obligation, and

(2) any interest payable on the obligation (other than interest taken into account in determining the amount of the acquisition discount) shall be included in gross income as it accrues.

[Sec. 1281(b)]

(b) SHORT-TERM OBLIGATIONS TO WHICH SECTION APPLIES.—

(1) IN GENERAL.—This section shall apply to any short-term obligation which—

(A) is held by a taxpayer using an accrual method of accounting,

(B) is held primarily for sale to customers in the ordinary course of the taxpayer's trade or business,

(C) is held by a bank (as defined in section 581),

(D) is held by a regulated investment company or a common trust fund,

(E) is identified by the taxpayer under section 1256(e)(2) as being part of a hedging transaction, or

(F) is a stripped bond or stripped coupon held by the person who stripped the bond or coupon (or by any other person whose basis is determined by reference to the basis in the hands of such person).

(2) TREATMENT OF OBLIGATIONS HELD BY PASS-THRU ENTITIES.—

(A) IN GENERAL.—This section shall apply also to—

(i) any short-term obligation which is held by a pass-thru entity which is formed or availed of for purposes of avoiding the provisions of this section, and

(ii) any short-term obligation which is acquired by a pass-thru entity (not described in clause (i)) during the required accrual period.

(B) REQUIRED ACCRUAL PERIOD.—For purposes of subparagraph (A), the term "required accrual period" means the period—

(i) which begins with the first taxable year for which the ownership test of subparagraph (C) is met with respect to the pass-thru entity (or a predecessor), and

(ii) which ends with the first taxable year after the taxable year referred to in clause (i) for which the ownership test of subparagraph (C) is not met and with respect to which the Secretary consents to the termination of the required accrual period.

(C) OWNERSHIP TEST.—The ownership test of this subparagraph is met for any taxable year if, on at least 90 days during the taxable year, 20 percent or more of the value of the interests in the pass-thru entity are held by persons described in paragraph (1) or by other pass-thru entities to which subparagraph (A) applies.

(D) PASS-THRU ENTITY.—The term "pass-thru entity" means any partnership, S corporation, trust, or other pass-thru entity.

[Sec. 1281(c)]

(c) CROSS REFERENCE.—

For special rules limiting the application of this section to original issue discount in the case of nongovernmental obligations, see section 1283(c).

[Sec. 1282]

SEC. 1282. DEFERRAL OF INTEREST DEDUCTION ALLOCABLE TO ACCRUED DISCOUNT.

[Sec. 1282(a)]

(a) GENERAL RULE.—Except as otherwise provided in this section, the net direct interest expense with respect to any short-term obligation shall be allowed as a deduction for the taxable year only to the extent such expense exceeds the sum of—

(1) the daily portions of the acquisition discount for each day during the taxable year on which the taxpayer held such obligation, and

(2) the amount of any interest payable on the obligation (other than interest taken into account in determining the amount of the acquisition discount) which accrues during the taxable year while the taxpayer held such obligation (and is not included in the gross income of the taxpayer for such taxable year by reason of the taxpayer's method of accounting).

[Sec. 1282(b)]

(b) SECTION NOT TO APPLY TO OBLIGATIONS TO WHICH SECTION 1281 APPLIES.—

(1) IN GENERAL.—This section shall not apply to any short-term obligation to which section 1281 applies.

(2) ELECTION TO HAVE SECTION 1281 APPLY TO ALL OBLIGATIONS.—

(A) IN GENERAL.—A taxpayer may make an election under this paragraph to have section 1281 apply to all short-term obligations acquired by the taxpayer on or after the 1st day of the 1st taxable year to which such election applies.

(B) PERIOD TO WHICH ELECTION APPLIES.—An election under this paragraph shall apply to the taxable year for which it is made and for all subsequent taxable years, unless the taxpayer secures the consent of the Secretary to the revocation of such election.

[Sec. 1282(c)]

(c) CERTAIN RULES MADE APPLICABLE.—Rules similar to the rules of subsections (b) and (c) of section 1277 shall apply for purposes of this section.

[Sec. 1282(d)]

(d) CROSS REFERENCE.—

For special rules limiting the application of this section to original issue discount in the case of nongovernmental obligations, see section 1283(c).

[Sec. 1283]

SEC. 1283. DEFINITIONS AND SPECIAL RULES.

[Sec. 1283(a)]

(a) DEFINITIONS.—For purposes of this subpart—

(1) SHORT-TERM OBLIGATION.—

(A) IN GENERAL.—Except as provided in subparagraph (B), the term "short-term obligation" means any bond, debenture, note, certificate, or other evidence of indebtedness which has a fixed maturity date not more than 1 year from the date of issue.

(B) EXCEPTIONS FOR TAX-EXEMPT OBLIGATIONS.—The term "short-term obligation" shall not include any tax-exempt obligation (as defined in section 1275(a)(3)).

(2) ACQUISITION DISCOUNT.—The term "acquisition discount" means the excess of—

(A) the stated redemption price at maturity (as defined in section 1273), over

(B) the taxpayer's basis for the obligation.

[Sec. 1283(b)]

(b) DAILY PORTION.—For purposes of this subpart—

(1) RATABLE ACCRUAL.—Except as otherwise provided in this subsection, the daily portion of the acquisition discount is an amount equal to—

(A) the amount of such discount, divided by

(B) the number of days after the day on which the taxpayer acquired the obligation and up to (and including) the day of its maturity.

(2) ELECTION OF ACCRUAL ON BASIS OF CONSTANT INTEREST RATE (IN LIEU OF RATABLE ACCRUAL).—

(A) IN GENERAL.—At the election of the taxpayer with respect to any obligation, the daily portion of the acquisition discount for any day is the portion of the acquisition discount accruing on such day determined (under regulations prescribed by the Secretary) on the basis of—

(i) the taxpayer's yield to maturity based on the taxpayer's cost of acquiring the obligation, and

(ii) compounding daily.

(B) ELECTION IRREVOCABLE.—An election under subparagraph (A), once made with respect to any obligation, shall be irrevocable.

[Sec. 1283(c)]

(c) SPECIAL RULES FOR NONGOVERNMENTAL OBLIGATIONS.—

(1) IN GENERAL.—In the case of any short-term obligation which is not a short-term Government obligation (as defined in section 1271(a)(3)(B))—

(A) sections 1281 and 1282 shall be applied by taking into account original issue discount in lieu of acquisition discount, and

(B) appropriate adjustments shall be made in the application of subsection (b) of this section.

(2) ELECTION TO HAVE PARAGRAPH (1) NOT APPLY.—

(A) IN GENERAL.—A taxpayer may make an election under this paragraph to have paragraph (1) not apply to all obligations acquired by the taxpayer on or after the first day of the first taxable year to which such election applies.

(B) PERIOD TO WHICH ELECTION APPLIES.—An election under this paragraph shall apply to the taxable year for which it is made and for all subsequent taxable years, unless the taxpayer secures the consent of the Secretary to the revocation of such election.

[Sec. 1283(d)]

(d) OTHER SPECIAL RULES.—

(1) BASIS ADJUSTMENTS.—The basis of any short-term obligation in the hands of the holder thereof shall be increased by the amount included in his gross income pursuant to section 1281.

(2) DOUBLE INCLUSION IN INCOME NOT REQUIRED.—Section 1281 shall not require the inclusion of any amount previously includible in gross income.

(3) COORDINATION WITH OTHER PROVISIONS.—Section 454(b) and paragraphs (3) and (4) of section 1271(a) shall not apply to any short-term obligation to which section 1281 applies.

Subpart D—Miscellaneous Provisions

[Sec. 1286]

SEC. 1286. TAX TREATMENT OF STRIPPED BONDS.

[Sec. 1286(a)]

(a) INCLUSION IN INCOME AS IF BOND AND COUPONS WERE ORIGINAL ISSUE DISCOUNT BONDS.—If any person purchases a stripped bond or stripped coupon, then such bond or coupon while held by such purchaser (or by any other person whose basis is determined by reference to the basis in the hands of such purchaser) shall be treated for purposes of this part as a bond originally issued on the purchase date and having an original issue discount equal to the excess (if any) of—

(1) the stated redemption price at maturity (or, in the case of coupon, the amount payable on the due date of such coupon), over

(2) such bond's or coupon's ratable share of the purchase price.

For purposes of paragraph (2), ratable shares shall be determined on the basis of their respective fair market values on the date of purchase.

[Sec. 1286(b)]

(b) TAX TREATMENT OF PERSON STRIPPING BOND.—For purposes of this subtitle, if any person strips 1 or more coupons from a bond and disposes of the bond or such coupon—

(1) such person shall include in gross income an amount equal to the sum of—

(A) the interest accrued on such bond while held by such person and before the time such coupon or bond was disposed of (to the extent such interest has not theretofore been included in such person's gross income), and

(B) the accrued market discount on such bond determined as of the time such coupon or bond was disposed of (to the extent such discount has not theretofore been included in such person's gross income),

(2) the basis of the bond and coupons shall be increased by the amount included in gross income under paragraph (1),

(3) the basis of the bond and coupons immediately before the disposition (as adjusted pursuant to paragraph (2)) shall be allocated among the items retained by such person and the items disposed of by such person on the basis of their respective fair market values, and

(4) for purposes of subsection (a), such person shall be treated as having purchased on the date of such disposition each such item which he retains for an amount equal to the basis allocated to such item under paragraph (3).

A rule similar to the rule of paragraph (4) shall apply in the case of any person whose basis in any bond or coupon is determined by reference to the basis of the person described in the preceding sentence.

[Sec. 1286(c)]

(c) SPECIAL RULES FOR TAX-EXEMPT OBLIGATIONS.—

(1) IN GENERAL.—In the case of any tax-exempt obligation (as defined in section 1275(a)(3)) from which 1 or more coupons have been stripped—

(A) the amount of the original issue discount determined under subsection (a) with respect to any stripped bond or stripped coupon—

(i) shall be treated as original issue discount on a tax-exempt obligation to the extent such discount does not exceed the tax-exempt portion of such discount, and

(ii) shall be treated as original issue discount on an obligation which is not a tax-exempt obligation to the extent such discount exceeds the tax-exempt portion of such discount,

(B) subsection (b)(1)(A) shall not apply, and

(C) subsection (b)(2) shall be applied by increasing the basis of the bond or coupon by the sum of—

(i) the interest accrued but not paid before such bond or coupon was disposed of (and not previously reflected in basis), plus

(ii) the amount included in gross income under subsection (b)(1)(B).

(2) TAX-EXEMPT PORTION.—For purposes of paragraph (1), the tax-exempt portion of the original issue discount determined under subsection (a) is the excess of—

(A) the amount referred to in subsection (a)(1), over

(B) an issue price which would produce a yield to maturity as of the purchase date equal to the lower of—

(i) the coupon rate of interest on the obligation from which the coupons were separated, or

(ii) the yield to maturity (on the basis of the purchase price) of the stripped obligation or coupon.

The purchaser of any stripped obligation or coupon may elect to apply clause (i) by substituting "original yield to maturity of" for "coupon rate of interest on".

[Sec. 1286(d)]

(d) DEFINITIONS AND SPECIAL RULES.—For purposes of this section—

(1) BOND.—The term "bond" means a bond, debenture, note, or certificate or other evidence of indebtedness.

(2) STRIPPED BOND.—The term "stripped bond" means a bond issued at any time with interest coupons where there is a separation in ownership between the bond and any coupon which has not yet become payable.

(3) STRIPPED COUPON.—The term "stripped coupon" means any coupon relating to a stripped bond.

(4) STATED REDEMPTION PRICE AT MATURITY.—The term "stated redemption price at maturity" has the meaning given such term by section 1273(a)(2).

(5) COUPON.—The term "coupon" includes any right to receive interest on a bond (whether or not evidenced by a coupon).

(6) PURCHASE.—The term "purchase" has the meaning given such term by section 1272(d)(1).

[Sec. 1286(e)]

(e) TREATMENT OF STRIPPED INTERESTS IN BOND AND PREFERRED STOCK FUNDS, ETC.—In the case of an account or entity substantially all of the assets of which consist of bonds, preferred stock, or a combination thereof, the Secretary may by regulations provide that rules similar to the rules of this section and section 305(e), as appropriate, shall apply to interests in such account or entity to which (but for this subsection) this section or section 305(e), as the case may be, would not apply.

[Sec. 1286(f)]

(f) REGULATION AUTHORITY.—The Secretary may prescribe regulations providing that where, by reason of varying rates of interest, put or call options, or other circumstances, the tax treatment under this section does not accurately reflect the income of the holder of a stripped coupon or stripped bond, or of the person disposing of such bond or coupon, as the case may be, for any period, such treatment shall be modified to require that the proper amount of income be included for such period.

[Sec. 1288]

SEC. 1288. TREATMENT OF ORIGINAL ISSUE DISCOUNT ON TAX-EXEMPT OBLIGATIONS.

[Sec. 1288(a)]

(a) GENERAL RULE.—Original issue discount on any tax-exempt obligation shall be treated as accruing—

(1) for purposes of section 163, in the manner provided by section 1272(a) (determined without regard to paragraph (7) thereof), and

(2) for purposes of determining the adjusted basis of the holder, in the manner provided by section 1272(a) (determined with regard to paragraph (7) thereof).

[Sec. 1288(b)]

(b) DEFINITIONS AND SPECIAL RULES.—For purposes of this section—

(1) ORIGINAL ISSUE DISCOUNT.—The term "original issue discount" has the meaning given to such term by section 1273(a) without regard to paragraph (3) thereof. In applying section 483 or 1274, under regulations prescribed by the Secretary, appropriate adjustments shall be made to the applicable Federal rate to take into account the tax exemption for interest on the obligation.

(2) TAX-EXEMPT OBLIGATION.—The term "tax-exempt obligation" has the meaning given to such term by section 1275(a)(3).

(3) SHORT-TERM OBLIGATION.—In applying this section to obligations with maturity of 1 year or less, rules similar to the rules of section 1283(b) shall apply.

SUBCHAPTER Q—READJUSTMENT OF TAX BETWEEN YEARS AND SPECIAL LIMITATIONS

PART V—CLAIM OF RIGHT

[Sec. 1341]

SEC. 1341. COMPUTATION OF TAX WHERE TAXPAYER RESTORES SUBSTANTIAL AMOUNT HELD UNDER CLAIM OF RIGHT.

[Sec. 1341(a)]

(a) GENERAL RULE.—If—

(1) an item was included in gross income for a prior taxable year (or years) because it appeared that the taxpayer had an unrestricted right to such item;

(2) a deduction is allowable for the taxable year because it was established after the close of such prior taxable year (or years) that the taxpayer did not have an unrestricted right to such item or to a portion of such item; and

(3) the amount of such deduction exceeds $3,000,

then the tax imposed by this chapter for the taxable year shall be the lesser of the following:

(4) the tax for the taxable year computed with such deduction; or

(5) an amount equal to—

(A) the tax for the taxable year computed without such deduction, minus

(B) the decrease in tax under this chapter (or the corresponding provisions of prior revenue laws) for the prior taxable year (or years) which would result solely from the exclusion of such item (or portion thereof) from gross income for such prior taxable year (or years).

For purposes of paragraph (5)(B), the corresponding provisions of the Internal Revenue Code of 1939 shall be chapter 1 of such code (other than subchapter E, relating to self-employment income) and subchapter E of chapter 2 of such code.

[Sec. 1341(b)]

(b) SPECIAL RULES.—

(1) If the decrease in tax ascertained under subsection (a)(5)(B) exceeds the tax imposed by this chapter for the taxable year (computed without the deduction) such excess shall be considered to be a payment of tax on the last day prescribed by law for the payment of tax for the taxable year, and shall be refunded or credited in the same manner as if it were an overpayment for such taxable year.

(2) Subsection (a) does not apply to any deduction allowable with respect to an item which was included in gross income by reason of the sale or other disposition of stock in trade of the taxpayer (or other property of a kind which would properly have been included in the inventory of the taxpayer if on hand at the close of the prior taxable year) or property held by the taxpayer primarily for sale to customers in the ordinary course of his trade or business. This paragraph shall not apply if the deduction arises out of refunds or repayments with respect to rates made by a regulated public utility (as defined in section 7701(a)(33) without regard to the limitation contained in the last two sentences thereof) if such refunds or

repayments are required to be made by the Government, political subdivision, agency, or instrumentality referred to in such section, or by an order of a court, or are made in settlement of litigation or under threat or imminence of litigation.

(3) If the tax imposed by this chapter for the taxable year is the amount determined under subsection (a)(5), then the deduction referred to in subsection (a)(2) shall not be taken into account for any purpose of this subtitle other than this section.

(4) For purposes of determining whether paragraph (4) or paragraph (5) of subsection (a) applies—

(A) in any case where the deduction referred to in paragraph (4) of subsection (a) results in a net operating loss, such loss shall, for purposes of computing the tax for the taxable year under such paragraph (4), be carried back to the same extent and in the same manner as is provided under section 172; and

(B) in any case where the exclusion referred to in paragraph (5)(B) of subsection (a) results in a net operating loss or capital loss for the prior taxable year (or years), such loss shall, for purposes of computing the decrease in tax for the prior taxable year (or years) under such paragraph (5)(B), be carried back and carried over to the same extent and in the same manner as is provided under section 172 or section 1212, except that no carryover beyond the taxable year shall be taken into account.

(5) For purposes of this chapter, the net operating loss described in paragraph (4)(A) of this subsection, or the net operating loss or capital loss described in paragraph (4)(B) of this subsection, as the case may be, shall (after the application of paragraph (4) or (5)(B) of subsection (a) for the taxable year) be taken into account under section 172 or 1212 for taxable years after the taxable year to the same extent and in the same manner as—

(A) a net operating loss sustained for the taxable year, if paragraph (4) of subsection (a) applied, or

(B) a net operating loss or capital loss sustained for the prior taxable year (or years), if paragraph (5)(B) of subsection (a) applied.

SUBCHAPTER S—TAX TREATMENT OF S CORPORATIONS AND THEIR SHAREHOLDERS

PART I—IN GENERAL

[Sec. 1361]

SEC. 1361. S CORPORATION DEFINED.

[Sec. 1361(a)]

(a) S CORPORATION DEFINED.—

(1) IN GENERAL.—For purposes of this title, the term "S corporation" means, with respect to any taxable year, a small business corporation for which an election under section 1362(a) is in effect for such year.

(2) C CORPORATION.—For purposes of this title, the term "C corporation" means, with respect to any taxable year, a corporation which is not an S corporation for such year.

[Sec. 1361(b)]

(b) SMALL BUSINESS CORPORATION.—

(1) IN GENERAL.—For purposes of this subchapter, the term "small business corporation" means a domestic corporation which is not an ineligible corporation and which does not—

(A) have more than 100 shareholders,

(B) have as a shareholder a person (other than an estate, a trust described in subsection (c)(2), or an organization described in subsection (c)(6)) who is not an individual,

(C) have a nonresident alien as a shareholder, and

(D) have more than 1 class of stock.

(2) INELIGIBLE CORPORATION DEFINED.—For purposes of paragraph (1), the term "ineligible corporation" means any corporation which is—

(A) a financial institution which uses the reserve method of accounting for bad debts described in section 585,

(B) an insurance company subject to tax under subchapter L, or

(C) a DISC or former DISC.

(3) TREATMENT OF CERTAIN WHOLLY OWNED SUBSIDIARIES.—

(A) IN GENERAL.—Except as provided in regulations prescribed by the Secretary, for purposes of this title—

(i) a corporation which is a qualified subchapter S subsidiary shall not be treated as a separate corporation, and

(ii) all assets, liabilities, and items of income, deduction, and credit of a qualified subchapter S subsidiary shall be treated as assets, liabilities, and such items (as the case may be) of the S corporation.

(B) QUALIFIED SUBCHAPTER S SUBSIDIARY.—For purposes of this paragraph, the term "qualified subchapter S subsidiary" means any domestic corporation which is not an ineligible corporation (as defined in paragraph (2)), if—

(i) 100 percent of the stock of such corporation is held by the S corporation, and

(ii) the S corporation elects to treat such corporation as a qualified subchapter S subsidiary.

(C) TREATMENT OF TERMINATIONS OF QUALIFIED SUBCHAPTER S SUBSIDIARY STATUS.—

(i) IN GENERAL.—For purposes of this title, if any corporation which was a qualified subchapter S subsidiary ceases to meet the requirements of subparagraph (B), such corporation shall be treated as a new corporation acquiring all of its assets (and assuming all of its liabilities) immediately before such cessation from the S corporation in exchange for its stock.

(ii) TERMINATION BY REASON OF SALE OF STOCK.—If the failure to meet the requirements of subparagraph (B) is by reason of the sale of stock of a corporation which is a qualified subchapter S subsidiary, the sale of such stock shall be treated as if—

(I) the sale were a sale of an undivided interest in the assets of such corporation (based on the percentage of the corporation's stock sold), and

(II) the sale were followed by an acquisition by such corporation of all of its assets (and the assumption by such corporation of all of its liabilities) in a transaction to which section 351 applies.

(D) ELECTION AFTER TERMINATION.—If a corporation's status as a qualified subchapter S subsidiary terminates, such corporation (and any successor corporation) shall not be eligible to make—

(i) an election under subparagraph (B)(ii) to be treated as a qualified subchapter S subsidiary, or

(ii) an election under section 1362(a) to be treated as an S corporation,

before its 5th taxable year which begins after the 1st taxable year for which such termination was effective, unless the Secretary consents to such election.

(E) INFORMATION RETURNS.—Except to the extent provided by the Secretary, this paragraph shall not apply to part III of subchapter A of chapter 61 (relating to information returns).

[Sec. 1361(c)]

(c) SPECIAL RULES FOR APPLYING SUBSECTION (b).—

(1) MEMBERS OF A FAMILY TREATED AS 1 SHAREHOLDER.—

(A) IN GENERAL.—For purposes of subsection (b)(1)(A), there shall be treated as one shareholder—

(i) a husband and wife (and their estates), and

(ii) all members of a family (and their estates).

(B) MEMBERS OF A FAMILY.—For purposes of this paragraph—

(i) IN GENERAL.—The term "members of a family" means a common ancestor, any lineal descendant of such common ancestor, and any spouse or former spouse of such common ancestor or any such lineal descendant.

(ii) COMMON ANCESTOR.—An individual shall not be considered to be a common ancestor if, on the applicable date, the individual is more than 6 generations removed from the youngest generation of shareholders who would (but for this subparagraph) be members of the family. For purposes of the preceding sentence, a spouse (or former spouse) shall be treated as being of the same generation as the individual to whom such spouse is (or was) married.

(iii) APPLICABLE DATE.—The term "applicable date" means the latest of—

(I) the date the election under section 1362(a) is made,

(II) the earliest date that an individual described in clause (i) holds stock in the S corporation, or

(III) October 22, 2004.

(C) EFFECT OF ADOPTION, ETC.—Any legally adopted child of an individual, any child who is lawfully placed with an individual for legal adoption by the individual, and any eligible foster child of an individual (within the meaning of section 152(f)(1)(C)), shall be treated as a child of such individual by blood.

(2) CERTAIN TRUSTS PERMITTED AS SHAREHOLDERS.—

(A) IN GENERAL.—For purposes of subsection (b)(1)(B), the following trusts may be shareholders:

(i) A trust all of which is treated (under subpart E of part I of subchapter J of this chapter) as owned by an individual who is a citizen or resident of the United States.

(ii) A trust which was described in clause (i) immediately before the death of the deemed owner and which continues in existence after such death, but only for the 2-year period beginning on the day of the deemed owner's death.

(iii) A trust with respect to stock transferred to it pursuant to the terms of a will, but only for the 2-year period beginning on the day on which such stock is transferred to it.

(iv) A trust created primarily to exercise the voting power of stock transferred to it.

(v) An electing small business trust.

(vi) In the case of a corporation which is a bank (as defined in section 581) or a depository institution holding company (as defined in section 3(w)(1) of the Federal Deposit Insurance Act (12 U.S.C. 1813(w)(1)), a trust which constitutes an individual retirement account under section 408(a), including one designated as a Roth IRA under section 408A, but only to the extent of the stock held by such trust in such bank or company as of the date of the enactment of this clause.

This subparagraph shall not apply to any foreign trust.

(B) TREATMENT AS SHAREHOLDERS.—For purposes of subsection (b)(1)—

(i) In the case of a trust described in clause (i) of subparagraph (A), the deemed owner shall be treated as the shareholder.

(ii) In the case of a trust described in clause (ii) of subparagraph (A), the estate of the deemed owner shall be treated as the shareholder.

(iii) In the case of a trust described in clause (iii) of subparagraph (A), the estate of the testator shall be treated as the shareholder.

(iv) In the case of a trust described in clause (iv) of subparagraph (A), each beneficiary of the trust shall be treated as the shareholder.

(v) In the case of a trust described in clause (v) of subparagraph (A), each potential current beneficiary of such trust shall be treated as a shareholder; except that, if for any period there is no potential current beneficiary of such trust, such trust shall be treated as the shareholder during such period. This clause shall not apply for purposes of subsection (b) (1) (C).

(vi) In the case of a trust described in clause (vi) of subparagraph (A), the individual for whose benefit the trust was created shall be treated as a shareholder.

(3) ESTATE OF INDIVIDUAL IN BANKRUPTCY MAY BE SHAREHOLDER.—For purposes of subsection (b) (1) (B), the term "estate" includes the estate of an individual in a case under title 11 of the United States Code.

(4) DIFFERENCES IN COMMON STOCK VOTING RIGHTS DISREGARDED.—For purposes of subsection (b) (1) (D), a corporation shall not be treated as having more than 1 class of stock solely because there are differences in voting rights among the shares of common stock.

(5) STRAIGHT DEBT SAFE HARBOR.—

(A) IN GENERAL.—For purposes of subsection (b) (1) (D), straight debt shall not be treated as a second class of stock.

(B) STRAIGHT DEBT DEFINED.—For purposes of this paragraph, the term "straight debt" means any written unconditional promise to pay on demand or on a specified date a sum certain in money if—

(i) the interest rate (and interest payment dates) are not contingent on profits, the borrower's discretion, or similar factors,

(ii) there is no convertibility (directly or indirectly) into stock, and

(iii) the creditor is an individual (other than a nonresident alien), an estate, a trust described in paragraph (2), or a person which is actively and regularly engaged in the business of lending money.

(C) REGULATIONS.—The Secretary shall prescribe such regulations as may be necessary or appropriate to provide for the proper treatment of straight debt under this subchapter and for the coordination of such treatment with other provisions of this title.

(6) CERTAIN EXEMPT ORGANIZATIONS PERMITTED AS SHAREHOLDERS.—For purposes of subsection (b) (1) (B), an organization which is—

(A) described in section 401 (a) or 501 (c) (3), and

(B) exempt from taxation under section 501 (a),

may be a shareholder in an S corporation.

[Sec. 1361(d)]

(d) SPECIAL RULE FOR QUALIFIED SUBCHAPTER S TRUST.—

(1) IN GENERAL.—In the case of a qualified subchapter S trust with respect to which a beneficiary makes an election under paragraph (2)—

(A) such trust shall be treated as a trust described in subsection (c) (2) (A) (i),

(B) for purposes of section 678 (a), the beneficiary of such trust shall be treated as the owner of that portion of the trust which consists of stock in an S corporation with respect to which the election under paragraph (2) is made, and

(C) for purposes of applying sections 465 and 469 to the beneficiary of the trust, the disposition of the S corporation stock by the trust shall be treated as a disposition by such beneficiary.

(2) ELECTION.—

(A) IN GENERAL.—A beneficiary of a qualified subchapter S trust (or his legal representative) may elect to have this subsection apply.

(B) MANNER AND TIME OF ELECTION.—

(i) SEPARATE ELECTION WITH RESPECT TO EACH CORPORATION.—An election under this paragraph shall be made separately with respect to each corporation the stock of which is held by the trust.

(ii) ELECTIONS WITH RESPECT TO SUCCESSIVE INCOME BENEFICIARIES.—If there is an election under this paragraph with respect to any beneficiary, an election under this paragraph shall be treated as made by each successive beneficiary unless such beneficiary affirmatively refuses to consent to such election.

(iii) TIME, MANNER, AND FORM OF ELECTION.—Any election, or refusal, under this paragraph shall be made in such manner and form, and at such time, as the Secretary may prescribe.

(C) ELECTION IRREVOCABLE.—An election under this paragraph, once made, may be revoked only with the consent of the Secretary.

(D) GRACE PERIOD.—An election under this paragraph shall be effective up to 15 days and 2 months before the date of the election.

(3) QUALIFIED SUBCHAPTER S TRUST.—For purposes of this subsection, the term "qualified subchapter S trust" means a trust—

(A) the terms of which require that—

(i) during the life of the current income beneficiary, there shall be only 1 income beneficiary of the trust,

(ii) any corpus distributed during the life of the current income beneficiary may be distributed only to such beneficiary,

(iii) the income interest of the current income beneficiary in the trust shall terminate on the earlier of such beneficiary's death or the termination of the trust, and

(iv) upon the termination of the trust during the life of the current income beneficiary, the trust shall distribute all of its assets to such beneficiary, and

(B) all of the income (within the meaning of section 643(b)) of which is distributed (or required to be distributed) currently to 1 individual who is a citizen or resident of the United States.

A substantially separate and independent share of a trust within the meaning of 663(c) shall be treated as a separate trust for purposes of this subsection and subsection (c).

(4) TRUST CEASING TO BE QUALIFIED.—

(A) FAILURE TO MEET REQUIREMENTS OF PARAGRAPH (3)(A).—If a qualified subchapter S trust ceases to meet any requirement of paragraph (3)(A), the provisions of this subsection shall not apply to such trust as of the date it ceases to meet such requirement.

(B) FAILURE TO MEET REQUIREMENTS OF PARAGRAPH (3)(B).—If any qualified subchapter S trust ceases to meet any requirement of paragraph (3)(B) but continues to meet the requirements of paragraph (3)(A), the provisions of this subsection shall not apply to such trust as of the first day of the first taxable year beginning after the first taxable year for which it failed to meet the requirements of paragraph (3)(B).

[Sec. 1361(e)]

(e) ELECTING SMALL BUSINESS TRUST DEFINED.—

(1) ELECTING SMALL BUSINESS TRUST.—For purposes of this section—

(A) IN GENERAL.—Except as provided in subparagraph (B), the term "electing small business trust" means any trust if—

(i) such trust does not have as a beneficiary any person other than (I) an individual, (II) an estate, (III) an organization described in paragraph (2), (3), (4), or (5) of section 170(c), or (IV) an organization described in section 170(c)(1) which holds a contingent interest in such trust and is not a potential current beneficiary,

(ii) no interest in such trust was acquired by purchase, and

(iii) an election under this subsection applies to such trust.

(B) CERTAIN TRUSTS NOT ELIGIBLE.—The term "electing small business trust" shall not include—

(i) any qualified subchapter S trust (as defined in subsection (d)(3)) if an election under subsection (d)(2) applies to any corporation the stock of which is held by such trust,

(ii) any trust exempt from tax under this subtitle, and

(iii) any charitable remainder annuity trust or charitable remainder unitrust (as defined in section 664(d)).

(C) PURCHASE.—For purposes of subparagraph (A), the term "purchase" means any acquisition if the basis of the property acquired is determined under section 1012.

(2) POTENTIAL CURRENT BENEFICIARY.—For purposes of this section, the term "potential current beneficiary" means, with respect to any period, any person who at any time during such period is entitled to, or at the discretion of any person may receive, a distribution from the principal or income of the trust (determined without regard to any power of appointment to the extent such power remains unexercised at the end of such period). If a trust disposes of all of the stock which it holds in an S corporation, then, with respect to such corporation, the term "potential current beneficiary" does not include any person who first met the requirements of the preceding sentence during the 1-year period ending on the date of such disposition.

(3) ELECTION.—An election under this subsection shall be made by the trustee. Any such election shall apply to the taxable year of the trust for which made and all subsequent taxable years of such trust unless revoked with the consent of the Secretary.

(4) CROSS REFERENCE.—

For special treatment of electing small business trusts, see section 641(c).

* * *

[Sec. 1362]

SEC. 1362. ELECTION; REVOCATION; TERMINATION.

[Sec. 1362(a)]

(a) ELECTION.—

(1) IN GENERAL.—Except as provided in subsection (g), a small business corporation may elect, in accordance with the provisions of this section, to be an S corporation.

(2) ALL SHAREHOLDERS MUST CONSENT TO ELECTION.—An election under this subsection shall be valid only if all persons who are shareholders in such corporation on the day on which such election is made consent to such election.

[Sec. 1362(b)]

(b) WHEN MADE.—

(1) IN GENERAL.—An election under subsection (a) may be made by a small business corporation for any taxable year—

(A) at any time during the preceding taxable year, or

(B) at any time during the taxable year and on or before the 15th day of the 3d month of the taxable year.

(2) CERTAIN ELECTIONS MADE DURING 1ST 2½ MONTHS TREATED AS MADE FOR NEXT TAXABLE YEAR.—If—

(A) an election under subsection (a) is made for any taxable year during such year and on or before the 15th day of the 3d month of such year, but

(B) either—

(i) on 1 or more days in such taxable year before the day on which the election was made the corporation did not meet the requirements of subsection (b) of section 1361, or

(ii) 1 or more of the persons who held stock in the corporation during such taxable year and before the election was made did not consent to the election,

then such election shall be treated as made for the following taxable year.

(3) ELECTION MADE AFTER 1ST 2½ MONTHS TREATED AS MADE FOR FOLLOWING TAXABLE YEAR.—If—

(A) a small business corporation makes an election under subsection (a) for any taxable year, and

(B) such election is made after the 15th day of the 3d month of the taxable year and on or before the 15th day of the 3rd month of the following taxable year,

then such election shall be treated as made for the following taxable year.

(4) TAXABLE YEARS OF 2½ MONTHS OR LESS.—For purposes of this subsection, an election for a taxable year made not later than 2 months and 15 days after the first day of the taxable year shall be treated as timely made during such year.

(5) AUTHORITY TO TREAT LATE ELECTIONS, ETC., AS TIMELY.—If—

(A) an election under subsection (a) is made for any taxable year (determined without regard to paragraph (3)) after the date prescribed by this subsection for making such election for such taxable year or no such election is made for any taxable year, and

(B) the Secretary determines that there was reasonable cause for the failure to timely make such election,

the Secretary may treat such an election as timely made for such taxable year (and paragraph (3) shall not apply).

[Sec. 1362(c)]

(c) YEARS FOR WHICH EFFECTIVE.—An election under subsection (a) shall be effective for the taxable year of the corporation for which it is made and for all succeeding taxable years of the corporation, until such election is terminated under subsection (d).

[Sec. 1362(d)]

(d) TERMINATION.—

(1) BY REVOCATION.—

(A) IN GENERAL.—An election under subsection (a) may be terminated by revocation.

(B) MORE THAN ONE-HALF OF SHARES MUST CONSENT TO REVOCATION.—An election may be revoked only if shareholders holding more than one-half of the shares of stock of the corporation on the day on which the revocation is made consent to the revocation.

(C) WHEN EFFECTIVE.—Except as provided in subparagraph (D)—

(i) a revocation made during the taxable year and on or before the 15th day of the 3d month thereof shall be effective on the 1st day of such taxable year, and

(ii) a revocation made during the taxable year but after such 15th day shall be effective on the 1st day of the following taxable year.

(D) REVOCATION MAY SPECIFY PROSPECTIVE DATE.—If the revocation specifies a date for revocation which is on or after the day on which the revocation is made, the revocation shall be effective on and after the date so specified.

(2) BY CORPORATION CEASING TO BE SMALL BUSINESS CORPORATION.—

(A) IN GENERAL.—An election under subsection (a) shall be terminated whenever (at any time on or after the 1st day of the 1st taxable year for which the corporation is an S corporation) such corporation ceases to be a small business corporation.

(B) WHEN EFFECTIVE.—Any termination under this paragraph shall be effective on and after the date of cessation.

(3) WHERE PASSIVE INVESTMENT INCOME EXCEEDS 25 PERCENT OF GROSS RECEIPTS FOR 3 CONSECUTIVE TAXABLE YEARS AND CORPORATION HAS ACCUMULATED EARNINGS AND PROFITS.—

(A) TERMINATION.—

(i) IN GENERAL.—An election under subsection (a) shall be terminated whenever the corporation—

(I) has accumulated earnings and profits at the close of each of 3 consecutive taxable years, and

(II) has gross receipts for each of such taxable years more than 25 percent of which are passive investment income.

(ii) WHEN EFFECTIVE.—Any termination under this paragraph shall be effective on and after the first day of the first taxable year beginning after the third consecutive taxable year referred to in clause (i).

(iii) YEARS TAKEN INTO ACCOUNT.—A prior taxable year shall not be taken into account under clause (i) unless the corporation was an S corporation for such taxable year.

(B) GROSS RECEIPTS FROM THE SALES OF CERTAIN ASSETS.—For purposes of this paragraph—

(i) in the case of dispositions of capital assets (other than stock and securities), gross receipts from such dispositions shall be taken into account only to the extent of the capital gain net income therefrom, and

(ii) in the case of sales or exchanges of stock or securities, gross receipts shall be taken into account only to the extent of the gains therefrom.

(C) PASSIVE INVESTMENT INCOME DEFINED.—

(i) IN GENERAL.—Except as otherwise provided in this subparagraph, the term "passive investment income" means gross receipts derived from royalties, rents, dividends, interest, and annuities.

(ii) EXCEPTION FOR INTEREST ON NOTES FROM SALES OF INVENTORY.—The term "passive investment income" shall not include interest on any obligation acquired in the ordinary course of the corporation's trade or business from its sale of property described in section 1221(a)(1).

(iii) TREATMENT OF CERTAIN LENDING OR FINANCE COMPANIES.—If the S corporation meets the requirements of section 542(c)(6) for the taxable year, the term "passive investment income" shall not include gross receipts for the taxable year which are derived directly from the active and regular conduct of a lending or finance business (as defined in section 542(d)(1)).

(iv) TREATMENT OF CERTAIN DIVIDENDS.—If an S corporation holds stock in a C corporation meeting the requirements of section 1504(a)(2), the term "passive investment income" shall not include dividends from such C corporation to the extent such dividends are attributable to the earnings and profits of such C corporation derived from the active conduct of a trade or business.

* * *

[Sec. 1362(e)]

(e) TREATMENT OF S TERMINATION YEAR.—

(1) IN GENERAL.—In the case of an S termination year, for purposes of this title—

(A) S SHORT YEAR.—The portion of such year ending before the 1st day for which the termination is effective shall be treated as a short taxable year for which the corporation is an S corporation.

(B) C SHORT YEAR.—The portion of such year beginning on such 1st day shall be treated as a short taxable year for which the corporation is a C corporation.

(2) PRO RATA ALLOCATION.—Except as provided in paragraph (3) and subparagraphs (C) and (D) of paragraph (6), the determination of which items are to be taken into account for each of the short taxable years referred to in paragraph (1) shall be made—

(A) first by determining for the S termination year—

(i) the amount of each of the items of income, loss, deduction, or credit described in section 1366(a)(1)(A), and

(ii) the amount of the nonseparately computed income or loss, and

(B) then by assigning an equal portion of each amount determined under subparagraph (A) to each day of the S termination year.

(3) ELECTION TO HAVE ITEMS ASSIGNED TO EACH SHORT TAXABLE YEAR UNDER NORMAL TAX ACCOUNTING RULES.—

(A) IN GENERAL.—A corporation may elect to have paragraph (2) not apply.

(B) SHAREHOLDERS MUST CONSENT TO ELECTION.—An election under this subsection shall be valid only if all persons who are shareholders in the corporation at any time during the S short year and all persons who are shareholders in the corporation on the first day of the C short year consent to such election.

(4) S TERMINATION YEAR.—For purposes of this subsection, the term "S termination year" means any taxable year of a corporation (determined without regard to this subsection) in which a termination of an election made under subsection (a) takes effect (other than on the 1st day thereof).

(5) TAX FOR C SHORT YEAR DETERMINED ON ANNUALIZED BASIS.—

(A) IN GENERAL.—The taxable income for the short year described in subparagraph (B) of paragraph (1) shall be placed on an annual basis by multiplying the taxable income for such short year by the number of days in the S termination year and by dividing the result by the number of days in the short year. The tax shall be the same part of the tax computed on the annual basis as the number of days in such short year is of the number of days in the S termination year.

(B) SECTION 443(d)(2) TO APPLY.—Subsection (d) of section 443 shall apply to the short taxable year described in subparagraph (B) of paragraph (1).

(6) OTHER SPECIAL RULES.—For purposes of this title—

(A) SHORT YEARS TREATED AS 1 YEAR FOR CARRYOVER PURPOSES.—The short taxable year described in subparagraph (A) of paragraph (1) shall not be taken into account for purposes of determining the number of taxable years to which any item may be carried back or carried forward by the corporation.

(B) DUE DATE FOR S YEAR.—The due date for filing the return for the short taxable year described in subparagraph (A) of paragraph (1) shall be the same as the due date for filing the return for the short taxable year described in subparagraph (B) of paragraph (1) (including extensions thereof).

(C) PARAGRAPH (2) NOT TO APPLY TO ITEMS RESULTING FROM SECTION 338.—Paragraph (2) shall not apply with respect to any item resulting from the application of section 338.

(D) PRO RATA ALLOCATION FOR S TERMINATION YEAR NOT TO APPLY IF 50-PERCENT CHANGE IN OWNERSHIP.—Paragraph (2) shall not apply to an S termination year if there is a sale or exchange of 50 percent or more of the stock in such corporation during such year.

[Sec. 1362(f)]

(f) INADVERTENT INVALID ELECTIONS OR TERMINATIONS.—If—

(1) an election under subsection (a) or section 1361(b)(3)(B)(ii) by any corporation—

(A) was not effective for the taxable year for which made (determined without regard to subsection (b)(2)) by reason of a failure to meet the requirements of section 1361(b) or to obtain shareholder consents, or

(B) was terminated under paragraph (2) or (3) of subsection (d) or section 1361(b)(3)(C),

(2) the Secretary determines that the circumstances resulting in such ineffectiveness or termination were inadvertent,

(3) no later than a reasonable period of time after discovery of the circumstances resulting in such ineffectiveness or termination, steps were taken—

(A) so that the corporation for which the election was made or the termination occurred is a small business corporation or a qualified subchapter S subsidiary, as the case may be, or

(B) to acquire the required shareholder consents, and

(4) the corporation for which the election was made or the termination occurred, and each person who was a shareholder in such corporation at any time during the period

specified pursuant to this subsection, agrees to make such adjustments (consistent with the treatment of such corporation as an S corporation or a qualified subchapter S subsidiary, as the case may be) as may be required by the Secretary with respect to such period,

then, notwithstanding the circumstances resulting in such ineffectiveness or termination, such corporation shall be treated as an S corporation or a qualified subchapter S subsidiary, as the case may be, during the period specified by the Secretary.

[Sec. 1362(g)]

(g) ELECTION AFTER TERMINATION.—If a small business corporation has made an election under subsection (a) and if such election has been terminated under subsection (d), such corporation (and any successor corporation) shall not be eligible to make an election under subsection (a) for any taxable year before its 5th taxable year which begins after the 1st taxable year for which such termination is effective, unless the Secretary consents to such election.

[Sec. 1363]

SEC. 1363. EFFECT OF ELECTION ON CORPORATION.

[Sec. 1363(a)]

(a) GENERAL RULE.—Except as otherwise provided in this subchapter, an S corporation shall not be subject to the taxes imposed by this chapter.

[Sec. 1363(b)]

(b) COMPUTATION OF CORPORATION'S TAXABLE INCOME.—The taxable income of an S corporation shall be computed in the same manner as in the case of an individual, except that—

(1) the items described in section 1366(a)(1)(A) shall be separately stated,

(2) the deductions referred to in section 703(a)(2) shall not be allowed to the corporation,

(3) section 248 shall apply, and

(4) section 291 shall apply if the S corporation (or any predecessor) was a C corporation for any of the 3 immediately preceding taxable years.

[Sec. 1363(c)]

(c) ELECTIONS OF THE S CORPORATION.—

(1) IN GENERAL.—Except as provided in paragraph (2), any election affecting the computation of items derived from an S corporation shall be made by the corporation.

(2) EXCEPTIONS.—In the case of an S corporation, elections under the following provisions shall be made by each shareholder separately—

(A) section 617 (relating to deduction and recapture of certain mining exploration expenditures), and

(B) section 901 (relating to taxes of foreign countries and possessions of the United States).

* * *

PART II—TAX TREATMENT OF SHAREHOLDERS

[Sec. 1366]

SEC. 1366. PASS-THRU OF ITEMS TO SHAREHOLDERS.

[Sec. 1366(a)]

(a) DETERMINATION OF SHAREHOLDER'S TAX LIABILITY.—

(1) IN GENERAL.—In determining the tax under this chapter of a shareholder for the shareholder's taxable year in which the taxable year of the S corporation ends (or for the final taxable year of a shareholder who dies, or of a trust or estate which terminates, before the end of the corporation's taxable year), there shall be taken into account the shareholder's pro rata share of the corporation's—

(A) items of income (including tax-exempt income), loss, deduction, or credit the separate treatment of which could affect the liability for tax of any shareholder, and

(B) nonseparately computed income or loss.

For purposes of the preceding sentence, the items referred to in subparagraph (A) shall include amounts described in paragraph (4) or (6) of section 702(a).

(2) NONSEPARATELY COMPUTED INCOME OR LOSS DEFINED.—For purposes of this subchapter, the term "nonseparately computed income or loss" means gross income minus the deductions allowed to the corporation under this chapter, determined by excluding all items described in paragraph (1)(A).

[Sec. 1366(b)]

(b) CHARACTER PASSED THRU.—The character of any item included in a shareholder's pro rata share under paragraph (1) of subsection (a) shall be determined as if such item were realized directly from the source from which realized by the corporation, or incurred in the same manner as incurred by the corporation.

[Sec. 1366(c)]

(c) GROSS INCOME OF A SHAREHOLDER.—In any case where it is necessary to determine the gross income of a shareholder for purposes of this title, such gross income shall include the shareholder's pro rata share of the gross income of the corporation.

[Sec. 1366(d)]

(d) SPECIAL RULES FOR LOSSES AND DEDUCTIONS.—

(1) CANNOT EXCEED SHAREHOLDER'S BASIS IN STOCK AND DEBT.—The aggregate amount of losses and deductions taken into account by a shareholder under subsection (a) for any taxable year shall not exceed the sum of—

(A) the adjusted basis of the shareholder's stock in the S corporation (determined with regard to paragraphs (1) and (2)(A) of section 1367(a) for the taxable year), and

(B) the shareholder's adjusted basis of any indebtedness of the S corporation to the shareholder (determined without regard to any adjustment under paragraph (2) of section 1367(b) for the taxable year).

(2) INDEFINITE CARRYOVER OF DISALLOWED LOSSES AND DEDUCTIONS.—

(A) IN GENERAL.—Except as provided in subparagraph (B), any loss or deduction which is disallowed for any taxable year by reason of paragraph (1) shall be treated as incurred by the corporation in the succeeding taxable year with respect to that shareholder.

(B) TRANSFERS OF STOCK BETWEEN SPOUSES OR INCIDENT TO DIVORCE.—In the case of any transfer described in section 1041(a) of stock of an S corporation, any loss or deduction described in subparagraph (A) with respect [to] such stock shall be treated as incurred by the corporation in the succeeding taxable year with respect to the transferee.

(3) CARRYOVER OF DISALLOWED LOSSES AND DEDUCTIONS TO POST-TERMINATION TRANSITION PERIOD.—

(A) IN GENERAL.—If for the last taxable year of a corporation for which it was an S corporation a loss or deduction was disallowed by reason of paragraph (1), such loss or deduction shall be treated as incurred by the shareholder on the last day of any post-termination transition period.

(B) CANNOT EXCEED SHAREHOLDER'S BASIS IN STOCK.—The aggregate amount of losses and deductions taken into account by a shareholder under subparagraph (A) shall not exceed the adjusted basis of the shareholder's stock in the corporation (determined at the close of the last day of the post-termination transition period and without regard to this paragraph).

(C) ADJUSTMENT IN BASIS OF STOCK.—The shareholder's basis in the stock of the corporation shall be reduced by the amount allowed as a deduction by reason of this paragraph.

(D) AT-RISK LIMITATIONS.—To the extent that any increase in adjusted basis described in subparagraph (B) would have increased the shareholder's amount at risk under section 465 if such increase had occurred on the day preceding the commencement of the post-termination transition period, rules similar to the rules described in subparagraphs (A) through (C) shall apply to any losses disallowed by reason of section 465(a).

(4) APPLICATION OF LIMITATION ON CHARITABLE CONTRIBUTIONS.—In the case of any charitable contribution of property to which the second sentence of section 1367(a)(2) applies, paragraph (1) shall not apply to the extent of the excess (if any) of—

(A) the shareholder's pro rata share of such contribution, over

(B) the shareholder's pro rata share of the adjusted basis of such property.

[Sec. 1366(e)]

(e) TREATMENT OF FAMILY GROUP.—If an individual who is a member of the family (within the meaning of section 704(e)(2)) of one or more shareholders of an S corporation renders services for the corporation or furnishes capital to the corporation without receiving reasonable compensation therefor, the Secretary shall make such adjustments in the items taken into account by such individual and such shareholders as may be necessary in order to reflect the value of such services or capital.

[Sec. 1366(f)]

(f) SPECIAL RULES.—

(1) SUBSECTION (a) NOT TO APPLY TO CREDIT ALLOWABLE UNDER SECTION 34.—Subsection (a) shall not apply with respect to any credit allowable under section 34 (relating to certain uses of gasoline and special fuels).

(2) TREATMENT OF TAX IMPOSED ON BUILT-IN GAINS.—If any tax is imposed under section 1374 for any taxable year on an S corporation, for purposes of subsection (a), the amount so imposed shall be treated as a loss sustained by the S corporation during such taxable year. The character of such loss shall be determined by allocating the loss proportionately among the recognized built-in gains giving rise to such tax.

(3) REDUCTION IN PASS-THRU FOR TAX IMPOSED ON EXCESS NET PASSIVE INCOME.—If any tax is imposed under section 1375 for any taxable year on an S corporation, for purposes of subsection (a), each item of passive investment income shall be reduced by an amount which bears the same ratio to the amount of such tax as—

(A) the amount of such item, bears to

(B) the total passive investment income for the taxable year.

[Sec. 1367]

SEC. 1367. ADJUSTMENTS TO BASIS OF STOCK OF SHAREHOLDERS, ETC.

[Sec. 1367(a)]

(a) GENERAL RULE.—

(1) INCREASES IN BASIS.—The basis of each shareholder's stock in an S corporation shall be increased for any period by the sum of the following items determined with respect to that shareholder for such period:

(A) the items of income described in subparagraph (A) of section 1366(a)(1),

(B) any nonseparately computed income determined under subparagraph (B) of section 1366(a)(1), and

(C) the excess of the deductions for depletion over the basis of the property subject to depletion.

(2) DECREASES IN BASIS.—The basis of each shareholder's stock in an S corporation shall be decreased for any period (but not below zero) by the sum of the following items determined with respect to the shareholder for such period:

(A) distributions by the corporation which were not includible in the income of the shareholder by reason of section 1368,

(B) the items of loss and deduction described in subparagraph (A) of section 1366(a)(1),

(C) any nonseparately computed loss determined under subparagraph (B) of section 1366(a)(1),

(D) any expense of the corporation not deductible in computing its taxable income and not properly chargeable to capital account, and

(E) the amount of the shareholder's deduction for depletion for any oil and gas property held by the S corporation to the extent such deduction does not exceed the proportionate share of the adjusted basis of such property allocated to such shareholder under section 613A(c)(11)(B).

The decrease under subparagraph (B) by reason of a charitable contribution (as defined in section 170(c)) of property shall be the amount equal to the shareholder's pro rata share of the adjusted basis of such property.

[Sec. 1367(b)]

(b) SPECIAL RULES.—

(1) INCOME ITEMS.—An amount which is required to be included in the gross income of a shareholder and shown on his return shall be taken into account under subparagraph (A) or (B) of subsection (a)(1) only to the extent such amount is included in the shareholder's gross income on his return, increased or decreased by any adjustment of such amount in a redetermination of the shareholder's tax liability.

(2) ADJUSTMENTS IN BASIS OF INDEBTEDNESS.—

(A) REDUCTION OF BASIS.—If for any taxable year the amounts specified in subparagraphs (B), (C), (D), and (E) of subsection (a)(2) exceed the amount which reduces the shareholder's basis to zero, such excess shall be applied to reduce (but not below zero) the shareholder's basis in any indebtedness of the S corporation to the shareholder.

(B) RESTORATION OF BASIS.—If for any taxable year beginning after December 31, 1982, there is a reduction under subparagraph (A) in the shareholder's basis in the indebtedness of an S corporation to a shareholder, any net increase (after the application of paragraphs (1) and (2) of subsection (a)) for any subsequent taxable year shall be applied to restore such reduction in basis before any of it may be used to increase the shareholder's basis in the stock of the S corporation.

(3) COORDINATION WITH SECTIONS 165(g) AND 166(d).—This section and section 1366 shall be applied before the application of sections 165(g) and 166(d) to any taxable year of the shareholder or the corporation in which the security or debt becomes worthless.

(4) ADJUSTMENTS IN CASE OF INHERITED STOCK.—

(A) IN GENERAL.—If any person acquires stock in an S corporation by reason of the death of a decedent or by bequest, devise, or inheritance, section 691 shall be applied with respect to any item of income of the S corporation in the same manner as if the decedent had held directly his pro rata share of such item.

(B) ADJUSTMENTS TO BASIS.—The basis determined under section 1014 of any stock in an S corporation shall be reduced by the portion of the value of the stock which is attributable to items constituting income in respect of the decedent.

[Sec. 1368]

SEC. 1368. DISTRIBUTIONS.

[Sec. 1368(a)]

(a) GENERAL RULE.—A distribution of property made by an S corporation with respect to its stock to which (but for this subsection) section 301(c) would apply shall be treated in the manner provided in subsection (b) or (c), whichever applies.

[Sec. 1368(b)]

(b) S CORPORATION HAVING NO EARNINGS AND PROFITS.—In the case of a distribution described in subsection (a) by an S corporation which has no accumulated earnings and profits—

(1) AMOUNT APPLIED AGAINST BASIS.—The distribution shall not be included in gross income to the extent that it does not exceed the adjusted basis of the stock.

(2) AMOUNT IN EXCESS OF BASIS.—If the amount of the distribution exceeds the adjusted basis of the stock, such excess shall be treated as gain from the sale or exchange of property.

[Sec. 1368(c)]

(c) S CORPORATION HAVING EARNINGS AND PROFITS.—In the case of a distribution described in subsection (a) by an S corporation which has accumulated earnings and profits—

(1) ACCUMULATED ADJUSTMENTS ACCOUNT.—That portion of the distribution which does not exceed the accumulated adjustments account shall be treated in the manner provided by subsection (b).

(2) DIVIDEND.—That portion of the distribution which remains after the application of paragraph (1) shall be treated as a dividend to the extent it does not exceed the accumulated earnings and profits of the S corporation.

(3) TREATMENT OF REMAINDER.—Any portion of the distribution remaining after the application of paragraph (2) of this subsection shall be treated in the manner provided by subsection (b).

Except to the extent provided in regulations, if the distributions during the taxable year exceed the amount in the accumulated adjustments account at the close of the taxable year, for purposes of this subsection, the balance of such account shall be allocated among such distributions in proportion to their respective sizes.

[Sec. 1368(d)]

(d) CERTAIN ADJUSTMENTS TAKEN INTO ACCOUNT.—Subsections (b) and (c) shall be applied by taking into account (to the extent proper)—

(1) the adjustments to the basis of the shareholder's stock described in section 1367, and

(2) the adjustments to the accumulated adjustments account which are required by subsection (e)(1).

In the case of any distribution made during any taxable year, the adjusted basis of the stock shall be determined with regard to the adjustments provided in paragraph (1) of section 1367(a) for the taxable year.

[Sec. 1368(e)]

(e) DEFINITIONS AND SPECIAL RULES.—For purposes of this section—

(1) ACCUMULATED ADJUSTMENTS ACCOUNT.—

(A) IN GENERAL.—Except as otherwise provided in this paragraph, the term "accumulated adjustments account" means an account of the S corporation which is adjusted for the S period in a manner similar to the adjustments under section 1367 (except that no adjustment shall be made for income (and related expenses) which is exempt from tax under this title and the phrase "(but not below zero)" shall be disregarded in section 1367(a)(2)) and no adjustment shall be made for Federal taxes attributable to any taxable year in which the corporation was a C corporation.

(B) AMOUNT OF ADJUSTMENT IN THE CASE OF REDEMPTIONS.—In the case of any redemption which is treated as an exchange under section 302(a) or 303(a), the adjustment in the accumulated adjustments account shall be an amount which bears the same ratio to the balance in such account as the number of shares redeemed in such redemption bears to the number of shares of stock in the corporation immediately before such redemption.

(C) NET LOSS FOR YEAR DISREGARDED.—

(i) IN GENERAL.—In applying this section to distributions made during any taxable year, the amount in the accumulated adjustments account as of the close of such taxable year shall be determined without regard to any net negative adjustment for such taxable year.

(ii) NET NEGATIVE ADJUSTMENT.—For purposes of clause (i), the term "net negative adjustment" means, with respect to any taxable year, the excess (if any) of—

(I) the reductions in the account for the taxable year (other than for distributions), over

(II) the increases in such account for such taxable year.

(2) S PERIOD.—The term "S period" means the most recent continuous period during which the corporation has been an S corporation. Such period shall not include any taxable year beginning before January 1, 1983.

(3) ELECTION TO DISTRIBUTE EARNINGS FIRST.—

(A) IN GENERAL.—An S corporation may, with the consent of all of its affected shareholders, elect to have paragraph (1) of subsection (c) not apply to all distributions made during the taxable year for which the election is made.

(B) AFFECTED SHAREHOLDER.—For purposes of subparagraph (A), the term "affected shareholder" means any shareholder to whom a distribution is made by the S corporation during the taxable year.

* * *

PART III—SPECIAL RULES

[Sec. 1371]

SEC. 1371. COORDINATION WITH SUBCHAPTER C.

[Sec. 1371(a)]

(a) APPLICATION OF SUBCHAPTER C RULES.—Except as otherwise provided in this title, and except to the extent inconsistent with this subchapter, subchapter C shall apply to an S corporation and its shareholders.

[Sec. 1371(b)]

(b) NO CARRYOVER BETWEEN C YEAR AND S YEAR.—

(1) FROM C YEAR TO S YEAR.—No carryforward, and no carryback, arising for a taxable year for which a corporation is a C corporation may be carried to a taxable year for which such corporation is an S corporation.

(2) NO CARRYOVER FROM S YEAR.—No carryforward, and no carryback, shall arise at the corporate level for a taxable year for which a corporation is an S corporation.

(3) TREATMENT OF S YEAR AS ELAPSED YEAR.—Nothing in paragraphs (1) and (2) shall prevent treating a taxable year for which a corporation is an S corporation as a taxable year for purposes of determining the number of taxable years to which an item may be carried back or carried forward.

[Sec. 1371(c)]

(c) EARNINGS AND PROFITS.—

(1) IN GENERAL.—Except as provided in paragraphs (2) and (3) and subsection (d)(3), no adjustment shall be made to the earnings and profits of an S corporation.

(2) ADJUSTMENTS FOR REDEMPTIONS, LIQUIDATIONS, REORGANIZATIONS, DIVISIVES, ETC.—In the case of any transaction involving the application of subchapter C to any S corporation, proper adjustment to any accumulated earnings and profits of the corporation shall be made.

(3) ADJUSTMENTS IN CASE OF DISTRIBUTIONS TREATED AS DIVIDENDS UNDER SECTION 1368(c)(2).—Paragraph (1) shall not apply with respect to that portion of a distribution which is treated as a dividend under section 1368(c)(2).

* * *

[Sec. 1371(e)]

(e) CASH DISTRIBUTIONS DURING POST-TERMINATION TRANSITION PERIOD.—

(1) IN GENERAL.—Any distribution of money by a corporation with respect to its stock during a post-termination transition period shall be applied against and reduce the adjusted basis of the stock, to the extent that the amount of the distribution does not exceed the accumulated adjustments account (within the meaning of section 1368(e)).

(2) ELECTION TO DISTRIBUTE EARNINGS FIRST.—An S corporation may elect to have paragraph (1) not apply to all distributions made during a post-termination transition period described in section 1377(b)(1)(A). Such election shall not be effective unless all shareholders of the S corporation to whom distributions are made by the S corporation during such post-termination transition period consent to such election.

[Sec. 1371(f)]

(f) CASH DISTRIBUTIONS FOLLOWING POST-TERMINATION TRANSITION PERIOD.—In the case of a distribution of money by an eligible terminated S corporation (as defined in section 481(d)) after the post-termination transition period, the accumulated adjustments account shall be allocated to such distribution, and the distribution shall be chargeable to accumulated earnings and profits, in the same ratio as the amount of such accumulated adjustments account bears to the amount of such accumulated earnings and profits.

[Sec. 1372]

SEC. 1372. PARTNERSHIP RULES TO APPLY FOR FRINGE BENEFIT PURPOSES.

[Sec. 1372(a)]

(a) GENERAL RULE.—For purposes of applying the provisions of this subtitle which relate to employee fringe benefits—

(1) the S corporation shall be treated as a partnership, and

(2) any 2-percent shareholder of the S corporation shall be treated as a partner of such partnership.

[Sec. 1372(b)]

(b) 2-PERCENT SHAREHOLDER DEFINED.—For purposes of this section, the term "2-percent shareholder" means any person who owns (or is considered as owning within the meaning of section 318) on any day during the taxable year of the S corporation more than 2 percent of the outstanding stock of such corporation or stock possessing more than 2 percent of the total combined voting power of all stock of such corporation.

[Sec. 1374]

SEC. 1374. TAX IMPOSED ON CERTAIN BUILT-IN GAINS.

[Sec. 1374(a)]

(a) GENERAL RULE.—If for any taxable year beginning in the recognition period an S corporation has a net recognized built-in gain, there is hereby imposed a tax (computed under subsection (b)) on the income of such corporation for such taxable year.

[Sec. 1374(b)]

(b) AMOUNT OF TAX.—

(1) IN GENERAL.—The amount of the tax imposed by subsection (a) shall be computed by applying the highest rate of tax specified in section 11(b) to the net recognized built-in gain of the S corporation for the taxable year.

(2) NET OPERATING LOSS CARRYFORWARDS FROM C YEARS ALLOWED.—Notwithstanding section 1371(b)(1), any net operating loss carryforward arising in a taxable year for which the corporation was a C corporation shall be allowed for purposes of this section as a deduction against the net recognized built-in gain of the S corporation for the taxable year. For purposes of determining the amount of any such loss which may be carried to subsequent taxable years, the amount of the net recognized built-in gain shall be treated as taxable income. Rules similar to the rules of the preceding sentences of this paragraph shall apply in the case of a capital loss carryforward arising in a taxable year for which the corporation was a C corporation.

(3) CREDITS.—

(A) IN GENERAL.—Except as provided in subparagraph (B), no credit shall be allowable under part IV if subchapter A of this chapter (other than under section 34) against the tax imposed by subsection (a).

(B) BUSINESS CREDIT CARRYFORWARDS FROM C YEARS ALLOWED.—Notwithstanding section 1371(b)(1), any business credit carryforward under section 39 arising in a taxable year for which the corporation was a C corporation shall be allowed as a credit against the tax imposed by subsection (a) in the same manner as if it were imposed by section 11. A similar rule shall apply in the case of the minimum tax credit under section 53 to the extent attributable to taxable years for which the corporation was a C corporation.

[Sec. 1374(c)]

(c) LIMITATIONS.—

(1) CORPORATIONS WHICH WERE ALWAYS S CORPORATIONS.—Subsection (a) shall not apply to any corporation if an election under section 1362(a) has been in effect with respect to such corporation for each of its taxable years. Except as provided in regulations, an S corporation and any predecessor corporation shall be treated as 1 corporation for purposes of the preceding sentence.

(2) LIMITATION ON AMOUNT OF RECOGNIZED BUILT-IN GAINS.—The amount of the net recognized built-in gain taken into account under this section for any taxable year shall not exceed the excess (if any) of—

(A) the net unrealized built-in gain, over

(B) the net recognized built-in gain for prior taxable years beginning in the recognition period.

[Sec. 1374(d)]

(d) DEFINITIONS AND SPECIAL RULES.—For purposes of this section—

(1) NET UNREALIZED BUILT-IN GAIN.—The term "net unrealized built-in gain" means the amount (if any) by which—

(A) the fair market value of the assets of S corporation as of the beginning of its 1st taxable year for which an election under section 1362(a) is in effect, exceeds

(B) the aggregate adjusted bases of such assets at such time.

(2) NET RECOGNIZED BUILT-IN GAIN.—

(A) IN GENERAL.—The term "net recognized built-in gain" means, with respect to any taxable year in the recognition period, the lesser of—

(i) the amount which would be taxable income of the S corporation for such taxable year if only recognized built-in gains and recognized built-in losses were taken into account, or

(ii) such corporation's taxable income for such taxable year (determined as provided in section 1375(b)(1)(B)).

(B) CARRYOVER.—If, for any taxable year described in subparagraph (A), the amount referred to in clause (i) of subparagraph (A) exceeds the amount referred to in clause (ii) of subparagraph (A), such excess shall be treated as a recognized built-in gain in the succeeding taxable year.

(3) RECOGNIZED BUILT-IN GAIN.—The term "recognized built-in gain" means any gain recognized during the recognition period on the disposition of any asset except to the extent that the S corporation establishes that—

(A) such asset was not held by the S corporation as of the beginning of the 1st taxable year for which it was an S corporation, or

(B) such gain exceeds the excess (if any) of—

(i) the fair market value of such asset as of the beginning of such 1st taxable year, over

(ii) the adjusted basis of the asset as of such time.

(4) RECOGNIZED BUILT-IN LOSSES.—The term "recognized built-in loss" means any loss recognized during the recognition period on the disposition of any asset to the extent that the S corporation establishes that—

(A) such asset was held by the S corporation as of the beginning of the 1st taxable year referred to in paragraph (3), and

(B) such loss does not exceed the excess of—

(i) the adjusted basis of such asset as of the beginning of such 1st taxable year, over

(ii) the fair market value of such asset as of such time.

(5) TREATMENT OF CERTAIN BUILT-IN ITEMS.—

(A) INCOME ITEMS.—Any item of income which is properly taken into account during the recognition period but which is attributable to periods before the 1st taxable year for which the corporation was an S corporation shall be treated as a recognized built-in gain for the taxable year in which it is properly taken into account.

(B) DEDUCTION ITEMS.—Any amount which is allowable as a deduction during the recognition period (determined without regard to any carryover) but which is attributable to periods before the 1st taxable year referred to in subparagraph (A) shall be treated as a recognized built-in loss for the taxable year for which it is allowable as a deduction.

(C) ADJUSTMENT TO NET UNREALIZED BUILT-IN GAIN.—The amount of the net unrealized built-in gain shall be properly adjusted for amounts which would be treated as recognized built-in gains or losses under this paragraph if such amounts were properly taken into account (or allowable as a deduction) during the recognition period.

(6) TREATMENT OF CERTAIN PROPERTY.—If the adjusted basis of any asset is determined (in whole or in part) by reference to the adjusted basis of any other asset held by the S corporation as of the beginning of the 1st taxable year referred to in paragraph (3)—

(A) such asset shall be treated as held by the S corporation as of the beginning of such 1st taxable year, and

(B) any determination under paragraph (3)(B) or (4)(B) with respect to such asset shall be made by reference to the fair market value and adjusted basis of such other asset as of the beginning of such 1st taxable year.

(7) RECOGNITION PERIOD.—

(A) IN GENERAL.—The term "recognition period" means the 5-year period beginning with the 1st day of the 1st taxable year for which the corporation was an S corporation. For purposes of applying this section to any amount includible in income by reason of distributions to shareholders pursuant to section 593(e), the preceding sentence shall be applied without regard to the phrase "5-year".

(B) INSTALLMENT SALES.—If an S corporation sells an asset and reports the income from the sale using the installment method under section 453, the treatment of all payments received shall be governed by the provisions of this paragraph applicable to the taxable year in which such sale was made.

(8) TREATMENT OF TRANSFER OF ASSETS FROM C CORPORATION TO S CORPORATION.—

(A) IN GENERAL.—Except to the extent provided in regulations, if—

(i) an S corporation acquires any asset, and

(ii) the S corporation's basis in such asset is determined (in whole or in part) by reference to the basis of such asset (or any other property) in the hands of a C corporation,

then a tax is hereby imposed on any net recognized built-in gain attributable to any such assets for any taxable year beginning in the recognition period. The amount of such tax shall be determined under the rules of this section as modified by subparagraph (B).

(B) MODIFICATIONS.—For purposes of this paragraph, the modifications of this subparagraph are as follows:

(i) IN GENERAL.—The preceding paragraphs of this subsection shall be applied by taking into account the day on which the assets were acquired by the S corporation in lieu of the beginning of the 1st taxable year for which the corporation was an S corporation.

(ii) SUBSECTION (c)(1) NOT TO APPLY.—Subsection (c)(1) shall not apply.

(9) REFERENCE TO 1ST TAXABLE YEAR.—Any reference in this section to the 1st taxable year for which the corporation was an S corporation shall be treated as a reference to the 1st taxable year for which the corporation was an S corporation pursuant to its most recent election under section 1362.

[Sec. 1374(e)]

(e) REGULATIONS.—The Secretary shall prescribe such regulations as may be necessary to carry out the purposes of this section including regulations providing for the appropriate treatment of successor corporations.

[Sec. 1375]

SEC. 1375. TAX IMPOSED WHEN PASSIVE INVESTMENT INCOME OF CORPORATION HAVING ACCUMULATED EARNINGS AND PROFITS EXCEEDS 25 PERCENT OF GROSS RECEIPTS.

[Sec. 1375(a)]

(a) GENERAL RULE.—If for the taxable year an S corporation has—

(1) accumulated earnings and profits at the close of such taxable year, and

(2) gross receipts more than 25 percent of which are passive investment income,

then there is hereby imposed a tax on the income of such corporation for such taxable year. Such tax shall be computed by multiplying the excess net passive income by the highest rate of tax specified in section 11(b).

[Sec. 1375(b)]

(b) DEFINITIONS.—For purposes of this section—

(1) EXCESS NET PASSIVE INCOME.—

(A) IN GENERAL.—Except as provided in subparagraph (B), the term "excess net passive income" means an amount which bears the same ratio to the net passive income for the taxable year as—

(i) the amount by which the passive investment income for the taxable year exceeds 25 percent of the gross receipts for the taxable year, bears to

(ii) the passive investment income for the taxable year.

(B) LIMITATION.—The amount of the excess net passive income for any taxable year shall not exceed the amount of the corporation's taxable income for such taxable year as determined under section 63(a)—

(i) without regard to the deductions allowed by part VIII of subchapter B (other than the deduction allowed by section 248, relating to organization expenditures), and

(ii) without regard to the deduction under section 172.

(2) NET PASSIVE INCOME.—The term "net passive income" means—

(A) passive investment income, reduced by

(B) the deductions allowable under this chapter which are directly connected with the production of such income (other than deductions allowable under section 172 and part VIII of subchapter B).

(3) PASSIVE INVESTMENT INCOME, ETC.—The terms "passive investment income" and "gross receipts" have the same respective meanings as when used in paragraph (3) of section 1362(d).

(4) COORDINATION WITH SECTION 1374.—Notwithstanding paragraph (3), the amount of passive investment income shall be determined by not taking into account any recognized built-in gain or loss of the S corporation for any taxable year in the recognition period. Terms used in the preceding sentence shall have the same respective meanings as when used in section 1374.

[Sec. 1375(c)]

(c) CREDITS NOT ALLOWABLE.—No credit shall be allowed under part IV of subchapter A of this chapter (other than section 34) against the tax imposed by subsection (a).

[Sec. 1375(d)]

(d) WAIVER OF TAX IN CERTAIN CASES.—If the S corporation establishes to the satisfaction of the Secretary that—

(1) it determined in good faith that it had no accumulated earnings and profits at the close of a taxable year, and

(2) during a reasonable period of time after it was determined that it did have accumulated earnings and profits at the close of such taxable year such earnings and profits were distributed,

the Secretary may waive the tax imposed by subsection (a) for such taxable year.

PART IV—DEFINITIONS; MISCELLANEOUS

[Sec. 1377]

SEC. 1377. DEFINITIONS AND SPECIAL RULE.

[Sec. 1377(a)]

(a) PRO RATA SHARE.—For purposes of this subchapter—

(1) IN GENERAL.—Except as provided in paragraph (2), each shareholder's pro rata share of any item for any taxable year shall be the sum of the amounts determined with respect to the shareholder—

(A) by assigning an equal portion of such item to each day of the taxable year, and

(B) then by dividing that portion pro rata among the shares outstanding on such day.

(2) ELECTION TO TERMINATE YEAR.—

(A) IN GENERAL.—Under regulations prescribed by the Secretary, if any shareholder terminates the shareholder's interest in the corporation during the taxable year and all affected shareholders and the corporation agree to the application of this paragraph, paragraph (1) shall be applied to the affected shareholders as if the taxable year consisted of 2 taxable years the first of which ends on the date of the termination.

(B) AFFECTED SHAREHOLDERS.—For purposes of subparagraph (A), the term "affected shareholders" means the shareholder whose interest is terminated and all shareholders to whom such shareholder has transferred shares during the taxable year. If such shareholder has transferred shares to the corporation, the term "affected shareholders" shall include all persons who are shareholders during the taxable year.

[Sec. 1377(b)]

(b) POST-TERMINATION TRANSITION PERIOD.—

(1) IN GENERAL.—For purposes of this subchapter, the term "post-termination transition period" means—

(A) the period beginning on the day after the last day of the corporation's last taxable year as an S corporation and ending on the later of—

(i) the day which is 1 year after such last day, or

(ii) the due date for filing the return for such last year as an S corporation (including extensions),

(B) the 120-day period beginning on the date of any determination pursuant to an audit of the taxpayer which follows the termination of the corporation's election and which adjusts a subchapter S item of income, loss, or deduction of the corporation arising during the S period (as defined in section 1368(e)(2)), and

(C) the 120-day period beginning on the date of a determination that the corporation's election under section 1362(a) had terminated for a previous taxable year.

(2) DETERMINATION DEFINED.—For purposes of paragraph (1), the term "determination" means—

(A) a determination as defined in section 1313(a), or

(B) an agreement between the corporation and the Secretary that the corporation failed to qualify as an S corporation.

(3) SPECIAL RULES FOR AUDIT RELATED POST-TERMINATION TRANSITION PERIODS.—

(A) NO APPLICATION TO CARRYOVERS.—Paragraph (1)(B) shall not apply for purposes of section 1366(d)(3).

(B) LIMITATION ON APPLICATION TO DISTRIBUTIONS.—Paragraph (1)(B) shall apply to a distribution described in section 1371(e) only to the extent that the amount of such distribution does not exceed the aggregate increase (if any) in the accumulated adjustments account (within the meaning of section 1368(e)) by reason of the adjustments referred to in such paragraph.

[Sec. 1377(c)]

(c) MANNER OF MAKING ELECTIONS, ETC.—Any election under this subchapter, and any revocation under section 1362(d)(1), shall be made in such manner as the Secretary shall by regulations prescribe.

[Sec. 1378]

SEC. 1378. TAXABLE YEAR OF S CORPORATION.

[Sec. 1378(a)]

(a) GENERAL RULE.—For purposes of this subtitle, the taxable year of an S corporation shall be a permitted year.

[Sec. 1378(b)]

(b) PERMITTED YEAR DEFINED.—For purposes of this section, the term "permitted year" means a taxable year which—

(1) is a year ending December 31, or

(2) is any other accounting period for which the corporation establishes a business purpose to the satisfaction of the Secretary.

For purposes of paragraph (2), any deferral of income to shareholders shall not be treated as a business purpose.

SUBCHAPTER V—TITLE 11 CASES

[Sec. 1399]

SEC. 1399. NO SEPARATE TAXABLE ENTITIES FOR PARTNERSHIPS, CORPORATIONS, ETC.

Except in any case to which section 1398 applies, no separate taxable entity shall result from the commencement of a case under title 11 of the United States Code.

SUBCHAPTER Z—OPPORTUNITY ZONES

[Sec. 1400Z-1]

SEC. 1400Z-1. DESIGNATION.

[Sec. 1400Z-1(a)]

(a) QUALIFIED OPPORTUNITY ZONE DEFINED.—For the purposes of this subchapter, the term "qualified opportunity zone" means a population census tract that is a low-income community that is designated as a qualified opportunity zone.

[Sec. 1400Z-1(b)]

(b) DESIGNATION.—

(1) IN GENERAL.—For purposes of subsection (a), a population census tract that is a low-income community is designated as a qualified opportunity zone if—

(A) not later than the end of the determination period, the chief executive officer of the State in which the tract is located—

(i) nominates the tract for designation as a qualified opportunity zone, and

(ii) notifies the Secretary in writing of such nomination, and

(B) the Secretary certifies such nomination and designates such tract as a qualified opportunity zone before the end of the consideration period.

(2) EXTENSION OF PERIODS.—A chief executive officer of a State may request that the Secretary extend either the determination or consideration period, or both (determined without regard to this subparagraph), for an additional 30 days.

(3) SPECIAL RULE FOR PUERTO RICO.—Each population census tract in Puerto Rico that is a low-income community shall be deemed to be certified and designated as a qualified opportunity zone, effective on the date of the enactment of Public Law 115-97.

[Sec. 1400Z-1(c)]

(c) OTHER DEFINITIONS.—For purposes of this subsection—

(1) LOW-INCOME COMMUNITIES.—The term "low-income community" has the same meaning as when used in section 45D (e).

(2) DEFINITION OF PERIODS.—

(A) CONSIDERATION PERIOD.—The term "consideration period" means the 30-day period beginning on the date on which the Secretary receives notice under subsection (b) (1) (A) (ii), as extended under subsection (b) (2).

(B) DETERMINATION PERIOD.—The term "determination period" means the 90-day period beginning on the date of the enactment of the Tax Cuts and Jobs Act, as extended under subsection (b) (2).

(3) STATE.—For purposes of this section, the term "State" includes any possession of the United States.

[Sec. 1400Z-1(d)]

(d) NUMBER OF DESIGNATIONS.—

(1) IN GENERAL.—Except as provided by paragraph (2) and subsection (b) (3), the number of population census tracts in a State that may be designated as qualified opportunity

zones under this section may not exceed 25 percent of the number of low-income communities in the State.

(2) EXCEPTION.—If the number of low-income communities in a State is less than 100, then a total of 25 of such tracts may be designated as qualified opportunity zones.

[Sec. 1400Z-1(e)]

(e) DESIGNATION OF TRACTS CONTIGUOUS WITH LOW-INCOME COMMUNITIES.—

(1) IN GENERAL.—A population census tract that is not a low-income community may be designated as a qualified opportunity zone under this section if—

(A) the tract is contiguous with the low-income community that is designated as a qualified opportunity zone, and

(B) the median family income of the tract does not exceed 125 percent of the median family income of the low-income community with which the tract is contiguous.

(2) LIMITATION.—Not more than 5 percent of the population census tracts designated in a State as a qualified opportunity zone may be designated under paragraph (1).

[Sec. 1400Z-1(f)]

(f) PERIOD FOR WHICH DESIGNATION IS IN EFFECT.—A designation as a qualified opportunity zone shall remain in effect for the period beginning on the date of the designation and ending at the close of the 10th calendar year beginning on or after such date of designation.

[Sec. 1400Z-2]

SEC. 1400Z-2. SPECIAL RULES FOR CAPITAL GAINS INVESTED IN OPPORTUNITY ZONES.

[Sec. 1400Z-2(a)]

(a) IN GENERAL.—

(1) TREATMENT OF GAINS.—In the case of gain from the sale to, or exchange with, an unrelated person of any property held by the taxpayer, at the election of the taxpayer—

(A) gross income for the taxable year shall not include so much of such gain as does not exceed the aggregate amount invested by the taxpayer in a qualified opportunity fund during the 180-day period beginning on the date of such sale or exchange,

(B) the amount of gain excluded by subparagraph (A) shall be included in gross income as provided by subsection (b), and

(C) subsection (c) shall apply.

(2) ELECTION.—No election may be made under paragraph (1)—

(A) with respect to a sale or exchange if an election previously made with respect to such sale or exchange is in effect, or

(B) with respect to any sale or exchange after December 31, 2026.

[Sec. 1400Z-2(b)]

(b) DEFERRAL OF GAIN INVESTED IN OPPORTUNITY ZONE PROPERTY.—

(1) YEAR OF INCLUSION.—Gain to which subsection (a)(1)(B) applies shall be included in income in the taxable year which includes the earlier of—

(A) the date on which such investment is sold or exchanged, or

(B) December 31, 2026.

(2) AMOUNT INCLUDIBLE.—

(A) IN GENERAL.—The amount of gain included in gross income under subsection (a)(1)(A) shall be the excess of—

(i) the lesser of the amount of gain excluded under paragraph (1) or the fair market value of the investment as determined as of the date described in paragraph (1), over

(ii) the taxpayer's basis in the investment.

(B) DETERMINATION OF BASIS.—

(i) IN GENERAL.—Except as otherwise provided in this clause or subsection (c), the taxpayer's basis in the investment shall be zero.

(ii) INCREASE FOR GAIN RECOGNIZED UNDER SUBSECTION (a)(1)(B).—The basis in the investment shall be increased by the amount of gain recognized by reason of subsection (a)(1)(B) with respect to such property.

(iii) INVESTMENTS HELD FOR 5 YEARS.—In the case of any investment held for at least 5 years, the basis of such investment shall be increased by an amount equal to 10 percent of the amount of gain deferred by reason of subsection (a)(1)(A).

(iv) INVESTMENTS HELD FOR 7 YEARS.—In the case of any investment held by the taxpayer for at least 7 years, in addition to any adjustment made under clause (iii), the basis of such property shall be increased by an amount equal to 5 percent of the amount of gain deferred by reason of subsection (a)(1)(A).

[Sec. 1400Z-2(c)]

(c) SPECIAL RULE FOR INVESTMENTS HELD FOR AT LEAST 10 YEARS.—In the case of any investment held by the taxpayer for at least 10 years and with respect to which the taxpayer makes an election under this clause, the basis of such property shall be equal to the fair market value of such investment on the date that the investment is sold or exchanged.

[Sec. 1400Z-2(d)]

(d) QUALIFIED OPPORTUNITY FUND.—For purposes of this section—

(1) IN GENERAL.—The term "qualified opportunity fund" means any investment vehicle which is organized as a corporation or a partnership for the purpose of investing in qualified opportunity zone property (other than another qualified opportunity fund) that holds at least 90 percent of its assets in qualified opportunity zone property, determined by the average of the percentage of qualified opportunity zone property held in the fund as measured—

(A) on the last day of the first 6-month period of the taxable year of the fund, and

(B) on the last day of the taxable year of the fund.

(2) QUALIFIED OPPORTUNITY ZONE PROPERTY.—

(A) IN GENERAL.—The term "qualified opportunity zone property" means property which is—

(i) qualified opportunity zone stock,

(ii) qualified opportunity zone partnership interest, or

(iii) qualified opportunity zone business property.

(B) QUALIFIED OPPORTUNITY ZONE STOCK.—

(i) IN GENERAL.—Except as provided in clause (ii), the term "qualified opportunity zone stock" means any stock in a domestic corporation if—

(I) such stock is acquired by the qualified opportunity fund after December 31, 2017, at its original issue (directly or through an underwriter) from the corporation solely in exchange for cash,

(II) as of the time such stock was issued, such corporation was a qualified opportunity zone business (or, in the case of a new corporation, such corporation was being organized for purposes of being a qualified opportunity zone business), and

(III) during substantially all of the qualified opportunity fund's holding period for such stock, such corporation qualified as a qualified opportunity zone business.

(ii) REDEMPTIONS.—A rule similar to the rule of section 1202(c)(3) shall apply for purposes of this paragraph.

(C) QUALIFIED OPPORTUNITY ZONE PARTNERSHIP INTEREST.—The term "qualified opportunity zone partnership interest" means any capital or profits interest in a domestic partnership if—

(i) such interest is acquired by the qualified opportunity fund after December 31, 2017, from the partnership solely in exchange for cash,

(ii) as of the time such interest was acquired, such partnership was a qualified opportunity zone business (or, in the case of a new partnership, such partnership was being organized for purposes of being a qualified opportunity zone business), and

(iii) during substantially all of the qualified opportunity fund's holding period for such interest, such partnership qualified as a qualified opportunity zone business.

(D) QUALIFIED OPPORTUNITY ZONE BUSINESS PROPERTY.—

(i) IN GENERAL.—The term "qualified opportunity zone business property" means tangible property used in a trade or business of the qualified opportunity fund if—

(I) such property was acquired by the qualified opportunity fund by purchase (as defined in section 179(d)(2)) after December 31, 2017,

(II) the original use of such property in the qualified opportunity zone commences with the qualified opportunity fund or the qualified opportunity fund substantially improves the property, and

(III) during substantially all of the qualified opportunity fund's holding period for such property, substantially all of the use of such property was in a qualified opportunity zone.

(ii) SUBSTANTIAL IMPROVEMENT.—For purposes of subparagraph (A)(ii), property shall be treated as substantially improved by the qualified opportunity fund only if, during any 30-month period beginning after the date of acquisition of such property, additions to basis with respect to such property in the hands of the qualified opportunity fund exceed an amount equal to the adjusted basis of such property at the beginning of such 30-month period in the hands of the qualified opportunity fund.

(iii) RELATED PARTY.—For purposes of subparagraph (A)(i), the related person rule of section 179(d)(2) shall be applied pursuant to paragraph (8) of this subsection in lieu of the application of such rule in section 179(d)(2)(A).

(3) QUALIFIED OPPORTUNITY ZONE BUSINESS.—

(A) IN GENERAL.—The term "qualified opportunity zone business" means a trade or business—

(i) in which substantially all of the tangible property owned or leased by the taxpayer is qualified opportunity zone business property (determined by substituting "qualified opportunity zone business" for "qualified opportunity fund" each place it appears in paragraph (2)(D)),

(ii) which satisfies the requirements of paragraphs (2), (4), and (8) of section 1397C(b), and

(iii) which is not described in section 144(c)(6)(B).

(B) SPECIAL RULE.—For purposes of subparagraph (A), tangible property that ceases to be a qualified opportunity zone business property shall continue to be treated as a qualified opportunity zone business property for the lesser of—

(i) 5 years after the date on which such tangible property ceases to be so qualified, or

(ii) the date on which such tangible property is no longer held by the qualified opportunity zone business.

[Sec. 1400Z-2(e)]

(e) APPLICABLE RULES.—

(1) TREATMENT OF INVESTMENTS WITH MIXED FUNDS.—In the case of any investment in a qualified opportunity fund only a portion of which consists of investments of gain to which an election under subsection (a) is in effect—

(A) such investment shall be treated as 2 separate investments, consisting of—

(i) one investment that only includes amounts to which the election under subsection (a) applies, and

(ii) a separate investment consisting of other amounts, and

(B) subsections (a), (b), and (c) shall only apply to the investment described in subparagraph (A)(i).

(2) RELATED PERSONS.—For purposes of this section, persons are related to each other if such persons are described in section 267(b) or 707(b)(1), determined by substituting "20 percent" for "50 percent" each place it occurs in such sections.

(3) DECEDENTS.—In the case of a decedent, amounts recognized under this section shall, if not properly includible in the gross income of the decedent, be includible in gross income as provided by section 691.

(4) REGULATIONS.—The Secretary shall prescribe such regulations as may be necessary or appropriate to carry out the purposes of this section, including—

(A) rules for the certification of qualified opportunity funds for the purposes of this section,

(B) rules to ensure a qualified opportunity fund has a reasonable period of time to reinvest the return of capital from investments in qualified opportunity zone stock and qualified opportunity zone partnership interests, and to reinvest proceeds received from the sale or disposition of qualified opportunity zone property, and

(C) rules to prevent abuse.

[Sec. 1400Z-2(f)]

(f) FAILURE OF QUALIFIED OPPORTUNITY FUND TO MAINTAIN INVESTMENT STANDARD.—

(1) IN GENERAL.—If a qualified opportunity fund fails to meet the 90-percent requirement of subsection (c)(1), the qualified opportunity fund shall pay a penalty for each month it fails to meet the requirement in an amount equal to the product of—

(A) the excess of—

(i) the amount equal to 90 percent of its aggregate assets, over

(ii) the aggregate amount of qualified opportunity zone property held by the fund, multiplied by

(B) the underpayment rate established under section 6621(a)(2) for such month.

(2) SPECIAL RULE FOR PARTNERSHIPS.—In the case that the qualified opportunity fund is a partnership, the penalty imposed by paragraph (1) shall be taken into account proportionately as part of the distributive share of each partner of the partnership.

(3) REASONABLE CAUSE EXCEPTION.—No penalty shall be imposed under this subsection with respect to any failure if it is shown that such failure is due to reasonable cause.

CHAPTER 2—TAX ON SELF-EMPLOYMENT INCOME

[Sec. 1401]

SEC. 1401. RATE OF TAX.

[Sec. 1401(a)]

(a) OLD-AGE, SURVIVORS, AND DISABILITY INSURANCE.—In addition to other taxes, there shall be imposed for each taxable year, on the self-employment income of every individual, a tax equal to 12.4 percent of the amount of the self-employment income for such taxable year.

[Sec. 1401(b)]

(b) HOSPITAL INSURANCE.—

(1) IN GENERAL.—In addition to the tax imposed by the preceding subsection, there shall be imposed for each taxable year, on the self-employment income of every individual, a tax equal to 2.9 percent of the amount of the self-employment income for such taxable year.

(2) ADDITIONAL TAX.—

(A) IN GENERAL.—In addition to the tax imposed by paragraph (1) and the preceding subsection, there is hereby imposed on every taxpayer (other than a corporation, estate, or trust) for each taxable year beginning after December 31, 2012, a tax equal to 0.9 percent of the self-employment income for such taxable year which is in excess of—

(i) in the case of a joint return, $250,000,

(ii) in the case of a married taxpayer (as defined in section 7703) filing a separate return, ½ of the dollar amount determined under clause (i), and

(iii) in any other case, $200,000.

(B) COORDINATION WITH FICA.—The amounts under clause (i), (ii), or (iii) (whichever is applicable) of subparagraph (A) shall be reduced (but not below zero) by the amount of wages taken into account in determining the tax imposed under section 3121(b)(2) with respect to the taxpayer.

* * *

CHAPTER 2A—UNEARNED INCOME MEDICARE CONTRIBUTION

[Sec. 1411]

SEC. 1411. IMPOSITION OF TAX.

[Sec. 1411(a)]

(a) IN GENERAL.—Except as provided in subsection (e)—

(1) APPLICATION TO INDIVIDUALS.—In the case of an individual, there is hereby imposed (in addition to any other tax imposed by this subtitle) for each taxable year a tax equal to 3.8 percent of the lesser of—

(A) net investment income for such taxable year, or

(B) the excess (if any) of—

(i) the modified adjusted gross income for such taxable year, over

(ii) the threshold amount.

(2) APPLICATION TO ESTATES AND TRUSTS.—In the case of an estate or trust, there is hereby imposed (in addition to any other tax imposed by this subtitle) for each taxable year a tax of 3.8 percent of the lesser of—

(A) the undistributed net investment income for such taxable year, or

(B) the excess (if any) of—

(i) the adjusted gross income (as defined in section 67(e)) for such taxable year, over

(ii) the dollar amount at which the highest tax bracket in section 1(e) begins for such taxable year.

[Sec. 1411(b)]

(b) THRESHOLD AMOUNT.—For purposes of this chapter, the term "threshold amount" means—

(1) in the case of a taxpayer making a joint return under section 6013 or a surviving spouse (as defined in section 2(a)), $250,000,

(2) in the case of a married taxpayer (as defined in section 7703) filing a separate return, ½ of the dollar amount determined under paragraph (1), and

(3) in any other case, $200,000.

[Sec. 1411(c)]

(c) NET INVESTMENT INCOME.—For purposes of this chapter—

(1) IN GENERAL.—The term "net investment income" means the excess (if any) of—

(A) the sum of—

(i) gross income from interest, dividends, annuities, royalties, and rents, other than such income which is derived in the ordinary course of a trade or business not described in paragraph (2),

(ii) other gross income derived from a trade or business described in paragraph (2), and

(iii) net gain (to the extent taken into account in computing taxable income) attributable to the disposition of property other than property held in a trade or business not described in paragraph (2), over

(B) the deductions allowed by this subtitle which are properly allocable to such gross income or net gain.

(2) TRADES AND BUSINESSES TO WHICH TAX APPLIES.—A trade or business is described in this paragraph if such trade or business is—

(A) a passive activity (within the meaning of section 469) with respect to the taxpayer, or

(B) a trade or business of trading in financial instruments or commodities (as defined in section 475(e)(2)).

(3) INCOME ON INVESTMENT OF WORKING CAPITAL SUBJECT TO TAX.—A rule similar to the rule of section 469(e)(1)(B) shall apply for purposes of this subsection.

(4) EXCEPTION FOR CERTAIN ACTIVE INTERESTS IN PARTNERSHIPS AND S CORPORATIONS.—In the case of a disposition of an interest in a partnership or S corporation—

(A) gain from such disposition shall be taken into account under clause (iii) of paragraph (1)(A) only to the extent of the net gain which would be so taken into account by the transferor if all property of the partnership or S corporation were sold for fair market value immediately before the disposition of such interest, and

(B) a rule similar to the rule of subparagraph (A) shall apply to a loss from such disposition.

(5) EXCEPTION FOR DISTRIBUTIONS FROM QUALIFIED PLANS.—The term "net investment income" shall not include any distribution from a plan or arrangement described in section 401(a), 403(a), 403(b), 408, 408A, or 457(b).

(6) SPECIAL RULE.—Net investment income shall not include any item taken into account in determining self-employment income for such taxable year on which a tax is imposed by section 1401(b).

[Sec. 1411(d)]

(d) MODIFIED ADJUSTED GROSS INCOME.—For purposes of this chapter, the term "modified adjusted gross income" means adjusted gross income increased by the excess of—

(1) the amount excluded from gross income under section 911(a)(1), over

(2) the amount of any deductions (taken into account in computing adjusted gross income) or exclusions disallowed under section 911(d)(6) with respect to the amounts described in paragraph (1).

[Sec. 1411(e)]

(e) NONAPPLICATION OF SECTION.—This section shall not apply to—

(1) a nonresident alien, or

(2) a trust all of the unexpired interests in which are devoted to one or more of the purposes described in section 170(c)(2)(B).

CHAPTER 6—CONSOLIDATED RETURNS

SUBCHAPTER A—RETURNS AND PAYMENT OF TAX

[Sec. 1501]

SEC. 1501. PRIVILEGE TO FILE CONSOLIDATED RETURNS.

An affiliated group of corporations shall, subject to the provisions of this chapter, have the privilege of making a consolidated return with respect to the income tax imposed by chapter 1 for the taxable year in lieu of separate returns. The making of a consolidated return shall be upon the condition that all corporations which at any time during the taxable year have been members of the affiliated group consent to all the consolidated return regulations prescribed under section 1502 prior to the last day prescribed by law for the filing of such return. The making of a consolidated return shall be considered as such consent. In the case of a corporation which is a member of the affiliated group for a fractional part of the year, the consolidated return shall include the income of such corporation for such part of the year as it is a member of the affiliated group.

[Sec. 1502]

SEC. 1502. REGULATIONS.

The Secretary shall prescribe such regulations as he may deem necessary in order that the tax liability of any affiliated group of corporations making a consolidated return and of each corporation in the group, both during and after the period of affiliation, may be returned, determined, computed, assessed, collected, and adjusted, in such manner as clearly to reflect the income tax liability and the various factors necessary for the determination of such liability, and in order to prevent avoidance of such tax liability. In carrying out the preceding sentence, the Secretary may prescribe rules that are different from the provisions of chapter 1 that would apply if such corporations filed separate returns.

[Sec. 1503]

SEC. 1503. COMPUTATION AND PAYMENT OF TAX.

[Sec. 1503(a)]

(a) GENERAL RULE.—In any case in which a consolidated return is made or is required to be made, the tax shall be determined, computed, assessed, collected, and adjusted in accordance with the regulations under section 1502 prescribed before the last day prescribed by law for the filing of such return.

* * *

[Sec. 1504]

SEC. 1504. DEFINITIONS.

[Sec. 1504(a)]

(a) AFFILIATED GROUP DEFINED.—For purposes of this subtitle—

(1) IN GENERAL.—The term “affiliated group” means—

(A) 1 or more chains of includible corporations connected through stock ownership with a common parent corporation which is an includible corporation, but only if—

(B) (i) the common parent owns directly stock meeting the requirements of paragraph (2) in at least 1 of the other includible corporations, and

(ii) stock meeting the requirements of paragraph (2) in each of the includible corporations (except the common parent) is owned directly by 1 or more of the other includible corporations.

(2) 80-PERCENT VOTING AND VALUE TEST.—The ownership of stock of any corporation meets the requirements of this paragraph if it—

(A) possesses at least 80 percent of the total voting power of the stock of such corporation, and

(B) has a value equal to at least 80 percent of the total value of the stock of such corporation.

(3) 5 YEARS MUST ELAPSE BEFORE RECONSOLIDATION.—

(A) IN GENERAL.—If—

(i) a corporation is included (or required to be included) in a consolidated return filed by an affiliated group, and

(ii) such corporation ceases to be a member of such group,

with respect to periods after such cessation, such corporation (and any successor of such corporation) may not be included in any consolidated return filed by the affiliated group (or by another affiliated group with the same common parent or a successor of such common parent) before the 61st month beginning after its first taxable year in which it ceased to be a member of such affiliated group.

(B) SECRETARY MAY WAIVE APPLICATION OF SUBPARAGRAPH (A).—The Secretary may waive the application of subparagraph (A) to any corporation for any period subject to such conditions as the Secretary may prescribe.

(4) STOCK NOT TO INCLUDE CERTAIN PREFERRED STOCK.—For purposes of this subsection, the term "stock" does not include any stock which—

(A) is not entitled to vote,

(B) is limited and preferred as to dividends and does not participate in corporate growth to any significant extent,

(C) has redemption and liquidation rights which do not exceed the issue price of such stock (except for a reasonable redemption or liquidation premium), and

(D) is not convertible into another class of stock.

(5) REGULATIONS.—The Secretary shall prescribe such regulations as may be necessary or appropriate to carry out the purposes of this subsection, including (but not limited to) regulations—

(A) which treat warrants, obligations convertible into stock, and other similar interests as stock, and stock as not stock,

(B) which treat options to acquire or sell stock as having been exercised,

(C) which provide that the requirements of paragraph (2)(B) shall be treated as met if the affiliated group, in reliance on a good faith determination of value, treated such requirements as met,

(D) which disregard an inadvertent ceasing to meet the requirements of paragraph (2)(B) by reason of changes in relative values of different classes of stock,

(E) which provide that transfers of stock within the group shall not be taken into account in determining whether a corporation ceases to be a member of an affiliated group, and

(F) which disregard changes in voting power to the extent such changes are disproportionate to related changes in value.

[Sec. 1504(b)]

(b) DEFINITION OF "INCLUDIBLE CORPORATION".—As used in this chapter, the term "includible corporation" means any corporation except—

(1) Corporations exempt from taxation under section 501.

(2) Insurance companies subject to taxation under section 801.

(3) Foreign corporations.

(4) Regulated investment companies and real estate investment trusts subject to tax under subchapter M of chapter 1.

(5) A DISC (as defined in section 992(a)(1)).

(6) An S corporation.

* * *

SUBCHAPTER B—RELATED RULES

PART I—IN GENERAL

[Sec. 1552]

SEC. 1552. EARNINGS AND PROFITS.

[Sec. 1552(a)]

(a) GENERAL RULE.—Pursuant to regulations prescribed by the Secretary the earnings and profits of each member of an affiliated group required to be included in a consolidated return for such group filed for a taxable year shall be determined by allocating the tax liability of the group for such year among the members of the group in accord with whichever of the following methods the group shall elect in its first consolidated return filed for such a taxable year:

(1) The tax liability shall be apportioned among the members of the group in accordance with the ratio which that portion of the consolidated taxable income attributable to each member of the group having taxable income bears to the consolidated taxable income.

(2) The tax liability of the group shall be allocated to the several members of the group on the basis of the percentage of the total tax which the tax of such member if computed on a separate return would bear to the total amount of the taxes for all members of the group so computed.

(3) The tax liability of the group (excluding the tax increases arising from the consolidation) shall be allocated on the basis of the contribution of each member of the group to the consolidated taxable income of the group. Any tax increases arising from the consolidation shall be distributed to the several members in direct proportion to the reduction in tax liability resulting to such members from the filing of the consolidated return as measured by the difference between their tax liabilities determined on a separate return basis and their tax liabilities based on their contributions to the consolidated taxable income.

(4) The tax liability of the group shall be allocated in accord with any other method selected by the group with the approval of the Secretary.

[Sec. 1552(b)]

(b) FAILURE TO ELECT.—If no election is made in such first return, the tax liability shall be allocated among the several members of the group pursuant to the method prescribed in subsection (a)(1).

PART II—CERTAIN CONTROLLED CORPORATIONS

[Sec. 1561]

SEC. 1561. LIMITATIONS ON ACCUMULATED EARNINGS CREDIT IN THE CASE OF CERTAIN CONTROLLED CORPORATIONS.

[Sec. 1561(a)]

(a) IN GENERAL.—The component members of a controlled group of corporations on a December 31 shall, for their taxable years which include such December 31, be limited for purposes of this subtitle to one $250,000 ($150,000 if any component member is a corporation described in section 535(c)(2)(B)) amount for purposes of computing the accumulated earnings credit under section 535(c)(2) and (3). Such amount shall be divided equally among the component members of such group on such December 31 unless the Secretary prescribes regulations permitting an unequal allocation of such amount.

[Sec. 1561(b)]

(b) CERTAIN SHORT TAXABLE YEARS.—If a corporation has a short taxable year which does not include a December 31 and is a component member of a controlled group of corporations with respect to such taxable year, then for purposes of this subtitle, the amount to be used in computing the accumulated earnings credit under section 535(c)(2) and (3) of such corporation for such taxable year shall be the amount specified in subsection (a) with respect to such group, divided by the number of corporations which are component members of such group on the last day of such taxable year. For purposes of the preceding sentence, section 1563(b) shall be applied as if such last day were substituted for December 31.

[Sec. 1563]

SEC. 1563. DEFINITIONS AND SPECIAL RULES.

[Sec. 1563(a)]

(a) CONTROLLED GROUP OF CORPORATIONS.—For purposes of this part, the term "controlled group of corporations" means any group of—

(1) PARENT-SUBSIDIARY CONTROLLED GROUP.—One or more chains of corporations connected through stock ownership with a common parent corporation if—

(A) stock possessing at least 80 percent of the total combined voting power of all classes of stock entitled to vote or at least 80 percent of the total value of shares of all classes of stock of each of the corporations, except the common parent corporation, is owned (within the meaning of subsection (d) (1)) by one or more of the other corporations; and

(B) the common parent corporation owns (within the meaning of subsection (d) (1)) stock possessing at least 80 percent of the total combined voting power of all classes of stock entitled to vote or at least 80 percent of the total value of shares of all classes of stock of at least one of the other corporations, excluding, in computing such voting power or value, stock owned directly by such other corporations.

(2) BROTHER-SISTER CONTROLLED GROUP.—Two or more corporations if 5 or fewer persons who are individuals, estates, or trusts own (within the meaning of subsection (d) (2)) stock possessing more than 50 percent of the total combined voting power of all classes of stock entitled to vote or more than 50 percent of the total value of shares of all classes of stock of each corporation, taking into account the stock ownership of each such person only to the extent such stock ownership is identical with respect to each such corporation.

(3) COMBINED GROUP.—Three or more corporations each of which is a member of a group of corporations described in paragraph (1) or (2), and one of which—

(A) is a common parent corporation included in a group of corporations described in paragraph (1), and also

(B) is included in a group of corporations described in paragraph (2).

* * *

[Sec. 1563(b)]

(b) COMPONENT MEMBER.—

(1) GENERAL RULE.—For purposes of this part, a corporation is a component member of a controlled group of corporations on a December 31 of any taxable year (and with respect to the taxable year which includes such December 31) if such corporation—

(A) is a member of such controlled group of corporations on the December 31 included in such year and is not treated as an excluded member under paragraph (2), or

(B) is not a member of such controlled group of corporations on the December 31 included in such year but is treated as an additional member under paragraph (3).

(2) EXCLUDED MEMBERS.—A corporation which is a member of a controlled group of corporations on December 31 of any taxable year shall be treated as an excluded member of such group for the taxable year including such December 31 if such corporation—

(A) is a member of such group for less than one-half the number of days in such taxable year which precede such December 31,

(B) is exempt from taxation under section 501(a) (except a corporation which is subject to tax on its unrelated business taxable income under section 511) for such taxable year,

(C) is a foreign corporation subject to tax under section 881 for such taxable year,

(D) is an insurance company subject to taxation under section 801 (other than an insurance company which is a member of a controlled group described in subsection (a) (4)), or

(E) is a franchised corporation, as defined in subsection (f) (4).

(3) ADDITIONAL MEMBERS.—A corporation which—

(A) was a member of a controlled group of corporations at any time during a calendar year,

(B) is not a member of such group on December 31 of such calendar year, and

(C) is not described, with respect to such group, in subparagraph (B), (C), (D), or (E) of paragraph (2),

shall be treated as an additional member of such group on December 31 for its taxable year including such December 31 if it was a member of such group for one-half (or more) of the number of days in such taxable year which precede such December 31.

(4) OVERLAPPING GROUPS.—If a corporation is a component member of more than one controlled group of corporations with respect to any taxable year, such corporation shall be treated as a component member of only one controlled group. The determination as to the group of which such corporation is a component member shall be made under regulations prescribed by the Secretary which are consistent with the purposes of this part.

[Sec. 1563(c)]

(c) CERTAIN STOCK EXCLUDED.—

(1) GENERAL RULE.—For purposes of this part, the term "stock" does not include—

(A) nonvoting stock which is limited and preferred as to dividends,

(B) treasury stock, and

(C) stock which is treated as "excluded stock" under paragraph (2).

(2) STOCK TREATED AS "EXCLUDED STOCK".—

(A) PARENT-SUBSIDIARY CONTROLLED GROUP.—For purposes of subsection (a) (1), if a corporation (referred to in this paragraph as "parent corporation") owns (within the meaning of subsections (d) (1) and (e) (4)), 50 percent or more of the total combined voting power of all classes of stock entitled to vote or 50 percent or more of the total value of shares of all classes of stock in another corporation (referred to in this paragraph as "subsidiary corporation"), the following stock of the subsidiary corporation shall be treated as excluded stock—

(i) stock in the subsidiary corporation held by a trust which is part of a plan of deferred compensation for the benefit of the employees of the parent corporation or the subsidiary corporation,

(ii) stock in the subsidiary corporation owned by an individual (within the meaning of subsection (d) (2)) who is a principal stockholder or officer of the parent corporation. For purposes of this clause, the term "principal stockholder" of a corporation means an individual who owns (within the meaning of subsection (d) (2)) 5 percent or more of the total combined voting power of all classes of stock entitled to vote or 5 percent or more of the total value of shares of all classes of stock in such corporation,

(iii) stock in the subsidiary corporation owned (within the meaning of subsection (d) (2)) by an employee of the subsidiary corporation if such stock is subject to conditions which run in favor of such parent (or subsidiary) corporation and which substantially restrict or limit the employee's right (or if the employee constructively owns such stock, the direct owner's right) to dispose of such stock, or

(iv) stock in the subsidiary corporation owned (within the meaning of subsection (d) (2)) by an organization (other than the parent corporation) to which section 501 (relating to certain educational and charitable organizations which are exempt from tax) applies and which is controlled directly or indirectly by the parent corporation or subsidiary corporation, by an individual, estate, or trust that is a principal stockholder (within the meaning of clause (ii)) of the parent corporation, by an officer of the parent corporation, or by any combination thereof.

(B) BROTHER-SISTER CONTROLLED GROUP.—For purposes of subsection (a) (2), if 5 or fewer persons who are individuals, estates, or trusts (referred to in this subparagraph as "common owners") own (within the meaning of subsection (d) (2)), 50 percent or more of the total combined voting power of all classes of stock entitled to vote or 50 percent or more of the total value of shares of all classes of stock in a corporation, the following stock of such corporation shall be treated as excluded stock—

(i) stock in such corporation held by an employees' trust described in section 401(a) which is exempt from tax under section 501(a), if such trust is for the benefit of the employees of such corporation,

(ii) stock in such corporation owned (within the meaning of subsection (d)(2)) by an employee of the corporation if such stock is subject to conditions which run in favor of any of such common owners (or such corporation) and which substantially restrict or limit the employee's right (or if the employee constructively owns such stock, the direct owner's right) to dispose of such stock. If a condition which limits or restricts the employee's right (or the direct owner's right) to dispose of such stock also applies to the stock held by any of the common owners pursuant to a bona fide reciprocal stock purchase arrangement, such condition shall not be treated as one which restricts or limits the employee's right to dispose of such stock, or

(iii) stock in such corporation owned (within the meaning of subsection (d)(2)) by an organization to which section 501 (relating to certain educational and charitable organizations which are exempt from tax) applies and which is controlled directly or indirectly by such corporation, by an individual, estate, or trust that is a principal stockholder (within the meaning of subparagraph (A)(ii)) of such corporation, by an officer of such corporation, or by any combination thereof.

[Sec. 1563(d)]

(d) Rules for Determining Stock Ownership.—

(1) Parent-subsidiary controlled group.—For purposes of determining whether a corporation is a member of a parent-subsidiary controlled group of corporations (within the meaning of subsection (a)(1)), stock owned by a corporation means—

(A) stock owned directly by such corporation, and

(B) stock owned with the application of paragraphs (1), (2), and (3) of subsection (e).

(2) Brother-sister controlled group.—For purposes of determining whether a corporation is a member of a brother-sister controlled group of corporations (within the meaning of subsection (a)(2)), stock owned by a person who is an individual, estate, or trust means—

(A) stock owned directly by such person, and

(B) stock owned with the application of subsection (e).

[Sec. 1563(e)]

(e) Constructive Ownership.—

(1) Options.—If any person has an option to acquire stock, such stock shall be considered as owned by such person. For purposes of this paragraph, an option to acquire such an option, and each one of a series of such options, shall be considered as an option to acquire such stock.

(2) Attribution from partnerships.—Stock owned, directly or indirectly, by or for a partnership shall be considered as owned by any partner having an interest of 5 percent or more in either the capital or profits of the partnership in proportion to his interest in capital or profits, whichever such proportion is the greater.

(3) Attribution from estates or trusts.—

(A) Stock owned, directly or indirectly, by or for an estate or trust shall be considered as owned by any beneficiary who has an actuarial interest of 5 percent or more in such stock, to the extent of such actuarial interest. For purposes of this subparagraph, the actuarial interest of each beneficiary shall be determined by assuming the maximum exercise of discretion by the fiduciary in favor of such beneficiary and the maximum use of such stock to satisfy his rights as a beneficiary.

(B) Stock owned, directly or indirectly, by or for any portion of a trust of which a person is considered the owner under subpart E of part I of subchapter J (relating to grantors and others treated as substantial owners) shall be considered as owned by such person.

(C) This paragraph shall not apply to stock owned by any employees' trust described in section 401(a) which is exempt from tax under section 501(a).

(4) ATTRIBUTION FROM CORPORATIONS.—Stock owned, directly or indirectly, by or for a corporation shall be considered as owned by any person who owns (within the meaning of subsection (d)) 5 percent or more in value of its stock in that proportion which the value of the stock which such person so owns bears to the value of all the stock in such corporation.

(5) SPOUSE.—An individual shall be considered as owning stock in a corporation owned, directly or indirectly, by or for his spouse (other than a spouse who is legally separated from the individual under a decree of divorce whether interlocutory or final, or a decree of separate maintenance), except in the case of a corporation with respect to which each of the following conditions is satisfied for its taxable year—

(A) The individual does not, at any time during such taxable year, own directly any stock in such corporation;

(B) The individual is not a director or employee and does not participate in the management of such corporation at any time during such taxable year;

(C) Not more than 50 percent of such corporation's gross income for such taxable year was derived from royalties, rents, dividends, interest, and annuities; and

(D) Such stock in such corporation is not, at any time during such taxable year, subject to conditions which substantially restrict or limit the spouse's right to dispose of such stock and which run in favor of the individual or his children who have not attained the age of 21 years.

(6) CHILDREN, GRANDCHILDREN, PARENTS, AND GRANDPARENTS.—

(A) MINOR CHILDREN.—An individual shall be considered as owning stock owned, directly or indirectly, by or for his children who have not attained the age of 21 years, and, if the individual has not attained the age of 21 years, the stock owned, directly or indirectly, by or for his parents.

(B) ADULT CHILDREN AND GRANDCHILDREN.—An individual who owns (within the meaning of subsection (d)(2), but without regard to this subparagraph) more than 50 percent of the total combined voting power of all classes of stock entitled to vote or more than 50 percent of the total value of shares of all classes of stock in a corporation shall be considered as owning the stock in such corporation owned, directly or indirectly, by or for his parents, grandparents, grandchildren, and children who have attained the age of 21 years.

(C) ADOPTED CHILD.—For purposes of this section, a legally adopted child of an individual shall be treated as a child of such individual by blood.

[Sec. 1563(f)]

(f) OTHER DEFINITIONS AND RULES.—

(1) EMPLOYEE DEFINED.—For purposes of this section the term "employee" has the same meaning such term is given by paragraphs (1) and (2) of section 3121(d).

(2) OPERATING RULES.—

(A) IN GENERAL.—Except as provided in subparagraph (B), stock constructively owned by a person by reason of the application of paragraph (1), (2), (3), (4), (5), or (6) of subsection (e) shall, for purposes of applying such paragraphs, be treated as actually owned by such person.

(B) MEMBERS OF FAMILY.—Stock constructively owned by an individual by reason of the application of paragraph (5) or (6) of subsection (e) shall not be treated as owned by him for purposes of again applying such paragraphs in order to make another the constructive owner of such stock.

(3) SPECIAL RULES.—For purposes of this section—

(A) If stock may be considered as owned by a person under subsection (e)(1) and under any other paragraph of subsection (e), it shall be considered as owned by him under subsection (e)(1).

(B) If stock is owned (within the meaning of subsection (d)) by two or more persons, such stock shall be considered as owned by the person whose ownership of such stock results in the corporation being a component member of a controlled group. If by reason of the preceding sentence, a corporation would (but for this sentence) become a component member of two controlled groups, it shall be treated as a component member of one controlled group. The determination as to the group of which such corporation is a component member shall be made under regulations prescribed by the Secretary which are consistent with the purposes of this part.

(C) If stock is owned by a person within the meaning of subsection (d) and such ownership results in the corporation being a component member of a controlled group, such stock shall not be treated as excluded stock under subsection (c)(2), if by reason of treating such stock as excluded stock the result is that such corporation is not a component member of a controlled group of corporations.

* * *

(5) BROTHER-SISTER CONTROLLED GROUP DEFINITION FOR PROVISIONS OTHER THAN THIS PART.—

(A) IN GENERAL.—Except as specifically provided in an applicable provision, subsection (a)(2) shall be applied to an applicable provision as if it read as follows:

(2) "BROTHER-SISTER CONTROLLED GROUP.—Two or more corporations if 5 or fewer persons who are individuals, estates, or trusts own (within the meaning of subsection (d)(2) stock possessing—

(A) "at least 80 percent of the total combined voting power of all classes of stock entitled to vote, or at least 80 percent of the total value of shares of all classes of stock, of each corporation, and

(B) "more than 50 percent of the total combined voting power of all classes of stock entitled to vote or more than 50 percent of the total value of shares of all classes of stock of each corporation, taking into account the stock ownership of each such person only to the extent such stock ownership is identical with respect to each such corporation."

(B) APPLICABLE PROVISION.—For purposes of this paragraph, an applicable provision is any provision of law (other than this part) which incorporates the definition of controlled group of corporations under subsection (a).

SUBTITLE C—EMPLOYMENT TAXES

CHAPTER 21—FEDERAL INSURANCE CONTRIBUTIONS ACT

SUBCHAPTER A—TAX ON EMPLOYEES

[Sec. 3101]

SEC. 3101. RATE OF TAX.

[Sec. 3101(a)]

(a) OLD-AGE, SURVIVORS, AND DISABILITY INSURANCE.—In addition to other taxes, there is hereby imposed on the income of every individual a tax equal to 6.2 percent of the wages (as defined in section 3121(a)) received by the individual with respect to employment (as defined in section 3121(b)).

[Sec. 3101(b)]

(b) HOSPITAL INSURANCE.—

(1) IN GENERAL.—In addition to the tax imposed by the preceding subsection, there is hereby imposed on the income of every individual a tax equal to 1.45 percent of the wages (as defined in section 3121(a)) received by him with respect to employment (as defined in section 3121(b)).

(2) ADDITIONAL TAX.—In addition to the tax imposed by paragraph (1) and the preceding subsection, there is hereby imposed on every taxpayer (other than a corporation, estate, or trust) a tax equal to 0.9 percent of wages which are received with respect to employment (as

defined in section 3121(b)) during any taxable year beginning after December 31, 2012, and which are in excess of—

(A) in the case of a joint return, $250,000,

(B) in the case of a married taxpayer (as defined in section 7703) filing a separate return, ½ of the dollar amount determined under subparagraph (A), and

(C) in any other case, $200,000.

* * *

CHAPTER 24—COLLECTION OF INCOME TAX AT SOURCE ON WAGES

SUBCHAPTER A—WITHHOLDING FROM WAGES

[Sec. 3401]

SEC. 3401. DEFINITIONS.

[Sec. 3401(a)]

(a) WAGES.—For purposes of this chapter, the term "wages" means all remuneration (other than fees paid to a public official) for services performed by an employee for his employer, including the cash value of all remuneration (including benefits) paid in any medium other than cash; except that such term shall not include remuneration paid—

* * *

(3) for domestic service in a private home, local college club, or local chapter of a college fraternity or sorority,

(4) for service not in the course of the employer's trade or business performed in any calendar quarter by an employee, unless the cash remuneration paid for such service is $50 or more and such service is performed by an individual who is regularly employed by such employer to perform such service. For purposes of this paragraph, an individual shall be deemed to be regularly employed by an employer during a calendar quarter only if—

(A) on each of some 24 days during such quarter such individual performs for such employer for some portion of the day service not in the course of the employer's trade or business, or

(B) such individual was regularly employed (as determined under subparagraph (A)) by such employer in the performance of such service during the preceding calendar quarter,

* * *

(9) for services performed by a duly ordained, commissioned, or licensed minister of a church in the exercise of his ministry or by a member of a religious order in the exercise of duties required by such order,

(10)(A) for services performed by an individual under the age of 18 in the delivery or distribution of newspapers or shopping news, not including delivery or distribution to any point for subsequent delivery or distribution, or

(B) for services performed by an individual in, and at the time of, the sale of newspapers or magazines to ultimate consumers, under an arrangement under which the newspapers or magazines are to be sold by him at a fixed price, his compensation being based on the retention of the excess of such price over the amount at which the newspapers or magazines are charged to him, whether or not he is guaranteed a minimum amount of compensation for such services, or is entitled to be credited with the unsold newspapers or magazines turned back,

(11) for services not in the course of the employer's trade or business, to the extent paid in any medium other than cash,

* * *

(13) pursuant to any provision of law other than section 5(c) or 6(1) of the Peace Corps Act, for service performed as a volunteer or volunteer leader within the meaning of such Act,

(14) in the form of group-term life insurance on the life of an employee,

(15) to or on behalf of an employee if (and to the extent that) at the time of the payment of such remuneration it is reasonable to believe that a corresponding deduction is allowable under section 217 (determined without regard to section 274(n)),

(16) (A) as tips in any medium other than cash,

(B) as cash tips to an employee in any calendar month in the course of his employment by an employer unless the amount of such cash tips is $20 or more,

* * *

(18) for any payment made, or benefit furnished, to or for the benefit of an employee if at the time of such payment or such furnishing it is reasonable to believe that the employee will be able to exclude such payment or benefit from income under section 127, 129, 134(b)(4), or 134(b)(5),

(19) for any benefit provided to or on behalf of an employee if at the time such benefit is provided it is reasonable to believe that the employee will be able to exclude such benefit from income under section 74(c), 108(f)(4), 117 or 132,

(20) for any medical care reimbursement made to or for the benefit of an employee under a self-insured medical reimbursement plan (within the meaning of section 105(h)(6)),

(21) for any payment made to or for the benefit of an employee if at the time of such payment it is reasonable to believe that the employee will be able to exclude such payment from income under section 106(b),

(22) any payment made to or for the benefit of an employee if at the time of such payment it is reasonable to believe that the employee will be able to exclude such payment from income under section 106(d), or

* * *

The term "wages" includes any amount includible in gross income of an employee under section 409A and payment of such amount shall be treated as having been made in the taxable year in which the amount is so includible.

* * *

[Sec. 3402]

SEC. 3402. INCOME TAX COLLECTED AT SOURCE.

[Sec. 3402(a)]

(a) REQUIREMENT OF WITHHOLDING.—

(1) IN GENERAL.—Except as otherwise provided in this section, every employer making payment of wages shall deduct and withhold upon such wages a tax determined in accordance with tables or computational procedures prescribed by the Secretary. Any tables or procedures prescribed under this paragraph shall—

(A) apply with respect to the amount of wages paid during such periods as the Secretary may prescribe, and

(B) be in such form, and provide for such amounts to be deducted and withheld, as the Secretary determines to be most appropriate to carry out the purposes of this chapter and to reflect the provisions of chapter 1 applicable to such periods.

(2) AMOUNT OF WAGES.—For purposes of applying tables or procedures prescribed under paragraph (1), the term "the amount of wages" means the amount by which the wages exceed the taxpayer's withholding allowance, prorated to the payroll period.

* * *

[Sec. 3403]

SEC. 3403. LIABILITY FOR TAX.

The employer shall be liable for the payment of the tax required to be deducted and withheld under this chapter, and shall not be liable to any person for the amount of any such payment.

SUBTITLE D—MISCELLANEOUS EXCISE TAXES

CHAPTER 42—PRIVATE FOUNDATIONS AND CERTAIN OTHER TAX-EXEMPT ORGANIZATIONS

[Sec. 4960]

SEC. 4960. TAX ON EXCESS TAX-EXEMPT ORGANIZATION EXECUTIVE COMPENSATION.

[Sec. 4960(a)]

(a) TAX IMPOSED.—There is hereby imposed a tax equal to the product of the rate of tax under section 11 and the sum of—

(1) so much of the remuneration paid (other than any excess parachute payment) by an applicable tax-exempt organization for the taxable year with respect to employment of any covered employee in excess of $1,000,000, plus

(2) any excess parachute payment paid by such an organization to any covered employee.

For purposes of the preceding sentence, remuneration shall be treated as paid when there is no substantial risk of forfeiture (within the meaning of section 457(f)(3)(B)) of the rights to such remuneration.

[Sec. 4960(b)]

(b) LIABILITY FOR TAX.—The employer shall be liable for the tax imposed under subsection (a).

[Sec. 4960(c)]

(c) DEFINITIONS AND SPECIAL RULES.—For purposes of this section—

(1) APPLICABLE TAX-EXEMPT ORGANIZATION.—The term "applicable tax-exempt organization" means any organization which for the taxable year—

(A) is exempt from taxation under section 501(a),

(B) is a farmers' cooperative organization described in section 521(b)(1),

(C) has income excluded from taxation under section 115(1), or

(D) is a political organization described in section 527(e)(1).

(2) COVERED EMPLOYEE.—For purposes of this section, the term "covered employee" means any employee (including any former employee) of an applicable tax-exempt organization if the employee—

(A) is one of the 5 highest compensated employees of the organization for the taxable year, or

(B) was a covered employee of the organization (or any predecessor) for any preceding taxable year beginning after December 31, 2016.

(3) REMUNERATION.—For purposes of this section:

(A) IN GENERAL.—The term "remuneration" means wages (as defined in section 3401(a)), except that such term shall not include any designated Roth contribution (as defined in section 402A(c)) and shall include amounts required to be included in gross income under section 457(f).

(B) EXCEPTION FOR REMUNERATION FOR MEDICAL SERVICES.—The term "remuneration" shall not include the portion of any remuneration paid to a licensed medical professional (including a veterinarian) which is for the performance of medical or veterinary services by such professional.

(4) REMUNERATION FROM RELATED ORGANIZATIONS.—

(A) IN GENERAL.—Remuneration of a covered employee by an applicable tax-exempt organization shall include any remuneration paid with respect to employment of such employee by any related person or governmental entity.

(B) RELATED ORGANIZATIONS.—A person or governmental entity shall be treated as related to an applicable tax-exempt organization if such person or governmental entity—

(i) controls, or is controlled by, the organization,

(ii) is controlled by one or more persons which control the organization,

(iii) is a supported organization (as defined in section 509(f)(3)) during the taxable year with respect to the organization,

(iv) is a supporting organization described in section 509(a)(3) during the taxable year with respect to the organization, or

(v) in the case of an organization which is a voluntary employees' beneficiary association described in section 501(c)(9), establishes, maintains, or makes contributions to such voluntary employees' beneficiary association.

(C) LIABILITY FOR TAX.—In any case in which remuneration from more than one employer is taken into account under this paragraph in determining the tax imposed by subsection (a), each such employer shall be liable for such tax in an amount which bears the same ratio to the total tax determined under subsection (a) with respect to such remuneration as—

(i) the amount of remuneration paid by such employer with respect to such employee, bears to

(ii) the amount of remuneration paid by all such employers to such employee.

(5) EXCESS PARACHUTE PAYMENT.—For purposes of determining the tax imposed by subsection (a)(2)—

(A) IN GENERAL.—The term "excess parachute payment" means an amount equal to the excess of any parachute payment over the portion of the base amount allocated to such payment.

(B) PARACHUTE PAYMENT.—The term "parachute payment" means any payment in the nature of compensation to (or for the benefit of) a covered employee if—

(i) such payment is contingent on such employee's separation from employment with the employer, and

(ii) the aggregate present value of the payments in the nature of compensation to (or for the benefit of) such individual which are contingent on such separation equals or exceeds an amount equal to 3 times the base amount.

(C) EXCEPTION.—Such term does not include any payment—

(i) described in section 280G(b)(6) (relating to exemption for payments under qualified plans),

(ii) made under or to an annuity contract described in section 403(b) or a plan described in section 457(b),

(iii) to a licensed medical professional (including a veterinarian) to the extent that such payment is for the performance of medical or veterinary services by such professional, or

(iv) to an individual who is not a highly compensated employee as defined in section 414(q).

(D) BASE AMOUNT.—Rules similar to the rules of 280G(b)(3) shall apply for purposes of determining the base amount.

(E) PROPERTY TRANSFERS; PRESENT VALUE.—Rules similar to the rules of paragraphs (3) and (4) of section 280G(d) shall apply.

(6) COORDINATION WITH DEDUCTION LIMITATION.—Remuneration the deduction for which is not allowed by reason of section 162(m) shall not be taken into account for purposes of this section.

[Sec. 4960(d)]

(d) REGULATIONS.—The Secretary shall prescribe such regulations as may be necessary to prevent avoidance of the tax under this section, including regulations to prevent avoidance of such tax through the performance of services other than as an employee or by providing compensation through a pass-through or other entity to avoid such tax.

[Sec. 4968]

SEC. 4968. EXCISE TAX BASED ON INVESTMENT INCOME OF PRIVATE COLLEGES AND UNIVERSITIES.

[Sec. 4968(a)]

(a) TAX IMPOSED.—There is hereby imposed on each applicable educational institution for the taxable year a tax equal to 1.4 percent of the net investment income of such institution for the taxable year.

[Sec. 4968(b)]

(b) APPLICABLE EDUCATIONAL INSTITUTION.—For purposes of this subchapter—

(1) IN GENERAL.—The term "applicable educational institution" means an eligible educational institution (as defined in section 25A(f)(2))—

(A) which had at least 500 tuition-paying students during the preceding taxable year,

(B) more than 50 percent of the tuition-paying students of which are located in the United States,

(C) which is not described in the first sentence of section 511(a)(2)(B) (relating to State colleges and universities), and

(D) the aggregate fair market value of the assets of which at the end of the preceding taxable year (other than those assets which are used directly in carrying out the institution's exempt purpose) is at least $500,000 per student of the institution.

(2) STUDENTS.—For purposes of paragraph (1), the number of students of an institution (including for purposes of determining the number of students at a particular location) shall be based on the daily average number of full-time students attending such institution (with part-time students taken into account on a full-time student equivalent basis).

[Sec. 4968(c)]

(c) NET INVESTMENT INCOME.—For purposes of this section, net investment income shall be determined under rules similar to the rules of section 4940(c).

[Sec. 4968(d)]

(d) ASSETS AND NET INVESTMENT INCOME OF RELATED ORGANIZATIONS.—

(1) IN GENERAL.—For purposes of subsections (b)(1)(C) and (c), assets and net investment income of any related organization with respect to an educational institution shall be treated as assets and net investment income, respectively, of the educational institution, except that—

(A) no such amount shall be taken into account with respect to more than 1 educational institution, and

(B) unless such organization is controlled by such institution or is described in section 509(a)(3) with respect to such institution for the taxable year, assets and net investment income which are not intended or available for the use or benefit of the educational institution shall not be taken into account.

(2) RELATED ORGANIZATION.—For purposes of this subsection, the term "related organization" means, with respect to an educational institution, any organization which—

(A) controls, or is controlled by, such institution,

(B) is controlled by 1 or more persons which also control such institution, or

(C) is a supported organization (as defined in section 509(f)(3)), or an organization described in section 509(a)(3), during the taxable year with respect to such institution.

CHAPTER 46—GOLDEN PARACHUTE PAYMENTS

[Sec. 4999]

SEC. 4999. GOLDEN PARACHUTE PAYMENTS.

[Sec. 4999(a)]

(a) IMPOSITION OF TAX.— There is hereby imposed on any person who receives an excess parachute payment a tax equal to 20 percent of the amount of such payment.

[Sec. 4999(b)]

(b) EXCESS PARACHUTE PAYMENT DEFINED.—For purposes of this section, the term "Excess parachute payment" has the meaning given to such term by section 280G(b).

* * *

SUBTITLE F—PROCEDURE AND ADMINISTRATION

CHAPTER 61—INFORMATION AND RETURNS

SUBCHAPTER A—RETURNS AND RECORDS

PART I—RECORDS, STATEMENTS, AND SPECIAL RETURNS

[Sec. 6001]

SEC. 6001. NOTICE OR REGULATIONS REQUIRING RECORDS, STATEMENTS, AND SPECIAL RETURNS.

Every person liable for any tax imposed by this title, or for the collection thereof, shall keep such records, render such statements, make such returns, and comply with such rules and regulations as the Secretary may from time to time prescribe. Whenever in the judgment of the Secretary it is necessary, he may require any person, by notice served upon such person or by regulations, to make such returns, render such statements, or keep such records, as the Secretary deems sufficient to show whether or not such person is liable for tax under this title. The only records which an employer shall be required to keep under this section in connection with charged tips shall be charge receipts, records necessary to comply with section 6053(c), and copies of statements furnished by employees under section 6053(a).

PART II—TAX RETURNS OR STATEMENTS

Subpart B—Income Tax Returns

[Sec. 6012]

SEC. 6012. PERSONS REQUIRED TO MAKE RETURNS OF INCOME.

[Sec. 6012(a)]

(a) GENERAL RULE.—Returns with respect to income taxes under subtitle A shall be made by the following:

(1) (A) Every individual having for the taxable year gross income which equals or exceeds the exemption amount, except that a return shall not be required of an individual—

(i) who is not married (determined by applying section 7703), is not a surviving spouse (as defined in section 2(a)), is not a head of a household (as defined in section 2(b)), and for the taxable year has gross income of less than the sum of the exemption amount plus the basic standard deduction applicable to such an individual,

(ii) who is a head of a household (as so defined) and for the taxable year has gross income of less than the sum of the exemption amount plus the basic standard deduction applicable to such an individual,

(iii) who is a surviving spouse (as so defined) and for the taxable year has gross income of less than the sum of the exemption amount plus the basic standard deduction applicable to such an individual, or

(iv) who is entitled to make a joint return and whose gross income, when combined with the gross income of his spouse, is, for the taxable year, less than the sum of twice the exemption amount plus the basic standard deduction applicable to a joint return, but only if such individual and his spouse, at the close of the taxable year, had the same household as their home.

Clause (iv) shall not apply if for the taxable year such spouse makes a separate return or any other taxpayer is entitled to an exemption for such spouse under section 151(c).

(B) The amount specified in clause (i), (ii), or (iii) of subparagraph (A) shall be increased by the amount of 1 additional standard deduction (within the meaning of section 63(c)(3)) in the case of an individual entitled to such deduction by reason of section 63(f)(1)(A) (relating to individuals age 65 or more), and the amount specified in clause (iv) of subparagraph (A) shall be increased by the amount of the additional standard deduction for each additional standard deduction to which the individual or his spouse is entitled by reason of section 63(f)(1).

(C) The exception under subparagraph (A) shall not apply to any individual—

(i) who is described in section 63(c)(5) and who has—

(I) income (other than earned income) in excess of the sum of the amount in effect under section 63(c)(5)(A) plus the additional standard deduction (if any) to which the individual is entitled, or

(II) total gross income in excess of the standard deduction, or

(ii) for whom the standard deduction is zero under section 63(c)(6).

(D) For purposes of this subsection—

(i) The terms "standard deduction", "basic standard deduction" and "additional standard deduction" have the respective meanings given such terms by section 63(c).

(ii) The term "exemption amount" has the meaning given such term by section 151(d). In the case of an individual described in section 151(d)(2), the exemption amount shall be zero.

(2) Every corporation subject to taxation under subtitle A;

(3) Every estate the gross income of which for the taxable year is $600 or more;

(4) Every trust having for the taxable year any taxable income, or having gross income of $600 or over, regardless of the amount of taxable income;

(5) Every estate or trust of which any beneficiary is a nonresident alien;

(6) Every political organization (within the meaning of section 527(e)(1)), and every fund treated under section 527(g) as if it constituted a political organization, which has political organization taxable income (within the meaning of section 527(c)(1)) for the taxable year;

(7) Every homeowners association (within the meaning of section 528(c)(1)) which has homeowners association taxable income (within the meaning of section 528(d)) for the taxable year; and

(8) Every estate of an individual under chapter 7 or 11 of title 11 of the United States Code (relating to bankruptcy) the gross income of which for the taxable year is not less than the sum of the exemption amount plus the basic standard deduction under section 63(c)(2)(C).

except that subject to such conditions, limitations, and exceptions and under such regulations as may be prescribed by the Secretary, nonresident alien individuals subject to the tax imposed by section 871 and foreign corporations subject to the tax imposed by section 881 may be exempted from the requirement of making returns under this section.

[Sec. 6012(b)]

(b) RETURNS MADE BY FIDUCIARIES AND RECEIVERS.—

(1) RETURNS OF DECEDENTS.—If an individual is deceased, the return of such individual required under subsection (a) shall be made by his executor, administrator, or other person charged with the property of such decedent.

(2) PERSONS UNDER A DISABILITY.—If an individual is unable to make a return required under subsection (a), the return of such individual shall be made by a duly authorized agent,

his committee, guardian, fiduciary or other person charged with the care of the person or property of such individual. The preceding sentence shall not apply in the case of a receiver appointed by authority of law in possession of only a part of the property of an individual.

(3) RECEIVERS, TRUSTEES AND ASSIGNEES FOR CORPORATIONS.—In a case where a receiver, trustee in a case under title 11 of the United States Code or assignee, by order of a court of competent jurisdiction, by operation of law or otherwise, has possession of or holds title to all or substantially all the property or business of a corporation, whether or not such property or business is being operated, such receiver, trustee, or assignee shall make the return of income for such corporation in the same manner and form as corporations are required to make such returns.

(4) RETURNS OF ESTATES AND TRUSTS.—Returns of an estate, a trust, or an estate of an individual under chapter 7 or 11 of title 11 of the United States Code shall be made by the fiduciary thereof.

(5) JOINT FIDUCIARIES.—Under such regulations as the Secretary may prescribe, a return made by one of two or more joint fiduciaries shall be sufficient compliance with the requirements of this section. A return made pursuant to this paragraph shall contain a statement that the fiduciary has sufficient knowledge of the affairs of the person for whom the return is made to enable him to make the return, and that the return is, to the best of his knowledge and belief, true and correct.

(6) IRA SHARE OF PARTNERSHIP INCOME.—In the case of a trust which is exempt from taxation under section 408(e), for purposes of this section, the trust's distributive share of items of gross income and gain of any partnership to which subchapter C or D of chapter 63 applies shall be treated as equal to the trust's distributive share of the taxable income of such partnership.

[Sec. 6012(c)]

(c) CERTAIN INCOME EARNED ABROAD OR FROM SALE OF RESIDENCE.—For purposes of this section, gross income shall be computed without regard to the exclusion provided for in section 121 (relating to gain from sale of principal residence) and without regard to the exclusion provided for in section 911 (relating to citizens or residents of the United States living abroad).

[Sec. 6012(d)]

(d) TAX-EXEMPT INTEREST REQUIRED TO BE SHOWN ON RETURN.—Every person required to file a return under this section for the taxable year shall include on such return the amount of interest received or accrued during the taxable year which is exempt from the tax imposed by chapter 1.

[Sec. 6012(e)]

(e) CONSOLIDATED RETURNS.—

For provisions relating to consolidated returns by affiliated corporations, see chapter 6.

[Sec. 6012(f)]

(f) SPECIAL RULE FOR TAXABLE YEARS 2018 THROUGH 2025.—In the case of a taxable year beginning after December 31, 2017, and before January 1, 2026, subsection (a)(1) shall not apply, and every individual who has gross income for the taxable year shall be required to make returns with respect to income taxes under subtitle A, except that a return shall not be required of—

(1) an individual who is not married (determined by applying section 7703) and who has gross income for the taxable year which does not exceed the standard deduction applicable to such individual for such taxable year under section 63, or

(2) an individual entitled to make a joint return if—

(A) the gross income of such individual, when combined with the gross income of such individual's spouse, for the taxable year does not exceed the standard deduction which would be applicable to the taxpayer for such taxable year under section 63 if such individual and such individual's spouse made a joint return,

(B) such individual and such individual's spouse have the same household as their home at the close of the taxable year,

(C) such individual's spouse does not make a separate return, and

(D) neither such individual nor such individual's spouse is an individual described in section 63(c)(5) who has income (other than earned income) in excess of the amount in effect under section 63(c)(5)(A).

[Sec. 6013]

SEC. 6013. JOINT RETURNS OF INCOME TAX BY HUSBAND AND WIFE.

[Sec. 6013(a)]

(a) JOINT RETURNS.—A husband and wife may make a single return jointly of income taxes under subtitle A, even though one of the spouses has neither gross income nor deductions, except as provided below:

(1) no joint return shall be made if either the husband or wife at any time during the taxable year is a nonresident alien;

(2) no joint return shall be made if the husband and wife have different taxable years; except that if such taxable years begin on the same day and end on different days because of the death of either or both, then the joint return may be made with respect to the taxable year of each. The above exception shall not apply if the surviving spouse remarries before the close of his taxable year, nor if the taxable year of either spouse is a fractional part of a year under section 443(a)(1);

(3) in the case of death of one spouse or both spouses the joint return with respect to the decedent may be made only by his executor or administrator; except that in the case of the death of one spouse the joint return may be made by the surviving spouse with respect to both himself and the decedent if no return for the taxable year has been made by the decedent, no executor or administrator has been appointed, and no executor or administrator is appointed before the last day prescribed by law for filing the return of the surviving spouse. If an executor or administrator of the decedent is appointed after the making of the joint return by the surviving spouse, the executor or administrator may disaffirm such joint return by making, within 1 year after the last day prescribed by law for filing the return of the surviving spouse, a separate return for the taxable year of the decedent with respect to which the joint return was made, in which case the return made by the survivor shall constitute his separate return.

[Sec. 6013(b)]

(b) JOINT RETURN AFTER FILING SEPARATE RETURN.—

(1) IN GENERAL.—Except as provided in paragraph (2), if an individual has filed a separate return for a taxable year for which a joint return could have been made by him and his spouse under subsection (a) and the time prescribed by law for filing the return for such taxable year has expired, such individual and his spouse may nevertheless make a joint return for such taxable year. A joint return filed by the husband and wife under this subsection shall constitute the return of the husband and wife for such taxable year, and all payments, credits, refunds, or other repayments made or allowed with respect to the separate return of either spouse for such taxable year shall be taken into account in determining the extent to which the tax based upon the joint return has been paid. If a joint return is made under this subsection, any election (other than the election to file a separate return) made by either spouse in his separate return for such taxable year with respect to the treatment of any income, deduction, or credit of such spouse shall not be changed in the making of the joint return where such election would have been irrevocable if the joint return had not been made. If a joint return is made under this subsection after the death of either spouse, such return with respect to the decedent can be made only by his executor or administrator.

(2) LIMITATIONS FOR MAKING OF ELECTION.—The election provided for in paragraph (1) may not be made—

(A) after the expiration of 3 years from the last date prescribed by law for filing the return for such taxable year (determined without regard to any extension of time granted to either spouse); or

(B) after there has been mailed to either spouse, with respect to such taxable year, a notice of deficiency under section 6212, if the spouse, as to such notice, files a petition with the Tax Court within the time prescribed in section 6213; or

(C) after either spouse has commenced a suit in any court for the recovery of any part of the tax for such taxable year; or

(D) after either spouse has entered into a closing agreement under section 7121 with respect to such taxable year, or after any civil or criminal case arising against either spouse with respect to such taxable year has been compromised under section 7122.

(3) WHEN RETURN DEEMED FILED.—

(A) ASSESSMENT AND COLLECTION.—For purposes of section 6501 (relating to periods of limitations on assessment and collection), and for purposes of section 6651 (relating to delinquent returns), a joint return made under this subsection shall be deemed to have been filed—

(i) Where both spouses filed separate returns prior to making the joint return—on the date the last separate return was filed (but not earlier than the last date prescribed by law for filing the return of either spouse);

(ii) Where only one spouse filed a separate return prior to the making of the joint return, and the other spouse had less than the exemption amount of gross income for such taxable year—on the date of the filing of such separate return (but not earlier than the last date prescribed by law for the filing of such separate return); or

(iii) Where only one spouse filed a separate return prior to the making of the joint return, and the other spouse had gross income of the exemption amount or more for such taxable year—on the date of the filing of such joint return.

For purposes of this subparagraph, the term "exemption amount" has the meaning given to such term by section 151(d). For purposes of clauses (ii) and (iii), if the spouse whose gross income is being compared to the exemption amount is 65 or over, such clauses shall be applied by substituting "the sum of the exemption amount and the additional standard deduction under section 63(c)(2) by reason of section 63(f)(1)(A) for "the exemption amount".

(B) CREDIT OR REFUND.—For purposes of section 6511, a joint return made under this subsection shall be deemed to have been filed on the last date prescribed by law for filing the return for such taxable year (determined without regard to any extension of time granted to either spouse).

(4) ADDITIONAL TIME FOR ASSESSMENT.—If a joint return is made under this subsection, the periods of limitations provided in sections 6501 and 6502 on the making of assessments and the beginning of levy or a proceeding in court for collection shall with respect to such return include one year immediately after the date of the filing of such joint return (computed without regard to the provisions of paragraph (3)).

(5) ADDITIONS TO THE TAX AND PENALTIES.—

(A) COORDINATION WITH PART II OF SUBCHAPTER A OF CHAPTER 68.—For purposes of part II of subchapter A of chapter 68, where the sum of the amounts shown as tax on the separate returns of each spouse is less than the amount shown as tax on the joint return made under this subsection—

(i) such sum shall be treated as the amount shown on the joint return,

(ii) any negligence (or disregard of rules or regulations) on either separate return shall be treated as negligence (or such disregard) on the joint return, and

(iii) any fraud on either separate return shall be treated as fraud on the joint return.

(B) CRIMINAL PENALTY.—For purposes of section 7206(1) and (2) and section 7207 (relating to criminal penalties in the case of fraudulent returns) the term "return" includes a separate return filed by a spouse with respect to a taxable year for which a joint return is made under this subsection after the filing of such separate return.

[Sec. 6013(c)]

(c) TREATMENT OF JOINT RETURN AFTER DEATH OF EITHER SPOUSE.—For purposes of sections 15, 443, and 7851(a)(1)(A), where the husband and wife have different taxable years because of the death of either spouse, the joint return shall be treated as if the taxable years of both spouses ended on the date of the closing of the surviving spouse's taxable year.

[Sec. 6013(d)]

(d) SPECIAL RULES.—For purposes of this section—

(1) the status as husband and wife of two individuals having taxable years beginning on the same day shall be determined—

(A) if both have the same taxable year—as of the close of such year; or

(B) if one dies before the close of the taxable year of the other—as of the time of such death;

(2) an individual who is legally separated from his spouse under a decree of divorce or of separate maintenance shall not be considered as married; and

(3) if a joint return is made, the tax shall be computed on the aggregate income and the liability with respect to the tax shall be joint and several.

* * *

[Sec. 6015]

SEC. 6015. RELIEF FROM JOINT AND SEVERAL LIABILITY ON JOINT RETURN.

[Sec. 6015(a)]

(a) IN GENERAL.—Notwithstanding section 6013(d)(3)—

(1) an individual who has made a joint return may elect to seek relief under the procedures prescribed under subsection (b); and

(2) if such individual is eligible to elect the application of subsection (c), such individual may, in addition to any election under paragraph (1), elect to limit such individual's liability for any deficiency with respect to such joint return in the manner prescribed under subsection (c).

Any determination under this section shall be made without regard to community property laws.

[Sec. 6015(b)]

(b) PROCEDURES FOR RELIEF FROM LIABILITY APPLICABLE TO ALL JOINT FILERS.—

(1) IN GENERAL.—Under procedures prescribed by the Secretary, if—

(A) a joint return has been made for a taxable year;

(B) on such return there is an understatement of tax attributable to erroneous items of 1 individual filing the joint return;

(C) the other individual filing the joint return establishes that in signing the return he or she did not know, and had no reason to know, that there was such understatement;

(D) taking into account all the facts and circumstances, it is inequitable to hold the other individual liable for the deficiency in tax for such taxable year attributable to such understatement; and

(E) the other individual elects (in such form as the Secretary may prescribe) the benefits of this subsection not later than the date which is 2 years after the date the Secretary has begun collection activities with respect to the individual making the election,

then the other individual shall be relieved of liability for tax (including interest, penalties, and other amounts) for such taxable year to the extent such liability is attributable to such understatement.

(2) APPORTIONMENT OF RELIEF.—If an individual who, but for paragraph (1)(C), would be relieved of liability under paragraph (1), establishes that in signing the return such individual did not know, and had no reason to know, the extent of such understatement, then such individual shall be relieved of liability for tax (including interest, penalties, and other amounts) for such taxable year to the extent that such liability is attributable to the portion of such understatement of which such individual did not know and had no reason to know.

(3) UNDERSTATEMENT.—For purposes of this subsection, the term "understatement" has the meaning given to such term by section 6662(d)(2)(A).

(c) PROCEDURES TO LIMIT LIABILITY FOR TAXPAYERS NO LONGER MARRIED OR TAXPAYERS LEGALLY SEPARATED OR NOT LIVING TOGETHER.—

(1) IN GENERAL.—Except as provided in this subsection, if an individual who has made a joint return for any taxable year elects the application of this subsection, the individual's liability for any deficiency which is assessed with respect to the return shall not exceed the portion of such deficiency properly allocable to the individual under subsection (d).

(2) BURDEN OF PROOF.—Except as provided in subparagraph (A)(ii) or (C) of paragraph (3), each individual who elects the application of this subsection shall have the burden of proof with respect to establishing the portion of any deficiency allocable to such individual.

(3) ELECTION.—

(A) INDIVIDUALS ELIGIBLE TO MAKE ELECTION.—

(i) IN GENERAL.—An individual shall only be eligible to elect the application of this subsection if—

(I) at the time such election is filed, such individual is no longer married to, or is legally separated from, the individual with whom such individual filed the joint return to which the election relates; or

(II) such individual was not a member of the same household as the individual with whom such joint return was filed at any time during the 12-month period ending on the date such election is filed.

(ii) CERTAIN TAXPAYERS INELIGIBLE TO ELECT.—If the Secretary demonstrates that assets were transferred between individuals filing a joint return as part of a fraudulent scheme by such individuals, an election under this subsection by either individual shall be invalid (and section 6013(d)(3) shall apply to the joint return).

(B) TIME FOR ELECTION.—An election under this subsection for any taxable year may be made at any time after a deficiency for such year is asserted but not later than 2 years after the date on which the Secretary has begun collection activities with respect to the individual making the election.

(C) ELECTION NOT VALID WITH RESPECT TO CERTAIN DEFICIENCIES.—If the Secretary demonstrates that an individual making an election under this subsection had actual knowledge, at the time such individual signed the return, of any item giving rise to a deficiency (or portion thereof) which is not allocable to such individual under subsection (d), such election shall not apply to such deficiency (or portion). This subparagraph shall not apply where the individual with actual knowledge establishes that such individual signed the return under duress.

(4) LIABILITY INCREASED BY REASON OF TRANSFERS OF PROPERTY TO AVOID TAX.—

(A) IN GENERAL.—Notwithstanding any other provision of this subsection, the portion of the deficiency for which the individual electing the application of this subsection is liable (without regard to this paragraph) shall be increased by the value of any disqualified asset transferred to the individual.

(B) DISQUALIFIED ASSET.—For purposes of this paragraph—

(i) IN GENERAL.—The term "disqualified asset" means any property or right to property transferred to an individual making the election under this subsection with respect to a joint return by the other individual filing such joint return if the principal purpose of the transfer was the avoidance of tax or payment of tax.

(ii) PRESUMPTION.—

(I) IN GENERAL.—For purposes of clause (i), except as provided in subclause (II), any transfer which is made after the date which is 1 year before the date on which the first letter of proposed deficiency which allows the taxpayer an opportunity for administrative review in the Internal Revenue Service Independent Office of Appeals is sent shall be presumed to have as its principal purpose the avoidance of tax or payment of tax.

(II) EXCEPTIONS.—Subclause (I) shall not apply to any transfer pursuant to a decree of divorce or separate maintenance or a written instrument incident to such a decree or to any transfer which an individual establishes did not have as its principal purpose the avoidance of tax or payment of tax.

[Sec. 6015(d)]

(d) ALLOCATION OF DEFICIENCY.—For purposes of subsection (c)—

(1) IN GENERAL.—The portion of any deficiency on a joint return allocated to an individual shall be the amount which bears the same ratio to such deficiency as the net amount of items taken into account in computing the deficiency and allocable to the individual under paragraph (3) bears to the net amount of all items taken into account in computing the deficiency.

(2) SEPARATE TREATMENT OF CERTAIN ITEMS.—If a deficiency (or portion thereof) is attributable to—

(A) the disallowance of a credit; or

(B) any tax (other than tax imposed by section 1 or 55) required to be included with the joint return;

and such item is allocated to one individual under paragraph (3), such deficiency (or portion) shall be allocated to such individual. Any such item shall not be taken into account under paragraph (1).

(3) ALLOCATION OF ITEMS GIVING RISE TO THE DEFICIENCY.—For purposes of this subsection—

(A) IN GENERAL.—Except as provided in paragraphs (4) and (5), any item giving rise to a deficiency on a joint return shall be allocated to individuals filing the return in the same manner as it would have been allocated if the individuals had filed separate returns for the taxable year.

(B) EXCEPTION WHERE OTHER SPOUSE BENEFITS.—Under rules prescribed by the Secretary, an item otherwise allocable to an individual under subparagraph (A) shall be allocated to the other individual filing the joint return to the extent the item gave rise to a tax benefit on the joint return to the other individual.

(C) EXCEPTION FOR FRAUD.—The Secretary may provide for an allocation of any item in a manner not prescribed by subparagraph (A) if the Secretary establishes that such allocation is appropriate due to fraud of one or both individuals.

(4) LIMITATIONS ON SEPARATE RETURNS DISREGARDED.—If an item of deduction or credit is disallowed in its entirety solely because a separate return is filed, such disallowance shall be disregarded and the item shall be computed as if a joint return had been filed and then allocated between the spouses appropriately. A similar rule shall apply for purposes of section 86.

(5) CHILD'S LIABILITY.—If the liability of a child of a taxpayer is included on a joint return, such liability shall be disregarded in computing the separate liability of either spouse and such liability shall be allocated appropriately between the spouses.

[Sec. 6015(e)]

(e) PETITION FOR REVIEW BY TAX COURT.—

(1) IN GENERAL.—In the case of an individual against whom a deficiency has been asserted and who elects to have subsection (b) or (c) apply, or in the case of an individual who requests equitable relief under subsection (f)—

(A) IN GENERAL.—In addition to any other remedy provided by law, the individual may petition the Tax Court (and the Tax Court shall have jurisdiction) to determine the appropriate relief available to the individual under this section if such petition is filed—

(i) at any time after the earlier of—

(I) the date the Secretary mails, by certified or registered mail to the taxpayer's last known address, notice of the Secretary's final determination of relief available to the individual, or

(II) the date which is 6 months after the date such election is filed or request is made with the Secretary, and

(ii) not later than the close of the 90th day after the date described in clause (i)(I).

(B) RESTRICTIONS APPLICABLE TO COLLECTION OF ASSESSMENT.—

(i) IN GENERAL.—Except as otherwise provided in section 6851 or 6861, no levy or proceeding in court shall be made, begun, or prosecuted against the individual making an election under subsection (b) or (c) or requesting equitable relief under subsection (f) for collection of any assessment to which such election or request relates until the close of the 90th day referred to in subparagraph (A)(ii), or, if a petition has been filed with the Tax Court under subparagraph (A), until the decision of the Tax Court has become final. Rules similar to the rules of section 7485 shall apply with respect to the collection of such assessment.

(ii) AUTHORITY TO ENJOIN COLLECTION ACTIONS.—Notwithstanding the provisions of section 7421(a), the beginning of such levy or proceeding during the time the prohibition under clause (i) is in force may be enjoined by a proceeding in the proper court, including the Tax Court. The Tax Court shall have no jurisdiction under this subparagraph to enjoin any action or proceeding unless a timely petition has been filed under subparagraph (A) and then only in respect of the amount of the assessment to which the election under subsection (b) or (c) relates or to which the request under subsection (f) relates.

(2) SUSPENSION OF RUNNING OF PERIOD OF LIMITATIONS.—The running of the period of limitations in section 6502 on the collection of the assessment to which the petition under paragraph (1)(A) relates shall be suspended—

(A) for the period during which the Secretary is prohibited by paragraph (1)(B) from collecting by levy or a proceeding in court and for 60 days thereafter, and

(B) if a waiver under paragraph (5) is made, from the date the claim for relief was filed until 60 days after the waiver is filed with the Secretary.

(3) LIMITATION ON TAX COURT JURISDICTION.—If a suit for refund is begun by either individual filing the joint return pursuant to section 6532—

(A) the Tax Court shall lose jurisdiction of the individual's action under this section to whatever extent jurisdiction is acquired by the district court or the United States Court of Federal Claims over the taxable years that are the subject of the suit for refund, and

(B) the court acquiring jurisdiction shall have jurisdiction over the petition filed under this subsection.

(4) NOTICE TO OTHER SPOUSE.—The Tax Court shall establish rules which provide the individual filing a joint return but not making the election under subsection (b) or (c) or the request for equitable relief under subsection (f) with adequate notice and an opportunity to become a party to a proceeding under either such subsection.

(5) WAIVER.—An individual who elects the application of subsection (b) or (c) or who requests equitable relief under subsection (f) (and who agrees with the Secretary's determination of relief) may waive in writing at any time the restrictions in paragraph (1)(B) with respect to collection of the outstanding assessment (whether or not a notice of the Secretary's final determination of relief has been mailed).

(6) SUSPENSION OF RUNNING OF PERIOD FOR FILING PETITION IN TITLE 11 CASES.—In the case of a person who is prohibited by reason of a case under title 11, United States Code, from filing a petition under paragraph (1)(A) with respect to a final determination of relief under this section, the running of the period prescribed by such paragraph for filing such a petition with respect to such final determination shall be suspended for the period during which the person is so prohibited from filing such a petition, and for 60 days thereafter.

(7) STANDARD AND SCOPE OF REVIEW.—Any review of a determination made under this section shall be reviewed de novo by the Tax Court and shall be based upon—

(A) the administrative record established at the time of the determination, and

(B) any additional newly discovered or previously unavailable evidence.

[Sec. 6015(f)]

(f) EQUITABLE RELIEF.—

(1) IN GENERAL.—Under procedures prescribed by the Secretary, if—

(A) taking into account all the facts and circumstances, it is inequitable to hold the individual liable for any unpaid tax or any deficiency (or any portion of either), and

(B) relief is not available to such individual under subsection (b) or (c),

the Secretary may relieve such individual of such liability.

(2) LIMITATION.—A request for equitable relief under this subsection may be made with respect to any portion of any liability that—

(A) has not been paid, provided that such request is made before the expiration of the applicable period of limitation under section 6502, or

(B) has been paid, provided that such request is made during the period in which the individual could submit a timely claim for refund or credit of such payment.

[Sec. 6015(g)]

(g) CREDITS AND REFUNDS.—

(1) IN GENERAL.—Except as provided in paragraphs (2) and (3), notwithstanding any other law or rule of law (other than section 6511, 6512(b), 7121, or 7122), credit or refund shall be allowed or made to the extent attributable to the application of this section.

(2) RES JUDICATA.—In the case of any election under subsection (b) or (c) or of any request for equitable relief under subsection (f), if a decision of a court in any prior proceeding for the same taxable year has become final, such decision shall be conclusive except with respect to the qualification of the individual for relief which was not an issue in such proceeding. The exception contained in the preceding sentence shall not apply if the court determines that the individual participated meaningfully in such prior proceeding.

(3) CREDIT AND REFUND NOT ALLOWED UNDER SUBSECTION (c).—No credit or refund shall be allowed as a result of an election under subsection (c).

[Sec. 6015(h)]

(h) REGULATIONS.—The Secretary shall prescribe such regulations as are necessary to carry out the provisions of this section, including—

(1) regulations providing methods for allocation of items other than the methods under subsection (d)(3); and

(2) regulations providing the opportunity for an individual to have notice of, and an opportunity to participate in, any administrative proceeding with respect to an election made under subsection (b) or (c) or a request for equitable relief made under subsection (f) by the other individual filing the joint return.

PART III—INFORMATION RETURNS

Subpart A—Information Concerning Persons Subject to Special Provisions

[Sec. 6031]

SEC. 6031. RETURN OF PARTNERSHIP INCOME.

[Sec. 6031(a)]

(a) GENERAL RULE.—Every partnership (as defined in section 761(a)) shall make a return for each taxable year, stating specifically the items of its gross income and the deductions allowable by subtitle A, and such other information for the purpose of carrying out the provisions of subtitle A as the Secretary may by forms and regulations prescribe, and shall include in the return the names and addresses of the individuals who would be entitled to share in the taxable income if distributed and the amount of the distributive share of each individual.

[Sec. 6031(b)]

(b) COPIES TO PARTNERS.—Each partnership required to file a return under subsection (a) for any partnership taxable year shall (on or before the day on which the return for such taxable year was required to be filed) furnish to each person who is a partner or who holds an interest in such partnership as a nominee for another person at any time during such taxable year a copy of such information required to be shown on such return as may be required by regulations. Information required to be furnished by the partnership under this subsection may not be amended after the due date of the return under subsection (a) to which such information relates, except—

(1) in the case of a partnership which has elected the application of section 6221(b) for the taxable year,

(2) as provided in the procedures under section 6225(c),

(3) with respect to statements under section 6226, or

(4) as otherwise provided by the Secretary.

[Sec. 6031(c)]

(c) NOMINEE REPORTING.—Any person who holds an interest in a partnership as a nominee for another person—

(1) shall furnish to the partnership, in the manner prescribed by the Secretary, the name and address of such other person, and any other information for such taxable year as the Secretary may by form and regulation prescribe, and

(2) shall furnish in the manner prescribed by the Secretary such other person the information provided by such partnership under subsection (b).

[Sec. 6031(d)]

(d) SEPARATE STATEMENT OF ITEMS OF UNRELATED BUSINESS TAXABLE INCOME.—In the case of any partnership regularly carrying on a trade or business (within the meaning of section 512(c)(1)), the information required under subsection (b) to be furnished to its partners shall include such information as is necessary to enable each partner to compute its distributive share of partnership income or loss from such trade or business in accordance with section 512(a)(1), but without regard to the modifications described in paragraphs (8) through (15) of section 512(b).

* * *

[Sec. 6031(f)]

(f) ELECTING INVESTMENT PARTNERSHIPS.—In the case of any electing investment partnership (as defined in section 743(e)(6)), the information required under subsection (b) to be furnished to any partner to whom section 743(e)(2) applies shall include such information as is necessary to enable the partner to compute the amount of losses disallowed under section 743(e).

[Sec. 6037]

SEC. 6037. RETURN OF S CORPORATION.

[Sec. 6037(a)]

(a) IN GENERAL.—Every S corporation shall make a return for each taxable year, stating specifically the items of its gross income and the deductions allowable by subtitle A, the names and addresses of all persons owning stock in the corporation at any time during the taxable year, the number of shares of stock owned by each shareholder at all times during the taxable year, the amount of money and other property distributed by the corporation during the taxable year to each shareholder, the date of each such distribution, each shareholder's pro rata share of each item of the corporation for the taxable year, and such other information, for the purpose of carrying out the provisions of subchapter S of chapter 1, as the Secretary may by forms and regulations prescribe. Any return filed pursuant to this section shall, for purposes of chapter 66 (relating to limitations), be treated as a return filed by the corporation under section 6012.

[Sec. 6037(b)]

(b) COPIES TO SHAREHOLDERS.—Each S corporation required to file a return under subsection (a) for any taxable year shall (on or before the day on which the return for such taxable year was filed) furnish to each person who is a shareholder at any time during such taxable year a copy of such information shown on such return as may be required by regulations.

[Sec. 6037(c)]

(c) SHAREHOLDER'S RETURN MUST BE CONSISTENT WITH CORPORATE RETURN OR SECRETARY NOTIFIED OF INCONSISTENCY.—

(1) IN GENERAL.—A shareholder of an S corporation shall, on such shareholder's return, treat a subchapter S item in a manner which is consistent with the treatment of such item on the corporate return.

(2) NOTIFICATION OF INCONSISTENT TREATMENT.—

(A) IN GENERAL.—In the case of any subchapter S item, if—

(i) (I) the corporation has filed a return but the shareholder's treatment on his return is (or may be) inconsistent with the treatment of the item on the corporate return, or

(II) the corporation has not filed a return, and

(ii) the shareholder files with the Secretary a statement identifying the inconsistency,

paragraph (1) shall not apply to such item.

(B) SHAREHOLDER RECEIVING INCORRECT INFORMATION.—A shareholder shall be treated as having complied with clause (ii) of subparagraph (A) with respect to a subchapter S item if the shareholder—

(i) demonstrates to the satisfaction of the Secretary that the treatment of the subchapter S item on the shareholder's return is consistent with the treatment of the item on the schedule furnished to the shareholder by the corporation, and

(ii) elects to have this paragraph apply with respect to that item.

(3) EFFECT OF FAILURE TO NOTIFY.—In any case—

(A) described in subparagraph (A) (i) (I) of paragraph (2), and

(B) in which the shareholder does not comply with subparagraph (A) (ii) of paragraph (2),

any adjustment required to make the treatment of the items by such shareholder consistent with the treatment of the items on the corporate return shall be treated as arising out of mathematical or clerical errors and assessed according to section 6213 (b) (1). Paragraph (2) of section 6213 (b) shall not apply to any assessment referred to in the preceding sentence.

(4) SUBCHAPTER S ITEM.—For purposes of this subsection, the term "subchapter S item" means any item of an S corporation to the extent that regulations prescribed by the Secretary provide that, for purposes of this subtitle, such item is more appropriately determined at the corporation level than at the shareholder level.

(5) ADDITION TO TAX FOR FAILURE TO COMPLY WITH SECTION.—For addition to tax in the case of a shareholder's negligence in connection with, or disregard of, the requirements of this section, see part II of subchapter A of chapter 68.

Subpart B—Information Concerning Transactions With Other Persons

[Sec. 6041]

SEC. 6041. INFORMATION AT SOURCE.

[Sec. 6041(a)]

(a) PAYMENTS OF $600 OR MORE.—All persons engaged in a trade or business and making payment in the course of such trade or business to another person, of rent, salaries, wages, premiums, annuities, compensations, remunerations, emoluments, or other fixed or determinable gains, profits, and income (other than payments to which section 6042 (a) (1), 6044 (a) (1), 6047 (e) [d], 6049 (a), or 6050N (a) applies, and other than payments with respect to which a statement is required under the authority of section 6042 (a) (2), 6044 (a) (2), or 6045), of $600 or more in any taxable year, or, in the case of such payments made by the United States, the officers or employees of the United States having information as to such payments and required to make returns in regard thereto by the regulations hereinafter provided for, shall render a true and accurate return to the Secretary, under such regulations and in such form and manner and to such extent as may be prescribed by the Secretary, setting forth the amount of such gains, profits, and income, and the name and address of the recipient of such payment.

* * *

[Sec. 6042]

SEC. 6042. RETURNS REGARDING PAYMENTS OF DIVIDENDS AND CORPORATE EARNINGS AND PROFITS.

[Sec. 6042(a)]

(a) REQUIREMENT OF REPORTING.—

(1) IN GENERAL.—Every person—

(A) who makes payments of dividends aggregating $10 or more to any other person during any calendar year, or

(B) who receives payments of dividends as a nominee and who makes payments aggregating $10 or more during any calendar year to any other person with respect to the dividends so received,

shall make a return according to the forms or regulations prescribed by the Secretary, setting forth the aggregate amount of such payments and the name and address of the person to whom paid.

(2) RETURNS REQUIRED BY THE SECRETARY.—Every person who makes payments of dividends aggregating less than $10 to any other person during any calendar year shall, when required by the Secretary, make a return setting forth the aggregate amount of such payments, and the name and address of the person to whom paid.

* * *

[Sec. 6043]

SEC. 6043. LIQUIDATING, ETC., TRANSACTIONS.

[Sec. 6043(a)]

(a) CORPORATE LIQUIDATING, ETC., TRANSACTIONS.—Every corporation shall—

(1) Within 30 days after the adoption by the corporation of a resolution or plan for the dissolution of the corporation or for the liquidation of the whole or any part of its capital stock, make a return setting forth the terms of such resolution or plan and such other information as the Secretary shall by forms or regulations prescribe; and

(2) When required by the Secretary, make a return regarding its distributions in liquidation, stating the name and address of, the number and class of shares owned by, and the amount paid to, each shareholder, or, if the distribution is in property other than money, the fair market value (as of the date the distribution is made) of the property distributed to each shareholder.

* * *

[Sec. 6043(c)]

(c) CHANGES IN CONTROL AND RECAPITALIZATIONS.—If—

(1) control (as defined in section 304(c)(1)) of a corporation is acquired by any person (or group of persons) in a transaction (or series of related transactions), or

(2) there is a recapitalization of a corporation or other substantial change in the capital structure of a corporation,

when required by the Secretary, such corporation shall make a return (at such time and in such manner as the Secretary may prescribe) setting forth the identity of the parties to the transaction, the fees involved, the changes in the capital structure involved, and such other information as the Secretary may require with respect to such transaction.

* * *

[Sec. 6043A]

SEC. 6043A. RETURNS RELATING TO TAXABLE MERGERS AND ACQUISITIONS.

[Sec. 6043A(a)]

(a) IN GENERAL.—According to the forms or regulations prescribed by the Secretary, the acquiring corporation in any taxable acquisition shall make a return setting forth—

(1) a description of the acquisition,

(2) the name and address of each shareholder of the acquired corporation who is required to recognize gain (if any) as a result of the acquisition,

(3) the amount of money and the fair market value of other property transferred to each such shareholder as part of such acquisition, and

(4) such other information as the Secretary may prescribe.

To the extent provided by the Secretary, the requirements of this section applicable to the acquiring corporation shall be applicable to the acquired corporation and not to the acquiring corporation.

[Sec. 6043A(b)]

(b) NOMINEES.—According to the forms or regulations prescribed by the Secretary:

(1) REPORTING.—Any person who holds stock as a nominee for another person shall furnish in the manner prescribed by the Secretary to such other person the information provided by the corporation under subsection (d).

(2) REPORTING TO NOMINEES.—In the case of stock held by any person as a nominee, references in this section (other than in subsection (c)) to a shareholder shall be treated as a reference to the nominee.

[Sec. 6043A(c)]

(c) TAXABLE ACQUISITION.—For purposes of this section, the term "taxable acquisition" means any acquisition by a corporation of stock in or property of another corporation if any shareholder of the acquired corporation is required to recognize gain (if any) as a result of such acquisition.

[Sec. 6043A(d)]

(d) STATEMENTS TO BE FURNISHED TO SHAREHOLDERS.—According to the forms or regulations prescribed by the Secretary, every person required to make a return under subsection (a) shall furnish to each shareholder whose name is required to be set forth in such return a written statement showing—

(1) the name, address, and phone number of the information contact of the person required to make such return,

(2) the information required to be shown on such return with respect to such shareholder, and

(3) such other information as the Secretary may prescribe.

The written statement required under the preceding sentence shall be furnished to the shareholder on or before January 31 of the year following the calendar year during which the taxable acquisition occurred.

[Sec. 6049]

SEC. 6049. RETURNS REGARDING PAYMENTS OF INTEREST.

[Sec. 6049(a)]

(a) REQUIREMENT OF REPORTING.—Every person—

(1) who makes payments of interest (as defined in subsection (b)) aggregating $10 or more to any other person during any calendar year, or

(2) who receives payments of interest (as so defined) as a nominee and who makes payments aggregating $10 or more during any calendar year to any other person with respect to the interest so received,

shall make a return according to the forms or regulations prescribed by the Secretary, setting forth the aggregate amount of such payments and the name and address of the person to whom paid.

* * *

[Sec. 6050I]

SEC. 6050I. RETURNS RELATING TO CASH RECEIVED IN TRADE OR BUSINESS, ETC.

[Sec. 6050I(a)]

(a) CASH RECEIPTS OF MORE THAN $10,000.—Any person—

(1) who is engaged in a trade or business, and

(2) who, in the course of such trade or business, receives more than $10,000 in cash in 1 transaction (or 2 or more related transactions),

shall make the return described in subsection (b) with respect to such transaction (or related transactions) at such time as the Secretary may by regulations prescribe.

[Sec. 6050I(b)]

(b) FORM AND MANNER OF RETURNS.—A return is described in this subsection if such return—

(1) is in such form as the Secretary may prescribe,

(2) contains—

(A) the name, address, and TIN of the person from whom the cash was received,

(B) the amount of cash received,

(C) the date and nature of the transaction, and

(D) such other information as the Secretary may prescribe.

[Sec. 6050I(c)]

(c) EXCEPTIONS.—

(1) CASH RECEIVED BY FINANCIAL INSTITUTIONS.—Subsection (a) shall not apply to—

(A) cash received in a transaction reported under title 31, United States Code, if the Secretary determines that reporting under this section would duplicate the reporting to the Treasury under title 31, United States Code, or

(B) cash received by any financial institution (as defined in subparagraphs (A), (B), (C), (D), (E), (F), (G), (J), (K), (R), and (S) of section 5312(a)(2) of title 31, United States Code).

(2) TRANSACTIONS OCCURRING OUTSIDE THE UNITED STATES.—Except to the extent provided in regulations prescribed by the Secretary, subsection (a) shall not apply to any transaction if the entire transaction occurs outside the United States.

[Sec. 6050I(d)]

(d) CASH INCLUDES FOREIGN CURRENCY AND CERTAIN MONETARY INSTRUMENTS.—For purposes of this section, the term "cash" includes—

(1) foreign currency, and

(2) to the extent provided in regulations prescribed by the Secretary, any monetary instrument (whether or not in bearer form) with a face amount of not more than $10,000.

Paragraph (2) shall not apply to any check drawn on the account of the writer in a financial institution referred to in subsection (c)(1)(B).

[Sec. 6050I(e)]

(e) STATEMENTS TO BE FURNISHED TO PERSONS WITH RESPECT TO WHOM INFORMATION IS REQUIRED.—Every person required to make a return under subsection (a) shall furnish to each person whose name is required to be set forth in such return a written statement showing—

(1) the name, address, and phone number of the information contact of the person required to make such return, and

(2) the aggregate amount of cash described in subsection (a) received by the person required to make such return.

The written statement required under the preceding sentence shall be furnished to the person on or before January 31 of the year following the calendar year for which the return under subsection (a) was required to be made.

[Sec. 6050I(f)]

(f) STRUCTURING TRANSACTIONS TO EVADE REPORTING REQUIREMENTS PROHIBITED.—

(1) IN GENERAL.—No person shall for the purpose of evading the return requirements of this section—

(A) cause or attempt to cause a trade or business to fail to file a return required under this section,

(B) cause or attempt to cause a trade or business to file a return required under this section that contains a material omission or misstatement of fact, or

(C) structure or assist in structuring, or attempt to structure or assist in structuring, any transaction with one or more trades or businesses.

(2) PENALTIES.—A person violating paragraph (1) of this subsection shall be subject to the same civil and criminal sanctions applicable to a person which fails to file or completes a false or incorrect return under this section.

* * *

[Sec. 6050L]

SEC. 6050L. RETURNS RELATING TO CERTAIN DONATED PROPERTY.

[Sec. 6050L(a)]

(a) DISPOSITIONS OF DONATED PROPERTY.—

(1) IN GENERAL.—If the donee of any charitable deduction property sells, exchanges, or otherwise disposes of such property within 3 years after its receipt, the donee shall make a return (in accordance with forms and regulations prescribed by the Secretary) showing—

(A) the name, address, and TIN of the donor,

(B) a description of the property,

(C) the date of the contribution,

(D) the amount received on the disposition,

(E) the date of such disposition,

(F) a description of the donee's use of the property, and

(G) a statement indicating whether the use of the property was related to the purpose or function constituting the basis for the donee's exemption under section 501.

In any case in which the donee indicates that the use of applicable property (as defined in section 170(e)(7)(C)) was related to the purpose or function constituting the basis for the exemption of the donee under section 501 under subparagraph (G), the donee shall include with the return the certification described in section 170(e)(7)(D) if such certification is made under section 170(e)(7).

(2) DEFINITIONS.—For purposes of this subsection:

(A) CHARITABLE DEDUCTION PROPERTY.—The term "charitable deduction property" means any property (other than publicly traded securities) contributed in a contribution for which a deduction was claimed under section 170 if the claimed value of such property (plus the claimed value of all similar items of property donated by the donor to 1 or more donees) exceeds $5,000.

(B) PUBLICLY TRADED SECURITIES.—The term "publicly traded securities" means securities for which (as of the date of the contribution) market quotations are readily available on an established securities market.

* * *

[Sec. 6050N]

SEC. 6050N. RETURNS REGARDING PAYMENTS OF ROYALTIES.

[Sec. 6050N(a)]

(a) REQUIREMENT OF REPORTING.—Every person—

(1) who makes payments of royalties (or similar amounts) aggregating $10 or more to any other person during any calendar year, or

(2) who receives payments of royalties (or similar amounts) as a nominee and who makes payments aggregating $10 or more during any calendar year to any other person with respect to the royalties (or similar amounts) so received,

shall make a return according to the forms or regulations prescribed by the Secretary, setting forth the aggregate amount of such payments and the name and address of the person to whom paid.

* * *

Subpart C—Information Regarding Wages Paid Employees

[Sec. 6053]

SEC. 6053. REPORTING OF TIPS.

[Sec. 6053(a)]

(a) REPORTS BY EMPLOYEES.—Every employee who, in the course of his employment by an employer, receives in any calendar month tips which are wages (as defined in section 3121(a) or section 3401(a)) or which are compensation (as defined in section 3231(e)) shall report all such tips in one or more written statements furnished to his employer on or before the 10th day following such month. Such statements shall be furnished by the employee under such regulations, at such other times before such 10th day, and in such form and manner, as may be prescribed by the Secretary.

* * *

PART V—TIME FOR FILING RETURNS AND OTHER DOCUMENTS

[Sec. 6072]

SEC. 6072. TIME FOR FILING INCOME TAX RETURNS.

[Sec. 6072(a)]

(a) GENERAL RULE.—In the case of returns under section 6012, 6013, or 6017 (relating to income tax under subtitle A), returns made on the basis of the calendar year shall be filed on or before the 15th day of April following the close of the calendar year and returns made on the basis of a fiscal year shall be filed on or before the 15th day of the fourth month following the close of the fiscal year, except as otherwise provided in the following subsections of this section.

[Sec. 6072(b)]

(b) RETURNS OF PARTNERSHIPS AND S CORPORATIONS.—Returns of partnerships under section 6031 and returns of S corporations under sections 6012 and 6037 made on the basis of the calendar year shall be filed on or before the 15th day of March following the close of the calendar year, and such returns made on the basis of a fiscal year shall be filed on or before the 15th day of the third month following the close of the fiscal year. Returns required for a taxable year by section 6011(c)(2) (relating to returns of a DISC) shall be filed on or before the fifteenth day of the ninth month following the close of the taxable year.

* * *

PART VI—EXTENSION OF TIME FOR FILING RETURNS

[Sec. 6081]

SEC. 6081. EXTENSION OF TIME FOR FILING RETURNS.

[Sec. 6081(a)]

(a) GENERAL RULE.—The Secretary may grant a reasonable extension of time for filing any return, declaration, statement, or other document required by this title or by regulations. Except in the case of taxpayers who are abroad, no such extension shall be for more than 6 months.

[Sec. 6081(b)]

(b) AUTOMATIC EXTENSION FOR CORPORATION INCOME TAX RETURNS.—An extension of 6 months for the filing of the return of income taxes imposed by subtitle A shall be allowed any corporation if, in such manner and at such time as the Secretary may by regulations prescribe, there is filed on behalf of such corporation the form prescribed by the Secretary, and if such corporation pays, on or before the date prescribed for payment of the tax, the amount properly estimated as its tax; but this extension may be terminated at any time by the Secretary by mailing to the taxpayer notice of such termination at least 10 days prior to the date for termination fixed in such notice. In the case of any return for a taxable year of a C corporation which ends on December 31 and begins before January 1, 2026, the first sentence of this subsection shall be applied by substituting "5 months" for "6 months". In the case of any return for a taxable year of a C corporation which ends on June 30 and begins before January 1, 2026, the first sentence of this subsection shall be applied by substituting "7 months" for "6 months".

* * *

SUBCHAPTER B—MISCELLANEOUS PROVISIONS

[Sec. 6115]

SEC. 6115. DISCLOSURE RELATED TO QUID PRO QUO CONTRIBUTIONS.

[Sec. 6115(a)]

(a) DISCLOSURE REQUIREMENT.—If an organization described in section 170(c) (other than paragraph (1) thereof) receives a quid pro quo contribution in excess of $75, the organization shall, in connection with the solicitation or receipt of the contribution, provide a written statement which—

(1) informs the donor that the amount of the contribution that is deductible for Federal income tax purposes is limited to the excess of the amount of any money and the value of any property other than money contributed by the donor over the value of the goods or services provided by the organization, and

(2) provides the donor with a good faith estimate of the value of such goods or services.

[Sec. 6115(b)]

(b) QUID PRO QUO CONTRIBUTION.—For purposes of this section, the term "quid pro quo contribution" means a payment made partly as a contribution and partly in consideration for goods or services provided to the payor by the donee organization. A quid pro quo contribution does not include any payment made to an organization, organized exclusively for religious purposes, in return for which the taxpayer receives solely an intangible religious benefit that generally is not sold in a commercial transaction outside the donative context.

CHAPTER 62—TIME AND PLACE FOR PAYING TAX

SUBCHAPTER A—PLACE AND DUE DATE FOR PAYMENT OF TAX

[Sec. 6151]

SEC. 6151. TIME AND PLACE FOR PAYING TAX SHOWN ON RETURNS.

[Sec. 6151(a)]

(a) GENERAL RULE.—Except as otherwise provided in this subchapter, when a return of tax is required under this title or regulations, the person required to make such return shall, without assessment or notice and demand from the Secretary, pay such tax to the internal revenue officer with whom the return is filed, and shall pay such tax at the time and place fixed for filing the return (determined without regard to any extension of time for filing the return).

* * *

SUBCHAPTER B—EXTENSIONS OF TIME FOR PAYMENT

[Sec. 6161]

SEC. 6161. EXTENSION OF TIME FOR PAYING TAX.

[Sec. 6161(a)]

(a) AMOUNT DETERMINED BY TAXPAYER ON RETURN.—

(1) GENERAL RULE.—The Secretary, except as otherwise provided in this title, may extend the time for payment of the amount of the tax shown, or required to be shown, on any return or declaration required under authority of this title (or any installment thereof), for a reasonable period not to exceed 6 months (12 months in the case of estate tax) from the date fixed for payment thereof. Such extension may exceed 6 months in the case of a taxpayer who is abroad.

* * *

CHAPTER 63—ASSESSMENT

SUBCHAPTER B—DEFICIENCY PROCEDURES IN THE CASE OF INCOME, ESTATE, GIFT, AND CERTAIN EXCISE TAXES

[Sec. 6213]

SEC. 6213. RESTRICTIONS APPLICABLE TO DEFICIENCIES; PETITION TO TAX COURT.

[Sec. 6213(a)]

(a) TIME FOR FILING PETITION AND RESTRICTION ON ASSESSMENT.—Within 90 days, or 150 days if the notice is addressed to a person outside the United States, after the notice of deficiency authorized in section 6212 is mailed (not counting Saturday, Sunday, or a legal holiday in the District of Columbia as the last day), the taxpayer may file a petition with the Tax Court for a redetermination of the deficiency. Except as otherwise provided in section 6851, 6852, or 6861 no assessment of a deficiency in respect of any tax imposed by subtitle A or B, chapter 41, 42, 43, or 44 and no levy or proceeding in court for its collection shall be made, begun, or prosecuted until such notice has been mailed to the taxpayer, nor until the expiration of such 90-day or 150-day period, as the case may be, nor, if a petition has been filed with the Tax Court, until the decision of the Tax Court has become final. Notwithstanding the provisions of section 7421(a), the making of such assessment or the beginning of such proceeding or levy during the time such prohibition is in force may be enjoined by a proceeding in the proper court, including the Tax Court, and a refund may be ordered by such court of any amount collected within the period during which the Secretary is prohibited from collecting by levy or through a proceeding in court under the provisions of this subsection. The Tax Court shall have no jurisdiction to enjoin any action or proceeding or order any refund under this subsection unless a timely petition for a redetermination of the deficiency has been filed and then only in respect of the deficiency that is the subject of such petition. Any petition filed with the Tax Court on or before the last date specified for filing such petition by the Secretary in the notice of deficiency shall be treated as timely filed.

* * *

SUBCHAPTER C—TAX TREATMENT OF PARTNERSHIP ITEMS

[Sec. 6221]

SEC. 6221. DETERMINATION AT PARTNERSHIP LEVEL.

[Sec. 6221(a)]

(a) IN GENERAL.—Any adjustment to a partnership-related item shall be determined, and any tax attributable thereto shall be assessed and collected, and the applicability of any penalty, addition to tax, or additional amount which relates to an adjustment to any such item shall be determined, at the partnership level, except to the extent otherwise provided in this subchapter.

[Sec. 6221(b)]

(b) ELECTION OUT FOR CERTAIN PARTNERSHIPS WITH 100 OR FEWER PARTNERS, ETC.—

(1) IN GENERAL.—This subchapter shall not apply with respect to any partnership for any taxable year if—

(A) the partnership elects the application of this subsection for such taxable year,

(B) for such taxable year the partnership is required to furnish 100 or fewer statements under section 6031(b) with respect to its partners,

(C) each of the partners of such partnership is an individual, a C corporation, any foreign entity that would be treated as a C corporation were it domestic, an S corporation, or an estate of a deceased partner,

(D) the election—

(i) is made with a timely filed return for such taxable year, and

(ii) includes (in the manner prescribed by the Secretary) a disclosure of the name and taxpayer identification number of each partner of such partnership, and

(E) the partnership notifies each such partner of such election in the manner prescribed by the Secretary.

(2) SPECIAL RULES RELATING TO CERTAIN PARTNERS.—

(A) S CORPORATION PARTNERS.—In the case of a partner that is an S corporation—

(i) the partnership shall only be treated as meeting the requirements of paragraph (1)(C) with respect to such partner if such partnership includes (in the manner prescribed by the Secretary) a disclosure of the name and taxpayer identification number of each person with respect to whom such S corporation is required to furnish a statement under section 6037(b) for the taxable year of the S corporation ending with or within the partnership taxable year for which the application of this subsection is elected, and

(ii) the statements such S corporation is required to so furnish shall be treated as statements furnished by the partnership for purposes of paragraph (1)(B).

(B) FOREIGN PARTNERS.—For purposes of paragraph (1)(D)(ii), the Secretary may provide for alternative identification of any foreign partners.

(C) OTHER PARTNERS.—The Secretary may by regulation or other guidance prescribe rules similar to the rules of subparagraph (A) with respect to any partners not described in such subparagraph or paragraph (1)(C).

[Sec. 6222]

SEC. 6222. PARTNER'S RETURN MUST BE CONSISTENT WITH PARTNERSHIP RETURN.

[Sec. 6222(a)]

(a) IN GENERAL.—A partner shall, on the partner's return, treat any partnership-related item in a manner which is consistent with the treatment of such item on the partnership return.

[Sec. 6222(b)]

(b) UNDERPAYMENT DUE TO INCONSISTENT TREATMENT ASSESSED AS MATH ERROR.—Any underpayment of tax by a partner by reason of failing to comply with the requirements of subsection (a) shall be assessed and collected in the same manner as if such underpayment were on account of a mathematical or clerical error appearing on the partner's return. Paragraph (2) of section 6213(b) shall not apply to any assessment of an underpayment referred to in the preceding sentence.

[Sec. 6222(c)]

(c) Exception for Notification of Inconsistent Treatment.—

(1) In general.—In the case of any item referred to in subsection (a), if—

(A) (i) the partnership has filed a return but the partner's treatment on the partner's return is (or may be) inconsistent with the treatment of the item on the partnership return, or

(ii) the partnership has not filed a return, and

(B) the partner files with the Secretary a statement identifying the inconsistency,

subsections (a) and (b) shall not apply to such item.

(2) Partner receiving incorrect information.—A partner shall be treated as having complied with subparagraph (B) of paragraph (1) with respect to an item if the partner—

(A) demonstrates to the satisfaction of the Secretary that the treatment of the item on the partner's return is consistent with the treatment of the item on the statement furnished to the partner by the partnership, and

(B) elects to have this paragraph apply with respect to that item.

[Sec. 6222(d)]

(d) Final Decision on Certain Positions Not Binding on Partnership.—Any final decision with respect to an inconsistent position identified under subsection (c) in a proceeding to which the partnership is not a party shall not be binding on the partnership.

[Sec. 6222(e)]

(e) Addition to Tax for Failure to Comply With Section.—For addition to tax in the case of a partner's disregard of the requirements of this section, see part II of subchapter A of chapter 68.

CHAPTER 64—COLLECTION

SUBCHAPTER A—GENERAL PROVISIONS

[Sec. 6304]

SEC. 6304. FAIR TAX COLLECTION PRACTICES.

[Sec. 6304(a)]

(a) Communication With the Taxpayer.—Without the prior consent of the taxpayer given directly to the Secretary or the express permission of a court of competent jurisdiction, the Secretary may not communicate with a taxpayer in connection with the collection of any unpaid tax—

(1) at any unusual time or place or a time or place known or which should be known to be inconvenient to the taxpayer;

(2) if the Secretary knows the taxpayer is represented by any person authorized to practice before the Internal Revenue Service with respect to such unpaid tax and has knowledge of, or can readily ascertain, such person's name and address, unless such person fails to respond within a reasonable period of time to a communication from the Secretary or unless such person consents to direct communication with the taxpayer; or

(3) at the taxpayer's place of employment if the Secretary knows or has reason to know that the taxpayer's employer prohibits the taxpayer from receiving such communication.

In the absence of knowledge of circumstances to the contrary, the Secretary shall assume that the convenient time for communicating with a taxpayer is after 8 a.m. and before 9 p.m., local time at the taxpayer's location.

[Sec. 6304(b)]

(b) Prohibition of Harassment and Abuse.—The Secretary may not engage in any conduct the natural consequence of which is to harass, oppress, or abuse any person in connection with the collection of any unpaid tax. Without limiting the general application of the foregoing, the following conduct is a violation of this subsection:

(1) The use or threat of use of violence or other criminal means to harm the physical person, reputation, or property of any person.

(2) The use of obscene or profane language or language the natural consequence of which is to abuse the hearer or reader.

(3) Causing a telephone to ring or engaging any person in telephone conversation repeatedly or continuously with intent to annoy, abuse, or harass any person at the called number.

(4) Except as provided under rules similar to the rules in section 804 of the Fair Debt Collection Practices Act (15 U.S.C. 1692b), the placement of telephone calls without meaningful disclosure of the caller's identity.

* * *

SUBCHAPTER B—RECEIPT OF PAYMENT

[Sec. 6315]

SEC. 6315. PAYMENTS OF ESTIMATED INCOME TAX.

Payment of the estimated income tax, or any installment thereof, shall be considered payment on account of the income taxes imposed by subtitle A for the taxable year.

SUBCHAPTER C—LIEN FOR TAXES

PART I—DUE PROCESS FOR LIENS

[Sec. 6320]

SEC. 6320. NOTICE AND OPPORTUNITY FOR HEARING UPON FILING OF NOTICE OF LIEN.

[Sec. 6320(a)]

(a) REQUIREMENT OF NOTICE.—

(1) IN GENERAL.—The Secretary shall notify in writing the person described in section 6321 of the filing of a notice of lien under section 6323.

(2) TIME AND METHOD FOR NOTICE.—The notice required under paragraph (1) shall be—

(A) given in person;

(B) left at the dwelling or usual place of business of such person; or

(C) sent by certified or registered mail to such person's last known address,

not more than 5 business days after the day of the filing of the notice of lien.

(3) INFORMATION INCLUDED WITH NOTICE.—The notice required under paragraph (1) shall include in simple and nontechnical terms—

(A) the amount of unpaid tax;

(B) the right of the person to request a hearing during the 30-day period beginning on the day after the 5-day period described in paragraph (2);

(C) the administrative appeals available to the taxpayer with respect to such lien and the procedures relating to such appeals;

(D) the provisions of this title and procedures relating to the release of liens on property; and

(E) the provisions of section 7345 relating to the certification of seriously delinquent tax debts and the denial, revocation, or limitation of passports of individuals with such debts pursuant to section 32101 of the FAST Act.

[Sec. 6320(b)]

(b) RIGHT TO FAIR HEARING.—

(1) IN GENERAL.—If the person requests a hearing in writing under subsection (a)(3)(B) and states the grounds for the requested hearing, such hearing shall be held by the Internal Revenue Service Independent Office of Appeals.

(2) ONE HEARING PER PERIOD.—A person shall be entitled to only one hearing under this section with respect to the taxable period to which the unpaid tax specified in subsection (a)(3)(A) relates.

(3) IMPARTIAL OFFICER.—The hearing under this subsection shall be conducted by an officer or employee who has had no prior involvement with respect to the unpaid tax specified in subsection (a)(3)(A) before the first hearing under this section or section 6330. A taxpayer may waive the requirement of this paragraph.

(4) COORDINATION WITH SECTION 6330.—To the extent practicable, a hearing under this section shall be held in conjunction with a hearing under section 6330.

(c) CONDUCT OF HEARING; REVIEW; SUSPENSIONS.—For purposes of this section, subsections (c), (d) (other than paragraph (3)(B) thereof), (e), and (g) of section 6330 shall apply.

PART II—LIENS

[Sec. 6321]

SEC. 6321. LIEN FOR TAXES.

If any person liable to pay any tax neglects or refuses to pay the same after demand, the amount (including any interest, additional amount, addition to tax, or assessable penalty, together with any costs that may accrue in addition thereto) shall be a lien in favor of the United States upon all property and rights to property, whether real or personal, belonging to such person.

[Sec. 6322]

SEC. 6322. PERIOD OF LIEN.

Unless another date is specifically fixed by law, the lien imposed by section 6321 shall arise at the time the assessment is made and shall continue until the liability for the amount so assessed (or a judgment against the taxpayer arising out of such liability) is satisfied or becomes unenforceable by reason of lapse of time.

SUBCHAPTER D—SEIZURE OF PROPERTY FOR COLLECTION OF TAXES

PART I—DUE PROCESS FOR COLLECTIONS

[Sec. 6330]

SEC. 6330. NOTICE AND OPPORTUNITY FOR HEARING BEFORE LEVY.

[Sec. 6330(a)]

(a) REQUIREMENT OF NOTICE BEFORE LEVY.—

(1) IN GENERAL.—No levy may be made on any property or right to property of any person unless the Secretary has notified such person in writing of their right to a hearing under this section before such levy is made. Such notice shall be required only once for the taxable period to which the unpaid tax specified in paragraph (3)(A) relates.

(2) TIME AND METHOD FOR NOTICE.—The notice required under paragraph (1) shall be—

(A) given in person;

(B) left at the dwelling or usual place of business of such person; or

(C) sent by certified or registered mail, return receipt requested, to such person's last known address,

not less than 30 days before the day of the first levy with respect to the amount of the unpaid tax for the taxable period.

(3) INFORMATION INCLUDED WITH NOTICE.—The notice required under paragraph (1) shall include in simple and nontechnical terms—

(A) the amount of unpaid tax;

(B) the right of the person to request a hearing during the 30-day period under paragraph (2); and

(C) the proposed action by the Secretary and the rights of the person with respect to such action, including a brief statement which sets forth—

(i) the provisions of this title relating to levy and sale of property;

(ii) the procedures applicable to the levy and sale of property under this title;

(iii) the administrative appeals available to the taxpayer with respect to such levy and sale and the procedures relating to such appeals;

(iv) the alternatives available to taxpayers which could prevent levy on property (including installment agreements under section 6159); and

(v) the provisions of this title and procedures relating to redemption of property and release of liens on property.

[Sec. 6330(b)]

(b) RIGHT TO FAIR HEARING.—

(1) IN GENERAL.—If the person requests a hearing in writing under subsection (a) (3) (B) and states the grounds for the requested hearing, such hearing shall be held by the Internal Revenue Service Independent Office of Appeals.

(2) ONE HEARING PER PERIOD.—A person shall be entitled to only one hearing under this section with respect to the taxable period to which the unpaid tax specified in subsection (a) (3) (A) relates.

(3) IMPARTIAL OFFICER.—The hearing under this subsection shall be conducted by an officer or employee who has had no prior involvement with respect to the unpaid tax specified in subsection (a) (3) (A) before the first hearing under this section or section 6320. A taxpayer may waive the requirement of this paragraph.

[Sec. 6330(c)]

(c) MATTERS CONSIDERED AT HEARING.—In the case of any hearing conducted under this section—

(1) REQUIREMENT OF INVESTIGATION.—The appeals officer shall at the hearing obtain verification from the Secretary that the requirements of any applicable law or administrative procedure have been met.

(2) ISSUES AT HEARING.—

(A) IN GENERAL.—The person may raise at the hearing any relevant issue relating to the unpaid tax or the proposed levy, including—

(i) appropriate spousal defenses;

(ii) challenges to the appropriateness of collection actions; and

(iii) offers of collection alternatives, which may include the posting of a bond, the substitution of other assets, an installment agreement, or an offer-in-compromise.

(B) UNDERLYING LIABILITY.—The person may also raise at the hearing challenges to the existence or amount of the underlying tax liability for any tax period if the person did not receive any statutory notice of deficiency for such tax liability or did not otherwise have an opportunity to dispute such tax liability.

(3) BASIS FOR THE DETERMINATION.—The determination by an appeals officer under this subsection shall take into consideration—

(A) the verification presented under paragraph (1);

(B) the issues raised under paragraph (2); and

(C) whether any proposed collection action balances the need for the efficient collection of taxes with the legitimate concern of the person that any collection action be no more intrusive than necessary.

(4) CERTAIN ISSUES PRECLUDED.—An issue may not be raised at the hearing if—

(A) (i) the issue was raised and considered at a previous hearing under section 6320 or in any other previous administrative or judicial proceeding; and

(ii) the person seeking to raise the issue participated meaningfully in such hearing or proceeding;

(B) the issue meets the requirement of clause (i) or (ii) of section 6702(b)(2)(A); or

(C) a final determination has been made with respect to such issue in a proceeding brought under subchapter C of chapter 63.

This paragraph shall not apply to any issue with respect to which subsection (d)(3)(B) applies.

[Sec. 6330(d)]

(d) PROCEEDING AFTER HEARING.—

(1) PETITION FOR REVIEW BY TAX COURT.—The person may, within 30 days of a determination under this section, petition the Tax Court for review of such determination (and the Tax Court shall have jurisdiction with respect to such matter).

(2) SUSPENSION OF RUNNING OF PERIOD FOR FILING PETITION IN TITLE 11 CASES.—In the case of a person who is prohibited by reason of a case under title 11, United States Code, from filing a petition under paragraph (1) with respect to a determination under this section, the running of the period prescribed by such subsection for filing such a petition with respect to such determination shall be suspended for the period during which the person is so prohibited from filing such a petition, and for 30 days thereafter.

(3) JURISDICTION RETAINED AT IRS INDEPENDENT OFFICE OF APPEALS.—The Internal Revenue Service Independent Office of Appeals shall retain jurisdiction with respect to any determination made under this section, including subsequent hearings requested by the person who requested the original hearing on issues regarding—

(A) collection actions taken or proposed with respect to such determination; and

(B) after the person has exhausted all administrative remedies, a change in circumstances with respect to such person which affects such determination.

[Sec. 6330(e)]

(e) SUSPENSION OF COLLECTIONS AND STATUTE OF LIMITATIONS.—

(1) IN GENERAL.—Except as provided in paragraph (2), if a hearing is requested under subsection (a)(3)(B), the levy actions which are the subject of the requested hearing and the running of any period of limitations under section 6502 (relating to collection after assessment), section 6531 (relating to criminal prosecutions), or section 6532 (relating to other suits) shall be suspended for the period during which such hearing, and appeals therein, are pending. In no event shall any such period expire before the 90th day after the day on which there is a final determination in such hearing. Notwithstanding the provisions of section 7421(a), the beginning of a levy or proceeding during the time the suspension under this paragraph is in force may be enjoined by a proceeding in the proper court, including the Tax Court. The Tax Court shall have no jurisdiction under this paragraph to enjoin any action or proceeding unless a timely appeal has been filed under subsection (d)(1) and then only in respect of the unpaid tax or proposed levy to which the determination being appealed relates.

(2) LEVY UPON APPEAL.—Paragraph (1) shall not apply to a levy action while an appeal is pending if the underlying tax liability is not at issue in the appeal and the court determines that the Secretary has shown good cause not to suspend the levy.

* * *

[Sec. 6330(h)]

(h) DEFINITIONS RELATED TO EXCEPTIONS.—For purposes of subsection (f)—

(1) DISQUALIFIED EMPLOYMENT TAX LEVY.—A disqualified employment tax levy is any levy in connection with the collection of employment taxes for any taxable period if the person subject to the levy (or any predecessor thereof) requested a hearing under this section with respect to unpaid employment taxes arising in the most recent 2-year period before the beginning of the taxable period with respect to which the levy is served. For purposes of the preceding sentence, the term "employment taxes" means any taxes under chapter 21, 22, 23, or 24.

(2) FEDERAL CONTRACTOR LEVY.—A Federal contractor levy is any levy if the person whose property is subject to the levy (or any predecessor thereof) is a Federal contractor.

PART II—LEVY

[Sec. 6331]

SEC. 6331. LEVY AND DISTRAINT.

[Sec. 6331(a)]

(a) AUTHORITY OF SECRETARY.—If any person liable to pay any tax neglects or refuses to pay the same within 10 days after notice and demand, it shall be lawful for the Secretary to collect such tax (and such further sum as shall be sufficient to cover the expenses of the levy) by levy upon all property and rights to property (except such property as is exempt under section 6334) belonging to such person or on which there is a lien provided in this chapter for the payment of such tax. Levy may be made upon the accrued salary or wages of any officer, employee, or elected official, of the United States, the District of Columbia, or any agency or instrumentality of the United States or the District of Columbia, by serving a notice of levy on the employer (as defined in section 3401 (d)) of such officer, employee, or elected official. If the Secretary makes a finding that the collection of such tax is in jeopardy, notice and demand for immediate payment of such tax may be made by the Secretary and, upon failure or refusal to pay such tax, collection thereof by levy shall be lawful without regard to the 10-day period provided in this section.

[Sec. 6331(b)]

(b) SEIZURE AND SALE OF PROPERTY.—The term "levy" as used in this title includes the power of distraint and seizure by any means. Except as otherwise provided in subsection (e), a levy shall extend only to property possessed and obligations existing at the time thereof. In any case in which the Secretary may levy upon property or rights to property, he may seize and sell such property or rights to property (whether real or personal, tangible or intangible).

[Sec. 6331(c)]

(c) SUCCESSIVE SEIZURES.—Whenever any property or right to property upon which levy has been made by virtue of subsection (a) is not sufficient to satisfy the claim of the United States for which levy is made, the Secretary may, thereafter, and as often as may be necessary, proceed to levy in like manner upon any other property liable to levy of the person against whom such claim exists, until the amount due from him, together with all expenses, is fully paid.

[Sec. 6331(d)]

(d) REQUIREMENT OF NOTICE BEFORE LEVY.—

(1) IN GENERAL.—Levy may be made under subsection (a) upon the salary or wages or other property of any person with respect to any unpaid tax only after the Secretary has notified such person in writing of his intention to make such levy.

(2) 30-DAY REQUIREMENT.—The notice required under paragraph (1) shall be—

(A) given in person,

(B) left at the dwelling or usual place of business of such person, or

(C) sent by certified or registered mail to such person's last known address,

no less than 30 days before the day of the levy.

(3) JEOPARDY.—Paragraph (1) shall not apply to a levy if the Secretary has made a finding under the last sentence of subsection (a) that the collection of tax is in jeopardy.

(4) INFORMATION INCLUDED WITH NOTICE.—The notice required under paragraph (1) shall include a brief statement which sets forth in simple and nontechnical terms—

(A) the provisions of this title relating to levy and sale of property,

(B) the procedures applicable to the levy and sale of property under this title,

(C) the administrative appeals available to the taxpayer with respect to such levy and sale and the procedures relating to such appeals,

(D) the alternatives available to taxpayers which could prevent levy on the property (including installment agreements under section 6159),

(E) the provisions of this title relating to redemption of property and release of liens on property,

(F) the procedures applicable to the redemption of property and the release of a lien on property under this title, and

(G) the provisions of section 7345 relating to the certification of seriously delinquent tax debts and the denial, revocation, or limitation of passports of individuals with such debts pursuant to section 32101 of the FAST Act.

[Sec. 6331(e)]

(e) CONTINUING LEVY ON SALARY AND WAGES.—The effect of a levy on salary or wages payable to or received by a taxpayer shall be continuous from the date such levy is first made until such levy is released under section 6343.

* * *

[Sec. 6331(j)]

(j) NO LEVY BEFORE INVESTIGATION OF STATUS OF PROPERTY.—

(1) IN GENERAL.—For purposes of applying the provisions of this subchapter, no levy may be made on any property or right to property which is to be sold under section 6335 until a thorough investigation of the status of such property has been completed.

(2) ELEMENTS IN INVESTIGATION.—For purposes of paragraph (1), an investigation of the status of any property shall include—

(A) a verification of the taxpayer's liability;

(B) the completion of an analysis under subsection (f);

(C) the determination that the equity in such property is sufficient to yield net proceeds from the sale of such property to apply to such liability; and

(D) a thorough consideration of alternative collection methods.

[Sec. 6331(k)]

(k) NO LEVY WHILE CERTAIN OFFERS PENDING OR INSTALLMENT AGREEMENT PENDING OR IN EFFECT.—

(1) OFFER-IN-COMPROMISE PENDING.—No levy may be made under subsection (a) on the property or rights to property of any person with respect to any unpaid tax—

(A) during the period that an offer-in-compromise by such person under section 7122 of such unpaid tax is pending with the Secretary; and

(B) if such offer is rejected by the Secretary, during the 30 days thereafter (and, if an appeal of such rejection is filed within such 30 days, during the period that such appeal is pending).

For purposes of subparagraph (A), an offer is pending beginning on the date the Secretary accepts such offer for processing.

(2) INSTALLMENT AGREEMENTS.—No levy may be made under subsection (a) on the property or rights to property of any person with respect to any unpaid tax—

(A) during the period that an offer by such person for an installment agreement under section 6159 for payment of such unpaid tax is pending with the Secretary;

(B) if such offer is rejected by the Secretary, during the 30 days thereafter (and, if an appeal of such rejection is filed within such 30 days, during the period that such appeal is pending);

(C) during the period that such an installment agreement for payment of such unpaid tax is in effect; and

(D) if such agreement is terminated by the Secretary, during the 30 days thereafter (and, if an appeal of such termination is filed within such 30 days, during the period that such appeal is pending).

(3) CERTAIN RULES TO APPLY.—Rules similar to the rules of—

(A) paragraphs (3) and (4) of subsection (i), and

(B) except in the case of paragraph (2)(C), paragraph (5) of subsection (i),

shall apply for purposes of this subsection.

* * *

»»→ Caution: Pursuant to Section 6334(g), the amounts set forth in Sections 6334(a)(2) and (3) are adjusted for taxable years beginning after 1999 to reflect increases in the Chained Consumer Price Index. Pursuant to Section 6334(d)(4)(C), the amount set forth in Section 6334(d)(4)(B) is adjusted for taxable years beginning after 2020 to reflect increases in the Chained Consumer Price Index.

[Sec. 6334]

SEC. 6334. PROPERTY EXEMPT FROM LEVY.

[Sec. 6334(a)]

(a) ENUMERATION.—There shall be exempt from levy—

(1) WEARING APPAREL AND SCHOOL BOOKS.—Such items of wearing apparel and such school books as are necessary for the taxpayer or for members of his family;

(2) FUEL, PROVISIONS, FURNITURE, AND PERSONAL EFFECTS.—So much of the fuel, provisions, furniture, and personal effects in the taxpayer's household, and of the arms for personal use, livestock, and poultry of the taxpayer, as does not exceed $6,250 in value;

(3) BOOKS AND TOOLS OF A TRADE, BUSINESS, OR PROFESSION.—So many of the books and tools necessary for the trade, business, or profession of the taxpayer as do not exceed in the aggregate $3,125 in value.

(4) UNEMPLOYMENT BENEFITS.—Any amount payable to an individual with respect to his unemployment (including any portion thereof payable with respect to dependents) under an unemployment compensation law of the United States, of any State, or of the District of Columbia or of the Commonwealth of Puerto Rico.

(5) UNDELIVERED MAIL.—Mail, addressed to any person, which has not been delivered to the addressee.

(6) CERTAIN ANNUITY AND PENSION PAYMENTS.—Annuity or pension payments under the Railroad Retirement Act, benefits under the Railroad Unemployment Insurance Act, special pension payments received by a person whose name has been entered on the Army, Navy, Air Force, and Coast Guard Medal of Honor roll (38 U. S. C. 562), and annuities based on retired or retainer pay under chapter 73 of title 10 of the United States Code.

(7) WORKMEN'S COMPENSATION.—Any amount payable to an individual as workmen's compensation (including any portion thereof payable with respect to dependents) under a workmen's compensation law of the United States, any State, the District of Columbia, or the Commonwealth of Puerto Rico.

(8) JUDGMENTS FOR SUPPORT OF MINOR CHILDREN.—If the taxpayer is required by judgment of a court of competent jurisdiction, entered prior to the date of levy, to contribute to the support of his minor children, so much of his salary, wages, or other income as is necessary to comply with such judgment.

(9) MINIMUM EXEMPTION FOR WAGES, SALARY, AND OTHER INCOME.—Any amount payable to or received by an individual as wages or salary for personal services, or as income derived from other sources, during any period, to the extent that the total of such amounts payable to or received by him during such period does not exceed the applicable exempt amount determined under subsection (d).

(10) CERTAIN SERVICE-CONNECTED DISABILITY PAYMENTS.—Any amount payable to an individual as a service-connected (within the meaning of section 101(16) of title 38, United States Code) disability benefit under—

(A) subchapter II, III, IV, V, or VI of chapter 11 of such title 38, or

(B) chapter 13, 21, 23, 31, 32, 34, 35, 37, or 39 of such title 38.

(11) CERTAIN PUBLIC ASSISTANCE PAYMENTS.—Any amount payable to an individual as a recipient of public assistance under—

(A) title IV or title XVI (relating to supplemental security income for the aged, blind, and disabled) of the Social Security Act, or

(B) State or local government public assistance or public welfare programs for which eligibility is determined by a needs or income test.

(12) ASSISTANCE UNDER JOB TRAINING PARTNERSHIP ACT.—Any amount payable to a participant under the Job Training Partnership Act (29 U.S.C. 1501 et seq.) from funds appropriated pursuant to such Act.

(13) RESIDENCES EXEMPT IN SMALL DEFICIENCY CASES AND PRINCIPAL RESIDENCES AND CERTAIN BUSINESS ASSETS EXEMPT IN ABSENCE OF CERTAIN APPROVAL OR JEOPARDY.—(A) RESIDENCES IN SMALL DEFICIENCY CASES.—If the amount of the levy does not exceed $5,000—

(i) any real property used as a residence by the taxpayer; or

(ii) any real property of the taxpayer (other than real property which is rented) used by any other individual as a residence.

(B) PRINCIPAL RESIDENCES AND CERTAIN BUSINESS ASSETS.—Except to the extent provided in subsection (e)—

(i) the principal residence of the taxpayer (within the meaning of section 121); and

(ii) tangible personal property or real property (other than real property which is rented) used in the trade or business of an individual taxpayer.

* * *

[Sec. 6334(c)]

(c) NO OTHER PROPERTY EXEMPT.—Notwithstanding any other law of the United States (including section 207 of the Social Security Act), no property or rights to property shall be exempt from levy other than the property specifically made exempt by subsection (a).

[Sec. 6334(d)]

(d) EXEMPT AMOUNT OF WAGES, SALARY, OR OTHER INCOME.—

(1) INDIVIDUALS ON WEEKLY BASIS.—In the case of an individual who is paid or receives all of his wages, salary, and other income on a weekly basis, the amount of the wages, salary, and other income payable to or received by him during any week which is exempt from levy under subsection (a)(9) shall be the exempt amount.

(2) EXEMPT AMOUNT.—For purposes of paragraph (1), the term "exempt amount" means an amount equal to—

(A) the sum of—

(i) the standard deduction, and

(ii) the aggregate amount of the deductions for personal exemptions allowed the taxpayer under section 151 in the taxable year in which such levy occurs, divided by

(B) 52.

Unless the taxpayer submits to the Secretary a written and properly verified statement specifying the facts necessary to determine the proper amount under subparagraph (A), subparagraph (A) shall be applied as if the taxpayer were a married individual filing a separate return with only 1 personal exemption.

(3) INDIVIDUALS ON BASIS OTHER THAN WEEKLY.—In the case of any individual not described in paragraph (1), the amount of the wages, salary, and other income payable to or received by him during any applicable pay period or other fiscal period (as determined under regulations prescribed by the Secretary) which is exempt from levy under subsection (a)(9) shall be an amount (determined under such regulations) which as nearly as possible will result in the same total exemption from levy for such individual over a period of time as he would have under paragraph (1) if (during such period of time) he were paid or received such wages, salary, and other income on a regular weekly basis.

(4) YEARS WHEN PERSONAL EXEMPTION AMOUNT IS ZERO.—

(A) IN GENERAL.—In the case of any taxable year in which the exemption amount under section 151(d) is zero, paragraph (2) shall not apply and for purposes of paragraph (1) the term "exempt amount" means an amount equal to—

(i) the sum of the amount determined under subparagraph (B) and the standard deduction, divided by

(ii) 52.

(B) AMOUNT DETERMINED.—For purposes of subparagraph (A), the amount determined under this subparagraph is $4,150 multiplied by the number of the taxpayer's dependents for the taxable year in which the levy occurs.

(C) INFLATION ADJUSTMENT.—In the case of any taxable year beginning in a calendar year after 2018, the $4,150 amount in subparagraph (B) shall be increased by an amount equal to—

(i) such dollar amount, multiplied by

(ii) the cost-of-living adjustment determined under section 1(f)(3) for the calendar year in which the taxable year begins, determined by substituting "2017" for "2016" in subparagraph (A)(ii) thereof.

If any increase determined under the preceding sentence is not a multiple of $100, such increase shall be rounded to the next lowest multiple of $100.

(D) VERIFIED STATEMENT.—Unless the taxpayer submits to the Secretary a written and properly verified statement specifying the facts necessary to determine the proper amount under subparagraph (A), subparagraph (A) shall be applied as if the taxpayer were a married individual filing a separate return with no dependents.

[Sec. 6334(e)]

(e) LEVY ALLOWED ON PRINCIPAL RESIDENCES AND CERTAIN BUSINESS ASSETS IN CERTAIN CIRCUMSTANCES.—

(1) PRINCIPAL RESIDENCES.—

(A) APPROVAL REQUIRED.—A principal residence shall not be exempt from levy if a judge or magistrate of a district court of the United States approves (in writing) the levy of such residence.

(B) JURISDICTION.—The district courts of the United States shall have exclusive jurisdiction to approve a levy under subparagraph (A).

(2) CERTAIN BUSINESS ASSETS.—Property (other than a principal residence) described in subsection (a)(13)(B) shall not be exempt from levy if—

(A) a district director or assistant district director of the Internal Revenue Service personally approves (in writing) the levy of such property; or

(B) the Secretary finds that the collection of tax is in jeopardy.

An official may not approve a levy under subparagraph (A) unless the official determines that the taxpayer's other assets subject to collection are insufficient to pay the amount due, together with expenses of the proceedings.

* * *

[Sec. 6334(g)]

(g) INFLATION ADJUSTMENT.—

(1) IN GENERAL.—In the case of any calendar year beginning after 1999, each dollar amount referred to in paragraphs (2) and (3) of subsection (a) shall be increased by an amount equal to—

(A) such dollar amount, multiplied by

(B) the cost-of-living adjustment determined under section 1(f)(3) for such calendar year, by substituting "calendar year 1998" for "calendar year 2016" in subparagraph (A)(ii) thereof.

(2) ROUNDING.—If any dollar amount after being increased under paragraph (1) is not a multiple of $10, such dollar amount shall be rounded to the nearest multiple of $10.

CHAPTER 65—ABATEMENTS, CREDITS, AND REFUNDS

Subchapter B—Rules of Special Application

[Sec. 6428]

SEC. 6428. 2020 RECOVERY REBATES FOR INDIVIDUALS.

[Sec. 6428(a)]

(a) IN GENERAL.—In the case of an eligible individual, there shall be allowed as a credit against the tax imposed by subtitle A for the first taxable year beginning in 2020 an amount equal to the sum of—

(1) $1,200 ($2,400 in the case of eligible individuals filing a joint return), plus

(2) an amount equal to the product of $500 multiplied by the number of qualifying children (within the meaning of section 24(c)) of the taxpayer.

[Sec. 6428(b)]

(b) TREATMENT OF CREDIT.—The credit allowed by subsection (a) shall be treated as allowed by subpart C of part IV of subchapter A of chapter 1.

[Sec. 6428(c)]

(c) LIMITATION BASED ON ADJUSTED GROSS INCOME.—The amount of the credit allowed by subsection (a) (determined without regard to this subsection and subsection (e)) shall be reduced (but not below zero) by 5 percent of so much of the taxpayer's adjusted gross income as exceeds—

(1) $150,000 in the case of a joint return,

(2) $112,500 in the case of a head of household, and

(3) $75,000 in the case of a taxpayer not described in paragraph (1) or (2).

[Sec. 6428(d)]

(d) ELIGIBLE INDIVIDUAL.—For purposes of this section, the term "eligible individual" means any individual other than—

(1) any nonresident alien individual,

(2) any individual with respect to whom a deduction under section 151 is allowable to another taxpayer for a taxable year beginning in the calendar year in which the individual's taxable year begins, and

(3) an estate or trust.

[Sec. 6428(e)]

(e) COORDINATION WITH ADVANCE REFUNDS OF CREDIT.—

(1) IN GENERAL.—The amount of credit which would (but for this paragraph) be allowable under this section shall be reduced (but not below zero) by the aggregate refunds and credits made or allowed to the taxpayer under subsection (f). Any failure to so reduce the credit shall be treated as arising out of a mathematical or clerical error and assessed according to section 6213(b)(1).

(2) JOINT RETURNS.—In the case of a refund or credit made or allowed under subsection (f) with respect to a joint return, half of such refund or credit shall be treated as having been made or allowed to each individual filing such return.

[Sec. 6428(f)]

(f) ADVANCE REFUNDS AND CREDITS.—

(1) IN GENERAL.—Subject to paragraph (5), each individual who was an eligible individual for such individual's first taxable year beginning in 2019 shall be treated as having made a

payment against the tax imposed by chapter 1 for such taxable year in an amount equal to the advance refund amount for such taxable year.

(2) ADVANCE REFUND AMOUNT.—For purposes of paragraph (1), the advance refund amount is the amount that would have been allowed as a credit under this section for such taxable year if this section (other than subsection (e) and this subsection) had applied to such taxable year.

(3) TIMING AND MANNER OF PAYMENTS.—

(A) TIMING.—The Secretary shall, subject to the provisions of this title, refund or credit any overpayment attributable to this section as rapidly as possible. No refund or credit shall be made or allowed under this subsection after December 31, 2020.

(B) DELIVERY OF PAYMENTS.—Notwithstanding any other provision of law, the Secretary may certify and disburse refunds payable under this subsection electronically to any account to which the payee authorized, on or after January 1, 2018, the delivery of a refund of taxes under this title or of a Federal payment (as defined in section 3332 of title 31, United States Code).

(C) WAIVER OF CERTAIN RULES.—Notwithstanding section 3325 of title 31, United States Code, or any other provision of law, with respect to any payment of a refund under this subsection, a disbursing official in the executive branch of the United States Government may modify payment information received from an officer or employee described in section 3325(a)(1)(B) of such title for the purpose of facilitating the accurate and efficient delivery of such payment. Except in cases of fraud or reckless neglect, no liability under sections 3325, 3527, 3528, or 3529 of title 31, United States Code, shall be imposed with respect to payments made under this subparagraph.

(4) NO INTEREST.—No interest shall be allowed on any overpayment attributable to this section.

(5) ALTERNATE TAXABLE YEAR.—In the case of an individual who, at the time of any determination made pursuant to paragraph (3), has not filed a tax return for the year described in paragraph (1), the Secretary may—

(A) apply such paragraph by substituting "2018" for "2019", and

(B) if the individual has not filed a tax return for such individual's first taxable year beginning in 2018, use information with respect to such individual for calendar year 2019 provided in—

(i) Form SSA-1099, Social Security Benefit Statement, or

(ii) Form RRB-1099, Social Security Equivalent Benefit Statement.

(6) NOTICE TO TAXPAYER.—Not later than 15 days after the date on which the Secretary distributed any payment to an eligible taxpayer pursuant to this subsection, notice shall be sent by mail to such taxpayer's last known address. Such notice shall indicate the method by which such payment was made, the amount of such payment, and a phone number for the appropriate point of contact at the Internal Revenue Service to report any failure to receive such payment.

[Sec. 6428(g)]

(g) IDENTIFICATION NUMBER REQUIREMENT.—

(1) IN GENERAL.—No credit shall be allowed under subsection (a) to an eligible individual who does not include on the return of tax for the taxable year—

(A) such individual's valid identification number,

(B) in the case of a joint return, the valid identification number of such individual's spouse, and

(C) in the case of any qualifying child taken into account under subsection (a)(2), the valid identification number of such qualifying child.

(2) VALID IDENTIFICATION NUMBER.—

(A) IN GENERAL.—For purposes of paragraph (1), the term "valid identification number" means a social security number (as such term is defined in section 24(h)(7)).

(B) ADOPTION TAXPAYER IDENTIFICATION NUMBER.—For purposes of paragraph (1)(C), in the case of a qualifying child who is adopted or placed for adoption, the term "valid identification number" shall include the adoption taxpayer identification number of such child.

(3) SPECIAL RULE FOR MEMBERS OF THE ARMED FORCES.—Paragraph (1)(B) shall not apply in the case where at least 1 spouse was a member of the Armed Forces of the United States at any time during the taxable year and at least 1 spouse satisfies paragraph (1)(A).

(4) MATHEMATICAL OR CLERICAL ERROR AUTHORITY.—Any omission of a correct valid identification number required under this subsection shall be treated as a mathematical or clerical error for purposes of applying section 6213(g)(2) to such omission.

[Sec. 6428(h)]

(h) REGULATIONS.—The Secretary shall prescribe such regulations or other guidance as may be necessary to carry out the purposes of this section, including any such measures as are deemed appropriate to avoid allowing multiple credits or rebates to a taxpayer.

CHAPTER 66—LIMITATIONS

SUBCHAPTER A—LIMITATIONS ON ASSESSMENT AND COLLECTION

[Sec. 6501]

SEC. 6501. LIMITATIONS ON ASSESSMENT AND COLLECTION.

[Sec. 6501(a)]

(a) GENERAL RULE.—Except as otherwise provided in this section, the amount of any tax imposed by this title shall be assessed within 3 years after the return was filed (whether or not such return was filed on or after the date prescribed) or, if the tax is payable by stamp, at any time after such tax became due and before the expiration of 3 years after the date on which any part of such tax was paid, and no proceeding in court without assessment for the collection of such tax shall be begun after the expiration of such period. For purposes of this chapter, the term "return" means the return required to be filed by the taxpayer (and does not include a return of any person from whom the taxpayer has received an item of income, gain, loss, deduction, or credit).

[Sec. 6501(b)]

(b) TIME RETURN DEEMED FILED.—

(1) EARLY RETURN.—For purposes of this section, a return of tax imposed by this title, except tax imposed by chapter 3, 4, 21, or 24, filed before the last day prescribed by law or by regulations promulgated pursuant to law for the filing thereof, shall be considered as filed on such last day.

(2) RETURN OF CERTAIN EMPLOYMENT AND WITHHOLDING TAXES.—For purposes of this section, if a return of tax imposed by chapter 3, 4, 21 or 24 for any period ending with or within a calendar year is filed before April 15 of the succeeding calendar year, such return shall be considered filed on April 15 of such calendar year.

(3) RETURN EXECUTED BY SECRETARY.—Notwithstanding the provisions of paragraph (2) of section 6020(b), the execution of a return by the Secretary pursuant to the authority conferred by such section shall not start the running of the period of limitations on assessment and collection.

(4) RETURN OF EXCISE TAXES.—For purposes of this section, the filing of a return for a specified period on which an entry has been made with respect to a tax imposed under a provision of subtitle D (including a return on which an entry has been made showing no liability for such tax for such period) shall constitute the filing of a return of all amounts of such tax which, if properly paid, would be required to be reported on such return for such period.

[Sec. 6501(c)]

(c) EXCEPTIONS.—

(1) FALSE RETURN.—In the case of a false or fraudulent return with the intent to evade tax, the tax may be assessed, or a proceeding in court for collection of such tax may be begun without assessment, at any time.

(2) WILLFUL ATTEMPT TO EVADE TAX.—In case of a willful attempt in any manner to defeat or evade tax imposed by this title (other than tax imposed by subtitle A or B), the tax may be assessed, or a proceeding in court for the collection of such tax may be begun without assessment, at any time.

(3) NO RETURN.—In the case of failure to file a return, the tax may be assessed, or a proceeding in court for the collection of such tax may be begun without assessment, at any time.

(4) EXTENSION BY AGREEMENT.—

(A) IN GENERAL.—Where before the expiration of the time prescribed for the assessment of any tax imposed by this title, except the estate tax provided in chapter 11, both the Secretary and the taxpayer have consented in writing to its assessment after such time, the tax may be assessed at any time prior to the expiration of the period agreed upon. The period so agreed upon may be extended by subsequent agreements in writing made before the expiration of the period previously agreed upon.

(B) NOTICE TO TAXPAYER OF RIGHT TO REFUSE OR LIMIT EXTENSION.—The Secretary shall notify the taxpayer of the taxpayer's right to refuse to extend the period of limitations, or to limit such extension to particular issues or to a particular period of time, on each occasion when the taxpayer is requested to provide such consent.

(5) TAX RESULTING FROM CHANGES IN CERTAIN INCOME TAX OR ESTATE TAX CREDITS.—For special rules applicable in cases where the adjustment of certain taxes allowed as a credit against income taxes or estate taxes results in additional tax, see section 905(c) (relating to the foreign tax credit for income tax purposes) and section 2016 (relating to taxes of foreign countries, States, etc., claimed as credit against estate taxes).

(6) TERMINATION OF PRIVATE FOUNDATION STATUS.—In the case of a tax on termination of private foundation status under section 507, such tax may be assessed, or a proceeding in court for the collection of such tax may be begun without assessment, at any time.

(7) SPECIAL RULE FOR CERTAIN AMENDED RETURNS.—Where, within the 60-day period ending on the day on which the time prescribed in this section for the assessment of any tax imposed by subtitle A for any taxable year would otherwise expire, the Secretary receives a written document signed by the taxpayer showing that the taxpayer owes an additional amount of such tax for such taxable year, the period for the assessment of such additional amount shall not expire before the day 60 days after the day on which the Secretary receives such document.

* * *

[Sec. 6501(d)]

(d) REQUEST FOR PROMPT ASSESSMENT.—Except as otherwise provided in subsection (c), (e), or (f), in the case of any tax (other than the tax imposed by chapter 11 of subtitle B, relating to estate taxes) for which return is required in the case of a decedent, or by his estate during the period of administration, or by a corporation, the tax shall be assessed, and any proceeding in court without assessment for the collection of such tax shall be begun, within 18 months after written request therefor (filed after the return is made and filed in such manner and such form as may be prescribed by regulations of the Secretary) by the executor, administrator, or other fiduciary representing the estate of such decedent, or by the corporation, but not after the expiration of 3 years after the return was filed. This subsection shall not apply in the case of a corporation unless—

(1)(A) such written request notifies the Secretary that the corporation contemplates dissolution at or before the expiration of such 18-month period, (B) the dissolution is in good faith begun before the expiration of such 18-month period, and (C) the dissolution is completed;

(2) (A) such written request notifies the Secretary that a dissolution has in good faith been begun, and (B) the dissolution is completed; or

(3) a dissolution has been completed at the time such written request is made.

[Sec. 6501(e)]

(e) SUBSTANTIAL OMISSION OF ITEMS.—Except as otherwise provided in subsection (c)—

(1) INCOME TAXES.—In the case of any tax imposed by subtitle A—

(A) GENERAL RULE.—If the taxpayer omits from gross income an amount properly includible therein and—

(i) such amount is in excess of 25 percent of the amount of gross income stated in the return, or

(ii) such amount—

(I) is attributable to one or more assets with respect to which information is required to be reported under section 6038D (or would be so required if such section were applied without regard to the dollar threshold specified in subsection (a) thereof and without regard to any exceptions provided pursuant to subsection (h) (1) thereof), and

(II) is in excess of $5,000,

the tax may be assessed, or a proceeding in court for collection of such tax may be begun without assessment, at any time within 6 years after the return was filed.

(B) DETERMINATION OF GROSS INCOME.—For purposes of subparagraph (A)—

(i) In the case of a trade or business, the term "gross income" means the total of the amounts received or accrued from the sale of goods or services (if such amounts are required to be shown on the return) prior to diminution by the cost of such sales or services;

(ii) An understatement of gross income by reason of an overstatement of unrecovered cost or other basis is an omission from gross income; and

(iii) In determining the amount omitted from gross income (other than in the case of an overstatement of unrecovered cost or other basis), there shall not be taken into account any amount which is omitted from gross income stated in the return if such amount is disclosed in the return, or in a statement attached to the return, in a manner adequate to apprise the Secretary of the nature and amount of such item.

(C) CONSTRUCTIVE DIVIDENDS.—If the taxpayer omits from gross income an amount properly includible therein under section 951(a), the tax may be assessed, or a proceeding in court for the collection of such tax may be done without assessing, at any time within 6 years after the return was filed.

* * *

[Sec. 6501(f)]

(f) PERSONAL HOLDING COMPANY TAX.—If a corporation which is a personal holding company for any taxable year fails to file with its return under chapter 1 for such year a schedule setting forth—

(1) the items of gross income and adjusted ordinary gross income, described in section 543, received by the corporation during such year, and

(2) the names and addresses of the individuals who owned, within the meaning of section 544 (relating to rules for determining stock ownership), at any time during the last half of such year more than 50 percent in value of the outstanding capital stock of the corporation,

the personal holding company tax for such year may be assessed, or a proceeding in court for the collection of such tax may be begun without assessment, at any time within 6 years after the return for such year was filed.

[Sec. 6501(g)]

(g) CERTAIN INCOME TAX RETURNS OF CORPORATIONS.—

(1) TRUSTS OR PARTNERSHIPS.—If a taxpayer determines in good faith that it is a trust or partnership and files a return as such under subtitle A, and if such taxpayer is thereafter held to be a corporation for the taxable year for which the return is filed, such return shall be deemed the return of the corporation for purposes of this section.

(2) EXEMPT ORGANIZATIONS.—If a taxpayer determines in good faith that it is an exempt organization and files a return as such under section 6033, and if such taxpayer is thereafter held to be a taxable organization for the taxable year for which the return is filed, such return shall be deemed the return of the organization for purposes of this section.

* * *

[Sec. 6501(h)]

(h) NET OPERATING LOSS OR CAPITAL LOSS CARRYBACKS.—In the case of a deficiency attributable to the application to the taxpayer of a net operating loss carryback or a capital loss carryback (including deficiencies which may be assessed pursuant to the provisions of section 6213(b)(3)), such deficiency may be assessed at any time before the expiration of the period within which a deficiency for the taxable year of the net operating loss or net capital loss which results in such carryback may be assessed.

* * *

SUBCHAPTER B—LIMITATIONS ON CREDIT OR REFUND

[Sec. 6511]

SEC. 6511. LIMITATIONS ON CREDIT OR REFUND.

[Sec. 6511(a)]

(a) PERIOD OF LIMITATION ON FILING CLAIM.—Claim for credit or refund of an overpayment of any tax imposed by this title in respect of which tax the taxpayer is required to file a return shall be filed by the taxpayer within 3 years from the time the return was filed or 2 years from the time the tax was paid, whichever of such periods expires the later, or if no return was filed by the taxpayer, within 2 years from the time the tax was paid. Claim for credit or refund of an overpayment of any tax imposed by this title which is required to be paid by means of a stamp shall be filed by the taxpayer within 3 years from the time the tax was paid.

[Sec. 6511(b)]

(b) LIMITATION ON ALLOWANCE OF CREDITS AND REFUNDS.—

(1) FILING OF CLAIM WITHIN PRESCRIBED PERIOD.—No credit or refund shall be allowed or made after the expiration of the period of limitation prescribed in subsection (a) for the filing of a claim for credit or refund, unless a claim for credit or refund is filed by the taxpayer within such period.

(2) LIMIT ON AMOUNT OF CREDIT OR REFUND.—

(A) LIMIT WHERE CLAIM FILED WITHIN 3-YEAR PERIOD.—If the claim was filed by the taxpayer during the 3-year period prescribed in subsection (a), the amount of the credit or refund shall not exceed the portion of the tax paid within the period, immediately preceding the filing of the claim, equal to 3 years plus the period of any extension of time for filing the return. If the tax was required to be paid by means of a stamp, the amount of the credit or refund shall not exceed the portion of the tax paid within the 3 years immediately preceding the filing of the claim.

(B) LIMIT WHERE CLAIM NOT FILED WITHIN 3-YEAR PERIOD.—If the claim was not filed within such 3-year period, the amount of the credit or refund shall not exceed the portion of the tax paid during the 2 years immediately preceding the filing of the claim.

(C) LIMIT IF NO CLAIM FILED.—If no claim was filed, the credit or refund shall not exceed the amount which would be allowable under subparagraph (A) or (B), as the case may be, if claim was filed on the date the credit or refund is allowed.

* * *

[Sec. 6511(d)]

(d) SPECIAL RULES APPLICABLE TO INCOME TAXES.—

(1) SEVEN-YEAR PERIOD OF LIMITATION WITH RESPECT TO BAD DEBTS AND WORTHLESS SECURITIES.—If the claim for credit or refund relates to an overpayment of tax imposed by subtitle A on account of—

(A) The deductibility by the taxpayer, under section 166 or section 832(c), of a debt as a debt which became worthless, or, under section 165(g), of a loss from worthlessness of a security, or

(B) The effect that the deductibility of a debt or loss described in subparagraph (A) has on the application to the taxpayer of a carryover,

in lieu of the 3-year period of limitation prescribed in subsection (a), the period shall be 7 years from the date prescribed by law for filing the return for the year with respect to which the claim is made. If the claim for credit or refund relates to an overpayment on account of the effect that the deductibility of such a debt or loss has on the application to the taxpayer of a carryback, the period shall be either 7 years from the date prescribed by law for filing the return for the year of the net operating loss which results in such carryback or the period prescribed in paragaph (2) of this subsection, whichever expires the later. In the case of a claim described in this paragraph the amount of the credit or refund may exceed the portion of the tax paid within the period prescribed in subsection (b)(2) or (c), whichever is applicable, to the extent of the amount of the overpayment attributable to the deductibility of items described in this paragraph.

(2) SPECIAL PERIOD OF LIMITATION WITH RESPECT TO NET OPERATING LOSS OR CAPITAL LOSS CARRYBACKS.—

(A) PERIOD OF LIMITATION.—If the claim for credit or refund relates to an overpayment attributable to a net operating loss carryback or a capital loss carryback, in lieu of the 3-year period of limitation prescribed in subsection (a), the period shall be that period which ends 3 years after the time prescribed by law for filing the return (including extensions thereof) for the taxable year of the net operating loss or net capital loss which results in such carryback, or the period prescribed in subsection (c) in respect of such taxable year, whichever expires later.

In the case of such a claim, the amount of the credit or refund may exceed the portion of the tax paid within the period provided in subsection (b)(2) or (c), whichever is applicable, to the extent of the amount of the overpayment attributable to such carryback.

(B) APPLICABLE RULES.—

(i) IN GENERAL.—If the allowance of a credit or refund of an overpayment of tax attributable to a net operating loss carryback or a capital loss carryback is otherwise prevented by the operation of any law or rule of law other than section 7122 (relating to compromises), such credit or refund may be allowed or made, if claim therefor is filed within the period provided in subparagraph (A) of this paragraph.

(ii) TENTATIVE CARRYBACK ADJUSTMENTS.—If the allowance of an application, credit, or refund of a decrease in tax determined under section 6411(b) is otherwise prevented by the operation of any law or rule of law other than section 7122, such application, credit, or refund may be allowed or made if application for a tentative carryback adjustment is made within the period provided in section 6411(a).

(iii) DETERMINATIONS BY COURTS TO BE CONCLUSIVE.—In the case of any such claim for credit or refund or any such application for a tentative carryback adjustment, the determination by any court, including the Tax Court, in any proceeding in which the decision of the court has become final, shall be conclusive except with respect to—

(I) the net operating loss deduction and the effect of such deduction, and

(II) the determination of a short-term capital loss and the effect of such short-term capital loss, to the extent that such deduction or short-term capital loss is affected by a carryback which was not an issue in such proceeding.

* * *

[Sec. 6513]

SEC. 6513. TIME RETURN DEEMED FILED AND TAX CONSIDERED PAID.

[Sec. 6513(a)]

(a) EARLY RETURN OR ADVANCE PAYMENT OF TAX.—For purposes of section 6511, any return filed before the last day prescribed for the filing thereof shall be considered as filed on such last day. For purposes of section 6511(b)(2) and (c) and section 6512, payment of any portion of the tax made before the last day prescribed for the payment of the tax shall be considered made on such last day. For purposes of this subsection, the last day prescribed for filing the return or paying the tax shall be determined without regard to any extension of time granted the taxpayer and without regard to any election to pay the tax in installments.

[Sec. 6513(b)]

(b) PREPAID INCOME TAX.—For purposes of section 6511 or 6512—

(1) Any tax actually deducted and withheld at the source during any calendar year under chapter 24 shall, in respect of the recipient of the income, be deemed to have been paid by him on the 15th day of the fourth month following the close of his taxable year with respect to which such tax is allowable as a credit under section 31.

(2) Any amount paid as estimated income tax for any taxable year shall be deemed to have been paid on the last day prescribed for filing the return under section 6012 for such taxable year (determined without regard to any extension of time for filing such return).

(3) Any tax withheld at the source under chapter 3 or 4 shall, in respect of the recipient of the income, be deemed to have been paid by such recipient on the last day prescribed for filing the return under section 6012 for the taxable year (determined without regard to any extension of time for filing) with respect to which such tax is allowable as a credit under section 1462 or 1474(b). For this purpose, any exemption granted under section 6012 from the requirement of filing a return shall be disregarded.

* * *

SUBCHAPTER D—PERIODS OF LIMITATION IN JUDICIAL PROCEEDINGS

[Sec. 6531]

SEC. 6531. PERIODS OF LIMITATION ON CRIMINAL PROSECUTIONS.

No person shall be prosecuted, tried, or punished for any of the various offenses arising under the internal revenue laws unless the indictment is found or the information instituted within 3 years next after the commission of the offense, except that the period of limitation shall be 6 years—

(1) for offenses involving the defrauding or attempting to defraud the United States or any agency thereof, whether by conspiracy or not, and in any manner;

(2) for the offense of willfully attempting in any manner to evade or defeat any tax or the payment thereof;

(3) for the offense of willfully aiding or assisting in, or procuring, counseling, or advising, the preparation or presentation under, or in connection with any matter arising under, the internal revenue laws, of a false or fraudulent return, affidavit, claim, or document (whether or not such falsity or fraud is with the knowledge or consent of the person authorized or required to present such return, affidavit, claim, or document);

(4) for the offense of willfully failing to pay any tax, or make any return (other than a return required under authority of part III of subchapter A of chapter 61) at the time or times required by law or regulations;

(5) for offenses described in sections 7206 (1) and 7207 (relating to false statements and fraudulent documents);

(6) for the offense described in section 7212 (a) (relating to intimidation of officers and employees of the United States);

(7) for offenses described in section 7214 (a) committed by officers and employees of the United States; and

(8) for offenses arising under section 371 of Title 18 of the United States Code, where the object of the conspiracy is to attempt in any manner to evade or defeat any tax or the payment thereof.

The time during which the person committing any of the various offenses arising under the internal revenue laws is outside the United States or is a fugitive from justice within the meaning of section 3290 of Title 18 of the United States Code, shall not be taken as any part of the time limited by law for the commencement of such proceedings. (The preceding sentence shall also be deemed an amendment to section 3748 (a) of the Internal Revenue Code of 1939, and shall apply in lieu of the sentence in section 3748 (a) which relates to the time during which a person committing an offense is absent from the district wherein the same is committed, except that such amendment shall apply only if the period of limitations under section 3748 would, without the application of such amendment, expire more than 3 years after the date of enactment of this title, and except that such period shall not, with the application of this amendment, expire prior to the date which is 3 years after the date of enactment of this title.) Where a complaint is instituted before a commissioner of the United States within the period above limited, the time shall be extended until the date which is 9 months after the date of the making of the complaint before the commissioner of the United States. For the purpose of determining the periods of limitation on criminal prosecutions, the rules of section 6513 shall be applicable.

CHAPTER 67—INTEREST

SUBCHAPTER A—INTEREST ON UNDERPAYMENTS

[Sec. 6601]

SEC. 6601. INTEREST ON UNDERPAYMENT, NONPAYMENT, OR EXTENSIONS OF TIME FOR PAYMENT, OF TAX.

[Sec. 6601(a)]

(a) GENERAL RULE.—If any amount of tax imposed by this title (whether required to be shown on a return, or to be paid by stamp or by some other method) is not paid on or before the last date prescribed for payment, interest on such amount at the underpayment rate established under section 6621 shall be paid for the period from such last date to the date paid.

[Sec. 6601(b)]

(b) LAST DATE PRESCRIBED FOR PAYMENT.—For purposes of this section, the last date prescribed for payment of the tax shall be determined under chapter 62 with the application of the following rules:

(1) EXTENSIONS OF TIME DISREGARDED.—The last date prescribed for payment shall be determined without regard to any extension of time for payment or any installment agreement entered into under section 6159.

(2) JEOPARDY.—The last date prescribed for payment shall be determined without regard to any notice and demand for payment issued, by reason of jeopardy (as provided in chapter 70), prior to the last date otherwise prescribed for such payment.

(3) ACCUMULATED EARNINGS TAX.—In the case of the tax imposed by section 531 for any taxable year, the last date prescribed for payment shall be deemed to be the due date (without regard to extensions) for the return of tax imposed by subtitle A for such taxable year.

(4) LAST DATE FOR PAYMENT NOT OTHERWISE PRESCRIBED.—In the case of taxes payable by stamp and in all other cases in which the last date for payment is not otherwise prescribed, the last date for payment shall be deemed to be the date the liability for tax arises (and in no event shall be later than the date notice and demand for the tax is made by the Secretary).

* * *

[Sec. 6601(e)]

(e) APPLICABLE RULES.—Except as otherwise provided in this title—

(1) INTEREST TREATED AS TAX.—Interest prescribed under this section on any tax shall be paid upon notice and demand, and shall be assessed, collected, and paid in the same manner

as taxes. Any reference in this title (except subchapter B of chapter 63, relating to deficiency procedures) to any tax imposed by this title shall be deemed also to refer to interest imposed by this section on such tax.

(2) INTEREST ON PENALTIES, ADDITIONAL AMOUNTS, OR ADDITIONS TO THE TAX.—

(A) IN GENERAL.—Interest shall be imposed under subsection (a) in respect of any assessable penalty, additional amount, or addition to the tax (other than an addition to tax imposed under section 6651(a)(1) or 6653 or under part II of subchapter A of chapter 68) only if such assessable penalty, additional amount, or addition to the tax is not paid within 21 calendar days from the date of notice and demand therefor (10 business days if the amount for which such notice and demand is made equals or exceeds $100,000), and in such case interest shall be imposed only for the period from the date of the notice and demand to the date of payment.

(B) INTEREST ON CERTAIN ADDITIONS TO TAX.—Interest shall be imposed under this section with respect to any addition to tax imposed by section 6651(a)(1) or 6653 or under part II of subchapter A of chapter 68 for the period which—

(i) begins on the date on which the return of the tax with respect to which such addition to tax is imposed is required to be filed (including any extensions), and

(ii) ends on the date of payment of such addition to tax.

(3) PAYMENTS MADE WITHIN SPECIFIED PERIOD AFTER NOTICE AND DEMAND.—If notice and demand is made for payment of any amount and if such amount is paid within 21 calendar days (10 business days if the amount for which such notice and demand is made equals or exceeds $100,000) after the date of such notice and demand, interest under this section on the amount so paid shall not be imposed for the period after the date of such notice and demand.

* * *

SUBCHAPTER B—INTEREST ON OVERPAYMENTS

[Sec. 6611]

SEC. 6611. INTEREST ON OVERPAYMENTS.

[Sec. 6611(a)]

(a) RATE.—Interest shall be allowed and paid upon any overpayment in respect of any internal revenue tax at the overpayment rate established under section 6621.

[Sec. 6611(b)]

(b) PERIOD.—Such interest shall be allowed and paid as follows:

(1) CREDITS.—In the case of a credit, from the date of the overpayment to the due date of the amount against which the credit is taken.

(2) REFUNDS.—In the case of a refund, from the date of the overpayment to a date (to be determined by the Secretary) preceding the date of the refund check by not more than 30 days, whether or not such refund check is accepted by the taxpayer after tender of such check to the taxpayer. The acceptance of such check shall be without prejudice to any right of the taxpayer to claim any additional overpayment and interest thereon.

(3) LATE RETURNS.—Notwithstanding paragraph (1) or (2) in the case of a return of tax which is filed after the last date prescribed for filing such return (determined with regard to extentions), no interest shall be allowed or paid for any day before the date on which the return is filed.

* * *

[Sec. 6611(f)]

(f) REFUND OF INCOME TAX CAUSED BY CARRYBACK OR ADJUSTMENT FOR CERTAIN UNUSED DEDUCTIONS.—

(1) NET OPERATING LOSS OR CAPITAL LOSS CARRYBACK.—For purposes of subsection (a), if any overpayment of tax imposed by subtitle A results from a carryback of a net operating loss or net capital loss, such overpayment shall be deemed not to have been made prior to the filing date for the taxable year in which such net operating loss or net capital loss arises.

* * *

SUBCHAPTER C—DETERMINATION OF INTEREST RATE; COMPOUNDING OF INTEREST

[Sec. 6621]

SEC. 6621. DETERMINATION OF RATE OF INTEREST.

[Sec. 6621(a)]

(a) GENERAL RULE.—

(1) OVERPAYMENT RATE.—The overpayment rate established under this section shall be the sum of—

(A) the Federal short-term rate determined under subsection (b), plus

(B) 3 percentage points (2 percentage points in the case of a corporation).

To the extent that an overpayment of tax by a corporation for any taxable period (as defined in subsection (c)(3), applied by substituting "overpayment" for "underpayment") exceeds $10,000, subparagraph (B) shall be applied by substituting "0.5 percentage point" for "2 percentage points".

(2) UNDERPAYMENT RATE.—The underpayment rate established under this section shall be the sum of—

(A) the Federal short-term rate determined under subsection (b), plus

(B) 3 percentage points.

[Sec. 6621(b)]

(b) FEDERAL SHORT-TERM RATE.—For purposes of this section—

(1) GENERAL RULE.—The Secretary shall determine the Federal short-term rate for the first month in each calendar quarter.

(2) PERIOD DURING WHICH RATE APPLIES.—

(A) IN GENERAL.—Except as provided in subparagraph (B), the Federal short-term rate determined under paragraph (1) for any month shall apply during the first calendar quarter beginning after such month.

(B) SPECIAL RULE FOR INDIVIDUAL ESTIMATED TAX.—In determining the addition to tax under section 6654 for failure to pay estimated tax for any taxable year, the Federal short-term rate which applies during the 3rd month following such taxable year shall also apply during the first 15 days of the 4th month following such taxable year.

(3) FEDERAL SHORT-TERM RATE.—The Federal short-term rate for any month shall be the Federal short-term rate determined during such month by the Secretary in accordance with section 1274(d). Any such rate shall be rounded to the nearest full percent (or, if a multiple of ½ of 1 percent, such rate shall be increased to the next highest full percent).

[Sec. 6621(c)]

(c) INCREASE IN UNDERPAYMENT RATE FOR LARGE CORPORATE UNDERPAYMENTS.—

(1) IN GENERAL.—For purposes of determining the amount of interest payable under section 6601 on any large corporate underpayment for periods after the applicable date, paragraph (2) of subsection (a) shall be applied by substituting "5 percentage points" for "3 percentage points".

(2) APPLICABLE RATE.—For purposes of this subsection—

(A) IN GENERAL.—The applicable date is the 30th day after the earlier of—

(i) the date on which the 1st letter of proposed deficiency which allows the taxpayer an opportunity for administrative review in the Internal Revenue Service Independent Office of Appeals is sent, or

(ii) the date on which the deficiency notice under section 6212 is sent.

The preceding sentence shall be applied without regard to any such letter or notice which is withdrawn by the Secretary.

(B) SPECIAL RULES.—

(i) NONDEFICIENCY PROCEDURES.—In the case of any underpayment of any tax imposed by this title to which the deficiency procedures do not apply, subparagraph (A) shall be applied by taking into account any letter or notice provided by the Secretary which notifies the taxpayer of the assessment or proposed assessment of the tax.

(ii) EXCEPTION WHERE AMOUNTS PAID IN FULL.—For purposes of subparagraph (A), a letter or notice shall be disregarded if, during the 30-day period beginning on the day on which it was sent, the taxpayer makes a payment equal to the amount shown as due in such letter or notice, as the case may be.

(iii) EXCEPTION FOR LETTERS OR NOTICES INVOLVING SMALL AMOUNTS.—For purposes of this paragraph, any letter or notice shall be disregarded if the amount of the deficiency or proposed deficiency (or the assessment or proposed assessment) set forth in such letter or notice is not greater than $100,000 (determined by not taking into account any interest, penalties, or additions to tax).

(3) LARGE CORPORATE UNDERPAYMENT.—For purposes of this subsection—

(A) IN GENERAL.—The term "large corporate underpayment" means any underpayment of a tax by a C corporation for any taxable period if the amount of such underpayment for such period exceeds $100,000.

(B) TAXABLE PERIOD.—For purposes of subparagraph (A), the term "taxable period" means—

(i) in the case of any tax imposed by subtitle A, the taxable year, or

(ii) in the case of any other tax, the period to which the underpayment relates.

* * *

[Sec. 6622]

SEC. 6622. INTEREST COMPOUNDED DAILY.

[Sec. 6622(a)]

(a) GENERAL RULE.—In computing the amount of any interest required to be paid under this title or sections 1961(c)(1) or 2411 of title 28, United States Code, by the Secretary or by the taxpayer, or any other amount determined by reference to such amount of interest, such interest and such amount shall be compounded daily.

[Sec. 6622(b)]

(b) EXCEPTION FOR PENALTY FOR FAILURE TO FILE ESTIMATED TAX.—Subsection (a) shall not apply for purposes of computing the amount of any addition to tax under section 6654 or 6655.

CHAPTER 68—ADDITIONS TO THE TAX, ADDITIONAL AMOUNTS, AND ASSESSABLE PENALTIES

SUBCHAPTER A—ADDITIONS TO THE TAX AND ADDITIONAL AMOUNTS

PART I—GENERAL PROVISIONS

[Sec. 6651]

SEC. 6651. FAILURE TO FILE TAX RETURN OR TO PAY TAX.

[Sec. 6651(a)]

(a) ADDITION TO THE TAX.—In case of failure—

(1) to file any return required under authority of subchapter A of chapter 61 (other than part III thereof), subchapter A of chapter 51 (relating to distilled spirits, wines, and beer), or of subchapter A of chapter 52 (relating to tobacco, cigars, cigarettes, and cigarette papers and tubes) or of subchapter A of chapter 53 (relating to machine guns and certain other firearms), on the date prescribed therefor (determined with regard to any extension of time for filing), unless it is shown that such failure is due to reasonable cause and not due to willful neglect, there shall be added to the amount required to be shown as tax on such return 5 percent of the amount of such tax if the failure is for not more than 1 month, with an additional 5 percent for each additional month or fraction thereof during which such failure continues, not exceeding 25 percent in the aggregate;

(2) to pay the amount shown as tax on any return specified in paragraph (1) on or before the date prescribed for payment of such tax (determined with regard to any extension of time for payment), unless it is shown that such failure is due to reasonable cause and not due to willful neglect, there shall be added to the amount shown as tax on such return 0.5 percent of the amount of such tax if the failure is for not more than 1 month, with an additional 0.5 percent for each additional month or fraction thereof during which such failure continues, not exceeding 25 percent in the aggregate; or

(3) to pay any amount in respect of any tax required to be shown on a return specified in paragraph (1) which is not so shown (including an assessment made pursuant to section 6213(b)) within 21 calendar days from the date of notice and demand therefor (10 business days if the amount for which such notice and demand is made equals or exceeds $100,000), unless it is shown that such failure is due to reasonable cause and not due to willful neglect, there shall be added to the amount of tax stated in such notice and demand 0.5 percent of the amount of such tax if the failure is for not more than 1 month, with an additional 0.5 percent for each additional month or fraction thereof during which such failure continues, not exceeding 25 percent in the aggregate.

In the case of a failure to file a return of tax imposed by chapter 1 within 60 days of the date prescribed for filing of such return (determined with regard to any extensions of time for filing), unless it is shown that such failure is due to reasonable cause and not due to willful neglect, the addition to tax under paragraph (1) shall not be less than the lesser of $435 or 100 percent of the amount required to be shown as tax on such return.

* * *

[Sec. 6651(i)]

(i) APPLICATION TO IMPUTED UNDERPAYMENT.—For purposes of this section, any failure to comply with section 6226(b)(4)(A)(ii) shall be treated as a failure to pay the amount described in subclause (II) thereof and such amount shall be treated for purposes of this section as an amount shown as tax on a return specified in subsection (a)(1).

[Sec. 6651(j)]

(j) ADJUSTMENT FOR INFLATION.—

(1) IN GENERAL.—In the case of any return required to be filed in a calendar year beginning after 2020, the $435 dollar amount under subsection (a) shall be increased by an amount equal to such dollar amount multiplied by the cost-of-living adjustment determined under section 1(f)(3) for the calendar year determined by substituting "calendar year 2019" for "calendar year 2016" in subparagraph (A)(ii) thereof.

(2) ROUNDING.—If any amount adjusted under paragraph (1) is not a multiple of $5, such amount shall be rounded to the next lowest multiple of $5.

[Sec. 6654]

SEC. 6654. FAILURE BY INDIVIDUAL TO PAY ESTIMATED INCOME TAX.

[Sec. 6654(a)]

(a) ADDITION TO THE TAX.—Except as otherwise provided in this section, in the case of any underpayment of estimated tax by an individual, there shall be added to the tax under chapter 1, the tax under chapter 2, and the tax under chapter 2A for the taxable year an amount determined by applying—

(1) the underpayment rate established under section 6621,

(2) to the amount of the underpayment,

(3) for the period of the underpayment.

[Sec. 6654(b)]

(b) AMOUNT OF UNDERPAYMENT; PERIOD OF UNDERPAYMENT.—For purposes of subsection (a)—

(1) AMOUNT.—The amount of the underpayment shall be the excess of—

(A) the required installment, over

(B) the amount (if any) of the installment paid on or before the due date for the installment.

(2) PERIOD OF UNDERPAYMENT.—The period of the underpayment shall run from the due date for the installment to whichever of the following dates is the earlier—

(A) the 15th day of the 4th month following the close of the taxable year, or

(B) with respect to any portion of the underpayment, the date on which such portion is paid.

(3) ORDER OF CREDITING PAYMENTS.—For purposes of paragraph (2)(B), a payment of estimated tax shall be credited against unpaid required installments in the order in which such installments are required to be paid.

[Sec. 6654(c)]

(c) NUMBER OF REQUIRED INSTALLMENTS; DUE DATES.—For purposes of this section—

(1) PAYABLE IN 4 INSTALLMENTS.—There shall be 4 required installments for each taxable year.

(2) TIME FOR PAYMENT OF INSTALLMENTS.—

In the case of the following required installments:	*The due date is:*
1st	April 15
2nd	June 15
3rd	September 15
4th	January 15 of the following taxable year.

[Sec. 6654(d)]

(d) AMOUNT OF REQUIRED INSTALLMENTS.—For purposes of this section—

(1) AMOUNT.—

(A) IN GENERAL.—Except as provided in paragraph (2), the amount of any required installment shall be 25 percent of the required annual payment.

(B) REQUIRED ANNUAL PAYMENT.—For purposes of subparagraph (A), the term "required annual payment" means the lesser of—

(i) 90 percent of the tax shown on the return for the taxable year (or, if no return is filed, 90 percent of the tax for such year), or

(ii) 100 percent of the tax shown on the return of the individual for the preceding taxable year.

Clause (ii) shall not apply if the preceding taxable year was not a taxable year of 12 months or if the individual did not file a return for such preceding taxable year.

(C) LIMITATION ON USE OF PRECEDING YEAR'S TAX.—

(i) IN GENERAL.—If the adjusted gross income shown on the return of the individual for the preceding taxable year beginning in any calendar year exceeds $150,000, clause (ii) of subparagraph (B) shall be applied by substituting "110 percent". For purposes of the preceding sentence, the applicable percentage shall be determined in accordance with the following table:

If the preceding taxable year begins in:	*The applicable percentage is:*
1998	105
1999	108.6
2000	110
2001	112
2002 or thereafter	110

This clause shall not apply in the case of a preceding taxable year beginning in calendar year 1997.

(ii) SEPARATE RETURNS.—In the case of a married individual (within the meaning of section 7703) who files a separate return for the taxable year for which the amount of the installment is being determined, clause (i) shall be applied by substituting "$75,000" for "$150,000".

(iii) SPECIAL RULE.—In the case of an estate or trust, adjusted gross income shall be determined as provided in section 67(e).

(2) LOWER REQUIRED INSTALLMENT WHERE ANNUALIZED INCOME INSTALLMENT IS LESS THAN AMOUNT DETERMINED UNDER PARAGRAPH (1).—

(A) IN GENERAL.—In the case of any required installment, if the individual establishes that the annualized income installment is less than the amount determined under paragraph (1)—

(i) the amount of such required installment shall be the annualized income installment, and

(ii) any reduction in a required installment resulting from the application of this subparagraph shall be recaptured by increasing the amount of the next required installment determined under paragraph (1) by the amount of such reduction (and by increasing subsequent required installments to the extent that the reduction has not previously been recaptured under this clause).

(B) DETERMINATION OF ANNUALIZED INCOME INSTALLMENT.—In the case of any required installment, the annualized income installment is the excess (if any) of—

(i) an amount equal to the applicable percentage of the tax for the taxable year computed by placing on an annualized basis the taxable income, alternative minimum taxable income, and adjusted self-employment income for months in the taxable year ending before the due date for the installment, over

(ii) the aggregate amount of any prior required installments for the taxable year.

(C) SPECIAL RULES.—For purposes of this paragraph—

(i) ANNUALIZATION.—The taxable income, alternative minimum taxable income, and adjusted self-employment income shall be placed on an annualized basis under regulations prescribed by the Secretary.

(ii) APPLICABLE PERCENTAGE.—

In the case of the following required installments:	*The applicable percentage is:*
1st	22.5
2nd	45
3rd	67.5
4th	90

(iii) ADJUSTED SELF-EMPLOYMENT INCOME.—The term "adjusted self-employment income" means self-employment income (as defined in section 1402(b)); except that section 1402(b) shall be applied by placing wages (within the meaning of section 1402(b)) for months in the taxable year ending before the due date for the installment on an annualized basis consistent with clause (i).

* * *

[Sec. 6654(e)]

(e) EXCEPTIONS.—

(1) WHERE TAX IS SMALL AMOUNT.—No addition to tax shall be imposed under subsection (a) for any taxable year if the tax shown on the return for such taxable year (or, if no return is filed, the tax), reduced by the credit allowable under section 31, is less than $1,000.

(2) WHERE NO TAX LIABILITY FOR PRECEDING TAXABLE YEAR.—No addition to tax shall be imposed under subsection (a) for any taxable year if—

(A) the preceding taxable year was a taxable year of 12 months,

(B) the individual did not have any liability for tax for the preceding taxable year, and

(C) the individual was a citizen or resident of the United States throughout the preceding taxable year.

(3) WAIVER IN CERTAIN CASES.—

(A) IN GENERAL.—No addition to tax shall be imposed under subsection (a) with respect to any underpayment to the extent the Secretary determines that by reason of casualty, disaster, or other unusual circumstances the imposition of such addition to tax would be against equity and good conscience.

(B) NEWLY RETIRED OR DISABLED INDIVIDUALS.—No addition to tax shall be imposed under subsection (a) with respect to any underpayment if the Secretary determines that—

(i) the taxpayer—

(I) retired after having attained age 62, or

(II) became disabled,

in the taxable year for which estimated payments were required to be made or in the taxable year preceding such taxable year, and

(ii) such underpayment was due to reasonable cause and not to willful neglect.

[Sec. 6654(f)]

(f) TAX COMPUTED AFTER APPLICATION OF CREDITS AGAINST TAX.—For purposes of this section, the term "tax" means—

(1) the tax imposed by chapter 1 (other than any increase in such tax by reason of section 143(m)), plus

(2) the tax imposed by chapter 2, plus

(3) the tax imposed by chapter 2A, minus

(4) the credits against tax provided by part IV of subchapter A of chapter 1, other than the credit against tax provided by section 31 (relating to tax withheld on wages).

[Sec. 6654(g)]

(g) APPLICATION OF SECTION IN CASE OF TAX WITHHELD ON WAGES.—

(1) IN GENERAL.—For purposes of applying this section, the amount of the credit allowed under section 31 for the taxable year shall be deemed a payment of estimated tax, and an equal part of such amount shall be deemed paid on each due date for such taxable year, unless the taxpayer establishes the dates on which all amounts were actually withheld, in which case the amounts so withheld shall be deemed payments of estimated tax on the dates on which such amounts were actually withheld.

(2) SEPARATE APPLICATION.—The taxpayer may apply paragraph (1) separately with respect to—

(A) wage withholding, and

(B) all other amounts withheld for which credit is allowed under section 31.

[Sec. 6654(h)]

(h) SPECIAL RULE WHERE RETURN FILED ON OR BEFORE JANUARY 31.—If, on or before January 31 of the following taxable year, the taxpayer files a return for the taxable year and pays in full the amount computed on the return as payable, then no addition to tax shall be imposed under subsection (a) with respect to any underpayment of the 4th required installment for the taxable year.

[Sec. 6654(i)]

(i) SPECIAL RULES FOR FARMERS AND FISHERMEN.—For purposes of this section—

(1) IN GENERAL.—If an individual is a farmer or fisherman for any taxable year—

(A) there shall be only 1 required installment for the taxable year,

(B) the due date for such installment shall be January 15 of the following taxable year,

(C) the amount of such installment shall be equal to the required annual payment determined under subsection (d)(1)(B) by substituting "66⅔ percent" for "90 percent" and without regard to subparagraph (C) of subsection (d)(1), and

(D) subsection (h) shall be applied—

(i) by substituting "March 1" for "January 31", and

(ii) by treating the required installment described in subparagraph (A) of this paragraph as the 4th required installment.

(2) FARMER OR FISHERMAN DEFINED.—An individual is a farmer or fisherman for any taxable year if—

(A) the individual's gross income from farming or fishing (including oyster farming) for the taxable year is at least 66⅔ percent of the total gross income from all sources for the taxable year, or

(B) such individual's gross income from farming or fishing (including oyster farming) shown on the return of the individual for the preceding taxable year is at least 66⅔ percent of the total gross income from all sources shown on such return.

* * *

[Sec. 6655]

SEC. 6655. FAILURE BY CORPORATION TO PAY ESTIMATED INCOME TAX.

[Sec. 6655(a)]

(a) ADDITION TO TAX.—Except as otherwise provided in this section, in the case of any underpayment of estimated tax by a corporation, there shall be added to the tax under chapter 1 for the taxable year an amount determined by applying—

(1) the underpayment rate established under section 6621,

(2) to the amount of the underpayment,

(3) for the period of the underpayment.

[Sec. 6655(b)]

(b) AMOUNT OF UNDERPAYMENT; PERIOD OF UNDERPAYMENT.—For purposes of subsection (a)—

(1) AMOUNT.—The amount of the underpayment shall be the excess of

(A) the required installment, over

(B) the amount (if any) of the installment paid on or before the due date for the installment.

(2) PERIOD OF UNDERPAYMENT.—The period of the underpayment shall run from the due date for the installment to whichever of the following dates is the earlier—

(A) the 15th day of the 4th month following the close of the taxable year, or

(B) with respect to any portion of the underpayment, the date on which such portion is paid.

(3) ORDER OF CREDITING PAYMENTS.—For purposes of paragraph (2)(B), a payment of estimated tax shall be credited against unpaid required installments in the order in which such installments are required to be paid.

[Sec. 6655(c)]

(c) NUMBER OF REQUIRED INSTALLMENTS; DUE DATES.—For purposes of this section—

(1) PAYABLE IN 4 INSTALLMENTS.—There shall be 4 required installments for each taxable year.

(2) TIME FOR PAYMENT OF INSTALLMENTS.—

In the case of the following required installments:	*The due date is:*
1st	April 15
2nd	June 15
3rd	September 15
4th	December 15.

[Sec. 6655(d)]

(d) AMOUNT OF REQUIRED INSTALLMENTS.—For purposes of this section—

(1) AMOUNT.—

(A) IN GENERAL.—Except as otherwise provided in this section, the amount of any required installment shall be 25 percent of the required annual payment.

(B) REQUIRED ANNUAL PAYMENT.—Except as otherwise provided in this subsection, the term "required annual payment" means the lesser of—

(i) 100 percent of the tax shown on the return for the taxable year (or, if no return is filed, 100 percent of the tax for such year), or

(ii) 100 percent of the tax shown on the return of the corporation for the preceding taxable year.

Clause (ii) shall not apply if the preceding taxable year was not a taxable year of 12 months, or the corporation did not file a return for such preceding taxable year showing a liability for tax.

(2) LARGE CORPORATIONS REQUIRED TO PAY 100 PERCENT OF CURRENT YEAR TAX.—

(A) IN GENERAL.—Except as provided in subparagraph (B), clause (ii) of paragraph (1)(B) shall not apply in the case of a large corporation.

(B) MAY USE LAST YEAR'S TAX FOR 1ST INSTALLMENT.—Subparagraph (A) shall not apply for purposes of determining the amount of the 1st required installment for any taxable year. Any reduction in such 1st installment by reason of the preceding sentence shall be recaptured by increasing the amount of the next required installment determined under paragraph (1) by the amount of such reduction.

[Sec. 6655(e)]

(e) Lower Required Installment Where Annualized Income Installment or Adjusted Seasonal Installment is Less Than Amount Determined Under Subsection (d).—

(1) In general.—In the case of any required installment, if the corporation establishes that the annualized income installment or the adjusted seasonal installment is less than the amount determined under subsection (d)(1) (as modified by paragraphs (2) and (3) of subsection (d))—

(A) the amount of such required installment shall be the annualized income installment (or, if lesser, the adjusted seasonal installment), and

(B) any reduction in a required installment resulting from the application of this paragraph shall be recaptured by increasing the amount of the next required installment determined under subsection (d)(1) (as so modified) by the amount of such reduction (and by increasing subsequent required installments to the extent that the reduction has not previously been recaptured under this subparagraph).

(2) Determination of annualized income installment.—

(A) In general.—In the case of any required installment, the annualized income installment is the excess (if any) of—

(i) an amount equal to the applicable percentage of the tax for the taxable year computed by placing on an annualized basis the taxable income and modified taxable income—

(I) for the first 3 months of the taxable year, in the case of the 1st required installment,

(II) for the first 3 months of the taxable year, in the case of the 2nd required installment,

(III) for the first 6 months of the taxable year in the case of the 3rd required installment, and

(IV) for the first 9 months of the taxable year, in the case of the 4th required installment, over

(ii) the aggregate amount of any prior required installments for the taxable year.

(B) Special rules.—For purposes of this paragraph—

(i) Annualization.—The taxable income and modified taxable income shall be placed on an annualized basis under regulations prescribed by the Secretary.

(ii) Applicable percentage.—

In the case of the following required installments:	*The applicable percentage is:*
1st	25
2nd	50
3rd	75
4th	100.

(iii) Modified taxable income.—The term "modified taxable income" has the meaning given such term by section 59A(c)(1).

(C) Election for different annualization periods.—

(i) If the taxpayer makes an election under this clause—

(I) subclause (I) of subparagraph (A)(i) shall be applied by substituting "2 months" for "3 months",

(II) subclause (II) of subparagraph (A)(i) shall be applied by substituting "4 months" for "3 months",

(III) subclause (III) of subparagraph (A)(i) shall be applied by substituting "7 months" for "6 months", and

(IV) subclause (IV) of subparagraph (A)(i) shall be applied by substituting "10 months" for "9 months".

(ii) If the taxpayer makes an election under this clause—

(I) subclause (II) of subparagraph (A)(i) shall be applied by substituting "5 months" for "3 months",

(II) subclause (III) of subparagraph (A)(i) shall be applied by substituting "8 months" for "6 months",

(III) subclause (IV) of subparagraph (A)(i) shall be applied by substituting "11 months" for "9 months".

(iii) An election under clause (i) or (ii) shall apply to the taxable year for which made and such an election shall be effective only if made on or before the date required for the payment of the first required installment for such taxable year.

(3) DETERMINATION OF ADJUSTED SEASONAL INSTALLMENT.—

(A) IN GENERAL.—In the case of any required installment, the amount of the adjusted seasonal installment is the excess (if any) of—

(i) 100 percent of the amount determined under subparagraph (C), over

(ii) the aggregate amount of all prior required installments for the taxable year.

(B) LIMITATION ON APPLICATION OF PARAGRAPH.—This paragraph shall apply only if the base period percentage for any 6 consecutive months of the taxable year equals or exceeds 70 percent.

(C) DETERMINATION OF AMOUNT.—The amount determined under this subparagraph for any installment shall be determined in the following manner—

(i) take the taxable income for all months during the taxable year preceding the filing month,

(ii) divide such amount by the base period percentage for all months during the taxable year preceding the filing month,

(iii) determine the tax on the amount determined under clause (ii), and

(iv) multiply the tax computed under clause (iii) by the base period percentage for the filing month and all months during the taxable year preceding the filing month.

(D) DEFINITIONS AND SPECIAL RULES.—For purposes of this paragraph—

(i) BASE PERIOD PERCENTAGE.—The base period percentage for any period of months shall be the average percent which the taxable income for the corresponding months in each of the 3 preceding taxable years bears to the taxable income for the 3 preceding taxable years.

(ii) FILING MONTH.—The term "filing month" means the month in which the installment is required to be paid.

(iii) REORGANIZATION, ETC.—The Secretary may by regulations provide for the determination of the base period percentage in the case of reorganizations, new corporations, and other similar circumstances.

* * *

[Sec. 6655(f)]

(f) EXCEPTION WHERE TAX IS SMALL AMOUNT.—No addition to tax shall be imposed under subsection (a) for any taxable year if the tax shown on the return for such taxable year (or, if no return is filed, the tax) is less than $500.

[Sec. 6655(g)]

(g) DEFINITIONS AND SPECIAL RULES.—

(1) TAX.—For purposes of this section, the term "tax" means the excess of—

(A) the sum of—

(i) the tax imposed by section 11 or subchapter L of chapter 1, whichever applies,

(ii) the tax imposed by section 59A, plus

(iii) the tax imposed by section 887, over

(B) the credits against tax provided by part IV of subchapter A of chapter 1.

For purposes of the preceding sentence, in the case of a foreign corporation subject to taxation under section 11 or 1201(a), or under subchapter L of chapter 1, the tax imposed by section 881 shall be treated as a tax imposed by section 11.

(2) LARGE CORPORATION.—

(A) IN GENERAL.—For purposes of this section, the term "large corporation" means any corporation if such corporation (or any predecessor corporation) had taxable income of $1,000,000 or more for any taxable year during the testing period.

(B) RULES FOR APPLYING SUBPARAGRAPH (A).—

(i) TESTING PERIOD.—For purposes of subparagraph (A), the term "testing period" means the 3 taxable years immediately preceding the taxable year involved.

(ii) MEMBERS OF CONTROLLED GROUP.—For purposes of applying subparagraph (A) to any taxable year in the testing period with respect to corporations which are component members of a controlled group of corporations for such taxable year, the $1,000,000 amount specified in subparagraph (A) shall be divided among such members under rules similar to the rules of section 1561.

(iii) CERTAIN CARRYBACKS AND CARRYOVERS NOT TAKEN INTO ACCOUNT.—For purposes of subparagraph (A), taxable income shall be determined without regard to any amount carried to the taxable year under section 172 or 1212(a).

(3) CERTAIN TAX-EXEMPT ORGANIZATIONS.—For purposes of this section—

(A) Any organization subject to the tax imposed by section 511, and any private foundation, shall be treated as a corporation subject to tax under section 11.

(B) Any tax imposed by section 511, and any tax imposed by section 1 or 4940 on a private foundation, shall be treated as a tax imposed by section 11.

(C) Any reference to taxable income shall be treated as including a reference to unrelated business taxable income or net investment income (as the case may be).

In the case of any organization described in subparagraph (A), subsection (b)(2)(A) shall be applied by substituting "5th month" for "4th month", subsection (e)(2)(A) shall be applied by substituting "2 months" for "3 months" in clause (i)(I), the election under clause (i) of subsection (e)(2)(C) may be made separately for each installment, and clause (ii) of subsection (e)(2)(C) shall not apply. In the case of a private foundation, subsection (c)(2) shall be applied by substituting "May 15" for "April 15".

(4) APPLICATION OF SECTION TO CERTAIN TAXES IMPOSED ON S CORPORATIONS.—In the case of an S corporation, for purposes of this section—

(A) The following taxes shall be treated as imposed by section 11:

(i) The tax imposed by section 1374(a).

(ii) The tax imposed by section 1375(a).

(iii) Any tax for which the S corporation is liable by reason of section 1371(d)(2).

(B) Paragraph (2) of subsection (d) shall not apply.

(C) Clause (ii) of subsection (d)(1)(B) shall be applied as if it read as follows:

"(ii) the sum of—

"(I) the amount determined under clause (i) by only taking into account the taxes referred to in clauses (i) and (iii) of subsection (g)(4)(A), and

"(II) 100 percent of the tax imposed by section 1375(a) which was shown on the return of the corporation for the preceding taxable year."

(D) The requirement in the last sentence of subsection (d)(1)(B) that the return for the preceding taxable year show a liability for tax shall not apply.

(E) Subsection (b)(2)(A) shall be applied by substituting "3rd month" for "4th month".

(F) Any reference in subsection (e) to taxable income shall be treated as including a reference to the net recognized built-in gain or the excess passive income (as the case may be).

* * *

PART II—ACCURACY-RELATED AND FRAUD PENALTIES

[Sec. 6662]

SEC. 6662. IMPOSITION OF ACCURACY-RELATED PENALTY ON UNDERPAYMENTS.

[Sec. 6662(a)]

(a) IMPOSITION OF PENALTY.—If this section applies to any portion of an underpayment of tax required to be shown on a return, there shall be added to the tax an amount equal to 20 percent of the portion of the underpayment to which this section applies.

[Sec. 6662(b)]

(b) PORTION OF UNDERPAYMENT TO WHICH SECTION APPLIES.—This section shall apply to the portion of any underpayment which is attributable to 1 or more of the following:

(1) Negligence or disregard of rules or regulations.

(2) Any substantial understatement of income tax.

(3) Any substantial valuation misstatement under chapter 1.

(4) Any substantial overstatement of pension liabilities.

(5) Any substantial estate or gift tax valuation understatement.

(6) Any disallowance of claimed tax benefits by reason of a transaction lacking economic substance (within the meaning of section 7701(o)) or failing to meet the requirements of any similar rule of law.

(7) Any undisclosed foreign financial asset understatement.

(8) Any inconsistent estate basis.

This section shall not apply to any portion of an underpayment on which a penalty is imposed under section 6663. Except as provided in paragraph (1) or (2)(B) of section 6662A(e), this section shall not apply to the portion of any underpayment which is attributable to a reportable transaction understatement on which a penalty is imposed under section 6662A.

[Sec. 6662(c)]

(c) NEGLIGENCE.—For purposes of this section, the term "negligence" includes any failure to make a reasonable attempt to comply with the provisions of this title, and the term "disregard" includes any careless, reckless, or intentional disregard.

[Sec. 6662(d)]

(d) SUBSTANTIAL UNDERSTATEMENT OF INCOME TAX.—

(1) SUBSTANTIAL UNDERSTATEMENT.—

(A) IN GENERAL.—For purposes of this section, there is a substantial understatement of income tax for any taxable year if the amount of the understatement for the taxable year exceeds the greater of—

(i) 10 percent of the tax required to be shown on the return for the taxable year, or

(ii) $5,000.

(B) SPECIAL RULE FOR CORPORATIONS.—In the case of a corporation other than an S corporation or a personal holding company (as defined in section 542), there is a substantial understatement of income tax for any taxable year if the amount of the understatement for the taxable year exceeds the lesser of—

(i) 10 percent of the tax required to be shown on the return for the taxable year (or, if greater, $10,000), or

(ii) $10,000,000.

(C) SPECIAL RULE FOR TAXPAYERS CLAIMING SECTION 199A DEDUCTION.—In the case of any taxpayer who claims any deduction allowed under section 199A for the taxable year, subparagraph (A) shall be applied by substituting "5 percent" for "10 percent".

(2) UNDERSTATEMENT.—

(A) IN GENERAL.—For purposes of paragraph (1), the term "understatement" means the excess of—

(i) the amount of the tax required to be shown on the return for the taxable year, over

(ii) the amount of the tax imposed which is shown on the return, reduced by any rebate (within the meaning of section 6211(b)(2)).

The excess under the preceding sentence shall be determined without regard to items to which section 6662A applies.

(B) REDUCTION FOR UNDERSTATEMENT DUE TO POSITION OF TAXPAYER OR DISCLOSED ITEM.—The amount of the understatement under subparagraph (A) shall be reduced by that portion of the understatement which is attributable to—

(i) the tax treatment of any item by the taxpayer if there is or was substantial authority for such treatment, or

(ii) any item if—

(I) the relevant facts affecting the item's tax treatment are adequately disclosed in the return or in a statement attached to the return, and

(II) there is a reasonable basis for the tax treatment of such item by the taxpayer.

For purposes of clause (ii)(II), in no event shall a corporation be treated as having a reasonable basis for its tax treatment of an item attributable to a multiple-party financing transaction if such treatment does not clearly reflect the income of the corporation.

(C) REDUCTION NOT TO APPLY TO TAX SHELTERS.—

(i) IN GENERAL.—Subparagraph (B) shall not apply to any item attributable to a tax shelter.

(ii) TAX SHELTER.—For purposes of clause (i), the term "tax shelter" means—

(I) a partnership or other entity,

(II) any investment plan or arrangement, or

(III) any other plan or arrangement,

if a significant purpose of such partnership, entity, plan, or arrangement is the avoidance or evasion of Federal income tax.

(3) SECRETARIAL LIST.—The Secretary may prescribe a list of positions which the Secretary believes do not meet 1 or more of the standards specified in paragraph (2)(B)(i), section 6664(d)(3), and section 6694(a)(1). Such list (and any revisions thereof) shall be published in the Federal Register or the Internal Revenue Bulletin.

[Sec. 6662(e)]

(e) SUBSTANTIAL VALUATION MISSTATEMENT UNDER CHAPTER 1.—

(1) IN GENERAL.—For purposes of this section, there is a substantial valuation misstatement under chapter 1 if—

(A) the value of any property (or the adjusted basis of any property) claimed on any return of tax imposed by chapter 1 is 150 percent or more of the amount determined to be the correct amount of such valuation or adjusted basis (as the case may be), or

(B)(i) the price for any property or services (or for the use of property) claimed on any such return in connection with any transaction between persons described in section 482 is 200 percent or more (or 50 percent or less) of the amount determined under section 482 to be the correct amount of such price, or

(ii) the net section 482 transfer price adjustment for the taxable year exceeds the lesser of $5,000,000 or 10 percent of the taxpayer's gross receipts.

(2) LIMITATION.—No penalty shall be imposed by reason of subsection (b)(3) unless the portion of the underpayment for the taxable year attributable to substantial valuation misstatements under chapter 1 exceeds $5,000 ($10,000 in the case of a corporation other than an S corporation or a personal holding company (as defined in section 542)).

(3) NET SECTION 482 TRANSFER PRICE ADJUSTMENT.—For purposes of this subsection—

(A) IN GENERAL.—The term "net section 482 transfer price adjustment" means, with respect to any taxable year, the net increase in taxable income for the taxable year (determined without regard to any amount carried to such taxable year from another taxable year) resulting from adjustments under section 482 in the price for any property or services (or for the use of property).

(B) CERTAIN ADJUSTMENTS EXCLUDED IN DETERMINING THRESHOLD.—For purposes of determining whether the threshold requirements of paragraph (1)(B)(ii) are met, the following shall be excluded:

(i) Any portion of the net increase in taxable income referred to in subparagraph (A) which is attributable to any redetermination of a price if—

(I) it is established that the taxpayer determined such price in accordance with a specific pricing method set forth in the regulations prescribed under section 482 and that the taxpayer's use of such method was reasonable,

(II) the taxpayer has documentation (which was in existence as of the time of filing the return) which sets forth the determination of such price in accordance with such a method and which establishes that the use of such method was reasonable, and

(III) the taxpayer provides such documentation to the Secretary within 30 days of a request for such documentation.

(ii) Any portion of the net increase in taxable income referred to in subparagraph (A) which is attributable to a redetermination of price where such price was not determined in accordance with such a specific pricing method if—

(I) the taxpayer establishes that none of such pricing methods was likely to result in a price that would clearly reflect income, the taxpayer used another pricing method to determine such price, and such other pricing method was likely to result in a price that would clearly reflect income,

(II) the taxpayer has documentation (which was in existence as of the time of filing the return) which sets forth the determination of such price in accordance with such other method and which establishes that the requirements of subclause (I) were satisfied, and

(III) the taxpayer provides such documentation to the Secretary within 30 days of a request for such documentation.

(iii) Any portion of such net increase which is attributable to any transaction solely between foreign corporations unless, in the case of any such corporations, the treatment of such transaction affects the determination of income from sources within the United States or taxable income effectively connected with the conduct of a trade or business within the United States.

(C) SPECIAL RULE.—If the regular tax (as defined in section 55(c)) imposed by chapter 1 on the taxpayer is determined by reference to an amount other than taxable income, such amount shall be treated as the taxable income of such taxpayer for purposes of this paragraph.

* * *

[Sec. 6662(h)]

(h) INCREASE IN PENALTY IN CASE OF GROSS VALUATION MISSTATEMENTS.—

(1) IN GENERAL.—To the extent that a portion of the underpayment to which this section applies is attributable to one or more gross valuation misstatements, subsection (a) shall be applied with respect to such portion by substituting "40 percent" for "20 percent".

(2) GROSS VALUATION MISSTATEMENTS.—The term "gross valuation misstatements" means—

(A) any substantial valuation misstatement under chapter 1 as determined under subsection (e) by substituting—

(i) in paragraph (1)(A), "200 percent" for "150 percent",

(ii) in paragraph (1)(B)(i)—

(I) "400 percent" for "200 percent", and

(II) "25 percent" for "50 percent", and

(iii) in paragraph (1)(B)(ii)—

(I) "$20,000,000" for "$5,000,000", and

(II) "20 percent" for "10 percent".

(B) any substantial overstatement of pension liabilities as determined under subsection (f) by substituting "400 percent" for "200 percent", and

(C) any substantial estate or gift tax valuation understatement as determined under subsection (g) by substituting "40 percent" for "65 percent".

[Sec. 6662(i)]

(i) INCREASE IN PENALTY IN CASE OF NONDISCLOSED NONECONOMIC SUBSTANCE TRANSACTIONS.—

(1) IN GENERAL.—In the case of any portion of an underpayment which is attributable to one or more nondisclosed noneconomic substance transactions, subsection (a) shall be applied with respect to such portion by substituting "40 percent" for "20 percent".

(2) NONDISCLOSED NONECONOMIC SUBSTANCE TRANSACTIONS.—For purposes of this subsection, the term "nondisclosed noneconomic substance transaction" means any portion of a transaction described in subsection (b)(6) with respect to which the relevant facts affecting the tax treatment are not adequately disclosed in the return nor in a statement attached to the return.

(3) SPECIAL RULE FOR AMENDED RETURNS.—In no event shall any amendment or supplement to a return of tax be taken into account for purposes of this subsection if the amendment or supplement is filed after the earlier of the date the taxpayer is first contacted by the Secretary regarding the examination of the return or such other date as is specified by the Secretary.

* * *

[Sec. 6662(k)]

(k) INCONSISTENT ESTATE BASIS REPORTING.—For purposes of this section, the term "inconsistent estate basis" means any portion of an underpayment attributable to the failure to comply with section 1014(f).

[Sec. 6663]

SEC. 6663. IMPOSITION OF FRAUD PENALTY.

[Sec. 6663(a)]

(a) IMPOSITION OF PENALTY.—If any part of any underpayment of tax required to be shown on a return is due to fraud, there shall be added to the tax an amount equal to 75 percent of the portion of the underpayment which is attributable to fraud.

[Sec. 6663(b)]

(b) DETERMINATION OF PORTION ATTRIBUTABLE TO FRAUD.—If the Secretary establishes that any portion of an underpayment is attributable to fraud, the entire underpayment shall be treated as attributable to fraud, except with respect to any portion of the underpayment which the taxpayer establishes (by a preponderance of the evidence) is not attributable to fraud.

[Sec. 6663(c)]

(c) SPECIAL RULE FOR JOINT RETURNS.—In the case of a joint return, this section shall not apply with respect to a spouse unless some part of the underpayment is due to the fraud of such spouse.

[Sec. 6664]

SEC. 6664. DEFINITIONS AND SPECIAL RULES.

[Sec. 6664(a)]

(a) UNDERPAYMENT.—For purposes of this part, the term "underpayment" means the amount by which any tax imposed by this title exceeds the excess of—

(1) the sum of—

(A) the amount shown as the tax by the taxpayer on his return, plus

(B) amounts not so shown previously assessed (or collected without assessment), over

(2) the amount of rebates made.

For purposes of paragraph (2), the term "rebate" means so much of an abatement, credit, refund, or other repayment, as was made on the ground that tax imposed was less than the excess of the amount specified in paragraph (1) over the rebates previously made. A rule similar to the rule of section 6211(b)(4) shall apply for purposes of this subsection.

[Sec. 6664(b)]

(b) PENALTIES APPLICABLE ONLY WHERE RETURN FILED.—The penalties provided in this part shall apply only in cases where a return of tax is filed (other than a return prepared by the Secretary under the authority of section 6020(b)).

[Sec. 6664(c)]

(c) REASONABLE CAUSE EXCEPTION FOR UNDERPAYMENTS.—

(1) IN GENERAL.—No penalty shall be imposed under section 6662 or 6663 with respect to any portion of an underpayment if it is shown that there was a reasonable cause for such portion and that the taxpayer acted in good faith with respect to such portion.

(2) EXCEPTION.—Paragraph (1) shall not apply to any portion of an underpayment which is attributable to one or more transactions described in section 6662(b)(6).

(3) SPECIAL RULE FOR CERTAIN VALUATION OVERSTATEMENTS.—In the case of any underpayment attributable to a substantial or gross valuation over statement under chapter 1 with respect to charitable deduction property, paragraph (1) shall not apply. The preceding sentence shall not apply to a substantial valuation overstatement under chapter 1 if—

(A) the claimed value of the property was based on a qualified appraisal made by a qualified appraiser, and

(B) in addition to obtaining such appraisal, the taxpayer made a good faith investigation of the value of the contributed property.

(4) DEFINITIONS.—For purposes of this subsection—

(A) CHARITABLE DEDUCTION PROPERTY.—The term "charitable deduction property" means any property contributed by the taxpayer in a contribution for which a deduction was claimed under section 170. For purposes of paragraph (3), such term shall not include any securities for which (as of the date of the contribution) market quotations are readily available on an established securities market.

(B) QUALIFIED APPRAISAL.—The term "qualified appraisal" has the meaning given such term by section 170(f)(11)(E)(i).

(C) QUALIFIED APPRAISER.—The term "qualified appraiser" has the meaning given such term by section 170(f)(11)(E)(ii).

* * *

PART III—APPLICABLE RULES

[Sec. 6665]

SEC. 6665. APPLICABLE RULES.

[Sec. 6665(a)]

(a) ADDITIONS TREATED AS TAX.—Except as otherwise provided in this title—

(1) the additions to the tax, additional amounts, and penalties provided by this chapter shall be paid upon notice and demand and shall be assessed, collected, and paid in the same manner as taxes; and

(2) any reference in this title to "tax" imposed by this title shall be deemed also to refer to the additions to the tax, additional amounts, and penalties provided by this chapter.

[Sec. 6665(b)]

(b) PROCEDURE FOR ASSESSING CERTAIN ADDITIONS TO TAX.—For purposes of subchapter B of chapter 63 (relating to deficiency procedures for income, estate, gift, and certain excise taxes), subsection (a) shall not apply to any addition to tax under section 6651, 6654, 6655; except that it shall apply—

(1) in the case of an addition described in section 6651, to that portion of such addition which is attributable to a deficiency in tax described in section 6211; or

(2) to an addition described in section 6654 or 6655, if no return is filed for the taxable year.

SUBCHAPTER B—ASSESSABLE PENALTIES

PART I—GENERAL PROVISIONS

[Sec. 6672]

SEC. 6672. FAILURE TO COLLECT AND PAY OVER TAX, OR ATTEMPT TO EVADE OR DEFEAT TAX.

[Sec. 6672(a)]

(a) GENERAL RULE.—Any person required to collect, truthfully account for, and pay over any tax imposed by this title who willfully fails to collect such tax, or truthfully account for and pay over such tax, or willfully attempts in any manner to evade or defeat any such tax or the payment thereof, shall, in addition to other penalties provided by law, be liable to a penalty equal to the total amount of the tax evaded, or not collected, or not accounted for and paid over. No penalty shall be imposed under section 6653 or part II of subchapter A of chapter 68 for any offense to which this section is applicable.

* * *

[Sec. 6676]

SEC. 6676. ERRONEOUS CLAIM FOR REFUND OR CREDIT.

[Sec. 6676(a)]

(a) CIVIL PENALTY.—If a claim for refund or credit with respect to income tax is made for an excessive amount, unless it is shown that the claim for such excessive amount is due to reasonable cause, the person making such claim shall be liable for a penalty in an amount equal to 20 percent of the excessive amount.

[Sec. 6676(b)]

(b) EXCESSIVE AMOUNT.—For purposes of this section, the term "excessive amount" means in the case of any person the amount by which the amount of the claim for refund or credit for any taxable year exceeds the amount of such claim allowable under this title for such taxable year.

[Sec. 6676(c)]

(c) NONECONOMIC SUBSTANCE TRANSACTIONS TREATED AS LACKING REASONABLE CAUSE.—For purposes of this section, any excessive amount which is attributable to any transaction described in section 6662(b)(6) shall not be treated as due to reasonable cause.

[Sec. 6676(d)]

(d) COORDINATION WITH OTHER PENALTIES.—This section shall not apply to any portion of the excessive amount of a claim for refund or credit which is subject to a penalty imposed under part II of subchapter A of chapter 68.

[Sec. 6694]

SEC. 6694. UNDERSTATEMENT OF TAXPAYER'S LIABILITY BY TAX RETURN PREPARER.

[Sec. 6694(a)]

(a) UNDERSTATEMENT DUE TO UNREASONABLE POSITIONS.—

(1) IN GENERAL.—If a tax return preparer—

(A) prepares any return or claim of refund with respect to which any part of an understatement of liability is due to a position described in paragraph (2), and

(B) knew (or reasonably should have known) of the position,

such tax return preparer shall pay a penalty with respect to each such return or claim in an amount equal to the greater of $1,000 or 50 percent of the income derived (or to be derived) by the tax return preparer with respect to the return or claim.

(2) UNREASONABLE POSITION.—

(A) IN GENERAL.—Except as otherwise provided in this paragraph, a position is described in this paragraph unless there is or was substantial authority for the position.

(B) DISCLOSED POSITIONS.—If the position was disclosed as provided in section 6662(d)(2)(B)(ii)(I) and is not a position to which subparagraph (C) applies, the position is described in this paragraph unless there is a reasonable basis for the position.

(C) TAX SHELTERS AND REPORTABLE TRANSACTIONS.—If the position is with respect to a tax shelter (as defined in section 6662(d)(2)(C)(ii)) or a reportable transaction to which section 6662A applies, the position is described in this paragraph unless it is reasonable to believe that the position would more likely than not be sustained on its merits.

(3) REASONABLE CAUSE EXCEPTION.—No penalty shall be imposed under this subsection if it is shown that there is reasonable cause for the understatement and the tax return preparer acted in good faith.

[Sec. 6694(b)]

(b) UNDERSTATEMENT DUE TO WILLFUL OR RECKLESS CONDUCT.—

(1) IN GENERAL.—Any tax return preparer who prepares any return or claim for refund with respect to which any part of an understatement of liability is due to a conduct described in paragraph (2) shall pay a penalty with respect to each such return or claim in an amount equal to the greater of—

(A) $5,000, or

(B) 75 percent of the income derived (or to be derived) by the tax return preparer with respect to the return or claim.

(2) WILLFUL OR RECKLESS CONDUCT.—Conduct described in this paragraph is conduct by the tax return preparer which is—

(A) a willful attempt in any manner to understate the liability for tax on the return or claim, or

(B) a reckless or intentional disregard of rules or regulations.

(3) REDUCTION IN PENALTY.—The amount of any penalty payable by any person by reason of this subsection for any return or claim for refund shall be reduced by the amount of the penalty paid by such person by reason of subsection (a).

[Sec. 6694(c)]

(c) EXTENSION OF PERIOD OF COLLECTION WHERE PREPARER PAYS 15 PERCENT OF PENALTY.—

(1) IN GENERAL.—If, within 30 days after the day on which notice and demand of any penalty under subsection (a) or (b) is made against any person who is a tax return preparer, such person pays an amount which is not less than 15 percent of the amount of such penalty and files a claim for refund of the amount so paid, no levy or proceeding in court for the collection of the remainder of such penalty shall be made, begun, or prosecuted until the final resolution of a proceeding begun as provided in paragraph (2). Notwithstanding the provisions of section 7421(a), the beginning of such proceeding or levy during the time such prohibition is in force may be enjoined by a proceeding in the proper court. Nothing in this paragraph shall be construed to prohibit any counterclaim for the remainder of such penalty in a proceeding begun as provided in paragraph (2).

(2) PREPARER MUST BRING SUIT IN DISTRICT COURT TO DETERMINE HIS LIABILITY FOR PENALTY.—If, within 30 days after the day on which his claim for refund of any partial payment of any penalty under subsection (a) or (b) is denied (or, if earlier, within 30 days after the expiration of 6 months after the day on which he filed the claim for refund), the tax return preparer fails to begin a proceeding in the appropriate United States district court for the determination of his liability for such penalty, paragraph (1) shall cease to apply with respect to such penalty, effective on the day following the close of the applicable 30-day period referred to in this paragraph.

(3) SUSPENSION OF RUNNING OF PERIOD OF LIMITATIONS ON COLLECTION.—The running of the period of limitations provided in section 6502 on the collection by levy or by a proceeding in court in respect of any penalty described in paragraph (1) shall be suspended for the period during which the Secretary is prohibited from collecting by levy or a proceeding in court.

[Sec. 6694(d)]

(d) ABATEMENT OF PENALTY WHERE TAXPAYER LIABILITY NOT UNDERSTATED.—If at any time there is a final administrative determination or a final judicial decision that there was no understatement of liability in the case of any return or claim for refund with respect to which a penalty under subsection (a) or (b) has been assessed, such assessment shall be abated, and if any portion of such penalty has been paid the amount so paid shall be refunded to the person who made such payment as an overpayment of tax without regard to any period of limitations which, but for this subsection, would apply to the making of such refund.

[Sec. 6694(e)]

(e) UNDERSTATEMENT OF LIABILITY DEFINED.—For purposes of this section, the term "understatement of liability" means any understatement of the net amount payable with respect to any tax imposed by this title or any overstatement of the net amount creditable or refundable with respect to any such tax. Except as otherwise provided in subsection (d), the determination of whether or not there is an understatement of liability shall be made without regard to any administrative or judicial action involving the taxpayer.

[Sec. 6694(f)]

(f) CROSS REFERENCE.—

For definition of tax return preparer, see section 7701(a)(36).

[Sec. 6701]

SEC. 6701. PENALTIES FOR AIDING AND ABETTING UNDERSTATEMENT OF TAX LIABILITY.

[Sec. 6701(a)]

(a) IMPOSITION OF PENALTY.—Any person—

(1) who aids or assists in, procures, or advises with respect to, the preparation or presentation of any portion of a return, affidavit, claim, or other document,

(2) who knows (or has reason to believe) that such portion will be used in connection with any material matter arising under the internal revenue laws, and

(3) who knows that such portion (if so used) would result in an understatement of the liability for tax of another person,

shall pay a penalty with respect to each such document in the amount determined under subsection (b).

[Sec. 6701(b)]

(b) AMOUNT OF PENALTY.—

(1) IN GENERAL.—Except as provided in paragraph (2), the amount of the penalty imposed by subsection (a) shall be $1,000.

(2) CORPORATIONS.—If the return, affidavit, claim, or other document relates to the tax liability of a corporation, the amount of the penalty imposed by subsection (a) shall be $10,000.

(3) ONLY 1 PENALTY PER PERSON PER PERIOD.—If any person is subject to a penalty under subsection (a) with respect to any document relating to any taxpayer for any taxable period (or where there is no taxable period, any taxable event), such person shall not be subject to a penalty under subsection (a) with respect to any other document relating to such taxpayer for such taxable period (or event).

* * *

[Sec. 6702]

SEC. 6702. FRIVOLOUS TAX SUBMISSIONS.

[Sec. 6702(a)]

(a) CIVIL PENALTY FOR FRIVOLOUS TAX RETURNS.—A person shall pay a penalty of $5,000 if—

(1) such person files what purports to be a return of a tax imposed by this title but which—

(A) does not contain information on which the substantial correctness of the self-assessment may be judged, or

(B) contains information that on its face indicates that the self-assessment is substantially incorrect, and

(2) the conduct referred to in paragraph (1)—

(A) is based on a position which the Secretary has identified as frivolous under subsection (c), or

(B) reflects a desire to delay or impede the administration of Federal tax laws.

[Sec. 6702(b)]

(b) CIVIL PENALTY FOR SPECIFIED FRIVOLOUS SUBMISSIONS.—

(1) IMPOSITION OF PENALTY.—Except as provided in paragraph (3), any person who submits a specified frivolous submission shall pay a penalty of $5,000.

(2) SPECIFIED FRIVOLOUS SUBMISSION.—For purposes of this section—

(A) SPECIFIED FRIVOLOUS SUBMISSION.—The term "specified frivolous submission" means a specified submission if any portion of such submission—

(i) is based on a position which the Secretary has identified as frivolous under subsection (c), or

(ii) reflects a desire to delay or impede the administration of Federal tax laws.

(B) SPECIFIED SUBMISSION.—The term "specified submission" means—

(i) a request for a hearing under—

(I) section 6320 (relating to notice and opportunity for hearing upon filing of notice of lien), or

(II) section 6330 (relating to notice and opportunity for hearing before levy), and

(ii) an application under—

(I) section 6159 (relating to agreements for payment of tax liability in installments),

(II) section 7122 (relating to compromises), or

(III) section 7811 (relating to taxpayer assistance orders).

(3) OPPORTUNITY TO WITHDRAW SUBMISSION.—If the Secretary provides a person with notice that a submission is a specified frivolous submission and such person withdraws such submission within 30 days after such notice, the penalty imposed under paragraph (1) shall not apply with respect to such submission.

[Sec. 6702(c)]

(c) LISTING OF FRIVOLOUS POSITIONS.—The Secretary shall prescribe (and periodically revise) a list of positions which the Secretary has identified as being frivolous for purposes of this subsection. The Secretary shall not include in such list any position that the Secretary determines meets the requirement of section 6662(d)(2)(B)(ii)(II).

[Sec. 6702(d)]

(d) REDUCTION OF PENALTY.—The Secretary may reduce the amount of any penalty imposed under this section if the Secretary determines that such reduction would promote compliance with and administration of the Federal tax laws.

[Sec. 6702(e)]

(e) PENALTIES IN ADDITION TO OTHER PENALTIES.—The penalties imposed by this section shall be in addition to any other penalty provided by law.

[Sec. 6702(f)]

(f) PARTNERSHIP ADJUSTMENTS.—An administrative adjustment request under section 6227 and a partnership adjustment tracking report under section 6226(b)(4)(A) shall be treated as a return for purposes of this section.

CHAPTER 71—TRANSFEREES AND FIDUCIARIES

[Sec. 6901]

SEC. 6901. TRANSFERRED ASSETS.

[Sec. 6901(a)]

(a) METHOD OF COLLECTION.—The amounts of the following liabilities shall, except as hereinafter in this section provided, be assessed, paid, and collected in the same manner and subject to the same provisions and limitations as in the case of the taxes with respect to which the liabilities were incurred:

(1) INCOME, ESTATE, AND GIFT TAXES.—

(A) TRANSFEREES.—The liability, at law or in equity, of a transferee of property—

(i) of a taxpayer in the case of a tax imposed by subtitle A (relating to income taxes),

(ii) of a decedent in the case of a tax imposed by chapter 11 (relating to estate taxes), or

(iii) of a donor in the case of a tax imposed by chapter 12 (relating to gift taxes),

in respect of the tax imposed by subtitle A or B.

(B) FIDUCIARIES.—The liability of a fiduciary under section 3713(b) of title 31, United States Code, in respect of the payment of any tax described in subparagraph (A) from the estate of the taxpayer, the decedent, or the donor, as the case may be.

(2) OTHER TAXES.—The liability, at law or in equity of a transferee of property of any person liable in respect of any tax imposed by this title (other than a tax imposed by subtitle A

or B), but only if such liability arises on the liquidation of a partnership or corporation, or on a reorganization within the meaning of section 368(a).

[Sec. 6901(b)]

(b) LIABILITY.—Any liability referred to in subsection (a) may be either as to the amount of tax shown on a return or as to any deficiency or underpayment of any tax.

* * *

[Sec. 6901(h)]

(h) DEFINITION OF TRANSFEREE.—As used in this section, the term "transferee" includes donee, heir, legatee, devisee, and distributee, and with respect to estate taxes, also includes any person who, under section 6324 (a) (2), is personally liable for any part of such tax.

* * *

CHAPTER 75—CRIMES, OTHER OFFENSES, AND FORFEITURES

SUBCHAPTER A—CRIMES

PART I—GENERAL PROVISIONS

→ Caution: See 18 U.S.C. § 3571, under which a larger fine may be imposed with respect to Section 7201.

[Sec. 7201]

SEC. 7201. ATTEMPT TO EVADE OR DEFEAT TAX.

Any person who willfully attempts in any manner to evade or defeat any tax imposed by this title or the payment thereof shall, in addition to other penalties provided by law, be guilty of a felony and, upon conviction thereof, shall be fined not more than $100,000 ($500,000 in the case of a corporation), or imprisoned not more than 5 years, or both, together with the costs of prosecution.

→ Caution: See 18 U.S.C. § 3571, under which a larger fine may be imposed with respect to Section 7202.

[Sec. 7202]

SEC. 7202. WILLFUL FAILURE TO COLLECT OR PAY OVER TAX.

Any person required under this title to collect, account for, and pay over any tax imposed by this title who willfully fails to collect or truthfully account for and pay over such tax shall, in addition to other penalties provided by law, be guilty of a felony and, upon conviction thereof, shall be fined not more than $10,000, or imprisoned not more than 5 years, or both, together with the costs of prosecution.

[Sec. 7203]

SEC. 7203. WILLFUL FAILURE TO FILE RETURN, SUPPLY INFORMATION, OR PAY TAX.

Any person required under this title to pay any estimated tax or tax, or required by this title or by regulations made under authority thereof to make a return, keep any records, or supply any information, who willfully fails to pay such estimated tax or tax, make such return, keep such records, or supply such information, at the time or times required by law or regulations, shall, in addition to other penalties provided by law, be guilty of a misdemeanor and, upon conviction thereof, shall be fined not more than $25,000 ($100,000 in the case of a corporation), or imprisoned not more than 1 year, or both, together with the costs of prosecution. In the case of any person with respect to whom there is a failure to pay any estimated tax, this section shall not apply to such person with respect to such failure if there is no addition to tax under section 6654 or 6655 with respect to such failure. In the case of a willful violation of any provision of section 6050 I, the first sentence of this section shall be applied by substituting "felony" for "misdemeanor" and "5 years" for "1 year".

[Sec. 7205]

SEC. 7205. FRAUDULENT WITHHOLDING EXEMPTION CERTIFICATE OR FAILURE TO SUPPLY INFORMATION.

[Sec. 7205(a)]

(a) WITHHOLDING ON WAGES.—Any individual required to supply information to his employer under section 3402 who willfully supplies false or fraudulent information, or who willfully fails to supply information thereunder which would require an increase in the tax to be withheld under section 3402, shall, in addition to any other penalty provided by law, upon conviction thereof, be fined not more than $1,000, or imprisoned not more than 1 year, or both.

[Sec. 7205(b)]

(b) BACKUP WITHHOLDING ON INTEREST AND DIVIDENDS.—If any individual willfully makes a false certification under paragraph (1) or (2)(C) of section 3406(d), then such individual shall, in addition to any other penalty provided by law, upon conviction thereof, be fined not more than $1,000, or imprisoned not more than 1 year, or both.

»»→ Caution: See 18 U.S.C. § 3571, under which a larger fine may be imposed with respect to Section 7206.

[Sec. 7206]

SEC. 7206. FRAUD AND FALSE STATEMENTS.

Any person who—

(1) DECLARATION UNDER PENALTIES OF PERJURY.—Willfully makes and subscribes any return, statement, or other document, which contains or is verified by a written declaration that it is made under the penalties of perjury, and which he does not believe to be true and correct as to every material matter; or

(2) AID OR ASSISTANCE.—Willfully aids or assists in, or procures, counsels, or advises the preparation or presentation under, or in connection with any matter arising under, the internal revenue laws, of a return, affidavit, claim, or other document, which is fraudulent or is false as to any material matter, whether or not such falsity or fraud is with the knowledge or consent of the person authorized or required to present such return, affidavit, claim, or document; or

(3) FRAUDULENT BONDS, PERMITS, AND ENTRIES.—Simulates or falsely or fraudulently executes or signs any bond, permit, entry, or other document required by the provisions of the internal revenue laws, or by any regulation made in pursuance thereof, or procures the same to be falsely or fraudulently executed or advises, aids in, or connives at such execution thereof; or

(4) REMOVAL OR CONCEALMENT WITH INTENT TO DEFRAUD.—Removes, deposits, or conceals, or is concerned in removing, depositing, or concealing, any goods or commodities for or in respect whereof any tax is or shall be imposed, or any property upon which levy is authorized by section 6331, with intent to evade or defeat the assessment or collection of any tax imposed by this title; or

(5) COMPROMISES AND CLOSING AGREEMENTS.—In connection with any compromise under section 7122, or offer of such compromise, or in connection with any closing agreement under section 7121, or offer to enter into any such agreement, willfully—

(A) CONCEALMENT OF PROPERTY.—Conceals from any officer or employee of the United States any property belonging to the estate of a taxpayer or other person liable in respect of the tax, or

(B) WITHHOLDING, FALSIFYING, AND DESTROYING RECORDS.—Receives, withholds, destroys, mutilates, or falsifies any book, document, or record, or makes any false statement, relating to the estate or financial condition of the taxpayer or other person liable in respect of the tax;

shall be guilty of a felony and, upon conviction thereof, shall be fined not more than $100,000 ($500,000 in the case of a corporation) or imprisoned not more than 3 years, or both, together with the costs of prosecution.

CHAPTER 76—JUDICIAL PROCEEDINGS

SUBCHAPTER B—PROCEEDINGS BY TAXPAYERS AND THIRD PARTIES

[Sec. 7421]

SEC. 7421. PROHIBITION OF SUITS TO RESTRAIN ASSESSMENT OR COLLECTION.

[Sec. 7421(a)]

(a) TAX.—Except as provided in sections 6015(e), 6212(a) and (c), 6213(a), 6232(c), 6330(e)(1), 6331(i), 6672(c), 6694(c), 7426(a) and (b)(1), 7429(b), and 7436, no suit for the purpose of restraining the assessment or collection of any tax shall be maintained in any court by any person, whether or not such person is the person against whom such tax was assessed.

[Sec. 7421(b)]

(b) LIABILITY OF TRANSFEREE OR FIDUCIARY.—No suit shall be maintained in any court for the purpose of restraining the assessment or collection (pursuant to the provisions of chapter 71) of—

(1) the amount of the liability, at law or in equity, of a transferee of property of a taxpayer in respect of any internal revenue tax, or

(2) the amount of the liability of a fiduciary under section 3713(b) of title 31, United States Code, in respect of any such tax.

[Sec. 7422]

SEC. 7422. CIVIL ACTIONS FOR REFUND.

[Sec. 7422(a)]

(a) NO SUIT PRIOR TO FILING CLAIM FOR REFUND.—No suit or proceeding shall be maintained in any court for the recovery of any internal revenue tax alleged to have been erroneously or illegally assessed or collected, or of any penalty claimed to have been collected without authority, or of any sum alleged to have been excessive or in any manner wrongfully collected, until a claim for refund or credit has been duly filed with the Secretary, according to the provisions of law in that regard, and the regulations of the Secretary established in pursuance thereof.

[Sec. 7422(b)]

(b) PROTEST OR DURESS.—Such suit or proceeding may be maintained whether or not such tax, penalty or sum has been paid under protest or duress.

* * *

»»→ Caution: As provided in Section 7430(c)(1), the dollar amount in Section 7430(c)(1)(B)(iii) is adjusted for taxable years beginning after 1996 to reflect increases in the Chained Consumer Price Index. The amount applicable to taxable years beginning in 2020 is provided in the material beginning at page ix.

[Sec. 7430]

SEC. 7430. AWARDING OF COSTS AND CERTAIN FEES.

[Sec. 7430(a)]

(a) IN GENERAL.—In any administrative or court proceeding which is brought by or against the United States in connection with the determination, collection, or refund of any tax, interest, or penalty under this title, the prevailing party may be awarded a judgment or a settlement for—

(1) reasonable administrative costs incurred in connection with such administrative proceeding within the Internal Revenue Service, and

(2) reasonable litigation costs incurred in connection with such court proceeding.

[Sec. 7430(b)]

(b) LIMITATIONS.—

(1) REQUIREMENT THAT ADMINISTRATIVE REMEDIES BE EXHAUSTED.—A judgment for reasonable litigation costs shall not be awarded under subsection (a) in any court proceeding unless the court determines that the prevailing party has exhausted the administrative remedies available to such party within the Internal Revenue Service. Any failure to agree to an extension of the time for the assessment of any tax shall not be taken into account for purposes of determining whether the prevailing party meets the requirements of the preceding sentence.

(2) ONLY COSTS ALLOCABLE TO THE UNITED STATES.—An award under subsection (a) shall be made only for reasonable litigation and administrative costs which are allocable to the United States and not to any other party.

(3) COSTS DENIED WHERE PARTY PREVAILING PROTRACTS PROCEEDINGS.—No award for reasonable litigation and administrative costs may be made under subsection (a) with respect to any portion of the administrative or court proceeding during which the prevailing party has unreasonably protracted such proceeding.

(4) PERIOD FOR APPLYING TO IRS FOR ADMINISTRATIVE COSTS.—An award may be made under subsection (a) by the Internal Revenue Service for reasonable administrative costs only if the prevailing party files an application with the Internal Revenue Service for such costs before the 91st day after the date on which the final decision of the Internal Revenue Service as to the determination of the tax, interest, or penalty is mailed to such party.

[Sec. 7430(c)]

(c) DEFINITIONS.—For purposes of this section—

(1) REASONABLE LITIGATION COSTS.—The term "reasonable litigation costs" includes—

(A) reasonable court costs, and

(B) based upon prevailing market rates for the kind or quality of services furnished—

(i) the reasonable expenses of expert witnesses in connection with a court proceeding, except that no expert witness shall be compensated at a rate in excess of the highest rate of compensation for expert witnesses paid by the United States,

(ii) the reasonable cost of any study, analysis, engineering report, test, or project which is found by the court to be necessary for the preparation of the party's case, and

(iii) reasonable fees paid or incurred for the services of attorneys in connection with the court proceeding, except that such fees shall not be in excess of $125 per hour unless the court determines that an increase in the cost of living or a special factor, such as the limited availability of qualified attorneys for such proceeding, the difficulty of the issues presented in the case, or the local availability of tax expertise, justifies a higher rate.

In the case of any calendar year beginning after 1996, the dollar amount referred to in clause (iii) shall be increased by an amount equal to such dollar amount multiplied by the cost-of-living adjustment determined under section 1(f)(3) for such calendar year, by substituting "calendar year 1995" for "calendar year 2016" in subparagraph (A)(ii) thereof. If any dollar amount after being increased under the preceding sentence is not a multiple of $10, such dollar amount shall be rounded to the nearest multiple of $10.

(2) REASONABLE ADMINISTRATIVE COSTS.—The term "reasonable administrative costs" means—

(A) any administrative fees or similar charges imposed by the Internal Revenue Service, and

(B) expenses, costs, and fees described in paragraph (1)(B), except that any determination made by the court under clause (ii) or (iii) thereof shall be made by the Internal Revenue Service in cases where the determination under paragraph (4)(C) of the awarding of reasonable administrative costs is made by the Internal Revenue Service.

Such term shall only include costs incurred on or after whichever of the following is the earliest: (i) the date of the receipt by the taxpayer of the notice of the decision of the Internal Revenue Service Independent Office of Appeals; (ii) the date of the notice of deficiency; or (iii) the date on which the 1st letter of proposed deficiency which allows the taxpayer an opportunity for administrative review in the Internal Revenue Service Independent Office of Appeals is sent.

(3) ATTORNEYS' FEES.—

(A) IN GENERAL.—For purposes of paragraphs (1) and (2), fees for the services of an individual (whether or not an attorney) who is authorized to practice before the Tax Court or before the Internal Revenue Service shall be treated as fees for the services of an attorney.

(B) PRO BONO SERVICES.—The court may award reasonable attorneys' fees under subsection (a) in excess of the attorneys' fees paid or incurred if such fees are less than the reasonable attorneys' fees because an individual is representing the prevailing party for no fee or for a fee which (taking into account all the facts and circumstances) is no more than a nominal fee. This subparagraph shall apply only if such award is paid to such individual or such individual's employer.

(4) PREVAILING PARTY.—

(A) IN GENERAL.—The term "prevailing party" means any party in any proceeding to which subsection (a) applies (other than the United States or any creditor of the taxpayer involved)—

(i) which—

(I) has substantially prevailed with respect to the amount in controversy, or

(II) has substantially prevailed with respect to the most significant issue or set of issues presented, and

(ii) which meets the requirements of the 1st sentence of section 2412(d)(1)(B) of title 28, United States Code (as in effect on October 22, 1986) except to the extent differing procedures are established by rule of court and meets the requirements of section 2412(d)(2)(B) of such title 28 (as so in effect).

(B) EXCEPTION IF UNITED STATES ESTABLISHES THAT ITS POSITION WAS SUBSTANTIALLY JUSTIFIED.—

(i) GENERAL RULE.—A party shall not be treated as the prevailing party in a proceeding to which subsection (a) applies if the United States establishes that the position of the United States in the proceeding was substantially justified.

(ii) PRESUMPTION OF NO JUSTIFICATION IF INTERNAL REVENUE SERVICE DID NOT FOLLOW CERTAIN PUBLISHED GUIDANCE.—For purposes of clause (i), the position of the United States shall be presumed not to be substantially justified if the Internal Revenue Service did not follow its applicable published guidance in the administrative proceeding. Such presumption may be rebutted.

(iii) EFFECT OF LOSING ON SUBSTANTIALLY SIMILAR ISSUES.—In determining for purposes of clause (i) whether the position of the United States was substantially justified, the court shall take into account whether the United States has lost in courts of appeal for other circuits on substantially similar issues.

(iv) APPLICABLE PUBLISHED GUIDANCE.—For purposes of clause (ii), the term "applicable published guidance" means—

(I) regulations, revenue rulings, revenue procedures, information releases, notices, and announcements, and

(II) any of the following which are issued to the taxpayer: private letter rulings, technical advice memoranda, and determination letters.

(C) DETERMINATION AS TO PREVAILING PARTY.—Any determination under this paragraph as to whether a party is a prevailing party shall be made by agreement of the parties or—

(i) in the case where the final determination with respect to the tax, interest, or penalty is made at the administrative level, by the Internal Revenue Service, or

(ii) in the case where such final determination is made by a court, the court.

(D) SPECIAL RULES FOR APPLYING NET WORTH REQUIREMENT.—In applying the requirements of section 2412(d)(2)(B) of title 28, United States Code, for purposes of subparagraph (A)(ii) of this paragraph—

(i) the net worth limitation in clause (i) of such section shall apply to—

(I) an estate but shall be determined as of the date of the decedent's death, and

(II) a trust but shall be determined as of the last day of the taxable year involved in the proceeding, and

(ii) individuals filing a joint return shall be treated as separate individuals for purposes of clause (i) of such section.

(E) SPECIAL RULES WHERE JUDGMENT LESS THAN TAXPAYER'S OFFER.—

(i) IN GENERAL.—A party to a court proceeding meeting the requirements of subparagraph (A)(ii) shall be treated as the prevailing party if the liability of the taxpayer pursuant to the judgment in the proceeding (determined without regard to interest) is equal to or less than the liability of the taxpayer which would have been so determined if the United States had accepted a qualified offer of the party under subsection (g).

(ii) EXCEPTIONS.—This subparagraph shall not apply to—

(I) any judgment issued pursuant to a settlement; or

(II) any proceeding in which the amount of tax liability is not in issue, including any declaratory judgment proceeding, any proceeding to enforce or quash any summons issued pursuant to this title, and any action to restrain disclosure under section 6110(f).

(iii) SPECIAL RULES.—If this subparagraph applies to any court proceeding—

(I) the determination under clause (i) shall be made by reference to the last qualified offer made with respect to the tax liability at issue in the proceeding; and

(II) reasonable administrative and litigation costs shall only include costs incurred on and after the date of such offer.

(iv) COORDINATION.—This subparagraph shall not apply to a party which is a prevailing party under any other provision of this paragraph.

(5) ADMINISTRATIVE PROCEEDINGS.—The term "administrative proceeding" means any procedure or other action before the Internal Revenue Service.

(6) COURT PROCEEDINGS.—The term "court proceeding" means any civil action brought in a court of the United States (including the Tax Court and the United States Court of Federal Claims).

(7) POSITION OF UNITED STATES.—The term "position of the United States" means—

(A) the position taken by the United States in a judicial proceeding to which subsection (a) applies, and

(B) the position taken in an administrative proceeding to which subsection (a) applies as of the earlier of—

(i) the date of the receipt by the taxpayer of the notice of the decision of the Internal Revenue Service Independent Office of Appeals, or

(ii) the date of the notice of deficiency.

* * *

SUBCHAPTER C—THE TAX COURT

PART II—PROCEDURE

[Sec. 7463]

SEC. 7463. DISPUTES INVOLVING $50,000 OR LESS.

[Sec. 7463(a)]

(a) IN GENERAL.—In the case of any petition filed with the Tax Court for a redetermination of a deficiency where neither the amount of the deficiency placed in dispute, nor the amount of any claimed overpayment, exceeds—

(1) $50,000 for any one taxable year, in the case of the taxes imposed by subtitle A,

(2) $50,000, in the case of the tax imposed by chapter 11,

(3) $50,000 for any one calendar year, in the case of the tax imposed by chapter 12, or

(4) $50,000 for any 1 taxable period (or, if there is no taxable period, taxable event) in the case of any tax imposed by subtitle D which is described in section 6212(a) (relating to a notice of deficiency),

at the option of the taxpayer concurred in by the Tax Court or a division thereof before the hearing of the case, proceedings in the case shall be conducted under this section. Notwithstanding the provisions of section 7453, such proceedings shall be conducted in accordance with such rules of evidence, practice, and procedure as the Tax Court may prescribe. A decision, together with a brief summary of the reasons therefor, in any such case shall satisfy the requirements of sections 7459(b) and 7460.

[Sec. 7463(b)]

(b) FINALITY OF DECISIONS.—A decision entered in any case in which the proceedings are conducted under this section shall not be reviewed in any other court and shall not be treated as a precedent for any other case.

[Sec. 7463(c)]

(c) LIMITATION OF JURISDICTION.—In any case in which the proceedings are conducted under this section, notwithstanding the provisions of sections 6214(a) and 6512(b), no decision shall be entered redetermining the amount of a deficiency, or determining an overpayment, except with respect to amounts placed in dispute within the limits described in subsection (a) and with respect to amounts conceded by the parties.

[Sec. 7463(d)]

(d) DISCONTINUANCE OF PROCEEDINGS.—At any time before a decision entered in a case in which the proceedings are conducted under this section becomes final, the taxpayer or the Secretary may request that further proceedings under this section in such case be discontinued. The Tax Court, or the division thereof hearing such case, may, if it finds that (1) there are reasonable grounds for believing that the amount of the deficiency placed in dispute, or the amount of an overpayment, exceeds the applicable jurisdictional amount described in subsection (a), and (2) the amount of such excess is large enough to justify granting such request, discontinue further proceedings in such case under this section. Upon any such discontinuance, proceedings in such case shall be conducted in the same manner as cases to which the provisions of sections 6214(a) and 6512(b) apply.

[Sec. 7463(e)]

(e) AMOUNT OF DEFICIENCY IN DISPUTE.—For purposes of this section, the amount of any deficiency placed in dispute includes additions to the tax, additional amounts, and penalties imposed by chapter 68, to the extent that the procedures described in subchapter B of chapter 63 apply.

[Sec. 7463(f)]

(f) ADDITIONAL CASES IN WHICH PROCEEDINGS MAY BE CONDUCTED UNDER THIS SECTION.—At the option of the taxpayer concurred in by the Tax Court or a division thereof before the hearing of the case, proceedings may be conducted under this section (in the same manner as a case described in subsection (a)) in the case of—

(1) a petition to the Tax Court under section 6015(e) in which the amount of relief sought does not exceed $50,000,

(2) an appeal under section 6330(d)(1)(A) to the Tax Court of a determination in which the unpaid tax does not exceed $50,000, and

(3) a petition to the Tax Court under section 6404(h) in which the amount of the abatement sought does not exceed $50,000.

[Sec. 7463(g)—Repealed]

SUBCHAPTER E—BURDEN OF PROOF

[Sec. 7491]

SEC. 7491. BURDEN OF PROOF.

[Sec. 7491(a)]

(a) BURDEN SHIFTS WHERE TAXPAYER PRODUCES CREDIBLE EVIDENCE.—

(1) GENERAL RULE.—If, in any court proceeding, a taxpayer introduces credible evidence with respect to any factual issue relevant to ascertaining the liability of the taxpayer for any tax imposed by subtitle A or B, the Secretary shall have the burden of proof with respect to such issue.

(2) LIMITATIONS.—Paragraph (1) shall apply with respect to an issue only if—

(A) the taxpayer has complied with the requirements under this title to substantiate any item;

(B) the taxpayer has maintained all records required under this title and has cooperated with reasonable requests by the Secretary for witnesses, information, documents, meetings, and interviews; and

(C) in the case of a partnership, corporation, or trust, the taxpayer is described in section 7430(c)(4)(A)(ii).

Subparagraph (C) shall not apply to any qualified revocable trust (as defined in section 645(b)(1)) with respect to liability for tax for any taxable year ending after the date of the decedent's death and before the applicable date (as defined in section 645(b)(2)).

(3) COORDINATION.—Paragraph (1) shall not apply to any issue if any other provision of this title provides for a specific burden of proof with respect to such issue.

[Sec. 7491(b)]

(b) USE OF STATISTICAL INFORMATION ON UNRELATED TAXPAYERS.—In the case of an individual taxpayer, the Secretary shall have the burden of proof in any court proceeding with respect to any item of income which was reconstructed by the Secretary solely through the use of statistical information on unrelated taxpayers.

[Sec. 7491(c)]

(c) PENALTIES.—Notwithstanding any other provision of this title, the Secretary shall have the burden of production in any court proceeding with respect to the liability of any individual for any penalty, addition to tax, or additional amount imposed by this title.

CHAPTER 77—MISCELLANEOUS PROVISIONS

[Sec. 7502]

SEC. 7502. TIMELY MAILING TREATED AS TIMELY FILING AND PAYING.

[Sec. 7502(a)]

(a) GENERAL RULE.—

(1) DATE OF DELIVERY.—If any return, claim, statement, or other document required to be filed, or any payment required to be made, within a prescribed period or on or before a prescribed date under authority of any provision of the internal revenue laws is, after such period or such date, delivered by United States mail to the agency, officer, or office with which such return, claim, statement, or other document is required to be filed, or to which

such payment is required to be made, the date of the United States postmark stamped on the cover in which such return, claim, statement, or other document, or payment, is mailed shall be deemed to be the date of delivery or the date of payment, as the case may be.

(2) MAILING REQUIREMENTS.—This subsection shall apply only if—

(A) the postmark date falls within the prescribed period or on or before the prescribed date—

(i) for the filing (including any extension granted for such filing) of the return, claim, statement, or other document, or

(ii) for making the payment (including any extension granted for making such payment), and

(B) the return, claim, statement, or other document, or payment was, within the time prescribed in subparagraph (A), deposited in the mail in the United States in an envelope or other appropriate wrapper, postage prepaid, properly addressed to the agency, officer, or office with which the return, claim, statement, or other document is required to be filed, or to which such payment is required to be made.

[Sec. 7502(b)]

(b) POSTMARKS.—This section shall apply in the case of postmarks not made by the United States Postal Service only if and to the extent provided by regulations prescribed by the Secretary.

[Sec. 7502(c)]

(c) REGISTERED AND CERTIFIED MAILING; ELECTRONIC FILING.—

(1) REGISTERED MAIL.—For purposes of this section, if any return, claim, statement, or other document, or payment, is sent by United States registered mail—

(A) such registration shall be prima facie evidence that the return, claim, statement, or other document was delivered to the agency, officer, or office to which addressed; and

(B) the date of registration shall be deemed the postmark date.

(2) CERTIFIED MAIL; ELECTRONIC FILING.—The Secretary is authorized to provide by regulations the extent to which the provisions of paragraph (1) with respect to prima facie evidence of delivery and the postmark date shall apply to certified mail and electronic filing.

[Sec. 7502(d)]

(d) EXCEPTIONS.—This section shall not apply with respect to—

(1) the filing of a document in, or the making of a payment to, any court other than the Tax Court,

(2) currency or other medium of payment unless actually received and accounted for, or

(3) returns, claims, statements, or other documents, or payments, which are required under any provision of the internal revenue laws or the regulations thereunder to be delivered by any method other than by mailing.

* * *

[Sec. 7502(f)]

(f) TREATMENT OF PRIVATE DELIVERY SERVICES.—

(1) IN GENERAL.—Any reference in this section to the United States mail shall be treated as including a reference to any designated delivery service, and any reference in this section to a postmark by the United States Postal Service shall be treated as including a reference to any date recorded or marked as described in paragraph (2)(C) by any designated delivery service.

(2) DESIGNATED DELIVERY SERVICE.—For purposes of this subsection, the term "designated delivery service" means any delivery service provided by a trade or business if such service is designated by the Secretary for purposes of this section. The Secretary may designate a delivery service under the preceding sentence only if the Secretary determines that such service—

(A) is available to the general public,

(B) is at least as timely and reliable on a regular basis as the United States mail,

(C) records electronically to its data base, kept in the regular course of its business, or marks on the cover in which any item referred to in this section is to be delivered, the date on which such item was given to such trade or business for delivery, and

(D) meets such other criteria as the Secretary may prescribe.

(3) EQUIVALENTS OF REGISTERED AND CERTIFIED MAIL.—The Secretary may provide a rule similar to the rule of paragraph (1) with respect to any service provided by a designated delivery service which is substantially equivalent to United States registered or certified mail.

[Sec. 7519]

SEC. 7519. REQUIRED PAYMENTS FOR ENTITIES ELECTING NOT TO HAVE REQUIRED TAXABLE YEAR.

[Sec. 7519(a)]

(a) GENERAL RULE.—This section applies to a partnership or S corporation for any taxable year, if—

(1) an election under section 444 is in effect for the taxable year, and

(2) the required payment determined under subsection (b) for such taxable year (or any preceding taxable year) exceeds $500.

[Sec. 7519(b)]

(b) REQUIRED PAYMENT.—For purposes of this section, the term "required payment" means, with respect to any applicable election year of a partnership or S corporation, an amount equal to—

(1) the excess of the product of—

(A) the applicable percentage of the adjusted highest section 1 rate, multiplied by

(B) the net base year income of the entity, over

(2) the net required payment balance.

For purposes of paragraph (1)(A), the term "adjusted highest section 1 rate" means the highest rate of tax in effect under section 1 as of the end of the base year plus 1 percentage point (or, in the case of applicable election years beginning in 1987, 36 percent).

[Sec. 7519(c)]

(c) REFUND OF PAYMENTS.—

(1) IN GENERAL.—If, for any applicable election year, the amount determined under subsection (b)(2) exceeds the amount determined under subsection (b)(1), the entity shall be entitled to a refund of such excess for such year.

(2) TERMINATION OF ELECTIONS, ETC.—If—

(A) an election under section 444 is terminated effective with respect to any year, or

(B) the entity is liquidated during any year, the entity shall be entitled to a refund of the net required payment balance.

(3) DATE ON WHICH REFUND PAYABLE.—Any refund under this subsection shall be payable on the later of—

(A) April 15 of the calendar year following—

(i) in the case of the year referred to in paragraph (1), the calendar year in which it begins,

(ii) in the case of the year referred to in paragraph (2), the calendar year in which it ends, or

(B) the day 90 days after the day on which claim therefor is filed with the Secretary.

[Sec. 7519(d)]

(d) NET BASE YEAR INCOME.—For purposes of this section—

(1) IN GENERAL.—An entity's net base year income shall be equal to the sum of—

(A) the deferral ratio multiplied by the entity's net income for the base year, plus

(B) the excess (if any) of—

(i) the deferral ratio multiplied by the aggregate amount of applicable payments made by the entity during the base year, over

(ii) the aggregate amount of such applicable payments made during the deferral period of the base year.

For purposes of this paragraph, the term "deferral ratio" means the ratio which the number of months in the deferral period of the base year bears to the number of months in the partnership's or S corporation's taxable year.

(2) NET INCOME.—Net income is determined by taking into account the aggregate amount of the following items—

(A) PARTNERSHIPS .—In the case of a partnership, net income shall be the amount (not below zero) determined by taking into account the aggregate amount of the partnership's items described in section 702(a) (other than credits and tax-exempt income).

(B) S CORPORATIONS.—In the case of an S corporation, net income shall be the amount (not below zero) determined by taking into account the aggregate amount of the S corporation's items described in section 1366(a) (other than credits and tax-exempt income). If the S corporation was a C corporation for the base year, its taxable income for such year shall be treated as its net income for such year (and such corporation shall be treated as an S corporation for such taxable year for purposes of paragraph (3)).

(C) CERTAIN LIMITATIONS DISREGARDED.—For purposes of subparagraph (A) or (B), any limitation on the amount of any item described in either such paragraph which may be taken into account for purposes of computing the taxable income of a partner or shareholder shall be disregarded.

(3) APPLICABLE PAYMENTS.—

(A) IN GENERAL.—The term "applicable payment" means amounts paid by a partnership or S corporation which are includible in gross income of a partner or shareholder.

(B) EXCEPTIONS.—The term "applicable payment" shall not include any—

(i) gain from the sale or exchange of property between the partner or shareholder and the partnership or S corporation, and

(ii) dividend paid by the S corporation.

(4) APPLICABLE PERCENTAGE.—The applicable percentage is the percentage determined in accordance with the following table:

If the applicable election year of the partnership or S corporation begins during:	*The applicable percentage is:*
1987	25
1988	50
1989	75
1990 or thereafter	100

Notwithstanding the preceding provisions of this paragraph, the applicable percentage for any partnership or S corporation shall be 100 percent unless more than 50 percent of such entity's net income for the short taxable year which would have resulted if the entity had not made an election under section 444 would have been allocated to partners or shareholders who would have been entitled to the benefits of section 806(e)(2)(C) of the Tax Reform Act of 1986 with respect to such income.

(5) TREATMENT OF GUARANTEED PAYMENTS.—

(A) IN GENERAL.—Any guaranteed payment by a partnership shall not be treated as an applicable payment, and the amount of the net income of the partnership shall be determined by not taking such guaranteed payment into account.

(B) GUARANTEED PAYMENT.—For purposes of subparagraph (A), the term "guaranteed payment" means any payment referred to in section 707(c).

[Sec. 7519(e)]

(e) OTHER DEFINITIONS AND SPECIAL RULES.— For purposes of this section—

(1) DEFERRAL PERIOD.—The term "deferral period" has the meaning given to such term by section 444(b)(4).

(2) YEARS.—

(A) BASE YEAR.—The term "base year" means, with respect to any applicable election year, the taxable year of the partnership or S corporation preceding such applicable election year.

(B) APPLICABLE ELECTION YEAR.—The term "applicable election year" means any taxable year of a partnership or S corporation with respect to which an election is in effect under section 444.

(3) REQUIREMENT OF REPORTING.—Each partnership or S corporation which makes an election under section 444 shall include on any required return or statement such information as the Secretary shall prescribe as is necessary to carry out the provisions of this section.

(4) NET REQUIRED PAYMENT BALANCE.—The term "net required payment balance" means the excess (if any) of—

(A) the aggregate of the required payments under this section for all preceding applicable election years, over

(B) the aggregate amount allowable as a refund to the entity under subsection (c) for all preceding applicable election years.

[Sec. 7519(f)]

(f) ADMINISTRATIVE PROVISIONS.—

(1) IN GENERAL.—Except as otherwise provided in this subsection or in regulations prescribed by the Secretary, any payment required by this section shall be assessed and collected in the same manner as if it were a tax imposed by subtitle C.

(2) DUE DATE.—The amount of any payment required by this section shall be paid on or before April 15 of the calendar year following the calendar year in which the applicable election year begins (or such later date as may be prescribed by the Secretary).

(3) INTEREST.—For purposes of determining interest, any payment required by this section shall be treated as a tax; except that no interest shall be allowed with respect to any refund of a payment made under this section.

* * *

[Sec. 7520]

SEC. 7520. VALUATION TABLES.

[Sec. 7520(a)]

(a) GENERAL RULE.—For purposes of this title, the value of any annuity, any interest for life or a term of years, or any remainder or reversionary interest shall be determined—

(1) under tables prescribed by the Secretary, and

(2) by using an interest rate (rounded to the nearest 2/10ths of 1 percent) equal to 120 percent of the Federal midterm rate in effect under section 1274(d)(1) for the month in which the valuation date falls.

If an income, estate, or gift tax charitable contribution is allowable for any part of the property transferred, the taxpayer may elect to use such Federal midterm rate for either of the 2 months preceding the month in which the valuation date falls for purposes of paragraph (2). In the case of transfers of more than 1 interest in the same property with respect to which the taxpayer may use the same rate under paragraph (2), the taxpayer shall use the same rate with respect to each such interest.

[Sec. 7520(b)]

(b) SECTION NOT TO APPLY FOR CERTAIN PURPOSES.—This section shall not apply for purposes of part I of subchapter D of chapter 1 or any other provision specified in regulations.

[Sec. 7520(c)]

(c) TABLES.—

(1) IN GENERAL.—The tables prescribed by the Secretary for purposes of subsection (a) shall contain valuation factors for a series of interest rate categories.

(2) REVISION FOR RECENT MORTALITY CHARGES.—The Secretary shall revise the initial tables prescribed for purposes of subsection (a) to take into account the most recent mortality experience available as of the time of such revision. Such tables shall be revised not less frequently than once each 10 years to take into account the most recent mortality experience available as of the time of the revision.

[Sec. 7520(d)]

(d) VALUATION DATE.—For purposes of this section, the term "valuation date" means the date as of which the valuation is made.

[Sec. 7520(e)]

(e) TABLES TO INCLUDE FORMULAS.—For purposes of this section, the term "tables" includes formulas.

CHAPTER 79—DEFINITIONS

[Sec. 7701]

SEC. 7701. DEFINITIONS.

[Sec. 7701(a)]

(a) When used in this title, where not otherwise distinctly expressed or manifestly incompatible with the intent thereof—

(1) PERSON.—The term "person" shall be construed to mean and include an individual, a trust, estate, partnership, association, company or corporation.

(2) PARTNERSHIP AND PARTNER.—The term "partnership" includes a syndicate, group, pool, joint venture, or other unincorporated organization, through or by means of which any business, financial operation, or venture is carried on, and which is not, within the meaning of this title, a trust or estate or a corporation; and the term "partner" includes a member in such a syndicate, group, pool, joint venture, or organization.

(3) CORPORATION.—The term "corporation" includes associations, joint-stock companies, and insurance companies.

(4) DOMESTIC.—The term "domestic" when applied to a corporation or partnership means created or organized in the United States or under the law of the United States or of any State unless, in the case of a partnership, the Secretary provides otherwise by regulations.

(5) FOREIGN.—The term "foreign" when applied to a corporation or partnership means a corporation or partnership which is not domestic.

(6) FIDUCIARY.—The term "fiduciary" means a guardian, trustee, executor, administrator, receiver, conservator, or any person acting in any fiduciary capacity for any person.

(7) STOCK.—The term "stock" includes shares in an association, joint-stock company, or insurance company.

(8) SHAREHOLDER.—The term "shareholder" includes a member in an association, joint-stock company, or insurance company.

(9) UNITED STATES.—The term "United States" when used in a geographical sense includes only the States and the District of Columbia.

(10) STATE.—The term "State" shall be construed to include the District of Columbia, where such construction is necessary to carry out provisions of this title.

(11) SECRETARY OF THE TREASURY AND SECRETARY.—

(A) SECRETARY OF THE TREASURY.—The term "Secretary of the Treasury" means the Secretary of the Treasury, personally, and shall not include any delegate of his.

(B) SECRETARY.—The term "Secretary" means the Secretary of the Treasury or his delegate.

(12) DELEGATE.—

(A) IN GENERAL.—The term "or his delegate"—

(i) when used with reference to the Secretary of the Treasury, means any officer, employee, or agency of the Treasury Department duly authorized by the Secretary of the Treasury directly, or indirectly by one or more redelegations of authority, to perform the function mentioned or described in the context; and

(ii) when used with reference to any other official of the United States, shall be similarly construed.

* * *

(13) COMMISSIONER.—The term "Commissioner" means the Commissioner of Internal Revenue.

(14) TAXPAYER.—The term "taxpayer" means any person subject to any internal revenue tax.

(15) MILITARY OR NAVAL FORCES AND ARMED FORCES OF THE UNITED STATES.—The term "military or naval forces of the United States" and the term "Armed Forces of the United States" each includes all regular and reserve components of the uniformed services which are subject to the jurisdiction of the Secretary of Defense, the Secretary of the Army, the Secretary of the Navy, or the Secretary of the Air Force, and each term also includes the Coast Guard. The members of such forces include commissioned officers and personnel below the grade of commissioned officers in such forces.

(16) WITHHOLDING AGENT.—The term "withholding agent" means any person required to deduct and withhold any tax under the provisions of section 1441, 1442, 1443, or 1461.

(17) HUSBAND AND WIFE.—As used in section 2516, if the husband and wife therein referred to are divorced, wherever appropriate to the meaning of such section, the term "wife" shall be read "former wife" and the term "husband" shall be read "former husband"; and, if the payments described in such section are made by or on behalf of the wife or former wife to the husband or former husband instead of vice versa, wherever appropriate to the meaning of such section, the term "husband" shall be read "wife" and the term "wife" shall be read "husband."

* * *

(20) EMPLOYEE.—For the purpose of applying the provisions of section 79 with respect to group-term life insurance purchased for employees, for the purpose of applying the provisions of sections 104, 105, and 106 with respect to accident and health insurance or accident and health plans, and for the purpose of applying the provisions of subtitle A with respect to contributions to or under a stock bonus, pension, profit-sharing, or annuity plan, and with respect to distributions under such a plan, or by a trust forming part of such a plan, and for purposes of applying section 125 with respect to cafeteria plans, the term "employee" shall include a full-time life insurance salesman who is considered an employee for the purpose of chapter 21.

(21) LEVY.—The term "levy" includes the power of distraint and seizure by any means.

(22) ATTORNEY GENERAL.—The term "Attorney General" means the Attorney General of the United States.

(23) TAXABLE YEAR.—The term "taxable year" means the calendar year, or the fiscal year ending during such calendar year, upon the basis of which the taxable income is computed

under subtitle A. "Taxable year" means, in the case of a return made for a fractional part of a year under the provisions of subtitle A or under regulations prescribed by the Secretary, the period for which such return is made.

(24) FISCAL YEAR.—The term "fiscal year" means an accounting period of 12 months ending on the last day of any month other than December.

(25) PAID OR INCURRED, PAID OR ACCRUED.—The terms "paid or incurred" and "paid or accrued" shall be construed according to the method of accounting upon the basis of which the taxable income is computed under subtitle A.

(26) TRADE OR BUSINESS.—The term "trade or business" includes the performance of the functions of a public office.

(27) TAX COURT.—The term "Tax Court" means the United States Tax Court.

(28) OTHER TERMS.—Any term used in this subtitle with respect to the application of, or in connection with, the provisions of any other subtitle of this title shall have the same meaning as in such provisions.

(29) INTERNAL REVENUE CODE.—The term "Internal Revenue Code of 1986" means this title, and the term "Internal Revenue Code of 1939" means the Internal Revenue Code enacted February 10, 1939, as amended.

(30) UNITED STATES PERSON.—The term "United States person" means—

(A) a citizen or resident of the United States,

(B) a domestic partnership,

(C) a domestic corporation,

(D) any estate (other than a foreign estate, within the meaning of paragraph (31)), and

(E) any trust if—

(i) a court within the United States is able to exercise primary supervision over the administration of the trust, and

(ii) one or more United States persons have the authority to control all substantial decisions of the trust.

* * *

(36) TAX RETURN PREPARER.—

(A) IN GENERAL.—The term "tax return preparer" means any person who prepares for compensation, or who employs one or more persons to prepare for compensation, any return of tax imposed by this title or any claim for refund of tax imposed by this title. For purposes of the preceding sentence, the preparation of a substantial portion of a return or claim for refund shall be treated as if it were the preparation of such return or claim for refund.

(B) EXCEPTIONS.—A person shall not be a "tax return preparer" merely because such person—

(i) furnishes typing, reproducing, or other mechanical assistance,

(ii) prepares a return or claim for refund of the employer (or of an officer or employee of the employer) by whom he is regularly and continuously employed,

(iii) prepares as a fiduciary a return or claim for refund for any person, or

(iv) prepares a claim for refund for a taxpayer in response to any notice of deficiency issued to such taxpayer or in response to any waiver of restriction after the commencement of an audit of such taxpayer or another taxpayer if a determination in such audit of such other taxpayer directly or indirectly affects the tax liability of such taxpayer.

(37) INDIVIDUAL RETIREMENT PLAN.—The term "individual retirement plan" means—

(A) an individual retirement account described in section 408(a), and

(B) an individual retirement annuity described in section 408(b).

(38) JOINT RETURN.—The term "joint return" means a single return made jointly under section 6013 by a husband and wife.

* * *

(41) TIN.—The term "TIN" means the identifying number assigned to a person under section 6109.

(42) SUBSTITUTED BASIS PROPERTY.—The term "substituted basis property" means property which is—

(A) transferred basis property, or

(B) exchanged basis property.

(43) TRANSFERRED BASIS PROPERTY.—The term "transferred basis property" means property having a basis determined under any provision of subtitle A (or under any corresponding provision of prior income tax law) providing that the basis shall be determined in whole or in part by reference to the basis in the hands of the donor, grantor, or other transferor.

(44) EXCHANGED BASIS PROPERTY.—The term "exchanged basis property" means property having a basis determined under any provision of subtitle A (or under any corresponding provision of prior income tax law) providing that the basis shall be determined in whole or in part by reference to other property held at any time by the person for whom the basis is to be determined.

(45) NONRECOGNITION TRANSACTION.—The term "nonrecognition transaction" means any disposition of property in a transaction in which gain or loss is not recognized in whole or in part for purposes of subtitle A.

* * *

[Sec. 7701(c)]

(c) INCLUDES AND INCLUDING.—The terms "includes" and "including" when used in a definition contained in this title shall not be deemed to exclude other things otherwise within the meaning of the term defined.

* * *

[Sec. 7701(g)]

(g) CLARIFICATION OF FAIR MARKET VALUE IN THE CASE OF NONRECOURSE INDEBTEDNESS.—For purposes of subtitle A, in determining the amount of gain or loss (or deemed gain or loss) with respect to any property, the fair market value of such property shall be treated as being not less than the amount of any nonrecourse indebtedness to which such property is subject.

* * *

[Sec. 7701(o)]

(o) CLARIFICATION OF ECONOMIC SUBSTANCE DOCTRINE.—

(1) APPLICATION OF DOCTRINE.—In the case of any transaction to which the economic substance doctrine is relevant, such transaction shall be treated as having economic substance only if—

(A) the transaction changes in a meaningful way (apart from Federal income tax effects) the taxpayer's economic position, and

(B) the taxpayer has a substantial purpose (apart from Federal income tax effects) for entering into such transaction.

(2) SPECIAL RULE WHERE TAXPAYER RELIES ON PROFIT POTENTIAL.—

(A) IN GENERAL.—The potential for profit of a transaction shall be taken into account in determining whether the requirements of subparagraphs (A) and (B) of paragraph (1) are met with respect to the transaction only if the present value of the reasonably expected pre-tax profit from the transaction is substantial in relation to the present value of the expected net tax benefits that would be allowed if the transaction were respected.

(B) TREATMENT OF FEES AND FOREIGN TAXES.—Fees and other transaction expenses shall be taken into account as expenses in determining pre-tax profit under subparagraph

(A). The Secretary shall issue regulations requiring foreign taxes to be treated as expenses in determining pre-tax profit in appropriate cases.

(3) STATE AND LOCAL TAX BENEFITS.—For purposes of paragraph (1), any State or local income tax effect which is related to a Federal income tax effect shall be treated in the same manner as a Federal income tax effect.

(4) FINANCIAL ACCOUNTING BENEFITS.—For purposes of paragraph (1)(B), achieving a financial accounting benefit shall not be taken into account as a purpose for entering into a transaction if the origin of such financial accounting benefit is a reduction of Federal income tax.

(5) DEFINITIONS AND SPECIAL RULES.—For purposes of this subsection—

(A) ECONOMIC SUBSTANCE DOCTRINE.—The term "economic substance doctrine" means the common law doctrine under which tax benefits under subtitle A with respect to a transaction are not allowable if the transaction does not have economic substance or lacks a business purpose.

(B) EXCEPTION FOR PERSONAL TRANSACTIONS OF INDIVIDUALS.—In the case of an individual, paragraph (1) shall apply only to transactions entered into in connection with a trade or business or an activity engaged in for the production of income.

(C) DETERMINATION OF APPLICATION OF DOCTRINE NOT AFFECTED.—The determination of whether the economic substance doctrine is relevant to a transaction shall be made in the same manner as if this subsection had never been enacted.

(D) TRANSACTION.—The term "transaction" includes a series of transactions.

* * *

[Sec. 7702B]

SEC. 7702B. TREATMENT OF QUALIFIED LONG-TERM CARE INSURANCE.

[Sec. 7702B(a)]

(a) IN GENERAL.—For purposes of this title—

(1) a qualified long-term care insurance contract shall be treated as an accident and health insurance contract,

(2) amounts (other than policyholder dividends, as defined in section 808, or premium refunds) received under a qualified long-term care insurance contract shall be treated as amounts received for personal injuries and sickness and shall be treated as reimbursement for expenses actually incurred for medical care (as defined in section 213(d)),

(3) any plan of an employer providing coverage under a qualified long-term care insurance contract shall be treated as an accident and health plan with respect to such coverage,

(4) except as provided in subsection (e)(3), amounts paid for a qualified long-term care insurance contract providing the benefits described in subsection (b)(2)(A) shall be treated as payments made for insurance for purposes of section 213(d)(1)(D), and

(5) a qualified long-term care insurance contract shall be treated as a guaranteed renewable contract subject to the rules of section 816(e).

[Sec. 7702B(b)]

(b) QUALIFIED LONG-TERM CARE INSURANCE CONTRACT.—For purposes of this title—

(1) IN GENERAL.—The term "qualified long-term care insurance contract" means any insurance contract if—

(A) the only insurance protection provided under such contract is coverage of qualified long-term care services,

(B) such contract does not pay or reimburse expenses incurred for services or items to the extent that such expenses are reimbursable under title XVIII of the Social Security Act or would be so reimbursable but for the application of a deductible or coinsurance amount,

(C) such contract is guaranteed renewable,

(D) such contract does not provide for a cash surrender value or other money that can be—

(i) paid, assigned, or pledged as collateral for a loan, or

(ii) borrowed,

other than as provided in subparagraph (E) or paragraph (2)(C),

(E) all refunds of premiums, and all policyholder dividends or similar amounts, under such contract are to be applied as a reduction in future premiums or to increase future benefits, and

(F) such contract meets the requirements of subsection (g).

* * *

[Sec. 7702B(c)]

(c) QUALIFIED LONG-TERM CARE SERVICES.—For purposes of this section—

(1) IN GENERAL.—The term "qualified long-term care services" means necessary diagnostic, preventive, therapeutic, curing, treating, mitigating, and rehabilitative services, and maintenance or personal care services, which—

(A) are required by a chronically ill individual, and

(B) are provided pursuant to a plan of care prescribed by a licensed health care practitioner.

(2) CHRONICALLY ILL INDIVIDUAL.—

(A) IN GENERAL.—The term "chronically ill individual" means any individual who has been certified by a licensed health care practitioner as—

(i) being unable to perform (without substantial assistance from another individual) at least 2 activities of daily living for a period of at least 90 days due to a loss of functional capacity,

(ii) having a level of disability similar (as determined under regulations prescribed by the Secretary in consultation with the Secretary of Health and Human Services) to the level of disability described in clause (i), or

(iii) requiring substantial supervision to protect such individual from threats to health and safety due to severe cognitive impairment.

Such term shall not include any individual otherwise meeting the requirements of the preceding sentence unless within the preceding 12-month period a licensed health care practitioner has certified that such individual meets such requirements.

(B) ACTIVITIES OF DAILY LIVING.—For purposes of subparagraph (A), each of the following is an activity of daily living:

(i) Eating.

(ii) Toileting.

(iii) Transferring.

(iv) Bathing.

(v) Dressing.

(vi) Continence.

A contract shall not be treated as a qualified long-term care insurance contract unless the determination of whether an individual is a chronically ill individual described in subparagraph (A)(i) takes into account at least 5 of such activities.

(3) MAINTENANCE OR PERSONAL CARE SERVICES.—The term "maintenance or personal care services" means any care the primary purpose of which is the provision of needed assistance with any of the disabilities as a result of which the individual is a chronically ill individual (including the protection from threats to health and safety due to severe cognitive impairment).

(4) LICENSED HEALTH CARE PRACTITIONER.—The term "licensed health care practitioner" means any physician (as defined in section 1861(r)(1) of the Social Security Act) and any

registered professional nurse, licensed social worker, or other individual who meets such requirements as may be prescribed by the Secretary.

* * *

[Sec. 7703]

SEC. 7703. DETERMINATION OF MARITAL STATUS.

[Sec. 7703(a)]

(a) GENERAL RULE.—For purposes of part v of subchapter B of chapter 1 and those provisions of this title which refer to this subsection—

(1) the determination of whether an individual is married shall be made as of the close of his taxable year; except that if his spouse dies during his taxable year such determination shall be made as of the time of such death; and

(2) an individual legally separated from his spouse under a decree of divorce or of separate maintenance shall not be considered as married.

[Sec. 7703(b)]

(b) CERTAIN MARRIED INDIVIDUALS LIVING APART.—For purposes of those provisions of this title which refer to this subsection, if—

(1) an individual who is married (within the meaning of subsection (a)) and who files a separate return maintains as his home a household which constitutes for more than one-half of the taxable year the principal place of abode of a child (within the meaning of section 152(f)(1)) with respect to whom such individual is entitled to a deduction for the taxable year under section 151 (or would be so entitled but for section 152(e)),

(2) such individual furnishes over one-half of the cost of maintaining such household during the taxable year, and

(3) during the last 6 months of the taxable year, such individual's spouse is not a member of such household,

such individual shall not be considered as married.

[Sec. 7704]

SEC. 7704. CERTAIN PUBLICLY TRADED PARTNERSHIPS TREATED AS CORPORATIONS.

[Sec. 7704(a)]

(a) GENERAL RULE.—For purposes of this title, except as provided in subsection (c), a publicly traded partnership shall be treated as a corporation.

[Sec. 7704(b)]

(b) PUBLICLY TRADED PARTNERSHIP.—For purposes of this section, the term "publicly traded partnership" means any partnership if—

(1) interests in such partnership are traded on an established securities market, or

(2) interests in such partnership are readily tradable on a secondary market (or the substantial equivalent thereof).

[Sec. 7704(c)]

(c) EXCEPTION FOR PARTNERSHIPS WITH PASSIVE-TYPE INCOME.—

(1) IN GENERAL.—Subsection (a) shall not apply to any publicly traded partnership for any taxable year if such partnership met the gross income requirements of paragraph (2) for such taxable year and each preceding taxable year beginning after December 31, 1987, during which the partnership (or any predecessor) was in existence. For purposes of the preceding sentence, a partnership shall not be treated as being in existence during any period before the 1st taxable year in which such partnership (or a predecessor) was a publicly traded partnership.

(2) GROSS INCOME REQUIREMENTS.—A partnership meets the gross income requirements of this paragraph for any taxable year if 90 percent or more of the gross income of such partnership for such taxable year consists of qualifying income.

(3) EXCEPTION NOT TO APPLY TO CERTAIN PARTNERSHIPS WHICH COULD QUALIFY AS REGULATED INVESTMENT COMPANIES.—This subsection shall not apply to any partnership which would be described in section 851(a) if such partnership were a domestic corporation. To the extent provided in regulations, the preceding sentence shall not apply to any partnership a principal activity of which is the buying and selling of commodities (not described in section 1221(a)(1)), or options, futures, or forwards with respect to commodities.

[Sec. 7704(d)]

(d) QUALIFYING INCOME.—For purposes of this section—

(1) IN GENERAL.—Except as otherwise provided in this subsection, the term "qualifying income" means—

(A) interest,

(B) dividends,

(C) real property rents,

(D) gain from the sale or other disposition of real property (including property described in section 1221(a)(1)),

(E) income and gains derived from the exploration, development, mining or production, processing, refining, transportation (including pipelines transporting gas, oil, or products thereof), or the marketing of any mineral or natural resource (including fertilizer, geothermal energy, and timber), [or] industrial source carbon dioxide, or the transportation or storage of any fuel described in subsection (b), (c), (d), or (e) of section 6426, or any alcohol fuel defined in section 6426(b)(4)(A) or any biodiesel fuel as defined in section 40A(d)(1),

(F) any gain from the sale or disposition of a capital asset (or property described in section 1231(b)) held for the production of income described in any of the foregoing subparagraphs of this paragraph, and

(G) in the case of a partnership described in the second sentence of subsection (c)(3), income and gains from commodities (not described in section 1221(a)(1)) or futures, forwards, and options with respect to commodities.

For purposes of subparagraph (E), the term "mineral or natural resource" means any product of a character with respect to which a deduction for depletion is allowable under section 611; except that such term shall not include any product described in subparagraph (A) or (B) of section 613(b)(7).

(2) CERTAIN INTEREST NOT QUALIFIED.—Interest shall not be treated as qualifying income if—

(A) such interest is derived in the conduct of a financial or insurance business, or

(B) such interest would be excluded from the term "interest" under section 856(f).

(3) REAL PROPERTY RENT.—The term "real property rent" means amounts which would qualify as rent from real property under section 856(d) if—

(A) such section were applied without regard to paragraph (2)(C) thereof (relating to independent contractor requirements), and

(B) stock owned, directly or indirectly, by or for a partner would not be considered as owned under section 318(a)(3)(A) by the partnership unless 5 percent or more (by value) of the interests in such partnership are owned, directly or indirectly, by or for such partner.

(4) CERTAIN INCOME QUALIFYING UNDER REGULATED INVESTMENT COMPANY OR REAL ESTATE TRUST PROVISIONS.—The term "qualifying income" also includes any income which would qualify under section 851(b)(2)(A) or 856(c)(2).

(5) SPECIAL RULE FOR DETERMINING GROSS INCOME FROM CERTAIN REAL PROPERTY SALES.—In the case of the sale or other disposition of real property described in section 1221(a)(1), gross income shall not be reduced by inventory costs.

[Sec. 7704(e)]

(e) INADVERTENT TERMINATIONS.—If—

(1) A partnership fails to meet the gross income requirements of subsection (c) (2),

(2) the Secretary determines that such failure was inadvertent,

(3) no later than a reasonable time after the discovery of such failure, steps are taken so that such partnership once more meets such gross income requirements, and

(4) such partnership agrees to make such adjustments (including adjustments with respect to the partners) or to pay such amounts as may be required by the Secretary with respect to such period,

then, notwithstanding such failure, such entity shall be treated as continuing to meet such gross income requirements for such period.

[Sec. 7704(f)]

(f) EFFECT OF BECOMING CORPORATION.—As of the 1st day that a partnership is treated as a corporation under this section, for purposes of this title, such partnership shall be treated as—

(1) transferring all of its assets (subject to its liabilities) to a newly formed corporation in exchange for the stock of the corporation, and

(2) distributing such stock to its partners in liquidation of their interests in the partnership.

* * *

CHAPTER 80—GENERAL RULES

SUBCHAPTER A—APPLICATION OF INTERNAL REVENUE LAWS

[Sec. 7805]

SEC. 7805. RULES AND REGULATIONS.

[Sec. 7805(a)]

(a) AUTHORIZATION.—Except where such authority is expressly given by this title to any person other than an officer or employee of the Treasury Department, the Secretary shall prescribe all needful rules and regulations for the enforcement of this title, including all rules and regulations as may be necessary by reason of any alteration of law in relation to internal revenue.

[Sec. 7805(b)]

(b) RETROACTIVITY OF REGULATIONS.—

(1) IN GENERAL.—Except as otherwise provided in this subsection, no temporary, proposed, or final regulation relating to the internal revenue laws shall apply to any taxable period ending before the earliest of the following dates:

(A) The date on which such regulation is filed with the Federal Register.

(B) In the case of any final regulation, the date on which any proposed or temporary regulation to which such final regulation relates was filed with the Federal Register.

(C) The date on which any notice substantially describing the expected contents of any temporary, proposed, or final regulation is issued to the public.

(2) EXCEPTION FOR PROMPTLY ISSUED REGULATIONS.—Paragraph (1) shall not apply to regulations filed or issued within 18 months of the date of the enactment of the statutory provision to which the regulation relates.

(3) PREVENTION OF ABUSE.—The Secretary may provide that any regulation may take effect or apply retroactively to prevent abuse.

(4) CORRECTION OF PROCEDURAL DEFECTS.—The Secretary may provide that any regulation may apply retroactively to correct a procedural defect in the issuance of any prior regulation.

(5) INTERNAL REGULATIONS.—The limitation of paragraph (1) shall not apply to any regulation relating to internal Treasury Department policies, practices, or procedures.

(6) CONGRESSIONAL AUTHORIZATION.—The limitation of paragraph (1) may be superseded by a legislative grant from Congress authorizing the Secretary to prescribe the effective date with respect to any regulation.

(7) ELECTION TO APPLY RETROACTIVELY.—The Secretary may provide for any taxpayer to elect to apply any regulation before the dates specified in paragraph (1).

(8) APPLICATION TO RULINGS.—The Secretary may prescribe the extent, if any, to which any ruling (including any judicial decision or any administrative determination other than by regulation) relating to the internal revenue laws shall be applied without retroactive effect.

* * *

[Sec. 7805(d)]

(d) MANNER OF MAKING ELECTIONS PRESCRIBED BY SECRETARY.—Except to the extent otherwise provided by this title, any election under this title shall be made at such time and in such manner as the Secretary shall prescribe.

[Sec. 7805(e)]

(e) TEMPORARY REGULATIONS.—

(1) ISSUANCE.—Any temporary regulation issued by the Secretary shall also be issued as a proposed regulation.

(2) 3-YEAR DURATION.—Any temporary regulation shall expire within 3 years after the date of issuance of such regulation.

* * *

[Sec. 7806]

SEC. 7806. CONSTRUCTION OF TITLE.

[Sec. 7806(a)]

(a) CROSS REFERENCES.—The cross references in this title to other portions of the title, or other provisions of law, where the word "see" is used, are made only for convenience, and shall be given no legal effect.

[Sec. 7806(b)]

(b) ARRANGEMENT AND CLASSIFICATION.—No inference, implication, or presumption of legislative construction shall be drawn or made by reason of the location or grouping of any particular section or provision or portion of this title, nor shall any table of contents, table of cross references, or similar outline, analysis, or descriptive matter relating to the contents of this title be given any legal effect. The preceding sentence also applies to the sidenotes and ancillary tables contained in the various prints of this Act before its enactment into law.

SUBCHAPTER C—PROVISIONS AFFECTING MORE THAN ONE SUBTITLE

[Sec. 7872]

SEC. 7872. TREATMENT OF LOANS WITH BELOW-MARKET INTEREST RATES.

[Sec. 7872(a)]

(a) TREATMENT OF GIFT LOANS AND DEMAND LOANS.—

(1) IN GENERAL.—For purposes of this title, in the case of any below-market loan to which this section applies and which is a gift loan or a demand loan, the forgone interest shall be treated as—

(A) transferred from the lender to the borrower, and

(B) retransferred by the borrower to the lender as interest.

(2) TIME WHEN TRANSFERS MADE.—Except as otherwise provided in regulations prescribed by the Secretary, any forgone interest attributable to periods during any calendar year shall be treated as transferred (and retransferred) under paragraph (1) on the last day of such calendar year.

[Sec. 7872(b)]

(b) TREATMENT OF OTHER BELOW-MARKET LOANS.—

(1) IN GENERAL.—For purposes of this title, in the case of any below-market loan to which this section applies and to which subsection (a)(1) does not apply, the lender shall be treated as having transferred on the date the loan was made (or, if later, on the first day on which this section applies to such loan), and the borrower shall be treated as having received on such date, cash in an amount equal to the excess of—

(A) the amount loaned, over

(B) the present value of all payments which are required to be made under the terms of the loan.

(2) OBLIGATION TREATED AS HAVING ORIGINAL ISSUE DISCOUNT.—For purposes of this title—

(A) IN GENERAL.—Any below-market loan to which paragraph (1) applies shall be treated as having original issue discount in an amount equal to the excess described in paragraph (1).

(B) AMOUNT IN ADDITION TO OTHER ORIGINAL ISSUE DISCOUNT.—Any original issue discount which a loan is treated as having by reason of subparagraph (A) shall be in addition to any other original issue discount on such loan (determined without regard to subparagraph (A)).

[Sec. 7872(c)]

(c) BELOW-MARKET LOANS TO WHICH SECTION APPLIES.—

(1) IN GENERAL.—Except as otherwise provided in this subsection and subsection (g), this section shall apply to—

(A) GIFTS.—Any below-market loan which is a gift loan.

(B) COMPENSATION-RELATED LOANS.—Any below-market loan directly or indirectly between—

(i) an employer and an employee, or

(ii) an independent contractor and a person for whom such independent contractor provides services.

(C) CORPORATION-SHAREHOLDER LOANS.—Any below-market loan directly or indirectly between a corporation and any shareholder of such corporation.

(D) TAX AVOIDANCE LOANS.—Any below-market loan 1 of the principal purposes of the interest arrangements of which is the avoidance of any Federal tax.

(E) OTHER BELOW-MARKET LOANS.—To the extent provided in regulations, any below-market loan which is not described in subparagraph (A), (B), (C), or (F) if the interest arrangements of such loan have a significant effect on any Federal tax liability of the lender or the borrower.

(F) LOANS TO QUALIFIED CONTINUING CARE FACILITIES.—Any loan to any qualified continuing care facility pursuant to a continuing care contract.

(2) $10,000 DE MINIMIS EXCEPTION FOR GIFT LOANS BETWEEN INDIVIDUALS.—

(A) IN GENERAL.—In the case of any gift loan directly between individuals, this section shall not apply to any day on which the aggregate outstanding amount of loans between such individuals does not exceed $10,000.

(B) DE MINIMIS EXCEPTION NOT TO APPLY TO LOANS ATTRIBUTABLE TO ACQUISITION OF INCOME-PRODUCING ASSETS.—Subparagraph (A) shall not apply to any gift loan directly attributable to the purchase or carrying of income-producing assets.

(C) CROSS REFERENCE.—

For limitation on amount treated as interest where loans do not exceed $100,000, see subsection (d)(1).

(3) $10,000 DE MINIMIS EXCEPTION FOR COMPENSATION-RELATED AND CORPORATE-SHAREHOLDER LOANS.—

(A) IN GENERAL.—In the case of any loan described in subparagraph (B) or (C) of paragraph (1), this section shall not apply to any day on which the aggregate outstanding amount of loans between the borrower and lender does not exceed $10,000.

(B) EXCEPTION NOT TO APPLY WHERE 1 OF PRINCIPAL PURPOSES IS TAX AVOIDANCE.—Subparagraph (A) shall not apply to any loan the interest arrangements of which have as 1 of their principal purposes the avoidance of any Federal tax.

[Sec. 7872(d)]

(d) SPECIAL RULES FOR GIFT LOANS.—

(1) LIMITATION ON INTEREST ACCRUAL FOR PURPOSES OF INCOME TAXES WHERE LOANS DO NOT EXCEED $100,000.—

(A) IN GENERAL.—For purposes of subtitle A, in the case of a gift loan directly between individuals, the amount treated as retransferred by the borrower to the lender as of the close of any year shall not exceed the borrower's net investment income for such year.

(B) LIMITATION NOT TO APPLY WHERE 1 OF PRINCIPAL PURPOSES IS TAX AVOIDANCE.—Subparagraph (A) shall not apply to any loan the interest arrangements of which have as 1 of their principal purposes the avoidance of any Federal tax.

(C) SPECIAL RULE WHERE MORE THAN 1 GIFT LOAN OUTSTANDING.—For purposes of subparagraph (A), in any case in which a borrower has outstanding more than 1 gift loan, the net investment income of such borrower shall be allocated among such loans in proportion to the respective amounts which would be treated as retransferred by the borrower without regard to this paragraph.

(D) LIMITATION NOT TO APPLY WHERE AGGREGATE AMOUNT OF LOANS EXCEED $100,000.—This paragraph shall not apply to any loan made by a lender to a borrower for any day on which the aggregate outstanding amount of loans between the borrower and lender exceeds $100,000.

(E) NET INVESTMENT INCOME.—For purposes of this paragraph—

(i) IN GENERAL.—The term "net investment income" has the meaning given such term by section 163(d)(4).

(ii) DE MINIMIS RULE.—If the net investment income of any borrower for any year does not exceed $1,000, the net investment income of such borrower for such year shall be treated as zero.

(iii) ADDITIONAL AMOUNTS TREATED AS INTEREST.—In determining the net investment income of a person for any year, any amount which would be included in the gross income of such person for such year by reason of section 1272 if such section applied to all deferred payment obligations shall be treated as interest received by such person for such year.

(iv) DEFERRED PAYMENT OBLIGATIONS.—The term "deferred payment obligation" includes any market discount bond, short-term obligation, United States savings bond, annuity, or similar obligation.

(2) SPECIAL RULE FOR GIFT TAX.—In the case of any gift loan which is a term loan, subsection (b)(1) (and not subsection (a)) shall apply for purposes of chapter 12.

[Sec. 7872(e)]

(e) DEFINITIONS OF BELOW-MARKET LOAN AND FORGONE INTEREST.—For purposes of this section—

(1) BELOW-MARKET LOAN.—The term "below-market loan" means any loan if—

(A) in the case of a demand loan, interest is payable on the loan at a rate less than the applicable Federal rate, or

(B) in the case of a term loan, the amount loaned exceeds the present value of all payments due under the loan.

(2) FORGONE INTEREST.—The term "forgone interest" means, with respect to any period during which the loan is outstanding, the excess of—

(A) the amount of interest which would have been payable on the loan for the period if interest accrued on the loan at the applicable Federal rate and were payable annually on the day referred to in subsection (a)(2), over

(B) any interest payable on the loan properly allocable to such period.

[Sec. 7872(f)]

(f) OTHER DEFINITIONS AND SPECIAL RULES.—For purposes of this section—

(1) PRESENT VALUE.—The present value of any payment shall be determined in the manner provided by regulations prescribed by the Secretary—

(A) as of the date of the loan, and

(B) by using a discount rate equal to the applicable Federal rate.

(2) APPLICABLE FEDERAL RATE.—

(A) TERM LOANS.—In the case of any term loan, the applicable Federal rate shall be the applicable Federal rate in effect under section 1274(d) (as of the day on which the loan was made), compounded semiannually.

(B) DEMAND LOANS.—In the case of a demand loan, the applicable Federal rate shall be the Federal short-term rate in effect under section 1274(d) for the period for which the amount of forgone interest is being determined, compounded semiannually.

(3) GIFT LOAN.—The term "gift loan" means any below-market loan where the forgoing of interest is in the nature of a gift.

(4) AMOUNT LOANED.—The term "amount loaned" means the amount received by the borrower.

(5) DEMAND LOAN.—The term "demand loan" means any loan which is payable in full at any time on the demand of the lender. Such term also includes (for purposes other than determining the applicable Federal rate under paragraph (2)) any loan if the benefits of the interest arrangements of such loan are not transferable and are conditioned on the future performance of substantial services by an individual. To the extent provided in regulations, such term also includes any loan with an indefinite maturity.

(6) TERM LOAN.—The term "term loan" means any loan which is not a demand loan.

(7) HUSBAND AND WIFE TREATED AS 1 PERSON.—A husband and wife shall be treated as 1 person.

(8) LOANS TO WHICH SECTION 483, 643(i), OR 1274 APPLIES.—This section shall not apply to any loan to which section 483, 643(i), or 1274 applies.

* * *

(10) SPECIAL RULE FOR TERM LOANS.—If this section applies to any term loan on any day, this section shall continue to apply to such loan notwithstanding paragraphs (2) and (3) of subsection (c). In the case of a gift loan, the preceding sentence shall only apply for purposes of chapter 12.

* * *

[Sec. 7872(i)]

(i) REGULATIONS.—

(1) IN GENERAL.—The Secretary shall prescribe such regulations as may be necessary or appropriate to carry out the purposes of this section, including—

(A) regulations providing that where, by reason of varying rates of interest, conditional interest payments, waivers of interest, disposition of the lender's or borrower's interest in the loan, or other circumstances, the provisions of this section do not carry out the purposes of this section, adjustments to the provisions of this section will be made to the extent necessary to carry out the purposes of this section,

(B) regulations for the purpose of assuring that the positions of the borrower and lender are consistent as to the application (or nonapplication) of this section, and

(C) regulations exempting from the application of this section any class of transactions the interest arrangements of which have no significant effect on any Federal tax liability of the lender or the borrower.

(2) ESTATE TAX COORDINATION.—Under regulations prescribed by the Secretary, any loan which is made with donative intent and which is a term loan shall be taken into account for purposes of chapter 11 in a manner consistent with the provisions of subsection (b).

Income Tax Regulations

Tax on Individuals

§ 1.1(h)-1. Capital gains look-through rule for sales or exchanges of interests in a partnership, S corporation, or trust.—(a) *In general.*—When an interest in a partnership held for more than one year is sold or exchanged, the transferor may recognize ordinary income (e.g., under section 751(a)), collectibles gain, section 1250 capital gain, and residual long-term capital gain or loss. When stock in an S corporation held for more than one year is sold or exchanged, the transferor may recognize ordinary income (e.g., under sections 304, 306, 341, 1254), collectibles gain, and residual long-term capital gain or loss. When an interest in a trust held for more than one year is sold or exchanged, a transferor who is not treated as the owner of the portion of the trust attributable to the interest sold or exchanged (sections 673 through 679) (a non-grantor transferor) may recognize collectibles gain and residual long-term capital gain or loss.

(b) *Look-through capital gain.*—(1) *In general.*—Look-through capital gain is the share of collectibles gain allocable to an interest in a partnership, S corporation, or trust, plus the share of section 1250 capital gain allocable to an interest in a partnership, determined under paragraphs (b)(2) and (3) of this section.

(2) *Collectibles gain.*—(i) *Definition.*—For purposes of this section, *collectibles gain* shall be treated as gain from the sale or exchange of a collectible (as defined in section 408(m) without regard to section 408(m)(3)) that is a capital asset held for more than 1 year.

(ii) *Share of collectibles gain allocable to an interest in a partnership, S corporation, or a trust.*—When an interest in a partnership, S corporation, or trust held for more than one year is sold or exchanged in a transaction in which all realized gain is recognized, the transferor shall recognize as collectibles gain the amount of net gain (but not net loss) that would be allocated to that partner (taking into account any remedial allocation under § 1.704-3(d)), shareholder, or beneficiary (to the extent attributable to the portion of the partnership interest, S corporation stock, or trust interest transferred that was held for more than one year) if the partnership, S corporation, or trust transferred all of its collectibles for cash equal to the fair market value of the assets in a fully taxable transaction immediately before the transfer of the interest in the partnership, S corporation, or trust. If less than all of the realized gain is recognized upon the sale or exchange of an interest in a partnership, S corporation, or trust, the same methodology shall apply to determine the collectibles gain recognized by the transferor, except that the partnership, S corporation, or trust shall be treated as transferring only a proportionate amount of each of its collectibles determined as a fraction that is the amount of gain recognized in the sale or exchange over the amount of gain realized in the sale or exchange. With respect to the transfer of an interest in a trust, this paragraph (b)(2) applies only to transfers by non-grantor transferors (as defined in paragraph (a) of this section). This paragraph (b)(2) does not apply to a transaction that is treated, for Federal income tax purposes, as a redemption of an interest in a partnership, S corporation, or trust.

(3) *Section 1250 capital gain.*—(i) *Definition.*—For purposes of this section, *section 1250 capital gain* means the capital gain (not otherwise treated as ordinary income) that would be treated as ordinary income if section 1250(b)(1) included all depreciation and the applicable percentage under section 1250(a) were 100 percent.

(ii) *Share of section 1250 capital gain allocable to interest in partnership.*—When an interest in a partnership held for more than one year is sold or exchanged in a transaction in which all realized gain is recognized, there shall be taken into account under section 1(h)(7)(A)(i) in determining the partner's unrecaptured section 1250 gain the amount of section 1250 capital gain that would be allocated (taking into account any remedial allocation under § 1.704-3(d)) to that partner (to the extent attributable to the portion of the partnership interest transferred that was held for more than one year) if the partnership transferred all of its section 1250 property in a fully taxable transaction for cash equal to the fair market value of the assets immediately before the transfer of the interest in the partnership. If less than all of the realized gain is recognized upon the sale or exchange of an interest in a partnership, the same methodology shall apply to determine the section 1250 capital gain recognized by the transferor, except that the partnership shall be treated as transferring only a proportionate amount of each section 1250 property determined as a fraction that is the amount of gain recognized in the sale or exchange over the amount of gain realized in the sale or exchange. This paragraph (b)(3) does not apply to a transaction that is treated, for Federal income tax purposes, as a redemption of a partnership interest.

(iii) *Limitation with respect to net section 1231 gain.*—In determining a transferor partner's net section 1231 gain (as defined in section 1231(c)(3)) for purposes of section 1(h)(7)(B), the transferor partner's allocable share of section 1250 capital gain in partnership property shall not be treated as section 1231 gain, regardless of whether the partnership property is used in the trade or business (as defined in section 1231(b)).

(c) *Residual long-term capital gain or loss.*—The amount of residual long-term capital gain or loss recognized by a partner, shareholder of an S corporation, or beneficiary of a trust on account of the sale or exchange of an interest in a partnership, S corporation, or trust shall equal the amount of long-term capital gain or loss that the partner would recognize under section 741, that the shareholder would recognize upon the sale or exchange of stock of an S corporation, or that the beneficiary would recognize upon the sale or exchange of an interest in a trust (pre-look-through long-term capital gain or loss) minus the amount of look-through capital gain determined under paragraph (b) of this section.

(d) *Special rule for tiered entities.*—In determining whether a partnership, S corporation, or trust has gain from collectibles, such partnership, S corporation, or trust shall be treated as owning its proportionate share of the collectibles of any partnership, S corporation, or trust in which it owns an interest either directly or indirectly through a chain of such entities. In determining whether a partnership has section 1250 capital gain, such partnership shall be treated as owning its proportionate share of the section 1250 property of any partnership in which it owns an interest, either directly or indirectly through a chain of partnerships.

(e) *Notification requirements.*—Reporting rules similar to those that apply to the partners and the partnership under section 751(a) shall apply in the case of sales or exchanges of interests in a partnership, S corporation, or trust that cause holders of such interests to recognize collectibles gain and in the case of sales or exchanges of interests in a partnership that cause holders of such interests to recognize section 1250 capital gain. See § 1.751-1(a)(3).

(f) *Examples.*—The following examples illustrate the requirements of this section:

Example 1. Collectibles gain. (i) *A* and *B* are equal partners in a personal service partnership (*PRS*). *B* transfers *B*'s interest in *PRS* to *T* for $15,000 when *PRS*'s balance sheet (reflecting a cash receipts and disbursements method of accounting) is as follows:

	Adjusted Basis	*Market Value*
ASSETS		
Cash	$3,000	$3,000
Loans Owed to Partnership	10,000	10,000
Collectibles	1,000	3,000
Other Capital Assets	6,000	2,000
Capital Assets	7,000	5,000
Unrealized Receivables	0	14,000
Total	$20,000	$32,000
LIABILITIES AND CAPITAL		
Liabilities	$2,000	$2,000
Capital:		
A	9,000	15,000
B	9,000	15,000
Total	$20,000	$32,000

(ii) At the time of the transfer, *B* has held the interest in *PRS* for more than one year, and *B*'s basis for the partnership interest is $10,000 ($9,000 plus $1,000, *B*'s share of partnership liabilities). None of the property owned by *PRS* is section 704(c) property. The total amount realized by *B* is $16,000, consisting of the cash received, $15,000, plus $1,000, *B*'s share of the partnership liabilities assumed by *T*. See section 752. *B*'s undivided one-half interest in *PRS* includes a one-half interest in the partnership's unrealized receivables and a one-half interest in the partnership's collectibles.

(iii) If *PRS* were to sell all of its section 751 property in a fully taxable transaction for cash equal to the fair market value of the assets immediately prior to the transfer of *B*'s partnership interest to *T*, *B* would be allocated $7,000 of ordinary income from the sale of *PRS*'s unrealized receivables. Therefore, *B* will recognize $7,000 of ordinary income with respect to the unrealized receivables. The difference between the amount of capital gain or loss that the partner would realize in the absence of section 751 ($6,000) and the amount of ordinary income or loss determined under § 1.751-1(a)(2) ($7,000) is the partner's capital gain or loss on the sale of the partnership interest under section 741. In this case, the transferor has a $1,000 pre-look-through long-term capital loss.

(iv) If *PRS* were to sell all of its collectibles in a fully taxable transaction for cash equal to the fair market value of the assets immediately prior to the transfer of *B*'s partnership interest to *T*, *B* would be allocated $1,000 of gain from the sale of the collectibles. Therefore, *B* will recognize $1,000 of collectibles gain on account of the collectibles held by *PRS*.

(v) The difference between the transferor's pre-look-through long-term capital gain or loss (–$1,000) and the look-through capital gain determined under this section ($1,000) is the transferor's residual long-term capital gain or loss on the sale of the partnership interest. Under these facts, *B* will recognize a $2,000 residual long-term capital loss on account of the sale or exchange of the interest in *PRS*.

Example 2. Special allocations. Assume the same facts as in *Example 1*, except that under the partnership agreement, all gain from the sale of the collectibles is specially allocated to *B*, and *B* transfers *B*'s interest to *T* for $16,000. All items of income, gain, loss, or deduction of *PRS*, other than the gain from the collectibles, are divided equally between *A* and *B*. Under these facts, *B*'s amount realized is $17,000, consisting of the cash received, $16,000, plus $1,000, *B*'s share of the partnership liabilities assumed by *T*. See section 752. *B* will recognize $7,000 of ordinary income with respect to the unrealized receivables (determined under § 1.751-1 (a) (2)). Accordingly, *B*'s pre-look-through long-term capital gain would be $0. If *PRS* were to sell all of its collectibles in a fully taxable transaction for cash equal to the fair market value of the assets immediately prior to the transfer of *B*'s partnership interest to *T*, *B* would be allocated $2,000 of gain from the sale of the collectibles. Therefore, *B* will recognize $2,000 of collectibles gain on account of the collectibles held by *PRS*. *B* will recognize a $2,000 residual long-term capital loss on account of the sale of *B*'s interest in *PRS*.

* * *

[Reg. § 1.1(h)-1.]

☐ [*T.D.* 8902, 9-20-2000.]

»»→ Caution: Reg. § 1.1(i)-1T does not reflect 2006 and 2007 changes in the age specified in Section 1(g)(2)(A).

»»→ Note: Section 1(i) as referred to in Reg. § 1.1(i)-1T was renumbered as Section 1(g) in 1990.

§ 1.1(i)-1T. Questions and answers relating to the tax on unearned income of certain minor children (Temporary).

In general.

Q-1. To whom does section 1(i) apply?

A-1. Section 1(i) applies to any child who is under 14 years of age at the close of the taxable year, who has at least one living parent at the close of the taxable year, and who recognizes over $1,000 of unearned income during the taxable year.

Q-2. What is the effective date of section 1(i)?

A-2. Section 1(i) applies to taxable years of the child beginning after December 31, 1986.

Computation of tax.

Q-3. What is the amount of tax imposed by section 1 on a child to whom section 1(i) applies?

A-3. In the case of a child to whom section 1(i) applies, the amount of tax imposed by section 1 equals the greater of (A) the tax imposed by section 1 without regard to section 1(i) or (B) the sum of the tax that would be imposed by section 1 if the child's taxable income was reduced by the child's net unearned income, plus the child's share of the allocable parental tax.

Q-4. What is the allocable parental tax?

A-4. The allocable parental tax is the excess of (A) the tax that would be imposed by section 1 on the sum of the parent's taxable income plus the net unearned income of all children of such parent to whom section 1(i) applies, over (B) the tax imposed by section 1 on the parent's taxable income. Thus, the allocable parental tax is not computed with reference to unearned income of a child over 14 or a child under 14 with less than $1,000 of unearned income. *See* A-10 through A-13 for rules regarding the determination of the parent(s) whose taxable income is taken into account under section 1(i). *See* A-14 for rules regarding the determination of children of the parent whose net unearned income is taken into account under section 1(i).

Q-5. What is the child's share of the allocable parental tax?

A-5. The child's share of the allocable parental tax is an amount that bears the same ratio to the total allocable parental tax as the child's net unearned income bears to the total net unearned income of all children of such parent to whom section 1(i) applies. See A-14.

Example (1). During 1988, D, a 12 year old, receives $5,000 of unearned income and no earned income. D has no itemized deductions and is not eligible for a personal exemption. D's parents have two other children, E, a 15 year old, and F, a 10 year old. E has $10,000 of unearned income and F has $100 of unearned income. D's parents file a joint return for 1988 and report taxable income of $70,000. Neither D's nor his parent's taxable income is attributable to net capital gain. D's tax liability for 1988, determined without regard to section 1(i), is $675 on $4,500 of taxable income ($5,000 less

$500 allowable standard deduction). In applying section 1(i), D's tax would be equal to the sum of (A) the tax that would be imposed on D's taxable income if it were reduced by any net unearned income, plus (B) D's share of the allocable parental tax. Only D's unearned income is taken into account in determining the allocable parental tax because E is over 14 and F has less than $1,000 of unearned income. *See* A-4. D's net unearned income is $4,000 ($4,500 taxable unearned income less $500). The tax imposed on D's taxable income as reduced by D's net unearned income is $75 ($500 × 15%). The allocable parental tax is $1,225, the excess of $16,957.50 (the tax on $74,000, the parent's taxable income plus D's net unearned income) over $15,732.50 (the tax on $70,000, the parent's taxable income). *See* A-4. Thus, D's tax under section 1(i)(1)(B) is $1,300 ($1,225 + $75). Since this amount is greater than the amount of D's tax liability as determined without regard to section 1(i), the amount of tax imposed on D for 1988 is $1,300. *See* A-3.

Example (2). H and W have 3 children, A, B, and C, who are all under 14 years of age. For the taxable year 1988, H and W file a joint return and report taxable income of $129,750. The tax imposed by section 1 on H and W is $35,355. A has $5,000 of net unearned income and B and C each have $2,500 of net unearned income during 1988. The allocable parental tax imposed on A, B, and C's combined net unearned income of $10,000 is $3,300. This tax is the excess of $38,655, which is the tax imposed by section 1 on $139,750 ($129, 750 + 10,000), over $35,355 (the tax imposed by section 1 on H and W's taxable income of $129,750). *See* A-4. Each child's share of the allocable parental tax is an amount that bears the same ratio to the total allocable parental tax as the child's net unearned income bears to the total net unearned income of A, B, and C. Thus, A's share of the allocable parental tax is $1,650 (5,000 ÷ 10,000 × 3,300) and B and C's share of the tax is $825 (2,500 ÷ 10,000 × 3,300) each. *See* A-5.

Definition of net unearned income.

Q-6. What is net unearned income?

A-6. Net unearned income is the excess of the portion of adjusted gross income for the taxable year that is not "earned income" as defined in section 911(d)(2) (income that is not attributable to wages, salaries, or other amounts received as compensation for personal services), over the sum of the standard deduction amount provided for under section 63(c)(5)(A) ($500 for 1987 and 1988; adjusted for inflation thereafter), plus the greater of (A) $500 (adjusted for inflation after 1988) or (B) the amount of allowable itemized deductions that are directly connected with the production of unearned income. A child's net unearned income for any taxable year shall not exceed the child's taxable income for such year.

Example (3). A is a child who is under 14 years of age at the end of the taxable year 1987. Both of A's parents are alive at this time. During 1987, A receives $3,000 of interest from a bank savings account and earns $1,000 from a paper route and performing odd jobs. A has no itemized deductions for 1987. A's standard deduction is $1,000, which is an amount equal to A's earned income for 1987. Of this amount, $500 is applied against A's unearned income and the remaining $500 is applied against A's earned income. Thus, A's $500 of taxable earned income ($1,000 less the remaining $500 of the standard deduction) is taxed without regard to section 1(i); A has $2,500 of taxable unearned income ($3,000 gross unearned income less $500 of the standard deduction) of which $500 is taxed without regard to section 1(i). The remaining $2,000 of taxable unearned income is A's net unearned income and is taxed under section 1(i).

Example (4). B is a child who is subject to tax under section 1(i). B has $400 of earned income and $2,000 of unearned income. B has itemized deductions of $800 (net of the 2 percent of adjusted gross income (AGI) floor on miscellaneous itemized deductions under section 67) of which $200 are directly connected with the production of unearned income. The amount of itemized deductions that B may apply against unearned income is equal to the greater of $500 or the deductions directly connected with the production of unearned income. *See* A-6. Thus, $500 of B's itemized deductions are applied against the $2,000 of unearned income and the remaining $300 of deductions are applied against earned income. As a result, B has taxable earned income of $100 and taxable unearned income of $1,500. Of these amounts, all of the earned income and $500 of the unearned income are taxed without regard to section 1(i). The remaining $1,000 of unearned income is net unearned income and is taxed under section 1(i).

Unearned income subject to tax under section 1(i).

Q-7. Will a child be subject to tax under section 1(i) on net unearned income (as defined in section 1(i)(4) and A-6 of this section) that is attributable to property transferred to the child prior to 1987?

A-7. Yes. the tax imposed by section 1(i) on a child's net unearned income applies to any net unearned income of the child for taxable years beginning after December 31, 1986, regardless of when the underlying assets were transferred to the child.

Q-8. Will a child be subject to tax under section 1(i) on net unearned income that is attributable to gifts from persons other than the child's parents or attributable to assets resulting from the child's earned income?

A-8. Yes. The tax imposed by section 1(i) applies to all net unearned income of the child, regardless of the source of the assets that produced such income. Thus, the rules of section 1(i) apply to income attributable to gifts not only from the parents but also from any other source, such as the child's grandparents. Section 1(i) also applies to unearned income derived with respect to assets resulting from earned income of the child, such as interest earned on bank deposits.

Example (5). A is a child who is under 14 years of age at the end of the taxable year beginning on January 1, 1987. Both of A's parents are alive at the end of the taxable year. During 1987, A receives $2,000 in interest from his bank account and $1,500 from a paper route. Some of the interest earned by A from the bank account is attributable to A's paper route earnings that were deposited in the account. The balance of the account is attributable to cash gifts from A's parents and grandparents and interest earned prior to 1987. Some cash gifts were received by A prior to 1987. A has no itemized deductions and is eligible to be claimed as a dependent on his parent's return. Therefore, for the taxable year 1987, A's standard deduction is $1,500, the amount of A's earned income. Of this standard deduction amount, $500 is allocated against unearned income and $1,000 is allocated against earned income. A's taxable unearned income is $1,500 of which $500 is taxed without regard to section 1(i). The remaining taxable unearned income of $1,000 is net unearned income and is taxed under section 1(i). The fact that some of A's unearned income is attributable to interest on principal created by earned income and gifts from persons other than A's parents or that some of the unearned income is attributable to property transferred to A prior to 1987, will not affect the tax treatment of this income under section 1(i). *See* A-8.

Q-9. For purposes of section 1(i), does income which is not earned income (as defined in section 911(d)(2)) include social security benefits or pension benefits that are paid to the child?

A-9. Yes. For purposes of section 1(i), earned income (as defined in section 911(d)(2)) does not include any social security or pension benefits paid to the child. Thus, such amounts are included in unearned income to the extent they are includible in the child's gross income.

Determination of the parent's taxable income.

Q-10. If a child's parents file a joint return, what is the taxable income that must be taken into account by the child in determining tax liability under section 1(i)?

A-10. In the case of parents who file a joint return, the parental taxable income to be taken into account in determining the tax liability of a child is the total taxable income shown on the joint return.

Q-11. If a child's parents are married and file separate tax returns, which parent's taxable income must be taken into account by the child in determining tax liability under section 1(i)?

A-11. For purposes of determining the tax liability of a child under section 1(i), where such child's parents are married and file separate tax returns, the parent whose taxable income is the greater of the two for the taxable year shall be taken into account.

Q-12. If the parents of a child are divorced, legally separated, or treated as not married under section 7703(b), which parent's taxable income is taken into account in computing the child's tax liability?

A-12. If the child's parents are divorced, legally separated, or treated as not married under section 7703(b), the taxable income of the custodial parent (within the meaning of section 152(e)) of the child is taken into account under section 1(i) in determining the child's tax liability.

Q-13. If a parent whose taxable income must be taken into account in determining a child's tax liability under section 1(i) files a joint return with a spouse who is not a parent of the child, what taxable income must the child take into account?

A-13. The amount of a parent's taxable income that a child must take into account for purposes of section 1(i) where the parent files a joint return with a spouse who is not a parent of the child is the total taxable income shown on such joint return.

Children of the parent.

Q-14. In determining a child's share of the allocable parental tax, is the net unearned income of legally adopted children, children related to such child by half-blood, or children from a prior marriage of the spouse of such child's parent taken into account in addition to the natural children of such child's parent?

A-14. Yes. In determining a child's share of the allocable parental tax, the net unearned income of all children subject to tax under section 1(i) and who use the same parent's taxable income as such child to determine their tax liability under section 1(i) must be taken into account. Such children are taken into account regardless of whether they are adopted by the parent, related to such child by half-blood, or are children from a prior marriage of the spouse of such child's parent.

Rules regarding income from a trust or similar instrument.

Q-15. Will the unearned income of a child who is subject to section 1(i) that is attributable to gifts given to the child under the Uniform Gift to Minors Act (UGMA) be subject to tax under section 1(i)?

A-15. Yes. A gift under the UGMA vests legal title to the property in the child although an adult custodian is given certain rights to deal with the property until the child attains majority. Any unearned income attributable to such a gift is the child's unearned income and is subject to tax under section 1(i), whether distributed to the child or not.

Q-16. Will a child who is a beneficiary of a trust be required to take into account the income of a trust in determining the child's tax liability under section 1(i)?

A-16. The income of a trust must be taken into account for purposes of determining the tax liability of a beneficiary who is subject to section 1(i) only to the extent it is included in the child's gross income for the taxable year under sections 652(a) or 662(a). Thus, income from a trust for the fiscal taxable year of a trust ending during 1987, that is included in the gross income of a child who is subject to section 1(i) and who has a calendar taxable year, will be subject to tax under section 1(i) for the child's 1987 taxable year.

* * *

[Temporary Reg. § 1.1(i)-1T.]

□ [*T.D.* 8158, 9-3-87.]

§ 1.2-2. Definitions and special rules.

* * *

(d) *Cost of maintaining a household.*—A taxpayer shall be considered as maintaining a household only if he pays more than one-half the cost thereof for his taxable year. The cost of maintaining a household shall be the expenses incurred for the mutual benefit of the occupants thereof by reason of its operation as the principal place of abode of such occupants for such taxable year. The cost of maintaining a household shall not include expenses otherwise incurred. The expenses of maintaining a household include property taxes, mortgage interest, rent, utility charges, upkeep and repairs, property insurance, and food consumed on the premises. Such expenses do not include the cost of clothing, education, medical treatment, vacations, life insurance, and transportation. In addition, the cost of maintaining a household shall not include any amount which represents the value of services rendered in the household by the taxpayer or by a person qualifying the taxpayer as a head of a household or as a surviving spouse.

* * *

[Reg. § 1.2-2.]

□ [*T.D.* 6161, 2-3-56. *Amended by T.D.* 6792, 1-14-65 *and T.D.* 7117, 5-24-71.]

Credits Against Tax

1.21-1. Expenses for household and dependent care services necessary for gainful employment.—(a) *In general.*—(1) Section 21 allows a credit to a taxpayer against the tax imposed by chapter 1 for employment-related expenses for household services and care (as defined in paragraph (d) of this section) of a qualifying individual (as defined in paragraph (b) of this section). The purpose of the expenses must be to enable the taxpayer to be gainfully employed (as defined in paragraph (c) of this section). For taxable years beginning after December 31, 2004, a qualifying individual must have the same principal place of abode (as defined in paragraph (g) of this section) as the taxpayer for more than one-half of the taxable year. For taxable years beginning before January 1, 2005, the taxpayer must maintain a household (as defined in paragraph (h) of this section) that includes one or more qualifying individuals.

(2) The amount of the credit is equal to the applicable percentage of the employment-related expenses that may be taken into account by the taxpayer during the taxable year (but subject to the limits prescribed in 1.21-2). *Applicable percentage* means 35 percent reduced by 1 percentage point for each $2,000 (or fraction thereof) by which the taxpayer's adjusted gross income for the taxable year exceeds $15,000, but not less than 20 percent. For example, if a taxpayer's adjusted gross income is $31,850, the applicable percentage is 26 percent.

(3) Expenses may be taken as a credit under section 21, regardless of the taxpayer's method of accounting, only in the taxable year the services are performed or the taxable year the expenses are paid, whichever is later.

(4) The requirements of section 21 and 1.21-1 through 1.21-4 are applied at the time the services are performed, regardless of when the expenses are paid.

(5) *Examples.*—The provisions of this paragraph (a) are illustrated by the following examples.

Example 1. In December 2007, B pays for the care of her child for January 2008. Under paragraph (a)(3) of this section, B may claim the credit in 2008, the later of the years in which the expenses are paid and the services are performed.

Example 2. The facts are the same as in *Example 1,* except that B's child turns 13 on February 1, 2008, and B pays for the care provided in January 2008 on February 3, 2008. Under paragraph (a)(4) of this section, the determination of whether the expenses are employment-related expenses is made when the services are performed. Assuming other requirements are met, the amount B pays will be an employment-related expense under section 21, because B's child is a qualifying individual when the services are performed, even though the child is not a qualifying individual when B pays the expenses.

(b) *Qualifying individual.*—(1) *In general.*— For taxable years beginning after December 31, 2004, a qualifying individual is

(i) The taxpayer's dependent (who is a qualifying child within the meaning of section 152) who has not attained age 13;

(ii) The taxpayer's dependent (as defined in section 152, determined without regard to subsections (b)(1), (b)(2), and (d)(1)(B)) who is physically or mentally incapable of self-care and who has the same principal place of abode as the taxpayer for more than one-half of the taxable year; or

(iii) The taxpayer's spouse who is physically or mentally incapable of self-care and who has the same principal place of abode as the taxpayer for more than one-half of the taxable year.

* * *

(3) *Qualification on a daily basis.*—The status of an individual as a qualifying individual is determined on a daily basis. An individual is not a qualifying individual on the day the status terminates.

(4) *Physical or mental incapacity.*—An individual is physically or mentally incapable of self-care if, as a result of a physical or mental defect, the individual is incapable of caring for the individual's hygiene or nutritional needs, or requires full-time attention of another person for the individual's own safety or the safety of others. The inability of an individual to engage in any substantial gainful activity or to perform the normal household functions of a homemaker or care for minor children by reason of a physical or mental condition does not of itself establish that the individual is physically or mentally incapable of self-care.

(5) *Special test for divorced or separated parents or parents living apart.*—(i) *Scope.*— This paragraph (b)(5) applies to a child (as defined in section 152(f)(1) for taxable years beginning after December 31, 2004, and in section 151(c)(3) for taxable years beginning before January 1, 2005) who

(A) Is under age 13 or is physically or mentally incapable of self-care;

(B) Receives over one-half of his or her support during the calendar year from one or both parents who are divorced or legally separated under a decree of divorce or separate maintenance, are separated under a written separation agreement, or live apart at all times during the last 6 months of the calendar year; and

(C) Is in the custody of one or both parents for more than one-half of the calendar year.

(ii) *Custodial parent allowed the credit.*—A child to whom this paragraph (b)(5) applies is the qualifying individual of only one parent in any taxable year and is the qualifying child of the custodial parent even if the noncustodial parent may claim the dependency exemption for that child for that taxable year. See section 21(e)(5). The custodial parent is the parent having custody for the greater portion of the calendar year. See section 152(e)(4)(A).

(6) *Example.*—The provisions of this paragraph (b) are illustrated by the following examples.

Example. C pays $420 for the care of her child, a qualifying individual, to be provided from January 2 through January 31, 2008 (21 days of care). On January 20, 2008, C's child turns 13 years old. Under paragraph (b)(3) of this section, C's child is a qualifying individual from January 2 through January 19, 2008 (13 days of care). C may take into account $260, the pro rata amount C pays for the care of her child for 13 days, under section 21. See 1.21-2(a)(4).

(c) *Gainful employment.*—(1) *In general.*— Expenses are employment-related expenses only if they are for the purpose of enabling the taxpayer to be gainfully employed. The expenses must be for the care of a qualifying individual or household services performed during periods in which the taxpayer is gainfully employed or is in active search of gainful employment. Employment may consist of service within or outside the taxpayer's home and includes self-employment. An expense is not employment-related merely because it is paid or incurred while the taxpayer is gainfully employed. The purpose of the expense must be to enable the taxpayer to be gainfully employed. Whether the purpose of an expense is to enable the taxpayer to be gainfully employed depends on the facts and circumstances of the particular case. Work as a volunteer or for a nominal consideration is not gainful employment.

(2) *Determination of period of employment on a daily basis.*—(i) *In general.*—Expenses paid for a period during only part of which the taxpayer is gainfully employed or in active search of gainful employment must be allocated on a daily basis.

* * *

(d) *Care of qualifying individual and household services.*—(1) *In general.*—To qualify for the dependent care credit, expenses must be for the care of a qualifying individual. Expenses are for the care of a qualifying individual if the primary function is to assure the individual's well-being and protection. Not all expenses relating to a qualifying individual are for the individual's care. Amounts paid for food, lodging, clothing, or education are not for the care of a qualifying individual. If, however, the care is provided in such a manner that the expenses cover other goods or services that are incidental to and inseparably a part of the care, the full amount is for care.

(2) *Allocation of expenses.*—If an expense is partly for household services or for the care of a qualifying individual and partly for other goods or services, a reasonable allocation must be made. Only so much of the expense that is allocable to the household services or care of a qualifying individual is an employment-related expense. An allocation must be made if a housekeeper or other domestic employee performs household duties and cares for the qualifying children of the taxpayer and also performs other services for the taxpayer. No allocation is required, however, if the expense for the other purpose is minimal or insignificant or if an expense is partly attributable to the care of a qualifying individual and partly to household services.

(3) *Household services.*—Expenses for household services may be employment-related expenses if the services are performed in connection with the care of a qualifying individual. The household services must be the performance in and about the taxpayer's home of ordinary and usual services necessary to the maintenance of the household and attributable to the care of the qualifying individual. Services of a housekeeper are household services within the meaning of this paragraph (d)(3) if the services are provided, at least in part, to the qualifying individual. Such services as are performed by chauffeurs, bartenders, or gardeners are not household services.

(4) *Manner of providing care.*—The manner of providing care need not be the least expensive alternative available to the taxpayer. The cost of a paid caregiver may be an expense for the care of a qualifying individual even if another caregiver is available at no cost.

(5) *School or similar program.*—Expenses for a child in nursery school, pre-school, or similar programs for children below the level of kindergarten are for the care of a qualifying individual and may be employment-related expenses. Expenses for a child in kindergarten or a higher grade are not for the care of a qualifying individual. However, expenses for before-or after-school care of a child in kindergarten or a higher grade may be for the care of a qualifying individual.

(6) *Overnight camps.*—Expenses for overnight camps are not employment-related expenses.

(7) *Day camps.*—(i) The cost of a day camp or similar program may be for the care of a qualifying individual and an employment-related expense, without allocation under paragraph (d)(2) of this section, even if the day camp specializes in a particular activity. Summer school and tutoring programs are not for the care of a qualifying individual and the costs are not employment-related expenses.

(ii) A day camp that meets the definition of *dependent care center* in section 21(b)(2)(D) and paragraph (e)(2) of this section must comply with the requirements of section 21(b)(2)(C) and paragraph (e)(2) of this section.

(8) *Transportation.*—The cost of transportation by a dependent care provider of a qualifying individual to or from a place where care of that qualifying individual is provided may be for the care of the qualifying individual. The cost of transportation not provided by a dependent care provider is not for the care of the qualifying individual.

(9) *Employment taxes.*—Taxes under sections 3111 (relating to the Federal Insurance Contributions Act) and 3301 (relating to the Federal Unemployment Tax Act) and similar state payroll taxes are employment-related expenses if paid in respect of wages that are employment-related expenses.

(10) *Room and board.*—The additional cost of providing room and board for a caregiver over usual household expenditures may be an employment-related expense.

(11) *Indirect expenses.*—Expenses that relate to, but are not directly for, the care of a qualifying individual, such as application fees, agency fees, and deposits, may be for the care of a qualifying individual and may be employment-related expenses if the taxpayer is required to pay the expenses to obtain the related

care. However, forfeited deposits and other payments are not for the care of a qualifying individual if care is not provided.

(12) *Examples.*—The provisions of this paragraph (d) are illustrated by the following examples:

Example 1. To be gainfully employed, K sends his 3-year old child to a pre-school. The pre-school provides lunch and snacks. Under paragraph (d)(1) of this section, K is not required to allocate expenses between care and the lunch and snacks, because the lunch and snacks are incidental to and inseparably a part of the care. Therefore, K may treat the full amount paid to the pre-school as for the care of his child.

Example 2. L, a member of the armed forces, is ordered to a combat zone. To be able to comply with the orders, L places her 10-year old child in boarding school. The school provides education, meals, and housing to L's child in addition to care. Under paragraph (d)(2) of this section, L must allocate the cost of the boarding school between expenses for care and expenses for education and other services not constituting care. Only the part of the cost of the boarding school that is for the care of L's child is an employment-related expense under section 21.

Example 3. To be gainfully employed, M employs a full-time housekeeper to care for M's two children, aged 9 and 13 years. The housekeeper regularly performs household services of cleaning and cooking and drives M to and from M's place of employment, a trip of 15 minutes each way. Under paragraph (d)(3) of this section, the chauffeur services are not household services. M is not required to allocate a portion of the expense of the housekeeper to the chauffeur services under paragraph (d)(2) of this section, however, because the chauffeur services are minimal and insignificant. Further, no allocation under paragraph (d)(2) of this section is required to determine the portion of the expenses attributable to the care of the 13-year old child (not a qualifying individual) because the household expenses are in part attributable to the care of the 9-year old child. Accordingly, the entire expense of employing the housekeeper is an employment-related expense. The amount that M may take into account as an employment-related expense under section 21, however, is limited to the amount allowable for one qualifying individual.

Example 4. To be gainfully employed, N sends her 9-year old child to a summer day camp that offers computer activities and recreational activities such as swimming and arts and crafts. Under paragraph (d)(7)(i) of this section, the full cost of the summer day camp may be for care.

Example 5. To be gainfully employed, O sends her 9-year old child to a math tutoring program for two hours per day during the summer. Under paragraph (d)(7)(i) of this section, the cost of the tutoring program is not for care.

Example 6. To be gainfully employed, P hires a full-time housekeeper to care for her 8-year old child. In order to accommodate the housekeeper, P moves from a 2-bedroom apartment to a 3-bedroom apartment that otherwise is comparable to the 2-bedroom apartment. Under paragraph (d)(10) of this section, the additional cost to rent the 3-bedroom apartment over the cost of the 2-bedroom apartment and any additional utilities attributable to the housekeeper's residence in the household may be employment-related expenses under section 21.

Example 7. Q pays a fee to an agency to obtain the services of an au pair to care for Q's children, qualifying individuals, to enable Q to be gainfully employed. An au pair from the agency subsequently provides care for Q's children. Under paragraph (d)(11) of this section, the fee may be an employment-related expense.

Example 8. R places a deposit with a pre-school to reserve a place for her child. R sends the child to a different pre-school and forfeits the deposit. Under paragraph (d)(11) of this section, the forfeited deposit is not an employment-related expense.

(e) *Services outside the taxpayer's household.*—(1) *In general.*—The credit is allowable for expenses for services performed outside the taxpayer's household only if the care is for one or more qualifying individuals who are described in this section at

(i) Paragraph (b)(1)(i) or (b)(2)(i); or

(ii) Paragraph (b)(1)(ii), (b)(2)(ii), (b)(1)(iii), or (b)(2)(iii) and regularly spend at least 8 hours each day in the taxpayer's household.

(2) *Dependent care centers.*—(i) *In general.*—The credit is allowable for services performed by a dependent care center only if

(A) The center complies with all applicable laws and regulations, if any, of a state or local government, such as state or local licensing requirements and building and fire code regulations; and

(B) The requirements provided in this paragraph (e) are met.

(ii) *Definition.*—The term *dependent care center* means any facility that provides full-time or part-time care for more than six individuals (other than individuals who reside at the facility) on a regular basis during the taxpayer's taxable year, and receives a fee, payment, or grant for providing services for the individuals (regardless of whether the facility is operated for profit). For purposes of the preceding sentence, a facility is presumed to provide full-time or part-time care for six or fewer individuals on a regular basis during the taxpayer's taxable year if the facility has six or fewer individuals (including the taxpayer's qualifying individual) enrolled for full-time or part-time care on the day the qualifying individual is enrolled in the facility (or on the first day of the taxable year the qualifying individual attends the facility if the qualifying individual was enrolled in the facility in the preceding taxable year) unless the Internal Revenue Service demonstrates that the facility provides full-time or part-time care for more than six individuals on a regular basis during the taxpayer's taxable year.

* * *

[Reg. 1.21-1.]

[*T.D.* 9354, 8-13-2007.]

§ 1.21-2. Limitations on amount creditable.—(a) *Annual dollar limitation.*—(1) The amount of employment-related expenses that may be taken into account under § 1.21-1(a) for any taxable year cannot exceed—

(i) $2,400 ($3,000 for taxable years beginning after December 31, 2002, and before January 1, 2011) if there is one qualifying individual with respect to the taxpayer at any time during the taxable year; or

(ii) $4,800 ($6,000 for taxable years beginning after December 31, 2002, and before January 1, 2011) if there are two or more qualifying individuals with respect to the taxpayer at any time during the taxable year.

(2) The amount determined under paragraph (a)(1) of this section is reduced by the aggregate amount excludable from gross income under section 129 for the taxable year.

(3) A taxpayer may take into account the total amount of employment-related expenses that do not exceed the annual dollar limitation although the amount of employment-related expenses attributable to one qualifying individual is disproportionate to the total employment-related expenses. For example, a taxpayer with expenses in 2007 of $4,000 for one qualifying individual and $1,500 for a second qualifying individual may take into account the full $5,500.

(4) A taxpayer is not required to prorate the annual dollar limitation if a qualifying individual ceases to qualify (for example, by turning age 13) during the taxable year. However, the taxpayer may take into account only amounts that qualify as employment-related expenses before the disqualifying event. See also § 1.21-1(b)(6).

(b) *Earned income limitation.*—(1) *In general.*—The amount of employment-related expenses that may be taken into account under section 21 for any taxable year cannot exceed—

(i) For a taxpayer who is not married at the close of the taxable year, the taxpayer's earned income for the taxable year; or

(ii) For a taxpayer who is married at the close of the taxable year, the lesser of the taxpayer's earned income or the earned income of the taxpayer's spouse for the taxable year.

(2) *Determination of spouse.*—For purposes of this paragraph (b), a taxpayer must take into account only the earned income of a spouse to whom the taxpayer is married at the close of the taxable year. The spouse's earned income for the entire taxable year is taken into account, however, even though the taxpayer and the spouse were married for only part of the taxable year. The taxpayer is not required to take into account the earned income of a spouse who died or was divorced or separated from the taxpayer during the taxable year. See § 1.21-3(b) for rules providing that certain married taxpayers legally separated or living apart are treated as not married.

(3) *Definition of earned income.*—For purposes of this section, the term *earned income* has the same meaning as in section 32(c)(2) and the regulations thereunder.

(4) *Attribution of earned income to student or incapacitated spouse.*—(i) For purposes of this section, a spouse is deemed, for each month during which the spouse is a full-time student or is a qualifying individual described in § 1.21-1(b)(1)(iii) or (b)(2)(iii), to be gainfully employed and to have earned income of not less than—

(A) $200 ($250 for taxable years beginning after December 31, 2002, and before January 1, 2011) if there is one qualifying individual with respect to the taxpayer at any time during the taxable year; or

(B) $400 ($500 for taxable years beginning after December 31, 2002, and before January 1, 2011) if there are two or more qualifying individuals with respect to the taxpayer at any time during the taxable year.

(ii) For purposes of this paragraph (b)(4), a full-time student is an individual who, during each of 5 calendar months of the taxpayer's taxable year, is enrolled as a student for the number of course hours considered to be a full-time course of study at an educational organization as defined in section

170(b)(1)(A)(ii). The enrollment for 5 calendar months need not be consecutive.

(iii) Earned income may be attributed under this paragraph (b)(4), in the case of any husband and wife, to only one spouse in any month.

(c) *Examples.*—The provisions of this section are illustrated by the following examples:

Example 1. In 2007, T, who is married to U, pays employment-related expenses of $5,000 for the care of one qualifying individual. T's earned income for the taxable year is $40,000 and her husband's earned income is $2,000. T did not exclude any dependent care assistance under section 129. Under paragraph (b)(1) of this section, T may take into account under section 21 only the amount of employment-related expenses that does not exceed the lesser of her earned income or the earned income of U, or $2,000.

Example 2. The facts are the same as in *Example 1* except that U is a full-time student at an educational organization within the meaning of section 170(b)(1)(A)(ii) for 9 months of the taxable year and has no earned income. Under paragraph (b)(4) of this section, U is deemed to have earned income of $2,250. T may take into account $2,250 of employment-related expenses under section 21.

Example 3. For all of 2007, V is a full-time student and W, V's husband, is an individual who is incapable of self-care (as defined in §1.21-1(b)(1)(iii)). V and W have no earned income and pay expenses of $5,000 for W's care. Under paragraph (b)(4) of this section, either V or W may be deemed to have $3,000 of earned income. However, earned income may be attributed to only one spouse under paragraph (b)(4)(iii) of this section. Under the limitation in paragraph (b)(1)(ii) of this section, the lesser of V's and W's earned income is zero. V and W may not take the expenses into account under section 21.

(d) *Cross-reference.*—For an additional limitation on the credit under section 21, see section 26. [Reg. §1.21-2.]

☐ [*T.D.* 9354, 8-13-2007.]

§1.25A-1. Calculation of education tax credit and general eligibility requirements.—(a) *Amount of education tax credit.*—An individual taxpayer is allowed a nonrefundable education tax credit against income tax imposed by chapter 1 of the Internal Revenue Code for the taxable year. The amount of the education tax credit is the total of the Hope Scholarship Credit (as described in §1.25A-3) plus the Lifetime Learning Credit (as described in §1.25A-4). For limitations on the credits allowed by subpart A of part IV of subchapter A of chapter 1 of the Internal Revenue Code, see section 26.

(b) *Coordination of Hope Scholarship Credit and Lifetime Learning Credit.*—(1) *In general.*—In the same taxable year, a taxpayer may claim a Hope Scholarship Credit for each eligible student's qualified tuition and related expenses (as defined in §1.25A-2(d)) and a Lifetime Learning Credit for one or more other students' qualified tuition and related expenses. However, a taxpayer may not claim both a Hope Scholarship Credit and a Lifetime Learning Credit with respect to the same student in the same taxable year.

(2) *Hope Scholarship Credit.*—Subject to certain limitations, a Hope Scholarship Credit may be claimed for the qualified tuition and related expenses paid during a taxable year with respect to each eligible student (as defined in §1.25A-3(d)). Qualified tuition and related expenses paid during a taxable year with respect to one student may not be taken into account in computing the amount of the Hope Scholarship Credit with respect to any other student. In addition, qualified tuition and related expenses paid during a taxable year with respect to any student for whom a Hope Scholarship Credit is claimed may not be taken into account in computing the amount of the Lifetime Learning Credit.

(3) *Lifetime Learning Credit.*—Subject to certain limitations, a Lifetime Learning Credit may be claimed for the aggregate amount of qualified tuition and related expenses paid during a taxable year with respect to students for whom no Hope Scholarship Credit is claimed.

(4) *Examples.*—The following examples illustrate the rules of this paragraph (b):

Example 1. In 1999, Taxpayer A pays qualified tuition and related expenses for his dependent, B, to attend College Y during 1999. Assuming all other relevant requirements are met, Taxpayer A may claim either a Hope Scholarship Credit or a Lifetime Learning Credit with respect to dependent B, but not both. See §1.25A-3(a) and §1.25A-4(a).

Example 2. In 1999, Taxpayer C pays $2,000 in qualified tuition and related expenses for her dependent, D, to attend College Z during 1999. In 1999, Taxpayer C also pays $500 in qualified tuition and related expenses to attend a computer course during 1999 to improve Taxpayer C's job skills. Assuming all other relevant requirements are met, Taxpayer C may claim a Hope Scholarship Credit for the $2,000 of qualified tuition and related expenses attributable to dependent D (see §1.25A-3(a)) and a Lifetime Learning Credit (see §1.25A-4(a))for the $500 of qualified tuition and related expenses incurred to improve her job skills.

Example 3. The facts are the same as in *Example 2,* except that Taxpayer C pays $3,000 in qualified tuition and related expenses for her dependent, D, to attend College Z during 1999. Although a Hope Scholarship Credit is available only with respect to the first $2,000 of qualified tuition and related expenses paid with respect to D (see § 1.25A-3(a)), Taxpayer C may not add the $1,000 of excess expenses to her $500 of qualified tuition and related expenses in computing the amount of the Lifetime Learning Credit.

(c) *Limitation based on modified adjusted gross income.*—(1) *In general.*—The education tax credit that a taxpayer may otherwise claim is phased out ratably for taxpayers with modified adjusted gross income between $40,000 and $50,000 ($80,000 and $100,000 for married individuals who file a joint return). Thus, taxpayers with modified adjusted gross income above $50,000 (or $100,000 for joint filers) may not claim an education tax credit.

(2) *Modified adjusted gross income defined.*—The term *modified adjusted gross income* means the adjusted gross income (as defined in section 62) of the taxpayer for the taxable year increased by any amount excluded from gross income under section 911, 931, or 933 (relating to income earned abroad or from certain U.S. possessions or Puerto Rico).

(3) *Inflation adjustment.*—For taxable years beginning after 2001, the amounts in paragraph (c) (1) of this section will be increased for inflation occurring after 2000 in accordance with section 1(f) (3). If any amount adjusted under this paragraph (c) (3) is not a multiple of $1,000, the amount will be rounded to the next lowest multiple of $1,000.

(d) *Election.*—No education tax credit is allowed unless a taxpayer elects to claim the credit on the taxpayer's federal income tax return for the taxable year in which the credit is claimed. The election is made by attaching Form 8863, "Education Credits (Hope and Lifetime Learning Credits)," to the Federal income tax return.

(e) *Identification requirement.*—No education tax credit is allowed unless a taxpayer includes on the federal income tax return claiming the credit the name and the taxpayer identification number of the student for whom the credit is claimed. For rules relating to assessment for an omission of a correct taxpayer identification number, see section 6213(b) and (g) (2) (J).

(f) *Claiming the credit in the case of a dependent.*—(1) *In general.*—If a student is a claimed dependent of another taxpayer, only that taxpayer may claim the education tax credit for the student's qualified tuition and related expenses. However, if another taxpayer is eligible to, but does not, claim the student as a dependent, only the student may claim the education tax credit for the student's qualified tuition and related expenses.

(2) *Examples.*—The following examples illustrate the rules of this paragraph (f):

Example 1. In 1999, Taxpayer A pays qualified tuition and related expenses for his dependent, B, to attend University Y during 1999. Taxpayer A claims B as a dependent on his federal income tax return. Therefore, assuming all other relevant requirements are met, Taxpayer A is allowed an education tax credit on his federal income tax return, and B is not allowed an education tax credit on B's federal income tax return. The result would be the same if B paid the qualified tuition and related expenses. See § 1.25A-5(a).

Example 2. In 1999, Taxpayer C has one dependent, D. In 1999, D pays qualified tuition and related expenses to attend University Z during 1999. Although Taxpayer C is eligible to claim D as a dependent on her federal income tax return, she does not do so. Therefore, assuming all other relevant requirements are met, D is allowed an education tax credit on D's federal income tax return, and Taxpayer C is not allowed an education tax credit on her federal income tax return, with respect to D's education expenses. The result would be the same if C paid the qualified tuition and related expenses on behalf of D. See § 1.25A-5(b).

(g) *Married taxpayers.*—If a taxpayer is married (within the meaning of section 7703), no education tax credit is allowed to the taxpayer unless the taxpayer and the taxpayer's spouse file a joint Federal income tax return for the taxable year.

* * *

[Reg. § 1.25A-1.]

☐ [*T.D.* 9034, 12-24-2002.]

Proposed Amendment to Regulation

§ 1.25A-1. Calculation of education tax credit and general eligibility requirements.

* * *

(e) *Identification requirements.*—(1) *In general.*—No education tax credit is allowed unless a taxpayer includes on the federal income tax return claiming the credit the name and the taxpayer identification number (TIN) of the student for whom the credit is claimed. For rules relating to assessment for an omission of a correct taxpayer identification number, see section 6213(b) and (g)(2)(J).

(2) *Additional identification requirements for the American Opportunity Tax Credit (AOTC).*—(i) *TIN must be issued on or before the due date of the original return.*—For any federal income tax return (including an amended return) filed after December 18, 2015, no AOTC is allowed unless the TIN of the student and the TIN for the taxpayer claiming the credit are issued on or before the due date, or the extended due date if the extension request is timely filed, for filing the return for the taxable year for which the credit is claimed.

(ii) *Return must include the eligible educational institution's employer identification number (EIN).*—For taxable years beginning after December 31, 2015, no AOTC is allowed unless the taxpayer includes the EIN of each eligible educational institution to which qualified tuition and related expenses were paid.

(3) *Applicability dates.*—(i) Except as provided in paragraphs (e)(3)(ii) and (iii) of this section, this paragraph (e) applies on or after December 26, 2002.

(ii) Paragraph (e)(2)(i) of this section applies to federal income tax returns (including amended returns) filed after December 18, 2015.

(iii) Paragraph (e)(2)(ii) of this section applies to taxable years beginning after December 31, 2015.

* * *

[Prop. Reg. § 1.25A-1.]

[Proposed 8-2-2016.]

§ 1.25A-2. Definitions.—(a) *Claimed dependent.*—A *claimed dependent* means a dependent (as defined in section 152) for whom a deduction under section 151 is allowed on a taxpayer's federal income tax return for the taxable year. Among other requirements under section 152, a nonresident alien student must be a resident of a country contiguous to the United States in order to be treated as a dependent.

(b) *Eligible educational institution.*—(1) *In general.*—In general, an *eligible educational institution* means a college, university, vocational school, or other postsecondary educational institution that is—

(i) Described in section 481 of the Higher Education Act of 1965 (20 U.S.C. 1088) as in effect on August 5, 1997, (generally all accredited public, nonprofit, and proprietary postsecondary institutions); and

(ii) Participating in a federal financial aid program under title IV of the Higher Education Act of 1965 or is certified by the Department of Education as eligible to participate in such a program but chooses not to participate.

(2) *Rules on federal financial aid programs.*—For rules governing an educational institution's eligibility to participate in federal financial aid programs, see 20 U.S.C. 1070; 20 U.S.C. 1094; and 34 CFR 600 and 668.

(c) *Academic period.*— *Academic period* means a quarter, semester, trimester, or other period of study as reasonably determined by an eligible educational institution. In the case of an eligible educational institution that uses credit hours or clock hours, and does not have academic terms, each payment period (as defined in 34 CFR 668.4, revised as of July 1, 2002) may be treated as an academic period.

(d) *Qualified tuition and related expenses.*—(1) *In general.*— *Qualified tuition and related expenses* means tuition and fees required for the enrollment or attendance of a student for courses of instruction at an eligible educational institution.

(2) *Required fees.*—(i) *In general.*—Except as provided in paragraph (d)(3) of this section, the test for determining whether any fee is a qualified tuition and related expense is whether the fee is required to be paid to the eligible educational institution as a condition of the student's enrollment or attendance at the institution.

(ii) *Books, supplies, and equipment.*—Qualified tuition and related expenses include fees for books, supplies, and equipment used in a course of study only if the fees must be paid to the eligible educational institution for the enrollment or attendance of the student at the institution.

(iii) *Nonacademic fees.*—Except as provided in paragraph (d)(3) of this section, qualified tuition and related expenses include fees charged by an eligible educational institution that are not used directly for, or allocated to, an academic course of instruction only if the fee must be paid to the eligible educational institution for the enrollment or attendance of the student at the institution.

(3) *Personal expenses.*—Qualified tuition and related expenses do not include the costs of room and board, insurance, medical expenses (including student health fees), transportation, and similar personal, living, or family expenses, regardless of whether the fee must be paid to the eligible educational institution for the enrollment or attendance of the student at the institution.

(4) *Treatment of a comprehensive or bundled fee.*—If a student is required to pay a fee

(such as a comprehensive fee or a bundled fee) to an eligible educational institution that combines charges for qualified tuition and related expenses with charges for personal expenses described in paragraph (d)(3) of this section, the portion of the fee that is allocable to personal expenses is not included in qualified tuition and related expenses. The determination of what portion of the fee relates to qualified tuition and related expenses and what portion relates to personal expenses must be made by the institution using a reasonable method of allocation.

(5) *Hobby courses.*—Qualified tuition and related expenses do not include expenses that relate to any course of instruction or other education that involves sports, games, or hobbies, or any noncredit course, unless the course or other education is part of the student's degree program, or in the case of the Lifetime Learning Credit, the student takes the course to acquire or improve job skills.

(6) *Examples.*—The following examples illustrate the rules of this paragraph (d). In each example, assume that the institution is an eligible educational institution and that all other relevant requirements to claim an education tax credit are met. The examples are as follows:

Example 1. University V offers a degree program in dentistry. In addition to tuition, all students enrolled in the program are required to pay a fee to University V for the rental of dental equipment. Because the equipment rental fee must be paid to University V for enrollment and attendance, the tuition and the equipment rental fee are qualified tuition and related expenses.

Example 2. First-year students at College W are required to obtain books and other reading materials used in its mandatory first-year curriculum. The books and other reading materials are not required to be purchased from College W and may be borrowed from other students or purchased from off-campus bookstores, as well as from College W's bookstore. College W bills students for any books and materials purchased from College W's bookstore. The fee that College W charges for the first-year books and materials purchased at its bookstore is not a qualified tuition and related expense because the books and materials are not required to be purchased from College W for enrollment or attendance at the institution.

Example 3. All students who attend College X are required to pay a separate student activity fee in addition to their tuition. The student activity fee is used solely to fund on-campus organizations and activities run by students, such as the student newspaper and the student government (no portion of the fee covers personal expenses). Although labeled as a student activity fee, the fee is required for enrollment or attendance at College X. Therefore, the fee is a qualified tuition and related expense.

Example 4. The facts are the same as in *Example 3,* except that College X offers an optional athletic fee that students may pay to receive discounted tickets to sports events. The athletic fee is not required for enrollment or attendance at College X. Therefore, the fee is not a qualified tuition and related expense.

Example 5. College Y requires all students to live on campus. It charges a single comprehensive fee to cover tuition, required fees, and room and board. Based on College Y's reasonable allocation, sixty percent of the comprehensive fee is allocable to tuition and other required fees not allocable to personal expenses, and the remaining forty percent of the comprehensive fee is allocable to charges for room and board and other personal expenses. Therefore, only sixty percent of College Y's comprehensive fee is a qualified tuition and related expense.

Example 6. As a degree student at College Z, Student A is required to take a certain number of courses outside of her chosen major in Economics. To fulfill this requirement, Student A enrolls in a square dancing class offered by the Physical Education Department. Because Student A receives credit toward her degree program for the square dancing class, the tuition for the square dancing class is included in qualified tuition and related expenses.

[Reg. § 1.25A-2.]

□ [*T.D.* 9034, 12-24-2002.]

§ 1.25A-3. Hope Scholarship Credit.—(a) *Amount of the credit.*—(1) *In general.*—Subject to the phaseout of the education tax credit described in § 1.25A-1(c), the Hope Scholarship Credit amount is the total of—

(i) 100 percent of the first $1,000 of qualified tuition and related expenses paid during the taxable year for education furnished to an eligible student (as defined in paragraph (d) of this section) who is the taxpayer, the taxpayer's spouse, or any claimed dependent during any academic period beginning in the taxable year (or treated as beginning in the taxable year, see § 1.25A-5(e)(2)); plus

(ii) 50 percent of the next $1,000 of such expenses paid with respect to that student.

(2) *Maximum credit.*—For taxable years beginning before 2002, the maximum Hope Scholarship Credit allowed for each eligible student is $1,500. For taxable years beginning after 2001, the amounts used in paragraph

(a)(1) of this section to determine the maximum credit will be increased for inflation occurring after 2000 in accordance with section 1(f)(3). If any amount adjusted under this paragraph (a)(2) is not a multiple of $100, the amount will be rounded to the next lowest multiple of $100.

(b) *Per student credit.*—(1) *In general.*—A Hope Scholarship Credit may be claimed for the qualified tuition and related expenses of each eligible student (as defined in paragraph (d) of this section).

(2) *Example.*—The following example illustrates the rule of this paragraph (b). In the example, assume that all the requirements to claim an education tax credit are met. The example is as follows:

Example. In 1999, Taxpayer A has two dependents, B and C, both of whom are eligible students. Taxpayer A pays $1,600 in qualified tuition and related expenses for dependent B to attend a community college. Taxpayer A pays $5,000 in qualified tuition and related expenses for dependent C to attend University X. Taxpayer A may claim a Hope Scholarship Credit of $1,300 ($1,000 + (.50 × $600)) for dependent B, and the maximum $1,500 Hope Scholarship Credit for dependent C, for a total Hope Scholarship Credit of $2,800.

(c) *Credit allowed for only two taxable years.*—For each eligible student, the Hope Scholarship Credit may be claimed for no more than two taxable years.

(d) *Eligible student.*—(1) *Eligible student defined.*—For purposes of the Hope Scholarship Credit, the term *eligible student* means a student who satisfies all of the following requirements—

(i) *Degree requirement.*—For at least one academic period that begins during the taxable year, the student enrolls at an eligible educational institution in a program leading toward a postsecondary degree, certificate, or other recognized postsecondary educational credential;

(ii) *Work load requirement.*—For at least one academic period that begins during the taxable year, the student enrolls for at least one-half of the normal full-time work load for the course of study the student is pursuing. The standard for what is half of the normal full-time work load is determined by each eligible educational institution. However, the standard for half-time may not be lower than the applicable standard for half-time established by the Department of Education under the Higher Education Act of 1965 and set forth in 34 CFR 674.2(b) (revised as of July 1, 2002) for a half-time undergraduate student;

(iii) *Year of study requirement.*—As of the beginning of the taxable year, the student has not completed the first two years of postsecondary education at an eligible educational institution. Whether a student has completed the first two years of postsecondary education at an eligible educational institution as of the beginning of a taxable year is determined based on whether the institution in which the student is enrolled in a degree program (as described in paragraph (d)(1)(i) of this section) awards the student two years of academic credit at that institution for postsecondary course work completed by the student prior to the beginning of the taxable year. Any academic credit awarded by the eligible educational institution solely on the basis of the student's performance on proficiency examinations is disregarded in determining whether the student has completed two years of postsecondary education; and

(iv) *No felony drug conviction.*—The student has not been convicted of a federal or state felony offense for possession or distribution of a controlled substance as of the end of the taxable year for which the credit is claimed.

* * *

(e) *Academic period for prepayments.*—(1) *In general.*—For purposes of determining whether a student meets the requirements in paragraph (d) of this section for a taxable year, if qualified tuition and related expenses are paid during one taxable year for an academic period that begins during January, February or March of the next taxable year (for taxpayers on a fiscal taxable year, use the first three months of the next taxable year), the academic period is treated as beginning during the taxable year in which the payment is made.

(2) *Example.*—The following example illustrates the rule of this paragraph (e). In the example, assume that all the requirements to claim a Hope Scholarship Credit are met. The example is as follows:

Example. Student G graduates from high school in June 1998. After graduation, Student G works full-time for several months to earn money for college. Student G is enrolled on a full-time basis in an undergraduate degree program at University W, an eligible educational institution, for the 1999 Spring semester, which begins in January 1999. Student G pays tuition to University W for the 1999 Spring semester in December 1998. Because the tuition paid by Student G in 1998 relates to an academic period that begins during the first three months of 1999, Student G's eligibility to claim a Hope

Scholarship Credit in 1998 is determined as if the 1999 Spring semester began in 1998. Thus, assuming Student G has not been convicted of a felony drug offense as of December 31, 1998, Student G is an eligible student for 1998.

* * *

[Reg. § 1.25A-3.]

☐ [*T.D.* 9034, 12-24-2002 (*corrected* 4-1-2003).]

§ 1.25A-4. Lifetime Learning Credit.—(a) *Amount of the credit.*

* * *

(2) *Taxable years beginning after December 31, 2002.*—Subject to the phaseout of the education tax credit described in § 1.25A-1(c), for taxable years beginning after 2002, the Lifetime Learning Credit amount is 20 percent of up to $10,000 of qualified tuition and related expenses paid during the taxable year for education furnished to the taxpayer, the taxpayer's spouse, and any claimed dependent during any academic period beginning in the taxable year (or treated as beginning in the taxable year, see § 1.25A-5(e)(2)).

(3) *Coordination with the Hope Scholarship Credit.*—Expenses paid with respect to a student for whom the Hope Scholarship Credit is claimed are not eligible for the Lifetime Learning Credit.

(4) *Examples.*—The following examples illustrate the rules of this paragraph (a). In each example, assume that all the requirements to claim a Lifetime Learning Credit or a Hope Scholarship Credit, as applicable, are met. The examples are as follows:

Example 1. In 1999, Taxpayer A pays qualified tuition and related expenses of $3,000 for dependent B to attend an eligible educational institution, and Taxpayer A pays qualified tuition and related expenses of $4,000 for dependent C to attend an eligible educational institution. Taxpayer A does not claim a Hope Scholarship Credit with respect to either B or C. Although Taxpayer A paid $7,000 of qualified tuition and related expenses during the taxable year, Taxpayer A may claim the Lifetime Learning Credit with respect to only $5,000 of such expenses. Therefore, the maximum Lifetime Learning Credit Taxpayer A may claim for 1999 is $1,000 (.20 × $5,000).

Example 2. In 1999, Taxpayer D pays $6,000 of qualified tuition and related expenses for dependent E, and $2,000 of qualified tuition and related expenses for dependent F, to attend eligible educational institutions. Dependent F has already completed the first two years of postsecondary education. For 1999, Taxpayer D claims the maximum $1,500 Hope Scholarship Credit with respect to dependent E. In computing the amount of the Lifetime Learning Credit, Taxpayer D may not include any of the $6,000 of qualified tuition and related expenses paid on behalf of dependent E but may include the $2,000 of qualified tuition and related expenses of dependent F.

(b) *Credit allowed for unlimited number of taxable years.*—There is no limit to the number of taxable years that a taxpayer may claim a Lifetime Learning Credit with respect to any student.

(c) *Both degree and nondegree courses are eligible for the credit.*—(1) *In general.*—For purposes of the Lifetime Learning Credit, amounts paid for a course at an eligible educational institution are qualified tuition and related expenses if the course is either part of a postsecondary degree program or is not part of a postsecondary degree program but is taken by the student to acquire or improve job skills.

(2) *Examples.*—The following examples illustrate the rule of this paragraph (c). In each example, assume that all the requirements to claim a Lifetime Learning Credit are met. The examples are as follows:

Example 1. Taxpayer A, a professional photographer, enrolls in an advanced photography course at a local community college. Although the course is not part of a degree program, Taxpayer A enrolls in the course to improve her job skills. The course fee paid by Taxpayer A is a qualified tuition and related expense for purposes of the Lifetime Learning Credit.

Example 2. Taxpayer B, a stockbroker, plans to travel abroad on a "photo-safari" for his next vacation. In preparation for the trip, Taxpayer B enrolls in a noncredit photography class at a local community college. Because Taxpayer B is not taking the photography course as part of a degree program or to acquire or improve his job skills, amounts paid by Taxpayer B for the course are not qualified tuition and related expenses for purposes of the Lifetime Learning Credit.

* * *

[Reg. § 1.25A-4.]

☐ [*T.D.* 9034, 12-24-2002.]

§ 1.25A-5. Special rules relating to characterization and timing of payments.—(a) *Educational expenses paid by claimed dependent.*—For any taxable year for which the student is a claimed dependent of another taxpayer, qualified tuition and related expenses paid by the student are treated as paid by the taxpayer to whom the deduction under section 151 is allowed.

(b) *Educational expenses paid by a third party.*—(1) *In general.*—Solely for purposes of section 25A, if a third party (someone other than the taxpayer, the taxpayer's spouse if the taxpayer is treated as married within the meaning of section 7703, or a claimed dependent) makes a payment directly to an eligible educational institution to pay for a student's qualified tuition and related expenses, the student is treated as receiving the payment from the third party and, in turn, paying the qualified tuition and related expenses to the institution.

(2) *Special rule for tuition reduction included in gross income of employee.*—Solely for purposes of section 25A, if an eligible educational institution provides a reduction in tuition to an employee of the institution (or to the spouse or dependent child of an employee, as described in section 132(h)(2)) and the amount of the tuition reduction is included in the employee's gross income, the employee is treated as receiving payment of an amount equal to the tuition reduction and, in turn, paying such amount to the institution.

(3) *Examples.*—The following examples illustrate the rules of this paragraph (b). In each example, assume that all the requirements to claim an education tax credit are met. The examples are as follows:

Example 1. Grandparent D makes a direct payment to an eligible educational institution for Student E's qualified tuition and related expenses. Student E is not a claimed dependent in 1999. For purposes of claiming an education tax credit, Student E is treated as receiving the money from her grandparent and, in turn, paying her qualified tuition and related expenses.

Example 2. Under a court-approved divorce decree, Parent A is required to pay Student C's college tuition. Parent A makes a direct payment to an eligible educational institution for Student C's 1999 tuition. Under paragraph (b)(1) of this section, Student C is treated as receiving the money from Parent A and, in turn, paying the qualified tuition and related expenses. Under the divorce decree, Parent B has custody of Student C for 1999. Parent B properly claims Student C as a dependent on Parent B's 1999 federal income tax return. Under paragraph (a) of this section, expenses paid by Student C are treated as paid by Parent B. Thus, Parent B may claim an education tax credit for the qualified tuition and related expenses paid directly to the institution by Parent A.

Example 3. University A, an eligible educational institution, offers reduced tuition charges to its employees and their dependent children. F is an employee of University A. F's dependent child, G, enrolls in a graduate-level course at University A. Section 117(d) does not apply, because it is limited to tuition reductions provided for education below the graduate level. Therefore, the amount of the tuition reduction received by G is treated as additional compensation from University A to F and is included in F's gross income. For purposes of claiming a Lifetime Learning Credit, F is treated as receiving payment of an amount equal to the tuition reduction from University A and, in turn, paying such amount to University A on behalf of F's child, G.

(c) *Adjustment to qualified tuition and related expenses for certain excludable educational assistance.*—(1) *In general.*—In determining the amount of an education tax credit, qualified tuition and related expenses for any academic period must be reduced by the amount of any tax-free educational assistance allocable to such period. For this purpose, *tax-free educational assistance* means—

(i) A qualified scholarship that is excludable from income under section 117;

(ii) A veterans' or member of the armed forces' educational assistance allowance under chapter 30, 31, 32, 34 or 35 of title 38, United States Code, or under chapter 1606 of title 10, United States Code;

(iii) Employer-provided educational assistance that is excludable from income under section 127; or

(iv) Any other educational assistance that is excludable from gross income (other than as a gift, bequest, devise, or inheritance within the meaning of section 102(a)).

(2) *No adjustment for excludable educational assistance attributable to expenses paid in a prior year.*—A reduction is not required under paragraph (c)(1) of this section if the amount of excludable educational assistance received during the taxable year is treated as a refund of qualified tuition and related expenses paid in a prior taxable year. See paragraph (f)(5) of this section.

(3) *Scholarships and fellowship grants.*—For purposes of paragraph (c)(1)(i) of this section, a scholarship or fellowship grant is treated as a qualified scholarship excludable under section 117 except to the extent—

(i) The scholarship or fellowship grant (or any portion thereof) may be applied, by its terms, to expenses other than qualified tuition and related expenses within the meaning of section 117(b)(2) (such as room and board) and the student reports the grant (or the appropriate portion thereof) as income on the student's federal income tax return if the student is required to file a return; or

(ii) The scholarship or fellowship grant (or any portion thereof) must be applied, by its terms, to expenses other than qualified tuition and related expenses within the meaning of section 117(b)(2) (such as room and board) and the student reports the grant (or the appropriate portion thereof) as income on the student's federal income tax return if the student is required to file a return.

* * *

(d) *No double benefit.*—Qualified tuition and related expenses do not include any expense for which a deduction is allowed under section 162, section 222, or any other provision of chapter 1 of the Internal Revenue Code.

(e) *Timing rules.*—(1) *In general.*—Except as provided in paragraph (e)(2) of this section, an education tax credit is allowed only for payments of qualified tuition and related expenses for an academic period beginning in the same taxable year as the year the payment is made. Except for certain individuals who do not use the cash receipts and disbursements method of accounting, qualified tuition and related expenses are treated as paid in the year in which the expenses are actually paid. See §1.461-1(a)(1).

(2) *Prepayment rule.*—(i) *In general.*—If qualified tuition and related expenses are paid during one taxable year for an academic period that begins during the first three months of the taxpayer's next taxable year (i.e., in January, February, or March of the next taxable year for calendar year taxpayers), an education tax credit is allowed with respect to the qualified tuition and related expenses only in the taxable year in which the expenses are paid.

(ii) *Example.*—The following example illustrates the rule of this paragraph (e)(2). In the example, assume that all the requirements to claim an education tax credit are met. The example is as follows:

Example. In December 1998, Taxpayer A, a calendar year taxpayer, pays College Z $1,000 in qualified tuition and related expenses to attend classes during the 1999 Spring semester, which begins in January 1999. Taxpayer A may claim an education tax credit only in 1998 for payments made in 1998 for the 1999 Spring semester.

* * *

[Reg. §1.25A-5.]

□ [*T.D.* 9034, 12-24-2002 (*corrected* 4-1-2003).]

Alternative Minimum Tax

§1.55-1. Alternative minimum taxable income.—(a) *General rule for computing alternative minimum taxable income.*—Except as otherwise provided by statute, regulations, or other published guidance issued by the Commissioner, all Internal Revenue Code provisions that apply in determining the regular taxable income of a taxpayer also apply in determining the alternative minimum taxable income of the taxpayer.

(b) *Items based on adjusted gross income or modified adjusted gross income.*—In determining the alternative minimum taxable income of a taxpayer other than a corporation, all references to the taxpayer's adjusted gross income or modified adjusted gross income in determining the amount of items of income, exclusion, or deduction must be treated as references to the taxpayer's adjusted gross income or modified adjusted gross income as determined for regular tax purposes.

* * *

[Reg. §1.55-1.]

□ [*T.D.* 8569, 11-23-94.]

§1.56(g)-1. Adjusted current earnings.—(a) *Adjustment for adjusted current earnings.*—(1) *Positive adjustment.*—For taxable years beginning after December 31, 1989, the alternative minimum taxable income of any taxpayer described in paragraph (a)(4) of this section is increased by the adjustment for adjusted current earnings. The adjustment for adjusted current earnings is 75 percent of the excess, if any, of—

(i) The adjusted current earnings (as defined in paragraph (a)(6)(ii) of this section) of the inventories to compute adjusted current earnings.taxpayer for the taxable year over

(ii) The pre-adjustment alternative minimum taxable income (as defined in paragraph (a)(6)(i) of this section) of the taxpayer for the taxable year.

(2) *Negative adjustment.*—(i) *In general.*—For taxable years beginning after December 31, 1989, the alternative minimum taxable income of any taxpayer is decreased, subject to the limitation of paragraph (a)(2)(ii) of this section, by 75 percent of the excess, if any, of pre-adjustment alternative minimum taxable income (as defined in paragraph (a)(6)(i) of this section), over adjusted current earnings (as defined in paragraph (a)(6)(ii) of this section).

(ii) *Limitation on negative adjustments.*—The amount of the negative adjustment for any taxable year is limited to the excess, if any, of—

(A) The aggregate increases in alternative minimum taxable income in prior years under paragraph (a)(1) of this section over

(B) The aggregate decreases in alternative minimum taxable income in prior years under this paragraph (a)(2).

Any excess of pre-adjustment alternative minimum taxable income over adjusted current earnings that is not allowed as a negative adjustment for the taxable year because of the limitation in this paragraph (a)(2)(ii) is not applied to reduce any positive adjustment in any other taxable year.

(iii) *Example.*—The following example illustrates the provisions of this paragraph (a)(2):

(A) Corporation P is a calendar-year taxpayer and has pre-adjustment alternative minimum taxable income and adjusted current earnings in the following amounts for 1990 through 1993:

Year	*Pre-adjustment alternative minimum taxable income*	*Adjusted current earnings*
1990	$800,000	$700,000
1991	600,000	900,000
1992	500,000	400,000
1993	500,000	100,000

(B) Under these facts, corporation P has the following positive and negative adjustments for adjusted current earnings:

Year	*Negative adjustment*	*Positive adjustment*
1990	–0–	–0–
1991	–0–	$225,000
1992	$75,000	–0–
1993	150,000	–0–

(C) In 1990, P has a potential negative adjustment (before the cumulative limitation) of $75,000 (75 percent of the $100,000 excess of pre-adjustment alternative minimum taxable income over adjusted current earnings). Nonetheless, P is not permitted a negative adjustment because P had no prior increases in its alternative minimum taxable income due to an adjustment for adjusted current earnings.

(D) In 1991, P has a positive adjustment of $225,000 (75 percent of the $300,000 excess of adjusted current earnings over pre-adjustment alternative minimum taxable income). P is not allowed to use the prior year's excess of pre-adjustment alternative minimum taxable income over adjusted current earnings to reduce its 1991 positive adjustment.

(E) In 1992, P is permitted a negative adjustment of $75,000, the full amount of 75 percent of the $100,000 excess of pre-adjustment alternative minimum taxable income over adjusted current earnings for the taxable year. This is because P's prior cumulative increases in alternative minimum taxable income due to the positive adjustments for adjusted current earnings exceed the negative adjustment for the year.

(F) In 1993, P has a potential negative adjustment (before the cumulative limitation) of $300,000 (75 percent of the $400,000 excess of pre-adjustment alternative minimum taxable income over adjusted current earnings). P's net cumulative increases in alternative minimum taxable income due to the adjustment for adjusted current earnings are $150,000 ($225,000 increase in 1991, less $75,000 decrease in 1992). Thus, P's Positive adjustment negative adjustment in 1993 is limited to $150,000. P may not use the remaining portion ($150,000) of the negative adjustment for 1993 to reduce positive adjustments in other taxable years.

(3) *Negative amounts.*—In determining whether an excess exists under paragraph (a)(1) or (a)(2) of this section, a positive amount exceeds a negative amount by the sum of the absolute numbers, and a smaller negative amount exceeds a larger negative amount by the difference between the absolute numbers. Thus, for example, a positive amount of adjusted current earnings of $30 exceeds a negative amount (or loss) of pre-adjustment AMTI of $10 by the sum of the absolute numbers, or $40 (30 + 10). Accordingly, the adjustment for adjusted current earnings would be 75 percent of $40, or $30. In contrast, a negative amount of adjusted current earnings of $10 exceeds a negative amount (or loss) of pre-adjustment alternative minimum taxable income of $30 by the difference between the absolute numbers, or $20 (30 - 10). Accordingly, the adjustment for adjusted current earnings would be 75 percent of $20, or $15.

(4) *Taxpayers subject to adjustment for adjusted current earnings.*—The adjustment for adjusted current earnings applies to any corporation other than—

(i) An S corporation as defined in section 1361,

(ii) A regulated investment company as defined in section 851,

(iii) A real estate investment trust as defined in section 856, or

(iv) A real estate mortgage investment conduit as defined in section 860A.

(5) *General rule for applying Internal Revenue Code provisions in determining adjusted current earnings.*—(i) *In general.*—Except as otherwise provided by regulations or other guidance issued by the Internal Revenue Service, all Internal Revenue Code provisions that apply in determining the regular taxable income of a taxpayer also apply in determining adjusted

current earnings. For example, the rules of part V of subchapter P (relating to original issue discount and similar matters) of the Code apply in determining the amount (and the timing) of any interest income included in adjusted current earnings under this section. In applying Code provisions, however, the adjustments of section 56(g) and this section are also taken into account. For example, in applying the capitalization provisions of section 263A, the amount of depreciation to be capitalized is based on the amount of depreciation allowed in computing adjusted current earnings.

(ii) *Example.*—The following example illustrates the provisions of this paragraph (a)(5):

(A) Corporation N is a calendar year manufacturer of golf clubs. N places new manufacturing equipment in service in 1990. The regular tax depreciation allowable for this equipment is $80,000; the pre-adjustment alternative minimum taxable income depreciation is $60,000; and the adjusted current earnings depreciation is $40,000. All of the golf clubs N produces in 1990 are unsold and are in ending inventory.

(B) Pursuant to section 263A and § 1.263A-1(e)(3)(ii)(I), N must capitalize the depreciation allowed for the year for the new manufacturing equipment in the ending inventory of golf clubs. Thus, when N sells the golf clubs (or is deemed to have sold them under its normal method of accounting), the cost of goods sold attributable to the capitalized depreciation will be $80,000 in computing regular taxable income; $60,000 in computing pre-adjustment alternative minimum taxable income; and $40,000 in computing adjusted current earnings.

(6) *Definitions.*—The following terms have the following meanings for purposes of this section.

(i) *Pre-adjustment alternative minimum taxable income.*—Pre-adjustment alternative minimum taxable income is the alternative minimum taxable income of the taxpayer for the taxable year, determined under section 55(b)(2), but without the adjustment for adjusted current earnings under section 56(g) and this section, without the alternative tax net operating loss deduction under section 56(a)(4), and without the alternative tax energy preference deduction under section 56(h).

(ii) *Adjusted current earnings.*—Adjusted current earnings is the pre-adjustment alternative minimum taxable income of the taxpayer for the taxable year, adjusted as provided in section 56(g) and this section. To the extent an amount is included (or deducted) in computing pre-adjustment alternative minimum taxable income for the taxable year (whether because an adjustment is made under section 56 or 58, because of a tax preference item under section 57, or because the item is reflected in taxable income), that amount is not again included (or deducted) in computing adjusted current earnings for the taxable year.

(iii) *Earnings and profits.*—Earnings and profits means current earnings and profits within the meaning of section 316(a)(2), that is, earnings and profits for the taxable year computed as of the close of the taxable year of the corporation without diminution by reason of any distributions made during the taxable year.

* * *

(b) *Depreciation allowed.*—The depreciation deduction allowed in computing adjusted current earnings is determined under the rules of this paragraph (b). Generally, the rules for computing the adjusted current earnings depreciation deduction differ depending on the taxable year in which the property is placed in service and the method used in computing the depreciation deduction for taxable income purposes. See § 1.168(i)-1(k) for an election to use general asset accounts.

(1) *Property placed in service after 1989.*—The depreciation deduction for property placed in service in a taxable year beginning after December 31, 1989, is the amount determined by using the alternative depreciation system of section 168(g). This paragraph (b)(1) does not apply to property to which paragraph (b)(4) of this section applies (relating to certain property described in sections 168(f)(1) through (f)(4)).

* * *

(4) *Special rule for certain section 168(f) property.*—The depreciation or amortization deduction for property described in section 168(f)(1) through (4) is determined in the same manner as used in computing taxable income, without regard to when the property is placed in service.

* * *

(c) *Inclusion in adjusted current earnings of items included in earnings and profits.*—(1) *In general.*—Except as otherwise provided in paragraph (c)(4) of this section, adjusted current earnings includes all income items that are permanently excluded from (*i.e.,* not taken into account in determining) pre-adjustment alternative minimum taxable income but that are taken into account in determining earnings and profits. An income item is considered taken into account in determining pre-adjustment alternative minimum taxable income without regard to the timing of its inclusion. Thus, this paragraph (c)(1) does not apply to any income item that is, has been, or will be included in pre-adjustment alternative minimum taxable income. For example, a taxpayer eligible to use the completed contract method of accounting for long-term construction contracts does not take income (or expenses) into account in determining pre-adjustment alternative minimum taxable income for taxable years before the taxable year the contract is completed. The taxpayer is required under section 312(n)(6) to include income (and expenses) in earnings and profits throughout the term of the contract under the percentage of completion method. This paragraph (c)(1) does not require the income on the contract to be included in adjusted current earnings, however, because the income will be taken into account in the taxable year the contract is completed and therefore is considered to be taken into account in determining pre-adjustment alternative minimum taxable income.

(2) *Certain amounts not taken into account in determining whether an item is permanently excluded.*—The fact that proceeds from an income item may eventually be reflected in pre-adjustment alternative minimum taxable income of another taxpayer on the liquidation or disposal of a business, or similar circumstances, is not taken into account in determining whether the item is permanently excluded from pre-adjustment alternative minimum taxable income. Thus, for example, a corporation's adjusted current earnings include interest excluded from pre-adjustment alternative minimum taxable income under section 103 even though the interest might eventually be reflected in the pre-adjustment alternative minimum taxable income of a corporate shareholder as gain on the liquidation of the corporation.

(3) *Allowance of offsetting deductions.*—In determining adjusted current earnings under this paragraph (c), a deduction is allowed for all items that relate to income required to be included in adjusted current earnings under this paragraph (c) and that would be deductible in computing pre-adjustment alternative minimum taxable income if the income items to which the items of deduction relate were included in pre-adjustment alternative minimum taxable income for any taxable year. For example, deductions disallowed under section 265(a)(2) for the costs of carrying tax-exempt obligations, the interest on which is excluded from pre-adjustment alternative minimum taxable income under section 103 but is included in adjusted current earnings under this paragraph (c), are generally allowed as deductions in computing adjusted current earnings. Amounts deductible under this paragraph (c)(3) are taken into account using the taxpayer's method of accounting and are subject to any provisions or limitations of the Code that would have applied if the amounts had been deductible in determining pre-adjustment alternative minimum taxable income. For example, section 267(a)(2) may affect the timing of a deduction otherwise disallowed under section 265(a)(2).

(4) *Special rules.*—Adjusted current earnings does not include the following amounts.

(i) *Income from the discharge of indebtedness.*—Amounts that are excluded from gross income under section 108 of the Internal Revenue Code of 1986 or any corresponding provision of prior law (including the Bankruptcy Tax Act of 1980, case law, income tax regulations and administrative pronouncements).

(ii) *Federal income tax refunds.*—Refunds of federal income taxes.

(iii) *Income earned on behalf of states and municipalities.*—Amounts that are excluded from gross income under section 115.

* * *

(6) *Partial list of income items excluded from gross income but included in earnings and profits.*—The following is a partial list of items that are permanently excluded from pre-adjustment alternative minimum taxable income but that are included in earnings and profits, and are therefore included in adjusted current earnings under this paragraph (c).

(i) Proceeds of life insurance contracts that are excluded under section 101, to the extent provided in paragraph (c)(5)(v) or (c)(5)(vi) of this section.

(ii) Interest that is excluded under section 103.

(iii) Amounts received as compensation for injuries or sickness that are excluded under section 104.

(iv) Income taxes of a lessor of property that are paid by a lessee and are excluded under section 110.

(v) Income attributable to the recovery of an item deducted in computing earnings and profits in a prior year that is excluded under section 111.

(vi) Amounts received as proceeds from sports programs that are excluded under section 114.

(vii) Cost-sharing payments that are excluded under section 126, to the extent section 126(e) does not apply.

(viii) Interest on loans used to acquire employer securities that is excluded under section 133.

(ix) Financial assistance that is excluded under section 597.

(x) Amounts that are excluded from pre-adjustment alternative minimum taxable income as a result of an election under section 831(b) (allowing certain insurance companies to compute their pre-adjustment alternative minimum taxable income using only their investment income).

Items described in paragraph (c)(1) of this section must be included in earnings and profits (and therefore in adjusted current earnings) even if they are not identified in this paragraph (c)(6). The Commissioner may identify additional items described in paragraph (c)(1) in other published guidance.

(7) *Partial list of items excluded from both pre-adjustment alternative minimum taxable income and adjusted current earnings.*—The following is a partial list of items that are excluded from both pre-adjustment alternative minimum taxable income and adjusted current earnings, and for which no adjustment is allowed under this section.

(i) The value of improvements made by a lessee to a lessor's property that is excluded from the lessor's income under section 109.

(ii) Contributions to the capital of a corporation by a non-shareholder that are excluded from the corporation's income under section 118.

The Commissioner may identify additional items described in this paragraph (c)(7) in other published guidance.

(d) *Disallowance of items not deductible in computing earnings and profits—.*—(1) *In general.*—Except as otherwise provided in this paragraph (d), no deduction is allowed in computing adjusted current earnings for any items that are not taken into account in determining earnings and profits for any taxable year, even if the items are taken into account in determining pre-adjustment alternative minimum taxable income. These items therefore increase adjusted current earnings to the extent they are deducted in computing pre-adjustment alternative minimum taxable income. An item of deduction is considered taken into account without regard to the timing of its deductibility in computing earnings and profits. Thus, to the extent an item is, has been, or will be deducted for purposes of determining earnings and profits, it does not increase adjusted current earnings in the taxable year in which it is deducted for purposes of determining pre-adjustment alternative minimum taxable income. For example, a deduction allowed (in determining pre-adjustment alternative minimum taxable income) under section 196 for unused research credits allowable under section 41 is taken into account in computing earnings and profits because the costs that gave rise to the credit were deductible in computing earnings and profits when incurred. Therefore, the deduction does not increase adjusted current earnings. As a further example, payments by a United States parent corporation with respect to employees of certain foreign subsidiaries, which are deductible under section 176, are considered contributions to the capital of the foreign subsidiary for purposes of computing earnings and profits. Although the payments are not deductible in computing the earnings and profits of the United States parent corporation in the year incurred, the payments do increase the parent's basis in its stock in the foreign subsidiary. This basis increase will reduce any gain the parent may later realize for purposes of computing earnings and profits on the disposition of the stock of the foreign subsidiary. Therefore, the amount of the payment by the parent is considered taken into account in computing the earnings and profits of the parent and does not increase adjusted current earnings. Thus, only deduction items that are never taken into account in computing earnings and profits are disallowed in computing adjusted current earnings under this paragraph (d).

(2) *Deductions for certain dividends received.*—(i) *Certain amounts deducted under sections 243 and 245.*—Paragraph (d)(1) of this section does not apply to, and adjusted current earnings therefore are not increased by, amounts deducted under sections 243 and 245 that qualify as 100-percent deductible dividends under sections 243(a), 245(b) or 245(c), or to any dividend received from a 20-percent owned corporation (as defined in section 243(c)(2)), to the extent that the dividend giving rise to the deductions is attributable to earnings of the paying corporation that are subject to federal income tax. Earnings are considered subject to federal income tax if the earnings are included on the federal income tax return (that is filed or, if not, that should be filed) of an entity subject to United States taxation, even if there is no resulting United States tax liability (*e.g.*, because of net operating losses or tax credits, other than the credit provided for in section 936).

* * *

(3) *Partial list of items not deductible in computing earnings and profits.*—The following is a partial list of items that are not taken into account in computing earnings and profits and thus are not deductible in computing adjusted current earnings.

(i) Unrecovered losses attributable to certain damages that are deductible under section 186, to the extent those damages were previously deducted in computing earnings and profits.

(ii) The deduction for small life insurance companies allowed under section 806.

(iii) Dividends deductible under the following sections of the Code:

(A) Dividends received by corporations that are deductible under section 243, to the extent paragraph (d)(2)(i) of this section does not apply.

(B) Dividends received on certain preferred stock that are deductible under section 244.

(C) Dividends received from certain foreign corporations that are deductible under section 245, to the extent neither paragraph (d)(2)(i) nor (d)(2)(iii) of this section applies.

(D) Dividends paid on certain preferred stock of public utilities that are deductible under section 247.

(E) Dividends paid to an employee stock ownership plan that are deductible under section 404(k).

(F) Non-patronage dividends that are paid and deductible under section 1382(c)(1).

Items described in paragraph (d)(1) of this section are not taken into account in computing earnings and profits (and thus are not deductible in computing adjusted current earnings) even if they are not identified in this paragraph (d)(3). The Commissioner may identify additional items described in paragraph (d)(1) of this section in other published guidance.

(4) *Partial list of items deductible for purposes of computing both pre-adjustment alternative minimum taxable income and adjusted current earnings.*—The following is a partial list of items that are deductible for purposes of computing both pre-adjustment alternative minimum taxable income and adjusted current earnings, and for which no adjustment is allowed under this section.

(i) Payments by a United States corporation with respect to employees of certain foreign corporations that are deductible under section 176.

(ii) Dividends paid on deposits by thrift institutions that are deductible under section 591.

(iii) Life insurance policyholder dividends that are deductible under section 808.

(iv) Dividends paid by cooperatives that are deductible under sections 1382(b) or 1382(c)(2) and that are not paid with respect to stock.

The Commissioner may identify additional items described in this paragraph (d)(4) in other published guidance.

(e) *Treatment of income items included, and deduction items not allowed, in computing pre-adjustment alternative minimum taxable income.*—Adjusted current earnings includes any income item that is included in pre-adjustment alternative minimum taxable income, even if that income item is not included in earnings and profits for the taxable year. Except as specifically provided in paragraph (c)(3) or (c)(5) of this section, no deduction is allowed for an item in computing adjusted current earnings if the item is not deductible in computing pre-adjustment alternative minimum taxable income for the taxable year, even if the item is deductible in computing earnings and profits for the year. Thus, for example, capital losses in excess of capital gains for the taxable year are not deductible in computing adjusted current earnings for the taxable year.

(f) *Certain other earnings and profits adjustments.*—(1) *Intangible drilling costs.*—For purposes of computing adjusted current earnings, the amount allowable as a deduction for intangible drilling costs (as defined in section 263(c)) for amounts paid or incurred in taxable years beginning after December 31, 1989, is determined as provided in section 312(n)(2)(A). See section 56(h) for an additional adjustment to alternative minimum taxable income based on energy preferences for taxable years beginning after 1990.

(2) *Certain amortization provisions do not apply.*—For purposes of computing adjusted current earnings, sections 173 (relating to circulation expenditures) and 248 (relating to organizational expenditures) do not apply to amounts paid or incurred in taxable years beginning after December 31, 1989. If an election is made under section 59(e) to amortize circulation expenditures described in section 173 over a three-year period, the expenditures to which the election applies are deducted ratably over the three-year period for purposes of computing taxable income, pre-adjustment alternative minimum taxable income, and adjusted current earnings.

* * *

(q) *Treatment of distributions of property to shareholders.*—(1) *In general.*—If a distribution of an item of property by a corporation with respect to its stock gives rise to more than one adjustment to earnings and profits under section 312, all of the adjustments with respect to that item of property (including the adjustment described in section 312(c) with respect to liabilities to which the item is subject or which are assumed in connection with the distribution) are combined for purposes of determining the corporation's adjusted current earnings for the taxable year. If the amount included in pre-adjustment alternative minimum taxable income with respect to a distribution of an item of property exceeds the net increase in earnings and profits caused by the distribution, pre-adjustment alternative minimum taxable income is not reduced in computing adjusted current earnings. If the net increase in earnings and profits caused by a distribution of an item of property exceeds the amount included in pre-adjustment alternative minimum taxable income with respect to the distribution, that excess is added to pre-adjustment alternative minimum taxable income in computing adjusted current earnings.

(2) *Examples.*—The following examples illustrate the provisions of this paragraph (q).

(i) *Example 1.*—K corporation distributes property with a fair market value of $150 and an adjusted basis of $100. The adjusted basis is the same for purposes of computing taxable income, pre-adjustment alternative minimum taxable income, adjusted current earnings, and earnings and profits. Under section 312(a)(3), as modified by section 312(b)(2), K decreases its earnings and profits by the fair market value of the property, or $150. Under section 312(b)(1), K increases its earnings and profits by the excess of the fair market value of the property over its adjusted basis, or $50. As a result of the distribution, there is a net decrease in K's earnings and profits of $100. K recognizes $50 of gain under section 311(b) as a result of the distribution as if K sold the property for $150. K thus has no amount permanently excluded from pre-adjustment alternative minimum taxable income that is taken into account in determining current earnings and profits, and thus has no adjustment under paragraph (c)(1) of this section.

(ii) *Example 2.*—The facts are the same as in example 1, except that the distributee shareholder assumes a $190 liability in connection with the distribution. Under section 312(c)(1), K must adjust the adjustments to its earnings and profits under section 312(a) and (b) to account for the liability the shareholder assumes. K adjusts the $100 net decrease in its earnings and profits to reflect the $190 liability, resulting in an increase in its earnings and profits of $90. Because section 311(b)(2) makes the rules of section 336(b) apply, the fair market value of the property is not less than the amount of the liability, or $190. K therefore is treated as if it sold the property for $190, recognizing $90 of gain. K thus has no amount permanently excluded from pre-adjustment alternative minimum taxable income that is taken into account in determining current earnings and profits, and thus has no adjustment under paragraph (c)(1) of this section.

* * *

[Reg. § 1.56(g)-1.]

☐ [*T.D.* 8340, 3-14-91. *Amended by T.D.* 8352, 6-26-91; *T.D.* 8454, 12-18-92; *T.D.* 8482, 8-6-93; *T.D.* 8566, 10-7-94; *T.D.* 8858, 1-5-2000, *T.D.* 8940, 2-12-2001 *and T.D.* 9849, 3-11-2019.]

Definition of Gross Income, Taxable Income, Etc.

§ 1.61-1. Gross income.—(a) *General definition.*—Gross income means all income from whatever source derived, unless excluded by law. Gross income includes income realized in any form, whether in money, property, or services. Income may be realized, therefore, in the form of services, meals, accommodations, stock, or other property, as well as in cash. Section 61 lists the more common items of gross income for purposes of illustration. For purposes of further illustration, § 1.61-14 mentions several miscellaneous items of gross income not listed specifically in section 61. Gross income, however, is not limited to the items so enumerated.

* * *

[Reg. § 1.61-1.]

☐ [*T.D.* 6272, 11-25-57.]

§ 1.61-2. Compensation for services, including fees, commissions, and similar items.—(a) *In general.*—(1) Wages, salaries, commissions paid salesmen, compensation for services on the basis of a percentage of profits, commissions on insurance premiums, tips, bonuses (including Christmas bonuses), termination or severance pay, rewards, jury fees, marriage fees and other contributions received by a clergyman for services, pay of persons in the military or naval forces of the United States, retired pay of employees, pensions, and retirement allowances are income to the recipients unless excluded by law. Several special rules apply to members of the Armed Forces, National Oceanic and Atmospheric Administration, and Public Health Service of the United States; see paragraph (b) of this section.

(2) The Internal Revenue Code provides special rules including the following items in gross income:

(i) Distributions from employees' trusts, see sections 72, 402, and 403, and the regulations thereunder;

(ii) Compensation for child's services (in child's gross income), see section 73 and the regulations thereunder;

(iii) Prizes and awards, see section 74 and the regulations thereunder.

(3) Similarly, the Code provides special rules excluding the following items from gross income in whole or in part:

(i) Gifts, see section 102 and the regulations thereunder;

(ii) Compensation for injuries or sickness, see section 104 and the regulations thereunder;

(iii) Amounts received under accident and health plans, see section 105 and the regulations thereunder;

(iv) Scholarship and fellowship grants, see section 117 and the regulations thereunder;

(v) Miscellaneous items, see section 122.

(b) *Members of the Armed Forces, National Oceanic and Atmospheric Administration, and Public Health Service.*—(1) Subsistence and uniform allowances granted commissioned officers, chief warrant officers, warrant officers, and enlisted personnel of the Armed Forces, National Oceanic and Atmospheric Administration, and Public Health Service of the United States, and amounts received by them as commutation of quarters, are excluded from gross income. Similarly, the value of quarters or subsistence furnished to such persons is excluded from gross income.

(2) For purposes of this section, quarters or subsistence includes the following allowances for expenses incurred after December 31, 1993, by members of the Armed Forces, members of the commissioned corps of the National Oceanic and Atmospheric Administration, and members of the commissioned corps of the Public Health Service, to the extent that the allowances are not otherwise excluded from gross income under another provision of the Internal Revenue Code: a dislocation allowance, authorized by 37 U.S.C. 407; a temporary lodging allowance, authorized by 37 U.S.C. 405; a temporary lodging expense, authorized by 37 U.S.C. 404a; and a move-in housing allowance, authorized by 37 U.S.C. 405. No deduction is allowed under this chapter for any expenses reimbursed by such excluded allowances. For the exclusion from gross income of—

(i) Disability pensions, see section 104(a)(4) and the regulations thereunder;

(ii) Miscellaneous items, see section 122.

(3) The per diem or actual expense allowance, the monetary allowance in lieu of transportation, and the mileage allowance received by members of the Armed Forces, National Oceanic and Atmospheric Administration, and the Public Health Service, while in a travel status or on temporary duty away fron their permanent stations, are included in their gross income except to the extent excluded under the accountable plan provisions of § 1.62-2.

(c) *Payment to charitable, etc., organization on behalf of person rendering services.*—The value of services is not includible in gross income when such services are rendered directly and gratuitously to an organization described in section 170(c). Where, however, pursuant to an agreement or understanding, services are rendered to a person for the benefit of an organization described in section 170(c) and an amount for such services is paid to such organization by the person to whom the services are rendered, the amount so paid constitutes income to the person performing the services.

(d) *Compensation paid other than in cash.*—(1) *In general.*—Except as otherwise provided in paragraph (d)(6)(i) of this section (relating to certain property transferred after June 30, 1969), if services are paid for in property, the fair market value of the property taken in payment must be included in income as compensation. If services are paid for in exchange for other services, the fair market value of such other services taken in payment must be included in income as compensation. If the services are rendered at a stipulated price, such price will be presumed to be the fair market value of the compensation received in the absence of evidence to the contrary. For special rules relating to certain options received as compensation, see §§ 1.61-15, 1.83-7, and section 421 and the regulations thereunder. For special rules relating to premiums paid by an employer for an annuity contract which is not subject to section 403(a), see section 403(c) and the regulations thereunder and § 1.83-8(a). For special rules relating to contributions made to an employees' trust which is not exempt under section 501, see section 402(b) and the regulations thereunder and § 1.83-8(a).

(2) *Property transferred to employee or independent contractor.*—(i) Except as otherwise provided in section 421 and the regulations thereunder and § 1.61-15 (relating to stock options), and paragraph (d)(6)(i) of this section, if property is transferred by an employer to an employee or if property is transferred to an independent contractor, as compensation for services, for an amount less than its fair market value, then regardless of whether the transfer is in the form of a sale or exchange, the difference between the amount paid for the property and the amount of its fair market value at the time of the transfer is compensation and shall be included in the gross income of the employee or independent contractor. In computing the gain or loss from the subsequent sale of such property, its basis shall be the amount

paid for the property increased by the amount of such difference included in gross income.

(ii) (A) *Cost of life insurance on the life of the employee.*—Generally, life insurance premiums paid by an employer on the life of his employee where the proceeds of such insurance are payable to the beneficiary of such employee are part of the gross income of the employee. However, the amount includible in the employee's gross income is determined with regard to the provisions of section 403 and the regulations thereunder in the case of an individual contract issued after December 31, 1962, or a group contract, which provides incidental life insurance protection and which satisfies the requirements of section 401(g) and § 1.401-9, relating to the nontransferability of annuity contracts. For example, if an employee or independent contractor is the owner (as defined in § 1.61-22(c) (1)) of a life insurance contract and the payments with regard to such contract are not split-dollar loans under § 1.7872-15(b) (1), the employee or independent contractor must include in income the amount of any such payments by the employer or service recipient with respect to such contract during any year to the extent that the employee's or independent contractor's rights to the life insurance contract are substantially vested (within the meaning of § 1.83-3(b)). This result is the same regardless of whether the employee or independent contractor has at all times been the owner of the life insurance contract or the contract previously has been owned by the employer or service recipient as part of a split-dollar life insurance arrangement (as defined in § 1.61-22(b) (1) or (2)) and was transferred by the employer or service recipient to the employee or independent contractor under § 1.61-22(g). For the special rules relating to the includibility in an employee's gross income of an amount equal to the cost of certain group-term life insurance on the employee's life which is carried directly or indirectly by his employer, see section 79 and the regulations thereunder. For special rules relating to the exclusion of contributions by an employer to accident and health plans for the employees, see section 106 and the regulations thereunder.

(B) *Cost of group-term life insurance on the life of an individual other than an employee.*—The cost (determined under paragraph (d) (2) of § 1.79-3) of group-term life insurance on the life of an individual other than an employee (such as the spouse or dependent of the employee) provided in connection with the performance of services by the employee is includible in the gross income of the employee.

(3) *Meals and living quarters.*—The value of living quarters or meals which an employee receives in addition to his salary constitutes gross income unless they are furnished for the convenience of the employer and meet the conditions specified in section 119 and the regulations thereunder. For the treatment of rental value of parsonages or rental allowance paid to ministers, see section 107 and the regulations thereunder; for the treatment of statutory subsistence allowances received by police, see section 120 and the regulations thereunder.

(4) *Stock and notes transferred to employee or independent contractor.*—Except as otherwise provided by section 421 and the regulations thereunder and § 1.61-15 (relating to stock options), and paragraph (d) (6) (i) of this section, if a corporation transfers its own stock to an employee or independent contractor as compensation for services, the fair market value of the stock at the time of transfer shall be included in the gross income of the employee or independent contractor. Notes or other evidences of indebtedness received in payment for services constitute income in the amount of their fair market value at the time of the transfer. A taxpayer receiving as compensation a note regarded as good for its face value at maturity, but not bearing interest, shall treat as income as of the time of receipts its fair discounted value computed at the prevailing rate. As payments are received on such a note, there shall be included in income that portion of each payment which represents the proportionate part of the discount originally taken on the entire note.

* * *

(6) *Certain property transferred, premiums paid, and contributions made in connection with the performance of services after June 30, 1969.*—(i) *Exception.*—Paragraph (d) (1), (2), (4), and (5) of this section and § 1.61-15 do not apply to the transfer of property (as defined in § 1.83-3(e)) after June 30, 1969, unless § 1.83-8 (relating to the applicability of section 83 and transitional rules) applies. If section 83 applies to a transfer of property, and the property is not subject to a restriction that has a significant effect on the fair market value of such property, then the rules contained in paragraph (d) (1), (2), and (4) of this section and § 1.61-15 shall also apply to such transfer to the extent such rules are not inconsistent with section 83.

* * *

[Reg. § 1.61-2.]

☐ [*T.D.* 6272, 11-25-57. *Amended by T.D.* 6416, 9-24-59; *T.D.* 6696, 12-11-63; *T.D.* 6856, 10-19-65; *T.D.* 6888, 7-5-66; *T.D.* 7554, 7-21-78; *T.D.* 7623, 5-14-79; *T.D.* 8256, 7-5-89; *T.D.* 8607, 8-4-95 *and T.D.* 9092, 9-11-2003.]

§ 1.61-3. Gross income derived from business.—(a) *In general.*—In a manufacturing, merchandising, or mining business, "gross income" means the total sales, less the cost of goods sold, plus any income from investments and from incidental or outside operations or sources. Gross income is determined without subtraction of depletion allowances based on a percentage of income to the extent that it exceeds cost depletion which may be required to be included in the amount of inventoriable costs as provided in § 1.471-11 and without subtraction of selling expenses, losses or other items not ordinarily used in computing costs of goods sold or amounts which are of a type for which a deduction would be disallowed under section 162(c), (f), or (g) in the case of a business expense. The cost of goods sold should be determined in accordance with the method of accounting consistently used by the taxpayer. Thus, for example, an amount cannot be taken into account in the computation of cost of goods sold any earlier than the taxable year in which economic performance occurs with respect to the amount (see § 1.446-1(c) (1) (ii)).

(b) *State contracts.*—The profit from a contract with a State or policitcal subdivision thereof must be included in gross income. If warrants are issued by a city, town, or other political subdivision of a State, and are accepted by the contractor in payment for public work done, the fair market value of such warrants should be returned as income. If, upon conversion of the warrants into cash, the contractor does not receive and cannot recover the full value of the warrants so returned, he may deduct any loss sustained from his gross income for the year in which the warrants are so converted. If, however, he realizes more than the value of the warrants so returned, he must include the excess in his gross income for the year in which realized. [Reg. § 1.61-3.]

☐ [*T.D.* 6272, 11-25-57. *Amended by T.D.* 7207, 10-3-72; *T.D.* 7285, 9-14-73 *and T.D.* 8408, 4-9-92.]

§ 1.61-4. Gross income of farmers.—(a) *Farmers using the cash method of accounting.*—A farmer using the cash receipts and disbursements method of accounting shall include in his gross income for the taxable year—

(1) The amount of cash and the value of merchandise or other property received during the taxable year from the sale of livestock and produce which he raised,

(2) The profits from the sale of any livestock or other items which were purchased,

(3) All amounts received from breeding fees, fees from rent of teams, machinery, or land, and other incidental farm income,

(4) All subsidy and conservation payments received which must be considered as income, and

(5) Gross income from all other sources.

The profit from the sale of livestock or other items which were purchased is to be ascertained by deducting the cost from the sales price in the year in which the sale occurs, except that in the case of the sale of purchased animals held for draft, breeding, or dairy purposes, the profits shall be the amount of any excess of the sales price over the amount representing the difference between the cost and the depreciation allowed or allowable (determined in accordance with the rules applicable under section 1016(a) and the regulations thereunder). However, see section 162 and the regulations thereunder with respect of the computation of taxable income on other than the crop method where the cost of seeds or young plants purchased for further development and cultivation prior to the sale is involved. Crop shares (whether or not considered rent under State law) shall be included in gross income as of the year in which the crop shares are reduced to money or the equivalent of money. See section 263A for rules regarding costs that are required to be capitalized.

(b) *Farmers using an accrual method of accounting.*—A farmer using an accrual method of accounting must use inventories to determine his gross income. His gross income on an accrual method is determined by adding the total of the items described in subparagraphs (1) through (5) of this paragraph and subtracting therefrom the total of the items described in subparagraphs (6) and (7) of this paragraph. These items are as follows:

(1) The sales price of all livestock and other products held for sale and sold during the year;

(2) The inventory value of livestock and products on hand and not sold at the end of the year;

(3) All miscellaneous items of income, such as breeding fees, fees from the rent of teams, machinery, or land, or other incidental farm income;

(4) Any subsidy or conservation payments which must be considered as income;

(5) Gross income from all other sources;

(6) The inventory value of the livestock and products on hand and not sold at the beginning of the year; and

(7) The cost of any livestock or products purchased during the year (except livestock held for draft, dairy, or breeding purposes, unless included in inventory).

All livestock raised or purchased for sale shall be added in the inventory at their proper valuation determined in accordance with the method authorized and adopted for the purpose. Livestock acquired for draft, breeding, or dairy purposes and not for sale may be included in the inventory (see subparagraphs (2), (6), and (7) of this paragraph) instead of being treated as capital assets subject to depreciation, provided such practice is followed consistently from year to year by the taxpayer. When any livestock included in an inventory are sold, their cost must not be taken as an additional deduction in computing taxable income, because such deduction is reflected in the inventory. See the regulations under section 471. See section 263A for rules regarding costs that are required to be capitalized. Crop shares (whether or not considered rent under State law) shall be included in gross income as of the year in which the crop shares are reduced to money or the equivalent of money.

(c) *Special rules for certain receipts.*—In the case of the sale of machinery, farm equipment, or any other property (except stock in trade of the taxpayer, or property of a kind which would properly be included in the inventory of the taxpayer if on hand at the close of the taxable year, or property held by the taxpayer primarily for sale to customers in the ordinary course of his trade or business), any excess of the proceeds of the sale over the adjusted basis of such property shall be included in the taxpayer's gross income for the taxable year in which such sale is made. See, however, section 453 and the regulations thereunder for special rules relating to certain installment sales. If farm produce is exchanged for merchandise, groceries, or the like, the market value of the article received in exchange is to be included in gross income. Proceeds of insurance, such as hail or fire insurance on growing crops, should be included in gross income to the extent of the amount received in cash or its equivalent for the crop injured or destroyed. See section 451(d) for special rule relating to election to include crop insurance proceeds in income for taxable year following taxable year of destruction. For taxable years beginning after July 12, 1972, where a farmer is engaged in producing crops and the process of gathering and disposing of such crops is not completed within the taxable year in which such crops are planted, the income therefrom may, with the consent of the Commissioner (see section 446 and the regulations thereunder), be computed upon the crop method. For taxable years beginning on or before July 12, 1972, where a farmer is engaged in producing crops which take more than a year from the time of planting to the time of gathering and disposing, the income therefrom may, with the consent of the Commissioner (see section 446 and the regulations thereunder), be computed upon the crop method. In any case in which the crop method is used, the entire cost of producing the crop must be taken as a deduction for the year in which the gross income from the crop is realized, and not earlier.

(d) *Definition of "farm"*.—As used in this section, the term "farm" embraces the farm in the ordinarily accepted sense, and includes stock, dairy, poultry, fruit, and truck farms; also plantations, ranches, and all land used for farming operations. All individuals, partnerships, or corporations that cultivate, operate, or manage farms for gain or profit, either as owners or tenants, are designated as farmers. For more detailed rules with respect to the determination of whether or not an individual is engaged in farming, see § 1.175-3. For rules applicable to persons cultivating or operating a farm for recreation or pleasure, see sections 162 and 165, and the regulations thereunder.

(e) *Cross references.*—(1) For election to include Commodity Credit Corporation loans as income, see section 77 and regulations thereunder.

(2) For definition of gross income derived from farming for purposes of limiting deductibility of soil and water conservation expenditures, see section 175 and regulations thereunder.

(3) For definition of gross income from farming in connection with declarations of estimated income tax, see section 6073 and regulations thereunder. [Reg. § 1.61-4.]

□ [*T.D.* 6272, 11-25-57. *Amended by T.D.* 7198, 7-12-72 *and T.D.* 8729, 8-21-97.]

§ 1.61-6. Gains derived from dealings in property.—(a) *In general.*—Gain realized on the sale or exchange of property is included in gross income, unless excluded by law. For this purpose property includes tangible items, such as a building, and intangible items, such as goodwill. Generally, the gain is the excess of the amount realized over the unrecovered cost or other basis for the property sold or exchanged. The specific rules for computing the amount of gain or loss are contained in section 1001 and the regulations thereunder. When a part of a larger property is sold, the cost or other basis of the entire property shall be equitably apportioned among the several parts, and the gain realized or loss sustained on the part of the entire property sold is the difference between the selling price and the cost or other basis allocated to such part. The sale of each part is treated as a separate transaction and gain or loss shall be computed separately on each part. Thus, gain or loss shall be determined at the time of sale of each part and not deferred until the entire property has been disposed of. This rule may be illustrated by the following examples:

Example (1). A, a dealer in real estate, acquires a 10-acre tract for $10,000, which he divides into 20 lots. The $10,000 cost must be equitably apportioned among the lots so that on the sale of each A can determine his taxable gain or deductible loss.

Example (2). B purchases for $25,000 property consisting of a used car lot and adjoining filling station. At the time, the fair market value of the filling station is $15,000 and the fair market value of the used car lot is $10,000. Five years later B sells the filling station for $20,000 at a time when $2,000 has been properly allowed as depreciation thereon. B's gain on this sale is $7,000, since $7,000 is the amount by which the selling price of the filling station exceeds the portion of the cost equitably allocable to the filling station at the time of purchase reduced by the depreciation properly allowed.

(b) *Nontaxable exchanges.*—Certain realized gains or losses on the sale or exchange of property are not "recognized", that is, are not included in or deducted from gross income at the time the transaction occurs. Gain or loss from such sales or exchanges is generally recognized at some later time. Examples of such sales or exchanges are the following:

(1) Certain formations, reorganizations, and liquidations of corporations, see sections 331, 333, 337, 351, 354, 355, and 361;

(2) Certain formations and distributions of partnerships, see sections 721 and 731;

(3) Exchange of certain property held for productive use or investment for property of like kind, see section 1031;

(4) A corporation's exchange of its stock for property, see section 1032;

(5) Certain involuntary conversions of property if replaced, see section 1033;

(6) Sale or exchange of residence if replaced, see section 1034;

(7) Certain exchanges of insurance policies and annuity contracts, see section 1035; and

(8) Certain exchanges of stock for stock in the same corporation, see section 1036.

* * *

[Reg. § 1.61-6.]

□ [*T.D.* 6272, 11-25-57.]

§ 1.61-7. Interest.—(a) *In general.*—As a general rule, interest received by or credited to the taxpayer constitutes gross income and is fully taxable. Interest income includes interest on savings or other bank deposits; interest on coupon bonds; interest on an open account, a promissory note, a mortgage, or a corporate bond or debenture; the interest portion of a condemnation award; usurious interest (unless by State law it is automatically converted to a payment on the principal); interest on legacies; interest on life insurance proceeds held under an agreement to pay interest thereon; and interest on refunds of Federal taxes. For rules determining the taxable year in which interest, including interest accrued or constructively received, is included in gross income, see section 451 and the regulations thereunder. For the inclusion of interest in income for the purpose of the retirement income credit, see section 37 and the regulations thereunder. For credit of tax withheld at source on interest on tax-free covenant bonds, see section 32 and the regulations thereunder. For rules relating to interest on certain deferred payments, see section 483 and the regulations thereunder.

* * *

[Reg. § 1.61-7.]

□ [*T.D.* 6272, 11-25-57. *Amended by T.D.* 6723, 4-20-64; *and T.D.* 6873, 1-24-66.]

§ 1.61-8. Rents and royalties.—(a) *In general.*—Gross income includes rentals received or accrued for the occupancy of real estate or the use of personal property. For the inclusion of rents in income for the purpose of the retirement income credit, see section 37 and the regulations thereunder. Gross income includes royalties. Royalties may be received from books, stories, plays, copyrights, trademarks, formulas, patents, and from the exploitation of natural resources, such as coal, gas, oil, copper, or timber. Payments received as a result of the transfer of patent rights may under some circumstances constitute capital gain instead of ordinary income. See section 1235 and the regulations thereunder. For special rules for certain income from natural resources, see subchapter I (611 and following), chapter 1 of the Code, and the regulations thereunder.

(b) *Advance rentals; cancellation payments.*—Except as provided in section 467 and the regulations thereunder, and except as otherwise provided by the Commissioner in published guidance (see § 601.601(d)(2) of this chapter), gross income includes advance rentals, which must be included in income for the year of receipt regardless of the period covered or the method of accounting employed by the taxpayer. An amount received by a lessor from a lessee for cancelling a lease constitutes gross income for the year in which it is received, since it is essentially a substitute for rental payments. As to amounts received by a lessee for the cancellation of a lease, see section 1241 and the regulations thereunder.

(c) *Expenditures by lessee.*—As a general rule, if a lessee pays any of the expenses of his lessor such payments are additional rental income of the lessor. If a lessee places improvements on real estate which constitute, in whole or in part, a substitute for rent, such improvements constitute rental income to the lessor. Whether or not improvements made by a lessee result in rental income to the lessor in a particular case depends upon the intention of the parties, which may be indicated either by the terms of the lease or by the surrounding circumstances. For the exclusion from gross income of income (other than rent) derived by a lessor of real property on the termination of a lease, representing the value of such property attributable to buildings erected or other improvements made by a lessee, see section 109 and the regulations thereunder. For the exclusion from gross income of a lessor corporation of certain of its income taxes on rental income paid by a lessee corporation under a lease entered into before January 1, 1954, see section 110 and the regulations thereunder. [Reg. § 1.61-8.]

☐ [*T.D.* 6272, 11-25-57. *Amended by T.D.* 8820, 5-17-99 *and T.D.* 9135, 7-7-2004.]

§ 1.61-9. Dividends.—(a) *In general.*—Except as otherwise specifically provided, dividends are included in gross income under sections 61 and 301. For the principal rules with respect to dividends includible in gross income, see section 316 and the regulations thereunder. As to distributions made or deemed to be made by regulated investment companies, see sections 851 through 855, and the regulations thereunder. As to distributions made by real estate investment trusts, see sections 856 through 858, and the regulations thereunder. See section 116 for the exclusion from gross income of $100 ($50 for dividends received in taxable years beginning before January 1, 1964) of dividends received by an individual, except those from certain corporations. Furthermore, dividends may give rise to a credit against tax under section 34, relating to dividends received by individuals (for dividends received on or before December 31, 1964), and under section 37, relating to retirement income.

(b) *Dividends in kind; stock dividends; stock redemptions.*—Gross income includes dividends in property other than cash, as well as cash dividends. For amounts to be included in gross income when distributions of property are made, see section 301 and the regulations thereunder. A distribution of stock, or rights to acquire stock, in the corporation making the distribution is not a dividend except under the circumstances described in section 305(b). However, the term "dividend" includes a distribution of stock, or rights to acquire stock, in a corporation other than the corporation making the distribution. For determining when distributions in complete liquidation shall be treated as dividends, see section 333 and the regulations thereunder. For rules determining when amounts received in exchanges under section 354 or exchanges and distributions under section 355 shall be treated as dividends, see section 356 and the regulations thereunder.

(c) *Dividends on stock sold.*—When stock is sold, and a dividend is both declared and paid after the sale, such dividend is not gross income to the seller. When stock is sold after the declaration of a dividend and after the date as of which the seller becomes entitled to the dividend, the dividend ordinarily is income to the seller. When stock is sold between the time of declaration and the time of payment of the dividend, and the sale takes place at such time that the purchaser becomes entitled to the dividend, the dividend ordinarily is income to him. The fact that the purchaser may have included the amount of the dividend in his purchase price in contemplation of receiving the dividend does not exempt him from tax. Nor can the purchaser deduct the added amount he advanced to the seller in anticipation of the dividend. That added amount is merely part of the purchase price of the stock. In some cases, however, the purchaser may be considered to be the recipient of the dividend even though he has not received the legal title to the stock itself and does not himself receive the dividend. For example, if the seller retains the legal title to the stock as trustee solely for the purpose of securing the payment of the purchase price, with the understanding that he is to apply the dividends received from time to time in reduction of the purchase price, the dividends are considered to be income to the purchaser. [Reg. § 1.61-9.]

☐ [*T.D.* 6272, 11-25-57. *Amended by T.D.* 6598, 4-25-62; *and T.D.* 6777, 12-15-64.]

§ 1.61-12. Income from discharge of indebtedness.—(a) *In general.*—The discharge of indebtedness, in whole or in part, may result in the realization of income. If, for example, an individual performs services for a creditor, who in consideration thereof cancels the debt, the debtor realizes income in the amount of the debt as compensation for his services. A taxpayer may realize income by the payment or purchase of his obligations at less than their face value. In general, if a shareholder in a corporation which is indebted to him gratuitously forgives the debt, the transaction amounts to a contribution to the capital of the corporation to the extent of the principal of the debt.

* * *

[Reg. § 1.61-12.]

☐ [*T.D.* 6272, 11-25-57. *Amended by T.D.* 6653, 5-22-63; *T.D.* 6984, 12-23-68; *T.D.* 7741, 12-11-80 *and T.D.* 8746, 12-30-97.]

§ 1.61-14. Miscellaneous items of gross income.—(a) *In general.*—In addition to the items enumerated in section 61(a), there are many other kinds of gross income. For example, punitive damages such as treble damages under the antitrust laws and exemplary damages for fraud are gross income. Another person's payment of the taxpayer's income taxes constitutes gross income to the taxpayer unless excluded by law. Illegal gains constitute gross income. Treasure trove, to the extent of its value in United States currency, constitutes gross income for the taxable year in which it is reduced to undisputed possession.

* * *

[Reg. § 1.61-14.]

☐ [*T.D.* 6272, 11-25-57. *Amended by T.D.* 6856, 10-19-65 *and T.D.* 8491, 10-8-93.]

§ 1.61-21. Taxation of fringe benefits.—(a) *Fringe benefits.*—(1) *In general.*—Section 61(a)(1) provides that, except as otherwise provided in subtitle A of the Internal Revenue Code of 1986, gross income includes compensation for services, including fees, commissions, fringe benefits, and similar items. For an outline of the regulations under this section relating to fringe benefits, see paragraph (a)(7) of this section. Examples of fringe benefits include: an employer-provided automobile, a flight on an employer-provided aircraft, an employer-provided free or discounted commercial airline flight, an employer-provided vacation, an employer-provided discount on property or services, an employer-provided membership in a country club or other social club, and an employer-provided ticket to an entertainment or sporting event.

(2) *Fringe benefits excluded from income.*—To the extent that a particular fringe benefit is specifically excluded from gross income pursuant to another section of subtitle A of the Internal Revenue Code of 1986, that section shall govern the treatment of that fringe benefit. Thus, if the requirements of the governing section are satisfied, the fringe benefits may be excludable from gross income. Examples of excludable fringe benefits include qualified tuition reductions provided to an employee (section 117(d)); meals or lodging furnished to an employee for the convenience of the employer (section 119); benefits provided under a dependent care assistance program (section 129); and no-additional-cost services, qualified employee discounts, working condition fringes, and de minimis fringes (section 132) [illegible] the value of the use by an emplo[illegible] employer-provided vehicle or a flight provided to an employee on an employer-provided aircraft may be excludable from income under section 105 (because, for example, the transportation is provided for medical reasons) if and to the extent that the requirements of that section are satisfied. Section 134 excludes from gross income "qualified military benefits." An example of a benefit that is not a qualified military benefit is the personal use of an employer-provided vehicle. The fact that another section of subtitle A of the Internal Revenue Code addresses the taxation of a particular fringe benefit will not preclude section 61 and the regulations thereunder from applying, to the extent that they are not inconsistent with such other section. For example, many fringe benefits specifically addressed in other sections of subtitle A of the Internal Revenue Code are excluded from gross income only to the extent that they do not exceed specific dollar or percentage limits, or only if certain other requirements are met. If the limits are exceeded or the requirements are not met, some or all of the fringe benefit may be includible in gross income pursuant to section 61. See paragraph (b)(3) of this section.

(3) *Compensation for services.*—A fringe benefit provided in connection with the performance of services shall be considered to have been provided as compensation for such services. Refraining from the performance of services (such as pursuant to a covenant not to compete) is deemed to be the performance of services for purposes of this section.

(4) *Person to whom fringe benefit is taxable.*—(i) *In general.*—A taxable fringe benefit is included in the income of the person performing the services in connection with which the fringe benefit is furnished. Thus, a fringe benefit may be taxable to a person even though that person did not actually receive the fringe benefit. If a fringe benefit is furnished to someone other than the service provider such benefit is considered in this section as furnished to the service provider, and use by the other person is considered use by the service provider. For example, the provision of an automobile by an employer to an employee's spouse in connection with the performance of services by the employee is taxable to the employee. The automobile is considered available to the employee and use by the employee's spouse is considered use by the employee.

(ii) *All persons to whom benefits are taxable referred to as employees.*—The person to whom a fringe benefit is taxable need not be an employee of the provider of the fringe benefit, but may be, for example, a partner, director, or an independent contractor. For convenience, the term "employee" includes any person performing services in connection with which a fringe benefit is furnished, unless otherwise specifically provided in this section.

(5) *Provider of a fringe benefit referred to as an employer.*—The "provider" of a fringe benefit is that person for whom the services are performed, regardless of whether that person actually provides the fringe benefit to the recipient. The provider of a fringe benefit need not be the employer of the recipient of the fringe benefit, but may be, for example, a client or customer of the employer or of an independent contractor. For convenience, the term "employer" includes any provider of a fringe benefit in connection with payment for the performance of services, unless otherwise specifically provided in this section.

* * *

(b) *Valuation of fringe benefits.*—(1) *In general.*—An employee must include in gross income the amount by which the fair market value of the fringe benefit exceeds the sum of—

(i) The amount, if any, paid for the benefit by or on behalf of the recipient, and

(ii) The amount, if any, specifically excluded from gross income by some other section of subtitle A of the Internal Revenue Code of 1986.

Therefore, for example, if the employee pays fair market value for what is received, no amount is includible in the gross income of the employee. In general, the determination of the fair market value of a fringe benefit must be made before subtracting out the amount, if any, paid for the benefit and the amount, if any, specifically excluded from gross income by another section of subtitle A. See paragraphs (d)(2)(ii) and (e)(1)(iii) of this section.

(2) *Fair market value.*—In general, fair market value is determined on the basis of all the facts and circumstances. Specifically, the fair market value of a fringe benefit is the amount that an individual would have to pay for the particular fringe benefit in an arm's-length transaction. Thus, for example, the effect of any special relationship that may exist between the employer and the employee must be disregarded. Similarly, an employee's subjective perception of the value of a fringe benefit is not relevant to the determination of the fringe benefit's fair market value nor is the cost incurred by the employer determinative of its fair market value. For special rules relating to the valuation of certain fringe benefits, see paragraph (c) of this section.

(3) *Exclusion from income based on cost.*—If a statutory exclusion phrased in terms of cost applies to the provision of a fringe benefit, section 61 does not require the inclusion in the recipient's gross income of the difference between the fair market value and the excludable cost of that fringe benefit. For example, section 129 provides an exclusion from an employee's gross income for amounts contributed by an employer to a dependent care assistance program for employees. Even if the fair market value of the dependent care assistance exceeds the employer's cost, the excess is not subject to inclusion under section 61 and this section. However, if the statutory cost exclusion is a limited amount, the fair market value of the fringe benefit attributable to any excess cost is subject to inclusion. This would be the case, for example, where an employer pays or incurs a cost of more than $5,000 to provide dependent care assistance to an employee.

* * *

[Reg. § 1.61-21.]

☐ [*T.D.* 8256, 7-5-89. *Amended by T.D.* 8389, 1-15-92; *T.D.* 8457, 12-29-92; *T.D.* 9597, 7-31-2012; *T.D.* 9849, 3-11-2019; *and T.D.* 9893, 2-4-2020.]

»»→ Caution: Reg. § 1.62-1T(a) does not reflect numerous sections that have been made dependent on adjusted gross income since the 1992 promulgation of Reg. § 1.62-1T. Reg. § 1.62-1T(c) does not reflect the addition of several pre-AGI deductions since the 1992 promulgation of Reg. § 1.62-1T.

§ 1.62-1T. Adjusted gross income (temporary).—(a) *Basis for determining the amount of certain deductions.*—The term "adjusted gross income" means the gross income computed under section 61 minus such of the deductions allowed by chapter 1 of the Code as are specified in section 62(a). Adjusted gross income is used as the basis for determining the following:

(1) The limitation on the amount of miscellaneous itemized deductions (under section 67).

(2) The limitation on the amount of the deduction for casualty losses (under section 165(h)(2)),

(3) The limitation on the amount of the deduction for charitable contributions (under section 170(b)(1)),

(4) The limitation on the amount of the deduction for medical and dental expenses (under section 213),

(5) The limitation on the amount of the deduction for qualified retirement contributions for active participants in certain pension plans (under section 219(g)), and

(6) The phase-out of the exemption from the disallowance of passive activity losses and credits (under section 469(i)(3)).

(b) *Double deduction not permitted.*—Section 62(a) merely specifies which of the deductions provided in chapter 1 of the Code shall be allowed in computing adjusted gross income. It does not create any new deductions. The fact that a particular item may be described in more than one of the paragraphs under section 62(a) does not permit the item to be deducted twice in computing adjusted gross income or taxable income.

(c) *Deductions allowable in computing adjusted gross income.*—The deductions specified in section 62(a) for purposes of computing adjusted gross income are:

(1) Deductions allowable under chapter 1 of the Code (other than by part VII (section 211 and following), subchapter B of such chapter) that are attributable to a trade or business carried on by the taxpayer not consisting of services performed as an employee;

(2) [Reserved]

(3) For taxable years beginning after December 31, 1986, deductions allowable under section 162 that consist of expenses paid or incurred by a qualified performing artist (as defined in section 62 (b)) in connection with the performance by him or her of services in the performing arts as an employee;

(4) Deductions allowable under part VI as losses from the sale or exchange of property;

(5) Deductions allowable under part VI, section 212, or section 611 that are attributable to property held for the production of rents or royalties;

(6) Deductions for depreciation or depletion allowable under sections 167 or 611 to a life tenant of property or to an income beneficiary of property held in trust or to an heir, legatee, or devisee of an estate;

(7) Deductions allowed by section 404 for contributions on behalf of a self-employed individual;

(8) Deductions allowed by section 219 for contributions to an individual retirement account described in section 408(a), or for an individual retirement annuity described in section 408(b);

(9) Deductions allowed by section 402(e)(3) with respect to a lump-sum distribution;

(10) For taxable years beginning after December 31, 1972, deductions allowed by section 165 for losses incurred in any transaction entered into for profit though not connected with a trade or business, to the extent that such losses include amounts forfeited to a bank, mutual savings bank, savings and loan association, building and loan association, cooperative bank or homestead association as a penalty for premature withdrawal of funds from a time savings account, certificate of deposit, or similar class of deposit;

(11) For taxable years beginning after December 31, 1976, deductions for alimony and separate maintenance payments allowed by section 215;

(12) Deductions allowed by section 194 for the amortization of reforestation expenditures; and

(13) Deductions allowed by section 165 for the repayment (made in a taxable year beginning after December 28, 1980) to a trust described in paragraph (9) or (17) of section 501(c) of supplemental unemployment compensation benefits received from such trust if such repayment is required because of the receipt of trade readjustment allowances under section 231 or 232 of the Trade Act of 1974 (19 U.S.C. 2291 and 2292).

(d) *Expenses directly related to a trade or business.*—For the purpose of the deductions specified in section 62, the performance of personal services as an employee does not constitute the carrying on of a trade or business, except as otherwise expressly provided. The practice of a profession, not as an employee, is considered the conduct of a trade or business within the meaning of such section. To be deductible for the purposes of determining adjusted gross income, expenses must be those directly, and not those merely remotely, connected with the conduct of a trade or business. For example, taxes are deductible in arriving at adjusted gross income only if they constitute expenditures directly attributable to a trade or business or to property from which rents or royalties are derived. Thus, property taxes paid or incurred on real property used in a trade or business are deductible, but state taxes on net income are not deductible even though the taxpayer's income is derived from the conduct of a trade or business.

(e) *Reimbursed and unreimbursed employee expenses.*—(1) *In general.*—Expenses paid or incurred by an employee that are deductible from gross income under part VI in computing taxable income (determined without regard to section 67) and for which the employee is reimbursed by the employer, its agent, or third party (for whom the employee performs a benefit as an employee of the employer) under an express agreement for reimbursement or pursuant to an *express* expense allowance arrangement may be deducted from gross income in computing adjusted gross income. Except as provided in paragraph (e)(2) and (e)(4) of this section, for taxable years beginning after December 31, 1986, if the amount of a reimbursement made by an employer, its agent, or third party to an employee is less than the total amount of the business expenses paid or incurred by the employee, the determination of to which of the employee's business expenses the reimbursement applies and the amount of each expense that is covered by the reimbursement is made on the basis of all of the facts and circumstances of the particular case.

(2) *Facts and circumstances unclear on business expenses for meals and entertainment.*—If—

(i) The facts and circumstances do not make clear—

(A) That a reimbursement does not apply to business expenses for meals or entertainment, or

(B) The amount of business expenses for meals or entertainment that is covered by the reimbursement, and

(ii) the employee pays or incurs business expenses for meals or entertainment,

the amount of the reimbursement that applies to such expenses (or portion thereof with respect to which the facts and circumstances are unclear) shall be determined by multiplying the amount of the employee's business expenses for meals and entertainment (or portion thereof with respect to which the facts and circumstances are unclear) by a fraction, the numerator of which is the total amount of the reimbursement (or portion thereof with respect to which the facts and circumstances are unclear) and the denominator of which is the aggregate amount of all the business expenses of the employee (or portion thereof with respect to which the facts and circumstances are unclear).

(3) *Deductibility of unreimbursed expenses.*—The amount of expenses that is determined not to be reimbursed pursuant to paragraph (e)(1) or (2) of this section is deductible from adjusted gross income in determining the employee's taxable income subject to the limitations applicable to such expenses (*e.g.,* the 2-percent floor of section 67 and the 80-percent limitation on meal and entertainment expenses provided for in section 274(n)).

* * *

(5) *Expenses paid directly by an employer, its agent, or third party.*—In the case of an employer, its agent, or a third party who provides property or services to an employee or who pays an employee's expenses directly instead of reimbursing the employee, see section 132 and the regulations thereunder for the income tax treatment of such expenses.

* * *

(f) [Reserved]

(g) *Moving expenses.*—For taxable years beginning after December 31, 1986, a taxpayer described in section 217(a) shall not take into account the deduction described in section 217 relating to moving expenses in computing adjusted gross income under section 62 even if the taxpayer is reimbursed for his or her moving expenses. Such a taxpayer shall include the amount of any reimbursement for moving expenses in income pursuant to section 82. The deduction described in section 217 shall be taken into account in computing the taxable income of the taxpayer under section 63. Pursuant to section 67(b)(6), the 2-percent floor described in section 67(a) does not apply to moving expenses.

* * *

[Temporary Reg. § 1.62-1T.]

☐ [*T.D.* 8189, 3-25-88. *Amended by T.D.* 8276, 12-7-89; *T.D.* 8324, 12-14-90 *and T.D.* 8451, 12-4-92.]

§ 1.62-2. Reimbursements and other expense allowance arrangements.—

* * *

(b) *Scope.*—For purposes of determining "adjusted gross income," section 62(a)(2)(A) allows an employee a deduction for expenses allowed by Part VI (section 161 and following), subchapter B, chapter 1 of the Code, paid by the employee, in connection with the performance of services as an employee of the employer, under a reimbursement or other expense allowance arrangement with a payor (the employer, its agent, or a third party). Section 62(c) provides that an arrangement will not be treated as a reimbursement or other expense allowance arrangement for purposes of section 62(a)(2)(A) if (1) such arrangement does not require the employee to substantiate the expenses covered by the arrangement to the payor, or (2) such arrangement provides the employee the right to retain any amount in excess of the substantiated expenses covered under the arrangement. This section prescribes rules relating to the requirements of section 62(c).

(c) *Reimbursement or other expense allowance arrangement.*—(1) *Defined.*—For purposes of §§ 1.62-1, 1.62-1T and 1.62-2, the phrase "reimbursement or other expense allowance arrangement" means an arrangement that meets the requirements of paragraphs (d) (business connection), (e) (substantiation), and (f) (returning amounts in excess of expenses) of this section. A payor may have more than one arrangement with respect to a particular employee, depending on the facts and circumstances. See paragraph (d)(2) of this section (payor treated as having two arrangements under certain circumstances).

(2) *Accountable plans.*—(i) *In general.*—Except as provided in paragraph (c)(2)(ii) of this section, if an arrangement meets the requirements of paragraphs (d), (e), and (f) of this section, all amounts paid under the arrangement are treated as paid under an "accountable plan."

(ii) *Special rule for failure to return excess.*—If an arrangement meets the requirements of paragraphs (d), (e), and (f) of this section, but the employee fails to return, within a reasonable period of time, any amount in excess of the amount of the expenses substantiated in accordance with paragraph (e) of this section, only the amounts paid under the arrangement that are not in excess of the substantiated expenses are treated as paid under an accountable plan.

(3) *Nonaccountable plans.*—(i) *In general.*—If an arrangement does not satisfy one or more of the requirements of paragraphs (d), (e), or (f) of this section, all amounts paid under the arrangement are treated as paid under a "nonaccountable plan." If a payor provides a nonaccountable plan, an employee who receives payments under the plan cannot compel the payor to treat the payments as paid under an accountable plan by voluntarily substantiating the expenses and returning any excess to the payor.

(ii) *Special rule for failure to return excess.*—If an arrangement meets the requirements of paragraphs (d), (e), and (f) of this section, but the employee fails to return, within a reasonable period of time, any amount in excess of the amount of the expenses substantiated in accordance with paragraph (e) of this section, the amounts paid under the arrangement that are in excess of the substantiated expenses are treated as paid under a nonaccountable plan.

(4) *Treatment of payments under accountable plans.*—Amounts treated as paid under an accountable plan are excluded from the employee's gross income, are not reported as wages or other compensation on the employee's Form W-2, and are exempt from the withholding and payment of employment taxes (Federal Insurance Contributions Act (FICA), Federal Unemployment Tax Act (FUTA), Railroad Retirement Tax Act (RRTA), Railroad Unemployment Repayment Tax (RURT), and income tax). See paragraph (l) of this section for cross references.

(5) *Treatment of payments under nonaccountable plans.*—Amounts treated as paid under a nonaccountable plan are included in the employee's gross income, must be reported as wages or other compensation on the employee's Form W-2, and are subject to withholding and payment of employment taxes (FICA, FUTA, RRTA, RURT, and income tax). See paragraph (h) of this section. Expenses attributable to amounts included in the employee's gross income may be deducted, provided the employee can substantiate the full amount of his or her expenses (i.e., the amount of the expenses, if any, the reimbursement for which is treated as paid under an accountable plan as well as those for which the employee is claiming the deduction) in accordance with § 1.274-5T and 1.274(d)-1 or § 1.162-17, but only as a miscellaneous itemized deduction subject to the limitations applicable to such expenses (e.g., the 80-percent limitation on meal and entertainment expenses provided in section 274(n) and the 2-percent floor provided in section 67).

(d) *Business connection.*—(1) *In general.*—Except as provided in paragraphs (d)(2) and (d)(3) of this section, an arrangement meets the requirements of this paragraph (d) if it provides advances, allowances (including per diem allowances, allowances only for meals and incidental expenses, and mileage allowances), or reimbursements only for business expenses that are allowable as deductions by Part VI (section 161 and the following), subchapter B, chapter 1 of the Code, and that are paid or incurred by the employee in connection with the performance of services as an employee of the employer. The payment may be actually received from the employer, its agent, or a third party for whom the employee performs a service as an employee of the employer, and may include amounts charged directly or indirectly to the payor through credit card systems or otherwise. In addition, if both wages and the reimbursement or other expense allowance are combined in a single payment, the reimbursement or other expense allowance must be identified either by making a separate payment or by specifically identifying the amount of the reimbursement or other expense allowance.

(2) *Other bona fide expenses.*—If an arrangement provides advances, allowances, or reimbursements for business expenses described in paragraph (d)(1) of this section (i.e., deductible employee business expenses) and for other bona fide expenses related to the employer's business (e.g., travel that is not away from home) that are not deductible under Part VI (section 161 and the following), subchapter B, chapter 1 of the Code, the payor is treated as maintaining two arrangements. The portion of the arrangement that provides payments for the deductible employee business

expenses is treated as one arrangement that satisfies this paragraph (d). The portion of the arrangement that provides payments for the nondeductible employee expenses is treated as a second arrangement that does not satisfy this paragraph (d) and all amounts paid under this second arrangement will be treated as paid under a nonaccountable plan. See paragraphs (c)(5) and (h) of this section.

(3) *Reimbursement requirement.*—(i) *In general.*—If a payor arranges to pay an amount to an employee regardless of whether the employee incurs (or is reasonably expected to incur) business expenses of a type described in paragraph (d)(1) or (d)(2) of this section, the arrangement does not satisfy this paragraph (d) and all amounts paid under the arrangement are treated as paid under a nonaccountable plan. See paragraphs (c)(5) and (h) of this section.

(ii) *Per diem allowances.*—An arrangement providing a per diem allowance for travel expenses of a type described in paragraph (d)(1) or (d)(2) of this section that is computed on a basis similar to that used in computing the employee's wages or other compensation (e.g., the number of hours worked, miles traveled, or pieces produced) meets the requirements of this paragraph (d) only if, on December 12, 1989, the per diem allowance was identified by the payor either by making a separate payment or by specifically identifying the amount of the per diem allowance, or a per diem allowance computed on that basis was commonly used in the industry in which the employee is employed. See section 274(d) and § 1.274(d)-1. A per diem allowance described in this paragraph (d)(3)(ii) may be adjusted in a manner that reasonably reflects actual increases in employee business expenses occurring after December 12, 1989.

(e) *Substantiation.*—(1) *In general.*—An arrangement meets the requirements of this paragraph (e) if it requires each business expense to be substantiated to the payor in accordance with paragraph (e)(2) or (e)(3) of this section, whichever is applicable, within a reasonable period of time. See § 1.274-5T or § 1.162-17.

(2) *Expenses governed by section 274(d).*—An arrangement that reimburses travel, entertainment, use of a passenger automobile or other listed property, or other business expenses governed by section 274(d) meets the requirements of this paragraph (e)(2) if information sufficient to satisfy the substantiation requirements of section 274(d) and the regulations thereunder is submitted to the payor. See § 1.274-5. Under section 274(d), information sufficient to substantiate the requisite elements of each expenditure or use must be submitted to the payor. For example, with respect to travel away from home, § 1.274-5(b)(2) requires that information sufficient to substantiate the amount, time, place, and business purpose of the expense must be submitted to the payor. Similarly, with respect to use of a passenger automobile or other listed property, § 1.274-5(b)(6) requires that information sufficient to substantiate the amount, time, use, and business purpose of the expense must be submitted to the payor. See § 1.274-5(g) and (j), which grant the Commissioner the authority to establish optional methods of substantiating certain expenses. Substantiation of the amount of a business expense in accordance with rules prescribed pursuant to the authority granted by § 1.274-5(g) or (j) will be treated as substantiation of the amount of such expense for purposes of this section.

(3) *Expenses not governed by section 274(d).*—An arrangement that reimburses business expenses not governed by section 274(d) meets the requirements of this paragraph (e)(3) if information is submitted to the payor sufficient to enable the payor to identify the specific nature of each expense and to conclude that the expense is attributable to the payor's business activities. Therefore, each of the elements of an expenditure or use must be substantiated to the payor. It is not sufficient if an employee merely aggregates expenses into broad categories (such as "travel") or reports individual expenses through the use of vague, nondescriptive terms (such as "miscellaneous business expenses"). See § 1.162-17(b).

* * *

(h) *Withholding and payment of employment taxes.*—(1) *When excluded from wages.*—If an arrangement meets the requirements of paragraphs (d), (e), and (f) of this section, the amounts paid under the arrangement that are not in excess of the expenses substantiated in accordance with paragraph (e) of this section (i.e., the amounts treated as paid under an accountable plan) are not wages and are not subject to withholding and payment of employment taxes. If an arrangement provides advances, allowances, or reimbursements for meal and entertainment expenses and a portion of the payment is treated as paid under a nonaccountable plan under paragraph (d)(2) of this section due solely to section 274(n), then notwithstanding paragraph (h)(2)(ii) of this section, these nondeductible amounts are neither treated as gross income nor subject to withholding and payment of employment taxes.

(2) *When included in wages.*—(i) *Accountable plans.*—(A) *General rule.*—Except as provided in paragraph (h)(2)(i)(B) of

this section, if the expenses covered under an arrangement that meets the requirements of paragraphs (d), (e), and (f) of this section are not substantiated to the payor in accordance with paragraph (e) of this section within a reasonable period of time or if any amounts in excess of the substantiated expenses are not returned to the payor in accordance with paragraph (f) of this section within a reasonable period of time, the amount which is treated as paid under a nonaccountable plan under paragraph (c)(3)(ii) of this section is subject to withholding and payment of employment taxes no later than the first payroll period following the end of the reasonable period. A payor may treat any amount not substantiated or returned within the periods specified in paragraph (g)(2) of this section as not substantiated or returned within a reasonable period of time.

(B) *Per diem or mileage allowances.*—*(1) In general.*—If a payor pays a per diem or mileage allowance under an arrangement that meets the requirements of paragraphs (d), (e), and (f) of this section, the portion, if any, of the allowance paid that relates to days or miles of travel substantiated in accordance with paragraph (e) of this section and that exceeds the amount of the employee's expenses deemed substantiated for such travel pursuant to rules prescribed under section 274(d) and §1.274(d)-1 or §1.274-5T(j) is treated as paid under a nonaccountable plan. See paragraph (c)(3)(ii) of this section. Because the employee is not required to return this excess portion, the reasonable period of time provisions of paragraph (g) of this section (relating to the return of excess amounts) do not apply to this excess portion.

(2) Reimbursements.—Except as provided in paragraph (h)(2)(i)(B)(*4*) of this section, in the case of a per diem or mileage allowance paid as a reimbursement at a rate for each day or mile of travel that exceeds the amount of the employee's expenses deemed substantiated for a day or mile of travel, the excess portion described in paragraph (h)(2)(i) of this section is subject to withholding and payment of employment taxes in the payroll period in which the payor reimburses the expenses for the days or miles of travel substantiated in accordance with paragraph (e) of this section.

(3) Advances.—Except as provided in paragraph (h)(2)(i)(B)(*4*) of this section, in the case of a per diem or mileage allowance paid as an advance at a rate for each day or mile of travel that exceeds the amount of the employee's expenses deemed substantiated for a day or mile of travel, the excess portion described in paragraph (h)(2)(i) of this section is subject to withholding and payment of employment taxes no later than the first payroll period following the payroll period in which the expenses with respect to which the advance was paid (i.e., the days or miles of travel) are substantiated in accordance with paragraph (e) of this section. The expenses with respect to which the advance was paid must be substantiated within a reasonable period of time. See paragraph (g) of this section.

(4) Special rules.—The Commissioner may, in his discretion, prescribe special rules in pronouncements of general applicability regarding the timing of withholding and payment of employment taxes on per diem and mileage allowances.

(ii) *Nonaccountable plans.*—If an arrangement does not satisfy one or more of the requirements of paragraphs (d), (e), or (f) of this section, all amounts paid under the arrangement are wages and are subject to withholding and payment of employment taxes when paid.

* * *

[Reg. §1.62-2.]

☐ [*T.D.* 8324, 12-14-90. *Amended by T.D.* 8451, 12-4-92; *T.D.* 8666, 5-29-96; *T.D.* 8784, 9-30-98; *T.D.* 8864, 1-21-2000 *and T.D.* 9064, 6-30-2003.]

Items Specifically Included in Gross Income

§1.72-1. Introduction.—(a) *General principle.*—Section 72 prescribes rules relating to the inclusion in gross income of amounts received under a life insurance, endowment, or annuity contract unless such amounts are specifically excluded from gross income under other provisions of chapter 1 of the Code. In general, these rules provide that amounts subject to the provisions of section 72 are includible in the gross income of the recipient except to the extent that they are considered to represent a reduction or return of premiums or other consideration paid.

(b) *Amounts to be considered as a return of premiums.*—For the purpose of determining the extent to which amounts received represent a reduction or return of premiums or other consideration paid, the provisions of section 72 distinguish between "amounts received as an annuity" and "amounts not received as an annuity". In general, "amounts received as an annuity" are amounts which are payable at regular intervals over a period of more than one full year from the date on which they are deemed to begin, provided the total of the amounts so payable or the period for which they are to be paid can be determined as of that date. See paragraph (b)(2) and (3) of §1.72.2. Any other amounts to which the provisions of section 72 apply are considered to be "amounts not received as an annuity." See §1.72-11.

(c) *"Amounts received as an annuity."*.—(1) In the case of "amounts received as an annuity" (other than certain employees' annuities described in section 72(d) and in §1.72-13), a proportionate part of each amount so received is considered to represent a return of premiums or other consideration paid. The proportionate part of each annuity payment which is thus excludable from gross income is determined by the ratio which the investment in the contract as of the date on which the annuity is deemed to begin bears to the expected return under the contract as of that date. See §1.72-4.

(2) In the case of employees' annuities of the type described in section 72(d), no amount received as an annuity in a taxable year to which the Internal Revenue Code of 1954 applies is includible in the gross income of a recipient until the aggregate of all amounts received thereunder and excluded from gross income under the applicable income tax law exceeds the consideration contributed (or deemed contributed) by the employee under §1.72-8. Thereafter, all amounts so received are includible in the gross income of the recipient. See §1.72-13.

(d) *"Amounts not received as an annuity"*.—In the case of "amounts not received as an annuity", if such amounts are received after an annuity has begun and during its continuance, amounts so received are generally includible in the gross income of the recipient. Amounts not received as an annuity which are received at any other time are generally includible in the gross income of the recipient only to the extent that such amounts, when added to all amounts previously received under the contract which were excludable from the gross income of the recipient under the income tax law applicable at the time of receipt, exceed the premiums or other consideration paid (see §1.72-11). However, if the aggregate of premiums or other consideration paid for the contract includes amounts for which a deduction was allowed under section 404 as contributions on behalf of an owner-employee, the amounts received under the circumstances of the preceding sentence shall be includible in gross income until the amount so included equals the amount for which the deduction was so allowed. See paragraph (b) of §1.72-17.

(e) *Classification of recipients.*—For the purpose of the regulations under section 72, a recipient shall be considered an "annuitant" if he receives amounts under an annuity contract during the period that the annuity payments are to continue, whether for a term certain or during the continuing life or lives of the person or persons whose lives measure the duration of such annuity. However, a recipient shall be considered a "beneficiary" rather than an "annuitant" if the amounts he receives under a contract are received after the term of the annuity for a life or lives has expired and such amounts are paid by reason of the fact that the contract guarantees that payments of some minimum amount or for some minimum period shall be made. For special rules with respect to beneficiaries, see paragraphs (a)(1)(ii) and (c) of §1.72-11. [Reg. §1.72-1.]

☐ [*T.D.* 6211, 11-14-56. *Amended by T.D.* 6676, 9-16-63.]

§1.72-4. Exclusion ratio.—(a) *General rule.*—(1)(i) To determine the proportionate part of the total amount received each year as an annuity which is excludable from the gross income of a recipient in the taxable year of receipt (other than amounts received under (*a*) certain employee annuities described in section 72(d) and §1.72-13, or (*b*) certain annuities described in section 72(o) and §1.122-1), an exclusion ratio is to be determined for each contract. In general, this ratio is determined by dividing the investment in the contract as found under §1.72-6 by the expected return under such contract as found under §1.72-5. Where a single consideration is given for a particular contract which provides for two or more annuity elements, an exclusion ratio shall be determined for the contract as a whole by dividing the investment in such contract by the aggregate of the expected returns under all the annuity elements provided thereunder. However, where the provisions of paragraph (b)(3) of §1.72-2 apply to payments received under such a contract, see paragraph (b)(3) of §1.72-6. In the case of a contract to which §1.72-6(d) (relating to contracts in which amounts were invested both before July 1, 1986, and after June 30, 1986) applies, the exclusion ratio for purposes of this paragraph (a) is determined in accordance with §1.72-6(d) and, in particular, §1.72-6(d)(5)(i).

(ii) The exclusion ratio for the particular contract is then applied to the total amount received as an annuity during the taxable year by each recipient. See, however, paragraph (e)(3) of §1.72-5. Any excess of the total amount received as an annuity during the taxable year over the amount determined by the application of the exclusion ratio to such total amount shall be included in the gross income of the recipient for the taxable year of receipt.

(2) The principles of subparagraph (1) may be illustrated by the following example:

Example. Taxpayer A purchased an annuity contract providing for payments of $100 per month for a consideration of $12,650. Assuming that the expected return under this contract is $16,000 the exclusion ratio to be used by A is $12,650 ÷ [$]16,000; or 79.1 percent (79.06 rounded to the nearest tenth). If 12 such monthly payments are received by A during his taxable year, the total amount he may exclude from his gross income in such year is $949.20 ($1,200 × 79.1 percent). The balance of $250.80 ($1,200 less $949.20) is the amount to be included in gross income. If A instead received only five such payments during the year, he should exclude $395.50 ([$]500 × 79.1 percent) of the total amounts received.

For examples of the computation of the exclusion ratio in cases where two annuity elements are acquired for a single consideration, see paragraph (b) (1) of § 1.72-6.

(3) The exclusion ratio shall be applied only to amounts received as an annuity within the meaning of that term under paragraph (b) (2) and (3) of § 1.72-2. Where the periodic payments increase in amount after the annuity starting date in a manner not provided by the terms of the contract at such date, the portion of such payments representing the increase is not an amount received as an annuity. For the treatment of amounts not received as an annuity, see section 72(e) and § 1.72-11. For special rules where paragraph (b) (3) of § 1.72-2 applies to amounts received, see paragraph (d) (3) of this section.

(4) After an exclusion ratio has been determined for a particular contract, it shall be applied to any amounts received as an annuity thereunder unless or until one of the following occurs:

(i) The contract is assigned or transferred for a valuable consideration (see section 72(g) and paragraph (a) of § 1.72-10);

(ii) The contract matures or is surrendered, redeemed, or discharged in accordance with the provisions of paragraph (c) or (d) of § 1.72-11;

(iii) The contract is exchanged (or is considered to have been exchanged) in a manner described in paragraph (e) of § 1.72-11.

(b) *Annuity starting date.*—(1) Except as provided in subparagraph (2) of this paragraph, the annuity starting date is the first day of the first period for which an amount is received as an annuity, except that if such date was before January 1, 1954, then the annuity starting date is January 1, 1954. The first day of the first period for which an amount is received as an annuity shall be whichever of the following is the later:

(i) The date upon which the obligations under the contract became fixed, or

(ii) The first day of the period (year, half-year, quarter, month, or otherwise, depending on whether payments are to be made annually, semi-annually, quarterly, monthly, or otherwise) which ends on the date of the first annuity payment.

(2) Notwithstanding the provisions of paragraph (b) (1) of this section, the annuity starting date shall be determined in accordance with whichever of the following provisions is appropriate:

(i) In the case of a joint and survivor annuity contract described in section 72(i) and paragraph (b) (3) of § 1.72-5, the annuity starting date is January 1, 1954, or the first day of the first period for which an amount is received as an annuity by the surviving annuitant, whichever is the later;

(ii) In the case of the transfer of an annuity contract for a valuable consideration, as described in section 72(g) and paragraph (a) of § 1.72-10, the annuity starting date shall be January 1, 1954, or the first day of the first period for which the transferee received an amount as an annuity, whichever is the later;

(iii) If the provisions of paragraph (e) of § 1.72-11 apply to an exchange of one contract for another, or to a transaction deemed to be such an exchange, the annuity starting date of the contract received (or deemed received) in exchange shall be January 1, 1954, or the first day of the first period for which an amount is received as an annuity under such contract, whichever is the later; and

(iv) In the case of an employee who has retired from work because of personal injuries or sickness, and who is receiving amounts under a plan that is a wage continuation plan under section 105(d) and § 1.105-4, the annuity starting date shall be the date the employee reaches mandatory retirement age, as defined in § 1.105-4(a) (3) (i) (B). (See, also §§ 1.72-15 and 1.105-6 for transitional and other special rules.)

* * *

[Reg. § 1.72-4.]

☐ [*T.D.* 6211, 11-14-56. *Amended by T.D.* 7043, 6-1-70, *T.D.* 7352, 4-9-75, *and T.D.* 8115, 12-16-86.]

§ 1.72-5. Expected return.—(a) *Expected return for but one life.*—(1) If a contract to which section 72 applies provides that one annuitant is to receive a fixed monthly income for life, the expected return is determined by multiplying the total of the annuity payments to be received annually by the multiple shown in Table I or V (whichever is applicable) of § 1.79-9 under the age (as of the annuity starting date) and, if applicable, sex of the measuring life (usually the annuitant's). Thus, where a male purchases a contract before July 1, 1986, providing for an immediate annuity of $100 per month for his life and, as of the annuity starting date (in this case the date of purchase), the annuitant's age at his nearest birthday is 66, the expected return is computed as follows:

Monthly payment of $100 × 12 months equals annual payment of	$1,200
Multiple shown in Table I, male, age 66	14.4
Expected return ($1,200 × 14.4)	17,280

If, however, the taxpayer had purchased the contract after June 30, 1986, the expected return would be $23,040, determined by multiplying 19.2 (multiple shown in Table V, age 66) by $1,200.

* * *

(b) *Expected return under joint and survivor and joint annuities.*—(1) In the case of a joint and survivor annuity contract involving two annuitants which provides the first annuitant with a fixed monthly income for life and, after the death of the first annuitant, provides an identical monthly income for life to a second annuitant, the expected return shall be determined by multiplying the total amount of the payments to be received annually by the multiple obtained from Table II or VI (whichever is applicable) of § 1.72-9 under the ages (as of the annuity starting date) and, if applicable, sexes of the living annuitants. For example, a husband purchases a joint and survivor annuity contract providing for payments of $100 per month for life and, after his death, for the same amount to his wife for the remainder of her life. As of the annuity starting date his age at his nearest birthday is 70 and that of his wife at her nearest birthday is 67. If there is no post-June 1986 investment in the contract, the expected return is computed as follows:

Monthly payments of $100 × 12 months equals annual payment of	$1,200
Multiple shown in Table II (male, age 70, female, age 67)	19.7
Expected return ($1,200 × 19.7)	$23,640

If the annuitants purchased the same contract after June 30, 1986, the expected return would be $26,400, computed as follows:

Monthly payments of $100 × 12 months equals annual payment of	$1,200
Multiple shown in Table VI (ages 70, 67)	22.0
Expected return ($1,200 × 22.0)	$26,400

If payments are to be made quarterly, semiannually, or annually, an appropriate adjustment of the multiple found in Table II or VI (whichever is applicable) should be made in accordance with paragraph (a)(2) of this section.

* * *

(c) *Expected return for term certain.*—In the case of a contract providing for specific periodic payments which are to be paid for a term certain such as a fixed number of months or years, without regard to life expectancy, the expected return is determined by multiplying the fixed number of years or months for which payments are to be on or after the annuity starting date by the amount of the payment provided in the contract for each such period.

* * *

[Reg. § 1.72-5.]

☐ [*T.D.* 6211, 11-14-56. *Amended by T.D.* 8115, 12-16-86.]

§ 1.72-6. Investment in the contract.—(a) *General rule.*—(1) For the purpose of computing the "investment in the contract", it is first necessary to determine the "aggregate amount of premiums or other consideration paid" for such contract. See section 72(c)(1). This determination is made as of the later of the annuity starting date of the contract or the date on which an amount is first received thereunder as an annuity. The amount so found is then reduced by the sum of the following amounts in order to find the investment in the contract:

(i) The total amount of any return of premiums or dividends received (including unrepaid loans or dividends applied against the principal or interest on such loans) on or before the date on which the foregoing determination is made, and

(ii) The total of any other amounts received with respect to the contract on or before such date which were excludable from the gross income for the recipient under the income tax law applicable at the time of receipt.

Amounts to which subdivision (ii) of this subparagraph applies shall include, for example, amounts considered to be return of premiums or other consideration paid under section 22(b)(2) of the Internal Revenue Code of 1939 and amounts considered to be an employer-provided death benefit under section 22(b)(1)(B) of such Code. For rules relating to the extent to which an employee or his beneficiary may include employer contributions in the aggregate amount of premiums or other consideration paid, see § 1.72-8. If the aggregate amount of premiums or other consideration paid for the contract includes amounts for which deductions were allowed under section 404 as contributions on behalf of a self-employed individual, such amounts shall not be included in the investment in the contract.

* * *

[Reg. § 1.72-6.]

☐ [*T.D.* 6211, 11-14-56. *Amended by T.D.* 6676, 9-16-63, *T.D.* 7311, 3-29-74 *and T.D.* 8115, 12-16-86.]

§ 1.72-9. Tables.—The following tables are to be used in connection with computations under section 72 and the regulations thereunder. Tables I, II, IIA, III, and IV are to be used if the investment in the contract does not include a post-June 1986 investment in the contract (as defined in § 1.72-6(d)(3)). Tables V, VI, VIA, VII, and VIII are to be used if the investment in the contract includes a post-June 1986 investment in the contract (as defined in § 1.72-6(d)(3)).

In the case of a contract under which amounts are received as an annuity after June 30, 1986, a taxpayer receiving such amounts may elect to treat the entire investment in the contract as post-June 1986 investment in the contract and thus apply Tables V through VIII. A taxpayer may make the election for any taxable year in which such amounts are received by attaching to the taxpayer's return for such taxable year a statement that the taxpayer is electing under § 1.72-9 to treat the entire investment in the contract as post-June 1986 investment in the contract. The statement must contain the taxpayer's name, address, and taxpayer identification number. The election is irrevocable and applies with respect to all amounts that the taxpayer receives as an annuity under the contract in the taxable year for which the election is made or in any subsequent taxable year. (Note that for purposes of the examples in §§ 1.72-4 through 1.72-11 the election described in this section is disregarded, (i.e., it is assumed that the taxpayer does not make an election under this section).)

* * *

TABLE I.—ORDINARY LIFE ANNUITIES—ONE LIFE—
EXPECTED RETURN MULTIPLES

Ages		Multiples	Ages		Multiples	Ages		Multiples
Male	Female		Male	Female		Male	Female	
6	11	65.0	41	46	33.0	76	81	9.1
7	12	64.1	42	47	32.1	77	82	8.7
8	13	63.2	43	48	31.2	78	83	8.3
9	14	62.3	44	49	30.4	79	84	7.8
10	15	61.4	45	50	29.6	80	85	7.5
11	16	60.4	46	51	28.7	81	86	7.1
12	17	59.5	47	52	27.9	82	87	6.7
13	18	58.6	48	53	27.1	83	88	6.3
14	19	57.7	49	54	26.3	84	89	6.0
15	20	56.7	50	55	25.5	85	90	5.7
16	21	55.8	51	56	24.7	86	91	5.4
17	22	54.9	52	57	24.0	87	92	5.1
18	23	53.9	53	58	23.2	88	93	4.8
19	24	53.0	54	59	22.4	89	94	4.5
20	25	52.1	55	60	21.7	90	95	4.2
21	26	51.1	56	61	21.0	91	96	4.0
22	27	50.2	57	62	20.3	92	97	3.7
23	28	49.3	58	63	19.6	93	98	3.5
24	29	48.3	59	64	18.9	94	99	3.3
25	30	47.4	60	65	18.2	95	100	3.1
26	31	46.5	61	66	17.5	96	101	2.9
27	32	45.6	62	67	16.9	97	102	2.7
28	33	44.6	63	68	16.2	98	103	2.5
29	34	43.7	64	69	15.6	99	104	2.3
30	35	42.8	65	70	15.0	100	105	2.1
31	36	41.9	66	71	14.4	101	106	1.9
32	37	41.0	67	72	13.8	102	107	1.7
33	38	40.0	68	73	13.2	103	108	1.5
34	39	39.1	69	74	12.6	104	109	1.3
35	40	38.2	70	75	12.1	105	110	1.2
						106	111	1.0
36	41	37.3	71	76	11.6	107	112	.8
37	42	36.5	72	77	11.0	108	113	.7
38	43	35.6	73	78	10.5	109	114	.6
39	44	34.7	74	79	10.1	110	115	.5
40	45	33.8	75	80	9.6	111	116	0.0

* * *

TABLE V.—ORDINARY LIFE ANNUITIES; ONE LIFE—EXPECTED RETURN MULTIPLES

Age	Multiple
5	76.6
6	75.6
7	74.7
8	73.7
9	72.7
10	71.7
11	70.7
12	69.7
13	68.8
14	67.8
15	66.8
16	65.8
17	64.8
18	63.9
19	62.9
20	61.9
21	60.9
22	59.9
23	59.9
24	58.9
25	57.9
26	56.0
27	55.1
28	54.1
29	53.1
30	52.2
31	51.2
32	50.2
33	49.3
34	48.3
35	47.3
36	46.4
37	45.4
38	44.4
39	43.5
40	42.5
41	41.5
42	40.6
43	39.6
44	38.7
45	37.7
46	36.8
47	35.9
48	34.9
49	34.0
50	33.1
51	32.2
52	31.3
53	30.4
54	29.5
55	28.6
56	27.7
57	26.8
58	25.9
59	25.0
60	24.2
61	23.3
62	22.5
63	21.6
64	20.8
65	20.0
66	19.2
67	18.4
68	17.6
69	16.8
70	16.0
71	15.3
72	14.6
73	13.9
74	13.2
75	12.5
76	11.9
77	11.2
78	10.6
79	10.0
80	9.5
81	8.9
82	8.4
83	7.9
84	7.4
85	6.9
86	6.5
87	6.1
88	5.7
89	5.3
90	5.0
91	4.7
92	4.4
93	4.1
94	3.9
95	3.7
96	3.4
97	3.2
98	3.0
99	2.8
100	2.7
101	2.5
102	2.3
103	2.1
104	1.9
105	1.8
106	1.6
107	1.4
108	1.3
109	1.1
110	1.0
111	.9
112	.8
113	.7
114	.6
115	.5

* * *

[Reg. § 1.72-9.]

□ [*T.D.* 6211, 11-14-56. *Amended by T.D.* 6233, 5-14-57 *and T.D.* 8115, 12-16-86.]

§ 1.73-1. Services of child.—(a) Compensation for personal services of a child shall, regardless of the provisions of State law relating to who is entitled to the earnings of the child, and regardless of whether the income is in fact received by the child, be deemed to be the gross income of the child and not the gross income of the parent of the child. Such compensation, therefore, shall be included in the gross income of the child and shall be reflected in the return rendered by or for such child. The income of a minor child is not required to be included in the gross income of the parent for income tax purposes. For requirements for making the return by such child, or for such child by his guardian, or other person charged with the care of his person or property, see section 6012.

(b) In the determination of taxable income or adjusted gross income, as the case may be, all expenditures made by the parent or the child attributable to amounts which are includible in the gross income of the child and not of the parent solely by reason of section 73 are deemed to have been paid or incurred by the child. In such determination, the child is entitled to take deductions not only for expenditures made on his behalf by his parent which would be commonly considered as business expenses, but also for other expenditures such as charitable contributions made by the parent in the name of the child and out of the child's earnings.

(c) For purposes of section 73, the term "parent" includes any individual who is entitled to the services of the child by reason of having parental rights and duties in respect of the child. See section 6201(c) and the regulations in Part 301 of this chapter (Regulations on Procedure and Administration) for assessment of tax against the parent in certain cases. [Reg. § 1.73-1.]

□ [*T.D.* 6211, 11-14-56.]

§ 1.79-3. Determination of amount equal to cost of group-term life insurance.—(a) *In general.*—This section prescribes the rules for determining the amount equal to the cost of group-term life insurance on an employee's life which is to be included in his gross income pursuant to the rule of inclusion set forth in section 79(a). Such amount is determined by—

(1) Computing the cost of the portion of the group-term life insurance on the employee's life to be taken into account (determined in accordance with the rules set forth in paragraph (b) of this section) for each "period of coverage" (as defined in paragraph (c) of this section) and aggregating the costs so determined, then

(2) Reducing the amount determined under subparagraph (1) of this paragraph by the amount determined in accordance with the rules set forth in paragraph (e) of this section, relating to the amount paid by the employee toward the purchase of group-term life insurance.

(b) *Determination of the portion of the group-term life insurance on the employee's life to be taken into account.*—(1) For each "period of coverage" (as defined in paragraph (c) of this section), the portion of the group-term life insurance to be taken into account in computing the amount includible in an employee's gross income for purposes of paragraph (a)(1) of this section is the sum of the proceeds payable upon the death of the employee under each policy, or portion of a policy, of group-term life insurance on such employee's life to which the rule of inclusion set forth in section 79(a) applies, less $50,000 of such insurance. Thus, the amount of any proceeds payable under a policy, or portion of a policy, which qualifies for one of the exceptions to the rule of inclusion provided by section 79(b) is not taken into account. For the regulations relating to such exceptions to the rule of inclusion, see § 1.79-2.

(2) For purposes of making the computation required by subparagraph (1) of this paragraph in any case in which the amount payable under the policy, or portion thereof, varies during the period of coverage, the amount payable under such policy during such period is considered to be the average of the amount payable under such policy at the beginning and the end of such period.

(3) (i) For purposes of making the computation required by subparagraph (1) of this paragraph in any case in which the amount payable under the policy is not payable as a specific amount upon the death of the employee in full discharge of the liability of the insurer, and such form of payment is not one of alternative methods of payment, the amount payable under such policy is the present value of the agreement by the insurer under the policy to make the payments to the beneficiary or beneficiaries entitled to such amounts upon the employee's death. For each period of coverage, such present value is to be determined as if the first and last day of such period is the date of death of the employee.

(ii) The present value of the agreement by the insurer under the policy to make payments shall be determined by the use of the mortality tables and interest rate employed by the insurer with respect to such a policy in calculating the amount held by the insurer (as defined in section 101(d)(2)), unless the Commissioner otherwise determines that a particular mortality table and interest rate, representative of the mortality table and interest rate used by commercial insurance companies with respect to such policies, shall be used to determine the present value of the policy for purposes of this subdivision.

(iii) For purposes of making the computation required by subdivision (i) of this subparagraph in any case in which it is necessary to determine the age of an employee's beneficiary and such beneficiary remains the same (under the policy, or the portion of the policy, with respect to which the determination of the present value of the agreement of the insurer to pay benefits is being made) for the entire period during the employee's taxable year for which such policy is in effect, the age of such beneficiary is such beneficiary's age at his nearest birthday on June 30th of the calendar year.

(iv) If the policy of group-term life insurance on the employee's life is such that the present value of the agreement by the insurer under the policy to pay benefits cannot be determined by the rules prescribed in this subparagraph, the taxpayer may submit with his return a computation of such present value, consistent with the actuarial and other assumptions set forth in this subparagraph, showing the appropriate factors applied in his case. Such computation shall be subject to the approval of the Commissioner upon examination of such return.

(c) *Period of coverage.*—For purposes of this section, the phrase "period of coverage" means any one calendar month period, or part thereof, during the employee's taxable year during which the employee is provided group-term life insurance on his life to which the rule of inclusion set forth in section 79(a) applies. The phrase "part thereof" as used in the preceding sentence means any continuous period which is less than the one calendar month period referred to in the preceding sentence for which premiums are charged by the insurer.

(d) *The cost of the portion of the group-term life insurance on an employee's life.*—(1) This paragraph sets forth the rules for determining the cost, for each period of coverage, of the portion of the group-term life insurance on the employee's life to be taken into account in computing the amount includible in the employee's gross income for purposes of paragraph (a)(1) of this section. The portion of the group-term life insurance on the employee's life to be taken into account is determined in accordance with the provisions of paragraph (b) of this section. Table I, which is set forth in subparagraph (2) of this paragraph, determines the cost for each $1,000 of such portion of the group-term life insurance on the employee's life for each one-month period. The cost of the portion of the group-term life insurance on the employee's life for each period of coverage of one month is obtained by multiplying the number of thousand dollars of such insurance computed to the nearest tenth which is provided during such period by the appropriate amount set forth in Table 1. In any case in which group-term life insurance is provided for a period of coverage of less than one month, the amount set forth in Table I is prorated over such period of coverage.

(2) For the cost of group-term life insurance provided after June 30, 1999, the following table sets forth the cost of $1,000 of group-term life insurance provided for one month, computed on the basis of 5-year age brackets. See 26 CFR 1.79-3(d)(2) in effect prior to July 1, 1999, and contained in the 26 CFR part 1 edition revised as of April 1, 1999, for a table setting forth the cost of group-term life insurance provided before July 1, 1999. For purposes of Table I, the age of the employee is the employee's attained age on the last day of the employee's taxable year.

TABLE I.—UNIFORM PREMIUMS FOR $1,000 OF GROUP-TERM LIFE INSURANCE PROTECTION

5-year age bracket	*Cost per $1,000 of protection for one month*
Under 25	$0.05
25 to 29	.06
30 to 34	.08
35 to 39	.09
40 to 44	.10
45 to 49	.15
50 to 54	.23
55 to 59	.43
60 to 64	.66
65 to 69	1.27
70 and above	2.06

(3) The net premium cost of group-term life insurance as provided in Table I of subparagraph (2) of this paragraph applies only to the cost of group-term life insurance subject to the rule of inclusion set forth in section 79(a). Therefore, such net premium cost is not applicable to the determination of the cost of group-term life insurance provided under a policy which is not subject to such rule of inclusion.

* * *

[Reg. § 1.79-3.]

☐ [*T.D.* 6888, 7-5-66. *Amended by T.D.* 7623, 5-14-79; *T.D.* 7924, 12-1-83; *T.D.* 8273, 11-17-89; *T.D.* 8424, 7-29-92 *and T.D.* 8821, 5-28-99.]

Caution: Reg. § 1.82-1 does not reflect changes made in Section 217 by the Omnibus Budget Reconciliation Act of 1993.

§ 1.82-1. Payments for or reimbursements of expenses of moving from one residence to another residence attributable to employment or self-employment.—

(a) *Reimbursements in gross income.*—(1) *In general.*—Any amount received or accrued, directly or indirectly, by an individual as a payment for or reimbursement of expenses of moving from one residence to another residence attributable to employment or self-employment is includible in gross income under section 82 as compensation for services in the taxable year received or accrued. For rules relating to the year a deduction may be allowed for expenses of moving from one residence to another residence, see section 217 and the regulations thereunder.

(2) *Amounts received or accrued as reimbursement or payment.*—For purposes of this section, amounts are considered as being received or accrued by an individual as reimbursement or payment whether received in the form of money, property, or services. A cash basis taxpayer will include amounts in gross income under section 82 when they are received or treated as received by him. Thus, for example, if an employer moves an employee's household goods and personal effects from the employee's old residence to his new residence using the employer's facilities, the employee is considered as having received a payment in the amount of the fair market value of the services furnished at the time the services are furnished by the employer. If the employer pays a mover for moving the employee's household goods and personal effects, the employee is considered as having received the payment at the time the employer pays the mover, rather than at the time the mover moves the employee's household goods and effects. Where an employee receives a loan or advance from an employer to enable him to pay his moving expenses, the employee will not be deemed to have received a reimbursement of moving expenses until such time as he accounts to his employer if he is not required to repay such loan or advance and if he makes such accounting within a reasonable time. Such loan or advance will be deemed to be a reimbursement of moving expenses at the time of such accounting to the extent used by the employee for such moving expenses.

(3) *Direct or indirect payments or reimbursements.*—For purposes of this section amounts are considered as being received or accrued whether received directly (paid or provided to an individual by an employer, a client, a customer, or similar person) or indirectly (paid to a third party on behalf of an individual by an employer, a client, a customer, or similar person). Thus, if an employer pays a mover for the expenses of moving an employee's household goods and personal effects from one residence to another residence, the employee has indirectly received a payment which is includible in his gross income under section 82.

(4) *Expenses of moving from one residence to another residence.*—An expense of moving from one residence to another residence is any expenditure, cost, loss, or similar item paid or incurred in connection with a move from one residence to another residence. Moving expenses include (but are not limited to) any expenditure, cost, loss, or similar item directly or indirectly resulting from the acquisition, sale, or exchange of property, the transportation of goods or property, or travel (by the taxpayer or any other person) in connection with a change in residence. Such expenses include items described in section 217(b) (relating to the definition of moving expenses), irrespective of the dollar limitations contained in section 217(b)(3) and the conditions contained in section 217(c), as well as items not described in section 217(b), such as a loss sustained on the sale or exchange of personal property, storage charges, taxes, or expenses of refitting rugs or draperies.

(5) *Attributable to employment or self-employment.*—Any amount received or accrued from an employer, a client, a customer, or similar person in connection with the performance of services for such employer, client, customer, or similar person, is attributable to employment or self-employment. Thus, for example, if an employer reimburses an employee for a loss incurred on the sale of the employee's house, reimbursement is attributable to the performance of services if made because of the employer-employee relationship. Similarly, if an employer in order to prevent an employee's sustaining a loss on a sale of a house acquires the property from the employee at a price in excess of fair market value, the employee is considered to have received a payment attributable to employment to the extent that such payment exceeds the fair market value of the property.

* * *

[Reg. § 1.82-1.]

□ [*T.D.* 7195, 7-10-72. *Amended by T.D.* 7578, 12-19-78.]

§ 1.83-1. Property transferred in connection with the performance of services.—(a) *Inclusion in gross income.*—(1) *General rule.*—Section 83 provides rules for the taxation of property transferred to an employee or independent contractor (or beneficiary thereof) in connection with the performance of services by such employee or independent contractor. In general, such property is not taxable under section 83(a) until it has been transferred (as defined in § 1.83-3(a)) to such person and become substantially vested (as defined in

§ 1.83-3(b)) in such person. In that case, the excess of—

(i) The fair market value of such property (determined without regard to any lapse restriction, as defined in § 1.83-3(i)) at the time that the property becomes substantially vested, over

(ii) The amount (if any) paid for such property,

shall be included as compensation in the gross income of such employee or independent contractor for the taxable year in which the property becomes substantially vested. Until such property becomes substantially vested, the transferor shall be regarded as the owner of such property, and any income from such property received by the employee or independent contractor (or beneficiary thereof) or the right to the use of such property by the employee or independent contractor constitutes additional compensation and shall be included in the gross income of such employee or independent contractor for the taxable year in which such income is received or such use is made available. This paragraph applies to a transfer of property in connection with the performance of services even though the transferor is not the person for whom such services are performed.

(2) *Life insurance.*—The cost of life insurance protection under a life insurance contract, retirement income contract, endowment contract, or other contract providing life insurance protection is taxable generally under section 61 and the regulations thereunder during the period such contract remains substantially nonvested (as defined in § 1.83-3(b)). For the taxation of life insurance protection under a split-dollar life insurance arrangement (as defined in § 1.61-22(b)(1) or (2)), see § 1.61-22.

(3) *Cross references.*—For rules concerning the treatment of employers and other transferors of property in connection with the performance of services, see section 83(h) and § 1.83-6. For rules concerning the taxation of beneficiaries of an employees' trust that is not exempt under section 501(a), see section 402(b) and the regulations thereunder.

(b) *Subsequent sale, forfeiture, or other disposition of nonvested property.*—(1) If substantially nonvested property (that has been transferred in connection with the performance of services) is subsequently sold or otherwise disposed of to a third party in an arm's length transaction while still substantially nonvested, the person who performed such services shall realize compensation in an amount equal to the excess of—

(i) The amount realized on such sale or other disposition, over

(ii) The amount (if any) paid for such property.

Such amount of compensation is includible in his gross income in accordance with his method of accounting. Two preceding sentences also apply when the person disposing of the property has received it in a non-arm's length transaction described in paragraph (c) of this section. In addition, section 83(a) and paragraph (a) of this section shall thereafter cease to apply with respect to such property.

(2) If substantially nonvested property that has been transferred in connection with the performance of services to the person performing such services is forfeited while still substantially nonvested and held by such person, the difference between the amount paid (if any) and the amount received upon forfeiture (if any) shall be treated as an ordinary gain or loss. This paragraph (b)(2) does not apply to property to which § 1.83-2(a) applies.

(3) This paragraph (b) shall not apply to, and no gain shall be recognized on, any sale, forfeiture, or other disposition described in this paragraph to the extent that any property received in exchange therefor is substantially nonvested. Instead, section 83 and this section shall apply with respect to such property received (as if it were substituted for the property disposed of).

(c) *Dispositions of nonvested property not at arm's length.*—If substantially nonvested property (that has been transferred in connection with the performance of services) is disposed of in a transaction which is not at arm's length and the property remains substantially nonvested, the person who performed such services realizes compensation equal in amount to the sum of any money and the fair market value of any substantially vested property received in such disposition. Such amount of compensation is includible in his gross income in accordance with his method of accounting. However, such amount of compensation shall not exceed the fair market value of the property disposed of at the time of disposition (determined without regard to any lapse restriction), reduced by the amount paid for such property. In addition, section 83 and these regulations shall continue to apply with respect to such property, except that any amount previously includible in gross income under this paragraph (c) shall thereafter be treated as an amount paid for such property. For example, if in 1971 an employee pays $50 for a share of stock which has a fair market value of $100 and is substantially nonvested at that time and later in 1971 (at a time when the property still has a fair market value of $100 and is still substantially nonvested) the employee disposes of, in a transaction not at arm's length, the share of stock to his wife for $10, the employee realizes compensation of $10 in 1971. If in 1972, when the share of stock has a fair market value of $120, it becomes substantially vested, the employee realizes additional compensation in 1972 in the amount of $60 (the $120 fair market value of the stock less both the $50 price paid for the stock and the $10 taxed as compensation in 1971). For purposes of this paragraph, if substantially nonvested property has been transferred to a person other than the person who performed the services, and the transferee dies holding the property while the property is still substantially nonvested and while the person who performed the services is alive, the transfer which results by reason of the death of such transferee is a transfer not at arm's length.

(d) *Certain transfers upon death.*—If substantially nonvested property has been transferred in connection with the performance of services and the person who performed such services dies while the property is still substantially nonvested, any income realized on or after such death with respect to such property under this section is income in respect of a decedent to which the rules of section 691 apply. In such a case the income in respect of such property shall be taxable under section 691 (except to the extent not includible under section 101(b)) to the estate or beneficiary of the person who performed the services, in accordance with section 83 and the regulations thereunder. However, if an item of income is realized upon such death before July 21, 1978, because the property became substantially vested upon death, the person responsible for filing decedent's income tax return for decedent's last taxable year may elect to treat such item as includible in gross income for decedent's last taxable year by including such item in gross income on the return or amended return filed for decedent's last taxable year.

(e) *Forfeiture after substantial vesting.*—If a person is taxable under section 83(a) when the property transferred becomes substantially vested and thereafter the person's beneficial interest in such property is nevertheless forfeited pursuant to a lapse restriction, any loss incurred by such person (but not by a beneficiary of such person) upon such forfeiture shall be an ordinary loss to the extent the basis in such property has been increased as a result of the recognition of income by such person under section 83(a) with respect to such property.

(f) *Examples.*—The provisions of this section may be illustrated by the following examples:

Example (1). On November 1, 1978, X corporation sells to E, an employee, 100 shares of X corporation stock at $10 per share. At the time of such sale the fair market value of the X corporation stock is $100 per share. Under the terms of the sale each share of stock is subject to a substantial risk of forfeiture which will not lapse until November 1, 1988. Evidence of this restriction is stamped on the face of E's stock certificates, which are therefore nontransferable (within the meaning of § 1.83-3(d)). Since in 1978 E's stock is substantially nonvested, E does not include any of such amount in his gross income as compensation in 1978. On November 1, 1988, the fair market value of the X corporation stock is $250 per share. Since the X corporation stock becomes substantially vested in 1988, E must include $24,000 (100 shares of X corporation stock × $250 fair market value per share less $10 price paid by E for each share) as compensation for 1988. Dividends paid by X to E on E's stock after it was transferred to E on November 1, 1973, are taxable to E as additional compensation during the period E's stock is substantially nonvested and are deductible as such by X.

Example (2). Assume the facts are the same as in example (1), except that on November 1, 1985, each share of stock of X corporation in E's hands could as a matter of law be transferred to a bona fide purchaser who would not be required to forfeit the stock if the risk of forfeiture materialized. In the event, however, that the risk materializes, E would be liable in damages to X. On November 1, 1985, the fair market value of the X corporation stock is $230 per share. Since E's stock is transferable within the meaning of § 1.83-3(d) in 1985, the stock is substantially vested and E must include $22,000 (100 shares of X corporation stock × $230 fair market value per share less $10 price paid by E for each share) as compensation for 1985.

Example (3). Assume the facts are the same as in example (1) except that, in 1984 E sells his 100 shares of X corporation stock in an arm's length sale to I, an investment company, for $120 per share. At the time of this sale each share of X corporation's stock has a fair market value of $200. Under paragraph (b) of this section, E must include $11,000 (100 shares of X corporation stock × $120 amount realized per share less $10 price paid by E per share) as compensation for 1984 notwithstanding that the stock remains nontransferable and is still subject to a substantial risk of forfeiture at the time of such sale. Under § 1.83-4(b)(2), I's basis in the X corporation stock is $120 per share. [Reg. § 1.83-1.]

☐ [*T.D.* 7554, 7-21-78. *Amended by T.D.* 9092, 9-11-2003.]

§1.83-2. Election to include in gross income in year of transfer.—(a) *In general.*—If property is transferred (within the meaning of §1.83-3(a)) in connection with the performance of services, the person performing such services may elect to include in gross income under section 83(b) the excess (if any) of the fair market value of the property at the time of transfer (determined without regard to any lapse restriction, as defined in §1.83-3(i)) over the amount (if any) paid for such property, as compensation for services. The fact that the transferee has paid full value for the property transferred, realizing no bargain element in the transaction, does not preclude the use of the election as provided for in this section. If this election is made, the substantial vesting rules of section 83(a) and the regulations thereunder do not apply with respect to such property, and except as otherwise provided in section 83(d)(2) and the regulations thereunder (relating to the cancellation of a nonlapse restriction), any subsequent appreciation in the value of the property is not taxable as compensation to the person who performed the services. Thus, property with respect to which this election is made shall be includible in gross income as of the time of transfer, even though such property is substantially nonvested (as defined in §1.83-3(b)) at the time of transfer, and no compensation will be includible in gross income when such property becomes substantially vested (as defined in §1.83-3(b)). In computing the gain or loss from the subsequent sale or exchange of such property, its basis shall be the amount paid for the property increased by the amount included in gross income under section 83(b). If property for which a section 83(b) election is in effect is forfeited while substantially nonvested, such forfeiture shall be treated as a sale or exchange upon which there is realized a loss equal to the excess (if any) of—

(1) The amount paid (if any) for such property, over,

(2) The amount realized (if any) upon such forfeiture.

If such property is a capital asset in the hands of the taxpayer, such loss shall be a capital loss. A sale or other disposition of the property that is in substance a forfeiture, or is made in contemplation of a forfeiture, shall be treated as a forfeiture under the two immediately preceding sentences.

* * *

[Reg. §1.83-2.]

☐ [*T.D.* 7554, 7-21-78. *Amended by T.D.* 9779, 7-25-2016.]

§1.83-3. Meaning and use of certain terms.—(a) *Transfer.*—(1) *In general.*—For purposes of section 83 and the regulations thereunder, a transfer of property occurs when a person acquires a beneficial ownership interest in such property (disregarding any lapse restriction, as defined in §1.83-3(i)). For special rules applying to the transfer of a life insurance contract (or an undivided interest therein) that is part of a split-dollar life insurance arrangement (as defined in §1.61-22(b)(1) or (2)), see §1.61-22(g).

(2) *Option.*—The grant of an option to purchase certain property does not constitute a transfer of such property. However, see §1.83-7 for the extent to which the grant of the option itself is subject to section 83. In addition, if the amount paid for the transfer of property is an indebtedness secured by the transferred property, on which there is no personal liability to pay all or a substantial part of such indebtedness, such transaction may be in substance the same as the grant of an option. The determination of the substance of the transaction shall be based upon all the facts and circumstances. The factors to be taken into account include the type of property involved, the extent to which the risk that the property will decline in value has been transferred, and the likelihood that the purchase price will, in fact, be paid. See also §1.83-4(c) for the treatment of forgiveness of indebtedness that has constituted an amount paid.

(3) *Requirement that property be returned.*—Similarly, no transfer may have occurred where property is transferred under conditions that require its return upon the happening of an event that is certain to occur, such as the termination of employment. In such a case, whether there is, in fact, a transfer depends upon all the facts and circumstances. Factors which indicate that no transfer has occurred are described in paragraph (a)(4), (5) and (6) of this section.

(4) *Similarity to option.*—An indication that no transfer has occurred is the extent to which the conditions relating to a transfer are similar to an option.

(5) *Relationship to fair market value.*—An indication that no transfer has occurred is the extent to which the consideration to be paid the transferee upon surrendering the property does not approach the fair market value of the property at the time of surrender. For purposes of paragraph (a)(5) and (6) of this section, fair market value includes fair market value determined under the rules of §1.83-5(a)(1), relating to the valuation of property subject to nonlapse restrictions. Therefore, the existence of a nonlapse restriction referred to in §1.83-5(a)(1) is not a factor indicating no transfer has occurred.

(6) *Risk of loss.*—An indication that no transfer has occurred is the extent to which the transferee does not incur the risk of a beneficial owner that the value of the property at the time of transfer will decline substantially. Therefore, for purposes of this (6), risk of decline in property value is not limited to the risk that any amount paid for the property may be lost.

(7) *Examples.*—The provisions of this paragraph may be illustrated by the following examples:

Example (1). On January 3, 1971, X corporation sells for $500 to S, a salesman of X, 10 shares of stock in X corporation with a fair market value of $1,000. The stock is nontransferable and subject to return to the corporation (for $500) if S's sales do not reach a certain level by December 31, 1971. Disregarding the restriction concerning S's sales (since the restriction is a lapse restriction), S's interest in the stock is that of a beneficial owner and therefore a transfer occurs on January 3, 1971.

Example (2). On November 17, 1972, W sells to E 100 shares of stock in W corporation with a fair market value of $10,000 in exchange for a $10,000 note without personal liability. The note requires E to make yearly payments of $2,000 commencing in 1973. E collects the dividends, votes the stock and pays the interest on the note. However, he makes no payments towards the face amount of the note. Because E has no personal liability on the note, and since E is making no payments towards the face amount of the note, the likelihood of E paying the full purchase price is in substantial doubt. As a result, E has not incurred the risks of a beneficial owner that the value of the stock will decline. Therefore, no transfer of the stock has occurred on November 17, 1972, but an option to purchase the stock has been granted to E.

Example (3). On January 3, 1971, X corporation purports to transfer to E, an employee, 100 shares of stock in X corporation. The X stock is subject to the sole restriction that E must sell such stock to X on termination of employment for any reason for an amount which is equal to the excess (if any) of the book value of the X stock at termination of employment over book value on January 3, 1971. The stock is not transferable by E and the restrictions on transfer are stamped on the certificate. Under these facts and circumstances, there is no transfer of the X stock within the meaning of section 83.

Example (4). Assume the same facts as in example (3) except that E paid $3,000 for the stock and that the restriction required E upon termination of employment to sell the stock to M for the total amount of dividends that have been declared on the stock since September 2, 1971, or $3,000 whichever is higher. Again, under the facts and circumstances, no transfer of the X stock has occurred.

Example (5). On July 4, 1971, X corporation purports to transfer to G an employee, 100 shares of X stock. The stock is subject to the sole restriction that upon termination of employment G must sell the stock to X for the greater of its fair market value at such time or $100, the amount G paid for the stock. On July 4, 1971 the X stock has a fair market value of $100. Therefore, G does not incur the risk of a beneficial owner that the value of the stock at the time of transfer ($100) will decline substantially. Under these facts and circumstances, no transfer has occurred.

(b) *Substantially vested and substantially nonvested property.*—For purposes of section 83 and the regulations thereunder, property is substantially nonvested when it is subject to a substantial risk of forfeiture, within the meaning of paragraph (c) of this section, and is nontransferable, within the meaning of paragraph (d) of this section. Property is substantially vested for such purposes when it is either transferable or not subject to a substantial risk of forfeiture.

(c) *Substantial risk of forfeiture.*—(1) *In general.*—For purposes of section 83 and these regulations, whether a risk of forfeiture is substantial or not depends upon the facts and circumstances. Except as set forth in paragraphs (j) and (k) of this section, a substantial risk of forfeiture exists only if rights in property that are transferred are conditioned, directly or indirectly, upon the future performance (or refraining from performance) of substantial services by any person, or upon the occurrence of a condition related to a purpose of the transfer if the possibility of forfeiture is substantial. Property is not transferred subject to a substantial risk of forfeiture if at the time of transfer the facts and circumstances demonstrate that the forfeiture condition is unlikely to be enforced. Further, property is not transferred subject to a substantial risk of forfeiture to the extent that the employer is required to pay the fair market value of a portion of such property to the employee upon the return of such property. The risk that the value of property will decline during a certain period of time does not constitute a substantial risk of forfeiture. A nonlapse restriction, standing by itself, will not result in a substantial risk of forfeiture. A restriction on the transfer of property, whether contractual or by operation of applicable law, will result in a substantial risk of forfeiture only if and to the extent that the restriction is described in paragraph (j) or (k) of this section. For this purpose, transfer restrictions that will not result in a substantial risk of forfeiture include, but are not limited to, restrictions that if violated, whether by transfer or attempted transfer of the property, would result in the forfeiture of some or all of the property, or liability by the employee for any damages, penalties, fees, or other amount.

(2) *Illustrations of substantial risks of forfeiture.*—The regularity of the performance of services and the time spent in performing such services tend to indicate whether services required by a condition are substantial. The fact that the person performing services has the right to decline to perform such services without forfeiture may tend to establish that services are insubstantial. Where stock is transferred to an underwriter prior to a public offering and the full enjoyment of such stock is expressly or impliedly conditioned upon the successful completion of the underwriting, the stock is subject to a substantial risk of forfeiture. Where an employee receives property from an employer subject to a requirement that it be returned if the total earnings of the employer do not increase, such property is subject to a substantial risk of forfeiture. On the other hand, requirements that the property be returned to the employer if the employee is discharged for cause or for committing a crime will not be considered to result in a substantial risk of forfeiture. An enforceable requirement that the property be returned to the employer if the employee accepts a job with a competing firm will not ordinarily be considered to result in a substantial risk of forfeiture unless the particular facts and circumstances indicate to the contrary. Factors which may be taken into account in determining whether a covenant not to compete constitutes a substantial risk of forfeiture are the age of the employee, the availability of alternative employment opportunities, the likelihood of the employee's obtaining such other employment, the degree of skill possessed by the employee, the employee's health, and the practice (if any) of the employer to enforce such covenants. Similarly, rights in property transferred to a retiring employee subject to the sole requirement that it be returned unless he renders consulting services upon the request of his former employer will not be considered subject to a substantial risk of forfeiture unless he is in fact expected to perform substantial services.

(3) *Enforcement of forfeiture condition.*—In determining whether the possibility of forfeiture is substantial in the case of rights in property transferred to an employee of a corporation who owns a significant amount of the total combined voting power or value of all classes of stock of the employer corporation or of its parent corporation, there will be taken into account (i) the employee's relationship to other stockholders and the extent of their control, potential control and possible loss of control of the corporation, (ii) the position of the employee in the corporation and the extent to which he is subordinate to other employees, (iii) the employee's relationship to the officers and directors of the corporation, (iv) the person or persons who must approve the employee's discharge, and (v) past actions of the employer in enforcing the provisions of the restrictions. For example, if an employee would be considered as having received rights in property subject to a substantial risk of forfeiture, but for the fact that the employee owns 20 percent of the single class of stock in the transferor corporation, and if the remaining 80 percent of the class of stock is owned by an unrelated individual (or members of such an individual's family) so that the possibility of the corporation enforcing a restriction on such rights is substantial, then such rights are subject to a substantial risk of forfeiture. On the other hand, if 4 percent of the voting power of all the stock of a corporation is owned by the president of such corporation and the remaining stock is so diversely held by the public that the president, in effect, controls the corporation, then the possibility of the corporation enforcing a restriction on rights in property transferred to the president is not substantial, and such rights are not subject to a substantial risk of forfeiture.

* * *

(d) *Transferability of property.*—For purposes of section 83 and the regulations thereunder, the rights of a person in property are transferable if such person can transfer any interest in the property to any person other than the transferor of the property, but only if the rights in such property of such transferee are not subject to a substantial risk of forfeiture. Accordingly, property is transferable if the person performing the services or receiving the property can sell, assign, or pledge (as collateral for a loan, or as security for the performance of an obligation, or for any other purpose) his interest in the property to any person other than the transferor of such property and if the transferee is not required to give up the property or its value in the event the substantial risk of forfeiture materializes. On the other hand, property is not considered to be transferable merely because the person performing the services or receiving the property may designate a beneficiary to receive the property in the event of his death.

(e) *Property.*—For purposes of section 83 and the regulations thereunder, the term "property" includes real and personal property other than either money or an unfunded and unsecured promise to pay money or property in the future. The term also includes a beneficial interest in assets (including money) which are transferred or set aside from the claims of creditors of the transferor, for example, in a trust or escrow account. See, however, § 1.83-8(a) with respect to employee trusts and annuity plans subject to section 402(b) and section 403(c). In the case of a transfer of a life insurance contract, retirement income contract, endowment contract, or other contract providing life insurance protection, or any undivided interest therein, the policy cash value and all other rights under such contract (including any supplemental agreements thereto and whether or not guaranteed), other than current life insurance protection, are treated as property for purposes of this section. However, in the case of the transfer of a life insurance contract, retirement income contract, endowment contract, or other contract providing life insurance protection, which was part of a split-dollar arrangement (as defined in § 1.61-22(b)) entered into (as defined in § 1.61-22(j)) on or before September 17, 2003, and which is not materially modified (as defined in § 1.61-22(j)(2)) after September 17, 2003, only the cash surrender value of the contract is considered to be property. Where rights in a contract providing life insurance protection are substantially nonvested, see § 1.83-1(a)(2) for rules relating to the taxation of the cost of life insurance protection.

(f) *Property transferred in connection with the performance of services.*—Property transferred to an employee or an independent contractor (or beneficiary thereof) in recognition of the performance of, or the refraining from performance of, services is considered transferred in connection with the performance of services within the meaning of section 83. The existence of other persons entitled to buy stock on the same terms and conditions as an employee, whether pursuant to a public or private offering may, however, indicate that in such circumstances a transfer to the employee is not in recognition of the performance of, or the refraining from performance of, services. The transfer of property is subject to section 83 whether such transfer is in respect of past, present, or future services.

(g) *Amount paid.*—For purposes of section 83 and the regulations thereunder, the term "amount paid" refers to the value of any money or property paid for the transfer of property to which section 83 applies, and does not refer to any amount paid for the right to use such property or to receive the income therefrom. Such value does not include any stated or unstated interest payments. For rules regarding the calculation of the amount of unstated interest payments, see § 1.483-1(c). When section 83 applies to the transfer of property pursuant to the exercise of an option, the term "amount paid" refers to any amount paid for the grant of the option plus any amount paid as the exercise price of the option. For rules regarding the forgiveness of indebtedness treated as an amount paid, see § 1.83-4(c).

(h) *Nonlapse restriction.*—For purposes of section 83 and the regulations thereunder, a restriction which by its terms will never lapse (also referred to as a "nonlapse restriction") is a permanent limitation on the transferability of property—

(i) Which will require the transferee of the property to sell, or offer to sell, such property at a price determined under a formula, and

(ii) Which will continue to apply to and be enforced against the transferee or any subsequent holder (other than the transferor).

A limitation subjecting the property to a permanent right of first refusal in a particular person at a price determined under a formula is a permanent nonlapse restriction. Limitations imposed by registration requirements of State or Federal security laws or similar laws imposed with respect to sales or other dispositions of stock or securities are not nonlapse restrictions. An obligation to resell or to offer to sell property transferred in connection with the performance of services to a specific person or persons at its fair market value at the time of such sale is not a nonlapse restriction. See § 1.83-5(c) for examples of nonlapse restrictions.

(i) *Lapse restriction.*—For purposes of section 83 and the regulations thereunder, the term "lapse restriction" means a restriction other than a nonlapse restriction as defined in paragraph (h) of this section, and includes (but is not limited to) a restriction that carries a substantial risk of forfeiture.

* * *

(k) For purposes of section 83 and the regulations thereunder, property is subject to substantial risk of forfeiture and is not transferable so long as the property is subject to a restriction on transfer to comply with the "Pooling-of-Interests Accounting" rules set forth in Accounting Series Release Numbered 130 ((10/5/72) 37 FR 20937; 17 CFR 211.130) and Accounting Series Release Numbered 135 ((1/18/73) 38 FR 1734; 17 CFR 211.135).

* * *

[Reg. § 1.83-3.]

☐ [*T.D.* 7554, 7-21-78. *Amended by T.D.* 8042, 8-5-85; *T.D.* 9092, 9-11-2003; *T.D.* 9223, 8-26-2005 *and T.D.* 9659, 2-25-2014.]

§1.83-4. Special rules.—(a) *Holding period.*—Under section 83(f), the holding period of transferred property to which section 83(a) applies shall begin just after such property is substantially vested. However, if the person who has performed the services in connection with which property is transferred has made an election under section 83(b), the holding period of such property shall begin just after the date such property is transferred. If property to which section 83 and the regulations thereunder apply is transferred at arm's length, the holding period of such property in the hands of the transferee shall be determined in accordance with the rules provided in section 1223.

(b) *Basis.*—(1) Except as provided in paragraph (b) (2) of this section, if property to which section 83 and the regulations thereunder apply is acquired by any person (including a person who acquires such property in a subsequent transfer which is not at arm's length), while such property is still substantially nonvested, such person's basis for the property shall reflect any amount paid for such property and any amount includible in the gross income of the person who performed the services (including any amount so includible as a result of a disposition by the person who acquired such property). Such basis shall also reflect any adjustments to basis provided under sections 1015, 1016, and 1022.

(2) If property to which §1.83-1 applies is transferred at arm's length, the basis of the property in the hands of the transferee shall be determined under section 1012 and the regulations thereunder.

(c) *Forgiveness of indebtedness treated as an amount paid.*—If an indebtedness that has been treated as an amount paid under §1.83-1 (a) (1) (ii) is subsequently cancelled, forgiven or satisfied for an amount less than the amount of such indebtedness, the amount that is not, in fact, paid shall be includible in the gross income of the service provider in the taxable year in which such cancellation, forgiveness or satisfaction occurs.

(d) *Effective/applicability date.*—The provisions in this section are applicable for taxable years beginning on or after July 21, 1978. The provisions of paragraph (b)(1) of this section relating to section 1022 are effective on and after January 19, 2017. [Reg. §1.83-4.]

☐ [*T.D.* 7554, 7-21-78. *Amended by T.D.* 9811, 1-18-2017.]

§1.83-5. Restrictions that will never lapse.—(a) *Valuation.*—For purposes of section 83 and the regulations thereunder, in the case of property subject to a nonlapse restriction (as defined in §1.83-3(h)), the price determined under the formula price will be considered to be the fair market value of the property unless established to the contrary by the Commissioner, and the burden of proof shall be on the Commissioner with respect to such value. If stock in a corporation is subject to a nonlapse restriction which requires the transferee to sell such stock only at a formula price based on book value, a reasonable multiple of earnings or a reaasonable combination thereof, the price so determined will ordinarily be regarded as determinative of the fair market value of such property for purposes of section 83. However, in certain circumstances the formula price will not be considered to be the fair market value of property subject to such a formula price restriction, even though the formula price restriction is a substantial factor in determining such value. For example, where the formula price is the current book value of stock, the book value of the stock at some time in the future may be a more accurate measure of the value of the stock than the current book value of the stock for purposes of determining the fair market value of the stock at the time the stock becomes substantially vested.

(b) *Cancellation.*—(1) *In general.*—Under section 83(d) (2), if a nonlapse restriction imposed on property that is subject to section 83 is cancelled, then, unless the taxpayer establishes—

(i) That such cancellation was not compensatory, and

(ii) That the person who would be allowed a deduction, if any, if the cancellation were treated as compensatory, will treat the transaction as not compensatory, as provided in paragraph (c) (2) of this section, the excess of the fair market value of such property (computed without regard to such restriction) at the time of cancellation, over the sum of—

(iii) The fair market value of such property (computed by taking the restriction into account) immediately before the cancellation, and

(iv) The amount, if any, paid for the cancellation,

shall be treated as compensation for the taxable year in which such cancellation occurs. Whether there has been a noncompensatory cancellation of a nonlapse restriction under section 83 (d) (2) depends upon the particular facts and circumstances. Ordinarily the fact that the employee or independent contractor is required to perform additional services or that the salary or payment of such a person is adjusted to take the cancellation into account indicates that such cancellation has a compensatory purpose. On the other hand, the fact that the original purpose of a restriction no longer exists may indicate that the purpose of such cancellation is noncompensatory. Thus, for example, if a so-called "buy-sell" restriction was imposed on a corporation's stock to limit ownership of such stock and is being cancelled in connection with a public offering of the stock, such cancellation will generally be regarded as noncompensatory. However, the mere fact that the employer is willing to forego a deduction under section 83(h) is insufficient evidence to establish a noncompensatory cancellation of a nonlapse restriction. The refusal by a corporation or shareholder to repurchase stock of the corporation which is subject to a permanent right of first refusal will generally be treated as a cancellation of a nonlapse restriction. The preceding sentence shall not apply where there is no nonlapse restriction, for example, where the price to be paid for the stock subject to the right of first refusal is the fair market value of the stock. Section 83 (d) (2) and this (1) do not apply where immediately after the cancellation of a nonlapse restriction the property is still substantially nonvested and no section 83 (b) election has been made with respect to such property. In such a case the rules of section 83 (a) and § 1.83-1 shall apply to such property.

(2) *Evidence of noncompensatory cancellation.*—In addition to the information necessary to establish the factors described in paragraph (b) (1) of this section, the taxpayer shall request the employer to furnish the taxpayer with a written statement indicating that the employer will not treat the cancellation of the nonlapse restriction as a compensatory event, and that no deduction will be taken with respect to such cancellation. The taxpayer shall file such written statement with his income tax return for the taxable year in which or with which such cancellation occurs.

(c) *Examples.*—The provisions of this section may be illustrated by the following examples:

Example (1). On November 1, 1971, X corporation whose shares are closely held and not regularly traded, transfers to E, an employee, 100 shares of X corporation stock subject to the condition that, if he desires to dispose of such stock during the period of his employment, he must resell the stock to his employer at its then existing book value. In addition, E or E's estate is obligated to offer to sell the stock at his retirement or death to his employer at its then existing book value. Under these facts and circumstances, the restriction to which the shares of X corporation stock are subject is a nonlapse restriction. Consequently, the fair market value of the X stock is includible in E's gross income as compensation for taxable year 1971. However, in determining the fair market value of the X stock, the book value formula price will ordinarily be regarded as being determinative of such value.

Example (2). Assume the facts are the same as in example (1), except that the X stock is subject to the condition that if E desires to dispose of the stock during the period of his employment he must resell the stock to his employer at a multiple of earnings per share that is in this case a reasonable approximation of value at the time of transfer to E. In addition, E or E's estate is obligated to offer to sell the stock at his retirement or death to his employer at the same multiple of earnings. Under these facts and circumstances, the restriction to which the X corporation stock is subject is a nonlapse restriction. Consequently, the fair market value of the X stock is includible in E's gross income for taxable year 1971. However, in determining the fair market value of the X stock, the multiple-of-earnings formula price will ordinarily be regarded as determinative of such value.

Example (3). On January 4, 1971, X corporation transfers to E, an employee, 100 shares of stock in X corporation. Each such share of stock is subject to an agreement between X and E whereby E agrees that such shares are to be held solely for investment purposes and not for resale (a so-called investment letter restriction). E's rights in such stock are substantially vested upon transfer, causing the fair market value of each share of X corporation stock to be includible in E's gross income as compensation for taxable year 1971. Since such an investment letter restriction does not constitute a nonlapse restriction, in determining the fair market value of each share, the investment letter restriction is disregarded.

Example (4). On September 1, 1971, X corporation transfers to B, an independent contractor, 500 shares of common stock in X corporation in exchange for B's agreement to provide services in the construction of an office building on property owned by X corporation. X corporation has 100 shares of preferred stock outstanding and an additional 500 shares of common stock outstanding. The preferred stock has a liquidation value of $1,000*x*, which is equal to the value of all assets owned by X. Therefore, the book value of the common stock in X corporation is $0. Under the terms of the transfer, if B wishes to dispose of the stock, B must offer to sell the stock to X for 150 percent of the then existing book value of B's common stock. The stock is also subject to a substantial risk of forfeiture until B performs the agreed-upon services. B makes a timely election under section 83(b) to include the value of the stock in gross income in 1971. Under these facts and circumstances, the restriction to which the shares of X corporation common stock are subject is a nonlapse restriction. In determining the fair market value of the X common stock at the time of transfer, the book value formula price would ordinarily be regarded as determinative of such value. However, the fair market value of X common stock at the time of transfer, subject to the book value restriction, is greater than $0 since B was willing to agree to provide valuable personal services in exchange for the stock. In determining the fair market value of the stock, the expected book value after construction of the office building would be given great weight. The likelihood of completion of construction would be a factor in determining the expected book value after completion of construction. [Reg. § 1.83-5.]

☐ [*T.D.* 7554, 7-21-78.]

§ 1.83-6. Deduction by employer.—(a) *Allowance of deduction.*—(1) *General rule.*—In the case of a transfer of property in connection with the performance of services, or a compensatory cancellation of a nonlapse restriction described in section 83(d) and § 1.83-5, a deduction is allowable under section 162 or 212 to the person for whom the services were performed. The amount of the deduction is equal to the amount included as compensation in the gross income of the service provider under section 83(a), (b), or (d)(2), but only to the extent the amount meets the requirements of section 162 or 212 and the regulations thereunder. The deduction is allowed only for the taxable year of that person in which or with which ends the taxable year of the service provider in which the amount is included as compensation. For purposes of this paragraph, any amount excluded from gross income under section 79 or section 101(b) or subchapter N is considered to have been included in gross income.

(2) *Special rule.*—For purposes of paragraph (a)(1) of this section, the service provider is deemed to have included the amount as compensation in gross income if the person for whom the services were performed satisfies in a timely manner all requirements of section 6041 or section 6041A, and the regulations thereunder, with respect to that amount of compensation. For purposes of the preceding sentence, whether a person for whom services were performed satisfies all requirements of section 6041 or section 6041A, and the regulations thereunder, is determined without regard to § 1.6041-3(c) (exception for payments to corporations). In the case of a disqualifying disposition of stock described in section 421(b), an employer that otherwise satisfies all requirements of section 6041 and the regulations thereunder will be considered to have done so timely for purposes of this paragraph (a)(2) if Form W-2 or Form W-2c, as appropriate, is furnished to the employee or former employee, and is filed with the federal government, on or before the date on which the employer files the tax return claiming the deduction relating to the disqualifying disposition.

(3) *Exceptions.*—Where property is substantially vested upon transfer, the deduction shall be allowed to such person in accordance with his method of accounting (in conformity with sections 446 and 461). In the case of a transfer to an employee benefit plan described in § 1.162-10(a) or a transfer to an employees' trust or annuity plan described in section 404(a)(5) and the regulations thereunder, section 83(h) and this section do not apply.

(4) *Capital expenditure, etc.*—No deduction is allowed under section 83(h) to the extent that the transfer of property constitutes a capital expenditure, an item of deferred expense, or an amount properly includible in the value of inventory items. In the case of a capital expenditure, for example, the basis of the property to which such capital expenditure relates shall be increased at the same time and to the same extent as any amount includible in the employee's gross income in respect of such transfer. Thus, for example, no deduction is allowed to a corporation in respect of a transfer of its stock to a promoter upon its organization, notwithstanding that such promoter must include the value of such stock in his gross income in accordance with the rules under section 83.

* * *

(b) *Recognition of gain or loss.*—Except as provided in section 1032, at the time of a transfer of property in connection with the performance of services the transferor recognizes gain to the extent that the transferor receives an amount that exceeds the transferor's basis in the property. In addition, at the time a deduction is allowed under section 83(h) and paragraph (a) of this section, gain or loss is recognized to the extent of the difference between (i) the sum of the amount paid plus the amount allowed as a deduction under section 83(h), and (ii) the sum of the taxpayer's basis in the property plus any amount recognized pursuant to the previous sentence.

(c) *Forfeitures.*—If, under section 83(h) and paragraph (a) of this section, a deduction, an increase in basis, or a reduction of gross income was allowable (disregarding the reasonableness of the amount of compensation) in respect of a transfer of property and such property is subsequently forfeited, the amount of such deduction, increase in basis or reduction of gross income shall be includible in the gross income of the person to whom it was allowable for the taxable year of forfeiture. The basis of such property in the hands of the person to whom it is forfeited shall include any such amount includible in the gross income of such person, as well as any amount such person pays upon forfeiture.

(d) *Special rules for transfers by shareholders.*—(1) *Transfers.*—If a shareholder of a corporation transfers property to an employee of such corporation or to an independent contractor (or to a beneficiary thereof), in consideration of services performed for the corporation, the transaction shall be considered to be a contribution of such property to the capital of such corporation by the shareholder, and immediately thereafter a transfer of such property by the corporation to the employee or independent contractor under paragraphs (a) and (b) of this section. For purposes of this (1), such a transfer will be considered to be in consideration for services performed for the corporation if either the property transferred is substantially nonvested at the time of transfer or an amount is includible in the gross income of the employee or independent contractor at the time of transfer under § 1.83-1(a)(1) or § 1.83-2(a). In the case of such a transfer, any money or other property paid to the shareholder for such stock shall be considered to be paid to the corporation and transferred immediately thereafter by the corporation to the shareholder as a distribution to which section 302 applies. For special rules that may apply to a corporation's transfer of its own stock to any person in consideration of services performed for another corporation or partnership, see § 1.1032-3. The preceding sentence applies to transfers of stock and amounts paid for such stock occurring on or after May 16, 2000.

(2) *Forfeiture.*—If, following a transaction described in paragraph (d)(1) of this section, the transferred property is forfeited to the shareholder, paragraph (c) of this section shall apply both with respect to the shareholder and with respect to the corporation. In addition, the corporation shall, in the taxable year of forfeiture be allowed a loss (or realize a gain) to offset any gain (or loss) realized under paragraph (b) of this section. For example, if a shareholder transfers property to an employee of the corporation as compensation, and as a result the shareholder's basis of $200x in such property is allocated to his stock in such corporation and such corporation recognizes a short-term capital gain of $800x, and is allowed a deduction of $1,000x on such transfer, upon a subsequent forfeiture of the property to the shareholder, the shareholder shall take $200x into gross income, and the corporation shall take $1,000x into gross income and be allowed a short-term capital loss of $800x.

* * *

[Reg. § 1.83-6.]

☐ [*T.D.* 7554, 7-21-78. *Amended by T.D.* 8599, 7-18-95; *T.D.* 8883, 5-11-2000 *and T.D.* 9092, 9-11-2003.]

§ 1.83-7. Taxation of nonqualified stock options.—(a) *In general.*—If there is granted to an employee or independent contractor (or beneficiary thereof) in connection with the performance of services, an option to which section 421 (relating generally to certain qualified and other options) does not apply, section 83(a) shall apply to such grant if the option has a readily ascertainable fair market value (determined in accordance with paragraph (b) of this section) at the time the option is granted. The person who performed such services realizes compensation upon such grant at the time and in the amount determined under section 83(a). If section 83(a) does not apply to the grant of such an option because the option does not have a readily ascertainable fair market value at the time of grant, sections 83(a) and 83(b) shall apply at the time the option is exercised or otherwise disposed of, even though the fair market value of such option may have become readily ascertainable before such time. If the option is exercised, sections 83(a) and 83(b) apply to the transfer of property pursuant to such exercise, and the employee or independent contractor realizes compensation upon such transfer at the time and in the amount determined under section 83(a) or 83(b). If the option is sold or otherwise disposed of in an arm's length transaction, sections 83(a) and 83(b) apply to the transfer of money or other property received in the same manner as sections 83(a) and 83(b) would have applied to the transfer of property pursuant to an exercise of the option. The preceding sentence does not apply to a sale or other disposition of the option to a person related to the service provider that occurs on or after July 2, 2003. For this purpose, a person is related to the service provider if—

(1) The person and the service provider bear a relationship to each other that is specified in section 267(b) or 707(b)(1), subject to the modifications that the language "20 percent" is used instead of "50 percent" each place it appears in sections 267(b) and 707(b)(1), and section 267(c)(4) is applied as if the family of an individual includes the spouse of any member of the family; or

(2) The person and the service provider are engaged in trades or businesses under common control (within the meaning of section 52(a) and (b)); provided that a person is not related to the service provider if the person is the service recipient with respect to the option or the grantor of the option.

(b) *Readily ascertainable defined.*—(1) *Actively traded on an established market.*—Options have a value at the time they are granted, but that value is ordinarily not readily ascertainable unless the option is actively traded on an established market. If an option is actively traded on an established market, the fair market value of such option is readily ascertainable for purposes of this section by applying the rules of valuation set forth in § 20.2031-2.

(2) *Not actively traded on an established market.*—When an option is not actively traded on an established market, it does not have a readily ascertainable fair market value unless its fair market value can otherwise be measured with reasonable accuracy. For purposes of this section, if an option is not actively traded on an established market, the option does not have a readily ascertainable fair market value when granted unless the taxpayer can show that all of the following conditions exist:

(i) The option is transferable by the optionee;

(ii) The option is exercisable immediately in full by the optionee;

(iii) The option or the property subject to the option is not subject to any restriction or condition (other than a lien or other condition to secure the payment of the purchase price) which has a significant effect upon the fair market value of the option; and

(iv) The fair market value of the option privilege is readily ascertainable in accordance with paragraph (b) (3) of this section.

(3) *Option privilege.*—The option privilege in the case of an option to buy is the opportunity to benefit during the option's exercise period from any increase in the value of property subject to the option during such period, without risking any capital. Similarly, the option privilege in the case of an option to sell is the opportunity to benefit during the exercise period from a decrease in the value of property subject to the option. For example, if at some time during the exercise period of an option to buy, the fair market value of the property subject to the option is greater than the option's exercise price, a profit may be realized by exercising the option and immediately selling the property so acquired for its higher fair market value. Irrespective of whether any such gain may be realized immediately at the time an option is granted, the fair market value of an option to buy includes the value of the right to benefit from any future increase in the value of the property subject to the option (relative to the option exercise price), without risking any capital. Therefore, the fair market value of an option is not merely the difference that may exist at a particular time between the option's exercise price and the value of the property subject to the option, but also includes the value of the option privilege for the remainder of the exercise period. Accordingly, for purposes of this section, in determining whether the fair market value of an option is readily ascertainable, it is necessary to consider whether the value of the entire option privilege can be measured with reasonable accuracy. In determining whether the value of the option privilege is readily ascertainable, and in determining the amount of such value when such value is readily ascertainable, it is necessary to consider—

(i) Whether the value of the property subject to the option can be ascertained;

(ii) The probability of any ascertainable value of such property increasing or decreasing; and

(iii) The length of the period during which the option can be exercised.

(c) *Reporting requirements.*—[Reserved]

* * *

[Reg. § 1.83-7.]

☐ [*T.D.* 7554, 7-21-78. *Amended by T.D.* 9067, 7-1-2003 *and T.D.* 9148, 8-9-2004.]

Items Specifically Excluded from Gross Income

§ 1.101-1. Exclusion from gross income of proceeds of life insurance contracts payable by reason of death.—(a) (1) *In general.*—Section 101 (a) (1) states the general rule that the proceeds of life insurance policies, if paid by reason of the death of the insured, are excluded from the gross income of the recipient. Death benefit payments having the characteristics of life insurance proceeds payable by reason of death under contracts, such as workmen's compensation insurance contracts, endowment contracts, or accident and health insurance contracts, issued on or before December 31, 1984, are covered by this provision. The exclusion from gross income allowed by section 101 (a) applies whether payment is made to the estate of the insured or to any beneficiary (individual, corporation, or partnership) and whether it is made directly or in trust. The extent to which this exclusion applies in cases where life insurance policies have been transferred for a valuable consideration is stated in section 101 (a) (2) and in paragraph (b) of this section. In cases where the proceeds of a life insurance policy, payable by reason of the death of the insured, are paid other than in a single sum at the time of such death, the amounts to be excluded from gross income may be affected by the provisions of section 101(c) (relating to amounts held under agreements to pay interest) or section 101(d) (relating to amounts payable at a date later than death). See §§1.101-3 and 1.101-4. However, neither section 101(c) nor section 101(d) applies to a single sum payment which does not exceed the amount payable at the time of death even though such amount is actually paid at a date later than death. If the life insurance contract is an employer-owned life insurance contract within the definition of section 101(j)(3), the amount to be excluded from gross income may be affected by the provisions of section 101(j).

(2) *Cross references.*—For rules governing the taxability of insurance proceeds constituting benefits payable on the death of an employee—

(i) Under pension, profit-sharing, or stock bonus plans described in section 401(a) and exempt from tax under section 501(a), or under annuity plans described in section 403(a), see section 72(m)(3) and paragraph (c) of §1.72-16;

(ii) Under annuity contracts to which §1.403(b)-3 applies, see §1.403(b)-7; or

(iii) Under eligible State deferred compensation plans described in section 457(b), see paragraph (c) of §1.457-1.

For the definition of a life insurance company, see section 801.

(b) *Transfers of life insurance policies.*—(1) *Transfer of an interest in a life insurance contract for valuable consideration.*—(i) *In general.*—In the case of a transfer of an interest in a life insurance contract for valuable consideration, including a reportable policy sale for valuable consideration, the amount of the proceeds attributable to the interest that is excludable from gross income under section 101(a)(1) is limited under section 101(a)(2) to the sum of the actual value of the consideration for the transfer paid by the transferee and the premiums and other amounts subsequently paid by the transferee with respect to the interest. For exceptions to this general rule for certain transfers for valuable consideration that are not reportable policy sales, see paragraph (b)(1)(ii) of this section. The application of section 101(d), (f) or (j), which is not addressed in paragraph (b) of this section, may further limit the amount of the proceeds excludable from gross income.

(ii) *Exceptions.*—(A) *Exception for carryover basis transfers.*—The limitation described in paragraph (b)(1)(i) of this section does not apply to the transfer of an interest in a life insurance contract for valuable consideration if each of the following requirements are satisfied. First, the transfer is not a reportable policy sale. Second, the basis of the interest, for the purpose of determining gain or loss with respect to the transferee, is determinable in whole or in part by reference to the basis of the interest in the hands of the transferor (see section 101(a)(2)(A)). Third, paragraph (b)(1)(ii)(B) of this section does not apply. In the case of a transfer described in this paragraph (b)(1)(ii)(A), the amount of the proceeds attributable to the interest that is excludable from gross income under section 101(a)(1) is limited to the sum of the amount that would have been excludable by the transferor if the transfer had not occurred and the premiums and other amounts subsequently paid by the transferee with respect to the interest. The preceding sentence applies without regard to whether the interest previously has been transferred and the nature of any prior transfer of the interest.

(B) *Exception for transfers to certain persons.*—*(1) In general.*—The limitation described in paragraph (b)(1)(i) of this section does not apply to the transfer of an interest in a life insurance contract for valuable consideration if both of the following requirements are satisfied. First, the transfer is not a reportable policy sale and the interest was not previously transferred for valuable consideration in a reportable policy sale. Second, the interest is transferred to the insured, a partner of the insured, a partnership in which the insured is a partner, or a corporation in which the insured is a shareholder or officer (see section 101(a)(2)(B)).

(2) Transfers to certain persons subsequent to a reportable policy sale.—Except as provided in paragraph (b)(1)(ii)(B)*(3)* of this section, if a transfer of an interest in a life insurance contract would be described in paragraph (b)(1)(ii)(B)*(1)* of this section, but for the fact that the interest previously was transferred for valuable consideration in a reportable policy sale (whether in the immediately preceding transfer or an earlier transfer), then the amount of the proceeds attributable to the interest that is excludable from gross income under section 101(a)(1) is limited to the sum of—

(i) The higher of the amount that would have been excludable by the transferor if the transfer had not occurred or the actual value of the consideration for the transfer paid by the transferee; and

(ii) The premiums and other amounts subsequently paid by the transferee with respect to the interest.

(3) Transfers to the insured subsequent to a reportable policy sale.—*(i)* Except as

provided in paragraph (b)(1)(ii)(B)(*3*)(*ii*) of this section, to the extent that an interest (or portion of an interest) in a life insurance contract that was transferred for valuable consideration in a reportable policy sale subsequently is transferred to the insured for valuable consideration, the limitations described in paragraph (b)(1)(i) of this section and paragraph (b)(1)(ii)(B)(*2*) of this section do not apply. To the extent that fair market value is not paid by the insured for the transferred interest, the transfer of the portion of the interest with a value in excess of the consideration paid will be treated as a gift under the bargain sale rule in paragraph (b)(2)(iii) of this section.

(*ii*) This paragraph (b)(1)(ii)(B)(*3*)(*ii*) applies with respect to an interest described in paragraph (b)(1)(ii)(B)(*3*)(*i*) of this section (or portion of such an interest) that subsequently is transferred by the insured to any other person. If all subsequent transfers of the interest (or portion of the interest) are gratuitous transfers that are not reportable policy sales, the amount of the proceeds excluded from gross income is determined under paragraph (b)(2)(i) of this section, taking into account the application of paragraph (b)(1)(ii)(B)(*3*)(*i*) of this section to the insured's acquisition of the interest. If any subsequent transfer of the interest (or portion of the interest) is for valuable consideration or is a reportable policy sale, the amount of the policy proceeds excludable from gross income is determined in accordance with paragraph (b) of this section; if the amount that would have been excludable from gross income by the insured following the transaction described in paragraph (b)(1)(ii)(B)(*3*)(*i*) of this section if no subsequent transfer had occurred is relevant, that amount is determined under paragraph (b)(1)(ii)(B)(*2*) of this section. Paragraph (g)(8) (*Example 8*) of this section and paragraph (g)(9) (*Example 9*) of this section illustrate the application of this paragraph (b)(1)(ii)(B)(*3*)(*ii*).

(2) *Other transfers.*—(i) *Gratuitous transfer of an interest in a life insurance contract.*—To the extent that a transfer of an interest in a life insurance contract is gratuitous, including a reportable policy sale that is not for valuable consideration, the amount of the proceeds attributable to the interest that is excludable from gross income under section 101(a)(1) is limited to the sum of the amount of the proceeds attributable to the gratuitously transferred interest that would have been excludable by the transferor if the transfer had not occurred and the premiums and other amounts subsequently paid by the transferee with respect to the interest. However, if an interest in a life insurance contract is transferred gratuitously to the insured, and that interest has not previously been transferred for value in a reportable policy sale, the entire amount of the proceeds attributable to the interest transferred to the insured is excludable from gross income.

(ii) *Partial transfers.*—When only part of an interest in a life insurance contract is transferred, the transferor's exclusion is ratably apportioned between or among the several parts. If multiple parts of an interest are transferred, the transfer of each part is treated as a separate transaction, with each transaction subject to the rule under paragraph (b) of this section that is applicable to the type of transfer involved.

(iii) *Bargain sales.*—When the transfer of an interest in a life insurance contract is in part a transfer for valuable consideration and in part a gratuitous transfer, the transfer of each part is treated as a separate transaction for purposes of determining the amount of the proceeds attributable to the interest that is excludable from gross income under section 101(a)(1). Each separate transaction is subject to the rule under paragraph (b) of this section that is applicable to the type of transfer involved.

(3) *Determination of amounts paid by the transferee.*—For purposes of paragraphs (b)(1) and (2) of this section, in determining the amounts, if any, of consideration paid by the transferee for the transfer of an interest in a life insurance contract and premiums and other amounts subsequently paid by the transferee with respect to that interest, the amounts paid by the transferee are reduced, but not below zero, by amounts received by the transferee under the life insurance contract that are not received as an annuity, to the extent excludable from gross income under section 72(e).

(c) *Reportable policy sale.*—(1) *In general.*—Except as provided in paragraph (c)(2) of this section, a reportable policy sale for purposes of this section and section 6050Y is any direct or indirect acquisition of an interest in a life insurance contract if the acquirer has, at the time of the acquisition, no substantial family, business, or financial relationship with the insured apart from the acquirer's interest in the life insurance contract.

(2) *Exceptions.*—None of the following transactions is a reportable policy sale:

(i) A transfer of an interest in a life insurance contract between entities with the same beneficial owners, if the ownership interest of each beneficial owner in the transferor entity does not vary by more than a 20 percent ownership interest from that beneficial owner's ownership interest in the transferee entity. In a series of transfers, the prior sentence is applied by comparing the beneficial owners' ownership interest in the first transferor entity and the last transferee entity. For purposes of this paragraph (c)(2)(i), each beneficial owner of a trust is deemed to have an ownership interest determined by the broadest possible exercise of a trustee's discretion in that beneficial owner's favor. Paragraph (g)(13) (*Example 13*) of this section provides an illustration of the application of this paragraph (c)(2)(i).

(ii) A transfer between corporations that are members of an affiliated group (as defined in section 1504(a)) that files a consolidated U.S. income tax return for the taxable year in which the transfer occurs.

(iii) The indirect acquisition of an interest in a life insurance contract by a person if—

(A) A partnership, trust, or other entity in which an ownership interest is being acquired directly or indirectly holds the interest in the life insurance contract and acquired that interest before January 1, 2019, or acquired that interest in a reportable policy sale reported in compliance with section 6050Y(a) and § 1.6050Y-2; or

(B) Immediately before the acquisition, no more than 50 percent of the gross value of the assets (as determined under paragraph (f)(4) of this section) of the partnership, trust, or other entity that directly or indirectly holds the interest in the life insurance contract, and in which an ownership interest is being directly acquired, consists of life insurance contracts, provided that, after the acquisition, with respect to that partnership, trust, or other entity, the person indirectly acquiring the interest in the life insurance contract and his or her family members own, in the aggregate—

(1) With respect to an S corporation, stock possessing 5 percent or less of the total combined voting power of all classes of stock entitled to vote and 5 percent or less of the total value of shares of all classes of stock of the S corporation;

(2) With respect to a trust or decedent's estate, 5 percent or less of the corpus and 5 percent or less of the annual income (taking into account, for the purpose of determining any person's ownership interest, the maximum amount of income and corpus that could be distributed to or held for the benefit of that person); or

(3) With respect to a partnership or other entity that is not a corporation or a trust, 5 percent or less of the capital interest and 5 percent or less of the profits interest.

(iv) The acquisition of a life insurance contract by an insurance company that issues a life insurance contract in an exchange pursuant to section 1035.

(v) The acquisition of a life insurance contract by a policyholder in an exchange pursuant to section 1035, if the policyholder has a substantial family, business, or financial relationship with the insured, apart from its interest in the life insurance contract, at the time of the exchange.

(d) *Substantial relationship.*—(1) *Substantial family relationship.*—For purposes of this section, a substantial family relationship means the relationship between an individual and any family member of that individual as defined in paragraph (f)(3) of this section. In addition, a substantial family relationship exists between an individual and his or her former spouse with regard to the transfer of an interest in a life insurance contract to (or in trust for the benefit of) that former spouse incident to divorce.

(2) *Substantial business relationship.*—For purposes of this section, a substantial business relationship between the insured and the acquirer exists in each of the following situations:

(i) The insured is a key person (as defined in section 264) of, or materially participates (within the meaning of section 469) in, an active trade or business as an owner, employee, or contractor, and at least 80 percent of that trade or business is owned (directly or indirectly, through one or more partnerships, trusts, or other entities) by the acquirer or the beneficial owners of the acquirer.

(ii) The acquirer acquires an active trade or business and acquires the interest in the life insurance contract either as part of that acquisition or from a person owning significant property leased to the acquired trade or business or life insurance policies held to facilitate the succession of the ownership of the business if—

(A) The insured—

(1) Is an employee within the meaning of section 101(j)(5)(A) of the acquired trade or business immediately preceding the acquisition (for purposes of this paragraph (d)(2)(ii)(A)(1), however, the reference in section 101(j)(5)(A) to highly compensated employee within the meaning of section 414(q) does not include a former employee); or

(2) Was a director, highly compensated employee, or highly compensated individual within the meaning of section 101(j)(2)(A)(ii) of the acquired trade or business, and the acquirer, immediately after the acquisition, has ongoing financial obligations to the insured with respect to the insured's employment by the trade or business (for example, the life insurance contract is maintained by the acquirer to fund current or future retire-

ment, pension, or survivorship obligations based on the insured's relationship with the entity or to fund a buy-out of the insured's interest in the acquired trade or business); and

(B) The acquirer either carries on the acquired trade or business or uses a significant portion of the acquired business assets in an active trade or business that does not include investing in interests in life insurance contracts.

(3) *Substantial financial relationship.*—For purposes of this section, a substantial financial relationship between the insured and the acquirer exists in each of the following situations:

(i) The acquirer (directly or indirectly, through one or more partnerships, trusts, or other entities of which it is a beneficial owner) has, or the beneficial owners of the acquirer have, a common investment (other than the interest in the life insurance contract) with the insured and a buy-out of the insured's interest in the common investment by the co-investor(s) after the insured's death is reasonably foreseeable.

(ii) The acquirer maintains the life insurance contract on the life of the insured to provide funds to purchase assets of or to satisfy liabilities of the insured or the insured's estate, heirs, legatees, or other successors in interest, or to satisfy other liabilities arising upon or by reason of the death of the insured.

(iii) The acquirer is an organization described in sections 170(c), 2055(a), and 2522(a) that previously received from the insured either financial support in a substantial amount or significant volunteer support or that meets other requirements prescribed in guidance published in the Internal Revenue Bulletin (see § 601.601(d)(2) of this chapter) for establishing that a substantial financial relationship exists between the insured and the organization.

(4) *Special rules.*—Paragraphs (d)(4)(i), (ii), and (iii) of this section apply for purposes of determining whether a substantial relationship (whether family, business, or financial) exists under paragraph (d)(1), (2), or (3) of this section, respectively.

(i) *Indirect acquisitions.*—The acquirer of an interest in a life insurance contract in an indirect acquisition is deemed to have a substantial business or financial relationship with the insured if the direct holder of the interest in the life insurance contract has a substantial business or financial relationship with the insured immediately before and after the date the acquirer acquires its interest.

(ii) *Acquisitions by certain persons.*—The sole fact that an acquirer is a partner of the insured, a partnership in which the insured is a partner, or a corporation in which the insured is a shareholder or officer, is not sufficient to establish a substantial business or financial relationship with the insured. In addition, an acquirer need not be a partner of the insured, a partnership in which the insured is a partner, or a corporation in which the insured is a shareholder or officer to have a substantial business or financial relationship with the insured.

(iii) *Acquisitions by those with differing types of substantial relationships.*—A substantial family, business, or financial relationship exists between the insured and a partnership, trust, or other entity if each beneficial owner of that partnership, trust, or other entity has a substantial family, business, or financial relationship with the insured. For example, a substantial family, business, or financial relationship exists between the insured and a trust if each trust beneficiary is a family member of the insured or an organization described in paragraph (d)(3)(iii) of this section.

(e) *Interest in a life insurance contract.*—(1) *Definition.*—For purposes of this section and section 6050Y, the term *interest in a life insurance contract* means the interest held by any person that has taken title to or possession of the life insurance contract (also referred to as a life insurance policy), in whole or part, for state law purposes, including any person that has taken title or possession as nominee for another person, and the interest held by any person that has an enforceable right to receive all or a part of the proceeds of a life insurance contract or to any other economic benefits of the policy as described in § 20.2042-1(c)(2) of this chapter, such as the enforceable right to designate a contract beneficiary. Any person named as the owner in the life insurance contract generally is the owner (or an owner) of the contract and holds an interest in the contract.

(2) *Transfer of an interest in a life insurance contract.*—For purposes of this section and section 6050Y, the term *transfer of an interest in a life insurance contract* means the transfer of any interest in the life insurance contract, including any transfer of title to, possession of, or legal or beneficial ownership of the life insurance contract itself. The creation of an enforceable right to receive all or a part of the proceeds of a life insurance contract constitutes the transfer of an interest in the life insurance contract. The following events are not a transfer of an interest in a life insurance contract: the revocable designation of a beneficiary of the policy proceeds (until the designation becomes irrevocable other than by reason of the death of the insured); the pledging or assign-

ment of a policy as collateral security; and the issuance of a life insurance contract to a policyholder, other than the issuance of a policy in an exchange pursuant to section 1035.

(3) *Acquisition of an interest in a life insurance contract.*—For purposes of this section and section 6050Y, the acquisition of an interest in a life insurance contract may be direct or indirect.

(i) *Direct acquisition of an interest in a life insurance contract.*—For purposes of this section and section 6050Y, the transfer of an interest in a life insurance contract results in the direct acquisition of the interest by the transferee (acquirer).

(ii) *Indirect acquisition of an interest in a life insurance contract.*—For purposes of this section and section 6050Y, an indirect acquisition of an interest in a life insurance contract occurs when a person (acquirer) becomes a beneficial owner of a partnership, trust, or other entity that holds (whether directly or indirectly) the interest (whether legal or beneficial) in the life insurance contract. For purposes of this paragraph (e)(3)(ii), the term *other entity* does not include a C corporation, unless more than 50 percent of the gross value of the assets of the C corporation consists of life insurance contracts (as determined under paragraph (f)(4) of this section) immediately before the indirect acquisition.

(f) *Definitions.*—The following definitions apply for purposes of this section:

(1) *Beneficial owner.*—A beneficial owner of a partnership, trust, or other entity is an individual or C corporation with an ownership interest in that entity. The interest may be held directly or indirectly, through one or more other partnerships, trusts, or other entities. For instance, an individual that directly owns an interest in a partnership (P1), which directly owns an interest in another partnership (P2), is an indirect beneficial owner of P2 and any assets or other entities owned by P2 directly or indirectly. For purposes of this paragraph (f)(1), the beneficial owners of a trust include those who may receive current distributions of trust income or corpus and those who could receive distributions if the trust were to terminate currently.

(2) *C corporation.*—The term *C corporation* has the meaning given to it in section 1361(a)(2).

(3) *Family member.*—With respect to any individual, the term *family member* refers to any person described in paragraphs (f)(3)(i) through (vi) of this section. For purposes of this paragraph (f)(3), full effect is given to a legal adoption, and a step-child is deemed to be a descendant. The family members of an individual include:

(i) The individual;

(ii) The individual's spouse or a person with whom the individual is in a registered domestic partnership, civil union, or other similar relationship established under state law;

(iii) Any parent, grandparent, or great-grandparent of the individual or of the person described in paragraph (f)(3)(ii) of this section and any spouse of such parent, grandparent, or great-grandparent, or person with whom the parent, grandparent, or great-grandparent is in a registered domestic partnership, civil union, or other similar relationship established under state law;

(iv) Any lineal descendant of the individual or of any person described in paragraph (f)(3)(ii) or (iii) of this section;

(v) Any spouse of a lineal descendant described in paragraph (f)(3)(iv) of this section and any person with whom such a lineal descendant is in a registered domestic partnership, civil union, or other similar relationship established under state law; and

(vi) Any lineal descendant of a person described in paragraph (f)(3)(v) of this section.

(4) *Gross value of assets.*—(i) *Determination of gross value of assets.*—Except as provided in paragraph (f)(4)(ii) or (iii) of this section, for purposes of paragraphs (c)(2)(iii)(B) and (e)(3)(ii) of this section, the term *gross value of assets* means, with respect to any entity, the fair market value of the entity's assets, including assets beneficially owned by the entity under paragraph (f)(1) of this section as a beneficial owner of a partnership, trust, or other entity.

(ii) *Determination of gross value of assets of publicly traded entity.*—For purposes of determining the gross value of assets of an entity that is publicly traded, if the entity's annual Form 10-K filed with the United States Securities and Exchange Commission (or equivalent annual filing if the entity is publicly traded in a non-U.S. jurisdiction) for the period immediately preceding a person's acquisition of an ownership interest in the entity does not contain information demonstrating that more than 50 percent of the gross value of the entity's assets consists of life insurance contracts, that person may assume that no more than 50 percent of the gross value of the entity's assets consists of life insurance contracts, unless that person has actual knowledge or reason to know that more than 50 percent of the gross value of the entity's assets consists of life insurance contracts.

(iii) *Safe harbor definition of gross value of assets.*—An entity may choose to determine the gross value of all the entity's assets for purposes of this section using the following alternative definition of *gross value of assets*:

(A) In the case of assets that are life insurance policies or annuity or endowment contracts that have cash values, the cash surrender value as defined in section 7702(f)(2)(A); and

(B) In the case of assets not described in paragraph (f)(4)(iii)(A) of this section, the adjusted bases (within the meaning of section 1016) of such assets.

(5) *Transfer for valuable consideration.*—A transfer for valuable consideration means any transfer of an interest in a life insurance contract for cash or other consideration reducible to a money value.

* * *

[Reg. § 1.101-1.]

☐ [*T.D.* 6280, 12-16-57. *Amended by T.D.* 6783, 12-23-64; *T.D.* 7836, 9-23-82; *T.D.* 9340, 7-23-2007; *and T.D.* 9879, 10-25-2019 (corrected 12-12-2019).]

§ 1.101-3. Interest payments.—(a) *Applicability of section 101(c).*—Section 101(c) provides that if any amount excluded from gross income by section 101(a) (relating to life insurance proceeds) or section 101(b) (relating to employees' death benefits) is held under an agreement to pay interest thereon, the interest payments shall be included in gross income. This provision applies to payments made (either by an insurer or by or on behalf of an employer) of interest earned on any amount so excluded from gross income which is held without substantial diminution of the principal amount during the period when such interest payments are being made or credited to the beneficiaries or estate of the insured or the employee. For example, if a monthly payment is $100, of which $99 represents interest and $1 represents diminution of the principal amount, the principal amount shall be considered held under an agreement to pay interest thereon and the interest payment shall be included in the gross income of the recipient. Section 101(c) applies whether the election to have an amount held under an agreement to pay interest thereon is made by the insured or employee or by his beneficiaries or estate, and whether or not an interest rate is explicitly stated in the agreement. Section 101(d), relating to the payment of life insurance proceeds at a date later than death, shall not apply to any amount to which section 101(c) applies. See section 101(d)(4). However, both section 101(c) and section 101(d) may apply to payments received under a single life insurance contract. For provisions relating to the application of this rule to payments received under a permanent life insurance policy with a family income rider attached, see paragraph (h) of § 1.101-4.

(b) *Determinations of "present value".*—For the purpose of determining whether section 101(c) or section 101(d) applies, the present value (at the time of the insured's death) of any amount which is to be paid at a date later than death shall be determined by the use of the interest rate and mortality tables used by the insurer in determining the size of the payments to be made. [Reg. § 1.101-3.]

☐ [*T.D.* 6280, 12-16-57. *Amended by T.D.* 6577, 10-27-61.]

§ 1.102-1. Gifts and inheritances.—(a) *General rule.*—Property received as a gift, or received under a will or under statutes of descent and distribution, is not includible in gross income, although the income from such property is includible in gross income. An amount of principal paid under a marriage settlement is a gift. However, see section 71 and the regulations thereunder for rules relating to alimony or allowances paid upon divorce or separation. Section 102 does not apply to prizes and awards (see section 74 and § 1.74-1) nor to scholarships and fellowship grants (see section 117 and the regulations thereunder).

(b) *Income from gifts and inheritances.*—The income from any property received as a gift, or under a will or statute of descent and distribution shall not be excluded from gross income under paragraph (a) of this section.

(c) *Gifts and inheritances of income.*—If the gift, bequest, devise, or inheritance is of income from property, it shall not be excluded from gross income under paragraph (a) of this section. Section 102 provides a special rule for the treatment of certain gifts, bequests, devises, or inheritances which by their terms are to be paid, credited, or distributed at intervals. Except as provided in section 663(a)(1) and paragraph (d) of this section, to the extent any such gift, bequest, devise, or inheritance is paid, credited, or to be distributed out of income from property, it shall be considered a gift, bequest, devise, or inheritance of income from property. Section 102 provides the same treatment for amounts of income from property which is paid, credited, or to be distributed under a gift or bequest whether the gift or bequest is in terms of a right to payments at intervals (regardless of income) or is in terms of a right to income. To the extent the amounts in either case are paid, credited, or to be distributed at intervals out of income, they are not to be excluded under section 102 from the taxpayer's gross income.

(d) *Effect of subchapter J.*—Any amount required to be included in the gross income of a beneficiary under sections 652, 662, or 668 shall be treated for purposes of this section as a gift, bequest, devise, or inheritance of income from property. On the other hand, any amount excluded from the gross income of a beneficiary under section 663(a)(1) shall be treated for purposes of this section as property acquired by gift, bequest, devise, or inheritance.

(e) *Income taxed to grantor or assignor.*—Section 102 is not intended to tax a donee upon the same income which is taxed to the grantor of a trust or assignor of income under section 61 or sections 671 through 677, inclusive. [Reg. § 1.102-1.]

☐ [*T.D.* 6220, 12-28-56.]

Proposed Amendment to Regulation

§ 1.102-1. Gifts and inheritances.

* * *

(f) *Exclusions.*—(1) *In general.*—Section 102 does not apply to prizes and awards (including employee achievement awards) (see section 74); certain de minimis fringe benefits (see section 132); any amount transferred by or for an employer to, or for the benefit of, an employee (see section 102(c)); or to qualified scholarships (see section 117).

(2) *Employer/Employee transfers.*—For purposes of section 102(c), extraordinary transfers to the natural objects of an employer's bounty will not be considered transfers to, or for the benefit of, an employee if the employee can show that the transfer was not made in recognition of the employee's employment. Accordingly, section 102(c) shall not apply to amounts transferred between related parties (*e.g.*, father and son) if the purpose of the transfer can be substantially attributed to the familial relationship of the parties and not to the circumstances of their employment. [Prop. Reg. § 1.102-1.]

[Proposed 1-9-89.]

§ 1.104-1. Compensation for injuries or sickness.—(a) *In general.*—Section 104(a) provides an exclusion from gross income with respect to certain amounts described in paragraphs (b), (c), (d) and (e) of this section, which are received for personal injuries or sickness, except to the extent that such amounts are attributable to (but not in excess of) deductions allowed under section 213 (relating to medical, etc., expenses) for any prior taxable year. See section 213 and the regulations thereunder.

(b) *Amounts received under workmen's compensation acts.*—Section 104(a)(1) excludes from gross income amounts which are received by an employee under a workmen's compensation act (such as the Longshoremen's and Harbor Workers' Compensation Act, 33 U.S.C., c. 18), or under a statute in the nature of a workmen's compensation act which provides compensation to employees for personal injuries or sickness incurred in the course of employment. Section 104(a)(1) also applies to compensation which is paid under a workmen's compensation act to the survivor or survivors of a deceased employee. However, section 104(a)(1) does not apply to a retirement pension or annuity to the extent that it is determined by reference to the employee's age or length of service, or the employee's prior contributions, even though the employee's retirement is occasioned by an occupational injury or sickness. Section 104(a)(1) also does not apply to amounts which are received as compensation for a nonoccupational injury or sickness nor to amounts received as compensation for an occupational injury or sickness to the extent that they are in excess of the amount provided in the applicable workmen's compensation act or acts. See, however, §§ 1.105-1 through 1.105-5 for rules relating to exclusion of such amounts from gross income.

(c) *Damages received on account of personal physical injuries or physical sickness.*—(1) *In general.*—Section 104(a)(2) excludes from gross income the amount of any damages (other than punitive damages) received (whether by suit or agreement and whether as lump sums or as periodic payments) on account of personal physical injuries or physical sickness. Emotional distress is not considered a physical injury or physical sickness. However, damages for emotional distress attributable to a physical injury or physical sickness are excluded from income under section 104(a)(2). Section 104(a)(2) also excludes damages not in excess of the amount paid for medical care (described in section 213(d)(1)(A) or (B)) for emotional distress. For purposes of this paragraph (c), the term *damages* means an amount received (other than workers' compensation) through prosecution of a legal suit or action, or through a settlement agreement entered into in lieu of prosecution.

(2) *Cause of action and remedies.*—The section 104(a)(2) exclusion may apply to damages recovered for a personal physical injury or physical sickness under a statute, even if that statute does not provide for a broad range of remedies. The injury need not be defined as a tort under state or common law.

* * *

(d) *Accident or health insurance.*—Section 104(a)(3) excludes from gross income amounts received through accident or health insurance for personal injuries or sickness (other than amounts received by an employee, to the extent that such amounts (1) are attributable to contributions of the employer which were not includible in the gross income of the employee, or (2) are paid by the employer). Similar treatment is also accorded to amounts received under accident or health plans and amounts received from sickness or disability funds. See section 105(e) and § 1.105-5. If, therefore, an individual purchases a policy of accident or health insurance out of his own funds, amounts received thereunder for personal injuries or sickness are excludable from his gross income under section 104(a)(3). See, however, section 213 and the regulations thereunder as to the inclusion in gross income of amounts attributable to deductions allowed under section 213 for any prior taxable year. Section 104(a)(3) also applies to amounts received by an employee for personal injuries or sickness from a fund which is maintained exclusively by employee contributions. Conversely, if an employer is either the sole contributor to such a fund, or is the sole purchaser of a policy of accident or health insurance for his employees (on either a group or individual basis), the exclusion provided under section 104(a)(3) does not apply to any amounts received by his employees through such fund or insurance. If the employer and his employees contribute to a fund or purchase insurance which pays accident or health benefits to employees, section 104(a)(3) does not apply to amounts received thereunder by employees to the extent that such amounts are attributable to the employer's contributions. See § 1.105-1 for rules relating to the determination of the amount attributable to employer contributions. Although amounts paid by or on behalf of an employer to an employee for personal injuries or sickness are not excludable from the employee's gross income under section 104(a)(3), they may be excludable therefrom under section 105. See §§ 1.105-1 through 1.105-5 , inclusive. For treatment of accident or health benefits paid to or on behalf of a self-employed individual by a trust described in section 401(a) which is exempt under section 501(a) or under a plan described in section 403(a), see paragraph (g) of § 1.72-15.

* * *

[Reg. § 1.104-1.]

□ [*T.D.* 6169, 4-13-56. *Amended by T.D.* 6722, 4-13-64; *T.D.* 7043, 6-1-70 *and T.D.* 9573, 1-20-2012.]

§ 1.105-2. Amounts expended for medical care.—Section 105(b) provides an exclusion from gross income with respect to the amounts referred to in section 105(a) (see § 1.105-1) which are paid, directly or indirectly, to the taxpayer to reimburse him for expenses incurred for the medical care (as defined in section 213(e)) of the taxpayer, his spouse, and his dependents (as defined in section 152). However, the exclusion does not apply to amounts which are attributable to (and not in excess of) deductions allowed under section 213 (relating to medical, etc., expenses) for any prior taxable year. See section 213 and the regulations thereunder. Section 105(b) applies only to amounts which are paid specifically to reimburse the taxpayer for expenses incurred by him for the prescribed medical care. Thus, section 105(b) does not apply to amounts which the taxpayer would be entitled to receive irrespective of whether or not he incurs expenses for medical care. For example, if under a wage continuation plan the taxpayer is entitled to regular wages during a period of absence from work due to sickness or injury, amounts received under such plan are not excludable from his gross income under section 105(b) even though the taxpayer may have incurred medical expenses during the period of illness. Such amounts may, however, be excludable from his gross income under section 105(d). See § 1.105-4. If the amounts are paid to the taxpayer solely to reimburse him for expenses which he incurred for the prescribed medical care, section 105(b) is applicable even though such amounts are paid without proof of the amount of the actual expenses incurred by the taxpayer, but section 105(b) is not applicable to the extent that such amounts exceed the amount of the actual expenses for such medical care. If the taxpayer incurs an obligation for medical care, payment to the obligee in discharge of such obligation shall constitute indirect payment to the taxpayer as reimbursement for medical care. Similarly, payment to or on behalf of the taxpayer's spouse or dependents shall constitute indirect payment to the taxpayer. [Reg. § 1.105-2.]

□ [*T.D.* 6169, 4-13-56.]

§ 1.106-1. Contributions by employer to accident and health plans.—(a) The gross income of an employee does not include the contributions that the employer makes to an accident or health plan for compensation (through insurance or otherwise) to the employee for personal injuries or sickness incurred by the employee, the employee's spouse, the employee's dependents (as defined in section 152 determined without regard to section 152(b)(1), (b)(2), or (d)(1)(B)), or any child (as defined in section 152(f)(1)) of the employee who as of the end of the taxable year has not attained age 27. The employer may contribute to an accident or health plan either by paying the premium (or a portion of the premium) on a policy of accident or health insurance covering one or more of his employees, or by contributing to a separate trust or fund (including a fund referred to in section 105(e)) which provides accident or health benefits directly or through insurance to one or more of his employees. However, if such insurance policy, trust, or fund provides other benefits in addition to accident or health benefits, section 106 applies only to the portion of the employer's contribution which is allocable to accident or health benefits. See paragraph (d) of § 1.104-1 and §§ 1.105-1 through 1.105-5, inclusive, for regulations relating to exclusion from an employee's gross income of amounts received through accident or health insurance and through accident or health plans. For the treatment of the payment of premiums for accident or health insurance from a qualified trust under section 401(a), see §§ 1.72-15 and 1.402(a)-1(e).

* * *

[Reg. § 1.106-1.]

□ [*T.D.* 6169, 4-13-56. *Amended by T.D.* 9665, 5-9-2014.]

§ 1.109-1. Exclusion from gross income of lessor of real property of value of improvements erected by lessee.—(a) Income derived by a lessor of real property upon the termination, through forfeiture or otherwise, of the lease of such property and attributable to buildings erected or other improvements made by the lessee upon the leased property is excluded from gross income. However, where the facts disclose that such buildings or improvements represent in whole or in part a liquidation in kind of lease rentals, the exclusion from gross income shall not apply to the extent that such buildings or improvements represent such liquidation. The exclusion applies only with respect to the income realized by the lessor upon the termination of the lease and has no application to income, if any, in the form of rent, which may be derived by a lessor during the period of the lease and attributable to buildings erected or other improvements made by the lessee. It has no application to income which may be realized by the lessor upon the termination of the lease but not attributable to the value of such buildings or improvements. Neither does it apply to income derived by the lessor subsequent to the termination of the lease incident to the ownership of such buildings or improvements.

(b) The provisions of this section may be illustrated by the following example:

Example. The A Corporation leased in 1945 for a period of 50 years unimproved real property to the B Corporation under a lease providing that the B Corporation erect on the leased premises an office building costing $500,000, in addition to paying the A Corporation a lease rental of $10,000 per annum beginning on the date of completion of the improvements, the sum of $100,000 being placed in escrow for the payment of the rental. The building was completed on January 1, 1950. The lease provided that all improvements made by the lessee on the leased property would become the absolute property of the A Corporation on the termination of the lease by forfeiture or otherwise and that the lessor would become entitled on such termination to the remainder of the sum, if any, remaining in the escrow fund. The B Corporation forfeited its lease on January 1, 1955, when the improvements had a value of $100,000. Under the provisions of section 109, the $100,000 is excluded from gross income. The amount of $50,000 representing the remainder in the escrow fund is forfeited to the A Corporation and is included in the gross income of that taxpayer. As to the basis of the property in the hands of the A Corporation, see § 1.1019-1.

[Reg. § 1.109-1.]

□ [*T.D.* 6220, 12-28-56.]

Proposed Regulation

§ 1.117-6. Qualified scholarships.—

* * *

(b) *Exclusion of qualified scholarships.*—(1) Gross income does not include any amount received as a qualified scholarship by an individual who is a candidate for a degree at an educational organization described in section 170(b)(1)(A)(ii), subject to the rules set forth in paragraph (d) of this section. Generally, any amount of a scholarship or fellowship grant that is not excludable under section 117 is includable in the gross income of the recipient for the taxable year in which such amount is received, notwithstanding the provisions of section 102 (relating to exclusion from gross income of gifts). However, see section 127 and the regulations thereunder for rules permitting an exclusion from gross income for certain educational assistance payments. See also section 162 and the regulations thereunder for the deductibility as a trade or business expense of the educational expenses of an individual who is not a candidate for a degree.

(2) If the amount of a scholarship or fellowship grant eligible to be excluded as a qualified scholarship under this paragraph cannot be determined when the grant is received because expenditures for qualified tuition and related expenses have not yet been incurred, then that portion of any amount received as a scholarship or fellowship grant that is not used for qualified tuition and related expenses within the academic period to which the scholarship or fellowship grant applies must be included in

the gross income of the recipient for the taxable year in which such academic period ends.

(c) *Definitions.*—(1) *Qualified scholarship.*—For purposes of this section, a qualified scholarship is any amount received by an individual as a scholarship or fellowship grant (as defined in paragraph (c)(3) of this section), to the extent the individual establishes that, in accordance with the conditions of the grant, such amount was used for qualified tuition and related expenses (as defined in paragraph (c)(2) of this section). To be considered a qualified scholarship, the terms of the scholarship or fellowship grant need not expressly require that the amounts received be used for tuition and related expenses. However, to the extent that the terms of the grant specify that any portion of the grant cannot be used for tuition and related expenses or designate any portion of the grant for purposes other than tuition and related expenses (such as for room and board, or for a meal allowance), such amounts are not amounts received as a qualified scholarship. See paragraph (e) of this section for rules relating to recordkeeping requirements for establishing amounts used for qualified tuition and related expenses.

(2) *Qualified tuition and related expenses.*—For purposes of this section, qualified tuition and related expenses are—

(i) Tuition and fees required for the enrollment or attendance of a student at an educational organization described in section 170(b)(1)(A)(ii); and

(ii) Fees, books, supplies, and equipment required for courses of instruction at such an educational organization.

In order to be treated as related expenses under this section, the fees, books, supplies, and equipment must be required of all students in the particular course of instruction. Incidental expenses are not considered related expenses. Incidental expenses include expenses incurred for room and board, travel, research, clerical help, and equipment and other expenses that are not required for either enrollment or attendance at an educational organization, or in a course of instruction at such educational organization. See paragraph (c)(6), Example (1) of this section.

(3) *Scholarship or fellowship grant.*—(i) *In general.*—Generally, a scholarship or fellowship grant is a cash amount paid or allowed to, or for the benefit of, an individual to aid such individual in the pursuit of study or research. A scholarship or fellowship grant also may be in the form of a reduction in the amount owed by the recipient to an educational organization for tuition, room and board, or any other fee. A scholarship or fellowship grant may be funded by a governmental agency, college or university, charitable organization, business, or any other source. To be considered a scholarship or fellowship grant for purposes of this section, any amount received need not be formally designated as a scholarship. For example, an "allowance" is treated as a scholarship if it meets the definition set forth in this paragraph. However, a scholarship or fellowship grant does not include any amount provided by an individual to aid a relative, friend, or other individual in the pursuit of study or research if the grantor is motivated by family or philanthropic considerations.

(ii) *Items not considered as scholarships or fellowship grants.*—The following payments or allowances are not considered to be amounts received as a scholarship or fellowship grant for purposes of section 117:

(A) Educational and training allowances to a veteran pursuant to section 400 of the Servicemen's Readjustment Act of 1944 (58 Stat. 287) or pursuant to 38 U.S.C. 1631 (formerly section 231 of the Veterans' Readjustment Assistance Act of 1952).

(B) Tuition and subsistence allowances to members of the Armed Forces of the United States who are students at an educational institution operated by the United States or approved by the United States for their education and training, such as the United States Naval Academy and the United States Military Academy.

(4) *Candidate for a degree.*—For purposes of this section, a candidate for a degree is—

(i) A primary or secondary school student;

(ii) An undergraduate or graduate student at a college or university who is pursuing studies or conducting research to meet the requirement for an academic or professional degree; or

(iii) A full-time or part-time student at an educational organization described in section 170(b)(1)(A)(ii) that—

(A) Provides an educational program that is acceptable for full credit towards a bachelor's or higher degree, or offers a program of training to prepare students for gainful employment in a recognized occupation, and

(B) Is authorized under Federal or State law to provide such a program and is accredited by a nationally recognized accreditation agency.

The student may pursue studies or conduct research at an educational organization other than the one conferring the degree provided that such study or research meets the requirements of the educational organization granting the degree. See paragraph (c)(6), Examples (2) and (3) of this section.

(5) *Educational organization.*—For purposes of this section, an educational organization is an organization described under section 170(b)(1)(A)(ii) and the regulations thereunder. An educational organization is described in section 170(b)(1)(A)(ii) if it has as its primary function the presentation of formal instruction, and it normally maintains a regular faculty and curriculum and normally has a regularly enrolled body of pupils or students in attendance at the place where its educational activities are regularly carried on. See paragraph (c)(6), Example (4) of this section.

(6) *Examples.*—The provisions of this paragraph may be illustrated by the following examples:

Example (1). On September 1, 1987, A receives a scholarship from University U for academic year 1987-1988. A is enrolled in a writing course at U. Suggested supplies for the writing course in which A is enrolled include a word processor, but students in the course are not required to obtain a word processor. Any amount used for suggested supplies is not an amount used for qualified tuition and related expenses for purposes of this section. Thus, A may not include the cost of a word processor in determining the amount received by A as a qualified scholarship.

Example (2). B is a scholarship student during academic year 1987-1988 at Technical School V located in State W. B is enrolled in a program to train individuals to become data processors. V is authorized by State W to provide this program and is accredited by an appropriate accreditation agency. B is a candidate for a degree for purposes of this section. Thus, B may exclude from gross income any amount received as a qualified scholarship, subject to the rules set forth in paragraph (d) of this section.

Example (3). C holds a Ph.D. in chemistry. On January 31, 1988, Foundation X awards C a fellowship. During 1988 C pursues chemistry research at Research Foundation Y, supported by the fellowship grant from X. C is not an employee of either foundation. C is not a candidate for a degree for purposes of this section. Thus, the fellowship grant from X must be included in C's gross income.

Example (4). On July 1, 1987, D receives a $500 scholarship to take a correspondence course from School Z. D receives and returns all lessons to Z through the mail. No students are in attendance at Z's place of business. D is not attending an educational organization described in section 170(b)(1)(A)(ii) for purposes of this section. Thus, the $500 scholarship must be included in D's gross income.

(d) *Inclusion of qualified scholarships and qualified tuition reductions representing payment for services.*—(1) *In general.*—The exclusion from gross income under this section does not apply to that portion of any amount received as a qualified scholarship or qualified tuition reduction (as defined under section 117(d)) that represents payment for teaching, research, or other services by the student required as a condition to receiving the qualified scholarship or qualified tuition reduction, regardless of whether all candidates for the degree are required to perform such services. The provisions of this paragraph (d) apply not only to cash amounts received in return for such services, but also to amounts by which the tuition or related expenses of the person who performs services are reduced, whether or not pursuant to a tuition reduction plan described in section 117(d).

(2) *Payment for services.*—For purposes of this section, a scholarship or fellowship grant represents payment for services when the grantor requires the recipient to perform services in return for the granting of the scholarship or fellowship. A requirement that the recipient pursue studies, research, or other activities primarily for the benefit of the grantor is treated as a requirement to perform services. A requirement that a recipient furnish periodic reports to the grantor for the purpose of keeping the grantor informed as to the general progress of the individual, however, does not constitute the performance of services. A scholarship or fellowship grant conditioned upon either past, present, or future teaching, research, or other services by the recipient represents payment for services under this section. See paragraph (d)(5), Examples (1), (2), (3) and (4) of this section.

(3) *Determination of amount of scholarship or fellowship grant representing payment for services.*—If only a portion of a scholarship or fellowship grant represents payment for services, the grantor must determine the amount of the scholarship or fellowship grant (including any reduction in tuition or related expenses) to be allocated to payment for services. Factors to be taken into account in making this allocation include, but are not limited to, compensation paid by—

(i) The grantor for similar services performed by students with qualifications comparable to those of the scholarship recipient, but who do not receive scholarship or fellowship grants;

(ii) The grantor for similar services performed by full-time or part-time employees of the grantor who are not students; and

(iii) Educational organizations, other than the grantor of the scholarship or fellowship, for similar services performed either by students or other employees.

If the recipient includes in gross income the amount allocated by the grantor to payment for services and such amount represents reasonable compensation for those services, then any additional amount of a scholarship or fellowship grant received from the same grantor that meets the requirements of paragraph (b) of this section is excludable from gross income. See paragraph (d)(5), Examples (5) and (6) of this section.

(4) *Characterization of scholarship or fellowship grants representing payment for services for purposes of the reporting and withholding requirements.*—Any amount of a scholarship or fellowship grant that represents payment for services (as defined in paragraph (d)(2) of this section) is considered wages for purposes of sections 3401 and 3402 (relating to withholding for income taxes), section 6041 (relating to returns of information), and section 6051 (relating to reporting wages of employees). The application of sections 3101 and 3111 (relating to the Federal Insurance Contributions Act (FICA)), or section 3301 (relating to the Federal Unemployment Tax Act (FUTA)) depends upon the nature of the employment and the status of the organization. See sections 3121(b), 3306(c), and the regulations thereunder.

(5) *Examples.*—The provisions of this paragraph may be illustrated by the following examples:

Example (1). On November 15, 1987, A receives a $5,000 qualified scholarship (as defined in paragraph (c)(1) of this section) for academic year 1988-1989 under a federal program requiring A's future service as a federal employee. The $5,000 scholarship represents payment for services for purposes of this section. Thus, the $5,000 must be included in A's gross income as wages.

Example (2). B receives a $10,000 scholarship from V Corporation on June 4, 1987, for academic year 1987-1988. As a condition to receiving the scholarship, B agrees to work for V after graduation. B has no previous relationship with V. The $10,000 scholarship represents payment for future services for purposes of this section. Thus, the $10,000 scholarship must be included in B's gross income as wages.

Example (3). On March 15, 1987, C is awarded a fellowship for academic year 1987-1988 to pursue a research project the nature of which is determined by the grantor, University W. C must submit a paper to W that describes the research results. The paper does not fulfill any course requirements. Under the terms of the grant, W may publish C's results, or otherwise use the results of C's research. C is treated as performing services for W. Thus, C's fellowship from W represents payment for services and must be included in C's gross income as wages.

Example (4). On September 27, 1987, D receives a qualified scholarship (as defined in paragraph (c)(1) of this section) from University X for academic year 1987-1988. As a condition to receiving the scholarship, D performs services as a teaching assistant for X. Such services are required of all candidates for a degree at X. The amount of D's scholarship from X is equal to the compensation paid by X to teaching assistants who are part-time employees and not students at X. D's scholarship from X represents payment for services. Thus, the entire amount of D's scholarship from X must be included in D's gross income as wages.

Example (5). On June 11, 1987, E receives a $6,000 scholarship for academic year 1987-1988 from University Y. As a condition to receiving the scholarship, E performs services as a researcher for Y. Other researchers who are not scholarship recipients receive $2,000 for similar services for the year. Therefore, Y allocates $2,000 of the scholarship amount to compensation for services performed by E. Thus, the portion of the scholarship that represents payment for services, $2,000, must be included in E's gross income as wages. However, if E establishes expenditures of $4,000 for qualified tuition and related expenses (as defined in paragraph (c)(2) of this section), then $4,000 of E's scholarship is excludable from E's gross income as a qualified scholarship.

Example (6). During 1987 F is employed as a research assistant to a faculty member at University Z. F receives a salary from Z that represents reasonable compensation for the position of research assistant. In addition to salary, F receives from Z a qualified tuition reduction (as defined in section 117(d)) to be used to enroll in an undergraduate course at Z. F includes the salary in gross income. Thus, the qualified tuition reduction does not represent payment for services and therefore, is not includable in F's gross income.

* * *

(h) *Characterization of scholarship or fellowship grants exceeding amounts permitted to be excluded from gross income for purposes of the standard deduction and filing requirements for dependents.*—For purposes of section 63(c)(5) (relating to the standard deduction for dependents) and section 6012(a)(1)(C)(i) (relating to dependents required to make returns of income), any amount of a scholarship or fellowship grant in excess of the amount permitted to be excluded from gross income under paragraph (b) of this section is considered earned income. For example, on June 11, 1987, A, a student who has no other earned or unearned income for the year and can be claimed as a dependent on another taxpayer's return of tax, receives a $1,000 scholarship for room and board. The $1,000 must be included in A's gross income because it is not a qualified scholarship under paragraph (b) of this section. However, for purposes of sections 63(c)(5) and 6012(a)(1)(C)(i), the $1,000 is earned income. Accordingly, A is not required to file a return of tax for 1987 because A's gross income ($1,000) does not exceed A's standard deduction ($1,000) and A has no unearned income. [Prop. Reg. § 1.117-6.]

[Proposed 6-9-88.]

§ 1.118-1. Contributions to the capital of a corporation.—In the case of a corporation, section 118 provides an exclusion from gross income with respect to any contribution of money or property to the capital of the taxpayer. Thus, if a corporation requires additional funds for conducting its business and obtains such funds through voluntary pro rata payments by its shareholders, the amounts so received being credited to its surplus account or to a special account, such amounts do not constitute income, although there is no increase in the outstanding shares of stock of the corporation. In such a case the payments are in the nature of assessments upon, and represent an additional price paid for, the shares of stock held by the individual shareholders, and will be treated as an addition to and as a part of the operating capital of the company. Section 118 also applies to contributions to capital made by persons other than shareholders. For example, the exclusion applies to the value of land or other property contributed to a corporation by a governmental unit or by a civic group for the purpose of inducing the corporation to locate its business in a particular community, or for the purpose of enabling the corporation to expand its operating facilities. However, the exclusion does not apply to any money or property transferred to the corporation in consideration for goods or services rendered, or to subsidies paid for the purpose of inducing the taxpayer to limit production. See section 362 for the basis of property acquired by a corporation through a contribution to its capital by its stockholders or by nonstockholders. [Reg. § 1.118-1.]

□ [*T.D.* 6220, 12-28-56.]

§ 1.119-1. Meals and lodging furnished for the convenience of the employer.—(a) *Meals.*—(1) *In general.*—The value of meals furnished to an employee by his employer shall be excluded from the employee's gross income if two tests are met: (i) The meals are furnished on the business premises of the employer, and (ii) the meals are furnished for the convenience of the employer. The question of whether meals are furnished for the convenience of the employer is one of fact to be determined by analysis of all the facts and circumstances in each case. If the tests described in subdivisions (i) and (ii) of this subparagraph are met, the exclusion shall apply irrespective of whether under an employment contract or a statute fixing the terms of employment such meals are furnished as compensation.

(2) *Meals furnished without a charge.*—(i) Meals furnished by an employer without charge to the employee will be regarded as furnished for the convenience of the employer if such meals are furnished for a substantial noncompensatory business reason of the employer. If an employer furnishes meals as a means of providing additional compensation to his employee (and not for a substantial noncompensatory business reason of the employer), the meals so furnished will not be regarded as furnished for the convenience of the employer. Conversely, if the employer furnishes meals to his employee for a substantial noncompensatory business reason, the meals so furnished will be regarded as furnished for the convenience of the employer, even though such meals are also furnished for a compensatory reason. In determining the reason of an employer for furnishing meals, the mere declaration that meals are furnished for a noncompensatory business reason is not sufficient to prove that meals are furnished for the convenience of the employer, but such determination will be based upon an examination of all the surrounding facts and circumstances. In subdivision (ii) of this subparagraph, there are set forth some of the substantial noncompensatory business reasons which occur frequently and which justify the conclusion that meals furnished for such a reason are furnished for the convenience of the employer. In subdivision (iii) of this subparagraph, there are set forth some of the business reasons which are considered to be compensatory and which, in the absence of a substantial noncompensatory business reason, justify the conclusion that meals furnished for such a reason are not furnished for the convenience of the employer. Generally, meals furnished before or after the working hours of the employee will not be regarded as furnished for the convenience of the employer, but see subdivision (ii)(*d*) and (*f*) of this sub-

paragraph for some exceptions to this general rule. Meals furnished on nonworking days do not qualify for the exclusion under section 119. If the employee is required to occupy living quarters on the business premises of his employer as a condition of his employment (as defined in paragraph (b) of this section), the exclusion applies to the value of any meal furnished without charge to the employee on such premises.

(ii) *(a)* Meals will be regarded as furnished for a substantial noncompensatory business reason of the employer when the meals are furnished to the employee during his working hours to have the employee available for emergency call during his meal period. In order to demonstrate that meals are furnished to the employee to have the employee available for emergency call during the meal period, it must be shown that emergencies have actually occurred, or can reasonably be expected to occur, in the employer's business which have resulted, or will result, in the employer calling on the employee to perform his job during his meal period.

(b) Meals will be regarded as furnished for a substantial noncompensatory business reason of the employer when the meals are furnished to the employee during his working hours because the employer's business is such that the employee must be restricted to a short meal period, such as 30 or 45 minutes, and because the employee could not be expected to eat elsewhere in such a short meal period. For example, meals may qualify under this subdivision when the employer is engaged in a business in which the peak workload occurs during the normal lunch hours. However, meals cannot qualify under this subdivision *(b)* when the reason for restricting the time of the meal period is so that the employee can be let off earlier in the day.

(c) Meals will be regarded as furnished for a substantial noncompensatory business reason of the employer when the meals are furnished to the employee during his working hours because the employee could not otherwise secure proper meals within a reasonable meal period. For example, meals may qualify under this subdivision *(c)* when there are insufficient eating facilities in the vicinity of the employer's premises.

(d) A meal furnished to a restaurant employee or other food service employee for each meal period in which the employee works will be regarded as furnished for a substantial noncompensatory business reason of the employer, irrespective of whether the meal is furnished during, immediately before, or immediately after the working hours of the employee.

(e) If the employer furnishes meals to employees at a place of business and the reason for furnishing the meals to each of substantially all of the employees who are furnished the meals is a substantial noncompensatory business reason of the employer, the meals furnished to each other employee will also be regarded as furnished for a substantial noncompensatory business reason of the employer.

(f) If an employer would have furnished a meal to an employee during his working hours for a substantial noncompensatory business reason, a meal furnished to such an employee immediately after his working hours because his duties prevented him from obtaining a meal during his working hours will be regarded as furnished for a substantial noncompensatory business reason.

(iii) Meals will be regarded as furnished for a compensatory business reason of the employer when the meals are furnished to the employee to promote the morale or goodwill of the employee, or to attract prospective employees.

(3) *Meals furnished with a charge.*—(i) If an employer provides meals which an employee may or may not purchase, the meals will not be regarded as furnished for the convenience of the employer. Thus, meals for which a charge is made by the employer will not be regarded as furnished for the convenience of the employer if the employee has a choice of accepting the meals and paying for them or of not paying for them and providing his meals in another manner.

(ii) If an employer furnishes an employee meals for which the employee is charged an unvarying amount (for example, by subtraction from his stated compensation) irrespective of whether he accepts the meals, the amount of such flat charge made by the employer for such meals is not, as such, part of the compensation includible in the gross income of the employee; whether the value of the meals so furnished is excludable under section 119 is determined by applying the rules of subparagraph (2) of this paragraph. If meals furnished for an unvarying amount are not furnished for the convenience of the employer in accordance with the rules of subparagraph (2) of this paragraph, the employee shall include in gross income the value of the meals regardless of whether the value exceeds or is less than the amount charged for such meals. In the absence of evidence to the contrary, the value of the meals may be deemed to be equal to the amount charged for them.

(b) *Lodging.*—The value of lodging furnished to an employee by the employer shall be excluded from the employee's gross income if three tests are met:

(1) The lodging is furnished on the business premises of the employer,

(2) The lodging is furnished for the convenience of the employer, and

(3) The employee is required to accept such lodging as a condition of his employment. The requirement of subparagraph (3) of this paragraph that the employee is required to accept such lodging as a condition of his employment means that he be required to accept the lodging in order to enable him properly to perform the duties of his employment. Lodging will be regarded as furnished to enable the employee properly to perform the duties of his employment when, for example, the lodging is furnished because the employee is required to be available for duty at all times or because the employee could not perform the services required of him unless he is furnished such lodging. If the tests described in subparagraphs (1), (2), and (3) of this paragraph are met, the exclusion shall apply irrespective of whether a charge is made, or whether, under an employment contract or statute fixing the terms of employment, such lodging is furnished as compensation. If the employer furnishes the employee lodging for which the employee is charged an unvarying amount irrespective of whether he accepts the lodging, the amount of the charge made by the employer for such lodging is not, as such, part of the compensation includible in the gross income of the employee; whether the value of the lodging is excludable from gross income under section 119 is determined by applying the other rules of this paragraph. If the tests described in subparagraphs (1), (2), and (3) of this paragraph are not met, the employee shall include in gross income the value of the lodging regardless of whether it exceeds or is less than the amount charged. In the absence of evidence to the contrary, the value of the lodging may be deemed to be equal to the amount charged.

(c) *Business premises of the employer.*—(1) *In general.*—For purposes of this section, the term "business premises of the employer" generally means the place of employment of the employee. For example, meals and lodging furnished in the employer's home to a domestic servant would constitute meals and lodging furnished on the business premises of the employer. Similarly, meals furnished to cowhands while herding their employer's cattle on leased land would be regarded as furnished on the business premises of the employer.

* * *

(e) *Rules.*—The exclusion provided by section 119 applies only to meals and lodging furnished in kind by or on behalf of an employer to his employee. If the employee has an option to receive additional compensation in lieu of meals or lodging in kind, the value of such meals and lodging is not excludable from gross income under section 119. However, the mere fact that an employee, at his option, may decline to accept meals tendered in kind will not of itself require inclusion of the value thereof in gross income. Cash allowances for meals or lodging received by an employee are includible in gross income to the extent that such allowances constitute compensation.

(f) *Examples.*—The provisions of section 119 may be illustrated by the following examples:

Example (1). A waitress who works from 7 a.m. to 4 p.m. is furnished without charge two meals a work day. The employer encourages the waitress to have her breakfast on his business premises before starting work, but does not require her to have breakfast there. She is required, however, to have her lunch on such premises. Since the waitress is a food service employee and works during the normal breakfast and lunch periods, the waitress is permitted to exclude from her gross income both the value of the breakfast and the value of the lunch.

Example (2). The waitress in example (1) is allowed to have meals on the employer's premises without charge on her days off. The waitress is not permitted to exclude the value of such meals from her gross income.

Example (3). A bank teller who works from 9 a.m. to 5 p.m. is furnished his lunch without charge in a cafeteria which the bank maintains on its premises. The bank furnishes the teller such meals in order to limit his lunch period to 30 minutes since the bank's peak work load occurs during the normal lunch period. If the teller had to obtain his lunch elsewhere, it would take him considerably longer than 30 minutes for lunch, and the bank strictly enforces the 30-minute time limit. The bank teller may exclude from his gross income the value of such meals obtained in the bank cafeteria.

Example (4). Assume the same facts as in example (3), except that the bank charges the bank teller an unvarying rate per meal regardless of whether he eats in the cafeteria. The bank teller is not required to include in gross income such flat amount charged as part of his compensation, and he is entitled to exclude from his gross income the value of the meals he receives for such flat charge.

Example (5). A Civil Service employee of a State is employed at an institution and is required by his employer to be available for duty at all times. The employer furnishes the employee with meals and lodging at the institution without charge. Under the applicable State statute, his meals and lodging are regarded as part of the employee's compensation. The employee would nevertheless be entitled to exclude the value of such meals and lodging from his gross income.

Example (6). An employee of an institution is given the choice of residing at the institution free of charge, or of residing elsewhere and receiving a cash allowance in addition to his regular salary. If he elects to reside at the institution, the value to the employee of the lodging furnished by the employer will be includible in the employee's gross income because his residence at the institution is not required in order for him to perform properly the duties of his employment.

Example (7). A construction worker is employed at a construction project at a remote job site in Alaska. Due to the inaccessibility of facilities for the employees who are working at the job site to obtain food and lodging and the prevailing weather conditions, the employer is required to furnish meals and lodging to the employee at the camp site in order to carry on the construction project. The employee is required to pay $40 a week for the meals and lodging. The weekly charge of $40 is not, as such, part of the compensation includible in the gross income of the employee, and under paragraphs (a) and (b) of this section the value of the meals and lodging is excludable from his gross income.

Example (8). A manufacturing company provides a cafeteria on its premises at which its employees can purchase their lunch. There is no other eating facility located near the company's premises, but the employee can furnish his own meal by bringing his lunch. The amount of compensation which any employee is required to include in gross income is not reduced by the amount charged for the meals, and the meals are not considered to be furnished for the convenience of the employer.

Example (9). A hospital maintains a cafeteria on its premises where all of its 230 employees may obtain a meal during their working hours. No charge is made for these meals. The hospital furnishes such meals in order to have each of 210 of the employees available for any emergencies that may occur, and it is shown that each such employee is at times called upon to perform services during his meal period. Although the hospital does not require such employees to remain on the premises during meal periods, they rarely leave the hospital during their meal period. Since the hospital furnishes meals to each of substantially all of its employees in order to have each of them available for emergency call during his meal period, all of the hospital employees who obtain their meals in the hospital cafeteria may exclude from their gross income the value of such meals. [Reg. § 1.119-1.]

☐ [*T.D.* 6220, 12-28-56. *Amended by T.D.* 6745, 7-8-64 *and T.D.* 8006, 1-17-85.]

§ 1.121-1. Exclusion of gain from sale or exchange of a principal residence.—(a) *In general.*—Section 121 provides that, under certain circumstances, gross income does not include gain realized on the sale or exchange of property that was owned and used by a taxpayer as the taxpayer's principal residence. Subject to the other provisions of section 121, a taxpayer may exclude gain only if, during the 5-year period ending on the date of the sale or exchange, the taxpayer owned and used the property as the taxpayer's principal residence for periods aggregating 2 years or more.

(b) *Residence.*—(1) *In general.*—Whether property is used by the taxpayer as the taxpayer's residence depends upon all the facts and circumstances. A property used by the taxpayer as the taxpayer's residence may include a houseboat, a house trailer, or the house or apartment that the taxpayer is entitled to occupy as a tenant-stockholder in a cooperative housing corporation (as those terms are defined in section 216(b)(1) and (2)). Property used by the taxpayer as the taxpayer's residence does not include personal property that is not a fixture under local law.

(2) *Principal residence.*—In the case of a taxpayer using more than one property as a residence, whether property is used by the taxpayer as the taxpayer's principal residence depends upon all the facts and circumstances. If a taxpayer alternates between 2 properties, using each as a residence for successive periods of time, the property that the taxpayer uses a majority of the time during the year ordinarily will be considered the taxpayer's principal residence. In addition to the taxpayer's use of the property, relevant factors in determining a taxpayer's principal residence, include, but are not limited to—

(i) The taxpayer's place of employment;

(ii) The principal place of abode of the taxpayer's family members;

(iii) The address listed on the taxpayer's federal and state tax returns, driver's license, automobile registration, and voter registration card;

(iv) The taxpayer's mailing address for bills and correspondence;

(v) The location of the taxpayer's banks; and

(vi) The location of religious organizations and recreational clubs with which the taxpayer is affiliated.

(3) *Vacant land.*—(i) *In general.*—The sale or exchange of vacant land is not a sale or exchange of the taxpayer's principal residence unless—

(A) The vacant land is adjacent to land containing the dwelling unit of the taxpayer's principal residence;

(B) The taxpayer owned and used the vacant land as part of the taxpayer's principal residence;

(C) The taxpayer sells or exchanges the dwelling unit in a sale or exchange that meets the requirements of section 121 within 2 years before or 2 years after the date of the sale or exchange of the vacant land; and

(D) The requirements of section 121 have otherwise been met with respect to the vacant land.

(ii) *Limitations.*—(A) *Maximum limitation amount.*—For purposes of section 121(b)(1) and (2) (relating to the maximum limitation amount of the section 121 exclusion), the sale or exchange of the dwelling unit and the vacant land are treated as one sale or exchange. Therefore, only one maximum limitation amount of $250,000 ($500,000 for certain joint returns) applies to the combined sales or exchanges of vacant land and the dwelling unit. In applying the maximum limitation amount to sales or exchanges that occur in different taxable years, gain from the sale or exchange of the dwelling unit, up to the maximum limitation amount under section 121(b)(1) or (2), is excluded first and each spouse is treated as excluding one-half of the gain from a sale or exchange to which section 121(b)(2)(A) and § 1.121-2(a)(3)(i) (relating to the limitation for certain joint returns) apply.

(B) *Sale or exchange of more than one principal residence in 2-year period.*—If a dwelling unit and vacant land are sold or exchanged in separate transactions that qualify for the section 121 exclusion under this paragraph (b)(3), each of the transactions is disregarded in applying section 121(b)(3) (restricting the application of section 121 to only 1 sale or exchange every 2 years) to the other transactions but is taken into account as a sale or exchange of a principal residence on the date of the transaction in applying section 121(b)(3) to that transaction and the sale or exchange of any other principal residence.

(C) *Sale or exchange of vacant land before dwelling unit.*—If the sale or exchange of the dwelling unit occurs in a later taxable year than the sale or exchange of the vacant land and after the date prescribed by law (including extensions) for the filing of the return for the taxable year of the sale or exchange of the vacant land, any gain from the sale or exchange of the vacant land must be treated as taxable on the taxpayer's return for the taxable year of the sale or exchange of the vacant land. If the taxpayer has reported gain from the sale or exchange of the vacant land as taxable, after satisfying the requirements of this paragraph (b)(3) the taxpayer may claim the section 121 exclusion with regard to the sale or exchange of the vacant land (for any period for which the period of limitation under section 6511 has not expired) by filing an amended return.

(4) *Examples.*—The provisions of this paragraph (b) are illustrated by the following examples:

Example 1. Taxpayer A owns 2 residences, one in New York and one in Florida. From 1999 through 2004, he lives in the New York residence for 7 months and the Florida residence for 5 months of each year. In the absence of facts and circumstances indicating otherwise, the New York residence is A's principal residence. A would be eligible for the section 121 exclusion of gain from the sale or exchange of the New York residence, but not the Florida residence.

Example 2. Taxpayer B owns 2 residences, one in Virginia and one in Maine. During 1999 and 2000, she lives in the Virginia residence. During 2001 and 2002, she lives in the Maine residence. During 2003, she lives in the Virginia residence. B's principal residence during 1999, 2000, and 2003 is the Virginia residence. B's principal residence during 2001 and 2002 is the Maine residence. B would be eligible for the 121 exclusion of gain from the sale or exchange of either residence (but not both) during 2003.

Example 3. In 1991 Taxpayer C buys property consisting of a house and 10 acres that she uses as her principal residence. In May 2005 C sells 8 acres of the land and realizes a gain of $110,000. C does not sell the dwelling unit before the due date for filing C's 2005 return, therefore C is not eligible to exclude the $110,000 of gain. In March 2007 C sells the house and remaining 2 acres realizing a gain of $180,000 from the sale of the house. C may exclude the $180,000 of gain. Because the sale of the 8 acres occurred within 2 years from the date of the sale of the dwelling unit, the sale of the 8 acres is treated as a sale of the taxpayer's principal residence under paragraph (b)(3) of this section. C may file an amended return for 2005 to claim an exclusion for $70,000 ($250,000 – $180,000 gain previously excluded) of the $110,000 gain from the sale of the 8 acres.

Example 4. In 1998 Taxpayer D buys a house and 1 acre that he uses as his principal residence. In 1999 D buys 29 acres adjacent to his house and uses the vacant land as part of his principal residence. In 2003 D sells the house and 1 acre and the 29 acres in 2 separate transactions. D sells the house and 1 acre at a loss of $25,000. D realizes $270,000 of gain from the sale of the 29 acres. D may exclude the $245,000 gain from the 2 sales.

(c) *Ownership and use requirements.*—(1) *In general.*—The requirements of ownership and use for periods aggregating 2 years or more may be satisfied by establishing ownership and use for 24 full months or for 730 days (365 × 2). The requirements of ownership and use may be satisfied during nonconcurrent periods if both the ownership and use tests are met during the 5-year period ending on the date of the sale or exchange.

(2) *Use.*—(i) In establishing whether a taxpayer has satisfied the 2-year use requirement, occupancy of the residence is required. However, short temporary absences, such as for vacation or other seasonal absence (although accompanied with rental of the residence), are counted as periods of use.

(ii) *Determination of use during periods of out-of-residence care.*—If a taxpayer has become physically or mentally incapable of self-care and the taxpayer sells or exchanges property that the taxpayer owned and used as the taxpayer's principal residence for periods aggregating at least 1 year during the 5-year period preceding the sale or exchange, the taxpayer is treated as using the property as the taxpayer's principal residence for any period of time during the 5-year period in which the taxpayer owns the property and resides in any facility (including a nursing home) licensed by a State or political subdivision to care for an individual in the taxpayer's condition.

(3) *Ownership.*—(i) *Trusts.*—If a residence is owned by a trust, for the period that a taxpayer is treated under sections 671 through 679 (relating to the treatment of grantors and others as substantial owners) as the owner of the trust or the portion of the trust that includes the residence, the taxpayer will be treated as owning the residence for purposes of satisfying the 2-year ownership requirement of section 121, and the sale or exchange by the trust will be treated as if made by the taxpayer.

(ii) *Certain single owner entities.*—If a residence is owned by an eligible entity (within the meaning of § 301.7701-3(a) of this chapter) that has a single owner and is disregarded for federal tax purposes as an entity separate from its owner under § 301.7701-3 of this chapter, the owner will be treated as owning the residence for purposes of satisfying the 2-year ownership requirement of section 121, and the sale or exchange by the entity will be treated as if made by the owner.

(4) *Examples.*—The provisions of this paragraph (c) are illustrated by the following examples. The examples assume that § 1.121-3 (relating to the reduced maximum exclusion) does not apply to the sale of the property. The examples are as follows:

Example 1. Taxpayer A has owned and used his house as his principal residence since 1986. On January 31, 1998, A moves to another state. A rents his house to tenants from that date until April 18, 2000, when he sells it. A is eligible for the section 121 exclusion because he has owned and used the house as his principal residence for at least 2 of the 5 years preceding the sale.

Example 2. Taxpayer B owns and uses a house as her principal residence from 1986 to the end of 1997. On January 4, 1998, B moves to another state and ceases to use the house. B's son moves into the house in March 1999 and uses the residence until it is sold on July 1, 2001. B may not exclude gain from the sale under section 121 because she did not use the property as her principal residence for at least 2 years out of the 5 years preceding the sale.

Example 3. Taxpayer C lives in a townhouse that he rents from 1993 through 1996. On January 18, 1997, he purchases the townhouse. On February 1, 1998, C moves into his daughter's home. On May 25, 2000, while still living in his daughter's home, C sells his townhouse. The section 121 exclusion will apply to gain from the sale because C owned the townhouse for at least 2 years out of the 5 years preceding the sale (from January 19, 1997 until May 25, 2000) and he used the townhouse as his principal residence for at least 2 years during the 5-year period preceding the sale (from May 25, 1995 until February 1, 1998).

Example 4. Taxpayer D, a college professor, purchases and moves into a house on May 1, 1997. He uses the house as his principal residence continuously until September 1, 1998, when he goes abroad for a 1-year sabbatical leave. On October 1, 1999, 1 month after returning from the leave, D sells the house. Because his leave is not considered to be a short temporary absence under paragraph (c)(2) of this section, the period of the sabbatical leave may not be included in determining whether D used the house for periods aggregating 2 years during the 5-year period ending on the date of the sale. Consequently, D is not entitled to exclude gain under section 121 because he did not use the residence for the requisite period.

Example 5. Taxpayer E purchases a house on February 1, 1998, that he uses as his principal residence. During 1998 and 1999, E leaves his residence for a 2-month summer vacation. E sells the house on March 1, 2000. Although, in the 5-year period preceding the date of sale, the total time E used his residence is less than 2 years (21 months), the section 121 exclusion will apply to gain from the sale of the residence because, under paragraph (c)(2) of this section, the 2-month vacations are short temporary absences and are counted as periods of use in determining whether E used the residence for the requisite period.

(d) *Depreciation taken after May 6, 1997.*—(1) *In general.*—The section 121 exclusion does not apply to so much of the gain from the sale or exchange of property as does not exceed the portion of the depreciation adjustments (as defined in section 1250(b)(3)) attributable to the property for periods after May 6, 1997. Depreciation adjustments allocable to any portion of the property to which the section 121 exclusion does not apply under paragraph (e) of this section are not taken into account for this purpose.

(2) *Example.*—The provisions of this paragraph (d) are illustrated by the following example:

Example. On July 1, 1999, Taxpayer A moves into a house that he owns and had rented to tenants since July 1, 1997. A took depreciation deductions totaling $14,000 for the period that he rented the property. After using the residence as his principal residence for 2 full years, A sells the property on August 1, 2001. A's gain realized from the sale is $40,000. A has no other section 1231 or capital gains or losses for 2001. Only $26,000 ($40,000 gain realized - $14,000 depreciation deductions) may be excluded under section 121. Under section 121(d)(6) and paragraph (d)(1) of this section, A must recognize $14,000 of the gain as unrecaptured section 1250 gain within the meaning of section 1(h).

* * *

[Reg. § 1.121-1.]

☐ [*T.D.* 6856, 10-19-65. *Amended by T.D.* 7614, 4-26-79 *and T.D.* 9030, 12-23-2002.]

§ 1.121-2. Limitations.—(a) *Dollar limitations.*—(1) *In general.*—A taxpayer may exclude from gross income up to $250,000 of gain from the sale or exchange of the taxpayer's principal residence. A taxpayer is eligible for only one maximum exclusion per principal residence.

(2) *Joint owners.*—If taxpayers jointly own a principal residence but file separate returns, each taxpayer may exclude from gross income up to $250,000 of gain that is attributable to each taxpayer's interest in the property, if the requirements of section 121 have otherwise been met.

(3) *Special rules for joint returns.*—(i) *In general.*—A husband and wife who make a joint return for the year of the sale or exchange of a principal residence may exclude up to $500,000 of gain if—

(A) Either spouse meets the 2-year ownership requirements of § 1.121-1(a) and (c);

(B) Both spouses meet the 2-year use requirements of § 1.121-1(a) and (c); and

(C) Neither spouse excluded gain from a prior sale or exchange of property under section 121 within the last 2 years (as determined under paragraph (b) of this section).

(ii) *Other joint returns.*—For taxpayers filing jointly, if either spouse fails to meet the requirements of paragraph (a)(3)(i) of this section, the maximum limitation amount to be claimed by the couple is the sum of each spouse's limitation amount determined on a separate basis as if they had not been married. For this purpose, each spouse is treated as owning the property during the period that either spouse owned the property.

(4) *Examples.*—The provisions of this paragraph (a) are illustrated by the following examples. The examples assume that § 1.121-3 (relating to the reduced maximum exclusion) does not apply to the sale of the property. The examples are as follows:

Example 1. Unmarried Taxpayers A and B own a house as joint owners, each owning a 50 percent interest in the house. They sell the house after owning and using it as their principal residence for 2 full years. The gain realized from the sale is $256,000. A and B are each eligible to exclude $128,000 of gain because the amount of realized gain allocable to each of them from the sale does not exceed each taxpayer's available limitation amount of $250,000.

Example 2. The facts are the same as in *Example 1*, except that A and B are married taxpayers who file a joint return for the taxable year of the sale. A and B are eligible to exclude the entire amount of realized gain ($256,000) from gross income because the gain realized from the sale does not exceed the limitation amount of $500,000 available to A and B as taxpayers filing a joint return.

Example 3. During 1999, married Taxpayers H and W each sell a residence that each had separately owned and used as a principal residence before their marriage. Each spouse meets the ownership and use tests for his or her respective residence. Neither spouse meets the use requirement for the other spouse's residence. H and W file a joint return for the year of the sales. The gain realized from the sale of

H's residence is $200,000. The gain realized from the sale of W's residence is $300,000. Because the ownership and use requirements are met for each residence by each respective spouse, H and W are each eligible to exclude up to $250,000 of gain from the sale of their individual residences. However, W may not use H's unused exclusion to exclude gain in excess of her limitation amount. Therefore, H and W must recognize $50,000 of the gain realized on the sale of W's residence.

Example 4. Married Taxpayers H and W sell their residence and file a joint return for the year of the sale. W, but not H, satisfies the requirements of section 121. They are eligible to exclude up to $250,000 of the gain from the sale of the residence because that is the sum of each spouse's dollar limitation amount determined on a separate basis as if they had not been married ($0 for H, $250,000 for W).

Example 5. Married Taxpayers H and W have owned and used their principal residence since 1998. On February 16, 2001, H dies. On September 24, 2001, W sells the residence and realizes a gain of $350,000. Pursuant to section 6013(a)(3), W and H's executor make a joint return for 2001. All $350,000 of the gain from the sale of the residence may be excluded.

Example 6. Assume the same facts as *Example 5,* except that W does not sell the residence until January 31, 2002. Because W's filing status for the taxable year of the sale is single, the special rules for joint returns under paragraph (a)(3) of this section do not apply and W may exclude only $250,000 of the gain.

(b) *Application of section 121 to only 1 sale or exchange every 2 years.*—(1) *In general.*—Except as otherwise provided in § 1.121-3 (relating to the reduced maximum exclusion), a taxpayer may not exclude from gross income gain from the sale or exchange of a principal residence if, during the 2-year period ending on the date of the sale or exchange, the taxpayer sold or exchanged other property for which gain was excluded under section 121. For purposes of this paragraph (b)(1), any sale or exchange before May 7, 1997, is disregarded.

(2) *Example.*—The following example illustrates the rules of this paragraph (b). The example assumes that § 1.121-3 (relating to the reduced maximum exclusion) does not apply to the sale of the property. The example is as follows:

Example. Taxpayer A owns a townhouse that he uses as his principal residence for 2 full years, 1998 and 1999. A buys a house in 2000 that he owns and uses as his principal residence. A sells the townhouse in 2002 and excludes gain realized on its sale under section 121. A sells the house in 2003. Although A meets the 2-year ownership and use requirements of section 121, A is not eligible to exclude gain from the sale of the house because A excluded gain within the last 2 years under section 121 from the sale of the townhouse.

* * *

[Reg. § 1.121-2.]

☐ [*T.D.* 6856, 10-19-65. *Amended by T.D.* 7614, 4-26-79 *and T.D.* 9030, 12-23-2002.]

§ 1.121-3. Reduced maximum exclusion for taxpayers failing to meet certain requirements.—(a) *In general.*—In lieu of the limitation under section 121(b) and § 1.121-2, a reduced maximum exclusion limitation may be available for a taxpayer who sells or exchanges property used as the taxpayer's principal residence but fails to satisfy the ownership and use requirements described in § 1.121-1(a) and (c) or the 2-year limitation described in § 1.121-2(b).

(b) *Primary reason for sale or exchange.*—In order for a taxpayer to claim a reduced maximum exclusion under section 121 (c), the sale or exchange must be by reason of a change in place of employment, health, or unforeseen circumstances. If a safe harbor described in this section applies, a sale or exchange is deemed to be by reason of a change in place of employment, health, or unforeseen circumstances. If a safe harbor described in this section does not apply, a sale or exchange is by reason of a change in place of employment, health, or unforeseen circumstances only if the primary reason for the sale or exchange is a change in place of employment (within the meaning of paragraph (c) of this section), health (within the meaning of paragraph (d) of this section), or unforeseen circumstances (within the meaning of paragraph (e) of this section). Whether the requirements of this section are satisfied depends upon all the facts and circumstances. Factors that may be relevant in determining the taxpayer's primary reason for the sale or exchange include (but are not limited to) the extent to which—

(1) The sale or exchange and the circumstances giving rise to the sale or exchange are proximate in time;

(2) The suitability of the property as the taxpayer's principal residence materially changes;

(3) The taxpayer's financial ability to maintain the property is materially impaired;

(4) The taxpayer uses the property as the taxpayer's residence during the period of the taxpayer's ownership of the property;

(5) The circumstances giving rise to the sale or exchange are not reasonably foreseeable when the taxpayer begins using the property as the taxpayer's principal residence; and

(6) The circumstances giving rise to the sale or exchange occur during the period of the taxpayer's ownership and use of the property as the taxpayer's principal residence.

(c) *Sale or exchange by reason of a change in place of employment.*—(1) *In general.*—A sale or exchange is by reason of a change in place of employment if, in the case of a qualified individual described in paragraph (f) of this section, the primary reason for the sale or exchange is a change in the location of the individual's employment.

(2) *Distance safe harbor.*—A sale or exchange is deemed to be by reason of a change in place of employment (within the meaning of paragraph (c) (1) of this section) if—

(i) The change in place of employment occurs during the period of the taxpayer's ownership and use of the property as the taxpayer's principal residence; and

(ii) The qualified individual's new place of employment is at least 50 miles farther from the residence sold or exchanged than was the former place of employment, or, if there was no forner place of employment, the distance between the qualified individual's new place of employment and the residence sold or exchanged is at least 50 miles.

(3) *Employment.*—For purposes of this paragraph (c), *employment* includes the commencement of employment with a new employer, the continuation of employment with the same employer, and the commencement or continuation of self-employment.

(4) *Examples.*—The following examples illustrate the rules of this paragraph (c):

Example 1. A is unemployed and owns a townhouse that she has owned and used as her principal residence since 2003. In 2004 A obtains a job that is 54 miles from her townhouse, and she sells the townhouse. Because the distance between A's new place of employment and the townhouse is at least 50 miles, the sale is within the safe harbor of paragraph (c) (2) of this section and A is entitled to claim a reduced maximum exclusion under section 121(c) (2).

Example 2. B is an officer in the United States Air Force stationed in Florida. B purchases a house in Florida in 2002. In May 2003 B moves out of his house to take a 3-year assignment in Germany. B sells his house in January 2004. Because B's new place of employment in Germany is at least 50 miles farther from the residence sold than is B's former place of employment in Florida, the sale is within the safe harbor of paragraph (c)(2) of this section and B is entitled to claim a reduced maximum exclusion under section 121(c)(2).

Example 3. C is employed by Employer R at R's Philadelphia office. C purchases a house in February 2002 that is 35 miles from R's Philadelphia office. In May 2003 C begins a temporary assignment at R's Wilmington office that is 72 miles from C's house, and moves out of the house. In June 2005 C is assigned to work in R's London office. C sells her house in August 2005 as a result of the assignment to London. The sale of the house is not within the safe harbor of paragraph (c)(2) of this section by reason of the change in place of employment from Philadelphia to Wilmington because the Wilmington office is not 50 miles farther from C's house than is the Philadelphia office. Furthermore, the sale is not within the safe harbor by reason of the change in place of employment to London because C is not using the house as her principal residence when she moves to London. However, C is entitled to claim a reduced maximum exclusion under section 121(c)(2) because, under the facts and circumstances, the primary reason for the sale is the change in C's place of employment.

Example 4. In July 2003 D, who works as an emergency medicine physician, buys a condominium that is 5 miles from her place of employment and uses it as her principal residence. In February 2004, D obtains a job that is located 51 miles from D's condominium. D may be called in to work unscheduled hours and, when called, must be able to arrive at work quickly. Because of the demands of the new job, D sells her condominium and buys a townhouse that is 4 miles from her new place of employment. Because D's new place of employment is only 46 miles farther from the condominium than is D's former place of employment, the sale is not within the safe harbor of paragraph (c)(2) of this section. However, D is entitled to claim a reduced maximum exclusion under section 121(c)(2) because, under the facts and circumstances, the primary reason for the sale is the change in D's place of employment.

(d) *Sale or exchange by reason of health.*—(1) *In general.*—A sale or exchange is by reason of health if the primary reason for the sale or exchange is to obtain, provide, or facilitate the diagnosis, cure, mitigation, or treatment of disease, illness, or injury of a qualified individual described in paragraph (f) of this section, or to obtain or provide medical or personal care for a qualified individual suffering from a disease, illness, or injury. A sale or exchange that is merely beneficial to the general health or well-being of an individual is not a sale or exchange by reason of health.

(2) *Physician's recommendation safe harbor.*—A sale or exchange is deemed to be by reason of health if a physician (as defined in

section 213(d)(4)) recommends a change of residence for reasons of health (as defined in paragraph (d)(1) of this section).

* * *

(e) *Sale or exchange by reason of unforeseen circumstances.*—(1) *In general.*—A sale or exchange is by reason of unforeseen circumstances if the primary reason for the sale or exchange is the occurrence of an event that the taxpayer could not reasonably have anticipated before purchasing and occupying the residence. A sale or exchange by reason of unforeseen circumstances (other than a sale or exchange deemed to be by reason of unforeseen circumstances under paragraph (e)(2) or (3) of this section) does not qualify for the reduced maximum exclusion if the primary reason for the sale or exchange is a preference for a different residence or an improvement in financial circumstances.

(2) *Specific event safe harbors.*—A sale or exchange is deemed to be by reason of unforeseen circumstances (within the meaning of paragraph (e)(1) of this section) if any of the events specified in paragraphs (e)(2)(i) through (iii) of this section occur during the period of the taxpayer's ownership and use of the residence as the taxpayer's principal residence:

(i) The involuntary conversion of the residence.

(ii) Natural or man-made disasters or acts of war or terrorism resulting in a casualty to the residence (without regard to deductibility under section 165(h)).

(iii) In the case of a qualified individual described in paragraph (f) of this section—

(A) Death;

(B) The cessation of employment as a result of which the qualified individual is eligible for unemployment compensation (as defined in section 85(b));

(C) A change in employment or self-employment status that results in the taxpayer's inability to pay housing costs and reasonable basic living expenses for the taxpayer's household (including amounts for food, clothing, medical expenses, taxes, transportation, court-ordered payments, and expenses reasonably necessary to the production of income, but not for the maintenance of an affluent or luxurious standard of living);

(D) Divorce or legal separation under a decree of divorce or separate maintenance; or

(E) Multiple births resulting from the same pregnancy.

(3) *Designation of additional events as unforeseen circumstances.*—The Commissioner may designate other events or situations as unforeseen circumstances in published guidance of general applicability and may issue rulings addressed to specific taxpayers identifying other events or situations as unforeseen circumstances with regard to those taxpayers (see § 601.601(d)(2) of this chapter).

* * *

(f) *Qualified individual.*—For purposes of this section, *qualified individual* means—

(1) The taxpayer;

(2) The taxpayer's spouse;

(3) A co-owner of the residence;

(4) A person whose principal place of abode is in the same household as the taxpayer; or

(5) For purposes of paragraph (d) of this section, a person bearing a relationship specified in sections 152(a)(1) through 152(a)(8) (without regard to qualification as a dependent) to a qualified individual described in paragraphs (f)(1) through (4) of this section, or a descendant of the taxpayer's grandparent.

(g) *Computation of reduced maximum exclusion.*—(1) The reduced maximum exclusion is computed by multiplying the maximum dollar limitation of $250,000 ($500,000 for certain joint filers) by a fraction. The numerator of the fraction is the shortest of the period of time that the taxpayer owned the property during the 5-year period ending on the date of the sale or exchange; the period of time that the taxpayer used the property as the taxpayer's principal residence during the 5-year period ending on the date of the sale or exchange; or the period of time between the date of a prior sale or exchange of property for which the taxpayer excluded gain under section 121 and the date of the current sale or exchange. The numerator of the fraction may be expressed in days or months. The denominator of the fraction is 730 days or 24 months (depending on the measure of time used in the numerator).

(2) *Examples.*—The following examples illustrate the rules of this paragraph (g):

Example 1. Taxpayer A purchases a house that she uses as her principal residence. Twelve months after the purchase, A sells the house due to a change in place of her employment. A has not excluded gain under section 121 on a prior sale or exchange of property within the last 2 years. A is eligible to exclude up to $125,000 of the gain from the sale of her house (12/24 × $250,000).

Example 2. (i) Taxpayer H owns a house that he has used as his principal residence since 1996. On January 15, 1999, H and W marry and W begins to use H's house as her principal residence. On January 15, 2000, H sells the house due to a change in W's place of employment. Neither H nor W has excluded gain under section 121 on a prior sale or exchange of property within the last 2 years.

(ii) Because H and W have not each used the house as their principal residence for at least 2 years during the 5-year period preceding its sale, the maximum dollar limitation amount that may be claimed by H and W will not be $500,000, but the sum of each spouse's limitation amount determined on a separate basis as if they had not been married. (See § 1.121-2(a)(3)(ii).)

(iii) H is eligible to exclude up to $250,000 of gain because he meets the requirements of section 121. W is not eligible to exclude the maximum dollar limitation amount. Instead, because the sale of the house is due to a change in place of employment, W is eligible to claim a reduced maximum exclusion of up to $125,000 of the gain (365/730 × $250,000). Therefore, H and W are eligible to exclude up to $375,000 of gain ($250,000 + $125,000) from the sale of the house.

* * *

[Reg. § 1.121-3.]

□ [*T.D.* 6856, 10-19-65. *Amended by T.D.* 7614, 4-26-79; *T.D.* 9030, 12-23-2002 *and T.D.* 9152, 8-13-2004.]

Proposed Regulation

§ 1.125-1. Cafeteria plans; general rules.—(a) *Definitions.*—The definitions set forth in this paragraph (a) apply for purposes of section 125 and the regulations.

(1) The term *cafeteria plan* means a separate written plan that complies with the requirements of section 125 and the regulations, that is maintained by an employer for the benefit of its employees and that is operated in compliance with the requirements of section 125 and the regulations. All participants in a cafeteria plan must be employees. A cafeteria plan must offer at least one permitted taxable benefit (as defined in paragraph (a)(2) of this section) and at least one qualified benefit (as defined in paragraph (a)(3) of this section). A cafeteria plan must not provide for deferral of compensation (except as specifically permitted in paragraph (o) of this section).

(2) The term *permitted taxable benefit* means cash and certain other taxable benefits treated as cash for purposes of section 125. For purposes of section 125, *cash* means cash compensation (including salary reduction), payments for annual leave, sick leave, or other paid time off and severance pay. A distribution from a trust described in section 401(a) is not cash for purposes of section 125. *Other taxable benefits treated as cash* for purposes of section 125 are:

(i) Property;

(ii) Benefits attributable to employer contributions that are currently taxable to the employee upon receipt by the employee; and

(iii) Benefits purchased with after-tax employee contributions, as described in paragraph (h) of this section.

(3) *Qualified benefit.*—Except as otherwise provided in section 125(f) and paragraph (q) of this section, the term *qualified benefit* means any benefit attributable to employer contributions to the extent that such benefit is not currently taxable to the employee by reason of an express provision of the Internal Revenue Code (Code) and which does not defer compensation (except as provided in paragraph (o) of this section). The following benefits are qualified benefits that may be offered under a cafeteria plan and are excludible from employees' gross income when provided in accordance with the applicable provisions of the Code—

(A) Group-term life insurance on the life of an employee in an amount that is less than or equal to the $50,000 excludible from gross income under section 79(a), but not combined with any permanent benefit within the meaning of § 1.79-0;

(B) An accident and health plan excludible from gross income under section 105 or 106, including self-insured medical reimbursement plans (such as health FSAs described in § 1.125-5);

(C) Premiums for COBRA continuation coverage (if excludible under section 106) under the accident and health plan of the employer sponsoring the cafeteria plan or premiums for COBRA continuation coverage of an employee of the employer sponsoring the cafeteria plan under an accident and health plan sponsored by a different employer;

(D) An accidental death and dismemberment insurance policy (section 106);

(E) Long-term or short-term disability coverage (section 106);

(F) Dependent care assistance program (section 129);

(G) Adoption assistance (section 137);

(H) A qualified cash or deferred arrangement that is part of a profit-sharing plan or stock bonus plan, as described in paragraph (o)(3) of this section (section 401(k));

(I) Certain plans maintained by educational organizations (section 125(d)(2)(C) and paragraph (o)(3)(iii) of this section); and

(J) Contributions to Health Savings Accounts (HSAs) (sections 223 and 125(d)(2)(D)).

(4) *Dependent.*—The term *dependent* generally means a dependent as defined in section 152. However, the definition of dependent is

modified to conform with the underlying Code section for the qualified benefit. For example, for purposes of a benefit under section 105, the term dependent means a dependent as defined in section 152, determined without regard to section 152(b)(1), (b)(2) or (d)(1)(B).

(5) *Premium-only-plan.*—A *premium-only-plan* is a cafeteria plan that offers as its sole benefit an election between cash (for example, salary) and payment of the employee share of the employer-provided accident and health insurance premium (excludible from the employee's gross income under section 106).

(b) *General rules.*—(1) *Cafeteria plans.*—Section 125 is the exclusive means by which an employer can offer employees an election between taxable and nontaxable benefits without the election itself resulting in inclusion in gross income by the employees. Section 125 provides that cash (including certain taxable benefits) offered to an employee through a nondiscriminatory cafeteria plan is not includible in the employee's gross income merely because the employee has the opportunity to choose among cash and qualified benefits (within the meaning of section 125(e)) through the cafeteria plan. Section 125(a), (d)(1). However, if a plan offering an employee an election between taxable benefits (including cash) and nontaxable qualified benefits does not meet the section 125 requirements, the election between taxable and nontaxable benefits results in gross income to the employee, regardless of what benefit is elected and when the election is made. An employee who has an election among nontaxable bénefits and taxable benefits (including cash) that is not through a cafeteria plan that satisfies section 125 must include in gross income the value of the taxable benefit with the greatest value that the employee could have elected to receive, even if the employee elects to receive only the nontaxable benefits offered. The amount of the taxable benefit is includible in the employee's income in the year in which the employee would have actually received the taxable benefit if the employee had elected such benefit. This is the result even if the employee's election between the nontaxable benefits and taxable benefits is made prior to the year in which the employee would actually have received the taxable benefits. See paragraph (q) in § 1.125-1 for nonqualified benefits.

* * *

(4) *Election by participants.*—(i) *In general.*—A cafeteria plan must offer participants the opportunity to elect between at least one permitted taxable benefit and at least one qualified benefit. For example, if employees are given the opportunity to elect only among two or more nontaxable benefits, the plan is not a cafeteria plan. Similarly, a plan that only offers the election among salary, permitted taxable benefits, paid time off or other taxable benefits is not a cafeteria plan. See section 125(a), (d). See § 1.125-2 for rules on elections.

* * *

(d) *Plan year requirements.*—(1) *Twelve consecutive months.*—The plan year must be specified in the cafeteria plan. The plan year of a cafeteria plan must be twelve consecutive months, unless a short plan year is allowed under this paragraph (d). A plan year is permitted to begin on any day of any calendar month and must end on the preceding day in the immediately following year (for example, a plan year that begins on October 15, 2007, must end on October 14, 2008). A calendar year plan year is a period of twelve consecutive months beginning on January 1 and ending on December 31 of the same calendar year. A plan year specified in the cafeteria plan is effective for the first plan year of a cafeteria plan and for all subsequent plan years, unless changed as provided in paragraph (d)(2) of this section.

* * *

(e) *Grace period.*—(1) *In general.*—A cafeteria plan may, at the employer's option, include a grace period of up to the fifteenth day of the third month immediately following the end of each plan year. If a cafeteria plan provides for a grace period, an employee who has unused benefits or contributions relating to a qualified benefit (for example, health flexible spending arrangement (health FSA) or dependent care assistance) from the immediately preceding plan year, and who incurs expenses for that same qualified benefit during the grace period, may be paid or reimbursed for those expenses from the unused benefits or contributions as if the expenses had been incurred in the immediately preceding plan year. A grace period is available for all qualified benefits described in paragraph (a)(3) of this section, except that the grace period does not apply to paid time off and elective contributions under a section 401(k) plan. The effect of the grace period is that the employee may have as long as 14 months and 15 days (that is, the 12 months in the current cafeteria plan year plus the grace period) to use the benefits or contributions for a plan year before those amounts are *forfeited* under the *use-or-lose* rule in paragraph (c) in § 1.125-5. If the grace period is added to a cafeteria plan through an amendment, all requirements in paragraph (c) of this section must be satisfied.

* * *

(i) *Prohibited taxable benefits.*—Any taxable benefit not described in paragraph (a)(2) of this section and not treated as cash for purposes of section 125 in paragraph (h) of this section is not permitted to be included in a cafeteria plan. A plan that offers taxable benefits other than the taxable benefits described in paragraph (a)(2) and (h) of this section is not a cafeteria plan.

* * *

[Prop. Reg. § 1.125-1.]

[Proposed 8-6-2007.]

Proposed Regulation

§ 1.125-5. Flexible spending arrangements.—(a) *Definition of flexible spending arrangement.*—(1) *In general.*—An FSA generally is a benefit program that provides employees with coverage which reimburses specified, incurred expenses (subject to reimbursement maximums and any other reasonable conditions). An expense for qualified benefits must not be reimbursed from the FSA unless it is incurred during a period of coverage. See paragraph (e) of this section. After an expense for a qualified benefit has been incurred, the expense must first be substantiated before the expense is reimbursed. See paragraphs (a) through (f) in § 1.125-6.

(2) *Maximum amount of reimbursement.*—The maximum amount of reimbursement that is reasonably available to an employee for a period of coverage must not be substantially in excess of the total salary reduction and employer flex-credit for such participant's coverage. A maximum amount of reimbursement is not substantially in excess of the total salary reduction and employer flex-credit if such maximum amount is less than 500 percent of the combined salary reduction and employer flex-credit. A single FSA may provide participants with different levels of coverage and maximum amounts of reimbursement. See paragraph (r) in § 1.125-1 and paragraphs (b) and (d) in this section for the definition of salary reduction, employer flex-credit, and uniform coverage rule.

(b) *Flex-credits allowed.*—(1) *In general.*—An FSA in a cafeteria plan must include an election between cash or taxable benefits (including salary reduction) and one or more qualified benefits, and may include, in addition, "employer flex-credits." For this purpose, flex-credits are non-elective employer contributions that the employer makes for every employee eligible to participate in the employer's cafeteria plan, to be used at the employee's election only for one or more qualified benefits (but not as cash or a taxable benefit). See § 1.125-1 for definitions of qualified benefits, cash and taxable benefits.

(2) *Example.*—The following example illustrates the rules in this paragraph (b):

Example. Flex-credit. Contribution to health FSA for employees electing employer-provided accident and health plan. Employer A maintains a cafeteria plan offering employees an election between cash or taxable benefits and premiums for employer-provided accident and health insurance or coverage through an HMO. The plan also provides an employer contribution of $200 to the health FSA of every employee who elects accident and health insurance or HMO coverage. In addition, these employees may elect to reduce their salary to make additional contributions to their health FSAs. The benefits offered in this cafeteria plan are consistent with the requirements of section 125 and this paragraph (b).

(c) *Use-or-lose rule.*—(1) *In general.*—An FSA may not defer compensation. No contribution or benefit from an FSA may be carried over to any subsequent plan year or period of coverage. See paragraph (k)(3) in this section for specific exceptions. Unused benefits or contributions remaining at the end of the plan year (or at the end of a grace period, if applicable) are forfeited.

(2) *Example.*—The following example illustrates the rules in this paragraph (c):

Example. Use-or-lose rule. (i) Employer B maintains a calendar year cafeteria plan, offering an election between cash and a health FSA. The cafeteria plan has no grace period.

(ii) Employee A plans to have eye surgery in 2009. For the 2009 plan year, Employee A timely elects salary reduction of $3,000 for a health FSA. During the 2009 plan year, Employee A learns that she cannot have eye surgery performed, but incurs other section 213(d) medical expenses totaling $1,200. As of December 31, 2009, she has $1,800 of unused benefits and contributions in the health FSA. Consistent with the rules in this paragraph (c), she forfeits $1,800.

* * *

[Prop. Reg. § 1.125-5.]

[Proposed 8-6-2007.]

§ 1.132-1. Exclusion from gross income for certain fringe benefits.—(a) *In general.*—Gross income does not include any fringe benefit which qualifies as a—

(1) No-additional-cost service,

(2) Qualified employee discount,

(3) Working condition fringe, or

(4) De minimis fringe.

Special rules apply with respect to certain on-premises gyms and other athletic facilities (§ 1.132-1(e)), demonstration use of employer-provided automobiles by full-time automobile salesmen (§ 1.132-5(o)), parking provided to an employee on or near the business premises of the employer (§ 1.132-5(p)), and on-premises eating facilities (§ 1.132-7).

(b) *Definition of employee.*—(1) *No-additional-cost services and qualified employee discounts.*—For purposes of section 132(a)(1) (relating to no-additional-cost services) and section 132(a)(2) (relating to qualified employee discounts), the term "employee" (with respect to a line of business of an employer) means—

(i) Any individual who is currently employed by the employer in the line of business,

(ii) Any individual who was formerly employed by the employer in the line of business and who separated from service with the employer in the line of business by reason of retirement or disability, and

(iii) Any widow or widower of an individual who died while employed by the employer in the line of business or who separated from service with the employer in the line of business by reason of retirement or disability.

For purposes of this paragraph (b)(1), any partner who performs services for a partnership is considered employed by the partnership. In addition, any use by the spouse or dependent child (as defined in paragraph (b)(5) of this section) of the employee will be treated as use by the employee. For purposes of section 132(a)(1) (relating to no-additional-cost services), any use of air transportation by a parent of an employee (determined without regard to section 132(f)(1)(B) and paragraph (b)(1)(iii) of this section) will be treated as use by the employee.

(2) *Working condition fringes.*—For purposes of section 132(a)(3) (relating to working condition fringes), the term "employee" means—

(i) Any individual who is currently employed by the employer,

(ii) Any partner who performs services for the partnership,

(iii) Any director of the employer, and

(iv) Any independent contractor who performs services for the employer.

Notwithstanding anything in this paragraph (b)(2) to the contrary, an independent contractor who performs services for the employer cannot exclude the value of parking or the use of consumer goods provided pursuant to a product testing program under § 1.132-5(n); in addition, any director of the employer cannot exclude the value of the use of consumer goods provided pursuant to a product testing program under § 1.132-5(n).

(3) *On-premises athletic facilities.*—For purposes of section 132(h)(5) (relating to on-premises athletic facilities), the term "employee" means—

(i) Any individual who is currently employed by the employer,

(ii) Any individual who was formerly employed by the employer and who separated from service with the employer by reason of retirement or disability, and

(iii) Any widow or widower of an individual who died while employed by the employer or who separated from service with the employer by reason of retirement or disability.

For purposes of this paragraph (b)(3), any partner who performs services for a partnership is considered employed by the partnership. In addition, any use by the spouse or dependent child (as defined in paragraph (b)(5) of this section) of the employee will be treated as use by the employee.

(4) *De minimis fringes.*—For purposes of section 132(a)(4) (relating to de minimis fringes), the term "employee" means any recipient of a fringe benefit.

(5) *Dependent child.*—The term "dependent child" means any son, stepson, daughter, or stepdaughter of the employee who is a dependent of the employee, or both of whose parents are deceased and who has not attained age 25. Any child to whom section 152(e) applies will be treated as the dependent of both parents.

* * *

(d) *Customers not to include employees.*—For purposes of section 132 and the regulations thereunder, the term "customer" means any customer who is not an employee. However, the preceding sentence does not apply to section 132(c)(2) (relating to the gross profit percentage for determining a qualified employee discount). Thus, an employer that provides employee discounts cannot exclude sales made to employees in determining the aggregate sales to customers.

(e) *Treatment of on-premises athletic facilities.*—(1) *In general.*—Gross income does not include the value of any on-premises athletic facility provided by an employer to its employees. For purposes of section 132(h)(5) and this paragraph (e), the term "on-premises athletic facility" means any gym or other athletic facility (such as a pool, tennis court, or golf course)—

(i) Which is located on the premises of the employer,

(ii) Which is operated by the employer, and

(iii) Substantially all of the use of which during the calendar year is by employees of the employer, their spouses, and their dependent children.

For purposes of paragraph (e)(1)(iii) of this section, the term "dependent children" has the same meaning as the plural of the term "dependent child" in paragraph (b)(5) of this section. The exclusion of this paragraph (e) does not apply to any athletic facility if access to the facility is made available to the general public through the sale of memberships, the rental of the facility, or a similar arrangement.

(2) *Premises of the employer.*—The athletic facility need not be located on the employer's business premises. However, the athletic facility must be located on premises of the employer. The exclusion provided in this paragraph (e) applies whether the premises are owned or leased by the employer; in addition, the exclusion is available even if the employer is not a named lessee on the lease so long as the employer pays reasonable rent. The exclusion provided in this paragraph (e) does not apply to any athletic facility that is a facility for residential use. Thus, for example, a resort with accompanying athletic facilities (such as tennis courts, pool, and gym) would not qualify for the exclusion provided in this paragraph (e). An athletic facility is considered to be located on the employer's premises if the facility is located on the premises of a voluntary employees' beneficiary association funded by the employer.

(3) *Application of rules to membership in an athletic facility* .—The exclusion provided in this paragraph (e) does not apply to any membership in an athletic facility (including health clubs or country clubs) unless the facility is owned (or leased) and operated by the employer and substantially all the use of the facility is by employees of the employer, their spouses, and their dependent children. Therefore, membership in a health club or country club not meeting the rules provided in this paragraph (e) would not qualify for the exclusion.

(4) *Operation by the employer.*—An employer is considered to operate the athletic facility if the employer operates the facility through its own employees, or if the employer contracts out to another to operate the athletic facility. For example, if an employer hires an independent contractor to operate the athletic facility for the employer's employees, the facility is considered to be operated by the employer. In addition, if an athletic facility is operated by more than one employer, it is considered to be operated by each employer. For purposes of paragraph (e)(1)(iii) of this section, substantially all of the use of a facility that is operated by more than one employer must be by employees of the various employers, their spouses, and their dependent children. Where the facility is operated by more than one employer, an employer that pays rent either directly to the owner of the premises or to a sublessor of the premises is eligible for the exclusion. If an athletic facility is operated by a voluntary employees' beneficiary association funded by an employer, the employer is considered to operate the facility.

(5) *Nonapplicability of nondiscrimination rules.*—The nondiscrimination rules of section 132 and § 1.132-8 do not apply to on-premises athletic facilities.

(f) *Nonapplicability of section 132 in certain cases.*—(1) *Tax treatment provided for in another section.*—If the tax treatment of a particular fringe benefit is expressly provided for in another section of Chapter 1 of the Internal Revenue Code of 1986, section 132 and the applicable regulations (except for section 132(e) and the regulations thereunder) do not apply to such fringe benefit. For example, because section 129 provides an exclusion from gross income for amounts paid or incurred by an employer for dependent care assistance for an employee, the exclusions under section 132 and this section do not apply to the provision by an employer to an employee of dependent care assistance. Similarly, because section 117(d) applies to tuition reductions, the exclusions under section 132 do not apply to free or discounted tuition provided to an employee by an organization operated by the employer, whether the tuition is for study at or below the graduate level. Of course, if the amounts paid by the employer are for education relating to the employee's trade or business of being an employee of the employer so that, if the employee paid for the education, the amount paid could be deducted under section 162, the costs of the education may be eligible for exclusion as a working condition fringe.

(2) *Limited statutory exclusions.*—If another section of Chapter 1 of the Internal Revenue Code of 1986 provides an exclusion from gross income based on the cost of the benefit provided to the employee and such exclusion is a limited amount, section 132 and the regulations thereunder may apply to the extent the cost of the benefit exceeds the statutory exclusion.

* * *

[Reg. § 1.132-1.]

☐ [*T.D.* 8256, 7-5-89. *Amended by T.D.* 8457, 12-29-92 *and T.D.* 8949, 3-11-2019.]

§ 1.132-2. No-additional-cost services.—(a) *In general.*—(1) *Definition.*—Gross income does not include the value of a no-additional-cost service. A "no-additional-cost service" is any service provided by an employer to an employee for the employee's personal use if—

(i) The service is offered for sale by the employer to its customers in the ordinary course of the line of business of the employer in which the employee performs substantial services, and

(ii) The employer incurs no substantial additional cost in providing the service to the employee (including foregone revenue and excluding any amount paid by or on behalf of the employee for the service).

For rules relating to the line of business limitation, see § 1.132-4. For purposes of this section, a service will not be considered to be offered for sale by the employer to its customers if that service is primarily provided to employees and not to the employer's customers.

(2) *Excess capacity services.*—Services that are eligible for treatment as no-additional-cost services include excess capacity services such as hotel accommodations; transportation by aircraft, train, bus, subway, or cruise line; and telephone services. Services that are not eligible for treatment as no-additional-cost services are non-excess capacity services such as the facilitation by a stock brokerage firm of the purchase of stock. Employees who receive non-excess capacity services may, however, be eligible for a qualified employee discount of up to 20 percent of the value of the service provided. See § 1.132-3.

(3) *Cash rebates.*—The exclusion for a no-additional-cost service applies whether the service is provided at no charge or at a reduced price. The exclusion also applies if the benefit is provided through a partial or total cash rebate of an amount paid for the service.

(4) *Applicability of nondiscrimination rules.*—The exclusion for a no-additional-cost service applies to highly compensated employees only if the service is available on substantially the same terms to each member of a group of employees that is defined under a reasonable classification set up by the employer that does not discriminate in favor of highly compensated employees. See § 1.132-8.

(5) *No substantial additional cost.*—(i) *In general.*—The exclusion for a no-additional-cost service applies only if the employer does not incur substantial additional cost in providing the service to the employee. For purposes of the preceding sentence, the term "cost" includes revenue that is forgone because the service is provided to an employee rather than a nonemployee. (For purposes of determining whether any revenue is forgone, it is assumed that the employee would not have purchased the service unless it were available to the employee at the actual price charged to the employee.) Whether an employer incurs substantial additional cost must be determined without regard to any amount paid by the employee for the service. Thus, any reimbursement by the employee for the cost of providing the service does not affect the determination of whether the employer incurs substantial additional cost.

(ii) *Labor intensive services.*—An employer must include the cost of labor incurred in providing services to employees when determining whether the employer has incurred substantial additional cost. An employer incurs substantial additional cost, whether [or not] non-labor costs are incurred, if a substantial amount of time is spent by the employer or its employees in providing the service to employees. This would be the result whether the time spent by the employer or its employees in providing the services would have been "idle," or if the services were provided outside normal business hours. An employer generally incurs no substantial additional cost, however, if the services provided to the employee are merely incidental to the primary service being provided by the employer. For example, the in-flight services of a flight attendant and the cost of in-flight meals provided to airline employees traveling on a space-available basis are merely incidental to the primary service being provided (i.e., air transportation). Similarly, maid service provided to hotel employees renting hotel rooms on a space-available basis is merely incidental to the primary service being provided (i.e., hotel accommodations).

(6) *Payments for telephone service.*—Payment made by an entity subject to the modified final judgment (as defined in section 559(c)(5) of the Tax Reform Act of 1984) of all or part of the cost of local telephone service provided to an employee by a person other than an entity subject to the modified final judgment shall be treated as telephone service provided to the employee by the entity making the payment for purposes of this section. The preceding sentence also applies to a rebate of the amount paid by the employee for the service and a payment to the person providing the service. This paragraph (a)(6) applies only to services and employees described in § 1.132-4(c). For a special line of business rule relating to such services and employees, see § 1.132-4(c).

(b) *Reciprocal agreements.*—For purposes of the exclusion from gross income for a no-additional-cost service, an exclusion is available to an employee of one employer for a no-additional-cost service provided by an unrelated employer only if all of the following requirements are satisfied—

(1) The service provided to such employee by the unrelated employer is the same type of service generally provided to nonemployee customers by both the line of business in which the employee works and the line of business in which the service is provided to such employee (so that the employee would be permitted to exclude from gross income the value of the service if such service were provided directly by the employee's employer);

(2) Both employers are parties to a written reciprocal agreement under which a group of employees of each employer, all of whom perform substantial services in the same line of business, may receive no-additional-cost services from the other employer; and

(3) Neither employer incurs any substantial additional cost (including forgone revenue) in providing such service to the employees of the other employer, or pursuant to such agreement. If one employer receives a substantial payment from the other employer with respect to the reciprocal agreement, the paying employer will be considered to have incurred a substantial additional cost pursuant to the agreement, and consequently services performed under the reciprocal agreement will not qualify for exclusion as no-additional-cost services.

(c) *Example.*—The rules of this section are illustrated by the following example:

Example. Assume that a commercial airline permits its employees to take personal flights on the airline at no charge and receive reserved seating. Because the employer forgoes potential revenue by permitting the employees to reserve seats, employees receiving such free flights are not eligible for the no-additional-cost exclusion. [Reg. § 1.132-2.]

□ [*T.D.* 8256, 7-5-89.]

§ 1.132-3. Qualified employee discounts.—(a) *In general.*—(1) *Definition.*—Gross income does not include the value of a qualified employee discount. A "qualified employee discount" is any employee discount with respect to qualified property or services provided by an employer to an employee for use by the employee to the extent the discount does not exceed—

(i) The gross profit percentage multiplied by the price at which the property is offered to customers in the ordinary course of the employer's line of business, for discounts on property, or

(ii) Twenty percent of the price at which the service is offered to customers, for discounts on services.

(2) *Qualified property or services.*—(i) *In general.*—The term "qualified property or services" means any property or services that are offered for sale to customers in the ordinary course of the line of business of the employer in which the employee performs substantial services. For rules relating to the line of business limitation, see § 1.132-4.

(ii) *Exception for certain property.*—The term "qualified property" does not include real property and it does not include personal property (whether tangible or intangible) of a kind commonly held for investment. Thus, an employee may not exclude from gross income the amount of an employee discount provided on the purchase of securities, commodities, or currency, or of either residential or commercial real estate, whether or not the particular purchase is made for investment purposes.

(iii) *Property and services not offered in ordinary course of business.*—The term "qualified property or services" does not include any property or services of a kind that is not offered for sale to customers in the ordinary course of the line of business of the employer. For example, employee discounts provided on property or services that are offered for sale primarily to employees and their families (such as merchandise sold at an employee store or through an employer-provided catalog service) may not be excluded from gross income. For rules relating to employer-operated eating facilities, see § 1.132-7, and for rules relating to employer-operated on-premises athletic facilities, see § 1.132-1(e).

(3) *No reciprocal agreement exception.*—The exclusion for a qualified employee discount does not apply to property or services provided by another employer pursuant to a written reciprocal agreement that exists between employers to provide discounts on property and services to employees of the other employer.

(4) *Property or services provided without charge, at a reduced price, or by rebates.*—The exclusion for a qualified employee discount applies whether the property or service is provided at no charge (in which case only part of the discount may be excludable as a qualified employee discount) or at a reduced price. The exclusion also applies if the benefit is provided through a partial or total cash rebate of an amount paid for the property or service.

(5) *Property or services provided directly by the employer or indirectly through a third party.*—A qualified employee discount may be provided either directly by the employer or indirectly through a third party. For example, an employee of an appliance manufacturer may

receive a qualified employee discount on the manufacturer's appliances purchased at a retail store that offers such appliances for sale to customers. The employee may exclude the amount of the qualified employee discount whether the employee is provided the appliance at no charge or purchases it at a reduced price, or whether the employee receives a partial or total cash rebate from either the employer-manufacturer or the retailer. If an employee receives additional rights associated with the property that are not provided by the employee's employer to customers in the ordinary course of the line of business in which the employee performs substantial services (such as the right to return or exchange the property or special warranty rights), the employee may only receive a qualified employee discount with respect to the property and not the additional rights. Receipt of such additional rights may occur, for example, when an employee of a manufacturer purchases property manufactured by the employee's employer at a retail outlet.

(6) *Applicability of nondiscrimination rules.*—The exclusion for a qualified employee discount applies to highly compensated employees only if the discount is available on substantially the same terms to each member of a group of employees that is defined under a reasonable classification set up by the employer that does not discriminate in favor of highly compensated employees. See § 1.132-8.

(b) *Employee discount.*—(1) *Definition.*—The term "employee discount" means the excess of—

(i) The price at which the property or service is being offered by the employer for sale to customers, over

(ii) The price at which the property or service is provided by the employer to an employee for use by the employee. A transfer of property by an employee without consideration is treated as use by the employee for purposes of this section. Thus, for example, if an employee receives a discount on property offered for sale by his employer to customers and the employee makes a gift of the property to his parent, the property will be considered to be provided for use by the employee; thus, the discount will be eligible for exclusion as a qualified employee discount.

(2) *Price to customers.*—(i) *Determined at time of sale.*—In determining the amount of an employee discount, the price at which the property or service is being offered to customers at the time of the employee's purchase is controlling. For example, assume that an employer offers a product to customers for $20 during the first six months of a calendar year, but at the time the employee purchases the product at a discount, the price at which the product is being offered to customers is $25. In this case, the price from which the employee discount is measured is $25. Assume instead that, at the time the employee purchases the product at a discount, the price at which the product is being offered to customers is $15 and the price charged the employee is $12. The employee discount is measured from $15, the price at which the product is offered for sale to customers at the time of the employee purchase. Thus, the employee discount is $15 - $12, or $3.

(ii) *Quantity discount not reflected.*—The price at which a property or service is being offered to customers cannot reflect any quantity discount unless the employee actually purchases the requisite quantity of the property or service.

(iii) *Price to employer's customers controls.*—In determining the amount of an employee discount, the price at which a property or service is offered to customers of the employee's employer is controlling. Thus, the price at which the property is sold to the wholesale customers of a manufacturer will generally be lower than the price at which the same property is sold to the customers of a retailer. However, see paragraph (a)(5) of this section regarding the effect of a wholesaler providing to its employees additional rights not provided to customers of the wholesaler in the ordinary course of its business.

(iv) *Discounts to discrete customer or consumer groups.*—Subject to paragraph (2)(ii) of this section, if an employer offers for sale property or services at one or more discounted prices to discrete customer or consumer groups, and sales at all such discounted prices comprise at least 35 percent of the employer's gross sales for a representative period, then in determining the amount of an employee discount, the price at which such property or service is being offered to customers for purposes of this section is a discounted price. The applicable discounted price is the current undiscounted price, reduced by the percentage discount at which the greatest percentage of the employer's discounted gross sales are made for such representative period. If sales at different percentage discounts equal the same percentage of the employer's gross sales, the price at which the property or service is being provided to customers may be reduced by the average of the discounts offered to each of the two groups. For purposes of this section, a representative period is the taxable year of the employer immediately preceding the taxable year in which the property or service is provided to the employee at a discount. If more than one employer would be aggregated under section 414(b), (c), (m), or (o), and not all of the employers have the same taxable year, the employers required to be aggregated must designate the 12-month period to be used in determining gross sales for a representative period. The 12-month period designated, however, must be used on a consistent basis.

(v) *Examples.*—The rules provided in this paragraph (b)(2) are illustrated by the following examples:

Example (1). Assume that a wholesale employer offers property for sale to two discrete customer groups at differing prices. Assume further that during the prior taxable year of the employer, 70 percent of the employer's gross sales are made at a 15 percent discount and 30 percent at no discount. For purposes of this paragraph (b)(2), the current undiscounted price at which the property or service is being offered by the employer for sale to customers may be reduced by the 15 percent discount.

Example (2). Assume that a retail employer offers a 20 percent discount to members of the American Bar Association, a 15 percent discount to members of the American Medical Association, and a ten percent discount to employees of the Federal Government. Assume further that during the prior taxable year of the employer, sales to American Bar Association members equal 15 percent of the employer's gross sales, sales to American Medical Association members equal 20 percent of the employer's gross sales, and sales to Federal Government employees equal 25 percent of the employer's gross sales. For purposes of this paragraph (b)(2), the current undiscounted price at which the property or service is being offered by the employer for sale to customers may be reduced by the ten percent Federal Government discount.

(3) *Damaged, distressed, or returned goods.*—If an employee pays at least fair market value for damaged, distressed, or returned property, such employee will not have income attributable to such purchase.

(c) *Gross profit percentage.*—(1) *In general.*—(i) *General rule.*—An exclusion from gross income for an employee discount on qualified property is limited to the price at which the property is being offered to customers in the ordinary course of the employer's line of business, multiplied by the employer's gross profit percentage. The term "gross profit percentage" means the excess of the aggregate sales price of the property sold by the employer to customers (including employees) over the employer's aggregate cost of the property, then divided by the aggregate sales price.

(ii) *Calculation of gross profit percentage.*—The gross profit percentage must be calculated separately for each line of business based on the aggregate sales price and aggregate cost of property in that line of business for a representative period. For purposes of this section, a representative period is the taxable year of the employer immediately preceding the taxable year in which the discount is available. For example, if the aggregate amount of sales of property in an employer's line of business for the prior taxable year was $800,000, and the aggregate cost of the property for the year was $600,000, the gross profit percentage would be 25 percent ($800,000 minus $600,000, then divided by $800,000). If two or more employers are required to aggregate under section 414(b), (c), (m), or (o) (aggregated employer), and if all of the aggregated employers do not share the same taxable year, then the aggregated employers must designate the 12-month period to be used in determining the gross profit percentage. The 12-month period designated, however, must be used on a consistent basis. If an employee performs substantial services in more than one line of business, the gross profit percentage of the line of business in which the property is sold determines the amount of the excludable employee discount.

(iii) *Special rule for employers in their first year of existence.*—An employer in its first year of existence may estimate the gross profit percentage of a line of business based on its mark-up from cost. Alternatively, an employer in its first year of existence may determine the gross profit percentage by reference to an appropriate industry average.

(iv) *Redetermination of gross profit percentage.*—If substantial changes in an employer's business indicate at any time that it is inappropriate for the prior year's gross profit percentage to be used for the current year, the employer must, within a reasonable period, redetermine the gross profit percentage for the remaining portion of the current year as if such portion of the year were the first year of the employer's existence.

(2) *Line of business.*—In general, an employer must determine the gross profit percentage on the basis of all property offered to customers (including employees) in each separate line of business. An employer may instead select a classification of property that is narrower than the applicable line of business. However, the classification must be reasonable. For example, if an employer computes gross profit percentage according to the department in which products are sold, such classification is reasonable. Similarly, it is reasonable to compute gross profit percentage on the basis of the

type of merchandise sold (such as high mark-up and low mark-up classifications). It is not reasonable, however, for an employer to classify certain low mark-up products preferred by certain employees (such as highly compensated employees) with high mark-up products or to classify certain high mark-up products preferred by other employees with low mark-up products.

(3) *Generally accepted accounting principles.*—In general, the aggregate sales price of property must be determined in accordance with generally accepted accounting principles. An employer must compute the aggregate cost of property in the same manner in which it is computed for the employer's Federal income tax liability; thus, for example, section 263A and the regulations thereunder apply in determining the cost of property.

* * *

(e) *Excess discounts.*—Unless excludable under a provision of the Internal Revenue Code of 1986 other than section 132(a)(2), an employee discount provided on property is excludable to the extent of the gross profit percentage multiplied by the price at which the property is being offered for sale to customers. If an employee discount exceeds the gross profit percentage, the excess discount is includible in the employee's income. For example, if the discount on employer-purchased property is 30 percent and the employer's gross profit percentage for the period in the relevant line of business is 25 percent, then 5 percent of the price at which the property is being offered for sale to customers is includible in the employee's income. With respect to services, an employee discount of up to 20 percent may be excludable. If an employee discount exceeds 20 percent, the excess discount is includible in the employee's income. For example, assume that a commercial airline provides a pass to each of its employees permitting the employees to obtain a free roundtrip coach ticket with a confirmed seat to any destination the airline services. Neither the exclusion of section 132(a)(1) (relating to no-additional-cost services) nor any other statutory exclusion applies to a flight taken primarily for personal purposes by an employee under this program. However, an employee discount of up to 20 percent may be excluded as a qualified employee discount. Thus, if the price charged to customers for the flight taken is $300 (under restrictions comparable to those actually placed on travel associated with the employee airline ticket), $60 is excludible from gross income as a qualified employee discount and $240 is includible in gross income. [Reg. § 1.132-3.]

☐ [*T.D.* 8256, 7-5-89.]

§ 1.132-4. Line of business limitation.—(a) *In general.*—(1) *Applicability.*—(i) *General rule.*—A no-additional-cost service or a qualified employee discount provided to an employee is only available with respect to property or services that are offered for sale to customers in the ordinary course of the same line of business in which the employee receiving the property or service performs substantial services. Thus, an employee who does not perform substantial services in a particular line of business of the employer may not exclude from income under section 132(a)(1) or (a)(2) the value of services or employee discounts received on property or services in that line of business. For rules that relax the line of business requirement, see paragraphs (b) through (g) of this section.

(ii) *Property and services sold to employees rather than customers.*—Because the property or services must be offered for sale to customers in the ordinary course of the same line of business in which the employee performs substantial services, the line of business limitation is not satisfied if the employer's products or services are sold primarily to employees of the employer, rather than to customers. Thus, for example, an employer in the banking line of business is not considered in the variety store line of business if the employer establishes an employee store that offers variety store items for sale to the employer's employees. See § 1.132-7 for rules relating to employer-operated eating facilities, and see § 1.132-1(e) for rules relating to employer-operated on-premises athletic facilities.

(iii) *Performance of substantial services in more than one line of business.*—An employee who performs services in more than one of the employer's lines of business may only exclude no-additional-cost services and qualified employee discounts in the lines of business in which the employee performs substantial services.

(iv) *Performance of services that directly benefit more than one line of business.*—(A) *In general.*—An employee who performs substantial services that directly benefit more than one line of business of an employer is treated as performing substantial services in all such lines of business. For example, an employee who maintains accounting records for an employer's three lines of business may receive qualified employee discounts in all three lines of business. Similarly, if an employee of a minor line of business of an employer that is significantly interrelated with a major line of business of the employer performs substantial services that directly benefit both the major and the minor lines of business, the employee is treated as performing substantial services for both the major and the minor lines of business.

(B) *Examples.*—The rules provided in this paragraph (a)(1)(iv) are illustrated by the following examples:

Example (1). Assume that employees of units of an employer provide repair or financing services, or sell by catalog, with respect to retail merchandise sold by the employer. Such employees may be considered to perform substantial services for the retail merchandise line of business under paragraph (a)(1)(iv)(A) of this section.

Example (2). Assume that an employer operates a hospital and a laundry service. Assume further that some of the gross receipts of the laundry service line of business are from laundry services sold to customers other than the hospital employer. Only the employees of the laundry service who perform substantial services which directly benefit the hospital line of business (through the provision of laundry services to the hospital) will be treated as performing substantial services for the hospital line of business. Other employees of the laundry service line of business will not be treated as employees of the hospital line of business.

Example (3). Assume the same facts as in example (2), except that the employer also operates a chain of dry cleaning stores. Employees who perform substantial services which directly benefit the dry cleaning stores but who do not perform substantial services that directly benefit the hospital line of business will not be treated as performing substantial services for the hospital line of business.

(2) *Definition.*—(i) *In general.*—An employer's line of business is determined by reference to the Enterprise Standard Industrial Classification Manual (ESIC Manual) prepared by the Statistical Policy Division of the U.S. Office of Management and Budget. An employer is considered to have more than one line of business if the employer offers for sale to customers property or services in more than one two-digit code classification referred to in the ESIC Manual.

(ii) *Examples.*—Examples of two-digit classifications are general retail merchandise stores; hotels and other lodging places; auto repair, services, and garages; and food stores.

(3) *Aggregation of two-digit classifications.*—If, pursuant to paragraph (a)(2) of this section, an employer has more than one line of business, such lines of business will be treated as a single line of business where and to the extent that one or more of the following aggregation rules apply:

(i) If it is uncommon in the industry of the employer for any of the separate lines of business of the employer to be operated without the others, the separate lines of business are treated as one line of business.

(ii) If it is common for a substantial number of employees (other than those employees who work at the headquarters or main office of the employer) to perform substantial services for more than one line of business of the employer, so that determination of which employees perform substantial services for which line or lines of business would be difficult, then the separate lines of business of the employer in which such employees perform substantial services are treated as one line of business. For example, assume that an employer operates a delicatessen with an attached service counter at which food is sold for consumption on the premises. Assume further that most but not all employees work both at the delicatessen and at the service counter. Under the aggregation rule of this paragraph (a)(3)(ii), the delicatessen and the service counter are treated as one line of business.

(iii) If the retail operations of an employer that are located on the same premises are in separate lines of business but would be considered to be within one line of business under paragraph (a)(2) of this section if the merchandise offered for sale in such lines of business were offered for sale at a department store, then the operations are treated as one line of business. For example, assume that on the same premises an employer sells both women's apparel and jewelry. Because, if sold together at a department store, the operations would be part of the same line of business, the operations are treated as one line of business.

* * *

(h) *Line of business requirement does not expand benefits eligible for exclusion.*—The line of business requirement limits the benefits eligible for the no-additional-cost service and qualified employee discount exclusions to property or services provided by an employer to its customers in the ordinary course of the line of business of the employer in which the employee performs substantial services. The requirement is intended to ensure that employers do not offer, on a tax-free or reduced basis, property or services to employees that are not offered to the employer's customers, even if the property or services offered to the customers and the employees are within the same line of business (as defined in this section). [Reg. § 1.132-4.]

☐ [*T.D.* 8256, 7-5-89.]

§1.132-5. Working condition fringes.—(a) *In general.*—(1) *Definition.*—Gross income does not include the value of a working condition fringe. A "working condition fringe" is any property or service provided to an employee of an employer to the extent that, if the employee paid for the property or service, the amount paid would be allowable as a deduction under section 162 or 167.

(i) A service or property offered by an employer in connection with a flexible spending account is not excludable from gross income as a working condition fringe. For purposes of the preceding sentence, a flexible spending account is an agreement (whether or not written) entered into between an employer and an employee that makes available to the employee over a time period a certain level of unspecified non-cash benefits with a pre-determined cash value.

(ii) If, under section 274 or any other section, certain substantiation requirements must be met in order for a deduction under section 162 or 167 to be allowable, then those substantiation requirements apply when determining whether a property or service is excludable as a working condition fringe.

(iii) An amount that would be deductible by the employee under a section other than section 162 or 167, such as section 212, is not a working condition fringe.

(iv) A physical examination program provided by the employer is not excludable as a working condition fringe even if the value of such program might be deductible to the employee under section 213. The previous sentence applies without regard to whether the employer makes the program mandatory to some or all employees.

(v) A cash payment made by an employer to an employee will not qualify as a working condition fringe unless the employer requires the employee to—

(A) Use the payment for expenses in connection with a specific or pre-arranged activity or undertaking for which a deduction is allowable under section 162 or 167,

(B) Verify that the payment is actually used for such expenses, and

(C) Return to the employer any part of the payment not so used.

(vi) The limitation of section 67(a) (relating to the two-percent floor on miscellaneous itemized deductions) is not considered when determining the amount of a working condition fringe. For example, assume that an employer provides a $1,000 cash advance to Employee A and that the conditions of paragraph (a)(1)(v) of this section are not satisfied. Even to the extent A uses the allowance for expenses for which a deduction is allowable under section 162 or 167, because such cash payment is not a working condition fringe, section 67(a) applies. The $1,000 payment is includible in A's gross income and subject to income and employment tax withholding. If, however, the conditions of paragraph (a)(1)(v) of this section are satisfied with respect to the payment, then the amount of A's working condition fringe is determined without regard to section 67(a). The $1,000 payment is excludible from A's gross income and not subject to income and employment tax reporting and withholding.

(2) *Trade or business of the employee.*—(i) *General.*—If the hypothetical payment for a property or service would be allowable as a deduction with respect to a trade or business of an employee other than the employee's trade or business of being an employee of the employer, it cannot be taken into account for purposes of determining the amount, if any, of the working condition fringe.

(ii) *Examples.*—The rule of paragraph (a)(2)(i) of this section may be illustrated by the following examples:

Example (1). Assume that, unrelated to company X's trade or business and unrelated to employee A's trade or business of being an employee of company X, A is a member of the board of directors of company Y. Assume further that company X provides A with air transportation to a company Y board of director's meeting. A may not exclude from gross income the value of the air transportation to the meeting as a working condition fringe. A may, however, deduct such amount under section 162 if the section 162 requirements are satisfied. The result would be the same whether the air transportation was provided in the form of a flight on a commercial airline or a seat on a company X airplane.

Example (2). Assume the same facts as in example (1) except that A serves on the board of directors of company Z and company Z regularly purchases a significant amount of goods and services from company X. Because of the relationship between Company Z and A's employer, A's membership on Company Z's board of directors is related to A's trade or business of being an employee of Company X. Thus, A may exclude from gross income the value of air transportation to board meetings as a working condition fringe.

Example (3). Assume the same facts as in example (1) except that A serves on the board of directors of a charitable organization. Assume further that the service by A on the charity's board is substantially related to company X's trade or business. In this case, A may exclude from gross income the value of air transportation to board meetings as a working condition fringe.

Example (4). Assume the same facts as in example (3) except that company X also provides A with the use of a company X conference room which A uses for monthly meetings relating to the charitable organization. Also assume that A uses company X's copy machine and word processor each month in connection with functions of the charitable organization. Because of the substantial business benefit that company X derives from A's service on the board of the charity, A may exclude as a working condition fringe the value of the use of company X property in connection with the charitable organization.

* * *

[Reg. § 1.132-5.]

□ [*T.D.* 8256, 7-5-89. *Amended by T.D.* 8451, 12-4-92; *T.D.* 8457, 12-29-92; *T.D.* 8666, 5-29-96; *T.D.* 8933, 1-10-2001 *and T.D.* 9483, 5-18-2010.]

§ 1.132-6. De minimis fringes.—(a) *In general.*—Gross income does not include the value of a de minimis fringe provided to an employee. The term "de minimis fringe" means any property or service the value of which is (after taking into account the frequency with which similar fringes are provided by the employer to the employer's employees) so small as to make accounting for it unreasonable or administratively impracticable.

(b) *Frequency.*—(1) *Employee-measured frequency.*—Generally, the frequency with which similar fringes are provided by the employer to the employer's employees is determined by reference to the frequency with which the employer provides the fringes to each individual employee. For example, if an employer provides a free meal in kind to one employee on a daily basis, but not to any other employee, the value of the meals is not de minimis with respect to that one employee even though with respect to the employer's entire workforce the meals are provided "infrequently."

(2) *Employer-measured frequency.*—Notwithstanding the rule of paragraph (b)(1) of this section, except for purposes of applying the special rules of paragraph (d)(2) of this section, where it would be administratively difficult to determine frequency with respect to individual employees, the frequency with which similar fringes are provided by the employer to the employer's employees is determined by reference to the frequency with which the employer provides the fringes to the workforce as a whole. Therefore, under this rule, the frequency with which any individual employee receives such a fringe benefit is not relevant and in some circumstances, the de minimis fringe exclusion may apply with respect to a benefit even though a particular employee receives the benefit frequently. For example, if an employer exercises sufficient control and imposes significant restrictions on the personal use of a company copying machine so that at least 85 percent of the use of the machine is for business purposes, any personal use of the copying machine by particular employees is considered to be a de minimis fringe.

(c) *Administrability.*—Unless excluded by a provision of chapter 1 of the Internal Revenue Code of 1986 other than section 132(a)(4), the value of any fringe benefit that would not be unreasonable or administratively impracticable to account for is includible in the employee's gross income. Thus, except as provided in paragraph (d)(2) of this section, the provision of any cash fringe benefit is never excludable under section 132(a) as a de minimis fringe benefit. Similarly except as otherwise provided in paragraph (d) of this section, a cash equivalent fringe benefit (such as a fringe benefit provided to an employee through the use of a gift certificate or charge or credit card) is generally not excludable under § 132(a) even if the same property or service acquired (if provided in kind) would be excludable as a de minimis fringe benefit. For example, the provision of cash to an employee for a theatre ticket that would itself be excludable as a de minimis fringe (see paragraph (e)(1) of this section) is not excludable as a de minimis fringe.

(d) *Special rules.*—

* * *

(2) *Occasional meal money or local transportation fare.*—(i) *General rule.*—Meals, meal money or local transportation fare provided to an employee is excluded as a de minimis fringe benefit if the benefit provided is reasonable and is provided in a manner that satisfies the following three conditions:

(A) *Occasional basis.*—The meals, meal money or local transportation fare is provided to the employee on an occasional basis. Whether meal money or local transportation fare is provided to an employee on an occasional basis will depend upon the frequency i.e. the availability of the benefit and regularity with which the benefit is provided by the employer to the employee. Thus, meals, meal money, or local transportation fare or a combination of such benefits provided to an employee on a regular or routine basis is not provided on an occasional basis.

(B) *Overtime.*—The meals, meal money or local transportation fare is provided to an employee because overtime work necessitates an extension of the employee's normal work schedule. This condition does not fail to be satisfied merely because the circumstances giving rise to the need for overtime work are reasonably foreseeable.

(C) *Meal money.*—In the case of a meal or meal money, the meal or meal money is provided to enable the employee to work overtime. Thus, for example, meals provided on the employer's premises that are consumed during the period that the employee works overtime or meal money provided for meals consumed during such period satisfy this condition.

In no event shall meal money or local transportation fare calculated on the basis of the number of hours worked (e.g., $1.00 per hour for each hour over eight hours) be considered a de minimis fringe benefit.

(ii) *Applicability of other exclusions for certain meals and for transportation provided for security concerns.*—The value of meals furnished to an employee, an employee's spouse, or any of the employee's dependents by or on behalf of the employee's employer for the convenience of the employer is excluded from the employee's gross income if the meals are furnished on the business premises of the employer (see section 119). (For purposes of the exclusion under section 119, the definitions of an employee under § 1.132-1(b) do not apply.) If, for a bona fide business-oriented security concern, an employer provides an employee vehicle transportation that is specially designed for security (for example, the vehicle is equipped with bulletproof glass and armor plating), and the conditions of § 1.132-5(m) are satisfied, the value of the special security design is excludable from gross income as a working condition fringe if the employee would not have had such special security design but for the bona fide business-oriented security concern.

(iii) *Special rule for employer-provided transportation provided in certain circumstances.*—(A) *Partial exclusion of value.*—If an employer provides transportation (such as taxi fare) to an employee for use in commuting to and/or from work because of unusual circumstances and because, based on the facts and circumstances, it is unsafe for the employee to use other available means of transportation, the excess of the value of each one-way trip over $1.50 per one-way commute is excluded from gross income. The rule of this paragraph (d)(2)(iii) is not available to a control employee as defined in § 1.61-21(f)(5) and (6).

(B) *"Unusual circumstances"*.—Unusual circumstances are determined with respect to the employee receiving the transportation and are based on all facts and circumstances. An example of unusual circumstances would be when an employee is asked to work outside of his normal work hours (such as being called to the workplace at 1:00 am when the employee normally works from 8:00 am to 4:00 pm). Another example of unusual circumstances is a temporary change in the employee's work schedule (such as working from 12 midnight to 8:00 am rather than from 8:00 am to 4:00 pm for a two-week period).

(C) *"Unsafe conditions"*.—Factors indicating whether it is unsafe for an employee to use other available means of transportation are the history of crime in the geographic area surrounding the employee's workplace or residence and the time of day during which the employee must commute.

(3) *Use of special rules or examples to establish a general rule.*—The special rules provided in this paragraph (d) or examples provided in paragraph (e) of this section may not be used to establish any general rule permitting exclusion as a de minimis fringe. For example, the fact that $252 (i.e., $21 per month for 12 months) worth of public transit passes can be excluded from gross income as a de minimis fringe in 1992 does not mean that any fringe benefit with a value equal to or less than $252 may be excluded as a de minimis fringe. As another example, the fact that the commuting use of an employer-provided vehicle more than one day a month is an example of a benefit not excludable as a de minimis fringe (see paragraph (e)(2) of this section) does not mean that the commuting use of a vehicle up to 12 times per year is excludable from gross income as a de minimis fringe.

(4) *Benefits exceeding value and frequency limits.*—If a benefit provided to an employee is not de minimis because either the value or frequency exceeds a limit provided in this paragraph (d), no amount of the benefit is considered to be a de minimis fringe. For example, if, in 1992, an employer provides a $50 monthly public transit pass, the entire $50 must be included in income, not just the excess value over $21.

(e) *Examples.*—(1) *Benefits excludable from income.*—Examples of de minimis fringe benefits are occasional typing of personal letters by a company secretary; occasional personal use of an employer's copying machine, provided that the employer exercises sufficient control and imposes significant restrictions on the personal use of the machine so that at least 85 percent of the use of the machine is for business purposes; occasional cocktail parties, group meals, or picnics for employees and their guests; traditional birthday or holiday gifts of property (not cash) with a low fair market value; occasional theater or sporting event tickets; coffee, doughnuts, and soft drinks; local telephone calls; and flowers, fruit, books, or similar property provided to employees under special circumstances (e.g., on account of illness, outstanding performance, or family crisis).

(2) *Benefits not excludable as de minimis fringes.*—Examples of fringe benefits that are not excludable from gross income as de minimis fringes are: season tickets to sporting or theatrical events; the commuting use of an employer-provided automobile or other vehicle more than one day a month; membership in a private country club or athletic facility, regardless of the frequency with which the employee uses the facility; employer-provided group-term life insurance on the life of the spouse or child of an employee; and use of employer-owned or leased facilities (such as an apartment, hunting lodge, boat, etc.) for a weekend. Some amount of the value of certain of these fringe benefits may be excluded from income under other statutory provisions, such as the exclusion for working condition fringes. See § 1.132-5.

(f) *Nonapplicability of nondiscrimination rules.*—Except to the extent provided in § 1.132-7, the nondiscrimination rules of section 132(h)(1) and § 1.132-8 do not apply in determining the amount, if any, of a de minimis fringe. Thus, a fringe benefit may be excludable as a de minimis fringe even if the benefit is provided exclusively to highly compensated employees of the employer. [Reg. § 1.132-6.]

☐ [*T.D.* 8256, 7-5-89. *Amended by T.D.* 8389, 1-15-92.]

§ 1.132-8. Fringe benefit nondiscrimination rules.—(a) *Application of nondiscrimination rules.*—(1) *General rule.*—A highly compensated employee who receives a no-additional cost service, a qualified employee discount or a meal provided at an employer-operated eating facility for employees shall not be permitted to exclude such benefit from his or her income unless the benefit is available on substantially the same terms to:

(i) All employees of the employer; or

(ii) A group of employees of the employer which is defined under a reasonable classification set up by the employer that does not discriminate in favor of highly compensated employees. See paragraph (f) of this section for the definition of a highly compensated employee.

(2) *Consequences of discrimination.*—(i) *In general.*—If an employer maintains more than one fringe benefit program, i.e., either different fringe benefits being provided to the same group of employees, or different classifications of employees or the same fringe benefit being provided to two or more classifications of employees, the nondiscrimination requirements of section 132 will generally be applied separately to each such program. Thus, a determination that one fringe benefit program discriminates in favor of highly compensated employees generally will not cause other fringe benefit programs covering the same highly compensated employees to be treated as discriminatory. If the fringe benefits provided to a highly compensated individual do not satisfy the nondiscrimination rules provided in this section, such individual shall be unable to exclude from gross income any portion of the benefit. For example, if an employer offers a 20 percent discount (which otherwise satisfies the requirements for a qualified employee discount) to all non-highly compensated employees and a 35 percent discount to all highly compensated employees, the entire value of the 35 percent discount (not just the excess over 20 percent) is includible in the gross income and wages of the highly compensated employees who make purchases at a discount.

(ii) *Exception.*—(A) *Related fringe benefit programs.*—If one of a group of fringe benefit programs discriminates in favor of highly compensated employees, no related fringe benefit provided to such highly compensated employees under any other fringe benefit program may be excluded from the gross income of such highly compensated employees. For example, assume a department store provides a 20 percent merchandise discount to all employees under one fringe benefit program. Assume further that under a second fringe benefit program, the department store provides an additional 15 percent merchandise discount to a group of employees defined under a classification which discriminates in favor of highly compensated employees. Because the second fringe benefit program is discriminatory, the 15 percent merchandise discount provided to the highly compensated employees is not a qualified employee discount. In addition, because the 20 percent merchandise discount provided under the first fringe benefit program is related to the fringe benefit provided under the second fringe benefit program, the 20 percent merchandise discount provided the highly compensated employees is not a qualified employee discount. Thus, the entire 35 percent merchandise discount provided to the highly compensated employees is includible in such employees' gross incomes.

(B) *Employer-operated eating facilities for employees.*—For purposes of paragraph (a)(2)(ii)(A) of this section, meals at different employer-operated eating facilities for employees are not related fringe benefits, so that a highly compensated employee may exclude from gross income the value of a meal at a nondiscriminatory facility even though any meals provided to him or her at a discriminatory facility cannot be excluded.

(3) *Scope of the nondiscrimination rules provided in this section.*—The nondiscrimination rules provided in this section apply only to fringe benefits provided pursuant to section 132(a)(1), (a)(2), and (e)(2). These rules have no application to any other employee benefit that may be subject to nondiscrimination requirements under any other section of the Code.

* * *

(f) *Highly compensated employee.*—(1) *Government and nongovernment employees.*—A highly compensated employee of any employer is any employee who, during the year or the preceding year—

(i) Was a 5-percent owner,

(ii) Received compensation from the employer in excess of $75,000,

(iii) Received compensation from the employer in excess of $50,000 and was in the top-paid group of employees for such year, or

(iv) Was at any time an officer and received compensation greater than 150 percent of the amount in effect under section 415(c)(1)(A) for such year.

For purposes of determining whether an employee is a highly compensated employee, the rules of sections 414(q), (s), and (t) apply.

(2) *Former employees.*—A former employee shall be treated as a highly compensated employee if—

(i) The employee was a highly compensated employee when the employee separated from service, or

(ii) The employee was a highly compensated employee at any time after attaining age 55. [Reg. § 1.132-8.]

☐ [*T.D.* 8256, 7-5-89.]

Deductions for Personal Exemptions

§ 1.152-1. General definition of a dependent.—(a)

* * *

(2)(i) For purposes of determining whether or not an individual received, for a given calendar year, over half of his support from the taxpayer, there shall be taken into account the amount of support received from the taxpayer as compared to the entire amount of support which the individual received from all sources, including support which the individual himself supplied. The term "support" includes food, shelter, clothing, medical and dental care, education, and the like. Generally, the amount of an item of support will be the amount of expense incurred by the one furnishing such item. If the item of support furnished an individual is in the form of property or lodging, it will be necessary to measure the amount of such item of support in terms of its fair market value.

(ii) In computing the amount which is contributed for the support of an individual, there must be included any amount which is contributed by such individual for his own support, including income which is ordinarily excludable from gross income, such as benefits received under the Social Security Act. For example, a father receives $800 social security benefits, $400 interest, and $1,000 from his son during 1955, all of which sums represent his sole support during that year. The fact that the social security benefits of $800 are not includible in the father's gross income does not prevent such amount from entering into the computation of the total amount contributed for the father's support. Consequently, since the son's contribution of $1,000 was less than one-half of the father's support ($2,200) he may not claim his father as a dependent.

(iii)(*a*) For purposes of determining the amount of support furnished for a child (or children) by a taxpayer for a given calendar year, an arrearage payment made in a year subsequent to a calendar year for which there is an unpaid liability shall not be treated as paid either during that calendar year or in the year of payment, but no amount shall be treated as an arrearage payment to the extent that there is an unpaid liability (determined without regard to such payment) with respect to the support of a child for the taxable year of payment; and

(*b*) Similarly, payments made prior to any calendar year (whether or not made in the form of a lump sum payment in settlement of the parent's liability for support) shall not be treated as made during such calendar year, but payments made during any calendar year from amounts set aside in trust by a parent in a prior year, shall be treated as made during the calendar year in which paid.

* * *

[Reg. § 1.152-1.]

☐ [*T.D.* 6231, 4-25-57. *Amended by T.D.* 6304, 8-22-58, *T.D.* 6441, 1-4-60, *T.D.* 6663, 7-10-63, *T.D.* 7099, 3-19-71 *and T.D.* 7114, 5-17-71.]

§ 1.152-4. Special rule for a child of divorced or separated parents or parents who live apart.—(a) *In general.*—A taxpayer may claim a dependency deduction for a child (as defined in section 152(f)(1)) only if the child is the qualifying child of the taxpayer under section 152(c) or the qualifying relative of the taxpayer under section 152(d). Section 152(c)(4)(B) provides that a child who is claimed as a qualifying child by parents who do not file a joint return together is treated as the qualifying child of the parent with whom the child resides for a longer period of time during the taxable year or, if the child resides with both parents for an equal period of time, of the parent with the higher adjusted gross income. However, a child is treated as the qualifying child or qualifying relative of the noncustodial parent if the custodial parent releases a claim to the exemption under section 152(e) and this section.

(b) *Release of claim by custodial parent.*—(1) *In general.*—Under section 152(e)(1), notwithstanding section 152(c)(1)(B), (c)(4), or (d)(1)(C), a child is treated as the qualifying child or qualifying relative of the noncustodial parent (as defined in paragraph (d) of this section) if the requirements of paragraphs (b)(2) and (b)(3) of this section are met.

(2) *Support, custody, and parental status.*—(i) *In general.*—The requirements of this paragraph (b)(2) are met if the parents of the child provide over one-half of the child's support for the calendar year, the child is in the custody of one or both parents for more than one-half of the calendar year, and the parents—

(A) Are divorced or legally separated under a decree of divorce or separate maintenance;

(B) Are separated under a written separation agreement; or

(C) Live apart at all times during the last 6 months of the calendar year whether or not they are or were married.

(ii) *Multiple support agreement.*—The requirements of this paragraph (b)(2) are not met if over one-half of the support of the child is treated as having been received from a taxpayer under section 152(d)(3).

(3) *Release of claim to child.*—The requirements of this paragraph (b)(3) are met for a calendar year if—

(i) The custodial parent signs a written declaration that the custodial parent will not claim the child as a dependent for any taxable year beginning in that calendar year and the noncustodial parent attaches the declaration to the noncustodial parent's return for the taxable year; or

(ii) A qualified pre-1985 instrument, as defined in section 152(e)(3)(B), applicable to the taxable year beginning in that calendar year, provides that the noncustodial parent is entitled to the dependency exemption for the child and the noncustodial parent provides at least $600 for the support of the child during the calendar year.

(c) *Custody.*—A child is in the custody of one or both parents for more than one-half of the calendar year if one or both parents have the right under state law to physical custody of the child for more than one-half of the calendar year.

(d) *Custodial parent.*—(1) *In general.*—The *custodial parent* is the parent with whom the child resides for the greater number of nights during the calendar year, and the *noncustodial parent* is the parent who is not the custodial parent. A child is treated as residing with neither parent if the child is emancipated under state law. For purposes of this section, a child resides with a parent for a night if the child sleeps—

(i) At the residence of that parent (whether or not the parent is present); or

(ii) In the company of the parent, when the child does not sleep at a parent's residence (for example, the parent and child are on vacation together).

(2) *Night straddling taxable years.*—A night that extends over two taxable years is allocated to the taxable year in which the night begins.

(3) *Absences.*—(i) Except as provided in paragraph (d)(3)(ii) of this section, for purposes of this paragraph (d), a child who does not reside (within the meaning of paragraph (d)(1) of this section) with a parent for a night is treated as residing with the parent with whom the child would have resided for the night but for the absence.

(ii) A child who does not reside (within the meaning of paragraph (d)(1) of this section) with a parent for a night is treated as not residing with either parent for that night if it cannot be determined with which parent the child would have resided or if the child would not have resided with either parent for the night.

(4) *Special rule for equal number of nights.*—If a child is in the custody of one or both parents for more than one-half of the calendar year and the child resides with each parent for an equal number of nights during the calendar year, the parent with the higher adjusted gross income for the calendar year is treated as the custodial parent.

(5) *Exception for a parent who works at night.*—If, in a calendar year, due to a parent's nighttime work schedule, a child resides for a greater number of days but not nights with the

parent who works at night, that parent is treated as the custodial parent. On a school day, the child is treated as residing at the primary residence registered with the school.

* * *

[Reg. § 1.152-4.]

□ [*T.D.* 7099, 3-19-71. *Amended by T.D.* 7145, 10-14-71; *T.D.* 7639, 8-17-79 *and T.D.* 9408, 7-1-2008.]

Itemized Deductions for Individuals and Corporations

§ 1.162-1. Business expenses.—(a) *In general.*—Business expenses deductible from gross income include the ordinary and necessary expenditures directly connected with or pertaining to the taxpayer's trade or business, except items which are used as the basis for a deduction or a credit under provisions of law other than section 162. The cost of goods purchased for resale, with proper adjustment for opening and closing inventories, is deducted from gross sales in computing gross income. See paragraph (a) of § 1.61-3. Among the items included in business expenses are management expenses, commissions (but see section 263 and the regulations thereunder), labor, supplies, incidental repairs, operating expenses of automobiles used in the trade or business, traveling expenses while away from home solely in the pursuit of a trade or business (see § 1.162-2), advertising and other selling expenses, together with insurance premiums against fire, storm, theft, accident, or other similar losses in the case of a business, and rental for the use of business property. No such item shall be included in business expenses, however, to the extent that it is used by the taxpayer in computing the cost of property included in its inventory or used in determining the gain or loss basis of its plant, equipment, or other property. See section 1054 and the regulations thereunder. A deduction for an expense paid or incurred after December 30, 1969, which would otherwise be allowable under section 162 shall not be denied on the grounds that allowance of such deduction would frustrate a sharply defined public policy. See section 162(c), (f), and (g) and the regulations thereunder. The full amount of the allowable deduction for ordinary and necessary expenses in carrying on a business is deductible, even though such expenses exceed the gross income derived during the taxable year from such business. In the case of any sports program to which section 114 (relating to sports programs conducted for the American National Red Cross) applies, expenses described in section 114(a)(2) shall be allowable as deductions under section 162(a) only to the extent that such expenses exceed the amount excluded from gross income under section 114(a).

* * *

[Reg. § 1.162-1.]

□ [*T.D.* 6291, 4-3-58. *Amended by T.D.* 6690, 11-18-63; *T.D.* 6996, 1-17-69; *T.D.* 7315, 6-6-74; *T.D.* 7345, 2-19-75; *T.D.* 8189, 3-25-88 *and T.D.* 8491, 10-8-93.]

§ 1.162-2. Traveling expenses.—(a) Traveling expenses include travel fares, meals and lodging, and expenses incident to travel such as expenses for sample rooms, telephone and telegraph, public stenographers, etc. Only such traveling expenses as are reasonable and necessary in the conduct of the taxpayer's business and directly attributable to it may be deducted. If the trip is undertaken for other than business purposes, the travel fares and expenses incident to travel are personal expenses and the meals and lodging are living expenses. If the trip is solely on business, the reasonable and necessary traveling expenses, including travel fares, meals and lodging, and expenses incident to travel, are business expenses. For the allowance of traveling expenses as deductions in determining adjusted gross income, see section 62(2)(B) and the regulations thereunder.

(b)(1) If a taxpayer travels to a destination and while at such destination engages in both business and personal activities, traveling expenses to and from such destination are deductible only if the trip is related primarily to the taxpayer's trade or business. If the trip is primarily personal in nature, the traveling expenses to and from the destination are not deductible even though the taxpayer engages in business activities while at such destination. However, expenses while at the destination which are properly allocable to the taxpayer's trade or business are deductible even though the traveling expenses to and from the destination are not deductible.

(2) Whether a trip is related primarily to the taxpayer's trade or business or is primarily personal in nature depends on the facts and circumstances in each case. The amount of time during the period of the trip which is spent on personal activity compared to the amount of time spent on activities directly relating to the taxpayer's trade or business is an important factor in determining whether the trip is primarily personal. If, for example, a taxpayer spends one week while at a destination on activities which are directly related to his trade or business and subsequently spends an additional five weeks for vacation or other personal activities, the trip will be considered

primarily personal in nature in the absence of a clear showing to the contrary.

* * *

(d) Expenses paid or incurred by a taxpayer in attending a convention or other meeting may constitute an ordinary and necessary business expense under section 162 depending upon the facts and circumstances of each case. No distinction will be made between self-employed persons and employees. The fact that an employee uses vacation or leave time or that his attendance at the convention is voluntary will not necessarily prohibit the allowance of the deduction. The allowance of deductions for such expenses will depend upon whether there is a sufficient relationship between the taxpayer's trade or business and his attendance at the convention or other meeting so that he is benefiting or advancing the interests of his trade or business by such attendance. If the convention is for political, social or other purposes unrelated to the taxpayer's trade or business, the expenses are not deductible.

(e) Commuters' fares are not considered as business expenses and are not deductible.

(f) For rules with respect to the reporting and substantiation of traveling and other business expenses of employees for taxable years beginning after December 31, 1957, see § 1.162-17. [Reg. § 1.162-2.]

☐ [*T.D.* 6291, 4-3-58. *Amended by T.D.* 6306, 8-27-58.]

§ 1.162-3. Materials and supplies.—(a) *In general.*—(1) *Non-incidental materials and supplies.*—Except as provided in paragraphs (d), (e), and (f) of this section, amounts paid to acquire or produce materials and supplies (as defined in paragraph (c) of this section) are deductible in the taxable year in which the materials and supplies are first used in the taxpayer's operations or are consumed in the taxpayer's operations.

(2) *Incidental materials and supplies.*—Amounts paid to acquire or produce incidental materials and supplies (as defined in paragraph (c) of this section) that are carried on hand and for which no record of consumption is kept or of which physical inventories at the beginning and end of the taxable year are not taken, are deductible in the taxable year in which these amounts are paid, provided taxable income is clearly reflected.

(3) *Use or consumption of rotable and temporary spare parts.*—Except as provided in paragraphs (d), (e), and (f) of this section, for purposes of paragraph (a)(1) of this section, rotable and temporary spare parts (defined under paragraph (c)(2) of this section) are first used in the taxpayer's operations or are consumed in the taxpayer's operations in the taxable year in which the taxpayer disposes of the parts.

(b) *Coordination with other provisions of the Internal Revenue Code.*—Nothing in this section changes the treatment of any amount that is specifically provided for under any provision of the Internal Revenue Code (Code) or regulations other than section 162(a) or section 212 and the regulations under those sections. For example, see § 1.263(a)-3, which requires taxpayers to capitalize amounts paid to improve tangible property and section 263A and the regulations under section 263A, which require taxpayers to capitalize the direct and allocable indirect costs, including the cost of materials and supplies, of property produced by the taxpayer and property acquired for resale. See also § 1.471-1, which requires taxpayers to include in inventory certain materials and supplies.

(c) *Definitions.*—(1) *Materials and supplies.*—For purposes of this section, *materials and supplies* means tangible property that is used or consumed in the taxpayer's operations that is not inventory and that—

(i) Is a component acquired to maintain, repair, or improve a unit of tangible property (as determined under § 1.263(a)-3(e)) owned, leased, or serviced by the taxpayer and that is not acquired as part of any single unit of tangible property;

(ii) Consists of fuel, lubricants, water, and similar items, reasonably expected to be consumed in 12 months or less, beginning when used in the taxpayer's operations;

(iii) Is a unit of property as determined under § 1.263(a)-3(e) that has an economic useful life of 12 months or less, beginning when the property is used or consumed in the taxpayer's operations;

(iv) Is a unit of property as determined under § 1.263(a)-3(e) that has an acquisition cost or production cost (as determined under section 263A) of $200 or less (or other amount as identified in published guidance in the Federal Register or in the Internal Revenue Bulletin (see § 601.601(d)(2)(ii)(*b*) of this chapter); or

(v) Is identified in published guidance in the Federal Register or in the Internal Revenue Bulletin (see § 601.601(d)(2)(ii)(*b*) of this chapter) as materials and supplies for which treatment is permitted under this section.

(2) *Rotable and temporary spare parts.*—For purposes of this section, rotable spare parts are materials and supplies under paragraph (c)(1)(i) of this section that are acquired for installation on a unit of property, removable

from that unit of property, generally repaired or improved, and either reinstalled on the same or other property or stored for later installation. Temporary spare parts are materials and supplies under paragraph (c)(1)(i) of this section that are used temporarily until a new or repaired part can be installed and then are removed and stored for later installation.

(3) *Standby emergency spare parts.*—Standby emergency spare parts are materials and supplies under paragraph (c)(1)(i) of this section that are—

(i) Acquired when particular machinery or equipment is acquired (or later acquired and set aside for use in particular machinery or equipment);

(ii) Set aside for use as replacements to avoid substantial operational time loss caused by emergencies due to particular machinery or equipment failure;

(iii) Located at or near the site of the installed related machinery or equipment so as to be readily available when needed;

(iv) Directly related to the particular machinery or piece of equipment they serve;

(v) Normally expensive;

(vi) Only available on special order and not readily available from a vendor or manufacturer;

(vii) Not subject to normal periodic replacement;

(viii) Not interchangeable in other machines or equipment;

(x) Not acquired in quantity (generally only one is on hand for each piece of machinery or equipment); and

(xi) Not repaired and reused.

(4) *Economic useful life.*—(i) *General rule.*—The economic useful life of a unit of property is not necessarily the useful life inherent in the property but is the period over which the property may reasonably be expected to be useful to the taxpayer or, if the taxpayer is engaged in a trade or business or an activity for the production of income, the period over which the property may reasonably be expected to be useful to the taxpayer in its trade or business or for the production of income, as applicable. The factors that must be considered in determining this period are provided under § 1.167(a)-1(b).

(ii) *Taxpayers with an applicable financial statement.*—For taxpayers with an applicable financial statement (as defined in paragraph (c)(4)(iii) of this section), the economic useful life of a unit of property, solely for the purposes of applying the provisions of this paragraph (c), is the useful life initially used by the taxpayer for purposes of determining depreciation in its applicable financial statement, regardless of any salvage value of the property. If a taxpayer does not have an applicable financial statement for the taxable year in which a unit of property was originally acquired or produced, the economic useful life of the unit of property must be determined under paragraph (c)(4)(i) of this section. Further, if a taxpayer treats amounts paid for a unit of property as an expense in its applicable financial statement on a basis other than the useful life of the property or if a taxpayer does not depreciate the unit of property on its applicable financial statement, the economic useful life of the unit of property must be determined under paragraph (c)(4)(i) of this section. For example, if a taxpayer has a policy of treating as an expense on its applicable financial statement amounts paid for a unit of property costing less than a certain dollar amount, notwithstanding that the unit of property has a useful life of more than one year, the economic useful life of the unit of property must be determined under paragraph (c)(4)(i) of this section.

(iii) *Definition of applicable financial statement.*—The taxpayer's applicable financial statement is the taxpayer's financial statement listed in paragraphs (c)(4)(iii)(A) through (C) of this section that has the highest priority (including within paragraph (c)(4)(iii)(B) of this section). The financial statements are, in descending priority—

(A) A financial statement required to be filed with the Securities and Exchange Commission (SEC) (the 10-K or the Annual Statement to Shareholders);

(B) A certified audited financial statement that is accompanied by the report of an independent certified public accountant (or in the case of a foreign entity, by the report of a similarly qualified independent professional), that is used for—

(1) Credit purposes;

(2) Reporting to shareholders, partners, or similar persons; or

(3) Any other substantial non-tax purpose; or

(C) A financial statement (other than a tax return) required to be provided to the federal or a state government or any federal or state agency (other than the SEC or the Internal Revenue Service).

(5) *Amount paid.*—For purposes of this section, in the case of a taxpayer using an accrual method of accounting, the terms *amount paid* and *payment* mean a liability incurred (within the meaning of § 1.446-1(c)(1)(ii)). A liability may not be taken into account under this section prior to the

taxable year during which the liability is incurred.

(6) *Produce.*—For purposes of this section, *produce* means construct, build, install, manufacture, develop, create, raise, or grow. This definition is intended to have the same meaning as the definition used for purposes of section 263A(g)(1) and § 1.263A-2(a)(1)(i), except that improvements are excluded from the definition in this paragraph (c)(6) and are separately defined and addressed in § 1.263(a)-3. Amounts paid to produce materials and supplies are subject to section 263A.

(d) *Election to capitalize and depreciate certain materials and supplies.*—(1) *In general.*—A taxpayer may elect to treat as a capital expenditure and to treat as an asset subject to the allowance for depreciation the cost of any rotable spare part, temporary spare part, or standby emergency spare part as defined in paragraph (c)(2) or (c)(3) of this section. Except as specified in paragraph (d)(2) of this section, an election made under this paragraph (d) applies to amounts paid during the taxable year to acquire or produce any rotable, temporary, or standby emergency spare part to which paragraph (a) of this section would apply (but for the election under this paragraph (d)). Any property for which this election is made shall not be treated as a material or a supply.

(2) *Exceptions.*—A taxpayer may not elect to capitalize and depreciate under this paragraph (d) any amount paid to acquire or produce a rotable, temporary, or standby emergency spare part defined in paragraph (c)(2) or (c)(3) of this section if—

(i) The rotable, temporary, or standby emergency spare part is intended to be used as a component of a unit of property under paragraph (c)(1)(iii), (iv), or (v) of this section;

(ii) The rotable, temporary, or standby emergency spare part is intended to be used as a component of a property described in paragraph (c)(1)(i) and the taxpayer cannot or has not elected to capitalize and depreciate that property under this paragraph (d); or

(iii) The amount is paid to acquire or produce a rotable or temporary spare part and the taxpayer uses the optional method of accounting for rotable and temporary spare parts under paragraph (e) to of this section.

(3) *Manner of electing.*—A taxpayer makes the election under this paragraph (d) by capitalizing the amounts paid to acquire or produce a rotable, temporary, or standby emergency spare part in the taxable year the amounts are paid and by beginning to depreciate the costs when the asset is placed in service by the taxpayer for purposes of determining depreciation under the applicable provisions of the Internal Revenue Code and the Treasury Regulations. Section 1.263(a)-2 provides for the treatment of amounts paid to acquire or produce real or personal tangible property. A taxpayer must make the election under this paragraph (d) in its timely filed original Federal tax return (including extensions) for the taxable year the asset is placed in service by the taxpayer for purposes of determining depreciation. Sections 301.9100-1 through 301.9100-3 of this chapter provide the rules governing extensions of the time to make regulatory elections. In the case of an S corporation or a partnership, the election is made by the S corporation or partnership, and not by the shareholders or partners. A taxpayer may make an election for each rotable, temporary, or standby emergency spare part that qualifies for the election under this paragraph (d). This election does not apply to an asset or a portion thereof placed in service and disposed of in the same taxable year. A taxpayer may revoke an election made under this paragraph (d) or made under § 1.162-3T(d), as contained in 26 CFR part 1, revised as of April 1, 2013, only by filing a request for a private letter ruling and obtaining the Commissioner's consent to revoke the election. The Commissioner may grant a request to revoke this election if the taxpayer acted reasonably and in good faith and the revocation will not prejudice the interests of the Government. See generally § 301.9100-3 of this chapter. The manner of electing and revoking the election to capitalize under this paragraph (d) or under § 1.162-3T(d), as contained in 26 CFR part 1, revised as of April 1, 2013, may be modified through guidance of general applicability (see §§ 601.601(d)(2) and 601.602 of this chapter). An election may not be made or revoked through the filing of an application for change in accounting method or, before obtaining the Commissioner's consent to make the late election or to revoke the election, by filing an amended Federal tax return.

(e) *Optional method of accounting for rotable and temporary spare parts.*—(1) *In general.*—This paragraph (e) provides an optional method of accounting for rotable and temporary spare parts (the optional method for rotable parts). A taxpayer may use the optional method for rotable parts, instead of the general rule under paragraph (a)(3) of this section, to account for its rotable and temporary spare parts as defined in paragraph (c)(2) of this section. A taxpayer that uses the optional method for rotable parts must use this method for all of its pools of rotable and temporary spare parts used in the same trade or business and for which it uses this method for its books and records. If a taxpayer uses the optional method for rotable parts for pools of rotable and temporary spare parts for which the taxpayer does not use the optional method for its books and records, then the taxpayer must use the optional method for all its pools in the same trade or business, whether rotable or temporary. The optional method for rotable parts is a method of accounting under section 446(a). Under the optional method for rotable parts, the taxpayer must apply the rules in this paragraph (e) to each rotable or temporary spare part (part) upon the taxpayer's initial installation, removal, repair, maintenance or improvement, reinstallation, and disposal of each part.

(2) *Description of optional method for rotable parts.*—(i) *Initial installation.*—The taxpayer must deduct the amount paid to acquire or produce the part in the taxable year that the part is first installed on a unit of property for use in the taxpayer's operations.

(ii) *Removal from unit of property.*—In each taxable year in which the part is removed from a unit of property to which it was initially or subsequently installed, the taxpayer must—

(A) Include in gross income the fair market value of the part; and

(B) Include in the basis of the part the fair market value of the part included in income under paragraph (e)(2)(ii)(A) of this section and the amount paid to remove the part from the unit of property.

(iii) *Repair, maintenance, or improvement of part.*—The taxpayer may not currently deduct and must include in the basis of the part any amounts paid to maintain, repair, or improve the part in the taxable year these amounts are paid.

(iv) *Reinstallation of part.*—The taxpayer must deduct the amounts paid to reinstall the part and those amounts included in the basis of the part under paragraphs (e)(2)(ii)(B) and (e)(2)(iii) of this section, to the extent that those amounts have not been previously deducted under this paragraph (e)(2)(iv), in the taxable year that the part is reinstalled on a unit of property.

(v) *Disposal of the part.*—The taxpayer must deduct the amounts included in the basis of the part under paragraphs (e)(2)(ii)(B) and (e)(2)(iii) of this section, to the extent that those amounts have not been previously deducted under paragraph (e)(2)(iv) of this section, in the taxable year in which the part is disposed of by the taxpayer.

(f) *Application of de minimis safe harbor.*—If a taxpayer elects to apply the de minimis safe harbor under §1.263(a)-1(f) to amounts paid for the production or acquisition of tangible property, then the taxpayer must apply the de minimis safe harbor to amounts paid for all materials and supplies that meet the requirements of §1.263(a)-1(f), except for those materials and supplies that the taxpayer elects to capitalize and depreciate under paragraph (d) of this section or for which the taxpayer properly uses the optional method of accounting for rotable and temporary spare parts under paragraph (e) of this section. If the taxpayer properly applies the de minimis safe harbor under §1.263(a)-1(f) to amounts paid for materials and supplies, then these amounts are not treated as amounts paid for materials and supplies under this section. See §1.263(a)-1(f)(5) for the time and manner of electing the de minimis safe harbor and §1.263(a)-1(f)(3)(iv) for the treatment of safe harbor amounts.

(g) *Sale or disposition of materials and supplies.*—Upon sale or other disposition, materials and supplies as defined in this section are not treated as a capital asset under section 1221 or as property used in the trade or business under section 1231. Any asset for which the taxpayer makes the election to capitalize and depreciate under paragraph (d) of this section shall not be treated as a material or supply, and the recognition and character of the gain or loss for such depreciable asset are determined under other applicable provisions of the Code.

* * *

[Reg. §1.162-3.]

☐ [*T.D.* 6291, 4-3-58. *Amended by T.D.* 9564, 12-23-2011 (*corrected* 3-27-2012) *and T.D.* 9636, 9-13-2013 (*corrected* 7-18-2014).]

§1.162-4. Repairs.—(a) *In general.*—A taxpayer may deduct amounts paid for repairs and maintenance to tangible property if the amounts paid are not otherwise required to be capitalized. Optionally, §1.263(a)-3(n) provides an election to capitalize amounts paid for repair and maintenance consistent with the taxpayer's books and records.

* * *

[Reg. §1.162-4.]

☐ [*T.D.* 6291, 4-3-58. *Amended by T.D.* 9564, 12-23-2011 *and T.D.* 9636, 9-13-2013 (*corrected* 7-18-2014).]

§1.162-5. Expenses for education.—(a) *General rule.*—Expenditures made by an individual for education (including research undertaken as part of his educational program) which are not expenditures of a type described in paragraph (b)(2) or (3) of this section are deductible as ordinary and necessary business expenses (even though the education may lead to a degree) if the education—

(1) Maintains or improves skills required by the individual in his employment or other trade or business, or

(2) Meets the express requirements of the individual's employer, or the requirements of applicable law or regulations, imposed as a condition to the retention by the individual of an established employment relationship, status, or rate of compensation.

(b) *Nondeductible educational expenditures.*—(1) *In general.*—Educational expenditures described in subparagraphs (2) and (3) of this paragraph are personal expenditures or constitute an inseparable aggregate of personal and capital expenditures and, therefore, are not deductible as ordinary and necessary business expenses even though the education may maintain or improve skills required by the individual in his employment or other trade or business or may meet the express requirements of the individual's employer or of applicable law or regulations.

(2) *Minimum educational requirements.*—(i) The first category of nondeductible educational expenses within the scope of subparagraph (1) of this paragraph are expenditures made by an individual for education which is required of him in order to meet the minimum educational requirements for qualification in his employment or other trade or business. The minimum education necessary to qualify for a position or other trade or business must be determined from a consideration of such factors as the requirements of the employer, the applicable law and regulations, and the standards of the profession, trade, or business involved. The fact that an individual is already performing service in an employment status does not establish that he has met the minimum educational requirements for qualification in that employment. Once an individual has met the minimum educational requirements for qualification in his employment or other trade or business (as in effect when he enters the employment or trade or business), he shall be treated as continuing to meet those requirements even though they are changed.

(ii) The minimum educational requirements for qualification of a particular individual in a position in an educational institution is the minimum level of education (in terms of aggregate college hours or degree) which under the applicable laws or regulations, in effect at the time this individual is first employed in such position, is normally required of an individual initially being employed in such a position. If there are no normal requirements as to the minimum level of education required for a position in an educational institution, then an individual in such a position shall be considered to have met the minimum educational requirements for qualification in that position when he becomes a member of the faculty of the educational institution. The determination of whether an individual is a member of the faculty of an educational institution must be made on the basis of the particular practices of the institution. However, an individual will ordinarily be considered to be a member of the faculty of an institution if (*a*) he has tenure or his years of service are being counted toward obtaining tenure; (*b*) the institution is making contributions to a retirement plan (other than Social Security or a similar program) in respect of his employment; or (*c*) he has a vote in faculty affairs.

(iii) The application of this subparagraph may be illustrated by the following examples:

Example (1). *General facts:* State X requires a bachelor's degree for beginning secondary school teachers which must include 30 credit hours of professional educational courses. In addition, in order to retain his position, a secondary school teacher must complete a fifth year of preparation within 10 years after beginning his employment. If an employing school official certifies to the State Department of Education that applicants having a bachelor's degree and the required courses in professional education cannot be found, he may hire individuals as secondary school teachers if they have completed a minimum of 90 semester hours of college work. However, to be retained in his position, such an individual must obtain his bachelor's degree and complete the required professional educational courses within 3 years after his employment commences. Under these facts, a bachelor's degree, without regard to whether it includes 30 credit hours of professional educational courses, is considered to be the minimum educational requirement for qualification as a secondary school teacher in State X. This is the case notwithstanding the number of teachers who are actually hired without such a degree. The following are examples of the application of these facts in particular situations:

Situation 1. A, at the time he is employed as a secondary school teacher in State X, has a bachelor's degree including 30 credit hours of professional educational courses. After his employment, A completes a fifth college year of education and, as a result, is issued a standard certificate. The fifth college year of education undertaken by A is not education required to meet the minimum educational requirements for qualification as a secondary school teacher. Accordingly, the expenditures for such education are deductible unless the expenditures are for education which is part of a program of study being pursued by A which will lead to qualifying him in a new trade or business.

Situation 2. Because of a shortage of applicants meeting the stated requirements, B, who has a bachelor's degree, is employed as a secondary school teacher in State X even though he has only 20 credit hours of professional educational courses. After his employment, B takes an additional 10 credit hours of professional educational courses. Since these courses do not constitute education required to meet the minimum educational requirements for qualification as a secondary school teacher which is a bachelor's degree and will not lead to qualifying B in a new trade or business, the expenditures for such courses are deductible.

Situation 3. Because of a shortage of applicants meeting the requirements, C is employed as a secondary school teacher in State X although he has only 90 semester hours of college work towards his bachelor's degree. After his employment, C undertakes courses leading to a bachelor's degree. These courses (including any courses in professional education) constitute education required to meet the minimum educational requirements for qualification as a secondary school teacher. Accordingly, the expenditures for such education are not deductible.

Situation 4. Subsequent to the employment of A, B, and C, but before they have completed a fifth college year of education, State X changes its requirements affecting secondary school teachers to provide that beginning teachers must have completed 5 college years of preparation. In the cases of A, B, and C, a fifth college year of education is not considered to be education undertaken to meet the minimum educational requirements for qualification as a secondary school teacher. Accordingly, expenditures for a fifth year of college will be deductible unless the expenditures are for education which is part of a program being pursued by A, B, or C which will lead to qualifying him in a new trade or business.

Example (2). D, who holds a bachelor's degree, obtains temporary employment as an instructor at University Y and undertakes graduate courses as a candidate for a graduate degree. D may become a faculty member only if he obtains a graduate degree and may continue to hold a position as instructor only so long as he shows satisfactory progress towards obtaining this graduate degree. The graduate courses taken by D constitute education required to meet the minimum educational requirements for qualification in D's trade or business and, thus, the expenditures for such courses are not deductible.

Example (3). E, who has completed 2 years of a normal 3-year law school course leading to a bachelor of laws degree (LL.B.), is hired by a law firm to do legal research and perform other functions on a full-time basis. As a condition to continued employment, E is required to obtain an LL.B. and pass the State bar examination. E completes his law school education by attending night law school, and he takes a bar review course in order to prepare for the State bar examination. The law courses and bar review course constitute education required to meet the minimum educational requirements for qualification in E's trade or business and, thus, the expenditures for such courses are not deductible.

(3) *Qualification for new trade or business.*—(i) The second category of nondeductible educational expenses within the scope of subparagraph (1) of this paragraph are expenditures made by an individual for education which is part of a program of study being pursued by him which will lead to qualifying him in a new trade or business. In the case of an employee, a change of duties does not constitute a new trade or business if the new duties involve the same general type of work as is involved in the individual's present employment. For this purpose, all teaching and related duties shall be considered to involve the same general type of work. The following are examples of changes in duties which do not constitute new trades or businesses:

(a) Elementary to secondary school classroom teacher.

(b) Classroom teacher in one subject (such as mathematics) to classroom teacher in another subject (such as science).

(c) Classroom teacher to guidance counselor.

(d) Classroom teacher to principal.

(ii) The application of this subparagraph to individuals other than teachers may be illustrated by the following examples:

Example (1). A, a self-employed individual practicing a profession other than law, for example, engineering, accounting, etc., attends law school at night and after completing his law school studies receives a bachelor of laws degree. The expenditures made by A in attending law school are nondeductible because this course of study qualifies him for a new trade or business.

Example (2). Assume the same facts as in example (1) except that A has the status of an employee rather than a self-employed individual, and that his employer requires him to obtain a bachelor of laws degree. A intends to continue practicing his nonlegal profession as an employee of such employer. Nevertheless, the expenditures made by A in attending law school are not deductible since this course of study qualifies him for a new trade or business.

Example (3). B, a general practitioner of medicine, takes a 2-week course reviewing new developments in several specialized fields of medicine. B's expenses for the course are deductible because the course maintains or improves skills required by him in his trade or business and does not qualify him for a new trade or business.

Example (4). C, while engaged in the private practice of psychiatry, undertakes a program of study and training at an accredited psychoanalytic institute which will lead to qualifying him to practice psychoanalysis. C's expenditures for such study and training are deductible because the study and training maintains or improves skills required by him in his trade or business and does not qualify him for a new trade or business.

(c) *Deductible educational expenditures.*—(1) *Maintaining or improving skills.*—The deduction under the category of expenditures for education which maintains or improves skills required by the individual in his employment or other trade or business includes refresher courses or courses dealing with current developments as well as academic or vocational courses provided the expenditures for the courses are not within either category of nondeductible expenditures described in paragraph (b) (2) or (3) of this section.

(2) *Meeting requirements of employer.*—An individual is considered to have undertaken education in order to meet the express requirements of his employer, or the requirements of applicable law or regulations, imposed as a condition to the retention by the taxpayer of his established employment relationship, status, or rate of compensation only if such requirements are imposed for a bona fide business purpose of the individual's employer. Only the minimum education necessary to the retention by the individual of his established employment relationship, status, or rate of compensation may be considered as undertaken to meet the express requirements of the taxpayer's employer. However, education in excess of such minimum education may qualify as education undertaken in order to maintain or improve the skills required by the taxpayer in his employment or other trade or business (see subparagraph (1) of this paragraph). In no event, however, is a deduction allowable for expenditures for education which, even though for education required by the employer or applicable law or regulations, are within one of the categories of nondeductible expenditures described in paragraph (b)(2) and (3) of this section.

* * *

(e) *Travel away from home.*—(1) If an individual travels away from home primarily to obtain education the expenses of which are deductible under this section, his expenditures for travel, meals, and lodging while away from home are deductible. However, if as an incident of such trip the individual engages in some personal activity such as sightseeing, social visiting, or entertaining, or other recreation, the portion of the expenses attributable to such personal activity constitutes nondeductible personal or living expenses and is not allowable as a deduction. If the individual's travel away from home is primarily personal, the individual's expenditures for travel, meals and lodging (other than meals and lodging during the time spent in participating in deductible educational pursuits) are not deductible. Whether a particular trip is primarily personal or primarily to obtain education the expenses of which are deductible under this section depends upon all the facts and circumstances of each case. An important factor to be taken into consideration in making the determination is the relative amount of time devoted to personal activity as compared with the time devoted to educational pursuits. The rules set forth in this paragraph are subject to the provisions of section 162(a)(2), relating to deductibility of certain traveling expenses, and section 274(c) and (d), relating to allocation of certain foreign travel expenses and substantiation required, respectively, and the regulations thereunder.

(2) *Examples.*—The application of this subsection may be illustrated by the following examples:

Example (1). A, a self-employed tax practitioner, decides to take a 1-week course in new developments in taxation, which is offered in City X, 500 miles away from his home. His primary purpose in going to X is to take the course, but he also takes a side trip to City Y (50 miles from X) for 1 day, takes a sightseeing trip while in X, and entertains some personal friends. A's transportation expenses to City X and return to his home are deductible but his transportation expenses to City Y are not deductible. A's expenses for meals and lodging while away from home will be allocated between his educational pursuits and his personal activities. Those expenses which are entirely personal, such as sightseeing and entertaining friends, are not deductible to any extent.

Example (2). The facts are the same as in example (1) except that A's primary purpose in going to City X is to take a vacation. This purpose is indicated by several factors, one of which is the fact that he spends only 1 week attending the tax course and devotes 5 weeks entirely to personal activities. None of A's transportation expenses are deductible and his expenses for meals and lodging while away from home are not deductible to the extent attributable to personal activities. His expenses for meals and lodging allocable to the week attending the tax course are, however, deductible.

Example (3). B, a high school mathematics teacher in New York City, in the summertime travels to a university in California in order to take a mathematics course the expense of which is deductible under this section. B pursues only one-fourth of a full course of study and the remainder of her time is devoted to personal activities the expense of which is not deductible. Absent a showing by B of a substantial nonpersonal reason for taking the course in the university in California, the trip is considered taken primarily for personal reasons and the cost of traveling from New York City to California and return would not be deductible. However, one-fourth of the cost of B's meals and lodging while attending the university in California may be considered properly allocable to deductible educational pursuits and, therefore, is deductible. [Reg. § 1.162-5.]

☐ [*T.D.* 6291, 4-3-58. *Amended by T.D.* 6918, 5-1-67.]

§ 1.162-7. Compensation for personal services.—(a) There may be included among the ordinary and necessary expenses paid or incurred in carrying on any trade or business a reasonable allowance for salaries or other compensation for personal services actually rendered. The test of deductibility in the case of compensation payments is whether they are reasonable and are in fact payments purely for services.

(b) The test set forth in paragraph (a) of this section and its practical application may be further stated and illustrated as follows:

(1) Any amount paid in the form of compensation, but not in fact as the purchase price of services is not deductible. An ostensible salary paid by a corporation may be a distribution of a dividend on stock. This is likely to occur in the case of a corporation having few shareholders, practically all of whom draw salaries. If in such a case the salaries are in excess of those ordinarily paid for similar services and the excessive payments correspond or bear a close relationship to the stockholdings of the officers or employees, it would seem likely that the salaries are not paid wholly for services rendered, but that the excessive payments are a distribution of earnings upon the stock. An ostensible salary may be in part payment for property. This may occur, for example, where a partnership sells out to a corporation, the former partners agreeing to continue in the service of the corporation. In such a case it may be found that the salaries of the former partners are not merely for services, but in part constitute payment for the transfer of their business.

(2) The form or method of fixing compensation is not decisive as to deductibility. While any form of contingent compensation invites scrutiny as a possible distribution of earnings of the enterprise, it does not follow that payments on a contingent basis are to be treated fundamentally on any basis different from that applying to compensation at a flat rate. Generally speaking, if contingent compensation is paid pursuant to a free bargain between the employer and the individual made before the services are rendered, not influenced by any consideration on the part of the employer other than that of securing on fair and advantageous terms the services of the individual, it should be allowed as a deduction even though in the actual working out of the contract it may prove to be greater than the amount which would ordinarily be paid.

(3) In any event the allowance for the compensation paid may not exceed what is reasonable under all the circumstances. It is, in general, just to assume that reasonable and true compensation is only such amount as would ordinarily be paid for like services by like enterprises under like circumstances. The circumstances to be taken into consideration are those existing at the date when the contract for services was made, not those existing at the date when the contract is questioned.

(4) For disallowance of deduction in the case of certain transfers of stock pursuant to employees stock options, see section 421 and the regulations thereunder. [Reg. § 1.162-7.]

☐ [*T.D.* 6291, 4-3-58.]

§ 1.162-8. Treatment of excessive compensation.—The income tax liability of the recipient in respect of an amount ostensibly paid to him as compensation, but not allowed to be deducted as such by the payor, will depend upon the circumstances of each case. Thus, in the case of excessive payments by corporations, if such payments correspond or bear a close relationship to stockholders, and are found to be a distribution of earnings or profits, the excessive payments will be treated as a dividend. If such payments constitute payment for property, they should be treated by the payor as a capital expenditure and by the recipient as part of the purchase price. In the absence of evidence to justify other treatment, excessive payments for salaries or other compensation for personal services will be included in gross income of the recipient. [Reg. § 1.162-8.]

☐ [*T.D.* 6291, 4-3-58.]

§ 1.162-9. Bonuses to employees.—Bonuses to employees will constitute allowable deductions from gross income when such payments are made in good faith and as additional compensation for the services actually rendered by the employees, provided such payments, when added to the stipulated salaries, do not exceed a reasonable compensation for the services rendered. It is immaterial whether such bonuses are paid in cash or in kind or partly in cash and partly in kind. Donations made to employees and others, which do not have in them the element of compensation or which are in excess of reasonable compensation for services, are not deductible from gross income. [Reg. § 1.162-9.]

☐ [*T.D.* 6291, 4-3-58.]

§ 1.162-11. Rentals.—(a) *Acquisition of a leasehold.*—If a leasehold is acquired for business purposes for a specified sum, the purchaser may take as a deduction in his return an aliquot part of such sum each year, based on the number of years the lease has to run. Taxes paid by a tenant to or for a landlord for business property are additional rent and constitute a deductible item to the tenant and taxable income to the landlord, the amount of the tax being deductible by the latter. For disallowance of deduction for income taxes paid by a lessee corporation pursuant to a lease arrangement with the lessor corporation, see section 110 and the regulations thereunder. See section 178 and the regulations thereunder for rules governing the effect to be given renewal options in amortizing the costs incurred after July 28, 1958, of acquiring a lease. See § 1.197-2 for rules governing the amortization of costs to acquire limited interests in section 197 intangibles.

(b) *Improvements by lessee on lessor's property.*—(1) *In general.*—The cost to a taxpayer of erecting buildings or making permanent improvements on property of which the taxpayer is a lessee is a capital expenditure. For the rules regarding improvements to leased property when the improvements are tangible property, see § 1.263(a)-3(f). For the rules regarding depreciation or amortization deductions for leasehold improvements, see § 1.167(a)-4.

* * *

[Reg. § 1.162-11.]

☐ [*T.D.* 6291, 4-3-58. *Amended by T.D.* 6520, 12-30-60; *T.D.* 8865, 1-20-2000; *T.D.* 9564, 12-23-2011 *and T.D.* 9636, 9-13-2013.]

§ 1.162-15. Contributions, dues, etc.—(a) *Contributions to organizations described in section 170.*—(1) *In general.*—No deduction is allowable under section 162(a) for a contribution or gift by an individual or a corporation if any part thereof is deductible under section 170. For example, if a taxpayer makes a contribution of $5,000 and only $4,000 of this amount is deductible under section 170(a) (whether because of the percentage limitation under either section 170(b)(1) or (2), the requirement as to time of payment, or both) no deduction is allowable under section 162(a) for the remaining $1,000.

(2) *Scope of limitations.*—The limitations provided in section 162(b) and this paragraph apply only to payments which are in fact contributions or gifts to organizations described in section 170. For example, payments by a transit company to a local hospital (which is a charitable organization within the meaning of section 170) in consideration of a binding obligation on the part of the hospital to provide hospital services and facilities for the company's employees are not contributions or gifts within the meaning of section 170 and may be deductible under section 162(a) if the requirements of section 162(a) are otherwise satisfied.

(b) *Other contributions.*—Donations to organizations other than those described in section 170 which bear a direct relationship to the taxpayer's business and are made with a reasonable expectation of a financial return commensurate with the amount of the donation may constitute allowable deductions as business expenses, provided the donation is not made for a purpose for which a deduction is not allowable by reason of the provisions of paragraph (b)(1)(i) or (c) of § 1.162-20. For example, a transit company may donate a sum of money to an organization (of a class not referred to in section 170) intending to hold a convention in the city in which it operates, with a reasonable expectation that the holding of such convention will augment its income through a greater number of people using its transportation facilities.

(c) *Dues.*—Dues and other payments to an organization, such as a labor union or a trade association, which otherwise meet the requirements of the regulations under section 162, are deductible in full. For limitations on the deductibility of dues and other payments, see paragraph (b) and (c) of § 1.162-20.

(d) *Cross reference.*—For provisions dealing with expenditures for institutional or "good will" advertising, see § 1.162-20. [Reg. § 1.162-15.]

☐ [*T.D.* 6291, 4-3-58. *Amended by T.D.* 6435, 12-28-59 *and T.D.* 6819, 4-19-65.]

Proposed Amendments to Regulation

§ 1.162-15. Contributions, dues, etc.—(a) *Payments and transfers to entities described in section 170(c).*—(1) *In general.*—A payment or transfer to or for the use of an entity described in section 170(c) that bears a direct relationship to the taxpayer's trade or business and that is made with a reasonable expectation of financial return commensurate with the amount of the payment or transfer may constitute an allowable deduction as a trade or business expense rather than a charitable contribution deduction under section 170. For payments or transfers in excess of the amount deductible under section 162(a), see § 1.170A-1(h).

(2) *Examples.*—The following examples illustrate the rules of paragraph (a)(1) of this section:

(i) *Example 1. A,* an individual, is a sole proprietor who manufactures musical instruments and sells them through a website. *A* makes a $1,000 payment to a local church (which is a charitable organization described in section 170(c)) for a half-page advertisement in the church's program for a concert. In the program, the church thanks its concert sponsors, including *A. A*'s advertisement includes the URL for the website through which *A* sells its instruments. *A* reasonably expects that the advertisement will attract new customers to *A*'s website and will help *A* to sell more musical instruments. *A* may treat the $1,000 payment as an expense of carrying on a trade or business under section 162.

(ii) *Example 2. P,* a partnership, operates a chain of supermarkets, some of which are located in State N. *P* operates a promotional program in which it sets aside the proceeds from one percent of its sales each year, which it pays to one or more charities described in section 170(c). The funds are earmarked for use in projects that improve conditions in State N. *P* makes the final determination on which charities receive payments. *P* advertises the program. *P* reasonably believes the program will generate a significant degree of name recognition and goodwill in the communities where it operates and thereby increase its revenue. As part of the program, *P* makes a $1,000 payment to a charity described in section 170(c). *P* may treat the $1,000 payment as an expense of carrying on a trade or business under section 162. This result is unchanged if, under State N's tax credit program, *P* expects to receive a $1,000 income tax credit on account of *P*'s payment, and under State N law, the credit can be passed through to *P*'s partners.

(3) *Safe harbors for C corporations and specified passthrough entities making payments in exchange for state or local tax credits.*—(i) *Safe harbor for C corporations.*—If a C corporation makes a payment to or for the use of an entity described in section 170(c) and receives or expects to receive in return a state or local tax credit that reduces a state or local tax imposed on the C corporation, the C corporation may treat such payment as meeting the requirements of an ordinary and necessary business expense for purposes of section 162(a) to the extent of the amount of the credit received or expected to be received.

(ii) *Safe harbor for specified passthrough entities.*—(A) *Definition of specified passthrough entity.*—For purposes of this paragraph (a)(3)(ii), an entity is a specified passthrough entity if each of the following requirements is satisfied—

(1) The entity is a business entity other than a C corporation and is regarded for all Federal income tax purposes as separate from its owners under § 301.7701-3 of this chapter;

(2) The entity operates a trade or business within the meaning of section 162;

(3) The entity is subject to a state or local tax incurred in carrying on its trade or business that is imposed directly on the entity; and

(4) In return for a payment to an entity described in section 170(c), the entity described in paragraph (a)(3)(ii)(A)(*1*) of this section receives or expects to receive a state or local tax credit that this entity applies or expects to apply to offset a state or local tax described in paragraph (a)(3)(ii)(A)(*3*) of this section.

(B) *Safe harbor.*—Except as provided in paragraph (a)(3)(ii)(C) of this section, if a specified passthrough entity makes a payment to or for the use of an entity described in section 170(c), and receives or expects to receive in return a state or local tax credit that reduces a state or local tax described in paragraph (a)(3)(ii)(A)(*3*) of this section, the specified passthrough entity may treat such payment as meeting the requirements of an ordinary and necessary business expense for purposes of section 162(a) to the extent of the amount of credit received or expected to be received.

(C) *Exception.*—The safe harbor described in this paragraph (a)(3)(ii) does not apply if the credit received or expected to be received reduces a state or local income tax.

(iii) *Definition of payment.*—For purposes of this paragraph (a)(3), payment is defined as a payment of cash or cash equivalent.

(iv) *Examples.*—The following examples illustrate the rules of paragraph (a)(3) of this section.

(A) *Example 1: C corporation that receives or expects to receive dollar-for-dollar state or local tax credit. A,* a C corporation engaged in a trade or business, makes a payment of $1,000 to an entity described in section 170(c). In return for the payment, *A* expects to receive a dollar-for-dollar state tax credit to be applied to *A*'s state corporate income tax liability. Under paragraph (a)(3)(i) of this section, *A* may treat the $1,000 payment as an expense of carrying on a trade or business under section 162.

(B) *Example 2: C corporation that receives or expects to receive percentage-based state or local tax credit. B*, a C corporation engaged in a trade or business, makes a payment of $1,000 to an entity described in section 170(c). In return for the payment, *B* expects to receive a local tax credit equal to 80 percent of the amount of this payment ($800) to be applied to *B*'s local real property tax liability. Under paragraph (a)(3)(i) of this section, *B* may treat $800 as an expense of carrying on a trade or business under section 162. The treatment of the remaining $200 will depend upon the facts and circumstances and is not affected by paragraph (a)(3)(i) of this section.

(C) *Example 3: Partnership that receives or expects to receive dollar-for-dollar state or local tax credit. P* is a limited liability company classified as a partnership for Federal income tax purposes under § 301.7701-3 of this chapter. *P* is engaged in a trade or business and makes a payment of $1,000 to an entity described in section 170(c). In return for the payment, *P* expects to receive a dollar-for-dollar state tax credit to be applied to *P*'s state excise tax liability incurred by *P* in carrying on its trade or business. Under applicable state law, the state's excise tax is imposed at the entity level (not the owner level). Under paragraph (a)(3)(ii) of this section, *P* may treat the $1,000 as an expense of carrying on a trade or business under section 162.

(D) *Example 4: S corporation that receives or expects to receive percentage-based state or local tax credit. S* is an S corporation engaged in a trade or business and is owned by individuals *C* and *D*. *S* makes a payment of $1,000 to an entity described in section 170(c). In return for the payment, *S* expects to receive a local tax credit equal to 80 percent of the amount of this payment ($800) to be applied to *S*'s local real property tax liability incurred by *S* in carrying on its trade or business. Under applicable state and local law, the real property tax is imposed at the entity level (not the owner level). Under paragraph (a)(3)(ii) of this section, *S* may treat $800 of the payment as an expense of carrying on a trade or business under section 162. The treatment of the remaining $200 will depend upon the facts and circumstances and is not affected by paragraph (a)(3)(ii) of this section.

(v) *Applicability of section 170 to payments in exchange for state or local tax benefits.*—For rules regarding the availability of a charitable contribution deduction under section 170 where a taxpayer makes a payment or transfers property to or for the use of an entity described in section 170(c) and receives or expects to receive a state or local tax benefit in return for such payment, see § 1.170A-1(h)(3).

* * *

[Prop. Reg. § 1.162-15.]

[Proposed 12-17-2019.]

§ 1.162-17. Reporting and substantiation of certain business expenses of employees.—(a) *Introductory.*—The purpose of the regulations in this section is to provide rules for the reporting of information on income tax returns by taxpayers who pay or incur ordinary and necessary business expenses in connection with the performance of services as an employee and to furnish guidance as to the type of records which will be useful in compiling such information and in its substantiation, if required. The rules prescribed in this section do not apply to expenses paid or incurred for incidentals, such as office supplies for the employer or local transportation in connection with an errand. Employees incurring such incidental expenses are not required to provide substantiation for such amounts. The term "ordinary and necessary business expenses" means only those expenses which are ordinary and necessary in the conduct of the taxpayer's business and are directly attributable to such business. The term does not include nondeductible personal, living or family expenses.

(b) *Expenses for which the employee is required to account to his employer.*—(1) *Reimbursements equal to expenses.*—The employee need not report on his tax return (either itemized or in total amount) expenses for travel, transportation, entertainment, and similar purposes paid or incurred by him solely for the benefit of his employer for which he is required to account and does account to his employer and which are charged directly or indirectly to the employer (for example, through credit cards) or for which the employee is paid through advances, reimbursements, or otherwise, provided the total amount of such advances, reimbursements, and charges is equal to such expenses. In such a case the taxpayer need only state in his return that the total of amounts charged directly or indirectly to his employer through credit cards or otherwise and received from the employer as advances or reimbursements did not exceed the ordinary and necessary business expenses paid or incurred by the employee.

(2) *Reimbursements in excess of expenses.*—In case the total of amounts charged directly or indirectly to the employer and received from the employer as advances, reimbursements, or otherwise, exceeds the ordinary and necessary business expenses paid or incurred by the employee and the employee is required to and

does account to his employer for such expenses, the taxpayer must include such excess in income and state on his return that he has done so.

(3) *Expenses in excess of reimbursements.*—If the employee's ordinary and necessary business expenses exceed the total of the amounts charged directly or indirectly to the employer and received from the employer as advances, reimbursements, or otherwise, and the employee is required to and does account to his employer for such expenses, the taxpayer may make the statement in his return required by subparagraph (1) of this paragraph unless he wishes to claim a deduction for such excess. If, however, he wishes to secure a deduction for such excess, he must submit a statement showing the following information as part of his tax return:

(i) The total of any charges paid or borne by the employer and of any other amounts received from the employer for payment of expenses, whether by means of advances, reimbursements or otherwise; and

(ii) The nature of his occupation, the number of days away from home on business, and the total amount of ordinary and necessary business expenses paid or incurred by him (including those charged directly or indirectly to the employer through credit cards or otherwise) broken down into such broad categories as transportation, meals and lodging while away from home overnight, entertainment expenses, and other business expenses.

(4) To "account" to his employer as used in this section means to submit an expense account or other required written statement to the employer showing the business nature and the amount of all the employee's expenses (including those charged directly or indirectly to the employer through credit cards or otherwise) broken down into such broad categories as transportation, meals and lodging while away from home overnight, entertainment expenses, and other business expenses. For this purpose, the Commissioner in his discretion may approve reasonable business practices under which mileage, per diem in lieu of subsistence, and similar allowances providing for ordinary and necessary business expenses in accordance with a fixed scale may be regarded as equivalent to an accounting to the employer.

(c) *Expenses for which the employee is not required to account to his employer.*—If the employee is not required to account to his employer for his ordinary and necessary business expenses, e.g., travel, transportation, entertainment, and similar items, or, though required, fails to account for such expenses, he must submit, as a part of his tax return, a statement showing the following information:

(1) The total of all amounts received as advances or reimbursements from his employer in connection with the ordinary and necessary business expenses of the employee, including amounts charged directly or indirectly to the employer through credit cards or otherwise; and

(2) The nature of his occupation, the number of days away from home on business, and the total amount of ordinary and necessary business expenses paid or incurred by him (including those charged directly or indirectly to the employer through credit cards or otherwise) broken down into such broad categories as transportation, meals and lodging while away from home overnight, entertainment expenses, and other business expenses.

(d) *Substantiation of items of expense.*—(1) Although the Commissioner may require any taxpayer to substantiate such information concerning expense accounts as may appear to be pertinent in determining tax liability, taxpayers ordinarily will not be called upon to substantiate expense account information except those in the following categories:

(i) A taxpayer who is not required to account to his employer, or who does not account;

(ii) A taxpayer whose expenses exceed the total of amounts charged to his employer and amounts received through advances, reimbursements or otherwise and who claims a deduction on his return for such excess;

(iii) A taxpayer who is related to his employer within the meaning of section 267(b); and

(iv) Other taxpayers in cases where it is determined that the accounting procedures used by the employer for the reporting and substantiation of expenses by employees are not adequate.

(2) The Code contemplates that taxpayers keep such records as will be sufficient to enable the Commissioner to correctly determine income tax liability. Accordingly, it is to the advantage of taxpayers who may be called upon to substantiate expense account information to maintain as adequate and detailed records of travel, transportation, entertainment, and similar business expenses as practical since the burden of proof is upon the taxpayer to show that such expenses were not only paid or incurred but also that they constitute ordinary and necessary business expenses. One method for substantiating expenses incurred by an employee in connection with his employment is through the preparation of a daily diary or record of expenditures, maintained in sufficient detail to enable him to readily identify the

amount and nature of any expenditure, and the preservation of supporting documents, especially in connection with large or exceptional expenditures. Nevertheless, it is recognized that by reason of the nature of certain expenses or the circumstances under which they are incurred, it is often difficult for an employee to maintain detailed records or to preserve supporting documents for all his expenses. Detailed records of small expenditures incurred in traveling or for transportation, as for example, tips, will not be required.

(3) Where records are incomplete or documentary proof is unavailable, it may be possible to establish the amount of the expenditures by approximations based upon reliable secondary sources of information and collateral evidence. For example, in connection with an item of traveling expense a taxpayer might establish that he was in a travel status a certain number of days but that it was impracticable for him to establish the details of all his various items of travel expense. In such a case rail fares or plane fares can usually be ascertained with exactness and automobile costs approximated on the basis of mileage covered. A reasonable approximation of meals and lodging might be based upon receipted hotel bills or upon average daily rates for such accommodations and meals prevailing in the particular community for comparable accommodations. Since detailed records of incidental items are not required, deductions for these items may be based upon a reasonable approximation. In cases where a taxpayer is called upon to substantiate expense account information, the burden is on the taxpayer to establish that the amounts claimed as a deduction are reasonably accurate and constitute ordinary and necessary business expenses paid or incurred by him in connection with his trade or business. In connection with the determination of factual matters of this type, due consideration will be given to the reasonableness of the stated expenditures for the claimed purposes in relation to the taxpayer's circumstances (such as his income and the nature of his occupation), to the reliability and accuracy of records in connection with other items more readily lending themselves to detailed record-keeping, and to all of the facts and circumstances in the particular case.

* * *

[Reg. § 1.162-17.]

□ [*T.D.* 6306, 8-27-58. *Amended by T.D.* 6630, 12-27-62; *T.D.* 8276, 12-7-89 *and T.D.* 8324, 12-14-90.]

§ 1.162-18. Illegal bribes and kickbacks.—(a) *Illegal payments to government officials or employees.*—(1) *In general.*—No deduction shall be allowed under section 162(a) for any amount paid or incurred, directly or indirectly, to an official or employee of any government, or of any agency or other instrumentality of any government, if—

(i) In the case of a payment made to an official or employee of a government other than a foreign government described in subparagraph (3)(ii) or (iii) of this paragraph, the payment constitutes an illegal bribe or kickback, or

(ii) In the case of a payment made to an official or employee of a foreign government described in subparagraph (3)(ii) or (iii) of this paragraph, the making of the payment would be unlawful under the laws of the United States (if such laws were applicable to the payment and to the official or employee at the time the expenses were paid or incurred).

No deduction shall be allowed for an accrued expense if the eventual payment thereof would fall within the prohibition of this section. The place where the expenses are paid or incurred is immaterial. For purposes of subdivision (ii) of this subparagraph, lawfulness or unlawfulness of the payment under the laws of the foreign country is immaterial.

(2) *Indirect payment.*—For purposes of this paragraph, an indirect payment to an individual shall include any payment which inures to his benefit or promotes his interests, regardless of the medium in which the payment is made and regardless of the identity of the immediate recipient or payor. Thus, for example, payment made to an agent, relative, or independent contractor of an official or employee, or even directly into the general treasury of a foreign country of which the beneficiary is an official or employee, may be treated as an indirect payment to the official or employee, if in fact such payment inures or will inure to his benefit or promotes or will promote his financial or other interests. A payment made by an agent or independent contractor of the taxpayer which benefits the taxpayer shall be treated as an indirect payment by the taxpayer to the official or employee.

(3) *Official or employee of a government.*—Any individual officially connected with—

(i) The government of the United States, a State, a territory or possession of the United States, the District of Columbia, or the Commonwealth of Puerto Rico,

(ii) The government of a foreign country, or

(iii) A political subdivision of, or a corporation or other entity serving as an agency or instrumentality of, any of the above,

in whatever capacity, whether on a permanent or temporary basis, and whether or not serving for compensation, shall be included within the term "official or employee of a government", regardless of the place of residence or post of duty of such individual. An independent contractor would not ordinarily be considered to be an official or employee. For purposes of section 162(c) and this paragraph, the term "foreign country" shall include any foreign nation, whether or not such nation has been accorded diplomatic recognition by the United States. Individuals who purport to act on behalf of or as the government of a foreign nation, or an agency or instrumentality thereof, shall be treated under this section as officials or employees of a foreign government, whether or not such individuals in fact control such foreign nation, agency, or instrumentality, and whether or not such individuals are accorded diplomatic recognition. Accordingly, a group in rebellion against an established government ment shall be treated as officials or employees of a foreign government, as shall officials or employees of the government against which the group is in rebellion.

(4) *Laws of the United States.*—The term "laws of the United States", to which reference is made in paragraph (a)(1)(ii) of this section, shall be deemed to include only Federal statutes, including State laws which are assimilated into Federal law by Federal statute, and legislative and interpretative regulations thereunder. The term shall also be limited to statutes which prohibit some act or acts, for the violation of which there is a civil or criminal penalty.

(5) *Burden of proof.*—In any proceeding involving the issue of whether, for purposes of section 162(c)(1), a payment made to a government official or employee constitutes an illegal bribe or kickback (or would be unlawful under the laws of the United States) the burden of proof in respect of such issue shall be upon the Commissioner to the same extent as he bears the burden of proof in civil fraud cases under section 7454 (*i.e.,* he must prove the illegality of the payment by clear and convincing evidence).

(6) *Example.*—The application of this paragraph may be illustrated by the following example:

Example. X Corp. is in the business of selling hospital equipment in State Y. During 1970, X Corp. employed A who at the time was employed full time by State Y as Superintendent of Hospitals. The purpose of A's employment by X Corp. was to procure for it an improper advantage over other concerns in the making of sales to hospitals in respect of which A, as Superintendent, had authority. X Corp. paid A $5,000 during 1970. The making of this payment was illegal under the laws of State Y. Under section 162(c)(1), X Corp. is precluded from deducting as a trade or business expense the $5,000 paid to A.

(b) *Other illegal payments.*—(1) *In general.*—No deduction shall be allowed under section 162(a) for any payment (other than a payment described in paragraph (a) of this section) made, directly or indirectly, to any person, if the payment constitutes an illegal bribe, illegal kickback, or other illegal payment under the laws of the United States (as defined in paragraph (a)(4) of this section), or under any State law (but only if such State law is generally enforced), which subjects the payor to a criminal penalty or the loss (including a suspension) of license or privilege to engage in a trade or business (whether or not such penalty or loss is actually imposed upon the taxpayer). For purposes of this paragraph, a kickback includes a payment in consideration of the referral of a client, patient, or customer. This paragraph applies only to payments made after December 30, 1969.

(2) *State law.*—For purposes of this paragraph, State law means a statute of a State or the District of Columbia.

(3) *Generally enforced.*—For purposes of this paragraph, a State law shall be considered to be generally enforced unless it is never enforced or the only persons normally charged with violations thereof in the State (or the District of Columbia) enacting the law are infamous or those whose violations are extraordinarily flagrant. For example, a criminal statute of a State shall be considered to be generally enforced unless violations of the statute which are brought to the attention of appropriate enforcement authorities do not result in any enforcement action in the absence of unusual circumstances.

(4) *Burden of proof.*—In any proceeding involving the issue of whether, for purposes of section 162(c)(2), a payment constitutes an illegal bribe, illegal kickback, or other illegal payment the burden of proof in respect of such issue shall be upon the Commissioner to the same extent as he bears the burden of proof in civil fraud cases under section 7454 (*i.e.,* he must prove the illegality of the payment by clear and convincing evidence).

(5) *Example.*—The application of this paragraph may be illustrated by the following example:

Example. X Corp., a calendar-year taxpayer, is engaged in the ship repair business in State Y. During 1970, repairs on foreign ships accounted for a substantial part of its total business. It was X Corp.'s practice to kick back approximately 10 percent of the repair bill to the captain and chief engineer of all foreign-owned vessels, which kickbacks are illegal under a law of State Y (which is generally enforced) and potentially subject X Corp. to fines. During 1970, X Corp. paid $50,000 in such kickbacks. On X Corp.'s return for 1970, a deduction under section 162 was taken for the $50,000. The deduction of the $50,000 of illegal kickbacks during 1970 is disallowed under section 162(c)(2), whether or not X Corp. is prosecuted with respect to the kickbacks.

(c) *Kickbacks, rebates, and bribes under medicare and medicaid.*—No deduction shall be allowed under section 162(a) for any kickback, rebate, or bribe (whether or not illegal) made on or after December 10, 1971, by any provider of services, supplier, physician, or other person who furnishes items or services for which payment is or may be made under the Social Security Act, as amended, or in whole or in part out of Federal funds under a State plan approved under such Act, if such kickback, rebate, or bribe is made in connection with the furnishing of such items or services or the making or receipt of such payments. For purposes of this paragraph, a kickback includes a payment in consideration of the referral of a client, patient, or customer. [Reg. § 1.162-18.]

□ [*T.D.* 6448, 1-26-60. *Amended by T.D.* 7345, 2-19-75.]

§ 1.162-21. Fines and penalties.—(a) *In general.*—No deduction shall be allowed under section 162(a) for any fine or similar penalty paid to—

(1) The government of the United States, a State, a territory or possession of the United States, the District of Columbia, or the Commonwealth of Puerto Rico;

(2) The government of a foreign country; or

(3) A political subdivision of, or corporation or other entity serving as an agency or instrumentality of, any of the above.

(b) *Definition.*—(1) For purposes of this section a fine or similar penalty includes an amount—

(i) Paid pursuant to conviction or a plea of guilty or *nolo contendere* for a crime (felony or misdemeanor) in a criminal proceeding;

(ii) Paid as a civil penalty imposed by Federal, State, or local law, including additions to tax and additional amounts and assessable penalties imposed by chapter 68 of the Internal Revenue Code of 1954;

(iii) Paid in settlement of the taxpayer's actual or potential liability for a fine or penalty (civil or criminal); or

(iv) Forfeited as collateral posted in connection with a proceeding which could result in imposition of such a fine or penalty.

(2) The amount of a fine or penalty does not include legal fees and related expenses paid or incurred in the defense of a prosecution or civil action arising from a violation of the law imposing the fine or civil penalty, nor court costs assessed against the taxpayer, or stenographic and printing charges. Compensatory damages (including damages under section 4A of the Clayton Act (15 U.S.C. 15a), as amended) paid to a government do not constitute a fine or penalty.

* * *

[Reg. § 1.162-21.]

□ [*T.D.* 7345, 2-19-75. *Amended by T.D.* 7366, 7-10-75.]

Proposed Amendments to Regulation

§ 1.162-21. Denial of deduction for certain fines, penalties, and other amounts.—(a) *Deduction Disallowed.*—Except as otherwise provided in this section, no deduction is allowed under chapter 1 of the Internal Revenue Code (Code) for any amount that is paid or incurred—

(1) By suit, settlement agreement (agreement), or otherwise;

(2) To or at the direction of a government or governmental entity, as defined in paragraph (f)(1) of this section, or a nongovernmental entity, as defined in paragraph (f)(2) of this section; and

(3) In relation to the violation, or investigation or inquiry into the potential violation, of any civil or criminal law.

(b) *Exception for restitution, remediation, and amounts paid to come into compliance with a law.*—(1) *In general.*—Paragraph (a) of this section does not apply to amounts paid or incurred for restitution, remediation, or to come into compliance with a law, as defined in paragraph (f)(3) of this section, provided that both the identification and the establishment requirements of paragraphs (b)(2) and (b)(3) of this section are met.

(2) *Identification requirement.*—(i) *In general.*—A court order (order) or an agreement identifies a payment by stating the nature of, or purpose for, each payment each taxpayer is obligated to pay and the amount of each payment identified.

(ii) *Meeting the identification requirement.*—The identification requirement is presumed to be met if an order or agreement specifically states that the payment, and the amount of the payment, described in paragraph (b)(2)(i) of this section, constitutes restitution, remediation, or an amount paid to come into compliance with a law or if the order or agreement uses a different form of the required words, such as, "remediate" or "comply with a law." Meeting the establishment requirement of paragraph (b)(3) of this section alone is not sufficient to meet the identification requirement of paragraph (b)(2) of this section.

(iii) *Payment amount not identified.*—If the order or agreement identifies a payment as restitution, remediation, or to come into compliance with a law but does not identify some or all of the aggregate amount the taxpayer must pay, the identification requirement may be met, with respect to any payment amount not identified, if the order or agreement describes the damage done, harm suffered, or manner of noncompliance with a law, and describes the action required of the taxpayer, such as paying or incurring costs to provide services or to provide property.

(iv) *Challenge by the IRS.*—The IRS may challenge the characterization of an amount identified under paragraph (b)(2) of this section. To rebut the presumption described in paragraph (b)(2)(ii) of this section, the IRS must develop sufficient contrary evidence that the amount paid or incurred was not for the purpose identified in the order or agreement.

(3) *Establishment requirement.*—(i) *Meeting the establishment requirement.*—The establishment requirement is met if the taxpayer substantiates, with documentary evidence, the taxpayer's legal obligation, pursuant to the order or agreement, to pay the amount identified as restitution, remediation, or to come into compliance with a law, the amount paid, and the date the amount was paid or incurred. Meeting the identification requirement of paragraph (b)(2) of this section alone is not sufficient to meet the establishment requirement of paragraph (b)(3) of this section.

(ii) *Substantiating the establishment requirement.*—The documentary evidence described in paragraph (b)(3)(i) of this section includes, but is not limited to, receipts; the legal or regulatory provision related to the violation or potential violation of a law; documents issued by the government or governmental entity relating to the investigation or inquiry; documents describing how the amount to be paid was determined; and correspondence exchanged between the taxpayer and the government or governmental entity before the order or agreement became binding under applicable law.

(c) *Other Exceptions.*—(1) *Suits between private parties.*—Paragraph (a) of this section does not apply to any amount paid or incurred by reason of any order or agreement in a suit in which no government or governmental entity is a party.

(2) *Taxes and related interest.*—Paragraph (a) of this section does not apply to amounts paid or incurred as otherwise deductible taxes or related interest. However, if penalties are imposed with respect to these taxes, paragraph (a) of this section applies to disallow a deduction for any interest payments related to the penalties imposed.

(3) *Failure to pay Title 26 tax.*—In the case of any amount paid or incurred as restitution for failure to pay tax imposed under Title 26 of the United States Code, paragraph (a) of this section does not disallow a deduction for Title 26 taxes which is otherwise allowed under chapter 1 of the Code.

(d) *Application of general principles of Federal income tax law.*—(1) *Taxable year of deduction.*—If, under paragraph (b) or (c) of this section, the taxpayer is allowed a deduction for the amount paid or incurred pursuant to an order or agreement, the deduction is taken into account under the rules of section 461 and the related regulations, or under a provision specifically applicable to the allowed deduction, such as § 1.468B-3(c).

(2) *Tax benefit rule applies.*—If the deduction allowed under paragraphs (b) or (c) of this section results in a tax benefit to the taxpayer, the taxpayer must include in income, under sections 61 and 111, the recovery of any amount deducted in a prior taxable year to the extent the prior year's deduction reduced the taxpayer's tax liability.

(i) A tax benefit to the taxpayer includes a reduction in the taxpayer's tax liability for that year or the creation of a net operating loss carryback or carryover.

(ii) A taxpayer's recovery of any amount deducted in a prior taxable year includes, but is not limited to—

(A) Receiving a refund, recoupment, rebate, reimbursement, or otherwise recovering some or all of the amount the taxpayer paid or incurred, or

(B) Being relieved of some or all of the payment liability under the order or agreement.

(e) *Material change to order or agreement.*—(1) *In general.*—If the parties to an order or agreement, entered before December 22, 2017, make a material change to the terms of that order or agreement on or after the applicability date in paragraph (h) of this section, paragraph (a) of this section applies to any amounts paid or incurred, or any obligation to provide property or services, after the date of the material change.

(2) *Material change.*—A material change to the terms of an order or agreement under para-

graph (e)(1) of this section may include: changing the nature or purpose of a payment obligation; or changing, adding to, or removing a payment obligation, an obligation to provide services, or an obligation to provide property. A material change does not include changing a payment date or changing the address of a party to the order or agreement.

(f) *Definitions.*—For purposes of section 162(f) and § 1.162-21, the following definitions apply:

(1) *Government or governmental entity.*—A government or governmental entity means—

(i) The government of the United States, a State, or the District of Columbia;

(ii) The government of a territory of the United States, including American Samoa, Guam, the Northern Mariana Islands, Puerto Rico, or the U.S. Virgin Islands;

(iii) The government of a foreign country;

(iv) An Indian tribal government, as defined in section 7701(a)(40), or a subdivision of an Indian tribal government, as determined in accordance with section 7871(d); or

(v) A political subdivision of (i), (ii), or (iii), or a corporation or other entity serving as an agency or instrumentality of any of paragraph (f)(1)(i)-(f)(iv) of this section.

(2) *Nongovernmental entity treated as a governmental entity.*—(i) A nongovernmental entity described in paragraph (f)(2)(ii) of this section is treated as a governmental entity.

(ii) A nongovernmental entity treated as governmental entity is an entity that—

(A) Exercises self-regulatory powers (including imposing sanctions) in connection with a qualified board or exchange (as defined in section 1256(g)(7)); or

(B) Exercises self-regulatory powers, including adopting; administering; or enforcing laws and imposing sanctions, as part of performing an essential governmental function.

(3) *Restitution, remediation of property, and amounts paid to come into compliance with a law.*—(i) An amount is paid or incurred for restitution or remediation pursuant to paragraph (b)(1) of this section if it restores, in whole or in part, the person, as defined in section 7701(a)(1); the government; the governmental entity; or property harmed by the violation or potential violation of a law described in paragraph (a)(3) of this section.

(ii) An amount is paid or incurred to come into compliance with a law that the taxpayer has violated, or is alleged to have violated, by performing services; taking action, such as modifying equipment; providing property; or doing any combination thereof.

(iii) Regardless of whether the order or agreement identifies them as such, restitution, remediation, and amounts paid to come into compliance with a law do not include any amount paid or incurred—

(A) To reimburse the government or governmental entity for investigation costs or litigation costs;

(B) At the payor's election, in lieu of a fine or penalty;

(C) As forfeiture or disgorgement; or

(D) To the extent the payment or contribution does not meet the requirements of paragraph (f)(3)(i) or (ii) of this section, to an entity; fund, including a restitution, remediation, or other fund; group; government or governmental entity.

(4) *Suit, agreement, or otherwise.*—A suit, agreement, or otherwise includes, but is not limited to, settlement agreements, non-prosecution agreements, deferred prosecution agreements, judicial proceedings, administrative adjudications, decisions issued by officials, committees, commissions, boards of a government or governmental entity, and any legal actions or hearings which impose a liability on the taxpayer or pursuant to which the taxpayer assumes liability.

(g) *Examples.*—The application of this section may be illustrated by the following examples.

(1) *Example 1. Identification and establishment requirements.*—(i) *Facts.* Corp. A enters into an agreement with State Y's environmental enforcement agency (Agency) for violating state environmental laws. Under the terms of the agreement, Corp. A must pay $40,000 to the Agency in civil penalties, $80,000 in restitution for environmental harm, $50,000 for remediation of contaminated sites, and $60,000 to conduct comprehensive upgrades to Corp. A's operations to come into compliance with the state environmental laws.

(ii) *Analysis.* The identification requirement is satisfied for those amounts the agreement identifies as restitution, remediation, or to come into compliance with a law. If Corp. A establishes, as provided in paragraph (b)(3) of this section, that the amounts it paid or incurred are for restitution, remediation, and to come into compliance with state environmental laws, paragraph (a) of this section does not preclude Corp. A from deducting $190,000. Under paragraph (a) of this section, Corp. A may not deduct the $40,000 in civil penalties. Section 162(f) and § 1.162-21(a) will not disallow Corp. A's deduction for the $60,000 paid to come into compliance with the state environmental laws. However, Corp. A may deduct the $60,000 paid only if, under the facts and circumstances, the payment would be otherwise deductible under chapter 1 of the Code. See section 161, concerning items allowed as deductions, and section 261, concerning items for which no deduction is allowed, and the regulations related to sections 161 and 261.

(2) *Example 2. Restitution.*—(i) *Facts.* Corp. A enters into an agreement with State T's securities agency (Agency) for violating a securities law by inducing B to make a $100,000 investment in Corp. C stock, which B lost when the Corp. C stock became worthless. As part of the agreement, Corp. A agrees to pay $100,000 to B as restitution for B's investment loss, incurred as a result of Corp. A's actions. The agreement specifically states that the $100,000 payment by Corp. A to B is restitution. The agreement also requires Corp. A to pay a $40,000 fine to the Agency as a result of Corp. A's misconduct.

(ii) *Analysis.* Corp. A's $100,000 payment to B is identified in the agreement as restitution. If Corp. A establishes, as provided in paragraph (b)(3) of this section, that the amount paid was for that purpose, Corp. A may deduct the $100,000 payment. Paragraph (a) of this section precludes Corp. A from deducting its payment of $40,000 to the Agency because the payment of a fine is not treated as restitution, remediation, or as paid to come into compliance with a law.

(3) *Example 3. Amount paid to come into compliance with a law.*—(i) *Facts.* Corp. B, an accrual method taxpayer, is under investigation by State X's environmental enforcement agency for a potential violation of State X's law governing emissions standards. Corp. B enters into an agreement with State X under which it agrees to upgrade the engines in a fleet of vehicles that Corp. B operates to come into compliance with State X's law. Although the agreement does not provide the specific amount Corp. B will incur to upgrade the engines to come into compliance with State X's law, it identifies that Corp. B must upgrade existing engines to lower certain emissions. Under the agreement, Corp. B also agrees to bring certain machinery, already in compliance with State X law, up to a standard higher than that which the law requires, and to construct a nature center in a local park for the benefit of the community. Corp. B presents evidence, as described in paragraph (b)(3)(ii) of this section, to substantiate that the expenses Corp. B will incur to upgrade the engines will be amounts paid to come into compliance with State X's law.

(ii) *Analysis.* Because the agreement describes the specific action Corp. B must take to come into compliance with State X's law, and Corp. B presents invoices to establish that the agreement obligates it to incur costs to come into compliance with a law, paragraph (a) of this section would not preclude a deduction for the amounts Corp. B incurs to come into compliance. However, Corp. B may not deduct the amounts paid to bring its machinery up to a higher standard than required by State X's law or to construct the nature center because no facts exist to establish that either amount was paid to come into compliance with a law or as restitution or remediation.

(4) *Example 4. At the direction of a government.*—(i) *Facts.* Corp. D enters into an agreement with governmental entity, Consumer Board, for violating consumer protection laws by failing to provide debt-relief services it promised its customers. The agreement requires Corp. D to pay $60,000 as restitution to the customers harmed by Corp. D's violation of the law.

(ii) *Analysis.* At the direction of Consumer Board, Corp. D must pay $60,000 to its customers as a result of its violation of the law. The agreement identifies the $60,000 as restitution. Provided Corp. D establishes, under paragraph (b)(3) of this section, that the $60,000 constitutes restitution, paragraph (a) does not apply.

* * *

[Prop. Reg. § 1.162-21.]

[Proposed 5-13-2020.]

§ 1.162-25T. Deductions with respect to noncash fringe benefits (temporary).—(a) *Employer.*—If an employer includes the value of a noncash fringe benefit in an employee's gross income, the employer may not deduct this amount as compensation for services, but rather may deduct only the costs incurred by the employer in providing the benefit to the employee. The employer may be allowed a cost recovery deduction under section 168 or a deduction under section 179 for an expense not chargeable to capital account, or, if the noncash fringe benefit is property leased by the employer, a deduction for the ordinary and necessary business expense of leasing the property.

(b) [Reserved]

(c) *Examples.*—The following examples illustrate the provisions of this section.

(1) *Example (1).* On January 1, 1986, X Company owns and provides the use of an automobile with a fair market value of $20,000 to E, an employee, for the entire calendar year. Both X and E compute taxable income on the basis of the calendar year. Seventy percent of the use of the automobile by E is in connection with X's trade or business. If X uses the special rule provided in § 1.61-21(d) for valuing the availability of the automobile and takes into

account the amount excludable as a working condition fringe, X would include $1,680 ($5,600, the Annual Lease Value, less 70 percent of $5,600) in E's gross income for 1986. X may not deduct the amount included in E's income as compensation for services. X may, however, determine a cost recovery deduction under section 168, subject to the limitations under section 280F, for taxable year 1986.

(2) *Example (2)*. The facts are the same as in *Example 1* of paragraph (c)(1) of this section, except that X includes $5,600 in E's gross income, the value of the noncash fringe benefit without taking into account the amount excludable as a working condition fringe. X may not deduct that amount as compensation for services, but may determine a cost recovery deduction under section 168, subject to the limitations under section 280F. For purposes of determining adjusted gross income, E may deduct $3,920 ($5,600 multiplied by the percent of business use). [Temporary Reg. § 1.162-25T.]

☐ [*T.D.* 8004, 1-2-85. *Amended by T.D.* 8061, 11-1-85; *T.D.* 8063, 12-18-85; *T.D.* 8276, 12-7-89; *T.D.* 8451, 12-4-92 *and T.D.* 9849, 3-11-2019.]

§ 1.162-29. Influencing legislation.— (a) *Scope.*—This section provides rules for determining whether an activity is influencing legislation for purposes of section 162(e)(1)(A). This section does not apply for purposes of sections 4911 and 4945 and the regulations thereunder.

(b) *Definitions.*—For purposes of this section—

(1) *Influencing legislation.*—Influencing legislation means—

(i) Any attempt to influence any legislation through a lobbying communication; and

(ii) All activities, such as research, preparation, planning, and coordination, including deciding whether to make a lobbying communication, engaged in for a purpose of making or supporting a lobbying communication, even if not yet made. See paragraph (c) of this section for rules for determining the purposes for engaging in an activity.

(2) *Attempt to influence legislation.*—An attempt to influence any legislation through a lobbying communication is making the lobbying communication.

(3) *Lobbying communication.*—A lobbying communication is any communication (other than any communication compelled by subpoena, or otherwise compelled by Federal or State law) with any member or employee of a legislative body or any other government official or employee who may participate in the formulation of the legislation that—

(i) Refers to specific legislation and reflects a view on that legislation; or

(ii) Clarifies, amplifies, modifies, or provides support for views reflected in a prior lobbying communication.

(4) *Legislation.*—Legislation includes any action with respect to Acts, bills, resolutions, or other similar items by a legislative body. Legislation includes a proposed treaty required to be submitted by the President to the Senate for its advice and consent from the time the President's representative begins to negotiate its position with the prospective parties to the proposed treaty.

(5) *Specific legislation.*—Specific legislation includes a specific legislative proposal that has not been introduced in a legislative body.

(6) *Legislative bodies.*—Legislative bodies are Congress, state legislatures, and other similar governing bodies, excluding local councils (and similar governing bodies), and executive, judicial, or administrative bodies. For this purpose, administrative bodies include school boards, housing authorities, sewer and water districts, zoning boards, and other similar Federal, State, or local special purpose bodies, whether elective or appointive.

* * *

(c) *Purpose for engaging in an activity.*— (1) *In general.*—The purposes for engaging in an activity are determined based on all the facts and circumstances. Facts and circumstances include, but are not limited to—

(i) Whether the activity and the lobbying communication are proximate in time;

(ii) Whether the activity and the lobbying communication relate to similar subject matter;

(iii) Whether the activity is performed at the request of, under the direction of, or on behalf of a person making the lobbying communication;

(iv) Whether the results of the activity are also used for a nonlobbying purpose; and

(v) Whether, at the time the taxpayer engages in the activity, there is specific legislation to which the activity relates.

(2) *Multiple purposes.*—If a taxpayer engages in an activity both for the purpose of making or supporting a lobbying communication and for some nonlobbying purpose, the taxpayer must treat the activity as engaged in partially for a lobbying purpose and partially for a nonlobbying purpose. This division of the activity must result in a reasonable allocation of costs to influencing legislation. See § 1.162-28 (allocation rules for certain expenditures to which section 162(e)(1) applies). A taxpayer's

treatment of these multiple-purpose activities will, in general, not result in a reasonable allocation if it allocates to influencing legislation—

(i) Only the incremental amount of costs that would not have been incurred but for the lobbying purpose; or

(ii) An amount based solely on the number of purposes for engaging in that activity without regard to the relative importance of those purposes.

(3) *Activities treated as having no purpose to influence legislation.*—A taxpayer that engages in any of the following activities is treated as having done so without a purpose of making or supporting a lobbying communication—

(i) Before evidencing a purpose to influence any specific legislation referred to in paragraph (c)(3)(i)(A) or (B) of this section (or similar legislation)—

(A) Determining the existence or procedural status of specific legislation, or the time, place, and subject of any hearing to be held by a legislative body with respect to specific legislation; or

(B) Preparing routine, brief summaries of the provisions of specific legislation;

(ii) Performing an activity for purposes of complying with the requirements of any law (for example, satisfying state or federal securities law filing requirements);

(iii) Reading any publications available to the general public or viewing or listening to other mass media communications; and

(iv) Merely attending a widely attended speech.

* * *

[Reg. § 1.162-29.]

☐ [*T.D.* 8602, 7-20-95.]

§ 1.162-32. Expenses paid or incurred for lodging when not traveling away from home.—(a) *In general.*—Expenses paid or incurred for lodging of an individual who is not traveling away from home (local lodging) generally are personal, living, or family expenses that are nondeductible by the individual under section 262(a). Under certain circumstances, however, local lodging expenses may be deductible under section 162(a) as ordinary and necessary expenses paid or incurred in connection with carrying on a taxpayer's trade or business, including a trade or business as an employee. Whether local lodging expenses are paid or incurred in carrying on a taxpayer's trade or business is determined under all the facts and circumstances. One factor is whether the taxpayer incurs an expense because of a bona fide condition or requirement of employment imposed by the taxpayer's employer. Expenses paid or incurred for local lodging that is lavish or extravagant under the circumstances or that primarily provides an individual with a social or personal benefit are not incurred in carrying on a taxpayer's trade or business.

(b) *Safe harbor for local lodging at business meetings and conferences.*—An individual's local lodging expenses will be treated as ordinary and necessary business expenses if—

(1) The lodging is necessary for the individual to participate fully in or be available for a bona fide business meeting, conference, training activity, or other business function;

(2) The lodging is for a period that does not exceed five calendar days and does not recur more frequently than once per calendar quarter;

(3) If the individual is an employee, the employee's employer requires the employee to remain at the activity or function overnight; and

(4) The lodging is not lavish or extravagant under the circumstances and does not provide any significant element of personal pleasure, recreation, or benefit.

(c) *Examples.*—The provisions of the facts and circumstances test of paragraph (a) of this section are illustrated by the following examples. In each example the employer and the employees meet all other requirements (such as substantiation) for deductibility of the expense and for exclusion from income of the value of the lodging as a working condition fringe or of reimbursements under an accountable plan.

Example 1. (i) Employer conducts a seven-day training session for its employees at a hotel near Employer's main office. The training is directly connected with Employer's trade or business. Some employees attending the training are traveling away from home and some employees are not traveling away from home. Employer requires all employees attending the training to remain at the hotel overnight for the bona fide purpose of facilitating the training. Employer pays the costs of the lodging at the hotel directly to the hotel and does not treat the value as compensation to the employees.

(ii) Because the training is longer than five calendar days, the safe harbor in paragraph (b) of this section does not apply. However, the value of the lodging may be excluded from income if the facts and circumstances test in paragraph (a) of this section is satisfied.

(iii) The training is a bona fide condition or requirement of employment and Employer has a noncompensatory business purpose for paying the lodging expenses. Employer is not paying the expenses primarily to provide a social or personal benefit to the employees, and the lodging Employer provides is not lavish or extravagant. If the employees who are not traveling away from home had paid for their own lodging, the expenses would have been deductible by the employees under section 162(a) as ordinary and necessary business expenses. Therefore, the value of the lodging is excluded from the employees' income as a working condition fringe under section 132(a) and (d).

(iv) Employer may deduct the lodging expenses, including lodging for employees who are not traveling away from home, as ordinary and necessary business expenses under section 162(a).

Example 2. (i) The facts are the same as in *Example 1,* except that the employees pay the cost of their lodging at the hotel directly to the hotel, Employer reimburses the employees for the cost of the lodging, and Employer does not treat the reimbursement as compensation to the employees.

(ii) Because the training is longer than five calendar days, the safe harbor in paragraph (b) of this section does not apply. However, the reimbursement of the expenses for the lodging may be excluded from income if the facts and circumstances test in paragraph (a) of this section is satisfied.

(iii) The training is a bona fide condition or requirement of employment and Employer is reimbursing the lodging expenses for a noncompensatory business purpose and not primarily to provide a social or personal benefit to the employees and the lodging Employer provides is not lavish or extravagant. The employees incur the expenses in performing services for the employer. If Employer had not reimbursed the employees who are not traveling away from home for the cost of the lodging, the expenses would have been deductible by the employees under section 162(a) as ordinary and necessary business expenses. Therefore, the reimbursements to the employees are made under an accountable plan and are excluded from the employees' gross income.

(iv) Employer may deduct the lodging expense reimbursements, including reimbursements for employees who are not traveling away from home, as ordinary and necessary business expenses under section 162(a).

Example 3. (i) Employer is a professional sports team. Employer requires its employees (for example, players and coaches) to stay at a local hotel the night before a home game to conduct last minute training and ensure the physical preparedness of the players. Employer pays the lodging expenses directly to the hotel and does not treat the value as compensation to the employees.

(ii) Because the overnight stays occur more than once per calendar quarter, the safe harbor in paragraph (b) of this section does not apply. However, the value of the lodging may be excluded from income if the facts and circumstances test in paragraph (a) of this section is satisfied.

(iii) The overnight stays are a bona fide condition or requirement of employment and Employer has a noncompensatory business purpose for paying the lodging expenses. Employer is not paying the lodging expenses primarily to provide a social or personal benefit to the employees and the lodging Employer provides is not lavish or extravagant. If the employees had paid for their own lodging, the expenses would have been deductible by the employees under section 162(a) as ordinary and necessary business expenses. Therefore, the value of the lodging is excluded from the employees' income as a working condition fringe.

(iv) Employer may deduct the expenses for lodging the employees at the hotel as ordinary and necessary business expenses under section 162(a).

* * *

[Reg. § 1.162-32.]

□ [*T.D.* 9696, 9-30-2014.]

§ 1.163-1. Interest deduction in general.—(a) Except as otherwise provided in sections 264 to 267, inclusive, interest paid or accrued within the taxable year on indebtedness shall be allowed as a deduction in computing taxable income. For rules relating to interest on certain deferred payments, see section 483 and the regulations thereunder.

(b) Interest paid by the taxpayer on a mortgage upon real estate of which he is the legal or equitable owner, even though the taxpayer is not directly liable upon the bond or note secured by such mortgage, may be deducted as interest on his indebtedness. Pursuant to the provisions of section 163(c), any annual or periodic rental payment made by a taxpayer on or after January 1, 1962, under a redeemable ground rent, as defined in section 1055(c) and paragraph (b) of § 1.1055-1, is required to be treated as interest on an indebtedness secured by a mortgage and, accordingly, may be deducted by the taxpayer as interest on his indebtedness. Section 163(c) has no application in respect of any annual or periodic rental payment made prior to January 1, 1962, or pursuant to an arrangement which does not constitute a "redeemable ground rent" as defined in section 1055(c) and paragraph (b) of § 1.1055-1. Accordingly, annual or periodic payments of Pennsylvania ground rents made before, on, or after January 1, 1962, are deductible as interest if the ground rent is redeemable. An annual or periodic rental payment under a Maryland redeemable ground rent made prior to January 1, 1962, is deductible in accordance with the rules and regulations applicable at the time such payment was made. Any annual or periodic rental payment under a Maryland redeemable ground rent made by the taxpayer on or after January 1, 1962, is, pursuant to the provisions of section 163(c), treated as interest on an indebtedness secured by a mortgage and, accordingly, is deductible by the taxpayer as interest on his indebtedness. In any case where the ground rent is irredeemable, any annual or periodic ground rent payment shall be treated as rent and shall be deductible only to the extent that the payment constitutes a proper business expense. Amounts paid in redemption of a ground rent shall not be treated as interest. For treatment of redeemable ground rents and real property held subject to liabilities under redeemable ground rents, see section 1055 and the regulations thereunder.

(c) Interest calculated for costkeeping or other purposes on account of capital or surplus invested in the business which does not represent a charge arising under an interest-bearing obligation, is not an allowable deduction from gross income. Interest paid by a corporation on scrip dividends is an allowable deduction. So-called interest on preferred stock, which is in reality a dividend thereon, cannot be deducted in computing taxable income. (See, however, section 583). In case of banks and loan or trust companies, interest paid within the year on deposits, such as interest paid on moneys received for investment and secured by interest-bearing certificates of indebtedness issued by such bank or loan or trust company, may be deducted from gross income.

(d) To the extent of assistance payments made in respect of an indebtedness of the taxpayer during the taxable year by the Department of Housing and Urban Development under section 235 of the National Housing Act (12 U.S.C. §1715z), as amended, no deduction shall be allowed under section 163 and this section for interest paid or accrued with respect to such indebtedness. However, such payments shall not affect the amount of any deduction under any section of the Code other than section 163. The provisions of this paragraph shall apply to taxable years beginning after December 31, 1974. [Reg. §1.163-1.]

□ [*T.D.* 6223, 1-23-57. *Amended by T.D.* 6593, 2-28-62; *T.D.* 6821, 5-3-65; *T.D.* 6873, 1-24-66 *and T.D.* 7408, 3-4-76.]

§1.163-7. Deduction for OID on certain debt instruments.—(a) *General rule.*—Except as otherwise provided in paragraph (b) of this section, an issuer (including a transferee) determines the amount of OID that is deductible each year under section 163(e)(1) by using the constant yield method described in §1.1272-1(b). This determination, however, is made without regard to section 1272(a)(7) (relating to acquisition premium) and §1.1273-1(d) (relating to de minimis OID). An issuer is permitted a deduction under section 163(e)(1) only to the extent the issuer is primarily liable on the debt instrument. For certain limitations on the deductibility of OID, see sections 163(e) and 1275(b)(2). To determine the amount of interest (OID) that is deductible each year on a debt instrument that provides for contingent payments, see §1.1275-4.

* * *

[Reg. §1.163-7.]

□ [*T.D.* 8517, 1-27-94. *Amended by T.D.* 8674, 6-11-96 *and T.D.* 8934, 1-11-2001.]

§1.163-8T. Allocation of interest expense among expenditures (temporary).—(a) *In general.*—(1) *Application.*—This section prescribes rules for allocating interest expense for purposes of applying sections 469 (the "passive loss limitation") and 163(d) and (h) (the "nonbusiness interest limitations").

* * *

(3) *Manner of allocation.*—In general, interest expense on a debt is allocated in the same manner as the debt to which such interest expense relates is allocated. Debt is allocated by tracing disbursements of the debt proceeds to specific expenditures. This section prescribes rules for tracing debt proceeds to specific expenditures.

(4) *Treatment of interest expense.*—(i) *General rule.*—Except as otherwise provided in paragraph (m) of this section (relating to limitations on interest expense other than the passive loss and nonbusiness interest limitations), interest expense allocated under the rules of this section is treated in the following manner:

(A) Interest expense allocated to a trade or business expenditure (as defined in paragraph (b)(7) of this section) is taken into account under section 163(h)(2)(A);

(B) Interest expense allocated to a passive activity expenditure (as defined in paragraph (b)(4) of this section) or a former passive activity expenditure (as defined in paragraph (b)(2) of this section) is taken into account for purposes of section 469 in determining the income or loss from the activity to which such expenditure relates;

(C) Interest expense allocated to an investment expenditure (as defined in paragraph (b)(3) of this section) is treated for purposes of section 163(d) as investment interest;

(D) Interest expense allocated to a personal expenditure (as defined in paragraph (b)(5) of this section) is treated for purposes of section 163(h) as personal interest; and

(E) Interest expense allocated to a portfolio expenditure (as defined in paragraph (b)(6) of this section) is treated for purposes of section 469(e)(2)(B)(ii) as interest expense described in section 469(e)(1)(A)(i)(III).

* * *

(c) *Allocation of debt and interest expense.*—(1) *Allocation in accordance with use of proceeds.*—Debt is allocated to expenditures in accordance with the use of the debt proceeds and, except as provided in paragraph (m) of this section, interest expense accruing on a debt during any period is allocated to expenditures in the same manner as the debt is allocated from time to time during such period. Except as provided in paragraph (m) of this section, debt proceeds and related interest expense are allocated solely by reference to the use of such proceeds, and the allocation is not affected by the use of an interest in any property to secure the repayment of such debt or interest. The following example illustrates the principles of this paragraph (c)(1):

Example. Taxpayer A, an individual, pledges corporate stock held for investment as security for a loan and uses the debt proceeds to purchase an automobile for personal use. Interest expense accruing on the debt is allocated to the personal expenditure to purchase the automobile even though the debt is secured by investment property.

* * *

(4) *Allocation of debt; proceeds deposited in borrower's account.*—(i) *Treatment of deposit.*—For purposes of this section, a deposit of debt proceeds in an account is treated as an investment expenditure, and amounts held in an account (whether or not interest bearing) are treated as property held for investment. Debt allocated to an account under this paragraph (c)(4)(i) must be reallocated as required by paragraph (j) of this section whenever debt proceeds held in the account are used for another expenditure. This paragraph (c)(4) provides rules for determining when debt proceeds are expended from the account. The following example illustrates the principles of this paragraph (c)(4)(i):

Example. Taxpayer C, a calendar year taxpayer, borrows $100,000 on January 1 and immediately uses the proceeds to open a noninterest-bearing checking account. No other amounts are deposited in the account during the year, and no portion of the principal amount of the debt is repaid during the year. On April 1, C uses $20,000 of the debt proceeds held in the account for a passive activity expenditure. On September 1, C uses an additional $40,000 of the debt proceeds held in the account for a personal expenditure. Under this paragraph (c)(4)(i), from January 1 through March 31 the entire $100,000 debt is allocated to an investment expenditure for the account. From April 1 through August 31, $20,000 of the debt is allocated to the passive activity expenditure, and $80,000 of the debt is allocated to the investment expenditure for the account. From September 1 through December 31, $40,000 of the debt is allocated to the personal expenditure, $20,000 is allocated to the passive activity expenditure, and $40,000 is allocated to an investment expenditure for the account.

(ii) *Expenditures from account; general ordering rule.*—Except as provided in paragraph (c)(4)(iii)(B) or (C) of this section, debt proceeds deposited in an account are treated as expended before—

(A) Any unborrowed amounts held in the account at the time such debt proceeds are deposited; and

(B) Any amounts (borrowed or unborrowed) that are deposited in the account after such debt proceeds are deposited.

The following example illustrates the application of this paragraph (c)(4)(ii):

Example. On January 10, taxpayer E opens a checking account, depositing $500 of proceeds of Debt A and $1,000 of unborrowed funds. The following chart summarizes the transactions which occur during the year with respect to the account:

Date		*Transaction*
January 10	$500	proceeds of Debt A and $1,000 unborrowed funds deposited
January 11	$500	proceeds of Debt B deposited
February 17	$800	personal expenditure
February 26	$700	passive activity expenditure
June 21	$1,000	proceeds of Debt C deposited
November 24	$800	investment expenditure
December 20	$600	personal expenditure

The $800 personal expenditure is treated as made from the $500 proceeds of Debt A and $300 of the proceeds of Debt B. The $700 passive activity expenditure is treated as made from the remaining $200 proceeds of Debt B and $500 of unborrowed funds. The $800 investment expenditure is treated as made entirely from the proceeds of Debt C. The $600 personal expenditure is treated as made from the remaining $200 proceeds of Debt C and $400 of unborrowed funds. Under paragraph (c)(4)(i) of this section, debt is allocated to an investment expenditure for periods during which debt proceeds are held in the account.

(iii) *Expenditures from account; supplemental ordering rules.*—(A) *Checking or similar accounts.*—Except as otherwise provided in this paragraph (c)(4)(iii), an expenditure from a checking or similar account is treated as made at the time the check is written on the account, provided the check is delivered or mailed to the payee within a reasonable period after the writing of the check. For this purpose, the taxpayer may treat checks written on the same day as written in any order. In the absence of evidence to the contrary, a check is presumed to be written on the date appearing on the check and to be delivered or mailed to the payee within a reasonable period thereafter. Evidence to the contrary may include the fact that a check does not clear within a reasonable period after the date appearing on the check.

(B) *Expenditures within 15 days after deposit of borrowed funds.*—The taxpayer may treat any expenditure made from an account within 15 days after debt proceeds are deposited in such account as made from such proceeds to the extent thereof even if under paragraph (c)(4)(ii) of this section the debt proceeds would be treated as used to make one or more other expenditures. Any such expenditures and the debt proceeds from which such expenditures are treated as made are disregarded in applying paragraph (c)(4)(ii) of this section. The following examples illustrate the application of this paragraph (c)(4)(iii)(B):

Example (1). Taxpayer D incurs a $1,000 debt on June 5 and immediately deposits the proceeds in an account ("Account A"). On June 17, D transfers $2,000 from Account A to another account ("Account B"). On June 30, D writes a $1,500 check on Account B for a passive activity expenditure. In addition, numerous deposits of borrowed and unborrowed amounts and expenditures occur with respect to both accounts throughout the month of June. Notwithstanding these other transactions, D may treat $1,000 of the deposit to Account B on June 17 as an expenditure from the debt proceeds deposited in Account A on June 5. In addition, D may similarly treat $1,000 of the passive activity expenditure on June 30 as made from debt proceeds treated as deposited in Account B on June 17.

Example (2). The facts are the same as in the example in paragraph (c)(4)(ii) of this section, except that the proceeds of Debt B are deposited on February 11 rather than on January 11. Since the $700 passive activity expenditure occurs within 15 days after the proceeds of Debt B are deposited in the account, E may treat such expenditure as being made from the proceeds of Debt B to the extent thereof. If E treats the passive activity expenditure in this manner, the expenditures from the account are treated as follows: The $800 personal expenditure is treated as made from the $500 proceeds of Debt A and $300 of unborrowed funds. The $700 passive activity expenditure is treated as made from the $500 proceeds of Debt B and $200 of unborrowed funds. The remaining expenditures are treated as in the example in paragraph (c)(4)(ii) of this section.

(C) *Interest on segregated account.*—In the case of an account consisting solely of the proceeds of a debt and interest earned on such account, the taxpayer may treat any expenditure from such account as made first from amounts constituting interest (rather than debt proceeds) to the extent of the balance of such interest in the account at the time of the expenditure, determined by applying the rules in this paragraph (c)(4). To the extent any expenditure is treated as made from interest under this paragraph (c)(4)(iii)(C), the expenditure is disregarded in applying paragraph (c)(4)(ii) of this section.

(iv) *Optional method for determining date of reallocation.*—Solely for the purpose of determining the date on which debt allocated to an account under paragraph (c)(4)(i) of this section is reallocated, the taxpayer may treat all expenditures made during any calendar month from debt proceeds in the account as occurring on the later of the first day of such month or the date on which such debt proceeds are deposited in the account. This paragraph (c)(4)(iv) applies only if all expenditures from an account during the same calendar month are similarly treated. The following example illustrates the application of this paragraph (c)(4)(iv):

Example. On January 10, taxpayer G opens a checking account, depositing $500 of proceeds of Debt A and $1,000 of unborrowed funds. The following chart summarizes the transactions which occur during the year with respect to the account (note that these facts are the same as the facts of the example in paragraph (c)(4)(ii) of this section):

Date		*Transaction*
January 10	$500	proceeds of Debt A and $1,000 unborrowed funds deposited
January 11	$500	proceeds of Debt B deposited
February 17	$800	personal expenditure
February 26	$700	passive activity expenditure
June 21	$1,000	proceeds of Debt C deposited
November 24	$800	investment expenditure
December 20	$600	personal expenditure

Assume that G chooses to apply the optional rule of this paragraph (c)(4)(iv) to all expenditures. For purposes of determining the date on which debt is allocated to the $800 personal expenditure made on February 17, the $500 treated as made from the proceeds of Debt A and the $300 treated as made from the proceeds of Debt B are treated as expenditures occurring on February 1. Accordingly, Debt A is allocated to an investment expenditure for the account from January 10 through January 31 and to the personal expenditure from February 1 through December 31, and $300 of Debt B is allocated to an investment expenditure for the account from January 11 through January 31 and to the personal expenditure from February 1 through December 31. The remaining $200 of Debt B is allocated to an investment expenditure for the account from January 11 through January 31 and to the passive activity expenditure from February 1 through December 31. The $800 of Debt C used to make the investment expenditure on November 24 is allocated to an investment expenditure for the account from June 21 through October 31 and to an investment expenditure from November 1 through December 31. The remaining $200 of Debt C is allocated to an investment expenditure for the account from June 21 through November 30 and to a personal expenditure from December 1 through December 31.

(v) *Simultaneous deposits.*—(A) *In general.*—If the proceeds of two or more debts are deposited in an account simultaneously, such proceeds are treated for purposes of this paragraph (c)(4) as deposited in the order in which the debts were incurred.

(B) *Order in which debts incurred.*—If two or more debts are incurred simultaneously or are treated under applicable law as incurred simultaneously, the debts are treated for purposes of this paragraph (c)(4)(v) as incurred in any order the taxpayer selects.

(C) *Borrowings on which interest accrues at different rates.*—If interest does not accrue at the same fixed or variable rate on the entire amount of a borrowing, each portion of the borrowing on which interest accrues at a different fixed or variable rate is treated as a separate debt for purposes of this paragraph (c)(4)(v).

(vi) *Multiple accounts.*—The rules in this paragraph (c)(4) apply separately to each account of a taxpayer.

* * *

(d) *Debt repayments.*—(1) *General ordering rule.*—If, at the time any portion of a debt is repaid, such debt is allocated to more than one expenditure, the debt is treated for purposes of this section as repaid in the following order:

(i) Amounts allocated to personal expenditures;

(ii) Amounts allocated to investment expenditures and passive activity expenditures (other than passive activity expenditures described in paragraph (d)(1)(iii) of this section).

(iii) Amounts allocated to passive activity expenditures in connection with a rental real estate activity with respect to which the taxpayer actively participates (within the meaning of section 469(i));

(iv) Amounts allocated to former passive activity expenditures; and

(v) Amounts allocated to trade or business expenditures and to expenditures described in the last sentence of paragraph (b)(4) of this section.

* * *

(m) *Coordination with other provisions.*—(1) *Effect of other limitations.*—(i) *In general.*—All debt is allocated among expenditures pursuant to the rules in this section, without regard to any limitations on the deductibility of interest expense on such debt. The applicability of the passive loss and nonbusiness interest limitations to interest on such debt, however, may be affected by other limitations on the deductibility of interest expense.

(ii) *Disallowance provisions.*—Interest expense that is not allowable as a deduction by reason of a disallowance provision (within the meaning of paragraph (m)(7)(ii) of this section) is not taken into account for any taxable year for purposes of applying the passive loss and nonbusiness interest limitations.

(iii) *Deferral provisions.*—Interest expense that is not allowable as a deduction for the taxable year in which paid or accrued by reason of a deferral provision (within the meaning of paragraph (m)(7)(iii) of this section) is allocated in the same manner as the debt giving rise to the interest expense is allocated for such taxable year. Such interest expense is taken into account for purposes of applying the passive loss and nonbusiness interest limitations for the taxable year in which such interest expense is allowable under such deferral provision.

(iv) *Capitalization provisions.*—Interest expense that is capitalized pursuant to a capitalization provision (within the meaning of paragraph (m)(7)(i) of this section) is not taken into account as interest for any taxable year for purposes of applying the passive loss and nonbusiness interest limitations.

(2) *Effect on other limitations.*—(i) *General rule.*—Except as provided in paragraph (m)(2)(ii) of this section, any limitation

on the deductibility of an item (other than the passive loss and nonbusiness interest limitations) applies without regard to the manner in which debt is allocated under this section. Thus, for example, interest expense treated under section 265(a)(2) as interest on indebtedness incurred or continued to purchase or carry obligations the interest on which is wholly exempt from Federal income tax is not deductible regardless of the expenditure to which the underlying debt is allocated under this section.

(ii) *Exception.*—Capitalization provisions (within the meaning of paragraph (m)(7)(i) of this section) do not apply to interest expense allocated to any personal expenditure under the rules of this section.

(3) *Qualified residence interest.*—Qualified residence interest (within the meaning of section 163 (h)(3)) is allowable as a deduction without regard to the manner in which such interest expense is allocated under the rules of this section. In addition, qualified residence interest is not taken into account in determining the income or loss from any activity for purposes of section 469 or in determining the amount of investment interest for purposes of section 163(d). The following example illustrates the rule in this paragraph (m)(3):

Example. Taxpayer E, an individual, incurs a $20,000 debt secured by a residence and immediately uses the proceeds to purchase an automobile exclusively for E's personal use. Under the rules in this section, the debt and interest expense on the debt are allocated to a personal expenditure. If, however, the interest on the debt is qualified residence interest within the meaning of section 163(h)(3), the interest is not treated as personal interest for purposes of section 163(h).

* * *

[Temporary Reg. § 1.163-8T.]

☐ [*T.D.* 8145, 7-1-87.]

»→ *Caution: Reg. § 1.163-10T does not reflect changes made by the Tax Cuts and Jobs Act of 2017, eliminating the deduction for home equity indebtedness and reducing the amount of allowable acquisition indebtedness.*

§ 1.163-10T. Qualified residence interest (temporary).—

* * *

(b) *Treatment of qualified residence interest.*—Except as provided below, qualified residence interest is deductible under section 163(a). Qualified residence interest is not subject to limitation or otherwise taken into account under section 163(d) (limitation on investment interest), section 163(h)(1) (disallowance of deduction for personal interest), section 263A (capitalization and inclusion in inventory costs of certain expenses) or section 469 (limitations on losses from passive activities). Qualified residence interest is subject to the limitation imposed by section 263(g) (certain interest in the case of straddles), section 264(a)(2) and (4) (interest paid in connection with certain insurance), section 265(a)(2) (interest relating to tax-exempt income), section 266 (carrying charges), section 267(a)(2) (interest with respect to transactions between related taxpayers), section 465 (deductions limited to amount at risk), section 1277 (deferral of interest deduction allocable to accrued market discount), and section 1282 (deferral of interest deduction allocable to accrued discount).

(c) *Determination of qualified residence interest when secured debt does not exceed adjusted purchase price.*—(1) *In general.*—If the sum of the average balances for the taxable year of all secured debts on a qualified residence does not exceed the adjusted purchase price (determined as of the end of the taxable year) of the qualified residence, all of the interest paid or accrued during the taxable year with respect to the secured debts is qualified residence interest. If the sum of the average balances for the taxable year of all secured debts exceeds the adjusted purchase price of the qualified residences (determined as of the end of the taxable year), the taxpayer must use either the simplified method (see paragraph (d) of this section) or the exact method (see paragraph (e) of this section) to determine the amount of interest that is qualified residence interest.

(2) *Examples.*

Example (1). T purchases a qualified residence in 1987 for $65,000. T pays $6,500 in cash and finances the remainder of the purchase with a mortgage of $58,500. In 1988, the average balance of the mortgage is $58,000. Because the average balance of the mortgage is less than the adjusted purchase price of the residence ($65,000), all of the interest paid or accrued during 1988 on the mortgage is qualified residence interest.

Example (2). The facts are the same as in example (1), except that T incurs a second mortgage on January 1, 1988, with an initial principal balance of $2,000. The average balance of the second mortgage in 1988 is $1,900. Because the sum of the average balance of the first and second mortgages ($59,900) is less than the adjusted purchase price of the residence ($65,000), all of the interest paid or accrued during 1988 on both the first and second mortgages is qualified residence interest.

Example (3). P borrows $50,000 on January 1, 1988 and secures the debt by a qualified residence. P pays the interest on the debt monthly, but makes no principal payments in 1988. There are no other debts secured by the residence during 1988. On December 31, 1988, the adjusted purchase price of the residence is $40,000. The average balance of the debt in 1988 is $50,000. Because the average balance of the debt exceeds the adjusted purchase price ($10,000), some of the interest on the debt is not qualified residence interest. The portion of the total interest that is qualified residence interest must be determined in accordance with the rules of paragraph (d) or paragraph (e) of this section.

(d) *Determination of qualified residence interest when secured debt exceeds adjusted purchase price—Simplified method.*—(1) *In general.*—Under the simplified method, the amount of qualified residence interest for the taxable year is equal to the total interest paid or accrued during the taxable year with respect to all secured debts multiplied by a fraction (not in excess of one), the numerator of which is the adjusted purchase price (determined as of the end of the taxable year) of the qualified residence and the denominator of which is the sum of the average balances of all secured debts.

(2) *Treatment of interest paid or accrued on secured debt that is not qualified residence interest.*—Under the simplified method, the excess of the total interest paid or accrued during the taxable year with respect to all secured debts over the amount of qualified residence interest is personal interest.

(3) *Example.*—R's principal residence has an adjusted purchase price on December 31, 1988, of $105,000. R has two debts secured by the residence, with the following average balances and interest payments:

Debt	*Date Secured*	*Average Balance*	*Interest*
Debt 1 . . .	June 1983	$80,000	$8,000
Debt 2 . . .	May 1987	$40,000	$4,800
Total . . .		$120,000	$12,800

The amount of qualified residence interest is determined under the simplified method by multiplying the total interest ($12,800) by a fraction (expressed as a decimal amount) equal to the adjusted purchase price ($105,000) of the residence divided by the combined average balances ($120,000). For 1988, this fraction is equal to 0.875 ($105,000/$120,000). Therefore, $11,200 ($12,800 × 0.875) of the total interest is qualified residence interest. The remaining $1,600 in interest ($12,800 - $11,200) is personal interest, even if (under the rules of § 1.163-8T) such remaining interest would be allocated to some other category of interest.

* * *

(o) *Secured debt.*—(1) *In general.*—For purposes of this section, the term "secured debt" means a debt that is on the security of any instrument (such as a mortgage, deed of trust, or land contract)—

(i) That makes the interest of the debtor in the qualified residence specific security for the payment of the debt,

(ii) Under which, in the event of default, the residence could be subjected to the satisfaction of the debt with the same priority as a mortgage or deed of trust in the jurisdiction in which the property is situated, and

(iii) That is recorded, where permitted, or is otherwise perfected in accordance with applicable State law.

A debt will not be considered to be secured by a qualified residence if it is secured solely by virtue of a lien upon the general assets of the taxpayer or by a security interest, such as a mechanic's lien or judgment lien, that attaches to the property without the consent of the debtor.

(2) *Special rule for debt in certain States.*—Debt will not fail to be treated as secured solely because, under an applicable State or local homestead law or other debtor protection law in effect on August 16, 1986, the security interest is ineffective or the enforceability of the security interest is restricted.

(3) *Time at which debt is treated as secured.*—For purposes of this section, a debt is treated as secured as of the date on which each of the requirements of paragraph (o)(1) of this section are satisfied, regardless of when amounts are actually borrowed with respect to the debt. For purposes of this paragraph (o)(3), if the instrument is recorded within a commercially reasonable time after the security interest is granted, the instrument will be treated as recorded on the date that the security interest was granted.

(4) *Partially secured debt.*—(i) *In general.*—If the security interest is limited to a prescribed maximum amount or portion of the residence, and the average balance of the debt exceeds such amount or the value of such portion, such excess shall not be treated as secured debt for purposes of this section.

(ii) *Example.*—T borrows $80,000 on January 1, 1991. T secures the debt with a principal residence. The security in the residence for the debt, however, is limited to $20,000. T pays $8,000 in interest on the debt in 1991 and the average balance of the debt in that year is $80,000. Because the average balance of the debt exceeds the maximum amount of the security interest, such excess is not treated as secured debt. Therefore, for purposes of applying the limitation on qualified residence interest, the average balance of the secured debt is $20,000 (the maximum amount of the security interest) and the interest paid or accrued on the secured debt is $2,000 (the total interest paid on the debt multiplied by the ratio of the average balance of the secured debt ($20,000) and the average balance of the total debt ($80,000)).

(5) *Election to treat debt as not secured by a qualified residence.*—(i) *In general.*—For purposes of this section, a taxpayer may elect to treat any debt that is secured by a qualified residence as not secured by the qualified residence. An election made under this paragraph shall be effective for the taxable year for which the election is made and for all subsequent taxable years unless revoked with the consent of the Commissioner.

(ii) *Example.*—T owns a principal residence with a fair market value of $75,000 and an adjusted purchase price of $40,000. In 1988, debt A, the proceeds of which were used to purchase the residence, has an average balance of $15,000. The proceeds of debt B, which is secured by a second mortgage on the property, are allocable to T's trade or business under § 1.163-8T and has an average balance of $25,000. In 1988, T incurs debt C, which is also secured by T's principal residence and which has an average balance in 1988 of $5,000. In the absence of an election to treat debt B as unsecured, the applicable debt limit for debt C in 1988 under paragraph (e) of this section would be zero dollars ($40,000 - $15,000 - $25,000) and none of the interest paid on debt C would be qualified residence interest. If, however, T makes or has previously made an election pursuant to paragraph (o) (5) (i) of this section to treat debt B as not secured by the residence, the applicable debt limit for debt C would be $25,000 ($40,000 - $15,000), and all of the interest paid on debt C during the taxable year would be qualified residence interest. Since the proceeds of debt B are allocable to T's trade or business under § 1.163-8T, interest on debt B may be deductible under other sections of the Internal Revenue Code.

(iii) *Allocation of debt secured by two qualified residences.*—[Reserved.]

(p) *Definition of qualified residence.*—(1) *In general.*—The term "qualified residence" means the taxpayer's principal residence (as defined in paragraph (p) (2) of this section), or the taxpayer's second residence (as defined in paragraph (p) (3) of this section).

(2) *Principal residence.*—The term "principal residence" means the taxpayer's principal residence within the meaning of section 1034. For purposes of this section, a taxpayer cannot have more than one principal residence at any one time.

(3) *Second residence.*—(i) *In general.*—The term "second residence" means—

(A) A residence within the meaning of paragraph (p) (3) (ii) of this section,

(B) That the taxpayer uses as a residence within the meaning of paragraph (p) (3) (iii) of this section, and

(C) That the taxpayer elects to treat as a second residence pursuant to paragraph (p) (3) (iv) of this section.

A taxpayer cannot have more than one second residence at any time.

(ii) *Definition of residence.*—Whether property is a residence shall be determined based on all the facts and circumstances, including the good faith of the taxpayer. A residence generally includes a house, condominium, mobile home, boat, or house trailer, that contains sleeping space and toilet and cooking facilities. A residence does not include personal property, such as furniture or a television, that, in accordance with the applicable local law, is not a fixture.

(iii) *Use as a residence.*—If a residence is rented at any time during the taxable year, it is considered to be used as a residence only if the taxpayer uses it during the taxable year as a residence within the meaning of section 280A(d). If a residence is not rented at any time during the taxable year, it shall be considered to be used as a residence. For purposes of the preceding sentence, a residence will be deemed to be rented during any period that the taxpayer holds the residence out for rental or resale or repairs or renovates the residence with the intention of holding it out for rental or resale.

(iv) *Election of second residence.*—A taxpayer may elect a different residence (other than the taxpayer's principal residence) to be the taxpayer's second residence for each taxable year. A taxpayer may not elect different residences as second residences at different times of the same taxable year except as provided below—

(A) If the taxpayer acquires a new residence during the taxable year, the taxpayer may elect the new residence as the taxpayer's second residence as of the date acquired;

(B) If property that was the taxpayer's principal residence during the taxable year ceases to qualify as the taxpayer's principal residence, the taxpayer may elect that property as the taxpayer's second residence as of the date that the property ceases to be the taxpayer's principal residence; or

(C) If property that was the taxpayer's second residence is sold during the taxable year or becomes the taxpayer's principal residence, the taxpayer may elect a new second residence as of such day.

(4) *Allocations between residence and other property.*—(i) *In general.*—For purposes of this section, the adjusted purchase price and fair market value of property must be allocated between the portion of the property that is a qualified residence and the portion that is not a qualified residence. Neither the average balance of the secured debt nor the interest paid or accrued on secured debt is so allocated. Property that is not used for residential purposes does not qualify as a residence. For example, if a portion of the property is used as an office in the taxpayer's trade or business, that portion of the property does not qualify as a residence.

(ii) *Special rule for rental of residence.*—If a taxpayer rents a portion of his or her principal or second residence to another person (a "tenant"), such portion may be treated as used by the taxpayer for residential purposes if, but only if—

(A) Such rented portion is used by the tenant primarily for residential purposes,

(B) The rented portion is not a self-contained residential unit containing separate sleeping space and toilet and cooking facilities, and

(C) The total number of tenants renting (directly or by sublease) the same or different portions of the residence at any time during the taxable year does not exceed two. For this purpose, if two persons (and the dependents, as defined by section 152, of either of them) share the same sleeping quarters, they shall be treated as a single tenant.

(iii) *Examples.*— *Example (1).* D, a dentist, uses a room in D's principal residence as an office which qualifies under section 280A(c)(1)(B) as a portion of the dwelling unit used exclusively on a regular basis as a place of business for meeting with patients in the normal course of D's trade or business. D's adjusted purchase price of the property is $65,000; $10,000 of which is allocable under paragraph (o)(4)(i) of this section to the room used as an office. For purposes of this section, D's residence does not include the room used as an office. The adjusted purchase price of the residence is, accordingly, $55,000. Similarly, the fair market value of D's residence must be allocated between the office and the remainder of the property.

Example (2). J rents out the basement of property that is otherwise used as J's principal residence. The basement is a self-contained residential unit, with sleeping space and toilet and cooking facilities. The adjusted purchase price of the property is $100,000; $15,000 of which is allocable under paragraph (o)(4)(i) of this section to the basement. For purposes of this section, J's residence does not include the basement and the adjusted purchase price of the residence is $85,000. Similarly, the fair market value of the residence must be allocated between the basement unit and the remainder of the property.

(5) *Residence under construction.*—(i) *In general.*—A taxpayer may treat a residence under construction as a qualified residence for a period of up to 24 months, but only if the residence becomes a qualified residence, without regard to this paragraph (p)(5)(i), as of the time that the residence is ready for occupancy.

(ii) *Example.*—X owns a residential lot suitable for the construction of a vacation home. On April 20, 1987, X obtains a mortgage secured by the lot and any property to be constructed on the lot. On August 9, 1987, X begins construction of a residence on the lot. The residence is ready for occupancy on November 9, 1989. The residence is used as a residence within the meaning of paragraph (p)(3)(iii) of this section during 1989 and X elects to treat the residence as his second residence for the period November 9, 1989, through December 31, 1989. Since the residence under construction is a qualified residence as of the first day that the residence is ready for occupancy (November 9, 1987), X may treat the residence as his second residence under paragraph (p)(5)(i) of this section for up to 24 months of the period during which the residence is under construction, commencing on or after the date that construction is begun (August 9, 1987). If X treats the residence under construction as X's second residence beginning on August 9, 1987, the residence under construction would cease to qualify as a qualified residence under paragraph (p)(5)(i) on August 8, 1989. The residence's status as a qualified residence for future periods would be determined without regard to paragraph (p)(5)(i) of this section.

(6) *Special rule for time-sharing arrangements.*—Property that is otherwise a qualified residence will not fail to qualify as such solely because the taxpayer's interest in or right to use the property is restricted by an arrangement whereby two or more persons with interests in the property agree to exercise control over the property for different periods during the taxable year. For purposes of determining the use of a residence under paragraph

(p)(3)(iii) of this section, a taxpayer will not be considered to have used or rented a residence during any period that the taxpayer does not have the right to use the property or to receive any benefits from the rental of the property.

* * *

[Temporary Reg. § 1.163-10T.]

□ [*T.D.* 8168, 12-21-87.]

§ 1.164-3. Definitions and special rules.—For purposes of section 164 and § 1.164-1 to § 1.164-8, inclusive—

(a) *State or local taxes.*—A State or local tax includes only a tax imposed by a State, a possession of the United States, or a political subdivision of any of the foregoing, or by the District of Columbia.

(b) *Real property taxes.*—The term "real property taxes" means taxes imposed on interests in real property and levied for the general public welfare, but it does not include taxes assessed against local benefits. See § 1.164-4.

(c) *Personal property taxes.*—The term "personal property tax" means an ad valorem tax which is imposed on an annual basis in respect of personal property. To qualify as a personal property tax, a tax must meet the following three tests:

(1) The tax must be ad valorem—that is, substantially in proportion to the value of the personal property. A tax which is based on criteria other than value does not qualify as ad valorem. For example, a motor vehicle tax based on weight, model year, and horsepower, or any of these characteristics is not an ad valorem tax. However, a tax which is partly based on value and partly based on other criteria may qualify in part. For example, in the case of a motor vehicle tax of 1 per cent of value plus 40 cents per hundredweight, the part of the tax equal to 1 percent of value qualifies as an ad valorem tax and the balance does not qualify.

(2) The tax must be imposed on an annual basis, even if collected more frequently or less frequently.

(3) The tax must be imposed in respect of personal property. A tax may be considered to be imposed in respect of personal property even if in form it is imposed on the exercise of a privilege. Thus, for taxable years beginning after December 31, 1963, State and local taxes on the registration or licensing of highway motor vehicles are not deductible as personal property taxes unless and to the extent that the tests prescribed in this subparagraph are met. For example, an annual ad valorem tax qualifies as a personal property tax although it is denominated a registration fee imposed for the privilege of registering motor vehicles or of using them on the highways.

(d) *Foreign taxes.*—The term "foreign tax" includes only a tax imposed by the authority of a foreign country. A tax imposed by a political subdivision of a foreign country is considered to be imposed by the authority of that foreign country.

* * *

[Reg. § 1.164-3.]

□ [*T.D.* 6256, 10-7-57. *Amended by T.D.* 6780, 12-21-64.]

Proposed Amendments to Regulation

§ 1.164-3. Definitions and special rules.

* * *

(j) *Safe harbor for payments by individuals in exchange for state or local tax credits.*—(1) *In general.*—An individual who itemizes deductions and who makes a payment to or for the use of an entity described in section 170(c) in consideration for a state or local tax credit may treat as a payment of state or local tax for purposes of section 164 the portion of such payment for which a charitable contribution deduction under section 170 is disallowed under § 1.170A-1(h)(3). This treatment as payment of state or local tax under section 164(a) is allowed in the taxable year in which the payment is made to the extent that the resulting credit is applied, consistent with applicable state or local law, to offset the individual's state or local tax liability for such taxable year or the preceding taxable year.

(2) *Credits carried forward.*—To the extent that a state or local tax credit described in paragraph (j)(1) of this section is not applied to offset the individual's applicable state or local tax liability for the taxable year of the payment or the preceding taxable year, any excess state or local tax credit permitted to be carried forward may be treated as a payment of state or local tax under section 164(a) in the taxable year or years for which the carryover credit is applied in accordance with state or local law.

(3) *Limitation on individual deductions.*—Nothing in this paragraph (j) may be construed as permitting a taxpayer who applies this safe harbor to avoid the limitations of section 164(b)(6) for any amount paid as a tax or treated under this paragraph (j) as a payment of tax.

(4) *No safe harbor for transfers of property.*—The safe harbor provided in this paragraph (j) applies only to a payment of cash or cash equivalent.

(5) *Coordination with other deductions.*—An individual who deducts a payment under section 164 may not also deduct the same payment under any other Code section.

(6) *Examples.*—In the following examples, assume that the taxpayer is an individual who itemizes deductions for Federal income tax purposes.

(i) *Example 1.* In year 1, Taxpayer *A* makes a payment of $500 to an entity described in section 170(c). In return for the payment, *A* receives a dollar-for-dollar state income tax credit. Prior to application of the credit, *A*'s state income tax liability for year 1 was more than $500. *A* applies the $500 credit to *A*'s year 1 state income tax liability. Under paragraph (j)(1) of this section, *A* treats the $500 payment as a payment of state income tax in year 1. To determine *A*'s deduction amount, *A* must apply the provisions of section 164 applicable to payments of state and local taxes, including the limitation in section 164(b)(6). See paragraph (j)(3) of this section.

(ii) *Example 2.* In year 1, Taxpayer *B* makes a payment of $7,000 to an entity described in section 170(c). In return for the payment, *B* receives a dollar-for-dollar state income tax credit, which under state law may be carried forward for three taxable years. Prior to application of the credit, *B*'s state income tax liability for year 1 was $5,000; *B* applies $5,000 of the $7,000 credit to *B*'s year 1 state income tax liability. Under paragraph (j)(1) of this section, *B* treats $5,000 of the $7,000 payment as a payment of state income tax in year 1. Prior to application of the remaining credit, *B*'s state income tax liability for year 2 exceeds $2,000. *B* applies the excess credit of $2,000 to *B*'s year 2 state income tax liability. For year 2, under paragraph (j)(2) of this section, *B* treats the $2,000 as a payment of state income tax under section 164. To determine *B*'s deduction amounts in years 1 and 2, *B* must apply the provisions of section 164 applicable to payments of state and local taxes, including the limitation under section 164(b)(6). See paragraph (j)(3) of this section.

(iii) *Example 3.* In year 1, Taxpayer *C* makes a payment of $7,000 to an entity described in section 170(c). In return for the payment, *C* receives a local real property tax credit equal to 25 percent of the amount of this payment ($1,750). Prior to application of the credit, *C*'s local real property tax liability in year 1 was more than $1,750. *C* applies the $1,750 credit to *C*'s year 1 local real property tax liability. Under paragraph (j)(1) of this section, for year 1, *C* treats $1,750 of her $7,000 payment as a payment of local real property tax for purposes of section 164. To determine *C*'s deduction amount, *C* must apply the provisions of section 164 applicable to payments of state and local taxes, including the limitation under section 164(b)(6). See paragraph (j)(3) of this section.

* * *

[Prop. Reg. § 1.164-3.]

[Proposed 12-17-2019.]

§ 1.164-4. Taxes for local benefits.—(a) So-called taxes for local benefits referred to in paragraph (g) of § 1.164-2 more properly assessments, paid for local benefits such as street, sidewalks, and other like improvements, imposed because of and measured by some benefit inuring directly to the property against which the assessment is levied are not deductible as taxes. A tax is considered assessed against local benefits when the property subject to the tax is limited to property benefited. Special assessments are not deductible, even though an incidental benefit may inure to the public welfare. The real property taxes deductible are those levied for the general public welfare by the proper taxing authorities at a like rate against all property in the territory over which such authorities have jurisdiction. Assessments under the statutes of California relating to irrigation, and of Iowa relating to drainage, and under certain statutes of Tennessee relating to levees, are limited to property benefited, and if the assessments are so limited, the amounts paid thereunder are not deductible as taxes. For treatment of assessments for local benefits as adjustments to the basis of property, see section 1016(a)(1) and the regulations thereunder.

(b)(1) Insofar as assessments against local benefits are made for the purpose of maintenance or repair or for the purpose of meeting interest charges with respect to such benefits, they are deductible. In such cases, the burden is on the taxpayer to show the allocation of the amounts assessed to the different purposes. If the allocation cannot be made, none of the amount so paid is deductible.

(2) Taxes levied by a special taxing district which was in existence on December 31, 1963, for the purpose of retiring indebtedness existing on such date, are deductible, to the extent levied for such purpose, if (i) the district covers the whole of at least one county, (ii) if at least 1,000 persons are subject to the taxes levied by the district, and (iii) if the district levies its assessments annually at a uniform rate on the same assessed value of real property, including improvements, as is used for purposes of the real property tax generally. [Reg. § 1.164-4.]

☐ [*T.D.* 6256, 10-7-57. *Amended by T.D.* 6780, 12-21-64.]

§ 1.164-6. Apportionment of taxes on real property between seller and purchaser.—(a) *Scope.*—Except as provided otherwise in section 164(f) and § 1.164-8, when real property is sold, section 164(d)(1) governs the deduction by the seller and the purchaser of current real property taxes. Section 164(d)(1) performs two functions: (1) It provides a method by which a portion of the taxes for the real property tax year in which the property is sold may be deducted by the seller and a portion by the purchaser; and (2) it limits the deduction of the seller and the purchaser to the portion of the taxes corresponding to the part of the real property tax year during which each was the owner of the property. These functions are accomplished by treating a portion of the taxes for the real property tax year in which the property is sold as imposed on the seller and a portion as imposed on the purchaser. To the extent that the taxes are treated as imposed on the seller and the purchaser, each shall be allowed a deduction, under section 164(a), in the taxable year such tax is paid or accrued, or treated as paid or accrued under section 164(d)(2)(A) or (D) and this section. No deduction is allowed for taxes on real property to the extent that they are imposed on another taxpayer, or are treated as imposed on another taxpayer under section 164(d). For the election to accrue real property taxes ratably see section 461(c) and the regulations thereunder.

(b) *Application of rule of apportionment.*—(1)(i) For purposes of the deduction provided by section 164(a), if real property is sold during any real property tax year, the portion of the real property tax properly allocable to that part of the real property tax year which ends on the day before the date of the sale shall be treated as a tax imposed on the seller, and the portion of such tax properly allocable to that part of such real property tax year which begins on the date of the sale shall be treated as a tax imposed on the purchaser. For definition of "real property tax year" see paragraph (c) of this section. This rule shall apply whether or not the seller and the purchaser apportion such tax. The rule of apportionment contained in section 164(d)(1) applies even though the same real property is sold more than once during the real property tax year. (See paragraph (d)(5) of this section for rule requiring inclusion in gross income of excess deductions.)

* * *

(c) *Real property tax year.*—As used in section 164(d), the term "real property tax year" refers to the period which, under the law imposing the tax, is regarded as the period to which the tax imposed relates. Where the State and one or more local governmental units each imposes a tax on real property, the real property tax year for each tax must be determined for purposes of applying the rule of apportionment of section 164(d)(1) to each tax. The time when the tax rate is determined, the time when the assessment is made, the time when the tax becomes a lien, or the time when the tax becomes due or delinquent does not necessarily determine the real property tax year. The real property tax year may or may not correspond to the fiscal year of the governmental unit imposing the tax. In each case the State or local law determines what constitutes the real property tax year. Although the seller and the purchaser may or may not make an allocation of real property taxes, the meaning of "real property tax year" in section 164(d) and the application of section 164(d) do not depend upon what real property taxes were allocated nor the method of allocation used by the parties.

* * *

[Reg. § 1.164-6.]

□ [*T.D.* 6256, 10-7-57. *Amended by T.D.* 6293, 5-20-58 *and T.D.* 6406, 8-14-59.]

§ 1.165-1. Losses.—(a) *Allowance of deduction.*—Section 165(a) provides that, in computing taxable income under section 63, any loss actually sustained during the taxable year and not made good by insurance or some other form of compensation shall be allowed as a deduction subject to any provision of the internal revenue laws which prohibits or limits the amount of the deduction. This deduction for losses sustained shall be taken in accordance with section 165 and the regulations thereunder. For the disallowance of deductions for worthless securities issued by a political party, see § 1.271-1.

(b) *Nature of loss allowable.*—To be allowable as a deduction under section 165(a), a loss must be evidenced by closed and completed transactions, fixed by identifiable events, and, except as otherwise provided in section 165(h) and § 1.165-11, relating to disaster losses, actually sustained during the taxable year. Only a bona fide loss is allowable. Substance and not mere form shall govern in determining a deductible loss.

(c) *Amount deductible.*—(1) The amount of loss allowable as a deduction under section 165(a) shall not exceed the amount prescribed by § 1.1011-1 as the adjusted basis for determining the loss from the sale or other disposition of the property involved. In the case of each such deduction claimed, therefore, the basis of the property must be properly adjusted as prescribed by § 1.1011-1 for such items as expenditures, receipts, or losses, properly chargeable to capital account, and for such items as depreciation, obsolescence, amortization, and depletion, in order to determine the amount of loss allowable as a deduction. To determine the allowable loss in the case of property acquired before March 1, 1913, see also paragraph (b) of § 1.1053-1.

(2) The amount of loss recognized upon the sale or exchange of property shall be determined for purposes of section 165(a) in accordance with § 1.1002-1.

(3) A loss from the sale or exchange of a capital asset shall be allowed as a deduction under section 165(a) but only to the extent allowed in section 1211 (relating to limitation on capital losses) and section 1212 (relating to capital loss carrybacks and carryovers), and in the regulations under those sections.

(4) In determining the amount of loss actually sustained for purposes of section 165(a), proper adjustment shall be made for any salvage value and for any insurance or other compensation received.

(d) *Year of deduction.*—(1) A loss shall be allowed as a deduction under section 165(a) only for the taxable year in which the loss is sustained. For this purpose, a loss shall be treated as sustained during the taxable year in which the loss occurs as evidenced by closed and completed transactions and as fixed by identifiable events occurring in such taxable year. For provisions relating to situations where a loss attributable to a disaster will be treated as sustained in the taxable year immediately preceding the taxable year in which the disaster actually occurred, see section 165(h) and § 1.165-11.

(2) (i) If a casualty or other event occurs which may result in a loss and, in the year of such casualty or event, there exists a claim for reimbursement with respect to which there is a reasonable prospect of recovery, no portion of the loss with respect to which reimbursement may be received is sustained, for purposes of section 165, until it can be ascertained with reasonable certainty whether or not such reimbursement will be received. Whether a reasonable prospect of recovery exists with respect to a claim for reimbursement of a loss is a question of fact to be determined upon an examination of all facts and circumstances. Whether or not such reimbursement will be received may be ascertained with reasonable certainty, for example, by a settlement of the claim, by an adjudication of the claim, or by an abandonment of the claim. When a taxpayer claims that the taxable year in which a loss is sustained is fixed by his abandonment of the claim for reimbursement, he must be able to produce objective evidence of his having abandoned the claim, such as the execution of a release.

(ii) If in the year of the casualty or other event a portion of the loss is not covered by a claim for reimbursement with respect to which there is a reasonable prospect of recovery, then such portion of the loss is sustained during the taxable year in which the casualty or other event occurs. For example, if property having an adjusted basis of $10,000 is completely destroyed by fire in 1961, and if the taxpayer's only claim for reimbursement consists of an insurance claim for $8,000 which is settled in 1962, the taxpayer sustains a loss of $2,000 in 1961. However, if the taxpayer's automobile is completely destroyed in 1961 as a result of the negligence of another person and there exists a reasonable prospect of recovery on a claim for the full value of the automobile against such person, the taxpayer does not sustain any loss until the taxable year in which the claim is adjudicated or otherwise settled. If the automobile had an adjusted basis of $5,000 and the taxpayer secures a judgment of $4,000 in 1962, $1,000 is deductible for the taxable year 1962. If in 1963 it becomes reasonably certain that only $3,500 can ever be collected on such judgment, $500 is deductible for the taxable year 1963.

(iii) If the taxpayer deducted a loss in accordance with the provisions of this paragraph and in a subsequent taxable year receives reimbursement for such loss, he does not recompute the tax for the taxable year in which the deduction was taken but includes the amount of such reimbursement in his gross income for the taxable year in which received, subject to the provisions of section 111, relating to recovery of amounts previously deducted.

(3) Any loss arising from theft shall be treated as sustained during the taxable year in which the taxpayer discovers the loss (see § 1.165-8, relating to theft losses). However, if in the year of discovery there exists a claim for reimbursement with respect to which there is a reasonable prospect of recovery, no portion of the loss with respect to which reimbursement may be received is sustained, for purposes of section 165, until the taxable year in which it can be ascertained with reasonable certainty whether or not such reimbursement will be received.

* * *

(e) *Limitation on losses of individuals.*—In the case of an individual, the deduction for losses granted by section 165(a) shall, subject to the provisions of section 165(c) and paragraph (a) of this section, be limited to:

(1) Losses incurred in a trade or business;

(2) Losses incurred in any transaction entered into for profit, though not connected with a trade or business; and

(3) Losses of property not connected with a trade or business and not incurred in any transaction entered into for profit, if such losses arise from fire, storm, shipwreck, or other casualty, or from theft, and if the loss involved has not been allowed for estate tax purposes in the estate tax return. For additional

provisions pertaining to the allowance of casualty and theft losses, see § § 1.165-7 and 1.165-8, respectively. For special rules relating to an election by a taxpayer to deduct disaster losses in the taxable year immediately preceding the taxable year in which the disaster occurred, see section 165(h) and § 1.165-11. [Reg. § 1.165-1.]

□ [*T.D.* 6445, 1-15-60. *Amended by T.D.* 6753, 5-18-64, *T.D.* 6996, 1-17-69, *T.D.* 7301, 1-3-74 *and T.D.* 7522, 12-15-77.]

§ 1.165-2. Obsolescence of nondepreciable property.—(a) *Allowance of deduction.*—A loss incurred in a business or in a transaction entered into for profit and arising from the sudden termination of the usefulness in such business or transaction of any nondepreciable property, in a case where such business or transaction is discontinued or where such property is permanently discarded from use therein, shall be allowed as a deduction under section 165(a) for the taxable year in which the loss is actually sustained. For this purpose, the taxable year in which the loss is sustained is not necessarily the taxable year in which the overt act of abandonment, or the loss of title to the property, occurs.

(b) *Exceptions.*—This section does not apply to losses sustained upon the sale or exchange of property, losses sustained upon the obsolescence or worthlessness of depreciable property, casualty losses, or losses reflected in inventories required to be taken under section 471. The limitations contained in sections 1211 and 1212 upon losses from the sale or exchange of capital assets do not apply to losses allowable under this section.

* * *

[Reg. § 1.165-2.]

□ [*T.D.* 6445, 1-15-60. *Amended by T.D.* 9564, 12-23-2011; *T.D.* 9636, 9-13-2013 *and T.D.* 9689, 8-14-2014.]

§ 1.165-4. Decline in value of stock.—(a) *Deduction disallowed.*—No deduction shall be allowed under section 165(a) solely on account of a decline in the value of stock owned by the taxpayer when the decline is due to a fluctuation in the market price of the stock or to other similar cause. A mere shrinkage in the value of stock owned by the taxpayer, even though extensive, does not give rise to a deduction under section 165(a) if the stock has any recognizable value on the date claimed as the date of loss. No loss for a decline in the value of stock owned by the taxpayer shall be allowed as a deduction under section 165(a) except insofar as the loss is recognized under § 1.1002-1 upon the sale or exchange of the stock and except as otherwise provided in § 1.165-5 with respect to stock which becomes worthless during the taxable year.

* * *

(c) *Application to inventories.*—This section does not apply to a decline in the value of corporate stock reflected in inventories required to be taken by a dealer in securities under section 471. See § 1.471-5.

(d) *Definition.*—As used in this section, the term "stock" means a share of stock in a corporation or a right to subscribe for, or to receive, a share of stock in a corporation. [Reg. § 1.165-4.]

□ [*T.D.* 6445, 1-15-60.]

§ 1.165-5. Worthless securities.—(a) *Definition of security.*—As used in section 165(g) and this section, the term "security" means:

(1) A share of stock in a corporation;

(2) A right to subscribe for, or to receive, a share of stock in a corporation; or

(3) A bond, debenture, note, or certificate, or other evidence of indebtedness to pay a fixed or determinable sum of money, which has been issued with interest coupons or in registered form by a domestic or foreign corporation or by any government or political subdivision thereof.

(b) *Ordinary loss.*—If any security which is not a capital asset becomes wholly worthless during the taxable year, the loss resulting therefrom may be deducted under section 165(a) as an ordinary loss.

(c) *Capital loss.*—If any security which is a capital asset becomes wholly worthless at any time during the taxable year, the loss resulting therefrom may be deducted under section 165(a) but only as though it were a loss from a sale or exchange, on the last day of the taxable year, of a capital asset. See section 165(g)(1). The amount so allowed as a deduction shall be subject to the limitations upon capital losses described in paragraph (c)(3) of § 1.165-1.

(d) *Loss on worthless securities of an affiliated corporation.*—(1) *Deductible as an ordinary loss.*—If a taxpayer which is a domestic corporation owns any security of a domestic or foreign corporation which is affiliated with the taxpayer within the meaning of subparagraph (2) of this paragraph and such security becomes wholly worthless during the taxable year, the loss resulting therefrom may be deducted under section 165(a) as an ordinary loss in accordance with paragraph (b) of this section. The fact that the security is in fact a capital asset of the taxpayer is immaterial for this purpose, since section 165(g)(3) provides that such security shall be treated as though it were not a capital asset for the purposes of section 165(g)(1). A debt which becomes wholly worthless during the taxable year shall be allowed as an ordinary loss in accordance with the provisions of this subparagraph, to the extent that such debt is a security within the meaning of paragraph (a)(3) of this section.

(2) *Affiliated corporation defined.*—For purposes of this paragraph, a corporation shall be treated as affiliated with the taxpayer owning the security if—

(i) *(a)* In the case of a taxable year beginning on or after January 1, 1970, the taxpayer owns directly—

(1) Stock possessing at least 80 percent of the voting power of all classes of such corporation's stock, and

(2) At least 80 percent of each class of such corporation's nonvoting stock excluding for purposes of this subdivision (i)(*a*) nonvoting stock which is limited and preferred as to dividends (see section 1504(a)), or

(b) In the case of a taxable year beginning before January 1, 1970, the taxpayer owns directly at least 95 percent of each class of the stock of such corporation;

(ii) None of the stock of such corporation was acquired by the taxpayer solely for the purpose of converting a capital loss sustained by reason of the worthlessness of any such stock into an ordinary loss under section 165(g)(3), and

(iii) More than 90 percent of the aggregate of the gross receipts of such corporation for all the taxable years during which it has been in existence has been from sources other than royalties, rents (except rents derived from rental of properties to employees of such corporation in the ordinary course of its operating business), dividends, interest (except interest received on the deferred purchase price of operating assets sold), annuities and gains from sales or exchanges of stocks and securities. For this purpose, the term "gross receipts" means total receipts determined without any deduction for cost of goods sold, and gross receipts from sales or exchanges of stocks and securities shall be taken into account only to the extent of gains from such sales or exchanges.

(e) *Bonds issued by an insolvent corporation.*—A bond of an insolvent corporation secured only by a mortgage from which nothing is realized for the bondholders on foreclosure shall be regarded as having become worthless not later than the year of the foreclosure sale, and no deduction in respect of the loss shall be allowed under section 165(a) in computing a bondholder's taxable income for a subsequent year. See also paragraph (d) of § 1.165-1.

(f) *Decline in market value.*—A taxpayer possessing a security to which this section relates shall not be allowed any deduction under section 165(a) on account of mere market fluctuation in the value of such security. See also § 1.165-4.

(g) *Application to inventories.*—This section does not apply to any loss upon the worthlessness of any security reflected in inventories required to be taken by a dealer in securities under section 471. See § 1.471-5.

(h) *Special rules for banks.*—For special rules applicable under this section to worthless securities of a bank, including securities issued by an affiliated bank, see § 1.582-1.

(i) *Abandonment of securities.*—(1) *In general.*—For purposes of section 165 and this section, a security that becomes wholly worthless includes a security described in paragraph (a) of this section that is abandoned and otherwise satisfies the requirements for a deductible loss under section 165. If the abandoned security is a capital asset and is not described in section 165(g)(3) and paragraph (d) of this section (concerning worthless securities of certain affiliated corporations), the resulting loss is treated as a loss from the sale or exchange, on the last day of the taxable year, of a capital asset. See section 165(g)(1) and paragraph (c) of this section. To abandon a security, a taxpayer must permanently surrender and relinquish all rights in the security and receive no consideration in exchange for the security. For purposes of this section, all the facts and circumstances determine whether the transaction is properly characterized as an abandonment or other type of transaction, such as an actual sale or exchange, contribution to capital, dividend, or gift.

* * *

[Reg. § 1.165-5.]

☐ [*T.D.* 6445, 1-15-60. *Amended by T.D.* 7224, 12-5-72 *and T.D.* 9386, 3-11-2008.]

§ 1.165-6. Farming losses.—(a) *Allowance of losses.*—(1) Except as otherwise provided in this section, any loss incurred in the operation of a farm as a trade or business shall be allowed as a deduction under section 165(a) or as a net operating loss deduction in accordance with the provisions of section 172. See § 1.172-1.

(2) If the taxpayer owns and operates a farm for profit in addition to being engaged in another trade or business, but sustains a loss from the operation of the farming business, then the amount of loss sustained in the opera-

tion of the farm may be deducted from gross income, if any, from all other sources.

(3) Loss incurred in the operation of a farm for recreation or pleasure shall not be allowed as a deduction from gross income. See § 1.162-12.

(b) *Loss from shrinkage.*—If, in the course of the business of farming, farm products are held for a favorable market, no deduction shall be allowed under section 165(a) in respect of such products merely because of shrinkage in weight, decline in value, or deterioration in storage.

(c) *Loss of prospective crop.*—The total loss by frost, storm, flood, or fire of a prospective crop being grown in the business of farming shall not be allowed as a deduction under section 165(a).

(d) *Loss of livestock.*—(1) *Raised stock.*—A taxpayer engaged in the business of raising and selling livestock, such as cattle, sheep, or horses, may not deduct as a loss under section 165(a) the value of animals that perish from among those which were raised on the farm.

(2) *Purchased stock.*—The loss sustained upon the death by disease, exposure, or injury of any livestock purchased and used in the trade or business of farming shall be allowed as a deduction under section 165(a). See, also, paragraph (e) of this section.

(e) *Loss due to compliance with orders of governmental authority.*—The loss sustained upon the destruction by order of the United States, a State, or any other governmental authority, of any livestock, or other property, purchased and used in the trade or business of farming shall be allowed as a deduction under section 165(a).

(f) *Amount deductible.*—(1) *Expenses of operation.*—The cost of any feed, pasture, or care which is allowed under section 162 as an expense of operating a farm for profit shall not be included as a part of the cost of livestock for purposes of determining the amount of loss deductible under section 165(a) and this section. For the deduction of farming expenses, see § 1.162-12.

(2) *Losses reflected in inventories.*—If inventories are taken into account in determining the income from the trade or business of farming, no deduction shall be allowed under this section for losses sustained during the taxable year upon livestock or other products, whether purchased for resale or produced on the farm, to the extent such losses are reflected in the inventory on hand at the close of the taxable year. Nothing in this section shall be construed to disallow the deduction of any loss reflected in the inventories of the taxpayer. For provisions relating to inventories of farmers, see section 471 and the regulations thereunder.

(3) *Other limitations.*—For other provisions relating to the amount deductible under this section, see paragraph (c) of § 1.165-1, relating to the amount deductible under section 165(a); § 1.165-7, relating to casualty losses; and § 1.1231-1, relating to gains and losses from the sale or exchange of certain property used in the trade or business.

(g) *Other provisions applicable to farmers.*—For other provisions relating to farmers, see § 1.61-4, relating to gross income of farmers; paragraph (b) of § 1.167(a)-6, relating to depreciation in the case of farmers; and § 1.175-1, relating to soil and water conservation expenditures. [Reg. § 1.165-6.]

☐ [*T.D.* 6445, 1-15-60.]

»»→ Note: Reg. § 1.165-7 does not reflect the limitations imposed by Section 165(h)(2), added in 1984.

§ 1.165-7. Casualty losses.—(a) *In general.*—(1) *Allowance of deduction.*—Except as otherwise provided in paragraphs (b)(4) and (c) of this section, any loss arising from fire, storm, shipwreck, or other casualty is allowable as a deduction under section 165(a) for the taxable year in which the loss is sustained. However, see § 1.165-6, relating to farming losses, and § 1.165-11, relating to an election by a taxpayer to deduct disaster losses in the taxable year immediately preceding the taxable year in which the disaster occurred. The manner of determining the amount of a casualty loss allowable as a deduction in computing taxable income under section 63 is the same whether the loss has been incurred in a trade or business or in any transaction entered into for profit, or whether it has been a loss of property not connected with a trade or business and not incurred in any transaction entered into for profit. The amount of a casualty loss shall be determined in accordance with paragraph (b) of this section. For other rules relating to the treatment of deductible casualty losses, see § 1.1231-1, relating to the involuntary conversion of property.

(2) *Method of valuation.*—(i) In determining the amount of loss deductible under this section, the fair market value of the property immediately before and immediately after the casualty shall generally be ascertained by competent appraisal. This appraisal must recognize the effects of any general market decline affecting undamaged as well as damaged property which may occur simultaneously with the casualty, in order that any deduction under this

section shall be limited to the actual loss resulting from damage to the property.

(ii) The cost of repairs to the property damaged is acceptable as evidence of the loss of value if the taxpayer shows that *(a)* the repairs are necessary to restore the property to its condition immediately before the casualty, *(b)* the amount spent for such repairs is not excessive, *(c)* the repairs do not care for more than the damage suffered, and *(d)* the value of the property after the repairs does not as a result of the repairs exceed the value of the property immediately before the casualty.

(3) *Damage to automobiles.*—An automobile owned by the taxpayer, whether used for business purposes or maintained for recreation or pleasure, may be the subject of a casualty loss, including those losses specifically referred to in subparagraph (1) of this paragraph. In addition, a casualty loss occurs when an automobile owned by the taxpayer is damaged and when:

(i) The damage results from the faulty driving of the taxpayer or other person operating the automobile but is not due to the willful act or willful negligence of the taxpayer or of one acting in his behalf, or

(ii) The damage results from the faulty driving of the operator of the vehicle with which the automobile of the taxpayer collides.

(4) *Application to inventories.*—This section does not apply to a casualty loss reflected in the inventories of the taxpayer. For provisions relating to inventories, see section 471 and the regulations thereunder.

(5) *Property converted from personal use.*—In the case of property which originally was not used in the trade or business or for income-producing purposes and which is thereafter converted to either of such uses, the fair market value of the property on the date of conversion, if less than the adjusted basis of the property at such time, shall be used, after making proper adjustments in respect of basis, as the basis for determining the amount of loss under paragraph (b)(1) of this section. See paragraph (b) of § 1.165-9, and § 1.167(g)-1.

(6) *Theft losses.*—A loss which arises from theft is not considered a casualty loss for purposes of this section. See § 1.165-8, relating to theft losses.

(b) *Amount deductible.*—(1) *General rule.*—In the case of any casualty loss whether or not incurred in a trade or business or in any transaction entered into for profit, the amount of loss to be taken into account for purposes of section 165(a) shall be the lesser of either—

(i) The amount which is equal to the fair market value of the property immediately before the casualty reduced by the fair market value of the property immediately after the casualty; or

(ii) The amount of the adjusted basis prescribed in § 1.1011-1 for determining the loss from the sale or other disposition of the property involved. However, if the property used in a trade or business or held for the production of income is totally destroyed by casualty, and if the fair market value of such property immediately before the casualty is less than the adjusted basis of such property, the amount of the adjusted basis of such property shall be treated as the amount of the loss for purposes of section 165(a).

(2) *Aggregation of property for computing loss.*—(i) A loss incurred in a trade or business or in any transaction entered into for profit shall be determined under subparagraph (1) of this paragraph by reference to the single, identifiable property damaged or destroyed. Thus, for example, in determining the fair market value of the property before and after the casualty in a case where damage by casualty has occurred to a building and ornamental or fruit trees used in a trade or business, the decrease in value shall be measured by taking the building and trees into account separately, and not together as an integral part of the realty, and separate losses shall be determined for such building and trees.

(ii) In determining a casualty loss involving real property and improvements thereon not used in a trade or business or in any transaction entered into for profit, the improvements (such as buildings and ornamental trees and shrubbery) to the property damaged or destroyed shall be considered an integral part of the property, for purposes of subparagraph (1) of this paragraph, and no separate basis need by apportioned to such improvements.

(3) *Examples.*—The application of this paragraph may be illustrated by the following examples:

Example (1). In 1956 B purchases for $3,600 an automobile which he uses for nonbusiness purposes. In 1959 the automobile is damaged in an accidental collision with another automobile. The fair market value of B's automobile is $2,000 immediately before the collision and $1,500 immediately after the collision. B receives insurance proceeds of $300 to cover the loss. The amount of the deduction allowable under section 165(a) for the taxable year 1959 is $200, computed as follows:

Value of automobile immediately before casualty	$2,000
Less: Value of automobile immediately after casualty	1,500
Value of property actually destroyed	500
Loss to be taken into account for purposes of section 165(a): Lesser amount of property actually destroyed ($500) or adjusted basis of property ($3,600)	$500
Less: Insurance received	300
Deduction allowable	200

Example (2). In 1958 A purchases land containing an office building for the lump sum of $90,000. The purchase price is allocated between the land ($18,000) and the building ($72,000) for purposes of determining basis. After the purchase A planted trees and ornamental shrubs on the grounds surrounding the building. In 1961 the land, building, trees, and shrubs are damaged by hurricane. At the time of the casualty the adjusted basis of the land is $18,000 and the adjusted basis of the building is $66,000. At that time the trees and shrubs have an adjusted basis of $1,200. The fair market value of the land and building immediately before the casualty is $18,000 and $70,000, respectively, and immediately after the casualty is $18,000 and $52,000, respectively. The fair market value of the trees and shrubs immediately before the casualty is $2,000 and immediately after the casualty is $400. In 1961 insurance of $5,000 is received to cover the loss to the building. A has no other gains or losses in 1961 subject to section 1231 and §1.1231-1. The amount of the deduction allowable under section 165(a) with respect to the building for the taxable year 1961 is $13,000, computed as follows:

Value of property immediately before casualty	$70,000
Less: Value of property immediately after casualty	52,000
Value of property actually destroyed	18,000
Loss to be taken into account for purposes of section 165(a): Lesser amount of property actually destroyed ($18,000) or adjusted basis of property ($66,000)	$18,000
Less: Insurance received	5,000
Deduction allowable	13,000

The amount of the deduction allowable under section 165(a) with respect to the trees and shrubs for the taxable year 1961 is $1,200, computed as follows:

Value of property immediately before casualty	$2,000
Less: Value of property immediately after casualty	400
Value of property actually destroyed	1,600
Loss to be taken into account for purposes of section 165(a): Lesser amount of property actually destroyed ($1,600) or adjusted basis of property ($1,200)	$1,200

Example (3). Assume the same facts as in example (2) except that A purchases land containing a house instead of an office building. The house is used as his private residence. Since the property is used for personal purposes, no allocation of the purchase price is necessary for the land and house. Likewise, no individual determination of the fair market values of the land, house, trees, and shrubs is necessary. The amount of the deduction allowable under section 165(a) with respect to the land, house, trees, and shrubs for the taxable year 1961 is $14,600, computed as follows:

Value of property immediately before casualty	$90,000
Less: Value of property immediately after casualty	70,400
Value of property actually destroyed	$19,600
Loss to be taken into account for purposes of section 165(a): Lesser amount of property actually destroyed ($19,600) or adjusted basis of property ($91,200)	$19,600
Less: Insurance received	5,000
Deduction allowable	14,600

(4) *Limitation on certain losses sustained by individuals after December 31, 1963.*—(i) Pursuant to section 165(c)(3), the deduction allowable under section 165(a) in respect of a loss sustained—

(*a*) After December 31, 1963, in a taxable year ending after such date,

(*b*) In respect of property not used in a trade or business or for income producing purposes, and

(*c*) From a single casualty

shall be limited to that portion of the loss which is in excess of $100. The nondeductibility of the first $100 of loss applies to a loss sustained after December 31, 1963, without regard to when the casualty occurred. Thus, if property not used in a trade or business or for income producing purposes is damaged or destroyed by a casualty which occurred prior to January 1, 1964, and loss resulting therefrom is sustained after December 31, 1963, the $100 limitation applies.

(ii) The $100 limitation applies separately in respect of each casualty and applies to the entire loss sustained from each casualty. Thus, if as a result of a particular casualty occurring in 1964, a taxpayer sustains in 1964 a loss of $40 and in 1965 a loss of $250, no deduction is allowable for the loss sustained in 1964 and the loss sustained in 1965 must be reduced by $60 ($100–$40). The determination of whether damage to, or destruction of, property resulted from a single casualty or from two or more separate casualties will be made upon the basis of the particular facts of each case. However, events which are closely related in origin generally give rise to a single casualty. For example, if a storm damages a taxpayer's residence and his automobile parked in his driveway, any loss sustained results from a single casualty. Similarly, if a hurricane causes high waves, all wind and flood damage to a taxpayer's property caused by the hurricane and the waves results from a single casualty.

(iii) Except as otherwise provided in this subdivision, the $100 limitation applies separately to each individual taxpayer who sustains a loss even though the property damaged or destroyed is owned by two or more individuals. Thus, if a house occupied by two sisters and jointly owned by them is damaged or destroyed, the $100 limitation applies separately to each sister in respect of any loss sustained by her. However, for purposes of applying the $100 limitation, a husband and wife who file a joint return for the first taxable year in which the loss is allowable as a deduction are treated as one individual taxpayer. Accordingly, if property jointly owned by a husband and wife, or property separately owned by the husband or by the wife, is damaged or destroyed by a single casualty in 1964, and a loss is sustained in that year by either or both the husband or wife, only one $100 limitation applies if a joint return is filed for 1964. If, however, the husband and wife file separate returns for 1964, the $100 limitation applies separately in respect of any loss sustained by the husband and in respect of any loss sustained by the wife. Where losses from a single casualty are sustained in two or more separate tax years, the husband and wife shall, for purposes of applying the $100 limitation to such losses, be treated as one individual for all such years if they file a joint return for the first year in which a loss is sustained from the casualty; they shall be treated as separate individuals for all such years if they file separate returns for the first such year. If a joint return is filed in the first loss year but separate returns are filed in a subsequent year, any unused portion of the $100 limitation shall be allocated equally between the husband and wife in the latter year.

(iv) If a loss is sustained in respect of property used partially for business and partially for nonbusiness purposes, the $100 limitation applies only to that portion of the loss properly attributable to the nonbusiness use. For example, if a taxpayer sustains a $1,000 loss in respect of an automobile which he uses 60 percent for business and 40 percent for nonbusiness, the loss is allocated 60 percent to business use and 40 percent to nonbusiness use. The $100 limitation applies to the portion of the loss allocable to the nonbusiness loss.

(c) *Loss sustained by an estate.*—A casualty loss of property not connected with a trade or business and not incurred in any transaction entered into for profit which is sustained during the settlement of an estate shall be allowed as a deduction under sections 165(a) and 641(b) in computing the taxable income of the estate if the loss has not been allowed under section 2054 in computing the taxable estate of the decedent and if the statement has been filed in accordance with § 1.642(g)-1. See section 165(c)(3).

(d) *Loss treated as though attributable to a trade or business.*—For the rule treating a casualty loss not connected with a trade or business as though it were a deduction attributable to a trade or business for purposes of computing a net operating loss, see paragraph (a)(3)(iii) of § 1.172-3.

* * *

[Reg. § 1.165-7.]

☐ [*T.D.* 6445, 1-15-60. *Amended by T.D.* 6712, 3-23-64, *T.D.* 6735, 5-18-64, *T.D.* 6786, 12-28-64 *and T.D.* 7522, 12-15-77.]

§ 1.165-8. Theft losses.—(a) *Allowance of deduction.*—(1) Except as otherwise provided in paragraphs (b) and (c) of this section, any loss arising from theft is allowable as a deduction under section 165(a) for the taxable year in which the loss is sustained. See section 165(c)(3).

(2) A loss arising from theft shall be treated under section 165(a) as sustained during the taxable year in which the taxpayer discovers the loss. See section 165(e). Thus, a theft loss is not deductible under section 165(a) for the taxable year in which the theft actually

occurs unless that is also the year in which the taxpayer discovers the loss. However, if in the year of discovery there exists a claim for reimbursement with respect to which there is a reasonable prospect of recovery, see paragraph (d) of § 1.165-1.

(3) The same theft loss shall not be taken into account both in computing a tax under chapter 1, relating to the income tax, or chapter 2, relating to additional income taxes, of the Internal Revenue Code of 1939 and in computing the income tax under the Internal Revenue Code of 1954. See section 7852(c), relating to items not to be twice deducted from income.

(b) *Loss sustained by an estate.*—A theft loss of property not connected with a trade or business and not incurred in any transaction entered into for profit which is discovered during the settlement of an estate, even though the theft actually occurred during a taxable year of the decedent, shall be allowed as a deduction under sections 165(a) and 641(b) in computing the taxable income of the estate if the loss has not been allowed under section 2054 in computing the taxable estate of the decedent and if the statement has been filed in accordance with § 1.642(g)-1. See section 165(c)(3). For purposes of determining the year of deduction, see paragraph (a)(2) of this section.

(c) *Amount deductible.*—The amount deductible under this section in respect of a theft loss shall be determined consistently with the manner prescribed in § 1.165-7 for determining the amount of casualty loss allowable as a deduction under section 165(a). In applying the provisions of paragraph (b) of § 1.165-7 for this purpose, the fair market value of the property immediately after the theft shall be considered to be zero. In the case of a loss sustained after December 31, 1963, in a taxable year ending after such date, in respect of property not used in a trade or business or for income producing purposes, the amount deductible shall be limited to that portion of the loss which is in excess of $100. For rules applicable in applying the $100 limitation, see subparagraph (b)(4) of § 1.165-7. For other rules relating to the treatment of deductible theft losses, see § 1.1231-1, relating to the involuntary conversion of property.

(d) *Definition.*—For purposes of this section the term "theft" shall be deemed to include, but shall not necessarily be limited to, larceny, embezzlement, and robbery.

(e) *Application to inventories.*—This section does not apply to a theft loss reflected in the inventories of the taxpayer. For provisions relating to inventories, see section 471 and the regulations thereunder.

(f) *Example.*—The application of this section may be illustrated by the following example:

Example. In 1955 B, who makes her return on the basis of the calendar year, purchases for personal use a diamond brooch costing $4,000. On November 30, 1961, at which time it has a fair market value of $3,500, the brooch is stolen; but B does not discover the loss until January 1962. The brooch was fully insured against theft. A controversy develops with the insurance company over its liability in respect of the loss. However, in 1962, B has a reasonable prospect of recovery of the fair market value of the brooch from the insurance company. The controversy is settled in March 1963, at which time B receives $2,000 in insurance proceeds to cover the loss from theft. No deduction for the loss is allowable for 1961 or 1962; but the amount of the deduction allowable under section 165(a) for the taxable year 1963 is $1,500, computed as follows:

Value of property immediately before theft	$3,500
Less: Value of property immediately after the theft	0
Balance	$3,500
Loss to be taken into account for purposes of section 165(a): ($3,500 but not to exceed adjusted basis of $4,000 at time of theft) .	$3,500
Less: Insurance received in 1963 . .	2,000
Deduction allowable for 1963	$1,500

[Reg. § 1.165-8.]

☐ [*T.D.* 6445, 1-15-60. *Amended by T.D.* 6786, 12-28-64.]

§ 1.165-9. Sale of residential property.—(a) *Losses not allowed.*—A loss sustained on the sale of residential property purchased or constructed by the taxpayer for use as his personal residence and so used by him up to the time of the sale is not deductible under section 165(a).

(b) *Property converted from personal use.*—(1) If property purchased or constructed by the taxpayer for use as his personal residence is, prior to its sale, rented or otherwise appropriated to income-producing purposes and is used for such purposes up to the time of its sale, a loss sustained on the sale of the property shall be allowed as a deduction under section 165(a).

(2) The loss allowed under this paragraph upon the sale of the property shall be the excess of the adjusted basis prescribed in § 1.1011-1 for determining loss over the amount realized from the sale. For this purpose, the adjusted basis for determining loss shall be the lesser of either of the following amounts, adjusted as prescribed in § 1.1011-1 for the period

subsequent to the conversion of the property to income-producing purposes:

(i) The fair market value of the property at the time of conversion, or

(ii) The adjusted basis for loss, at the time of conversion, determined under § 1.1011-1 but without reference to the fair market value.

(3) For rules relating to casualty losses of property converted from personal use, see paragraph (a)(5) of § 1.165-7. To determine the basis for depreciation in the case of such property, see § 1.167(g)-1. For limitations on the loss from the sale of a capital asset, see paragraph (c)(3) of § 1.165-1.

(c) *Examples.*—The application of paragraph (b) of this section may be illustrated by the following examples:

Example (1). Residential property is purchased by the taxpayer in 1943 for use as his personal residence at a cost of $25,000, of which $15,000 is allocable to the building. The taxpayer uses the property as his personal residence until January 1, 1952, at which time its fair market value is $22,000, of which $12,000 is allocable to the building. The taxpayer rents the property from January 1, 1952, until January 1, 1955, at which time it is sold for $16,000. On January 1, 1952, the building has an estimated useful life of 20 years. It is assumed that the building has no estimated salvage value and that there are no adjustments in respect of basis other than depreciation, which is computed on the straight-line method. The loss to be taken into account for purposes of section 165(a) for the taxable year 1955 is $4,200, computed as follows:

Basis of property at time of conversion for purposes of this section (that is, the lesser of $25,000 cost or $22,000 fair market value)	$22,000
Less: Depreciation allowable from January 1, 1952, to January 1, 1955 (3 years at 5 percent based on $12,000, the value of the building at time of conversion, as prescribed by § 1.167(g)-1)	$1,800
Adjusted basis prescribed in § 1.1011-1 for determining loss on sale of the property	$20,200
Less: Amount realized on sale . . .	16,000
Loss to be taken into account for purposes of section 165(a)	$4,200

In this example the value of the building at the time of conversion is used as the basis for computing depreciation. See example (2) of this paragraph wherein the adjusted basis of the building is required to be used for such purpose.

Example (2). Residential property is purchased by the taxpayer in 1940 for use as his personal residence at a cost of $23,000, of which $10,000 is allocable to the building. The taxpayer uses the property as his personal residence until January 1, 1953, at which time its fair market value is $20,000, of which $12,000 is allocable to the building. The taxpayer rents the property from January 1, 1953, until January 1, 1957, at which time it is sold for $17,000. On January 1, 1953, the building has an estimated useful life of 20 years. It is assumed that the building has no estimated salvage value and that there are no adjustments in respect of basis other than depreciation, which is computed on the straight-line method. The loss to be taken into account for purposes of section 165(a) for the taxable year 1957 is $1,000, computed as follows:

Basis of property at time of conversion for purposes of this section (that is, the lesser of $23,000 cost or $20,000 fair market value)	$20,000
Less: Depreciation allowable from January 1, 1953, to January 1, 1957 (4 years at 5% based on $10,000, the cost of the building, as prescribed by § 1.167(g)-1)	2,000
Adjusted basis prescribed in § 1.1011-1 for determining loss on sale of the property	$18,000
Less: Amount realized on sale . . .	17,000
Loss to be taken into account for purposes of section 165(a)	$1,000

[Reg. § 1.165-9.]

☐ [*T.D.* 6445, 1-15-60. *Amended by T.D.* 6712, 3-23-64.]

§ 1.165-10. Wagering losses.—Losses sustained during the taxable year on wagering transactions shall be allowed as a deduction but only to the extent of the gains during the taxable year from such transactions. In the case of a husband and wife making a joint return for the taxable year, the combined losses of the spouses from wagering transactions shall be allowed to the extent of the combined gains of the spouses from wagering transactions. [Reg. § 1.165-10.]

☐ [*T.D.* 6445, 1-15-60.]

§ 1.166-1. Bad debts.—(a) *Allowance of deduction.*—Section 166 provides that, in computing taxable income under section 63, a deduction shall be allowed in respect of bad debts owed to the taxpayer. For this purpose, bad debts shall, subject to the provisions of section 166 and the regulations thereunder, be taken into account either as—

(1) A deduction in respect of debts which become worthless in whole or in part; or as

(2) A deduction for a reasonable addition to a reserve for bad debts.

(b) *Manner of selecting method.*—(1) A taxpayer filing a return of income for the first taxable year for which he is entitled to a bad debt deduction may select either of the two methods prescribed by paragraph (a) of this section for treating bad debts, but such selection is subject to the approval of the district director upon examination of the return. If the method so selected is approved, it shall be used in returns for all subsequent taxable years unless the Commissioner grants permission to use the other method. A statement of facts substantiating any deduction claimed under section 166 on account of bad debts shall accompany each return of income.

(2) Taxpayers who have properly selected one of the two methods for treating bad debts under provisions of prior law corresponding to section 166 shall continue to use that method for all subsequent taxable years unless the Commissioner grants permission to use the other method.

(3) (i) For taxable years beginning after December 31, 1959, application for permission to change the method of treating bad debts shall be made in accordance with section 446(e) and paragraph (e) (3) of § 1.446-1.

(ii) For taxable years beginning before January 1, 1960, application for permission to change the method of treating bad debts shall be made at least 30 days before the close of the taxable year for which the change is effective.

(4) Notwithstanding paragraph (b) (1), (2), and (3) of this section, a dealer in property currently employing the accrual method of accounting and currently maintaining a reserve for bad debts under section 166(c) (which may have included guaranteed debt obligations described in section 166(f) (1) (A)) may establish a reserve for section 166(f) (1) (A) guaranteed debt obligations for a taxable year ending after October 21, 1965 under section 166(f) and § 1.166-10 by filing on or before April 17, 1986, an amended return indicating that such a reserve has been established. The establishment of such a reserve will not be considered a change in method of accounting for purposes of section 446(e). However, an election by a taxpayer to establish a reserve for bad debts under section 166(c) shall be treated as a change in method of accounting. See also § 1.166-4, relating to reserve for bad debts, and § 1.166-10, relating to reserve for guaranteed debt obligations.

(c) *Bona fide debt required.*—Only a bona fide debt qualifies for purposes of section 166. A bona fide debt is a debt which arises from a debtor-creditor relationship based upon a valid and enforceable obligation to pay a fixed or determinable sum of money. A debt arising out of the receivables of an accrual method taxpayer is deemed to be an enforceable obligation for purposes of the preceding sentence to the extent that the income such debt represents has been included in the return of income for the year for which the deduction as a bad debt is claimed or for a prior taxable year. For example, a debt arising out of gambling receivables that are unenforceable under state or local law, which an accrual method taxpayer includes in income under section 61, is an enforceable obligation for purposes of this paragraph. A gift or contribution to capital shall not be considered a debt for purposes of section 166. The fact that a bad debt is not due at the time of deduction shall not of itself prevent its allowance under section 166. For the disallowance of deductions for bad debts owed by a political party, see § 1.271-1.

(d) *Amount deductible.*—(1) *General rule.*—Except in the case of a deduction for a reasonable addition to a reserve for bad debts, the basis for determining the amount of deduction under section 166 in respect of a bad debt shall be the same as the adjusted basis prescribed by § 1.1011-1 for determining the loss from the sale or other disposition of property. To determine the allowable deduction in the case of obligations acquired before March 1, 1913, see also paragraph (b) of § 1.1053-1.

(2) *Specific cases.*—Subject to any provision of section 166 and the regulations thereunder which provides to the contrary, the following amounts are deductible as bad debts:

(i) *Notes or accounts receivable.*

(a) If, in computing taxable income, a taxpayer values his notes or accounts receivable at their fair market value when received, the amount deductible as a bad debt under section 166 in respect of such receivables shall be limited to such fair market value even though it is less than their face value.

(b) A purchaser of accounts receivable which become worthless during the taxable year shall be entitled under section 166 to a deduction which is based upon the price he paid for such receivables but not upon their face value.

(ii) *Bankruptcy claim.*—Only the difference between the amount received in distribution of the assets of a bankrupt and the amount of the claim may be deducted under section 166 as a bad debt.

(iii) *Claim against decedent's estate.*—The excess of the amount of the claim over the amount received by a creditor of a decedent in distribution of the assets of the decedent's estate may be considered a worthless debt under section 166.

(e) *Prior inclusion in income required.*—Worthless debts arising from unpaid wages, salaries, fees, rents, and similar items of taxable income shall not be allowed as a deduction under section 166 unless the income such items represent has been included in the return of income for the year for which the deduction as a bad debt is claimed or for a prior taxable year.

(f) *Recovery of bad debts.*—Any amount attributable to the recovery during the taxable year of a bad debt, or of a part of a bad debt, which was allowed as a deduction from gross income in a prior taxable year shall be included in gross income for the taxable year of recovery, except to the extent that the recovery is excluded from gross income under the provisions of § 1.111-1, relating to the recovery of certain items previously deducted or credited. This paragraph shall not apply, however, to a bad debt which was previously charged against a reserve by a taxpayer on the reserve method of treating bad debts.

(g) *Worthless securities.*—(1) Section 166 and the regulations thereunder do not apply to a debt which is evidenced by a bond, debenture, note, or certificate, or other evidence of indebtedness, issued by a corporation, or by a government or political subdivision thereof, with interest coupons or in registered form. See section 166(e). For provisions allowing the deduction of a loss resulting from the worthlessness of such a debt, see § 1.165-5.

(2) The provisions of subparagraph (1) of this paragraph do not apply to any loss sustained by a bank and resulting from the worthlessness of a security described in section 165(g)(2)(C). See paragraph (a) of § 1.582-1. [Reg. § 1.166-1.]

□ [*T.D.* 6403, 7-30-59. *Amended by T.D.* 6996, 1-17-69, *T.D.* 7902, 7-20-83 *and T.D.* 8071, 1-17-86.]

§ 1.166-2. Evidence of worthlessness.—(a) *General rule.*—In determining whether a debt is worthless in whole or in part the district director will consider all pertinent evidence, including the value of the collateral, if any, securing the debt and the financial condition of the debtor.

(b) *Legal action not required.*—Where the surrounding circumstances indicate that a debt is worthless and uncollectible and that legal action to enforce payment would in all probability not result in the satisfaction of execution on a judgment, a showing of these facts will be sufficient evidence of the worthlessness of the debt for purposes of the deduction under section 166.

(c) *Bankruptcy.*—(1) *General rule.*—Bankruptcy is generally an indication of the worthlessness of at least a part of an unsecured and unpreferred debt.

(2) *Year of deduction.*—In bankruptcy cases a debt may become worthless before settlement in some instances; and in others, only when a settlement in bankruptcy has been reached. In either case, the mere fact that bankruptcy proceedings instituted against the debtor are terminated in a later year, thereby confirming the conclusion that the debt is worthless, shall not authorize the shifting of the deduction under section 166 to such later year.

* * *

[Reg. § 1.166-2.]

□ [*T.D.* 6403, 7-30-59. *Amended by T.D.* 7254, 1-24-73; *T.D.* 8396, 2-21-92; *T.D.* 8441, 10-1-92 *and T.D.* 8492, 10-15-93.]

§ 1.166-3. Partial or total worthlessness.—(a) *Partial worthlessness.*—(1) *Applicable to specific debts only.*—A deduction under section 166 (a)(2) on account of partially worthless debts shall be allowed with respect to specific debts only.

(2) *Charge-off required.*—(i) If, from all the surrounding and attending circumstances, the district director is satisfied that a debt is partially worthless, the amount which has become worthless shall be allowed as a deduction under section 166(a)(2) but only to the extent charged off during the taxable year.

(ii) If a taxpayer claims a deduction for a part of a debt for the taxable year within which that part of the debt is charged off and the deduction is disallowed for that taxable year, then, in a case where the debt becomes partially worthless after the close of that taxable year, a deduction under section 166(a)(2) shall be allowed for a subsequent taxable year but not in excess of the amount charged off in the prior taxable year plus any amount charged off in the subsequent taxable year. In such instance, the charge-off in the prior taxable year shall, if consistently maintained as such, be sufficient to that extent to meet the charge-off requirement of section 166(a)(2) with respect to the subsequent taxable year.

(iii) Before a taxpayer may deduct a debt in part, he must be able to demonstrate to the satisfaction of the district director the amount thereof which is worthless and the part thereof which has been charged off.

(3) *Significantly modified debt.*—(i) *Deemed charge-off.*—If a significant modifi-

cation of a debt instrument (within the meaning of § 1.1001-3) during a taxable year results in the recognition of gain by a taxpayer under § 1.1001-1(a), and if the requirements of paragraph (a)(3)(ii) of this section are met, there is a deemed charge-off of the debt during that taxable year in the amount specified in paragraph (a)(3)(iii) of this section.

(ii) *Requirements for deemed charge-off.*—A debt is deemed to have been charged off only if—

(A) The taxpayer (or, in the case of a debt that constitutes transferred basis property within the meaning of section 7701(a)(43), a transferor taxpayer) has claimed a deduction for partial worthlessness of the debt in any prior taxable year; and

(B) Each prior charge-off and deduction for partial worthlessness satisfied the requirements of paragraphs (a)(1) and (2) of this section.

(iii) *Amount of deemed charge-off.*—The amount of the deemed charge-off, if any, is the amount by which the tax basis of the debt exceeds the greater of the fair market value of the debt or the amount of the debt recorded on the taxpayer's books and records reduced as appropriate for a specific allowance for loan losses. The amount of the deemed charge-off, however, may not exceed the amount of recognized gain described in paragraph (a)(3)(i) of this section.

* * *

(b) *Total worthlessness.*—If a debt becomes wholly worthless during the taxable year, the amount thereof which has not been allowed as a deduction from gross income for any prior taxable year shall be allowed as a deduction for the current taxable year. [Reg. § 1.166-3.]

□ [*T.D.* 6403, 7-30-59. *Amended by T.D.* 8763, 1-28-98.]

§ 1.166-5. Nonbusiness debts.—(a) *Allowance of deduction as capital loss.*—(1) The loss resulting from any nonbusiness debt's becoming partially or wholly worthless within the taxable year shall not be allowed as a deduction under either section 166(a) or section 166(c) in determining the taxable income of a taxpayer other than a corporation. See section 166(d)(1)(A).

(2) If, in the case of a taxpayer other than a corporation, a non-business debt becomes wholly worthless within the taxable year, the loss resulting therefrom shall be treated as a loss from the sale or exchange, during the taxable year, of a capital asset held for not more than 1 year (6 months for taxable years beginning before 1977; 9 months for taxable years beginning in 1977). Such a loss is subject to the limitations provided in section 1211, relating to the limitation on capital losses, and section 1212, relating to the capital loss carryover, and in the regulations under those sections. A loss on a nonbusiness debt shall be treated as sustained only if and when the debt has become totally worthless, and no deduction shall be allowed for a nonbusiness debt which is recoverable in part during the taxable year.

(b) *Nonbusiness debt defined.*—For purposes of section 166 and this section, a nonbusiness debt is any debt other than —

(1) A debt which is created, or acquired, in the course of a trade or business of the taxpayer, determined without regard to the relationship of the debt to a trade or business of the taxpayer at the time when the debt becomes worthless; or

(2) A debt the loss from the worthlessness of which is incurred in the taxpayer's trade or business.

The question whether a debt is a nonbusiness debt is a question of fact in each particular case. The determination of whether the loss on a debt's becoming worthless has been incurred in a trade or business of the taxpayer shall, for this pupose, be made in substantially the same manner for determining whether a loss has been incurred in a trade or business for purposes of section 165(c)(1). For purposes of subparagraph (2) of this paragraph, the character of the debt is to be determined by the relation which the loss resulting from the debt's becoming worthless bears to the trade or business of the taxpayer. If that relation is a proximate one in the conduct of the trade or business in which the taxpayer is engaged at the time the debt becomes worthless, the debt comes within the exception provided by that subparagraph. The use to which the borrowed funds are put by the debtor is of no consequence in making a determination under this paragraph. For purposes of section 166 and this section, a nonbusiness debt does not include a debt described in section 165(g)(2)(C). See § 1.165-5, relating to losses on worthless securities.

(c) *Guaranty of obligations.*—For provisions treating a loss sustained by a guarantor of obligations as a loss resulting from the worthlessness of a debt, see §§ 1.166-8 and 1.166-9.

(d) *Examples.*—The application of this section may be illustrated by the following examples involving a case where A, an individual who is engaged in the grocery business and who makes his return on the basis of the calendar year, extends credit to B in 1955 on an open account:

Example (1). In 1956 A sells the business but retains the claim against B. The claim becomes worthless in A's hands in 1957. A's loss is not controlled by the nonbusiness debt provisions, since the original consideration has been advanced by A in his trade or business.

Example (2). In 1956 A sells the business to C but sells the claim against B to the taxpayer, D. The claim becomes worthless in D's hands in 1957. During 1956 and 1957, D is not engaged in any trade or business. D's loss is controlled by the nonbusiness debt provisions even though the original consideration has been advanced by A in his trade or business, since the debt has not been created or acquired in connection with a trade or business of D and since in 1957 D is not engaged in a trade or business incident to the conduct of which a loss from the worthlessness of such claims is a proximate result.

Example (3). In 1956 A dies, leaving the business, including the accounts receivable, to his son, C, the taxpayer. The claim against B becomes worthless in C's hands in 1957. C's loss is not controlled by the nonbusiness debt provisions. While C does not advance any consideration for the claim, or create or acquire it in connection with his trade or business, the loss is sustained as a proximate incident to the conduct of the trade or business in which he is engaged at the time the debt becomes worthless.

Example (4). In 1956 A dies, leaving the business to his son, C, but leaving the claim against B to his son, D, the taxpayer. The claim against B becomes worthless in D's hands in 1957. During 1956 and 1957, D is not engaged in any trade or business. D's loss is controlled by the nonbusiness debt provisions even though the original consideration has been advanced by A in his trade or business, since the debt has not been created or acquired in connection with a trade or business of D and since in 1957 D is not engaged in a trade or business incident to the conduct of which a loss from the worthlessness of such claims is a proximate result.

Example (5). In 1956 A dies, and, while his executor, C, is carrying on the business, the claim against B becomes worthless in 1957. The loss sustained by A's estate is not controlled by the nonbusiness debt provisions. While C does not advance any consideration for the claim on behalf of the estate, or create or acquire it in connection with a trade or business in which the estate is engaged, the loss is sustained as a proximate incident to the conduct of the trade or business in which the estate is engaged at the time the debt becomes worthless.

Example (6). In 1956, A, in liquidating the business, attempts to collect the claim against B but finds that it has become worthless. A's loss is not controlled by the nonbusiness debt provisions, since the original consideration has been advanced by A in his trade or business and since a loss incurred in liquidating a trade or business is a proximate incident to the conduct thereof. [Reg. § 1.166-5.]

□ [*T.D.* 6403, 7-23-59. *Amended by T.D.* 7657, 11-28-79 *and T.D.* 7728, 10-31-80.]

§ 1.166-6. Sale of mortgaged or pledged property.—(a) *Deficiency deductible as bad debts.*—(1) *Principal amount.*—If mortgaged or pledged property is lawfully sold (whether to the creditor or another purchaser) for less than the amount of the debt, and the portion of the indebtedness remaining unsatisfied after the sale is wholly or partially uncollectible, the mortgagee or pledgee may deduct such amount under section 166(a) (to the extent that it constitutes capital or represents an item the income from which has been returned by him) as a bad debt for the taxable year in which it becomes wholly worthless or is charged off as partially worthless. See § 1.166-3.

(2) *Accrued interest.*—Accrued interest may be included as part of the deduction allowable under this paragraph, but only if it has previously been returned as income.

(b) *Realization of gain or loss.*—(1) *Determination of amount.*—If, in the case of a sale described in paragraph (a) of this section, the creditor buys in the mortgaged or pledged property, loss or gain is also realized, measured by the difference between the amount of those obligations of the debtor which are applied to the purchase or bid price of the property (to the extent that such obligations constitute capital or represent an item the income from which has been returned by the creditor) and the fair market value of the property.

(2) *Fair market value defined.*—The fair market value of the property for this purpose shall, in the absence of clear and convincing proof to the contrary, be presumed to be the amount for which it is bid in by the taxpayer.

(c) *Basis of property purchased.*—If the creditor subsequently sells the property so acquired, the basis for determining gain or loss upon the subsequent sale is the fair market value of the property at the date of its acquisition by the creditor.

* * *

[Reg. § 1.166-6.]

□ [*T.D.* 6403, 7-30-59. *Amended by T.D.* 6814, 4-6-65 *and T.D.* 6916, 4-12-67.]

§ 1.167(a)-2. Tangible property.—The depreciation allowance in the case of tangible property applies only to that part of the property which is subject to wear and tear, to decay or decline from natural causes, to exhaustion, and to obsolescence. The allowance does not apply to inventories or stock in trade, or to land apart from the improvements of physical development added to it. The allowance does not apply to natural resources which are subject to the allowance for depletion provided in section 611. No deduction for depreciation shall be allowed on automobiles or other vehicles used solely for pleasure, on a building used by the taxpayer solely as his residence, or on furniture or furnishings therein, personal effects, or clothing; but properties and costumes used exclusively in a business, such as a theatrical business, may be depreciated. [Reg. § 1.167(a)-2.]

☐ [*T.D.* 6182, 6-11-56.]

§ 1.167(a)-3. Intangibles.—(a) *In general.*—If an intangible asset is known from experience or other factors to be of use in the business or in the production of income for only a limited period, the length of which can be estimated with reasonable accuracy, such an intangible asset may be the subject of a depreciation allowance. Examples are patents and copyrights. An intangible asset, the useful life of which is not limited, is not subject to the allowance for depreciation. No allowance will be permitted merely because, in the unsupported opinion of the taxpayer, the intangible asset has a limited useful life. No deduction for depreciation is allowable with respect to good will. For rules with respect to organizational expenditures, see section 248 and the regulations thereunder. For rules with respect to trademark and trade name expenditures, see section 177 and the regulations thereunder. See sections 197 and 167(f) and, to the extent applicable, § § 1.197-2 and 1.167(a)-14 for amortization of goodwill and certain other intangibles acquired after August 10, 1993, or after July 25, 1991, if a valid retroactive election under § 1.197-1T has been made.

(b) *Safe harbor amortization for certain intangible assets.*—(1) *Useful life.*—Solely for purposes of determining the depreciation allowance referred to in paragraph (a) of this section, a taxpayer may treat an intangible asset as having a useful life equal to 15 years unless—

(i) An amortization period or useful life for the intangible asset is specifically prescribed or prohibited by the Internal Revenue Code, the regulations thereunder (other than by this paragraph (b)), or other published guidance in the Internal Revenue Bulletin (see § 601.601(d)(2) of this chapter);

(ii) The intangible asset is described in § 1.263(a)-4(c) (relating to intangibles acquired from another person) or § 1.263(a)-4(d)(2) (relating to created financial interests);

(iii) The intangible asset has a useful life the length of which can be estimated with reasonable accuracy; or

(iv) The intangible asset is described in § 1.263(a)-4(d)(8) (relating to certain benefits arising from the provision, production, or improvement of real property), in which case the taxpayer may treat the intangible asset as having a useful life equal to 25 years solely for purposes of determining the depreciation allowance referred to in paragraph (a) of this section.

(2) *Applicability to acquisitions of a trade or business, changes in the capital structure of a business entity, and certain other transactions.*—The safe harbor useful life provided by paragraph (b)(1) of this section does not apply to an amount required to be capitalized by § 1.263(a)-5 (relating to amounts paid to facilitate an acquisition of a trade or business, a change in the capital structure of a business entity, and certain other transactions).

(3) *Depreciation method.*—A taxpayer that determines its depreciation allowance for an intangible asset using the 15-year useful life prescribed by paragraph (b)(1) of this section (or the 25-year useful life in the case of an intangible asset described in § 1.263(a)-4(d)(8)) must determine the allowance by amortizing the basis of the intangible asset (as determined under section 167(c) and without regard to salvage value) ratably over the useful life beginning on the first day of the month in which the intangible asset is placed in service by the taxpayer. The intangible asset is not eligible for amortization in the month of disposition.

* * *

[Reg. § 1.167(a)-3.]

☐ [*T.D.* 6182, 6-11-56. *Amended by T.D.* 6452, 2-3-60; *T.D.* 8865, 1-20-2000 *and T.D.* 9107, 12-31-2003.]

§ 1.167(a)-4. Leased property.—(a) *In general.*—Capital expenditures made by either a lessee or lessor for the erection of a building or for other permanent improvements on leased property are recovered by the lessee or lessor under the provisions of the Internal Revenue Code (Code) applicable to the cost recovery of the building or improvements, if subject to depreciation or amortization, without regard to the period of the lease. For example, if the building or improvement is property to which section 168 applies, the lessee or lessor determines the depreciation deduction for the building or improvement under section 168. See section 168(i)(8)(A). If the improvement is property to which section 167 or section 197 applies, the lessee or lessor determines the depreciation or amortization deduction for the improvement under section 167 or section 197, as applicable.

* * *

[Reg. § 1.167(a)-4.]

□ [*T.D.* 6182, 6-11-56. *Amended by T.D.* 6520, 12-23-60; *T.D.* 9564, 12-23-2011 *and T.D.* 9636, 9-13-2013.]

§ 1.167(a)-5. Apportionment of basis.— In the case of the acquisition on or after March 1, 1913, of a combination of depreciable and nondepreciable property for a lump sum, as for example, buildings and land, the basis for depreciation cannot exceed an amount which bears the same proportion to the lump sum as the value of the depreciable property at the time of acquisition bears to the value of the entire property at that time. In the case of property which is subject to both the allowance for depreciation and amortization, depreciation is allowable only with respect to the portion of the depreciable property which is not subject to the allowance for amortization and may be taken concurrently with the allowance for amortization. After the close of the amortization period or after amortization deductions have been discontinued with respect to any such property, the unrecovered cost or other basis of the depreciable portion of such property will be subject to depreciation. For adjustments to basis, see section 1016 and other applicable provisions of law. For the adjustment to the basis of a structure in the case of a donation of a qualified conservation contribution under section 170(h), see § 1.170A-14(h)(3)(iii). [Reg. § 1.167(a)-5.]

□ [*T.D.* 6182, 6-11-56. *Amended by T.D.* 8069, 1-13-86.]

§ 1.167(a)-9. Obsolescence.—The depreciation allowance includes an allowance for normal obsolescence which should be taken into account to the extent that the expected useful life of property will be shortened by reason thereof. Obsolescence may render an asset economically useless to the taxpayer regardless of its physical condition. Obsolescence is attributable to many causes, including technological improvements and reasonably foreseeable economic changes. Among these causes are normal progress of the arts and sciences, supersession or inadequacy brought about by developments in the industry, products, methods, markets, sources of supply, and other like changes, and legislative or regulatory action. In any case in which the taxpayer shows that the estimated useful life previously used should be shortened by reason of obsolescence greater than had been assumed in computing such estimated useful life, a change to a new and shorter estimated useful life computed in accordance with such showing will be permitted. No such change will be permitted merely because in the unsupported opinion of the taxpayer the property may become obsolete. For rules governing the allowance of a loss when the usefulness of depreciable property is suddenly terminated, see § 1.167(a)-8. If the estimated useful life and the depreciation rates have been the subject of a previous agreement, see section 167(d) and § 1.167(d)-1. [Reg. § 1.167(a)-9.]

□ [*T.D.* 6182, 6-11-56. *Amended by T.D.* 6445, 1-15-60.]

§ 1.167(a)-10. When depreciation deduction is allowable.—(a) A taxpayer should deduct the proper depreciation allowance each year and may not increase his depreciation allowances in later years by reason of his failure to deduct any depreciation allowance or of his action in deducting an allowance plainly inadequate under the known facts in prior years. The inadequacy of the depreciation allowance for property in prior years shall be determined on the basis of the allowable method of depreciation used by the taxpayer for such property or under the straight line method if no allowance has ever been claimed for such property. The preceding sentence shall not be construed as precluding application of any method provided in section 167 (b) if taxpayer's failure to claim any allowance for depreciation was due solely to erroneously treating as a deductible expense an item properly chargeable to capital account. For rules relating to adjustments to basis, see section 1016 and the regulations thereunder.

* * *

[Reg. § 1.167(a)-10.]

□ [*T.D.* 6182, 6-11-56.]

§ 1.167(a)-14. Treatment of certain intangible property excluded from section 197.—(a) *Overview.*—This section provides rules for the amortization of certain intangibles that are excluded from section 197 (relating to the amortization of goodwill and certain other intangibles). These excluded intangibles are specifically described in § 1.197-2(c)(4), (6), (7), (11), and (13) and include certain computer software and certain other separately acquired rights, such as rights to receive tangible property or services, patents and copyrights, certain mortgage servicing rights, and rights of fixed duration or amount. Intangibles for which an amortization amount is determined under section 167(f) and intangibles otherwise excluded from section 197 are amortizable only if they qualify as property subject to the allowance for depreciation under section 167(a).

(b) *Computer software.*—(1) *In general.*—The amount of the deduction for computer software described in section 167(f)(1) and § 1.197-2(c)(4) is determined by amortizing the cost or other basis of the computer software using the straight line method described in § 1.167(b)-1 (except that its salvage value is treated as zero) and an amortization period of 36 months beginning on the first day of the month that the computer software is placed in service. Before determining the amortization deduction allowable under this paragraph (b), the cost or other basis of computer software that is section 179 property, as defined in section 179(d)(1)(A)(ii), must be reduced for any portion of the basis the taxpayer properly elects to treat as an expense under section 179. In addition, the cost or other basis of computer software that is qualified property under section 168(k)(2) and § 1.168(k)-1 or § 1.168(k)-2, as applicable, 50-percent bonus depreciation property under section 168(k)(4) or § 1.168(k)-1, or qualified New York Liberty Zone property under section 1400L(b) or § 1.1400L(b)-1, must be reduced by the amount of the additional first year depreciation deduction allowed or allowable, whichever is greater, under section 168(k) or section 1400L(b) for the computer software. If costs for developing computer software that the taxpayer properly elects to defer under section 174(b) result in the development of property subject to the allowance for depreciation under section 167, the rules of this paragraph (b) will apply to the unrecovered costs. In addition, this paragraph (b) applies to the cost of separately acquired computer software if the cost to acquire the software is separately stated and the cost is required to be capitalized under section 263(a).

(2) *Exceptions.*—Paragraph (b)(1) of this section does not apply to the cost of computer software properly and consistently taken into account under § 1.162-11. The cost of acquiring an interest in computer software that is included, without being separately stated, in the cost of the hardware or other tangible property is treated as part of the cost of the hardware or other tangible property that is capitalized and depreciated under other applicable sections of the Internal Revenue Code.

(3) *Additional rules.*—Rules similar to those in § 1.197-2(f)(1)(iii), (f)(1)(iv), and (f)(2) (relating to the computation of amortization deductions and the treatment of contingent amounts) apply for purposes of this paragraph (b).

(c) *Certain interests or rights not acquired as part of a purchase of a trade or business.*—(1) *Certain rights to receive tangible property or services.*—The amount of the deduction for a right (other than a right acquired as part of a purchase of a trade or business) to receive tangible property or services under a contract or from a governmental unit (as specified in section 167(f)(2) and § 1.197-2(c)(6)) is determined as follows:

(i) *Amortization of fixed amounts.*—The basis of a right to receive a fixed amount of tangible property or services is amortized for each taxable year by multiplying the basis of the right by a fraction, the numerator of which is the amount of tangible property or services received during the taxable year and the denominator of which is the total amount of tangible property or services received or to be received under the terms of the contract or governmental grant. For example, if a taxpayer acquires a favorable contract right to receive a fixed amount of raw materials during an unspecified period, the taxpayer must amortize the cost of acquiring the contract right by multiplying the total cost by a fraction, the numerator of which is the amount of raw materials received under the contract during the taxable year and the denominator of which is the total amount of raw materials received or to be received under the contract.

(ii) *Amortization of unspecified amount over fixed period.*—The cost or other basis of a right to receive an unspecified amount of tangible property or services over a fixed period is amortized ratably over the period of the right. (See paragraph (c)(3) of this section regarding renewals).

(iii) *Amortization in other cases.*—[Reserved]

(2) *Rights of fixed duration or amount.*—The amount of the deduction for a right (other than a right acquired as part of a purchase of a trade or business) of fixed duration or amount received under a contract or granted by a governmental unit (specified in section 167(f)(2) and § 1.197-2(c)(13)) and not covered by paragraph (c)(1) of this section is determined as follows:

(i) *Rights to a fixed amount.*—The basis of a right to a fixed amount is amortized for each taxable year by multiplying the basis by a fraction, the numerator of which is the amount received during the taxable year and the denominator of which is the total amount received or to be received under the terms of the contract or governmental grant.

(ii) *Rights to an unspecified amount over fixed duration of less than 15 years.*—The basis of a right to an unspecified amount over a fixed duration of less than 15 years is amortized ratably over the period of the right.

(3) *Application of renewals.*—(i) For purposes of paragraphs (c)(1) and (2) of this section, the duration of a right under a contract (or granted by a governmental unit) includes any renewal period if, based on all of the facts and circumstances in existence at any time during the taxable year in which the right is acquired, the facts clearly indicate a reasonable expectancy of renewal.

(ii) The mere fact that a taxpayer will have the opportunity to renew a contract right or other right on the same terms as are available to others, in a competitive auction or similar process that is designed to reflect fair market value and in which the taxpayer is not contractually advantaged, will generally not be taken into account in determining the duration of such right provided that the bidding produces a fair market value price comparable to the price that would be obtained if the rights were purchased immediately after renewal from a person (other than the person granting the renewal) in an arm's-length transaction.

(iii) The cost of a renewal not included in the terms of the contract or governmental grant is treated as the acquisition of a separate intangible asset.

(4) *Patents and copyrights.*—If the purchase price of a interest (other than an interest acquired as part of a purchase of a trade or business) in a patent or copyright described in section 167(f)(2) and § 1.197-2(c)(7) is payable on at least an annual basis as either a fixed amount per use or a fixed percentage of the revenue derived from the use of the patent or copyright, the depreciation deduction for a taxable year is equal to the amount of the purchase price paid or incurred during the year. Otherwise, the basis of such patent or copyright (or an interest therein) is depreciated either ratably over its remaining useful life or under section 167(g) (income forecast method). If a patent or copyright becomes valueless in any year before its legal expiration, the adjusted basis may be deducted in that year.

(5) *Additional rules.*—The period of amortization under paragraphs (c)(1) through (4) of this section begins when the intangible is placed in service, and rules similar to those in § 1.197-2(f)(2) apply for purposes of this paragraph (c).

* * *

[Reg. § 1.167(a)-14.]

☐ [*T.D.* 8865, 1-20-2000. *Amended by T.D.* 9091, 9-5-2003; *T.D.* 9283, 8-28-2006; *and T.D.* 9874, 9-17-2019.]

§ 1.167(b)-1. Straight line method.—(a) *Application of method.*—Under the straight line method the cost or other basis of the property less its estimated salvage value is deductible in equal annual amounts over the period of the estimated useful life of the property. The allowance for depreciation for the taxable year is determined by dividing the adjusted basis of the property at the beginning of the taxable year, less salvage value, by the remaining useful life of the property at such time. For convenience, the allowance so determined may be reduced to a percentage or fraction. The straight line method may be used in determining a reasonable allowance for depreciation for any property which is subject to depreciation under section 167 and it shall be used in all cases where the taxpayer has not adopted a different acceptable method with respect to such property.

* * *

[Reg. § 1.167(b)-1.]

☐ [*T.D.* 6182, 6-11-56.]

§ 1.167(b)-2. Declining balance method.—(a) *Application of method.*—Under the declining balance method a uniform rate is applied each year to the unrecovered cost or other basis of the property. The unrecovered cost or other basis is the basis provided by section 167(g), adjusted for depreciation previously allowed or allowable, and for all other adjustments provided by section 1016 and other applicable provisions of law. The declining balance rate may be determined without resort to formula. Such rate determined under section 167(b)(2) shall not exceed twice the appropriate straight line rate computed without adjustment for salvage. While salvage is not taken into account in determining the annual allowances under this method, in no event shall an asset (or an account) be depreciated below a reasonable salvage value. However, see section 167(f) and § 1.167(f)-1 for rules which permit a reduction in the amount of salvage value to be taken into account for certain personal property acquired after October 16, 1962. Also, see section 167(c) and § 1.167(c)-1 for restrictions on the use of the declining balance method.

(b) *Illustrations.*—The declining balance method is illustrated by the following examples:

Example (1). A new asset having an estimated useful life of 20 years was purchased on January 1, 1954, for $1,000. The normal straight line rate (without adjustment for salvage) is 5 percent, and the declining balance rate at twice the normal straight line rate is 10 percent. The annual depreciation allowances for 1954, 1955, and 1956 are as follows:

Year	Basis	Declining balance rate (percent)	Depreciation allowance
1954 . . .	$1,000	10	$100
1955 . . .	900	10	90
1956 . . .	810	10	81

* * *

[Reg. § 1.167(b)-2.]

☐ [*T.D.* 6182, 6-11-56. *Amended by T.D.* 6712, 3-23-64.]

§ 1.167(g)-1. Basis for depreciation.—The basis upon which the allowance for depreciation is to be computed with respect to any property shall be the adjusted basis provided in section 1011 for the purpose of determining gain on the sale or other disposition of such property. In the case of property which has not been used in the trade or business or held for the production of income and which is thereafter converted to such use, the fair market value on the date of such conversion, if less than the adjusted basis of the property at that time, is the basis for computing depreciation. [Reg. § 1.167(g)-1.]

☐ [*T.D.* 6182, 6-11-56. *Amended by T.D.* 6712, 3-23-64.]

§ 1.167(h)-1. Life tenants and beneficiaries of trusts and estates.—(a) *Life tenants.*—In the case of property held by one person for life with remainder to another person, the deduction for depreciation shall be computed as if the life tenant were the absolute owner of the property so that he will be entitled to the deduction during his life, and thereafter the deduction, if any, shall be allowed to the remainderman.

(b) *Trusts.*—If property is held in trust, the allowable deduction is to be apportioned between the income beneficiaries and the trustee on the basis of the trust income allocable to each, unless the governing instrument (or local law) requires or permits the trustee to maintain a reserve for depreciation in any amount. In the latter case, the deduction is first allocated to the trustee to the extent that income is set aside for a depreciation reserve, and any part of the deduction in excess of the income set aside for the reserve shall be apportioned between the income beneficiaries and the trustee on the basis of the trust income (in excess of the income set aside for the reserve) allocable to each. For example:

(1) If under the trust instrument or local law the income of a trust computed without regard to depreciation is to be distributed to a named beneficiary, the beneficiary is entitled to the deduction to the exclusion of the trustee.

(2) If under the trust instrument or local law the income of a trust is to be distributed to a named beneficiary, but the trustee is directed to maintain a reserve for depreciation in any amount, the deduction is allowed to the trustee (except to the extent that income set aside for the reserve is less than the allowable deduction). The same result would follow if the trustee sets aside income for a depreciation reserve pursuant to discretionary authority to do so in the governing instrument.

No effect shall be given to any allocation of the depreciation deduction which gives any beneficiary or the trustee a share of such deduction greater than his pro rata share of the trust income, irrespective of any provisions in the trust instrument, except as otherwise provided in this paragraph when the trust instrument or local law requires or permits the trustee to maintain a reserve for depreciation.

(c) *Estates.*—In the case of an estate, the allowable deduction shall be apportioned between the estate and the heirs, legatees, and devisees on the basis of income of the estate which is allocable to each. [Reg. § 1.167(h)-1.]

☐ [*T.D.* 6182, 6-11-56. *Amended by T.D.* 6712, 3-23-64.]

§ 1.168(a)-1. Modified accelerated cost recovery system.—(a) Section 168 determines the depreciation allowance for tangible property that is of a character subject to the allowance for depreciation provided in section 167(a) and that is placed in service after December 31, 1986 (or after July 31, 1986, if the taxpayer made an election under section 203(a)(1)(B) of the Tax Reform Act of 1986; 100 Stat. 2143). Except for property excluded from the application of section 168 as a result of section 168(f) or as a result of a transitional rule, the provisions of section 168 are mandatory for all eligible property. The allowance for depreciation under section 168 constitutes the amount of depreciation allowable under section 167(a). The determination of whether tangible property is property of a character subject to the allowance for depreciation is made under section 167 and the regulations under section 167.

(b) This section is applicable on and after February 27, 2004. [Reg. § 1.168(a)-1.]

☐ [*T.D.* 9314, 2-26-2007.]

§ 1.168(b)-1. Definitions.—(a) *Definitions.*—For purposes of section 168 and the regulations under section 168, the following definitions apply:

(1) *Depreciable property* is property that is of a character subject to the allowance for depreciation as determined under section 167 and the regulations under section 167.

(2) *MACRS property* is tangible, depreciable property that is placed in service after De-

cember 31, 1986 (or after July 31, 1986, if the taxpayer made an election under section 203(a)(1)(B) of the Tax Reform Act of 1986; 100 Stat. 2143) and subject to section 168, except for property excluded from the application of section 168 as a result of section 168(f) or as a result of a transitional rule.

(3) *Unadjusted depreciable basis* is the basis of property for purposes of section 1011 without regard to any adjustments described in section 1016(a)(2) and (3). This basis reflects the reduction in basis for the percentage of the taxpayer's use of property for the taxable year other than in the taxpayer's trade or business (or for the production of income), for any portion of the basis the taxpayer properly elects to treat as an expense under section 179, section 179C, section 181, or any similar provision, and for any adjustments to basis provided by other provisions of the Internal Revenue Code and the regulations under the Code (other than section 1016(a)(2) and (3)) (for example, a reduction in basis by the amount of the disabled access credit pursuant to section 44(d)(7)). For property subject to a lease, see section 167(c)(2).

(4) *Adjusted depreciable basis* is the unadjusted depreciable basis of the property, as defined in § 1.168(b)-1(a)(3), less the adjustments described in section 1016(a)(2) and (3).

* * *

(b) *Applicability date.*—(1) *In general.*—Except as provided in paragraph (b)(2) of this section, this section is applicable on or after February 27, 2004.

* * *

[Reg. § 1.168(b)-1.]

☐ [*T.D.* 9314, 2-26-2007. *Amended by T.D.* 9874, 9-17-2019.]

§ 1.168(d)-1. Applicable conventions—half-year and mid-quarter conventions.—(a) *In general.*—Under section 168(d), the half-year convention applies to depreciable property (other than certain real property described in section 168(d)(2)) placed in service during a taxable year, unless the mid-quarter convention applies to the property. Under section 168(d)(3)(A), the mid-quarter convention applies to depreciable property (other than certain real property described in section 168(d)(2)) placed in service during a taxable year if the aggregate basis of property placed in service during the last three months of the taxable year exceeds 40 percent of the aggregate basis of property placed in service during the taxable year ("the 40-percent test"). Thus, if the depreciable property is placed in service during a taxable year that consists of three months or less, the mid-quarter convention applies to the property. Under section 168(d)(3)(B)(i), the depreciable basis of nonresidential real property, residential rental property, and any railroad grading or tunnel bore is disregarded in applying the 40-percent test. For rules regarding property that is placed in service and disposed of in the same taxable year, see paragraph (b)(3) of this section. For the definition of "aggregate basis of property," see paragraph (b)(4) of this section.

(b) *Additional rules for determining whether the mid-quarter convention applies and for applying the applicable convention.*—(1) *Property described in section 168(f).*—In determining whether the 40-percent test is satisfied for a taxable year, the depreciable basis of property described in section 168(f) (property to which section 168 does not apply) is not taken into account.

(2) *Listed property.*—The depreciable basis of listed property (as defined in section 280F(d)(4) and the regulations thereunder) placed in service during a taxable year is taken into account (unless otherwise excluded) in applying the 40-percent test.

(3) *Property placed in service and disposed of in the same taxable year.*—(i) Under section 168(d)(3)(B)(ii), the depreciable basis of property placed in service and disposed of in the same taxable year is not taken into account in determining whether the 40-percent test is satisfied. However, the depreciable basis of property placed in service, disposed of, subsequently reacquired, and again placed in service, by the taxpayer in the same taxable year must be taken into account in applying the 40-percent test, but the basis of the property is only taken into account on the later of the dates that the property is placed in service by the taxpayer during the taxable year. Further, see §§ 1.168(i)-6(c)(4)(v)(B) and 1.168(i)-6(f) for rules relating to property placed in service and exchanged or involuntarily converted during the same taxable year.

(ii) The applicable convention, as determined under this section, applies to all depreciable property (except nonresidential real property, residential rental property, and any railroad grading or tunnel bore) placed in service by the taxpayer during the taxable year, excluding property placed in service and disposed of in the same taxable year. However, see §§ 1.168(i)-6(c)(4)(v)(A) and 1.168(i)-6(f) for rules relating to MACRS property that has a basis determined under section 1031(d) or section 1033(b). No depreciation deduction is allowed for property placed in service and disposed of during the same taxable year. However, see § 1.168(k)-1(f)(1) for rules relating to qualified property or 50-percent bonus depreciation property, and § 1.1400L(b)-1(f)(1) for rules relating to qualified New York Liberty Zone property, that is placed in service by the taxpayer in the same taxable year in which either a partnership is terminated as a result of a technical termination under section 708(b)(1)(B) or the property is transferred in a transaction described in section 168(i)(7).

* * *

(4) *Aggregate basis of property.*—For purposes of the 40-percent test, the term "aggregate basis of property" means the sum of the depreciable bases of all items of depreciable property that are taken into account in applying the 40-percent test. "Depreciable basis" means the basis of depreciable property for purposes of determining gain under sections 1011 through 1024. The depreciable basis for the taxable year the property is placed in service reflects the reduction in basis for—

(i) Any portion of the basis the taxpayer properly elects to treat as an expense under section 179;

(ii) Any adjustment to basis under section 48(q); and

(iii) The percentage of the taxpayer's use of property for the taxable year other than in the taxpayer's trade or business (or for the production of income), but is determined before any reduction for depreciation under section 167(a) for that taxable year.

* * *

(6) *Special rule for partnerships and S corporations.*—In the case of property placed in service by a partnership or an S corporation, the 40-percent test is generally applied at the partnership or corporate level. However, if a partnership or an S corporation is formed or availed of for the principal purpose of either avoiding the application of the mid-quarter convention or having the mid-quarter convention apply where it otherwise would not, the 40-percent test is applied at the partner, shareholder, or other appropriate level.

* * *

(c) *Disposition of property subject to the half-year or mid-quarter convention.*—(1) *In general.*—If depreciable property is subject to the half-year (or mid-quarter) convention in the taxable year in which it is placed in service, it also is subject to the half-year (or mid-quarter) convention in the taxable year in which it is disposed of.

(2) *Example.*—The provisions of paragraph (c)(1) of this section are illustrated by the following example.

Example. In October 1991, B, a calendar-year taxpayer, purchases and places in service a light general purpose truck costing $10,000. B does not elect to expense any part of the cost of the truck, and this is the only item of depreciable property placed in service by B during 1991. The 40-percent test is satisfied and the mid-quarter convention applies, because the truck is placed in service during the last three months of the taxable year and no other assets are placed in service in that year. In April 1993 (prior to the end of the truck's recovery period), B sells the truck. The mid-quarter convention applies in determining the depreciation deduction for the truck in 1993, the year of disposition.

* * *

[Reg. § 1.168(d)-1.]

☐ [*T.D.* 8444, 10-28-92. *Amended by T.D.* 9091, 9-5-2003; *T.D.* 9115, 2-27-2004; *T.D.* 9283, 8-28-2006; *T.D.* 9314, 2-26-2007; *and T.D.* 9874, 9-17-2019.]

§ 1.168(k)-2. Additional first year depreciation deduction for property acquired and placed in service after September 27, 2017.—(a) *Scope and definitions.*—(1) *Scope.*—This section provides rules for determining the additional first year depreciation deduction allowable under section 168(k) for qualified property acquired and placed in service after September 27, 2017.

(2) *Definitions.*—For purposes of this section—

(i) *Act* is the Tax Cuts and Jobs Act, Public Law 115-97 (131 Stat. 2054 (December 22, 2017));

(ii) *Applicable percentage* is the percentage provided in section 168(k)(6);

(iii) *Initial live staged performance* is the first commercial exhibition of a production to an audience. However, the term *initial live staged performance* does not include limited exhibition prior to commercial exhibition to general audiences if the limited exhibition is primarily for purposes of publicity, determining the need for further production activity, or raising funds for the completion of production. For example, an initial live staged performance does not include a preview of the production if the preview is primarily to determine the need for further production activity; and

(iv) *Predecessor* includes—

(A) A transferor of an asset to a transferee in a transaction to which section 381(a) applies;

(B) A transferor of an asset to a transferee in a transaction in which the transferee's basis in the asset is determined, in whole or in part, by reference to the basis of the asset in the hands of the transferor;

(C) A partnership that is considered as continuing under section 708(b)(2) and §1.708-1;

(D) The decedent in the case of an asset acquired by the estate; or

(E) A transferor of an asset to a trust.

(b) *Qualified property.*—(1) *In general.*—Qualified property is depreciable property, as defined in §1.168(b)-1(a)(1), that meets all the following requirements in the first taxable year in which the property is subject to depreciation by the taxpayer whether or not depreciation deductions for the property are allowable:

(i) The requirements in §1.168(k)-2(b)(2) (description of qualified property);

(ii) The requirements in §1.168(k)-2(b)(3) (original use or used property acquisition requirements);

(iii) The requirements in §1.168(k)-2(b)(4) (placed-in-service date); and

(iv) The requirements in §1.168(k)-2(b)(5) (acquisition of property).

(2) *Description of qualified property.*—(i) *In general.*—Depreciable property will meet the requirements of this paragraph (b)(2) if the property is—

(A) MACRS property, as defined in §1.168(b)-1(a)(2), that has a recovery period of 20 years or less. For purposes of this paragraph (b)(2)(i)(A) and section 168(k)(2)(A)(i)(I), the recovery period is determined in accordance with section 168(c) regardless of any election made by the taxpayer under section 168(g)(7). This paragraph (b)(2)(i)(A) includes the following MACRS property that is acquired by the taxpayer after September 27, 2017, and placed in service by the taxpayer after September 27, 2017, and before January 1, 2018:

(1) Qualified leasehold improvement property as defined in section 168(e)(6) as in effect on the day before amendment by section 13204(a)(1) of the Act;

(2) Qualified restaurant property, as defined in section 168(e)(7) as in effect on the day before amendment by section 13204(a)(1) of the Act, that is qualified improvement property as defined in §1.168(b)-1(a)(5)(i)(C) and (a)(5)(ii); and

(3) Qualified retail improvement property as defined in section 168(e)(8) as in effect on the day before amendment by section 13204(a)(1) of the Act;

(B) Computer software as defined in, and depreciated under, section 167(f)(1) and §1.167(a)-14;

(C) Water utility property as defined in section 168(e)(5) and depreciated under section 168;

(D) Qualified improvement property as defined in §1.168(b)-1(a)(5)(i)(C) and (a)(5)(ii) and depreciated under section 168;

(E) A qualified film or television production, as defined in section 181(d) and §1.181-3, for which a deduction would have been allowable under section 181 and §§1.181-1 through 1.181-6 without regard to section 181(a)(2) and (g), §1.181-1(b)(1)(i) and (ii), and (b)(2)(i), or section 168(k). Only production costs of a qualified film or television production are allowable as a deduction under section 181 and §§1.181-1 through 1.181-6 without regard, for purposes of section 168(k), to section 181(a)(2) and (g), §1.181-1(b)(1)(i) and (ii), and (b)(2)(i). The taxpayer that claims the additional first year depreciation deduction under this section for the production costs of a qualified film or television production must be the owner, as defined in §1.181-1(a)(2), of the qualified film or television production. See §1.181-1(a)(3) for the definition of production costs;

(F) A qualified live theatrical production, as defined in section 181(e), for which a deduction would have been allowable under section 181 and §§1.181-1 through 1.181-6 without regard to section 181(a)(2) and (g), §1.181-1(b)(1)(i) and (ii), and (b)(2)(i), or section 168(k). Only production costs of a qualified live theatrical production are allowable as a deduction under section 181 and §§1.181-1 through 1.181-6 without regard, for purposes of section 168(k), to section 181(a)(2) and (g), §1.181-1(b)(1)(i) and (ii), and (b)(2)(i). The taxpayer that claims the additional first year depreciation deduction under this section for the production costs of a qualified live theatrical production must be the owner, as defined in §1.181-1(a)(2), of the qualified live theatrical production. In applying §1.181-1(a)(2)(ii) to a person that acquires a finished or partially-finished qualified live theatrical production, such person is treated as an owner of that production, but only if the production is acquired prior to its initial live staged performance. Rules similar to the rules in §1.181-1(a)(3) for the definition of production costs of a qualified film or television production apply for defining production costs of a qualified live theatrical production; or

(G) A specified plant, as defined in section 168(k)(5)(B), for which the taxpayer has properly made an election to apply section 168(k)(5) for the taxable year in which the specified plant is planted, or grafted to a plant that has already been planted, by the taxpayer in the ordinary course of the taxpayer's farming business, as defined in section 263A(e)(4) (for further guidance, see paragraph (f) of this section).

(ii) *Property not eligible for additional first year depreciation deduction.*—Depreciable property will not meet the requirements of this paragraph (b)(2) if the property is—

(A) Described in section 168(f) (for example, automobiles for which the taxpayer uses the optional business standard mileage rate);

(B) Required to be depreciated under the alternative depreciation system of section 168(g) pursuant to section 168(g)(1)(A), (B), (C), (D), (F), or (G), or other provisions of the Internal Revenue Code (for example, property described in section 263A(e)(2)(A) if the taxpayer or any related person, as defined in section 263A(e)(2)(B), has made an election under section 263A(d)(3), or property described in section 280F(b)(1)). If section 168(h)(6) applies to the property, only the tax-exempt entity's proportionate share of the property, as determined under section 168(h)(6), is treated as tax-exempt use property described in section 168(g)(1)(B) and in this paragraph (b)(2)(ii)(B). This paragraph (b)(2)(ii)(B) does not apply to property for which the adjusted basis is required to be determined using the alternative depreciation system of section 168(g) pursuant to section 250(b)(2)(B) or 951A(d)(3), as applicable, or to property for which the adjusted basis is required to be determined using the alternative depreciation system of section 168(g) for allocating business interest expense between excepted and non-excepted trades or businesses under section 163(j), but only if the property is not required to be depreciated under the alternative depreciation system of section 168(g) pursuant to section 168(g)(1)(A), (B), (C), (D), (F), or (G), or other provisions of the Code, other than section 163(j), 250(b)(2)(B), or 951A(d)(3), as applicable;

(C) Included in any class of property for which the taxpayer elects not to deduct the additional first year depreciation (for further guidance, see paragraph (f) of this section);

(D) A specified plant that is placed in service by the taxpayer during the taxable year and for which the taxpayer made an election to apply section 168(k)(5) for a prior taxable year;

(E) Included in any class of property for which the taxpayer elects to apply section 168(k)(4). This paragraph (b)(2)(ii)(E) applies to property placed in service by the taxpayer in any taxable year beginning before January 1, 2018;

(F) Primarily used in a trade or business described in section 163(j)(7)(A)(iv), and placed in service by the taxpayer in any taxable year beginning after December 31, 2017; or

(G) Used in a trade or business that has had floor plan financing indebtedness, as defined in section 163(j)(9), if the floor plan financing interest, as defined in section 163(j)(9), related to such indebtedness is taken into account under section 163(j)(1)(C) for the taxable year. Such property also must be placed in service by the taxpayer in any taxable year beginning after December 31, 2017.

* * *

(3) *Original use or used property acquisition requirements.*—(i) *In general.*—Depreciable property will meet the requirements of this paragraph (b)(3) if the property meets the original use requirements in paragraph (b)(3)(ii) of this section or if the property meets the used property acquisition requirements in paragraph (b)(3)(iii) of this section.

(ii) *Original use.*—(A) *In general.*—Depreciable property will meet the requirements of this paragraph (b)(3)(ii) if the original use of the property commences with the taxpayer. Except as provided in paragraphs (b)(3)(ii)(B) and (C) of this section, original use means the first use to which the property is put, whether or not that use corresponds to the use of the property by the taxpayer. Additional capital expenditures paid or incurred by a taxpayer to recondition or rebuild property acquired or owned by the taxpayer satisfy the original use requirement. However, the cost of reconditioned or rebuilt property does not satisfy the original use requirement (but may satisfy the used property acquisition requirements in paragraph (b)(3)(iii) of this section). The question of whether property is reconditioned or rebuilt property is a question of fact. For purposes of this paragraph (b)(3)(ii)(A), property that contains used parts will not be treated as reconditioned or rebuilt if the cost of the used parts is not more than 20 percent of the total cost of the property, whether acquired or self-constructed.

(B) *Conversion to business or income-producing use.*—*(1) Personal use to business or income-producing use.*—If a taxpayer initially acquires new property for personal use and subsequently uses the property in the taxpayer's trade or business or for the taxpayer's production of income, the taxpayer is considered the original user of the property. If a person initially acquires new property for personal use and a taxpayer subsequently acquires the property from the person for use in the taxpayer's trade or business or for the taxpayer's production of income, the taxpayer is not considered the original user of the property.

(2) Inventory to business or income-producing use.—If a taxpayer initially acquires new property and holds the property primarily for sale to customers in the ordinary course of the taxpayer's business and subsequently with-

draws the property from inventory and uses the property primarily in the taxpayer's trade or business or primarily for the taxpayer's production of income, the taxpayer is considered the original user of the property. If a person initially acquires new property and holds the property primarily for sale to customers in the ordinary course of the person's business and a taxpayer subsequently acquires the property from the person for use primarily in the taxpayer's trade or business or primarily for the taxpayer's production of income, the taxpayer is considered the original user of the property. For purposes of this paragraph (b) (3) (ii) (B) (*2*), the original use of the property by the taxpayer commences on the date on which the taxpayer uses the property primarily in the taxpayer's trade or business or primarily for the taxpayer's production of income.

(C) *Fractional interests in property.*—If, in the ordinary course of its business, a taxpayer sells fractional interests in new property to third parties unrelated to the taxpayer, each first fractional owner of the property is considered as the original user of its proportionate share of the property. Furthermore, if the taxpayer uses the property before all of the fractional interests of the property are sold but the property continues to be held primarily for sale by the taxpayer, the original use of any fractional interest sold to a third party unrelated to the taxpayer subsequent to the taxpayer's use of the property begins with the first purchaser of that fractional interest. For purposes of this paragraph (b) (3) (ii) (C), persons are not related if they do not have a relationship described in section 267(b) and § 1.267(b)-1, or section 707(b) and § 1.707-1.

(iii) *Used property acquisition requirements.*—(A) *In general.*—Depreciable property will meet the requirements of this paragraph (b) (3) (iii) if the acquisition of the used property meets the following requirements:

(1) Such property was not used by the taxpayer or a predecessor at any time prior to such acquisition;

(2) The acquisition of such property meets the requirements of section 179(d) (2) (A), (B), and (C), and § 1.179-4(c) (1) (ii), (iii), and (iv); or § 1.179-4(c) (2) (property is acquired by purchase); and

(3) The acquisition of such property meets the requirements of section 179(d) (3) and § 1.179-4(d) (cost of property) (for further guidance regarding like-kind exchanges and involuntary conversions, see paragraph (g) (5) of this section).

(B) *Property was not used by the taxpayer at any time prior to acquisition.*—*(1)* In *general*. Solely for purposes of paragraph (b) (3) (iii) (A) (*1*) of this section, the property is treated as used by the taxpayer or a predecessor at any time prior to acquisition by the taxpayer or predecessor if the taxpayer or the predecessor had a depreciable interest in the property at any time prior to such acquisition, whether or not the taxpayer or the predecessor claimed depreciation deductions for the property. To determine if the taxpayer or a predecessor had a depreciable interest in the property at any time prior to acquisition, only the five calendar years immediately prior to the taxpayer's current placed-in-service year of the property is taken into account. If the taxpayer and a predecessor have not been in existence for this entire five-year period, only the number of calendar years the taxpayer and the predecessor have been in existence is taken into account. If a lessee has a depreciable interest in the improvements made to leased property and subsequently the lessee acquires the leased property of which the improvements are a part, the unadjusted depreciable basis, as defined in § 1.168(b)-1(a) (3), of the acquired property that is eligible for the additional first year depreciation deduction, assuming all other requirements are met, must not include the unadjusted depreciable basis attributable to the improvements.

(2) Taxpayer has a depreciable interest in a portion of the property.—If a taxpayer initially acquires a depreciable interest in a portion of the property and subsequently acquires a depreciable interest in an additional portion of the same property, such additional depreciable interest is not treated as used by the taxpayer at any time prior to its acquisition by the taxpayer under paragraphs (b) (3) (iii) (A) (*1*) and (b) (3) (iii) (B) (*1*) of this section. This paragraph (b) (3) (iii) (B) (*2*) does not apply if the taxpayer or a predecessor previously had a depreciable interest in the subsequently acquired additional portion. For purposes of this paragraph (b) (3) (iii) (B) (*2*), a portion of the property is considered to be the percentage interest in the property. If a taxpayer holds a depreciable interest in a portion of the property, sells that portion or a part of that portion, and subsequently acquires a depreciable interest in another portion of the same property, the taxpayer will be treated as previously having a depreciable interest in the property up to the amount of the portion for which the taxpayer held a depreciable interest in the property before the sale.

(3) Substantial renovation of property.—If a taxpayer acquires and places in service substantially renovated property and the taxpayer or a predecessor previously had a depreciable interest in the property before it

was substantially renovated, the taxpayer's or predecessor's depreciable interest in the property before it was substantially renovated is not taken into account for determining whether the substantially renovated property was used by the taxpayer or a predecessor at any time prior to its acquisition by the taxpayer under paragraphs (b)(3)(iii)(A)(*1*) and (b)(3)(iii)(B)(*1*) of this section. For purposes of this paragraph (b)(3)(iii)(B)(*3*), property is substantially renovated if the cost of the used parts is not more than 20 percent of the total cost of the substantially renovated property, whether acquired or self-constructed.

(C) [Reserved]

(iv) *Application to partnerships.*—(A) *Section 704(c) remedial allocations.*—Remedial allocations under section 704(c) do not satisfy the requirements of paragraph (b)(3) of this section. See § 1.704-3(d)(2).

(B) *Basis determined under section 732.*—Any basis of distributed property determined under section 732 does not satisfy the requirements of paragraph (b)(3) of this section.

(C) *Section 734(b) adjustments.*—Any increase in basis of depreciable property under section 734(b) does not satisfy the requirements of paragraph (b)(3) of this section.

(D) *Section 743(b) adjustments.*—*(1) In general.*—For purposes of determining whether the transfer of a partnership interest meets the requirements of paragraph (b)(3)(iii)(A) of this section, each partner is treated as having a depreciable interest in the partner's proportionate share of partnership property. Any increase in basis of depreciable property under section 743(b) satisfies the requirements of paragraph (b)(3)(iii)(A) of this section if—

(i) At any time prior to the transfer of the partnership interest that gave rise to such basis increase, neither the transferee partner nor a predecessor of the transferee partner had any depreciable interest in the portion of the property deemed acquired to which the section 743(b) adjustment is allocated under section 755 and § 1.755-1; and

(ii) The transfer of the partnership interest that gave rise to such basis increase satisfies the requirements of paragraphs (b)(3)(iii)(A)(*2*) and (*3*) of this section.

(2) Relatedness tested at partner level.—Solely for purposes of paragraph (b)(3)(iv)(D)(*1*)(*ii*) of this section, whether the parties are related or unrelated is determined by comparing the transferor and the transferee of the transferred partnership interest.

(v) [Reserved]

(vi) *Syndication transaction.*—If new property is acquired and placed in service by a lessor, or if used property is acquired and placed in service by a lessor and the lessor or a predecessor did not previously have a depreciable interest in the used property, and the property is sold by the lessor or any subsequent purchaser within three months after the date the property was originally placed in service by the lessor (or, in the case of multiple units of property subject to the same lease, within three months after the date the final unit is placed in service, so long as the period between the time the first unit is placed in service and the time the last unit is placed in service does not exceed 12 months), and the user of the property after the last sale during the three-month period remains the same as when the property was originally placed in service by the lessor, the purchaser of the property in the last sale during the three-month period is considered the taxpayer that acquired the property for purposes of applying paragraphs (b)(3)(ii) and (iii) of this section. The purchaser of the property in the last sale during the three-month period is treated, for purposes of applying paragraph (b)(3) of this section, as—

(A) The original user of the property in this transaction if the lessor acquired and placed in service new property; or

(B) The taxpayer having the depreciable interest in the property in this transaction if the lessor acquired and placed in service used property.

* * *

(4) *Placed-in-service date.*—(i) *In general.*—Depreciable property will meet the requirements of this paragraph (b)(4) if the property is placed in service by the taxpayer for use in its trade or business or for production of income after September 27, 2017; and, except as provided in paragraphs (b)(2)(i)(A) and (D) of this section, before January 1, 2027, or, in the case of property described in section 168(k)(2)(B) or (C), before January 1, 2028.

(ii) *Specified plant.*—If the taxpayer has properly made an election to apply section 168(k)(5) for a specified plant, the requirements of this paragraph (b)(4) are satisfied only if the specified plant is planted before January 1, 2027, or is grafted before January 1, 2027, to a plant that has already been planted, by the taxpayer in the ordinary course of the taxpayer's farming business, as defined in section 263A(e)(4).

(iii) *Qualified film, television, or live theatrical production.*—(A) *Qualified film or television production.*—For purposes of this paragraph (b)(4), a qualified film or television production is treated as placed in service at the time of initial release or broadcast as defined under § 1.181-1(a)(7). The taxpayer that places in service a qualified film or television production must be the owner, as defined in § 1.181-1(a)(2), of the qualified film or television production.

(B) *Qualified live theatrical production.*—For purposes of this paragraph (b)(4), a qualified live theatrical production is treated as placed in service at the time of the initial live staged performance. The taxpayer that places in service a qualified live theatrical production must be the owner, as defined in paragraph (b)(2)(i)(F) of this section and in § 1.181-1(a)(2), of the qualified live theatrical production.

(iv) *Syndication transaction.*—If new property is acquired and placed in service by a lessor, or if used property is acquired and placed in service by a lessor and the lessor and any predecessor did not previously have a depreciable interest in the used property, and the property is sold by the lessor or any subsequent purchaser within three months after the date the property was originally placed in service by the lessor (or, in the case of multiple units of property subject to the same lease, within three months after the date the final unit is placed in service, so long as the period between the time the first unit is placed in service and the time the last unit is placed in service does not exceed 12 months), and the user of the property after the last sale during this three-month period remains the same as when the property was originally placed in service by the lessor, the property is treated as originally placed in service by the purchaser of the property in the last sale during the three-month period but not earlier than the date of the last sale for purposes of sections 167 and 168, and §§ 1.46-3(d) and 1.167(a)-11(e)(1).

(v) *Technical termination of a partnership.*—For purposes of this paragraph (b)(4), in the case of a technical termination of a partnership under section 708(b)(1)(B) occurring in a taxable year beginning before January 1, 2018, qualified property placed in service by the terminated partnership during the taxable year of termination is treated as originally placed in service by the new partnership on the date the qualified property is contributed by the terminated partnership to the new partnership.

(vi) *Section 168(i)(7) transactions.*—For purposes of this paragraph (b)(4), if qualified property is transferred in a transaction described in section 168(i)(7) in the same taxable year that the qualified property is placed in service by the transferor, the transferred property is treated as originally placed in service on the date the transferor placed in service the qualified property. In the case of multiple transfers of qualified property in multiple transactions described in section 168(i)(7) in the same taxable year, the placed-in-service date of the transferred property is deemed to be the date on which the first transferor placed in service the qualified property.

* * *

(d) *Property described in section 168(k)(2)(B) or (C).*—(1) *In general.*—Property described in section 168(k)(2)(B) or (C) will meet the acquisition requirements of section 168(k)(2)(B)(i)(III) or (k)(2)(C)(i) if the property is acquired by the taxpayer before January 1, 2027, or acquired by the taxpayer pursuant to a written binding contract that is entered into before January 1, 2027. Property described in section 168(k)(2)(B) or (C), including its components, also must meet the acquisition requirement in section 13201(h)(1)(A) of the Act (for further guidance, see paragraph (b)(5) of this section).

(2) *Definition of binding contract.*—For purposes of this paragraph (d), the rules in paragraph (b)(5)(iii) of this section for a binding contract apply.

(3) *Self-constructed property.*—(i) *In general.*—If a taxpayer manufactures, constructs, or produces property for use by the taxpayer in its trade or business or for its production of income, the acquisition rules in paragraph (d)(1) of this section are treated as met for the property if the taxpayer begins manufacturing, constructing, or producing the property before January 1, 2027. Property that is manufactured, constructed, or produced for the taxpayer by another person under a written binding contract, as defined in paragraph (b)(5)(iii) of this section, that is entered into prior to the manufacture, construction, or production of the property for use by the taxpayer in its trade or business or for its production of income is considered to be manufactured, constructed, or produced by the taxpayer. If a taxpayer enters into a written binding contract, as defined in paragraph (b)(5)(iii) of this section, before January 1, 2027, with another person to manufacture, construct, or produce property described in section 168(k)(2)(B) or (C) and the manufacture, construction, or production of this property begins after December 31, 2026, the acquisition rule in paragraph (d)(1) of this section is met.

(ii) *When does manufacture, construction, or production begin.*—(A) *In general.*—For purposes of this paragraph (d)(3), manufacture, construction, or production of property begins when physical work of a significant nature begins. Physical work does not include preliminary activities such as planning or designing, securing financing, exploring, or researching. The determination of when physical work of a significant nature begins depends on the facts and circumstances. For example, if a retail motor fuels outlet is to be constructed on-site, construction begins when physical work of a significant nature commences at the site; that is, when work begins on the excavation for footings, pouring the pads for the outlet, or the driving of foundation pilings into the ground. Preliminary work, such as clearing a site, test drilling to determine soil condition, or excavation to change the contour of the land (as distinguished from excavation for footings) does not constitute the beginning of construction. However, if a retail motor fuels outlet is to be assembled on-site from modular units manufactured off-site and delivered to the site where the outlet will be used, manufacturing begins when physical work of a significant nature commences at the off-site location.

(B) *Safe harbor.*—For purposes of paragraph (d)(3)(ii)(A) of this section, a taxpayer may choose to determine when physical work of a significant nature begins in accordance with this paragraph (d)(3)(ii)(B). Physical work of a significant nature will be considered to begin at the time the taxpayer incurs (in the case of an accrual basis taxpayer) or pays (in the case of a cash basis taxpayer) more than 10 percent of the total cost of the property, excluding the cost of any land and preliminary activities such as planning or designing, securing financing, exploring, or researching. When property is manufactured, constructed, or produced for the taxpayer by another person, this safe harbor test must be satisfied by the taxpayer. For example, if a retail motor fuels outlet is to be constructed for an accrual basis taxpayer by another person for the total cost of $200,000, excluding the cost of any land and preliminary activities such as planning or designing, securing financing, exploring, or researching, construction is deemed to begin for purposes of this paragraph (d)(3)(ii)(B) when the taxpayer has incurred more than 10 percent (more than $20,000) of the total cost of the property. A taxpayer chooses to apply this paragraph (d)(3)(ii)(B) by filing a Federal income tax return for the placed-in-service year of the property that determines when physical work of a significant nature begins consistent with this paragraph (d)(3)(ii)(B).

(iii) *Components of self-constructed property.*—(A) *Acquired components.*—If a binding contract, as defined in paragraph (b)(5)(iii) of this section, to acquire a component does not satisfy the requirements of paragraph (d)(1) of this section, the component does not qualify for the additional first year depreciation deduction under this section. A binding contract described in the preceding sentence to acquire one or more components of a larger self-constructed property will not preclude the larger self-constructed property from satisfying the acquisition rules in paragraph (d)(3)(i) of this section. Accordingly, the unadjusted depreciable basis of the larger self-constructed property that is eligible for the additional first year depreciation deduction under this section, assuming all other requirements are met, must not include the unadjusted depreciable basis of any component that does not satisfy the requirements of paragraph (d)(1) of this section. If a binding contract to acquire the component is entered into before January 1, 2027, but the manufacture, construction, or production of the larger self-constructed property does not begin before January 1, 2027, the component qualifies for the additional first year depreciation deduction under this section, assuming all other requirements are met, but the larger self-constructed property does not.

(B) *Self-constructed components.*—If the manufacture, construction, or production of a component by the taxpayer does not satisfy the requirements of paragraph (d)(3)(i) of this section, the component does not qualify for the additional first year depreciation deduction under this section. However, if the manufacture, construction, or production of a component does not satisfy the requirements of paragraph (d)(3)(i) of this section, but the manufacture, construction, or production of the larger self-constructed property satisfies the requirements of paragraph (d)(3)(i) of this section, the larger self-constructed property qualifies for the additional first year depreciation deduction under this section, assuming all other requirements are met, even though the component does not qualify for the additional first year depreciation deduction under this section. Accordingly, the unadjusted depreciable basis of the larger self-constructed property that is eligible for the additional first year depreciation deduction under this section, assuming all other requirements are met, must not include the unadjusted depreciable basis of any component that does not qualify for the additional first year depreciation deduction under this section. If the manufacture, construction, or production of a component begins before January 1, 2027, but the manufacture, construction, or production of the larger self-constructed property does not begin before January 1, 2027, the component qualifies for the additional first year depreciation deduction under this section, assuming all other requirements are met, but the larger self-constructed property does not.

* * *

(e) *Computation of depreciation deduction for qualified property.*—(1) *Additional first year depreciation deduction.*—(i) *Allowable taxable year.*—The additional first year depreciation deduction is allowable—

(A) Except as provided in paragraph (e)(1)(i)(B) or (g) of this section, in the taxable year in which the qualified property is placed in service by the taxpayer for use in its trade or business or for the production of income; or

(B) In the taxable year in which the specified plant is planted, or grafted to a plant that has already been planted, by the taxpayer in the ordinary course of the taxpayer's farming business, as defined in section 263A(e)(4), if the taxpayer properly made the election to apply section 168(k)(5) (for further guidance, see paragraph (f) of this section).

(ii) *Computation.*—Except as provided in paragraph (g)(5) of this section, the allowable additional first year depreciation deduction for qualified property is determined by multiplying the unadjusted depreciable basis, as defined in § 1.168(b)-1(a)(3), of the qualified property by the applicable percentage. Except as provided in paragraph (g)(1) of this section, the additional first year depreciation deduction is not affected by a taxable year of less than 12 months. See paragraph (g)(1) of this section for qualified property placed in service or planted or grafted, as applicable, and disposed of during the same taxable year. See paragraph (g)(5) of this section for qualified property acquired in a like-kind exchange or as a result of an involuntary conversion.

(iii) *Property described in section 168(k)(2)(B).*—For purposes of paragraph (e)(1)(ii) of this section, the unadjusted depreciable basis, as defined in § 1.168(b)-1(a)(3), of qualified property described in section 168(k)(2)(B) is limited to the property's unadjusted depreciable basis attributable to the property's manufacture, construction, or production before January 1, 2027.

(iv) *Alternative minimum tax.*—(A) *In general.*—The additional first year depreciation deduction is allowable for alternative minimum tax purposes—

(1) Except as provided in paragraph (e)(1)(iv)(A)*(2)* of this section, in the taxable year in which the qualified property is placed in service by the taxpayer; or

(2) In the taxable year in which a specified plant is planted by the taxpayer, or grafted by the taxpayer to a plant that was previously planted, if the taxpayer properly made the election to apply section 168(k)(5) (for further guidance, see paragraph (f) of this section).

(B) *Special rules.*—In general, the additional first year depreciation deduction for alternative minimum tax purposes is based on the unadjusted depreciable basis of the property for alternative minimum tax purposes. However, see paragraph (g)(5)(iii)(E) of this section for qualified property acquired in a like-kind exchange or as a result of an involuntary conversion.

(2) *Otherwise allowable depreciation deduction.*—(i) *In general.*—Before determining the amount otherwise allowable as a depreciation deduction for the qualified property for the placed-in-service year and any subsequent taxable year, the taxpayer must determine the remaining adjusted depreciable basis of the qualified property. This remaining adjusted depreciable basis is equal to the unadjusted depreciable basis, as defined in § 1.168(b)-1(a)(3), of the qualified property reduced by the amount of the additional first year depreciation allowed or allowable, whichever is greater. The remaining adjusted depreciable basis of the qualified property is then depreciated using the applicable depreciation provisions under the Internal Revenue Code for the qualified property. The remaining adjusted depreciable basis of the qualified property that is MACRS property is also the basis to which the annual depreciation rates in the optional depreciation tables apply (for further guidance, see section 8 of Rev. Proc. 87-57 (1987-2 C.B. 687) and § 601.601(d)(2)(ii)(*b*) of this chapter). The depreciation deduction allowable for the remaining adjusted depreciable basis of the qualified property is affected by a taxable year of less than 12 months.

(ii) *Alternative minimum tax.*—For alternative minimum tax purposes, the depreciation deduction allowable for the remaining adjusted depreciable basis of the qualified property is based on the remaining adjusted depreciable basis for alternative minimum tax purposes. The remaining adjusted depreciable basis of the qualified property for alternative minimum tax purposes is depreciated using the same depreciation method, recovery period (or useful life in the case of computer software), and convention that apply to the qualified property for regular tax purposes.

* * *

(f) *Elections under section 168(k).*—(1) *Election not to deduct additional first year depreciation.*—(i) *In general.*—A taxpayer may make an election not to deduct the additional first year depreciation for any class of property that is qualified property placed in service during the taxable year. If this election is made, the election applies to all qualified property that is in the same class of property and placed in service in the same taxable year, and no additional first year depreciation deduction is allowable for the property placed in service during the taxable year in the class of property, except as provided in § 1.743-1(j)(4)(i)(B)(*1*).

(ii) *Definition of class of property.*—For purposes of this paragraph (f)(1), the term *class of property* means:

(A) Except for the property described in paragraphs (f)(1)(ii)(B) and (D), and (f)(2) of this section, each class of property described in section 168(e) (for example, 5-year property);

(B) Water utility property as defined in section 168(e)(5) and depreciated under section 168;

(C) Computer software as defined in, and depreciated under, section 167(f)(1) and § 1.167(a)-14(b);

(D) Qualified improvement property as defined in § 1.168(b)-1(a)(5)(i)(C) and (a)(5)(ii), and depreciated under section 168;

(E) Each separate production, as defined in § 1.181-3(b), of a qualified film or television production;

(F) Each separate production, as defined in section 181(e)(2), of a qualified live theatrical production; or

(G) A partner's basis adjustment in partnership assets under section 743(b) for each class of property described in paragraphs (f)(1)(ii)(A) through (F), and (f)(2) of this section (for further guidance, see § 1.743-1(j)(4)(i)(B)(*1*)).

(iii) *Time and manner for making election.*—(A) *Time for making election.*—Except as provided in paragraph (f)(6) of this section, any election specified in paragraph (f)(1)(i) of this section must be made by the due date, including extensions, of the Federal tax return for the taxable year in which the qualified property is placed in service by the taxpayer.

(B) *Manner of making election.*—Except as provided in paragraph (f)(6) of this section, any election specified in paragraph (f)(1)(i) of this section must be made in the manner prescribed on Form 4562, "Depreciation and Amortization," and its instructions. The election is made separately by each person owning qualified property (for example, for each member of a consolidated group by the common parent of the group, by the partnership (including a lower-tier partnership; also including basis adjustments in the partnership assets under section 743(b)), or by the S corporation). If Form 4562 is revised or renumbered, any reference in this section to that form shall be treated as a reference to the revised or renumbered form.

(iv) *Failure to make election.*—If a taxpayer does not make the election specified in paragraph (f)(1)(i) of this section within the time and in the manner prescribed in paragraph (f)(1)(iii) of this section, the amount of depreciation allowable for that property under section 167 or 168, as applicable, must be determined for the placed-in-service year and for all subsequent taxable years by taking into account the additional first year depreciation deduction. Thus, any election specified in paragraph (f)(1)(i) of this section shall not be made by the taxpayer in any other manner (for example, the election cannot be made through a request under section 446(e) to change the taxpayer's method of accounting).

* * *

(g) *Special rules.*—

* * *

(3) *Sections 1245 and 1250 depreciation recapture.*—For purposes of section 1245 and §§ 1.1245-1 through -6, the additional first year depreciation deduction is an amount allowed or allowable for depreciation. Further, for purposes of section 1250(b) and § 1.1250-2, the additional first year depreciation deduction is not a straight line method.

* * *

[Reg. § 1.168(k)-2.]

☐ [*T.D.* 9874, 9-17-2019.]

§ 1.170A-1. Charitable, etc., contributions and gifts; allowance of deduction.—(a) *Allowance of deduction.*—Any charitable contribution, as defined in section 170(c), actually paid during the taxable year is allowable as a deduction in computing taxable income irrespective of the method of accounting employed or of the date on which the contribution is pledged. However, charitable contributions by corporations may under certain circumstances be deductible even though not paid during the taxable year, as provided in section 170(a)(2) and § 1.170A-11. For rules relating to record keeping and return requirements in support of deductions for charitable contributions (whether by an itemizing or nonitemizing taxpayer), see §§ 1.170A-13 (generally applicable to contributions on or before July 30, 2018), 1.170A-14, 1.170A-15, 1.170A-16, 1.170A-17, and 1.170A-18. The deduction is subject to the limitations of section 170(b) and § 1.170A-8 or § 1.170A-11. Subject to the provisions of section 170(d) and §§ 1.170A-10 and 1.170A-11, certain excess charitable contributions made by individuals and corporations shall be treated as paid in certain succeeding taxable years. For provisions relating to direct charitable deductions under section 63 by nonitemizers, see section 63(b)(1)(C) and (i) and section 170(i). For rules relating to the determination of, and the deduction for, amounts paid to maintain certain students as members of the taxpayer's household and treated under section 170(g) as paid for the use of an organization described in section 170(c)(2), (3), or (4), see § 1.170A-2. For the reduction of any charitable contributions for interest on certain indebtedness, see section 170(f)(5) and § 1.170A-3. For a special rule relating to the computation of the amount of the deduction with respect to a charitable contribution of certain ordinary income or capital gain property, see section 170(e) and § 1.170A-4 and § 1.170A-4A. For rules for postponing the time for deduction of a charitable contribution of a future interest in tangible personal property, see section 170(a)(3) and § 1.170A-5. For rules with respect to transfers in trust and of partial interests in property, see section 170(e), section 170(f)(2) and (3), § 1.170A-4, § 1.170A-6, and § 1.170A-7. For definition of the term "section 170(b)(1)(A) organization," see § 1.170A-9. For valuation of a remainder interest in real property, see section 170(f)(4) and the regulations thereunder. The deduction for charitable contributions is subject to verification by the district director.

(b) *Time of making contribution.*—Ordinarily, a contribution is made at the time delivery is effected. The unconditional delivery or mailing of a check which subsequently clears in due course will constitute an effective contribution on the date of delivery or mailing. If a taxpayer unconditionally delivers or mails a properly endorsed stock certificate to a charitable donee or the donee's agent, the gift is completed on the date of delivery or, if such certificate is received in the ordinary course of the mails, on the date of mailing. If the donor delivers the stock certificate to his bank or broker as the donor's agent, or to the issuing corporation or its agent, for transfer into the name of the donee, the gift is completed on the date the stock is transferred on the books of the corporation. For rules relating to the date of payment of a contribution consisting of a future interest in tangible personal property, see section 170(a)(3) and § 1.170A-5.

(c) *Value of a contribution in property.*—(1) If a charitable contribution is made in property other than money, the amount of the contribution is the fair market value of the property at the time of the contribution reduced as provided in section 170(e)(1) and paragraph (a) of § 1.170A-4, or section 170(e)(3) and paragraph (c) of § 1.170A-4A.

(2) The fair market value is the price at which the property would change hands between a willing buyer and a willing seller, neither being under any compulsion to buy or sell and both having reasonable knowledge of relevant facts. If the contribution is made in property of a type which the taxpayer sells in the course of his business, the fair market value is the price which the taxpayer would have received if he had sold the contributed property in the usual market in which he customarily sells, at the time and place of the contribution and, in the case of a contribution of goods in quantity, in the quantity contributed. The usual market of a manufacturer or other producer consists of the wholesalers or other distributors to or through whom he customarily sells, but if he sells only at retail the usual market consists of his retail customers.

(3) If the donor makes a charitable contribution of property, such as stock in trade, at a time when he could not reasonably have been expected to realize its usual selling price, the value of the gift is not the usual selling price but is the amount for which the quantity of property contributed would have been sold by the donor at the time of the contribution.

(4) Any costs and expenses pertaining to the contributed property which were incurred in taxable years preceding the year of contribution and are properly reflected in the opening inventory for the year of contribution must be removed from inventory and are not a part of the cost of goods sold for purposes of determining gross income for the year of contribution. Any costs and expenses pertaining to the contributed property which are incurred in the year of contribution and would, under the method of accounting used, be properly reflected in the cost of goods sold for such year are to be treated as part of the cost of goods sold for such year. If costs and expenses incurred in producing or acquiring the contributed property are, under the method of accounting used, properly deducted under section 162 or other section of the Code, such costs and expenses will be allowed as deductions for the taxable year in which they are paid or incurred, whether or not such year is the year of the contribution. Any such costs and expenses which are treated as part of the cost of goods sold for the year of contribution, and any such costs and expenses which are properly deducted under section 162 or other section of the Code, are not to be treated under any section of the Code as resulting in any basis for the contributed property. Thus, for example, the contributed property has no basis for purposes of determining under section 170(e)(1)(A) and paragraph (a) of § 1.170A-4 the amount of gain which would have been recognized if such property had been sold by

the donor at its fair market value at the time of its contribution. The amount of any charitable contribution for the taxable year is not to be reduced by the amount of any costs or expenses pertaining to the contributed property which was properly deducted under section 162 or other section of the Code for any taxable year preceding the year of the contribution. This subparagraph applies only to property which was held by the taxpayer for sale in the course of a trade or business. The application of this subparagraph may be illustrated by the following examples:

Example (1). In 1970, A, an individual using the calendar year as the taxable year and the accrual method of accounting, contributed to a church property from inventory having a fair market value of $600. The closing inventory at the end of 1969 properly included $400 of costs attributable to the acquisition of such property, and in 1969 A properly deducted under section 162 $50 of administrative and other expenses attributable to such property. Under section 170(e)(1)(A) and paragraph (a) of § 1.170A-4, the amount of the charitable contribution allowed for 1970 is $400 ($600 – [$600 – $400]). Pursuant to this subparagraph, the cost of goods sold to be used in determining gross income for 1970 may not include the $400 which was included in opening inventory for that year.

Example (2). The facts are the same as in example (1) except that the contributed property was acquired in 1970 at a cost of $400. The $400 cost of the property is included in determining the cost of goods sold for 1970, and $50 is allowed as a deduction for that year under section 162. A is not allowed any deduction under section 170 for the contributed property, since under section 170(e)(1)(A) and paragraph (a) of § 1.170A-4 the amount of the charitable contribution is reduced to zero ($600 – [$600 – $0]).

Example (3). In 1970, B, an individual using the calendar year as the taxable year and the accrual method of accounting, contributed to a church property from inventory having a fair market value of $600. Under § 1.471-3(c), the closing inventory at the end of 1969 properly included $450 costs attributable to the production of such property, including $50 of administrative and other indirect expenses which, under his method of accounting, was properly added to inventory rather than deducted as a business expense. Under section 170(e)(1)(A) and paragraph (a) of § 1.170A-4, the amount of the charitable contribution allowed for 1970 is $450 ($600 – [$600 – $450]). Pursuant to this subparagraph, the cost of goods sold to be used in determining gross income for 1970 may not include the $450 which was included in opening inventory for that year.

Example (4). The facts are the same as in example (3) except that the contributed property was produced in 1970 at a cost of $450, including $50 of administrative and other indirect expenses. The $450 cost of the property is included in determining the cost of goods sold for 1970. B is not allowed any deduction under section 170 for the contributed property, since under section 170(e)(1)(A) and paragraph (a) of § 1.170A-4 the amount of the charitable contribution is reduced to zero ($600 – [$600 – $0]).

Example (5). In 1970, C, a farmer using the cash method of accounting and the calendar year as the taxable year, contributed to a church a quantity of grain which he had raised having a fair market value of $600. In 1969, C paid expenses of $450 in raising the property which he properly deducted for such year under section 162. Under section 170(e)(1)(A) and paragraph (a) of § 1.170A-4, the amount of the charitable contribution in 1970 is reduced to zero ($600 – [$600 – $0]). Accordingly, C is not allowed any deduction under section 170 for the contributed property.

Example (6). The facts are the same as in example (5) except that the $450 expenses incurred in raising the contributed property were paid in 1970. The result is the same as in example (5), except the amount of $450 is deductible under section 162 for 1970.

(5) Transfers of property to an organization described in section 170(c) which bear a direct relationship to the taxpayer's trade or business and which are made with a reasonable expectation of financial return commensurate with the amount of the transfer may constitute allowable deductions as trade or business expenses rather than as charitable contributions. See section 162 and the regulations thereunder.

(d) *Purchase of an annuity.*—(1) In the case of an annuity or portion thereof purchased from an organization described in section 170(c), there shall be allowed as a deduction the excess of the amount paid over the value at the time of purchase of the annuity or portion purchased.

(2) The value of the annuity or portion is the value of the annuity determined in accordance with paragraph (e)(1)(iii)(*b*)(*2*) of § 1.101-2.

(3) For determining gain on any such transaction constituting a bargain sale, see section 1011(b) and § 1.1011-2.

(e) *Transfers subject to a condition or power.*—If as of the date of a gift a transfer for charitable purposes is dependent upon the performance of some act or the happening of a precedent event in order that it might become effective, no deduction is allowable unless the possibility that the charitable transfer will not become effective is so remote as to be negligible. If an interest in property passes to, or is vested in, charity on the date of the gift and the interest would be defeated by the subsequent performance of some act or the happening of some event, the possibility of occurrence of which appears on the date of the gift to be so remote as to be negligible, the deduction is allowable. For example, A transfers land to a city government for as long as the land is used by the city for a public park. If on the date of the gift the city does plan to use the land for a park and the possibility that the city will not use the land for a public park is so remote as to be negligible, A is entitled to a deduction under section 170 for his charitable contribution.

* * *

(g) *Contributions of services.*—No deduction is allowable under section 170 for a contribution of services. However, unreimbursed expenditures made incident to the rendition of services to an organization contributions to which are deductible may constitute a deductible contribution. For example, the cost of a uniform without general utility which is required to be worn in performing donated services is deductible. Similarly, out-of-pocket transportation expenses necessarily incurred in performing donated services are deductible. Reasonable expenditures for meals and lodging necessarily incurred while away from home in the course of performing donated services also are deductible. For the purposes of this paragraph, the phrase "while away from home" has the same meaning as that phrase is used for purposes of section 162 and the regulations thereunder.

(h) *Payment in exchange for consideration.*—(1) *Burden on taxpayer to show that all or part of payment is a charitable contribution or gift.*—No part of a payment that a taxpayer makes to or for the use of an organization described in section 170(c) that is in consideration for (as defined in § 1.170A-13(f)(6)) goods or services (as defined in § 1.170A-13(f)(5)) is a contribution or gift within the meaning of section 170(c) unless the taxpayer—

(i) Intends to make a payment in an amount that exceeds the fair market value of the goods or services; and

(ii) Makes a payment in an amount that exceeds the fair market value of the goods or services.

(2) *Limitation on amount deductible.*—(i) *In general.*—The charitable contribution deduction under section 170(a) for a payment a taxpayer makes partly in consideration for goods or services may not exceed the excess of—

(A) The amount of any cash paid and the fair market value of any property (other than cash) transferred by the taxpayer to an organization described in section 170(c); over

(B) The fair market value of the goods or services the organization provides in return.

(ii) *Special rules.*—For special limits on the deduction for charitable contributions of ordinary income and capital gain property, see section 170(e) and §§ 1.170A-4 and 1.170A-4A.

(3) *Payments resulting in state or local tax benefits.*—(i) *State or local tax credits.*—Except as provided in paragraph (h)(3)(vi) of this section, if a taxpayer makes a payment or transfers property to or for the use of an entity described in section 170(c), the amount of the taxpayer's charitable contribution deduction under section 170(a) is reduced by the amount of any state or local tax credit that the taxpayer receives or expects to receive in consideration for the taxpayer's payment or transfer.

(ii) *State or local tax deductions.*—(A) *In general.*—If a taxpayer makes a payment or transfers property to or for the use of an entity described in section 170(c), and the taxpayer receives or expects to receive state or local tax deductions that do not exceed the amount of the taxpayer's payment or the fair market value of the property transferred by the taxpayer to the entity, the taxpayer is not required to reduce its charitable contribution deduction under section 170(a) on account of the state or local tax deductions.

(B) *Excess state or local tax deductions.*—If the taxpayer receives or expects to receive a state or local tax deduction that exceeds the amount of the taxpayer's payment or the fair market value of the property transferred, the taxpayer's charitable contribution deduction under section 170(a) is reduced.

(iii) *In consideration for.*—For purposes of paragraph (h)(3)(i) of this section, the term *in consideration for* shall have the meaning set forth in § 1.170A-13(f)(6), except that the state or local tax credit need not be provided by the donee organization.

(iv) *Amount of reduction.*—For purposes of paragraph (h)(3)(i) of this section, the amount of any state or local tax credit is the maximum credit allowable that corresponds to the amount of the taxpayer's payment or transfer to the entity described in section 170(c).

(v) *State or local tax.*—For purposes of paragraph (h)(3) of this section, the term *state or local tax* means a tax imposed by a State, a possession of the United States, or by a political subdivision of any of the foregoing, or by the District of Columbia.

(vi) *Exception.*—Paragraph (h)(3)(i) of this section shall not apply to any payment or transfer of property if the total amount of the state and local tax credits received or expected to be received by the taxpayer is 15 percent or less of the taxpayer's payment, or 15 percent or less of the fair market value of the property transferred by the taxpayer.

(vii) *Examples.*—The following examples illustrate the provisions of this paragraph (h)(3). The examples in paragraph (h)(6) of this section are not illustrative for purposes of this paragraph (h)(3).

(A) *Example 1.* A, an individual, makes a payment of $1,000 to X, an entity described in section 170(c). In exchange for the payment, A receives or expects to receive a state tax credit of 70 percent of the amount of A's payment to X. Under paragraph (h)(3)(i) of this section, A's charitable contribution deduction is reduced by $700 (0.70 x $1,000). This reduction occurs regardless of whether A is able to claim the state tax credit in that year. Thus, A's charitable contribution deduction for the $1,000 payment to X may not exceed $300.

(B) *Example 2.* B, an individual, transfers a painting to Y, an entity described in section 170(c). At the time of the transfer, the painting has a fair market value of $100,000. In exchange for the painting, B receives or expects to receive a state tax credit equal to 10 percent of the fair market value of the painting. Under paragraph (h)(3)(vi) of this section, B is not required to apply the general rule of paragraph (h)(3)(i) of this section because the amount of the tax credit received or expected to be received by B does not exceed 15 percent of the fair market value of the property transferred to Y. Accordingly, the amount of B's charitable contribution deduction for the transfer of the painting is not reduced under paragraph (h)(3)(i) of this section.

(C) *Example 3.* C, an individual, makes a payment of $1,000 to Z, an entity described in section 170(c). In exchange for the payment, under state M law, C is entitled to receive a state tax deduction equal to the amount paid by C to Z. Under paragraph (h)(3)(ii)(A) of this section, C's charitable contribution deduction under section 170(a) is not required to be reduced on account of C's state tax deduction for C's payment to Z.

(viii) *Effective/applicability date.*—This paragraph (h)(3) applies to amounts paid or property transferred by a taxpayer after August 27, 2018.

(4) *Donee estimates of the value of goods or services may be treated as fair market value.*—(i) *In general.*—For purposes of section 170(a), a taxpayer may rely on either a contemporaneous written acknowledgment provided under section 170(f)(8) and § 1.170A-13(f) or a written disclosure statement provided under section 6115 for the fair market value of any goods or services provided to the taxpayer by the donee organization.

(ii) *Exception.*—A taxpayer may not treat an estimate of the value of goods or services as their fair market value if the taxpayer knows, or has reason to know, that such treatment is unreasonable. For example, if a taxpayer knows, or has reason to know, that there is an error in an estimate provided by an organization described in section 170(c) pertaining to goods or services that have a readily ascertainable value, it is unreasonable for the taxpayer to treat the estimate as the fair market value of the goods or services. Similarly, if a taxpayer is a dealer in the type of goods or services provided in consideration for the taxpayer's payment and knows, or has reason to know, that the estimate is in error, it is unreasonable for the taxpayer to treat the estimate as the fair market value of the goods or services.

(5) *Examples.*—The following examples illustrate the rules of this paragraph (h).

Example 1. Certain goods or services disregarded. Taxpayer makes a $50 payment to Charity *B*, an organization described in section 170(c), in exchange for a family membership. The family membership entitles Taxpayer and members of Taxpayer's family to certain benefits. These benefits include free admission to weekly poetry readings, discounts on merchandise sold by *B* in its gift shop or by mail order, and invitations to special events for members only, such as lectures or informal receptions. When *B* first offers its membership package for the year, *B* reasonably projects that each special event for members will have a cost to *B*, excluding any allocable overhead, of $5 or less per person attending the event. Because the family membership benefits are disregarded pursuant to § 1.170A-13(f)(8)(i), Taxpayer may treat the $50 payment as a contribution or gift within the meaning of section 170(c), regardless of Taxpayer's intent and whether or not the payment exceeds the fair market value of the goods or services. Furthermore, any charitable contribution deduction available to Taxpayer may be calculated without regard to the membership benefits.

Example 2. Treatment of good faith estimate at auction as the fair market value. Taxpayer attends an auction held by Charity *C*, an organization described in section 170(c). Prior to the auction, *C* publishes a catalog that meets the requirements for a written disclosure statement under section 6115(a) (including *C*'s good faith estimate of the value of items that will be available for bidding). A representative of *C* gives a copy of the catalog to each individual (including Taxpayer) who attends the auction. Taxpayer notes that in the catalog *C*'s estimate of the value of a vase is $100. Taxpayer has no reason to doubt the accuracy of this estimate. Taxpayer successfully bids and pays $500 for the vase. Because Taxpayer knew, prior to making her payment, that the estimate in the catalog was less than the amount of her payment, Taxpayer satisfies the requirement of paragraph (h)(1)(i) of this section. Because Taxpayer makes a payment in an amount that exceeds that estimate, Taxpayer satisfies the requirements of paragraph (h)(1)(ii) of this section. Taxpayer may treat *C*'s estimate of the value of the vase as its fair market value in determining the amount of her charitable contribution deduction.

Example 3. Good faith estimate not in error. Taxpayer makes a $200 payment to Charity *D*, an organization described in section 170(c). In return for Taxpayer's payment, *D* gives Taxpayer a book that Taxpayer could buy at retail prices typically ranging from $18 to $25. *D* provides Taxpayer with a good faith estimate, in a written disclosure statement under section 6115(a), of $20 for the value of the book. Because the estimate is within the range of typical retail prices for the book, the estimate contained in the written disclosure statement is not in error. Although Taxpayer knows that the book is sold for as much as $25, Taxpayer may treat the estimate of $20 as the fair market value of the book in determining the amount of his charitable contribution deduction.

(i) [Reserved]

(j) *Exceptions and other rules.*—(1) The provisions of section 170 do not apply to contributions by an estate; nor do they apply to a trust unless the trust is a private foundation which, pursuant to section 642(c)(6) and § 1.642(c)-4, is allowed a deduction under section 170 subject to the provisions applicable to individuals.

(2) No deduction shall be allowed under section 170 for a charitable contribution to or for the use of an organization or trust described in section 508(d) or 4948(c)(4), subject to the conditions specified in such sections and the regulations thereunder.

(3) For disallowance of deductions for contributions to or for the use of communist controlled organizations, see section 11(a) of the Internal Security Act of 1950, as amended (50 U.S.C. 790).

(4) For denial of deductions for charitable contributions as trade or business expenses and rules with respect to treatment of payments to organizations other than those described in section 170(c), see section 162 and the regulations thereunder.

(5) No deduction shall be allowed under section 170 for amounts paid to an organization:

(i) Which is disqualified for tax exemption under section 501(c)(3) by reason of attempting to influence legislation, or

(ii) Which participates in, or intervenes in (including the publishing or distributing of statements), any political campaign on behalf of or in opposition to any candidate for public office.

For purposes of determining whether an organization is attempting to influence legislation or is engaging in political activities, see sections 501(c)(3), 501(h), 4911 and the regulations thereunder.

(6) No deduction shall be allowed under section 170 for expenditures for lobbying purposes, the promotion or defeat of legislation, etc. See also the regulations under sections 162 and 4945.

(7) No deduction for charitable contributions is allowed in computing the taxable income of a common trust fund or of a partnership. See sections 584(d)(3) and 703(a)(2)(D). However, a partner's distributive share of charitable contributions actually paid by a partnership during its taxable year may be allowed as a deduction in the partner's separate return for his taxable year with or within which the taxable year of the partnership ends, to the extent that the aggregate of his share of the partnership contributions and his own contributions does not exceed the limitations in section 170(b).

(8) For charitable contributions paid by a nonresident alien individual or a foreign corporation, see § 1.170A-4(b)(5) and sections 873, 876, 877, and 882(c), and the regulations thereunder.

(9) Charitable contributions paid by bona fide residents of a section 931 possession as defined in § 1.931-1(c)(1) or Puerto Rico are deductible only to the extent allocable to income that is not excluded under section 931 or 933. For the rules for allocating deductions for charitable contributions, see the regulations under section 861.

(10) For carryover of excess charitable contributions in certain corporate acquisitions, see section 381(c)(19) and the regulations thereunder.

(11) No deduction shall be allowed under section 170 for out-of-pocket expenditures on behalf of an eligible organization (within the

meaning of § 1.501(h)-2(b)(1)) if the expenditure is made in connection with influencing legislation (within the meaning of section 501(c)(3) or § 56.4911-2), or in connection with the payment of the organization's tax liability under section 4911. For the treatment of similar expenditures on behalf of other organizations see paragraph (h)(6) of this section.

* * *

[Reg. § 1.170A-1.]

☐ [*T.D.* 7207, 10-3-72. *Amended by T.D.* 7340, 1-6-75; *T.D.* 7807, 1-29-82; *T.D.* 8002, 12-26-84; *T.D.* 8308, 8-30-90; *T.D.* 8690, 12-13-96; *T.D.* 9194, 4-6-2005; *T.D.* 9391, 4-4-2008; *T.D.* 9836, 7-27-2018 (corrected 9-10-2018); *and T.D.* 9864, 6-11-2019.]

Proposed Amendments to Regulation

§ 1.170A-1. Charitable, etc., contributions and gifts; allowance of deduction.

* * *

(c) * * *

(5) For payments or transfers to an entity described in section 170(c) by a taxpayer carrying on a trade or business, see § 1.162-15(a).

* * *

(h) * * *

(2) * * *

(i) * * *

(B) The fair market value of the goods or services received or expected to be received in return.

* * *

(3) * * *

(iii) *In consideration for.*—For purposes of paragraph (h) of this section, the term *in consideration for* has the meaning set forth in paragraph (h)(4)(i) of this section.

* * *

(viii) *Safe harbor for payments by C corporations and specified passthrough entities.*—For payments by a C corporation or by a specified passthrough entity to an entity described in section 170(c), where the C corporation or specified passthrough entity receives or expects to receive a state or local tax credit that reduces the charitable contribution deduction for such payments under paragraph (h)(3) of this section, see § 1.162-15(a)(3) (providing safe harbors under section 162(a) to the extent of that reduction).

(ix) *Safe harbor for individuals.*—Under certain circumstances, an individual who itemizes deductions and makes a payment to an entity described in section 170(c) in consideration for a state or local tax credit may treat the portion of such payment for which a charitable contribution deduction is disallowed under paragraph (h)(3) of this section as a payment of state or local taxes under section 164. See § 1.164-3(j), providing a safe harbor for certain payments by individuals in exchange for state or local tax.

* * *

(4) *Definitions.*—For purposes of this paragraph (h), the following definitions apply:

(i) *In consideration for.*—A taxpayer receives goods or services in consideration for a taxpayer's payment or transfer to an entity described in section 170(c) if, at the time the taxpayer makes the payment to such entity, the taxpayer receives or expects to receive goods or services from that entity or any other party in return.

(ii) *Goods or services.*—Goods or services means cash, property, services, benefits, and privileges.

* * *

[Prop. Reg. § 1.170A-1.]

[Proposed 12-17-2019.]

»»→ Caution: Reg. § 1.170A-4 does not reflect changes in Section 170(e) made in 2006.

§ 1.170A-4. Reduction in amount of charitable contributions of certain appreciated property.—

* * *

(b) *Definitions and other rules.*—For purposes of this section—

(1) *Ordinary income property.*—The term "ordinary income property" means property any portion of the gain on which would not have been long-term capital gain if the property had been sold by the donor at its fair market value at the time of its contribution to the charitable organization. Such term includes, for example, property held by the donor primarily for sale to customers in the ordinary course of his trade or business, a work of art created by the donor, a manuscript prepared by the donor, letters and memorandums prepared by or for the donor, a capital asset held by the donor for not more than 1 year (6 months for taxable years beginning before 1977; 9 months for taxable years beginning in 1977), and stock described in section 306(a), 341(a), or 1248(a) to the extent that, after applying such section, gain on its disposition would not have been long-term capital gain. The term does not include an income interest in respect of which a deduction is allowed under section 170(f)(2)(B) and paragraph (c) of § 1.170A-6.

(2) *Section 170(e) capital gain property.*—The term "section 170(e) capital gain property"

means property any portion of the gain on which would have been treated as long-term capital gain if the property had been sold by the donor at its fair market value at the time of its contribution to the charitable organization and which—

(i) Is contributed to or for the use of a private foundation, as defined in section 509(a) and the regulations thereunder, other than a private foundation described in section 170(b)(1)(E),

(ii) Constitutes tangible personal property contributed to or for the use of a charitable organization, other than a private foundation to which subdivision (i) of this subparagraph applies, which is put to an unrelated use by the charitable organization within the meaning of subparagraph (3) of this paragraph, or

(iii) Constitutes property not described in subdivision (i) or (ii) of this subparagraph which is 30-percent capital gain property to which an election under paragraph (d)(2) of § 1.170A-8 applies.

For purposes of this subparagraph a fixture which is intended to be severed from real property shall be treated as tangible personal property.

(3) *Unrelated use.*—(i) *In general.*—The term "unrelated use" means a use which is unrelated to the purpose or function constituting the basis of the charitable organization's exemption under section 501 or, in the case of a contribution of property to a governmental unit, the use of such property by such unit for other than exclusively public purposes. For example, if a painting contributed to an educational institution is used by that organization for educational purposes by being placed in its library for display and study by art students, the use is not an unrelated use; but if the painting is sold and the proceeds used by the organization for educational purposes, the use of the property is an unrelated use. If furnishings contributed to a charitable organization are used by it in its offices and buildings in the course of carrying out its functions, the use of the property is not an unrelated use. If a set or collection of items of tangible personal property is contributed to a charitable organization or governmental unit, the use of the set or collection is not an unrelated use if the donee sells or otherwise disposes of only an insubstantial portion of the set or collection. The use by a trust of tangible personal property contributed to it for the benefit of a charitable organization is an unrelated use if the use by the trust is one which would have been unrelated if made by the charitable organization.

(ii) *Proof of use.*—For purposes of applying subparagraph (2)(ii) of this paragraph, a taxpayer who makes a charitable contribution of tangible personal property to or for the use of a charitable organization or governmental unit may treat such property as not being put to an unrelated use by the donee if—

(a) He establishes that the property is not in fact put to an unrelated use by the donee, or

(b) At the time of the contribution or at the time the contribution is treated as made, it is reasonable to anticipate that the property will not be put to an unrelated use by the donee. In the case of a contribution of tangible personal property to or for the use of a museum, if the object donated is of a general type normally retained by such museum or other museums for museum purposes, it will be reasonable for the donor to anticipate, unless he has actual knowledge to the contrary, that the object will not be put to an unrelated use by the donee, whether or not the object is later sold or exchanged by the donee.

(4) *Property used in trade or business.*—For purposes of applying subparagraphs (1) and (2) of this paragraph, property which is used in the trade or business, as defined in section 1231(b), shall be treated as a capital asset, except that any gain in respect of such property which would have been recognized if the property had been sold by the donor at its fair market value at the time of its contribution to the charitable organization shall be treated as ordinary income to the extent that such gain would have constituted ordinary income by reason of the application of section 617(d)(1), 1245(a), 1250(a), 1251(c), 1252(a), or 1254(a).

* * *

[Reg. § 1.170A-4.]

☐ [*T.D.* 7207, 10-3-72. *Amended by T.D.* 7728, 10-31-80, *T.D.* 7807, 1-29-82, *T.D.* 8176, 2-24-88 *and T.D.* 8540, 6-9-94.]

§ 1.170A-5. Future interests in tangible personal property.—(a) *In general.*—(1) A contribution consisting of a transfer of a future interest in tangible personal property shall be treated as made only when all intervening interests in, and rights to the actual possession or enjoyment of, the property—

(i) Have expired, or

(ii) Are held by persons other than the taxpayer or those standing in a relationship to the taxpayer described in section 267(b) and the regulations thereunder, relating to losses, expenses, and interest with respect to transactions between related taxpayers.

(2) Section 170(a)(3) and this section have no application in respect of a transfer of an undivided present interest in property. For example, a contribution of an undivided one-quarter interest in a painting with respect to

which the donee is entitled to possession during three months of each year shall be treated as made upon the receipt by the donee of a formally executed and acknowledged deed of gift. However, the period of initial possession by the donee may not be deferred in time for more than one year.

(3) Section 170(a)(3) and this section have no application in respect of a transfer of a future interest in intangible personal property or in real property. However, a fixture which is intended to be severed from real property shall be treated as tangible personal property. For example, a contribution of a future interest in a chandelier which is attached to a building is considered a contribution which consists of a future interest in tangible personal property if the transferor intends that it be detached from the building at or prior to the time when the charitable organization's right to possession or enjoyment of the chandelier is to commence.

(4) For purposes of section 170(a)(3) and this section, the term "future interest" has generally the same meaning as it has when used in section 2503 and §25.2503-3 of this chapter (Gift Tax Regulations); it includes reversions, remainders, and other interests or estates, whether vested or contingent, and whether or not supported by a particular interest or estate, which are limited to commence in use, possession, or enjoyment at some future date or time. The term "future interest" includes situations in which a donor purports to give tangible personal property to a charitable organization, but has an understanding, arrangement, agreement, etc., whether written or oral, with the charitable organization which has the effect of reserving to, or retaining in, such donor a right to the use, possession, or enjoyment of the property.

(5) In the case of a charitable contribution of a future interest to which section 170(a)(3) and this section apply, the other provisions of section 170 and the regulations thereunder are inapplicable to the contribution until such time as the contribution is treated as made under section 170(a)(3).

(b) *Illustrations.*—The application of this section may be illustrated by the following examples:

Example (1). On December 31, 1970, A, an individual who reports his income on the calendar year basis, conveys by deed of gift to a museum title to a painting, but reserves to himself the right to use, possession, and enjoyment of the painting during his lifetime. It is assumed that there was no intention to avoid the application of section 170(f)(3)(A) by the conveyance. At the time of the gift the value of the painting is $90,000. Since the contribution consists of a future interest in tangible personal property in which the donor has retained an intervening interest, no contribution is considered to have been made in 1970.

Example (2). Assume the same facts as in example (1) except that on December 31, 1971, A relinquishes all of his right to the use, possession, and enjoyment of the painting and delivers the painting to the museum. Assuming that the value of the painting has increased to $95,000, A is treated as having made a charitable contribution of $95,000 in 1971 for which a deduction is allowable without regard to section 170(f)(3)(A).

Example (3). Assume the same facts as in example (1) except A dies without relinquishing his right to the use, possession, and enjoyment of the painting. Since A did not relinquish his right to the use, possession, and enjoyment of the property during his life, A is treated as not having made a charitable contribution of the painting for income tax purposes.

Example (4). Assume the same facts as in example (1) except A, on December 31, 1971, transfers his interest in the painting to his son, B, who reports his income on the calendar year basis. Since the relationship between A and B is one described in section 267(b), no contribution of the remainder interest in the painting is considered to have been made in 1971.

Example (5). Assume the same facts as in example (4). Also assume that on December 31, 1972, B conveys to the museum the interest measured by A's life. B has made a charitable contribution of the present interest in the painting conveyed to the museum. In addition, since all intervening interests in, and rights to the actual possession or enjoyment of the property, have expired, a charitable contribution of the remainder interest is treated as having been made by A in 1972 for which a deduction is allowable without regard to section 170(f)(3)(A). Such remainder interest is valued according to §20.2031-7A(c) of this chapter (Estate Tax Regulations), determined by subtracting the value of B's interest measured by A's life expectancy in 1972, and B receives a deduction in 1972 for the life interest measured by A's life expectancy and valued according to Table A (1) in such section.

Example (6). On December 31, 1970, C, an individual who reports his income on the calendar year basis, transfers a valuable painting to a pooled income fund described in section 642(c)(5), which is maintained by a university. C retains for himself for life an income interest in the painting, the remainder interest in the painting being contributed to the university. Since the contribution consists of a future interest in tangible personal property in which the donor has retained an intervening interest, no charitable contribution is considered to have been made in 1970.

Example (7). On January 15, 1972, D, an individual who reports his income on the calendar year basis, transfers a capital asset held for more than 6 months consisting of a valuable painting to a pooled income fund described in section 642(c)(5), which is maintained by a university, and creates an income interest in such painting for E for life. E is an individual not standing in a relationship to D described in section 267(b). The remainder interest in the property is contributed by D to the university. The trustee of the pooled income fund puts the painting to an unrelated use within the meaning of paragraph (b)(3) of § 1.170A-4. Accordingly, D is allowed a deduction under section 170 in 1972 for the present value of the remainder interest in the painting, after reducing such amount under section 170(e)(1)(B)(i) and paragraph (a)(2) of § 1.170A-4. This reduction in the amount of the contribution is required since under paragraph (b)(3) of that section the use by the pooled income fund of the painting is a use which would have been an unrelated use if it had been made by the university.

* * *

[Reg. § 1.170A-5.]

☐ [*T.D.* 7207, 10-3-72. *Amended by T.D.* 8540, 6-9-94.]

»→ Caution: Reg. 1.170A-7 does not reflect adoption of Section 170(o) in 2006.

§ 1.170A-7. Contributions not in trust of partial interests in property.—(a) *In general.*—(1) In the case of a charitable contribution, not made by a transfer in trust, of any interest in property which consists of less than the donor's entire interest in such property, no deduction is allowed under section 170 for the value of such interest unless the interest is an interest described in paragraph (b) of this section. See section 170(f)(3)(A). For purposes of this section, a contribution of the right to use property which the donor owns, for example, a rent-free lease, shall be treated as a contribution of less than the taxpayer's entire interest in property.

(2)(i) A deduction is allowed without regard to this section for a contribution of a partial interest in property if such interest is the taxpayer's entire interest in the property, such as an income interest or a remainder interest. Thus, if securities are given to A for life, with the remainder over to B, and B makes a charitable contribution of his remainder interest to an organization described in section 170(c), a deduction is allowed under section 170 for the present value of B's remainder interest in the securities. If, however, the property in which such partial interest exists was divided in order to create such interest and thus avoid section 170(f)(3)(A), the deduction will not be allowed. Thus, for example, assume that a taxpayer desires to contribute to a charitable organization an income interest in property held by him, which is not of a type described in paragraph (b)(2) of this section. If the taxpayer transfers the remainder interest in such property to his son and immediately thereafter contributes the income interest to a charitable organization, no deduction shall be allowed under section 170 for the contribution of the taxpayer's entire interest consisting of the retained income interest. In further illustration, assume that a taxpayer desires to contribute to a charitable organization the reversionary interest in certain stocks and bonds held by him, which is not of a type described in paragraph (b)(2) of this section. If the taxpayer grants a life estate in such property to his son and immediately thereafter contributes the reversionary interest to a charitable organization, no deduction will be allowed under section 170 for the contribution of the taxpayer's entire interest consisting of the reversionary interest.

(ii) A deduction is allowed without regard to this section for a contribution of a partial interest in property if such contribution constitutes part of a charitable contribution not in trust in which all interests of the taxpayer in the property are given to a charitable organization described in section 170(c). Thus, if on March 1, 1971, an income interest in property is given not in trust to a church and the remainder interest in the property is given not in trust to an educational organization described in section 170(b)(1)(A), a deduction is allowed for the value of such property.

(3) A deduction shall not be disallowed under section 170(f)(3)(A) and this section merely because the interest which passes to, or is vested in, the charity may be defeated by the performance of some act or the happening of some event, if on the date of the gift it appears that the possibility that such act or event will occur is so remote as to be negligible. See paragraph (e) of § 1.170A-1.

(b) *Contributions of certain partial interests in property for which a deduction is allowed.*—A deduction is allowed under section 170 for a contribution not in trust of a partial interest which is less than the donor's entire interest in property and which qualifies under one of the following subparagraphs:

(1) *Undivided portion of donor's entire interest.*—(i) A deduction is allowed under section 170 for the value of a charitable contribution not in trust of an undivided portion of a donor's entire interest in property. An undivided portion of a donor's entire interest in

property must consist of a fraction or percentage or each and every substantial interest or right owned by the donor in such property and must extend over the entire term of the donor's interest in such property and in other property into which such property is converted. For example, assuming that in 1967 B has been given a life estate in an office building for the life of A and that B has no other interest in the office building, B will be allowed a deduction under section 170 for his contribution in 1972 to charity of a one-half interest in such life estate in a transfer which is not made in trust. Such contribution by B will be considered a contribution of an undivided portion of the donor's entire interest in property. In further illustration, assuming that in 1968 C has been given the remainder interest in a trust created under the will of his father and C has no other interest in the trust, C will be allowed a deduction under section 170 for his contribution in 1972 to charity of a 20-percent interest in such remainder interest in a transfer which is not made in trust. Such contribution by C will be considered a contribution of an undivided portion of the donor's entire interest in property. If a taxpayer owns 100 acres of land and makes a contribution of 50 acres to a charitable organization, the charitable contribution is allowed as a deduction under section 170. A deduction is allowed under section 170 for a contribution of property to a charitable organization whereby such organization is given the right, as a tenant in common with the donor, to possession, dominion, and control of the property for a portion of each year appropriate to its interest in such property. However, for purposes of this subparagraph a charitable contribution in perpetuity of an interest in property not in trust where the donor transfers some specific rights and retains other substantial rights will not be considered a contribution of an undivided portion of the donor's entire interest in property to which section 170(f)(3)(A) does not apply. Thus, for example, a deduction is not allowable for the value of an immediate and perpetual gift not in trust of an interest in original historic motion picture films to a charitable organization where the donor retains the exclusive right to make reproductions of such films and to exploit such reproductions commercially.

* * *

(2) *Partial interests in property which would be deductible in trust.*—A deduction is allowed under section 170 for the value of a charitable contribution not in trust of a partial interest in property which is less than the donor's entire interest in the property and which would be deductible under section 170(f)(2) and § 1.170A-6 if such interest had been transferred in trust.

(3) *Contribution of a remainder interest in a personal residence.*—A deduction is allowed under section 170 for the value of a charitable contribution not in trust of an irrevocable remainder interest in a personal residence which is not the donor's entire interest in such property. Thus, for example, if a taxpayer contributes not in trust to an organization described in section 170(c) a remainder interest in a personal residence and retains an estate in such property for life or for a term of years, a deduction is allowed under section 170 for the value of such remainder interest not transferred in trust. For purposes of section 170(f)(3)(B)(i) and this subparagraph, the term "personal residence" means any property used by the taxpayer as his personal residence even though it is not used as his principal residence. For example, the taxpayer's vacation home may be a personal residence for purposes of this subparagraph. The term "personal residence" also includes stock owned by a taxpayer as a tenant-stockholder in a cooperative housing corporation (as those terms are defined in section 216(b)(1) and (2)) if the dwelling which the taxpayer is entitled to occupy as such stockholder is used by him as his personal residence.

(4) *Contribution of a remainder interest in a farm.*—A deduction is allowed under section 170 for the value of a charitable contribution not in trust of an irrevocable remainder interest in a farm which is not the donor's entire interest in such property. Thus, for example, if a taxpayer contributes not in trust to an organization described in section 170(c) a remainder interest in a farm and retains an estate in such farm for life or for a term of years, a deduction is allowed under section 170 for the value of such remainder interest not transferred in trust. For purposes of section 170(f)(3)(B)(i) and this subparagraph, the term "farm" means any land used by the taxpayer or his tenant for the production of crops, fruits, or other agricultural products or for the sustenance of livestock. The term "livestock" includes cattle, hogs, horses, mules, donkeys, sheep, goats, captive fur-bearing animals, chickens, turkeys, pigeons, and other poultry. A farm includes the improvements thereon.

(5) *Qualified conservation contribution.*—A deduction is allowed under section 170 for the value of a qualified conservation contribution. For the definition of a qualified conservation contribution, see § 1.170A-14.

(c) *Valuation of a partial interest in property.*—Except as provided in § 1.170A-14, the amount of the deduction under section 170 in the case of a charitable contribution of a partial interest in property to which paragraph (b) of this section applies is the fair market value of the partial interest at the time of the contribution. See § 1.170A-1(c). the fair market value of such partial interest must be determined in accordance with § 20.2031-7 of this chapter (Estate Tax Regulations), except that, in the case of a charitable contribution of a remainder interest in real property which is not transferred in trust, the fair market value of such interest must be determined in accordance with section 170(f)(4) and § 1.170A-12. In the case of a charitable contribution of a remainder interest in the form of a remainder interest in a pooled income fund, a charitable remainder annuity trust, or a charitable remainder unitrust, the fair market value of the remainder interest must be determined as provided in paragraph (b)(2) of § 1.170A-6. However, in some cases a reduction in the amount of a charitable contribution of the remainder interest may be required. See section 170(e) and paragraph (a) of § 1.170A-4.

(d) *Illustrations.*—The application of this section may be illustrated by the following examples:

Example (1). A, an individual owning a 10-story office building, donates the rent-free use of the top floor of the building for the year 1971 to a charitable organization. Since A's contribution consists of a partial interest to which section 170(f)(3)(A) applies, he is not entitled to a charitable contributions deduction for the contribution of such partial interest.

Example (2). In 1971, B contributes to a charitable organization an undivided one-half interest in 100 acres of land, whereby as tenants in common they share in the economic benefits from the property. The present value of the contributed property is $50,000. Since B's contribution consists of an undivided portion of his entire interest in the property to which section 170(f)(3)(B) applies, he is allowed a deduction in 1971 for his charitable contribution of $50,000.

Example (3). In 1971, D loans $10,000 in cash to a charitable organization and does not require the organization to pay any interest for the use of the money. Since D's contribution consists of a partial interest to which section 170(f)(3)(A) applies, he is not entitled to a charitable contributions deduction for the contribution of such partial interest.

* * *

[Reg. § 1.170A-7.]

☐ [*T.D.* 7207, 10-3-72. *Amended by T.D.* 7955, 5-10-84; *T.D.* 8069, 1-14-86 *and T.D.* 8540, 6-9-94.]

§ 1.172-1. Net operating loss deduction.—(a) *Allowance of deduction.*—Section 172(a) allows as a deduction in computing taxable income for any taxable year subject to the Code the aggregate of the net operating loss carryovers and net operating loss carrybacks to such taxable year. This deduction is referred to as the net operating loss deduction. The net operating loss is the basis for the computation of the net operating loss carryovers and net operating loss carrybacks and ultimately for the net operating loss deduction itself. The net operating loss deduction shall not be disallowed for any taxable year merely because the taxpayer has no income from a trade or business for the taxable year.

(b) *Steps in computation of net operating loss deduction.*—The three steps to be taken in the ascertainment of the net operating loss deduction for any taxable year subject to the Code are as follows:

(1) Compute the net operating loss for any preceding or succeeding taxable year from which a net operating loss may be carried over or carried back to such taxable year.

(2) Compute the net operating loss carryovers to such taxable year from such preceding taxable years and the net operating loss carrybacks to such taxable year from such succeeding taxable years.

(3) Add such net operating loss carryovers and carrybacks in order to determine the net operating loss deduction for such taxable year.

(c) *Statement with tax return.*—Every taxpayer claiming a net operating loss deduction for any taxable year shall file with his return for such year a concise statement setting forth the amount of the net operating loss deduction claimed and all material and pertinent facts relative thereto, including a detailed schedule showing the computation of the net operating loss deduction.

(d) *Ascertainment of deduction dependent upon net operating loss carryback.*—If the taxpayer is entitled in computing his net operating loss deduction to a carryback which he is not able to ascertain at the time his return is due, he shall compute the net operating loss deduction on his return without regard to such net operating loss carryback. When the taxpayer ascertains the net operating loss carryback, he may within the applicable period of limitations file a claim for credit or refund of the overpayment, if any, resulting from the failure to compute the net operating loss deduction for the taxable year with the inclusion of such carryback; or he may file an application under the provisions of section 6411 for a tentative carryback adjustment.

(e) *Law applicable to computations.*—(1) In determining the amount of any net operating loss carryback or carryover to any taxable year, the necessary computations involving any other taxable year shall be made under the law applicable to such other taxable year.

(2) The net operating loss for any taxable year shall be determined under the law applicable to that year without regard to the year to which it is to be carried and in which, in effect, it is to be deducted as part of the net operating loss deduction.

(3) The amount of the net operating loss deduction which shall be allowed for any taxable year shall be determined under the law applicable to that year.

(f) *Electing small business corporations.*—In determining the amount of the net operating loss deduction of any corporation, there shall be disregarded the net operating loss of such corporation for any taxable year for which such corporation was an electing small business corporation under subchapter S (section 1371 and following), chapter 1 of the Code. In applying section 172(b)(1) and (2) to a net operating loss sustained in a taxable year in which the corporation was not an electing small business corporation, a taxable year in which the corporation was an electing small business corporation is counted as a taxable year to which such net operating loss is carried back or over. However, the taxable income for such year as determined under section 172(b)(2) is treated as if it were zero for purposes of computing the balance of the loss available to the corporation as a carryback or carryover to other taxable years in which the corporation is not an electing small business corporation. See section 1374 and the regulations thereunder for allowance of a deduction to shareholders for a net operating loss sustained by an electing small business corporation.

(g) *Husband and wife.*—The net operating loss deduction of a husband and wife shall be determined in accordance with this section, but subject also to the provisions of § 1.172-7. [Reg. § 1.172-1.]

□ [*T.D.* 6192, 7-23-56. *Amended by T.D.* 6486, 8-12-60 *and T.D.* 8107, 12-1-86.]

§ 1.172-3. Net operating loss in case of a taxpayer other than a corporation.—

(a) *Modification of deductions.*—A net operating loss is sustained by a taxpayer other than a corporation in any taxable year if and to the extent that, for such year, there is an excess of deductions allowed by chapter 1 of the Internal Revenue Code over gross income computed thereunder. In determining the excess of deductions over gross income for such purpose—

(1) *Items not deductible.*—No deduction shall be allowed under—

(i) Section 151 for the personal exemptions or under any other section which grants a deduction in lieu of the deductions allowed by section 151,

(ii) Section 172 for the net operating loss deduction, and

(iii) Section 1202 in respect of net long-term capital gain.

(2) *Capital losses.*—(i) The amount deductible on account of business capital losses shall not exceed the sum of the amount includible on account of business capital gains and that portion of nonbusiness capital gains which is computed in accordance with paragraph (c) of this section.

(ii) The amount deductible on account of nonbusiness capital losses shall not exceed the amount includible on account of nonbusiness capital gains.

(3) *Nonbusiness deductions.*—(i) *Ordinary deductions.*—Ordinary nonbusiness deductions shall be taken into account without regard to the amount of business deductions and shall be allowed in full to the extent, but not in excess, of that amount which is the sum of the ordinary nonbusiness gross income and the excess of nonbusiness capital gains over nonbusiness capital losses. See paragraph (c) of this section. For purposes of section 172, nonbusiness deductions and income are those deductions and that income which are not attributable to, or derived from, a taxpayer's trade or business. Wages and salary constitute income attributable to the taxpayer's trade or business for such purposes.

(ii) *Sale of business property.*—Any gain or loss on the sale or other disposition of property which is used in the taxpayer's trade or business and which is of a character that is subject to the allowance for depreciation provided in section 167, or of real property used in the taxpayer's trade or business, shall be considered, for purposes of section 172(d)(4), as attributable to, or derived from, the taxpayer's trade or business. Such gains and losses are to be taken into account fully in computing a net operating loss without regard to the limitation on nonbusiness deductions. Thus, a farmer who sells at a loss land used in the business of farming may, in computing a net operating loss, include in full the deduction otherwise allowable with respect to such loss, without regard to the amount of his nonbusiness income and without regard to whether he is engaged in the trade or business of selling farms. Similarly, an individual who sells at a loss machinery which is used in his trade or business and which is of a character that is subject to the allowance for depreciation may, in computing the net operating loss, include in full the deduction otherwise allowable with respect to such loss.

(iii) *Casualty losses.*—Any deduction allowable under section 165(c)(3) for losses of property not connected with a trade or business shall not be considered, for purposes of section 172(d)(4), to be a nonbusiness deduction but shall be treated as a deduction attributable to the taxpayer's trade or business.

(iv) *Self-employed retirement plans.*—Any deduction allowed under section 404, relating to contributions of an employer to an employees' trust or annuity plan, or under section 405(c), relating to contributions to a bond purchase plan, to the extent attributable to contributions made on behalf of an individual while he is an employee within the meaning of section 401(c)(1), shall not be treated, for purposes of section 172(d)(4), as attributable to, or derived from, the taxpayer's trade or business, but shall be treated as a nonbusiness deduction.

(v) *Limitation.*—The provisions of this subparagraph shall not be construed to permit the deduction of items disallowed by subparagraph (1) of this paragraph.

(b) *Treatment of capital loss carryovers.*—Because of the distinction between business and nonbusiness capital gains and losses, a taxpayer who has a capital loss carryover from a preceding taxable year, includible by virtue of section 1212 among the capital losses for the taxable year in issue, is required to determine how much of such capital loss carryover is a business capital loss and how much is a nonbusiness capital loss. In order to make this determination, the taxpayer shall first ascertain what proportion of the net capital loss for such preceding taxable year was attributable to an excess of business capital losses over business capital gains for such year, and what proportion was attributable to an excess of nonbusiness capital losses over nonbusiness capital gains. The same proportion of the capital loss carryover from such preceding taxable year shall be treated as a business capital loss and a nonbusiness capital loss, respectively. In order to determine the composition (business—nonbusiness) of a net capital loss for a taxable year, for purposes of this paragraph, if such net capital loss is computed under paragraph (b) of § 1.1212-1 and takes into account a capital loss carryover from a preceding taxable year, the composition (business—nonbusiness) of the net capital loss for such preceding taxable year must also be determined. For purposes of this paragraph, the term "capital loss carryover" means the sum of the short-term and long-term capital loss carryovers from such year This paragaraph may be illustrated by the following examples:

Example (1). (i) A, an individual, has $5,000 ordinary taxable income (computed without regard to the deductions for personal exemptions) for the calendar year 1954 and also has the following capital gains and losses for such year: Business capital gains of $2,000; business capital losses of $3,200; nonbusiness capital gains of $1,000; and nonbusiness capital losses of $1,200.

(ii) A's net capital loss for the taxable year 1954 is $400, computed as follows:

Capital losses	$4,400
Capital gains	3,000
Excess of capital losses over capital gains	$1,400
Less: $1,000 of such ordinary taxable income	1,000
Net capital loss for 1954	$400

(iii) A's capital losses for 1954 exceeded his capital gains for such year by $1,400. Since A's business capital losses for 1954 exceeded his business capital gains for such year by $1,200, 6/7ths ($1,200/$1,400) of A's net capital loss for 1954 is attributable to an excess of his business capital losses over his business capital gains for such year. Similarly, 1/7th of the net capital loss is attributable to the excess of nonbusiness capital losses over nonbusiness capital gains. Since the capital loss carryover for 1954 to 1955 is $400, 6/7ths of $400, or $342.86, shall be treated as a business capital loss in 1955; and 1/7th of $400, or $57.14, as a nonbusiness capital loss.

Example (2). (i) A, an individual who is computing a net operating loss for the calendar year 1966, has a capital loss carryover from 1965 of $8,000. In order to apply the provisions of this paragraph, A must determine what portion of the $8,000 carryover is attributable to the excess of business capital losses over business capital gains and what portion thereof is attributable to the excess of nonbusiness capital losses over nonbusiness capital gains. For 1965, A had $10,000 ordinary taxable income (computed without regard to the deductions for personal exemptions), and a short-term capital loss carryover of $6,000 from 1964. In order to determine the composition (business—nonbusiness) of the $8,000 carryover from 1965, A first determines that of the $6,000 carryover from 1964, $5,000 is a business capital loss and $1,000 is a nonbusiness capital loss. This must be done since, under paragraph (b) of § 1.1212-1, the net capital loss for 1965 is computed by taking into account the capital loss carryover from 1964. A's capital gains and losses for 1965 are as follows:

	1965	Carried over from 1964
Business capital gains	$2,000	
Business capital losses	3,000	$5,000
Nonbusiness capital gains . .	4,000	
Nonbusiness capital losses . .	6,000	1,000

(ii) A's net capital loss for the taxable year 1965 is $8,000, computed as follows:

Capital losses (including carryovers)	$15,000
Capital gains	6,000
Excess of capital losses over capital gains . . .	$9,000
Less: $1,000 of such ordinary taxable income .	1,000
Net capital loss for 1965	$8,000

(iii) A's capital losses, including carryovers, for 1965 exceeded his capital gains for such year by $9,000. Since A's business capital losses for 1965 exceeded his business capital gains for such year by $6,000, 2/3rds ($6,000/$9,000) of A's net capital loss for 1965 is attributable to an excess of his business capital losses over his business capital gains for such year. Similarly, 1/3rd of the net capital loss is attributable to the excess of nonbusiness capital losses over nonbusiness capital gains. Since the total capital loss carryover from 1965 to 1966 is $8,000, 2/3rds of $8,000, or $5,333.33, shall be treated as a business capital loss in 1966; and 1/3rd of $8,000, or $2,666.67, as a nonbusiness capital loss.

(c) *Determination of portion of nonbusiness capital gains available for the deduction of business capital losses.*—In the computation of a net operating loss a taxpayer other than a corporation must use his nonbusiness capital gains for the deduction of his nonbusiness capital losses. Any amount not necessary for this purpose shall then be used for the deduction of any excess of ordinary nonbusiness deductions over ordinary nonbusiness gross income. The remainder, computed by applying the excess ordinary nonbusiness deductions against the excess nonbusiness capital gains, shall be treated as nonbusiness capital gains and used for the purpose of determining the deductibility of business capital losses under paragraph (a)(2)(i) of this section. This principle may be illustrated by the following example:

Example. (1) A, an individual, has a total nonbusiness gross income of $20,500, computed as follows:

Ordinary gross income	$7,500
Capital gains	13,000
Total gross income	20,500

(2) A also has total nonbusiness deductions of $16,000, computed as follows:

Ordinary deductions	$9,000
Capital loss	7,000
Total deductions	16,000

(3) The portion of nonbusiness capital gains to be used for the purpose of determining the deductibility of business capital losses is $4,500, computed as follows:

Nonbusiness capital gains		$13,000
Less: Nonbusiness capital loss		7,000
Excess to be taken into account for purposes of paragraph (a)(3)(i) of this section		6,000
Ordinary nonbusiness deductions	$9,000	
Less: Ordinary nonbusiness gross income	7,500	1,500
Portion of nonbusiness capital gains to be used for purposes of paragraph (a)(2)(i) of this section		4,500

(d) *Joint net operating loss of husband and wife.*—In the case of a husband and wife, the joint net operating loss for any taxable year for which a joint return is filed is to be computed on the basis of the combined income and deductions of both spouses, and the modifications prescribed in paragraph (a) of this section are to be computed as if the combined income and deductions of both spouses were the income and deductions of one individual.

(e) *Illustration of computation of net operating loss of a taxpayer other than a corporation.*—(1) *Facts.*—For the calendar year 1954, A, an individual, has gross income of $483,000 and allowable deductions of $540,000. The latter amount does not include the net operating loss deduction or any deduction on account of the sale or exchange of capital assets. Included in gross income are business capital gains of $50,000 and ordinary nonbusiness income of $10,000. Included among the deductions are ordinary nonbusiness deductions of $12,000 and a deduction of $600 for his personal exemption. A has a business capital loss of $60,000 in 1954. A has no other items of income or deductions to which section 172(d) applies.

(2) *Computation.*—On the basis of these facts, A has a net operating loss for 1954 of $104,400, computed as follows:

Deductions for 1954 (as specified in first sentence of subparagraph (1))		$540,000
Plus: Amount of business capital loss ($60,000) to extent such amount does not exceed business capital gains ($50,000) . . .		50,000
Total		590,000
Less: Excess of ordinary nonbusiness deductions over ordinary nonbusiness gross income ($12,000 minus $10,000)	$2,000	
Deduction for personal exemption	600	2,600
Deductions for 1954 adjusted as required by section 172(d)		587,400
Gross income for 1954		483,000
Net operating loss for 1954		104,400

[Reg. § 1.172-3.]

□ [*T.D.* 6192, 7-23-56. *Amended by T.D.* 6828, 6-16-65, *T.D.* 6862, 11-17-65 *and T.D.* 8107, 12-1-86.]

§1.174-1. Research and experimental expenditures; in general.—Section 174 provides two methods for treating research or experimental expenditures paid or incurred by the taxpayer in connection with his trade or business. These expenditures may be treated as expenses not chargeable to capital account and deducted in the year in which they are paid or incurred (see §1.174-3), or they may be deferred and amortized (see §1.174-4). Research or experimental expenditures which are neither treated as expenses nor deferred and amortized under section 174 must be charged to capital account. The expenditures to which section 174 applies may relate either to a general research program or to a particular project. See §1.174-2 for the definition of research and experimental expenditures. The term "paid or incurred", as used in section 174 and in §§1.174-1 to 1.174-4, inclusive, is to be construed according to the method of accounting used by the taxpayer in computing taxable income. See section 7701(a)(25). [Reg. §1.174-1.]

□ [*T.D.* 6255, 10-3-57.]

§1.174-2. Definition of research and experimental expenditures.—(a) *In general.*—(1) *Research or experimental expenditures defined.*—The term *research or experimental expenditures,* as used in section 174, means expenditures incurred in connection with the taxpayer's trade or business which represent research and development costs in the experimental or laboratory sense. The term generally includes all such costs incident to the development or improvement of a product. The term includes the costs of obtaining a patent, such as attorneys' fees expended in making and perfecting a patent application. Expenditures represent research and development costs in the experimental or laboratory sense if they are for activities intended to discover information that would eliminate uncertainty concerning the development or improvement of a product. Uncertainty exists if the information available to the taxpayer does not establish the capability or method for developing or improving the product or the appropriate design of the product. Whether expenditures qualify as research or experimental expenditures depends on the nature of the activity to which the expenditures relate, not the nature of the product or improvement being developed or the level of technological advancement the product or improvement represents. The ultimate success, failure, sale, or use of the product is not relevant to a determination of eligibility under section 174. Costs may be eligible under section 174 if paid or incurred after production begins but before uncertainty concerning the development or improvement of the product is eliminated.

(2) *Production costs.*—Except as provided in paragraph (a)(5) of this section (the rule concerning the application of section 174 to components of a product), costs paid or incurred in the production of a product after the elimination of uncertainty concerning the development or improvement of the product are not eligible under section 174.

(3) *Product defined.*—For purposes of this section, the term *product* includes any pilot model, process, formula, invention, technique, patent, or similar property, and includes products to be used by the taxpayer in its trade or business as well as products to be held for sale, lease, or license.

(4) *Pilot model defined.*—For purposes of this section, the term *pilot model* means any representation or model of a product that is produced to evaluate and resolve uncertainty concerning the product during the development or improvement of the product. The term includes a fully-functional representation or model of the product or, to the extent paragraph (a)(5) of this section applies, a component of the product.

(5) *Application of section 174 to components of a product.*—If the requirements of paragraph (a)(1) of this section are not met at the level of a product (as defined in paragraph (a)(3) of this section), then whether expenditures represent research and development costs is determined at the level of the component or subcomponent of the product. The presence of uncertainty concerning the development or improvement of certain components of a product does not necessarily indicate the presence of uncertainty concerning the development or improvement of other components of the product or the product as a whole. The rule in this paragraph (a)(5) is not itself applied as a reason to exclude research or experimental expenditures from section 174 eligibility.

(6) *Research or experimental expenditures—exclusions.*—The term *research or experimental expenditures* does not include expenditures for—

(i) The ordinary testing or inspection of materials or products for quality control (quality control testing);

(ii) Efficiency surveys;

(iii) Management studies;

(iv) Consumer surveys;

(v) Advertising or promotions;

(vi) The acquisition of another's patent, model, production or process; or

(vii) Research in connection with literary, historical, or similar projects.

(7) *Quality control testing.*—For purposes of paragraph (a)(6)(i) of this section, testing or inspection to determine whether particular units of materials or products conform to specified parameters is quality control testing. However, quality control testing does not include testing to determine if the design of the product is appropriate.

(8) *Expenditures for literary, historical, or similar research—cross reference.*—See section 263A and the regulations thereunder for cost capitalization rules which apply to expenditures paid or incurred for research in connection with literary, historical, or similar projects involving the production of property, including the production of films, sound recordings, video tapes, books, or similar properties.

(9) *Research or experimental expenditures limited to reasonable amounts.*—Section 174 applies to a research or experimental expenditure only to the extent that the amount of the expenditure is reasonable under the circumstances. In general, the amount of an expenditure for research or experimental activities is reasonable if the amount would ordinarily be paid for like activities by like enterprises under like circumstances. Amounts supposedly paid for research that are not reasonable under the circumstances may be characterized as disguised dividends, gifts, loans, or similar payments. The reasonableness requirement of this paragraph (a)(9) does not apply to the reasonableness of the type or nature of the activities themselves.

(10) *Amounts paid to others for research or experimentation.*—The provisions of this section apply not only to costs paid or incurred by the taxpayer for research or experimentation undertaken directly by him but also to expenditures paid or incurred for research or experimentation carried on in his behalf by another person or organization (such as a research institute, foundation, engineering company, or similar contractor). However, any expenditures for research or experimentation carried on in the taxpayer's behalf by another person are not expenditures to which section 174 relates, to the extent that they represent expenditures for the acquisition or improvement of land or depreciable property, used in connection with the research or experimentation, to which the taxpayer acquires rights of ownership.

(11) *Examples.*—The following examples illustrate the application of this paragraph (a).

Example 1. Amounts paid to others for research or experimentation allowed as a deduction. A engages B to undertake research and experimental work in order to create a particular product. B will be paid annually a fixed sum plus an amount equivalent to his actual expenditures. In 1957, A pays to B in respect of the project the sum of $150,000 of which $25,000 represents an addition to B's laboratory and the balance represents charges for research and experimentation on the project. It is agreed between the parties that A will absorb the entire cost of this addition to B's laboratory which will be retained by B. A may treat the entire $150,000 as expenditures under section 174.

Example 2. Amounts paid to others not allowable as a deduction. S Corporation, a manufacturer of explosives, contracts with the T research organization to attempt through research and experimentation the creation of a new process for making certain explosives. Because of the danger involved in such an undertaking, T is compelled to acquire an isolated tract of land on which to conduct the research and experimentation. It is agreed that upon completion of the project T will transfer this tract, including any improvements thereon, to S. Section 174 does not apply to the amount paid to T representing the costs of the tract of land and improvements.

Example 3. Pilot model. U is engaged in the manufacture and sale of custom machines. U contracts to design and produce a machine to meet a customer's specifications. Because U has never designed a machine with these specifications, U is uncertain regarding the appropriate design of the machine, and particularly whether features desired by the customer can be designed and integrated into a functional machine. U incurs a total of $31,000 on the project. Of the $31,000, U incurs $10,000 of costs on materials and labor to produce a model that is used to evaluate and resolve the uncertainty concerning the appropriate design. U also incurs $1,000 of costs using the model to test whether certain features can be integrated into the design of the machine. This $11,000 of costs represents research and development costs in the experimental or laboratory sense. After uncertainty is eliminated, U incurs $20,000 to produce the machine for sale to the customer based on the appropriate design. The model produced and used to evaluate and resolve uncertainty is a pilot model within the meaning of paragraph (a)(4) of this section. Therefore, the $10,000 incurred to produce the model and the $1,000 incurred on design testing activities qualifies as research or experimental expenditures under section 174. However, section 174 does not apply to the $20,000 that U incurred to produce the machine for sale to the customer based on the appropriate design. See paragraph (a)(2) of this section (relating to production costs).

Example 4. Product component redesign. Assume the same facts as *Example 3*, except that during a quality control test of the machine, a component of the machine fails to function due to the component's inappropriate design. U incurs an additional $8,000 (including design retesting) to reconfigure the component's design. The $8,000 of costs represents research and development costs in the experimental or laboratory sense. After the elimination of uncertainty regarding the appropriate design of the component, U incurs an additional $2,000 on its production. The reconfigured component produced and used to evaluate and resolve uncertainty with respect to the component is a pilot model within the meaning of paragraph (a)(4) of this section. Therefore, in addition to the $11,000 of research and experimental expenditures previously incurred, the $8,000 incurred on design activities to establish the appropriate design of the component qualifies as research or experimental expenditures under section 174. However, section 174 does not apply to the additional $2,000 that U incurred for the production after the elimination of uncertainty of the re-designed component based on the appropriate design or to the $20,000 previously incurred to produce the machine. See paragraph (a)(2) of this section (relating to production costs).

Example 5. Multiple pilot models. V is a manufacturer that designs a new product. V incurs $5,000 to produce a number of models of the product that are to be used in testing the appropriate design before the product is mass-produced for sale. The $5,000 of costs represents research and development costs in the experimental or laboratory sense. Multiple models are necessary to test the design in a variety of different environments (exposure to extreme heat, exposure to extreme cold, submersion, and vibration). In some cases, V uses more than one model to test in a particular environment. Upon completion of several years of testing, V enters into a contract to sell one of the models to a customer and uses another model in its trade or business. The remaining models were rendered inoperable as a result of the testing process. Because V produced the models to resolve uncertainty regarding the appropriate design of the product, the models are pilot models under paragraph (a)(4) of this section. Therefore, the $5,000 that V incurred in producing the models qualifies as research or experimental expenditures under section 174. See also paragraph (a)(1) of this section (ultimate use is not relevant).

Example 6. Development of a new component; pilot model. W wants to improve a machine for use in its trade or business and incurs $20,000 to develop a new component for the machine. The $20,000 is incurred for engineering labor and materials to produce a model of the new component that is used to eliminate uncertainty regarding the development of the new component for the machine. The $20,000 of costs represents research and experimental costs in the experimental or laboratory sense. After W completes its research and experimentation on the new component, W incurs $10,000 for materials and labor to produce the component and incorporate it into the machine. The model produced and used to evaluate and resolve uncertainty with respect to the new component is a pilot model within the meaning of paragraph (a)(4) of this section. Therefore, the $20,000 incurred to produce the model and eliminate uncertainty regarding the development of the new component qualifies as research or experimental expenditures under section 174. However, section 174 does not apply to the $10,000 of production costs of the component because those costs were not incurred for research or experimentation. See paragraph (a)(2) of this section (relating to production costs).

* * *

(b) *Certain expenditures with respect to land and other property.*—(1) *Land and other property.*—Expenditures by the taxpayer for the acquisition or improvement of land, or for the acquisition or improvement of property which is subject to an allowance for depreciation under section 167 or depletion under section 611, are not deductible under section 174, irrespective of the fact that the property or improvements may be used by the taxpayer in connection with research or experimentation. However, allowances for depreciation or depletion of property are considered as research or experimental expenditures, for purposes of section 174, to the extent that the property to which the allowances relate is used in connection with research or experimentation. If any part of the cost of acquisition or improvement of depreciable property is attributable to research or experimentation (whether made by the taxpayer or another), see subparagraphs (2), (3), and (4) of this paragraph.

(2) *Expenditure resulting in depreciable property.*—Expenditures for research or experimentation which result, as an end product of the research or experimentation, in depreciable property to be used in the taxpayer's trade or business may, subject to the limitations of subparagraph (4) of this paragraph, be allowable as a current expense deduction under section 174(a). Such expenditures cannot be amortized under section 174(b) except to the extent provided in paragraph (a)(4) of § 1.174-4.

(3) *Amounts paid to others for research or experimentation resulting in depreciable prop-*

erty.—If expenditures for research or experimentation are incurred in connection with the construction or manufacture of depreciable property by another, they are deductible under section 174(a) only if made upon the taxpayer's order and at his risk. No deduction will be allowed (i) if the taxpayer purchases another's product under a performance guarantee (whether express, implied, or imposed by local law) unless the guarantee is limited, to engineering specifications or otherwise, in such a way that economic utility is not taken into account; or (ii) for any part of the purchase price of a product in regular production. For example, if a taxpayer orders a specially-built automatic milling machine under a guarantee that the machine will be capable of producing a given number of units per hour, no portion of the expenditure is deductible since none of it is made at the taxpayer's risk. Similarly, no deductible expense is incurred if a taxpayer enters into a contract for the construction of a new type of chemical processing plant under a turn-key contract guaranteeing a given annual production and a given consumption of raw material and fuel per unit. On the other hand, if the contract contained no guarantee of quality of production and of quantity of units in relation to consumption of raw material and fuel, and if real doubt existed as to the capabilities of the process, expenses for research or experimentation under the contract are at the taxpayer's risk and are deductible under section 174(a). However, see subparagraph (4) of this paragraph.

(4) *Deductions limited to amounts expended for research or experimentation.*—The deductions referred to in paragraphs (b)(2) and (3) of this section for expenditures in connection with the acquisition or production of depreciable property to be used in the taxpayer's trade or business are limited to amounts expended for research or experimentation within the meaning of section 174 and paragraph (a) of this section.

* * *

(c) *Exploration expenditures.*—The provisions of section 174 are not applicable to any expenditures paid or incurred for the purpose of ascertaining the existence, location, extent, or quality of any deposit of ore, oil, gas or other mineral. See sections 617 and 263. [Reg. § 1.174-2.]

* * *

□ [*T.D.* 6255, 10-3-57. *Amended by T.D.* 8131, 3-24-87; *T.D.* 8562, 9-30-94 *and T.D.* 9680, 7-18-2014.]

§ 1.179-1. Election to expense certain depreciable assets.—(a) *In general.*—Section 179(a) allows a taxpayer to elect to expense the cost (as defined in § 1.179-4(d)), or a portion of the cost, of section 179 property (as defined in § 1.179-4(a)) for the taxable year in which the property is placed in service (as defined in § 1.179-4(e)). The election is not available for trusts, estates, and certain noncorporate lessors. See paragraph (i)(2) of this section for rules concerning noncorporate lessors. However, section 179(b) provides certain limitations on the amount that a taxpayer may elect to expense in any one taxable year. See §§ 1.179-2 and 1.179-3 for rules relating to the dollar and taxable income limitations and the carryover of disallowed deduction rules. For rules describing the time and manner of making an election under section 179, see § 1.179-5. For the effective date, see § 1.179-6.

(b) *Cost subject to expense.*—The expense deduction under section 179 is allowed for the entire cost or a portion of the cost of one or more items of section 179 property. This expense deduction is subject to the limitations of section 179(b) and § 1.179-2. The taxpayer may select the properties that are subject to the election as well as the portion of each property's cost to expense.

(c) *Proration not required.*—(1) *In general.*—The expense deduction under section 179 is determined without any proration based on—

(i) The period of time the section 179 property has been in service during the taxable year; or

(ii) The length of the taxable year in which the property is placed in service.

(2) *Example.*—The following example illustrates the provisions of paragraph (c)(1) of this section.

Example. On December 1, 1991, X, a calendar-year corporation, purchases and places in service section 179 property costing $20,000. For the taxable year ending December 31, 1991, X may elect to claim a section 179 expense deduction on the property (subject to the limitations imposed under section 179(b)) without proration of its cost for the number of days in 1991 during which the property was in service.

(d) *Partial business use.*—(1) *In general.*—If a taxpayer uses section 179 property for trade or business as well as other purposes, the portion of the cost of the property attributable to the trade or business use is eligible for expensing under section 179 provided that more than 50 percent of the property's use in the taxable year is for trade or business purposes. The limitations of section 179(b) and § 1.179-2 are applied to the portion of the cost attributable to the trade or business use.

(2) *Example.*—The following example illustrates the provisions of paragraph (d)(1) of this section.

Example. A purchases section 179 property costing $10,000 in 1991 for which 80 percent of its use will be in A's trade or business. The cost of the property adjusted to reflect the business use of the property is $8,000 (80 percent × $10,000). Thus, A may elect to expense up to $8,000 of the cost of the property (subject to the limitations imposed under section 179(b) and § 1.179-2).

(3) *Additional rules that may apply.*—If a section 179 election is made for "listed property" within the meaning of section 280F(d)(4) and there is personal use of the property, section 280F (d)(1), which provides rules that coordinate section 179 with the section 280F limitation on the amount of depreciation, may apply. If section 179 property is no longer predominantly used in the taxpayer's trade or business, paragraphs (e)(1) through (4) of this section, relating to recapture of the section 179 deduction, may apply.

(e) *Change in use; recapture.*—(1) *In general.*—If a taxpayer's section 179 property is not used predominantly in a trade or business of the taxpayer at any time before the end of the property's recovery period, the taxpayer must recapture in the taxable year in which the section 179 property is not used predominantly in a trade or business any benefit derived from expensing such property. The benefit derived from expensing the property is equal to the excess of the amount expensed under this section over the total amount that would have been allowable for prior taxable years and the taxable year of recapture as a deduction under section 168 (had section 179 not been elected) for the portion of the cost of the property to which the expensing relates (regardless of whether such excess reduced the taxpayer's tax liability). For purposes of the preceding sentence, (i) the "amount expensed under this section" shall not include any amount that was not allowed as a deduction to a taxpayer because the taxpayer's aggregate amount of allowable section 179 expenses exceeded the section 179(b) dollar limitation, and (ii) in the case of an individual who does not elect to itemize deductions under section 63(g) in the taxable year of recapture, the amount allowable as a deduction under section 168 in the taxable year of recapture shall be determined by treating property used in the production of income other than rents or royalties as being property used for personal purposes. The amount to be recaptured shall be treated as ordinary income for the taxable year in which the property is no longer used predominantly in a trade or business of the taxpayer. For taxable years following the year of recapture, the taxpayer's deductions under section 168(a) shall be determined as if no section 179 election with respect to the property had been made. However, see section 280F(d)(1) relating to the coordination of section 179 with the limitation on the amount of depreciation for luxury automobiles and where certain property is used for personal purposes. If the recapture rules of both section 280F(b)(2) and this paragraph (e)(1) apply to an item of section 179 property, the amount of recapture for such property shall be determined only under the rules of section 280F(b)(2).

(2) *Predominant use.*—Property will be treated as not used predominantly in a trade or business of the taxpayer if 50 percent or more of the use of such property during any taxable year within the recapture period is for a use other than in a trade or business of the taxpayer. If during any taxable year of the recapture period the taxpayer disposes of the property (other than in a disposition to which section 1245(a) applies) or ceases to use the property in a trade or business in a manner that had the taxpayer claimed a credit under section 38 for such property such disposition or cessation in use would cause recapture under section 47, the property will be treated as not used in a trade or business of the taxpayer. However, for purposes of applying the recapture rules of section 47 pursuant to the preceding sentence, converting the use of the property from use in a trade or business to use in the production of income will be treated as a conversion to personal use.

(3) *Basis; application with section 1245.*—The basis of property with respect to which there is recapture under paragraph (e)(1) of this section shall be increased immediately before the event resulting in such recapture by the amount recaptured. If section 1245(a) applies to a disposition of property, there is no recapture under paragraph (e)(1) of this section.

(4) *Carryover of disallowed deduction.*—See § 1.179-3 for rules on applying the recapture provisions of this paragraph (e) when a taxpayer has a carryover of disallowed deduction.

(5) *Example.*—The following example illustrates the provisions of paragraphs (e)(1) through (e)(4) of this section.

Example. A, a calendar-year taxpayer, purchases and places in service on January 1, 1991, section 179 property costing $15,000. The property is 5-year property for section 168 purposes and is the only item of depreciable property placed in service by A during 1991. A properly elects to expense $10,000 of the cost and elects under section 168(b)(5) to depreciate the remaining cost under the straight-line method. On January 1, 1992, A converts the property from use in A's business to use for the production of income, and A uses the property in the latter capacity for the entire year. A elects to itemize deductions for 1992. Because the property was not predominantly used in A's trade or business in 1992, A must recapture any benefit derived from expensing the property under section 179. Had A not elected to expense the $10,000 in 1991, A would have been entitled to deduct, under section 168, 10 percent of the $10,000 in 1991, and 20 percent of the $10,000 in 1992. Therefore, A must include $7,000 in ordinary income for the 1992 taxable year, the excess of $10,000 (the section 179 expense amount) over $3,000 (30 percent of $10,000).

(f) *Basis.*—(1) *In general.*—A taxpayer who elects to expense under section 179 must reduce the depreciable basis of the section 179 property by the amount of the section 179 expense deduction.

(2) *Special rules for partnerships and S Corporations.*—Generally the basis of a partnership or S corporation's section 179 property must be reduced to reflect the amount of section 179 expense elected by the partnership or S corporation. This reduction must be made in the basis of partnership or S corporation property even if the limitations of section 179(b) and § 1.179-2 prevent a partner in a partnership or a shareholder in an S corporation from deducting all or a portion of the amount of the section 179 expense allocated by the partnership or S corporation. See § 1.179-3 for rules on applying the basis provisions of this paragraph (f) when a person has a carryover of disallowed deduction.

* * *

(h) *Partnerships and S corporations.*—(1) *In general.*—In the case of property purchased and placed in service by a partnership or an S corporation, the determination of whether the property is section 179 property is made at the partnership or S corporation level. The election to expense the cost of section 179 property is made by the partnership or the S corporation. See sections 703(b), 1363(c), 6221, 6231(a)(3), 6241, and 6245.

(2) *Example.*—The following example illustrates the provisions of paragraph (h)(1) of this section.

Example. A owns certain residential rental property as an investment. A and others form ABC partnership whose function is to rent and manage such property. A and ABC partnership file their income tax returns on a calendar-year basis. In 1991, ABC partnership purchases and places in service office furniture costing $20,000 to be used in the active conduct of ABC's business. Although the office furniture is used with respect to an investment activity of A, the furniture is being used in the active conduct of ABC's trade or business. Therefore, because the determination of whether property is section 179 property is made at the partnership level, the office furniture is section 179 property and ABC may elect to expense a portion of its cost under section 179.

(i) *Leasing of section 179 property.*—(1) *In general.*—A lessor of section 179 property who is treated as the owner of the property for Federal tax purposes will be entitled to the section 179 expense deduction if the requirements of section 179 and the regulations thereunder are met. These requirements will not be met if the lessor merely holds the property for the production of income. For certain leases entered prior to January 1, 1984, the safe harbor provisions of section 168(f)(8) apply in determining whether an agreement is treated as a lease for Federal tax purposes.

(2) *Noncorporate lessor.*—In determining the class of taxpayers (other than an estate or trust) for which section 179 is applicable, section 179(d)(5) provides that if a taxpayer is a noncorporate lessor (*i.e.*, a person who is not a corporation and is a lessor), the taxpayer shall not be entitled to claim a section 179 expense for section 179 property purchased and leased by the taxpayer unless the taxpayer has satisfied all of the requirements of section 179(d)(5)(A) or (B).

(j) *Application of sections 263 and 263A.*—Under section 263(a)(1)(G), expenditures for which a deduction is allowed under section 179 and this section are excluded from capitalization under section 263(a). Under this paragraph (j), amounts allowed as a deduction under section 179 and this section are excluded from the application of the uniform capitalization rules of section 263A.

(k) *Cross references.*—See section 453(i) and the regulations thereunder with respect to installment sales of section 179 property. See section 1033(g)(3) and the regulations thereunder relating to the condemnation of outdoor advertising displays. See section 1245(a) and the regulations thereunder with respect to recapture rules for section 179 property. [Reg. § 1.179-1.]

☐ [*T.D.* 8121, 1-5-87. *Amended by T.D.* 8455, 12-23-92.]

§1.183-1. Activities not engaged in for profit.—(a) *In general.*—Section 183 provides rules relating to the allowance of deductions in the case of activities (whether active or passive in character) not engaged in for profit by individuals and electing small business corporations, creates a presumption that an activity is engaged in for profit if certain requirements are met, and permits the taxpayer to elect to postpone determination of whether such presumption applies until he has engaged in the activity for at least five taxable years, or, in certain cases, seven taxable years. Whether an activity is engaged in for profit is determined under section 162 and section 212(1) and (2) except insofar as section 183(d) creates a presumption that the activity is engaged in for profit. If deductions are not allowable under sections 162 and 212(1) and (2), the deduction allowance rules of section 183(b) and this section apply. Pursuant to section 641(b), the taxable income of an estate or trust is computed in the same manner as in the case of an individual, with certain exceptions not here relevant. Accordingly, where an estate or trust engages in an activity or activities which are not for profit, the rules of section 183 and this section apply in computing the allowable deductions of such trust or estate. No inference is to be drawn from the provisions of section 183 and the regulations thereunder that any activity of a corporation (other than an electing small business corporation) is or is not a business or engaged in for profit. For rules relating to the deductions that may be taken into account by taxable membership organizations which are operated primarily to furnish services, facilities, or goods to members, see section 277 and the regulations thereunder. For the definition of an activity not engaged in for profit, see §1.183-2. For rules relating to the election contained in section 183(e), see §1.183-3.

(b) *Deductions allowable.*—(1) *Manner and extent.*—If an activity is not engaged in for profit, deductions are allowable under section 183(b) in the following order and only to the following extent:

(i) Amounts allowable as deductions during the taxable year under chapter 1 of the Code without regard to whether the activity giving rise to such amounts was engaged in for profit are allowable to the full extent allowed by the relevant sections of the Code, determined after taking into account any limitations or exceptions with respect to the allowability of such amounts. For example, the allowability-of-interest expenses incurred with respect to activities not engaged in for profit is limited by the rules contained in section 163(d).

(ii) Amounts otherwise allowable as deductions during the taxable year under chapter 1 of the Code, but only if such allowance does not result in an adjustment to the basis of property, determined as if the activity giving rise to such amounts was engaged in for profit, are allowed only to the extent the gross income attributable to such activity exceeds the deductions allowed or allowable under subdivision (i) of this subparagraph.

(iii) Amounts otherwise allowable as deductions for the taxable year under chapter 1 of the Code which result in (or if otherwise allowed would have resulted in) an adjustment to the basis of property, determined as if the activity giving rise to such deductions was engaged in for profit, are allowed only to the extent the gross income attributable to such activity exceeds the deductions allowed or allowable under subdivisions (i) and (ii) of this subparagraph. Deductions falling within this subdivision include such items as depreciation, partial losses with respect to property, partially worthless debts, amortization, and amortizable bond premium.

(2) *Rule for deductions involving basis adjustments.*—(i) *In general.*—If deductions are allowed under subparagraph, (1)(iii) of this paragraph, and such deductions are allowed with respect to more than one asset, the deduction allowed with respect to each asset shall be determined separately in accordance with the computation set forth in subdivision (ii) of this paragraph.

(ii) *Basis adjustment fraction.*—The deduction allowed under subparagraph (1)(iii) of this paragraph is computed by multiplying the amount which would have been allowed, had the activity been engaged in for profit, as a deduction with respect to each particular asset which involves a basis adjustment, by the basis adjustment fraction—

(a) The numerator of which is the total of deductions allowable under subparagraph (1)(iii) of this paragraph, and

(b) The denominator of which is the total of deductions which involve basis adjustments which would have been allowed with respect to the activity had the activity been engaged in for profit.

The amount resulting from this computation is the deduction allowed under subparagraph (1)(iii) of this paragraph with respect to the particular asset. The basis of such asset is adjusted only to the extent of such deduction.

* * *

(5) *Cross reference.*—For rules relating to section 183(e) which permits a taxpayer to elect to postpone determination of whether any

activity shall be presumed to be "an activity engaged in for profit" by operation of the presumption described in section 183(d) and this paragraph until after the close of the fourth taxable year (sixth taxable year, in the case of activity which consists in major part of breeding, training, showing, or racing of horses) following the taxable year in which the taxpayer first engages in the activity, see § 1.183-3.

(d) *Activity defined.*—(1) *Ascertainment of activity.*—In order to determine whether, and to what extent, section 183 and the regulations thereunder apply, the activity or activities of the taxpayer must be ascertained. For instance, where the taxpayer is engaged in several undertakings, each of these may be a separate activity, or several undertakings may constitute one activity. In ascertaining the activity or activities of the taxpayer, all the facts and circumstances of the case must be taken into account. Generally, the most significant facts and circumstances in making this determination are the degree of organizational and economic interrelationship of various undertakings, the business purpose which is (or might be) served by carrying on the various undertakings separately or together in a trade or business or in an investment setting, and the similarity of various undertakings. Generally, the Commissioner will accept the characterization by the taxpayer of several undertakings either as a single activity or as separate activities. The taxpayer's characterization will not be accepted, however, when it appears that his characterization is artificial and cannot be reasonably supported under the facts and circumstances of the case. If the taxpayer engages in two or more separate activities, deductions and income from each separate activity are not aggregated either in determining whether a particular activity is engaged in for profit or in applying section 183. Where land is purchased or held primarily with the intent to profit from increase in its value, and the taxpayer also engages in farming on such land, the farming and the holding of the land will ordinarily be considered a single activity only if the farming activity reduces the net cost of carrying the land for its appreciation in value. Thus, the farming and holding of the land will be considered a single activity only if the income derived from farming exceeds the deductions attributable to the farming activity which are not directly attributable to the holding of the land (that is, deductions other than those directly attributable to the holding of the land such as interest on a mortgage secured by the land, annual property taxes attributable to the land and improvements, and depreciation of improvements to the land).

(2) *Rules for allocation of expenses.*—If the taxpayer is engaged in more than one activity, an item of deduction or income may be allocated between two or more of these activities. Where property is used in several activities, and one or more of such activities is determined not to be engaged in for profit, deductions relating to such property must be allocated between the various activities on a reasonable and consistently applied basis.

* * *

(e) *Gross income from activity not engaged in for profit defined.*—For purposes of section 183 and the regulations thereunder, gross income derived from an activity not engaged in for profit includes the total of all gains from the sale, exchange, or other disposition of property, and all other gross receipts derived from such activity. Such gross income shall include, for instance, capital gains, and rents received for the use of property which is held in connection with the activity. The taxpayer may determine gross income from any activity by subtracting the cost of goods sold from the gross receipts so long as he consistently does so and follows generally accepted methods of accounting in determining such gross income.

(f) *Rule for electing small business corporations.*—Section 183 and this section shall be applied at the corporate level in determining the allowable deductions of an electing small business corporation. [Reg. § 1.183-1.]

□ [*T.D.* 7198, 7-12-72.]

§ 1.183-2. Activity not engaged in for profit defined.—(a) *In general.*—For purposes of section 183 and the regulations thereunder, the term "activity not engaged in for profit" means any activity other than one with respect to which deductions are allowable for the taxable year under section 162 or under paragraph (1) or (2) of section 212. Deductions are allowable under section 162 for expenses of carrying on activities which constitute a trade or business of the taxpayer and under section 212 for expenses incurred in connection with activities engaged in for the production or collection of income or for the management, conservation, or maintenance of property held for the production of income. Except as provided in section 183 and § 1.183-1, no deductions are allowable for expenses incurred in connection with activities which are not engaged in for profit. Thus, for example, deductions are not allowable under section 162 or 212 for activities which are carried on primarily as a sport, hobby, or for recreation. The determination whether an activity is engaged in for profit is to be made by reference to objective standards, taking into account all of the facts and circumstances of each case. Although a reasonable expectation of profit is not required, the facts and circumstances must indicate that the taxpayer entered into the activity, or continued the activity, with the objective of making a profit. In determining whether such an objective exists, it may be sufficient that there is a small chance of making a large profit. Thus it may be found that an investor in a wildcat oil well who incurs very substantial expenditures is in the venture for profit even though the expectation of a profit might be considered unreasonable. In determining whether an activity is engaged in for profit, greater weight is given to objective facts than to the taxpayer's mere statement of his intent.

(b) *Relevant factors.*—In determining whether an activity is engaged in for profit, all facts and circumstances with respect to the activity are to be taken into account. No one factor is determinative in making this determination. In addition, it is not intended that only the factors described in this paragraph are to be taken into account in making the determination, or that a determination is to be made on the basis that the number of factors (whether or not listed in this paragraph) indicating a lack of profit objective exceeds the number of factors indicating a profit objective, or vice versa. Among the factors which should normally be taken into account are the following:

(1) *Manner in which the taxpayer carries on the activity.*—The fact that the taxpayer carries on the activity in a businesslike manner and maintains complete and accurate books and records may indicate that the activity is engaged in for profit. Similarly, where an activity is carried on in a manner substantially similar to other activities of the same nature which are profitable, a profit motive may be indicated. A change of operating methods, adoption of new techniques or abandonment of unprofitable methods in a manner consistent with an intent to improve profitability may also indicate a profit motive.

(2) *The expertise of the taxpayer or his advisors.*—Preparation for the activity by extensive study of its accepted business, economic, and scientific practices, or consultation with those who are expert therein, may indicate that the taxpayer has a profit motive where the taxpayer carries on the activity in accordance with such practices. Where a taxpayer has such preparation or procures such expert advice, but does not carry on the activity in accordance with such practices, a lack of intent to derive profit may be indicated unless it appears that the taxpayer is attempting to develop new or superior techniques which may result in profits from the activity.

(3) *The time and effort expended by the taxpayer in carrying on the activity.*—The fact that the taxpayer devotes much of his personal time and effort to carrying on an activity, particularly if the activity does not have substantial personal or recreational aspects, may indicate an intention to derive a profit. A taxpayer's withdrawal from another occupation to devote most of his energies to the activity may also be evidence that the activity is engaged in for profit. The fact that the taxpayer devotes a limited amount of time to an activity does not necessarily indicate a lack of profit motive where the taxpayer employs competent and qualified persons to carry on such activity.

(4) *Expectation that assets used in activity may appreciate in value.*—The term "profit" encompasses appreciation in the value of assets, such as land, used in the activity. Thus, the taxpayer may intend to derive a profit from the operation of the activity, and may also intend that, even if no profit from current operations is derived, an overall profit will result when appreciation in the value of land used in the activity is realized since income from the activity together with the appreciation of land will exceed expenses of operation. See, however, paragraph (d) of § 1.183-1 for definition of an activity in this connection.

(5) *The success of the taxpayer in carrying on other similar or dissimilar activities.*—The fact that the taxpayer has engaged in similar activities in the past and converted them from unprofitable to profitable enterprises may indicate that he is engaged in the present activity for profit, even though the activity is presently unprofitable.

(6) *The taxpayer's history of income or losses with respect to the activity.*—A series of losses during the initial or start-up stage of an activity may not necessarily be an indication that the activity is not engaged in for profit. However, where losses continue to be sustained beyond the period which customarily is necessary to bring the operation to profitable status such continued losses, if not explainable, as due to customary business risks or reverses, may be indicative that the activity is not being engaged in for profit. If losses are sustained because of unforeseen or fortuitous circumstances which are beyond the control of the taxpayer, such as drought, disease, fire, theft, weather damages, other involuntary conversions, or depressed market conditions, such losses would not be an indication that the activity is not engaged in for profit. A series of years in which net income was realized would of course be strong evidence that the activity is engaged in for profit.

(7) *The amount of occasional profits, if any, which are earned.*—The amount of profits in relation to the amount of losses incurred, and in relation to the amount of the taxpayer's investment and the value of the assets used in the activity, may provide useful criteria in determining the taxpayer's intent. An occasional small profit from an activity generating large losses, or from an activity in which the taxpayer has made a large investment, would not generally be determinative that the activity is engaged in for profit. However, substantial profit, though only occasional, would generally be indicative that an activity is engaged in for profit, where the investment or losses are comparatively small. Moreover, an opportunity to earn a substantial ultimate profit in a highly speculative venture is ordinarily sufficient to indicate that the activity is engaged in for profit even though losses or only occasional small profits are actually generated.

(8) *The financial status of the taxpayer.*—The fact that the taxpayer does not have substantial income or capital from sources other than the activity may indicate that an activity is engaged in for profit. Substantial income from sources other than the activity (particularly if the losses from the activity generate substantial tax benefits) may indicate that the activity is not engaged in for profit especially if there are personal or recreational elements involved.

(9) *Elements of personal pleasure or recreation.*—The presence of personal motives in carrying on of an activity may indicate that the activity is not engaged in for profit, especially where there are recreational or personal elements involved. On the other hand, a profit motivation may be indicated where an activity lacks any appeal other than profit. It is not, however, necessary that an activity be engaged in with the exclusive intention of deriving a profit or with the intention of maximizing profits. For example, the availability of other investments which would yield a higher return, or which would be more likely to be profitable, is not evidence that an activity is not engaged in for profit. An activity will not be treated as not engaged in for profit merely because the taxpayer has purposes or motivations other than solely to make a profit. Also, the fact that the taxpayer derives personal pleasure from engaging in the activity is not sufficient to cause the activity to be classified as not engaged in for profit if the activity is in fact engaged in for profit as evidenced by other factors whether or not listed in this paragraph.

(c) *Examples.*—The provisions of this section may be illustrated by the following examples:

Example (1). The taxpayer inherited a farm from her husband in an area which was becoming largely residential, and is now nearly all so. The farm had never made a profit before the taxpayer inherited it, and the farm has since had substantial losses in each year. The decedent from whom the taxpayer inherited the farm was a stockbroker, and he also left the taxpayer substantial stock holdings which yield large income from dividends. The taxpayer lives on an area of the farm which is set aside exclusively for living purposes. A farm manager is employed to operate the farm, but modern methods are not used in operating the farm. The taxpayer was born and raised on a farm, and expresses a strong preference for living on a farm. The taxpayer's activity of farming, based on all the facts and circumstances, could be found not to be engaged in for profit.

Example (2). The taxpayer is a wealthy individual who is greatly interested in philosophy. During the past thirty years he has written and published at his own expense several pamphlets, and he has engaged in extensive lecturing activity, advocating and disseminating his ideas. He has made a profit from these activities in only occasional years, and the profits in those years were small in relation to the amounts of the losses in all other years. The taxpayer has very sizable income from securities (dividends and capital gains) which constitutes the principal source of his livelihood. The activity of lecturing, publishing pamphlets, and disseminating his ideas is not an activity engaged in by the taxpayer for profit.

Example (3). The taxpayer, very successful in the business of retailing soft drinks, raises dogs and horses. He began raising a particular breed of dogs many years ago in the belief that the breed was in danger of declining, and he has raised and sold the dogs in each year since. The taxpayer recently began raising and racing thoroughbred horses. The losses from the taxpayer's dog and horse activities have increased in magnitude over the years, and he has not made a profit on these operations during any of the last 15 years. The taxpayer generally sells the dogs only to friends, does not advertise the dogs for sale, and shows the dogs only infrequently. The taxpayer races his horses only at the "prestige" tracks at which he combines his racing activities with social and recreational activities. The horse and dog operations are conducted at a large residential property on which the taxpayer also lives, which includes substantial living quarters and attractive recreational facilities for the taxpayer and his family. Since (i) the activity of raising dogs and horses and racing the horses is of a sporting and recreational nature, (ii) the taxpayer has substantial income from his business activities of retailing soft drinks, (iii) the horse and dog operations are not conducted in a businesslike manner, and (iv) such operations have a continuous record of losses, it could be determined that the horse and dog activities of the taxpayer are not engaged in for profit.

Example (4). The taxpayer inherited a farm of 65 acres from his parents when they died 6 years ago. The taxpayer moved to the farm from his house in a small nearby town, and he operates it in the same manner as his parents operated the farm before they died. The taxpayer is employed as a skilled machine operator in a nearby factory, for which he is paid approximately $8,500 per year. The farm has not been profitable for the past 15 years because of rising costs of operating farms in general, and because of the decline in the price of the produce of this farm in particular. The taxpayer consults the local agent of the State agricultural service from time-to-time, and the suggestions of the agent have generally been followed. The manner in which the farm is operated by the taxpayer is substantially similar to the manner in which farms of similar size, and which grow similar crops in the area are operated. Many of these other farms do not make profits. The taxpayer does much of the required labor around the farm himself, such as fixing fences, planting crops, etc. The activity of farming could be found, based on all the facts and circumstances, to be engaged in by the taxpayer for profit.

Example (5). A, an independent oil and gas operator, frequently engages in the activity of searching for oil on undeveloped and unexplored land which is not near proven fields. He does so in a manner substantially similar to that of others who engage in the same activity. The chances, based on the experience of A and others who engaged in this activity, are strong that A will not find a commercially profitable oil deposit when he drills on land not established geologically to be proven oil bearing land. However, on the rare occasions that these activities do result in discovering a well, the operator generally realizes a very large return from such activity. Thus, there is a small chance that A will make a large profit from his oil exploration activity. Under these circumstances, A is engaged in the activity of oil drilling for profit.

Example (6). C, a chemist, is employed by a large chemical company and is engaged in a wide variety of basic research projects for his employer. Although he does no work for his employer with respect to the development of new plastics, he has always been interested in such development and has outfitted a workshop in his home at his own expense which he uses to experiment in the field. He has patented several developments at his own expense but as yet has realized no income from his inventions or from such patents. C conducts his research on a regular, systematic basis, incurs fees to secure consultation on his projects from time to time, and makes extensive efforts to "market" his developments. C has devoted substantial time and expense in an effort to develop a plastic sufficiently hard, durable, and malleable that it could be used in lieu of sheet steel in many major applications, such as automobile bodies. Although there may be only a small chance that C will invent new plastics, the return from any such development would be so large that it induces C to incur the costs of his experimental work. C is sufficiently qualified by his background that there is some reasonable basis for his experimental activities. C's experimental work does not involve substantial personal or recreational aspects and is conducted in an effort to find practical applications for his work. Under these circumstances, C may be found to be engaged in the experimental activities for profit. [Reg. § 1.183-2.]

□ [*T.D.* 7198, 7-12-72.]

§ 1.195-1. Election to amortize start-up expenditures.—(a) *In general.*—Under section 195(b), a taxpayer may elect to amortize start-up expenditures as defined in section 195(c)(1). In the taxable year in which a taxpayer begins an active trade or business, an electing taxpayer may deduct an amount equal to the lesser of the amount of the start-up expenditures that relate to the active trade or business, or $5,000 (reduced (but not below zero) by the amount by which the start-up expenditures exceed $50,000). The remainder of the start-up expenditures is deductible ratably over the 180-month period beginning with the month in which the active trade or business begins. All start-up expenditures that relate to the active trade or business are considered in determining whether the start-up expenditures exceed $50,000, including expenditures incurred on or before October 22, 2004.

(b) *Time and manner of making election.*—A taxpayer is deemed to have made an election under section 195(b) to amortize start-up expenditures as defined in section 195(c)(1) for the taxable year in which the active trade or business to which the expenditures relate begins. A taxpayer may choose to forgo the deemed election by affirmatively electing to capitalize its start-up expenditures on a timely filed Federal income tax return (including extensions) for the taxable year in which the active trade or business to which the expenditures relate begins. The election either to amortize startup expenditures under section 195(b) or to capitalize start-up expenditures is irrevocable and applies to all start-up expenditures that are related to the active trade or business. A change in the characterization of an item as a start-up expenditure is a change in method of accounting to which sections 446 and 481(a) apply if the taxpayer treated the item consistently for two or more taxable years. A change in the determination of the taxable year in which the active trade or business begins also is treated as a change in method of accounting if the taxpayer amortized start-up expenditures for two or more taxable years.

(c) *Examples*.—The following examples illustrate the application of this section:

Example 1. Expenditures of $5,000 or less. Corporation X, a calendar year taxpayer, incurs $3,000 of start-up expenditures after October 22, 2004, that relate to an active trade or business that begins on July 1, 2011. Under paragraph (b) of this section, Corporation X is deemed to have elected to amortize start-up expenditures under section 195(b) in 2011. Therefore, Corporation X may deduct the entire amount of the start-up expenditures in 2011, the taxable year in which the active trade or business begins.

Example 2. Expenditures of more than $5,000 but less than or equal to $50,000. The facts are the same as in *Example 1* except that Corporation X incurs start-up expenditures of $41,000. Under paragraph (b) of this section, Corporation X is deemed to have elected to amortize start-up expenditures under section 195(b) in 2011. Therefore, Corporation X may deduct $5,000 and the portion of the remaining $36,000 that is allocable to July through December of 2011 ($36,000/180 × 6 = $1,200) in 2011, the taxable year in which the active trade or business begins. Corporation X may amortize the remaining $34,800 ($36,000 - $1,200 = $34,800) ratably over the remaining 174 months.

Example 3. Subsequent change in the characterization of an item. The facts are the same as in *Example 2* except that Corporation X determines in 2013 that Corporation X incurred $10,000 for an additional start-up expenditure erroneously deducted in 2011 under section 162 as a business expense. Under paragraph (b) of this section, Corporation X is deemed to have elected to amortize start-up expenditures under section 195(b) in 2011, including the additional $10,000 of start-up expenditures. Corporation X is using an impermissible method of accounting for the additional $10,000 of start-up expenditures and must change its method under § 1.446-1(e) and the applicable general administrative procedures in effect in 2013.

Example 4. Subsequent redetermination of year in which business begins. The facts are the same as in *Example 2* except that, in 2012, Corporation X deducted the start-up expenditures allocable to January through December of 2012 ($36,000/180 x 12 = $2,400). In addition, in 2013 it is determined that Corporation X actually began business in 2012. Under paragraph (b) of this section, Corporation X is deemed to have elected to amortize start-up expenditures under section 195(b) in 2012. Corporation X impermissibly deducted start-up expenditures in 2011, and incorrectly determined the amount of start-up expenditures deducted in 2012. Therefore, Corporation X is using an impermissible method of accounting for the start-up expenditures and must change its method under § 1.446-1(e) and the applicable general administrative procedures in effect in 2013.

Example 5. Expenditures of more than $50,000 but less than or equal to $55,000. The facts are the same as in *Example 1* except that Corporation X incurs start-up expenditures of $54,500. Under paragraph (b) of this section, Corporation X is deemed to have elected to amortize start-up expenditures under section 195(b) in 2011. Therefore, Corporation X may deduct $500 ($5,000 - $4,500) and the portion of the remaining $54,000 that is allocable to July through December of 2011 ($54,000/180 × 6 = $1,800) in 2011, the taxable year in which the active trade or business begins. Corporation X may amortize the remaining $52,200 ($54,000 - $1,800 = $52,200) ratably over the remaining 174 months.

Example 6. Expenditures of more than $55,000. The facts are the same as in *Example 1* except that Corporation X incurs start-up expenditures of $450,000. Under paragraph (b) of this section, Corporation X is deemed to have elected to amortize startup expenditures under section 195(b) in 2011. Therefore, Corporation X may deduct the amounts allocable to July through December of 2011 ($450,000/180 × 6 = $15,000) in 2011, the taxable year in which the active trade or business begins. Corporation X may amortize the remaining $435,000 ($450,000 - $15,000 = $435,000) ratably over the remaining 174 months.

* * *

[Reg. § 1.195-1.]

☐ [*T.D.* 8797, 12-16-98. *Amended by T.D.* 9411, 7-7-2008 *and T.D.* 9542, 8-16-2011.]

§ 1.197-2. Amortization of goodwill and certain other intangibles.—(a) *Overview.*—(1) *In general.*—Section 197 allows an amortization deduction for the capitalized costs of an amortizable section 197 intangible and prohibits any other depreciation or amortization with respect to that property. Paragraphs (b), (c), and (e) of this section provide rules and definitions for determining whether property is a section 197 intangible, and paragraphs (d) and (e) of this section provide rules and definitions for determining whether a section 197 intangible is an amortizable section 197 intangible. The amortization deduction under section 197 is determined by amortizing basis ratably over a 15-year period under the rules of paragraph (f) of this section. Section 197 also includes various special rules pertaining to the disposition of amortizable section 197 intangibles, nonrecognition transactions, anti-churning rules, and anti-abuse rules. Rules relating to these provisions are contained in paragraphs (g), (h), and (j) of this section. Examples demonstrating the application of these provisions are contained in paragraph (k) of this section. The effective date of the rules in this section is contained in paragraph (l) of this section.

(2) *Section 167(f) property.*—Section 167(f) prescribes rules for computing the depreciation deduction for certain property to which section 197 does not apply. See § 1.167(a)-14 for rules under section 167(f) and paragraphs (c)(4), (6), (7), (11), and (13) of this section for a description of the property subject to section 167(f).

(3) *Amounts otherwise deductible.*—Section 197 does not apply to amounts that are not chargeable to capital account under paragraph (f)(3) (relating to basis determinations for covenants not to compete and certain contracts for the use of section 197 intangibles) of this section and are otherwise currently deductible. For this purpose, an amount described in § 1.162-11 is not currently deductible if, without regard to § 1.162-11, such amount is properly chargeable to capital account.

(b) *Section 197 intangibles; in general.*—Except as otherwise provided in paragraph (c) of this section, the term *section 197 intangible* means any property described in section 197(d)(1). The following rules and definitions provide guidance concerning property that is a section 197 intangible unless an exception applies:

(1) *Goodwill.*—Section 197 intangibles include goodwill. Goodwill is the value of a trade or business attributable to the expectancy of continued customer patronage. This expectancy may be due to the name or reputation of a trade or business or any other factor.

(2) *Going concern value.*—Section 197 intangibles include going concern value. Going concern value is the additional value that attaches to property by reason of its existence as an integral part of an ongoing business activity. Going concern value includes the value attributable to the ability of a trade or business (or a part of a trade or business) to continue functioning or generating income without interruption notwithstanding a change in ownership, but does not include any of the intangibles described in any other provision of this paragraph (b). It also includes the value that is attributable to the immediate use or availability of an acquired trade or business, such as, for example, the use of the revenues or net earnings that otherwise would not be received during any period if the acquired trade or business were not available or operational.

(3) *Workforce in place.*—Section 197 intangibles include workforce in place. Workforce in place (sometimes referred to as agency force or assembled workforce) includes the composition of a workforce (for example, the experience, education, or training of a workforce), the terms and conditions of employment whether contractual or otherwise, and any other value placed on employees or any of their attributes. Thus, the amount paid or incurred for workforce in place includes, for example, any portion of the purchase price of an acquired trade or business attributable to the existence of a highly-skilled workforce, an existing employment contract (or contracts), or a relationship with employees or consultants (including, but not limited to, any key employee contract or relationship). Workforce in place does not include any covenant not to compete or other similar arrangement described in paragraph (b)(9) of this section.

(4) *Information base.*—Section 197 intangibles include any information base, including a customer-related information base. For this purpose, an information base includes business books and records, operating systems, and any other information base (regardless of the method of recording the information) and a customer-related information base is any information base that includes lists or other information with respect to current or prospective customers. Thus, the amount paid or incurred for information base includes, for example, any portion of the purchase price of an acquired trade or business attributable to the intangible value of technical manuals, training manuals or programs, data files, and accounting or inventory control systems. Other examples include the cost of acquiring customer lists, subscription lists, insurance expirations, patient or client files, or lists of newspaper, magazine, radio, or television advertisers.

(5) *Know-how, etc.*—Section 197 intangibles include any patent, copyright, formula, process, design, pattern, know-how, format, package design, computer software (as defined in paragraph (c)(4)(iv) of this section), or interest in a film, sound recording, video tape, book, or other similar property. (See, however, the exceptions in paragraph (c) of this section.)

(6) *Customer-based intangibles.*—Section 197 intangibles include any customer-based in-

tangible. A customer-based intangible is any composition of market, market share, or other value resulting from the future provision of goods or services pursuant to contractual or other relationships in the ordinary course of business with customers. Thus, the amount paid or incurred for customer-based intangibles includes, for example, any portion of the purchase price of an acquired trade or business attributable to the existence of a customer base, a circulation base, an undeveloped market or market growth, insurance in force, the existence of a qualification to supply goods or services to a particular customer, a mortgage servicing contract (as defined in paragraph (c)(11) of this section), an investment management contract, or other relationship with customers involving the future provision of goods or services. (See, however, the exceptions in paragraph (c) of this section.) In addition, customer-based intangibles include the deposit base and any similar asset of a financial institution. Thus, the amount paid or incurred for customer-based intangibles also includes any portion of the purchase price of an acquired financial institution attributable to the value represented by existing checking accounts, savings accounts, escrow accounts, and other similar items of the financial institution. However, any portion of the purchase price of an acquired trade or business attributable to accounts receivable or other similar rights to income for goods or services provided to customers prior to the acquisition of a trade or business is not an amount paid or incurred for a customer-based intangible.

* * *

(8) *Licenses, permits, and other rights granted by governmental units.*—Section 197 intangibles include any license, permit, or other right granted by a governmental unit (including, for purposes of section 197, an agency or instrumentality thereof) even if the right is granted for an indefinite period or is reasonably expected to be renewed for an indefinite period. These rights include, for example, a liquor license, a taxi-cab medallion (or license), an airport landing or takeoff right (sometimes referred to as a slot), a regulated airline route, or a television or radio broadcasting license. The issuance or renewal of a license, permit, or other right granted by a governmental unit is considered an acquisition of the license, permit, or other right. (See, however, the exceptions in paragraph (c) of this section, including the exceptions in paragraph (c)(3) of this section for an interest in land, paragraph (c)(6) of this section for certain rights to receive tangible property or services, paragraph (c)(8) of this section for an interest under a lease of tangible property, and paragraph (c)(13) of this section for certain rights granted by a governmental unit. See paragraph (b)(10) of this section for the treatment of franchises.)

(9) *Covenants not to compete and other similar arrangements.*—Section 197 intangibles include any covenant not to compete, or agreement having substantially the same effect, entered into in connection with the direct or indirect acquisition of an interest in a trade or business or a substantial portion thereof. For purposes of this paragraph (b)(9), an acquisition may be made in the form of an asset acquisition (including a qualified stock purchase that is treated as a purchase of assets under section 338), a stock acquisition or redemption, and the acquisition or redemption of a partnership interest. An agreement requiring the performance of services for the acquiring taxpayer or the provision of property or its use to the acquiring taxpayer does not have substantially the same effect as a covenant not to compete to the extent that the amount paid under the agreement represents reasonable compensation for the services actually rendered or for the property or use of the property actually provided.

(10) *Franchises, trademarks, and trade names.*—(i) Section 197 intangibles include any franchise, trademark, or trade name. The term *franchise* has the meaning given in section 1253(b)(1) and includes any agreement that provides one of the parties to the agreement with the right to distribute, sell, or provide goods, services, or facilities, within a specified area. The term *trademark* includes any word, name, symbol, or device, or any combination thereof, adopted and used to identify goods or services and distinguish them from those provided by others. The term *trade name* includes any name used to identify or designate a particular trade or business or the name or title used by a person or organization engaged in a trade or business. A license, permit, or other right granted by a governmental unit is a franchise if it otherwise meets the definition of a franchise. A trademark or trade name includes any trademark or trade name arising under statute or applicable common law, and any similar right granted by contract. The renewal of a franchise, trademark, or trade name is treated as an acquisition of the franchise, trademark, or trade name.

(ii) Notwithstanding the definitions provided in paragraph (b)(10)(i) of this section, any amount that is paid or incurred on account of a transfer, sale, or other disposition of a franchise, trademark, or trade name and that is subject to section 1253(d)(1) is not included in the basis of a section 197 intangible. (See paragraph (g)(6) of this section.)

(11) *Contracts for the use of, and term interests in, section 197 intangibles.*—Section 197 intangibles include any right under a license, contract, or other arrangement providing for the use of property that would be a section 197 intangible under any provision of this paragraph (b) (including this paragraph (b)(11)) after giving effect to all of the exceptions provided in paragraph (c) of this section. Section 197 intangibles also include any term interest (whether outright or in trust) in such property.

(12) *Other similar items.*—Section 197 intangibles include any other intangible property that is similar in all material respects to the property specifically described in section 197(d)(1)(C)(i) through (v) and paragraphs (b)(3) through (7) of this section. (See paragraph (g)(5) of this section for special rules regarding certain reinsurance transactions.)

(c) *Section 197 intangibles; exceptions.*—The term *section 197 intangible* does not include property described in section 197(e). The following rules and definitions provide guidance concerning property to which the exceptions apply:

(1) *Interests in a corporation, partnership, trust, or estate.*—Section 197 intangibles do not include an interest in a corporation, partnership, trust, or estate. Thus, for example, amortization under section 197 is not available for the cost of acquiring stock, partnership interests, or interests in a trust or estate, whether or not the interests are regularly traded on an established market. (See paragraph (g)(3) of this section for special rules applicable to property of a partnership when a section 754 election is in effect for the partnership.)

(2) *Interests under certain financial contracts.*—Section 197 intangibles do not include an interest under an existing futures contract, foreign currency contract, notional principal contract, interest rate swap, or other similar financial contract, whether or not the interest is regularly traded on an established market. However, this exception does not apply to an interest under a mortgage servicing contract, credit card servicing contract, or other contract to service another person's indebtedness, or an interest under an assumption reinsurance contract. (See paragraph (g)(5) of this section for the treatment of assumption reinsurance contracts. See paragraph (c)(11) of this section and § 1.167(a)-14(d) for the treatment of mortgage servicing rights.)

(3) *Interests in land.*—Section 197 intangibles do not include any interest in land. For this purpose, an interest in land includes a fee interest, life estate, remainder, easement, mineral right, timber right, grazing right, riparian right, air right, zoning variance, and any other similar right, such as a farm allotment, quota for farm commodities, or crop acreage base. An interest in land does not include an airport landing or takeoff right, a regulated airline route, or a franchise to provide cable television service. The cost of acquiring a license, permit, or other land improvement right, such as a building construction or use permit, is taken into account in the same manner as the underlying improvement.

(4) *Certain computer software.*—(i) *Publicly available.*—Section 197 intangibles do not include any interest in computer software that is (or has been) readily available to the general public on similar terms, is subject to a nonexclusive license, and has not been substantially modified. Computer software will be treated as readily available to the general public if the software may be obtained on substantially the same terms by a significant number of persons that would reasonably be expected to use the software. This requirement can be met even though the software is not available through a system of retail distribution. Computer software will not be considered to have been substantially modified if the cost of all modifications to the version of the software that is readily available to the general public does not exceed the greater of 25 percent of the price at which the unmodified version of the software is readily available to the general public or $2,000. For the purpose of determining whether computer software has been substantially modified—

(A) Integrated programs acquired in a package from a single source are treated as a single computer program; and

(B) Any cost incurred to install the computer software on a system is not treated as a cost of the software. However, the costs for customization, such as tailoring to a user's specifications (other than embedded programming options) are costs of modifying the software.

(ii) *Not acquired as part of trade or business.*—Section 197 intangibles do not include an interest in computer software that is not acquired as part of a purchase of a trade or business.

(iii) *Other exceptions.*—For other exceptions applicable to computer software, see paragraph (a)(3) of this section (relating to otherwise deductible amounts) and paragraph (g)(7) of this section (relating to amounts properly taken into account in determining the cost of property that is not a section 197 intangible).

(iv) *Computer software defined.*—For purposes of this section, computer software is any program or routine (that is, any sequence of machine-readable code) that is designed to cause a computer to perform a desired function or set of functions, and the documentation required to describe and maintain that program or routine. It includes all forms and media in which the software is contained, whether written, magnetic, or otherwise. Computer programs of all classes, for example, operating systems, executive systems, monitors, compilers and translators, assembly routines, and utility programs as well as application programs, are included. Computer software also includes any incidental and ancillary rights that are necessary to effect the acquisition of the title to, the ownership of, or the right to use the computer software, and that are used only in connection with that specific computer software. Such incidental and ancillary rights are not included in the definition of trademark or trade name under paragraph (b)(10)(i) of this section. For example, a trademark or trade name that is ancillary to the ownership or use of a specific computer software program in the taxpayer's trade or business and is not acquired for the purpose of marketing the computer software is included in the definition of computer software and is not included in the definition of trademark or trade name. Computer software does not include any data or information base described in paragraph (b)(4) of this section unless the data base or item is in the public domain and is incidental to a computer program. For this purpose, a copyrighted or proprietary data or information base is treated as in the public domain if its availability through the computer program does not contribute significantly to the cost of the program. For example, if a word-processing program includes a dictionary feature used to spell-check a document or any portion thereof, the entire program (including the dictionary feature) is computer software regardless of the form in which the feature is maintained or stored.

(5) *Certain interests in films, sound recordings, video tapes, books, or other similar property.*—Section 197 intangibles do not include any interest (including an interest as a licensee) in a film, sound recording, video tape, book, or other similar property (such as the right to broadcast or transmit a live event) if the interest is not acquired as part of a purchase of a trade or business. A film, sound recording, video tape, book, or other similar property includes any incidental and ancillary rights (such as a trademark or trade name) that are necessary to effect the acquisition of title to, the ownership of, or the right to use the property and are used only in connection with that property. Such incidental and ancillary rights are not included in the definition of trademark or trade name under paragraph (b)(10)(i) of this section. For purposes of this paragraph (c)(5), computer software (as defined in paragraph (c)(4)(iv) of this section) is not treated as other property similar to a film, sound recording, video tape, or book. (See section 167 for amortization of excluded intangible property or interests.)

(6) *Certain rights to receive tangible property or services.*—Section 197 intangibles do not include any right to receive tangible property or services under a contract or from a governmental unit if the right is not acquired as part of a purchase of a trade or business. Any right that is described in the preceding sentence is not treated as a section 197 intangible even though the right is also described in section 197(d)(1)(D) and paragraph (b)(8) of this section (relating to certain governmental licenses, permits, and other rights) and even though the right fails to meet one or more of the requirements of paragraph (c)(13) of this section (relating to certain rights of fixed duration or amount). (See § 1.167(a)-14(c)(1) and (3) for applicable rules.)

(7) *Certain interests in patents or copyrights.*—Section 197 intangibles do not include any interest (including an interest as a licensee) in a patent, patent application, or copyright that is not acquired as part of a purchase of a trade or business. A patent or copyright includes any incidental and ancillary rights (such as a trademark or trade name) that are necessary to effect the acquisition of title to, the ownership of, or the right to use the property and are used only in connection with that property. Such incidental and ancillary rights are not included in the definition of trademark or trade name under paragraph (b)(10)(i) of this section. (See § 1.167(a)-14(c)(4) for applicable rules.)

(8) *Interests under leases of tangible property.*—(i) *Interest as a lessor.*—Section 197 intangibles do not include any interest as a lessor under an existing lease or sublease of tangible real or personal property. In addition, the cost of acquiring an interest as a lessor in connection with the acquisition of tangible property is taken into account as part of the cost of the tangible property. For example, if a taxpayer acquires a shopping center that is leased to tenants operating retail stores, any portion of the purchase price attributable to favorable lease terms is taken into account as part of the basis of the shopping center and in determining the depreciation deduction allowed with respect to the shopping center. (See section 167(c)(2).)

(ii) *Interest as a lessee.*—Section 197 intangibles do not include any interest as a lessee under an existing lease of tangible real or personal property. For this purpose, an airline lease of an airport passenger or cargo gate is a lease of tangible property. The cost of acquiring such an interest is taken into account under section 178 and § 1.162-11(a). If an interest as a lessee under a lease of tangible property is acquired in a transaction with any other intangible property, a portion of the total purchase price may be allocable to the interest as a lessee based on all of the relevant facts and circumstances.

(9) *Interests under indebtedness.*—(i) *In general.*—Section 197 intangibles do not include any interest (whether as a creditor or debtor) under an indebtedness in existence when the interest was acquired. Thus, for example, the value attributable to the assumption of an indebtedness with a below-market interest rate is not amortizable under section 197. In addition, the premium paid for acquiring a debt instrument with an above-market interest rate is not amortizable under section 197. See section 171 for rules concerning the treatment of amortizable bond premium.

(ii) *Exceptions.*—For purposes of this paragraph (c)(9), an interest under an existing indebtedness does not include the deposit base (and other similar items) of a financial institution. An interest under an existing indebtedness includes mortgage servicing rights, however, to the extent the rights are stripped coupons under section 1286.

(10) *Professional sports franchises.*—Section 197 intangibles do not include any franchise to engage in professional baseball, basketball, football, or any other professional sport, and any item (even though otherwise qualifying as a section 197 intangible) acquired in connection with such a franchise.

(11) *Mortgage servicing rights.*—Section 197 intangibles do not include any right described in section 197(e)(7) (concerning rights to service indebtedness secured by residential real property that are not acquired as part of a purchase of a trade or business). (See § 1.167(a)-14(d) for applicable rules.)

(12) *Certain transaction costs.*—Section 197 intangibles do not include any fees for professional services and any transaction costs incurred by parties to a transaction in which all or any portion of the gain or loss is not recognized under part III of subchapter C of the Internal Revenue Code.

(13) *Rights of fixed duration or amount.*—(i) Section 197 intangibles do not include any right under a contract or any license, permit, or other right granted by a governmental unit if the right—

(A) Is acquired in the ordinary course of a trade or business (or an activity described in section 212) and not as part of a purchase of a trade or business;

(B) Is not described in section 197(d)(1)(A), (B), (E), or (F);

(C) Is not a customer-based intangible, a customer-related information base, or any other similar item; and

(D) Either—

(1) Has a fixed duration of less than 15 years; or

(2) Is fixed as to amount and the adjusted basis thereof is properly recoverable (without regard to this section) under a method similar to the unit-of-production method.

(ii) See § 1.167(a)-14(c)(2) and (3) for applicable rules.

(d) *Amortizable section 197 intangibles.*—(1) *Definition.*—Except as otherwise provided in this paragraph (d), the term *amortizable section 197 intangible* means any section 197 intangible acquired after August 10, 1993 (or after July 25, 1991, if a valid retroactive election under § 1.197-1T has been made), and held in connection with the conduct of a trade or business or an activity described in section 212.

(2) *Exception for self-created intangibles.*—(i) *In general.*—Except as provided in paragraph (d)(2)(iii) of this section, amortizable section 197 intangibles do not include any section 197 intangible created by the taxpayer (a self-created intangible).

(ii) *Created by the taxpayer.*—(A) *Defined.*—A section 197 intangible is created by the taxpayer to the extent the taxpayer makes payments or otherwise incurs costs for its creation, production, development, or improvement, whether the actual work is performed by the taxpayer or by another person under a contract with the taxpayer entered into before the contracted creation, production, development, or improvement occurs. For example, a technological process developed specifically for a taxpayer under an arrangement with another person pursuant to which the taxpayer retains all rights to the process is created by the taxpayer.

(B) *Contracts for the use of intangibles.*—A section 197 intangible is not a self-created intangible to the extent that it results from the entry into (or renewal of) a contract for the use of an existing section 197 intangible. Thus, for example, the exception for self-created intangibles does not apply to capitalized costs, such as legal and other professional fees, incurred by a licensee in connection with the entry into (or renewal of) a contract for the use of know-how or similar property.

(C) *Improvements and modifications.*—If an existing section 197 intangible is improved or otherwise modified by the taxpayer or by another person under a contract with the taxpayer, the existing intangible and the capitalized costs (if any) of the improvements or other modifications are each treated as a separate section 197 intangible for purposes of this paragraph (d).

(iii) *Exceptions.*—(A) The exception for self-created intangibles does not apply to any section 197 intangible described in section 197(d)(1)(D) (relating to licenses, permits or other rights granted by a governmental unit), 197(d)(1)(E) (relating to covenants not to compete), or 197(d)(1)(F) (relating to franchises, trademarks, and trade names). Thus, for example, capitalized costs incurred in the development, registration, or defense of a trademark or trade name do not qualify for the exception and are amortized over 15 years under section 197.

(B) The exception for self-created intangibles does not apply to any section 197 intangible created in connection with the purchase of a trade or business (as defined in paragraph (e) of this section).

(C) If a taxpayer disposes of a self-created intangible and subsequently reacquires the intangible in an acquisition described in paragraph (h)(5)(ii) of this section, the exception for self-created intangibles does not apply to the reacquired intangible.

(3) *Exception for property subject to anti-churning rules.*—Amortizable section 197 intangibles do not include any property to which the anti-churning rules of section 197(f)(9) and paragraph (h) of this section apply.

(e) *Purchase of a trade or business.*—Several of the exceptions in section 197 apply only to property that is not acquired in (or created in connection with) a transaction or series of related transactions involving the acquisition of assets constituting a trade or business or a substantial portion thereof. Property acquired in (or created in connection with) such a transaction or series of related transactions is referred to in this section as property acquired as part of (or created in connection with) a purchase of a trade or business. For purposes of section 197 and this section, the applicability of the limitation is determined under the following rules:

(1) *Goodwill or going concern value.*—An asset or group of assets constitutes a trade or business or a substantial portion thereof if their use would constitute a trade or business under section 1060 (that is, if goodwill or going concern value could under any circumstances attach to the assets). See §1.1060-1(b)(2). For this purpose, all the facts and circumstances, including any employee relationships that continue (or covenants not to compete that are entered into) as part of the transfer of the assets, are taken into account in determining whether goodwill or going concern value could attach to the assets.

(2) *Franchise, trademark, or trade name.*—(i) *In general.*—The acquisition of a franchise, trademark, or trade name constitutes the acquisition of a trade or business or a substantial portion thereof.

(ii) *Exceptions.*—For purposes of this paragraph (e)(2)—

(A) A trademark or trade name is disregarded if it is included in computer software under paragraph (c)(4) of this section or in an interest in a film, sound recording, video tape, book, or other similar property under paragraph (c)(5) of this section;

(B) A franchise, trademark, or trade name is disregarded if its value is nominal or the taxpayer irrevocably disposes of it immediately after its acquisition; and

(C) The acquisition of a right or interest in a trademark or trade name is disregarded if the grant of the right or interest is not, under the principles of section 1253, a transfer of all substantial rights to such property or of an undivided interest in all substantial rights to such property.

(3) *Acquisitions to be included.*—The assets acquired in a transaction (or series of related transactions) include only assets (including a beneficial or other indirect interest in assets where the interest is of a type described in paragraph (c)(1) of this section) acquired by the taxpayer and persons related to the taxpayer from another person and persons related to that other person. For purposes of this paragraph (e)(3), persons are related only if their relationship is described in section 267(b) or 707(b) or they are engaged in trades or businesses under common control within the meaning of section 41(f)(1).

(4) *Substantial portion.*—The determination of whether acquired assets constitute a substantial portion of a trade or business is to be based on all of the facts and circumstances, including the nature and the amount of the assets acquired as well as the nature and amount of the assets retained by the transferor.

The value of the assets acquired relative to the value of the assets retained by the transferor is not determinative of whether the acquired assets constitute a substantial portion of a trade or business.

(5) *Deemed asset purchases under section 338.*—A qualified stock purchase that is treated as a purchase of assets under section 338 is treated as a transaction involving the acquisition of assets constituting a trade or business only if the direct acquisition of the assets of the corporation would have been treated as the acquisition of assets constituting a trade or business or a substantial portion thereof.

(6) *Mortgage servicing rights.*—Mortgage servicing rights acquired in a transaction or series of related transactions are disregarded in determining for purposes of paragraph (c)(11) of this section whether the assets acquired in the transaction or transactions constitute a trade or business or substantial portion thereof.

(7) *Computer software acquired for internal use.*—Computer software acquired in a transaction or series of related transactions solely for internal use in an existing trade or business is disregarded in determining for purposes of paragraph (c)(4) of this section whether the assets acquired in the transaction or series of related transactions constitute a trade or business or substantial portion thereof.

(f) *Computation of amortization deduction.*—(1) *In general.*—Except as provided in paragraph (f)(2) of this section, the amortization deduction allowable under section 197(a) is computed as follows:

(i) The basis of an amortizable section 197 intangible is amortized ratably over the 15-year period beginning on the later of—

(A) The first day of the month in which the property is acquired; or

(B) In the case of property held in connection with the conduct of a trade or business or in an activity described in section 212, the first day of the month in which the conduct of the trade or business or the activity begins.

(ii) Except as otherwise provided in this section, basis is determined under section 1011 and salvage value is disregarded.

(iii) Property is not eligible for amortization in the month of disposition.

(iv) The amortization deduction for a short taxable year is based on the number of months in the short taxable year.

(2) *Treatment of contingent amounts.*—(i) *Amounts added to basis during 15-year period.*—Any amount that is properly included in the basis of an amortizable section 197 intangible after the first month of the 15-year period described in paragraph (f)(1)(i) of this section and before the expiration of that period is amortized ratably over the remainder of the 15-year period. For this purpose, the remainder of the 15-year period begins on the first day of the month in which the basis increase occurs.

(ii) *Amounts becoming fixed after expiration of 15-year period.*—Any amount that is not properly included in the basis of an amortizable section 197 intangible until after the expiration of the 15-year period described in paragraph (f)(1)(i) of this section is amortized in full immediately upon the inclusion of the amount in the basis of the intangible.

(iii) *Rules for including amounts in basis.*—See §§1.1275-4(c)(4) and 1.483-4(a) for rules governing the extent to which contingent amounts payable under a debt instrument given in consideration for the sale or exchange of an amortizable section 197 intangible are treated as payments of principal and the time at which the amount treated as principal is included in basis. See §1.461-1(a)(1) and (2) for rules governing the time at which other contingent amounts are taken into account in determining the basis of an amortizable section 197 intangible.

(3) *Basis determinations for certain assets.*—(i) *Covenants not to compete.*—In the case of a covenant not to compete or other similar arrangement described in paragraph (b)(9) of this section (a covenant), the amount chargeable to capital account includes, except as provided in this paragraph (f)(3), all amounts that are required to be paid pursuant to the covenant, whether or not any such amount would be deductible under section 162 if the covenant were not a section 197 intangible.

(ii) *Contracts for the use of section 197 intangibles; acquired as part of a trade or business.*—(A) *In general.*—Except as provided in this paragraph (f)(3), any amount paid or incurred by the transferee on account of the transfer of a right or term interest described in paragraph (b)(11) of this section (relating to contracts for the use of, and term interests in, section 197 intangibles) by the owner of the property to which such right or interest relates and as part of a purchase of a trade or business is chargeable to capital account, whether or not such amount would be deductible under section 162 if the property were not a section 197 intangible.

(B) *Know-how and certain information base.*—The amount chargeable to capital account with respect to a right or term interest described in paragraph (b)(11) of this section is determined without regard to the rule in paragraph (f)(3)(ii)(A) of this section if the right or interest relates to property (other than a customer-related information base) described in paragraph (b)(4) or (5) of this section and the acquiring taxpayer establishes that—

(1) The transfer of the right or interest is not, under the principles of section 1235, a transfer of all substantial rights to such property or of an individed interest in all substantial rights to such property; and

(2) The right or interest was transferred for an arm's-length consideration.

(iii) *Contracts for the use of section 197 intangibles; not acquired as part of a trade or business.*—The transfer of a right or term interest described in paragraph (b)(11) of this section by the owner of the property to which such right or interest relates but not as part of a purchase of a trade or business will be closely scrutinized under the principles of section 1235 for purposes of determining whether the transfer is a sale or exchange and, accordingly, whether amounts paid on account of the transfer are chargeable to capital account. If under the principles of section 1235 the transaction is not a sale or exchange, amounts paid on account of the transfer are not chargeable to capital account under this paragraph (f)(3).

(iv) *Applicable rules.*—(A) *Franchises, trademarks, and trade names.*—For purposes of this paragraph (f)(3), section 197 intangibles described in paragraph (b)(11) of this section do not include any property that is also described in paragraph (b)(10) of this section (relating to franchises, trademarks, and trade names).

(B) *Certain amounts treated as payable under a debt instrument.—(1) In general.*—For purposes of applying any provision of the Internal Revenue Code to a person making payments of amounts that are otherwise chargeable to capital account under this paragraph (f)(3) and are payable after the acquisition of the section 197 intangible to which they relate, such amounts are treated as payable under a debt instrument given in consideration for the sale or exchange of the section 197 intangible.

(2) Rights granted by governmental units.—For purposes of applying any provision of the Internal Revenue Code to any amounts that are otherwise chargeable to capital account with respect to a license, permit, or other right described in paragraph (b)(8) of this section (relating to rights granted by a governmental unit or agency or instrumentality thereof) and are payable after the acquisition of the section 197 intangible to which they relate, such amounts are treated, except as provided in paragraph (f)(4)(i) of this section (relating to renewal transactions), as payable under a debt instrument given in consideration for the sale or exchange of the section 197 intangible.

(3) Treatment of other parties to transaction.—No person shall be treated as having sold, exchanged, or otherwise disposed of property in a transaction for purposes of any provision of the Internal Revenue Code solely by reason of the application of this paragraph (f)(3) to any other party to the transaction.

(4) Basis determinations in certain transactions.—(i) Certain renewal transactions.—The costs paid or incurred for the renewal of a franchise, trademark, or trade name or any license, permit, or other right granted by a governmental unit or an agency or instrumentality thereof are amortized over the 15-year period that begins with the month of renewal. Any costs paid or incurred for the issuance, or earlier renewal, continue to be taken into account over the remaining portion of the amortization period that began at the time of the issuance, or earlier renewal. Any amount paid or incurred for the protection, expansion, or defense of a trademark or trade name and chargeable to capital account is treated as an amount paid or incurred for a renewal.

(ii) Transactions subject to section 338 or 1060.—In the case of a section 197 intangible deemed to have been acquired as the result of a qualified stock purchase within the meaning of section 338(d)(3), the basis shall be determined pursuant to section 338(b)(5) and the regulations thereunder. In the case of a section 197 intangible acquired in an applicable asset acquisition within the meaning of section 1060(c), the basis shall be determined pursuant to section 1060(a) and the regulations thereunder.

(iii) Certain reinsurance transactions.—See paragraph (g)(5)(ii) of this section for special rules regarding the adjusted basis of an insurance contract acquired through an assumption reinsurance transaction.

(g) *Special rules.*—* * *

(8) *Treatment of amortizable section 197 intangibles as depreciable property.*—An amortizable section 197 intangible is treated as property of a character subject to the allowance for depreciation under section 167. Thus, for example, an amortizable section 197 intangible is not a capital asset for purposes of section 1221, but if used in a trade or business and held for more than one year, gain or loss on its disposition generally qualifies as section 1231 gain or loss. Also, an amortizable section 197 intangible is section 1245 property and section 1239 applies

to any gain recognized upon its sale or exchange between related persons (as defined in section 1239(b)).

* * *

(k) *Examples.*—The following examples illustrate the application of this section:

Example 1. Advertising costs. (i) Q manufactures and sells consumer products through a series of wholesalers and distributors. In order to increase sales of its products by encouraging consumer loyalty to its products and to enhance the value of the goodwill, trademarks, and trade names of the business, Q advertises its products to the consuming public. It regularly incurs costs to develop radio, television, and print advertisements. These costs generally consist of employee costs and amounts paid to independent advertising agencies. Q also incurs costs to run these advertisements in the various media for which they were developed.

(ii) The advertising costs are not chargeable to capital account under paragraph (f)(3) of this section (relating to costs incurred for covenants not to compete, rights granted by governmental units, and contracts for the use of section 197 intangibles) and are currently deductible as ordinary and necessary expenses under section 162. Accordingly, under paragraph (a)(3) of this section, section 197 does not apply to these costs.

Example 2. Computer software. (i) X purchases all of the assets of an existing trade or business from Y. One of the assets acquired is all of Y's rights in certain computer software previously used by Y under the terms of a nonexclusive license from the software developer. The software was developed for use by manufacturers to maintain a comprehensive accounting system, including general and subsidiary ledgers, payroll, accounts receivable and payable, cash receipts and disbursements, fixed asset accounting, and inventory cost accounting and controls. The developer modified the software for use by Y at a cost of $1,000 and Y made additional modifications at a cost of $500. The developer does not maintain wholesale or retail outlets but markets the software directly to ultimate users. Y's license of the software is limited to an entity that is actively engaged in business as a manufacturer.

(ii) Notwithstanding these limitations, the software is considered to be readily available to the general public for purposes of paragraph (c)(4)(i) of this section. In addition, the software is not substantially modified because the cost of the modifications by the developer and Y to the version of the software that is readily available to the general public does not exceed $2,000. Accordingly, the software is not a section 197 intangible.

Example 3. Acquisition of software for internal use. (i) B, the owner and operator of a worldwide package-delivery service, purchases from S all rights to software developed by S. The software will be used by B for the sole purpose of improving its package-tracking operations. B does not purchase any other assets in the transaction or any related transaction.

(ii) Because B acquired the software solely for internal use, it is disregarded in determining for purposes of paragraph (c)(4)(ii) of this section whether the assets acquired in the transaction or series of related transactions constitute a trade or business or substantial portion thereof. Since no other assets were acquired, the software is not acquired as part of a purchase of a trade or business and under paragraph (c)(4)(ii) of this section is not a section 197 intangible.

* * *

Example 6. Acquisition and amortization of covenant not to compete. (i) As part of the acquisition of a trade or business from C, B and C enter into an agreement containing a covenant not to compete. Under this agreement, C agrees that it will not compete with the business acquired by B within a prescribed geographical territory for a period of three years after the date on which the business is sold to B. In exchange for this agreement, B agrees to pay C $90,000 per year for each year in the term of the agreement. The agreement further provides that, in the event of a breach by C of his obligations under the agreement, B may terminate the agreement, cease making any of the payments due thereafter, and pursue any other legal or equitable remedies available under applicable law. The amounts payable to C under the agreement are not contingent payments for purposes of § 1.1275-4. The present fair market value of B's rights under the agreement is $225,000. The aggregate consideration paid excluding any amount treated as interest or original issue discount under applicable provisions of the Internal Revenue Code, for all assets acquired in the transaction (including the covenant not to compete) exceeds the sum of the amount of Class I assets and the aggregate fair market value of all Class II, Class III, Class IV, Class V, and Class VI assets by $50,000. See § 1.338-6(b) for rules for determining the assets in each class.

(ii) Because the covenant is acquired in an applicable asset acquisition (within the meaning of section 1060(c)), paragraph (f)(4)(ii) of this section applies and the basis of B in the covenant is determined pursuant to section 1060(a) and the regulations thereunder. Under §§ 1.1060-1(c)(2) and 1.338-6(c)(1), B's basis in the covenant cannot exceed its fair market value. Thus, B's basis in the covenant immediately after the acquisition is $225,000. This basis is amortized ratably over the 15-year period beginning on the first day of the month in which the agreement is entered into. All of the remaining consideration after allocation to the covenant and other Class VI assets, ($50,000) is allocated to Class VII assets (goodwill and going concern value). See §§1.1060-1(c)(2) and 1.338-6(b).

* * *

[Reg. §1.197-2.]

□ [*T.D.* 8865, 1-20-2000 (*corrected* 3-27-2000 *and* 10-11-2000). *Amended by T.D.* 8907, 11-17-2000; *T.D.* 8940, 2-12-2001; *T.D.* 9257, 4-7-2006; *T.D.* 9377, 1-22-2008; *T.D.* 9533, 7-1-2011; *T.D.* 9637, 9-5-2013; *T.D.* 9811, 1-18-2017; *T.D.* 9814, 1-18-2017; *and T.D.* 9891, 1-17-2020.]

§1.199A-1. Operational rules.—(a) *Overview.*—(1) *In general.*—This section provides operational rules for calculating the section 199A(a) qualified business income deduction (section 199A deduction) under section 199A of the Internal Revenue Code (Code). This section refers to the rules in §§1.199A-2 through 1.199A-6. This paragraph (a) provides an overview of this section. Paragraph (b) of this section provides definitions that apply for purposes of section 199A and §§1.199A-1 through 1.199A-6. Paragraph (c) of this section provides computational rules and examples for individuals whose taxable income does not exceed the threshold amount. Paragraph (d) of this section provides computational rules and examples for individuals whose taxable income exceeds the threshold amount. Paragraph (e) of this section provides special rules for purposes of section 199A and §§1.199A-1 through 1.199A-6. This section and §§1.199A-2 through 1.199A-6 do not apply for purposes of calculating the deduction in section 199A(g) for specified agricultural and horticultural cooperatives.

(2) *Usage of term individual.*—For purposes of applying the rules of §§1.199A-1 through 1.199A-6, a reference to an individual includes a reference to a trust (other than a grantor trust) or an estate to the extent that the section 199A deduction is determined by the trust or estate under the rules of §1.199A-6.

(b) *Definitions.*—For purposes of section 199A and §§1.199A-1 through 1.199A-6, the following definitions apply:

(1) *Aggregated trade or business* means two or more trades or businesses that have been aggregated pursuant to §1.199A-4.

(2) *Applicable percentage* means, with respect to any taxable year, 100 percent reduced (not below zero) by the percentage equal to the ratio that the taxable income of the individual for the taxable year in excess of the threshold amount, bears to $50,000 (or $100,000 in the case of a joint return).

(3) *Net capital gain* means *net capital gain* as defined in section 1222(11) plus any *qualified dividend income* (as defined in section 1(h)(11)(B)) for the taxable year.

(4) *Phase-in range* means a range of taxable income between the threshold amount and the threshold amount plus $50,000 (or $100,000 in the case of a joint return).

(5) *Qualified business income (QBI)* means the net amount of qualified items of income, gain, deduction, and loss with respect to any trade or business (or aggregated trade or business) as determined under the rules of §1.199A-3(b).

(6) *QBI component* means the amount determined under paragraph (d)(2) of this section.

(7) *Qualified PTP income* is defined in §1.199A-3(c)(3).

(8) *Qualified REIT dividends* are defined in §1.199A-3(c)(2).

(9) *Reduction amount* means, with respect to any taxable year, the excess amount multiplied by the ratio that the taxable income of the individual for the taxable year in excess of the threshold amount, bears to $50,000 (or $100,000 in the case of a joint return). For purposes of this paragraph (b)(9), the *excess amount* is the amount by which 20 percent of QBI exceeds the greater of 50 percent of W-2 wages or the sum of 25 percent of W-2 wages plus 2.5 percent of the UBIA of qualified property.

(10) *Relevant passthrough entity (RPE)* means a partnership (other than a PTP) or an S corporation that is owned, directly or indirectly, by at least one individual, estate, or trust. Other passthrough entities including common trust funds as described in §1.6032-1T and religious or apostolic organizations described in section 501(d) are also treated as RPEs if the entity files a Form 1065, *U.S. Return of Partnership Income,* and is owned, directly or indirectly, by at least one individual, estate, or trust. A trust or estate is treated as an RPE to the extent it passes through QBI, W-2 wages, UBIA of qualified property, qualified REIT dividends, or qualified PTP income.

(11) *Specified service trade or business (SSTB)* means a specified service trade or business as defined in §1.199A-5(b).

(12) *Threshold amount* means, for any taxable year beginning before 2019, $157,500 (or $315,000 in the case of a taxpayer filing a joint return). In the case of any taxable year beginning after 2018, the threshold amount is the dollar amount in the preceding sentence increased by an amount equal to such dollar

amount, multiplied by the cost-of-living adjustment determined under section 1(f)(3) of the Code for the calendar year in which the taxable year begins, determined by substituting "calendar year 2017" for "calendar year 2016" in section 1(f)(3)(A)(ii). The amount of any increase under the preceding sentence is rounded as provided in section 1(f)(7) of the Code.

(13) *Total QBI amount* means the net total QBI from all trades or businesses (including the individual's share of QBI from trades or business conducted by RPEs).

(14) *Trade or business* means a trade or business that is a trade or business under section 162 (a section 162 trade or business) other than the trade or business of performing services as an employee. In addition, rental or licensing of tangible or intangible property (rental activity) that does not rise to the level of a section 162 trade or business is nevertheless treated as a trade or business for purposes of section 199A, if the property is rented or licensed to a trade or business conducted by the individual or an RPE which is commonly controlled under § 1.199A-4(b)(1)(i) (regardless of whether the rental activity and the trade or business are otherwise eligible to be aggregated under § 1.199A-4(b)(1)).

(15) *Unadjusted basis immediately after acquisition of qualified property* (*UBIA of qualified property*) is defined in § 1.199A-2(c).

(16) *W-2 wages* means W-2 wages of a trade or business (or aggregated trade or business) properly allocable to QBI as determined under § 1.199A-2(b).

(c) *Computation of the section 199A deduction for individuals with taxable income not exceeding threshold amount.*—(1) *In general.*— The section 199A deduction is determined for individuals with taxable income for the taxable year that does not exceed the threshold amount by adding 20 percent of the total QBI amount (including the individual's share of QBI from an RPE and QBI attributable to an SSTB) and 20 percent of the combined amount of qualified REIT dividends and qualified PTP income (including the individual's share of qualified REIT dividends and qualified PTP income from RPEs and qualified PTP income attributable to an SSTB). That sum is then compared to 20 percent of the amount by which the individual's taxable income exceeds net capital gain. The lesser of these two amounts is the individual's section 199A deduction.

(2) *Carryover rules.*—(i) *Negative total QBI amount.*—If the total QBI amount is less than zero, the portion of the individual's section 199A deduction related to QBI is zero for the taxable year. The negative total QBI amount is treated as negative QBI from a separate trade or business in the succeeding taxable years of the individual for purposes of section 199A and this section. This carryover rule does not affect the deductibility of the loss for purposes of other provisions of the Code.

(ii) *Negative combined qualified REIT dividends/qualified PTP income.*—If the combined amount of REIT dividends and qualified PTP income is less than zero, the portion of the individual's section 199A deduction related to qualified REIT dividends and qualified PTP income is zero for the taxable year. The negative combined amount must be carried forward and used to offset the combined amount of REIT dividends and qualified PTP income in the succeeding taxable years of the individual for purposes of section 199A and this section. This carryover rule does not affect the deductibility of the loss for purposes of other provisions of the Code.

(3) *Examples.*—The following examples illustrate the provisions of this paragraph (c). For purposes of these examples, unless indicated otherwise, assume that all of the trades or businesses are trades or businesses as defined in paragraph (b)(14) of this section and all of the tax items are effectively connected to a trade or business within the United States within the meaning of section 864(c). Total taxable income does not include the section 199A deduction.

(i) *Example 1.* A, an unmarried individual, owns and operates a computer repair shop as a sole proprietorship. The business generates $100,000 in net taxable income from operations in 2018. A has no capital gains or losses. After allowable deductions not relating to the business, A's total taxable income for 2018 is $81,000. The business's QBI is $100,000, the net amount of its qualified items of income, gain, deduction, and loss. A's section 199A deduction for 2018 is equal to $16,200, the lesser of 20% of A's QBI from the business ($100,000 x 20% = $20,000) and 20% of A's total taxable income for the taxable year ($81,000 x 20% = $16,200).

(ii) *Example 2.* Assume the same facts as in *Example 1* of paragraph (c)(3)(i) of this section, except that A also has $7,000 in net capital gain for 2018 and that, after allowable deductions not relating to the business, A's taxable income for 2018 is $74,000. A's taxable income minus net capital gain is $67,000 ($74,000 - $7,000). A's section 199A deduction is equal to $13,400, the lesser of 20% of A's QBI from the business ($100,000 x 20% = $20,000) and 20% of A's total taxable income minus net capital gain for the taxable year ($67,000 x 20% = $13,400).

* * *

(d) *Computation of the section 199A deduction for individuals with taxable income above threshold amount.*—(1) *In general.*—The section 199A deduction is determined for individuals with taxable income for the taxable year that exceeds the threshold amount by adding the QBI component described in paragraph (d)(2) of this section and the qualified REIT dividends/qualified PTP income component described in paragraph (d)(3) of this section (including the individual's share of qualified REIT dividends and qualified PTP income from RPEs). That sum is then compared to 20 percent of the amount by which the individual's taxable income exceeds net capital gain. The lesser of these two amounts is the individual's section 199A deduction.

(2) *QBI component.*—An individual with taxable income for the taxable year that exceeds the threshold amount determines the QBI component using the following computational rules, which are to be applied in the order they appear.

(i) *SSTB exclusion.*—If the individual's taxable income is within the phase-in range, then only the applicable percentage of QBI, W-2 wages, and UBIA of qualified property for each SSTB is taken into account for all purposes of determining the individual's section 199A deduction, including the application of the netting and carryover rules described in paragraph (d)(2)(iii) of this section. If the individual's taxable income exceeds the phase-in range, then none of the individual's share of QBI, W-2 wages, or UBIA of qualified property attributable to an SSTB may be taken into account for purposes of determining the individual's section 199A deduction.

(ii) *Aggregated trade or business.*—If an individual chooses to aggregate trades or businesses under the rules of § 1.199A-4, the individual must combine the QBI, W-2 wages, and UBIA of qualified property of each trade or business within an aggregated trade or business prior to applying the netting and carryover rules described in paragraph (d)(2)(iii) of this section and the W-2 wage and UBIA of qualified property limitations described in paragraph (d)(2)(iv) of this section.

(iii) *Netting and carryover.*—(A) *Netting.*—If an individual's QBI from at least one trade or business (including an aggregated trade or business) is less than zero, the individual must offset the QBI attributable to each trade or business (or aggregated trade or business) that produced net positive QBI with the QBI from each trade or business (or aggregated trade or business) that produced net negative QBI in proportion to the relative amounts of net QBI in the trades or businesses (or aggregated trades or businesses) with positive QBI. The adjusted QBI is then used in paragraph (d)(2)(iv) of this section. The W-2 wages and UBIA of qualified property from the trades or businesses (including aggregated trades or businesses) that produced net negative QBI are not taken into account for purposes of this paragraph (d) and are not carried over to the subsequent year.

(B) *Carryover of negative total QBI amount.*—If an individual's QBI from all trades or businesses (including aggregated trades or businesses) combined is less than zero, the QBI component is zero for the taxable year. This negative amount is treated as negative QBI from a separate trade or business in the succeeding taxable years of the individual for purposes of section 199A and this section. This carryover rule does not affect the deductibility of the loss for purposes of other provisions of the Code. The W-2 wages and UBIA of qualified property from the trades or businesses (including aggregated trades or businesses) that produced net negative QBI are not taken into account for purposes of this paragraph (d) and are not carried over to the subsequent year.

(iv) *QBI component calculation.*—(A) *General rule.*—Except as provided in paragraph (d)(2)(iv)(B) of this section, the QBI component is the sum of the amounts determined under this paragraph (d)(2)(iv)(A) for each trade or business (or aggregated trade or business). For each trade or business (or aggregated trade or business) (including trades or businesses operated through RPEs) the individual must determine the lesser of—

(1) 20 percent of the QBI for that trade or business (or aggregated trade or business); or

(2) The greater of—

(i) 50 percent of W-2 wages with respect to that trade or business (or aggregated trade or business); or

(ii) The sum of 25 percent of W-2 wages with respect to that trade or business (or aggregated trade or business) plus 2.5 percent of the UBIA of qualified property with respect to that trade or business (or aggregated trade or business).

(B) *Taxpayers with taxable income within phase-in range.*—If the individual's taxable income is within the phase-in range and the amount determined under paragraph (d)(2)(iv)(A)*(2)* of this section for a trade or business (or aggregated trade or business) is less than the amount determined under paragraph (d)(2)(iv)(A)*(1)* of this section for that trade or business (or aggregated trade or business), the amount determined under paragraph (d)(2)(iv)(A) of this section for such trade or business (or aggregated trade or business) is modified. Instead of the amount determined under paragraph (d)(2)(iv)(A)(*2*) of this section, the QBI component for the trade or business (or aggregated trade or business) is the amount determined under paragraph (d)(2)(iv)(A)(*1*) of this section reduced by the reduction amount as defined in paragraph (b)(9) of this section. This reduction amount does not apply if the amount determined in paragraph (d)(2)(iv)(A)(*2*) of this section is greater than the amount determined under paragraph (d)(2)(iv)(A)(*1*) of this section (in which circumstance the QBI component for the trade or business (or aggregated trade or business) will be the unreduced amount determined in paragraph (d)(2)(iv)(A)(*1*) of this section).

(3) *Qualified REIT dividends/qualified PTP income component.*—(i) *In general.*—The qualified REIT dividend/qualified PTP income component is 20 percent of the combined amount of qualified REIT dividends and qualified PTP income received by the individual (including the individual's share of qualified REIT dividends and qualified PTP income from RPEs).

(ii) *SSTB exclusion.*—If the individual's taxable income is within the phase-in range, then only the applicable percentage of qualified PTP income generated by an SSTB is taken into account for purposes of determining the individual's section 199A deduction, including the determination of the combined amount of qualified REIT dividends and qualified PTP income described in paragraph (d)(1) of this section. If the individual's taxable income exceeds the phase-in range, then none of the individual's share of qualified PTP income generated by an SSTB may be taken into account for purposes of determining the individual's section 199A deduction.

(iii) *Negative combined qualified REIT dividends/qualified PTP income.*—If the combined amount of REIT dividends and qualified PTP income is less than zero, the portion of the individual's section 199A deduction related to qualified REIT dividends and qualified PTP income is zero for the taxable year. The negative combined amount must be carried forward and used to offset the combined amount of REIT dividends/qualified PTP income in the succeeding taxable years of the individual for purposes of section 199A and this section. This carryover rule does not affect the deductibility of the loss for purposes of other provisions of the Code.

* * *

(e) *Special rules.*—(1) *Effect of deduction.*—In the case of a partnership or S corporation, section 199A is applied at the partner or shareholder level. The rules of subchapter K and subchapter S of the Code apply in their entirety for purposes of determining each partner's or shareholder's share of QBI, W-2 wages, UBIA of qualified property, qualified REIT dividends, and qualified PTP income or loss. The section 199A deduction has no effect on the adjusted basis of a partner's interest in the partnership, the adjusted basis of a shareholder's stock in an S corporation, or an S corporation's accumulated adjustments account.

(2) *Disregarded entities.*—An entity with a single owner that is treated as disregarded as an entity separate from its owner under any provision of the Code is disregarded for purposes of section 199A and §§1.199A-1 through 1.199A-6.

(3) *Self-employment tax and net investment income tax.*—The deduction allowed under section 199A does not reduce net earnings from self-employment under section 1402 or net investment income under section 1411.

* * *

(5) *Coordination with alternative minimum tax.*—For purposes of determining alternative minimum taxable income under section 55, the deduction allowed under section 199A(a) for a taxable year is equal in amount to the deduction allowed under section 199A(a) in determining taxable income for that taxable year (that is, without regard to any adjustments under sections 56 through 59).

(6) *Imposition of accuracy-related penalty on underpayments.*—For rules related to the imposition of the accuracy-related penalty on underpayments for taxpayers who claim the deduction allowed under section 199A, see section 6662(d)(1)(C).

* * *

[Reg. §1.199A-1.]

□ [T.D. 9847, 2-4-2019 (*corrected* 4-16-2019.]

§1.199A-2. Determination of W-2 wages and unadjusted basis immediately after acquisition of qualified property.—(a) *Scope.*—(1) *In general.*—This section provides guidance on calculating a trade or business's W-2 wages properly allocable to QBI (W-2 wages) and the trade or business's unadjusted basis immediately after acquisition of all qualified property (UBIA of qualified property). The provisions of this section apply solely for purposes of section 199A of the Internal Revenue Code (Code).

(2) *W-2 wages.*—Paragraph (b) of this section provides guidance on the determination of W-2 wages. The determination of W-2 wages must be made for each trade or business by the individual or RPE that directly conducts the trade or business (or aggregated trade or business). In the case of W-2 wages paid by an RPE, the RPE must determine and report W-2 wages for each trade or business (or aggregated trade or business) conducted by the RPE. W-2 wages are presumed to be zero if not determined and reported for each trade or business (or aggregated trade or business).

* * *

(b) *W-2 wages.*—(1) *In general.*—Section 199A(b)(2)(B) provides limitations on the section 199A deduction based on the W-2 wages paid with respect to each trade or business (or aggregated trade or business). Section 199A(b)(4)(B) provides that W-2 wages do not include any amount which is not properly allocable to QBI for purposes of section 199A(c)(1). This section provides a three step process for determining the W-2 wages paid with respect to a trade or business that are properly allocable to QBI. First, each individual or RPE must determine its total W-2 wages paid for the taxable year under the rules in paragraph (b)(2) of this section. Second, each individual or RPE must allocate its W-2 wages between or among one or more trades or businesses under the rules in paragraph (b)(3) of this section. Third, each individual or RPE must determine the amount of such wages with respect to each trade or business, which are allocable to the QBI of the trade or business (or aggregated trade or business) under the rules in paragraph (b)(4) of this section.

(2) *Definition of W-2 wages.*—(i) *In general.*—Section 199A(b)(4)(A) provides that the term W-2 wages means with respect to any person for any taxable year of such person, the amounts described in section 6051(a)(3) and (8) paid by such person with respect to employment of employees by such person during the calendar year ending during such taxable year. Thus, the term W-2 wages includes the total amount of wages as defined in section 3401(a) plus the total amount of elective deferrals (within the meaning of section 402(g)(3)), the compensation deferred under section 457, and the amount of designated Roth contributions (as defined in section 402A). For this purpose, except as provided in paragraphs (b)(2)(iv)(C)(*2*) and (b)(2)(iv)(D) of this section, the Forms W-2, "Wage and Tax Statement," or any subsequent form or document used in determining the amount of W-2 wages, are those issued for the calendar year ending during the individual's or RPE's taxable year for wages paid to employees (or former employees) of the individual or RPE for employment by the individual or RPE. For purposes of this section, employees of the individual or RPE are limited to employees of the individual or RPE as defined in section 3121(d)(1) and (2). (For purposes of section 199A, this includes officers of an S corporation and employees of an individual or RPE under common law.)

(ii) *Wages paid by a person other than a common law employer.*—In determining W-2 wages, an individual or RPE may take into account any W-2 wages paid by another person and reported by the other person on Forms W-2 with the other person as the employer listed in Box c of the Forms W-2, provided that the W-2 wages were paid to common law employees or officers of the individual or RPE for employment by the individual or RPE. In such cases, the person paying the W-2 wages and reporting the W-2 wages on Forms W-2 is precluded from taking into account such wages for purposes of determining W-2 wages with respect to that person. For purposes of this paragraph (b)(2)(ii), persons that pay and report W-2 wages on behalf of or with respect to others can include, but are not limited to, certified professional employer organizations under section 7705, statutory employers under section 3401(d)(1), and agents under section 3504.

(iii) *Requirement that wages must be reported on return filed with the Social Security Administration (SSA).*—(A) *In general.*—Pursuant to section 199A(b)(4)(C), the term W-2 wages does not include any amount that is not properly included in a return filed with SSA on or before the 60th day after the due date (including extensions) for such return. Under § 31.6051-2 of this chapter, each Form W-2 and the transmittal Form W-3, "Transmittal of Wage and Tax Statements," together constitute an information return to be filed with SSA. Similarly, each Form W-2c, "Corrected Wage and Tax Statement," and the transmittal Form W-3 or W-3c, "Transmittal of Corrected Wage and Tax Statements," together constitute an information return to be filed with SSA. In determining whether any amount has been properly included in a return filed with SSA on or before the 60th day after the due date (including extensions) for such return, each Form W-2 together with its accompanying Form W-3 will be considered a separate information return and each Form W-2c together with its accompanying Form W-3 or Form W-3c will be considered a separate information return. Section 6071(c) provides that Forms W-2 and W-3 must be filed on or before January 31 of the year following the calendar year to which such returns relate (but see the special rule in

§31.6071(a)-1T(a)(3)(i) of this chapter for monthly returns filed under §31.6011(a)-5(a) of this chapter). Corrected Forms W-2 are required to be filed with SSA on or before January 31 of the year following the year in which the correction is made.

* * *

(iv) *Methods for calculating W-2 wages.*—(A) *In general.*—The Secretary may provide for methods to be used in calculating W-2 wages, including W-2 wages for short taxable years by publication in the Internal Revenue Bulletin (see §601.601(d)(2)(ii)*(b)* of this chapter).

(B) *Acquisition or disposition of a trade or business.—(1) In general.*—In the case of an acquisition or disposition of a trade or business, the major portion of a trade or business, or the major portion of a separate unit of a trade or business that causes more than one individual or entity to be an employer of the employees of the acquired or disposed of trade or business during the calendar year, the W-2 wages of the individual or entity for the calendar year of the acquisition or disposition are allocated between each individual or entity based on the period during which the employees of the acquired or disposed of trade or business were employed by the individual or entity, regardless of which permissible method is used for reporting predecessor and successor wages on Form W-2, "Wage and Tax Statement." For this purpose, the period of employment is determined consistently with the principles for determining whether an individual is an employee described in paragraph (b) of this section.

(2) Acquisition or disposition.—For purposes of this paragraph (b)(2)(iv)(B), the term *acquisition or disposition* includes an incorporation, a formation, a liquidation, a reorganization, or a purchase or sale of assets.

(C) *Application in the case of a person with a short taxable year.—(1) In general.*—In the case of an individual or RPE with a short taxable year, subject to the rules of paragraph (b)(2) of this section, the W-2 wages of the individual or RPE for the short taxable year include only those wages paid during the short taxable year to employees of the individuals or RPE, only those elective deferrals (within the meaning of section 402(g)(3)) made during the short taxable year by employees of the individual or RPE and only compensation actually deferred under section 457 during the short taxable year with respect to employees of the individual or RPE.

(2) Short taxable year that does not include December 31.—If an individual or RPE has a short taxable year that does not contain a calendar year ending during such short taxable year, wages paid to employees for employment by such individual or RPE during the short taxable year are treated as W-2 wages for such short taxable year for purposes of paragraph (b) of this section (if the wages would otherwise meet the requirements to be W-2 wages under this section but for the requirement that a calendar year must end during the short taxable year).

* * *

(3) *Allocation of wages to trades or businesses.*—After calculating total W-2 wages for a taxable year, each individual or RPE that directly conducts more than one trade or business must allocate those wages among its various trades or businesses. W-2 wages must be allocated to the trade or business that generated those wages. In the case of W-2 wages that are allocable to more than one trade or business, the portion of the W-2 wages allocable to each trade or business is determined in the same manner as the expenses associated with those wages are allocated among the trades or businesses under §1.199A-3(b)(5).

(4) *Allocation of wages to QBI.*—Once W-2 wages for each trade or business have been determined, each individual or RPE must identify the amount of W-2 wages properly allocable to QBI for each trade or business (or aggregated trade or business). W-2 wages are properly allocable to QBI if the associated wage expense is taken into account in computing QBI under §1.199A-3. In the case of an RPE, the wage expense must be allocated and reported to the partners or shareholders of the RPE as required by the Code, including subchapters K and S of chapter 1 of subtitle A of the Code. The RPE must also identify and report the associated W-2 wages to its partners or shareholders.

(5) *Non-duplication rule.*—Amounts that are treated as W-2 wages for a taxable year under any method cannot be treated as W-2 wages of any other taxable year. Also, an amount cannot be treated as W-2 wages by more than one trade or business (or aggregated trade or business).

(c) *UBIA of qualified property.*—(1) *Qualified property.*—(i) *In general.*—The term *qualified property* means, with respect to any trade or business (or aggregated trade or business) of an individual or RPE for a taxable year, tangible property of a character subject to the allowance for depreciation under section 167(a)—

(A) Which is held by, and available for use in, the trade or business (or aggregated trade or business) at the close of the taxable year;

(B) Which is used at any point during the taxable year in the trade or business's (or aggregated trade or business's) production of QBI; and

(C) The depreciable period for which has not ended before the close of the individual's or RPE's taxable year.

(ii) *Improvements to qualified property.*—In the case of any addition to, or improvement of, qualified property that has already been placed in service by the individual or RPE, such addition or improvement is treated as separate qualified property first placed in service on the date such addition or improvement is placed in service for purposes of paragraph (c)(2) of this section.

(iii) *Adjustments under sections 734(b) and 743(b).*—Excess section 743(b) basis adjustments as defined in paragraph (a)(3)(iv)(B) of this section are treated as qualified property. Otherwise, basis adjustments under sections 734(b) and 743(b) are not treated as qualified property.

(iv) *Property acquired at end of year.*—Property is not qualified property if the property is acquired within 60 days of the end of the taxable year and disposed of within 120 days of acquisition without having been used in a trade or business for at least 45 days prior to disposition, unless the taxpayer demonstrates that the principal purpose of the acquisition and disposition was a purpose other than increasing the section 199A deduction.

(2) *Depreciable period.*—(i) *In general.*—The term *depreciable period* means, with respect to qualified property of a trade or business, the period beginning on the date the property was first placed in service by the individual or RPE and ending on the later of—

(A) The date that is 10 years after such date; or

(B) The last day of the last full year in the applicable recovery period that would apply to the property under section 168(c), regardless of any application of section 168(g).

(ii) *Additional first-year depreciation under section 168.*—The additional first-year depreciation deduction allowable under section 168 (for example, under section 168(k) or (m)) does not affect the applicable recovery period under this paragraph for the qualified property.

(iii) *Qualified property acquired in transactions subject to section 1031 or section 1033.*—Solely for purposes of paragraph (c)(2)(i) of this section, the following rules apply to qualified property acquired in a like-kind exchange or in an involuntary conversion (replacement property).

(A) *Replacement property received in a section 1031 or 1033 transaction.*—The date on which replacement property that is of like-kind to relinquished property or is similar or related in service or use to involuntarily converted property was first placed in service by the individual or RPE is determined as follows—

(1) For the portion of the individual's or RPE's UBIA, as defined in paragraph (c)(3) of this section, in such replacement property that does not exceed the individual's or RPE's UBIA in the relinquished property or involuntarily converted property, the date such portion in the replacement property was first placed in service by the individual or RPE is the date on which the relinquished property or involuntarily converted property was first placed in service by the individual or RPE; and

(2) For the portion of the individual's or RPE's UBIA, as defined in paragraph (c)(3) of this section, in such replacement property that exceeds the individual's or RPE's UBIA in the relinquished property or involuntarily converted property, such portion in the replacement property is treated as separate qualified property that the individual or RPE first placed in service on the date on which the replacement property was first placed in service by the individual or RPE.

(B) *Other property received in a section 1031 or 1033 transaction.*—Other property, as defined in paragraph (c)(3)(ii) or (iii) of this section, that is qualified property is treated as separate qualified property that the individual or RPE first placed in service on the date on which such other property was first placed in service by the individual or RPE.

(iv) *Qualified property acquired in transactions described in section 168(i)(7)(B).*—If an individual or RPE acquires qualified property in a transaction described in section 168(i)(7)(B) (pertaining to treatment of transferees in certain nonrecognition transactions), the individual or RPE must determine the date on which the qualified property was first placed in service solely for purposes of paragraph (c)(2)(i) of this section as follows—

(A) For the portion of the transferee's UBIA in the qualified property that does not exceed the transferor's UBIA in such property, the date such portion was first placed in service by the transferee is the date on which the transferor first placed the qualified property in service; and

(B) For the portion of the transferee's UBIA in the qualified property that exceeds the transferor's UBIA in such property, such portion is treated as separate qualified property that the transferee first placed in service on the date of the transfer.

(v) *Excess section 743(b) basis adjustment.*—Solely for purposes of paragraph (c)(2)(i) of this section, an excess section 743(b) basis adjustment with respect to an item of partnership property that is qualified property is treated as being placed in service when the transfer of the partnership interest occurs, and the recovery period for such property is determined under § 1.743-1(j)(4)(i)(B) with respect to positive basis adjustments and § 1.743-1(j)(4)(ii)(B) with respect to negative basis adjustments.

(3) *Unadjusted basis immediately after acquisition.*—(i) *In general.*—Except as provided in paragraphs (c)(3)(ii) through (v) of this section, the term *unadjusted basis immediately after acquisition* (UBIA) means the basis on the placed in service date of the property as determined under section 1012 or other applicable sections of chapter 1 of the Code, including the provisions of subchapters O (relating to gain or loss on dispositions of property), C (relating to corporate distributions and adjustments), K (relating to partners and partnerships), and P (relating to capital gains and losses). UBIA is determined without regard to any adjustments described in section 1016(a)(2) or (3), to any adjustments for tax credits claimed by the individual or RPE (for example, under section 50(c)), or to any adjustments for any portion of the basis which the individual or RPE has elected to treat as an expense (for example, under sections 179, 179B, or 179C). However, UBIA does reflect the reduction in basis for the percentage of the individual's or RPE's use of property for the taxable year other than in the trade or business.

(ii) *Qualified property acquired in a like-kind exchange.*—(A) *In general.*—Solely for purposes of this section, if property that is qualified property (replacement property) is acquired in a like-kind exchange that qualifies for deferral of gain or loss under section 1031, then the UBIA of such property is the same as the UBIA of the qualified property exchanged (relinquished property), decreased by excess boot or increased by the amount of money paid or the fair market value of property not of a like kind to the relinquished property (other property) transferred by the taxpayer to acquire the replacement property. If the taxpayer acquires more than one piece of qualified property as replacement property that is of a like kind to the relinquished property in an exchange described in section 1031, UBIA is apportioned between or among the qualified replacement properties in proportion to their relative fair market values. Other property received by the taxpayer in a section 1031 transaction that is qualified property has a UBIA equal to the fair market value of such other property.

(B) *Excess boot.*—For purposes of paragraph (c)(3)(ii)(A) of this section, *excess boot* is the amount of any money or the fair market value of other property received by the taxpayer in the exchange over the amount of appreciation in the relinquished property. Appreciation for this purpose is the excess of the fair market value of the relinquished property on the date of the exchange over the fair market value of the relinquished property on the date of the acquisition by the taxpayer.

(iii) *Qualified property acquired pursuant to an involuntary conversion.*—(A) *In general.*—Solely for purposes of this section, if qualified property is compulsorily or involuntarily converted (converted property) within the meaning of section 1033 and qualified replacement property is acquired in a transaction that qualifies for deferral of gain under section 1033, then the UBIA of the replacement property is the same as the UBIA of the converted property, decreased by excess boot or increased by the amount of money paid or the fair market value of property not similar or related in service or use to the converted property (other property) transferred by the taxpayer to acquire the replacement property. If the taxpayer acquires more than one piece of qualified replacement property that meets the similar or related in service or use requirements in section 1033, UBIA is apportioned between the qualified replacement properties in proportion to their relative fair market values. Other property acquired by the taxpayer with the proceeds of an involuntary conversion that is qualified property has a UBIA equal to the fair market value of such other property.

(B) *Excess boot.*—For purposes of paragraph (c)(3)(iii)(A) of this section, *excess boot* is the amount of any money or the fair market value of other property received by the taxpayer in the conversion over the amount of appreciation in the converted property. Appreciation for this purpose is the excess of the fair market value of the converted property on the date of the conversion over the fair market value of the converted property on the date of the acquisition by the taxpayer.

(iv) *Qualified property acquired in transactions described in section 168(i)(7)(B).*—Solely for purposes of this section, if qualified property is acquired in a transaction described in section 168(i)(7)(B) (pertaining to treatment of transferees in certain nonrecognition transactions), the transferee's UBIA in the qualified property shall be the same as the transferor's UBIA in the property, decreased by the amount of money received by the transferor in the transaction or increased by the amount of money paid by the transferee to acquire the property in the transaction.

(v) *Qualified property acquired from a decedent.*—In the case of qualified property acquired from a decedent and immediately placed in service, the UBIA of the property will generally be the fair market value at the date of the decedent's death under section 1014. See section 1014 and the regulations thereunder. Solely for purposes of paragraph (c)(2)(i) of this section, a new depreciable period for the property commences as of the date of the decedent's death.

(vi) *Property acquired in a nonrecognition transaction with principal purpose of increasing UBIA.*—If qualified property is acquired in a transaction described in section 1031, 1033, or 168(i)(7) with the principal purpose of increasing the UBIA of the qualified property, the UBIA of the acquired qualified property is its basis as determined under relevant Code sections and not under the rules described in paragraphs (c)(3)(i) through (iv) of this section. For example, in a section 1031 transaction undertaken with the principal purpose of increasing the UBIA of the replacement property, the UBIA of the replacement property is its basis as determined under section 1031(d).

* * *

[Reg. § 1.199A-2.]

☐ [T.D. 9847, 2-4-2019 (*corrected* 4-16-2019).]

§ 1.199A-3. Qualified business income, qualified REIT dividends, and qualified PTP income.—(a) *In general.*—This section provides rules on the determination of a trade or business's qualified business income (QBI), as well as the determination of qualified real estate investment trust (REIT) dividends and qualified publicly traded partnership (PTP) income. The provisions of this section apply solely for purposes of section 199A of the Internal Revenue Code (Code). Paragraph (b) of this section provides rules for the determination of QBI. Paragraph (c) of this section provides rules for the determination of qualified REIT dividends and qualified PTP income. QBI must be determined and reported for each trade or business by the individual or relevant passthrough entity (RPE) that directly conducts the trade or business before applying the aggregation rules of § 1.199A-4.

(b) *Definition of qualified business income.*—(1) *In general.*—For purposes of this section, the term *qualified business income* or *QBI* means, for any taxable year, the net amount of qualified items of income, gain, deduction, and loss with respect to any trade or business of the taxpayer as described in paragraph (b)(2) of this section, provided the other requirements of this section and section 199A are satisfied (including, for example, the exclusion of income not effectively connected with a United States trade or business).

(i) *Section 751 gain.*—With respect to a partnership, if section 751(a) or (b) applies, then gain or loss attributable to assets of the partnership giving rise to ordinary income under section 751(a) or (b) is considered attributable to the trades or businesses conducted by the partnership, and is taken into account for purposes of computing QBI.

(ii) *Guaranteed payments for the use of capital.*—Income attributable to a guaranteed payment for the use of capital is not considered to be attributable to a trade or business, and thus is not taken into account for purposes of computing QBI except to the extent properly allocable to a trade or business of the recipient. The partnership's deduction associated with the guaranteed payment will be taken into account for purposes of computing QBI if such deduction is properly allocable to the trade or business and is otherwise deductible for Federal income tax purposes.

(iii) *Section 481 adjustments.*—Section 481 adjustments (whether positive or negative) are taken into account for purposes of computing QBI to the extent that the requirements of this section and section 199A are otherwise satisfied, but only if the adjustment arises in taxable years ending after December 31, 2017.

(iv) *Previously disallowed losses.*—Generally, previously disallowed losses or deductions (including under sections 465, 469, 704(d), and 1366(d)) allowed in the taxable year are taken into account for purposes of computing QBI. These losses shall be used, for purposes of section 199A and these regulations, in order from the oldest to the most recent on a first-in, first-out (FIFO) basis. However, losses or deductions that were disallowed, suspended, limited, or carried over from taxable years ending before January 1, 2018 (including under sections 465, 469, 704(d), and 1366(d)), are not taken into account in a later taxable year for purposes of computing QBI.

(v) *Net operating losses.*—Generally, a net operating loss deduction under section 172 is not considered with respect to a trade or business and therefore, is not taken into account in computing QBI. However, an excess business loss under section 461(l) is treated as a net operating loss carryover to the following taxable year and is taken into account for purposes of computing QBI in the subsequent taxable year in which it is deducted.

(vi) *Other deductions.*—Generally, deductions attributable to a trade or business are taken into account for purposes of computing QBI to the extent that the requirements of section 199A and this section are otherwise satisfied. For purposes of section 199A only, deductions such as the deductible portion of the tax on self-employment income under section 164(f), the self-employed health insurance deduction under section 162(l), and the deduction for contributions to qualified retirement plans under section 404 are considered attributable to a trade or business to the extent that the individual's gross income from the trade or business is taken into account in calculating the allowable deduction, on a proportionate basis to the gross income received from the trade or business.

(2) *Qualified items of income, gain, deduction, and loss.*—(i) *In general.*—The term *qualified items of income, gain, deduction, and loss* means items of gross income, gain, deduction, and loss to the extent such items are—

(A) Effectively connected with the conduct of a trade or business within the United States (within the meaning of section 864(c), determined by substituting "trade or business (within the meaning of section 199A)" for "nonresident alien individual or a foreign corporation" or for "a foreign corporation" each place it appears); and

(B) Included or allowed in determining taxable income for the taxable year.

(ii) *Items not taken into account.*—Notwithstanding paragraph (b)(2)(i) of this section and in accordance with section 199A(c)(3)(B) and (c)(4), the following items are not taken into account as qualified items of income, gain, deduction, or loss and thus are not included in determining QBI:

(A) Any item of short-term capital gain, short-term capital loss, long-term capital gain, or long-term capital loss, including any item treated as one of such items under any other provision of the Code. This provision does not apply to the extent an item is treated as anything other than short-term capital gain, short-term capital loss, long-term capital gain, or long-term capital loss.

(B) Any dividend, income equivalent to a dividend, or payment in lieu of dividends described in section 954(c)(1)(G). Any amount described in section 1385(a)(1) is not treated as described in this clause.

(C) Any interest income other than interest income which is properly allocable to a trade or business. For purposes of section 199A and this section, interest income attributable to an investment of working capital, reserves, or similar accounts is not properly allocable to a trade or business.

(D) Any item of gain or loss described in section 954(c)(1)(C) (transactions in commodities) or section 954(c)(1)(D) (excess foreign currency gains) applied in each case by substituting "trade or business (within the meaning of section 199A)" for "controlled foreign corporation."

(E) Any item of income, gain, deduction, or loss described in section 954(c)(1)(F) (income from notional principal contracts) determined without regard to section 954(c)(1)(F)(ii) and other than items attributable to notional principal contracts entered into in transactions qualifying under section 1221(a)(7).

(F) Any amount received from an annuity which is not received in connection with the trade or business.

(G) Any qualified REIT dividends as defined in paragraph (c)(2) of this section or qualified PTP income as defined in paragraph (c)(3) of this section.

(H) Reasonable compensation received by a shareholder from an S corporation. However, the S corporation's deduction for such reasonable compensation will reduce QBI if such deduction is properly allocable to the trade or business and is otherwise deductible for Federal income tax purposes.

(I) Any guaranteed payment described in section 707(c) received by a partner for services rendered with respect to the trade or business, regardless of whether the partner is an individual or an RPE. However, the partnership's deduction for such guaranteed payment will reduce QBI if such deduction is properly allocable to the trade or business and is otherwise deductible for Federal income tax purposes.

(J) Any payment described in section 707(a) received by a partner for services rendered with respect to the trade or business, regardless of whether the partner is an individual or an RPE. However, the partnership's deduction for such payment will reduce QBI if such deduction is properly allocable to the trade or business and is otherwise deductible for Federal income tax purposes.

* * *

(4) *Wages.*—Expenses for all wages paid (or incurred in the case of an accrual method taxpayer) must be taken into account in computing QBI (if the requirements of this section

and section 199A are satisfied) regardless of the application of the W-2 wage limitation described in § 1.199A-1 (d) (2) (iv).

(5) *Allocation of items among directly-conducted trades or businesses.*—If an individual or an RPE directly conducts multiple trades or businesses, and has items of QBI that are properly attributable to more than one trade or business, the individual or RPE must allocate those items among the several trades or businesses to which they are attributable using a reasonable method based on all the facts and circumstances. The individual or RPE may use a different reasonable method with respect to different items of income, gain, deduction, and loss. The chosen reasonable method for each item must be consistently applied from one taxable year to another and must clearly reflect the income and expenses of each trade or business. The overall combination of methods must also be reasonable based on all facts and circumstances. The books and records maintained for a trade or business must be consistent with any allocations under this paragraph (b) (5).

(c) *Qualified REIT Dividends and Qualified PTP Income.*—(1) *In general.*—Qualified REIT dividends and qualified PTP income are the sum of qualified REIT dividends as defined in paragraph (c) (2) of this section earned directly or through an RPE and the net amount of qualified PTP income as defined in paragraph (c) (3) of this section earned directly or through an RPE.

(2) *Qualified REIT dividend.*—(i) The term *qualified REIT dividend* means any dividend from a REIT received during the taxable year which—

(A) Is not a capital gain dividend, as defined in section 857 (b) (3); and

(B) Is not qualified dividend income, as defined in section 1 (h) (11).

(ii) The term qualified REIT dividend does not include any REIT dividend received with respect to any share of REIT stock—

(A) That is held by the shareholder for 45 days or less (taking into account the principles of section 246 (c) (3) and (4)) during the 91-day period beginning on the date which is 45 days before the date on which such share becomes ex-dividend with respect to such dividend; or

(B) To the extent that the shareholder is under an obligation (whether pursuant to a short sale or otherwise) to make related payments with respect to positions in substantially similar or related property.

(3) *Qualified PTP income.*—(i) *In general.*—The term *qualified PTP income* means the sum of—

(A) The net amount of such taxpayer's allocable share of income, gain, deduction, and loss from a PTP as defined in section 7704 (b) that is not taxed as a corporation under section 7704 (a); plus

(B) Any gain or loss attributable to assets of the PTP giving rise to ordinary income under section 751 (a) or (b) that is considered attributable to the trades or businesses conducted by the partnership.

(ii) *Special rules.*—The rules applicable to the determination of QBI described in paragraph (b) of this section also apply to the determination of a taxpayer's allocable share of income, gain, deduction, and loss from a PTP. An individual's allocable share of income from a PTP, and any section 751 gain or loss is qualified PTP income only to the extent the items meet the qualifications of section 199A and this section, including the requirement that the item is included or allowed in determining taxable income for the taxable year, and the requirement that the item be effectively connected with the conduct of a trade or business within the United States. For example, if an individual owns an interest in a PTP, and for the taxable year is allocated a distributive share of net loss which is disallowed under the passive activity rules of section 469, such loss is not taken into account for purposes of section 199A. The specified service trade or business limitations described in §§ 1.199A-1 (d) (3) and 1.199A-5 also apply to income earned from a PTP. Furthermore, each PTP is required to determine its qualified PTP income for each trade or business and report that information to its owners as described in § 1.199A-6 (b) (3).

* * *

[Reg. § 1.199A-3.]

☐ [T.D. 9847, 2-4-2019.]

§ 1.199A-4. Aggregation.—(a) *Scope and purpose.*—An individual or RPE may be engaged in more than one trade or business. Except as provided in this section, each trade or business is a separate trade or business for purposes of applying the limitations described in § 1.199A-1 (d) (2) (iv). This section sets forth rules to allow individuals and RPEs to aggregate trades or businesses, treating the aggregate as a single trade or business for purposes of applying the limitations described in § 1.199A-1 (d) (2) (iv). Trades or businesses may be aggregated only to the extent provided in this section, but aggregation by taxpayers is not required.

(b) *Aggregation rules.*—(1) *General rule.*—Trades or businesses may be aggregated only if an individual or RPE can demonstrate that—

(i) The same person or group of persons, directly or by attribution under sections 267(b) or 707(b), owns 50 percent or more of each trade or business to be aggregated, meaning in the case of such trades or businesses owned by an S corporation, 50 percent or more of the issued and outstanding shares of the corporation, or, in the case of such trades or businesses owned by a partnership, 50 percent or more of the capital or profits in the partnership;

(ii) The ownership described in paragraph (b)(1)(i) of this section exists for a majority of the taxable year, including the last day of the taxable year, in which the items attributable to each trade or business to be aggregated are included in income;

(iii) All of the items attributable to each trade or business to be aggregated are reported on returns with the same taxable year, not taking into account short taxable years;

(iv) None of the trades or businesses to be aggregated is a *specified service trade or business* (SSTB) as defined in § 1.199A-5; and

(v) The trades or businesses to be aggregated satisfy at least two of the following factors (based on all of the facts and circumstances):

(A) The trades or businesses provide products, property, or services that are the same or customarily offered together.

(B) The trades or businesses share facilities or share significant centralized business elements, such as personnel, accounting, legal, manufacturing, purchasing, human resources, or information technology resources.

(C) The trades or businesses are operated in coordination with, or reliance upon, one or more of the businesses in the aggregated group (for example, supply chain interdependencies).

(2) *Operating rules.*—(i) *Individuals.*—An individual may aggregate trades or businesses operated directly or through an RPE to the extent an aggregation is not inconsistent with the aggregation of an RPE. If an individual aggregates multiple trades or businesses under paragraph (b)(1) of this section, QBI, W-2 wages, and UBIA of qualified property must be combined for the aggregated trades or businesses for purposes of applying the W-2 wage and UBIA of qualified property limitations described in § 1.199A-1(d)(2)(iv). An individual may not subtract from the trades or businesses aggregated by an RPE but may aggregate additional trades or businesses with the RPE's aggregation if the rules of this section are otherwise satisfied.

(ii) *RPEs.*—An RPE may aggregate trades or businesses operated directly or through a lower-tier RPE to the extent an aggregation is not inconsistent with the aggregation of a lower-tier RPE. If an RPE itself does not aggregate, multiple owners of an RPE need not aggregate in the same manner. If an RPE aggregates multiple trades or businesses under paragraph (b)(1) of this section, the RPE must compute and report QBI, W-2 wages, and UBIA of qualified property for the aggregated trade or business under the rules described in § 1.199A-6(b). An RPE may not subtract from the trades or businesses aggregated by a lower-tier RPE but may aggregate additional trades or businesses with a lower-tier RPE's aggregation if the rules of this section are otherwise satisfied.

(c) *Reporting and consistency requirements.*—(1) *Individuals.*—Once an individual chooses to aggregate two or more trades or businesses, the individual must consistently report the aggregated trades or businesses in all subsequent taxable years. A failure to aggregate will not be considered to be an aggregation for purposes of this rule. An individual that fails to aggregate may not aggregate trades or businesses on an amended return (other than an amended return for the 2018 taxable year). However, an individual may add a newly created or newly acquired (including through nonrecognition transfers) trade or business to an existing aggregated trade or business (including the aggregated trade or business of an RPE) if the requirements of paragraph (b)(1) of this section are satisfied. In a subsequent year, if there is a significant change in facts and circumstances such that an individual's prior aggregation of trades or businesses no longer qualifies for aggregation under the rules of this section, then the trades or businesses will no longer be aggregated within the meaning of this section, and the individual must reapply the rules in paragraph (b)(1) of this section to determine a new permissible aggregation (if any). An individual also must report aggregated trades or businesses of an RPE in which the individual holds a direct or indirect interest.

(2) *Individual disclosure.*—(i) *Required annual disclosure.*—For each taxable year, individuals must attach a statement to their returns identifying each trade or business aggregated under paragraph (b)(1) of this section. The statement must contain —

(A) A description of each trade or business;

(B) The name and EIN of each entity in which a trade or business is operated;

(C) Information identifying any trade or business that was formed, ceased operations, was acquired, or was disposed of during the taxable year;

(D) Information identifying any aggregated trade or business of an RPE in which the individual holds an ownership interest; and

(E) Such other information as the Commissioner may require in forms, instructions, or other published guidance.

(ii) *Failure to disclose.*—If an individual fails to attach the statement required in paragraph (c)(2)(i) of this section, the Commissioner may disaggregate the individual's trades or businesses. The individual may not aggregate trades or businesses that are disaggregated by the Commissioner for the subsequent three taxable years.

(3) *RPEs.*—Once an RPE chooses to aggregate two or more trades or businesses, the RPE must consistently report the aggregated trades or businesses in all subsequent taxable years. A failure to aggregate will not be considered to be an aggregation for purposes of this rule. An RPE that fails to aggregate may not aggregate trades or businesses on an amended return (other than an amended return for the 2018 taxable year). However, an RPE may add a newly created or newly acquired (including through non-recognition transfers) trade or business to an existing aggregated trade or business (including the aggregated trade or business of a lower-tier RPE) if the requirements of paragraph (b)(1) of this section are satisfied. In a subsequent year, if there is a significant change in facts and circumstances such that an RPE's prior aggregation of trades or businesses no longer qualifies for aggregation under the rules of this section, then the trades or businesses will no longer be aggregated within the meaning of this section, and the RPE must reapply the rules in paragraph (b)(1) of this section to determine a new permissible aggregation (if any). An RPE also must report aggregated trades or businesses of a lower-tier RPE in which the RPE holds a direct or indirect interest.

(4) *RPE disclosure.*—(i) *Required annual disclosure.*—For each taxable year, RPEs (including each RPE in a tiered structure) must attach a statement to each owner's Schedule K-1 identifying each trade or business aggregated under paragraph (b)(1) of this section. The statement must contain —

(A) A description of each trade or business;

(B) The name and EIN of each entity in which a trade or business is operated;

(C) Information identifying any trade or business that was formed, ceased operations, was acquired, or was disposed of during the taxable year;

(D) Information identifying any aggregated trade or business of an RPE in which the RPE holds an ownership interest; and

(E) Such other information as the Commissioner may require in forms, instructions, or other published guidance.

(ii) *Failure to disclose.*—If an RPE fails to attach the statement required in paragraph (c)(4)(i) of this section, the Commissioner may disaggregate the RPE's trades or businesses. The RPE may not aggregate trades or businesses that are disaggregated by the Commissioner for the subsequent three taxable years.

* * *

[Reg. § 1.199A-4.]

☐ [T.D. 9847, 2-4-2019 (*corrected* 4-16-2019).]

§ 1.199A-5. Specified service trades or businesses and the trade or business of performing services as an employee.—(a) *Scope and effect.*—(1) *Scope.*—This section provides guidance on specified service trades or businesses (SSTBs) and the trade or business of performing services as an employee. This paragraph (a) describes the effect of a trade or business being an SSTB and the trade or business of performing services as an employee. Paragraph (b) of this section provides definitional guidance on SSTBs. Paragraph (c) of this section provides special rules related to SSTBs. Paragraph (d) of this section provides guidance on the trade or business of performing services as an employee. The provisions of this section apply solely for purposes of section 199A of the Internal Revenue Code (Code).

(2) *Effect of being an SSTB.*—If a trade or business is an SSTB, no qualified business income (QBI), W-2 wages, or unadjusted basis immediately after acquisition (UBIA) of qualified property from the SSTB may be taken into account by any individual whose taxable income exceeds the phase-in range as defined in § 1.199A-1(b)(4), even if the item is derived from an activity that is not itself a specified service activity. The SSTB limitation also applies to income earned from a publicly traded partnership (PTP). If a trade or business conducted by a relevant passthrough entity (RPE) or PTP is an SSTB, this limitation applies to any direct or indirect individual owners of the business, regardless of whether the owner is passive or participated in any specified service activity. However, the SSTB limitation does not apply to individuals with taxable income below the threshold amount as defined in § 1.199A-1(b)(12). A phase-in rule, provided in

§ 1.199A-1 (d) (2), applies to individuals with taxable income within the phase-in range, allowing them to take into account a certain "applicable percentage" of QBI, W-2 wages, and UBIA of qualified property from an SSTB. The phase-in rule also applies to income earned from a PTP. A direct or indirect owner of a trade or business engaged in the performance of a specified service is engaged in the performance of the specified service for purposes of section 199A and this section, regardless of whether the owner is passive or participated in the specified service activity.

(3) *Trade or business of performing services as an employee.*—The trade or business of performing services as an employee is not a trade or business for purposes of section 199A and the regulations thereunder. Therefore, no items of income, gain, deduction, or loss from the trade or business of performing services as an employee constitute QBI within the meaning of section 199A and § 1.199A-3. No taxpayer may claim a section 199A deduction for wage income, regardless of the amount of taxable income.

(b) *Definition of specified service trade or business.*—Except as provided in paragraph (c) (1) of this section, the term *specified service trade or business (SSTB)* means any of the following:

(1) *Listed SSTBs.*—Any trade or business involving the performance of services in one or more of the following fields:

(i) *Health* as described in paragraph (b) (2) (ii) of this section;

(ii) *Law* as described in paragraph (b) (2) (iii) of this section;

(iii) *Accounting* as described in paragraph (b) (2) (iv) of this section;

(iv) *Actuarial science* as described in paragraph (b) (2) (v) of this section;

(v) *Performing arts* as described in paragraph (b) (2) (vi) of this section;

(vi) *Consulting* as described in paragraph (b) (2) (vii) of this section;

(vii) *Athletics* as described in paragraph (b) (2) (viii) of this section;

(viii) *Financial services* as described in paragraph (b) (2) (ix) of this section;

(ix) *Brokerage services* as described in paragraph (b) (2) (x) of this section;

(x) *Investing and investment management* as described in paragraph (b) (2) (xi) of this section;

(xi) *Trading* as described in paragraph (b) (2) (xii) of this section;

(xii) *Dealing in securities (as defined in section 475(c) (2)), partnership interests, or commodities (as defined in section 475(e) (2))* as described in paragraph (b) (2) (xiii) of this section; or

(xiii) *Any trade or business where the principal asset of such trade or business is the reputation or skill of one or more of its employees or owners* as defined in paragraph (b) (2) (xiv) of this section.

(2) *Additional rules for applying section 199A(d) (2) and paragraph (b) of this section.*—(i) *In general.*—(A) *No effect on other tax rules.*—This paragraph (b) (2) provides additional rules for determining whether a business is an SSTB within the meaning of section 199A(d) (2) and paragraph (b) of this section only. The rules of this paragraph (b) (2) apply solely for purposes of section 199A and therefore may not be taken into account for purposes of applying any provision of law or regulation other than section 199A and the regulations thereunder, except to the extent such provision expressly refers to section 199A(d) or this section.

(B) *Hedging transactions.*—Income, deduction, gain or loss from a *hedging transaction* (as defined in § 1.1221-2(b)) entered into by an individual or RPE in the normal course of the individual's or RPE's trade or business is treated as income, deduction, gain, or loss from that trade or business for purposes of this paragraph (b) (2). See also § 1.446-4.

(ii) *Meaning of services performed in the field of health.*—For purposes of section 199A(d) (2) and paragraph (b) (1) (i) of this section only, the *performance of services in the field of health* means the provision of medical services by individuals such as physicians, pharmacists, nurses, dentists, veterinarians, physical therapists, psychologists, and other similar healthcare professionals performing services in their capacity as such. The performance of services in the field of health does not include the provision of services not directly related to a medical services field, even though the services provided may purportedly relate to the health of the service recipient. For example, the performance of services in the field of health does not include the operation of health clubs or health spas that provide physical exercise or conditioning to their customers, payment processing, or the research, testing, and manufacture and/or sales of pharmaceuticals or medical devices.

(iii) *Meaning of services performed in the field of law.*—For purposes of section 199A(d) (2) and paragraph (b) (1) (ii) of this section only, the *performance of services in the field of law* means the performance of legal services by individuals such as lawyers, paralegals, legal arbitrators, mediators, and similar professionals performing services in their capacity as such. The performance of services in the field of law does not include the provision of services that do not require skills unique to the field of law; for example, the provision of services in the field of law does not include the provision of services by printers, delivery services, or stenography services.

(iv) *Meaning of services performed in the field of accounting.*—For purposes of section 199A(d)(2) and paragraph (b)(1)(iii) of this section only, the *performance of services in the field of accounting* means the provision of services by individuals such as accountants, enrolled agents, return preparers, financial auditors, and similar professionals performing services in their capacity as such.

(v) *Meaning of services performed in the field of actuarial science.*—For purposes of section 199A(d)(2) and paragraph (b)(1)(iv) of this section only, the *performance of services in the field of actuarial science* means the provision of services by individuals such as actuaries and similar professionals performing services in their capacity as such.

(vi) *Meaning of services performed in the field of performing arts.*—For purposes of section 199A(d)(2) and paragraph (b)(1)(v) of this section only, the *performance of services in the field of the performing arts* means the performance of services by individuals who participate in the creation of performing arts, such as actors, singers, musicians, entertainers, directors, and similar professionals performing services in their capacity as such. The performance of services in the field of performing arts does not include the provision of services that do not require skills unique to the creation of performing arts, such as the maintenance and operation of equipment or facilities for use in the performing arts. Similarly, the performance of services in the field of the performing arts does not include the provision of services by persons who broadcast or otherwise disseminate video or audio of performing arts to the public.

(vii) *Meaning of services performed in the field of consulting.*—For purposes of section 199A(d)(2) and paragraph (b)(1)(vi) of this section only, the *performance of services in the field of consulting* means the provision of professional advice and counsel to clients to assist the client in achieving goals and solving problems. Consulting includes providing advice and counsel regarding advocacy with the intention of influencing decisions made by a government or governmental agency and all attempts to influence legislators and other government officials on behalf of a client by lobbyists and other similar professionals performing services in their capacity as such. The performance of services in the field of consulting does not include the performance of services other than advice and counsel, such as sales (or economically similar services) or the provision of training and educational courses. For purposes of the preceding sentence, the determination of whether a person's services are sales or economically similar services will be based on all the facts and circumstances of that person's business. Such facts and circumstances include, for example, the manner in which the taxpayer is compensated for the services provided. Performance of services in the field of consulting does not include the performance of consulting services embedded in, or ancillary to, the sale of goods or performance of services on behalf of a trade or business that is otherwise not an SSTB (such as typical services provided by a building contractor) if there is no separate payment for the consulting services. Services within the fields of architecture and engineering are not treated as consulting services.

(viii) *Meaning of services performed in the field of athletics.*—For purposes of section 199A(d)(2) and paragraph (b)(1)(vii) of this section only, the *performance of services in the field of athletics* means the performance of services by individuals who participate in athletic competition such as athletes, coaches, and team managers in sports such as baseball, basketball, football, soccer, hockey, martial arts, boxing, bowling, tennis, golf, skiing, snowboarding, track and field, billiards, and racing. The performance of services in the field of athletics does not include the provision of services that do not require skills unique to athletic competition, such as the maintenance and operation of equipment or facilities for use in athletic events. Similarly, the performance of services in the field of athletics does not include the provision of services by persons who broadcast or otherwise disseminate video or audio of athletic events to the public.

(ix) *Meaning of services performed in the field of financial services.*—For purposes of section 199A(d)(2) and paragraph (b)(1)(viii) of this section only, the *performance of services in the field of financial services* means the provision of financial services to clients including managing wealth, advising clients with respect to finances, developing retirement plans, developing wealth transition plans, the provision of advisory and other similar services regarding valuations, mergers, acquisitions, dispositions, restructurings (including in title 11 of the Code or similar cases), and raising financial capital by underwriting, or acting as a client's agent in the issuance of securities and similar services. This includes services provided by financial advisors, investment bankers, wealth planners, retirement advisors, and other similar professionals performing services in their capacity as such. Solely for purposes of section 199A, the performance of services in the field of financial services does not include taking deposits or making loans, but does include arranging lending transactions between a lender and borrower.

(x) *Meaning of services performed in the field of brokerage services.*—For purposes of section 199A(d)(2) and paragraph (b)(1)(ix) of this section only, the *performance of services in the field of brokerage services* includes services in which a person arranges transactions between a buyer and a seller with respect to securities (as defined in section 475(c)(2)) for a commission or fee. This includes services provided by stock brokers and other similar professionals, but does not include services provided by real estate agents and brokers, or insurance agents and brokers.

(xi) *Meaning of the provision of services in investing and investment management.*—For purposes of section 199A(d)(2) and paragraph (b)(1)(x) of this section only, the *performance of services that consist of investing and investment management* refers to a trade or business involving the receipt of fees for providing investing, asset management, or investment management services, including providing advice with respect to buying and selling investments. The performance of services of investing and investment management does not include directly managing real property.

(xii) *Meaning of the provision of services in trading.*—For purposes of section 199A(d)(2) and paragraph (b)(1)(xi) of this section only, the *performance of services that consist of trading* means a trade or business of trading in securities (as defined in section 475(c)(2)), commodities (as defined in section 475(e)(2)), or partnership interests. Whether a person is a trader in securities, commodities, or partnership interests is determined by taking into account all relevant facts and circumstances, including the source and type of profit that is associated with engaging in the activity regardless of whether that person trades for the person's own account, for the account of others, or any combination thereof.

(xiii) *Meaning of the provision of services in dealing.*—(A) *Dealing in securities.*—For purposes of section 199A(d)(2) and paragraph (b)(1)(xii) of this section only, *the performance of services that consist of dealing in securities (as defined in section 475(c)(2))* means regularly purchasing securities from and selling securities to customers in the ordinary course of a trade or business or regularly offering to enter into, assume, offset, assign, or otherwise terminate positions in securities with customers in the ordinary course of a trade or business. Solely for purposes of the preceding sentence, the performance of services to originate a loan is not treated as the purchase of a security from the borrower in determining whether the lender is dealing in securities.

(B) *Dealing in commodities.*—For purposes of section 199A(d)(2) and paragraph (b)(1)(xii) of this section only, *the performance of services that consist of dealing in commodities (as defined in section 475(e)(2))* means regularly purchasing commodities from and selling commodities to customers in the ordinary course of a trade or business or regularly offering to enter into, assume, offset, assign, or otherwise terminate positions in commodities with customers in the ordinary course of a trade or business. Solely for purposes of the preceding sentence, gains and losses from qualified active sales as defined in paragraph (b)(2)(xiii)(B)(*1*) of this section are not taken into account in determining whether a person is engaged in the trade or business of dealing in commodities.

(1) Qualified active sale.—The term *qualified active sale* means the sale of commodities in the active conduct of a commodities business as a producer, processor, merchant, or handler of commodities if the trade or business is as an active producer, processor, merchant or handler of commodities. A hedging transaction described in paragraph (b)(2)(i)(B) of this section is treated as a qualified active sale. The sale of commodities held by a trade or business other than in its capacity as an active producer, processor, merchant, or handler of commodities is not a qualified active sale. For example, the sale by a trade or business of commodities that were held for investment or speculation would not be a qualified active sale.

(2) Active conduct of a commodities business.—For purposes of paragraph (b)(2)(xiii)(B)(*1*) of this section, a trade or business is engaged in the active conduct of a commodities business as a producer, processor, merchant, or handler of commodities only with respect to commodities for which each of the conditions described in paragraphs (b)(2)(xiii)(B)(*3*) through (*5*) of this section are satisfied.

(3) Directly holds commodities as inventory or similar property.—The commodities trade or business holds the commodities directly, and not through an agent or independent contractor, as inventory or similar prop-

erty. The term inventory or similar property means property that is stock in trade of the trade or business or other property of a kind that would properly be included in the inventory of the trade or business if on hand at the close of the taxable year, or property held by the trade or business primarily for sale to customers in the ordinary course of its trade or business.

(4) *Directly incurs substantial expenses in the ordinary course.*—The commodities trade or business incurs substantial expenses in the ordinary course of the commodities trade or business from engaging in one or more of the following activities directly, and not through an agent or independent contractor—

(i) Substantial activities in the production of the commodities, including planting, tending or harvesting crops, raising or slaughtering livestock, or extracting minerals;

(ii) Substantial processing activities prior to the sale of the commodities, including the blending and drying of agricultural commodities, or the concentrating, refining, mixing, crushing, aerating or milling of commodities; or

(iii) Significant activities as described in paragraph (b)(2)(xiii)(B)(*5*) of this section.

(5) *Significant activities for purposes of paragraph (b)(2)(xiii)(B)(4)(iii) of this section.*—The commodities trade or business performs significant activities with respect to the commodities that consists of—

(i) The physical movement, handling and storage of the commodities, including preparation of contracts and invoices, arranging transportation, insurance and credit, arranging for receipt, transfer or negotiation of shipping documents, arranging storage or warehousing, and dealing with quality claims;

(ii) Owning and operating facilities for storage or warehousing; or

(iii) Owning, chartering, or leasing vessels or vehicles for the transportation of the commodities.

(C) *Dealing in partnership interests.*—For purposes of section 199A(d)(2) and paragraph (b)(1)(xii) of this section only, *the performance of services that consist of dealing in partnership interests* means regularly purchasing partnership interests from and selling partnership interests to customers in the ordinary course of a trade or business or regularly offering to enter into, assume, offset, assign, or otherwise terminate positions in partnership interests with customers in the ordinary course of a trade or business.

(xiv) *Meaning of trade or business where the principal asset of such trade or business is the reputation or skill of one or more employees or owners.*—For purposes of section 199A(d)(2) and paragraph (b)(1)(xiii) of this section only, the term *any trade or business where the principal asset of such trade or business is the reputation or skill of one or more of its employees or owners* means any trade or business that consists of any of the following (or any combination thereof):

(A) A trade or business in which a person receives fees, compensation, or other income for endorsing products or services;

(B) A trade or business in which a person licenses or receives fees, compensation, or other income for the use of an individual's image, likeness, name, signature, voice, trademark, or any other symbols associated with the individual's identity; or

(C) Receiving fees, compensation, or other income for appearing at an event or on radio, television, or another media format.

(D) For purposes of paragraphs (b)(2)(xiv)(A) through (C) of this section, the term *fees, compensation, or other income* includes the receipt of a partnership interest and the corresponding distributive share of income, deduction, gain, or loss from the partnership, or the receipt of stock of an S corporation and the corresponding income, deduction, gain, or loss from the S corporation stock.

* * *

(c) *Special rules.*—(1) *De minimis rule.*—(i) *Gross receipts of $25 million or less.*—For a trade or business with gross receipts of $25 million or less for the taxable year, a trade or business is not an SSTB if less than 10 percent of the gross receipts of the trade or business are attributable to the performance of services in a field described in paragraph (b) of this section. For purposes of determining whether this 10 percent test is satisfied, the performance of any activity incident to the actual performance of services in the field is considered the performance of services in that field.

(ii) *Gross receipts of greater than $25 million.*—For a trade or business with gross receipts of greater than $25 million for the taxable year, the rules of paragraph (c)(1)(i) of this section are applied by substituting "5 percent" for "10 percent" each place it appears.

(iii) *Examples.*—The following examples illustrate the provisions of paragraph (c)(1) of this section.

(A) *Example 1.* Landscape LLC sells lawn care and landscaping equipment and also provides advice and counsel on landscape design for large office parks and residential buildings. The landscape design services include advice on the selection and placement of trees, shrubs, and flowers and are considered to be the performance of services in the field of consulting under paragraphs (b)(1)(vi) and (b)(2)(vii) of this section. Landscape LLC separately invoices for its landscape design services and does not sell the trees, shrubs, or flowers it recommends for use in the landscape design. Landscape LLC maintains one set of books and records and treats the equipment sales and design services as a single trade or business for purposes of sections 162 and 199A. Landscape LLC has gross receipts of $2 million. $250,000 of the gross receipts is attributable to the landscape design services, an SSTB. Because the gross receipts from the consulting services exceed 10 percent of Landscape LLC's total gross receipts, the entirety of Landscape LLC's trade or business is considered an SSTB.

(B) *Example 2.* Animal Care LLC provides veterinarian services performed by licensed staff and also develops and sells its own line of organic dog food at its veterinarian clinic and online. The veterinarian services are considered to be the performance of services in the field of health under paragraphs (b)(1)(i) and (b)(2)(ii) of this section. Animal Care LLC separately invoices for its veterinarian services and the sale of its organic dog food. Animal Care LLC maintains separate books and records for its veterinarian clinic and its development and sale of its dog food. Animal Care LLC also has separate employees who are unaffiliated with the veterinary clinic and who only work on the formulation, marketing, sales, and distribution of the organic dog food products. Animal Care LLC treats its veterinary practice and the dog food development and sales as separate trades or businesses for purposes of section 162 and 199A. Animal Care LLC has gross receipts of $3,000,000. $1,000,000 of the gross receipts is attributable to the veterinary services, an SSTB. Although the gross receipts from the services in the field of health exceed 10 percent of Animal Care LLC's total gross receipts, the dog food development and sales business is not considered an SSTB due to the fact that the veterinary practice and the dog food development and sales are separate trades or businesses under section 162.

(2) *Services or property provided to an SSTB.*—(i) *In general.*—If a trade or business provides property or services to an SSTB within the meaning of this section and there is 50 percent or more common ownership of the trades or businesses, that portion of the trade or business of providing property or services to the 50 percent or more commonly-owned SSTB will be treated as a separate SSTB with respect to the related parties.

(ii) *50 percent or more common ownership.*—For purposes of paragraph (c)(2)(i) and (ii) of this section, 50 percent or more common ownership includes direct or indirect ownership by related parties within the meaning of sections 267(b) or 707(b).

(iii) *Examples.*—The following examples illustrate the provisions of paragraph (c)(2) of this section.

(A) *Example 1.* Law Firm is a partnership that provides legal services to clients, owns its own office building and employs its own administrative staff. Law Firm divides into three partnerships. Partnership 1 performs legal services to clients. Partnership 2 owns the office building and rents the entire building to Partnership 1. Partnership 3 employs the administrative staff and through a contract with Partnership 1 provides administrative services to Partnership 1 in exchange for fees. All three of the partnerships are owned by the same people (the original owners of Law Firm). Because Partnership 2 provides all of its property to Partnership 1, and Partnership 3 provides all of its services to Partnership 1, Partnerships 2 and 3 will each be treated as an SSTB under paragraph (c)(2) of this section.

(B) *Example 2.* Assume the same facts as in Example 1 of this paragraph (c)(2), except that Partnership 2, which owns the office building, rents 50 percent of the building to Partnership 1, which provides legal services, and the other 50 percent to various unrelated third party tenants. Because Partnership 2 is owned by the same people as Partnership 1, the portion of Partnership 2's leasing activity related to the lease of the building to Partnership 1 will be treated as a separate SSTB. The remaining 50 percent of Partnership 2's leasing activity will not be treated as an SSTB.

(d) *Trade or business of performing services as an employee.*—(1) *In general.*—The trade or business of performing services as an employee is not a trade or business for purposes of section 199A and the regulations thereunder. Therefore, no items of income, gain, deduction, and loss from the trade or business of performing services as an employee constitute QBI within the meaning of section 199A and § 1.199A-3. Except as provided in paragraph (d)(3) of this section, income from the trade or business of performing services as an employee refers to all wages (within the meaning of section 3401(a)) and other income earned in a capacity as an employee, including payments described in § 1.6041-2(a)(1) (other than payments to individuals described in section 3121(d)(3)) and § 1.6041-2(b)(1).

(2) *Employer's Federal employment tax classification of employee immaterial.*—For pur-

poses of determining whether wages are earned in a capacity as an employee as provided in paragraph (d)(1) of this section, the treatment of an employee by an employer as anything other than an employee for Federal employment tax purposes is immaterial. Thus, if a worker should be properly classified as an employee, it is of no consequence that the employee is treated as a non-employee by the employer for Federal employment tax purposes.

* * *

[Reg. § 1.199A-5.]

☐ [T.D. 9847, 2-4-2019 (*corrected* 4-16-2019).]

§ 1.199A-6. Relevant passthrough entities (RPEs), publicly traded partnerships (PTPs), trusts, and estates.—(a) *Overview.*—This section provides special rules for RPEs, PTPs, trusts, and estates necessary for the computation of the section 199A deduction of their owners or beneficiaries. Paragraph (b) of this section provides computational and reporting rules for RPEs necessary for individuals who own interests in RPEs to calculate their section 199A deduction. Paragraph (c) of this section provides computational and reporting rules for PTPs necessary for individuals who own interests in PTPs to calculate their section 199A deduction. Paragraph (d) of this section provides computational and reporting rules for trusts (other than grantor trusts) and estates necessary for their beneficiaries to calculate their section 199A deduction.

(b) *Computational and reporting rules for RPEs.*—(1) *In general.*—An RPE must determine and report information attributable to any trades or businesses it is engaged in necessary for its owners to determine their section 199A deduction.

(2) *Computational rules.*—Using the following four rules, an RPE must determine the items necessary for individuals who own interests in the RPE to calculate their section 199A deduction under § 1.199A-1(c) or (d). An RPE that chooses to aggregate trades or businesses under the rules of § 1.199A-4 may determine these items for the aggregated trade or business.

(i) First, the RPE must determine if it is engaged in one or more trades or businesses. The RPE must also determine whether any of its trades or businesses is an SSTB under the rules of § 1.199A-5.

(ii) Second, the RPE must apply the rules in § 1.199A-3 to determine the QBI for each trade or business engaged in directly.

(iii) Third, the RPE must apply the rules in § 1.199A-2 to determine the W-2 wages and UBIA of qualified property for each trade or business engaged in directly.

(iv) Fourth, the RPE must determine whether it has any qualified REIT dividends as defined in § 1.199A-3(c)(1) earned directly or through another RPE. The RPE must also determine the amount of qualified PTP income as defined in § 1.199A-3(c)(2) earned directly or indirectly through investments in PTPs.

(3) *Reporting rules for RPEs.*—(i) *Trade or business directly engaged in.*—An RPE must separately identify and report on the Schedule K-1 issued to its owners for any trade or business (including an aggregated trade or business) engaged in directly by the RPE—

(A) Each owner's allocable share of QBI, W-2 wages, and UBIA of qualified property attributable to each such trade or business; and

(B) Whether any of the trades or businesses described in paragraph (b)(3)(i) of this section is an SSTB.

(ii) *Other items.*—An RPE must also report on an attachment to the Schedule K-1, any QBI, W-2 wages, UBIA of qualified property, or SSTB determinations, reported to it by any RPE in which the RPE owns a direct or indirect interest. The RPE must also report each owner's allocated share of any qualified REIT dividends received by the RPE (including through another RPE) as well as any qualified PTP income or loss received by the RPE for each PTP in which the RPE holds an interest (including through another RPE). Such information can be reported on an amended or late filed return to the extent that the period of limitations remains open.

(iii) *Failure to report information.*—If an RPE fails to separately identify or report on the Schedule K-1 (or any attachments thereto) issued to an owner an item described in paragraph (b)(3)(i) of this section, the owner's share (and the share of any upper-tier indirect owner) of each unreported item of positive QBI, W-2 wages, or UBIA of qualified property attributable to trades or businesses engaged in by that RPE will be presumed to be zero.

(c) *Computational and reporting rules for PTPs.*—(1) *Computational rules.*—Each PTP must determine its QBI under the rules of § 1.199A-3 for each trade or business in which the PTP is engaged in directly. The PTP must also determine whether any of the trades or businesses it is engaged in directly is an SSTB.

(2) *Reporting rules.*—Each PTP is required to separately identify and report the information described in paragraph (c)(1) of this section on Schedules K-1 issued to its part-

ners. Each PTP must also determine and report any qualified REIT dividends or qualified PTP income or loss received by the PTP including through an RPE, a REIT, or another PTP. A PTP is not required to determine or report W-2 wages or the UBIA of qualified property attributable to trades or businesses it is engaged in directly.

(d) *Application to trusts, estates, and beneficiaries.*—(1) *In general.*—A trust or estate computes its section 199A deduction based on the QBI, W-2 wages, UBIA of qualified property, qualified REIT dividends, and qualified PTP income that are allocated to the trust or estate. An individual beneficiary of a trust or estate takes into account any QBI, W-2 wages, UBIA of qualified property, qualified REIT dividends, and qualified PTP income allocated from a trust or estate in calculating the beneficiary's section 199A deduction, in the same manner as though the items had been allocated from an RPE. For purposes of this section and §§1.199A-1 through 1.199A-5, a trust or estate is treated as an RPE to the extent it allocates QBI and other items to its beneficiaries, and is treated as an individual to the extent it retains the QBI and other items.

(2) *Grantor trusts.*—To the extent that the grantor or another person is treated as owning all or part of a trust under sections 671 through 679, such person computes its section 199A deduction as if that person directly conducted the activities of the trust with respect to the portion of the trust treated as owned by the grantor or other person.

(3) *Non-grantor trusts and estates.*—(i) *Calculation at entity level.*—A trust or estate must calculate its QBI, W-2 wages, UBIA of qualified property, qualified REIT dividends, and qualified PTP income. The QBI of a trust or estate must be computed by allocating qualified items of deduction described in section 199A(c)(3) in accordance with the classification of those deductions under §1.652(b)-3(a), and deductions not directly attributable within the meaning of §1.652(b)-3(b) (other deductions) are allocated in a manner consistent with the rules in §1.652(b)-3(b). Any depletion and depreciation deductions described in section 642(e) and any amortization deductions described in section 642(f) that otherwise are properly included in the computation of QBI are included in the computation of QBI of the trust or estate, regardless of how those deductions may otherwise be allocated between the trust or estate and its beneficiaries for other purposes of the Code.

(ii) *Allocation among trust or estate and beneficiaries.*—The QBI (including any amounts that may be less than zero as calculated at the trust or estate level), W-2 wages, UBIA of qualified property, qualified REIT dividends, and qualified PTP income of a trust or estate are allocated to each beneficiary and to the trust or estate based on the relative proportion of the trust's or estate's *distributable net income (DNI)*, as defined by section 643(a), for the taxable year that is distributed or required to be distributed to the beneficiary or is retained by the trust or estate. For this purpose, the trust's or estate's DNI is determined with regard to the separate share rule of section 663(c), but without regard to section 199A. If the trust or estate has no DNI for the taxable year, any QBI, W-2 wages, UBIA of qualified property, qualified REIT dividends, and qualified PTP income are allocated entirely to the trust or estate.

(iii) [Reserved]

(iv) *Threshold amount.*—The threshold amount applicable to a trust or estate is $157,500 for any taxable year beginning before 2019. For taxable years beginning after 2018, the threshold amount shall be $157,500 increased by the cost-of-living adjustment as outlined in §1.199A-1(b)(12). For purposes of determining whether a trust or estate has taxable income in excess of the threshold amount, the taxable income of the trust or estate is determined after taking into account any distribution deduction under sections 651 or 661.

(v) [Reserved]

(vi) *Electing small business trusts.*—An electing small business trust (ESBT) is entitled to the deduction under section 199A. Any section 199A deduction attributable to the assets in the S portion of the ESBT is to be taken into account by the S portion. The S portion of the ESBT must take into account the QBI and other items from any S corporation owned by the ESBT, the grantor portion of the ESBT must take into account the QBI and other items from any assets treated as owned by a grantor or another person (owned portion) of a trust under sections 671 through 679, and the non-S portion of the ESBT must take into account any QBI and other items from any other entities or assets owned by the ESBT. For purposes of determining whether the taxable income of an ESBT exceeds the threshold amount, the S portion and the non-S portion of an ESBT are treated as a single trust. *See* §1.641(c)-1.

(vii) *Anti-abuse rule for creation of a trust to avoid exceeding the threshold amount.*—A trust formed or funded with a principal purpose of avoiding, or of using more than one, threshold amount for purposes of calculating the deduction under section 199A will not be respected as a separate trust entity for purposes of determining the threshold amount for purposes of section 199A. *See also* § 1.643(f)-1 of the regulations.

* * *

[Reg. § 1.199A-6.]

☐ [T.D. 9847, 2-4-2019.]

Additional Itemized Deductions for Individuals

§ 1.212-1. Nontrade or nonbusiness expenses.—(a) An expense may be deducted under section 212 only if—

(1) It has been paid or incurred by the taxpayer during the taxable year (i) for the production or collection of income which, if and when realized, will be required to be included in income for Federal income tax purposes, or (ii) for the management, conservation, or maintenance of property held for the production of such income, or (iii) in connection with the determination, collection, or refund of any tax; and

(2) It is an ordinary and necessary expense for any of the purposes stated in subparagraph (1) of this paragraph.

(b) The term "income" for the purpose of section 212 includes not merely income of the taxable year but also income which the taxpayer has realized in a prior taxable year or may realize in subsequent taxable years; and is not confined to recurring income but applies as well to gains from the disposition of property. For example, if defaulted bonds, the interest from which if received would be includible in income, are purchased with the expectation of realizing capital gain on their resale, even though no current yield thereon is anticipated, ordinary and necessary expenses thereafter paid or incurred in connection with such bonds are deductible. Similarly, ordinary and necessary expenses paid or incurred in the management, conservation, or maintenance of a building devoted to rental purposes are deductible notwithstanding that there is actually no income therefrom in the taxable year, and regardless of the manner in which or the purpose for which the property in question was acquired. Expenses paid or incurred in managing, conserving, or maintaining property held for investment may be deductible under section 212 even though the property is not currently productive and there is no likelihood that the property will be sold at a profit or will otherwise be productive of income and even though the property is held merely to minimize a loss with respect thereto.

* * *

(d) Expenses, to be deductible under section 212, must be "ordinary and necessary". Thus, such expenses must be reasonable in amount and must bear a reasonable and proximate relation to the production or collection of taxable income or to the management, conservation, or maintenance of property held for the production of income.

(e) A deduction under section 212 is subject to the restrictions and limitations in part IX (section 261 and following), subchapter B, chapter 1 of the Code, relating to items not deductible. Thus, no deduction is allowable under section 212 for any amount allocable to the production or collection of one or more classes of income which are not includible in gross income, or for any amount allocable to the management, conservation, or maintenance of property held for the production of income which is not included in gross income. See section 265. Nor does section 212 allow the deduction of any expenses which are disallowed by any of the provisions of subtitle A of the Code, even though such expenses may be paid or incurred for one of the purposes specified in section 212.

(f) Among expenditures not allowable as deductions under section 212 are the following: Commuter's expenses; expenses of taking special courses or training; expenses for improving personal appearance; the cost of rental of a safe-deposit box for storing jewelry and other personal effects; expenses such as those paid or incurred in seeking employment or in placing oneself in a position to begin rendering personal services for compensation, campaign expenses of a candidate for public office, bar examination fees and other expenses paid or incurred in securing admission to the bar, and corresponding fees and expenses paid or incurred by physicians, dentists, accountants, and other taxpayers for securing the right to practice their respective professions. See, however, section 162 and the regulations thereunder.

(g) Fees for services of investment counsel, custodial fees, clerical help, office rent, and similar expenses paid or incurred by a taxpayer in connection with investments held by him are deductible under section 212 only if (1) they are paid or incurred by the taxpayer for the production or collection of income or for the management, conservation, or maintenance of investments held by him for the production of income; and (2) they are ordinary and necessary under all the circumstances, having regard to the type of investment and to the relation of the taxpayer to such investment.

(h) Ordinary and necessary expenses paid or incurred in connection with the management, conservation, or maintenance of property held for use as a residence by the taxpayer are not deductible. However, ordinary and necessary expenses paid or incurred in connection with the management, conservation, or maintenance of property held by the taxpayer as rental property are deductible even though such property was formerly held by the taxpayer for use as a home.

(i) Reasonable amounts paid or incurred by the fiduciary of an estate or trust on account of administration expenses, including fiduciaries' fees and expenses of litigation, which are ordinary and necessary in connection with the performance of the duties of administration are deductible under section 212 notwithstanding that the estate or trust is not engaged in a trade or business, except to the extent that such expenses are allocable to the production or collection of tax-exempt income. But see section 642(g) and the regulations thereunder for disallowance of such deductions to an estate where such items are allowed as a deduction under section 2053 or 2054 in computing the net estate subject to the estate tax.

(j) Reasonable amounts paid or incurred for the services of a guardian or committee for a ward or minor, and other expenses of guardians and committees which are ordinary and necessary, in connection with the production or collection of income inuring to the ward or minor, or in connection with the management, conservation, or maintenance of property, held for the production of income, belonging to the ward or minor, are deductible.

(k) Expenses paid or incurred in defending or perfecting title to property, in recovering property (other than investment property and amounts of income which, if and when recovered, must be included in gross income), or in developing or improving property, constitute a part of the cost of the property and are not deductible expenses. Attorneys' fees paid in a suit to quiet title to lands are not deductible; but if the suit is also to collect accrued rents thereon, that portion of such fees is deductible which is properly allocable to the services rendered in collecting such rents. Expenses paid or incurred in protecting or asserting one's rights to property of a decedent as heir or legatee, or as beneficiary under a testamentary trust, are not deductible.

(l) Expenses paid or incurred by an individual in connection with the determination, collection, or refund of any tax, whether the taxing authority be Federal, State, or municipal, and whether the tax be income, estate, gift, property, or any other tax, are deductible. Thus, expenses paid or incurred by a taxpayer for tax counsel or expenses paid or incurred in connection with the preparation of his tax returns or in connection with any proceedings involved in determining the extent of tax liability or in contesting his tax liability are deductible.

(m) An expense (not otherwise deductible) paid or incurred by an individual in determining or contesting a liability asserted against him does not become deductible by reason of the fact that property held by him for the production of income may be required to be used or sold for the purpose of satisfying such liability.

(n) Capital expenditures are not allowable as nontrade or nonbusiness expenses. The deduction of an item otherwise allowable under section 212 will not be disallowed simply because the taxpayer was entitled under subtitle A of the Code to treat such item as a capital expenditure, rather than to deduct it as an expense. For example, see section 266. Where, however, the item may properly be treated only as a capital expenditure or where it was properly so treated under an option granted in subtitle A, no deduction is allowable under section 212; and this is true regardless of whether any basis adjustment is allowed under any other provision of the Code.

(o) The provisions of section 212 are not intended in any way to disallow expenses which would otherwise be allowable under section 162 and the regulations thereunder. Double deductions are not permitted. Amounts deducted under one provision of the Internal Revenue Code of 1954 cannot again be deducted under any other provision thereof.

(p) *Frustration of public policy.*—The deduction of a payment will be disallowed under section 212 if the payment is of a type for which a deduction would be disallowed under section 162(c), (f), or (g) and the regulations thereunder in the case of a business expense. [Reg. § 1.212-1.]

□ [*T.D.* 6279, 12-13-57. *Amended by T.D.* 7198, 7-12-72 *and T.D.* 7345, 2-19-75.]

§ 1.213-1. Medical, dental, etc., expenses.—(a) *Allowance of deduction.*—(1) Section 213 permits a deduction of payments for certain medical expenses (including expenses for medicine and drugs). Except as provided in paragraph (d) of this section (relating to special rule for decedents) a deduction is allowable only to individuals and only with respect to medical expenses actually paid during the taxable year, regardless of when the incident or event which occasioned the expenses occurred and regardless of the method of accounting employed by the taxpayer in making his income tax return. Thus, if the medical expenses are incurred but not paid during the taxable year, no deduction for such expenses shall be allowed for such year.

* * *

(e) *Definitions.*—(1) *General.*—(i) The term "medical care" includes the diagnosis, cure, mitigation, treatment, or prevention of disease. Expenses paid for "medical care" shall include those paid for the purpose of affecting any structure or function of the body or for transportation primarily for and essential to medical care. See subparagraph (4) of this paragraph for provisions relating to medical insurance.

(ii) Amounts paid for operations or treatments affecting any portion of the body, including obstetrical expenses and expenses of therapy or X- ray treatments, are deemed to be for the purpose of affecting any structure or function of the body and are therefore paid for medical care. Amounts expended for illegal operations or treatments are not deductible. Deductions for expenditures for medical care allowable under section 213 will be confined strictly to expenses incurred primarily for the prevention or alleviation of a physical or mental defect or illness. Thus, payments for the following are payments for medical care: Hospital services, nursing services (including nurses' board where paid by the taxpayer), medical, laboratory, surgical, dental and other diagnostic and healing services, X-rays, medicine and drugs (as defined in subparagraph (2) of this paragraph, subject to the 1 percent limitation in paragraph (b) of this section), artificial teeth or limbs, and ambulance hire. However, an expenditure which is merely beneficial to the general health of an individual, such as an expenditure for a vacation, is not an expenditure for medical care.

(iii) Capital expenditures are generally not deductible for Federal income tax purposes. See section 263 and the regulations thereunder. However, an expenditure which otherwise qualifies as a medical expense under section 213 shall not be disqualified merely because it is a capital expenditure. For purposes of section 213 and this paragraph, a capital expenditure made by the taxpayer may qualify as a medical expense, if it has as its primary purpose the medical care (as defined in subdivisions (i) and (ii) of this subparagraph) of the taxpayer, his spouse, or his dependent. Thus, a capital expenditure which is related only to the sick person and is not related to permanent improvement or betterment of property, if it otherwise qualifies as an expenditure for medical care, shall be deductible; for example, an expenditure for eye glasses, a seeing eye dog, artificial teeth and limbs, a wheel chair, crutches, an inclinator or an air conditioner which is detachable from the property and purchased only for the use of a sick person, etc. Moreover, a capital expenditure for permanent improvement or betterment of property which would not ordinarily be for the purpose of medical care (within the meaning of this paragraph) may, nevertheless, qualify as a medical expense to the extent that the expenditure exceeds the increase in the value of the related property, if the particular expenditure is related directly to medical care. Such a situation could arise, for example, where a taxpayer is advised by a physician to install an elevator in his residence so that the taxpayer's wife who is afflicted with heart disease will not be required to climb stairs. If the cost of installing the elevator is $1,000 and the increase in the value of the residence is determined to be only $700, the difference of $300, which is the amount in excess of the value enhancement, is deductible as a medical expense. If, however, by reason of this expenditure, it is determined that the value of the residence has not been increased, the entire cost of installing the elevator would qualify as a medical expense. Expenditures made for the operation or maintenance of a capital asset are likewise deductible medical expenses if they have as their primary purpose the medical care (as defined in subdivisions (i) and (ii) of this subparagraph) of the taxpayer, his spouse, or his dependent. Normally, if a capital expenditure qualifies as a medical expense, expenditures for the operation or maintenance of the capital asset would also qualify provided that the medical reason for the capital expenditure still exists. The entire amount of such operation and maintenance expenditures qualifies, even if none or only a portion of the original cost of the capital asset itself qualified.

(iv) Expenses paid for transportation primarily for and essential to the rendition of the medical care are expenses paid for medical care. However, an amount allowable as a deduction for "transportation primarily for and essential to medical care" shall not include the cost of any meals and lodging while away from home receiving medical treatment. For example, if a doctor prescribes that a taxpayer go to a warm climate in order to alleviate a specific chronic ailment, the cost of meals and lodging while there would not be deductible. On the other hand, if the travel is undertaken merely for the general improvement of a taxpayer's health, neither the cost of transportation nor the cost of meals and lodging would be deductible. If a doctor prescribes an operation or other medical care, and the taxpayer chooses for purely personal considerations to travel to another locality (such as a resort area) for the operation or the other medical care, neither the cost of transportation nor the cost of meals and lodging (except where paid as part of a hospital bill) is deductible.

(v) The cost of in-patient hospital care (including the cost of meals and lodging therein) is an expenditure for medical care.

The extent to which expenses for care in an institution other than a hospital shall constitute medical care is primarily a question of fact which depends upon the condition of the individual and the nature of the services he receives (rather than the nature of the institution). A private establishment which is regularly engaged in providing the types of care or services outlined in this subdivision shall be considered an institution for purposes of the rules provided herein. In general, the following rules will be applied:

(a) Where an individual is in an institution because his condition is such that the availability of medical care (as defined in subdivisions (i) and (ii) of this subparagraph) in such institution is a principal reason for his presence there, and meals and lodging are furnished as a necessary incident to such care, the entire cost of medical care and meals and lodging at the institution, which are furnished while the individual requires continual medical care, shall constitute an expense for medical care. For example, medical care includes the entire cost of institutional care for a person who is mentally ill and unsafe when left alone. While ordinary education is not medical care, the cost of medical care includes the cost of attending a special school for a mentally or physically handicapped individual, if his condition is such that the resources of the institution for alleviating such mental or physical handicap are a principal reason for his presence there. In such a case, the cost of attending such a special school will include the cost of meals and lodging, if supplied, and the cost of ordinary education furnished which is incidental to the special services furnished by the school. Thus, the cost of medical care includes the cost of attending a special school designed to compensate for or overcome a physical handicap, in order to qualify the individual for future normal education or for normal living, such as a school for the teaching of braille or lip reading. Similarly, the cost of care and supervision, or of treatment and training, of a mentally retarded or physically handicapped individual at an institution is within the meaning of the term "medical care."

(b) Where an individual is in an institution, and his condition is such that the availability of medical care in such institution is not a principal reason for his presence there, only that part of the cost of care in the institution as is attributable to medical care (as defined in subdivisions (i) and (ii) of this subparagraph) shall be considered as a cost of medical care; meals and lodging at the institution in such a case are not considered a cost of medical care for purposes of this section. For example, an individual is in a home for the aged for personal or family considerations and not because he requires medical or nursing attention. In such case, medical care consists only of that part of the cost for care in the home which is attributable to medical care or nursing attention furnished to him; his meals and lodging at the home are not considered a cost of medical care.

(c) It is immaterial for purposes of this subdivision whether the medical care is furnished in a Federal or State institution or in a private institution.

(vi) See section 262 and the regulations thereunder for disallowance of deduction for personal, living, and family expenses not falling within the definition of medical care.

* * *

[Reg. § 1.213-1.]

☐ [*T.D.* 6279, 12-13-57. *Amended by T.D.* 6451, 2-3-60; *T.D.* 6604, 7-23-62; *T.D.* 6661, 6-26-63; *T.D.* 6761, 9-28-64; *T.D.* 6946, 2-12-68; *T.D.* 6985, 12-26-68; *T.D.* 7114, 5-17-71; *T.D.* 7317, 6-27-74 *and T.D.* 7643, 8-27-79.]

§ 1.221-1. Deduction for interest paid on qualified education loans after December 31, 2001.—(a) *In general.*—(1) *Applicability.*—Under section 221, an individual taxpayer may deduct from gross income certain interest paid by the taxpayer during the taxable year on a qualified education loan. See paragraph (b)(4) of this section for rules on payments of interest by third parties. The rules of this section are applicable to periods governed by section 221 as amended in 2001, which relates to deductions for interest paid on qualified education loans after December 31, 2001, in taxable years ending after December 31, 2001, and on or before December 31, 2010. For rules applicable to interest due and paid on qualified education loans after January 21, 1999, if paid before January 1, 2002, see § 1.221-2. Taxpayers also may apply § 1.221-2 to interest due and paid on qualified education loans after December 31, 1997, but before January 21, 1999. To the extent that the effective date limitation (sunset) of the 2001 amendment remains in force unchanged, section 221 before amendment in 2001, to which § 1.221-2 relates, also applies to interest due and paid on qualified education loans in taxable years beginning after December 31, 2010.

* * *

(b) *Eligibility.*—(1) *Taxpayer must have a legal obligation to make interest payments.*—A taxpayer is entitled to a deduction under section 221 only if the taxpayer has a legal obligation to make interest payments under the terms of the qualified education loan.

(2) *Claimed dependents not eligible.*—(i) *In general.*—An individual is not entitled to

a deduction under section 221 for a taxable year if the individual is a dependent (as defined in section 152) for whom another taxpayer is allowed a deduction under section 151 on a Federal income tax return for the same taxable year (or, in the case of a fiscal year taxpayer, the taxable year beginning in the same calendar year as the individual's taxable year).

(ii) *Examples.*—The following examples illustrate the rules of this paragraph (b)(2):

Example 1. Student not claimed as dependent. Student B pays $750 of interest on qualified education loans during 2003. Student B's parents are not allowed a deduction for her as a dependent for 2003. Assuming fulfillment of all other relevant requirements, Student B may deduct under section 221 the $750 of interest paid in 2003.

Example 2. Student claimed as dependent. Student C pays $750 of interest on qualified education loans during 2003. Only Student C has the legal obligation to make the payments. Student C's parent claims him as a dependent and is allowed a deduction under section 151 with respect to Student C in computing the parent's 2003 Federal income tax. Student C is not entitled to a deduction under section 221 for the $750 of interest paid in 2003. Because Student C's parent was not legally obligated to make the payments, Student C's parent also is not entitled to a deduction for the interest.

(3) *Married taxpayers.*—If a taxpayer is married as of the close of a taxable year, he or she is entitled to a deduction under this section only if the taxpayer and the taxpayer's spouse file a joint return for that taxable year.

(4) *Payments of interest by a third party.*—(i) *In general.*—If a third party who is not legally obligated to make a payment of interest on a qualified education loan makes a payment of interest on behalf of a taxpayer who is legally obligated to make the payment, then the taxpayer is treated as receiving the payment from the third party and, in turn, paying the interest.

(ii) *Examples.*—The following examples illustrate the rules of this paragraph (b)(4):

Example 1. Payment by employer. Student D obtains a qualified education loan to attend college. Upon Student D's graduation from college, Student D works as an intern for a non-profit organization during which time Student D's loan is in deferment and Student D makes no interest payments. As part of the internship program, the non-profit organization makes an interest payment on behalf of Student D after the deferment period. This payment is not excluded from Student D's income under section 108(f) and is treated as additional compensation includible in Student D's gross income. Assuming fulfillment of all other requirements of section 221, Student D may deduct this payment of interest for Federal income tax purposes.

Example 2. Payment by parent. Student E obtains a qualified education loan to attend college. Upon graduation from college, Student E makes legally required monthly payments of principal and interest. Student E's mother makes a required monthly payment of interest as a gift to Student E. A deduction for Student E as a dependent is not allowed on another taxpayer's tax return for that taxable year. Assuming fulfillment of all other requirements of section 221, Student E may deduct this payment of interest for Federal income tax purposes.

(c) *Maximum deduction.*—The amount allowed as a deduction under section 221 for any taxable year may not exceed $2,500.

(d) *Limitation based on modified adjusted gross income.*—(1) *In general.*—The deduction allowed under section 221 is phased out ratably for taxpayers with modified adjusted gross income between $50,000 and $65,000 ($100,000 and $130,000 for married individuals who file a joint return). Section 221 does not allow a deduction for taxpayers with modified adjusted gross income of $65,000 or above ($130,000 or above for married individuals who file a joint return). See paragraph (d)(3) of this section for inflation adjustment of amounts in this paragraph (d)(1).

(2) *Modified adjusted gross income defined.*—The term *modified adjusted gross income* means the adjusted gross income (as defined in section 62) of the taxpayer for the taxable year increased by any amount excluded from gross income under section 911, 931, or 933 (relating to income earned abroad or from certain United States possessions or Puerto Rico). Modified adjusted gross income must be determined under this section after taking into account the inclusions, exclusions, deductions, and limitations provided by sections 86 (social security and tier 1 railroad retirement benefits), 135 (redemption of qualified United States savings bonds), 137 (adoption assistance programs), 219 (deductible qualified retirement contributions), and 469 (limitation on passive activity losses and credits), but before taking into account the deductions provided by sections 221 and 222 (qualified tuition and related expenses).

(3) *Inflation adjustment.*—For taxable years beginning after 2002, the amounts in paragraph (d)(1) of this section will be increased for inflation occurring after 2001 in accordance

with section 221(f)(1). If any amount adjusted under section 221(f)(1) is not a multiple of $5,000, the amount will be rounded to the next lowest multiple of $5,000.

(e) *Definitions.*—(1) *Eligible educational institution.*—In general, an *eligible educational institution* means any college, university, vocational school, or other postsecondary educational institution described in section 481 of the Higher Education Act of 1965 (20 U.S.C. 1088), as in effect on August 5, 1997, and certified by the U.S. Department of Education as eligible to participate in student aid programs administered by the Department, as described in section 25A(f)(2) and § 1.25A-2(b). For purposes of this section, an eligible educational institution also includes an institution that conducts an internship or residency program leading to a degree or certificate awarded by an institution, a hospital, or a health care facility that offers postgraduate training.

(2) *Qualified higher education expenses.*—(i) *In general.*— *Qualified higher education expenses* means the cost of attendance (as defined in section 472 of the Higher Education Act of 1965, 20 U.S.C. 1087II, as in effect on August 4, 1997), at an eligible educational institution, reduced by the amounts described in paragraph (e)(2)(ii) of this section. Consistent with section 472 of the Higher Education Act of 1965, a student's cost of attendance is determined by the eligible educational institution and includes tuition and fees normally assessed a student carrying the same academic workload as the student, an allowance for room and board, and an allowance for books, supplies, transportation, and miscellaneous expenses of the student.

(ii) *Reductions.*—Qualified higher education expenses are reduced by any amount that is paid to or on behalf of a student with respect to such expenses and that is—

(A) A qualified scholarship that is excludable from income under section 117;

(B) An educational assistance allowance for a veteran or member of the armed forces under chapter 30, 31, 32, 34 or 35 of title 38, United States Code, or under chapter 1606 of title 10, United States Code;

(C) Employer-provided educational assistance that is excludable from income under section 127;

(D) Any other amount that is described in section 25A(g)(2)(C) (relating to amounts excludable from gross income as educational assistance);

(E) Any otherwise includible amount excluded from gross income under section 135 (relating to the redemption of United States savings bonds);

(F) Any otherwise includible amount distributed from a Coverdell education savings account and excluded from gross income under section 530(d)(2); or

(G) Any otherwise includible amount distributed from a qualified tuition program and excluded from gross income under section 529(c)(3)(B).

(3) *Qualified education loan.*—(i) *In general.*—A *qualified education loan* means indebtedness incurred by a taxpayer solely to pay qualified higher education expenses that are—

(A) Incurred on behalf of a student who is the taxpayer, the taxpayer's spouse, or a dependent (as defined in section 152) of the taxpayer at the time the taxpayer incurs the indebtedness;

(B) Attributable to education provided during an academic period, as described in section 25A and the regulations thereunder, when the student is an eligible student as defined in section 25A(b)(3) (requiring that the student be a degree candidate carrying at least half the normal full-time workload); and

(C) Paid or incurred within a reasonable period of time before or after the taxpayer incurs the indebtedness.

(ii) *Reasonable period.*—Except as otherwise provided in this paragraph (e)(3)(ii), what constitutes a reasonable period of time for purposes of paragraph (e)(3)(i)(C) of this section generally is determined based on all the relevant facts and circumstances. However, qualified higher education expenses are treated as paid or incurred within a reasonable period of time before or after the taxpayer incurs the indebtedness if—

(A) The expenses are paid with the proceeds of education loans that are part of a Federal postsecondary education loan program; or

(B) The expenses relate to a particular academic period and the loan proceeds used to pay the expenses are disbursed within a period that begins 90 days prior to the start of that academic period and ends 90 days after the end of that academic period.

(iii) *Related party.*—A qualified education loan does not include any indebtedness owed to a person who is related to the taxpayer, within the meaning of section 267(b) or 707(b)(1). For example, a parent or grandparent of the taxpayer is a related person. In addition, a qualified education loan does not include a loan made under any qualified employer plan as defined in section 72(p)(4) or under any contract referred to in section 72(p)(5).

(iv) *Federal issuance or guarantee not required.*—A loan does not have to be issued or guaranteed under a Federal postsecondary education loan program to be a qualified education loan.

(v) *Refinanced and consolidated indebtedness.*—(A) *In general.*—A qualified education loan includes indebtedness incurred solely to refinance a qualified education loan. A qualified education loan includes a single, consolidated indebtedness incurred solely to refinance two or more qualified education loans of a borrower.

(B) *Treatment of refinanced and consolidated indebtedness.*—[*Reserved.*]

(4) *Examples.*—The following examples illustrate the rules of this paragraph (e):

Example 1. Eligible educational institution. University F is a postsecondary educational institution described in section 481 of the Higher Education Act of 1965. The U.S. Department of Education has certified that University F is eligible to participate in federal financial aid programs administered by that Department, although University F chooses not to participate. University F is an eligible educational institution.

Example 2. Qualified higher education expenses. Student G receives a $3,000 qualified scholarship for the 2003 fall semester that is excludable from Student G's gross income under section 117. Student G receives no other forms of financial assistance with respect to the 2003 fall semester. Student G's cost of attendance for the 2003 fall semester, as determined by Student G's eligible educational institution for purposes of calculating a student's financial need in accordance with section 472 of the Higher Education Act, is $16,000. For the 2003 fall semester, Student G has qualified higher education expenses of $13,000 (the cost of attendance as determined by the institution ($16,000) reduced by the qualified scholarship proceeds excludable from gross income ($3,000)).

Example 3. Qualified education loan. Student H borrows money from a commercial bank to pay qualified higher education expenses related to his enrollment on a half-time basis in a graduate program at an eligible educational institution. Student H uses all the loan proceeds to pay qualified higher education expenses incurred within a reasonable period of time after incurring the indebtedness. The loan is not federally guaranteed. The commercial bank is not related to Student H within the meaning of section 267(b) or 707(b)(1). Student H's loan is a qualified education loan within the meaning of section 221.

Example 4. Qualified education loan. Student I signs a promissory note for a loan on August 15, 2003, to pay for qualified higher education expenses for the 2003 fall and 2004 spring semesters. On August 20, 2003, the lender disburses loan proceeds to Student I's college. The college credits them to Student I's account to pay qualified higher education expenses for the 2003 fall semester, which begins on August 25, 2003. On January 26, 2004, the lender disburses additional loan proceeds to Student I's college. The college credits them to Student I's account to pay qualified higher education expenses for the 2004 spring semester, which began on January 12, 2004. Student I's qualified higher education expenses for the two semesters are paid within a reasonable period of time, as the first loan disbursement occurred within the 90 days prior to the start of the fall 2003 semester and the second loan disbursement occurred during the spring 2004 semester.

Example 5. Qualified education loan. The facts are the same as in *Example 4* except that in 2005 the college is not an eligible educational institution because it loses its eligibility to participate in certain federal financial aid programs administered by the U.S. Department of Education. The qualification of Student I's loan, which was used to pay for qualified higher education expenses for the 2003 fall and 2004 spring semesters, as a qualified education loan is not affected by the college's subsequent loss of eligibility.

Example 6. Mixed-use loans. Student J signs a promissory note for a loan secured by Student J's personal residence. Student J will use part of the loan proceeds to pay for certain improvements to Student J's residence and part of the loan proceeds to pay qualified higher education expenses of Student J's spouse. Because Student J obtains the loan not solely to pay qualified higher education expenses, the loan is not a qualified education loan.

(f) *Interest.*—(1) *In general.*—Amounts paid on a qualified education loan are deductible under section 221 if the amounts are interest for Federal income tax purposes. For example, interest includes—

(i) Qualified stated interest (as defined in § 1.1273-1(c)); and

(ii) Original issue discount, which generally includes capitalized interest. For purposes of section 221, capitalized interest means any accrued and unpaid interest on a qualified education loan that, in accordance with the terms of the loan, is added by the lender to the outstanding principal balance of the loan.

(2) *Operative rules for original issue discount.*—(i) *In general.*—The rules to deter-

mine the amount of original issue discount on a loan and the accruals of the discount are in sections 163(e), 1271 through 1275, and the regulations thereunder. In general, original issue discount is the excess of a loan's stated redemption price at maturity (all payments due under the loan other than qualified stated interest payments) over its issue price (the amount loaned). Although original issue discount generally is deductible as it accrues under section 163(e) and § 1.163-7, original issue discount on a qualified education loan is not deductible until paid. See paragraph (f)(3) of this section to determine when original issue discount is paid.

(ii) *Treatment of loan origination fees by the borrower.*—If a loan origination fee is paid by the borrower other than for property or services provided by the lender, the fee reduces the issue price of the loan, which creates original issue discount (or additional original issue discount) on the loan in an amount equal to the fee. See § 1.1273-2(g). For an example of how a loan origination fee is taken into account, see *Example 2* of paragraph (f)(4) of this section.

(3) *Allocation of payments.*—See §§ 1.446-2(e) and 1.1275-2(a) for rules on allocating payments between interest and principal. In general, these rules treat a payment first as a payment of interest to the extent of the interest that has accrued and remains unpaid as of the date the payment is due, and second as a payment of principal. The characterization of a payment as either interest or principal under these rules applies regardless of how the parties label the payment (either as interest or principal). Accordingly, the taxpayer may deduct the portion of a payment labeled as principal that these rules treat as a payment of interest on the loan, including any portion attributable to capitalized interest or loan origination fees.

(4) *Examples.*—The following examples illustrate the rules of this paragraph (f). In the examples, assume that the institution the student attends is an eligible educational institution, the loan is a qualified education loan, the student is legally obligated to make interest payments under the terms of the loan, and any other applicable requirements, if not otherwise specified, are fulfilled. The examples are as follows:

Example 1. Capitalized interest. Interest on Student K's loan accrues while Student K is in school, but Student K is not required to make any payments on the loan until six months after he graduates or otherwise leaves school. At that time, the lender capitalizes all accrued but unpaid interest and adds it to the outstanding principal amount of the loan. Thereafter, Student K is required to make monthly payments of interest and principal on the loan. The interest payable on the loan, including the capitalized interest, is original issue discount. See section 1273 and the regulations thereunder. Therefore, in determining the total amount of interest paid on the loan each taxable year, Student K may deduct any payments that § 1.1275-2(a) treats as payments of interest, including any principal payments that are treated as payments of capitalized interest. See paragraph (f)(3) of this section.

Example 2. Allocation of payments. The facts are the same as in *Example 1*, except that, in addition, the lender charges Student K a loan origination fee, which is not for any property or services provided by the lender. Under § 1.1273-2(g), the loan origination fee reduces the issue price of the loan, which reduction increases the amount of original issue discount on the loan by the amount of the fee. The amount of original issue discount (which includes the capitalized interest and loan origination fee) that accrues each year is determined under section 1272 and § 1.1272-1. In effect, the loan origination fee accrues over the entire term of the loan. Because the loan has original issue discount, the payment ordering rules in § 1.1275-2(a) must be used to determine how much of each payment is interest for federal tax purposes. See paragraph (f)(3) of this section. Under § 1.1275-2(a), each payment (regardless of its designation by the parties as either interest or principal) generally is treated first as a payment of original issue discount, to the extent of the original issue discount that has accrued as of the date the payment is due and has not been allocated to prior payments, and second as a payment of principal. Therefore, in determining the total amount of interest paid on the qualified education loan for a taxable year, Student K may deduct any payments that the parties label as principal but that are treated as payments of original issue discount under § 1.1275-2(a).

(g) *Additional rules.*—(1) *Payment of interest made during period when interest payment not required.*—Payments of interestion a qualified education loan to which this section is applicable are deductible even if the payments are made during a period when interest payments are not required because, for example, the loan has not yet entered repayment status or is in a period of deferment or forbearance.

(2) *Denial of double benefit.*—No deduction is allowed under this section for any amount for which a deduction is allowable under another provision of Chapter 1 of the Internal Revenue Code. No deduction is allowed under this section for any amount for which an exclusion is allowable under section

108(f) (relating to cancellation of indebtedness).

(3) *Examples.*—The following examples illustrate the rules of this paragraph (g). In the examples, assume that the institution the student attends is an eligible educational institution, the loan is a qualified education loan, and the student is legally obligated to make interest payments under the terms of the loan:

Example 1. Voluntary payment of interest before loan has entered repayment status. Student L obtains a loan to attend college. The terms of the loan provide that interest accrues on the loan while Student L earns his undergraduate degree but that Student L is not required to begin making payments of interest until six full calendar months after he graduates or otherwise leaves school. Nevertheless, Student L voluntarily pays interest on the loan during 2003, while enrolled in college. Assuming all other relevant requirements are met, Student L is allowed a deduction for interest paid while attending college even though the payments were made before interest payments were required.

Example 2. Voluntary payment during period of deferment or forbearance. The facts are the same as in *Example 2,* except that Student L makes no payments on the loan while enrolled in college. Student L graduates in June 2003 and begins making monthly payments of principal and interest on the loan in January 2004, as required by the terms of the loan. In August 2004, Student L enrolls in graduate school on a fulltime basis. Under the terms of the loan, Student L may apply for deferment of the loan payments while Student L is enrolled in graduate school. Student L applies for and receives a deferment on the outstanding loan. However, Student L continues to make some monthly payments of interest during graduate school. Student L may deduct interest paid on the loan during the period beginning in January 2004, including interest paid while Student L is enrolled in graduate school.

(h) *Effective date.*—This section is applicable to periods governed by section 221 as amended in 2001, which relates to interest paid on a qualified education loan after December 31, 2001, in taxable years ending after December 31, 2001, and on or before December 31, 2010. [Reg. § 1.221-1.]

☐ [*T.D.* 9125, 5-6-2004.]

Special Deductions for Corporations

§ 1.248-1. Election to amortize organizational expenditures.—(a) *In general.*—Under section 248(a), a corporation may elect to amortize organizational expenditures as defined in section 248(b) and § 1.248-1(b). In the taxable year in which a corporation begins business, an electing corporation may deduct an amount equal to the lesser of the amount of the organizational expenditures of the corporation, or $5,000 (reduced (but not below zero) by the amount by which the organizational expenditures exceed $50,000). The remainder of the organizational expenditures is deducted ratably over the 180-month period beginning with the month in which the corporation begins business. All organizational expenditures of the corporation are considered in determining whether the organizational expenditures exceed $50,000, including expenditures incurred on or before October 22, 2004.

(b) *Organizational expenditures defined.*—(1) Section 248(b) defines the term "organization expenditures." Such expenditures for purposes of section 248 and this section, are those expenditures which are directly incident to the creation of the corporation. An expenditure, in order to qualify as an organizational expenditure, must be (i) incident to the creation of the corporation, (ii) chargeable to the capital account of the corporation, and (iii) of a character which, if expended incident to the creation of a corporation having a limited life, would be amortizable over such life. An expenditure which fails to meet each of these three tests may not be considered an organizational expenditure for purposes of section 248 and this section.

(2) The following are examples of organizational expenditures within the meaning of section 248 and this section: legal services incident to the organization of the corporation, such as drafting the corporate charter, by-laws, minutes of organizational meetings, terms of original stock certificates, and the like; necessary accounting services; expenses of temporary directors and of organizational meetings of directors or stockholders; and fees paid to State of incorporation.

(3) The following expenditures are not organizational expenditures within the meaning of section 248 and this section:

(i) Expenditures connected with issuing or selling shares of stock or other securities, such as commissions, professional fees, and printing costs. This is so even where the particular issue of stock to which the expenditures relate is for a fixed term of years;

(ii) Expenditures connected with the transfer of assets to a corporation.

(4) Expenditures connected with the reorganization of a corporation, unless directly incident to the creation of a corporation, are not

organizational expenditures within the meaning of section 248 and this section.

(c) *Time and manner of making election.*—A corporation is deemed to have made an election under section 248(a) to amortize organizational expenditures as defined in section 248(b) and § 1.248-1(b) for the taxable year in which the corporation begins business. A corporation may choose to forgo the deemed election by affirmatively electing to capitalize its organizational expenditures on a timely filed Federal income tax return (including extensions) for the taxable year in which the corporation begins business. The election either to amortize organizational expenditures under section 248(a) or to capitalize organizational expenditures is irrevocable and applies to all organizational expenditures of the corporation. A change in the characterization of an item as an organizational expenditure is a change in method of accounting to which sections 446 and 481(a) apply if the corporation treated the item consistently for two or more taxable years. A change in the determination of the taxable year in which the corporation begins business also is treated as a change in method of accounting if the corporation amortized organizational expenditures for two or more taxable years.

(d) *Determination of when corporation begins business.*—The deduction allowed under section 248 must be spread over a period beginning with the month in which the corporation begins business. The determination of the date the corporation begins business presents a question of fact which must be determined in each case in light of all the circumstances of the particular case. The words "begins business," however, do not have the same meaning as "in existence." Ordinarily, a corporation begins business when it starts the business operations for which it was organized; a corporation comes into existence on the date of its incorporation. Mere organizational activities, such as the obtaining of the corporate charter, are not alone sufficient to show the beginning of business. If the activities of the corporation have advanced to the extent necessary to establish the nature of its business operations, however, it will be deemed to have begun business. For example, the acquisition of operating assets which are necessary to the type of business contemplated may constitute the beginning of business.

(e) *Examples.*—The following examples illustrate the application of this section:

Example 1. Expenditures of $5,000 or less. Corporation X, a calendar year taxpayer, incurs $3,000 of organizational expenditures after October 22, 2004, and begins business on July 1, 2011. Under paragraph (c) of this section, Corporation X is deemed to have elected to amortize organizational expenditures under section 248(a) in 2011. Therefore, Corporation X may deduct the entire amount of the organizational expenditures in 2011, the taxable year in which Corporation X begins business.

Example 2. Expenditures of more than $5,000 but less than or equal to $50,000. The facts are the same as in *Example 1* except that Corporation X incurs organizational expenditures of $41,000. Under paragraph (c) of this section, Corporation X is deemed to have elected to amortize organizational expenditures under section 248(a) in 2011. Therefore, Corporation X may deduct $5,000 and the portion of the remaining $36,000 that is allocable to July through December of 2011 ($36,000/180 × 6 = $1,200) in 2011, the taxable year in which Corporation X begins business. Corporation X may amortize the remaining $34,800 ($36,000 - $1,200 = $34,800) ratably over the remaining 174 months.

* * *

[Reg. § 1.248-1.]

☐ [*T.D.* 6183, 6-13-56. *Amended by T.D.* 9411, 7-7-2008 *and T.D.* 9542, 8-16-2011.]

Items Not Deductible

§ 1.262-1. Personal, living, and family expenses.—(a) *In general.*—In computing taxable income, no deduction shall be allowed, except as otherwise expressly provided in chapter 1 of the Code, for personal, living, and family expenses.

(b) *Examples of personal, living, and family expenses.*—Personal, living, and family expenses are illustrated in the following examples:

(1) Premiums paid for life insurance by the insured are not deductible. See also section 264 and the regulations thereunder.

(2) The cost of insuring a dwelling owned and occupied by the taxpayer as a personal residence is not deductible.

(3) Expenses of maintaining a household, including amounts paid for rent, water, utilities, domestic service, and the like, are not deductible. A taxpayer who rents a property for residential purposes, but incidentally conducts business there (his place of business being elsewhere) shall not deduct any part of the rent. If, however, he uses part of the house as his place of business, such portion of the rent and other similar expenses as is properly attributable to such place of business is deductible as a business expense. [But see Code Sec. 280A.]

(4) Losses sustained by the taxpayer upon the sale or other disposition of property held for personal, living, and family purposes are not deductible. But see section 165 and the regulations thereunder for deduction of losses sustained to such property by reason of casualty, etc.

(5) Expenses incurred in traveling away from home (which include transportation expenses, meals, and lodging) and any other transportation expenses are not deductible unless they qualify as expenses deductible under section 162 (relating to trade or business expenses), section 170 (relating to charitable contributions), section 212 (relating to expenses for production of income), section 213 (relating to medical expenses), or section 217 (relating to moving expenses), and the regulations under those sections. The taxpayer's costs of commuting to his place of business or employment are personal expenses and do not qualify as deductible expenses. For expenses paid or incurred before October 1, 2014, a taxpayer's expenses for lodging when not traveling away from home (local lodging) are nondeductible personal expenses. However, taxpayers may deduct local lodging expenses that qualify under section 162 and are paid or incurred in taxable years for which the period of limitation on credit or refund under section 6511 has not expired. For expenses paid or incurred on or after October 1, 2014, a taxpayer's local lodging expenses are personal expenses and are not deductible unless they qualify as deductible expenses under section 162. Except as permitted under section 162 or 212, the costs of a taxpayer's meals not incurred in traveling away from home are nondeductible personal expenses.

(6) Amounts paid as damages for breach of promise to marry, and attorney's fees and other costs of suit to recover such damages, are not deductible.

(7) Generally, attorney's fees and other costs paid in connection with a divorce, separation, or decree for support are not deductible by either the husband or the wife. However, the part of an attorney's fee and the part of the other costs paid in connection with a divorce, legal separation, written separation agreement, or a decree for support, which are properly attributable to the production or collection of amounts includible in gross income under section 71 are deductible by the wife under section 212.

(8) The cost of equipment of a member of the armed services is deductible only to the extent that it exceeds nontaxable allowances received for such equipment and to the extent that such equipment is especially required by his profession and does not merely take the place of articles required in civilian life. For example, the cost of a sword is an allowable deduction in computing taxable income, but the cost of a uniform is not. However, amounts expended by a reservist for the purchase and maintenance of uniforms which may be worn only when on active duty for training for temporary periods, when attending service school courses, or when attending training assemblies are deductible except to the extent that nontaxable allowances are received for such amounts.

(9) Expenditures made by a taxpayer in obtaining an education or in furthering his education are not deductible unless they qualify under section 162 and § 1.162-5 (relating to trade or business expenses).

(c) *Cross references.*—Certain items of a personal, living, or family nature are deductible to the extent expressly provided under the following sections, and the regulations under those sections:

(1) Section 163 (interest).

(2) Section 164 (taxes).

(3) Section 165 (losses).

(4) Section 166 (bad debts).

(5) Section 170 (charitable, etc., contributions and gifts).

(6) Section 213 (medical, dental, etc., expenses).

(7) Section 214 (expenses for care of certain dependents). [Now a credit under Code § 44A.]

(8) Section 215 (alimony, etc., payments).

(9) Section 216 (amounts representing taxes and interest paid to cooperative housing corporation).

(10) Section 217 (moving expenses). [Reg. § 1.262-1.]

□ [*T.D.* 6313, 9-16-58. *Amended by T.D.* 6796, 1-29-65; *T.D.* 6918, 5-1-67; *T.D.* 7207, 10-3-72 *and T.D.* 9696, 9-30-2014.]

§ 1.263(a)-1. Capital expenditures; in general.—(a) *General rule for capital expenditures.*—Except as provided in chapter 1 of the Internal Revenue Code, no deduction is allowed for—

(1) Any amount paid for new buildings or for permanent improvements or betterments made to increase the value of any property or estate; or

(2) Any amount paid in restoring property or in making good the exhaustion thereof for which an allowance is or has been made.

(b) *Coordination with other provisions of the Internal Revenue Code.*—Nothing in this section changes the treatment of any amount that is specifically provided for under any provision of the Internal Revenue Code or the Treasury Regulations other than section 162(a) or section 212 and the regulations under those sections. For example, see section 263A, which requires taxpayers to capitalize the direct and allocable indirect costs to property produced by the taxpayer and property acquired for resale. See also section 195 requiring taxpayers to capitalize certain costs as start-up expenditures.

(c) *Definitions.*—For purposes of this section, the following definitions apply:

(1) *Amount paid.*—In the case of a taxpayer using an accrual method of accounting, the terms *amount paid* and *payment* mean a liability incurred (within the meaning of § 1.446-1(c)(1)(ii)). A liability may not be taken into account under this section prior to the taxable year during which the liability is incurred.

(2) *Produce* means construct, build, install, manufacture, develop, create, raise, or grow. This definition is intended to have the same meaning as the definition used for purposes of section 263A(g)(1) and § 1.263A-2(a)(1)(i), except that improvements are excluded from the definition in this paragraph (c)(2) and are separately defined and addressed in § 1.263(a)-3.

(d) *Examples of capital expenditures.*—The following amounts paid are examples of capital expenditures:

(1) An amount paid to acquire or produce a unit of real or personal tangible property. See § 1.263(a)-2.

(2) An amount paid to improve a unit of real or personal tangible property. See § 1.263(a)-3.

(3) An amount paid to acquire or create intangibles. See § 1.263(a)-4.

(4) An amount paid or incurred to facilitate an acquisition of a trade or business, a change in capital structure of a business entity, and certain other transactions. See § 1.263(a)-5.

(5) An amount paid to acquire or create interests in land, such as easements, life estates, mineral interests, timber rights, zoning variances, or other interests in land.

(6) An amount assessed and paid under an agreement between bondholders or shareholders of a corporation to be used in a reorganization of the corporation or voluntary contributions by shareholders to the capital of the corporation for any corporate purpose. See section 118 and § 1.118-1.

(7) An amount paid by a holding company to carry out a guaranty of dividends at a specified rate on the stock of a subsidiary corporation for the purpose of securing new capital for the subsidiary and increasing the value of its stockholdings in the subsidiary. This amount must be added to the cost of the stock in the subsidiary.

(e) *Amounts paid to sell property.*—(1) *In general.*—Commissions and other transaction costs paid to facilitate the sale of property are not currently deductible under section 162 or 212. Instead, the amounts are capitalized costs that reduce the amount realized in the taxable year in which the sale occurs or are taken into account in the taxable year in which the sale is abandoned if a deduction is permissible. These amounts are not added to the basis of the property sold or treated as an intangible asset under § 1.263(a)-4. See § 1.263(a)-5(g) for the treatment of amounts paid to facilitate the disposition of assets that constitute a trade or business.

(2) *Dealer in property.*—In the case of a dealer in property, amounts paid to facilitate the sale of such property are treated as ordinary and necessary business expenses.

(3) *Examples.*—The following examples, which assume the sale is not an installment sale under section 453, illustrate the rules of this paragraph (e):

Example 1. Sales costs of real property. A owns a parcel of real estate. A sells the real estate and pays legal fees, recording fees, and sales commissions to facilitate the sale. A must capitalize the fees and commissions and, in the taxable year of the sale, must reduce the amount realized from the sale of the real estate by the fees and commissions.

Example 2. Sales costs of dealers. Assume the same facts as in *Example 1*, except that A is a dealer in real estate. The commissions and fees paid to facilitate the sale of the real estate may be deducted as ordinary and necessary business expenses under section 162.

Example 3. Sales costs of personal property used in a trade or business. B owns a truck for use in B's trade or business. B decides to sell the truck on November 15, Year 1. B pays for an appraisal to determine a reasonable asking price. On February 15, Year 2, B sells the truck to C. In Year 1, B must capitalize the amount paid to appraise the truck, and in Year 2, must reduce the amount realized from the sale of the truck by the amount paid for the appraisal.

Example 4. Costs of abandoned sale of personal property used in a trade or business. Assume the same facts as in *Example 3*, except that, instead of selling the truck on February 15, Year 2, B decides on that date not to sell the truck and takes the truck off the market. In Year 1, B must capitalize the amount paid to appraise the truck. However, B may recognize the amount paid to appraise the truck as a loss under section 165 in Year 2, the taxable year when the sale is abandoned.

Example 5. Sales costs of personal property not used in a trade or business. Assume the same facts as in *Example 3,* except that B does not use the truck in B's trade or business but instead uses it for personal purposes. In Year 1, B must capitalize the amount paid to appraise the truck, and in Year 2, must reduce the amount realized from the sale of the truck by the amount paid for the appraisal.

Example 6. Costs of abandoned sale of personal property not used in a trade or business. Assume the same facts as in *Example 5,* except that, instead of selling the truck on February 15, Year 2, B decides on that date not to sell the truck and takes the truck off the market. In Year 1, B must capitalize the amount paid to appraise the truck. Although B abandons the sale in Year 2, B may not treat the amount paid to appraise the truck as a loss under section 165 because the truck was not used in B's trade or business or in a transaction entered into for profit.

(f) *De minimis safe harbor election.*—(1) *In general.*—Except as otherwise provided in paragraph (f)(2) of this section, a taxpayer electing to apply the de minimis safe harbor under this paragraph (f) may not capitalize under § 1.263(a)-2(d)(1) or § 1.263(a)-3(d) any amount paid in the taxable year for the acquisition or production of a unit of tangible property nor treat as a material or supply under § 1.162-3(a) any amount paid in the taxable year for tangible property if the amount specified under this paragraph (f)(1) meets the requirements of paragraph (f)(1)(i) or (f)(1)(ii) of this section. However, section 263A and the regulations under section 263A require taxpayers to capitalize the direct and allocable indirect costs of property produced by the taxpayer (for example, property improved by the taxpayer) and property acquired for resale.

(i) *Taxpayer with applicable financial statement.*—A taxpayer electing to apply the de minimis safe harbor may not capitalize under § 1.263(a)-2(d)(1) or § 1.263(a)-3(d) nor treat as a material or supply under § 1.162-3(a) any amount paid in the taxable year for property described in paragraph (f)(1) of this section if—

(A) The taxpayer has an applicable financial statement (as defined in paragraph (f)(4) of this section);

(B) The taxpayer has at the beginning of the taxable year written accounting procedures treating as an expense for non-tax purposes—

(1) Amounts paid for property costing less than a specified dollar amount; or

(2) Amounts paid for property with an economic useful life (as defined in § 1.162-3(c)(4)) of 12 months or less;

(C) The taxpayer treats the amount paid for the property as an expense on its applicable financial statement in accordance with its written accounting procedures; and

(D) The amount paid for the property does not exceed $5,000 per invoice (or per item as substantiated by the invoice) or other amount as identified in published guidance in the Federal Register or in the Internal Revenue Bulletin (see § 601.601(d)(2)(ii)(*b*) of this chapter).

(ii) *Taxpayer without applicable financial statement.*—A taxpayer electing to apply the de minimis safe harbor may not capitalize under § 1.263(a)-2(d)(1) or § 1.263(a)-3(d) nor treat as a material or supply under § 1.162-3(a) any amount paid in the taxable year for property described in paragraph (f)(1) of this section if—

(A) The taxpayer does not have an applicable financial statement (as defined in paragraph (f)(4) of this section);

(B) The taxpayer has at the beginning of the taxable year accounting procedures treating as an expense for non-tax purposes—

(1) Amounts paid for property costing less than a specified dollar amount; or

(2) Amounts paid for property with an economic useful life (as defined in § 1.162-3(c)(4)) of 12 months or less;

(C) The taxpayer treats the amount paid for the property as an expense on its books and records in accordance with these accounting procedures; and

(D) The amount paid for the property does not exceed $500 per invoice (or per item as substantiated by the invoice) or other amount as identified in published guidance in the Federal Register or in the Internal Revenue Bulletin (see § 601.601(d)(2)(ii)(*b*) of this chapter).

(iii) *Taxpayer with both an applicable financial statement and a non-qualifying financial statement.*—For purposes of this paragraph (f)(1), if a taxpayer has an applicable financial statement defined in paragraph (f)(4) of this section in addition to a financial statement that does not meet requirements of paragraph (f)(4) of this section, the taxpayer must meet the requirements of paragraph (f)(1)(i) of this section to qualify to elect the de minimis safe harbor under this paragraph (f).

(2) *Exceptions to de minimis safe harbor.*—The de minimis safe harbor in paragraph (f)(1) of this section does not apply to the following:

(i) Amounts paid for property that is or is intended to be included in inventory property;

(ii) Amounts paid for land;

(iii) Amounts paid for rotable, temporary, and standby emergency spare parts that the taxpayer elects to capitalize and depreciate under § 1.162-3(d); and

(iv) Amounts paid for rotable and temporary spare parts that the taxpayer accounts for under the optional method of accounting for rotable parts pursuant to § 1.162-3(e).

(3) *Additional rules.*—(i) *Transaction and other additional costs.*—A taxpayer electing to apply the de minimis safe harbor under paragraph (f)(1) of this section is not required to include in the cost of the tangible property the additional costs of acquiring or producing such property if these costs are not included in the same invoice as the tangible property. However, the taxpayer electing to apply the de minimis safe harbor under paragraph (f)(1) of this section must include in the cost of such property all additional costs (for example, delivery fees, installation services, or similar costs) if these additional costs are included on the same invoice with the tangible property. For purposes of this paragraph, if the invoice includes amounts paid for multiple tangible properties and such invoice includes additional invoice costs related to these multiple properties, then the taxpayer must allocate the additional invoice costs to each property using a reasonable method, and each property, including allocable labor and overhead, must meet the requirements of paragraph (f)(1)(i) or paragraph (f)(1)(ii) of this section, whichever is applicable. Reasonable allocation methods include, but are not limited to specific identification, a pro rata allocation, or a weighted average method based on the property's relative cost. For purposes of this paragraph (f)(3)(i), additional costs consist of the costs of facilitating the acquisition or production of such tangible property under § 1.263(a)-2(f) and the costs for work performed prior to the date that the tangible property is placed in service under § 1.263(a)-2(d).

(ii) *Materials and supplies.*—If a taxpayer elects to apply the de minimis safe harbor provided under this paragraph (f), then the taxpayer must also apply the de minimis safe harbor to amounts paid for all materials and supplies (as defined under § 1.162-3) that meet the requirements of § 1.263(a)-1(f). See paragraph (f)(3)(iv) of this section for treatment of materials and supplies under the de minimis safe harbor.

(iii) *Sale or disposition.*—Property to which a taxpayer applies the de minimis safe harbor contained in this paragraph (f) is not treated upon sale or other disposition as a capital asset under section 1221 or as property used in the trade or business under section 1231.

(iv) *Treatment of de minimis amounts.*—An amount paid for property to which a taxpayer properly applies the de minimis safe harbor contained in this paragraph (f) is not treated as a capital expenditure under § 1.263(a)-2(d)(1) or § 1.263(a)-3(d) or as a material and supply under § 1.162-3, and may be deducted under § 1.162-1 in the taxable year the amount is paid provided the amount otherwise constitutes an ordinary and necessary expense incurred in carrying on a trade or business.

(v) *Coordination with section 263A.*—Amounts paid for tangible property described in paragraph (f)(1) of this section may be subject to capitalization under section 263A if the amounts paid for tangible property comprise the direct or allocable indirect costs of other property produced by the taxpayer or property acquired for resale. See, for example, § 1.263A-1(e)(3)(ii)(R) requiring taxpayers to capitalize the cost of tools and equipment allocable to property produced or property acquired for resale.

(vi) *Written accounting procedures for groups of entities.*—If the taxpayer's financial results are reported on the applicable financial statement (as defined in paragraph (f)(4) of this section) for a group of entities then, for purposes of paragraph (f)(1)(i)(A) of this section, the group's applicable financial statement may be treated as the applicable financial statement of the taxpayer, and for purposes of paragraphs (f)(1)(i)(B) and (f)(1)(i)(C) of this section, the written accounting procedures provided for the group and utilized for the group's applicable financial statement may be treated as the written accounting procedures of the taxpayer.

(vii) *Combined expensing accounting procedures.*—For purposes of paragraphs (f)(1)(i) and (f)(1)(ii) of this section, if the taxpayer has, at the beginning of the taxable year, accounting procedures treating as an expense for non-tax purposes amounts paid for property costing less than a specified dollar amount and amounts paid for property with an economic useful life (as defined in § 1.162-3(c)(4)) of 12 months or less, then a taxpayer electing to apply the de minimis safe harbor under this paragraph (f) must apply the provisions of this paragraph (f) to amounts qualifying under either accounting procedure.

(4) *Definition of applicable financial statement.*—For purposes of this paragraph (f), the

taxpayer's applicable financial statement (AFS) is the taxpayer's financial statement listed in paragraphs (f)(4)(i) through (iii) of this section that has the highest priority (including within paragraph (f)(4)(ii) of this section). The financial statements are, in descending priority—

(i) A financial statement required to be filed with the Securities and Exchange Commission (SEC) (the 10-K or the Annual Statement to Shareholders);

(ii) A certified audited financial statement that is accompanied by the report of an independent certified public accountant (or in the case of a foreign entity, by the report of a similarly qualified independent professional) that is used for—

(A) Credit purposes;

(B) Reporting to shareholders, partners, or similar persons; or

(C) Any other substantial non-tax purpose; or

(iii) A financial statement (other than a tax return) required to be provided to the federal or a state government or any federal or state agency (other than the SEC or the Internal Revenue Service).

(5) *Time and manner of election.*—A taxpayer that makes the election under this paragraph (f) must make the election for all amounts paid during the taxable year for property described in paragraph (f)(1) of this section and meeting the requirements of paragraph (f)(1)(i) or paragraph (f)(1)(ii) of this section, as applicable. A taxpayer makes the election by attaching a statement to the taxpayer's timely filed original Federal tax return (including extensions) for the taxable year in which these amounts are paid. Sections 301.9100-1 through 301.9100-3 of this chapter provide the rules governing extensions of the time to make regulatory elections. The statement must be titled "Section 1.263(a)-1(f) de minimis safe harbor election" and include the taxpayer's name, address, taxpayer identification number, and a statement that the taxpayer is making the de minimis safe harbor election under §1.263(a)-1(f). In the case of a consolidated group filing a consolidated income tax return, the election is made for each member of the consolidated group by the common parent, and the statement must also include the names and taxpayer identification numbers of each member for which the election is made. In the case of an S corporation or a partnership, the election is made by the S corporation or the partnership and not by the shareholders or partners. An election may not be made through the filing of an application for change in accounting method or, before obtaining the Commissioner's consent to make a late election, by filing an amended Federal tax return. A taxpayer may not revoke an election made under this paragraph (f). The manner of electing the de minimis safe harbor under this paragraph (f) may be modified through guidance of general applicability (see §§601.601(d)(2) and 601.602 of this chapter).

(6) *Anti-abuse rule.*—If a taxpayer acts to manipulate transactions with the intent to achieve a tax benefit or to avoid the application of the limitations provided under paragraphs (f)(1)(i)(B)(*1*), (f)(1)(i)(D), (f)(1)(ii)(B)(*1*), and (f)(1)(ii)(D) of this section, appropriate adjustments will be made to carry out the purposes of this section. For example, a taxpayer is deemed to act to manipulate transactions with an intent to avoid the purposes and requirements of this section if—

(i) The taxpayer applies the de minimis safe harbor to amounts substantiated with invoices created to componentize property that is generally acquired or produced by the taxpayer (or other taxpayers in the same or similar trade or business) as a single unit of tangible property; and

(ii) This property, if treated as a single unit, would exceed any of the limitations provided under paragraphs (f)(1)(i)(B)(*1*), (f)(1)(i)(D), (f)(1)(ii)(B)(*1*), and (f)(1)(ii)(D) of this section, as applicable.

* * *

[Reg. §1.263(a)-1.]

□ [*T.D.* 6313, 9-16-58. *Amended by T.D.* 6548, 2-21-61; *T.D.* 6794, 1-25-65; *T.D.* 8121, 1-5-87; *T.D.* 8131, 3-24-87; *T.D.* 8408, 4-9-92; *T.D.* 8482, 8-6-93; *T.D.* 9564, 12-23-2011 *and T.D.* 9636, 9-13-2013 (*corrected* 7-18-2014).]

§1.263(a)-2. Amounts paid to acquire or produce tangible property.—(a) *Overview.*—This section provides rules for applying section 263(a) to amounts paid to acquire or produce a unit of real or personal property. Paragraph (b) of this section contains definitions. Paragraph (c) of this section contains the rules for coordinating this section with other provisions of the Internal Revenue Code (Code). Paragraph (d) of this section provides the general requirement to capitalize amounts paid to acquire or produce a unit of real or personal property. Paragraph (e) of this section provides the requirement to capitalize amounts paid to defend or perfect title to real or personal property. Paragraph (f) of this section provides the rules for determining the extent to which taxpayers must capitalize transaction costs related to the acquisition of tangible property. Paragraphs (g) and (h) of this section address the treatment and recovery of capital expenditures. Paragraph (i) of this section provides for changes in methods of accounting to comply with this section, and paragraph (j) of this section provides the effective and applicability dates for the rules under this section.

(b) *Definitions.*—For purposes of this section, the following definitions apply:

(1) *Amount paid.*—In the case of a taxpayer using an accrual method of accounting, the terms *amount paid* and *payment* mean a liability incurred (within the meaning of § 1.446-1(c)(1)(ii)). A liability may not be taken into account under this section prior to the taxable year during which the liability is incurred.

(2) *Personal property* means tangible personal property as defined in § 1.48-1(c).

(3) *Real property* means land and improvements thereto, such as buildings or other inherently permanent structures (including items that are structural components of the buildings or structures) that are not personal property as defined in paragraph (b)(2) of this section. Any property that constitutes other tangible property under § 1.48-1(d) is treated as real property for purposes of this section. Local law is not controlling in determining whether property is real property for purposes of this section.

(4) *Produce* means construct, build, install, manufacture, develop, create, raise, or grow. This definition is intended to have the same meaning as the definition used for purposes of section 263A(g)(1) and § 1.263A-2(a)(1)(i), except that improvements are excluded from the definition in this paragraph (b)(4) and are separately defined and addressed in § 1.263(a)-3.

(c) *Coordination with other provisions of the Code.*—(1) *In general.*—Nothing in this section changes the treatment of any amount that is specifically provided for under any provision of the Code or the Treasury Regulations other than section 162(a) or section 212 and the regulations under those sections. For example, see section 263A requiring taxpayers to capitalize the direct and allocable indirect costs of property produced by the taxpayer and property acquired for resale. See also section 195 requiring taxpayers to capitalize certain costs as start-up expenditures.

(2) *Materials and supplies.*—Nothing in this section changes the treatment of amounts paid to acquire or produce property that is properly treated as materials and supplies under § 1.162-3.

(d) *Acquired or produced tangible property.*—(1) *Requirement to capitalize.*—Except as provided in § 1.162-3 (relating to materials and supplies) and in § 1.263(a)-1(f) (providing a de minimis safe harbor election), a taxpayer must capitalize amounts paid to acquire or produce a unit of real or personal property (as determined under § 1.263(a)-3(e)), including leasehold improvements, land and land improvements, buildings, machinery and equipment, and furniture and fixtures. Section 1.263(a)-3(f) provides the rules for determining whether amounts are for leasehold improvements. Amounts paid to acquire or produce a unit of real or personal property include the invoice price, transaction costs as determined under paragraph (f) of this section, and costs for work performed prior to the date that the unit of property is placed in service by the taxpayer (without regard to any applicable convention under section 168(d)). A taxpayer also must capitalize amounts paid to acquire real or personal property for resale.

(2) *Examples.*—The following examples illustrate the rules of this paragraph (d). Unless otherwise provided, assume that the taxpayer does not elect the de minimis safe harbor under § 1.263(a)-1(f) and that the property is not acquired for resale under section 263A.

Example 1. Acquisition of personal property. A purchases new cash registers for use in its retail store located in leased space in a shopping mall. Assume each cash register is a unit of property as determined under § 1.263(a)-3(e) and is not a material or supply under § 1.162-3. A must capitalize under paragraph (d)(1) of this section the amount paid to acquire each cash register.

Example 2. Acquisition of personal property that is a material or supply; coordination with § 1.162-3. B operates a fleet of aircraft. In Year 1, B acquires a stock of component parts, which it intends to use to maintain and repair its aircraft. Assume that each component part is a material or supply under § 1.162-3(c)(1) and B does not make elections under § 1.162-3(d) to treat the materials and supplies as capital expenditures. In Year 2, B uses the component parts in the repair and maintenance of its aircraft. Because the parts are materials and supplies under § 1.162-3, B is not required to capitalize the amounts paid for the parts under paragraph (d)(1) of this section. Rather, to determine the treatment of these amounts, B must apply the rules under § 1.162-3, governing the treatment of materials and supplies.

Example 3. Acquisition of unit of personal property; coordination with § 1.162-3. C operates a rental business that rents out a variety of small individual items to customers (rental items). C maintains a supply of rental items on hand to replace worn or damaged items. C purchases a large quantity of rental items to be used in its business. Assume that each of these rental items is a unit of property under § 1.263(a)-3(e). Also assume that a portion of the rental items are materials and supplies under § 1.162-3(c)(1). Under paragraph (d)(1) of this section, C must capitalize the amounts paid for the rental items that are not materials and supplies under § 1.162-3(c)(1). However, C must apply the rules in § 1.162-3 to determine the treatment of the rental items that are materials and supplies under § 1.162-3(c)(1).

Example 4. Acquisition or production cost. D purchases and produces jigs, dies, molds, and patterns for use in the manufacture of D's products. Assume that each of these items is a unit of property as determined under § 1.263(a)-3(e) and is not a material and supply under § 1.162-3(c)(1). D is required to capitalize under paragraph (d)(1) of this section the amounts paid to acquire and produce the jigs, dies, molds, and patterns.

Example 5. Acquisition of land. F purchases a parcel of undeveloped real estate. F must capitalize under paragraph (d)(1) of this section the amount paid to acquire the real estate. See paragraph (f) of this section for the treatment of amounts paid to facilitate the acquisition of real property.

Example 6. Acquisition of building. G purchases a building. G must capitalize under paragraph (d)(1) of this section the amount paid to acquire the building. See paragraph (f) of this section for the treatment of amounts paid to facilitate the acquisition of real property.

Example 7. Acquisition of property for resale and production of property for sale; coordination with section 263A. H purchases goods for resale and produces other goods for sale. H must capitalize under paragraph (d)(1) of this section the amounts paid to acquire and produce the goods. See section 263A for the amounts required to be capitalized to the property produced or to the property acquired for resale.

Example 8. Production of building; coordination with section 263A. J constructs a building. J must capitalize under paragraph (d)(1) of this section the amount paid to construct the building. See section 263A for the costs required to be capitalized to the real property produced by J.

Example 9. Acquisition of assets constituting a trade or business. K owns tangible and intangible assets that constitute a trade or business. L purchases all the assets of K in a taxable transaction. L must capitalize under paragraph (d)(1) of this section the amount paid for the tangible assets of K. See § 1.263(a)-4 for the treatment of amounts paid to acquire or create intangibles and § 1.263(a)-5 for the treatment of amounts paid to facilitate the acquisition of assets that constitute a trade or business. See section 1060 for special allocation rules for certain asset acquisitions.

Example 10. Work performed prior to placing the property in service. In Year 1, M purchases a building for use as a business office. Prior to placing the building in service, M pays amounts to repair cement steps, refinish wood floors, patch holes in walls, and paint the interiors and exteriors of the building. In Year 2, M places the building in service and begins using the building as its business office. Assume that the work that M performs does not constitute an improvement to the building or its structural components under § 1.263(a)-3. Under § 1.263-3(e)(2)(i), the building and its structural components is a single unit of property. Under paragraph (d)(1) of this section, the amounts paid must be capitalized as amounts to acquire the building unit of property because they were for work performed prior to M's placing the building in service.

Example 11. Work performed prior to placing the property in service. In January Year 1, N purchases a new machine for use in an existing production line of its manufacturing business. Assume that the machine is a unit of property under § 1.263(a)-3(e) and is not a material or supply under § 1.162-3. N pays amounts to install the machine, and after the machine is installed, N pays amounts to perform a critical test on the machine to ensure that it will operate in accordance with quality standards. On November 1, Year 1, the critical test is complete, and N places the machine in service on the production line. N pays amounts to perform periodic quality control testing after the machine is placed in service. Under paragraph (d)(1) of this section, the amounts paid for the installation and the critical test performed before the machine is placed in service must be capitalized by N as amounts to acquire the machine. However, amounts paid for periodic quality control testing after N placed the machine in service are not required to be capitalized as amounts paid to acquire the machine.

(e) *Defense or perfection of title to property.*—(1) *In general.*—Amounts paid to defend or perfect title to real or personal property are amounts paid to acquire or produce property within the meaning of this section and must be capitalized.

(2) *Examples.*—The following examples illustrate the rule of this paragraph (e):

Example 1. Amounts paid to contest condemnation. X owns real property located in County. County files an eminent domain complaint condemning a portion of X's property to use as a roadway. X hires an attorney to contest the condemnation. The amounts that X paid to the attorney must be capitalized because they were to defend X's title to the property.

Example 2. Amounts paid to invalidate ordinance. Y is in the business of quarrying and supplying for sale sand and stone in a certain municipality. Several years after Y establishes its business, the municipality in which it is located passes an ordinance that prohibits the operation of Y's business. Y incurs attorney's fees in a successful prosecution of a suit to invalidate the municipal ordinance. Y prosecutes the suit to preserve its business activities and not to defend Y's title in the property. Therefore, the attorney's fees that Y paid are not required to be capitalized under paragraph (e)(1) of this section.

Example 3. Amounts paid to challenge building line. The board of public works of a municipality establishes a building line across Z's business property, adversely affecting the value of the property. Z incurs legal fees in unsuccessfully litigating the establishment of the building line. The amounts Z paid to the attorney must be capitalized because they were to defend Z's title to the property.

(f) *Transaction costs.*—(1) *In general.*—Except as provided in § 1.263(a)-1(f)(3)(i) (for purposes of the de minimis safe harbor), a taxpayer must capitalize amounts paid to facilitate the acquisition of real or personal property. See § 1.263(a)-5 for the treatment of amounts paid to facilitate the acquisition of assets that constitute a trade or business. See § 1.167(a)-5 for allocations of facilitative costs between depreciable and non-depreciable property.

(2) *Scope of facilitate.*—(i) *In general.*—Except as otherwise provided in this section, an amount is paid to facilitate the acquisition of real or personal property if the amount is paid in the process of investigating or otherwise pursuing the acquisition. Whether an amount is paid in the process of investigating or otherwise pursuing the acquisition is determined based on all of the facts and circumstances. In determining whether an amount is paid to facilitate an acquisition, the fact that the amount would (or would not) have been paid but for the acquisition is relevant but is not determinative. Amounts paid to facilitate an acquisition include, but are not limited to, inherently facilitative amounts specified in paragraph (f)(2)(ii) of this section.

(ii) *Inherently facilitative amounts.*—An amount is paid in the process of investigating or otherwise pursuing the acquisition of real or personal property if the amount is inherently facilitative. An amount is inherently facilitative if the amount is paid for—

(A) Transporting the property (for example, shipping fees and moving costs);

(B) Securing an appraisal or determining the value or price of property;

(C) Negotiating the terms or structure of the acquisition and obtaining tax advice on the acquisition;

(D) Application fees, bidding costs, or similar expenses;

(E) Preparing and reviewing the documents that effectuate the acquisition of the property (for example, preparing the bid, offer, sales contract, or purchase agreement);

(F) Examining and evaluating the title of property;

(G) Obtaining regulatory approval of the acquisition or securing permits related to the acquisition, including application fees;

(H) Conveying property between the parties, including sales and transfer taxes, and title registration costs;

(I) Finders' fees or brokers' commissions, including contingency fees (defined in paragraph (f)(3)(iii) of this section);

(J) Architectural, geological, survey, engineering, environmental, or inspection services pertaining to particular properties; or

(K) Services provided by a qualified intermediary or other facilitator of an exchange under section 1031.

(iii) *Special rule for acquisitions of real property.*—(A) *In general.*—Except as provided in paragraph (f)(2)(ii) of this section (relating to inherently facilitative amounts), an amount paid by the taxpayer in the process of investigating or otherwise pursuing the acquisition of real property does not facilitate the acquisition if it relates to activities performed in the process of determining whether to acquire real property and which real property to acquire.

(B) *Acquisitions of real and personal property in a single transaction.*—An amount paid by the taxpayer in the process of investigating or otherwise pursuing the acquisition of personal property facilitates the acquisition of such personal property, even if such property is acquired in a single transaction that also includes the acquisition of real property subject to the special rule set out in paragraph (f)(2)(iii)(A) of this section. A taxpayer may use a reasonable allocation method to determine which costs facilitate the acquisition of personal property and which costs relate to the acquisition of real property and are subject to the special rule of paragraph (f)(2)(iii)(A) of this section.

(iv) *Employee compensation and overhead costs.*—(A) *In general.*—For purposes of paragraph (f) of this section, amounts paid for employee compensation (within the meaning of § 1.263(a)-4(e)(4)(ii)) and overhead are treated as amounts that do not facilitate the acquisition of real or personal property. However, section

263A provides rules for employee compensation and overhead costs required to be capitalized to property produced by the taxpayer or to property acquired for resale.

(B) *Election to capitalize.*—A taxpayer may elect to treat amounts paid for employee compensation or overhead as amounts that facilitate the acquisition of property. The election is made separately for each acquisition and applies to employee compensation or overhead, or both. For example, a taxpayer may elect to treat overhead, but not employee compensation, as amounts that facilitate the acquisition of property. A taxpayer makes the election by treating the amounts to which the election applies as amounts that facilitate the acquisition in the taxpayer's timely filed original Federal tax return (including extensions) for the taxable year during which the amounts are paid. Sections 301.9100-1 through 301.9100-3 of this chapter provide the rules governing extensions of the time to make regulatory elections. In the case of an S corporation or a partnership, the election is made by the S corporation or by the partnership, and not by the shareholders or partners. A taxpayer may revoke an election made under this paragraph (f)(2)(iv)(B) with respect to each acquisition only by filing a request for a private letter ruling and obtaining the Commissioner's consent to revoke the election. The Commissioner may grant a request to revoke this election if the taxpayer acted reasonably and in good faith and the revocation will not prejudice the interests of Government. See generally §301.9100-3 of this chapter. The manner of electing and revoking the election to capitalize under this paragraph (f)(2)(iv)(B) may be modified through guidance of general applicability (see §§606.601(d)(2) and 601.602 of this section). An election may not be made or revoked through the filing of an application for change in accounting method or, before obtaining the Commissioner's consent to make the late election or to revoke the election, by filing an amended Federal tax return.

(3) *Treatment of transaction costs.*—(i) *In general.*—Except as provided under §1.263(a)-1(f)(3)(i) (for purposes of the de minimis safe harbor), all amounts paid to facilitate the acquisition of real or personal property are capital expenditures. Facilitative amounts allocable to real or personal property must be included in the basis of the property acquired.

(ii) *Treatment of inherently facilitative amounts allocable to property not acquired.*—Inherently facilitative amounts allocable to real or personal property are capital expenditures related to such property, even if the property is not eventually acquired. Except for contingency fees as defined in paragraph (f)(3)(iii) of this section, inherently facilitative amounts allocable to real or personal property not acquired may be allocated to those properties and recovered as appropriate in accordance with the applicable provisions of the Code and the Treasury Regulations (for example, sections 165, 167, or 168). See paragraph (h) of this section for the recovery of capitalized amounts.

(iii) *Contingency Fees.*—For purposes of this section, a contingency fee is an amount paid that is contingent on the successful closing of the acquisition of real or personal property. Contingency fees must be included in the basis of the property acquired and may not be allocated to the property not acquired.

(4) *Examples.*—The following examples illustrate the rules of paragraph (f) of this section. For purposes of these examples, assume that the taxpayer does not elect the de minimis safe harbor under §1.263(a)-1(f):

Example 1. Broker's fees to facilitate an acquisition. A decides to purchase a building in which to relocate its offices and hires a real estate broker to find a suitable building. A pays fees to the broker to find property for A to acquire. Under paragraph (f)(2)(ii)(I) of this section, A must capitalize the amounts paid to the broker because these costs are inherently facilitative of the acquisition of real property.

Example 2. Inspection and survey costs to facilitate an acquisition. B decides to purchase Building X and pays amounts to third-party contractors for a termite inspection and an environmental survey of Building X. Under paragraph (f)(2)(ii)(J) of this section, B must capitalize the amounts paid for the inspection and the survey of the building because these costs are inherently facilitative of the acquisition of real property.

Example 3. Moving costs to facilitate an acquisition. C purchases all the assets of D and, in connection with the purchase, hires a transportation company to move storage tanks from D's plant to C's plant. Under paragraph (f)(2)(ii)(A) of this section, C must capitalize the amount paid to move the storage tanks from D's plant to C's plant because this cost is inherently facilitative to the acquisition of personal property.

Example 4. Geological and geophysical costs; coordination with other provisions. E is in the business of exploring, purchasing, and developing properties in the United States for the production of oil and gas. E considers acquiring a particular property but first incurs costs for the services of an engineering firm to perform geological and geophysical studies to determine if the property is suitable for oil or gas production. Assume that the amounts that E paid to the engineering firm constitute geological and geophysical expenditures under section 167(h). Although the amounts that E paid for the geological and geophysical services are inherently facilitative to the acquisition of real property under paragraph (f)(2)(ii)(J) of this section, E is not required to include those amounts in the basis of the real property acquired. Rather, under paragraph (c) of this section, E must capitalize these costs separately and amortize such costs as required under section 167(h) (addressing the amortization of geological and geophysical expenditures).

Example 5. Scope of facilitate. F is in the business of providing legal services to clients. F is interested in acquiring a new conference table for its office. F hires and incurs fees for an interior designer to shop for, evaluate, and make recommendations to F regarding which new table to acquire. Under paragraphs (f)(1) and (2) of this section, F must capitalize the amounts paid to the interior designer to provide these services because they are paid in the process of investigating or otherwise pursuing the acquisition of personal property.

Example 6. Transaction costs allocable to multiple properties. G, a retailer, wants to acquire land for the purpose of building a new distribution facility for its products. G considers various properties on Highway X in State Y. G incurs fees for the services of an architect to advise and evaluate the suitability of the sites for the type of facility that G intends to construct on the selected site. G must capitalize the architect fees as amounts paid to acquire land because these amounts are inherently facilitative to the acquisition of land under paragraph (f)(2)(ii)(J) of this section.

Example 7. Transaction costs; coordination with section 263A. H, a retailer, wants to acquire land for the purpose of building a new distribution facility for its products. H considers various properties on Highway X in State Y. H incurs fees for the services of an architect to prepare preliminary floor plans for a building that H could construct at any of the sites. Under these facts, the architect's fees are not facilitative to the acquisition of land under paragraph (f) of this section. Therefore, H is not required to capitalize the architect fees as amounts paid to acquire land. However, the amounts paid for the architect's fees may be subject to capitalization under section 263A if these amounts comprise the direct or allocable indirect cost of property produced by H, such as the building.

Example 8. Special rule for acquisitions of real property. J owns several retail stores. J decides to examine the feasibility of opening a new store in City X. In October, Year 1, J hires and incurs costs for a development consulting firm to study City X and perform market surveys, evaluate zoning and environmental requirements, and make preliminary reports and recommendations as to areas that J should consider for purposes of locating a new store. In December, Year 1, J continues to consider whether to purchase real property in City X and which property to acquire. J hires, and incurs fees for, an appraiser to perform appraisals on two different sites to determine a fair offering price for each site. In March, Year 2, J decides to acquire one of these two sites for the location of its new store. At the same time, J determines not to acquire the other site. Under paragraph (f)(2)(iii) of this section, J is not required to capitalize amounts paid to the development consultant in Year 1 because the amounts relate to activities performed in the process of determining whether to acquire real property and which real property to acquire, and the amounts are not inherently facilitative costs under paragraph (f)(2)(ii) of this section. However, J must capitalize amounts paid to the appraiser in Year 1 because the appraisal costs are inherently facilitative costs under paragraph (f)(2)(ii)(B) of this section. In Year 2, J must include the appraisal costs allocable to property acquired in the basis of the property acquired. In addition, J may recover the appraisal costs allocable to the property not acquired in accordance with paragraphs (f)(3)(ii) and (h) of this section. See, for example, §1.165-2 for losses on the permanent withdrawal of non-depreciable property.

Example 9. Contingency fee. K owns several restaurant properties. K decides to open a new restaurant in City X. In October, Year 1, K hires a real estate consultant to identify potential property upon which K may locate its restaurant, and is obligated to compensate the consultant upon the acquisition of property. The real estate consultant identifies three properties, and K decides to acquire one of those properties. Upon closing of the acquisition of that property, K pays the consultant its fee. The amount paid to the consultant constitutes a contingency fee under paragraph (f)(3)(iii) of this section because the payment is contingent on the successful closing of the acquisition of property. Accordingly, under paragraph (f)(3)(iii) of this section, K must include the amount paid to the consultant in the basis of the property acquired. K is not permitted to allocate the amount paid between the properties acquired and not acquired.

Example 10. Employee compensation and overhead. L, a freight carrier, maintains an acquisition department whose sole function is to arrange for the purchase of vehicles and aircraft from manufacturers or other parties to be used in its freight carrying business. As provided in paragraph (f)(2)(iv)(A) of this section, L is not required to capitalize any portion of the compensation paid to employees in its acquisition department or any portion of its overhead allocable to its acquisition department. However, under paragraph (f)(2)(iv)(B) of this section, L may elect to capitalize the compensation and/or overhead costs allocable to the acquisition of a vehicle or aircraft by treating these amounts as costs that facilitate the acquisition of that property in its timely filed original Federal tax return for the year the amounts are paid.

(g) *Treatment of capital expenditures.*—Amounts required to be capitalized under this section are capital expenditures and must be taken into account through a charge to capital account or basis, or in the case of property that is inventory in the hands of a taxpayer, through inclusion in inventory costs.

(h) *Recovery of capitalized amounts.*—(1) *In general.*—Amounts that are capitalized under this section are recovered through depreciation, cost of goods sold, or by an adjustment to basis at the time the property is placed in service, sold, used, or otherwise disposed of by the taxpayer. Cost recovery is determined by the applicable provisions of the Code and regulations relating to the use, sale, or disposition of property.

(2) *Examples.*—The following examples illustrate the rule of paragraph (h)(1) of this section. For purposes of these examples, assume that the taxpayer does not elect the de minimis safe harbor under § 1.263(a)-1(f).

Example 1. Recovery when property placed in service. X owns a 10-unit apartment building. The refrigerator in one of the apartments stops functioning, and X purchases a new refrigerator to replace the old one. X pays for the acquisition, delivery, and installation of the new refrigerator. Assume that the refrigerator is the unit of property, as determined under § 1.263(a)-3(e), and is not a material or supply under § 1.162-3. Under paragraph (d)(1) of this section, X is required to capitalize the amounts paid for the acquisition, delivery, and installation of the refrigerator. Under this paragraph (h), the capitalized amounts are recovered through depreciation, which begins when the refrigerator is placed in service by X.

Example 2. Recovery when property used in the production of property. Y operates a plant where it manufactures widgets. Y purchases a tractor loader to move raw materials into and around the plant for use in the manufacturing process. Assume that the tractor loader is a unit of property, as determined under § 1.263(a)-3(e), and is not a material or supply under § 1.162-3. Under paragraph (d)(1) of this section, Y is required to capitalize the amounts paid to acquire the tractor loader. Under this paragraph (h), the capitalized amounts are recovered through depreciation, which begins when Y places the tractor loader in service. However, because the tractor loader is used in the production of property, under section 263A the cost recovery (that is, the depreciation) may also be capitalized to Y's property produced, and, consequently, recovered through cost of goods sold. See § 1.263A-1(e)(3)(ii)(I).

* * *

[Reg. § 1.263(a)-2.]

☐ [*T.D.* 6313, 9-16-58. *Amended by T.D.* 8131, 3-24-87; *T.D.* 9564, 12-23-2011 *and T.D.* 9636, 9-13-2013 (*corrected* 7-18-2014).]

§ 1.263(a)-3. Amounts paid to improve tangible property.—(a) *Overview.*—This section provides rules for applying section 263(a) to amounts paid to improve tangible property. Paragraph (b) of this section provides definitions. Paragraph (c) of this section provides rules for coordinating this section with other provisions of the Internal Revenue Code (Code). Paragraph (d) of this section provides the requirement to capitalize amounts paid to improve tangible property and provides the general rules for determining whether a unit of property is improved. Paragraph (e) of this section provides the rules for determining the appropriate unit of property. Paragraph (f) of this section provides rules for leasehold improvements. Paragraph (g) of this section provides special rules for determining improvement costs in particular contexts, including indirect costs incurred during an improvement, removal costs, aggregation of related costs, and regulatory compliance costs. Paragraph (h) of this section provides a safe harbor for small taxpayers. Paragraph (i) provides a safe harbor for routine maintenance costs. Paragraph (j) of this section provides rules for determining whether amounts are paid for betterments to the unit of property. Paragraph (k) of this section provides rules for determining whether amounts are paid to restore the unit of property. Paragraph (l) of this section provides rules for amounts paid to adapt the unit of property to a new or different use. Paragraph (m) of this section provides an optional regulatory accounting method. Paragraph (n) of this section provides an election to capitalize repair and maintenance costs consistent with books and records. Paragraphs (o) and (p) of this section provide for the treatment and recovery of amounts capitalized under this section. Paragraphs (q) and (r) of this section provide for accounting method changes and state the effective/applicability date for the rules in this section.

(b) *Definitions.*—For purposes of this section, the following definitions apply:

(1) *Amount paid.*—In the case of a taxpayer using an accrual method of accounting, the terms *amounts paid* and *payment* mean a liability incurred (within the meaning of § 1.446-1(c)(1)(ii)). A liability may not be taken into account under this section prior to the taxable year during which the liability is incurred.

(2) *Personal property* means tangible personal property as defined in § 1.48-1(c).

(3) *Real property* means land and improvements thereto, such as buildings or other inherently permanent structures (including items that are structural components of the buildings or structures) that are not personal property as defined in paragraph (b)(2) of this section. Any property that constitutes other tangible property under § 1.48-1(d) is also treated as real property for purposes of this section. Local law is not controlling in determining whether property is real property for purposes of this section.

(4) *Owner* means the taxpayer that has the benefits and burdens of ownership of the unit of property for Federal income tax purposes.

(c) *Coordination with other provisions of the Code.*—(1) *In general.*—Nothing in this section changes the treatment of any amount that is specifically provided for under any provision of the Code or the regulations other than section 162(a) or section 212 and the regulations under those sections. For example, see section 263A requiring taxpayers to capitalize the direct and allocable indirect costs of property produced and property acquired for resale.

(2) *Materials and supplies.*—A material or supply as defined in § 1.162-3(c)(1) that is acquired and used to improve a unit of tangible property is subject to this section and is not treated as a material or supply under § 1.162-3.

(3) *Example.*—The following example illustrates the rules of this paragraph (c):

Example. Railroad rolling stock. X is a railroad that properly treats amounts paid for the rehabilitation of railroad rolling stock as deductible expenses under section 263(d). X is not required to capitalize the amounts paid because nothing in this section changes the treatment of amounts specifically provided for under section 263(d).

(d) *Requirement to capitalize amounts paid for improvements.*—Except as provided in paragraph (h) or paragraph (n) of this section or under § 1.263(a)-1(f), a taxpayer generally must capitalize the related amounts (as defined in paragraph (g)(3) of this section) paid to improve a unit of property owned by the taxpayer. However, paragraph (f) of this section applies to the treatment of amounts paid to improve leased property. Section 263A provides the requirement to capitalize the direct and allocable indirect costs of property produced by the taxpayer and property acquired for resale. Section 1016 provides for the addition of capitalized amounts to the basis of the property, and section 168 governs the treatment of additions or improvements for depreciation purposes. For purposes of this section, a unit of property is improved if the amounts paid for activities performed after the property is placed in service by the taxpayer—

(1) Are for a betterment to the unit of property (see paragraph (j) of this section);

(2) Restore the unit of property (see paragraph (k) of this section); or

(3) Adapt the unit of property to a new or different use (see paragraph (l) of this section).

(e) *Determining the unit of property.*—(1) *In general.*—The unit of property rules in this paragraph (e) apply only for purposes of section 263(a) and §§ 1.263(a)-1, 1.263(a)-2, 1.263(a)-3, and 1.162-3. Unless otherwise specified, the unit of property determination is based upon the functional interdependence standard provided in paragraph (e)(3)(i) of this section. However, special rules are provided for buildings (see paragraph (e)(2) of this section), plant property (see paragraph (e)(3)(ii) of this section), network assets (see paragraph (e)(3)(iii) of this section), leased property (see paragraph (e)(2)(v) of this section for leased buildings and paragraph (e)(3)(iv) of this section for leased property other than buildings), and improvements to property (see paragraph (e)(4) of this section). Additional rules are provided if a taxpayer has assigned different MACRS classes or depreciation methods to components of property or subsequently changes the class or depreciation method of a component or other item of property (see paragraph (e)(5) of this section). Property that is aggregated or subject to a general asset account election or accounted for in a multiple asset account (that is, pooled) may not be treated as a single unit of property.

(2) *Building.*—(i) *In general.*—Except as otherwise provided in paragraphs (e)(4), and (e)(5)(ii) of this section, in the case of a building (as defined in § 1.48-1(e)(1)), each building and its structural components (as defined in § 1.48-1(e)(2)) is a single unit of property ("building"). Paragraph (e)(2)(iii) of this section provides the unit of property for condominiums, paragraph (e)(2)(iv) of this section provides the unit of property for cooperatives, and paragraph (e)(2)(v) of this section provides the unit of property for leased buildings.

(ii) *Application of improvement rules to a building.*—An amount is paid to improve a building under paragraph (d) of this section if the amount is paid for an improvement under paragraphs (j), (k), or paragraph (l) of this section to any of the following:

(A) *Building structure.*—A building structure consists of the building (as defined in § 1.48-1(e)(1)), and its structural components (as defined in § 1.48-1(e)(2)), other than the structural components designated as buildings systems in paragraph (e)(2)(ii)(B) of this section.

(B) *Building system.*—Each of the following structural components (as defined in § 1.48-1(e)(2)), including the components thereof, constitutes a building system that is separate from the building structure, and to which the improvement rules must be applied—

(1) Heating, ventilation, and air conditioning ("HVAC") systems (including motors, compressors, boilers, furnace, chillers, pipes, ducts, radiators);

(2) Plumbing systems (including pipes, drains, valves, sinks, bathtubs, toilets, water and sanitary sewer collection equipment, and site utility equipment used to distribute water and waste to and from the property line and between buildings and other permanent structures);

(3) Electrical systems (including wiring, outlets, junction boxes, lighting fixtures and associated connectors, and site utility equipment used to distribute electricity from the property line to and between buildings and other permanent structures);

(4) All escalators;

(5) All elevators;

(6) Fire-protection and alarm systems (including sensing devices, computer controls, sprinkler heads, sprinkler mains, associated piping or plumbing, pumps, visual and audible alarms, alarm control panels, heat and smoke detection devices, fire escapes, fire doors, emergency exit lighting and signage, and fire fighting equipment, such as extinguishers, and hoses);

(7) Security systems for the protection of the building and its occupants (including window and door locks, security cameras, recorders, monitors, motion detectors, security lighting, alarm systems, entry and access systems, related junction boxes, associated wiring and conduit);

(8) Gas distribution system (including associated pipes and equipment used to distribute gas to and from the property line and between buildings or permanent structures); and

(9) Other structural components identified in published guidance in the Federal Register or in the Internal Revenue Bulletin (see § 601.601(d)(2)(ii)(*b*) of this chapter) that are excepted from the building structure under paragraph (e)(2)(ii)(A) of this section and are specifically designated as building systems under this section.

(iii) *Condominium.*—(A) *In general.*—In the case of a taxpayer that is the owner of an individual unit in a building with multiple units (such as a condominium), the unit of property ("condominium") is the individual unit owned by the taxpayer and the structural components (as defined in § 1.48-1(e)(2)) that are part of the unit.

(B) *Application of improvement rules to a condominium.*—An amount is paid to improve a condominium under paragraph (d) of this section if the amount is paid for an improvement under paragraphs (j), (k), or paragraph (l) of this section to the building structure (as defined in paragraph (e)(2)(ii)(A) of this section) that is part of the condominium or to the portion of any building system (as defined in paragraph (e)(2)(ii)(B) of this section) that is part of the condominium. In the case of the condominium management association, the association must apply the improvement rules to the building structure or to any building system described under paragraphs (e)(2)(ii)(A) and (e)(2)(ii)(B) of this section.

(iv) *Cooperative.*—(A) *In general.*—In the case of a taxpayer that has an ownership interest in a cooperative housing corporation, the unit of property ("cooperative") is the portion of the building in which the taxpayer has possessory rights and the structural components (as defined in § 1.48-1(e)(2)) that are part of the portion of the building subject to the taxpayer's possessory rights (cooperative).

(B) *Application of improvement rules to a cooperative.*—An amount is paid to improve a cooperative under paragraph (d) of this section if the amount is paid for an improvement under paragraphs (j), (k), or (l) of this section to the portion of the building structure (as defined in paragraph (e)(2)(ii)(A) of this section) in which the taxpayer has possessory rights or to the portion of any building system (as defined in paragraph (e)(2)(ii)(B) of this section) that is part of the portion of the building structure subject to the taxpayer's possessory rights. In the case of a cooperative housing corporation, the corporation must apply the improvement rules to the building structure or to any building system as described under paragraphs (e)(2)(ii)(A) and (e)(2)(ii)(B) of this section.

(v) *Leased building.*—(A) *In general.*—In the case of a taxpayer that is a lessee of all or a portion of a building (such as an office, floor, or certain square footage), the unit of property ("leased building property") is each building and its structural components or the portion of each building subject to the lease and the structural components associated with the leased portion.

(B) *Application of improvement rules to a leased building.*—An amount is paid to improve a leased building property under paragraphs (d) and (f)(2) of this section if the amount is paid for an improvement, under paragraphs (j), (k), or (l) of this section, to any of the following:

(1) Entire building.—In the case of a taxpayer that is a lessee of an entire building, the building structure (as defined under paragraph (e)(2)(ii)(A) of this section) or any building system (as defined under paragraph (e)(2)(ii)(B) of this section) that is part of the leased building.

(2) Portion of a building.—In the case of a taxpayer that is a lessee of a portion of a building (such as an office, floor, or certain square footage), the portion of the building structure (as defined under paragraph (e)(2)(ii)(A) of this section) subject to the lease or the portion of any building system (as defined under paragraph (e)(2)(ii)(B) of this section) subject to the lease.

(3) *Property other than building.*—(i) *In general.*—Except as otherwise provided in paragraphs (e)(3), (e)(4), (e)(5), and (f)(1) of this section, in the case of real or personal property other than property described in paragraph (e)(2) of this section, all the components that are functionally interdependent comprise a single unit of property. Components of property are functionally interdependent if the placing in service of one component by the taxpayer is dependent on the placing in service of the other component by the taxpayer.

(ii) *Plant property.*—(A) *Definition.*—For purposes of this paragraph (e), the term *plant property* means functionally interdependent machinery or equipment, other than network assets, used to perform an industrial process, such as manufacturing, generation, warehousing, distribution, automated materials handling in service industries, or other similar activities.

(B) *Unit of property for plant property.*—In the case of plant property, the unit of property determined under the general rule of paragraph (e)(3)(i) of this section is further divided into smaller units comprised of each component (or group of components) that performs a discrete and major function or operation within the functionally interdependent machinery or equipment.

(iii) *Network assets.*—(A) *Definition.*—For purposes of this paragraph (e), the term *network assets* means railroad track, oil and gas pipelines, water and sewage pipelines, power transmission and distribution lines, and telephone and cable lines that are owned or leased by taxpayers in each of those respective industries. The term includes, for example, trunk and feeder lines, pole lines, and buried conduit. It does not include property that would be included as building structure or building systems under paragraphs (e)(2)(ii)(A) and (e)(2)(ii)(B) of this section, nor does it include separate property that is adjacent to, but not part of a network asset, such as bridges, culverts, or tunnels.

(B) *Unit of property for network assets.*—In the case of network assets, the unit of property is determined by the taxpayer's particular facts and circumstances except as otherwise provided in published guidance in the Federal Register or in the Internal Revenue Bulletin (see § 601.601(d)(2)(ii)(*b*) of this chapter). For these purposes, the functional interdependence standard provided in paragraph (e)(3)(i) of this section is not determinative.

(iv) *Leased property other than buildings.*—In the case of a taxpayer that is a lessee of real or personal property other than property described in paragraph (e)(2) of this section, the unit of property for the leased property is determined under paragraphs (e)(3)(i),(ii), (iii), and (e)(5) of this section except that, after applying the applicable rules under those paragraphs, the unit of property may not be larger than the property subject to the lease.

(4) *Improvements to property.*—An improvement to a unit of property generally is not a unit of property separate from the unit of property improved. For the unit of property for lessee improvements, see also paragraph (f)(2)(ii)) of this section. If a taxpayer elects to treat as a capital expenditure under § 1.162-3(d) the amount paid for a rotable spare part, temporary spare part, or standby emergency spare part, and such part is used in an improvement to a unit of property, then for purposes of applying paragraph (d) of this section to the unit of property improved, the part is not a unit of property separate from the unit of property improved.

(5) *Additional rules.*—(i) *Year placed in service.*—Notwithstanding the unit of property determination under paragraph (e)(3) of this section, a component (or a group of compo-

nents) of a unit property must be treated as a separate unit of property if, at the time the unit of property is initially placed in service by the taxpayer, the taxpayer has properly treated the component as being within a different class of property under section 168(e) (MACRS classes) than the class of the unit of property of which the component is a part, or the taxpayer has properly depreciated the component using a different depreciation method than the depreciation method of the unit of property of which the component is a part.

(ii) *Change in subsequent taxable year.*—Notwithstanding the unit of property determination under paragraphs (e)(2), (3), (4), or (5)(i) of this section, in any taxable year after the unit of property is initially placed in service by the taxpayer, if the taxpayer or the Internal Revenue Service changes the treatment of that property (or any portion thereof) to a proper MACRS class or a proper depreciation method (for example, as a result of a cost segregation study or a change in the use of the property), then the taxpayer must change the unit of property determination for that property (or the portion thereof) under this section to be consistent with the change in treatment for depreciation purposes. Thus, for example, if a portion of a unit of property is properly reclassified to a MACRS class different from the MACRS class of the unit of property of which it was previously treated as a part, then the reclassified portion of the property should be treated as a separate unit of property for purposes of this section.

* * *

(f) *Improvements to leased property.*—(1) *In general.*—Except as provided in paragraph (h) of this section (safe harbor for small taxpayers) and under § 1.263(a)-1(f) (de minimis safe harbor), this paragraph (f) provides the exclusive rules for determining whether amounts paid by a taxpayer are for an improvement to a leased property and must be capitalized. In the case of a leased building or a leased portion of a building, an amount is paid to improve a leased property if the amount is paid for an improvement to any of the properties specified in paragraph (e)(2)(ii) of this section (for lessor improvements) or in paragraph (e)(2)(v)(B) of this section (for lessee improvements, except as provided in paragraph (f)(2)(ii) of this section). Section 1.263(a)-4 does not apply to amounts paid for improvements to leased property or to amounts paid for the acquisition or production of leasehold improvement property.

(2) *Lessee improvements.*—(i) *Requirement to capitalize.*—A taxpayer lessee must capitalize the related amounts, as determined under paragraph (g)(3) of this section, that it pays to improve, as defined under paragraph (d) of this section, a leased property except to the extent that section 110 applies to a construction allowance received by the lessee for the purpose of such improvement or when the improvement constitutes a substitute for rent. See § 1.61-8(c) for the treatment of lessee expenditures that constitute a substitute for rent. A taxpayer lessee must also capitalize the related amounts that a lessor pays to improve, as defined under paragraph (d) of this section, a leased property if the lessee is the owner of the improvement, except to the extent that section 110 applies to a construction allowance received by the lessee for the purpose of such improvement. An amount paid for a lessee improvement under this paragraph (f)(2)(i) is treated as an amount paid to acquire or produce a unit of real or personal property under § 1.263(a)-2(d)(1) of the regulations.

(ii) *Unit of property for lessee improvements.*—For purposes of determining whether an amount paid by a lessee constitutes a lessee improvement to a leased property under paragraph (f)(2)(i) of this section, the unit of property and the improvement rules are applied to the leased property in accordance with paragraph (e)(2)(v) (leased buildings) or paragraph (e)(3)(iv) (leased property other than buildings) of this section and include previous lessee improvements. However, if a lessee improvement is comprised of an entire building erected on leased property, then the unit of property for the building and the application of the improvement rules to the building are determined under paragraphs (e)(2)(i) and (e)(2)(ii) of this section.

(3) *Lessor improvements.*—(i) *Requirement to capitalize.*—A taxpayer lessor must capitalize the related amounts, as determined under paragraph (g)(3) of this section, that it pays directly, or indirectly through a construction allowance to the lessee, to improve, as defined in paragraph (d) of this section, a leased property when the lessor is the owner of the improvement or to the extent that section 110 applies to the construction allowance. A lessor must also capitalize the related amounts that the lessee pays to improve a leased property, as defined in paragraph (e) of this section, when the lessee's improvement constitutes a substitute for rent. See § 1.61-8(c) for treatment of expenditures by lessees that constitute a substitute for rent. Amounts capitalized by the lessor under this paragraph (f)(3)(i) may not be capitalized by the lessee. If a lessor improvement is comprised of an entire building erected on leased property, then the amount paid for the building is treated as an amount paid by the lessor to acquire or produce a unit of property under

§ 1.263(a)-2(d)(1). See paragraph (e)(2) of this section for the unit of property for a building and paragraph (e)(3) of this section for the unit of property for real or personal property other than a building.

(ii) *Unit of property for lessor improvements.*—In general, an amount capitalized as a lessor improvement under paragraph (f)(3)(i) of this section is not a unit of property separate from the unit of property improved. See paragraph (e)(4) of this section. However, if a lessor improvement is comprised of an entire building erected on leased property, then the unit of property for the building and the application of the improvement rules to the building are determined under paragraphs (e)(2)(i) and (e)(2)(ii) of this section.

* * *

(g) *Special rules for determining improvement costs.*—(1) *Certain costs incurred during an improvement.*—(i) *In general.*—A taxpayer must capitalize all the direct costs of an improvement and all the indirect costs (including, for example, otherwise deductible repair costs) that directly benefit or are incurred by reason of an improvement. Indirect costs arising from activities that do not directly benefit and are not incurred by reason of an improvement are not required to be capitalized under section 263(a), regardless of whether the activities are performed at the same time as an improvement.

(ii) *Exception for individuals' residences.*—A taxpayer who is an individual may capitalize amounts paid for repairs and maintenance that are made at the same time as capital improvements to units of property not used in the taxpayer's trade or business or for the production of income if the amounts are paid as part of an improvement (for example, a remodeling) of the taxpayer's residence.

(2) *Removal Costs.*—(i) *In general.*—If a taxpayer disposes of a depreciable asset, including a partial disposition under Prop. Reg. § 1.168(i)-1(e)(2)(ix) (September 19, 2013), or Prop. Reg. § 1.168(i)-8(d) (September 19, 2013), for Federal income tax purposes and has taken into account the adjusted basis of the asset or component of the asset in realizing gain or loss, then the costs of removing the asset or component are not required to be capitalized under this section. If a depreciable asset is included in a general asset account under section 168(i)(4), and neither the regulations under section 168(i)(4) and § 1.168(i)-1T(e)(3) nor Prop. Reg. § 1.168(i)-1(e)(3) (September 19, 2013), apply to a disposition of such asset, or a portion of such asset under Prop. Reg. § 1.168(i)-1(e)(2)(ix) (September 19, 2013), a loss is treated as being realized in the amount of zero upon the disposition of the asset solely for purposes of this paragraph (g)(2)(i). If a taxpayer disposes of a component of a unit of property, but the disposal of the component is not a disposition for Federal tax purposes, then the taxpayer must deduct or capitalize the costs of removing the component based on whether the removal costs directly benefit or are incurred by reason of a repair to the unit of property or an improvement to the unit of property. But see § 1.280B-1 for the rules applicable to demolition of structures.

* * *

(h) *Safe harbor for small taxpayers.*—(1) *In general.*—A qualifying taxpayer (as defined in paragraph (h)(3) of this section) may elect to not apply paragraph (d) or paragraph (f) of this section to an eligible building property (as defined in paragraph (h)(4) of this section) if the total amount paid during the taxable year for repairs, maintenance, improvements, and similar activities performed on the eligible building property does not exceed the lesser of—

(i) 2 percent of the unadjusted basis (as defined under paragraph (h)(5) of this section) of the eligible building property; or

(ii) $10,000.

(2) *Application with other safe harbor provisions.*—For purposes of paragraph (h)(1) of this section, amounts paid for repairs, maintenance, improvements, and similar activities performed on eligible building property include those amounts not capitalized under the de minimis safe harbor election under § 1.263(a)-1(f) and those amounts deemed not to improve property under the safe harbor for routine maintenance under paragraph (i) of this section.

(3) *Qualifying taxpayer.*—(i) *In general.*—For purposes of this paragraph (h), the term *qualifying taxpayer* means a taxpayer whose average annual gross receipts as determined under this paragraph (h)(3) for the three preceding taxable years is less than or equal to $10,000,000.

(ii) *Application to new taxpayers.*—If a taxpayer has been in existence for less than three taxable years, the taxpayer determines its average annual gross receipts for the number of taxable years (including short taxable years) that the taxpayer (or its predecessor) has been in existence.

(iii) *Treatment of short taxable year.*—In the case of any taxable year of less than 12 months (a short taxable year), the gross receipts shall be annualized by—

(A) Multiplying the gross receipts for the short period by 12; and

(B) Dividing the product determined in paragraph (h)(3)(iii)(A) of this section by the number of months in the short period.

(iv) *Definition of gross receipts*.—For purposes of applying paragraph (h)(3)(i) of this section, the term *gross receipts* means the taxpayer's receipts for the taxable year that are properly recognized under the taxpayer's methods of accounting used for Federal income tax purposes for the taxable year. For this purpose, gross receipts include total sales (net of returns and allowances) and all amounts received for services. In addition, gross receipts include any income from investments and from incidental or outside sources. For example, gross receipts include interest (including original issue discount and tax-exempt interest within the meaning of section 103), dividends, rents, royalties, and annuities, regardless of whether such amounts are derived in the ordinary course of the taxpayer's trade of business. Gross receipts are not reduced by cost of goods sold or by the cost of property sold if such property is described in section 1221(a)(1), (3), (4), or (5). With respect to sales of capital assets as defined in section 1221, or sales of property described in section 1221(a)(2) (relating to property used in a trade or business), gross receipts shall be reduced by the taxpayer's adjusted basis in such property. Gross receipts do not include the repayment of a loan or similar instrument (for example, a repayment of the principal amount of a loan held by a commercial lender) and, except to the extent of gain recognized, do not include gross receipts derived from a non-recognition transaction, such as a section 1031 exchange. Finally, gross receipts do not include amounts received by the taxpayer with respect to sales tax or other similar state and local taxes if, under the applicable state or local law, the tax is legally imposed on the purchaser of the good or service, and the taxpayer merely collects and remits the tax to the taxing authority. If, in contrast, the tax is imposed on the taxpayer under the applicable law, then gross receipts include the amounts received that are allocable to the payment of such tax.

(4) *Eligible building property*.—For purposes of this section, the term *eligible building property* refers to each unit of property defined in paragraph (e)(2)(i) (building), paragraph (e)(2)(iii)(A) (condominium), paragraph (e)(2)(iv)(A) (cooperative), or paragraph (e)(2)(v)(A) (leased building or portion of building) of this section, as applicable, that has an unadjusted basis of $1,000,000 or less.

(5) *Unadjusted basis*.—(i) *Eligible building property owned by taxpayer*.—For purposes of this section, the unadjusted basis of eligible building property owned by the taxpayer means the basis as determined under section 1012, or other applicable sections of Chapter 1, including subchapters O (relating to gain or loss on dispositions of property), C (relating to corporate distributions and adjustments), K (relating to partners and partnerships), and P (relating to capital gains and losses). Unadjusted basis is determined without regard to any adjustments described in section 1016(a)(2) or (3) or to amounts for which the taxpayer has elected to treat as an expense (for example, under sections 179, 179B, or 179C).

(ii) *Eligible building property leased to the taxpayer*.—For purposes of this section, the unadjusted basis of eligible building property leased to the taxpayer is the total amount of (undiscounted) rent paid or expected to be paid by the lessee under the lease for the entire term of the lease, including renewal periods if all the facts and circumstances in existence during the taxable year in which the lease is entered indicate a reasonable expectancy of renewal. Section 1.263(a)-4(f)(5)(ii) provides the factors that are significant in determining whether there exists a reasonable expectancy of renewal for purposes of this paragraph.

(6) *Time and manner of election*.—A taxpayer makes the election described in paragraph (h)(1) of this section by attaching a statement to the taxpayer's timely filed original Federal tax return (including extensions) for the taxable year in which amounts are paid for repairs, maintenance, improvements, and similar activities performed on the eligible building property providing that such amounts qualify under the safe harbor provided in paragraph (h)(1) of this section. Sections 301.9100-1 through Reg. § 301.9100-3 of this chapter provide the rules governing extensions of the time to make regulatory elections. The statement must be titled, "Section 1.263(a)-3(h) Safe Harbor Election for Small Taxpayers" and include the taxpayer's name, address, taxpayer identification number, and a description of each eligible building property to which the taxpayer is applying the election. In the case of an S corporation or a partnership, the election is made by the S corporation or by the partnership, and not by the shareholders or partners. An election may not be made through the filing of an application for change in accounting method or, before obtaining the Commissioner's consent to make a late election, by filing an amended Federal tax return. A taxpayer may not revoke an election made under this paragraph (h). The time and manner of making the election under this paragraph (h) may be modified through

guidance of general applicability (see §§601.601(d)(2) and 601.602 of this chapter).

(7) *Treatment of safe harbor amounts.*—Amounts paid by the taxpayer for repairs, maintenance, improvements, and similar activities to which the taxpayer properly applies the safe harbor under paragraph (h)(1) of this section and for which the taxpayer properly makes the election under paragraph (h)(6) of this section are not treated as improvements under paragraph (d) or (f) of this section and may be deducted under §1.162-1 or §1.212-1, as applicable, in the taxable year these amounts are paid, provided the amounts otherwise qualify for a deduction under these sections.

(8) *Safe harbor exceeded.*—If total amounts paid by a qualifying taxpayer during the taxable year for repairs, maintenance, improvements, and similar activities performed on an eligible building property exceed the safe harbor limitations specified in paragraph (h)(1) of this section, then the safe harbor election is not available for that eligible building property and the taxpayer must apply the general improvement rules under this section to determine whether amounts are for improvements to the unit of property, including the safe harbor for routine maintenance under paragraph (i) of this section. The taxpayer may also elect to apply the de minimis safe harbor under §1.263(a)-1(f) to amounts qualifying under that safe harbor irrespective of the application of this paragraph (h).

* * *

(i) *Safe harbor for routine maintenance on property.*—(1) *In general.*—An amount paid for routine maintenance (as defined in paragraph (i)(1)(i) or (i)(1)(ii) of this section, as applicable) on a unit of tangible property, or in the case of a building, on any of the properties designated in paragraphs (e)(2)(ii), (e)(2)(iii)(B), (e)(2)(iv)(B), or paragraph (e)(2)(v)(B) of this section, is deemed not to improve that unit of property.

(i) *Routine maintenance for buildings.*—Routine maintenance for a building unit of property is the recurring activities that a taxpayer expects to perform as a result of the taxpayer's use of any of the properties designated in paragraphs (e)(2)(ii), (e)(2)(iii)(B), (e)(2)(iv)(B), or (e)(2)(v)(B) of this section to keep the building structure or each building system in its ordinarily efficient operating condition. Routine maintenance activities include, for example, the inspection, cleaning, and testing of the building structure or each building system, and the replacement of damaged or worn parts with comparable and commercially available replacement parts. Routine maintenance may be performed any time during the useful life of the building structure or building systems. However, the activities are routine only if the taxpayer reasonably expects to perform the activities more than once during the 10-year period beginning at the time the building structure or the building system upon which the routine maintenance is performed is placed in service by the taxpayer. A taxpayer's expectation will not be deemed unreasonable merely because the taxpayer does not actually perform the maintenance a second time during the 10-year period, provided that the taxpayer can otherwise substantiate that its expectation was reasonable at the time the property was placed in service. Factors to be considered in determining whether maintenance is routine and whether a taxpayer's expectation is reasonable include the recurring nature of the activity, industry practice, manufacturers' recommendations, and the taxpayer's experience with similar or identical property. With respect to a taxpayer that is a lessor of a building or a part of the building, the taxpayer's use of the building unit of property includes the lessee's use of its unit of property.

(ii) *Routine maintenance for property other than buildings.*—Routine maintenance for property other than buildings is the recurring activities that a taxpayer expects to perform as a result of the taxpayer's use of the unit of property to keep the unit of property in its ordinarily efficient operating condition. Routine maintenance activities include, for example, the inspection, cleaning, and testing of the unit of property, and the replacement of damaged or worn parts of the unit of property with comparable and commercially available replacement parts. Routine maintenance may be performed any time during the useful life of the unit of property. However, the activities are routine only if, at the time the unit of property is placed in service by the taxpayer, the taxpayer reasonably expects to perform the activities more than once during the class life (as defined in paragraph (i)(4) of this section) of the unit of property. A taxpayer's expectation will not be deemed unreasonable merely because the taxpayer does not actually perform the maintenance a second time during the class life of the unit of property, provided that the taxpayer can otherwise substantiate that its expectation was reasonable at the time the property was placed in service. Factors to be considered in determining whether maintenance is routine and whether the taxpayer's expectation is reasonable include the recurring nature of the activity, industry practice, manufacturers' recommendations, and the taxpayer's experience with similar or identical property. With respect to a taxpayer that is a lessor of a unit of property, the taxpayer's use of the unit of property includes the lessee's use of the unit of property.

(2) *Rotable and temporary spare parts.*—Except as provided in paragraph (i)(3) of this section, for purposes of paragraph (i)(1)(ii) of this section, amounts paid for routine maintenance include routine maintenance performed on (and with regard to) rotable and temporary spare parts.

(3) *Exceptions.*—Routine maintenance does not include the following:

(i) Amounts paid for a betterment to a unit of property under paragraph (j) of this section;

(ii) Amounts paid for the replacement of a component of a unit of property for which the taxpayer has properly deducted a loss for that component (other than a casualty loss under § 1.165-7) (see paragraph (k)(1)(i) of this section);

(iii) Amounts paid for the replacement of a component of a unit of property for which the taxpayer has properly taken into account the adjusted basis of the component in realizing gain or loss resulting from the sale or exchange of the component (see paragraph (k)(1)(ii) of this section);

(iv) Amounts paid for the restoration of damage to a unit of property for which the taxpayer is required to take a basis adjustment as a result of a casualty loss under section 165, or relating to a casualty event described in section 165, subject to the limitation in paragraph (k)(4) of this section (see paragraph (k)(1)(iii) of this section);

(v) Amounts paid to return a unit of property to its ordinarily efficient operating condition, if the property has deteriorated to a state of disrepair and is no longer functional for its intended use (see paragraph (k)(1)(iv) of this section);

(vi) Amounts paid to adapt a unit of property to a new or different use under paragraph (l) of this section;

(vii) Amounts paid for repairs, maintenance, or improvement of network assets (as defined in paragraph (e)(3)(iii)(A) of this section); or

(viii) Amounts paid for repairs, maintenance, or improvement of rotable and temporary spare parts to which the taxpayer applies the optional method of accounting for rotable and temporary spare parts under § 1.162-3(e).

(4) *Class life.*—The class life of a unit of property is the recovery period prescribed for the property under sections 168(g)(2) and (3) for purposes of the alternative depreciation system, regardless of whether the property is depreciated under section 168(g). For purposes of determining class life under this section, section 168(g)(3)(A) (relating to tax-exempt use property subject to lease) does not apply. If the unit of property is comprised of components with different class lives, then the class life of the unit of property is deemed to be the same as the component with the longest class life.

(5) *Coordination with section 263A.*—Amounts paid for routine maintenance under this paragraph (i) may be subject to capitalization under section 263A if these amounts comprise the direct or allocable indirect costs of other property produced by the taxpayer or property acquired for resale. See, for example, § 1.263A-1(e)(3)(ii)(O) requiring taxpayers to capitalize the cost of repairing equipment or facilities allocable to property produced or property acquired for resale.

* * *

(j) *Capitalization of betterments.*—(1) *In general.*—A taxpayer must capitalize as an improvement an amount paid for a betterment to a unit of property. An amount is paid for a betterment to a unit of property only if it—

(i) Ameliorates a material condition or defect that either existed prior to the taxpayer's acquisition of the unit of property or arose during the production of the unit of property, whether or not the taxpayer was aware of the condition or defect at the time of acquisition or production;

(ii) Is for a material addition, including a physical enlargement, expansion, extension, or addition of a major component (as defined in paragraph (k)(6) of this section) to the unit of property or a material increase in the capacity, including additional cubic or linear space, of the unit of property; or

(iii) Is reasonably expected to materially increase the productivity, efficiency, strength, quality, or output of the unit of property.

(2) *Application of betterment rules.*—(i) *In general.*—The applicability of each quantitative and qualitative factor provided in paragraphs (j)(1)(ii) and (j)(1)(iii) of this section to a particular unit of property depends on the nature of the unit of property. For example, if an addition or an increase in a particular factor cannot be measured in the context of a specific type of property, this factor is not relevant in the determination of whether an amount has been paid for a betterment to the unit of property.

(ii) *Application of betterment rules to buildings.*—An amount is paid to improve a building if it is paid for a betterment, as defined under paragraph (j)(1) of this section, to a property specified under paragraph (e)(2)(ii) (building), paragraph (e)(2)(iii)(B) (condominium), paragraph (e)(2)(iv)(B) (cooperative), or paragraph (e)(2)(v)(B) (leased building or leased portion of building) of this section. For example, an amount is paid to improve a building if it is paid for an increase in the efficiency of the building structure or any one of its building systems (for example, the HVAC system).

(iii) *Unavailability of replacement parts.*—If a taxpayer replaces a part of a unit of property that cannot reasonably be replaced with the same type of part (for example, because of technological advancements or product enhancements), the replacement of the part with an improved, but comparable, part does not, by itself, result in a betterment to the unit of property.

(iv) *Appropriate comparison.*—(A) *In general.*—In cases in which an expenditure is necessitated by normal wear and tear or damage to the unit of property that occurred during the taxpayer's use of the unit of property, the determination of whether an expenditure is for the betterment of the unit of property is made by comparing the condition of the property immediately after the expenditure with the condition of the property immediately prior to the circumstances necessitating the expenditure.

(B) *Normal wear and tear.*—If the expenditure is made to correct the effects of normal wear and tear to the unit of property that occurred during the taxpayer's use of the unit of property, the condition of the property immediately prior to the circumstances necessitating the expenditure is the condition of the property after the last time the taxpayer corrected the effects of normal wear and tear (whether the amounts paid were for maintenance or improvements) or, if the taxpayer has not previously corrected the effects of normal wear and tear, the condition of the property when placed in service by the taxpayer.

(C) *Damage to property.*—If the expenditure is made to correct damage to a unit of property that occurred during the taxpayer's use of the unit of property, the condition of the property immediately prior to the circumstances necessitating the expenditure is the condition of the property immediately prior to damage.

(3) *Examples.*—The following examples illustrate the application of this paragraph (j) only and do not address whether capitalization is required under another provision of this section or another provision of the Internal Revenue Code (for example, section 263A). Unless otherwise provided, assume that the appropriate comparison in paragraph (j)(2)(iv) of this section is not applicable under the facts.

Example 1. Amelioration of pre-existing material condition or defect. In Year 1, A purchases a store located on a parcel of land that contains underground gasoline storage tanks left by prior occupants. Assume that the parcel of land is the unit of property. The tanks had leaked prior to A's purchase, causing soil contamination. A is not aware of the contamination at the time of purchase. In Year 2, A discovers the contamination and incurs costs to remediate the soil. The remediation costs are for a betterment to the land under paragraph (j)(1)(i) of this section because A incurred the costs to ameliorate a material condition or defect that existed prior to A's acquisition of the land.

Example 2. Not amelioration of pre-existing condition or defect. B owns an office building that was constructed with insulation that contained asbestos. The health dangers of asbestos were not widely known when the building was constructed. Several years after B places the building into service, B determines that certain areas of asbestos-containing insulation have begun to deteriorate and could eventually pose a health risk to employees. Therefore, B pays an amount to remove the asbestos-containing insulation from the building structure and replace it with new insulation that is safer to employees, but no more efficient or effective than the asbestos insulation. Under paragraphs (e)(2)(ii) and (j)(2)(ii) of this section, an amount is paid to improve a building unit of property if the amount is paid for a betterment to the building structure or any building system. Although the asbestos is determined to be unsafe under certain circumstances, the presence of asbestos insulation in a building, by itself, is not a preexisting material condition or defect of the building structure under paragraph (j)(1)(i) of this section. In addition, the removal and replacement of the asbestos is not for a material addition to the building structure or a material increase in the capacity of the building structure under paragraphs (j)(1)(ii) and (j)(2)(iv) of this section as compared to the condition of the property prior to the deterioration of the insulation. Similarly, the removal and replacement of asbestos is not reasonably expected to materially increase the productivity, efficiency, strength, quality, or output of the building structure under paragraphs (j)(1)(iii) and (j)(2)(iv) of this section as compared to the condition of the property prior to the deterioration of the insulation. Therefore, the amount paid to remove and replace the asbestos insulation is not for a betterment to the building structure or an improvement to the building under paragraph (j) of this section.

* * *

(l) *Capitalization of amounts to adapt property to a new or different use.*—(1) *In general.*—

A taxpayer must capitalize as an improvement an amount paid to adapt a unit of property to a new or different use. In general, an amount is paid to adapt a unit of property to a new or different use if the adaptation is not consistent with the taxpayer's ordinary use of the unit of property at the time originally placed in service by the taxpayer.

(2) *Application of adaption rule to buildings.*—In the case of a building, an amount is paid to improve a building if it is paid to adapt to a new or different use a property specified under paragraph (e)(2)(ii) (building), paragraph (e)(2)(iii)(B) (condominium), paragraph (e)(2)(iv)(B) (cooperative), or paragraph (e)(2)(v)(B) (leased building or leased portion of building) of this section. For example, an amount is paid to improve a building if it is paid to adapt the building structure or any one of its buildings systems to a new or different use.

(3) *Examples.*—The following examples illustrate the application of this paragraph (l) only and do not address whether capitalization is required under another provision of this section or under another provision of the Code (for example, section 263A). Unless otherwise stated, assume that the taxpayer has not properly deducted a loss for any unit of property, asset, or component of a unit of property that is removed and replaced.

Example 1. New or different use; change in building use. A is a manufacturer and owns a manufacturing building that it has used for manufacturing since Year 1, when A placed it in service. In Year 30, A pays an amount to convert its manufacturing building into a showroom for its business. To convert the facility, A removes and replaces various structural components to provide a better layout for the showroom and its offices. A also repaints the building interiors as part of the conversion. When building materials are removed and replaced, A uses comparable and commercially available replacement materials. Under paragraphs (l)(2) and (e)(2)(ii) of this section, an amount is paid to improve A's manufacturing building if the amount adapts the building structure or any designated building system to a new or different use. Under paragraph (l)(1) of this section, the amount paid to convert the manufacturing building into a showroom adapts the building structure to a new or different use because the conversion to a showroom is not consistent with A's ordinary use of the building structure at the time it was placed in service. Therefore, A must capitalize the amount paid to convert the building into a showroom as an improvement to the building under paragraphs (d)(3) and (l) of this section.

Example 2. Not a new or different use; leased building. B owns and leases out space in a building consisting of twenty retail spaces. The space was designed to be reconfigured; that is, adjoining spaces could be combined into one space. One of the tenants expands its occupancy by leasing two adjoining retail spaces. To facilitate the new lease, B pays an amount to remove the walls between the three retail spaces. Assume that the walls between spaces are part of the building and its structural components. Under paragraphs (l)(2) and (e)(2)(ii) of this section, an amount is paid to improve B's building if it adapts the building structure or any of the building systems to a new or different use. Under paragraph (l)(1) of this section, the amount paid to convert three retail spaces into one larger space for an existing tenant does not adapt B's building structure to a new or different use because the combination of retail spaces is consistent with B's intended, ordinary use of the building structure. Therefore, the amount paid by B to remove the walls does not improve the building under paragraph (l) of this section and is not required to be capitalized under paragraph (d)(3) of this section.

Example 3. Not a new or different use; preparing building for sale. C owns a building consisting of twenty retail spaces. C decides to sell the building. In anticipation of selling the building, C pays an amount to repaint the interior walls and to refinish the hardwood floors. Under paragraphs (l)(2) and (e)(2)(ii) of this section, an amount is paid to improve C's building to a new or different use if it adapts the building structure or any of the building systems to a new or different use. Preparing the building for sale does not constitute a new or different use for the building structure under paragraph (l)(1) of this section. Therefore, the amount paid by C to prepare the building structure for sale does not improve the building under paragraph (l) of this section and is not required to be capitalized under paragraph (d)(3) of this section.

Example 4. New or different use; land. D owns a parcel of land on which it previously operated a manufacturing facility. Assume that the land is the unit of property. During the course of D's operation of the manufacturing facility, the land became contaminated with wastes from its manufacturing processes. D discontinues manufacturing operations at the site and decides to develop the property for residential housing. In anticipation of building residential property, D pays an amount to remediate the contamination caused by D's manufacturing process. In addition, D pays an amount to regrade the land so that it can be used for residential purposes. Amounts that D pays to clean up wastes do not adapt the land to a new or different use, regardless of the extent to which the land was cleaned, because this cleanup merely returns the land to the condition it was in before the land was contaminated in D's operations. Therefore, D is not required to capitalize the amount paid for the cleanup under paragraph (l)(1) of this section. However, the amount paid to regrade the land so that it can be used for residential purposes adapts the land to a new or different use that is inconsistent with D's intended ordinary use of the property at the time it was placed in service. Accordingly, the amounts paid to regrade the land must be capitalized as improvements to the land under paragraphs (d)(3) and (l) of this section.

* * *

(m) *Optional regulatory accounting method.*—(1) *In general.*—This paragraph (m) provides an optional simplified method (the regulatory accounting method) for regulated taxpayers to determine whether amounts paid to repair, maintain, or improve tangible property are to be treated as deductible expenses or capital expenditures. A taxpayer that uses the regulatory accounting method described in paragraph (m)(3) of this section must use that method for property subject to regulatory accounting instead of determining whether amounts paid to repair, maintain, or improve property are capital expenditures or deductible expenses under the general principles of sections 162(a), 212, and 263(a). Thus, the capitalization rules in paragraph (d) (and the routine maintenance safe harbor described in paragraph (i)) of this section do not apply to amounts paid to repair, maintain, or improve property subject to regulatory accounting by taxpayers that use the regulatory accounting method under this paragraph (m).

(2) *Eligibility for regulatory accounting method.*—A taxpayer that is engaged in a trade or business in a regulated industry is a regulated taxpayer and may use the regulatory accounting method under this paragraph (m). For purposes of this paragraph (m), a taxpayer is in a regulated industry only if the taxpayer is subject to the regulatory accounting rules of the Federal Energy Regulatory Commission (FERC), the Federal Communications Commission (FCC), or the Surface Transportation Board (STB).

(3) *Description of regulatory accounting method.*—Under the regulatory accounting method, a taxpayer must follow the method of accounting for regulatory accounting purposes that it is required to follow for FERC, FCC, or STB (whichever is applicable) in determining whether an amount paid repairs, maintains, or improves property under this section. Therefore, a taxpayer must capitalize for Federal income tax purposes an amount paid that is capitalized as an improvement for regulatory accounting purposes. A taxpayer may not capitalize for Federal income tax purposes under this section an amount paid that is not capitalized as an improvement for regulatory accounting purposes. A taxpayer that uses the regulatory accounting method must use that method for all of its tangible property that is subject to regulatory accounting rules. The method does not apply to tangible property that is not subject to regulatory accounting rules. The method also does not apply to property for the taxable years in which the taxpayer elected to apply the repair allowance under § 1.167(a)-11(d)(2). The regulatory accounting method is a method of accounting under section 446(a).

(4) *Examples.*—The following examples illustrate the application of this paragraph (m):

Example 1. Taxpayer subject to regulatory accounting rules of FERC. W is an electric utility company that operates a power plant that generates electricity and that owns and operates network assets to transmit and distribute the electricity to its customers. W is subject to the regulatory accounting rules of FERC, and W uses the regulatory accounting method under paragraph (m) of this section. W does not capitalize on its books and records for regulatory accounting purposes the cost of repairs and maintenance performed on its turbines or its network assets. Under the regulatory accounting method, W may not capitalize for Federal income tax purposes amounts paid for repairs performed on its turbines or its network assets.

Example 2. Taxpayer not subject to regulatory accounting rules of FERC. X is an electric utility company that operates a power plant to generate electricity. X previously was subject to the regulatory accounting rules of FERC, but currently X is not required to use FERC's regulatory accounting rules. X cannot use the regulatory accounting method provided in this paragraph (m).

Example 3. Taxpayer subject to regulatory accounting rules of FCC. Y is a telecommunications company that is subject to the regulatory accounting rules of the FCC. Y uses the regulatory accounting method under this paragraph (m). Y's assets include a telephone central office switching center, which contains numerous switches and various switching equipment. Y capitalizes on its books and records for regulatory accounting purposes the cost of replacing each switch. Under the regulatory accounting method, Y is required to capitalize for Federal income tax purposes amounts paid to replace each switch.

Example 4. Taxpayer subject to regulatory accounting rules of STB. Z is a Class I railroad that is subject to the regulatory accounting rules of the STB. Z uses the regulatory accounting method under this paragraph (m). Z capitalizes on its books and records for regulatory accounting purposes the cost of locomotive rebuilds. Under the regulatory accounting method, Z is required to capitalize for Federal income tax purposes amounts paid to rebuild its locomotives.

(n) *Election to capitalize repair and maintenance costs.*—(1) *In general.*—A taxpayer may elect to treat amounts paid during the taxable year for repair and maintenance (as defined under § 1.162-4) to tangible property as amounts paid to improve that property under this section and as an asset subject to the allowance for depreciation if the taxpayer incurs these amounts in carrying on the taxpayer's trade or business and if the taxpayer treats these amounts as capital expenditures on its books and records regularly used in computing income ("books and records"). A taxpayer that elects to apply this paragraph (n) in a taxable year must apply this paragraph to all amounts paid for repair and maintenance to tangible property that it treats as capital expenditures on its books and records in that taxable year. Any amounts for which this election is made shall not be treated as amounts paid for repair or maintenance under § 1.162-4.

(2) *Time and manner of election.*—A taxpayer makes this election under this paragraph (n) by attaching a statement to the taxpayer's timely filed original Federal tax return (including extensions) for the taxable year in which the taxpayer pays amounts described under paragraph (n)(1) of this paragraph. Sections 301.9100-1 through 301.9100-3 of this chapter provide the rules governing extensions of the time to make regulatory elections. The statement must be titled "Section 1.263(a)-3(n) Election" and include the taxpayer's name, address, taxpayer identification number, and a statement that the taxpayer is making the election to capitalize repair and maintenance costs under § 1.263(a)-3(n). In the case of a consolidated group filing a consolidated income tax return, the election is made for each member of the consolidated group by the common parent, and the statement must also include the names and taxpayer identification numbers of each member for which the election is made. In the case of an S corporation or a partnership, the election is made by the S corporation or partnership and not by the shareholders or partners. A taxpayer making this election for a taxable year must treat any amounts paid for repairs and maintenance during the taxable year that are capitalized on the taxpayer's books and records as improvements to tangible property. The taxpayer must begin to depreciate the cost of such improvements amounts when they are placed in service by the taxpayer under the applicable provisions of the Code and regulations. An election may not be made through the filing of an application for change in accounting method or, before obtaining the Commissioner's consent to make a late election, by filing an amended Federal tax return. The time and manner of electing to capitalize repair and maintenance costs under this paragraph (n) may be modified through guidance of general applicability (see §§ 601.601(d)(2) and 601.602 of this chapter).

* * *

(o) *Treatment of capital expenditures.*—Amounts required to be capitalized under this section are capital expenditures and must be taken into account through a charge to capital account or basis, or in the case of property that is inventory in the hands of a taxpayer, through inclusion in inventory costs.

(p) *Recovery of capitalized amounts.*—Amounts that are capitalized under this section are recovered through depreciation, cost of goods sold, or by an adjustment to basis at the time the property is placed in service, sold, used, or otherwise disposed of by the taxpayer. Cost recovery is determined by the applicable Code and regulation provisions relating to the use, sale, or disposition of property.

* * *

[Reg. § 1.263(a)-3.]

☐ [*T.D.* 6313, 9-16-58. *Amended by T.D.* 6548, 2-21-61; *T.D.* 6794, 1-25-65; *T.D.* 8121, 1-15-87; *T.D.* 9564, 12-23-2011; *T.D.* 9636, 9-13-2013 (*corrected* 7-18-2014) *and T.D.* 9689, 8-14-2014.]

§ 1.263(a)-4. Amounts paid to acquire or create intangibles.—(a) *Overview.*—This section provides rules for applying section 263(a) to amounts paid to acquire or create intangibles. Except to the extent provided in paragraph (d)(8) of this section, the rules provided by this section do not apply to amounts paid to acquire or create tangible assets. Paragraph (b) of this section provides a general principle of capitalization. Paragraphs (c) and (d) of this section identify intangibles for which capitalization is specifically required under the general principle. Paragraph (e) of this section provides rules for determining the extent to which taxpayers must capitalize transaction costs. Paragraph (f) of this section provides a 12-month rule intended to simplify the application of the general principle to certain payments that create benefits of a brief duration. Additional rules and examples relating to these provisions are provided in paragraphs (g) through (n) of this section. The applicability date of the rulesin this section is provided in paragraph (o) of this section. Paragraph (p) of this section provides rules applicable to changes in methods of accounting made to comply with this section.

(b) *Capitalization with respect to intangibles.*—(1) *In general.*—Except as otherwise provided in this section, a taxpayer must capitalize—

(i) An amount paid to acquire an intangible (see paragraph (c) of this section);

(ii) An amount paid to create an intangible described in paragraph (d) of this section;

(iii) An amount paid to create or enhance a separate and distinct intangible asset within the meaning of paragraph (b)(3) of this section;

(iv) An amount paid to create or enhance a future benefit identified in published guidance in the Federal Register or in the Internal Revenue Bulletin (see § 601.601(d)(2)(ii) of this chapter) as an intangible for which capitalization is required under this section; and

(v) An amount paid to facilitate (within the meaning of paragraph (e)(1) of this section) an acquisition or creation of an intangible described in paragraph (b)(1)(i), (ii), (iii) or (iv) of this section.

(2) *Published guidance.*—Any published guidance identifying a future benefit as an intangible for which capitalization is required under paragraph (b)(1)(iv) of this section applies only to amounts paid on or after the date of publication of the guidance.

(3) *Separate and distinct intangible asset.*—(i) *Definition.*—The term *separate and distinct intangible asset* means a property interest of ascertainable and measurable value in money's worth that is subject to protection under applicable state, federal or foreign law and the possession and control of which is intrinsically capable of being sold, transferred or pledged (ignoring any restrictions imposed on assignability) separate and apart from a trade or business. In addition, for purposes of this section, a fund (or similar account) is treated as a separate and distinct intangible asset of the taxpayer if amounts in the fund (or account) may revert to the taxpayer. The determination of whether a payment creates a separate and distinct intangible asset is made based on all of the facts and circumstances existing during the taxable year in which the payment is made.

(ii) *Creation or termination of contract rights.*—Amounts paid to another party to create, originate, enter into, renew or renegotiate an agreement with that party that produces rights or benefits for the taxpayer (and amounts paid to facilitate the creation, origination, enhancement, renewal or renegotiation of such an agreement) are treated as amounts that do not create (or facilitate the creation of) a separate and distinct intangible asset within the meaning of this paragraph (b)(3). Further, amounts paid to another party to terminate (or facilitate the termination of) an agreement with that party are treated as amounts that do not create a separate and distinct intangible asset within the meaning of this paragraph (b)(3). See paragraphs (d)(2), (d)(6), and (d)(7) of this section for rules that specifically require capitalization of amounts paid to create or terminate certain agreements.

(iii) *Amounts paid in performing services.*—Amounts paid in performing services under an agreement are treated as amounts that do not create a separate and distinct intangible asset within the meaning of this paragraph (b)(3), regardless of whether the amounts result in the creation of an income stream under the agreement.

(iv) *Creation of computer software.*—Except as otherwise provided in the Internal Revenue Code, the regulations thereunder, or other published guidance in the Federal Register or in the Internal Revenue Bulletin (see § 601.601(d)(2)(ii) of this chapter), amounts paid to develop computer software are treated as amounts that do not create a separate and distinct intangible asset within the meaning of this paragraph (b)(3).

(v) *Creation of package design.*—Amounts paid to develop a package design are treated as amounts that do not create a separate and distinct intangible asset within the meaning of this paragraph (b)(3). For purposes of this section, the term *package design* means the specific graphic arrangement or design of shapes, colors, words, pictures, lettering, and other elements on a given product package, or the design of a container with respect to its shape or function.

(4) *Coordination with other provisions of the Internal Revenue Code.*—(i) *In general.*—Nothing in this section changes the treatment of an amount that is specifically provided for under any other provision of the Internal Revenue Code (other than section 162(a) or 212) or the regulations thereunder.

(ii) *Example.*—The following example illustrates the rule of this paragraph (b)(4):

Example. On January 1, 2004, G enters into an interest rate swap agreement with unrelated counterparty H under which, for a term of five years, G is obligated to make annual payments at 11% and H is obligated to make annual payments at LIBOR on a notional principal amount of $100 million. At the time G and H enter into this swap agreement, the rate for similar on-market swaps is LIBOR to 10%. To compensate for this difference, on January 1, 2004, H pays G a yield adjustment fee of $3,790,786. This yield adjustment fee constitutes an amount paid to create an intangible and would be capitalized under paragraph (d)(2) of this section. However, because the yield adjustment fee is a nonperiodic payment on a notional principal contract as defined in § 1.446-3(c), the treatment of this fee is governed by § 1.446-3 and not this section.

(c) *Acquired intangibles.*—(1) *In general.*—A taxpayer must capitalize amounts paid to another party to acquire any intangible from that party in a purchase or similar transaction. Examples of intangibles within the scope of this paragraph (c) include, but are not limited to, the following (if acquired from another party in a purchase or similar transaction):

(i) An ownership interest in a corporation, partnership, trust, estate, limited liability company, or other entity.

(ii) A debt instrument, deposit, stripped bond, stripped coupon (including a servicing right treated for federal income tax purposes as a stripped coupon), regular interest in a REMIC or FASIT, or any other intangible treated as debt for federal income tax purposes.

(iii) A financial instrument, such as—

(A) A notional principal contract;

(B) A foreign currency contract;

(C) A futures contract;

(D) A forward contract (including an agreement under which the taxpayer has the right and obligation to provide or to acquire property (or to be compensated for such property, regardless of whether the taxpayer provides or acquires the property));

(E) An option (including an agreement under which the taxpayer has the right to provide or to acquire property (or to be compensated for such property, regardless of whether the taxpayer provides or acquires the property)); and

(F) Any other financial derivative.

(iv) An endowment contract, annuity contract, or insurance contract.

(v) Non-functional currency.

(vi) A lease.

(vii) A patent or copyright.

(viii) A franchise, trademark or tradename (as defined in § 1.197-2(b)(10)).

(ix) An assembled workforce (as defined in § 1.197-2(b)(3)).

(x) Goodwill (as defined in § 1.197-2(b)(1)) or going concern value (as defined in § 1.197-2(b)(2)).

(xi) A customer list.

(xii) A servicing right (for example, a mortgage servicing right that is not treated for federal income tax purposes as a stripped coupon).

(xiii) A customer-based intangible (as defined in § 1.197-2(b)(6)) or supplier-based intangible (as defined in § 1.197-2(b)(7)).

(xiv) Computer software.

(xv) An agreement providing either party the right to use, possess or sell an intangible described in paragraphs (c)(1)(i) through (v) of this section.

(2) *Readily available software.*—An amount paid to obtain a nonexclusive license for software that is (or has been) readily available to the general public on similar terms and has not been substantially modified (within the meaning of § 1.197-2(c)(4)) is treated for purposes of this paragraph (c) as an amount paid to another party to acquire an intangible from that party in a purchase or similar transaction.

(3) *Intangibles acquired from an employee.*—Amounts paid to an employee to acquire an intangible from that employee are not required to be capitalized under this section if the amounts are includible in the employee's income in connection with the performance of services under section 61 or 83. For purposes of this section, whether an individual is an employee is determined in accordance with the rules contained in section 3401(c) and the regulations thereunder.

(4) *Examples.*—The following examples illustrate the rules of this paragraph (c):

Example 1. Debt instrument. X corporation, a commercial bank, purchases a portfolio of existing loans from Y corporation, another financial institution. X pays Y $2,000,000 in exchange for the portfolio. The $2,000,000 paid to Y constitutes an amount paid to acquire an intangible from Y and must be capitalized.

Example 2. Option. W corporation owns all of the outstanding stock of X corporation. Y corporation holds a call option entitling it to purchase from W all of the outstanding stock of X at a certain price per share. Z corporation acquires the call option from Y in exchange for $5,000,000. The $5,000,000 paid to Y constitutes an amount paid to acquire an intangible from Y and must be capitalized.

Example 3. Ownership interest in a corporation. Same as *Example 2,* but assume Z exercises its option and purchases from W all of the outstanding stock of X in exchange for $100,000,000. The $100,000,000 paid to W constitutes an amount paid to acquire an intangible from W and must be capitalized.

Example 4. Customer list. N corporation, a retailer, sells its products through its catalog and mail order system. N purchases a customer list from R corporation. N pays R $100,000 in exchange for the customer list. The $100,000 paid to R constitutes an amount paid to acquire an intangible from R and must be capitalized.

Example 5. Goodwill. Z corporation pays W corporation $10,000,000 to purchase all of the assets of W in a transaction that constitutes an applicable asset acquisition under section 1060(c). Of the $10,000,000 consideration paid in the transaction, $9,000,000 is allocable to tangible assets purchased from W and $1,000,000 is allocable to goodwill. The $1,000,000 allocable to goodwill constitutes an amount paid to W to acquire an intangible from W and must be capitalized.

(d) *Created intangibles.*—(1) *In general.*—Except as provided in paragraph (f) of this section (relating to the 12-month rule), a taxpayer must capitalize amounts paid to create an intangible described in this paragraph (d). The determination of whether an amount is paid to create an intangible described in this paragraph (d) is to be made based on all of the facts and circumstances, disregarding distinctions between the labels used in this paragraph (d) to describe the intangible and the labels used by the taxpayer and other parties to the transaction.

(2) *Financial interests.*—(i) *In general.*—A taxpayer must capitalize amounts paid to another party to create, originate, enter into, renew or renegotiate with that party any of the following financial interests, whether or not the interest is regularly traded on an established market:

(A) An ownership interest in a corporation, partnership, trust, estate, limited liability company, or other entity.

(B) A debt instrument, deposit, stripped bond, stripped coupon (including a servicing right treated for federal income tax purposes as a stripped coupon), regular interest in a REMIC or FASIT, or any other intangible treated as debt for federal income tax purposes.

(C) A financial instrument, such as—

(1) A letter of credit;

(2) A credit card agreement;

(3) A notional principal contract;

(4) A foreign currency contract;

(5) A futures contract;

(6) A forward contract (including an agreement under which the taxpayer has the right and obligation to provide or to acquire property (or to be compensated for such property, regardless of whether the taxpayer provides or acquires the property));

(7) An option (including an agreement under which the taxpayer has the right to provide or to acquire property (or to be compensated for such property, regardless of whether the taxpayer provides or acquires the property)); and

(8) Any other financial derivative.

(D) An endowment contract, annuity contract, or insurance contract that has or may have cash value.

(E) Non-functional currency.

(F) An agreement providing either party the right to use, possess or sell a financial interest described in this paragraph (d)(2).

(ii) *Amounts paid to create, originate, enter into, renew or renegotiate.*—An amount paid to another party is not paid to create, originate, enter into, renew or renegotiate a financial interest with that party if the payment is made with the mere hope or expectation of developing or maintaining a business relationship with that party and is not contingent on the origination, renewal or renegotiation of a financial interest with that party.

(iii) *Renegotiate.*—A taxpayer is treated as renegotiating a financial interest if the terms of the financial interest are modified. A taxpayer also is treated as renegotiating a financial interest if the taxpayer enters into a new financial interest with the same party (or substantially the same parties) to a terminated financial interest, the taxpayer could not cancel the terminated financial interest without the consent of the other party (or parties), and the other party (or parties) would not have consented to the cancellation unless the taxpayer entered into the new financial interest. A taxpayer is treated as unable to cancel a financial interest without the consent of the other party (or parties) if, under the terms of the financial interest, the taxpayer is subject to a termination penalty and the other party (or parties) to the financial interest modifies the terms of the penalty.

(iv) *Coordination with other provisions of this paragraph (d).*—An amount described in this paragraph (d)(2) that is also described elsewhere in paragraph (d) of this section is treated as described only in this paragraph (d)(2).

(v) *Coordination with § 1.263(a)-5.*—See § 1.263(a)-5 for the treatment of borrowing costs and the treatment of amounts paid by an option writer.

(vi) *Examples.*—The following examples illustrate the rules of this paragraph (d)(2):

Example 1. Loan. X corporation, a commercial bank, makes a loan to A in the principal amount of $250,000. The $250,000 principal amount of the loan paid to A constitutes an amount paid to another party to create a debt instrument with that party under paragraph (d)(2)(i)(B) of this section and must be capitalized.

Example 2. Option. W corporation owns all of the outstanding stock of X corporation. Y corporation pays W $1,000,000 in exchange for W's grant of a 3-year call option to Y permitting Y to purchase all of the outstanding stock of X at a certain price per share. Y's payment of $1,000,000 to W constitutes an amount paid to another party to create an option with that party under paragraph (d)(2)(i)(C)(*7*) of this section and must be capitalized.

Example 3. Partnership interest. Z corporation pays $10,000 to P, a partnership, in exchange for an ownership interest in P. Z's payment of $10,000 to P constitutes an amount paid to another party to create an ownership interest in a partnership with that party under paragraph (d)(2)(i)(A) of this section and must be capitalized.

Example 4. Take or pay contract. Q corporation, a producer of natural gas, pays $1,000,000 to R during 2005 to induce R corporation to enter into a 5-year "take or pay" gas purchase contract. Under the contract, R is liable to pay for a specified minimum amount of gas, whether or not R takes such gas. Q's payment of $1,000,000 is an amount paid to another party to induce that party to enter into an agreement providing Q the right and obligation to provide property or be compensated for such property (regardless of whether the property is provided) under paragraph (d)(2)(i)(C)(*6*) of this section and must be capitalized.

Example 5. Agreement to provide property. P corporation pays R corporation $1,000,000 in exchange for R's agreement to purchase 1,000 units of P's product at any time within the three succeeding calendar years. The agreement describes P's $1,000,000 as a sales discount. P's $1,000,000 payment is an amount paid to induce R to enter into an agreement providing P the right and obligation to provide property under paragraph (d)(2)(i)(C)(*6*) of this section and must be capitalized.

Example 6. Customer incentive payment. S corporation, a computer manufacturer, seeks to develop a business relationship with V corporation, a computer retailer. As an incentive to encourage V to purchase computers from S, S enters into an agreement with V under which S agrees that, if V purchases $20,000,000 of computers from S within 3 years from the date of the agreement, S will pay V $2,000,000 on the date that V reaches the $20,000,000 threshold. V reaches the $20,000,000 threshold during the third year of the agreement, and S pays V $2,000,000. S is not required to capitalize its payment to V under this paragraph (d)(2) because the payment does not provide S the right or obligation to provide property and does not create a separate and distinct intangible asset for S within the meaning of paragraph (b)(3)(i) of this section.

(3) *Prepaid expenses.*—(i) *In general.*—A taxpayer must capitalize prepaid expenses.

(ii) *Examples.*—The following examples illustrate the rules of this paragraph (d)(3):

Example 1. Prepaid insurance. N corporation, an accrual method taxpayer, pays $10,000 to an insurer to obtain three years of coverage under a property and casualty insurance policy. The $10,000 is a prepaid expense and must be capitalized under this paragraph (d)(3). Paragraph (d)(2) of this section does not apply to the payment because the policy has no cash value.

Example 2. Prepaid rent. X corporation, a cash method taxpayer, enters into a 24-month lease of office space. At the time of the lease signing, X prepays $240,000. No other amounts are due under the lease. The $240,000 is a prepaid expense and must be capitalized under this paragraph (d)(3).

(4) *Certain memberships and privileges.*—(i) *In general.*—A taxpayer must capitalize amounts paid to an organization to obtain, renew, renegotiate, or upgrade a membership or privilege from that organization. A taxpayer is not required to capitalize under this paragraph (d)(4) an amount paid to obtain, renew, renegotiate or upgrade certification of the taxpayer's products, services, or business processes.

(ii) *Examples.*—The following examples illustrate the rules of this paragraph (d)(4):

Example 1. Hospital privilege. B, a physician, pays $10,000 to Y corporation to obtain lifetime staff privileges at a hospital operated by Y. B must capitalize the $10,000 payment under this paragraph (d)(4).

Example 2. Initiation fee. X corporation pays a $50,000 initiation fee to obtain membership in a trade association. X must capitalize the $50,000 payment under this paragraph (d)(4).

Example 3. Product rating. V corporation, an automobile manufacturer, pays W corporation, a national quality ratings association, $100,000 to conduct a study and provide a rating of the quality and safety of a line of V's automobiles. V's payment is an amount paid to obtain a certification of V's product and is not required to be capitalized under this paragraph (d)(4).

Example 4. Business process certification. Z corporation, a manufacturer, seeks to obtain a certification that its quality control standards meet a series of international standards known as ISO 9000. Z pays $50,000 to an independent registrar to obtain a certification from the registrar that Z's quality management system conforms to the ISO 9000 standard. Z's payment is an amount paid to obtain a certification of Z's business processes and is not required to be capitalized under this paragraph (d)(4).

(5) *Certain rights obtained from a governmental agency.*—(i) *In general.*—A taxpayer must capitalize amounts paid to a governmental agency to obtain, renew, renegotiate, or upgrade its rights under a trademark, trade name, copyright, license, permit, franchise, or other similar right granted by that governmental agency.

(ii) *Examples.*—The following examples illustrate the rules of this paragraph (d)(5):

Example 1. Business license. X corporation pays $15,000 to state Y to obtain a business license that is valid indefinitely. Under this paragraph (d)(5), the amount paid to state Y is an amount paid to a government agency for a right granted by that agency. Accordingly, X must capitalize the $15,000 payment.

Example 2. Bar admission. A, an individual, pays $1,000 to an agency of state Z to obtain a license to practice law in state Z that is valid indefinitely, provided A adheres to the requirements governing the practice of law in state Z. Under this paragraph (d)(5), the amount paid to state Z is an amount paid to a government agency for a right granted by that agency. Accordingly, A must capitalize the $1,000 payment.

(6) *Certain contract rights.*—(i) *In general.*—Except as otherwise provided in this paragraph (d)(6), a taxpayer must capitalize amounts paid to another party to create, originate, enter into, renew or renegotiate with that party—

(A) An agreement providing the taxpayer the right to use tangible or intangible property or the right to be compensated for the use of tangible or intangible property;

(B) An agreement providing the taxpayer the right to provide or to receive services (or the right to be compensated for services regardless of whether the taxpayer provides such services);

(C) A covenant not to compete or an agreement having substantially the same effect as a covenant not to compete (except, in the case of an agreement that requires the performance of services, to the extent that the amount represents reasonable compensation for services actually rendered);

(D) An agreement not to acquire additional ownership interests in the taxpayer; or

(E) An agreement providing the taxpayer (as the covered party) with an annuity, an endowment, or insurance coverage.

(ii) *Amounts paid to create, originate, enter into, renew or renegotiate.*—An amount paid to another party is not paid to create, originate, enter into, renew or renegotiate an agreement with that party if the payment is made with the mere hope or expectation of developing or maintaining a business relationship with that party and is not contingent on the origination, renewal or renegotiation of an agreement with that party.

(iii) *Renegotiate.*—A taxpayer is treated as renegotiating an agreement if the terms of the agreement are modified. A taxpayer also is treated as renegotiating an agreement if the taxpayer enters into a new agreement with the same party (or substantially the same parties) to a terminated agreement, the taxpayer could not cancel the terminated agreement without the consent of the other party (or parties), and the other party (or parties) would not have consented to the cancellation unless the taxpayer entered into the new agreement. A taxpayer is treated as unable to cancel an agreement without the consent of the other party (or parties) if, under the terms of the agreement, the taxpayer is subject to a termination penalty and the other party (or parties) to the agreement modifies the terms of the penalty.

(iv) *Right.*—An agreement does not provide the taxpayer a right to use property or to provide or receive services if the agreement may be terminated at will by the other party (or parties) to the agreement before the end of the period prescribed by paragraph (f)(1) of this section. An agreement is not terminable at will if the other party (or parties) to the agreement is economically compelled not to terminate the agreement until the end of the period prescribed by paragraph (f)(1) of this section. All of the facts and circumstances will be considered in determining whether the other party (or parties) to an agreement is economically compelled not to terminate the agreement. An agreement also does not provide the taxpayer the right to provide services if the agreement merely provides that the taxpayer will stand ready to provide services if requested, but places no obligation on another person to request or pay for the taxpayer's services.

(v) *De minimis amounts.*—A taxpayer is not required to capitalize amounts paid to another party (or parties) to create, originate, enter into, renew or renegotiate with that party (or those parties) an agreement described in paragraph (d)(6)(i) of this section if the aggregate of all amounts paid to that party (or those parties) with respect to the agreement does not exceed $5,000. If the aggregate of all amounts paid to the other party (or parties) with respect to that agreement exceeds $5,000, then all amounts must be capitalized. For purposes of this paragraph (d)(6), an amount paid in the form of property is valued at its fair market value at the time of the payment. In general, a taxpayer must determine whether the rules of this paragraph (d)(6)(v) apply by accounting for the specific amounts paid with respect to each agreement. However, a taxpayer that reasonably expects to create, originate, enter into, renew or renegotiate at least 25 similar agreements during the taxable year may establish a pool of agreements for purposes of determining the amounts paid with respect to the agreements in the pool. Under this pooling method, the amount paid with respect to each agreement included in the pool is equal to the average amount paid with respect to all agreements included in the pool. A taxpayer computes the average amount paid with respect to all agreements included in the pool by dividing the sum of all amounts paid with respect to all agreements included in the pool by the number of agreements included in the pool. See paragraph (h) of this section for additional rules relating to pooling.

(vi) *Exception for lessee construction allowances.*—Paragraph (d)(6)(i) of this section does not apply to amounts paid by a lessor to a lessee as a construction allowance to the extent the lessee expends the amount for the tangible property that is owned by the lessor for federal income tax purposes (see, for example, section 110).

* * *

(7) *Certain contract terminations.*—(i) *In general.*—A taxpayer must capitalize amounts paid to another party to terminate—

(A) A lease of real or tangible personal property between the taxpayer (as lessor) and that party (as lessee);

(B) An agreement that grants that party the exclusive right to acquire or use the taxpayer's property or services or to conduct the taxpayer's business (other than an intangible described in paragraph (c)(1)(i) through (iv) of this section or a financial interest described in paragraph (d)(2) of this section); or

(C) An agreement that prohibits the taxpayer from competing with that party or from acquiring property or services from a competitor of that party.

(ii) *Certain break-up fees.*—Paragraph (d)(7)(i) of this section does not apply to the termination of a transaction described in § 1.263(a)-5(a) (relating to an acquisition of a trade or business, a change in the capital structure of a business entity, and certain other transactions). See § 1.263(a)-5(c)(8) for rules governing the treatment of amounts paid to terminate a transaction to which that section applies.

* * *

(e) *Transaction costs.*—(1) *Scope of facilitate.*—(i) *In general.*—Except as otherwise provided in this section, an amount is paid to facilitate the acquisition or creation of an intangible (the transaction) if the amount is paid in the process of investigating or otherwise pursuing the transaction. Whether an amount is paid in the process of investigating or otherwise pursuing the transaction is determined based on all of the facts and circumstances. In determining whether an amount is paid to facilitate a transaction, the fact that the amount would (or would not) have been paid but for the transaction is relevant, but is not determinative. An amount paid to determine the value or price of an intangible is an amount paid in the process of investigating or otherwise pursuing the transaction.

(ii) *Treatment of termination payments.*—An amount paid to terminate (or facilitate the termination of) an existing agreement does not facilitate the acquisition or creation of another agreement under this section. See paragraph (d)(6)(iii) of this section for the treatment of termination fees paid to the other party (or parties) of a renegotiated agreement.

(iii) *Special rule for contracts.*—An amount is treated as not paid in the process of investigating or otherwise pursuing the creation of an agreement described in paragraph (d)(2) or (d)(6) of this section if the amount relates to activities performed before the earlier of the date the taxpayer begins preparing its bid for the agreement or the date the taxpayer begins discussing or negotiating the agreement with another party to the agreement.

(iv) *Borrowing costs.*—An amount paid to facilitate a borrowing does not facilitate an acquisition or creation of an intangible described in paragraphs (b)(1)(i) through (iv) of this section. See §§ 1.263(a)-5 and 1.446-5 for the treatment of an amount paid to facilitate a borrowing.

(v) *Special rule for stock redemption costs of open-end regulated investment companies.*—An amount paid by an open-end regulated investment company (within the meaning of section 851) to facilitate a redemption of its stock is treated as an amount that does not facilitate the acquisition of an intangible under this section.

(2) *Coordination with paragraph (d) of this section.*—In the case of an amount paid to facilitate the creation of an intangible described in paragraph (d) of this section, the provisions of this paragraph (e) apply regardless of whether a payment described in paragraph (d) is made.

(3) *Transaction.*—For purposes of this section, the term *transaction* means all of the factual elements comprising an acquisition or creation of an intangible and includes a series of steps carried out as part of a single plan. Thus, a transaction can involve more than one invoice and more than one intangible. For example, a purchase of intangibles under one purchase agreement constitutes a single transaction, notwithstanding the fact that the acquisition involves multiple intangibles and the amounts paid to facilitate the acquisition are capable of being allocated among the various intangibles acquired.

(4) *Simplifying conventions.*—(i) *In general.*—For purposes of this section, employee compensation (within the meaning of paragraph (e)(4)(ii) of this section), overhead, and de minimis costs (within the meaning of paragraph (e)(4)(iii) of this section) are treated as amounts that do not facilitate the acquisition or creation of an intangible.

(ii) *Employee compensation.*—(A) *In general.*—The term *employee compensation* means compensation (including salary, bonuses and commissions) paid to an employee of the taxpayer. For purposes of this section, whether an individual is an employee is determined in accordance with the rules contained in section 3401(c) and the regulations thereunder.

(B) *Certain amounts treated as employee compensation.*—For purposes of this section, a guaranteed payment to a partner in a partnership is treated as employee compensation. For purposes of this section, annual compensation paid to a director of a corporation is treated as employee compensation. For example, an amount paid to a director of a corporation for attendance at a regular meeting of the board of directors (or committee thereof) is treated as employee compensation for purposes of this section. However, an amount paid to a director for attendance at a special meeting of the board of directors (or committee thereof) is not treated as employee compensation. An amount paid to a person that is not an employee of the taxpayer (including the employer of the individual who performs the services) is treated as employee compensation for purposes of this section only if the amount is paid for secretarial, clerical, or similar administrative support services. In the case of an affiliated group of corporations filing a consolidated federal income tax return, a payment by one member of the group to a second member of the group for services performed by an employee of the second member is treated as employee compensation if the services provided by the employee are provided at a time during which both members are affiliated.

(iii) *De minimis costs.*—(A) *In general.*—Except as provided in paragraph (e)(4)(iii)(B) of this section, the term *de minimis costs* means amounts (other than employee compensation and overhead) paid in the process of investigating or otherwise pursuing a transaction if, in the aggregate, the amounts do not exceed $5,000 (or such greater amount as may be set forth in published guidance). If the amounts exceed $5,000 (or such greater amount as may be set forth in published guidance), none of the amounts are de minimis costs within the meaning of this paragraph (e)(4)(iii)(A). For purposes of this paragraph (e)(4)(iii), an amount paid in the form of property is valued at its fair market value at the time of the payment. In determining the amount of transaction costs paid in the process of investigating or otherwise pursuing a transaction, a taxpayer generally must account for the specific costs paid with respect to each transaction. However, a taxpayer that reasonably expects to enter into at least 25 similar transactions during the taxable year may establish a pool of similar transactions for purposes of determining the amount of transaction costs paid in the process of investigating or otherwise pursuing the transactions in the pool. Under this pooling method, the amount of transaction costs paid in the process of investigating or otherwise pursuing each transaction included in the pool is equal to the average transaction costs paid in the process of investigating or otherwise pursuing all transactions included in the pool. A taxpayer computes the average transaction costs paid in the process of investigating or otherwise pursuing all transactions included in the pool by dividing the sum of all transaction costs paid in the process of investigating or otherwise pursuing all transactions included in the pool by the number of transactions included in the pool. See paragraph (h) of this section for additional rules relating to pooling.

(B) *Treatment of commissions.*—The term *de minimis costs* does not include commissions paid to facilitate the acquisition of an intangible described in paragraphs (c)(1)(i) through (v) of this section or to facilitate the creation, origination, entrance into, renewal or renegotiation of an intangible described in paragraph (d)(2)(i) of this section.

(iv) *Election to capitalize.*—A taxpayer may elect to treat employee compensation, overhead, or de minimis costs paid in the process of investigating or otherwise pursuing a transaction as amounts that facilitate the transaction. The election is made separately for each transaction and applies to employee compensation, overhead, or de minimis costs, or to any combination thereof. For example, a taxpayer may elect to treat overhead and de minimis costs, but not employee compensation, as amounts that facilitate the transaction. A taxpayer makes the election by treating the amounts to which the election applies as amounts that facilitate the transaction in the taxpayer's timely filed original federal income tax return (including extensions) for the taxable year during which the amounts are paid. In the case of an affiliated group of corporations filing a consolidated return, the election is made separately with respect to each member of the group, and not with respect to the group as a whole. In the case of an S corporation or partnership, the election is made by the S corporation or by the partnership, and not by the shareholders or partners. An election made under this paragraph (e)(4)(iv) is revocable with respect to each taxable year for which made only with the consent of the Commissioner.

* * *

(f) *12-month rule.*—(1) *In general.*—Except as otherwise provided in this paragraph (f), a taxpayer is not required to capitalize under this section amounts paid to create (or to facilitate the creation of) any right or benefit for the taxpayer that does not extend beyond the earlier of—

(i) 12 months after the first date on which the taxpayer realizes the right or benefit; or

(ii) The end of the taxable year following the taxable year in which the payment is made.

(2) *Duration of benefit for contract terminations.*—For purposes of this paragraph (f), amounts paid to terminate a contract or other agreement described in paragraph (d)(7)(i) of this section prior to its expiration date (or amounts paid to facilitate such termination) create a benefit for the taxpayer that lasts for the unexpired term of the agreement immediately before the date of the termination. If the terms of a contract or other agreement described in paragraph (d)(7)(i) of this section permit the taxpayer to terminate the contract or agreement after a notice period, amounts paid by the taxpayer to terminate the contract or agreement before the end of the notice period create a benefit for the taxpayer that lasts for the amount of time by which the notice period is shortened.

(3) *Inapplicability to created financial interests and self-created amortizable section 197 intangibles.*—Paragraph (f)(1) of this section does not apply to amounts paid to create (or facilitate the creation of) an intangible described in paragraph (d)(2) of this section (relating to amounts paid to create financial interests) or to amounts paid to create (or facilitate the creation of) an intangible that constitutes an amortizable section 197 intangible within the meaning of section 197(c).

(4) *Inapplicability to rights of indefinite duration.*—Paragraph (f)(1) of this section does not apply to amounts paid to create (or facilitate the creation of) an intangible of indefinite duration. A right has an indefinite duration if it has no period of duration fixed by agreement or by law, or if it is not based on a period of time, such as a right attributable to an agreement to provide or receive a fixed amount of goods or services. For example, a license granted by a governmental agency that permits the taxpayer to operate a business conveys a right of indefinite duration if the license may be revoked only upon the taxpayer's violation of the terms of the license.

(5) *Rights subject to renewal.*—(i) *In general.*—For purposes of paragraph (f)(1) of this section, the duration of a right includes any renewal period if all of the facts and circumstances in existence during the taxable year in which the right is created indicate a reasonable expectancy of renewal.

(ii) *Reasonable expectancy of renewal.*—The following factors are significant in determining whether there exists a reasonable expectancy of renewal:

(A) *Renewal history.*—The fact that similar rights are historically renewed is evidence of a reasonable expectancy of renewal. On the other hand, the fact that similar rights are rarely renewed is evidence of a lack of a reasonable expectancy of renewal. Where the taxpayer has no experience with similar rights, or where the taxpayer holds similar rights only occasionally, this factor is less indicative of a reasonable expectancy of renewal.

(B) *Economics of the transaction.*—The fact that renewal is necessary for the taxpayer to earn back its investment in the right is evidence of a reasonable expectancy of renewal. For example, if a taxpayer pays $14,000 to enter into a renewable contract with an initial 9-month term that is expected to general income to the taxpayer of $1,000 per month, the fact that renewal is necessary for the taxpayer to earn back its $14,000 payment is evidence of a reasonable expectancy of renewal.

(C) *Likelihood of renewal by other party.*—Evidence that indicates a likelihood of renewal by the other party to a right, such as a bargain renewal option or similar arrangement, is evidence of a reasonable expectancy of renewal. However, the mere fact that the other party will have the opportunity to renew on the same terms as are available to others is not evidence of a reasonable expectancy of renewal.

(D) *Terms of renewal.*—The fact that material terms of the right are subject to renegotiation at the end of the initial term is evidence of a lack of a reasonable expectancy of renewal. For example, if the parties to an agreement must renegotiate price or amount, the renegotiation requirement is evidence of a lack of a reasonable expectancy of renewal.

(E) *Terminations.*—The fact that similar rights are typically terminated prior to renewal is evidence of a lack of a reasonably expectancy of renewal.

(iii) *Safe harbor pooling method.*—In lieu of applying the reasonable expectancy of renewal test described in paragraph (f)(5)(ii) of this section to each separate right created during a taxable year, a taxpayer that reasonably expects to enter into at least 25 similar rights during the taxable year may establish a pool of similar rights for which the initial term does not extend beyond the period prescribed in paragraph (f)(1) of this section and may elect to apply the reasonable expectancy of renewal test to that pool. See paragraph (h) of this section for additional rules relating to pooling. The application of paragraph (f)(1) of this section to each pool is determined in the following manner:

(A) All amounts (except de minimis costs described in paragraph (d)(6)(v) of this section) paid to create the rights included in the pool and all amounts paid to facilitate the creation of the rights included in the pool are aggregated.

(B) If less than 20 percent of the rights in the pool are reasonably expected to be renewed beyond the period prescribed in paragraph (f)(1) of this section, all rights in the pool are treated as having a duration that does not extend beyond the period prescribed in paragraph (f)(1) of this section, and the taxpayer is not required to capitalize under this section any portion of the aggregate amount described in paragraph (f)(5)(iii)(A) of this section.

(C) If more than 80 percent of the rights in the pool are reasonably expected to be renewed beyond the period prescribed in paragraph (f)(1) of this section, all rights in the pool are treated as having a duration that extends beyond the period prescribed in paragraph (f)(1) of this section, and the taxpayer is required to capitalize under this section the aggregate amount described in paragraph (f)(5)(iii)(A) of this section.

(D) If 20 percent or more, but 80 percent or less, of the rights in the pool are reasonably expected to be renewed beyond the period prescribed in paragraph (f)(1) of this section, the aggregate amount described in paragraph (f)(5)(iii)(A) of this section is multiplied by the percentage of the rights in the pool that are reasonably expected to be renewed beyond the period prescribed in paragraph (f)(1) of this section and the taxpayer must capitalize the resulting amount under this section by treating such amount as creating a separate intangible. The amount determined by multiplying the aggregate amount described in paragraph (f)(5)(iii)(A) of this section by the percentage of rights in the pool that are not reasonably expected to be renewed beyond the period prescribed in paragraph (f)(1) of this section is not required to be capitalized under this section.

(6) *Coordination with section 461.*—In the case of a taxpayer using an accrual method of accounting, the rules of this paragraph (f) do not affect the determination of whether a liability is incurred during the taxable year, including the determination of whether economic performance has occurred with respect to the liability. See §1.461-4 for rules relating to economic performance.

(7) *Election to capitalize.*—A taxpayer may elect not to apply the rule contained in paragraph (f)(1) of this section. An election made under this paragraph (f)(7) applies to all similar transactions during the taxable year to which paragraph (f)(1) of this section would apply (but for the election under this paragraph (f)(7)). For example, a taxpayer may elect under this paragraph (f)(7) to capitalize its costs of prepaying insurance contracts for 12 months, but may continue to apply the rule in paragraph (f)(1) to its costs of entering into non-renewable, 12-month service contracts. A taxpayer makes the election by treating the amounts as capital expenditures in its timely filed original federal income tax return (including extensions) for the taxable year during which the amounts are paid. In the case of an

affiliated group of corporations filing a consolidated return, the election is made separately with respect to each member of the group, and not with respect to the group as a whole. In the case of an S corporation or partnership, the election is made by the S corporation or by the partnership, and not by the shareholders or partners. An election made under this paragraph (f)(7) is revocable with respect to each taxable year for which made only with the consent of the Commissioner.

* * *

(g) *Treatment of capitalized costs.*—(1) *In general.*—An amount required to be capitalized by this section is not currently deductible under section 162. Instead, the amount generally is added to the basis of the intangible acquired or created. See section 1012.

(2) *Financial instruments.*—In the case of a financial instrument described in paragraph (c)(1)(iii) or (d)(2)(i)(C) of this section, notwithstanding paragraph (g)(1) of this section, if under other provisions of law the amount required to be capitalized is not required to be added to the basis of the intangible acquired or created, then the other provisions of law will govern the tax treatment of the amount.

* * *

[Reg. § 1.263(a)-4.]

☐ [*T.D.* 9107, 12-31-2003.]

§ 1.263(a)-5. Amounts paid or incurred to facilitate an acquisition of a trade or business, a change in the capital structure of a business entity, and certain other transactions.—(a) *General rule.*—A taxpayer must capitalize an amount paid to facilitate (within the meaning of paragraph (b) of this section) each of the following transactions, without regard to whether the transaction is comprised of a single step or a series of steps carried out as part of a single plan and without regard to whether gain or loss is recognized in the transaction:

(1) An acquisition of assets that constitute a trade or business (whether the taxpayer is the acquirer in the acquisition or the target of the acquisition).

(2) An acquisition by the taxpayer of an ownership interest in a business entity if, immediately after the acquisition, the taxpayer and the business entity are related within the meaning of section 267(b) or 707(b) (see § 1.263(a)-4 for rules requiring capitalization of amounts paid by the taxpayer to acquire an ownership interest in a business entity, or to facilitate the acquisition of an ownership interest in a business entity, where the taxpayer and the business entity are not related within the meaning of section 267(b) or 707(b) immediately after the acquisition).

(3) An acquisition of an ownership interest in the taxpayer (other than an acquisition by the taxpayer of an ownership interest in the taxpayer, whether by redemption or otherwise).

(4) A restructuring, recapitalization, or reorganization of the capital structure of a business entity (including reorganizations described in section 368 and distributions of stock by the taxpayer as described in section 355).

(5) A transfer described in section 351 or section 721 (whether the taxpayer is the transferor or transferee).

(6) A formation or organization of a disregarded entity.

(7) An acquisition of capital.

(8) A stock issuance.

(9) A borrowing. For purposes of this section, a borrowing means any issuance of debt, including an issuance of debt in an acquisition of capital or in a recapitalization. A borrowing also includes debt issued in a debt for debt exchange under § 1.1001-3.

(10) Writing an option.

(b) *Scope of facilitate.*—(1) *In general.*—Except as otherwise provided in this section, an amount is paid to facilitate a transaction described in paragraph (a) of this section if the amount is paid in the process of investigating or otherwise pursuing the transaction. Whether an amount is paid in the process of investigating or otherwise pursuing the transaction is determined based on all of the facts and circumstances. In determining whether an amount is paid to facilitate a transaction, the fact that the amount would (or would not) have been paid but for the transaction is relevant, but is not determinative. An amount paid to determine the value or price of a transaction is an amount paid in the process of investigating or otherwise pursuing the transaction. An amount paid to another party in exchange for tangible or intangible property is not an amount paid to facilitate the exchange. For example, the purchase price paid to the target of an asset acquisition in exchange for its assets is not an amount paid to facilitate the acquisition. Similarly, the purchase price paid by an acquirer to the target's shareholders in exchange for their stock in a stock acquisition is not an amount paid to facilitate the acquisition of the stock. See § 1.263(a)-1, § 1.263(a)-2, and § 1.263(a)-4 for rules requiring capitalization of the purchase price paid to acquire property.

(2) *Ordering rules.*—An amount paid in the process of investigating or otherwise pursuing both a transaction described in paragraph

(a) of this section and an acquisition or creation of an intangible described in § 1.263(a)-4 is subject to the rules contained in this section, and not to the rules contained in § 1.263(a)-4. In addition, an amount required to be capitalized by § 1.263(a)-1, § 1.263(a)-2, or § 1.263(a)-4 does not facilitate a transaction described in paragraph (a) of this section.

(c) *Special rules for certain costs.*—(1) *Borrowing costs.*—An amount paid to facilitate a borrowing does not facilitate another transaction (other than the borrowing) described in paragraph (a) of this section.

(2) *Costs of asset sales.*—An amount paid by a taxpayer to facilitate a sale of its assets does not facilitate another transaction (other than the sale) described in paragraph (a) of this section. For example, where a target corporation, in preparation for a merger with an acquiring corporation, sells assets that are not desired by the acquiring corporation, amounts paid to facilitate the sale of the unwanted assets are not required to be capitalized as amounts paid to facilitate the merger.

(3) *Mandatory stock distributions.*—An amount paid in the process of investigating or otherwise pursuing a distribution of stock by a taxpayer to its shareholders does not facilitate a transaction described in paragraph (a) of this section if the divestiture of the stock (or of properties transferred to an entity whose stock is distributed) is required by law, regulatory mandate, or court order. A taxpayer is not required to capitalize (under this section or § 1.263(a)-4) an amount paid to organize (or facilitate the organization of) an entity if the entity is organized solely to receive properties that the taxpayer is required to divest by law, regulatory mandate, or court order and if the taxpayer distributes the stock of the entity to its shareholders. A taxpayer also is not required to capitalize (under this section or § 1.263(a)-4) an amount paid to transfer property to an entity if the taxpayer is required to divest itself of that property by law, regulatory mandate, or court order and if the stock of the recipient entity is distributed to the taxpayer's shareholders.

(4) *Bankruptcy reorganization costs.*—An amount paid to institute or administer a proceeding under Chapter 11 of the Bankruptcy Code by a taxpayer that is the debtor under the proceeding constitutes an amount paid to facilitate a reorganization within the meaning of paragraph (a)(4) of this section, regardless of the purpose for which the proceeding is instituted. For example, an amount paid to prepare and file a petition under Chapter 11, to obtain an extension of the exclusivity period under Chapter 11, to formulate plans of reorganization under Chapter 11, to analyze plans of reorganization formulated by another party in interest, or to contest or obtain approval of a plan of reorganization under Chapter 11 facilitates a reorganization within the meaning of this section. However, amounts specifically paid to formulate, analyze, contest or obtain approval of the portion of a plan of reorganization under Chapter 11 that resolves tort liabilities of the taxpayer do not facilitate a reorganization within the meaning of paragraph (a)(4) of this section if the amounts would have been treated as ordinary and necessary business expenses under section 162 had the bankruptcy proceeding not been instituted. In addition, an amount paid by the taxpayer to defend against the commencement of an involuntary bankruptcy proceeding against the taxpayer does not facilitate a reorganization within the meaning of paragraph (a)(4) of this section. An amount paid by the debtor to operate its business during a Chapter 11 bankruptcy proceeding is not an amount paid to institute or administer the bankruptcy proceeding and does not facilitate a reorganization. Such amount is treated in the same manner as it would have been treated had the bankruptcy proceeding not been instituted.

(5) *Stock issuance costs of open-end regulated investment companies.*—Amounts paid by an open-end regulated investment company (within the meaning of section 851) to facilitate an issuance of its stock are treated as amounts that do not facilitate a transaction described in paragraph (a) of this section unless the amounts are paid during the initial stock offering period.

(6) *Integration costs.*—An amount paid to integrate the business operations of the taxpayer with the business operations of another does not facilitate a transaction described in paragraph (a) of this section, regardless of when the integration activities occur.

(7) *Registrar and transfer agent fees for the maintenance of capital stock records.*—An amount paid by a taxpayer to a registrar or transfer agent in connection with the transfer of the taxpayer's capital stock does not facilitate a transaction described in paragraph (a) of this section unless the amount is paid with respect to a specific transaction described in paragraph (a). For example, a taxpayer is not required to capitalize periodic payments to a transfer agent for maintaining records of the names and addresses of shareholders who trade the taxpayer's shares on a national exchange. By comparison, a taxpayer is required to capitalize an amount paid to the transfer agent for distributing proxy statements requesting shareholder

approval of a transaction described in paragraph (a) of this section.

(8) *Termination payments and amounts paid to facilitate mutually exclusive transactions.*—An amount paid to terminate (or facilitate the termination of) an agreement to enter into a transaction described in paragraph (a) of this section constitutes an amount paid to facilitate a second transaction described in paragraph (a) of this section only if the transactions are mutually exclusive. An amount paid to facilitate a transaction described in paragraph (a) of this section is treated as an amount paid to facilitate a second transaction described in paragraph (a) of this section only if the transactions are mutually exclusive.

(d) *Simplifying conventions.*—(1) *In general.*—For purposes of this section, employee compensation (within the meaning of paragraph (d)(2) of this section), overhead, and de minimis costs (within the meaning of paragraph (d)(3) of this section) are treated as amounts that do not facilitate a transaction described in paragraph (a) of this section.

(2) *Employee compensation.*—(i) *In general.*—The term *employee compensation* means compensation (including salary, bonuses and commissions) paid to an employee of the taxpayer. For purposes of this section, whether an individual is an employee is determined in accordance with the rules contained in section 3401(c) and the regulations thereunder.

(ii) *Certain amounts treated as employee compensation.*—For purposes of this section, a guaranteed payment to a partner in a partnership is treated as employee compensation. For purposes of this section, annual compensation paid to a director of a corporation is treated as employee compensation. For example, an amount paid to a director of a corporation for attendance at a regular meeting of the board of directors (or committee thereof) is treated as employee compensation for purposes of this section. However, an amount paid to the director for attendance at a special meeting of the board of directors (or committee thereof) is not treated as employee compensation. An amount paid to a person that is not an employee of the taxpayer (including the employer of the individual who performs the services) is treated as employee compensation for purposes of this section only if the amount is paid for secretarial, clerical, or similar administrative support services (other than services involving the preparation and distribution of proxy solicitations and other documents seeking shareholder approval of a transaction described in paragraph (a) of this section). In the case of an affiliated group of corporations filing a consolidated federal income tax return, a payment by one member of the group to a second member of the group for services performed by an employee of the second member is treated as employee compensation if the services provided by the employee are provided at a time during which both members are affiliated.

(3) *De minimis costs.*—(i) *In general.*—The term *de minimis costs* means amounts (other than employee compensation and overhead) paid in the process of investigating or otherwise pursuing a transaction described in paragraph (a) of this section if, in the aggregate, the amounts do not exceed $5,000 (or such greater amount as may be set forth in published guidance). If the amounts exceed $5,000 (or such greater amount as may be set forth in published guidance), none of the amounts are de minimis costs within the meaning of this paragraph (d)(3). For purposes of this paragraph (d)(3), an amount paid in the form of property is valued at its fair market value at the time of the payment.

(ii) *Treatment of commissions.*—The term *de minimis costs* does not include commissions paid to facilitate a transaction described in paragraph (a) of this section.

(4) *Election to capitalize.*—A taxpayer may elect to treat employee compensation, overhead, or de minimis costs paid in the process of investigating or otherwise pursuing a transaction described in paragraph (a) of this section as amounts that facilitate the transaction. The election is made separately for each transaction and applies to employee compensation, overhead, or de minimis costs, or to any combination thereof. For example, a taxpayer may elect to treat overhead and de minimis costs, but not employee compensation, as amounts that facilitate the transaction. A taxpayer makes the election by treating the amounts to which the election applies as amounts that facilitate the transaction in the taxpayer's timely filed original federal income tax return (including extensions) for the taxable year during which the amounts are paid. In the case of an affiliated group of corporations filing a consolidated return, the election is made separately with respect to each member of the group, and not with respect to the group as a whole. In the case of an S corporation or partnership, the election is made by the S corporation or by the partnership, and not by the shareholders or partners. An election made under this paragraph (d)(4) is revocable with respect to each taxable year for which made only with the consent of the Commissioner.

(e) *Certain acquisitive transactions.*—(1) *In general.*—Except as provided in paragraph (e)(2) of this section (relating to inherently facilitative amounts), an amount paid by the taxpayer in the process of investigating or otherwise pursuing a covered transaction (as described in paragraph (e)(3) of this section) facilitates the transaction within the meaning of this section only if the amount relates to activities performed on or after the earlier of—

(i) The date on which a letter of intent, exclusivity agreement, or similar written communication (other than a confidentiality agreement) is executed by representatives of the acquirer and the target; or

(ii) The date on which the material terms of the transaction (as tentatively agreed to by representatives of the acquirer and the target) are authorized or approved by the taxpayer's board of directors (or committee of the board of directors) or, in the case of a taxpayer that is not a corporation, the date on which the material terms of the transaction (as tentatively agreed to by representatives of the acquirer and the target) are authorized or approved by the appropriate governing officials of the taxpayer. In the case of a transaction that does not require authorization or approval of the taxpayer's board of directors (or appropriate governing officials in the case of a taxpayer that is not a corporation) the date determined under this paragraph (e)(1)(ii) is the date on which the acquirer and the target execute a binding written contract reflecting the terms of the transaction.

(2) *Exception for inherently facilitative amounts.*—An amount paid in the process of investigating or otherwise pursuing a covered transaction facilitates that transaction if the amount is inherently facilitative, regardless of whether the amount is paid for activities performed prior to the date determined under paragraph (e)(1) of this section. An amount is inherently facilitative if the amount is paid for—

(i) Securing an appraisal, formal written evaluation, or fairness opinion related to the transaction;

(ii) Structuring the transaction, including negotiating the structure of the transaction and obtaining tax advice on the structure of the transaction (for example, obtaining tax advice on the application of section 368);

(iii) Preparing and reviewing the documents that effectuate the transaction (for example, a merger agreement or purchase agreement);

(iv) Obtaining regulatory approval of the transaction, including preparing and reviewing regulatory filings;

(v) Obtaining shareholder approval of the transaction (for example, proxy costs, solicitation costs, and costs to promote the transaction to shareholders); or

(vi) Conveying property between the parties to the transaction (for example, transfer taxes and title registration costs).

(3) *Covered transactions.*—For purposes of this paragraph (e), the term *covered transaction* means the following transactions:

(i) A taxable acquisition by the taxpayer of assets that constitute a trade or business.

(ii) A taxable acquisition of an ownership interest in a business entity (whether the taxpayer is the acquirer in the acquisition or the target of the acquisition) if, immediately after the acquisition, the acquirer and the target are related within the meaning of section 267(b) or 707(b).

(iii) A reorganization described in section 368(a)(1)(A), (B), or (C) or a reorganization described in section 368(a)(1)(D) in which stock or securities of the corporation to which the assets are transferred are distributed in a transaction which qualifies under section 354 or 356 (whether the taxpayer is the acquirer or the target in the reorganization).

(f) *Documentation of success-based fees.*—An amount paid that is contingent on the successful closing of a transaction described in paragraph (a) of this section is an amount paid to facilitate the transaction except to the extent the taxpayer maintains sufficient documentation to establish that a portion of the fee is allocable to activities that do not facilitate the transaction. This documentation must be completed on or before the due date of the taxpayer's timely filed original federal income tax return (including extensions) for the taxable year during which the transaction closes. For purposes of this paragraph (f), documentation must consist of more than merely an allocation between activities that facilitate the transaction and activities that do not facilitate the transaction, and must consist of supporting records (for example, time records, itemized invoices, or other records) that identify—

(1) The various activities performed by the service provider;

(2) The amount of the fee (or percentage of time) that is allocable to each of the various activities performed;

(3) Where the date the activity was performed is relevant to understanding whether the activity facilitated the transaction, the amount of the fee (or percentage of time) that is allocable to the performance of that activity before and after the relevant date; and

(4) The name, business address, and business telephone number of the service provider.

(g) *Treatment of capitalized costs.*—(1) *Tax-free acquisitive transactions.*—[Reserved].

(2) *Taxable acquisitive transactions.*—(i) *Acquirer.*—In the case of an acquisition, merger, or consolidation that is not described in section 368, an amount required to be capitalized under this section by the acquirer is added to the basis of the acquired assets (in the case of a transaction that is treated as an acquisition of the assets of the target for federal income tax purposes) or the acquired stock (in the case of a transaction that is treated as an acquisition of the stock of the target for federal income tax purposes).

(ii) *Target.*—(A) *Asset acquisition.*—In the case of an acquisition, merger, or consolidation that is not described in section 368 and that is treated as an acquisition of the assets of the target for federal income tax purposes, an amount required to be capitalized under this section by the target is treated as a reduction of the target's amount realized on the disposition of its assets.

(B) *Stock acquisition.*—[Reserved].

(3) *Stock issuance transactions.*—[Reserved].

(4) *Borrowings.*—For the treatment of amounts required to be capitalized under this section with respect to a borrowing, see § 1.446-5.

(5) *Treatment of capitalized amounts by option writer.*—An amount required to be capitalized by an option writer under paragraph (a)(10) of this section is not currently deductible under section 162 or 212. Instead, the amount required to be capitalized generally reduces the total premium received by the option writer. However, other provisions of law may limit the reduction of the premium by the capitalized amount (for example, if the capitalized amount is never deductible by the option writer).

(h) *Application to accrual method taxpayers.*—For purposes of this section, the terms *amount paid* and *payment* mean, in the case of a taxpayer using an accrual method of accounting, a liability incurred (within the meaning of § 1.446-1(c)(1)(ii)). A liability may not be taken into account under this section prior to the taxable year during which the liability is incurred.

(i) [Reserved].

(j) *Coordination with other provisions of the Internal Revenue Code.*—Nothing in this section changes the treatment of an amount that is specifically provided for under any other provision of the Internal Revenue Code (other than section 162(a) or 212) or regulations thereunder.

(k) *Treatment of indirect payments.*—For purposes of this section, references to an amount paid to or by a party include an amount paid on behalf of that party.

* * *

[Reg. § 1.263(a)-5.]

□ [*T.D.* 9107, 12-31-2003.]

§ 1.265-1. Expenses relating to tax-exempt income.—(a) *Nondeductibility of expenses allocable to exempt income.*—(1) No amount shall be allowed as a deduction under any provision of the Internal Revenue Code of 1954 for any expense or amount which is otherwise allowable as a deduction and which is allocable to a class or classes of exempt income other than a class or classes of exempt interest income.

(2) No amount shall be allowed as a deduction under section 212 (relating to expenses for production of income) for any expense or amount which is otherwise allowable as a deduction and which is allocable to a class or classes of exempt interest income.

(b) *Exempt income and nonexempt income.*—(1) As used in this section, the term "class of exempt income" means any class of income (whether or not any amount of income of such class is received or accrued) wholly exempt from the taxes imposed by subtitle A of the Code. For purposes of this section, a class of income which is considered as wholly exempt from the taxes imposed by subtitle A includes any class of income which is—

(i) Wholly excluded from gross income under any provision of subtitle A, or

(ii) Wholly exempt from the taxes imposed by subtitle A under the provisions of any other law.

(2) As used in this section the term "nonexempt income" means any income which is required to be included in gross income.

(c) *Allocation of expenses to a class or classes of exempt income.*—Expenses and amounts otherwise allowable which are directly allocable to any class or classes of exempt income shall be allocated thereto; and expenses and amounts directly allocable to any class or classes of nonexempt income shall be allocated thereto. If an expense or amount otherwise allowable is indirectly allocable to both a class of nonexempt income and a class of exempt income, a reasonable proportion thereof determined in the light of all the facts and circumstances in each case shall be allocated to each.

(d) *Statement of classes of exempt income; records.*—(1) A taxpayer receiving any class of exempt income or holding any property or engaging in any activity the income from which is exempt shall submit with his return as a part thereof an itemized statement, in detail, showing (i) the amount of each class of exempt income, and (ii) the amount of expenses and amounts otherwise allowable allocated to each such class (the amount allocated by apportionment being shown separately) as required by paragraph (c) of this section. If an item is apportioned between a class of exempt income and a class of nonexempt income, the statement shall show the basis of the apportionment. Such statement shall also recite that each deduction claimed in the return is not in any way attributable to a class of exempt income.

(2) The taxpayer shall keep such records as will enable him to make the allocations required by this section. See section 6001 and the regulations thereunder. [Reg. § 1.265-1.]

□ [*T.D.* 6313, 9-16-58.]

§ 1.266-1. Taxes and carrying charges chargeable to capital account and treated as capital items.—(a) (1) *In general.*—In accordance with section 266, items enumerated in paragraph (b) (1) of this section may be capitalized at the election of the taxpayer. Thus, taxes and carrying charges with respect to property of the type described in this section are chargeable to capital account at the election of the taxpayer, notwithstanding that they are otherwise expressly deductible under provisions of subtitle A of the Code. No deduction is allowable for any items so treated.

(2) See § § 1.263A-8 through 1.263A-15 for rules regarding the requirement to capitalize interest, that apply prior to the application of this section. After applying § § 1.263A-8 through 1.263A-15, a taxpayer may elect to capitalize interest under section 266 with respect to designated property within the meaning of § 1.263A-8(b), provided a computation under any provision of the Internal Revenue Code is not thereby materially distorted, including computations relating to the source of deductions.

(b) *Taxes and carrying charges.*—(1) The taxpayer may elect, as provided in paragraph (c) of this section, to treat the items enumerated in this subparagraph which are otherwise expressly deductible under the provisions of subtitle A of the Code as chargeable to capital account either as a component of original cost or other basis, for the purposes of section 1012, or as an adjustment to basis, for the purpose of section 1016(a) (1). The items thus chargeable to capital account are—

(i) In the case of unimproved and unproductive real property: Annual taxes, interest on a mortgage, and other carrying charges.

(ii) In the case of real property, whether improved or unimproved and whether productive or unproductive:

(a) Interest on a loan (but not theoretical interest of a taxpayer using his own funds),

(b) Taxes of the owner of such real property measured by compensation paid to his employees,

(c) Taxes of such owner imposed on the purchase of materials, or on the storage, use, or other consumption of materials, and

(d) Other necessary expenditures,

paid or incurred for the development of the real property or for the construction of an improvement or additional improvement to such real property, up to the time the development or construction work has been completed. The development or construction work with respect to which such items are incurred may relate to unimproved and unproductive real estate whether the construction work will make the property productive of income subject to tax (as in the case of a factory) or not (as in the case of a personal residence), or may relate to property already improved or productive (as in the case of a plant addition or improvement, such as the construction of another floor on a factory or the installation of insulation therein).

(iii) In the case of personal property:

(a) Taxes of an employer measured by compensation for services rendered in transporting machinery or other fixed assets to the plant or installing them therein,

(b) Interest on a loan to purchase such property or to pay for transporting or installing the same, and

(c) Taxes of the owner thereof imposed on the purchase of such property or on the storage, use, or other consumption of such property, paid or incurred up to the date of installation or the date when such property is first put into use by the taxpayer, whichever date is later.

(iv) Any other taxes and carrying charges with respect to property, otherwise deductible, which in the opinion of the Commissioner are, under sound accounting principles, chargeable to capital account.

(2) The sole effect of section 266 is to permit the items enumerated in subparagraph (1) of this paragraph to be chargeable to capital account notwithstanding that such items are otherwise expressly deductible under the provisions of subtitle A of the Code. An item not otherwise deductible may not be capitalized under section 266.

(3) In the absence of a provision in this section for treating a given item as a capital item, this section has no effect on the treatment otherwise accorded such item. Thus, items

which are otherwise deductible are deductible notwithstanding the provisions of this section, and items which are otherwise treated as capital items are to be so treated. Similarly, an item not otherwise deductible is not made deductible by this section. Nor is the absence of a provision in this section for treating a given item as a capital item to be construed as withdrawing or modifying the right now given to the taxpayer under any other provisions of subtitle A of the Code, or of the regulations thereunder, to elect to capitalize or to deduct a given item.

(c) *Election to charge taxes and carrying charges to capital account.*—(1) If for any taxable year there are two or more items of the type described in paragraph (b)(1) of this section, which relate to the same project to which the election is applicable, the taxpayer may elect to capitalize any one or more of such items even though he does not elect to capitalize the remaining items or to capitalize items of the same type relating to other projects. However, if expenditures for several items of the same type are incurred with respect to a single project, the election to capitalize must, if exercised, be exercised as to all items of that type. For purposes of this section, a "project" means, in the case of items described in paragraph (b)(1)(ii) of this section, a particular development of, or construction of an improvement to, real property, and in the case of items described in paragraph (b)(1)(iii) of this section, the transportation and installation of machinery or other fixed assets.

(2)(i) An election with respect to an item described in paragraph (b)(1)(i) of this section is effective only for the year for which it is made.

(ii) An election with respect to an item described in—

(a) Paragraph (b)(1)(ii) of this section is effective until the development or construction work described in that subdivision has been completed;

(b) Paragraph (b)(1)(iii) of this section is effective until the later of either the date of installation of the property described in that subdivision, or the date when such property is first put into use by the taxpayer;

(c) Paragraph (b)(1)(iv) of this section is effective as determined by the Commissioner.

Thus, an item chargeable to capital account under this section must continue to be capitalized for the entire period described in this subdivision applicable to such election although such period may consist of more than one taxable year.

(3) If the taxpayer elects to capitalize an item or items under this section, such election shall be exercised by filing with the original return for the year for which the election is made a statement indicating the item or items (whether with respect to the same project or to different projects) which the taxpayer elects to treat as chargeable to capital account. Elections filed for taxable years beginning before January 1, 1954, and for taxable years ending before August 17, 1954, under section 24(a)(7) of the Internal Revenue Code of 1939, and the regulations thereunder, shall have the same effect as if they were filed under this section. See section 7807(b)(2).

* * *

[Reg. § 1.266-1.]

□ [*T.D.* 6313, 9-16-58. *Amended by T.D.* 6380, 5-26-59 *and T.D.* 8584, 12-28-94.]

§ 1.267(a)-1. Deductions disallowed.—(a) *Losses.*—Except in cases of distributions in corporate liquidations, no deduction shall be allowed for losses arising from direct or indirect sales or exchanges of property between persons who, on the date of the sale or exchange, are within any one of the relationships specified in section 267(b). See § 1.267(b)-1.

* * *

(c) *Scope of section.*—Section 267(a) requires that deductions for losses or unpaid expenses or interest described therein be disallowed even though the transaction in which such losses, expenses, or interest were incurred was a bona fide transaction. However, section 267 is not exclusive. No deduction for losses or unpaid expenses or interest arising in a transaction which is not bona fide will be allowed even though section 267 does not apply to the transaction. [Reg. § 1.267(a)-1.]

□ [*T.D.* 6312, 9-10-58.]

§ 1.267(b)-1. Relationships.—(a) *In general.*—(1) The persons referred to in section 267(a) and § 1.267(a)-1 are specified in section 267(b).

(2) Under section 267(b)(3), it is not necessary that either of the two corporations be a personal holding company or a foreign personal holding company for the taxable year in which the sale or exchange occurs or in which the expenses or interest are properly accruable, but either one of them must be such a company for the taxable year next preceding the taxable year in which the sale or exchange occurs or in which the expenses or interest are accrued.

(3) Under section 267(b)(9), the control of certain educational and charitable organizations exempt from tax under section 501 includes any kind of control, direct or indirect, by means of which a person in fact controls such an organization, whether or not the control is

legally enforceable and regardless of the method by which the control is exercised or exercisable. In the case of an individual, control possessed by the individual's family, as defined in section 267(c)(4) and paragraph (a)(4) of § 1.267(c)-1, shall be taken into account.

(b) *Partnerships.*—(1) Since section 267 does not include members of a partnership and the partnership as related persons, transactions between partners and partnerships do not come within the scope of section 267. Such transactions are governed by section 707 for the purposes of which the partnership is considered to be an entity separate from the partners. See section 707 and § 1.707-1. Any transaction described in section 267(a) between a partnership and a person other than a partner shall be considered as occurring between the other person and the members of the partnership separately. Therefore, if the other person and a partner are within any one of the relationships specified in section 267(b), no deductions with respect to such transactions between the other person and the partnership shall be allowed—

(i) To the related partner to the extent of his distributive share of partnership deductions for losses or unpaid expenses or interest resulting from such transactions, and

(ii) To the other person to the extent the related partner acquires an interest in any property sold to or exchanged with the partnership by such other person at a loss, or to the extent of the related partner's distributive share of the unpaid expenses or interest payable to the partnership by the other person as a result of such transaction.

(2) The provisions of this paragraph may be illustrated by the following examples:

Example (1). A, an equal partner in the ABC partnership, personally owns all the stock of M Corporation. B and C are not related to A. The partnership and all the partners use an accrual method of accounting, and are on a calendar year. M Corporation uses the cash receipts and disbursements method of accounting and is also on a calendar year. During 1956 the partnership borrowed money from M Corporation and also sold property to M Corporation, sustaining a loss on the sale. On December 31, 1956, the partnership accrued its interest liability to the M Corporation and on April 1, 1957 (more than 2½ months after the close of its taxable year), it paid the M Corporation the amount of such accrued interest. Applying the rules of this paragraph, the transactions are considered as occurring between M Corporation and the partners separately. The sale and interest transactions considered as occurring between A and the M Corporation fall within the scope of section 267(a) and (b), but the transactions considered as occurring between partners B and C and the M Corporation do not. The latter two partners may, therefore, deduct their distributive shares of partnership deductions for the loss and the accrued interest. However, no deduction shall be allowed to A for his distributive shares of these partnership deductions. Furthermore, A's adjusted basis for his partnership interest must be decreased by the amount of his distributive share of such deductions. See section 705(a)(2).

Example (2). Assume the same facts as in example (1) of this subparagraph except that the partnership and all the partners use the cash receipts and disbursements method of accounting, and that M Corporation uses an accrual method. Assume further, that during 1956 M Corporation borrowed money from the partnership and that on a sale of property to the partnership during that year M Corporation sustained a loss. On December 31, 1956, the M Corporation accrued its interest liability on the borrowed money and on April 1, 1957 (more than 2½ months after the close of its taxable year) it paid the accrued interest to the partnership. The corporation's deduction for the accrued interest is not allowed to the extent of A's distributive share (one-third) of such interest income. M Corporation's deduction for the loss on the sale of the property to the partnership is not allowed to the extent of A's one-third interest in the purchased property. [Reg. § 1.267(b)-1.]

□ [*T.D.* 6312, 9-10-58.]

§ 1.267(c)-1. Constructive ownership of stock.—(a) *In general.*—(1) The determination of stock ownership for purposes of section 267(b) shall be in accordance with the rules in section 267(c).

(2) For an individual to be considered under section 267(c)(2) as constructively owning the stock of a corporation which is owned, directly or indirectly, by or for members of his family it is not necessary that he own stock in the corporation either directly or indirectly. On the other hand, for an individual to be considered under section 267(c)(3) as owning the stock of a corporation owned either actually, or constructively under section 267(c)(1), by or for his partner, such individual must himself actually own, or constructively own under section 267(c)(1), stock of such corporation.

(3) An individual's constructive ownership, under section 267(c)(2) or (3), of stock owned directly or indirectly by or for a member of his family, or by or for his partner, is not to be considered as actual ownership of such stock, and the individual's constructive ownership of the stock is not to be attributed to another member of his family or to another

partner. However, an individual's constructive ownership, under section 267(c)(1), of stock owned directly or indirectly by or for a corporation, partnership, estate, or trust shall be considered as actual ownership of the stock, and the individual's ownership may be attributed to a member of his family or to his partner.

(4) The family of an individual shall include only his brothers and sisters, spouse, ancestors, and lineal descendants. In determining whether any of these relationships exist, full effect shall be given to a legal adoption. The term "ancestors" includes parents and grandparents, and the term "lineal descendants" includes children and grandchildren.

(b) *Examples.*—The application of section 267(c) may be illustrated by the following examples:

Example (1). On July 1, 1957, A owned 75 percent, and AW, his wife, owned 25 percent, of the outstanding stock of the M Corporation. The M Corporation in turn owned 80 percent of the outstanding stock of the O Corporation. Under section 267(c)(1), A and AW are each considered as owning an amount of the O Corporation stock actually owned by M Corporation in proportion to their respective ownership of M Corporation stock. Therefore, A constructively owns 60 percent (75 percent of 80 percent) of the O Corporation stock and AW constructively owns 20 percent (25 percent of 80 percent) of such stock. Under the family ownership rule of section 267(c)(2), an individual is considered as constructively owning the stock actually owned by his spouse. A and AW, therefore, are each considered as constructively owning the M Corporation stock actually owned by the other. For the purpose of applying this family ownership rule, A's and AW's constructive ownership of O Corporation stock is considered as actual ownership under section 267(c)(5). Thus, A constructively owns the 20 percent of the O Corporation stock constructively owned by AW, and AW constructively owns the 60 percent of the O Corporation stock constructively owned by A. In addition, the family ownership rule may be applied to make AWF, AW's father, the constructive owner of the 25 percent of the M Corporation stock actually owned by AW. As noted above, AW's constructive ownership of 20 percent of the O Corporation stock is considered as actual ownership for purposes of applying the family ownership rule, and AWF is thereby considered the constructive owner of this stock also. However, AW's constructive ownership of the stock constructively and actually owned by A may not be considered as actual ownership for the purpose of again applying the family ownership rule to make AWF the constructive owner of these shares. The ownership of the stock in the M and O Corporations may be tabulated as follows:

Person	Stock ownership in M Corporation		Total under Section 267	Stock ownership in O Corporation		Total under Section 267
	Actual Percent	Constructive Percent	Percent	Actual Percent	Constructive Percent	Percent
A	75	25	100	None	{60} {20}	80
AW (A's wife)	25	75	100	None	{20} {60}	80
AWF (AW's father) . .	None	25	25	None	20	20
M Corporation	. . .	. . .	. . .	80	None	80
O Corporation	None	None	None	. . .	. . .	. . .

Assuming that the M Corporation and the O Corporation make their income tax returns for calendar years, and that there was no distribution in liquidation of the M or O Corporation, and further assuming that either corporation was a personal holding company under section 542 for the calendar year 1956, no deduction is allowable with respect to losses from sales or exchanges of property made on July 1, 1957, between the two corporations. Moreover, whether or not either corporation was a personal holding company, no loss would be allowable on a sale or exchange between A or AW and either corporation. A deduction would be allowed, however, for a loss sustained in an arm's length sale or exchange between A and AWF, and between AWF and the M or O Corporation.

Example (2). On June 15, 1957, all of the stock of the N Corporation was owned in equal proportions by A and his partner, AP. Except in the case of distributions in liquidation by the N Corporation, no deduction is allowable with respect to losses from sales or exchanges of property made on June 15, 1957, between A and the N Corporation or AP and the N Corporation since each partner is considered as owning the stock owned by the other; therefore, each is considered as owning more than 50 percent in value of the outstanding stock of the N Corporation.

Example (3). On June 7, 1957, A owned no stock in X Corporation, but his wife, AW, owned 20 percent in value of the outstanding stock of X, and A's partner, AP, owned 60 percent in value of the outstanding stock of X. The partnership firm of A and AP owned no stock in X Corporation. The ownership of AW's stock is attributed to A, but not that of AP since A does not own any X Corporation stock either actually, or constructively under section 267(c)(1). A's constructive ownership of AW's stock is not the ownership required for the attribution of AP's stock. Therefore, deductions for losses from sales or exchanges of property made on June 7, 1957, between X Corporation and A or AW are allowable since neither person owned more than 50 percent in value of the outstanding stock of X, but deductions for losses from sales or exchanges between X Corporation and AP would not be allowable by section 267(a) (except for distributions in liquidation of X Corporation). [Reg. § 1.267(c)-1.]

☐ [*T.D.* 6312, 9-10-58.]

§ 1.267(d)-1. Amount of gain where loss previously disallowed.—(a) *General rule.*—(1) If a taxpayer acquires property by purchase or exchange from a transferor who, on the transaction, sustained a loss not allowable as a deduction by reason of section 267(a)(1) (or by reason of section 24(b) of the Internal Revenue Code of 1939), then any gain realized by the taxpayer on a sale or other disposition of the property after December 31, 1953, shall be recognized only to the extent that the gain exceeds the amount of such loss as is properly allocable to the property sold or otherwise disposed of by the taxpayer.

(2) The general rule is also applicable to a sale or other disposition of property by a taxpayer when the basis of such property in the taxpayer's hands is determined directly or indirectly by reference to other property acquired by the taxpayer from a transferor through a sale or exchange in which a loss sustained by the transferor was not allowable. Therefore, section 267(d) applies to a sale or other disposition of property after a series of transactions if the basis of the property acquired in each transaction is determined by reference to the basis of the property transferred, and if the original property was acquired in a transaction in which a loss to a transferor was not allowable by reason of section 267(a)(1) (or by reason of section 24(b) of the Internal Revenue Code of 1939).

(3) The benefit of the general rule is available only to the original transferee but does not apply to any original transferee (for example, a donee or a person acquiring property from a decedent where the basis of property is determined under section 1014 or 1022) who acquired the property in any manner other than by purchase or exchange.

(4) The application of the provisions of this paragraph may be illustrated by the following examples:

Example (1). He sells to his wife, W, for $500, certain corporate stock with an adjusted basis for determining loss to him of $800. The loss of $300 is not allowable to H by reason of section 267(a)(1) and paragraph (a) of § 1.267(a)-1. W later sells this stock for $1,000. Although W's realized gain is $500 ($1,000 minus $500, her basis), her recognized gain under section 267(d) is only $200, the excess of the realized gain of $500 over the loss of $300 not allowable to H. In determining capital gain or loss W's holding period commences on the date of the sale from H to W.

Example (2). Assume the same facts as in example (1) except that W later sells her stock for $300 instead of $1,000. Her recognized loss is $200 and not $500 since section 267(d) applies only to the nonrecognition of gain and does not affect basis.

Example (3). Assume the same facts as in example (1) except that W transfers her stock as a gift to X. The basis of the stock in the hands of X for the purpose of determining gain, under the provisions of section 1015, is the same as W's, or $500. If X later sells the stock for $1,000 the entire $500 gain is taxed to him.

Example (4). H sells to his wife, W, for $5,500, farmland, with an adjusted basis for determining loss to him of $8,000. The loss of $2,500 is not allowable to H by reason of section 267(a)(1) and paragraph (a) of § 1.267(a)-1. W exchanges the farmland, held for investment purposes, with S, an unrelated individual, for two city lots, also held for investment purposes. The basis of the city lots in the hands of W ($5,500) is a substituted basis determined under section 1031(d) by reference to the basis of the farmland. Later W sells the city lots for $10,000. Although W's realized gain is $4,500 ($10,000 minus $5,500), her recognized gain under section 267(d) is only $2,000, the excess of the realized gain of $4,500 over the loss of $2,500 not allowable to H.

* * *

(c) *Special rules.*—(1) Section 267(d) does not affect the basis of property for determining gain. Depreciation and other items which depend on such basis are also not affected.

(2) The provisions of section 267(d) shall not apply if the loss sustained by the transferor is not allowable to the transferor as a deduction by reason of section 1091, or section 118 of the Internal Revenue Code of 1939, which relate to losses from wash sales of stock or securities.

(3) In determining the holding period in the hands of the transferee of property received in an exchange with a transferor with respect to whom a loss on the exchange is not allowable by reason of section 267, section 1223(2) does not apply to include the period during which the property was held by the transferor.

In determining such holding period, however, section 1223(1) may apply to include the period during which the transferee held the property which he exchanged where, for example, he exchanged a capital asset in a transaction which, as to him, was nontaxable under section 1031 and the property received in the exchange has the same basis as the property exchanged. [Reg. § 1.267(d)-1.]

□ [*T.D.* 6312, 9-10-58. *Amended by T.D.* 9811, 1-18-2017.]

§ 1.269-1. Meaning and use of terms.—As used in section 269 and §§ 1.269-2 through 1.269-7—

(a) *Allowance.*—The term "allowance" refers to anything in the internal revenue laws which has the effect of diminishing tax liability. The term includes, among other things, a deduction, a credit, an adjustment, an exemption, or an exclusion.

(b) *Evasion or avoidance.*—The phrase "evasion or avoidance" is not limited to cases involving criminal penalties, or civil penalties for fraud.

(c) *Control.*—The term "control" means the ownership of stock possessing at least 50 percent of the total combined voting power of all classes of stock entitled to vote, or at least 50 percent of the total value of shares of all classes of stock of the corporation. For control to be "acquired on or after October 8, 1940", it is not necessary that all of such stock be acquired on or after October 8, 1940. Thus, if A, on October 7, 1940, and at all times thereafter, owns 40 percent of the stock of X Corporation and acquires on October 8, 1940, an additional 10 percent of such stock, an acquisition within the meaning of such phrase is made by A on October 8, 1940. Similarly, if B, on October 7, 1940, owns certain assets and transfers on October 8, 1940, such assets to a newly organized Y Corporation in exchange for all the stock of Y Corporation, an acquisition within the meaning of such phrase is made by B on October 8, 1940. If, under the facts stated in the preceding sentence, B is a corporation, all of whose stock is owned by Z Corporation, then an acquisition within the meaning of such phrase is also made by Z Corporation on October 8, 1940, as well as by the shareholders of Z Corporation taken as a group on such date, and by any of such shareholders if such shareholders as a group own 50 percent of the stock of Z on such date.

(d) *Person.*—The term "person" includes an individual, a trust, an estate, a partnership, an association, a company, or a corporation. [Reg. § 1.269-1.]

□ [*T.D.* 6595, 4-13-62. *Amended by T.D.* 8388, 12-31-91.]

§ 1.269-2. Purpose and scope of section 269.—(a) *General.*—Section 269 is designed to prevent in the instances specified therein the use of the sections of the Internal Revenue Code providing deductions, credits, or allowances in evading or avoiding Federal income tax. See § 1.269-3.

(b) *Disallowance of deduction, credit, or other allowance.*—Under the Code, an amount otherwise constituting a deduction, credit, or other allowance becomes unavailable as such under certain circumstances. Characteristic of such circumstances are those in which the effect of the deduction, credit, or other allowance would be to distort the liability of the particular taxpayer when the essential nature of the transaction or situation is examined in the light of the basic purpose or plan which the deduction, credit, or other allowance was designed by the Congress to effectuate. The distortion may be evidenced, for example, by the fact that the transaction was not undertaken for reasons germane to the conduct of the business of the taxpayer, by the unreal nature of the transaction such as its sham character, or by the unreal or unreasonable relation which the deduction, credit, or other allowance bears to the transaction. The principle of law making an amount unavailable as a deduction, credit, or other allowance in cases in which the effect of making an amount so available would be to distort the liability of the taxpayer has been judicially recognized and applied in several cases. Included in these cases are *Gregory v. Helvering* (1935) (293 U.S. 465; Ct. D. 911, C.B. XIV-1, 193); *Griffiths v. Helvering* (1939) (308 U.S. 355; Ct. D. 1431, C.B. 1940-1, 136); *Higgins v. Smith* (1940) (308 U.S. 473; Ct. D. 1434, C.B. 1940-1, 127); and *J.D. & A.B.* Spreckels Co. v. Commissioner (1940) (41 B.T.A. 370). In order to give effect to such principle, but not in limitation thereof, several provisions of the Code, for example, section 267 and section 270, specify with some particularity instances in which disallowance of the deduction, credit, or other allowance is required. Section 269 is also included in such provisions of the Code. The principle of law and the particular sections of the Code are not mutually exclusive and in appropriate circumstances they may operate together or they may operate separately. See, for example, § 1.269-6. [Reg. § 1.269-2.]

□ [*T.D.* 6595, 4-13-62.]

§ 1.269-3. Instances in which section 269(a) disallows a deduction, credit, or other allowance.—(a) *Instances of disallowance.*—Section 269 specifies two instances in which a deduction, credit, or other allowance is to be disallowed. These instances, described in paragraphs (1) and (2) of section 269(a), are those in which—

(1) Any person or persons acquire, or acquired on or after October 8, 1940, directly or indirectly, control of a corporation, or

(2) Any corporation acquires, or acquired on or after October 8, 1940, directly or indirectly, property of another corporation (not controlled, directly or indirectly, immediately before such acquisition by such acquiring corporation or its stockholders), the basis of which property in the hands of the acquiring corporation is determined by reference to the basis in the hands of the transferor corporation.

In either instance the principal purpose for which the acquisition was made must have been the evasion or avoidance of Federal income tax by securing the benefit of a deduction, credit, or other allowance which such other person, or persons, or corporation, would not otherwise enjoy. If this requirement is satisfied, it is immaterial by what method or by what conjunction of events the benefit was sought. Thus, an acquiring person or corporation can secure the benefit of a deduction, credit, or other allowance within the meaning of section 269 even though it is the acquired corporation that is entitled to such deduction, credit, or other allowance in the determination of its tax. If the purpose to evade or avoid Federal income tax exceeds in importance any other purpose, it is the principal purpose. This does not mean that only those acquisitions fall within the provisions of section 269 which would not have been made if the evasion or avoidance purpose was not present. The determination of the purpose for which an acquisition was made requires a scrutiny of the entire circumstances in which the transaction or course of conduct occurred, in connection with the tax result claimed to arise therefrom.

(b) *Acquisition of control; transactions indicative of purpose to evade or avoid tax.*—If the requisite acquisition of control within the meaning of paragraph (1) of section 269(a) exists, the transactions set forth in the following subparagraphs are among those which, in the absence of additional evidence to the contrary, ordinarily are indicative that the principal purpose for acquiring control was evasion or avoidance of Federal income tax:

(1) A corporation or other business enterprise (or the interest controlling such corporation or enterprise) with large profits acquires control of a corporation with current, past, or prospective credits, deductions, net operating losses, or other allowances and the acquisition is followed by such transfers or other action as is necessary to bring the deduction, credit, or other allowance into conjunction with the income (see further § 1.259-6). This subparagraph may be illustrated by the following example:

Example. Individual A acquires all of the stock of L Corporation which has been engaged in the business of operating retail drug stores. At the time of the acquisition, L Corporation has net operating loss carryovers aggregating $100,000 and its net worth is $100,000. After the acquisition, L Corporation continues to engage in the business of operating retail drug stores but the profits attributable to such business after the acquisition are not sufficient to absorb any substantial portion of the net operating loss carryovers. Shortly after the acquisition, individual A causes to be transferred to L Corporation the assets of a hardware business previously controlled by A which business produces profits sufficient to absorb a substantial portion of L Corporation's net operating loss carryovers. The transfer of the profitable business, which has the effect of using net operating loss carryovers to offset gains of a business unrelated to that which produced the losses, indicates that the principal purpose for which the acquisition of control was made is evasion or avoidance of Federal income tax.

(2) A person or persons organize two or more corporations instead of a single corporation in order to secure the benefit of multiple surtax exemptions (see section 11(c)) or multiple minimum accumulated earnings credits (see section 535(c)(2) and (3)).

(3) A person or persons with high earning assets transfer them to a newly organized controlled corporation retaining assets producing net operating losses which are utilized in an attempt to secure refunds.

(c) *Acquisition of property; transactions indicative of purpose to evade or avoid tax.*—If the requisite acquisition of property within the meaning of paragraph (2) of section 269(a) exists, the transactions set forth in the following subparagraphs are among those which, in the absence of additional evidence to the contrary, ordinarily are indicative that the principal purpose for acquiring such property was evasion or avoidance of Federal income tax:

(1) A corporation acquires property having in its hands an aggregate carryover basis which is materially greater than its aggregate fair market value at the time of such acquisition and utilizes the property to create tax-reducing losses or deductions.

(2) A subsidiary corporation, which has sustained large net operating losses in the operation of business X and which has filed separate returns for the taxable years in which the losses were sustained, acquires high earning assets, comprising business Y, from its parent corporation. The acquisition occurs at a time

when the parent would not succeed to the net operating loss carryovers of the subsidiary if the subsidiary were liquidated, and the profits of business Y are sufficient to offset a substantial portion of the net operating loss carryovers attributable to business X (see further example (3) of § 1.269-6).

(d) *Ownership changes to which section 382(l)(5) applies; transactions indicative of purpose to evade or avoid tax.*—(1) *In general.*—Absent strong evidence to the contrary, a requisite acquisition of control or property in connection with an ownership change to which section 382(l)(5) applies is considered to be made for the principal purpose of evasion or avoidance of Federal income tax unless the corporation carries on more than an insignificant amount of an active trade or business during and subsequent to the title 11 or similar case (as defined in section 382(l)(5)(G)). The determination of whether the corporation carries on more than an insignificant amount of an active trade or business is made without regard to the continuity of business enterprise requirement set forth in § 1.368-1(d). The determination is based on all the facts and circumstances, including, for example, the amount of business assets that continue to be used, or the number of employees in the work force who continue employment, in an active trade or business (although not necessarily the historic trade or business). Where the corporation continues to utilize a significant amount of its business assets or work force, the requirement of carrying on more than an insignificant amount of an active trade or business may be met even though all trade or business activities temporarily cease for a period of time in order to address business exigencies.

* * *

[Reg. § 1.269-3.]

☐ [*T.D.* 6595, 4-13-62. *Amended by T.D.* 8388, 12-31-91.]

§ 1.269-5. Time of acquisition of control.—(a) *In general.*—For purposes of section 269, an acquisition of control occurs when one or more persons acquire beneficial ownership of stock possessing at least 50 percent of the total combined voting power of all classes of stock entitled to vote or at least 50 percent of the total value of shares of all classes of stock of the corporation.

(b) *Application of general rule to certain creditor acquisitions.*—(1) For purposes of section 269, creditors of an insolvent or bankrupt corporation (by themselves or in conjunction with other persons) acquire control of the corporation when they acquire beneficial ownership of the requisite amount of stock. Although insolvency or bankruptcy may cause the interests of creditors to predominate as a practical matter, creditor interests do not constitute beneficial ownership of the corporation's stock. Solely for purposes of section 269, creditors of a bankrupt corporation are treated as acquiring beneficial ownership of stock of the corporation no earlier than the time a bankruptcy court confirms a plan of reorganization.

(2) The provisions of this section are illustrated by the following example.

Example. Corporation *L* files a petition under chapter 11 of the Bankruptcy Code on January 5, 1987. A creditors' committee is formed. On February 22, 1987, and upon the request of the creditors, the bankruptcy court removes the debtor-in-possession from business management and operations and appoints a trustee. The trustee consults regularly with the creditors' committee in formulating both short-term and long-term management decisions. After three years, the creditors approve a plan of reorganization in which the outstanding stock of Corporation *L* is cancelled and its creditors receive shares of stock constituting all of the outstanding shares. The bankruptcy court confirms the plan of reorganization on March 23, 1990, and the plan is put into effect on May 25, 1990. For purposes of section 269, the creditors acquired control of Corporation *L* no earlier than March 23, 1990. Similarly, the determination of whether the creditors acquired control of Corporation *L* with the principal purpose of evasion or avoidance of Federal income tax is made by reference to the creditors' purposes as of no earlier than March 23, 1990. [Reg. § 1.269-5.]

☐ [*T.D.* 6595, 4-13-62. *Amended by T.D.* 8388, 12-31-91.]

§ 1.269-7. Relationship of section 269 to sections 382 and 383 after the Tax Reform Act of 1986.—Section 269 and §§ 1.269-1 through 1.269-5 may be applied to disallow a deduction, credit, or other allowance notwithstanding that the utilization or amount of a deduction, credit, or other allowance is limited or reduced under section 382 or 383 and the regulations thereunder. However, the fact that the amount of taxable income or tax that may be offset by a deduction, credit, or other allowance is limited under section 382(a) or 383 and the regulations thereunder is relevant to the determination of whether the principal purpose of an acquisition is the evasion or avoidance of Federal income tax. [Reg. § 1.269-7.]

☐ [*T.D.* 8388, 12-31-91.]

§ 1.273-1. Life or terminable interests.—(a) *In general.*—Amounts paid as income to the holder of a life or a terminable interest acquired by gift, bequest, or inheritance shall not be subject to any deduction for shrinkage (whether called by depreciation or any other name) in the value of such interest due to the lapse of time. In other words, the holder of such an interest so acquired may not set up the value of the expected future payments as corpus or principal and claim deduction for shrinkage or exhaustion thereof due to the passage of time. For the treatment generally of distributions to beneficiaries of an estate or trust, see Subparts A, B, C, and D (section 641 and following), Subchapter J, Chapter 1 of the Code, and the regulations thereunder. For basis of property acquired from a decedent and by gifts and transfers in trust, see sections 1014, 1015, and 1022, and the regulations thereunder.

* * *

[Reg. § 1.273-1.]

☐ [*T.D.* 6313, 9-16-58. *Amended by T.D.* 9811, 1-18-2017.]

§ 1.274-1. Disallowance of certain entertainment, gift and travel expenses.—Section 274 disallows in whole, or in part, certain expenditures for entertainment, gifts and travel which would otherwise be allowable under chapter 1 of the Code. The requirements imposed by section 274 are in addition to the requirements for deductibility imposed by other provisions of the Code. If a deduction is claimed for an expenditure for entertainment, gifts, or travel, the taxpayer must first establish that it is otherwise allowable as a deduction under chapter 1 of the Code before the provisions of section 274 become applicable. An expenditure for entertainment, to the extent it is lavish or extravagant, shall not be allowable as a deduction. The taxpayer should then substantiate such an expenditure in accordance with the rules under section 274(d). See § 1.274-5. Section 274 is a disallowance provision exclusively, and does not make deductible any expense which is disallowed under any other provision of the Code. Similarly, section 274 does not affect the includability of an item in, or the excludability of an item from, the gross income of any taxpayer. For specific provisions with respect to the deductibility of expenditures: for an activity of a type generally considered to constitute entertainment, amusement, or recreation, and for a facility used in connection with such an activity, as well as certain travel expenses of a spouse, etc., see § 1.274-2; for expenses for gifts, see § 1.274-3; for expenses for foreign travel, see § 1.274-4; for expenditures deductible without regard to business activity, see § 1.274-6; and for treatment of personal portion of entertainment facility, see § 1.274-7. [Reg. § 1.274-1.]

☐ [*T.D.* 6659, 6-24-63. *Amended by T.D.* 8666, 5-29-96.]

»»→ Caution: Reg. § 1.274-2 does not reflect changes in Section 274 made by the Tax Cuts and Jobs Act of 2017.

§ 1.274-2. Disallowance of deductions for certain expenses for entertainment, amusement, recreation, or travel.—(a) *General rules.*—(1) *Entertainment activity.*—Except as provided in this section, no deduction otherwise allowable under chapter 1 of the Code shall be allowed for any expenditure with respect to entertainment unless the taxpayer establishes—

(i) That the expenditure was directly related to the active conduct of the taxpayer's trade or business, or

(ii) In the case of an expenditure directly preceding or following a substantial and bona fide business discussion (including business meetings at a convention or otherwise), that the expenditure was associated with the active conduct of the taxpayer's trade or business.

Such deduction shall not exceed the portion of the expenditure directly related to (or in the case of an expenditure described in subdivision (ii) above, the portion of the expenditure associated with) the active conduct of the taxpayer's trade or business.

(2) *Entertainment facilities.*—(i) *Expenditures paid or incurred after December 31, 1978, and not with respect to a club.*—Except as provided in this section with respect to a club, no deduction otherwise allowable under chapter 1 of the Code shall be allowed for any expenditure paid or incurred after December 31, 1978, with respect to a facility used in connection with entertainment.

* * *

(iii) *Expenditures paid or incurred after December 31, 1993, with respect to a club.*—*(a) In general.*—No deduction otherwise allowable under chapter 1 of the Internal Revenue Code shall be allowed for amounts paid or incurred after December 31, 1993, for membership in any club organized for business, pleasure, recreation, or other social purpose. The purposes and activities of a club, and not its name, determine whether it is organized for business, pleasure, recreation, or other social purpose. Clubs organized for business, pleasure, recreation, or other social purpose include any membership organization if a principal purpose of the organization is to conduct entertainment activities for members of the organization or their guests or to provide members or their guests with access to entertainment facilities within the meaning of paragraph (e)(2) of this section. Clubs organized for business, pleasure, recreation, or other social purpose include, but are not limited to, country clubs, golf and athletic clubs, airline clubs, hotel clubs, and clubs operated to provide meals under circumstances generally considered to be conducive to business discussion.

(b) Exceptions.—Unless a principal purpose of the organization is to conduct entertainment activities for members or their guests or to provide members or their guests with access to entertainment facilities, business leagues, trade associations, chambers of commerce, boards of trade, real estate boards, professional organizations (such as bar associations and medical associations), and civic or public service organizations will not be treated as clubs organized for business, pleasure, recreation, or other social purpose.

(3) *Cross references.*—For definition of the term "entertainment," see paragraph (b)(1) of this section. For the disallowance of deductions for the cost of admission to a dinner or program any part of the proceeds of which inures to the use of a political party or political candidate, and cost of admission to an inaugural event or similar event identified with any political party or political candidate, see §1.276-1. For rules and definitions with respect to—

(i) "Directly related entertainment", see paragraph (c) of this section,

(ii) "Associated entertainment", see paragraph (d) of this section,

(iii) "Expenditures paid or incurred before January 1, 1979, with respect to entertainment facilities or before January 1, 1994, with respect to clubs", see paragraph (e) of this section, and

(iv) "Specific exceptions" to the disallowance rules of this section, see paragraph (f) of this section.

(b) *Definitions.*—(1) *Entertainment defined.*—(i) *In general.*—For purposes of this section, the term "entertainment" means any activity which is of a type generally considered to constitute entertainment, amusement, or recreation, such as entertaining at night clubs, cocktail lounges, theaters, country clubs, golf and athletic clubs, sporting events, and on hunting, fishing, vacation and similar trips, including such activity relating solely to the taxpayer or the taxpayer's family. The term "entertainment" may include an activity, the cost of which is claimed as a business expense by the taxpayer, which satisfies the personal, living, or family needs of any individual, such as providing food and beverages, a hotel suite, or an automobile to a business customer or his family. The term "entertainment" does not include activities which, although satisfying personal, living, or family needs of an individual, are clearly not regarded as constituting entertainment, such as *(a)* supper money provided by an employer to his employee working overtime, *(b)* a hotel room maintained by an employer for lodging of his employees while in business travel status, or *(c)* an automobile used in the active conduct of trade or business even though used for routine personal purposes such as commuting to and from work. On the other hand, the providing of a hotel room or an automobile by an employer to his employee who is on vacation would constitute entertainment of the employee.

(ii) *Objective test.*—An objective test shall be used to determine whether an activity is of a type generally considered to constitute entertainment. Thus, if an activity is generally considered to be entertainment, it will constitute entertainment for purposes of this section and section 274(a) regardless of whether the expenditure can also be described otherwise, and even though the expenditure relates to the taxpayer alone. This objective test precludes arguments such as that "entertainment" means only entertainment of others or that an expenditure for entertainment should be characterized as an expenditure for advertising or public relations. However, in applying this test the taxpayer's trade or business shall be considered. Thus, although attending a theatrical performance would generally be considered entertainment, it would not be so considered in the case of a professional theater critic, attending in his professional capacity. Similarly, if a manufacturer of dresses conducts a fashion show to introduce his products to a group of store buyers, the show would not be generally considered to constitute entertainment. However, if an appliance distributor conducts a fashion show for the wives of his retailers, the fashion show would be generally considered to constitute entertainment.

(iii) *Special definitional rules.*—*(a) In general.*—Except as otherwise provided in *(b)* or *(c)* of this subdivision, any expenditure which might generally be considered either for a gift or entertainment, or considered either for travel or entertainment, shall be considered an expenditure for entertainment rather than for a gift or travel.

(b) Expenditures deemed gifts.—An expenditure described in *(a)* of this subdivision shall be deemed for a gift to which this section does not apply if it is:

(1) An expenditure for packaged food or beverages transferred directly or indirectly to another person intended for consumption at a later time.

(2) An expenditure for tickets of admission to a place of entertainment transferred to another person if the taxpayer does

not accompany the recipient to the entertainment unless the taxpayer treats the expenditure as entertainment. The taxpayer may change his treatment of such an expenditure as either a gift or entertainment at any time within the period prescribed for assessment of tax as provided in section 6501 of the Code and the regulations thereunder.

(3) Such other specific classes of expenditure generally considered to be for a gift as the Commissioner, in his discretion, may prescribe.

(c) Expenditures deemed travel.—An expenditure described in *(a)* of this subdivision shall be deemed for travel to which this section does not apply if it is:

(1) With respect to a transportation type facility (such as an automobile or an airplane), even though used on other occasions in connection with an activity of a type generally considered to constitute entertainment, to the extent the facility is used in pursuit of a trade or business for purposes of transportation not in connection with entertainment. See also paragraph (e) (3) (iii) (*b*) of this section for provisions covering non-entertainment expenditures with respect to such facilities.

(2) Such other specific classes of expenditure generally considered to be for travel as the Commissioner, in his discretion, may prescribe.

(2) *Other definitions.*—(i) *Expenditure.*—The term "expenditure" as used in this section shall include expenses paid or incurred for goods, services, facilities, and items (including items such as losses and depreciation).

(ii) *Expenses for production of income.*—For purposes of this section, any reference to "trade or business" shall include any activity described in section 212.

(iii) *Business associate.*—The term "business associate" as used in this section means a person with whom the taxpayer could reasonably expect to engage or deal in the active conduct of the taxpayer's trade or business such as the taxpayer's customer, client, supplier, employee, agent, partner, or professional adviser, whether established or prospective.

(c) *Directly related entertainment.*—(1) *In general.*—Except as otherwise provided in paragraph (d) of this section (relating to associated entertainment) or under paragraph (f) of this section (relating to business meals and other specific exceptions), no deduction shall be allowed for any expenditure for entertainment unless the taxpayer establishes that the expenditure was directly related to the active conduct of his trade or business within the meaning of this paragraph.

(2) *Directly related entertainment defined.*—Any expenditure for entertainment, if it is otherwise allowable as a deduction under chapter 1 of the Code, shall be considered directly related to the active conduct of the taxpayer's trade or business if it meets the requirements of any one of subparagraphs (3), (4), (5), or (6) of this paragraph.

(3) *Directly related in general.*—Except as provided in subparagraph (7) of this paragraph, an expenditure for entertainment shall be considered directly related to the active conduct of the taxpayer's trade or business if it is established that it meets all of the requirements of subdivisions (i), (ii), (iii) and (iv) of this subparagraph.

(i) At the time the taxpayer made the entertainment expenditure (or committed himself to make the expenditure), the taxpayer had more than a general expectation of deriving some income or other specific trade or business benefit (other than the goodwill of the person or persons entertained) at some indefinite future time from the making of the expenditure. A taxpayer, however, shall not be required to show that income or other business benefit actually resulted from each and every expenditure for which a deduction is claimed.

(ii) During the entertainment period to which the expenditure related, the taxpayer actively engaged in a business meeting, negotiation, discussion, or other bona fide business transaction, other than entertainment, for the purpose of obtaining such income or other specific trade or business benefit (or, at the time the taxpayer made the expenditure or committed himself to the expenditure, it was reasonable for the taxpayer to expect that he would have done so, although such was not the case solely for reasons beyond the taxpayer's control).

(iii) In light of all the facts and circumstances of the case, the principal character or aspect of the combined business and entertainment to which the expenditure related was the active conduct of the taxpayer's trade or business (or at the time the taxpayer made the expenditure or committed himself to the expenditure, it was reasonable for the taxpayer to expect that the active conduct of trade or business would have been the principal character or aspect of the entertainment, although such was not the case solely for reasons beyond the taxpayer's control). It is not necessary that more time be devoted to business than to entertainment to meet this requirement. The active conduct of trade or business is considered not to be the principal character or aspect of combined business and entertainment activity on hunting or fishing trips or on yachts and other pleasure boats unless the taxpayer clearly establishes to the contrary.

(iv) The expenditure was allocable to the taxpayer and a person or persons with whom the taxpayer engaged in the active conduct of trade or business during the entertainment or with whom the taxpayer establishes he would have engaged in such active conduct of trade or business if it were not for circumstances beyond the taxpayer's control. For expenditures closely connected with directly related entertainment, see paragraph (d)(4) of this section.

(4) *Expenditures in clear business setting.*—An expenditure for entertainment shall be considered directly related to the active conduct of the taxpayer's trade or business if it is established that the expenditure was for entertainment occurring in a clear business setting directly in furtherance of the taxpayer's trade or business. Generally, entertainment shall not be considered to have occurred in a clear business setting unless the taxpayer clearly establishes that any recipient of the entertainment would have reasonably known that the taxpayer had no significant motive, in incurring the expenditure, other than directly furthering his trade or business. Objective rather than subjective standards will be determinative. Thus, entertainment which occurred under any circumstances described in subparagraph (7)(ii) of this paragraph ordinarily will not be considered as occurring in a clear business setting. Such entertainment will generally be considered to be socially rather than commercially motivated. Expenditures made for the furtherance of a taxpayer's trade or business in providing a "hospitality room" at a convention (described in paragraph (d)(3)(i)(*b*) of this section) at which goodwill is created through display or discussion of the taxpayer's products, will, however, be treated as directly related. In addition, entertainment of a clear business nature which occurred under circumstances where there was no meaningful personal or social relationship between the taxpayer and the recipients of the entertainment may be considered to have occurred in a clear business setting. For example, entertainment of business representatives and civic leaders at the opening of a new hotel or theatrical production, where the clear purpose of the taxpayer is to obtain business publicity rather than to create or maintain the goodwill of the recipients of the entertainment, would generally be considered to be in a clear business setting. Also, entertainment which has the principal effect of a price rebate in connection with the sale of the taxpayer's products generally will be considered to have occurred in a clear business setting. Such would be the case, for example, if a taxpayer owning a hotel were to provide occasional free dinners at the hotel for a customer who patronized the hotel.

(5) *Expenditures for services performed.*—An expenditure shall be considered directly related to the active conduct of the taxpayer's trade or business if it is established that the expenditure was made directly or indirectly by the taxpayer for the benefit of an individual (other than an employee), and if such expenditure was in the nature of compensation for services rendered or was paid as a prize or award which is required to be included in gross income under section 74 and the regulations thereunder. For example, if a manufacturer of products provides a vacation trip for retailers of his products who exceed sales quotas, as a prize or award includible in gross income, the expenditure will be considered directly related to the active conduct of the taxpayer's trade or business.

(6) *Club dues, etc., allocable to business meals.* An expenditure shall be considered directly related to the active conduct of the taxpayer's trade or business if it is established that the expenditure was with respect to a facility (as described in paragraph (e) of this section) used by the taxpayer for the furnishing of food or beverages under circumstances described in paragraph (f)(2)(i) of this section (relating to business meals and similar expenditures), to the extent allocable to the furnishing of such food or beverages. This paragraph (c)(6) applies to club dues paid or incurred before January 1, 1987.

(7) *Expenditures generally considered not directly related.*—Expenditures for entertainment, even if connected with the taxpayer's trade or business, will generally be considered not directly related to the active conduct of the taxpayer's trade or business, if the entertainment occurred under circumstances where there was little or no possibility of engaging in the active conduct of trade or business. The following circumstances will generally be considered circumstances where there was little or no possibility of engaging in the active conduct of a trade or business:

(i) The taxpayer was not present;

(ii) The distractions were substantial, such as—

(a) A meeting or discussion at night clubs, theaters, and sporting events, or during essentially social gatherings such as cocktail parties, or

(b) A meeting or discussion, if the taxpayer meets with a group which includes persons other than business associates, at

places such as cocktail lounges, country clubs, golf and athletic clubs, or at vacation resorts. An expenditure for entertainment in any such case is considered not to be directly related to the active conduct of the taxpayer's trade or business unless the taxpayer clearly establishes to the contrary.

(d) *Associated entertainment.*—(1) *In general.*—Except as provided in paragraph (f) of this section (relating to business meals and other specific exceptions) and subparagraph (4) of this paragraph (relating to expenditures closely connected with directly related entertainment), any expenditure for entertainment which is not directly related to the active conduct of the taxpayer's trade or business will not be allowable as a deduction unless—

(i) It was associated with the active conduct of trade or business as defined in subparagraph (2) of this paragraph, and

(ii) The entertainment directly preceded or followed a substantial and bona fide business discussion as defined in subparagraph (3) of this paragraph.

(2) *Associated entertainment defined.*—Generally, any expenditure for entertainment, if it is otherwise allowable under chapter 1 of the Code, shall be considered associated with the active conduct of the taxpayer's trade or business if the taxpayer establishes that he had a clear business purpose in making the expenditure, such as to obtain new business or to encourage the continuation of an existing business relationship. However, any portion of an expenditure allocable to a person who was not closely connected with a person who engaged in the substantial and bona fide business discussion (as defined in subparagraph (3)(i) of this paragraph) shall not be considered associated with the active conduct of the taxpayer's trade or business. The portion of an expenditure allocable to the spouse of a person who engaged in the discussion will, if it is otherwise allowable under chapter 1 of the Code, be considered associated with the active conduct of the taxpayer's trade or business.

(3) *Directly preceding or following a substantial and bona fide business discussion defined.*—(i) *Substantial and bona fide business discussion.*—*(a) In general.*—Whether any meeting, negotiation or discussion constitutes a "substantial and bona fide business discussion" within the meaning of this section depends upon the facts and circumstances of each case. It must be established, however, that the taxpayer actively engaged in a business meeting, negotiation, discussion, or other bona fide business transaction, other than entertainment, for the purpose of obtaining income or other specific trade or business benefit. In addition, it must be established that such a business meeting, negotiation, discussion, or transaction was substantial in relation to the entertainment. This requirement will be satisfied if the principal character or aspect of the combined entertainment and business activity was the active conduct of business. However, it is not necessary that more time be devoted to business than to entertainment to meet this requirement.

(b) Meetings at conventions, etc..—Any meeting officially scheduled in connection with a program at a convention or similar general assembly, or at a bona fide trade or business meeting sponsored and conducted by business or professional organizations, shall be considered to constitute a substantial and bona fide business discussion within the meaning of this section provided—

(1) Expenses necessary to taxpayer's attendance.—The expenses necessary to the attendance of the taxpayer at the convention, general assembly, or trade or business meeting, were ordinary and necessary within the meaning of section 162 or 212;

(2) Convention program.—The organization which sponsored the convention, or trade or business meeting had scheduled a program of business activities (including committee meetings or presentation of lectures, panel discussions, display of products, or other similar activities), and that such program was the principal activity of the convention, general assembly, or trade or business meeting.

(ii) *Directly preceding or following.*—Entertainment which occurs on the same day as a substantial and bona fide business discussion (as defined in subdivision (i) of this subparagraph) will be considered to directly precede or follow such discussion. If the entertainment and the business discussion do not occur on the same day, the facts and circumstances of each case are to be considered, including the place, date and duration of the business discussion, whether the taxpayer or his business associates are from out of town, and, if so, the date of arrival and departure, and the reasons the entertainment did not take place on the day of the business discussion. For example, if a group of business associates comes from out of town to the taxpayer's place of business to hold a substantial business discussion, the entertainment of such business guests and their wives on the evening prior to, or on the evening of the day following, the business discussion would generally be regarded as directly preceding or following such discussion.

(4) *Expenses closely connected with directly related entertainment.*—If any portion of an ex-

penditure meets the requirements of paragraph (c) (3) of this section (relating to directly related entertainment in general), the remaining portion of the expenditure, if it is otherwise allowable under chapter 1 of the Code, shall be considered associated with the active conduct of the taxpayer's trade or business to the extent allocable to a person or persons closely connected with a person referred to in paragraph (c) (3) (iv) of this section. The spouse of a person referred to in paragraph (c) (3) (iv) of this section will be considered closely connected to such a person for purposes of this subparagraph. Thus, if a taxpayer and his wife entertain a business customer and the customer's wife under circumstances where the entertainment of the customer is considered directly related to the active conduct of the taxpayer's trade or business (within the meaning of paragraph (c) (3) of this section) the portion of the expenditure allocable to both wives will be considered associated with the active conduct of the taxpayer's trade or business under this subparagraph.

* * *

(f) *Specific exceptions to application of this section.*—(1) *In general.*—The provisions of paragraphs (a) through (e) of this section (imposing limitations on deductions for entertainment expenses) are not applicable in the case of expenditures set forth in subparagraph (2) of this paragraph. Such expenditures are deductible to the extent allowable under Chapter 1 of the Code. This paragraph shall not be construed to affect the allowability or nonallowability of a deduction under section 162 or 212 and the regulations thereunder. The fact that an expenditure is not covered by a specific exception provided for in this paragraph shall not be determinative of the allowability or nonallowability of the expenditure under paragraphs (a) through (e) of this section. Expenditures described in subparagraph (2) of this paragraph are subject to the substantiation requirements of section 274(d) to the extent provided in § 1.274-5.

(2) *Exceptions.*—The expenditures referred to in subparagraph (1) of this paragraph are set forth in subdivisions (i) through (ix) of this subparagraph.

* * *

(ii) *Food and beverages for employees.*—Any expenditure by a taxpayer for food and beverages (or for use of a facility in connection therewith) furnished on the taxpayer's business premises primarily for employees is not subject to the limitations on allowability of deductions provided for in paragraphs (a) through (e) of this section. This exception applies not only to expenditures for food or beverages furnished in a typical company cafeteria or an executive dining room, but also to expenditures with respect to the operation of such facilities. This exception applies even though guests are occasionally served in the cafeteria or dining room.

(iii) *Certain entertainment and travel expenses treated as compensation.*—(A) *In general.*—Any expenditure by a taxpayer for entertainment (or for use of a facility in connection therewith) or for travel described in section 274(m) (3), if an employee is the recipient of the entertainment or travel, is not subject to the limitations on allowability of deductions provided for in paragraphs (a) through (e) of this section to the extent that the expenditure is treated by the taxpayer—

(1) On the taxpayer's income tax return as originally filed, as compensation paid to the employee; and

(2) As wages to the employee for purposes of withholding under chapter 24 (relating to collection of income tax at source on wages).

(B) *Expenses includible in income of persons who are not employees.*—Any expenditure by a taxpayer for entertainment (or for use of a facility in connection therewith), or for travel described in section 274(m) (3), is not subject to the limitations on allowability of deductions provided for in paragraphs (a) through (e) of this section to the extent the expenditure is includible in gross income as compensation for services rendered, or as a prize or award under section 74, by a recipient of the expenditure who is not an employee of the taxpayer. The preceding sentence shall not apply to any amount paid or incurred by the taxpayer if such amount is required to be included (or would be so required except that the amount is less that $600) in any information return filed by such taxpayer under part III of subchapter A of chapter 61 and is not so included. See section 274(e) (9).

(C) *Example.*—The following example illustrates the provisions this paragraph (f):

Example. If an employer rewards the employee (and the employee's spouse) with an expense paid vacation trip, the expense is deductible by the employer (if otherwise allowable under section 162 and the regulations thereunder) to the extent the employer treats the expenses as compensation and as wages. On the other hand, if a taxpayer owns a yacht which the taxpayer uses for the entertainment of business customers, the portion of salary paid to employee members of the crew which is allocable to use of the yacht for entertainment purposes (even though treated on the taxpayer's tax return as compensation and treated as wages for withholding tax purposes) would not come within this exception since the members of the crew were not recipients of the entertainment. If an expenditure of a type described in this subdivision properly constitutes a dividend paid to a shareholder or if it constitutes unreasonable compensation paid to an employee, nothing in this exception prevents disallowance of the expenditure to the taxpayer under other provisions of the Internal Revenue Code.

(iv) *Reimbursed entertainment, food, or beverage expenses.*—(A) *Introduction.*—In the case of any expenditure for entertainment, amusement, recreation, food, or beverages made by one person in performing services for another person (whether or not the other person is an employer) under a reimbursement or other expense allowance arrangement, the limitations on deductions in paragraphs (a) through (e) of this section and section 274(n)(1) apply either to the person who makes the expenditure or to the person who actually bears the expense, but not to both. If an expenditure of a type described in this paragraph (f)(2)(iv) properly constitutes a dividend paid to a shareholder, unreasonable compensation paid to an employee, a personal expense, or other nondeductible expense, nothing in this exception prevents disallowance of the expenditure to the taxpayer under other provisions of the Code.

(B) *Reimbursement arrangements involving employees.*—In the case of an employee's expenditure for entertainment, amusement, recreation, food, or beverages in performing services as an employee under a reimbursement or other expense allowance arrangement with a payor (the employer, its agent, or a third party), the limitations on deductions in paragraphs (a) through (e) of this section and section 274(n)(1) apply—

(1) To the employee to the extent the employer treats the reimbursement or other payment of the expense on the employer's income tax return as originally filed as compensation paid to the employee and as wages to the employee for purposes of withholding under chapter 24 (relating to collection of income tax at source on wages); or

(2) To the payor to the extent the reimbursement or other payment of the expense is not treated as compensation and wages paid to the employee in the manner provided in paragraph (f)(2)(iv)(B)(1) of this section (however, see paragraph (f)(2)(iv)(C) of this section if the payor receives a payment from a third party that may be treated as a reimbursement arrangement under that paragraph).

(C) *Reimbursement arrangements involving persons that are not employees.*—In the case of an expense for entertainment, amusement, recreation, food, or beverages of a person who is not an employee (referred to as an independent contractor) in performing services for another person (a client or customer) under a reimbursement or other expense allowance arrangement with the person, the limitations on deductions in paragraphs (a) through (e) of this section and section 274(n)(1) apply to the party expressly identified in an agreement between the parties as subject to the limitations. If an agreement between the parties does not expressly identify the party subject to the limitations, the limitations apply—

(1) To the independent contractor (which may be a payor described in paragraph (f)(2)(iv)(B) of this section) to the extent the independent contractor does not account to the client or customer within the meaning of section 274(d) and the associated regulations; or

(2) To the client or customer if the independent contractor accounts to the client or customer within the meaning of section 274(d) and the associated regulations. See also §1.274-5.

(D) *Reimbursement or other expense allowance arrangement.*—The term *reimbursement or other expense allowance arrangement* means—

(1) For purposes of paragraph (f)(2)(iv)(B) of this section, an arrangement under which an employee receives an advance, allowance, or reimbursement from a payor (the employer, its agent, or a third party) for expenses the employee pays or incurs; and

(2) For purposes of paragraph (f)(2)(iv)(C) of this section, an arrangement under which an independent contractor receives an advance, allowance, or reimbursement from a client or customer for expenses the independent contractor pays or incurs if either—

(a) A written agreement between the parties expressly states that the client or customer will reimburse the independent contractor for expenses that are subject to the limitations on deductions in paragraphs (a) through (e) of this section and section 274(n)(1); or

(b) A written agreement between the parties expressly identifies the party subject to the limitations.

(E) *Examples.*—The following examples illustrate the application of this paragraph (f)(2)(iv).

Example 1. (i) Y, an employee, performs services under an arrangement in which L, an employee leasing company, pays Y a per diem allowance of $10x for each day that Y performs services for L's client, C, while traveling away from home. The per diem allowance is a reimbursement of travel expenses for food and beverages that Y pays in performing services as an employee. L enters into a written agreement with C under which C agrees to reimburse L for any substantiated reimbursements for travel expenses, including meals, that L pays to Y. The agreement does not expressly identify the party that is subject to the deduction limitations. Y performs services for C while traveling away from home for 10 days and provides L with substantiation that satisfies the requirements of section 274(d) of $100x of meal expenses incurred by Y while traveling away from home. L pays Y $100x to reimburse those expenses pursuant to their arrangement. L delivers a copy of Y's substantiation to C. C pays L $300x, which includes $200x compensation for services and $100x as reimbursement of L's payment of Y's travel expenses for meals. Neither L nor C treats the $100x paid to Y as compensation or wages.

(ii) Under paragraph (f)(2)(iv)(D)(*1*) of this section, Y and L have established a reimbursement or other expense allowance arrangement for purposes of paragraph (f)(2)(iv)(B) of this section. Because the reimbursement payment is not treated as compensation and wages paid to Y, under section 274(e)(3)(A) and paragraph (f)(2)(iv)(B)(*1*) of this section, Y is not subject to the section 274 deduction limitations. Instead, under paragraph (f)(2)(iv)(B)(*2*) of this section, L, the payor, is subject to the section 274 deduction limitations unless L can meet the requirements of section 274(e)(3)(B) and paragraph (f)(2)(iv)(C) of this section.

(iii) Because the agreement between L and C expressly states that C will reimburse L for substantiated reimbursements for travel expenses that L pays to Y, under paragraph (f)(2)(iv)(D)(*2*)(*a*) of this section, L and C have established a reimbursement or other expense allowance arrangement for purposes of paragraph (f)(2)(iv)(C) of this section. L accounts to C for C's reimbursement in the manner required by section 274(d) by delivering to C a copy of the substantiation L received from Y. Therefore, under section 274(e)(3)(B) and paragraph (f)(2)(iv)(C)(*2*) of this section, C and not L is subject to the section 274 deduction limitations.

Example 2. (i) The facts are the same as in *Example 1* except that, under the arrangements between Y and L and between L and C, Y provides the substantiation of the expenses directly to C, and C pays the per diem directly to Y.

(ii) Under paragraph (f)(2)(iv)(D)(*1*) of this section, Y and C have established a reimbursement or other expense allowance arrangement for purposes of paragraph (f)(2)(iv)(C) of this section. Because Y substantiates directly to C and the reimbursement payment was not treated as compensation and wages paid to Y, under section 274(e)(3)(A) and paragraph (f)(2)(iv)(C)(*1*) of this section Y is not subject to the section 274 deduction limitations. Under paragraph (f)(2)(iv)(C)(*2*) of this section, C, the payor, is subject to the section 274 deduction limitations.

Example 3. (i) The facts are the same as in *Example 1*, except that the written agreement between L and C expressly provides that the limitations of this section will apply to C.

(ii) Under paragraph (f)(2)(iv)(D)(*2*)(*b*) of this section, L and C have established a reimbursement or other expense allowance arrangement for purposes of paragraph (f)(2)(iv)(C) of this section. Because the agreement provides that the 274 deduction limitations apply to C, under section 274(e)(3)(B) and paragraph (f)(2)(iv)(C) of this section, C and not L is subject to the section 274 deduction limitations.

Example 4. (i) The facts are the same as in *Example 1*, except that the agreement between L and C does not provide that C will reimburse L for travel expenses.

(ii) The arrangement between L and C is not a reimbursement or other expense allowance arrangement within the meaning of section 274(e)(3)(B) and paragraph (f)(2)(iv)(D)(*2*) of this section. Therefore, even though L accounts to C for the expenses, L is subject to the section 274 deduction limitations.

(F) *Effective/applicability date.*—This paragraph (f)(2)(iv) applies to expenses paid or incurred in taxable years beginning after August 1, 2013.

(v) *Recreational expenses for employees generally.*—Any expenditure by a taxpayer for a recreational, social, or similar activity (or for use of a facility in connection therewith), primarily for the benefit of his employees generally, is not subject to the limitations on allowability of deductions provided for in paragraphs (a) through (e) of this section. This exception applies only to expenditures made primarily for the benefit of employees of the taxpayer other than employees who are officers, shareholders or other owners who own a 10-percent or greater interest in the business, or other highly compensated employees. For purposes of the preceding sentence, an employee shall be treated as owning any interest owned by a member of his family (within the meaning of section 267(c)(4) and the regulations thereunder). Ordinarily, this exception applies to usual employee benefit programs such as expenses of a taxpayer (*a*) in holding Christmas parties, annual picnics, or summer outings, for his employees generally, or (*b*) of maintaining a swimming pool, baseball diamond, bowling alley, or golf course available to his employees generally. Any expenditure for an activity which is made under circumstances which discriminate in favor of employees who are officers, shareholders or other owners, or highly compensated employees shall not be considered made primarily for the benefit of employees generally. On the other hand, an expenditure for an activity will not be considered outside of this exception merely because, due to the large number of employees involved, the activity is intended to benefit only a limited number of such employees at one time, provided the activity does not discriminate in favor of officers, shareholders, other owners, or highly compensated employees.

(vi) *Employee, stockholder, etc., business meetings.* Any expenditure by a taxpayer for entertainment which is directly related to bona fide business meetings of the taxpayer's employees, stockholders, agents, or directors held principally for discussion of trade or business is not subject to the limitations on allowability of deductions provided for in paragraphs (a) through (e) of this section. For purposes of this exception, a partnership is to be considered a taxpayer and a member of a partnership is to be considered an agent. For example, an expenditure by a taxpayer to furnish refreshments to his employees at a bona fide meeting, sponsored by the taxpayer for the principal purpose of instructing them with respect to a new procedure for conducting his business, would be within the provisions of this exception. A similar expenditure made at a bona fide meeting of stockholders of the taxpayer for the election of directors and discussion of corporate affairs would also be within the provisions of this exception. While this exception will apply to bona fide business meetings even though some social activities are provided, it will not apply to meetings which are primarily for social or nonbusiness purposes rather than for the transaction of the taxpayer's business. A meeting under circumstances where there was little or no possibility of engaging in the active conduct of trade or business (as described in paragraph (c)(7) of this section) generally will not be considered a business meeting for purposes of this subdivision. This exception will not apply to a meeting or convention of employees or agents, or similar meeting for directors, partners or others for the principal purpose of rewarding them for their services to the taxpayer. However, such a meeting or convention of employees might come within the scope of subdivisions (iii) or (v) of this subparagraph.

(vii) *Meetings of business leagues, etc.*—Any expenditure for entertainment directly related and necessary to attendance at bona fide business meetings or conventions of organizations exempt from taxation under section 501(c)(6) of the Code, such as business leagues, chambers of commerce, real estate boards, boards of trade, and certain professional associations, is not subject to the limitations on allowability of deductions provided in paragraphs (a) through (e) of this section.

(viii) *Items available to the public.*—Any expenditure by a taxpayer for entertainment (or for a facility in connection therewith) to the extent the entertainment is made available to the general public is not subject to the limitations on allowability of deductions provided for in paragraphs (a) through (e) of this section. Expenditures for entertainment of the general public by means of television, radio, newspapers and the like, will come within this exception, as will expenditures for distributing samples to the general public. Similarly, expenditures for maintaining private parks, golf courses and similar facilities, to the extent that they are available for public use, will come within this exception. For example, if a corporation maintains a swimming pool which it makes available for a period of time each week to children participating in a local public recreational program, the portion of the expense relating to such public use of the pool will come within this exception.

(ix) *Entertainment sold to customers.*—Any expenditure by a taxpayer for entertainment (or for use of a facility in connection therewith) to the extent the entertainment is sold to customers in a bona fide transaction for an adequate and full consideration in money or money's worth is not subject to the limitations on allowability of deductions provided for in paragraphs (a) through (e) of this section. Thus, the cost of producing night club entertainment (such as salaries paid to employees of night clubs and amounts paid to performers) for sale to customers or the cost of operating a pleasure cruise ship as a business will come within this exception.

(g) *Additional provisions of section 274—travel of spouse, dependent or others.*—Section 274(m)(3) provides that no deduction shall be allowed under this chapter (except section 217) for travel expenses paid or incurred with respect to a spouse, dependent, or other individual accompanying the taxpayer (or an officer or employee of the taxpayer) on business travel, unless certain conditions are met. As provided in section 274(m)(3), the term *other individual* does not include a business associate (as defined in paragraph (b)(2)(iii) of this section) who otherwise meets the requirements of sections 274(m)(3)(B) and (C). [Reg. § 1.274-2.]

□ [*T.D.* 6659, 6-24-63. *Amended by T.D.* 6996, 1-17-69; *T.D.* 8051, 9-6-85; *T.D.* 8601, 7-18-95; *T.D.* 8666, 5-29-96 *and T.D.* 9625, 7-31-2013.]

§ 1.274-5T. Substantiation requirements (temporary).—(a) *In general.*—For taxable years beginning on or after January 1, 1986, no deduction or credit shall be allowed with respect to—

(1) Traveling away from home (including meals and lodging),

(2) Any activity which is of a type generally considered to constitute entertainment, amusement, or recreation, or with respect to a facility used in connection with such an activity, including the items specified in section 274(e),

(3) Gifts defined in section 274(b), or

(4) Any listed property (as defined in section 280F(d)(4) and § 1.280F-6T(b)),

unless the taxpayer substantiates each element of the expenditure or use (as described in paragraph (b) of this section) in the manner provided in paragraph (c) of this section. This limitation supersedes the doctrine founded in *Cohan v. Commissioner*, 39 F.2d 540 (2d Cir. 1930). The decision held that, where the evidence indicated a taxpayer incurred deductible travel or entertainment expenses but the exact amount could not be determined, the court should make a close approximation and not disallow the deduction entirely. Section 274(d) contemplates that no deduction or credit shall be allowed a taxpayer on the basis of such approximations or unsupported testimony of the taxpayer. For purposes of this section, the term "entertainment" means entertainment, amusement, or recreation, and use of a facility therefor; and the term "expenditure" includes expenses and items (including items such as loss and depreciation).

(b) *Elements of an expenditure or use.*—(1) *In general.*—Section 274(d) and this section contemplate that no deduction or credit shall be allowed for travel, entertainment, a gift, or with respect to listed property unless the taxpayer substantiates the requisite elements of each expenditure or use as set forth in this paragraph (b).

(2) *Travel away from home.*—The elements to be proved with respect to an expenditure for travel away from home are—

(i) *Amount.*—Amount of each separate expenditure for traveling away from home, such as cost of transportation or lodging, except that the daily cost of the traveler's own breakfast, lunch, and dinner and of expenditures incidental to such travel may be aggregated, if set forth in reasonable categories, such as for meals, for gasoline and oil, and for taxi fares;

(ii) *Time.*—Dates of departure and return for each trip away from home, and number of days away from home spent on business;

(iii) *Place.*—Destinations or locality of travel, described by name of city or town or other similar designation; and

(iv) *Business purpose.*—Business reason for travel or nature of the business benefit derived or expected to be derived as a result of travel.

(3) *Entertainment in general.*—The elements to be proved with respect to an expenditure for entertainment are—

(i) *Amount.*—Amount of each separate expenditure for entertainment, except that such incidental items as taxi fares or telephone calls may be aggregated on a daily basis;

(ii) *Time.*—Date of entertainment;

(iii) *Place.*—Name, if any, address or location, and designation of type of entertainment, such as dinner or theater, if such information is not apparent from the designation of the place;

(iv) *Business purpose.*—Business reason for the entertainment or nature of business benefit derived or expected to be derived as a result of the entertainment and, except in the case of business meals described in section 274(e)(1), the nature of any business discussion or activity;

(v) *Business relationship.*—Occupation or other information relating to the person or persons entertained, including name, title, or other designation, sufficient to establish business relationship to the taxpayer.

(4) *Entertainment directly preceding or following a substantial and bona fide business discussion.*—If a taxpayer claims a deduction for entertainment directly preceding or following a substantial and bona fide business discussion on the ground that such entertainment was associated with the active conduct of the taxpayer's trade or business, the elements to be proved with respect to such expenditure, in addition to those enumerated in paragraph (b)(3)(i), (ii), (iii), and (v) of this section are—

(i) *Time.*—Date and duration of business discussion;

(ii) *Place.*—Place of business discussion;

(iii) *Business purpose.*—Nature of business discussion, and business reason for the entertainment or nature of business benefit derived or expected to be derived as the result of the entertainment;

(iv) *Business relationship.*—Identification of those persons entertained who participated in the business discussion.

(5) *Gifts.*—The elements to be proved with respect to an expenditure for a gift are—

(i) *Amount.*—Cost of the gift to the taxpayer;

(ii) *Time.*—Date of the gift;

(iii) *Description.*—Description of the gift;

(iv) *Business purpose.*—Business reason for the gift or nature of business benefit derived or expected to be derived as a result of the gift; and

(v) *Business relationship.*—Occupation or other information relating to the recipient of the gift, including name, title, or other designation, sufficient to establish business relationship to the taxpayer.

(6) *Listed property.*—The elements to be proved with respect to any listed property are—

(i) *Amount.*—(A) *Expenditures.*—The amount of each separate expenditure with respect to an item of listed property, such as the cost of acquisition, the cost of capital improvements, lease payments, the cost of maintenance and repairs, or other expenditures, and

(B) *Uses.*—The amount of each business/investment use (as defined in § 1.280F-6T(d)(3) and (e)), based on the appropriate measure (i.e., mileage for automobiles and other means of transportation and time for other listed property, unless the Commissioner approves an alternative method), and the total use of the listed property for the taxable period.

(ii) *Time.*—Date of the expenditure or use with respect to listed property, and

(iii) *Business or investment purpose.*—The business purpose for an expenditure or use with respect to any listed property (*see* § 1.274-5T(c)(6)(i)(B) and (C) for special rules for the aggregation of expenditures and business use and § 1.280F-6T(d)(2) for the distinction between qualified business use and business/investment use).

See also § 1.274-5T(e) relating to the substantiation of business use of employer-provided listed property and § 1.274-6T for special rules for substantiating the business/investment use of certain types of listed property.

(c) *Rules of substantiation.*—(1) *In general.*—Except as otherwise provided in this section and § 1.274-6T, a taxpayer must substantiate each element of an expenditure or use (described in paragraph (b) of this section) by adequate records or by sufficient evidence corroborating his own statement. Section 274(d) contemplates that a taxpayer will maintain and produce such substantiation as will constitute proof of each expenditure or use referred to in section 274. Written evidence has considerably more probative value than oral evidence alone. In addition, the probative value of written evidence is greater the closer in time it relates to the expenditure or use. A contemporaneous log is not required, but a record of the elements of an expenditure or of a business use of listed property made at or near the time of the expenditure or use, supported by sufficient documentary evidence, has a high degree of credibility not present with respect to a statement prepared subsequent thereto when generally there is a lack of accurate recall. Thus, the corroborative evidence required to support a statement not made at or near the time of the expenditure or use must have a high degree of probative value to elevate such statement and evidence to the level of credibility reflected by a record made at or near the time of the expenditure or use supported by sufficient documentary evidence. The substantiation requirements of section 274(d) are designed to encourage taxpayers to maintain the records, together with documentary evidence, as provided in paragraph (c)(2) of this section.

(2) *Substantiation by adequate records.*—(i) *In general.*—To meet the "adequate records" requirements of section 274(d), a taxpayer shall maintain an account book, diary, log, statement of expense, trip sheets, or similar record (as provided in paragraph (c)(2)(ii) of this section), and documentary evidence (as provided in paragraph (c)(2)(iii) of this section) which, in combination, are sufficient to establish each element of an expenditure or use specified in paragraph (b) of this section. It is not necessary to record information in an account book, diary, log, statement of expense, trip sheet, or similar record which duplicates information reflected on a receipt so long as the account book, etc., and receipt complement each other in an orderly manner.

(ii) *Account book, diary, etc.*—An account book, diary, log, statement of expense, trip sheet, or similar record must be prepared or maintained in such manner that each recording of an element of an expenditure or use is made at or near the time of the expenditure or use.

(A) *Made at or near the time of the expenditure or use.*—For purposes of this section, the phrase "made at or near the time of the expenditure or use" means the elements of an expenditure or use are recorded at a time when, in relation to the use or making of an expenditure, the taxpayer has full present knowledge of each element of the expenditure or use, such as the amount, time, place, and business purpose of the expenditure and business relationship. An expense account statement which is a transcription of an account book, diary, log, or similar record prepared or maintained in accordance with the provisions of this paragraph (c)(2)(ii) shall be considered a record prepared or maintained in the manner prescribed in the preceding sentence if such expense account statement is submitted by an employee to his employer or by an independent contractor to his client or customer in the regular course of good business practice. For example, a log maintained on a weekly basis, which accounts for use during the week, shall be considered a record made at or near the time of such use.

(B) *Substantiation of business purpose.*—In order to constitute an adequate record of business purpose within the meaning of section 274(d) and this paragraph (c)(2), a written statement of business purpose generally is required. However, the degree of substantiation necessary to establish business purpose will vary depending upon the facts and circumstances of each case. Where the business purpose is evident from the surrounding facts and circumstances, a written explanation of such business purpose will not be required. For example, in the case of a salesman calling on customers on an established sales route, a written explanation of the business purpose of such travel ordinarily will not be required. Similarly, in the case of a business meal described in section 274(e)(1), if the business purpose of such meal is evident from the business relationship to the taxpayer of the persons entertained and other surrounding circumstances, a written explanation of such business purpose will not be required.

(C) *Substantiation of business use of listed property.—(1) Degree of substantiation.*—In order to constitute an adequate record (within the meaning of section 274(d) and this paragraph (c)(2)(ii)), which substantiates business/investment use of listed property (as defined in §1.280F-6T(d)(3)), the record must contain sufficient information as to each element of every business/investment use. However, the level of detail required in an adequate record to substantiate business/investment use may vary depending upon the facts and circumstances. For example, a taxpayer who uses a truck for both business and personal purposes and whose only business use of a truck is to make deliveries to customers on an established route may satisfy the adequate record requirement by recording the total number [of] miles driven during the taxable year, the length of the delivery route once, and the date of each trip at or near the time of the trips. Alternatively, the taxpayer may establish the date of each trip with a receipt, record of delivery, or other documentary evidence.

(2) Written record.—Generally, an adequate record must be written. However, a record of the business use of listed property, such as a computer or automobile, prepared in a computer memory device with the aid of a logging program will constitute an adequate record.

* * *

(f) *Reporting and substantiation of expenses of certain employees for travel, entertainment, gifts, and with respect to listed property.*—(1) *In general.*—The purpose of this paragraph is to provide rules for reporting and substantiation of certain expenses paid or incurred by employees in connection with the performance of services as employees. For purposes of this paragraph, the term "business expenses" means ordinary and necessary expenses for travel, entertainment, gifts, or with respect to listed property which are deductible under section 162, and the regulations thereunder, to the extent not disallowed by sections 262, 274(c), and 280F. Thus, the term "business expenses" does not include personal, living, or family expenses disallowed by section 262, travel expenses disallowed by section 274(c), or cost recovery deductions and credits with respect to listed property disallowed by section 280F(d)(3) because the use of such property is not for the convenience of the employer and required as a condition of employment. Except as provided in paragraph (f)(2), advances, reimbursements, or allowances for such expenditures must be reported as income by the employee.

(2) *Reporting of expenses for which the employee is required to make an adequate accounting to his employer.*—(i) *Reimbursements equal to expenses.*—For purposes of computing tax liability, an employee need not report on his tax return business expenses for travel, transportation, entertainment, gifts, or with respect to listed property, paid or incurred by him solely for the benefit of his employer for which he is required to, and does, make an adequate accounting to his employer (as defined in para-

graph (f)(4) of this section) and which are charged directly or indirectly to the employer (for example, through credit cards) or for which the employee is paid through advances, reimbursements, or otherwise, provided that the total amount of such advances, reimbursements, and charges is equal to such expenses.

(ii) *Reimbursements in excess of expenses.*—In case the total of the amounts charged directly or indirectly to the employer or received from the employer as advances, reimbursements, or otherwise, exceeds the business expenses paid or incurred by the employee and the employee is required to, and does, make an adequate accounting to his employer for such expenses, the employee must include such excess (including amounts received for expenditures not deductible by him) in income.

(iii) *Expenses in excess of reimbursement.*—If an employee incurs deductible business expenses on behalf of his employer which exceed the total of the amounts charged directly or indirectly to the employer and received from the employer as advances, reimbursements, or otherwise, and the employee makes an adequate accounting to his employer, the employee must be able to substantiate any deduction for such excess with such records and supporting evidence as will substantiate each element of an expenditure (described in paragraph (b) of this section) in accordance with paragraph (c) of this section.

(3) *Reporting of expenses for which the employee is not required to make an adequate accounting to his employer.*—If the employee is not required to make an adequate accounting to his employer for his business expenses or, though required, fails to make an adequate accounting for such expenses, he must submit, as a part of his tax return, the appropriate form issued by the Internal Revenue Service for claiming deductions for employee business expenses (e.g., Form 2106, Employee Business Expenses, for 1985) and provide the information requested on that form, including the information required by paragraph (d)(2) and (3) of this section if the employee's business expenses are with respect to the use of listed property. In addition, the employee must maintain such records and supporting evidence as will substantiate each element of an expenditure or use (described in paragraph (b) of this section) in accordance with paragraph (c) of this section.

(4) [Reserved]. For further guidance, see §1.274-5(f)(4).

(5) *Substantiation of expenditures by certain employees.*—An employee who makes an adequate accounting to his employer within the meaning of this paragraph will not again be required to substantiate such expense account information except in the following cases:

(i) An employee whose business expenses exceed the total of amounts charged to his employer and amounts received through advances, reimbursements or otherwise and who claims a deduction on his return for such excess,

(ii) An employee who is related to his employer within the meaning of section 267(b), but for this purpose the percentage referred to in section 267(b)(2) shall be 10 percent, and

(iii) Employees in cases where it is determined that the accounting procedures used by the employer for the reporting and substantiation of expenses by such employees are not adequate, or where it cannot be determined that such procedures are adequate. The district director will determine whether the employer's accounting procedures are adequate by considering the facts and circumstances of each case, including the use of proper internal controls. For example, an employer should require that an expense account be verified and approved by a reasonable person other than the person incurring such expenses. Accounting procedures will be considered inadequate to the extent that the employer does not require an adequate accounting from his employees as defined in paragraph (f)(4) of this section, or does not maintain such substantiation. To the extent an employer fails to maintain adequate accounting procedures he will thereby obligate his employees to substantiate separately their expense account information.

* * *

[Temporary Reg. §1.274-5T.]

☐ [*T.D.* 8061, 10-31-85. *Amended by T.D.* 8063, 12-18-85; *T.D.* 8276, 12-7-89; *T.D.* 8451, 12-4-92; *T.D.* 8601, 7-18-95; *T.D.* 8715, 3-24-97; *T.D.* 8864, 1-21-2000; *T.D.* 9020, 11-8-2002; *T.D.* 9064, 6-30-2003 *and T.D.* 9483, 5-18-2010.]

§1.274-6. Expenditures deductible without regard to trade or business or other income producing activity.—The provisions of §§1.274-1 through 1.274-5, inclusive, do not apply to any deduction allowable to the taxpayer without regard to its connection with the taxpayer's trade or business or other income producing activity. Examples of such items are interest, taxes such as real property taxes, and casualty losses. Thus, if a taxpayer owned a fishing camp, the taxpayer could still deduct mortgage interest and real property taxes in full even if deductions for its use are not allowable under section 274(a) and §1.274-2. In the case of a taxpayer which is not an individual, the provisions of this section shall be applied as if it were an individual. Thus, if a corporation sustains a casualty loss on an entertainment facility used in its trade or business, it could deduct the loss even though deductions for the use of the facility are not allowable. [Reg. § 1.274-6.]

☐ [*T.D.* 6659, 6-24-63. *Amended by T.D.* 8051, 9-6-85.]

§ 1.274-7. Treatment of certain expenditures with respect to entertainment-type facilities.—If deductions are disallowed under § 1.274-2 with respect to any portion of a facility, such portion shall be treated as an asset which is used for personal, living, and family purposes (and not as an asset used in a trade or business). Thus, the basis of such a facility will be adjusted for purposes of computing depreciation deductions and determining gain or loss on the sale of such facility in the same manner as other property (for example, a residence) which is regarded as used partly for business and partly for personal purposes. [Reg. § 1.274-7.]

☐ [*T.D.* 6659, 6-24-63.]

Proposed Regulation

§ 1.274-11. Disallowance of deductions for certain entertainment, amusement, or recreation expenditures paid or incurred after December 31, 2017.—(a) *In general.*—Except as provided in this section, no deduction otherwise allowable under chapter 1 of the Internal Revenue Code (Code) is allowed for any expenditure with respect to an activity that is of a type generally considered to be entertainment, or with respect to a facility used in connection with an entertainment activity. For purposes of this paragraph (a), dues or fees to any social, athletic, or sporting club or organization are treated as items with respect to facilities and, thus, are not deductible. In addition, no deduction otherwise allowable under chapter 1 of the Code is allowed for amounts paid or incurred for membership in any club organized for business, pleasure, recreation, or other social purpose.

(b) *Definitions.*—(1) *Entertainment.*—(i) *In general.*—For section 274 purposes, the term *entertainment* means any activity which is of a type generally considered to constitute entertainment, amusement, or recreation, such as entertaining at bars, theaters, country clubs, golf and athletic clubs, sporting events, and on hunting, fishing, vacation and similar trips, including such activity relating solely to the taxpayer or the taxpayer's family. These activities are treated as entertainment under this section, subject to the objective test, regardless of whether the expenditure for the activity is related to or associated with the active conduct of the taxpayer's trade or business. The term *entertainment* may include an activity, the cost of which otherwise is a business expense of the taxpayer, which satisfies the personal, living, or family needs of any individual, such as a hotel suite or an automobile to a business customer or the customer's family. The term *entertainment* does not include activities which, although satisfying personal, living, or family needs of an individual, are clearly not regarded as constituting entertainment, such as a hotel room maintained by an employer for lodging of employees while in business travel status or an automobile used in the active conduct of trade or business even though used for routine personal purposes such as commuting to and from work. On the other hand, the providing of a hotel room or an automobile by an employer to an employee who is on vacation would constitute entertainment of the employee.

(ii) *Food or beverages.*—Under this section, the term *entertainment* does not include food or beverages unless the food or beverages are provided during or at an entertainment activity. Food or beverages provided during or at an entertainment activity generally are treated as part of the entertainment activity. However, in the case of food or beverages provided during or at an entertainment activity, the food or beverages are not considered entertainment if the food or beverages are purchased separately from the entertainment, or the cost of the food or beverages is stated separately from the cost of the entertainment on one or more bills, invoices, or receipts. The amount charged for food or beverages on a bill, invoice, or receipt must reflect the venue's usual selling cost for those items if they were to be purchased separately from the entertainment, or must approximate the reasonable value of those items. Unless the food or beverages are purchased separately from the entertainment, or the cost of the food or beverages is stated separately from the cost of the entertainment on one or more bills, invoices, or receipts, no allocation can be made and the entire amount is a nondeductible entertainment expenditure.

(iii) *Objective test.*—An objective test is used to determine whether an activity is of a type generally considered to be entertainment. Thus, if an activity is generally considered to be entertainment, it will be treated as entertainment for purposes of this section and section 274(a) regardless of whether the expenditure can also be described otherwise, and even though the expenditure relates to the taxpayer alone. This objective test precludes arguments that *entertainment* means only entertainment of others or that an expenditure for entertainment should be characterized as an expenditure for advertising or public relations. However, in applying this test the taxpayer's trade or business is considered. Thus, although attending a theatrical performance generally would be considered entertainment, it would not be so considered in the case of a professional theater critic, attending in a professional capacity. Similarly, if a manufacturer of dresses conducts a fashion show to introduce its products to a group of store buyers, the show generally would not be considered entertainment. However, if an appliance distributor sponsors a fashion show, the fashion show generally would be considered to be entertainment.

(2) *Expenditure.*—The term *expenditure* as used in this section includes amounts paid or incurred for goods, services, facilities, and other items, including items such as losses and depreciation.

(3) *Expenditures for production of income.*—For purposes of this section, any reference to *trade or business* includes an activity described in section 212.

(c) *Exceptions.*—Paragraph (a) of this section does not apply to any expenditure described in section 274(e)(1), (2), (3), (4), (5), (6), (7), (8), or (9).

(d) *Examples.*—The following examples illustrate the application of paragraphs (a) and (b) of this section. In each example, neither the taxpayer nor the business associate is engaged in a trade or business that relates to the entertainment activity.

(1) *Example 1.*—Taxpayer A invites, B, a business associate, to a baseball game to discuss a proposed business deal. A purchases tickets for A and B to attend the game. The baseball game is entertainment as defined in paragraph (b)(1) of this section and thus, the cost of the game tickets is an entertainment expenditure and is not deductible by A.

(2) *Example 2.*—Assume the same facts as in paragraph (d)(1) of this section (*Example 1*), except that A also buys hot dogs and drinks for A and B from a concession stand. The cost of the hot dogs and drinks, which are purchased separately from the game tickets, is not an entertainment expenditure and is not subject to the section 274(a)(1) disallowance. Therefore, A may deduct 50 percent of the expenses associated with the hot dogs and drinks purchased at the game if they meet the requirements of section 162 and § 1.274-12.

(3) *Example 3.*—Taxpayer C invites D, a business associate, to a basketball game. C purchases tickets for C and D to attend the game in a suite, where they have access to food and beverages. The cost of the basketball game tickets, as stated on the invoice, includes the food or beverages. The basketball game is entertainment as defined in paragraph (b)(1) of this section and, thus, the cost of the game tickets is an entertainment expenditure and is not deductible by C. The cost of the food and beverages, which are not purchased separately from the game tickets, is not stated separately on the invoice. Thus, the cost of the food and beverages is an entertainment expenditure that is subject to the section 274(a)(1) disallowance. Therefore, C may not deduct the cost of the tickets or the food and beverages associated with the basketball game.

(4) *Example 4.*—Assume the same facts as in paragraph (d)(3) of this section (*Example 3*), except that the invoice for the basketball game tickets separately states the cost of the food and beverages and reflects the venue's usual selling price if purchased separately. As in paragraph (d)(3) (*Example 3*), the basketball game is entertainment as defined in paragraph (b)(1) of this section and, thus, the cost of the game tickets, other than the cost of the food and beverages, is an entertainment expenditure and is not deductible by C. However, the cost of the food and beverages, which is stated separately on the invoice for the game tickets, is not an entertainment expenditure and is not subject to the section 274(a)(1) disallowance. Therefore, C may deduct 50 percent of the expenses associated with the food and beverages provided at the game if they meet the requirements of section 162 and § 1.274-12.

* * *

[Prop. Reg. § 1.274-11.]
[Proposed 2-26-2020.]

Proposed Regulation

§ 1.274-12. Limitation on deductions for certain food or beverage expenses paid or incurred after December 31, 2017.—(a) *Food or beverage expenses.*—(1) *In general.*—Except as provided in this section, no deduction is allowed for the expense of any food or beverages provided by the taxpayer (or an employee of the taxpayer) to another person or persons unless—

(i) The expense is not lavish or extravagant under the circumstances;

(ii) The taxpayer, or an employee of the taxpayer, is present at the furnishing of such food or beverages; and

(iii) The food or beverages are provided to a business associate.

(2) *Only 50 percent of food or beverage expenses allowed as deduction.*—Except as provided in this section, the amount allowable as a deduction for any expense for food or beverages provided by the taxpayer, or an employee of the taxpayer, to a business associate may not

exceed 50 percent of the amount of the expense that otherwise would be allowable.

(3) *Examples.*—The following examples illustrate the application of paragraph (a)(1) and (2) of this section. In each example, the food or beverage expenses are ordinary and necessary expenses under section 162(a) that are paid or incurred during the taxable year in carrying on a trade or business and are not lavish or extravagant under the circumstances.

(i) *Example 1.*—Taxpayer A takes client B out to lunch. While eating lunch, A and B discuss A's trade or business activities. Under section 274(k) and (n) and paragraph (a) of this section, A may deduct 50 percent of the food or beverage expenses.

(ii) *Example 2.*—Taxpayer C takes employee D out to lunch. While eating lunch, C and D discuss D's annual performance review. Under section 274(k) and (n) and paragraph (a) of this section, C may deduct 50 percent of the food and beverage expenses.

(4) *Special rules for travel meals.*—(i) *In general.*—Food or beverage expenses paid or incurred while traveling away from home in pursuit of a trade or business generally are subject to the deduction limitations in section 274(k) and (n) and paragraph (a)(1) and (2) of this section, as well as the substantiation requirements in section 274(d). In addition, travel expenses generally are subject to the limitations in section 274(m)(1), (2) and (3).

(ii) *Substantiation.*—Except as provided in this section, no deduction is allowed for the expense of any food or beverages paid or incurred while traveling away from home in pursuit of a trade or business unless the taxpayer meets the substantiation requirements in section 274(d).

(iii) *Travel meal expenses of spouse, dependent, or others.*—No deduction is allowed under chapter 1 of the Internal Revenue Code (Code), except under section 217 for certain members of the Armed Forces of the United States, for the expense of any food or beverages paid or incurred with respect to a spouse, dependent, or other individual accompanying the taxpayer, or an officer or employee of the taxpayer, on business travel, unless—

(A) The spouse, dependent, or other individual is an employee of the taxpayer;

(B) The travel of the spouse, dependent, or other individual is for a bona fide business purpose of the taxpayer; and

(C) The expenses would otherwise be deductible by the spouse, dependent or other individual.

(D) The following example illustrates the application of paragraph (a)(4)(iii) of this section. Taxpayer E and Taxpayer E's spouse travel from New York to Boston to attend a series of business meetings. E's spouse is not an employee of E, does not travel to Boston for a bona fide business purpose of E, and the expenses would not otherwise be deductible. While in Boston, E and E's spouse go out to dinner. Under section 274(m)(3) and paragraph (a)(4)(iii) of this section, the expenses associated with the food and beverages consumed by E's spouse are not deductible. Therefore, the cost of E's spouse's dinner is not deductible. E may deduct 50 percent of the expense associated with the food and beverages E consumed while on business travel if E meets the requirements in sections 162 and 274, including section 274(k) and (d).

(b) *Definitions.*—Except as otherwise provided in this section, the following definitions apply for purposes of section 274(k) and (n), § 1.274-11(b)(1)(ii) and (d), and this section:

(1) *Food or beverages.*—*Food or beverages* means all food and beverage items, regardless of whether characterized as meals, snacks, or other types of food and beverages, and regardless of whether the food and beverages are treated as *de minimis* fringes under section 132(e).

(2) *Food or beverage expenses.*—*Food or beverage expenses* mean the full cost of food or beverages, including any delivery fees, tips, and sales tax. In the case of employer-provided meals furnished at an eating facility on the employer's business premises, *food or beverage expenses* do not include expenses for the operation of the eating facility such as salaries of employees preparing and serving meals, and other overhead costs.

(3) *Business associate.*—*Business associate* means a person with whom the taxpayer could reasonably expect to engage or deal in the active conduct of the taxpayer's trade or business such as the taxpayer's customer, client, supplier, employee, agent, partner, or professional adviser, whether established or prospective.

(4) *Independent contractor.*—For purposes of the reimbursement or other expense allowance arrangements described in paragraph (c)(2)(ii) of this section, *independent contractor* means a person who is not an employee of the payor.

(5) *Client or customer.*—For purposes of the reimbursement or other expense allowance arrangements described in paragraph (c)(2)(ii) of this section, *client* or *customer* means a per-

son who receives services from an independent contractor and enters into a reimbursement or other expense allowance arrangement with the independent contractor.

(6) *Payor.*—For purposes of the reimbursement or other expense allowance arrangements described in paragraph (c)(2)(ii) of this section, *payor* means a person that enters into a reimbursement or other expense allowance arrangement with an employee and may include an employer, its agent, or a third party.

(7) *Reimbursement or other expense allowance arrangement.*—For purposes of the reimbursement or other expense allowance arrangements described in paragraph (c)(2)(ii) of this section, *reimbursement or other expense allowance arrangement* means—

(i) For purposes of paragraph (c)(2)(ii)(B) of this section, an arrangement under which an employee receives an advance, allowance, or reimbursement from a payor (the employer, its agent, or a third party) for expenses the employee pays or incurs; and

(ii) For purposes of paragraph (c)(2)(ii)(C) of this section, an arrangement under which an independent contractor receives an advance, allowance, or reimbursement from a client or customer for expenses the independent contractor pays or incurs if either—

(A) A written agreement between the parties expressly states that the client or customer will reimburse the independent contractor for expenses that are subject to the limitations on deductions in paragraph (a) of this section; or

(B) A written agreement between the parties expressly identifies the party subject to the limitations.

(8) *Primarily consumed.*—For purposes of paragraph (c)(2)(iv) of this section, *primarily consumed* means greater than 50 percent of actual or reasonably estimated consumption.

(9) *General public.*—For purposes of paragraph (c)(2)(iv) of this section, the *general public* includes, but is not limited to, customers, clients, and visitors. The *general public* does not include employees, partners or independent contractors of the taxpayer. Also, an exclusive list of guests is not the *general public*.

(c) *Exceptions.*—(1) *In general.*—The limitations on the deduction of food or beverage expenses in paragraph (a) of this section do not apply to any expense described in paragraph (c)(2) of this section. These expenses are deductible to the extent allowable under chapter 1 of the Code.

(2) *Exceptions.*—(i) *Expenses treated as compensation.*—(A) *In general.*—Any expense paid or incurred by a taxpayer for food or beverages, including food or beverages provided during travel described in section 274(m)(3), if an employee is the recipient of the food or beverages, is not subject to the deduction limitations in paragraph (a) of this section to the extent that the expense is treated by the taxpayer—

(1) On the taxpayer's income tax return as originally filed, as compensation paid to the employee; and

(2) As wages to the employee for purposes of withholding under chapter 24 of the Code, relating to collection of income tax at source on wages.

(B) *Expenses includible in income of persons who are not employees.*—An expense paid or incurred by a taxpayer for food or beverages, including food or beverages provided during travel described in section 274(m)(3), is not subject to the deduction limitations in paragraph (a) of this section to the extent the expenditure is includible in gross income as compensation for services rendered, or as a prize or award under section 74 by a recipient of the expense who is not an employee of the taxpayer. The preceding sentence does not apply to any amount paid or incurred by the taxpayer if the amount is required to be included, or would be so required except that the amount is less than $600, in any information return filed by such taxpayer under part III of subchapter A of chapter 61 of the Code and is not so included.

(C) *Expenses for which value is improperly included or for which amount required to be included is zero.*—The exception in section 274(e)(2) and (e)(9) and paragraph (c)(2)(i) of this section does not apply to expenses paid or incurred for food or beverages for which the value that is included in gross income is less than the amount required to be included in gross income under § 1.61-21. Furthermore, if the amount required to be included in gross income under § 1.61-21 is zero, the exception in section 274(e)(2) and (e)(9) and paragraph (c)(2)(i) of this section does not apply.

(D) *Examples.*—The following examples illustrate the application of paragraph (c)(2)(i) of this section. In each example, the food or beverage expenses are ordinary and necessary expenses under section 162(a) that are paid or incurred during the taxable year in carrying on a trade or business and that are not lavish or extravagant under the circumstances.

(1) Example 1.—Employer F provides food and beverages to its employees with-

out charge at a company cafeteria on its premises. The food and beverages do not meet the definition of a *de minimis* fringe under section 132(e). F treats the food and beverage expenses as compensation and wages, and determines the amount of the inclusion under § 1.61-21. Under section 274(e)(2) and paragraph (c)(2)(i) of this section, the expenses associated with the food and beverages provided to the employees are not subject to the 50 percent deduction limitations in paragraph (a) of this section. Thus, F may deduct 100 percent of the food and beverage expenses.

(2) Example 2.—Employer G provides meals to its employees without charge. The meals are properly excluded from the employees' income under section 119 as meals provided for the convenience of the employer. Under § 1.61-21(b)(1), an employee must include in gross income the amount by which the fair market value of a fringe benefit exceeds the sum of the amount, if any, paid for the benefit by or on behalf of the recipient, and the amount, if any, specifically excluded from gross income by some other section of subtitle A of the Code. Because the entire value of the employees' meals is excluded from the employees' income under section 119, the fair market value of the fringe benefit does not exceed the amount excluded from gross income under subtitle A of the Code, so there is nothing to be included in the employees' income under § 1.61-21. Thus, the exception in section 274(e)(2) and paragraph (c)(2)(i) of this section does not apply and G may only deduct 50 percent of the expenses for the food and beverages provided to employees.

(ii) *Reimbursed food or beverage expenses.*—(A) *In general.*—In the case of expenses for food or beverages paid or incurred by one person in connection with the performance of services for another person, whether or not the other person is an employer, under a reimbursement or other expense allowance arrangement, the deduction limitations in paragraph (a) of this section apply either to the person who makes the expenditure or to the person who actually bears the expense, but not to both. If an expense of a type described in paragraph (c)(2)(ii) of this section properly constitutes a dividend paid to a shareholder, unreasonable compensation paid to an employee, a personal expense, or other nondeductible expense, nothing in this paragraph (c)(2)(ii)(A) prevents disallowance of the deduction to the taxpayer under other provisions of the Code.

(B) *Reimbursement arrangements involving employees.*—In the case of expenses paid or incurred by an employee for food or beverages in performing services as an employee under a reimbursement or other expense allowance arrangement with a payor (the employer, its agent, or a third party) the limitations on deductions in paragraph (a) of this section apply—

(1) To the employee to the extent the employer treats the reimbursement or other payment of the expense on the employer's income tax return as originally filed as compensation paid to the employee and as wages to the employee for purposes of withholding under chapter 24 relating to collection of income tax at source on wages; or

(2) To the payor to the extent the reimbursement or other payment of the expense is not treated as compensation and wages paid to the employee in the manner provided in paragraph (c)(2)(ii)(B)(*1*) of this section. However, see paragraph (c)(2)(ii)(C) of this section if the payor receives a payment from a third party that may be treated as a reimbursement arrangement under paragraph (c)(2)(ii)(C).

(C) *Reimbursement arrangements involving persons that are not employees.*—In the case of expenses for food or beverages paid or incurred by an independent contractor in connection with the performance of services for a client or customer under a reimbursement or other expense allowance arrangement with the independent contractor, the limitations on deductions in paragraph (a) of this section apply to the party expressly identified in an agreement between the parties as subject to the limitations. If an agreement between the parties does not expressly identify the party subject to the limitations, then the deduction limitations in paragraph (a) of this section apply—

(1) To the independent contractor (which may be a payor) to the extent the independent contractor does not account to the client or customer within the meaning of section 274(d); or

(2) To the client or customer if the independent contractor accounts to the client or customer within the meaning of section 274(d).

(D) *Section 274(d) substantiation.*—If the reimbursement or other expense allowance arrangement involves persons who are not employees and the agreement between the parties does not expressly identify the party subject to the limitations on deductions in paragraph (a) of this section, the limitations on deductions in paragraph (a) of this section apply to the independent contractor unless the independent contractor accounts to the client or customer with substantiation that satisfies the requirements of section 274(d).

(E) *Examples.*—The following examples illustrate the application of paragraph (c)(2)(ii) of this section.

(1) Example 1.—(*i*) Employee I performs services under an arrangement in which J, an employee leasing company, pays I a per diem allowance of $10x for each day that I performs services for J's client, K, while traveling away from home. The per diem allowance is a reimbursement of travel expenses for food or beverages that I pays in performing services as an employee. J enters into a written agreement with K under which K agrees to reimburse J for any substantiated reimbursements for travel expenses, including meal expenses, that J pays to I. The agreement does not expressly identify the party that is subject to the limitations on deductions in paragraph (a) of this section. I performs services for K while traveling away from home for 10 days and provides J with substantiation that satisfies the requirements of section 274(d) of $100x of meal expenses incurred by I while traveling away from home. J pays I $100x to reimburse those expenses pursuant to their arrangement. J delivers a copy of I's substantiation to K. K pays J $300x, which includes $200x compensation for services and $100x as reimbursement of J's payment of I's travel expenses for meals. Neither J nor K treats the $100x paid to I as compensation or wages.

(*ii*) Under paragraph (b)(7)(i) of this section, I and J have established a reimbursement or other expense allowance arrangement for purposes of paragraph (c)(2)(ii)(B) of this section. Because the reimbursement payment is not treated as compensation and wages paid to I, under section 274(e)(3)(A) and paragraph (c)(2)(ii)(B)(*1*) of this section, I is not subject to the limitations on deductions in paragraph (a) of this section. Instead, under paragraph (c)(2)(ii)(B)(*2*) of this section, J, the payor, is subject to limitations on deductions in paragraph (a) of this section unless J can meet the requirements of section 274(e)(3)(B) and paragraph (c)(2)(ii)(C) of this section.

(*iii*) Because the agreement between J and K expressly states that K will reimburse J for substantiated reimbursements for travel expenses that J pays to I, under paragraph (b)(7)(ii)(A) of this section, J and K have established a reimbursement or other expense allowance arrangement for purposes of paragraph (c)(2)(ii)(C) of this section. J accounts to K for K's reimbursement in the manner required by section 274(d) by delivering to K a copy of the substantiation J received from I. Therefore, under section 274(e)(3)(B) and paragraph (c)(2)(ii)(C)(*2*) of this section, K and not J is subject to the deduction limitations in paragraph (a) of this section.

(2) Example 2.—(*i*) The facts are the same as in paragraph (c)(2)(ii)(E)(*1*) of this section *(Example 1)* except that, under the arrangements between I and J and between J and K, I provides the substantiation of the expenses directly to K, and K pays the per diem directly to I.

(*ii*) Under paragraph (b)(7)(i) of this section, I and K have established a reimbursement or other expense allowance arrangement for purposes of paragraph (c)(2)(ii)(C) of this section. Because I substantiates directly to K and the reimbursement payment was not treated as compensation and wages paid to I, under section 274(e)(3)(A) and paragraph (c)(2)(ii)(C)(*1*) of this section I is not subject to the limitations on deductions in paragraph (a) of this section. Under paragraph (c)(2)(ii)(C)(*2*) of this section, K, the payor, is subject to the limitations on deductions in paragraph (a) of this section.

(3) Example 3.—(*i*) The facts are the same as in paragraph (c)(2)(ii)(E)(*1*) of this section (*Example 1*), except that the written agreement between J and K expressly provides that the limitations of this section will apply to K.

(*ii*) Under paragraph (b)(7)(ii)(B) of this section, J and K have established a reimbursement or other expense allowance arrangement for purposes of paragraph (c)(2)(ii)(C) of this section. Because the agreement provides that the 274 deduction limitations apply to K, under section 274(e)(3)(B) and paragraph (c)(2)(ii)(C) of this section, K and not J is subject to the limitations on deductions in paragraph (a) of this section.

(4) Example 4.—(*i*) The facts are the same as in paragraph (c)(2)(ii)(E)(*1*) of this section (*Example 1*), except that the agreement between J and K does not provide that K will reimburse J for travel expenses.

(*ii*) The arrangement between J and K is not a reimbursement or other expense allowance arrangement within the meaning of section 274(e)(3)(B) and paragraph (b)(7)(ii) of this section. Therefore, even though J accounts to K for the expenses, J is subject to the limitations on deductions in paragraph (a) of this section.

(iii) *Recreational expenses for employees.*—(A) *In general.*—Any food or beverage expense paid or incurred by a taxpayer for a recreational, social, or similar activity, primarily for the benefit of taxpayer's employees (other than employees who are highly compensated employees (within the meaning of paragraph (c)(2)(iii)(B) of this section)) is not subject to the deduction limitations in paragraph (a) of this section. This paragraph (c)(2)(iii)(A) applies to expenses paid or incurred for events such as holiday parties, annual picnics, or summer outings. This paragraph (c)(2)(iii)(A) does not apply to expenses for meals the value of which is excluded from employees' income under section 119 because the meals are provided for the convenience of the employer.

(B) *Highly compensated employees.*—The exception in this paragraph (c)(2)(iii) applies only to expenses for food or beverages made primarily for the benefit of employees of the taxpayer other than employees who are officers, shareholders or other owners who own a 10-percent or greater interest in the business, or other highly compensated employees. For purposes of the preceding sentence, an employee is treated as owning any interest owned by a member of the employee's family, within the meaning of section 267(c)(4). Any expense for food or beverages that is made under circumstances which discriminate in favor of employees who are officers, shareholders or other owners, or highly compensated employees is not considered to be made primarily for the benefit of employees generally. An expense for food or beverages is not to be considered outside of the exception of this paragraph (c)(2)(iii) merely because, due to the large number of employees involved, the provision of food or beverages is intended to benefit only a limited number of employees at one time, provided the provision of food or beverages does not discriminate in favor of officers, shareholders, other owners, or highly compensated employees.

(C) *Examples.*—The following examples illustrate the application of this paragraph (c)(2)(iii). In each example, the food or beverage expenses are ordinary and necessary expenses under section 162(a) that are paid or incurred during the taxable year in carrying on a trade or business and that are not lavish or extravagant under the circumstances.

(1) Example 1.—Employer L invites all employees to a holiday party in a hotel ballroom that includes a buffet dinner and an open bar. Under section 274(e)(4), this paragraph (c)(2)(iii), and § 1.274-11(c), the cost of the party, including food and beverage expenses, is not subject to the deduction limitations in paragraph (a) of this section because the holiday party is a recreational, social, or similar activity primarily for the benefit of non-highly compensated employees. Thus, L may deduct 100 percent of the cost of the party.

(2) Example 2.—The facts are the same as in paragraph (c)(2)(iii)(C)(*1*) of this section (*Example 1*), except that Employer L invites only highly-compensated employees to the holiday party, and the invoice provided by the hotel lists the costs for food and beverages separately from the cost of the rental of the ballroom. The costs reflect the venue's usual selling price for food or beverages. The exception in this paragraph (c)(2)(iii) does not apply because L invited only highly-compensated employees to the holiday party. However, under § 1.274-11(b)(1)(ii), the food and beverage expenses are not treated as entertainment. L may deduct 50 percent of the food and beverage costs that are separately stated on the invoice under paragraph (a)(2) of this section.

(3) Example 3.—Employer M provides free coffee, soda, bottled water, chips, donuts, and other snacks in a break room available to all employees. The expenses associated with the food and beverages are subject to the deduction limitations in paragraph (a) of this section because the break room is not a recreational, social, or similar activity primarily for the benefit of the employees. Thus, the exception in section 274(e)(4) and this paragraph (c)(2)(iii) does not apply and M may only deduct 50 percent of the expenses for food and beverages provided in the break room.

(4) Example 4.—Employer N has a written policy that employees in a certain medical services-related position must be available for emergency calls due to the nature of the position that requires frequent emergency response. Because these emergencies can and do occur during meal periods, N furnishes food and beverages to employees in this position without charge in a cafeteria on N's premises. N excludes food and beverage expenses from the employees' income as meals provided for the convenience of the employer excludable under section 119. Because these food and beverages are furnished for the employer's convenience, and therefore are not primarily for the benefit of the employees, the exception in section 274(e)(4) and this paragraph (c)(2)(iii) does not apply, even if some socializing related to the food and beverages provided occurs. Thus, N may only deduct 50 percent of the expenses for food and beverages provided to employees in the cafeteria.

(5) Example 5.—Employer O invites an employee and a client to dinner at a restaurant. Because it is the birthday of the employee, O orders a special dessert in celebration. Because the meal is a business meal, and therefore not primarily for the benefit of the employee, the exception in section 274(e)(4) and this paragraph (c)(2)(iii) does

not apply, even though an employee social activity in the form of a birthday celebration occurred during the meal. Thus, O may only deduct 50 percent of the meal expenses.

(iv) *Items available to the public.*—(A) *In general.*—Any expense paid or incurred by a taxpayer for food or beverages to the extent the food or beverages are made available to the general public is not subject to the deduction limitations in paragraph (a) of this section. If a taxpayer provides food or beverages to employees, this paragraph (c) (2) (iv) (A) applies to the entire amount of expenses for those food or beverages if the same types of food or beverages are provided to, and are primarily consumed by, the general public.

(B) *Examples.*—The following examples illustrate the application of this paragraph (c) (2) (iv). In each example, the food and beverage expenses are ordinary and necessary expenses under section 162(a) that are paid or incurred during the taxable year in carrying on a trade or business and that are not lavish or extravagant under the circumstances.

(1) Example 1.—Employer P is a real estate agent and provides refreshments at an open house for a home available for sale to the public. The refreshments are consumed by P's employees, potential buyers of the property, and other real estate agents. Under section 274(e) (7) and this paragraph (c) (2) (iv), the expenses associated with the refreshments are not subject to the deduction limitations in paragraph (a) of this section if over 50 percent of the food and beverages are primarily consumed by potential buyers and other real estate agents. If the food and beverages are not primarily consumed by the general public, only the costs attributable to the food and beverages provided to the general public are excepted under section 274(e) (7) and this paragraph (c) (2) (iv).

(2) *Example 2.*—Employer Q is an automobile service center and provides refreshments in its waiting area. The refreshments are consumed by Q's employees and customers. Under section 274(e) (7) and this paragraph (c) (2) (iv), the expenses associated with the refreshments are not subject to the deduction limitations provided for in paragraph (a) of this section if over 50 percent of the food and beverages are primarily consumed by customers. If the food and beverages are not primarily consumed by the general public, only the costs attributable to the food and beverages provided to the general public are excepted under section 274(e) (7) and this paragraph (c) (2) (iv).

(3) Example 3.—Employer R operates a summer camp open to the general public for children and provides breakfast and lunch, as part of the fee to attend camp, both to camp counselors, who are employees, and to camp attendees, who are customers. There are 20 camp counselors and 100 camp attendees. The same type of meal is available to each counselor and attendee, and attendees consume more than 50 percent of the food and beverages. Under section 274(e) (7) and this paragraph (c) (2) (iv), the expenses associated with the food and beverages are not subject to the deduction limitations in paragraph (a) of this section, because over 50 percent of the food and beverages are primarily consumed by camp attendees. Thus, R may deduct 100 percent of the food and beverage expenses.

(4) Example 4.—Employer S provides food and beverages to its employees without charge at a company cafeteria on its premises. Occasionally, customers or other visitors also eat without charge in the cafeteria. The occasional consumption of food and beverages at the company cafeteria by customers and visitors is less than 50 percent of the total amount of food and beverages consumed at the cafeteria. Therefore, only the costs attributable to the food and beverages provided to the general public are excepted under section 274(e) (7) and this paragraph (c) (2) (iv).

(v) *Goods or services sold to customers.*—(A) *In general.*—An expense paid or incurred for food or beverages, to the extent the food or beverages are sold to customers in a bona fide transaction for an adequate and full consideration in money or money's worth, is not subject to the deduction limitations in paragraph (a) of this section. However, *money or money's worth* does not include payment through services provided. Under this paragraph (c) (2) (v), a restaurant or catering business may deduct 100 percent of its costs for food or beverage items, purchased in connection with preparing and providing meals to its paying customers, which are also consumed at the worksite by employees who work in the employer's restaurant or catering business. In addition, for purposes of this paragraph (c) (2) (v), the term *customer* includes anyone, including an employee of the taxpayer, who is sold food or beverages in a bona fide transaction for an adequate and full consideration in money or money's worth.

(B) *Example.*—The following example illustrates the application of this paragraph (c) (2) (v). Employer T operates a restaurant. T provides food and beverages to its food service employees before, during, and after their shifts for no consideration. Under section 274(e) (8) and this paragraph (c) (2) (v), the expenses associated with the food and beverages provided to the employees are not subject to the 50 percent deduction limitation in paragraph (a) of this section because the restaurant sells food and beverages to customers in a bona fide transaction for an adequate and full consideration in money or money's worth. Thus, T may deduct 100 percent of the food and beverage expenses.

* * *

[Prop. Reg. § 1.274-12.]

[Proposed 2-26-2020.]

Proposed Regulation

§ 1.280A-1. Limitations on deductions with respect to a dwelling unit which is used by the taxpayer during the taxable year as a residence.—

* * *

(c) *Dwelling unit.*—(1) *In general.*—For purposes of this section and §§ 1.280A-2 and 1.280A-3, the term "dwelling unit" includes a house, apartment, condominium, mobile home, boat, or similar property, which provides basic living accommodations such as sleeping space, toilet, and cooking facilities. A single structure may contain more than one dwelling unit. For example, each apartment in an apartment building is a separate dwelling unit. Similarly, if the basement of a house contains basic living accommodations, the basement constitutes a separate dwelling unit. All structures and other property appurtenant to a dwelling unit which do not themselves constitute dwelling units are considered part of the unit. For example, an individual who rents to another person space in a garage which is appurtenant to a house which the individual owns and occupies may claim deductions with respect to that rental activity only to the extent allowed under section 280A, paragraph (b) of this section, and § 1.280A-3.

(2) *Exception.*—Notwithstanding the provisions of paragraph (c)(1) of this section, the term "dwelling unit" does not include any unit or portion of a unit which is used exclusively as a hotel, motel, inn, or similar establishment. Property is so used only if it is regularly available for occupancy by paying customers and only if no person having an interest in the property is deemed under the rules of this section to have used the unit (or the portion of the unit) as a residence during the taxable year. Thus, this exception may apply to a portion of a home used to furnish lodging to tourists or to long-term boarders such as students. This exception may also apply to a unit entered in a rental pool (see 1.280A-3 (e)) if the owner of the unit does not use it as a residence during the taxable year.

* * *

[Prop. Reg. § 1.280A-1.]

[Proposed 8-7-80 and 7-21-83.]

Proposed Regulation

§ 1.280A-2. Deductibility of expenses attributable to business use of a dwelling unit used as a residence.—(a) *Scope.*—This section describes the business uses of a dwelling unit used as a residence for which items may be deductible under an exception to the general rule of section 280A and explains the general conditions for the deductibility of items attributable to those uses. Deductions are allowable only to the extent provided in section 280A(c)(5) and in paragraph (i) of this section. See § 1.280A-1 for the general rules under section 280A.

(b) *Use as the taxpayer's principal place of business.*—(1) *In general.*—Section 280A(c)(1)(A) provides an exception to the general rule of section 280A(a) for any item to the extent that the item is allocable to a portion of the dwelling unit which is used exclusively and on a regular basis as the principal place of business for any trade or business of the taxpayer.

(2) [*Withdrawn by the IRS on 5-20-94.*]

(3) [*Withdrawn by the IRS on 5-20-94.*]

(c) *Use by patients, clients, or customers in meeting or dealing with the taxpayer in the normal course of business.*—Section 280A(c)(1)(B) provides an exception to the general rule of section 280A for any item to the extent the item is allocable to a portion of the dwelling unit which is used exclusively and on a regular basis as a place of business in which patients, clients, or customers meet or deal with the taxpayer in the normal course of the taxpayer's business. Property is so used only if the patients, clients, or customers are physically present on the premises; conversations with the taxpayer by telephone do not constitute use of the premises by patients, clients or customers. This exception applies only if the use of the dwelling unit by patients, clients, or customers is substantial and integral to the conduct of the taxpayer's business. Occasional meetings are insufficient to make this exception applicable.

(d) *Use of a separate structure not attached to the dwelling unit in connection with the taxpayer's trade or business.*—Section 280A(c)(1)(C) provides an exception to the general rule of section 280A(a) for any item to the extent that the item is allocable to a separate structure which is appurtenant to, but not attached to, the dwelling unit and is used exclusively and on a regular basis in connection with the taxpayer's trade or business. An artist's studio, a florist's greenhouse, and a carpenter's workshop are examples of structures that may be within the description of this paragraph.

(e) *Use as a storage unit for taxpayer's inventory.*—Section 280A(c)(2) provides an exception to the general rule of section 280A(a) for any item to the extent such item is allocable to space within the dwelling unit which is used on a regular basis as a storage unit for the inventory of the taxpayer held for use in the taxpayer's trade or business of selling products at retail or wholesale. The storage unit includes only the space actually used for storage; thus, if a taxpayer stores inventory in one portion of a basement, the storage unit includes only that portion even if the taxpayer makes no use of the rest of the basement. The exception provided under section 280A(c)(2) applies only if—

(1) The dwelling unit is the sole fixed location of that trade or business, and

(2) The space used is a separately identifiable space suitable for storage.

(f) *Use in providing day care services.*—(1) *In general.*—Section 280A(c)(4) provides an exception to the general rule of section 280A(a) for any item to the extent that the item is allocable to the use of any portion of the dwelling unit on a regular basis in the taxpayer's trade or business of providing day care services for children, for individuals who have attained age 65, or for individuals who are physically or mentally incapable of caring for themselves.

(2) *Day care services.*—Day care services are services which are primarily custodial in nature and which, unlike foster care, are provided for only certain hours during the day. Day care services may include educational, developmental, or enrichment activities which are incidental to the primary custodial services. If the services performed in the home are primarily educational or instructional in nature, however, they do not qualify as day care services. The determination whether particular activities are incidental to the primary custodial services generally depends upon all the facts and circumstances of the case. Educational instruction to children of nursery school age shall be considered incidental to the custodial services. Further, educational instruction to children of kindergarten age would ordinarily be considered incidental to the custodial services if the instruction is not in lieu of public instruction under a State compulsory education requirement. In addition, enrichment instruction in arts and crafts to children, handicapped individuals, or the elderly would ordinarily be considered incidental to the custodial services rendered.

(3) *State law requirements.*—This paragraph, applies to items accruing after August 31, 1977, only if the owner or operator of the day care business is, at the time the item accrues, acting in accordance with the applicable State law relating to the licensing, certification, registration, or approval of day care centers or family or group day care homes. A person satisfies the condition stated in the preceding sentence for any period for which—

(i) There is no applicable State law of the type described;

(ii) The person is exempt from the requirements of the applicable State law;

(iii) The person has whatever license, etc., is required under the applicable State law; or

(iv) The person has applied for whatever license, etc., is required under the applicable State law, provided, that the application has not been rejected, and provided that the person has corrected or removed any deficiencies that resulted in the revocation of any previous license, etc., or in the rejection of any previous application.

(g) *Exclusive use requirement.*—(1) *In general.*—Paragraph (b), (c), or (d) of this section may apply to the use of a portion of a dwelling unit for a taxable year only if there is no use of that portion of the unit at any time during the taxable year other than for business purposes. For purposes of section 280A(c)(1) and this section, the phrase "a portion of the dwelling unit" refers to a room or other separately identifiable space; it is not necessary that the portion be marked off by a permanent partition. Paragraph (b), (c), or (d) of this section may apply to a portion of a unit which is used for more than one business purpose. Necessary repair or maintenance does not constitute use for purposes of this paragraph.

(2) *Convenience of the employer.*—In the case of an employee, paragraph (b), (c), or (d) shall apply to a use of a portion of a dwelling unit only if that use is for the convenience of the employer.

(h) *Use on a regular basis.*—The determination whether a taxpayer has used a portion of a dwelling unit for a particular purpose on a regular basis must be made in light of all the facts and circumstances.

(i) *Limitation on deductions.*—(1) *In general.*—The deductions allowable under chapter 1 of the Code for a taxable year with respect to the use of a dwelling unit for one of the purposes described in paragraphs (b) through (f) of this section shall not exceed the gross income derived from such use of the unit during the taxable year, as determined under subparagraph (2) of this paragraph. Subparagraphs (3) and (4) of this paragraph provide rules for determining the expenses allocable to the business use of a unit. Subparagraph (5) of this paragraph prescribes the order in which deductions are allowable.

(2) *Gross income derived from use of unit.*—(i) *Only income from qualifying business use to be taken into account.*—For purposes of section 280A and this section, the taxpayer shall take into account, in applying the limitation on deductions, only gross income from a business use described in section 280A(c). For example, a taxpayer who teaches at school may also be engaged in a retail sales business. If the taxpayer uses a home office on a regular basis as the principal place of business for the retail sales business (a use described in section 280A(c) (1) (A)) and makes no non-business use of the office, the taxpayer shall take the gross income from the use of the office for the retail sales business into account in applying the limitation on deductions. Even if the taxpayer also corrects student papers and prepares class presentations in the home office (not a use described in section 280A(c)), no portion of the taxpayer's gross income from teaching may be taken into account in applying the limitation on deductions.

(ii) *More than one location.*—If the taxpayer engages in a business in the dwelling unit and in one or more other locations, the taxpayer shall allocate the gross income from the business to the different locations on a reasonable basis. In making this determination, the taxpayer shall take into account the amount of time that the taxpayer engages in activity related to the business at each location, the capital investment related to the business at each location, and any other facts and circumstances that may be relevant.

(iii) *Exclusion of certain amounts.*—For purposes of section 280A(c) (5) (A) and this section, gross income derived from use of a unit means gross income from the business activity in the unit reduced by expenditures required for the activity but not allocable to use of the unit itself, such as expenditures for supplies and compensation paid to other persons. For example, a physician who uses a portion of a dwelling unit for treating patients shall compute gross income derived from use of the unit by subtracting from the gross income attributable to the business activity in the unit any expenditures for nursing and secretarial services, supplies, etc.

(3) *Expenses allocable to portion of unit.*—The taxpayer may determine the expenses allocable to the portion of the unit used for business purposes by any method that is reasonable under the circumstances. If the rooms in the dwelling unit are of approximately equal size, the taxpayer may ordinarily allocate the general expenses for the unit according to the number of rooms used for the business purpose. The taxpayer may also allocate general expenses according to the percentage of the total floor space in the unit that is used for the business purpose. Expenses which are attributable only to certain portions of the unit, *e.g.,* repairs to kitchen fixtures, shall be allocated in full to those portions of the unit. Expenses which are not related to the use of the unit for business purposes, *e.g.,* expenditures for lawn care, are not taken into account for purposes of section 280A.

(4) *Time allocation for use in providing day care services.*—If the taxpayer uses a portion of a dwelling unit in providing day care services, as described in paragraph (f) of this section, and the taxpayer makes any use of that portion of the unit for nonbusiness purposes during the taxable year, the taxpayer shall make further allocation of the amounts determined under subparagraph (3) of this paragraph to be allocable to the portion of the unit used in providing day care services. The amounts allocated to the business use of the unit under this subparagraph shall bear the same proportion to the amounts determined under subparagraph (3) of this paragraph as the length of time that the portion of the unit is used for day care services bears to the length of time that the portion of the unit is available for all purposes. For example, if a portion of the unit is used for day care services for an average of 36 hours each week during the taxable year, the fraction to be used for making the allocation required under this subparagraph is 36/168 the ratio of the number of hours of day care use in a week to the total number of hours in a week.

(5) *Order of deductions.*—Business deductions with respect to the business use of a dwelling unit are allowable in the following order and only to the following extent:

(i) The allocable portions of amounts allowable as deductions for the taxable year under chapter 1 of the Code with respect to the dwelling unit without regard to any use of the unit in trade or business, *e.g.,* mortgage interest and real estate taxes, are allowable as business deductions to the extent of the gross income derived from use of the unit.

(ii) Amounts otherwise allowable as deductions for the taxable year under chapter 1 of the Code by reason of the business use of the dwelling unit (other than those which would result in an adjustment to the basis of property) are allowable to the extent the gross income derived from use of the unit exceeds the deductions allowed or allowable under subdivision (i) of this subparagraph.

(iii) Amounts otherwise allowable as deductions for the taxable year under chapter 1 of the Code by reason of the business use of the dwelling unit which would result in an adjustment to the basis of property are allowable to the extent the gross income derived from use of the unit exceeds the deductions allowed or allowable under subdivisions (i) and (ii) of this subparagraph.

(6) *Cross reference.*—For rules with respect to the deductions to be taken into account in computing adjusted gross income in the case of employees, see section 62 and the regulations prescribed thereunder.

(7) *Example.*—The provisions of this subparagraph may be illustrated by the following example:

Example. A, a self-employed individual, uses an office in the home on a regular basis as a place of business for meeting with clients of A's consulting service. A makes no other use of the office during the taxable year and uses no other premises for the consulting activity. A has a special telephone line for the office and occasionally employs secretarial assistance. A also has a gardener care for the lawn around the home during the year. A determines that 10% of the general expenses for the dwelling unit are allocable to the office. On the basis of the following figures, A determines that the sum of the allowable business deductions for the use of the office is $1,050.

	Total	Allocable to Office	
Gross income from consulting services			$1,900
Expense for secretary		$500	
Business telephone		150	
Supplies		200	
Total expenditures not allocable to use of unit			850
Gross income derived from use of unit			$1,050
Deductions allowable under subparagraph (5) (i) of this paragraph			
Mortgage interest	$5,000	$500	
Real estate taxes	2,000	200	
Amount allowable			700
Limit on further deductions			$350
Deductions allowable under subparagraph (5) (ii) of this paragraph			
Insurance	$600	$60	
Utilities (other than residential telephone)	900	90	
Lawn care	500	0	
Amount allowable			150
Limit on further deductions			$200
Deductions allowable under subparagraph (5) (iii) of this paragraph			
Depreciation	$3,200	$320	
Amount allowable			200

No portion of the lawn care expense is allocable to the business use of the dwelling unit. A may claim the remaining $6,300 paid for mortgage interest and real estate taxes as itemized deductions. [Prop. Reg. § 1.280A-2.]

[Proposed 8-7-80, 7-21-83 and 5-20-94.]

Distributions by Corporations

§ 1.301-1. Rules applicable with respect to distributions of money and other property.—(a) *General.*—Section 301 provides the general rule for treatment of distributions on or after June 22, 1954, of property by a corporation to a shareholder with respect to its stock. The term "property" is defined in section 317(a). Such distributions, except as otherwise provided in this chapter, shall be treated as provided in section 301(c). Under section 301(c), distributions may be included in gross income, applied against and reduce the adjusted basis of the stock, treated as gain from the sale or exchange of property, or (in the case of certain distributions out of increase in value accrued before March 1, 1913) may be exempt from tax.

The amount of the distributions to which section 301 applies is determined in accordance with the provisions of section 301(b). The basis of property received in a distribution to which section 301 applies is determined in accordance with the provisions of section 301(d). Accordingly, except as otherwise provided in this chapter, a distribution on or after June 22, 1954, of property by a corporation to a shareholder with respect to its stock shall be included in gross income to the extent the amount distributed is considered a dividend under section 316. For examples of distributions treated otherwise, see sections 116, 301(c)(2), 301(c)(3)(B), 301(e), 302(b), 303, and 305. See also Part II (relating to distributions in partial or complete liquidation), Part III (relating to corporate organizations and reorganizations), and Part IV (relating to insolvency reorganizations) subchapter C, chapter 1 of the Code.

(b) *Time of inclusion in gross income and of determination of fair market value.*—A distribution made by a corporation to its shareholders shall be included in the gross income of the distributees when the cash or other property is unqualifiedly made subject to their demands. However, if such distribution is a distribution other than in cash, the fair market value of the property shall be determined as of the date of distribution without regard to whether such date is the same as that on which the distribution is includible in gross income. For example, if a corporation distributes a taxable dividend in property (the adjusted basis of which exceeds its fair market value on December 31, 1955) on December 31, 1955, which is received by, or unqualifiedly made subject to the demand of, its shareholders on January 2, 1956, the amount to be included in the gross income of the shareholders will be the fair market value of such property on December 31, 1955, although such amount will not be includible in the gross income of the shareholders until January 2, 1956.

(c) *Application of section to shareholders.*—Section 301 is not applicable to an amount paid by a corporation to a shareholder unless the amount is paid to the shareholder in his capacity as such.

(d) *Distributions to corporate shareholders.*—(1) If the shareholder is a corporation, the amount of any distribution to be taken into account under section 301(c) shall be:

(i) The amount of money distributed,

(ii) An amount equal to the fair market value of any property distributed which consists of any obligations of the distributing corporation, stock of the distributing corporation treated as property under section 305(b), or rights to acquire such stock treated as property under section 305(b), plus

(iii) In the case of a distribution not described in subdivision (iv) of this subparagraph, an amount equal to (*a*) the fair market value of any other property distributed or, if lesser, (*b*) the adjusted basis of such other property in the hands of the distributing corporation (determined immediately before the distribution and increased for any gain recognized to the distributing corporation under section 311(b), (c), or (d), or under section 341(f), 617(d), 1245(a), 1250(a), 1251(c), 1252(a), or 1254(a)), or

(iv) In the case of a distribution made after November 8, 1971, to a shareholder which is a foreign corporation, an amount equal to the fair market value of any other property distributed, but only if the distribution received by such shareholder is not effectively connected for the taxable year with the conduct of a trade or business in the United States by such shareholder.

(2) In the case of a distribution the amount of which is determined by reference to the adjusted basis described in subparagraph (1)(iii)(*b*) or this paragraph:

(i) That portion of the distribution which is a dividend under section 301(c)(1) may not exceed such adjusted basis, or

(ii) If the distribution is not out of earnings and profits, the amount of the reduction in basis of the shareholder's stock, and the amount of any gain resulting from such distribution, are to be determined by reference to such adjusted basis of the property which is distributed.

(3) Notwithstanding paragraph (d)(1)(iii), if a distribution of property described in such paragraph is made after December 31, 1962, by a foreign corporation to a shareholder which is a corporation, the amount of the distribution to be taken into account under section 301(c) shall be determined under section 301(b)(1)(C) and paragraph (n) of this section.

(e) *Adjusted basis.*—In determining the adjusted basis of property distributed in the hands of the distributing corporation immediately before the distribution for purposes of section 301(b)(1)(B)(ii), (b)(1)(C)(i), and (d)(2)(B), the basis to be used shall be the basis for determining gain upon a sale or exchange.

(f) *Examples.*—The application of this section (except paragraph (n)) may be illustrated by the following examples:

Example (1). On January 1, 1955, A, an individual owned all of the stock of Corporation M with an adjusted basis of $2,000. During 1955, A received distributions from Corporation M totaling $30,000, consisting of $10,000 in cash and listed securities having a basis in the hands of Corporation M and a fair market value on the date distributed of $20,000. Corporation M's taxable year is the calendar year. As of December 31, 1954, Corporation M had earnings and profits accumulated after February 28, 1913, in the amount of $26,000, and it had no earnings and profits and no deficit for 1955. Of the $30,000 received by A, $26,000 will be treated as an ordinary dividend; the remaining $4,000 will be applied against the adjusted basis of his stock; the $2,000 in excess of the adjusted basis of his stock will either be treated as gain from the sale or exchange of property (under section 301(c)(3)(A)) or, if out of increase in value accrued before March 1, 1913, will (under section 301(c)(3)(B)) be exempt from tax. If A subsequently sells his stock in Corporation M, the basis for determining gain or loss on the sale will be zero.

Example (2). The facts are the same as in *Example 1* with the exceptions that the sole shareholder of Corporation M is Corporation W and that the securities which were distributed had an adjusted basis to Corporation M of $15,000. The distribution received by Corporation W totals $25,000 consisting of $10,000 in cash and securities with an adjusted basis of $15,000. The total $25,000 will be treated as a dividend to Corporation W since the earnings and profits of Corporation M ($26,000) are in excess of the amount of the distribution.

Example (3). Corporation X owns timber land which it acquired prior to March 1, 1913, at a cost of $50,000 with $5,000 allocated as the separate cost of the land. On March 1, 1913, this property had a fair market value of $150,000 of which $135,000 was attributable to the timber and $15,000 to the land. All of the timber was cut prior to 1955 and the full appreciation in the value thereof, $90,000 ($135,000 – $45,000), realized through depletion allowances based on March 1, 1913, value. None of this surplus from realized appreciation had been distributed. In 1955, Corporation X sold the land for $20,000 thereby realizing a gain of $15,000. Of this gain, $10,000 is due to realized appreciation in value which accrued before March 1, 1913 ($15,000 – $5,000). Of the gain of $15,000, $5,000 is taxable. Therefore, at December 31, 1955, Corporation X had a surplus from realized appreciation in the amount of $100,000. It had no accumulated earnings and profits and no deficit at January 1, 1955. The net earnings for 1955 (including the $5,000 gain on the sale of the land) were $20,000. During 1955, Corporation X distributed $75,000 to its stockholders. Of this amount, $20,000 will be treated as a dividend. The remaining $55,000, which is a distribution of realized appreciation, will be applied against and reduce the adjusted basis of the shareholder's stock. If any part of the $55,000 is in excess of the adjusted basis of a shareholder's stock, such part will be exempt from tax.

(g) *Reduction for liabilities.*—(1) *General rule.*—For the purpose of section 301, no reduction shall be made for the amount of any liability, unless the liability is assumed by the shareholder within the meaning of section 357(d).

(2) *No reduction below zero.*—Any reduction pursuant to paragraph (g)(1) of this section shall not cause the amount of the distribution to be reduced below zero.

* * *

(h) *Basis.*—The basis of property received in the distribution to which section 301 applies shall be—

(1) If the shareholder is not a corporation, the fair market value of such property;

(2) If the shareholder is a corporation—

(i) In the case of a distribution of the obligations of the distributing corporation or of the stock of such corporation or rights to acquire such stock (if such stock or rights are treated as property under section 305(b)), the fair market value of such obligations, stock, or rights;

(ii) In the case of the distribution of any other property, except as provided in subdivision (iii) (relating to certain distributions by a foreign corporation) or subdivision (iv) (relating to certain distributions to foreign corporate distributees) of this subparagraph, whichever of the following is the lesser—

(a) The fair market value of such property; or

(b) The adjusted basis (in the hands of the distributing corporation immediately before the distribution) of such property increased in the amount of gain to the distributing corporation which is recognized under section 311(b) (relating to distributions of LIFO inventory), section 311(c) (relating to distributions of property subject to liabilities in excess of basis), section 311(d) (relating to appreciated property used to redeem stock), section 341(f) (relating to certain sales of stock of consenting corporations), section 617(d) (relating to gain from dispositions of certain mining property, section 1245(a) or 1250(a) (relating to gain from dispositions of certain depreciable property), section 1251(c) (relating to gain from disposition of farm recapture property), section 1252(a) (relating to gain from disposition of farm land), or section 1254(a) (relating to gain from disposition of interest in natural resource recapture property);

(iii) In the case of the distribution by a foreign corporation of any other property after December 31, 1962, in a distribution not described in subdivision (iv) of this subparagraph, the amount determined under paragraph (n) of this section;

(iv) In the case of the distribution of any other property made after November 8, 1971, to a shareholder which is a foreign corporation, the fair market value of such property, but only if the distribution received by such shareholder is not effectively connected for the taxable year with the conduct of a trade or business in the United States by such shareholder.

[There is no "(i)" in the official Regulations.— CCH.]

(j) *Transfers for less than fair market value.*—If property is transferred by a corporation to a shareholder which is not a corporation for an amount less than its fair market value in a sale or exchange, such shareholder shall be treated as having received a distribution to which section 301 applies. In such case, the amount of the distribution shall be the difference between the amount paid for the property and its fair market value. If property is transferred in a sale or exchange by a corporation to a shareholder which is a corporation, for an amount less than its fair market value and also less than its adjusted basis, such shareholder shall be treated as having received a distribution to which section 301 applies, and—

(1) Where the fair market value of the property equals or exceeds its adjusted basis in the hands of the distributing corporation the amount of the distribution shall be the excess of the adjusted basis (increased by the amount of gain recognized under section 311(b), (c), or (d), or under section 341(f), 617(d), 1245(a), 1250(a), 1251(c), 1252(a), or 1254(a) to the distributing corporation) over the amount paid for the property;

(2) Where the fair market value of the property is less than its adjusted basis in the hands of the distributing corporation, the amount of the distribution shall be the excess of such fair market value over the amount paid for the property.

* * *

(l) *Transactions treated as distributions.*—A distribution to shareholders with respect to their stock is within the terms of section 301 although it takes place at the same time as another transaction if the distribution is in substance a separate transaction whether or not connected in a formal sense. This is most likely to occur in the case of a recapitalization, a reincorporation, or a merger of a corporation with a newly organized corporation having substantially no property. For example, if a corporation having only common stock outstanding, exchanges one share of newly issued common stock and one bond in the principal amount of $10 for each share of outstanding common stock, the distribution of the bonds will be a distribution of property (to the extent of their fair market value) to which section 301 applies, even though the exchange of common stock for common stock may be pursuant to a plan of reorganization under the terms of section 368(a)(1)(E) (recapitalization) and even though the exchange of common stock for common stock may be tax free by virtue of section 354.

(m) *Cancellation of indebtedness.*—The cancellation of indebtedness of a shareholder by a corporation shall be treated as a distribution of property.

* * *

(p) *Cross references.*—For certain rules relating to adjustments to earnings and profits and for determining the extent to which a distribution is a dividend, see sections 312 and 316 and regulations thereunder.

* * *

[Reg. § 1.301-1.]

☐ [*T.D.* 6152, 12-2-55. *Amended by T.D.* 6752, 9-8-64; *T.D.* 7084, 1-7-71; *T.D.* 7209, 10-3-72; *T.D.* 7283, 8-2-73; *T.D.* 7293, 11-27-73; *T.D.* 7587, 1-4-79; *T.D.* 8474, 4-26-93; *T.D.* 8586, 1-9-95; *T.D.* 8924, 1-3-2001; *T.D.* 8964, 9-26-2001 *and T.D.* 9092, 9-11-2003.]

Proposed Amendments to Regulation

§ 1.301-1. Rules applicable with respect to distributions of money and other property.

(a) *General.*—Section 301 provides the general rule for treatment of distributions made in taxable years beginning after December 31, 1986, of property by a corporation to a shareholder with respect to its stock. The term *property* is defined in section 317(a). Such distributions, except as otherwise provided in this chapter, shall be treated as provided in section 301(c). Under section 301(c), distributions may be included in gross income to the extent the amount distributed is considered a dividend under section 316, applied against and reduce the adjusted basis of the stock, treated as gain from the sale or exchange of property, or (in the case of certain distributions out of increase in value accrued before March 1, 1913) may be exempt from tax. The amount of the distributions to which section 301 applies is determined in accordance with the provisions of section 301(b). The basis of property received in a distribution to which section 301 applies is determined in accordance with the provisions of section 301(d).

(b) *Amount of distribution and determination of fair market value.*—The amount of a distribution to which section 301 applies shall be the amount of money received in the distribution, plus the fair market value of other property received in the distribution. The fair market value of any property distributed shall be determined as of the date of the distribution.

(c) *Time of inclusion in gross income and time of determination of fair market value.*—A distribution made by a corporation to its shareholders shall be included in the gross income of the distributees when the cash or other property is unqualifiedly made subject to their demands without regard to whether such date is the same as that on which the corporation made the distribution. For example, if a corporation distributes a taxable dividend in property on December 30, 2018, which is received by, or unqualifiedly made subject to the demand of, its shareholders on January 3, 2019, the amount to be included in the gross income of the shareholders will be the fair market value of such property on December 30, 2018, although such amount will not be includible in the gross income of the shareholders until January 3, 2019.

(d) *Application of section to shareholders.*—Section 301 is not applicable to an amount paid by a corporation to a shareholder unless the amount is paid to the shareholder in the shareholder's capacity as such.

(e) *Example.*—Corporation M, formed in 1998, has never been an acquiring corporation in a transaction to which section 381(a) applies. On January 1, 2019, A, an individual owned all of the stock of Corporation M, consisting of a single share, with an adjusted basis of $2,000. During 2019, A received distributions from Corporation M totaling $30,000, consisting of $10,000 in cash and listed securities having a basis in the hands of Corporation M and a fair market value on the date distributed of $20,000. Corporation M's taxable year is the calendar year. As of December 31, 2018, Corporation M had accumulated earnings and profits in the amount of $26,000, and it had no earnings and profits and no deficit for 2019. Of the $30,000 received by A, $26,000 will be treated as an ordinary dividend; the remaining $4,000 will be applied against the adjusted basis of his stock; the $2,000 in excess of the adjusted basis of his stock will be treated as gain from the sale or exchange of property under section 301(c)(3)(A). If A subsequently sells his stock in Corporation M, the basis for determining gain or loss on the sale will be zero.

(f) *Reduction for liabilities.*—(1) *General rule.*—For purposes of section 301(b)(2), no reduction in the amount of a distribution shall be made for the amount of any liability, except to the extent the liability is assumed by the shareholder within the meaning of section 357(d).

(2) *No reduction below zero.*—Any reduction pursuant to paragraph (f)(1) of this section shall not cause the amount of the distribution to be reduced below zero.

(3) *Effective dates.*—(i) *In general.*—This paragraph (f) applies to distributions occurring after January 4, 2001.

(ii) *Retroactive application.*—This paragraph (f) also applies to distributions made on or before January 4, 2001, if the distribution is made as part of a transaction described in, or substantially similar to the transaction in, Notice 99-59 (1999-2 C.B. 761), including transactions designed to reduce gain (*see* § 601.601(d)(2) of this chapter). For rules for distributions on or before January 4, 2001 (other than distributions on or before that date to which this paragraph (f) applies), see rules in effect on January 4, 2001 (see § 1.301-1(g) as contained in 26 CFR part 1 revised April 1, 2001).

(g) *Basis.*—The basis of property received in a distribution to which section 301 applies shall be the fair market value of such property. See paragraph (b) of this section.

(h) *Transfers for less than fair market value.*—If property is transferred by a corporation to a shareholder for an amount less than its fair market value in a sale or exchange, such shareholder shall be treated as having received a distribution to which section 301 applies. In such case, the amount of the distribution shall be the excess of the fair market value of the property over the amount paid for such property at the time of the transfer. For example, on January 3, 2019, A, a shareholder of Corporation X, purchased property from X for $20. The fair market value of such property on January 3, 2019 was $100. The amount of the distribution to A determined under section 301(b) is $80.

(i) [Reserved]

(j) *Transactions treated as distributions.*—A distribution to shareholders with respect to their stock is within the terms of section 301 although it takes place at the same time as another transaction if the distribution is in substance a separate transaction whether or not connected in a formal sense. This is most likely to occur in the case of a recapitalization, a reincorporation, or a merger of a corporation with a newly organized corporation having substantially no property. For example, if a corporation having only common stock outstanding, exchanges one share of newly issued common stock and one bond in the principal amount of $10 for each share of outstanding common stock, the distribution of the bonds will be a distribution of property (to the extent of their fair market value) to which section 301 applies, even though the exchange of common stock for common stock may be pursuant to a plan of reorganization under the terms of section 368(a)(1)(E) (recapitalization) and even though the exchange of common stock for common stock may be tax free by virtue of section 354.

(k) *Cancellation of indebtedness.*—The cancellation of indebtedness of a shareholder by a corporation shall be treated as a distribution of property.

(l) *Cross references.*—For certain rules relating to adjustments to earnings and profits and for determining the extent to which a distribution is a dividend, see sections 312 and 316 and regulations thereunder.

* * *

[Prop. Reg. § 1.301-1.]

[Proposed 3-26-2019 (corrected 4-23-2019).]

»»→ Note: Reg. § 1.302-1 does not reflect the 1982 change in location of the partial liquidation rules. The partial liquidation provisions formerly embodied in Section 346 are now set forth, with some modification, in Sections 302(b)(4) and 302(e).

§ 1.302-1. General.—(a) Under section 302(d), unless otherwise provided in subchapter C, chapter 1 of the Code, a distribution in redemption of stock shall be treated as a distribution of property to which section 301 applies if the distribution is not within any of the provisions of section 302(b). A distribution in redemption of stock shall be considered a distribution in part or full payment in exchange for the stock under section 302(a) provided paragraph (1), (2), (3), or (4) of section 302(b) applies. Section 318(a) (relating to constructive ownership of stock) applies to all redemptions under section 302 except that in the termination of a shareholder's interest certain limitations are placed on the application of section 318(a)(1) by section 302(c)(2). The term "redemption of stock" is defined in section 317(b). Section 302 does not apply to that portion of any distribution which qualifies as a distribution in partial liquidation under section 346. For special rules relating to redemption of stock to pay death taxes see section 303. For special rules relating to redemption of section 306 stock see section 306. For special rules relating to redemption of stock in partial or complete liquidation see section 331.

* * *

[Reg. § 1.302-1.]

□ [*T.D.* 6152, 12-2-55.]

§ 1.302-2. Redemptions not taxable as dividends.—(a) *In general.*—The fact that a redemption fails to meet the requirements of paragraph (2), (3) or (4) of section 302(b) shall not be taken into account in determining whether the redemption is not essentially equivalent to a dividend under section 302(b)(1). See, however, paragraph (b) of this section. For example, if a shareholder owns only nonvoting stock of a corporation which is not section 306 stock and which is limited and preferred as to dividends and in liquidation, and one-half of such stock is redeemed, the distribution will ordinarily meet the requirements of paragraph (1) of section 302(b) but will not meet the requirements of paragraph (2), (3) or (4) of such section. The determination of whether or not a distribution is within the phrase "essentially equivalent to a dividend" (that is, having the same effect as a distribution without any redemption of stock) shall be made without regard to the earnings and profits of the corporation at the time of the distribution. For example, if A owns all the stock of a corporation and the corporation redeems part of his stock at a time when it has no earnings and profits, the distribution shall be treated as a distribution under section 301 pursuant to section 302(d).

(b) *Redemption not essentially equivalent to a dividend.*—(1) *In general.*—The question whether a distribution in redemption of stock of a shareholder is not essentially equivalent to a dividend under section 302(b)(1) depends upon the facts and circumstances of each case. One of the facts to be considered in making this determination is the constructive stock ownership of such shareholder under section 318(a). All distributions in pro rata redemptions of a part of the stock of a corporation generally will be treated as distributions under section 301 if the corporation has only one class of stock outstanding. However, for distributions in partial liquidation, see section 302(e). The redemption of all of one class of stock (except section 306 stock) either at one time or in a series of redemptions generally will be considered as a distribution under section 301 if all classes of stock outstanding at the time of the redemption are held in the same proportion. Distributions in redemption of stock may be treated as distributions under section 301 regardless of the provisions of the stock certificate and regardless of whether all stock being redeemed was acquired by the stockholders from whom the stock was redeemed by purchase or otherwise.

* * *

(c) *Basis adjustments.*—In any case in which an amount received in redemption of stock is treated as a distribution of a dividend, proper adjustment of the basis of the remaining stock will be made with respect to the stock redeemed. (For adjustments to basis required for certain redemptions of corporate shareholders that are treated as extraordinary dividends, see section 1059 and the regulations thereunder.) The following examples illustrate the application of this rule:

Example (1). A, an individual, purchased all of the stock of Corporation X for $100,000. In 1955 the corporation redeems half of the stock for $150,000, and it is determined that this amount constitutes a dividend. The remaining stock of Corporation X held by A has a basis of $100,000.

Example (2). H and W, husband and wife, each own half of the stock of Corporation X. All of the stock was purchased by H for $100,000 cash. In 1950 H gave one-half of the stock to W, the stock transferred having a value in excess of $50,000. In 1955 all of the stock of H is redeemed for $150,000, and it is determined that the distribution to H in redemption of his shares constitutes the distribution of a dividend. Immediately after the transaction, W holds the remaining stock of Corporation X with a basis of $100,000.

Example (3). The facts are the same as in Example (2) with the additional facts that the outstanding stock of Corporation X consists of 1,000 shares and all but 10 shares of the stock of H is redeemed. Immediately after the transaction, H holds 10 shares of the stock of Corporation X with a basis of $50,000, and W holds 500 shares with a basis of $50,000.

* * *

[Reg. § 1.302-2.]

☐ [*T.D.* 6152, 12-2-55. *Amended by T.D.* 8724, 7-15-97; *T.D.* 9264, 5-26-2006 *and T.D.* 9329, 6-13-2007.]

§ 1.302-3. Substantially disproportionate redemption.—(a) Section 302(b)(2) provides for the treatment of an amount received in redemption of stock as an amount received in exchange for such stock if—

(1) Immediately after the redemption the shareholder owns less than 50 percent of the total combined voting power of all classes of stock as provided in section 302(b)(2)(B),

(2) The redemption is a substantially disproportionate redemption within the meaning of section 302(b)(2)(C), and

(3) The redemption is not pursuant to a plan described in section 302(b)(2)(D).

Section 318(a) (relating to constructive ownership of stock) shall apply both in making the disproportionate redemption test and in determining the percentage of stock ownership after the redemption. The requirements under section 302(b)(2) shall be applied to each shareholder separately and shall be applied only with respect to stock which is issued and outstanding in the hands of the shareholders. Section 302(b)(2) only applies to a redemption of voting stock or to a redemption of both voting stock and other stock. Section 302(b)(2) does not apply to the redemption solely of nonvoting stock (common or preferred). However, if a redemption is treated as an exchange to a particular shareholder under the terms of section 302(b)(2), such section will apply to the simultaneous redemption of nonvoting preferred stock (which is not section 306 stock) owned by such shareholder and such redemption will also be treated as an exchange. Generally, for purposes of this section, stock which does not have voting rights until the happening of an event, such as a default in the payment of dividends on preferred stock, is not voting stock until the happening of the specified event. Subsection 302(b)(2)(D) provides that a redemption will not be treated as substantially disproportionate if made pursuant to a plan the purpose or effect of which is a series of redemptions which result in the aggregate in a distribution which is not substantially disproportionate. Whether or not such a plan exists will be determined from all the facts and circumstances.

(b) The application of paragraph (a) of this section is illustrated by the following example:

Example. Corporation M has outstanding 400 shares of common stock of which A, B, C and D each own 100 shares or 25 percent. No stock is considered constructively owned by A, B, C or D under section 318. Corporation M redeems 55 shares from A, 25 shares from B, and 20 shares from C. For the redemption to be disproportionate as to any shareholder, such shareholder must own after the redemptions less than 20 percent (80 percent of 25 percent) of the 300 shares of stock then outstanding. After the redemptions, A owns 45 shares (15 percent), B owns 75 shares (25 percent), and C owns 80 shares (26⅔ percent). The distribution is disproportionate only with respect to A.

[Reg. § 1.302-3.]

☐ [*T.D.* 6152, 12-2-55.]

§ 1.302-4. Termination of shareholder's interest.—Section 302(b)(3) provides that a distribution in redemption of all of the stock of the corporation owned by a shareholder shall be treated as a distribution in part or full payment in exchange for the stock of such shareholder. In determining whether all of the stock of the shareholder has been redeemed, the general rule of section 302(c)(1) requires that the rules of constructive ownership provided in section 318(a) shall apply. Section 302(c)(2), however, provides that section 318(a)(1) (relating to constructive ownership of stock owned by members of a family) shall not apply where the specific requirements of section 302(c)(2) are met. The following rules shall be applicable in determining whether the specific requirements of section 302(c)(2) are met:

(a) *Statement.*—The agreement specified in section 302(c)(2)(A)(iii) shall be in the form of a statement entitled, "STATEMENT PURSUANT TO SECTION 302(c)(2)(A)(iii) BY [INSERT NAME AND TAXPAYER IDENTIFICATION NUMBER (IF ANY) OF TAXPAYER OR RELATED PERSON, AS THE CASE MAY BE], A DISTRIBUTEE (OR RELATED PERSON) OF [INSERT NAME AND EMPLOYER IDENTIFICATION NUMBER (IF ANY) OF DISTRIBUTING CORPORATION]." The distributee must include such statement on or with the distributee's first return for the taxable year in which the distribution described in section 302(b)(3) occurs. If the distributee is a controlled foreign corporation (within the meaning of section 957), each United States shareholder (within the meaning of section 951(b)) with respect thereto must include this statement on or with its return. The distributee must represent in the statement—

(1) THE DISTRIBUTEE (OR RELATED PERSON) HAS NOT ACQUIRED, OTHER THAN BY BEQUEST OR INHERITANCE, ANY INTEREST IN THE CORPORATION (AS DESCRIBED IN SECTION 302(c)(2)(A)(i)) SINCE THE DISTRIBUTION; and

(2) THE DISTRIBUTEE (OR RELATED PERSON) WILL NOTIFY THE INTERNAL REVENUE SERVICE OF ANY ACQUISITION, OTHER THAN BY BEQUEST OR INHERITANCE, OF SUCH AN INTEREST IN THE CORPORATION WITHIN 30 DAYS AFTER THE ACQUISITION, IF THE ACQUISITION OCCURS WITHIN 10 YEARS FROM THE DATE OF THE DISTRIBUTION.

(b) *Substantiation information.*—The distributee who files an agreement under section 302(c)(2)(A)(iii) shall retain copies of income tax returns and any other records indicating fully the amount of tax which would have been payable had the redemption been treated as a distribution subject to section 301.

(c) *Stock of parent, subsidiary or successor corporation redeemed.*—If stock of a parent corporation is redeemed, section 302(c)(2)(A), relating to acquisition of an interest in the corporation within 10 years after termination shall be applied with reference to an interest both in the parent corporation and any subsidiary of such parent corporation. If stock of a parent corporation is sold to a subsidiary in a transaction described in section 304, section 302(c)(2)(A) shall be applicable to the acquisition of an interest in such subsidiary corporation or in the parent corporation. If stock of a subsidiary corporation is redeemed, section 302(c)(2)(A) shall be applied with reference to an interest both in such subsidiary corporation and its parent. Section 302(c)(2)(A) shall also be applied with respect to an interest in a corporation which is a successor corporation to the corporation the interest in which has been terminated.

(d) *Redeemed shareholder as creditor.*—For the purpose of section 302(c)(2)(A)(i), a person will be considered to be a creditor only if the rights of such person with respect to the corporation are not greater or broader in scope than necessary for the enforcement of his claim. Such claim must not in any sense be proprietary and must not be subordinate to the claims of general creditors. An obligation in the form of a debt may thus constitute a proprietary interest. For example, if under the terms of the instrument the corporation may discharge the principal amount of its obligation to a person by payments, the amount or certainty of which are dependent upon the earnings of the corporation, such a person is not a creditor of the corporation. Furthermore, if under the terms of the instrument the rate of purported interest is dependent upon earnings, the holder of such instrument may not, in some cases, be a creditor.

(e) *Acquisition of assets pursuant to creditor's rights.*—In the case of a distributee to whom section 302(b)(3) is applicable, who is a creditor after such transaction, the acquisition of the assets of the corporation in the enforcement of the rights of such creditor shall not be considered an acquisition of an interest in the corporation for purposes of section 302(c)(2) unless stock of the corporation, its parent corporation, or, in the case of a redemption of stock of a parent corporation, of a subsidiary of such corporation is acquired.

(f) *Constructive ownership rules applicable.*—In determining whether an entire interest in the corporation has been terminated under section 302(b)(3), under all circumstances paragraphs (2), (3), (4), and (5) of section 318(a) (relating to constructive ownership of stock) shall be applicable.

(g) *Avoidance of Federal income tax.*—Section 302(c)(2)(B) provides that section 302(c)(2)(A) shall not apply—

(1) If any portion of the stock redeemed was acquired directly or indirectly within the 10-year period ending on the date of the distribution by the distributee from a person, the ownership of whose stock would (at the time of distribution) be attributable to the distributee under section 318(a), or

(2) If any person owns (at the time of the distribution) stock, the ownership of which is attributable to the distributee under section 318(a), such person acquired any stock in the corporation directly or indirectly from the distributee within the 10-year period ending on the date of the distribution, and such stock so acquired from the distributee is not redeemed in the same transaction,

unless the acquisition (described in (1) of this paragraph) or the disposition by the distributee (described in subparagraph (2)) did not have as one of its principal purposes the avoidance of Federal income tax. A transfer of stock by the transferor, within the 10-year period ending on the date of the distribution, to a person whose stock would be attributable to the transferor shall not be deemed to have as one of its principal purposes the avoidance of Federal income tax merely because the transferee is in a lower income tax bracket than the transferor.

* * *

[Reg. § 1.302-4.]

☐ [*T.D.* 6152, 12-2-55. *Amended by T.D.* 6969, 8-22-68; *T.D.* 7535, 3-14-78; *T.D.* 9264, 5-26-2006 *and T.D.* 9329, 6-13-2007.]

»»→ Note: The alternative qualification requirement relating to "50 percent of the taxable estate" referred to in Reg. § 1.303-2 was deleted in 1976. The 75 percent stock ownership requirement relating to multiple corporations, also referred to in Reg. § 1.303-2, was reduced to 20 percent in 1981.

§ 1.303-2. Requirements.—(a) Section 303 applies only where the distribution is with respect to stock of a corporation the value of whose stock in the gross estate of the decedent for Federal estate tax purposes is an amount in excess of (1) 35 percent of the value of the gross estate of such decedent, or (2) 50 percent of the taxable estate of such decedent. For the purposes of such 35 percent and 50 percent requirements, stock of two or more corporations shall be treated as the stock of a single corporation if more than 75 percent in value of the outstanding stock of each such corporation is included in determining the value of the decedent's gross estate. For the purpose of the 75 percent requirement, stock which, at the decedent's death, represents the surviving spouse's interest in community property shall be considered as having been included in determining the value of the decedent's gross estate.

(b) For the purpose of section 303(b)(2)(A)(i), the term "gross estate" means the gross estate as computed in accordance with section 2031 (or, in the case of the estate of a decedent nonresident not a citizen of the United States, in accordance with section 2103). For the purpose of section 303(b)(2)(A)(ii), the term "taxable estate" means the taxable estate as computed in accordance with section 2051 (or, in the case of the estate of a decedent non-resident not a citizen of the United States, in accordance with section 2106). In case the value of an estate is determined for Federal estate tax purposes under section 2032 (relating to alternate valuation), then, for purposes of section 303(b)(2), the value of the gross estate, the taxable estate, and the stock shall each be determined on the applicable date prescribed in section 2032.

(c)(1) In determining whether the estate of the decedent is comprised of stock of a corporation of sufficient value to satisfy the percentage requirements of section 303(b)(2)(A) and section 303(b)(2)(B), the total value, in the aggregate, of all classes of stock of the corporation includible in determining the value of the gross estate is taken into account. A distribution under section 303(a) may be in redemption of the stock of the corporation includible in determining the value of the gross estate, without regard to the class of such stock.

(2) The above may be illustrated by the following example:

Example. The gross estate of the decedent has a value of $1,000,000, the taxable estate is $700,000, and the sum of the death taxes and funeral and administration expenses is $275,000. Included in determining the gross estate of the decedent is stock of three corporations which, for Federal estate tax purposes, is valued as follows:

Corporation A:	
Common stock	$100,000
Preferred stock	100,000
Corporation B:	
Common stock	50,000
Preferred stock	350,000
Corporation C:	
Common stock	200,000

The stock of Corporation A and Corporation C included in the estate of the decedent constitutes all of the outstanding stock of both corporations. The stock of Corporation A and the stock of Corporation C, treated as the stock of a single corporation under section 303(b)(2)(B), has a value in excess of $350,000 (35 percent of the gross estate or 50 percent of the taxable estate). Likewise, the stock of Corporation B has a value in excess of $350,000. The distribution by one or more of the above corporations, within the period prescribed in section 303(b)(1), of amounts not exceeding, in the aggregate, $275,000, in redemption of preferred stock or common stock of such corporation or corporations, will be treated as in full payment in exchange for the stock so redeemed.

(d) If stock includible in determining the value of the gross estate of a decedent is exchanged for new stock, the basis of which is determined by reference to the basis of the old stock, the redemption of the new stock will be treated the same under section 303 as the redemption of the old stock would have been. Thus, section 303 shall apply with respect to a distribution in redemption of stock received by the estate of a decedent (1) in connection with a reorganization under section 368, (2) in a distribution or exchange under section 355 (or so much of section 356 as relates to section 355), (3) in an exchange under section 1036 or (4) in a distribution to which section 305(a) applies. Similarly, a distribution in redemption of stock will qualify under section 303, notwithstanding the fact that the stock redeemed is section 306 stock to the extent that the conditions of section 303 are met.

(e) Section 303 applies to distributions made after the death of the decedent and (1) before the expiration of the 3-year period of limitations for the assessment of estate tax provided in section 6501(a) (determined without the application of any provisions of law extending or suspending the running of such period of limitations), or within 90 days after the expiration of such period, or (2) if a petition for redetermination of a deficiency in such estate tax has been filed with the Tax Court within the time prescribed in section 6213, at any time before the expiration of 60 days after the decision of the Tax Court becomes final. The extension of the period of distribution provided in section 303(b)(1)(B) has reference solely to bona fide contests in the Tax Court and will not apply in the case of a petition for redetermination of a deficiency which is initiated solely for the purpose of extending the period within which section 303 would otherwise be applicable.

(f) While section 303 will most frequently have application in the case where stock is redeemed from the executor or administrator of an estate, the section is also applicable to distributions in redemption of stock included in the decedent's gross estate and held at the time of the redemption by any person who acquired the stock by any of the means comprehended by Part III, Subchapter A, Chapter 11 of the Code, including the heir, legatee, or donee of the decedent, a surviving joint tenant, surviving spouse, appointee, or taker in default of appointment, or a trustee of a trust created by the decedent. Thus, section 303 may apply with respect to a distribution in redemption of stock from a donee to whom the decedent has transferred stock in contemplation of death where the value of such stock is included in the decedent's gross estate under section 2035. Similarly, section 303 may apply to the redemption of stock from a beneficiary of the estate to whom an executor has distributed the stock pursuant to the terms of the will of the decedent. However, section 303 is not applicable to the case where stock is redeemed from a stockholder who has acquired the stock by gift or purchase from any person to whom such stock has passed from the decedent. Nor is section 303 applicable to the case where stock is redeemed from a stockholder who has acquired the stock from the executor in satisfaction of a specific monetary bequest.

(g)(1) The total amount of the distributions to which section 303 may apply with respect to redemptions of stock included in the gross estate of a decedent may not exceed the sum of the estate, inheritance, legacy, and succession taxes (including any interest collected as a part of such taxes) imposed because of the decedent's death and the amount of funeral and administration expenses allowable as deductions to the estate. Where there is more than one distribution in redemption of stock described in section 303(b)(2) during the period of time prescribed in section 303(b)(1), the distributions shall be applied against the total amount which qualifies for treatment under section 303 in the order in which the distributions are made. For this purpose, all distributions in redemption of such stock shall be taken into account, including distributions which under another provision of the Code are treated as in part or full payment in exchange for the stock redeemed.

(2) Subparagraph (1) of this paragraph may be illustrated by the following example:

Example. (i) The gross estate of the decedent has a value of $800,000, the taxable estate is $500,000, and the sum of the death taxes and funeral and administrative expenses is $225,000. Included in determining the gross estate of the decedent is the stock of a corporation which for Federal estate tax purposes is valued at $450,000. During the first year of administration, one-third of such stock is distributed to a legatee and shortly thereafter this stock is redeemed by the corporation for $150,000. During the second year of administration, another one-third of such stock includible in the estate is redeemed for $150,000.

(ii) The first distribution of $150,000 is applied against the amount that qualifies for treatment under section 303, regardless of whether the first distribution was treated as in payment in exchange for stock under section 302(a). Thus, only $75,000 of the second distribution may be treated as in full payment in exchange for stock under section 303. The tax treatment of the remaining $75,000 would be determined under other provisions of the Code.

(h) For the purpose of section 303, the Federal estate tax or any other estate, inheritance, legacy, or succession tax shall be ascertained after the allowance of any credit, relief, discount, refund, remission or reduction of tax. [Reg. § 1.303-2.]

□ [*T.D.* 6152, 12-2-55. *Amended by T.D.* 6724, 4-20-64 *and T.D.* 7346, 3-6-75.]

§ 1.303-3. Application of other sections.—(a) The sole effect of section 303 is to exempt from tax as a dividend a distribution to which such section is applicable when made in redemption of stock includible in a decedent's gross estate. Such section does not, however, in any other manner affect the principles set forth in sections 302 and 306. Thus, if stock of a corporation is owned equally by A, B, and the C Estate, and the corporation redeems one-half of the stock of each shareholder, the determination of whether the distributions to A and B are essentially equivalent to dividends shall be made without regard to the effect which section 303 may have upon the taxability of the distribution to the C Estate.

(b) See section 304 relative to redemption of stock through the use of related corporations. [Reg. § 1.303-3.]

□ [*T.D.* 6152, 12-2-55.]

§ 1.304-1. General.—(a) Except as provided in paragraph (b) of this section, section 304 is applicable where a shareholder sells stock of one corporation to a related corporation as defined in section 304. Sales to which section 304 is applicable shall be treated as redemptions subject to sections 302 and 303.

* * *

[Reg. § 1.304-1.]

□ [*T.D.* 6152, 12-2-55. *Amended by T.D.* 6533, 1-18-61.]

§ 1.304-2. Acquisition by related corporation (other than subsidiary).—(a) If a corporation, in return for property, acquires stock of another corporation from one or more persons, and the person or persons from whom the stock was acquired were in control of both such corporations before the acquisition, then such property shall be treated as received in redemption of stock of the acquiring corporation. The stock received by the acquiring corporation shall be treated as a contribution to the capital of such corporation. See section 362(a) for determination of the basis of such stock. The transferor's basis for his stock in the acquiring corporation shall be increased by the basis of stock surrendered by him. (But see below in this paragraph for subsequent reductions of basis in certain cases.) As to each person transferring stock, the amount received shall be treated as a distribution of property under section 302(d), unless as to such person such amount is to be treated as received in exchange for the stock under the terms of section 302(a) or section 303. In applying section 302(b), reference shall be had to the shareholder's ownership of stock in the issuing corporation and not to his ownership of stock in the acquiring corporation (except for purposes of applying section 318(a)). In determining control and applying section 302(b), section 318(a) (relating to the constructive ownership of stock) shall be applied without regard to the 50-percent limitation contained in section 318(a)(2)(C) and (3)(C). A series of redemptions referred to in section 302(b)(2)(D) shall include acquisitions by either of the corporations of stock of the other and stock redemptions by both corporations. If section 302(d) applies to the surrender of stock by a shareholder, his basis for his stock in the acquiring corporation after the transaction (increased as stated above in this paragraph) shall not be decreased except as provided in section 301. If section 302(d) does not apply, the property received shall be treated as received in a distribution in payment in exchange for stock of the acquiring corporation under section 302(a), which stock has a basis equal to the amount by which the shareholder's basis for his stock in the acquiring corporation was increased on account of the contribution to capital as provided for above in this paragraph. Accordingly, such amount shall be applied in reduction of the shareholder's basis for his stock in the acquiring corporation. Thus, the basis of each share of the shareholder's stock in the acquiring corporation will be the same as the basis of such share before the entire transaction. The holding period of the stock which is considered to have been redeemed shall be the same as the holding period of the stock actually surrendered.

(b) In any case in which two or more persons, in the aggregate, control two corporations, section 304(a)(1) will apply to sales by such persons of stock in either corporation to the other (whether or not made simultaneously) provided the sales by each of such persons are related to each other. The determination of whether the sales are related to each other shall be dependent upon the facts and circumstances surrounding all of the sales. For this purpose, the fact that the sales may occur during a period of one or more years (such as in the case of a series of sales by persons who together control each of such corporations immediately prior to the first of such sales and immediately subsequent to the last of such sales) shall be disregarded, provided the other facts and circumstances indicate related transactions.

(c) The application of section 304(a)(1) may be illustrated by the following examples:

Example (1). Corporation X and corporation Y each have outstanding 200 shares of common stock. One-half of the stock of each corporation is owned by an individual, A, and one-half by another individual, B, who is unrelated to A. On or after August 31, 1964, A sells 30 shares of corporation X stock to corporation Y for $50,000, such stock having an adjusted basis of $10,000 to A. After the sale, A is considered as owning corporation X stock as follows: (i) 70 shares directly, and (ii) 15 shares constructively, since by virtue of his 50-percent ownership of Y he constructively owns 50 percent of the 30 shares owned directly by Y. Since A's percentage of ownership of X's voting stock after the sale (85 out of 200 shares, or 42.5%) is not less than 80 percent of his percentage of ownership of X's voting stock before the sale (100 out of 200 shares, or 50%), the transfer is not "substantially disproportionate" as to him as provided in section 302(b)(2). Under these facts, and assuming that section 302(b)(1) is not applicable, the entire $50,000 is treated as a dividend to A to the extent of the earnings and profits of corporation Y. The basis of the corporation X stock to corporation Y is $10,000, its adjusted basis to A. The amount of $10,000 is added to the basis of the stock of corporation Y in the hands of A.

Example (2). The facts are the same as in example (1) except that A sells 80 shares of corporation X stock to corporation Y, and the sale occurs before August 31, 1964. After the sale, A is considered as owning corporation X stock as follows: (i) 20 shares directly, and (ii) 90 shares indirectly, since by virtue of his 50-percent ownership of Y he constructively owns 50 percent of the 80 shares owned directly by Y and 50 percent of the 100 shares attributed to Y because they are owned by Y's stockholder, B. Since after the sale A owns a total of more than 50 percent of the voting power of all of the outstanding stock of X (110 out of 200 shares, or 55%), the transfer is not "substantially disproportionate" as to him as provided in section 302(b)(2).

Example (3). Corporation X and corporation Y each have outstanding 100 shares of common stock. A, an individual, owns one-half the stock of each corporation. B owns one-half the stock of corporation X, and C owns one-half the stock of corporation Y. A, B, and C are unrelated. A sells 30 shares of the stock of corporation X to corporation Y for $50,000, such stock having an adjusted basis of $10,000 to him. After the sale, A is considered as owning 35 shares of the stock of corporation X (20 shares directly and 15 constructively because one-half of the 30 shares owned by corporation Y are attributed to him). Since before the sale he owned 50 percent of the stock of corporation X and after the sale he owned directly and constructively only 35 percent of such stock, the redemption is substantially disproportionate as to him pursuant to the provisions of section 302(b)(2). He, therefore, realizes a gain of $40,000 ($50,000 minus $10,000). If the stock surrendered is a capital asset, such gain is long-term or short-term capital gain depending on the period of time that such stock was held. The basis to A for the stock of corporation Y is not changed as a result of the entire transaction. The basis to corporation Y for the stock of corporation X is $50,000, *i.e.,* the basis of the transferor ($10,000), increased in the amount of gain recognized to the transferor ($40,000) on the transfer.

Example (4). Corporation X and corporation Y each have outstanding 100 shares of common stock. H, an individual, W, his wife, S, his son, and G, his grandson, each own 25 shares of stock of each corporation. H sells all of his 25 shares of stock of corporation X to corporation Y. Since both before and after the transaction H owned directly and constructively 100 percent of the stock of corporation X, and assuming that section 302(b)(1) is not applicable, the amount received by him for his stock of corporation X is treated as a dividend to him to the extent of the earnings and profits of corporation Y. [Reg. § 1.304-2.]

□ [*T.D.* 6152, 12-2-55. *Amended by T.D.* 6533, 1-18-61 *and T.D.* 6969, 8-22-68.]

§ 1.304-3. Acquisition by a subsidiary.—(a) If a subsidiary acquires stock of its parent corporation from a shareholder of the parent corporation, the acquisition of such stock shall be treated as though the parent corporation had redeemed its own stock. For the purpose of this section, a corporation is a parent corporation if it meets the 50 percent ownership requirements of section 304(c). The determination whether the amount received shall be treated as an amount received in payment in exchange for the stock shall be made by applying section 303, or by applying section 302(b) with reference to the stock of the issuing parent corporation. If such distribution would have been treated as a distribution of property (pursuant to section 302(d) under section 301, the entire amount of the selling price of the stock shall be treated as a dividend to the seller to the extent of the earnings and profits of the parent corporation determined as if the distribution had been made to it of the property that the subsidiary exchanged for the stock. In such cases, the transferor's basis for his remaining stock in the parent corporation will be determined by including the amount of the basis of the stock of the parent corporation sold to the subsidiary.

(b) Section 304(a)(2) may be illustrated by the following example:

Example. Corporation M has outstanding 100 shares of common stock which are owned as follows: B, 75 shares, C, son of B, 20 shares, and D, daughter of B, 5 shares. Corporation M owns the stock of Corporation X. B sells his 75 shares of Corporation M stock to Corporation X. Under section 302(b)(3) this is a termination of B's entire interest in Corporation M and the full amount received from the sale of his stock will be treated as payment in exchange for this stock, provided he fulfills the requirements of section 302(c)(2) (relating to an acquisition of an interest in the corporations). [Reg. § 1.304-3.]

□ [*T.D.* 6152, 12-2-55.]

§ 1.304-4. Special rules for the use of related corporations to avoid the application of section 304.—(a) *Scope and purpose.*—This section applies to determine the amount of a property distribution constituting a dividend (and the source thereof) under section 304(b)(2), for certain transactions involving controlled corporations. The purpose of this section is to prevent the avoidance of the application of section 304 to a controlled corporation.

(b) *Amount and source of dividend.*—For purposes of determining the amount constituting a dividend (and source thereof) under section 304(b)(2), the following rules shall apply:

(1) *Deemed acquiring corporation.*—A corporation (deemed acquiring corporation) shall be treated as acquiring for property the stock of a corporation (issuing corporation) acquired for property by another corporation (acquiring corporation) that is controlled by the deemed acquiring corporation, if a principal purpose for creating, organizing, or funding the acquiring corporation by any means (including through capital contributions or debt) is to avoid the application of section 304 to the deemed acquiring corporation. See paragraph (c) *Example 1* of this section for an illustration of this paragraph.

(2) *Deemed issuing corporation.*—The acquiring corporation shall be treated as acquiring for property the stock of a corporation (deemed issuing corporation) controlled by the issuing corporation if, in connection with the acquisition for property of stock of the issuing corporation by the acquiring corporation, the issuing corporation acquired stock of the deemed issuing corporation with a principal purpose of avoiding the application of section 304 to the deemed issuing corporation. See paragraph (c) *Example 2* of this section for an illustration of this paragraph.

(c) *Examples.*—The rules of this section are illustrated by the following examples:

Example 1. (i) *Facts.* P, a domestic corporation, wholly owns CFC1, a controlled foreign corporation with substantial accumulated earnings and profits. CFC1 is organized in Country X, which imposes a high rate of tax on the income of CFC1. P also wholly owns CFC2, a controlled foreign corporation with accumulated earnings and profits of $200x. CFC2 is organized in Country Y, which imposes a low rate of tax on the income of CFC2. P wishes to own all of its foreign corporations in a direct chain and to repatriate the cash of CFC2. In order to avoid having to obtain Country X approval for the acquisition of CFC1 (a Country X corporation) by CFC2 (a Country Y corporation) and to avoid the dividend distribution from CFC2 to P that would result if CFC2 were the acquiring corporation, P causes CFC2 to form CFC3 in Country X and to contribute $100x to CFC3. CFC3 then acquires all of the stock of CFC1 from P for $100x.

(ii) *Result.* Because a principal purpose for creating, organizing, or funding CFC3 (acquiring corporation) is to avoid the application of section 304 to CFC2 (deemed acquiring corporation), under paragraph (b)(1) of this section, for purposes of determining the amount of the $100x distribution constituting a dividend (and source thereof) under section 304(b)(2), CFC2 shall be treated as acquiring the stock of CFC1 (issuing corporation) from P for $100x. As a result, P receives a $100x distribution out of the earnings and profits of CFC2 to which section 301(c)(1) applies.

Example 2. (i) *Facts.* P, a domestic corporation, wholly owns CFC1, a controlled foreign corporation with substantial accumulated earnings and profits. The CFC1 stock has a basis of $100x. CFC1 is organized in Country X. P also wholly owns CFC2, a controlled foreign corporation with zero accumulated earnings and profits. CFC2 is organized in Country Y. P wishes to own all of its foreign corporations in a direct chain and to repatriate the cash of CFC2. In order to avoid having to obtain Country X approval for the acquisition of CFC1 (a Country X corporation) by CFC2 (a Country Y corporation) and to avoid a dividend distribution from CFC1 to P, P forms a new corporation (CFC3) in Country X and transfers the stock of CFC1 to CFC3 in exchange for CFC3 stock. P then transfers the stock of CFC3 to CFC2 in exchange for $100x.

(ii) *Result*. Because a principal purpose for the transfer of the stock of CFC1 (deemed issuing corporation) by P to CFC3 (issuing corporation) is to avoid the application of section 304 to CFC1, under paragraph (b)(2) of this section, for purposes of determining the amount of the $100x distribution constituting a dividend (and source thereof) under section 304(b)(2), CFC2 (acquiring corporation) shall be treated as acquiring the stock of CFC1 from P for $100x. As a result, P receives a $100x distribution out of the earnings and profits of CFC1 to which section 301(c)(1) applies.

* * *

[Reg. § 1.304-4.]

□ [*T.D.* 9477, 12-29-2009. *Amended by T.D.* 9606, 12-21-2012.]

§ 1.304-5. Control.—(a) *Control requirement in general.*—Section 304(c)(1) provides that, for purposes of section 304, control means the ownership of stock possessing at least 50 percent of the total combined voting power of all classes of stock entitled to vote or at least 50 percent of the total value of shares of all classes of stock. Section 304(c)(3) makes section 318(a) (relating to constructive ownership of stock), as modified by section 304(c)(3)(B), applicable to section 304 for purposes of determining control under section 304(c)(1).

(b) *Effect of section 304(c)(2)(B).*—(1) *In general.*—In determining whether the control test with respect to both the issuing and acquiring corporations is satisfied, section 304(a)(1) considers only the person or persons that—

(i) Control the issuing corporation before the transaction;

(ii) Transfer issuing corporation stock to the acquiring corporation for property; and

(iii) Control the acquiring corporation thereafter.

(2) *Application.*—Section 317 defines property to include money, securities, and any other property except stock (or stock rights) in the distributing corporation. However, section 304(c)(2)(B) provides a special rule to extend the relevant group of persons to be tested for control of both the issuing and acquiring corporations to include the person or persons that do not acquire property, but rather solely stock from the acquiring corporation in the transaction. Section 304(c)(2)(B) provides that if two or more persons in control of the issuing corporation transfer stock of such corporation to the acquiring corporation, and if the transferors are in control of the acquiring corporation after the transfer, the person or persons in control of each corporation include each of those transferors. Because the purpose of section 304(c)(2)(B) is to include in the relevant control group the person or persons that retain or acquire acquiring corporation stock in the transaction, only the person or persons transferring stock of the issuing corporation that retain or acquire any proprietary interest in the acquiring corporation are taken into account for purposes of applying section 304(c)(2)(B).

(3) *Example.*—This section may be illustrated by the following example.

Example. (a) A, the owner of 20% of T's only class of stock, transfers that stock to P solely in exchange for all of the P stock. Pursuant to the same transaction, P, solely in exchange for cash, acquires the remaining 80% of the T stock from T's other shareholder, B, who is unrelated to A and P.

(b) Although A and B together were in control of T (the issuing corporation) before the transaction and A and B each transferred T stock to P (the acquiring corporation), sections 304(a)(1) and (c)(2)(B) do not apply to B because B did not retain or acquire any proprietary interest in P in the transaction. Section 304(a)(1) also does not apply to A because A (or any control group of which A was a member) did not control T before the transaction and P after the transaction.

* * *

[Reg. § 1.304-5.]

□ [*T.D.* 8515, 1-12-94.]

§ 1.305-1. Stock dividends.—(a) *In general.*—Under section 305, a distribution made by a corporation to its shareholders in its stock or in rights to acquire its stock is not included in gross income except as provided in section 305(b) and the regulations promulgated under the authority of section 305(c). A distribution made by a corporation to its shareholders in its stock or rights to acquire its stock which would not otherwise be included in gross income by reason of section 305 shall not be so included merely because such distribution was made out of Treasury stock or consisted of rights to acquire Treasury stock. See section 307 for rules as to basis of stock and stock rights acquired in a distribution.

(b) *Amount of distribution.*—(1) In general, where a distribution of stock or rights to acquire stock of a corporation is treated as a distribution of property to which section 301 applies by reason of section 305(b), the amount of the distribution, in accordance with section 301(b) and § 1.301-1, is the fair market value of such stock or rights on the date of distribution. See example (1) of § 1.305-2(b).

(2) Where a corporation which regularly distributes its earnings and profits, such as a

regulated investment company, declares a dividend pursuant to which the shareholders may elect to receive either money or stock of the distributing corporation of equivalent value, the amount of the distribution of the stock received by any shareholder electing to receive stock will be considered to equal the amount of the money which could have been received instead. See example (2) of § 1.305-2(b).

(3) For rules for determining the amount of the distribution where certain transactions, such as changes in conversion ratios or periodic redemptions, are treated as distributions under section 305(c), see examples (6), (8), (9), and (15) of § 1.305-3(e).

(c) *Adjustment in purchase price.*—A transfer of stock (or rights to acquire stock) or an increase or decrease in the conversion ratio or redemption price of stock which represents an adjustment of the price to be paid by the distributing corporation in acquiring property (within the meaning of section 317(a)) is not within the purview of section 305 because it is not a distribution with respect to its stock. For example, assume that on January 1, 1970, pursuant to a reorganization, corporation X acquires all the stock of corporation Y solely in exchange for its convertible preferred class B stock. Under the terms of the class B stock, its conversion ratio is to be adjusted in 1976 under a formula based upon the earnings of corporation Y over the 6-year period ending on December 31, 1975. Such an adjustment in 1976 is not covered by section 305.

(d) *Definitions.*—(1) For purposes of this section and §§ 1.305-2 through 1.305-7, the term "stock" includes rights or warrants to acquire such stock.

(2) For purposes of §§ 1.305-2 through 1.305-7, the term "shareholder" includes a holder of rights or warrants or a holder of convertible securities. [Reg. § 1.305-1.]

□ [*T.D.* 6152, 12-2-55. *Amended by T.D.* 7281, 7-11-73.]

§ 1.305-2. Distributions in lieu of money.—(a) *In general.*—Under section 305(b)(1), if any shareholder has the right to an election or option with respect to whether a distribution shall be made either in money or any other property, or in stock or rights to acquire stock of the distributing corporation, then, with respect to all shareholders, the distribution of stock or rights to acquire stock is treated as a distribution of property to which section 301 applies regardless of—

(1) Whether the distribution is actually made in whole or in part in stock or in stock rights;

(2) Whether the election or option is exercised or exercisable before or after the declaration of the distribution;

(3) Whether the declaration of the distribution provides that the distribution will be made in one medium unless the shareholder specifically requests payment in the other;

(4) Whether the election governing the nature of the distribution is provided in the declaration of the distribution or in the corporate charter or arises from the circumstances of the distribution; or

(5) Whether all or part of the shareholders have the election.

(b) *Examples.*—The application of section 305(b)(1) may be illustrated by the following examples:

Example (1). (i) Corporation X declared a dividend payable in additional shares of its common stock to the holders of its outstanding common stock on the basis of two additional shares for each share held on the record date but with the provision that, at the election of any shareholder made within a specified period prior to the distribution date, he may receive one additional share for each share held on the record date plus $12 principal amount of securities of corporation Y owned by corporation X. The fair market value of the stock of corporation X on the distribution date was $10 per share. The fair market value of $12 principal amount of securities of corporation Y on the distribution date was $11 but such securities had a cost basis to corporation X of $9.

(ii) The distribution to all shareholders of one additional share of stock of corporation X (with respect to which no election applies) for each share outstanding is not a distribution to which section 301 applies.

(iii) The distribution of the second share of stock of corporation X to those shareholders who do not elect to receive securities of corporation Y is a distribution of property to which section 301 applies, whether such shareholders are individuals or corporations. The amount of the distribution to which section 301 applies is $10 per share of stock of corporation X held on the record date (the fair market value of the stock of corporation X on the distribution date).

(iv) The distribution of securities of corporation Y in lieu of the second share of stock of corporation X to the shareholders of corporation X whether individuals or corporations, who elect to receive such securities, is also a distribution of property to which section 301 applies.

(v) In the case of the individual shareholders of corporation X who elect to receive such securities, the amount of the distribution to which section 301 applies is $11 per share of stock of corporation X held on the record date (the fair market value of the $12 principal amount of securities of corporation Y on the distribution date).

(vi) In the case of the corporate shareholders of corporation X electing to receive such securities, the amount of the distribution to which section 301 applies is $9 per share of stock of corporation X held on the record date (the basis of the securities of corporation Y in the hands of corporation X).

Example (2). On January 10, 1970, corporation X, a regulated investment company, declared a dividend of $1 per share on its common stock payable on February 11, 1970, in cash or in stock of corporation X of equivalent value determined as of January 22, 1970, at the election of the shareholder made on or before January 22, 1970. The amount of the distribution to which section 301 applies is $1 per share whether the shareholder elects to take cash or stock and whether the shareholder is an individual or a corporation. Such amount will also be used in determining the dividend paid deduction of corporation X and the reduction in earnings and profits of corporation X. [Reg. § 1.305-2.]

□ [*T.D.* 6152, 12-2-55. *Amended by T.D.* 6476, 6-3-60; *T.D.* 6990, 1-10-69; *T.D.* 7004, 2-7-69 *and T.D.* 7281, 7-11-73.]

§ 1.305-3. Disproportionate distributions.—(a) *In general.*—Under section 305(b)(2), a distribution (including a deemed distribution) by a corporation of its stock or rights to acquire its stock is treated as a distribution of property to which section 301 applies if the distribution (or a series of distributions of which such distribution is one) has the result of (1) the receipt of money or other property by some shareholders, and (2) an increase in the proportionate interests of other shareholders in the assets or earnings and profits of the corporation. Thus, if a corporation has two classes of common stock outstanding and cash dividends are paid on one class and stock dividends are paid on the other class, the stock dividends are treated as distributions to which section 301 applies.

(b) *Special rules.*—(1) As used in section 305(b)(2), the term "a series of distributions" encompasses all distributions of stock made or deemed made by a corporation which have the result of a receipt of cash or property by some shareholders and an increase in the proportionate interests of other shareholders.

(2) In order for a distribution of stock to be considered as one of a series of distributions it is not necessary that such distribution be pursuant to a plan to distribute cash or property to some shareholders and to increase the proportionate interests of other shareholders. It is sufficient if there is an actual or deemed distribution of stock (of which such distribution is one) and as a result of such distribution or distributions some shareholders receive cash or property and other shareholders increase their proportionate interests. For example, if a corporation pays quarterly stock dividends to one class of common shareholders and annual cash dividends to another class of common shareholders the quarterly stock dividends constitute a series of distributions of stock having the result of the receipt of cash or property by some shareholders and an increase in the proportionate interests of other shareholders. This is so whether or not the stock distributions and the cash distributions are steps in an overall plan or are independent and unrelated. Accordingly, all the quarterly stock dividends are distributions to which section 301 applies.

(3) There is no requirement that both elements of section 305(b)(2) (*i.e.,* receipt of cash or property by some shareholders and an increase in proportionate interests of other shareholders) occur in the form of a distribution or series of distributions as long as the result of a distribution or distributions of stock is that some shareholders' proportionate interests increase and other shareholders in fact receive cash or property. Thus, there is no requirement that the shareholders receiving cash or property acquire the cash or property by way of a corporate distribution with respect to their shares, so long as they receive such cash or property in their capacity as shareholders, if there is a stock distribution which results in a change in the proportionate interests of some shareholders and other shareholders receive cash or property. However, in order for a distribution of property to meet the requirements of section 305(b)(2), such distribution must be made to a shareholder in his capacity as a shareholder, and must be a distribution to which section 301, 356(a)(2), 871(a)(1)(A), 881(a)(1), 852(b), or 857(b) applies. (Under section 305(d)(2), the payment of interest to a holder of a convertible debenture is treated as a distribution of property to a shareholder for purposes of section 305(b)(2).) For example if a corporation makes a stock distribution to its shareholders, and, pursuant to a prearranged plan with such corporation, a related corporation purchases such stock from those shareholders who want cash, in a transaction to which section 301 applies by virtue of section 304, the requirements of section 305(b)(2) are satisfied. In addition, a distribution of property incident to an isolated redemption of stock (for example, pursuant to a tender offer) will not cause section 305(b)(2) to apply even though the redemption distribution is treated as a dis-

tribution of property to which section 301, 871(a)(1)(A), 881(a)(1), or 356(a)(2) applies.

(4) Where the receipt of cash or property occurs more than 36 months following a distribution or series of distributions of stock, or where a distribution or series of distributions of stock is made more than 36 months following the receipt of cash or property, such distribution or distributions will be presumed not to result in the receipt of cash or property by some shareholders and an increase in the proportionate interest of other shareholders, unless the receipt of cash or property and the distribution or series of distributions of stock are made pursuant to a plan. For example, if, pursuant to a plan, a corporation pays cash dividends to some shareholders on January 1, 1971 and increases the proportionate interests of other shareholders on March 1, 1974, such increases in proportionate interests are distributions to which section 301 applies.

(5) In determining whether a distribution or a series of distributions has the result of a disproportionate distribution, there shall be treated as outstanding stock of the distributing corporation (i) any right to acquire such stock (whether or not exercisable during the taxable year), and (ii) any security convertible into stock of the distributing corporation (whether or not convertible during the taxable year).

(6) In cases where there is more than one class of stock outstanding, each class of stock is to be considered separately in determining whether a shareholder has increased his proportionate interest in the assets or earnings and profits of a corporation. The individual shareholders of a class of stock will be deemed to have an increased interest if the class of stock as a whole has an increased interest in the corporation.

(c) *Distributions of cash in lieu of fractional shares.*—(1) Section 305(b)(2) will not apply if—

(i) A corporation declares a dividend payable in stock of the corporation and distributes cash in lieu of fractional shares to which shareholders would otherwise be entitled, or

(ii) Upon a conversion of convertible stock or securities a corporation distributes cash in lieu of fractional shares to which shareholders would otherwise be entitled.

Provided the purpose of the distribution of cash is to save the corporation the trouble, expense, and inconvenience of issuing and transferring fractional shares (or scrip representing fractional shares), or issuing full shares representing the sum of fractional shares, and not to give any particular group of shareholders an increased interest in the asset or earnings and profits of the corporation. For purposes of paragraph (c)(1)(i) of this section, if the total amount of cash distributed in lieu of fractional shares is 5 percent or less of the total fair market value of the stock distributed (determined as of the date of declaration), the distribution shall be considered to be for such valid purpose.

(2) In a case to which subparagraph (1) of this paragraph applies, the transaction will be treated as though the fractional shares were distributed as part of the stock distribution and then were redeemed by the corporation. The treatment of the cash received by a shareholder will be determined under section 302.

(d) *Adjustment in conversion ratio.*—(1)(i) Except as provided in subparagraph (2) of this paragraph, if a corporation has convertible stock or convertible securities outstanding (upon which it pays or is deemed to pay dividends or interest in money or other property) and distributes a stock dividend (or rights to acquire such stock) with respect to the stock into which the convertible stock or securities are convertible, an increase in proportionate interest in the assets or earnings and profits of the corporation by reason of such stock dividend shall be considered to have occurred unless a full adjustment in the conversion ratio or conversion price to reflect such stock dividend is made. Under certain circumstances, however, the application of an adjustment formula which in effect provides for a "credit" where stock is issued for consideration in excess of the conversion price may not satisfy the requirement for a "full adjustment". Thus, if under a "conversion price" antidilution formula the formula provides for a "credit" where stock is issued for consideration in excess of the conversion price (in effect as an offset against any decrease in the conversion price which would otherwise be required when stock is subsequently issued for consideration below the conversion price) there may still be an increase in proportionate interest by reason of a stock dividend after application of the formula, since any downward adjustment of the conversion price that would otherwise be required to reflect the stock dividend may be offset, in whole or in part, by the effect of prior sales made at prices above the conversion price. On the other hand, if there were no prior sales of stock above the conversion price then a full adjustment would occur upon the application of such an adjustment formula and there would be no change in proportionate interest. Similarly, if consideration is to be received in connection with the issuance of stock, such as in the case of a rights offering or a distribution of warrants, the fact that such consideration is taken into account in making the antidilution adjustment will not preclude a full adjustment. See paragraph *(b)* of the example in this subparagraph for a case where the application of an adjustment formula with a cumulative feature does not result in a full adjustment and where a change in proportionate interest therefore occurs. See paragraph *(c)* for a case where the application of an adjustment formula with a cumulative feature does result in a full adjustment and where no change in proportionate interest therefore occurs. See paragraph *(d)* for an application of an antidilution formula in the case of a rights offering. See paragraph *(e)* for a case where the application of a noncumulative type adjustment formula will in all cases prevent a change in proportionate interest from occurring in the case of a stock dividend, because of the omission of the cumulative feature.

(ii) The principles of this subparagraph may be illustrated by the following example:

Example. (a) Corporation S has two classes of securities outstanding, convertible debentures and common stock. At the time of issuance of the debentures the corporation had 100 shares of common stock outstanding. Each debenture is interest-paying and is convertible into common stock at a conversion price of $2. The debenture's conversion price is subject to reduction pursuant to the following formula:

(Number of common shares outstanding at date of issue of debentures times initial conversion price)

plus

(Consideration received upon issuance of additional common shares)

divided by

(Number of common shares outstanding at date of issue of debentures)

plus

(Number of additional common shares issued)

Under the formula, common stock dividends are treated as an issue of common stock for zero consideration. If the computation results in a figure which is less than the existing conversion price the conversion price is reduced. However, under the formula, the existing conversion price is never increased. The formula works upon a cumulative basis since the numerator includes the consideration received upon the issuance of all common shares subsequent to the issuance of the debentures, and the reduction effected by the formula because of a sale or issuance of common stock below the existing conversion price is thus limited by any prior sales made above the existing conversion price.

(b) In 1972 corporation S sells 100 common shares at $3 per share. In 1973 the corporation declares a stock dividend of 20 shares to all holders of common stock. Under the antidilution formula no adjustment will be made to the conversion price of the debentures to reflect the stock dividend to common stockholders since the prior sale of common stock in excess of the conversion price in 1972 offsets the reduction in the conversion price which would otherwise result, as follows:

$$100 \times \$2 + \$300 \div 100 + 120 = \frac{\$500}{220} = \$2.27$$

Since $2.27 is greater than the existing conversion price of $2 no adjustment is required. As a result, there is an increase in proportionate interest of the common stockholders by reason of the stock dividend and the additional shares of common stock will be treated, pursuant to section 305(b)(2), as a distribution of property to which section 301 applies.

(c) Assume the same facts as above, but instead of selling 100 common shares at $3 per share in 1972, assume corporation S sold no shares. Application of the antidilution formula would give rise to an adjustment in the conversion price as follows:

$$100 \times \$2 + \$0 \div 100 + 20 = \frac{\$200}{220} = \$1.67$$

The conversion price, being reduced from $2 to $1.67, fully reflects the stock dividend distributed to the common stockholders. Hence, the distribution of common stock is not treated under section 305(b)(2) as one to which section 301 applies because the distribution does not increase the proportionate interests of the common shareholders as a class.

(d) Corporation S distributes to its shareholders rights entitling the shareholders to purchase a total of 20 shares at $1 per share. Application of the antidilution formula would produce an adjustment in the conversion price as follows:

$$100 \times \$2 + 20 \times \$1 \div 100 + 20 = \frac{\$220}{120} = \$1.83$$

The conversion price, being reduced from $2 to $1.83, fully reflects the distribution of rights to purchase stock at a price lower than the conversion price. Hence, the distribution of the rights is not treated under section 305(b)(2) as one to which section 301 applies because the distribution does not increase the proportionate interests of the common shareholders as a class.

(e) Assume the same facts as in *(b)* above, but instead of using a "conversion price" antidilution formula which operates on a cumulative basis, assume corporation S has employed a formula which operates as follows with respect to all stock dividends: The conversion price in effect at the opening of business on the day following the dividend record date is reduced by multiplying such conversion price

by a fraction the numerator of which is the number of shares of common stock outstanding at the close of business on the record date and the denominator of which is the sum of such shares so outstanding and the number of shares constituting the stock dividend. Under such a formula the following adjustment would be made to the conversion price upon the declaration of a stock dividend of 20 shares in 1973:

$$200 \div 200 + 20 = \frac{200}{220} \times \$2 = \$1.82$$

The conversion price, being reduced from $2 to $1.82, fully reflects the stock dividend distributed to the common stockholders. Hence, the distribution of common stock is not treated under section 305(b)(2) as one to which section 301 applies because the distribution does not increase the proportionate interests of the common shareholders as a class.

(2)(i) A distributing corporation either must make the adjustment required by subparagraph (1) of this paragraph as of the date of the distribution of the stock dividend, or must elect (in the manner provided in subdivision (iii) of this subparagraph) to make such adjustment within the time provided in subdivision (ii) of this subparagraph.

(ii) If the distributing corporation elects to make such adjustment, such adjustment must be made no later than the earlier of *(a)* 3 years after the date of the stock dividend, or *(b)* that date as of which the aggregate stock dividends for which adjustment of the conversion ratio has not previously been made total at least 3 percent of the issued and outstanding stock with respect to which such stock dividends were distributed.

(iii) The election provided by subdivision (ii) of this subparagraph shall be made by filing with the income tax return for the taxable year during which the stock dividend is distributed—

(a) A statement that an adjustment will be made as provided by that subdivision, and

(b) A description of the antidilution provisions under which the adjustment will be made.

(3) Notwithstanding the preceding subparagraph, if a distribution has been made before July 12, 1973, and the adjustment required by subparagraph (1) or the election to make such adjustment was not made before such date, the adjustment or the election to make such adjustment, as the case may be, shall be considered valid if made no later than 15 days following the date of the first annual meeting of the shareholders after July 12, 1973, or July 12, 1974, whichever is earlier. If the election is made within such period, and if the income tax return has been filed before the time of such election, the statement of adjustment and the description of the antidilution provisions required by subparagraph (2)(iii) shall be filed with the Internal Revenue Service Center with which the income tax return was filed.

(4) See § 1.305-7(b) for a discussion of antidilution adjustments in connection with the application of section 305(c) in conjunction with section 305(b).

(e) *Examples.*—The application of section 305(b)(2) to distributions of stock and section 305(c) to deemed distributions of stock may be illustrated by the following examples:

Example 1. Corporation X is organized with two classes of common stock, class A and class B. Each share of stock is entitled to share equally in the assets and earnings and profits of the corporation. Dividends may be paid in stock or in cash on either class of stock without regard to the medium of payment of dividends on the other class. A dividend is declared on the class A stock payable in additional shares of class A stock and a dividend is declared on class B stock payable in cash. Since the class A shareholders as a class will have increased their proportionate interests in the assets and earnings and profits of the corporation and the class B shareholders will have received cash, the additional shares of class A stock are distributions of property to which section 301 applies. This is true even with respect to those shareholders who may own class A stock and class B stock in the same proportion.

Example 2. Corporation Y is organized with two classes of stock, class A common, and class B, which is nonconvertible and limited and preferred as to dividends. A dividend is declared upon the class A stock payable in additional shares of class A stock and a dividend is declared on the class B stock payable in cash. The distribution of class A stock is not one to which section 301 applies because the distribution does not increase the proportionate interests of the class A shareholders as a class.

Example 3. Corporation K is organized with two classes of stock, class A common, and class B, which is nonconvertible preferred stock. A dividend is declared upon the class A stock payable in shares of class B stock and a dividend is declared on the class B stock payable in cash. Since the class A shareholders as a class have an increased interest in the assets and earnings and profits of the corporation, the stock distribution is treated as a distribution to which section 301 applies. If, however, a dividend were declared upon the class A stock payable in a new class of preferred stock that is subordinated in all respects to the class B stock, the distribution would not increase the proportionate interests of the class A shareholders in the assets or earnings and profits of the corporation and would not be treated as a distribution to which section 301 applies.

Example 4. (i) Corporation W has one class of stock outstanding, class A common. The corporation also has outstanding interest paying securities convertible into class A common stock which have a fixed conversion ratio that is not subject to a full adjustment in the event stock dividends or rights are distributed to the class A shareholders. Corporation W distributes to the class A shareholders rights to acquire additional shares of class A stock. During the year, interest is paid on the convertible securities.

(ii) The stock rights and convertible securities are considered to be outstanding stock of the corporation and the distribution increases the proportionate interests of the class A shareholders in the assets and earnings and profits of the corporation. Therefore, the distribution is treated as a distribution to which section 301 applies. The same result would follow if, instead of convertible securities, the corporation had outstanding convertible stock. If, however, the conversion ratio of the securities or stock were fully adjusted to reflect the distribution of rights to the class A shareholders, the rights to acquire class A stock would not increase the proportionate interests of the class A shareholders in the assets or earnings and profits of the corporation and would not be treated as a distribution to which section 301 applies.

Example 5. (i) Corporation S is organized with two classes of stock, class A common and class B convertible preferred. The class B is fully protected against dilution in the event of a stock dividend or stock split with respect to the class A stock; however, no adjustment in the conversion ratio is required to be made until the stock dividends equal 3 percent of the common stock issued and outstanding on the date of the first such stock dividend except that such adjustment must be made no later than 3 years after the date of the stock dividend. Cash dividends are paid annually on the class B stock.

(ii) Corporation S pays a 1 percent stock dividend on the class A stock in 1973. In 1974, another 1 percent stock dividend is paid and in 1975 another 1 percent stock dividend is paid. The conversion ratio of the class B stock is increased in 1975 to reflect the three stock dividends paid on the class A stock. The distributions of class A stock are not distributions to which section 301 applies because they do not increase the proportionate interests of the class A shareholders in the assets or earnings and profits of the corporation.

Example 6. (i) Corporation M is organized with two classes of stock outstanding, class A and class B. Each class B share may be converted, at the option of the holder, into class A shares. During the first year, the conversion ratio is one share of class A stock for each share of class B stock. At the beginning of each subsequent year, the conversion ratio is increased by 0.05 share of class A stock for each share of class B stock. Thus, during the second year, the conversion ratio would be 1.05 shares of class A stock for each share of class B stock, during the third year, the ratio would be 1.10 shares, etc.

(ii) M pays an annual cash dividend on the class A stock. At the beginning of the second year, when the conversion ratio is increased to 1.05 shares of class A stock for each share of class B stock, a distribution of 0.05 shares of class A stock is deemed made under section 305(c) with respect to each share of class B stock, since the proportionate interests of the class B shareholders in the assets or earnings and profits of M are increased and the transaction has the effect described in section 305(b)(2). Accordingly, sections 305(b)(2) and 301 apply to the transaction.

Example 7. (i) Corporation N has two classes of stock outstanding, class A and class B. Each class B share is convertible into class A stock. However, in accordance with a specified formula, the conversion ratio is decreased each time a cash dividend is paid on the class B stock to reflect the amount of the cash dividend. The conversion ratio is also adjusted in the event that cash dividends are paid on the class A stock to increase the number of class A shares into which the class B shares are convertible to compensate the class B shareholders for the cash dividend paid on the class A stock.

(ii) In 1972, a $1 cash dividend per share is declared and paid on the class B stock. On the date of payment, the conversion ratio of the class B stock is decreased. A distribution of stock is deemed made under section 305(c) to the class A shareholders, since the proportionate interest of the class A shareholders in the assets or earnings and profits of the corporation is increased and the transaction has the effect described in section 305(b)(2). Accordingly, sections 305(b)(2) and 301 apply to the transaction.

(iii) In the following year a cash dividend is paid on the class A stock and none is paid on the class B stock. The increase in conversion rights of the class B shares is deemed to be a distribution under section 305(c) to the class B shareholders since their proportionate interest in the assets or earnings and profits of the corporation is increased and since the transaction has the effect described in section

305(b)(2). Accordingly, sections 305(b)(2) and 301 apply to the transaction.

Example 8. Corporation T has 1,000 shares of stock outstanding. C owns 100 shares. Nine other shareholders each owns 100 shares. Pursuant to a plan for periodic redemptions, T redeems up to 5 percent of each shareholder's stock each year. During the year, each of the nine other shareholders has five shares of his stock redeemed for cash. Thus, C's proportionate interest in the assets and earnings and profits of T is increased. Assuming that the cash received by the nine other shareholders is taxable under section 301, C is deemed under section 305(c) to have received a distribution under section 305(b)(2) of 5.25 shares of T stock to which section 301 applies. The amount of C's distribution is measured by the fair market value of the number of shares which would have been distributed to C had the corporation sought to increase his interest by 0.47 percentage points (C owned 10 percent of the T stock immediately before the redemption and 10.47 percent immediately thereafter) and the other shareholders continued to hold 900 shares (*i.e.*,

(a) $\frac{100}{955}$ = 10.47% (percent of C's ownership after redemption);

(b) $\frac{100 + X}{1000 + X}$ = 10.47%; X = 5.25 (additional shares considered to be distributed to C)).

Since in computing the amount of additional shares deemed to be distributed to C the redemption of shares is disregarded, the redemption of shares will be similarly disregarded in determining the value of the stock of the corporation which is deemed to be distributed. Thus, in the example, 1,005.25 shares of stock are considered as outstanding after the redemption. The value of each share deemed to be distributed to C is then determined by dividing the 1,005.25 shares into the aggregate fair market value of the actual shares outstanding (955) after the redemption.

* * *

Example 10. Corporation P has 1,000 shares of stock outstanding. T owns 700 shares of the P stock and G owns 300 shares of the P stock. In a single and isolated redemption to which section 301 applies, the corporation redeems 150 shares of T's stock. Since this is an isolated redemption and is not a part of a periodic redemption plan, G is not treated as having received a deemed distribution under section 305(c) to which sections 305(b)(2) and 301 apply even though he has an increased proportionate interest in the assets and earnings and profits of the corporation.

* * *

Example 12. Corporation R has 2,000 shares of class A stock outstanding. Five shareholders own 300 shares each and five shareholders own 100 shares each. In preparation for the retirement of the five major shareholders, corporation R, in a single and isolated transaction, has a recapitalization in which each share of class A stock may be exchanged either for five shares of new class B nonconvertible preferred stock plus 0.4 share of new class C common stock, or for two shares of new class C common stock. As a result of the exchanges, each of the five major shareholders receives 1,500 shares of class B nonconvertible preferred stock and 120 shares of class C common stock. The remaining shareholders each receives 200 shares of class C common stock. None of the exchanges are within the purview of section 305.

Example 13. Corporation P is a widely-held company whose shares are listed for trading on a stock exchange. P distributes annual cash dividends to its shareholders. P purchases shares of its common stock directly from small stockholders (holders of record of 100 shares or less) or through brokers where the holders may not be known at the time of purchase. Where such purchases are made through brokers, they are pursuant to the rules and regulations of the Securities and Exchange Commission. The shares are purchased for the purpose of issuance to employee stock investment plans, to holders of convertible stock or debt, to holders of stock options, or for future acquisitions. Provided the purchases are not pursuant to a plan to increase the proportionate interest of some shareholders and distribute property to other shareholders, thus the remaining shareholders of P are not treated as having received a deemed distribution under section 305 to which section 305(b)(2) and 301 apply, even though they have an increased proportionate interest in the assets and earnings and profits of the corporation.

* * *

Example 15. (i) *Facts.* Corporation V is organized with two classes of stock, class A common and class B convertible preferred. The class B stock is issued for $100 per share and is convertible at the holder's option into class A at a fixed ratio that is not subject to full adjustment in the event stock dividends or rights are distributed to the class A shareholders. The class B stock pays no dividends but it is mandatorily redeemable in 10 years for $200. Under sections 305(c) and 305(b)(4), the entire redemption premium (i.e., the excess of the redemption price over the issue price) is deemed to be a distribution of preferred stock on preferred stock which is taxable as a distribution of property under section 301. This amount is considered to be distributed over the 10-year period under principles similar to the principles of section 1272(a). During the year, the corporation declares a dividend on the class A stock payable in additional shares of class A stock.

(ii) *Analysis.* The distribution on the class A stock is a distribution to which sections 305(b)(2) and 301 apply since it increases the proportionate interests of the class A shareholders in the assets and earnings and profits of the corporation and the class B shareholders have received property (i.e., the constructive distribution described above). If, however, the conversion ratio of the class B stock were subject to full adjustment to reflect the distribution of stock to class A shareholders, the distribution of stock dividends on the class A stock would not increase the proportionate interest of the class A shareholders in the assets and earnings and profits of the corporation and such distribution would not be a distribution to which section 301 applies.

* * *

[Reg. § 1.305-3.]

☐ [*T.D.* 6152, 12-2-55. *Amended by T.D.* 6990, 1-10-69, *T.D.* 7004, 2-7-69, *T.D.* 7281, 7-11-73, *T.D.* 7329, 10-11-74 *and T.D.* 8643, 12-20-95.]

§ 1.305-4. Distributions of common and preferred stock.—(a) *In general.*—Under section 305(b)(3), a distribution (or a series of distributions) by a corporation which results in the receipt of preferred stock (whether or not convertible into common stock) by some common shareholders and the receipt of common stock by other common shareholders is treated as a distribution of property to which section 301 applies. For the meaning of the term "a series of distributions", see subparagraphs (1) through (6) of § 1.305-3(b).

(b) *Examples.*—The application of section 305(b)(3) may be illustrated by the following examples:

Example (1). Corporation X is organized with two classes of common stock, class A and class B. Dividends may be paid in stock or in cash on either class of stock without regard to the medium of payment of dividends on the other class. A dividend is declared on the class A stock payable in additional shares of class A stock and a dividend is declared on class B stock payable in newly authorized class C stock which is nonconvertible and limited and preferred as to dividends. Both the distribution of class A shares and the distribution of new class C shares are distributions to which section 301 applies.

Example (2). Corporation Y is organized with one class of stock, class A common. During the year the corporation declares a dividend on the class A stock payable in newly authorized class B preferred stock which is convertible into class A stock no later than 6 months from the date of distribution at a price that is only slightly higher than the market price of class A stock on the date of distribution. Taking into account the dividend rate, redemption provisions, the marketability of the convertible stock, and the conversion price, it is reasonable to anticipate that within a relatively short period of time some shareholders will exercise their conversion rights and some will not. Since the distribution can reasonably be expected to result in the receipt of preferred stock by some common shareholders and the receipt of common stock by other common shareholders, the distribution is a distribution of property to which section 301 applies. [Reg. § 1.305-4.]

☐ [*T.D.* 7281, 7-11-73.]

§ 1.305-5. Distributions on preferred stock.—(a) *In general.*—Under section 305(b)(4), a distribution by a corporation of its stock (or rights to acquire its stock) made (or deemed made under section 305(c)) with respect to its preferred stock is treated as a distribution of property to which section 301 applies unless the distribution is made with respect to convertible preferred stock to take into account a stock dividend, stock split, or any similar event (such as the sale of stock at less than the fair market value pursuant to a rights offering) which would otherwise result in the dilution of the conversion right. For purposes of the preceding sentence, an adjustment in the conversion ratio of convertible preferred stock made solely to take into account the distribution by a closed-end regulated investment company of a capital gain dividend with respect to the stock into which such stock is convertible shall not be considered a "similar event". The term "preferred stock" generally refers to stock which, in relation to other classes of stock outstanding enjoys certain limited rights and privileges (generally associated with specified dividend and liquidation priorities) but does not participate in corporate growth to any significant extent. The distinguishing feature of "preferred stock" for the purposes of section 305(b)(4) is not its privileged position as such, but that such privileged position is limited and that such stock does not participate in corporate growth to any significant extent. However, a right to participate which lacks substance will not prevent a class of stock from being treated as preferred stock. Thus, stock which enjoys a priority as to dividends and on liquidation but which is entitled to participate, over and above such priority, with another less privileged class of stock in earnings and profits and upon liquidation, may nevertheless be treated as preferred stock for purposes of section 305 if, taking into account all the facts and circumstances, it is reasonable to anticipate at the time a distribution is made (or is deemed to have been made) with respect to such stock that there is little or no likelihood of such stock actually participating in current and anticipated earnings and upon liquidation beyond its preferred interest. Among the facts and circumstances to be considered are the prior and anticipated earnings per share, the cash dividends per share, the book value per share, the extent of preference and of participation of each class, both absolutely and relative to each other, and any other facts which indicate whether or not the stock has a real and meaningful probability of actually participating in the earnings and growth of the corporation. The determination of whether stock is preferred for purposes of section 305 shall be made without regard to any right to convert such stock into another class of stock of the corporation. The term "preferred stock", however, does not include convertible debentures.

(b) *Redemption premium.*—(1) *In general.*—If a corporation issues preferred stock that may be redeemed under the circumstances described in this paragraph (b) at a price higher than the issue price, the difference (the redemption premium) is treated under section 305(c) as a constructive distribution (or series of constructive distributions) of additional stock on preferred stock that is taken into account under principles similar to the principles of section 1272(a). However, constructive distribution treatment does not result under this paragraph (b) if the redemption premium does not exceed a de minimis amount, as determined under the principles of section 1273(a)(3). For purposes of this paragraph (b), preferred stock that may be acquired by a person other than the issuer (the third person) is deemed to be redeemable under the circumstances described in this paragraph (b), and references to the issuer include the third person, if—

(i) this paragraph (b) would apply to the stock if the third person were the issuer; and

(ii) either—

(A) the acquisition of the stock by the third person would be treated as a redemption for federal income tax purposes (under section 304 or otherwise); or

(B) the third person and the issuer are members of the same affiliated group (having the meaning for this purpose given the term by section 1504(a), except that section 1504(b) shall not apply) and a principal purpose of the arrangement for the third person to acquire the stock is to avoid the application of section 305 and paragraph (b)(1) of this section.

(2) *Mandatory redemption or holder put.*—Paragraph (b)(1) of this section applies to stock if the issuer is required to redeem the stock at a specified time or the holder has the option (whether or not currently exercisable) to require the issuer to redeem the stock. However, paragraph (b)(1) of this section will not apply if the issuer's obligation to redeem or the holder's ability to require the issuer to redeem is subject to a contingency that is beyond the legal or practical control of either the holder or the holders as a group (or through a related party within the meaning of section 267(b) or 707(b)), and that, based on all of the facts and circumstances as of the issue date, renders remote the likelihood of redemption. For purposes of this paragraph, a contingency does not include the possibility of default, insolvency, or similar circumstances, or that a redemption may be precluded by applicable law which requires that the issuer have a particular level of capital, surplus, or similar items. A contingency also does not include an issuer's option to require earlier redemption of the stock. For rules applicable if stock may be redeemed at more than one time, see paragraph (b)(4) of this section.

(3) *Issuer call.*—(i) *In general.*—Paragraph (b)(1) of this section applies to stock by reason of the issuer's right to redeem the stock (even if the right is immediately exercisable), but only if, based on all of the facts and circumstances as of the issue date, redemption pursuant to that right is more likely than not to occur. However, even if redemption is more likely than not to occur, paragraph (b)(1) of this section does not apply if the redemption premium is solely in the nature of a penalty for premature redemption. A redemption premium is not a penalty for premature redemption unless it is a premium paid as a result of changes in economic or market conditions over which neither the issuer nor the holder has legal or practical control.

(ii) *Safe harbor.*—For purposes of this paragraph (b)(3), redemption pursuant to an issuer's right to redeem is not treated as more likely than not to occur if—

(A) The issuer and the holder are not related within the meaning of section 267(b) or 707(b) (for purposes of applying sections 267(b) and 707(b) (including section 267(f)(1)), the phrase "20 percent" shall be substituted for the phrase "50 percent");

(B) There are no plans, arrangements, or agreements that effectively require or are intended to compel the issuer to redeem the stock (disregarding, for this purpose, a separate mandatory redemption obligation described in paragraph (b)(2) of this section); and

(C) Exercise of the right to redeem would not reduce the yield of the stock, as determined under principles similar to the principles of section 1272(a) and the regulations under sections 1271 through 1275.

(iii) *Effect of not satisfying safe harbor.*—The fact that a redemption right is not described in paragraph (b)(3)(ii) of this section does not affect the determination of whether a redemption pursuant to the right to redeem is more likely than not to occur.

(4) *Coordination of multiple redemption provisions.*—If stock may be redeemed at more than one time, the time and price at which redemption is most likely to occur must be determined based on all of the facts and circumstances as of the issue date. Any constructive distribution under paragraph (b)(1) of this section will result only with respect to the time and price identified in the preceding sentence. However, if redemption does not occur at that identified time, the amount of any additional premium payable on any later redemption date, to the extent not previously treated as distributed, is treated as a constructive distribution over the period from the missed call or put date to that later date, to the extent required under the principles of this paragraph (b).

(5) *Consistency.*—The issuer's determination as to whether there is a constructive distribution under this paragraph (b) is binding on all holders of the stock, other than a holder that explicitly discloses that its determination as to whether there is a constructive distribution under this paragraph (b) differs from that of the issuer. Unless otherwise prescribed by the Commissioner, the disclosure must be made on a statement attached to the holder's timely filed federal income tax return for the taxable year that includes the date the holder acquired the stock. The issuer must provide the relevant information to the holder in a reasonable manner. For example, the issuer may provide the name or title and either the address or telephone number of a representative of the issuer who will make available to holders upon request the information required for holders to comply with this provision of this paragraph (b).

* * *

[Reg. § 1.305-5.]

☐ [*T.D.* 7281, 7-11-73. *Amended by T.D.* 7329, 10-11-74 *and T.D.* 8643, 12-20-95.]

§ 1.305-6. Distributions of convertible preferred.—(a) *In general.*—(1) Under section 305(b)(5), a distribution by a corporation of its convertible preferred stock or rights to acquire such stock made or considered as made with respect to its stock is treated as a distribution of property to which section 301 applies unless the corporation establishes that such distribution will not result in a disproportionate distribution as described in § 1.305-3.

(2) The distribution of convertible preferred stock is likely to result in a disproportionate distribution when both of the following conditions exist: (i) The conversion right must be exercised within a relatively short period of time after the date of distribution of the stock; and (ii) taking into account such factors as the dividend rate, the redemption provisions, the marketability of the convertible stock, and the conversion price, it may be anticipated that some shareholders will exercise their conversion rights and some will not. On the other hand, where the conversion right may be exercised over a period of many years and the dividend rate is consistent with market conditions at the time of distribution of the stock, there is no basis for predicting at what time and the extent to which the stock will be converted and it is unlikely that a disproportionate distribution will result.

(b) *Examples.*—The application of section 305(b)(5) may be illustrated by the following examples:

Example (1). Corporation Z is organized with one class of stock, class A common. During the year the corporation declares a dividend on the class A stock payable in newly authorized class B preferred stock which is convertible into class A stock for a period of 20 years from the date of issuance. Assuming dividend rates are normal in light of existing conditions so that there is no basis for predicting the extent to which the stock will be converted, these circumstances will ordinarily be sufficient to establish that a disproportionate distribution will not result since it is impossible to predict the extent to which the class B stock will be converted into class A stock. Accordingly, the distribution of class B stock is not one to which section 301 applies.

Example (2). Corporation X is organized with one class of stock, class A common. During the year the corporation declares a dividend on the class A stock payable in newly authorized redeemable class C preferred stock which is convertible into class A common stock no later than 4 months from the date of distribution at a price slightly higher than the market price of class A stock on the date of distribution. By prearrangement with corporation X, corporation Y, an insurance company, agrees to purchase class C stock from any shareholder who does not wish to convert. By reason of this prearrangement, it is anticipated that the shareholders will either sell the class C stock to the insurance company (which expects to retain the shares for investment purposes) or will convert. As a result, some of the shareholders exercise their conversion privilege and receive additional shares of class A stock, while other shareholders sell their class C stock to corporation Y and receive cash. The distribution is a distribution to which section 301 applies since it results in the receipt of property by some shareholders and an increase in the proportionate interests of other shareholders. [Reg. § 1.305-6.]

□ [*T.D.* 7281, 7-11-73.]

§ 1.305-7. Certain transactions treated as distributions.—(a) *In general.*—Under section 305(c), a change in conversion ratio, a change in redemption price, a difference between redemption price and issue price, a redemption which is treated as a distribution to which section 301 applies, or any transaction (including a recapitalization) having a similar effect on the interest of any shareholder may be treated as a distribution with respect to any shareholder whose proportionate interest in the earnings and profits or assets of the corporation is increased by such change, difference, redemption, or similar transaction. In general, such change, difference, redemption, or similar transaction will be treated as a distribution to which sections 305(b) and 301 apply where—

(1) The proportionate interest of any shareholder in the earnings and profits or assets of the corporation deemed to have made such distribution is increased by such change, difference, redemption, or similar transaction; and

(2) Such distribution has the result described in paragraph (2), (3), (4), or (5) of section 305(b).

Where such change, difference, redemption, or similar transaction is treated as a distribution under the provisions of this section, such distribution will be deemed made with respect to any shareholder whose interest in the earnings and profits or assets of the distributing corporation is increased thereby. Such distribution will be deemed to be a distribution of the stock of such corporation made by the corporation to such shareholder with respect to his stock. Depending upon the facts presented, the distribution may be deemed to be made in common or preferred stock. For example, where a redemption premium exists with respect to a class of preferred stock under the circumstances described in § 1.305-5(b) and the other requirements of this section are also met, the distribution will be deemed made with respect to such preferred stock, in stock of the same class. Accordingly, the preferred shareholders are considered under sections 305(b)(4) and 305(c) to have received a distribution of preferred stock to which section 301 applies. See the examples in §§ 1.305-3(e) and 1.305-5(d) for further illustrations of the application of section 305(c).

(b) *Antidilution provisions.*—(1) For purposes of applying section 305(c) in conjunction with section 305(b), a change in the conversion ratio or conversion price of convertible preferred stock (or securities), or in the exercise price of rights or warrants, made pursuant to a bona fide, reasonable, adjustment formula (including, but not limited to, either the so-called "market price" or "conversion price" type of formulas) which has the effect of preventing dilution of the interest of the holders of such stock (or securities) will not be considered to result in a deemed distribution of stock. An adjustment in the conversion ratio or price to compensate for cash or property distributions to other shareholders that are taxable under section 301, 356(a)(2), 871(a)(1)(A), 881(a)(1), 852(b), or 857(b) will not be considered as made pursuant to a bona fide adjustment formula.

(2) The principles of this paragraph may be illustrated by the following example:

Example. (i) Corporation U has two classes of stock outstanding, class A and class B. Each class B share is convertible into class A stock. In accordance with a bona fide, reasonable, antidilution provision, the conversion price is adjusted if the corporation transfers class A stock to anyone for a consideration that is below the conversion price.

(ii) The corporation sells class A stock to the public at the current market price but below the conversion price. Pursuant to the antidilution provision, the conversion price is adjusted downward. Such a change in conversion price will not be deemed to be a distribution under section 305(c) for the purposes of section 305(b).

(c) *Recapitalizations.*—(1) A recapitalization (whether or not an isolated transaction) will be deemed to result in a distribution to which section 305(c) and this section apply if—

(i) It is pursuant to a plan to periodically increase a shareholder's proportionate interest in the assets or earnings and profits of the corporation, or

(ii) A shareholder owning preferred stock with dividends in arrears exchanges his stock for other stock and, as a result, increases his proportionate interest in the assets or earnings and profits of the corporation. An increase in a preferred shareholder's proportionate interest occurs in any case where the fair market value or the liquidation preference, whichever is greater, of the stock received in the exchange (determined immediately following the recapitalization), exceeds the issue price of the preferred stock surrendered.

(2) In a case to which subparagraph (1)(ii) of this paragraph applies, the amount of the distribution deemed under section 305(c) to result from the recapitalization is the lesser of (i) the amount by which the fair market value or the liquidation preference, whichever is greater, of the stock received in the exchange (determined immediately following the recapitalization) exceeds the issue price of the preferred stock surrendered, or (ii) the amount of the dividends in arrears.

(3) For purposes of applying subparagraphs (1) and (2) of this paragraph with respect to stock issued before July 12, 1973, the term "issue price of the preferred stock surrendered" shall mean the greater of the issue price or the liquidation preference (not including dividends in arrears) of the stock surrendered.

(4) For an illustration of the application of this paragraph, see example (12) of § 1.305-3(e) and examples (1), (2), (3), and (6) of § 1.305-5(d).

(5) For rules relating to redemption premiums on preferred stock, see § 1.305-5(b) [Reg. § 1.305-7.]

□ [*T.D.* 7281, 7-11-73. *Amended by T.D.* 8643, 12-20-95.]

§ 1.306-1. General.—(a) Section 306 provides, in general, that the proceeds from the sale or redemption of certain stock (referred to as "section 306 stock") shall be treated either as ordinary income or as a distribution of property to which section 301 applies. Section 306 stock is defined in section 306(c) and is usually preferred stock received either as a nontaxable dividend or in a transaction in which no gain or loss is recognized. Section 306(b) lists certain circumstances in which the special rules of section 306(a) shall not apply.

(b)(1) If a shareholder sells or otherwise disposes of section 306 stock (other than by redemption or within the exceptions listed in section 306(b)), the entire proceeds received from such disposition shall be treated as ordinary income to the extent that the fair market value of the stock sold, on the date distributed to the shareholder, would have been a dividend to such shareholder had the distributing corporation distributed cash in lieu of stock. Any excess of the amount received over the sum of the amount treated as ordinary income plus the adjusted basis of the stock disposed of shall be treated as gain from the sale of a capital asset or noncapital asset as the case may be. No loss shall be recognized. No reduction of earnings and profits results from any disposition of stock other than a redemption. The term "disposition" under section 306(a)(1) includes, among other things, pledges of stock under certain circumstances, particularly where the pledgee can look only to the stock itself as its security.

(2) Section 306(a)(1) may be illustrated by the following examples:

Example (1). On December 15, 1954, A and B owned equally all of the stock of Corporation X which files its income tax return on a calendar year basis. On that date Corporation X distributed pro rata 100 shares of preferred stock as a dividend on its outstanding common stock. On December 15, 1954, the preferred stock had a fair market value of $10,000. On December 31, 1954, the earnings and profits of Corporation X were $20,000. The 50 shares of preferred stock so distributed to A had an allocated basis to him of $10 per share or a total of $500 for the 50 shares. Such shares had a fair market value of $5,000 when issued. A sold the 50 shares of preferred stock on July 1, 1955, for $6,000. Of this amount $5,000 will be treated as ordinary income; $500 ($6,000 minus $5,500) will be treated as gain from the sale of a capital or noncapital asset as the case may be.

Example (2). The facts are the same as in example 1 except that A sold his 50 shares of preferred stock for $5,100. Of this amount $5,000 will be treated as ordinary income. No loss will be allowed. There will be added back to the basis of the common stock of Corporation X with respect to which the preferred stock was distributed, $400, the allocated basis of $500 reduced by the $100 received.

Example (3). The facts are the same as in example 1 except that A sold 25 of his shares of preferred stock for $2,600. Of this amount $2,500 will be treated as ordinary income. No loss will be allowed. There will be added back to the basis of the common stock of Corporation X with respect to which the preferred stock was distributed, $150, the allocated basis of $250 reduced by the $100 received.

(c) The entire amount received by a shareholder from the redemption of section 306 stock shall be treated as a distribution of property under section 301. See also section 303 (relating to distribution in redemption of stock to pay death taxes). [Reg. § 1.306-1.]

□ [*T.D.* 6152, 12-2-55. *Amended by T.D.* 7556, 8-2-78.]

§ 1.307-1. General.—(a) If a shareholder receives stock or stock rights as a distribution on stock previously held and under section 305 such distribution is not includible in gross income then, except as provided in section 307(b) and § 1.307-2, the basis of the stock with respect to which the distribution was made shall be allocated between the old and new stocks or rights in proportion to the fair market values of each on the date of distribution. If a shareholder receives stock or stock rights as a distribution on stock previously held and pursuant to section 305 part of the distribution is not includible in gross income, then (except as provided in section 307(b) and § 1.307-2) the basis of the stock with respect to which the distribution is made shall be allocated between (1) the old stock and (2) that part of the new stock or rights which is not includible in gross income, in proportion to the fair market values of each on the date of distribution. The date of distribution in each case shall be the date the stock or the rights are distributed to the stockholder and not the record date. The general rule will apply with respect to stock rights only if such rights are exercised or sold.

(b) The application of paragraph (a) of this section is illustrated by the following example:

Example. A taxpayer in 1947 purchased 100 shares of common stock at $100 per share and in 1954 by reason of the ownership of such stock acquired 100 rights entitling him to subscribe to 100 additional shares of such stock at $90 a share. Immediately after the issuance of the rights, each of the shares of stock in respect of which the rights were acquired had a fair market value, ex-rights, of $110 and the rights had a fair market value of $19 each. The basis of the rights and the common stock for the purpose of determining the basis for gain or loss on a subsequent sale or exercise of the rights or a sale of the old stock is computed as follows:

100 (shares) × $100	=	$10,000, cost of old stock (stock in respect of which the rights were acquired).
100 (shares) × $110	=	$11,000, market value of old stock.
100 (rights) × $ 19	=	$ 1,900, market value of rights.
11,000/12,900 of $10,000	=	$ 8,527.13, cost of old stock apportioned to such stock.
1,900/12,900 of $10,000	=	$ 1,472.87, cost of old stock apportioned to rights.

If the rights are sold, the basis for determining gain or loss will be $14.7287 per right. If the rights are exercised, the basis of the new stock acquired will be the subscription price paid therefor ($90) plus the basis of the rights exercised ($14.7287 each) or $104.7287 per share. The remaining basis of the old stock for the purpose of determining gain or loss on a subsequent sale will be $85.2713 per share. [Reg. § 1.307-1.]

□ [*T.D.* 6152, 12-2-55.]

§ 1.312-1. Adjustment to earnings and profits reflecting distributions by corporations.—(a) In general, on the distribution of property by a corporation with respect to its stock, its earnings and profits (to the extent thereof) shall be decreased by—

(1) The amount of money,

(2) The principal amount of the obligations of such corporation issued in such distribution, and

(3) The adjusted basis of other property.

For special rule with respect to distributions to which section 312(e) applies, see § 1.312-5.

(b) The adjustment provided in section 312(a)(3) and paragraph (a)(3) of this section with respect to a distribution of property (other than money or its own obligations) shall be made notwithstanding the fact that such property has appreciated or depreciated in value since acquisition.

(c) The application of paragraphs (a) and (b) of this section may be illustrated by the following examples:

Example (1). Corporation A distributes to its sole shareholder property with a value of $10,000 and a basis of $5,000. It has $12,500 in earnings and profits. The reduction in earnings and profits by reason of such distribution is $5,000. Such is the reduction even though the amount of $10,000 is includible in the income of the shareholder (other than a corporation) as a dividend.

Example (2). The facts are the same as in example (1) above except that the property has a basis of $15,000 and the earnings and profits of the corporation are $20,000. The reduction in earnings and profits is $15,000. Such is the reduction even though only the amount of $10,000 is includible in the income of the shareholder as a dividend.

(d) In the case of a distribution of stock or rights to acquire stock a portion of which is includible in income by reason of section 305(b), the earnings and profits shall be reduced by the fair market value of such portion. No reduction shall be made if a distribution of stock or rights to acquire stock is not includible in income under the provisions of section 305.

(e) No adjustment shall be made in the amount of the earnings and profits of the issuing corporation upon a disposition of section 306 stock unless such disposition is a redemption. [Reg. § 1.312-1.]

□ [*T.D.* 6152, 12-2-55.]

§ 1.312-2. Distributions of inventory assets.—Section 312(b) provides for the increase and the decrease of the earnings and profits of a corporation which distributes, with respect to its stock, inventory assets as defined in section 312(b)(2), where the fair market value of such assets exceeds their adjusted basis. The rules provided in section 312(b) (relating to distributions of certain inventory assets) shall be applicable without regard to the method used in computing inventories for the purpose of the computation of taxable income. Section 312(b) does not apply to distributions described in section 312(e). [Reg. § 1.312-2.]

□ [*T.D.* 6152, 12-2-55.]

§ 1.312-3. Liabilities.—The amount of any reductions in earnings and profits described in section 312(a) or (b) shall be (a) reduced by the amount of any liability to which the property distributed was subject and by the amount of any other liability of the corporation assumed by the shareholder in connection with such distribution, and (b) increased by the amount of gain recognized to the corporation under section 311(b), (c), or (d), or under section 341(f), 617(d), 1245(a), 1250(a), 1251(c), 1252(a), or 1254(a). [Reg. § 1.312-3.]

□ [*T.D.* 6152, 12-2-55. *Amended by T.D.* 6832, 7-6-65, *T.D.* 7084, 1-7-71; *T.D.* 7209, 10-3-72 *and T.D.* 8586, 1-9-95.]

➾ Caution: Reg. § 1.312-6 does not reflect the 1984 enactment of Section 312(n)(5) regarding the installment method.

§ 1.312-6. Earnings and profits.—(a) In determining the amount of earnings and profits (whether of the taxable year, or accumulated since February 28, 1913, or accumulated before March 1, 1913) due consideration must be given to the facts, and, while mere bookkeeping entries increasing or decreasing surplus will not be conclusive, the amount of the earnings and profits in any case will be dependent upon the method of accounting properly employed in computing taxable income (or net income, as the case may be). For instance, a corporation keeping its books and filing its income tax returns under subchapter E, chapter 1 of the Code, on the cash receipts and disbursements basis may not use the accrual basis in determining earnings and profits; a corporation computing income on the installment basis as provided in section 453 shall, with respect to the installment transactions, compute earnings and profits on such basis; and an insurance company subject to taxation under section 831 shall exclude from earnings and profits that portion of any premium which is unearned under the provisions of section 832(b)(4) and which is segregated accordingly in the unearned premium reserve.

(b) Among the items entering into the computation of corporate earnings and profits for a particular period are all income exempted by statute, income not taxable by the Federal Government under the Constitution, as well as all items includible in gross income under section 61 or corresponding provisions of prior revenue acts. Gains and losses within the purview of section 1002 or corresponding provisions of prior revenue acts are brought into the earnings and profits at the time and to the extent such gains and losses are recognized under that section. Interest on State bonds and certain other obligations, although not taxable when received by a corporation, is taxable to the same extent as other dividends when distributed to shareholders in the form of dividends.

(c)(1) In the case of a corporation in which depletion or depreciation is a factor in the determination of income, the only depletion or depreciation deductions to be considered in the computation of the total earnings and profits are those based on cost or other basis without regard to March 1, 1913, value. In computing the earnings and profits for any period beginning after February 28, 1913, the only depletion or depreciation deductions to be considered are those based on (i) cost or other basis, if the depletable or depreciable asset was acquired subsequent to February 28, 1913, or (ii) adjusted cost or March 1, 1913, value, whichever is higher, if acquired before March 1, 1913. Thus, discovery or percentage depletion under all revenue acts for mines and oil and gas wells is not to be taken into consideration in computing the earnings and profits of a corporation. Similarly, where the basis of property in the hands of a corporation is a substituted basis, such basis, and not the fair market value of the property at the time of the acquisition by the corporation, is the basis for computing depletion and depreciation for the purpose of determining earnings and profits of the corporation.

(2) The application of subparagraph (1) of this paragraph may be illustrated by the following example:

Example. Oil producing property which A had acquired in 1949 at a cost of $28,000 was transferred to Corporation Y in December 1951, in exchange for all of its capital stock. The fair market value of the stock and of the property as of the date of the transfer was $247,000. Corporation Y, after four years' operation, effected in 1955 a cash distribution to A in the amount of $165,000. In determining the extent to which the earnings and profits of Corporation Y available for dividend distributions have been increased as the result of production and sale of oil, the depletion to be taken into account is to be computed upon the basis of $28,000 established in the nontaxable exchange in 1951 regardless of the fair market value of the property or of the stock issued in exchange therefor.

(d) A loss sustained for a year before the taxable year does not affect the earnings and profits of the taxable year. However, in determining the earnings and profits accumulated since February 28, 1913, the excess of a loss sustained for a year subsequent to February 28, 1913, over the undistributed earnings and profits accumulated since February 28, 1913, and before the year for which the loss was sustained, reduces surplus as of March 1, 1913, to the extent of such excess. If the surplus as of March 1, 1913, was sufficient to absorb such excess, distributions to shareholders after the year of the loss are out of earnings and profits accumulated since the year of the loss to the extent of such earnings.

(e) With respect to the effect on the earnings and profits accumulated since February 28, 1913, of distributions made on or after January 1, 1916, and before August 6, 1917, out of earnings or profits accumulated before March 1, 1913, which distributions were specifically declared to be out of earnings and profits accumulated before March 1, 1913, see section 31(b) of the Revenue Act of 1916, as amended by section 1211 of the Revenue Act of 1917 (40 Stat. 336). [Reg. § 1.312-6.].

□ [*T.D.* 6152, 12-2-55.]

§ 1.312-7. Effect on earnings and profits of gain or loss realized after February 28, 1913.—(a) In order to determine the effect on earnings and profits of gain or loss realized from the sale or other disposition (after February 28, 1913) of property by a corporation, section 312(f)(1) prescribes certain rules for—

(1) The computation of the total earnings and profits of the corporation of most frequent application in determining invested capital; and

(2) The computation of earnings and profits of the corporation for any period beginning after February 28, 1913, of most frequent application in determining the source of dividend distributions.

Such rules are applicable whenever under any provision of subtitle A of the Code it is necessary to compute either the total earnings and profits of the corporation or the earnings and profits for any period beginning after February 28, 1913. For example, since the earnings and profits accumulated after February 28, 1913, or the earnings and profits of the taxable year, are earnings and profits for a period beginning after February 28, 1913, the determination of either must be in accordance with the regulations prescribed by this section, for the ascertainment of earnings and profits for any period beginning after February 28, 1913. Under subparagraph (1) of this paragraph, such gain or loss is determined by using the adjusted basis (under the law applicable to the year in which the sale or other disposition was made) for determining gain, but disregarding value as of March 1, 1913. Under subparagraph (2) of this paragraph, there is used such adjusted basis for determining gain, giving effect to the value as of March 1, 1913, whenever applicable. In both cases the rules are the same as those governing depreciation and depletion in computing earnings and profits (see § 1.312-6). Under both subparagraphs (1) and (2) of this paragraph, the adjusted basis is subject to the limitations of the third sentence of section 312(f)(1) requiring the use of adjustments proper in determining earnings and profits. The proper adjustments may differ under section 312(f)(1)(A) and (B) depending upon the basis to which the adjustments are to be made. If the application of section 312(f)(1)(B) results in a loss and if the application of section 312(f)(1)(A) to the same transaction reaches a different result, then the loss under section 312(f)(1)(B) will be subject to the adjustment thereto required by section 312(g)(2). (See § 1.312-9.)

(b)(1) The gain or loss so realized increases or decreases the earnings and profits to, but not beyond, the extent to which such gain or loss was recognized in computing taxable income (or net income, as the case may be) under the law applicable to the year in which such sale or disposition was made. As used in this paragraph, the term "recognized" has reference to that kind of realized gain or loss which is recognized for income tax purposes by the statute applicable to the year in which the gain or loss was realized. For example, see section 356. A loss (other than a wash sale loss with respect to which a deduction is disallowed under the provisions of section 1091 or corresponding provisions of prior revenue laws) may be recognized though not allowed as a deduction (by reason, for example, of the operation of sections 267 and 1211 and corresponding provisions of prior revenue laws) but the mere fact that it is not allowed does not prevent decrease in earnings and profits by the amount of such disallowed loss. Wash sale losses, however, disallowed under section 1091 and corresponding provisions of prior revenue laws, are deemed nonrecognized losses and do not reduce earnings or profits. The "recognized" gain or loss for the purpose of computing earnings and profits is determined by applying the recognition provisions to the realized gain or loss computed under the provisions of section 312(f)(1) as distinguished from the realized gain or loss used in computing taxable income (or net income, as the case may be).

(2) The application of subparagraph (1) of this paragraph may be illustrated by the following examples:

Example (1). Corporation X on January 1, 1952, owned stock in Corporation Y which it had acquired from Corporation Y in December 1951, in an exchange transaction in which no gain or loss was recognized. The adjusted basis to Corporation X of the property exchanged by it for the stock in Corporation Y was $30,000. The fair market value of the stock in Corporation Y when received by Corporation X was

$930,000. On April 9, 1955, Corporation X made a cash distribution of $900,000 and, except for the possible effect of the transaction in 1951, had no earnings or profits accumulated after February 28, 1913, and had no earnings or profits for the taxable year. The amount of $900,000 representing the excess of the fair market value of the stock of Corporation Y over the adjusted basis of the property exchanged therefor was not recognized gain to Corporation X under the provisions of section 112 of the Internal Revenue Code of 1939. Accordingly, the earnings and profits of Corporation X are not increased by $900,000, the amount of the gain realized but not recognized in the exchange, and the distribution was not a taxable dividend. The basis in the hands of Corporation Y of the property acquired by it from Corporation X is $30,000. If such property is thereafter sold by Corporation Y, gain or loss will be computed on such basis of $30,000, and earnings and profits will be increased or decreased accordingly.

Example (2). On January 2, 1910, Corporation M acquired nondepreciable property at a cost of $1,000. On March 1, 1913, the fair market value of such property in the hands of Corporation M was $2,200. On December 31, 1952, Corporation M transfers such property to Corporation N in exchange for $1,900 in cash and all Corporation N's stock, which has a fair market value of $1,100. For the purpose of computing the total earnings and profits of Corporation M, the gain on such transaction is $2,000 (the sum of $1,900 in cash and stock worth $1,100 minus $1,000, the adjusted basis for computing gain, determined without regard to March 1, 1913, value), $1,900 of which is recognized under section 356, since this was the amount of money received, although for the purpose of computing net income the gain is only $800 (the sum of $1,900 in cash and stock worth $1,100, minus $2,200, the adjusted basis for computing gain determined by giving effect to March 1, 1913, value). Such earnings and profits will therefore be increased by $1,900. In computing the earnings and profits of Corporation M for any period beginning after February 28, 1913, however, the gain arising from the transaction, like the taxable gain, is only $800, all of which is recognized under section 112(c) of the Internal Revenue Code of 1939, the money received being in excess of such amount. Such earnings and profits will therefore be increased by only $800 as a result of the transaction. For increase in that part of the earnings and profits consisting of increase in value of property accrued before, but realized on or after March 1, 1913, see § 1.312-9.

Example (3). On July 31, 1955, Corporation R owned oil-producing property acquired after February 28, 1913, at a cost of $200,000, but having an adjusted basis (by reason of taking percentage depletion) of $100,000 for determining gain. However, the adjusted basis of such property to be used in computing gain or loss for the purpose of earnings and profits is, because of the provisions of the third sentence of section 312(f)(1), $150,000. On such day Corporation R transferred such property to Corporation S in exchange for $25,000 in cash and all of the stock of Corporation S, which had a fair market value of $100,000. For the purpose of computing taxable income, Corporation R has realized a gain of $25,000 as a result of this transaction, all of which is recognized under section 356. For the purpose of computing earnings and profits, however, Corporation R has realized a loss of $25,000, none of which is recognized owing to the provisions of section 356(c). The earnings and profits of Corporation R are therefore neither increased nor decreased as a result of the transaction. The adjusted basis of the Corporation S stock in the hands of Corporation R for purposes of computing earnings and profits, however, will be $125,000 (though only $100,000 for the purpose of computing taxable income), computed as follows:

Basis of property transferred	$200,000
Less money received on exchange	25,000
Plus gain or minus loss recognized on exchange	None
Basis of stock	$175,000
Less adjustments (same as those used in determining adjusted basis of property transferred)	$50,000
Adjusted basis of stock	$125,000

If, therefore, Corporation R should subsequently sell the Corporation S stock for $100,000, a loss of $25,000 will again be realized for the purpose of computing earnings and profits, all of which will be recognized and will be applied to decrease the earnings and profits of Corporation R.

(c)(1) The third sentence of section 312(f)(1) provides for cases in which the adjustments, prescribed in section 1016, to the basis indicated in section 312(f)(1)(A) or (B), as the case may be, differ from the adjustments to such basis proper for the purpose of determining earnings or profits. The adjustments provided by such third sentence reflect the treatment provided by §§ 1.312-6 and 1.312-15 relative to cases where the deductions for depletion and depreciation in computing taxable income (or net income, as the case may be) differ from the deductions proper for the purpose of computing earnings and profits.

(2) The effect of the third sentence of section 312(f)(1) may be illustrated by the following examples:

Example (1). Corporation X purchased on January 2, 1931, an oil lease at a cost of $10,000. The lease was operated only for the years 1931 and 1932. The deduction for depletion in each of the years 1931 and 1932 amounted to $2,750, of which amount $1,750 represented percentage depletion in excess of depletion based on cost. The lease was sold in 1955 for $15,000. Under section 1016(a)(2), in determining the gain or loss from the sale of the property, the basis must be adjusted for cost depletion of $1,000 in 1931 and percentage depletion of $2,750 in 1932. However, the adjustment of such basis, proper for the determination of earnings and profits, is $1,000 for each year, or $2,000. Hence, the cost is to be adjusted only to the extent of $2,000, leaving an adjusted basis of $8,000 and the earnings and profits will be increased by $7,000, and not by $8,750. The difference of $1,750 is equal to the amount by which the percentage depletion for the year 1932 ($2,750) exceeds the depletion on cost for that year ($1,000) and has already been applied in the computation of earnings and profits for the year 1932 by taking into account only $1,000 instead of $2,750 for depletion in the computation of such earnings and profits. (See § 1.316-1.)

Example (2). If, in example (1), above, the property, instead of being sold, is exchanged in a transaction described in section 1031 for like property having a fair market value of $7,750 and cash of $7,250, then the increase in earnings and profits amounts to $7,000, that is, $15,000 ($7,750 plus $7,250) minus the basis of $8,000. However, in computing taxable income of Corporation X, the gain is $8,750, that is, $15,000 minus $6,250 ($10,000 less depletion of $3,750), of which only $7,250 is recognized because the recognized gain cannot exceed the sum of money received in the transaction. See section 1031(b) and the corresponding provisions of prior revenue laws. If, however, the cash received was only $2,250 and the value of the property received was $12,750, then the increase in earnings and profits would be $2,250, that amount being the gain recognized under section 1031.

Example (3). On January 1, 1973, corporation X purchased for $10,000 a depreciable asset with an estimated useful life of 20 years and no salvage value. In computing depreciation on the asset, corporation X used the declining balance method with a rate twice the straight line rate. On December 31, 1976, the asset was sold for $9,000. Under section 1016(a)(2), the basis of the asset is adjusted for depreciation allowed for the years 1973 through 1976, or a total of $3,439. Thus, X realizes a gain of $2,439 (the excess of the amount realized, $9,000, over the adjusted basis, $6,561). However, the proper adjustment to basis for the purpose of determining earnings and profits is only $2,000, i.e., the total amount which, under § 1.312-15, was applied in the computation of earnings and profits for the years 1973-76. Hence, upon sale of the asset, earnings and profits are increased by only $1,000, i.e., the excess of the amount realized, $9,000, over the adjusted basis for earnings and profits purposes, $8,000.

(d) For adjustment and allocation of the earnings and profits of the transferor as between the transferor and the transferee in cases where the transfer of property by one corporation to another corporation results in the nonrecognition in whole or in part of gain or loss, see § 1.312-10; and see section 381 for earnings and profits of successor corporations in certain transactions. [Reg. § 1.312-7.]

☐ [*T.D.* 6152, 12-2-55. *Amended by T.D.* 7221, 11-20-72.]

§ 1.312-10. Allocation of earnings in certain corporate separations.—(a) If one corporation transfers part of its assets constituting an active trade or business to another corporation in a transaction to which section 368(a)(1)(D) applies and immediately thereafter the stock and securities of the controlled corporation are distributed in a distribution or exchange to which section 355 (or so much of section 356 as relates to section 355) applies, the earnings and profits of the distributing corporation immediately before the transaction shall be allocated between the distributing corporation and the controlled corporation. In the case of a newly created controlled corporation, such allocation generally shall be made in proportion to the fair market value of the business or businesses (and interests in any other properties) retained by the distributing corporation and the business or businesses (and interests in any other properties) of the controlled corporation immediately after the transaction. In a proper case, allocation shall be made between the distributing corporation and the controlled corporation in proportion to the net basis of the assets transferred and of the assets retained or by such other method as may be appropriate under the facts and circumstances of the case. The term "net basis" means the basis of the assets less liabilities assumed or liabilities to which such assets are subject. The part of the earnings and profits of the taxable year of the distributing corporation in which the transaction occurs allocable to the controlled corporation shall be included in the computation of the earnings and profits of the first taxable year of the controlled corporation ending after the date of the transaction.

(b) If a distribution or exchange to which section 355 applies (or so much of section 356 as relates to section 355) is not in pursuance of a plan meeting the requirements of a reorganization as defined in section 368(a)(1)(D), the earnings and profits of the distributing corporation shall be decreased by the lesser of the following amounts:

(1) The amount by which the earnings and profits of the distributing corporation would have been decreased if it had transferred the stock of the controlled corporation to a new corporation in a reorganization to which section 368(a)(1)(D) applied and immediately thereafter distributed the stock of such new corporation or,

(2) The net worth of the controlled corporation. (For this purpose the term "net worth" means the sum of the bases of all of the properties plus cash minus all liabilities.) If the earnings and profits of the controlled corporation immediately before the transaction are less than the amount of the decrease in earnings and profits of the distributing corporation (including a case in which the controlled corporation has a deficit) the earnings and profits of the controlled corporation, after the transaction, shall be equal to the amount of such decrease. If the earnings and profits of the controlled corporation immediately before the transaction are more than the amount of the decrease in the earnings and profits of the distributing corporation, they shall remain unchanged.

(c) In no case shall any part of a deficit of a distributing corporation within the meaning of section 355 be allocated to a controlled corporation. [Reg. § 1.312-10.]

□ [*T.D.* 6152, 12-2-55.]

§ 1.312-11. Effect on earnings and profits of certain other tax-free exchanges, tax-free distributions, and tax-free transfers from one corporation to another.—(a) In a transfer described in section 381(a), the acquiring corporation, as defined in § 1.381(a)-1(b)(2), and only that corporation, succeeds to the earnings and profits of the distributor or transferor corporation (within the meaning of § 1.381(a)-1(a)). Except as provided in § 1.312-10, in all other cases in which property is transferred from one corporation to another, no allocation of the earnings and profits of the transferor is made to the transferee.

(b) The general rule provided in section 316 that every distribution is made out of earnings or profits to the extent thereof and from the most recently accumulated earnings or profits does not apply to:

(1) The distribution, in pursuance of a plan of reorganization, by or on behalf of a corporation a party to the reorganization, or in a transaction subject to section 355, to its shareholders—

(i) Of stock or securities in such corporation or in another corporation a party to the reorganization in any taxable year beginning before January 1, 1934, without the surrender by the distributees of stock or securities in such corporation (see section 112(g) of the Revenue Act of 1932 (47 Stat. 197)); or

(ii) Of stock (other than preferred stock) in another corporation which is a party to the reorganization without the surrender by the distributees of stock in the distributing corporation if the distribution occurs after October 20, 1951, and is subject to section 112(b)(11) of the Internal Revenue Code of 1939; or

(iii) Of stock or securities in such corporation or in another corporation a party to the reorganization in any taxable year beginning before January 1, 1939, or on or after such date, in exchange for its stock or securities in a transaction to which section 112(b)(3) of the Internal Revenue Code of 1939 was applicable; or

(iv) Of stock or securities in such corporation or in another corporation in exchange for its stock or securities in a transaction subject to section 354 or 355,

if no gain to the distributees from the receipt of such stock or securities was recognzied by law.

(2) The distribution in any taxable year (beginning before January 1, 1939, or on or after such date) of stock or securities, or other property or money, to a corporation in complete liquidation of another corporation, under the circumstances described in section 112(b)(6) of the Revenue Act of 1936 (49 Stat. 1679), the Revenue Act of 1938 (52 Stat. 485), of the Internal Revenue Code of 1939, or section 332 of the Internal Revenue Code of 1954.

(3) The distribution in any taxable year (beginning after December 31, 1939 [1938]), of stock or securities, or other property or money, in the case of an exchange or distribution described in section 371 of the Internal Revenue Code of 1939 or in section 1081 of the Internal Revenue Code of 1954 (relating to exchanges and distributions in obedience to orders of the Securities and Exchange Commission), if no gain to the distributee from the receipt of such stock, securities, or other property or money was recognized by law.

(4) A stock dividend which was not subject to tax in the hands of the distributee because either it did not constitute income to him within the meaning of the sixteenth amendment to the Constitution or because exempt to him under section 115(f) of the Revenue Act of

1934 (48 Stat. 712) or a corresponding provision of a prior revenue act, or section 305 of the Code.

(5) The distribution, in a taxable year of the distributee beginning after December 31, 1931, by or on behalf of an insolvent corporation, in connection with a section 112(b)(10) reorganization under the Internal Revenue Code of 1939, or in a transaction subject to section 371 of the Internal Revenue Code of 1954, of stock or securities in a corporation organized or made use of to effectuate the plan of reorganization, if under section 112(I) of the Internal Revenue Code of 1939 or sections 371 of the Internal Revenue Code of 1954 no gain to the distributee from the receipt of such stock or securities was recognized by law.

(c) A distribution described in paragraph (b) of this section does not diminish the earnings or profits of any corporation. In such cases, the earnings or profits remain intact and available for distribution as dividends by the corporation making such distribution, or by another corporation to which the earnings or profits are transferred upon such reorganization or other exchange. In the case, however, of amounts distributed in liquidation (other than a tax-free liquidation or reorganization described in paragraph (b)(1), (2), (3), or (5) of this section) the earnings or profits of the corporation making the distribution are diminished by the portion of such distribution properly chargeable to earnings or profits accumulated after February 28, 1913, after first deducting from the amount of such distribution the portion thereof allocable to capital account.

* * *

[Reg. § 1.312-11.]

□ [*T.D.* 6152, 12-2-55. *Amended by T.D.* 6476, 6-30-60 *and T.D.* 9700, 11-7-2014.]

§ 1.312-15. Effect of depreciation on earnings and profits.—(a) *Depreciation for taxable years beginning after June 30, 1972.*—(1) *In general.*—Except as provided in subparagraph (2) of this paragraph and paragraph (c) of this section, for purposes of computing the earnings and profits of a corporation (including a real estate investment trust as defined in section 856) for any taxable year beginning after June 30, 1972, the allowance for depreciation (and amortization, if any) shall be deemed to be the amount which would be allowable for such year if the straight line method of depreciation had been used for all property for which depreciation is allowable for each taxable year beginning after June 30, 1972. Thus, for taxable years beginning after June 30, 1972, in determining the earnings and profits of a corporation, depreciation must be computed under the straight line method, notwithstanding that in determining taxable income the corporation uses an accelerated method of depreciation described in subparagraph (A), (B), or (C) of section 312(m)(2) or elects to amortize the basis of property under section 169, 184, 187, or 188, or any similar provision. See § 1.168(k)-1(f)(7) with respect to the treatment of the additional first year depreciation deduction allowable under section 168(k) for qualified property or 50-percent bonus depreciation property, and § 1.1400L(b)-1(f)(7) with respect to the treatment of the additional first year depreciation deduction allowable under section 1400L(b) for qualified New York Liberty Zone property, for purposes of computing the earnings and profits of a corporation. Further, see § 1.168(k)-2(g)(7) with respect to the treatment of the additional first year depreciation deduction allowable under section 168(k), as amended by the Tax Cuts and Jobs Act, Public Law 115-97 (131 Stat. 2054 (December 22, 2017)), for purposes of computing the earnings and profits of a corporation.

(2) *Exception.*—(i) If, for any taxable year beginning after June 30, 1972, a method of depreciation is used by a corporation in computing taxable income which the Secretary or his delegate has determined results in a reasonable allowance under section 167(a) and which is not a declining balance method of depreciation (described in § 1.167(b)-2), the sum of the years-digits methods (described in § 1.167(b)-3), or any other method allowed solely by reason of the application of subsection (b)(4) or (j)(1)(C) of section 167, then the adjustment to earnings and profits for depreciation for such year shall be determined under the method so used (in lieu of the straight line method).

(ii) The Commissioner has determined that the "unit of production" (see § 1.167(b)-0 (b)), and the "machine hour" methods of depreciation, when properly used under appropriate circumstances, meet the requirements of subdivision (i) of this subparagraph. Thus, the adjustment to earnings and profits for depreciation (for the taxable year for which either of such methods is properly used under appropriate circumstances) shall be determined under whichever of such methods is used to compute taxable income.

(3) *Determinations under straight line method.*—(i) In the case of property with respect to which an allowance for depreciation is claimed in computing taxable income, the determination of the amount which would be allowable under the straight line method shall be based on the manner in which the corporation computes depreciation in determining taxable income. Thus, if an election under § 1.167(a)-11 is in effect with respect to the property, the amount of depreciation which would be allowa-

ble under the straight line method shall be determined under § 1.167(a)-11(g)(3). On the other hand, if property is not depreciated under the provisions of § 1.167(a)-11, the amount of depreciation which would be allowable under the straight line method shall be determined under § 1.167(b)-1. Any election made under section 167(f), with respect to reducing the amount of salvage value taken into account in computing the depreciation allowance for certain property, or any convention adopted under § 1.167(a)-10(b) or § 1.167(a)-11(c)(2), with respect to additions and retirements from multiple asset accounts, which is used in computing depreciation for taxable income shall be used in computing depreciation for earnings and profits purposes.

(ii) In the case of property with respect to which an election to amortize is in effect under section 169, 184, 187, or 188, or any similar provision, the amount which would be allowable under the straight line method of depreciation shall be determined under the provisions of § 1.167(b)-1. Thus, the cost or other basis of the property, less its estimated salvage value, is to be deducted in equal annual amounts over the period of the estimated useful life of the property. In computing the amount of depreciation for earnings and profits purposes, a taxpayer may utilize the provisions of section 167(f) (relating to the reduction in the amount of salvage value taken into account in computing the depreciation allowance for certain property) and any convention which could have been adopted for such property under § 1.167(a)-10(b) (relating to additions and retirements from multiple asset accounts).

* * *

(d) *Books and records.*—Wherever different methods of depreciation are used for taxable income and earnings and profits purposes, records shall be maintained which show the depreciation taken for earnings and profits purposes each year and which will allow computation of the adjusted basis of the property in each account using the depreciation taken for earnings and profits purposes. [Reg. § 1.312-15.]

* * *

☐ [*T.D.* 7221, 11-20-72. *Amended by T.D.* 9283, 8-28-2006 *and T.D.* 9874, 9-17-2019.]

§ 1.316-1. Dividends.—(a)(1) The term "dividend" for the purpose of subtitle A of the Code (except when used in subchapter L, chapter 1 of the Code, in any case where the reference is to dividends and similar distributions of insurance companies paid to policyholders as such) comprises any distribution of property as defined in section 317 in the ordinary course of business, even though extraordinary in amount, made by a domestic or foreign corporation to its shareholders out of either—

(i) Earnings and profits accumulated since February 28, 1913, or

(ii) Earnings and profits of the taxable year computed without regard to the amount of the earnings and profits (whether of such year or accumulated since February 28, 1913) at the time the distribution was made.

The earnings and profits of the taxable year shall be computed as of the close of such year, without diminution by reason of any distributions made during the taxable year. For the purpose of determining whether a distribution constitutes a dividend, it is unnecessary to ascertain the amount of the earnings and profits accumulated since February 28, 1913, if the earnings and profits of the taxable year are equal to or in excess of the total amount of the distributions made within such year.

* * *

(e) The application of section 316 may be illustrated by the following examples:

Example (1). At the beginning of the calendar year 1955, Corporation M had an operating deficit of $200,000 and the earnings and profits for the year amounted to $100,000. Beginning on March 16, 1955, the corporation made quarterly distributions of $25,000 during the taxable year to its shareholders. Each distribution is a taxable dividend in full, irrespective of the actual or the pro rata amount of the earnings and profits on hand at any of the dates of distribution, since the total distributions made during the year ($100,000) did not exceed the total earnings and profits of the year ($100,000).

* * *

[Reg. § 1.316-1.]

☐ [*T.D.* 6152, 12-2-55. *Amended by T.D.* 6625, 12-18-62, *T.D.* 6949, 4-8-68, *T.D.* 7767, 2-3-81 and *T.D.* 7936, 1-17-84.]

§ 1.316-2. Sources of distribution in general.—(a) For the purpose of income taxation every distribution made by a corporation is made out of earnings and profits to the extent thereof and from the most recently accumulated earnings and profits. In determining the source of a distribution, consideration should be given first, to the earnings and profits of the taxable year; second, to the earnings and profits accumulated since February 28, 1913, only in the case where, and to the extent that, the distributions made during the taxable year are not regarded as out of the earnings and profits of that year; third, to the earnings and profits accumulated before March 1, 1913, only after all the earnings and profits of the taxable year and all the earnings and profits accumulated since February 28, 1913, have been distributed; and, fourth, to sources other than earnings and profits only after the earnings and profits have been distributed.

(b) If the earnings and profits of the taxable year (computed as of the close of the year without diminution by reason of any distributions made during the year and without regard to the amount of earnings and profits at the time of the distribution) are sufficient in amount to cover all the distributions made during that year, then each distribution is a taxable dividend. See § 1.316-1. If the distributions made during the taxable year consist only of money and exceed the earnings and profits of such year, then that proportion of each distribution which the total of the earnings and profits of the year bears to the total distributions made during the year shall be regarded as out of the earnings and profits of that year. The portion of each such distribution which is not regarded as out of earnings and profits of the taxable year shall be considered a taxable dividend to the extent of the earnings and profits accumulated since February 28, 1913, and available on the date of the distribution. In any case in which it is necessary to determine the amount of earnings and profits accumulated since February 28, 1913, and the actual earnings and profits to the date of a distribution within any taxable year (whether beginning before January 1, 1936, or, in the case of an operating deficit, on or after that date) cannot be shown, the earnings and profits for the year (or accounting period, if less than a year) in which the distribution was made shall be prorated to the date of the distribution not counting the date on which the distribution was made.

(c) The provisions of the section may be illustrated by the following example:

Example. At the beginning of the calendar year 1955, Corporation M had $12,000 in earnings and profits accumulated since February 28, 1913. Its earnings and profits for 1955 amounted to $30,000. During the year it made quarterly cash distributions of $15,000 each. Of each of the four distributions made, $7,500 (that portion of $15,000 which the amount of $30,000, the total earnings and profits of the taxable year, bears to $60,000, the total distributions made during the year) was paid out of the earnings and profits of the taxable year; and of the first and second distributions, $7,500 and $4,500, respectively, were paid out of the earnings and profits accumulated after February 28, 1913, and before the taxable year, as follows:

Distributions during 1955		*Portion out of earnings and profits of the taxable year*	*Portion out of earnings accumulated since Feb. 28, 1913, and before the taxable year*	*Taxable amount of each distribution*
Date	*Amount*			
March 10	$15,000	$7,500	$7,500	$15,000
June 10	15,000	7,500	4,500	12,000
September 10	15,000	7,500	...	7,500
December 10	15,000	7,500	...	7,500
Total amount taxable as dividends				42,000

(d) Any distribution by a corporation out of earnings and profits accumulated before March 1, 1913, or out of increase in value of property accrued before March 1, 1913 (whether or not realized by sale or other disposition, and, if realized, whether before, on, or after March 1, 1913), is not a dividend within the meaning of subtitle A of the Code.

(e) A reserve set up out of gross income by a corporation and maintained for the purpose of making good any loss of capital assets on account of depletion or depreciation is not a part of surplus out of which ordinary dividends may be paid. A distribution made from a depletion or a depreciation reserve based upon the cost or other basis of the property will not be considered as having been paid out of earnings and profits, but the amount thereof shall be applied against and reduce the cost or other basis of the stock upon which declared. If such a distribution is in excess of the basis, the excess shall be taxed as a gain from the sale or other disposition of property as provided in section 301 (c) (3) (A). A distribution from a depletion reserve based upon discovery value to the extent that such reserve represents the excess of the discovery value over the cost or other basis for determining gain or loss, is, when received by the shareholders, taxable as an ordinary dividend. The amount by which a corporation's percentage depletion allowance for any year exceeds depletion sustained on cost or other basis, that is, determined without regard to discovery or percentage depletion allowances for the year of distribution or prior years, constitutes a part of the corporation's "earnings and profits accumulated after February 28, 1913," within the meaning of section 316, and, upon distribution to shareholders, is taxable to them as a dividend. A distribution made from that portion of a depletion reserve based upon a valuation as of March 1, 1913, which is in excess of the depletion reserve based upon cost, will not be considered as having been paid out of earnings and profits, but the amount of the distribution shall be applied against and reduce the cost or other basis of the stock upon which declared. See section 301. No distribution, however, can be made from such a reserve until all the earnings and profits of the corporation have first been distributed. [Reg. § 1.316-2.]

☐ [*T.D.* 6152, 12-2-55.]

§ 1.317-1. Property defined.—The term "property", for purposes of Part 1, subchapter C, chapter 1 of the Code, means any property (including money, securities, and indebtedness to the corporation) other than stock, or rights to acquire stock, in the corporation making the distribution. [Reg. § 1.317-1.]

☐ [*T.D.* 6152, 12-2-55.]

§ 1.318-1. Constructive ownership of stock; introduction.—(a) For the purposes of certain provisions of chapter 1 of the Code, section 318(a) provides that stock owned by a taxpayer includes stock constructively owned by such taxpayer under the rules set forth in such section. An individual is considered to own the stock owned, directly or indirectly, by or for his spouse (other than a spouse who is legally separated from the individual under a decree of divorce or separate maintenance), and by or for his children, grandchildren, and parents. Under section 318(a)(2) and (3), constructive ownership rules are established for partnerships and partners, estates and beneficiaries, trusts and beneficiaries, and corporations and stockholders. If any person has an option to acquire stock, such stock is considered as owned by such person. The term "option" includes an option to acquire such an option and each of a series of such options.

(b) In applying section 318(a) to determine the stock ownership of any person for any one purpose—

(1) A corporation shall not be considered to own its own stock by reason of section 318(a)(3)(C);

(2) In any case in which an amount of stock owned by any person may be included in the computation more than one time, such stock shall be included only once, in the manner in which it will impute to the person concerned the largest total stock ownership; and

(3) In determining the 50-percent requirement of section 318(a)(2)(C) and (3)(C) all of the stock owned actually and constructively by the person concerned shall be aggregated. [Reg. § 1.318-1.]

☐ [*T.D.* 6152, 12-2-55. *Amended by T.D.* 6598, 4-25-62, *T.D.* 6621, 11-30-62 *and T.D.* 6969, 8-22-68.]

§ 1.318-2. Application of general rules.—(a) The application of paragraph (b) of § 1.318-1 may be illustrated by the following examples:

Example (1). H, an individual owns all of the stock of Corporation A. Corporationo A is not considered to own the stock owned by H in Corporation A.

Example (2). H, an individual, his wife, W, and his son, S, each own one-third of the stock of the Green Corporation. For purposes of determining the amount of stock owned by H, W, or S for the purpose of section 318(a)(2)(C) and (3)(C), the amount of stock held by the other members of the family shall be added pursuant to paragraph (b)(3) of § 1.318-1 in applying the 50-percent requirement of such section. H, W, or S, as the case may be, is for this purpose deemed to own 100 percent of the stock of the Green Corporation.

(b) The application of section 318(a)(1), relating to members of a family, may be illustrated by the following example:

Example. An individual, H, his wife, W, his son, S, and his grandson (S's son), G, own the 100 outstanding shares of stock of a corporation, each owning 25 shares. H, W, and S are each considered as owning 100 shares. G is considered as owning only 50 shares, that is, his own and his father's.

(c) The application of section 318(a)(2) and (3), relating to partnerships, trusts and corporations, may be illustrated by the following examples:

Example (1). A, an individual, has a 50 percent interest in a partnership. The partnership owns 50 of the 100 outstanding shares of stock of a corporation, the remaining 50 shares being owned by A. The partnership is considered as owning 100 shares. A is considered as owning 75 shares.

Example (2). A testamentary trust owns 25 of the outstanding 100 shares of stock of a corporation. A, an individual, who holds a vested remainder in the trust having a value, computed actuarially equal to 4 percent of the value of the trust property, owns the remaining 75 shares. Since the interest of A in the trust is a vested interest rather than a contingent interest (whether or not remote), the trust is considered as owning 100 shares. A is considered as owning 76 shares.

Example (3). The facts are the same as in (2), above, except that A's interest in the trust is a contingent remainder. A is considered as owning 76 shares. However, since A's interest in the trust is a remote contingent interest, the trust is not considered as owning any of the shares owned by A.

Example (4). A and B, unrelated individuals, own 70 percent and 30 percent, respectively, in value of the stock of Corporation M. Corporation M owns 50 of the 100 outstanding shares of stock of Corporation O, the remaining 50 shares being owned by A. Corporation M is considered as owning 100 shares of Corporation O, and A is considered as owning 85 shares.

Example (5). A and B, unrelated individuals, own 70 percent and 30 percent, respectively, of the stock of corporation M. A, B, and corporation M all own stock of corporation O. Since B owns less than 50 percent in value of the stock of corporation M, neither B nor corporation M constructively owns the stock of corporation O owned by the other. However, for purposes of certain sections of the Code, such as sections 304 and 856(d), the 50-percent limitation of section 318(a)(2)(C) and (3)(C) is disregarded or is reduced to less than 30 percent. For such purposes, B constructively owns his proportionate share of the stock of corporation O owned directly by corporation M, and corporation M constructively owns the stock of corporation O owned by B. [Reg. § 1.318-2.]

□ [*T.D.* 6152, 12-2-55. *Amended by T.D.* 6969, 8-22-68.]

§ 1.318-3. Estates, trusts, and options.—(a) For the purpose of applying section 318(a), relating to estates, property of a decedent shall be considered as owned by his estate if such property is subject to administration by the executor or administrator for the purpose of paying claims against the estate and expenses of administration notwithstanding that, under local law, legal title to such property vests in the decedent's heirs, legatees or devisees immediately upon death. The term "beneficiary" includes any person entitled to receive property of a decedent pursuant to a will or pursuant to laws of descent and distribution. A person shall no longer be considered a beneficiary of an estate when all the property to which he is entitled has been received by him, when he no longer has a claim against the estate arising out of having been a beneficiary, and when there is only a remote possibility that it will be necessary for the estate to seek the return of property or to seek payment from him by contribution or otherwise to satisfy claims against the estate or expenses of administration. When, pursuant to the preceding sentence, a person ceases to be a beneficiary, stock owned by him shall not thereafter be considered owned by the estate, and stock owned by the estate shall not thereafter be considered owned by him. The application of section 318(a) relating to estates may be illustrated by the following examples:

Example (1). (a) A decedent's estate owns 50 of the 100 outstanding shares of stock of corporation X. The remaining shares are owned by three unrelated individuals, A, B, and C, who together own the entire interest in the estate. A owns 12 shares of stock of corporation X directly and is entitled to 50 percent of the estate. B owns 18 shares directly and has a life estate in the remaining 50 percent of the estate. C owns 20 shares directly and also owns the remainder interest after B's life estate.

(b) If section 318(a)(5)(C) applies (see paragraph (c)(3) of § 1.318-4), the stock of corporation X is considered to be owned as follows: the estate is considered as owning 80 shares, 50 shares directly, 12 shares constructively through A, and 18 shares constructively through B; A is considered as owning 37 shares, 12 shares directly, and 25 shares constructively (50 percent of the 50 shares owned directly by the estate); B is considered as owning 43 shares, 18 shares directly and 25 shares constructively (50 percent of the 50 shares owned directly by the estate); C is considered as owning 20 shares directly and no shares constructively. C is not considered a beneficiary of the estate under section 318(a) since he has no direct present interest in the property held by the estate nor in the income produced by such property.

(c) If section 318(a)(5)(C) does not apply, A is considered as owning nine additional shares (50 percent of the 18 shares owned constuctively by the estate through B), and B is considered as owning six additional shares (50 percent of the 12 shares owned constructively by the estate through A).

Example (2). Under the will of A, Blackacre is left to B for life, remainder to C, an unrelated individual. The residue of the estate consisting of stock of a corporation is left to D. B and D are beneficiaries of the estate under section 318(a). C is not considered a beneficiary since he has no direct present interest in Blackacre nor in the income produced by such property. The stock owned by the estate is considered as owned proportionately by B and D.

(b) For the purpose of section 318(a)(2)(B) stock owned by a trust will be considered as being owned by its beneficiaries only to the extent of the interest of such beneficiaries in the trust. Accordingly, the interest of income beneficiaries, remainder beneficiaries, and other beneficiaries will be computed on an actuarial basis. Thus, if a trust owns 100 percent of the stock of Corporation A, and if, on an actuarial basis, W's life interest in the trust is 15 percent, Y's life interest is 25 percent, and Z's remainder interest is 60 percent, under this provision W will be considered to be the owner of 15 percent of the stock of Corporation A, Y will be considered to be the owner of 25 percent of such stock, and Z will be considered to be the owner of 60 percent of such stock. The factors and methods prescribed in § 20.2031-7 of this chapter (Estate Tax Regulations) for use in ascertaining the value of an interest in property for estate tax purposes shall be used in determining a beneficiary's actuarial interest in a trust for purposes of this section. See § 20.2031-7 of this chapter (Estate Tax Regulations) for examples illustrating the use of these factors and methods.

(c) The application of section 318(a) relating to options may be illustrated by the following example:

Example. A and B, unrelated individuals, own all of the 100 outstanding shares of stock of a corporation, each owning 50 shares. A has an option to acquire 25 of B's shares and has an option to acquire a further option to acquire the remaining 25 of B's shares. A is considered as owning the entire 100 shares of stock of the corporation. [Reg. § 1.318-3.]

□ [*T.D.* 6152, 12-2-55. *Amended by T.D.* 6462, 5-5-60 *and T.D.* 6969, 8-22-68.]

§ 1.318-4. Constructive ownership as actual ownership; exceptions.—(a) *In general.*—Section 318(a)(5)(A) provides that, except as provided in section 318(a)(5)(B) and (C), stock constructively owned by a person by reason of the application of section 318(a)(1), (2), (3), or (4) shall be considered as actually owned by such person for purposes of applying section 318(a)(1), (2), (3), and (4). For example, if a trust owns 50 percent of the stock of corporation X, stock of corporation Y owned by corporation X which is attributed to the trust may be further attributed to the beneficiaries of the trust.

(b) *Constructive family ownership.*—Section 318(a)(5)(B) provides that stock constructively owned by an individual by reason of ownership by a member of his family shall not be considered as owned by him for purposes of making another family member the constructive owner of such stock under section 318(a)(1). For example, if F and his two sons, A and B, each own one-third of the stock of a corporation, under section 381(a)(1), A is treated as owning constructively the stock owned by his father but is not treated as owning the stock owned by B. Section 318(a)(5)(B) prevents the attribution of the stock of one brother through the father to the other brother, an attribution beyond the scope of section 318(a)(1) directly.

(c) *Reattribution.*—(1) Section 318(a)(5)(C) provides that stock constructively owned by a partnership, estate, trust, or corporation by reason of the application of section 318(a)(3) shall not be considered as owned by it for purposes of applying section 318(a)(2) in order to make another the constructive owner of such stock. For example, if two unrelated individuals are beneficiaries of the same trust, stock held by one which is attributed to the trust under section 318(a)(3) is not reattributed from the trust to the other beneficiary. However, stock constructively owned by reason of section 318(a)(2) may be reattributed under section 318(a)(3). Thus, for example, if all the stock of corporations X and Y is owned by A, stock of corporation Z held by X is attributed to Y through A.

(2) Section 318(a)(5)(C) does not prevent reattribution under section 318(a)(2) of stock constructively owned by an entity under section 318(a)(3) if the stock is also constructively owned by the entity under section 318(a)(4). For example, if individuals A and B are beneficiaries of a trust and the trust has an option to buy stock from A, B is considered under section 318(a)(2)(B) as owning a proportionate part of such stock.

* * *

[Reg. § 1.318-4.]

□ [*T.D.* 6152, 12-2-55. *Amended by T.D.* 6969, 8-22-68.]

Corporate Liquidations

»→ Note: Reg. § 1.331-1 does not reflect the 1982 changes in Section 331 deleting all references to partial liquidations.

§ 1.331-1. Corporate liquidations.—(a) *In general.*—Section 331 contains rules governing the extent to which gain or loss is recognized to a shareholder receiving a distribution in complete or partial liquidation of a corporation. Under section 331(a)(1), it is provided that amounts distributed in complete liquidation of a corporation shall be treated as in full payment in exchange for the stock. Under section 331(a)(2), it is provided that amounts distributed in partial liquidation of a corporation shall be treated as in full or part payment in exchange for the stock. For this purpose, the term "partial liquidation" shall have the meaning ascribed in section 346. If section 331 is applicable to the distribution of property by a corporation, section 301 (relating to the effects on a shareholder of distributions of property) has no application other than to a distribution in complete liquidation to which section 316(b)(2)(B) applies. See paragraph (b)(2) of § 1.316-1.

(b) *Gain or loss.*—The gain or loss to a shareholder from a distribution in partial or complete liquidation is to be determined under section 1001 by comparing the amount of the distribution with the cost or other basis of the stock. The gain or loss will be recognized to the extent provided in section 1002 and will be subject to the provisions of parts I, II, and III (section 1201 and following), subchapter P, chapter 1 of the Code.

(c) *Recharacterization.*—A liquidation which is followed by a transfer to another corporation of all or part of the assets of the liquidating corporation or which is preceded by such a transfer may, however, have the effect of the distribution of a dividend or of a transaction in which no loss is recognized and gain is recognized only to the extent of "other property." See sections 301 and 356.

* * *

(e) *Example.*—The provisions of this section may be illustrated by the following example:

Example. A, an individual who makes his income tax returns on the calendar year basis, owns 20 shares of stock of the P Corporation, a domestic corporation, 10 shares of which were acquired in 1951 at a cost of $1,500 and the remainder of 10 shares in December 1954 at a cost of $2,900. He receives in April 1955 a distribution of $250 per share in complete liquidation, or $2,500 on the 10 shares acquired in 1951, and $2,500 on the 10 shares acquired in December 1954. The gain of $1,000 on the shares acquired in 1951 is a long-term capital gain to be treated as provided in parts I, II, and III (section 1201 and following), subchapter P, chapter 1 of the Code. The loss of $400 on the shares acquired in 1954 is a short-term capital loss to be treated as provided in parts I, II, and III (section 1201 and following), subchapter P, chapter 1 of the Code.

[Reg. § 1.331-1.]

* * *

□ [*T.D.* 6152, 12-2-55. *Amended by T.D.* 6949, 4-8-68; *T.D.* 9264, 5-26-2006 *and T.D.* 9329, 6-13-2007.]

§ 1.332-1. Distributions in liquidation of subsidiary corporation; general.—Under the general rule prescribed by section 331 for the treatment of distributions in liquidation of a corporation, amounts received by one corporation in complete liquidation of another corporation are treated as in full payment in exchange for stock in such other corporation, and gain or loss from the receipt of such amounts is to be determined as provided in section 1001. Section 332 excepts from the general rule property received, under certain specifically described circumstances, by one corporation as a distribution in complete liquidation of the stock of another corporation and provides for the nonrecognition of gain or loss in those cases which meet the statutory requirements. Section 367 places a limitation on the application of section 332 in the case of foreign corporations. See section 334(b) for the basis for determining gain or loss from the subsequent sale of property received upon complete liquidations such as described in this section. See section 453(d)(4)(A) relative to distribution of installment obligations by subsidiary. [Reg. § 1.332-1.]

□ [*T.D.* 6152, 12-2-55.]

§ 1.332-2. Requirements for nonrecognition of gain or loss.—(a) The nonrecognition of gain or loss under section 332 is limited to the receipt of property by a corporation that is the actual owner of stock (in the liquidating corporation) meeting the requirements of section 1504(a)(2). The recipient corporation must have been the owner of the specified amount of such stock on the date of the adoption of the plan of liquidation and have continued so to be at all times until the receipt of the property. If the recipient corporation does not continue qualified with respect to the ownership of stock of the liquidating corporation and if the failure to continue qualified occurs at any time prior to the completion of the transfer of all the property, the provisions for the nonrecognition of gain or loss do not apply to any distribution received under the plan.

(b) Section 332 applies only to those cases in which the recipient corporation receives at least partial payment for the stock which it owns in the liquidating corporation. If section 332 is not applicable, see section 165(g) relative to allowance of losses on worthless securities.

(c) To constitute a distribution in complete liquidation within the meaning of section 332, the distribution must be (1) made by the liquidating corporation in complete cancellation or redemption of all of its stock in accordance with a plan of liquidation, or (2) one of a series of distributions in complete cancellation or redemption of all its stock in accordance with a plan of liquidation. Where there is more than one distribution, it is essential that a status of liquidation exist at the time the first distribution is made under the plan and that such status continue until the liquidation is completed. Liquidation is completed when the liquidating corporation and the receiver or trustees in liquidation are finally divested of all the property (both tangible and intangible). A status of liquidation exists when the corporation ceases to be a going concern and its activities are merely for the purpose of winding up its affairs, paying its debts and distributing any remaining balance to its shareholders. A liquidation may be completed prior to the actual dissolution of the liquidating corporation. However, legal dissolution of the corporation is not required. Nor will the mere retention of a nominal amount of assets for the sole purpose of preserving the corporation's legal existence disqualify the transaction. (See 26 CFR (1939) 39.22(a)-20 (Regulations 118).)

(d) If a transaction constitutes a distribution in complete liquidation within the meaning of the Internal Revenue Code of 1954 and satisfies the requirements of section 332, it is not material that it is otherwise described under the local law. If a liquidating corporation distributes all of its property in complete liquidation and if pursuant to the plan for such complete liquidation a corporation owning the specified amount of stock in the liquidating corporation receives property constituting amounts distributed in complete liquidation within the meaning of the Code and also receives other property attributable to shares not owned by it, the transfer of the property to the recipient corporation shall not be treated, by reason of the receipt of such other property, as not being a distribution (or one of a series of distributions) in complete cancellation or redemption of all of the stock of the liquidating corporation within the meaning of section 332, even though for purposes of those provisions relating to corporate reorganizations the amount received by the recipient corporation in excess of its ratable share is regarded as acquired upon the issuance of its stock or securities in a tax-free exchange as described in section 361 and the cancellation or redemption of the stock not owned by the recipient corporation is treated as occurring as a result of a tax-free exchange described in section 354.

(e) The application of these rules may be illustrated by the following example:

Example. On September 1, 1954, the M Corporation had outstanding capital stock consisting of 3,000 shares of common stock, par value $100 a share, and 1,000 shares of preferred stock, par value $100 a share, which preferred stock was limited and preferred as to dividends and had no voting rights. On that date, and thereafter until the date of dissolution of the M Corporation, the O Corporation owned 2,500 shares of common stock of the M Corporation. By statutory merger consummated on October 1, 1954, pursuant to a plan of liquidation adopted on September 1, 1954, the M Corporation was merged into the O Corporation, the O Corporation under the plan issuing stock which was received by the other holders of the stock of the M Corporation. The receipt by the O Corporation of the properties of the M Corporation is a distribution received by the O Corporation in complete liquidation of the M Corporation within the meaning of section 332, and no gain or loss is recognized as the result of the receipt of such properties.

* * *

[Reg. § 1.332-2.]

□ [*T.D.* 6152, 12-2-55. *Amended by T.D.* 9759, 3-25-2016.]

§ 1.332-3. Liquidations completed within one taxable year.—If in a liquidation completed within one taxable year pursuant to a plan of complete liquidation, distributions in complete liquidation are received by a corporation which owns the specified amount of stock in the liquidating corporation and which continues qualified with respect to the ownership of such stock until the transfer of all the property within such year is completed (see paragraph (a) of § 1.332-2), then no gain or loss shall be recognized with respect to the distributions received by the recipient corporation. In such case no waiver or bond is required of the recipient corporation under section 332. [Reg. § 1.332-3.]

□ [*T.D.* 6152, 12-2-55.]

§ 1.332-4. Liquidations covering more than one taxable year.—(a) If the plan of liquidation is consummated by a series of distributions extending over a period of more than one taxable year, the nonrecognition of gain or loss with respect to the distributions in liquidation shall, in addition to the requirements of § 1.332-2, be subject to the following requirements:

(1) In order for the distribution in liquidation to be brought within the exception provided in section 332 to the general rule for computing gain or loss with respect to amounts received in liquidation of a corporation, the entire property of the corporation shall be transferred in accordance with a plan of liquidation, which plan shall include a statement showing the period within which the transfer of the property of the liquidating corporation to the recipient corporation is to be completed. The transfer of all the property under the liquidation must be completed within three years from the close of the taxable year during which is made the first of the series of distributions under the plan.

(2) For each of the taxable years which falls wholly or partly within the period of liquidation, the recipient corporation shall, at the time of filing its return, file with the district director of internal revenue a waiver of the statute of limitations on assessment. The waiver shall be executed on such form as may be prescribed by the Commissioner and shall extend the period of assessment of all income and profits taxes for each such year to a date not earlier than one year after the last date of the period for assessment of such taxes for the last taxable year in which the transfer of the property of such liquidating corporation to the controlling corporation may be completed in accordance with section 332. Such waiver shall

also contain such other terms with respect to assessment as may be considered by the Commissioner to be necessary to insure the assessment and collection of the correct tax liability for each year within the period of liquidation.

(3) For each of the taxable years which falls wholly or partly within the period of liquidation, the recipient corporation may be required to file a bond, the amount of which shall be fixed by the district director. The bond shall contain all terms specified by the Commissioner, including provisions unequivocally assuring prompt payment of the excess of income and profits taxes (plus penalty, if any, and interest) as computed by the district director without regard to the provisions of sections 332 and 334(b) over such taxes computed with regard to such provisions, regardless of whether such excess may or may not be made the subject of a notice of deficiency under section 6212 and regardless of whether it may or may not be assessed. Any bond required under section 332 shall have such surety or sureties as the Commissioner may require. However, see 6 U.S.C.15, providing that where a bond is required by law or regulations, in lieu of surety or sureties there may be deposited bonds or notes of the United States. Only surety companies holding certificates of authority from the Secretary as acceptable sureties on Federal bonds will be approved as sureties. The bonds shall be executed in triplicate so that the Commissioner, the taxpayer, and the surety or the depository may each have a copy. On and after September 1, 1953, the functions of the Commissioner with respect to such bonds shall be performed by the district director for the internal revenue district in which the return was filed and any bond filed on or after such date shall be filed with such district director.

(b) Pending the completion of the liquidation, if there is a compliance with paragraph (a)(1), (2), and (3) of this section and § 1.332-2 with respect to the nonrecognition of gain or loss, the income and profits tax liability of the recipient corporation for each of the years covered in whole or in part by the liquidation shall be determined without the recognition of any gain or loss on account of the receipt of the distributions in liquidation. In such determination, the basis of the property or properties received by the recipient corporation shall be determined in accordance with section 334(b). However, if the transfer of the property is not completed within the three-year period allowed by section 332 or if the recipient corporation does not continue qualified with respect to the ownership of stock of the liquidating corporation as required by that section, gain or loss shall be recognized with respect to each distribution and the tax liability for each of the years covered in whole or in part by the liquidation shall be recomputed without regard to the provisions of section 332 or section 334(b) and the amount of any additional tax due upon such recomputation shall be promptly paid. [Reg. § 1.332-4.]

☐ [*T.D.* 6152, 12-2-55.]

§ 1.332-5. Distributions in liquidation as affecting minority interests.—Upon the liquidation of a corporation in pursuance of a plan of complete liquidation, the gain or loss of minority shareholders shall be determined without regard to section 332, since it does not apply to that part of distributions in liquidation received by minority shareholders. [Reg. § 1.332-5.]

☐ [*T.D.* 6152, 12-2-55.]

§ 1.332-7. Indebtedness of subsidiary to parent.—If section 332(a) is applicable to the receipt of the subsidiary's property in complete liquidation, then no gain or loss shall be recognized to the subsidiary upon the transfer of such properties even though some of the properties are transferred in satisfaction of the subsidiary's indebtedness to its parent. See section 337(b)(1). However, any gain or loss realized by the parent corporation on such satisfaction of indebtedness, shall be recognized to the parent corporation at the time of the liquidation. For example, if the parent corporation purchased its subsidiary's bonds at a discount and upon liquidation of the subsidiary the parent corporation receives payment for the face amount of such bonds, gain shall be recognized to the parent corporation. Such gain shall be measured by the difference between the cost or other basis of the bonds to the parent and the amount received in payment of the bonds. [Reg. § 1.332-7.]

☐ [*T.D.* 6152, 12-2-55. *Amended by T.D.* 9759, 3-25-2016.]

§ 1.334-1. Basis of property received in liquidations.—(a) *In general.*—Section 334 sets forth rules for determining a distributee's basis in property received in a distribution in complete liquidation of a corporation. The general rule is set forth in section 334(a) and provides that, if property is received in a distribution in complete liquidation of a corporation and if gain or loss is recognized on the receipt of the property, then the distributee's basis in the property is the fair market value of the property at the time of the distribution. However, if property is received in a complete liquidation to which section 332 applies, including property received in satisfaction of an indebtedness described in section 337(b)(1), see section 334(b)(1) and paragraph (b) of this section.

(b) *Liquidations under section 332.*—(1) *General rule.*—Except as otherwise provided in paragraph (b)(2) or (3) of this section, if a corporation (P) meeting the ownership requirements of section 332(b)(1) receives property from a subsidiary (S) in a complete liquidation to which section 332 applies (section 332 liquidation), including property received in a transfer in satisfaction of indebtedness that satisfies the requirements of section 337(b)(1), P's basis in the property received is the same as S's basis in the property immediately before the property was distributed. However, see § 1.460-4(k)(3)(iv)(B)(*2*) for rules relating to adjustments to the basis of certain contracts accounted for using a long-term contract method of accounting that are acquired in a section 332 liquidation.

(2) *Basis in property with respect to which gain or loss was recognized.*—Except as otherwise provided in Subtitle A of the Internal Revenue Code (Code) and this subchapter of the Income Tax Regulations, if S recognizes gain or loss on the distribution of property to P in a section 332 liquidation, P's basis in that property is the fair market value of the property at the time of the distribution. Section 334(b)(1)(A) (certain tax-exempt distributions under section 337(b)(2)); see also, for example, § 1.367(e)-2(b)(3)(i).

(3) *Basis in importation property received in loss importation transaction.*—(i) *Purpose.*—The purpose of section 334(b)(1)(B) and this paragraph (b)(3) is to modify the application of this section to prevent P from importing a net built-in loss in a transaction described in section 332. See paragraph (b)(3)(iii)(A) of this section for definitions of terms used in this paragraph (b)(3).

(ii) *Determination of basis.*—Notwithstanding paragraph (b)(1) of this section, if a section 332 liquidation is a loss importation transaction, P's basis in each importation property received from S in the liquidation is an amount that is equal to the value of the property. The basis of property received in a section 332 liquidation that is not importation property received in a loss importation transaction is determined under generally applicable basis rules without regard to whether the liquidation also involves the receipt of importation property in a loss importation transaction.

(iii) *Operating rules.*—(A) *In general.*—For purposes of section 334(b)(1)(B) and this paragraph (b)(3), the provisions of § 1.362-3 (basis of importation property received in a loss importation transaction) apply, adjusted as appropriate to apply to section 332 liquidations. Thus, when used in this paragraph (b)(3), the terms "importation property," "loss importation transaction," and "value" have the same meaning as in § 1.362-3(c)(2), (3), and (4), respectively, except that "the section 332(b)(1) distributee corporation" is substituted for "Acquiring" and "section 332 liquidation" is substituted for "section 362 transaction." Similarly, when gain or loss on property would be owned or treated as owned by multiple persons, the provisions of § 1.362-3(d)(2) apply to tentatively divide the property in applying this section, substituting "section 332 liquidation" for "section 362 transaction" and making such other adjustments as necessary.

(B) *Time for making determinations.*—For purposes of section 334(b)(1)(B) and this paragraph (b)(3)—

(1) P's basis in distributed property.—P's basis in each property S distributes to P in the section 332 liquidation is determined immediately after S distributes each such property;

(2) Value of distributed property.—The value of each property S distributes to P in the section 332 liquidation is determined immediately after S distributes the property;

(3) Importation property.—The determination of whether each property distributed by S is importation property is made as of the time S distributes each such property;

(4) Loss importation transaction.—The determination of whether a section 332 liquidation is a loss importation transaction is made immediately after S makes the final liquidating distribution to P.

(C) *Effect of basis determination under this paragraph (b)(3).*—*(1) Determination by reference to transferor's basis.*—A determination of basis under section 334(b)(1)(B) and this paragraph (b)(3) is a determination by reference to the transferor's basis, including for purposes of sections 1223(2) and 7701(a)(43). However, solely for purposes of applying section 755, a determination of basis under this paragraph (b)(3) is treated as a determination not by reference to the transferor's basis.

(2) Not tax-exempt income or noncapital, nondeductible expense.—The application of this paragraph (b)(3) does not give rise to an item treated as tax-exempt income under § 1.1502-32(b)(2)(ii) or as a noncapital, nondeductible expense under § 1.1502-32(b)(2)(iii).

(3) No effect on earnings and profits.—Any determination of basis under this paragraph (b)(3) does not reduce or otherwise affect the calculation of the all earnings and profits amount provided in § 1.367(b)-2(d).

* * *

[Reg. § 1.334-1.]

□ [*T.D.* 6152, 12-2-55. *Amended by T.D.* 6298, 6-23-58; *T.D.* 7231, 12-21-72; *T.D.* 8474, 4-26-93, *T.D.* 8995, 5-14-2002 *and T.D.* 9759, 3-25-2016.]

§ 1.336-1. General principles, nomenclature, and definitions for a section 336(e) election.—(a) *Overview*.—(1) *In general*.—Section 336(e) authorizes the promulgation of regulations under which, in certain circumstances, a sale, exchange, or distribution of the stock of a corporation may be treated as an asset sale. This section and §§ 1.336-2 through 1.336-5 provide the rules for and consequences of making such election. This section provides the definitions and nomenclature. Generally, except to the extent inconsistent with section 336(e), the results of section 336(e) should coincide with those of section 338(h)(10). Accordingly, to the extent not inconsistent with section 336(e) or these regulations, the principles of section 338 and the regulations under section 338 apply for purposes of these regulations. For example, § 1.338(h)(10)-1(d)(8), concerning the availability of the section 453 installment method, may apply with respect to section 336(e).

(2) *Consistency rules*.—In general, the principles of § 1.338-8, concerning asset and stock consistency, apply with respect to section 336(e). However, for this purpose, the application of § 1.338-8(b)(1) is modified such that § 1.338-8(b)(1)(iii) applies to an asset if the asset is owned, immediately after its acquisition and on the disposition date, by a person or by a related person (as defined in § 1.336-1(b)(12)) to a person that acquires, by sale, exchange, distribution, or any combination thereof, five percent or more, by value, of the stock of target in the qualified stock disposition.

(b) *Definitions*.—For purposes of §§ 1.336-1 through 1.336-5 (except as otherwise provided):

(1) *Seller*.—The term *seller* means any domestic corporation that makes a qualified stock disposition of stock of another corporation. Seller includes both a transferor and a distributor of target stock. Generally, all members of a consolidated group that dispose of target stock are treated as a single seller. See § 1.336-2(g)(2).

(2) *Purchaser*.—The term *purchaser* means one or more persons that acquire or receive the stock of another corporation in a qualified stock disposition. A purchaser includes both a transferee and a distributee of target stock.

(3) *Target; S corporation target; old target; new target*.—The term *target* means any domestic corporation the stock of which is sold, exchanged, or distributed in a qualified stock disposition. An *S corporation target* is a target that is an S corporation immediately before the disposition date; any other target is a *non-S corporation target*. Except as the context otherwise requires, a reference to target includes a reference to an S corporation target. In the case of a transaction not described in section 355(d)(2) or (e)(2), *old target* refers to target for periods ending on or before the close of target's disposition date and *new target* refers to target for subsequent periods. In the case of a transaction described in section 355(d)(2) or (e)(2), *old target* refers to target for periods ending on or before the disposition date as well as for subsequent periods.

(4) *S corporation shareholders*.—*S corporation shareholders* are the S corporation target's shareholders. Unless otherwise provided, a reference to S corporation shareholders refers both to S corporation shareholders who dispose of and those who do not dispose of their S corporation target stock.

(5) *Disposed of; disposition*.—(i) *In general*.—The term *disposed of* refers to a transfer of stock in a disposition. The term *disposition* means any sale, exchange, or distribution of stock, but only if—

(A) The basis of the stock in the hands of the purchaser is not determined in whole or in part by reference to the adjusted basis of such stock in the hands of the person from whom the stock is acquired, is not determined under section 1014(a) (relating to property acquired from a decedent), or is not determined under section 1022 (relating to the basis of property acquired from certain decedents who died in 2010);

(B) Except as provided in paragraph (b)(5)(ii) of this section, the stock is not sold, exchanged, or distributed in a transaction to which section 351, 354, 355, or 356 applies and is not sold, exchanged, or distributed in any transaction described in regulations in which the transferor does not recognize the entire amount of the gain or loss realized in the transaction; and

(C) The stock is not sold, exchanged, or distributed to a related person.

(ii) *Exception for disposition of stock in certain section 355 transactions*.—Notwithstanding paragraph (b)(5)(i)(B) of this section, a distribution of stock to a person who is not a related person in a transaction in which the full amount of stock gain would be recognized pursuant to section 355(d)(2) or (e)(2) shall be considered a disposition.

(iii) *Transactions with related persons.*—In determining whether stock is sold, exchanged, or distributed to a related person, the principles of section 338(h)(3)(C) and § 1.338-3(b)(3) shall apply.

(iv) *No consideration paid.*—Stock in target may be considered disposed of if, under general principles of tax law, seller is considered to sell, exchange, or distribute stock of target notwithstanding that no amount may be paid for (or allocated to) the stock.

(v) *Disposed of stock reacquired by certain persons.*—Stock disposed of by seller to another person under this section that is reacquired by seller or a member of seller's consolidated group during the 12-month disposition period shall not be considered as disposed of. Similarly, stock disposed of by an S corporation shareholder to another person under this section that is reacquired by the S corporation shareholder or by a person related (within the meaning of paragraph (b)(12) of this section) to the S corporation shareholder during the 12-month disposition period shall not be considered as disposed of.

(6) *Qualified stock disposition.*—(i) *In general.*—The term *qualified stock disposition* means any transaction or series of transactions in which stock meeting the requirements of section 1504(a)(2) of a domestic corporation is either sold, exchanged, or distributed, or any combination thereof, by another domestic corporation or by the S corporation shareholders in a disposition, within the meaning of paragraph (b)(5) of this section, during the 12-month disposition period.

(ii) *Overlap with qualified stock purchase.*—(A) *In general.*—Except as provided in paragraph (b)(6)(ii)(B) of this section, a transaction satisfying the definition of a qualified stock disposition under paragraph (b)(6)(i) of this section, which also qualifies as a qualified stock purchase (as defined in section 338(d)(3)), will not be treated as a qualified stock disposition.

(B) *Exception.*—If, as a result of the deemed sale of old target's assets pursuant to a section 336(e) election, there would be, but for paragraph (b)(6)(ii)(A) of this section, a qualified stock disposition of the stock of a subsidiary of target, then paragraph (b)(6)(ii)(A) shall not apply to the disposition of the stock of the subsidiary.

(7) *12-month disposition period.*—The term *12-month disposition period* means the 12-month period beginning with the date of the first sale, exchange, or distribution of stock included in a qualified stock disposition.

(8) *Disposition date.*—The term *disposition date* means, with respect to any corporation, the first day on which there is a qualified stock disposition with respect to the stock of such corporation.

(9) *Disposition date assets.*—*Disposition date assets* are the assets of target held at the beginning of the day after the disposition date (but see § 1.338-1(d) (regarding certain transactions on the disposition date)).

(10) *Domestic corporation.*—The term *domestic corporation* has the same meaning as in § 1.338-2(c)(9).

(11) *Section 336(e) election.*—A section 336(e) election is an election to apply section 336(e) to target. A section 336(e) election is made by making an election for target under § 1.336-2(h).

(12) *Related persons.*—Two persons are related if stock of a corporation owned by one of the persons would be attributed under section 318(a), other than section 318(a)(4), to the other. However, neither section 318(a)(2)(A) nor section 318(a)(3)(A) apply to attribute stock ownership from a partnership to a partner, or from a partner to a partnership, if such partner owns, directly or indirectly, interests representing less than five percent of the value of the partnership.

(13) *Liquidation.*—Any reference to a liquidation is treated as a reference to the transfer described in § 1.336-2(b)(1)(iii) notwithstanding its ultimate characterization for Federal income tax purposes.

(14) *Deemed asset disposition.*—The deemed sale of old target's assets is, without regard to its characterization for Federal income tax purposes, referred to as the deemed asset disposition.

(15) *Deemed disposition tax consequences.*—Deemed disposition tax consequences refers to, in the aggregate, the Federal income tax consequences (generally, the income, gain, deduction, and loss) of the deemed asset disposition. Deemed disposition tax consequences also refers to the Federal income tax consequences of the transfer of a particular asset in the deemed asset disposition.

(16) *80-percent purchaser.*—An 80-percent purchaser is any purchaser that, after application of the attribution rules of section 318(a), other than section 318(a)(4), owns 80 percent or more of the voting power or value of target stock.

(17) *Recently disposed stock.*—The term *recently disposed stock* means any stock in target

that is not held by seller, a member of seller's consolidated group, or an S corporation shareholder immediately after the close of the disposition date and that was disposed of by seller, a member of seller's consolidated group, or an S corporation shareholder during the 12-month disposition period.

(18) *Nonrecently disposed stock*.—The term *nonrecently disposed stock* means stock in target that is held on the disposition date by a purchaser or a person related (as described in § 1.336-1(b)(12)) to the purchaser who owns, on the disposition date, with the application of section 318(a), other than section 318(a)(4), at least 10 percent of the total voting power or value of the stock of target and that is not recently disposed stock.

(c) *Nomenclature*.—For purposes of §§ 1.336-1 through 1.336-5, except as otherwise provided, Parent, Seller, Target, Sub, S Corporation Target, and Target Subsidiary are domestic corporations and A, B, C, and D are individuals, none of whom are related to Parent, Seller, Target, Sub, S Corporation Target, Target Subsidiary, or each other. [Reg. § 1.336-1.]

☐ [*T.D.* 9619, 5-10-2013. *Amended by T.D.* 9811, 1-18-2017.]

§ 1.336-2. Availability, mechanics, and consequences of section 336(e) election.—(a) *Availability of election*.—A section 336(e) election is available if seller or S corporation shareholder(s) dispose of stock of another corporation (target) in a qualified stock disposition (as defined in § 1.336-1(b)(6)). A section 336(e) election is irrevocable. A section 336(e) election is not available for transactions described in section 336(e) that do not constitute qualified stock dispositions.

(b) *Deemed transaction*.—(1) *Dispositions not described in section 355(d)(2) or (e)(2)*.—(i) *Old target—deemed asset disposition*.—(A) *In general*.—This paragraph (b)(1) provides the Federal income tax consequences of a section 336(e) election made with respect to a qualified stock disposition not described, in whole or in part, in section 355(d)(2) or (e)(2). For the Federal income tax consequences of a section 336(e) election made with respect to a qualified stock disposition described, in whole or in part, in section 355(d)(2) or (e)(2), see paragraph (b)(2) of this section. In general, if a section 336(e) election is made, seller (or S corporation shareholders) are treated as not having sold, exchanged, or distributed the stock disposed of in the qualified stock disposition. Instead, old target is treated as selling its assets to an unrelated person in a single transaction at the close of the disposition date (but before the deemed liquidation described in paragraph (b)(1)(iii) of this section) in exchange for the aggregate deemed asset disposition price (ADADP) as determined under § 1.336-3. ADADP is allocated among the disposition date assets in the same manner as the aggregate deemed sale price (ADSP) is allocated under §§ 1.338-6 and 1.338-7 in order to determine the amount realized from each of the sold assets. Old target realizes the deemed disposition tax consequences from the deemed asset disposition before the close of the disposition date while old target is owned by seller or the S corporation shareholders. If old target is an S corporation target, old target's S election continues in effect through the close of the disposition date (including the time of the deemed asset disposition and the deemed liquidation) notwithstanding section 1362(d)(2)(B). Also, if old target is an S corporation target (but not a qualified subchapter S subsidiary), any direct or indirect subsidiaries of old target that old target has elected to treat as qualified subchapter S subsidiaries under section 1361(b)(3) remain qualified subchapter S subsidiaries through the close of the disposition date.

(B) *Gains and losses*.—*(1) Gains*.—Except as provided in § 1.338(h)(10)-1(d)(8) (regarding the installment method), old target shall recognize all of the gains realized on the deemed asset disposition.

(2) Losses.—*(i) In general*.—Except as provided in paragraphs (b)(1)(i)(B)*(2)*(*ii*), (*iii*), and (*iv*) of this section, old target shall recognize all of the losses realized on the deemed asset disposition.

(ii) Stock distributions.—Notwithstanding paragraphs (b)(1)(i)(A) and (b)(1)(iii)(A) of this section, for purposes of determining the amount of target's losses that are disallowed on the deemed asset disposition, seller is still treated as selling, exchanging, or distributing its target stock disposed of in the 12-month disposition period. If target's losses realized on the deemed sale of all of its assets exceed target's gains realized (a net loss), the portion of such net loss attributable to a distribution of target stock during the 12-month disposition period is disallowed. The total amount of disallowed loss and the allocation of disallowed loss is determined in the manner provided in paragraphs (b)(1)(i)(B)*(2)*(*iii*) and (*iv*) of this section.

(iii) Amount and allocation of disallowed loss.—The total disallowed loss pursuant to paragraph (b)(1)(i)(B)*(2)*(*ii*) of this section shall be determined by multiplying the net loss realized on the deemed asset disposi-

tion by the disallowed loss fraction. The numerator of the disallowed loss fraction is the value of target stock, determined on the disposition date, distributed by seller during the 12-month disposition period, whether or not a part of the qualified stock disposition (for example, stock distributed to a related person), and the denominator of the disallowed loss fraction is the sum of the value of target stock, determined on the disposition date, disposed of by sale or exchange in the qualified stock disposition during the 12-month disposition period and the value of target stock, determined on the disposition date, distributed by seller during the 12-month disposition period, whether or not a part of the qualified stock disposition. The amount of the disallowed loss allocated to each asset disposed of in the deemed asset disposition is determined by multiplying the total amount of the disallowed loss by the loss allocation fraction. The numerator of the loss allocation fraction is the amount of loss realized with respect to the asset and the denominator of the loss allocation fraction is the sum of the amount of losses realized with respect to each loss asset disposed of in the deemed asset disposition. To the extent old target's losses from the deemed asset disposition are not disallowed under this paragraph, such losses may be disallowed under other provisions of the Internal Revenue Code or general principles of tax law, in the same manner as if such assets were actually sold to an unrelated person.

(iv) Tiered targets.—If an asset of target is the stock of a subsidiary corporation of target for which a section 336(e) election is made, any gain or loss realized on the deemed sale of the stock of the subsidiary corporation is disregarded in determining the amount of disallowed loss. For purposes of determining the amount of disallowed loss on the deemed asset disposition by a subsidiary of target for which a section 336(e) election is made, the amount of subsidiary stock deemed sold in the deemed asset disposition of target's assets multiplied by the disallowed loss fraction with respect to the corporation that is deemed to have disposed of stock of the subsidiary is considered to have been distributed. In determining the disallowed loss fraction with respect to the deemed asset disposition of any subsidiary of target, disregard any sale, exchange, or distribution of its stock that was made after the disposition date if such stock was included in the deemed asset disposition of the corporation deemed to have disposed of the subsidiary stock.

(3) Examples.—The following examples illustrate this paragraph (b)(1)(i)(B).

Example 1. (i) *Facts.* Parent owns 60 of the 100 outstanding shares of the common stock of Seller, Seller's only class of stock outstanding. The remaining 40 shares of the common stock of Seller are held by shareholders unrelated to Seller or each other. Seller owns 95 of the 100 outstanding shares of Target common stock, and all 100 shares of Target preferred stock that is described in section 1504(a)(4). The remaining 5 shares of Target common stock are owned by A. On January 1 of Year 1, Seller sells 72 shares of Target common stock to B for $3,520. On July 1 of Year 1, Seller distributes 12 shares of Target common stock to Parent and 8 shares to its unrelated shareholders in a distribution described in section 301. Seller retains 3 shares of Target common stock and all 100 shares of Target preferred stock immediately after July 1. The value of Target common stock on July 1 is $60 per share. The value of Target preferred stock on July 1 is $36 per share. Target has three assets, Asset 1, a Class IV asset, with a basis of $1,776 and a fair market value of $2,000, Asset 2, a Class V asset, with a basis of $2,600 and a fair market value of $2,750, and Asset 3, a Class V asset, with a basis of $3,900 and a fair market value of $3,850. Seller incurred no selling costs on the sale of the 72 shares of Target common stock to B. Target has no liabilities. A section 336(e) election is made.

(ii) *Consequences—Deemed Asset Sale.* Because at least 80 percent ((72 + 8)/100) of Target stock, other than stock described in section 1504(a)(4), was disposed of (within the meaning of § 1.336-1(b)(5)) by Seller during the 12-month disposition period, a qualified stock disposition occurred. July 1 of Year 1, the first day on which there was a qualified stock disposition with respect to Target stock, is the disposition date. Accordingly, pursuant to the section 336(e) election, for Federal income tax purposes, Seller generally is not treated as selling the 72 shares of Target common stock sold to B or distributing the 8 shares of Target common stock distributed to its unrelated shareholders. However, Seller is still treated as distributing the 12 shares of Target common stock distributed to Parent because Seller and Parent are related persons within the meaning of § 1.336-1(b)(12) and accordingly the 12 shares are not part of the qualified stock disposition. Target is treated as if, on July 1, it sold all of its assets to an unrelated person in exchange for the ADADP, $8,000, which is allocated $2,000 to Asset 1, $2,500 to Asset 2, and $3,500 to Asset 3 (see *Example 1* of § 1.336-3(g) for the determination and allocation of ADADP).

(iii) *Consequences—Amount and Allocation of Disallowed Loss.* Old Target realized a net loss of $276 on the deemed asset disposition ($224 gain realized on Asset 1, $100 loss realized on Asset 2, and $400 loss realized on

Asset 3). However, 20 shares of Target common stock were distributed by Seller during the 12-month disposition period (8 shares distributed to Seller's unrelated shareholders in the qualified stock disposition plus 12 shares distributed to Parent that were not part of the qualified stock disposition). Therefore, because there was a net loss realized on the deemed asset disposition and a portion of the stock of Target was distributed during the 12-month disposition period, a portion of the loss on the deemed sale of each of Target's loss assets is disallowed. The total amount of disallowed loss equals $60 ($276 net loss realized on the deemed disposition of Assets 1, 2, and 3 multiplied by the disallowed loss fraction, the numerator of which is $1,200, the value on July 1, the disposition date, of the 20 shares of Target common stock distributed during the 12-month disposition period, and the denominator of which is $5,520, the sum of $4,320, the value on July 1 of the 72 shares of Target common stock sold to B and $1,200, the value on July 1 of the 20 shares of Target common stock distributed during the 12-month disposition period). The portion of the disallowed loss allocated to Asset 2 is $12 ($60 total disallowed loss multiplied by the loss allocation fraction, the numerator of which is $100, the loss realized on the deemed disposition of Asset 2 and the denominator of which is $500, the sum of the losses realized on the deemed disposition of Assets 2 and 3). The portion of the disallowed loss allocated to Asset 3 is $48 ($60 total disallowed loss multiplied by the loss allocation fraction, the numerator of which is $400, the loss realized on the deemed disposition of Asset 3 and the denominator of which is $500, the sum of the losses realized on the deemed disposition of Assets 2 and 3). Accordingly, Old Target recognizes $224 of gain on Asset 1, recognizes $88 of loss on Asset 2 (realized loss of $100 less allocated disallowed loss of $12), and recognizes $352 of loss on Asset 3 (realized loss of $400 less allocated disallowed loss of $48) or a recognized net loss of $216 on the deemed asset disposition.

Example 2. (i) *Facts.* The facts are the same as in *Example 1* except that Asset 2 is the stock of Target Subsidiary, a corporation of which Target owns 100 of the 110 shares of common stock, the only outstanding class of Target Subsidiary stock. The remaining 10 shares of Target Subsidiary stock are owned by D. The value of Target Subsidiary stock on July 1 is $27.50 per share. Target Subsidiary has two assets, Asset 4, a Class IV asset, with a basis of $800 and a fair market value of $1,000, and Asset 5, a Class IV asset, with a basis of $2,200 and a fair market value of $2,025. Target Subsidiary has no liabilities. A section 336(e) election with respect to Target Subsidiary is also made.

(ii) *Consequences—Target.* The ADADP on the deemed sale of Target's assets is determined and allocated in the same manner as in *Example 1.* However, Target's loss realized on the deemed sale of Target Subsidiary is disregarded in determining the amount of disallowed loss on the deemed asset disposition of Target's assets. Thus, the net loss is only $176 ($224 gain realized on Asset 1 and $400 loss realized on Asset 3), and the amount of disallowed loss equals $38.26 ($176 net loss multiplied by the disallowed loss fraction with respect to Target stock, $1,200/$5,520). The entire disallowed loss is allocated to Asset 3.

(iii) *Consequences—Target Subsidiary.* The deemed sale of the stock of Target Subsidiary is disregarded and instead Target Subsidiary is deemed to sell all of its assets to an unrelated person. The ADADP on the deemed asset disposition of Target Subsidiary is $2,750, which is allocated $909 to Asset 4 and $1,841 to Asset 5 (see *Example 2* of § 1.336-3(g) for the determination and allocation of ADADP). Old Target Subsidiary realized $109 of gain on Asset 4 and realized $359 of loss on Asset 5 in the deemed asset disposition. Although Old Target Subsidiary realized a net loss of $250 on the deemed asset disposition ($109 gain on Asset 4 and $359 loss on Asset 5), a portion of this net loss is disallowed because a portion of Target stock was distributed during the 12-month disposition period. For purposes of determining the amount of disallowed loss on the deemed sale of the assets of Target Subsidiary, the portion of the 100 shares of Target Subsidiary stock deemed sold by Target pursuant to the section 336(e) election for Target Subsidiary multiplied by the disallowed loss fraction with respect to Target stock is treated as having been distributed. Thus, for purposes of determining the amount of disallowed loss on the deemed asset disposition of Target Subsidiary's assets, 21.74 shares of Target Subsidiary stock (100 shares of Target Subsidiary stock owned by Target multiplied by the disallowed loss fraction with respect to Target stock, $1,200/$5,520) are treated as having been distributed by Target during the 12-month disposition period. The total amount of disallowed loss with respect to the deemed asset disposition of Target Subsidiary's assets equals $54 ($250 net loss realized on the deemed disposition of Assets 4 and 5 multiplied by the disallowed loss fraction with respect to Target Subsidiary, the numerator of which is $598, the value on July 1, the disposition date, of the 21.74 shares of Target Subsidiary stock deemed distributed during the 12-month disposition period (21.74 shares × $27.50) and the denominator of which is $2,750 (the sum of $2,152, the value on July 1 of the 78.26 shares of Target Subsidiary stock deemed sold in the qualified stock disposition pursuant to the section 336(e) election for Target Subsidiary (78.26 shares × $27.50) and $598, the value on July 1 of the 21.74 shares of Target Subsidiary stock deemed distributed during the 12-month disposition period)). (The 10 shares of Target Subsidiary owned by D are not part of the qualified stock disposition and therefore are not included in the denominator of the disallowed loss fraction.) All of the disallowed loss is allocated to Asset 5, the only loss asset. Accordingly, Old Target Subsidiary recognizes $109 of gain on Asset 4 and recognizes $305 of loss on Asset 5 (realized loss of $359 less disallowed loss of $54) or a net loss of $196 on the deemed asset disposition.

Example 3. (i) *Facts.* The facts are the same as in *Example 2* except that on August 1 of Year 1, Target sells 50 of its shares of Target Subsidiary stock and distributes the remaining 50 shares.

(ii) *Consequences.* Because the 100 shares of Target Subsidiary stock that were sold and distributed on August 1 were deemed disposed of on July 1 in the deemed asset disposition of Target, the August 1 sale and distribution of Target Subsidiary stock are disregarded in determining the amount of disallowed loss. Accordingly, the consequences are the same as in *Example 2.*

(C) *Tiered targets.*—In the case of parent-subsidiary chains of corporations making section 336(e) elections, the deemed asset disposition of a higher-tier subsidiary is considered to precede the deemed asset disposition of a lower-tier subsidiary.

(ii) *New target—deemed purchase.*—New target is treated as acquiring all of its assets from an unrelated person in a single transaction at the close of the disposition date (but before the deemed liquidation) in exchange for an amount equal to the adjusted grossed-up basis (AGUB) as determined under § 1.336-4. New target allocates the consideration deemed paid in the transaction in the same manner as new target would under §§ 1.338-6 and 1.338-7 in order to determine the basis in each of the purchased assets. If new target qualifies as a small business corporation within the meaning of section 1361(b) and wants to be an S corporation, a new election under section 1362(a) must be made. Notwithstanding paragraph (b)(1)(iii) of this section (deemed liquidation of old target), new target remains liable for the tax liabilities of old target (including the tax liability for the deemed disposition tax consequences). For example, new target remains liable for the tax liabilities of the members of any consolidated group that are attributable to taxable years in which those corporations and old target joined in the same consolidated return. See § 1.1502-6(a).

(iii) *Old target and seller—deemed liquidation.*—(A) *In general.*—If old target is an S corporation, S corporation shareholders (whether or not they sell or exchange their stock) take their pro rata share of the deemed disposition tax consequences into account under section 1366 and increase or decrease their basis in target stock under section 1367. Old target and seller (or S corporation shareholders) are treated as if, before the close of the disposition date, after the deemed asset disposition described in paragraph (b)(1)(i)(A) of this section, and while target is owned by seller or S corporation shareholders, old target transferred all of the consideration deemed received from new target in the deemed asset disposition to seller or S corporation shareholders, any S corporation election for old target terminated, and old target ceased to exist. The transfer from old target to seller or S corporation shareholders is characterized for Federal income tax purposes in the same manner as if the parties had actually engaged in the transactions deemed to occur because of this section and taking into account other transactions that actually occurred or are deemed to occur. For example, the transfer may be treated as a distribution in pursuance of a plan of reorganization, a distribution in complete cancellation or redemption of all of its stock, one of a series of distributions in complete cancellation or redemption of all of its stock in accordance with a plan of liquidation, or part of a circular flow of cash. In most cases, the transfer will be treated as a distribution in complete liquidation to which sections 331 or 332 and sections 336 or 337 apply.

(B) *Tiered targets.*—In the case of parent-subsidiary chains of corporations making section 336(e) elections, the deemed liquidation of a lower-tier subsidiary corporation is considered to precede the deemed liquidation of a higher-tier subsidiary.

(iv) *Seller—distribution of target stock.*—In the case of a distribution of target stock in a qualified stock disposition, seller (the distributor) is deemed to purchase from an unrelated person, on the disposition date, immediately after the deemed liquidation of old target, the amount of stock distributed in the qualified stock disposition (new target stock) and to have distributed such new target stock to its shareholders. Seller recognizes no gain or loss on the distribution of such stock.

(v) *Seller—retention of target stock.*—If seller or an S corporation shareholder retains any target stock after the disposition date, seller or the S corporation shareholder is treated as purchasing the stock so retained from an unrelated person (new target stock) on the day after the disposition date for its fair market value. The holding period for the retained stock starts on the day after the disposition date. For purposes of this paragraph (b)(1)(v), the fair market value of all of the target stock equals the grossed-up amount realized on the sale, exchange, or distribution of recently disposed stock of target (see § 1.336-3(c)).

* * *

(c) *Purchaser.*—Generally, the making of a section 336(e) election will not affect the Federal income tax consequences to which purchaser would have been subject with respect to the acquisition of target stock if a section 336(e) election was not made. Thus, notwithstanding § § 1.336-2(b)(1)(i)(A), 1.336-2(b)(1)(iv), and 1.336-2(b)(2)(iii)(A), purchaser will still be treated as having purchased, received in an exchange, or received in a distribution, the stock of target so acquired on the date actually acquired. However, see section 1223(1)(B) with respect to the holding period for stock acquired pursuant to a distribution qualifying under section 355 (or so much of section 356 that relates to section 355). The Federal income tax consequences of the deemed asset disposition and liquidation of target may affect purchaser's consequences. For example, if seller distributes the stock of target to its shareholders in a qualified stock disposition for which a section 336(e) election is made, any increase in seller's earnings and profits as a result of old target's deemed asset disposition and liquidation into seller may increase the amount of a distribution to the shareholders constituting a dividend under section 301(c)(1).

(d) *Minority shareholders.*—(1) *In general.*—This paragraph (d) describes the treatment of shareholders of old target other than seller, a member of seller's consolidated group, and S corporation shareholders (whether or not they sell or exchange their stock of target). A shareholder to which this paragraph (d) applies is referred to as a minority shareholder.

(2) *Sale, exchange, or distribution of target stock by a minority shareholder.*—A minority shareholder recognizes gain or loss (as permitted under the general principles of tax law) on its sale, exchange, or distribution of target stock.

(3) *Retention of target stock by a minority shareholder.*—A minority shareholder who retains its target stock does not recognize gain or loss under this section with respect to its shares of target stock. The minority shareholder's basis and holding period for that target stock are not affected by the section 336(e) election. Notwithstanding this treatment of the minority shareholder, if a section 336(e) election is made, target will still be treated as disposing of all of its assets in the deemed asset disposition.

(e) *Treatment consistent with an actual asset disposition.*—Except as otherwise provided, no provision in this section shall produce a Federal income tax result under subtitle A of the Internal Revenue Code that would not occur if the parties had actually engaged in the transactions deemed to occur because of this section, taking into account other transactions that actually occurred or are deemed to occur. See § 1.338-1(a)(2) regarding the application of other rules of law.

(f) *Treatment of target under other provisions of the Internal Revenue Code.*—The provisions § 1.338-1(b) apply with respect to the treatment of new target after a section 336(e) election, treating any reference to section 338 or 338(h)(10) as a reference to section 336(e).

* * *

(k) *Examples.*—The following examples illustrate the provisions of this section.

Example 1. Sale of 100 percent of Target stock. (i) *Facts.* Parent owns all 100 shares of Target's only class of stock. Target's only assets are two parcels of land. Parcel 1 has a basis of $5,000 and Parcel 2 has a basis of $4,000. Target has no liabilities. On July 1 of Year 1, Parent sells all 100 shares of Target stock to A for $100 per share. Parent incurs no selling costs and A incurs no acquisition costs. On July 1, the value of Parcel 1 is $7,000 and the value of Parcel 2 is $3,000. A section 336(e) election is made.

(ii) *Consequences.* The sale of Target stock constitutes a qualified stock disposition. July 1 of Year 1 is the disposition date. Accordingly, pursuant to the section 336(e) election, for Federal income tax purposes, rather than treating Parent as selling the stock of Target to A, the following events are deemed to occur. Target is treated as if, on July 1, it sold all of its assets to an unrelated person in exchange for the ADADP of $10,000, which is allocated $7,000 to Parcel 1 and $3,000 to Parcel 2 (see § § 1.336-3 and 1.338-6 for determination of amount and allocation of ADADP). Target recognizes gain of $2,000 on Parcel 1 and loss of $1,000 on Parcel 2. New Target is then treated as acquiring all its assets from an unrelated person in a single transaction in exchange for the amount of the AGUB of $10,000, which is allocated $7,000 to Parcel 1 and $3,000 to Parcel 2 (see § § 1.336-4, 1.338-5, and 1.338-6 for determination of amount and allocation of AGUB). Old

Target is treated as liquidating into Parent immediately thereafter, distributing the $10,000 deemed received in exchange for Parcel 1 and Parcel 2 in a transaction qualifying under section 332. Parent recognizes no gain or loss on the liquidation. A's basis in New Target stock is $100 per share, the amount paid for the stock.

Example 2. Sale of 80 percent of Target stock. (i) *Facts.* The facts are the same as in Example 1 except that Parent only sells 80 shares of its Target stock to A and retains the other 20 shares.

(ii) *Consequences.* The results are the same as in *Example 1* except that Parent also is treated as purchasing from an unrelated person on July 2, the day after the disposition date, the 20 shares of Target stock (New Target stock) not sold to A, for their fair market value as determined under § 1.336-2(b)(1)(v) of $2,000 ($100 per share).

Example 3. Distribution of 100 percent of Target stock. (i) *Facts.* The facts are the same as in *Example 1* except that instead of on July 1 Parent selling 100 shares of Target stock to A, Parent distributes 100 shares to its shareholders, all of whom are unrelated to Parent, in a transaction that does not qualify under section 355. The value of Target stock on July 1 is $100 per share.

(ii) *Consequences.* The distribution of Target stock constitutes a qualified stock disposition. July 1 of Year 1 is the disposition date. Accordingly, pursuant to the section 336(e) election, for Federal income tax purposes, rather than treating Parent as distributing the stock of Target to its shareholders, the following events are deemed to occur. Target is treated as if, on July 1, it sold all of its assets to an unrelated person in exchange for the ADADP of $10,000, which is allocated $7,000 to Parcel 1 and $3,000 to Parcel 2 (see §§ 1.336-3 and 1.338-6 for determination of amount and allocation of ADADP). Target recognizes gain of $2,000 on Parcel 1 and loss of $1,000 on Parcel 2. Because Target's losses realized on the deemed asset disposition do not exceed Target's gains realized on the deemed asset disposition, Target can recognize all of the losses from the deemed asset disposition (see § 1.336-2(b)(1)(i)(B)). New Target is then treated as acquiring all its assets from an unrelated person in a single transaction in exchange for the amount of the AGUB of $10,000, which is allocated $7,000 to Parcel 1 and $3,000 to Parcel 2 (see §§ 1.336-4, 1.338-5, and 1.338-6 for determination of amount and allocation of AGUB). Old Target is treated as liquidating into Parent immediately thereafter, distributing the $10,000 deemed received in exchange for Parcel 1 and Parcel 2 in a transaction qualifying under section 332. Parent recognizes no gain or loss on the liquidation. On July 1, immediately after the deemed liquidation of Target, Parent is deemed to purchase from an unrelated person 100 shares of New Target stock and distribute those New Target shares to its shareholders. Parent recognizes no gain or loss on the deemed distribution of the shares under § 1.336-2(b)(1)(iv). The shareholders receive New Target stock as a distribution pursuant to section 301 and their basis in New Target stock received is its fair market value pursuant to section 301(d).

Example 4. Distribution of 80 percent of Target stock. (i) *Facts.* The facts are the same as in *Example 3* except that Parent distributes only 80 shares of Target stock to its shareholders and retains the other 20 shares.

(ii) *Consequences.* The results are the same as in *Example 3* except that Parent is treated as purchasing on July 1 only 80 shares of New Target stock and as distributing only 80 shares of New Target stock to its shareholders and then as purchasing (and retaining) on July 2, the day after the disposition date, 20 shares of New Target stock at their fair market value as determined under § 1.336-2(b)(1)(v), $2,000 ($100 per share).

* * *

[Reg. § 1.336-2.]

☐ [*T.D.* 9619, 5-10-2013 (*corrected* 8-27-2013).]

§ 1.336-3. Aggregate deemed asset disposition price; various aspects of taxation of the deemed asset disposition.—(a) *Scope.*—This section provides rules under section 336(e) to determine the aggregate deemed asset disposition price (ADADP) for target. ADADP is the amount for which old target is deemed to have sold all of its assets in the deemed asset disposition. ADADP is allocated among target's assets in the same manner as the aggregate deemed sale price (ADSP) is allocated under § 1.338-6 to determine the amount for which each asset is deemed to have been sold. If a subsequent increase or decrease is required under general principles of tax law with respect to an element of ADADP, the redetermined ADADP is allocated among target's assets in the same manner as redetermined ADSP is allocated under § 1.338-7.

(b) *Determination of ADADP.*—(1) *General rule.*—ADADP is the sum of—

(i) The grossed-up amount realized on the sale, exchange, or distribution of recently disposed stock of target; and

(ii) The liabilities of old target.

(2) *Time and amount of ADADP.*—(i) *Original determination.*—ADADP is initially determined at the beginning of the day after the disposition date of target. General princi-

ples of tax law apply in determining the timing and amount of the elements of ADADP.

(ii) *Redetermination of ADADP.*—ADADP is redetermined at such time and in such amount as an increase or decrease would be required, under general principles of tax law, for the elements of ADADP. For example, ADADP is redetermined because of an increase or decrease in the amount realized on the sale or exchange of recently disposed stock of target or because liabilities not originally taken into account in determining ADADP are subsequently taken into account. Increases or decreases with respect to the elements of ADADP result in the reallocation of ADADP among target's assets in the same manner as ADSP under § 1.338-7.

(c) *Grossed-up amount realized on the disposition of recently disposed stock of target.*—(1) *Determination of amount.*—The grossed-up amount realized on the disposition of recently disposed stock of target is an amount equal to—

(i) The sum of—

(A) With respect to recently disposed of stock of target that is not distributed in the qualified stock disposition, the amount realized on the sale or exchange of such recently disposed stock of target, determined as if seller or S corporation shareholders were required to use old target's accounting methods and characteristics and the installment method were not available and determined without regard to the selling costs taken into account under paragraph (c) (1) (iii) of this section, and

(B) With respect to recently disposed of stock of target that is distributed in the qualified stock disposition, the fair market value of such recently disposed stock of target determined on the date of each distribution;

(ii) Divided by the percentage of target stock (by value, determined on the disposition date) attributable to the recently disposed stock;

(iii) Less the selling costs incurred by seller or S corporation shareholders in connection with the sale or exchange of recently disposed stock that reduce its amount realized on the sale or exchange of the stock (for example, brokerage commissions and any similar costs to sell the stock).

(2) *Example.*—The following example illustrates this paragraph (c):

Example. Target has two classes of stock outstanding, voting common stock and preferred stock described in section 1504(a) (4). Seller owns all 100 shares of each class of stock. On March 1 of Year 1, Seller sells 10 shares of Target voting common stock to A for $75. On April 1 of Year 2, Seller distributes 15 shares of Target voting common stock with a fair market value of $120 to B. On May 1 of Year 2, Seller distributes 10 shares of Target voting common stock with a fair market value of $110 to C. On July 1 of Year 2, Seller sells 55 shares of Target voting common stock to D for $550. On July 1 of Year 2, the fair market value of all the Target voting common stock is $1,000 ($10 per share) and the fair market value of all the preferred stock is $600 ($6 per share). Seller incurs $20 of selling costs with respect to the sale to A and $60 of selling costs with respect to the sale to D. The grossed-up amount realized on the sale, exchange, or distribution of recently disposed stock of Target is calculated as follows: The sum of the amount realized on the sale or exchange of recently disposed stock sold or exchanged (without regard to selling costs) and the fair market value of the recently disposed stock distributed is $780 ($120 + $110 + $550) (the 10 shares sold to A on March 1 of Year 1 is not recently disposed stock because it was not disposed of during the 12-month disposition period). The percentage of Target stock by value on the disposition date attributable to recently disposed stock equals 50% ($800 (80 shares of recently disposed stock × $10, the fair market value of each share of Target common stock on the disposition date) / $1,600 ($1,000 (the total value of Target's common stock on the disposition date) + $600 (the total value of Target's preferred stock on the disposition date))). The grossed-up amount realized equals $1,500 (($780/.50) - $60 selling costs).

(d) *Liabilities of old target.*—(1) *In general.*—In general, the liabilities of old target are measured as of the beginning of the day after the disposition date. However, if a target for which a section 336(e) election is made engages in a transaction outside the ordinary course of business on the disposition date after the event resulting in the qualified stock disposition of target or a higher-tier corporation, target and all persons related thereto (either before or after the qualified stock disposition) under section 267(b) or section 707 must treat the transaction for all Federal income tax purposes as occurring at the beginning of the day following the transaction and after the deemed disposition by old target. In order to be taken into account in ADADP, a liability must be a liability of target that is properly taken into account in amount realized under general principles of tax law that would apply if old target had sold its assets to an unrelated person for consideration that included the discharge of its liabilities. See § 1.1001-2(a). Such liabilities may include liabilities for the tax consequences resulting from the deemed asset disposition.

(2) *Time and amount of liabilities.*—The time for taking into account liabilities of old target in determining ADADP and the amount of the liabilities taken into account is determined as if old target had sold its assets to an unrelated person for consideration that included the discharge of the liabilities by the unrelated person. For example, if no amount of a target liability is properly taken into account in amount realized as of the beginning of the day after the disposition date, the liability is not initially taken into account in determining ADADP, but it may be taken into account at some later date.

(e) *Deemed disposition tax consequences.*—Gain or loss on each asset in the deemed asset disposition is computed by reference to the ADADP allocated to that asset. ADADP is allocated in the same manner as is ADSP under § 1.338-6. Although deemed disposition tax consequences may increase or decrease ADADP by creating or reducing a tax liability, the amount of the tax liability itself may be a function of the size of the deemed disposition tax consequences. Thus, these determinations may require trial and error computations.

(f) *Other rules apply in determining ADADP.*—ADADP may not be applied in such a way as to contravene other applicable rules. For example, a capital loss cannot be applied to reduce ordinary income in calculating the tax liability on the deemed asset disposition for purposes of determining ADADP.

(g) *Examples.*—The following examples illustrate this section.

Example 1. (i) *Facts.* The facts are the same as in *Example 1* of § 1.336-2(b)(1)(i)(B)(3), that is, Parent owns 60 of the 100 outstanding shares of the common stock of Seller, Seller's only class of stock outstanding. The remaining 40 shares of the common stock of Seller are held by shareholders unrelated to Seller or each other. Seller owns 95 of the 100 outstanding shares of Target common stock, and all 100 shares of Target preferred stock that is described in section 1504(a)(4). The remaining 5 shares of Target common stock are owned by A. On January 1 of Year 1, Seller sells 72 shares of Target common stock to B for $3,520. On July 1 of Year 1, Seller distributes 12 shares of Target common stock to Parent and 8 shares to its unrelated shareholders in a distribution described in section 301. Seller retains 3 shares of Target common stock and all 100 shares of Target preferred stock immediately after July 1. The value of Target common stock on July 1 is $60 per share. The value of Target preferred stock on July 1 is $36 per share. Target has three assets, Asset 1, a Class IV asset, with a basis of $1,776 and a fair market value of $2,000, Asset 2, a Class V asset, with a basis of $2,600 and a fair market value of $2,750, and Asset 3, a Class V asset, with a basis of $3,900 and a fair market value of $3,850. Seller incurred no selling costs on the sale of the 72 shares of Target common stock to B. Target has no liabilities. A section 336(e) election is made.

(ii) *Determination of ADADP.* The ADADP on the deemed asset disposition of Target is determined as follows. The grossed-up amount realized on the sale, exchange, or distribution of recently disposed stock of Target is $8,000, the sum of $3,520, the amount realized on the sale to B of the 72 shares of Target common stock and $480, the fair market value on the date distributed of the 8 shares of Target common stock distributed to Seller's unrelated shareholders in the qualified stock disposition, divided by .50, the percentage of Target stock by value, determined on the disposition date, attributable to the recently disposed stock ($4,800 (80 shares of Target common stock disposed of in the qualified stock disposition × $60, the value of a share of Target common stock on the disposition date) divided by $9,600 ((100, the total number of shares of Target common stock × $60, the value of a share of Target common stock on the disposition date) + (100, the total number of shares of Target preferred stock × $36, the value of a share of Target preferred stock on the disposition date))), minus $0, Seller's selling costs in connection with the sale of the 72 shares of Target common stock sold to B. The $8,000 grossed-up amount realized on the sale, exchange, or distribution of recently disposed stock of Target is then added to the liabilities of Old Target, $0, to arrive at the ADADP, $8,000.

(iii) *Allocation of ADADP.* The ADADP of $8,000 is allocated first to Asset 1, the Class IV asset, but not in excess of Asset 1's fair market value, $2,000. The remaining ADADP of $6,000 is allocated between Assets 2 and 3, both Class V assets, in proportion to their fair market values, but not in excess of their fair market values. Because the total fair market value of Assets 2 and 3, $6,600, exceeds the ADADP remaining after allocation of a portion of the ADADP to Asset 1, the $6,000 remaining ADADP is allocated to Assets 2 and 3 in proportion to their respective fair market values. Accordingly, $2,500 is allocated to Asset 2 ($6,000 × ($2,750/($2,750 + $3,850))) and $3,500 is allocated to Asset 3 ($6,000 × ($3,850/($2,750 + $3,850))).

Example 2. (i) *Facts.* The facts are the same as in *Example 1* except that Asset 2 is the stock of Target Subsidiary, a corporation of which Target owns 100 of the 110 shares of common stock, the only outstanding class of Target Subsidiary stock. The remaining 10 shares of Target Subsidiary stock are owned by D. The value of Target Subsidiary stock on July 1 is $27.50 per share. Target Subsidiary has two assets, Asset 4, a Class IV asset, with a basis of $800 and a fair market value of $1,000, and Asset 5, a Class IV asset, with a basis of $2,200 and a fair market value of $2,025. Target Subsidiary has no liabilities. A section 336(e) election with respect to Target Subsidiary is also made.

(ii) *Determination of ADADP*. The ADADP on the deemed asset disposition of Target Subsidiary is determined as follows. The grossed-up amount realized on the sale, exchange, or distribution of recently disposed stock of Target Subsidiary is $2,750, ($2,500 ADADP allocable to Asset 2, the 100 shares of the stock of Target Subsidiary owned by Target, divided by .909, the percentage of Target Subsidiary stock by value, determined on the disposition date, attributable to the recently disposed stock ($2,750 (100 shares of the stock of Target Subsidiary deemed disposed in the qualified stock disposition × $27.50, the value of a share of Target Subsidiary stock on the disposition date) divided by $3,025 (110, the total number of shares of Target Subsidiary stock × $27.50, the value of a share of Target Subsidiary stock on the disposition date)), minus $0, Seller's selling costs in connection with the deemed sale of the 100 shares of Target Subsidiary stock). The $2,750 grossed-up amount realized on the sale, exchange, or distribution of recently disposed stock of Target Subsidiary is then added to the liabilities of Old Target Subsidiary, $0, to arrive at the ADADP of Target Subsidiary, $2,750.

(iii) *Allocation of ADADP*. Because Assets 4 and 5 are each assets of the same class, and the total fair market value of Assets 4 and 5 exceeds the $2,750 ADADP of Target Subsidiary, the $2,750 ADADP is allocated to Assets 4 and 5 in proportion to their respective fair market values. Accordingly, $909 is allocated to Asset 4 ($2,750 × ($1,000/($1,000 + $2,025))) and $1,841 is allocated to Asset 5 ($2,750 × ($2,025/($1,000 + $2,025))).

* * *

[Reg. § 1.336-3.]

□ [*T.D.* 9619, 5-10-2013.]

§ 1.336-4. Adjusted grossed-up basis.—(a) *Scope*.—Except as provided in paragraphs (b) and (c) of this section or as the context otherwise requires, the principles of paragraphs (b) through (g) of § 1.338-5 apply in determining the adjusted grossed-up basis (AGUB) for target and the consequences of a gain recognition election. AGUB is the amount for which new target is deemed to have purchased all of its assets in the deemed purchase under § 1.336-2(b)(1)(ii) or the amount for which old target is deemed to have purchased all of its assets in the deemed purchase under § 1.336-2(b)(2)(ii). AGUB is allocated among target's assets in accordance with § 1.338-6 to determine the price at which the assets are deemed to have been purchased. If a subsequent increase or decrease with respect to an element of AGUB is required under general principles of tax law, redetermined AGUB is allocated among target's assets in accordance with § 1.338-7.

(b) *Modifications to the principles in § 1.338-5*.—Solely for purposes of applying §§ 1.336-1 through 1.336-4, the principles of § 1.338-5 are modified as follows—

(1) *Purchasing corporation; purchaser*.—Any reference to the *purchasing corporation* shall be treated as a reference to a purchaser, as defined in § 1.336-1(b)(2).

(2) *Acquisition date; disposition date*.—Any reference to the *acquisition date* shall be treated as a reference to the disposition date, as defined in § 1.336-1(b)(8).

(3) *Section 338 election; section 338(h)(10) election; section 336(e) election*.—Any reference to a *section 338 election* or a *section 338(h)(10) election* shall be treated as a reference to a section 336(e) election, as defined in § 1.336-1(b)(11).

(4) *New target; old target*.—In the case of a disposition described in section 355(d)(2) or (e)(2), any reference to *new target* shall be treated as a reference to *old target* in its capacity as the purchaser of assets pursuant to the section 336(e) election.

(5) *Recently purchased stock; recently disposed stock*.—Any reference to *recently purchased stock* shall be treated as a reference to recently disposed stock, as defined in § 1.336-1(b)(17). In the case of a distribution of stock, for purposes of determining the purchaser's grossed-up basis of recently disposed stock, the purchaser's basis in recently disposed stock shall be deemed to be such stock's fair market value on the date it was acquired.

(6) *Nonrecently purchased stock; nonrecently disposed stock*.—Any reference to *nonrecently purchased stock* shall be treated as a reference to nonrecently disposed stock, as defined in § 1.336-1(b)(18).

(c) *Gain recognition election*.—(1) *In general*.—Any holder of nonrecently disposed stock of target may make a gain recognition election. The gain recognition election is irrevocable. Each owner of nonrecently disposed stock determines its basis amount, and therefore the gain recognized pursuant to the gain recognition election, by applying §§1.338-5(c) and 1.338-5(d)(3)(ii) by reference to its own recently disposed stock and nonrecently disposed stock, and not by reference to all recently disposed stock and nonrecently disposed stock.

(2) *80-percent purchaser.*—If a section 336(e) election is made for target, any 80-percent purchaser and all persons related to the 80-percent purchaser are automatically deemed to have made a gain recognition election for its nonrecently disposed target stock.

(3) *Non-80-percent purchaser.*—If not automatically deemed made under paragraph (c)(2) of this section, a gain recognition election is made by a non-80-percent purchaser providing, on or before the due date for filing the section 336(e) election statement by the appropriate party, a gain recognition election statement, as described in paragraph (c)(4) of this section, to the appropriate party. If seller and target are members of the same consolidated group, seller is the appropriate party and the common parent of the consolidated group must retain the gain recognition election statement. If seller and target are members of the same affiliated group but do not join in the filing of a consolidated Federal income tax return, or if target is an S corporation, target is the appropriate party and target must retain the gain recognition election statement. If a non-80-percent purchaser makes a gain recognition election, all related persons to the non-80-percent purchaser must also make a gain recognition election. Otherwise, the gain recognition election for the non-80-percent purchaser will have no effect.

(4) *Gain recognition election statement.*—A gain recognition election statement must include the following declarations (or substantially similar declarations):

(i) [Insert name, address, and taxpayer identifying number of person for whom gain recognition election is actually being made] has elected to recognize gain under §1.336-4(c) with respect to [his, hers, or its] nonrecently disposed stock.

(ii) [Insert name of person for whom gain recognition election is actually being made] agrees to report any gain under the gain recognition election on [his, hers, or its] Federal income tax return (including an amended return, if necessary) for the taxable year that includes the disposition date of [insert name and employer identification number of target].

(d) *Examples.*—The following examples illustrate the provisions of this section.

Example 1. On January 1 of Year 1, Seller owns 85 shares of Target stock, A owns 8 shares, B owns 4 shares, and C owns the remaining 3 shares. Each of A's 8 shares, B's 4 shares, and C's 3 shares have a $5 basis. Assume that Target has no liabilities. On July 1 of Year 2, Seller sells 70 shares of Target stock to A for $10 per share. On September 1 of Year 2, Seller sells 5 shares of Target stock to B and 5 shares of Target stock to C for $14 per share. A section 336(e) election is made. A does not make a gain recognition election. A incurs $25 of acquisition costs and B and C each incur $10 of acquisition costs in connection with their respective Year 2 purchases. These costs are capitalized in the basis of Target stock. September 1 of Year 2 is the disposition date. Because A owns at least 10 percent of Target stock on September 1, the disposition date, and A's original 8 shares of Target stock owned on January 1 of Year 1 were not disposed of in the qualified stock disposition, A's original 8 shares of Target stock are nonrecently disposed stock. Although B's original 4 shares and C's original 3 shares were not disposed of in the qualified stock disposition, because neither B nor C owns, with the application of section 318(a), other than section 318(a)(4), at least 10 percent of the total voting power or value of Target stock on the disposition date, their original shares are not nonrecently disposed stock. The grossedup basis of recently disposed Target stock is $1,011, determined as follows: The purchasers' (A, B, and C) aggregate basis in the recently disposed target stock, determined without regard to acquisition costs, is $840 ((70 × $10) + (5 × $14) + (5 × $14)). This amount is multiplied by a fraction, the numerator of which is 100 minus 8, the percentage of Target stock that is nonrecently disposed stock, and the denominator of which is 80, the percentage of Target stock attributable to recently disposed stock ($840 × 92/80 = $966). This amount is then increased by the $45 of acquisition costs incurred by A, B, and C to arrive at the $1,011 grossed-up basis of recently disposed Target stock ($966 + $45 = $1,011). New Target's AGUB is $1,051, the sum of $1,011, the grossed-up basis of recently disposed Target stock and $40 (8 × $5), A's basis in his nonrecently disposed Target stock.

Example 2. The facts are the same as in *Example 1* except that A makes a gain recognition election. Pursuant to the gain recognition election, A is treated as if he sold on September 1 of Year 2, the disposition date, his 8 shares of nonrecently disposed Target stock for the basis amount, and A's basis in nonrecently disposed target stock immediately after the deemed sale is the basis amount. A's basis amount equals his basis in his recently disposed Target stock without regard to acquisition costs, $700 (70 × $10), multiplied by a fraction, the numerator of which is 100 minus 8, the percentage of Target stock, by value, determined on the disposition date, which is A's nonrecently disposed Target stock, and the denominator of which is 70, the percentage of Target stock, by value, determined on the disposition date, which is A's recently disposed stock, which is then multiplied by a fraction, the numerator of which is 8, the percentage of Target stock, by value, determined on the disposition date, attributable to A's nonrecently disposed Target stock and the denominator of which is 100 minus the numerator amount. Accordingly, A's basis amount is $80 ($700 × 92/70 × 8/92). A therefore recognizes gain of $40 under the gain recognition election ($80 basis amount minus A's $40 basis in his nonrecently disposed stock prior to the gain recognition election). New Target's AGUB is $1,091, the sum of $1,011, the grossed-up basis of all recently disposed Target stock and $80, A's basis in his nonrecently disposed Target stock pursuant to the gain recognition election.

Example 3. (i) The facts are the same as in *Example 3* of § 1.336-3(g), that is, Seller owns all 100 of the outstanding shares of the common stock of Target, the only class of Target stock outstanding. On January 1 of Year 1, Seller sells 10 shares of Target stock to A for $6,000 ($600 per share). On August 1 of Year 1, Seller distributes the remaining 90 shares of Target stock to its unrelated shareholders in a transaction described in section 355(d)(2) or (e)(2). The value of Target stock on August 1 is $560 per share. Target has two assets, Asset 1, which is stock in trade of Target, a Class IV asset, with a basis of $15,000 and a value of $50,000, and Asset 2, which is stock in a publicly traded, unrelated corporation, a Class II asset, with a basis of $38,000 and a value of $16,000. Target has no liabilities other than any liabilities for Federal tax on account of the deemed asset disposition. Assume Target's Federal tax rate for any gain or income on the deemed asset disposition is 34 percent. Seller had no selling costs in connection with its sale of the 10 shares of Target stock. A section 336(e) election is made. In addition, A incurred $100 of acquisition costs with respect to the purchase of the 10 shares of Target stock. Target's AGUB in the assets deemed acquired pursuant to § 1.336-2(b)(2)(ii)(B) is determined as follows (for purposes of this *Example 3,* GRD is the grossed-up basis of recently disposed stock, BND is the basis in nonrecently disposed stock, TotL is Target's total liabilities, including Target's tax liability, and X is the A's total acquisition costs):

AGUB = GRD + BND + TotL

GRD = ($6,000 + ($560 × 90)) × ((100 - 0) / 100) + X

GRD = ($6,000 + $50,400) × (100/100) + $100

GRD = $56,500

BND = $0

TotL = .34 × ($27,152 (Target's gain recognized on deemed disposition of Asset 1) - $22,000 (Target's loss recognized on deemed disposition of Asset 2)) (see *Example 3* of § 1.336-3(g) for determination of Target's gain and loss recognized on deemed disposition of Assets 1 and 2)

TotL = $1,752

AGUB = $56,500 + $0 + $1,752

AGUB = $58,252

(ii) The AGUB allocated to Asset 2 is $16,000, the value of Asset 2. Because the excess of the total AGUB, $58,252, over the portion of the AGUB allocated to Asset 2, $16,000, does not exceed the value of Asset 1, the AGUB allocated to Asset 1 is such excess, $42,252. [Reg. § 1.336-4.]

□ [*T.D.* 9619, 5-10-2013.]

§ 1.337(d)-3. Gain recognition upon certain partnership transactions involving a partner's stock.—(a) *Purpose.*—The purpose of this section is to prevent corporate taxpayers from using a partnership to circumvent gain required to be recognized under section 311(b) or section 336(a). The rules of this section, including the determination of the amount of gain, must be applied in a manner that is consistent with and reasonably carries out this purpose.

(b) *In general.*—This section applies when a partnership, either directly or indirectly, owns, acquires, or distributes Stock of the Corporate Partner (within the meaning of paragraph (c)(2) of this section). Under paragraphs (d) or (e) of this section, a Corporate Partner (within the meaning of paragraph (c)(1) of this section) is required to recognize gain when a transaction has the effect of the Corporate Partner acquiring or increasing an interest in its own stock in exchange for appreciated property in a manner that contravenes the purpose of this section as set forth in paragraph (a) of this section. Paragraph (f) of this section sets forth exceptions under which a Corporate Partner does not recognize gain.

(c) *Definitions.*—The following definitions apply for purposes of this section:

(1) *Corporate Partner.*—A *Corporate Partner* is a person that is classified as a corporation for federal income tax purposes and holds or acquires an interest in a partnership.

(2) *Stock of the Corporate Partner.*—(i) *In general.*—With respect to a Corporate Partner, *Stock of the Corporate Partner* includes the Corporate Partner's stock, or other equity interests, including options, warrants, and similar

interests, in the Corporate Partner or a corporation that controls the Corporate Partner within the meaning of section 304(c) (except that section 318(a)(1) and (3) shall not apply). *Stock of the Corporate Partner* also includes interests in any entity to the extent that the value of the interest is attributable to Stock of the Corporate Partner.

(ii) *Affiliated partner exception.*—Stock of the Corporate Partner does not include any stock or other equity interests held or acquired by a partnership if all interests in the partnership's capital and profits are held by members of an affiliated group as defined in section 1504(a) that includes the Corporate Partner.

(3) *Section 337(d) Transaction.*—A *Section 337(d) Transaction* is a transaction (or series of transactions) that has the effect of an exchange by a Corporate Partner of its interest in appreciated property for an interest in Stock of the Corporate Partner owned, acquired, or distributed by a partnership. For example, a Section 337(d) Transaction may occur when —

(i) A Corporate Partner contributes appreciated property to a partnership that owns Stock of the Corporate Partner;

(ii) A partnership acquires Stock of the Corporate Partner;

(iii) A partnership that owns Stock of the Corporate Partner distributes appreciated property to a partner other than a Corporate Partner;

(iv) A partnership distributes Stock of the Corporate Partner to the Corporate Partner; or

(v) A partnership agreement is amended in a manner that increases a Corporate Partner's interest in Stock of the Corporate Partner (including in connection with a contribution to, or distribution from, a partnership).

(4) *Gain Percentage.*—A Corporate Partner's *Gain Percentage* equals a fraction, the numerator of which is the Corporate Partner's interest (by value) in appreciated property effectively exchanged for Stock of the Corporate Partner under the test described in paragraphs (d)(1) and (2) of this section, and the denominator of which is the Corporate Partner's interest (by value) in that appreciated property immediately before the Section 337(d) Transaction. Paragraph (d) of this section requires a partnership to multiply the Gain Percentage by the Corporate Partner's aggregate gain in appreciated property to determine gain recognized under this section.

(d) *Deemed redemption rule.*—(1) *In general.*—A Corporate Partner in a partnership that engages in a Section 337(d) Transaction recognizes gain at the time, and to the extent, that the Corporate Partner's interest in appreciated property (other than Stock of the Corporate Partner) is reduced in exchange for an increased interest in Stock of the Corporate Partner, as determined under paragraph (d)(2) of this section. This section does not apply to the extent a transaction has the effect of an exchange by a Corporate Partner of non-appreciated property for Stock of the Corporate Partner, or has the effect of an exchange by a Corporate Partner for property other than Stock of the Corporate Partner.

(2) *Corporate Partner's interest in partnership property.*—The Corporate Partner's interest with respect to both Stock of the Corporate Partner and the appreciated property that is the subject of the exchange is determined based on all facts and circumstances, including the allocation and distribution rights set forth in the partnership agreement. The Corporate Partner's interest in an identified share of Stock of the Corporate Partner will never be less than the Corporate Partner's largest interest (by value) in that share of Stock of the Corporate Partner that was taken into account when the partnership previously determined whether there had been a Section 337(d) Transaction with respect to such share (regardless of whether the Corporate Partner recognized gain in the earlier transaction). See *Example 7* of paragraph (h) of this section. However, this limitation will not apply if any reduction in the Corporate Partner's interest in the identified share of Stock of the Corporate Partner occurred as part of a plan or arrangement to circumvent the purpose of this section. See *Example 8* of paragraph (h) of this section.

(3) *Amount and character of gain recognized on the exchange.*—(i) *Amount of gain.*—The amount of gain the Corporate Partner recognizes under paragraph (d)(1) of this section equals the product of the Corporate Partner's Gain Percentage and the gain from the appreciated property that is the subject of the exchange that the Corporate Partner would recognize if, immediately before the Section 337(d) Transaction, all assets of the partnership and any assets contributed to the partnership in the Section 337(d) Transaction were sold in a fully taxable transaction for cash in an amount equal to the fair market value of such property (taking into account section 7701(g)), reduced, but not below zero, by any gain the Corporate Partner is required to recognize with respect to the appreciated property in the Section 337(d) Transaction under any other provision of this chapter. This gain is computed taking into account allocations of tax items applying the principles of section 704(c), including any remedial allocations under § 1.704-3(d), and also taking into account any basis adjust-

ments including adjustments made pursuant to section 743(b).

(ii) *Character of gain.*—The character of the gain that the Corporate Partner recognizes under paragraph (d)(1) of this section from the appreciated property that is the subject of the exchange shall be the character of the gain that the Corporate Partner would recognize if, immediately before the Section 337(d) Transaction, the Corporate Partner had disposed of the appreciated property that is the subject of the exchange in a fully taxable transaction for cash in an amount equal to the fair market value of such property (taking into account section 7701(g)).

(4) *Basis adjustments.*—(i) *Corporate Partner's basis in the partnership interest.*—The basis of the Corporate Partner's interest in the partnership is increased by the amount of gain that the Corporate Partner recognizes under this paragraph (d).

(ii) *Partnership's basis in partnership property.*—The partnership's adjusted tax basis in the appreciated property that is treated as the subject of the exchange under this paragraph (d) is increased by the amount of gain recognized with respect to that property by the Corporate Partner as a result of that exchange, regardless of whether the partnership has an election in effect under section 754. For basis recovery purposes, this basis increase is treated as property that is placed in service by the partnership in the taxable year of the Section 337(d) Transaction.

(e) *Distribution of Stock of the Corporate Partner.*—(1) *In general.*—This paragraph (e) applies to distributions to the Corporate Partner of Stock of the Corporate Partner to which section 732(f) does not apply and that have previously been the subject of a Section 337(d) Transaction or become the subject of a Section 337(d) Transaction as a result of the distribution. Upon the distribution of Stock of the Corporate Partner to the Corporate Partner, paragraph (d) of this section will apply as though immediately before the distribution the partners amended the partnership agreement to allocate to the Corporate Partner a 100 percent interest in that portion of the Stock of the Corporate Partner that is distributed, and to allocate an appropriately reduced interest in other partnership property away from the Corporate Partner.

(2) *Basis rules.*—(i) *Basis allocation on distributions of stock and other property.*—If, as part of the same transaction, a partnership distributes Stock of the Corporate Partner and other property (other than cash) to the Corporate Partner, see § 1.732-1(c)(1)(iii) for a rule allocating basis first to the Stock of the Corporate Partner before the distribution of the other property.

(ii) *Computation of basis.*—For purposes of determining the basis of property distributed to a partner in a transaction that includes the distribution of Stock of the Corporate Partner (other than the basis of the Corporate Partner in its own stock), the basis of the partner's remaining partnership interest, and the partnership's basis in undistributed Stock of the Corporate Partner, and for purposes of computing gain under paragraph (e)(3) of this section, the partnership's basis of Stock of the Corporate Partner distributed to the partner equals the greater of—

(A) The partnership's basis of that distributed Stock of the Corporate Partner immediately before the distribution; or

(B) The fair market value of that distributed Stock of the Corporate Partner immediately before the distribution less the partner's allocable share of gain from all of the Stock of the Corporate Partner if the partnership sold all of its assets in a fully taxable transaction for cash in an amount equal to the fair market value of such property (taking into account section 7701(g)) immediately before the distribution.

(iii) *Section 732(f) basis reduction.*—For purposes of determining the amount of the decrease to the basis of property held by a distributed corporation pursuant to section 732(f), the amount of this decrease shall be reduced by the amount of gain that a Corporate Partner has recognized under this section in the same Section 337(d) Transaction or in a prior Section 337(d) Transaction involving the property.

(3) *Gain recognition.*—The Corporate Partner will recognize gain on a distribution of Stock of the Corporate Partner to the Corporate Partner to the extent that the partnership's adjusted basis in the distributed Stock of the Corporate Partner (as determined under paragraph (e)(2)(ii) of this section) immediately before the distribution exceeds the Corporate Partner's adjusted basis in its partnership interest immediately after the distribution.

(f) *Exceptions.*—(1) *De minimis rule.*—(i) *In general.*—Unless Stock of the Corporate Partner is acquired as part of a plan to circumvent the purpose of this section, this section does not apply to a Corporate Partner if at the time that the partnership acquires Stock of the Corporate Partner or at the time of a revaluation event as described in § 1.704-1(b)(2)(iv)(*f*) (without regard to whether or not the partnership revalues its assets) —

(A) The Corporate Partner and any persons related to the Corporate Partner under section 267(b) or section 707(b) own in the aggregate less than 5 percent of the partnership;

(B) The partnership holds Stock of the Corporate Partner with a value of less than 2 percent of the partnership's gross assets (including the Stock of the Corporate Partner); and

(C) The partnership has never, at any point in time, held in the aggregate—

(1) Stock of the Corporate Partner with a fair market value greater than $1,000,000; or

(2) More than 2 percent of any particular class of Stock of the Corporate Partner.

(ii) *De minimis rule ceases to apply.*—If a partnership satisfies the conditions of the de minimis rule of paragraph (f)(1) of this section upon an acquisition of Stock of the Corporate Partner or revaluation event as described in § 1.704-1(b)(2)(iv)*(f)*, but later fails to satisfy the conditions of the de minimis rule upon a subsequent acquisition or revaluation event, then solely for purposes of paragraph (d) of this section, the Corporate Partner may compute its gain on the subsequent acquisition or revaluation event as if it had already recognized gain at the previous event. Neither the Corporate Partner nor the partnership increases its basis by the gain the Corporate Partner would have recognized if the de minimis rule of paragraph (f)(1) of this section did not apply to the prior acquisition or revaluation event.

(2) *Certain dispositions of stock.*—Unless acquired as part of a plan to circumvent the purpose of this section, this section does not apply to Stock of the Corporate Partner that —

(i) Is disposed of (by sale or distribution) by the partnership before the due date (including extensions) of its federal income tax return for the taxable year during which the Stock of the Corporate Partner is acquired (or for the taxable year in which the Corporate Partner becomes a partner, whichever is applicable); and

(ii) Is not distributed to the Corporate Partner or a corporation that controls the Corporate Partner within the meaning of section 304(c), except that section 318(a)(1) and (3) shall not apply.

(g) *Tiered partnerships.*—The rules of this section shall apply to tiered partnerships in a manner that is consistent with the purpose set forth in paragraph (a) of this section.

(h) *Examples.*—The following examples illustrate the principles of this section. All amounts in the following examples are reported in millions of dollars:

Example 1. Deemed redemption rule – contribution of Stock of the Corporate Partner. (i) In Year 1, X, a corporation, and A, an individual, form partnership AX as equal partners in all respects. X contributes Asset 1 with a fair market value of $100 and a basis of $20. A contributes X stock, which is Stock of the Corporate Partner, with a basis and fair market value of $100.

(ii) Because A and X are equal partners in AX in all respects, the partnership formation causes X's interest in X stock to increase from $0 to $50 and its interest in Asset 1 to decrease from $100 to $50. Thus, the partnership formation is a Section 337(d) Transaction because the formation has the effect of an exchange by X of $50 of Asset 1 for $50 of X stock.

(iii) X must recognize gain under paragraph (d) of this section with respect to Asset 1 to prevent the circumvention of section 311(b) principles. X's gain equals the product of X's Gain Percentage and the gain from Asset 1 that X would recognize (decreased, but not below zero, by any gain that X recognized with respect to Asset 1 in the Section 337(d) Transaction under any other provision of this chapter) if, immediately before the Section 337(d) Transaction, all assets were sold in a fully taxable transaction for cash in an amount equal to the fair market value of such property. If Asset 1 had been sold in a fully taxable transaction immediately before the formation of partnership AX, X's allocable share of gain would have been $80. X's Gain Percentage is 50 percent (equal to a fraction, the numerator of which is X's $50 interest in Asset 1 effectively exchanged for X stock, and the denominator of which is X's $100 interest in Asset 1 immediately before the Section 337(d) Transaction). Thus, X recognizes $40 of gain ($80 multiplied by 50 percent) under the deemed redemption rule in paragraph (d) of this section. Under paragraph (d)(4)(i) of this section, X's basis in its AX partnership interest increases from $20 to $60. Under paragraph (d)(4)(ii) of this section, AX's basis in Asset 1 increases from $20 to $60 because Asset 1 is the appreciated property treated as the subject of the exchange.

Example 2. Deemed redemption rule – contribution of stock in a corporation that controls the Corporate Partner. (i) In Year 1, X, a corporation, and A, an individual, form partnership AX as equal partners in all respects. X contributes Asset 1 with a fair market value of $100 and a basis of $20. A contributes stock in P, with a basis and fair market value of $100. P is the sole owner of X. P's interest in X constitutes 10 percent of P's total assets.

(ii) Because P controls X within the meaning of section 304(c), stock in P is Stock of the Corporate Partner under paragraph (c)(2)(i) of this section.

(iii) Because A and X are equal partners in AX in all respects, the partnership formation causes X's interest in Stock of the Corporate Partner stock to increase from $0 to $50 and its interest in Asset 1 to decrease from $100 to $50. Thus, the partnership formation is a Section 337(d) Transaction because the formation has the effect of an exchange by X of $50 of Asset 1 for $50 of Stock of the Corporate Partner.

(iv) X must recognize gain under paragraph (d) of this section with respect to Asset 1 to prevent the circumvention of section 311(b) principles. X's gain equals the product of X's Gain Percentage and the gain from Asset 1 that X would recognize (decreased, but not below zero, by any gain that X recognized with respect to Asset 1 in the Section 337(d) Transaction under any other provision of this chapter) if, immediately before the Section 337(d) Transaction, all assets were sold in a fully taxable transaction for cash in an amount equal to the fair market value of such property. If Asset 1 had been sold in a fully taxable transaction immediately before the formation of partnership AX, X's allocable share of gain would have been $80. X's Gain Percentage is 50 percent (equal to a fraction, the numerator of which is X's $50 interest in Asset 1 effectively exchanged for Stock of the Corporate Partner, and the denominator of which is X's $100 interest in Asset 1 immediately before the Section 337(d) Transaction). Thus, X recognizes $40 of gain ($80 multiplied by 50 percent) under the deemed redemption rule in paragraph (d) of this section. Under paragraph (d)(4)(i) of this section, X's basis in its AX partnership interest increases from $20 to $60. Under paragraph (d)(4)(ii) of this section, AX's basis in Asset 1 increases from $20 to $60 because Asset 1 is the appreciated property treated as the subject of the exchange.

Example 3. Distribution of Stock of the Corporate Partner – pro rata distribution. (i) The facts are the same as in *Example 1(i)* of this paragraph (h). AX liquidates in Year 9, when Asset 1 and the X stock each have a fair market value of $200. X and A each receive 50 percent of Asset 1 and 50 percent of the X stock in the liquidation. At the time AX liquidates, X's basis in its AX partnership interest is $60 and A's basis in its AX partnership interest is $100.

(ii) When AX liquidates, X's interests in its stock and in Asset 1 do not change. Thus, the liquidation is not a Section 337(d) Transaction because it does not have the effect of an exchange by X of appreciated property for Stock of the Corporate Partner.

(iii) Paragraph (e) of this section applies because the distributed X stock was the subject of a previous Section 337(d) Transaction and because section 732(f) does not apply. Under § 1.732-1(c)(1)(iii), the distribution to X of X stock is deemed to immediately precede the distribution of 50 percent of Asset 1 to X for purposes of determining X's basis in the distributed property. For purposes of determining X's basis in Asset 1 and X's gain on distribution, the basis of the distributed X stock is treated as $50, the greater of $50 (50 percent of the stock's $100 basis in the hands of the partnership), or $50, the fair market value of that distributed X stock ($100) less X's allocable share of gain from the distributed X stock if AX had sold all of its assets in a fully taxable transaction for cash in an amount equal to the fair market value of such property immediately before the distribution ($50). Thus, X reduces its basis in its partnership interest by $50 prior to the distribution of Asset 1. Accordingly, X's basis in the distributed portion of Asset 1 is $10. Because AX's basis in the distributed X stock immediately before the distribution ($50) does not exceed X's basis in its AX partnership interest immediately before the distribution ($60), X recognizes no gain under paragraph (e)(3) of this section.

Example 4. Distribution of Stock of the Corporate Partner – non pro rata distribution. (i) The facts are the same as *Example 3(i)* of this paragraph (h), except that when AX liquidates, X receives 75 percent of the X stock and 25 percent of Asset 1 and A receives 25 percent of the X stock and 75 percent of Asset 1.

(ii) The liquidation of AX causes X's interest in X stock to increase from $100 to $150 and its interest in Asset 1 to decrease from $100 to $50. Thus, AX's liquidating distributions of X stock and Asset 1 to X are a Section 337(d) Transaction because the distributions have the effect of an exchange by X of $50 of Asset 1 for $50 of X stock.

(iii) (A) X must recognize gain with respect to Asset 1 to prevent the circumvention of section 311(b) principles. Under paragraph (e)(1) of this section, paragraph (d) of this section is applied as if X and A amended the AX partnership agreement to allocate to X a 100 percent interest in the distributed portion of the X stock. X must recognize gain equal to the product of X's Gain Percentage and the gain from Asset 1 that X would have recognized (decreased, but not below zero, by any gain X recognized with respect to Asset 1 in the Section 337(d) Transaction under any other provision of this chapter) if, immediately before the Section 337(d) Transaction, AX had sold all of its assets in a fully taxable transaction for cash in an amount equal to the fair market value of such property.

(B) If Asset 1 had been sold in a fully taxable transaction immediately before the amendment of the AX partnership agreement, X's allocable share of gain would have been $90, or the sum of X's $40 remaining gain under section 704(c) and $50 of the $100 post-contribution appreciation. X's Gain Percentage is 50 percent (equal to a fraction, the numerator of which is X's $50 interest in Asset 1 effectively exchanged for X stock, and the denominator of which is X's $100 interest in Asset 1 immediately before the Section 337(d) Transaction). Thus, X recognizes $45 of gain ($90 multiplied by 50 percent) under the deemed redemption rule in paragraph (d) of this section. Under paragraph (d)(4)(i) of this section, X's basis in its AX partnership interest increases from $60 to $105. Under paragraph (d)(4)(ii) of this section, AX's basis in Asset 1 increases from $60 to $105 because Asset 1 is the appreciated property treated as the subject of the exchange.

(iv)(A) Paragraph (e) of this section applies because the distributed X stock was the subject of a previous Section 337(d) Transaction and because section 732(f) does not apply. Under § 1.732-1(c)(1)(iii), AX is treated as first distributing the X stock to X before the distribution of 25 percent of Asset 1. For purposes of determining X's basis in Asset 1 and X's gain on distribution, the basis of the distributed X stock is treated as $100, the greater of $75 (75 percent of the stock's $100 basis in the hands of the partnership) or $100, the fair market value of the distributed X stock ($150) less X's allocable share of gain if the partnership had sold all of the X stock immediately before the distribution for cash in an amount equal to its fair market value ($50). Thus, X will reduce its basis in its partnership interest by $100 prior to the distribution of Asset 1. Accordingly, X's basis in the distributed portion of Asset 1 is $5. Because AX's basis in the distributed X stock immediately before the distribution as computed for purposes of this section ($100) does not exceed X's basis in its AX partnership interest immediately before the distribution ($105), X recognizes no additional gain under paragraph (e)(3) of this section.

(B) For purposes of determining A's basis in Asset 1 and A's gain on distribution, the basis of the distributed X stock is treated as $25, the greater of $25 (25 percent of the stock's $100 basis in the hands of the partnership) or $0, the fair market value of the distributed X stock ($50) less A's allocable share of gain if the partnership had sold all of the X stock immediately before the distribution for cash in an amount equal to its fair market value ($50). Thus, A will reduce its basis in its partnership interest by $25 prior to the distribution of Asset 1. Accordingly, A's basis in the distributed portion of Asset 1 is $75. Because AX's basis in the distributed X stock immediately before the distribution as computed for purposes of this section ($100) does not exceed A's basis in its AX partnership interest immediately before the distribution ($100), A recognizes no additional gain under paragraph (e)(3) of this section.

Example 5. Deemed redemption rule – subsequent purchase of Stock of the Corporate Partner. The facts are the same as *Example 1(i)* of this paragraph (h), except that A contributes cash of $100 instead of X stock. In a later year, when the value of Asset 1 has not changed, AX uses the contributed cash to purchase X stock for $100. AX's purchase of X stock has the effect of an exchange by X of appreciated property for X stock, and thus, is a Section 337(d) Transaction. X must recognize gain at the time, and to the extent, that X's share of appreciated property (other than X stock) is reduced in exchange for X stock. Thus, the consequences of the partnership's purchase of X stock are the same as those described in *Example 1(ii)* and *(iii)* of this paragraph (h), resulting in X recognizing $40 of gain.

Example 6. Change in allocation ratios – amendment of partnership agreement. (i) The facts are the same as *Example 3(i)* of this paragraph (h), except that in Year 9, AX does not liquidate, and the AX partnership agreement is amended to allocate to X 80 percent of the income, gain, loss, and deduction from the X stock and to allocate to A 80 percent of the income, gain, loss, and deduction from Asset 1. If AX had sold the partnership assets immediately before the change to the partnership agreement, X would have been allocated $90 of gain from Asset 1 and $50 of gain from the X stock.

(ii) The amendment to the AX partnership agreement causes X's interest in its stock to increase from $100 (50 percent of the stock value immediately before the amendment of the agreement) to $160 (80 percent of stock value immediately following amendment of agreement) and its interest in Asset 1 to decrease from $100 to $40. Thus, the amendment of the partnership agreement is a Section 337(d) Transaction because the amendment has the effect of an exchange by X of $60 of Asset 1 for $60 of its stock.

(iii) X must recognize gain equal to the product of X's Gain Percentage and the gain from Asset 1 that X would have recognized (decreased, but not below zero, by any gain X recognized with respect to Asset 1 in the Section 337(d) Transaction under any other provision of this chapter) if, immediately before the Section 337(d) Transaction, AX had sold all of its assets in a fully taxable transaction for cash in an amount equal to the fair market value of such property. If Asset 1 had been sold in a fully taxable transaction immediately before the amendment of the AX partnership agreement, X's allocable share of gain would have been $90, or the sum of X's $40 remaining gain under section 704(c) and 50 percent of the $100 post-contribution appreciation. X's Gain Percentage is 60 percent (equal to a fraction, the numerator of which is X's $60 interest in Asset 1 effectively exchanged for X stock, and the denominator of which is X's $100 interest in Asset 1 immediately before the Section 337(d) Transaction). Thus, X recognizes $54 of gain ($90 multiplied by 60 percent) under the deemed redemption rule in paragraph (d) of this section. Under paragraph (d)(4)(i) of this section, X's basis in its AX partnership interest increases from $60 to $114. Under paragraph (d)(4)(ii) of this section, AX's basis in Asset 1 increases from $60 to $114 because Asset 1 is the appreciated property treated as the subject of the exchange.

Example 7. Change in allocation ratios – admission and exit of a partner. (i) The facts are the same as *Example 1(i)* of this paragraph (h). In addition, in Year 2, when the values of Asset 1 and the X stock have not changed, B contributes $100 of cash to AX in exchange for a one-third interest in the partnership. Upon the admission of B as a partner, X's interest in Asset 1 decreases from $50 to $33.33, and its interest in B's contributed cash increases. B's admission is not a Section 337(d) Transaction because it does not have the effect of an exchange by X of its interest in Asset 1 for X stock. Accordingly, X does not recognize gain under paragraph (d) of this section.

(ii) In Year 9, when the values of Asset 1 and the X stock have not changed, the partnership distributes $50 of cash and 50 percent of Asset 1 (valued at $50) to B in liquidation of B's interest. X and A are equal partners in all respects after the distribution. Upon the liquidation of B's interest, X's interest in Asset 1 decreases from $33.33 to $25, and its interest in X stock increases from $33.33 to $50. AX's liquidation of B's interest has the effect of an exchange by X of appreciated property for X stock, and thus, is a Section 337(d) Transaction.

(iii) Pursuant to paragraph (d)(2) of this section, X's interest in X stock and other appreciated property held by the partnership is determined based on all facts and circumstances, including allocation and distribution rights in the partnership agreement. However, paragraph (d)(2) of this section also requires that X's interest in its stock for purposes of paragraph (d) will never be less than the Corporate Partner's largest interest (by value) in those shares of Stock of the Corporate Partner taken into account when the partnership previously determined whether there had been a Section 337(d) Transaction (regardless of whether the Corporate Partner recognized gain in the earlier transaction). Although X's interest in X stock increases to $50 upon AX's liquidation of B's interest, X's largest interest previously taken into account under paragraph (d)(1) of this section was $50. Thus, X's interest in its stock is not considered to be increased, and X therefore recognizes no gain under paragraph (d) of this section, provided that the transactions did not occur as part of a plan or arrangement to circumvent the purpose of this section.

Example 8. Change in allocation ratios – plan to circumvent purpose of this section. (i) In Year 1, X, a corporation, and A, an individual, contribute $99 and $1, respectively, to newly-formed partnership AX, with X receiving a 99 percent interest in AX and A receiving a 1 percent interest in AX. AX borrows $100,000 from a third-party lender and uses the proceeds to purchase X stock, which is Stock of the Corporate Partner. Later, as part of a plan or arrangement to circumvent the purposes of this section, A contributes $99,999 of cash, which AX uses to repay the loan, and X contributes Asset 1 with a fair market value of $99,901 and basis of $20,000. After these contributions, A and X are equal partners in AX in all respects.

(ii) Pursuant to paragraph (d)(2) of this section, X's interest in X stock and other appreciated property held by the partnership is determined based on all facts and circumstances, including allocation and distribution rights in the partnership agreement. Generally, pursuant to paragraph (d)(2) of this section, X's interest in X stock for purposes of paragraph (d) of this section will never be less than the Corporate Partner's largest interest (by value) in those shares of Stock of the Corporate Partner taken into account when the partnership previously determined whether there had been a Section 337(d) Transaction (regardless of whether the Corporate Partner recognized gain in the earlier transaction). This limitation does not apply, however, if the reduction in X's interest in X's stock occurred as part of a plan or arrangement to circumvent the purpose of this section. Because the transactions described in this example are part of a plan or arrangement to circumvent the purpose of this section, the limitation in paragraph (d)(2) of this section does not apply. Accordingly, the deemed redemption rule under paragraph (d) of this section applies to the transactions with the consequences described in *Example 1(iii)* of this paragraph (h), resulting in X recognizing $39,950.50 of gain.

Example 9. Tiered partnership. (i) In Year 1, X, a corporation, and A, an individual, form partnership UTP. X contributes Asset 1 with a fair market value of $80 and a basis of $0 in exchange for an 80 percent interest in UTP. A contributes $20 of cash in exchange for a 20 percent interest in UTP. UTP and B, an individual, form partnership LTP as equal partners. UTP contributes Asset 1 and $20 of cash. B contributes X stock, which is Stock of the Corporate Partner, with a basis and fair market value of $100.

(ii) Pursuant to paragraph (g) of this section, the rules of this section shall apply to tiered partnerships in a manner that is consistent with the purpose set forth in paragraph (a) of this section. Pursuant to paragraph (d)(1) of this section, if X is in a partnership that engages in a Section 337(d) Transaction, X must recognize gain at the time, and to the extent, that X's share of appreciated property is reduced in exchange for X stock. The formation of LTP causes X's interest in X stock to increase from $0 to $40 and its interest in Asset 1 to decrease from $64 to $32. Thus, LTP's formation is a Section 337(d) Transaction because the formation has the effect of an exchange by X of $32 of Asset 1 for $32 of X stock.

(iii) X must recognize gain with respect to Asset 1 to prevent the circumvention of section 311(b) principles. X must recognize gain equal to the product of X's Gain Percentage and the gain from Asset 1 (decreased, but not below zero, by any gain X recognized with respect to Asset 1 in the Section 337(d) Transaction under any other provision of this chapter) that X would recognize if, immediately before the Section 337(d) Transaction, all assets were sold in a fully taxable transaction for cash in an amount equal to the fair market value of such property. If Asset 1 had been sold in a fully taxable transaction immediately before LTP's formation, X's allocable share of gain would have been $80 pursuant to section 704(c). X's Gain Percentage is 50 percent (equal to a fraction, the numerator of which is X's $32 interest in Asset 1 effectively exchanged for X stock, and the denominator of which is X's $64 interest in Asset 1 immediately before the Section 337(d) Transaction). Thus, X recognizes $40 of gain ($80 multiplied by 50 percent) under the deemed redemption rule in paragraph (d) of this section. Under paragraphs (d)(4)(i) and (ii) of this section, X's basis in its UTP partnership interest increases from $0 to $40, UTP's basis in its LTP partnership interest increases from $20 to $60, and LTP's basis in Asset 1 increases from $0 to $40 pursuant to paragraph (g) of this section.

* * *

[Reg. § 1.337(d)-3.]

□ [*T.D.* 9833, 6-7-18.]

§ 1.338-1. General principles; status of old target and new target.—(a) *In general.*—(1) *Deemed transaction.*—Elections are available under section 338 when a purchasing corporation acquires the stock of another corporation (the target) in a qualified stock purchase. One type of election, under section 338(g), is available to the purchasing corporation. Another type of election, under section 338(h)(10), is, in more limited circumstances, available jointly to the purchasing corporation and the sellers of the stock. (Rules concerning eligibility for these elections are contained in §§ 1.338-2, 1.338-3, and 1.338(h)(10)-1.) However, if, as a result of the deemed purchase of old target's assets pursuant to a section 336(e) election, there would be both a qualified stock purchase and a qualified stock disposition (as defined in § 1.336-1(b)(6)) of the stock of a subsidiary of target, neither a section 338(g) election nor a section 338(h)(10) election may be made with respect to the qualified stock purchase of the subsidiary. Instead, a section 336(e) election may be made with respect to such purchase. See § 1.336-1(b)(6)(ii). Although target is a single corporation under corporate law, if a section 338 election is made, then two separate corporations, old target and new target, generally are considered to exist for purposes of subtitle A of the Internal Revenue Code. Old target is treated as transferring all of its assets to an unrelated person in exchange for consideration that includes the discharge of its liabilities (see § 1.1001-2(a)), and new target is treated as acquiring all of its assets from an unrelated person in exchange for consideration that includes the assumption of those liabilities. (Such transaction is, without regard to its characterization for Federal income tax purposes, referred to as the deemed asset sale and the income tax consequences thereof as the deemed sale tax consequences.) If a section 338(h)(10) election is made, old target is deemed to liquidate following the deemed asset sale.

(2) *Application of other rules of law.*—Other rules of law apply to determine the tax consequences to the parties as if they had actually engaged in the transactions deemed to occur under section 338 and the regulations thereunder except to the extent otherwise provided in those regulations. See also § 1.338-6(c)(2). Other rules of law may characterize the transaction as something other than or in addition to a sale and purchase of assets; however, the transaction between old and new target must be a taxable transaction. For example, if the target is an insurance company for which a section 338 election is made, the deemed asset sale results in an assumption reinsurance transaction for the insurance contracts deemed transferred from old target to new target. See, generally, § 1.817-4(d), and for special rules regarding the acquisition of insurance company targets, § 1.338-11. See also

§ 1.367(a)-8(k)(13) for a rule applicable to gain recognition agreements (filed under section §§ 1.367(a)-3(b)(1)(ii) and 1.367(a)-8) and deemed asset sales as a result of an election under section 338(g).

(3) *Overview.*—Definitions and special nomenclature and rules for making the section 338 election are provided in § 1.338-2. Qualification for the section 338 election is addressed in § 1.338-3. The amount for which old target is treated as selling all of its assets (the aggregate deemed sale price, or ADSP) is addressed in § 1.338-4. The amount for which new target is deemed to have purchased all its assets (the adjusted grossed-up basis, or AGUB) is addressed in § 1.338-5. Section 1.338-6 addresses allocation both of ADSP among the assets old target is deemed to have sold and of AGUB among the assets new target is deemed to have purchased. Section 1.338-7 addresses allocation of ADSP or AGUB when those amounts subsequently change. Asset and stock consistency are addressed in § 1.338-8. International aspects of section 338 are covered in § 1.338-9. Rules for the filing of returns are provided in § 1.338-10. Section 1.338-11 provides special rules for insurance company targets. Eligibility for and treatment of section 338(h)(10) elections is addressed in § 1.338(h)(10)-1.

(b) *Treatment of target under other provisions of the Internal Revenue Code.*—(1) *General rule for subtitle A.*—Except as provided in this section, new target is treated as a new corporation that is unrelated to old target for purposes of subtitle A of the Internal Revenue Code. Thus—

(i) New target is not considered related to old target for purposes of section 168 and may make new elections under section 168 without taking into account the elections made by old target; and

(ii) New target may adopt, without obtaining prior approval from the Commissioner, any taxable year that meets the requirements of section 441 and any method of accounting that meets the requirements of section 446. Notwithstanding § 1.441-1T(b)(2), a new target may adopt a taxable year on or before the last day for making the election under section 338 by filing its first return for the desired taxable year on or before that date.

(2) *Exceptions for subtitle A.*—New target and old target are treated as the same corporation for purposes of—

(i) The rules applicable to employee benefit plans (including those plans described in sections 79, 104, 105, 106, 125, 127, 129, 132, 137, and 220), qualified pension, profit-sharing, stock bonus and annuity plans (sections 401(a) and 403(a)), simplified employee pensions (section 408(k)), tax qualified stock option plans (sections 422 and 423), welfare benefit funds (sections 419, 419A, 512(a)(3), and 4976), and voluntary employee benefit associations (section 501(a)(9) and the regulations thereunder);

(ii) Sections 1311 through 1314 (relating to the mitigation of the effect of limitations), if a section 338(h)(10) election is not made for target;

(iii) Section 108(e)(5) (relating to the reduction of purchase money debt);

(iv) Section 45A (relating to the Indian Employment Credit), section 51 (relating to the Work Opportunity Credit), section 51A (relating to the Welfare to Work Credit), and section 1396 (relating to the Empowerment Zone Act);

(v) Sections 401(h) and 420 (relating to medical benefits for retirees);

(vi) Section 414 (relating to definitions and special rules); and

(vii) Section 846(e) (relating to an election to use an insurance company's historical loss payment pattern).

(viii) Any other provision designated in the Internal Revenue Bulletin by the Internal Revenue Service. See § 601.601(d)(2)(ii) of this chapter. See, for example, § 1.1001-3(e)(4)(i)(F) providing that an election under section 338 does not result in the substitution of a new obligor on target's debt. See also, for example, § 1.1502–77(c)(8), providing that an election under section 338 does not result in a deemed termination of target's existence for purposes of the rules applicable to the agent for a consolidated group.

(3) *General rule for other provisions of the Internal Revenue Code.*—Except as provided in the regulations under section 338 or in the Internal Revenue Bulletin by the Internal Revenue Service (see § 601.601(d)(2)(ii) of this chapter), new target is treated as a continuation of old target for purposes other than subtitle A of the Internal Revenue Code. For example—

(i) New target is liable for old target's Federal income tax liabilities, including the tax liability for the deemed sale tax consequences and those tax liabilities of the other members of any consolidated group that included old target that are attributable to taxable years in which those corporations and old target joined in the same consolidated return (see § 1.1502-6(a));

(ii) Wages earned by the employees of old target are considered wages earned by such employees from new target for purposes of sections 3101 and 3111 (Federal Insurance Contributions Act) and section 3301 (Federal Unemployment Tax Act); and

(iii) Old target and new target must use the same employer identification number.

(c) *Anti-abuse rule.*—(1) *In general.*—The rules of this paragraph (c) apply for purposes of applying the regulations under sections 336(e), 338, and 1060. The Commissioner is authorized to treat any property (including cash) transferred by old target in connection with the transactions resulting in the application of the residual method (and not held by target at the close of the acquisition date) as, nonetheless, property of target at the close of the acquisition date if the property so transferred is, within 24 months after the deemed asset sale, owned by new target, or is owned, directly or indirectly, by a member of the affiliated group of which new target is a member and continues after the acquisition date to be held or used primarily in connection with one or more of the activities of new target. In addition, the Commissioner is authorized to treat any property (including cash) transferred to old target in connection with the transactions resulting in the application of the residual method (and held by target at the close of the acquisition date) as, nonetheless, not being property of target at the close of the acquisition date if the property so transferred is, within 24 months after the deemed asset sale, not owned by new target but owned, directly or indirectly, by a member of the affiliated group of which new target is a member, or owned by new target but held or used primarily in connection with an activity conducted, directly or indirectly, by another member of the affiliated group of which new target is a member in combination with other property retained by or acquired, directly or indirectly, from the transferor of the property (or a member of the same affiliated group) to old target. For purposes of this paragraph (c)(1), an interest in an entity is considered held or used in connection with an activity if property of the entity is so held or used. The authority of the Commissioner under this paragraph (c)(1) includes the making of any appropriate correlative adjustments (avoiding, to the extent possible, the duplication or omission of any item of income, gain, loss, deduction, or basis).

(2) *Examples.*—The following examples illustrate this paragraph (c):

Example 1. Prior to a qualified stock purchase under section 338, target transfers one of its assets to a related party. The purchasing corporation then purchases the target stock and also purchases the transferred asset from the related party. After its purchase of target, the purchasing corporation and target are members of the same affiliated group. A section 338 election is made. Under an arrangement with the purchaser, the separately transferred asset is used primarily in connection with target's activities. Applying the anti-abuse rule of this paragraph (c), the Commissioner may consider target to own the transferred asset for purposes of applying the residual method under section 338.

Example 2. T owns all the stock of T1. T1 leases intellectual property to T, which T uses in connection with its own activities. P, a purchasing corporation, wishes to buy the T-T1 chain of corporations. P, in connection with its planned purchase of the T stock, contracts to consummate a purchase of all the stock of T1 on March 1 and of all the stock of T on March 2. Section 338 elections are thereafter made for both T and T1. Immediately after the purchases, P, T and T1 are members of the same affiliated group. T continues to lease the intellectual property from T1 and that is the primary use of the intellectual property. Thus, an asset of T, the T1 stock, was removed from T's own assets prior to the qualified stock purchase of the T stock, T1's own assets are used after the deemed asset sale in connection with T's own activities, and the T1 stock is after the deemed asset sale owned by P, a member of the same affiliated group of which T is a member. Applying the anti-abuse rule of this paragraph (c), the Commissioner may, for purposes of application of the residual method under section 338 both to T and to T1, consider P to have bought only the stock of T, with T at the time of the qualified stock purchases of both T and T1 (the qualified stock purchase of T1 being triggered by the deemed sale under section 338 of T's assets) owning T1. The Commissioner accordingly would allocate consideration to T's assets as though the T1 stock were one of those assets, and then allocate consideration within T1 based on the amount allocated to the T1 stock at the T level.

(d) *Next day rule for post-closing transactions.*—If a target corporation for which an election under section 338 is made engages in a transaction outside the ordinary course of business on the acquisition date after the event resulting in the qualified stock purchase of the target or a higher tier corporation, the target and all persons related thereto (either before or after the qualified stock purchase) under section 267(b) or section 707 must treat the transaction for all Federal income tax purposes as occurring at the beginning of the day following the transaction and after the deemed purchase by new target.

* * *

[Reg. § 1.338-1.]

☐ [*T.D.* 8940, 2-12-2001. *Amended by T.D.* 9002, 6-27-2002; *T.D.* 9257, 4-7-2006; *T.D.* 9377, 1-22-2008; *T.D.* 9446, 2-9-2009; *T.D.* 9619, 5-10-2013 *and T.D.* 9715, 3-31-2015.]

§ 1.338-2. Nomenclature and definitions; mechanics of the section 338 election.—(a) *Scope*.—This section prescribes rules relating to elections under section 338.

(b) *Nomenclature*.—For purposes of the regulations under section 338 (except as otherwise provided):

(1) T is a domestic target corporation that has only one class of stock outstanding. Old T refers to T for periods ending on or before the close of T's acquisition date; new T refers to T for subsequent periods.

(2) P is the purchasing corporation.

(3) The P group is an affiliated group of which P is a member.

(4) P1, P2, etc., are domestic corporations that are members of the P group.

(5) T1, T2, etc., are domestic corporations that are target affiliates of T. These corporations (T1, T2, etc.) have only one class of stock outstanding and may also be targets.

(6) S is a domestic corporation (unrelated to P and B) that owns T prior to the purchase of T by P. (S is referred to in cases in which it is appropriate to consider the effects of having all of the outstanding stock of T owned by a domestic corporation.)

(7) A, a U.S. citizen or resident, is an individual (unrelated to P and B) who owns T prior to the purchase of T by P. (A is referred to in cases in which it is appropriate to consider the effects of having all of the outstanding stock of T owned by an individual who is a U.S. citizen or resident. Ownership of T by A and ownership of T by S are mutually exclusive circumstances.)

(8) B, a U.S. citizen or resident, is an individual (unrelated to T, S, and A) who owns the stock of P.

(9) F, used as a prefix with the other terms in this paragraph (b), connotes foreign, rather than domestic, status. For example, FT is a foreign corporation (as defined in section 7701(a)(5)) and FA is an individual other than a U.S. citizen or resident.

(10) CFC, used as a prefix with the other terms in this paragraph (b) referring to a corporation, connotes a controlled foreign corporation (as defined in section 957, taking into account section 953(c)). A corporation identified with the prefix F may be a controlled foreign corporation. (The prefix CFC is used when the corporation's status as a controlled foreign corporation is significant.)

(c) *Definitions*.—For purposes of the regulations under section 338 (except as otherwise provided):

(1) *Acquisition date*.—The term *acquisition date* has the same meaning as in section 338(h)(2).

(2) *Acquisition date assets*.— *Acquisition date assets* are the assets of the target held at the beginning of the day after the acquisition date (but see § 1.338-1(d) (regarding certain transactions on the acquisition date)).

(3) *Affiliated group*.—The term *affiliated group* has the same meaning as in section 338(h)(5). Corporations are affiliated on any day they are members of the same affiliated group.

(4) *Common parent*.—The term *common parent* has the same meaning as in section 1504.

(5) *Consistency period*.—The *consistency period* is the period described in section 338(h)(4)(A) unless extended pursuant to § 1.338-8(j)(1).

(6) *Deemed asset sale*.—The *deemed asset sale* is the transaction described in § 1.338-1(a)(1) that is deemed to occur for purposes of subtitle A of the Internal Revenue Code if a section 338 election is made.

(7) *Deemed sale tax consequences*.—*Deemed sale tax consequences* refers to, in the aggregate, the Federal income tax consequences (generally, the income, gain, deduction, and loss) of the deemed asset sale. Deemed sale tax consequences also refers to the Federal income tax consequences of the transfer of a particular asset in the deemed asset sale.

(8) *Deemed sale return*.—The *deemed sale return* is the return on which target's deemed sale tax consequences are reported that does not include any other items of target. Target files a deemed sale return when a section 338 election (but not a section 338(h)(10) election) is filed for target and target is a member of a selling group (defined in paragraph (c)(16) of this section) that files a consolidated return for the period that includes the acquisition date. See § 1.338-10. If target is an S corporation for the period that ends on the day before the acquisition date and a section 338 election (but not a section 338(h)(10) election) is filed for target, see § 1.338-10(a)(3).

(9) *Domestic corporation*.—A *domestic corporation* is a corporation—

(i) That is domestic within the meaning of section 7701(a)(4) or that is treated as domestic for purposes of subtitle A of the Internal Revenue Code (e.g., to which an election under section 953(d) or 1504(d) applies); and

(ii) That is not a DISC, a corporation described in section 1248(e), or a corporation to which an election under section 936 applies.

(10) *Old target's final return.— Old target's final return* is the income tax return of old target for the taxable year ending at the close of the acquisition date that includes the deemed sale tax consequences. However, if a deemed sale return is filed for old target, the deemed sale return is considered old target's final return.

(11) *Purchasing corporation.*—The term *purchasing corporation* has the same meaning as in section 338(d)(1). The purchasing corporation may also be referred to as purchaser. Unless otherwise provided, any reference to the purchasing corporation is a reference to all members of the affiliated group of which the purchasing corporation is a member. See sections 338(h)(5) and (8). Also, unless otherwise provided, any reference to the purchasing corporation is, with respect to a deemed purchase of stock under section 338(a)(2), a reference to new target with respect to its own deemed purchase of stock in another target.

(12) *Qualified stock purchase.*—The term *qualified stock purchase* has the same meaning as in section 338(d)(3).

(13) *Related persons.*—Two persons are related if stock in a corporation owned by one of the persons would be attributed under section 318(a) (other than section 318(a)(4)) to the other.

(14) *Section 338 election.*—A *section 338 election* is an election to apply section 338(a) to target. A section 338 election is made by filing a statement of section 338 election pursuant to paragraph (d) of this section. The form on which this statement is filed is referred to in the regulations under section 338 as the Form 8023, "Elections Under Section 338 For Corporations Making Qualified Stock Purchases."

(15) *Section 338(h)(10) election.*—A *section 338(h)(10) election* is an election to apply section 338(h)(10) to target. A section 338(h)(10) election is made by making a joint election for target under §1.338(h)(10)-1 on Form 8023.

(16) *Selling group.*—The *selling group* is the affiliated group (as defined in section 1504) eligible to file a consolidated return that includes target for the taxable period in which the acquisition date occurs. However, a selling group is not an affiliated group of which target is the common parent on the acquisition date.

(17) *Target; old target; new target.— Target* is the target corporation as defined in section 338(d)(2). *Old target* refers to target for periods ending on or before the close of target's acquisition date. *New target* refers to target for subsequent periods.

(18) *Target affiliate.*—The term *target affiliate* has the same meaning as in section 338(h)(6) (applied without section 338(h)(6)(B)(i)). Thus, a corporation described in section 338(h)(6)(B)(i) is considered a target affiliate for all purposes of section 338. If a target affiliate is acquired in a qualified stock purchase, it is also a target.

(19) *12-month acquisition period.*—The *12-month acquisition period* is the period described in section 338(h)(1), unless extended pursuant to §1.338-8(j)(2).

* * *

[Reg. §1.338-2.]

☐ [*T.D.* 8940, 2-12-2001.]

§1.338-3. Qualification for the section 338 election.—(a) *Scope.*—This section provides rules on whether certain acquisitions of stock are qualified stock purchases and on other miscellaneous issues under section 338.

(b) *Rules relating to qualified stock purchases.*—(1) *Purchasing corporation requirement.*—An individual cannot make a qualified stock purchase of target. Section 338(d)(3) requires, as a condition of a qualified stock purchase, that a corporation purchase the stock of target. If an individual forms a corporation (new P) to acquire target stock, new P can make a qualified stock purchase of target if new P is considered for tax purposes to purchase the target stock. Facts that may indicate that new P does not purchase the target stock include new P's merging downstream into target, liquidating, or otherwise disposing of the target stock following the purported qualified stock purchase.

(2) *Purchase.*—The term *purchase* has the same meaning as in section 338(h)(3). Stock in a target (or target affiliate) may be considered purchased if, under general principles of tax law, the purchasing corporation is considered to own stock of the target (or target affiliate) meeting the requirements of section 1504(a)(2), notwithstanding that no amount may be paid for (or allocated to) the stock.

(3) *Acquisitions of stock from related corporations.*—(i) *In general.*—Stock acquired by a purchasing corporation from a related corporation (R) is generally not considered acquired by purchase. See section 338(h)(3)(A)(iii).

(ii) *Time for testing relationship.*—For purposes of section 338(h)(3)(A)(iii), a purchasing corporation is treated as related to another person if the relationship specified in section 338(h)(3)(A)(iii) exists—

(A) In the case of a single transaction, immediately after the purchase of target stock;

(B) In the case of a series of acquisitions otherwise constituting a qualified stock purchase within the meaning of section 338(d)(3), immediately after the last acquisition in such series; and

(C) In the case of a series of transactions effected pursuant to an integrated plan to dispose of target stock, immediately after the last transaction in such series.

(iii) *Cases where section 338(h)(3)(C) applies—acquisitions treated as purchases.*—If section 338(h)(3)(C) applies and the purchasing corporation is treated as acquiring stock by purchase from R, solely for purposes of determining when the stock is considered acquired, target stock acquired from R is considered to have been acquired by the purchasing corporation on the day on which the purchasing corporation is first considered to own that stock under section 318(a) (other than section 318(a)(4)).

(iv) *Examples.*—The following examples illustrate this paragraph (b)(3):

Example 1. (i) S is the parent of a group of corporations that are engaged in various businesses. Prior to January 1, Year 1, S decided to discontinue its involvement in one line of business. To accomplish this, S forms a new corporation, Newco, with a nominal amount of cash. Shortly thereafter, on January 1, Year 1, S transfers all the stock of the subsidiary conducting the unwanted business (T) to Newco in exchange for 100 shares of Newco common stock and a Newco promissory note. Prior to January 1, Year 1, S and Underwriter (U) had entered into a binding agreement pursuant to which U would purchase 60 shares of Newco common stock from S and then sell those shares in an Initial Public Offering (IPO). On January 6, Year 1, the IPO closes.

(ii) Newco's acquisition of T stock is one of a series of transactions undertaken pursuant to one integrated plan. The series of transactions ends with the closing of the IPO and the transfer of all the shares of stock in accordance with the agreements. Immediately after the last transaction effected pursuant to the plan, S owns 40 percent of Newco, which does not give rise to a relationship described in section 338(h)(3)(A)(iii). See § 1.338-3(b)(3)(ii)(C). Accordingly, S and Newco are not related for purposes of section 338(h)(3)(A)(iii).

(iii) Further, because Newco's basis in the T stock is not determined by reference to S's basis in the T stock and because the transaction is not an exchange to which section 351, 354, 355, or 356 applies, Newco's acquisition of the T stock is a purchase within the meaning of section 338(h)(3).

Example 2. (i) On January 1 of Year 1, P purchases 75 percent in value of the R stock. On that date, R owns 4 of the 100 shares of T stock. On June 1 of Year 1, R acquires an additional 16 shares of T stock. On December 1 of Year 1, P purchases 70 shares of T stock from an unrelated person and 12 of the 20 shares of T stock held by R.

(ii) Of the 12 shares of T stock purchased by P from R on December 1 of Year 1, 3 of those shares are deemed to have been acquired by P on January 1 of Year 1, the date on which 3 of the 4 shares of T stock held by R on that date were first considered owned by P under section 318(a)(2)(C) (i.e., 4 × .75). The remaining 9 shares of T stock purchased by P from R on December 1 of Year 1 are deemed to have been acquired by P on June 1 of Year 1, the date on which an additional 12 of the 20 shares of T stock owned by R on that date were first considered owned by P under section 318(a)(2)(C) (i.e., (20 × .75) − 3). Because stock acquisitions by P sufficient for a qualified stock purchase of T occur within a 12-month period (i.e., 3 shares constructively on January 1 of Year 1, 9 shares constructively on June 1 of Year 1, and 70 shares actually on December 1 of Year 1), a qualified stock purchase is made on December 1 of Year 1.

Example 3. (i) On February 1 of Year 1, P acquires 25 percent in value of the R stock from B (the sole shareholder of P). That R stock is not acquired by purchase. See section 338(h)(3)(A)(iii). On that date, R owns 4 of the 100 shares of T stock. On June 1 of Year 1, P purchases an additional 25 percent in value of the R stock, and on January 1 of Year 2, P purchases another 25 percent in value of the R stock. On June 1 of Year 2, R acquires an additional 16 shares of the T stock. On December 1 of Year 2, P purchases 68 shares of the T stock from an unrelated person and 12 of the 20 shares of the T stock held by R.

(ii) Of the 12 shares of the T stock purchased by P from R on December 1 of Year 2, 2 of those shares are deemed to have been acquired by P on June 1 of Year 1, the date on which 2 of the 4 shares of the T stock held by R on that date were first considered owned by P under section 318(a)(2)(C) (i.e., 4 × .5). For purposes of this attribution, the R stock need not be acquired by P by purchase. See section 338(h)(1). (By contrast, the acquisition of the T stock by P from R does not qualify as a purchase unless P has acquired at least 50 percent in value of the R stock by purchase. Section 338(h)(3)(C)(i).) Of the remaining 10 shares of the T stock purchased by P from R on

December 1 of Year 2, 1 of those shares is deemed to have been acquired by P on January 1 of Year 2, the date on which an additional 1 share of the 4 shares of the T stock held by R on that date was first considered owned by P under section 318(a)(2)(C) (i.e., (4 × .75) − 2). The remaining 9 shares of the T stock purchased by P from R on December 1 of Year 2, are deemed to have been acquired by P on June 1 of Year 2, the date on which an additional 12 shares of the T stock held by R on that date were first considered owned by P under section 318(a)(2)(C) (i.e., (20 × .75) − 3). Because a qualified stock purchase of T by P is made on December 1 of Year 2 only if all 12 shares of the T stock purchased by P from R on that date are considered acquired during a 12-month period ending on that date (so that, in conjunction with the 68 shares of the T stock P purchased on that date from the unrelated person, 80 of T's 100 shares are acquired by P during a 12-month period) and because 2 of those 12 shares are considered to have been acquired by P more than 12 months before December 1 of Year 2 (i.e., on June 1 of Year 1), a qualified stock purchase is not made. (Under § 1.338-8(j)(2), for purposes of applying the consistency rules, P is treated as making a qualified stock purchase of T if, pursuant to an arrangement, P purchases T stock satisfying the requirements of section 1504(a)(2) over a period of more than 12 months.)

Example 4. Assume the same facts as in *Example 3*, except that on February 1 of Year 1, P acquires 25 percent in value of the R stock by purchase. The result is the same as in *Example 3.*

(4) *Acquisition date for tiered targets.*—(i) *Stock sold in deemed asset sale.*—If an election under section 338 is made for target, old target is deemed to sell target's assets and new target is deemed to acquire those assets. Under section 338(h)(3)(B), new target's deemed purchase of stock of another corporation is a purchase for purposes of section 338(d)(3) on the acquisition date of target. If new target's deemed purchase causes a qualified stock purchase of the other corporation and if a section 338 election is made for the other corporation, the acquisition date for the other corporation is the same as the acquisition date of target. However, the deemed sale and purchase of the other corporation's assets is considered to take place after the deemed sale and purchase of target's assets.

(ii) *Example.*—The following example illustrates this paragraph (b)(4):

Example. A owns all of the T stock. T owns 50 of the 100 shares of X stock. The other 50 shares of X stock are owned by corporation Y, which is unrelated to A, T, or P. On January 1 of Year 1, P makes a qualified stock purchase of T from A and makes a section 338 election for T. On December 1 of Year 1, P purchases the 50 shares of X stock held by Y. A qualified stock purchase of X is made on December 1 of Year 1, because the deemed purchase of 50 shares of X stock by new T because of the section 338 election for T and the actual purchase of 50 shares of X stock by P are treated as purchases made by one corporation. Section 338(h)(8). For purposes of determining whether those purchases occur within a 12-month acquisition period as required by section 338(d)(3), T is deemed to purchase its X stock on T's acquisition date, i.e., January 1 of Year 1.

(5) *Effect of redemptions.*—(i) *General rule.*—Except as provided in this paragraph (b)(5), a qualified stock purchase is made on the first day on which the percentage ownership requirements of section 338(d)(3) are satisfied by reference to target stock that is both—

(A) Held on that day by the purchasing corporation; and

(B) Purchased by the purchasing corporation during the 12-month period ending on that day.

(ii) *Redemptions from persons unrelated to the purchasing corporation.*—Target stock redemptions from persons unrelated to the purchasing corporation that occur during the 12-month acquisition period are taken into account as reductions in target's outstanding stock for purposes of determining whether target stock purchased by the purchasing corporation in the 12-month acquisition period satisfies the percentage ownership requirements of section 338(d)(3).

(iii) *Redemptions from the purchasing corporation or related persons during 12-month acquisition period.*—(A) *General rule.*—For purposes of the percentage ownership requirements of section 338(d)(3), a redemption of target stock during the 12-month acquisition period from the purchasing corporation or from any person related to the purchasing corporation is not taken into account as a reduction in target's outstanding stock.

(B) *Exception for certain redemptions from related corporations.*—A redemption of target stock during the 12-month acquisition period from a corporation related to the purchasing corporation is taken into account as a reduction in target's outstanding stock to the extent that the redeemed stock would have been considered purchased by the purchasing corporation (because of section 338(h)(3)(C)) during the 12-month acquisition period if the redeemed stock had been acquired by the purchasing corporation from the related corporation On the day of the redemption. See paragraph (b)(3) of this section.

* * *

(c) *Effect of post-acquisition events on eligibility for section 338 election.*—(1) *Post-acquisition elimination of target.*—(i) The purchasing corporation may make an election under section 338 for target even though target is liquidated on or after the acquisition date. If target liquidates on the acquisition date, the liquidation is considered to occur on the following day and immediately after new target's deemed purchase of assets. The purchasing corporation may also make an election under section 338 for target even though target is merged into another corporation, or otherwise disposed of by the purchasing corporation provided that, under the facts and circumstances, the purchasing corporation is considered for tax purposes as the purchaser of the target stock. See §1.338(h)(10)-1(c)(2) for special rules concerning section 338(h)(10) elections in certain multi-step transactions.

(ii) The following examples illustrate this paragraph (c)(1):

Example 1. On January 1 of Year 1, P purchases 100 percent of the outstanding common stock of T. On June 1 of Year 1, P sells the T stock to an unrelated person. Assuming that P is considered for tax purposes as the purchaser of the T stock, P remains eligible, after June 1 of Year 1, to make a section 338 election for T that results in a deemed asset sale of T's assets on January 1 of Year 1.

Example 2. On January 1 of Year 1, P makes a qualified stock purchase of T. On that date, T owns the stock of T1. On March 1 of Year 1, T sells the T1 stock to an unrelated person. On April 1 of Year 1, P makes a section 338 election for T. Notwithstanding that the T1 stock was sold on March 1 of Year 1, the section 338 election for T on April 1 of Year 1 results in a qualified stock purchase by T of T1 on January 1 of Year 1. See paragraph (b)(4)(i) of this section.

(2) *Post-acquisition elimination of the purchasing corporation.*—An election under section 338 may be made for target after the acquisition of assets of the purchasing corporation by another corporation in a transaction described in section 381(a), provided that the purchasing corporation is considered for tax purposes as the purchaser of the target stock. The acquiring corporation in the section 381(a) transaction may make an election under section 338 for target.

(d) *Consequences of post-acquisition elimination of target where section 338 election not made.*—(1) *Scope.*—The rules of this paragraph (d) apply to the transfer of target assets to the purchasing corporation (or another member of the same affiliated group as the purchasing corporation) (the transferee) following a qualified stock purchase of target stock, if the purchasing corporation does not make a section 338 election for target. Notwithstanding the rules of this paragraph (d), section 354(a) (and so much of section 356 as relates to section 354) cannot apply to any person other than the purchasing corporation or another member of the same affiliated group as the purchasing corporation unless the transfer of target assets is pursuant to a reorganization as determined without regard to this paragraph (d).

(2) *Continuity of interest.*—By virtue of section 338, in determining whether the continuity of interest requirement of §1.368-1(b) is satisfied on the transfer of assets from target to the transferee, the purchasing corporation's target stock acquired in the qualified stock purchase represents an interest on the part of a person who was an owner of the target's business enterprise prior to the transfer that can be continued in a reorganization.

(3) *Control requirement.*—By virtue of section 338, the acquisition of target stock in the qualified stock purchase will not prevent the purchasing corporation from qualifying as a shareholder of the target transferor for the purpose of determining whether, immediately after the transfer of target assets, a shareholder of the transferor is in control of the corporation to which the assets are transferred within the meaning of section 368(a)(1)(D).

(4) *Solely for voting stock requirement.*—By virtue of section 338, the acquisition of target stock in the qualified stock purchase for consideration other than voting stock will not prevent the subsequent transfer of target assets from satisfying the solely for voting stock requirement for purposes of determining if the transfer of target assets qualifies as a reorganization under section 368(a)(1)(C).

(5) *Example.*—The following example illustrates this paragraph (d):

Example. (i) *Facts.* P, T, and X are domestic corporations. T and X each operate a trade or business. A and K, individuals unrelated to P, own 85 and 15 percent, respectively, of the stock of T. P owns all of the stock of X. The total adjusted basis of T's property exceeds the sum of T's liabilities plus the amount of liabilities to which T's property is subject. P purchases all of A's T stock for cash in a qualified stock purchase. P does not make an election under section 338(g) with respect to its acquisition of T stock. Shortly after the acquisition date, and as part of the same plan, T merges under applicable state law into X in a transaction that, but for the question of continuity of interest, satisfies all the requirements of section 368(a)(1)(A). In the merger, all of T's assets are transferred to X. P and K receive X stock in exchange for their T stock. P intends to retain the stock of X indefinitely.

(ii) *Status of transfer as a reorganization.* By virtue of section 338, for the purpose of determining whether the continuity of interest requirement of §1.368-1(b) is satisfied, P's T stock acquired in the qualified stock purchase represents an interest on the part of a person who was an owner of T's business enterprise prior to the transfer that can be continued in a reorganization through P's continuing ownership of X. Thus, the continuity of interest requirement is satisfied and the merger of T into X is a reorganization within the meaning of section 368(a)(1)(A). Moreover, by virtue of section 338, the requirement of section 368(a)(1)(D) that a target shareholder control the transferee immediately after the transfer is satisfied because P controls X immediately after the transfer. In addition, all of T's assets are transferred to X in the merger and P and K receive the X stock exchanged therefor in pursuance of the plan of reorganization. Thus, the merger of T into X is also a reorganization within the meaning of section 368(a)(1)(D).

(iii) *Treatment of T and X.* Under section 361(a), T recognizes no gain or loss in the merger. Under section 362(b), X's basis in the assets received in the merger is the same as the basis of the assets in T's hands. X succeeds to and takes into account the items of T as provided in section 381.

(iv) *Treatment of P.* By virtue of section 338, the transfer of T assets to X is a reorganization. Pursuant to that reorganization, P exchanges its T stock solely for stock of X, a party to the reorganization. Because P is the purchasing corporation, section 354 applies to P's exchange of T stock for X stock in the merger of T into X. Thus, P recognizes no gain or loss on the exchange. Under section 358, P's basis in the X stock received in the exchange is the same as the basis of P's T stock exchanged therefor.

(v) *Treatment of K.* Because K is not the purchasing corporation (or an affiliate thereof), section 354 cannot apply to K's exchange of T stock for X stock in the merger of T into X unless the transfer of T's assets is pursuant to a reorganization as determined without regard to this paragraph (d). Under general principles of tax law applicable to reorganizations, the continuity of interest requirement is not satisfied because P's stock purchase and the merger of T into X are pursuant to an integrated transaction in which A, the owner of 85 percent of the stock of T, received solely cash in exchange for A's T stock. See, e.g., §1.368-1(e)(1)(i); *Yoc Heating v. Commissioner*, 61 T.C. 168 (1973); *Kass v. Commissioner*, 60 T.C. 218 (1973), aff'd, 491 F.2d 749 (3d Cir. 1974). Thus, the requisite continuity of interest under §1.368-1(b) is lacking and section 354 does not apply to K's exchange of T stock for X stock. K recognizes gain or loss, if any, pursuant to section 1001(c) with respect to its T stock.

[Reg. §1.338-3.]

☐ [*T.D.* 8940, 2-12-2001 (*corrected* 3-29-2001). *Amended by T.D.* 9071, 7-8-2003 *and T.D.* 9271, 7-3-2006.]

§1.338-4. Aggregate deemed sale price; various aspects of taxation of the deemed asset sale.—(a) *Scope.*—This section provides rules under section 338(a)(1) to determine the aggregate deemed sale price (ADSP) for target. ADSP is the amount for which old target is deemed to have sold all of its assets in the deemed asset sale. ADSP is allocated among target's assets in accordance with §1.338-6 to determine the amount for which each asset is deemed to have been sold. When a subsequent increase or decrease is required under general principles of tax law with respect to an element of ADSP, the redetermined ADSP is allocated among target's assets in accordance with §1.338-7. This §1.338-4 also provides rules regarding the recognition of gain or loss on the deemed sale of target affiliate stock. Notwithstanding section 338(h)(6)(B)(ii), stock held by a target affiliate in a foreign corporation or in a corporation that is a DISC or that is described in section 1248(e) is not excluded from the operation of section 338.

(b) *Determination of ADSP.*—(1) *General rule.*—ADSP is the sum of—

(i) The grossed-up amount realized on the sale to the purchasing corporation of the purchasing corporation's recently purchased target stock (as defined in section 338(b)(6)(A)); and

(ii) The liabilities of old target.

(2) *Time and amount of ADSP.*—(i) *Original termination.*—ADSP is initially determined at the beginning of the day after the acquisition date of target. General principles of tax law apply in determining the timing and amount of the elements of ADSP.

(ii) *Redetermination of ADSP.*—ADSP is redetermined at such time and in such amount as an increase or decrease would be required, under general principles of tax law, for the elements of ADSP. For example, ADSP is redetermined because of an increase or decrease in the amount realized for recently purchased stock or because liabilities not originally taken into account in determining ADSP are subsequently taken into account. Increases or decreases with respect to the elements of ADSP result in the reallocation of ADSP among target's assets under § 1.338-7.

(iii) *Example.*—The following example illustrates this paragraph (b) (2):

Example. In Year 1, T, a manufacturer, purchases a customized delivery truck from X with purchase money indebtedness having a stated principal amount of $100,000. P acquires all of the stock of T in Year 3 for $700,000 and makes a section 338 election for T. Assume T has no liabilities other than its purchase money indebtedness to X. In Year 4, when T is neither insolvent nor in a title 11 case, T and X agree to reduce the amount of the purchase money indebtedness to $80,000. Assume further that the reduction would be a purchase price reduction under section 108(e) (5). T and X's agreement to reduce the amount of the purchase money indebtedness would not, under general principles of tax law that would apply if the deemed asset sale had actually occurred, change the amount of liabilities of old target taken into account in determining its amount realized. Accordingly, ADSP is not redetermined at the time of the reduction. See § 1.338-5(b) (2) (iii) *Example 1* for the effect on AGUB.

(c) *Grossed-up amount realized on the sale to the purchasing corporation of the purchasing corporation's recently purchased target stock.*—(1) *Determination of amount.*—The grossed-up amount realized on the sale to the purchasing corporation of the purchasing corporation's recently purchased target stock is an amount equal to—

(i) The amount realized on the sale to the purchasing corporation of the purchasing corporation's recently purchased target stock determined as if the selling shareholder(s) were required to use old target's accounting methods and characteristics and the installment method were not available and determined without regard to the selling costs taken into account under paragraph (c) (1) (iii) of this section;

(ii) Divided by the percentage of target stock (by value, determined on the acquisition date) attributable to that recently purchased target stock;

(iii) Less the selling costs incurred by the selling shareholders in connection with the sale to the purchasing corporation of the purchasing corporation's recently purchased target stock that reduce their amount realized on the sale of the stock (e.g., brokerage commissions and any similar costs to sell the stock).

(2) *Example.*—The following example illustrates this paragraph (c):

Example. T has two classes of stock outstanding, voting common stock and preferred stock described in section 1504(a) (4). On March 1 of Year 1, P purchases 40 percent of the outstanding T stock from S1 for $500, 20 percent of the outstanding T stock from S2 for $225, and 20 percent of the outstanding T stock from S3 for $275. On that date, the fair market value of all the T voting common stock is $1,250 and the preferred stock $750. S1, S2, and S3 incur $40, $35, and $25 respectively of selling costs. S1 continues to own the remaining 20 percent of the outstanding T stock. The grossed-up amount realized on the sale to P of P's recently purchased T stock is calculated as follows: The total amount realized (without regard to selling costs) is $1,000 (500 + 225 + 275). The percentage of T stock by value on the acquisition date attributable to the recently purchased T stock is 50% (1,000/(1,250 + 750)). The selling costs are $100 (40 + 35 + 25). The grossed-up amount realized is $1,900 (1,000/.5 - 100).

(d) *Liabilities of old target.*—(1) *In general.*—In general, the liabilities of old target are measured as of the beginning of the day after the acquisition date. (But see § 1.338-1(d) (regarding certain transactions on the acquisition date).) In order to be taken into account in ADSP, a liability must be a liability of target that is properly taken into account in amount realized under general principles of tax law that would apply if old target had sold its assets to an unrelated person for consideration that included the discharge of its liabilities. See § 1.1001-2(a). Such liabilities may include liabilities for the tax consequences resulting from the deemed sale.

(2) *Time and amount of liabilities.*—The time for taking into account liabilities of old target in determining ADSP and the amount of the liabilities taken into account is determined as if old target had sold its assets to an unrelated person for consideration that included the discharge of the liabilities by the unrelated person. For example, if no amount of a target liability is properly taken into account in amount realized as of the beginning of the day after the acquisition date, the liability is not initially taken into account in determining ADSP (although it may be taken into account at some later date).

(e) *Deemed sale tax consequences.*—Gain or loss on each asset in the deemed sale is computed by reference to the ADSP allocated to that asset. ADSP is allocated under the rules of § 1.338-6. Though deemed sale tax consequences may increase or decrease ADSP by creating or reducing a tax liability, the amount of the tax liability itself may be a function of the size of the deemed sale tax consequences. Thus, these determinations may require trial and error computations.

(f) *Other rules apply in determining ADSP.*—ADSP may not be applied in such a way as to contravene other applicable rules. For example, a capital loss cannot be applied to reduce ordinary income in calculating the tax liability on the deemed sale for purposes of determining ADSP.

(g) *Examples.*—The following examples illustrate this section. For purposes of the examples in this paragraph (g), unless otherwise stated, T is a calendar year taxpayer that files separate returns and that has no loss, tax credit, or other carryovers to Year 1. Depreciation for Year 1 is not taken into account. T has no liabilities other than the Federal income tax liability resulting from the deemed asset sale, and the T shareholders have no selling costs. Assume that T's tax rate for any ordinary income or net capital gain resulting from the deemed sale of assets is 34 percent and that any capital loss is offset by capital gain. On July 1 of Year 1, P purchases all of the stock of T and makes a section 338 election for T. The examples are as follows:

Example 1. One class. (i) On July 1 of Year 1, T's only asset is an item of section 1245 property with an adjusted basis to T of $50,400, a recomputed basis of $80,000, and a fair market value of $100,000. P purchases all of the T stock for $75,000, which also equals the amount realized for the stock determined as if the selling shareholder(s) were required to use old target's accounting methods and characteristics.

(ii) ADSP is determined as follows (for purposes of this section (g), G is the grossed-up amount realized on the sale to P of P's recently purchased T stock, L is T's liabilities other than T's tax liability for the deemed sale tax consequences, T_R is the applicable tax rate, and B is the adjusted basis of the asset deemed sold):

ADSP = G + L + T_R × (ADSP − B)

ADSP = ($75,000/1) + $0 + .34 × (ADSP − $50,400)

ADSP = $75,000 + .34ADSP − $17,136

.66ADSP = $57,864

ADSP = $87,672.72

(iii) Because ADSP for T ($87,672.72) does not exceed the fair market value of T's asset ($100,000), a Class V asset, T's entire ADSP is allocated to that asset. Thus, T's deemed sale results in $37,272.72 of taxable income (consisting of $29,600 of ordinary income and $7,672.72 of capital gain).

(iv) The facts are the same as in paragraph (i) of this *Example 1*, except that on July 1 of Year 1, P purchases only 80 of the 100 shares of T stock for $60,000. The grossed-up amount realized on the sale to P of P's recently purchased T stock (G) is $75,000 ($60,000/.8). Consequently, ADSP and the deemed sale tax consequences are the same as in paragraphs (ii) and (iii) of this *Example 1*.

(v) The facts are the same as in paragraph (i) of this *Example 1*, except that T also has goodwill (a Class VII asset) with an appraised value of $10,000. The results are the same as in paragraphs (ii) and (iii) of this *Example 1*. Because ADSP does not exceed the fair market value of the Class V asset, no amount is allocated to the Class VII asset (goodwill).

Example 2. More than one class. (i) P purchases all of the T stock for $140,000, which also equals the amount realized for the stock determined as if the selling shareholder(s) were required to use old target's accounting methods and characteristics. On July 1 of Year 1, T has liabilities (not including the tax liability for the deemed sale tax consequences) of $50,000, cash (a Class I asset) of $10,000, actively traded securities (a Class II asset) with a basis of $4,000 and a fair market value of $10,000, goodwill (a Class VII asset) with a basis of $3,000, and the following Class V assets:

Asset	*Basis*	*FMV*	*Ratio of asset FMV to total Class V FMV*
Land	$5,000	$35,000	.14
Building	10,000	50,000	.20
Equipment A (Recomputed basis $80,000)	5,000	90,000	.36
Equipment B (Recomputed basis $20,000)	10,000	75,000	.30
Totals	$30,000	$250,000	1.00

(ii) ADSP exceeds $20,000. Thus, $10,000 of ADSP is allocated to the cash and $10,000 to the actively traded securities. The amount allocated to an asset (other than a Class VII asset) cannot exceed its fair market value (however, the fair market value of any property subject to nonrecourse indebtedness is treated as being not less than the amount of such indebtedness;

see § 1.338-6(a)(2)). See § 1.338-6(c)(1) (relating to fair market value limitation).

(iii) The portion of ADSP allocable to the Class V assets is preliminarily determined as follows (in the formula, the amount allocated to the Class I assets is referred to as I and the amount allocated to the Class II assets as II):

$ADSP_V = (G - (I + II)) + L + T_R \times [(II - B_{II}) + (ADSP_V - B_V)]$

$ADSP_V = (\$140,000 - (\$10,000 + \$10,000)) + \$50,000 + .34 \times [(\$10,000 - \$4,000) + (ADSP_V - (\$5,000 + \$10,000 + \$5,000 + \$10,000))]$

$ADSP_V = \$161,840 + .34\ ADSP_V$

$.66\ ADSP_V = \$161,840$

$ADSP_V = \$245,212.12$

(iv) Because, under the preliminary calculations of ADSP, the amount to be allocated to the Class I, II, III, IV, V, and VI assets does not exceed their aggregate fair market value, no ADSP amount is allocated to goodwill. Accordingly, the deemed sale of the goodwill results in a capital loss of $3,000. The portion of ADSP allocable to the Class V assets is finally determined by taking into account this loss as follows:

$ADSP_V = (G - (I + II)) + L + T_R \times [(II - B_{II}) + (ADSP_V - B_V) + (ADSP_{VII} - B_{VII})]$

$ADSP_V = (\$140,000 - (\$10,000 + \$10,000)) + \$50,000 + .34 \times [(\$10,000 - \$4,000) + (ADSP_V - \$30,000) + (\$0 - \$3,000)]$

$ADSP_V = \$160,820 + .34\ ADSP_V$

$.66\ ADSP_V = \$160,820$

$ADSP_V = \$243,666.67$

(v) The allocation of $ADSP_V$ among the Class V assets is in proportion to their fair market values, as follows:

Asset	*ADSP*	*Gain*
Land	$34,113.33	$29,113.33 (capital gain)
Building	48,733.34	38,733.34 (capital gain)
Equipment A	87,720.00	82,720.00 (75,000 ordinary income 7,720 capital gain)
Equipment B	73,100.00	63,100.00 (10,000 ordinary income 53,100 capital gain)
Totals	$243,666.67	$213,666.67

Example 3. More than one class. (i) The facts are the same as in *Example 2,* except that P purchases the T stock for $150,000, rather than $140,000. The amount realized for the stock determined as if the selling shareholder(s) were required to use old target's accounting methods and characteristics is also $150,000.

(ii) As in *Example 2,* ADSP exceeds $20,000. Thus, $10,000 of ADSP is allocated to the cash and $10,000 to the actively traded securities.

(iii) The portion of ADSP allocable to the Class V assets as preliminarily determined under the formula set forth in paragraph (iii) of *Example 2* is $260,363.64. The amount allocated to the Class V assets cannot exceed their aggregate fair market value ($250,000). Thus, preliminarily, the ADSP amount allocated to Class V assets is $250,000.

(iv) Based on the preliminary allocation, the ADSP is determined as follows (in the formula, the amount allocated to the Class I assets is referred to as I, the amount allocated to the Class II assets as II, and the amount allocated to the Class V assets as V):

$ADSP = G + L + T_R \times [(II - B_{II}) + (V - B_V) + (ADSP - (I + II + V + B_{VII}))]$

$ADSP = \$150,000 + \$50,000 + .34 \times [(\$10,000 - \$4,000) + (\$250,000 - \$30,000) + (ADSP - (\$10,000 + \$10,000 + \$250,000 + \$3,000))]$

$ADSP = \$200,000 + .34ADSP - \$15,980$

$.66ADSP = \$184,020$

$ADSP = \$278,818.18$

(v) Because ADSP as determined exceeds the aggregate fair market value of the Class I, II, III, IV, V, and VI assets, the $250,000 amount preliminarily allocated to the Class V assets is appropriate. Thus, the amount of ADSP allocated to Class V assets equals their aggregate fair market value ($250,000), and the allocated ADSP amount for each Class V asset is its fair market value. Further, because there are no Class VI assets, the allocable ADSP amount for the Class VII asset (goodwill) is $8,818.18 (the excess of ADSP over the aggregate ADSP amounts for the Class I, II, III, IV, V and VI assets).

Example 4. Amount allocated to T1 stock. (i) The facts are the same as in *Example 2,* except that T owns all of the T1 stock (instead of the building), and T1's only asset is the building. The T1 stock and the building each have a fair market value of $50,000, and the building has a basis of $10,000. A section 338 election is made for T1 (as well as T), and T1 has no liabilities other than the tax liability for the deemed sale tax consequences. T is the common parent of a consolidated group filing a final consolidated return described in § 1.338-10(a)(1).

(ii) ADSP exceeds $20,000. Thus, $10,000 of ADSP is allocated to the cash and $10,000 to the actively traded securities.

(iii) Because T does not recognize any gain on the deemed sale of the T1 stock under paragraph (h)(2) of this section, appropriate adjustments must be made to reflect accurately the fair market value of the T and T1 assets in determining the allocation of ADSP among T's Class V assets (including the T1 stock). In preliminarily calculating ADSPv in this case, the T1 stock can be disregarded and, because T owns all of the T1 stock, the T1 asset can be treated as a T asset. Under this assumption, ADSPV is $243,666.67. See paragraph (iv) of *Example 2.*

(iv) Because the portion of the preliminary ADSP allocable to Class V assets ($243,666.67) does not exceed their fair market value ($250,000), no amount is allocated to Class VII assets for T. Further, this amount ($243,666.67) is allocated among T's Class V assets in proportion to their fair market values. See paragraph (v) of *Example 2.* Tentatively, $48,733.34 of this amount is allocated to the T1 stock.

(v) The amount tentatively allocated to the T1 stock, however, reflects the tax incurred on the deemed sale of the T1 asset equal to $13,169.34 (.34 × ($48,733.34 - $10,000)). Thus, the ADSP allocable to the Class V assets of T, and the ADSP allocable to the T1 stock, as preliminarily calculated, each must be reduced by $13,169.34. Consequently, these amounts, respectively, are $230,497.33 and $35,564.00. In determining ADSP for T1, the grossed-up amount realized on the deemed sale to new T of new T's recently purchased T1 stock is $35,564.00.

(vi) The facts are the same as in paragraph (i) of this *Example 4,* except that the T1 building has a $12,500 basis and a $62,500 value, all of the outstanding T1 stock has a $62,500 value, and T owns 80 percent of the T1 stock. In preliminarily calculating $ADSP_V$, the T1 stock can be disregarded but, because T owns only 80 percent of the T1 stock, only 80 percent of T1 asset basis and value should be taken into account in calculating T's ADSP. By taking into account 80 percent of these amounts, the remaining calculations and results are the same as in paragraphs (ii), (iii), (iv), and (v) of this *Example 4,* except that the grossed-up amount realized on the sale of the recently purchased T1 stock is $44,455.00 ($35,564.00/0.8).

(h) *Deemed sale of target affiliate stock.*—(1) *Scope.*—This paragraph (h) prescribes rules relating to the treatment of gain or loss realized on the deemed sale of stock of a target affiliate when a section 338 election (but not a section 338(h)(10) election) is made for the target affiliate. For purposes of this paragraph (h), the definition of domestic corporation in § 1.338-2(c)(9) is applied without the exclusion therein for DISCs, corporations described in section 1248(e), and corporations to which an election under section 936 applies.

(2) *In general.*—Except as otherwise provided in this paragraph (h), if a section 338 election is made for target, target recognizes no gain or loss on the deemed sale of stock of a target affiliate having the same acquisition date and for which a section 338 election is made if—

(i) Target directly owns stock in the target affiliate satisfying the requirements of section 1504(a)(2);

(ii) Target and the target affiliate are members of a consolidated group filing a final consolidated return described in § 1.338-10(a)(1); or

(iii) Target and the target affiliate file a combined return under § 1.338-10(a)(4).

(3) *Deemed sale of foreign target affiliate by a domestic target.*—A domestic target recognizes gain or loss on the deemed sale of stock of a foreign target affiliate. For the proper treatment of such gain or loss, see, e.g., sections 1246, 1248, 1291 et seq., and 338(h)(16) and § 1.338-9.

(4) *Deemed sale producing effectively connected income.*—A foreign target recognizes gain or loss on the deemed sale of stock of a foreign target affiliate to the extent that such gain or loss is effectively connected (or treated

as effectively connected) with the conduct of a trade or business in the United States.

(5) *Deemed sale of insurance company target affiliate electing under section 953(d).*—A domestic target recognizes gain (but not loss) on the deemed sale of stock of a target affiliate that has in effect an election under section 953(d) in an amount equal to the lesser of the gain realized or the earnings and profits described in section 953(d)(4)(B).

(6) *Deemed sale of DISC target affiliate.*—A foreign or domestic target recognizes gain (but not loss) on the deemed sale of stock of a target affiliate that is a DISC or a former DISC (as defined in section 992(a)) in an amount equal to the lesser of the gain realized or the amount of accumulated DISC income determined with respect to such stock under section 995(c). Such gain is included in gross income as a dividend as provided in sections 995(c)(2) and 996(g).

(7) *Anti-stuffing rule.*—If an asset the adjusted basis of which exceeds its fair market value is contributed or transferred to a target affiliate as transferred basis property (within the meaning of section 7701(a)(43)) and a purpose of such transaction is to reduce the gain (or increase the loss) recognized on the deemed sale of such target affiliate's stock, the gain or loss recognized by target on the deemed sale of stock of the target affiliate is determined as if such asset had not been contributed or transferred.

(8) *Examples.*—The following examples illustrate this paragraph (h):

Example 1. (i) P makes a qualified stock purchase of T and makes a section 338 election for T. T's sole asset, all of the T1 stock, has a basis of $50 and a fair market value of $150. T's deemed purchase of the T1 stock results in a qualified stock purchase of T1 and a section 338 election is made for T1. T1's assets have a basis of $50 and a fair market value of $150.

(ii) T realizes $100 of gain on the deemed sale of the T1 stock, but the gain is not recognized because T directly owns stock in T1 satisfying the requirements of section 1504(a)(2) and a section 338 election is made for T1.

(iii) T1 recognizes gain of $100 on the deemed sale of its assets.

Example 2. The facts are the same as in *Example 1,* except that P does not make a section 338 election for T1. Because a section 338 election is not made for T1, the $100 gain realized by T on the deemed sale of the T1 stock is recognized.

Example 3. (i) P makes a qualified stock purchase of T and makes a section 338 election for T. T owns all of the stock of T1 and T2. T's deemed purchase of the T1 and T2 stock results in a qualified stock purchase of T1 and T2 and section 338 elections are made for T1 and T2. T1 and T2 each own 50 percent of the vote and value of T3 stock. The deemed purchases by T1 and T2 of the T3 stock result in a qualified stock purchase of T3 and a section 338 election is made for T3. T is the common parent of a consolidated group and all of the deemed asset sales are reported on the T group's final consolidated return. See § 1.338-10(a)(1).

(ii) Because T, T1, T2 and T3 are members of a consolidated group filing a final consolidated return, no gain or loss is recognized by T, T1 or T2 on their respective deemed sales of target affiliate stock.

Example 4. (i) T's sole asset, all of the FT1 stock, has a basis of $25 and a fair market value of $150. FT1's sole asset, all of the FT2 stock, has a basis of $75 and a fair market value of $150. FT1 and FT2 each have $50 of accumulated earnings and profits for purposes of section 1248(c) and (d). FT2's assets have a basis of $125 and a fair market value of $150, and their sale would not generate subpart F income under section 951. The sale of the FT2 stock or assets would not generate income effectively connected with the conduct of a trade or business within the United States. FT1 does not have an election in effect under section 953(d) and neither FT1 nor FT2 is a passive foreign investment company.

(ii) P makes a qualified stock purchase of T and makes a section 338 election for T. T's deemed purchase of the FT1 stock results in a qualified stock purchase of FT1 and a section 338 election is made for M. Similarly, FT1's deemed purchase of the FT2 stock results in a qualified stock purchase of FT2 and a section 338 election is made for FT2.

(iii) T recognizes $125 of gain on the deemed sale of the FT1 stock under paragraph (h)(3) of this section. FT1 does not recognize $75 of gain on the deemed sale of the FT2 stock under paragraph (h)(2) of this section. FT2 recognizes $25 of gain on the deemed sale of its assets. The $125 gain T recognizes on the deemed sale of the FT1 stock is included in T's income as a dividend under section 1248, because FT1 and FT2 have sufficient earnings and profits for full recharacterization ($50 of accumulated earnings and profits in FT1, $50 of accumulated earnings and profits in FT2, and $25 of deemed sale earnings and profits in FT2). Section 1.338-9(b). For purposes of sections 901 through 908, the source and foreign tax credit limitation basket of $25 of the recharacterized gain on the deemed sale of the FT1 stock is determined under section 338(h)(16).

[Reg. § 1.338-4.]

□ [*T.D.* 8940, 2-12-2001.]

§ 1.338-5. Adjusted grossed-up basis.—(a) *Scope.*—This section provides rules under section 338(b) to determine the adjusted grossed-up basis (AGUB) for target. AGUB is the amount for which new target is deemed to have purchased all of its assets in the deemed purchase under section 338(a)(2). AGUB is allocated among target's assets in accordance with § 1.338-6 to determine the price at which the assets are deemed to have been purchased. When a subsequent increase or decrease with respect to an element of AGUB is required under general principles of tax law, redetermined AGUB is allocated among target's assets in accordance with § 1.338-7.

(b) *Determination of AGUB.*—(1) *General rule.*—AGUB is the sum of—

(i) The grossed-up basis in the purchasing corporation's recently purchased target stock;

(ii) The purchasing corporation's basis in nonrecently purchased target stock; and

(iii) The liabilities of new target.

(2) *Time and amount of AGUB.*—(i) *Original determination.*—AGUB is initially determined at the beginning of the day after the acquisition date of target. General principles of tax law apply in determining the timing and amount of the elements of AGUB.

(ii) *Redetermination of AGUB.*—AGUB is redetermined at such time and in such amount as an increase or decrease would be required, under general principles of tax law, with respect to an element of AGUB. For example, AGUB is redetermined because of an increase or decrease in the amount paid or incurred for recently purchased stock or nonrecently purchased stock or because liabilities not originally taken into account in determining AGUB are subsequently taken into account. An increase or decrease to one element of AGUB also may cause an increase or decrease to another element of AGUB. For example, if there is an increase in the amount paid or incurred for recently purchased stock after the acquisition date, any increase in the basis of nonrecently purchased stock because a gain recognition election was made is also taken into account when AGUB is redetermined. Increases or decreases with respect to the elements of AGUB result in the reallocation of AGUB among target's assets under § 1.338-7.

(iii) *Examples.*—The following examples illustrate this paragraph (b)(2):

Example 1. In Year 1, T, a manufacturer, purchases a customized delivery truck from X with purchase money indebtedness having a stated principal amount of $100,000. P acquires all of the stock of T in Year 3 for $700,000 and makes a section 338 election for T. Assume T has no liabilities other than its purchase money indebtedness to X. In Year 4, when T is neither insolvent nor in a title 11 case, T and X agree to reduce the amount of the purchase money indebtedness to $80,000. Assume that the reduction would be a purchase price reduction under section 108(e)(5). T and X's agreement to reduce the amount of the purchase money indebtedness would, under general principles of tax law that would apply if the deemed asset sale had actually occurred, change the amount of liabilities of old target taken into account in determining its basis. Accordingly, AGUB is redetermined at the time of the reduction. See paragraph (e)(2) of this section. Thus the purchase price reduction affects the basis of the truck only indirectly, through the mechanism of §§ 1.338-6 and 1.338-7. See § 1.338-4(b)(2)(iii) *Example* for the effect on ADSP.

Example 2. T, an accrual basis taxpayer, is a chemical manufacturer. In Year 1, T is obligated to remediate environmental contamination at the site of one of its plants. Assume that all the events have occurred that establish the fact of the liability and the amount of the liability can be determined with reasonable accuracy but economic performance has not occurred with respect to the liability within the meaning of section 461(h). P acquires all of the stock of T in Year 1 and makes a section 338 election for T. Assume that, if a corporation unrelated to T had actually purchased T's assets and assumed T's obligation to remediate the contamination, the corporation would not satisfy the economic performance requirements until Year 5. Under section 461(h), the assumed liability would not be treated as incurred and taken into account in basis until that time. The incurrence of the liability in Year 5 under the economic performance rules is an increase in the amount of liabilities properly taken into account in basis and results in the redetermination of AGUB. (Respecting ADSP, compare § 1.461-4(d)(5), which provides that economic performance occurs for old T as the amount of the liability is properly taken into account in amount realized on the deemed asset sale. Thus ADSP is not redetermined when new T satisfies the economic performance requirements.)

(c) *Grossed-up basis of recently purchased stock.*—The purchasing corporation's grossed-up basis of recently purchased target stock (as defined in section 338(b)(6)(A)) is an amount equal to—

(1) The purchasing corporation's basis in recently purchased target stock at the beginning of the day after the acquisition date determined without regard to the acquisition costs taken into account in paragraph (c)(3) of this section;

(2) Multiplied by a fraction, the numerator of which is 100 minus the number that is the percentage of target stock (by value, determined on the acquisition date) attributable to the purchasing corporation's nonrecently purchased target stock, and the denominator of which is the number equal to the percentage of target stock (by value, determined on the acquisition date) attributable to the purchasing corporation's recently purchased target stock;

(3) Plus the acquisition costs the purchasing corporation incurred in connection with its purchase of the recently purchased stock that are capitalized in the basis of such stock (e.g., brokerage commissions and any similar costs incurred by the purchasing corporation to acquire the stock).

(d) *Basis of nonrecently purchased stock; gain recognition election.*—(1) *No gain recognition election.*—In the absence of a gain recognition election under section 338(b)(3) and this section, the purchasing corporation retains its basis in the nonrecently purchased stock.

(2) *Procedure for making gain recognition election.*—A gain recognition election may be made for nonrecently purchased stock of target (or a target affiliate) only if a section 338 election is made for target (or the target affiliate). The gain recognition election is made by attaching a gain recognition statement to a timely filed Form 8023 for target. The gain recognition statement must contain the information specified in the form and its instructions. The gain recognition election is irrevocable. If a section 338(h)(10) election is made for target, see § 1.338(h)(10)-1(d)(1) (providing that the purchasing corporation is automatically deemed to have made a gain recognition election for its nonrecently purchased T stock).

(3) *Effect of gain recognition election.*—(i) *In general.*—If the purchasing corporation makes a gain recognition election, then for all purposes of the Internal Revenue Code—

(A) The purchasing corporation is treated as if it sold on the acquisition date the nonrecently purchased target stock for the basis amount determined under paragraph (d)(3)(ii) of this section; and

(B) The purchasing corporation's basis on the acquisition date in nonrecently purchased target stock immediately following the deemed sale in paragraph (d)(3)(i)(A) of this section is the basis amount.

(ii) *Basis amount.*—The basis amount is equal to the amount in paragraphs (c)(1) and (2) of this section (the purchasing corporation's grossed-up basis in recently purchased target stock at the beginning of the day after the acquisition date determined without regard to the acquisition costs taken into account in paragraph (c)(3) of this section) multiplied by a fraction the numerator of which is the percentage of target stock (by value, determined on the acquisition date) attributable to the purchasing corporation's nonrecently purchased target stock and the denominator of which is 100 percent minus the numerator amount. Thus, if target has a single class of outstanding stock, the purchasing corporation's basis in each share of nonrecently purchased target stock after the gain recognition election is equal to the average price per share of the purchasing corporation's recently purchased target stock.

(iii) *Losses not recognized.*—Only gains (unreduced by losses) on the nonrecently purchased target stock are recognized.

(iv) *Stock subject to election.*—The gain recognition election applies to—

(A) All nonrecently purchased target stock; and

(B) Any nonrecently purchased stock in a target affiliate having the same acquisition date as target if such target affiliate stock is held by the purchasing corporation on such date.

(e) *Liabilities of new target.*—(1) *In general.*—The liabilities of new target are the liabilities of target as of the beginning of the day after the acquisition date (but see § 1.338-1(d)(regarding certain transactions on the acquisition date)). In order to be taken into account in AGUB, a liability must be a liability of target that is properly taken into account in basis under general principles of tax law that would apply if new target had acquired its assets from an unrelated person for consideration that included discharge of the liabilities of that unrelated person. Such liabilities may include liabilities for the tax consequences resulting from the deemed sale.

(2) *Time and amount of liabilities.*—The time for taking into account liabilities of old target in determining AGUB and the amount of the liabilities taken into account is determined as if new target had acquired its assets from an unrelated person for consideration that included the discharge of its liabilities.

(3) *Interaction with deemed sale tax consequences.*—In general, see § 1.338-4(e). Although ADSP and AGUB are not necessarily

linked, if an increase in the amount realized for recently purchased stock of target is taken into account after the acquisition date, and if the tax on the deemed sale tax consequences is a liability of target, any increase in that liability is also taken into account in redetermining AGUB.

(f) *Adjustments by the Internal Revenue Service.*—In connection with the examination of a return, the Commissioner may increase (or decrease) AGUB under the authority of section 338(b)(2) and allocate such amounts to target's assets under the authority of section 338(b)(5) so that AGUB and the basis of target's assets properly reflect the cost to the purchasing corporation of its interest in target's assets. Such items may include distributions from target to the purchasing corporation, capital contributions from the purchasing corporation to target during the 12-month acquisition period, or acquisitions of target stock by the purchasing corporation after the acquisition date from minority shareholders. See also § 1.338-1(d) (regarding certain transactions on the acquisition date).

(g) *Examples.*—The following examples illustrate this section. For purposes of the examples in this paragraph (g), T has no liabilities other than the tax liability for the deemed sale tax consequences, T shareholders incur no costs in selling the T stock, and P incurs no costs in acquiring the T stock. The examples are as follows:

Example 1. (i) Before July 1 of Year 1, P purchases 10 of the 100 shares of T stock for $5,000. On July 1 of Year 2, P purchases 80 shares of T stock for $60,000 and makes a section 338 election for T. As of July 1 of Year 2, T's only asset is raw land with an adjusted basis to T of $50,400 and a fair market value of $100,000. T has no loss or tax credit carryovers to Year 2. T's marginal tax rate for any ordinary income or net capital gain resulting from the deemed asset sale is 34 percent. The 10 shares purchased before July 1 of Year 1 constitute nonrecently purchased T stock with respect to P's qualified stock purchase of T stock on July 1 of Year 2.

(ii) The ADSP formula as applied to these facts is the same as in § 1.338-4(g) *Example 1.* Accordingly, the ADSP for T is $87,672.72. The existence of nonrecently purchased T stock is irrelevant for purposes of the ADSP formula, because that formula treats P's nonrecently purchased T stock in the same manner as T stock not held by P.

(iii) The total tax liability resulting from T's deemed asset sale, as calculated under the ADSP formula, is $12,672.72.

(iv) If P does not make a gain recognition election, the AGUB of new T's assets is $85,172.72, determined as follows (in the following formula below, GRP is the grossed-up basis in P's recently purchased T stock, BNP is P's basis in nonrecently purchased T stock, L is T's liabilities, and X is P's acquisition costs for the recently purchased T stock):

AGUB = GRP + BNP + L + X

AGUB = $60,000 × [(1 – .1)/.8] + $5,000 + $12,672.72 + 0

AGUB = $85,172.72

(v) If P makes a gain recognition election, the AGUB of new T's assets is $87,672.72, determined as follows:

AGUB = $60,000 × [(1 – .1)/.8] + $60,000 × [(1 – .1)/.8] × [.1/(1 – .1)] + $12,672.72

AGUB = $87,672.72

(vi) The calculation of AGUB if P makes a gain recognition election may be simplified as follows:

AGUB = $60,000/.8 + $12,672.72

AGUB = $87,672.72

(vii) As a result of the gain recognition election, P's basis in its nonrecently purchased T stock is increased from $5,000 to $7,500 (i.e., $60,000 × [(1 – .1)/.8] × [.1/(1 – .1)]). Thus, P recognizes a gain in Year 2 with respect to its nonrecently purchased T stock of $2,500 (i.e., $7,500 – $5,000).

Example 2. On January 1 of Year 1, P purchases one-third of the T stock. On March 1 of Year 1, T distributes a dividend to all of its shareholders. On April 15 of Year 1, P purchases the remaining T stock and makes a section 338 election for T. In appropriate circumstances, the Commissioner may decrease the AGUB of T to take into account the payment of the dividend and properly reflect the fair market value of T's assets deemed purchased.

Example 3. (i) T's sole asset is a building worth $100,000. At this time, T has 100 shares of stock outstanding. On August 1 of Year 1, P purchases 10 of the 100 shares of T stock for $8,000. On June 1 of Year 2, P purchases 50 shares of T stock for $50,000. On June 15 of Year 2, P contributes a tract of land to the capital of T and receives 10 additional shares of T stock as a result of the contribution. Both the basis and fair market value of the land at that time are $10,800. On June 30 of Year 2, P purchases the remaining 40 shares of T stock for $40,000 and makes a section 338 election for T. The AGUB of T is $108,800.

(ii) To prevent the shifting of basis from the contributed property to other assets of T, the Commissioner may allocate $10,800 of the AGUB to the land, leaving $98,000 to be allocated to the building. See paragraph (f) of this section. Otherwise, applying the allocation rules of § 1.338-6 would, on these facts, result in an allocation to the recently contributed land of an amount less than its value of $10,800, with the difference being allocated to the building already held by T.

* * *

[Reg. § 1.338-5.]

☐ [*T.D.* 8940, 2-12-2001. *Amended by T.D.* 9619, 5-10-2013.]

§ 1.338-6. Allocation of ADSP and AGUB among target assets.—(a) *Scope.*—(1) *In general.*—This section prescribes rules for allocating ADSP and AGUB among the acquisition date assets of a target for which a section 338 election is made.

(2) *Fair market value.*—(i) *In general.*—Generally, the fair market value of an asset is its gross fair market value (i.e., fair market value determined without regard to mortgages, liens, pledges, or other liabilities). However, for purposes of determining the amount of old target's deemed sale tax consequences, the fair market value of any property subject to a nonrecourse indebtedness will be treated as being not less than the amount of such indebtedness. (For purposes of the preceding sentence, a liability that was incurred because of the acquisition of the property is disregarded to the extent that such liability was not taken into account in determining old target's basis in such property.)

(ii) *Transaction costs.*—Transaction costs are not taken into account in allocating ADSP or AGUB to assets in the deemed sale (except indirectly through their effect on the total ADSP or AGUB to be allocated).

(iii) *Internal Revenue Service authority.*—In connection with the examination of a return, the Internal Revenue Service may challenge the taxpayers determination of the fair market value of any asset by any appropriate method and take into account all factors, including any lack of adverse tax interests between the parties.

(b) *General rule for allocating ADSP and AGUB.*—(1) *Reduction in the amount of consideration for Class I assets.*—Both ADSP and AGUB, in the respective allocation of each, are first reduced by the amount of Class I assets. Class I assets are cash and general deposit accounts (including savings and checking accounts) other than certificates of deposit held in banks, savings and loan associations, and other depository institutions. If the amount of Class I assets exceeds AGUB, new target will immediately realize ordinary income in an amount equal to such excess. The amount of ADSP or AGUB remaining after the reduction is to be allocated to the remaining acquisition date assets.

(2) *Other assets.*—(i) *In general.*—Subject to the limitations and other rules of paragraph (c) of this section, ADSP and AGUB (as reduced by the amount of Class I assets) are allocated among Class II acquisition date assets of target in proportion to the fair market values of such Class II assets at such time, then among Class III assets so held in such proportion, then among Class IV assets so held in such proportion, then among Class V assets so held in such proportion, then among Class VI assets so held in such proportion, and finally to Class VII assets. If an asset is described below as includible in more than one class, then it is included in such class with the lower or lowest class number (for instance, Class III has a lower class number than Class IV).

(ii) *Class II assets.*—Class II assets are actively traded personal property within the meaning of section 1092(d)(1) and § 1.1092(d)-1 (determined without regard to section 1092(d)(3)). In addition, Class II assets include certificates of deposit and foreign currency even if they are not actively traded personal property. Class II assets do not include stock of target affiliates, whether or not of a class that is actively traded, other than actively traded stock described in section 1504(a)(4). Examples of Class II assets include U.S. government securities and publicly traded stock.

(iii) *Class III assets.*—Class III assets are assets that the taxpayer marks to market at least annually for Federal income tax purposes and debt instruments (including accounts receivable). However, Class III assets do not include—

(A) Debt instruments issued by persons related at the beginning of the day following the acquisition date to the target under section 267(b) or 707;

(B) Contingent debt instruments subject to § 1.1275-4, § 1.483-4, or section 988, unless the instrument is subject to the noncontingent bond method of § 1.1275-4(b) or is described in § 1.988-2(b)(2)(i)(B)(*2*); and

(C) Debt instruments convertible into the stock of the issuer or other property.

(iv) *Class IV assets.*—Class IV assets are stock in trade of the taxpayer or other property of a kind that would properly be included in the inventory of taxpayer if on hand at the close of the taxable year, or property held by the taxpayer primarily for sale to customers in the ordinary course of its trade or business.

(v) *Class V assets.*—Class V assets are all assets other than Class I, II, III, IV, VI, and VII assets.

(vi) *Class VI assets.*—Class VI assets are all section 197 intangibles, as defined in section 197, except goodwill and going concern value.

(vii) *Class VII assets.*—Class VII assets are goodwill and going concern value (whether or not the goodwill or going concern value qualifies as a section 197 intangible).

(3) *Other items designated by the Internal Revenue Service.*—Similar items may be added to any class described in this paragraph (b) by designation in the Internal Revenue Bulletin by the Internal Revenue Service (see § 601.601(d)(2) of this chapter).

(c) *Certain limitations and other rules for allocation to an asset.*—(1) *Allocation not to exceed fair market value.*—The amount of ADSP or AGUB allocated to an asset (other than Class VII assets) cannot exceed the fair market value of that asset at the beginning of the day after the acquisition date.

(2) *Allocation subject to other rules.*—The amount of ADSP or AGUB allocated to an asset is subject to other provisions of the Internal Revenue Code or general principles of tax law in the same manner as if such asset were transferred to or acquired from an unrelated person in a sale or exchange. For example, if the deemed asset sale is a transaction described in section 1056(a) (relating to basis limitation for player contracts transferred in connection with the sale of a franchise), the amount of AGUB allocated to a contract for the services of an athlete cannot exceed the limitation imposed by that section. As another example, section 197(f)(5) applies in determining the amount of AGUB allocated to an amortizable section 197 intangible resulting from an assumption-reinsurance transaction.

(3) *Special rule for allocating AGUB when purchasing corporation has nonrecently purchased stock.*—(i) *Scope.*—This paragraph (c)(3) applies if at the beginning of the day after the acquisition date—

(A) The purchasing corporation holds nonrecently purchased stock for which a gain recognition election under section 338(b)(3) and § 1.338-5(d) is not made; and

(B) The hypothetical purchase price determined under paragraph (c)(3)(ii) of this section exceeds the AGUB determined under § 1.338-5(b).

(ii) *Determination of hypothetical purchase price.*—Hypothetical purchase price is the AGUB that would result if a gain recognition election were made.

(iii) *Allocation of AGUB.*—Subject to the limitations in paragraphs (c)(1) and (2) of this section, the portion of AGUB (after reduction by the amount of Class I assets) to be allocated to each Class II, III, IV, V, VI, and VII asset of target held at the beginning of the day after the acquisition date is determined by multiplying—

(A) The amount that would be allocated to such asset under the general rules of this section were AGUB equal to the hypothetical purchase price; by

(B) A fraction, the numerator of which is actual AGUB (after reduction by the amount of Class I assets) and the denominator of which is the hypothetical purchase price (after reduction by the amount of Class I assets).

(4) *Liabilities taken into account in determining amount realized on subsequent disposition.*—In determining the amount realized on a subsequent sale or other disposition of property deemed purchased by new target, § 1.1001-2(a)(3) shall not apply to any liability that was taken into account in AGUB.

* * *

(d) *Examples.*—The following examples illustrate §§ 1.338-4, 1.338-5, and this section:

Example 1. (i) T owns 90 percent of the outstanding T1 stock. P purchases 100 percent of the outstanding T stock for $2,000. There are no acquisition costs. P makes a section 338 election for T and, as a result, T1 is considered acquired in a qualified stock purchase. A section 338 election is made for T1. The grossed-up basis of the T stock is $2,000 (i.e., $2,000 × 1/1).

(ii) The liabilities of T as of the beginning of the day after the acquisition date (including the tax liability for the deemed sale tax consequences) that would, under general principles of tax law, properly be taken into account at that time, are as follows:

Liabilities (nonrecourse mortgage plus unsecured liabilities)	$700
Taxes Payable	300
Total	$1,000

(iii) The AGUB of T is determined as follows:

Grossed-up basis	$2,000
Total liabilities	1,000
AGUB	$3,000

(iv) Assume that ADSP is also $3,000.

(v) Assume that, at the beginning of the day after the acquisition date, T's cash and the fair market values of T's Class II, III, IV, and V assets are as follows:

Asset Class	Asset	Fair market value
I	Cash	$200 *
II	Portfolio of actively traded securities	300
III	Accounts receivable	600
IV	Inventory	300
V	Building	800
V	Land	200
V	Investment in T1	450
	Total	$2,850

* Amount

(vi) Under paragraph (b)(1) of this section, the amount of ADSP and AGUB allocable to T's Class II, III, IV, and V assets is reduced by the amount of cash to $2,800, i.e., $3,000 – $200. $300 of ADSP and of AGUB is then allocated to actively traded securities. $600 of ADSP and of AGUB is then allocated to accounts receivable. $300 of ADSP and of AGUB is then allocated to the inventory. Since the remaining amount of ADSP and of AGUB is $1,600 (i.e., $3,000 – ($200 + $300 + $600 + $300)), an amount which exceeds the sum of the fair market values of T's Class V assets, the amount of ADSP and of AGUB allocated to each Class V asset is its fair market value:

Building	800
Land	200
Investment in T1	450
Total	$1,450

(vii) T has no Class VI assets. The amount of ADSP and of AGUB allocated to T's Class VII assets (goodwill and going concern value) is $150, i.e., $1,600 – $1,450.

(viii) The grossed-up basis of the T1 stock is $500, i.e., $450 × 1/.9.

(ix) The liabilities of T1 as of the beginning of the day after the acquisition date (including the tax liability for the deemed sale tax consequences) that would, under general principles of tax law, properly be taken into account at that time, are as follows:

General Liabilities	$100
Taxes Payable	20
Total	$120

(x) The AGUB of T1 is determined as follows:

Grossed-up basis of T1 Stock	$500
Liabilities	120
AGUB	$620

(xi) Assume that ADSP is also $620.

(xii) Assume that at the beginning of the day after the acquisition date, T1's cash and the fair market values of its Class IV and VI assets are as follows:

Asset Class	Asset	Fair Market Value
I	Cash	$ 50 *
IV	Inventory	200
VI	Patent	350
	Total	$600

* Amount.

(xiii) The amount of ADSP and of AGUB allocable to T1's Class IV and VI assets is first reduced by the $50 of cash.

(xiv) Because the remaining amount of ADSP and of AGUB ($570) is an amount which exceeds the fair market value of T1's only Class IV asset, the inventory, the amount allocated to the inventory is its fair market value ($200). After that, the remaining amount of ADSP and of AGUB ($370) exceeds the fair market value of T1's only Class VI asset, the patent. Thus, the amount of ADSP and of AGUB allocated to the patent is its fair market value ($350).

(xv) The amount of ADSP and of AGUB allocated to T1's Class VII assets (goodwill and going concern value) is $20, i.e., $570 – $550.

Example 2. (i) Assume that the facts are the same as in *Example 1* except that P has, for five years, owned 20 percent of T's stock, which has a basis in P's hands at the beginning of the day after the acquisition date of $100, and P purchases the remaining 80 percent of T's stock for $1,600. P does not make a gain recognition election under section 338(b)(3).

(ii) Under § 1.338-5(c), the grossed-up basis of recently purchased T stock is $1,600, i.e., $1,600 × (1 – .2)/.8.

(iii) The AGUB of T is determined as follows:

Grossed-up basis of recently purchased stock as determined under § 1.338-5(c) ($1,600 × (1 – .2)/.8)	$1,600
Basis of nonrecently purchased stock	100
Liabilities	1,000
AGUB	$2,700

(iv) Since P holds nonrecently purchased stock, the hypothetical purchase price of the T stock must be computed and is determined as follows:

Grossed-up basis of recently purchased stock as determined under § 1.338-5(c) ($1,600 × (1 – .2)/.8)	$1,600
Basis of nonrecently purchased stock as if the gain recognition election under § 1.338-5(d)(2) had been made ($1,600 × .2/(1 – .2))	400
Liabilities	1,000
Total	$3,000

(v) Since the hypothetical purchase price ($3,000) exceeds the AGUB ($2,700) and no gain recognition election is made under section 338(b)(3), AGUB is allocated under paragraph (c)(3) of this section.

(vi) First, an AGUB amount equal to the hypothetical purchase price ($3,000) is allocated among the assets under the general rules of this section. The allocation is set forth in the column below entitled *Original Allocation.* Next, the allocation to each asset in Class II through Class VII is multiplied by a fraction having a numerator equal to the actual AGUB reduced by the amount of Class I assets ($2,700 – $200 = $2,500) and a denominator equal to the hypothetical purchase price reduced by the amount of Class I assets ($3,000 – $200 = $2,800), or 2,500/2,800. This produces the *Final Allocation*:

Class	*Asset*	*Original Allocation*	*Final Allocation*
I	Cash	$200	$200
II	Portfolio of actively traded securities	300	268 *
III	Accounts receivable	600	536
IV	Inventory	300	268
V	Building	800	714
V	Land	200	178
V	Investment in T1	450	402
VII	Goodwill and going concern value	150	134
	Total	$3,000	$2,700

* All numbers rounded for convenience.

[Reg. § 1.338-6.]

☐ [*T.D.* 8940, 2-12-2001 (*corrected* 3-29-2001). *Amended by T.D.* 9158, 9-15-2004 *and T.D.* 9358, 9-10-2007.]

§ 1.338-7. Allocation of redetermined ADSP and AGUB among target assets.—(a) *Scope.*—ADSP and AGUB are redetermined at such time and in such amount as an increase or decrease would be required under general principles of tax law for the elements of ADSP or AGUB. This section provides rules for allocating redetermined ADSP or AGUB.

(b) *Allocation of redetermined ADSP and AGUB.*—When ADSP or AGUB is redetermined, a new allocation of ADSP or AGUB is made by allocating the redetermined ADSP or AGUB amount under the rules of § 1.338-6. If the allocation of the redetermined ADSP or AGUB amount under § 1.338-6 to a given asset is different from the original allocation to it, the difference is added to or subtracted from the original allocation to the asset, as appropriate. (See paragraph (d) of this section for new target's treatment of the amount so allocated.) Amounts allocable to an acquisition date asset (or with respect to a disposed-of acquisition date asset) are subject to all the asset allocation rules (for example, the fair market value limitation in § 1.338-6(c)(1)) as if the redetermined ADSP or AGUB were the ADSP or AGUB on the acquisition date.

(c) *Special rules for ADSP.*—(1) *Increases or decreases in deemed sale tax consequences taxable notwithstanding old target ceases to exist.*—To the extent general principles of tax law would require a seller in an actual asset sale to account for events relating to the sale that occur after the sale date, target must make such an accounting. Target is not precluded from realizing additional deemed sale tax consequences because the target is treated as a new corporation after the acquisition date.

(2) *Procedure for transactions in which section 338(h)(10) is not elected.*—(i) *Deemed sale tax consequences included in new target's return.*—If an election under section 338(h)(10)

is not made, any additional deemed sale tax consequences of old target resulting from an increase or decrease in the ADSP are included in new target's income tax return for new target's taxable year in which the increase or decrease is taken into account. For example, if after the acquisition date there is an increase in the allocable ADSP of section 1245 property for which the recomputed basis (but not the adjusted basis) exceeds the portion of the ADSP allocable to that particular asset on the acquisition date, the additional gain is treated as ordinary income to the extent it does not exceed such excess amount. See paragraph (c)(2)(ii) of this section for the special treatment of old target's carryovers and carrybacks. Although included in new target's income tax return, the deemed sale tax consequences are separately accounted for as an item of old target and may not be offset by income, gain, deduction, loss, credit, or other amount of new target. The amount of tax on income of old target resulting from an increase or decrease in the ADSP is determined as if such deemed sale tax consequences had been recognized in old target's taxable year ending at the close of the acquisition date. However, because the income resulting from the increase or decrease in ADSP is reportable in new target's taxable year of the increase or decrease, not in old target's taxable year ending at the close of the acquisition date, there is not a resulting underpayment of tax in that past taxable year of old target for purposes of calculation of interest due.

(ii) *Carryovers and carrybacks.*—(A) *Loss carryovers to new target taxable years.*—A net operating loss or net capital loss of old target may be carried forward to a taxable year of new target, under the principles of section 172 or 1212, as applicable, but is allowed as a deduction only to the extent of any recognized income of old target for such taxable year, as described in paragraph (c)(2)(i) of this section. For this purpose, however, taxable years of new target are not taken into account in applying the limitations in section 172(b)(1) or 1212(a)(1)(B) (or other similar limitations). In applying sections 172(b) and 1212(a)(1), only income, gain, loss, deduction, credit, and other amounts of old target are taken into account. Thus, if old target has an unexpired net operating loss at the close of its taxable year in which the deemed asset sale occurred that could be carried forward to a subsequent taxable year, such loss may be carried forward until it is absorbed by old target's income.

(B) *Loss carrybacks to taxable years of old target.*—An ordinary loss or capital loss accounted for as a separate item of old target under paragraph (c)(2)(i) of this section may be carried back to a taxable year of old target under the principles of section 172 or 1212, as applicable. For this purpose, taxable years of new target are not taken into account in applying the limitations in section 172(b) or 1212(a) (or other similar limitations).

(C) *Credit carryovers and carrybacks.*—The principles described in paragraphs (c)(2)(ii)(A) and (B) of this section apply to carryovers and carrybacks of amounts for purposes of determining the amount of a credit allowable under part IV, subchapter A, chapter 1 of the Internal Revenue Code. Thus, for example, credit carryovers of old target may offset only income tax attributable to items described in paragraph (c)(2)(i) of this section.

(3) *Procedure for transactions in which section 338(h)(10) is elected.*—If an election under section 338(h)(10) is made, any changes in the deemed sale tax consequences caused by an increase or decrease in the ADSP are accounted for in determining the taxable income (or other amount) of the member of the selling consolidated group, the selling affiliate, or the S corporation shareholders to which such income, loss, or other amount is attributable for the taxable year in which such increase or decrease is taken into account.

(d) *Special rules for AGUB.*—(1) *Effect of disposition or depreciation of acquisition date assets.*—If an acquisition date asset has been disposed of, depreciated, amortized, or depleted by new target before an amount is added to the original allocation to the asset, the increased amount otherwise allocable to such asset is taken into account under general principles of tax law that apply when part of the cost of an asset not previously taken into account in basis is paid or incurred after the asset has been disposed of, depreciated, amortized, or depleted. A similar rule applies when an amount is subtracted from the original allocation to the asset. For purposes of the preceding sentence, an asset is considered to have been disposed of to the extent that its allocable portion of the decrease in AGUB would reduce its basis below zero.

(2) *Section 38 property.*—Section 1.47-2(c) applies to a reduction in basis of section 38 property under this section.

* * *

[Reg. § 1.338-7.]

□ [*T.D.* 8940, 2-12-2001.]

§ 1.338(h)(10)-1. Deemed asset sale and liquidation.—(a) *Scope.*—This section prescribes rules for qualification for a section 338(h)(10) election and for making a section 338(h)(10) election. This section also prescribes the consequences of such election.

The rules of this section are in addition to the rules of §§1.338-1 through 1.338-10 and, in appropriate cases, apply instead of the rules of §§1.338-1 through 1.338-10.

(b) *Definitions.*—(1) *Consolidated target.*—A *consolidated target* is a target that is a member of a consolidated group within the meaning of §1.1502-1(h) on the acquisition date and is not the common parent of the group on that date.

(2) *Selling consolidated group.*—A *selling consolidated group* is the consolidated group of which the consolidated target is a member on the acquisition date.

(3) *Selling affiliate; affiliated target.*—A *selling affiliate* is a domestic corporation that owns on the acquisition date an amount of stock in a domestic target, which amount of stock is described in section 1504(a)(2), and does not join in filing a consolidated return with the target. In such case, the target is an *affiliated target.*

(4) *S corporation target.*—An *S corporation target* is a target that is an S corporation immediately before the acquisition date.

(5) *S corporation shareholders.*— *S corporation shareholders* are the S corporation target's shareholders. Unless otherwise indicated, a reference to S corporation shareholders refers both to S corporation shareholders who do and those who do not sell their target stock.

(6) *Liquidation.*—Any reference in this section to a liquidation is treated as a reference to the transfer described in paragraph (d)(4) of this section notwithstanding its ultimate characterization for Federal income tax purposes.

(c) *Section 338(h)(10) election.*—(1) *In general.*—A section 338(h)(10) election may be made for T if P acquires stock meeting the requirements of section 1504(a)(2) from a selling consolidated group, a selling affiliate, or the S corporation shareholders in a qualified stock purchase.

(2) *Availability of section 338(h)(10) election in certain multi-step transactions.*—Notwithstanding anything to the contrary in §1.338-3(c)(1)(i), a section 338(h)(10) election may be made for T where P's acquisition of T stock, viewed independently, constitutes a qualified stock purchase and, after the stock acquisition, T merges or liquidates into P (or another member of the affiliated group that includes P), whether or not, under relevant provisions of law, including the step transaction doctrine, the acquisition of the T stock and the merger or liquidation of T qualify as a reorganization described in section 368(a). If a section 338(h)(10) election is made in a case where the acquisition of T stock followed by a merger or liquidation of T into P qualifies as a reorganization described in section 368(a), for all Federal tax purposes, P's acquisition of T stock is treated as a qualified stock purchase and is not treated as part of a reorganization described in section 368(a).

(3) *Simultaneous joint election requirement.*—A section 338(h)(10) election is made jointly by P and the selling consolidated group (or the selling affiliate or the S corporation shareholders) on Form 8023 in accordance with the instructions to the form. S corporation shareholders who do not sell their stock must also consent to the election. The section 338(h)(10) election must be made not later than the 15th day of the 9th month beginning after the month in which the acquisition date occurs.

(4) *Irrevocability.*—A section 338(h)(10) election is irrevocable. If a section 338(h)(10) election is made for T, a section 338 election is deemed made for T.

(5) *Effect of invalid election.*—If a section 338(h)(10) election for T is not valid, the section 338 election for T is also not valid.

(d) *Certain consequences of section 338(h)(10) election.*—For purposes of subtitle A of the Internal Revenue Code (except as provided in §1.338-1(b)(2)), the consequences to the parties of making a section 338(h)(10) election for T are as follows:

(1) *P.*—P is automatically deemed to have made a gain recognition election for its nonrecently purchased T stock, if any. The effect of a gain recognition election includes a taxable deemed sale by P on the acquisition date of any nonrecently purchased target stock. See §1.338-5(d).

(2) *New T.*—The AGUB for new T's assets is determined under §1.338-5 and is allocated among the acquisition date assets under §§1.338-6 and 1.338-7. Notwithstanding paragraph (d)(4) of this section (deemed liquidation of old T), new T remains liable for the tax liabilities of old T (including the tax liability for the deemed sale tax consequences). For example, new T remains liable for the tax liabilities of the members of any consolidated group that are attributable to taxable years in which those corporations and old T joined in the same consolidated return. See §1.1502-6(a).

(3) *Old T—deemed sale.*—(i) *In general.*—Old T is treated as transferring all of its assets to an unrelated person in exchange for consideration that includes the discharge of its liabilities in a single transaction at the close of the

acquisition date (but before the deemed liquidation). See § 1.338-1(a) regarding the tax characterization of the deemed asset sale. Except as provided in § 1.338(h)(10)-1(d)(8) (regarding the installment method), old T recognizes all of the gain realized on the deemed transfer of its assets in consideration for the ADSP. ADSP for old T is determined under § 1.338-4 and allocated among the acquisition date assets under §§ 1.338-6 and 1.338-7. Old T realizes the deemed sale tax consequences from the deemed asset sale before the close of the acquisition date while old T is a member of the selling consolidated group (or owned by the selling affiliate or owned by the S corporation shareholders). If T is an affiliated target, or an S corporation target, the principles of §§ 1.338-2(c)(10) and 1.338-10(a)(1), (5), and (6)(i) apply to the return on which the deemed sale tax consequences are reported. When T is an S corporation target, T's S election continues in effect through the close of the acquisition date (including the time of the deemed asset sale and the deemed liquidation) notwithstanding section 1362(d)(2)(B). Also, when T is an S corporation target (but not a qualified subchapter S subsidiary), any direct and indirect subsidiaries of T which T has elected to treat as qualified subchapter S subsidiaries under section 1361(b)(3) remain qualified subchapter S subsidiaries through the close of the acquisition date.

(ii) *Tiered targets.*—In the case of parent-subsidiary chains of corporations making elections under section 338(h)(10), the deemed asset sale of a parent corporation is considered to precede that of its subsidiary. See § 1.338-3(b)(4)(i).

(4) *Old T and selling consolidated group, selling affiliate, or S corporation shareholders—deemed liquidation; tax characterization.*—(i) *In general.*—Old T is treated as if, before the close of the acquisition date, after the deemed asset sale in paragraph (d)(3) of this section, and while old T is a member of the selling consolidated group (or owned by the selling affiliate or owned by the S corporation shareholders), it transferred all of its assets to members of the selling consolidated group, the selling affiliate, or S corporation shareholders and ceased to exist. The transfer from old T is characterized for Federal income tax purposes in the same manner as if the parties had actually engaged in the transactions deemed to occur because of this section and taking into account other transactions that actually occurred or are deemed to occur. For example, the transfer may be treated as a distribution in pursuance of a plan of reorganization, a distribution in complete cancellation or redemption of all its stock, one of a series of distributions in complete cancellation or redemption of all its stock in accordance with a plan of liquidation, or part of a circular flow of cash. In most cases, the transfer will be treated as a distribution in complete liquidation to which section 336 or 337 applies.

(ii) *Tiered targets.*—In the case of parent-subsidiary chains of corporations making elections under section 338(h)(10), the deemed liquidation of a subsidiary corporation is considered to precede the deemed liquidation of its parent.

(5) *Selling consolidated group, selling affiliate, or S corporation shareholders.*—(i) *In general.*—If T is an S corporation target, S corporation shareholders (whether or not they sell their stock) take their pro rata share of the deemed sale tax consequences into account under section 1366 and increase or decrease their basis in T stock under section 1367. Members of the selling consolidated group, the selling affiliate, or S corporation shareholders are treated as if, after the deemed asset sale in paragraph (d)(3) of this section and before the close of the acquisition date, they received the assets transferred by old T in the transaction described in paragraph (d)(4)(i) of this section. In most cases, the transfer will be treated as a distribution in complete liquidation to which section 331 or 332 applies.

(ii) *Basis and holding period of T stock not acquired.*—A member of the selling consolidated group (or the selling affiliate or an S corporation shareholder) retaining T stock is treated as acquiring the stock so retained on the day after the acquisition date for its fair market value. The holding period for the retained stock starts on the day after the acquisition date. For purposes of this paragraph, the fair market value of all of the T stock equals the grossed-up amount realized on the sale to P of P's recently purchased target stock. See § 1.338-4(c).

(iii) *T stock sale.*—Members of the selling consolidated group (or the selling affiliate or S corporation shareholders) recognize no gain or loss on the sale or exchange of T stock included in the qualified stock purchase (although they may recognize gain or loss on the T stock in the deemed liquidation).

(6) *Nonselling minority shareholders other than nonselling S corporation shareholders.*—(i) *In general.*—This paragraph (d)(6) describes the treatment of shareholders of old T other than the following: members of the selling consolidated group, the selling affiliate, S corporation shareholders (whether or not they sell their stock), and P. For a description of the treatment of S corporation shareholders, see

paragraph (d)(5) of this section. A shareholder to which this paragraph (d)(6) applies is called a minority shareholder.

(ii) *T stock sale.*—A minority shareholder recognizes gain or loss on the shareholder's sale or exchange of T stock included in the qualified stock purchase.

(iii) *T stock not acquired.*—A minority shareholder does not recognize gain or loss under this section with respect to shares of T stock retained by the shareholder. The shareholder's basis and holding period for that T stock is not affected by the section 338(h)(10) election.

(7) *Consolidated return of selling consolidated group.*—If P acquires T in a qualified stock purchase from a selling consolidated group—

(i) The selling consolidated group must file a consolidated return for the taxable period that includes the acquisition date;

(ii) A consolidated return for the selling consolidated group for that period may not be withdrawn on or after the day that a section 338(h)(10) election is made for T; and

(iii) Permission to discontinue filing consolidated returns cannot be granted for, and cannot apply to, that period or any of the immediately preceding taxable periods during which consolidated returns continuously have been filed.

(8) *Availability of the section 453 installment method.*—Solely for purposes of applying sections 453, 453A, and 453B, and the regulations thereunder (the installment method) to determine the consequences to old T in the deemed asset sale and to old T (and its shareholders, if relevant) in the deemed liquidation, the rules in paragraphs (d)(1) through (7) of this section are modified as follows:

(i) *In deemed asset sale.*—Old T is treated as receiving in the deemed asset sale new T installment obligations, the terms of which are identical (except as to the obligor) to P installment obligations issued in exchange for recently purchased stock of T. Old T is treated as receiving in cash all other consideration in the deemed asset sale other than the assumption of, or taking subject to, old T liabilities. For example, old T is treated as receiving in cash any amounts attributable to the grossing-up of amount realized under § 1.338-4(c). The amount realized for recently purchased stock taken into account in determining ADSP is adjusted (and, thus, ADSP is redetermined) to reflect the amounts paid under an installment obligation for the stock when the total payments under the installment obligation are greater or less than the amount realized.

(ii) *In deemed liquidation.*—Old T is treated as distributing in the deemed liquidation the new T installment obligations that it is treated as receiving in the deemed asset sale. The members of the selling consolidated group, the selling affiliate, or the S corporation shareholders are treated as receiving in the deemed liquidation the new T installment obligations that correspond to the P installment obligations they actually received individually in exchange for their recently purchased stock. The new T installment obligations may be recharacterized under other rules. See for example § 1.453-11(a)(2) which, in certain circumstances, treats the new T installment obligations deemed distributed by old T as if they were issued by new T in exchange for the stock in old T owned by members of the selling consolidated group, the selling affiliate, or the S corporation shareholders. The members of the selling consolidated group, the selling affiliate, or the S corporation shareholders are treated as receiving all other consideration in the deemed liquidation in cash.

(9) *Treatment consistent with an actual asset sale.*—No provision in section 338(h)(10) or this section shall produce a Federal income tax result under subtitle A of the Internal Revenue Code that would not occur if the parties had actually engaged in the transactions deemed to occur because of this section and taking into account other transactions that actually occurred or are deemed to occur. See, however, § 1.338-1(b)(2) for certain exceptions to this rule.

(e) *Examples.*—The following examples illustrate the provisions of this section:

Example 1. (i) S1 owns all of the T stock and T owns all of the stock of T1 and T2. S1 is the common parent of a consolidated group that includes T, T1, and T2. P makes a qualified stock purchase of all of the T stock from S1. S1 joins with P in making a section 338(h)(10) election for T and for the deemed purchase of T1. A section 338 election is not made for T2.

(ii) S1 does not recognize gain or loss on the sale of the T stock and T does not recognize gain or loss on the sale of the T1 stock because section 338(h)(10) elections are made for T and T1. Thus, for example, gain or loss realized on the sale of the T or T1 stock is not taken into account in earnings and profits. However, because a section 338 election is not made for T2, T must recognize any gain or loss realized on the deemed sale of the T2 stock. See § 1.338-4(h).

(iii) The results would be the same if S1, T, T1, and T2 are not members of any consolidated group, because S1 and T are selling affiliates.

Example 2. (i) S and T are solvent corporations. S owns all of the outstanding stock of T. S and P agree to undertake the following transaction: T will distribute half its assets to S, and S will assume half of T's liabilities. Then, P will purchase the stock of T from S. S and P will jointly make a section 338(h)(10) election with respect to the sale of T. The corporations then complete the transaction as agreed.

(ii) Under section 338(a), the assets present in T at the close of the acquisition date are deemed sold by old T to new T. Under paragraph (d)(4) of this section, the transactions described in paragraph (d) of this section are treated in the same manner as if they had actually occurred. Because S and P had agreed that, after T's actual distribution to S of part of its assets, S would sell T to P pursuant to an election under section 338(h)(10), and because paragraph (d)(4) of this section deems T subsequently to have transferred all its assets to its shareholder, T is deemed to have adopted a plan of complete liquidation under section 332. T's actual transfer of assets to S is treated as a distribution pursuant to that plan of complete liquidation.

Example 3. (i) S1 owns all of the outstanding stock of both T and S2. All three are corporations. S1 and P agree to undertake the following transaction. T will transfer substantially all of its assets and liabilities to S2, with S2 issuing no stock in exchange therefor, and retaining its other assets and liabilities. Then, P will purchase the stock of T from S1. S1 and P will jointly make a section 338(h)(10) election with respect to the sale of T. The corporations then complete the transaction as agreed.

(ii) Under section 338(a), the remaining assets present in T at the close of the acquisition date are deemed sold by old T to new T. Under paragraph (d)(4) of this section, the transactions described in this section are treated in the same manner as if they had actually occurred. Because old T transferred substantially all of its assets to S2, and is deemed to have distributed all its remaining assets and gone out of existence, the transfer of assets to S2, taking into account the related transfers, deemed and actual, qualifies as a reorganization under section 368(a)(1)(D). Section 361(c)(1) and not section 332 applies to T's deemed liquidation.

* * *

[Reg. § 1.338(h)(10)-1.]

□ [*T.D.* 8940, 2-12-2001. *Amended by T.D.* 9071, 7-8-2003; *T.D.* 9264, 5-26-2006; *T.D.* 9271, 7-3-2006 *and T.D.* 9329, 6-13-2007.]

»»→ Note: Reg. § 1.346-1 was issued under the prior version of Section 346, which covered partial liquidations until 1982. The partial liquidation provisions formerly embodied in Section 346 are now set forth, with some modifications, in Sections 302(b)(4) and 302(e). No regulations have been issued under Sections 302(b)(4) and 302(e).

§ 1.346-1. Partial liquidation.—(a) *General.*—This section defines a partial liquidation. If amounts are distributed in partial liquidation such amounts are treated under section 331(a)(2) as received in part or full payment in exchange for the stock. A distribution is treated as in partial liquidation of a corporation if:

(1) The distribution is one of a series of distributions in redemption of all the stock of the corporation pursuant to a plan of complete liquidation or

(2) The distribution:

(i) Is not essentially equivalent to a dividend,

(ii) Is in redemption of a part of the stock of the corporation pursuant to a plan, and

(iii) Occurs within the taxable year in which the plan is adopted or within the succeeding taxable year.

An example of a distribution which will qualify as a partial liquidation under subparagraph (2) of this paragraph and section 346(a) is a distribution resulting from a genuine contraction of the corporate business such as the distribution of unused insurance proceeds recovered as a result of a fire which destroyed part of the business causing a cessation of a part of its activities. On the other hand, the distribution of funds attributable to a reserve for an expansion program which has been abandoned does not qualify as a partial liquidation within the meaning of section 346(a). A distribution to which section 355 applies (or so much of section 356 as relates to section 355) is not a distribution in partial liquidation within the meaning of section 346(a).

(b) *Special requirements on termination of business.*—A distribution which occurs within the taxable year in which the plan is adopted or within the succeeding taxable year and which meets the requirements of subsection (b) of section 346 falls within paragraph (a)(2) of this section and within section 346(a)(2). The requirements which a distribution must meet to fall within subsection (b) of section 346 are:

(1) Such distribution is attributable to the corporation's ceasing to conduct, or consists of assets of, a trade or business which has been actively conducted throughout the five-year period immediately before the distribution, which

trade or business was not acquired by the corporation within such period in a transaction in which gain or loss was recognized in whole or in part, and

(2) Immediately after such distribution by the corporation it is actively engaged in the conduct of a trade or business, which trade or business was actively conducted throughout the five-year period ending on the date of such distribution and was not acquired by the corporation within such period in a transaction in which gain or loss was recognized in whole or in part.

A distribution shall be treated as having been made in partial liquidation pursuant to section 346(b) if it consists of the proceeds of the sale of the assets of a trade or business which has been actively conducted for the five-year period and has been terminated, or if it is a distribution in kind of the assets of such a business, or if it is a distribution in kind of some of the assets of such a business and of the proceeds of the sale of the remainder of the assets of such a business. In general, a distribution which will qualify under section 346(b) may consist of, *but is not limited to*—

(i) Assets (other than inventory or property described in subdivision (ii) of this subparagraph) used in the trade or business throughout the five-year period immediately before the distribution (for this purpose an asset shall be considered used in the trade or business during the period of time the asset which it replaced was so used), or

(ii) Proceeds from the sale of assets described in (i), and, in addition,

(iii) The inventory of such trade or business or property held primarily for sale to customers in the ordinary course of business, if:

(a) The items constituting such inventory or such property were substantially similar to the items constituting such inventory or property during the five-year period immediately before the distribution, and

(b) The quantity of such items on the date of distribution was not substantially in excess of the quantity of similar items regularly on hand in the conduct of such business during such five-year period, or

(iv) Proceeds from the sale of inventory or property described in subdivision (iii) of this subparagraph, if such inventory or property is sold in bulk in the course of termination of such trade or business and if with respect to such inventory the conditions of subdivision (iii) *(a)* and *(b)* of this subparagraph would have been met had such inventory or property been distributed on the date of such sale.

(c) *Active conduct of a trade or business.*—For the purpose of section 346(b) (1), a corporation shall be deemed to have actively conducted a trade or business immediately before the distribution, if:

(1) In the case of a business the assets of which have been distributed in kind, the business was operated by such corporation until the date of distribution, or

(2) In the case of a business the proceeds of the sale of the assets of which are distributed, such business was actively conducted until the date of sale and the proceeds of such sale were distributed as soon thereafter as reasonably possible.

The term "active conduct of a trade or business" shall have the same meaning in this section as in paragraph (c) of § 1.355-1. [Reg. § 1.346-1.]

☐ [*T.D.* 6152, 12-2-55.]

Corporate Organizations and Reorganizations

»»→ Caution: Reg. §§ 1.351-1 and 1.351-2 do not reflect changes made by the Revenue Reconciliation Act of 1989, which deleted the words "or securities" after the word "stock" throughout Section 351.

§ 1.351-1. Transfer to corporation controlled by transferor.—(a) *In general.*—(1) *Nonrecognition of gain or loss.*—Section 351(a) provides, in general, for the nonrecognition of gain or loss upon the transfer by one or more persons of property to a corporation solely in exchange for stock of such corporation if, immediately after the exchange, such person or persons are in control of the corporation to which the property was transferred. As used in section 351, the phrase "one or more persons" includes individuals, trusts, estates, partnerships, associations, companies, or corporations (see section 7701(a)(1)). To be in control of the transferee corporation, such person or persons must own immediately after the transfer stock possessing at least 80 percent of the total combined voting power of all classes of stock entitled to vote and at least 80 per cent of the total number of shares of all other classes of stock of such corporation (see section 368(c)). In determining control under this section, the fact that any corporate transferor distributes part or all of the stock which it receives in the exchange to its shareholders shall not be taken into account. The phrase "immediately after the exchange" does not necessarily require simultaneous exchanges by two or more persons, but comprehends a situation where the rights of the parties have been previously defined and the execution of the agreement proceeds with an expedition consistent with orderly procedure. For purposes of this section, stock rights and stock warrants are not included in the term *stock*. In addition, for purposes of this section—

(i) Stock will not be treated as issued for property if it is issued for services rendered or to be rendered to or for the benefit of the issuing corporation; and

(ii) Stock will not be treated as issued for property if it is issued for property which is of relatively small value in comparison to the value of the stock already owned (or to be received for services) by the person who transferred such property and the primary purpose of the transfer is to qualify under this section the exchanges of property by other persons transferring property.

(2) *Application.*—The application of section 351(a) is illustrated by the following examples:

Example (1). C owns a patent right worth $25,000 and D owns a manufacturing plant worth $75,000. C and D organize the R Corporation with an authorized capital stock of $100,000. C transfers his patent right to the R Corporation for $25,000 of its stock and D transfers his plant to the new corporation for $75,000 of its stock. No gain or loss to C or D is recognized.

Example (2). B owns certain real estate which cost him $50,000 in 1930, but which has a fair market value of $200,000 in 1955. He transfers the property to the N Corporation in 1955 for 78 percent of each class of stock of the corporation having a fair market value of $200,000, the remaining 22 percent of the stock of the corporation having been issued by the corporation in 1940 to other persons for cash. B realized a taxable gain of $150,000 on this transaction.

Example (3). E, an individual, owns property with a basis of $10,000 but which has a fair market value of $18,000. E also had rendered services valued at $2,000 to Corporation F. Corporation F has outstanding 100 shares of common stock all of which are held by G. Corporation F issues 400 shares of its common stock (having a fair market value of $20,000) to E in exchange for his property worth $18,000 and in compensation for the services he has rendered worth $2,000. Since immediately after the transaction, E owns 80 percent of the outstanding stock of Corporation F, no gain is recognized upon the exchange of the property for the stock. However, E realized $2,000 of ordinary income as compensation for services rendered to Corporation F.

(3) *Underwritings of stock.*—(i) *In general.*—For the purpose of section 351, if a person acquires stock of a corporation from an underwriter in exchange for cash in a qualified underwriting transaction, the person who acquires stock from the underwriter is treated as transferring cash directly to the corporation in exchange for stock of the corporation and the underwriter is disregarded. A qualified underwriting transaction is a transaction in which a corporation issues stock for cash in an underwriting in which either the underwriter is an agent of the corporation or the underwriter's ownership of the stock is transitory.

* * *

(b) *Multiple transferors.*—(1) *Disproportionate transfers.*—When property is transferred to a corporation by two or more persons in exchange for stock, as described in paragraph (a) of this section, and the stock received is disproportionate to the transferor's prior interest in such property, the entire transaction will be given tax effect in accordance with its true nature, and the transaction may be treated as if the stock had first been received in proportion and then some of such stock had been used to make gifts (section 2501 and following), to pay compensation (sections 61(a)(1) and 83(a)), or to satisfy obligations of the transferor of any kind.

(2) *Application.*—The application of paragraph (b)(1) of this section may be illustrated as follows:

Example (1). Individuals A and B, father and son, organize a corporation with 100 shares of common stock to which A transfers property worth $8,000 in exchange for 20 shares of stock, and B transfers property worth $2,000 in exchange for 80 shares of stock. No gain or loss will be recognized under section 351. However, if it is determined that A in fact made a gift to B, such gift will be subject to tax under section 2501 and following. Similarly, if B had rendered services to A (such services having no relation to the assets transferred or to the business of the corporation) and the disproportion in the amount of stock received constituted the payment of compensation by A to B, B will be taxable upon the fair market value of the 60 shares of stock received as compensation for services rendered, and A will realize gain or loss upon the difference between the basis to him of the 60 shares and their fair market value at the time of the exchange.

Example (2). Individuals C and D each transferred, to a newly organized corporation, property having a fair market value of $4,500 in exchange for the issuance by the corporation of 45 shares of its capital stock to each transferor. At the same time, the corporation issued to E, an individual, 10 shares of its capital stock in payment for organizational and promotional services rendered by E for the benefit of the corporation. E transferred no property to the corporation. C and D were under no obligation to pay for E's services. No gain or loss is recognized to C or D. E received compensation taxable as ordinary income to the extent of the fair market value of the 10 shares of stock received by him.

(c) (1) The general rule of section 351 does not apply, and consequently gain or loss will be recognized, where property is transferred to an investment company after June 30, 1967. A transfer of property after June 30, 1967, will be considered to be a transfer to an investment company if—

(i) The transfer results, directly or indirectly, in diversification of the transferors' interests, and

(ii) The transferee is (*a*) a regulated investment company, (*b*) a real estate investment trust, or (*c*) a corporation more than 80 percent of the value of whose assets (excluding cash and nonconvertible debt obligations from consideration) are held for investment and are readily marketable stocks or securities, or interests in regulated investment companies or real estate investment trusts.

(2) The determination of whether a corporation is an investment company shall ordinarily be made by reference to the circumstances in existence immediately after the transfer in question. However, where circumstances change thereafter pursuant to a plan in existence at the time of the transfer, this determination shall be made by reference to the later circumstances.

(3) Stocks and securities will be considered readily marketable if (and only if) they are part of a class of stock or securities which is traded on a securities exchange or traded or quoted regularly in the over-the-counter market. For purposes of subparagraph (1) (ii) (*c*) of this paragraph, the term "readily marketable stocks or securities" includes convertible debentures, convertible preferred stock, warrants, and other stock rights if the stock for which they may be converted or exchanged is readily marketable. Stocks and securities will be considered to be held for investment unless they are (i) held primarily for sale to customers in the ordinary course of business, or (ii) used in the trade or business of banking, insurance, brokerage, or a similar trade or business.

(4) In making the determination required under subparagraph (1) (ii) (*c*) of this paragraph, stock and securities in subsidiary corporations shall be disregarded and the parent corporation shall be deemed to own its ratable share of its subsidiaries' assets. A corporation shall be considered a subsidiary if the parent owns 50 percent or more of (i) the combined voting power of all classes of stock entitled to vote, or (ii) the total value of shares of all classes of stock outstanding.

(5) A transfer ordinarily results in the diversification of the transferors' interests if two or more persons transfer nonidentical assets to a corporation in the exchange. For this purpose, if any transaction involves one or more transfers of nonidentical assets which, taken in the aggregate, constitute an insignificant portion of the total value of assets transferred, such transfers shall be disregarded in determining whether diversification has occurred. If there is only one transferor (or two or more transferors of identical assets) to a newly organized corporation, the transfer will generally be treated as not resulting in diversification. If a transfer is part of a plan to achieve diversification without recognition of gain, such as a plan which contemplates a subsequent transfer, however delayed, of the corporate assets (or of the stock or securities received in the earlier exchange) to an investment company in a transaction purporting to qualify for nonrecognition treatment, the original transfer will be treated as resulting in diversification.

(6) (i) For purposes of paragraph (c) (5) of this section, a transfer of stocks and securities will not be treated as resulting in a diversification of the transferors' interests if each transferor transfers a diversified portfolio of stocks and securities. For purposes of this paragraph (c) (6), a portfolio of stocks and securities is diversified if it satisfies the 25 and 50-percent tests of section 368(a) (2) (F) (ii), applying the relevant provisions of section 368(a) (2) (F). However, Government securities are included in total assets for purposes of the denominator of the 25 and 50-percent tests (unless the Government securities are acquired to meet the 25 and 50-percent tests), but are not treated as securities of an issuer for purposes of the numerator of the 25 and 50-percent tests.

* * *

(7) The application of subparagraph (5) of this paragraph may be illustrated as follows:

Example (1). Individuals A, B, and C organize a corporation with 101 shares of common stock. A and B each transfers to it $10,000 worth of the only class of stock of corporation X, listed on the New York Stock Exchange, in exchanges for 50 shares of stock. C transfers $200 worth of readily marketable securities in corporation Y for one share of stock. In determining whether or not diversification has occurred, C's participation in the transaction will be disregarded. There is, therefore, no diversification, and gain or loss will not be recognized.

Example (2). A, together with 50 other transferors, organizes a corporation with 100 shares of stock. A transfers $10,000 worth of stock in corporation X, listed on the New York

Stock Exchange, in exchange for 50 shares of stock. Each of the other 50 transferors transfers $200 worth of readily marketable securities in corporations other than X in exchange for one share of stock. In determining whether or not diversification has occurred, all transfers will be taken into account. Therefore, diversification is present, and gain or loss will be recognized.

* * *

[Reg. § 1.351-1.]

□ [*T.D.* 6152, 12-2-55. *Amended by T.D.* 6942, 12-28-67; *T.D.* 8663, 5-1-96, *T.D.* 8665, 4-30-96 *and T.D.* 9759, 3-25-2016.]

§ 1.351-2. Receipt of property.—(a) If an exchange would be within the provisions of section 351(a) if it were not for the fact that the property received in exchange consists not only of property permitted by such subsection to be received without the recognition of gain, but also of other property or money, then the gain, if any, to the recipient shall be recognized, but in an amount not in excess of the sum of such money and the fair market value of such other property. No loss to the recipient shall be recognized.

(b) See section 357 and the regulations pertaining to that section for applicable rules as to the treatment of liabilities as "other property" in cases subject to section 351, where another party to the exchange assumes a liability, or acquires property subject to a liability.

(c) See sections 358 and 362 and the regulations pertaining to those sections for applicable rules with respect to the determination of the basis of stock, securities, or other property received in exchanges subject to section 351.

(d) See part 1 (section 301 and following), subchapter C, chapter 1 of the Code, and the regulations thereunder for applicable rules with respect to the taxation of dividends where a distribution by a corporation of its stock or securities in connection with an exchange subject to section 351(a) has the effect of the distribution of a taxable dividend.

* * *

[Reg. § 1.351-2.]

□ [*T.D.* 6152, 12-2-55. *Amended by T.D.* 8904, 9-29-2000.]

§ 1.354-1. Exchanges of stock and securities in certain reorganizations.—(a) Section 354 provides that under certain circumstances no gain or loss is recognized to a shareholder who surrenders his stock in exchange for other stock or to a security holder who surrenders his securities in exchange for stock. Section 354 also provides that under certain circumstances a security holder may surrender securities and receive securities in the same principal amount or in a lesser principal amount without the recognition of gain or loss to him. The exchanges to which section 354 applies must be pursuant to a plan of reorganization as provided in section 368(a) and the stock and securities surrendered as well as the stock and securities received must be those of a corporation which is a party to the reorganization. Section 354 does not apply to exchanges pursuant to a reorganization described in section 368(a)(1)(D) unless the transferor corporation—

(1) Transfers all or substantially all of its assets to a single corporation, and

(2) Distributes all of its remaining properties (if any) and the stock, securities and other properties received in the exchange to its shareholders or security holders in pursuance of the plan of reorganization. The fact that properties retained by the transferor corporation, or received in exchange for the properties transferred in the reorganization, are used to satisfy existing liabilities not represented by securities and which were incurred in the ordinary course of business before the reorganization does not prevent the application of section 354 to an exchange pursuant to a plan of reorganization defined in section 368(a)(1)(D).

(b) Except as provided in section 354(c) and (d), section 354 is not applicable to an exchange of stock or securities if a greater principal amount of securities is received than the principal amount of securities the recipient surrenders, or if securities are received and the recipient surrenders no securities. See, however, section 356 and regulations pertaining to such section. See also section 306 with respect to the receipt of preferred stock in a transaction to which section 354 is applicable.

(c) An exchange of stock or securities shall be subject to section 354(a)(1) even though—

(1) Such exchange is not pursuant to a plan of reorganization described in section 368(a), and

(2) The principal amount of the securities received exceeds the principal amount of the securities surrendered or if securities are received and no securities are surrendered—

if such exchange is pursuant to a plan of reorganization for a railroad corporation as defined in section 77(m) of the Bankruptcy Act (11 U.S.C. 205(m)) and is approved by the Interstate Commerce Commission under section 77 of such Act or under section 20b of the Interstate Commerce Act (49 U.S.C. 20b) as being in the public interest. Section 354 is not applicable to such exchanges if there is received property other than stock or securities. See, however, section 356 and regulations pertaining to such section.

(d) The rules of section 354 may be illustrated by the following examples:

Example 1. Pursuant to a reorganization under section 368(a) to which Corporations T and W are parties, A, a shareholder in Corporation T, surrenders all his common stock in Corporation T in exchange for common stock of Corporation W. No gain or loss is recognized to A.

Example 2. Pursuant to a reorganization under section 368(a) to which Corporations X and Y (which are not railroad corporations) are parties, B, a shareholder in Corporation X, surrenders all his stock in X for stock and securities in Y. Section 354 does not apply to this exchange. See, however, section 356.

Example 3. C, a shareholder in Corporation Z (which is not a railroad corporation), surrenders all his stock in Corporation Z in exchange for securities in Corporation Z. Whether or not this exchange is in connection with a recapitalization under section 368(a)(1)(E), section 354 does not apply. See, however, section 302.

Example 4. The facts are the same as in *Example 3* of this paragraph (d), except that C receives solely rights to acquire stock in Corporation Z. Section 354 does not apply.

(e) Except as provided in § 1.356-6, for purposes of section 354, the term *securities* includes rights issued by a party to the reorganization to acquire its stock. For purposes of this section and section 356(d)(2)(B), a right to acquire stock has no principal amount. For this purpose, rights to acquire stock has the same meaning as it does under sections 305 and 317(a). Other Internal Revenue Code provisions governing the treatment of rights to acquire stock may also apply to certain exchanges occurring in connection with a reorganization. See, for example, sections 83 and 421 through 424 and the regulations thereunder. This paragraph (e) applies to exchanges occurring on or after March 9, 1998.

(f) See § 1.356-7(a) and (b) for the treatment of nonqualified preferred stock (as defined in section 351(g)(2)) received in certain exchanges for nonqualified preferred stock or preferred stock. See § 1.356-7(c) for the treatment of preferred stock received in certain exchanges for common or preferred stock described in section 351(g)(2)(C)(i)(II). [Reg. § 1.354-1.]

☐ [*T.D.* 6152, 12-2-55. *Amended by T.D.* 7616, 5-7-79; *T.D.* 8752, 1-5-98; *T.D.* 8882, 5-15-2000 *and T.D.* 8904, 9-29-2000.]

§ 1.355-1. Distribution of stock and securities of a controlled corporation.—

* * *

(b) *Application of section.*—Section 355 provides for the separation, without recognition of gain or loss to (or the inclusion in income of) the shareholders and security holders, of one or more existing businesses formerly operated, directly or indirectly, by a single corporation (the "distributing corporation"). It applies only to the separation of existing businesses that have been in active operation for at least five years (or a business that has been in active operation for at least five years into separate businesses), and which, in general, have been owned, directly or indirectly, for at least five years by the distributing corporation. A separation is achieved through the distribution by the distributing corporation of stock, or stock and securities, of one or more subsidiaries (the "controlled corporations") to its shareholders with respect to its stock or to its security holders in exchange for its securities. The controlled corporations may be preexisting or newly created subsidiaries. Throughout the regulations under section 355, the term "distribution" refers to a distribution by the distributing corporation of stock, or stock and securities, of one or more controlled corporations, unless the context indicates otherwise. Section 355 contemplates the continued operation of the business or businesses existing prior to the separation. See § 1.355-4 for types of distributions that may qualify under section 355, including pro-rata distributions and non-pro-rata distributions.

(c) *Stock rights.*—Except as provided in § 1.356-6, for purposes of section 355, the term *securities* includes rights issued by the distributing corporation or the controlled corporation to acquire the stock of that corporation. For purposes of this section and section 356(d)(2)(B), a right to acquire stock has no principal amount. For this purpose, rights to acquire stock has the same meaning as it does under sections 305 and 317(a). Other Internal Revenue Code provisions governing the treatment of rights to acquire stock may also apply to certain distributions occurring in connection with a transaction described in section 355. See, for example, sections 83 and 421 through 424 and the regulations thereunder. This paragraph (c) applies to distributions occurring on or after March 9, 1998.

(d) *Nonqualified preferred stock.*—See § 1.356-7(a) and (b) for the treatment of nonqualified preferred stock (as defined in section 351(g)(2)) received in certain exchanges for (or in certain distributions with respect to) nonqualified preferred stock or preferred stock. See § 1.356-7(c) for the treatment of the receipt of preferred stock in certain exchanges for (or in certain distributions with respect to) common or preferred stock described in section 351(g)(2)(C)(i)(II). [Reg. § 1.355-1.]

□ [*T.D.* 6152, 12-2-55. *Amended by T.D.* 8238, 1-4-89; *T.D.* 8752, 1-5-98; *T.D.* 8882, 5-15-2000 *T.D.* 8904, 9-29-2000; *T.D.* 9435, 12-12-2008 (*corrected* 1-16-2009) *and T.D.* 9548, 10-19-2011.]

§ 1.355-2. Limitations.—(a) *Property distributed.*—Section 355 applies to a distribution only if the property distributed consists solely of stock, or stock and securities, of a controlled corporation. If additional property (including an excess principal amount of securities received over securities surrendered) is received, see section 356.

(b) *Independent business purpose.*—(1) *Independent business purpose requirement.*—Section 355 applies to a transaction only if it is carried out for one or more corporate business purposes. A transaction is carried out for a corporate business purpose if it is motivated, in whole or substantial part, by one or more corporate business purposes. The potential for the avoidance of Federal taxes by the distributing or controlled corporations (or a corporation controlled by either) is relevant in determining the extent to which an existing corporate business purpose motivated the distribution. The principal reason for this business purpose requirement is to provide nonrecognition treatment only to distributions that are incident to readjustments of corporate structures required by business exigencies and that effect only readjustments of continuing interests in property under modified corporate forms. This business purpose requirement is independent of the other requirements under section 355.

(2) *Corporate business purpose.*—A corporate business purpose is a real and substantial non-Federal tax purpose germane to the business of the distributing corporation, the controlled corporation, or the affiliated group (as defined in § 1.355-3(b)(4)(iv)) to which the distributing corporation belongs. A purpose of reducing non-Federal taxes is not a corporate business purpose if (i) the transaction will effect a reduction in both Federal and non-Federal taxes because of similarities between Federal tax law and the tax law of the other jurisdiction and (ii) the reduction of Federal taxes is greater than or substantially coextensive with the reduction of non-Federal taxes. See examples (7) and (8) of paragraph (b)(5) of this section. A shareholder purpose (for example, the personal planning purposes of a shareholder) is not a corporate business purpose. Depending upon the facts of a particular case, however, a shareholder purpose for a transaction may be so nearly coextensive with a corporate business purpose as to preclude any distinction between them. In such a case, the transaction is carried out for one or more corporate business purposes. See example (2) of paragraph (b)(5) of this section.

(3) *Business purpose for distribution.*—The distribution must be carried out for one or more corporate business purposes. See example (3) of paragraph (b)(5) of this section. If a corporate business purpose can be achieved through a nontaxable transaction that does not involve the distribution of stock of a controlled corporation and which is neither impractical nor unduly expensive, then, for purposes of paragraph (b)(1) of this section, the separation is not carried out for that corporate business purpose. See examples (3) and (4) of paragraph (b)(5) of this section. For rules with respect to the requirement of a business purpose for a transfer of assets to a controlled corporation in connection with a reorganization described in section 368(a)(1)(D), see § 1.368-1(b).

(4) *Business purpose as evidence of nondevice.*—The corporate business purpose or purposes for a transaction are evidence that the transaction was not used principally as a device for the distribution of earnings and profits within the meaning of section 355(a)(1)(B). See paragraph (d)(3)(ii) of this section.

(5) *Examples.*—The provisions of this paragraph (b) may be illustrated by the following examples:

Example (1). Corporation X is engaged in the production, transportation, and refining of petroleum products. In 1985, X acquires all of the properties of corporation Z, which is also engaged in the production, transportation, and refining of petroleum products. In 1991, as a result of antitrust litigation, X is ordered to divest itself of all of the properties acquired from Z. X transfers those properties to new corporation Y and distributes the stock of Y pro rata to X's shareholders. In view of the divestiture order, the distribution is carried out for a corporate business purpose. See paragraph (b)(1) of this section.

Example (2). Corporation X is engaged in two businesses: the manufacture and sale of furniture and the sale of jewelry. The businesses are of equal value. The outstanding stock of X is owned equally by unrelated individuals A and B. A is more interested in the furniture business, while B is more interested in the jewelry business. A and B decide to split up the businesses and go their separate ways. A and B anticipate that the operations of each business will be enhanced by the separation because each shareholder will be able to devote his undivided attention to the business in which he is more interested and more proficient. Accordingly, X transfers the jewelry business to new corporation Y and distributes the stock of Y to B in exchange for all of B's stock in X. The distribution is carried out for a corporate business purpose, notwithstanding that it is also carried out in part for shareholder purposes. See paragraph (b) (2) of this section.

Example (3). Corporation X is engaged in the manufacture and sale of toys and the manufacture and sale of candy. The shareholders of X wish to protect the candy business from the risks and vicissitudes of the toy business. Accordingly, X transfers the toy business to new corporation Y and distributes the stock of Y to X's shareholders. Under applicable law, the purpose of protecting the candy business from the risks and vicissitudes of the toy business is achieved as soon as X transfers the toy business to Y. Therefore, the distribution is not carried out for a corporate business purpose. See paragraph (b) (3) of this section.

Example (4). Corporation X is engaged in a regulated business in State T. X owns all of the stock of corporation Y, a profitable corporation that is not engaged in a regulated business. Commission C sets the rates that X may charge its customers, based on its total income. C has recently adopted rules according to which the total income of a corporation includes the income of a business if, and only if, the business is operated, directly or indirectly, by the corporation. Total income, for this purpose, includes the income of a wholly owned subsidiary corporation but does not include the income of a parent or "brother/sister" corporation. Under C's new rule, X's total income includes the income of Y, with the result that X has suffered a reduction of the rates that it may charge its customers. It would not be impractical or unduly expensive to create in a nontaxable transaction (such as a transaction qualifying under section 351) a holding company to hold the stock of X and Y. X distributes the stock of Y to X's shareholders. The distribution is not carried out for the purpose of increasing the rates that X may charge its customers because that purpose could be achieved through a nontaxable transaction, the creation of a holding company, that does not involve the distribution of stock of a controlled corporation and which is neither impractical nor unduly expensive. See paragraph (b) (3) of this section.

Example (5). The facts are the same as in example (4), except that C has recently adopted rules according to which the total income of a corporation includes not only the income included in example (3), but also the income of any member of the affiliated group to which the corporation belongs. In order to avoid a reduction in the rates that it may charge its customers, X distributes the stock of Y to X's shareholders. The distribution is carried out for a corporate business purpose. See paragraph (b) (3) of this section.

Example (6). (i) Corporation X owns all of the one class of stock of corporation Y. X distributes the stock of Y pro rata to its five shareholders, all of whom are individuals, for the sole purpose of enabling X and/or Y to elect to become an S corporation. The distribution does not meet the corporate business purpose requirement. See paragraph (b) (1) and (2) of this section.

(ii) The facts are the same as in Example (6) (i), except that the business of Y is operated as a division of X. X transfers this division to new corporation Y and distributes the stock of Y pro rata to its shareholders, all of whom are individuals, for the sole purpose of enabling X and/or Y to elect to become an S corporation. The distribution does not meet the corporate business purpose requirement. See paragraph (b) (1) and (2) of this section.

Example (7). The facts are the same as in example (6) (i), except that the distribution is made to enable X to elect to become an S corporation both for Federal tax purposes and for purposes of the income tax imposed by State M. State M has tax law provisions similar to subchapter S of the Internal Revenue Code of 1986. An election to be an S corporation for Federal tax purposes will effect a substantial reduction in Federal taxes that is greater than the reduction of State M taxes pursuant to an election to be an S corporation for State M purposes. The purpose of reducing State M taxes is not a corporate business purpose. The distribution does not meet the corporate business purpose requirement. See paragraph (b) (1) and (2) of this section.

Example (8). The facts are the same as Example (7), except that the distribution also is made to enable *A*, a key employee of Y, to acquire stock of Y without investing in X. *A* is considered to be critical to the success of Y and he has indicated that he will seriously consider leaving the company if he is not given the opportunity to purchase a significant amount of stock of Y. As a matter of state law, Y could not issue stock to the employee while it was a subsidiary of X. As in Example (7), the purpose of reducing State M taxes is not a corporate business purpose. In order to determine whether the issuance of stock to the key employee, in fact, motivated the distribution of the Y stock, the potential avoidance of Federal taxes is a relevant factor to take into account. If the facts and circumstances establish that the distribution was substantially motivated by the need to issue stock to the employee, the distribution will meet the corporate business purpose requirement.

(c) *Continuity of interest requirement.*—(1) *Requirement.*—Section 355 applies to a separation that effects only a readjustment of continuing interests in the property of the distributing and controlled corporations. In this regard section 355 requires that one or more persons who, directly or indirectly, were the owners of the enterprise prior to the distribution or exchange own, in the aggregate, an amount of stock establishing a continuity of interest in each of the modified corporate forms in which the enterprise is conducted after the separation. This continuity of interest requirement is independent of the other requirements under section 355.

(2) *Examples.*—

Example (1). For more than five years, corporation X has been engaged directly in one business, and indirectly in a different business through its wholly owned subsidiary, S. The businesses are equal in value. At all times, the outstanding stock of X has been owned equally by unrelated individuals A and B. For valid business reasons, A and B cause X to distribute all of the stock of S to B in exchange for all of B's stock in X. After the transaction, A owns all the stock of X and B owns all the stock of S. The continuity of interest requirement is met because one or more persons who were the owners of X prior to the distribution (A and B) own, in the aggregate, an amount of stock establishing a continuity of interest in each of X and S after the distribution.

Example (2). Assume the same facts as in Example (1), except that pursuant to a plan to acquire a stock interest in X without acquiring, directly or indirectly, an interest in S, C purchased one-half of the X stock owned by A and immediately thereafter X distributed all of the S stock to B in exchange for all of B's stock in X. After the transactions, A owns 50 percent of X and B owns 100 percent of S. The distribution by X of all of the stock of S to B in exchange for all of B's stock in X will satisfy the continuity of interest requirement for section 355 because one or more persons who were the owners of X prior to the distribution (A and B) own, in the aggregate, an amount of stock establishing a continuity of interest in each of X and S after the distribution.

Example (3). Assume the same facts as in Example (1) and (2), except that C purchased all of the X stock owned by A. After the transactions, neither A nor B own any of the stock of X, and B owns all the stock of S. The continuity of interest requirement is not met because the owners of X prior to the distribution (A and B) do not, in the aggregate, own an amount of stock establishing a continuity of interest in each of X and S after the distribution, *i.e.*, although A and B collectively have retained 50 percent of their equity interest in the former combined enterprise, they have failed to continue to own the minimum stock interest in the distributing corporation, X, that would be required in order to meet the continuity of interest requirement.

Example (4). Assume the same facts as in Examples (1) and (2), except that C purchased 80 percent of the X stock owned by A. After the transactions, A owns 20 percent of the stock of X, B owns no X stock, and B owns 100 percent of the S stock. The continuity of interest requirement is not met because the owners of X prior to the distribution (A and B) do not, in the aggregate, have a continuity of interest in each of X and S after the distribution, *i.e.*, although A and B collectively have retained 60 percent of their equity interest in the former combined enterprise, the 20 percent interest of A in X is less than the minimum equity interest in the distributing corporation, X, that would be required in order to meet the continuity of interest requirement.

(d) *Device for distribution of earnings and profits.*—(1) *In general.*—Section 355 does not apply to a transaction used principally as a device for the distribution of the earnings and profits of the distributing corporation, the controlled corporation, or both (a "device"). Section 355 recognizes that a tax-free distribution of the stock of a controlled corporation presents a potential for tax avoidance by facilitating the avoidance of the dividend provisions of the Code through the subsequent sale or exchange of stock of one corporation and the retention of the stock of another corporation. A device can include a transaction that effects a recovery of basis. In this paragraph (d), "exchange" includes transactions, such as redemptions, treated as exchanges under the Code. Generally, the determination of whether a transaction was used principally as a device will be made from all of the facts and circumstances, including, but not limited to, the presence of the device factors specified in paragraph (d)(2) of this section ("evidence of device"), and the presence of the nondevice factors specified in paragraph (d)(3) of this section ("evidence of nondevice"). However, if a transaction is specified in paragraph (d)(5) of this section, then it is ordinarily considered not to have been used principally as a device.

(2) *Device factors.*—(i) *In general.*—The presence of any of the device factors specified in this subparagraph (2) is evidence of device. The strength of this evidence depends on the facts and circumstances.

(ii) *Pro rata distribution.*—A distribution that is pro rata or substantially pro rata among the shareholders of the distributing corporation presents the greatest potential for the avoidance of the dividend provisions of the Code and, in contrast to other types of distributions, is more likely to be used principally as a device. Accordingly, the fact that a distribution is pro rata or substantially pro rata is evidence of device.

(iii) *Subsequent sale or exchange of stock.*—(A) *In general.*—A sale or exchange of stock of the distributing or the controlled corporation after the distribution (a "subsequent sale or exchange") is evidence of device. Generally, the greater the percentage of the stock sold or exchanged after the distribution, the stronger the evidence of device. In addition, the shorter the period of time between the distribution and the sale or exchange, the stronger the evidence of device.

(B) *Sale or exchange negotiated or agreed upon before the distribution.*—A subsequent sale or exchange pursuant to an arrangement negotiated or agreed upon before the distribution is substantial evidence of device.

(C) *Sale or exchange not negotiated or agreed upon before the distribution.*—A subsequent sale or exchange not pursuant to an arrangement negotiated or agreed upon before the distribution is evidence of device.

(D) *Negotiated or agreed upon before the distribution.*—For purposes of this subparagraph (2), a sale or exchange is always pursuant to an arrangement negotiated or agreed upon before the distribution if enforceable rights to buy or sell existed before the distribution. If a sale or exchange was discussed by the buyer and the seller before the distribution and was reasonably to be anticipated by both parties, then the sale or exchange will ordinarily be considered to be pursuant to an arrangement negotiated or agreed upon before the distribution.

(E) *Exchange in pursuance of a plan of reorganization.*—For purposes of this subparagraph (2), if stock is exchanged for stock in pursuance of a plan of reorganization, and either no gain or loss or only an insubstantial amount of gain is recognized on the exchange, then the exchange is not treated as a subsequent sale or exchange, but the stock received in the exchange is treated as the stock surrendered in the exchange. For this purpose, gain treated as a dividend pursuant to sections 356(a)(2) and 316 shall be disregarded.

(iv) *Nature and use of assets.*—(A) *In general.*—The determination of whether a transaction was used principally as a device will take into account the nature, kind, amount, and use of the assets of the distributing and the controlled corporations (and corporations controlled by them) immediately after the transaction.

(B) *Assets not used in a trade or business meeting the requirement of section 355(b).*—The existence of assets that are not used in a trade or business that satisfies the requirements of section 355(b) is evidence of device. For this purpose, assets that are not used in a trade or business that satisfies the requirements of section 355(b) include, but are not limited to, cash and other liquid assets that are not related to the reasonable needs of a business satisfying such section. The strength of the evidence of device depends on all the facts and circumstances, including, but not limited to, the ratio for each corporation of the value of assets not used in a trade or business that satisfies the requirements of section 355(b) to the value of its business that satisfies such requirements. A difference in the ratio described in the preceding sentence for the distributing and controlled corporation is ordinarily not evidence of device if the distribution is not pro rata among the shareholders of the distributing corporation and such difference is attributable to a need to equalize the value of the stock distributed and the value of the stock or securities exchanged by the distributees.

(C) *Related function.*—There is evidence of device if a business of either the distributing or controlled corporation (or a corporation controlled by it) is (*1*) a "secondary business" that continues as a secondary business for a significant period after the separation, and (*2*) can be sold without adversely affecting the business of the other corporation (or a corporation controlled by it). A secondary business is a business of either the distributing or controlled corporation, if its principal function is to serve the business of the other corporation (or a corporation controlled by it). A secondary business can include a business transferred to a newly-created subsidiary or a business which serves a business transferred to a newly-created subsidiary. The activities of the secondary business may consist of providing property or performing services. Thus, in example (11) of § 1.355-3(c), evidence of device would be presented if the principal function of the coal mine (satisfying the requirements of the steel business) continued after the separation and the coal mine could be sold without adversely affecting the steel business. Similarly, in example (10) of § 1.355-3(c), evidence of device would be presented if the principal function of the sales operation after the separation is to sell the output from the manufacturing operation and the sales operation could be sold without adversely affecting the manufacturing operation.

(3) *Nondevice factors.*—(i) *In general.*—The presence of any of the nondevice factors specified in this subparagraph (3) is evidence of nondevice. The strength of this evidence depends on all of the facts and circumstances.

(ii) *Corporate business purpose.*—The corporate business purpose for the transaction is evidence of nondevice. The stronger the evidence of device (such as the presence of the device factors specified in paragraph (d)(2) of this section), the stronger the corporate business purpose required to prevent the determination that the transaction was used principally as a device. Evidence of device presented by the transfer or retention of assets not used in a trade or business that satisfies the requirements of section 355(b) can be outweighed by the existence of a corporate business purpose for those transfers or retentions. The assessment of the strength of a corporate business purpose will be based on all of the facts and circumstances, including, but not limited to, the following factors:

(A) The importance of achieving the purpose to the success of the business;

(B) The extent to which the transaction is prompted by a person not having a proprietary interest in either corporation, or by other outside factors beyond the control of the distributing corporation; and

(C) The immediacy of the conditions prompting the transaction.

(iii) *Distributing corporation publicly traded and widely held.*—The fact that the distributing corporation is publicly traded and has no shareholder who is directly or indirectly the beneficial owner of more than five percent of any class of stock is evidence of nondevice.

(iv) *Distribution to domestic corporate shareholders.*—The fact that the stock of the controlled corporation is distributed to one or more domestic corporations that, if section 355 did not apply, would be entitled to a deduction under section 243(a)(1) available to corporations meeting the stock ownership requirements of section 243(c), or a deduction under section 243(a)(2) or (3) or 245(b) is evidence of nondevice.

(4) *Examples.*—The provisions of paragraph (d)(1) through (3) of this section may be illustrated by the following examples:

Example (1). Individual A owns all of the stock of corporation X, which is engaged in the warehousing business. X owns all of the stock of corporation Y, which is engaged in the transportation business. X employs individual B, who is extremely knowledgeable of the warehousing business in general and the operations of X in particular. B has informed A that he will seriously consider leaving the company if he is not given the opportunity to purchase a significant amount of stock of X. Because of his knowledge and experience, the loss of B would seriously damage the business of X. B cannot afford to purchase any significant amount of stock of X as long as X owns Y. Accordingly, X distributes the stock of Y to A and A subsequently sells a portion of his X stock to B. However, X could have issued additional shares to B sufficient to give B an equivalent ownership interest in X. There is no other evidence of device or evidence of nondevice. In light of the fact that X could have issued additional shares to B, the sale of X stock by A is substantial evidence of device. The transaction is considered to have been used principally as a device. See paragraph (d)(1), (2)(ii), (iii)(A), (B) and (D), and (3)(i) and (ii) of this section.

Example (2). Corporation X owns and operates a fast food restaurant in State M and owns all of the stock of corporation Y, which owns and operates a fast food restaurant in State N. X and Y operate their businesses under franchises granted by D and E, respectively. X owns cash and marketable securities that exceed the reasonable needs of its business but whose value is small relative to the value of its business. E has recently changed its franchise policy and will no longer grant or renew franchises to subsidiaries (or other members of the same affiliated group) of corporations operating businesses under franchises granted by its competitors. Thus, Y will lose its franchise if it remains a subsidiary of X. The franchise is about to expire. Accordingly, X distributes the stock of Y pro rata among X's shareholders. X retains its business and transfers cash and marketable securities to Y in an amount proportional to the value of Y's business. There is no other evidence of device or evidence of nondevice. The transfer by X to Y and the retention by X of cash and marketable securities is relatively weak evidence of device because after the transfer X and Y hold cash and marketable securities in amounts proportional to the values of their businesses. The fact that the distribution is pro rata is evidence of device. A strong corporate business purpose is relatively strong evidence of nondevice. Accordingly, the transaction is considered not to have been used principally as a device. See paragraph (d)(1), (2)(ii), (iv)(A), and (B) and (3)(i) and (ii)(A), (B), and (C) of this section.

Example (3). Corporation X is engaged in a regulated business in State M and owns all of the stock of corporation Y, which is not engaged in a regulated business in State M. State M has recently amended its laws to provide that affiliated corporations operating in M may not conduct both regulated and unregulated businesses. X transfers cash not related to the reasonable needs of the business of X or Y to Y and then distributes the stock of Y pro rata among X's shareholders. As a result of the transfer of cash, the ratio of the value of its assets not used in a trade or business that satisfies the requirements of section 355(b) to the value of its business is substantially greater for Y than for X. There is no other evidence of device or evidence of nondevice. The transfer of cash by X to Y is relatively strong evidence of device because after the transfer Y holds disproportionately many assets that are not used in a trade or business that satisfies the requirements of section 355(b). The fact that the distribution is pro rata is evidence of device. The strong business purpose is relatively strong evidence of nondevice, but it does not pertain to the transfer. Accordingly, the transaction is considered to have been used principally as a device. See paragraph (d)(1), (2)(ii), (iv)(A) and (B), and (3)(i) and (ii) of this section.

Example (4). The facts are the same as in example (3), except that, instead of transferring cash to Y, X purchases operating assets unrelated to the business of Y and transfers them to Y prior to the distribution. There is no other evidence of device or evidence of nondevice. The transaction is considered to have been used principally as a device. See paragraph (d)(1), (2)(ii), (iv)(A) and (B), and (3)(i) and (ii) of this section.

(5) *Transactions ordinarily not considered as a device.*—(i) *In general.*—This subparagraph (5) specifies three distributions that ordinarily do not present the potential for tax avoidance described in paragraph (d)(1) of this section. Accordingly, such distributions are ordinarily considered not to have been used principally as a device, notwithstanding the presence of any of the device factors described in paragraph (d)(2) of this section. A transaction described in paragraph (d)(5)(iii) or (iv) of this section is not protected by this subparagraph (5) from a determination that it was used principally as a device if it involves the distribution of the stock of more than one controlled corporation and facilitates the avoidance of the dividend provisions of the Code through the subsequent sale or exchange of stock of one corporation and the retention of the stock of another corporation.

(ii) *Absence of earnings and profits.*—A distribution is ordinarily considered not to have been used principally as a device if—

(A) The distributing and controlled corporations have no accumulated earnings and profits at the beginning of their respective taxable years,

(B) The distributing and controlled corporations have no current earnings and profits as of the date of the distribution, and

(C) No distribution of property by the distributing corporation immediately before the separation would require recognition of gain resulting in current earnings and profits for the taxable year of the distribution.

(iii) *Section 303(a) transactions.*—A distribution is ordinarily considered not to have been used principally as a device if, in the absence of section 355, with respect to each shareholder distributee, the distribution would be a redemption to which section 303(a) applied.

(iv) *Section 302(a) transactions.*—A distribution is ordinarily considered not to have been used principally as a device if, in the absence of section 355, with respect to each shareholder distributee, the distribution would be a redemption to which section 302(a) applied. For purposes of the preceding sentence, section 302(c)(2)(A)(ii) and (iii) shall not apply.

(v) *Examples.*—The provisions of this subparagraph (5) may be illustrated by the following examples:

Example (1). The facts are the same as in example (3) of paragraph (d)(4) of this section, except that X and Y had no accumulated earnings and profits at the beginning of its taxable year, X and Y have no current earnings and profits as of the date of the distribution, and no distribution of property by X immediately before the separation would require recognition of gain that would result in earnings and profits for the taxable year of the distribution. The transaction is considered not to have been used principally as a device. See paragraph (d)(5)(i) and (ii) of this section.

Example (2). Corporation X is engaged in three businesses: a hotel business, a restaurant business, and a rental real estate business. Individuals A, B, and C own all of the stock of X. X transfers the restaurant business to new corporation Y and transfers the rental real estate business to new corporation Z. X then distributes the stock of Y and Z pro rata between B and C in exchange for all of their stock in X. In the absence of section 355, the distribution would be a redemption to which section 302(a) applied. Since this distribution involves the stock of more than one controlled corporation and facilitates the avoidance of the dividend provisions of the Code through the subsequent sale or exchange of stock in one corporation and the retention of the stock of another corporation, it is not protected by paragraph (d)(5)(i) and (iv) of this section from a determination that it was used principally as a device. Thus, the determination of whether the transaction was used principally as a device must be made from all the facts and circumstances, including the presence of the device factors and nondevice factors specified in paragraph (d)(2) and (3) of this section.

(e) *Stock and securities distributed.*—(1) *In general.*—Section 355 applies to a distribution only if the distributing corporation distributes—

(i) All of the stock and securities of the controlled corporation that it owns, or

(ii) At least an amount of the stock of the controlled corporation that constitutes control as defined in section 368(c). In such a case, all, or any part, of the securities of the controlled corporation may be distributed, and paragraph (e)(2) of this section shall apply.

(2) *Additional rules.*—Where a part of either the stock or the securities of the controlled corporation is retained under paragraph (e)(1)(ii) of this section, it must be established to the satisfaction of the Commissioner that the retention by the distributing corporation was not in pursuance of a plan having as one of its principal purposes the avoidance of Federal income tax. Ordinarily, the corporate business purpose or purposes for the distribution will require the distribution of all of the stock and securities of the controlled corporation. If the distribution of all of the stock and securities of a controlled corporation would be treated to any extent as a distribution of "other property" under section 356, this fact tends to establish that the retention of stock or securities is in pursuance of a plan having as one of its principal purposes the avoidance of Federal income tax.

(f) *Principal amount of securities.*—(1) *Securities received.*—Section 355 does not apply to a distribution if, with respect to any shareholder or security holder, the principal amount of securities received exceeds the principal amount of securities surrendered, or securities are received but no securities are surrendered. In such cases, see section 356.

(2) *Only stock received.*—If only stock is received in a distribution to which section 355(a)(1)(A) applies, the principal amount of the securities surrendered, if any, and the par value or stated value of the stock surrendered, if any, are not relevant to the application of that section.

(g) *Recently acquired controlled stock under section 355(a)(3)(B).*—(1) *Other property.*—Except as provided in paragraph (g)(2) of this section, for purposes of section 355(a)(1)(A), section 355(c), and so much of section 356 as relates to section 355, stock of a controlled corporation acquired by the DSAG in a taxable transaction (as defined in paragraph (g)(4) of this section) within the five-year period ending on the date of the distribution (pre-distribution period) shall not be treated as stock of the controlled corporation but shall be treated as "other property." Transfers of controlled corporation stock that is owned by the DSAG immediately before and immediately after the transfer are disregarded and are not acquisitions for purposes of this paragraph (g)(1).

(2) *Exceptions.*—Paragraph (g)(1) of this section does not apply to an acquisition of stock of the controlled corporation—

(i) If the controlled corporation is a DSAG member at any time after the acquisition (but prior to the distribution); or

(ii) Described in § 1.355-3(b)(4)(iii).

(3) *DSAG.*—For purposes of this paragraph (g), a *DSAG* is the distributing corporation's separate affiliated group (the affiliated group which would be determined under section 1504(a) if such corporation were the common parent and section 1504(b) did not apply) that consists of the distributing corporation as the common parent and all corporations affiliated with the distributing corporation through stock ownership described in section 1504(a)(1)(B) (regardless of whether the corporations are includible corporations under section 1504(b)). For purposes of paragraph (g)(1) of this section, any reference to the DSAG is a reference to the distributing corporation if it is not the common parent of a separate affiliated group.

(4) *Taxable transaction.*—(i) *Generally.*—For purposes of this paragraph (g), a *taxable transaction* is a transaction in which gain or loss was recognized in whole or in part.

(ii) *Dunn Trust and predecessor issues.*—[Reserved].

(5) *Examples.*—The following examples illustrate this paragraph (g). Assume that C, D, P, and S are corporations, X is an unrelated individual, each of the transactions is unrelated to any other transaction and, but for the issue of whether C stock is treated as "other property" under section 355(a)(3)(B), the distributions satisfy all of the requirements of section 355. No inference should be drawn from any of these examples as to whether any requirements of section 355 other than section 355(a)(3)(B), as specified, are satisfied. Furthermore, the following definitions apply:

(i) *Purchase* is an acquisition that is a taxable transaction.

(ii) *Section 368(c) stock* is stock constituting control within the meaning of section 368(c).

(iii) *Section 1504(a)(2) stock* is stock meeting the requirements of section 1504(a)(2).

Example 1. Hot stock. For more than five years, D has owned section 368(c) stock but not section 1504(a)(2) stock of C. In year 6, D purchases additional C stock from X. However, D does not own section 1504(a)(2) stock of C after the year 6 purchase. If D distributes all of its C stock within five years after the year 6 purchase, for purposes of section 355(a)(1)(A), section 355(c), and so much of section 356 as relates to section 355, the C stock purchased in year 6 would be treated as "other property." See paragraph (g)(1) of this section.

Example 2. C becomes a DSAG member. For more than five years, D has owned section 368(c) stock but not section 1504(a)(2) stock of C. In year 6, D purchases additional C stock from X such that D's total ownership of C is section 1504(a)(2) stock. If D distributes all of its C stock within five years after the year 6 purchase, the distribution of the C stock purchased in year 6 would not be treated as "other property" because C becomes a DSAG member. See paragraph (g)(2)(i) of this section. The result would be the same if D did not own any C stock prior to year 6 and D purchased all of the C stock in year 6. See paragraph (g)(2)(i) of this section. Similarly, if D did not own any C stock prior to year 6, D purchased 20 percent of the C stock in year 6, and then acquired all of the remaining C stock in year 7, the C stock purchased in year 6 and the C stock acquired in year 7 (even if purchased) would not be treated as "other property" because C becomes a DSAG member. See paragraph (g)(2)(i) of this section.

Example 3. Intra-SAG transaction. For more than five years, D has owned all of the stock of S. D and S, in the aggregate, have owned section 368(c) stock but not section 1504(a)(2) stock of C. Therefore, D and S are DSAG members, but C is not. In year 6, D purchases S's C stock. If D distributes all of its C stock within five years after the year 6 purchase, the distribution of the C stock purchased in year 6 would not be treated as "other property". D's purchase of the C stock from S is disregarded for purposes of paragraph (g)(1) of this section because that C stock was owned by the DSAG immediately before and immediately after the purchase. See paragraph (g)(1) of this section.

Example 4. Affiliate exception. For more than five years, P has owned 90 percent of the sole outstanding class of the stock of D and a portion of the stock of C, and X has owned the remaining 10 percent of the D stock. Throughout this period, D has owned section 368(c) stock but not section 1504(a)(2) stock of C. In year 6, D purchases P's C stock. However, D does not own section 1504(a)(2) stock of C after the year 6 purchase. If D distributes all of its C stock to X in exchange for X's D stock within five years after the year 6 purchase, the distribution of the C stock purchased in year 6 would not be treated as "other property" because the C stock was purchased from a member (P) of the affiliated group (as defined in § 1.355-3(b)(4)(iv)) of which D is a member, and P did not purchase that C stock within the pre-distribution period. See paragraph (g)(2)(ii) of this section.

(h) *Active conduct of a trade or business.*—Section 355 applies to a distribution only if the requirements of § 1.355-3 (relating to the active conduct of a trade or business) are satisfied.

* * *

[Reg. § 1.355-2.]

☐ [*T.D.* 6152, 12-2-55. *Amended by T.D.* 8238, 1-4-89; *T.D.* 9435, 12-12-2008 *and T.D.* 9548, 10-19-2011.]

§ 1.355-3. Active conduct of a trade or business.—(a) *General requirements.*—(1) *Application of section 355.*—Under section 355(b)(1), a distribution of stock, or stock and securities, of a controlled corporation qualifies under section 355 only if—

(i) The distributing and the controlled corporations are each engaged in the active conduct of a trade or business immediately after the distribution (section 355(b)(1)(A)), or

(ii) Immediately before the distribution, the distributing corporation had no assets other than stock or securities of the controlled corporations, and each of the controlled corporations is engaged in the active conduct of a trade or business immediately after the distribution (section 355(b)(1)(B)). A *de minimis* amount of assets held by the distributing corporation shall be disregarded for purposes of this paragraph (a)(1)(ii).

(2) *Examples.*—Paragraph (a)(1) of this section may be illustrated by the following examples:

Example (1). Prior to the distribution, corporation X is engaged in the active conduct of a trade or business and owns all of the stock of corporation Y, which also is engaged in the active conduct of a trade or business. X distributes all of the stock of Y to X's shareholders, and each corporation continues the active conduct of its trade or business. The active business requirement of section 355(b)(1)(A) is satisfied.

Example (2). The facts are the same as in example (1), except that X transfers all of its assets other than the stock of Y to a new corporation in exchange for all of the stock of the new corporation and then distributes the stock of both controlled corporations to X's shareholders. The active business requirement of section 355(b)(1)(B) is satisfied.

(b) *Active conduct of a trade or business defined.*—(1) *In general.*—Section 355(b)(2) provides rules for determining whether a corporation is treated as engaged in the active conduct of a trade or business for purposes of section 355(b)(1). Under section 355(b)(2)(A), a corporation is treated as engaged in the active conduct of a trade or business if it is itself engaged in the active conduct of a trade or business or if substantially all of its assets consist of the stock, or stock and securities, of a corporation or corporations controlled by it (immediately after the distribution) each of which is engaged in the active conduct of a trade or business.

(2) *Active conduct of a trade or business immediately after distribution.*—(i) *In general.*—For purposes of section 355(b), a corporation shall be treated as engaged in the "active conduct of a trade or business" immediately after the distribution if the assets and activities of the corporation satisfy the requirements and limitations described in paragraph (b)(2)(ii), (iii), and (iv) of this section.

(ii) *Trade or business.*—A corporation shall be treated as engaged in a trade or business immediately after the distribution if a specific group of activities are being carried on by the corporation for the purpose of earning income or profit, and the activities included in such group include every operation that forms a part of, or a step in, the process of earning income or profit. Such group of activities ordinarily must include the collection of income and the payment of expenses.

(iii) *Active conduct.*—For purposes of section 355(b), the determination whether a trade or business is actively conducted will be made from all of the facts and circumstances. Generally, the corporation is required itself to perform active and substantial management and operational functions. Generally, activities performed by the corporation itself do not include activities performed by persons outside the corporation, including independent contractors. A corporation may satisfy the requirements of this subdivision (iii) through the activities that it performs itself, even though some of its activities are performed by others. Separations of real property all or substantially all of which is occupied prior to the distribution by the distributing or the controlled corporation (or by any corporation controlled directly or indirectly by either of those corporations) will be carefully scrutinized with respect to the requirements of section 355(b) and this § 1.355-3.

(iv) *Limitations.*—The active conduct of a trade or business does not include—

(A) The holding for investment purposes of stock, securities, land, or other property, or

(B) The ownership and operation (including leasing) of real or personal property used in a trade or business, unless the owner performs significant services with respect to the operation and management of the property.

(3) *Active conduct for five-year period preceding distribution.*—Under section 355(b)(2)(B), a trade or business that is relied upon to meet the requirements of section 355(b) must have been actively conducted throughout the five-year period ending on the date of the distribution. For purposes of this subparagraph (3)—

(i) activities which constitute a trade or business under the tests described in paragraph (b)(2) of this section shall be treated as meeting the requirement of the preceding sentence if such activities were actively conducted throughout the 5-year period ending on the date of distribution, and

(ii) the fact that a trade or business underwent change during the five-year period preceding the distribution (for example, by the addition of new or the dropping of old products, changes in production capacity, and the like) shall be disregarded, provided that the changes are not of such a character as to constitute the acquisition of a new or different business. In particular, if a corporation engaged in the active conduct of one trade or business during that five-year period purchased, created, or otherwise acquired another trade or business in the same line of business, then the acquisition of that other business is ordinarily treated as an expansion of the original business, all of which is treated as having been actively conducted during that five-year period, unless that purchase, creation, or other acquisition effects a change of such a character as to constitute the acquisition of a new or different business.

* * *

(c) *Examples.*—The following examples illustrate section 355(b)(2)(A) and (B) and paragraph (b)(1), (2), and (3) of this section. However, a transaction that satisfies these active business requirements will qualify under section 355 only if it satisfies the other requirements of section 355(a) and (b).

Example (1). Corporation X is engaged in the manufacture and sale of soap and detergents and also owns investment securities. X transfers the investment securities to new subsidiary Y and distributes the stock of Y to X's shareholders. Y does not satisfy the requirements of section 355(b) because the holding of investment securities does not constitute the active conduct of a trade or business. See paragraph (b)(2)(iv)(A) of this section.

Example (2). Corporation X owns, manages, and derives rental income from an office building and also owns vacant land. X transfers the land to new subsidiary Y and distributes the stock of Y to X's shareholders. Y will subdivide the land, install streets and utilities, and sell the developed lots to various homebuilders. Y does not satisfy the requirements of section 355(b) because no significant development activities were conducted with respect to the land during the five-year period ending on the date of the distribution. See paragraph (b)(3) of this section.

Example (3). Corporation X owns land on which it conducts a ranching business. Oil has been discovered in the area, and it is apparent that oil may be found under the land on which the ranching business is conducted. X has engaged in no significant activities in connection with its mineral rights. X transfers its mineral rights to new subsidiary Y and distributes the stock of Y to X's shareholders. Y will actively pursue the development of the oil producing potential of the property. Y does not satisfy the requirements of section 355(b) because X engaged in no significant exploitation activities with respect to the mineral rights during the five-year period ending on the date of the distribution. See paragraph (b)(3) of this section.

Example (4). For more than five years, corporation X has conducted a single business of constructing sewage disposal plants and other facilities. X transfers one half of its assets to new subsidiary Y. These assets include a contract for the construction of a sewage disposal plant in State M, construction equipment, cash, and other tangible assets. X retains a contract for the construction of a sewage disposal plant in State N, construction equipment, cash, and other intangible assets. X then distributes the stock of Y to one of X's shareholders in exchange for all of his stock of X. X and Y both satisfy the requirements of section 355(b). See paragraph (b)(3)(i) of this section.

Example (5). For the past six years, corporation X has owned and operated two factories devoted to the production of edible pork skins. The entire output of one factory is sold to one customer, C, while the output of the second factory is sold to C and a number of other customers. To eliminate errors in packaging, X opens a new factory. Thereafter, orders from C are processed and packaged at the two original factories, while the new factory handles only orders from other customers. Eight months after opening the new factory, X transfers it and related business assets to new subsidiary Y and distributes the stock of Y to X's shareholders. X and Y both satisfy the requirements of section 355(b). See paragraph (b)(3)(i) and (ii) of this section.

Example (6). Corporation X has owned and operated a men's retail clothing store in the downtown area of the City of G for nine years and has owned and operated another men's retail clothing store in a suburban area of G for seven years. X transfers the store building, fixtures, inventory, and other assets related to the operations of the suburban store to new subsidiary Y. X also transfers to Y the delivery trucks and delivery personnel that formerly served both stores. Henceforth, X will contract with a local public delivery service to make its deliveries. X retains the warehouses that formerly served both stores. Henceforth, Y will lease warehouse space from an unrelated public warehouse company. X then distributes the stock of Y to X's shareholders. X and Y both satisfy the requirements of section 355(b). See paragraph (b)(3)(i) of this section.

Example (7). For the past nine years, corporation X has owned and operated a department store in the downtown area of the City of G. Three years ago, X acquired a parcel of land in a suburban area of G and constructed a new department store on it. X transfers the suburban store and related business assets to new subsidiary Y and distributes the stock of Y to X's shareholders. After the distribution, each store has its own manager and is operated independently of the other store. X and Y both satisfy the requirements of section 355(b). See paragraph (b)(3)(i) and (ii) of this section.

Example (8). For the past six years, corporation X has owned and operated hardware stores in several states. Two years ago, X purchased all of the assets of a hardware store in State M, where X had not previously conducted business. X transfers the State M store and related business assets to new subsidiary Y and distributes the stock of Y to X's shareholders. After the distribution, the State M store has its own manager and is operated independently of the other stores. X and Y both satisfy the requirements of section 355(b). See paragraph (b)(3)(i) and (ii) of this section.

Example (9). For the past eight years, corporation X has engaged in the manufacture and sale of household products. Throughout this period, X has maintained a research department for use in connection with its manufacturing activities. The research department has 30 employees actively engaged in the development of new products. X transfers the research department to new subsidiary Y and distributes the stock of Y to X's shareholders. After the distribution, Y continues its research operations on a contractual basis with several corporations, including X. X and Y both satisfy the requirements of section 355(b). See paragraph (b)(3)(i) of this section. The result in this example is the same if, after the distribution, Y continues its research operations but furnishes its services only to X. See paragraph (b)(3)(i) of this section. However, see § 1.355-2(d)(2)(iv)(C) (related function device factor) for possible evidence of device.

Example (10). For the past six years, corporation X has processed and sold meat products. X derives income from no other source. X separates the sales function from the processing function by transferring the business assets related to the sales function and cash for working capital to new subsidiary Y. X then distributes the stock of Y to X's shareholders. After the distribution, Y purchases for resale the meat products processed by X. X and Y both satisfy the requirements of section 355(b). See paragraph (b)(3)(i) of this section. However, see § 1.355-2(d)(2)(iv)(C) (related function device factor) for possible evidence of device.

Example (11). For the past eight years, corporation X has been engaged in the manufacture and sale of steel and steel products. X owns all of the stock of corporation Y, which, for the past six years, has owned and operated a coal mine for the sole purpose of supplying X's coal requirements in the manufacture of steel. X distributes the stock of Y to X's shareholders. X and Y both satisfy the requirements of section 355(b). See paragraph (b)(3)(i) of this section. However, see § 1.355-2(d)(2)(iv)(C) (related function device factor) for possible evidence of device.

Example (12). For the past seven years, corporation X, a bank, has owned an eleven-story office building, the ground floor of which X has occupied in the conduct of its banking business. The remaining ten floors are rented to various tenants. Throughout this seven-year period, the building has been managed and maintained by employees of the bank. X transfers the building to new subsidiary Y and distributes the stock of Y to X's shareholders. Henceforth, Y will manage the building, negotiate leases, seek new tenants, and repair and maintain the building. X and Y both satisfy the requirements of section 355(b). See paragraph (b)(3) of this section.

Example (13). For the past nine years, corporation X, a bank, has owned a two-story building, the ground floor and one half of the second floor of which X has occupied in the conduct of its banking business. The other half of the second floor has been rented as storage space to a neighboring retail merchant. X transfers the building to new subsidiary Y and distributes the stock of Y to X's shareholders. After the distribution, X leases from Y the space in the building that it formerly occupied. Under the lease, X will repair and maintain its portion of the building and pay property taxes and insurance. Y does not satisfy the requirements of section 355(b) because it is not engaged in the active conduct of a trade or business immediately after the distribution. See paragraph (b)(2)(iv)(A) of this section. This example does not address the question of whether the activities of X with respect to the building prior to the separation would constitute the active conduct of a trade or business. [Reg. § 1.355-3.]

□ [*T.D.* 6152, 12-2-55. *Amended by T.D.* 8238, 1-5-89.]

Proposed Amendments to Regulation

§ 1.355-3. Active conduct of a trade or business.—(a) *General requirements.*—Under section 355(b)(1), a distribution of stock, or stock and securities, of controlled (as defined in paragraph (c)(2) of this section) qualifies under section 355 only if—

(1) Distributing (as defined in paragraph (c)(3) of this section) and controlled are each engaged in the active conduct of a trade or business immediately after the distribution (section 355(b)(1)(A)); or

(2) Immediately before the distribution, distributing had no assets other than stock or securities of the controlled corporations (without regard to paragraph (b)(1)(ii) of this section), and each of the controlled corporations is engaged in the active conduct of a trade or business immediately after the distribution (section 355(b)(1)(B)). A *de minimis* amount of assets held by distributing shall be disregarded for purposes of this paragraph (a)(2).

(b) *Active conduct of a trade or business defined.*—(1) *In general.*—(i) *Directly engaged in a trade or business.*—Section 355(b)(2) provides rules for determining whether a corporation is treated as engaged in the active conduct of a trade or business under section 355(b)(1). Section 355(b)(2)(A) and (b)(3)(A) provides that a corporation is treated as engaged in the active conduct of a trade or business if and only if such corporation is engaged in the active conduct of a trade or business. Accordingly, except as provided in paragraph (b)(1)(ii) of this section, a corporation is not treated as engaged in the active conduct of a trade or business under such Internal Revenue Code section solely as a result of substantially all of its assets consisting of stock, or stock and securities, of one or more corporations controlled by it (immediately after the distribution) each of which is engaged in the active conduct of a trade or business.

(ii) *Treatment of a separate affiliated group.*—Under section 355(b)(3)(B), solely for purposes of determining whether a corporation is engaged in the active conduct of a trade or business, all members of a corporation's separate affiliated group (SAG) (as defined in paragraph (b)(1)(iii) of this section) shall be treated as one corporation. This treatment applies for all purposes of determining whether a corporation is engaged in the active conduct of a trade or business. Accordingly, for this purpose, transfers of assets (or activities) that are owned (or performed) by the SAG immediately before and immediately after the transfer are disregarded and are not acquisitions under paragraph (b)(4) of this section. Further, a transaction that results in a corporation becoming a subsidiary SAG member (a SAG member that is not the common parent of such SAG) is treated as an acquisition of any assets (or activities) that are owned (or performed) by the acquired corporation at such time. Therefore, the acquisition of additional stock of a current subsidiary SAG member has no effect for purposes of applying paragraph (b)(4)(i)(A) of this section.

(iii) *Separate affiliated group defined.*—A corporation's SAG is the affiliated group which would be determined under section 1504(a) if such corporation were the common parent and section 1504(b) did not apply. Thus, the separate affiliated group of distributing (DSAG) is the affiliated group that consists of distributing as the common parent and all corporations affiliated with distributing through stock ownership described in section 1504(a)(1)(B) (regardless of whether the corporations are includible corporations under section 1504(b)). The separate affiliated group of controlled (CSAG) is determined in a similar manner (with controlled as the common parent). Accordingly, prior to a distribution, the DSAG may include CSAG members if the applicable ownership requirements are met. Further, the determination of whether a corporation is a DSAG or CSAG member shall be made separately for each distribution, and without regard to whether such corporation is a SAG member with respect to any other distribution. Any reference to DSAG or CSAG is a reference to distributing or controlled, respectively, if such corporation is not the common parent of a SAG (that is, such corporation does not own stock in any corporation that is a subsidiary member of its SAG). Further, any reference to a SAG is a reference to distributing or controlled, as the context may require, if such corporation is not the common parent of a SAG.

(2) *Active conduct of a trade or business immediately after the distribution.*—(i) *In general.*—For purposes of section 355(b), a corporation shall be treated as engaged in the active conduct of a trade or business immediately after the distribution if the assets and activities of the corporation satisfy the requirements and limitations described in paragraphs (b)(2)(ii), (b)(2)(iii), and (b)(2)(iv) of this section. See paragraph (b)(2)(v) of this section for additional special rules that apply to determine whether a corporation is attributed the trade or business assets and activities of a partnership.

(ii) *Trade or business.*—A corporation shall be treated as engaged in a trade or business immediately after the distribution if a specific group of activities is being carried on by the corporation for the purpose of earning income or profit, and the activities included in such group include every operation that forms a part of, or a step in, the process of earning income or profit. Such group of activities ordinarily must include the collection of income and the payment of expenses.

(iii) *Active conduct.*—For purposes of section 355(b), the determination of whether a trade or business is actively conducted will be made from all of the facts and circumstances. Generally, the corporation is required itself to perform active and substantial management and operational functions. Activities performed by a corporation include activities performed by employees of an affiliate (as defined in paragraph (c)(1) of this section), and in certain cases by shareholders of a closely held corporation, if such activities are performed for the corporation. For example, activities performed by a corporation include activities performed for the corporation by its sole shareholder. However, the activities of employees of affiliates (or, in certain cases, shareholders) are only taken into account during the period such corporations are affiliates (or persons are shareholders) of the corporation. A corporation will not be treated as engaged in the active conduct of a trade or business unless it (or its SAG, or a partnership from which the trade or business assets and activities are attributed) is the principal owner of the goodwill and significant assets of the trade or business for Federal income tax purposes. Activities performed by a corporation generally do not include activities performed by persons outside the corporation, including independent contractors, unless those activities are performed by employees of an affiliate (or, in certain cases, by shareholders). However, a corporation may satisfy the requirements of this paragraph (b)(2)(iii) through the activities that it performs itself, even though some of its activities are performed by persons that are not its employees, or employees of an affiliate (or, in certain cases, shareholders). Separations of real property all or substantially all of which is occupied before the distribution by the DSAG or CSAG will be carefully scrutinized in applying the requirements of section 355(b) and this section.

(iv) *Limitations.*—The active conduct of a trade or business does not include—

(A) The holding for investment purposes of stock, securities, land, or other property; or

(B) The ownership and operation (including leasing) of real or personal property used in a trade or business, unless the owner performs significant services with respect to the operation and management of the property.

(v) *Partner attributed the trade or business assets and activities of a partnership.*—(A) *In general.*—For purposes of section 355(b), a partner in a partnership will be attributed the trade or business assets and activities of that partnership during the period that such partner satisfies the requirements of paragraph (b)(2)(v)(B) or (b)(2)(v)(C) of this section. However, for purposes of this paragraph (b)(2)(v), the stock of a corporation owned by the partnership is not attributed to a partner. For purposes of determining the activities that are conducted by the partnership that may be attributed to the partner under this paragraph (b)(2)(v), the activities of independent contractors, and partners that are not affiliates (or, in certain cases, shareholders) of the partner, are not taken into account. For this purpose, the activities of partners that are affiliates (or, in certain cases, shareholders) of the partner are only taken into account during the period that such partners are affiliates (or, in certain cases, shareholders) of the partner.

(B) *Significant interest.*—The trade or business assets and activities of a partnership will be attributed to a partner if the partner (or its SAG) directly (or indirectly through one or more other partnerships) owns a significant interest in the partnership.

(C) *Meaningful interest.*—The trade or business assets and activities of a partnership will be attributed to a partner if the partner or affiliates (or, in certain cases, shareholders) of the partner performs active and substantial management functions for the partnership with respect to the trade or business assets and activities (for example, makes decisions regarding significant business issues of the partnership and regularly participates in the overall supervision, direction, and control of the employees performing the operational functions for the partnership), and the partner (or its SAG) directly (or indirectly through one or more other partnerships) owns a meaningful interest in the partnership. Whether such active and substantial management functions are performed with respect to the trade or business assets and activities of the partnership will be determined from all of the facts and circumstances. The number of partners providing management functions will not be determinative.

(D) *Other factors.*—In deciding whether the requirements of paragraph (b)(2)(v)(B) or (b)(2)(v)(C) of this section are satisfied, the formal description of the partnership interest (for example, general or limited) will not be determinative and the extent to which the partner is responsible for liabilities of the partnership will not be relevant.

(3) *Active conduct for the pre-distribution period.*—(i) *In general.*—Under section 355(b)(2), a trade or business that is relied upon to meet the requirements of section 355(b) must have been actively conducted throughout the pre-distribution period (as defined in paragraph (c)(4) of this section) by the DSAG or CSAG, or actively conducted throughout the pre-distribution period and acquired during such period by the DSAG or CSAG in a transaction in which no gain or loss is recognized as provided in paragraph (b)(4) of this section. For purposes of section 355(b)(2)(B), activities that constitute a trade or business under paragraph (b)(2) of this section shall be treated as described in the preceding sentence if such activities were actively conducted throughout the pre-distribution period.

(ii) *Change and expansion.*—The fact that a trade or business underwent change during the pre-distribution period (for example, by the addition of new or the dropping of old products, changes in production capacity, and the like) shall be disregarded, provided that the changes are not of such a character as to constitute the acquisition of a new or different business. In particular, if a SAG engaged in the active conduct of one trade or business during the pre-distribution period (the original business) purchased, created, or otherwise acquired (either directly, through an interest in a partnership, or as a result of a corporation becoming a subsidiary SAG member) another trade or business (the acquired business) in the same line of business, the acquisition of the acquired business is ordinarily treated as an expansion of the original business, all of which is treated as having been actively conducted by the acquiring SAG during the pre-distribution period, unless the acquired business effects a change of such a character as to constitute the acquisition of a new or different business. For purposes of this paragraph (b)(3)(ii), in determining whether an acquired business is in the same line of business as the original business, all facts and circumstances shall be considered, including the following—

(A) Whether the product of the acquired business is similar to that of the original business;

(B) Whether the business activities associated with the operation of the acquired business are the same as the business activities associated with the operation of the original business; and

(C) Whether the operation of the acquired business involves the use of the experience and know-how that the owner of the original business developed in the operation of the original business or, alternatively, whether the operation of the acquired business draws to a significant extent on the existing experience and know-how of the owner of the original business and the success of the acquired business will depend in large measure on the goodwill associated with the original business and the name of the original business.

(iii) *Certain transactions with partnerships that do not constitute acquisitions.*—If a partner is attributed the trade or business assets and activities of a partnership under paragraph (b)(2)(v) of this section, the partner's acquisition of such trade or business assets and activities from the partnership is not, in and of itself, the acquisition of a new or different trade or business. In addition, if a partner transfers to a partnership trade or business assets and activities that the partner actively conducted immediately before the transfer and, immediately after the transfer, the partner is attributed the trade or business assets and activities of the partnership under paragraph (b)(2)(v) of this section, such transfer is not, in and of itself, the acquisition of a new or different trade or business by the transferor partner.

(4) *Special rules for an acquisition of a trade or business.*—(i) *In general.*—(A) *Application of section 355(b)(2)(C).*—Under section 355(b)(2)(C) and (b)(3), a trade or business or an interest in a partnership engaged in a trade or business relied on to meet the requirements of section 355(b) must not have been acquired by either the DSAG or CSAG during the pre-distribution period unless it was acquired in a transaction in which no gain or loss was recognized. Further, a trade or business must not have been acquired by either the DSAG or CSAG during the pre-distribution period as a result of a corporation becoming a subsidiary SAG member unless such corporation became a subsidiary SAG member as a result of one or more transactions in which no gain or loss was recognized or by reason of such transactions combined with acquisitions before the pre-distribution period. This paragraph (b)(4)(i)(A) also applies with respect to any acquisition during the pre-distribution period of a trade or business, an interest in a partnership engaged in a trade or business, or stock of a corporation engaged in a trade or business by a corporation that later becomes a subsidiary SAG member. See paragraphs (b)(4)(iv)(C) and (b)(4)(iv)(D) of this section regarding the application of this paragraph (b)(4)(i)(A) to certain multi-step acquisitions.

(B) *Application of section 355(b)(2)(D).*—Under section 355(b)(2)(D), control of distributing must not have been acquired (at the time it was conducting the trade or business to be relied on) directly or indirectly by any distributee corporation, and control of controlled must not have been acquired (at the time it was conducting the trade or business to be relied on) directly or indirectly by the DSAG, during the pre-distribution period in one or more transactions in which gain or loss was recognized. This paragraph (b)(4)(i)(B) also applies with respect to any acquisition of stock of controlled during the pre-distribution period by a corporation that later becomes a DSAG member. For purposes of this paragraph (b)(4)(i)(B), and paragraphs (b)(4)(iii)(C) and (b)(4)(iv)(B) of this section, all distributee corporations that are affiliates shall be treated as one distributee corporation. This paragraph (b)(4)(i)(B) does not apply with respect to an acquisition of stock of any corporation other than distributing or controlled. See paragraph (b)(4)(iv)(B) of this section regarding the application of this paragraph (b)(4)(i)(B) to certain multi-step acquisitions of control. Further, see paragraph (b)(4)(iv)(F) of this section regarding certain acquisitions of stock in controlled to which paragraph (b)(4)(i)(A) of this section (and not this paragraph (b)(4)(i)(B)) applies.

(C) *Gain or loss recognized.*—Any reference to gain or loss recognized includes gain or loss treated as recognized under paragraphs (b)(4)(ii) or (b)(4)(iv) of this section.

(ii) *Certain transactions treated as transactions in which gain or loss is recognized.*—The common purpose of section 355(b)(2)(C) and (D) is to prevent the direct or indirect acquisition of the trade or business to be relied on by a corporation in exchange for assets in anticipation of a distribution to which section 355 would otherwise apply. Generally, if a DSAG member or controlled acquires the trade or business solely in exchange for distributing stock, distributing acquires control of controlled solely in exchange for distributing stock, or controlled acquires the trade or business from distributing solely in exchange for stock of controlled, in a transaction in which no gain or loss was recognized, the requirements of section 355(b)(2)(C) and (D) are satisfied. On the other hand, if the trade or business is acquired in exchange for assets of distributing (other than stock of a corporation in control of distributing used in a reorganization) the requirements of section 355(b)(2)(C) and (D) are generally not satisfied. For example, acquisitions by controlled (while controlled by distributing) from an unrelated party made in exchange for controlled stock have the effect of an indirect acquisition by distributing in exchange for distributing's assets. Such acquisitions violate the purpose of section 355(b)(2)(C) even if no gain or loss is recognized. Therefore, as provided in paragraphs (b)(4)(ii)(A) and (b)(4)(ii)(B) of this section, if the DSAG or CSAG acquires a trade or business, an interest in a partnership engaged in a trade or business, or stock of a corporation engaged in a trade or business in exchange for assets of the DSAG in a transaction in which no gain or loss is recognized, for purposes of paragraph (b)(4)(i) of this section such acquisition will be treated as one in which gain or loss is recognized.

(A) *Certain tax-free acquisitions made in exchange for assets.*—An acquisition paid for in whole or in part, directly or indirectly, with assets of the DSAG will be treated as an acquisition in which gain or loss is recognized even if no gain or loss is actually recognized. Acquisitions described in this paragraph (b)(4)(ii)(A) include for example, a transaction in which the DSAG or CSAG acquires stock of a corporation engaged in the trade or business to be relied on by transferring assets not constituting the trade or business to be relied on to such corporation in exchange for stock of such corporation, the DSAG or CSAG acquires an interest in a partnership engaged in the trade or business to be relied on by contributing assets not constituting the trade or business to be relied on to the partnership, the DSAG or CSAG acquires stock of a corporation engaged in the trade or business in an exchange to which section 304(a)(1) applies, or distributing acquires a trade or business in exchange for its stock and assets in a transaction in which no loss is recognized by virtue of section 351(b). See also paragraph (b)(4)(iv)(E) of this section regarding the extent to which an acquisition involving the issuance of subsidiary stock constitutes an acquisition paid for with assets. However, the assumption by the DSAG or CSAG of liabilities of a transferor shall not, in and of itself, be treated as the payment of assets if such assumption is not treated as the payment of money or other property under any other applicable provision. In addition, an acquisition in which no gain or loss is recognized consisting of a pro rata distribution to which section 355 applies (to the extent the stock with respect to which the distribution is made was not acquired during the pre-distribution period in a transaction in which gain or loss was recognized), a distribution from a partnership that is explicitly excluded from paragraph (b)(4)(ii)(B) of this section, a reorganization described in section 368(a)(1)(E) or (F), and an exchange to which section 1036 applies, are not acquisitions described in this paragraph (b)(4)(ii)(A).

(B) *Distributions from partnerships.*—An acquisition consisting of a distribution from a partnership is generally an acquisition paid for with assets of the DSAG, and will be treated as an acquisition in which gain or loss is recognized even if no gain or loss is actually recognized. However, an acquisition consisting of a pro rata distribution from a partnership of stock or an interest in lower-tier partnership is not an acquisition described in this paragraph (b)(4)(ii)(B) (and consequently not described in paragraph (b)(4)(ii)(A) of this section) to the extent the distributee partner did not acquire the interest in the distributing partnership during the pre-distribution period in a transaction in which gain or loss was recognized and to the extent the distributing partnership did not acquire the distributed stock or partnership interest within such period. This paragraph (b)(4)(ii)(B) (and consequently paragraph (b)(4)(ii)(A) of this section) does not apply to any partnership distribution to which paragraph (b)(3)(iii) of this section (regarding distributions from partnerships that are not, in and of themselves, the acquisition of a new or different trade or business) applies.

(iii) *Certain transactions in which recognized gain or loss is disregarded.*—The common purpose of section 355(b)(2)(C) and (D) is to prevent the direct or indirect acquisition of the trade or business to be relied on by a corporation in exchange for assets in anticipation of a distribution to which section 355 would otherwise apply. An additional purpose of section 355(b)(2)(D) is to prevent a distributee corporation from acquiring control of distributing in anticipation of a distribution to which section 355 would otherwise apply, enabling the disposition of controlled stock without recognizing the appropriate amount of gain. The acquisitions described in paragraphs (b)(4)(iii)(A) through (b)(4)(iii)(C) of this section are not the types of acquisitions to which section 355(b)(2)(C) or (D) is intended to apply. Therefore, for purposes of paragraph (b)(4)(i) of this section, the recognition of gain or loss is disregarded if a trade or business, an interest in a partnership engaged in a trade or business, or stock of a corporation engaged in a trade or business is acquired in a transaction described in any of paragraphs (b)(4)(iii)(A) through (b)(4)(iii)(C) of this section.

(A) *Transfers to controlled.*—An acquisition by the CSAG from the DSAG provided the DSAG controls controlled immediately after the acquisition.

(B) *Cash for fractional shares.*—An acquisition that would satisfy the requirements of paragraph (b)(4)(i) of this section but for the payment of cash to shareholders for fractional shares in the transaction, provided that the cash paid represents a mere rounding off of the fractional shares in the exchange and is not separately bargained for consideration.

(C) *Certain acquisitions of control of distributing.*—A direct or indirect acquisition by a distributee corporation of control of distributing, in one or more transactions, where the basis of the acquired distributing stock in the hands of the distributee corporation is determined in whole by reference to the transferor's basis. This paragraph (b)(4)(iii)(C) is only applicable with respect to a distribution by the acquired distributing, and does not apply for purposes of any subsequent distribution by any distributee corporation.

(iv) *Operating rules for acquisitions.*—(A) *Predecessors.*—References to a corporation shall include references to a predecessor of such corporation. For this purpose, a predecessor of a corporation is a corporation that transfers its assets to such corporation in a transaction to which section 381 applies.

(B) *Certain multi-step acquisitions of control of distributing or controlled.*—A distributee corporation's acquisition of stock in distributing or a DSAG's acquisition of stock in controlled in one or more transactions in which gain or loss was recognized during the pre-distribution period will not prevent a distributee corporation's acquisition of distributing stock or a DSAG's acquisition of controlled stock constituting control of distributing or controlled in one or more separate transactions in which no gain or loss is recognized from satisfying the requirements of paragraph (b)(4)(i)(B) of this section, provided that, at the time control of distributing or controlled is first acquired, the acquiring distributee corporation owns an amount of distributing stock or the acquiring DSAG owns an amount of controlled stock, as the case may be, constituting control that was acquired in one or more transactions in which no gain or loss was recognized or by reason of such transactions combined with acquisitions before the pre-distribution period. The principles of this paragraph (b)(4)(iv)(B) will be applied with respect to an indirect acquisition of distributing or controlled stock.

(C) *Certain multi-step acquisitions of a subsidiary SAG member.*—An acquisition of stock in a corporation (target) by a SAG in one or more transactions in which gain or loss was recognized during the pre-distribution period will not prevent a SAG's acquisition of target stock resulting in target becoming a subsidiary SAG member in one or more separate transactions in which no gain or loss is recognized from satisfying the requirements of paragraph (b)(4)(i)(A) of this section, provided that, at the time that target first becomes a subsidiary SAG member, the SAG owns an amount of target stock meeting the requirements of section 1504(a)(2) that was acquired in one or more transactions in which no gain or loss was recognized or by reason of such transactions combined with acquisitions before the pre-distribution period. The principles of this paragraph (b)(4)(iv)(C) will be applied with respect to an indirect acquisition of target stock by the SAG.

(D) *Certain multi-step asset acquisitions.*—Notwithstanding paragraph (b)(4)(i)(A) of this section, if immediately before a SAG's direct acquisition of a trade or business (or an interest in a partnership engaged in a trade or business) held by a corporation (owner) in a transaction to which section 381 applies and in which no gain or loss is recognized, the SAG owns an amount of stock of the owner that it acquired in one or more transactions during the pre-distribution period in which gain or loss was recognized such that all of the other stock of the owner does not meet the requirements of section 1504(a)(2), such direct acquisition shall be treated as a transaction in which gain or loss was recognized. The principles of this paragraph (b)(4)(iv)(D) will be applied with respect to an indirect acquisition of the owner stock by the SAG.

(E) *Acquisitions involving the issuance of subsidiary stock.*—If a SAG directly or indirectly owns stock of a subsidiary (including a subsidiary SAG member) and the subsidiary directly or indirectly acquires a trade or business, an interest in a partnership engaged in a trade or business, or stock of a corporation engaged in a trade or business from a person other than such SAG in exchange for stock of such subsidiary in a transaction in which no gain or loss is recognized (the acquisition), solely for purposes of applying this paragraph (b)(4) with respect to the trade or business, partnership interest, or stock acquired by the subsidiary in the acquisition, the subsidiary's stock directly or indirectly owned by the SAG immediately after the acquisition is treated as acquired at the time of the acquisition in a transaction in which gain or loss is recognized.

(F) *Acquisitions of controlled stock where controlled is or becomes a DSAG member.*—With respect to an acquisition of stock in controlled, if controlled is or becomes a DSAG member, paragraph (b)(4)(i)(A) of this section applies and paragraph (b)(4)(i)(B) of this section does not apply for purposes of determining whether the requirements of section 355(b) are satisfied with respect to controlled.

(G) *Treatment of stock received in certain tax-free exchanges.*—Any stock received in a reorganization described in section 368(a)(1)(E) or (F), or in an exchange to which section 1036 applies, in which no gain or loss is recognized is treated as acquired in the same manner as the stock surrendered.

(H) *Situations where the separate existence of a subsidiary SAG member is respected.*—The separate existence of a subsidiary SAG member will be respected for purposes of determining whether a transaction qualifies for nonrecognition treatment under other provisions of the Internal Revenue Code. For example, for purposes of determining whether section 351 applies or whether the transaction qualifies as a reorganization described in section 368(a), the separate existence of the subsidiary SAG member is respected.

(c) *Definitions.*—For purposes of this section the following definitions apply:

(1) *Affiliate.*—An affiliate is any member of an affiliated group as defined in section 1504(a) (without regard to section 1504(b)).

(2) *Controlled.*—*Controlled* is the controlled corporation.

(3) *Distributing.*—*Distributing* is the distributing corporation.

(4) *Pre-distribution period.*—The *pre-distribution period* is the five-year period ending on the date of the distribution.

(d) *Conventions and examples.*—(1) *Conventions.*—The examples in paragraph (d)(2) of this section illustrate section 355(b) and this section. No inference should be drawn from any of these examples as to whether any requirements of section 355 other than those of section 355(b), as specified, are satisfied. Throughout these examples, C, D, D2, P, S, S1, S2, S3, T, X, Y, and Z are corporations, and Partnership is an entity that is treated as a partnership for Federal income tax purposes under § 301.7701-3 of this chapter. Further, assume any transfer described in *Examples 1* through *25* that is not identified as a purchase (defined in paragraph (d)(1)(iii) of this section) satisfies all the requirements of paragraph (b)(4) of this section as a transaction in which no gain or loss is recognized. Except as otherwise provided, for more than five years D has owned section 368(c) stock (as defined in paragraph (d)(1)(iv) of this section) but not section 1504(a)(2) stock (as defined in paragraph (d)(1)(v) of this section) of C. Furthermore, the following definitions apply:

(i) *ATB.*—*ATB* is any active trade or business. ATB1 and ATB2 are not in the same line of business under paragraph (b)(3)(ii) of this section.

(ii) *New subsidiary.*—A *new subsidiary* is a newly formed wholly owned corporation.

(iii) *Purchase.*—A *purchase* is an acquisition for cash.

(iv) *Section 368(c) stock.*—*Section 368(c) stock* is stock constituting control within the meeting of section 368(c).

(v) *Section 1504(a)(2) stock.*—*Section 1504(a)(2) stock* is stock meeting the requirements of section 1504(a)(2).

(2) *Examples.*—Generally, *Examples 1* and *2* illustrate the general requirements in paragraph (a) of this section, *Examples 3* through *9* illustrate the SAG rules in paragraphs (b)(1)(ii) and (b)(1)(iii) of this section, *Examples 10* through *25* illustrate the rules regarding the active trade or business and active conduct for the pre-distribution period in paragraphs (b)(2) and (b)(3) of this section, *Examples 26* through *40* illustrate the acquisition rules in paragraphs (b)(4)(i) through (b)(4)(iii) of this section, and *Examples 41* through *51* illustrate the operating rules for acquisitions in paragraph (b)(4)(iv) of this section. The examples are as follows:

Example 1. Spin-off. For more than five years, D and C have engaged in the active conduct of ATB1 and ATB2, respectively. D distributes the C stock to the D shareholders, and each corporation continues the active conduct of its respective trade or business. Because both D and C are engaged in the active conduct of a trade or business immediately after the distribution and such trades or businesses have been actively conducted by such corporations throughout the pre-distribution period, the requirements of section 355(b) have been satisfied. See paragraphs (a)(1) and (b)(3) of this section.

Example 2. Split-up. The facts are the same as *Example 1* except that D transfers all of its assets (including ATB1) other than the C stock to new subsidiary S, and then distributes the C stock and S stock to the D shareholders. Because C and S are respectively engaged in the active conduct of ATB2 and ATB1 immediately after the distribution, ATB2 has been actively conducted by C throughout the pre-distribution period, and together D (prior to the transfer to S) and S (after the transfer to S) have actively conducted ATB1 throughout the pre-distribution period, the requirements of section 355(b) have been satisfied. See paragraphs (a)(2) and (b)(3) of this section.

* * *

Example 16. Horizontal division - research. For more than five years, D has engaged in the active conduct of manufacturing and sale of household products. Throughout this period, D has maintained a research department for use in connection with its manufacturing activities. The research department has 30 employees actively engaged in the development of new products. D transfers the research department (which has significant assets and goodwill) to new subsidiary C and distributes the C stock to the D shareholders. After the distribution, C continues its research operations on a contractual basis with several corporations, including D. D and C both satisfy the requirements of section 355(b). See paragraphs (b)(2) and (b)(3)(i) of this section. The result is the same if, after the distribution, C continues its research operations but furnishes its services only to D. See paragraphs (b)(2) and (b)(3)(i) of this section. However, see §1.355-2(d)(2)(iv)(C) (related function device factor) for possible evidence of device.

Example 17. Horizontal division - sales. For more than five years, D has engaged in the active conduct of processing and selling meat products. D derives income from no other source. D separates the sales function from the processing function by transferring the significant business assets related to the sales function, the goodwill associated with the sales function, and cash for working capital to new subsidiary C. D then distributes the C stock to the D shareholders. After the distribution, C purchases for resale the meat products processed by D. D and C both satisfy the requirements of section 355(b). See paragraphs (b)(2) and (b)(3)(i) of this section. However, see §1.355-2(d)(2)(iv)(C) (related function device factor) for possible evidence of device.

Example 18. Expansion and vertical division - location. For more than five years, D has engaged in the active conduct of owning and operating hardware stores in several states. In year 6, D purchased all of the assets of a hardware store in State M, where D had not previously conducted business. In year 8, D transfers the State M hardware store and related significant assets and goodwill to new subsidiary C and distributes the C stock to the D shareholders. After the distribution, the State M hardware store has its own manager and is operated independently of the other stores. Because—

(i) The product of the State M hardware store is similar to the product of D's hardware stores in the other states;

(ii) The business activities associated with the operation of the State M hardware store are the same as the business activities associated with the operation of D's hardware stores in the other states; and

(iii) The operation of a hardware store in State M involves the use of the experience and know-how that D developed in the operation of the hardware stores in the other states, the hardware store in State M is in the same line of business as the hardware stores in the other states. Therefore, the acquisition of the State M hardware store constitutes an expansion of D's existing business and its acquisition does not constitute the acquisition of a new or different business under paragraph (b)(3)(ii) of this section. Accordingly, D and C both satisfy the requirements of section 355(b).

Example 19. Expansion and horizontal division - Internet. For more than five years, D has engaged in the active conduct of operating a retail shoe store business, under the name D. Throughout this period, D's sales are made exclusively to customers who frequent its retail stores in shopping malls and other locations. D's business enjoys favorable name recognition, customer loyalty, and other elements of goodwill in the retail shoe market. D creates an Internet web site and begins selling shoes at retail on the web site. To a significant extent, the operation of the web site draws upon D's existing experience and know-how. The web site is named "D.com" to take advantage of the name recognition, customer loyalty, and other elements of goodwill associated with D and the D name and to enhance the web site's chances for success in its initial stages. Eight months after beginning to sell shoes on the web site, D transfers all of the web site's assets and liabilities (all of which include the significant assets and goodwill associated with the web site's business) to new subsidiary C and distributes the C stock to the D shareholders. The product of the retail shoe store business and the product of the web site are the same (shoes), and the principal business activities of the retail shoe store business are the same as those of the web site (purchasing shoes at wholesale and reselling them at retail). Although selling shoes on a web site requires some know-how not associated with operating a retail store, such as familiarity with different marketing approaches, distribution chains, and technical operations issues, the web site's operation does draw to a significant extent on D's existing experience and know-how, and the web site's success will depend in large measure on the goodwill associated with D and the D name. Therefore, the creation by D of the Internet web site does not constitute the acquisition of a new or different business under paragraph (b)(3)(ii) of this section. Accordingly, it is an expansion of D's retail shoe store business, all of which is treated as having been actively conducted throughout the pre-distribution period. Therefore, D and C both satisfy the requirements of section 355(b).

* * *

[Prop. Reg. § 1.355-3.]

[Proposed 5-8-2007 (corrected 6-5-2007).]

§ 1.355-4. Non pro rata distributions, etc.—Section 355 provides for nonrecognition of gain or loss with respect to a distribution whether or not (a) the distribution is pro rata with respect to all of the shareholders of the distributing corporation, (b) the distribution is pursuant to a plan of reorganization within the meaning of section 368(a)(1)(D), or (c) the shareholder surrenders stock in the distributing corporation. Under section 355, the stock of a controlled corporation may consist of common stock or preferred stock. (See, however, section 306 and the regulations thereunder.) Section 355 does not apply, however, if the substance of a transaction is merely an exchange between shareholders or security holders of stock or securities in one corporation for stock or securities in another corporation. For example, if two individuals, A and B, each own directly 50 percent of the stock of corporation X and 50 percent of the stock of corporation Y, section 355 would not apply to a transaction in which A and B transfer all of their stock of X and Y to a new corporation Z, for all of the stock of Z, and Z then distributes the stock of X to A and the stock of Y to B. [Reg. § 1.355-4.]

□ [*T.D.* 6152, 12-2-55. *Amended by T.D.* 8238, 1-5-89.]

§ 1.355-6. Recognition of gain on certain distributions of stock or securities in controlled corporation.—(a) *Conventions.*—(1) *Examples.*—For purposes of the examples in this section, unless otherwise stated, assume that P, S, T, X, Y, N, HC, D, D1, D2, D3, and C are corporations, A and B are individuals, shareholders are not treated as one person under section 355(d)(7), stock has been owned for more than five years and section 355(d)(6) and paragraph (e)(4) of this section do not apply, no election under section 338 (if available) is made, and all transactions described are respected under general tax principles, including the step transaction doctrine. No inference should be drawn from any example as to whether any requirements of section 355 other than those of section 355(d), as specified, are satisfied.

(2) *Five-year period.*—For purposes of this section, the term five-year period means the five-year period (determined after applying section 355(d)(6) and paragraph (e)(4) of this section) ending on the date of the distribution, but in no event beginning earlier than October 10, 1990.

(3) *Distributing securities.*—For purposes of determining if stock of any controlled corporation received in the distribution is disqualified stock described in section 355(d)(3)(B)(ii)(II) (relating to a distribution of controlled corporation stock on any securities in the distributing corporation acquired by purchase during the five-year period), references in this section to stock of a corporation that is or becomes a distributing corporation includes securities of the corporation. Similarly, a reference to stock in paragraph (c)(4) of this section (relating to a plan or arrangement) includes securities.

(4) *Marketable securities.*—Unless otherwise stated, any reference in this section to marketable stock includes marketable securities.

(b) *General rules and purposes of section 355(d).*—(1) *Disqualified distributions in general.*—In the case of a disqualified distribution, any stock or securities in the controlled corporation shall not be treated as qualified property for purposes of section 355(c)(2) or 361(c)(2). In general, a disqualified distribution is any distribution to which section 355 (or so much of section 356 as relates thereto) applies if, immediately after the distribution—

(i) Any person holds disqualified stock in the distributing corporation that constitutes a 50 percent or greater interest in such corporation; or

(ii) Any person holds disqualified stock in the controlled corporation (or, if stock of more than one controlled corporation is distributed, in any controlled corporation) that constitutes a 50 percent or greater interest in such corporation.

(2) *Disqualified stock.*—(i) *In general.*—*Disqualified stock* is—

(A) Any stock in the distributing corporation acquired by purchase during the five-year period; and

(B) Any stock in any controlled corporation—

(1) Acquired by purchase during the five-year period; or

(2) Received in the distribution to the extent attributable to distributions on any stock in the distributing corporation acquired by purchase during the five-year period.

(ii) *Purchase.*—For the definition of a purchase for purposes of section 355(d) and this section, see section 355(d)(5) and paragraph (d) of this section.

(iii) *Exceptions.*—(A) *Purchase eliminated.*—Stock (or an interest in another entity) that is acquired by purchase (including stock (or another interest) that is treated as acquired by purchase under paragraph (e)(2), (3), or (4) of this section) ceases to be acquired by that purchase if (and when) the basis resulting from the purchase is eliminated. For purposes of this paragraph (b)(2)(iii), basis resulting from the purchase is basis in the stock (or in an interest in another entity) that is directly purchased during the five-year period or that is treated as acquired by purchase during such period under paragraph (e)(2), (3), or (4) of this section.

(B) *Deemed purchase eliminated.*—Stock (or an interest in another entity) that is deemed purchased under section 355(d)(8) or paragraph (e)(1) of this section shall cease to be treated as purchased if (and when) the basis resulting from the purchase that effects the deemed purchase is eliminated.

(C) *Elimination of basis.*—*(1) General rule.* Basis in the stock of a corporation (or in an interest in another entity) is eliminated if (and when) it would no longer be taken into account by any person in determining gain or loss on a sale or exchange of any stock of such corporation (or an interest in the other entity). Basis is not eliminated, however, if it is allocated between stock of two corporations under § 1.358-2(a).

(2) Special rule for transferred and exchanged basis property. Basis of stock (or an interest in another entity) resulting from a purchase (the first purchase) is eliminated if (and when) such stock (or other interest) is subsequently transferred to another person in an exchange or other transfer to which paragraph (e)(2) or (3) of this section applies (the second purchase). The elimination of basis in stock (or in another interest) resulting from the first purchase, however, does not eliminate the basis resulting from the second purchase in the stock (or other interest) that is treated as acquired by purchase by the acquirer in a transaction to which paragraph (e)(2) of this section applies or by the person making the exchange in a transaction to which paragraph (e)(3) of this section applies.

(3) Special rule for split-offs and split-ups.—Under section 355(d)(3)(B)(ii) and paragraph (b)(2)(i)(B)(*2*) of this section, disqualified stock includes controlled corporation stock received in exchange for distributing corporation stock acquired by purchase. Solely for purposes of determining whether controlled corporation stock received in a distribution in exchange for distributing corporation stock is disqualified stock described in that section and paragraph immediately after the distribution, paragraph (b)(2)(iii)(C)(*2*) of this section does not apply to the exchange to eliminate basis resulting from a purchase of that distributing corporation stock (notwithstanding that paragraph (e)(3) of this section applies to the exchange).

(D) *Special rule if basis allocated between two corporations.*—If the shareholder of a distributing corporation, pursuant to § 1.358-2, allocates basis resulting from a purchase between the stock of two or more corporations then, following such allocation, the determination of whether such basis has been eliminated shall be made separately with respect to the stock of each such corporation.

(3) *Certain distributions not disqualified distributions because purposes of section 355(d) not violated.*—(i) *In general.*—Notwithstanding the provisions of section 355(d)(2) and this paragraph (b), a distribution is not a disqualified distribution if the distribution does not violate the purposes of section 355(d) as provided in this paragraph (b)(3). A distribution does not violate the purposes of section 355(d) if the effect of the distribution is neither—

(A) To increase ownership (combined direct and indirect) in the distributing corporation or any controlled corporation by a disqualified person; nor

(B) To provide a disqualified person with a purchased basis in the stock of any controlled corporation.

(ii) *Disqualified person.*—A disqualified person is any person (taking into account section 355(d)(7) and paragraph (c)(4) of this section) that, immediately after a distribution, holds (directly or indirectly under section 355(d)(8) and paragraph (e)(1) of this section) disqualified stock in the distributing corporation or controlled corporation that—

(A) The person—

(1) Acquired by purchase under section 355(d)(5) or (8) and paragraphs (d) and (e) of this section during the five-year period, or

(2) Received in the distribution to the extent attributable to distributions on any stock in the distributing corporation acquired

by purchase under section 355(d)(5) or (8) and paragraphs (d) and (e) of this section by that person during the five-year period; and

(B) Constitutes a 50 percent or greater interest in such corporation (under section 355(d)(4) and paragraph (c) of this section).

(iii) *Purchased basis.*—In general, a purchased basis is basis in controlled corporation stock that is disqualified stock. However, basis in controlled corporation stock that is disqualified stock will not be treated as purchased basis if the controlled corporation stock and any distributing corporation stock with respect to which the controlled corporation stock is distributed are treated as acquired by purchase solely under the attribution rules of section 355(d)(8) and paragraph (e)(1) of this section. The prior sentence will not apply, however, if the distributing corporation stock is treated as acquired by purchase under the attribution rules as a result of the acquisition of an interest in a partnership (the purchased partnership), and following the distribution, the controlled corporation stock is directly held by the purchased partnership (or a chain of partnerships that includes the purchased partnership).

(iv) *Increase in interest because of payment of cash in lieu of fractional shares.*—Any increase in direct or indirect ownership in the distributing corporation or any controlled corporation by a disqualified person because of a payment of cash in lieu of issuing fractional shares will be disregarded for purposes of paragraph (b)(3)(i)(A) of this section if the payment of the cash is solely to avoid the expense and inconvenience of issuing fractional share interests, and does not represent separately bargained for consideration.

(v) *Other exceptions.*—The Commissioner may provide by guidance published in the Internal Revenue Bulletin that other distributions are not disqualified distributions because they do not violate the purposes of section 355(d).

(vi) *Examples.*—The following examples illustrate this paragraph (b)(3):

Example 1. Stock distributed in spin-off; no purchased basis. D owns all of the stock of D1, and D1 owns all the stock of C. A purchases 60 percent of the D stock for cash. Within five years of A's purchase, D1 distributes the C stock to D. A is treated as having purchased 60 percent of the stock of both D1 and C on the date A purchases 60 percent of the D stock under the attribution rules of section 355(d)(8) and paragraph (e)(1) of this section. The C stock received by D is attributable to a distribution on purchased D1 stock under section 355(d)(3)(B)(ii). Accordingly, the D1 and C stock each is disqualified stock under section 355(d)(3) and paragraph (b)(2) of this section, and A is a disqualified person under paragraph (b)(3)(ii) of this section. However, the purposes of section 355(d) under paragraph (b)(3)(i) of this section are not violated. A did not increase direct or indirect ownership in D1 or C. In addition, D's basis in the C stock is not a purchased basis under paragraph (b)(3)(iii) of this section because both the D1 and the C stock are treated as acquired by purchase solely under the attribution rules of section 355(d)(8) and paragraph (e)(1) of this section. Accordingly, D1's distribution of the C stock to D is not a disqualified distribution under section 355(d)(2) and paragraph (b)(1) of this section.

Example 2. Stock distributed in spin-off; purchased basis. The facts are the same as *Example 1,* except that D immediately further distributes the C stock to its shareholders (including A) pro rata. The D and C stock each is disqualified stock under section 355(d)(3) and paragraph (b)(2) of this section, and A is a disqualified person under paragraph (b)(3)(ii) of this section. The purposes of section 355(d) under paragraph (b)(3)(i) of this section are violated. A did not increase direct or indirect ownership in D or C. However, A's basis in the C stock is a purchased basis under paragraph (b)(3)(iii) of this section because the D stock is not treated as acquired by purchase solely under the attribution rules of section 355(d)(8) and paragraph (e)(1) of this section. Accordingly, the further distribution is a disqualified distribution under section 355(d)(2) and paragraph (b)(1) of this section.

Example 3. Stock distributed in split-off with ownership increase; purchased basis. The facts are the same as *Example 1,* except that D immediately further distributes the C stock to A in exchange for A's purchased stock in D. The C stock received by A is attributable to a distribution on purchased D stock under section 355(d)(3)(B)(ii), and A's basis in the C stock is determined by reference to the adjusted basis of A's purchased D stock under paragraph (e)(3) of this section. (Under paragraph (b)(2)(iii)(B)(*3*) of this section, the basis resulting from A's purchase of D stock is not eliminated solely for purposes of determining if the C stock acquired by A is disqualified stock immediately after the distribution, notwithstanding that paragraph (e)(3) of this section applies to the exchange.) Accordingly, the D stock and the C stock each is disqualified stock under section 355(d)(3) and paragraph (b)(2) of this section, and A is a disqualified person under paragraph (b)(3)(ii) of this section. The purposes of section 355(d) under paragraph (b)(3)(i) of this section are violated because A increased its ownership in C from a 60 percent indirect interest to a 100 percent direct interest, and because A's basis in the C stock is a purchased basis under paragraph (b)(3)(iii) of this section. Accordingly, the further distribution is a disqualified distribution under section 355(d)(2) and paragraph (b)(1) of this section.

Example 4. Stock distributed in spin-off; purchased basis. D1 owns all the stock of C. D purchases all of the stock of D1 for cash Within five years of D's purchase of D1, P acquires all of the stock of D1 from D in a section 368(a)(i)(B) reorganization that is not a reorganization under section 368(a)(1)(A) by reason of section 368(a)(2)(E), and D1 distributes all of its C stock to P. P is treated as having acquired the D1 stock by purchase on the date D acquired it under the transferred basis rule of section 355(d)(5)(C) and paragraph (e)(2) of this section. P is treated as having purchased all of the C stock on the date D purchased the D1 stock under the attribution rules of section 355(d)(8) and paragraph (e)(1) of this section, and the C stock received by P is attributable to a distribution on purchased D1 stock under section 355(d)(3)(B)(ii). Accordingly, the D1 and C stock each is disqualified stock under section 355(d)(3) and paragraph (b)(2) of this section, and P is a disqualified person under paragraph (b)(3)(ii) of this section. The purposes of section 355(d) under paragraph (b)(3)(i) of this section are violated. P did not increase direct or indirect ownership in D1 or C. However, P's basis in the C stock is a purchased basis under paragraph (b)(3)(iii) of this section because the D1 stock is not treated as acquired by purchase solely under the attribution rules of section 355(d)(8) and paragraph (e)(1) of this section. Accordingly, D1's distribution of the C stock to P is a disqualified distribution under section 355(d)(2) and paragraph (b)(1) of this section.

Example 5. Stock distributed in split-off with ownership increase; no purchased basis. P owns 50 percent of the stock of D, the remaining D stock is owned by unrelated persons, D owns all the stock of C, and A purchases all of the P stock from the P shareholders. Within five years of A's purchase, D distributes all of the C stock to P in exchange for P's D stock. A is treated as having purchased 50 percent of the stock of both D and C on the date A purchases the P stock under the attribution rules of section 355(d)(8) and paragraph (e)(1) of this section. The C stock received by P is attributable to a distribution on purchased D stock under section 355(d)(3)(B)(ii). Accordingly, the D stock and the C stock each is disqualified stock under section 355(d)(3) and paragraph (b)(2) of this section, and A is a disqualified person under paragraph (b)(3)(ii) of this section. The purposes of section 355(d) under paragraph (b)(3)(i) of this section are violated because, even though P's basis in the C stock is not a purchased basis under paragraph (b)(3)(iii) of this section, A increased its direct or indirect ownership in C from a 50 percent indirect interest to a 100 percent indirect interest. Accordingly, D's distribution of the C stock to P is a disqualified distribution under section 355(d)(2) and paragraph (b)(1) of this section.

Example 6. Stock distributed in split-off with no ownership increase; no purchased basis. A purchases all of the stock of T. T later merges into D in a section 368(a)(1)(A) reorganization and A exchanges its purchased T stock for 60 percent of the stock of D. D owns all of the stock of D1 and D2, D1 and D2 each owns 50 percent of the stock of D3, and D3 owns all of the stock of C. Within five years of A's purchase of the T stock, D3 distributes the C stock to D1 in exchange for all of D1's D3 stock. A is treated as having acquired 60 percent of the D stock by purchase on the date A purchases the T stock under paragraph (e)(3) of this section. A is treated as having purchased 60 percent of the stock of D1, D2, D3, and C on the date A purchases the T stock under the attribution rules of section 355(d)(8) and paragraph (e)(1) of this section. The C stock received by D1 is attributable to a distribution on purchased D3 stock under section 355(d)(3)(B)(ii). Accordingly, the D3 stock and the C stock each is disqualified stock under section 355(d)(3) and paragraph (b)(2) of this section, and A is a disqualified person under paragraph (b)(3)(ii) of this section. However, the purposes of section 355(d) under paragraph (b)(3)(i) of this section are not violated. A did not increase direct or indirect ownership in D3 or C, and D1's basis in the C stock is not a purchased basis under paragraph (b)(3)(iii) of this section because the D3 stock is treated as acquired by purchase solely under the attribution rules of section 355(d)(8) and paragraph (e)(1) of this section. Accordingly, D3's distribution of the C stock to D1 is not a disqualified distribution under section 355(d)(2) and paragraph (b)(1) of this section.

Example 7. Purchased basis eliminated by liquidation; stock distributed in spin-off. P owns 30 percent of the stock of D, D owns all of the stock of D1, and D1 owns all of the stock of C. P purchases the remaining 70 percent of the D stock for cash. Within five years of P's purchase, P liquidates D in a transaction qualifying under sections 332 and 337(a), and D1 then distributes the stock of C to P. Prior to the liquidation, P is treated as having purchased 70 percent of the stock of D1 and C on the date P purchases the D stock under the attribution rules of section 355(d)(8)(B) and paragraph (e)(1) of this section. After the liquidation, however, under paragraph (b)(2)(iii) of this section, P is not treated as having acquired by purchase the D1 or the C stock under section 355(d)(8)(B) and paragraph (e)(1) of this section because P's basis in the D stock is eliminated in the liquidation of D. Under section 334(b)(1), P's basis in the D1 stock is determined by reference to D's basis in the D1 stock and not by reference to P's basis in D. Paragraph (d)(2)(i)(B) of this section does not treat the D1 stock as newly purchased in P's hands because no gain or loss was recognized by D in the liquidation. Accordingly, neither the D1 stock nor the C stock is disqualified stock under section 355(d)(3) and paragraph (b)(2) of this section in P's hands, and the distribution is not a disqualified distribution under section 355(d)(2) and paragraph (b)(1) of this section.

Example 8. Purchased basis eliminated by upstream merger; stock distributed in spin-off. D owns all of the stock of D1, and D1 owns all of the stock of C. P purchases 60 percent of the D stock for cash. Within five years of P's purchase, D merges into P in a section 368(a)(1)(A) reorganization, with the D shareholders other than P receiving solely P stock in exchange for their D stock, and D1 then distributes the stock of C to P. Prior to the merger, P is treated as having purchased 60 percent of the stock of D1 and C on the date P purchases the D stock under the attribution rules of section 355(d)(8) and paragraph (e)(1) of this section. After the merger, however, under paragraph (b)(2)(iii) of this section, P is not treated as having acquired by purchase the D1 or the C stock under section 355(d)(8)(B) and paragraph (e)(1) of this section because P's basis in the D stock is eliminated in the merger. Under section 362(b), P's basis in the D1 stock is determined by reference to D's basis in the D1 stock and not by reference to P's basis in D. Paragraph (d)(2)(i)(B) of this section does not treat the D1 stock as newly purchased in P's hands because no gain or loss was recognized by D in the merger. Accordingly, neither the D1 stock nor the C stock is disqualified stock under section 355(d)(3) and paragraph (b)(2) of this section in P's hands, and the distribution is not a disqualified distribution under section 355(d)(2) and paragraph (b)(1) of this section.

Example 9. Purchased basis eliminated by distribution; stock distributed in spin-off. A purchases all the stock of C for cash on Date 1. D acquires all of the stock of C from A in a section 368(a)(1)(B) reorganization that is not a reorganization under section 368(a)(1)(A) by reason of section 368(A)(1)(E). A receives ten percent of the D stock in the transaction. The remaining D stock is owned by B. Within five years of A's purchase of the C stock, D distributes all the stock of C pro rata to A and B. Under the transferred basis rule of paragraph (e)(2) of this section, D is treated as having purchased all of the C stock on the date A acquired it. Under the exchanged basis rule of paragraph (e)(3) of this section, A is treated as having purchased its D stock on Date 1 and A is treated as having purchased ten percent of the C stock on Date 1 under the attribution rules of section 355(d)(8) and paragraph (e)(3) of this section. Moreover, under paragraph (b)(2)(iii)(C) of this section, A's basis in the C stock resulting from A's Date 1 purchase of C stock is eliminated. After the distribution, A's and B's bases in their C stock are determined by reference to the bases of their D stock under § 1.358-2(a)(2) (and not by reference to D's basis in the C stock). D's basis in the stock of C resulting from its deemed purchase of that stock under paragraph (e)(2) of this section is eliminated by the distribution of the C stock because it would no longer be taken into account by any person in determining gain or loss on the sale of C stock. Therefore, the C stock distributed to A and B is not disqualified stock as a result of D's purchase of C. However, A's basis in its D stock resulting from its deemed purchase of that stock under paragraph (e)(3) of this section is not eliminated. Therefore, A's ten percent interest in the stock of D is disqualified stock. Furthermore, A's ten percent interest in the stock of C is disqualified stock because the distribution of the C stock is attributable to A's D stock that was acquired by purchase. However, there has not been a disqualified distribution because no person, immediately after the distribution, holds disqualified stock in either D or C that constitutes a 50 percent or greater interest in such corporation.

* * *

(4) *Anti-avoidance rule.*—(i) *In general.*—Notwithstanding any provision of section 355(d) or this section, the Commissioner may treat any distribution as a disqualified distribution under section 355(d)(2) and paragraph (b)(1) of this section if the distribution or another transaction or transactions are engaged in or structured with a principal purpose to avoid the purposes of section 355(d) or this section with respect to the distribution. Without limiting the preceding sentence, the Commissioner may determine that the existence of a related person, intermediary, pass-through entity, or similar person (an intermediary) should be disregarded, in whole or in part, if the intermediary is formed or availed of with a principal purpose to avoid the purposes of section 355(d) or this section.

(ii) *Example.*—The following example illustrates this paragraph (b)(4):

Example. Post-distribution redemption. B wholly owns D, which wholly owns C. With a principal purpose to avoid the purposes of section 355(d), A, B, D, and C engage in the following transactions. A purchases 45 of 100 shares of the only class of D stock. Within five years after A's purchase, D distributes all of its 100 shares in C to A and B pro rata. D then redeems 20 shares of B's D stock, and C redeems 20 shares of B's C stock. After the redemption, A owns 45 shares and B owns 35 shares in each of D and C. Under paragraph (b)(4)(i) of this section, the Commissioner may treat A as owning disqualified stock in D and C that constitutes a 50 percent or greater interest in D and C immediately after the distribution. Under that treatment, the distribution is a disqualified distribution under section 355(d)(2) and paragraph (b)(1) of this section.

(c) *Whether a person holds a 50 percent or greater interest.*—(1) *In general.*—Under section 355(d)(4), 50 percent or greater interest means stock possessing at least 50 percent of the total combined voting power of all classes of stock entitled to vote or at least 50 percent of the total value of shares of all classes of stock.

(2) *Valuation.*—For purposes of section 355(d)(4) and this section, all shares of stock within a single class are considered to have the same value. But see paragraph (c)(3)(vii)(A) of this section (determination of whether it is reasonably certain that an option will be exercised).

* * *

(4) *Plan or arrangement.*—(i) *In general.*—Under section 355(d)(7)(B), if two or more persons act pursuant to a plan or arrangement with respect to acquisitions of stock in the distributing corporation or controlled corporation, those persons are treated as one person for purposes of section 355(d).

(ii) *Understanding.*—For purposes of section 355(d)(7)(B), two or more persons who are (or will after an acquisition become) shareholders (or are treated as shareholders under paragraph (c)(3)(ii) of this section) act pursuant to a plan or arrangement with respect to an acquisition of stock only if they have a formal or informal understanding among themselves to make a coordinated acquisition of stock. A principal element in determining if such an understanding exists is whether the investment decision of each person is based on the investment decision of one or more other existing or prospective shareholders. However, the participation by creditors in formulating a plan for an insolvency workout or a reorganization in a title 11 or similar case (whether as members of a creditors' committee or otherwise) and the receipt of stock by creditors in satisfaction of indebtedness pursuant to the workout or reorganization do not cause the creditors to be considered as acting pursuant to a plan or arrangement.

(iii) *Examples.*—The following examples illustrate paragraph (c)(4)(ii) of this section:

Example 1. D has 1,000 shares of common stock outstanding. A group of 20 unrelated individuals who previously owned no D stock (the Group) agree among themselves to acquire 50 percent or more of D's stock. The Group is not a person under section 7701(a)(1). Subsequently, pursuant to their understanding, the members of the Group purchase 600 shares of D common stock from the existing D shareholders (a total of 60 percent of the D stock), with each member purchasing 30 shares. Under paragraph (c)(4)(ii) of this section, the members of the Group have a formal or informal understanding among themselves to make a coordinated acquisition of stock. Their interests are therefore aggregated under section 355(d)(7)(B), and they are treated as one person that purchased 600 shares of D's stock for purposes of section 355(d).

Example 2. D has 1,000 shares of outstanding stock owned by unrelated individuals. D's management is concerned that D may become subject to a takeover bid. In separate meetings, D's management meets with potential investors who own no stock and are friendly to management to convince them to acquire D's stock based on an understanding that D will assemble a group that in the aggregate will acquire more than 50 percent of D's stock. Subsequently, 15 of these investors each purchases four percent of D's outstanding stock. Under paragraph (c)(4)(ii) of this section, the 15 investors have a formal or informal understanding among themselves to make a coordinated acquisition of stock. Their interests are therefore aggregated under section 355(d)(7)(B), and they are treated as one person that purchased 600 shares of D stock for purposes of section 355(d).

Example 3. (i) D has 1,000 shares of outstanding stock owned by unrelated individuals. An investment advisor advises its clients that it believes D's stock is undervalued and recommends that they acquire D stock. Acting on the investment advisor's recommendation, 20 unrelated individuals each purchases 30 shares of the outstanding D stock. Each client's decision was not based on the investment decisions made by one or more other clients. Because there is no formal or informal understanding among the clients to make a coordinated acquisition of D stock, their interests are not aggregated under section

355(d)(7)(B) and they are treated as making separate purchases.

(ii) The facts are the same as in paragraph (i) of this *Example 3*, except that the investment advisor is also the underwriter (without regard to whether it is a firm commitment or best efforts underwriting) for a primary or secondary offering of D stock. The result is the same.

(iii) The facts are the same as in paragraph (i) of this *Example 3*, except that, instead of an investment advisor recommending that clients purchase D stock, the trustee of several trusts qualified under section 401(a) sponsored by unrelated corporations causes each trust to purchase the D stock. The result is the same, provided that the trustee's investment decision made on behalf of each trust was not based on the investment decision made on behalf of one or more of the other trusts.

(iv) *Exception.*—(A) *Subsequent disposition.*—If two or more persons do not act pursuant to a plan or arrangement within the meaning of this paragraph (c)(4) with respect to an acquisition of stock in a corporation (the first corporation), a subsequent acquisition in which such persons exchange their stock in the first corporation for stock in another corporation (the second corporation) in a transaction in which the basis of the second corporation's stock in the hands of such persons is determined in whole or in part by reference to the basis of their stock in the first corporation, will not result in such persons being treated as one person, even if the acquisition of the second corporation's stock is pursuant to a plan or arrangement.

(B) *Example.*—The following example illustrates this paragraph (c)(4)(iv):

Example. In an initial public offering of D stock on Date 1, 100 investors independently purchase one percent each of the D stock. Two years later, D merges into P (in a reorganization described in section 368(a)(1)(A)) and, pursuant to the plan of reorganization, the D shareholders exchange their D stock for 50 percent of the stock of P. The D shareholders approve the plan by a two-thirds vote, as required by state law. Under section 358(a), each shareholder's basis in its P stock is determined by reference to the basis of the D stock it purchased. Under paragraph (e)(3) of this section, the former D shareholders are treated as purchasing their P stock on Date 1. The investors do not become a single person under paragraph (c)(4) of this section with respect to the deemed purchase of the P stock on Date 1 by virtue of their acquisition of the P stock pursuant to the merger on Date 2.

(d) *Purchase.*—(1) *In general.*—(i) *Definition of purchase under section 355(d)(5)(A).*—Under section 355(d)(5)(A), except as otherwise provided in section 355(d)(5)(B) and (C), a *purchase* means any acquisition, but only if—

(A) The basis of the property acquired in the hands of the acquirer is not determined—

(1) In whole or in part by reference to the adjusted basis of such property in the hands of the person from whom acquired; or

(2) Under section 1014(a) or 1022; and

(B) The property is not acquired in an exchange to which section 351, 354, 355, or 356 applies.

(ii) *Section 355 distributions.*—Paragraph (d)(1)(i)(B) of this section includes all section 355 distributions, whether in exchange (in whole or in part) for stock or pro rata.

(iii) *Example.*—The following example illustrates this paragraph (d)(1):

Example. Section 304(a)(1) acquisition. A, who owns all of the stock of P and T, sells the T stock to P for cash. The T stock is not marketable stock under section 355(d)(5)(B)(ii) and paragraph (d)(3)(ii) of this section. A is treated under section 304(a)(1) as receiving a distribution in redemption of the P stock. Under section 302(d). the deemed redemption is treated as a section 301 distribution. Assume that under sections 304(b)(2) and 301 (c)(1), all of the distribution is a dividend. A and P are treated in the same manner as if A had transferred the T stock to P in exchange for stock of P in a transaction to which section 351(a) applies, and P had then redeemed the stock P was treated as issuing in the transaction. Under section 362(a), P's basis in the T stock is determined by reference to A's adjusted basis in the T stock, and there is no basis increase in the T stock because A recognizes no gain on the deemed transfer. Accordingly, P's acquisition of the T stock from A is not a purchase by P under section 355(d)(5)(A)(i)(I) and paragraphs (d)(1)(i)(A)*(1)* and (d)(2)(i)(B) of this section.

(2) *Exceptions to definition of purchase under section 355(d)(5)(A).*—The following acquisitions are not treated as purchases under section 355(d)(5)(A):

(i) *Acquisition of stock in a transaction which includes other property or money.*—(A) *Transferors and shareholders of transferor or distributing corporations.*—*(1) In general.*—An acquisition of stock permitted to be received by a transferor of property without the recognition of gain under section 351(a), or permitted to be received without the recognition of gain under section 354, 355, or 356 is not a purchase to the extent section 358(a)(1) applies to determine the recipient's basis in the stock received, whether or not the recipient recognizes gain under section 351(b) or 356. But see paragraph (e)(3) of this section (interest received in exchange for purchased interest in exchanged basis transaction treated as purchased).

(2) Exception.—To the extent there is received in the exchange or distribution, in addition to stock described in paragraph (d)(2)(i)(A)(*1*) of this section, stock that is other property under section 351(b) or 356(a)(1), the stock is treated as purchased on the date of the exchange or distribution for purposes of section 355(d).

(B) *Transferee corporations.—(1) In general.*—An acquisition of stock by a corporation is not a purchase to the extent section 334(b) or 362(a) or (b) applies to determine the corporation's basis in the stock received. But see section 355(d)(5)(C) and paragraph (e)(2) of this section (purchased property transferred in transferred basis transaction is treated as purchased by transferee).

(2) Exception.—If a corporation acquires stock, the stock is treated as purchased on the date of the stock acquisition for purposes of section 355(d)—

(i) If the liquidating corporation recognizes gain or loss with respect to the transferred stock as described in section 334(b)(1); or

(ii) To the extent the basis of the transferred stock is increased through the recognition of gain by the transferor under section 362(a) or (b).

(C) *Examples.*—The following examples illustrate this paragraph (d)(2)(i):

Example 1. (i) A owns all the stock of T. T merges into D in a transaction qualifying under section 368(a)(1)(A), with A exchanging all of the T stock for D stock and $100 cash. Under section 356(a)(1), A recognizes $100 of the realized gain on the transaction. Under section 358(a)(1), A's basis in the D stock equals A's basis in the T stock, decreased by the $100 received and increased by the gain recognized, also $100. Under paragraph (d)(2)(i)(A) of this section, A is not treated as having purchased the D stock for purposes of section 355(d)(5).

(ii) The facts are the same as in paragraph (i) of this *Example 1*, except that rather than D stock and $100 cash, A receives D stock and stock in C, a corporation not a party to the reorganization, with a fair market value of $100. Under section 358(a)(2), A's basis in the C stock is its fair market value, or $100. Under paragraph (d)(2)(i)(A)(*2*) of this section, A is treated as having purchased the C stock, but not the D stock, for purposes of section 355(d)(5).

Example 2. A purchases all of the stock of D, which is not marketable stock, on Date 1 for $90. Within five years of A's purchase, on Date 2, A contributes the D stock to P in exchange for P stock worth $90 and $10 cash in a transaction qualifying under section 351. A recognizes a gain of $10 as a result of the transfer. Under section 362(a), P's basis in D is $100. P is treated as having purchased 90 percent ($90 worth) of the D stock on Date 1 under section 355(d)(5)(C) and paragraph (e)(2) of this section and as having purchased 10 percent ($10 worth) of the D stock on Date 2 under paragraph (d)(2)(i)(B)(*2*)(*ii*) of this section.

(ii) *Acquisition of stock in a distribution to which section 305(a) applies.*—An acquisition of stock in a distribution qualifying under section 305(a) is not a purchase to the extent section 307(a) applies to determine the recipient's basis. However, to the extent the distribution is of rights to acquire stock, see paragraph (c)(3) of this section for rules regarding options, warrants, convertible obligations, and other similar interests.

(iii) *Section 1036(a) exchange.*—An exchange of stock qualifying under section 1036(a) is not a purchase by either party to the exchange to the extent the basis of the property acquired equals that of the property exchanged under section 1031(d).

(iv) *Section 338 elections.*—(A) *In general.*—Stock acquired in a qualified stock purchase with respect to which a section 338 election (or a section 338(h)(10) election) is made is not treated as a purchase for purposes of section 355(d)(5)(A). However, any stock (or an interest in another entity) held by old target that is treated as purchased by new target is treated as acquired by purchase for purposes of section 355(d)(5)(A) unless a section 338 election or section 338(h)(10) election also is made for that stock. See § 1.338-2T(c) for the definitions of section 338 election, section 338(h)(10) election, old target, and new target.

(B) *Example.*—The following example illustrates this paragraph (d)(2)(iv):

Example. T owns all of the stock of S and no other assets. X acquires all of the T stock from the T shareholders for cash and makes an election under section 338. Under section 338(a) and (b), T, as Old T, is treated as having sold all of its assets at fair market value and purchased the assets as a new corporation,

New T, as of the beginning of the day after the acquisition date. Under paragraph (d)(2)(iv)(A) of this section, X is not treated as having purchased the T stock. Absent a section 338 election or a section 338(h)(10) election with respect to S, New T is treated as having purchased all of the S stock under section 355(d)(5)(A).

(v) *Partnership distributions.*—(A) *Section 732(b).*—An acquisition of stock (or an interest in another entity) in a liquidation of a partner's interest in a partnership in which basis is determined pursuant to section 732(b) is a purchase at the time of the liquidation.

(B) *Section 734(b).*—If the adjusted basis of stock (or an interest in another entity) held by a partnership is increased under section 734(b), a proportionate amount of the stock (or other interest) will be treated as purchased at the time of the basis adjustment, determined by reference to the amount of the basis adjustment (but not in excess of the fair market value of the stock (or other interest) at the time of the adjustment) over the fair market value of the stock (or other interest) at the time of the adjustment.

(3) *Certain section 351 exchanges treated as purchases.*—(i) *In general.*—(A) *Treatment of stock received by transferor.*—Under section 355(d)(5)(B), a purchase includes any acquisition of property in an exchange to which section 351 applies to the extent the property is acquired in exchange for any cash or cash item, any marketable stock, or any debt of the transferor. The property treated as acquired by purchase is the property received by the transferor in the exchange.

(B) *Multiple classes of stock.*—If the transferor in a transaction described in section 355(d)(5)(B) receives stock or securities of more than one class, or receives both stock and securities, then the amount of stock or securities purchased is determined in a manner that corresponds to the allocation of basis to the stock or securities under section 358. See §1.358-2(b).

(ii) *Cash item, marketable stock.*—For purposes of section 355(d)(5)(B) and this paragraph (d)(3), either or both of the terms cash item and marketable stock include personal property within the meaning of section 1092(d)(1) and §1.1092(d)-1, without giving effect to section 1092(d)(3).

(iii) *Exception for certain acquisitions.*—(A) *In general.*—Except to the extent provided in paragraph (e)(3) of this section (interest received in exchange for purchased interest in exchanged basis transaction treated as purchased), an acquisition of stock in a corporation in a section 351 transaction by one or more persons in exchange for an amount of stock in another corporation (the transferred corporation) that meets the requirements of section 1504(a)(2) is not a purchase by the transferor or transferors, regardless of whether the stock of the transferred corporation is marketable stock under section 355(d)(5)(B)(ii) and paragraph (d)(3)(ii) of this section.

(B) *Example.*—The following example illustrates this paragraph (d)(3)(iii):

Example. D's two classes of stock, voting common and nonvoting preferred, are both widely held and publicly traded. The nonvoting preferred stock is stock described in section 1504(a)(4). Assume that all of the D stock is marketable stock under section 355(d)(5)(B)(ii) and paragraph (d)(3)(ii) of this section. D's board of directors proposes that, for valid business purposes, D's common stock should be held by a holding company, HC, but its preferred stock should not be transferred to HC. As proposed, the D common shareholders exchange their D stock solely for HC common stock in a section 351(a) transaction. The D preferred shareholders retain their stock. HC acquires an amount of D stock that meets the requirements of section 1504(a)(2). Although the D common stock was marketable stock in the hands of the D shareholders immediately before the transfer, and the D nonvoting preferred stock is marketable stock after the transfer, the D shareholders are not treated as having acquired the HC stock by purchase (except to the extent the exchanged basis rule of paragraph (e)(3) of this section may apply to treat HC stock as purchased on the date the exchanged D stock was purchased).

(iv) *Exception for assets transferred as part of an active trade or business.*—(A) *In general.*—Except to the extent provided in paragraph (e)(3) of this section, an acquisition not described in paragraph (d)(3)(iii) of this section of stock in exchange for any cash or cash item, any marketable stock, or any debt of the transferor in a section 351 transaction is not a purchase if—

(1) The transferor is engaged in the active conduct of a trade or business under paragraph (d)(3)(iv)(B) of this section and the transferred items (including debt incurred in the ordinary course of the trade or business) are used in the trade or business;

(2) The transferred items do not exceed the reasonable needs of the trade or business under paragraph (d)(3)(iv)(C) of this section;

(3) The transferor transfers the items as part of the trade or business; and

(4) The transferee continues the active conduct of the trade or business.

(B) *Active conduct of a trade or business.*—For purposes of this paragraph (d)(3)(iv), whether, with respect to the trade or business at issue, the transferor and transferee are engaged in the active conduct of a trade or business is determined under § 1.355-3(b)(2) and (3), except that—

(1) Conduct is tested before the transfer (with respect to the transferor) and after the transfer (with respect to the transferee) rather than immediately after a distribution; and

(2) The trade or business need not have been conducted for five years before its transfer, but it must have been conducted for a sufficient period of time to establish that it is a viable and ongoing trade or business.

(C) *Reasonable needs of the trade or business.*—For purposes of this paragraph (d)(3)(iv), the reasonable needs of the trade or business include only the amount of cash or cash items, marketable stock, or debt of the transferor that a prudent business person apprised of all relevant facts would consider necessary for the present and reasonably anticipated future needs of the business. Transferred items may be considered necessary for reasonably anticipated future needs only if the transferor and transferee have specific, definite, and feasible plans for their use. Those plans must require that items intended for anticipated future needs rather than present needs be used as expeditiously as possible consistent with the business purpose for retention of the items. Future needs are not reasonably anticipated if they are uncertain or vague or where the execution of the plan for their use is substantially postponed. The reasonable needs of a trade or business are generally its needs at the time of the transfer of the business including the items. However, for purposes of applying section 355(d) to a distribution, events and conditions after the transfer and through the date immediately after the distribution (including whether plans for the use of transferred items have been consummated or substantially postponed) may be considered to determine whether at the time of the transfer the items were necessary for the present and reasonably anticipated future needs of the business.

(D) *Consideration of all facts and circumstances.*—All facts and circumstances are considered in determining whether this paragraph (d)(3)(iv) applies.

(E) *Successive transfers.*—A transfer of assets does not fail to meet the requirements of paragraph (d)(3)(iv)(A)*(4)* of this section solely because the transferee transfers the assets directly (or indirectly through other members) to another member of the transferee's affiliated group, as defined in § 1.355-3(b)(4)(iv) (the final transferee), if the requirements of paragraphs (d)(3)(iv)(A)*(1)*, *(2)*, *(3)* and *(4)* of this section would be met if the transferor had transferred the assets directly to the final transferee.

(v) *Exception for transfer between members of the same affiliated group.*—(A) *In general.*—Except to the extent provided in paragraph (e)(3) of this section, an acquisition of stock (whether actual or constructive) not described in paragraphs (d)(3)(iii) and (iv) of this section in exchange for any cash or cash item, marketable stock, or debt of the transferor in a section 351 transaction is not a purchase if—

(1) The transferor corporation or corporations and the transferee corporation (whether formed in the transaction or already existing) are members of the same affiliated group as defined in section 1504(a) before the section 351 transaction (if the transferee corporation is in existence before the transaction);

(2) The cash or cash item, marketable stock or debt of the transferor are not included in assets that are acquired (or treated as acquired) by the transferor (or another member of the transferor's affiliated group) from a nonmember in a related transaction in which section 362(a) or (b) applies to determine the basis in the acquired assets; and

(3) The transferor corporation or corporations, the transferee corporation, and any distributed controlled corporation of the transferee corporation do not cease to be members of such affiliated group in any transaction pursuant to a plan that includes the section 351 transaction (including any distribution of a controlled corporation by the transferee corporation). But see paragraph (b)(4) of this section where the transfer is made for a principal purpose to avoid the purposes of section 355(d).

(B) *Examples.*—The following examples illustrate this paragraph (d)(3)(v):

Example 1. Publicly traded P has wholly owned S since 1990. S is engaged in the telecommunications business and the business of computer software development. S is developing new software for use in the managed health care industry. Over a period of four years beginning on January 31, 2000, P contributes a substantial amount of cash to S solely for the purpose of funding the software development. On completion of the software in January of 2004, 60 percent of the value of the S stock is attributable to the cash contributions made within the last four years. The P group's primary lender requires that S separately incorporate the software and related assets and distribute the new subsidiary to P as a condition of providing required funding to market the Software. Accordingly, on February 1, 2004, S forms N, contributes the software and related assets to N, and distributes all of the N stock to P in a transaction intended to qualify under section 355(a). P, S, and N will not leave the affiliated group in any transaction related to the cash contributions. Under paragraph (d)(3)(v)(A) of this section, P's cash contributions to S are not treated as purchases of additional S stock, and the distribution of N from S to P is not a disqualified distribution under section 355(d)(2) and paragraph (b)(1) of this section.

Example 2. On Date 1, P contributes cash to its subsidiary S with a principal purpose to increase its stock basis in S. Sixty percent of the value of P's S stock is attributable to the cash contribution. Under paragraph (b)(4) of this section (anti-avoidance rule), 60 percent of the S stock is treated as purchased under section 355(d)(5)(B), notwithstanding paragraph (d)(3)(v)(A) of this section. Accordingly, any distribution of a subsidiary of S to P within the five-year period after Date 1 will be a disqualified distribution, regardless of whether P, S, and any distributed S subsidiary remain affiliated after the distribution and any transactions related to the cash contribution.

(4) *Triangular asset reorganizations.*—(i) *Definition.*—A *triangular asset reorganization* is a reorganization that qualifies under—

(A) Section 368(a)(1)(A) or (G) by reason of section 368(a)(2)(D);

(B) Section 368(a)(1)(A) by reason of section 368(a)(2)(E) (regardless of whether section 368(a)(3)(E) applies), unless the transaction also qualifies as either a section 351 transfer or a reorganization under section 368(a)(1)(B); or

(C) Section 368(a)(1)(C), and stock of the controlling corporation rather than the acquiring corporation is exchanged for the acquired corporation's properties.

(ii) *Treatment.*—Notwithstanding section 355(d)(5)(A), for purposes of section 355(d), the controlling corporation in a triangular asset reorganization is treated as having—

(A) Acquired the assets of the acquired corporation (and as having assumed any liabilities assumed by the controlling corporation's subsidiary corporation or to which the acquired corporation's assets were subject (the acquired liabilities)) in a transaction in which the controlling corporation's basis in the acquired corporation's assets was determined under section 362(b); and

(B) Transferred the acquired assets and acquired liabilities to its subsidiary corporation in a section 351 transfer.

(iii) *Example.*—The following example illustrates this paragraph (d)(4):

Example. Forward triangular reorganization. P forms S with $25 of cash and T merges into S in a reorganization qualifying under section 368(a)(1)(A) by reason of section 368(a)(2)(D) in which the T shareholders receive $70 of P stock and $15 of cash in exchange for their T stock. T is not a common parent of a consolidated group of corporations. The remaining $10 of cash with which P formed S will not be used in the acquired business. T's assets consist only of assets part of and used in its business with a value of $80, and $5 of cash that is not part of or used in T's business. T has no liabilities. S will use T's business assets in T's business (which will become S's business), but will invest the $5 of cash in an unrelated passive investment. Under paragraph (d)(4)(ii) of this section, P is treated as acquiring the T assets in a transaction in which P's basis in the T assets was determined under section 362(b) and contributing them to S in a section 351 transfer. Under paragraph (d)(3)(v) of this section, $10 (of the total $25) of cash contributed by P to S upon S's formation is not treated as a purchase of S stock. The $15 (of the total $25) of cash contributed by P to S upon S's formation that is paid to T's shareholders is not treated as a purchase of S stock. The exception in paragraph (d)(3)(v) of this section does not apply to the $5 of cash from T's business because P is treated as having acquired T's assets in a related transaction in which section 362(b) applies to determine P's basis in such assets. Accordingly, P is treated under section 355(d)(5)(B) and paragraph (d)(3)(iv) of this section as having purchased $5 of the S stock, but is not deemed to have purchased the remaining $80 of the S stock.

(5) *Reverse triangular reorganizations other than triangular asset reorganizations.*—(i) *In general.*—Except as provided in paragraph (d)(5)(ii) of this section, if a transaction qualifies as a reorganization under section 368(a)(1)(A) by reason of section 368(a)(2)(E) and also as either a reorganization under section 368(a)(1)(B) or a section 351 transfer, then either section 355(d)(5)(B) (and paragraphs (d)(3)(i) through (iv) of this section) or 355(d)(5)(C) (and paragraph (e)(2) of this section) applies. Regardless of which method the controlling corporation employs to determine its basis in the surviving corporation stock under § 1.358-6(c)(2)(ii) or § 1.1502-30(b), the total amount of surviving corporation stock

treated as purchased by the controlling corporation will equal the higher of—

(A) The amount of surviving corporation stock that would be treated as purchased (on the date of the deemed section 351 transfer) by the controlling corporation if the controlling corporation acquired the surviving corporation's assets and assumed its liabilities in a transaction in which the controlling corporation's basis in the surviving corporation assets was determined under section 362(b), and then transferred the acquired assets and liabilities to the surviving corporation in a section 351 transfer (see §§1.358-6(c)(1) and (2)(ii)(A), and 1.1502-30(b)); or

(B) The amount of surviving corporation stock that would be treated as purchased (on the date the surviving corporation shareholders purchased their surviving corporation stock) if the controlling corporation acquired the stock of the surviving corporation in a transaction in which the basis in the surviving corporation's stock was determined under section 362(b) (see §§1.358-6(c)(2)(ii)(B) and 1.1502-30(b)).

(ii) *Letter ruling and closing agreement.*—If a controlling corporation obtains a letter ruling and enters into a closing agreement under section 7121 in which it agrees to determine its basis in surviving corporation stock under §1.358-6(c)(2)(ii)(A), or under §1.1502-30(b) by applying §1.358-6(c)(2)(ii)(A) (deemed asset acquisition and transfer by controlling corporation), then section 355(d)(5)(B) and paragraphs (d)(3)(i) through (iv) of this section apply, and section 355(d)(5)(C) and paragraph (e)(2) of this section do not apply. If a controlling corporation obtains a letter ruling and enters into a closing agreement under section 7121 under which it agrees to determine its basis in surviving corporation stock under §1.358-6(c)(2)(ii)(B), or under §1.1502-30(b) by applying §1.358-6(c)(2)(ii)(B) (deemed stock acquisition), then section 355(d)(5)(C) and paragraph (e)(2) of this section apply, and section 355(d)(5)(B) and paragraphs (d)(3)(i) through (iv) of this section do not apply.

(iii) *Example.*—The following example illustrates this paragraph (d)(5):

Example. Reverse triangular reorganization; purchase. (i) A purchases 60 percent of the stock of D on Date 1. D owns no cash items, marketable stock, or transferor debt, but holds cash that is not part of or used in D's trade or business under paragraph (d)(3)(iv) of this section and that represents 20 percent of D's value. On Date 2, P forms S, and S merges into D in a reorganization qualifying under section 368(a)(1)(B) and under section 368(a)(1)(A) by reason of section 368(a)(2)(E). In the reorganization, P acquires all of the D stock in exchange solely for P stock. After Date 2, and within five years after Date 1, D distributes its wholly owned subsidiary C to P. P does not obtain a letter ruling and enter into a closing agreement under paragraph (d)(5)(ii) of this section. P would acquire 20 percent of the D stock by purchase on Date 2 under paragraph (d)(5)(i)(A) of this section by operation of section 355(d)(5)(B) and paragraph (d)(3)(iv) of this section. The exception in paragraph (d)(3)(v) of this section does not apply because D was not affiliated with P before the transaction in which the section 351 transfer is deemed to occur and D's assets are treated as acquired by P in a related transaction in which section 362(b) applies to determine P's basis in the D assets. P would acquire 60 percent of the D stock by purchase on Date 1 under paragraph (d)(5)(i)(B) of this section because, under the transferred basis rule of section 355(d)(5)(C) and paragraph (e)(2) of this section, P is treated as though P purchased the D stock on the date A purchased it. Accordingly, under paragraph (d)(5)(i) of this section, P is treated as acquiring the higher amount (60 percent) by purchase on Date 1. D's distribution of C to P is a disqualified distribution under section 355(d)(2) and paragraph (b)(1) of this section. In addition. A is treated as acquiring the P stock by purchase on Date 1 under paragraph (e)(3) of this section because A's basis in the P stock is determined by reference to A's basis in the D stock.

(ii) The facts are the same as in paragraph (i) of this *Example*, except that P obtains a letter ruling and enters into a closing agreement under which it agrees to determine its basis in the D stock under §1.358-6(c)(2)(ii)(A). Under paragraph (d)(5)(ii) of this section, section 355(d)(5)(B) (and paragraphs (d)(3)(i) through (iv) of this section) applies, and section 355(d)(5)(C) (and paragraph (e)(2) of this section) does not apply. Accordingly, P is treated as acquiring only 20 percent of the D stock by purchase on Date 2. D's distribution of C to P is not a disqualified distribution under section 355(d)(2) and paragraph (b)(1) of this section.

(6) *Treatment of group structure changes.*—(i) *In general.*—Notwithstanding section 355(d)(5)(A), for purposes of section 355(d), if a corporation succeeds another corporation as the common parent of a consolidated group in a group structure change to which §1.1502-31 applies, the new common parent is treated as having acquired the assets and assumed the liabilities of the former common parent in a transaction in which the new common parent's basis in the former common parent's assets was determined under section

362(b), and then transferred the acquired assets and liabilities to the former common parent (or, if the former common parent does not survive, to the new common parent's subsidiary) in a section 351 transfer, with the new common parent and former common parent being treated as not in the same affiliated group at the time of the transfer for purposes of applying paragraph (d)(3)(v) of this section (notwithstanding § 1.1502-31(c)(2)).

(ii) *Adjustments to basis of higher-tier members.*—A higher-tier member that indirectly owns all or part of the former common parent's stock after a group structure change is treated as having purchased the stock of an immediate subsidiary to the extent that the higher-tier member's basis in the subsidiary is increased under § 1.1502-31(d)(4).

(iii) *Example.*—The following example illustrates this paragraph (d)(6):

Example. P is the common parent of a consolidated group, and T is the common parent of another group. P has owned S for more than five years, and the fair market value of the S stock is $50. T's assets consist only of nonmarketable stock of direct and indirect wholly owned subsidiaries with a value of $50, assets used in its business with a value of $50, and $50 of marketable stock that is not part of or used in T's business. T has no liabilities. T merges into S with the T shareholders receiving solely P stock with a value of $150 in exchange for their T stock in a section 368(a)(2)(D) reorganization. S will use T's business assets in T's business (which will become S's business), but will hold the $50 of marketable stock for investment purposes. Assume that the transaction is a reverse acquisition under § 1.1502-75(d)(3) because the T shareholders, as a result of owning T stock, own more than 50 percent of the value of P's stock immediately after the transaction. Thus, the transaction is a group structure change under § 1.1502-33(f)(1). Under paragraph (d)(6) of this section, P is treated as having acquired the assets of T in a transaction in which P's basis in the T assets was determined under section 362(b), and then transferred the acquired assets to S in a section 351 transfer, with P and T being treated as not in the same affiliated group at the time of the transfer solely for purposes of paragraph (d)(3)(v) of this section. The exception in paragraph (d)(3)(v) of this section (transfers within an affiliated group) does not apply. Accordingly, P is treated under section 355(d)(5)(B) and paragraph (d)(3)(iv) of this section as having purchased $50 of the S stock (attributable to the marketable stock), but is not deemed to have purchased the remaining $150 of the S stock.

(7) *Special rules for triangular asset reorganizations, other reverse triangular reorganizations, and group structure changes.*—The amount of acquiring subsidiary, surviving corporation, or former common parent stock that is treated as purchased under paragraph (c)(4), (5)(i)(A), or (6) of this section (by operation of section 355(d)(5)(B) and paragraphs (d)(3)(i) through (iv) of this section) is adjusted to reflect any basis adjustment under—

(i) Section 1.358-6(c)(2)(i)(B) and (C) (reduction of basis adjustment in reverse triangular reorganization where controlling corporation acquires less than all of the surviving corporation stock), § 1.1502-30(b) (applying § 1.358-6(c)(2)(i)(B) and (C) to a consolidated group), and § 1.1502-31(d)(2)(ii) (reduction of basis adjustment in group structure change where new common parent acquires less than all of the former common parent stock); or

(ii) Section 1.358-6(d) (reduction of basis adjustment in any triangular reorganization to the extent controlling corporation does not provide consideration), § 1.1502-30(b) (applying § 1.358-6(d) (except § 1.358-6(d)(2)) to a consolidated group), and § 1.1502-31(d)(1) (reduction of basis adjustment in group structure change to the extent new common parent does not provide consideration).

(e) *Deemed purchase and timing rules.*—(1) *Attribution and aggregation.*—(i) *In general.*—Under section 355(d)(8)(B), if any person acquires by purchase an interest in any entity, and the person is treated under section 355(d)(8)(A) as holding any stock by reason of holding the interest, the stock shall be treated as acquired by purchase on the later of the date of the purchase of the interest in the entity or the date the stock is acquired by purchase by such entity.

(ii) *Purchase of additional interest.*—If a person and an entity are treated as a single person under section 355(d)(7), and the person later purchases an additional interest in the entity, the person is treated as purchasing on the date of the later purchase the amount of stock attributed from the entity to the person under section 355(d)(8)(A) as a result of the additional interest.

(iii) *Purchase between persons treated as one person.*—If two persons are treated as one person under section 355(d)(7), and one later purchases stock from the other, the date of the later purchase is used for purposes of determining when the five-year period commences.

(iv) *Purchase by a person already treated as holding stock under section 355(d)(8)(A).*—If a person who is already treated as holding stock under section 355(d)(8)(A) later directly purchases such stock, the date of the later direct purchase is used for purposes of determining when the five-year period commences.

(v) *Examples.*—The following examples illustrate this paragraph (e) (1):

Example 1. On Date 1, A purchases 10 percent of the stock of P, which has held 100 percent of the stock of T for more than five years at the time of A's purchase. A is deemed to have purchased 10 percent of P's T stock on Date 1. If A later purchases an additional 41 percent of the stock of P on Date 2, A is deemed to have purchased an additional 41 percent of P's T stock on Date 2. Because A and P are now related persons under section 267(b), they are treated as one person under section 355(d) (7) (A), and A is treated as owning all of P's T stock. A is treated as acquiring 51 percent of the T stock by purchase at the times of A's respective purchases of P stock on Date 1 and Date 2. The remaining 49 percent of T stock is treated as acquired when P acquired the T stock, more than five years before Date 1. If P distributes T after Date 2 and within five years after Date 1, the distribution will be a disqualified distribution under section 355(d) (2) and paragraph (b) (1) of this section.

Example 2. A has owned 60 percent of the stock of P for more than five years, and P has owned 40 percent of the stock of T for more than five years. A and P are treated as one person, and A is treated as owning 40 percent of the stock of T for more than five years. If P later purchases an additional 20 percent of the stock of T on Date 1, A is treated as acquiring by purchase the additional 20 percent of T stock on Date 1. If A then purchases an additional 10 percent of the stock of P on Date 2, under paragraph (e) (1) (i) of this section, A is deemed to have purchased on Date 2 an additional four percent of the T stock (10 percent of the 40 percent that P originally owned). In addition, even though A and P were already treated as one person under section 355(d) (7) (A), A also is deemed to have purchased two percent of the T stock on Date 2 (10 percent of the 20 percent of the T stock that it was treated as purchasing on Date 1). A is still treated as owning all 60 percent of the T stock owned by P. However, of the 60 percent, A is treated as having purchased 18 percent of the T stock on Date 1 and 6 percent of the T stock on Date 2, for a total of 24 percent purchased stock.

Example 3. A purchases a 20 percent interest in partnership M on Date 1. M has owned 30 percent of the stock and 25 percent of the securities of P for more than five years. P has owned 40 percent of the stock and 100 percent of the securities of T for more than five years. Under section 318(a) (2) (C) as modified by section 355(d) (8) (A), M is deemed to own 12 percent of the stock (30 percent of the 40 percent P owns) and 30 percent of the securities (30 percent of the 100 percent P owns) of T. Under sections 318(a) (2) (A) and 355(d) (8) (B), A is deemed to have purchased 2.4 percent of the stock (20 percent of the 12 percent M is deemed to own) and 6 percent of the securities (20 percent of the 30 percent M is deemed to own) of T on Date 1. Similarly, A is deemed to have purchased 6 percent of the stock (20 percent of the 30 percent M owns) and five percent of the securities (20 percent of the 25 percent M owns) of P on Date 1. If M later purchases an additional 10 percent of P stock on Date 2, M is deemed to have purchased four percent of the stock (10 percent of the 40 percent P owns) and 10 percent of the securities (10 percent of the 100 percent. P owns) of T on Date 2. A is deemed to have purchased two percent of the stock of P on Date 2 (20 percent of the 10 percent M purchased). A is also deemed to have purchased 0.8 percent of the stock (20 percent of the four percent M is deemed to have purchased) and two percent of the securities (20 percent of the 10 percent M is deemed to have purchased) of T on Date 2.

Example 4. A and B are brother and sister. For more than five years, A has owned 75 percent of the stock of P, and B has owned 25 percent of the stock of P. A and B are treated as one person under section 267(b), and the stock of each is treated as purchased on the date it was purchased by A and B, respectively. If B later purchases 50 percent of the P stock from A on Date 1, A and B are still treated as one person. However, under paragraph (e) (3) (iii) of this section, the 50 percent of P stock that B purchased from A is treated as purchased on Date 1.

(2) *Transferred basis rule.*—If any person acquires property from another person who acquired the property by purchase (determined with regard to section 355(d) (5) and paragraphs (d) and (e) (2), (3) and (4) of this section, but without regard to section 355(d) (8) and paragraph (e) (1) of this section), and the adjusted basis of the property in the hands of the acquirer is determined in whole or in part by reference to the adjusted basis of the property in the hands of the other person, the acquirer is treated as having acquired the property by purchase on the date it was so acquired by the other person. The rule in this paragraph (e) (2) applies, for example, where stock of a corporation acquired by purchase is subsequently acquired in a section 351 transfer or a reorganization qualifying under section 368(a) (1) (B), but does not apply if the stock of a former common parent is acquired in a group

structure change to which § 1.1502-31 applies. But see paragraph (d)(2)(i)(B)(*2*) of this section for situations where the stock is treated as purchased on the date of a transfer.

(3) *Exchanged basis rule.*—(i) *In general.*—If any person acquires an interest in an entity (the first interest) by purchase (determined with regard to section 355(d)(5) and paragraphs (d) and (e)(2), (3) and (4) of this section, but without regard to section 355(d)(8) and paragraph (e)(1) of this section), and the first interest is exchanged for an interest in the same or another entity (the second interest) where the adjusted basis of the second interest is determined in whole or in part by reference to the adjusted basis of the first interest, then the second interest is treated as having been purchased on the date the first interest was purchased. The rule in this paragraph (e)(3) applies only to exchanges that are not otherwise treated as purchases under section 355(d)(5) and paragraph (d) of this section. The rule in this paragraph (e)(3) applies, for example, where stock of a corporation acquired by purchase is subsequently exchanged for other stock in a section 351,354, or 1036(a) exchange. But see paragraph (d)(2)(i)(A)(*2*) of this section for situations where the stock is treated as purchased on the date of an exchange or distribution.

(ii) *Example.*—The following example illustrates this paragraph (e)(3):

Example. A purchases 50 percent of the stock of T on Date 1. On Date 2, T merges into D in a section 368(a)(1)(A) reorganization, with A exchanging all of the T stock solely for stock of D. Under section 358(a), A's basis in the D stock is determined by reference to the basis of the T stock it purchased. Accordingly, A is treated as having purchased the D stock on Date 1, and has a purchased basis in the D stock under paragraph (b)(3)(iii) of this section.

(4) *Certain section 355 or section 305 distributions.*—(i) *Section 355.*—If a distributing corporation distributes any stock of a controlled corporation with respect to recently purchased distributing stock in a distribution that qualifies under section 355 (or so much of section 356 as relates to section 355), such controlled corporation stock is deemed to be acquired by purchase by the distributee on the date the distributee acquired the recently purchased distributing stock. Recently purchased distributing stock is stock in the distributing corporation acquired by purchase (determined with regard to section 355(d)(5) and paragraphs (d) and (e)(2), (3), and (4) of this section, but without regard to section 355(d)(8) and paragraph (e)(1) of this section) by the distributee during the five-year period with respect to that distribution.

(ii) *Section 305.*—If a corporation distributes its stock in a distribution that qualifies under section 305(a), the stock received in the distribution (to the extent section 307(a) applies to determine the recipient's basis) is deemed to be acquired by purchase by the recipient on the date (if any) that the recipient acquired by purchase (determined with regard to section 355(d)(5) and paragraphs (d) and (e)(2), (3), and (4) of this section), the stock with respect to which the distribution is made.

(5) *Substantial diminution of risk.*—(i) *In general.*—If section 355(d)(6) applies to any stock for any period, the running of any five-year period set forth in section 355(d)(3) is suspended during such period.

(ii) *Property to which suspension applies.*—Section 355(d)(6) applies to any stock for any period during which the holder's risk of loss with respect to such stock, or with respect to any portion of the activities of the corporation, is (directly or indirectly) substantially diminished by an option, a short sale, any special class of stock, or any other device or transaction.

(iii) *Risk of loss substantially diminished.*—Whether a holder's risk of loss is substantially diminished under section 355(d)(6) and paragraph (e)(5)(ii) of this section will be determined based on all facts and circumstances relating to the stock, the corporate activities, and arrangements for holding the stock.

(iv) *Special class of stock.*—For purposes of section 355(d)(6) and paragraph (e)(5)(ii) of this section, the term special class of stock includes a class of stock that grants particular rights to, or bears particular risks for, the holder or the issuer with respect to the earnings, assets, or attributes of less than all the assets or activities of a corporation or any of its subsidiaries. The term includes, for example, tracking stock and stock (or any related instruments or arrangements) the terms of which provide for the distribution (whether or not at the option of any party or in the event of any contingency) of any controlled corporation or other specified assets to the holder or to one or more persons other than the holder.

(f) *Duty to determine stockholders.*—(1) *In general.*—In determining whether section 355(d) applies to a distribution of controlled corporation stock, a distributing corporation must determine whether a disqualified person holds its stock or the stock of any distributed controlled corporation. This paragraph (f) provides rules regarding this determination and the extent to which a distributing corporation must investigate whether a disqualified person holds stock.

(2) *Deemed knowledge of contents of securities filings.*—A distributing corporation is deemed to have knowledge of the existence and contents of all schedules, forms, and other documents filed with or under the rules of the Securities and Exchange Commission, including without limitation any Schedule 13D or 13G (or any similar schedules) and amendments, with respect to any relevant corporation.

(3) *Presumption as to securities filings.*—Absent actual knowledge to the contrary, in determining whether section 355(d) applies to a distribution, a distributing corporation may presume, with respect to stock that is reporting stock (while such stock is reporting stock), that every shareholder or other person required to file a schedule, form, or other document with or under the rules of the Securities and Exchange Commission as of a given date has filed the schedule, form, or other document as of that date and that the contents of filed schedules, forms, or other documents are accurate and complete. Reporting stock is stock that is described in Rule 13d-1(i) of Regulation 13D (17 CFR 240.13d-1(i)) (or any rule or regulation to generally the same effect) promulgated by the Securities and Exchange Commission under the Securities Exchange Act of 1934 (15 U.S.C. 78a et seq.).

(4) *Presumption as to less-than-five-percent shareholders.*—Absent actual knowledge (or deemed knowledge under paragraph (f)(2) of this section) immediately after the distribution to the contrary with regard to a particular shareholder, a distributing corporation may presume that no less-than-five-percent shareholder of a corporation acquired stock or securities by purchase under section 355(d)(5) or (8) and paragraphs (d) and (e) of this section during the five-year period. For purposes of this paragraph (f), a less-than-five-percent shareholder is a person that, at no time during the five-year period, holds directly (or by application of paragraph (c)(3)(ii) of this section, but not by application of section 355(d)(7) or (8)) stock possessing five percent or more of the total combined voting power of all classes of stock entitled to vote or the total value of shares of all classes of stock of a corporation. However, this presumption does not apply to any less-than-five-percent shareholder that, at any time during the five-year period—

(i) Is related under section 355(d)(7)(A) to a shareholder in the corporation that is at any time during the five-year period, not a less-than-five-percent shareholder;

(ii) Acted pursuant to a plan or arrangement, with respect to acquisitions of the corporation's stock or securities under section 355(d)(7)(B) and paragraph (c)(4) of this section, with a shareholder in the corporation that is, at any time during the five-year period, not a less-than-five-percent shareholder; or

(iii) Holds stock or securities that is attributed under section 355(d)(8)(A) to a shareholder in the corporation that is, at any time during the five-year period, not a less-than-five-percent shareholder.

(5) *Examples.*—The following examples illustrate this paragraph (f):

Example 1. Publicly traded corporation; no schedules filed. D is a widely held and publicly traded corporation with a single class of reporting stock and no other class of stock. Assume that applicable federal law requires any person that directly holds five percent or more of the D stock to file a schedule with the Securities and Exchange Commission within 10 days after an acquisition. D distributes its wholly owned subsidiary C pro rata. D determines that no schedule, form, or other document has been filed with respect to its stock or the stock of any other relevant corporation during the five-year period or within 10 days after the distribution. Immediately after the distribution, D has no knowledge that any of its shareholders are (or were at any time during the five-year period) not less-than-five-percent shareholders, or that any particular shareholder acquired D stock by purchase under section 355(d)(5) or (8) and paragraphs (d) and (e) of this section during the five-year period. Under paragraph (f)(3) of this section, D may presume it has no shareholder that is or was not a less-than-five-percent shareholder during the five-year period due to the absence of any filed schedules, forms, or other documents. Under paragraph (f)(4) of this section, D may presume that none of its less-than-five-percent shareholders acquired D's stock by purchase during the five-year period. Accordingly, D may presume that section 355(d) does not apply to the distribution of C.

Example 2. Publicly traded corporation; schedule filed. The facts are the same as those in *Example 1*, except that D determines that, as of 10 days after the distribution, only one schedule has been filed with respect to its stock. That schedule discloses that X acquired 15 percent of the D stock one year before the distribution. Absent contrary knowledge, D may rely on the presumptions in paragraph (f)(3) of this section and so may presume that X is its only shareholder that is or was not a less-than-five-percent shareholder during the five-year period. D may not rely on the presumption in paragraph (f)(4) of this section with respect to X. In addition, D may not rely on the presumption in paragraph (f)(4) of this section with respect to any less-than-five-percent shareholder that, at any time during the five-year period, is related to X under section 355(d)(7)(A), acted pursuant to a plan or arrangement with X under section 355(d)(7)(B) and paragraph (c)(4) of this section with respect to acquisitions of D stock, or holds stock that is attributed to X under section 355(d)(8)(A). Accordingly, under paragraph (f)(1) of this section, to determine whether section 355(d) applies, D must determine: whether X acquired its directly held D stock by purchase under section 355(d)(5) and paragraphs (d) and (e)(2) and (3) of this section during the five-year period; whether X is treated as having purchased any additional D stock under section 355(d)(8) and paragraph (e)(1) of this section during the five-year period; and whether X is related to, or acquired its D stock pursuant to a plan or arrangement with, one or more of D's other shareholders during the five-year period under section 355(d)(7)(A) or (B) and paragraph (c)(4) of this section, and if so, whether those shareholders acquired their D stock by purchase under section 355(d)(5) or (8) and paragraphs (d) and (e) of this section during the five-year period.

Example 3. Acquisition of publicly traded corporation. The facts are the same as those in *Example 1*, except that P acquires all of the D stock in a section 368(a)(1)(B) reorganization that is not also a reorganization under section 368(a)(1)(A) by reason of section 368(a)(2)(E), and D distributes C to P one year later. Because D was widely held, P applies statistical sampling procedures that involve less than 50% of D's outstanding shares, to estimate the basis of all shares acquired, instead of surveying each shareholder. Under the deemed purchase rule of section 355(d)(5)(C) and paragraph (e)(2) of this section, P is treated as having acquired the D stock by purchase on the date the D shareholders acquired the D stock by purchase. Even though D has no less-than-five-percent shareholder immediately after the distribution, D may rely on the presumptions in paragraphs (f)(3) and (4) of this section to determine whether and to what extent the D stock is treated as purchased during the five-year period in P's hands under the deemed purchase rule of section 355(d)(5)(C) and paragraph (e)(2) of this section. Accordingly, D may presume that section 355(d) does not apply to the distribution of C to P. This result would not change even if the statistical sampling that involves less than 50 percent of D's outstanding shares indicated that more than 50% of D's shares were acquired by purchase during the five-year period.

Example 4. Non-publicly traded corporation. D is owned by 20 shareholders and has a single class of stock that is not reporting stock. D knows that A owns 40 percent of the D stock, and D does not know that any other shareholder has owned as much as five percent of the D stock at any time during the five-year period. D may not rely on the presumption in paragraph (f)(3) of this section because its stock is not reporting stock. D may not rely on the presumption in paragraph (f)(4) of this section with respect to A. In addition, D may not rely on the presumption in paragraph (f)(4) of this section for any less-than-five-percent shareholder that, at any time during the five-year period, is related to A under section 355(d)(7)(A), acted pursuant to a plan or arrangement with A under section 355(d)(7)(B) and paragraph (c)(4) of this section with respect to acquisitions of D stock, or holds stock that is attributed to A under section 355(d)(8)(A). D may rely on the presumption in paragraph (f)(4) of this section for less-than-five-percent shareholders that during the five-year period are not related to A, did not act pursuant to a plan or arrangement with A, and do not hold stock attributed to A. Accordingly, under paragraph (f)(1) of this section, to determine whether section 355(d) applies, D must determine: that A is its only shareholder that is (or was at any time during the five-year period) not a less-than-five-percent shareholder; whether A acquired its directly held D stock by purchase under section 355(d)(5) and paragraphs (d) and (e)(2) and (3) of this section during the five-year period; whether A is treated as having purchased any additional D stock under section 355(d)(8) and paragraph (e)(1) of this section during the five-year period; and whether A is related to, or acquired its D stock pursuant to a plan or arrangement with, one or more of D's other shareholders during the five-year period under section 355(d)(7)(A) or (B) and paragraph (c)(4) of this section, and if so, whether those shareholders acquired their D stock by purchase under section 355(d)(5) or (8) and paragraphs (d) and (e) of this section during the five-year period.

* * *

[Reg. § 1.355-6.]

☐ [*T.D.* 8238, 1-5-89. *Amended by T.D.* 8913, 12-19-2000 (*corrected* 2-5-2001) *and T.D.* 9811, 1-18-2017.]

§ 1.355-7. Recognition of gain on certain distributions of stock or securities in connection with an acquisition.—(a) *In general.*—Except as provided in section 355(e) and in this section, section 355(e) applies to any distribution—

(1) To which section 355 (or so much of section 356 as relates to section 355) applies; and

(2) That is part of a plan (or series of related transactions) (hereinafter, plan) pursuant to which 1 or more persons acquire directly or indirectly stock representing a 50-percent or greater interest in the distributing corporation (Distributing) or any controlled corporation (Controlled).

(b) *Plan.*—(1) *In general.*—Whether a distribution and an acquisition are part of a plan is determined based on all the facts and circumstances. The facts and circumstances to be considered in demonstrating whether a distribution and an acquisition are part of a plan include, but are not limited to, the facts and circumstances set forth in paragraphs (b)(3) and (4) of this section. In general, the weight to be given each of the facts and circumstances depends on the particular case. Whether a distribution and an acquisition are part of a plan does not depend on the relative number of facts and circumstances set forth in paragraph (b)(3) that evidence that a distribution and an acquisition are part of a plan as compared to the relative number of facts and circumstances set forth in paragraph (b)(4) that evidence that a distribution and an acquisition are not part of a plan.

(2) *Certain post-distribution acquisitions.*—In the case of an acquisition (other than involving a public offering) after a distribution, the distribution and the acquisition can be part of a plan only if there was an agreement, understanding, arrangement, or substantial negotiations regarding the acquisition or a similar acquisition at some time during the two-year period ending on the date of the distribution. In the case of an acquisition (other than involving a public offering) after a distribution, the existence of an agreement, understanding, arrangement, or substantial negotiations regarding the acquisition or a similar acquisition at some time during the two-year period ending on the date of the distribution tends to show that the distribution and the acquisition are part of a plan. See paragraph (b)(3)(i) of this section. However, all facts and circumstances must be considered to determine whether the distribution and the acquisition are part of a plan. For example, in the case of an acquisition (other than involving a public offering) after a distribution, if the distribution was motivated in whole or substantial part by a corporate business purpose (within the meaning of § 1.355-2(b)) other than a business purpose to facilitate the acquisition or a similar acquisition of Distributing or Controlled (see paragraph (b)(4)(v) of this section) and would have occurred at approximately the same time and in similar form regardless of whether the acquisition or a similar acquisition was effected (see paragraph (b)(4)(vi) of this section), the taxpayer may be able to establish that the distribution and the acquisition are not part of a plan.

(3) *Plan factors.*—Among the facts and circumstances tending to show that a distribution and an acquisition are part of a plan are the following:

(i) In the case of an acquisition (other than involving a public offering) after a distribution, at some time during the two-year period ending on the date of the distribution, there was an agreement, understanding, arrangement, or substantial negotiations regarding the acquisition or a similar acquisition. The weight to be accorded this fact depends on the nature, extent, and timing of the agreement, understanding, arrangement, or substantial negotiations. The existence of an agreement, understanding, or arrangement at the time of the distribution is given substantial weight.

(ii) In the case of an acquisition involving a public offering after a distribution, at some time during the two-year period ending on the date of the distribution, there were discussions by Distributing or Controlled with an investment banker regarding the acquisition or a similar acquisition. The weight to be accorded this fact depends on the nature, extent, and timing of the discussions.

(iii) In the case of an acquisition (other than involving a public offering) before a distribution, at some time during the two-year period ending on the date of the acquisition, there were discussions by Distributing or Controlled with the acquirer regarding a distribution. The weight to be accorded this fact depends on the nature, extent, and timing of the discussions. In addition, in the case of an acquisition (other than involving a public offering) before a distribution, the acquirer intends to cause a distribution and, immediately after the acquisition, can meaningfully participate in the decision regarding whether to make a distribution.

(iv) In the case of an acquisition involving a public offering before a distribution, at some time during the two-year period ending on the date of the acquisition, there were discussions by Distributing or Controlled with an investment banker regarding a distribution. The weight to be accorded this fact depends on the nature, extent, and timing of the discussions.

(v) In the case of an acquisition either before or after a distribution, the distribution was motivated by a business purpose to facilitate the acquisition or a similar acquisition.

(4) *Non-plan factors.*—Among the facts and circumstances tending to show that a dis-

tribution and an acquisition are not part of a plan are the following:

(i) In the case of an acquisition involving a public offering after a distribution, during the two-year period ending on the date of the distribution, there were no discussions by Distributing or Controlled with an investment banker regarding the acquisition or a similar acquisition.

(ii) In the case of an acquisition after a distribution, there was an identifiable, unexpected change in market or business conditions occurring after the distribution that resulted in the acquisition that was otherwise unexpected at the time of the distribution.

(iii) In the case of an acquisition (other than involving a public offering) before a distribution, during the two-year period ending on the date of the earlier to occur of the acquisition or the first public announcement regarding the distribution, there were no discussions by Distributing or Controlled with the acquirer regarding a distribution. Paragraph (b)(4)(iii) of this section does not apply to an acquisition where the acquirer intends to cause a distribution and, immediately after the acquisition, can meaningfully participate in the decision regarding whether to make a distribution.

(iv) In the case of an acquisition before a distribution, there was an identifiable, unexpected change in market or business conditions occurring after the acquisition that resulted in a distribution that was otherwise unexpected.

(v) In the case of an acquisition either before or after a distribution, the distribution was motivated in whole or substantial part by a corporate business purpose (within the meaning of § 1.355-2(b)) other than a business purpose to facilitate the acquisition or a similar acquisition.

(vi) In the case of an acquisition either before or after a distribution, the distribution would have occurred at approximately the same time and in similar form regardless of the acquisition or a similar acquisition.

(c) *Operating rules.*—The operating rules contained in this paragraph (c) apply for all purposes of this section.

(1) *Internal discussions and discussions with outside advisors evidence of business purpose.*—Discussions by Distributing or Controlled with outside advisors and internal discussions may be indicative of one or more business purposes for the distribution and the relative importance of such purposes.

(2) *Takeover defense.*—If Distributing engages in discussions with a potential acquirer regarding an acquisition of Distributing or Controlled and distributes Controlled stock intending, in whole or substantial part, to decrease the likelihood of the acquisition of Distributing or Controlled by separating it from another corporation that is likely to be acquired, Distributing will be treated as having a business purpose to facilitate the acquisition of the corporation that was likely to be acquired.

(3) *Effect of distribution on trading in stock.*—The fact that the distribution made all or a part of the stock of Controlled available for trading or made Distributing's or Controlled's stock trade more actively is not taken into account in determining whether the distribution and an acquisition of Distributing or Controlled stock were part of a plan.

(4) *Consequences of section 355(e) disregarded for certain purposes.*—For purposes of determining the intentions of the relevant parties under this section, the consequences of the application of section 355(e), and the existence of any contractual indemnity by Controlled for tax resulting from the application of section 355(e) caused by an acquisition of Controlled, are disregarded.

(5) *Multiple acquisitions.*—All acquisitions of stock of Distributing or Controlled that are considered to be part of a plan with a distribution pursuant to paragraph (b) of this section will be aggregated for purposes of the 50-percent test of paragraph (a)(2) of this section.

(d) *Safe harbors.*—(1) *Safe Harbor I.*—A distribution and an acquisition occurring after the distribution will not be considered part of a plan if—

(i) The distribution was motivated in whole or substantial part by a corporate business purpose (within the meaning of § 1.355-2(b)), other than a business purpose to facilitate an acquisition of the acquired corporation (Distributing or Controlled); and

(ii) The acquisition occurred more than six months after the distribution and there was no agreement, understanding, arrangement, or substantial negotiations concerning the acquisition or a similar acquisition during the period that begins one year before the distribution and ends six months thereafter.

(2) *Safe Harbor II.*—(i) *In general.*—A distribution and an acquisition occurring after the distribution will not be considered part of a plan if—

(A) The distribution was not motivated by a business purpose to facilitate the acquisition or a similar acquisition;

(B) The acquisition occurred more than six months after the distribution and there was no agreement, understanding, arrangement, or substantial negotiations concerning the acquisition or a similar acquisition during the period that begins one year before the distribution and ends six months thereafter; and

(C) No more than 25 percent of the stock of the acquired corporation (Distributing or Controlled) was either acquired or the subject of an agreement, understanding, arrangement, or substantial negotiations during the period that begins one year before the distribution and ends six months thereafter.

(ii) *Special rule.*—For purposes of paragraph (d)(2)(i)(C) of this section, acquisitions of stock that are treated as not part of a plan pursuant to Safe Harbor VII, Safe Harbor VIII, or Safe Harbor IX are disregarded.

(3) *Safe Harbor III.*—If an acquisition occurs after a distribution, there was no agreement, understanding, or arrangement concerning the acquisition or a similar acquisition at the time of the distribution, and there was no agreement, understanding, arrangement, or substantial negotiations concerning the acquisition or a similar acquisition within one year after the distribution, the acquisition and the distribution will not be considered part of a plan.

(4) *Safe Harbor IV.*—(i) *In general.*—A distribution and an acquisition (other than involving a public offering) occurring before the distribution will not be considered part of a plan if the acquisition occurs before the date of the first disclosure event regarding the distribution.

(ii) *Special rules.*—(A) Paragraph (d)(4)(i) of this section does not apply to a stock acquisition if the acquirer or a coordinating group of which the acquirer is a member is a controlling shareholder or a ten-percent shareholder of the acquired corporation (Distributing or Controlled) at any time during the period beginning immediately after the acquisition and ending on the date of the distribution.

(B) Paragraph (d)(4)(i) of this section does not apply to an acquisition that occurs in connection with a transaction in which the aggregate acquisitions are of stock possessing 20 percent or more of the total voting power of the stock of the acquired corporation (Distributing or Controlled) or stock having a value of 20 percent or more of the total value of the stock of the acquired corporation (Distributing or Controlled).

(5) *Safe Harbor V.*—(i) *In general* .—A distribution that is pro rata among the Distributing shareholders and an acquisition (other than involving a public offering) of Distributing stock occurring before the distribution will not be considered part of a plan if—

(A) The acquisition occurs after the date of a public announcement regarding the distribution; and

(B) There were no discussions by Distributing or Controlled with the acquirer regarding a distribution on or before the date of the first public announcement regarding the distribution.

(ii) *Special rules.*—(A) Paragraph (d)(5)(i) of this section does not apply to a stock acquisition if the acquirer or a coordinating group of which the acquirer is a member is a controlling shareholder or a ten-percent shareholder of Distributing at any time during the period beginning immediately after the acquisition and ending on the date of the distribution.

(B) Paragraph (d)(5)(i) of this section does not apply to an acquisition that occurs in connection with a transaction in which the aggregate acquisitions are of stock possessing 20 percent or more of the total voting power of the stock of Distributing or stock having a value of 20 percent or more of the total value of the stock of Distributing.

(6) *Safe Harbor VI.*—A distribution and an acquisition involving a public offering occurring before the distribution will not be considered part of a plan if the acquisition occurs before the date of the first disclosure event regarding the distribution in the case of an acquisition of stock that is not listed on an established market immediately after the acquisition, or before the date of the first public announcement regarding the distribution in the case of an acquisition of stock that is listed on an established market immediately after the acquisition.

(7) *Safe Harbor VII.*—(i) *In general.*—An acquisition (other than involving a public offering) of Distributing or Controlled stock that is listed on an established market is not part of a plan if, immediately before or immediately after the transfer, none of the transferor, the transferee, and any coordinating group of which either the transferor or the transferee is a member is—

(A) The acquired corporation (Distributing or Controlled);

(B) A corporation that the acquired corporation (Distributing or Controlled) controls within the meaning of section 368(c);

(C) A member of a controlled group of corporations within the meaning of section 1563 of which the acquired corporation (Distributing or Controlled) is a member;

(D) A controlling shareholder of the acquired corporation (Distributing or Controlled); or

(E) A ten-percent shareholder of the acquired corporation (Distributing or Controlled).

(ii) *Special rules.*—(A) Paragraph (d)(7)(i) of this section does not apply to a transfer of stock by or to a person if the corporation the stock of which is being transferred knows, or has reason to know, that the person or a coordinating group of which such person is a member intends to become a controlling shareholder or a tenpercent shareholder of the acquired corporation (Distributing or Controlled) at any time after the acquisition and before the date that is two years after the distribution.

(B) If a transfer of stock to which paragraph (d)(7)(i) of this section applies results immediately, or upon a subsequent event or the passage of time, in an indirect acquisition of voting power by a person other than the transferee, paragraph (d)(7)(i) of this section does not prevent an acquisition of stock (with the voting power such stock represents after the transfer to which paragraph (d)(7)(i) of this section applies) by such other person from being treated as part of a plan.

(8) *Safe Harbor VIII.*—(i) *In general.*—If, in a transaction to which section 83 or section 421(a) or (b) applies, stock of Distributing or Controlled is acquired by a person in connection with such person's performance of services as an employee, director, or independent contractor for Distributing, Controlled, a related person, a corporation the assets of which Distributing, Controlled, or a related person acquires in a reorganization under section 368(a), or a corporation that acquires the assets of Distributing or Controlled in such a reorganization (and the stock acquired is not excessive by reference to the services performed), the acquisition and the distribution will not be considered part of a plan. For purposes of this paragraph (d)(8)(i), a related person is a person related to Distributing or Controlled under section 355(d)(7)(A).

(ii) *Special rule.*—Paragraph (d)(8)(i) of this section does not apply to a stock acquisition if the acquirer or a coordinating group of which the acquirer is a member is a controlling shareholder or a ten-percent shareholder of the acquired corporation (Distributing or Controlled) immediately after the acquisition.

(9) *Safe Harbor IX.*—(i) *In general.*—If stock of Distributing or Controlled is acquired by a retirement plan of Distributing or Controlled (or a retirement plan of any other person that is treated as the same employer as Distributing or Controlled under section 414(b), (c), (m), or (o)) that qualifies under section 401(a) or 403(a), the acquisition and the distribution will not be considered part of a plan.

(ii) *Special rule.*—Paragraph (d)(9)(i) of this section does not apply to the extent that the stock acquired pursuant to acquisitions by all of the qualified plans of the persons described in paragraph (d)(9)(i) of this section during the four-year period beginning two years before the distribution, in the aggregate, represents more than ten percent of the total combined voting power of all classes of stock entitled to vote, or more than ten percent of the total value of shares of all classes of stock, of the acquired corporation (Distributing or Controlled).

(e) *Options, warrants, convertible obligations, and other similar interests.*—(1) *Treatment of options.*—(i) *General rule.*—For purposes of this section, if stock of Distributing or Controlled is acquired pursuant to an option that is written by Distributing, Controlled, or a person that is a controlling shareholder of Distributing or Controlled at the time the option is written, or that is acquired by a person that is a controlling shareholder of Distributing or Controlled immediately after the option is written, the option will be treated as an agreement, understanding, or arrangement to acquire the stock on the earliest of the following dates: the date that the option is written, if the option was more likely than not to be exercised as of such date; the date that the option is transferred if, immediately before or immediately after the transfer, the transferor or transferee was Distributing, Controlled, a corporation that Distributing or Controlled controls within the meaning of section 368(c), a member of a controlled group of corporations within the meaning of section 1563 of which Distributing or Controlled is a member, or a controlling shareholder or a ten-percent shareholder of Distributing or Controlled and the option was more likely than not to be exercised as of such date; and the date that the option is modified in a manner that materially increases the likelihood of exercise, if the option was more likely than not to be exercised as of such date; provided, however, if the writing, transfer, or modification had a principal purpose of avoiding section 355(e), the option will be treated as an agreement, understanding, arrangement, or substantial negotiations to acquire the stock on the date of the distribution. The determination of whether an option was more likely than not to be exercised is based on all the facts and circumstances, taking control premiums and minority and blockage discounts into account in determining the fair market value of stock underlying an option.

(ii) *Agreement, understanding, or arrangement to write, transfer, or modify an option.*—If there is an agreement, understanding, or arrangement to write an option, the option will be treated as written on the date of the agreement, understanding, or arrangement. If there is an agreement, understanding, or arrangement to transfer an option, the option will be treated as transferred on the date of the agreement, understanding, or arrangement. If there is an agreement, understanding, or arrangement to modify an option in a manner that materially increases the likelihood of exercise, the option will be treated as so modified on the date of the agreement, understanding, or arrangement.

(iii) *Substantial negotiations related to options.*—If an option is treated as an agreement, understanding, or arrangement to acquire the stock on the date that the option is written, substantial negotiations to acquire the option will be treated as substantial negotiations to acquire the stock subject to such option. If an option is treated as an agreement, understanding, or arrangement to acquire the stock on the date that the option is transferred, substantial negotiations regarding the transfer of the option will be treated as substantial negotiations to acquire the stock subject to such option. If an option is treated as an agreement, understanding, or arrangement to acquire the stock on the date that the option is modified in a manner that materially increases the likelihood of exercise, substantial negotiations regarding such modifications to the option will be treated as substantial negotiations to acquire the stock subject to such option.

(2) *Stock acquired pursuant to options.*—For purposes of this section, if an option is issued for cash, the terms of the acquisition of the option and the terms of the option are established by the corporation the stock of which is subject to the option (Distributing or Controlled) or the writer with the involvement of one or more investment bankers, and the potential acquirers of the option have no opportunity to negotiate the terms of the acquisition of the option or the terms of the option, then an acquisition pursuant to such option shall be treated as an acquisition involving a public offering occurring after the distribution if the option is exercised after the distribution or an acquisition involving a public offering before a distribution if the option is exercised before the distribution. Otherwise, an acquisition pursuant to an option shall be treated as an acquisition not involving a public offering.

(3) *Instruments treated as options.*—For purposes of this section, except to the extent provided in paragraph (e)(4) of this section, call options, warrants, convertible obligations, the conversion feature of convertible stock, put options, redemption agreements (including rights to cause the redemption of stock), any other instruments that provide for the right or possibility to issue, redeem, or transfer stock (including an option on an option), or any other similar interests are treated as options.

(4) *Instruments generally not treated as options.*—For purposes of this section, the following are not treated as options unless (in the case of paragraphs (e)(4)(i), (ii), and (iii) of this section) written, transferred (directly or indirectly), modified, or listed with a principal purpose of avoiding the application of section 355(e) or this section.

(i) *Escrow, pledge, or other security agreements.*—An option that is part of a security arrangement in a typical lending transaction (including a purchase money loan), if the arrangement is subject to customary commercial conditions. For this purpose, a security arrangement includes, for example, an agreement for holding stock in escrow or under a pledge or other security agreement, or an option to acquire stock contingent upon a default under a loan.

(ii) *Options exercisable only upon death, disability, mental incompetency, or separation from service.*—Any option entered into between shareholders of a corporation (or a shareholder and the corporation) that is exercisable only upon the death, disability, or mental incompetency of the shareholder, or, in the case of stock acquired in connection with the performance of services for the corporation or a person related to it under section 355(d)(7)(A) (and that is not excessive by reference to the services performed), the shareholder's separation from service.

(iii) *Rights of first refusal.*—A bona fide right of first refusal regarding the corporation's stock with customary terms, entered into between shareholders of a corporation (or between the corporation and a shareholder).

(iv) *Other enumerated instruments.*—Any other instrument the Commissioner may designate in revenue procedures, notices, or other guidance published in the Internal Revenue Bulletin (see §601.601(d)(2) of this chapter).

* * *

(g) *Valuation.*—Except as provided in paragraph (e)(1)(i) of this section, for purposes of section 355(e) and this section, all shares of stock within a single class are considered to have the same value. Thus, control premiums and minority and blockage discounts within a single class are not taken into account.

(h) *Definitions.*—For purposes of this section, the following definitions shall apply:

(1) *Agreement, understanding, arrangement, or substantial negotiations.*—(i) An agreement, understanding, or arrangement generally requires either—

(A) an agreement, understanding, or arrangement by one or more officers or directors acting on behalf of Distributing or Controlled, by controlling shareholders of Distributing or Controlled, or by another person or persons with the implicit or explicit permission of one or more of such officers, directors, or controlling shareholders, with the acquirer or with a person or persons with the implicit or explicit permission of the acquirer; or

(B) an agreement, understanding, or arrangement by an acquirer that is a controlling shareholder of Distributing or Controlled immediately after the acquisition that is the subject of the agreement, understanding, or arrangement, or by a person or persons with the implicit or explicit permission of such acquirer, with the transferor or with a person or persons with the implicit or explicit permission of the transferor.

(ii) In the case of an acquisition by a corporation, an agreement, understanding, or arrangement with the acquiring corporation generally requires an agreement, understanding, or arrangement with one or more officers or directors acting on behalf of the acquiring corporation, with controlling shareholders of the acquiring corporation, or with another person or persons with the implicit or explicit permission of one or more of such officers, directors, or controlling shareholders.

(iii) Whether an agreement, understanding, or arrangement exists depends on the facts and circumstances. The parties do not necessarily have to have entered into a binding contract or have reached agreement on all significant economic terms to have an agreement, understanding, or arrangement. However, an agreement, understanding, or arrangement clearly exists if a binding contract to acquire stock exists.

(iv) Substantial negotiations in the case of an acquisition (other than involving a public offering) generally require discussions of significant economic terms, e.g., the exchange ratio in a reorganization, either—

(A) by one or more officers or directors acting on behalf of Distributing or Controlled, by controlling shareholders of Distributing or Controlled, or by another person or persons with the implicit or explicit permission of one or more of such officers, directors, or controlling shareholders, with the acquirer or with a person or persons with the implicit or explicit permission of the acquirer; or

(B) if the acquirer is a controlling shareholder of Distributing or Controlled immediately after the acquisition that is the subject of substantial negotiations, by the acquirer or by a person or persons with the implicit or explicit permission of the acquirer, with the transferor or with a person or persons with the implicit or explicit permission of the transferor.

(v) In the case of an acquisition (other than involving a public offering) by a corporation, substantial negotiations generally require discussions of significant economic terms with one or more officers or directors acting on behalf of the acquiring corporation, with controlling shareholders of the acquiring corporation, or with another person or persons with the implicit or explicit permission of one or more of such officers, directors, or controlling shareholders.

(vi) In the case of an acquisition involving a public offering, the existence of an agreement, understanding, arrangement, or substantial negotiations will be based on discussions by one or more officers or directors acting on behalf of Distributing or Controlled, by controlling shareholders of Distributing or Controlled, or by another person or persons with the implicit or explicit permission of one or more of such officers, directors, or controlling shareholders, with an investment banker.

(2) *Controlled corporation.*—A controlled corporation is a corporation the stock of which is distributed in a distribution to which section 355 (or so much of section 356 as relates to section 355) applies.

(3) *Controlling shareholder.*—(i) A controlling shareholder of a corporation the stock of which is listed on an established market is a five-percent shareholder who actively participates in the management or operation of the corporation. For purposes of this paragraph (h)(3)(i), a corporate director will be treated as actively participating in the management of the corporation.

(ii) A controlling shareholder of a corporation the stock of which is not listed on an established market is any person that owns stock possessing voting power representing a meaningful voice in the governance of the corporation. For purposes of determining whether a person owns stock possessing voting power representing a meaningful voice in the governance of the corporation, the person shall be treated as owning the stock that such person owns actually and constructively under the rules of section 318 (without regard to section 318(a)(4)). In addition, if the exercise of an option (whether by itself or in conjunction with the deemed exercise of one or more other options) would cause the holder to own stock possessing voting power representing a meaningful voice in the governance of the corporation, then the option will be treated as exercised.

(iii) If a distribution precedes an acquisition, Controlled's controlling shareholders immediately after the distribution and Distributing are included among Controlled's controlling shareholders at the time of the distribution.

(4) *Coordinating group.*—A coordinating group includes two or more persons that, pursuant to a formal or informal understanding, join in one or more coordinated acquisitions or dispositions of stock of Distributing or Controlled. A principal element in determining if such an understanding exists is whether the investment decision of each person is based on the investment decision of one or more other existing or prospective shareholders. A coordinating group is treated as a single shareholder for purposes of determining whether the coordinating group is treated as a controlling shareholder, a five-percent shareholder, or a ten-percent shareholder.

(5) *Disclosure event.*—A disclosure event regarding the distribution means any communication by an officer, director, controlling shareholder, or employee of Distributing, Controlled, or a corporation related to Distributing or Controlled, or an outside advisor of any of those persons (where such advisor makes the communication on behalf of such person), regarding the distribution, or the possibility thereof, to the acquirer or any other person (other than an officer, director, controlling shareholder, or employee of Distributing, Controlled, or a corporation related to Distributing or Controlled, or an outside advisor of any of those persons). For purposes of this paragraph (h)(5), a corporation is related to Distributing or Controlled if it is a member of an affiliated group (as defined in section 1504(a) without regard to section 1504(b)) that includes either Distributing or Controlled or it is a member of a qualified group (as defined in §1.368-1(d)(4)(ii)) that includes either Distributing or Controlled.

(6) *Discussions.*—Discussions by Distributing or Controlled generally require discussions by one or more officers or directors acting on behalf of Distributing or Controlled, by controlling shareholders of Distributing or Controlled, or by another person or persons with the implicit or explicit permission of one or more of such officers, directors, or controlling shareholders. Discussions with the acquirer generally require discussions with the acquirer or with a person or persons with the implicit or explicit permission of the acquirer. In the case of an acquisition by a corporation, discussions with the acquiring corporation generally require discussions with one or more officers or directors acting on behalf of the acquiring corporation, with controlling shareholders of the acquiring corporation, or with another person or persons with the implicit or explicit permission of one or more of such officers, directors, or controlling shareholders.

(7) *Established market.*—An established market is—

(i) A national securities exchange registered under section 6 of the Securities Exchange Act of 1934 (15 U.S.C. 78f);

(ii) An interdealer quotation system sponsored by a national securities association registered under section 15A of the Securities Act of 1934 (15 U.S.C. 78o-3); or

(iii) Any additional market that the Commissioner may designate in revenue procedures, notices, or other guidance published in the Internal Revenue Bulletin (see §601.601(d)(2) of this chapter).

(8) *Five-percent shareholder.*—A person will be considered a five-percent shareholder of a corporation the stock of which is listed on an established market if the person owns five percent or more of any class of stock of the corporation whose stock is transferred. For purposes of determining whether a person owns five percent or more of any class of stock of the corporation whose stock is transferred, the person shall be treated as owning the stock that such person owns actually and constructively under the rules of section 318 (without regard to section 318(a)(4)). In addition, if the exercise of an option (whether by itself or in conjunction with the deemed exercise of one or more other options) would cause the holder to become a five-percent shareholder, then the option will be treated as exercised. Absent actual knowledge that a person is a five-percent shareholder, a corporation can rely on Schedules 13D and 13G (or any similar schedules) filed with the Securities and Exchange Commission to identify its five-percent shareholders.

(9) *Implicit permission.*—A corporation is treated as having the implicit permission of its shareholders when it engages in discussions or negotiations, or enters into an agreement, understanding, or arrangement.

(10) *Public announcement.*—A public announcement regarding the distribution means any communication by Distributing or Controlled regarding Distributing's intention to effect the distribution where the communication is generally available to the public.

(11) *Public offering.*—An acquisition involving a public offering means an acquisition of stock for cash where the terms of the acquisition are established by the acquired corporation (Distributing or Controlled) or the seller with the involvement of one or more investment bankers and the potential acquirers have no opportunity to negotiate the terms of the acquisition. For example, a public offering includes an underwritten offering of registered stock for cash.

(12) *Similar acquisition (not involving a public offering).*—In general, an actual acquisition (other than involving a public offering) is similar to another potential acquisition if the actual acquisition effects a direct or indirect combination of all or a significant portion of the same business operations as the combination that would have been effected by such other potential acquisition. Thus, an actual acquisition may be similar to another acquisition even if the timing or terms of the actual acquisition are different from the timing or terms of the other acquisition. For example, an actual acquisition of Distributing by shareholders of another corporation in connection with a merger of such other corporation with and into Distributing is similar to another acquisition of Distributing by merger into such other corporation or into a subsidiary of such other corporation. However, in general, an actual acquisition (other than involving a public offering) is not similar to another acquisition if the ultimate owners of the business operations with which Distributing or Controlled is combined in the actual acquisition are substantially different from the ultimate owners of the business operations with which Distributing or Controlled was to be combined in such other acquisition.

(13) *Similar acquisition involving a public offering.*—(i) *One public offering.*—In general, an actual acquisition involving a public offering may be similar to a potential acquisition involving a public offering, even though there are changes in the terms of the stock, the class of stock being offered, the size of the offering, the timing of the offering, the price of the stock, or the participants in the offering.

(ii) *More than one public offering.*—More than one actual acquisition involving a public offering may be similar to a potential acquisition involving a public offering. If there is an actual acquisition involving a public offering (the first public offering) that is the same as, or similar to, a potential acquisition involving a public offering, then another actual acquisition involving a public offering (the second public offering) cannot be similar to the potential acquisition unless the purpose of the second public offering is similar to that of the potential acquisition and occurs close in time to the first public offering.

(iii) *Potential acquisition involving a public offering.*—For purposes of paragraph (h)(13)(i) and (ii) of this section, as the context may require, a potential acquisition involving a public offering means a potential acquisition involving a public offering that was discussed by Distributing or Controlled with an investment banker, that motivated the distribution, or that was the subject of an agreement, understanding, arrangement, or substantial negotiations.

(14) *Ten-percent shareholder.*—A person will be considered a ten-percent shareholder of a corporation the stock of which is listed on an established market if the person owns, actually or constructively under the rules of section 318 (without regard to section 318(a)(4)), ten percent or more of any class of stock of the corporation whose stock is transferred. A person will be considered a ten-percent shareholder of a corporation the stock of which is not listed on an established market if the person owns stock possessing ten percent or more of the total voting power of the stock of the corporation whose stock is transferred or stock having a value equal to ten percent or more of the total value of the stock of the corporation whose stock is transferred. For purposes of determining whether a person owns ten percent or more of the total voting power or value of the stock of the corporation whose stock is transferred, the person shall be treated as owning the stock that such person owns actually and constructively under the rules of section 318 (without regard to section 318(a)(4)). In addition, if the exercise of an option (whether by itself or in conjunction with the deemed exercise of one or more other options) would cause the holder to become a ten-percent shareholder, then the option will be treated as exercised. Absent actual knowledge that a person is a ten-percent shareholder, a corporation the stock of which is listed on an established market can rely on Schedules 13D and 13G (or any similar schedules) filed with the Securities and Exchange Commission to identify its ten-percent shareholders.

(i) [Reserved]

(j) *Examples.*—The following examples illustrate paragraphs (a) through (h) of this section.

Throughout these examples, assume that Distributing (D) owns all of the stock of Controlled (C). Assume further that D distributes the stock of C in a distribution to which section 355 applies and to which section 355(d) does not apply. Unless otherwise stated, assume the corporations do not have controlling shareholders. No inference should be drawn from any example concerning whether any requirements of section 355 other than those of section 355(e) are satisfied. The examples are as follows:

Example 1. Unwanted assets. (i) D is in business 1. C is in business 2. D is relatively small in its industry. D wants to combine with X, a larger corporation also engaged in business 1. X and D begin negotiating for X to acquire D, but X does not want to acquire C. To facilitate the acquisition of D by X, D agrees to distribute all the stock of C pro rata before the acquisition. Prior to the distribution, D and X enter into a contract for D to merge into X subject to several conditions. One month after D and X enter into the contract, D distributes C and, on the day after the distribution, D merges into X. As a result of the merger, D's former shareholders own less than 50 percent of the stock of X.

(ii) The issue is whether the distribution of C and the merger of D into X are part of a plan. No Safe Harbor applies to this acquisition. To determine whether the distribution of C and the merger of D into X are part of a plan, D must consider all the facts and circumstances, including those described in paragraph (b) of this section.

(iii) The following tends to show that the distribution of C and the merger of D into X are part of a plan: X and D had an agreement regarding the acquisition during the two-year period ending on the date of the distribution (paragraph (b)(3)(i) of this section), and the distribution was motivated by a business purpose to facilitate the merger (paragraph (b)(3)(v) of this section). Because the merger was agreed to at the time of the distribution, the fact described in paragraph (b)(3)(i) of this section is given substantial weight.

(iv) None of the facts and circumstances listed in paragraph (b)(4) of this section, tending to show that a distribution and an acquisition are not part of a plan, exist in this case.

(v) The distribution of C and the merger of D into X are part of a plan under paragraph (b) of this section.

Example 2. Public offering. (i) D's managers, directors, and investment banker discuss the possibility of offering D stock to the public. They decide a public offering of 20 percent of D's stock with D as a stand-alone corporation would be in D's best interest. One month later, to facilitate a stock offering by D of 20 percent of its stock, D distributes all the stock of C pro rata to D's shareholders. D issues new shares amounting to 20 percent of its stock to the public in a public offering seven months after the distribution.

(ii) The issue is whether the distribution of C and the public offering by D are part of a plan. No Safe Harbor applies to this acquisition. Safe Harbor VII, relating to public trading, does not apply to public offerings (see paragraph (d)(7)(i) of this section). To determine whether the distribution of C and the public offering by D are part of a plan, D must consider all the facts and circumstances, including those described in paragraph (b) of this section.

(iii) The following tends to show that the distribution of C and the public offering by D are part of a plan: D discussed the public offering with its investment banker during the two-year period ending on the date of the distribution (paragraph (b)(3)(ii) of this section), and the distribution was motivated by a business purpose to facilitate the public offering (paragraph (b)(3)(v) of this section).

(iv) None of the facts and circumstances listed in paragraph (b)(4) of this section, tending to show that a distribution and an acquisition are not part of a plan, exist in this case.

(v) The distribution of C and the public offering by D are part of a plan under paragraph (b) of this section.

Example 3. Hot market. (i) D is a widely-held corporation the stock of which is listed on an established market. D announces a distribution of C and distributes C pro rata to D's shareholders. By contract, C agrees to indemnify D for any imposition of tax under section 355(e) caused by the acts of C. The distribution is motivated by a desire to improve D's access to financing at preferred customer interest rates, which will be more readily available if D separates from C. At the time of the distribution, although neither D nor C has been approached by any potential acquirer of C, it is reasonably certain that soon after the distribution either an acquisition of C will occur or there will be an agreement, understanding, arrangement, or substantial negotiations regarding an acquisition of C. Corporation Y acquires C in a merger described in section 368(a)(1)(A) by reason of section 368(a)(2)(E) within six months after the distribution. The C shareholders receive less than 50 percent of the stock of Y in the exchange.

(ii) The issue is whether the distribution of C and the acquisition of C by Y are part of a plan. No Safe Harbor applies to this acquisition. Under paragraph (b)(2) of this section, because prior to the distribution neither D nor C and Y had an agreement, understanding, arrangement, or substantial negotiations regarding the acquisition or a similar acquisition, the distribution of C by D and the acquisition of C by Y are not part of a plan under paragraph (b) of this section.

Example 4. Unexpected opportunity. (i) D, the stock of which is listed on an established market, makes a public announcement that it will distribute all the stock of C pro rata to D's shareholders. After the public announcement but before the distribution, widely-held X becomes available as an acquisition target. There were no discussions by D or C with X before the date of the public announcement. D negotiates with X and X merges into D before the distribution. In the merger, X's shareholders receive ten percent of D's stock. D distributes the stock of C pro rata within six months after the acquisition of X. No shareholder of X was a controlling shareholder or a ten-percent shareholder of D at any time during the period beginning immediately after the merger and ending on the date of the distribution

(ii) The issue is whether the acquisition of X by D and the distribution of C are part of a plan. Safe Harbor V applies to this acquisition because the distribution is pro rata among D's shareholders, the acquisition occurs after the date of a public announcement regarding the distribution, there were no discussions by D or C with X on or before the date of the public announcement, no acquirer was a controlling shareholder or a ten-percent shareholder of D during the period beginning immediately after the merger and ending on the date of the distribution, and not more than 20 percent of D's stock was acquired by the X shareholders in the merger.

Example 5. Vote shifting transaction. (i) D is in business 1. C is in business 2. D wants to combine with X, which is also engaged in business 1. The stock of X is closely held. X and D begin negotiating for D to acquire X, but the X shareholders do not want to acquire an indirect interest in C. To facilitate the acquisition of X by D, D agrees to distribute all the stock of C pro rata before the acquisition of X. D and X enter into a contract for X to merge into D subject to several conditions. Among those conditions is that D will amend its corporate charter to provide for two classes of stock: Class A and Class B. Under all circumstances, each share of Class A stock will be entitled to ten votes in the election of each director on D's board of directors. Upon issuance, each share of Class B stock will be entitled to ten votes in the election of each director on D's board of directors; however, a disposition of such share by its original holder will result in such share being entitled to only one vote, rather than ten votes, in the election of each director. Immediately after the merger, the Class B shares will be listed on an established market. One month after D and X enter into the contract, D distributes C. Immediately after the distribution, the shareholders of D exchange their D stock for the new Class B shares. On the day after the distribution, X merges into D. In the merger, the former shareholders of X exchange their X stock for Class A shares of D. Immediately after the merger, D's historic shareholders own stock of D representing 51 percent of the total combined voting power of all classes of stock of D entitled to vote and more than 50 percent of the total value of all classes of stock of D. During the 30-day period following the merger, none of the Class A shares are transferred, but a number of D's historic shareholders sell their Class B stock of D in public trading with the result that, at the end of that 30-day period, the Class A shares owned by the former X shareholders represent 52 percent of the total combined voting power of all classes of stock of D entitled to vote.

(ii) *X acquisition.* (A) The issue is whether the distribution of C and the merger of X into D are part of a plan. No Safe Harbor applies to this acquisition. To determine whether the distribution of C and the merger of X into D are part of a plan, D must consider all the facts and circumstances, including those described in paragraph (b) of this section.

(B) The following tends to show that the distribution of C and the merger of X into D are part of a plan: X and D had an agreement regarding the acquisition during the two-year period ending on the date of the distribution (paragraph (b)(3)(i) of this section), and the distribution was motivated by a business purpose to facilitate the merger (paragraph (b)(3)(v) of this section). Because the merger was agreed to at the time of the distribution, the fact described in paragraph (b)(3)(i) of this section is given substantial weight.

(C) None of the facts and circumstances listed in paragraph (b)(4) of this section, tending to show that a distribution and an acquisition are not part of a plan, exist in this case.

(D) The distribution of C and the merger of X into D are part of a plan under paragraph (b) of this section.

(iii) *Public trading of Class B shares.* (A) Assuming that each of the transferors and the transferees of the Class B stock of D in public trading is not one of the prohibited transferors or transferees listed in paragraph (d)(7)(i), Safe Harbor VII will apply to the acquisitions of the Class B stock during the 30-day period following the merger such that the distribution and those acquisitions will not be treated as part of a plan. However, to the extent that those acquisitions result in an indirect acquisition of voting power by a person other than the acquirer of the transferred stock, Safe Harbor VII does not prevent the acquisition of the D stock (with the voting power such stock represents after those acquisitions) by the former X shareholders from being treated as part of a plan.

(B) To the extent that the transfer of the Class B shares causes the voting power of D to shift to the Class A stock acquired by the former X shareholders, such shifted voting power will be treated as attributable to the stock acquired by the former X shareholders as part of a plan that includes the distribution and the X acquisition.

Example 6. Acquisition not involving a public offering that is not similar. (i) D, X, and Y are each corporations the stock of which is publicly traded and widely held. Each of D, X, and Y is engaged in the manufacture and sale of trucks. C is engaged in the manufacture and sale of buses. D and X engage in substantial negotiations concerning X's acquisition of the stock of D from the D shareholders in exchange for stock of X. D and X do not reach an agreement regarding that acquisition. Three months after D and X first began negotiations regarding that acquisition, D distributes the stock of C pro rata to its shareholders. Three months after the distribution, Y acquires the stock of D from the D shareholders in exchange for stock of Y. The ultimate owners of Y are substantially different from the ultimate owners of X.

(ii) Although both X and Y engage in the manufacture and sale of trucks, X's truck business and Y's truck business are not the same business operations. Therefore, because Y's acquisition of D does not effect a combination of the same business operations as X's acquisition of D would have effected, and because the ultimate owners of Y are substantially different from the ultimate owners of X, Y's acquisition of D is not similar to X's potential acquisition of D that was the subject of earlier negotiations.

Example 7. Acquisition not involving a public offering that is similar. (i) D is engaged in the business of writing custom software for several industries (industries 1 through 6). The software business of D related to industries 4, 5, and 6 is significant relative to the software business of D related to industries 3, 4, 5, and 6. X, an unrelated corporation, is engaged in the business of writing software and the business of manufacturing and selling hardware devices. X's business of writing software is significant relative to its total businesses. X and D engage in substantial negotiations regarding X's acquisition of D stock from the D shareholders in exchange for stock of X. Because X does not want to acquire the software businesses related to industries 1 and 2, these negotiations relate to an acquisition of D stock where D owns the software businesses related only to industries 3, 4, 5, and 6. Thereafter, D concludes that the intellectual property licenses central to the software business related to industries 1 and 2 are not transferable and that a separation of the software business related to industry 3 from the software business related to industry 2 is not desirable. One month after D begins negotiating with X, D contributes the software businesses related to industries 4, 5, and 6 to C, and distributes the stock of C pro rata to its shareholders. In addition, X sells its hardware businesses for cash. After the distribution, C and X negotiate for X's acquisition of the C stock from the C shareholders in exchange for X stock, and X acquires the stock of C.

(ii) Although D and C are different corporations, C does not own the custom software business related to industry 3, and X sold its hardware business prior to the acquisition of C, because X's acquisition of C involves a combination of a significant portion of the same business operations as the combination that would have been effected by the acquisition of D that was the subject of negotiations between D and X, X's acquisition of C is the same as, or similar to, X's potential acquisition of D that was the subject of earlier negotiations.

* * *

[Reg. § 1.355-7.]

□ [*T.D.* 9198, 4-18-2005.]

§ 1.355-8. Definition of predecessor and successor and limitations on gain recognition under section 355(e) and section 355(f).—(a) *In general.*—(1) *Scope.*—For purposes of section 355(e), this section provides rules under section 355(e)(4)(D) to determine whether a corporation is treated as a predecessor or successor of a distributing corporation (Distributing) or a controlled corporation (Controlled) with respect to a distribution by Distributing of stock (or stock and securities) of Controlled that qualifies under section 355(a) (or so much of section 356 as relates to section 355) (Distribution). This section also provides rules limiting the amount of Distributing's gain recognized under section 355(e) on a Distribution if section 355(e) applies to an acquisition by one or more persons, as part of a Plan, of stock that in the aggregate represents a 50-percent or greater interest (Planned 50-percent Acquisition) of a Predecessor of Distributing, or a Planned 50-percent Acquisition of Distributing. In addition, this section provides rules regarding the application of section 336(e) to a Distribution to which this section applies. This section also provides rules regarding the application of section 355(f) to a Distribution in certain cases.

(2) *Overview.*—(i) *Purposes and conceptual overview.*—Paragraph (a)(3) of this section summarizes the two principal purposes of this

section and sets forth a brief conceptual overview of the scenarios in which a corporation may be a Predecessor of Distributing.

(ii) *References to and definitions of terms used in this section.*—Paragraph (a)(4) of this section provides rules regarding references to the terms *Distributing, Controlled, Distribution, Plan,* and *Plan Period* for purposes of section 355(e), § 1.355-7, and this section. Paragraph (a)(5) of this section lists the terms used in this section and indicates where each term is defined. Paragraph (b) of this section defines the term *Predecessor of Distributing* and several related terms. Paragraph (c) of this section defines the terms *Predecessor of Controlled, Successor* (of Distributing or Controlled), and *Section 381 Transaction.*

(iii) *Special rules and examples.*—Paragraph (d) of this section provides guidance with regard to acquisitions and deemed acquisitions of stock if there is a Predecessor of Distributing or a Successor of either Distributing or Controlled. Paragraph (e) of this section provides two rules that may limit the amount of Distributing's gain on a Distribution if there is a Predecessor of Distributing, as well as an overall gain limitation. Paragraph (e) of this section also provides guidance with respect to the application of section 336(e). Regardless of whether there is a Predecessor of Distributing, Predecessor of Controlled, or Successor of either Distributing or Controlled, paragraph (f) of this section provides a special rule relating to section 355(e)(2)(C), which provides that section 355(e) does not apply to certain transactions within an Expanded Affiliated Group. Paragraph (g) of this section provides rules coordinating the application of section 355(f) with the rules of this section. Paragraph (h) of this section contains examples that illustrate the rules of this section.

(3) *Purposes of section; Predecessor of Distributing overview.*—(i) *Purposes.*—The rules in this section have two principal purposes. The first is to ensure that section 355(e) applies to a Distribution if, as part of a Plan, some of the assets of a Predecessor of Distributing are transferred directly or indirectly to Controlled without full recognition of gain, and the Distribution accomplishes a division of the assets of the Predecessor of Distributing. The second is to ensure that section 355(e) applies when there is a Planned 50-percent Acquisition of a Successor of Distributing or Successor of Controlled. The rules of this section must be interpreted and applied in a manner that is consistent with and reasonably carries out the purposes of this section.

(ii) *Predecessor of Distributing overview.*—The term Predecessor of Distributing is defined in paragraph (b) of this section. Only a Potential Predecessor can be a Predecessor of Distributing. See paragraph (b)(1)(i) of this section. A Potential Predecessor can be a Predecessor of Distributing only if, as part of a Plan, the Distribution accomplishes a division of the assets of the Potential Predecessor. See paragraph (b)(1)(iii) of this section. Accordingly, in the absence of that Plan, a Predecessor of Distributing cannot exist for purposes of section 355(e). The detailed rules set forth in paragraph (b) of this section provide that a Potential Predecessor the assets of which are divided as part of a Plan may be a Predecessor of Distributing in either of the following two scenarios:

(A) *Relevant Property transferred to Controlled.*—As part of the Plan, one or more of the Potential Predecessor's assets were transferred to Controlled in one or more tax-deferred transactions prior to the Distribution.

(B) *Relevant Property includes Controlled Stock.*—The Potential Predecessor's assets included Controlled stock that, as part of the Plan, was transferred to Distributing in one or more tax-deferred transactions prior to the Distribution.

(4) *References.*—(i) *References to Distributing or Controlled.*—For purposes of section 355(e), except as otherwise provided in this section, any reference to Distributing or Controlled includes, as the context may require, a reference to any Predecessor of Distributing or any Predecessor of Controlled, respectively, or any Successor of Distributing or Controlled, respectively. However, except as otherwise provided in this section, a reference to a Predecessor of Distributing or to a Successor of Distributing does not include a reference to Distributing, and a reference to a Predecessor of Controlled or to a Successor of Controlled does not include a reference to Controlled.

(ii) *References to Plan or Distribution.*—Except as otherwise provided in this section, references to a *Plan* in this section are references to a plan within the meaning of § 1.355-7. References to a distribution in § 1.355-7 include a reference to a Distribution and other related pre-Distribution transactions that together effect a division of the assets of a Predecessor of Distributing. In determining whether a Distribution and a Planned 50-percent Acquisition of a Predecessor of Distributing, Distributing (including any Successor thereof), or Controlled (including any Successor thereof) are part of a Plan, the rules of § 1.355-7 apply. In applying those rules, references to Distributing or Controlled in § 1.355-7 generally include references to any Predecessor of Distributing and any Successor of Distributing, or any Successor of Controlled, as appropriate. However, with regard to any possible Planned 50-percent Acquisition of a Predecessor of Distributing, any agreement, understanding, arrangement, or substantial negotiations with regard to the acquisition of the stock of the Predecessor of Distributing is analyzed under § 1.355-7 with regard to the actions of officers or directors of Distributing or Controlled, controlling shareholders (as defined in § 1.355-7(h)(3)) of Distributing or Controlled, or a person acting with permission of one of those parties. For purposes of the preceding sentence, references in § 1.355-7 to Distributing do not include references to a Predecessor of Distributing. Therefore, the actions of officers, directors, or controlling shareholders of a Predecessor of Distributing, or of a person acting with the implicit or explicit permission of one of those parties, are not considered unless those parties otherwise would be treated as acting on behalf of Distributing or Controlled under § 1.355-7 (for example, if a Predecessor of Distributing is a controlling shareholder of Distributing).

(iii) *Plan Period.*—For purposes of this section, the term *Plan Period* means the period that ends immediately after the Distribution and begins on the earliest date on which any pre-Distribution step that is part of the Plan is agreed to or understood, arranged, or substantially negotiated by one or more officers or directors acting on behalf of Distributing or Controlled, by controlling shareholders of Distributing or Controlled, or by another person or persons with the implicit or explicit permission of one or more of such officers, directors, or controlling shareholders. For purposes of the preceding sentence, references to Distributing and Controlled do not include references to any Predecessor of Distributing, Predecessor of Controlled, or Successor of Distributing or Controlled.

(5) *List of definitions.*—This section uses the following terms, which are defined where indicated—

(i) *Acquiring Owner.*—Paragraph (d)(1)(i) of this section.

(ii) *Controlled.*—Paragraph (a)(1) of this section.

(iii) *Distributing.*—Paragraph (a)(1) of this section.

(iv) *Distributing Gain Limitation Rule.*—Paragraph (e)(1)(ii) of this section.

(v) *Distribution.*—Paragraph (a)(1) of this section.

(vi) *Division of Relevant Property Requirement.*—Paragraph (b)(1)(iii) of this section.

(vii) *Expanded Affiliated Group.*—Paragraph (b)(2)(ii)(B) of this section.

(viii) *Hypothetical Controlled.*—Paragraph (e)(2)(i) of this section.

(ix) *Hypothetical D/355(e) Reorganization.*—Paragraph (e)(2)(i) of this section.

(x) *Plan.*—Paragraph (a)(4)(ii) of this section.

(xi) *Plan Period.*—Paragraph (a)(4)(iii) of this section.

(xii) *Planned 50-percent Acquisition.*—Paragraph (a)(1) of this section.

(xiii) *POD Gain Limitation Rule.*—Paragraph (e)(1)(ii) of this section.

(xiv) *Potential Predecessor.*—Paragraph (b)(2)(ii)(A) of this section.

(xv) *Predecessor of Controlled.*—Paragraph (c)(1) of this section.

(xvi) *Predecessor of Distributing.*—Paragraph (b)(1) of this section.

(xvii) *Reflection of Basis Requirement.*—Paragraph (b)(1)(ii)(B) of this section.

(xviii) *Relevant Equity.*—Paragraph (b)(2)(iv)(A) of this section.

(xix) *Relevant Property.*—Paragraph (b)(2)(iv)(A) of this section.

(xx) *Relevant Property Requirement.*—Paragraph (b)(1)(ii)(A) of this section.

(xxi) *Section 381 Transaction.*—Paragraph (c)(3) of this section.

(xxii) *Separated Property.*—Paragraph (b)(2)(vii) of this section.

(xxiii) *Statutory Recognition Amount.*—Paragraph (e)(1)(i) of this section.

(xxiv) *Substitute Asset.*—Paragraph (b)(2)(vi)(A) of this section.

(xxv) *Successor.*—Paragraph (c)(2)(i) of this section.

(xxvi) *Successor Transaction.*—Paragraph (c)(2)(i) of this section.

(xxvii) *Underlying Property.*—Paragraph (b)(2)(viii) of this section.

(b) *Predecessor of Distributing.*—(1) *Definition.*—(i) *In general.*—For purposes of section 355(e), a Potential Predecessor is a predecessor of Distributing (Predecessor of Distributing) if, taking into account the special rules of paragraph (b)(2) of this section—

(A) Both pre-Distribution requirements of paragraph (b)(1)(ii) of this section are satisfied; and

(B) The post-Distribution requirement of paragraph (b)(1)(iii) of this section is satisfied.

(ii) *Pre-Distribution requirements.*—(A) *Relevant Property requirement.*—The requirement set forth in this paragraph (b)(1)(ii)(A) (Relevant Property Requirement) is satisfied if, before the Distribution, and as part of a Plan, either—

(1) Any Controlled stock distributed in the Distribution was directly or indirectly acquired (or deemed acquired under the rules set forth in paragraph (b)(2)(x) of this section) by Distributing in exchange for any direct or indirect interest in Relevant Property—

(i) That is held directly or indirectly by Controlled immediately before the Distribution; and

(ii) The gain on which (if any) was not recognized in full at any point during the Plan Period; or

(2) Any Controlled stock that is distributed in the Distribution is Relevant Property of the Potential Predecessor.

(B) *Reflection of basis requirement.*—The requirement set forth in this paragraph (b)(1)(ii)(B) (Reflection of Basis Requirement) is satisfied if any Controlled stock that satisfies the Relevant Property Requirement—

(1) Either—

(i) Had a basis prior to the Distribution that was determined in whole or in part by reference to the basis of any Separated Property; or

(ii) Is Relevant Property of the Potential Predecessor; and

(2) During the Plan Period prior to the Distribution, was neither distributed in a distribution to which section 355(e) applied nor transferred in a transaction in which the gain (if any) on that Controlled stock was recognized in full.

(iii) *Post-Distribution requirement.*—The requirement set forth in this paragraph (b)(1)(iii) (Division of Relevant Property Requirement) is satisfied if, immediately after the Distribution, and as part of a Plan, direct or indirect ownership of the Potential Predecessor's Relevant Property has been divided between Controlled on the one hand, and Distributing or the Potential Predecessor (or a successor to the Potential Predecessor) on the other hand. For purposes of this paragraph (b)(1)(iii), if Controlled stock that is distributed in the Distribution is Relevant Property of a Potential Predecessor, then Controlled is deemed to have received Relevant Property of the Potential Predecessor.

(2) *Additional definitions and rules related to paragraph (b)(1) of this section.*—(i) *References to Distributing and Controlled.*—For purposes of the Relevant Property Requirement, the Reflection of Basis Requirement, and the Division of Relevant Property Requirement, references to Distributing and Controlled do not include references to any Predecessor of Distributing, Predecessor of Controlled, or Successor of Distributing or Controlled.

(ii) *Potential Predecessor.*—(A) *Potential Predecessor definition.*—The term *Potential Predecessor* means a corporation, other than Distributing or Controlled, if—

(1) As part of a Plan, the corporation transfers property to a Potential Predecessor, Distributing, or a member of the same Expanded Affiliated Group as Distributing in a Section 381 Transaction; or

(2) Immediately after completion of the Plan, the corporation is a member of the same Expanded Affiliated Group as Distributing.

(B) *Expanded Affiliated Group definition.*—The term *Expanded Affiliated Group* means an affiliated group (as defined in section 1504 without regard to section 1504(b)).

(iii) *Successors of Potential Predecessors.*—For purposes of the Division of Relevant Property Requirement, if a Potential Predecessor transfers property in a Section 381 Transaction to a corporation (other than Distributing or Controlled) during the Plan Period, the corporation is a successor to the Potential Predecessor.

(iv) *Relevant Property; Relevant Equity.*—(A) *In general.*—Except as otherwise provided in this paragraph (b)(2)(iv) or in paragraph (b)(2)(v) of this section, the term *Relevant Property* means any property that was held, directly or indirectly, by the Potential Predecessor during the Plan Period. The term *Relevant Equity* means Relevant Property that is an equity interest in a corporation or a partnership.

(B) *Property held by Distributing.*—Except as provided in paragraph (b)(2)(iv)(C) of this section, property held directly or indirectly by Distributing (including Controlled stock) is Relevant Property of a Potential Predecessor only to the extent that the property was transferred directly or indirectly to Distributing during the Plan Period, and it was Relevant Property of the Potential Predecessor before the direct or indirect transfer(s). For example, if during the Plan Period a subsidiary corporation of a Potential Predecessor merges into Controlled in a reorganization under section 368(a)(1)(A) and (2)(D), and, as a result, the Potential Predecessor directly or indirectly owns Distributing stock received in the merger, the subsidiary's assets held by Controlled are Relevant Property of that Potential Predecessor.

(C) *F reorganizations.*—For purposes of paragraph (b)(2)(iv)(B) of this section, the transferor and transferee in any reorganization described in section 368(a)(1)(F) (F reorganization) are treated as a single corporation. Therefore, for example, Relevant Property acquired during the Plan Period by a corporation that is a transferor (as to a later F reorganization) is treated as having been acquired directly (and from the same source) by the transferee (as to the later F reorganization) during the Plan Period. In addition, any transfer (or deemed transfer) of assets to Distributing in an F reorganization will not cause the transferred assets to be treated as Relevant Property.

(v) *Stock of Distributing as Relevant Property.*—(A) *In general.*—For purposes of the Division of Relevant Property Requirement, except as provided in paragraph (b)(2)(v)(B) of this section, stock of Distributing is not Relevant Property (and thus is not Relevant Equity) to the extent that the Potential Predecessor becomes, as part of a Plan, the direct or indirect owner of that stock as the result of the transfer to Distributing of direct or indirect interests in the Potential Predecessor's Relevant Property. For example, stock of Distributing is not Relevant Property if it is acquired by a Potential Predecessor as part of a Plan in an exchange to which section 351(a) applies.

(B) *Certain reorganizations.*—For purposes of the Division of Relevant Property Requirement, stock of Distributing is Relevant Property (and thus Relevant Equity) to the extent that the Potential Predecessor becomes, as part of the Plan, the direct or indirect owner of that stock as the result of a transaction described in section 368(a)(1)(E).

(vi) *Substitute Asset.*—(A) *In general.*—Subject to paragraph (b)(2)(vi)(B) of this section, the term *Substitute Asset* means any property that is held directly or indirectly by Distributing during the Plan Period and was received, during the Plan Period, in exchange for Relevant Property that was acquired directly or indirectly by Distributing if all gain on the transferred Relevant Property is not recognized on the exchange. For example, property received by Controlled in exchange for Relevant Property in a transaction qualifying under section 1031 is a Substitute Asset. In addition, stock received by Distributing in a distribution qualifying under section 305(a) or section 355(a) on Relevant Equity is a Substitute Asset.

(B) *Controlled stock received by Distributing.*—*(1) In general.*—Except as provided in paragraph (b)(2)(vi)(B)(*2*) of this section, stock of Controlled received in exchange for a direct or indirect transfer of Relevant Property by Distributing is not a Substitute Asset.

(2) Exception.—If the basis in Controlled stock received or deemed received in an exchange described in paragraph (b)(2)(vi)(B)(*1*) of this section is determined in whole or in part by reference to the basis of Relevant Equity the issuer of which ceases to exist for Federal income tax purposes under the Plan, that Controlled stock constitutes a Substitute Asset. See paragraph (b)(2)(x) of this section.

(C) *Treatment as Relevant Property.*—For purposes of this section, a Substitute Asset is treated as Relevant Property with the same ownership and transfer history as the Relevant Property for which (or with respect to which) it was received.

(vii) *Separated Property.*—The term *Separated Property* means each item of Relevant Property that is described in the Relevant Property Requirement (regardless of whether the fair market value of the Relevant Property exceeds its adjusted basis). However, if Relevant Equity is Separated Property, Underlying Property associated with that Relevant Equity is not treated as Separated Property. In addition, if Distributing directly or indirectly acquires Relevant Equity in a transaction in which gain is recognized in full, Underlying Property associated with that Relevant Equity is not treated as Separated Property.

(viii) *Underlying Property.*—The term *Underlying Property* means property directly or indirectly held by a corporation or partnership any equity interest in which is Relevant Equity.

(ix) *Multiple Predecessors of Distributing.*—If there are multiple Potential Predecessors that satisfy the pre-Distribution requirements and post-Distribution requirement of paragraph (b)(1) of this section, each of those Potential Predecessors is a Predecessor of Distributing. For example, a Potential Predecessor that transfers property to a Predecessor of Distributing without full recognition of gain (and that otherwise meets the requirements of paragraph (b)(1) of this section) is also a Predecessor of Distributing if the applicable transfer occurred as part of a Plan that existed at the time of such transfer.

(x) *Deemed exchanges.*—For purposes of paragraph (b)(1)(ii) of this section (regarding the Relevant Property Requirement and the Reflection of Basis Requirement) and paragraph (b)(2)(vi) of this section (regarding Substitute Assets), Distributing is treated as acquiring Controlled stock in exchange for a direct or indirect interest in Relevant Property if the basis of Distributing in that Controlled stock, immediately after a transfer of the Relevant Property, is determined in whole or in part by reference to the basis of that Relevant Property immediately before the transfer. For example, if a corporation transfers Relevant Property to Controlled in exchange for Distributing stock in a transaction that qualifies as a reorganization under section 368(a)(1)(C), then, for purposes of paragraphs (b)(1)(ii) and (b)(2)(vi) of this section, Distributing is treated as acquiring Controlled stock in exchange for a direct or indirect interest in Relevant Property. See § 1.358-6(c)(1).

(c) *Additional definitions.*—(1) *Predecessor of Controlled.*—Solely for purposes of applying paragraph (f) of this section, a corporation is a predecessor of Controlled (Predecessor of Controlled) if, before the Distribution, it transfers property to Controlled in a Section 381 Transaction as part of a Plan. Other than for the purpose described in the preceding sentence, no corporation can be a Predecessor of Controlled. If multiple corporations satisfy the requirements of this paragraph (c)(1), each of those corporations is a Predecessor of Controlled. For example, a corporation that transfers property to a Predecessor of Controlled in a Section 381 Transaction is also a Predecessor of Controlled if the Section 381 Transaction occurred as part of a Plan that existed at the time of such transaction.

(2) *Successors.*—(i) *In general.*—For purposes of section 355(e), a successor (Successor) of Distributing or of Controlled is a corporation to which Distributing or Controlled, respectively, transfers property in a Section 381 Transaction after the Distribution (Successor Transaction).

(ii) *Determination of Successor status.*—More than one corporation may be a Successor of Distributing or Controlled. For example, if Distributing transfers property to another corporation (X) in a Section 381 Transaction, and X transfers property to another corporation (Y) in a Section 381 Transaction, then each of X and Y is a Successor of Distributing. In this case, the determination of whether Y is a Successor of Distributing is made after the determination of whether X is a Successor of Distributing.

(3) *Section 381 Transaction.*—The term *Section 381 Transaction* means a transaction to which section 381 applies.

(d) *Special acquisition rules.*—(1) *Deemed acquisitions of stock in Section 381 Transactions.*—(i) *Rule.*—This paragraph (d)(1)(i) applies to each shareholder of the acquiring corporation immediately before a Section 381 Transaction (Acquiring Owner). Each Acquiring Owner is treated for purposes of this section as acquiring, in the Section 381 Transaction, stock representing an interest in the distributor or transferor corporation, to the extent that the Acquiring Owner's interest in the acquiring corporation immediately after the Section 381 Transaction exceeds the Acquiring Owner's direct or indirect interest in the distributor or transferor corporation immediately before the Section 381 Transaction.

(ii) *Example.*—The example set forth in this paragraph (d)(1)(ii) illustrates the application of the deemed acquisition rule in paragraph (d)(1)(i) of this section. Assume that A held all of the stock of Distributing, Distributing held a 25-percent interest in a Predecessor of Distributing, and A held no direct interest, or other indirect interest, in the Predecessor of Distributing immediately before a Section 381 Transaction in which the Predecessor of Distributing transfers its assets to Distributing. In the Section 381 Transaction, the Predecessor of Distributing's shareholders (other than Distributing) collectively receive a 10-percent interest in Distributing (reducing A's interest in Distributing to 90 percent). Under paragraph (d)(1)(i) of this section, A is treated as acquiring in the Section 381 Transaction stock representing a 65-percent interest in the Predecessor of Distributing. This is because A's 90-percent interest in Distributing (the acquiring corporation in the Section 381 Transaction) immediately after the Section 381 Transaction exceeds A's 25-percent interest (held indirectly through Distributing) in the Predecessor of Distributing (the transferor corporation in the Section 381 Transaction) immediately before the Section 381 Transaction by 65 percent. Similarly, each Acquiring Owner of a Successor of Distributing is treated as acquiring, in the Successor Transaction, stock of Distributing, to the extent that the Acquiring Owner's interest in the Successor of Distributing immediately after the Successor Transaction exceeds the Acquiring Owner's direct or indirect interest in Distributing immediately before the Successor Transaction.

(2) *Deemed acquisitions of stock after Section 381 Transactions.*—For purposes of this section, after a Section 381 Transaction (including a Successor Transaction), an acquisition of stock of an acquiring corporation (including a deemed stock acquisition under paragraph (d)(1)(i) of this section) is treated also as an acquisition of an interest in the stock of the distributor or transferor corporation. For example, an acquisition of the stock of Distributing that occurs after a Section 381 Transaction is treated not only as an acquisition of the stock of Distributing, but also as an acquisition of the stock of any Predecessor of Distributing whose assets were acquired by Distributing in the prior Section 381 Transaction. Similarly, an acquisition of the stock of a Successor of Distributing that occurs after the Successor Transaction is treated not only as an acquisition of the stock of the Successor of Distributing, but also as an acquisition of the stock of Distributing.

(3) *Separate counting for Distributing and each Predecessor of Distributing.*—The measurement of whether one or more persons have acquired stock of any specific corporation in a Planned 50-percent Acquisition is made separately from the measurement of any potential Planned 50-percent Acquisition of any other corporation. Therefore, there may be a Planned 50-percent Acquisition of a Predecessor of Distributing even if there is no Planned 50-percent Acquisition of Distributing. Similarly, there may be a Planned 50-percent Acquisition of Distributing even if there is no Planned 50-percent Acquisition of a Predecessor of Distributing.

(e) *Special rules for limiting gain recognition.*—(1) *Overview.*—(i) *Gain limitation.*—This paragraph (e) provides rules that limit the amount of gain that must be recognized by Distributing by reason of section 355(e) to an amount that is less than the amount that Distributing otherwise would be required to recognize under section 355(c)(2) or section 361(c)(2) (Statutory Recognition Amount) in certain cases involving one or more Predecessors of Distributing.

(ii) *Multiple Planned 50-percent Acquisitions.*—If there are Planned 50-percent Acquisitions of multiple corporations (for example, two Predecessors of Distributing), Distributing must recognize the Statutory Recognition Amount with respect to each such corporation, subject to the limitations in paragraph (e)(2) of this section relating to a Planned 50-percent Acquisition of a Predecessor of Distributing (POD Gain Limitation Rule) and paragraph (e)(3) of this section relating to a Planned 50-percent Acquisition of Distributing (Distributing Gain Limitation Rule), if applicable. The POD Gain Limitation Rule and the Distributing Gain Limitation Rule are applied separately to the Planned 50-percent Acquisition of each such corporation to determine the amount of gain required to be recognized.

(iii) *Statutory Recognition Amount limit; Section 336(e).*—Paragraph (e)(4) of this section sets forth an overall gain limitation based on the Statutory Recognition Amount. Paragraph (e)(5) of this section clarifies the availability of an election under section 336(e) with regard to certain Distributions.

(2) *Planned 50-percent Acquisition of a Predecessor of Distributing.*—(i) *In general.*—If there is a Planned 50-percent Acquisition of a Predecessor of Distributing, the amount of gain recognized by Distributing by reason of section 355(e) as a result of the Planned 50-percent Acquisition is limited to the amount of gain, if any, that Distributing would have recognized if, immediately before the Distribution, Distributing had engaged in the following transaction: Distributing transferred all Separated Property received from the Predecessor of Distributing to a newly formed corporation (Hypothetical Controlled) in exchange solely for stock of Hypothetical Controlled in a reorganization under section 368(a)(1)(D) and then distributed the stock of Hypothetical Controlled to the shareholders of Distributing in a transaction to which section 355(e) applied (Hypothetical D/355(e) Reorganization). The computation in this paragraph (e)(2)(i) is applied regardless of whether Distributing actually directly held the Separated Property.

(ii) *Operating rules.*—For purposes of applying paragraph (e)(2)(i) of this section, the following rules apply:

(A) *Separated Property other than Controlled stock.*—Each of the basis and the fair market value of Separated Property other than stock of Controlled treated as transferred by Distributing to a Hypothetical Controlled in a Hypothetical D/355(e) Reorganization equals the basis and the fair market value, respectively, of such property in the hands of Controlled immediately before the Distribution.

(B) *Controlled stock that is Separated Property.*—Each of the basis and the fair market value of the stock of Controlled that is Separated Property treated as transferred by Distributing to a Hypothetical Controlled in a Hypothetical D/355(e) Reorganization equals the basis and the fair market value, respectively, of such stock in the hands of Distributing immediately before the Distribution.

(C) *Anti-duplication rule.*—A Predecessor of Distributing's Separated Property is taken into account for purposes of applying this paragraph (e)(2) only to the extent such property was not taken into account by Distributing in a Hypothetical D/355(e) Reorganization with respect to another Predecessor of Distributing. Further, appropriate adjustments must be made to prevent other duplicative inclusions of section 355(e) gain under this paragraph (e) reflecting the same economic gain.

(3) *Planned 50-percent Acquisition of Distributing.*—This paragraph (e)(3) applies if there is a Planned 50-percent Acquisition of Distributing. In that case, the amount of gain recognized by Distributing by reason of section 355(e) as a result of the Planned 50-percent Acquisition is limited to the excess, if any, of the Statutory Recognition Amount over the amount of gain, if any, that Distributing would have been required to recognize under paragraphs (e)(1)(ii) and (e)(2) of this section if there had been a Planned 50-percent Acquisition of every Predecessor of Distributing, but not of Distributing or Controlled. For purposes of this paragraph (e)(3), references to Distributing are not references to a Predecessor of Distributing.

(4) *Gain recognition limited to Statutory Recognition Amount.*—The sum of the amounts required to be recognized by Distributing under section 355(e) (taking into account the POD Gain Limitation Rule and the Distributing Gain Limitation Rule) with regard to a single Distribution cannot exceed the Statutory Recognition Amount. In addition, Distributing may choose not to apply the POD Gain Limitation Rule or the Distributing Gain Limitation Rule to a Distribution, and instead may recognize the Statutory Recognition Amount. Distributing indicates its choice to apply the preceding sentence by reporting the Statutory Recognition Amount on its original or amended Federal income tax return for the year of the Distribution.

(5) *Section 336(e) election.*—Distributing is not eligible to make a section 336(e) election (as defined in § 1.336-1(b)(11)) with respect to a Distribution to which this section applies unless Distributing would, absent the making of a section 336(e) election, recognize the Statutory Recognition Amount with respect to the Distribution (taking into account the POD Gain Limitation Rule and the Distributing Gain Limitation Rule) without regard to the final two sentences of paragraph (e)(4) of this section. See §§ 1.336-1 through 1.336-5 for additional requirements with regard to a section 336(e) election.

(f) *Predecessor or Successor as a member of the affiliated group.*—For purposes of section 355(e)(2)(C), if a corporation transfers its assets to a member of the same Expanded Affiliated Group in a Section 381 Transaction, the transferor will be treated as continuing in existence within the same Expanded Affiliated Group.

(g) *Inapplicability of section 355(f) to certain intra-group Distributions.*—(1) *In general.*—Section 355(f) does not apply to a Distribution if there is a Planned 50-percent Acquisition of a Predecessor of Distributing (but not of Distributing, Controlled, or their Successors), except as provided in paragraph (g)(2) of this section. Therefore, except as provided in paragraph (g)(2) of this section, section 355 (or so much of section 356 as relates to section 355) and the regulations under sections 355 and 356, including the POD Gain Limitation Rule, apply, without regard to section 355(f), to a Distribution within an affiliated group (as defined in section 1504(a)) if the Distribution and the Planned 50-percent Acquisition of the Predecessor of Distributing are part of a Plan. For purposes of this paragraph (g)(1), references to a Distribution (and Distributing and Controlled) include references to a distribution (and Distributing and Controlled) to which section 355 would apply but for the application of section 355(f).

(2) *Alternative application of section 355(f).*—Distributing may choose not to apply paragraph (g)(1) of this section to each Distribution (that occurs under a Plan) to which section 355(f) would otherwise apply absent paragraph (g)(1) of this section. Instead, Distributing may apply section 355(f) to all such Distributions according to its terms, but only if all members of the same Expanded Affiliated Group report consistently the Federal income tax consequences of the Distributions that are part of the Plan (determined without regard to section 355(f)). In such a case, neither the POD Gain Limitation Rule nor the Distributing Gain Limitation Rule is available with regard to any applicable Distribution. Distributing indicates its choice to apply section 355(f) consistently to all applicable Distributions by reporting the Federal income tax consequences of each Distribution in accordance with section 355(f) on its Federal income tax return for the year of the Distribution.

(h) *Examples.*—The following examples illustrate the principles of this section. Unless the facts indicate otherwise, assume throughout these examples that: Distributing (D) owns all the stock of Controlled (C), and none of the shares of C held by D has a built-in loss; D distributes the stock of C in a Distribution to which section 355(d) does not apply; X, Y, and Z are individuals; each of D, D1, C, P, P1, P2, and R is a corporation having one class of stock outstanding, and none is a member of a consolidated group; and each transaction that is part of a Plan defined in this section is respected as a separate transaction under general Federal income tax principles. No inference should be drawn from any example concerning whether any requirements of section 355 are satisfied other than those of section 355(e) or whether any general Federal income tax principles (including the step transaction doctrine) are implicated by the example:

(1) *Example 1: Predecessor of D and Planned 50-Percent Acquisition of P*—(i) *Facts*. X owns 100% of the stock of P, which holds multiple assets. Y owns 100% of the stock of D. The following steps occur as part of a Plan: P merges into D in a reorganization under section 368(a)(1)(A). Immediately after the merger, X and Y own 10% and 90%, respectively, of the stock of D. D then contributes to C one of the assets (Asset 1) acquired from P in the merger. At the time of the contribution, Asset 1 has a basis of $40x and a fair market value of $110x. In exchange for Asset 1, D receives additional C stock and $10x. D distributes the stock of C (but not the cash) to X and Y, pro rata. The contribution and Distribution constitute a reorganization under section 368(a)(1)(D), and D recognizes $10x of gain under section 361(b) on the contribution. Immediately before the Distribution, taking into account the $10x of gain recognized by D on the contribution, Asset 1 has an adjusted basis of $50x under section 362(b) and a fair market value of $110x, and the stock of C held by D has a basis of $100x and a fair market value of $200x.

(ii) *Analysis*—(A) *P is a Predecessor of D*. Under paragraph (b)(1) of this section, P is a Predecessor of D. First, P is a Potential Predecessor because, as part of a Plan, P transferred property to D in a Section 381 Transaction. See paragraph (b)(2)(ii)(A)(*1*) of this section. Second, both of the pre-Distribution requirements and the post-Distribution requirement are satisfied. The Relevant Property Requirement is satisfied because, immediately before the Distribution and as part of a Plan, C holds P Relevant Property (Asset 1) the gain on which was not recognized in full at any point during the Plan Period, and some of the C stock distributed in the Distribution was acquired by D in exchange for Asset 1. See paragraph (b)(1)(ii)(A)(*1*) of this section. The Reflection of Basis Requirement is satisfied because that C stock had a basis prior to the Distribution that was determined in whole or in part by reference to the basis of Separated Property (Asset 1), and was neither distributed in a distribution to which section 355(e) applied nor transferred in a transaction in which the gain on that C stock was recognized in full during the Plan Period prior to the Distribution. See paragraph (b)(1)(ii)(B) of this section. The Division of Relevant Property Requirement is satisfied because immediately after the Distribution, D continues to hold Relevant Property of P, and therefore, as part of a Plan, P's Relevant Property has been divided between C and D. See paragraph (b)(1)(iii) of this section.

(B) *Planned 50-percent Acquisition of P*. Under paragraph (d)(1)(i) of this section, Y is treated as acquiring stock representing 90% of the voting power and value of P as a result of the merger of P into D. Accordingly, there has been a Planned 50-percent Acquisition of P.

(C) *Gain limited*. Without regard to the limitations in paragraph (e) of this section, D would be required to recognize $100x of gain ($200x of aggregate fair market value minus $100x of aggregate basis of the C stock held by D), the Statutory Recognition Amount described in section 361(c)(2). However, under the POD Gain Limitation Rule, D's gain recognized by reason of the Planned 50-percent Acquisition of P will not exceed $60x, an amount equal to the amount of gain D would have recognized had D transferred Asset 1 (Separated Property) to a newly formed corporation (C1) solely for C1 stock and distributed the C1 stock to D's shareholders in a Hypothetical D/355(e) Reorganization. See paragraph (e)(2)(i) of this section. For purposes of the computation in this paragraph (h)(1)(ii)(C), the basis and fair market value of Asset 1 equal the basis and fair market value of Asset 1 in the hands of C immediately before the Distribution. See paragraph (e)(2)(ii)(A) of this section. Under section 361(c)(2), D would recognize $60x of gain, an amount equal to the gain in the hypothetical C1 stock (excess of the $110x fair market value over the $50x basis). Therefore, D recognizes $60x of gain (in addition to the $10x of gain recognized under section 361(b)).

(iii) *Plan not in existence at time of acquisition of Potential Predecessor's property*. The facts are the same as in paragraph (h)(1)(i) of this section (*Example 1*) except that the merger of P into D occurred before the existence of a Plan. Even though D transferred P property (Asset 1) to C, Asset 1 was not Relevant Property of P because P did not hold Asset 1 during the Plan Period. See paragraphs (b)(2)(iv) and (a)(4)(iii) of this section. Because Asset 1 is not Relevant Property, D did not receive C stock distributed in the Distribution in exchange for Relevant Property when it contributed Asset 1 to C, none of the distributed C stock had a basis prior to the Distribution that was determined in whole or in part by reference to the basis of Separated Property, and C did not hold Relevant Property immediately before the Distribution. Further, Relevant Property of P has not been divided. Therefore, P is not a Predecessor of D.

(2) *Example 2: Planned 50-percent Acquisition of D, but not Predecessor of D*—(i) *Facts*. X owns 100% of the stock of P, which holds multiple assets. Y owns 100% of the stock of D. The following steps occur as part of a Plan: P merges into D in a reorganization under section 368(a)(1)(A). Immediately after the merger, X and Y own 90% and 10%, respectively, of the stock of D. D then contributes to C one of the assets (Asset 1) acquired from P in the merger. In exchange for Asset 1, D receives additional C stock. D distributes the stock of C to X and Y, pro rata. The contribution and Distribution constitute a reorganization under section 368(a)(1)(D). Immediately before the Distribution, Asset 1 has a basis of $50x and a fair market value of $110x, and the stock of C held by D has a basis of $120x and a fair market value of $200x.

(ii) *Analysis*—(A) *P is a Predecessor of D*. Under paragraph (b)(1) of this section, P is a Predecessor of D. First, P is a Potential Predecessor because, as part of a Plan, P transferred property to D in a Section 381 Transaction. See paragraph (b)(2)(ii)(A)(*1*) of this section. Second, both of the pre-Distribution requirements and the post-Distribution requirement are satisfied. The Relevant Property Requirement is satisfied because, immediately before the Distribution and as part of a Plan, C holds P Relevant Property (Asset 1) the gain on which was not recognized in full at any point during the Plan Period, and some of the C stock distributed in the Distribution was acquired by D in exchange for Asset 1. See paragraph (b)(1)(ii)(A)(*1*) of this section. The Reflection of Basis Requirement is satisfied because that C stock had a basis prior to the Distribution that was determined in whole or in part by reference to the basis of Separated Property (Asset 1), and was neither distributed in a distribution to which section 355(e) applied nor transferred in a transaction in which the gain on that C stock was recognized in full during the Plan Period prior to the Distribution. See paragraph (b)(1)(ii)(B) of this section. The Division of Relevant Property Requirement is satisfied because immediately after the Distribution, D continues to hold Relevant Property of P, and therefore, as part of a Plan, P's Relevant Property has been divided between C and D. See paragraph (b)(1)(iii) of this section.

(B) *Planned 50-percent Acquisition of D*. Under paragraph (d)(1)(i) of this section, Y is treated as acquiring stock representing 10% of the voting power and value of P as a result of the merger of P into D. The 10% acquisition of P stock does not cause section 355(e) gain recognition or cause application of the POD Gain Limitation Rule because there has not been a Planned 50-percent Acquisition of P. X acquires 90% of the voting power and value of D as a result of the merger of P into D. Accordingly, there has been a Planned 50-percent Acquisition of D. This Planned 50-percent Acquisition implicates section 355(e) and results in gain recognition, subject to the rules of paragraph (e) of this section.

(C) *Gain limited*. Without regard to the limitations in paragraph (e) of this section, D would be required to recognize $80x of gain ($200x of fair market value minus $120x of basis of the C stock held by D), the Statutory Recognition Amount described in section 361(c)(2). However, under the Distributing Gain Limitation Rule, D's gain recognized by reason of the Planned 50-percent Acquisition of D will not exceed $20x, the excess of the Statutory Recognition Amount ($80x) over the amount of gain that D would have been required to recognize under the POD Gain Limitation Rule if there had been a Planned 50-percent Acquisition of P but not D or C ($60x). See paragraph (e)(3) of this section. The hypothetical gain limitation under the POD Gain Limitation Rule equals the amount D would have recognized had it transferred Asset 1 (Separated Property) to a newly formed corporation (C1) solely for stock and distributed the C1 stock in a Hypothetical D/355(e) Reorganization. See paragraph (e)(2)(i) of this section. Under section 361(c)(2), D would recognize $60x of gain, an amount equal to the gain in the hypothetical C1 stock (excess of the $110x fair market value over the $50x basis). Therefore, D recognizes $20x of gain ($80x - $60x).

(3) *Example 3: Predecessor of D owns C stock*—(i) *Facts*. X owns 100% of the stock of P, which holds multiple assets, including Asset 2. Y owns 100% of the stock of D. P owns 35% of the stock of C (Block 1), and D owns the remaining 65% of the C stock (Block 2). The following steps occur as part of a Plan: P merges into D in a reorganization under section 368(a)(1)(A), and D immediately thereafter distributes all of the C stock to X and Y pro rata. Immediately after the merger, X and Y own 10% and 90%, respectively, of the D stock, and, prior to the Distribution, D owns Block 1 with a basis of $30x and a fair market value of $35x, and Block 2 with a basis of $10x and a fair market value of $65x. D continues to hold Asset 2.

(ii) *Analysis*—(A) *P is a Predecessor of D.* Under paragraph (b)(1) of this section, P is a Predecessor of D. First, P is a Potential Predecessor because, as part of a Plan, P transferred property to D in a Section 381 Transaction. See paragraph (b)(2)(ii)(A)(*1*) of this section. Second, both of the pre-Distribution requirements and the post-Distribution requirement are satisfied. The Relevant Property Requirement is satisfied because some of the C stock distributed in the Distribution (Block 1) was Relevant Property of P. See paragraph (b)(1)(ii)(A)(*2*) of this section. The Reflection of Basis Requirement is satisfied because Block 1 of the C stock is Relevant Property of P, and was neither distributed in a distribution to which section 355(e) applied nor transferred in a transaction in which the gain on that C stock was recognized in full during the Plan Period prior to the Distribution. See paragraph (b)(1)(ii)(B) of this section. The Division of Relevant Property Requirement is satisfied because some of the C stock distributed in the Distribution was Relevant Property of P, and therefore C is deemed to have received Relevant Property of P, and D continues to hold Relevant Property of P immediately after the Distribution. See paragraph (b)(1)(iii) of this section. Therefore, as part of a Plan, P's Relevant Property has been divided between C and D.

(B) *Planned 50-percent Acquisition of P.* Under paragraph (d)(1)(i) of this section, Y is treated as acquiring stock representing 90% of the voting power and value of P as a result of the merger of P into D. Accordingly, there has been a Planned 50-percent Acquisition of P.

(C) *Gain limited.* Without regard to the limitations in paragraph (e) of this section, D would be required to recognize $60x of gain ($100x of fair market value minus $40x of basis of the C stock held by D), the Statutory Recognition Amount under section 355(c)(2). However, under the POD Gain Limitation Rule, D's gain recognized by reason of the Planned 50-percent Acquisition of P will not exceed $5x, an amount equal to the amount D would have recognized had it transferred Block 1 of the C stock (Separated Property) to a newly formed corporation (C1) solely for stock and distributed the C1 stock to D shareholders in a Hypothetical D/355(e) Reorganization. See paragraph (e)(2)(i) of this section. Because Relevant Equity (Block 1 of the C stock) is Separated Property, Underlying Property associated with that Relevant Equity is not treated as Separated Property. See paragraph (b)(2)(vii) of this section. For purposes of the computation in this paragraph (h)(3)(ii)(C), the basis and fair market value of the Block 1 C stock equal its basis and fair market value in the hands of D immediately before the Distribution. See paragraph (e)(2)(ii)(A) of this section. Under section 361(c)(2), D would recognize $5x of gain, an amount equal to the gain in the hypothetical C1 stock ($35x fair market value - $30x basis). Therefore, D recognizes $5x of gain.

(4) *Example 4: C stock as Substitute Asset*—(i) *Facts.* X owns 100% of the stock of P, which owns multiple assets, including 100% of the stock of R and Asset 2. Y owns 100% of the stock of D. The following steps occur as part of a Plan: P merges into D in a reorganization under section 368(a)(1)(A) (P-D reorganization). Immediately after the merger, X and Y own 10% and 90%, respectively, of the stock of D. D then causes R to transfer all of its assets to C and liquidate in a reorganization under section 368(a)(1) (R-C reorganization). At the time of the P-D reorganization, the R stock has a basis of $40x and a fair market value of $110x. D distributes the stock of C to X and Y, pro rata. D continues to directly hold Asset 2. Immediately before the Distribution, the C stock held by D that was deemed received in the R-C reorganization (Block 1) has a basis of $40x and a fair market value of $110x, and all of the stock of C held by D has a basis of $100x and a fair market value of $200x.

(ii) *Analysis*—(A) *P is a Predecessor of D.* Under paragraph (b)(1) of this section, P is a Predecessor of D. First, P is a Potential Predecessor because, as part of a Plan, P transferred property to D in a Section 381 Transaction. See paragraph (b)(2)(ii)(A)(*1*) of this section. Second, both pre-Distribution requirements and the post-Distribution requirement are satisfied. The Relevant Property Requirement is satisfied because, for the following two reasons, some of the C stock distributed in the Distribution (Block 1) was Relevant Property of P. D is treated as acquiring Block 1 of the C stock in exchange for a direct or indirect interest in R stock (that is, Relevant Property) in the R-C reorganization because the basis of D in that C stock immediately after a transfer of the R stock (in the liquidation of R) is determined in whole or in part by reference to the basis of the R stock immediately before the transfer. See paragraph (b)(2)(x) of this section. Further, because the basis in Block 1 of the C stock is determined in whole or in part by reference to the basis of Relevant Equity (the R stock) the issuer of which ceases to exist for Federal income tax purposes under the Plan, Block 1 of the C stock is a Substitute Asset, and is therefore treated as Relevant Property with the same ownership and transfer history as the R stock. See paragraph (b)(2)(vi)(B)(*2*) of this section. The Reflection of Basis Requirement is satisfied because Block 1 of the C stock is Relevant Property of P, and was neither distributed in a distribution to which section 355(e) applied nor transferred in a transaction in which the gain on that C stock was recognized in full during the Plan Period prior to the Distribution. See paragraph (b)(1)(ii)(B) of this section. The Division of Relevant Property Requirement is satisfied because some of the C stock distributed in the Distribution was Relevant Property of P, and therefore C is deemed to have received Relevant Property of P, and immediately after the Distribution, D continues to hold Asset 2, which is Relevant Property of P. See paragraph (b)(1)(iii) of this section. Therefore, as part of a Plan, P's Relevant Property has been divided between C and D.

(B) *Planned 50-percent Acquisition of P.* Under paragraph (d)(1)(i) of this section, Y is treated as acquiring stock representing 90% of the voting power and value of P as a result of the P-D reorganization. Accordingly, there has been a Planned 50-percent Acquisition of P.

(C) *Gain limited.* Without regard to the limitations in paragraph (e) of this section, D would be required to recognize $100x of gain ($200x of fair market value minus $100x of basis of all C stock held by D), the Statutory Recognition Amount described in section 355(c)(2). However, under the POD Gain Limitation Rule, D's gain recognized by reason of the Planned 50-percent Acquisition of P will not exceed $70x, an amount equal to the amount D would have recognized had it transferred Block 1 of the C stock (Separated Property) to a newly formed corporation (C1) solely for stock and distributed the C1 stock to D shareholders in a Hypothetical D/355(e) Reorganization. See paragraph (e)(2)(i) of this section. Because Relevant Equity (Block 1 of the C stock) is Separated Property, Underlying Property associated with that Relevant Equity is not treated as Separated Property. See paragraph (b)(2)(vii) of this section. Under section 361(c)(2), D would recognize $70x of gain, an amount equal to the gain in the hypothetical C1 stock (excess of the $110x fair market value over the $40x basis). Therefore, D recognizes $70x of gain.

(5) *Example 5: Section 351 transaction*—(i) *Facts.* X owns 100% of the stock of P, which holds multiple assets, including Asset 1, Asset 2, and Asset 3. Y owns 100% of the stock of D. The following steps occur as part of a Plan: P transfers Asset 1 and Asset 2 to D and Y transfers property to D in an exchange qualifying under section 351. Immediately after the exchange, P and Y own 10% and 90%, respectively, of the stock of D. D then contributes Asset 1 to C in exchange for additional C stock. D distributes all of the stock of C to P and Y, pro rata. D continues to directly hold Asset 2, and P continues to directly hold Asset 3. The contribution and Distribution constitute a reorganization under section 368(a)(1)(D). Immediately before the Distribution, Asset 1 has a basis of $40x and a fair market value of $110x, and the stock of C held by D has a basis of $100x and a fair market value of $200x. Following the Distribution, and as part of the same Plan, Z acquires 51% of the P stock.

(ii) *Analysis—P is not a Predecessor of D.* Under paragraph (b)(1) of this section, P is not a Predecessor of D. P is not a Potential Predecessor because P did not transfer property to a Potential Predecessor, D, or a member of the same Expanded Affiliated Group as D in a Section 381 Transaction and P is not a member of the same Expanded Affiliated Group as D immediately after completion of the Plan. See paragraph (b)(2)(ii) of this section. Thus, P cannot be a Predecessor of D. See paragraph (b)(1)(i) of this section.

* * *

(7) *Example 7: Sequential Predecessors*—(i) *Facts.* X owns 100% of P1, which holds multiple assets, including Asset 1 and Asset 2. Y owns 100% of P2, which holds Asset 3, and Z owns 100% of D. The following steps occur as part of a Plan: P1 merges into P2 in a reorganization under 368(a)(1)(A) (P1-P2 reorganization). Immediately after the merger, X and Y own 10% and 90%, respectively, of the stock of P2. P2 then merges into D in a reorganization under 368(a)(1)(A) (P2-D reorganization). Immediately after the merger, X, Y, and Z own 1%, 9%, and 90%, respectively, of the stock of D. D then contributes Asset 1 to C in exchange for additional C stock, and retains Asset 2 and Asset 3. D distributes all of the stock of C to X, Y, and Z, pro rata. Immediately before the Distribution, Asset 1 has a basis of $40x and a fair market value of $100x, and the stock of C held by D has a basis of $100x and a fair market value of $200x.

(ii) *Analysis*—(A) *P2 is a Predecessor of D.* Under paragraph (b)(1) of this section, P2 is a Predecessor of D. First, P2 is a Potential Predecessor because, as part of a Plan, P2 transferred property to D in a Section 381 Transaction. See paragraph (b)(2)(ii)(A)(*1*) of this section. Second, both pre-Distribution requirements and the post-Distribution requirement are satisfied. The Relevant Property Requirement is satisfied because, immediately before the Distribution and as part of a Plan, C holds P2 Relevant Property (Asset 1) the gain on which was not recognized in full at any point during the Plan Period, and some of the C stock distributed in the Distribution was acquired by D in exchange for Asset 1. See paragraph (b)(1)(ii)(A)(*1*) of this section. The Reflection of Basis Requirement is satisfied because that C stock had a basis prior to the Distribution that was determined in whole or in part by reference to the basis of Separated Property (Asset 1), and was neither distributed in a distribution to which section 355(e) applied nor transferred in a transaction in which the gain on that C stock was recognized in full during the Plan Period prior to the Distribution. See paragraph (b)(1)(ii)(B) of this section. The Division of Relevant Property Requirement is satisfied because immediately after the Distribution, D continues to hold P2 Relevant Property (Asset 2 and Asset 3), and therefore, as part of a Plan, P2's Relevant Property has been divided between C and D. See paragraph (b)(1)(iii) of this section.

(B) *P1 is a Predecessor of D*. Under paragraph (b)(1) of this section, P1 is a Predecessor of D. First, P1 is a Potential Predecessor because, as part of a Plan, P1 transferred property to a Potential Predecessor (P2) in a Section 381 Transaction. See paragraph (b)(2)(ii)(A)(*1*) of this section. Second, both pre-Distribution requirements and the post-Distribution requirement are satisfied. The Relevant Property Requirement is satisfied because, immediately before the Distribution and as part of a Plan, C holds P1 Relevant Property (Asset 1) the gain on which was not recognized in full at any point during the Plan Period, and some of the C stock distributed in the Distribution was acquired by D in exchange for Asset 1. See paragraph (b)(1)(ii)(A)(*1*) of this section. The Reflection of Basis Requirement is satisfied because that C stock had a basis prior to the Distribution that was determined in whole or in part by reference to the basis of Separated Property (Asset 1), and was neither distributed in a distribution to which section 355(e) applied nor transferred in a transaction in which the gain on that C stock was recognized in full during the Plan Period prior to the Distribution. See paragraph (b)(1)(ii)(B) of this section. The Division of Relevant Property Requirement is satisfied because immediately after the Distribution, D continues to hold Relevant Property of P1 (Asset 2), and therefore, as part of a Plan, P1's Relevant Property has been divided between C and D. See paragraph (b)(1)(iii) of this section.

(C) *Planned 50-percent Acquisitions of P1 and P2*. Under paragraph (d)(1)(i) of this section, Y is treated as acquiring stock representing 90% of the voting power and value of P1 as a result of the P1-P2 merger. In addition, under paragraph (d)(1)(i) of this section, Z is treated as acquiring stock representing 90% of the voting power and value of P2 in the P2-D merger. Accordingly, there have been Planned 50-percent Acquisitions of P1 and P2.

(D) *Gain limited*. Without regard to the limitations in paragraph (e) of this section, D would be required to recognize $100x of gain ($200x of aggregate fair market value minus $100x of aggregate basis of the C stock held by D), the Statutory Recognition Amount described in section 361(c)(2), because there have been Planned 50-percent Acquisitions of P1 and P2, both Predecessors of D. However, under paragraph (e) of this section, D's gain recognized by reason of the Planned 50-percent Acquisitions of P1 and P2 will not exceed $60x, an amount equal to the amount D would have recognized had it transferred Asset 1 (Separated Property) to a newly formed corporation (C1) solely for stock and distributed the C1 stock to D shareholders in a Hypothetical D/355(e) Reorganization. Under section 361(c)(2), D would recognize $60x, an amount equal to the gain in the hypothetical C1 stock (excess of the $100x fair market value over the $40x basis). Paragraph (e)(1)(ii) of this section provides that if there are Planned 50-percent Acquisitions of multiple corporations, Distributing must recognize the Statutory Recognition Amount with respect to each such corporation, subject to the POD Gain Limitation Rule and the Distributing Gain Limitation Rule, if applicable. In this case, the POD Gain Limitation Rule limits the amount of gain required to be recognized by D with respect to each of the Planned 50-percent Acquisitions of P1 and P2 to $60x. See paragraph (e)(2)(i) of this section. Ordinarily, each $60x limitation would be added together, and the total gain limitation provided by paragraph (e) of this section would be $120x. However, the anti-duplication rule set forth in paragraph (e)(2)(ii)(C) of this section provides that, for purposes of applying the POD Gain Limitation Rule, a Predecessor of Distributing's Separated Property is taken into account only to the extent such property was not taken into account with respect to another Predecessor of Distributing. Thus, Asset 1 may not be taken into account more than once in determining the total gain limitation. Therefore, D recognizes $60x of gain.

* * *

(9) *Example 9: Successor of C*—(i) *Facts*. X owns 100% of the stock of each of D and R. The following steps occur as part of a Plan: D distributes all of its C stock to X. Immediately before the Distribution, D's C stock has a basis of $10x and a fair market value of $30x. C then merges into R in a reorganization under section 368(a)(1)(D). Immediately after the merger, X owns all of the R stock. As part of the same Plan, Z acquires 51% of the stock of R from X.

(ii) *Analysis*—(A) *R is a Successor of C*. Under paragraph (c)(2)(i) of this section, R is a Successor of C because, after the Distribution, C transfers property to R in a Section 381 Transaction.

(B) *Planned 50-percent Acquisition of C*. Under paragraph (d)(2) of this section, Z's acquisition of stock of R is treated as an acquisition of stock of C. Therefore, Z is treated as acquiring 51% of the stock of C. Accordingly, there has been a Planned 50-percent Acquisition of C.

(C) *Gain not limited.* Section 355(e) applies to the Distribution because there has been a Planned 50-percent Acquisition of C. Neither the POD Gain Limitation Rule nor the Distributing Gain Limitation Rule applies because there has been no Planned 50-percent Acquisition of a Predecessor of D, and no Planned 50-percent Acquisition of D. Therefore, D recognizes $20x of gain ($30x fair market value minus $10x basis of the C stock held by D) under section 355(c)(2).

* * *

(i) *Applicability date.*—This section applies to Distributions occurring after December 15, 2019. For Distributions occurring on or before December 15, 2019, see §1.355-8T as contained in 26 CFR part 1 revised as of April 1, 2019. [Reg. §1.355-8.]

☐ [*T.D.* 9888, 12-16-2019 (*corrected* 3-16-2020).]

§1.356-1. Receipt of additional consideration in connection with an exchange.—(a) If in any exchange to which the provisions of section 354 or section 355 would apply except for the fact that there is received by the shareholders or security holders other property (in addition to property permitted to be received without recognition of gain by such sections) or money, then—

(1) The gain, if any, to the taxpayer shall be recognized in an amount not in excess of the sum of the money and the fair market value of the other property, but,

(2) The loss, if any, to the taxpayer from the exchange or distribution shall not be recognized to any extent.

(b) For purposes of computing the gain, if any, recognized pursuant to section 356 and paragraph (a)(1) of this section, to the extent the terms of the exchange specify the other property or money that is received in exchange for a particular share of stock or security surrendered or a particular class of stock or securities surrendered, such terms shall control provided that such terms are economically reasonable. To the extent the terms of the exchange do not specify the other property or money that is received in exchange for a particular share of stock or security surrendered or a particular class of stock or securities surrendered, a pro rata portion of the other property and money received shall be treated as received in exchange for each share of stock and security surrendered, based on the fair market value of such surrendered share of stock or security.

(c) If the distribution of such other property or money by or on behalf of a corporation has the effect of the distribution of a dividend, then there shall be chargeable to each distributee (either an individual or a corporation)—

(1) As a dividend, such an amount of the gain recognized as is not in excess of the distributee's ratable share of the undistributed earnings and profits of the corporation accumulated after February 28, 1913, and

(2) As a gain from the exchange of property, the remainder of the gain so recognized.

(d) The rules of this section may be illustrated by the following examples:

Example 1. In an exchange to which the provisions of section 356 apply and to which section 354 would apply but for the receipt of property not permitted to be received without the recognition of gain or loss, A (either an individual or a corporation), received the following in exchange for a share of stock having an adjusted basis to A of $85:

One share of stock worth	$100
Cash	25
Other property (basis $25) fair market value	50
Total fair market value of consideration received	$175
Adjusted basis of stock surrendered in exchange	$85
Total gain	90
Gain to be recognized, limited to cash and other property received	$75
A's pro rata share of earnings and profits accumulated after February 28, 1913 (taxable dividend)	$30
Remainder to be treated as a gain from the exchange of property	45

Example 2. If, in *Example 1*, A's stock had an adjusted basis to A of $200, A would have realized a loss of $25 on the exchange, which loss would not be recognized.

Example 3. (i) *Facts.* J, an individual, acquired 10 shares of Class A stock of Corporation X on Date 1 for $3 each and 10 shares of Class B stock of Corporation X on Date 2 for $9 each. On Date 3, Corporation Y acquires the assets of Corporation X in a reorganization under section 368(a)(1)(A). Pursuant to the terms of the plan of reorganization, J surrenders all of J's shares of Corporation X stock for 10 shares of Corporation Y stock and $100 of cash. On the date of the exchange, the fair market value of each share of Class A stock of Corporation X is $10, the fair market value of each share of Class B stock of Corporation X is $10, and the fair market value of each share of Corporation Y stock is $10. The terms of the exchange do not specify that shares of Corporation Y stock or cash are received in exchange for particular shares of Class A stock or Class B stock of Corporation X.

(ii) *Analysis.* Under paragraph (b) of this section, because the terms of the exchange do not specify that the cash is received in exchange for shares of Class A or Class B stock of Corporation X, a pro rata portion of the cash received is treated as received in exchange for each share of Class A stock of Corporation X and each share of Class B stock of Corporation X based on the fair market value of the surrendered shares. Therefore, J is treated as receiving shares of Corporation Y stock with a fair market value of $50 and $50 of cash in exchange for its shares of Class A stock of Corporation X and shares of Corporation Y stock with a fair market value of $50 and $50 of cash in exchange for its shares of Class B stock of Corporation X. J realizes a gain of $70 on the exchange of shares of Class A stock, $50 of which is recognized under section 356 and paragraph (a) of this section, and J realizes a gain of $10 on the exchange of shares of Class B stock of Corporation X, all of which is recognized under section 356 and paragraph (a) of this section. Assuming that J's gain recognized is not treated as a dividend under section 356(a)(2), such gain shall be treated as gain from the exchange of property.

Example 4. (i) *Facts.* The facts are the same as in *Example 3*, except that the terms of the plan of reorganization specify that J receives 10 shares of stock of Corporation Y in exchange for J's shares of Class A stock of Corporation X and $100 of cash in exchange for J's shares of Class B stock of Corporation X.

(ii) *Analysis.* Under paragraph (b) of this section, because the terms of the exchange specify that J receives 10 shares of stock of Corporation Y in exchange for J's shares of Class A stock of Corporation X and $100 of cash in exchange for J's shares of Class B stock of Corporation X and such terms are economically reasonable, such terms control. J realizes a gain of $70 on the exchange of shares of Class A stock, none of which is recognized under section 356 and paragraph (a) of this section, and J realizes a gain of $10 on the exchange of shares of Class B stock of Corporation X, all of which is recognized under section 356 and paragraph (a) of this section.

(e) Section 301(b)(1)(B) and section 301(d)(2) do not apply to a distribution of "other property" to a corporate shareholder if such distribution is within the provisions of section 356.

(f) See paragraph (l) of § 1.301-1 for certain transactions which are not within the scope of section 356.

(g) This section applies to exchanges and distributions of stock and securities occurring on or after January 23, 2006. [Reg. § 1.356-1.]

☐ [*T.D.* 6152, 12-2-55. *Amended by T.D.* 9244, 1-23-2006.]

§ 1.356-2. Receipt of additional consideration not in connection with an exchange.—(a) If, in a transaction to which section 355 would apply except for the fact that a shareholder (individual or corporate) receives property permitted by section 355 to be received without the recognition of gain, together with other property or money, without the surrender of any stock or securities of the distributing corporation, then the sum of the money and the fair market value of the other property as of the date of the distribution shall be treated as a distribution of property to which the rules of section 301 (other than section 301(b) and section 301(d) apply. See section 358 for determination of basis of such other property.

(b) Paragraph (a) of this section may be illustrated by the following examples:

Example (1). Individuals A and B each own 50 of the 100 outstanding shares of common stock of Corporation X. Corporation X owns all of the stock of Corporation Y, 100 shares. Corporation X distributes to each shareholder 50 shares of the stock of Corporation Y plus $100 cash without requiring the surrender of any shares of its own stock. The $100 cash received by each is treated as a distribution of property to which the rules of section 301 apply.

Example (2). If, in the above example, Corporation X distributes 50 shares of stock of Corporation Y to A and 30 shares of such stock plus $100 cash to B without requiring the surrender of any of its own stock, the amount of cash received by B is treated as a distribution of property to which the rules of section 301 apply. [Reg. § 1.356-2.]

☐ [*T.D.* 6152, 12-2-55.]

§ 1.356-3. Rules for treatment of securities as "other property".—(a) As a general rule, for purposes of section 356, the term "other property" includes securities. However, it does not include securities permitted under section 354 or section 355 to be received tax free. Thus, when securities are surrendered in a transaction to which section 354 or section 355 is applicable, the characterization of the securities received as "other property" does not include securities received where the principal amount of such securities does not exceed the principal amount of securities surrendered in the transaction. If a greater principal amount of securities is received in an exchange described in section 354(other than subsection (c) or (d) thereof) or section 355 over the principal amount of securities surrendered, the term "other property" includes the fair market value of such excess principal amount as of the date of the exchange. If no securities are surrendered in exchange, the term "other property" includes the fair market value, as of the date of receipt, of the entire principal amount of the securities received.

(b) Except as provided in § 1.356-6, for purposes of this section, a right to acquire stock that is treated as a security for purposes of section 354 or 355 has no principal amount. Thus, such right is not *other property* when received in a transaction to which section 356 applies (regardless of whether securities are surrendered in the exchange). This paragraph (b) applies to transactions occurring on or after March 9, 1998.

(c) In the examples in this paragraph (c), *stock* means common stock and *warrants* means rights to acquire common stock. The following examples illustrate the rules of paragraph (a) of this section:—

Example 1. A, an individual, exchanged 100 shares of stock for 100 shares of stock and a security in the principal amount of $1,000 with a fair market value of $990. The amount of $990 is treated as "other property."

Example 2. B, an individual, exchanged 100 shares of stock and a security in the principal amount of $1,000 for 300 shares of stock and a security in the principal amount of $1,500. The security had a fair market value on the date of receipt of $1,575. The fair market value of the excess principal amount, or $525, is treated as "other property."

Example 3. C, an individual, exchanged a security in a principal amount of $1,000 for 100 shares of stock and a security in the principal amount of $900. No part of the security received is treated as "other property."

Example 4. D, an individual, exchanged a security in the principal amount of $1,000 for 100 shares of stock and a security in the principal amount of $1,200 with a fair market value of $1,100. The fair market value of the excess principal amount, or $183.33, is treated as "other property."

Example 5. E, an individual, exchanged a security in the principal amount of $1,000 for another security in the principal amount of $1,200 with a fair market value of $1,080. The fair market value of the excess principal amount, or $180, is treated as "other property."

Example 6. F, an individual, exchanged a security in the principal amount of $1,000 for two different securities each in the principal amount of $750. One of the securities had a fair market value of $750, the other had a fair market value of $600. One-third of the fair market value of each security ($250 and $200) is treated as "other property."

Example 7. G, an individual, exchanged stock for stock and a warrant. The warrant had no principal amount. Thus, G received no excess principal amount within the meaning of section 356(d).

Example 8. H, an individual, exchanged a warrant for stock and a warrant. The warrants had no principal amount. Thus, H received no excess principal amount within the meaning of section 356(d).

Example 9. I, an individual, exchanged a warrant for stock and a debt security. The warrant had no principal amount. The debt security had a $100 principal amount. I received $100 of excess principal amount within the meaning of section 356(d).

[Reg. § 1.356-3.]

☐ [*T.D.* 6152, 12-2-55. *Amended by T.D.* 7616, 5-7-79; *T.D.* 8752, 1-5-98 *and T.D.* 8882, 5-15-2000.]

§ 1.356-4. Exchanges for section 306 stock.—If, in a transaction to which section 356 is applicable, other property or money is received in exchange for section 306 stock, an amount equal to the fair market value of the property plus the money, if any, shall be treated as a distribution of property to which section 301 is applicable. The determination of whether section 306 stock is surrendered for other property (including money) is a question of fact to be decided under all of the circumstances of each case. Ordinarily, the other property (including money) received will first be treated as received in exchange for any section 306 stock owned by a shareholder prior to such transaction. For example, if a shareholder who owns a share of common stock (having a basis to him of $100) and a share of preferred stock which is section 306 stock (having a basis to him of $100) surrenders both shares in a transaction to which section 356 is applicable for one share of common stock having a fair market value of $80 and one $100 bond having a fair market value of $100, the bond will be deemed received in exchange for the section 306 stock and it will be treated as a distribution to which section 301 is applicable to the extent of its entire fair market value ($100). [Reg. § 1.356-4.]

☐ [*T.D.* 6152, 12-2-55.]

§ 1.356-5. Transactions involving gift or compensation.—With respect to transactions described in sections 354, 355, or 356, but which—

(a) Result in a gift, see section 2501 and following, and the regulations pertaining thereto, or

(b) Have the effect of the payment of compensation, see section 61(a)(1), and the regulations pertaining thereto. [Reg. § 1.356-5.]

☐ [*T.D.* 6152, 12-2-55.]

§ 1.356-6. Rules for treatment of nonqualified preferred stock as other property.—(a) *In general.*—For purposes of §§ 1.354-1(e), 1.355-1(c), and 1.356-3(b), the terms *stock* and *securities* do not include—

(1) Nonqualified preferred stock, as defined in section 351(g)(2), received in exchange for (or in a distribution with respect to) stock, or a right to acquire stock, other than nonqualified preferred stock; or

(2) A right to acquire such nonqualified preferred stock, received in exchange for (or in a distribution with respect to) stock, or a right to acquire stock, other than nonqualified preferred stock.

(b) *Exceptions.*—The following exceptions apply:

(1) *Certain recapitalizations.*—Paragraph (a) of this section does not apply in the case of a recapitalization under section 368(a)(1)(E) of a family-owned corporation as described in section 354(a)(2)(C)(ii)(II).

(2) *Transition rule.*—Paragraph (a) of this section does not apply to a transaction described in section 1014(f)(2) of the Taxpayer Relief Act of 1997 (111 Stat. 921).

* * *

[Reg. § 1.356-6.]

☐ [*T.D.* 8753, 1-5-98. *Redesignated by T.D.* 8882, 5-15-2000.]

§ 1.357-1. Assumption of liability.—(a) *General rule.*—Section 357(a) does not affect the rule that liabilities assumed are to be taken into account for the purpose of computing the amount of gain or loss realized under section 1001 upon an exchange. Section 357(a) provides, subject to the exceptions and limitations specified in section 357(b) and (c), that:

(1) Liabilities assumed are not to be treated as "other property or money" for the purpose of determining the amount of realized gain which is to be recognized under section 351, 361, 371, or 374, if the transactions would, but for the receipt of "other property or money" have been exchanges of the type described in any one of such sections; and

(2) If the only type of consideration received by the transferor in addition to that permitted to be received by section 351, 361, 371, or 374, consists of an assumption of liabilities, the transaction, if otherwise qualified, will be deemed to be within the provisions of section 351, 361, 371, or 374.

(b) *Application of general rule.*—The application of paragraph (a) of this section may be illustrated by the following example:

Example. A, an individual, transfers to a controlled corporation property with an adjusted basis of $10,000 in exchange for stock of the corporation with a fair market value of $8,000, $3,000 cash, and the assumption by the corporation of indebtedness of A amounting to $4,000. A's gain is $5,000, computed as follows:

Stock received, fair market value	$8,000
Cash received	3,000
Liability assumed by transferee	4,000
Total consideration received	15,000
Less: Adjusted basis of property transferred	10,000
Gain realized	$5,000

Assuming that the exchange falls within section 351 as a transaction in which the gain to be recognized is limited to "other property or money" received, the gain recognized to A will be limited to the $3,000 cash received, since, under the general rule of section 357(a), the assumption of the $4,000 liability does not constitute "other property."

(c) *Tax avoidance purpose.*—The benefits of section 357(a) do not extend to any exchange involving an assumption of liabilities where it appears that the principal purpose of the taxpayer with respect to such assumption was to avoid Federal income tax on the exchange, or, if not such purpose, was not a bona fide business purpose. In such cases, the total amount of liabilities assumed or acquired pursuant to such exchange (and not merely a particular liability with respect to which the tax avoidance purpose existed) shall, for the purpose of determining the amount of gain to be recognized upon the exchange in which the liabilities are assumed or acquired, be treated as money received by the taxpayer upon the exchange. Thus, if in the example set forth in paragraph (b) of this section, the principal purpose of the assumption of the $4,000 liability was to avoid tax on the exchange, or was not a bona fide business purpose, then the amount of gain recognized would be $5,000. In any suit or proceeding where the burden is on the taxpayer to prove that an assumption of liabilities is not to be treated as "other property or money" under section 357, which is the case if the Commissioner determines that the taxpayer's purpose with respect thereto was a purpose to avoid Federal income tax on the exchange or was not a bona fide business purpose, and the taxpayer contests such determination by litigation, the taxpayer must sustain such burden by the clear preponderance of the evidence. Thus, the taxpayer must prove his case by such a clear preponderance of all the evidence that the absence of a purpose to avoid Federal income tax on the exchange, or the presence of a bona fide business purpose, is unmistakable. [Reg. § 1.357-1.]

☐ [*T.D.* 6152, 12-2-55. *Amended by T.D.* 6528, 1-18-61.]

§ 1.357-2. Liabilities in excess of basis.—(a) Section 357(c) provides in general that in an exchange to which section 351 (relating to a transfer to a corporation controlled by the transferor) is applicable, or to which section 361 (relating to the nonrecognition of gain or loss to corporations) is applicable by reason of a section 368(a)(1)(D) reorganization, if the sum of the amount of liabilities assumed plus the amount of liabilities to which the property is subject exceeds the total of the adjusted basis of the property transferred pursuant to such exchange, then such excess shall be considered as a gain from the sale or exchange of a capital asset or of property which is not a capital asset as the case may be. Thus, if an individual transfers, under section 351, properties having a total basis in his hands of $20,000, one of which has a basis of $10,000 but is subject to a mortgage of $30,000, to a corporation controlled by him, such individual will be subject to tax with respect to $10,000, the excess of the amount of the liability over the total adjusted basis of all the properties in his hands. The same result will follow whether or not the liability is assumed by the transferee. The determination of whether a gain resulting from the transfer of capital assets is long-term or short-term capital gain shall be made by reference to the holding period to the transferor of the assets transferred. An exception to the general rule of section 357(c) is made (1) for any exchange as to which under section 357(b) (relating to assumption of liabilities for tax-avoidance purposes) the entire amount of the liabilities is treated as money received and (2) for an exchange to which section 371 (relating to reorganizations in certain receivership and bankruptcy proceedings) or section 374 (relating to gain or loss not recognized in certain railroad reorganizations) is applicable.

(b) The application of paragraph (a) of this section may be illustrated by the following examples:

Example (1). If all such assets transferred are capital assets and if half the assets (ascertained by reference to their fair market value at the time of the transfer) have been held for less than 1 year (6 months for taxable years beginning before 1977; 9 months for taxable years beginning in 1977) and the remaining half for more than 1 year (6 months for taxable years beginning before 1977; 9 months for taxable years beginning in 1977), half the excess of the amount of the liability over the total of the adjusted basis of the property transferred pursuant to the exchange shall be treated as short-term capital gain, and the remaining half shall be treated as long-term capital gain.

Example (2). If half of the assets (ascertained by reference to their fair market value at the time of the transfer) transferred are capital assets and half are assets other than capital assets, then half of the excess of the amount of the liability over the total of the adjusted basis of the property transferred pursuant to the exchange shall be treated as capital gain, and the remaining half shall be treated as gain from the sale or exchange of assets other than capital assets. [Reg. § 1.357-2.]

☐ [*T.D.* 6152, 12-2-55. *Amended by T.D.* 6528, 1-18-61 *and by T.D.* 7728, 10-31-80.]

§ 1.358-1. Basis to distributees.—(a) In the case of an exchange to which section 354 or 355 applies in which, under the law applicable to the year in which the exchange is made, only nonrecognition property is received, immediately after the transaction, the sum of the basis of all of the stock and securities received in the transaction shall be the same as the basis of all the stock and securities in such corporation surrendered in the transaction, allocated in the manner described in § 1.358-2. In the case of a distribution to which section 355 applies in which, under the law applicable to the year in which the distribution is made, only nonrecognition property is received, immediately after the transaction, the sum of the basis of all of the stock and securities with respect to which the distribution is made plus the basis of all stock and securities received in the distribution with respect to such stock and securities shall be the same as the basis of the stock and securities with respect to which the distribution is made immediately before the transaction, allocated in the manner described in § 1.358-2. In the case of an exchange to which section 351 or 361 applies in which, under the law applicable to the year in which the exchange was made, only nonrecognition property is received, the basis of all the stock and securities received in the exchange shall be the same as the basis of all property exchanged therefor. If in an exchange or distribution to which section 351, 356, or 361 applies both nonrecognition property and "other property" are received, the basis of all the property except "other property" held after the transaction shall be determined as described in the preceding three sentences decreased by the sum of the money and the fair market value of the "other property" (as of the date of the transaction) and increased by the sum of the amount treated as a dividend (if any) and the amount of the gain recognized on the exchange, but the term gain as here used does not include any portion of the recognized gain that was treated as a dividend. In any case in which a taxpayer transfers property with respect to which loss is recognized, such loss shall be reflected in determining the basis of the property received in the exchange. The basis of the "other property" is its fair market value as of the date of the transaction. See § 1.460- 4(k)(3)(iv)(A) for rules relating to stock basis adjustments required where a contract accounted for using a long-term contract method of accounting is transferred in a transaction described in section 351 or a reorganization described in section 368(a)(1)(D) with respect to which the requirements of section 355 (or so much of section 356 as relates to section 355) are met.

(b) The application of paragraph (a) of this section may be illustrated by the following example:

Example. A purchased a share of stock in Corporation X in 1935 for $150. Since that date A has received distributions out of other than earnings and profits (as defined in section 316) totaling $60, so that A's adjusted basis for the stock is $90. In a transaction qualifying under section 356, A exchanged this share for one share in Corporation Y, worth $100, cash in the amount of $10, and other property with a fair market value of $30. The exchange had the effect of the distribution of a dividend. A's ratable share of the earnings and profits of Corporation X accumulated after February 28, 1913, was $5. A realized a gain of $50 on the exchange, but the amount recognized is limited to $40, the sum of the cash received and the fair market value of the other property. Of the gain recognized, $5 is taxable as a dividend, and $35 is taxable as a gain from the exchange of property. The basis to A of the one share of stock of Corporation Y is $90, that is, the adjusted basis of the one share of stock of Corporation X ($90), decreased by the sum of the cash received ($10) and the fair market value of the other property received ($30) and increased by the sum of the amount treated as a dividend ($5) and the amount treated as a gain from the exchange of property ($35). The basis of the other property received is $30.

(c) This section applies to exchanges and distributions of stock and securities occurring on or after January 23, 2006. [Reg. § 1.358-1.]

□ [*T.D.* 6152, 12-2-55. *Amended by T.D.* 6533, 1-18-61; *T.D.* 7616, 5-7-79; *T.D.* 8995, 5-14-2002 *and T.D.* 9244, 1-23-2006 (*corrected* 4-12-2006 *and* 10-25-2006).]

§ 1.358-2. Allocation of basis among nonrecognition property.—(a) *Allocation of basis in exchanges or distributions to which section 354, 355, or 356 applies.*—(1) As used in this paragraph the term *stock* means stock which is not "other property" under section 356. The term *securities* means securities (including, where appropriate, fractional parts of securities) which are not "other property" under section 356. Stock, or securities, as the case may be, which differ either because they are in different corporations or because the rights attributable to them differ (although they are in the same corporation) are considered different classes of stock or securities, as the case may be, for purposes of this section.

(2)(i) If a shareholder or security holder surrenders a share of stock or a security in an exchange under the terms of section 354, 355, or 356, the basis of each share of stock or security received in the exchange shall be the same as the basis of the share or shares of stock or security or securities (or allocable portions thereof) exchanged therefor (as adjusted under § 1.358-1). If more than one share of stock or security is received in exchange for one share of stock or one security, the basis of the share of stock or security surrendered shall be allocated to the shares of stock or securities received in the exchange in proportion to the fair market value of the shares of stock or securities received. If one share of stock or security is received in exchange for more than one share of stock or security or if a fraction of a share of stock or security is received, then the basis of the shares of stock or securities surrendered must be allocated to the shares of stock or securities (or allocable portions thereof) received in a manner that reflects, to the greatest extent possible, that a share of stock or security received is received in respect of shares of stock or securities that were acquired on the same date and at the same price. To the extent it is not possible to allocate basis in this manner, the basis of the shares of stock or securities surrendered must be allocated to the shares of stock or securities (or allocable portions thereof) received in a manner that minimizes the disparity in the holding periods of the surrendered shares of stock or securities whose basis is allocated to any particular share of stock or security received.

(ii) If a shareholder or security holder surrenders a share of stock or a security in an exchange under the terms of section 354, 355, or 356, and receives shares of stock or securities of more than one class, or receives "other property" or money in addition to shares of stock or securities, then, to the extent the terms of the exchange specify that shares of stock or securities of a particular class or "other property" or money is received in exchange for a particular share of stock or security or a particular class of stock or securities, for purposes of applying the rules of this section, such terms shall control provided such terms are economically reasonable. To the extent the terms of the exchange do not specify that shares of stock or securities of a particular class or "other property" or money is received in exchange for a particular share of stock or security or a particular class of stock or securities, then, for purposes of applying the rules of paragraph (a)(2)(i) of this section, a pro rata portion of the shares of stock and securities of each class received and a pro rata portion of the "other property" and money received shall be treated as received in exchange for each share of stock and security surrendered, based on the fair market value of the stock and securities surrendered.

(iii)(A) For purposes of this section, if a shareholder or security holder surrenders a share of stock or a security in a transaction under the terms of section 354 (or so much of section 356 as relates to section 354) in which the shareholder or security holder receives no property or property (including property permitted by section 354 to be received without the recognition of gain or "other property" or money) with a fair market value less than that of the stock or securities surrendered in the transaction:

(1) Such shareholder or security holder shall be treated as receiving the stock, securities, other property, and money actually received by the shareholder or security holder in the transaction and an amount of stock of the issuing corporation (as defined in § 1.368-1(b)) that has a value equal to the excess of the value of the stock or securities the shareholder or security holder surrendered in the transaction over the value of the stock, securities, other property, and money the shareholder or security holder actually received in the transaction. If the shareholder owns only one class of stock of the issuing corporation the receipt of which would be consistent with the economic rights associated with each class of stock of the issuing corporation, the stock deemed received by the shareholder pursuant to the previous sentence shall be stock of such class. If the shareholder owns multiple classes of stock of the issuing corporation the receipt of which would be consistent with the economic rights associated with each class of stock of the issuing corporation, the stock deemed received by the shareholder shall be stock of each such class owned by the shareholder immediately prior to the transaction, in proportion to the value of the stock of each such class owned by the shareholder at that time. The basis of each share of stock or security of the issuing corporation deemed received and actually received shall be determined under the rules of this section. If and to the extent necessary to reflect the actual ownership of the issuing corporation immediately after the exchange to which section 354 (or so much of section 356 as relates to section 354) applies, an appropriate amount of the stock of the issuing corporation treated as issued to the shareholder or security holder in the exchange is deemed further transferred in accordance with § 1.368-2(l) to reflect the actual ownership of the issuing corporation. Paragraph (a)(2)(iii)(A)(*2*) of this section is only applied to any shareholder of the issuing corporation after all of the deemed transfers pursuant to § 1.368-2(l) are completed. The transferred shares' basis shall be adjusted for all deemed transfers required by § 1.368-2(l).

(2) A direct shareholder of the issuing corporation that receives the shares deemed issued as part of the transaction, as described in paragraph (a)(2)(iii)(A)(*1*) of this section, shall then be treated as surrendering all of its shares of stock and securities in the issuing corporation, including those shares of stock or securities held immediately prior to the transaction, those shares of stock or securities actually received in the transaction, and those shares of stock deemed received as described in paragraph (a)(2)(iii)(A)(*1*) of this section, in a reorganization under section 368(a)(1)(E) in exchange for the shares of stock and securities of the issuing corporation that the shareholder or security holder actually holds immediately after the transaction. The basis of each share of stock and security deemed received in the reorganization under section 368(a)(1)(E) shall be determined under the rules of this section.

(B) For purposes of this section, if an actual shareholder of the issuing corporation is deemed to receive a nominal share of stock of the issuing corporation as provided in § 1.368-2(l), then that shareholder must, after allocating and adjusting the basis of the nominal share in accordance with the rules of this section and § 1.358-1, designate the share of stock of the issuing corporation that it owns to which the basis, if any, of the nominal share will attach. If the shareholder does not actually own any shares of stock in the issuing corporation immediately after the exchange to which section 354 (or so much of section 356 as relates to section 354) applies, the nominal share of stock of the issuing corporation received by the shareholder in the exchange is deemed further transferred in accordance with §1.368-2(l) without applying the designation rule set forth in the first sentence of this paragraph until it is transferred to a person that actually owns stock in the issuing corporation. The transferred share's basis shall be adjusted for all deemed transfers required by §1.368-2(l).

(iv) If a shareholder or security holder receives one or more shares of stock or one or more securities in a distribution under the terms of section 355 (or so much of section 356 as relates to section 355), the basis of each share of stock or security of the distributing corporation (as defined in §1.355-1(b)), as adjusted under §1.358-1, shall be allocated between the share of stock or security of the distributing corporation with respect to which the distribution is made and the share or shares of stock or security or securities (or allocable portions thereof) received with respect to the share of stock or security of the distributing corporation in proportion to their fair market values. If one share of stock or security is received with respect to more than one share of stock or security or if a fraction of a share of stock or security is received, then the basis of each share of stock or security of the distributing corporation must be allocated to the shares of stock or securities (or allocable portions thereof) received in a manner that reflects that, to the greatest extent possible, a share of stock or security received is received with respect to shares of stock or securities acquired on the same date and at the same price. To the extent it is not possible to allocate basis in this manner, the basis of each share of stock or security of the distributing corporation must be allocated to the shares of stock or securities (or allocable portions thereof) received in a manner that minimizes the disparity in the holding periods of the shares of stock or securities with respect to which such shares of stock or securities are received.

(v) If a shareholder or security holder receives shares of stock or securities of more than one class, or receives "other property" or money in addition to stock or securities in a distribution under the terms of section 355 (or so much of section 356 as relates to section 355), then, to the extent the terms of the distribution specify that shares of stock or securities of a particular class or "other property" or money is received with respect to a particular share of stock or security of the distributing corporation or a particular class of stock or securities of the distributing corporation, for purposes of applying the rules of this section, such terms shall control provided that such terms are economically reasonable. To the extent the terms of the distribution do not specify that shares of stock or securities of a particular class or "other property" or money is received with respect to a particular share of stock or security of the distributing corporation or a particular class of stock or securities of the distributing corporation, then, for purposes of applying the rules of this section, a pro rata portion of the shares of stock and securities of each class received and a pro rata portion of the "other property" and money received shall be treated as received with respect to each share of stock and security of the distributing corporation with respect to which the distribution is made, based on the fair market value of each such share of stock or security.

(vi) If a share of stock or a security is received in exchange for, or with respect to, more than one share of stock or security and such shares or securities were acquired on different dates or at different prices, the share of stock or security received shall be divided into segments based on the relative fair market values of the shares of stock or securities surrendered in exchange for such share or security or the relative fair market values of the shares of stock or securities with respect to which the share of stock or security is received in a distribution under the terms of section 355 (or so much of section 356 as relates to section 355)). Each segment shall have a basis determined under the rules of paragraph (a)(2) of this section and a corresponding holding period.

(vii) If a shareholder or security holder that purchased or acquired shares of stock or securities in a corporation on different dates or at different prices exchanges such shares of stock or securities under the terms of section 354, 355, or 356, or receives a distribution of shares of stock or securities under the terms of section 355 (or so much of section 356 as relates to section 355), and the shareholder or security holder is not able to identify which particular share of stock or security (or allocable portion of a share of stock or security) is received (or deemed received) in exchange for, or with respect to, a particular share of stock or security, the shareholder or security holder may designate which share of stock or security is received in exchange for, or with respect to, a particular share of stock or security, provided that such designation is consistent with the terms of the exchange or distribution (or an exchange deemed to have occurred pursuant to paragraph (a)(2)(iii) of this section), and the other rules of this section. In the case of an exchange under the terms of section 354 or 356 (including a deemed exchange as a result of the application of paragraph (a)(2)(iii) of this section), the designation must be made on or before the first date on which the basis of a share of stock or a security received (or deemed received in the reorganization under section 368(a)(1)(E) in the case of a transaction to which paragraph (a)(2)(iii) of this section applies) is relevant. In the case of an exchange or distribution under the terms of section 355 (or so much of section 356 as relates to section 355), the designation must be made on or before the first date on which the basis of a share of stock or a security of the distributing corporation or the controlled corporation (as defined in § 1.355-1(b)) is relevant. The basis of the shares or securities received in an exchange under the terms of section 354 or section 356, for example, is relevant when such shares or securities are sold or otherwise transferred. The designation will be binding for purposes of determining the Federal tax consequences of any sale or transfer of, or distribution with respect to, the shares or securities received. If the shareholder fails to make a designation in a case in which the shareholder is not able to identify which share of stock is received in exchange for, or with respect to, a particular share of stock, then the shareholder will not be able to identify which shares are sold or transferred for purposes of determining the basis of property sold or transferred under section 1012 and § 1.1012-1(c) and, instead, will be treated as selling or transferring the share received in respect of the earliest share purchased or acquired.

(viii) This paragraph (a)(2) shall not apply to determine the basis of a share of stock or security received by a shareholder or security holder in an exchange described in both section 351 and either section 354 or 356, if, in connection with the exchange—

(A) The shareholder or security holder exchanges property for stock or securities in an exchange to which neither section 354 nor section 356 applies;

(B) The shareholder or security holder exchanges property for stock or securities in a transaction for which an election to apply section 362(e)(2)(C) is in effect; or

(C) Liabilities of the shareholder or security holder are assumed.

(ix) This paragraph (a)(2) shall apply to determine the basis of a share of stock or security received by a shareholder or security holder in an exchange described in both section 1036 and section 354 or section 356.

(b) *Allocation of basis in exchanges to which section 351 or 361 applies.*—(1) As used in this paragraph (b), the term *stock* refers only to stock which is not "other property" under section 351 or 361 and the term *securities* refers only to securities which are not "other property" under section 351 or 361.

(2) If in an exchange to which section 351 or 361 applies property is transferred to a corporation and the transferor receives stock or securities of more than one class or receives both stock and securities, then the basis of the property transferred (as adjusted under § 1.358-1) shall be allocated among all of the stock and securities received in proportion to the fair market values of the stock of each class and the securities of each class.

(c) *Examples.*—The application of paragraphs (a) and (b) of this section is illustrated by the following examples:

Example 1. (i) *Facts.* J, an individual, acquired 20 shares of Corporation X stock on Date 1 for $3 each and 10 shares of Corporation X stock on Date 2 for $6 each. On Date 3, Corporation Y acquires the assets of Corporation X in a reorganization under section 368(a)(1)(A). Pursuant to the terms of the plan of reorganization, J receives 2 shares of Corporation Y stock in exchange for each share of Corporation X stock. Therefore, J receives 60 shares of Corporation Y stock. Pursuant to section 354, J recognizes no gain or loss on the exchange. J is not able to identify which shares of Corporation Y stock are received in exchange for each share of Corporation X stock.

(ii) *Analysis.* Under paragraph (a)(2)(i) of this section, J has 40 shares of Corporation Y stock each of which has a basis of $1.50 and is treated as having been acquired on Date 1 and 20 shares of Corporation Y stock each of which has a basis of $3 and is treated as having been acquired on Date 2. Under paragraph (a)(2)(vii) of this section, on or before the date on which the basis of a share of Corporation Y stock received becomes relevant, J may designate which of the shares of Corporation Y stock have a basis of $1.50 and which have a basis of $3.

Example 2. (i) *Facts.* The facts are the same as in *Example 1*, except that instead of receiving 2 shares of Corporation Y stock in exchange for each share of Corporation X stock, J receives 11/2 shares of Corporation Y stock in exchange for each share of Corporation X stock. Therefore, J receives 45 shares of Corporation Y stock. Again, J is not able to identify which shares (or portions of shares) of Corporation Y stock are received in exchange for each share of Corporation X stock.

(ii) *Analysis.* Under paragraph (a)(2)(i) of this section, J has 30 shares of Corporation Y stock each of which has a basis of $2 and is treated as having been acquired on Date 1 and

15 shares of Corporation Y stock each of which has a basis of $4 and is treated as having been acquired on Date 2. Under paragraph (a)(2)(vii) of this section, on or before the date on which the basis of a share of Corporation Y stock received becomes relevant, J may designate which of the shares of Corporation Y stock received have a basis of $2 and which have a basis of $4.

Example 3. (i) *Facts*. J, an individual, acquired 10 shares of Class A stock of Corporation X on Date 1 for $3 each, 10 shares of Class A stock of Corporation X on Date 2 for $9 each, and 10 shares of Class B stock of Corporation X on Date 3 for $3 each. On Date 4, J surrenders all of J's shares of Class A stock in exchange for 20 shares of new Class C stock and 20 shares of new Class D stock in a reorganization under section 368(a)(1)(E). Pursuant to section 354, J recognizes no gain or loss on the exchange. On the date of the exchange, the fair market value of each share of Class A stock is $6, the fair market value of each share of Class C stock is $2, and the fair market value of each share of Class D stock is $4. The terms of the exchange do not specify that shares of Class C stock or shares of Class D stock of Corporation X are received in exchange for particular shares of Class A stock of Corporation X.

(ii) *Analysis*. Under paragraph (a)(2)(ii) of this section, because the terms of the exchange do not specify that shares of Class C stock or shares of Class D stock of Corporation X are received in exchange for particular shares of Class A stock of Corporation X, a pro rata portion of the shares of Class C stock and shares of Class D stock received will be treated as received in exchange for each share of Class A stock based on the fair market value of the surrendered shares of Class A stock. Therefore, J is treated as receiving one share of Class C stock and one share of Class D stock in exchange for each share of Class A stock. Under paragraph (a)(2)(i) of this section, J has 10 shares of Class C stock, each of which has a basis of $1 and is treated as having been acquired on Date 1 and 10 shares of Class C stock, each of which has a basis of $3 and is treated as having been acquired on Date 2. In addition, J has 10 shares of Class D stock, each of which has a basis of $2 and is treated as having been acquired on Date 1 and 10 shares of Class D stock, each of which has a basis of $6 and is treated as having been acquired on Date 2. J's basis in each share of Class B stock remains $3. Under paragraph (a)(2)(vii) of this section, on or before the date on which the basis of a share of Class C stock or Class D stock received becomes relevant, J may designate which of the shares of Class C stock have a basis of $1 and which have a basis of $3, and which of the shares of Class D stock have a basis of $2 and which have a basis of $6.

Example 4. (i) *Facts*. J, an individual, acquired 10 shares of Class A stock of Corporation X on Date 1 for $2 each, 10 shares of Class A stock of Corporation X on Date 2 for $4 each, and 20 shares of Class B stock of Corporation X on Date 3 for $6 each. On Date 4, Corporation Y acquires the assets of Corporation X in a reorganization under section 368(a)(1)(A). Pursuant to the terms of the plan of reorganization, J surrenders all of J's shares of Corporation X stock for 40 shares of Corporation Y stock and $200 of cash. On the date of the exchange, the fair market value of each share of Class A stock of Corporation X is $10, the fair market value of each share of Class B stock of Corporation X is $10, and the fair market value of each share of Corporation Y stock is $5. The terms of the exchange do not specify that shares of Corporation Y stock or cash are received in exchange for particular shares of Class A stock or Class B stock of Corporation X.

(ii) *Analysis*. Under paragraph (a)(2)(ii) of this section and under § 1.356-1(b), because the terms of the exchange do not specify that shares of Corporation Y stock or cash are received in exchange for particular shares of Class A stock or Class B stock of Corporation X, a pro rata portion of the shares of Corporation Y stock and cash received will be treated as received in exchange for each share of Class A stock and Class B stock of Corporation X surrendered based on the fair market value of such stock. Therefore, J is treated as receiving one share of Corporation Y stock and $5 of cash in exchange for each share of Class A stock of Corporation X and one share of Corporation Y stock and $5 of cash in exchange for each share of Class B stock of Corporation X. J realizes a gain of $140 on the exchange of shares of Class A stock of Corporation X, $100 of which is recognized under § 1.356-1(a). J realizes a gain of $80 on the exchange of Class B stock of Corporation X, all of which is recognized under § 1.356-1(a). Under paragraph (a)(2)(i) of this section, J has 10 shares of Corporation Y stock, each of which has a basis of $2 and is treated as having been acquired on Date 1, 10 shares of Corporation Y stock, each of which has a basis of $4 and is treated as having been acquired on Date 2, and 20 shares of Corporation Y stock, each of which has a basis of $5 and is treated as having been acquired on Date 3. Under paragraph (a)(2)(vii) of this section, on or before the date on which the basis of a share of Corporation Y stock received becomes relevant, J may designate which of the shares of Corporation Y stock received have a basis of $2, which have a basis of $4, and which have a basis of $5.

Example 5. (i) *Facts.* The facts are the same as in *Example 4,* except that the terms of the plan of reorganization specify that J receives 40 shares of stock of Corporation Y in exchange for J's shares of Class A stock of Corporation X and $200 of cash in exchange for J's shares of Class B stock of Corporation X.

(ii) *Analysis.* Under paragraph (a)(2)(ii) of this section and under § 1.356-1(b), because the terms of the exchange specify that J receives 40 shares of stock of Corporation Y in exchange for J's shares of Class A stock of Corporation X and $200 of cash in exchange for J's shares of Class B stock of Corporation X and such terms are economically reasonable, such terms control. J realizes a gain of $140 on the exchange of shares of Class A stock of Corporation X, none of which is recognized under § 1.356-1(a). J realizes a gain of $80 on the exchange of shares of Class B stock of Corporation X, all of which is recognized under § 1.356-1(a). Under paragraph (a)(2)(i) of this section, J has 20 shares of Corporation Y stock, each of which has a basis of $1 and is treated as having been acquired on Date 1, and 20 shares of Corporation Y stock, each of which has a basis of $2 and is treated as having been acquired on Date 2. Under paragraph (a)(2)(vii) of this section, on or before the date on which the basis of a share of Corporation Y stock received becomes relevant, J may designate which of the shares of Corporation Y stock received have a basis of $1 and which have a basis of $2.

Example 6. (i) *Facts.* J, an individual, acquired 10 shares of stock of Corporation X on Date 1 for $2 each, and a security issued by Corporation X to J on Date 2 with a principal amount of $100 and a basis of $100. On Date 3, Corporation Y acquires the assets of Corporation X in a reorganization under section 368(a)(1)(A). Pursuant to the terms of the plan of reorganization, J surrenders all of J's shares of Corporation X stock in exchange for 10 shares of Corporation Y stock and surrenders J's Corporation X security in exchange for a Corporation Y security. On the date of the exchange, the fair market value of each share of stock of Corporation X is $10, the fair market value of J's Corporation X security is $100, the fair market value of each share of Corporation Y stock is $10, and the fair market value and principal amount of the Corporation Y security received by J is $100.

(ii) *Analysis.* Under paragraph (a)(2)(ii) of this section and under § 1.354-1(a), because the terms of the exchange specify that J receives 10 shares of stock of Corporation Y in exchange for J's shares of Class A stock of Corporation X and a Corporation Y security in exchange for its Corporation X security and such terms are economically reasonable, such terms control. Pursuant to section 354, J recognizes no gain on either exchange. Under paragraph (a)(2)(i) of this section, J has 10 shares of Corporation Y stock, each of which has a basis of $2 and is treated as having been acquired on Date 1, and a security that has a basis of $100 and is treated as having been acquired on Date 2.

Example 7. (i) *Facts.* J, an individual, acquired 10 shares of Corporation X stock on Date 1 for $2 each and 10 shares of Corporation X stock on Date 2 for $5 each. On Date 3, Corporation Y acquires the stock of Corporation X in a reorganization under section 368(a)(1)(B). Pursuant to the terms of the plan of reorganization, J receives one share of Corporation Y stock in exchange for every 2 shares of Corporation X stock. Pursuant to section 354, J recognizes no gain or loss on the exchange. J is not able to identify which portion of each share of Corporation Y stock is received in exchange for each share of Corporation X stock.

(ii) *Analysis.* Under paragraph (a)(2)(i) of this section, J has 5 shares of Corporation Y stock each of which has a basis of $4 and is treated as having been acquired on Date 1 and 5 shares of Corporation Y stock each of which has a basis of $10 and is treated as having been acquired on Date 2. Under paragraph (a)(2)(vii) of this section, on or before the date on which the basis of a share of Corporation Y stock received becomes relevant, J may designate which of the shares of Corporation Y stock received have a basis of $4 and which have a basis of $10.

Example 8. (i) *Facts.* The facts are the same as in *Example 7,* except that, in addition to transferring the stock of Corporation X to Corporation Y, J transfers land to Corporation Y. In addition, after the transaction, J owns stock of Corporation Y satisfying the requirements of section 368(c). J's transfer of the Corporation X stock to Corporation Y is an exchange described in sections 351 and 354. J's transfer of land to Corporation Y is an exchange described in section 351.

(ii) *Analysis.* Under paragraph (a)(2)(viii) of this section, because neither section 354 nor section 356 applies to the transfer of land to Corporation Y, the rules of paragraph (a)(2) of this section do not apply to determine J's basis in the Corporation Y stock received in the transaction.

Example 9. (i) *Facts.* J, an individual, acquired 10 shares of Corporation X stock on Date 1 for $3 each and 10 shares of Corporation X stock on Date 2 for $6 each. On Date 3, Corporation Z, a newly formed, wholly owned subsidiary of Corporation Y, merges with and into Corporation X with Corporation X surviving. As part of the plan of merger, J receives one share of Corporation Y stock in exchange for each share of Corporation X stock. In connection with the transaction, Corporation Y assumes a liability of J. In addition, after the transaction, J owns stock of Corporation Y satisfying the requirements of section 368(c). J's transfer of the Corporation X stock to Corporation Y is an exchange described in sections 351 and 354.

(ii) *Analysis.* Under paragraph (a)(2)(viii) of this section, because, in connection with the transfer of the Corporation X stock to Corporation Y, Corporation Y assumed a liability of J, the rules of paragraph (a)(2) of this section do not apply to determine J's basis in the Corporation Y stock received in the transaction.

Example 10. (i) *Facts.* Each of Corporation X and Corporation Y has a single class of stock outstanding, all of which is owned by J, an individual. J acquired 100 shares of Corporation X stock on Date 1 for $1 each and 100 shares of Corporation Y stock on Date 2 for $2 each. On Date 3, Corporation Y acquires the assets of Corporation X in a reorganization under section 368(a)(1)(D). Pursuant to the terms of the plan of reorganization, J surrenders J's 100 shares of Corporation X stock but does not receive any additional Corporation Y stock. Immediately before the effective time of the reorganization, the fair market value of each share of Corporation X stock and each share of Corporation Y stock is $1. Pursuant to section 354, J recognizes no gain or loss.

(ii) *Analysis.* Under paragraph (a)(2)(iii) of this section, J is deemed to have received shares of Corporation Y stock with an aggregate fair market value of $100 in exchange for J's Corporation X shares. Given the number of outstanding shares of stock of Corporation Y and their value immediately before the effective time of the reorganization, J is deemed to have received 100 shares of stock of Corporation Y in the reorganization. Under paragraph (a)(2)(i) of this section, each of those shares has a basis of $1 and is treated as having been acquired on Date 1. Then, the stock of Corporation Y is deemed to be recapitalized in a reorganization under section 368(a)(1)(E) in which J receives 100 shares of Corporation Y stock in exchange for those shares of Corporation Y stock that J held immediately prior to the reorganization and those shares J is deemed to have received in the reorganization. Under paragraph (a)(2)(i), immediately after the reorganization, J holds 50 shares of Corporation Y stock each of which has a basis of $2 and is treated as having been acquired on Date 1 and 50 shares of Corporation Y stock each of which has a basis of $4 and is treated as having been acquired on Date 2. Under paragraph (a)(2)(vii) of this section, on or before the date on which the basis of any share of J's Corporation Y stock becomes relevant, J may designate which of the shares of Corporation Y have a basis of $2 and which have a basis of $4.

Example 11. (i) *Facts.* Corporation X has a single class of stock outstanding, all of which is owned by J, an individual. J acquired 100 shares of Corporation X stock on Date 1 for $1 each. Corporation Y has two classes of stock outstanding, common stock and nonvoting preferred stock. On Date 2, J acquired 100 shares of Corporation Y common stock for $2 each and 100 shares of Corporation Y preferred stock for $4 each. On Date 3, Corporation Y acquires the assets of Corporation X in a reorganization under section 368(a)(1)(D). Pursuant to the terms of the plan of reorganization, J surrenders J's 100 shares of Corporation X stock but does not receive any additional Corporation Y stock. Immediately before the effective time of the reorganization, the fair market value of each share of Corporation X stock is $10, the fair market value of each share of Corporation Y common stock is $10, and the fair market value of each share of Corporation Y preferred stock is $20. Pursuant to section 354, J recognizes no gain or loss.

(ii) *Analysis.* Under paragraph (a)(2)(iii) of this section, J is deemed to have received shares of Corporation Y stock with an aggregate fair market value of $1,000 in exchange for J's Corporation X shares. Consistent with the economics of the transaction and the rights associated with each class of stock of Corporation Y owned by J, J is deemed to receive additional shares of Corporation Y common stock. Because the value of the common stock indicates that the liquidation preference associated with the Corporation Y preferred stock could be satisfied even if the reorganization did not occur, it is not appropriate to deem the issuance of additional Corporation Y preferred stock. Given the number of outstanding shares of common stock of Corporation Y and their value immediately before the effective time of the reorganization, J is deemed to have received 100 shares of common stock of Corporation Y in the reorganization. Under paragraph (a)(2)(i) of this section, each of those shares has a basis of $1 and is treated as having been acquired on Date 1. Then, the common stock of Corporation Y is deemed to be recapitalized in a reorganization under section 368(a)(1)(E) in which J receives 100 shares of Corporation Y common stock in exchange for those shares of Corporation Y common stock that J held immediately prior to the reorganization and those shares of Corporation Y common stock that J is deemed to have received in the reorganization. Under paragraph (a)(2)(i), immediately after the reorganization, J holds 50 shares of Corporation Y common stock, each of which has a basis of $2 and is treated as having been acquired on Date 1, and 50 shares of Corporation Y common stock, each of which has a basis of $4 and is treated as having been acquired on Date 2. Under paragraph (a)(2)(vii) of this section, on or before the date on which the basis of any share of J's Corporation Y common stock becomes relevant, J may designate which of those shares have a basis of $2 and which have a basis of $4.

Example 12. (i) *Facts.* J, an individual, acquired 5 shares of Corporation X stock on Date 1 for $4 each and 5 shares of Corporation X stock on Date 2 for $8 each. Corporation X owns all of the outstanding stock of Corporation Y. The fair market value of the stock of Corporation X is $1800. The fair market value of the stock of Corporation Y is $900. In a distribution to which section 355 applies, Corporation X distributes all of the stock of Corporation Y pro rata to its shareholders. No stock of Corporation X is surrendered in connection with the distribution. In the distribution, J receives 2 shares of Corporation Y stock with respect to each share of Corporation X stock. Pursuant to section 355, J recognizes no gain or loss on the receipt of the shares of Corporation Y stock. J is not able to identify which share of Corporation Y stock is received in respect of each share of Corporation X stock.

(ii) *Analysis.* Under paragraph (a)(2)(iv) of this section, because J receives 2 shares of Corporation Y stock with respect to each share of Corporation X stock, the basis of each share of Corporation X stock is allocated between such share of Corporation X stock and two shares of Corporation Y stock in proportion to the fair market value of those shares. Therefore, each of the 5 shares of Corporation X stock acquired on Date 1 will have a basis of $2 and each of the 10 shares of Corporation Y stock received with respect to those shares will have a basis of $1. In addition, each of the 5 shares of Corporation X stock acquired on Date 2 will have a basis of $4 and each of the 10 shares of Corporation Y stock received with respect to those shares will have a basis of $2. Under paragraph (a)(2)(vii) of this section, on or before the date on which the basis of a share of Corporation Y stock received becomes relevant, J may designate which of the shares of Corporation Y stock have a basis of $1 and which have a basis of $2.

* * *

Example 15. (i) *Facts.* Each of Corporation X and Corporation Y has a single class of stock outstanding, all of which is owned by J, an individual. J purchased 100 shares of Corporation X stock on Date 1 for $1.50 each, resulting in J having an aggregate basis in the stock of Corporation X of $150. On Date 2, Corporation Y acquires the assets of Corporation X for $100 of cash, their fair market value, in a transaction described in § 1.368-2(l). Pursuant to the terms of the exchange, Corporation X does not receive any Corporation Y stock. Corporation X distributes the $100 of cash to J and retains no assets.

(ii) *Analysis.* Pursuant to § 1.368-2(l), Corporation Y will be deemed to issue a nominal share of Corporation Y stock to Corporation X in addition to the $100 of cash actually exchanged for the Corporation X assets. Corporation X will then be deemed to distribute the nominal share of Corporation Y stock to J in addition to the $100 of cash actually distributed to J. Pursuant to § 1.368-2(l), J, the actual shareholder of Corporation Y, the issuing corporation, is deemed to receive the nominal share of Corporation Y stock described in § 1.368-2(l). J will have a basis of $50 in the nominal share of Corporation Y stock under section 358(a)(1). Therefore, under paragraph (a)(2)(iii)(B) of this section, J must designate a share of Corporation Y stock to which J's basis of $50 in the nominal share of Corporation Y stock will attach.

Example 16. (i) *Facts.* Each of Corporation X and Corporation Y has a single class of stock outstanding, all of which is owned by Corporation P. Corporation T has a single class of stock outstanding, all of which is owned by Corporation X. The corporations do not join in the filing of a consolidated return. Corporation X purchased 100 shares of Corporation T stock on Date 1 for $1.50 each, resulting in Corporation X having an aggregate basis in the stock of Corporation T of $150. On Date 2, Corporation Y acquires the assets of Corporation T for $100 of cash, their fair market value, in a transaction described in § 1.368-2(l). Pursuant to the terms of the exchange, Corporation T does not receive any Corporation Y stock. Corporation T distributes the $100 of cash to Corporation X and retains no assets.

(ii) *Analysis.* Pursuant to § 1.368-2(l), Corporation Y will be deemed to issue a nominal share of Corporation Y stock to Corporation T in addition to the $100 of cash actually exchanged for the Corporation T assets. Corporation T will be deemed to distribute the nominal share of Corporation Y stock to Corporation X in addition to the $100 of cash actually distributed. Corporation X will have a basis of $50 in the nominal share of Corporation Y stock under section 358(a). However, Corporation X is not an actual shareholder of Corporation Y, the issuing corporation. Therefore, Corporation X cannot designate any share of Corporation Y stock under paragraph (a)(2)(iii)(B) of this section to which the basis of the nominal share of Corporation Y stock will attach and Corporation X will be deemed to distribute the nominal share of Corporation Y stock to Corporation P as required by § 1.368-2(l). Corporation X does not recognize the loss on the deemed distribution of the nominal share to Corporation P under section 311(a). Corporation P's basis in the nominal share it receives is zero, its fair market value, under section 301(d). Under paragraph (a)(2)(iii)(B) of this section, Corporation P must designate a share of Corporation Y stock to which the nominal share's zero basis will attach.

* * *

[Reg. § 1.358-2.]

☐ [*T.D.* 6152, 12-2-55. *Amended by T.D.* 7616, 5-7-79; *T.D.* 8648, 12-20-95; *T.D.* 9244, 1-23-2006 (corrected 4-12-2006 and 10-25-2006); *T.D.* 9475, 12-17-2009; *T.D.* 9558, 11-18-2011; *T.D.* 9633, 8-30-2013 *and T.D.* 9702, 11-10-2014.]

§ 1.358-3. Treatment of assumption of liabilities.—(a) For purposes of section 358, where a party to the exchange assumes a liability of a distributee or acquires from him property subject to a liability, the amount of such liability is to be treated as money received by the distributee upon the exchange, whether or not the assumption of liabilities resulted in a recognition of gain or loss to the taxpayer under the law applicable to the year in which the exchange was made.

(b) The application of paragraph (a) of this section may be illustrated by the following examples:

Example (1). A, an individual, owns property with an adjusted basis of $100,000 on which there is a purchase money mortgage of $25,000. On December 1, 1954, A organizes Corporation X to which he transfers the property in exchange for all the stock of Corporation X and the assumption by Corporation X of the mortgage. The capital stock of the Corporation X has a fair market value of $150,000. Under sections 351 and 357, no gain or loss is recognized to A. The basis in A's hands of the stock of Corporation X is $75,000, computed as follows:

Adjusted basis of property transferred	$100,000
Less: Amount of money received (amount of liabilities assumed)	25,000
Basis of Corporation X stock to A	$75,000

Example (2). A, an individual, owns property with an adjusted basis of $25,000 on which there is a mortgage of $50,000. On December 1, 1954, A organizes Corporation X to which he transfers the property in exchange for all the stock of Corporation X and the assumption by Corporation X of the mortgage. The stock of Corporation X has a fair market value of $50,000. Under sections 351 and 357, gain is recognized to A in the amount of $25,000. The basis in A's hands of the stock of Corporation X is zero, computed as follows:

Adjusted basis of property transferred	$25,000
Less: Amount of money received (amount of liabilities)	-50,000
Plus: Amount of gain recognized to taxpayer	$25,000
Basis of Corporation X stock to A	$0

[Reg. § 1.358-3.]

☐ [*T.D.* 6152, 12-2-55.]

§ 1.358-6. Stock basis in certain triangular reorganizations.—(a) *Scope.*—This section provides rules for computing the basis of a controlling corporation in the stock of a controlled corporation as the result of certain reorganizations involving the stock of the controlling corporation as described in paragraph (b) of this section. The rules of this section are in addition to rules under other provisions of the Internal Revenue Code and principles of law. See, e.g., section 1001 for the recognition of gain or loss by the controlled corporation on the exchange of property for the assets or stock of a target corporation in a reorganization described in section 368. See also sections 362(e)(1) and 362(e)(2) for further adjustments to basis that may be necessary under either or both of those sections.

(b) *Triangular reorganizations.*—(1) *Nomenclature.*—For purposes of this section—

(i) *P* is a corporation—

(A) That is a party to a reorganization,

(B) That is in control (within the meaning of section 368(c)) of another party to the reorganization, and

(C) Whose stock is transferred pursuant to the reorganization.

(ii) *S* is a corporation—

(A) That is a party to the reorganization, and

(B) That is controlled by *P*.

(iii) *T* is a corporation that is another party to the reorganization.

(2) *Definitions of triangular reorganizations.*—This section applies to the following reorganizations (which are referred to collectively as *triangular reorganizations*):

(i) *Forward triangular merger.*—A forward triangular merger is a statutory merger of *T* and *S*, with *S* surviving, that qualifies as a reorganization under section 368(a)(1)(A) or

(G) by reason of the application of section 368(a)(2)(D).

(ii) *Triangular C reorganization.*—A triangular C reorganization is an acquisition by *S* of substantially all of *T*'s assets in exchange for *P* stock in a transaction that qualifies as a reorganization under section 368(a)(1)(C).

(iii) *Reverse triangular merger.*—A reverse triangular merger is a statutory merger of *S* and *T*, with *T* surviving, that qualifies as a reorganization under section 368(a)(1)(A) by reason of the application of section 368(a)(2)(E).

(iv) *Triangular B reorganization.*—A triangular B reorganization is an acquisition by *S* of *T* stock in exchange for *P* stock in a transaction that qualifies as a reorganization under section 368(a)(1)(B).

(v) *Triangular G reorganization.*—A triangular G reorganization is an acquisition by S (other than by statutory merger) of substantially all of T's assets in a title 11 or similar case in exchange for P stock in a transaction that qualifies as a reorganization under section 368(a)(1)(G) by reason of the application of section 368(a)(2)(D).

(c) *General rules.*—Subject to the special rule provided in paragraph (d) of this section, *P*'s basis in the stock of *S* or *T*, as applicable, as a result of a triangular reorganization, is adjusted under the following rules—

(1) *Forward triangular merger or triangular C reorganization.*—(i) *In general.*—In a forward triangular merger or a triangular C reorganization *P*'s basis in its *S* stock is adjusted as if—

(A) *P* acquired the *T* assets acquired by *S* in the reorganization (and *P* assumed any liabilities which *S* assumed or to which the *T* assets acquired by *S* were subject) directly from *T* in a transaction in which *P*'s basis in the *T* assets was determined under section 362(b); and

(B) *P* transferred the *T* assets (and liabilities which *S* assumed or to which the *T* assets acquired by *S* were subject) to *S* in a transaction in which *P*'s basis in *S* stock was determined under section 358.

(ii) *Limitation.*—If, in applying section 358, the amount of *T* liabilities assumed by *S* or to which the *T* assets acquired *by S* are subject equals or exceeds *T*'s aggregate adjusted basis in its assets, the amount of the adjustment under paragraph (c)(1)(i) of this section is zero. *P* recognizes no gain under section 357(c) as a result of a triangular reorganization.

(2) *Reverse triangular merger.*—(i) *In general.*—(A) *Treated as a forward triangular merger.*—Except as otherwise provided in this paragraph (c)(2), *P*'s basis in its *T* stock acquired in a reverse triangular merger equals its basis in its *S* stock immediately before the transaction adjusted as if *T* had merged into *S* in a forward triangular merger to which paragraph (c)(1) of this section applies.

(B) *Allocable share.*—If *P* acquires less than all of the *T* stock in the transaction, the basis adjustment described in paragraph (c)(2)(i)(A) of this section is reduced in proportion to the percentage of *T* stock not acquired in the transaction. The percentage of *T* stock not acquired in the transaction is determined by taking into account the fair market value of all classes of *T* stock.

(C) *Special rule if P owns T stock before the transaction.*—Solely for purposes of paragraphs (c)(2)(i)(A) and (B) of this section, if *P* owns *T* stock before the transaction, *P* may treat that stock as acquired in the transaction or not, without regard to the form of the transaction.

(ii) *Reverse triangular merger that qualifies as a section 351 transfer or section 368(a)(1)(B) reorganization.*—Notwithstanding paragraph (c)(2)(i) of this section, if a reorganization qualifies as both a reverse triangular merger and as a section 351 transfer or as both a reverse triangular merger and a reorganization under section 368(a)(1)(B), P can—

(A) Determine the basis in its *T* stock as if paragraph (c)(2)(i) of this section applies; or

(B) Determine the basis in the *T* stock acquired as if *P* acquired such stock from the former *T* shareholders in a transaction in which *P*'s basis in the *T* stock was determined under section 362(b).

(3) *Triangular B reorganization.*—In a triangular B reorganization *P*'s basis in its *S* stock is adjusted as if—

(i) *P* acquired the *T* stock acquired by *S* in the reorganization directly from the *T* shareholders in a transaction in which *P*'s basis in the *T* stock was determined under section 362(b); and

(ii) *P* transferred the *T* stock to *S* in a transaction in which *P*'s basis in its *S* stock was determined under section 358.

(4) *Examples.*—The rules of this paragraph (c) are illustrated by the following examples. For purposes of these examples, P, S, and T are domestic corporations, the property transferred is not importation property within the meaning of § 1.362-3(c)(2) or loss duplica-

tion property within the meaning of § 1.362-4(g)(1), P and S do not file consolidated returns, P owns all of the shares of the only class of S stock, the P stock exchanged in the transaction satisfies the requirements of the applicable triangular reorganization provisions, and the facts set forth the only corporate activity.

Example 1. Forward triangular merger. (a) *Facts. T* has assets with an aggregate basis of $60 and fair market value of $100 and no liabilities. Pursuant to a plan, *P* forms *S* with $5 cash (which S retains), and *T* merges into *S.* In the merger, the *T* shareholders receive *P* stock worth $100 in exchange for their *T* stock. The transaction is a reorganization to which sections 368(a)(1)(A) and (a)(2)(D) apply.

(b) *Basis adjustment.* Under § 1.358-6(c)(1), *P*'s $5 basis in its *S* stock is adjusted as if *P* acquired the *T* assets acquired by *S* in the reorganization directly from *T* in a transaction in which *P*'s basis in the *T* assets was determined under section 362(b). Under section 362(b), *P* would have an aggregate basis of $60 in the *T* assets. *P* is then treated as if it transferred the *T* assets to *S* in a transaction in which *P*'s basis in the *S* stock was determined under section 358. Under section 358, *P*'s $5 basis in its *S* stock would be increased by the $60 basis in the *T* assets deemed transferred. Consequently, *P* has a $65 basis in its *S* stock as a result of the reorganization.

(c) *Use of pre-existing S.* The facts are the same as paragraph (a) of this *Example 1,* except that *S* is an operating company with substantial assets that has been in existence for several years. *P* has a $110 basis in the *S* stock. Under § 1.358-6(c)(1), *P*'s $110 basis in its *S* stock is increased by the $60 basis in the *T* assets deemed transferred. Consequently, *P* has a $170 basis in its *S* stock as a result of the reorganization.

(d) *Mixed consideration.* The facts are the same as paragraph (a) of this *Example 1,* except that the *T* shareholders receive *P* stock worth $80 and $20 cash from *P.* Under section 358, *P*'s $5 basis in its *S* stock is increased by the $60 basis in the *T* assets deemed transferred. Consequently, *P* has a $65 basis in its *S* stock as a result of the reorganization.

(e) *Liabilities.* The facts are the same as paragraph (a) of this *Example 1,* except that T's assets are subject to $50 of liabilities, and the *T* shareholders receive $50 of *P* stock in exchange for their *T* stock. Under section 358, *P*'s basis in its *S* stock is increased by the $60 basis in the *T* assets deemed transferred and decreased by the $50 of liabilities to which the *T* assets acquired by *S* are subject. Consequently, *P* has a net basis adjustment of $10, and a $15 basis in its *S* stock as a result of the reorganization.

(f) *Liabilities in excess of basis.* The facts are the same as in paragraph (a) of this *Example 1,* except that *T*'s assets are subject to liabilities of $90, and the *T* shareholders receive $10 of *P* stock in exchange for their *T* stock in the reorganization. Under § 1.358-6(c)(1)(ii), the adjustment under § 1.358-6(c) is zero if the amount of the liabilities which *S* assumed or to which the *T* assets acquired by *S* are subject exceeds the aggregate adjusted basis in T's assets. Consequently, *P* has no adjustment in its *S* stock, and *P* has a $5 basis in its *S* stock as a result of the reorganization.

Example 2. Reverse triangular merger. (a) *Facts. T* has assets with an aggregate basis of $60 and a fair market value of $100 and no liabilities. *P* has a $110 basis in its *S* stock. Pursuant to a plan, *S* merges into *T* with *T* surviving. In the merger, the *T* shareholders receive $10 cash from *P* and *P* stock worth $90 in exchange for their *T* stock. The transaction is a reorganization to which sections 368(a)(1)(A) and (a)(2)(E) apply.

(b) *Basis adjustment.* Under § 1.358-6(c)(2)(i)(A), *P*'s basis in the *T* stock acquired is *P*'s $110 basis in its *S* stock before the transaction, adjusted as if *T* had merged into *S* in a forward triangular merger to which § 1.358-6(c)(1) applies. In such a case, *P*'s $110 basis in its *S* stock before the transaction would have been increased by the $60 basis of the *T* assets deemed transferred. Consequently, *P* has a $170 basis in its *T* stock immediately after the transaction.

(c) *Reverse triangular merger that also qualifies under section 368(a)(1)(B).* The facts relating to *T* are the same as in paragraph (a) of this *Example 2. P,* however, forms *S* pursuant to the plan of reorganization. The *T* shareholders receive $100 worth of *P* stock (and no cash) in exchange for their *T* stock. The *T* shareholders have an aggregate basis in their *T* stock of $85 immediately before the reorganization. The reorganization qualifies as both a reverse triangular merger and a reorganization under section 368(a)(1)(B). Under § 1.358-6(c)(2)(ii), *P* may determine its basis in its *T* stock either as if § 1.358-6(c)(2)(i) applied to the *T* stock acquired, or as if *P* acquired the *T* stock from the former *T* shareholders in a transaction in which *P*'s basis in the *T* stock was determined under section 362(b). Accordingly, *P* may determine a basis in its *T* stock of $60 (*T*'s net asset basis) or $85 (the *T* shareholders' aggregate basis in the *T* stock immediately before the reorganization).

(d) *Allocable share in a reverse triangular merger.* The facts are the same as in paragraph

(a) of this *Example 2,* except that *X*, a 10% shareholder of *T*, does not participate in the transaction. The remaining *T* shareholders receive $10 cash from *P* and *P* stock worth $80 for their *T* stock. *P* owns 90% of the *T* stock after the transaction. Under § 1.358-6(c) (2) (i) (A), *P*'s basis in its *T* stock is *P*'s $110 basis in its *S* stock before the reorganization, adjusted as if *T* had merged into *S* in a forward triangular merger. In such a case, *P*'s basis would have been adjusted by the $60 basis in the *T* assets deemed transferred. Under § 1.358-6(c) (2) (i) (B), however, the basis adjustment determined under § 1.358-6(c) (2) (i) (A) is reduced in proportion to the percentage of *T* stock not acquired by *P* in the transaction. The percentage of *T* stock not acquired in the transaction is 10%. Therefore, *P* reduces its $60 basis adjustment by 10%, resulting in a net basis adjustment of $54. Consequently, *P* has a $164 basis in its *T* stock as a result of the transaction.

(e) *P's ownership of T stock.* The facts are the same as in paragraph (a) of this *Example 2,* except that *P* owns 10% of the *T* stock before the transaction. *P*'s basis in that *T* stock is $8. All the *T* shareholders other than *P* surrender their *T* stock for $10 cash from *P* and *P* stock worth $80. *P* does not surrender the stock in the transaction. Under § 1.358-6(c) (i) (C), *P* may treat its *T* stock owned before the transaction as acquired in the transaction or not. If *P* treats that *T* stock as acquired in the transaction, *P*'s basis in that *T* stock and the *T* stock actually acquired in the transaction equals P's $110 basis in its *S* stock before the transaction, adjusted by the $60 basis of the *T* assets deemed transferred, for a total basis of $170. If *P* treats its *T* stock as not acquired, *P* retains its $8 pre-transaction basis in that stock. *P*'s basis in its other *T* shares equals *P*'s $110 basis in its *S* stock before the transaction, adjusted by $54 (the $60 basis in the *T* assets deemed transferred, reduced by 10%), for a total basis of $164 in those shares. See § 1.358-6(c) (2) (i) (A) and (B). Consequently, if *P* treats its *T* shares as not acquired, *P*'s total basis in all of its *T* shares is $172.

Example 3. Triangular B reorganization. (a) *Facts. T* has assets with a fair market value of $100 and no liabilities. The *T* shareholders have an aggregate basis in their *T* stock of $85 immediately before the reorganization. Pursuant to a plan, *P* forms *S* with $5 cash and *S* acquires all of the *T* stock in exchange for $100 of *P* stock. The transaction is a reorganization to which section 368(a) (1) (B) applies.

(b) *Basis adjustment.* Under § 1.358-6(c) (3), P adjusts its $5 basis in its *S* stock by treating *P* as if it acquired the *T* stock acquired by *S* in the reorganization directly from the *T* shareholders in exchange for the *P* stock in a transaction in which *P*'s basis in the *T* stock was determined under section 362(b). Under section 362(b), *P* would have an aggregate basis of $85 in the *T* stock received by *S* in the reorganization. *P* is then treated as if it transferred the *T* stock to *S* in a transaction in which *P*'s basis in the *S* stock was determined under section 358. Under section 358, *P*'s basis in its *S* stock would be increased by the $85 basis in the *T* stock deemed transferred. Consequently, P has a $90 basis in its *S* stock as a result of the reorganization.

(d) *Special rule for consideration not provided by P.*—(1) *In general.*—The amount of *P*'s adjustment to basis in its *S* or *T* stock, as applicable, described in paragraph (c) of this section is decreased by the fair market value of any consideration (including *P* stock in which gain or loss is recognized, see § 1.1032-2(c)) that is exchanged in the reorganization and that is not provided by P pursuant to the plan of reorganization. This paragraph (d) does not apply to the amount of *T* liabilities assumed by *S* or to which the *T* assets acquired by *S* are subject under paragraph (c) (1) of this section (or deemed assumed or taken subject to by S under paragraph (c) (2) (i) of this section).

(2) *Limitation.*—*P* makes no adjustment to basis under this section if the decrease required under paragraph (d) (1) of this section equals or exceeds the amount of the adjustment described in paragraph (c) of this section.

(3) *Example.*—The rules of this paragraph (d) are illustrated by the following example. For purposes of this example, *P, S,* and *T* are domestic corporations, *P* and *S* do not file consolidated returns, *P* owns all of the only class of *S* stock, the *P* stock exchanged in the transaction satisfies the requirements of the applicable triangular reorganization provisions, and the facts set forth the only corporate activity.

Example. (a) *Facts. T* has assets with an aggregate basis of $60 and fair market value of $100 and no liabilities. *S* is an operating company with substantial assets that has been in existence for several years. *P* has a $100 basis in its *S* stock. Pursuant to a plan, *T* merges into *S* and the *T* shareholders receive $70 of *P* stock provided by *P* pursuant to the plan and $30 of cash provided by *S* in exchange for their *T* stock. The transaction is a reorganization to which sections 368(a) (1) (A) and (a) (2) (D) apply.

(b) *Basis adjustment.* Under § 1.358-6(c) (1), P's $100 basis in its *S* stock is increased by the $60 basis in the *T* assets deemed transferred. Under § 1.358-6(d) (1), the $60 adjustment is decreased by the $30 of cash provided by *S* in the reorganization. Consequently, *P* has a net adjustment of $30 in its *S* stock, and *P* has a $130 basis in its *S* stock as a result of the reorganization.

(c) *Appreciated asset.* The facts are the same as in paragraph (a) of this *Example,* except that in the reorganization *S* provides an asset with a $20 adjusted basis and $30 fair market value instead of $30 of cash. The basis results are the same as in paragraph (b) of this *Example.* In addition *S* recognizes $10 of gain under section 1001 on its disposition of the asset in the reorganization.

(d) *Depreciated asset.* The facts are the same as in paragraph (c) of this *Example,* except that *S* has a $60 adjusted basis in the asset. The basis results are the same as in paragraph (b) of this *Example.* In addition, *S* recognizes $30 of loss under section 1001 on its disposition of the asset in the reorganization.

(e) *P stock.* The facts are the same as in paragraph (a) of this *Example,* except that in the reorganization *S* provides *P* stock with a fair market value of $30 instead of $30 of cash. *S* acquired the *P* stock in an unrelated transaction several years before the reorganization. *S* has a $20 adjusted basis in the *P* stock. The basis results are the same as in paragraph (b) of this *Example.* In addition, *S* recognizes $10 of gain on its disposition of the *P* stock in the reorganization. See § 1.1032-2(c).

* * *

[Reg. § 1.358-6.]

☐ [*T.D.* 8648, 12-20-95. *Amended by T.D.* 9243, 1-23-2006, *T.D.* 9424, 9-9-2008 (*corrected* 10-17-2008) *and T.D.* 9759, 3-25-2016.]

§ 1.358-7. Transfers by partners and partnerships to corporations.—(a) *Transfers by partners of partnership interests.*—For purposes of section 358(h), a transfer of a partnership interest to a corporation is treated as a transfer of the partner's share of each of the partnership's assets and an assumption by the corporation of the partner's share of partnership liabilities (including section 358(h) liabilities, as defined in paragraph (d) of this section). See paragraph (e) *Example 2* of this section.

(b) *Transfers by partnerships.*—If a corporation assumes a section 358(h) liability from a partnership in an exchange to which section 358(a) applies, then, for purposes of applying section 705 (determination of basis of partner's interest) and § 1.704-1(b), any reduction, under section 358(h)(1), in the partnership's basis in corporate stock received in the transaction is treated as an expenditure of the partnership described in section 705(a)(2)(B). See paragraph (e) *Example 1* of this section. This expenditure must be allocated among the partners in accordance with section 704(b) and (c) and § 1.752-7(c). If a partner's share of the reduction, under section 358(h)(1), in the partnership's basis in corporate stock exceeds the partner's basis in the partnership interest, then the partner recognizes gain equal to the excess, which is treated as gain from the sale or exchange of a partnership interest. This paragraph does not apply to the extent that § 1.752-7(j)(4) applies to the assumption of the § 1.752-7 liability by the corporation.

(c) *Assumption of section 358(h) liability by partnership followed by transfer of partnership interest or partnership property to a corporation—trade or business exception.*—Where a partnership assumes a section 358(h) liability from a partner and, subsequently, the partner transfers all or part of the partner's partnership interest to a corporation in an exchange to which section 358(a) applies, then, for purposes of applying section 358(h)(2), the section 358(h) liability is treated as associated only with the contribution made to the partnership by that partner. See paragraph (e) *Example 2* of this section. Similar rules apply where a partnership assumes a section 358(h) liability of a partner and a corporation subsequently assumes that section 358(h) liability from the partnership in an exchange to which section 358(a) applies.

(d) *Section 358(h) liabilities defined.*—For purposes of this section, section 358(h) liabilities are liabilities described in section 358(h)(3).

(e) *Examples.*—The following examples illustrate the provisions of this section. Assume, for purposes of these examples, that the obligation assumed by the corporation does not reduce the shareholder's basis in the corporate stock under section 358(d). The examples are as follows:

Example 1. Transfer of partnership property to corporation. In 2004, in an exchange to which section 351(a) applies, PRS, a cash basis taxpayer, transfers $2,000,000 cash to Corporation X, also a cash basis taxpayer, in exchange for Corporation X shares and the assumption by Corporation X of $1,000,000 of accounts payable incurred by PRS. At the time of the exchange, PRS has two partners, A, a 90% partner, who has a $2,000,000 basis in the PRS interest, and B, a 10% partner, who has a $50,000 basis in the PRS interest. Assume that, under section 358(h)(1), PRS's basis in the Corporation X stock is reduced by the accounts payable assumed by Corporation X ($1,000,000). Under paragraph (b) of this section, A's and B's bases in PRS must be reduced, but not below zero, by their respective shares of the section 358(h)(1) basis reduction. If either partner's share of the section 358(h)(1) basis reduction exceeds the partner's basis in the partnership interest, then the partner recognizes gain equal to the excess. A's share of the section 358(h) basis reduction is $900,000 (90% of $1,000,000). Therefore, A's basis in the PRS interest is reduced to $1,100,000 ($2,000,000 - $900,000). B's share of the section 358(h) basis reduction is $100,000 (10% of $1,000,000). Because B's share of the section 358(h) basis reduction ($100,000) exceeds B's basis in the PRS interest ($50,000), B's basis in the PRS interest is reduced to $0 and B recognizes $50,000 of gain. This gain is treated as gain from the sale of the PRS interest.

Example 2. Transfer of partnership interest to corporation. In 2004, A contributes undeveloped land with a value and basis of $4,000,000 in exchange for a 50% interest in PRS and an assumption by PRS of $2,000,000 of pension liabilities from a separate business that A conducts. A's basis in the PRS interest immediately after the contribution is A's basis in the land, $4,000,000, unreduced by the amount of the pension liabilities. PRS develops the land as a landfill. Before PRS has economically performed with respect to the pension liabilities, A transfers A's interest in PRS to Corporation X, in an exchange to which section 351 applies. At the time of the exchange, the value of A's PRS interest is $2,000,000, A's basis in PRS is $4,000,000, and A has no share of partnership liabilities other than the pension liabilities. For purposes of applying section 358(h), the transfer of the PRS interest to Corporation X is treated as a transfer to Corporation X of A's share of PRS assets and an assumption by Corporation X of A's share of the pension liabilities of PRS ($2,000,000). Because the pension liabilities were not assumed by PRS from A in an exchange in which the trade or business associated with the liability was transferred to PRS, the transfer of the PRS interest to Corporation X is not excepted from section 358(h) under section 358(h)(2). See paragraph (c) of this section. Under section 358(h), A's basis in the Corporation X stock is reduced by the $2,000,000 of pension liabilities.

(f) *Effective date.*—This section applies to assumptions of liabilities by a corporation occurring on or after June 24, 2003. [Reg. § 1.358-7.]

□ [*T.D.* 9207, 5-23-2005.]

§ 1.361-1. Nonrecognition of gain or loss to corporations.—Section 361 provides the general rule that no gain or loss shall be recognized if a corporation, a party to a reorganization, exchanges property in pursuance of the plan of reorganization solely for stock or securities in another corporation, a party to the reorganization. This provision includes only stock and securities received in connection with a reorganization defined in section 368(a). It also includes nonvoting stock and securities in a corporation, a party to a reorganization, received in a transaction to which section 368(a)(1)(C) is applicable only by reason of section 368(a)(2)(B). [Reg. § 1.361-1.]

□ [*T.D.* 6152, 12-2-55.]

§ 1.362-1. Basis to corporations.—(a) *In general.*—Section 362 provides, as a general rule, that if property was acquired on or after June 22, 1954, by a corporation (1) in connection with a transaction to which section 351 (relating to transfer of property to corporation controlled by transferor) applies, (2) as paid-in surplus or as a contribution to capital, or (3) in connection with a reorganization to which part III, subchapter C, chapter 1 of the Code applies, then the basis shall be the same as it would be in the hands of the transferor, increased in the amount of gain recognized to the transferor on such transfer. (See also § 1.362-2.) See § 1.460-4(k)(3)(iv)(B)(*2*) for rules relating to adjustments to the basis of certain contracts accounted for using a long-term contract method of accounting that are acquired in certain liquidations described in section 332.

(b) *Exceptions.*—(1) In the case of a plan of reorganization adopted after October 22, 1968, section 362 does not apply if the property acquired in connection with such reorganization consists of stock or securities in a corporation a party to the reorganization, unless acquired by the exchange of stock or securities of the transferee (or of a corporation which is in control of the transferee) as the consideration in whole or in part for the transfer.

* * *

[Reg. § 1.362-1.]

□ [*T.D.* 6152, 12-2-55. *Amended by T.D.* 7422, 6-25-76 *and T.D.* 8995, 5-14-2002.]

§ 1.362-2. Certain contributions to capital.—The following regulations shall be used in the application of section 362(c):

(a) Property deemed to be acquired with contributed money shall be that property, if any, the acquisition of which was the purpose motivating the contribution;

(b) In the case of an excess of the amount of money contributed over the cost of the property deemed to be acquired with such money (as defined in (a) above) such excess shall be applied to the reduction of the basis (but not below zero) of other properties held by the corporation, on the last day of the 12-month period beginning on the day the contribution is received, in the following order—

(1) All property of a character subject to an allowance for depreciation (not including

any properties as to which a deduction for amortization is allowable),

(2) Property with respect to which a deduction for amortization is allowable,

(3) Property with respect to which a deduction for depletion is allowable under section 611 but not under section 613, and

(4) All other remaining properties.

The reduction of the basis of each of the properties within each of the above categories shall be made in proportion to the relative bases of such properties.

(c) With the consent of the Commissioner, the taxpayer may, however, have the basis of the various units of property within a particular category adjusted in a manner different from the general rule set forth in paragraph (b) of this section. Variations from such rule may, for example, involve adjusting the basis of only certain units of the taxpayer's property within a given category. A request for variations from the general rule should be filed by the taxpayer with its return for the taxable year for which the transfer of the property has occurred. [Reg. § 1.362-2.]

□ [*T.D.* 6152, 12-2-55.]

§ 1.362-3. Basis of importation property acquired in loss importation transaction.—(a) *Purpose.*—The purpose of section 362(e)(1) and this section is to modify the application of section 362(a) (section 351 transfers, contributions to capital, or paid-in surplus) and section 362(b) (reorganizations) to prevent a corporation (Acquiring) from importing a net built-in loss in a transaction described in either section. See paragraph (c) of this section for definitions of terms used in this section.

(b) *Basis determinations under this section.*—(1) *Basis of importation property received in loss importation transaction.*—Notwithstanding the general rules of section 362(a) and (b), Acquiring's basis in importation property (as defined in paragraph (c)(2) of this section) acquired in a loss importation transaction (as defined in paragraph (c)(3) of this section) is equal to the value of the property immediately after the transaction.

(2) *Adjustment to basis of subsidiary stock in triangular reorganizations.*—If a corporation (P) computes its basis in stock of a subsidiary (whether S or T) under § 1.358-6 (stock basis in certain triangular reorganizations), P's basis in property treated as acquired by P in § 1.358-6(c) is determined under section 362(e)(1) and this section to the extent such property, if actually acquired by P, would be importation property acquired in a loss importation transaction. See § 1.358-6(c)(1)(i)(A), (c)(2)(ii)(B), and (c)(3)(i). The subsidiary's basis in the property actually acquired in the transaction is determined under applicable law (including this section), without regard to the amount of any adjustment to P's basis in the subsidiary's stock. Thus, the basis of the property in S's or T's hands may differ from the amount of the adjustment to P's basis in its stock of S or T.

(3) *Acquiring's basis in other property transferred.*—In general, Acquiring's basis in property received in a section 362 transaction (as defined in paragraph (c)(1) of this section) that is not determined under section 362(e)(1) and this section is determined under section 362(a) or section 362(b). However, if the transaction is described in section 362(a) (without regard to whether it is also described in any other section), further adjustment may be required under section 362(e)(2). See § 1.362-4.

(4) *Other effects of basis determination under this section.*—(i) *Determination by reference to transferor's basis.*—A determination of basis under this section is a determination by reference to the transferor's basis, including for purposes of sections 1223(2) and 7701(a)(43). However, solely for purposes of applying section 755, a determination of basis under this section is treated as a determination not by reference to the transferor's basis.

(ii) *Not tax-exempt income or noncapital, nondeductible expense.*—The application of this section does not give rise to an item treated as tax-exempt income under § 1.1502-32(b)(2)(ii) or as a noncapital, nondeductible expense under § 1.1502-32(b)(2)(iii).

(iii) *No effect on earnings and profits.*—Any determination of basis under this section does not reduce or otherwise affect the calculation of the all earnings and profits amount provided in § 1.367(b)-2(d).

(c) *Definitions.*—For purposes of this section, the following definitions apply:

(1) *Section 362 transaction.*—The term *section 362 transaction* means any transaction described in section 362(a) or in section 362(b).

(2) *Importation property.*—(i) *General rule.*—The term *importation property* means any property (including separate portions determined under paragraph (d)(4) of this section and separate portions of property tentatively divided under paragraph (e)(2) of this section) with respect to which—

(A) Any gain or loss that would be recognized on its sale by the transferor immediately before the transaction (the transferor's hypothetical sale) would not be subject to tax imposed under any provision of subtitle A of the Internal Revenue Code (federal income tax) (taking into account the provisions of paragraph (d) of this section); and

(B) Any gain or loss that would be recognized on its sale by Acquiring immediately after the transaction (Acquiring's hypothetical sale) would be subject to federal income tax (taking into account the provisions of paragraph (d) of this section).

(ii) *Special rules for applying this paragraph (c)(2).*—See paragraph (d) of this section for rules for determining whether gain or loss on a hypothetical sale would be taken into account in determining a federal income tax liability and paragraph (e) of this section for rules applicable when more than one person would take such gain or loss into account.

(3) *Loss importation transaction.*—The term *loss importation transaction* means any section 362 transaction in which Acquiring's aggregate basis in all importation property received from all transferors in the transaction would exceed the aggregate value of such property immediately after the transaction. For this purpose, Acquiring's basis in property received is determined without regard to this section or section 362(e)(2).

(4) *Value.*—(i) *General rule.*—The term *value* means fair market value.

(ii) *Special rule for transfers of partnership interests.*—Notwithstanding the general rule in paragraph (c)(4)(i) of this section, when referring to a partnership interest, for purposes of this section, the term *value* means the sum of the cash that Acquiring would receive for the interest, assuming an exchange between a willing buyer and a willing seller (neither being under any compulsion to buy or sell and both having reasonable knowledge of relevant facts), increased by any § 1.752-1 liabilities (as defined in § 1.752-1(a)(4)) of the partnership allocated to Acquiring with regard to such transferred interest under section 752 immediately after the transfer to Acquiring. If a partnership has elected under section 754, or if section 743(b) would require a downward basis adjustment to the partnership property, the partnership must apply the rules of § 1.743-1 to determine the amount of the basis adjustment to the partnership property.

(d) *Rules for determining whether gain or loss would be taken into account in determining a federal income tax liability.*—(1) *General rule.*—In general, any gain or loss that would be recognized on a hypothetical sale described in paragraph (c)(2) of this section is considered to be subject to federal income tax if, taking into account all relevant facts and circumstances, such gain or loss would affect or be taken into account in determining the federal income tax liability of the transferor or Acquiring, respectively. This determination is made without regard to whether such person has or would have any actual federal income tax liability for the taxable year of the transaction.

(2) *Look-through rule in the case of certain pass-through entities.*—Notwithstanding the general rule in paragraph (d)(1) of this section, the determination of whether any gain or loss on a hypothetical sale would be treated as subject to federal income tax is made by reference to the person that would be required to include such gain or loss in its taxable income if the hypothetical seller is—

(i) A trust treated as owned by its grantors or others (see section 671);

(ii) A partnership (see section 701); or

(iii) An S corporation (see sections 1363 and 1366).

(3) *Controlled foreign corporation (CFC), passive foreign investment company (PFIC).*—For purposes of this section, gain or loss that would be recognized by a CFC (as defined in section 957(a)) or a PFIC (as defined in section 1297(a)) is not deemed taken into account in determining a federal income tax liability solely because it could affect an inclusion under section 951(a) or section 1293(a).

(4) *Special rule for debt-financed property subject to section 512.*—If property is debt-financed property (as defined in section 514(b)) owned by an organization subject to the unrelated business income tax described in section 511(a)(2) and, as a result, a portion of any gain or loss on a sale of the property would be included in unrelated taxable business income (UBTI) under section 512, such property is treated as divided into separate portions in proportion to the amount of such gain or loss that would be includible in UBTI. The rules of paragraph (e) of this section apply to determine the characterization of such portions (as includible in the determination of a federal income tax liability or not), and the tax treatment and consequences of the transaction in which such portions are transferred.

(5) *Look-through treatment in the case of certain avoidance transactions.*—(i) *Application of this paragraph (d)(5).*—This paragraph (d)(5) applies if—

(A) The transferor is a domestic entity that is a trust (other than a trust described in paragraph (d)(2)(i) of this section), estate, regulated investment company (as defined in section 851(a)), a real estate investment trust (as defined in section 856(a)), or a cooperative (as described in section 1381); and

(B) The transferor transfers, directly or indirectly, property that was transferred to or acquired by it as part of a plan (whether of transferor, Acquiring, or any other person) to avoid the application of section 362(e)(1) and this section to a section 362 transaction.

(ii) *Effect of application of this paragraph (d)(5)*.—Notwithstanding paragraph (d)(1) of this section, if a transferor is described in both paragraphs (d)(5)(i)(A) and (B) of this section—

(A) The transferor is treated as though it distributes the proceeds of the hypothetical sale (which, for this purpose, are presumed to be an amount greater than zero);

(B) To the fullest extent possible under the transferor's organizing instrument, the deemed distribution is treated as made to a distributee or distributees that would not take distributions from the transferor into account in determining a federal income tax liability; and

(C) The determination of whether the gain or loss on the hypothetical sale is treated as subject to federal income tax is made by reference to the deemed distributee or distributees.

(iii) *Tiered entities*.—If a deemed distributee is an entity described in paragraph (d)(5)(i)(A) of this section, the determination of whether gain or loss on the hypothetical sale is taken into account in determining a federal income tax liability is made by treating the deemed distributee, and any successive such deemed distributees, as a transferor and applying the rules in paragraphs (d)(5)(i) and (ii) of this section to its deemed distribution (and to all successive deemed distributions), until no deemed distributee or successive deemed distributee is an entity described in paragraph (d)(5)(i)(A) of this section.

* * *

(f) *Examples*.—The examples in this paragraph (f) illustrate the application of section 362(e)(1) and the provisions of this section. Unless otherwise indicated, the examples use the following nomenclature and assumptions: A and B are U.S. citizens. DC, DC1, and P are domestic corporations that have not elected to be S corporations within the meaning of section 1361(a)(1) and that are not members of a consolidated group. F is a foreign individual. FP is a foreign partnership. FC, FC1, and FC2 are foreign corporations. Unless the facts indicate otherwise, the foreign individuals, corporations, and partnerships are not engaged in a U.S. trade or business, have no U.S. real property interests, and have no other relationships, activities, or interests that would cause them, their shareholders, their partners, or their property to be subject to federal income tax. There is no applicable income tax treaty, all persons' tax years are calendar years, and all persons and transactions are unrelated unless the facts indicate otherwise.

Example 1. Basic application of section. (i) *Section 351 transfer of importation property in a loss importation transaction.* (A) *Facts.* FC owns three assets, A1 (basis $40, value $150), A2 (basis $120, value $30), and A3 (basis $140, value $20). On Date 1, FC transfers A1, A2, and A3 to DC in a transaction to which section 351 applies.

(B) *Importation property.* If FC had sold A1, A2, or A3 immediately before the transaction, no gain or loss recognized on the sale would have been taken into account in determining a federal income tax liability. Further, if DC had sold A1, A2, or A3 immediately after the transaction, DC would take into account any gain or loss recognized on the sale in determining its federal income tax liability. Therefore, A1, A2, and A3 are all importation properties. See paragraph (c)(2) of this section.

(C) *Loss importation transaction.* FC's transfer of A1, A2, and A3 is a section 362 transaction. Furthermore, but for section 362(e)(1) and this section and section 362(e)(2), DC's aggregate basis in the importation properties, A1, A2, and A3, would be $300 ($40 + $120 + $140) under section 362(a) and the properties' aggregate value would be $200 ($150 + $30 + $20). Therefore, the importation properties' aggregate basis would exceed their aggregate value and the transaction is a loss importation transaction. See paragraph (c)(3) of this section.

(D) *Application of section 362(e)(1) and this section to importation property received in loss importation transaction.* Because the importation properties, A1, A2, and A3, were transferred in a loss importation transaction, paragraph (b)(1) of this section applies and DC's basis in A1, A2, and A3 will each be equal to the property's value ($150, $30, and $20, respectively) immediately after the transfer.

(E) *Basis of property received in transaction.* Following the application of section 362(e)(1) and this section, the provisions of section 362(e)(2) must be taken into account because the transfer is a section 362(a) transaction. Taking into account the application of section 362(e)(1) and this section, DC's aggregate basis in the transferred properties would not exceed their aggregate value immediately after the transfer. Therefore, FC does not have a net built-in loss, FC's transfer is not a loss duplication transaction, and section 362(e)(2) does not apply to this transaction. DC's bases in A1, A2, and A3, as determined under paragraph (i)(D) of this *Example 1*, are $150, $30, and $20, respectively. Under section 358(a), FC receives the DC stock with a basis of $300 (the sum of FC's bases in A1, A2, and A3 immediately before the exchange).

(ii) *Reorganization*. The facts are the same as in paragraph (i)(A) of this *Example 1* except that, instead of transferring property to DC in a section 351 exchange, FC merges with and into DC in a transaction described in section 368(a)(1)(A). The analysis and results are the same as set forth in paragraphs (i)(B), (C), and (D) of this *Example 1*. However, the analysis in paragraph (i)(E) of this *Example 1* does not apply to these facts because the transaction is not subject to 362(e)(2) and § 1.362-4. Under section 358(a), FC's shareholders will take the DC stock with a basis determined by reference to their FC stock basis.

(iii) *FC's property used in U.S. trade or business*. (A) *Facts*. The facts are the same as in paragraph (i)(A) of this *Example 1*, except that FC is engaged in a U.S. trade or business and uses all the properties in that U.S. trade or business. In this case, none of the properties would be importation property because FC would take any gain or loss on the disposition of the properties into account in determining its federal income tax liability. Accordingly, this section does not apply to the transaction.

(B) *Basis of property received in transaction*. Following the application of section 362(e)(1) and this section, the provisions of section 362(e)(2) must be taken into account because the transfer is a section 362(a) transaction. Taking into account the application of section 362(e)(1) and this section but without taking into account the provisions of section 362(e)(2), DC's aggregate basis in the transferred properties would be $300 ($40 + $120 + $140) under section 362(a) and the properties' aggregate value immediately after the transfer would be $200 ($150 + $30 + $20). Therefore, FC has a net built-in loss and FC's transfer of A1, A2, and A3 is a loss duplication transaction. Accordingly, under the general rule of section 362(e)(2), FC's $100 net built-in loss ($300 aggregate basis over $200 aggregate value) would be allocated proportionately (by the amount of built-in loss in each property) to reduce DC's basis in the loss properties, A2 and A3. See § 1.362-4. As a result, DC's basis in A2 would be $77.14 ($120 basis under section 362(a) reduced by $42.86, A2's proportionate share of FC's net built-in loss, computed as $90/$210 x $100) and DC's basis in A3 would be $82.86 ($140 basis under section 362(a) reduced by $57.14, A3's proportionate share of FC's net built-in loss, computed as $120/$210 x $100). However, if FC and DC were to elect under section 362(e)(2)(C) to apply the $100 basis reduction to FC's basis in the DC stock received in the transaction, DC's bases in A2 and A3 would remain their section 362(a) bases of $120 and $140, respectively. Under section 362(a), DC's basis in A1 is $40 (irrespective of whether the section 362(e)(2)(C) election is made). If FC and DC do not make a section 362(e)(2)(C) election, FC's basis in the DC stock received in the exchange will be $300; if FC and DC do make the election, FC's basis in the DC stock will be $200 ($300 - $100 net built-in loss). See § 1.362-4(b).

* * *

[Reg. § 1.362-3.]

□ [*T.D.* 9759, 3-25-2016.]

§ 1.368-1. Purpose and scope of exception of reorganization exchanges.—(a) *Reorganizations.*—As used in the regulations under parts I, II, and III (section 301 and following), subchapter C of the Code, the terms "reorganization" and "party to a reorganization" mean only a reorganization or a party to a reorganization as defined in subsections (a) and (b) of section 368. In determining whether a transaction qualifies as a reorganization under section 368(a), the transaction must be evaluated under relevant provisions of law, including the step transaction doctrine. But see §§ 1.368-2(f) and (k) and 1.338-3(d). The preceding two sentences apply to transactions occurring after January 28, 1998, except that they do not apply to any transaction occurring pursuant to a written agreement which is binding on January 28, 1998, and at all times thereafter. With respect to insolvency reorganizations, see part IV of subchapter C, chapter 1 of the Code.

(b) *Purpose.*—Under the general rule, upon the exchange of property, gain or loss must be accounted for if the new property differs in a material particular, either in kind or in extent, from the old property. The purpose of the reorganization provisions of the Code is to except from the general rule certain specifically described exchanges incident to such readjustments of corporate structures made in one of the particular ways specified in the Code, as are required by business exigencies and which effect only a readjustment of continuing interest in property under modified corporate forms. Requisite to a reorganization under the Internal Revenue Code are a continuity of the business enterprise through the issuing corporation under the modified corporate form as described in paragraph (d) of this section, and (except as provided in section 368(a)(1)(D)) a continuity of interest as described in paragraph (e) of this section. (For rules regarding the continuity of interest requirement under section 355, see § 1.355-2(c).) For purposes of this section, the term *issuing corporation* means the acquiring corporation (as that term is used in section 368(a)), except that, in determining whether a reorganization qualifies as a triangular reorganization (as defined in §1.358-6(b)(2)), the issuing corporation means the corporation in control of the acquiring corporation. The preceding three sentences apply to transactions occurring after January 28, 1998, except that they do not apply to any transaction occurring pursuant to a written agreement which is binding on January 28, 1998, and at all times thereafter. The continuity of business enterprise requirement is described in paragraph (d) of this section. Notwithstanding the requirements of this paragraph (b), for transactions occurring on or after February 25, 2005, a continuity of the business enterprise and a continuity of interest are not required for the transaction to qualify as a reorganization under section 368(a)(1)(E) or (F). The Code recognizes as a reorganization the amalgamation (occurring in a specified way) of two corporate enterprises under a single corporate structure if there exists among the holders of the stock and securities of either of the old corporations the requisite continuity of interest in the new corporation, but there is not a reorganization if the holders of the stock and securities of the old corporation are merely the holders of short-term notes in the new corporation. In order to exclude transactions not intended to be included, the specifications of the reorganization provisions of the law are precise. Both the terms of the specifications and their underlying assumptions and purposes must be satisfied in order to entitle the taxpayer to the benefit of the exception from the general rule. Accordingly, under the Code, a short-term purchase money note is not a security of a party to a reorganization, an ordinary dividend is to be treated as an ordinary dividend, and a sale is nevertheless to be treated as a sale even though the mechanics of a reorganization have been set up.

(c) *Scope.*—The nonrecognition of gain or loss is prescribed for two specifically described types of exchanges, viz.: The exchange that is provided for in section 354(a)(1) in which stock or securities in a corporation, a party to a reorganization, are, in pursuance of a plan of reorganization, exchanged for the stock or securities in a corporation, a party to the same reorganization; and the exchange that is provided for in section 361(a) in which a corporation, a party to a reorganization, exchanges property, in pursuance of a plan of reorganization, for stock or securities in another corporation, a party to the same reorganization. Section 368(a)(1) limits the definition of the term "reorganization" to six kinds of transactions and excludes all others. From its context, the term "a party to a reorganization" can only mean a party to a transaction specifically defined as a reorganization by section 368(a). Certain rules respecting boot received in either of the two types of exchanges provided for in section 354(a)(1) and section 361(a) are prescribed in sections 356, 357, and 361(b). A special rule respecting a transfer of property with a liability in excess of its basis is prescribed in section 357(c). Under section 367 a limitation is placed on all these provisions by providing that except under specified conditions foreign corporations shall not be deemed within their scope. The provisions of the Code referred to in this paragraph are inapplicable unless there is a plan of reorganization. A plan of reorganization must contemplate the bona fide execution of one of the transactions specifically described as a reorganization in section 368(a) and for the bona fide consummation of each of the requisite acts under which nonrecognition of gain is claimed. Such transaction and such acts must be an ordinary and necessary incident of the conduct of the enterprise and must provide for a continuation of the enterprise. A scheme, which involves an abrupt departure from normal reorganization procedure in connection with a transaction on which the imposition of tax is imminent, such as a mere device that puts on the form of a corporate reorganization as a disguise for concealing its real character, and the object and accomplishment of which is the consummation of a preconceived plan having no business or corporate purpose, is not a plan of reorganization.

(d) *Continuity of business enterprise.*—(1) *General rule.*—Continuity of business enterprise (COBE) requires that the issuing corporation (P), as defined in paragraph (b) of this section, either continue the target corporation's (T's) historic business or use a significant portion of T's historic business assets in a business. The preceding sentence applies to transactions occurring after January 28, 1998, except that it does not apply to any transaction occurring pursuant to a written agreement which is binding on January 28, 1998, and at all times thereafter. The application of this general rule to certain transactions, such as mergers of holding companies, will depend on all facts and circumstances. The policy underlying this general rule, which is to ensure that reorganizations are limited to readjustments of continuing interests in property under modified corporate form, provides the guidance necessary to make these facts and circumstances determinations.

(2) *Business continuity.*—(i) The continuity of business enterprise requirement is satisfied if *P* continues *T*' s historic business. The fact *P* is in the same line of business as *T*

tends to establish the requisite continuity, but is not alone sufficient.

(ii) If *T* has more than one line of business, continuity of business enterprise requires only that *P* continue a significant line of business.

(iii) In general, a corporation's historic business is the business it has conducted most recently. However, a corporation's historic business is not one the corporation enters into as part of a plan of reorganization.

(iv) All facts and circumstances are considered in determining the time when the plan comes into existence and in determining whether a line of business is "significant".

(3) *Asset continuity.*—(i) The continuity of business enterprise requirement is satisfied if *P* uses a significant portion of *T*'s historic business assets in a business.

(ii) A corporation's historic business assets are the assets used in its historic business. Business assets may include stock and securities and intangible operating assets such as good will, patents, and trademarks, whether or not they have a tax basis.

(iii) In general, the determination of the portion of a corporation's assets considered "significant" is based on the relative importance of the assets to operation of the business. However, all other facts and circumstances, such as the net fair market value of those assets, will be considered.

(4) *Acquired assets or stock held by members of the qualified group or partnerships.*—The following rules apply in determining whether the COBE requirement of paragraph (d)(1) of this section is satisfied:

(i) *Businesses and assets of members of a qualified group.*—The issuing corporation is treated as holding all of the businesses and assets of all of the members of the qualified group, as defined in paragraph (d)(4)(ii) of this section.

(ii) *Qualified group.*—A qualified group is one or more chains of corporations connected through stock ownership with the issuing corporation, but only if the issuing corporation owns directly stock meeting the requirements of section 368(c) in at least one other corporation, and stock meeting the requirements of section 368(c) in each of the corporations (except the issuing corporation) is owned directly (or indirectly as provided in paragraph (d)(4)(iii)(D) of this section) by one or more of the other corporations.

(iii) *Partnerships.*—(A) *Partnership assets.*—Each partner of a partnership will be treated as owning the T business assets used in a business of the partnership in accordance with that partner's interest in the partnership.

(B) *Partnership businesses.*—The issuing corporation will be treated as conducting a business of a partnership if—

(1) Members of the qualified group, in the aggregate, own an interest in the partnership representing a significant interest in that partnership business; or

(2) One or more members of the qualified group have active and substantial management functions as a partner with respect to that partnership business.

(C) *Conduct of the historic T business in a partnership.*—If a significant historic T business is conducted in a partnership, the fact that P is treated as conducting such T business under paragraph (d)(4)(iii)(B) of this section tends to establish the requisite continuity, but is not alone sufficient.

(D) *Stock attributed from certain partnerships.*—Solely for purposes of paragraph (d)(4)(ii) of this section, if members of the qualified group own interests in a partnership meeting requirements equivalent to section 368(c) (a section 368(c) controlled partnership), any stock owned by the section 368(c) controlled partnership shall be treated as owned by members of the qualified group. Solely for purposes of determining whether a lower-tier partnership is a section 368(c) controlled partnership, any interest in a lower-tier partnership that is owned by a section 368(c) controlled partnership shall be treated as owned by members of the qualified group.

* * *

(5) *Examples.*—The following examples illustrate this paragraph (d). All the corporations have only one class of stock outstanding. The preceding sentence and paragraph (d)(5) *Example 6* and *Example 8* through *Example 13* apply to transactions occurring after January 28, 1998, except that they do not apply to any transaction occurring pursuant to a written agreement which is binding on January 28, 1998, and at all times thereafter. Paragraph (d)(5) *Example 7*, *Example 14*, and *Example 15* apply to transactions occurring on or after October 25, 2007, except that they do not apply to any transaction occurring pursuant to a written agreement which is binding before October 25, 2007, and at all times after that. The examples read as follows:

Example 1. *T* conducts three lines of business: manufacture of synthetic resins, manufacture of chemicals for the textile industry, and distribution of chemicals. The three lines of business are approximately equal in value. On July 1, 1981, *T* sells the synthetic resin and chemical distribution businesses to a third party for cash and marketable securities. On December 31, 1981, *T* transfers all of its assets to *P* solely for *P* voting stock. *P* continues the chemical manufacturing business without interruption. The continuity of business enterprise requirement is met. Continuity of business enterprise requires only that *P* continue one of *T*' s three significant lines of business.

Example 2. P manufactures computers and *T* manufactures components for computers. *T* sells all of its output to *P.* On January 1, 1981, *P* decides to buy imported components only. On March 1, 1981, *T* merges into *P. P* continues buying imported components but retains *T*' s equipment as a backup source of supply. The use of the equipment as a backup source of supply constitutes use of a significant portion of *T*' s historic business assets, thus establishing continuity of business enterprise. *P* is not required to continue *T*' s business.

Example 3. T is a manufacturer of boys' and men's trousers. On January 1, 1978, as part of a plan of reorganization, *T* sold all of its assets to a third party for cash and purchased a highly diversified portfolio of stocks and bonds. As part of the plan *T* operates an investment business until July 1, 1981. On that date, the plan of reorganization culminates in a transfer by *T* of all its assets to *P,* a regulated investment company, solely in exchange for *P* voting stock. The continuity of business enterprise requirement is not met. *T*' s investment activity is not its historic business, and the stocks and bonds are not *T*' s historic business assets.

Example 4. T manufactures children's toys and *P* distributes steel and allied products. On January 1, 1981, *T* sells all of its assets to a third party for $100,000 cash and $900,000 in notes. On March 1, 1981, *T* merges into *P.* Continuity of business enterprise is lacking. The use of the sales proceeds in *P*' s business is not sufficient.

Example 5. T manufactures farm machinery and *P* operates a lumber mill. *T* merges into *P. P* disposes of *T*' s assets immediately after the merger as part of the plan of reorganization. *P* does not continue *T*' s farm machinery manufacturing business. Continuity of business enterprise is lacking.

Example 6. Use of a significant portion of T's historic business assets by the qualified group. (i) *Facts.* T operates an auto parts distributorship. P owns 80 percent of the stock of a holding company (HC). HC owns 80 percent of the stock of ten subsidiaries, S-1 through S-10. S-1 through S-10 each separately operate a full service gas station. Pursuant to a plan of reorganization, T merges into P and the T shareholders receive solely P stock. As part of the plan of reorganization, P transfers T's assets to HC, which in turn transfers some of the T assets to each of the ten subsidiaries. No one subsidiary receives a significant portion of T's historic business assets. Each of the subsidiaries will use the T assets in the operation of its full service gas station. No P subsidiary will be an auto parts distributor.

(ii) *Continuity of business enterprise.* Under paragraph (d) (4) (i) of this section, P is treated as conducting the ten gas station businesses of S-1 through S-10 and as holding the historic T assets used in those businesses. P is treated as holding all the assets and conducting the businesses of all of the members of the qualified group, which includes S-1 through S-10 (paragraphs (d) (4) (i) and (ii) of this section). No member of the qualified group continues T's historic distributorship business. However, subsidiaries S-1 through S-10 continue to use the historic T assets in a business. Even though no one corporation of the qualified group is using a significant portion of T's historic business assets in a business, the COBE requirement of paragraph (d) (1) of this section is satisfied because, in the aggregate, the qualified group is using a significant portion of T's historic business assets in a business.

Example 7. Transfers of acquired stock to members of the qualified group - continuity of business enterprise satisfied. (i) *Facts.* The facts are the same as *Example 6*, except that, instead of P acquiring the assets of T, HC acquires all of the outstanding stock of T in exchange solely for stock of P. In addition, as part of the plan of reorganization, HC transfers 10 percent of the stock of T to each of subsidiaries S-1 through S-10. T will continue to operate an auto parts distributorship. Without regard to whether the transaction satisfies the COBE requirement, the transaction qualifies as a triangular B reorganization (as defined in § 1.358-6(b) (2) (iv)).

(ii) *Continuity of business enterprise.* Under paragraph (d) (4) (i) of this section, P is treated as holding the assets and conducting the business of T because T is a member of the qualified group (as defined in paragraph (d) (4) (ii) of this section). The COBE requirement of paragraph (d) (1) of this section is satisfied.

Example 8. Continuation of the historic T business in a Partnership satisfies continuity of business enterprise. (i) *Facts.* T manufactures ski boots. P owns all of the stock of S-1. S-1 owns all of the stock of S-2, and S-2 owns all of the stock of S-3. T merges into P and the T shareholders receive consideration consisting of P stock and cash. The T ski boot business is to be continued and expanded. In anticipation of this expansion, P transfers all of the T assets to S-1, S-1 transfers all of the T assets to S-2, and S-2 transfers all of the T assets to S-3. S-3 and X (an unrelated party) form a new partnership (PRS). As part of the plan of reorganization, S-3 transfers all the T assets to PRS, and S-3, in its capacity as a partner, performs active and substantial management functions for the PRS ski boot business, including making significant business decisions and regularly participating in the overall supervision, direction, and control of the employees of the ski boot business. S-3 receives a 20 percent interest in PRS. X transfers cash in exchange for an 80 percent interest in PRS.

(ii) *Continuity of business enterprise.* Under paragraph (d)(4)(iii)(B)(*2*) of this section, P is treated as conducting T's historic business because S-3 performs active and substantial management functions for the ski boot business in S-3's capacity as a partner. P is treated as holding all the assets and conducting the businesses of all of the members of the qualified group, which includes S-3 (paragraphs (d)(4)(i) and (ii) of this section). The COBE requirement of paragraph (d)(1) of this section is satisfied.

Example 9. Continuation of the historic T business in a partnership does not satisfy continuity of business enterprise. (i) *Facts.* The facts are the same as *Example 8*, except that S-3 transfers the historic T business to PRS in exchange for a 1 percent interest in PRS.

(ii) *Continuity of business enterprise.* Under paragraph (d)(4)(iii)(B)(*2*) of this section, P is treated as conducting T's historic business because S-3 performs active and substantial management functions for the ski boot business in S-3's capacity as a partner. The fact that a significant historic T business is conducted in PRS, and P is treated as conducting such T business under (d)(4)(iii)(B) tends to establish the requisite continuity, but is not alone sufficient (paragraph (d)(4)(iii)(C) of this section). The COBE requirement of paragraph (d)(1) of this section is not satisfied.

Example 10. Continuation of the T historic business in a partnership satisfies continuity of business enterprise. (i) *Facts.* The facts are the same as *Example 8*, except that S-3 transfers the historic T business to PRS in exchange for a 33 1/3 percent interest in PRS, and no member of P's qualified group performs active and substantial management functions for the ski boot business operated in PRS.

(ii) *Continuity of business enterprise.* Under paragraph (d)(4)(iii)(B)(*1*) of this section, P is treated as conducting T's historic business because S-3 owns an interest in the partnership representing a significant interest in that partnership business. P is treated as holding all the assets and conducting the businesses of all of the members of the qualified group, which includes S-3 (paragraphs (d)(4)(i) and (ii) of this section). The COBE requirement of paragraph (d)(1) of this section is satisfied.

Example 11. Use of T's historic business assets in a partnership business. (i) *Facts.* T is a fabric distributor. P owns all of the stock of S-1. T merges into P and the T shareholders receive solely P stock. S-1 and X (an unrelated party) own interests in a partnership (PRS). As part of the plan of reorganization, P transfers all of the T assets to S-1, and S-1 transfers all the T assets to PRS, increasing S-1's percentage interest in PRS from 5 to 33 1/3 percent. After the transfer, X owns the remaining 66 2/3 percent interest in PRS. Almost all of the T assets consist of T's large inventory of fabric, which PRS uses to manufacture sportswear. All of the T assets are used in the sportswear business. No member of P's qualified group performs active and substantial management functions for the sportswear business operated in PRS.

(ii) *Continuity of business enterprise.* Under paragraph (d)(4)(iii)(A) of this section, S-1 is treated as owning 33 1/3 percent of the T assets used in the PRS sportswear manufacturing business. Under paragraph (d)(4)(iii)(B)(*1*) of this section, P is treated as conducting the sportswear manufacturing business because S-1 owns an interest in the partnership representing a significant interest in that partnership business. P is treated as holding all the assets and conducting the businesses of all of the members of the qualified group, which includes S-1 (paragraphs (d)(4)(i) and (ii) of this section). The COBE requirement of paragraph (d)(1) of this section is satisfied.

Example 12. Aggregation of partnership interests among members of the qualified group: use of T's historic business assets in a partnership business. (i) *Facts.* The facts are the same as *Example 11*, except that S-1 transfers all the T assets to PRS, and P and X each transfer cash to PRS in exchange for partnership interests. After the transfers, P owns 11 percent, S-1 owns 22 1/3 percent, and X owns 66 2/3 percent of PRS.

(ii) *Continuity of business enterprise.* Under paragraph (d)(4)(iii)(B)(*1*) of this section, P is treated as conducting the sportswear manufacturing business because members of the qualified group, in the aggregate, own an interest in the partnership representing a significant interest in that business. P is treated as owning 11 percent of the assets directly, and S-1 is treated as owning 22 1/3 percent of the assets, used in the PRS sportswear business (paragraph (d)(4)(iii)(A) of this section). P is treated as holding all the assets of all of the members of the qualified group, which includes S-1, and thus in the aggregate, P is treated as owning 33 1/3 of the T assets (paragraph (d)(4)(i) and (ii) of this section). The COBE requirement of paragraph (d)(1) of this section is satisfied because P is treated as using a significant portion of T's historic business assets in its sportswear manufacturing business.

Example 13. Tiered partnerships: use of T's historic business assets in a partnership business. (i) *Facts.* T owns and manages a commercial office building in state Z. Pursuant to a plan of reorganization, T merges into P, solely in exchange for P stock, which is distributed to the T shareholders. P-transfers all of the T assets to a partnership, PRS-1, which owns and operates television stations nationwide. After the transfer, P owns a 50 percent interest in PRS-1. P does not have active and substantial management functions as a partner with respect to the PRS-1 business. X, not a member of P's qualified group, owns the remaining 50 percent interest in PRS-1. PRS-1, in an effort to expand its state Z television operation, enters into a joint venture with U, an unrelated party. As part of the plan of reorganization, PRS-1 transfers all the T assets and its state Z television station to PRS-2, in exchange for a 75 percent partnership interest. U contributes cash to PRS-2 in exchange for a 25 percent partnership interest and oversees the management of the state Z television operation. PRS-1 does not actively and substantially manage PRS-2's business. PRS-2's state Z operations are moved into the acquired T office building. All of the assets that P acquired from T are used in PRS-2's business.

(ii) *Continuity of business enterprise.* Under paragraph (d)(4)(iii)(A) of this section, PRS-1 is treated as owning 75 percent of the T assets used in PRS-2's business. P, in turn, is treated as owning 50 percent of PRS-1's interest the T assets. Thus, P is treated as owning 37 1/2 percent (50 percent×75 percent) of the T assets used in the PRS-2 business. Under paragraph (d)(4)(iii)(B)(1) of this section, P is treated as conducting PRS-2's business, the operation of the state Z television station, and under paragraph (d)(4)(iii)(A) of this section, P is treated as using 37 1/2 percent of the historic T business assets in that business. The COBE requirement of paragraph (d)(1) of this section is satisfied because P is treated as using a significant portion of T's historic business assets in its television business.

Example 14. Transfer of acquired stock to a partnership - continuity of business enterprise satisfied. (i) *Facts.* Pursuant to a plan of reorganization, the T shareholders transfer all of their T stock to a subsidiary of P, S-1, solely in exchange for P stock. In addition, as part of the plan of reorganization, S-1 transfers the T stock to its subsidiary, S-2, and S-2 transfers the T stock to its subsidiary, S-3. S-2 and S-3 form a new partnership, PRS. Immediately thereafter, S-3 transfers all of the T stock to PRS in exchange for an 80 percent interest in PRS, and S-2 transfers cash to PRS in exchange for a 20 percent interest in PRS.

(ii) *Continuity of business enterprise.* Members of the qualified group, in the aggregate, own all of the interests in PRS. Because these interests in PRS meet requirements equivalent to section 368(c), under paragraph (d)(4)(iii)(D) of this section, the T stock owned by PRS is treated as owned by members of the qualified group. P is treated as holding all of the businesses and assets of T because T is a member of the qualified group (as defined in paragraph (d)(4)(ii) of this section). The COBE requirement of paragraph (d)(1) of this section is satisfied because P is treated as continuing T's business.

Example 15. Transfer of acquired stock to a partnership - continuity of business enterprise not satisfied. (i) *Facts.* The facts are the same as in *Example 14,* except that S-3 and U, an unrelated corporation, form a new partnership, PRS, and, immediately thereafter, S-3 transfers all of the T stock to PRS in exchange for a 50 percent interest in PRS, and U transfers cash to PRS in exchange for a 50 percent interest in PRS.

(ii) *Continuity of business enterprise.* Members of the qualified group, in the aggregate, own 50 percent of the interests in PRS. Because these interests in PRS do not meet requirements equivalent to section 368(c), the T stock owned by PRS is not treated as owned by members of the qualified group under paragraph (d)(4)(iii)(D) of this section. P is not treated as holding all of the businesses and assets of T because T has ceased to be a member of the qualified group (as defined in paragraph (d)(4)(ii) of this section). The COBE requirement of paragraph (d)(1) of this section is not satisfied because P is not treated as continuing T's business or using T's historic business assets in a business.

(e) *Continuity of interest.*—(1) *General rule.*—(i) The purpose of the continuity of interest requirement is to prevent transactions that resemble sales from qualifying for nonrecognition of gain or loss available to corporate reorganizations. Continuity of interest requires that in substance a substantial part of the value of the proprietary interests in the target corporation be preserved in the reorganization. A proprietary interest in the target corporation is preserved if, in a potential reorganization, it is exchanged for a proprietary interest in the issuing corporation (as defined in paragraph (b) of this section), it is exchanged by the acquiring corporation for a direct interest in the target corporation enterprise, or it otherwise continues as a proprietary interest in the target corporation. However, a proprietary interest in the target corporation is not preserved if, in connection with the potential reorganization, it is acquired by the issuing corporation for consideration other than stock of the issuing corporation, or stock of the issuing corporation furnished in exchange for a proprietary interest in the target corporation in the potential reorganization is redeemed. All facts and circumstances must be considered in determining whether, in substance, a proprietary interest in the target corporation is preserved. See paragraph (e)(6) of this section for rules related to when a creditor's claim against a target corporation is a proprietary interest in the corporation. For purposes of the continuity of interest requirement, a mere disposition of stock of the target corporation prior to a potential reorganization to persons not related (as defined in paragraph (e)(4) of this section determined without regard to paragraph (e)(4)(i)(A) of this section) to the target corporation or to persons not related (as defined in paragraph (e)(4) of this section) to the issuing corporation is disregarded and a mere disposition of stock of the issuing corporation received in a potential reorganization to persons not related (as defined in paragraph (e)(4) of this section) to the issuing corporation is disregarded.

(ii) For purposes of paragraph (e)(1)(i) of this section, a proprietary interest in the target corporation (other than one held by the acquiring corporation) is not preserved to the extent that consideration received prior to a potential reorganization, either in a redemption of the target corporation stock or in a distribution with respect to the target corporation stock, is treated as other property or money received in the exchange for purposes of section 356, or would be so treated if the target shareholder also had received stock of the issuing corporation in exchange for stock owned by the shareholder in the target corporation. A proprietary interest in the target corporation is not preserved to the extent that creditors (or former creditors) of the target corporation that own a proprietary interest in the corporation under paragraph (e)(6) of this section (or would be so treated if they had received the consideration in the potential reorganization) receive payment for the claim prior to the potential reorganization and such payment would be treated as other property or money received in the exchange for purposes of section 356 had it been a distribution with respect to stock.

(2) *Measuring continuity of interest.*—(i) *In general.*—In determining whether a proprietary interest in the target corporation is preserved, the consideration to be exchanged for the proprietary interests in the target corporation pursuant to a contract to effect the potential reorganization shall be valued on the last business day before the first date such contract is a binding contract (the pre-signing date), if such contract provides for fixed consideration. If a portion of the consideration provided for in such a contract consists of other property identified by value, then this specified value of such other property is used for purposes of determining the extent to which a proprietary interest in the target corporation is preserved. If the contract does not provide for fixed consideration, this paragraph (e)(2)(i) is not applicable.

(ii) *Binding contract.*—(A) *In general.*—A binding contract is an instrument enforceable under applicable law against the parties to the instrument. The presence of a condition outside the control of the parties (including, for example, regulatory agency approval) shall not prevent an instrument from being a binding contract. Further, the fact that insubstantial terms remain to be negotiated by the parties to the contract, or that customary conditions remain to be satisfied, shall not prevent an instrument from being a binding contract.

(B) *Modifications.*—*(1) In general.*—If a term of a binding contract that relates to the amount or type of the consideration the target shareholders will receive in a potential reorganization is modified before the closing date of the potential reorganization, and the contract as modified is a binding contract, the date of the modification shall be treated as the first date there is a binding contract.

(2) Modification of a transaction that preserves continuity of interest.—Notwithstanding paragraph (e)(2)(ii)(B)(*1*) of this section, a modification of a term that relates to the amount or type of consideration the target shareholders will receive in a transaction that would have resulted in the preservation of a substantial part of the value of the target corporation shareholders' proprietary interests in the target corporation if there had been no modification will not be treated as a modification if—

(i) The modification has the sole effect of providing for the issuance of additional shares of issuing corporation stock to the target corporation shareholders;

(ii) The modification has the sole effect of decreasing the amount of money or other property to be delivered to the target corporation shareholders; or

(iii) The modification has the effect of decreasing the amount of money or other property to be delivered to the target corporation shareholders and providing for the issuance of additional shares of issuing corporation stock to the target corporation shareholders.

(3) Modification of a transaction that does not preserve continuity of interest.—Notwithstanding paragraph (e)(2)(ii)(B)(*1*) of this section, a modification of a term that relates to the amount or type of consideration the target shareholders will receive in a transaction that would not have resulted in the preservation of a substantial part of the value of the target corporation shareholders' proprietary interests in the target corporation if there had been no modification will not be treated as a modification if—

(i) The modification has the sole effect of providing for the issuance of fewer shares of issuing corporation stock to the target corporation shareholders;

(ii) The modification has the sole effect of increasing the amount of money or other property to be delivered to the target corporation shareholders; or

(iii) The modification has the effect of increasing the amount of money or other property to be delivered to the target corporation shareholders and providing for the issuance of fewer shares of issuing corporation stock to the target corporation shareholders.

(C) *Tender offers.*—For purposes of this paragraph (e)(2), a tender offer that is subject to section 14(d) of the Securities and Exchange Act of 1934 [15 U.S.C. 78n(d)(1)] and Regulation 14D (17 CFR 240.14d-1 through 240.14d-101) and is not pursuant to a binding contract, is treated as a binding contract made on the date of its announcement, notwithstanding that it may be modified by the offeror or that it is not enforceable against the offerees. If a modification (not pursuant to a binding contract) of such a tender offer is subject to the provisions of Regulation 14d-6(c) (17 CFR 240.14d-6(c)) and relates to the amount or type of the consideration received in the tender offer, then the date of the modification shall be treated as the first date there is a binding contract.

(iii) *Fixed consideration.*—(A) *In general.*—A contract provides for fixed consideration if it provides the number of shares of each class of stock of the issuing corporation, the amount of money, and the other property (identified either by value or by specific description), if any, to be exchanged for all the proprietary interests in the target corporation, or to be exchanged for each proprietary interest in the target corporation. A shareholder's election to receive a number of shares of stock of the issuing corporation, money, or other property (or some combination of stock of the issuing corporation, money, or other property) in exchange for all of the shareholder's proprietary interests in the target corporation, or each of the shareholder's proprietary interests in the target corporation, will not prevent a contract from satisfying the definition of fixed consideration provided for in this paragraph (e)(2)(iii)(A).

(B) *Shareholder elections.*—A contract that provides a target corporation shareholder with an election to receive a number of shares of stock of the issuing corporation, money, or other property (or some combination of stock of the issuing corporation, money, or other property) in exchange for all of the shareholder's proprietary interests in the target corporation, or each of the shareholder's proprietary interests in the target corporation, provides for fixed consideration if the determination of the number of shares of issuing corporation stock to be provided to the target corporation shareholder is determined using the value of the issuing corporation stock on the last business day before the first date there is a binding contract. This is the case even though the shareholder election may preclude a determination, prior to the closing date, of the number of shares of each class of the issuing corporation, the amount of money, and the other property (or the combination of shares, money and other property) to be exchanged for each proprietary interest in the target corporation.

(C) *Contingent adjustments to the consideration.*—*(1) In general.*—Except as provided in paragraph (e)(2)(iii)(C)(*2*) of this section, a contract that provides for contingent adjustments to the consideration will be treated as providing for fixed consideration if it would satisfy the requirements of paragraph (e)(2)(iii)(A) of this section without the contingent adjustment provision.

(2) Exceptions.—A contract will not be treated as providing for fixed consideration if the contract provides for contingent adjustments to the consideration that prevent (to any extent) the target corporation shareholders from being subject to the economic benefits and burdens of ownership of the issuing corporation stock after the last business day before the first date the contract is a binding contract. For example, a contract will not be treated as providing for fixed consideration if the contract provides for contingent adjustments to the consideration in the event that the value of the stock of the issuing corporation, the value of the assets of the issuing corporation, or the value of any surrogate for either the value of the stock of the issuing corporation or the assets of the issuing corporation increases or decreases after the last business day before the first date there is a binding contract. Similarly, a contract will not be treated as providing for

fixed consideration if the contract provides for contingent adjustments to the number of shares of the issuing corporation stock to be provided to the target corporation shareholders computed using any value of the issuing corporation shares after the last business day before the first date there is a binding contract.

(D) *Escrows*.—Placing part of the consideration to be exchanged for proprietary interests in the target corporation in escrow to secure target's performance of customary pre-closing covenants or customary target representations and warranties will not prevent a contract from being treated as providing for fixed consideration.

(E) *Anti-dilution clauses*.—The presence of a customary anti-dilution clause will not prevent a contract from being treated as providing for fixed consideration. However, the absence of such a clause will prevent a contract from being treated as providing for fixed consideration if the issuing corporation alters its capital structure between the first date there is an otherwise binding contract to effect the transaction and the effective date of the transaction in a manner that materially alters the economic arrangement of the parties to the binding contract. If the number of shares of the issuing corporation to be issued to the target corporation shareholders is altered pursuant to a customary anti-dilution clause, the value of the shares determined under paragraph (e)(2)(i) of this section must be adjusted accordingly.

(F) *Dissenters' rights*.—The possibility that some shareholders may exercise dissenters' rights and receive consideration other than that provided for in the binding contract will not prevent the contract from being treated as providing for fixed consideration.

(G) *Fractional shares*.—The fact that money may be paid in lieu of issuing fractional shares will not prevent a contract from being treated as providing for fixed consideration.

(iv) *New issuances*.—For purposes of applying paragraph (e)(2)(i) of this section, any class of stock, securities, or indebtedness that the issuing corporation issues to the target corporation shareholders pursuant to the potential reorganization and that does not exist before the first date there is a binding contract to effect the potential reorganization is deemed to have been issued on the last business day before the first date there is a binding contract to effect the potential reorganization.

(v) *Examples*.—For purposes of the examples in this paragraph (e)(2)(v), P is the issuing corporation, T is the target corporation, S is a wholly owned subsidiary of P, all corporations have only one class of stock outstanding, A is an individual, no transactions other than those described occur, and the transactions are not otherwise subject to recharacterization. The following examples illustrate the application of this paragraph (e)(2):

Example 1. Application of signing date rule. On January 3 of year 1, P and T sign a binding contract pursuant to which T will be merged with and into P on June 1 of year 1. Pursuant to the contract, the T shareholders will receive 40 P shares and $60 of cash in exchange for all of the outstanding stock of T. Twenty of the P shares, however, will be placed in escrow to secure customary target representations and warranties. The P stock is listed on an established market. On January 2 of year 1, the value of the P stock is $1 per share. On June 1 of year 1, T merges with and into P pursuant to the terms of the contract. On that date, the value of the P stock is $.25 per share. None of the stock placed in escrow is returned to P. Because the contract provides for the number of shares of P and the amount of money to be exchanged for all of the proprietary interests in T, under this paragraph (e)(2), there is a binding contract providing for fixed consideration as of January 3 of year 1. Therefore, whether the transaction satisfies the continuity of interest requirement is determined by reference to the value of the P stock on the pre-signing date. Because, for continuity of interest purposes, the T stock is exchanged for $40 of P stock and $60 of cash, the transaction preserves a substantial part of the value of the proprietary interest in T. Therefore, the transaction satisfies the continuity of interest requirement.

Example 2. Treatment of forfeited escrowed stock. (i) Escrowed stock. The facts are the same as in *Example 1* except that T's breach of a representation results in the escrowed consideration being returned to P. Because the contract provides for the number of shares of P and the amount of money to be exchanged for all of the proprietary interests in T, under this paragraph (e)(2), there is a binding contract providing for fixed consideration as of January 3 of year 1. Therefore, whether the transaction satisfies the continuity of interest requirement is determined by reference to the value of the P stock on the pre-signing date. Pursuant to paragraph (e)(1)(i) of this section, for continuity of interest purposes, the T stock is exchanged for $20 of P stock and $60 of cash, and the transaction does not preserve a substantial part of the value of the proprietary interest in T. Therefore, the transaction does not satisfy the continuity of interest requirement.

(ii) *Escrowed stock and cash.* The facts are the same as in paragraph (i) of this *Example 2* except that the consideration placed in escrow consists solely of eight of the P shares and $12 of the cash. Because the contract provides for the number of shares of P and the amount of money to be exchanged for all of the proprietary interests in T, under this paragraph (e)(2), there is a binding contract providing for fixed consideration as of January 3 of year 1. Therefore, whether the transaction satisfies the continuity of interest requirement is determined by reference to the value of the P stock on the pre-signing date. Pursuant to paragraph (e)(1)(i) of this section, for continuity of interest purposes, the T stock is exchanged for $32 of P stock and $48 of cash, and the transaction preserves a substantial part of the value of the proprietary interest in T. Therefore, the transaction satisfies the continuity of interest requirement.

Example 3. Redemption of stock received pursuant to binding contract. The facts are the same as in *Example 1* except that A owns 50 percent of the outstanding stock of T immediately prior to the merger and receives 10 P shares and $30 in the merger and an additional 10 P shares upon the release of the stock placed in escrow. In connection with the merger, A and S agree that, immediately after the merger, S will purchase any P shares that A acquires in the merger for $1 per share. Shortly after the merger, S purchases A's P shares for $20. Because the contract provides for the number of shares of P and the amount of money to be exchanged for all of the proprietary interests in T, under this paragraph (e)(2), there is a binding contract providing for fixed consideration as of January 3 of year 1. Therefore, whether the transaction satisfies the continuity of interest requirement is determined by reference to the value of the P stock on the pre-signing date. In addition, S is a person related to P under paragraph (e)(4)(i)(A) of this section. Accordingly, A is treated as exchanging his T shares for $50 of cash. Because, for continuity of interest purposes, the T stock is exchanged for $20 of P stock and $80 of cash, the transaction does not preserve a substantial part of the value of the proprietary interest in T. Therefore, the transaction does not satisfy the continuity of interest requirement.

Example 4. Modification of binding contract—continuity not preserved. The facts are the same as in *Example 1* except that on April 1 of year 1, the parties modify their contract. Pursuant to the modified contract, which is a binding contract, the T shareholders will receive 50 P shares (an additional 10 shares) and $75 of cash (an additional $15 of cash) in exchange for all of the outstanding T stock. On March 31 of year 1, the value of the P stock is $.50 per share. Under this paragraph (e)(2), although there was a binding contract providing for fixed consideration as of January 3 of year 1, terms of that contract relating to the consideration to be provided to the target shareholders were modified on April 1 of year 1. The execution of the transaction without modification would have resulted in the preservation of a substantial part of the value of the target corporation shareholders' proprietary interests in the target corporation if there had been no modification. However, because the modified contract provides for additional P stock and cash to be exchanged for all the proprietary interests in T, the exception in paragraph (e)(2)(ii)(B)(2) of this section does not apply to preserve the original signing date. Therefore, whether the transaction satisfies the continuity of interest requirement is determined by reference to the value of the P stock on March 31 of year 1. Because, for continuity of interest purposes, the T stock is exchanged for $25 of P stock and $75 of cash, the transaction does not preserve a substantial part of the value of the proprietary interest in T. Therefore, the transaction does not satisfy the continuity of interest requirement.

Example 5. Modification of binding contract disregarded—continuity preserved. The facts are the same as in *Example 4* except that, pursuant to the modified contract, which is a binding contract, the T shareholders will receive 60 P shares (an additional 20 shares as compared to the original contract) and $60 of cash in exchange for all of the outstanding T stock. In addition, on March 31 of year 1, the value of the P stock is $.40 per share. Under this paragraph (e)(2), although there was a binding contract providing for fixed consideration as of January 3 of year 1, terms of that contract relating to the consideration to be provided to the target shareholders were modified on April 1 of year 1. Nonetheless, the modification has the sole effect of providing for the issuance of additional P shares to the T shareholders. In addition, the execution of the terms of the contract without regard to the modification would have resulted in the preservation of a substantial part of the value of the T shareholders' proprietary interest in T because, for continuity of interest purposes, the T stock would have been exchanged for $40 of P stock and $60 of cash. Pursuant to paragraph (e)(2)(ii)(B)(*2*) of this section, the modification is not treated as a modification for purposes of paragraph (e)(2)(ii)(B)(*1*) of this section. Accordingly, whether the transaction satisfies the continuity of interest requirement is determined by reference to the value of the P stock on the pre-signing date. Because, for continuity of interest purposes, the T stock is exchanged for $60 of P stock and $60 of cash, the transaction preserves a substantial part of the value of the proprietary interest in T. Therefore the transaction satisfies the continuity of interest requirement.

Example 6. New issuance. The facts are the same as in *Example 1,* except that, instead of cash, the T shareholders will receive a new class of P securities that will be publicly traded. In the aggregate, the securities will have a stated principal amount of $60 and bear interest at the average LIBOR (London Interbank Offered Rates) during the 10 days prior to the potential reorganization. If the T shareholders had been issued the P securities on January 2 of year 1, the P securities would have had a value of $60 (determined by reference to the value of comparable publicly traded securities). Whether the transaction satisfies the continuity of interest requirement is determined by reference to the value of the P stock and the P securities to be issued to the T shareholders on January 2 of year 1. Under paragraph (e)(2)(iv) of this section, for purposes of valuing the new P securities, they will be treated as having been issued on the pre-signing date. Because, for continuity of interest purposes, the T stock is exchanged for $40 of P stock and $60 of other property, the transaction preserves a substantial part of the value of the proprietary interest in T. Therefore, the transaction satisfies the continuity of interest requirement.

Example 7. Fixed consideration—continuity not preserved. On January 3 of year 1, P and T sign a binding contract pursuant to which T will be merged with and into P on June 1 of year 1. Pursuant to the contract, 60 shares of the T stock will be exchanged for $80 of cash and 40 shares of the T stock will be exchanged for 20 shares of P stock. On January 2 of year 1, the value of the P stock is $1 per share. On June 1 of year 1, T merges with and into P pursuant to the terms of the contract. This contract provides for fixed consideration and therefore whether the transaction satisfies the continuity of interest requirement is determined by reference to the value of the P stock on the pre-signing date. However, applying the signing date rule, the P stock represents only 20 percent of the value of the total consideration to be received by the T shareholders. Accordingly, based on the economic realities of the exchange, the transaction does not preserve a substantial part of the value of the proprietary interest in T. Therefore, the transaction does not satisfy the continuity of interest requirement.

Example 8. Anti-dilution clause. (i) *Absence of anti-dilution clause.* On January 3 of year 1, P and T sign a binding contract pursuant to which T will be merged with and into P on June 1 of year 1. Pursuant to the contract, the T shareholders will receive 40 P shares and $60 of cash in exchange for all of the outstanding stock of T. The contract does not contain a customary anti-dilution provision. The P stock is listed on an established market. On January 2 of year 1, the value of the P stock is $1 per share. On April 10 of year 1, P issues its stock to effect a stock split; each shareholder of P receives an additional share of P for each P share that it holds. On April 11 of year 1, the value of the P stock is $.50 per share. Because P altered its capital structure between January 3 and June 1 of year 1 in a manner that materially alters the economic arrangement of the parties, under paragraph (e)(2)(iii)(E) of this section, the contract is not treated as a binding contract that provides for fixed consideration. Accordingly, whether the transaction satisfies the continuity of interest requirement cannot be determined by reference to the value of the P stock on January 2 of year 1.

(ii) *Adjustment for anti-dilution clause.* The facts are the same as in paragraph (i) of this *Example 8* except that the contract contains a customary anti-dilution provision, and the T shareholders receive 80 P shares and $60 of cash in exchange for all of the outstanding stock of T. Under paragraph (e)(2)(iii)(E) of this section, the contract is treated as a binding contract that provides for fixed consideration as of January 3 of year 1. Therefore, whether the transaction satisfies the continuity of interest requirement is generally determined by reference to the value of the P stock on January 2 of year 1. However, under paragraph (e)(2)(iii)(E) of this section, the value of the P stock on the pre-signing date must be adjusted to take the stock split into account. For continuity of interest purposes, the T stock is exchanged for $40 of P stock (($1/2) × 80) and $60 of cash. Therefore, the transaction satisfies the continuity of interest requirement.

Example 9. Shareholder election. On January 3 of year 1, P and T sign a binding contract pursuant to which T will be merged with and into P on June 1 of year 1. On January 2 of year 1, the value of the P stock and the T stock is $1 per share. Pursuant to the contract, at the shareholders' election, each share of T's 100 shares will be exchanged for cash of $1, or alternatively, P stock. The contract provides that the determination of the number of shares of P stock to be exchanged for a share of T stock is made using the value of the P stock on the last business day before the first date there is a binding contract (that is, $1 per share). The contract further provides that, in the aggregate, 40 shares of P stock and $60 will be delivered, and contains a proration mechanism in the event that either item of consideration is oversubscribed. On the closing date, the value of the P stock is $.20 per share, and all target shareholders elect to receive cash. Pursuant to the proration provision, each target share is exchanged for \$.60 of cash and \$.08 of P stock. Pursuant to paragraph (e)(2)(iii)(A) of this section, the contract provides for fixed consideration because it provides for the number of shares of P stock and the amount of money to be exchanged for all the proprietary interests in the target corporation. Furthermore, pursuant to paragraph (e)(2)(iii)(B) of this section, the contract provides for fixed consideration because the number of shares of issuing corporation stock to be provided to the target corporation shareholders is determined using the presigning date value of P stock. Accordingly, whether the transaction satisfies the continuity of interest requirement is determined by reference to the value of the P stock on January 2 of year 1. Because, for continuity purposes, the T stock is exchanged for \$40 of P stock and \$60 of cash, the transaction preserves a substantial part of the value of the proprietary interest in T. Therefore, the transaction satisfies the continuity of interest requirement.

Example 10. Contingent adjustment based on the value of the issuing corporation stock—continuity not preserved. On January 3 of year 1, P and T sign a binding contract pursuant to which T will be merged with and into P on June 1 of year 1. On January 2 of year 1, the value of the P stock is \$1 per share. Pursuant to the contract, if the value of the P stock does not decrease after January 2 of year 1, the T shareholders will receive 40 P shares and \$60 of cash in exchange for all of the outstanding stock of T. Furthermore, the contract provides that the T shareholders will receive \$.16 of additional P shares and \$.24 for every \$.01 decrease in the value of one share of P stock after January 2 of year 1. On June 1 of year 1, T merges with and into P pursuant to the terms of the contract. On that date, the value of the P stock is \$.40 per share. Pursuant to the terms of the contract, the consideration is adjusted so that the T shareholders receive 24 more P shares ((60 × \$.16)/\$.40) and \$14.40 more cash (60 × \$.24) than they would absent an adjustment. Accordingly, at closing the T shareholders receive 64 P shares and \$74.40 of cash. Because the contract provides that additional P shares and cash will be delivered to the T shareholders if the value of the stock of P decreases after January 2 of year 1, under paragraph (e)(2)(iii)(C)(*2*) of this section, the contract is not treated as providing for fixed consideration, and therefore whether the transaction satisfies the continuity of interest requirement cannot be determined by reference to the value of the P stock on January 2 of year 1. For continuity of interest purposes, the T stock is exchanged for \$25.60 of P stock (64 × \$.40) and \$74.40 of cash and the transaction does not preserve a substantial part of the value of the proprietary interest in T. Therefore, the transaction does not satisfy the continuity of interest requirement.

Example 11. Contingent adjustment to boot based on the value of the target corporation stock—continuity not preserved. On January 3 of year 1, P and T sign a binding contract pursuant to which T will be merged with and into P on June 1 of year 1. On January 2 of year 1, T has 100 shares outstanding, and each T share is worth \$1. On January 2 of year 1, each P share is worth \$1. Pursuant to the contract, if the value of the T stock does not increase after January 3 of year 1, the T shareholders will receive 40 P shares and \$60 of cash in exchange for all of the outstanding stock of T. Furthermore, the contract provides that the T shareholders will receive \$1 of additional cash for every \$.01 increase in the value of one share of T stock after January 3 of year 1. On June 1 of year 1, the value of the T stock is \$1.40 per share and the value of the P stock is \$.75 per share. Pursuant to the terms of the contract, the consideration is adjusted so that the T shareholders receive \$40 more cash (40 x \$1) than they would absent an adjustment. Accordingly, at closing the T shareholders receive 40 P shares and \$100 of cash. Because the contract provides the number of shares of P stock and the amount of money to be exchanged for all the proprietary interests in T, and the contingent adjustment to the cash consideration is not based on changes in the value of the P stock, P assets, or any surrogate thereof, after January 2 of year 1, there is a binding contract providing for fixed consideration as of January 3 of year 1. Therefore, whether the transaction satisfies the continuity of interest requirement is determined by reference to the value of the P stock on January 2 of year 1. For continuity of interest purposes, the T stock is exchanged for \$40 of P stock (40 × \$1) and \$100 of cash. Therefore, the transaction does not satisfy the continuity of interest requirement.

Example 12. Contingent adjustment to stock based on the value of the target corporation stock—continuity preserved. On January 3 of year 1, P and T sign a binding contract pursuant to which T will be merged with and into P on June 1 of year 1. On that date T has 100 shares outstanding, and each T share is worth \$1. On January 2 of year 1, each P share is worth \$1. Pursuant to the contract, if the value of the T stock does not decrease after January 3 of year 1, the T shareholders will receive 40 P shares and \$60 of cash in exchange for all of the outstanding stock of T. Furthermore, the contract provides that the T shareholders will receive \$.40 less P stock and \$.60 less cash for every \$.01 decrease in the value of one share of T stock after January 3 of year 1. The contract also provides that the number of P shares by which the consideration will be reduced as a result of this adjustment will be determined based on the value of the P stock on January 2 of year 1. On June 1 of year 1, T merges with and into P pursuant to the terms of the contract. On that date, the value of the T stock is $.70 per share and the value of the P stock is $.75 per share. Pursuant to the terms of the contract, the consideration is adjusted so that the T shareholders receive 12 fewer P shares ((30 × $.40)/$1) and $18 less cash (30 × $.60) than they would absent an adjustment. Accordingly, at closing the T shareholders receive 28 P shares and $42 of cash. Because the contract provides for the number of shares of P stock and the amount of money to be exchanged for all of the proprietary interests in T, the contract does not provide for contingent adjustments to the consideration based on a change in value of the P stock, P assets, or any surrogate thereof, after January 2 of year 1, and the adjustment to the number of P shares the T shareholders receive is determined based on the value of the P shares on January 2 of year 1, there is a binding contract providing for fixed consideration as of January 3 of year 1. Therefore, whether the transaction satisfies the continuity of interest requirement is determined by reference to the value of the P stock on January 2 of year 1. For continuity of interest purposes, the T stock is exchanged for $28 of P stock (28 × $1) and $42 of cash. Accordingly, the transaction satisfies the continuity of interest requirement.

(3) *Related person acquisitions.*—A proprietary interest in the target corporation is not preserved if, in connection with a potential reorganization, a person related (as defined in paragraph (e)(4) of this section) to the issuing corporation acquires, for consideration other than stock of the issuing corporation, either a proprietary interest in the target corporation or stock of the issuing corporation that was furnished in exchange for a proprietary interest in the target corporation. The preceding sentence does not apply to the extent those persons who were the direct or indirect owners of the target corporation prior to the potential reorganization maintain a direct or indirect proprietary interest in the issuing corporation.

(4) *Definition of related person.*—(i) *In general.*—For purposes of this paragraph (e), two corporations are related persons if either—

(A) The corporations are members of the same affiliated group as defined in section 1504 (determined without regard to section 1504(b)); or

(B) A purchase of the stock of one corporation by another corporation would be treated as a distribution in redemption of the stock of the first corporation under section 304(a)(2) (determined without regard to § 1.1502-80(b)).

(ii) *Special rules.*—The following rules apply solely for purposes of this paragraph (e)(4):

(A) A corporation will be treated as related to another corporation if such relationship exists immediately before or immediately after the acquisition of the stock involved.

(B) A corporation, other than the target corporation or a person related (as defined in paragraph (e)(4) of this section determined without regard to paragraph (e)(4)(i)(A) of this section) to the target corporation, will be treated as related to the issuing corporation if the relationship is created in connection with the potential reorganization.

(5) *Acquisitions by partnerships.*—For purposes of this paragraph (e), each partner of a partnership will be treated as owning or acquiring any stock owned or acquired, as the case may be, by the partnership in accordance with that partner's interest in the partnership. If a partner is treated as acquiring any stock by reason of the application of this paragraph (e)(5), the partner is also treated as having furnished its share of any consideration furnished by the partnership to acquire the stock in accordance with that partner's interest in the partnership.

(6) *Creditors' claims as proprietary interests.*—(i) *In general.*—A creditor's claim against a target corporation may be a proprietary interest in the target corporation if the target corporation is in a title 11 or similar case (as defined in section 368(a)(3)) or the amount of the target corporation's liabilities exceeds the fair market value of its assets immediately prior to the potential reorganization. In such cases, if any creditor receives a proprietary interest in the issuing corporation in exchange for its claim, every claim of that class of creditors and every claim of all equal and junior classes of creditors (in addition to the claims of shareholders) is a proprietary interest in the target corporation immediately prior to the potential reorganization to the extent provided in paragraph (e)(6)(ii) of this section.

(ii) *Value of proprietary interest.*—(A) *Claims of most senior class of creditor receiving stock.*—A claim of the most senior class of creditors receiving a proprietary interest in the issuing corporation and a claim of any equal class of creditors will be treated as a proprietary interest in accordance with the rules of this paragraph (e)(6)(ii). For a claim of the most senior class of creditors receiving a proprietary interest in the issuing corporation and a claim of any equal class of creditors, the value of the proprietary interest in the target corporation represented by the claim is determined by multiplying the fair market value of the claim by a fraction, the numerator of which is the fair market value of the proprietary interests in the issuing corporation that are received in the aggregate in exchange for the claims of those classes of creditors, and the denominator of which is the sum of the amount of money and the fair market value of all other consideration (including the proprietary interests in the issuing corporation) received in the aggregate in exchange for such claims. If only one class (or one set of equal classes) of creditors receives stock, such class (or set of equal classes) is treated as the most senior class of creditors receiving stock. When only one class (or one set of equal classes) of creditors receives issuing corporation stock in exchange for a creditor's proprietary interest in the target corporation, such stock will be counted for measuring continuity of interest provided that the stock issued by the issuing corporation is not de minimis in relation to the total consideration received by the insolvent target corporation, its shareholders, and its creditors.

(B) *Claims of junior classes of creditor receiving stock.*—The value of a proprietary interest in the target corporation held by a creditor whose claim is junior to the claims of other classes of target claims which are receiving proprietary interests in the issuing corporation is the fair market value of the junior creditor's claim.

(iii) *Bifurcated claims.*—If a creditor's claim is bifurcated into a secured claim and an unsecured claim pursuant to an order in a title 11 or similar case (as defined in section 368(a)(3)) or pursuant to an agreement between the creditor and the debtor, the bifurcation of the claim and the allocation of consideration to each of the resulting claims will be respected in applying the rules of this paragraph (e)(6).

(iv) *Effect of treating creditors as proprietors.*—The treatment of a creditor's claim as a proprietary interest in the target corporation shall not preclude treating shares of the target corporation as proprietary interests in the target corporation.

(7) *Successors and predecessors.*—For purposes of this paragraph (e), any reference to the issuing corporation or the target corporation includes a reference to any successor or predecessor of such corporation, except that the target corporation is not treated as a predecessor of the issuing corporation and the issuing corporation is not treated as a successor of the target corporation.

(8) *Examples.*—For purposes of the examples in this paragraph (e)(7), P is the issuing corporation, T is the target corporation, S is a wholly owned subsidiary of P, all corporations have only one class of stock outstanding, A and B are individuals, PRS is a partnership, all reorganization requirements other than the continuity of interest requirement are satisfied, and the transaction is not otherwise subject to recharacterization. The following examples illustrate the application of this paragraph (e):

Example 1. Sale of stock to third party. (i) *Sale-of issuing corporation stock after merger.* A owns all of the stock of T. T merges into P. In the merger, A receives P stock having a fair market value of $50x and cash of $50x. Immediately after the merger, and pursuant to a preexisting binding contract, A sells all of the P stock received by A in the merger to B. Assume that there are no facts and circumstances indicating that the cash used by B to purchase A's P stock was in substance exchanged by P for T stock. Under paragraphs (e)(1) and (3) of this section, the sale to B is disregarded because B is not a person related to P within the meaning of paragraph (e)(4) of this section. Thus, the transaction satisfies the continuity of interest requirement because 50 percent of A's T stock was exchanged for P stock, preserving a substantial part of the value of the proprietary interest in T.

(ii) *Sale of target corporation stock before merger.* The facts are the same as paragraph (i) of this *Example 1,* except that B buys A's T stock prior to the merger of T into P and then exchanges the T stock for P stock having a fair market value of $50x and cash of $50x. The sale by A is disregarded. The continuity of interest requirement is satisfied because B's T stock was exchanged for P stock, preserving a substantial part of the value of the proprietary interest in T.

Example 2. Relationship created in connection with potential reorganization. Corporation X owns 60 percent of the stock of P and 30 percent of the stock of T. A owns the remaining 70 percent of the stock of T. X buys A's T stock for cash in a transaction which is not a qualified stock purchase within the meaning of section 338. T then merges into P. In the merger, X exchanges all of its T stock for additional stock of P. As a result of the issuance of the additional stock to X in the merger, X's ownership interest in P increases from 60 to 80 percent of the stock of P. X is not a person related to P under paragraph (e)(4)(i)(B) of this section, because a purchase of stock of P by X would not be treated as a distribution in redemption of the stock of P under section 304(a)(2). However, X is a person related to P under paragraphs (e)(4)(i)(A) and (ii)(B) of this section, because X becomes affiliated with P in the merger. The continuity of interest requirement is not satisfied, because X acquired a proprietary interest in T for consideration other than P stock, and a substantial part of the value of the proprietary interest in T is not preserved. See paragraph (e)(3) of this section.

Example 3. Participation by issuing corporation in post-merger sale. A owns 80 percent of the T stock and none of the P stock, which is widely held. T merges into P. In the merger, A receives P stock. In addition, A obtains rights pursuant to an arrangement with P to have P register the P stock under the Securities Act of 1933, as amended. P registers A's stock, and A sells the stock shortly after the merger. No person who purchased the P stock from A is a person related to P within the meaning of paragraph (e)(4) of this section. Under paragraphs (e)(1) and (3) of this section, the sale of the P stock by A is disregarded because no person who purchased the P stock from A is a person related to P within the meaning of paragraph (e)(4) of this section. The transaction satisfies the continuity of interest requirement because A's T stock was exchanged for P stock, preserving a substantial part of the value of the proprietary interest in T.

Example 4. Redemptions and purchases by issuing corporation or related persons. (i) *Redemption by issuing corporation.* A owns 100 percent of the stock of T and none of the stock of P. T merges into S. In the merger, A receives P stock. In connection with the merger, P redeems all of the P stock received by A in the merger for cash. The continuity of interest requirement is not satisfied, because, in connection with the merger, P redeemed the stock exchanged for a proprietary interest in T, and a substantial part of the value of the proprietary interest in T is not preserved. See paragraph (e)(1) of this section.

(ii) *Purchase of target corporation stock by issuing corporation.* The facts are the same as paragraph (i) of this *Example 4*, except that, instead of P redeeming its stock, prior to and in connection with the merger of T into S, P purchases 90 percent of the T stock from A for cash. The continuity of interest requirement is not satisfied, because in connection with the merger, P acquired a proprietary interest in T for consideration other than P stock, and a substantial part of the value of the proprietary interest in T is not preserved. See paragraph (e)(1) of this section. However, see § 1.338-3(d) (which may change the result in this case by providing that, by virtue of section 338, continuity of interest is satisfied for certain parties after a qualified stock purchase).

(iii) *Purchase of issuing corporation stock by person related to issuing corporation.* The facts are the same as paragraph (i) of this *Example 4*, except that, instead of P redeeming its stock, S buys all of the P stock received by A in the merger for cash. S is a person related to P under paragraphs (e)(4)(i)(A) and (B) of this section. The continuity of interest requirement is not satisfied, because S acquired P stock issued in the merger, and a substantial part of the value of the proprietary interest in T is not preserved. See paragraph (e)(3) of this section.

Example 5. Redemption in substance by issuing corporation. A owns 100 percent of the stock of T and none of the stock of P. T merges into P. In the merger, A receives P stock. In connection with the merger, B buys all of the P stock received by A in the merger for cash. Shortly thereafter, in connection with the merger, P redeems the stock held by B for cash. Based on all the facts and circumstances, P in substance has exchanged solely cash for T stock in the merger. The continuity of interest requirement is not satisfied, because in substance P redeemed the stock exchanged for a proprietary interest in T, and a substantial part of the value of the proprietary interest in T is not preserved. See paragraph (e)(1) of this section.

Example 6. Purchase of issuing corporation stock through partnership. A owns 100 percent of the stock of T and none of the stock of P. S is an 85 percent partner in PRS. The other 15 percent of PRS is owned by unrelated persons. T merges into P. In the merger, A receives P stock. In connection with the merger, PRS purchases all of the P stock received by A in the merger for cash. Under paragraph (e)(5) of this section, S, as an 85 percent partner of PRS, is treated as having acquired 85 percent of the P stock exchanged for A's T stock in the merger, and as having furnished 85 percent of the cash paid by PRS to acquire the P stock. S is a person related to P under paragraphs (e)(4)(i)(A) and (B) of this section. The continuity of interest requirement is not satisfied, because S is treated as acquiring 85 percent of the P stock issued in the merger, and a substantial part of the value of the proprietary interest in T is not preserved. See paragraph (e)(3) of this section.

Example 7. Exchange by acquiring corporation for direct interest. A owns 30 percent of the stock of T. P owns 70 percent of the stock of T, which was not acquired by P in connection with the acquisition of T's assets. T merges into P. A receives cash in the merger. The continuity of interest requirement is satisfied, because P's 70 percent proprietary interest in T is exchanged by P for a direct interest in the assets of the target corporation enterprise.

Example 8. Maintenance of direct or indirect interest in issuing corporation. X, a corporation, owns all of the stock of each of corporations P and Z. Z owns all of the stock of T. T merges into P. Z receives P stock in the merger. Immediately thereafter and in connection with the merger, Z distributes the P stock received in the merger to X. X is a person related to P under paragraph (e)(4)(i)(A) of this section. The continuity of interest requirement is satisfied, because X was an indirect owner of T prior to the merger who maintains a direct or indirect proprietary interest in P, preserving a substantial part of the value of the proprietary interest in T. See paragraph (e)(3) of this section.

Example 9. Preacquisition redemption by target corporation. T has two shareholders, A and B. P expresses an interest in acquiring the stock of T. A does not wish to own P stock. T redeems A's shares in T in exchange for cash. No funds have been or will be provided by P for this purpose. P subsequently acquires all the outstanding stock of T from B solely in exchange for voting stock of P. The cash received by A in the prereorganization redemption is not treated as other property or money under section 356, and would not be so treated even if A had received some stock of P in exchange for his T stock. The prereorganization redemption by T does not affect continuity of interest, because B's proprietary interest in T is unaffected, and the value of the proprietary interest in T is preserved.

* * *

[Reg. § 1.368-1.]

☐ [*T.D.* 6152, 12-2-55. *Amended by T.D.* 7745, 12-29-80; *T.D.* 8760, 1-23-98; *T.D.* 8783, 9-22-98; *T.D.* 8858, 1-5-2000; *T.D.* 8898, 8-30-2000; *T.D.* 8940, 2-12-2001; *T.D.* 9182, 2-24-2005; *T.D.* 9225, 9-15-2005; *T.D.* 9316, 3-19-2007; *T.D.* 9361, 10-24-2007; *T.D.* 9434, 12-11-2008 (*corrected* 12-23-2008) *and T.D.* 9565, 12-16-2011.]

§ 1.368-2. Definition of terms.—(a) The application of the term "reorganization" is to be strictly limited to the specific transactions set forth in section 368(a). The term does not embrace the mere purchase by one corporation of the properties of another corporation. The preceding sentence applies to transactions occurring after January 28, 1998, except that it does not apply to any transaction occurring pursuant to a written agreement which is binding on January 28, 1998, and at all times thereafter. If the properties are transferred for cash and deferred payment obligations of the transferee evidenced by short-term notes, the transaction is a sale and not an exchange in which gain or loss is not recognized.

(b)(1)(i) *Definitions.*—For purposes of this paragraph (b)(1), the following terms shall have the following meanings:

(A) *Disregarded entity.*—A disregarded entity is a business entity (as defined in § 301.7701-2(a) of this chapter) that is disregarded as an entity separate from its owner for Federal income tax purposes. Examples of disregarded entities include a domestic single member limited liability company that does not elect to be classified as a corporation for Federal income tax purposes, a corporation (as defined in § 301.7701-2(b) of this chapter) that is a qualified REIT subsidiary (within the meaning of section 856(i)(2)), and a corporation that is a qualified subchapter S subsidiary (within the meaning of section 1361(b)(3)(B)).

(B) *Combining entity.*—A combining entity is a business entity that is a corporation (as defined in § 301.7701-2(b) of this chapter) that is not a disregarded entity.

(C) *Combining unit.*—A combining unit is composed solely of a combining entity and all disregarded entities, if any, the assets of which are treated as owned by such combining entity for Federal income tax purposes.

(ii) *Statutory merger or consolidation generally.*—For purposes of section 368(a)(1)(A), a statutory merger or consolidation is a transaction effected pursuant to the statute or statutes necessary to effect the merger or consolidation, in which transaction, as a result of the operation of such statute or statutes, the following events occur simultaneously at the effective time of the transaction—

(A) All of the assets (other than those distributed in the transaction) and liabilities (except to the extent such liabilities are satisfied or discharged in the transaction or are nonrecourse liabilities to which assets distributed in the transaction are subject) of each member of one or more combining units (each a transferor unit) become the assets and liabilities of one or more members of one other combining unit (the transferee unit); and

(B) The combining entity of each transferor unit ceases its separate legal existence for all purposes; provided, however, that this requirement will be satisfied even if, under applicable law, after the effective time of the transaction, the combining entity of the transferor unit (or its officers, directors, or agents) may act or be acted against, or a member of the transferee unit (or its officers, directors, or agents) may act or be acted against in the name of the combining entity of the transferor unit, provided that such actions relate to assets or obligations of the combining entity of the transferor unit that arose, or relate to activities engaged in by such entity, prior to the effective time of the transaction, and such actions are not inconsistent with the requirements of paragraph (b)(1)(ii)(A) of this section.

(iii) *Examples.*—The following examples illustrate the rules of paragraph (b)(1) of this section. In each of the examples, except as otherwise provided, each of R, V, Y, and Z is a C corporation. X is a domestic limited liability company. Except as otherwise provided, X is wholly owned by Y and is disregarded as an entity separate from Y for Federal income tax purposes. The examples are as follows:

Example 1. Divisive transaction pursuant to a merger statute. (i) *Facts.* Under State W law, Z transfers some of its assets and liabilities to Y, retains the remainder of its assets and liabilities, and remains in existence for Federal income tax purposes following the transaction. The transaction qualifies as a merger under State W corporate law.

(ii) *Analysis.* The transaction does not satisfy the requirements of paragraph (b)(1)(ii)(A) of this section because all of the assets and liabilities of Z, the combining entity of the transferor unit, do not become the assets and liabilities of Y, the combining entity and sole member of the transferee unit. In addition, the transaction does not satisfy the requirements of paragraph (b)(1)(ii)(B) of this section because the separate legal existence of Z does not cease for all purposes. Accordingly, the transaction does not qualify as a statutory merger or consolidation under section 368(a)(1)(A).

Example 2. Merger of a target corporation into a disregarded entity in exchange for stock of the owner. (i) *Facts.* Under State W law, Z merges into X. Pursuant to such law, the following events occur simultaneously at the effective time of the transaction: all of the assets and liabilities of Z become the assets and liabilities of X and Z's separate legal existence ceases for all purposes. In the merger, the Z shareholders exchange their stock of Z for stock of Y.

(ii) *Analysis.* The transaction satisfies the requirements of paragraph (b)(1)(ii) of this section because the transaction is effected pursuant to State W law and the following events occur simultaneously at the effective time of the transaction: all of the assets and liabilities of Z, the combining entity and sole member of the transferor unit, become the assets and liabilities of one or more members of the transferee unit that is comprised of Y, the combining entity of the transferee unit, and X, a disregarded entity the assets of which Y is treated as owning for Federal income tax purposes, and Z ceases its separate legal existence for all purposes. Accordingly, the transaction qualifies as a statutory merger or consolidation for purposes of section 368(a)(1)(A).

Example 3. Merger of a target S corporation that owns a QSub into a disregarded entity. (i) *Facts.* The facts are the same as in *Example 2*, except that Z is an S corporation and owns all of the stock of U, a QSub.

(ii) *Analysis.* The deemed formation by Z of U pursuant to § 1.1361-5(b)(1) (as a consequence of the termination of U's QSub election) is disregarded for Federal income tax purposes. The transaction is treated as a transfer of the assets of U to X, followed by X's transfer of these assets to U in exchange for stock of U. See § 1.1361-5(b)(3) *Example 9.* The transaction will, therefore, satisfy the requirements of paragraph (b)(1)(ii) of this section because the transaction is effected pursuant to State W law and the following events occur simultaneously at the effective time of the transaction: all of the assets and liabilities of Z and U, the sole members of the transferor unit, become the assets and liabilities of one or more members of the transferee unit that is comprised of Y, the combining entity of the transferee unit, and X, a disregarded entity the assets of which Y is treated as owning for Federal income tax purposes, and Z ceases its separate legal existence for all purposes. Moreover, the deemed transfer of the assets of U in exchange for U stock does not cause the transaction to fail to qualify as a statutory merger or consolidation. See § 368(a)(2)(C). Accordingly, the transaction qualifies as a statutory merger or consolidation for purposes of section 368(a)(1)(A).

Example 4. Triangular merger of a target corporation into a disregarded entity. (i) *Facts.* The facts are the same as in *Example 2*, except that V owns 100 percent of the outstanding stock of Y and, in the merger of Z into X, the Z shareholders exchange their stock of Z for stock of V. In the transaction, Z transfers substantially all of its properties to X.

(ii) *Analysis.* The transaction is not prevented from qualifying as a statutory merger or consolidation under section 368(a)(1)(A), provided the requirements of section 368(a)(2)(D) are satisfied. Because the assets of X are treated for Federal income tax purposes as the assets of Y, Y will be treated as acquiring substantially all of the properties of Z in the merger for purposes of determining whether the merger satisfies the requirements of section 368(a)(2)(D). As a result, the Z shareholders that receive stock of V will be treated as receiving stock of a corporation that is in control of Y, the combining entity of the transferee unit that is the acquiring corporation for purposes of section 368(a)(2)(D). Accordingly, the merger will satisfy the requirements of section 368(a)(2)(D).

Example 5. Merger of a target corporation into a disregarded entity owned by a partnership. (i) *Facts.* The facts are the same as in *Example 2*, except that Y is organized as a partnership under the laws of State W and is classified as a partnership for Federal income tax purposes.

(ii) *Analysis.* The transaction does not satisfy the requirements of paragraph (b)(1)(ii)(A) of this section. All of the assets and liabilities of Z, the combining entity and sole member of the transferor unit, do not become the assets and liabilities of one or more members of a transferee unit because neither X nor Y qualifies as a combining entity. Accordingly, the transaction cannot qualify as a statutory merger or consolidation for purposes of section 368(a)(1)(A).

Example 6. Merger of a disregarded entity into a corporation. (i) *Facts.* Under State W law, X merges into Z. Pursuant to such law, the following events occur simultaneously at the effective time of the transaction: all of the assets and liabilities of X (but not the assets and liabilities of Y other than those of X) become the assets and liabilities of Z and X's separate legal existence ceases for all purposes.

(ii) *Analysis.* The transaction does not satisfy the requirements of paragraph (b)(1)(ii)(A) of this section because all of the assets and liabilities of a transferor unit do not become the assets and liabilities of one or more members of the transferee unit. The transaction also does not satisfy the requirements of paragraph (b)(1)(ii)(B) of this section because X does not qualify as a combining entity. Accordingly, the transaction cannot qualify as a statutory merger or consolidation for purposes of section 368(a)(1)(A).

Example 7. Merger of a corporation into a disregarded entity in exchange for interests in the disregarded entity. (i) *Facts.* Under State W law, Z merges into X. Pursuant to such law, the following events occur simultaneously at the effective time of the transaction: all of the assets and liabilities of Z become the assets and liabilities of X and Z's separate legal existence ceases for all purposes. In the merger of Z into X, the Z shareholders exchange their stock of Z for interests in X so that, immediately after the merger, X is not disregarded as an entity separate from Y for Federal income tax purposes. Following the merger, pursuant to §301.7701-3(b)(1)(i) of this chapter, X is classified as a partnership for Federal income tax purposes.

(ii) *Analysis.* The transaction does not satisfy the requirements of paragraph (b)(1)(ii)(A) of this section because immediately after the merger X is not disregarded as an entity separate from Y and, consequently, all of the assets and liabilities of Z, the combining entity of the transferor unit, do not become the assets and liabilities of one or more members of a transferee unit. Accordingly, the transaction cannot qualify as a statutory merger or consolidation for purposes of section 368(a)(1)(A).

Example 8. Merger transaction preceded by distribution. (i) *Facts.* Z operates two unrelated businesses, Business P and Business Q, each of which represents 50 percent of the value of the assets of Z. Y desires to acquire and continue operating Business P, but does not want to acquire Business Q. Pursuant to a single plan, Z sells Business Q for cash to parties unrelated to Z and Y in a taxable transaction, and then distributes the proceeds of the sale pro rata to its shareholders. Then, pursuant to State W law, Z merges into Y. Pursuant to such law, the following events occur simultaneously at the effective time of the transaction: all of the assets and liabilities of Z related to Business P become the assets and liabilities of Y and Z's separate legal existence ceases for all purposes. In the merger, the Z shareholders exchange their Z stock for Y stock.

(ii) *Analysis.* The transaction satisfies the requirements of paragraph (b)(1)(ii) of this section because the transaction is effected pursuant to State W law and the following events occur simultaneously at the effective time of the transaction: all of the assets and liabilities of Z, the combining entity and sole member of the transferor unit, become the assets and liabilities of Y, the combining entity and sole member of the transferee unit, and Z ceases its separate legal existence for all purposes. Accordingly, the transaction qualifies as a statutory merger or consolidation for purposes of section 368(a)(1)(A).

Example 9. State law conversion of target corporation into a limited liability company. (i) *Facts.* Y acquires the stock of V from the V shareholders in exchange for consideration that consists of 50 percent voting stock of Y and 50 percent cash. Immediately after the stock acquisition, V files the necessary documents to convert from a corporation to a limited liability company under State W law. Y's acquisition of the stock of V and the conversion of V to a limited liability company are steps in a single integrated acquisition by Y of the assets of V.

(ii) *Analysis.* The acquisition by Y of the assets of V does not satisfy the requirements of paragraph (b)(1)(ii)(B) of this section because V, the combining entity of the transferor unit, does not cease its separate legal existence. Although V is an entity disregarded from its owner for Federal income tax purposes, it continues to exist as a juridical entity after the conversion. Accordingly, Y's acquisition of the assets of V does not qualify as a statutory merger or consolidation for purposes of section 368(a)(1)(A).

Example 10. Dissolution of target corporation. (i) *Facts.* Y acquires the stock of Z from the Z shareholders in exchange for consideration that consists of 50 percent voting stock of Y and 50 percent cash. Immediately after the stock acquisition, Z files a certificate of dissolution pursuant to State W law and commences winding up its activities. Under State W dissolution law, ownership and title to Z's assets does not automatically vest in Y upon dissolution. Instead, Z transfers assets to its creditors in satisfaction of its liabilities and transfers its remaining assets to Y in the liquidation stage of the dissolution. Y's acquisition of the stock of Z and the dissolution of Z are steps in a single integrated acquisition by Y of the assets of Z.

(ii) *Analysis.* The acquisition by Y of the assets of Z does not satisfy the requirements of paragraph (b)(1)(ii) of this section because Y does not acquire all of the assets of Z as a result of Z filing the certificate of dissolution or simultaneously with Z ceasing its separate legal existence. Instead, Y acquires the assets of Z by reason of Z's transfer of its assets to Y. Accordingly, Y's acquisition of the assets of Z does not qualify as a statutory merger or consolidation for purposes of section 368(a)(1)(A).

Example 11. Merger of corporate partner into a partnership. (i) *Facts.* Y owns an interest in X, an entity classified as a partnership for Federal income tax purposes, that represents a 60 percent capital and profits interest in X. Z owns an interest in X that represents a 40 percent capital and profits interest. Under State W law, Z merges into X. Pursuant to such law, the following events occur simultaneously at the effective time of the transaction: all of the assets and liabilities of Z become the assets and liabilities of X and Z ceases its separate legal existence for all purposes. In the merger, the Z shareholders exchange their stock of Z for stock of Y. As a result of the merger, X becomes an entity that is disregarded as an entity separate from Y for Federal income tax purposes.

(ii) *Analysis.* The transaction satisfies the requirements of paragraph (b)(1)(ii) of this section because the transaction is effected pursuant to State W law and the following events occur simultaneously at the effective time of the transaction: all of the assets and liabilities of Z, the combining entity and sole member of the transferor unit, become the assets and liabilities of one or more members of the transferee unit that is comprised of Y, the combining entity of the transferee unit, and X, a disregarded entity the assets of which Y is treated as owning for Federal income tax purposes immediately after the transaction, and Z ceases its separate legal existence for all purposes. Accordingly, the transaction qualifies as a statutory merger or consolidation for purposes of section 368(a)(1)(A).

Example 12. State law consolidation. (i) *Facts.* Under State W law, Z and V consolidate. Pursuant to such law, the following events occur simultaneously at the effective time of the transaction: all of the assets and liabilities of Z and V become the assets and liabilities of Y, an entity that is created in the transaction, and the existence of Z and V continues in Y. In the consolidation, the Z shareholders and the V shareholders exchange their stock of Z and V, respectively, for stock of Y.

(ii) *Analysis.* With respect to each of Z and V, the transaction satisfies the requirements of paragraph (b)(1)(ii) of this section because the transaction is effected pursuant to State W law and the following events occur simultaneously at the effective time of the transaction: all of the assets and liabilities of Z and V, respectively, each of which is the combining entity of a transferor unit, become the assets and liabilities of Y, the combining entity and sole member of the transferee unit, and Z and V each ceases its separate legal existence for all purposes. Accordingly, the transaction qualifies as the statutory merger or consolidation of each of Z and V into Y for purposes of section 368(a)(1)(A).

* * *

(2) In order for the transaction to qualify under section 368(a)(1)(A) by reason of the application of section 368(a)(2)(D), one corporation (the acquiring corporation) must acquire substantially all of the properties of another corporation (the acquired corporation) partly or entirely in exchange for stock of a corporation which is in control of the acquiring corporation (the controlling corporation), provided that (i) the transaction would have qualified under section 368(a)(1)(A) if the merger had been into the controlling corporation, and (ii) no stock of the acquiring corporation is used in the transaction. The foregoing test of whether the transaction would have qualified under section 368(a)(1)(A) if the merger had been into the controlling corporation means that the general requirements of a reorganization under section 368(a)(1)(A) (such as a business purpose, continuity of business enterprise, and continuity of interest) must be met in addition to the special requirements of section 368(a)(2)(D). Under this test, it is not relevant whether the merger into the controlling corporation could have been effected pursuant to State or Federal corporation law. The term "substantially all" has the same meaning as it has in section 368(a)(1)(C). Although no stock of the acquiring corporation can be used in the transaction, there is no prohibition (other than the continuity of interest requirement) against

using other property, such as cash or securities, of either the acquiring corporation or the parent or both. In addition, the controlling corporation may assume liabilities of the acquired corporation without disqualifying the transaction under section 368(a)(2)(D), and for purposes of section 357(a) the controlling corporation is considered a party to the exchange. For example, if the controlling corporation agrees to substitute its stock for stock of the acquired corporation under an outstanding employee stock option agreement, this assumption of liability will not prevent the transaction from qualifying as a reorganization under section 368(a)(2)(D) and the assumption of liability is not treated as money or other property for purposes of section 361(b). Section 368(a)(2)(D) applies whether or not the controlling corporation (or the acquiring corporation) is formed immediately before the merger, in anticipation of the merger, or after preliminary steps have been taken to merge directly into the controlling corporation. Section 368(a)(2)(D) applies only to statutory mergers occurring after October 22, 1968.

(3) For regulations under section 368(a)(2)(E), see paragraph (j) of this section.

(c) In order to qualify as a "reorganization" under section 368(a)(1)(B), the acquisition by the acquiring corporation of stock of another corporation must be in exchange solely for all or a part of the voting stock of the acquiring corporation (or, in the case of transactions occurring after December 31, 1963, solely for all or a part of the voting stock of a corporation which is in control of the acquiring corporation), and the acquiring corporation must be in control of the other corporation immediately after the transaction. If, for example, corporation X in one transaction exchanges nonvoting preferred stock or bonds in addition to all or a part of its voting stock in the acquisition of stock of corporation Y, the transaction is not a reorganization under section 368(a)(1)(B). Nor is a transaction a reorganization described in section 368(a)(1)(B) if stock is acquired in exchange for voting stock both of the acquiring corporation and of a corporation which is in control of the acquiring corporation. The acquisition of the stock of another corporation by the acquiring corporation solely for its voting stock (or solely for voting stock of a corporation which is in control of the acquiring corporation) is permitted tax free even though the acquiring corporation already owns some of the stock of the other corporation. Such an acquisition is permitted tax free in a single transaction or in a series of transactions taking place over a relatively short period of time such as 12 months. For example, corporation A purchased 30 percent of the common stock of corporation W (the only class of stock outstanding) for cash in 1939. On March 1, 1955, corporation A offers to exchange its own voting stock for all the stock of corporation W tendered within 6 months from the date of the offer. Within the 6 months' period corporation A acquires an additional 60 percent of stock of corporation W solely for its own voting stock, so that it owns 90 percent of the stock of corporation W. No gain or loss is recognized with respect to the exchanges of stock of corporation A for stock of corporation W. For this purpose, it is immaterial whether such exchanges occurred before corporation A acquired control (80 percent) of corporation W or after such control was acquired. If corporation A had acquired 80 percent of the stock of corporation W for cash in 1939, it could likewise acquire some or all of the remainder of such stock solely in exchange for its own voting stock without recognition of gain or loss.

(d) In order to qualify as a reorganization under section 368(a)(1)(C), the transaction must be one described in subparagraph (1) or (2) of this paragraph:

(1) One corporation must acquire substantially all the properties of another corporation solely in exchange for all or a part of its own voting stock, or solely in exchange for all or a part of the voting stock of a corporation which is in control of the acquiring corporation. For example, Corporation P owns all the stock of Corporation A. All the properties of Corporation W are transferred to Corporation A either solely in exchange for voting stock of Corporation P or solely in exchange for less than 80 percent of the voting stock of Corporation A. Either of such transactions constitutes a reorganization under section 368(a)(1)(C). However, if the properties of Corporation W are acquired in exchange for voting stock of both Corporation P and Corporation A, the transaction will not constitute a reorganization under section 368(a)(1)(C). In determining whether the exchange meets the requirement of "solely for voting stock", the assumption by the acquiring corporation of liabilities of the transferor corporation, or the fact that property acquired from the transferor corporation is subject to a liability, shall be disregarded. Though such an assumption does not prevent an exchange from being solely for voting stock for the purposes of the definition of a reorganization contained in section 368(a)(1)(C), it may in some cases, however, so alter the character of the transaction as to place the transaction outside the purposes and assumptions of the reorganization provisions. Section 368(a)(1)(C) does not prevent consideration of the effect of an assumption of liabilities on the general character of the transaction but merely provides that the requirement that the exchange be solely for

voting stock is satisfied if the only additional consideration is an assumption of liabilities.

(2) One corporation—

(i) Must acquire substantially all of the properties of another corporation in such manner that the acquisition would qualify under (1) above, but for the fact that the acquiring corporation exchanges money, or other property in addition to such voting stock, and

(ii) Must acquire solely for voting stock (either of the acquiring corporation or of a corporation which is in control of the acquiring corporation) properties of the other corporation having a fair market value which is at least 80 percent of the fair market value of all the properties of the other corporation.

(3) For the purposes of subparagraph (2) (ii) only, a liability assumed or to which the properties are subject is considered money paid for the properties. For example, Corporation A has properties with a fair market value of $100,000 and liabilities of $10,000. In exchange for these properties, Corporation Y transfers its own voting stock, assumes the $10,000 liabilities, and pays $8,000 in cash. The transaction is a reorganization even though a part of the properties of Corporation A is acquired for cash. On the other hand, if the properties of Corporation A worth $100,000, were subject to $50,000 in liabilities, an acquisition of all the properties, subject to the liabilities, for any consideration other than solely voting stock would not qualify as a reorganization under this section since the liabilities alone are in excess of 20 percent of the fair market value of the properties. If the transaction would qualify under either subparagraph (1) or (2) of this paragraph and also under section 368(a) (1) (D), such transaction shall not be treated as a reorganization under section 368(a) (1) (C).

(4) (i) For purposes of paragraphs (d) (1) and (2) (ii) of this section, prior ownership of stock of the target corporation by an acquiring corporation will not by itself prevent the solely for voting stock requirement of such paragraphs from being satisfied. In a transaction in which the acquiring corporation has prior ownership of stock of the target corporation, the requirement of paragraph (d) (2) (ii) of this section is satisfied only if the sum of the money or other property that is distributed in pursuance of the plan of reorganization to the shareholders of the target corporation other than the acquiring corporation and to the creditors of the target corporation pursuant to section 361(b) (3), and all of the liabilities of the target corporation assumed by the acquiring corporation (including liabilities to which the properties of the target corporation are subject), does not exceed 20 percent of the value of all of the properties of the target corporation. If, in connection with a potential acquisition by an acquiring corporation of substantially all of a target corporation's properties, the acquiring corporation acquires the target corporation's stock for consideration other than the acquiring corporation's own voting stock (or voting stock of a corporation in control of the acquiring corporation if such stock is used in the acquisition of the target corporation's properties), whether from a shareholder of the target corporation or the target corporation itself, such consideration is treated, for purposes of paragraphs (d) (1) and (2) of this section, as money or other property exchanged by the acquiring corporation for the target corporation's properties. Accordingly, the transaction will not qualify under section 368(a) (1) (C) unless, treating such consideration as money or other property, the requirements of section 368(a) (2) (B) and paragraph (d) (2) (ii) of this section are met. The determination of whether there has been an acquisition in connection with a potential reorganization under section 368(a) (1) (C) of a target corporation's stock for consideration other than an acquiring corporation's own voting stock (or voting stock of a corporation in control of the acquiring corporation if such stock is used in the acquisition of the target corporation's properties) will be made on the basis of all of the facts and circumstances.

(ii) The following examples illustrate the principles of this paragraph (d) (4):

Example 1. Corporation P (P) holds 60 percent of the Corporation T (T) stock that P purchased several years ago in an unrelated transaction. T has 100 shares of stock outstanding. The other 40 percent of the T stock is owned by Corporation X (X), an unrelated corporation. T has properties with a fair market value of $110 and liabilities of $10. T transfers all of its properties to P. In exchange, P assumes the $10 of liabilities, and transfers to T $30 of P voting stock and $10 of cash. T distributes the P voting stock and $10 of cash to X and liquidates. The transaction satisfies the solely for voting stock requirement of paragraph (d) (2) (ii) of this section because the sum of $10 of cash paid to X and the assumption by P of $10 of liabilities does not exceed 20% of the value of the properties of T.

Example 2. The facts are the same as in *Example 1* except that P purchased the 60 shares of T for $60 in cash in connection with the acquisition of T's assets. The transaction does not satisfy the solely for voting stock requirement of paragraph (d) (2) (ii) of this section because P is treated as having acquired all of the T assets for consideration consisting of $70 of cash, $10 of liability assumption and $30 of P voting stock, and the sum of $70 of cash and the assumption by P of $10 of liabilities exceeds 20% of the value of the properties of T.

(iii) This paragraph (d)(4) applies to transactions occurring after December 31, 1999, unless the transaction occurs pursuant to a written agreement that is (subject to customary conditions) binding on that date and at all times thereafter.

(e) A "recapitalization", and therefore a reorganization, takes place if, for example:

(1) A corporation with $200,000 par value of bonds outstanding, instead of paying them off in cash, discharges them by issuing preferred shares to the bondholders;

(2) There is surrendered to a corporation for cancellation 25 percent of its preferred stock in exchange for no par value common stock;

(3) A corporation issues preferred stock, previously authorized but unissued, for outstanding common stock;

(4) An exchange is made of a corporation's outstanding preferred stock, having certain priorities with reference to the amount and time of payment of dividends and the distribution of the corporate assets upon liquidation, for a new issue of such corporation's common stock having no such rights;

(5) An exchange is made of an amount of a corporation's outstanding preferred stock with dividends in arrears for other stock of the corporation. However, if pursuant to such an exchange there is an increase in the proportionate interest of the preferred shareholders in the assets or earnings and profits of the corporation, then under §1.305-7(c)(2), an amount equal to the lesser of (i) the amount by which the fair market value or liquidation preference, whichever is greater, of the stock received in the exchange (determined immediately following the recapitalization) exceeds the issue price of the preferred stock surrendered, or (ii) the amount of the dividends in arrears, shall be treated under section 305(c) as a deemed distribution to which sections 305(b)(4) and 301 apply.

(f) The term "a party to a reorganization" includes a corporation resulting from a reorganization, and both corporations in a transaction qualifying as a reorganization where one corporation acquires stock or properties of another corporation. If a transaction otherwise qualifies as a reorganization, a corporation remains a party to the reorganization even though stock or assets acquired in the reorganization are transferred in a transaction described in paragraph (k) of this section. If a transaction otherwise qualifies as a reorganization, a corporation shall not cease to be a party to the reorganization solely by reason of the fact that part or all of the assets acquired in the reorganization are transferred to a partnership in which the transferor is a partner if the continuity of business enterprise requirement is satisfied. See §1.368-1(d). The preceding three sentences apply to transactions occurring after January 28, 1998, except that they do not apply to any transaction occurring pursuant to a written agreement which is binding on January 28, 1998, and at all times thereafter. A corporation controlling an acquiring corporation is a party to the reorganization when the stock of such controlling corporation is used in the acquisition of properties. Both corporations are parties to the reorganization if, under statutory authority, Corporation A is merged into Corporation B. All three of the corporations are parties to the reorganization if, pursuant to statutory authority, Corporation C and Corporation D are consolidated into Corporation E. Both corporations are parties to the reorganization if Corporation F transfers substantially all its assets to Corporation G in exchange for all or a part of the voting stock of Corporation G. All three corporations are parties to the reorganization if Corporation H transfers substantially all its assets to Corporation K in exchange for all or part of the voting stock of Corporation L, which is in control of Corporation K. Both corporations are parties to the reorganization if Corporation M transfers all or a part of its assets to Corporation N in exchange for all or a part of the stock and securities of Corporation N, but only if (1) immediately after such transfer, Corporation M, or one or more of its shareholders (including persons who were shareholders immediately before such transfer), or any combination thereof, is in control of Corporation N, and (2) in pursuance of the plan, the stock and securities of Corporation N are transferred or distributed by Corporation M in a transaction in which gain or loss is not recognized under section 354 or 355, or is recognized only to the extent provided in section 356. Both Corporation O and Corporation P, but not Corporation S, are parties to the reorganization if Corporation O acquires stock of Corporation P from Corporation S in exchange solely for a part of the voting stock of Corporation O, if (1) the stock of Corporation P does not constitute substantially all of the assets of Corporation S, (2) Corporation S is not in control of Corporation O immediately after the acquisition, and (3) Corporation O is in control of Corporation P immediately after the acquisition. If a transaction otherwise qualifies as a reorganization under section 368(a)(1)(B) or as a reverse triangular merger (as defined in §1.358-6(b)(2)(iii)), the target corporation (in the case of a transaction that otherwise qualifies as a reorganization under section 368(a)(1)(B)) or the surviving corporation (in the case of a transaction that otherwise qualifies as a reverse triangular merger) remains a party to the reorganization even though its stock or assets are transferred in a transaction described in paragraph (k) of this section. If a transaction otherwise qualifies as a forward triangular merger (as defined in § 1.358-6(b)(2)(i)), a triangular B reorganization (as defined in § 1.358-6(b)(2)(iv)), a triangular C reorganization (as defined in § 1.358-6(b)(2)(ii)), or a reorganization under section 368(a)(1)(G) by reason of section 368(a)(2)(D), the acquiring corporation remains a party to the reorganization even though its stock is transferred in a transaction described in paragraph (k) of this section. The two preceding sentences apply to transactions occurring on or after October 25, 2007, except that they do not apply to any transaction occurring pursuant to a written agreement which is binding before October 25, 2007, and at all times after that.

(g) The term "plan of reorganization" has reference to a consummated transaction specifically defined as a reorganization under section 368(a). The term is not to be construed as broadening the definition of "reorganization" as set forth in section 368(a), but is to be taken as limiting the nonrecognition of gain or loss to such exchanges or distributions as are directly a part of the transaction specifically described as a reorganization in section 368(a). Moreover, the transaction, or series of transactions, embraced in a plan of reorganization must not only come within the specific language of section 368(a), but the readjustments involved in the exchanges or distributions effected in the consummation thereof must be undertaken for reasons germane to the continuance of the business of a corporation a party to the reorganization. Section 368(a) contemplates genuine corporate reorganizations which are designed to effect a readjustment of continuing interests under modified corporate forms.

(h) As used in section 368, as well as in other provisions of the Internal Revenue Code, if the context so requires, the conjunction "or" denotes both the conjunctive and the disjunctive, and the singular includes the plural. For example, the provisions of the statute are complied with if "stock and securities" are received in exchange as well as if "stock or securities" are received.

(i) [Reserved]

(j)(1) This paragraph (j) prescribes rules relating to the application of section 368(a)(2)(E).

(2) Section 368(a)(2)(E) does not apply to a consolidation.

(3) A transaction otherwise qualifying under section 368(a)(1)(A) is not disqualified by reason of the fact that stock of a corporation (the controlling corporation) which before the merger was in control of the merged corporation is used in the transaction, if the conditions of section 368(a)(2)(E) are satisfied. Those conditions are as follows:

(i) In the transaction, shareholders of the surviving corporation must surrender stock in exchange for voting stock of the controlling corporation. Further, the stock so surrendered must constitute control of the surviving corporation. Control is defined in section 368(c). The amount of stock constituting control is measured immediately before the transaction. For purposes of this subdivision (i), stock in the surviving corporation which is surrendered in the transaction (by any shareholder except the controlling corporation) in exchange for consideration furnished by the surviving corporation (and not by the controlling corporation or the merged corporation) is considered not to be outstanding immediately before the transaction. For effect on "substantially all" test of consideration furnished by the surviving corporation, see paragraph (j)(3)(iii) of this section.

(ii) Except as provided in paragraph (k) of this section, the controlling corporation must control the surviving corporation immediately after the transaction.

(iii) After the transaction, the surviving corporation must hold substantially all of its own properties and substantially all of the properties of the merged corporation (other than stock of the controlling corporation distributed in the transaction). The surviving corporation may transfer such properties as provided in paragraph (k) of this section. The term "substantially all" has the same meaning as in section 368(a)(1)(C). The "substantially all" test applies separately to the merged corporation and to the surviving corporation. In applying the "substantially all" test to the surviving corporation, consideration furnished in the transaction by the surviving corporation in exchange for its stock is property of the surviving corporation which it does not hold after the transaction. In applying the "substantially all" test to the merged corporation, assets transferred from the controlling corporation to the merged corporation in pursuance of the plan of reorganization are not taken into account. Thus, for example, money transferred from the controlling corporation to the merged corporation to be used for the following purposes is not taken into account for purposes of the "substantially all" test:

(A) To pay additional consideration to shareholders of the surviving corporation;

(B) To pay dissenting shareholders of the surviving corporation;

(C) To pay creditors of the surviving corporation;

(D) To pay reorganization expenses; or

(E) To enable the merged corporation to satisfy state minimum capitalization requirements (where the money is returned to the controlling corporation as part of the transaction).

(iv) Paragraph (j)(3)(ii) and the first two sentences of paragraph (j)(3)(iii) of this section apply to transactions occurring on or after October 25, 2007, except that they do not apply to any transaction occurring pursuant to a written agreement which is binding before October 25, 2007, and at all times thereafter. The remainder of paragraph (j)(3)(iii) of this section applies to transactions occurring after January 28, 1998, except that it does not apply to any transaction occurring pursuant to a written agreement which is binding on January 28, 1998, and at all times after that.

(4) The controlling corporation may assume liabilities of the surviving corporation without disqualifying the transaction under section 368(a)(2)(E). An assumption of liabilities of the surviving corporation by the controlling corporation is a contribution to capital by the controlling corporation to the surviving corporation. If, in pursuance of the plan of reorganization, securities of the surviving corporation are exchanged for securities of the controlling corporation, or for other securities of the surviving corporation, see sections 354 and 356.

(5) In applying section 368(a)(2)(E), it makes no difference if the merged corporation is an existing corporation, or is formed immediately before the merger, in anticipation of the merger, or after preliminary steps have been taken to otherwise acquire control of the surviving corporation.

(6) The following examples illustrate the application of this paragraph (j). In each of the examples, Corporation P owns all of the stock of Corporation S and, except as otherwise stated, Corporation T has outstanding 1,000 shares of common stock and no shares of any other class. In each of the examples, it is also assumed that the transaction qualifies under section 368(a)(1)(A) if the conditions of section 368(a)(2)(E) are satisfied.

Example 1. P owns no T stock. On January 1, 1981, S merges into T. In the merger, T's shareholders surrender 950 shares of common stock in exchange for P voting stock. The holders of the other 50 shares (who dissent from the merger) are paid in cash with funds supplied by P. After the transaction, T holds all of its own assets and all of S's assets. Based on these facts, the transaction qualifies under section 368(a)(1)(A) by reason of the application of section 368(a)(2)(E). In the transaction, former shareholders of T surrender, in exchange for P voting stock, an amount of T stock (950/1,000 shares or 95 percent) which constitutes control of T.

Example 2. The facts are the same as in example (1) except that holders of 100 shares in corporation T, who dissented from the merger, are paid in cash with funds supplied by T (and not by P or S) and, in the merger, T's remaining shareholders surrender 720 shares of common stock in exchange for P voting stock and 180 shares of common stock for cash supplied by P. The requirements of section 368(a)(2)(E)(ii) are satisfied since, in the transaction, former shareholders of T surrender, in exchange for P voting stock, an amount of T stock (720/900 shares or 80 percent) which constitutes control of T. The T stock surrendered in exchange for consideration furnished by T is not considered outstanding for purposes of determining whether the amount of T stock surrendered by T shareholders for P stock constitutes control of T.

Example 3. T has outstanding 1,000 shares of common stock, 100 shares of nonvoting preferred stock, and no shares of any other class. On January 1, 1981, S merges into T. Prior to the merger, as part of the transaction, T distributes its own cash in redemption of the 100 shares of preferred stock. In the transaction, T's remaining shareholders surrender their 1,000 shares of common stock in exchange for P voting stock. The requirements of section 368(a)(2)(E)(ii) are satisfied since, in the transaction, former shareholders of T surrender, in exchange for P voting stock, an amount of T stock (1,000/1,000 shares or 100 percent) which constitutes control of T. The preferred stock surrendered in exchange for consideration furnished by T is not considered outstanding for purposes of determining whether the amount of T stock surrendered by T shareholders for P stock constitutes control of T. However, the consideration furnished by T for its stock is property of T which does not hold after the transaction for purposes of the substantially all test in paragraph (j)(3)(iii) of this section.

Example 4. On January 1, 1971, P purchased 201 shares of T's stock. On January 1, 1981, S merges into T. In the merger, T's shareholders (other than P) surrender 799 shares of T stock in exchange for P voting stock. Based on these facts, in the transaction, former shareholders of T do not surrender, in exchange for P voting stock, an amount of T stock which constitutes control of T (799/1,000 shares being less than 80 percent). Therefore, the transaction does not qualify under section 368(a)(1)(A). However, if S is a transitory corporation, formed solely for purposes of effectuating the transaction, the transaction may qualify as a reorganization described in section 368(a)(1)(B) provided all of the applicable requirements are satisfied.

Example 5. On January 1, 1971, P purchased 200 shares of T's stock. On January 1, 1981, S merges into T. Prior to the merger, as part of the transaction, T distributes its own cash in redemption of 1 share of T stock from a T shareholder other than P. In the merger, T's remaining shareholders (other than P) surrender 799 shares of T stock in exchange for P voting stock. Based on these facts, in the transaction, former shareholders of T do not surrender, in exchange for P voting stock, an amount of T stock which constitutes control of T (799/999 shares being less than 80 percent). Therefore, the transaction does not qualify under section 368(a)(1)(A). However, if S is a transitory corporation, formed for purposes of effectuating the transaction, the transaction may qualify as a reorganization described in section 368(a)(1)(B) provided all of the applicable requirements are satisfied.

Example 6. The stock of S has a value of $25,000. The stock of T has a value of $75,000. On January 1, 1984, S merges into T. In the merger, T's shareholders surrender all of their T stock in exchange for P voting stock. After the transaction, T holds all of its own assets and all of S's assets. Based on these facts, the transaction qualifies under section 368(a)(1)(A) by reason of the application of section 368(a)(2)(E). In the transaction, former shareholders of T surrender, in exchange for P voting stock, an amount of T stock (1,000/1,000 shares or 100 percent) which constitutes control of T. The stock of T received by P in exchange for P's prior interest in S is not taken into account for purposes of section 368(a)(2)(E)(ii) since the amount of T stock constituting control of T is measured before the transaction.

Example 7. The stock of T has a value of $75,000. On January 1, 1984, S merges into T. In the merger, T's shareholders surrender all of their T stock in exchange for P voting stock. As part of the transaction, P contributes $25,000 to T in exchange for new shares of T stock. None of the cash received by T is distributed or otherwise paid out to former T shareholders. After the transaction, T holds all of its own assets and all of S's assets. Based on these facts, the transaction qualifies under section 368(a)(1)(A) by reason of the application of section 368(a)(2)(E). In the transaction, former shareholders of T surrender, in exchange for P voting stock, an amount of T stock (1,000/1,000 shares or 100 percent) which constitutes control of T. The T stock received by P in exchange for its contribution to T is not taken into account for purposes of section 368(a)(2)(E)(ii) since the amount of T stock constituting control of T is measured before the transaction.

Example 8. The facts are the same as in example (7) except that, as part of the transaction, corporation R, instead of P, contributes $25,000 to T in exchange for T stock. Based on these facts, the transaction does not qualify under section 368(a)(1)(A) by reason of section 368(a)(2)(E) since P does not control T immediately after the transaction.

Example 9. T stock has a value of $75,000. P owns 500 shares (1/2) of that stock with a value of $37,500. The stock of S has a value of $125,000. On January 1, 1984, S merges into T. In the merger, T's shareholders (other than P) surrender their T stock in exchange for P voting stock. Based on these facts, in the transaction, former shareholders of T do not surrender, in exchange for P voting stock, an amount of T stock which constitutes control of T (500/1,000 shares being less than 80 percent). Therefore, the transaction does not qualify under section 368(a)(1)(A). The stock of T received by P in exchange for P's prior interest in S does not contribute to satisfaction of the requirement of section 368(a)(2)(E)(ii).

(k) *Certain transfers of assets or stock in reorganizations.*—(1) *General rule.*—A transaction otherwise qualifying as a reorganization under section 368(a) shall not be disqualified or recharacterized as a result of one or more subsequent transfers (or successive transfers) of assets or stock, provided that the requirements of § 1.368-1(d) are satisfied and the transfer(s) are described in either paragraph (k)(1)(i) or (k)(1)(ii) of this section. However, this paragraph (k) shall not apply to a transfer to the former shareholders of the acquired corporation (other than a former shareholder that is also the acquiring corporation) or the surviving corporation, as the case may be, to the extent it constitutes the receipt of consideration for a proprietary interest in the acquired corporation or the surviving corporation, as the case may be. Similarly, this paragraph (k) shall not apply to a transfer by the former shareholders of the acquired corporation (other than a former shareholder that is also the acquiring corporation) or the surviving corporation, as the case may be, of consideration initially received in the potential reorganization to the issuing corporation or a person related to the issuing corporation (see definition of "related person" in § 1.368-1(e)).

(i) *Distributions.*—One or more distributions to shareholders (including distribution(s) that involve the assumption of liabilities) are described in this paragraph (k)(1)(i) if—

(A) The property distributed consists of—

(1) Assets of the acquired corporation, the acquiring corporation, or the surviving corporation, as the case may be, or an interest in an entity received in exchange for such assets in a transfer described in paragraph (k)(1)(ii) of this section;

(2) Stock of the acquired corporation provided that such distribution(s) of stock do not cause the acquired corporation to cease to be a member of the qualified group (as defined in § 1.368-1(d)(4)(ii)); or

(3) A combination thereof; and

(B) The aggregate of such distributions does not consist of—

(1) An amount of assets of the acquired corporation, the acquiring corporation (disregarding assets held prior to the potential reorganization), or the surviving corporation (disregarding assets of the merged corporation), as the case may be, that would result in a liquidation of such corporation for Federal income tax purposes; or

(2) All of the stock of the acquired corporation that was acquired in the transaction.

(ii) *Transfers Other Than Distributions.*—One or more other transfers are described in this paragraph (k)(1)(ii) if—

(A) The transfer(s) do not consist of one or more distributions to shareholders;

(B) The property transferred consists of—

(1) Part or all of the assets of the acquired corporation, the acquiring corporation, or the surviving corporation, as the case may be;

(2) Part or all of the stock of the acquired corporation, the acquiring corporation, or the surviving corporation, as the case may be, provided that such transfer(s) of stock do not cause such corporation to cease to be a member of the qualified group (as defined in § 1.368-1(d)(4)(ii)); or

(3) A combination thereof; and

(C) The acquired corporation, the acquiring corporation, or the surviving corporation, as the case may be, does not terminate its corporate existence for Federal income tax purposes in connection with the transfer(s).

(2) *Examples.*—The following examples illustrate the application of this paragraph (k). Except as otherwise noted, P is the issuing corporation, and T is an unrelated target corporation. All corporations have only one class of stock outstanding. T operates a bakery that supplies delectable pastries and cookies to local retail stores. The acquiring corporate group produces a variety of baked goods for nationwide distribution. Except as otherwise noted, P owns all of the stock of S-1 and 80 percent of the stock of S-4, S-1 owns 80 percent of the stock of S-2 and 50 percent of the stock of S-5, S-2 owns 80 percent of the stock of S-3, and S-4 owns the remaining 50 percent of the stock of S-5. The examples are as follows:

Example 1. Transfers of acquired assets to members of the qualified group after a reorganization under section 368(a)(1)(C). (i) *Facts.* Pursuant to a plan of reorganization, T transfers all of its assets to S-1 solely in exchange for P stock, which T distributes to its shareholders, and S-1's assumption of T's liabilities. In addition, pursuant to the plan, S-1 transfers all of the T assets to S-2, and S-2 transfers all of the T assets to S-3.

(ii) *Analysis.* Under this paragraph (k), the transaction, which otherwise qualifies as a reorganization under section 368(a)(1)(C), is not disqualified by the successive transfers of all of the T assets to S-2 and from S-2 to S-3 because the transfers are not one or more distributions to shareholders, the transfers consist of part or all of the assets of the acquiring corporation, the acquiring corporation does not terminate its corporate existence for Federal income tax purposes in connection with the transfers, and the transaction satisfies the requirements of § 1.368-1(d).

Example 2. Distribution of acquired assets to a member of the qualified group after a reorganization under section 368(a)(1)(C). (i) *Facts.* Pursuant to a plan of reorganization, T transfers all of its assets to S-1 solely in exchange for P stock, which T distributes to its shareholders, and S-1's assumption of T's liabilities. In addition, pursuant to the plan, S-1 distributes half of the T assets to P, and P assumes half of the T liabilities.

(ii) *Analysis.* Under this paragraph (k), the transaction, which otherwise qualifies as a reorganization under section 368(a)(1)(C), is not disqualified by the distribution of half of the T assets from S-1 to P, or P's assumption of half of the T liabilities from S-1, because the distribution consists of assets of the acquiring corporation, the distribution does not consist of an amount of S-1's assets that would result in a liquidation of S-1 for Federal income tax purposes (disregarding S-1's assets held prior to the acquisition of T), and the transaction satisfies the requirements of § 1.368-1(d).

Example 3. Indirect distribution of acquired assets to a member of the qualified group after a reorganization under section 368(a)(1)(C). (i) *Facts.* The facts are the same as *Example 2*, except that, instead of S-1 distributing half of the T assets to P and having P assume half of the T liabilities, S-1 contributes half of the T assets to newly formed S-6, S-6 assumes half of the T liabilities, and S-1 distributes all of the S-6 stock to P.

(ii) *Analysis.* Under this paragraph (k), the transaction, which otherwise qualifies as a reorganization under section 368(a)(1)(C), is not disqualified by the transfer of half of the T assets to S-6 and the distribution of the S-6 stock to P because the transfer of half of the T assets to S-6 is described in paragraph (k)(1)(ii) of this section, the distribution of the S-6 stock to P is an indirect distribution of assets of the acquiring corporation, the distribution does not consist of an amount of S-1's assets that would result in a liquidation of S-1 for Federal income tax purposes (disregarding S-1's assets held prior to the acquisition of T), and the transaction satisfies the requirements of § 1.368-1(d).

Example 4. Distribution of acquired stock to a controlled partnership after a reorganization under section 368(a)(1)(B). (i) *Facts.* P owns 80 percent of the stock of S-1, and an 80-percent interest in PRS, a partnership. S-4 owns the remaining 20-percent interest in PRS. PRS owns the remaining 20 percent of the stock of S-1. Pursuant to a plan of reorganization, the T shareholders transfer all of their T stock to S-1 solely in exchange for P stock. In addition, pursuant to the plan, S-1 distributes 90 percent of the T stock to PRS in redemption of 5 percent of the stock of S-1 owned by PRS.

(ii) *Analysis.* Under this paragraph (k), the transaction, which otherwise qualifies as a reorganization under section 368(a)(1)(B), is not disqualified by the distribution of 90 percent of the T stock from S-1 to PRS because the distribution consists of less than all of the stock of the acquired corporation that was acquired in the transaction, the distribution does not cause T to cease to be a member of the qualified group (as defined in § 1.368-1(d)(4)(ii)), and the transaction satisfies the requirements of § 1.368-1(d).

Example 5. Transfer of acquired stock to a non-controlled partnership. (i) *Facts.* Pursuant to a plan, the T shareholders transfer all of their T stock to S-1 solely in exchange for P stock. In addition, as part of the plan, T distributes half of its assets to S-1, S-1 assumes half of the T liabilities, and S-1 transfers the T stock to S-2. S-2 and U, an unrelated corporation, form a new partnership, PRS. Immediately thereafter, S-2 transfers all of the T stock to PRS in exchange for a 50 percent interest in PRS, and U transfers cash to PRS in exchange for a 50 percent interest in PRS.

(ii) *Analysis.* Under this paragraph (k), the transaction, which otherwise qualifies as a reorganization under section 368(a)(1)(B), is not disqualified by the distribution of half of the T assets from T to S-1, or S-1's assumption of half of the T liabilities from T, because the distribution consists of assets of the acquired corporation, the distribution does not consist of an amount of T's assets that would result in a liquidation of T for Federal income tax purposes, and the transaction satisfies the requirements of § 1.368-1(d). Further, this paragraph (k) describes the transfer of the acquired stock from S-1 to S-2, but does not describe the transfer of the acquired stock from S-2 to PRS because such transfer causes T to cease to be a member of the qualified group (as defined in § 1.368-1(d)(4)(ii)). Therefore, the characterization of this transaction must be determined under the relevant provisions of law, including the step transaction doctrine. See § 1.368-1(a). The transaction fails to meet the control requirement of a reorganization described in section 368(a)(1)(B) because immediately after the acquisition of the T stock, the acquiring corporation does not have control of T.

Example 6. Transfers of acquired assets to members of the qualified group after a reorganization under section 368(a)(1)(D). (i) *Facts.* P owns all of the stock of T. Pursuant to a plan of reorganization, T transfers all of its assets to S-1 solely in exchange for S-1 stock, which T distributes to P, and S-1's assumption of T's liabilities. In addition, pursuant to the plan, S-1 transfers all of the T assets to S-2, and S-2 transfers all of the T assets to S-3.

(ii) *Analysis.* Under this paragraph (k), the transaction, which otherwise qualifies as a reorganization under section 368(a)(1)(D), is not disqualified by the successive transfers of all the T assets from S-1 to S-2 and from S-2 to S-3 because the transfers are not one or more distributions to shareholders, the transfers consist of part or all of the assets of the acquiring corporation, the acquiring corporation does not terminate its corporate existence for Federal income tax purposes in connection with the transfers, and the transaction satisfies the requirements of § 1.368-1(d).

Example 7. Transfer of stock of the acquiring corporation to a member of the qualified group after a reorganization under section 368(a)(1)(A) by reason of section 368(a)(2)(D). (i) *Facts.* Pursuant to a plan of reorganization, S-1 acquires all of the T assets in the merger of T into S-1. In the merger, the T shareholders receive solely P stock. Also, pursuant to the plan, P transfers all of the S-1 stock to S-4.

(ii) *Analysis.* Under this paragraph (k), the transaction, which otherwise qualifies as a reorganization under section 368(a)(1)(A) by reason of section 368(a)(2)(D), is not disqualified by the transfer of all of the S-1 stock to S-4 because the transfer is not a distribution to shareholders, the transfer consists of part or all of the stock of the acquiring corporation, the transfer does not cause S-1 to cease to be a member of the qualified group (as defined in § 1.368-1(d)(4)(ii)), the acquiring corporation does not terminate its corporate existence for Federal income tax purposes in connection with the transfer, and the transaction satisfies the requirements of § 1.368-1(d).

Example 8. Transfer of acquired assets to a partnership after a reorganization under section 368(a)(1)(A) by reason of section 368(a)(2)(D). (i) *Facts.* Pursuant to a plan of reorganization, S-1 acquires all of the T assets in the merger of T into S-1. In the merger, the T shareholders receive solely P stock. In addition, pursuant to the plan, S-1 transfers all of the T assets to PRS, a partnership in which S-1 owns a 33 1/3-percent interest. PRS continues T's historic business. S-1 does not perform active and substantial management functions as a partner with respect to PRS' business.

(ii) *Analysis.* Under this paragraph (k), the transaction, which otherwise qualifies as a reorganization under section 368(a)(1)(A) by reason of section 368(a)(2)(D), is not disqualified by the transfer of T assets from S-1 to PRS because the transfer is not a distribution to shareholders, the transfer consists of part or all of the assets of the acquiring corporation, the acquiring corporation does not terminate its corporate existence for Federal income tax purposes in connection with the transfers, and the transaction satisfies the requirements of § 1.368-1(d).

Example 9. Sale of acquired assets to a member of the qualified group after a reorganization under section 368(a)(1)(C). (i) *Facts.* Pursuant to a plan of reorganization, T transfers all of its assets to S-1 in exchange for P stock, which T distributes to its shareholders, and S-1's assumption of T's liabilities. In addition, pursuant to the plan, S-1 sells all of the T assets to S-5 for cash equal to the fair market value of those assets.

(ii) *Analysis.* Under this paragraph (k), the transaction, which otherwise qualifies as a reorganization under section 368(a)(1)(C), is not disqualified by the sale of all of the T assets from S-1 to S-5 because the transfer is not a distribution to shareholders, the transfer consists of part or all of the assets of the acquiring corporation, the acquiring corporation does not terminate its corporate existence for Federal income tax purposes in connection with the transfer, and the transaction satisfies the requirements of § 1.368-1(d).

(3) *Effective/applicability dates.*—This paragraph (k) applies to transactions occurring on or after May 9, 2008, except that it does not apply to any transaction occurring pursuant to a written agreement which is binding before May 9, 2008, and at all times after that.

(l) *Certain transactions treated as reorganizations described in section 368(a)(1)(D).*—(1) *General rule.*—In order to qualify as a reorganization under section 368(a)(1)(D), a corporation (transferor corporation) must transfer all or part of its assets to another corporation (transferee corporation) and immediately after the transfer the transferor corporation, or one or more of its shareholders (including persons who were shareholders immediately before the transfer), or any combination thereof, must be in control of the transferee corporation; but only if, in pursuance of the plan, stock or securities of the transferee are distributed in a transaction which qualifies under section 354, 355, or 356.

(2) *Distribution requirement.*—(i) *In general.*—For purposes of paragraph (l)(1) of this section, a transaction otherwise described in section 368(a)(1)(D) will be treated as satisfying the requirements of sections 368(a)(1)(D) and 354(b)(1)(B) notwithstanding that there is no actual issuance of stock and/or securities of the transferee corporation if the same person or persons own, directly or indirectly, all of the stock of the transferor and transferee corporations in identical proportions. In cases where no consideration is received or the value of the consideration received in the transaction is less than the fair market value of the transferor corporation's assets, the transferee corporation will be treated as issuing stock with a value equal to the excess of the fair market value of the transferor corporation's assets over the value of the consideration actually received in the transaction. In cases where the value of the consideration received in the transaction is equal to the fair market value of the transferor corporation's assets, the transferee corporation will be deemed to issue a nominal share of stock to the transferor corporation in addition to the actual consideration exchanged for the transferor corporation's assets. The nominal share of stock in the transferee corporation will then be deemed distributed by the transferor corporation to the shareholders of the transferor corporation, as part of the exchange for the stock of such shareholders. Where appropriate, the nominal share will be further transferred through chains of ownership to the extent necessary to reflect the actual ownership of the transferor and transferee corporations. Similar treatment to that of the preceding two sentences shall apply where the transferee corporation is treated as issuing stock with a value equal to the excess of the fair market value of the transferor corporation's assets over the value of the consideration actually received in the transaction.

(ii) *Attribution.*—For purposes of paragraph (l)(2)(i) of this section, ownership of stock will be determined by applying the principles of section 318(a)(2) without regard to the 50 percent limitation in section 318(a)(2)(C). In addition, an individual and all members of his family described in section 318(a)(1) shall be treated as one individual.

(iii) *De minimis variations in ownership and certain stock not taken into account.*—For purposes of paragraph (l)(2)(i) of this section, the same person or persons will be treated as owning, directly or indirectly, all of the stock of the transferor and transferee corporations in identical proportions notwithstanding the fact that there is a de minimis variation in shareholder identity or proportionality of ownership. Additionally, for purposes of paragraph (l)(2)(i) of this section, stock described in section 1504(a)(4) is not taken into account.

(iv) *Exception.*—Paragraph (l)(2) of this section does not apply to a transaction otherwise described in § 1.358-6(b)(2).

(3) *Examples.*—The following examples illustrate the principles of paragraph (l) of this section. For purposes of these examples, each of A, B, C, and D is an individual, T is the acquired corporation, S is the acquiring corporation, P is the parent corporation, and each of S1, S2, S3, and S4 is a direct or indirect subsidiary of P. Further, all of the requirements of section 368(a)(1)(D) other than the requirement that stock or securities be distributed in a transaction to which section 354 or 356 applies are satisfied. The examples are as follows:

Example 1. A owns all the stock of T and S. The T stock has a fair market value of $100x. T sells all of its assets to S in exchange for $100x of cash and immediately liquidates. Because there is complete shareholder identity and proportionality of ownership in T and S, under paragraph (l)(2)(i) of this section, the requirements of sections 368(a)(1)(D) and 354(b)(1)(B) are treated as satisfied notwithstanding the fact that no S stock is issued. Pursuant to paragraph (l)(2)(i) of this section, S will be deemed to issue a nominal share of S stock to T in addition to the $100x of cash actually exchanged for the T assets, and T will be deemed to distribute all such consideration to A. The transaction qualifies as a reorganization described in section 368(a)(1)(D).

Example 2. The facts are the same as in *Example 1* except that C, A's son, owns all of the stock of S. Under paragraph (l)(2)(ii) of this section, A and C are treated as one individual. Accordingly, there is complete shareholder identity and proportionality of ownership in T and S. Therefore, under paragraph (l)(2)(i) of this section, the requirements of sections 368(a)(1)(D) and 354(b)(1)(B) are treated as satisfied notwithstanding the fact that no S stock is issued. Pursuant to paragraph (l)(2)(i) of this section, S will be deemed to issue a nominal share of S stock to T in addition to the $100x of cash actually exchanged for the T assets, and T will be deemed to distribute all such consideration to A. A will be deemed to transfer the nominal share of S stock to C. The transaction qualifies as a reorganization described in section 368(a)(1)(D).

Example 3. P owns all of the stock of S1 and S2. S1 owns all of the stock of S3, which owns all of the stock of T. S2 owns all of the stock of S4, which owns all of the stock of S. The T stock has a fair market value of $70x. T sells all of its assets to S in exchange for $70x of cash and immediately liquidates. Under paragraph (l)(2)(ii) of this section, there is indirect, complete shareholder identity and proportionality of ownership in T and S. Accordingly, the requirements of sections 368(a)(1)(D) and 354(b)(1)(B) are treated as satisfied notwithstanding the fact that no S stock is issued. Pursuant to paragraph (l)(2)(i) of this section, S will be deemed to issue a nominal share of S stock to T in addition to the $70x of cash actually exchanged for the T assets, and T will be deemed to distribute all such consideration to S3. S3 will be deemed to distribute the nominal share of S stock to S1, which, in turn, will be deemed to distribute the nominal share of S stock to P. P will be deemed to transfer the nominal share of S stock to S2, which, in turn, will be deemed to transfer such share of S stock to S4. The transaction qualifies as a reorganization described in section 368(a)(1)(D).

Example 4. A, B, and C own 34%, 33%, and 33%, respectively, of the stock of T. The T stock has a fair market value of $100x. A, B, and C each own 33% of the stock of S. D owns the remaining 1% of the stock of S. T sells all of its assets to S in exchange for $100x of cash and immediately liquidates. For purposes of determining whether the distribution requirement of sections 368(a)(1)(D) and 354(b)(1)(B) is met, under paragraph (l)(2)(iii) of this section, D's ownership of a de minimis amount of stock of S is disregarded and the transaction is treated as if there is complete shareholder identity and proportionality of ownership in T and S. Because there is complete shareholder identity and proportionality of ownership in T and S, under paragraph (l)(2)(i) of this section, the requirements of sections 368(a)(1)(D) and 354(b)(1)(B) are treated as satisfied notwithstanding the fact that no S stock is issued. Pursuant to paragraph (l)(2)(i) of this section, S will be deemed to issue a nominal share of S stock to T in addition to the $100x of cash actually exchanged for the T assets, T will be deemed to distribute all such consideration to A, B, and C, and the nominal S stock will be deemed transferred among the S shareholders to the extent necessary to reflect their actual ownership of S. The transaction qualifies as a reorganization described in section 368(a)(1)(D).

Example 5. The facts are the same as in *Example 4* except that A, B, and C own 34%, 33%, and 33%, respectively, of the common stock of T and S. D owns preferred stock in S described in section 1504(a)(4). For purposes of determining whether the distribution requirement of sections 368(a)(1)(D) and 354(b)(1)(B) is met, under paragraph (l)(2)(iii) of this section, D's ownership of S stock described in section 1504(a)(4) is ignored and the transaction is treated as if there is complete shareholder identity and proportionality of ownership in T and S. Because there is complete shareholder identity and proportionality of ownership in T and S, under paragraph (l)(2)(i) of this section, the requirements of sections 368(a)(1)(D) and 354(b)(1)(B) are treated as satisfied notwithstanding the fact that no S stock is issued. Pursuant to paragraph (l)(2)(i) of this section, S will be deemed to issue a nominal share of S stock to T in addition to the $100x of cash actually exchanged for the T assets, and T will be deemed to distribute all such consideration to A, B, and C. The transaction qualifies as a reorganization described in section 368(a)(1)(D).

Example 6. A and B each own 50% of the stock of T. The T stock has a fair market value of $100x. B and C own 90% and 10%, respectively, of the stock of S. T sells all of its assets to S in exchange for $100x of cash and immediately liquidates. Because complete shareholder identity and proportionality of ownership in T and S does not exist, paragraph (l)(2)(i) of this section does not apply. The requirements of sections 368(a)(1)(D) and 354(b)(1)(B) are not satisfied, and the transaction does not qualify as a reorganization described in section 368(a)(1)(D).

* * *

(m) *Qualification as a reorganization under section 368(a)(1)(F).*—(1) *Mere change.*—To qualify as a reorganization under section 368(a)(1)(F), a transaction must result in a mere change in identity, form, or place of organization of one corporation, however effected (a mere change). A mere change can consist of a transaction that involves an actual or deemed transfer of property from one corporation (a transferor corporation) to one other corporation (a resulting corporation). Such a transaction is a mere change and qualifies as a reorganization under section 368(a)(1)(F) only if all the requirements set forth in paragraphs (m)(1)(i) through (vi) of this section are satisfied. For purposes of this paragraph (m), a transaction or a series of related transactions that can be tested against the requirements set forth in paragraphs (m)(1)(i) through (vi) of this section (a potential F reorganization) begins when the transferor corporation begins transferring (or is deemed to begin transferring) its assets, directly or indirectly, to the resulting corporation, and it ends when the transferor corporation has distributed (or is deemed to have distributed) to its shareholders the consideration it receives (or is deemed to receive) from the resulting corporation and has completely liquidated for federal income tax purposes. For purposes of this paragraph (m), deemed transfers include, for example, those provided in § 301.7701-3(g)(1)(iv) of this chapter (when an entity disregarded as separate from its owner elects under paragraph § 301.7701-3(c)(1)(i) of this chapter to be classified as an association, the owner of the entity is deemed to transfer all of the assets and liabilities of the entity to the association in exchange for stock of the association). Deemed transfers also include those resulting from the application of step transaction principles. For example, step transaction principles may disregard a transitory holding of property by an individual after a liquidation of the transferor corporation and before a subsequent transfer of the transferor corporation's property to the resulting corporation. Step transaction principles may also treat a contribution of all the stock of the transferor corporation to the resulting corporation, followed by a liquidation (or deemed liquidation) of the transferor corporation, as a deemed transfer of the transferor corporation's property to the resulting corporation, followed by a distribution of stock of the resulting corporation in complete liquidation of the transferor corporation.

(i) *Resulting corporation stock distributed in exchange for transferor corporation stock.*—Immediately after the potential F reorganization, all the stock of the resulting corporation, including any stock of the resulting corporation issued before the potential F reorganization, must have been distributed (or deemed distributed) in exchange for stock of the transferor corporation in the potential F reorganization. However, for purposes of this paragraph (m)(1)(i) and paragraph (m)(1)(ii) of this section, a de minimis amount of stock issued by the resulting corporation other than in respect of stock of the transferor corporation to facilitate the organization of the resulting corporation or maintain its legal existence is disregarded.

(ii) *Identity of stock ownership.*—The same person or persons must own all of the stock of the transferor corporation, determined immediately before the potential F reorganization, and of the resulting corporation, determined immediately after the potential F reorganization, in identical proportions. However, this requirement is not violated if one or more holders of stock in the transferor corporation exchange stock in the transferor corporation for stock of equivalent value in the resulting corporation, but having different terms from those of the stock in the transferor corporation, or receive a distribution of money or other property from either the transferor corporation or the resulting corporation, whether or not in exchange for stock in the transferor corporation or the resulting corporation.

(iii) *Prior assets or attributes of resulting corporation.*—The resulting corporation may not hold any property or have any tax attributes (including those specified in section 381(c)) immediately before the potential F reorganization. However, this requirement is not violated if the resulting corporation holds or has held a de minimis amount of assets to facilitate its organization or maintain its legal existence, and has tax attributes related to holding those assets, or holds the proceeds of borrowings undertaken in connection with the potential F reorganization.

(iv) *Liquidation of transferor corporation.*—The transferor corporation must completely liquidate, for federal income tax purposes, in the potential F reorganization. However, the transferor corporation is not required to dissolve under applicable law and may retain a de minimis amount of assets for the sole purpose of preserving its legal existence.

(v) *Resulting corporation is the only acquiring corporation.*—Immediately after the potential F reorganization, no corporation other than the resulting corporation may hold property that was held by the transferor corporation immediately before the potential F reorganization, if such other corporation would, as a result, succeed to and take into account the items of the transferor corporation described in section 381(c).

(vi) *Transferor corporation is the only acquired corporation.*—Immediately after the potential F reorganization, the resulting corporation may not hold property acquired from a corporation other than the transferor corporation if the resulting corporation would, as a result, succeed to and take into account the items of such other corporation described in section 381(c).

(2) *Non-application of continuity of interest and continuity of business enterprise requirements.*—A continuity of the business enterprise and a continuity of interest are not required for a potential F reorganization to qualify as a reorganization under section 368(a)(1)(F). *See* §1.368-1(b).

(3) *Related transactions.*—(i) *Series of transactions.*—A potential F reorganization consisting of a series of related transactions that together result in a mere change of one corporation may qualify as a reorganization under section 368(a)(1)(F), whether or not certain steps in the series, viewed in isolation, could be subject to other Code provisions, such as sections 304(a), 331, 332, or 351. However, *see* paragraph (k) of this section for transactions that qualify as reorganizations under section 368(a) and will not be recharacterized as a mere change as a result of one or more subsequent transfers of assets or stock.

(ii) *Mere change within a larger transaction.*—A potential F reorganization that qualifies as a reorganization under section 368(a)(1)(F) may occur before, within, or after other transactions that effect more than a mere change, even if the resulting corporation has only transitory existence. Related events that precede or follow the potential F reorganization generally will not cause that potential F reorganization to fail to qualify as a reorganization under section 368(a)(1)(F). Qualification of a potential F reorganization as a reorganization under section 368(a)(1)(F) will not alter the character of other transactions for federal income tax purposes, and step transaction principles may be applied to other transactions without regard to whether certain steps qualify as a reorganization or part of a reorganization under section 368(a)(1)(F).

(iii) *Distributions treated as separate transactions.*—As provided in paragraph (m)(1)(ii) of this section, a potential F reorganization may qualify as a mere change even though a holder of stock in the transferor corporation receives a distribution of money or other property from either the transferor corporation or the resulting corporation. If a shareholder receives money or other property (including in exchange for its shares) from the transferor corporation or the resulting corporation in a potential F reorganization that qualifies as a reorganization under section 368(a)(1)(F), then the receipt of money or other property (including any exchanged for shares) is treated as an unrelated, separate transaction from the reorganization, whether or not connected in a formal sense. *See* §1.301-1(l).

(iv) *Transactions also qualifying under other provisions of section 368(a)(1).*—In certain cases, a potential F reorganization would (but for this paragraph (m)(3)(iv)) qualify both as a reorganization under section 368(a)(1)(F) and as a reorganization or part of a reorganization under another provision of section 368(a)(1). The following rules determine which of these overlapping qualifications applies.

(A) If the potential F reorganization or a step thereof qualifies as a reorganization or part of a reorganization under another provision of section 368(a)(1), and if a corporation in control (within the meaning of section 368(c)) of the resulting corporation is a party to such other reorganization (within the meaning of section 368(b)), the potential F reorganization will not qualify as a reorganization under section 368(a)(1)(F).

(B) Except as provided in paragraph (m)(3)(iv)(A) of this section, if, but for this paragraph (m)(3)(iv)(B), the potential F reorganization would qualify as a reorganization under both section 368(a)(1)(F) and one or more of sections 368(a)(1)(A), 368(a)(1)(C), or 368(a)(1)(D), then for all federal income tax purposes the potential F reorganization will qualify as a reorganization only under section 368(a)(1)(F).

(4) *Examples.*—The following examples illustrate the application of this paragraph (m). Unless the facts otherwise indicate, A, B, and C are domestic individuals; P, S, T, X, Y, and Z (and similar designations) are domestic corporations; each transaction is entered into for a valid business purpose; all persons and transactions are unrelated; and all other relevant facts are set forth in the examples.

Example 1. Cash contribution and redemption – no mere change. C owns all of the stock of X, a State A corporation. The net value of X's assets and liabilities is $1,000,000. Y, a State B corporation, seeks to acquire the assets of X for cash. To effect the acquisition, Y and X enter into an agreement under which Y will contribute $1,000,000 to Z, a newly formed corporation of which Y is the sole shareholder, in exchange for Z stock and X will merge into Z. In the merger, C surrenders all of the X stock and receives the $1,000,000 Y contributed to Z. C receives no Z stock in the transaction. After the merger, Y holds all of the Z stock, and Z holds all of the assets and liabilities previously held by X. Z stock is not distributed to the shareholders of X in exchange for their stock in X as required by paragraph (m)(1)(i) of this section, and the transaction results in a change in the ownership of X that does not result from an exchange or distribution described in paragraph (m)(1)(ii) of this section. Therefore, the merger of X into Z is not a mere change of X and does not qualify as a reorganization under section 368(a)(1)(F).

Example 2. Cash redemption – mere change. A owns 75%, and B owns 25%, of the stock of X, a State A corporation. The management of X determines that it would be in the best interest of X to reorganize under the laws of State B. Accordingly, X forms Y, a State B corporation, and X and Y enter into an agreement under which X will merge into Y. A does not wish to own stock in Y. In the merger, A surrenders A's X stock and receives cash, and B surrenders all of B's X stock and receives all the stock of Y. The change in ownership caused by A's surrender of X stock results from a distribution and exchange described in paragraph (m)(1)(ii) of this section. Therefore, the merger of X into Y is a mere change of X and qualifies as a reorganization under section 368(a)(1)(F). Under paragraph (m)(3)(iii) of this section, A's surrender of X stock for cash is treated as a transaction, separate from the reorganization, to which section 302(a) applies.

Example 3. Pre-transaction de minimis stock issuance – mere change – other provisions of section 368(a)(1). P owns all of the stock of S, a Country A corporation. The management of P determines that it would be in the best interest of S to change its place of incorporation to Country B. Under Country B law, a corporation must have at least two shareholders to enjoy limited liability. P is advised by its Country B advisors that the new corporation should issue 1% of its stock to a shareholder that is not P's nominee to assure satisfaction of the two-shareholder requirement. As part of an integrated plan, C, an officer of S, organizes Y, a Country B corporation with 1,000 shares of common stock authorized, and contributes cash to Y in exchange for ten of the common shares. S then merges into Y under the laws of Country A and Country B. Pursuant to the plan of merger, P surrenders its shares of S stock and receives 990 shares of Y common stock. The ten shares of Y stock issued to C not in respect of the S stock are de minimis and are used to facilitate the organization of Y within the meaning of paragraph (m)(1)(i) of this section. Therefore, the issuance of this stock to a new shareholder does not prevent the merger of S into Y from qualifying as a mere change of S. Accordingly, the merger is a reorganization under section 368(a)(1)(F). Without regard to the merger's qualification under section 368(a)(1)(F), the merger would also qualify as a reorganization under both section 368(a)(1)(A) and section 368(a)(1)(D). Under paragraph (m)(3)(iv)(B) of this section, if a potential F reorganization qualifies as a reorganization under section 368(a)(1)(F), and would also qualify under one or more of sections 368(a)(1)(A) or 368(a)(1)(D), the potential F reorganization qualifies only as a reorganization under 368(a)(1)(F), and neither section 368(a)(1)(A) nor section 368(a)(1)(D) will apply.

Example 4. Pre-transaction assets, attributes – no mere change. A owns all of the stock of P, and P owns all of the stock of S, which is engaged in a manufacturing business. P has owned the stock of S for many years. P owns no assets other than the stock of S. A decides to eliminate the holding company structure by merging P into S. Because it operates a manufacturing business, the potential resulting corporation, S, holds property and has tax attributes immediately before the potential F reorganization. Therefore, under paragraph (m)(1)(iii) of this section, the merger of P into S is not a mere change of P and does not qualify as a reorganization under section 368(a)(1)(F). The same result would occur under paragraph (m)(1)(iii) of this section if, instead of P merging into S, S merged into P, because P, the potential resulting corporation, holds property (the stock of S) and has tax attributes immediately before the potential F reorganization.

Example 5. Series of related transactions – mere change. P owns all of the stock of S1, a State A corporation. The management of P determines that it would be in the best interest of S1 to change its place of incorporation to State B. Accordingly, under an integrated plan, P forms S2, a new State B corporation; P contributes the S1 stock to S2; and S1 merges into S2 under the laws of State A and State B. Under paragraph (m)(3)(i) of this section, a series of transactions that together result in a mere change of one corporation may qualify as a reorganization under section 368(a)(1)(F). The contribution of S1 stock to S2 and the merger of S1 into S2 together constitute a mere change of S1. Therefore, the potential F reorganization qualifies as a reorganization under section 368(a)(1)(F). Without regard to its qualification under section 368(a)(1)(F), the potential F reorganization would also qualify as a reorganization under both section 368(a)(1)(A) and section 368(a)(1)(D). Under paragraph (m)(3)(iv)(B) of this section, if a potential F reorganization qualifies as a reorganization under section 368(a)(1)(F) and would also qualify under one or more of sections 368(a)(1)(A) or 368(a)(1)(D), it qualifies only as a reorganization under 368(a)(1)(F), and neither section 368(a)(1)(A) nor section 368(a)(1)(D) will apply. The result would be the same with respect to qualification under section 368(a)(1)(F) if, instead of merging into S2, S1 completely liquidates or is deemed to liquidate by reason of a conversion in an entity disregarded as separate from its owner under §301.7701-3 of this chapter.

Example 6. Post-transaction stock sale – mere change. P owns all of the stock of S1, a State A corporation. The management of P determines that it would be in the best interest of S1 to change its place of incorporation to State B. Accordingly, P forms S2, a new State B corporation. S1 then merges into S2 under the laws of State A and State B. Immediately thereafter, and as part of the same plan, P sells all of its stock in S2 to an unrelated party. Without regard to P's sale of S2 stock, the merger of S1 into S2 is a potential F reorganization that qualifies as a mere change of S1 within the meaning of paragraph (m)(1) of this section. Under paragraph (m)(3)(ii) of this section, related events that occur before or after a potential F reorganization that qualifies as a mere change generally do not cause that potential F reorganization to fail to qualify as a reorganization under section 368(a)(1)(F). Therefore, P's sale of the S2 stock is disregarded in determining whether the merger of S1 into S2 is a mere change of S1. Accordingly, the merger of S1 into S2 qualifies as a reorganization under section 368(a)(1)(F). The result would be the same if, instead of the S2 stock being sold by P, S2 merges into a previously unrelated corporation and terminates its separate existence.

Example 7. Post-transaction redemption – mere change. A owns all of the stock of T. P owns all of the stock of S. Each of T, P, and S is a State A corporation engaged in a manufacturing business. The following transactions occur pursuant to a single plan. First, T merges into S with A receiving solely stock in P. Second, P changes its state of incorporation to State B by merging into newly incorporated New P under the laws of State A and State B. Third, New P redeems all the New P stock issued to A in respect of A's P stock (initially issued to A in respect of A's T stock) for cash. Without regard to the other steps, the merger of P into New P is a potential F reorganization that qualifies as a reorganization under section 368(a)(1)(F). Under paragraph (m)(3)(ii) of this section, related events that occur before or after a potential F reorganization that qualifies as a mere change generally do not prevent that potential F reorganization from qualifying as a reorganization under section 368(a)(1)(F). Therefore, the merger of P into New P qualifies as a reorganization under section 368(a)(1)(F). Under paragraph (m)(3)(ii) of this section, the qualification of the merger of P into New P as a reorganization under section 368(a)(1)(F) does not alter the tax treatment of the merger of T into S. Because the P shares received by A in respect of the T shares (exchanged for New P shares in the mere change of P into New P) are redeemed for cash pursuant to the plan, the merger of T into S does not satisfy the continuity of interest requirement of §1.368-1(e) and therefore does not qualify as a reorganization under section 368(a).

Example 8. Series of related transactions – mere change. P owns all of the stock of S, a

State A corporation. The management of P determines that it would be in the best interest of S to change its form from a State A corporation to a State A limited partnership but to continue to be treated as a corporation for federal tax purposes. Accordingly, P contributes 1% of the S stock to newly formed LLC, a limited liability company, in exchange for all of the membership interests in LLC. P is the sole member of LLC. Under § 301.7701-3 of this chapter, LLC is disregarded as an entity separate from its owner, P. Then, under a State A statute, S converts to a State A limited partnership. In the conversion, P's interest as a 99% shareholder of S is converted into a 99% limited partner interest, and LLC's interest as a 1% shareholder of S is converted into a 1% general partner interest. S also elects, under § 301.7701-3(c) of this chapter, to be classified as a corporation for federal income tax purposes, effective on the same day as the conversion. Under paragraph (m)(3)(i) of this section, the conversion of S from a State A corporation to a State A limited partnership, together with the election to treat S as a corporation for federal tax purposes, results in a mere change of S and qualifies as a reorganization under section 368(a)(1)(F).

Example 9. Other acquiring corporation – no mere change. P owns 80%, and A owns 20%, of the stock of S. A and the management of P determine that it would be in the best interest of S to completely liquidate while A continues to operate part of the business of S in corporate form. Accordingly, S distributes 80% of its assets to P and 20% of its assets to A; S dissolves; and A contributes the assets it receives from S to newly incorporated New S in exchange for all of the stock of New S. S's distribution of 80% of its property to P as part of the complete liquidation of S meets the requirements of section 332. Thus, section 381(a)(1) applies to P's acquisition of 80% of the property held by S immediately before the transaction. Under paragraph (m)(1)(v) of this section, the potential F reorganization in which 20% of the property held by S immediately before the transaction is transferred to New S cannot be a mere change of S, because section 381(a) applies to P's acquisition of property held by S immediately before the potential F reorganization. Accordingly, sections 331 and 336 apply to A's acquisition of property from S and S's distribution of property to A, and section 351 applies to A's contribution of that property to New S.

Example 10. Other acquiring corporation – no mere change. P owns all of the stock of S1. The management of P determines that it would be in the best interest of S1 to merge S1 into P. Accordingly, pursuant to a state merger statute, S1 merges into P. Immediately afterward and as part of the same plan, P contributes 50% of the former assets of S1 to newly incorporated S2 in exchange for all of the stock of S2. The transaction does not qualify as a complete liquidation of S1 under section 332 (because of the reincorporation of some of S1's assets) but does qualify as a reorganization under section 368(a)(1)(A) by reason of section 368(a)(2)(C) and paragraph (k) of this section. Under paragraph (m)(1)(v) of this section, the potential F reorganization in which some of the former assets of S1 are transferred (in form) first to P, and then to S2, is not a mere change of S1, because section 381(a) applies to P's acquisition of property held by S1 immediately before the potential F reorganization. Furthermore, under paragraph (m)(3)(iv)(A) of this section, P, the corporation in control of S2 within the meaning of section 368(c), is a party to the reorganization within the meaning of section 368(b). Thus, the indirect transfer of property from S1 to S2 does not qualify under section 368(a)(1)(F).

Example 11. Other acquiring corporation – mere change. P owns all of the stock of S1. S1's only asset is all of the equity interest in LLC2, a domestic limited liability company. Under § 301.7701-3 of this chapter, LLC2 is disregarded as an entity separate from its owner, S1. Pursuant to an integrated plan to undergo a reorganization under 368(a)(1)(F), S1 and LLC2 undergo the following two state law conversions. First, under state law LLC2 converts into S2, a corporation. Second, under state law S1 converts into LLC1, a domestic limited liability company. Under § 301.7701-3 of this chapter, LLC1 is disregarded as an entity separate from its owner, P. As a result of the two conversions, S1 is deemed to transfer its assets to S2 in exchange for all of the stock in S2 and then distribute the S2 stock to P in complete liquidation of S1. The two conversions, viewed as a potential F reorganization, constitute a mere change of S1, and that potential F reorganization qualifies as a reorganization under section 368(a)(1)(F). The result would be the same if, instead of converting into S2 pursuant to state law, LLC2 elected under § 301.7701-3(c) to change its classification for federal tax purposes and be treated as an association taxable as a corporation, provided the effective date of the election (and its resulting deemed transactions) occurs before the conversion of S1.

Example 12. Other acquiring corporation – no mere change. The facts are the same facts as in *Example 11*, except that S1 converts into LLC1 prior to the conversion of LLC2 into S2. As a result of these conversions, S1 is deemed to distribute all of its assets to P in exchange for all of P's S1 stock, and P is deemed to transfer all of those assets to S2 in exchange for all of the stock in S2. The transaction does not qualify as a complete liquidation of S1 under section 332 (because of the reincorporation of S1's assets), but does qualify as a reorganization under section 368(a)(1)(C) by reason of section 368(a)(2)(C) and paragraph (k) of this section. Under paragraph (m)(1)(v) of this section, the potential F reorganization in which the former assets of S1 are deemed transferred, first by S1 to P, and then by P to S2, is not a mere change of S1 because section 381(a) applies to P's acquisition of property held by S1 immediately before the potential F reorganization. Furthermore, the corporation in control of S2, within the meaning of section 368(c), is a party to the reorganization within the meaning of section 368(b). Thus, the indirect transfer of property from S1 to S2 does not qualify under section 368(a)(1)(F).

Example 13. *Series of related transactions – no mere change.* X owns all of the stock of T. P acquires all of the stock of T in exchange for consideration consisting of $50 cash and P voting stock with $50 value. No election is made under section 338. Immediately thereafter and as part of the same plan, P forms S as a wholly-owned subsidiary, and T is merged into S. Viewed in isolation as a potential F reorganization, the merger of T into S appears to constitute a mere change of T. However, the acquisition of the T stock by P and the merger of T into S, viewed together, qualify as a reorganization under section 368(a)(1)(A) by reason of section 368(a)(2)(D). The step transaction doctrine is applied treat the transaction as a statutory merger of T into S in exchange for $50 cash and $50 of P's voting stock (and S's assumption of T's liabilities), P's momentary ownership of T stock is disregarded. Under paragraph (m)(3)(iv)(A) of this section, P, the corporation in control of S, is a party to the reorganization within the meaning of section 368(b). Thus, the transfer of property from T to S does not qualify under section 368(a)(1)(F).

Example 14. *Multiple transferor corporations – no mere change.* P owns all the stock of S1 and S2. The management of P determines it would be in the best interest of S1 and S2 to operate as a single corporation. P forms S3 and, under applicable corporate law,S1 and S2 simultaneously merge into S3. Immediately after the merger, P owns all the stock of S3. Each of the mergers can be tested as a potential F reorganization. However, immediately after the simultaneous mergers. the resulting corporation, S3, holds property acquired from a corporation other than the transferor corporation, and section 381(a) would apply to the acquisition of such property. Therefore, under paragraph (m)(1)(vi) of this section, neither potential F reorganization is a mere change, and neither merger into S3 qualifies as a reorganization under section 386(a)(1)(F). The result would be different if the mergers were not simultaneous. If S1 completed its merger into S3 before S2 began its merger into S3, the merger of S1 into S3 would qualify as a reorganization under section 368(a)(1)(F), but the merger of S2 into S3 would not so qualify (although it would qualify as a reorganization under sections 368(a)(1)(A) and 368(a)(1)(D)).

* * *

[Reg. § 1.368-2.]

☐ [*T.D.* 6152, 12-2-55. *Amended by T.D.* 7281, 7-11-73; *T.D.* 7422, 6-25-76; *T.D.* 8059, 10-21-85; *T.D.* 8760, 1-23-98; *T.D.* 8885, 5-18-2000; *T.D.* 9038, 1-23-2003; *T.D.* 9242, 1-23-2006; *T.D.* 9259, 4-24-2006; *T.D.* 9303, 12-18-2006; *T.D.* 9361, 10-24-2007; *T.D.* 9396, 5-8-2008, *T.D.* 9475, 12-17-2009 *(corrected* 1-19-2010) *and T.D.* 9739, 9-18-2015 (*corrected* 12-7-2015).]

Carryovers

§ 1.381(a)-1. General rule relating to carryovers in certain corporate acquisitions.—(a) *Allowance of carryovers.*—Section 381 provides that a corporation which acquires the assets of another corporation in certain liquidations and reorganizations shall succeed to, and take into account, as of the close of the date of distribution or transfer, the items described in section 381(c) of the distributor or transferor corporation. These items shall be taken into account by the acquiring corporation subject to the conditions and limitations specified in sections 381, 382(b) and 383 and the regulations thereunder.

(b) *Determination of transactions and items to which section 381 applies.*—(1) *Qualified transactions.*—Except to the extent provided in section 381(c)(20), relating to the carryover of unused pension trust deductions in certain liquidations, the items described in section 381(c) are required by section 381 to be carried over to the acquiring corporation (as defined in subparagraph (2) of this paragraph) only in the following liquidations and reorganizations:

(i) The complete liquidation of a subsidiary corporation upon which no gain or loss is recognized in accordance with the provisions of section 332;

(ii) A statutory merger or consolidation qualifying under section 368(a)(1)(A) to which section 361 applies;

(iii) A reorganization qualifying under section 368(a)(1)(C);

(iv) A reorganization qualifying under section 368(a)(1)(D) if the requirements of section 354(b)(1)(A) and (B) are satisfied; and

(v) A mere change in identify, form, or place of organization qualifying under section 368(a)(1)(F).

(2) *Acquiring corporation defined.*—(i) Only a single corporation may be an acquiring corporation for purposes of section 381 and the regulations thereunder. The corporation which acquires the assets of its subsidiary corporation in a complete liquidation to which section 381(a)(1) applies is the acquiring corporation for purposes of section 381. In a transaction to which section 381(a)(2) applies, the acquiring corporation is the corporation that, pursuant to the plan of reorganization, directly acquires the assets transferred by the transferor corporation, even if that corporation ultimately retains none of the assets so transferred.

(ii) The application of this subparagraph may be illustrated by the following examples:

Example (1). Y Corporation, a wholly-owned subsidiary of X Corporation, directly acquired all the assets of Z Corporation solely in exchange for voting stock of X Corporation in a transaction qualifying under section 368(a)(1)(C). Y Corporation is the acquiring corporation for purposes of section 381.

Example (2). X Corporation acquired all the assets of Z Corporation solely in exchange for voting stock of X Corporation in a transaction qualifying under section 368(a)(1)(C). Thereafter, pursuant to the plan of reorganization X Corporation transferred all the assets so acquired to Y Corporation, its wholly-owned subsidiary (see section 368(a)(2)(C)). X Corporation is the acquiring corporation for purposes of section 381.

Example (3). X Corporation acquired all the assets of Z Corporation solely in exchange for the voting stock of X Corporation in a transaction qualifying under section 368(a)(1)(C). Thereafter, pursuant to the plan of reorganization X Corporation transferred one-half of the assets so acquired to Y Corporation, its wholly-owned subsidiary, and retained the other half of such assets. X Corporation is the acquiring corporation for purposes of section 381.

Example (4). X Corporation acquired all the assets of Z Corporation solely in exchange for voting stock of X Corporation in a transaction qualifying under section 368(a)(1)(C). Thereafter, pursuant to the plan of reorganization X Corporation transferred one-half of the assets so acquired to Y Corporation, its wholly-owned subsidiary, and the other half of such assets to M Corporation, another wholly-owned subsidiary of X Corporation. X Corporation is the acquiring corporation for purposes of section 381.

(3) *Transactions and items not covered by section 381.*—Section 381 does not apply to partial liquidations, divisive reorganizations, or other transactions not described in subparagraph (1) of this paragraph. Moreover, section 381 does not apply to the carryover of an item or tax attribute not specified in subsection (c) thereof. In a case where section 381 does not apply to a transaction, item, or tax attribute by reason of either of the preceding sentences, no inference is to be drawn from the provisions of section 381 as to whether any item or tax attribute shall be taken into account by the successor corporation.

* * *

[Reg. § 1.381(a)-1.]

☐ [*T.D.* 6480, 7-12-60. *Amended by T.D.* 7343, 1-8-75; *T.D.* 9273, 8-7-2006; *T.D.* 9534, 7-29-2011 *and T.D.* 9700, 11-7-2014.]

§ 1.381(b)-1. Operating rules applicable to carryovers in certain corporate acquisitions.—(a) *Closing of taxable year.*—(1) *In general.*—Except in the case of certain reorganizations qualifying under section 368(a)(1)(F), the taxable year of the distributor or transferor corporation shall end with the close of the date of distribution or transfer. With regard to the closing of the taxable year of the transferor corporation in certain reorganizations under section 368(a)(1)(F) involving a foreign corporation after December 31, 1986, see §§ 1.367(a)-1(e) and 1.367(b)-2(f).

(2) *Reorganizations under section 368(a)(1)(F).*—In the case of a reorganization qualifying under section 368(a)(1)(F) (whether or not such reorganization also qualifies under any other provision of section 368(a)(1)), the acquiring corporation shall be treated (for purposes of section 381) just as the transferor corporation would have been treated if there had been no reorganization. Thus, the taxable year of the transferor corporation shall not end on the date of transfer merely because of the transfer; a net operating loss of the acquiring corporation for any taxable year ending after the date of transfer shall be carried back in accordance with section 172(b) in computing the taxable income of the transferor corporation for a taxable year ending before the date of transfer; and the tax attributes of the transferor corporation enumerated in section 381(c) shall be taken into account by the acquiring corporation as if there had been no reorganization.

(b) *Date of distribution or transfer.*—(1) The date of distribution or transfer shall be that day on which are distributed or transferred all those properties of the distributor or transferor corporation which are to be distributed or transferred pursuant to a liquidation or reorganization described in paragraph (b)(1) of

§1.381(a)-1. If the distribution or transfer of all such properties is not made on one day, then, except as provided in subparagraph (2) of this paragraph, the date of distribution or transfer shall be that day on which the distribution or transfer of all such properties is completed.

(2) If the distributor or transferor and acquiring corporations file the statements described in subparagraph (3) of this paragraph, the date of distribution or transfer shall be that day as of which (i) substantially all of the properties to be distributed or transferred have been distributed or transferred, and (ii) the distributor or transferor corporation has ceased all operations (other than liquidating activities). Such day also shall be the date of distribution or transfer if the completion of the distribution or transfer is unreasonably postponed beyond the date as of which substantially all the properties to be distributed or transferred have been distributed or transferred and the distributor or transferor corporation has ceased all operations other than liquidating activities. A corporation shall be considered to have distributed or transferred substantially all of its properties to be distributed or transferred even though it retains money or other property in a reasonable amount to pay outstanding debts or preserve the corporation's legal existence. A corporation shall be considered to have ceased all operations, other than liquidating activities, when it ceases to be a going concern and its activities are merely for the purpose of winding up its affairs, paying its debts, and distributing any remaining balance of its money or other properties to its shareholders.

* * *

(4) If—

(i) The last day of the acquiring corporation's taxable year is a Saturday, Sunday, or legal holiday, and

(ii) The day specified in subparagraph (1) and (2) of this paragraph as the date of distribution or transfer is the last business day before such Saturday, Sunday, or holiday,

then the last day of the acquiring corporation's taxable year shall be the date of distribution or transfer for purposes of section 381(b) and this section. For purposes of this subparagraph, the term "business day" means a day which is not a Saturday, Sunday, or legal holiday, and also means a Saturday, Sunday, or legal holiday if the date of distribution or transfer determined under subparagraph (1) or (2) of this paragraph is such Saturday, Sunday, or holiday.

(c) *Return of distributor or transferor corporation.*—The distributor or transferor corporation shall file an income tax return for the taxable year ending with the date of distribution or transfer described in paragraph (b) of this section. If the distributor or transferor corporation remains in existence after such date of distribution or transfer, it shall file an income tax return for the taxable year beginning on the day following the date of distribution or transfer and ending with the date on which the distributor or transferor corporation's taxable year would have ended if there had been no distribution or transfer.

(d) *Carryback of net operating losses.*—For provisions relating to the carryback of net operating losses of the acquiring corporation, see paragraph (b) of §1.381(c)(1)-1.

* * *

[Reg. §1.381(b)-1.]

☐ [*T.D.* 6480, 7-12-60. *Amended by T.D.* 8280, 1-12-90; *T.D.* 8862, 1-21-2000; *T.D.* 9264, 5-26-2006, *T.D.* 9329, 6-13-2007 *and T.D.* 9739, 9-18-2015.]

§1.381(c)(2)-1. Earnings and profits.—(a) *In general.*—(1) Section 381(c)(2) requires the acquiring corporation in a transaction to which section 381(a) applies to succeed to, and take into account, the earnings and profits, or deficit in earnings and profits, of the distributor or transferor corporation as of the close of the date of distribution or transfer. In determining the amount of such earnings and profits, or deficit, to be carried over, and the manner in which they are to be used by the acquiring corporation after such date, the provisions of section 381(c)(2) and this section shall apply. For purposes of section 381(c)(2) and this section, if the distributor or transferor corporation accumulates earnings and profits, or incurs a deficit in earnings and profits, after the date of distribution or transfer and before the completion of the reorganization or liquidation, such earnings and profits, or deficit, shall be deemed to have been accumulated or incurred as of the close of the date of distribution or transfer.

(2) If the distributor or transferor corporation has accumulated earnings and profits as of the close of the date of distribution or transfer, such earnings and profits shall (except as hereinafter provided in this section) be deemed to be received by, and to become a part of the accumulated earnings and profits of, the acquiring corporation as of such time. Similarly, if the distributor or transferor corporation has a deficit in accumulated earnings and profits as of the close of the date of distribution or transfer, such deficit shall (except as hereinafter provided in this section) be deemed to be incurred by the acquiring corporation as of such time. In no event, however, shall the accumulated earnings and profits, or deficit, of the distributor or transferor corporation be taken into account in determining earnings and profits of the acquiring corporation for the taxable year during which occurs the date of distribution or transfer.

(3) Any part of the accumulated earnings and profits, or deficit in accumulated earnings and profits, of the distributor or transferor corporation which consists of earnings and profits, or deficits, accumulated before March 1, 1913, shall be deemed to become earnings and profits, or deficits, of the acquiring corporation accumulated before March 1, 1913, and any part of the accumulated earnings and profits of the distributor or transferor corporation which consists of increase in value of property accrued before March 1, 1913, shall be deemed to become earnings and profits of the acquiring corporation consisting of increase in value of property accrued before March 1, 1913.

(4) If the acquiring corporation and each distributor or transferor corporation has accumulated earnings and profits as of the close of the date of distribution or transfer, or if each of such corporations has a deficit in accumulated earnings and profits as of such time, then the accumulated earnings and profits (or deficit) of each such corporation shall be consolidated as of the close of the date of distribution or transfer in the accumulated earnings and profits account of the acquiring corporation. See subparagraph (6) of this paragraph for determination of the accumulated earnings and profits (or deficit) of the acquiring corporation as of the close of the date of distribution or transfer.

(5) If (i) one or more corporations a party to a distribution or transfer has accumulated earnings and profits as of the close of the date of distribution or transfer, and (ii) one or more of such corporations has a deficit in accumulated earnings and profits as of such time, the total of any such deficits shall be used only to offset earnings and profits accumulated, or deemed to have been accumulated under subparagraph (6) of this paragraph, by the acquiring corporation after the date of distribution or transfer. In such instance, the acquiring corporation will be considered as maintaining two separate earnings and profits accounts after the date of distribution or transfer. The first such account shall contain the total of the accumulated earnings and profits as of the close of the date of distribution or transfer of each corporation which has accumulated earnings and profits as of such time, and the second such account shall contain the total of the deficits in accumulated earnings and profits of each corporation which has a deficit as of such time. The total deficit in the second account may not be used to reduce the accumulated earnings and profits in the first account (although such earnings and profits may be offset by deficits incurred, or deemed to have been incurred, after the date of distribution or transfer) but shall be used only to offset earnings and profits accumulated, or deemed to have been accumulated under subparagraph (6) of this paragraph, by the acquiring corporation after the date of distribution or transfer.

(6) In any case in which it is necessary to compute the accumulated earnings and profits, or the deficit in accumulated earnings and profits, of the acquiring corporation as of the close of the date of distribution or transfer and such date is a day other than the last day of a taxable year of the acquiring corporation—

(i) If the acquiring corporation has earnings and profits for its taxable year during which occurs the date of distribution or transfer, such earnings and profits (*a*) shall be deemed to have accumulated as of the close of such date in an amount which bears the same ratio to the undistributed earnings and profits of such corporation for such year as the number of days in the taxable year preceding the date following the date of distribution or transfer bears to the total number of days in the taxable year, and (*b*) shall be deemed to have accumulated after the date of distribution or transfer in an amount which bears the same ratio to the undistributed earnings and profits of such corporation for such year as the number of days in the taxable year following such date bears to the total number of days in such taxable year. For purposes of the preceding sentence, the undistributed earnings and profits of the acquiring corporation for such taxable year shall be the earnings and profits for such taxable year reduced by any distributions made therefrom during such taxable year.

(ii) If the acquiring corporation has an operating deficit for its taxable year during which occurs the date of distribution or transfer, then, unless the actual accumulated earnings and profits, or deficit, as of such date can be shown, such operating deficit shall be deemed to have accumulated in a manner similar to that described in subdivision (i) of this subparagraph.

* * *

(c) *Distribution of earnings and profits pursuant to reorganization or liquidation.*—(1) If, in a reorganization to which section 381(a)(2) applies, the transferor corporation pursuant to the plan of reorganization distributes to its stockholders property consisting not only of property permitted by section 354 to be received without recognition of gain, but also of other property or money, then the accumulated earnings and profits of the transferor corporation as of the close of the date of transfer shall be computed by taking into account the amount of earnings and profits properly applicable to the distribution, regardless of whether such distribution occurs before or after the close of the date of transfer.

(2) If, in a distribution to which section 381(a)(1) (relating to certain liquidations of subsidiaries) applies, the acquiring corporation receives less than 100 percent of the assets distributed by the distributor corporation, then the accumulated earnings and profits of the distributor corporation as of the close of the date of distribution shall be computed by taking into account the amount of earnings and profits properly applicable to the distributions to minority stockholders, regardless of whether such distributions occur before or after the close of the date of distribution. [Reg. § 1.381(c)(2)-1.]

□ [*T.D.* 6586, 12-27-61. *Amended by T.D.* 6692, 12-2-63 *and T.D.* 9700, 11-7-2014.]

Pension, Profit-Sharing, Stock Bonus Plans, Etc.

§ 1.408A-1. Roth IRAs in general.—This section sets forth the following questions and answers that discuss the background and general features of Roth IRAs:

Q-1 What is a Roth IRA?

A-1. (a) A Roth IRA is a new type of individual retirement plan that individuals can use, beginning in 1998. Roth IRAs are described in section 408A, which was added by the Taxpayer Relief Act of 1997 (TRA 97), Public Law 105-34 (111 Stat. 788).

(b) Roth IRAs are treated like traditional IRAs except where the Internal Revenue Code specifies different treatment. For example, aggregate contributions (other than by a conversion or other rollover) to all an individual's Roth IRAs are not permitted to exceed $2,000 for a taxable year. Further, income earned on funds held in a Roth IRA is generally not taxable. Similarly, the rules of section 408(e), such as the loss of exemption of the account where the owner engages in a prohibited transaction, apply to Roth IRAs in the same manner as to traditional IRAs.

Q-2. What are the significant differences between traditional IRAs and Roth IRAs?

A-2. There are several significant differences between traditional IRAs and Roth IRAs under the Internal Revenue Code. For example, eligibility to contribute to a Roth IRA is subject to special modified AGI (adjusted gross income) limits; contributions to a Roth IRA are never deductible; qualified distributions from a Roth IRA are not includible in gross income; the required minimum distribution rules under section 408(a)(6) and (b)(3) (which generally incorporate the provisions of section 401(a)(9)) do not apply to a Roth IRA during the lifetime of the owner; and contributions to a Roth IRA can be made after the owner has attained age 70 1/2.

[Reg. § 1.408A-1.]

□ [*T.D.* 8816, 2-3-99.]

§ 1.408A-2. Establishing Roth IRAs.—This section sets forth the following questions and answers that provide rules applicable to establishing Roth IRAs:

Q-1. Who can establish a Roth IRA?

A-1. Except as provided in A-3 of this section, only an individual can establish a Roth IRA. In addition, in order to be eligible to contribute to a Roth IRA for a particular year, an individual must satisfy certain compensation requirements and adjusted gross income limits (see § 1.408A-3 A-3).

Q-2. How is a Roth IRA established?

A-2. A Roth IRA can be established with any bank, insurance company, or other person authorized in accordance with § 1.408-2(e) to serve as a trustee with respect to IRAs. The document establishing the Roth IRA must clearly designate the IRA as a Roth IRA, and this designation cannot be changed at a later date. Thus, an IRA that is designated as a Roth IRA cannot later be treated as a traditional IRA. However, see § 1.408A-4 A-1(b)(3) for certain rules for converting a traditional IRA to a Roth IRA with the same trustee by redesignating the traditional IRA as a Roth IRA, and see § 1.408A-5 for rules for recharacterizing certain IRA contributions.

Q-3. Can an employer or an association of employees establish a Roth IRA to hold contributions of employees or members?

A-3. Yes. Pursuant to section 408(c), an employer or an association of employees can establish a trust to hold contributions of employees or members made under a Roth IRA. Each employee's or member's account in the trust is treated as a separate Roth IRA that is subject to the generally applicable Roth IRA rules. The employer or association of employees may do certain acts otherwise required by an individual, for example, establishing and designating a trust as a Roth IRA.

Q-4. What is the effect of a surviving spouse of a Roth IRA owner treating an IRA as his or her own?

A-4. If the surviving spouse of a Roth IRA owner treats a Roth IRA as his or her own as of a date, the Roth IRA is treated from that date forward as though it were established for the benefit of the surviving spouse and not the original Roth IRA owner. Thus, for example, the surviving spouse is treated as the Roth IRA owner for purposes of applying the minimum distribution requirements under section 408(a)(6) and (b)(3). Similarly, the surviving spouse is treated as the Roth IRA owner rather than a beneficiary for purposes of determining the amount of any distribution from the Roth IRA that is includible in gross income and whether the distribution is subject to the 10-percent additional tax under section 72(t).

[Reg. § 1.408A-2.]

☐ [*T.D.* 8816, 2-3-99.]

§ 1.408A-3. Contributions to Roth IRAs.—This section sets forth the following questions and answers that provide rules regarding contributions to Roth IRAs:

Q-1. What types of contributions are permitted to be made to a Roth IRA?

A-1. There are two types of contributions that are permitted to be made to a Roth IRA: regular contributions and qualified rollover contributions (including conversion contributions). The term regular contributions means contributions other than qualified rollover contributions.

Q-2. When are contributions permitted to be made to a Roth IRA?

A-2. (a) The provisions of section 408A are effective for taxable years beginning on or after January 1, 1998. Thus, the first taxable year for which contributions are permitted to be made to a Roth IRA by an individual is the individual's taxable year beginning in 1998.

(b) Regular contributions for a particular taxable year must generally be contributed by the due date (not including extensions) for filing a Federal income tax return for that taxable year. (See § 1.408A-5 regarding recharacterization of certain contributions.)

Q-3. What is the maximum aggregate amount of regular contributions an individual is eligible to contribute to a Roth IRA for a taxable year?

A-3. (a) The maximum aggregate amount that an individual is eligible to contribute to all his or her Roth IRAs as a regular contribution for a taxable year is the same as the maximum for traditional IRAs: $2,000 or, if less, that individual's compensation for the year.

(b) For Roth IRAs, the maximum amount described in paragraph (a) of this A-3 is phased out between certain levels of modified AGI. For an individual who is not married, the dollar amount is phased out ratably between modified AGI of $95,000 and $110,000; for a married individual filing a joint return, between modified AGI of $150,000 and $160,000; and for a married individual filing separately, between modified AGI of $0 and $10,000. For this purpose, a married individual who has lived apart from his or her spouse for the entire taxable year and who files separately is treated as not married. Under section 408A(c)(3)(A), in applying the phase-out, the maximum amount is rounded up to the next higher multiple of $10 and is not reduced below $200 until completely phased out.

(c) If an individual makes regular contributions to both traditional IRAs and Roth IRAs for a taxable year, the maximum limit for the Roth IRA is the lesser of—

(1) The amount described in paragraph (a) of this A-3 reduced by the amount contributed to traditional IRAs for the taxable year; and

(2) The amount described in paragraph (b) of this A-3. Employer contributions, including elective deferrals, made under a SEP or SIMPLE IRA Plan on behalf of an individual (including a self-employed individual) do not reduce the amount of the individual's maximum regular contribution.

(d) The rules in this A-3 are illustrated by the following examples:

Example 1. In 1998, unmarried, calendar-year taxpayer B, age 60, has modified AGI of $40,000 and compensation of $5,000. For 1998, B can contribute a maximum of $2,000 to a traditional IRA, a Roth IRA or a combination of traditional and Roth IRAs.

Example 2. The facts are the same as in *Example 1.* However, assume that B violates the maximum regular contribution limit by contributing $2,000 to a traditional IRA and $2,000 to a Roth IRA for 1998. The $2,000 to B's Roth IRA would be an excess contribution to B's Roth IRA for 1998 because an individual's contributions are applied first to a traditional IRA, then to a Roth IRA.

Example 3. The facts are the same as in *Example 1*, except that B's compensation is $900. The maximum amount B can contribute to either a traditional IRA or a Roth (or a combination of the two) for 1998 is $900.

Example 4. In 1998, unmarried, calendar-year taxpayer C, age 60, has modified AGI of $100,000 and compensation of $5,000. For 1998, C contributes $800 to a traditional IRA and $1,200 to a Roth IRA. Because C's $1,200 Roth IRA contribution does not exceed the phased-out maximum Roth IRA contribution of $1,340 and because C's total IRA contributions do not exceed $2,000, C's Roth IRA contribution does not exceed the maximum permissible contribution.

Q-4. How is compensation defined for purposes of the Roth IRA contribution limit?

A-4. For purposes of the contribution limit described in A-3 of this section, an individual's compensation is the same as that used to determine the maximum contribution an individual can make to a traditional IRA. This amount is defined in section 219(f)(1) to include wages, commissions, professional fees, tips, and other amounts received for personal services, as well as taxable alimony and separate maintenance payments received under a decree of divorce or separate maintenance. Compensation also includes earned income as defined in section 401(c)(2), but does not include any amount received as a pension or annuity or as deferred compensation. In addition, under section 219(c), a married individual filing a joint return is permitted to make an IRA contribution by treating his or her spouse's higher compensation as his or her own, but only to the extent that the spouse's compensation is not being used for purposes of the spouse making a contribution to a Roth IRA or a deductible contribution to a traditional IRA.

Q-5. What is the significance of modified AGI and how is it determined?

A-5. Modified AGI is used for purposes of the phase-out rules described in A-3 of this section and for purposes of the $100,000 modified AGI limitation described in § 1.408A-4 A-2(a) (relating to eligibility for conversion). As defined in section 408A(c)(3)(C)(i), modified AGI is the same as adjusted gross income under section 219(g)(3)(A) (used to determine the amount of deductible contributions that can be made to a traditional IRA by an individual who is an active participant in an employer-sponsored retirement plan), except that any conversion is disregarded in determining modified AGI. For example, the deduction for contributions to an IRA is not taken into account for purposes of determining adjusted gross income under section 219 and thus does not apply in determining modified AGI for Roth IRA purposes.

Q-6. Is a required minimum distribution from an IRA for a year included in income for purposes of determining modified AGI?

A-6. (a) Yes. For taxable years beginning before January 1, 2005, any required minimum distribution from an IRA under section 408(a)(6) and (b)(3) (which generally incorporate the provisions of section 401(a)(9)) is included in income for purposes of determining modified AGI.

(b) For taxable years beginning after December 31, 2004, and solely for purposes of the $100,000 limitation applicable to conversions, modified AGI does not include any required minimum distributions from an IRA under section 408(a)(6) and (b)(3).

Q-7. Does an excise tax apply if an individual exceeds the aggregate regular contribution limits for Roth IRAs?

A-7. Yes. Section 4973 imposes an annual 6-percent excise tax on aggregate amounts contributed to Roth IRAs that exceed the maximum contribution limits described in A-3 of this section. Any contribution that is distributed, together with net income, from a Roth IRA on or before the tax return due date (plus extensions) for the taxable year of the contribution is treated as not contributed. Net income described in the previous sentence is includible in gross income for the taxable year in which the contribution is made. Aggregate excess contributions that are not distributed from a Roth IRA on or before the tax return due date (with extensions) for the taxable year of the contributions are reduced as a deemed Roth IRA contribution for each subsequent taxable year to the extent that the Roth IRA owner does not actually make regular IRA contributions for such years. Section 4973 applies separately to an individual's Roth IRAs and other types of IRAs.

[Reg. § 1.408A-3.]

☐ [*T.D.* 8816, 2-3-99.]

§ 1.408A-4. Converting amounts to Roth IRAs.—This section sets forth the following questions and answers that provide rules applicable to Roth IRA conversions:

Q-1. Can an individual convert an amount in his or her traditional IRA to a Roth IRA?

A-1. (a) Yes. An amount in a traditional IRA may be converted to an amount in a Roth IRA if two requirements are satisfied. First, the IRA owner must satisfy the modified AGI limitation described in A-2(a) of this section and, if married, the joint filing requirement described in A-2(b) of this section. Second, the amount contributed to the Roth IRA must satisfy the definition of a qualified rollover contribution in section 408A(e) (i.e., it must satisfy the requirements for a rollover contribution as defined in section 408(d)(3), except that the one-rollover-per-year limitation in section 408(d)(3)(B) does not apply).

(b) An amount can be converted by any of three methods—

(1) An amount distributed from a traditional IRA is contributed (rolled over) to a Roth IRA within the 60-day period described in section 408(d)(3)(A)(i);

(2) An amount in a traditional IRA is transferred in a trustee-to-trustee transfer from the trustee of the traditional IRA to the trustee of the Roth IRA; or

(3) An amount in a traditional IRA is transferred to a Roth IRA maintained by the same trustee. For purposes of sections 408 and 408A, redesignating a traditional IRA as a Roth IRA is treated as a transfer of the entire account balance from a traditional IRA to a Roth IRA.

(c) Any converted amount is treated as a distribution from the traditional IRA and a qualified rollover contribution to the Roth IRA for purposes of section 408 and section 408A, even if the conversion is accomplished by means of a trustee-to-trustee transfer or a transfer between IRAs of the same trustee.

(d) A transaction that is treated as a failed conversion under § 1.408A-5 A-9(a)(1) is not a conversion.

Q-2. What are the modified AGI limitation and joint filing requirements for conversions?

A-2. (a) An individual with modified AGI in excess of $100,000 for a taxable year is not permitted to convert an amount to a Roth IRA during that taxable year. This $100,000 limitation applies to the taxable year that the funds are paid from the traditional IRA, rather than the year they are contributed to the Roth IRA.

(b) If the individual is married, he or she is permitted to convert an amount to a Roth IRA during a taxable year only if the individual and the individual's spouse file a joint return for the taxable year that the funds are paid from the traditional IRA. In this case, the modified AGI subject to the $100,000 limit is the modified AGI derived from the joint return using the couple's combined income. The only exception to this joint filing requirement is for an individual who has lived apart from his or her spouse for the entire taxable year. If the married individual has lived apart from his or her spouse for the entire taxable year, then such individual can treat himself or herself as not married for purposes of this paragraph, file a separate return and be subject to the $100,000 limit on his or her separate modified AGI. In all other cases, a married individual filing a separate return is not permitted to convert an amount to a Roth IRA, regardless of the individual's modified AGI.

* * *

Q-7. What are the tax consequences when an amount is converted to a Roth IRA?

A-7. (a) Any amount that is converted to a Roth IRA is includible in gross income as a distribution according to the rules of section 408(d)(1) and (2) for the taxable year in which the amount is distributed or transferred from the traditional IRA. Thus, any portion of the distribution or transfer that is treated as a return of basis under section 408(d)(1) and (2) is not includible in gross income as a result of the conversion.

(b) The 10-percent additional tax under section 72(t) generally does not apply to the taxable conversion amount. But see § 1.408A-6 A-5 for circumstances under which the taxable conversion amount would be subject to the additional tax under section 72(t).

(c) Pursuant to section 408A(e), a conversion is not treated as a rollover for purposes of the one-rollover-per-year rule of section 408(d)(3)(B).

* * *

Q-9. Is the taxable conversion amount included in income for all purposes?

A-9. Except as provided below, any taxable conversion amount includible in gross income for a year as a result of the conversion (regardless of whether the individual is using a 4-year spread) is included in income for all purposes. Thus, for example, it is counted for purposes of determining the taxable portion of social security payments under section 86 and for purposes of determining the phase-out of the $25,000 exemption under section 469(i) relating to the disallowance of passive activity losses from rental real estate activities. However, as provided in § 1.408A-3 A-5, the taxable conversion amount (and any resulting change in other elements of adjusted gross income) is disregarded for purposes of determining modified AGI for section 408A.

* * *

[Reg. § 1.408A-4.]

☐ [*T.D.* 8816, 2-3-99. *Amended by T.D.* 9220, 8-19-2005 *and T.D.* 9418, 7-28-2008.]

§ 1.408A-6. Distributions.—This section sets forth the following questions and answers that provide rules regarding distributions from Roth IRAs:

Q-1. How are distributions from Roth IRAs taxed?

A-1. (a) The taxability of a distribution from a Roth IRA generally depends on whether or not the distribution is a qualified distribution. This A-1 provides rules for qualified distributions and certain other nontaxable distributions. A-4 of this section provides rules for the taxability of distributions that are not qualified distributions.

(b) A distribution from a Roth IRA is not includible in the owner's gross income if it is a qualified distribution or to the extent that it is a return of the owner's contributions to the Roth IRA (determined in accordance with A-8 of this section). A qualified distribution is one that is both—

(1) Made after a 5-taxable-year period (defined in A-2 of this section); and

(2) Made on or after the date on which the owner attains age 59 1/2, made to a beneficiary or the estate of the owner on or after the date of the owner's death, attributable to the owner's being disabled within the meaning of section 72(m)(7), or to which section 72(t)(2)(F) applies (exception for first-time home purchase).

(c) An amount distributed from a Roth IRA will not be included in gross income to the extent it is rolled over to another Roth IRA on a tax-free basis under the rules of sections 408(d)(3) and 408A(e).

(d) Contributions that are returned to the Roth IRA owner in accordance with section 408(d)(4) (corrective distributions) are not includible in gross income, but any net income required to be distributed under section 408(d)(4) together with the contributions is includible in gross income for the taxable year in which the contributions were made.

Q-2. When does the 5-taxable-year period described in A-1 of this section (relating to qualified distributions) begin and end?

A-2. The 5-taxable-year period described in A-1 of this section begins on the first day of the individual's taxable year for which the first regular contribution is made to any Roth IRA of the individual or, if earlier, the first day of the individual's taxable year in which the first conversion contribution is made to any Roth IRA of the individual. The 5-taxable-year period ends on the last day of the individual's fifth consecutive taxable year beginning with the taxable year described in the preceding sentence. For example, if an individual whose taxable year is the calendar year makes a first-time regular Roth IRA contribution any time between January 1, 1998, and April 15, 1999, for 1998, the 5-taxable-year period begins on January 1, 1998. Thus, each Roth IRA owner has only one 5-taxable-year period described in A-1 of this section for all the Roth IRAs of which he or she is the owner. Further, because of the requirement of the 5-taxable-year period, no qualified distributions can occur before taxable years beginning in 2003. For purposes of this A-2, the amount of any contribution distributed as a corrective distribution under A-1(d) of this section is treated as if it was never contributed.

Q-3. If a distribution is made to an individual who is the sole beneficiary of his or her deceased spouse's Roth IRA and the individual is treating the Roth IRA as his or her own, can the distribution be a qualified distribution based on being made to a beneficiary on or after the owner's death?

A-3. No. If a distribution is made to an individual who is the sole beneficiary of his or her deceased spouse's Roth IRA and the individual is treating the Roth IRA as his or her own, then, in accordance with § 1.408A-2 A-4, the distribution is treated as coming from the individual's own Roth IRA and not the deceased spouse's Roth IRA. Therefore, for purposes of determining whether the distribution is a qualified distribution, it is not treated as made to a beneficiary on or after the owner's death.

Q-4. How is a distribution from a Roth IRA taxed if it is not a qualified distribution?

A-4. A distribution that is not a qualified distribution, and is neither contributed to another Roth IRA in a qualified rollover contribution nor constitutes a corrective distribution, is includible in the owner's gross income to the extent that the amount of the distribution, when added to the amount of all prior distributions from the owner's Roth IRAs (whether or not they were qualified distributions) and reduced by the amount of those prior distributions previously includible in gross income, exceeds the owner's contributions to all his or her Roth IRAs. For purposes of this A-4, any amount distributed as a corrective distribution is treated as if it was never contributed.

Q-5. Will the additional tax under 72(t) apply to the amount of a distribution that is not a qualified distribution?

A-5. (a) The 10-percent additional tax under section 72(t) will apply (unless the distribution is excepted under section 72(t)) to any distribution from a Roth IRA includible in gross income.

(b) The 10-percent additional tax under section 72(t) also applies to a nonqualified distribution, even if it is not then includible in gross income, to the extent it is allocable to a conversion contribution, if the distribution is made within the 5-taxable-year period beginning with the first day of the individual's taxable year in which the conversion contribution was made. The 5-taxable-year period ends on the last day of the individual's fifth consecutive taxable year beginning with the taxable year described in the preceding sentence. For purposes of applying the tax, only the amount of the conversion contribution includible in gross income as a result of the conversion is taken into account. The exceptions under section 72(t) also apply to such a distribution.

(c) The 5-taxable-year period described in this A-5 for purposes of determining whether section 72(t) applies to a distribution allocable to a conversion contribution is separately determined for each conversion contribution, and need not be the same as the 5-taxable-year period used for purposes of determining whether a distribution is a qualified distribution under A-1(b) of this section. For example, if a calendar-year taxpayer who received a distribution from a traditional IRA on December 31, 1998, makes a conversion contribution by contributing the distributed amount to a Roth IRA on February 25, 1999 in a qualifying rollover contribution and makes a regular contribution for 1998 on the same date, the 5-taxable-year period for purposes of this A-5 begins on January 1, 1999, while the 5-taxable-year period for purposes of A-1(b) of this section begins on January 1, 1998.

* * *

Q-7. Is the 5-taxable-year period described in A-1 of this section redetermined when a Roth IRA owner dies?

A-7. (a) No. The beginning of the 5-taxable-year period described in A-1 of this section is not redetermined when the Roth IRA owner dies. Thus, in determining the 5-taxable-year period, the period the Roth IRA is held in the name of a beneficiary, or in the name of a surviving spouse who treats the decedent's Roth IRA as his or her own, includes the period it was held by the decedent.

(b) The 5-taxable-year period for a Roth IRA held by an individual as a beneficiary of a deceased Roth IRA owner is determined independently of the 5-taxable-year period for the beneficiary's own Roth IRA. However, if a surviving spouse treats the Roth IRA as his or her own, the 5-taxable-year period with respect to any of the surviving spouse's Roth IRAs (including the one that the surviving spouse treats as his or her own) ends at the earlier of the end of either the 5-taxable-year period for the decedent or the 5-taxable-year period applicable to the spouse's own Roth IRAs.

* * *

Q-14. What minimum distribution rules apply to a Roth IRA?

A-14. (a) No minimum distributions are required to be made from a Roth IRA under section 408(a)(6) and (b)(3) (which generally incorporate the provisions of section 401(a)(9)) while the owner is alive. The post-death minimum distribution rules under section 401(a)(9)(B) that apply to traditional IRAs, with the exception of the at-least-as-rapidly rule described in section 401(a)(9)(B)(i), also apply to Roth IRAs.

(b) The minimum distribution rules apply to the Roth IRA as though the Roth IRA owner died before his or her required beginning date. Thus, generally, the entire interest in the Roth IRA must be distributed by the end of the fifth calendar year after the year of the owner's death unless the interest is payable to a designated beneficiary over a period not greater than that beneficiary's life expectancy and distribution commences before the end of the calendar year following the year of death. If the sole beneficiary is the decedent's spouse, such spouse may delay distributions until the decedent would have attained age 70 1/2 or may treat the Roth IRA as his or her own.

(c) Distributions to a beneficiary that are not qualified distributions will be includible in the beneficiary's gross income according to the rules in A-4 of this section.

(d) The special rules in A-3 of § 1.401(a)(9)-5 and A-12 of § 1.408-8 for a qualifying longevity annuity contract (QLAC), defined in A-17 of § 1.401(a)(9)-6, do not apply to a Roth IRA.

Q-15. Does section 401(a)(9) apply separately to Roth IRAs and individual retirement plans that are not Roth IRAs?

A-15. Yes. An individual required to receive minimum distributions from his or her own traditional or SIMPLE IRA cannot choose to take the amount of the minimum distributions from any Roth IRA. Similarly, an individual required to receive minimum distributions from a Roth IRA cannot choose to take the amount of the minimum distributions from a traditional or SIMPLE IRA. In addition, an individual required to receive minimum distributions as a beneficiary under a Roth IRA can only satisfy the minimum distributions for one Roth IRA by distributing from another Roth IRA if the Roth IRAs were inherited from the same decedent.

Q-16. How is the basis of property distributed from a Roth IRA determined for purposes of a subsequent disposition?

A-16. The basis of property distributed from a Roth IRA is its fair market value (FMV) on the date of distribution, whether or not the distribution is a qualified distribution. Thus, for example, if a distribution consists of a share of stock in XYZ Corp. with an FMV of $40.00 on the date of distribution, for purposes of determining gain or loss on the subsequent sale of the share of XYZ Corp. stock, it has a basis of $40.00.

Q-17. What is the effect of distributing an amount from a Roth IRA and contributing it to another type of retirement plan other than a Roth IRA?

A-17. Any amount distributed from a Roth IRA and contributed to another type of retirement plan (other than a Roth IRA) is treated as a distribution from the Roth IRA that is neither a rollover contribution for purposes of section 408(d)(3) nor a qualified rollover contribution within the meaning of section 408A(e) to the other type of retirement plan. This treatment also applies to any amount transferred from a Roth IRA to any other type of retirement plan unless the transfer is a recharacterization described in § 1.408A-5.

Q-18. Can an amount be transferred directly from an education IRA to a Roth IRA (or distributed from an education IRA and rolled over to a Roth IRA)?

A-18. No amount may be transferred directly from an education IRA to a Roth IRA. A transfer of funds (or distribution and rollover) from an education IRA to a Roth IRA constitutes a distribution from the education IRA and a regular contribution to the Roth IRA (rather than a qualified rollover contribution to the Roth IRA).

Q-19. What are the Federal income tax consequences of a Roth IRA owner transferring his or her Roth IRA to another individual by gift?

A-19. A Roth IRA owner's transfer of his or her Roth IRA to another individual by gift constitutes an assignment of the owner's rights under the Roth IRA. At the time of the gift, the assets of the Roth IRA are deemed to be distributed to the owner and, accordingly, are treated as no longer held in a Roth IRA. In the case of any such gift of a Roth IRA made prior to October 1, 1998, if the entire interest in the Roth IRA is reconveyed to the Roth IRA owner prior to January 1, 1999, the Internal Revenue Service will treat the gift and reconveyance as never having occurred for estate tax, gift tax, and generation-skipping tax purposes and for purposes of this A-19.

[Reg. § 1.408A-6.]

□ [*T.D.* 8816, 2-3-99. *Amended by T.D.* 9673, 7-1-2014.]

§ 1.408A-8. Definitions.—This section sets forth the following question and answer that provides definitions of terms used in the provisions of § § 1.408A-1 through 1.408A-7 and this section:

Q-1. Are there any special definitions that govern in applying the provisions of § § 1.408A-1 through 1.408A-7 and this section?

A-1. Yes, the following definitions govern in applying the provisions of § § 1.408A-1 through 1.408A-7 and this section. Unless the context indicates otherwise, the use of a particular term excludes the use of the other terms.

(a) *Different types of IRAs.*—(1) *IRA.*—Sections 408(a) and (b), respectively, describe an individual retirement account and an individual retirement annuity. The term IRA means an IRA described in either section 408(a) or (b), including each IRA described in paragraphs (a)(2) through (5) of this A-1. However, the term IRA does not include an education IRA described in section 530.

(2) *Traditional IRA.*—The term traditional IRA means an individual retirement account or individual retirement annuity described in section 408(a) or (b), respectively. This term includes a SEP IRA but does not include a SIMPLE IRA or a Roth IRA.

(3) *SEP IRA.*—Section 408(k) describes a simplified employee pension (SEP) as an employer-sponsored plan under which an employer can make contributions to IRAs established for its employees. The term SEP IRA means an IRA that receives contributions made under a SEP. The term SEP includes a salary reduction SEP (SARSEP) described in section 408(k)(6).

(4) *SIMPLE IRA.*—Section 408(p) describes a SIMPLE IRA Plan as an employer-sponsored plan under which an employer can make contributions to SIMPLE IRAs established for its employees. The term SIMPLE IRA means an IRA to which the only contributions that can be made are contributions under a SIMPLE IRA Plan or rollovers or transfers from another SIMPLE IRA.

(5) *Roth IRA.*—The term Roth IRA means an IRA that meets the requirements of section 408A.

(b) *Other defined terms or phrases.*—(1) *4-year spread.*—The term 4-year spread is described in § 1.408A-4 A-8.

(2) *Conversion.*—The term conversion means a transaction satisfying the requirements of § 1.408A-4 A-1.

(3) *Conversion amount or conversion contribution.*—The term conversion amount or conversion contribution is the amount of a distribution and contribution with respect to which a conversion described in § 1.408A-4 A-1 is made.

(4) *Failed conversion.*—The term failed conversion means a transaction in which an individual contributes to a Roth IRA an amount transferred or distributed from a traditional IRA or SIMPLE IRA (including a transfer by redesignation) in a transaction that does not constitute a conversion under § 1.408A-4 A-1.

(5) *Modified AGI.*—The term modified AGI is defined in § 1.408A-3 A-5.

(6) *Recharacterization.*—The term recharacterization means a transaction described in § 1.408A-5 A-1.

(7) *Recharacterized amount or recharacterized contribution.*—The term recharacterized amount or recharacterized contribution means an amount or contribution treated as contributed to an IRA other than the one to which it was originally contributed pursuant to a recharacterization described in § 1.408A-5 A-1.

(8) *Taxable conversion amount.*—The term taxable conversion amount means the portion of a conversion amount includible in income on account of a conversion, determined under the rules of section 408(d)(1) and (2).

(9) *Tax-free transfer.*—The term tax-free transfer means a tax-free rollover described in section 402(c), 402(e)(6), 403(a)(4), 403(a)(5), 403(b)(8), 403(b)(10) or 408(d)(3), or a tax-free trustee-to-trustee transfer.

(10) *Treat an IRA as his or her own.*—The phrase treat an IRA as his or her own means to treat an IRA for which a surviving spouse is the sole beneficiary as his or her own IRA after the death of the IRA owner in accordance with the terms of the IRA instrument or in the manner provided in the regulations under section 408(a)(6) or (b)(3).

(11) *Trustee.*—The term trustee includes a custodian or issuer (in the case of an annuity) of an IRA (except where the context clearly indicates otherwise).

[Reg. § 1.408A-8.]

□ [*T.D.* 8816, 2-3-99.]

Accounting Periods

§ 1.441-1. Period for computation of taxable income.—(a) *Computation of taxable income.*—(1) *In general.*—Taxable income must be computed and a return must be made for a period known as the taxable year. For rules relating to methods of accounting, the taxable year for which items of gross income are included and deductions are taken, inventories, and adjustments, see parts II and III (section 446 and following), subchapter E, chapter 1 of the Internal Revenue Code, and the regulations thereunder.

(2) *Length of taxable year.*—Except as otherwise provided in the Internal Revenue Code and the regulations thereunder (e.g., § 1.441-2 regarding 52-53-week taxable years), a taxable year may not cover a period of more than 12 calendar months.

(b) *General rules and definitions.*—The general rules and definitions in this paragraph (b) apply for purposes of sections 441 and 442 and the regulations thereunder.

(1) *Taxable year.*—*Taxable year* means—

(i) The period for which a return is made, if a return is made for a period of less than 12 months (short period). See section 443 and the regulations thereunder;

(ii) Except as provided in paragraph (b) (1) (i) of this section, the taxpayer's required taxable year (as defined in paragraph (b) (2) of this section), if applicable;

(iii) Except as provided in paragraphs (b) (1) (i) and (ii) of this section, the taxpayer's annual accounting period (as defined in paragraph (b) (3) of this section), if it is a calendar year or a fiscal year; or

(iv) Except as provided in paragraphs (b) (1) (i) and (ii) of this section, the calendar year, if the taxpayer keeps no books, does not have an annual accounting period, or has an annual accounting period that does not qualify as a fiscal year.

(2) *Required taxable year.*—(i) *In general.*—Certain taxpayers must use the particular taxable year that is required under the Internal Revenue Code and the regulations thereunder (the required taxable year). For example, the required taxable year is—

(A) [Reserved]

(B) In the case of a personal service corporation (PSC), the taxable year determined under section 441 (i) and § 1.441-3;

(C) In the case of a nuclear decommissioning fund, the taxable year determined under § 1.468A-4 (c) (1);

(D) In the case of a designated settlement fund or a qualified settlement fund, the taxable year determined under § 1.468B-2 (j);

(E) In the case of a common trust fund, the taxable year determined under section 584 (i);

(F) In the case of certain trusts, the taxable year determined under section 644;

(G) In the case of a partnership, the taxable year determined under section 706 and § 1.706-1;

(H) In the case of an insurance company, the taxable year determined under section 843 and § 1.1502-76 (a) (2);

(I) In the case of a real estate investment trust, the taxable year determined under section 859;

(J) In the case of a real estate mortgage investment conduit, the taxable year determined under section 860D (a) (5) and § 1.860D-1 (b) (6);

(K) In the case of a specified foreign corporation, the taxable year determined under section 898 (c) (1) (A);

(L) In the case of an S corporation, the taxable year determined under section 1378 and § 1.1378-1; or

(M) In the case of a member of an affiliated group that makes a consolidated return, the taxable year determined under § 1.1502-76.

(ii) *Exceptions.*—Notwithstanding paragraph (b) (2) (i) of this section, the following taxpayers may have a taxable year other than their required taxable year:

(A) *52-53-week taxable years.*—Certain taxpayers may elect to use a 52-53-week taxable year that ends with reference to their required taxable year. See, for example, §§ 1.441-3 (PSCs), 1.706-1 (partnerships), 1.1378-1 (S corporations), and 1.1502-76 (a) (1) (members of a consolidated group).

(B) *Partnerships, S corporations, and PSCs.*—A partnership, S corporation, or PSC may use a taxable year other than its required taxable year if the taxpayer elects to use a taxable year other than its required taxable year under section 444, elects a 52-53-week taxable year that ends with reference to its required taxable year as provided in paragraph (b) (2) (ii) (A) of this section or to a taxable year elected under section 444, or establishes a business purpose to the satisfaction of the Commissioner under section 442 (such as a grandfathered fiscal year).

(C) *Specified foreign corporations.*—A specified foreign corporation (as defined in section 898(b)) may use a taxable year other than its required taxable year if it elects a 52-53-week taxable year that ends with reference to its required taxable year as provided in paragraph (b)(2)(ii)(A) of this section or makes a one-month deferral election under section 898(c)(1)(B).

(3) *Annual accounting period.—Annual accounting period* means the annual period (calendar year or fiscal year) on the basis of which the taxpayer regularly computes its income in keeping its books.

(4) *Calendar year.—Calendar year* means a period of 12 consecutive months ending on December 31. A taxpayer who has not established a fiscal year must make its return on the basis of a calendar year.

(5) *Fiscal year.*—(i) *Definition.—Fiscal year* means—

(A) A period of 12 consecutive months ending on the last day of any month other than December; or

(B) A 52-53-week taxable year, if such period has been elected by the taxpayer. See § 1.441-2.

(ii) *Recognition.*—A fiscal year will be recognized only if the books of the taxpayer are kept in accordance with such fiscal year.

(6) *Grandfathered fiscal year.—Grandfathered fiscal year* means a fiscal year (other than a year that resulted in a three month or less deferral of income) that a partnership or an S corporation received permission to use on or after July 1, 1974, by a letter ruling (i.e., not by automatic approval).

(7) *Books.—Books* include the taxpayer's regular books of account and such other records and data as may be necessary to support the entries on the taxpayer's books and on the taxpayer's return, as for example, a reconciliation of any difference between such books and the taxpayer's return. Records that are sufficient to reflect income adequately and clearly on the basis of an annual accounting period will be regarded as the keeping of books. See section 6001 and the regulations thereunder for rules relating to the keeping of books and records.

(8) *Taxpayer.—Taxpayer* has the same meaning as the term *person* as defined in section 7701(a)(1) (*e.g.*, an individual, trust, estate, partnership, association, or corporation) rather than the meaning of the term taxpayer as defined in section 7701(a)(14) (any person subject to tax).

(c) *Adoption of taxable year.*—(1) *In general.*—Except as provided in paragraph (c)(2) of this section, a new taxpayer may adopt any taxable year that satisfies the requirements of section 441 and the regulations thereunder without the approval of the Commissioner. A taxable year of a new taxpayer is adopted by filing its first Federal income tax return using that taxable year. The filing of an application for automatic extension of time to file a Federal income tax return (e.g., Form 7004, "Application for Automatic Extension of Time To File Corporation Income Tax Return"), the filing of an application for an employer identification number (i.e., Form SS-4, "Application for Employer Identification Number"), or the payment of estimated taxes, for a particular taxable year do not constitute an adoption of that taxable year.

(2) *Approval required.*—(i) *Taxpayers with required taxable years.*—A newly-formed partnership, S corporation, or PSC that wants to adopt a taxable year other than its required taxable year, a taxable year elected under section 444, or a 52-53-week taxable year that ends with reference to its required taxable year or a taxable year elected under section 444 must establish a business purpose and obtain the approval of the Commissioner under section 442.

(ii) *Taxpayers without books.*—A taxpayer that must use a calendar year under section 441(g) and paragraph (f) of this section may not adopt a fiscal year without obtaining the approval of the Commissioner.

(d) *Retention of taxable year.*—In certain cases, a partnership, S corporation, electing S corporation, or PSC will be required to change its taxable year unless it obtains the approval of the Commissioner under section 442, or makes an election under section 444, to retain its current taxable year. For example, a corporation using a June 30 fiscal year that either becomes a PSC or elects to be an S corporation and, as a result, is required to use the calendar year under section 441(i) or 1378, respectively, must obtain the approval of the Commissioner to retain its current fiscal year. Similarly, a partnership using a taxable year that corresponds to its required taxable year must obtain the approval of the Commissioner to retain such taxable year if its required taxable year changes as a result of a change in ownership. However, a partnership that previously established a business purpose to the satisfaction of the Commissioner to use a taxable year is not required to obtain the approval of the Commissioner if its required taxable year changes as a result of a change in ownership.

(e) *Change of taxable year.*—Once a taxpayer has adopted a taxable year, such taxable year must be used in computing taxable income and making returns for all subsequent years unless the taxpayer obtains approval from the Commissioner to make a change or the taxpayer is otherwise authorized to change without the approval of the Commissioner under the Internal Revenue Code (e.g., section 444 or 859) or the regulations thereunder.

(f) *Obtaining approval of the Commissioner or making a section 444 election.*—See § 1.442-1(b) for procedures for obtaining approval of the Commissioner (automatically or otherwise) to adopt, change, or retain an annual accounting period. See §§ 1.444-1T and 1.444-2T for qualifications, and 1.444-3T for procedures, for making an election under section 444. [Reg. § 1.441-1.]

☐ [*T.D.* 8996, 5-16-2002. *Amended by T.D.* 9849, 3-11-2019.]

§ 1.442-1. Change of annual accounting period.—(a) *Approval of the Commissioner.*—A taxpayer that has adopted an annual accounting period (as defined in § 1.441-1(b)(3)) as its taxable year generally must continue to use that annual accounting period in computing its taxable income and for making its Federal income tax returns. If the taxpayer wants to change its annual accounting period and use a new taxable year, it must obtain the approval of the Commissioner, unless it is otherwise authorized to change without the approval of the Commissioner under either the Internal Revenue Code (e.g., section 444 and section 859) or the regulations thereunder (e.g., paragraph (c) of this section). In addition, as described in § 1.441-1(c) and (d), a partnership, S corporation, electing S corporation, or personal service corporation (PSC) generally is required to secure the approval of the Commissioner to adopt or retain an annual accounting period other than its required taxable year. The manner of obtaining approval from the Commissioner to adopt, change, or retain an annual accounting period is provided in paragraph (b) of this section. However, special rules for obtaining approval may be provided in other sections.

(b) *Obtaining approval.*—(1) *Time and manner for requesting approval.*—In order to secure the approval of the Commissioner to adopt, change, or retain an annual accounting period, a taxpayer must file an application, generally on Form 1128, "Application To Adopt, Change, or Retain a Tax Year," with the Commissioner within such time and in such manner as is provided in administrative procedures published by the Commissioner.

(2) *General requirements for approval.*—An adoption, change, or retention in annual accounting period will be approved where the taxpayer establishes a business purpose for the requested annual accounting period and agrees to the Commissioner's prescribed terms, conditions, and adjustments for effecting the adoption, change, or retention. In determining whether a taxpayer has established a business purpose and which terms, conditions, and adjustments will be required, consideration will be given to all the facts and circumstances relating to the adoption, change, or retention, including the tax consequences resulting therefrom. Generally, the requirement of a business purpose will be satisfied, and adjustments to neutralize any tax consequences will not be required, if the requested annual accounting period coincides with the taxpayer's required taxable year (as defined in § 1.441-1(b)(2)), ownership taxable year, or natural business year. In the case of a partnership, S corporation, electing S corporation, or PSC, deferral of income to partners, shareholders, or employee-owners will not be treated as a business purpose.

* * *

[Reg. § 1.442-1.]

☐ [*T.D.* 6226, 2-27-57. *Amended by T.D.* 6432, 12-18-59, *T.D.* 6614, 10-12-62, *T.D.* 7235, 12-27-72, *T.D.* 7286, 9-26-73, *T.D.* 7323, 9-24-74, *T.D.* 7470, 2-28-77, *T.D.* 7767, 2-3-81, *T.D.* 7936, 1-17-84; *T.D.* 8123, 2-5-87 *and T.D.* 8996, 5-16-2002.]

Methods of Accounting

§ 1.446-1. General rule for methods of accounting.—(a) *General rule.*—(1) Section 446(a) provides that taxable income shall be computed under the method of accounting on the basis of which a taxpayer regularly computes his income in keeping his books. The term "method of accounting" includes not only the over-all method of accounting of the taxpayer but also the accounting treatment of any item. Examples of such over-all methods are the cash receipts and disbursements method, an accrual method, combinations of such methods, and combinations of the foregoing with various methods provided for the accounting treatment of special items. These methods of accounting for special items include the accounting treatment prescribed for research and experimental expenditures, soil and water conservation expenditures, depreciation, net operating losses, etc. Except for deviations permitted or required by such special accounting treatment, taxable income shall be computed under the method of accounting on the basis of which the taxpayer regularly computes his income in keeping his books. For requirement respecting the adoption or change of accounting method, see section 446(e) and paragraph (e) of this section.

(2) It is recognized that no uniform method of accounting can be prescribed for all taxpayers. Each taxpayer shall adopt such forms and systems as are, in his judgment, best suited to his needs. However, no method of accounting is acceptable unless, in the opinion of the Commissioner, it clearly reflects income. A method of accounting which reflects the consistent application of generally accepted accounting principles in a particular trade or business in accordance with accepted conditions or practices in that trade or business will ordinarily be regarded as clearly reflecting income, provided all items of gross income and expense are treated consistently from year to year.

(3) Items of gross income and expenditures which are elements in the computation of taxable income need not be in the form of cash. It is sufficient that such items can be valued in terms of money. For general rules relating to the taxable year for inclusion of income and for taking deductions, see sections 451 and 461, and the regulations thereunder.

(4) Each taxpayer is required to make a return of his taxable income for each taxable year and must maintain such accounting records as will enable him to file a correct return. See section 6001 and the regulations thereunder. Accounting records include the taxpayer's regular books of account and such other records and data as may be necessary to support the entries on his books of account and on his return, as for example, a reconciliation of any differences between such books and his return. The following are among the essential features that must be considered in maintaining such records:

(i) In all cases in which the production, purchase, or sale of merchandise of any kind in an income-producing factor, merchandise on hand (including finished goods, work in process, raw materials, and supplies) at the beginning and end of the year shall be taken into account in computing the taxable income of the year. (For rules relating to computation of inventories, see sections 263A, 471 and 472, and the regulations thereunder.)

(ii) Expenditures made during the year shall be properly classified as between capital and expense. For example, expenditures for such items as plant and equipment, which have a useful life extending substantially beyond the taxable year, shall be charged to a capital account and not to an expense account.

(iii) In any case in which there is allowable with respect to an asset a deduction for depreciation, amortization, or depletion, any expenditures (other than ordinary repairs) made to restore the asset or prolong its useful life shall be added to the asset account or charged against the appropriate reserve.

(b) *Exceptions.*—(1) If the taxpayer does not regularly employ a method of accounting which clearly reflects his income, the computation of taxable income shall be made in a manner which, in the opinion of the Commissioner, does clearly reflect income.

(2) A taxpayer whose sole source of income is wages need not keep formal books in order to have an accounting method. Tax returns, copies thereof, or other records may be sufficient to establish the use of the method of accounting used in the preparation of the taxpayer's income tax returns.

(c) *Permissible methods.*—(1) *In general.*—Subject to the provisions of paragraphs (a) and (b) of this section, a taxpayer may compute his taxable income under any of the following methods of accounting:

(i) *Cash receipts and disbursements method.*—Generally, under the cash receipts and disbursements method in the computation of taxable income, all items which constitute gross income (whether in the form of cash, property, or services) are to be included for the taxable year in which actually or constructively received. Expenditures are to be deducted for the taxable year in which actually made. For rules relating to constructive receipt, see § 1.451-2. For treatment of an expenditure attributable to more than one taxable year, see section 461(a) and paragraph (a)(1) of § 1.461-1.

(ii) *Accrual method.*—(A) Generally, under an accrual method, income is to be included for the taxable year when all the events have occurred that fix the right to receive the income and the amount of the income can be determined with reasonable accuracy. Under such a method, a liability is incurred, and generally is taken into account for Federal income tax purposes, in the taxable year in which all the events have occurred that establish the fact of the liability, the amount of the liability can be determined with reasonable accuracy, and economic performance has occurred with respect to the liability. (See paragraph (a)(2)(iii)(A) of §1.461-1 for examples of liabilities that may not be taken into account until after the taxable year incurred, and see §§1.461-4 through 1.461-6 for rules relating to economic performance.) Applicable provisions of the Code, the Income Tax Regulations, and other guidance published by the Secretary prescribe the manner in which a liability that has been incurred is taken into account. For example, section 162 provides that a deductible liability generally is taken into account in the taxable year incurred through a deduction from gross income. As a further example, under section 263 or 263A, a liability that relates to the creation of an asset having a useful life extending substantially beyond the close of the taxable year is taken into account in the taxable year incurred through capitalization (within the meaning of §1.263A-1(c)(3)), and may later affect the computation of taxable income through depreciation or otherwise over a period including subsequent taxable years, in accordance with applicable Internal Revenue Code sections and related guidance.

(B) The term "liability" includes any item allowable as a deduction, cost, or expense for Federal income tax purposes. In addition to allowable deductions, the term includes any amount otherwise allowable as a capitalized cost, as a cost taken into account in computing cost of goods sold, as a cost allocable to a long-term contract, or as any other cost or expense. Thus, for example, an amount that a taxpayer expends or will expend for capital improvements to property must be incurred before the taxpayer may take the amount into account in computing its basis in the property. The term "liability" is not limited to items for which a legal obligation to pay exists at the time of payment. Thus, for example, amounts prepaid for goods or services and amounts paid without a legal obligation to do so may not be taken into account by an accrual basis taxpayer any earlier than the taxable year in which those amounts are incurred.

(C) No method of accounting is acceptable unless, in the opinion of the Commissioner, it clearly reflects income. The method used by the taxpayer in determining when income is to be accounted for will generally be acceptable if it accords with generally accepted accounting principles, is consistently used by the taxpayer from year to year, and is consistent with the Income Tax Regulations. For example, a taxpayer engaged in a manufacturing business may account for sales of the taxpayer's product when the goods are shipped, when the product is delivered or accepted, or when title to the goods passes to the customers, whether or not billed, depending on the method regularly employed in keeping the taxpayer's books.

(iii) *Other permissible methods.*—Special methods of accounting are described elsewhere in chapter 1 of the Code and the regulations thereunder. For example, see the following sections and the regulations thereunder: Sections 61 and 162, relating to the crop method of accounting; section 453, relating to the installment method; section 460, relating to the long-term contract methods. In addition, special methods of accounting for particular items of income and expense are provided under other sections of chapter 1. For example, see section 174, relating to research and experimental expenditures, and section 175, relating to soil and water conservation expenditures.

(iv) *Combinations of the foregoing methods.*—*(a)* In accordance with the following rules, any combination of the foregoing methods of accounting will be permitted in connection with a trade or business if such combination clearly reflects income and is consistently used. Where a combination of methods of accounting includes any special methods, such as those referred to in subdivision (iii) of this subparagraph, the taxpayer must comply with the requirements relating to such special methods. A taxpayer using an accrual method of accounting with respect to purchases and sales may use the cash method in computing all other items of income and expense. However, a taxpayer who uses the cash method of accounting in computing gross income from his trade or business shall use the cash method in computing expenses of such trade or business. Similarly, a taxpayer who uses an accrual method of accounting in computing business expenses shall use an accrual method in computing items affecting gross income from his trade or business.

(b) A taxpayer using one method of accounting in computing items of income and deductions of his trade or business may compute other items of income and deductions not connected with his trade or business under a different method of accounting.

(2) *Special rules.*—(i) In any case in which it is necessary to use an inventory the accrual method of accounting must be used with regard to purchases and sales unless otherwise authorized under subdivision (ii) of this subparagraph.

(ii) No method of accounting will be regarded as clearly reflecting income unless all items of gross profit and deductions are treated with consistency from year to year. The Commissioner may authorize a taxpayer to adopt or change to a method of accounting permitted by this chapter although the method is not specifically described in this part if, in the opinion of the Commissioner, income is clearly reflected by the use of such method. Further, the Commissioner may authorize a taxpayer to continue the use of a method of accounting consistently used by the taxpayer, even though not specifically authorized by the regulations in this part, if, in the opinion of the Commissioner, income is clearly reflected by the use of such method. See section 446(a) and paragraph (a) of this section, which require that taxable income shall be computed under the method of accounting on the basis of which the taxpayer regularly computes his income in keeping his books, and section 446(e) and paragraph (e) of this section, which require the prior approval of the Commissioner in the case of changes in accounting method.

(iii) The timing rules of § 1.1502-13 are a method of accounting for intercompany transactions (as defined in § 1.1502-13(b)(1)(i)), to be applied by each member of a consolidated group in addition to the member's other methods of accounting. See § 1.1502-13(a)(3)(i). This paragraph (c)(2)(iii) is applicable to consolidated return years beginning on or after November 7, 2001.

(d) *Taxpayer engaged in more than one business.*—(1) Where a taxpayer has two or more separate and distinct trades or businesses, a different method of accounting may be used for each trade or business, provided the method used for each trade or business clearly reflects the income of that particular trade or business. For example, a taxpayer may account for the operations of a personal service business on the cash receipts and disbursements method and of a manufacturing business on an accrual method, provided such businesses are separate and distinct and the methods used for each clearly reflect income. The method first used in accounting for business income and deductions in connection with each trade or business, as evidenced in the taxpayer's income tax return in which such income or deductions are first reported, must be consistently followed thereafter.

(2) No trade or business will be considered separate and distinct for purposes of this paragraph unless a complete and separable set of books and records is kept for such trade or business.

(3) If, by reason of maintaining different methods of accounting, there is a creation or shifting of profits or losses between the trades or businesses of the taxpayer (for example, through inventory adjustments, sales, purchases, or expenses) so that income of the taxpayer is not clearly reflected, the trades or businesses of the taxpayer will not be considered to be separate and distinct.

* * *

[Reg. § 1.446–1.]

☐ [*T.D.* 6282, 12-24-57. *Amended by T.D.* 6584, 12-20-61; *T.D.* 7073, 11-17-70; *T.D.* 7285, 9-14-73; *T.D.* 8067, 12-30-85; *T.D.* 8131, 3-24-87; *T.D.* 8408, 4-9-92; *T.D.* 8482, 8-6-93; *T.D.* 8608, 8-4-95; *T.D.* 8719, 5-14-97; *T.D.* 8742, 12-30-97; *T.D.* 8929, 1-10-2001; *T.D.* 9025, 12-13-2002; *T.D.* 9105, 12-30-2003; *T.D.* 9307, 12-22-2006 *and T.D.* 9534, 7-29-2011.]

§ 1.451-1. General rule for taxable year of inclusion.—(a) *General rule.*—Gains, profits, and income are to be included in gross income for the taxable year in which they are actually or constructively received by the taxpayer unless includible for a different year in accordance with the taxpayer's method of accounting. Under an accrual method of accounting, income is includible in gross income when all the events have occurred which fix the right to receive such income and the amount thereof can be determined with reasonable accuracy. Therefore, under such a method of accounting if, in the case of compensation for services, no determination can be made as to the right to such compensation or the amount thereof until the services are completed, the amount of compensation is ordinarily income from the taxable year in which the determination can be made. Under the cash receipts and disbursements method of accounting, such an amount is includible in gross income when actually or constructively received. Where an amount of income is properly accrued on the basis of a reasonable estimate and the exact amount is subsequently determined, the difference, if any, shall be taken into account for the taxable year in which such determination is made. To the extent that income is attributable to the recovery of bad debts for accounts charged off in prior years, it is includible in the year of recovery in accordance with the taxpayer's method of accounting, regardless of the date when the amounts were charged off. For treatment of bad debts and bad debt recoveries, see sections 166 and 111 and the regulations thereunder. For rules relating to the treatment of amounts received in crop shares, see section 61 and the regulations thereunder. For the year in which a partner must include his distributive share of partnership income, see section 706(a) and paragraph (a) of § 1.706-1. If a taxpayer ascertains that an item should have been included in gross income in a prior taxable year, he should, if within the period of limitation, file an amended return and pay any additional tax due. Similarly, if a taxpayer ascertains that an item was improperly included in gross income in a prior taxable year, he should, if within the period of limitation, file claim for credit or refund of any overpayment of tax arising therefrom.

(b) *Special rule in case of death.*—(1) A taxpayer's taxable year ends on the date of his death. See section 443(a)(2) and paragraph (a)(2) of §1.443-1. In computing taxable income for such year, there shall be included only amounts properly includible under the method of accounting used by the taxpayer. However, if the taxpayer used an accrual method of accounting, amounts accrued only by reason of his death shall not be included in computing taxable income for such year. If the taxpayer uses no regular accounting method, only amounts actually or constructively received during such year shall be included. (For rules relating to the inclusion of partnership income in the return of a decedent partner, see subchapter K of chapter 1 of the Code and the regulations thereunder.)

(2) If the decedent owned an installment obligation the income from which was taxable to him under section 453, no income is required to be reported in the return of the decedent by reason of the transmission at death of such obligation. See section 453(d)(3). For the treatment of installment obligations acquired by the decedent's estate or by any person by bequest, devise, or inheritance from the decedent, see section 691(a)(4) and the regulations thereunder.

(c) *Special rule for employee tips.*—Tips reported by an employee to his employer in a written statement furnished to the employer pursuant to section 6053(a) shall be included in gross income of the employee for the taxable year in which the written statement is furnished the employer. For provisions relating to the reporting of tips by an employee to his employer, see section 6053 and §31.6053-1 of this chapter (Employment Tax Regulations).

(d) *Special rule for ratable inclusion of original issue discount.*—For ratable inclusion of original issue discount in respect of certain corporate obligations issued after May 27, 1969, see section 1232(a)(3).

(e) *Special rule for inclusion of qualified tax refund effected by allocation.*—For rules relating to the inclusion in income of an amount paid by a taxpayer in respect of his liability for a qualified State individual income tax and allocated or reallocated in such a manner as to apply it toward the taxpayer's liability for the Federal income tax, see paragraph (f)(1) of §301.6361-1 of this chapter (Regulations on Procedure and Administration).

(f) *Timing of income from notional principal contracts.*—For the timing of income with respect to notional principal contracts, see §1.446-3.

(g) *Timing of income from section 467 rental agreements.*—For the timing of income with respect to section 467 rental agreements, see section 467 and the regulations thereunder. [Reg. §1.451-1.]

☐ [*T.D.* 6282, 12-24-57. *Amended by T.D.* 7001, 1-17-69; *T.D.* 7154, 12-27-71; *T.D.* 7577, 12-19-78; *T.D.* 8491, 10-8-93 *and T.D.* 8820, 5-17-99.]

§1.451-2. Constructive receipts of income.—(a) *General rule.*—Income although not actually reduced to a taxpayer's possession is constructively received by him in the taxable year during which it is credited to his account, set apart for him, or otherwise made available so that he may draw upon it at any time, or so that he could have drawn upon it during the taxable year if notice of intention to withdraw had been given. However, income is not constructively received if the taxpayer's control of its receipt is subject to substantial limitations or restrictions. Thus, if a corporation credits its employees with bonus stock, but the stock is not available to such employees until some future date, the mere crediting on the books of the corporation does not constitute receipt. In the case of interest, dividends, or other earnings (whether or not credited) payable in respect of any deposit or account in a bank, building and loan association, savings and loan association, or similar institution, the following are not substantial limitations or restrictions on the taxpayer's control over the receipt of such earnings:

(1) A requirement that the deposit or account, and the earnings thereon, must be withdrawn in multiples of even amounts;

(2) The fact that the taxpayer would, by withdrawing the earnings during the taxable year, receive earnings that are not substantially less in comparison with the earnings for the corresponding period to which the taxpayer would be entitled had he left the account on deposit until a later date (for example, if an amount equal to three months' interest must be forfeited upon withdrawal or redemption before maturity of a one year or less certificate of deposit, time deposit, bonus plan, or other deposit arrangement then the earnings payable on premature withdrawal or redemption would be substantially less when compared with the earnings available at maturity);

(3) A requirement that the earnings may be withdrawn only upon a withdrawal of all or part of the deposit or account. However, the mere fact that such institutions may pay earnings on withdrawals, total or partial, made during the last three business days of any calendar

month ending a regular quarterly or semiannual earnings period at the applicable rate calculated to the end of such calendar month shall not constitute constructive receipt of income by any depositor or account holder in any such institution who has not made a withdrawal during such period;

(4) A requirement that a notice of intention to withdraw must be given in advance of the withdrawal. In any case when the rate of earnings payable in respect of such a deposit or account depends on the amount of notice of intention to withdraw that is given, earnings at the maximum rate are constructively received during the taxable year regardless of how long the deposit or account was held during the year or whether, in fact, any notice of intention to withdraw is given during the year. However, if in the taxable year of withdrawal the depositor or account holder receives a lower rate of earnings because he failed to give the required notice of intention to withdraw, he shall be allowed an ordinary loss in such taxable year in an amount equal to the difference between the amount of earnings previously included in gross income and the amount of earnings actually received. See section 165 and the regulations thereunder.

(b) *Examples of constructive receipt.*—Amounts payable with respect to interest coupons which have matured and are payable but which have not been cashed are constructively received in the taxable year during which the coupons mature, unless it can be shown that there are no funds available for payment of the interest during such year. Dividends on corporate stock are constructively received when unqualifiedly made subject to the demand of the shareholder. However, if a dividend is declared payable on December 31 and the corporation followed its usual practice of paying the dividends by checks mailed so that the shareholders would not receive them until January of the following year, such dividends are not considered to have been constructively received in December. Generally, the amount of dividends or interest credited on savings bank deposits or to shareholders of organizations such as building and loan associations or cooperative banks is income to the depositors or shareholders for the taxable year when credited. However, if any portion of such dividends or interest is not subject to withdrawal at the time credited, such portion is not constructively received and does not constitute income to the depositor or shareholder until the taxable year in which the portion first may be withdrawn. Accordingly, if, under a bonus or forfeiture plan, a portion of the dividends or interest is accumulated and may not be withdrawn until the maturity of the plan, the crediting of such portion to the account of the shareholder or depositor does not constitute constructive receipt. In this case, such credited portion is income to the depositor or shareholder in the year in which the plan matures. However, in the case of certain deposits made after December 31, 1970, in banks, domestic building and loan associations, and similar financial institutions, the ratable inclusion rules of section 1232(a)(3) apply. See § 1.1232-3A. Accrued interest on unwithdrawn insurance policy dividends is gross income to the taxpayer for the first taxable year during which such interest may be withdrawn by him. [Reg. § 1.451-2.]

☐ [*T.D.* 6282, 12-24-57. *Amended by T.D.* 6723, 4-20-64; *T.D.* 7154, 12-27-71 *and T.D.* 7663, 12-21-79.]

§ 15A.453-1. Installment method reporting for sales of real property and casual sales of personal property (Temporary).—(a) *In general.*—Unless the taxpayer otherwise elects in the manner prescribed in paragraph (d)(3) of this section, income from a sale of real property or a casual sale of personal property, where any payment is to be received in a taxable year after the year of sale, is to be reported on the installment method.

(b) *Installment sale defined.*—(1) *In general.*—The term "installment sale" means a disposition of property (except as provided in paragraph (b)(4) of this section) where at least one payment is to be received after the close of the taxable year in which the disposition occurs. The term "installment sale" includes dispositions from which payment is to be received in a lump sum in a taxable year subsequent to the year of sale. For purposes of this paragraph, the taxable year in which payments are to be received is to be determined without regard to section 453(e) (relating to related party sales), section (f)(3) (relating to the definition of a "payment") and section (g) (relating to sales of depreciable property to a spouse or 80-percent-owned entity).

(2) *Installment method defined.*—(i) *In general.*—Under the installment method, the amount of any payment which is income to the taxpayer is that portion of the installment payment received in that year which the gross profit realized or to be realized bears to the total contract price (the "gross profit ratio"). See paragraph (c) of this section for rules describing installment method reporting of contingent payment sales.

(ii) *Selling price defined.*—The term "selling price" means the gross selling price without reduction to reflect any existing mortgage or other encumbrance on the property (whether assumed or taken subject to by the buyer) and, for installment sales in taxable years ending after October 19, 1980, without reduction to reflect any selling expenses. Neither interest, whether stated or unstated, nor original issue discount is considered to be a part of the selling price. See paragraph (c) of this section for rules describing installment method reporting of contingent payment sales.

(iii) *Contract price defined.*—The term "contract price" means the total contract price equal to selling price reduced by that portion of any qualifying indebtedness (as defined in paragraph (b)(2)(iv) of this section), assumed or taken subject to by the buyer, which does not exceed the seller's basis in the property (adjusted, for installment sales in taxable years ending after October 19, 1980, to reflect commissions and other selling expenses as provided in paragraph (b)(2)(v) of this section). See paragraph (c) of this section for rules describing installment method reporting of contingent payment sales.

(iv) *Qualifying indebtedness.*—The term "qualifying indebtedness" means a mortgage or other indebtedness encumbering the property and indebtedness, not secured by the property but incurred or assumed by the purchaser incident to the purchaser's acquisition, holding, or operation in the ordinary course of business or investment, of the property. The term "qualifying indebtedness" does not include an obligation of the taxpayer incurred incident to the disposition of the property (*e.g.,* legal fees relating to the taxpayer's sale of the property) or an obligation functionally unrelated to the acquisition, holding, or operating of the property (*e.g.,* the taxpayer's medical bill). Any obligation created subsequent to the taxpayer's acquisition of the property and incurred or assumed by the taxpayer or placed as an encumbrance on the property in contemplation of disposition of the property is not qualifying indebtedness if the arrangement results in accelerating recovery of the taxpayer's basis in the installment sale.

(v) *Gross profit defined.*—The term "gross profit" means the selling price less the adjusted basis as defined in section 1011 and the regulations thereunder. For sales in taxable years ending after October 19, 1980, in the case of sales of real property by a person other than a dealer and casual sales of personal property, commissions and other selling expenses shall be added to basis for purposes of determining the proportion of payments which is gross profit attributable to the disposition. Such additions to basis will not be deemed to affect the taxpayer's holding period in the transferred property.

(3) *Payment.*—(i) *In general.*—Except as provided in paragraph (e) of this section (relating to purchaser evidences of indebtedness payable on demand or readily tradable), the term "payment" does not include the receipt of evidences of indebtedness of the person acquiring the property ("installment obligation"), whether or not payment of such indebtedness is guaranteed by a third party (including a government agency). For special rules regarding the receipt of an evidence of indebtedness of a transferee of a qualified intermediary, see §§1.1031(b)-2(b) and 1.1031(k)-1(j)(2)(iii) of this chapter. A standby letter of credit (as defined in paragraph (b)(3)(iii) of this section) shall be treated as a third party guarantee. Payments include amounts actually or constructively received in the taxable year under an installment obligation. For a special rule regarding a transfer of property to a qualified intermediary followed by the sale of such property by the qualified intermediary, see §1.1031(k)-1(j)(2)(ii) of this chapter. Receipt of an evidence of indebtedness which is secured directly or indirectly by cash or a cash equivalent, such as a bank certificate of deposit or a treasury note, will be treated as the receipt of payment. For a special rule regarding a transfer of property in exchange for an obligation that is secured by cash or a cash equivalent held in a qualified escrow account or a qualified trust, see §1.1031(k)-1(j)(2)(i) of this chapter. Payment may be received in cash or other property, including foreign currency, marketable securities, and evidences of indebtedness which are payable on demand or readily tradable. However, for special rules relating to the receipt of certain property with respect to which gain is not recognized, see paragraph (f) of this section (relating to transactions described in sections 351, 356(a) and 1031). Except as provided in §15A.453-2 of these regulations (relating to distributions of installment obligations in corporate liquidations described in section 337), payment includes receipt of an evidence of indebtedness of a person other than the person acquiring the property from the taxpayer. For purposes of determining the amount of payment received in the taxable year, the amount of qualifying indebtedness (as defined in paragraph (b)(2)(iv) of this section) assumed or taken subject to by the person acquiring the property shall be included only to the extent that it exceeds the basis of the property (determined after adjustment to reflect selling expenses). For purposes of the preceding sentence, an arrangement under which the taxpayer's liability on qualifying indebtedness is eliminated incident to the disposition (*e.g.,* a novation) shall be treated as an assumption of the qualifying indebtedness. If the taxpayer sells property to a creditor of

the taxpayer and indebtedness of the taxpayer is cancelled in consideration of the sale, such cancellation shall be treated as payment. To the extent that cancellation is not in consideration of the sale, see §§1.61-12(b)(1) and 1.1001-2(a)(2) relating to discharges of indebtedness. If the taxpayer sells property which is encumbered by a mortgage or other indebtedness on which the taxpayer is not personally liable, and the person acquiring the property is the obligee, the taxpayer shall be treated as having received payment in the amount of such indebtedness.

(ii) *Wrap-around mortgage.*—This paragraph (b)(3)(ii) shall apply generally to any installment sale after March 4, 1981 unless the installment sale was completed before June 1, 1981 pursuant to a written obligation binding on the seller that was executed on or before March 4, 1981. A "wrap-around mortgage" means an agreement in which the buyer initially does not assume and purportedly does not take subject to part or all of the mortgage or other indebtedness encumbering the property ("wrapped indebtedness") and, instead, the buyer issues to the seller an installment obligation the principal amount of which reflects such wrapped indebtedness. Ordinarily, the seller will use payments received on the installment obligation to service the wrapped indebtedness. The wrapped indebtedness shall be deemed to have been taken subject to even though title to the property has not passed in the year of sale and even though the seller remains liable for payments on the wrapped indebtedness. In the hands of the seller, the wrap-around installment obligation shall have a basis equal to the seller's basis in the property which was the subject of the installment sale, increased by the amount of gain recognized in the year of sale, and decreased by the amount of cash and the fair market value of other nonqualifying property received in the year of sale. For purposes of this paragraph (b)(3)(ii), the amount of any indebtedness assumed or taken subject to by the buyer (other than wrapped indebtedness) is to be treated as cash received by the seller in the year of sale. Therefore, except as otherwise required by section 483 or 1232, the gross profit ratio with respect to the wrap-around installment obligation is a fraction, the numerator of which is the face value of the obligation less the taxpayer's basis in the obligation and the denominator of which is the face value of the obligation.

(iii) *Standby letter of credit.*—The term "standby letter of credit" means a non-negotiable, nontransferable (except together with the evidence of indebtedness which it secures) letter of credit, issued by a bank or other financial institution, which serves as a guarantee of the evidence of indebtedness which is secured by the letter of credit. Whether or not the letter of credit explicitly states it is non-negotiable and nontransferable, it will be treated as non-negotiable and nontransferable if applicable local law so provides. The mere right of the secured party (under applicable local law) to transfer the proceeds of a letter of credit shall be disregarded in determining whether the instrument qualifies as a standby letter of credit. A letter of credit is not a standby letter of credit if it may be drawn upon in the absence of default in payment of the underlying evidence of indebtedness.

(4) *Exceptions.*—The term "installment sale" does not include, and the provisions of section 453 do not apply to, dispositions of personal property on the installment plan by a person who regularly sells or otherwise disposes of personal property on the installment plan, or to dispositions of personal property of a kind which is required to be included in the inventory of the taxpayer if on hand at the close of the taxable year. See section 453A and the regulations thereunder for rules relating to installment sales by dealers in personal property. A dealer in real property or a farmer who is not required under his method of accounting to maintain inventories may report the gain on the installment method under section 453.

(5) *Examples.*—The following examples illustrate installment method reporting under this section:

Example (1). In 1980, A, a calendar year taxpayer, sells Blackacre, an unencumbered capital asset in A's hands, to B for $100,000: $10,000 down and the remainder payable in equal annual installments over the next 9 years, together with adequate stated interest. A's basis in Blackacre, exclusive of selling expenses, is $38,000. Selling expenses paid by A are $2,000. Therefore, the gross profit is $60,000 ($100,000 selling price - $40,000 basis inclusive of selling expenses). The gross profit ratio is 3/5 (gross profit of $60,000 divided by $100,000 contract price). Accordingly, $6,000 (3/5 of $10,000) of each $10,000 payment received is gain attributable to the sale and $4,000 ($10,000 - $6,000) is recovery of basis. The interest received in addition to principal is ordinary income to A.

Example (2). C sells Whiteacre to D for a selling price of $160,000. Whiteacre is encumbered by a longstanding mortgage in the principal amount of $60,000. D will assume or take subject to the $60,000 mortgage and pay the remaining $100,000 in 10 equal annual installments together with adequate stated interest. C's basis in Whiteacre is $90,000. There are no selling expenses. The contract price is

$100,000, the $160,000 selling price reduced by the mortgage of $60,000 assumed or taken subject to. Gross profit is $70,000 ($160,000 selling price less C's basis of $90,000). C's gross profit ratio is 7/10 (gross profit of $70,000 divided by $100,000 contract price). Thus, $7,000 (7/10 of $10,000) of each $10,000 annual payment is gain attributable to the sale, and $3,000 ($10,000 – $7,000) is recovery of basis.

Example (3). The facts are the same as in example (2), except that C's basis in the land is $40,000. In the year of the sale C is deemed to have received payment of $20,000 ($60,000 – $40,000, the amount by which the mortgage D assumed or took subject to exceeds C's basis). Since basis is fully recovered in the year of sale, the gross profit ratio is 1 ($120,000/$120,000) and C will report 100% of the $20,000 deemed payment in the year of sale and each $10,000 annual payment as gain attributable to the sale.

Example (4). E sells Blackacre, an unencumbered capital gain property in E's hands, to F on January 2, 1981. F makes a cash down payment of $500,000 and issues a note to E obliging F to pay an additional $500,000 on the fifth anniversary date. The note does not require a payment of interest. In determining selling price, section 483 will apply to recharacterize as interest a portion of the $500,000 future payment. Assume that under section 483 and the applicable regulations $193,045 is treated as total unstated interest, and the selling price is $806,955 ($1 million less unstated interest). Assuming E's basis (including selling expenses) in Blackacre is $200,000, gross profit is $606,955 ($806,955 – $200,000) and the gross profit ratio is 75.21547%. Accordingly, of the $500,000 cash down payment received by E in 1981, $376,077 (75.21547% of $500,000) is gain attributable to the sale and $123,923 is recovery of basis ($500,000 – $376,077).

Example (5). In 1982, G sells to H Blackacre, which is encumbered by a first mortgage with a principal amount of $500,000 and a second mortgage with a principal amount of $400,000, for a selling price of $2 million. G's basis in Blackacre is $700,000. Under the agreement between G and H, passage of title is deferred and H does not assume and purportedly does not take subject to either mortgage in the year of sale. H pays G $200,000 in cash and issues a wrap-around mortgage note with a principal amount of $1,800,000 bearing adequate stated interest. H is deemed to have acquired Blackacre subject to the first and second mortgages (wrapped indebtedness) totalling $900,000. The contract price is $1,300,000 (selling price of $2 million less $700,000 mortgages within the seller's basis assumed or taken subject to). Gross profit is also $1,300,000 (selling price of $2 million less $700,000 basis). Accordingly in the year of sale, the gross profit ratio is 1 ($1,300,000/$1,300,000). Payment in the year of sale is $400,000 ($200,000 cash received plus $200,000 mortgage in excess of basis ($900,000 – $700,000)). Therefore, G recognizes $400,000 gain in the year of sale ($400,000 × 1). In the hands of G the wrap-around installment obligation has a basis of $900,000, equal to G's basis in Blackacre ($700,000) increased by the gain recognized by G in the year of sale ($400,000) reduced by the cash received by G in the year of sale ($200,000). G's gross profit with respect to the note is $900,000 ($1,800,000 face amount less $900,000 basis in the note) and G's contract price with respect to the note is its face amount of $1,800,000. Therefore, the gross profit ratio with respect to the note is ½ ($900,000/$1,800,000).

Example (6). The facts are the same as example (5) except that under the terms of the agreement H assumes the $500,000 first mortgage on Blackacre. H does not assume and purportedly does not take subject to the $400,000 second mortgage on Blackacre. The wrap-around installment obligation issued by H to G has a face amount of $1,300,000. The tax results in the year of sale to G are the same as example (5) ($400,000 payment received and gain recognized). In the hands of G, basis in the wrap-around installment obligation is $400,000 ($700,000 basis in Blackacre plus $400,000 gain recognized in the year of sale minus $700,000 ($200,000 cash received and $500,000 treated as cash received as a result of H's assumption of the first mortgage)). G's gross profit with respect to the note is $900,000 ($1,300,000 face amount of the wrap-around installment obligation less $400,000 basis in that note) and G's contract price with respect to the note is its face value of $1,300,000. Therefore, the gross profit ratio with respect to the note is 9/13

$$\frac{(\$\ 900{,}000)}{(\$1{,}300{,}000)}.$$

* * *

(c) *Contingent payment sales.*—(1) *In general.*—Unless the taxpayer otherwise elects in the manner prescribed in paragraph (d)(3) of this section, contingent payment sales are to be reported on the installment method. As used in this section, the term "contingent payment sale" means a sale or other disposition of property in which the aggregate selling price cannot be determined by the close of the taxable year in which such sale or other disposition occurs.

The term "contingent payment sale" does not include transactions with respect to which the installment obligation represents, under applicable principles of tax law, a retained interest in the property which is the subject of the transaction, an interest in a joint venture or a partnership, an equity interest in a corporation or similar transactions, regardless of the existence of a stated maximum selling price or a fixed payment term. See paragraph (c)(8) of this section, describing the extent to which the regulations under section 385 apply to the determination of whether an installment obligation represents an equity interest in a corporation.

This paragraph prescribes the rules to be applied in allocating the taxpayer's basis (including selling expenses except for selling expenses of dealers in real estate) to payments received and to be received in a contingent payment sale. The rules are designed appropriately to distinguish contingent payment sales for which a maximum selling price is determinable, sales for which a maximum selling price is not determinable but the time over which payments will be received is determinable, and sales for which neither a maximum selling price nor a definite payment term is determinable. In addition, rules are prescribed under which, in appropriate circumstances, the taxpayer will be permitted to recover basis under an income forecast computation.

(2) *Stated maximum selling price.*—(i) *In general.*—(A) A contingent payment sale will be treated as having a stated maximum selling price if, under the terms of the agreement, the maximum amount of sale proceeds that may be received by the taxpayer can be determined as of the end of the taxable year in which the sale or other disposition occurs. The stated maximum selling price shall be determined by assuming that all of the contingencies contemplated by the agreement are met or otherwise resolved in a manner that will maximize the selling price and accelerate payments to the earliest date or dates permitted under the agreement. Except as provided in paragraph (c)(2)(ii) and (7) of this section (relating to certain payment recomputations), the taxpayer's basis shall be allocated to payments received and to be received under a stated maximum selling price agreement by treating the stated maximum selling price as the selling price for purposes of paragraph (b) of this section. The stated maximum selling price, as initially determined, shall thereafter be treated as the selling price unless and until that maximum amount is reduced, whether pursuant to the terms of the original agreement, by subsequent amendment, by application of the payment recharacterization rule (described in paragraph (c)(2)(ii) of this section), or by a subsequent supervening event such as bankruptcy of the obligor. When the maximum amount is subsequently reduced, the gross profit ratio will be recomputed with respect to payments received in or after the taxable year in which an event requiring reduction occurs. If, however, application of the foregoing rules in a particular case would substantially and inappropriately accelerate or defer recovery of the taxpayer's basis, a special rule will apply. See paragraph (c)(7) of this section.

(B) The following examples illustrate the provisions of paragraph (c)(2)(i) of this section. In each example, it is assumed that application of the rules illustrated will not substantially and inappropriately defer or accelerate recovery of the taxpayer's basis.

Example (1). A sells all of the stock of X corporation to B for $100,000 payable at closing plus an amount equal to 5% of the net profits of X for each of the next nine years, the contingent payments to be made annually together with adequate stated interest. The agreement provides that the maximum amount A may receive, inclusive of the $100,000 down payment but exclusive of interest, shall be $2,000,000. A's basis in the stock of X inclusive of selling expenses, is $200,000. Selling price and contract price are considered to be $2,000,000. Gross profit is $1,800,000, and the gross profit ratio is 9/10 ($1,800,000/$2,000,000). Accordingly, of the $100,000 received by A in the year of sale, $90,000 is reportable as gain attributable to the sale and $10,000 is recovery of basis.

Example (2). C owns Blackacre which is encumbered by a long-standing mortgage of $100,000. On January 15, 1981, C sells Blackacre to D under the following payment arrangement: $100,000 in cash on closing; nine equal annual installment payments of $100,000 commencing January 15, 1982; and nine annual payments (the first to be made on March 30, 1982) equal to 5% of the gross annual rental receipts from Blackacre generated during the preceding calendar year. The agreement provides that each deferred payment shall be accompanied by a payment of interest calculated at the rate of 12% per annum and that the maximum amount payable to C under the agreement (exclusive of interest) shall be $2,100,000. The agreement also specifies that D will assume the long-standing mortgage. C's basis (inclusive of selling expenses) in Blackacre is $300,000. Accordingly, selling price is $2,100,000 and contract price is $2,000,000 (selling price of $2,100,000 less the $100,000 mortgage). The gross profit ratio is 9/10 (gross profit of $1,800,000 divided by $2,000,000 contract price). Of the $100,000 cash payment received by C in 1981, $90,000 is gain attributable to the sale of Blackacre and $10,000 is recovery of basis.

(ii) *Certain interest recomputations.*—When interest is stated in the contingent price sale agreement at a rate equal to or greater than the applicable prescribed test rate referred to in § 1.483-1(d)(1)(ii) and such stated interest is payable in addition to the amounts otherwise payable under the agreement, such stated interest is not considered a part of the selling price. In other circumstances (i.e., section 483 is applicable because no interest is stated or interest is stated below the applicable test rate, or interest is stated under a payment recharacterization provision of the sale agreement), the special rule set forth in this (ii) shall be applied in the initial computation and subsequent recomputations of selling price, contract price, and gross profit ratio. The special rule is referred to in this section as the "price-interest recomputation rule." As used in this section, the term "payment recharacterization" refers to a contractual arrangement under which a computed amount otherwise payable as part of the selling price is denominated an interest payment. The amount of unstated interest determined under section 483 or (if section 483 is inapplicable in the particular case) the amount of interest determined under a payment recharacterization arrangement is collectively referred to in this section as "internal interest" amounts. The price-interest recomputation rule is applicable to any stated maximum selling price agreement which contemplates receipt of internal interest by the taxpayer. Under the rule, stated maximum selling price will be determined as of the end of the taxpayer's taxable year in which the sale or other disposition occurs, taking into account all events which have occurred and are subject to prompt subsequent calculation and verification and assuming that all amounts that may become payable under the agreement will be paid on the earliest date or dates permitted under the agreement. With respect to the year of sale, the amount (if any) of internal interest then shall be determined taking account of the respective components of that calculation. The maximum amount initially calculated, minus the internal interest so determined, is the initial stated maximum selling price under the price-interest recomputation rule. For each subsequent taxable year, stated maximum selling price (and thus selling price, contract price, and gross profit ratio) shall be recomputed, taking into account all events which have occurred and are subject to prompt subsequent calculation and verification and assuming that all amounts that may become payable under the agreement will be paid on the earliest date or dates permitted under the agreement. The redetermined gross profit ratio, adjusted to reflect payments received and gain recognized in prior taxable years, shall be applied to payments received in that taxable year.

(iii) *Examples.*—The following examples illustrate installment method reporting of a contingent payment sale under which there is a stated maximum selling price. In each example, it is assumed that application of the rules described will not substantially and inappropriately defer or accelerate recovery of the taxpayer's basis.

Example (1). A owns all of the stock of X corporation with a basis to A of $20 million. On July 1, 1981, A sells the stock of X to B under an agreement calling for fifteen annual payments respectively equal to 5% of the net profits of X earned in the immediately preceding fiscal year beginning with the fiscal year ending March 31, 1982. Each payment is to be made on the following June 15th, commencing June 15, 1982, together with adequate stated interest. The agreement specifies that the maximum amount (exclusive of interest) payable to A shall not exceed $60 million. Since stated interest is payable as an addition to the selling price and the specified rate is not below the section 483 test rate, there is no internal interest under the agreement. The stated maximum selling price is $60 million. The gross profit ratio is ⅔ (gross profit of $40 million divided by $60 million contract price). Thus, if on June 15, 1982, A receives a payment of $3 million (exclusive of interest) under the agreement, in that year A will report $2 million ($3 million × ⅔) as gain attributable to the sale, and $1 million as recovery of basis.

Example (2). (i) The facts are the same as in example (1) except that the agreement does not call for the payment of any stated interest but does provide for an initial cash payment of $3 million on July 1, 1981. The maximum amount payable, including the $3 million initial payment, remains $60 million. Since section 483 will apply to each payment received by A more than one year following the date of sale (section 483 is inapplicable to the contingent payment that will be received on June 15, 1982 since that date is within one year following the July 1, 1981 sale date), the agreement contemplates internal interest and the price-interest recomputation rule is applicable. Under the rule, an initial determination must be made for A's taxable year 1981. On December 31, 1981, the last day of the taxable year, no events with regard to the first fiscal year have occurred which are subject to prompt subsequent calculation and verification because that fiscal year will end March 31, 1982. Under the price-interest recomputation rule, on December 31, 1981 A is required to assume that the maximum amount subsequently payable under the agreement ($57 million, equal to $60 million less the $3 million initial cash payment received by A in 1981) will be paid on the earliest date permissible under the agreement, *i.e.,* on June 15, 1982. Since no part of a payment received on that date would be treated as interest under section 483, the initial stated maximum selling price, applicable to A's 1981 tax calculation, is deemed to be $60 million. Thus, the 1981 gross profit ratio is ⅔ and for the taxable year 1981 A will report $2 million as gain attributable to the sale.

(ii) The net profits of X for its fiscal year ending March 31, 1982 are $100 million. On June 15, 1982 A receives a payment from B equal to 5% of that amount, or $6 million. On December 31, 1982, A knows that the maximum amount he may subsequently receive under the agreement is $51 million, and A is required to assume that this amount will be paid to him on the earliest permissible date, June 15, 1983. Section 483 does not treat as interest any part of the $6 million received by A on June 15, 1982, but section 483 will treat as unstated interest a computed part of the $51 million it is assumed A will receive on June 15, 1983. Assuming that under the tables in the regulations under section 483, it is determined that the principal component of a payment received more than 21 months but less than 27 months after the date of sale is considered to be .82270, $41,957,700 of the presumed $51 million payment will be treated as principal. The balance of $9,042,300 is interest. Accordingly, in A's 1982 tax calculations stated maximum selling price will be $50,957,700, which amount is equal to the stated maximum selling price that was determined in the 1981 tax calculations ($60 million) reduced by the section 483 interest component of the $6 million payment received by A in 1982 ($0) and further reduced by the section 483 interest component of the $51 million presumed payment to be received by A on June 15, 1983 ($9,042,300). Similarly, in determining gross profit for 1982 tax calculations, the gross profit of $40 million determined in the 1981 tax calculations must be reduced by the same section 483 interest amounts, yielding a recomputed gross profit of $30,957,700 ($40,000,000 - $9,042,300). Further, since prior to 1982 A received payment under the agreement (1981 payment of $3 million of which $2 million was profit), the appropriate amounts must be subtracted in the 1982 tax calculation. The total previously received selling price payment of $3 million is subtracted from the recomputed maximum selling price of $50,957,700, yielding an adjusted selling price of $47,957,700. The total previously recognized gain of $2 million is subtracted from the recomputed maximum gross profit of $30,957,700, yielding an adjusted gross profit of $28,957,700. The gross profit percentage applicable to 1982 tax calculations thus is determined to be 60.38175%, equal to the quotient of dividing the adjusted gross profit of $28,957,700 by the adjusted selling price of $47,957,700. Accordingly, of the $6 million received by A in 1982, no part of which is unstated interest under section 483, A will report $3,622,905 (60.38175% of $6 million) as gain attributable to the sale and $2,377,095 ($6,000,000 - $3,622,905) as recovery of basis.

(iii) The net profits of X for its fiscal year ending March 31, 1983 are $200 million. On June 15, 1983 A receives a payment from B equal to $10 million. On December 31, 1983, A knows that the maximum amount he may subsequently receive under the agreement is $41 million, and A is required to assume that this amount will be paid to him on the earliest permissible date, June 15, 1984. Assuming that under the tables in the regulations under section 483 it is determined that the principal component of a payment received more than 33 months but less than 39 months after the date of sale is .74622, $30,595,020 of the presumed $41 million ($51 million - $10 million) payment will be treated as principal and $10,404,980 is interest. Based upon the assumed factor for 21 months but less than 27 months (.82270) $8,227,000 of the $10 million payment is principal and $1,733,000 is interest. Accordingly, in A's 1983 tax calculations stated maximum selling price will be $47,822,020, which amount is equal to the stated maximum selling price determined in the 1981 calculation ($60 million) reduced by the section 483 interest component of the $6 million 1982 payment ($0), the section 483 interest component of the 1983 payment ($1,773,000) and by the section 483 interest component of the presumed $41 million payment to be received in 1984 ($10,404,980). The recomputed gross profit is $27,822,020 ($40 million - $10,404,980 - $1,773,000). The previously reported payments must be deducted for the 1983 calculation. Selling price is reduced to $38,822,020 by subtracting the $3 million 1981 payment and the $6 million 1982 payment ($47,822,020 - $9 million) and gross profit is reduced to $22,199,115 by subtracting the 1981 profit of $2 million and the 1982 profit of $3,622,905 ($27,822,020 - $5,622,905), yielding a gross profit percentage of 57.18176% ($22,199,115/$38,822,020). Accordingly, of the $10 million received in 1983, A will report $1,773,000 as interest under section 483, and of the remaining principal component of $8,227,000, $4,704,343 as gain attributable to the sale ($8,227,000 × 57.18176%) and $3,522,657 ($8,227,000 - $4,704,343) as recovery of basis.

Example (3). The facts are the same as in example (2) except that X is a collapsible corporation as defined in section 341(b)(1) and no limitation or exception under section 341(d), (e), or (f) is applicable. Under section 341(a), all of A's gain on the sale will be ordinary income. Accordingly, section 483 will not apply to treat as interest any part of the payments to be received by A under his agreement with B. See section 483(f)(3). Therefore, the price-interest recomputation rule is inapplicable and the tax results to A in each year in which payment is received will be determined in a manner consistent with example (1).

Example (4). The facts are the same as in example (2) (maximum amount payable under the agreement $60 million) except that the agreement between A and B contains the following "payment recharacterization" provision:

"Any payment made more than one year after the (July 1, 1981) date of sale shall be composed of an interest element and a principal element, the interest element being computed on the principal element at an interest rate of 9% per annum computed from the date of sale to the date of payment."

The results reached in example (2), with respect to the $3 million initial cash payment received by A in 1981 remain the same because, under the payment recharacterization formula, no amount received or assumed to be received prior to July 1, 1982 is treated as interest. The 1982 tax computation method described in example (2) is equally applicable to the $6 million payment received in 1982. However, the adjusted gross profit ratio determined in this example (4) will differ from the ratio determined in example (2). The difference is attributable to the difference between a 9% stated interest rate calculation (in this example (4)) and the compound rate of unstated interest required under section 483 and used in calculating the results in example (2).

Example (5). The facts are the same as in example (1). In 1992 X is adjudged a bankrupt and it is determined that, in and after 1992, B will not be required to make any further payments under the agreement, *i.e.,* B's contingent payment obligation held by A now has become worthless. Assume that A previously received aggregate payments (exclusive of interest) of $45 million and out of those payments recovered $15 million of A's total $20 million basis. For 1992 A will report a loss of $5 million attributable to the sale, taken at the time determined to be appropriate under the rules generally applicable to worthless debts.

* * *

(3) *Fixed period.*—(i) *In general.*—When a stated maximum selling price cannot be determined as of the close of the taxable year in which the sale or other disposition occurs, but the maximum period over which payments may be received under the contingent sale price agreement is fixed, the taxpayer's basis (inclusive of selling expenses) shall be allocated to the taxable years in which payment may be received under the agreement in equal annual increments. In making the allocation it is not relevant whether the buyer is required to pay adequate stated interest. However, if the terms of the agreement incorporate an arithmetic component that is not identical for all taxable years, basis shall be allocated among the taxable years to accord with that component unless, taking into account all of the payment terms of the agreement, it is inappropriate to presume that payments under the contract are likely to accord with the variable component. If in any taxable year no payment is received or the amount of payment received (exclusive of interest) is less than the basis allocated to that taxable year, no loss shall be allowed unless the taxable year is the final payment year under the agreement or unless it is otherwise determined in accordance with the rules generally applicable to worthless debts that the future payment obligation under the agreement has become worthless. When no loss is allowed, the unrecovered portion of the basis allocated to the taxable year shall be carried forward to the next succeeding taxable year. If application of the foregoing rules to a particular case would substantially and inappropriately defer or accelerate recovery of the taxpayer's basis, a special rule will apply. See paragraph (c)(7) of this section.

(ii) *Examples.*—The following examples illustrate the rules for recovery of basis in a contingent payment sale in which stated maximum selling price cannot be determined but the period over which payments are to be received under the agreement is fixed. In each case, it is assumed that application of the described rules will not substantially and inappropriately defer or accelerate recovery of the taxpayer's basis.

Example (1). A sells Blackacre to B for 10 percent of Blackacre's gross yield for each of the next 5 years. A's basis in Blackacre is $5 million. Since the sales price is indefinite and the maximum selling price is not ascertainable from the terms of the contract, basis is recovered ratably over the period during which payment may be received under the contract. Thus, assuming A receives the payments (exclusive of interest) listed in the following table, A will report the following:

Year	*Payment*	*Basis Recovered*	*Gain Attributable to the Sale*
1	$1,300,000	$1,000,000	$300,000
2	$1,500,000	$1,000,000	$500,000
3	$1,400,000	$1,000,000	$400,000
4	$1,800,000	$1,000,000	$800,000
5	$2,100,000	$1,000,000	$1,100,000

Example (2). The facts are the same as in example (1), except that the payment in year 1 is only $900,000. Since the installment payment is less than the amount of basis allocated to that year, the unrecovered basis, $100,000, is carried forward to year 2.

Year	*Payment*	*Basis Recovered*	*Gain Attributable to the Sale*
1	$900,000	$900,000	—0—
2	$1,500,000	$1,100,000	$400,000
3	$1,400,000	$1,000,000	$400,000
4	$1,800,000	$1,000,000	$800,000
5	$2,100,000	$1,000,000	$1,100,000

Example (3). C owns all of the stock of X corporation with a basis of $100,000 (inclusive of selling expenses). D purchases the X stock from C and agrees to make four payments computed in accordance with the following formula: 40% of the net profits of X in year 1, 30% in year 2, 20% in year 3, and 10% in year 4. Accordingly, C's basis is allocated as follows: $40,000 to year 1, $30,000 to year 2, $20,000 to year 3, and $10,000 to year 4.

Example (4). The facts are the same as in example (3), but the agreement also requires that D make fixed installment payments in accordance with the following schedule: no payment in year 1, $100,000 in year 2, $200,000 in year 3, $300,000 in year 4, and $400,000 in year 5. Thus, while it is reasonable to project that the contingent component of the payments will decrease each year, the fixed component of the payments will increase each year. Accordingly, C is required to allocate $20,000 of basis to each of the taxable years 1 through 5.

(4) *Neither stated maximum selling price nor fixed period.*—If the agreement neither specifies a maximum selling price nor limits payments to a fixed period, a question arises whether a sale realistically has occurred or whether, in economic effect, payments received under the agreement are in the nature of rent or royalty income. Arrangements of this sort will be closely scrutinized. If, taking into account all of the pertinent facts, including the nature of the property, the arrangement is determined to qualify as a sale, the taxpayer's basis (including selling expenses) shall be recovered in equal annual increments over a period of 15 years commencing with the date of sale. However, if in any taxable year no payment is received or the amount of payment received (exclusive of interest) is less than basis allocated to the year, no loss shall be allowed unless it is otherwise determined in accordance with the timing rules generally applicable to worthless debts that the future payment obligation under the agreement has become worthless; instead the excess basis shall be reallocated in level amounts over the balance of the 15-year term. Any basis not recovered at the end of the 15th year shall be carried forward to the next succeeding year, and to the extent unrecovered thereafter shall be carried forward from year to year until all basis has been recovered or the future payment obligation is determined to be worthless. The general rule requiring initial level allocation of basis over 15 years shall not apply if the taxpayer can establish to the satisfaction of the Internal Revenue Service that application of the general rule would substantially and inappropriately defer recovery of the taxpayer's basis. See paragraph (c)(7) of this section. If the Service determines that initially allocating basis in level amounts over the first 15 years will substantially and inappropriately accelerate recovery of the taxpayer's basis in early years of that 15-year term, the Service may require that basis be reallocated within the 15-year term but the Service will not require that basis initially be allocated over more than 15 years. See paragraph (c)(7) of this section.

* * *

(d) *Election not to report an installment sale on the installment method.*—(1) *In general.*—An installment sale is to be reported on the installment method unless the taxpayer elects otherwise in accordance with the rules set forth in paragraph (d)(3) of this section.

(2) *Treatment of an installment sale when a taxpayer elects not to report on the installment method.*—(i) *In general.*—A taxpayer who elects not to report an installment sale on the installment method must recognize gain on the sale in accordance with the taxpayer's method of accounting. The fair market value of an installment obligation shall be determined in accordance with paragraph (d)(2)(ii) and (iii) of this section. In making such determination, any provision of contract or local law restricting the transferability of the installment obligation shall be disregarded. Receipt of an installment obligation shall be treated as a receipt of property, in an amount equal to the fair market value of the installment obligation, whether or not such obligation is the equivalent of cash. An installment obligation is considered to be property and is subject to valuation, as provided in paragraph (d)(2)(ii) and (iii) of this section, without regard to whether the obligation is embodied in a note, an executory contract, or any other instrument, or is an oral promise enforceable under local law.

(ii) *Fixed amount obligations.*—(A) A fixed amount obligation means an installment obligation the amount payable under which is fixed. Solely for the purpose of determining whether the amount payable under an installment obligation is fixed, the provisions of section 483 and any "payment recharacterization" arrangement (as defined in paragraph (c)(2)(ii) of this section) shall be disregarded. If the fixed amount payable is stated in identified, fungible units of property the value of which will or may vary over time in relation to the United States dollar (*e.g.,* foreign currency, ounces of gold, or bushels of wheat), such units shall be converted to United States dollars at the rate of exchange or dollar value on the date the installment sale is made. A taxpayer using the cash receipts and disbursements methods of accounting shall treat as an amount realized in the year of sale the fair market value of the installment obligation. In no event will the fair market value of the installment obligation be considered to be less than the fair market value of the property sold (minus any another consideration received by the taxpayer on the sale). A taxpayer using the accrual method of accounting shall treat as an amount realized in the year of sale the total amount payable under the installment obligation. For this purpose, neither interest (whether stated or unstated) nor original issue discount is considered to be part of the amount payable. If the amount payable is otherwise fixed, but because the time over which payments may be made is contingent, a portion of the fixed amount will or may be treated as internal interest (as defined in paragraph (c)(2)(ii) of this section), the amount payable shall be determined by applying the price interest recomputation rule (described in paragraph (c)(2)(ii) of this section). Under no circumstances will an installment sale for a fixed amount obligation be considered an "open" transaction. For purposes of this (ii) remote or incidental contingencies are not to be taken into account.

(B) The following examples illustrate the provisions of paragraph (d)(2) of this section.

Example (1). A, an accrual method taxpayer, owns all of the stock of X corporation with a basis of $20 million. On July 1, 1981, A sells the stock of X corporation to B for $60 million payable on June 15, 1992. The agreement also provides that, against this fixed amount, B shall make annual prepayments (on June 15) equal to 5% of the net profits of X earned in the immediately preceding fiscal year beginning with the fiscal year ending March 31, 1982. Thus, the first prepayment will be made on June 15, 1982. No stated interest is payable under the agreement and thus the unstated interest provisions of section 483 are applicable. Under section 483, no part of any payment made on June 15, 1982 (which is within one year following the July 1, 1981 sale date), will be treated as unstated interest. Under the price interest recomputation rule, it is presumed that the entire $60 million fixed amount will be paid on June 15, 1982. Accordingly, if A elects not to report the transaction on the installment method, in 1981 A must report $60 million as the amount realized on the sale and must report $40 million as gain on the sale in that year.

Example (2). The facts are the same as in example (1) except that A uses the cash receipts and disbursements method of accounting. In 1981 A must report as an amount realized on the sale the fair market value of the installment obligation and must report as gain on the sale in 1981 the excess of that amount realized over A's basis of $20 million. In no event will the fair market value of the installment obligation be considered to be less than the fair market value of the stock of X. In determining the fair market value of the installment obligation, any contractual or legal restrictions on the transferability of the installment obligation, and any remote or incidental contingencies otherwise affecting the amount payable or time of payments under the installment obligation, shall be disregarded.

(iii) *Contingent payment obligations.*—Any installment obligation which is not a fixed amount obligation (as defined in paragraph (d)(2)(ii) of this section) is a contingent payment obligation. If an installment obligation contains both a fixed amount component and a contingent payment component, the fixed amount component shall be treated under the rules of paragraph (d)(2)(ii) of this section and the contingent amount component shall be treated under the rules of this (iii). The fair market value of a contingent payment obligation shall be determined by disregarding any restrictions on transfer imposed by agreement or under local law. The fair market value of a contingent payment obligation may be ascertained from, and in no event shall be considered to be less than, the fair market value of the property sold (less the amount of any other consideration received in the sale). Only in those rare and extraordinary cases involving sales for a contingent payment obligation in which the fair market value of the obligation (determinable under the preceding sentences) cannot reasonably be ascertained will the taxpayer be entitled to assert that the transaction is "open." Any such transaction will be carefully scrutinized to determine whether a sale in fact has taken place. A taxpayer using the cash receipts and disbursements method of accounting must report as an amount realized in the year of sale the fair market value of the contingent payment obligation. A taxpayer using the accrual method of accounting must report an amount realized in the year of sale determined in accordance with that method of accounting, but in no event less than the fair market value of the contingent payment obligation.

(3) *Time and manner for making election.*—(i) *In general.*—An election under paragraph (d)(1) of this section must be made on or before the due date prescribed by law (including extensions) for filing the taxpayer's return for the taxable year in which the installment sale occurs. The election must be made in the manner prescribed by the appropriate forms for the taxpayer's return for the taxable year of the sale. A taxpayer who reports an amount realized equal to the selling price including the full face amount of any installment obligation on the tax return filed for the taxable year in which the installment sale occurs will be considered to have made an effective election under paragraph (d)(1) of this section. A cash method taxpayer receiving an obligation the fair market value of which is less than the face value must make the election in the manner prescribed by appropriate instructions for the return filed for the taxable year of the sale.

(ii) *Election made after the due date.*—Elections after the time specified in paragraph (d)(3)(i) of this section will be permitted only in those rare circumstances when the Internal Revenue Service concludes that the taxpayer had good cause for failing to make a timely election. A recharacterization of a transaction as a sale in a taxable year subsequent to the taxable year in which the transaction occurred (*e.g.,* a transaction initially reported as a lease later is determined to have been an installment sale) will not justify a late election. No conditional elections will be permitted. For a special transitional rule relating to certain taxable years for which a return is filed prior to February 19, 1981, see paragraph (d)(5) of this section.

(4) *Revoking an election.*—Generally, an election made under paragraph (d)(1) is irrevocable. An election may be revoked only with the consent of the Internal Revenue Service. A revocation is retroactive. A revocation will not be permitted when one of its purposes is the avoidance of federal income taxes, or when the taxable year in which any payment was received has closed. For a special transitional rule relating to certain taxable years for which a return is filed prior to February 19, 1981, see paragraph (d)(5) of this section.

* * *

(e) *Purchaser evidences of indebtedness payable on demand or readily tradable.*—(1) *Treatment as payment.*—(i) *In general.*—A bond or other evidence of indebtedness (hereinafter in this section referred to as an obligation) issued by any person and payable on demand shall be treated as a payment in the year received, not as installment obligations payable in future years. In addition, an obligation issued by a corporation or a government or political subdivision thereof—

(A) With interest coupons attached (whether or not the obligation is readily tradable in an established securities market),

(B) In registered form (other than an obligation issued in registered form which the taxpayer establishes will not be readily tradable in an established securities market), or

(C) In any other form designed to render such obligation readily tradable in an established securities market,

shall be treated as a payment in the year received, not as an installment obligation payable in future years. For purposes of this paragraph, an obligation is to be considered in registered form if it is registered as to principal, interest, or both and if its transfer must be effected by the surrender of the old instrument and either the reissuance by the corporation of the old instrument to the new holder or the issuance by the corporation of a new instrument to the new holder.

(ii) *Examples.*—The rules stated in this paragraph may be illustrated by the following examples:

Example (1). On July 1, 1981, A, an individual on the cash method of accounting reporting on a calendar year basis, transferred all of his stock in corporation X (traded on an established securities market and having a fair market value of $1,000,000) to corporation Y in exchange for 250 of Y's registered bonds (which are traded in an over-the-counter market) each with a principal amount and fair market value of $1,000 (with interest payable at the rate of 12 percent per year), and Y's unsecured promissory note with a principal amount of $750,000. At the time of such exchange A's basis in the X stock is $900,000. The promissory note is payable at the rate of $75,000 annually, due on July 1 of each year following 1981 until the principal balance is paid. The note provides for the payment of interest at the rate of 12 percent per year also payable on July 1 of each year. Under the rule stated in paragraph (e)(1)(i) of this section, the 250 registered bonds of Y are treated as a payment in 1981 in the amount of the value of the bonds, $250,000.

Example (2). Assume the same facts as in example (1). Assume further that on July 1, 1982, Y makes its first installment payment to A under the terms of the unsecured promissory note with 75 more of its $1,000 registered bonds. A must include $7,500 (*i.e.,* 10 percent gross profit percentage times $75,000), A's gross income for calendar year 1982. In addition, A includes the interest payment made by Y on July 1 in A's gross income for 1982.

(2) *Amounts treated as payment.*—If under paragraph (e)(1) of this section an obligation is treated as a payment in the year received, the amount realized by reason of such payment shall be determined in accordance with the taxpayer's method of accounting. If the taxpayer uses the cash receipts and disbursements method of accounting, the amount realized on such payment is the fair market value of the obligation. If the taxpayer uses the accrual method of accounting, the amount realized on receipt of an obligation payable on demand is the face amount of the obligation, and the amount realized on receipt of an obligation with coupons attached or a readily tradable obligation is the stated redemption price at maturity less any original issue discount (as defined in section 1232(b)(1)) or, if there is no original issue discount, the amount realized is the stated redemption price at maturity appropriately discounted to reflect total unstated interest (as defined in section 483(b)), if any.

(3) *Payable on demand.*—An obligation shall be treated as payable on demand only if the obligation is treated as payable on demand under applicable state or local law.

(4) *Designed to be readily tradable in an established securities market.*—(i) *In general.*—Obligations issued by a corporation or government or political subdivision thereof will be deemed to be in a form designed to render such obligations readily tradable in an established securities market if—

(A) Steps necessary to create a market for them are taken at the time of issuance (or later, if taken pursuant to an expressed or implied agreement or understanding which existed at the time of issuance),

(B) If they are treated as readily tradable in an established securities market under paragraph (e)(4)(ii) of this section, or

(C) If they are convertible obligations to which paragraph (e)(5) of this section applies.

(ii) *Readily tradable in an established securities market.*—An obligation will be treated as readily tradable in an established securities market if—

(A) The obligation is part of an issue or series of issues which are readily tradable in an established securities market, or

(B) The corporation issuing the obligation has other obligations of a comparable character which are described in paragraph (e)(4)(ii)(A) of this section.

For purposes of paragraph (e)(4)(ii)(B) of this section, the determination as to whether there exist obligations of a comparable character depends upon the particular facts and circumstances. Factors to be considered in making such determination include, but are not limited to, substantial similarity with respect to the presence and nature of security for the obligation, the number of obligations issued (or to be issued), the number of holders of such obligation, the principal amount of the obligation, and other relevant factors.

(iii) *Readily tradable.*—For purposes of paragraph (e)(4)(ii)(A) of this section, an obligation shall be treated as readily tradable if it is regularly quoted by brokers or dealers making a market in such obligation or is part of an issue a portion of which is in fact traded in an established securities market.

(iv) *Established securities market.*—For purposes of this paragraph, the term "established securities market" includes (A) a national securities exchange which is registered under section 6 of the Securities Exchange Act of 1934 (15 U.S.C. 78f), (B) an exchange which is exempted from registration under section 5 of the Securities Exchange Act of 1934 (15 U.S.C. 78e) because of its limited volume of transactions, and (C) any over-the-counter market. For purposes of this (iv), an over-the-counter market is reflected by the existence of an interdealer quotation system. An interdealer quotation system is any system of general circulation to brokers and dealers which regularly disseminates quotations of obligations by identified brokers or dealers, other than a quotation sheet prepared and distributed by a broker or dealer in the regular course of business and containing only quotations of such broker or dealer.

(v) *Examples.*—The rules stated in this paragraph may be illustrated by the following examples:

Example (1). On June 1, 1982, 25 individuals owning equal interests in a tract of land with a fair market value of $1 million sell the land to corporation Y. The $1 million sales price is represented by 25 bonds issued by Y, each having a face value of $40,000. The bonds are not in registered form and do not have interest coupons attached, and, in addition, are payable in 120 equal installments, each due on the first business day of each month. In addition, the bonds are negotiable and may be assigned by the holder to any other person. However, the bonds are not quoted by any brokers or dealers who deal in corporate bonds, and, furthermore, there are no comparable obligations of Y (determined with reference to the characteristics set forth in paragraph (e)(2) of this section) which are so quoted. Therefore, the bonds are not treated as readily tradable in an established securities market. In addition, under the particular facts and circumstances stated, the bonds will not be considered to be in a form designed to render them readily tradable in an established securities market. The receipt of such bonds by the holder is not treated as a payment for purposes of section 453(f)(4), notwithstanding that they are freely assignable.

Example (2). On April 1, 1981, corporation M purchases in a casual sale of personal property a fleet of trucks from corporation N in exchange for M's negotiable notes, not in registered form and without coupons attached. The M notes are comparable to earlier notes issued by M, which notes are quoted in the Eastern Bond section of the National Daily Quotation Sheet, which is an interdealer quotation system. Both issues of notes are unsecured, held by more than 100 holders, have a maturity date of more than 5 years, and were issued for a comparable principle [sic] amount. On the basis of these similar characteristics it appears that the latest notes will also be readily tradable. Since an interdealer system reflects an over-the-counter market, the earlier notes are treated as readily tradable in an established securities market. Since the later notes are obligations comparable to the earlier ones, which are treated as readily tradable in an established securities market, the later notes are also treated as readily tradable in an established securities market (whether or not such notes are actually traded).

(5) *Special rule for convertible securities.*—(i) *General rule.*—If an obligation contains a right whereby the holder of such obligation may convert it directly or indirectly into another obligation which would be treated as a payment under paragraph (e)(1) of this section or may convert it directly or indirectly into stock which would be treated as readily tradable or designed to be readily tradable in an established securities market under paragraph (e)(4) of this section, the convertible obligation shall be considered to be in a form designed to render such obligation readily tradable in an established securities market unless such obligation is convertible only at a substantial discount. In determining whether the stock or obligation into which an obligation is convertible is readily tradable or designed to be readily tradable in an established securities market, the rules stated in paragraph (e)(4) of this section shall apply, and for purposes of such paragraph (e)(4) if such obligation is convertible into stock then the term "stock" shall be substituted for the term "obligation" wherever it appears in such paragraph (e)(4).

(ii) *Substantial discount rule.*—Whether an obligation is convertible at a substantial discount depends upon the particular facts and circumstances. A substantial discount shall be considered to exist if at the time the convertible obligation is issued, the fair market value of the stock or obligation into which the obligation is convertible is less than 80 percent of the fair market value of the obligation (determined by taking into account all relevant factors, including proper discount to reflect the fact that the convertible obligation is not readily tradable in an established securities market and any additional consideration required to be paid by the taxpayer). Also, if a privilege to convert an obligation into stock or an obligation which is readily tradable in an established securities market may not be exercised within a period of one year from the date the obligation is issued, a substantial discount shall be considered to exist.

* * *

[Temporary Reg. § 15A.453-1.]

□ [*T.D.* 7768, 1-30-81. *Amended by T.D.* 7788, 9-30-81 *and T.D.* 8535, 4-19-94.]

Proposed Amendments to Regulation

§ 1.453-1. Installment method reporting for sales of real property and casual sales of personal property.—

* * *

(f) *Installment obligations received in certain nonrecognition exchanges.*—(1) *Exchanges described in section 1031(b).*—(i) *In general.*—The provisions of paragraph (f)(1) of this section apply to exchanges described in section 1031(b) ("section 1031(b) exchanges") in which the taxpayer receives as boot (property which is "other property" under section 1031(b)) an installment obligation issued by the other party to the exchange, as well as property with respect to which no gain or loss is recognized ("permitted property" for purposes of paragraph (f)(1) of this section). However, an exchange otherwise described in section 1036 in which the receipt of an installment obligation is treated as a dividend (or would be treated as a dividend if the issuing corporation had adequate earnings and profits) is not a section 1031(b) exchange for purposes of this section.

(ii) *Exclusion from payment.*—Receipt of permitted property will not be considered payment for purposes of paragraph (c) of this section.

(iii) *Installment method determinations.*—In a section 1031(b) exchange, the taxpayer's basis in the property transferred by the taxpayer, including nondeductible expenses of the exchange, will first be allocated to the permitted property received by the taxpayer up to, but not in excess of, the fair market value of such property. If the taxpayer's basis exceeds the fair market value of the permitted property, that excess amount of basis is "excess basis." In making all required installment method determinations, the exchange is treated as if the taxpayer had made an installment sale of appreciated property (with a basis equal to the amount of excess basis) in which the consideration received was the installment obligation and any other boot. In a section 1031(b) exchange, only net qualifying indebtedness is taken into account in determining the amount of qualifying indebtedness (as defined in § 1.453-1A(b)(2)(iv)). For this purpose, net qualifying indebtedness is the excess of—

(A) Liabilities of the taxpayer (or liabilities encumbering the property) assumed or taken subject to by the other party to the exchange as part of the consideration to the taxpayer, over

(B) The sum of any net cash paid (cash paid less any cash received) by the taxpayer in the exchange and any liability assumed or taken subject to by the taxpayer in the exchange.

Therefore, for purposes of installment method determinations, the selling price is the sum of the face value of the installment obligation (reduced by any portion of the obligation characterized as interest by section 483 or 1232), any net qualifying indebtedness, any cash received (in excess of any cash paid) by the taxpayer, and the fair market value of any other boot. The basis is the excess basis. The total contract price is the selling price less any net qualifying indebtedness that does not exceed the excess basis. Finally, payment in the year of exchange includes any net qualifying indebtedness that exceeds the excess basis.

* * *

(3) *Other partial recognition exchanges.*—(i) *In general.*—The provisions of paragraph (f)(3) of this section apply to exchanges not described in paragraph (f)(1) or (2) of this section in which a taxpayer, in exchange for appreciated property, receives both permitted property (*i.e.,* property with respect to which no gain or loss would be recognized but which, in the hands of the taxpayer, would have as basis for determining gain or loss the same basis in whole or in part as the property exchanged) and boot that includes an installment obligation issued by the other party to the exchange. Ordinarily, the installment method rules set forth in paragraph (f)(1)(ii) and (iii) of this section will apply to an exchange described in paragraph (f)(3) of this section subject to such variations, if any, as may be required under the applicable provisions of the Code.

(ii) *Exchanges to which section 351 applies.*—If a taxpayer receives, in an exchange to which section 351(b) applies (a "section 351(b) exchange"), an installment obligation that is not a security within the meaning of section 351(a), the installment obligation is boot and the stock and securities (within the meaning of section 351(a)) are permitted property (within the meaning of paragraph (f)(1)(ii) of this section). The taxpayer will report the installment obligation on the installment method and any other boot received will be treated as a payment made in the year of the exchange. In applying the rules of paragraph (f)(1)(iii) of this section to a section 351(b) exchange the excess basis is the amount, if any, by which the taxpayer's basis in the property transferred (plus any cash transferred) by the taxpayer exceeds the sum of the transferred liabilities which are not treated as money received under section 357 plus the fair market value of permitted property received by the taxpayer. In determining selling price and total contract price, transferred liabilities which are not treated as money received under section 357 shall be disregarded. For purposes of paragraph (f)(3)(ii) of this section, transferred liabilities are liabilities described in section 357(a)(2). Solely for the purpose of applying section 358(a)(1), the taxpayer shall be treated as if the taxpayer elected not to report receipt of the installment obligation on the installment method. Under section 362(a)(1) the corporation's basis in the property received from the taxpayer is the taxpayer's basis in the property increased by the gain recognized by the taxpayer at the time of the exchange. As the taxpayer recognizes gain on the installment method, the corporation will increase its basis in the property by an amount equal to the amount of gain recognized by the taxpayer.

* * *

[Prop. Reg. § 1.453-1.]

[Proposed 5-3-84.]

§ 1.461-1. General rule for taxable year of deduction.—(a) *General rule.*—(1) *Taxpayer using cash receipts and disbursements method.*—Under the cash receipts and disbursements method of accounting, amounts representing allowable deductions shall, as a general rule, be taken into account for the taxable year in which paid. Further, a taxpayer using this method may also be entitled to certain deductions in the computation of taxable income which do not involve cash disbursements during the taxable year, such as the deductions for depreciation, depletion, and losses under sections 167, 611, and 165, respectively. If an expenditure results in the creation of an asset having a useful life which extends substantially beyond the close of the taxable year, such an expenditure may not be deductible, or may be deductible only in part, for the taxable year in which made. An example is an expenditure for the construction of improvements by the lessee on leased property where the estimated life of the improvements is in excess of the remaining period of the lease. In such a case, in lieu of the allowance for depreciation provided by section 167, the basis shall be amortized ratably over the remaining period of the lease. See section 178 and the regulations thereunder for rules governing the effect to be given renewal options in determining whether the useful life of the improvements exceeds the remaining term of the lease where a lessee begins improvements on leased property after July 28, 1958, other than improvements which on such date and at all times thereafter, the lessee was under a binding legal obligation to make. See section 263 and the regulations thereunder for rules relating to capital expenditures. See section 467 and the regulations thereunder for rules under which a liability arising out of the use of property pursuant to a section 467 rental agreement is taken into account.

(2) *Taxpayer using an accrual method.*—(i) *In general.*—Under an accrual method of accounting, a liability (as defined in § 1.446-1(c)(1)(ii)(B)) is incurred, and generally is taken into account for Federal income tax purposes, in the taxable year in which all the events have occurred that establish the fact of the liability, the amount of the liability can be determined with reasonable accuracy, and economic performance has occurred with respect to the liability. (See paragraph (a)(2)(iii)(A) of this section for examples of liabilities that may not be taken into account until a taxable year subsequent to the taxable year incurred, and see § § 1.461-4 through 1.461-6 for rules relating to economic performance.) Applicable provisions of the Code, the Income Tax Regulations, and other guidance published by the Secretary prescribe the manner in which a liability that has been incurred is taken into account. For example, section 162 provides that a deductible liability generally is taken into account in the taxable year incurred through a deduction from gross income. As a further example, under section 263 or 263A, a liability that relates to the creation of an asset having a useful life extending substantially beyond the close of the taxable year is taken into account in the taxable year incurred through capitalization (within the meaning of § 1.263A-1(c)(3)), and may later affect the computation of taxable income through depreciation or otherwise over a period including subsequent taxable years, in accordance with applicable Internal Revenue Code sections and guidance published by the Secretary. The principles of this paragraph (a)(2) also apply in the calculation of earnings and profits and accumulated earnings and profits.

(ii) *Uncertainty as to the amount of a liability.*—While no liability shall be taken into account before economic performance and all of the events that fix the liability have occurred, the fact that the exact amount of the liability cannot be determined does not prevent a taxpayer from taking into account that portion of the amount of the liability which can be computed with reasonable accuracy within the taxable year. For example, A renders services to B during the taxable year for which A charges $10,000. B admits a liability to A for $6,000 but contests the remainder. B may take into account only $6,000 as an expense for the taxable year in which the services were rendered.

(iii) *Alternative timing rules.*—(A) If any provision of the Code requires a liability to be taken into account in a taxable year later than the taxable year provided in paragraph (a)(2)(i) of this section, the liability is taken into account as prescribed in that Code provision. See, for example, section 267 (transactions between related parties) and section 464 (farming syndicates).

(B) If the liability of a taxpayer is subject to section 170 (charitable contributions), section 192 (black lung benefit trusts), section 194A (employer liability trusts), section 468 (mining and solid waste disposal reclamation and closing costs), or section 468A(a) (certain nuclear decommissioning costs), the liability is taken into account as determined under that section and not under section 461 or the regulations thereunder. For special rules relating to certain loss deductions, see sections 165(e), 165(i), and 165(l), relating to theft losses, disaster losses, and losses from certain deposits in qualified financial institutions.

(C) Section 461 and the regulations thereunder do not apply to any amount allowable under a provision of the Code as a deduction for a reserve for estimated expenses.

(D) Except as otherwise provided in any Internal Revenue regulation, revenue procedure, or revenue ruling, the economic performance requirement of section 461(h) and the regulations thereunder is satisfied to the extent that any amount is otherwise deductible under section 404 (employer contributions to a plan of deferred compensation), section 404A (certain foreign deferred compensation plans), or section 419 (welfare benefit funds). See § 1.461-4(d)(2)(iii).

(E) Except as otherwise provided by regulations or other published guidance issued by the Commissioner (See § 601.601(b)(2) of this chapter), in the case of a liability arising out of the use of property pursuant to a section 467 rental agreement, the all events test (including economic performance) is considered met in the taxable year in which the liability is to be taken into account under section 467 and the regulations thereunder.

(3) *Effect in current taxable year of improperly accounting for a liability in a prior taxable year.*—Each year's return should be complete in itself, and taxpayers shall ascertain the facts necessary to make a correct return. The expenses, liabilities, or loss of one year generally cannot be used to reduce the income of a subsequent year. A taxpayer may not take into account in a return for a subsequent taxable year liabilities that, under the taxpayer's method of accounting, should have been taken into account in a prior taxable year. If a taxpayer ascertains that a liability should have been taken into account in a prior taxable year, the taxpayer should, if within the period of limitation, file a claim for credit or refund of any overpayment of tax arising therefrom. Similarly, if a taxpayer ascertains that a liability was improperly taken into account in a prior taxable year, the taxpayer should, if within the period of limitation, file an amended return and pay any additional tax due. However, except as provided in section 905(c) and the regulations thereunder, if a liability is properly taken into account in an amount based on a computation made with reasonable accuracy and the exact amount of the liability is subsequently determined in a later taxable year, the difference, if any, between such amounts shall be taken into account for the later taxable year.

* * *

(b) *Special rule in case of death.*—A taxpayer's taxable year ends on the date of his death. See section 443(a)(2) and paragraph (a)(2) of §1.443-1. In computing taxable income for such year, there shall be deducted only amounts properly deductible under the method of accounting used by the taxpayer. However, if the taxpayer used an accrual method of accounting, no deduction shall be allowed for amounts accrued only by reason of his death. For rules relating to the inclusion of items of partnership deduction, loss, or credit in the return of a decedent partner, see subchapter K, chapter 1 of the Code, and the regulations thereunder.

* * *

[Reg. §1.461-1.]

☐ [*T.D.* 6282, 12-24-57. *Amended by T.D.* 6520, 12-23-60; *T.D.* 6710, 3-17-64; *T.D.* 6735, 5-18-64; *T.D.* 6772, 11-23-64; *T.D.* 6917, 5-1-67; *T.D.* 8408, 4-9-92; *T.D.* 8482, 8-6-93; *T.D.* 8554, 7-13-94 *and T.D.* 8820, 5-17-99.]

§1.461-2. Contested liabilities.—(a) *General rule.*—(1) *Taxable year of deduction.*—If—

(i) The taxpayer contests an asserted liability,

(ii) The taxpayer transfers money or other property to provide for the satisfaction of the asserted liability,

(iii) The contest with respect to the asserted liability exists after the time of the transfer, and

(iv) But for the fact that the asserted liability is contested, a deduction would be allowed for the taxable year of the transfer (or, in the case of an accrual method taxpayer, for an earlier taxable year for which such amount would be accruable),

then the deduction with respect to the contested amount shall be allowed for the taxable year of the transfer.

(2) *Exception.*—Subparagraph (1) of this paragraph shall not apply in respect of the deduction for income, war profits, and excess profits taxes imposed by the authority of any foreign country or possession of the United States, including a tax paid in lieu of a tax on income, war profits, or excess profits otherwise generally imposed by any foreign country or by any possession of the United States.

(3) *Refunds includible in gross income.*—If any portion of the contested amount which is deducted under subparagraph (1) of this paragraph for the taxable year of transfer is refunded when the contest is settled, such portion is includible in gross income except as provided in §1.111-1, relating to recovery of certain items previously deducted or credited. Such refunded amount is includible in gross income for the taxable year of receipt, or for an earlier taxable year if properly accruable for such earlier year.

(4) *Examples.*—The provisions of this paragraph are illustrated by the following examples:

Example (1). X Corporation, which uses an accrual method of accounting, in 1964 contests $20 of a $100 asserted real property tax liability but pays the entire $100 to the taxing authority. In 1968, the contest is settled and X receives a refund of $5. X deducts $100 for the taxable year 1964, and includes $5 in gross income for the taxable year 1968 (assuming §1.111-1 does not apply to such amount). If in 1964 X pays only $80 to the taxing authority, X deducts only $80 for 1964. The result would be the same if X Corporation used the cash method of accounting.

Example (2). Y Corporation makes its return on the basis of a calendar year and uses an accrual method of accounting. Y's real property taxes are assessed and become a lien on December 1, but are not payable until March 1 of the following year. On December 10, 1964, Y contests $20 of the $100 asserted real property tax which was assessed and became a lien on December 1, 1964. On March 1, 1965, Y pays the entire $100 to the taxing authority. In 1968, the contest is settled and Y receives a refund of $5. Y deducts $80 for the taxable year 1964, deducts $20 for the taxable year 1965, and includes $5 in gross income for the taxable year 1968 (assuming § 1.111-1 does not apply to such amount).

(b) *Contest of asserted liability.*—(1) *Asserted liability.*—For purposes of paragraph (a)(1) of this section, the term "asserted liability" means an item with respect to which, but for the existence of any contest in respect of such item, a deduction would be allowable under an accrual method of accounting. For example, a notice of a local real estate tax assessment and a bill received for services may represent asserted liabilities.

(2) *Definition of the term "contest"*.—Any contest which would prevent accrual of a liability under section 461(a) shall be considered to be a contest in determining whether the taxpayer satisfies paragraph (a)(1)(i) of this section. A contest arises when there is a bona fide dispute as to the proper evaluation of the law or the facts necessary to determine the existence or correctness of the amount of an asserted liability. It is not necessary to institute suit in a court of law in order to contest an asserted liability. An affirmative act denying the validity or accuracy, or both, of an asserted liability to the person who is asserting such liability, such as including a written protest with payment of the asserted liability, is sufficient to commence a contest. Thus, lodging a protest in accordance with local law is sufficient to contest an asserted liability for taxes. It is not necessary that the affirmative act denying the validity or accuracy, or both, of an asserted liability be in writing if, upon examination of all the facts and circumstances, it can be established to the satisfaction of the Commissioner that a liability has been asserted and contested.

(3) *Example.*—The provisions of this paragraph are illustrated by the following example:

Example: O Corporation makes its return on the basis of a calendar year and uses an accrual method of accounting. O receives a large shipment of typewriter ribbons from S Company on January 30, 1964, which O pays for in full on February 10, 1964. Subsequent to their receipt, several of the ribbons prove defective because of inferior materials used by the manufacturer. On August 9, 1964, O orally notifies S and demands refund of the full purchase price of the ribbons. After negotiations prove futile and a written demand is rejected by S, O institutes an action for the full purchase price. For purposes of paragraph (a)(1)(i) of this section, S has asserted a liability against O which O contests on August 9, 1964. O deducts the contested amount for 1964.

(c) *Transfer to provide for the satisfaction of an asserted liability.*—(1) *In general.*—(i) A taxpayer may provide for the satisfaction of an asserted liability by transferring money or other property beyond his control to—

(A) The person who is asserting the liability;

(B) An escrowee or trustee pursuant to a written agreement (among the escrowee or trustee, the taxpayer, and the person who is asserting the liability) that the money or other property be delivered in accordance with the settlement of the contest;

(C) An escrowee or trustee pursuant to an order of the United States or of any State or political subdivision thereof or any agency or instrumentality of the foregoing, or of a court, that the money or other property be delivered in accordance with the settlement of the contest; or

(D) A court with jurisdiction over the contest.

(ii) In order for money or other property to be beyond the control of a taxpayer, the taxpayer must relinquish all authority over the money or other property.

(iii) The following are not transfers to provide for the satisfaction of an asserted liability—

(A) Purchasing a bond to guarantee payment of the asserted liability;

(B) An entry on the taxpayer's books of account;

(C) A transfer to an account that is within the control of the taxpayer;

(D) A transfer of any indebtedness of the taxpayer or of any promise by the taxpayer to provide services or property in the future; and

(E) A transfer to a person (other than the person asserting the liability) of any stock of the taxpayer or of any stock or indebtedness of a person related to the taxpayer (as defined in section 267(b)).

(2) *Examples.*—The provisions of this paragraph are illustrated by the following examples:

Example (1). M Corporation contests a $5,000 liability asserted against it by L Company for services rendered. To provide for the contingency that it might have to pay the liability, M establishes a separate bank account in its own name. M then transfers $5,000 from its general account to such separate account. Such transfer does not qualify as a transfer to provide for the satisfaction of an asserted liability because M has not transferred the money beyond its control.

Example (2). M Corporation contests a $5,000 liability asserted against it by L Company for services rendered. To provide for the contingency that it might have to pay the liability, M transfers $5,000 to an irrevocable trust pursuant to a written agreement among the trustee, M (the taxpayer), and L (the person who is asserting the liability) that the money shall be held until the contest is settled and then disbursed in accordance with the settlement. Such transfer qualifies as a transfer to provide for the satisfaction of an asserted liability.

(d) *Contest exists after transfer.*—In order for a contest with respect to an asserted liability to exist after the time of transfer, such contest must be pursued subsequent to such time. Thus, the contest must have been neither settled nor abandoned at the time of the transfer. A contest may be settled by a decision, judgment, decree, or other order of any court of competent jurisdiction which has become final, or by written or oral agreement between the parties. For example, Z Corporation, which uses an accrual method of accounting, in 1964 contests a $100 asserted liability. In 1967 the contested liability is settled as being $80 which Z accrues and deducts for such year. In 1968 Z pays the $80. Section 461(f) does not apply to Z with respect to the transfer because a contest did not exist after the time of such transfer.

(e) *Deduction otherwise allowed.*—(1) *In general.*—The existence of the contest with respect to an asserted liability must prevent (without regard to section 461(f)) and be the only factor preventing a deduction for the taxable year of the transfer (or, in the case of an accrual method taxpayer, for an earlier taxable year for which such amount would be accruable) to provide for the satisfaction of such liability. Nothing in section 461(f) or this section shall be construed to give rise to a deduction since section 461(f) and this section relate only to the timing of deductions which are otherwise allowable under the Code.

(2) *Application of economic performance rules to transfers under section 461(f).*—(i) A taxpayer using an accrual method of accounting is not allowed a deduction under section 461(f) in the taxable year of the transfer unless economic performance has occurred.

(ii) Economic performance occurs for liabilities requiring payment to another person arising out of any workers compensation act or any tort, or any other liability designated in § 1.461-4(g), as payments are made to the person to which the liability is owed. Except as provided in section 468B or the regulations thereunder, economic performance does not occur when a taxpayer transfers money or other property to a trust, an escrow account, or a court to provide for the satisfaction of an asserted workers compensation, tort, or other liability designated under § 1.461-4(g) that the taxpayer is contesting unless the trust, escrow account, or court is the person to which the liability is owed or the taxpayer's payment to the trust, escrow account, or court discharges the taxpayer's liability to the claimant. Rather, economic performance occurs in the taxable year the taxpayer transfers money or other property to the person that is asserting the workers compensation, tort, or other liability designated under § 1.461-4(g) that the taxpayer is contesting or in the taxable year that payment is made from a trust, an escrow account, or a court registry funded by the taxpayer to the person to which the liability is owed.

(3) *Examples.*—The provisions of this paragraph are illustrated by the following examples:

Example 1. A, an individual, makes a gift of certain property to B, an individual. A pays the entire amount of gift tax assessed against him but contests his liability for the tax. Section 275(a)(3) provides that gift taxes are not deductible. A does not satisfy the requirement of paragraph (a)(1)(iv) of this section because a deduction would not be allowed for the taxable year of the transfer even if A did not contest his liability to the tax.

Example 2. Corporation X is a defendant in a class action suit for tort liabilities. In 2002, X establishes a trust for the purpose of satisfying the asserted liability and transfers $10,000,000 to the trust. The trust does not satisfy the requirements of section 468B or the regulations thereunder. In 2004, the trustee pays $10,000,000 to the plaintiffs in settlement of the litigation. Under paragraph (e)(2) of this section, economic performance with respect to X's liability to the plaintiffs occurs in 2004. X may deduct the $10,000,000 payment to the plaintiffs in 2004.

* * *

[Reg. § 1.461-2.]

☐ [*T.D.* 6772, 11-23-64. *Amended by T.D.* 8408, 4-9-92; *T.D.* 9095, 11-19-2003 *and T.D.* 9140, 7-19-2004.]

§ 1.461-4. Economic performance.— (a) *Introduction.*—(1) *In general.*—For purposes of determining whether an accrual basis taxpayer can treat the amount of any liability (as defined in § 1.446-1(c)(1)(ii)(B)) as incurred, the all events test is not treated as met any earlier than the taxable year in which economic performance occurs with respect to the liability.

(2) *Overview.*—Paragraph (b) of this section lists exceptions to the economic performance requirement. Paragraph (c) of this section provides cross-references to the definitions of certain terms for purposes of section 461(h) and the regulations thereunder. Paragraphs (d) through (m) of this section and § 1.461-6 provide rules for determining when economic performance occurs. Section 1.461-5 provides rules relating to an exception under which certain recurring items may be incurred for the taxable year before the year during which economic performance occurs.

(b) *Exceptions to the economic performance requirement.*—Paragraph (a)(2)(iii)(B) of § 1.461-1 provides examples of liabilities that are taken into account under rules that operate without regard to the all events test (including economic performance).

(c) *Definitions.*—The following cross-references identify certain terms defined for purposes of section 461(h) and the regulations thereunder:

(1) *Liability.*—See paragraph (c)(1)(ii)(B) of § 1.446-1 for the definition of "liability."

(2) *Payment.*—See paragraph (g)(1)(ii) of this section for the definition of "payment."

(d) *Liabilities arising out of the provision of services, property, or the use of property.*—(1) *In general.*—The principles of this paragraph (d) determine when economic performance occurs with respect to liabilities arising out of the performance of services, the transfer of property, or the use of property. This paragraph (d) does not apply to liabilities described in paragraph (e) (relating to interest expense) or paragraph (g) (relating to breach of contract, workers compensation, tort, etc.) of this section. In addition, except as otherwise provided in Internal Revenue regulations, revenue procedures, or revenue rulings this paragraph (d) does not apply to amounts paid pursuant to a notional principal contract. The Commissioner may provide additional rules in regulations, revenue procedures, or revenue rulings concerning the time at which economic performance occurs for items described in this paragraph (d).

(2) *Services or property provided to the taxpayer.*—(i) *In general.*—Except as otherwise provided in paragraph (d)(5) of this section, if the liability of a taxpayer arises out of the providing of services or property to the taxpayer by another person, economic performance occurs as the services or property is provided.

(ii) *Long-term contracts.*—In the case of any liability of a taxpayer described in paragraph (d)(2)(i) of this section that is an expense attributable to a long-term contract with respect to which the taxpayer uses the percentage of completion method, economic performance occurs—

(A) As the services or property is provided; or, if earlier,

(B) As the taxpayer makes payment (as defined in paragraph (g)(1)(ii) of this section) in satisfaction of the liability to the person providing the services or property. See paragraph (k)(2) of this section for the effective date of this paragraph (d)(2)(ii).

(iii) *Employee benefits.*—(A) *In general.*—Except as otherwise provided in any Internal Revenue regulation, revenue procedure, or revenue ruling, the economic performance requirement is satisfied to the extent that any amount is otherwise deductible under section 404 (employer contributions to a plan of deferred compensation), section 404A (certain foreign deferred compensation plans), and section 419 (welfare benefit funds). See § 1.461-1(a)(2)(iii)(D).

(B) *Property transferred in connection with performance of services.*—[Reserved]

(iv) *Cross-references.*—See *Examples 4* through *6* of paragraph (d)(7) of this section. See paragraph (d)(6) of this section for rules relating to when a taxpayer may treat services or property as provided to the taxpayer.

(3) *Use of property provided to the taxpayer.*—(i) *In general.*—Except as otherwise provided in this paragraph (d)(3) and paragraph (d)(5) of this section, if the liability of a taxpayer arises out of the use of property by the taxpayer, economic performance occurs ratably over the period of time the taxpayer is entitled to the use of the property (taking into account any reasonably expected renewal periods when necessary to carry out the purposes of section 461(h)). See *Examples 6* through *9* of paragraph (d)(7) of this section.

(ii) *Exceptions.*—(A) *Volume, frequency of use, or income.*—If the liability of a taxpayer arises out of the use of property by the taxpayer and all or a portion of the liability is determined by reference to the frequency or volume of use of the property or the income from the property, economic performance occurs for the portion of the liability determined by reference to the frequency or volume of use of the property or the income from the property as the taxpayer uses the property or includes income from the property. See *Examples 8* and *9* of paragraph (d)(7) of this section. This paragraph (d)(3)(ii) shall not apply if the District Director determines, that based on the substance of the transaction, the liability of the taxpayer for use of the property is more appropriately measured ratably over the period of time the taxpayer is entitled to the use of the property.

(B) *Section 467 rental agreements.*—In the case of a liability arising out of the use of property pursuant to a section 467 rental agreement, economic performance occurs as provided in § 1.461-1(a)(2)(iii)(E).

(4) *Services or property provided by the taxpayer.*—(i) *In general.*—Except as otherwise provided in paragraph (d)(5) of this section, if the liability of a taxpayer requires the taxpayer to provide services or property to another person, economic performance occurs as the taxpayer incurs costs (within the meaning of § 1.446-1(c)(1)(ii)) in connection with the satisfaction of the liability. See *Examples 1* through *3* of paragraph (d)(7) of this section.

(ii) *Barter transactions.*—If the liability of a taxpayer requires the taxpayer to provide services, property, or the use of property, and arises out of the use of property by the taxpayer, or out of the provision of services or property to the taxpayer by another person, economic performance occurs to the extent of the lesser of—

(A) The cumulative extent to which the taxpayer incurs costs (within the meaning of § 1.446-1(c)(1)(ii)) in connection with its liability to provide the services or property; or

(B) The cumulative extent to which the services or property is provided to the taxpayer.

(5) *Liabilities that are assumed in connection with the sale of a trade or business.*—(i) *In general.*—If, in connection with the sale or exchange of a trade or business by a taxpayer, the purchaser expressly assumes a liability arising out of the trade or business that the taxpayer but for the economic performance requirement would have been entitled to incur as of the date of the sale, economic performance with respect to that liability occurs as the amount of the liability is properly included in the amount realized on the transaction by the taxpayer. See § 1.1001-2 for rules relating to the inclusion in amount realized from a discharge of liabilities resulting from a sale or exchange.

(ii) *Trade or business.*—For purposes of this paragraph (d)(5), a trade or business is a specific group of activities carried on by the taxpayer for the purpose of earning income or profit if every operation that is necessary to the process of earning income or profit is included in the group. Thus, for example, the group of activities generally must include the collection of income and the payment of expenses.

(iii) *Tax avoidance.*—This paragraph (d)(5) does not apply if the District Director determines that tax avoidance is one of the taxpayer's principal purposes for the sale or exchange.

(6) *Rules relating to the provision of services or property to a taxpayer.*—The following rules apply for purposes of this paragraph (d):

(i) Services or property provided to a taxpayer include services or property provided to another person at the direction of the taxpayer.

(ii) A taxpayer is permitted to treat services or property as provided to the taxpayer as the taxpayer makes payment to the person providing the services or property (as defined in paragraph (g)(1)(ii) of this section), if the taxpayer can reasonably expect the person to provide the services or property within 3 1/2 months after the date of payment.

(iii) A taxpayer is permitted to treat property as provided to the taxpayer when the property is delivered or accepted, or when title to the property passes. The method used by the taxpayer to determine when property is provided is a method of accounting that must comply with the rules of § 1.446-1(e). Thus, the method of determining when property is provided must be used consistently from year to year, and cannot be changed without the consent of the Commissioner.

(iv) If different services or items of property are required to be provided to a taxpayer under a single contract or agreement, economic performance generally occurs over the time each service is provided and as each item of property is provided. However, if a service or item of property to be provided to the taxpayer is incidental to other services or property to be provided under a contract or agreement, the taxpayer is not required to allocate any portion of the total contract price to the incidental service or property. For purposes of this paragraph (d)(6)(iv), services or property is treated as incidental only if—

(A) The cost of the services or property is treated on the taxpayer's books and records as part of the cost of the other services or property provided under the contract; and

(B) The aggregate cost of the services or property does not exceed 10 percent of the total contract price.

(7) *Examples.*—The following examples illustrate the principles of this paragraph (d).

For purposes of these examples, it is assumed that the requirements of the all events test other than economic performance have been met, and that the recurring item exception is not used. Assume further that the examples do not involve section 467 rental agreements and, therefore, section 467 is not applicable. The examples are as follows:

Example 1. Services or property provided by the taxpayer. (i) X corporation, a calendar year, accrual method taxpayer, is an oil company. During March 1990, X enters into an oil and gas lease with Y. In November 1990, X installs a platform and commences drilling. The lease obligates X to remove its offshore platform and well fixtures upon abandonment of the well or termination of the lease. During 1998, X removes the platform and well fixtures at a cost of $200,000.

(ii) Under paragraph (d)(4)(i) of this section, economic performance with respect to X's liability to remove the offshore platform and well fixtures occurs as X incurs costs in connection with that liability. X incurs these costs in 1998 as, for example, X's employees provide X with removal services (see paragraph (d)(2) of this section). Consequently, X incurs $200,000 for the 1998 taxable year. Alternatively, assume that during 1990 X pays Z $130,000 to remove the platform and fixtures, and that Z performs these removal services in 1998. Under paragraph (d)(2) of this section, X does not incur this cost until Z performs the services. Thus, economic performance with respect to the $130,000 X pays Z occurs in 1998.

Example 2. Services or property provided by the taxpayer. (i) W corporation, a calendar year, accrual method taxpayer, sells tractors under a three-year warranty that obligates W to make any reasonable repairs to each tractor it sells. During 1990, W sells ten tractors. In 1992 W repairs, at a cost of $5,000, two tractors sold during 1990.

(ii) Under paragraph (d)(4)(i) of this section, economic performance with respect to W's liability to perform services under the warranty occurs as W incurs costs in connection with that liability. W incurs these costs in 1992 as, for example, replacement parts are provided to W (see paragraph (d)(2) of this section). Consequently, $5,000 is incurred by W for the 1992 taxable year.

Example 3. Services or property provided by the taxpayer; Long-term contracts. (i) W corporation, a calendar year, accrual method taxpayer, manufactures machine tool equipment. In November 1992, W contracts to provide X corporation with certain equipment. The contract is not a long-term contract under section 460 or §1.451-3. In 1992, W pays Z corporation $50,000 to lease from Z, for the one-year period beginning on January 1, 1993, testing equipment to perform quality control tests required by the agreement with X. In 1992, pursuant to the terms of a contract, W pays Y corporation $100,000 for certain parts necessary to manufacture the equipment. The parts are provided to W in 1993. W's employees provide W with services necessary to manufacture the equipment during 1993, for which W pays $150,000 in 1993.

(ii) Under paragraph (d)(4) of this section, economic performance with respect to W's liability to provide the equipment to X occurs as W incurs costs in connection with that liability. W incurs these costs during 1993, as services, property, and the use of property necessary to manufacture the equipment are provided to W (see paragraphs (d)(2) and (d)(3) of this section). Thus, $300,000 is incurred by W for the 1993 taxable year. See section 263A and the regulations thereunder for rules relating to the capitalization and inclusion in inventory of these incurred costs.

(iii) Alternatively, assume that the agreement with X is a long-term contract as defined in section 460(f), and that W takes into account all items with respect to such contracts under the percentage of completion method as described in section 460 (b)(1). Under paragraph (d)(2)(ii) of this section, the $100,000 W pays in 1992 for parts is incurred for the 1992 taxable year, for purposes of determining the percentage of completion under section 460(b)(1)(A). W's other costs under the agreement are incurred for the 1993 taxable year for this purpose.

Example 4. Services or property provided to the taxpayer. (i) LP1, a calendar year, accrual method limited partnership, owns the working interest in a parcel of property containing oil and gas. During December 1990, LP1 enters into a turnkey contract with Z corporation pursuant to which LP1 pays Z $200,000 and Z is required to provide a completed well by the close of 1992. In May 1992, Z commences drilling the well, and, in December 1992, the well is completed.

(ii) Under paragraph (d)(2) of this section, economic performance with respect to LP1's liability for drilling and development services provided to LP1 by Z occurs as the services are provided. Consequently, $200,000 is incurred by LP1 for the 1992 taxable year.

Example 5. Services or property provided to the taxpayer. (i) X corporation, a calendar year, accrual method taxpayer, is an automobile dealer. On January 15, 1990, X agrees to pay an additional $10 to Y, the manufacturer of the automobiles, for each automobile purchased by X from Y. Y agrees to provide advertising and promotional activities to X.

(ii) During 1990, X purchases from Y 1,000 new automobiles and pays to Y an additional $10,000 as provided in the agreement. Y, in turn, uses this $10,000 to provide advertising and promotional activities during 1992.

(iii) Under paragraph (d)(2) of this section, economic performance with respect to X's liability for advertising and promotional services provided to X by Y occurs as the services are provided. Consequently, $10,000 is incurred by X for the 1992 taxable year.

Example 6. Use of property provided to the taxpayer; services or property provided to the taxpayer. (i) V corporation, a calendar year, accrual method taxpayer, charters aircraft. On December 20, 1990, V leases a jet aircraft from L for the four-year period that begins on January 1, 1991. The lease obligates V to pay L a base rental of $500,000 per year. In addition, the lease requires V to pay $25 to an escrow account for each hour that the aircraft is flown. The escrow account funds are held by V and are to be used by L to make necessary repairs to the aircraft. Any amount remaining in the escrow account upon termination of the lease is payable to V. During 1991, the aircraft is flown 1,000 hours and V pays $25,000 to the escrow account. The aircraft is repaired by L in 1993. In 1994, $20,000 is released from the escrow account to pay L for the repairs.

(ii) Under paragraph (d)(3)(i) of this section, economic performance with respect to V's base rental liability occurs ratably over the period of time V is entitled to use the jet aircraft. Consequently, the $500,000 rent is incurred by V for the 1991 taxable year and for each of the next three taxable years. Under paragraph (d)(2) of this section, economic performance with respect to the liability to place amounts in escrow occurs as the aircraft is repaired. Consequently, V incurs $20,000 for the 1993 taxable year.

Example 7. Use of property provided to the taxpayer. (i) X corporation, a calendar year, accrual method taxpayer, manufactures and sells electronic circuitry. On November 15, 1990, X enters into a contract with Y that entitles X to the exclusive use of a product owned by Y for the five-year period beginning on January 1, 1991. Pursuant to the contract, X pays Y $100,000 on December 30, 1990.

(ii) Under paragraph (d)(3)(i) of this section, economic performance with respect to X's liability for the use of property occurs ratably over the period of time X is entitled to use the product. Consequently, $20,000 is incurred by X for 1991 and for each of the succeeding four taxable years.

Example 8. Use of property provided to the taxpayer. (i) Y corporation, a calendar year, accrual method taxpayer, enters into a five-year lease with Z for the use of a copy machine on July 1, 1991. Y also receives delivery of the copy machine on July 1, 1991. The lease obligates Y to pay Z a base rental payment of $6,000 per year at the beginning of each lease year and an additional charge of 5 cents per copy 30 days after the end of each lease year. The machine is used to make 50,000 copies during the first lease year: 20,000 copies in 1991 and 30,000 copies from January 1, 1992, to July 1, 1992. Y pays the $6,000 base rental payment to Z on July 1, 1991, and the $2,500 variable use payment on July 30, 1992.

(ii) Under paragraph (d)(3)(i) of this section, economic performance with respect to Y's base rental liability occurs ratably over the period of time Y is entitled to use the copy machine. Consequently, $3,000 rent is incurred by Y for the 1991 taxable year. Under paragraph (d)(3)(ii) of this section, economic performance with respect to Y's variable use portion of the liability occurs as Y uses the machine. Thus, the $1,000 of the $2,500 variable-use liability that relates to the 20,000 copies made in 1991 is incurred by Y for the 1991 taxable year.

Example 9. Use of property provided to the taxpayer. (i) X corporation, a calendar year, accrual method taxpayer, enters into a five-year product distribution agreement with Y, on January 1, 1992. The agreement provides for a payment of $100,000 on January 1, 1992, plus 10 percent of the gross profits earned by X from distribution of the product. The variable income portion of X's liability is payable on April 1 of each subsequent year. On January 1, 1992, X pays Y $100,000. On April 1, 1993, X pays Y $3 million representing 10 percent of X's gross profits from January 1 through December 31, 1992.

(ii) Under paragraph (d)(3)(i) of this section, economic performance with respect to X's $100,000 payment occurs ratably over the period of time X is entitled to use the product. Consequently, $20,000 is incurred by X for each year of the agreement beginning with 1992. Under paragraph (d)(3)(ii) of this section, economic performance with respect to X's variable income portion of the liability occurs as the income is earned by X. Thus, the $3 million variable-income liability is incurred by X for the 1992 taxable year.

(e) *Interest.*—In the case of interest, economic performance occurs as the interest cost economically accrues, in accordance with the principles of relevant provisions of the Code.

(f) *Timing of deductions from notional principal contracts.*—Economic performance on a notional principal contract occurs as provided under § 1.446-3.

(g) *Certain liabilities for which payment is economic performance.*—(1) *In general.*—(i) *Person to which payment must be made.*—In the case of liabilities described in paragraphs (g)(2) through (7) of this section, economic performance occurs when, and to the extent that, payment is made to the person to which the liability is owed. Thus, except as otherwise provided in paragraph (g)(1)(iv) of this section and § 1.461-6, economic performance does not occur as a taxpayer makes payments in connection with such a liability to any other person, including a trust, escrow account, court-administered fund, or any similar arrangement, unless the payments constitute payment to the person to which the liability is owed under paragraph (g)(1)(ii)(B) of this section. Instead, economic performance occurs as payments are made from that other person or fund to the person to which the liability is owed. The amount of economic performance that occurs as payment is made from the other person or fund to the person to which the liability is owed may not exceed the amount the taxpayer transferred to the other person or fund. For special rules relating to the taxation of amounts transferred to "qualified settlement funds," see section 468B and the regulations thereunder. The Commissioner may provide additional rules in regulations, revenue procedures, and revenue rulings concerning the time at which economic performance occurs for items described in this paragraph (g).

(ii) *Payment to person to which liability is owed.*—Paragraph (d)(6) of this section provides that for purposes of paragraph (d) of this section (relating to the provision of services or property to the taxpayer) in certain cases a taxpayer may treat services or property as provided to the taxpayer as the taxpayer makes payments to the person providing the services or property. In addition, this paragraph (g) provides that in the case of certain liabilities of a taxpayer, economic performance occurs as the taxpayer makes payment to persons specified therein. For these and all other purposes of section 461(h) and the regulations thereunder:

(A) *Payment.*—The term "payment" has the same meaning as is used when determining whether a taxpayer using the cash receipts and disbursements method of accounting has made a payment. Thus, for example, payment includes the furnishing of cash or cash equivalents and the netting of offsetting accounts. Payment does not include the furnishing of a note or other evidence of indebtedness of the taxpayer, whether or not the evidence is guaranteed by any other instrument (including a standby letter of credit) or by any third party (including a government agency). As a further example, payment does not include a promise of the taxpayer to provide services or property in the future (whether or not the promise is evidenced by a contract or other written agreement). In addition, payment does not include an amount transferred as a loan, refundable deposit, or contingent payment.

(B) *Person to which payment is made.*—Payment to a particular person is accomplished if paragraph (g)(1)(ii)(A) of this section is satisfied and a cash basis taxpayer in the position of that person would be treated as having actually or constructively received the amount of the payment as gross income under the principles of section 451 (without regard to section 104(a) or any other provision that specifically excludes the amount from gross income). Thus, for example, the purchase of an annuity contract or any other asset generally does not constitute payment to the person to which a liability is owed unless the ownership of the contract or other asset is transferred to that person.

(C) *Liabilities that are assumed in connection with the sale of a trade or business.*—Paragraph (d)(5) of this section provides rules that determine when economic performance occurs in the case of liabilities that are assumed in connection with the sale of a trade or business. The provisions of paragraph (d)(5) of this section also apply to any liability described in paragraph (g)(2) through (7) of this section that the purchaser expressly assumes in connection with the sale or exchange of a trade or business by a taxpayer, provided the taxpayer (but for the economic performance requirement) would have been entitled to incur the liability as of the date of the sale.

(iii) *Person.*—For purposes of this paragraph (g), "person" has the same meaning as in section 7701(a)(1), except that it also includes any foreign state, the United States, any State or political subdivision thereof, any possession of the United States, and any agency or instrumentality of any of the foregoing.

(iv) *Assignments.*—If a person that has a right to receive payment in satisfaction of a liability described in paragraphs (g)(2) through (7) of this section makes a valid assignment of that right to a second person, or if the right is assigned to the second person through operation of law, then payment to the second person in satisfaction of that liability constitutes payment to the person to which the liability is owed.

(2) *Liabilities arising under a workers compensation act or out of any tort, breach of contract, or violation of law.*—If the liability of a taxpayer requires a payment or series of pay-

ments to another person and arises under any workers compensation act or out of any tort, breach of contract, or violation of law, economic performance occurs as payment is made to the person to which the liability is owed. See *Example 1* of paragraph (g)(8) of this section. For purposes of this paragraph (g)(2)—

(i) A liability to make payments for services, property, or other consideration provided under a contract is not a liability arising out of a breach of that contract unless the payments are in the nature of incidental, consequential, or liquidated damages; and

(ii) A liability arising out of a tort, breach of contract, or violation of law includes a liability arising out of the settlement of a dispute in which a tort, breach of contract, or violation of law, respectively, is alleged.

(3) *Rebates and refunds.*—If the liability of a taxpayer is to pay a rebate, refund, or similar payment to another person (whether paid in property, money, or as a reduction in the price of goods or services to be provided in the future by the taxpayer), economic performance occurs as payment is made to the person to which the liability is owed. This paragraph (g)(3) applies to all rebates, refunds, and payments or transfers in the nature of a rebate or refund regardless of whether they are characterized as a deduction from gross income, an adjustment to gross receipts or total sales, or an adjustment or addition to cost of goods sold. In the case of a rebate or refund made as a reduction in the price of goods or services to be provided in the future by the taxpayer, "payment" is deemed to occur as the taxpayer would otherwise be required to recognize income resulting from a disposition at an unreduced price. See *Example 2* of paragraph (g)(8) of this section. For purposes of determining whether the recurring item exception of § 1.461-5 applies, a liability that arises out of a tort, breach of contract, or violation of law is not considered a rebate or refund.

(4) *Awards, prizes, and jackpots.*—If the liability of a taxpayer is to provide an award, prize, jackpot, or other similar payment to another person, economic performance occurs as payment is made to the person to which the liability is owed. See *Examples 3* and *4* of paragraph (g)(8) of this section.

(5) *Insurance, warranty, and service contracts.*—If the liability of a taxpayer arises out of the provision to the taxpayer of insurance, or a warranty or service contract, economic performance occurs as payment is made to the person to which the liability is owed. See *Examples 5* through *7* of paragraph (g)(8) of this section. For purposes of this paragraph (g)(5)—

(i) A warranty or service contract is a contract that a taxpayer enters into in connection with property bought or leased by the taxpayer, pursuant to which the other party to the contract promises to replace or repair the property under specified circumstances.

(ii) The term "insurance" has the same meaning as is used when determining the deductibility of amounts paid or incurred for insurance under section 162.

(6) Taxes—

(i) *In general.*—Except as otherwise provided in this paragraph (g)(6), if the liability of a taxpayer is to pay a tax, economic performance occurs as the tax is paid to the governmental authority that imposed the tax. For purposes of this paragraph (g)(6), payment includes payments of estimated income tax and payments of tax where the taxpayer subsequently files a claim for credit or refund. In addition, for purposes of this paragraph (g)(6), a tax does not include a charge collected by a governmental authority for specific extraordinary services or property provided to a taxpayer by the governmental authority. Examples of such a charge include the purchase price of a parcel of land sold to a taxpayer by a governmental authority and a charge for labor engaged in by government employees to improve that parcel. In certain cases, a liability to pay a tax is permitted to be taken into account in the taxable year before the taxable year during which economic performance occurs under the recurring item exception of § 1.461-5. See *Example 8* of paragraph (g)(8) of this section.

(ii) *Licensing fees.*—If the liability of a taxpayer is to pay a licensing or permit fee required by a governmental authority, economic performance occurs as the fee is paid to the governmental authority, or as payment is made to any other person at the direction of the governmental authority.

(iii) *Exceptions.*—(A) *Real property taxes.*—If a taxpayer has made a valid election under section 461(c), the taxpayer's accrual for real property taxes is determined under section 461(c). Otherwise, economic performance with respect to a property tax liability occurs as the tax is paid, as specified in paragraph (g)(6)(i) of this section.

(B) *Certain foreign taxes.*—If the liability of a taxpayer is to pay an income, war profits, or excess profits tax that is imposed by the authority of any foreign country or possession of the United States and is creditable under section 901 (including a creditable tax described in section 903 that is paid in lieu of such a tax), economic performance occurs when the requirements of the all events test (as described in § 1.446-1(c)(1)(ii)) other than economic performance are met, whether or not the taxpayer elects to credit such taxes under section 901(a).

(7) *Other liabilities.*—In the case of a taxpayer's liability for which economic performance rules are not provided elsewhere in this section or in any other Internal Revenue regulation, revenue ruling or revenue procedure, economic performance occurs as the taxpayer makes payments in satisfaction of the liability to the person to which the liability is owed. This paragraph (g)(7) applies only if the liability cannot properly be characterized as a liability covered by rules provided elsewhere in this section. If a liability may properly be characterized as, for example, a liability arising from the provision of services or property to, or by, a taxpayer, the determination as to when economic performance occurs with respect to that liability is made under paragraph (d) of this section and not under this paragraph (g)(7).

(8) *Examples.*—The following examples illustrate the principles of this paragraph (g). For purposes of these examples, it is assumed that the requirements of the all events test other than economic performance have been met and, except as otherwise provided, that the recurring item exception is not used.

Example 1. Liabilities arising out of a tort. (i) During the period 1970 through 1975, Z corporation, a calendar year, accrual method taxpayer, manufactured and distributed industrial products that contained carcinogenic substances. In 1992, a number of lawsuits are filed against Z alleging damages due to exposure to these products. In settlement of a lawsuit maintained by A, Z agrees to purchase an annuity contract that will provide annual payments to A of $50,000 for a period of 25 years. On December 15, 1992, Z pays W, an unrelated life insurance company, $491,129 for such an annuity contract. Z retains ownership of the annuity contract.

(ii) Under paragraph (g)(2) of this section, economic performance with respect to Z's liability to A occurs as each payment is made to A. Consequently, $50,000 is incurred by Z for each taxable year that a payment is made to A under the annuity contract. (Z must also include in income a portion of amounts paid under the annuity, pursuant to section 72.) The result is the same if in 1992 Z secures its obligation with a standby letter of credit.

(iii) If Z later transfers ownership of the annuity contract to A, an amount equal to the fair market value of the annuity on the date of transfer is incurred by Z in the taxable year of the transfer (see paragraph (g)(1)(ii)(B) of this section). In addition, the transfer constitutes a transaction to which section 1001 applies.

Example 2. Rebates and refunds. (i) X corporation, a calendar year, accrual method taxpayer, manufactures and sells hardware products. X enters into agreements that entitle each of its distributors to a rebate (or discount on future purchases) from X based on the amount of purchases made by the distributor from X during any calendar year. During the 1992 calendar year, X becomes liable to pay a $2,000 rebate to distributor A. X pays A $1,200 of the rebate on January 15, 1993, and the remaining $800 on October 15, 1993. Assume the rebate is deductible (or allowable as an adjustment to gross receipts or cost of goods sold) when incurred.

(ii) If X does not adopt the recurring item exception described in § 1.461-5 with respect to rebates and refunds, then under paragraph (g)(3) of this section, economic performance with respect to the $2,000 rebate liability occurs in 1993. However, if X has made a proper election under § 1.461-5, and as of December 31, 1992, all events have occurred that determine the fact of the rebate liability, X incurs $1,200 for the 1992 taxable year. Because economic performance (payment) with respect to the remaining $800 does not occur until October 15, 1993 (more than 8½ months after the end of 1992), X cannot use the recurring item exception for this portion of the liability (see § 1.461-5). Thus, the $800 is not incurred by X until the 1993 taxable year. If, instead of making the cash payments to A during 1993, X adjusts the price of hardware purchased by A that is delivered to A during 1993, X's "payment" occurs as X would otherwise be required to recognize income resulting from a disposition at an unreduced price.

Example 3. Awards, prizes, and jackpots. (i) W corporation, a calendar year, accrual method taxpayer, produces and sells breakfast cereal. W conducts a contest pursuant to which the winner is entitled to $10,000 per year for a period of 20 years. On December 1, 1992, A is declared the winner of the contest and is paid $10,000 by W. In addition, on December 1 of each of the next nineteen years, W pays $10,000 to A.

(ii) Under paragraph (g)(4) of this section, economic performance with respect to the $200,000 contest liability occurs as each of the $10,000 payments is made by W to A. Consequently, $10,000 is incurred by W for the 1992 taxable year and for each of the succeeding nineteen taxable years.

Example 4. Awards, prizes, and jackpots. (i) Y corporation, a calendar year, accrual method taxpayer, owns a casino that contains progressive slot machines. A progressive slot machine provides a guaranteed jackpot amount that increases as money is gambled through the machine until the jackpot is won or until a maximum predetermined amount is reached. On July 1, 1993, the guaranteed jackpot amount on one of Y's slot machines reaches the maximum predetermined amount of $50,000. On October 1, 1994, the $50,000 jackpot is paid to B.

(ii) Under paragraph (g)(4) of this section, economic performance with respect to the $50,000 jackpot liability occurs on the date the jackpot is paid to B. Consequently, $50,000 is incurred by Y for the 1994 taxable year.

Example 5. Insurance, warranty, and service contracts. (i) V corporation, a calendar year, accrual method taxpayer, manufactures toys. V enters into a contract with W, an unrelated insurance company, on December 15, 1992. The contract obligates V to pay W a premium of $500,000 before the end of 1995. The contract obligates W to satisfy any liability of V resulting from claims made during 1993 or 1994 against V by any third party for damages attributable to defects in toys manufactured by V. Pursuant to the contract, V pays W a premium of $500,000 on October 1, 1995.

(ii) Assuming the arrangement constitutes insurance, under paragraph (g)(5) of this section economic performance occurs as the premium is paid. Thus, $500,000 is incurred by V for the 1995 taxable year.

Example 6. Insurance, warranty, and service contracts. (i) Y corporation, a calendar year, accrual method taxpayer, is a common carrier. On December 15, 1992, Y enters into a contract with Z, an unrelated insurance company, under which Z must satisfy any liability of Y that arises during the succeeding 5 years for damages under a workers compensation act or out of any tort, provided the event that causes the damages occurs during 1993 or 1994. Under the contract, Y pays $360,000 to Z on December 31, 1993.

(ii) Assuming the arrangement constitutes insurance, under paragraph (g)(5) of this section economic performance occurs as the premium is paid. Consequently, $360,000 is incurred by Y for the 1993 taxable year. The period for which the $360,000 amount is permitted to be taken into account is determined under the capitalization rules because the insurance contract is an asset having a useful life extending substantially beyond the close of the taxable year.

Example 7. Insurance, warranty, and service contracts. Assume the same facts as in *Example 6*, except that Y is obligated to pay the first $5,000 of any damages covered by the arrangement with Z. Y is, in effect, self-insured to the extent of this $5,000 "deductible." Thus, under paragraph (g)(2) of this section, economic performance with respect to the $5,000 liability does not occur until the amount is paid to the person to which the tort or workers compensation liability is owed.

Example 8. Taxes. (i) The laws of State A provide that every person owning personal property located in State A on the first day of January shall be liable for tax thereon and that a lien for the tax shall attach as of that date. In addition, the laws of State A provide that 60% of the tax is due on the first day of December following the lien date and the remaining 40% is due on the first day of July of the succeeding year. On January 1, 1992, X corporation, a calendar year, accrual method taxpayer, owns personal property located in State A. State A imposes a $10,000 tax on X with respect to that property on January 1, 1992. X pays State A $6,000 of the tax on December 1, 1992, and the remaining $4,000 on July 1, 1993.

(ii) Under paragraph (g)(6) of this section, economic performance with respect to $6,000 of the tax liability occurs on December 1, 1992. Consequently, $6,000 is incurred by X for the 1992 taxable year. Economic performance with respect to the remaining $4,000 of the tax liability occurs on July 1, 1993. If X has adopted the recurring item exception described in § 1.461-5 as a method of accounting for taxes, and as of December 31, 1992, all events have occurred that determine the liability of X for the remaining $4,000, X also incurs $4,000 for the 1992 taxable year. If X does not adopt the recurring item exception method, the $4,000 is not incurred by X until the 1993 taxable year.

* * *

[Reg. § 1.461-4.]

☐ [*T.D.* 8408, 4-9-92. *Amended by T.D.* 8491, 10-8-93; *T.D.* 8593, 4-7-95 *and T.D.* 8820, 5-17-99.]

Proposed Regulation

§ 1.465-1. General rules; limitation of deductions to amount at risk.—(a) *In general.*—For taxable years beginning after December 31, 1975, section 465 generally limits the amount of any loss described in section 465(d) that is otherwise deductible in connection with an activity described in section 465(c)(1). Under section 465 the amount of the loss is allowed as a deduction only to the extent that the taxpayer is at risk with respect to the activity at the close of the taxable year. The determination of the amount the taxpayer is at risk in cases where the activity is engaged in by an entity separate from the taxpayer is made as of the close of the taxable year of the entity engaging in the activity (for example, a partnership). For the purposes of these regulations, in cases where the activity is engaged in by an entity separate from the taxpayer references to a taxable year shall apply to the taxable year of the entity unless otherwise stated. For rules determining the amount at risk and for more specific rules regarding the effective dates, see §§1.465-20 through 1.465-25 and 1.465-95.

(b) *Substance over form.*—In applying section 465 and these regulations, substance will prevail over form. Regardless of the form a transaction may take, the taxpayer's amount at risk will not be increased if the transaction is inconsistent with normal commercial practices or is, in essence, a device to avoid section 465. See §1.465-4 for rules regarding attempts to avoid the at risk provisions.

(c) *Activities.*—See sections 465(c)(1)(A) through (D) and §§1.465-42 through 1.465-45 for the activities to which section 465 applies for taxable years beginning generally after December 31, 1975. These activities are holding, producing, or distributing movies and video tapes, farming, leasing of personal property, and exploring for or exploiting oil and gas resources. See section 465(c)(3) and section 465(c)(1)(E) for additional activities to which section 465 applies for taxable years beginning generally after December 31, 1978.

(d) *Taxpayers affected by at risk provisions.*—(1) For taxable years beginning generally after December 31, 1975, section 465 applies to all noncorporate taxpayers, to electing small business corporations (as defined in section 1371(b)), and to personal holding companies (as defined in section 542). For special rules relating to electing small business corporations, see §1.465-10.

(2) See section 465(a)(1)(C) for additional taxpayers to whom section 465 applies for taxable years beginning generally after December 31, 1978.

(e) *Basis.*—The provisions of section 465 and the regulations thereunder are only intended to limit the extent to which certain losses in connection with covered activities may be deducted in a given year by a taxpayer. Section 465 does not apply for other purposes, such as determining adjusted basis. Thus, for example, the adjusted basis of a partner in a partnership interest is not affected by section 465. [Prop. Reg. §1.465-1.]

[Proposed 6-5-79.]

Proposed Regulation

§1.465-2. General rules; allowance of deductions.—(a) *In general.*—In any taxable year, there are two ways in which deductions allocable to an activity to which section 465 applies will be allowable under section 465. First, deductions allocable to an activity and otherwise allowable will be allowable in a taxable year to the extent of income received or accrued from the activity in that taxable year. See the example at §1.465-11(c)(2). Thus, to the extent there is income from the activity in a taxable year, deductions allocable to that activity will be allowable without regard to the amount at risk. Second, losses from the activity (that is, the excess of deductions allocable to the activity over the income received or accrued from the activity) will be allowable to the extent the taxpayer is at risk with respect to that activity at the close of the taxable year. See the example at §1.465-11(a)(2). Also see §§1.465-11 through 1.465-13 for the definition of loss.

(b) *Carryover of loss.*—A loss which is disallowed by reason of section 465(a) shall be treated as a deduction for the succeeding taxable year with respect to the same activity to which it is allocable. In the succeeding taxable year there will again be two ways for the deduction to be allowable. There is no limit to the number of years to which a taxpayer may carry over a loss disallowed solely by reason of section 465(a). [Prop. Reg. §1.465-2.]

[Proposed 6-5-79.]

Proposed Regulation

§1.465-10. General rules; rules relating to subchapter S corporations and their shareholders.—(a) *In general.*—In the case of electing small business corporations (as defined in section 1371(b)) the at risk rules of section 465 apply at both the corporate level and the shareholder level. Therefore, losses from an activity can be deducted by the corporation only to the extent that the corporation is at risk in the activity. In addition, each shareholder will be allowed a loss in the activity only to the extent that the shareholder is at risk in the activity.

(b) *Determination of corporation's amount at risk.*—(1) *General rule.*—Except as provided in paragraph (b)(2) of this section, an electing small business corporation's amount at risk in an activity is determined in the same manner as that of any other taxpayer.

(2) *Special rule for certain borrowed amounts.*—Amounts borrowed by an electing small business corporation from one or more of its shareholders may increase the corporation's amount at risk, notwithstanding the fact that the shareholders have an interest in the activity other than that of a creditor.

(c) *Determination of shareholder's amount at risk.*—The amount at risk of a shareholder of an electing small business corporation (as described in section 1371(b)) shall be adjusted to reflect any increase or decrease in the adjusted basis of any indebtedness of the corporation to the shareholder described in section 1374(c)(2)(B).

(d) *Example.*—The provisions of this section may be illustrated by the following example:

Example. A is the single shareholder in X, an electing small business corporation engaged in an activity described in section 465(c)(1). A contributed $50,000 to X in exchange for its stock under section 351. In addition, A borrowed $40,000 for which A assumed personal liability A then loaned the entire amount to X for use in the activity. During its taxable year, X had a net operating loss of $75,000. At the close of the taxable year (without reduction for any losses of X) A's amount at risk is $90,000 ($50,000 + $40,000). However, it is also necessary to determine X's amount at risk in the activity. X is also at risk for the $40,000 borrowed from A and expended in the activity. Therefore, X's amount at risk in the activity is $90,000 ($50,000 + $40,000). Because X's amount at risk in the activity ($90,000) exceeds the net operating loss ($75,000), the entire loss is allowed to the corporation and allocated to A. Since A's amount at risk ($90,000) also exceeds the loss ($75,000) A will be allowed the entire loss deduction. [Prop. Reg. § 1.465-10.]

[Proposed 6-5-79.]

Proposed Regulation

§ 1.465-24. Effect on amount at risk of loans for which borrower is personally liable for repayment.—(a) *Creation of loan.*—(1) *General rule.*—A taxpayer's amount at risk in an activity is increased by the amount of any liability incurred in the conduct of an activity for use in the activity to the extent the taxpayer is personally liable for repayment of the liability.

(2) *Partnerships.*—(i) When a partnership incurs a liability in the conduct of an activity and under state law members of the partnership may be held personally liable for repayment of the liability, each partner's amount at risk is increased to the extent the partner is not protected against loss. To the extent the partner is protected against loss (such as through a right of contribution), the liability shall be treated in the same manner as amounts borrowed for which the taxpayer has no personal liability and for which no security is pledged. See § 1.465-25.

(ii) The application of this paragraph may be illustrated by the following example:

Example. A and B are equal general partners in partnership AB, which is engaged solely in an activity described in section 465(c)(1). AB borrows $25,000 from a bank to purchase equipment to be used in the activity. In addition to giving the bank a security interest in the newly purchased equipment, A and B each assumes personal liability for the loan. Although either A or B could be called upon by the bank to repay the entire $25,000, in such instance the partner who paid would be entitled to $12,500 from the other partner. Thus, although each is personally liable for $25,000, each is protected against loss in excess of $12,500. Accordingly, the loan increases the amount each is at risk with respect to the activity by $12,500.

(3) *Small business corporations.*—The amount at risk of a shareholder of an electing small business corporation (as defined in section 1371(b)) shall not be increased by indebtedness incurred by the corporation from persons other than that shareholder. For treatment of indebtedness described in section 1374(c)(2)(B) (relating to loans by shareholders to electing small business corporations), see § 1.465-10(c).

* * *

[Prop. Reg. § 1.465-24.]

[Proposed 6-5-79.]

§ 1.465-27. Qualified nonrecourse financing.—(a) *In general.*—Notwithstanding any provision of section 465(b) or the regulations under section 465(b), for an activity of holding real property, a taxpayer is considered at risk for the taxpayer's share of any qualified nonrecourse financing which is secured by real property used in such activity.

(b) *Qualified nonrecourse financing secured by real property.*—(1) *In general.*—For purposes of section 465(b)(6) and this section, the term *qualified nonrecourse financing* means any financing—

(i) Which is borrowed by the taxpayer with respect to the activity of holding real property;

(ii) Which is borrowed by the taxpayer from a qualified person or represents a loan from any federal, state, or local government or instrumentality thereof, or is guaranteed by any federal, state, or local government;

(iii) For which no person is personally liable for repayment, taking into account paragraphs (b)(3), (4), and (5) of this section; and

(iv) Which is not convertible debt.

(2) *Security for qualified nonrecourse financing.*—(i) *Types of property.*—For a taxpayer to be considered at risk under section 465(b)(6), qualified nonrecourse financing must be secured only by real property used in the activity of holding real property. For this

purpose, however, property that is incidental to the activity of holding real property will be disregarded. In addition, for this purpose, property that is neither real property used in the activity of holding real property nor incidental property will be disregarded if the aggregate gross fair market value of such property is less than 10 percent of the aggregate gross fair market value of all the property securing the financing.

(ii) *Look-through rule for partnerships.*—For purposes of paragraph (b)(2)(i) of this section, a borrower shall be treated as owning directly its proportional share of the assets in a partnership in which the borrower owns (directly or indirectly through a chain of partnerships) an equity interest.

(3) *Personal liability; partial liability.*—If one or more persons are personally liable for repayment of a portion of a financing, the portion of the financing for which no person is personally liable may qualify as qualified nonrecourse financing.

(4) *Partnership liability.*—For purposes of section 465(b)(6) and this paragraph (b), the personal liability of any partnership for repayment of a financing is disregarded and, provided the requirements contained in paragraphs (b)(1)(i), (ii), and (iv) of this section are satisfied, the financing will be treated as qualified nonrecourse financing secured by real property if—

(i) The only persons personally liable to repay the financing are partnerships;

(ii) Each partnership with personal liability holds only property described in paragraph (b)(2)(i) of this section (applying the principles of paragraph (b)(2)(ii) of this section in determining the property held by each partnership); and

(iii) In exercising its remedies to collect on the financing in a default or default-like situation, the lender may proceed only against property that is described in paragraph (b)(2)(i) of this section and that is held by the partnership or partnerships (applying the principles of paragraph (b)(2)(ii) of this section in determining the property held by the partnership or partnerships).

(5) *Disregarded entities.*—Principles similar to those described in paragraph (b)(4) of this section shall apply in determining whether a financing of an entity that is disregarded for federal tax purposes under § 301.7701-3 of this chapter is treated as qualified nonrecourse financing secured by real property.

* * *

[Reg. § 1.465-27.]

☐ [*T.D.* 8777, 8-3-98.]

Proposed Amendments to Regulation

§ 1.469-5. Material participation.—

(a) through (d) [Reserved].

(e) *Treatment of an interest in a limited partnership as a limited partner.*—(1) *In general.*—Except as otherwise provided in this paragraph (e), an individual shall not be treated as materially participating in any activity in which the individual owns an interest in a limited partnership as a limited partner (as defined in paragraph (e)(3)(i) of this section) for purposes of applying section 469 and the regulations thereunder to—

(i) The individual's share of any income, gain, loss, deduction, or credit from such activity that is attributable to an interest in a limited partnership as a limited partner; and

(ii) Any gain or loss from such activity recognized upon a sale or exchange of such an interest.

(2) *Exceptions.*—Paragraph (e)(1) of this section shall not apply to an individual's share of income, gain, loss, deduction, and credit for a taxable year from any activity in which the individual would be treated as materially participating for the taxable year under paragraphs (a)(1), (a)(5), or (a)(6) of § 1.469-5T if the individual did not own an interest in a limited partnership as a limited partner (as defined in paragraph (e)(3)(i) of this section) for such taxable year.

(3) *Interest in a limited partnership as a limited partner.*—(i) *In general.*—Except as provided in paragraph (e)(3)(ii) of this section, for purposes of section 469(h)(2) and this paragraph (e), an interest in an entity shall be treated as an interest in a limited partnership as a limited partner if—

(A) The entity in which such interest is held is classified as a partnership for Federal income tax purposes under § 301.7701-3; and

(B) The holder of such interest does not have rights to manage the entity at all times during the entity's taxable year under the law of the jurisdiction in which the entity is organized and under the governing agreement.

(ii) *Individual holding an interest other than an interest in a limited partnership as a limited partner.*—An individual shall not be treated as holding an interest in a limited partnership as a limited partner for the individual's taxable year if such individual also holds an interest in the partnership that is not an interest in a limited partnership as a limited partner (as defined in paragraph (e)(3)(i) of this section), such as a state-law general partnership interest, at all times during the entity's taxable year ending with or within the individual's taxable year (or the portion of the entity's taxable year during which the individual (directly or indirectly) owns such interest in a limited partnership as a limited partner).

(4) *Effective/applicability date.*—This section applies to taxable years beginning on or after the date of publication of the Treasury decision adopting these rules as a final regulation in the Federal Register.

* * *

[Prop. Reg. § 1.469-5.]

[Proposed 11-28-2011.]

§ 1.469-5T. Material participation (temporary).—(a) *In general.*—Except as provided in paragraphs (e) and ((h) (2) of this section, an individual shall be treated, for purposes of section 469 and the regulations thereunder, as materially participating in an activity for the taxable year if and only if—

(1) The individual participates in the activity for more than 500 hours during such year;

(2) The individual's participation in the activity for the taxable year constitutes substantially all of the participation in such activity of all individuals (including individuals who are not owners of interests in the activity) for such year;

(3) The individual participates in the activity for more than 100 hours during the taxable year, and such individual's participation in the activity for the taxable year is not less than the participation in the activity of any other individual (including individuals who are not owners of interests in the activity) for such year;

(4) The activity is a significant participation activity (within the meaning of paragraph (c) of this section) for the taxable year, and the individual's aggregate participation in all significant participation activities during such year exceeds 500 hours;

(5) The individual materially participated in the activity (determined without regard to this paragraph (a) (5)) for any five taxable years (whether or not consecutive) during the ten taxable years that immediately precede the taxable year;

(6) The activity is a personal service activity (within the meaning of paragraph (d) of this section), and the individual materially participated in the activity for any three taxable years (whether or not consecutive) preceding the taxable year; or

(7) Based on all of the facts and circumstances (taking into account the rules in paragraph (b) of this section), the individual participates in the activity on a regular, continuous, and substantial basis during such year.

(b) *Facts and circumstances.*—(1) *In general.*—[Reserved.]

(2) *Certain participation insufficient to constitute material participation under this paragraph (b).*—(i) *Participation satisfying standards not contained in section 469.*—Except as provided in section 469(h) (3) and paragraph (h) (2) of this section (relating to certain retired individuals and surviving spouses in the case of farming activities), the fact that an individual satisfies the requirements of any participation standard (whether or not referred to as "material participation") under any provision (including sections 1402 and 2032A and the regulations thereunder) other than section 469 and the regulations thereunder shall not be taken into account in determining whether such individual materially participates in any activity for any taxable year for purposes of section 469 and the regulations thereunder.

(ii) *Certain management activities.*—An individual's services performed in the management of an activity shall not be taken into account in determining whether such individual is treated as materially participating in such activity for the taxable year under paragraph (a) (7) of this section unless, for such taxable year—

(A) No person (other than such individual) who performs services in connection with the management of the activity receives compensation described in section 911(d) (2) (A) in consideration for such services; and

(B) No individual performs services in connection with the management of the activity that exceed (by hours) the amount of such services performed by such individual.

(iii) *Participation less than 100 hours.*—If an individual participates in an activity for 100 hours or less during the taxable year, such individual shall not be treated as materially participating in such activity for the taxable year under paragraph (a) (7) of this section.

(c) *Significant participation activity.*—(1) *In general.*—For purposes of paragraph (a) (4) of this section, an activity is a significant participation activity of an individual if and only if such activity—

(i) Is a trade or business activity (within the meaning of § 1.469-1T(e) (2)) in which the individual significantly participates for the taxable year; and

(ii) Would be an activity in which the individual does not materially participate for the taxable year if material participation for such year were determined without regard to paragraph (a) (4) of this section.

(2) *Significant participation.*—An individual is treated as significantly participating in an activity for a taxable year if and only if the individual participates in the activity for more than 100 hours during such year.

(d) *Personal service activity.*—An activity constitutes a personal service activity for purposes of paragraph (a)(6) of this section if such activity involves the performance of personal services in—

(1) The fields of health, law, engineering, architecture, accounting, actuarial science, performing arts, or consulting; or

(2) Any other trade or business in which capital is not a material income-producing factor.

(e) *Treatment of limited partners.*—(1) *General rule.*—Except as otherwise provided in this paragraph (e), an individual shall not be treated as materially participating in any activity of a limited partnership for purposes of applying section 469 and the regulations thereunder to—

(i) The individual's share of any income, gain, loss, deduction, or credit from such activity that is attributable to a limited partnership interest in the partnership; and

(ii) Any gain or loss from such activity recognized upon a sale or exchange of such an interest.

(2) *Exceptions.*—Paragraph (e)(1) of this section shall not apply to an individual's share of income, gain, loss, deduction, and credit for a taxable year from any activity in which the individual would be treated as materially participating for the taxable year under paragraph (a)(1), (5) or (6) of this section if the individual were not a limited partner for such taxable year.

(3) *Limited partnership interest.*—(i) *In general.*—Except as provided in paragraph (e)(3)(ii) of this section, for purposes of section 469(h)(2) and this paragraph (e), a partnership interest shall be treated as a limited partnership interest if—

(A) Such interest is designated a limited partnership interest in the limited partnership agreement or the certificate of limited partnership, without regard to whether the liability of the holder of such interest for obligations of the partnership is limited under the applicable State law; or

(B) The liability of the holder of such interest for obligations of the partnership is limited, under the law of the State in which the partnership is organized, to a determinable fixed amount (for example, the sum of the holder's capital contributions to the partnership and contractual obligations to make additional capital contributions to the partnership).

(ii) *Limited partner holding general partner interest.*—A partnership interest of an individual shall not be treated as a limited partnership interest for the individual's taxable year if the individual is a general partner in the partnership at all times during the partnership's taxable year ending with or within the individual's taxable year (or portion of the partnership's taxable year during which the individual (directly or indirectly) owns such limited partnership interest).

(f) *Participation.*—(1) [Reserved]See §1.469-5(f)(1) for rules relating to this paragraph.

(2) *Exceptions.*—(i) *Certain work not customarily done by owners.*—Work done in connection with an activity shall not be treated as participation in the activity for purposes of this section if—

(A) Such work is not of a type that is customarily done by an owner of such an activity; and

(B) One of the principal purposes for the performance of such work is to avoid the disallowance, under section 469 and the regulations thereunder, of any loss or credit from such activity.

(ii) *Participation as an investor.*—(A) *In general.*—Work done by an individual in the individual's capacity as an investor in an activity shall not be treated as participation in the activity for purposes of this section unless the individual is directly involved in the day-to-day management or operations of the activity.

(B) *Work done in individual's capacity as an investor.*—For purposes of this paragraph (f)(2)(ii), work done by an individual in the individual's capacity as an investor in an activity includes—

(1) Studying and reviewing financial statements or reports on operations of the activity;

(2) Preparing or compiling summaries or analyses of the finances or operations of the activity for the individual's own use; and

(3) Monitoring the finances or operations of the activity in a non-managerial capacity.

(3) *Participation of spouse.*—In the case of any person who is a married individual (within the meaning of section 7703) for the taxable year, any participation by such person's spouse in the activity during the taxable year (without regard to whether the spouse owns an interest in the activity and without regard to whether

the spouses file a joint return for the taxable year) shall be treated, for purposes of applying section 469 and the regulations thereunder to such person, as participation by such person in the activity during the taxable year.

(4) *Methods of proof.*—The extent of an individual's participation in an activity may be established by any reasonable means. Contemporaneous daily time reports, logs, or similar documents are not required if the extent of such participation may be established by other reasonable means. Reasonable means for purposes of this paragraph may include but are not limited to the identification of services performed over a period of time and the approximate number of hours spent performing such services during such period, based on appointment books, calendars, or narrative summaries.

* * *

[Temporary Reg. § 1.469-5T.]

☐ [*T.D.* 8175, 2-19-88. *Amended by T.D.* 8253, 5-11-89 *and T.D.* 8417, 5-11-92.]

§ 1.471-1. Need for inventories.—In order to reflect taxable income correctly, inventories at the beginning and end of each taxable year are necessary in every case in which the production, purchase, or sale of merchandise is an income-producing factor. The inventory should include all finished or partly finished goods and, in the case of raw materials and supplies, only those which have been acquired for sale or which will physically become a part of merchandise intended for sale, in which class fall containers, such as kegs, bottles, and cases, whether returnable or not, if title thereto will pass to the purchaser of the product to be sold therein. Merchandise should be included in the inventory only if title thereto is vested in the taxpayer. Accordingly, the seller should include in his inventory goods under contract for sale but not yet segregated and applied to the contract and goods out upon consignment, but should exclude from inventory goods sold (including containers) title to which has passed to the purchaser. A purchaser should include in inventory merchandise purchased (including containers), title to which has passed to him, although such merchandise is in transit or for other reasons has not been reduced to physical possession, but should not include goods ordered for future delivery, transfer of title to which has not yet been effected. (But see § 1.472-1.) [Reg. § 1.471-1.]

☐ [*T.D.* 6336, 12-1-58.]

§ 1.471-2. Valuation of inventories.—(a) Section 471 provides two tests to which each inventory must conform:

(1) It must conform as nearly as may be to the best accounting practice in the trade or business, and

(2) It must clearly reflect the income.

(b) It follows, therefore, that inventory rules cannot be uniform but must give effect to trade customs which come within the scope of the best accounting practice in the particular trade or business. In order clearly to reflect income, the inventory practice of a taxpayer should be consistent from year to year, and greater weight is to be given to consistency than to any particular method of inventorying or basis of valuation so long as the method or basis used is in accord with § § 1.471-1 through 1.471-11.

(c) The bases of valuation most commonly used by business concerns and which meet the requirements of section 471 are (1) cost and (2) cost or market, whichever is lower. (For inventories by dealers in securities, see § 1.471-5.) Any goods in an inventory which are unsalable at normal prices or unusable in the normal way because of damage, imperfections, shop wear, changes of style, odd or broken lots, or other similar causes, including second-hand goods taken in exchange, should be valued at bona fide selling prices less direct cost of disposition, whether subparagraph (1) or (2) of this paragraph is used, or if such goods consist of raw materials or partly finished goods held for use or consumption, they shall be valued upon a reasonable basis, taking into consideration the usability and the condition of the goods, but in no case shall such value be less than the scrap value. Bona fide selling price means actual offering of goods during a period ending not later than 30 days after inventory date. The burden of proof will rest upon the taxpayer to show that such exceptional goods as are valued upon such selling basis come within the classifications indicated above, and he shall maintain such records of the disposition of the goods as will enable a verification of the inventory to be made.

(d) In respect of normal goods, whichever method is adopted must be applied with reasonable consistency to the entire inventory of the taxpayer's trade or business except as to those goods inventoried under the last-in, first-out method authorized by section 472 or to animals inventoried under the elective unit-livestock-price-method authorized by § 1.471-6. See paragraph (d) of § 1.446-1 for rules permitting the use of different methods of accounting if the taxpayer has more than one trade or business. Where the taxpayer is engaged in more than one trade or business the Commissioner may require that the method of valuing inventories with respect to goods in one trade or business also be used with respect to similar goods in other trades or businesses if, in the opinion of the Commissioner, the use of such method with respect to such other goods is essential to a clear reflection of income. Taxpayers were given an option to adopt the basis of either (1) cost or (2) cost or market, whichever is lower, for their 1920 inventories. The basis properly adopted for that year or any subsequent year is controlling, and a change can now be made only after permission is secured from the Commissioner. Application for permission to change the basis of valuing inventories shall be made in writing and filed with the Commissioner as provided in paragraph (e) of § 1.446-1. Goods taken in the inventory which have been so intermingled that they cannot be identified with specific invoices will be deemed to be the goods most recently purchased or produced, and the cost thereof will be the actual cost of the goods purchased or produced during the period in which the quantity of goods in the inventory has been acquired. But see section 472 as to last-in, first-out inventories. Where the taxpayer maintains book inventories in accordance with a sound accounting system in which the respective inventory accounts are charged with the actual cost of the goods purchased or produced and credited with the value of goods used, transferred, or sold, calculated upon the basis of the actual cost of the goods acquired during the taxable year (including the inventory at the beginning of the year), the net value as shown by such inventory accounts will be deemed to be the cost of the goods on hand. The balances shown by such book inventories should be verified by physical inventories at reasonable intervals and adjusted to conform therewith.

(e) Inventories should be recorded in a legible manner, properly computed and summarized, and should be preserved as a part of the accounting records of the taxpayer. The inventories of taxpayers on whatever basis taken will be subject to investigation by the district director, and the taxpayer must satisfy the district director of the correctness of the prices adopted.

(f) The following methods, among others, are sometimes used in taking or valuing inventories, but are not in accord with the regulations in this part:

(1) Deducting from the inventory a reserve for price changes, or an estimated depreciation in the value thereof.

(2) Taking work in process, or other parts of the inventory, at a nominal price or at less than its proper value.

(3) Omitting portions of the stock on hand.

(4) Using a constant price or nominal value for so-called normal quantity of materials or goods in stock.

(5) Including stock in transit, shipped either to or from the taxpayer, the title to which is not vested in the taxpayer.

(6) Segregating indirect production costs into fixed and variable production cost classifications (as defined in § 1.471-11(b)(3)(ii)) and allocating only the variable costs to the cost of goods produced while treating fixed costs as period costs which are currently deductible. This method is commonly referred to as the "direct cost" method.

(7) Treating all or substantially all indirect production costs (whether classified as fixed or variable) as period costs which are currently deductible. This method is generally referred to as the "prime cost" method. [Reg. § 1.471-2.]

☐ [*T.D.* 6336, 12-1-58. *Amended by T.D.* 7285, 9-14-73.]

§ 1.471-3. Inventories at cost.—Cost means:

(a) In the case of merchandise on hand at the beginning of the taxable year, the inventory price of such goods.

(b) In the case of merchandise purchased since the beginning of the taxable year, the invoice price less trade or other discounts, except strictly cash discounts approximating a fair interest rate, which may be deducted or not at the option of the taxpayer, provided a consistent course is followed. To this net invoice price should be added transportation or other necessary charges incurred in acquiring possession of the goods. But see § 1.263A-1(d)(2)(iv)(C) for special rules for certain direct material costs that in certain cases are permitted to be capitalized as additional section 263A costs by taxpayers using a simplified method under § 1.263A-2(b) or (c) or § 1.263A-3(d). For taxpayers acquiring merchandise for resale that are subject to the provisions of section 263A, see §§ 1.263A-1 and 1.263A-3 for additional amounts that must be included in inventory costs.

(c) In the case of merchandise produced by the taxpayer since the beginning of the taxable year, (1) the cost of raw materials and supplies entering into or consumed in connection with the product, (2) expenditures for direct labor, and (3) indirect production costs incident to and necessary for the production of the particular article, including in such indirect production costs an appropriate portion of management expenses, but not including any cost of selling or return on capital, whether by way of interest or profit. See §§ 1.263A-1 and 1.263A-2 for more specific rules regarding the treatment of production costs.

(d) In any industry in which the usual rules for computation of cost of production are inapplicable, costs may be approximated upon such basis as may be reasonable and in conformity with established trade practice in the particular industry. Among such cases are: (1) Farmers and raisers of livestock (see § 1.471-6); (2) miners and manufacturers who by a single process or uniform series of processes derive a product of two or more kinds, sizes, or grades, the unit cost of which is substantially alike (see § 1.471-7); and (3) retail merchants who use what is known as the "retail method" in ascertaining approximate cost (see § 1.471-8).

(e) *Sales-based vendor allowances.*—(1) *Treatment of sales-based vendor chargebacks.*—(i) *In general.*—A sales-based vendor chargeback is an allowance, discount, or price rebate that a taxpayer becomes unconditionally entitled to by selling a vendor's merchandise to specific customers identified by the vendor at a price determined by the vendor. A sales-based vendor chargeback decreases cost of goods sold and does not reduce the cost of goods on hand at the end of the taxable year.

(ii) *Example.*—The following example illustrates the provisions of this paragraph (e)(1).

Example. (i) W is a wholesaler of pharmaceuticals. W purchases Drug X from the manufacturer, M, for $10x per unit. M has agreements with specific customers that allow those customers to acquire Drug X from M's wholesalers for $6x per unit. Under an agreement between W and M, W is required to sell Drug X to specific customers at the prices M has negotiated with such customers ($6x per unit) and, in exchange, M agrees to provide a price rebate to W equal to the difference between W's cost for Drug X and the price W is required to charge specific customers under the agreement (a difference of $4x per unit). W sells Drug X to specific customer Y for $6x. Under the agreement between W and M, the price rebate can be paid to W, credited against M's invoice to W for W's purchase of Drug X, or it can be credited to W's future purchases of drugs from M.

(ii) Under the terms of the agreement, W is unconditionally entitled to the price rebate of Drug X when it sells Drug X to specific customer Y, a specifically identified customer of M. The price rebate received by W for the sale of Drug X to Y is a sales-based vendor chargeback. Therefore, the amount of the sales-based vendor charge back, $4x per unit for Drug X, whether paid to W, credited against M's invoice to W for W's purchase of Drug X or credited against a future purchase, decreases cost of goods sold and does not reduce the cost of Drug X on hand at the end of the taxable year.

(2) *Treatment of other sales-based vendor allowances.*—[Reserved]

(f) Notwithstanding the other rules of this section, cost shall not include an amount which is of a type for which a deduction would be disallowed under section 162(c), (f), or (g) and the regulations thereunder in the case of a business expense.

(g) *Effective/applicability date.*—Paragraph (f) of this section applies to taxable years ending on or after January 13, 2014. [Reg. § 1.471-3.]

□ [*T.D.* 6336, 12-1-58. *Amended by T.D.* 7285, 9-14-73; *T.D.* 7345, 2-19-75; *T.D.* 8131, 3-24-87; *T.D.* 8482, 8-6-93; *T.D.* 9652, 1-10-2014 *and T.D.* 9843, 11-19-2018.]

§ 1.471-4. Inventories at cost or market, whichever is lower.—(a) *In general.*—(1) *Market definition.*—Under ordinary circumstances and for normal goods in an inventory, *market* means the aggregate of the current bid prices prevailing at the date of the inventory of the basic elements of cost reflected in inventories of goods purchased and on hand, goods in process of manufacture, and finished manufactured goods on hand. The basic elements of cost include direct materials, direct labor, and indirect costs required to be included in inventories by the taxpayer (e.g., under section 263A and its underlying regulations for taxpayers subject to that section). For taxpayers to which section 263A applies, for example, the basic elements of cost must reflect all direct costs and all indirect costs properly allocable to goods on hand at the inventory date at the current bid price of those costs, including but not limited to the cost of purchasing, handling, and storage activities conducted by the taxpayer, both prior to and subsequent to acquisition or production of the goods. The determination of the current bid price of the basic elements of costs reflected in goods on hand at the inventory date must be based on the usual volume of particular cost elements purchased (or incurred) by the taxpayer.

(2) *Fixed price contracts.*—Paragraph (a)(1) of this section does not apply to any goods on hand or in process of manufacture for delivery upon firm sales contracts (i.e., those not legally subject to cancellation by either party) at fixed prices entered into before the date of the inventory, under which the taxpayer is protected against actual loss. Any such goods must be inventoried at cost.

(3) *Examples.*—The valuation principles in paragraph (a)(1) of this section are illustrated by the following examples:

Example 1. (i) Taxpayer A manufactures tractors. A values its inventory using cost or market, whichever is lower, under paragraph (a)(1) of this section. At the end of 1994, the cost of one of A's tractors on hand is determined as follows:

Direct materials	$3,000
Direct labor	4,000
Indirect costs under section 263A	3,000
Total section 263A costs (cost)	$10,000

(ii) A determines that the aggregate of the current bid prices of the materials, labor, and overhead required to reproduce the tractor at the end of 1994 are as follows:

Direct materials	$3,100
Direct labor	4,100
Indirect costs under section 263A	3,100
Total section 263A costs (market)	$10,300

(iii) In determining the lower of cost or market value of the tractor, A compares the cost of the tractor, $10,000, with the market value of the tractor, $10,300, in accordance with paragraph (c) of this section. Thus, under this section, A values the tractor at $10,000.

Example 2. (i) Taxpayer B purchases and resells several lines of shoes and is subject to section 263A. B values its inventory using cost or market, whichever is lower, under paragraph (a) (1) of this section. At the end of 1994, the cost of one pair of shoes on hand is determined as follows:

Acquisition cost	$200
Indirect costs under section 263A	10
Total section 263A costs (cost)	$210

(ii) B determines the aggregate current bid prices prevailing at the end of 1994 for the elements of cost (both direct costs and indirect costs incurred prior and subsequent to acquisition of the shoes) based on the volume of the elements usually purchased (or incurred) by B as follows:

Acquisition cost	$178
Indirect costs under section 263A	12
Total [section] 263A costs (market)	$190

(iii) In determining the lower of cost or market value of the shoes, B compares the cost of the pair of shoes, $210, with the market value of the shoes, $190, in accordance with paragraph (c) of this section. Thus, under this section, B values the shoes at $190.

(b) *Inactive markets.*—Where no open market exists or where quotations are nominal, due to inactive market conditions, the taxpayer must use such evidence of a fair market price at the date or dates nearest the inventory as may be available, such as specific purchases or sales by the taxpayer or others in reasonable volume and made in good faith, or compensation paid for cancellation of contracts for purchase commitments. Where the taxpayer in the regular course of business has offered for sale such merchandise at prices lower than the current price as above defined, the inventory may be valued at such prices less direct cost of disposition, and the correctness of such prices will be determined by reference to the actual sales of the taxpayer for a reasonable period before and after the date of the inventory. Prices which vary materially from the actual prices so ascertained will not be accepted as reflecting the market.

(c) *Comparison of cost and market.*—Where the inventory is valued upon the basis of cost or market, whichever is lower, the market value of each article on hand at the inventory date shall be compared with the cost of the article, and the lower of such values shall be taken as the inventory value of the article.

* * *

[Reg. § 1.471-4.]

☐ [*T.D.* 6336, 12-1-58. *Amended by T.D.* 8482, 8-6-93.]

Adjustments

§1.483-1. Interest on certain deferred payments.—(a) *Amount constituting interest in certain deferred payment transactions.*—(1) *In general.*—Except as provided in paragraph (c) of this section, section 483 applies to a contract for the sale or exchange of property if the contract provides for one or more payments due more than 1 year after the date of the sale or exchange, and the contract does not provide for adequate stated interest. In general, a contract has adequate stated interest if the contract provides for a stated rate of interest that is at least equal to the test rate (determined under § 1.483-3) and the interest is paid or compounded at least annually. Section 483 may apply to a contract whether the contract is express (written or oral) or implied. For purposes of section 483, a sale or exchange is any transaction treated as a sale or exchange for tax purposes. In addition, for purposes of section 483, property includes debt instruments and investment units, but does not include money, services, or the right to use property. For the treatment of certain obligations given in exchange for services or the use of property, see sections 404 and 467. For purposes of this paragraph (a), money includes functional currency and, in certain circumstances, nonfunctional currency. See § 1.988-2(b)(2) for circumstances when nonfunctional currency is treated as money rather than as property.

(2) *Treatment of contracts to which section 483 applies.*—(i) *Treatment of unstated interest.*—If section 483 applies to a contract, unstated interest under the contract is treated as interest for tax purposes. Thus, for example, unstated interest is not treated as part of the amount realized from the sale or exchange of property (in the case of the seller), and is not included in the purchaser's basis in the property acquired in the sale or exchange.

(ii) *Method of accounting for interest on contracts subject to section 483.*—Any stated or unstated interest on a contract subject to section 483 is taken into account by a taxpayer under the taxpayer's regular method of accounting (e.g., an accrual method or the cash receipts and disbursements method). See §§ 1.446-1, 1.451-1, and 1.461-1. For purposes of the preceding sentence, the amount of interest (including unstated interest) allocable to a payment under a contract to which section 483 applies is determined under § 1.446-2(e).

(b) *Definitions.*—(1) *Deferred payments.*—For purposes of the regulations under section 483, a deferred payment means any payment that constitutes all or a part of the sales price (as defined in paragraph (b)(2) of this section), and that is due more than 6 months after the date of the sale or exchange. Except as provided in section 483(c)(2) (relating to the treatment of a debt instrument of the purchaser), a payment may be made in the form of cash, stock or securities, or other property.

(2) *Sales price.*—For purposes of section 483, the sales price for any sale or exchange is the sum of the amount due under the contract (other than stated interest) and the amount of any liability included in the amount realized from the sale or exchange. See § 1.1001-2. Thus, the sales price for any sale or exchange includes any amount of unstated interest under the contract.

(c) *Exceptions to and limitations on the application of section 483.*—(1) *In general.*—Sections 483(d), 1274(c)(4), and 1275(b) contain exceptions to and limitations on the application of section 483.

(2) *Sales price of $3,000 or less.*—Section 483(d)(2) applies only if it can be determined at the time of the sale or exchange that the sales price cannot exceed $3,000, regardless of whether the sales price eventually paid for the property is less than $3,000.

(3) *Other exceptions and limitations.*—(i) *Certain transfers subject to section 1041.*—Section 483 does not apply to any transfer of property subject to section 1041 (relating to transfers of property between spouses or incident to divorce).

(ii) *Treatment of certain obligees.*—Section 483 does not apply to an obligee under a contract for the sale or exchange of personal use property (within the meaning of section 1275(b)(3)) in the hands of the obligor and that evidences a below-market loan described in section 7872(c)(1).

(iii) *Transactions involving certain demand loans.*—Section 483 does not apply to any payment under a contract that evidences a demand loan that is a below-market loan described in section 7872(c)(1).

(iv) *Transactions involving certain annuity contracts.*—Section 483 does not apply to any payment under an annuity contract described in section 1275(a)(1)(B) (relating to annuity contracts excluded from the definition of debt instrument).

(v) *Options.*—Section 483 does not apply to any payment under an option to buy or sell property.

(d) *Assumptions.*—If a debt instrument is assumed, or property is taken subject to a debt instrument, in connection with a sale or exchange of property, the debt instrument is treated for purposes of section 483 in a manner consistent with the rules of § 1.1274-5.

(e) *Aggregation rule.*—For purposes of section 483, all sales or exchanges that are part of the same transaction (or a series of related transactions) are treated as a single sale or exchange and all contracts calling for deferred payments arising from the same transaction (or a series of related transactions) are treated as a single contract. This rule, however, generally only applies to contracts and to sales or exchanges involving a single buyer and a single seller.

* * *

[Reg. § 1.483-1.]

☐ [*T.D.* 6873, 1-24-66. *Amended by T.D.* 7154, 12-27-71; *T.D.* 7394, 12-31-75; *T.D.* 7781, 7-1-81 *and T.D.* 8517, 1-27-94.]

§ 1.483-2. Unstated interest.—(a) *In general.*—(1) *Adequate stated interest.*—For purposes of section 483, a contract has unstated interest if the contract does not provide for adequate stated interest. A contract does not provide for adequate stated interest if the sum of the deferred payments exceeds—

(i) The sum of the present values of the deferred payments and the present values of any stated interest payments due under the contract; or

(ii) In the case of a cash method debt instrument (within the meaning of section 1274A(c)(2)) received in exchange for property in a potentially abusive situation (as defined in § 1.1274-3), the fair market value of the property reduced by the fair market value of any consideration other than the debt instrument, and reduced by the sum of all principal payments that are not deferred payments.

(2) *Amount of unstated interest.*—For purposes of section 483, unstated interest means an amount equal to the excess of the sum of the deferred payments over the amount described in paragraph (a)(1)(i) or (a)(1)(ii) of this section, whichever is applicable.

(b) *Operational rules.*—(1) *In general.*—For purposes of paragraph (a) of this section, rules similar to those in § 1.1274-2 apply to determine whether a contract has adequate stated interest and the amount of unstated interest, if any, on the contract.

(2) *Present value.*—For purposes of paragraph (a) of this section, the present value of any deferred payment or interest payment is determined by discounting the payment from the date it becomes due to the date of the sale or exchange at the test rate of interest applicable to the contract in accordance with § 1.483-3.

(c) *Examples.*—The following examples illustrate the rules of this section.

Example 1. Contract that does not have adequate stated interest. On January 1, 1995, A sells B nonpublicly traded property under a contract that calls for a $100,000 payment of principal on January 1, 2005, and 10 annual interest payments of $9,000 on January 1 of each year, beginning on January 1, 1996. Assume that the test rate of interest is 9.2 percent, compounded annually. The contract does not provide for adequate stated interest because it does not provide for interest equal to 9.2 percent, compounded annually. The present value of the deferred payments is $98,727.69. As a result, the contract has unstated interest of $1,272.31 ($100,000 – $98,727.69)

Example 2. Contract that does not have adequate stated interest; no interest for initial short period. On May 1, 1996, A sells B nonpublicly traded property under a contract that calls for B to make a principal payment of $200,000 on December 31, 1998, and semiannual interest payments of $9,000, payable on June 30 and December 31 of each year, beginning on December 31, 1996. Assume that the test rate of interest is 9 percent, compounded semiannually. Even though the contract calls for a stated rate of interest no lower than the test rate of interest, the contract does not provide for adequate stated interest because the stated rate of interest does not apply for the short period from May 1, 1996, through June 30, 1996.

Example 3. Potentially abusive situation—(i) *Facts.* In a potentially abusive situation, a contract for the sale of nonpublicly traded personal property calls for the issuance of a cash method debt instrument (as defined in section 1274A(c)(2)) with a stated principal amount of $700,000, payable in 5 years. No other consideration is given. The debt instrument calls for annual payments of interest over its entire term at a rate of 9.2 percent, compounded annually (the test rate of interest applicable to the debt instrument). Thus, the present value of the deferred payment and the interest payments is $700,000. Assume that the fair market value of the properly is $500,000.

(ii) *Amount of unstated interest.* A cash method debt instrument received in exchange for property in a potentially abusive situation provides for adequate stated interest only if the sum of the deferred payments under the instrument does not exceed the fair market value of the property. Because the deferred payment ($700,000) exceeds the fair market value of the property ($500,000), the debt instrument does not provide for adequate stated interest. Therefore, the debt instrument has unstated interest of $200,000.

Example 4. Variable rate debt instrument with adequate stated interest; variable rate as of the issue date greater than the test rate—(i) *Facts.* A contract for the sale of nonpublicly traded property calls for the issuance of a debt instrument in the principal amount of $75,000 due in 10 years. The debt instrument calls for interest payable semiannually at a rate of 3 percentage points above the yield on 6-month Treasury bills at the mid-point of the semiannual period immediately preceding each interest payment date. Assume that the interest rate is a qualified floating rate and that the debt instrument is a variable rate debt instrument within the meaning of § 1.1275-5.

(ii) *Adequate stated interest.* Under paragraph (b)(1) of this section, rules similar to those in § 1.1274-2(f) apply to determine whether the debt instrument has adequate stated interest. Assume that the test rate of interest applicable to the debt instrument is 9 percent, compounded semiannually. Assume also that the yield on 6-month Treasury bills on the date of the sale is 8.89 percent, which is greater than the yield on 6-month Treasury bills on the first date on which there is a binding written contract that substantially sets forth the terms under which the sale is consummated. Under § 1.1274-2(f), the debt instrument is tested for adequate stated interest as if it provided for a stated rate of interest of 11.89 percent (3 percent plus 8.89 percent), compounded semiannually, payable over its entire term. Because the test rate of interest is 9 percent, compounded semiannually, and the debt instrument is treated as providing for stated interest of 11.89 percent, compounded semiannually, the debt instrument provides for adequate stated interest.

* * *

[Reg. § 1.483-2.]

□ [*T.D.* 6873, 1-24-66. *Amended by T.D.* 8517, 1-27-94.]

§ 1.483-3. Test rate of interest applicable to a contract.—(a) *General rule.*—For purposes of section 483, the test rate of interest for a contract is the same as the test rate that would apply under § 1.1274-4 if the contract were a debt instrument. Paragraph (b) of this section, however, provides for a lower test rate in the case of certain sales or exchanges of land between related individuals.

(b) *Lower rate for certain sales or exchanges of land between related individuals.*—(1) *Test rate.*—In the case of a qualified sale or exchange of land between related individuals (described in section 483(e)), the test rate is not greater than 6 percent, compounded semiannually, or an equivalent rate based on an appropriate compounding period.

(2) *Special rules.*—The following rules and definitions apply in determining whether a sale or exchange is a qualified sale under section 483(e):

(i) *Definition of family members.*—The members of an individual's family are determined as of the date of the sale or exchange. The members of an individual's family include those individuals described in section 267(c)(4) and the spouses of those individuals. In addition, for purposes of section 267(c)(4), full effect is given to a legal adoption, ancestor means parents and grandparents, and lineal descendants means children and grandchildren.

(ii) *$500,000 limitation.*—Section 483(e) does not apply to the extent that the stated principal amount of the debt instrument issued in the sale or exchange, when added to the aggregate stated principal amount of any other debt instruments to which section 483(e) applies that were issued in prior qualified sales between the same two individuals during the same calendar year, exceeds $500,000. See *Example 3* of paragraph (b)(3) of this section.

(iii) *Other limitations.*—Section 483(e) does not apply if the parties to a contract include persons other than the related individuals and the parties enter into the contract with an intent to circumvent the purposes of section 483(e). In addition, if the property sold or exchanged includes any property other than land, section 483(e) applies only to the extent that the stated principal amount of the debt instrument issued in the sale or exchange is attributable to the land (based on the relative fair market values of the land and the other property).

(3) *Examples.*—The following examples illustrate the rules of this paragraph (b).

Example 1. On January 1, 1995, A sells land to B, A's child, for $650,000. The contract for sale calls for B to make a $250,000 down payment and issue a debt instrument with a stated principal amount of $400,000. Because the stated principal amount of the debt instrument is less than $500,000, the sale is a qualified sale and section 483(e) applies to the debt instrument.

Example 2. The facts are the same as in *Example 1* of paragraph (b)(3) of this section, except that on June 1, 1995, A sells additional land to B under a contract that calls for B to issue a debt instrument with a stated principal amount of $100,000. The stated principal amount of this debt instrument ($100,000) when added to the stated principal amount of the prior debt instrument ($400,000) does not exceed $500,000. Thus, section 483(e) applies to both debt instruments.

Example 3. The facts are the same as in *Example 1* of paragraph (b)(3) of this section, except that on June 1, 1995, A sells additional land to B under a contract that calls for B to issue a debt instrument with a stated principal amount of $150,000. The stated principal amount of this debt instrument when added to the stated principal amount of the prior debt instrument ($400,000) exceeds $500,000. Thus, for purposes of section 483(e), the debt instrument issued in the sale of June 1, 1995, is treated as two separate debt instruments: a $100,000 debt instrument (to which section 483(e) applies) and a $50,000 debt instrument (to which section 1274, if otherwise applicable, applies).

* * *

[Reg. § 1.483-3.]

☐ [*T.D.* 8517, 1-27-94.]

General Rule

§ 1.501(c)(4)-1. Civic organizations and local associations of employees.—(a) *Civic organizations.*—(1) *In general.*—A civic league or organization may be exempt as an organization described in section 501(c)(4) if:

(i) It is not organized or operated for profit; and

(ii) It is operated exclusively for the promotion of social welfare.

(2) *Promotion of social welfare.*—(i) *In general.*—An organization is operated exclusively for the promotion of social welfare if it is primarily engaged in promoting in some way the common good and general welfare of the people of the community. An organization embraced within this section is one which is operated primarily for the purpose of bringing about civic betterments and social improvements. A "social welfare" organization will qualify for exemption as a charitable organization if it falls within the definition of "charitable" set forth in paragraph (d)(2) of § 1.501(c)(3)-1 and is not an "action" organization as set forth in paragraph (c)(3) of § 1.501(c)(3)-1.

(ii) *Political or social activities.*—The promotion of social welfare does not include direct or indirect participation or intervention in political campaigns on behalf of or in opposition to any candidate for public office. Nor is an organization operated primarily for the promotion of social welfare if its primary activity is operating a social club for the benefit, pleasure, or recreation of its members, or is carrying on a business with the general public in a manner similar to organizations which are operated for profit. See, however, section 501(c)(6) and § 1.501(c)(6)-1, relating to business leagues and similar organizations. A social welfare organization that is not, at any time after October 4, 1976, exempt from taxation as an organization described in section 501(c)(3) may qualify under section 501(c)(4) even though it is an "action" organization described in § 1.501(c)(3)-1(c)(3)(ii) or (iv), if it otherwise qualifies under this section. For rules relating to an organization that is, after October 4, 1976, exempt from taxation as an organization described in section 501(c)(3), see section 504 and § 1.504-1.

* * *

[Reg. § 1.501(c)(4)-1.]

☐ [*T.D.* 6391, 6-25-59. *Amended by T.D.* 8308, 8-30-90.]

Corporations Improperly Accumulating Surplus

§ 1.537-1. Reasonable needs of the business.—(a) *In general.*—The term "reasonable needs of the business" includes (1) the reasonable anticipated needs of the business (including product liability loss reserves, as defined in paragraph (f) of this section), (2) the section 303 redemption needs of the business, as defined in paragraph (c) of this section, and (3) the excess business holdings redemption needs of the business as described in paragraph (d) of this section. See paragraph (e) of this section for additional rules relating to the section 303 redemption needs and the excess business holdings redemption needs of the business. An accumulation of the earnings and profits (including the undistributed earnings and profits of prior years) is in excess of the reasonable needs of the business if it exceeds the amount that a prudent businessman would consider appropriate for the present business purposes and for the reasonably anticipated future needs of the business. The need to retain earnings and profits must be directly connected with the needs of the corporation itself and must be for bona fide business purposes. For purposes of this paragraph the section 303 redemption needs of the business and the excess business holdings redemption needs of the business are deemed to be directly connected with the needs of the business and for a bona fide business purpose. See § 1.537-3 for a discussion of what constitutes the business of the corporation. The extent to which earnings and profits have been distributed by the corporation may be taken into account in determining whether or not retained earnings and profits exceed the reasonable needs of the business. See § 1.537-2, relating to grounds for accumulation of earnings and profits.

(b) *Reasonably anticipated needs.*—(1) In order for a corporation to justify an accumulation of earnings and profits for reasonably anticipated future needs, there must be an indication that the future needs of the business require such accumulation, and the corporation must have specific, definite, and feasible plans for the use of such accumulation. Such an accumulation need not be used immediately, nor must the plans for its use be consummated within a short period after the close of the taxable year, provided that such accumulation will be used within a reasonable time depending upon all the facts and circumstances relating to the future needs of the business. Where the future needs of the business are uncertain or vague, where the plans for the future use of an accumulation are not specific, definite, and feasible, or where the execution of such a plan is postponed indefinitely, an accumulation cannot be justified on the grounds of reasonably anticipated needs of the business.

(2) Consideration shall be given to reasonably anticipated needs as they exist on the basis of the facts at the close of the taxable year. Thus, subsequent events shall not be used for the purpose of showing that the retention of earnings or profits was unreasonable at the close of the taxable year if all the elements of reasonable anticipation are present at the close of such taxable year. However, subsequent events may be considered to determine whether the taxpayer actually intended to consummate or has actually consummated the plans for which the earnings and profits were accumulated. In this connection, projected expansion or investment plans shall be reviewed in the light of the facts during each year and as they exist as of the close of the taxable year. If a corporation has justified an accumulation for future needs by plans never consummated, the amount of such an accumulation shall be taken into account in determining the reasonableness of subsequent accumulations.

(c) *Section 303 redemption needs of the business.*—(1) The term "section 303 redemption needs" means, with respect to the taxable year of the corporation in which a shareholder of the corporation died or any taxable year thereafter, the amount needed (or reasonably anticipated to be needed) to redeem stock included in the gross estate of such shareholder but not in excess of the amount necessary to effect a distribution to which section 303 applies. For purposes of this paragraph, the term "shareholder" includes an individual in whose gross estate stock of the corporation is includable upon his death for Federal estate tax purposes.

(2) This paragraph applies to a corporation to which section 303(c) would apply if a distribution described therein were made.

(3) If stock included in the gross estate of a decedent is stock of two or more corporations described in section 303(b)(2)(B), the amount needed by each such corporation for section 303 redemption purposes under this section shall, unless the particular facts and circumstances indicate otherwise, be that amount which bears the same ratio to the amount described in section 303(a) as the fair market value of such corporation's stock included in the gross estate of such decedent bears to the fair market value of all of the stock of such corporations included in the gross estate. For example, facts and circumstances indicating that the allocation prescribed by this subparagraph is not required would include notice given to the corporations by the executor or administrator of the decedent's estate that he intends to request the redemption of stock of only one of such corporations or the redemption of stock of such corporations in a ratio which is unrelated to the respective fair market values of the stock of the corporations included in the decedent's gross estate.

(4) The provisions of this paragraph apply only to taxable years ending after May 26, 1969.

* * *

(e)(1) A determination whether and to what extent an amount is needed (or reasonably anticipated to be needed) for the purpose described in subparagraph (1) of paragraph (c) or (d) of this section is dependent upon the particular circumstances of the case, including the total amount of earnings and profits accumulated in prior years which may be available for such purpose and the existence of a reasonable expectation that a redemption described in paragraph (c) or (d) of this section will in fact be effected. Although paragraph (c) or (d) of this section may apply even though no redemption of stock is in fact effected, the failure to effect such redemption may be taken into account in determining whether the accumulation was needed (or reasonably anticipated to be needed) for a purpose described in paragraph (c) or (d).

(2) In applying subparagraph (1) of paragraph (c) or (d) of this section, the discharge of an obligation incurred to make a redemption shall be treated as the making of the redemption.

(3) In determining whether an accumulation is in excess of the reasonable needs of the business for a particular year, the fact that one of the exceptions specified in paragraph (c) or (d) of this section applies in a subsequent year is not to give rise to an inference that the accumulation would not have been for the reasonable needs of the business in the prior year. Also, no inference is to be drawn from the enactment of section 537(a)(2) and (3) that accumulations in any prior year would not have been for the reasonable needs of the business in the absence of such provisions. Thus, the reasonableness of accumulations in years prior to a year in which one of the exceptions specified in paragraph (c) or (d) of this section applies is to be determined solely upon the

facts and circumstances existing at the times the accumulations occur.

(f) *Product liability loss reserves.*—(1) The term "product liability loss reserve" means, with respect to taxable years beginning after September 30, 1979, reasonable amounts accumulated for the payment of reasonably anticipated product liability losses, as defined in section 172(j) and § 1.172-13(b)(1).

(2) For purposes of this paragraph, whether an accumulation for anticipated product liability losses is reasonable in amount and whether such anticipated product liability losses are likely to occur shall be determined in light of all facts and circumstances of the taxpayer making such accumulation. Some of the factors to be considered in determining the reasonableness of the accumulation include the taxpayer's previous product liability experience, the extent of the taxpayer's coverage by commercial product liability insurance, the income tax consequences of the taxpayer's ability to deduct product liability losses and related expenses, and the taxpayer's potential future liability due to defective products in light of the taxpayer's plans to expand the production of products currently being manufactured, provided such plans are specific, definite and feasible. Additionally, a factor to be considered in determining whether the accumulation is reasonable in amount is whether the taxpayer, in accounting for its potential future liability, took into account the reasonably estimated present value of the potential future liability.

(3) Only those accumulations made with respect to products that have been manufactured, leased, or sold shall be considered as accumulations made under this paragraph. Thus, for example, accumulations with respect to a product which has not progressed beyond the development stage are not reasonable accumulations under this paragraph. [Reg. § 1.537-1.]

□ [*T.D.* 6377, 5-12-59. *Amended by T.D.* 7165, 3-8-72, *by T.D.* 7678, 2-25-80, *and by T.D.* 8096, 8-27-86.]

§ 1.537-2. Grounds for accumulation of earnings and profits.—(a) *In general.*—Whether a particular ground or grounds for the accumulation of earnings and profits indicate that the earnings and profits have been accumulated for the reasonable needs of the business or beyond such needs is dependent upon the particular circumstances of the case. Listed below in paragraphs (b) and (c) of this section are some of the grounds which may be used as guides under ordinary circumstances.

(b) *Reasonable accumulation of earnings and profits.*—Although the following grounds are not exclusive, one or more of such grounds, if supported by sufficient facts, may indicate that the earnings and profits of a corporation are being accumulated for the reasonable needs of the business provided the general requirements under §§ 1.537-1 and 1.537-3 are satisfied:

(1) To provide for bona fide expansion of business or replacement of plant;

(2) To acquire a business enterprise through purchasing stock or assets;

(3) To provide for the retirement of bona fide indebtedness created in connection with the trade or business, such as the establishment of a sinking fund for the purpose of retiring bonds issued by the corporation in accordance with contract obligations incurred on issue;

(4) To provide necessary working capital for the business, such as, for the procurement of inventories;

(5) To provide for investments or loans to suppliers or customers if necessary in order to maintain the business of the corporation; or

(6) To provide for the payment of reasonably anticipated product liability losses, as defined in section 172(j), § 1.172-13(b)(1), and § 1.537-1(f).

(c) *Unreasonable accumulations of earnings and profits.*—Although the following purposes are not exclusive, accumulations of earnings and profits to meet any one of such objectives may indicate that the earnings and profits of a corporation are being accumulated beyond the reasonable needs of the business:

(1) Loans to shareholders, or the expenditure of funds of the corporation for the personal benefit of the shareholders;

(2) Loans having no reasonable relation to the conduct of the business made to relatives or friends of shareholders, or to other persons;

(3) Loans to another corporation, the business of which is not that of the taxpayer corporation, if the capital stock of such other corporation is owned, directly or indirectly, by the shareholder or shareholders of the taxpayer corporation and such shareholder or shareholders are in control of both corporations;

(4) Investments in properties, or securities which are unrelated to the activities of the business of the taxpayer corporation; or

(5) Retention of earnings and profits to provide against unrealistic hazards. [Reg. § 1.537-2.]

□ [*T.D.* 6377, 5-12-59. *Amended by T.D.* 8096, 8-26-86.]

§ 1.537-3. Business of the corporation.—(a) The business of a corporation is not merely that which it has previously carried on but includes, in general, any line of business which it may undertake.

(b) If one corporation owns the stock of another corporation and, in effect, operates the other corporation, the business of the latter corporation may be considered in substance, although not in legal form, the business of the first corporation. However, investment by a corporation of its earnings and profits in stock and securities of another corporation is not, of itself, to be regarded as employment of the earnings and profits in its business. Earnings and profits of the first corporation put into the second corporation through the purchase of stock or securities or otherwise, may, if a subsidiary relationship is established, constitute employment of the earnings and profits in its own business. Thus, the business of one corporation may be regarded as including the business of another corporation if such other corporation is a mere instrumentality of the first corporation; that may be established by showing that the first corporation owns at least 80 percent of the voting stock of the second corporation. If the taxpayer's ownership of stock is less than 80 percent in the other corporation, the determination of whether the funds are employed in a business operated by the taxpayer will depend upon the particular circumstances of the case. Moreover, the business of one corporation does not include the business of another corporation if such other corporation is a personal holding company, an investment company, or a corporation not engaged in the active conduct of a trade or business. [Reg. § 1.537-3.]

□ [*T.D.* 6377, 5-12-59.]

Natural Resources—Deductions

§ 1.611-1. Allowance of deduction for depletion.—(a) *Depletion of mines, oil and gas wells, other natural deposits, and timber.*—(1) *In general.*—Section 611 provides that there shall be allowed as a deduction in computing taxable income in the case of mines, oil and gas wells, other natural deposits, and timber, a reasonable allowance for depletion. In the case of standing timber, the depletion allowance shall be computed solely upon the adjusted basis of the property. In the case of other exhaustible natural resources the allowance for depletion shall be computed upon either the adjusted depletion basis of the property (see section 612, relating to cost depletion) or upon a percentage of gross income from the property (see section 613, relating to percentage depletion), whichever results in the greater allowance for depletion for any taxable year. In no case will depletion based upon discovery value be allowed.

(2) See § 1.611-5 for methods of depreciation relating to improvements connected with mineral or timber properties.

(3) See paragraph (d) of this section for definition of terms.

(b) *Economic interest.*—(1) Annual depletion deductions are allowed only to the owner of an economic interest in mineral deposits or standing timber. An economic interest is possessed in every case in which the taxpayer has acquired by investment any interest in mineral in place or standing timber and secures, by any form of legal relationship, income derived from the extraction of the mineral or severance of the timber, to which he must look for a return of his capital. For an exception in the case of certain mineral production payments, see section 636 and the regulations thereunder. A person who has no capital investment in the mineral deposit or standing timber does not possess an economic interest merely because through a contractual relation he possesses a mere economic or pecuniary advantage derived from production. For example, an agreement between the owner of an economic interest and another entitling the latter to purchase or process the product upon production or entitling the latter to compensation for extraction or cutting does not convey a depletable economic interest. Further, depletion deductions with respect to an economic interest of a corporation are allowed to the corporation and not to its shareholders.

(2) No depletion deduction shall be allowed the owner with respect to any timber, coal, or domestic iron ore that such owner has disposed of under any form of contract by virtue of which he retains an economic interest in such timber, coal, or iron ore, if such disposal is considered a sale of timber, coal, or domestic iron ore under section 631(b) or (c).

(c) *Special rules.*—(1) *In general.*—For the purpose of the equitable apportionment of depletion among the several owners of economic interests in a mineral deposit or standing timber, if the value of any mineral or timber must be ascertained as of any specific date for the determination of the basis for depletion, the values of such several interests therein may be determined separately, but, when determined as of the same date, shall together never exceed the value at that date of the mineral or timber as a whole.

(2) *Leases.*—In the case of a lease, the deduction for depletion under section 611 shall be equitably apportioned between the lessor and lessee. In the case of a lease or other contract providing for the sharing of economic interest in a mineral deposit or standing tim-

ber, such deduction shall be computed by each taxpayer by reference to the adjusted basis of his property determined in accordance with sections 611 and 612, or computed in accordance with section 613, if applicable, and the regulations thereunder.

(3) *Life tenant and remainderman.*—In the case of property held by one person for life with remainder to another person, the deduction for depletion under section 611 shall be computed as if the life tenant were the absolute owner of the property so that he will be entitled to the deduction during his life, and thereafter the deduction, if any, shall be allowed to the remainderman.

(4) *Mineral or timber property held in trust.*—If a mineral property or timber property is held in trust, the allowable deduction for depletion is to be apportioned between the income beneficiaries and the trustee on the basis of the trust income from such property allocable to each, unless the governing instrument (or local law) requires or permits the trustee to maintain a reserve for depletion in any amount. In the latter case, the deduction is first allocated to the trustee to the extent that income is set aside for a depletion reserve, and any part of the deduction in excess of the income set aside for the reserve shall be apportioned between the income beneficiaries and the trustee on the basis of the trust income (in excess of the income set aside for the reserve) allocable to each. For example:

(i) If under the trust instrument or local law the income of a trust computed without regard to depletion is to be distributed to a named beneficiary, the beneficiary is entitled to the deduction to the exclusion of the trustee.

(ii) If under the trust instrument or local law the income of a trust is to be distributed to a named beneficiary, but the trustee is directed to maintain a reserve for depletion in any amount, the deduction is allowed to the trustee (except to the extent that income set aside for the reserve is less than the allowable deduction). The same result would follow if the trustee sets aside income for a depletion reserve pursuant to discretionary authority to do so in the governing instrument.

No effect shall be given to any allocation of the depletion deduction which gives any beneficiary or the trustee a share of such deduction greater than his pro rata share of the trust income, irrespective of any provisions in the trust instrument, except as otherwise provided in this paragraph when the trust instrument or local law requires or permits the trustee to maintain a reserve for depletion.

(5) *Mineral or timber property held by estate.*—In the case of mineral property or timber property held by an estate, the deduction for depletion under section 611 shall be apportioned between the estate and the heirs, legatees, and devisees on the basis of income of the estate from such property which is allocable to each.

(d) *Definitions.*—As used in this part, and the regulations thereunder, the term—

(1) "Property" means—(i) in the case of minerals, each separate economic interest owned in each mineral deposit in each separate tract or parcel of land or an aggregation or combination of such mineral interests permitted under section 614(b), (c), (d), or (e); and (ii) in the case of timber, an economic interest in standing timber in each tract or block representing a separate timber account (see paragraph (d) of § 1.611-3). For rules with respect to waste or residue of prior mining, see paragraph (c) of § 1.614-1. When, in the regulations under this part, either the word "mineral" or "timber" precedes the word "property", such adjectives are used only to classify the type of "property" involved. For further explanation of the term "property", see section 614 and the regulations thereunder.

(2) "Fair market value" of a property is that amount which would induce a willing seller to sell and a willing buyer to purchase.

(3) "Mineral enterprise" is the mineral deposit or deposits and improvements, if any, used in mining or in the production of oil and gas and only so much of the surface of the land as is necessary for purposes of mineral extraction. The value of the mineral enterprise is the combined value of its component parts.

(4) "Mineral deposit" refers to minerals in place. When a mineral enterprise is acquired as a unit, the cost of any interest in the mineral deposit or deposits is that proportion of the total cost of the mineral enterprise which the value of the interest in the deposit bears to the value of the entire enterprise at the time of its acquisition.

(5) "Minerals" includes ores of the metals, coal, oil, gas, and all other natural metallic and nonmetallic deposits, except minerals derived from sea water, the air, or from similar inexhaustible sources. It includes but is not limited to all of the minerals and other natural deposits subject to depletion based upon a percentage of gross income from the property under section 613 and the regulations thereunder. [Reg. § 1.611-1.]

☐ [*T.D.* 6446, 1-20-60. *Amended by T.D.* 6841, 7-26-65 *and by T.D.* 7261, 2-26-73.]

§ 1.611-2. Rules applicable to mines, oil and gas wells, and other natural deposits.—(a) *Computation of cost depletion of mines, oil and gas wells, and other natural deposits.*—

(1) The basis upon which cost depletion is to be allowed in respect of any mineral property is the basis provided for in section 612 and the regulations thereunder. After the amount of such basis applicable to the mineral property has been determined for the taxable year, the cost depletion for that year shall be computed by dividing such amount by the number of units of mineral remaining as of the taxable year (see subparagraph (3) of this paragraph), and by multiplying the depletion unit, so determined, by the number of units of mineral sold within the taxable year (see subparagraph (2) of this paragraph). In the selection of a unit of mineral for depletion, preference shall be given to the principal or customary unit or units paid for in the products sold, such as tons of ore, barrels of oil, or thousands of cubic feet of natural gas.

(2) As used in this paragraph the phrase "number of units sold within the taxable year"—

(i) In the case of a taxpayer reporting income on the cash receipts and disbursements method, includes units for which payments were received within the taxable year although produced or sold prior to the taxable year, and excludes units sold but not paid for in the taxable year, and

(ii) In the case of a taxpayer reporting income on the accrual method, shall be determined from the taxpayer's inventories kept in physical quantities and in a manner consistent with his method of inventory accounting under section 471 or 472.

The phrase does not include units with respect to which depletion deductions were allowed or allowable prior to the taxable year.

(3) "The number of units of mineral remaining as of the taxable year" is the number of units of mineral remaining at the end of the period to be recovered from the property (including units recovered but not sold) plus the "number of units sold within the taxable year" as defined in this section.

(4) In the case of a natural gas well where the annual production is not metered and is not capable of being estimated with reasonable accuracy, the taxpayer may compute the cost depletion allowance in respect of such property for the taxable year by multiplying the adjusted basis of the property by a fraction, the numerator of which is equal to the decline in rock pressure during the taxable year and the denominator of which is equal to the expected total decline in rock pressure from the beginning of the taxable year to the economic limit of production. Taxpayers computing depletion by this method must keep accurate records of periodical pressure determinations.

(5) If an aggregation of two or more separate mineral properties is made during a taxable year under section 614, cost depletion for each such property shall be computed separately for that portion of the taxable year ending immediately before the effective date of the aggregation. Cost depletion with respect to the aggregated property shall be computed for that portion of the taxable year beginning on such effective date. The allowance for cost depletion for the taxable year shall be the sum of such cost depletion computations. For purposes of this paragraph, each such portion of the taxable year shall be considered as a taxable year. Similar rules shall be applied where a separate mineral property is properly removed from an existing aggregation during a taxable year. See section 614 and the regulations thereunder for rules relating to the effective date of an aggregation of mineral interests and for rules relating to the adjusted basis of an aggregation.

(6) The apportionment of the deduction among the several owners of economic interests in the mineral deposit or deposits will be made as provided in paragraph (c) of § 1.611-1.

(b) *Depletion account of mineral property.*—(1) Every taxpayer claiming and making a deduction for depletion of mineral property shall keep a separate account in which shall be accurately recorded the cost or other basis provided by section 1012, of such property together with subsequent allowable capital additions to each account and all the other adjustments required by section 1016.

(2) Mineral property accounts shall thereafter be credited annually with amounts of the depletion computed in accordance with section 611 or 613 and the regulations thereunder; or the amounts of the depletion so computed shall be credited to depletion reserve accounts. No further deductions for cost depletion shall be allowed when the sum of the credits for depletion equals the cost or other basis of the property, plus allowable capital additions. However, depletion deductions may be allowable thereafter computed upon a percentage of gross income from the property. See section 613 and the regulations thereunder. In no event shall percentage depletion in excess of cost or other basis of the property be credited to the improvements account or the depreciation reserve account.

(c) *Determination of mineral contents of deposits.*—(1) If it is necessary to estimate or determine with respect to any mineral deposit as of any specific date the total recoverable units (tons, pounds, ounces, barrels, thousands of cubic feet, or other measure) of mineral products reasonably known, or on good evidence believed, to have existed in place as of that date, the estimate or determination must be made according to the method current in the industry and in the light of the most accurate and reliable information obtainable. In the selection of a unit of estimate, preference shall be given to the principal unit (or units) paid for in the product marketed. The estimate of the recoverable units of the mineral products in the deposit for the purposes of valuation and depletion shall include as to both quantity and grade:

(i) The ores and minerals "in sight", "blocked out", "developed", or "assured", in the usual or conventional meaning of these terms with respect to the type of the deposits, and

(ii) "Probable" or "prospective" ores or minerals (in the corresponding sense), that is, ores or minerals that are believed to exist on the basis of good evidence although not actually known to occur on the basis of existing development. Such "probable" or "prospective" ores or minerals may be estimated:

(a) As to quantity, only in case they are extensions of known deposits or are new bodies or masses whose existence is indicated by geological surveys or other evidence to a high degree of probability, and

(b) As to grade, only in accordance with the best indications available as to richness.

(2) If the number of recoverable units of mineral in the deposit has been previously estimated for the prior year or years, and if there has been no known change in the facts upon which the prior estimate was based, the number of recoverable units of mineral in the deposit as of the taxable year will be the number remaining from the prior estimate. However, for any taxable year for which it is ascertained either by the taxpayer or the district director from any source, such as operations or development work prior to the close of the taxable year, that the remaining recoverable mineral units as of the taxable year are materially greater or less than the number remaining from the prior estimate, then the estimate of the remaining recoverable units shall be revised, and the annual cost depletion allowance with respect to the property for the taxable year and for subsequent taxable years will be based upon the revised estimate until a change in the facts requires another revision. Such revised estimate will not, however, change the adjusted basis for depletion.

(d) *Determination of fair market value of mineral properties, and improvements, if any.*—(1) If the fair market value of the mineral property and improvements at a specified date is to be determined for the purpose of ascertaining the basis, such value must be determined, subject to approval or revision by the district director, by the owner of such property and improvements in the light of the conditions and circumstances known at that date, regardless of later discoveries or developments or subsequent improvements in methods of extraction and treatment of the mineral product. The district director will give due weight and consideration to any and all factors and evidence having a bearing on the market value, such as cost, actual sales and transfer of similar properties and improvements, bona fide offers, market value of stock or shares, royalties and rentals, valuation for local or State taxation, partnership accountings, records of litigation in which the value of the property and improvements was in question, the amount at which the property and improvements may have been inventoried or appraised in probate or similar proceedings, and disinterested appraisals by approved methods.

(2) If the fair market value must be ascertained as of a certain date, analytical appraisal methods of valuation, such as the present value method will not be used:

(i) If the value of a mineral property and improvements, if any, can be determined upon the basis of cost or comparative values and replacement value of equipment, or

(ii) If the fair market value can reasonably be determined by any other method.

(e) *Determination of the fair market value of mineral property by the present value method.*—(1) To determine the fair market value of a mineral property and improvements by the present value method, the essential factors must be determined for each mineral deposit. The essential factors in determining the fair market value of mineral deposits are:

(i) The total quantity of mineral in terms of the principal or customary unit (or units) paid for in the product marketed,

(ii) The quantity of mineral expected to be recovered during each operating period,

(iii) The average quality or grade of the mineral reserves,

(iv) The allocation of the total expected profit to the several processes or operations necessary for the preparation of the mineral for market,

(v) The probable operating life of the deposit in years,

(vi) The development cost,

(vii) The operating cost,

(viii) The total expected profit,

(ix) The rate at which this profit will be obtained, and

(x) The rate of interest commensurate with the risk for the particular deposit.

(2) If the mineral deposit has been sufficiently developed the valuation factors specified in subparagraph (1) of this paragraph may

be determined from past operating experience. In the application of factors derived from past experience, full allowance should be made for probable future variations in the rate of exhaustion, quality or grade of the mineral, percentage of recovery, cost of development, production, interest rate, and selling price of the product marketed during the expected operating life of the mineral deposit. Mineral deposits for which these factors cannot be determined with reasonable accuracy from past operating experience may also be valued by the present value method; but the factors must be deduced from concurrent evidence, such as the general type of the deposit, the characteristics of the district in which it occurs, the habit of the mineral deposits, the intensity of mineralization, the oil-gas ratio, the rate at which additional mineral has been disclosed by exploitation, the stage of the operating life of the deposit, and any other evidence tending to establish a reasonable estimate of the required factors.

(3) Mineral deposits of different grades, locations, and probable dates of extraction should be valued separately. The mineral content of a deposit shall be determined in accordance with paragraph (c) of this section. In estimating the average grade of the developed and prospective mineral, account should be taken of probable increases or decreases as indicated by the operating history. The rate of exhaustion of a mineral deposit should be determined with due regard to the limitations imposed by plant capacity, by the character of the deposit, by the ability to market the mineral product, by labor conditions, and by the operating program in force or reasonably to be expected for future operations. The operating life of a mineral deposit is that number of years necessary for the exhaustion of both the developed and prospective mineral content at the rate determined as above. The operating life of oil and gas wells is also influenced by the natural decline in pressure and flow, and by voluntary or enforced curtailment of production. The operating cost includes all current expense of producing, preparing, and marketing the mineral product sold (due consideration being given to taxes) exclusive of allowable capital additions, as described in §§1.612-2 and 1.612-4, and deductions for depreciation and depletion, but including cost of repairs. This cost of repairs is not to be confused with the depreciation deduction by which the cost of improvements is returned to the taxpayer free from tax. In general, no estimates of these factors will be approved by the district director which are not supported by the operating experience of the property or which are derived from different and arbitrarily selected periods.

(4) The value of each mineral deposit is measured by the expected gross income (the number of units of mineral recoverable in marketable form multiplied by the estimated market price per unit) less the estimated operating cost, reduced to a present value as of the date for which the valuation is made at the rate of interest commensurate with the risk for the operating life, and further reduced by the value at that date of the improvements and of the capital additions, if any, necessary to realize the profits. The degree of risk is generally lowest in cases where the factors of valuation are fully supported by the operating record of the mineral enterprise before the date for which the valuation is made. On the other hand, higher risks ordinarily attach to appraisals upon any other basis.

(f) *Revaluation of mineral property not allowed.*—No revaluation of a mineral property whose value as of any specific date has been determined and approved will be made or allowed during the continuance of the ownership under which the value was so determined and approved, except in the case of misrepresentation or fraud or gross error as to any facts known on the date as of which the valuation was made. Revaluation on account of misrepresentation or fraud or such gross error will be made only with the written approval of the Commissioner.

* * *

[Reg. §1.611-2.]

☐ [*T.D.* 6446, 1-20-60. *Amended by T.D.* 6938, 12-6-67 *and by T.D.* 7170, 3-10-72.]

§1.612-1. Basis for allowance of cost depletion.—(a) *In general.*—The basis upon which the deduction for cost depletion under section 611 is to be allowed in respect of any mineral or timber property is the adjusted basis provided in section 1011 for the purpose of determining gain upon the sale or other disposition of such property except as provided in paragraph (b) of this section. The adjusted basis of such property is the cost or other basis determined under section 1012, relating to the basis of property, adjusted as provided in section 1016, relating to adjustments to basis, and the regulations under such sections. In the case of the sale of a part of such property, the unrecovered basis thereof shall be allocated to the part sold and the part retained.

(b) *Special rules.*—(1) The basis for cost depletion of mineral or timber property does not include:

(i) Amounts recoverable through depreciation deductions, through deferred expenses, and through deductions other than depletion, and

(ii) The residual value of land and improvements at the end of operations.

In the case of any mineral property the basis for cost depletion does not include amounts representing the cost or value of land for purposes other than mineral production. Furthermore, in the case of certain mineral properties, such basis does not include exploration or development expenditures which are treated under section 615(b) or 616(b) as deferred expenses to be taken into account as deductions on a ratable basis as the units of minerals benefited thereby are produced and sold. However, there shall be included in the basis for cost depletion of oil and gas property the amounts of capitalized drilling and development costs which, as provided in § 1.612-4, are recoverable through depletion deductions. In the case of timber property, the basis for cost depletion does not include amounts representing the cost or value of land.

(2) Where a taxpayer elects to treat the cutting of timber as a sale or exchange of such timber, the basis for cost depletion shall be the fair market value of such timber as of the first day of the taxable year in which such timber is cut and such value shall be considered for such taxable year and all subsequent taxable years as the cost of such timber for all purposes for which such cost is a necessary factor. See section 631(a).

(c) *Cross references.*—In cases where the valuation, revaluation, or mineral content of deposits is a factor, see paragraphs (c), (d), (e), and (f) of § 1.611-2. In cases where the valuation, revaluation, or quantity of timber is a factor, see paragraphs (e), (f), and (g) of § 1.611-3. For definitions of the terms "property", "fair market value", "mineral enterprise", "mineral deposit", and "minerals", see paragraph (d) of § 1.611-1. For rules with respect to treatment of depletion accounts on taxpayer's books, see paragraph (b) of § 1.611-2 in the case of mineral property, and paragraph (c) of § 1.611-3 in the case of timber property. [Reg. § 1.612-1.]

☐ [*T.D.* 6446, 1-20-60.]

§ 1.612-3. Depletion; treatment of bonus and advanced royalty.—(a) *Bonus.*—(1) If a bonus in addition to royalties is received upon the grant of an economic interest in a mineral deposit, or standing timber, there shall be allowed to the payee as a cost depletion deduction in respect of the bonus an amount equal to that proportion of his basis for depletion as provided in section 612 and § 1.612-1 which the amount of the bonus bears to the sum of the bonus and the royalties expected to be received. Such allowance shall be deducted from the payee's basis for depletion and the remainder of the basis is recoverable through depletion deductions as the royalties are thereafter received. (But see paragraph (e) of this section.) For example, a taxpayer leases mineral property to another reserving a one-eighth royalty and in addition receives a bonus of $10,000. Assuming that the taxpayer's basis with respect to the mineral property is $21,000 and that the royalties expected to be received are estimated to total $20,000, the depletion on the bonus would be $7,000:

$$\frac{\$21{,}000 \text{ (basis)} \times \$10{,}000 \text{ (bonus)}}{\$30{,}000 \text{ (bonus plus estimated royalties)}}.$$

The remaining $14,000 of basis will be recovered through depletion as the royalties are received.

(2) If the grant of an economic interest in a mineral deposit or standing timber with respect to which a bonus was received expires, terminates, or is abandoned before there has been any income derived from the extraction of mineral or cutting of timber, the payee shall adjust his capital account by restoring thereto the depletion deduction taken on the bonus and a corresponding amount must be returned as income in the year of such expiration, termination, or abandonment.

(3) In the case of the payor, payment of the bonus constitutes a capital investment made for the acquisition of an economic interest in a mineral deposit or standing timber recoverable through the depletion allowance. See paragraph (c)(5)(ii) of § 1.613-2 in cases in which percentage depletion is used.

(b) *Advanced royalties.*—(1) If the owner of an operating interest in a mineral deposit or standing timber is required to pay royalties on a specified number of units of such mineral or timber annually whether or not extracted or cut within the year, and may apply any amounts paid on account of units not extracted or cut within the year against the royalty on the mineral or timber thereafter extracted or cut, the payee shall compute cost depletion on the number of units so paid for in advance of extraction or cutting and shall treat the amount so determined as an allowable deduction for depletion from the gross income of the year in which such payment or payments are made. No deduction for depletion by such payee shall be claimed or allowed in any subsequent year on account of the extraction or cutting in such year of any mineral or timber so paid for in advance and for which deduction has once been made. (But see paragraph (e) of this section.)

(2) If the right to extract minerals or to cut timber against which the advanced royalties may be applied expires, terminates, or is abandoned before all such minerals or timber have been extracted or cut, the payee shall

adjust his capital account by restoring thereto the depletion deductions made in prior years on account of any units of mineral or timber paid for in advance but not extracted or cut, and a corresponding amount must be returned as income for the year of such expiration, termination or abandonment. (But see paragraph (e) of this section.)

(3) The payor shall treat the advanced royalties paid or accrued in connection with mineral property as deductions from gross income for the year the mineral product, in respect of which the advanced royalties were paid or accrued, is sold. For purposes of the preceding sentence, in the case of mineral sold before production the mineral product is considered to be sold when the mineral is produced (*i.e.*, when a mineral product first exists). However, in the case of advanced mineral royalties paid or accrued in connection with mineral property as a result of a minimum royalty provision, the payor, at his option, may instead treat the advanced royalties as deductions from gross income for the year in which the advanced royalties are paid or accrued. See section 446 (relating to general rule for methods of accounting) and the regulations thereunder. For purposes of this paragraph, a minimum royalty provision requires that a substantially uniform amount of royalties be paid at least annually either over the life of the lease or for a period of at least 20 years, in the absence of mineral production requiring payment of aggregate royalties in a greater amount. For purposes of the preceding sentence, in the case of a lease which is subject to renewal or extension, the period for which it can be renewed or extended shall be treated as part of the term of the original lease. For special rules applicable when the payor is a sublessor of coal or domestic iron ore, see paragraph (b)(3) of § 1.631-3. Every taxpayer who pays or accrues advanced royalties resulting from a minimum royalty provision must make an election as to the treatment of all such advanced royalties in his return for the first taxable year ending after December 31, 1939, in which the advanced royalties are paid or accrued. The taxpayer's treatment of the advanced royalties for the first year shall be deemed to be the exercise of the election. Accordingly, a failure to deduct the advanced royalties for that year will constitute an election to have all the advanced royalties treated as deductions for the year of the sale of the mineral product in respect of which the advanced royalties are paid or accrued. See section 7807(b)(2). For additional rules relating to elections in the case of partners and partnerships, see section 703(b) and the regulations thereunder. The provisions of this subparagraph do not allow as deductions from gross income amounts disallowed as deductions under other provisions of the Code, such as section 461 (relating to general rule for taxable year of deduction), section 465 (relating to deductions limited to amount at risk in case of certain activities), or section 704(d) (relating to limitation on allowance to partners of partnership losses).

(4) The application of subparagraphs (2) and (3) of this paragraph may be illustrated by the following examples:

Example (1). B leased certain mineral lands from A under a lease in which A reserved a royalty of 10 cents a ton on minerals mined and sold by B. The lease also provided that B had to pay an annual minimum royalty of $10,000 representing the amount due on 100,000 tons of the particular mineral whether or not B mined and sold that amount. It was further provided that, if B did not mine and sell 100,000 tons in any year, he could mine and sell in any subsequent year the amount of mineral on which he had paid the royalty without the payment of any additional royalty. However, this right of recoupment was limited to minerals mined and sold in any later year in excess of the 100,000 tons represented by the $10,000 minimum royalty required to be paid for that later year. Assume that in 1956 B paid A the minimum royalty of $10,000, but mined and sold only 60,000 tons of the mineral and that in 1957 he abandoned the lease without any further production. Since the $10,000 represents royalties on 100,000 tons of mineral and only 60,000 tons were mined and sold, A must restore in 1957 to his capital account the depletion deductions taken in 1956 on $4,000 on account of the 40,000 tons paid for in advance but not mined and sold, and must also return the corresponding amount as income in 1957.

Example (2). Assume that B, under the lease in example (1), paid the $10,000 minimum royalty and mined no minerals in 1956 but that in 1957 B mined and sold 200,000 tons of mineral. If this is B's first such expenditure, B has an option, for the purpose of computing taxable income under section 63, to deduct in 1956 the $10,000 paid in that year although no mineral was mined, or to take the deduction in 1957 when the mineral, for which the $10,000 was paid in 1956, was mined and sold. (For treatment under percentage depletion, see example in paragraph (c)(5)(iii) of § 1.613-2.)

(c) *Delay rental.*—(1) A delay rental is an amount paid for the privilege of deferring development of the property and which could have been avoided by abandonment of the lease, or by commencement of development operations, or by obtaining production.

(2) Since a delay rental is in the nature of rent it is ordinary income to the payee and not subject to depletion. The payor may at his elec-

tion deduct such amount as an expense, or under section 266 and the regulations thereunder, charge it to depletable capital account.

(d) *Percentage depletion deduction with respect to bonus and advanced royalty.*—In lieu of the allowance based on cost depletion computed under paragraphs (a) and (b) of this section, the payees referred to therein may be allowed a depletion deduction in respect of any bonus or advanced royalty for the taxable year in an amount computed on the basis of the percentage of gross income from the property as provided in section 613 and the regulations thereunder. However, for special rules applicable to certain bonuses and advanced royalties received in connection with oil or gas properties, see paragraph (j) of § 1.613A-3.

(e) *Cross reference.*—In the case of bonuses and advanced royalties received in connection with a contract of disposal of timber covered by section 631(b) or coal or iron ore covered by section 631(c), see that section and the regulations thereunder. [Reg. § 1.612-3.]

☐ [*T.D.* 6446, 1-20-60. *Amended by T.D.* 6841, 7-26-65; *by T.D.* 7523, 12-14-77 *and T.D.* 8348, 5-10-91.]

§ 1.612-4. Charges to capital and to expense in case of oil and gas wells.—(a) *Option with respect to intangible drilling and development costs.*—In accordance with the provisions of section 263(c), intangible drilling and development costs incurred by an operator (one who holds a working or operating interest in any tract or parcel of land either as a fee owner or under a lease or any other form of contract granting working or operating rights) in the development of oil and gas properties may at his option be chargeable to capital or to expense. This option applies to all expenditures made by an operator for wages, fuel, repairs, hauling, supplies, etc., incident to and necessary for the drilling of wells and the preparation of wells for the production of oil or gas. Such expenditures have for convenience been termed intangible drilling and development costs. They include the cost to operators of any drilling or development work (excluding amounts payable only out of production or gross or net proceeds from production, if such amounts are depletable income to the recipient, and amounts properly allocable to cost of depreciable property) done for them by contractors under any form of contract, including turnkey contracts. Examples of items to which this option applies are, all amounts paid for labor, fuel, repairs, hauling, and supplies, or any of them, which are used—

(1) In the drilling, shooting, and cleaning of wells,

(2) In such clearing of ground, draining, road making, surveying, and geological works as are necessary in preparation for the drilling of wells, and

(3) In the construction of such derricks, tanks, pipelines, and other physical structures as are necessary for the drilling of wells and the preparation of wells for the production of oil or gas.

In general, this option applies only to expenditures for those drilling and developing items which in themselves do not have a salvage value. For the purpose of this option, labor, fuel, repairs, hauling, supplies, etc., are not considered as having a salvage value, even though used in connection with the installation of physical property which has a salvage value. Included in this option are all costs of drilling and development undertaken (directly or through a contract) by an operator of an oil and gas property whether incurred by him prior or subsequent to the formal grant or assignment to him of operating rights (a leasehold interest, or other form of operating rights, or working interest); except that in any case where any drilling or development project is undertaken for the grant or assignment of a fraction of the operating rights, only that part of the costs thereof which is attributable to such fractional interest is within this option. In the excepted cases, costs of the project undertaken, including depreciable equipment furnished, to the extent allocable to fractions of the operating rights held by others, must be capitalized as the depletable capital cost of the fractional interest thus acquired.

(b) *Recovery of optional items, if capitalized.*—(1) Items returnable through depletion: If the taxpayer charges such expenditures as fall within the option to capital account, the amounts so capitalized and not deducted as a loss are returnable through depletion insofar as they are not represented by physical property. For the purposes of this section the expenditures for clearing ground, draining, road making, surveying, geological work, excavation, grading, and the drilling, shooting, and cleaning of wells, are considered not to be represented by physical property, and when charged to capital account are returnable through depletion.

(2) Items returnable through depreciation: If the taxpayer charges such expenditures as fall within the option to capital account, the amounts so capitalized and not deducted as a loss are returnable through depreciation insofar as they are represented by physical property. Such expenditures are amounts paid for wages, fuel, repairs, hauling, supplies, etc., used in the installation of casing and equipment

and in the construction on the property of derricks and other physical structures.

(3) In the case of capitalized intangible drilling and development costs incurred under a contract, such costs shall be allocated between the foregoing classes of items specified in subparagraphs (1) and (2) for the purpose of determining the depletion and depreciation allowances.

(4) Option with respect to cost of nonproductive wells: If the operator has elected to capitalize intangible drilling and development costs, then an additional option is accorded with respect to intangible drilling and development costs incurred in drilling a nonproductive well. Such costs incurred in drilling a nonproductive well may be deducted by the taxpayer as an ordinary loss provided a proper election is made in the return for the first taxable year beginning after December 31, 1942, in which such a nonproductive well is completed. Such election with respect to intangible drilling and development costs of nonproductive wells is a new election, and, when made, shall be binding for all subsequent years. Any taxpayer who incurs optional drilling and development costs in drilling a nonproductive well must make a clear statement of election under this option in the return for the first taxable year beginning after December 31, 1942, in which such nonproductive well is completed. The absence of a clear indication in such return of an election to deduct as ordinary losses intangible drilling and development costs of nonproductive wells shall be deemed to be an election to recover such costs through depletion to the extent that they are not represented by physical property, and through depreciation to the extent that they are represented by physical property.

(c) *Nonoptional items distinguished.*—(1) Capital items: The option with respect to intangible drilling and development costs does not apply to expenditures by which the taxpayer acquires tangible property ordinarily considered as having a salvage value. Examples of such items are the costs of the actual materials in those structures which are constructed in the wells and on the property, and the cost of drilling tools, pipe, casing, tubing, tanks, engines, boilers, machines, etc. The option does not apply to any expenditure for wages, fuel, repairs, hauling, supplies, etc., in connection with equipment, facilities, or structures, not incident to or necessary for the drilling of wells, such as structures for storing or treating oil or gas. These are capital items and are returnable through depreciation.

(2) Expense items: Expenditures which must be charged off as expense, regardless of the option provided by this section, are those for labor, fuel, repairs, hauling, supplies, etc., in connection with the operation of the wells and of other facilities on the property for the production of oil or gas.

(d) *Manner of making election.*—The option granted in paragraph (a) of this section to charge intangible drilling and development costs to expense may be exercised by claiming intangible drilling and development costs as a deduction on the taxpayer's return for the first taxable year in which the taxpayer pays or incurs such costs; no formal statement is necessary. If the taxpayer fails to deduct such costs as expenses in such return, he shall be deemed to have elected to recover such costs through depletion to the extent that they are not represented by physical property, and through depreciation to the extent that they are represented by physical property.

* * *

[Reg. § 1.612-4.]

☐ [*T.D.* 6836, 7-14-65.]

Estates, Trusts, and Beneficiaries

§ 1.641(c)-1. Electing small business trust.—(a) *In general.*—An electing small business trust (ESBT) within the meaning of section 1361(e) is treated as two separate trusts for purposes of chapter 1 of the Internal Revenue Code. The portion of an ESBT that consists of stock in one or more S corporations is treated as one trust. The portion of an ESBT that consists of all the other assets in the trust is treated as a separate trust. The grantor or another person may be treated as the owner of all or a portion of either or both such trusts under subpart E, part I, subchapter J, chapter 1 of the Internal Revenue Code. The ESBT is treated as a single trust for administrative purposes, such as having one taxpayer identification number and filing one tax return. See § 1.1361-1(m).

(b) *Definitions.*—(1) *Grantor portion.*—(i) *In general.*—Subject to paragraph (b)(1)(ii) of this section, the grantor portion of an ESBT is the portion of the trust that is treated as owned by the grantor or another person under subpart E of the Code.

(ii) *Nonresident alien deemed owner.*—If, pursuant to section 672(f)(2)(A)(ii), the deemed owner of a grantor portion of the ESBT is a nonresident alien, as defined in section 7701(b)(1)(B) (NRA), the items of income, deduction, and credit from that grantor portion must be reallocated from the grantor portion to the S portion, as defined in paragraph (b)(2) of this section, of the ESBT.

(2) *S portion.*—(i) *In general.*—Subject to paragraph (b)(2)(ii) of this section, the S portion of an ESBT is the portion of the trust that consists of S corporation stock and that is not treated as owned by the grantor or another person under subpart E of the Code.

(ii) *Nonresident alien (NRA) deemed owner of grantor portion.*—The S portion of an ESBT also includes the grantor portion of the items of income, deduction, and credit reallocated under paragraph (b)(1)(ii) of this section from the grantor portion of the ESBT to the S portion of the ESBT.

(3) *Non-S portion.*—The non-S portion of an ESBT is the portion of the trust that consists of all assets other than S corporation stock and that is not treated as owned by the grantor or another person under subpart E.

(c) *Taxation of grantor portion.*—The grantor or another person who is treated as the owner of a portion of the ESBT includes in computing taxable income items of income, deductions, and credits against tax attributable to that portion of the ESBT under section 671.

(d) *Taxation of S portion.*—(1) *In general.*—The taxable income of the S portion is determined by taking into account only the items of income, loss, deduction, or credit specified in paragraphs (d)(2), (3), and (4) of this section, to the extent not attributable to the grantor portion.

(2) *Section 1366 amounts.*—(i) *In general.*—The S portion takes into account the items of income, loss, deduction, or credit that are taken into account by an S corporation shareholder pursuant to section 1366 and the regulations thereunder. Rules otherwise applicable to trusts apply in determining the extent to which any loss, deduction, or credit may be taken into account in determining the taxable income of the S portion. See § 1.1361-1(m)(3)(iv) for allocation of those items in the taxable year of the S corporation in which the trust is an ESBT for part of the year and an eligible shareholder under section 1361(a)(2)(A)(i) through (iv) for the rest of the year.

(ii) *Special rule for charitable contributions.*—If a deduction described in paragraph (d)(2)(i) of this section is attributable to an amount of the S corporation's gross income that is paid by the S corporation for a charitable purpose specified in section 170(c) (without regard to section 170(c)(2)(A)), the contribution will be deemed to be paid by the S portion pursuant to the terms of the trust's governing instrument within the meaning of section 642(c)(1). The limitations of section 681, regarding unrelated business income, apply in determining whether the contribution is deductible in computing the taxable income of the S portion.

(iii) *Multiple S corporations.*—If an ESBT owns stock in more than one S corporation, items of income, loss, deduction, or credit from all the S corporations are aggregated for purposes of determining the S portion's taxable income.

(3) *Gains and losses on disposition of S stock.*—(i) *In general.*—The S portion takes into account any gain or loss from the disposition of S corporation stock. No deduction is allowed under section 1211(b)(1) and (2) for capital losses that exceed capital gains.

(ii) *Installment method.*—If income from the sale or disposition of stock in an S corporation is reported by the trust on the installment method, the income recognized under this method is taken into account by the S portion. See paragraph (g)(3) of this section for the treatment of interest on the installment obligation. See § 1.1361-1(m)(5)(ii) regarding treatment of a trust as an ESBT upon the sale of all S corporation stock using the installment method.

(iii) *Distributions in excess of basis.*—Gain recognized under section 1368(b)(2) from distributions in excess of the ESBT's basis in its S corporation stock is taken into account by the S portion.

(4) *State and local income taxes and administrative expenses.*—(i) *In general.*—State and local income taxes and administrative expenses directly related to the S portion and those allocated to that portion in accordance with paragraph (h) are taken into account by the S portion.

(ii) *Special rule for certain interest.*—Interest paid by the trust on money borrowed by the trust to purchase stock in an S corporation is allocated to the S portion but is not a deductible administrative expense for purposes of determining the taxable income of the S portion.

(e) *Tax rates and exemption of S portion.*—(1) *Income tax rate.*—Except for capital gains, the highest marginal trust rate provided in section 1(e) is applied to the taxable income of the S portion. See section 1(h) for the rates that apply to the S portion's net capital gain.

(2) *Alternative minimum tax exemption.*—The exemption amount of the S portion under section 55(d) is zero.

(f) *Adjustments to basis of stock in the S portion under section 1367.*—The basis of S corporation stock in the S portion must be adjusted in accordance with section 1367 and the regulations thereunder. If the ESBT owns stock in more than one S corporation, the adjustments to the basis in the S corporation stock of each S corporation must be determined separately with respect to each S corporation. Accordingly, items of income, loss, deduction, or credit of an S corporation that are taken into account by the ESBT under section 1366 can only result in an adjustment to the basis of the stock of that S corporation and cannot affect the basis in the stock of the other S corporations held by the ESBT.

(g) *Taxation of non-S portion.*—(1) *In general.*—The taxable income of the non-S portion is determined by taking into account all items of income, deduction, and credit to the extent not taken into account by either the grantor portion or the S portion. The items attributable to the non-S portion are taxed under subparts A through D of part I, subchapter J, chapter 1 of the Internal Revenue Code. The non-S portion may consist of more than one share pursuant to section 663(c).

(2) *Dividend income under section 1368(c)(2).*—Any dividend income within the meaning of section 1368(c)(2) is includible in the gross income of the non-S portion.

(3) *Interest on installment obligations.*—If income from the sale or disposition of stock in an S corporation is reported by the trust on the installment method, the interest on the installment obligation is includible in the gross income of the non- S portion. See paragraph (d)(3)(ii) of this section for the treatment of income from such a sale or disposition.

(4) *Charitable deduction.*—For purposes of applying section 642(c)(1) to payments made by the trust for a charitable purpose, the amount of gross income of the trust is limited to the gross income of the non-S portion. See paragraph (d)(2)(ii) of this section for special rules concerning charitable contributions paid by the S corporation that are deemed to be paid by the S portion.

(h) *Allocation of state and local income taxes and administration expenses.*—Whenever state and local income taxes or administration expenses relate to more than one portion of an ESBT, they must be allocated between or among the portions to which they relate. These items may be allocated in any manner that is reasonable in light of all the circumstances, including the terms of the governing instrument, applicable local law, and the practice of the trustee with respect to the trust if it is reasonable and consistent. The taxes and expenses apportioned to each portion of the ESBT are taken into account by that portion.

(i) *Treatment of distributions from the trust.*—Distributions to beneficiaries from the S portion or the non-S portion, including distributions of the S corporation stock, are deductible under section 651 or 661 in determining the taxable income of the non-S portion, and are includible in the gross income of the beneficiaries under section 652 or 662. However, the amount of the deduction or inclusion cannot exceed the amount of the distributable net income of the non-S portion. Items of income, loss, deduction, or credit taken into account by the grantor portion or the S portion are excluded for purposes of determining the distributable net income of the non-S portion of the trust.

(j) *Termination or revocation of ESBT election.*—If the ESBT election of the trust terminates pursuant to § 1.1361-1(m)(5) or the ESBT election is revoked pursuant to § 1.1361-1(m)(6), the rules contained in this section are thereafter not applicable to the trust. If, upon termination or revocation, the S portion has a net operating loss under section 172; a capital loss carryover under section 1212; or deductions in excess of gross income; then any such loss, carryover, or excess deductions shall be allowed as a deduction, in accordance with the regulations under section 642(h), to the trust, or to the beneficiaries succeeding to the property of the trust if the entire trust terminates.

* * *

[Reg. § 1.641(c)-1.]

☐ [*T.D.* 8994, 5-13-2002. *Amended by T.D.* 9868, 6-13-2019.]

Income in Respect of Decedents

§ 1.691(a)-1. Income in respect of a decedent.—(a) *Scope of section 691.*—In general, the regulations under section 691 cover: (1) The provisions requiring that amounts which are not includible in gross income for the decedent's last taxable year or for a prior taxable year be included in the gross income of the estate or persons receiving such income to the extent that such amounts constitute "income in respect of a decedent"; (2) the taxable effect of a transfer of the right to such income; (3) the treatment of certain deductions and credit in respect of a decedent which are not allowable to the decedent for the taxable period ending with his death or for a prior taxable year; (4) the allowance to a recipient of income in respect of a decedent of a deduction for estate taxes attributable to the inclusion of the value of the right to such income in the decedent's estate; (5) special provisions with respect to installment obligations acquired from a decedent and with respect to the allowance of a deduction for estate taxes to a surviving annuitant under a joint and survivor annuity contract; and (6) special provisions relating to installment obligations transmitted at death when prior law applied to the transmission.

(b) *General definition.*—In general, the term "income in respect of a decedent" refers to those amounts to which a decedent was entitled as gross income but which were not properly includible in computing his taxable income for the taxable year ending with the date of his death or for a previous taxable year under the method of accounting employed by the decedent. See the regulations under section 451. Thus, the term includes—

(1) All accrued income of a decedent who reported his income by use of the cash receipts and disbursements method:

(2) Income accrued solely by reason of the decedent's death in case of a decedent who reports his income by use of an accrual method of accounting; and

(3) Income to which the decedent had a contingent claim at the time of his death.

See sections 736 and 753 and the regulations thereunder for "income in respect of a decedent" in the case of a deceased partner.

(c) *Prior decedent.*—The term "income in respect of a decedent" also includes the amount of all items of gross income in respect of a prior decedent, if (1) the right to receive such amount was acquired by the decedent by reason of the death of the prior decedent or by bequest, devise, or inheritance from the prior decedent and if (2) the amount of gross income in respect of the prior decedent was not properly includible in computing the decedent's taxable income for the taxable year ending with the date of his death or for a previous taxable year. See example (2) of paragraph (b) of § 1.691(a)-2.

(d) *Items excluded from gross income.*—Section 691 applies only to the amount of items of gross income in respect of a decedent, and items which are excluded from gross income under subtitle A of the Code are not within the provisions of section 691.

(e) *Cross reference.*—For items deemed to be income in respect of a decedent for purposes of the deduction for estate taxes provided by section 691(c), see paragraph (c) of § 1.691(c)-1. [Reg. § 1.691(a)-1.]

☐ [*T.D.* 6257, 10-7-57. *Amended by T.D.* 6808, 3-15-65.]

§ 1.691(a)-2. Inclusion in gross income by recipients.—(a) Under section 691(a)(1), income in respect of a decedent shall be included in the gross income, for the taxable year when received, of—

(1) The estate of the decedent, if the right to receive the amount is acquired by the decedent's estate from the decedent;

(2) The person who, by reason of the death of the decedent, acquires the right to receive the amount, if the right to receive the amount is not acquired by the decedent's estate from the decedent; or

(3) The person who acquires from the decedent the right to receive the amount by bequest, devise, or inheritance, if the amount is received after a distribution by the decedent's estate of such right.

These amounts are included in the income of the estate or of such persons when received by them whether or not they report income by use of the cash receipts and disbursements method.

(b) The application of paragraph (a) of this section may be illustrated by the following examples, in each of which it is assumed that the decedent kept his books by use of the cash receipts and disbursements method:

Example (1). The decedent was entitled at the date of his death to a large salary payment to be made in equal annual installments over five years. His estate, after collecting two installments, distributed the right to the remaining installment payments to the residuary legatee of the estate. The estate must include in its gross income the two installments received by it, and the legatee must include in his gross income each of the three installments received by him.

Example (2). A widow acquired, by bequest from her husband, the right to receive renewal commissions on life insurance sold by him in his lifetime, which commissions were payable over a period of years. The widow died before having received all of such commissions, and her son inherited the right to receive the rest of the commissions. The commissions received by the widow were includible in her gross income. The commissions received by the son were not includible in the widow's gross income but must be included in the gross income of the son.

Example (3). The decedent owned a Series E United States savings bond, with his wife as coowner or beneficiary, but died before the payment of such bond. The entire amount of interest accruing on the bond and not includible in income by the decedent, nor just the amount accruing after the death of the decedent, would be treated as income to his wife when the bond is paid.

Example (4). A, prior to his death, acquired 10,000 shares of the capital stock of the X Corporation at a cost of $100 per share. During his lifetime, A had entered into an agreement with X Corporation whereby X Corporation agreed to purchase and the decedent agreed that his executor would sell the 10,000 shares of X Corporation stock owned by him at the book value of the stock at the date of A's death. Upon A's death, the shares are sold by A's executor for $500 a share pursuant to the agreement. Since the sale of stock is consummated after A's death, there is no income in respect of a decedent with respect to the appreciation in value of A's stock to the date of his death. If, in this example, A had in fact sold the stock during his lifetime but payment had not been received before his death, any gain on the sale would constitute income in respect of a decedent when the proceeds were received.

Example (5). (1) A owned and operated an apple orchard. During his lifetime, A sold and delivered 1,000 bushels of apples to X, a canning factory, but did not receive payment before his death. A also entered into negotiations to sell 3,000 bushels of apples to Y, a canning factory, but did not complete the sale before his death. After A's death, the executor received payment from X. He also completed the sale to Y and transferred to Y 1,200 bushels of apples on hand at A's death and harvested and transferred an additional 1,800 bushels. The gain from the sale of apples by A to X constitutes income in respect of a decedent when received. On the other hand, the gain from the sale of apples by the executor to Y does not.

(2) Assume that, instead of the transaction entered into with Y, A had disposed of the 1,200 bushels of harvested apples by delivering them to Z, a cooperative association, for processing and sale. Each year the association commingles the fruit received from all of its members into a pool and assigns to each member a percentage interest in the pool based on the fruit delivered by him. After the fruit is processed and the products are sold, the association distributes the net proceeds from the pool to its members in proportion to their interests in the pool. After A's death, the association made distributions to the executor with respect to A's share of the proceeds from the pool in which A had an interest. Under such circumstances, the proceeds from the disposition of the 1,200 bushels of apples constitute income in respect of a decedent. [Reg. § 1.691(a)-2.]

□ [*T.D.* 6257, 10-7-57.]

§ 1.691(a)-3. Character of gross income.—(a) The right to receive an amount of income in respect of a decedent shall be treated in the hands of the estate, or by the person entitled to receive such amount by bequest, devise, or inheritance from the decedent or by reason of his death, as if it had been acquired in the transaction by which the decedent (or a prior decedent) acquired such right, and shall be considered as having the same character it would have had if the decedent (or a prior decedent) had lived and received such amount. The provisions of section 1014(a), relating to the basis of property acquired from a decedent, and section 1022, relating to the basis of property acquired from certain decedents who died in 2010, do not apply to these amounts in the hands of the estate and such persons. See sections 1014(c) and 1022(f).

(b) The application of paragraph (a) of this section may be illustrated by the following:

(1) If the income would have been capital gain to the decedent, if he had lived and had received it, from the sale of property held for more than 1 year (6 months for taxable years beginning before 1977; 9 months for taxable years beginning in 1977), the income, when received, shall be treated in the hands of the estate or of such person as capital gain from the sale of the property, held for more than 1 year (6 months for taxable years beginning before 1977; 9 months for taxable years beginning in 1977), in the same manner as if such person had held the property for the period the decedent held it, and had made the sale.

(2) If the income is interest on United States obligations which were owned by the decedent, such income shall be treated as interest on United States obligations in the hands of the person receiving it, for the purpose of determining the credit provided by section 35, as if such person had owned the obligations with respect to which such interest is paid.

(3) If the amounts received would be subject to special treatment under part I (section 1301 and following), subchapter Q, chapter 1 of the Code, relating to income attributable to several taxable years, as in effect for taxable years beginning before January 1, 1964, if the decedent had lived and included such amounts in his gross income, such sections apply with respect to the recipient of the income.

(4) The provisions of sections 632 and 1347, relating to the tax attributable to the sale of certain oil or gas property and to certain claims against the United States, apply to any amount included in gross income, the right to which was obtained by the decedent by a sale or claim within the provisions of those sections.

* * *

[Reg. § 1.691(a)-3.]

□ [*T.D.* 6257, 10-7-57. *Amended by T.D.* 6885, 6-1-66, *T.D.* 7728, 10-31-80 *and T.D.* 9811, 1-18-2017.]

§ 1.691(a)-4. Transfer of right to income in respect of a decedent.—(a) Section 691(a)(2) provides the rules governing the treatment of income in respect of a decedent (or a prior decedent) in the event a right to receive such income is transferred by the estate or person entitled thereto by bequest, devise, or inheritance, or by reason of the death of the decedent. In general, the transferor must include in his gross income for the taxable period in which the transfer occurs the amount of the consideration, if any, received for the right or the fair market value of the right at the time of the transfer, whichever is greater. Thus, upon a sale of such right by the estate or person entitled to receive it, the fair market value of the right or the amount received upon the sale, whichever is greater, is included in the gross income of the vendor. Similarly, if such right is disposed of by gift, the fair market value of the right at the time of the gift must be included in the gross income of the donor. In the case of a satisfaction of an installment obligation at other than face value, which is likewise considered a transfer under section 691(a)(2), see § 1.691(a)-5.

(b) If the estate of a decedent or any person transmits the right to income in respect of a decedent to another who would be required by section 691(a)(1) to include such income when received in his gross income, only the transferee will include such income when received in his gross income. In this situation, a transfer within the meaning of section 691(a)(2) has not occurred. This paragraph may be illustrated by the following:

(1) If a person entitled to income in respect of a decedent dies before receiving such income, only his estate or other person entitled to such income by bequest, devise, or inheritance from the latter decedent, or by reason of the death of the latter decedent, must include such amount in gross income when received.

(2) If a right to income in respect of a decedent is transferred by an estate to a specific or residuary legatee, only the specific or residuary legatee must include such income in gross income when received.

(3) If a trust to which is bequeathed a right of a decedent to certain payments of income terminates and transfers the right to a beneficiary, only the beneficiary must include such income in gross income when received. If the transferee described in subparagraphs (1), (2), and (3) of this paragraph transfers his right to receive the amounts in the manner described in paragraph (a) of this section, the principles contained in paragraph (a) are applied to such transfer. On the other hand, if the transferee transmits his right in the manner described in this paragraph, the principles of this paragraph are again applied to such transfer. [Reg. § 1.691(a)-4.]

□ [*T.D.* 6257, 10-7-57.]

§ 1.691(b)-1. Allowance of deductions and credit in respect of decedents.—(a) Under section 691(b), the expenses, interest, and taxes described in sections 162, 163, 164, and 212 for which the decedent (or a prior decedent) was liable, which were not properly allowable as a deduction in his last taxable year or any prior taxable year, are allowed when paid—

(1) As a deduction by the estate; or

(2) If the estate was not liable to pay such obligation, as a deduction by the person who by bequest, devise, or inheritance from the decedent or by reason of the death of the decedent acquires, subject to such obligation, an interest in property of the decedent (or the prior decedent).

Similar treatment is given to the foreign tax credit provided by section 33. For the purposes of subparagraph (2) of this paragraph, the right to receive an amount of gross income in respect of a decedent is considered property of the decedent; on the other hand, it is not necessary for a person, otherwise within the provisions of subparagraph (2) of this paragraph, to receive the right to any income in respect of a decedent. Thus, an heir who receives a right to income in respect of a decedent (by reason of the death of the decedent) subject to an income tax imposed by a foreign country during the decedent's life, which tax must be satisfied out of such income, is entitled to the credit provided by section 33 when he pays the tax. If a decedent who reported income by use of the cash receipts and disbursements method owned real property on which accrued taxes had become a lien, and if such property passed directly to the heir of the decedent in a jurisdiction in which real property does not become a part of a decedent's estate, the heir, upon paying such taxes, may take the same deduction under section 164 that would be allowed to the decedent if, while alive, he had made such payment.

(b) The deduction for percentage depletion is allowable only to the person (described in section 691(a)(1)) who receives the income in respect of the decedent to which the deduction relates, whether or not such person receives the property from which such income is derived. Thus, an heir who (by reason of the decedent's death) receives income derived from sales of units of mineral by the decedent (who reported income by use of the cash receipts and disbursements method) shall be allowed the deduction for percentage depletion, computed on the gross income from such number of units as if the heir had the same economic interest in the property as the decedent. Such heir need not also receive any interest in the mineral property other than such income. If the decedent did not compute his deduction for depletion on the basis of percentage depletion, any deduction for depletion to which the decedent was entitled at the date of his death would be allowable in computing his taxable income for his last taxable year, and there can be no deduction in respect of the decedent by any other person for such depletion. [Reg. § 1.691(b)-1.]

□ [*T.D.* 6257, 10-7-57.]

Partners and Partnerships—Determination of Tax Liability

§ 1.701-1. Partners, not partnership, subject to tax.—Partners are liable for income tax only in their separate capacities. Partnerships as such are not subject to the income tax imposed by subtitle A but are required to make returns of income under the provisions of section 6031 and the regulations thereunder. For definition of the terms "partner" and "partnership", see sections 761 and 7701(a)(2), and the regulations thereunder. For provisions relating to the election of certain partnerships to be taxed as domestic corporations, see section 1361 and the regulations thereunder. [Reg. § 1.701-1.]

□ [*T.D.* 6175, 5-23-56.]

§ 1.701-2. Anti-abuse rule.—(a) *Intent of subchapter K.*—Subchapter K is intended to permit taxpayers to conduct joint business (including investment) activities through a flexible economic arrangement without incurring an entity-level tax. Implicit in the intent of subchapter K are the following requirements—

(1) The partnership must be bona fide and each partnership transaction or series of related transactions (individually or collectively, the transaction) must be entered into for a substantial business purpose.

(2) The form of each partnership transaction must be respected under substance over form principles.

(3) Except as otherwise provided in this paragraph (a)(3), the tax consequences under subchapter K to each partner of partnership operations and of transactions between the partner and the partnership must accurately reflect the partners' economic agreement and clearly reflect the partner's income (collectively, *proper reflection of income*). However, certain provisions of subchapter K and the regulations thereunder were adopted to promote administrative convenience and other policy objectives, with the recognition that the application of those provisions to a transaction could, in some circumstances, produce tax results that do not properly reflect income. Thus, the proper reflection of income requirement of this paragraph (a)(3) is treated as satisfied with respect to a transaction that satisfies paragraphs (a)(1) and (2) of this section to the extent that the application of such a provision to the transaction and the ultimate tax results, taking into account all the relevant facts and circumstances, are clearly contemplated by that provision. See, for example, paragraph (d) *Example 6* of this section (relating to the value-equals-basis rule in § 1.704-1(b)(2)(iii)(*c*)), paragraph (d) *Example 9* of this section (relating to the election under section 754 to adjust basis in partnership property), and paragraph (d) *Examples 10 and 11* of this section (relating to the basis in property distributed by a partnership under section 732). See also, for example, §§ 1.704-3(e)(1) and 1.752-2(e)(4) (providing certain de minimis exceptions).

(b) *Application of subchapter K rules.*—The provisions of subchapter K and the regulations thereunder must be applied in a manner that is consistent with the intent of subchapter K as set forth in paragraph (a) of this section (*intent of subchapter K*). Accordingly, if a partnership is formed or availed of in connection with a transaction a principal purpose of which is to reduce substantially the present value of the partners' aggregate federal tax liability in a manner that is inconsistent with the intent of subchapter K, the Commissioner can recast the transaction for federal tax purposes, as appropriate to achieve tax results that are consistent with the intent of subchapter K, in light of the applicable statutory and regulatory provisions and the pertinent facts and circumstances. Thus, even though the transaction may fall within the literal words of a particular statutory or regulatory provision, the Commissioner can determine, based on the particular facts and circumstances, that to achieve tax results that are consistent with the intent of subchapter K—

(1) The purported partnership should be disregarded in whole or in part, and the partnership's assets and activities should be considered, in whole or in part, to be owned and conducted, respectively, by one or more of its purported partners;

(2) One or more of the purported partners of the partnership should not be treated as a partner;

(3) The methods of accounting used by the partnership or a partner should be adjusted

to reflect clearly the partnership's or the partner's income;

(4) The partnership's items of income, gain, loss, deduction, or credit should be reallocated; or

(5) The claimed tax treatment should otherwise be adjusted or modified.

(c) *Facts and circumstances analysis; factors.*—Whether a partnership was formed or availed of with a principal purpose to reduce substantially the present value of the partners' aggregate federal tax liability in a manner inconsistent with the intent of subchapter K is determined based on all of the facts and circumstances, including a comparison of the purported business purpose for a transaction and the claimed tax benefits resulting from the transaction. The factors set forth below may be indicative, but do not necessarily establish, that a partnership was used in such a manner. These factors are illustrative only, and therefore may not be the only factors taken into account in making the determination under this section. Moreover, the weight given to any factor (whether specified in this paragraph or otherwise) depends on all the facts and circumstances. The presence or absence of any factor described in this paragraph does not create a presumption that a partnership was (or was not) used in such a manner. Factors include:

(1) The present value of the partners' aggregate federal tax liability is substantially less than had the partners owned the partnership's assets and conducted the partnership's activities directly;

(2) The present value of the partners' aggregate federal tax liability is substantially less than would be the case if purportedly separate transactions that are designed to achieve a particular end result are integrated and treated as steps in a single transaction. For example, this analysis may indicate that it was contemplated that a partner who was necessary to achieve the intended tax results and whose interest in the partnership was liquidated or disposed of (in whole or in part) would be a partner only temporarily in order to provide the claimed tax benefits to the remaining partners;

(3) One or more partners who are necessary to achieve the claimed tax results either have a nominal interest in the partnership, are substantially protected from any risk of loss from the partnership's activities (through distribution preferences, indemnity or loss guaranty agreements, or other arrangements), or have little or no participation in the profits from the partnership's activities other than a preferred return that is in the nature of a payment for the use of capital;

(4) Substantially all of the partners (measured by number or interests in the partnership) are related (directly or indirectly) to one another;

(5) Partnership items are allocated in compliance with the literal language of §§1.704-1 and 1.704-2 but with results that are inconsistent with the purpose of section 704(b) and those regulations. In this regard, particular scrutiny will be paid to partnerships in which income or gain is specially allocated to one or more partners that may be legally or effectively exempt from federal taxation (for example, a foreign person, an exempt organization, an insolvent taxpayer, or a taxpayer with unused federal tax attributes such as net operating losses, capital losses, or foreign tax credits);

(6) The benefits and burdens of ownership of property nominally contributed to the partnership are in substantial part retained (directly or indirectly) by the contributing partner (or a related party); or

(7) The benefits and burdens of ownership of partnership property are in substantial part shifted (directly or indirectly) to the distributee partner before or after the property is actually distributed to the distributee partner (or a related party).

(d) *Examples.*—The following examples illustrate the principles of paragraphs (a), (b), and (c) of this section. The examples set forth below do not delineate the boundaries of either permissible or impermissible types of transactions. Further, the addition of any facts or circumstances that are not specifically set forth in an example (or the deletion of any facts or circumstances) may alter the outcome of the transaction described in the example. Unless otherwise indicated, parties to the transactions are not related to one another.

Example 1. Choice of entity; avoidance of entity-level tax; use of partnership consistent with the intent of subchapter K. (i) A and B form limited partnership PRS to conduct a bona fide business. A, the corporate general partner, has a 1% partnership interest. B, the individual limited partner, has a 99% interest. PRS is properly classified as a partnership under §§301.7701-2 and 301.7701-3. A and B chose limited partnership form as a means to provide B with limited liability without subjecting the income from the business operations to an entity-level tax.

(ii) Subchapter K is intended to permit taxpayers to conduct joint business activity through a flexible economic arrangement without incurring an entity-level tax. See paragraph (a) of this section. Although B has retained, indirectly, substantially all of the benefits and burdens of ownership of the money or property B contributed to PRS (see paragraph (c)(6) of this section), the decision to organize and conduct business through PRS under these circumstances is consistent with this intent. In addition, on these facts, the requirements of paragraphs (a)(1), (2), and (3) of this section have been satisfied. The Commissioner therefore cannot invoke paragraph (b) of this section to recast the transaction.

Example 2. Choice of entity; avoidance of subchapter S shareholder requirements; use of partnership consistent with the intent of subchapter K. (i) A and B form partnership PRS to conduct a bona fide business. A is a corporation that has elected to be treated as an S corporation under subchapter S. B is a nonresident alien. PRS is properly classified as a partnership under §§301.7701-2 and 301.7701-3. Because section 1361(b) prohibits B from being a shareholder in A, A and B chose partnership form, rather than admit B as a shareholder in A, as a means to retain the benefits of subchapter S treatment for A and its shareholders.

(ii) Subchapter K is intended to permit taxpayers to conduct joint business activity through a flexible economic arrangement without incurring an entity-level tax. See paragraph (a) of this section. The decision to organize and conduct business through PRS is consistent with this intent. In addition, on these facts, the requirements of paragraphs (a)(1), (2), and (3) of this section have been satisfied. Although it may be argued that the form of the partnership transaction should not be respected because it does not reflect its substance (inasmuch as application of the substance over form doctrine arguably could result in B being treated as a shareholder of A, thereby invalidating A's subchapter S election), the facts indicate otherwise. The shareholders of A are subject to tax on their pro rata shares of A's income (see section 1361 et. seq.), and B is subject to tax on B's distributive share of partnership income (see sections 871 and 875). Thus, the form in which this arrangement is cast accurately reflects its substance as a separate partnership and S corporation. The Commissioner therefore cannot invoke paragraph (b) of this section to recast the transaction.

* * *

Example 4. Choice of entity; avoidance of gain recognition under sections 351(e) and 357(c); use of partnership consistent with the intent of subchapter K. (i) X, ABC, and DEF form limited partnership PRS to conduct a bona fide real estate management business. PRS is properly classified as a partnership under §§301.7701-2 and 301.7701-3. X, the general partner, is a newly formed corporation that elects to be treated as a real estate investment trust as defined in section 856. X offers its stock to the public and contributes substantially all of the proceeds from the public offering to PRS. ABC and DEF, the limited partners, are existing partnerships with substantial real estate holdings. ABC and DEF contribute all of their real property assets to PRS, subject to liabilities that exceed their respective aggregate bases in the real property contributed, and terminate under section 708(b)(1)(A). In addition, some of the former partners of ABC and DEF each have the right, beginning two years after the formation of PRS, to require the redemption of their limited partnership interests in PRS in exchange for cash or X stock (at X's option) equal to the fair market value of their respective interests in PRS at the time of the redemption. These partners are not compelled, as a legal or practical matter, to exercise their exchange rights at any time. X, ABC, and DEF chose to form a partnership rather than have ABC and DEF invest directly in X to allow ABC and DEF to avoid recognition of gain under sections 351(e) and 357(c). Because PRS would not be treated as an investment company within the meaning of section 351(e) if PRS were incorporated (so long as it did not elect under section 856), section 721(a) applies to the contribution of the real property to PRS. See section 721(b).

(ii) Subchapter K is intended to permit taxpayers to conduct joint business activity through a flexible economic arrangement without incurring an entity-level tax. See paragraph (a) of this section. The decision to organize and conduct business through PRS, thereby avoiding the tax consequences that would have resulted from contributing the existing partnerships' real estate assets to X (by applying the rules of sections 721, 731, and 752 in lieu of the rules of sections 351(e) and 357(c)), is consistent with this intent. In addition, on these facts, the requirements of paragraphs (a)(1), (2), and (3) of this section have been satisfied. Although it may be argued that the form of the transaction should not be respected because it does not reflect its substance (inasmuch as the present value of the partners' aggregate federal tax liability is substantially less than would be the case if the transaction were integrated and treated as a contribution of the encumbered assets by ABC and DEF directly to X, see paragraph (c)(2) of this section), the facts indicate otherwise. For example, the right of some of the former ABC and DEF partners after two years to exchange their PRS interests for cash or X stock (at X's option) equal to the fair market value of their PRS interest at that time would not require that right to be considered as exercised prior to its actual exercise. Moreover, X may make other real estate investments and other business decisions, including the decision to raise additional capital for those purposes. Thus, although it may be likely that some or all of the partners with the right to do so will, at some point, exercise their exchange rights, and thereby receive either cash or X stock, the form of the transaction as a separate partnership and real estate investment trust is respected under substance over form principles (see paragraph (a)(2) of this section). The Commissioner therefore cannot invoke paragraph (b) of this section to recast the transaction.

Example 5. Special allocations; dividends received deductions; use of partnership consistent with the intent of subchapter K. (i) Corporations X and Y contribute equal amounts to PRS, a bona fide partnership formed to make joint investments. PRS pays $100*x* for a share of common stock of Z, an unrelated corporation, which has historically paid an annual dividend of $6*x*. PRS specially allocates the dividend income on the Z stock to X to the extent of the London Inter-Bank Offered Rate (LIBOR) on the record date, applied to X's contribution of $50*x*, and allocates the remainder of the dividend income to Y. All other items of partnership income and loss are allocated equally between X and Y. The allocations under the partnership agreement have substantial economic effect within the meaning of § 1.704-1(b)(2). In addition to avoiding an entity-level tax, a principal purpose for the formation of the partnership was to invest in the Z common stock and to allocate the dividend income from the stock to provide X with a floating-rate return based on LIBOR, while permitting X and Y to claim the dividends received deduction under section 243 on the dividends allocated to each of them.

(ii) Subchapter K is intended to permit taxpayers to conduct joint business activity through a flexible economic arrangement without incurring an entity-level tax. See paragraph (a) of this section. The decision to organize and conduct business through PRS is consistent with this intent. In addition, on these facts, the requirements of paragraphs (a)(1), (2), and (3) of this section have been satisfied. Section 704(b) and § 1.704-1(b)(2) permit income realized by the partnership to be allocated validly to the partners separate from the partners' respective ownership of the capital to which the allocations relate, provided that the allocations satisfy both the literal requirements of the statute and regulations and the purpose of those provisions (see paragraph (c)(5) of this section). Section 704(e)(2) is not applicable to the facts of this example (otherwise, the allocations would be required to be proportionate to the partners' ownership of contributed capital). The Commissioner therefore cannot invoke paragraph (b) of this section to recast the transaction.

Example 6. Special allocations; nonrecourse financing; low-income housing credit; use of partnership consistent with the intent of subchapter K. (i) A and B, high-bracket taxpayers, and X, a corporation with net operating loss carryforwards, form general partnership PRS to own and operate a building that qualifies for the low-income housing credit provided by section 42. The project is financed with both cash contributions from the partners and nonrecourse indebtedness. The partnership agreement provides for special allocations of income and deductions, including the allocation of all depreciation deductions attributable to the building to A and B equally in a manner that is reasonably consistent with allocations that have substantial economic effect of some other significant partnership item attributable to the building. The section 42 credits are allocated to A and B in accordance with the allocation of depreciation deductions. PRS's allocations comply with all applicable regulations, including the requirements of §§ 1.704-1(b)(2)(ii) (pertaining to economic effect) and 1.704-2(e) (requirements for allocations of nonrecourse deductions). The nonrecourse indebtedness is validly allocated to the partners under the rules of § 1.752-3, thereby increasing the basis of the partners' respective partnership interests. The basis increase created by the nonrecourse indebtedness enables A and B to deduct their distributive share of losses from the partnership (subject to all other applicable limitations under the Internal Revenue Code) against their nonpartnership income and to apply the credits against their tax liability.

(ii) At a time when the depreciation deductions attributable to the building are not treated as nonrecourse deductions under § 1.704-2(c) (because there is no net increase in partnership minimum gain during the year), the special allocation of depreciation deductions to A and B has substantial economic effect because of the value-equals-basis safe harbor contained in § 1.704-1(b)(2)(iii)(*c*) and the fact that A and B would bear the economic burden of any decline in the value of the building (to the extent of the partnership's investment in the building), notwithstanding that A and B believe it is unlikely that the building will decline in value (and, accordingly, they anticipate significant timing benefits through the special allocation). Moreover, in later years, when the depreciation deductions attributable to the building are treated as nonrecourse deductions under § 1.704-2(c), the special allocation of depreciation deductions to A and B is considered to be consistent with the partners' interests in the partnership under § 1.704-2(e).

(iii) Subchapter K is intended to permit taxpayers to conduct joint business activity through a flexible economic arrangement without incurring an entity-level tax. See paragraph (a) of this section. The decision to organize and conduct business through PRS is consistent with this intent. In addition, on these facts, the requirements of paragraphs (a)(1), (2), and (3) of this section have been satisfied. Section 704(b), § 1.704-1(b)(2), and § 1.704-2(e) allow partnership items of income, gain, loss, deduction, and credit to be allocated validly to the partners separate from the partners' respective ownership of the capital to which the allocations relate, provided that the allocations satisfy both the literal requirements of the statute and regulations and the purpose of those provisions (see paragraph (c)(5) of this section). Moreover, the application of the value-equals-basis safe harbor and the provisions of § 1.704-2(e) with respect to the allocations to A and B, and the tax results of the application of those provisions, taking into account all the facts and circumstances, are clearly contemplated. Accordingly, even if the allocations would not otherwise be considered to satisfy the proper reflection of income standard in paragraph (a)(3) of this section, that requirement will be treated as satisfied under these facts. Thus, even though the partners' aggregate federal tax liability may be substantially less than had the partners owned the partnership's assets directly (due to X's inability to use its allocable share of the partnership's losses and credits) (see paragraph (c)(1) of this section), the transaction is not inconsistent with the intent of subchapter K. The Commissioner therefore cannot invoke paragraph (b) of this section to recast the transaction.

Example 7. Partner with nominal interest; temporary partner; use of partnership not consistent with the intent of subchapter K. (i) Pursuant to a plan a principal purpose of which is to generate artificial losses and thereby shelter from federal taxation a substantial amount of income, X (a foreign corporation), Y (a domestic corporation), and Z (a promoter) form partnership PRS by contributing \$9,000*x*, \$990*x*, and \$10*x*, respectively, for proportionate interests (90.0%, 9.9%, and 0.1%, respectively) in the capital and profits of PRS. PRS purchases offshore equipment for \$10,000*x* and validly leases the equipment offshore for a term representing most of its projected useful life. Shortly thereafter, PRS sells its rights to receive income under the lease to a third party for \$9,000*x*, and allocates the resulting \$9,000*x* of income \$8,100*x* to X, \$891*x* to Y, and \$9*x* to Z. PRS thereafter makes a distribution of \$9,000*x* to X in complete liquidation of its interest. Under § 1.704-1(b)(2)(iv)(*f*), PRS restates the partners' capital accounts immediately before making the liquidating distribution to X to reflect its assets consisting of the offshore equipment worth \$1,000*x* and \$9,000*x* in cash. Thus, because the capital accounts immediately before the distribution reflect assets of \$19,000*x* (that is, the initial capital contributions of \$10,000*x* plus the \$9,000*x* of income realized from the sale of the lease), PRS allocates a \$9,000*x* book loss among the partners (for capital account purposes only), resulting in restated capital accounts for X, Y, and Z of \$9,000*x*, \$990*x*, and \$10*x*, respectively. Thereafter, PRS purchases real property by borrowing the \$8,000*x* purchase price on a recourse basis, which increases Y's and Z's bases in their respective partnership interests from \$1,881*x* and \$19*x*, to \$9,801*x* and \$99*x*, respectively (reflecting Y's and Z's adjusted interests in the partnership of 99% and 1%, respectively). PRS subsequently sells the offshore equipment, subject to the lease, for \$1,000*x* and allocates the \$9,000*x* tax loss \$8,910*x* to Y and \$90*x* to Z. Y's and Z's bases in their partnership interests are therefore reduced to \$891*x* and \$9*x*, respectively.

(ii) On these facts, any purported business purpose for the transaction is insignificant in comparison to the tax benefits that would result if the transaction were respected for federal tax purposes (see paragraph (c) of this section). Accordingly, the transaction lacks a substantial business purpose (see paragraph (a)(1) of this section). In addition, factors (1), (2), (3), and (5) of paragraph (c) of this section indicate that PRS was used with a principal purpose to reduce substantially the partners' tax liability in a manner inconsistent with the intent of subchapter K. On these facts, PRS is not bona fide (see paragraph (a)(1) of this section), and the transaction is not respected under applicable substance over form principles (see paragraph (a)(2) of this section) and does not properly reflect the income of Y (see paragraph (a)(3) of this section). Thus, PRS has been formed and availed of with a principal purpose of reducing substantially the present value of the partners' aggregate federal tax liability in a manner inconsistent with the intent of subchapter K. Therefore (in addition to possibly challenging the transaction under judicial principles or the validity of the allocations under § 1.704-1(b)(2) (see paragraph (h) of this section)), the Commissioner can recast the transaction as appropriate under paragraph (b) of this section.

* * *

Example 9. Absence of section 754 election; use of partnership consistent with the intent of subchapter K. (i) PRS is a bona fide partnership formed to engage in investment activities with contributions of cash from each partner. Several years after joining PRS, A, a partner with a capital account balance and basis in its partnership interest of \$100*x*, wishes to withdraw from PRS. The partnership agreement entitles A to receive the balance of A's capital account in cash or securities owned by PRS at the time of withdrawal, as mutually agreed to by A and the managing general partner, P. P and A agree to distribute to A \$100*x* worth of non-marketable securities (see section 731(c)) in which PRS has an aggregate basis of $20x. Upon distribution, A's aggregate basis in the securities is $100x under section 732(b). PRS does not make an election to adjust the basis in its remaining assets under section 754. Thus, PRS's basis in its remaining assets is unaffected by the distribution. In contrast, if a section 754 election had been in effect for the year of the distribution, under these facts section 734(b) would have required PRS to adjust the basis in its remaining assets downward by the amount of the untaxed appreciation in the distributed property, thus reflecting that gain in PRS's retained assets. In selecting the assets to be distributed, A and P had a principal purpose to take advantage of the facts that (i) A's basis in the securities will be determined by reference to A's basis in its partnership interest under section 732(b), and (ii) because PRS will not make an election under section 754, the remaining partners of PRS will likely enjoy a federal tax timing advantage (i.e., from the $80x of additional basis in its assets that would have been eliminated if the section 754 election had been made) that is inconsistent with proper reflection of income under paragraph (a)(3) of this section.

(ii) Subchapter K is intended to permit taxpayers to conduct joint business activity through a flexible economic arrangement without incurring an entity-level tax. See paragraph (a) of this section. The decision to organize and conduct business through PRS is consistent with this intent. In addition, on these facts, the requirements of paragraphs (a)(1) and (2) of this section have been satisfied. The validity of the tax treatment of this transaction is therefore dependent upon whether the transaction satisfies (or is treated as satisfying) the proper reflection of income standard under paragraph (a)(3) of this section. A's basis in the distributed securities is properly determined under section 732(b). The benefit to the remaining partners is a result of PRS not having made an election under section 754. Subchapter K is generally intended to produce tax consequences that achieve proper reflection of income. However, paragraph (a)(3) of this section provides that if the application of a provision of subchapter K produces tax results that do not properly reflect income, but application of that provision to the transaction and the ultimate tax results, taking into account all the relevant facts and circumstances, are clearly contemplated by that provision (and the transaction satisfies the requirements of paragraphs (a)(1) and (2) of this section), then the application of that provision to the transaction will be treated as satisfying the proper reflection of income standard.

(iii) In general, the adjustments that would be made if an election under section 754 were in effect are necessary to minimize distortions between the partners' bases in their partnership interests and the partnership's basis in its assets following, for example, a distribution to a partner. The electivity of section 754 is intended to provide administrative convenience for bona fide partnerships that are engaged in transactions for a substantial business purpose, by providing those partnerships the option of not adjusting their bases in their remaining assets following a distribution to a partner. Congress clearly recognized that if the section 754 election were not made, basis distortions may result. Taking into account all the facts and circumstances of the transaction, the electivity of section 754 in the context of the distribution from PRS to A, and the ultimate tax consequences that follow from the failure to make the election with respect to the transaction, are clearly contemplated by section 754. Thus, the tax consequences of this transaction will be treated as satisfying the proper reflection of income standard under paragraph (a)(3) of this section. The Commissioner therefore cannot invoke paragraph (b) of this section to recast the transaction.

Example 10. Basis adjustments under section 732; use of partnership consistent with the intent of subchapter K. (i) A, B, and C are partners in partnership PRS, which has for several years been engaged in substantial bona fide business activities. For valid business reasons, the partners agree that A's interest in PRS, which has a value and basis of $100x, will be liquidated with the following assets of PRS: a nondepreciable asset with a value of $60x and a basis to PRS of $40x, and related equipment with two years of cost recovery remaining and a value and basis to PRS of $40x. Neither asset is described in section 751 and the transaction is not described in section 732(d). Under section 732(b) and (c), A's $100x basis in A's partnership interest will be allocated between the nondepreciable asset and the equipment received in the liquidating distribution in proportion to PRS's bases in those assets, or $50x to the nondepreciable asset and $50x to the equipment. Thus, A will have a $10x built-in gain in the nondepreciable asset ($60x value less $50x basis) and a $10x built-in loss in the equipment ($50x basis less $40x value), which it expects to recover rapidly through cost recovery deductions. In selecting the assets to be distributed to A, the partners had a principal purpose to take advantage of the fact that A's basis in the assets will be determined by reference to A's basis in A's partnership interest, thus, in effect, shifting a portion of A's basis from the nondepreciable asset to the equipment, which in turn would allow A to recover that portion of its basis more rapidly. This shift provides a federal tax timing advantage to A, with no offsetting detriment to B or C.

(ii) Subchapter K is intended to permit taxpayers to conduct joint business activity through a flexible economic arrangement without incurring an entity-level tax. See paragraph (a) of this section. The decision to organize and conduct business through PRS is consistent with this intent. In addition, on these facts, the requirements of paragraphs (a)(1) and (2) of this section have been satisfied. The validity of the tax treatment of this transaction is therefore dependent upon whether the transaction satisfies (or is treated as satisfying) the proper reflection of income standard under paragraph (a)(3) of this section. Subchapter K is generally intended to produce tax consequences that achieve proper reflection of income. However, paragraph (a)(3) of this section provides that if the application of a provision of subchapter K produces tax results that do not properly reflect income, but the application of that provision to the transaction and the ultimate tax results, taking into account all the relevant facts and circumstances, are clearly contemplated by that provision (and the transaction satisfies the requirements of paragraphs (a)(1) and (2) of this section), then the application of that provision to the transaction will be treated as satisfying the proper reflection of income standard.

(iii) A's basis in the assets distributed to it was determined under section 732(b) and (c). The transaction does not properly reflect A's income due to the basis distortions caused by the distribution and the shifting of basis from a nondepreciable to a depreciable asset. However, the basis rules under section 732, which in some situations can produce tax results that are inconsistent with the proper reflection of income standard (see paragraph (a)(3) of this section), are intended to provide simplifying administrative rules for bona fide partnerships that are engaged in transactions with a substantial business purpose. Taking into account all the facts and circumstances of the transaction, the application of the basis rules under section 732 to the distribution from PRS to A, and the ultimate tax consequences of the application of that provision of subchapter K, are clearly contemplated. Thus, the application of section 732 to this transaction will be treated as satisfying the proper reflection of income standard under paragraph (a)(3) of this section. The Commissioner therefore cannot invoke paragraph (b) of this section to recast the transaction.

Example 11. Basis adjustments under section 732; plan or arrangement to distort basis allocations artificially; use of partnership not consistent with the intent of subchapter K. (i) Partnership PRS has for several years been engaged in the development and management of commercial real estate projects. X, an unrelated party, desires to acquire undeveloped land owned by PRS, which has a value of \$95*x* and a basis of \$5*x*. X expects to hold the land indefinitely after its acquisition. Pursuant to a plan a principal purpose of which is to permit X to acquire and hold the land but nevertheless to recover for tax purposes a substantial portion of the purchase price for the land, X contributes \$100*x* to PRS for an interest therein. Subsequently (at a time when the value of the partnership's assets have not materially changed), PRS distributes to X in liquidation of its interest in PRS the land and another asset with a value and basis to PRS of \$5*x*. The second asset is an insignificant part of the economic transaction but is important to achieve the desired tax results. Under section 732(b) and (c), X's \$100*x* basis in its partnership interest is allocated between the assets distributed to it in proportion to their bases to PRS, or \$50*x* each. Thereafter, X plans to sell the second asset for its value of \$5*x*, recognizing a loss of \$45*x*. In this manner, X will, in effect, recover a substantial portion of the purchase price of the land almost immediately. In selecting the assets to be distributed to X, the partners had a principal purpose to take advantage of the fact that X's basis in the assets will be determined under section 732(b) and (c), thus, in effect, shifting a portion of X's basis economically allocable to the land that X intends to retain to an inconsequential asset that X intends to dispose of quickly. This shift provides a federal tax timing advantage to X, with no offsetting detriment to any of PRS's other partners.

(ii) Although section 732 recognizes that basis distortions can occur in certain situations, which may produce tax results that do not satisfy the proper reflection of income standard of paragraph (a)(3) of this section, the provision is intended only to provide ancillary, simplifying tax results for bona fide partnership transactions that are engaged in for substantial business purposes. Section 732 is not intended to serve as the basis for plans or arrangements in which inconsequential or immaterial assets are included in the distribution with a principal purpose of obtaining substantially favorable tax results by virtue of the statute's simplifying rules. The transaction does not properly reflect X's income due to the basis distortions caused by the distribution that result in shifting a significant portion of X's basis to this inconsequential asset. Moreover, the proper reflection of income standard contained in paragraph (a)(3) of this section is not treated as satisfied, because, taking into account all the facts and circumstances, the application of section 732 to this arrangement, and the ultimate tax consequences that would thereby result, were not clearly contemplated by that provision of subchapter K. In addition, by using a partnership (if respected), the partners' aggregate federal tax liability would be substantially less than had they owned the partnership's assets directly (see paragraph (c)(1) of this section). On these facts, PRS has been formed and availed of with a principal purpose to reduce the taxpayers' aggregate federal tax liability in a manner that is inconsistent with the intent of subchapter K. Therefore (in addition to possibly challenging the transaction under applicable judicial principles and statutory authorities, such as the disguised sale rules under section 707, see paragraph (h) of this section), the Commissioner can recast the transaction as appropriate under paragraph (b) of this section.

(e) *Abuse of entity treatment.*—(1) *General rule.*—The Commissioner can treat a partnership as an aggregate of its partners in whole or in part as appropriate to carry out the purpose of any provision of the Internal Revenue Code or the regulations promulgated thereunder.

(2) *Clearly contemplated entity treatment.*—Paragraph (e)(1) of this section does not apply to the extent that—

(i) A provision of the Internal Revenue Code or the regulations promulgated thereunder prescribes the treatment of a partnership as an entity, in whole or in part, and

(ii) That treatment and the ultimate tax results, taking into account all the relevant facts and circumstances, are clearly contemplated by that provision.

* * *

(h) *Scope and application.*—This section applies solely with respect to taxes under subtitle A of the Internal Revenue Code, and for purposes of this section, any reference to a federal tax is limited to any tax imposed under subtitle A of the Internal Revenue Code.

* * *

[Reg. § 1.701-2.]

☐ [*T.D.* 8588, 12-29-94. *Amended by T.D.* 8592, 4-12-95.]

§ 1.702-1. Income and credits of partner.—(a) *General rule.*—Each partner is required to take into account separately in his return his distributive share, whether or not distributed, of each class or item of partnership income, gain, loss, deduction, or credit described in subparagraphs (1) through (9) of this paragraph. (For the taxable year in which a partner includes his distributive share of partnership taxable income, see section 706(a) and § 1.706-1(a). Such distributive share shall be determined as provided in section 704 and § 1.704-1.) Accordingly, in determining his income tax:

(1) Each partner shall take into account, as part of his gains and losses from sales or exchanges of capital assets held for not more than 1 year (6 months for taxable years beginning before 1977; 9 months for taxable years beginning in 1977), his distributive share of the combined net amount of such gains and losses of the partnership.

(2) Each partner shall take into account, as part of his gains and losses from sales or exchanges of capital assets held for more than 1 year (6 months for taxable years beginning before 1977; 9 months for taxable years beginning in 1977), his distributive share of the combined net amount of such gains and losses of the partnership.

(3) Each partner shall take into account, as part of his gains and losses from sales or exchanges of property described in section 1231 (relating to property used in the trade or business and involuntary conversions), his distributive share of the combined net amount of such gains and losses of the partnership. The partnership shall not combine such items with items set forth in subparagraph (1) or (2) of this paragraph.

(4) Each partner shall take into account, as part of the charitable contributions paid by him, his distributive share of each class of charitable contributions paid by the partnership within the partnership's taxable year. Section 170 determines the extent to which such amount may be allowed as a deduction to the partner. For the definition of the term "charitable contribution", see section 170(c).

(5) Each partner shall take into account, as part of the dividends received by him from domestic corporations, his distributive share of dividends received by the partnership, with respect to which the partner is entitled to a credit under section 34 (for dividends received on or before December 31, 1964), an exclusion under section 116, or a deduction under part VIII, subchapter B, chapter 1 of the Code.

(6) Each partner shall take into account, as part of his taxes described in section 901 which have been paid or accrued to foreign countries or to possessions of the United States, his distributive share of such taxes which have been paid or accrued by the partnership, according to its method of treating such taxes. A partner may elect to treat his total amount of such taxes, including his distributive share of such taxes of the partnership, as a deduction under section 164 or as a credit under section 901, the subject to the provisions of sections 901 through 905.

(7) Each partner shall take into account, as part of the partially tax-exempt interest received by him on obligations of the United States or on obligations of instrumentalities of

the United States, as described in section 35 or section 242, his distributive share of such partially tax-exempt interest received by the partnership. However, if the partnership elects to amortize premiums on bonds as provided in section 171, the amount received on such obligations by the partnership shall be reduced by the amortizable bond premium applicable to such obligations as provided in section 171(a)(3).

(8)(i) Each partner shall take into account separately, as part of any class of income, gain, loss, deduction, or credit, his distributive share of the following items: recoveries of bad debts, prior taxes, and delinquency amounts (section 111); gains and losses from wagering transactions (section 165(d)); soil and water conservation expenditures (section 175); nonbusiness expenses as described in section 212; medical, dental, etc., expenses (section 213); expenses for care of certain dependents (section 214); alimony, etc., payments (section 215); amounts representing taxes and interest paid to cooperative housing corporations (section 216); intangible drilling and developments costs (section 263(c)); pre-1970 exploration expenditures (section 615); certain mining exploration expenditures (section 617); income, gain, or loss to the partnership under section 751(b); and any items of income, gain, loss, deduction, or credit subject to a special allocation under the partnership agreement which differs from the allocation of partnership taxable income or loss generally.

(ii) Each partner must also take into account separately the partner's distributive share of any partnership item which, if separately taken into account by any partner, would result in an income tax liability for that partner, or for any other person, different from that which would result if that partner did not take the item into account separately. Thus, if any partner is a controlled foreign corporation, as defined in section 957, items of income that would be gross subpart F income if separately taken into account by the controlled foreign corporation must be separately stated for all partners. Under section 911(a), if any partner is a bona fide resident of a foreign country who may exclude from gross income the part of the partner's distributive share which qualifies as earned income, as defined in section 911(b), the earned income of the partnership for all partners must be separately stated. Similarly, all relevant items of income or deduction of the partnership must be separately stated for all partners in determining the applicability of section 183 (relating to activities not engaged in for profit) and the recomputation of tax thereunder for any partner. This paragraph (a)(8)(ii) applies to taxable years beginning on or after July 23, 2002.

(iii) Each partner shall aggregate the amount of his separate deductions or exclusions and his distributive share of partnership deductions or exclusions separately stated in determining the amount allowable to him of any deduction or exclusion under subtitle A of the Code as to which a limitation is imposed. For example, partner A has individual domestic exploration expenditures of $300,000. He is also a member of the AB partnership which in 1971, in its first year of operation has foreign exploration expenditures of $400,000. A's distributable share of this item is $200,000. However, the total amount of his distributable share that A can deduct as exploration expenditures under section 617(a) is limited to $100,000 in view of the limitation provided in section 617(h). Therefore, the excess of $100,000 ($200,000 minus $100,000) is not deductible by A.

(9) Each partner shall also take into account separately his distributive share of the taxable income or loss of the partnership, exclusive of items requiring separate computations under subparagraphs (1) through (8) of this paragraph. For limitation on allowance of a partner's distributive share of partnership losses, see section 704(d) and paragraph (d) of § 1.704-1.

(b) *Character of items constituting distributive share.*—The character in the hands of a partner of any item of income, gain, loss, deduction, or credit described in section 702(a)(1) through (8) shall be determined as if such item were realized directly from the source from which realized by the partnership or incurred in the same manner as incurred by the partnership. For example, a partner's distributive share of gain from the sale of depreciable property used in the trade or business of the partnership shall be considered as gain from the sale of such depreciable property in the hands of the partner. Similarly, a partner's distributive share of partnership "hobby losses" (section 270) or his distributive share of partnership charitable contributions to organizations qualifying under section 170(b)(1)(A) retains such character in the hands of the partner.

(c) *Gross income of a partner.*—(1) Where it is necessary to determine the amount or character of the gross income of a partner, his gross income shall include the partner's distributive share of the gross income of the partnership, that is, the amount of gross income of the partnership from which was derived the partner's distributive share of partnership taxable income or loss (including items described in section 702(a)(1) through (8)). For example, a partner is required to include his distributive share of partnership gross income:

(i) In computing his gross income for the purpose of determining the necessity of filing a return (section 6012(a));

(ii) In determining the application of the provisions permitting the spreading of income for services rendered over a 36-month period (section 1301, as in effect for taxable years beginning before January 1, 1964);

(iii) In computing the amount of gross income received from sources within possessions of the United States (section 937);

(iv) In determining a partner's "gross income from farming" (sections 175 and 6073); and

(v) In determining whether the de minimis or full inclusion rules of section 954(b)(3) apply.

(2) In determining the applicability of the 6-year period of limitation on assessment and collection provided in section 6501(e) (relating to omission of more than 25 percent of gross income), a partner's gross income includes his distributive share of partnership gross income (as described in section 6501(e)(1)(A)(i)). In this respect, the amount of partnership gross income from which was derived the partner's distributive share of any item of partnership income, gain, loss, deduction, or credit (as included or disclosed in the partner's return) is considered as an amount of gross income stated in the partner's return for the purposes of section 6501(e). For example, A, who is entitled to one-fourth of the profits of the ABCD partnership, which has $10,000 gross income and $2,000 taxable income, reports only $300 as his distributive share of partnership profits. A should have shown $500 as his distributive share of profits, which amount was derived from $2,500 of partnership gross income. However, since A included only $300 on his return without explaining in the return the difference of $200, he is regarded as having stated in his return only $1,500 ($300/$500 of $2,500) as gross income from the partnership.

(d) *Partners in community property States.*—If separate returns are made by a husband and wife domiciled in a community property State, and only one spouse is a member of the partnership, the part of his or her distributive share of any item or items listed in paragraph (a)(1) through (9) of this section which is community property, or which is derived from community property, should be reported by the husband and wife in equal proportions.

* * *

[Reg. § 1.702-1.]

☐ [*T.D.* 6175, 5-23-56. *Amended by T.D.* 6605, 8-14-62; *T.D.* 6777, 12-15-64; *T.D.* 6885, 6-1-66; *T.D.* 7192, 6-29-72; *T.D.* 7564, 9-11-78; *T.D.* 7728, 10-31-80; *T.D.* 8247, 4-5-89; *T.D.* 8348, 5-10-91; *T.D.* 9008, 7-22-2002 *and T.D.* 9194, 4-6-2005.]

§ 1.702-2. Net operating loss deduction of partner.—For the purpose of determining a net operating loss deduction under section 172, a partner shall take into account his distributive share of items of income, gain, loss, deduction, or credit of the partnership. The character of any such item shall be determined as if such item were realized directly from the source from which realized by the partnership, or incurred in the same manner as incurred by the partnership. See section 702(b) and paragraph (b) of § 1.702-1. To the extent necessary to determine the allowance under section 172(d)(4) of the nonbusiness deductions of a partner (arising from both partnership and nonpartnership sources), the partner shall separately take into account his distributive share of the deductions of the partnership which are not attributable to a trade or business and combine such amount with his nonbusiness deductions from nonpartnership sources. Such partner shall also separately take into account his distributive share of the gross income of the partnership not derived from a trade or business and combine such amount with his nonbusiness income from nonpartnership sources. See section 172 and the regulations thereunder. [Reg. § 1.702-2.]

☐ [*T.D.* 6175, 5-23-56.]

§ 1.703-1. Partnership computations.—(a) *Income and deductions.*—(1) The taxable income of a partnership shall be computed in the same manner as the taxable income of an individual, except as otherwise provided in this section. A partnership is required to state separately in its return the items described in section 702(a)(1) through (7) and, in addition, to attach to its return a statement setting forth separately those items described in section 702(a)(8) which the partner is required to take into account separately in determining his income tax. See paragraph (a)(8) of § 1.702-1. The partnership is further required to compute and to state separately in its return:

(i) As taxable income under section 702(a)(9), the total of all other items of gross income (not separately stated) over the total of all other allowable deductions (not separately stated), or

(ii) As loss under section 702(a)(9), the total of all other allowable deductions (not separately stated) over the total of all other items of gross income (not separately stated).

The taxable income or loss so computed shall be accounted for by the partners in accordance with their partnership agreement.

(2) The partnership is not allowed the following deductions:

(i) The standard deduction provided in section 141.

(ii) The deduction for personal exemptions provided in section 151.

(iii) The deduction provided in section 164(a) for taxes, described in section 901, paid or accrued to foreign countries or possessions of the United States. Each partner's distributive share of such taxes shall be accounted for separately by him as provided in section 702(a)(6).

(iv) The deduction for charitable contributions provided in section 170. Each partner is considered as having paid within his taxable year his distributive share of any contribution or gift, payment of which was actually made by the partnership within its taxable year ending within or with the partner's taxable year. This item shall be accounted for separately by the partners as provided in section 702(a)(4). See also paragraph (b) of § 1.702-1.

(v) The net operating loss deduction provided in section 172. See § 1.702-2.

(vi) The additional itemized deductions for individuals provided in Part VII of Subchapter B, Chapter 1 of the Code, as follows: expenses for production of income (section 212); medical, dental, etc., expenses (section 213); Expenses for care of certain dependents (section 214); alimony, etc., payments (section 215); and amounts representing taxes and interest paid to cooperative housing corporation (section 216). However, see paragraph (a)(8) of § 1.702-1.

(vii) The deduction for depletion under section 611 with respect to domestic oil or gas which is produced after December 31, 1974, and to which gross income from the property is attributable after such year.

(viii) The deduction for capital gains provided by section 1202 and the deduction for capital loss carryover provided by section 1212.

(b) *Elections of the partnership.*—(1) *General rule.*—Any elections (other than those described in subparagraph (2) of this paragraph) affecting the computation of income derived from a partnership shall be made by the partnership. For example, elections of methods of accounting, of computing depreciation, of treating soil and water conservation expenditures, and the option to deduct as expenses intangible drilling and development costs, shall be made by the partnership and not by the partners separately. All partnership elections are applicable to all partners equally, but any election made by a partnership shall not apply to any partner's nonpartnership interests.

(2) *Exceptions.*—(i) Each partner shall add his distributive share of taxes described in section 901 paid or accrued by the partnership to foreign countries or possessions of the United States (according to its method of treating such taxes) to any such taxes paid or accrued by him (according to his method of treating such taxes), and may elect to use the total amount either as a credit against tax or as a deduction from income.

(ii) Each partner shall add his distributive share of expenses described in section 615 or section 617 paid or accrued by the partnership to any such expenses paid or accrued by him and shall treat the total amount according to his method of treating such expenses, notwithstanding the treatment of the expenses by the partnership.

(iii) Each partner who is a nonresident alien individual or a foreign corporation shall add his distributive share of income derived by the partnership from real property located in the United States, as described in section 871(d)(1) or 882(d)(1), to any such income derived by him and may elect under § 1.871-10 to treat all such income as income which is effectively connected for the taxable year with the conduct of a trade or business in the United States. [Reg. § 1.703-1.]

☐ [*T.D.* 6175, 5-23-56. *Amended by T.D.* 7192, 6-29-72, *T.D.* 7332, 12-20-74 *and T.D.* 8348, 5-10-91.]

§ 1.704-1. Partner's distributive share.—(a) *Effect of partnership agreement.*—A partner's distributive share of any item or class of items of income, gain, loss, deduction, or credit of the partnership shall be determined by the partnership agreement, unless otherwise provided by section 704 and paragraphs (b) through (e) of this section. For definition of partnership agreement see section 761(c).

(b) *Determination of partner's distributive share.*—(0) *Cross-references.*

Table 1 to paragraph (b)(0)

Heading	*Section*
Cross-references	1.704-1(b)(0)
In general	1.704-1(b)(1)
Basic principles	1.704-1(b)(1)(i)
Effective dates	1.704-1(b)(1)(ii)
Generally	1.704-1(b)(1)(ii)*(a)*
Foreign tax expenditures	1.704-1(b)(1)(ii)*(b)*
In general	1.704-1(b)(1)(ii)*(b)*(*1*)
Special rules for certain interbranch payments	1.704-1(b)(1)(ii)*(b)*(*3*)
Effect of other sections	1.704-1(b)(1)(iii)
Other possible tax consequences	1.704-1(b)(1)(iv)
Purported allocations	1.704-1(b)(1)(v)
Section 704(c) determinations	1.704-1(b)(1)(vi)
Bottom line allocations	1.704-1(b)(1)(vii)
Substantial economic effect	1.704-1(b)(2)
Two-part analysis	1.704-1(b)(2)(i)
Economic effect	1.704-1(b)(2)(ii)
Fundamental principles	1.704-1(b)(2)(ii)*(a)*
Three requirements	1.704-1(b)(2)(ii)*(b)*

(0)(1) *In general.*—(i) *Basic principles.*—Under section 704(b) if a partnership agreement does not provide for the allocation of income, gain, loss, deduction, or credit (or item thereof) to a partner, or if the partnership agreement provides for the allocation of income, gain, loss, deduction, or credit (or item thereof) to a partner but such allocation does not have substantial economic effect, then the partner's distributive share of such income, gain, loss, deduction, or credit (or item thereof) shall be determined in accordance with such partner's interest in the partnership (taking into account all facts and circumstances). If the partnership agreement provides for the allocation of income, gain, loss, deduction, or credit (or item thereof) to a partner, there are three ways in which such allocation will be respected under section 704(b) and this paragraph. First, the allocation can have substantial economic effect in accordance with paragraph (b)(2) of this section. Second, taking into account all facts and circumstances, the allocation can be in accordance with the partner's interest in the partnership. See paragraph (b)(3) of this section. Third, the allocation can be deemed to be in accordance with the partner's interest in the partnership pursuant to one of the special rules contained in paragraph (b)(4) of this section and § 1.704-2. To the extent an allocation under the partnership agreement of income, gain, loss, deduction, or credit (or item thereof) to a partner does not have substantial economic effect, is not in accordance with the partner's interest in the partnership, and is not deemed to be in accordance with the partner's interest in the partnership, such income, gain, loss, deduction, or credit (or item thereof) will be reallocated in accordance with the partner's interest in the partnership (determined under paragraph (b)(3) of this section).

* * *

(iii) *Effect of other sections.*—The determination of a partner's distributive share of income, gain, loss, deduction, or credit (or item thereof) under section 704(b) and this paragraph is not conclusive as to the tax treatment of a partner with respect to such distributive share. For example, an allocation of loss or deduction to a partner that is respected under section 704(b) and this paragraph may not be deductible by such partner if the partner lacks the requisite motive for economic gain (see, *e.g.*, *Goldstein v. Commissioner*, 364 F.2d 734 (2d Cir. 1966)), or may be disallowed for that taxable year (and held in suspense) if the limitations of section 465 or section 704(d) are applicable. Similarly, an allocation that is respected under section 704(b) and this paragraph nevertheless may be reallocated under other provisions, such as section 482, section 704(e)(2), section 706(d) (and related assignment of income principles), and paragraph (b)(2)(ii) of § 1.751-1. If a partnership has a section 754 election in effect, a partner's distributive share of partnership income, gain, loss, or deduction may be affected as provided in § 1.743-1 (see paragraph (b)(2)(iv)(*m*)(*2*) of this section). A deduction that appears to be a nonrecourse deduction deemed to be in accordance with the partners' interests in the partnership may not be such because purported nonrecourse liabilities of the partnership in fact constitute equity rather than debt. The examples in paragraph (b)(5) of this section concern the validity of allocations under section 704(b) and this paragraph and, except as noted, do not address the effect of other sections or limitations on such allocations.

(iv) *Other possible tax consequences.*—Allocations that are respected under section 704(b) and this paragraph may give rise to other tax consequences, such as those resulting from the application of section 61, section 83, section 751, section 2501, paragraph (f) of § 1.46-3, § 1.47-6, paragraph (b)(1) of § 1.721-1 (and related principles), and paragraph (e) of § 1.752-1. The examples in paragraph (b)(5) of this section concern the validity of allocations under section 704(b) and this paragraph and, except as noted, do not address other tax consequences that may result from such allocations.

(v) *Purported allocations.*—Section 704(b) and this paragraph do not apply to a purported allocation if it is made to a person who is not a partner of the partnership (see section 7701(a)(2) and paragraph (d) of § 301.7701-3) or to a person who is not receiving the purported allocation in his capacity as a partner (see section 707(a) and paragraph (a) of § 1.707-1).

(vi) *Section 704(c) determinations.*—Section 704(c) and § 1.704-3 generally require that if property is contributed by a partner to a partnership, the partners' distributive shares of income, gain, loss, and deduction, as computed for tax purposes, with respect to the property are determined so as to take account of the variation between the adjusted tax basis and fair market value of the property. Although section 704(b) does not directly determine the partners' distributive shares of tax items governed by section 704(c), the partners' distributive shares of tax items may be determined under section 704(c) and § 1.704-3 (depending on the allocation method chosen by the partnership under § 1.704-3) with reference to the partners' distributive shares of the corresponding book items, as determined under section 704(b) and this paragraph. (See paragraphs (b)(2)(iv)(*d*) and (b)(4)(i) of this section.) See § 1.704-3 for methods of making allocations under section 704(c), and § 1.704-3(d)(2) for a special rule in determining the amount of book items if the remedial allocation method is chosen by the partnership. See also paragraph (b)(5) *Example (13)* (i) of this section.

(vii) *Bottom line allocations.*—Section 704(b) and this paragraph are applicable to allocations of income, gain, loss, deduction, and credit, allocations of specific items of income, gain, loss, deduction, and credit, and allocations of partnerhip net or"bottom line" taxable income and loss. An allocation to a partner of a share of partnership net or "bottom line" taxable income or loss shall be treated as an allocation to such partner of the same share of each item of income, gain, loss, and deduction that is taken into account in computing such net or "bottom line" taxable income or loss. See example (15) (i) of paragraph (b) (5) of this section.

(2) *Substantial economic effect.*—(i) *Two-part analysis.*—The determination of whether an allocation of income, gain, loss, or deduction (or item thereof) to a partner has substantial economic effect involves a two-part analysis that is made as of the end of the partnership taxable year to which the allocation relates. First, the allocation must have economic effect (within the meaning of paragraph (b) (2) (ii) of this section). Second, the economic efect of the allocation must be substantial (within the meaning of paragraph (b) (2) (iii) of this section).

(ii) *Economic effect.*—*(a) Fundamental principles.*—In order for an allocation to have economic effect, it must be consistent with the underlying economic arrangement of the partners. This means that in the event there is an economic benefit or economic burden that corresponds to an allocation, the partner to whom the allocation is made must receive such economic benefit or bear such economic burden.

(b) Three requirements.—Based on the principles contained in paragraph (b) (2) (ii) (*a*) of this section, and except as otherwise provided in this paragraph, an allocation of income, gain, loss, or deduction (or item thereof) to a partner will have economic effect if, and only if, throughout the full term of the partnership, the partnership agreement provides—

(1) For the determination and maintenance of the partners' capital accounts in accordance with the rules of paragraph (b) (2) (iv) of this section,

(2) Upon liquidation of the partnership (or any partner's interest in the partnership), liquidating distributions are required in all cases to be made in accordance with the positive capital account balances of the partners, as determined after taking into account all capital account adjustments for the partnership taxable year during which such liquidation occurs (other than those made pursuant to this requirement (*2*) and requirement (*3*) of this paragraph (b) (2) (ii) (*b*)), by the end of such taxable year (or, if later, within 90 days after the date of such liquidation), and

(3) If such partner has a deficit balance in his capital account following the liquidation of his interest in the partnership, as determined after taking into account all capital account adjustments for the partnership taxable year during which such liquidation occurs (other than those made pursuant to this requirement (*3*)), he is unconditionally obligated to restore the amount of such deficit balance to the partnership by the end of such taxable year (or, if later, within 90 days after the date of such liquidation), which amount shall, upon liquidation of the partnership, be paid to creditors of the partnership or distributed to other partners in accordance with their positive capital account balances (in accordance with requirement (*2*) of this paragraph (b) (2) (ii) (*b*)). Notwithstanding the partnership agreement, an obligation to restore a deficit balance in a partner's capital account, including an obligation described in paragraph (b) (2) (ii) (*c*) (*1*) of this section, will not be respected for purposes of this section to the extent the obligation is disregarded under paragraph (b) (2) (ii) (*c*) (*4*) of this section.

(4) For purposes of paragraphs (b) (2) (ii) (*b*) (*1*) through (*3*) of this section, a partnership taxable year shall be determined without regard to section 706 (c) (2) (A).

(5) The requirements in paragraphs (b) (2) (ii) (*b*) (*2*) and (*3*) of this section are not violated if all or part of the partnership interest of one or more partners is purchased (other than in connection with the liquidation of the partnership) by the partnership or by one or more partners (or one or more persons related, within the meaning of section 267 (b) (without modification by section 267 (e) (1)) or section 707 (b) (1), to a partner) pursuant to an agreement negotiated at arm's length by persons who at the time such agreement is entered into have materially adverse interests and if a principal purpose of such purchase and sale is not to avoid the principles of the second sentence of paragraph (b) (2) (ii) (*a*) of this section.

(6) The requirement in paragraph (b) (2) (ii) (*b*) (*2*) of this section is not violated if, upon the liquidation of the partnership, the capital accounts of the partners are increased or decreased pursuant to paragraph (b) (2) (iv) (*f*) of this section as of the date of such liquidation and the partnership makes liquidating distributions within the time set out in the requirement in paragraph (b) (2) (ii) (*b*) (*2*) of this section in the ratios of the partners' positive capital accounts, except that it does not distribute reserves reasonably required to provide for liabilities (contingent or otherwise) of the partnership and installment obligations owed to the partnership, so long as such withheld amounts are distributed as soon as practicable and in the ratios of the partners' positive capital account balances.

(7) See *Examples 1.(i)* and *(ii), 4.(i), 8.(i)*, and *16.(i)* of paragraph (b)(5) of this section for issues concerning paragraph (b)(2)(ii)(*b*) of this section.

(c) Obligation to restore deficit.—(1) Other arrangements treated as obligations to restore deficits.—If a partner is not expressly obligated to restore the deficit balance in such partner's capital account, such partner nevertheless will be treated as obligated to restore the deficit balance in his capital account (in accordance with the requirement in paragraph (b)(2)(ii)(*b*)(*3*) of this section and subject to paragraph (b)(2)(ii)(*c*)(*2*) of this section) to the extent of—

(A) The outstanding principal balance of any promissory note (of which such partner is the maker) contributed to the partnership by such partner (other than a promissory note that is readily tradable on an established securities market), and

(B) The amount of any unconditional obligation of such partner (whether imposed by the partnership agreement or by state or local law) to make subsequent contributions to the partnership (other than pursuant to a promissory note of which such partner is the maker).

(2) Satisfaction requirement.—For purposes of paragraph (b)(2)(ii)(*c*)(*1*) of this section, a promissory note or unconditional obligation is taken into account only if it is required to be satisfied at a time no later than the end of the partnership taxable year in which such partner's interest is liquidated (or, if later, within 90 days after the date of such liquidation). If a promissory note referred to in paragraph (b)(2)(ii)(*c*)(*1*) of this section is negotiable, a partner will be considered required to satisfy such note within the time period specified in this paragraph (b)(2)(ii)(*c*)(*2*) if the partnership agreement provides that, in lieu of actual satisfaction, the partnership will retain such note and such partner will contribute to the partnership the excess, if any, of the outstanding principal balance of such note over its fair market value at the time of liquidation. See paragraph (b)(2)(iv)(*d*)(*2*) of this section. See *Examples 1.(ix)* and *(x)* of paragraph (b)(5) of this section.

(3) Related party notes.—For purposes of paragraph (b)(2) of this section, if a partner contributes a promissory note to the partnership during a partnership taxable year beginning after December 29, 1988, and the maker of such note is a person related to such partner (within the meaning of § 1.752-4(b)(1)), then such promissory note shall be treated as a promissory note of which such partner is the maker.

(4) Obligations disregarded.—(A) General rule.—A partner in no event will be considered obligated to restore the deficit balance in his capital account to the partnership (in accordance with the requirement in paragraph (b)(2)(ii)(*b*)(*3*) of this section) to the extent such partner's obligation is a bottom dollar payment obligation that is not recognized under § 1.752-2(b)(3) or is not legally enforceable, or the facts and circumstances otherwise indicate a plan to circumvent or avoid such obligation. See paragraphs (b)(2)(ii)(*f*), (b)(2)(ii)(*h*), and (b)(4)(vi) of this section for other rules regarding such obligation. To the extent a partner is not considered obligated to restore the deficit balance in the partner's capital account to the partnership (in accordance with the requirement in paragraph (b)(2)(ii)(*b*)(*3*) of this section), the obligation is disregarded and paragraph (b)(2) of this section and § 1.752-2 are applied as if the obligation did not exist.

(B) Factors indicating plan to circumvent or avoid obligation.—In the case of an obligation to restore a deficit balance in a partner's capital account upon liquidation of a partnership, paragraphs (b)(2)(ii)(*c*)(*4*)(B)(i) through (iv) of this section provide a non-exclusive list of factors that may indicate a plan to circumvent or avoid the obligation. For purposes of making determinations under this paragraph (b)(2)(ii)(*c*)(*4*), the weight to be given to any particular factor depends on the particular case and the presence or absence of any particular factor is not, in itself, necessarily indicative of whether or not the obligation is respected. The following factors are taken into consideration for purposes of this paragraph (b)(2):

(i) The partner is not subject to commercially reasonable provisions for enforcement and collection of the obligation.

(ii) The partner is not required to provide (either at the time the obligation is made or periodically) commercially reasonable documentation regarding the partner's financial condition to the partnership.

(iii) The obligation ends or could, by its terms, be terminated before the liquidation of the partner's interest in the partnership or when the partner's capital account as provided in § 1.704-1(b)(2)(iv) is negative other than when a transferee partner assumes the obligation.

(iv) The terms of the obligation are not provided to all the partners in the partnership in a timely manner.

(d) Alternate test for economic effect.—If—

(1) Requirements *(1)* and *(2)* of paragraph (b)(2)(ii)(*b*) of this section are satisfied, and

(2) The partner to whom an allocation is made is not obligated to restore the deficit balance in his capital account to the partnership (in accordance with requirement *(3)* of paragraph (b)(2)(ii)(*b*) of this section), or is obligated to restore only a limited dollar amount of such deficit balance, and

(3) The partnership agreement contains a "qualified income offset,"

such allocation will be considered to have economic effect under this paragraph (b)(2)(ii)(*d*) to the extent such allocation does not cause or increase a deficit balance in such partner's capital account (in excess of any limited dollar amount of such deficit balance that such partner is obligated to restore) as of the end of the partnership taxable year to which such allocation relates. In determining the extent to which the previous sentence is satisfied, such partner's capital account also shall be reduced for—

(4) Adjustments that, as of the end of such year, reasonably are expected to be made to such partner's capital account under paragraph (b)(2)(iv)(*k*) of this section for depletion allowances with respect to oil and gas properties of the partnership, and

(5) Allocations of loss and deduction that, as of the end of such year, reasonably are expected to be made to such partner pursuant to section 704(e)(2), section 706(d), and paragraph (b)(2)(ii) of § 1.751-1, and

(6) Distributions that, as of the end of such year, reasonably are expected to be made to such partner to the extent they exceed offsetting increases to such partner's capital account that reasonably are expected to occur during (or prior to) the partnership taxable years in which such distributions reasonably are expected to be made (other than increases pursuant to a minimum gain chargeback under paragraph (b)(4)(iv)(*e*) of this section or under § 1.704-2(f); however, increases to a partner's capital account pursuant to a minimum gain chargeback requirement are taken into account as an offset to distributions of nonrecourse liability proceeds that are reasonably expected to be made and that are allocable to an increase in partnership minimum gain).

For purposes of determining the amount of expected distributions and expected capital account increases described in *(6)* above, the rule set out in paragraph (b)(2)(iii)(*c*) of this section concerning the presumed value of partnership property shall apply. The partnership agreement contains a "qualified income offset" if, and only if, it provides that a partner who unexpectedly receives an adjustment, allocation, or distribution described in *(4)*, *(5)*, or *(6)* above, will be allocated items of income and gain (consisting of a pro rata portion of each item of partnership income, including gross income, and gain for such year) in an amount and manner sufficient to eliminate such deficit balance as quickly as possible. Allocations of items of income and gain made pursuant to the immediately preceding sentence shall be deemed to be made in accordance with the partners' interests in the partnership if requirements *(1)* and *(2)* of paragraph (b)(2)(ii)(*b*) of this section are satisfied. See examples (1)(iii), (iv), (v), (vi), (viii), (ix), and (x), (15), and (16)(ii) of paragraph (b)(5) of this section.

(e) Partial economic effect.—If only a portion of an allocation made to a partner with respect to a partnership taxable year has economic effect, both the portion that has economic effect and the portion that is reallocated shall consist of a proportionate share of all items that made up the allocation to such partner for such year. See examples (15)(ii) and (iii) of paragraph (b)(5) of this section.

(f) Reduction of obligation to restore.—If requirements *(1)* and *(2)* of paragraph (b)(2)(ii)(*b*) of this section are satisfied, a partner's obligation to restore the deficit balance in his capital account (or any limited dollar amount thereof) to the partnership may be eliminated or reduced as of the end of a partnership taxable year without affecting the validity of prior allocations (see paragraph (b)(4)(vi) of this section) to the extent the deficit balance (if any) in such partner's capital account, after reduction for the items described in *(4)*, *(5)*, and *(6)* of paragraph (b)(2)(ii)(*d*) of this section, will not exceed the partner's remaining obligation (if any) to restore the deficit balance in his capital account. See example (l)(viii) of paragraph (b)(5) of this section.

(g) Liquidation defined.—For purposes of this paragraph, a liquidation of a partner's interest in the partnership occurs upon the earlier of *(1)* the date upon which there is a liquidation of the partnership, or *(2)* the date upon which there is a liquidation of the partner's interest in the partnership under paragraph (d) of § 1.761-1. For purposes of this paragraph, the liquidation of a partnership occurs upon the earlier of *(3)* the date upon which the partnership is terminated under section 708(b)(1), or *(4)* the date upon which the partnership ceases to be a going concern (even though it may continue in existence for the purpose of winding up its affairs, paying its debts, and distributing any remaining balance to its partners). Requirements *(2)* and *(3)* of

paragraph (b)(2)(ii)(*b*) of this section will be considered unsatisfied if the liquidation of a partner's interest in the partnership is delayed after its primary business activities have been terminated (for example, by continuing to engage in a relatively minor amount of business activity, if such actions themselves do not cause the partnership to terminate pursuant to section 708(b)(1)) for a principal purpose of deferring any distribution pursuant to requirement (*2*) of paragraph (b)(2)(ii)(*b*) of this section or deferring any partner's obligation under requirement (*3*) of paragraph (b)(2)(ii)(*b*) of this section.

(h) Partnership agreement defined.—For purposes of this paragraph, the partnership agreement includes all agreements among the partners, or between one or more partners and the partnership, concerning affairs of the partnership and responsibilities of partners, whether oral or written, and whether or not embodied in a document referred to by the partners as the partnership agreement. Thus, in determining whether distributions are required in all cases to be made in accordance with the partners' positive capital account balances (requirement (*2*) of paragraph (b)(2)(ii)(*b*) of this section), and in determining the extent to which a partner is obligated to restore a deficit balance in his capital account (requirement (*3*) of paragraph (b)(2)(ii)(*b*) of this section), all arrangements among partners, or between one or more partners and the partnership relating to the partnership, direct and indirect, including puts, options, and other buy-sell agreements, and any other "stop-loss" arrangement, are considered to be part of the partnership agreement. (Thus, for example, if one partner who assumes a liability of the partnership is indemnified by another partner for a portion of such liability, the indemnifying partner (depending upon the particular facts) may be viewed as in effect having a partial deficit makeup obligation as a result of such indemnity agreement.) In addition, the partnership agreement includes provisions of Federal, State, or local law that govern the affairs of the partnership or are considered under such law to be a part of the partnership agreement (see the last sentence of paragraph (c) of § 1.761-1). For purposes of this paragraph (b)(2)(ii)(*h*), an agreement with a partner or a partnership shall include an agreement with a person related, within the meaning of section 267(b) (without modification by section 267(e)(1)) or section 707(b)(1), to such partner or partnership. For purposes of the preceding sentence, sections 267(b) and 707(b)(1) shall be applied for partnership taxable years beginning after December 29, 1988, by (*1*) substituting "80 percent or more" for "more than 50 percent" each place it appears in such sections, (*2*) excluding brothers and sisters from the members of a person's family, and (*3*) disregarding section 267(f)(1)(A).

(i) Economic effect equivalence.—Allocations made to a partner that do not otherwise have economic effect under this paragraph (b)(2)(ii) shall nevertheless be deemed to have economic effect, provided that as of the end of each partnership taxable year a liquidation of the partnership at the end of such year or at the end of any future year would produce the same economic results to the partners as would occur if requirements (*1*), (*2*), and (*3*) of paragraph (b)(2)(ii)(*b*) of this section had been satisfied, regardless of the economic performance of the partnership. See examples (4)(ii) and (iii) of paragraph (b)(5) of this section.

(iii) *Substantiality.—(a) General rules.*—Except as otherwise provided in this paragraph (b)(2)(iii), the economic effect of an allocation (or allocations) is substantial if there is a reasonable possibility that the allocation (or allocations) will affect substantially the dollar amounts to be received by the partners from the partnership, independent of tax consequences. Notwithstanding the preceding sentence, the economic effect of an allocation (or allocations) is not substantial if, at the time the allocation becomes part of the partnership agreement, (*1*) the after-tax economic consequences of at least one partner may, in present value terms, be enhanced compared to such consequences if the allocation (or allocations) were not contained in the partnership agreement, and (*2*) there is a strong likelihood that the after-tax economic consequences of no partner will, in present value terms, be substantially diminished compared to such consequences if the allocation (or allocations) were not contained in the partnership agreement. In determining the after-tax economic benefit or detriment to a partner, tax consequences that result from the interaction of the allocation with such partner's tax attributes that are unrelated to the partnership will be taken into account. See examples (5) and (9) of paragraph (b)(5) of this section. The economic effect of an allocation is not substantial in the two situations described in paragraphs (b)(2)(iii)(*b*) and (*c*) of this section. However, even if an allocation is not described therein, its economic effect may be insubstantial under the general rules stated in this paragraph (b)(2)(iii)(*a*). References in this paragraph (b)(2)(iii) to allocations includes capital account adjustments made pursuant to paragraph (b)(2)(iv)(*k*) of this section. References in this paragraph (b)(2)(iii) to a comparison to consequences arising if an allocation (or allocations) were not contained in the partnership agreement mean that the allocation (or allocations) is determined in accordance with the partners' interests in the partnership (within the meaning of paragraph (b)(3) of this section), disregarding the allocation (or allocations) being tested under this paragraph (b)(2)(iii).

(b) Shifting tax consequences.—The economic effect of an allocation (or allocations) in a partnership taxable year is not substantial if, at the time the allocation (or allocations) becomes part of the partnership agreement, there is a strong likelihood that—

(1) The net increases and decreases that will be recorded in the partners' respective capital accounts for such taxable year will not differ substantially from the net increases and decreases that would be recorded in such partners' respective capital accounts for such year if the allocations were not contained in the partnership agreement, and

(2) The total tax liability of the partners (for their respective taxable years in which the allocations will be taken into account) will be less than if the allocations were not contained in the partnership agreement (taking into account tax consequences that result from the interaction of the allocation (or allocations) with partner tax attributes that are unrelated to the partnership).

If, at the end of a partnership taxable year to which an allocation (or allocations) relates, the net increases and decreases that are recorded in the partners' respective capital accounts do not differ substantially from the net increases and decreases that would have been recorded in such partners' respective capital accounts had the allocation (or allocations) not been contained in the partnership agreement, and the total tax liability of the partners is (as described in (*2*) above) less than it would have been had the allocation (or allocations) not been contained in the partnership agreement, it will be presumed that, at the time the allocation (or allocations) became part of such partnership agreement, there was a strong likelihood that these results would occur. This presumption may be overcome by a showing of facts and circumstances that prove otherwise. See examples (6), (7)(ii) and (iii), and (10)(ii) of paragraph (b)(5) of this section.

(c) Transitory allocations.—If a partnership agreement provides for the possibility that one or more allocations (the "original allocation(s)") will be largely offset by one or more other allocations (the "offsetting allocations(s)"), and, at the time the allocations become part of the partnership agreement, there is a strong likelihood that—

(1) The net increases and decreases that will be recorded in the partners' respective capital accounts for the taxable years to which the allocations relate will not differ substantially from the net increases and decreases that would be recorded in such partners' respective capital accounts for such years if the original allocation(s) and offsetting allocation(s) were not contained in the partnership agreement, and

(2) The total tax liability of the partners (for their respective taxable years in which the allocations will be taken into account) will be less than if the allocations were not contained in the partnership agreement (taking into account tax consequences that result from the interaction of the allocation (or allocations) with partner tax attributes that are unrelated to the partnership)

the economic effect of the original allocation(s) and offsetting allocation(s) will not be substantial. If, at the end of a partnership taxable year to which an offsetting allocation(s) relates, the net increases and decreases recorded in the partners' respective capital accounts do not differ substantially from the net increases and decreases that would have been recorded in such partners' respective capital accounts had the original allocation(s) and the offsetting allocation(s) not been contained in the partnership agreement, and the total tax liability of the partners is (as described in (*2*) above) less than it would have been had such allocations not been contained in the partnership agreement, it will be presumed that, at the time the allocations became part of the partnership agreement, there was a strong likelihood that these results would occur. This presumption may be overcome by a showing of facts and circumstances that prove otherwise. See examples (1)(xi), (2), (3), (7), (8)(ii), and (17) of paragraph (b)(5) of this section. Notwithstanding the foregoing, the original allocation(s) and the offsetting allocation(s) will not be insubstantial (under this paragraph (b)(2)(iii)(*c*)) and, for purposes of paragraph (b)(2)(iii)(*a*), it will be presumed that there is a reasonable possibility that the allocations will affect substantially the dollar amounts to be received by the partners from the partnership if, at the time the allocations become part of the partnership agreement, there is a strong likelihood that the offsetting allocation(s) will not, in large part, be made within five years after the original allocation(s) is made (determined on a first-in, first-out basis). See example (2) of paragraph (b)(5) of this section. For purposes of applying the provisions of this paragraph (b)(2)(iii) (and paragraphs (b)(2)(ii)(*d*)(*6*) and (b)(3)(iii) of this section), the adjusted tax basis of partnership property (or, if partnership property is properly reflected on the books of the partnership at a book value that differs from its adjusted tax basis, the book value of such property) will be presumed to be the fair market value of such property, and adjustments to the adjusted tax basis (or book value) of such property will be presumed to be matched by corresponding changes in such property's fair market value. Thus, there cannot be a strong likelihood that the economic effect of an allocation (or allocations) will be largely offset by an allocation (or allocations) of gain or loss from the disposition of partnership property. See examples (1)(vi) and (xi) of paragraph (b)(5) of this section.

(d) Partners that are look-through entities or members of a consolidated group.—(1) In general.—For purposes of applying paragraphs (b)(2)(iii)(*a*), (*b*), and (*c*) of this section to a partner that is a look-through entity, the tax consequences that result from the interaction of the allocation with the tax attributes of any person that is an owner, or in the case of a trust or estate, the beneficiary, of an interest in such a partner, whether directly or indirectly through one or more look-through entities, must be taken into account. For purposes of applying paragraphs (b)(2)(iii)(*a*), (*b*), and (*c*) of this section to a partner that is a member of a consolidated group (within the meaning of §1.1502- 1(h)), the tax consequences that result from the interaction of the allocation with the tax attributes of the consolidated group and with the tax attributes of another member with respect to a separate return year must be taken into account. See paragraph (b)(5) *Example 29* of this section.

(2) Look-through entity.—For purposes of this paragraph (b)(2)(iii)(*d*), a *look-through entity* means—

(i) A partnership;

(ii) A subchapter S corporation;

(iii) A trust or an estate;

(iv) An entity that is disregarded for Federal tax purposes, such as a qualified subchapter S subsidiary under section 1361(b)(3), an entity that is disregarded as an entity separate from its owner under §§301.7701-1 through 301.7701-3 of this chapter, or a qualified REIT subsidiary within the meaning of section 856(i)(2); or

(v) A controlled foreign corporation if United States shareholders of the controlled foreign corporation in the aggregate own, directly or indirectly, at least 10 percent of the capital or profits of the partnership on any day during the partnership's taxable year. In such case, the controlled foreign corporation shall be treated as a look-through entity, but only with respect to allocations of income, gain, loss, or deduction (or items thereof) that enter into the computation of a United States shareholder's inclusion under section 951(a) with respect to the controlled foreign corporation, enter into any person's income attributable to a United States shareholder's inclusion under section 951(a) with respect to the controlled foreign corporation, or would enter into the computations described in this paragraph if such items were allocated to the controlled foreign corporation. See paragraph (b)(2)(iii)(*d*)(*6*) for the definition of indirect ownership.

(3) Controlled foreign corporations.—For purposes of this section, the term *controlled foreign corporation* means a controlled foreign corporation as defined in section 957(a) or section 953(c). In the case of a controlled foreign corporation that is a look-through entity, the tax attributes to be taken into account are those of any person that is a United States shareholder (as defined in paragraph (b)(2)(iii)(*d*)(*5*) of this section) of the controlled foreign corporation, or, if the United States shareholder is a look-through entity, a United States person that owns an interest in such shareholder directly or indirectly through one or more look-through entities.

(4) United States person.—For purposes of this section, a *United States person* is a person described in section 7701(a)(30).

(5) United States shareholder.—For purposes of this section, a *United States shareholder* is a person described in section 951(b) or section 953(c).

(6) Indirect ownership.—For purposes of this section, indirect ownership of stock or another equity interest (such as an interest in a partnership) shall be determined in accordance with the principles of section 318, substituting the phrase "10 percent" for the phrase "50 percent" each time it appears.

* * *

(iv) *Maintenance of capital accounts.—(a) In general.*—The economic effect test described in paragraph (b)(2)(ii) of this section requires an examination of the capital accounts of the partners of a partnership, as maintained under the partnership agreement. Except as otherwise provided in paragraph (b)(2)(ii)(*i*) of this section, an allocation of income, gain, loss, or deduction will not have economic effect under paragraph (b)(2)(ii) of this section, and will not be deemed to be in accordance with a partner's interest in the partnership under paragraph (b)(4) of this section, unless the capital accounts of the partners are determined and maintained throughout the full term of the partnership in accordance with the capital accounting rules of this paragraph (b) (2) (iv).

(b) Basic rules.—Except as otherwise provided in this paragraph (b) (2) (iv), the partners' capital accounts will be considered to be determined and maintained in accordance with the rules of this paragraph (b) (2) (iv) if, and only if, each partner's capital account is increased by (*1*) the amount of money contributed by him to the partnership, (*2*) the fair market value of property contributed by him to the partnership (net of liabilities that the partnership is considered to assume or take subject to), and (*3*) allocations to him of partnership income and gain (or items thereof), including income and gain exempt from tax and income and gain described in paragraph (b) (2) (iv) (*g*) of this section, but excluding income and gain described in paragraph (b) (4) (i) of this section; and is decreased by (*4*) the amount of money distributed to him by the partnership, (*5*) the fair market value of property distributed to him by the partnership (net of liabilities that such partner is considered to assume or take subject to), (*6*) allocations to him of expenditures of the partnership described in section 705(a) (2) (B), and (*7*) allocations of partnership loss and deduction (or item thereof), including loss and deduction described in paragraph (b) (2) (iv) (*g*) of this section, but excluding items described in (*6*) above and loss or deduction described in paragraphs (b) (4) (i) or (b) (4) (iii) of this section; and is otherwise adjusted in accordance with the additional rules set forth in this paragraph (b) (2) (iv). For purposes of this paragraph, a partner who has more than one interest in a partnership shall have a single capital account that reflects all such interests, regardless of the class of interests owned by such partner (*e.g.,* general or limited) and regardless of the time or manner in which such interests were acquired. For liabilities assumed before June 24, 2003, references to liabilities in this paragraph (b) (2) (iv) (*b*) shall include only liabilities secured by the contributed or distributed property that are taken into account under section 752(a) and (b).

(c) Treatment of liabilities.—For purposes of this paragraph (b) (2) (iv), (*1*) money contributed by a partner to a partnership includes the amount of any partnership liabilities that are assumed by such partner (other than liabilities described in paragraph (b) (2) (iv) (*b*) (*5*) of this section that are assumed by a distributee partner) but does not include increases in such partner's share of partnership liabilities (see section 752(a)), and (*2*) money distributed to a partner by a partnership includes the amount of such partner's individual liabilities that are assumed by the partnership (other than liabilities described in paragraph (b) (2) (iv) (*b*) (*2*) of this section that are assumed by the partnership) but does not include decreases in such partner's share of partnership liabilities (see section 752(b)). For purposes of this paragraph (b) (2) (iv) (*c*), liabilities are considered assumed only to the extent the assuming party is thereby subjected to personal liability with respect to such obligation, the obligee is aware of the assumption and can directly enforce the assuming party's obligation, and, as between the assuming party and the party from whom the liability is assumed, the assuming party is ultimately liable.

(d) Contributed property.—(1) In general.—The basic capital accounting rules contained in paragraph (b) (2) (iv) (*b*) of this section require that a partner's capital account be increased by the fair market value of property contributed to the partnership by such partner on the date of contribution. See *Example 13*(i) of paragraph (b) (5) of this section. Consistent with section 752(c), section 7701(g) does not apply in determining such fair market value.

(2) Contribution of promissory notes.—Notwithstanding the general rule of paragraph (b) (2) (iv) (*b*) (*2*) of this section, except as provided in this paragraph (b) (2) (iv) (*d*) (*2*), if a promissory note is contributed to a partnership by a partner who is the maker of such note, such partner's capital account will be increased with respect to such note only when there is a taxable disposition of such note by the partnership or when the partner makes principal payments on such note. See example (1) (ix) of paragraph (b) (5) of this section. The first sentence of this paragraph (b) (2) (iv) (*d*) (*2*) shall not apply if the note referred to therein is readily tradable on an established securities market. See also paragraph (b) (2) (ii) (*c*) of this section. Furthermore, a partner whose interest is liquidated will be considered as satisfying his obligation to restore the deficit balance in his capital account to the extent of (*i*) the fair market value, at the time of contribution, of any negotiable promissory note (of which such partner is the maker) that such partner contributes to the partnership on or after the date his interest is liquidated and within the time specified in paragraph (b) (2) (ii) (*b*) (*3*) of this section, and (*ii*) the fair market value, at the time of liquidation, of the unsatisfied portion of any negotiable promissory note (of which such partner is the maker) that such partner previously contributed to the partnership. For purposes of the preceding sentence, the fair market value of a note will be no less than the outstanding principal balance of such note, provided that such note bears interest at a rate no less than the applicable federal rate at the time of valuation.

(3) Section 704(c) considerations.—Section 704(c) and § 1.704-3 govern the determination of the partners' distributive shares of income, gain, loss, and deduction, as computed for tax purposes, with respect to property contributed to a partnership (see paragraph (b)(1)(vi) of this section). In cases where section 704(c) and § 1.704-3 apply to partnership property, the capital accounts of the partners will not be considered to be determined and maintained in accordance with the rules of this paragraph (b)(2)(iv) unless the partnership agreement requires that the partners' capital accounts be adjusted in accordance with paragraph (b)(2)(iv)(*g*) of this section for allocations to them of income, gain, loss, and deduction (including depreciation, depletion, amortization, or other cost recovery) as computed for book purposes, with respect to the property. See, however, § 1.704-3(d)(2) for a special rule in determining the amount of book items if the partnership chooses the remedial allocation method. See also *Example (13)* (i) of paragraph (b)(5) of this section. Capital accounts are not adjusted to reflect allocations under section 704(c) and § 1.704-3 (e.g., tax allocations of precontribution gain or loss).

(4) Exercise of noncompensatory options.—Solely for purposes of paragraph (b)(2)(iv)(*b*)(*2*) of this section, the fair market value of the property contributed on the exercise of a noncompensatory option (as defined in § 1.721-2(f)) does not include the fair market value of the option privilege, but does include the consideration paid to the partnership to acquire the option and the fair market value of any property (other than the option) contributed to the partnership on the exercise of the option. With respect to convertible debt, the fair market value of the property contributed on the exercise of the option is the adjusted issue price of the debt and the accrued but unpaid qualified stated interest (as defined in § 1.1273-1(c)) on the debt immediately before the conversion, plus the fair market value of any property (other than the convertible debt) contributed to the partnership on the exercise of the option. See *Examples 31* through *35* of paragraph (b)(5) of this section.

(e) Distributed property.—(1) In general.—The basic capital accounting rules contained in paragraph (b)(2)(iv)(*b*) of this section require that a partner's capital account be decreased by the fair market value of property distributed by the partnership (without regard to section 7701(g)) to such partner (whether in connection with a liquidation or otherwise). To satisfy this requirement, the capital accounts of the partners first must be adjusted to reflect the manner in which the unrealized income, gain, loss, and deduction inherent in such property (that has not been reflected in the capital accounts previously) would be allocated among the partners if there were a taxable disposition of such property for the fair market value of such property (taking section 7701(g) into account) on the date of distribution. See example (14)(v) of paragraph (b)(5) of this section.

(2) Distribution of promissory notes.—Notwithstanding the general rule of paragraph (b)(2)(iv)(*b*)(*5*), except as provided in this paragraph (b)(2)(iv)(*e*)(*2*), if a promissory note is distributed to a partner by a partnership that is the maker of such note, such partner's capital account will be decreased with respect to such note only when there is a taxable disposition of such note by the partner or when the partnership makes principal payments on the note. The previous sentence shall not apply if a note distributed to a partner by a partnership who is the maker of such note is readily tradable on an established securities market. Furthermore, the capital account of a partner whose interest in a partnership is liquidated will be reduced to the extent of (*i*) the fair market value, at the time of distribution, of any negotiable promissory note (of which such partnership is the maker) that such partnership distributes to the partner on or after the date such partner's interest is liquidated and within the time specified in paragraph (b)(2)(ii)(*b*)(*2*) of this section, and (*ii*) the fair market value, at the time of liquidation, of the unsatisfied portion of any negotiable promissory note (of which such partnership is the maker) that such partnership previously distributed to the partner. For purposes of the preceding sentence, the fair market value of a note will be no less than the outstanding principal balance of such note, provided that such note bears interest at a rate no less than the applicable federal rate at the time of valuation.

(f) Revaluations of property.—A partnership agreement may, upon the occurrence of certain events, increase or decrease the capital accounts of the partners to reflect a revaluation of partnership property (including intangible assets such as goodwill) on the partnership's books. Capital accounts so adjusted will not be considered to be determined and maintained in accordance with the rules of this paragraph (b)(2)(iv) unless—

(1) The adjustments are based on the fair market value of partnership property (taking section 7701(g) into account) on the date of adjustment, as determined under paragraph (b)(2)(iv)(*h*) of this section. See *Example 33* of paragraph (b)(5) of this section.

(2) The adjustments reflect the manner in which the unrealized income, gain, loss, or deduction inherent in such property

(that has not been reflected in the capital accounts previously) would be allocated among the partners if there were a taxable disposition of such property for such fair market value on that date, and

(3) The partnership agreement requires that the partners' capital accounts be adjusted in accordance with paragraph (b)(2)(iv)(*g*) of this section for allocations to them of depreciation, depletion, amortization, and gain or loss, as computed for book purposes, with respect to such property, and

(4) The partnership agreement requires that the partners' distributive shares of depreciation, depletion, amortization, and gain or loss, as computed for tax purposes, with respect to such property be determined so as to take account of the variation between the adjusted tax basis and book value of such property in the same manner as under section 704(c) (see paragraph (b)(4)(i) of this section), and

(5) The adjustments are made principally for a substantial non-tax business purpose—

(i) In connection with a contribution of money or other property (other than a *de minimis* amount) to the partnership by a new or existing partner as consideration for an interest in the partnership, or

(ii) In connection with the liquidation of the partnership or a distribution of money or other property (other than a *de minimis* amount) by the partnership to a retiring or continuing partner as consideration for an interest in the partnership, or

(iii) In connection with the grant of an interest in the partnership (other than a *de minimis* interest) on or after May 6, 2004, as consideration for the provision of services to or for the benefit of the partnership by an existing partner acting in a partner capacity, or by a new partner acting in a partner capacity or in anticipation of being a partner, or

(iv) In connection with the issuance by the partnership of a noncompensatory option (other than an option for a de minimis partnership interest), or

(v) Under generally accepted industry accounting practices, provided substantially all of the partnership's property (excluding money) consists of stock, securities, commodities, options, warrants, futures, or similar instruments that are readily tradable on an established securities market.

See examples (14) and (18) of paragraph (b)(5) of this section. If the capital accounts of the partners are not adjusted to reflect the fair market value of partnership property when an interest in the partnership is acquired from or relinquished to the partnership, paragraphs (b)(1)(iii) and (b)(1)(iv) of this section should be consulted regarding the potential tax consequences that may arise if the principles of section 704(c) are not applied to determine the partners' distributive shares of depreciation, depletion, amortization, and gain or loss, as computed for tax purposes, with respect to such property.

* * *

(g) Adjustments to reflect book value.—(1) In general.—Under paragraphs (b)(2)(iv)(*d*) and (b)(2)(iv)(*f*) of this section, property may be properly reflected on the books of the partnership at a book value that differs from the adjusted tax basis of such property. In these circumstances, paragraphs (b)(2)(iv)(*d*)(*3*) and (b)(2)(iv)(*f*)(*3*) of this section provide that the capital accounts of the partners will not be considered to be determined and maintained in accordance with the rules of this paragraph (b)(2)(iv) unless the partnership agreement requires the partners' capital accounts to be adjusted in accordance with this paragraph (b)(2)(iv)(*g*) for allocations to them of depreciation, depletion, amortization, and gain or loss, as computed for book purposes, with respect to such property. In determining whether the economic effect of an allocation of book items is substantial, consideration will be given to the effect of such allocation on the determination of the partners' distributive shares of corresponding tax items under section 704(c) and paragraph (b)(4)(i) of this section. See example (17) of paragraph (b)(5) of this section. If an allocation of book items under the partnership agreement does not have substantial economic effect (as determined under paragraphs (b)(2)(ii) and (b)(2)(iii) of this section), or is not otherwise respected under this paragraph, such items will be reallocated in accordance with the partners' interests in the partnership, and such reallocation will be the basis upon which the partners' distributive shares of the corresponding tax items are determined under section 704(c) and paragraph (b)(4)(i) of this section. See examples (13), (14), and (18) of paragraph (b)(5) of this section.

(2) Payables and receivables.—References in this paragraph (b)(2)(iv) and paragraph (b)(4)(i) of this section to book and tax depreciation, depletion, amortization, and gain or loss with respect to property that has an adjusted tax basis that differs from book value include, under analogous rules and principles, the unrealized income or deduction with respect to accounts receivable, accounts payable, and other accrued but unpaid items.

(3) Determining amount of book items.—The partners' capital accounts will not

be considered adjusted in accordance with this paragraph (b)(2)(iv)(*g*) unless the amount of book depreciation, depletion, or amortization for a period with respect to an item of partnership property is the amount that bears the same relationship to the book value of such property as the depreciation (or cost recovery deduction), depletion, or amortization computed for tax purposes with respect to such property for such period bears to the adjusted tax basis of such property. If such property has a zero adjusted tax basis, the book depreciation, depletion, or amortization may be determined under any reasonable method selected by the partnership. For purposes of the preceding sentence, additional first year depreciation deduction under section 168(k) is not a reasonable method.

(h) Determinations of fair market value.—(1) In general.—For purposes of this paragraph (b)(2)(iv), the fair market value assigned to property contributed to a partnership, property distributed by a partnership, or property otherwise revalued by a partnership, will be regarded as correct, provided that (*1*) such value is reasonably agreed to among the partners in arm's-length negotiations, and (*2*) the partners have sufficiently adverse interests. If, however, these conditions are not satisfied and the value assigned to such property is overstated or understated (by more than an insignificant amount), the capital accounts of the partners will not be considered to be determined and maintained in accordance with the rules of this paragraph (b)(2)(iv). Valuation of property contributed to the partnership, distributed by the partnership, or otherwise revalued by the partnership shall be on a property-by-property basis, except to the extent the regulations under section 704(c) permit otherwise.

(2) Adjustments for noncompensatory options.—The value of partnership property as reflected on the books of the partnership must be adjusted to account for any outstanding noncompensatory options (as defined in § 1.721-2(f)) at the time of a revaluation of partnership property under paragraph (b)(2)(iv)(*f*) or (*s*) of this section. If the fair market value of outstanding noncompensatory options (as defined in § 1.721-2(f)) as of the date of the adjustment exceeds the consideration paid to the partnership to acquire the options, then the value of partnership property as reflected on the books of the partnership must be reduced by that excess to the extent of the unrealized income or gain in partnership property (that has not been reflected in the capital accounts previously). This reduction is allocated only to properties with unrealized appreciation in proportion to their respective amounts of unrealized appreciation. If the consideration paid to the partnership to acquire the outstanding noncompensatory options (as defined in § 1.721-2(f)) exceeds the fair market value of such options as of the date of the adjustment, then the value of partnership property as reflected on the books of the partnership must be increased by that excess to the extent of the unrealized loss in partnership property (that has not been reflected in the capital accounts previously). This increase is allocated only to properties with unrealized loss in proportion to their respective amounts of unrealized loss. However, any reduction or increase shall take into account the economic arrangement of the partners with respect to the property.

(i) Section 705(a)(2)(B) expenditures.—(1) In general.—The basic capital accounting rules contained in paragraph (b)(2)(iv)(*b*) of this section require that a partner's capital account be decreased by allocations made to such partner of expenditures described in section 705(a)(2)(B). See example (11) of paragraph (b)(5) of this section. If an allocation of these expenditures under the partnership agreement does not have substantial economic effect (as determined under paragraphs (b)(2)(ii) and (b)(2)(iii) of this section), or is not otherwise respected under this paragraph, such expenditures will be reallocated in accordance with the partners' interest in the partnership.

(2) Expenses described in section 709.—Except for amounts with respect to which an election is properly made under section 709(b), amounts paid or incurred to organize a partnership or to promote the sale of (or to sell) an interest in such a partnership shall, solely for purposes of this paragraph, be treated as section 705(a)(2)(B) expenditures, and upon liquidation of the partnership no further capital account adjustments will be made in respect thereof.

(3) Disallowed losses.—If a deduction for a loss incurred in connection with the sale or exchange of partnership property is disallowed to the partnership under section 267(a)(1) or section 707(b), that deduction shall, solely for purposes of this paragraph, be treated as a section 705(a)(2)(B) expenditure.

(j) Basis adjustments to section 38 property.—The capital accounts of the partners will not be considered to be determined and maintained in accordance with the rules of this paragraph (b)(2)(iv) unless such capital accounts are adjusted by the partners' shares of any upward or downward basis adjustments allocated to them under this paragraph (b)(2)(iv)(*j*). When there is a reduction in the

adjusted tax basis of partnership section 38 property under section 48(q)(1) or section 48(q)(3), section 48(q)(6) provides for an equivalent downward adjustment to the aggregate basis of partnership interests (and no additional adjustment is made under section 705(a)(2)(B)). These downward basis adjustments shall be shared among the partners in the same proportion as the adjusted tax basis or cost of (or the qualified investment in) such section 38 property is allocated among the partners under paragraph (f) of § 1.46-3 (or paragraph (a)(4)(iv) of § 1.48-8). Conversely, when there is an increase in the adjusted tax basis of partnership section 38 property under section 48(q)(2), section 48(q)(6) provides for an equivalent upward adjustment to the aggregate basis or partnership interests. These upward adjustments shall be allocated among the partners in the same proportion as the investment tax credit from such property is recaptured by the partners under § 1.47-6.

(k) Depletion of oil and gas properties.—(1) In general.—The capital accounts of the partners will not be considered to be determined and maintained in accordance with the rules of this paragraph (b)(2)(iv) unless such capital accounts are adjusted for depletion and gain or loss with respect to the oil or gas properties of the partnership in accordance with this paragraph (b)(2)(iv)(*k*).

(2) Simulated depletion.—Except as provided in paragraph (b)(2)(iv)(*k*)(*3*) of this section, a partnership shall, solely for purposes of maintaining capital accounts under this paragraph, compute simulated depletion allowances with respect to its oil and gas properties at the partnership level. These allowances shall be computed on each depletable oil or gas property of the partnership by using either the cost depletion method or the percentage depletion method (computed in accordance with section 613 at the rates specified in section 613A(c)(5) without regard to the limitations of section 613A, which theoretically could apply to any partner) for each partnership taxable year that the property is owned by the partnership and subject to depletion. The choice between the simulated cost depletion method and the simulated percentage depletion method shall be made on a property-by-property basis in the first partnership taxable year beginning after April 30, 1986, for which it is relevant for the property, and shall be binding for all partnership taxable years during which the oil or gas property is held by the partnership. The partnership shall make downward adjustments to the capital accounts of the partners for the simulated depletion allowance with respect to each oil or gas property of the partnership, in the same proportion as such partners (or their predecessors in interest) were properly allocated the adjusted tax basis of each such property. The aggregate capital account adjustments for simulated percentage depletion allowances with respect to an oil or gas property of the partnership shall not exceed the aggregate adjusted tax basis allocated to the partners with respect to such property. Upon the taxable disposition of an oil or gas property by a partnership, such partnership's simulated gain or loss shall be determined by subtracting its simulated adjusted basis in such property from the amount realized upon such disposition. (The partnership's simulated adjusted basis in an oil or gas property is determined in the same manner as adjusted tax basis except that simulated depletion allowances are taken into account instead of actual depletion allowances.) The capital accounts of the partners shall be adjusted upward by the amount of any simulated gain in proportion to such partners' allocable shares of the portion of the total amount realized from the disposition of such property that exceeds the partnership's simulated adjusted basis in such property. The capital accounts of such partners shall be adjusted downward by the amount of any simulated loss in proportion to such partners' allocable shares of the total amount realized from the disposition of such property that represents recovery of the partnership's simulated adjusted basis in such property. See section 613A(c)(7)(D) and the regulations thereunder and paragraph (b)(4)(v) of this section. See example (19)(iv) of paragraph (b)(5) of this section.

(3) Actual depletion.—Pursuant to section 613A(c)(7)(D) and the regulations thereunder, the depletion allowance under section 611 with respect to the oil and gas properties of a partnership is computed separately by the partners. Accordingly, in lieu of adjusting the partners' capital accounts as provided in paragraph (b)(2)(iv)(*k*)(*2*) of this section, the partnership may make downward adjustments to the capital account of each partner equal to such partner's depletion allowance with respect to each oil or gas property of the partnership (for the partner's taxable year that ends with or within the partnership's taxable year). The aggregate adjustments to the capital account of a partner for depletion allowances with respect to an oil or gas property of the partnership shall not exceed the adjusted tax basis allocated to such partner with respect to such property. Upon the taxable disposition of an oil or gas property by a partnership, the capital account of each partner shall be adjusted upward by the amount of any excess of such partner's allocable share of the total amount realized from the disposition of such property over such part-

ner's remaining adjusted tax basis in such property. If there is no such excess, the capital account of such partner shall be adjusted downward by the amount of any excess of such partner's remaining adjusted tax basis in such property over such partner's allocable share of the total amount realized from the disposition thereof. See section 613A(c)(7)(4)(D) and the regulations thereunder and paragraph (b)(4)(v) of this section.

(4) Effect of book values.—If an oil or gas property of the partnership is, under paragraphs (b)(2)(iv)(*d*) or (b)(2)(iv)(*f*) of this section, properly reflected on the books of the partnership at a book value that differs from the adjusted tax basis of such property, the rules contained in this paragraph (b)(2)(iv)(*k*) and paragraph (b)(4)(v) of this section shall be applied with reference to such book value. A revaluation of a partnership oil or gas property under paragraph (b)(2)(iv)(*f*) of this section may give rise to a reallocation of the adjusted tax basis of such property, or a change in the partners' relative shares of simulated depletion from such property, only to the extent permitted by section 613A(c)(7)(D) and the regulations thereunder.

(l) Transfers of partnership interests.—The capital accounts of the partners will not be considered to be determined and maintained in accordance with the rules of this paragraph (b)(2)(iv) unless, upon the transfer of all or a part of an interest in the partnership, the capital account of the transferor that is attributable to the transferred interest carries over to the transferee partner. (See paragraph (b)(2)(iv)(*m*) of this section for rules concerning the effect of a section 754 election on the capital accounts of the partners.) If the transfer of an interest in a partnership causes a termination of the partnership under section 708(b)(1)(B), the capital account of the transferee partner and the capital accounts of the other partners of the terminated partnership carry over to the new partnership that is formed as a result of the termination of the partnership under § 1.708-1(b)(1)(iv). Moreover, the deemed contribution of assets and liabilities by the terminated partnership to a new partnership and the deemed liquidation of the terminated partnership that occur under § 1.708-1(b)(1)(iv) are disregarded for purposes of paragraph (b)(2)(iv) of this section. See Example 13 of paragraph (b)(5) of this section and the example in § 1.708-1(b)(1)(iv). The previous three sentences apply to terminations of partnerships under section 708(b)(1)(B) occurring on or after May 9, 1997; however, the sentences may be applied to terminations occurring on or after May 9, 1996, provided that the partnership and its partners apply the sentences to the termination in a consistent manner.

(m) Section 754 elections.—*(1) In general.*—The capital accounts of the partners will not be considered to be determined and maintained in accordance with the rules of this paragraph (b)(2)(iv) unless, upon adjustment to the adjusted tax basis of partnership property under section 732, 734, or 743, the capital accounts of the partners are adjusted as provided in this paragraph (b)(2)(iv)(*m*).

(2) Section 743 adjustments.—In the case of a transfer of all or a part of an interest in a partnership that has a section 754 election in effect for the partnership taxable year in which such transfer occurs, adjustments to the adjusted tax basis of partnership property under section 743 shall not be reflected in the capital account of the transferee partner or on the books of the partnership, and subsequent capital account adjustments for distributions (see paragraph (b)(2)(iv)(*e*)(*1*) of this section) and for depreciation, depletion, amortization, and gain or loss with respect to such property will disregard the effect of such basis adjustment. The preceding sentence shall not apply to the extent such basis adjustment is allocated to the common basis of partnership property under paragraph (b)(1) of § 1.734-2; in these cases, such basis adjustment shall, except as provided in paragraph (b)(2)(iv)(*m*)(*5*) of this section, give rise to adjustments to the capital accounts of the partners in accordance with their interests in the partnership under paragraph (b)(3) of this section. See examples (13)(iii) and (iv) of paragraph (b)(5) of this section.

(3) Section 732 adjustments.—In the case of a transfer of all or a part of an interest in a partnership that does not have a section 754 election in effect for the partnership taxable year in which such transfer occurs, adjustments to the adjusted tax basis of partnership property under section 732(d) will be treated in the capital accounts of the partners in the same manner as section 743 basis adjustments are treated under paragraph (b)(2)(iv)(*m*)(*2*) of this section.

(4) Section 734 adjustments.—Except as provided in paragraph (b)(2)(iv)(*m*)(*5*) of this section, in the case of a distribution of property in liquidation of a partner's interest in the partnership by a partnership that has a section 754 election in effect for the partnership taxable year in which the distribution occurs, the partner who receives the distribution that gives rise to the adjustment to the adjusted tax basis of partnership property under section 734 shall have a corresponding adjustment made to

his capital account. If such distribution is made other than in liquidation of a partner's interest in the partnership, however, except as provided in paragraph (b)(2)(iv)(*m*)(*5*) of this section, the capital accounts of the partners shall be adjusted by the amount of the adjustment to the adjusted tax basis of partnership property under section 734, and such capital account adjustment shall be shared among the partners in the manner in which the unrealized income and gain that is displaced by such adjustment would have been shared if the property whose basis is adjusted were sold immediately prior to such adjustment for its recomputed adjusted tax basis.

(5) Limitations on adjustments.—Adjustments may be made to the capital account of a partner (or his successor in interest) in respect of basis adjustments to partnership property under sections 732, 734, and 743 only to the extent that such basis adjustments (i) are permitted to be made to one or more items of partnership property under section 755, and (ii) result in an increase or a decrease in the amount at which such property is carried on the partnership's balance sheet, as computed for book purposes. For example, if the book value of partnership property exceeds the adjusted tax basis of such property, a basis adjustment to such property may be reflected in a partner's capital account only to the extent such adjustment exceeds the difference between the book value of such property and the adjusted tax basis of such property prior to such adjustment.

(n) Partnership level characterization.—Except as otherwise provided in paragraph (b)(2)(iv)(*k*) of this section, the capital accounts of the partners will not be considered to be determined and maintained in accordance with the rules of this paragraph (b)(2)(iv) unless adjustments to such capital accounts in respect of partnership income, gain, loss, deduction, and section 705(a)(2)(B) expenditures (or item thereof) are made with reference to the Federal tax treatment of such items (and in the case of book items, with reference to the Federal tax treatment of the corresponding tax items) at the partnership level, without regard to any requisite or elective tax treatment of such items at the partner level (for example, under section 58(i)). However, a partnership that incurs mining exploration expenditures will determine the Federal tax treatment of income, gain, loss, and deduction with respect to the property to which such expenditures relate at the partnership level only after first taking into account the elections made by its partners under section 617 and section 703(b)(4).

(o) Guaranteed payments.—Guaranteed payments to a partner under section 707(c) cause the capital account of the recipient partner to be adjusted only to the extent of such partner's distributive share of any partnership deduction, loss, or other downward capital account adjustment resulting from such payment.

(p) Minor discrepancies.—Discrepancies between the balances in the respective capital accounts of the partners and the balances that would be in such respective capital accounts if they had been determined and maintained in accordance with this paragraph (b)(2)(iv) will not adversely affect the validity of an allocation, provided that such discrepancies are minor and are attributable to good faith error by the partnership.

(q) Adjustments where guidance is lacking.—If the rules of this paragraph (b)(2)(iv) fail to provide guidance on how adjustments to the capital accounts of the partners should be made to reflect particular adjustments to partnership capital on the books of the partnership, such capital accounts will not be considered to be determined and maintained in accordance with those rules unless such capital account adjustments are made in a manner that (*1*) maintains equality between the aggregate governing capital accounts of the partners and the amount of partnership capital reflected on the partnership's balance sheet, as computed for book purposes, (*2*) is consistent with the underlying economic arrangement of the partners, and (*3*) is based, wherever practicable, on Federal tax accounting principles.

(r) Restatement of capital accounts.—With respect to partnerships that began operating in a taxable year beginning before May 1, 1986, the capital accounts of the partners of which have not been determined and maintained in accordance with the rules of this paragraph (b)(2)(iv) since inception, such capital accounts shall not be considered to be determined and maintained in accordance with the rules of this paragraph (b)(2)(iv) for taxable years beginning after April 30, 1986, unless either—

(1) such capital accounts are adjusted, effective for the first partnership taxable year beginning after April 30, 1986, to reflect the fair market value of partnership property as of the first day of such taxable year, and in connection with such adjustment, the rules contained in paragraph (b)(2)(iv)(*f*)(*2*), (*3*), and (*4*) of this section are satisfied, or

(2) the differences between the balance in each partner's capital account and the balance that would be in such partner's capital account if capital accounts had been

determined and maintained in accordance with this paragraph (b)(2)(iv) throughout the full term of the partnership are not significant (for example, such differences are solely attributable to a failure to provide for treatment of section 709 expenses in accordance with the rules of paragraph (b)(2)(iv)(*i*)(*2*) of this section or to a failure to follow the rules in paragraph (b)(2)(iv)(*m*) of this section), and capital accounts are adjusted to bring them into conformity with the rules of this paragraph (b)(2)(iv) no later than the end of the first partnership taxable year beginning after April 30, 1986.

(3) With respect to a partnership that began operating in a taxable year beginning before May 1, 1986, modifications to the partnership agreement adopted on or before November 1, 1988, to make the capital account adjustments required to comply with this paragraph, and otherwise to satisfy the requirements of this paragraph, will be treated as if such modifications were included in the partnership agreement before the end of the first partnership taxable year beginning after April 30, 1986. However, compliance with the previous sentences will have no bearing on the validity of allocations that relate to partnership taxable years beginning before May 1, 1986.

(s) Adjustments on the exercise of a noncompensatory option.—A partnership agreement may grant a partner, on the exercise of a noncompensatory option (as defined in § 1.721-2(f)), a right to share in partnership capital that exceeds (or is less than) the sum of the consideration paid to the partnership to acquire and exercise such option. Where such an agreement exists, capital accounts will not be considered to be determined and maintained in accordance with the rules of this paragraph (b)(2)(iv) unless the following requirements are met:

(1) In lieu of revaluing partnership property under paragraph (b)(2)(iv)(*f*) of this section immediately before the exercise of the option, the partnership revalues partnership property in accordance with the provisions of paragraphs (b)(2)(iv)(*f*)(*1*) through (*f*)(*4*) of this section immediately after the exercise of the option.

(2) In determining the capital accounts of the partners (including the exercising partner) under paragraph (b)(2)(iv)(*s*)(*1*) of this section, the partnership first allocates any unrealized income, gain, or loss in partnership property (that has not been reflected in the capital accounts previously) to the exercising partner to the extent necessary to reflect that partner's right to share in partnership capital under the partnership agreement, and then allocates any remaining unrealized income, gain, or loss (that has not been reflected in the capital accounts previously) to the existing partners, to reflect the manner in which the unrealized income, gain, or loss in partnership property would be allocated among those partners if there were a taxable disposition of such property for its fair market value on that date. For purposes of the preceding sentence, if the exercising partner's initial capital account as determined under § 1.704-1(b)(2)(iv)(*b*) and (*d*)(*4*) of this section would be less than the amount that reflects the exercising partner's right to share in partnership capital under the partnership agreement, then only income or gain may be allocated to the exercising partner from partnership properties with unrealized appreciation, in proportion to their respective amounts of unrealized appreciation. If the exercising partner's initial capital account, as determined under § 1.704-1(b)(2)(iv)(*b*) and (*d*)(*4*) of this section, would be greater than the amount that reflects the exercising partner's right to share in partnership capital under the partnership agreement, then only loss may be allocated to the exercising partner from partnership properties with unrealized loss, in proportion to their respective amounts of unrealized loss. However, any allocation must take into account the economic arrangement of the partners with respect to the property.

(3) If, after making the allocations described in paragraph (b)(2)(iv)(*s*)(*2*) of this section, the exercising partner's capital account does not reflect that partner's right to share in partnership capital under the partnership agreement, then the partnership reallocates partnership capital between the existing partners and the exercising partner so that the exercising partner's capital account reflects the exercising partner's right to share in partnership capital under the partnership agreement (a capital account reallocation). Any increase or decrease in the capital accounts of existing partners that occurs as a result of a capital account reallocation under this paragraph (b)(2)(iv)(*s*)(*3*) must be allocated among the existing partners in accordance with the principles of this section. See *Example 32* of paragraph (b)(5) of this section.

(4) The partnership agreement requires corrective allocations so as to take into account all capital account reallocations made under paragraph (b)(2)(iv)(*s*)(*3*) of this section (see paragraph (b)(4)(x) of this section). See *Example 32* of paragraph (b)(5) of this section.

(3) *Partner's interest in the partnership.*—(i) *In general.*—References in section 704(b) and this paragraph to a partner's interest in the partnership, or to the partners' interests in the partnership, signify the manner in which the partners have agreed to share the economic

benefit or burden (if any) corresponding to the income, gain, loss, deduction, or credit (or item thereof) that is allocated. Except with respect to partnership items that cannot have economic effect (such as nonrecourse deductions of the partnership), this sharing arrangement may or may not correspond to the overall economic arrangement of the partners. (For example, in the case of an unexpected downward adjustment to the capital account of a partner who does not have a deficit makeup obligation that causes such partner to have a negative capital account, it may be necessary to allocate a disproportionate amount of gross income of the partnership to such partner for such year so as to bring that partner's capital account back up to zero.) Thus, a partner who has a 50 percent overall interest in the partnership may have a 90 percent interest in a particular item of income or deduction. The determination of a partner's interest in a partnership shall be made by taking into account all facts and circumstances relating to the economic arrangement of the partners.

(ii) *Factors considered.*—In determining a partner's interest in the partnership, the following factors are among those that will be considered:

(a) The partners' relative contributions to the partnership,

(b) The interests of the partners in economic profits and losses (if different than that in taxable income or loss),

(c) The interests of the partners in cash flow and other non-liquidating distributions, and

(d) The rights of the partners to distributions of capital upon liquidation.

The provisions of this subparagraph (b)(3) are illustrated by examples (1)(i) and (ii), (4)(i), (5)(i) and (ii), (6), (7)(i), (ii), and (iv), (8), (10)(ii), (16)(i), and (19)(iii) of paragraph (b)(5) of this section. See paragraph (b)(4)(i) of this section concerning rules for determining the partners' interests in the partnership with respect to certain tax items.

(iii) *Certain determinations.*—If—

(a) Requirements *(1)* and *(2)* of paragraph (b)(2)(ii)*(b)* of this section are satisfied, and

(b) All or a portion of an allocation of income, gain, loss, or deduction made to a partner for a partnership taxable year does not have economic effect under paragraph (b)(2)(ii) of this section,

the partners' interests in the partnership with respect to the portion of the allocation that lacks economic effect will be determined by comparing the manner in which distributions (and contributions) would be made if all partnership property were sold at book value and the partnership were liquidated immediately following the end of the taxable year to which the allocation relates with the manner in which distributions (and contributions) would be made if all partnership property were sold at book value and the partnership were liquidated immediately following the end of the prior taxable year, and adjusting the result for the items described in *(4)*, *(5)*, and *(6)* of paragraph (b)(2)(ii)*(d)* of this section. A determination made under this paragraph (b)(3)(iii) will have no force if the economic effect of valid allocations made in the same manner is insubstantial under paragraph (b)(2)(iii) of this section. See examples (1)(iv), (v), and (vi), and (15)(ii) and (iii) of paragraph (b)(5) of this section.

* * *

(4) *Special rules.*—(i) *Allocations to reflect revaluations.*—If partnership property is, under paragraphs (b)(2)(iv)*(d)* or (b)(2)(iv)*(f)* of this section, properly reflected in the capital accounts of the partners and on the books of the partnership at a book value that differs from the adjusted tax basis of such property, then depreciation, depletion, amortization, and gain or loss, as computed for book purposes, with respect to such property will be greater or less than the depreciation, depletion, amortization, and gain or loss, as computed for tax purposes, with respect to such property. In these cases the capital accounts of the partners are required to be adjusted solely for allocations of the book items to such partners (see paragraph (b)(2)(iv)*(g)* of this section), and the partners' shares of the corresponding tax items are not independently reflected by further adjustments to the partners' capital accounts. Thus, separate allocations of these tax items cannot have economic effect under paragraph (b)(2)(ii)*(b)*(*1*) of this section, and the partners' distributive shares of such tax items must (unless governed by section 704(c)) be determined in accordance with the partners' interests in the partnership. These tax items must be shared among the partners in a manner that takes account of the variation between the adjusted tax basis of such property and its book value in the same manner as variations between the adjusted tax basis and fair market value of property contributed to the partnership are taken into account in determining the partners' shares of tax items under section 704(c). See examples (14) and (18) of paragraph (b)(5) of this section.

(ii) *Credits.*—Allocations of tax credits and tax credit recapture are not reflected by adjustments to the partners' capital accounts (except to the extent that adjustments to the adjusted tax basis of partnership section 38 property in respect of tax credits and tax credit recapture give rise to capital account adjustments under paragraph (b)(2)(iv)(*j*) of this section). Thus, such allocations cannot have economic effect under paragraph (b)(2)(ii)(*b*)(*1*) of this section, and the tax credits and tax credit recapture must be allocated in accordance with the partners' interests in the partnership as of the time the tax credit or credit recapture arises. With respect to the investment tax credit provided by section 38, allocations of cost or qualified investment made in accordance with paragraph (f) of § 1.46-3 and paragraph (a)(4)(iv) of § 1.48-8 shall be deemed to be made in accordance with the partners' interests in the partnership. With respect to other tax credits, if a partnership expenditure (whether or not deductible) that gives rise to a tax credit in a partnership taxable year also gives rise to valid allocations of partnership loss or deduction (or other downward capital account adjustments) for such year, then the partners' interests in the partnership with respect to such credit (or the cost giving rise thereto) shall be in the same proportion as such partners' respective distributive shares of such loss or deduction (and adjustments). See example (11) of paragraph (b)(5) of this section. Identical principles shall apply in determining the partners' interests in the partnership with respect to tax credits that arise from receipts of the partnership (whether or not taxable).

(iii) *Excess percentage depletion*.—To the extent the percentage depletion in respect of an item of depletable property of the partnership exceeds the adjusted tax basis of such property, allocations of such excess percentage depletion are not reflected by adjustments to the partners' capital accounts. Thus, such allocations cannot have economic effect under paragraph (b)(2)(ii)(*b*)(*1*) of this section, and such excess percentage depletion must be allocated in accordance with the partners' interests in the partnership. The partners' interests in the partnership for a partnership taxable year with respect to such excess percentage depletion shall be in the same proportion as such partners' respective distributive shares of gross income from the depletable property (as determined under section 613(c)) for such year. See example (12) of paragraph (b)(5) of this section. See paragraphs (b)(2)(iv)(*k*) and (b)(4)(v) of this section for special rules concerning oil and gas properties of the partnership.

* * *

(5) *Examples*.—The operation of the rules in this paragraph is illustrated by the following examples:

Example (1). (i) A and B form a general partnership with cash contributions of $40,000 each, which cash is used to purchase depreciable personal property at a cost of $80,000. The partnership elects under section 48(q)(4) to reduce the amount of investment tax credit in lieu of adjusting the tax basis of such property. The partnership agreement provides that A and B will have equal shares of taxable income and loss (computed without regard to cost recovery deductions) and cash flow and that all cost recovery deductions on the property will be allocated to A. The agreement further provides that the partners' capital accounts will be determined and maintained in accordance with paragraph (b)(2)(iv) of this section, but that upon liquidation of the partnership, distributions will be made equally between the partners (regardless of capital account balances) and no partner will be required to restore the deficit balance in his capital account for distribution to partners with positive capital accounts balances. In the partnership's first taxable year, it recognizes operating income equal to its operating expenses and has an additional $20,000 cost recovery deduction, which is allocated entirely to A. That A and B will be entitled to equal distributions on liquidation, even though A is allocated the entire $20,000 cost recovery deduction, indicates A will not bear the full risk of the economic loss corresponding to such deduction if such loss occurs. Under paragraph (b)(2)(ii) of this section, the allocation lacks economic effect and will be disregarded. The partners made equal contributions to the partnership, share equally in other taxable income and loss and in cash flow, and will share equally in liquidation proceeds, indicating that their actual economic arrangement is to bear the risk imposed by the potential decrease in the value of the property equally. Thus, under paragraph (b)(3) of this section the partners' interests in the partnership are equal, and the cost recovery deduction will be reallocated equally between A and B.

(ii) Assume the same facts as in (i) except that the partnership agreement provides that liquidation proceeds will be distributed in accordance with capital account balances if the partnership is liquidated during the first five years of its existence but that liquidation proceeds will be distributed equally if the partnership is liquidated thereafter. Since the partnership agreement does not provide for the requirement contained in paragraph (b)(2)(ii)(*b*)(*2*) of this section to be satisfied throughout the term of the partnership, the partnership allocations do not have economic effect. Even if the partnership agreement provided for the requirement contained in paragraph (b)(2)(ii)(*b*)(*2*) to be satisfied throughout the term of the partnership, such allocations would not have economic effect unless the requirement contained in paragraph (b)(2)(ii)(*b*)(*3*) of this section or the alternate economic effect test contained in paragraph (b)(2)(ii)(*d*) of this section were satisfied.

(iii) Assume the same facts as in (i) except that distributions in liquidation of the partnership (or any partner's interest) are to be made in accordance with the partners' positive capital account balances throughout the term of the partnership (as set forth in paragraph (b)(2)(ii)(*b*)(*2*) of this section). Assume further that the partnership agreement contains a qualified income offset (as defined in paragraph (b)(2)(ii)(*d*) of this section) and that, as of the end of each partnership taxable year, the items described in paragraphs (b)(2)(ii)(*d*)(*4*), (*5*), and (*6*) of this section are not reasonably expected to cause or increase a deficit balance in A's capital account.

	A	*B*
Capital account upon formation	$40,000	$40,000
Less: year 1 cost recovery deduction	(20,000)	0
Capital account at end of year 1	$20,000	$40,000

Under the alternate economic effect test contained in paragraph (b)(2)(ii)(*d*) of this section, the allocation of the $20,000 cost recovery deduction to A has economic effect.

(iv) Assume the same facts as in (iii) and that in the partnership's second taxable year it recognizes operating income equal to its operating expenses and has a $25,000 cost recovery deduction which, under the partnership agreement, is allocated entirely to A.

	A	*B*
Capital account at beginning of year 2	$20,000	$40,000
Less: year 2 cost recovery deduction	(25,000)	0
Capital account at end of year 2	$(5,000)	$40,000

The allocation of the $25,000 cost recovery deduction to A satisfies the alternate economic effect test contained in paragraph (b)(2)(ii)(*d*) of this section only to the extent of $20,000. Therefore, only $20,000 of such allocation has economic effect, and the remaining $5,000 must be reallocated in accordance with the partners' interests in the partnership. Under the partnership agreement, if the property were sold immediately following the end of the partnership's second taxable year for $35,000 (its adjusted tax basis), the $35,000 would be distributed to B. Thus, B, and not A, bears the economic burden corresponding to $5,000 of the $25,000 cost recovery deduction allocated to A. Under paragraph (b)(3)(iii) of this section, $5,000 of such cost recovery deduction will be reallocated to B.

(v) Assume the same facts as in (iv) except that the cost recovery deduction for the partnership's second taxable year is $20,000 instead of $25,000. The allocation of such cost recovery deduction to A has economic effect under the alternate economic effect test contained in paragraph (b)(2)(ii)(*d*) of this section. Assume further that the property is sold for $35,000 immediately following the end of the partnership's second taxable year, resulting in a $5,000 taxable loss ($40,000 adjusted tax basis less $35,000 sales price), and the partnership is liquidated.

	A	*B*
Capital account at beginning of year 2	$20,000	$40,000
Less: year 2 cost recovery deduction	(20,000)	0
Capital account at end of year 2	0	$40,000
Less: loss on sale	(2,500)	(2,500)
Capital account before liquidation	$(2,500)	$37,500

Under the partnership agreement the $35,000 sales proceeds are distributed to B. Since B bears the entire economic burden corresponding to the $5,000 taxable loss from the sale of the property, the allocation of $2,500 of such loss to A does not have economic effect and must be reallocated in accordance with the partners' interests in the partnership. Under paragraph (b)(3)(iii) of this section, such $2,500 loss will be reallocated to B.

(vi) Assume the same facts as in (iv) except that the cost recovery deduction for the partnership's second taxable year is $20,000 instead of $25,000, and that as of the end of the partnership's second taxable year it is reasonably expected that during its third taxable year the partnership will (1) have operating income equal to its operating expenses (but will have no cost recovery deductions), (2) borrow $10,000 (recourse) and distribute such amount $5,000 to A and $5,000 to B, and (3) thereafter sell the partnership property, repay the $10,000 liability, and liquidate. In determining the extent to which the alternate economic effect test contained in paragraph (b)(2)(ii)(*d*) of this section is satisfied as of the end of the partnership's second taxable year, the fair market value of partnership property is presumed to be equal to its adjusted tax basis (in accordance with paragraph (b)(2)(iii)(*c*) of this section). Thus, it is presumed that the selling price of such property during the partnership's third taxable year will be its $40,000 adjusted tax basis. Accordingly, there can be no reasonable expectation that there will be increases to A's capital account in the partnership's third taxable year that will offset the expected $5,000 distribution to A. Therefore, the distribution of the loan proceeds must be taken into account in determining to what extent the alternate economic effect test contained in paragraph (b)(2)(ii)(*d*) is satisfied.

	A	*B*
Capital account at beginning of year 2	$20,000	$40,000
Less: expected future distribution	(5,000)	(5,000)
Less: year 2 cost recovery deduction	(20,000)	(0)
Hypothetical capital account at end of year 2	$(5,000)	$35,000

Upon sale of the partnership property, the $40,000 presumed sales proceeds would be used to repay the $10,000 liability, and the remaining $30,000 would be distributed to B. Under these circumstances the allocation of the $20,000 cost recovery deduction to A in the partnership's second taxable year satisfies the alternate economic effect test contained in paragraph (b)(2)(ii)(*d*) of this section only to the extent of $15,000. Under paragraph (b)(3)(iii) of this section, the remaining $5,000 of such deduction will be reallocated to B. The results in this example would be the same even if the partnership agreement also provided that any gain (whether ordinary income or capital gain) upon the sale of the property would be allocated to A to the extent of the prior allocations of cost recovery deductions to him, and, at end of the partnership's second taxable year, the partners were confident that the gain on the sale of the property in the partnership's third taxable year would be sufficient to offset the expected $5,000 distribution to A.

(vii) Assume the same facts as in (iv) except that the partnership agreement also provides that any partner with a deficit balance in his capital account following the liquidation of his interest must restore that deficit to the partnership (as set forth in paragraph (b)(2)(ii)(*b*)(*3*) of this section). Thus, if the property were sold for $35,000 immediately after the end of the partnership's second taxable year, the $35,000 would be distributed to B, A would contribute $5,000 (the deficit balance in his capital account) to the partnership, and that $5,000 would be distributed to B. The allocation of the entire $25,000 cost recovery deduction to A in the partnership's second taxable year has economic effect.

(viii) Assume the same facts as in (vii) except that A's obligation to restore the deficit balance in his capital account is limited to a maximum of $5,000. The allocation of the $25,000 cost recovery deduction to A in the partnership's second taxable year has economic effect under the alternate economic effect test contained in paragraph (b)(2)(ii)(*d*) of this section. At the end of such year, A makes an additional $5,000 contribution to the partnership (thereby eliminating the $5,000 deficit balance in his capital account). Under paragraph (b)(2)(ii)(*f*) of this section, A's obligation to restore up to $5,000 of the deficit balance in his capital account may be eliminated after he contributes the additional $5,000 without affecting the validity of prior allocations.

(ix) Assume the same facts as in (iv) except that upon formation of the partnership A also contributes to the partnership his negotiable promissory note with a $5,000 principal balance. The note unconditionally obligates A to pay an additional $5,000 to the partnership at the earlier of (a) the beginning of the partnership's fourth taxable year, or (b) the end of the partnership taxable year in which A's interest is liquidated. Under paragraph (b)(2)(ii)(*c*) of this section, A is considered obligated to restore up to $5,000 of the deficit balance in his capital account to the partnership. Accordingly, under the alternate economic effect test contained in paragraph (b)(2)(ii)(*d*) of this section, the allocation of the $25,000 cost recovery deduction to A in the partnership's second taxable year has economic effect. The results in this example would be the same if (1) the note A contributed to the partnership were payable only at the end of the partnership's fourth taxable year (so that A would not be required to satisfy the note upon liquidation of his interest in the partnership), and (2) the partnership agreement provided that upon liquidation of A's interest, the partnership would retain A's note, and A would contribute to the partnership the excess of the outstanding principal balance of the note over its then fair market value.

(x) Assume the same facts as in (ix) except that A's obligation to contribute an additional $5,000 to the partnership is not evidenced by a promissory note. Instead, the partnership agreement imposes upon A the obligation to make an additional $5,000 contribution to the partnership at the earlier of (a) the beginning of the partnership's fourth taxable year, or (b) the end of the partnership taxable year in which A's interest is liquidated. Under paragraph (b)(2)(ii)(*c*) of this section, as a result of A's deferred contribution requirement, A is considered obligated to restore up to $5,000 of the deficit balance in his capital account to the partnership. Accordingly, under the alternate economic effect test contained in paragraph (b)(2)(*ii*)(*d*) of this section, the allocation of the $25,000 cost recovery deduction to A in the partnership's second taxable year has economic effect.

(xi) Assume the same facts as in (vii) except that the partnership agreement also provides that any gain (whether ordinary income or capital gain) upon the sale of the property will be allocated to A to the extent of the prior allocations to A of cost recovery deductions from such property, and additional gain will be allocated equally between A and B. At the time the allocations of cost recovery deductions were made to A, the partners believed there would be gain on the sale of the property in an amount sufficient to offset the allocations of cost recovery deductions to A. Nevertheless, the existence of the gain chargeback provision will not cause the economic effect of the allocations to be insubstantial under paragraph (b)(2)(iii)(*c*) of this section, since in testing whether the economic effect of such allocations is substantial, the recovery property is presumed to decrease in value by the amount of such deductions.

Example (2). C and D form a general partnership solely to acquire and lease machinery that is 5-year recovery property under section 168. Each contributes $100,000, and the partnership obtains an $800,000 recourse loan to purchase the machinery. The partnership elects under section 48(q)(4) to reduce the amount of investment tax credit in lieu of adjusting the tax basis of such machinery. The partnership, C, and D have calendar taxable years. The partnership agreement provides that the partners' capital accounts will be determined and maintained in accordance with paragraph (b)(2)(iv) of this section, distributions in liquidation of the partnership (or any partner's interest) will be made in accordance with the partners' positive capital account balances, and any partner with a deficit balance in his capital account following the liquidation of his interest must restore that deficit to the partnership (as set forth in paragraphs (b)(2)(ii)(*b*)(*2*) and (*3*) of this section). The partnership agreement further provides that (a) partnership net taxable loss will be allocated 90 percent to C and 10 percent to D until such time as there is partnership net taxable income, and thereafter C will be allocated 90 percent of such taxable income until he has been allocated partnership net taxable income equal to the partnership net taxable loss previously allocated to him, (b) all further partnership net taxable income or loss will be allocated equally between C and D, and (c) distributions of operating cash flow will be made equally between C and D. The partnership enters into a 12-year lease with a financially secure corporation under which the partnership expects to have a net taxable loss in each of its first 5 partnership taxable years due to cost recovery deductions with respect to the machinery and net taxable income in each of its following 7 partnership taxable years, in part due to the absence of such cost recovery deductions. There is a strong likelihood that the partnership's net taxable loss in partnership taxable years 1 through 5 will be $100,000, $90,000, $80,000, $70,000, and $60,000, respectively, and the partnership's net taxable income in partnership taxable years 6 through 12 will be $40,000, $50,000, $60,000, $70,000, $80,000, $90,000, and $100,000, respectively. Even though there is a strong likelihood that the allocations of net taxable loss in years 1 through 5 will be largely offset by other allocations in partnership taxable years 6 through 12, and even if it is assumed that the total tax liability of the partners in years 1 through 12 will be less than if the allocations had not been provided in the partnership agreement, the economic effect of the allocations will not be insubstantial under paragraph (b)(2)(iii)(*c*) of this section. This is because at the time such allocations became part of the partnership agreement, there was a strong likelihood that the allocations of net taxable loss in years 1 through 5 would not be largely offset by allocations of income within 5 years (determined on a first-in, first-out basis). The year 1 allocation will not be offset until years 6, 7, and 8, the year 2 allocation will not be offset until years 8 and 9, the year 3 allocation will not be offset until years 9 and 10, the year 4 allocation will not be offset until years 10 and 11, and the year 5 allocation will not be offset until years 11 and 12.

Example (3). E and F enter into a partnership agreement to develop and market experimental electronic devices. E contributes $2,500 cash and agrees to devote his full-time services to the partnership. F contributes $100,000 cash and agrees to obtain a loan for the partnership for any additional capital needs. The partnership agreement provides that all deductions for research and experimental expenditures and interest on partnership loans are to be allocated to F. In addition, F will be allocated 90 percent, and E 10 percent, of partnership taxable income or loss, computed net of the deductions for such research and experimental expenditures and interest, until F has received allocations of such taxable income equal to the sum of such research and experimental expenditures, such interest expense, and his share of such taxable loss. Thereafter, E and F will share all taxable income and loss equally. Operating cash flow will be distributed equally between E and F. The partnership agreement also provides that E's and F's capital accounts will be determined and maintained in accordance with paragraph (b)(2)(iv) of this section, distributions in liquidation of the partnership (or any partner's interest) will be made in accordance with the partners' positive capital account balances, and any partner with a deficit balance in his capital account following the liquidation of his interest must restore that deficit to the partnership (as set forth in paragraphs (b)(2)(ii)(*b*)(*2*) and (*3*) of this section). These allocations have economic effect. In addition, in view of the nature of the partnership's activities, there is not a strong likelihood at the time the allocations become part of the partnership agreement that the economic effect of the allocations to F of deductions for research and experimental expenditures and interest on partnership loans will be largely offset by allocations to F of partnership net taxable income. The economic effect of the allocations is substantial.

Example (4). (i) G and H contribute $75,000 and $25,000, respectively, in forming a general partnership. The partnership agreement provides that all income, gain, loss, and deduction will be allocated equally between the partners, that the partners' capital accounts will be determined and maintained in accordance with paragraph (b)(2)(iv) of this section, but that all partnership distributions will, regardless of capital account balances, be made 75 percent to G and 25 percent to H. Following the liquidation of the partnership, neither partner is required to restore the deficit balance in his capital account to the partnership for distribution to partners with positive capital account balances. The allocations in the partnership agreement do not have economic effect. Since contributions were made in a 75/25 ratio and the partnership agreement indicates that all economic profits and losses of the partnership are to be shared in a 75/25 ratio, under paragraph (b)(3) of this section, partnership income, gain, loss, and deduction will be reallocated 75 percent to G and 25 percent to H.

(ii) Assume the same facts as in (i) except that the partnership maintains no capital accounts and the partnership agreement provides that all income, gain, loss, deduction, and credit will be allocated 75 percent to G and 25 percent to H. G and H are ultimately liable (under a State law right of contribution) for 75 percent and 25 percent, respectively, of any debts of the partnership. Although the allocations do not satisfy the requirements of paragraph (b)(2)(ii)(*b*) of this section, the allocations have economic effect under the economic effect equivalence test of paragraph (b)(2)(ii)(*i*) of this section.

(iii) Assume the same facts as in (i) except that the partnership agreement provides that any partner with a deficit balance in his capital account must restore that deficit to the partnership (as set forth in paragraph (b)(2)(ii)(*b*)(*2*) of this section). Although the allocations do not satisfy the requirements of paragraph (b)(2)(ii)(*b*) of this section, the allocations have economic effect under the economic effect equivalence test of paragraph (b)(2)(ii)(*i*) of this section.

Example (5). (i) Individuals I and J are the only partners of an investment partnership. The partnership owns corporate stocks, corporate debt instruments, and tax-exempt debt instruments. Over the next several years, I expects to be in the 50 percent marginal tax bracket, and J expects to be in the 15 percent marginal tax bracket. There is a strong likelihood that in each of the next several years the partnership will realize between $450 and $550 of tax-exempt interest and between $450 and $550 of a combination of taxable interest and dividends from its investments. I and J made equal capital contributions to the partnership, and they have agreed to share equally in gains and losses from the sale of the partnership's investment securities. I and J agree, however, that rather than share interest and dividends of the partnership equally, they will allocate the partnership's tax-exempt interest 80 percent to I and 20 percent to J and will distribute cash derived from interest received on the tax-exempt bonds in the same percentages. In addition, they agree to allocate 100 percent of the partnership's taxable interest and dividends to J and to distribute cash derived from interest and dividends received on the corporate stocks and debt instruments 100 percent to J. The partnership agreement further provides that the partners' capital accounts will be determined and maintained in accordance with paragraph (b)(2)(iv) of this section, distributions in liquidation of the partnership (or any partner's interest) will be made in accordance with the partner's positive capital account balances, and any partner with a deficit balance in his capital account following the liquidation of his interest must restore that deficit to the partnership (as set forth in paragraphs (b)(2)(ii)(*b*)(*2*) and (*3*) of this section). The allocation of taxable interest and dividends and tax-exempt interest has economic effect, but that economic effect is not substantial under the general rules set forth in paragraph (b)(2)(iii) of this section. Without the allocation I would be allocated between $225 and $275 of tax-exempt interest and between $225 and $275 of a combination of taxable interest and dividends, which (net of Federal income taxes he would owe on such income) would give I between $337.50 and $412.50 after tax. With the allocation, however, I will be allocated between $360 and $440 of tax-exempt interest and no taxable interest and dividends, which (net of Federal income taxes) will give I between $360 and $440 after tax. Thus, at the time the allocations became part of the partnership agreement, I is expected to enhance his after-tax economic consequences as a result of the allocations. On the other hand, there is a strong likelihood that neither I nor J will substantially diminish his after-tax economic consequences as a result of the allocations. Under the combination of likely investment outcomes least favorable for J, the partnership would realize $550 of tax-exempt interest and $450 of taxable interest and dividends, giving J $492.50 after tax (which is more than the $466.25 after tax J would have received if each of such amounts had been allocated equally between the partners). Under the combination of likely investment outcomes least favorable for I, the partnership would realize $450 of tax-exempt interest and $550 of taxable interest and dividends, giving I $360 after tax (which is not substantially less than the $362.50 he would have received if each of such amounts had been allocated equally between the partners). Accordingly, the allocations in the partnership agreement must be reallocated in accordance with the partners' interests in the partnership under paragraph (b)(3) of this section.

(ii) Assume the same facts as in (i). In addition, assume that in the first partnership taxable year in which the allocation arrangement described in (i) applies, the partnership realizes $450 of tax-exempt interest and $550 of taxable interest and dividends, so that, pursuant to the partnership agreement, I's capital account is credited with $360 (80 percent of the tax-exempt interest), and J's capital account is credited with $640 (20 percent of the tax-exempt interest and 100 percent of the taxable interest and dividends). The allocations of tax-exempt interest and taxable interest and dividends (which do not have substantial economic effect for the reasons stated in (i)) will be disregarded and will be reallocated. Since under the partnership agreement I will receive 36 percent (360/1,000) and J will receive 64 percent (640/1,000) of the partnership's total investment income in such year, under paragraph (b)(3) of this section the partnership's tax-exempt interest and taxable interest and dividends each will be reallocated 36 percent to I and 64 percent to J.

Example (6). K and L are equal partners in a general partnership formed to acquire and operate property described in section 1231(b). The partnership, K, and L have calendar taxable years. The partnership agreement provides that the partners' capital accounts will be determined and maintained in accordance with paragraph (b)(2)(iv) of this section, that distributions in liquidation of the partnership (or any partner's interest) will be made in accordance with the partners' positive capital account balances, and that any partner with a deficit balance in his capital account following the liquidation of his interest must restore that deficit to the partnership (as set forth in paragraphs (b)(2)(ii)(*b*) and (*3*) of this section). For a taxable year in which the partnership expects to incur a loss on the sale of a portion of such property, the partnership agreement is amended (at the beginning of the taxable year) to allocate such loss to K, who expects to have no gains from the sale of depreciable property described in section 1231(b) in that taxable year, and to allocate an equivalent amount of partnership loss and deduction for that year of a different character to L, who expects to have such gains. Any partnership loss and deduction in excess of these allocations will be allocated equally between K and L. The amendment is effective only for that taxable year. At the time the partnership agreement is amended, there is a strong likelihood that the partnership will incur deduction or loss in the taxable year other than loss from the sale of property described in section 1231(b) in an amount that will substantially equal or exceed the expected amount of the section 1231(b) loss. The allocations in such taxable year have economic effect. However, the economic effect of the allocations is insubstantial under the test described in paragraph (b)(2)(iii)(*b*) of this section because there is a stong likelihood, at the time the allocations become part of the partnership agreement, that the net increases and decreases to K's and L's capital accounts will be the same at the end of the taxable year to which they apply with such allocations in effect as they would have been in the absence of such allocations, and that the total taxes of K and L for such year will be reduced as a result of such allocations. If in fact the partnership incurs deduction or loss, other than loss from the sale of property described in section 1231(b), in an amount at least equal to the section 1231(b) loss, the loss and deduction in such taxable year will be reallocated equally between K and L under paragraph (b)(3) of this section. If not, the loss from the sale of property described in section 1231(b) and the items of deduction and other loss realized in such year will be reallocated between K and L in proportion to the net decreases in their capital accounts due to the allocation of such items under the partnership agreement.

Example (7). (i) M and N are partners in the MN general partnership, which is engaged in an active business. Income, gain, loss, and deduction from MN's business is allocated equally between M and N. The partnership, M, and N have calendar taxable years. Under the partnership agreement the partners' capital accounts will be determined and maintained in accordance with paragraph (b)(2)(iv) of this section, distributions in liquidation of the partnership (or any partner's interest) will be made in accordance with the partners' positive capital account balances, and any partner with a deficit balance in his capital account following the liquidation of his interest must restore that deficit to the partnership (as set forth in paragraphs (b)(2)(ii)(*b*)(*2*) and (*3*) of this section). In order to enhance the credit standing of the partnership, the partners contribute surplus funds to the partnership, which the partners agree to invest in equal dollar amounts of tax-exempt bonds and corporate stock for the partnership's first 3 taxable years. M is expected to be in a higher marginal tax bracket than N during those 3 years. At the time the decision to make these investments is made, it is agreed that, during the 3-year period of the investment, M will be allocated 90 percent and N 10 percent of the interest income from the tax-exempt bonds as well as any gain or loss from the sale thereof, and that M will be allocated 10 percent and N 90 percent of the dividend income from the corporate stock as well as any gain or loss from the sale thereof. At the time the allocations concerning the investments become part of the partnership agreement, there is not a strong likelihood that the gain or loss from the sale of the stock will be substantially equal to the gain or loss from the sale of the tax-exempt bonds, but there is a strong likelihood that the tax-exempt interest and the taxable dividends realized from these investments during the 3-year period will not differ substantially. These allocations have economic effect, and the economic effect of the allocations of the gain or loss on the sale of the tax-exempt bonds and corporate stock is substantial. The economic effect of the allocations of the tax-exempt interest and the taxable dividends, however, is not substantial under the test described in paragraph (b)(2)(iii)(*c*) of this section because there is a strong likelihood, at the time the allocations become part of the partnership agreement, that at the end of the 3-year period to which such allocations relate, the net increases and decreases to M's and N's capital accounts will be the same with such allocations as they would have been in the absence of such allocations, and that the total taxes of M and N for the taxable years to which such allocations relate will be reduced as a result of such allocations. If in fact the amounts of tax-exempt interest and taxable dividends earned by the partnership during the 3-year period are equal, the tax-exempt interest and taxable dividends will be reallocated to the partners in equal shares under paragraph (b)(3) of this section. If not, the tax-exempt interest and taxable dividends will be reallocated between M and N in proportion to the net increases in their capital accounts during such 3-year period due to the allocation of such items under the partnership agreement.

(ii) Assume the same facts as in (i) except that gain or loss from the sale of the tax-exempt bonds and corporate stock will be allocated equally between M and N and the partnership agreement provides that the 90/10 allocation arrangement with respect to the investment income applies only to the first $10,000 of interest income from the tax-exempt bonds and the first $10,000 of dividend income from the corporate stock, and only to the first taxable year of the partnership. There is a strong likelihood at the time the 90/10 allocation of the investment income became part of the partnership agreement that in the first taxable year of the partnership, the partnership will earn more than $10,000 of tax-exempt interest and more than $10,000 of taxable dividends. The allocations of tax-exempt interest and taxable dividends provided in the partnership agreement have economic effect, but under the test contained in paragraph (b)(2)(iii)(*b*) of this section, such economic effect is not substantial for the same reasons stated in (i) (but applied to the 1 taxable year, rather than to a 3-year period). If in fact the partnership realizes at least $10,000 of tax-exempt interest and at least $10,000 of taxable dividends in such year, the allocations of such interest income and dividend income will be reallocated equally between M and N under paragraph (b)(3) of this section. If not, the tax-exempt interest and taxable dividends will be reallocated between M and N in proportion to the net increases in their capital accounts due to the allocations of such items under the partnership agreement.

(iii) Assume the same facts as in (ii) except that at the time the 90/10 allocation of investment income becomes part of the partnership agreement, there is not a strong likelihood that (1) the partnership will earn $10,000 or more of tax-exempt interest and $10,000 or more of taxable dividends in the partnership's first taxable year, and (2) the amount of tax-exempt interest and taxable dividends earned during such year will be substantially the same. Under these facts the economic effect of the allocations generally will be substantial. (Additional facts may exist in certain cases, however, so that the allocation is insubstantial under the second sentence of paragraph (b)(2)(iii). See example (5) above.)

* * *

Example (12). (i) W and X form a general partnership for the purpose of mining iron ore. W makes an initial contribution of $75,000, and X makes an initial contribution of $25,000. The partnership agreement provides that non-liquidating distributions will be made 75 percent to W and 25 percent to X, and that all items of income, gain, loss, and deduction will be allocated 75 percent to W and 25 percent to X, except that all percentage depletion deductions will be allocated to W. The agreement further provides that the partners' capital accounts will be determined and maintained in accordance with paragraph (b)(2)(iv) of this section, distributions in liquidation of the partnership (or any partner's interest) will be made in accordance with the partners' positive capital account balances, and any partner with a deficit balance in his capital account following the liquidation of his interest must restore such deficit to the partnership (as set forth in paragraphs (b)(2)(ii)(*b*)(*2*) and (*3*) of this section). Assume that the adjusted tax basis of the partnership's only depletable iron ore property is $1,000 and that the percentage depletion deduction for the taxable year with respect to such property is $1,500. The allocation of partnership income, gain, loss, and deduction (excluding the percentage depletion deduction) as well as the allocation of $1,000 of the percentage depletion deduction have substantial economic effect. The allocation to W of the remaining $500 of the percentage depletion deduction, representing the excess of percentage depletion over adjusted tax basis of the iron ore property, cannot have economic effect since such amount cannot properly be reflected in the partners' capital accounts. Furthermore, the allocation to W of that $500 excess percentage depletion deduction is not in accordance with the special partners' interests in the partnership rule contained in paragraph (b)(4)(iii) of this section, under which such $500 excess depletion deduction (and all further percentage depletion deductions from the mine) will be reallocated 75 percent to W and 25 percent to X.

(ii) Assume the same facts as in (i) except that the partnership agreement provides that all percentage depletion deductions of the partnership will be allocated 75 percent to W and 25 percent to X. Once again, the allocation of partnership income, gain, loss, and deduction (excluding the percentage depletion deduction) as well as the allocation of $1,000 of the percentage depletion deduction have substantial economic effect. Furthermore, since the $500 portion of the percentage depletion deduction that exceeds the adjusted basis of such iron ore property is allocated in the same manner as valid allocations of the gross income from such property during the taxable year (*i.e.,* 75 percent to W and 25 percent to X), the allocation of the $500 excess percentage depletion contained in the partnership agreement is in accordance with the special partners' interests in the partnership rule contained in paragraph (b)(4)(iii) of this section.

Example (13). (i) Y and Z form a brokerage general partnership for the purpose of investing and trading in marketable securities. Y contributes cash of $10,000, and Z contributes securities of P corporation, which have an adjusted basis of $3,000 and a fair market value of $10,000. The partnership would not be an investment company under section 351(e) if it were incorporated. The partnership agreement provides that the partners' capital accounts will be determined and maintained in accordance with paragraph (b)(2)(iv) of this section, distributions in liquidation of the partnership (or any partner's interest) will be made in accordance with the partners' positive capital account balances, and any partner with a deficit balance in his capital account following the liquidation of his interest must restore that deficit to the partnership (as set forth in paragraphs (b)(2)(ii)(*b*)(*2*) and (*3*) of this section). The partnership uses the interim closing of the books method for purposes of section 706. The initial capital accounts of Y and Z are fixed at $10,000 each. The agreement further provides that all partnership distributions, income, gain, loss, deduction, and credit will be shared equally between Y and Z, except that the taxable gain attributable to the precontribution appreciation in the value of the securities of P corporation will be allocated to Z in accordance with section 704(c). During the partnership's first taxable year, it sells the securities of P corporation for $12,000, resulting in a $2,000 book gain ($12,000 less $10,000 book value) and a $9,000 taxable gain ($12,000 less $3,000 adjusted tax basis). The partnership has no other income, gain, loss, or deductions for the taxable year. The gain from the sale of the securities is allocated as follows:

	Y		Z	
	Tax	*Book*	*Tax*	*Book*
Capital account upon formation	$10,000	$10,000	$3,000	$10,000
Plus: gain	1,000	1,000	8,000	1,000
Capital account at end of year 1	$11,000	$11,000	$11,000	$11,000

The allocation of the $2,000 book gain, $1,000 each to Y and Z, has substantial economic effect. Furthermore, under section 704(c) the partners' distributive shares of the $9,000 taxable gain are $1,000 to Y and $8,000 to Z.

(ii) Assume the same facts as in (i) and that at the beginning of the partnership's second taxable year, it invests its $22,000 of cash in securities of G Corp. The G Corp. securities increase in value to $40,000, at which time Y sells 50 percent of his partnership interest (*i.e.*, a 25 percent interest in the partnership) to LK for $10,000. The partnership does not have a section 754 election in effect for the partnership taxable year during which such sale occurs. In accordance with paragraph (b)(2)(iv)(*l*) of this section, the partnership agreement provides that LK inherits 50 percent of Y's $11,000 capital account balance. Thus, following the sale, LK and Y each have a capital account of $5,500, and Z's capital account remains at $11,000. Prior to the end of the partnership's second taxable year, the securities are sold for their $40,000 fair market value, resulting in an $18,000 taxable gain ($40,000 less $22,000 adjusted tax basis). The partnership has no other income, gain, loss, or deduction in such taxable year. Under the partnership agreement the $18,000 taxable gain is allocated as follows:

	Y	*Z*	*LK*
Capital account before sale of securities	$5,500	$11,000	$5,500
Plus: gain	4,500	9,000	4,500
Capital account at end of year 2	$10,000	$20,000	$10,000

The allocation of the $18,000 taxable gain has substantial economic effect.

(iii) Assume the same facts as in (ii) except that the partnership has a section 754 election in effect for the partnership taxable year during which Y sells 50 percent of his interest to LK. Accordingly, under § 1.743-1 there is a $4,500 basis increase to the G Corp. securities with respect to LK. Notwithstanding this basis adjustment, as a result of the sale of the G Corp. securities, LK's capital account is, as in (ii), increased by $4,500. The fact that LK recognizes no taxable gain from such sale (due to his $4,500 section 743 basis adjustment) is irrelevant for capital accounting purposes since, in accordance with paragraph (b)(2)(iv)(*m*)(*2*) of this section, that basis adjustment is disregarded in the maintenance and computation of the partners' capital accounts.

(iv) Assume the same facts as in (iii) except that immediately following Y's sale of 50 percent of this interest to LK, the G Corp. securities decrease in value to $32,000 and are sold. The $10,000 taxable gain ($32,000 less $22,000 adjusted tax basis) is allocated as follows:

	Y	*Z*	*LK*
Capital account before sale of securities	$5,500	$11,000	$5,500
Plus: gain	2,500	5,000	2,500
Capital account at end of the year 2	$8,000	$16,000	$8,000

The fact that LK recognizes a $2,000 taxable loss from the sale of the G Corp. securities (due to his $4,500 section 743 basis adjustment) is irrelevant for capital accounting purposes since, in accordance with paragraph (b)(2)(iv)(*m*)(*2*) of this section, that basis adjustment is disregarded in the maintenance and computation of the partners' capital accounts.

(v) Assume the same facts as in (ii) except that Y sells 100 percent of his partnership interest (*i.e.*, a 50 percent interest in the partnership) to LK for $20,000. Under section 708(b)(1)(B) the partnership terminates. Under paragraph (b)(1)(iv) of § 1.708-1, there is a constructive liquidation of the partnership. Immediately preceding the constructive liquidation, the capital accounts of Z and LK equal $11,000 each (LK having inherited Y s $11,000 capital account) and the book value of the G Corp. securities is $22,000 (original purchase price of securities). Under paragraph (b)(2)(iv)(*l*) of this section, the deemed contribution of assets and liabilities by the terminated partnership to the new partnership and the deemed liquidation of the terminated partnership that occur under § 1.708-1(b)(1)(iv) in connection with the constructive liquidation of the terminated partnership are disregarded in the maintenance and computation of the partners' capital accounts. As a result, the capital accounts of Z and LK in the new partnership equal $11,000 each (their capital accounts in the terminated partnership immediately prior to the termination), and the book value of the G Corp. securities remains $22,000 (its book value immediately prior to the termination). This *Example 13*(v) applies to terminations of partnerships under section 708(b)(1)(B) occurring on or after May 9, 1997; however, this *Example 13*(v) may be applied to terminations occurring on or after May 9, 1996, provided that the partnership and its partners apply this *Example 13*(v) to the termination in a consistent manner.

Example (14). (i) MC and RW form a general partnership to which each contributes $10,000. The $20,000 is invested in securities of Ventureco (which are not readily tradable on an established securities market). In each of the partnership's taxable years, it recognizes operating income equal to its operating deductions (excluding gain or loss from the sale of securities). The partnership agreement provides that the partners' capital accounts will be determined and maintained in accordance with paragraph (b)(2)(iv) of this section, distributions in liquidation of the partnership (or any partner's interest) will be made in accordance with the partners' positive capital account balances, and any partner with a deficit balance in his capital account following the liquidation of his interest must restore that deficit to the partnership (as set forth in paragraphs (b)(2)(ii)(*b*)(*2*) and (*3*) of this section). The partnership uses the interim closing of the books method for purposes of section 706. Assume that the Ventureco securities subsequently appreciate in value to $50,000. At that time SK makes a $25,000 cash contribution to the partnership (thereby acquiring a one-third interest in the partnership), and the $25,000 is placed in a bank account. Upon SK's admission to the partnership, the capital accounts of MC and RW (which were $10,000 each prior to SK's admission) are, in accordance with paragraph (b)(2)(iv)(*f*) of this section, adjusted upward (to $25,000 each) to reflect their shares of the unrealized appreciation in the Ventureco securities that occurred before SK was admitted to the partnership. Immediately after SK's admission to the partnership, the securities are sold for their $50,000 fair market value, resulting in taxable gain of $30,000 ($50,000 less $20,000 adjusted tax basis) and no book gain or loss. An allocation of the $30,000 taxable gain cannot have economic effect since it cannot properly be reflected in the partners' book capital accounts. Under paragraph (b)(2)(iv)(*f*) of this section and the special partners' interests in the partnership rule contained in paragraph (b)(4)(i) of this section, unless the partnership agreement provides that the $30,000 taxable gain will, in accordance with section 704(c) principles, be shared $15,000 to MC and $15,000 to RW, the partners' capital accounts will not be considered maintained in accordance with paragraph (b)(2)(iv) of this section.

	MC		*RW*		*SK*	
	Tax	*Book*	*Tax*	*Book*	*Tax*	*Book*
Capital account following SK's admission	$10,000	$25,000	$10,000	$25,000	$25,000	$25,000
Plus: gain	15,000	0	15,000	0	0	0
Capital account following sale	$25,000	$25,000	$25,000	$25,000	$25,000	$25,000

(ii) Assume the same facts as (i), except that after SK's admission to the partnership, the Ventureco securities appreciate in value to $74,000 and are sold, resulting in taxable gain of $54,000 ($74,000 less $20,000 adjusted tax basis) and book gain of $24,000 ($74,000 less $50,000 book value). Under the partnership agreement the $24,000 book gain (the appreciation in value occurring after SK became a partner) is allocated equally among MC, RW, and SK, and such allocations have substantial economic effect. An allocation of the $54,000 taxable gain cannot have economic effect since it cannot properly be reflected in the partners' book capital accounts. Under paragraph (b)(2)(iv)(*f*) of this section and the special partners' interests in the partnership rule contained in paragraph (b)(4)(i) of this section, unless the partnership agreement provides that the taxable gain will, in accordance with section 704(c) principles, be shared $23,000 to MC, $23,000 to RW, and $8,000 to SK, the partners' capital accounts will not be considered maintained in accordance with paragraph (b)(2)(iv) of this section.

	MC		*RW*		*SK*	
	Tax	*Book*	*Tax*	*Book*	*Tax*	*Book*
Capital account following SK's admission	$10,000	$25,000	$10,000	$25,000	$25,000	$25,000
Plus: gain	23,000	8,000	23,000	8,000	8,000	8,000
Capital account following sale	$33,000	$33,000	$33,000	$33,000	$33,000	$33,000

(iii) Assume the same facts as (i) except that after SK's admission to the partnership, the Ventureco securities depreciate in value to $44,000 and are sold, resulting in taxable gain of $24,000 ($44,000 less $20,000 adjusted tax basis) and a book loss of $6,000 ($50,000 book value less $44,000). Under the partnership agreement the $6,000 book loss is allocated equally among MC, RW, and SK, and such allocations have substantial economic effect. An allocation of the $24,000 taxable gain cannot have economic effect since it cannot properly be reflected in the partners' book capital accounts. Under paragraph (b)(2)(iv)(*f*) of this section and the special partners' interests in the partnership rule contained in paragraph (b)(4)(i) of this section, unless the partnership agreement provides that the $24,000 taxable gain will, in accordance with section 704(c) principles, be shared equally between MC and RW, the partners' capital accounts will not be considered maintained in accordance with paragraph (b)(2)(iv) of this section.

	MC		RW		SK	
	Tax	*Book*	*Tax*	*Book*	*Tax*	*Book*
Capital account following SK's admission	$10,000	$25,000	$10,000	$25,000	$25,000	$25,000
Plus: gain	12,000	0	12,000	0	0	0
Less: loss	0	(2,000)	0	(2,000)	0	(2,000)
Capital account following sale	$22,000	$23,000	$22,000	$23,000	$25,000	$23,000

That SK bears an economic loss of $2,000 without a corresponding taxable loss is attributable entirely to the "ceiling rule." See paragraph (c) (2) of § 1.704-1.

(iv) Assume the same facts as in (ii) except that upon the admission of SK the capital accounts of MC and RW are not each adjusted upward from $10,000 to $25,000 to reflect the appreciation in the partnership's securities that occurred before SK was admitted to the partnership. Rather, upon SK's admission to the partnership, the partnership agreement is amended to provide that the first $30,000 of taxable gain upon the sale of such securities will be allocated equally between MC and RW, and that all other income, gain, loss, and deduction will be allocated equally between MC, RW, and SK. When the securities are sold for $74,000, the $54,000 of taxable gain is so allocated. These allocations of taxable gain have substantial economic effect. (If the agreement instead provides for all taxable gain (including the $30,000 taxable gain attributable to the appreciation in the securities prior to SK's admission to the partnership) to be allocated equally between MC, RW, and SK, the partners should consider whether, and to what extent, the provisions of paragraphs (b) (1) (iii) and (iv) of this section are applicable.)

(v) Assume the same facts as in (iv) except that instead of selling the securities, the partnership makes a distribution of the securities (which have a fair market value of $74,000). Assume the distribution does not give rise to a transaction described in section 707(a) (2) (B). In accordance with paragraph (b) (2) (iv) (*e*) of this section, the partners' capital accounts are adjusted immediately prior to the distribution to reflect how taxable gain ($54,000) would have been allocated had the securities been sold for their $74,000 fair market value, and capital account adjustments in respect of the distribution of the securities are made with reference to the $74,000 "booked-up" fair market value.

	MC	*RW*	*SK*
Capital account before adjustment	$10,000	$10,000	$25,000
Deemed sale adjustment	23,000	23,000	8,000
Less: distribution	(24,667)	(24,667)	(24,667)
Capital account after distribution	$8,333	$8,333	$8,333

(vi) Assume the same facts as in (i) except that the partnership does not sell the Ventureco securities. During the next 3 years the fair market value of the Ventureco securities remains at $50,000, and the partnership engages in no other investment activities. Thus, at the end of that period the balance sheet of the partnership and the partners' capital accounts are the same as they were at the beginning of such period. At the end of the 3 years, MC's interest in the partnership is liquidated for the $25,000 cash held by the partnership. Assume the distribution does not give rise to a transaction described in section 707(a) (2) (B). Assume further that the partnership has a section 754 election in effect for the taxable year during which such liquidation occurs. Under sections 734(b) and 755 the partnership increases the basis of the Ventureco securities by the $15,000 basis adjustment (the excess of $25,000 over the $10,000 adjusted tax basis of MC's partnership interest).

	MC		RW		SK	
	Tax	*Book*	*Tax*	*Book*	*Tax*	*Book*
Capital account before distribution	$10,000	$25,000	$10,000	$25,000	$25,000	$25,000
Plus: basis adjustment	15,000	0	0	0	0	0
Less: distribution	(25,000)	(25,000)	0	0	0	0
Capital account, account after liquidation	0	0	$10,000	$25,000	$25,000	$25,000

(vii) Assume the same facts as in (vi) except that the partnership has no section 754 election in effect for the taxable year during which such liquidation occurs.

	MC		RW		SK	
	Tax	*Book*	*Tax*	*Book*	*Tax*	*Book*
Capital account before distribution	$10,000	$25,000	$10,000	$25,000	$25,000	$25,000
Less: distribution	25,000	(25,000)	0	0	0	0
Capital account after liquidation	($15,000)	0	$10,000	$25,000	$25,000	$25,000

Following the liquidation of MC's interest in the partnership, the Ventureco securities are sold for their $50,000 fair market value, resulting in no book gain or loss but a $30,000 taxable gain. An allocation of this $30,000 taxable gain cannot have economic effect since it cannot properly be reflected in the partners' book capital accounts. Under paragraph (b)(2)(iv)(*f*) of this section and the special partners' interests in the partnership rule contained in paragraph (b)(4)(i) of this section, unless the partnership agreement provides that $15,000 of such taxable gain will, in accordance with section 704(c) principles, be included in RW's distributive share, the partners' capital accounts will not be considered maintained in accordance with paragraph (b)(2)(iv) of this section. The remaining $15,000 of such gain will, under paragraph (b)(3) of this section, be shared equally between RW and SK.

Example (15). (i) JB and DK form a limited partnership for the purpose of purchasing residential real estate to lease. JB, the limited partner, contributes $13,500, and DK, the general partner, contributes $1,500. The partnership, which uses the cash receipts and disbursements method of accounting, purchases a building for $100,000 (on leased land), incurring a recourse mortgage of $85,000 that requires the payment of interest only for a period of 3 years. The partnership agreement provides that partnership net taxable income and loss will be allocated 90 percent to JB and 10 percent to DK, the partners' capital accounts will be determined and maintained in accordance with paragraph (b)(2)(iv) of this section, distributions in liquidation of the partnership (or any partner's interest) will be made in accordance with the partners' positive capital account balances (as set forth in paragraph (b)(2)(ii)(*b*)(*2*) of this section), and JB is not required to restore any deficit balance in his capital account, but DK is so required. The partnership agreement contains a qualified income offset (as defined in paragraph (b)(2)(ii)(*d*) of this section). As of the end of each of the partnership's first 3 taxable years, the items described in paragraphs (b)(2)(ii)(*d*)(*4*), (*5*), and (*6*) of this section are not reasonably expected to cause or increase a deficit balance in JB's capital account. In the partnership's first taxable year, it has rental income of $10,000, operating expenses of $2,000, interest expense of $8,000, and cost recovery deductions of $12,000. Under the partnership agreement JB and DK are allocated $10,800 and $1,200, respectively, of the $12,000 net taxable loss incurred in the partnership's first taxable year.

	JB	*DK*
Capital account upon formation	$13,500	$1,500
Less: year 1 net loss	(10,800)	(1,200)
Capital account at end of year 1	$2,700	$300

The alternate economic effect test contained in paragraph (b)(2)(ii)(*d*) of this section is satisfied as of the end of the partnership's first taxable year. Thus, the allocation made in the partnership's first taxable year has economic effect.

(ii) Assume the same facts as in (i) and that in the partnership's second taxable year it again has rental income of $10,000, operating expenses of $2,000, interest expense of $8,000, and cost recovery deductions of $12,000. Under the partnership agreement JB and DK are allocated $10,800 and $1,200, respectively, of the $12,000 net taxable loss incurred in the partnership's second taxable year.

	JB	*DK*
Capital account at beginning of year 1	$2,700	$300
Less: year 2 net loss	(10,800)	(1,200)
Capital account at end of year 2	$(8,100)	$(900)

Only $2,700 of the $10,800 net taxable loss allocated to JB satisfies the alternate economic effect test contained in paragraph (b)(2)(ii)(*d*) of this section as of the end of the partnership's second taxable year. The allocation of such $2,700 net taxable loss to JB (consisting of $2,250 of rental income, $450 of operating expenses, $1,800 of interest expense, and $2,700 of cost recovery deductions) has economic effect. The remaining $8,100 of net taxable loss allocated by the partnership agreement to JB must be reallocated in accordance with the partners' interests in the partnership. Under paragraph (b)(3)(iii) of this section, the determination of the partners' interests in the remaining $8,100 net taxable loss is made by comparing how distributions (and contributions) would be made if the partnership sold its property at its adjusted tax basis and liquidated immediately following the end of the partnership's first taxable year with the results of such a sale and liquidation immediately following the end of the partnership's second taxable year. If the partnership's real property were sold for its $88,000 adjusted tax basis and the partnership were liquidated immediately following the end of the partnership's first taxable year, the $88,000 sales proceeds would be used to repay the $85,000 note, and there would be $3,000 remaining in the partnership, which would be used to make liquidating distributions to DK and JB of $300 and $2,700, respectively. If such property were sold for its $76,000 adjusted tax basis and the partnership were liquidated immediately following the end of the partnership's second taxable year, DK would be required to contribute $9,000 to the partnership in order for the partnership to repay the $85,000 note, and there would be no assets remaining in the partnership to distribute. A comparison of these outcomes indicates that JB bore $2,700 and DK $9,300 of the economic burden that corresponds to the $12,000 net taxable loss. Thus, in addition to the $1,200 net taxable loss allocated to DK under the partnership agreement, $8,100 of net taxable loss will be reallocated to DK under paragraph (b)(3)(iii) of this section. Similarly, for subsequent taxable years, absent an increase in JB's capital account, all net taxable loss allocated to JB under the partnership agreement will be reallocated to DK.

(iii) Assume the same facts as in (ii) and that in the partnership's third taxable year there is rental income of $35,000, operating expenses of $2,000, interest expense of $8,000, the cost recovery deductions of $10,000. The capital accounts of the partners maintained on the books of the partnership do not take into account the reallocation to DK of the $8,100 net taxable loss in the partnership's second taxable year. Thus, an allocation of the $15,000 net taxable income $13,500 to JB and $1,500 to DK (as dictated by the partnership agreement and as reflected in the capital accounts of the partners) does not have economic effect. The partners' interests in the partnership with respect to such $15,000 taxable gain again is made in the manner described in paragraph (b)(3)(iii) of this section. If the partnership's real property were sold for its $76,000 adjusted tax basis and the partnership were liquidated immediately following the end of the partnership's second taxable year, DK would be required to contribute $9,000 to the partnership in order for the partnership to repay the $85,000 note, and there would be no assets remaining to distribute. If such property were sold for its $66,000 adjusted tax basis and the partnership were liquidated immediately following the end of the partnership's third taxable year, the $91,000 ($66,000 sales proceeds plus $25,000 cash on hand) would be used to repay the $85,000 note and there would be $6,000 remaining in the partnership, which would be used to make liquidating distributions to DK and JB of $600 and $5,400, respectively. Accordingly, under paragraph (b)(3)(iii) of this section the $15,000 net taxable income in the partnership's third taxable year will be reallocated $9,600 to DK (minus $9,000 at end of the second taxable year to positive $600 at end of the third taxable year) and $5,400 to JB (zero at end of the second taxable year to positive $5,400 at end of the third taxable year).

Example (16). (i) KG and WN form a limited partnership for the purpose of investing in improved real estate. KG, the general partner, contributes $10,000 to the partnership, and WN, the limited partner, contributes $990,000 to the partnership. The $1,000,000 is used to purchase an apartment building on leased land. The partnership agreement provides that (1) the partners' capital accounts will be determined and maintained in accordance with paragraph (b)(2)(iv) of this section; (2) cash will be distributed first to WN until such time as he has received the amount of his original capital contribution ($990,000), next to KG until such time as he has received the amount of his original capital contribution ($10,000), and thereafter equally between WN and KG; (3) partnership net taxable income will be allocated 99 percent to WN and 1 percent to KG until the cumulative net taxable income allocated for all taxable years is equal to the cumulative net taxable loss previously allocated to the partners, and thereafter equally between WN and KG; (4) partnership net taxable loss will be allocated 99 percent to WN and 1 percent to KG, unless net taxable income has previously been allocated equally between WN and KG, in which case such net taxable loss first will be allocated equally until the cumulative net taxable loss allocated for all taxable years is equal to the cumulative net taxable income previously allocated to the partners; and (5) upon liquidation, WN is not required to restore any deficit balance in his capital account, but KG is so required. Since distributions in liquidation are not required to be made in accordance with the partners' positive capital account balances, and since WN is not required, upon the liquidation of his interest, to restore the deficit balance in his capital account to the partnership, the allocations provided by the partnership agreement do not have economic effect and will be reallocated in accordance with the partners' interests in the partnership under paragraph (b)(3) of this section.

(ii) Assume the same facts as in (i) except that the partnership agreement further provides that distributions in liquidation of the partnership (or any partner's interest) are to be made in accordance with the partners' positive capital account balances (as set forth in paragraph (b)(2)(ii)(*b*)(*2*) of this section). Assume further that the partnership agreement contains a qualified income offset (as defined in paragraph (b)(2)(ii)(*d*) of this section) and that, as of the end of each partnership taxable year, the items described in paragraphs (b)(2)(iii)(*d*)(*4*), (*5*), and (*6*) of this section are not reasonably expected to cause or increase a deficit balance in WN's capital account. The allocations provided by the partnership agreement have economic effect.

Example (17). FG and RP form a partnership with FG contributing cash of $100 and RP contributing property, with 2 years of cost recovery deductions remaining, that has an adjusted tax basis of $80 and a fair market value of $100. The partnership, FG, and RP have calendar taxable years. The partnership agreement provides that the partners' capital accounts will be determined and maintained in accordance with paragraph (b)(2)(iv) of this section, liquidation proceeds will be made in accordance with capital account balances, and each partner is liable to restore the deficit balance in his capital account to the partnership upon liquidation of his interest (as set forth in paragraphs (b)(2)(ii)(*b*)(*2*) and (*3*) of this section). FG expects to be in a substantially higher tax bracket than RP in the partnership's first taxable year. In the partnership's second taxable year, and in subsequent taxable years, it is expected that both will be in approximately equivalent tax brackets. The partnership agreement allocates all items equally except that all $50 of book depreciation is allocated to FG in the partnership's first taxable year and all $50 of book depreciation is allocated to RP in the partnership's second taxable year. If the allocation to FG of all book depreciation in the partnership's first taxable year is respected, FG would be entitled under section 704(c) to the entire cost recovery deduction ($40) for such year. Likewise, if the allocation to RP of all the book depreciation in the partnership's second taxable year is respected, RP would be entitled under section 704(c) to the entire cost recovery deduction ($40) for such year. The allocation of book depreciation to FG and RP in the partnership's first 2 taxable years has economic effect within the meaning of paragraph (b)(2)(ii) of this section. However, the economic effect of these allocations is not substantial under the test described in paragraph (b)(2)(iii)(*c*) of this section since there is a strong likelihood at the time such allocations became part of the partnership agreement that at the end of the 2-year period to which such allocations relate, the net increases and decreases to FG's and RP's capital accounts will be the same with such allocations as they would have been in the absence of such allocation, and the total tax liability of FG and RP for the taxable years to which the section 704(c) determinations relate would be reduced as a result of the allocations of book depreciation. As a result the allocations of book depreciation in the partnership agreement will be disregarded. FG and RP will be allocated such book depreciation in accordance with the partners' interests in the partnership under paragraph (b)(3) of this section. Under these facts the book depreciation deductions will be reallocated equally between the partners, and section 704(c) will be applied with reference to such reallocation of book depreciation.

* * *

Example (19). (i) DG and JC form a general partnership for the purpose of drilling oil wells. DG contributes an oil lease, which has a fair market value and adjusted tax basis of $100,000. JC contributes $100,000 in cash, which is used to finance the drilling operations. The partnership agreement provides that DG is credited with a capital account of $100,000, and JC is credited with a capital account of $100,000. The agreement further provides that the partners' capital accounts will be determined and maintained in accordance with paragraph (b)(2)(iv) of this section, distributions in liquidation of the partnership (or any partner's interest) will be made in accordance with the partners' positive capital account balances, and any partner with a deficit balance in his capital account following the liquidation of his interest must restore such deficit to the partnership (as set forth in paragraphs (b)(2)(ii)(b)(*2*) and (*3*) of this section). The partnership chooses to adjust capital accounts on a simulated cost depletion basis and elects under section 48(q)(4) to reduce the amount of investment tax credit in lieu of adjusting the basis of its section 38 property. The agreement further provides that (1) all additional cash requirements of the partnership will be borne equally by DG and JC, (2) the deductions attributable to the property (including money) contributed by each partner will be allocated to such partner, (3) all other income, gain, loss, and deductions (and item thereof) will be allocated equally between DG and JC, and (4) all cash from operations will be distributed equally between DG and JC. In the partnership's first taxable year $80,000 of partnership intangible drilling cost deductions and $20,000 of cost recovery deductions on partnership equipment are allocated to JC, and the $100,000 basis of the lease is, for purposes of the depletion allowance under sections 611 and 613A(c)(7)(D), allocated to DG. The allocations of income, gain, loss, and deduction provided in the partnership agreement have substantial economic effect. Furthermore, since the allocation of the entire basis of the lease to DG will not result in capital account adjustments (under paragraph (b)(2)(*iv*)(*k*) of this section) the economic effect of which is insubstantial, and since all other partnership allocations are recognized under this paragraph, the allocation of the $100,000 adjusted basis of the lease to DG is, under paragraph (b)(4)(v) of this section, recognized as being in accordance with the partners' interests in partnership capital for purposes of section 613A(c)(7)(D).

(ii) Assume the same facts as in (i) except that the partnership agreement provides that (1) all additional cash requirements of the partnership for additional expenses will be funded by additional contributions from JC, (2) all cash from operations will first be distributed to JC until the excess of such cash distributions over the amount of such additional expenses equals his initial $100,000 contribution, (3) all deductions attributable to such additional operating expenses will be allocated to JC, and (4) all income will be allocated to JC until the aggregate amount of income allocated to him equals the amount of partnership operating expenses funded by his initial $100,000 contribution plus the amount of additional operating expenses paid from contributions made solely by him. The allocations of income, gain, loss, and deduction provided in the partnership agreement have economic effect. In addition, the economic effect of the allocations provided in the agreement is substantial. Because the partnership's drilling activities are sufficiently speculative, there is not a strong likelihood at the time the disproportionate allocations of loss and deduction to JC are provided for by the partnership agreement that the economic effect of such allocations will be largely offset by allocations of income. In addition, since the allocation of the entire basis of the lease to DG will not result in capital account adjustments (under paragraph (b)(2)(*iv*)(*k*) of this section), the economic effect of which is insubstantial, and since all other partnership allocations are recognized under this paragraph, the allocation of the adjusted basis of the lease to DG is, under paragraph (b)(4)(v) of this section, recognized as being in accordance with the partners' interests in partnership capital under section 613A(c)(7)(D).

(iii) Assume the same facts as in (i) except that all distributions, including those made upon liquidation of the partnership, will be made equally between DG and JC, and no partner is obligated to restore the deficit balance in his capital account to the partnership following the liquidation of his interest for distribution to partners with positive capital account balances. Since liquidation proceeds will be distributed equally between DG and JC irrespective of their capital account balances, and since no partner is required to restore the deficit balance in his capital account to the partnership upon liquidation (in accordance with paragraph (b)(2)(ii)(*b*)(*3*) of this section), the allocations of income, gain, loss, and deduction provided in the partnership agreement do not have economic effect and must be reallocated in accordance with the partners' interests in the partnership under paragraph (b)(3) of this section. Under these facts all partnership income, gain, loss, and deduction (and item thereof) will be reallocated equally between JC and DG. Furthermore, the allocation of the $100,000 adjusted tax basis of the lease to DG is not, under paragraph (b)(4)(v) of this section, deemed to be in accordance with the partners' interests in partnership capital under section 613A(c)(7)(D), and such basis must be reallocated in accordance with the partners' interests in partnership capital or income as determined under section 613A(c)(7)(D). The results in this example would be the same if JC's initial cash contribution were $1,000,000 (instead of $100,000), but in such case the partners should consider whether, and to what extent, the provisions of paragraph (b)(1) of § 1.721-1, and principles related thereto, may be applicable.

(iv) Assume the same facts as in (i) and that for the partnership's first taxable year the simulated depletion deduction with respect to the lease is $10,000. Since DG properly was allocated the entire depletable basis of the lease (such allocation having been recognized as being in accordance with DG's interest in partnership capital with respect to such lease), under paragraph (b)(2)(iv)(*k*)(*1*) of this section the partnership's $10,000 simulated depletion deduction is allocated to DG and will reduce his capital account accordingly. If (prior to any additional simulated depletion deductions) the lease is sold for $100,000, paragraph (b)(4)(v) of this section requires that the first $90,000 (*i.e.,* the partnership's simulated adjusted basis in the lease) out of the $100,000 amount realized on such sale be allocated to DG (but does not directly affect his capital account). The partnersip agreement allocates the remaining $10,000 amount realized equally between JC and DG (but such allocation does not directly affect their capital accounts). This allocation of the $10,000 portion of amount realized that exceeds the partnership's simulated adjusted basis in the lease will be treated as being in accordance with the partners' allocable shares of such amount realized under section 613A(c)(7)(D) because such allocation will not result in capital account adjustments (under paragraph (b)(2)(iv)(*k*) of this section) the economic effect of which is insubstantial, and all other partnership allocations are recognized under this paragraph. Under paragraph (b)(2)(iv)(*k*) of this section, the partners' capital accounts are adjusted upward by the partnership's simulated gain of $10,000 ($100,000 sales price less $90,000 simulated adjusted basis) in proportion to such partners' allocable shares of the $10,000 portion of the total amount realized that exceeds the partnership's $90,000 simulated adjusted basis ($5,000 to JC and $5,000 to DG). If the lease is sold for $50,000, under paragraph (b)(4)(v) of this section the entire $50,000 amount realized on the sale of the lease will be allocated to DG (but will not directly affect his capital account). Under paragraph (b)(2)(iv)(*k*) of this section the partners' capital accounts will be adjusted downward by the partnership's $40,000 simulated loss ($50,000 sales price less $90,000 simulated adjusted basis) in proportion to the partners' allocable shares of the total amount realized from the property that represents recovery of the partnership's simulated adjusted basis therein. Accordingly, DG's capital account will be reduced by such $40,000.

* * *

Example 23. (i) The facts are the same as in *Example 21*, except that AB does not actually receive the $50,000 of income accrued in 2007 with respect to business N until 2008 and AB accrues and receives an additional $100,000 with respect to business N in 2008. Also assume that A, B, and AB each report taxable income on an accrual basis for U.S. tax purposes and AB reports taxable income using the cash receipts and disbursements method of accounting for country X and country Y purposes. In 2007, AB pays or accrues country X taxes of $40,000. In 2008, AB pays or accrues country Y taxes of $30,000. Pursuant to the partnership agreement, in 2007, A is allocated 75 percent of business M income ($75,000) and country X taxes ($30,000) and 50 percent of business N income ($25,000). B is allocated 25 percent of business M income ($25,000) and country X taxes ($10,000) and 50 percent of business N income ($25,000). In 2008, A and B are each allocated 50 percent of the business N income ($50,000) and country Y taxes ($15,000).

(ii) For 2007, the $40,000 of country X taxes paid or accrued by AB relates to the $100,000 of net income in the business M CFTE category. No portion of the country X taxes paid or accrued in 2007 relates to the $50,000 of net income in the business N CFTE category. For 2008, the net income in the business N CFTE category is the $100,000 attributable to business N. See paragraph (b)(4)(viii)(*c*)(*3*) of this section. Under paragraph (b)(4)(viii)(*d*)(*1*) of this section, $20,000 of the country Y tax paid or accrued in 2008 is allocated to the business N CFTE category. The remaining $10,000 of country Y tax is allocated to the business N CFTE category under paragraph (b)(4)(viii)(*d*)(*2*) of this section (relating to timing differences). Therefore, the $30,000 of country Y taxes paid or accrued by AB in 2008 is related to the $100,000 of net income in the business N CFTE category for 2008. See paragraph (b)(4)(viii)(*c*)(*1*) of this section. Because AB's partnership agreement allocates the $40,000 of country X taxes and the $30,000 of country Y taxes in proportion to the distributive shares of income to which the taxes relate, the allocations of the country X and country Y taxes satisfy the requirements of paragraphs (b)(4)(viii)(*a*)(*1*) and (*2*) of this section and the allocations of the country X and Y taxes are deemed to be in accordance with the partners' interests in the partnership under paragraph (b)(4)(viii) of this section.

* * *

(c) *Contributed property; cross-reference.*—See § 1.704-3 for methods of making allocations that take into account precontribution appreciation or diminution in value of property contributed by a partner to a partnership.

(d) *Limitation on allowance of losses.*—(1) A partner's distributive share of partnership loss will be allowed only to the extent of the adjusted basis (before reduction by current year's losses) of such partner's interest in the partnership at the end of the partnership taxable year in which such loss occurred. A partner's share of loss in excess of his adjusted basis at the end of the partnership taxable year will not be allowed for that year. However, any loss so disallowed shall be allowed as a deduction at the end of the first succeeding partnership taxable year, and subsequent partnership taxable years, to the extent that the partner's adjusted basis for his partnership interest at the end of any such year exceeds zero (before reduction by such loss for such year).

(2) In computing the adjusted basis of a partner's interest for the purpose of ascertaining the extent to which a partner's distributive share of partnership loss shall be allowed as a deduction for the taxable year, the basis shall first be increased under section 705(a)(1) and decreased under section 705(a)(2), except for losses of the taxable year and losses previously disallowed. If the partner's distributive share of the aggregate of items of loss specified in section 702(a)(1), (2), (3), (8), and (9) exceeds the basis of the partner's interest computed under the preceding sentence, the limitation on losses under section 704(d) must be allocated to his distributive share of each such loss. This allocation shall be determined by taking the proportion that each loss bears to the total of all such losses. For purposes of the preceding sentence, the total losses for the taxable year shall be the sum of his distributive share of losses for the current year and his losses disallowed and carried forward from prior years.

(3) For the treatment of certain liabilities of the partner or partnership, see section 752 and § 1.752-1.

(4) The provisions of this paragraph may be illustrated by the following examples:

Example (1). At the end of the partnership taxable year 1955, partnership AB has a loss of $20,000. Partner A's distributive share of this loss is $10,000. At the end [of] such year, A's adjusted basis for his interest in the partnership (not taking into account his distributive share of the loss) is $6,000. Under section 704(d), A's distributive share of partnership loss is allowed to him (in his taxable year within or with which the partnership taxable year ends) only to the extent of his adjusted basis of $6,000. The $6,000 loss allowed for 1955 decreases the adjusted basis of A's interest to zero. Assume that, at the end of partnership taxable year 1956, A's share of partnership income has increased the adjusted basis of A's interest in the partnership to $3,000 (not taking into account the $4,000 loss disallowed in 1955). Of the $4,000 loss disallowed for the partnership taxable year 1955, $3,000 is allowed A for the partnership taxable year 1956, thus again decreasing the adjusted basis of his interest to zero. If, at the end of partnership taxable year 1957, A has an adjusted basis of his interest of at least $1,000 (not taking into account the disallowed loss of $1,000), he will be allowed the $1,000 loss previously disallowed.

Example (2). At the end of partnership taxable year 1955, partnership CD has a loss of $20,000. Partner C's distributive share of this loss is $10,000. The adjusted basis of his interest in the partnership (not taking into account his distributive share of such loss) is $6,000. Therefore, $4,000 of the loss is disallowed. At the end of partnership taxable year 1956, the partnership has no taxable income or loss, but owes $8,000 to a bank for money borrowed. Since C's share of this liability is $4,000, the basis of his partnership interest is increased from zero to $4,000. (See sections 752 and 722, and §§1.752-1 and 1.722-1.) C is allowed the $4,000 loss, disallowed for the preceding year under section 704(d), for his taxable year within or with which partnership taxable year 1956 ends.

Example (3). At the end of partnership taxable year 1955, partner C has the following distributive share of partnership items described in section 702(a); long-term capital loss, $4,000; short-term capital loss, $2,000; income as described in section 702(a)(9), $4,000. Partner C's adjusted basis for his partnership interest at the end of 1955, before adjustment for any of the above items, is $1,000. As adjusted under section 705(a)(1)(A), C's basis is increased from $1,000 to $5,000 at the end of the year. C's total distributive share of partnership loss is $6,000. Since without regard to losses, C has a basis of only $5,000, C is allowed only $5,000/$6,000 of each loss, that is, $3,333 of his long-term capital loss, and $1,667 of his short-term capital loss. C must carry forward to succeeding taxable years $667 as a long-term capital loss and $333 as a short-term capital loss.

(e) *Family partnerships.*—(1) *In general.*—(i) *Introduction.*—The production of income by a partnership is attributable to the capital or services, or both, contributed by the partners. The provisions of subchapter K, chapter 1 of the Code, are to be read in the light of their relationship to section 61, which requires, inter alia, that income be taxed to the person who earns it through his own labor and skill and the utilization of his own capital.

(ii) *Recognition of donee as partner.*—With respect to partnerships in which capital is a material income-producing factor, section 704(e)(1) provides that a person shall be recognized as a partner for income tax purposes if he owns a capital interest in such a partnership whether or not such interest is derived by purchase or gift from any other person. If a capital interest in a partnership in which capital is a material income-producing factor is created by gift, section 704(e)(2) provides that the distributive share of the donee under the partnership agreement shall be includible in his gross income, except to the extent that such distributive share is determined without allowance of reasonable compensation for services rendered to the partnership by the donor, and except to the extent that the portion of such distributive share attributable to donated capital is proportionately greater than the share of the donor attributable to the donor's capital. For rules of allocation in such cases, see subparagraph (3) of this paragraph.

(iii) *Requirement of complete transfer to donee.*—A donee or purchaser of a capital interest in a partnership is not recognized as a partner under the principles of section 704(e)(1) unless such interest is acquired in a bona fide transaction, not a mere sham for tax avoidance or evasion purposes, and the donee or purchaser is the real owner of such interest. To be recognized, a transfer must vest dominion and control of the partnership interest in the transferee. The existence of such dominion and control in the donee is to be determined from all the facts and circumstances. A transfer is not recognized if the transferor retains such incidents of ownership that the transferee has not acquired full and complete ownership of the partnership interest. Transactions between members of a family will be closely scrutinized, and the circumstances, not only at the time of the purported transfer but also during the periods preceding and following it, will be taken into consideration in determining the bona fides or lack of bona fides of the purported gift or sale. A partnership may be recognized for income purposes as to some partners but not as to others.

(iv) *Capital as a material income-producing factor.*—For purposes of section 704(e)(1), the determination as to whether capital is a material income-producing factor must be made by reference to all the facts of each case. Capital is a material income-producing factor if a substantial portion of the gross income of the business is attributable to the employment of capital in the business conducted by the partnership. In general, capital is not a material income-producing factor where the income of the business consists principally of fees, commissions, or other compensation for personal services performed by members or employees of the partnership. On the other hand, capital is ordinarily a material income-producing factor if the operation of the business requires substantial inventories or a substantial investment in plant, machinery, or other equipment.

(v) *Capital interest in a partnership.*—For purposes of section 704(e), a capital interest in a partnership means an interest in the assets of the partnership, which is distributable to the owner of the capital interest upon his withdrawal from the partnership or upon liquidation of the partnership. The mere right to participate in the earnings and profits of a partnership is not a capital interest in the partnership.

(2) *Basic tests as to ownership.*—(i) *In general.*—Whether an alleged partner who is a donee of a capital interest in a partnership is the real owner of such capital interest, and whether the donee has dominion and control over such interest, must be ascertained from all the facts and circumstances of the particular case. Isolated facts are not determinative; the reality of the donee's ownership is to be determined in the light of the transaction as a whole. The execution of legally sufficient and irrevocable deeds or other instruments of gift under State law is a factor to be taken into account but is not determinative of ownership by the donee for the purposes of section 704(e). The reality of the transfer and of the donee's ownership of the property attributed to him are to be ascertained from the conduct of the parties with respect to the alleged gift and not by any mechanical or formal test. Some of the more important factors to be considered in determining whether the donee has acquired ownership of the capital interest in a partnership are indicated in subdivisions (ii) to (x), inclusive, of this subparagraph.

(ii) *Retained controls.*—The donor may have retained such controls of the interest which he has purported to transfer to the donee that the donor should be treated as remaining the substantial owner of the interest. Controls of particular significance include, for example, the following:

(a) Retention of control of the distribution of amounts of income or restrictions on the distributions of amounts of income (other than amounts retained in the partnership annually with the consent of the partners, including the donee partner, for the reasonable needs of the business). If there is a partnership agreement providing for a managing partner or partners, then amounts of income may be retained in the partnership without the acquiescence of all the partners if such amounts are retained for the reasonable needs of the business.

(b) Limitation of the right of the donee to liquidate or sell his interest in the partnership at his discretion without financial detriment.

(c) Retention of control of assets essential to the business (for example, through retention of assets leased to the alleged partnership).

(d) Retention of management powers inconsistent with normal relationships among partners. Retention by the donor of control of business management or of voting control, such as is common in ordinary business relationships, is not by itself to be considered as inconsistent with normal relationships among partners, provided the donee is free to liquidate his interest at his discretion without financial detriment. The donee shall not be considered free to liquidate his interest unless, considering all the facts, it is evident that the donee is independent of the donor and has such maturity and understanding of his rights as to be capable of deciding to exercise, and capable of exercising, his right to withdraw his capital interest from the partnership. The existence of some of the indicated controls, though amounting to less than substantial ownership retained by the donor, may be considered along with other facts and circumstances as tending to show the lack of reality of the partnership interest of the donee.

(iii) *Indirect controls.*—Controls inconsistent with ownership by the donee may be exercised indirectly as well as directly, for example, through a separate business organization, estate, trust, individual, or other partnership. Where such indirect controls exist, the reality of the donee's interest will be determined as if such controls were exercisable directly.

(iv) *Participation in management.*—Substantial participation by the donee in the control and management of the business (including participation in the major policy decisions affecting the business) is strong evidence of a donee partner's exercise of dominion and control over his interest. Such participation presupposes sufficient maturity and experience on the part of the donee to deal with the business problems of the partnership.

(v) *Income distributions.*—The actual distribution to a donee partner of the entire amount or a major portion of his distributive share of the business income for the sole benefit and use of the donee is substantial evidence of the reality of the donee's interest, provided the donor has not retained controls inconsistent with real ownership by the donee. Amounts distributed are not considered to be used for the donee's sole benefit if, for example, they are deposited, loaned, or invested in such manner that the donor controls or can control the use or enjoyment of such funds.

(vi) *Conduct of partnership business.*—In determining the reality of the donee's ownership of a capital interest in a partnership, consideration shall be given to whether the donee is actually treated as a partner in the operation of the business. Whether or not the donee has been held out publicly as a partner in the conduct of the business, in relations with customers, or with creditors or other sources of financing, is of primary significance. Other factors of significance in this connection include:

(a) Compliance with local partnership, fictitious names, and business registration statutes.

(b) Control of business bank accounts.

(c) Recognition of the donee's rights in distributions of partnership property and profits.

(d) Recognition of the donee's interest in insurance policies, leases, and other business contracts and in litigation affecting business.

(e) The existence of written agreements, records, or memoranda, contemporaneous with the taxable year or years concerned, establishing the nature of the partnership agreement and the rights and liabilities of the respective partners.

(f) Filing of partnership tax returns as required by law.

However, despite formal compliance with the above factors, other circumstances may indicate that the donor has retained substantial ownership of the interest purportedly transferred to the donee.

(vii) *Trustees as partners.*—A trustee may be recognized as a partner for income tax purposes under the principles relating to family partnerships generally as applied to the particular facts of the trust-partnership arrangement. A trustee who is unrelated to and independent of the grantor, and who participates as a partner and receives distribution of the income distributable to the trust, will ordinarily be recognized as the legal owner of the partnership interest which he holds in trust unless the grantor has retained controls inconsistent with such ownership. However, if the grantor is the trustee, or if the trustee is amenable to the will of the grantor, the provisions of the trust instrument (particularly as to whether the trustee is subject to the responsibilities of a fiduciary), the provisions of the partnership agreement, and the conduct of the parties must all be taken into account in determining whether the trustee in a fiduciary capacity has become the real owner of the partnership interest. Where the grantor (or person amenable to his will) is the trustee, the trust may be recognized as a partner only if the grantor (or such other person) in his participation in the affairs of the partnership actively represents and protects the interests of the beneficiaries in accordance with the obligations of a fiduciary and does not subordinate such interests to the interests of the grantor. Furthermore, if the grantor (or person amenable to his will) is the trustee, the following factors will be given particular consideration:

(a) Whether the trust is recognized as a partner in business dealings with customers and creditors, and

(b) Whether, if any amount of the partnership income is not properly retained for the reasonable needs of the business, the trust's share of such amount is distributed to the trust annually and paid to the beneficiaries or reinvested with regard solely to the interests of the beneficiaries.

(viii) *Interests (not held in trust) of minor children.*—Except where a minor child is shown to be competent to manage his own property and participate in the partnership activities in accordance with his interest in the property, a minor child generally will not be recognized as a member of a partnership unless control of the property is exercised by another person as fiduciary for the sole benefit of the child, and unless there is such judicial supervision of the conduct of the fiduciary as is required by law. The use of the child's property or income for support for which a parent is legally responsible will be considered a use for the parent's benefit. "Judicial supervision of the conduct of the fiduciary" includes filing of such accountings and reports as are required by law of the fiduciary who participates in the affairs of the partnership on behalf of the minor. A minor child will be considered as competent to manage his own property if he actually has sufficient maturity and experience to be treated by disinterested persons as competent to enter business dealings and otherwise to conduct his affairs on a basis of equality with adult persons, notwithstanding legal disabilities of the minor under State law.

(ix) *Donees as limited partners.*—The recognition of a donee's interest in a limited partnership will depend, as in the case of other donated interests, on whether the transfer of property is real and on whether the donee has acquired dominion and control over the interest purportedly transferred to him. To be recognized for Federal income tax purposes, a limited partnership must be organized and conducted in accordance with the requirements of the applicable State limited-partnership law. The absence of services and participation in management by a donee in a limited partnership is immaterial if the limited partnership meets all the other requirements prescribed in this paragraph. If the limited partner's right to transfer or liquidate his interest is subject to substantial restrictions (for example, where the interest of the limited partner is not assignable in a real sense or where such interest may be required to be left in the business for a long term of years), or if the general partner retains any other control which substantially limits any of the rights which would ordinarily be exercisable by unrelated limited partners in normal business relationships, such restrictions on the right to transfer or liquidate, or retention of other control, will be considered strong evidence as to the lack of reality of ownership by the donee.

(x) *Motive.*—If the reality of the transfer of interest is satisfactorily established, the motives for the transaction are generally immaterial. However, the presence or absence of a tax-avoidance motive is one of many factors to be considered in determining the reality of the ownership of a capital interest acquired by gift.

(3) *Allocation of family partnership income.*—(i) *In general.*—*(a)* Where a capital interest in a partnership in which capital is a material income-producing factor is created by gift, the donee's distributive share shall be includible in his gross income, except to the extent that such share is determined without allowance of reasonable compensation for services rendered to the partnership by the donor, and except to the extent that the portion of such distributive share attributable to donated capital is proportionately greater than the distributive share attributable to the donor's capital. For the purpose of section 704, a capital interest in a partnership purchased by one member of a family from another shall be considered to be created by gift from the seller, and the fair market value of the purchased interest shall be considered to be donated capital. The "family" of any individual, for the purpose of the preceding sentence, shall include only his spouse, ancestors, and lineal descendants, and any trust for the primary benefit of such persons.

(b) To the extent that the partnership agreement does not allocate the partnership income in accordance with subdivision *(a)* of this subdivision, the distributive shares of the partnership income of the donor and donee shall be reallocated by making a reasonable allowance for the services of the donor and by attributing the balance of such income (other than a reasonable allowance for the services, if any, rendered by the donee) to the partnership capital of the donor and donee. The portion of income, if any, thus attributable to partnership capital for the taxable year shall be allocated between the donor and donee in accordance with their respective interests in partnership capital.

(c) In determining a reasonable allowance for services rendered by the partners, consideration shall be given to all the facts and circumstances of the business, including the fact that some of the partners may have greater managerial responsibility than others. There shall also be considered the amount that would ordinarily be paid in order to obtain comparable services from a person not having an interest in the partnership.

(d) The distributive share of partnership income, as determined under subdivision *(b)* of this subdivision, of a partner who rendered services to the partnership before entering the Armed Forces of the United States shall not be diminished because of absence due to military service. Such distributive share shall be adjusted to reflect increases or decreases in the capital interest of the absent partner. However, the partners may by agreement allocate a smaller share to the absent partner due to his absence.

(ii) *Special rules.*—*(a)* The provisions of subdivision (i) of this subparagraph, relating to allocation of family partnership income, are applicable where the interest in the partnership is created by gift, indirectly or directly. Where the partnership interest is created indirectly, the term "donor" may include persons other than the nominal transferor. This rule may be illustrated by the following examples:

Example (1). A father gives property to his son who shortly thereafter conveys the property to a partnership consisting of the father and the son. The partnership interest of the son may be considered created by gift and the father may be considered the donor of the son's partnership interest.

Example (2). A father, the owner of a business conducted as a sole proprietorship, transfers the business to a partnership consisting of his wife and himself. The wife subsequently conveys her interest to their son. In such case, the father, as well as the mother, may be considered the donor of the son's partnership interest.

Example (3). A father makes a gift to his son of stock in the family corporation. The corporation is subsequently liquidated. The son later contributes the property received in the liquidation of the corporation to a partnership consisting of his father and himself. In such case, for purposes of section 704, the son's partnership interest may be considered created by gift and the father may be considered the donor of his son's partnership interest.

(b) The allocation rules set forth in section 704(e) and subdivision (i) of this subparagraph apply in any case in which the transfer or creation of the partnership interest has any of the substantial characteristics of a gift. Thus, allocation may be required where transfer of a partnership interest is made between members of a family (including collaterals) under a purported purchase agreement, if the characteristics of a gift are ascertained from the terms of the purchase agreement, the terms of any loan or credit arrangements made to finance the purchase, or from other relevant data.

(c) In the case of a limited partnership, for the purpose of the allocation provisions of subdivision (i) of this subparagraph, consideration shall be given to the fact that a general partner, unlike a limited partner, risks his credit in the partnership business.

(4) *Purchased interest.*—(i) *In general.*—If a purported purchase of a capital interest in a partnership does not meet the requirements of subdivision (ii) of this subparagraph, the ownership by the transferee of such capital interest will be recognized only if it qualifies under the requirements applicable to a transfer of a partnership interest by gifts. In a case not qualifying under subdivision (ii) of this subparagraph, if payment of any part of the purchase price is made out of partnership earnings, the transaction may be regarded in the same light as a purported gift subject to deferred enjoyment of income. Such a transaction may be lacking in reality either as a gift or as a bona fide purchase.

(ii) *Tests as to reality of purchased interests.*—A purchase of a capital interest in a partnership, either directly or by means of a loan or credit extended by a member of the family, will be recognized as bona fide if:

(a) It can be shown that the purchase has the usual characteristics of an arm's-length transaction, considering all relevant factors, including the terms of the purchase agreement (as to price, due date of payment, rate of interest, and security, if any) and the terms of any loan or credit arrangement collateral to the purchase agreement; the credit standing of the purchaser (apart from relationship to the seller) and the capacity of the purchaser to incur a legally binding obligation; or

(b) It can be shown, in the absence of characteristics of an arm's-length transaction, that the purchase was genuinely intended to promote the success of the business by securing participation of the purchaser in the business or by adding his credit to that of the other participants.

However, if the alleged purchase price or loan has not been paid or the obligation otherwise discharged, the factors indicated in *(a)* and *(b)* of this subdivision shall be taken into account only as an aid in determining whether a bona fide purchase or loan obligation existed.

* * *

[Reg. § 1.704-1.]

☐ [*T.D.* 6175, 5-23-56. *Amended by T.D.* 6771, 11-19-64; *T.D.* 8065, 12-24-85; *T.D.* 8099, 9-8-86; *T.D.* 8237, 12-29-88; *T.D.* 8385, 12-26-91; *T.D.* 8500, 12-21-93; *T.D.* 8585, 12-27-94; *T.D.* 8717, 5-8-97; *T.D.* 9121, 4-20-2004; *T.D.* 9126, 5-5-2004; *T.D.* 9207, 5-23-2005; *T.D.* 9292, 10-18-2006 (*corrected* 12-6-2006); *T.D.* 9398, 5-16-2008 (*corrected* 6-11-2008); *T.D.* 9577, 2-9-2012; *T.D.* 9607, 12-21-2012; *T.D.* 9612, 2-4-2013 (*corrected* 3-22-2013 *and* 6-12-2013); *T.D.* 9710, 2-9-2015; *T.D.* 9748, 2-3-2016; *T.D.* 9814, 1-18-2017; *T.D.* 9871, 7-23-2019; *T.D.* 9874, 9-17-2019; *T.D.* 9877, 10-4-2019; *T.D.* 9891, 1-17-2020 *and T.D.* 9895, 3-20-2020.]

§ 1.704-2. Allocations attributable to nonrecourse liabilities.—

* * *

(b) *General principles and definitions.*—(1) *Definition of and allocations of nonrecourse deductions.*—Allocations of losses, deductions, or section 705(a)(2)(B) expenditures attributable to partnership nonrecourse liabilities ("nonrecourse deductions") cannot have economic effect because the creditor alone bears any economic burden that corresponds to those allocations. Thus, nonrecourse deductions must be allocated in accordance with the partners' interests in the partnership. Paragraph (e) of this section provides a test that deems allocations of nonrecourse deductions to be in accordance with the partners' interests in the partnership. If that test is not satisfied, the partners' distributive shares of nonrecourse deductions are determined under § 1.704-1(b)(3), according to the partners' overall economic interests in the partnership. See also paragraph

(i) of this section for special rules regarding the allocation of deductions attributable to nonrecourse liabilities for which a partner bears the economic risk of loss (as described in paragraph (b)(4) of this section).

(2) *Definition of and allocations pursuant to a minimum gain chargeback.*—To the extent a nonrecourse liability exceeds the adjusted tax basis of the partnership property it encumbers, a disposition of that property will generate gain that at least equals that excess ("partnership minimum gain"). An increase in partnership minimum gain is created by a decrease in the adjusted tax basis of property encumbered by a nonrecourse liability below the amount of that liability and by a partnership nonrecourse borrowing that exceeds the adjusted tax basis of the property encumbered by the borrowing. Partnership minimum gain decreases as reductions occur in the amount by which the nonrecourse liability exceeds the adjusted tax basis of the property encumbered by the liability. Allocations of gain attributable to a decrease in partnership minimum gain (a "minimum gain chargeback," as required under paragraph (f) of this section) cannot have economic effect because the gain merely offsets nonrecourse deductions previously claimed by the partnership. Thus, to avoid impairing the economic effect of other allocations, allocations pursuant to a minimum gain chargeback must be made to the partners that either were allocated nonrecourse deductions or received distributions of proceeds attributable to a nonrecourse borrowing. Paragraph (e) of this section provides a test that, if met, deems allocations of partnership income pursuant to a minimum gain chargeback to be in accordance with the partners' interests in the partnership. If property encumbered by a nonrecourse liability is reflected on the partnership's books at a value that differs from its adjusted tax basis, paragraph (d)(3) of this section provides that minimum gain is determined with reference to the property's book basis. See also paragraph (i)(4) of this section for special rules regarding the minimum gain chargeback requirement for partner nonrecourse debt.

(3) *Definition of nonrecourse liability.*—"Nonrecourse liability" means a nonrecourse liability as defined in § 1.752-1(a)(2) or a § 1.752-7 liability (as defined in § 1.752-7(b)(3)(i)) assumed by the partnership from a partner on or after June 24, 2003.

(4) *Definition of partner nonrecourse debt.*—"Partner nonrecourse debt" or "partner nonrecourse liability" means any partnership liability to the extent the liability is nonrecourse for purposes of § 1.1001-2, and a partner or related person (within the meaning of § 1.752-4(b)) bears the economic risk of loss under § 1.752-2 because, for example, the partner or related person is the creditor or a guarantor.

(c) *Amount of nonrecourse deductions.*—The amount of nonrecourse deductions for a partnership taxable year equals the net increase in partnership minimum gain during the year (determined under paragraph (d) of this section), reduced (but not below zero) by the aggregate distributions made during the year of proceeds of a nonrecourse liability that are allocable to an increase in partnership minimum gain (determined under paragraph (h) of this section). See paragraph (m), *Examples* (1)(i) and (vi), (2), and (3) of this section. However, increases in partnership minimum gain resulting from conversions, refinancings, or other changes to a debt instrument (as described in paragraph (g)(3)) do not generate nonrecourse deductions. Generally, nonrecourse deductions consist first of certain depreciation or cost recovery deductions and then, if necessary, a pro rata portion of other partnership losses, deductions, and section 705(a)(2)(B) expenditures for that year, excess nonrecourse deductions are carried over. See paragraphs (j)(1)(ii) and (iii) of this section for more specific ordering rules. See also paragraph (m), *Example* (1)(vi) of this section.

(d) *Partnership minimum gain.*—(1) *Amount of partnership minimum gain.*—The amount of partnership minimum gain is determined by first computing for each partnership nonrecourse liability any gain the partnership would realize if it disposed of the property subject to that liability for no consideration other than full satisfaction of the liability, and then aggregating the separately computed gains. The amount of partnership minimum gain includes minimum gain arising from a conversion, refinancing, or other change to a debt instrument, as described in paragraph (g)(3) of this section, only to the extent a partner is allocated a share of that minimum gain. For any partnership taxable year, the net increase or decrease in partnership minimum gain is determined by comparing the partnership minimum gain on the last day of the immediately preceding taxable year with the partnership minimum gain on the last day of the current taxable year. See paragraph (m), *Examples* (l)(i) and (iv), (2), and (3) of this section.

(2) *Property subject to more than one liability.*—(i) *In general.*—If property is subject to more than one liability, only the portion of the property's adjusted tax basis that is allocated to a nonrecourse liability under paragraph

(d)(2)(ii) of this section is used to compute minimum gain with respect to that liability.

(ii) *Allocating liabilities.*—If property is subject to two or more liabilities of equal priority, the property's adjusted tax basis is allocated among the liabilities in proportion to their outstanding balances. If property is subject to two or more liabilities of unequal priority, the adjusted tax basis is allocated first to the liability of the highest priority to the extent of its outstanding balance and then to each liability in descending order of priority to the extent of its outstanding balance, until fully allocated. See paragraph (m), *Example* (1)(v) of this section.

(3) *Partnership minimum gain if there is a book/tax disparity.*—If partnership property subject to one or more nonrecourse liabilities is, under § 1.704-1(b)(2)(iv)(*d*), (*f*), or (*r*), reflected on the partnership's books at a value that differs from its adjusted tax basis, the determinations under this section are made with reference to the property's book value. See section 704(c) and § 1.704-1(b)(4)(i) for principles that govern the treatment of a partner's share of minimum gain that is eliminated by the revaluation. See also paragraph (m), *Example* (3) of this section.

(4) *Special rule for year of revaluation.*—If the partners' capital accounts are increased pursuant to § 1.704-1(b)(2)(iv)(*d*), (*f*), or (*r*) to reflect a revaluation of partnership property subject to a nonrecourse liability, the net increase or decrease in partnership minimum gain for the partnership taxable year of the revaluation is determined by:

(i) First calculating the net decrease or increase in partnership minimum gain using the current year's book values and the prior year's partnership minimum gain amount; and

(ii) Then adding back any decrease in minimum gain arising solely from the revaluation.

See paragraph (m), *Example* (3)(iii) of this section. If the partners' capital accounts are decreased to reflect a revaluation, the net increases or decreases in partnership minimum gain are determined in the same manner as in the year before the revaluation, but by using book values rather than adjusted tax bases. See section 7701(g) and § 1.704-1(b)(2)(iv)(*f*)(*1*) (property being revalued cannot be booked down below the amount of any nonrecourse liability to which the property is subject).

(e) *Requirements to be satisfied.*—Allocations of nonrecourse deductions are deemed to be in accordance with the partners' interests in the partnership only if—

(1) Throughout the full term of the partnership requirements (*1*) and (*2*) of § 1.704-1(b)(2)(ii)(*b*) are satisfied (*i.e.*, capital accounts are maintained in accordance with § 1.704-1(b)(2)(iv) and liquidating distributions are required to be made in accordance with positive capital account balances), and requirement (*3*) of either § 1.704-1(b)(2)(ii)(*b*) or § 1.704-1(b)(2)(ii)(*d*) is satisfied (*i.e.*, partners with deficit capital accounts have an unconditional deficit restoration obligation or agree to a qualified income offset);

(2) Beginning in the first taxable year of the partnership in which there are nonrecourse deductions and thereafter throughout the full term of the partnership, the partnership agreement provides for allocations of nonrecourse deductions in a manner that is reasonably consistent with allocations that have substantial economic effect of some other significant partnership item attributable to the property securing the nonrecourse liabilities;

(3) Beginning in the first taxable year of the partnership that it has nonrecourse deductions or makes a distribution of proceeds of a nonrecourse liability that are allocable to an increase in partnership minimum gain, and thereafter throughout the full term of the partnership, the partnership agreement contains a provision that complies with the minimum gain chargeback requirement of paragraph (f) of this section; and

(4) All other material allocations and capital account adjustments under the partnership agreement are recognized under § 1.704-1(b) (without regard to whether allocations of adjusted tax basis and amount realized under section 613A(c)(7)(D) are recognized under § 1.704-1(b)(4)(v)).

(f) *Minimum gain chargeback requirement.*—(1) *In general.*—If there is a net decrease in partnership minimum gain for a partnership taxable year, the minimum gain chargeback requirement applies and each partner must be allocated items of partnership income and gain for that year equal to that partner's share of the net decrease in partnership minimum gain (within the meaning of paragraph (g)(2)).

(2) *Exception for certain conversions and refinancings.*—A partner is not subject to the minimum gain chargeback requirement to the extent the partner's share of the net decrease in partnership minimum gain is caused by a recharacterization of nonrecourse partnership debt as partially or wholly recourse debt or partner nonrecourse debt, and the partner bears the economic risk of loss (within the meaning of § 1.752-2) for the liability.

(3) *Exception for certain capital contributions.*—A partner is not subject to the minimum gain chargeback requirement to the extent the

partner contributes capital to the partnership that is used to repay the nonrecourse liability or is used to increase the basis of the property subject to nonrecourse liability, and the partner's share of the net decrease in partnership minimum gain results from the repayment or the increase to the property's basis. See paragraph (m), *Example* (1) (iv) of this section.

(4) *Waiver for certain income allocations that fail to meet minimum gain chargeback requirement if minimum gain chargeback distorts economic arrangement.*—In any taxable year that a partnership has a net decrease in partnership minimum gain, if the minimum gain chargeback requirement would cause a distortion in the economic arrangement among the partners and it is not expected that the partnership will have sufficient other income to correct that distortion, the Commissioner has the discretion, if requested by the partnership, to waive the minimum gain chargeback requirement. The following facts must be demonstrated in order for a request for a waiver to be considered:

(i) The partners have made capital contributions or received net income allocations that have restored the previous nonrecourse deductions and the distributions attributable to proceeds of a nonrecourse liability; and

(ii) The minimum gain chargeback requirement would distort the partners' economic arrangement as reflected in the partnership agreement and as evidenced over the term of the partnership by the partnership's allocations and distributions and the partners' contributions.

(5) *Additional exceptions.*—The Commissioner may, by revenue ruling, provide additional exceptions to the minimum gain chargeback requirement.

(6) *Partnership items subject to the minimum gain chargeback requirement.*—Any minimum gain chargeback required for a partnership taxable year consists first of a pro rata portion of certain gains recognized from the disposition of partnership property subject to one or more partnership nonrecourse liabilities and income from the discharge of indebtedness relating to one or more partnership nonrecourse liabilities to which partnership property is subject, and then, if necessary, consists of a pro rata portion of the partnership's other items of income and gain for that year. If the amount of the minimum gain chargeback requirement exceeds the partnership's income and gains for the taxable year, the excess carries over. See paragraphs (j) (2) (i) and (j) (2) (iii) of this section for more specific ordering rules.

(7) *Examples.*—The following examples illustrate the provisions in § 1.704-2(f).

Example 1. Partnership AB consists of two partners, limited partner A and general partner B. Partner A contributes $90 and partner B contributes $10 to the partnership. The partnership agreement has a minimum gain chargeback provision and provides that, except as otherwise required by section 704(c), all losses will be allocated 90 percent to A and 10 percent to B; and that all income will be allocated first to restore previous losses and thereafter 50 percent to A and 50 percent to B. Distributions are made first to return initial capital to the partners and then 50 percent to A and 50 percent to B. Final distributions are made in accordance with capital account balances. The partnership borrows $200 on a nonrecourse basis from an unrelated third party and purchases an asset for $300. The partnership's only tax item for each of the first three years is $100 of depreciation on the asset. A's and B's shares of minimum gain (under paragraph (g) of this section) and deficit capital account balances are $180 and $20 respectively at the end of the third year. In the fourth year, the partnership earns $400 of net operating income and allocates the first $300 to restore the previous losses (*i.e.*, $270 to A and $30 to B); the last $100 is allocated $50 each. The partnership distributes $200 of the available cash that same year; the first $100 is distributed $90 to A and $10 to B to return their capital contributions; the last $100 is distributed $50 each to reflect their ratio for sharing profits.

	A	*B*
Capital account on formation	$90	$10
Less: net loss in years 1-3	($270)	($30)
Capital account at end of year 3	($180)	($20)
Allocation of operating income to restore nonrecourse deductions	$180	$20
Allocation of operating income to restore capital contributions	$90	$10
Allocation of operating income to reflect profits	$50	$50
Capital accounts after allocation of operating income	$140	$60
Distribution reflecting capital contribution	($90)	($10)
Distribution in profit-sharing ratio	($50)	($50)
Capital accounts following distribution	($0)	($0)

In the fifth year, the partnership sells the property for $300 and realizes $300 of gain. $200 of the proceeds are used to pay the nonrecourse lender. The partnership has $300 to distribute, and the partners expect to share that equally. Absent a waiver under paragraph (f)(4) of this section, the minimum gain chargeback would require the partnership to allocate the first $200 of the gain $180 to A and $20 to B, which would distort their economic arrangement. This allocation, together with the allocation of the $100 profit $50 to each partner, would result in A having a positive capital account balance of $230 and B having a positive capital account balance of $70. The allocation of income in year 4 in effect anticipated the minimum gain chargeback that did not occur until year 5. Assuming the partnership would not have sufficient other income to correct the distortion that would otherwise result, the partnership may request that the Commissioner exercise his or her discretion to waive the minimum gain chargeback requirement and recognize allocations that would allow A and B to share equally the gain on the sale of the property. These allocations would bring the partners' capital accounts to $150 each, allowing them to share the last $300 equally. The Commissioner may, in his or her discretion, permit this allocation pursuant to paragraph (f) (4) of this section because the minimum gain chargeback would distort the partners' economic arrangement over the term of the partnership as reflected in the partnership agreement and as evidenced by the partners' contributions and the partnership's allocations and distributions.

Example 2. A and B form a partnership, contribute $25 each to the partnership's capital, and agree to share all losses and profits 50 percent each. Neither partner has an unconditional deficit restoration obligation and all the requirements in paragraph (e) of this section are met. The partnership obtains a nonrecourse loan from an unrelated third party of $100 and purchases two assets, stock for $50 and depreciable property for $100. The nonrecourse loan is secured by the partnership's depreciable property. The partnership generates $20 of depreciation in each of the first five years as its only tax item. These deductions are properly treated as nonrecourse deductions and the allocation of these deductions 50 percent to A and 50 percent to B is deemed to be in accordance with the partners' interests in the partnership. At the end of year five, A and B each have a $25 deficit capital account and a $50 share of partnership minimum gain. In the beginning of year six, (at the lender's request), A guarantees the entire nonrecourse liability. Pursuant to paragraph (d)(1) of this section, the partnership has a net decrease in minimum gain of $100 and under paragraph (g)(2) of this section, A's and B's shares of that net decrease are $50 each. Under paragraph (f)(1) of this section (the minimum gain chargeback requirement), B is subject to a $50 minimum gain chargeback. Because the partnership has no gross income in year six, the entire $50 carries over as a minimum gain chargeback requirement to succeeding taxable years until there is enough income to cover the minimum gain chargeback requirement. Under the exception to the minimum gain chargeback in paragraph (f)(2) of this section, A is not subject to a minimum gain chargeback for A's $50 share of the net decrease because A bears the economic risk of loss for the liability. Instead, A's share of partner nonrecourse debt minimum gain is $50 pursuant to paragraph (i)(3) of this section. In year seven, the partnership earns $100 of net operating income and uses the money to repay the entire $100 nonrecourse debt (that A has guaranteed). Under paragraph (i)(3) of this section, the partnership has a net decrease in partner nonrecourse debt minimum gain of $50. B must be allocated $50 of the operating income pursuant to the carried over minimum gain chargeback requirement; pursuant to paragraph (i)(4) of this section, the other $50 of operating income must be allocated to A as a partner nonrecourse debt minimum gain chargeback.

(g) *Shares of partnership minimum gain.*—(1) *Partner's share of partnership minimum gain.*—Except as increased in paragraph (g)(3) of this section, a partner's share of partnership minimum gain at the end of any partnership taxable year equals:

(i) the sum of nonrecourse deductions allocated to that partner (and to that partner's predecessors in interest) up to that time and the distributions made to that partner (and to that partner's predecessors' in interest) up to that time of proceeds of a nonrecourse liability allocable to an increase in partnership minimum gain (see paragraph (h)(1) of this section); minus

(ii) the sum of that partner's (and that partner's predecessors' in interest) aggregate share of the net decreases in partnership minimum gain plus their aggregate share of decreases resulting from revaluations of partnership property subject to one or more partnership nonrecourse liabilities.

For purposes of § 1.704-1(b)(2)(ii)(*d*) a partner's share of partnership minimum gain is added to the limited dollar amount, if any, of the deficit balance in the partner's capital account that the partner is obligated to restore. See paragraph (m), *Examples* (1)(i) and (3)(i) of this section.

(2) *Partner's share of the net decrease in partnership minimum gain.*—A partner's share of the net decrease in partnership minimum gain is the amount of the total net decrease multiplied by the partner's percentage share of the partnership's minimum gain at the end of the immediately preceding taxable year. A partner's share of any decrease in partnership minimum gain resulting from a revaluation of partnership property equals the increase in the partner's capital account attributable to the revaluation to the extent the reduction in minimum gain is caused by the revaluation. See paragraph (m), *Example* (3) (ii) of this section.

(3) *Conversions of recourse or partner nonrecourse debt into nonrecourse debt.*—A partner's share of partnership minimum gain is increased to the extent provided in this paragraph (g) (3) if a recourse or partner nonrecourse liability becomes partially or wholly nonrecourse. If a recourse liability becomes a nonrecourse liability, a partner has a share of the partnership's minimum gain that results from the conversion equal to the partner's deficit capital account (determined under § 1.704-1(b) (2) (iv)) to the extent the partner no longer bears the economic burden for the entire deficit capital account as a result of the conversion. For purposes of the preceding sentence, the determination of the extent to which a partner bears the economic burden for a deficit capital account is made by determining the consequences to the partner in the case of a complete liquidation of the partnership immediately after the conversion applying the rules described in § 1.704-1(b) (2) (iii) (*c*) that deem the value of partnership property to equal its basis, taking into account section 7701(g) in the case of property that secures nonrecourse indebtedness. If a partner nonrecourse debt becomes a nonrecourse liability, the partner's share of partnership minimum gain is increased to the extent the partner is not subject to the minimum gain chargeback requirement under paragraph (i) (4) of this section.

(h) *Distribution of nonrecourse liability proceeds allocable to an increase in partnership minimum gain.*—(1) *In general.*—If during its taxable year a partnership makes a distribution to the partners allocable to the proceeds of a nonrecourse liability, the distribution is allocable to an increase in partnership minimum gain to the extent the increase results from encumbering partnership property with aggregate nonrecourse liabilities that exceed the property's adjusted tax basis. See paragraph (m), *Example* (1) (vi) of this section. If the net increase in partnership minimum gain for a partnership taxable year is allocable to more than one nonrecourse liability, the net increase is allocated among the liabilities in proportion to the amount each liability contributed to the increase in minimum gain.

(2) *Distribution allocable to nonrecourse liability proceeds.*—A partnership may use any reasonable method to determine whether a distribution by the partnership to one or more partners is allocable to proceeds of a nonrecourse liability. The rules prescribed under § 1.163-8T for allocating debt proceeds among expenditures (applying those rules to the partnership as if it were an individual) constitute a reasonable method for determining whether the nonrecourse liability proceeds are distributed to the partners and the partners to whom the proceeds are distributed.

(3) *Option when there is an obligation to restore.*—A partnership may treat any distribution to a partner of the proceeds of a nonrecourse liability (that would otherwise be allocable to an increase in partnership minimum gain) as a distribution that is not allocable to an increase in partnership minimum gain to the extent the distribution does not cause or increase a deficit balance in the partner's capital account that exceeds the amount the partner is otherwise obligated to restore (within the meaning of § 1.704-1(b) (2) (ii) (*c*)) as of the end of the partnership taxable year in which the distribution occurs.

(4) *Carryover to immediately succeeding taxable year.*—The carryover rule of this paragraph applies if the net increase in partnership minimum gain for a partnership taxable year that is allocable to a nonrecourse liability under paragraph (h) (2) of this section exceeds the distributions allocable to the proceeds of the liability ("excess allocable amount"), and all or part of the net increase in partnership minimum gain for the year is carried over as an increase in partnership minimum gain for the immediately succeeding taxable year (pursuant to paragraph (j) (1) (iii) of this section). If the carryover rule of this paragraph applies, the excess allocable amount (or the amount carried over under paragraph (j) (1) (iii) of this section, if less) is treated in the succeeding taxable year as an increase in partnership minimum gain that arose in that year as a result of incurring the nonrecourse liability to which the excess allocable amount is attributable. See paragraph (m), *Example* (1) (vi) of this section. If for a partnership taxable year there is an excess allocable amount with respect to more than one partnership nonrecourse liability, the excess allocable amount is allocated to each liability in proportion to the amount each liability contributed to the increase in minimum gain.

(i) *Partnership nonrecourse liabilities where a partner bears the economic risk of loss.*—(1) *In general.*—Partnership losses, deductions, or section 705(a)(2)(B) expenditures that are attributable to a particular partner nonrecourse liability ("partner nonrecourse deductions," as defined in paragraph (i)(2) of this section) must be allocated to the partner that bears the economic risk of loss for the liability. If more than one partner bears the economic risk of loss for a partner nonrecourse liability, any partner nonrecourse deductions attributable to that liability must be allocated among the partners according to the ratio in which they bear the economic risk of loss. If partners bear the economic risk of loss for different portions of a liability, each portion is treated as a separate partner nonrecourse liability.

(2) *Definition of and determination of partner nonrecourse deductions.*—For any partnership taxable year, the amount of partner nonrecourse deductions with respect to a partner nonrecourse debt equals the net increase during the year in minimum gain attributable to the partner nonrecourse debt ("partner nonrecourse debt minimum gain"), reduced (but not below zero) by proceeds of the liability distributed during the year to the partner bearing the economic risk of loss for the liability that are both attributable to the liability and allocable to an increase in the partner nonrecourse debt minimum gain. See paragraph (m), *Example* (1)(vii) and (viii) of this section. The determination of which partnership items constitute the partner nonrecourse deductions with respect to a partner nonrecourse debt must be made in a manner consistent with the provisions of paragraphs (c) and (j)(1)(i) and (iii) of this section.

(3) *Determination of partner nonrecourse debt minimum gain.*—For any partnership taxable year, the determination of partner nonrecourse debt minimum gain and the net increase or decrease in partner nonrecourse debt minimum gain must be made in a manner consistent with the provisions of paragraphs (d) and (g)(3) of this section.

(4) *Chargeback of partner nonrecourse debt minimum gain.*—If during a partnership taxable year there is a net decrease in partner nonrecourse debt minimum gain, any partner with a share of that partner nonrecourse debt minimum gain (determined under paragraph (i)(5) of this section) as of the beginning of the year must be allocated items of income and gain for the year (and, if necessary, for succeeding years) equal to that partner's share of the net decrease in the partner nonrecourse debt minimum gain. A partner's share of the net decrease in partner nonrecourse debt minimum gain is determined in a manner consistent with the provisions of paragraph (g)(2) of this section. A partner is not subject to this minimum gain chargeback, however, to the extent the net decrease in partner nonrecourse debt minimum gain arises because a partner nonrecourse liability becomes partially or wholly a nonrecourse liability. The amount that would otherwise be subject to the partner nonrecourse debt minimum gain chargeback is added to the partner's share of partnership minimum gain under paragraph (g)(3) of this section. In addition, rules consistent with the provisions of paragraphs (f)(2), (3), (4), and (5) of this section apply with respect to partner nonrecourse debt in appropriate circumstances. The determination of which items of partnership income and gain must be allocated pursuant to this paragraph (i)(4) is made in a manner that is consistent with the provisions of paragraph (f)(6) of this section. See paragraph (j)(2)(ii) and (iii) of this section for more specific rules.

(5) *Partner's share of partner nonrecourse debt minimum gain.*—A partner's share of partner nonrecourse debt minimum gain at the end of any partnership taxable year is determined in a manner consistent with the provisions of paragraphs (g)(1) and (g)(3) of this section with respect to each particular partner nonrecourse debt for which the partner bears the economic risk of loss. For purposes of §1.704-1(b)(2)(ii)(*d*), a partner's share of partner nonrecourse debt minimum gain is added to the limited dollar amount, if any, of the deficit balance in the partner's capital account that the partner is obligated to restore, and the partner is not otherwise considered to have a deficit restoration obligation as a result of bearing the economic risk of loss for any partner nonrecourse debt. See paragraph (m), *Example* (1)(vii) of this section.

(6) *Distribution of partner nonrecourse debt proceeds allocable to an increase in partner nonrecourse debt minimum gain.*—Rules consistent with the provisions of paragraph (h) of this section apply to distributions of the proceeds of partner nonrecourse debt.

(j) *Ordering Rules.*—For purposes of this section, the following ordering rules apply to partnership items. Notwithstanding any other provision in this section and §1.704-1, allocations of partner nonrecourse deductions, nonrecourse deductions, and minimum gain chargebacks are made before any other allocations.

(1) *Treatment of partnership losses and deductions.*—(i) *Partner nonrecourse deductions.*—Partnership losses, deductions, and section 705(a)(2)(B) expenditures are treated as partner nonrecourse deductions in the

amount determined under paragraph (i)(2) of this section (determining partner nonrecourse deductions) in the following order:

(A) First, depreciation or cost recovery deductions with respect to property that is subject to partner nonrecourse debt;

(B) Then, if necessary, a pro rata portion of the partnership's other deductions, losses, and section 705(a)(2)(B) items.

Depreciation or cost recovery deductions with respect to property that is subject to a partnership nonrecourse liability is first treated as a partnership nonrecourse deduction and any excess is treated as a partner nonrecourse deduction under this paragraph (j)(1)(i).

(ii) *Partnership nonrecourse deductions.*—Partnership losses, deductions, and section 705(a)(2)(B) expenditures are treated as partnership nonrecourse deductions in the amount determined under paragraph (c) of this section (determining nonrecourse deductions) in the following order:

(A) First, depreciation or cost recovery deductions with respect to property that is subject to partnership nonrecourse liabilities;

(B) Then, if necessary, a pro rata portion of the partnership's other deductions, losses, and section 705(a)(2)(B) items.

Depreciation or cost recovery deductions with respect to property that is subject to partner nonrecourse debt is first treated as a partner nonrecourse deduction and any excess is treated as a partnership nonrecourse deduction under this paragraph (j)(1)(ii). Any other item that is treated as a partner nonrecourse deduction will in no event be treated as a partnership nonrecourse deduction.

(iii) *Carryover to succeeding taxable year.*—If the amount of partner nonrecourse deductions or nonrecourse deductions exceeds the partnership's losses, deductions, and section 705(a)(2)(B) expenditures for the taxable year (determined under paragraphs (j)(1)(i) and (ii) of this section), the excess is treated as an increase in partner nonrecourse debt minimum gain or partnership minimum gain in the immediately succeeding partnership taxable year. See paragraph (m), *Example* (1)(vi) of this section.

(2) *Treatment of partnership income and gains.*—(i) *Minimum gain chargeback.*—Items of partnership income and gain equal to the minimum gain chargeback requirement (determined under paragraph (f) of this section) are allocated as a minimum gain chargeback in the following order:

(A) First, a pro rata portion of gain from the disposition of property subject to partnership nonrecourse liabilities and discharge of indebtedness income relating to partnership nonrecourse liabilities to which property is subject;

(B) Then, if necessary, a pro rata portion of the partnership's other items of income and gain for that year. Gain from the disposition of property subject to partner nonrecourse debt is allocated to satisfy a minimum gain chargeback requirement for partnership nonrecourse debt only to the extent not allocated under paragraph (j)(2)(ii) of this section.

(ii) *Chargeback attributable to decrease in partner nonrecourse debt minimum gain.*—Items of partnership income and gain equal to the partner nonrecourse debt minimum gain chargeback (determined under paragraph (i)(4) of this section) are allocated to satisfy a partner nonrecourse debt minimum gain chargeback in the following order:

(A) First, a pro rata portion of gain from the disposition of property subject to partner nonrecourse debt and discharge of indebtedness income relating to partner nonrecourse debt to which property is subject.

(B) Then, if necessary, a pro rata portion of the partnership's other items of income and gain for that year. Gain from the disposition of property subject to a partnership nonrecourse liability is allocated to satisfy a partner nonrecourse debt minimum gain chargeback only to the extent not allocated under paragraph (j)(2)(i) of this section. An item of partnership income and gain that is allocated to satisfy a minimum gain chargeback under paragraph (f) of this section is not allocated to satisfy a minimum gain chargeback under paragraph (i)(4).

(iii) *Carryover to succeeding taxable year.*—If a minimum gain chargeback requirement (determined under paragraphs (f) and (i)(4) of this section) exceeds the partnership's income and gains for the taxable year, the excess is treated as a minimum gain chargeback requirement in the immediately succeeding partnership taxable years until fully charged back.

(k) *Tiered partnerships.*—For purposes of this section, the following rules determine the effect on partnership minimum gain when a partnership ("upper-tier partnership") is a partner in another partnership ("lower-tier partnership").

(1) *Increase in upper-tier partnership's minimum gain.*—The sum of the nonrecourse deductions that the lower-tier partnership allocates to the upper-tier partnership for any taxable year of the upper-tier partnership, and the distributions made during that taxable year from the lower-tier partnership to the upper-tier

partnership of proceeds of nonrecourse debt that are allocable to an increase in the lower-tier partnership's minimum gain, is treated as an increase in the upper-tier partnership's minimum gain.

(2) *Decrease in upper-tier partnership's minimum gain.*—The upper-tier partnership's share for its taxable year of the lower-tier partnership's net decrease in its minimum gain is treated as a decrease in the upper-tier partnership's minimum gain for that taxable year.

(3) *Nonrecourse debt proceeds distributed from the lower-tier partnership to the upper-tier partnership.*—All distributions from the lower-tier partnership to the upper-tier partnership during the upper-tier partnership's taxable year of proceeds of a nonrecourse liability allocable to an increase in the lower-tier partnership's minimum gain are treated as proceeds of a nonrecourse liability of the upper-tier partnership. The increase in the upper-tier partnership's minimum gain (under paragraph (k)(1) of this section) attributable to the receipt of those distributions is, for purposes of paragraph (h) of this section, treated as an increase in the upper-tier partnership's minimum gain arising from encumbering property of the upper-tier partnership with a nonrecourse liability of the upper-tier partnership.

(4) *Nonrecourse deductions of lower-tier partnership treated as depreciation by upper-tier partnership.*—For purposes of paragraph (c) of this section, all nonrecourse deductions allocated by the lower-tier partnership to the upper-tier partnership for the upper-tier partnership's taxable year are treated as depreciation or cost recovery deductions with respect to property owned by the upper-tier partnership and subject to a nonrecourse liability of the upper-tier partnership with respect to which minimum gain increased during the year by the amount of the nonrecourse deductions.

* * *

(m) *Examples.*—The principles of this section are illustrated by the following examples:

Example 1. Nonrecourse deductions and partnership minimum gain. For *Example* 1, unless otherwise provided, the following facts are assumed. LP, the limited partner, and GP, the general partner, form a limited partnership to acquire and operate a commercial office building. LP contributes $180,000, and GP contributes $20,000. The partnership obtains an $800,000 nonrecourse loan and purchases the building (on leased land) for $1,000,000. The nonrecourse loan is secured only by the building, and no principal payments are due for 5 years. The partnership agreement provides that GP will be required to restore any deficit balance in GP's capital account following the liquidation of GP's interest (as set forth in § 1.704-1(b)(2)(ii)(*b*)(*3*)), and LP will not be required to restore any deficit balance in LP's capital account following the liquidation of LP's interest. The partnership agreement contains the following provisions required by paragraph (e) of this section: a qualified income offset (as defined in § 1.704-1(b)(2)(ii)(*d*)); a minimum gain chargeback (in accordance with paragraph (f) of this section); a provision that the partners' capital accounts will be determined and maintained in accordance with § 1.704-1(b)(2)(ii)(*b*)(*1*); and a provision that distributions will be made in accordance with partners' positive capital account balances (as set forth in § 1.704-1(b)(2)(ii)(*b*)(*2*)). In addition, as of the end of each partnership taxable year discussed herein, the items described in § 1.704-1(b)(2)(ii)(*d*)(*4*), (*5*), and (*6*) are not reasonably expected to cause or increase a deficit balance in LP's capital account. The partnership agreement provides that, except as otherwise required by its qualified income offset and minimum gain chargeback provisions, all partnership items will be allocated 90 percent to LP and 10 percent to GP until the first time when the partnership has recognized items of income and gain that exceed the items of loss and deduction it has recognized over its life, and all further partnership items will be allocated equally between LP and GP. Finally, the partnership agreement provides that all distributions, other than distributions in liquidation of the partnership or of a partner's interest in the partnership, will be made 90 percent to LP and 10 percent to GP until a total of $200,000 has been distributed, and thereafter all the distributions will be made equally to LP and GP. In each of the partnership's first 2 taxable years, it generates rental income of $95,000, operating expenses (including land lease payments) of $10,000, interest expense of $80,000, and a depreciation deduction of $90,000, resulting in a net taxable loss of $85,000 in each of those years. The allocations of these losses 90 percent to LP and 10 percent to GP have substantial economic effect.

	LP	*GP*
Capital account on formation	$180,000	$20,000
Less: net loss in years 1 and 2	(153,000)	(17,000)
Capital account at end of year 2	$27,000	$3,000

In the partnership's third taxable year, it again generates rental income of $95,000, operating expenses of $10,000, interest expense of $80,000, and a depreciation deduction of

$90,000, resulting in a net taxable loss of $85,000. The partnership makes no distributions.

(i) *Calculation of nonrecourse deductions and partnership minimum gain.* If the partnership were to dispose of the building in full satisfaction of the nonrecourse liability at the end of the third year, it would realize $70,000 of gain ($800,000 amount realized less $730,000 adjusted tax basis). Because the amount of partnership minimum gain at the end of the third year (and the net increase in partnership minimum gain during the year) is $70,000, there are partnership nonrecourse deductions for that year of $70,000, consisting of depreciation deductions allowable with respect to the building of $70,000. Pursuant to the partnership agreement, all partnership items comprising the net taxable loss of $85,000, including the $70,000 nonrecourse deduction, are allocated 90 percent to LP and 10 percent to GP. The allocation of these items, other than the nonrecourse deductions, has substantial economic effect.

	LP	*GP*
Capital account at end of year 2	$27,000	$3,000
Less: net loss in year 3 (without nonrecourse deductions)	(13,500)	(1,500)
Less: nonrecourse deductions in year 3	(63,000)	(7,000)
Capital account at end of year 3	($49,500)	($5,500)

The allocation of the $70,000 nonrecourse deduction satisfies requirement (2) of paragraph (e) of this section because it is consistent with allocations having substantial economic effect of other significant partnership items attributable to the building. Because the remaining requirements of paragraph (e) of this section are satisfied, the allocation of nonrecourse deductions is deemed to be in accordance with the partners' interests in the partnership. At the end of the partnership's third taxable year, LP's and GP's shares of partnership minimum gain are $63,000 and $7,000, respectively. Therefore, pursuant to paragraph (g)(1) of this section, LP is treated as obligated to restore a deficit capital account balance of $63,000, so that in the succeeding year LP could be allocated up to an additional $13,500 of partnership deductions, losses, and section 705(a)(2)(B) items that are not nonrecourse deductions. Even though this allocation would increase a deficit capital account balance, it would be considered to have economic effect under the alternate economic effect test contained in § 1.704-1(b)(2)(ii)(*d*). If the partnership were to dispose of the building in full satisfaction of the nonrecourse liability at the beginning of the partnership's fourth taxable year (and had no other economic activity in that year), the partnership minimum gain would be decreased from $70,000 to zero, and the minimum gain chargeback would require that LP and GP be allocated $63,000 and $7,000, respectively, of the gain from that disposition.

(ii) *Illustration of reasonable consistency requirement.* Assume instead that the partnership agreement provides that all nonrecourse deductions of the partnership will be allocated equally between LP and GP. Furthermore, at the time the partnership agreement is entered into, there is a reasonable likelihood that over the partnership's life it will realize amounts of income and gain significantly in excess of amounts of loss and deduction (other than nonrecourse deductions). The equal allocation of excess income and gain has substantial economic effect.

	LP	*GP*
Capital account on formation	$180,000	$20,000
Less: net loss years 1 and 2	(153,000)	(17,000)
Less: net loss in year 3 (without nonrecourse deductions)	(13,500)	(1,500)
Less: nonrecourse deductions in year 3	(35,000)	(35,000)
Capital account at end of year 3	($21,500)	($33,500)

The allocation of the $70,000 nonrecourse deduction equally between LP and GP satisfies requirement (2) of paragraph (e) of this section because the allocation is consistent with allocations, which will have substantial economic effect, of other significant partnership items attributable to the building. Because the remaining requirements of paragraph (e) of this section are satisfied, the allocation of nonrecourse deductions is deemed to be in accordance with the partners' interests in the partnership. The allocation of the nonrecourse deductions 75 percent to LP and 25 percent to GP (or in any other ratio between 90 percent to LP/10 percent to GP and 50 percent to LP/50 percent to GP) also would satisfy requirement (2) of paragraph (e) of this section.

(iii) *Allocation of nonrecourse deductions that fails reasonable consistency requirement.* Assume instead that the partnership agreement provides that LP will be allocated 99 percent, and GP 1 percent, of all nonrecourse deductions of the partnership. Allocating nonrecourse deductions this way does not satisfy requirement (2) of paragraph (e) of this section because the allocations are not reasonably consistent with allocations, having substantial economic effect, of any other significant partnership item attributable to the building. Therefore, the allocation of nonrecourse deductions will be disregarded, and the nonrecourse deductions of the partnership will be reallocated according to the partners' overall economic interests in the partnership, determined under § 1.704-1(b)(3)(ii).

(iv) *Capital contribution to pay down nonrecourse debt.* At the beginning of the partnership's fourth taxable year, LP contributes $144,000 and GP contributes $16,000 of additional capital to the partnership, which the partnership immediately uses to reduce the amount of its nonrecourse liability from $800,000 to $640,000. In addition, in the partnership's fourth taxable year, it generates rental income of $95,000, operating expenses of $10,000, interest expense of $64,000 (consistent with the debt reduction), and a depreciation deduction of $90,000, resulting in a net taxable loss of $69,000. If the partnership were to dispose of the building in full satisfaction of the nonrecourse liability at the end of that year, it would realize no gain ($640,000 amount realized less $640,000 adjusted tax basis). Therefore, the amount of partnership minimum gain at the end of the year is zero, which represents a net decrease in partnership minimum gain of $70,000 during the year. LP's and GP's shares of this net decrease are $63,000 and $7,000 respectively, so that at the end of the partnership's fourth taxable year, LP's and GP's shares of partnership minimum gain are zero. Although there has been a net decrease in partnership minimum gain, pursuant to paragraph (f)(3) of this section LP and GP are not subject to a minimum gain chargeback.

	LP	*GP*
Capital account at end of year 3	($49,500)	($5,500)
Plus: contribution	144,000	16,000
Less: net loss in year 4	(62,100)	(6,900)
Capital account at end of year 4	$32,400	$3,600
Minimum gain chargeback carryforward	$ 0000	$ 0

(v) *Loans of unequal priority.* Assume instead that the building acquired by the partnership is secured by a $700,000 nonrecourse loan and a $100,000 recourse loan, subordinate in priority to the nonrecourse loan. Under paragraph (d)(2) of this section, $700,000 of the adjusted basis of the building at the end of the partnership's third taxable year is allocated to the nonrecourse liability (with the remaining $30,000 allocated to the recourse liability) so that if the partnership disposed of the building in full satisfaction of the nonrecourse liability at the end of that year, it would realize no gain ($700,000 amount realized less $700,000 adjusted tax basis). Therefore, there is no minimum gain (or increase in minimum gain) at the end of the partnership's third taxable year. If, however, the $700,000 nonrecourse loan were subordinate in priority to the $100,000 recourse loan, under paragraph (d)(2) of this section, the first $100,000 of adjusted tax basis in the building would be allocated to the recourse liability leaving only $630,000 of the adjusted basis of the building to be allocated to the $700,000 nonrecourse loan. In that case, the balance of the $700,000 nonrecourse liability would exceed the adjusted tax basis of the building by $70,000, so that there would be $70,000 of minimum gain (and a $70,000 increase in partnership minimum gain) in the partnership's third taxable year.

(vi) *Nonrecourse borrowing; distribution of proceeds in subsequent year.* The partnership obtains an additional nonrecourse loan of $200,000 at the end of its fourth taxable year, secured by a second mortgage on the building, and distributes $180,000 of this cash to its partners at the beginning of its fifth taxable year. In addition, in its fourth and fifth taxable years, the partnership again generates rental income of $95,000, operating expenses of $10,000, interest expense of $80,000 ($100,000 in the fifth taxable year reflecting the interest paid on both liabilities), and a depreciation deduction of $90,000, resulting in a net taxable loss of $85,000 ($105,000 in the fifth taxable year reflecting the interest paid on both liabilities). The partnership has distributed its $5,000 of operating cash flow in each year ($95,000 of rental income less $10,000 of operating expense and $80,000 of interest expense) to LP and GP at the end of each year. If the partnership were to dispose of the building in full satisfaction of both nonrecourse liabilities at the end of its fourth taxable year, the partnership would realize $360,000 of gain ($1,000,000 amount realized less $640,000 adjusted tax basis). Thus, the net increase in partnership minimum gain during the partnership's fourth taxable year is $290,000 ($360,000 of minimum gain at the end of the fourth year less $70,000 of minimum gain at the end of the third year). Because the partnership did not distribute any of the proceeds of the loan it obtained in its fourth year during that year, the potential amount of partnership nonrecourse deductions for that year is $290,000. Under paragraph (c) of this section, if the partnership had distributed the proceeds of that loan to its partners at the end of its fourth year, the partnership's nonrecourse deductions for that year would have been reduced by the amount of that distribution because the proceeds of that loan are allocable to an increase in partnership minimum gain under paragraph (h)(1) of this section. Because the nonrecourse deductions of $290,000 for the partnership's fourth taxable year exceed its total deductions for that year, all $180,000 of the partnership's deductions for that year are treated as nonrecourse deductions, and the $110,000 excess nonrecourse deductions are treated as an increase in partnership minimum gain in the partnership's fifth taxable year under paragraph (c) of this section.

	LP	*GP*
Capital account at end of year 3 (including cash flow distributions)	($63,000)	($7,000)
Plus: rental income in year 4	85,500	9,500
Less: nonrecourse deductions in year 4	(162,000)	(18,000)
Less: cash flow distributions in year 4	(4,500)	(500)
Capital account at end of year 4	($144,000)	($16,000)

At the end of the partnership's fourth taxable year, LP's and GP's shares of partnership minimum gain are $225,000 and $25,000, respectively (because the $110,000 excess of nonrecourse deductions is carried forward to the next year). If the partnership were to dispose of the building in full satisfaction of the nonrecourse liabilities at the end of its fifth taxable year, the partnership would realize $450,000 of gain ($1,000,000 amount realized less $550,000 adjusted tax basis). Therefore, the net increase in partnership minimum gain during the partnership's fifth taxable year is $200,000 ($110,000 deemed increase plus the $90,000 by which minimum gain at the end of the fifth year exceeds minimum gain at the end of the fourth year ($450,000 less $360,000)). At the beginning of its fifth year, the partnership distributes $180,000 of the loan proceeds (retaining $20,000 to pay the additional interest expense). Under paragraph (h) of this section, the first $110,000 of this distribution (an amount equal to the deemed increase in partnership minimum gain for the year) is considered allocable to an increase in partnership minimum gain for the year. As a result, the amount of nonrecourse deductions for the partnership's fifth taxable year is $90,000 ($200,000 net increase in minimum gain less $110,000 distribution of nonrecourse liability proceeds allocable to an increase in partnership minimum gain), and the nonrecourse deductions consist solely of the $90,000 depreciation deduction allowable with respect to the building. As a result of the distributions during the partnership's fifth taxable year, the total distributions to the partners over the partnership's life equal $205,000. Therefore, the last $5,000 distributed to the partners during the fifth year will be divided equally between them under the partnership agreement. Thus, out of the $185,000 total distribution during the partnership's fifth taxable year, the first $180,000 is distributed 90 percent to LP and 10 percent to GP, and the last $5,000 is divided equally between them.

	LP	*GP*
Capital account at end of year 4	($144,000)	($16,000)
Less: net loss in year 5 (without nonrecourse deductions)	(13,500)	(1,500)
Less: nonrecourse deductions in year 5	(81,000)	(9,000)
Less: distribution of loan proceeds	(162,000)	(18,000)
Less: cash flow distribution in year 5	(2,500)	(2,500)
Capital account at end of year 5	($403,000)	($47,000)

At the end of the partnership's fifth taxable year, LP's share of partnership minimum gain is $405,000 ($225,000 share of minimum gain at the end of the fourth year plus $81,000 of nonrecourse deductions for the fifth year and a $99,000 distribution of nonrecourse liability proceeds that are allocable to an increase in minimum gain) and GP's share of partnership minimum gain is $45,000 ($25,000 share of minimum gain at the end of the fourth year plus $9,000 of nonrecourse deductions for the fifth year and an $11,000 distribution of nonrecourse liability proceeds that are allocable to an increase in minimum gain).

(vii) *Partner nonrecourse debt.* Assume instead that the $800,000 loan is made by LP, the limited partner. Under paragraph (b)(4) of this section, the $800,000 obligation does not constitute a nonrecourse liability of the partnership for purposes of this section because LP, a partner, bears the economic risk of loss for that loan within the meaning of § 1.752-2. Instead, the $800,000 loan constitutes a partner nonrecourse debt under paragraph (b)(4) of this section. In the partnership's third taxable year, partnership minimum gain would have increased by $70,000 if the debt were a nonrecourse liability of the partnership. Thus, under paragraph (i)(3) of this section, there is a net increase of $70,000 in the minimum gain attributable to the $800,000 partner nonrecourse debt for the partnership's third taxable year, and $70,000 of the $90,000 depreciation deduction from the building for the partnership's third taxable year constitutes a partner nonrecourse deduction with respect to the debt. See paragraph (i)(4) of this section. Under paragraph (i)(2) of this section, this partner nonrecourse deduction must be allocated to LP, the partner that bears the economic risk of loss for that liability.

(viii) *Nonrecourse debt and partner nonrecourse debt of differing priorities.* As in Example 1 (vii) of this paragraph (m), the $800,000 loan is made to the partnership by LP, the limited partner, but the loan is a purchase money loan that "wraps around" a $700,000 underlying nonrecourse note (also secured by the building) issued by LP to an unrelated person in connection with LP's acquisition of the building. Under these circumstances, LP bears the economic risk of loss with respect to only $100,000 of the liability within the meaning of § 1.752-2. See § 1.752-2(f) (*Example* 6). Therefore, for purposes of paragraph (d) of this section, the $800,000 liability is treated as a $700,000 nonrecourse liability of the partnership and a $100,000 partner nonrecourse debt (inferior in priority to the $700,000 liability) of the partnership for which LP bears the economic risk of loss. Under paragraph (i)(2) of this section, $70,000 of the $90,000 depreciation deduction realized in the partnership's third taxable year constitutes a partner nonrecourse deduction that must be allocated to LP.

Example 2. *Netting of increases and decreases in partnership minimum gain.* For *Example* 2 unless otherwise provided, the following facts are assumed. X and Y form a general partnership to acquire and operate residential real properties. Each partner contributes $150,000 to the partnership. The partnership obtains a $1,500,000 nonrecourse loan and purchases 3 apartment buildings (on leased land) for $720,000 ("Property A"), $540,000 ("Property B"), and $540,000 ("Property C"). The nonrecourse loan is secured only by the 3 buildings, and no principal payments are due for 5 years. In each of the partnership's first 3 taxable years, it generates rental income of $225,000, operating expenses (including land lease payments) of $50,000, interest expense of $175,000, and depreciation deductions on the 3 properties of $150,000 ($60,000 on Property A and $45,000 on each of Property B and Property C), resulting in a net taxable loss of $150,000 in each of those years. The partnership makes no distributions to X or Y.

(i) *Calculation of net increases and decreases in partnership minimum gain.* If the partnership were to dispose of the 3 apartment buildings in full satisfaction of its nonrecourse liability at the end of its third taxable year, it would realize $150,000 of gain ($1,500,000 amount realized less $1,350,000 adjusted tax basis). Because the amount of partnership minimum gain at the end of that year (and the net increase in partnership minimum gain during that year) is $150,000, the amount of partnership nonrecourse deductions for that year is $150,000, consisting of depreciation deductions allowable with respect to the 3 apartment buildings of $150,000. The result would be the same if the partnership obtained 3 separate nonrecourse loans that were "cross-collateralized" (*i.e.*, if each separate loan were secured by all 3 of the apartment buildings).

(ii) *Netting of increases and decreases in partnership minimum gain when there is a disposition.* At the beginning of the partnership's fourth taxable year, the partnership (with the permission of the nonrecourse lender) disposes of Property A for $835,000 and uses a portion of the proceeds to repay $600,000 of the nonrecourse liability (the principal amount attributable to Property A), reducing the balance to $900,000. As a result of the disposition, the partnership realizes gain of $295,000 ($835,000 amount realized less $540,000 adjusted tax basis). If the disposition is viewed in isolation, the partnership has generated minimum gain of $60,000 on the sale of Property A ($600,000 of debt reduction less $540,000 adjusted tax basis). However, during the partnership's fourth taxable year it also generates rental income of $135,000, operating expenses of $30,000, interest expense of $105,000, and depreciation deductions of $90,000 ($45,000 on each remaining building). If the partnership were to dispose of the remaining two buildings in full satisfaction of its nonrecourse liability at the end of the partnership's fourth taxable year, it would realize gain of $180,000 ($900,000 amount realized less $720,000 aggregate adjusted tax basis), which is the amount of partnership minimum gain at the end of the year. Because the partnership minimum gain increased from $150,000 to $180,000 during the partnership's fourth taxable year, the amount of partnership nonrecourse deductions for that year is $30,000, consisting of a ratable portion of depreciation deductions allowable with respect to the two remaining apartment buildings. No minimum gain chargeback is required for the taxable year, even though the partnership disposed of one of the properties subject to the nonrecourse liability during the year, because there is no net decrease in partnership minimum gain for the year. See paragraph (f)(1) of this section.

* * *

Example 4. *Allocations of increase in partnership minimum gain among partnership properties.* For *Example* 4, unless otherwise provided, the following facts are assumed. A partnership owns 4 properties, each of which is subject to a nonrecourse liability of the partnership. During a taxable year of the partnership, the following events take place. First, the partnership generates a depreciation deduction (for both book and tax purposes) with respect to Property W of $10,000 and repays $5,000 of the nonrecourse liability secured only by that property, resulting in an increase in minimum gain with respect to that liability of $5,000. Second, the partnership generates a depreciation deduction (for both book and tax purposes) with respect to Property X of $10,000 and repays none of the nonrecourse liability secured by that property, resulting in an increase in minimum gain with respect to that liability of $10,000. Third, the partnership generates a depreciation deduction (for both book and tax purposes) of $2,000 with respect to Property Y and repays $11,000 of the nonrecourse liability secured only by that property, resulting in a decrease in minimum gain with respect to that liability of $9,000 (although at the end of that year, there remains minimum gain with respect to that liability). Finally, the partnership borrows $5,000 on a nonrecourse basis, giving as the only security for that liability Property Z, a parcel of undeveloped land with an adjusted tax basis (and book value) of $2,000, resulting in a net increase in minimum gain with respect to that liability of $3,000.

(i) *Allocation of increase in partnership minimum gain*. The net increase in partnership minimum gain during that partnership taxable year is $9,000, so that the amount of nonrecourse deductions of the partnership for that taxable year is $9,000. Those nonrecourse deductions consist of $3,000 of depreciation deductions with respect to Property W and $6,000 of depreciation deductions with respect to Property X. See paragraph (c) of this section. The amount of nonrecourse deductions consisting of depreciation deductions is determined as follows. With respect to the nonrecourse liability secured by Property Z, for which there is no depreciation deduction, the amount of depreciation deductions that constitutes nonrecourse deductions is zero. Similarly, with respect to the nonrecourse liability secured by Property Y, for which there is no increase in minimum gain, the amount of depreciation deductions that constitutes nonrecourse deductions is zero. With respect to each of the nonrecourse liabilities secured by Properties W and X, which are secured by property for which there are depreciation deductions and for which there is an increase in minimum gain, the amount of depreciation deductions that constitutes nonrecourse deductions is determined by the following formula:

$$\text{net increase in partnership minimum gain} \times \frac{\text{total depreciation deductions for that taxable year on the specific property securing the nonrecourse liability to the extent gain increased on that liability}}{\text{total depreciation deductions for that taxable year on all properties securing nonrecourse liabilities to the extent of the aggregate increase in minimum gain on all those liabilities}}$$

Thus, for the liability secured by Property W, the amount is $9,000 times $5,000/$15,000, or $3,000. For the liability secured by Property X, the amount is $9,000 times $10,000/$15,000, or $6,000. (If one depreciable property secured two partnership nonrecourse liabilities, the amount of depreciation or book depreciation with respect to that property would be allocated among those liabilities in accordance with the method by which adjusted basis is allocated under paragraph (d)(2) of this section).

(ii) *Alternative allocation of increase in partnership minimum gain among partnership properties*. Assume instead that the loan secured by Property Z is $15,000 (rather than $5,000), resulting in a net increase in minimum gain with respect to that liability of $13,000. Thus, the net increase in partnership minimum gain is $19,000, and the amount of nonrecourse deductions of the partnership for that taxable year is $19,000. Those nonrecourse deductions consist of $5,000 of depreciation deductions with respect to Property W, $10,000 of depreciation deductions with respect to Property X, and a pro rata portion of the partnership's other items of deduction, loss, and section 705(a)(2)(B) expenditure for that year. The method for computing the amounts of depreciation deductions that constitute nonrecourse deductions is the same as in (i) of this *Example* 4 for the liabilities secured by Properties Y and Z. With respect to each of the nonrecourse liabilities secured by Properties W and X, the amount of depreciation deductions that constitutes nonrecourse deductions equals the total depreciation deductions with respect to the partnership property securing that particular liability to the extent of the increase in minimum gain with respect to that liability. [Reg. § 1.704-2.]

□ [*T.D.* 8385, 12-26-91. *Amended by T.D.* 9207, 5-23-2005; *T.D.* 9289, 10-10-2006; *T.D.* 9557, 11-15-2011 *and T.D.* 9787, 10-4-2016.]

§ 1.704-3. Contributed property.—(a) *In general.*—(1) *General principles.*—The purpose of section 704(c) is to prevent the shifting of tax consequences among partners with respect to precontribution gain or loss. Under section 704(c), a partnership must allocate income, gain, loss, and deduction with respect to property contributed by a partner to the partnership so as to take into account any variation between the adjusted tax basis of the property and its fair market value at the time of contribution. Notwithstanding any other provision of this section, the allocations must be made using a reasonable method that is consistent with the purpose of section 704(c). For this purpose, an allocation method includes the application of all of the rules of this section (e.g., aggregation rules). An allocation method is not necessarily unreasonable merely because another allocation method would result in a higher aggregate tax liability. Paragraphs (b), (c), and (d) of this section describe allocation methods that are generally reasonable. Other methods may be reasonable in appropriate circumstances. Nevertheless, in the absence of specific published guidance, it is not reasonable to use an allocation method in which the basis of property contributed to the partnership is increased (or decreased) to reflect built-in gain (or loss), or a method under which the partnership creates tax allocations of income, gain, loss, or deduction independent of allocations affecting book capital accounts. See § 1.704-3(d). Paragraph (e) of this section contains special rules and exceptions. The principles of this paragraph (a)(1), together with the methods described in paragraphs (b), (c) and (d) of this section, apply only to contributions of property that are otherwise respected. See for example § 1.701-2. Accordingly, even though a partnership's allocation method may be described in the literal language of paragraphs (b), (c) or (d) of this section, based on the particular facts and circumstances, the Commissioner can recast the contribution as appropriate to avoid tax results inconsistent with the intent of subchapter K. One factor that may be considered by the Commissioner is the use of the remedial allocation method by related partners in which allocations of remedial items of income, gain, loss or deduction are made to one partner and the allocations of offsetting remedial items are made to a related partner.

(2) *Operating rules.*—Except as provided in paragraphs (e)(2) and (e)(3) of this section, section 704(c) and this section apply on a property-by-property basis. Therefore, in determining whether there is a disparity between adjusted tax basis and fair market value, the built-in gains and built-in losses on items of contributed property cannot be aggregated. A partnership may use different methods with respect to different items of contributed property, provided that the partnership and the partners consistently apply a single reasonable method for each item of contributed property and that the overall method or combination of methods are reasonable based on the facts and circumstances and consistent with the purpose of section 704(c). It may be unreasonable to use one method for appreciated property and another method for depreciated property. Similarly, it may be unreasonable to use the traditional method for built-in gain property contributed by a partner with a high marginal tax rate while using curative allocations for built-in gain property contributed by a partner with a low marginal tax rate. A new partnership formed as the result of the termination of a partnership under section 708(b)(1)(B) is not required to use the same method as the terminated partnership with respect to section 704(c) property deemed contributed to the new partnership by the terminated partnership under § 1.7081(b)(1)(iv). The previous sentence applies to terminations of partnerships under section 708(b)(1)(B) occurring on or after May 9, 1997; however, the sentence may be applied to terminations occurring on or after May 9, 1996, provided that the partnership and its partners apply the sentence to the termination in a consistent manner.

(3) *Definitions.*—(i) *Section 704(c) property.*—Property contributed to a partnership is section 704(c) property if at the time of contribution its book value differs from the contributing partner's adjusted tax basis. For purposes of this section, book value is determined as contemplated by § 1.704-1(b). Therefore, book value is equal to fair market value at the time of contribution and is subsequently adjusted for cost recovery and other events that affect the basis of the property. For a partnership that maintains capital accounts in accordance with § 1.704-1(b)(2)(iv), the book value of property is initially the value used in determining the contributing partner's capital account under § 1.704-1(b)(2)(iv)(*d*), and is appropriately adjusted thereafter (e.g., for book cost recovery under §§ 1.704-1(b)(2)(iv)(*g*)(*3*) and 1.704-3(d)(2) and other events that affect the basis of the property). A partnership that does not maintain capital accounts under § 1.704-1(b)(2)(iv) must comply with this section using a book capital account based on the same principles (i.e., a book capital account that reflects the fair market value of property at the time of contribution and that is subsequently adjusted for cost recovery and other events that affect the basis of the property). Property deemed contributed to a new partnership as the result of the termination of a part-

nership under section 708(b)(1)(B) is treated as section 704(c) property in the hands of the new partnership only to the extent that the property was section 704(c) property in the hands of the terminated partnership immediately prior to the termination. See § 1.708-1(b)(1)(iv) for an example of the application of this rule. The previous two sentences apply to terminations of partnerships under section 708(b)(1)(B) occurring on or after May 9, 1997; however, the sentences may be applied to terminations occurring on or after May 9, 1996, provided that the partnership and its partners apply the sentences to the termination in a consistent manner.

(ii) *Built-in gain and built-in loss.*—The built-in gain on section 704(c) property is the excess of the property's book value over the contributing partner's adjusted tax basis upon contribution. The built-in gain is thereafter reduced by decreases in the difference between the property's book value and adjusted tax basis. The built-in loss on section 704(c) property is the excess of the contributing partner's adjusted tax basis over the property's book value upon contribution. The built-in loss is thereafter reduced by decreases in the difference between the property's adjusted tax basis and book value. See § 1.460-4(k)(3)(v)(A) for a rule relating to the amount of built-in income or built-in loss attributable to a contract accounted for under a long-term contract method of accounting.

(4) *Accounts payable and other accrued but unpaid items.*—Accounts payable and other accrued but unpaid items contributed by a partner using the cash receipts and disbursements method of accounting are treated as section 704(c) property for purposes of applying the rules of this section.

(5) *Other provisions of the Internal Revenue Code.*—Section 704(c) and this section apply to a contribution of property to the partnership only if the contribution is governed by section 721, taking into account other provisions of the Internal Revenue Code. For example, to the extent that a transfer of property to a partnership is a sale under section 707, the transfer is not a contribution of property to which section 704(c) applies.

(6) *Other applications of section 704(c) principles.*—(i) *Revaluations under section 704(b).*—The principles of this section apply to allocations with respect to property for which differences between book value and adjusted tax basis are created when a partnership revalues partnership property pursuant to § 1.704-1(b)(2)(iv)(*f*) or 1.704-1(b)(2)(iv)(*s*) (reverse section 704(c) allocations). Partnerships are not required to use the same allocation method for reverse section 704(c) allocations as for contributed property, even if at the time of revaluation the property is already subject to section 704(c) and paragraph (a) of this section. In addition, partnerships are not required to use the same allocation method for reverse section 704(c) allocations each time the partnership revalues its property. A partnership that makes allocations with respect to revalued property must use a reasonable method that is consistent with the purposes of section 704(b) and (c).

(ii) *Basis adjustments.*—A partnership making adjustments under § 1.743-1(b) or 1.751-1(a)(2) must account for built-in gain or loss under section 704(c) in accordance with the principles of this section.

(7) *Transfer of a partnership interest.*—If a contributing partner transfers a partnership interest, built-in gain or loss must be allocated to the transferee partner as it would have been allocated to the transferor partner. If the contributing partner transfers a portion of the partnership interest, the share of built-in gain or loss proportionate to the interest transferred must be allocated to the transferee partner. This rule does not apply to any person who acquired a partnership interest from a § 1.752-7 liability partner in a transaction to which paragraph (e)(1) of § 1.752-7 applies. See § 1.752-7(c)(1).

(8) *Special rules.*—(i) *Disposition in a nonrecognition transaction.*—If a partnership disposes of section 704(c) property in a nonrecognition transaction, the substituted basis property (within the meaning of section 7701(a)(42)) is treated as section 704(c) property with the same amount of built-in gain or loss as the section 704(c) property disposed of by the partnership. If gain or loss is recognized in such a transaction, appropriate adjustments must be made. The allocation method for the substituted basis property must be consistent with the allocation method chosen for the original property. If a partnership transfers an item of section 704(c) property together with other property to a corporation under section 351, in order to preserve that item's built-in gain or loss, the basis in the stock received in exchange for the section 704(c) property is determined as if each item of section 704(c) property had been the only property transferred to the corporation by the partnership.

(ii) *Disposition in an installment sale.*—If a partnership disposes of section 704(c) property in an installment sale as defined in section 453(b), the installment obligation received by the partnership is treated as the section 704(c) property with the same amount of built-in gain as the section 704(c) property disposed of by the partnership (with appropriate adjustments for any gain recognized on the installment sale). The allocation method for the installment obligation must be consistent with the allocation method chosen for the original property.

(iii) *Contributed contracts.*—If a partner contributes to a partnership a contract that is section 704(c) property, and the partnership subsequently acquires property pursuant to that contract in a transaction in which less than all of the gain or loss is recognized, then the acquired property is treated as the section 704(c) property with the same amount of built-in gain or loss as the contract (with appropriate adjustments for any gain or loss recognized on the acquisition). For this purpose, the term contract includes, but is not limited to, options, forward contracts, and futures contracts. The allocation method for the acquired property must be consistent with the allocation method chosen for the contributed contract.

(iv) *Capitalized amounts.*—To the extent that a partnership properly capitalizes all or a portion of an item as described in paragraph (a)(12) of this section, then the item or items to which such cost is properly capitalized is treated as section 704(c) property with the same amount of built-in loss as corresponds to the amount capitalized.

(9) *Tiered partnerships.*—If a partnership contributes section 704(c) property to a second partnership (the lower-tier partnership), or if a partner that has contributed section 704(c) property to a partnership contributes that partnership interest to a second partnership (the upper-tier partnership), the upper-tier partnership must allocate its distributive share of lower-tier partnership items with respect to that section 704(c) property in a manner that takes into account the contributing partner's remaining built-in gain or loss. Allocations made under this paragraph will be considered to be made in a manner that meets the requirements of § 1.704-1(b)(2)(iv)(*q*) (relating to capital account adjustments where guidance is lacking).

(10) *Anti-abuse rule.*—(i) *In general.*—An allocation method (or combination of methods) is not reasonable if the contribution of property (or event that results in reverse section 704(c) allocations) and the corresponding allocation of tax items with respect to the property are made with a view to shifting the tax consequences of built-in gain or loss among the partners in a manner that substantially reduces the present value of the partners' aggregate tax liability. For purposes of this paragraph (a)(10), all references to the partners shall include both direct and indirect partners.

(ii) *Definition of indirect partner.*—An *indirect partner* is any direct or indirect owner of a partnership, S corporation, or controlled foreign corporation (as defined in section 957(a) or 953(c)), or direct or indirect beneficiary of a trust or estate, that is a partner in the partnership, and any consolidated group of which the partner in the partnership is a member (within the meaning of § 1.1502-1(h)). An owner (whether directly or through tiers of entities) of a controlled foreign corporation is treated as an indirect partner only with respect to allocations of items of income, gain, loss, or deduction that enter into the computation of a United States shareholder's inclusion under section 951(a) with respect to the controlled foreign corporation, enter into any person's income attributable to a United States shareholder's inclusion under section 951(a) with respect to the controlled foreign corporation, or would enter into the computations described in this sentence if such items were allocated to the controlled foreign corporation.

(11) *Contributing and noncontributing partners' recapture shares.*—For special rules applicable to the allocation of depreciation recapture with respect to property contributed by a partner to a partnership, see §§ 1.1245-1(e)(2) and 1.1250-1(f).

(12) *§ 1.752-7 liabilities.*—Except as otherwise provided in § 1.752-7, § 1.752-7 liabilities (within the meaning of § 1.752-7(b)(2)) are section 704(c) property (built-in loss property that at the time of contribution has a book value that differs from the contributing partner's adjusted tax basis) for purposes of applying the rules of this section. See § 1.752-7(c). To the extent that the built-in loss associated with the § 1.752-7 liability exceeds the cost of satisfying the § 1.752-7 liability (as defined in § 1.752-7(b)(3)), the excess creates a "ceiling rule" limitation, within the meaning of § 1.704-3(b)(1), subject to the methods of allocation set forth in § 1.704-3(b), (c) and (d).

* * *

(b) *Traditional method.*—(1) *In general.*—This paragraph (b) describes the traditional method of making section 704(c) allocations. In general, the traditional method requires that when the partnership has income, gain, loss, or deduction attributable to section 704(c) property, it must make appropriate allocations to the partners to avoid shifting the tax consequences of the built-in gain or loss. Under this rule, if the partnership sells section 704(c) property and recognizes gain or loss, built-in gain or loss on the property is allocated to the contributing partner. If the partnership sells a portion of, or an interest in, section 704(c) property, a proportionate part of the built-in gain or loss is allocated to the contributing partner. For section 704(c) property subject to amortization, depletion, depreciation, or other cost recovery, the allocation of deductions attributable to these items takes into account built-in gain or loss on the property. For example, tax allocations to the noncontributing partners of cost recovery deductions with respect to section 704(c) property generally must, to the extent possible, equal book allocations to those partners. However, the total income, gain, loss, or deduction allocated to the partners for a taxable year with respect to a property cannot exceed the total partnership income, gain, loss, or deduction with respect to that property for the taxable year (the ceiling rule). If a partnership has no property the allocations from which are limited by the ceiling rule, the traditional method is reasonable when used for all contributed property.

(2) *Examples.*—The following examples illustrate the principles of the traditional method.

Example 1. Operation of the traditional method—(i) *Calculation of built-in gain on contribution.* A and B form partnership AB and agree that each will be allocated a 50 percent share of all partnership items and that AB will make allocations under section 704(c) using the traditional method under paragraph (b) of this section. A contributes depreciable property with an adjusted tax basis of $4,000 and a book value of $10,000, and B contributes $10,000 cash. Under paragraph (a)(3) of this section, A has built-in gain of $6,000, the excess of the partnership's book value for the property ($10,000) over A's adjusted tax basis in the property at the time of contribution ($4,000).

(ii) *Allocation of tax depreciation.* The property is depreciated using the straight-line method over a 10-year recovery period. Because the property depreciates at an annual rate of 10 percent, B would have been entitled to a depreciation deduction of $500 per year for both book and tax purposes if the adjusted tax basis of the property equalled its fair market value at the time of contribution. Although each partner is allocated $500 of book depreciation per year, the partnership is allowed a tax depreciation deduction of only $400 per year (10 percent of $4,000). The partnership can allocate only $400 of tax depreciation under the ceiling rule of paragraph (b)(1) of this section, and it must be allocated entirely to B. In AB's first year, the proceeds generated by the equipment exactly equal AB's operating expense. At the end of that year, the book value of the property is $9,000 ($10,000 less the $1,000 book depreciation deduction), and the adjusted tax basis is $3,600 ($4,000 less the $400 tax depreciation deduction). A's built-in gain with respect to the property decreases to $5,400 ($9,000 book value less $3,600 adjusted tax basis). Also, at the end of AB's first year, A has a $9,500 book capital account and a $4,000 tax basis in A's partnership interest. B has a $9,500 book capital account and a $9600 adjusted tax basis in B's partnership interest.

(iii) *Sale of the property.* If AB sells the property at the beginning of AB's second year for $9,000, AB realizes tax gain of $5,400 ($9,000, the amount realized, less the adjusted tax basis of $3,600). Under paragraph (b)(1) of this section, the entire $5,400 gain must be allocated to A because the property A contributed has that much built-in gain remaining. If AB sells the property at the beginning of AB's second year for $10,000, AB realizes tax gain of $6,400 ($10,000, the amount realized, less the adjusted tax basis of $3,600). Under paragraph (b)(1) of this section, only $5,400 of gain must be allocated to A to account for A's built-in gain. The remaining $1,000 of gain is allocated equally between A and B in accordance with the partnership agreement. If AB sells the property for less than the $9,000 book value, AB realizes tax gain of less than $5,400, and the entire gain must be allocated to A.

(iv) *Termination and liquidation of partnership.* If AB sells the property at the beginning of AB's second year for $9,000, and AB engages in no other transactions that year, A will recognize a gain of $5,400, and B will recognize no income or loss. A's adjusted tax basis for A's interest in AB will then be $9,400 ($4,000, A's original tax basis, increased by the gain of $5,400). B's adjusted tax basis for B's interest in AB will be $9,600 ($10,000, B's original tax basis, less the $400 depreciation deduction in he first partnership year). If the partnership then terminates and distributes its assets ($19,000 in cash) to A and B in proportion to their capital account balances, A will recognize a capital gain of $100 ($9,500, the amount distributed to A, less $9,400, the adjusted tax basis of A's interest). B will recognize a capital loss of $100 (the excess of B's adjusted tax basis, $9,600, over the amount received, $9,500).

Example 2. Unreasonable use of the traditional method—(i) *Facts.* C and D form partnership CD and agree that each will be allocated a 50 percent share of all partnership items and that CD will make allocations under section 704(c) using the traditional method under paragraph (b) of this section. C contributes equipment with an adjusted tax basis of $1,000 and a book value of $10,000, with a view to taking advantage of the fact that the equipment has only one year remaining on its cost recovery schedule although its remaining economic life is significantly longer. At the time of contribution, C has a built-in gain of $9,000 and the equipment is section 704(c) property. D contributes $10,000 of cash, which CD uses to buy securities. D has substantial net operating loss carryforwards that D anticipates will otherwise expire unused. Under § 1.704-1(b)(2)(iv)(*g*)(*3*), the partnership must allocate the $10,000 of book depreciation to the partners in the first year of the partnership. Thus, there is $10,000 of book depreciation and $1,000 of tax depreciation in the partnership's first year. CD sells the equipment during the second year for $10,000 and recognizes a $10,000 gain ($10,000, the amount realized, less the adjusted tax basis of $0).

(ii) *Unreasonable use of method*—(A) At the beginning of the second year, both the book value and adjusted tax basis of the equipment are $0. Therefore, there is no remaining built-in gain. The $10,000 gain on the sale of the equipment in the second year is allocated $5,000 each to C and D. The interaction of the partnership's one-year write-off of the entire book value of the equipment and the use of the traditional method results in a shift of $4,000 of the precontribution gain in the equipment from C to D (D's $5,000 share of CD's $10,000 gain, less the $1,000 tax depreciation deduction previously allocated to D).

(B) The traditional method is not reasonable under paragraph (a)(10) of this section because the contribution of property is made, and the traditional method is used, with a view to shifting a significant amount of taxable income to a partner with a low marginal tax rate and away from a partner with a high marginal tax rate.

(C) Under these facts, if the partnership agreement in effect for the year of contribution had provided that tax gain from the sale of the property (if any) would always be allocated first to C to offset the effect of the ceiling rule limitation, the allocation method would not violate the anti-abuse rule of paragraph (a)(10) of this section. See paragraph (c)(3) of this section. Under other facts, (for example, if the partnership holds multiple section 704(c) properties and either uses multiple allocation methods or uses a single allocation method where one or more of the properties are subject to the ceiling rule) the allocation to C may not be reasonable.

(c) *Traditional method with curative allocations.*—(1) *In general.*—To correct distortions created by the ceiling rule, a partnership using the traditional method under paragraph (b) of this section may make reasonable curative allocations to reduce or eliminate disparities between book and tax items of noncontributing partners. A curative allocation is an allocation of income, gain, loss, or deduction for tax purposes that differs from the partnership's allocation of the corresponding book item. For example, if a noncontributing partner is allocated less tax depreciation than book depreciation with respect to an item of section 704(c) property, the partnership may make a curative allocation to that partner of tax depreciation from another item of partnership property to make up the difference, notwithstanding that the corresponding book depreciation is allocated to the contributing partner. A partnership may limit its curative allocations to allocations of one or more particular tax items (e.g., only depreciation from a specific property or properties) even if the allocation of those available items does not offset fully the effect of the ceiling rule.

(2) *Consistency.*—A partnership must be consistent in its application of curative allocations with respect to each item of section 704(c) property from year to year.

(3) *Reasonable curative allocations.*—(i) *Amount.*—A curative allocation is not reasonable to the extent it exceeds the amount necessary to offset the effect of the ceiling rule for the current taxable year or, in the case of a curative allocation upon disposition of the property, for prior taxable years.

(ii) *Timing.*—The period of time over which the curative allocations are made is a factor in determining whether the allocations are reasonable. Notwithstanding paragraph (c)(3)(i) of this section, a partnership may make curative allocations in a taxable year to offset the effect of the ceiling rule for a prior taxable year if those allocations are made over a reasonable period of time, such as over the property's economic life, and are provided for under the partnership agreement in effect for the year of contribution. See paragraph (c)(4) *Example 3* (ii)(C) of this section.

(iii) *Type.*—(A) *In general.*—To be reasonable, a curative allocation of income, gain, loss, or deduction must be expected to have substantially the same effect on each partner's tax liability as the tax item limited by the ceiling rule. The expectation must exist at the time the section 704(c) property is obligated to be (or is) contributed to the partnership and the allocation with respect to that property becomes part of the partnership agreement. However, the expectation is tested at the time the allocation with respect to that property is actually made if the partnership agreement is not sufficiently specific as to the precise manner in which allocations are to be made with respect to that property. Under this paragraph (c), if the item limited by the ceiling rule is loss from the sale of property, a curative allocation of gain must be expected to have substantially the same effect as would an allocation to that partner of gain with respect to the sale of the property. If the item limited by the ceiling rule is depreciation or other cost recovery, a curative allocation of income to the contributing partner must be expected to have substantially the same effect as would an allocation to that partner of partnership income with respect to the contributed property. For example, if depreciation deductions with respect to leased equipment contributed by a tax-exempt partner are limited by the ceiling rule, a curative allocation of dividend or interest income to that partner generally is not reasonable, although a curative allocation of depreciation deductions from other leased equipment to the noncontributing partner is reasonable. Similarly, under this rule, if depreciation deductions apportioned to foreign source income in a particular statutory grouping under section 904(d) are limited by the ceiling rule, a curative allocation of income from another statutory grouping to the contributing partner generally is not reasonable, although a curative allocation of income from the same statutory grouping and of the same character is reasonable.

(B) *Exception for allocation from disposition of contributed property.*—If cost recovery has been limited by the ceiling rule, the general limitation on character does not apply to income from the disposition of contributed property subject to the ceiling rule, but only if properly provided for in the partnership agreement in effect for the year of contribution or revaluation. For example, if allocations of depreciation deductions to a noncontributing partner have been limited by the ceiling rule, a curative allocation to the contributing partner of gain from the sale of that property, if properly provided for in the partnership agreement, is reasonable for purposes of paragraph (c)(3)(iii)(A) of this section even if not of the same character.

(4) *Examples.*—The following examples illustrate the principles of this paragraph (c).

Example 1. Reasonable and unreasonable curative allocations—(i) *Facts.* E and F form partnership EF and agree that each will be allocated a 50 percent share of all partnership items and that EF will make allocations under section 704(c) using the traditional method with curative allocations under paragraph (c) of this section. E contributes equipment with an adjusted tax basis of $4,000 and a book value of $10,000. The equipment has 10 years remaining on its cost recovery schedule and is depreciable using the straight-line method. At the time of contribution, E has a built-in gain of $6,000, and therefore, the equipment is section 704(c) property. F contributes $10,000 of cash, which EF uses to buy inventory for resale. In EF's first year, the revenue generated by the equipment equals EF's operating expenses. The equipment generates $1,000 of book depreciation and $400 of tax depreciation for each of 10 years. At the end of the first year EF sells all the inventory for $10,700, recognizing $700 of income. The partners anticipate that the inventory income will have substantially the same effect on their tax liabilities as income from E's contributed equipment. Under the traditional method of paragraph (b) of this section, E and F would each be allocated $350 of income from the sale of inventory for book and tax purposes and $500 of depreciation for book purposes. The $400 of tax depreciation would all be allocated to F. Thus, at the end of the first year, E and F's book and tax capital accounts would be as follows:

E		F		
Book	*Tax*	*Book*	*Tax*	
$10,000	$4,000	$10,000	$10,000	Initial contribution
<500 >	<0 >	<500 >	<400 >	Depreciation
350	350	350	350	Sales income
$9,850	$4,350	$9,850	$9,950	

(ii) *Reasonable curative allocation.* Because the ceiling rule would cause a disparity of $100 between F's book and tax capital accounts, EF may properly allocate to E under paragraph (c) of this section an additional $100 of income from the sale of inventory for tax purposes. This allocation results in capital accounts at the end of EF's first year as follows:

E		F		
Book	*Tax*	*Book*	*Tax*	
$10,000	$4,000	$10,000	$10,000	Initial contribution
<500 >	<0 >	<500 >	<400 >	Depreciation
350	450	350	250	Sales income
$9,850	$4,450	$9,850	$9,850	

(iii) *Unreasonable curative allocation.* (A) The facts are the same as in paragraphs (i) and (ii) of this *Example 1*, except that E and F choose to allocate all the income from the sale of the inventory to E for tax purposes, although they share it equally for book purposes. This allocation results in capital accounts at the end of EF's first year as follows:

E		*F*		
Book	*Tax*	*Book*	*Tax*	
$10,000	$4,000	$10,000	$10,000	Initial contribution
<500 >	<0 >	<500 >	<400 >	Depreciation
350	700	350	0	Sales income
$9,850	$4,700	$9,850	$9,600	

(B) This curative allocation is not reasonable under paragraph (c)(3)(i) of this section because the allocation exceeds the amount necessary to offset the disparity caused by the ceiling rule.

Example 2. Curative allocations limited to depreciation—(i) *Facts.* G and H form partnership GH and agree that each will be allocated a 50 percent share of all partnership items and that GH will make allocations under section 704(c) using the traditional method with curative allocations under paragraph (c) of this section, but only to the extent that the partnership has sufficient tax depreciation deductions. G contributes property G1, with an adjusted tax basis of $3,000 and a fair market value of $10,000, and H contributes property H1, with an adjusted tax basis of $6,000 and a fair market value of $10,000. Both properties have 5 years remaining on their cost recovery schedules and are depreciable using the straight-line method. At the time of contribution, G1 has a built-in gain of $7,000 and H1 has a built-in gain of $4,000, and therefore, both properties are section 704(c) property. G1 generates $600 of tax depreciation and $2,000 of book depreciation for each of five years. H1 generates $1,200 of tax depreciation and $2,000 of book depreciation for each of 5 years. In addition, the properties each generate $500 of operating income annually. G and H are each allocated $1,000 of book depreciation for each property. Under the traditional method of paragraph (b) of this section, G would be allocated $0 of tax depreciation for G1 and $1,000 for H1, and H would be allocated $600 of tax depreciation for G1 and $200 for H1. Thus, at the end of the first year, G and H's book and tax capital accounts would be as follows:

G		*H*		
Book	*Tax*	*Book*	*Tax*	
$10,000	$3,000	$10,000	$6,000	Initial contribution
<1,000 >	<0 >	<1,000 >	<600 >	G1 depreciation
<1,000 >	<1,000 >	<1,000 >	<200 >	H1 depreciation
500	500	500	500	Operating income
$8,500	$2,500	$8,500	$5,700	

(ii) *Curative allocations.* Under the traditional method, G is allocated more depreciation deductions than H, even though H contributed property with a smaller disparity reflected on GH's book and tax capital accounts. GH makes curative allocations to H of an additional $400 of tax depreciation each year, which reduces the disparities between G and H's book and tax capital accounts ratably each year. These allocations are reasonable provided the allocations meet the other requirements of this section. As a result of their agreement, at the end of the first year, G and H's capital accounts are as follows:

G		*H*		
Book	*Tax*	*Book*	*Tax*	
$10,000	$3,000	$10,000	$6,000	Initial contribution
<1,000 >	<0 >	<1,000 >	<600 >	G1 depreciation
<1,000 >	<600 >	<1,000 >	<600 >	H1 depreciation
500	500	500	500	Operating income
$8,500	$2,900	$8,500	$5,300	

Example 3. Unreasonable use of curative allocations—(i) *Facts.* J and K form partnership JK and agree that each will receive a 50 percent share of all partnership items and that JK will make allocations under section 704(c) using the traditional method with curative allocations under paragraph (c) of this section. J contributes equipment with an adjusted tax basis of $1,000 and a book value of $10,000, with a view to taking advantage of the fact that the equipment has only one year remaining on its cost recovery schedule although it has an estimated remaining economic life of 10 years. J has substantial net operating loss carryforwards that J anticipates will otherwise expire unused. At the time of contribution, J has a built-in gain of

$9,000, and therefore, the equipment is section 704(c) property. K contributes $10,000 of cash, which JK uses to buy inventory for resale. In JK's first year, the revenues generated by the equipment exactly equal JK's operating expenses. Under § 1.704-1(b)(2)(iv)(*g*)(*3*), the partnership must allocate the $10,000 of book depreciation to the partners in the first year of the partnership. Thus, there is $10,000 of book depreciation and $1,000 of tax depreciation in the partnership's first year. In addition, at the end of the first year JK sells all of the inventory for $18,000, recognizing $8,000 of income. The partners anticipate that the inventory income will have substantially the same effect on their tax liabilities as income from J's contributed equipment. Under the traditional method of paragraph (b) of this section, J and K's book and tax capital accounts at the end of the first year would be as follows:

J Book	*J* Tax	*K* Book	*K* Tax	
$10,000	$1,000	$10,000	$10,000	Initial contribution
<5,000 >	<0 >	<5,000 >	<1,000 >	Depreciation
4,000	4,000	4,000	4,000	Sales income
$9,000	$5,000	$9,000	$13,000	

(ii) *Unreasonable use of method.* (A) The use of curative allocations under these facts to offset immediately the full effect of the ceiling rule would result in the following book and tax capital accounts at the end of JK's first year:

J Book	*J* Tax	*K* Book	*K* Tax	
$10,000	$1,000	$10,000	$10,000	Initial contribution
<5,000 >	<0 >	<5,000 >	<1,000 >	Depreciation
4,000	8,000	4,000	0	Sales income
$9,000	$9,000	$9,000	$9,000	

(B) This curative allocation is not reasonable under paragraph (a)(10) of this section because the contribution of property is made and the curative allocation method is used with a view to shifting a significant amount of partnership taxable income to a partner with a low marginal tax rate and away from a partner with a high marginal tax rate, within a period of time significantly shorter than the economic life of the property.

(C) The property has only one year remaining on its cost recovery schedule even though its economic life is considerably longer. Under these facts, if the partnership agreement had provided for curative allocations over a reasonable period of time, such as over the property's economic life, rather than over its remaining cost recovery period, the allocations would have been reasonable. See paragraph (c)(3)(ii) of this section. Thus, in this example, JK would make a curative allocation of $400 of sales income to J in the partnership's first year (10 percent of $4,000). J and K's book and tax capital accounts at the end of the first year would be as follows:

J Book	*J* Tax	*K* Book	*K* Tax	
$10,000	$1,000	$10,000	$10,000	Initial contribution
<5,000 >	<0 >	<5,000 >	<1,000 >	Depreciation
4,000	4,400	4,000	3,600	Sales income
$9,000	$5,400	$9,000	$12,600	

(d) *Remedial allocation method.*—(1) *In general.*—A partnership may adopt the remedial allocation method described in this paragraph to eliminate distortions caused by the ceiling rule. A partnership adopting the remedial allocation method eliminates those distortions by creating remedial items and allocating those items to its partners. Under the remedial allocation method, the partnership first determines the amount of book items under paragraph (d)(2) of this section and the partners' distributive shares of these items under section 704(b). The partnership then allocates the corresponding tax items recognized by the partnership, if any, using the traditional method described in paragraph (b)(1) of this section. If the ceiling rule (as defined in paragraph (b)(1) of this section) causes the book allocation of an item to a noncontributing partner to differ from the tax allocation of the same item to the noncontributing partner, the partnership creates a remedial item of income, gain, loss, or deduction equal to the full amount of the difference and allocates it to the noncontributing partner. The partnership simultaneously creates an offsetting remedial item in an identical amount and allocates it to the contributing partner.

(2) *Determining the amount of book items.*—Under the remedial allocation method, a partnership determines the amount of book items attributable to contributed property in the following manner rather than under the rules of § 1.704-1(b)(2)(iv)(*g*)(*3*). The portion of the partnership's book basis in the property equal to the adjusted tax basis in the property at the time of contribution is recovered in the same manner as the adjusted tax basis in the property is recovered (generally, over the property's remaining recovery period under section 168(i)(7) or other applicable Internal Revenue Code section). The remainder of the partnership's book basis in the property (the amount by which book basis exceeds adjusted tax basis) is recovered using any recovery period and depreciation (or other cost recovery) method (including first-year conventions) available to the partnership for newly purchased property (of the same type as the contributed property) that is placed in service at the time of contribution. However, the additional first year depreciation deduction under section 168(k) is not a permissible method for purposes of the preceding sentence and, if a partnership has acquired property in a taxable year for which the additional first year depreciation deduction under section 168(k) has been used of the same type as the contributed property, the portion of the contributed property's book basis that exceeds its adjusted tax basis must be recovered under a reasonable method. See § 1.168(k)-2(b)(3)(iv)(B).

(3) *Type.*—Remedial allocations of income, gain, loss, or deduction to the noncontributing partner have the same tax attributes as the tax item limited by the ceiling rule. The tax attributes of offsetting remedial allocations of income, gain, loss, or deduction to the contributing partner are determined by reference to the item limited by the ceiling rule. Thus, for example, if the ceiling rule limited item is loss from the sale of contributed property, the offsetting remedial allocation to the contributing partner must be gain from the sale of that property. Conversely, if the ceiling rule limited item is gain from the sale of contributed property, the offsetting remedial allocation to the contributing partner must be loss from the sale of that property. If the ceiling rule limited item is depreciation or other cost recovery from the contributed property, the offsetting remedial allocation to the contributing partner must be income of the type produced (directly or indirectly) by that property. Any partner level tax attributes are determined at the partner level. For example, if the ceiling rule limited item is depreciation from property used in a rental activity, the remedial allocation to the noncontributing partner is depreciation from property used in a rental activity and the offsetting remedial allocation to the contributing partner is ordinary income from that rental activity. Each partner then applies section 469 to the allocations as appropriate.

(4) *Effect of remedial items.*—(i) *Effect on partnership.*—Remedial items do not affect the partnership's computation of its taxable income under section 703 and do not affect the partnership's adjusted tax basis in partnership property.

(ii) *Effect on partners.*—Remedial items are notional tax items created by the partnership solely for tax purposes and do not affect the partners' book capital accounts. Remedial items have the same effect as actual tax items on a partner's tax liability and on the partner's adjusted tax basis in the partnership interest.

(5) *Limitations on use of methods involving remedial allocations.*—(i) *Limitation on taxpayers.*—In the absence of published guidance, the remedial allocation method described in this paragraph (d) is the only reasonable section 704(c) method permitting the creation of notional tax items.

(ii) *Limitation on Internal Revenue Service.*—In exercising its authority under paragraph (a)(10) of this section to make adjustments if a partnership's allocation method is not reasonable, the Internal Revenue Service will not require a partnership to use the remedial allocation method described in this paragraph (d) or any other method involving the creation of notional tax items.

* * *

(6) *Adjustments to application of method.*—The Commissioner may, by published guidance, prescribe adjustments to the remedial allocation method under this paragraph (d) as necessary or appropriate. This guidance may, for example, prescribe adjustments to the remedial allocation method to prevent the duplication or omission of items of income or deduction or to reflect more clearly the partners' income or the income of a transferee of a partner.

(7) *Examples.*—The following examples illustrate the principles of this paragraph (d).

Example 1. Remedial allocation method—(i) *Facts.* On January 1, L and M form partnership LM and agree that each will be allocated a 50 percent share of all partnership items. The partnership agreement provides that LM will make allocations under section 704(c) using the remedial allocation method under this paragraph (d) and that the straight-line method will be used to recover excess book basis. L contributes depreciable property with an adjusted tax basis of $4,000 and a fair market value of $10,000. The property is depreciated using the straight-line method with a 10-year recovery period and has 4 years remaining on its recovery period. M contributes $10,000, which the partnership uses to purchase land. Except for the depreciation deductions, LM's expenses equal its income in each year of the 10 years commencing with the year the partnership is formed.

(ii) *Years 1 through 4*. Under the remedial allocation method of this paragraph (d), LM has book depreciation for each of its first 4 years of $1,600 [$1,000 ($4,000 adjusted tax basis divided by the 4-year remaining recovery period) plus $600 ($6,000 excess of book value over tax basis, divided by the *new* 10-year recovery period)]. (For the purpose of simplifying the example, the partnership's book depreciation is determined without regard to any first-year depreciation conventions.) Under the partnership agreement, L and M are each allocated 50 percent ($800) of the book depreciation. M is allocated $800 of tax depreciation and L is allocated the remaining $200 of tax depreciation ($1,000 – $800). See paragraph (d)(1) of this section. No remedial allocations are made because the ceiling rule does not result in a book allocation of depreciation to M different from the tax allocation. The allocations result in capital accounts at the end of LM's first 4 years as follows:

L		*M*		
Book	*Tax*	*Book*	*Tax*	
$10,000	$4,000	$10,000	$10,000	Initial contribution
<3,200 >	<800 >	<3,200 >	<3,200 >	Depreciation
$6,800	$3,200	$6,800	$6,800	

(iii) *Subsequent years*. (A) For each of years 5 through 10, LM has $600 of book depreciation ($6,000 excess of initial book value over adjusted tax basis divided by the 10-year recovery period that commenced in year 1), but no tax depreciation. Under the partnership agreement, the $600 of book depreciation is allocated equally to L and M. Because of the application of the ceiling rule in year 5, M would be allocated $300 of book depreciation, but no tax depreciation. Thus, at the end of LM's fifth year L's and M's book and tax capital accounts would be as follows:

L		*M*		
Book	*Tax*	*Book*	*Tax*	
$6,800	$3,200	$6,800	$6,800	End of year 4
<300 >		<300 >		Depreciation
$6,500	$3,200	$6,500	$6,800	

(B) Because the ceiling rule would cause an annual disparity of $300 between M's allocations of book and tax depreciation, LM must make remedial allocations of $300 of tax depreciation deductions to M under the remedial allocation method for each of years 5 through 10. LM must also make an offsetting remedial allocation to L of $300 of taxable income, which must be of the same type as income produced by the property. At the end of year 5, LM's capital accounts are as follows:

L		*M*		
Book	*Tax*	*Book*	*Tax*	
$6,800	$3,200	$6,800	$6,800	End of year 4
<300 >		<300 >		Depreciation
	300		<300 >	Remedial allocations
$6,500	$3,500	$6,500	$6,500	

(C) At the end of year 10, LM's capital accounts are as follows:

L		*M*		
Book	*Tax*	*Book*	*Tax*	
$6,500	$3,500	$6,500	$6,500	End of year 5
<1,500 >		<1,500 >		Depreciation
	1,500		<1,500 >	Remedial allocations
$5,000	$5,000	$5,000	$5,000	

Example 2. Remedial allocations on sale—(i) *Facts*. N and P form partnership NP and agree that each will be allocated a 50 percent share of all partnership items. The partnership agreement provides that NP will make allocations under section 704(c) using the remedial allocation method under this paragraph (d). N contributes Blackacre (land) with an adjusted tax basis of $4,000 and a fair market value of $10,000. Because N has a built-in gain of

$6,000, Blackacre is section 704(c) property. P contributes Whiteacre (land) with an adjusted tax basis and fair market value of $10,000. At the end of NP's first year, NP sells Blackacre to Q for $9,000 and recognizes a capital gain of $5,000 ($9,000 amount realized less $4,000 adjusted tax basis) and a book loss of $1,000 ($9,000 amount realized less $10,000 book basis). NP has no other items of income, gain, loss, or deduction. If the ceiling rule were applied, N would be allocated the entire $5,000 of tax gain and N and P would each be allocated $500 of book loss. Thus, at the end of NP's first year N's and P's book and tax capital accounts would be as follows:

N Book	*N* Tax	*P* Book	*P* Tax	
$10,000	$4,000	$10,000	$10,000	Initial contribution
<500 >	5,000	<500 >		Sale of Blackacre
$9,500	$9,000	$9,500	$10,000	

(ii) *Remedial allocation.* Because the ceiling rule would cause a disparity of $500 between P's allocation of book and tax loss, NP must make a remedial allocation of $500 of capital loss to P and an offsetting remedial allocation to N of an additional $500 of capital gain. These allocations result in capital accounts at the end of NP's first year as follows:

N Book	*N* Tax	*P* Book	*P* Tax	
$10,000	$4,000	$10,000	$10,000	Initial contribution
<500 >	5,000	<500 >		Sale of Blackacre
	500		<500 >	Remedial allocations
$9,500	$9,500	$9,500	$9,500	

Example 3. Remedial allocation where built-in gain property sold for book and tax loss—(i) *Facts.* The facts are the same as in Example 2, except that at the end of NP's first year, NP sells Blackacre to Q for $3,000 and recognizes a capital loss of $1,000 ($3,000 amount realized less $4,000 adjusted tax basis) and a book loss of $7,000 ($3,000 amount realized less $10,000 book basis). If the ceiling rule were applied, P would be allocated the entire $1,000 of tax loss and N and P would each be allocated $3,500 of book loss. Thus, at the end of NP's first year, N's and P's book and tax capital accounts would be as follows:

N Book	*N* Tax	*P* Book	*P* Tax	
$10,000	$4,000	$10,000	$10,000	Initial contribution
<3,500 >	0	<3,500 >	<1,000 >	Sale of Blackacre
$6,500	$4,000	$6,500	$9,000	

(ii) *Remedial allocation.* Because the ceiling rule would cause a disparity of $2,500 between P's allocation of book and tax loss on the sale of Blackacre, NP must make a remedial allocation of $2,500 of capital loss to P and an offsetting remedial allocation to N of $2,500 of capital gain. These allocations result in capital accounts at the end of NP's first year as follows:

N Book	*N* Tax	*P* Book	*P* Tax	
$10,000	$4,000	$10,000	$10,000	Initial contribution
<3,500 >	0	<3,500 >	<1,000 >	Sale of Blackacre
	<2,500 >		<2,500 >	Remedial allocations
$6,500	$6,500	$6,500	$6,500	

(e) *Exceptions and special rules.*—(1) *Small disparities.*—(i) *General rule.*—If a partner contributes one or more items of property to a partnership within a single taxable year of the partnership, and the disparity between the book value of the property and the contributing partner's adjusted tax basis in the property is a small disparity, the partnership may—

(A) Use a reasonable section 704(c) method;

(B) Disregard the application of section 704(c) to the property; or

(C) Defer the application of section 704(c) to the property until the disposition of the property.

(ii) *Definition of small disparity.*—A disparity between book value and adjusted tax basis is a small disparity if the book value of all properties contributed by one partner during the partnership taxable year does not differ from the adjusted tax basis by more than 15 percent of the adjusted tax basis, and the total gross disparity does not exceed $20,000.

(2) *Aggregation.*—Each of the following types of property may be aggregated for purposes of making allocations under section 704(c) and this section if contributed by one partner during the partnership taxable year.

(i) *Depreciable property.*—All property, other than real property, that is included in the same general asset account of the contributing partner and the partnership under section 168.

(ii) *Zero-basis property.*—All property with a basis equal to zero, other than real property.

(iii) *Inventory.*—For partnerships that do not use a specific identification method of accounting, each item of inventory, other than qualified financial assets (as defined in paragraph (e)(3)(ii) of this section).

* * *

(4) *Aggregation as permitted by the Commissioner.*—The Commissioner may, by published guidance or by letter ruling, permit:

(i) Aggregation of properties other than those described in paragraphs (e)(2) and (e)(3) of this section;

(ii) Partnerships and partners not described in paragraph (e)(3) of this section to aggregate gain and loss from qualified financial assets; and

(iii) Aggregation of qualified financial assets for purposes of making section 704(c) allocations in the same manner as that described in paragraph (e)(3) of this section.

* * *

[Reg. § 1.704-3.]

☐ [*T.D.* 8500, 12-21-93. *Amended by T.D.* 8585, 12-27-94; *T.D.* 8717, 5-8-97; *T.D.* 8730, 8-19-97; *T.D.* 9137, 7-15-2004; *T.D.* 9193, 3-21-2005 (*corrected* 8-5-2005); *T.D.* 9207, 5-23-2005; *T.D.* 9485, 6-8-2010; *T.D.* 9612, 2-4-2013 *T.D.* 9814, 1-18-2017; *T.D.* 9874, 9-17-2019 *and T.D.* 9891, 1-17-2020.]

Proposed Amendments to Regulation

§ 1.704-3. Contributed property.—(a) * * *

(3) * * *

(ii) *Built-in gain and built-in loss.*—The built-in gain on section 704(c) property is the excess of the property's book value over the contributing partner's adjusted tax basis upon contribution. The built-in gain is thereafter reduced by decreases in the difference between the property's book value and adjusted tax basis (other than decreases to the property's book value pursuant to § 1.704-1(b)(2)(iv)(*f*) or § 1.704-1(b)(2)(iv)(*s*)). The built-in loss on section 704(c) property is the excess of the contributing partner's adjusted tax basis over the property's book value upon contribution. The built-in loss is thereafter reduced by decreases in the difference between the property's adjusted tax basis and book value (other than increases to the property's book value pursuant to § 1.704-1(b)(2)(iv)(*f*) or § 1.704-1(b)(2)(iv)(*s*)). For purposes of paragraph (a)(6)(iii) and (iv) of this section, a built-in gain or built-in loss referred to in this paragraph shall be referred to as a forward section 704(c) allocation. *See* § 1.460-4(k)(3)(v)(A) for a rule relating to the amount of built-in income or built-in loss attributable to a contract accounted for under a long-term contract method of accounting.

(iii) *Effective/applicability date.*—The provisions of paragraph (a)(3)(ii) of this section apply to partnership contributions and transactions occurring on or after the date of publication of the Treasury decision adopting these rules as final regulations in the Federal Register.

* * *

(6)(i) *Revaluations under section 704(b).*—The principles of this section apply with respect to property for which differences between book value and adjusted tax basis are created when a partnership revalues partnership property pursuant to § 1.704-1(b)(2)(iv)(*f*) or § 1.704-1(b)(2)(iv)(*s*) (reverse section 704(c) allocations). Each such revaluation creates a separate amount of built-in gain or built-in loss, as the case may be (a section 704(c) layer), that must be tracked separately from built-in gain or built-in loss arising from contribution (a forward section 704(c) layer) and any other revaluation (a reverse section 704(c) layer). For instance, one section 704(c) layer with respect to a particular property may be of built-in gain, and another section 704(c) layer with respect to the same property may be of built-in loss.

* * *

(iii) *Allocation method.*—A partnership may use any reasonable method to allocate the items of income, gain, loss, and deduction associated with an item of property among the property's forward and reverse section 704(c) layers.

(iv) *Effective/applicability date.*—The provisions of paragraph (a)(6)(iii) of this section apply to partnership contributions and transactions occurring on or after the date of publication of the Treasury decision adopting these rules as final regulations in the Federal Register.

* * *

(7) *Transfers of a partnership interest.*.—If a contributing partner transfers a partnership interest, built-in gain must be allocated to the transferee partner as it would have been allocated to the transferor partner. If the contributing partner transfers a portion of the partnership interest, the share of built-in gain proportionate to the interest transferred must be allocated to the transferee partner. Rules for the allocation of builtin loss are provided in paragraph (f) of this section.

* * *

(f) *Special rules for built-in loss property.*—(1) *General principles.*—(i) *Contributing partner.*—If a partner contributes section 704(c)(1)(C) property (as defined in paragraph (f)(2)(i) of this section) to a partnership, the excess of the adjusted basis of the section 704(c)(1)(C) property (determined without regard to paragraph (f)(1)(ii) of this section) over its fair market value immediately before the contribution will be taken into account only in determining the amount of items allocated to the section 704(c)(1)(C) partner (as defined in paragraph (f)(2)(ii) of this section) that contributed such section 704(c)(1)(C) property.

(ii) *Non-contributing partners.*—In determining the amount of items allocated to partners other than the section 704(c)(1)(C) partner, the initial basis of section 704(c)(1)(C) property in the hands of the partnership is equal to the property's fair market value at the time of contribution.

(2) *Definitions.*—For purposes of this section—

(i) *Section 704(c)(1)(C) property.*—The term *section 704(c)(1)(C) property* means section 704(c) property (as defined in paragraph (a)(3)(i) of this section) with a built-in loss at the time of contribution. Section 704(c)(1)(C) property does not include a § 1.752-7 liability (within the meaning of § 1.752-7(b)(3)) or property for which differences between book value and adjusted tax basis are created when a partnership revalues property pursuant to § 1.704-1(b)(2)(iv)(*f*) or § 1.704-1(b)(2)(iv)(*s*).

(ii) *Section 704(c)(1)(C) partner.*—The term *section 704(c)(1)(C) partner* means a partner that contributes section 704(c)(1)(C) property to a partnership.

(iii) *Section 704(c)(1)(C) basis adjustment.*—A property's section 704(c)(1)(C) basis adjustment is initially equal to the excess of the adjusted basis of section 704(c)(1)(C) property (determined without regard to paragraph (f)(1)(ii) of this section) over its fair market value immediately before the contribution, and is subsequently adjusted for the recovery of the section 704(c)(1)(C) basis adjustment under paragraph (f)(3)(ii)(D) of this section.

(3) *Operational rules.*—(i) *In general.*—Except as provided in this section, section 704(c)(1)(C) property is subject to the rules and regulations applicable to section 704(c) property. *See*, for example, § 1.704-3(a)(9).

(ii) *Effect of section 704(c)(1)(C) basis adjustment.*—(A) *In general.*—The section 704(c)(1)(C) basis adjustment is an adjustment to the basis of partnership property with respect to the section 704(c)(1)(C) partner only. A section 704(c)(1)(C) basis adjustment amount is excluded from the partnership's basis of section 704(c)(1)(C) property. Thus, for purposes of calculating income, deduction, gain, and loss, the section 704(c)(1)(C) partner will have a special basis for section 704(c)(1)(C) property in which the partner has a section 704(c)(1)(C) basis adjustment. The section 704(c)(1)(C) basis adjustment has no effect on the partnership's computation of any item under section 703.

(B) *Computation of section 704(c)(1)(C) partner's distributive share of partnership items.*—The partnership first computes its items of income, deduction, gain, or loss at the partnership level under section 703. The partnership then allocates the partnership items among the partners, including the section 704(c)(1)(C) partner, in accordance with section 704, and adjusts the partners' capital accounts accordingly. The partnership then adjusts the section 704(c)(1)(C) partner's distributive share of the items of partnership income, deduction, gain, or loss in accordance with paragraphs (f)(3)(ii)(C) and (D) of this section, to reflect the effects of the section 704(c)(1)(C) partner's section 704(c)(1)(C) basis adjustment. These adjustments to the section 704(c)(1)(C) partner's distributive share must be reflected on Schedules K and K-1 of the partnership's return (Form 1065). The adjustments to the section 704(c)(1)(C) partner's distributive shares do not affect the section 704(c)(1)(C) partner's capital account.

(C) *Effect of section 704(c)(1)(C) basis adjustment in determining items of income, gain, or loss.*—The amount of a section 704(c)(1)(C) partner's income, gain, or loss from the sale or exchange of partnership property in which the section 704(c)(1)(C) partner has a section 704(c)(1)(C) basis adjustment is equal to the section 704(c)(1)(C) partner's share of the partnership's gain or loss from the sale of the property (including any remedial allocations under § 1.704-3(d)), minus the section 704(c)(1)(C) partner's section 704(c)(1)(C) basis adjustment for the partnership property.

(D) *Effect of section 704(c)(1)(C) basis adjustment in determining items of deduction.—(1) In general.*—If section 704(c)(1)(C) property is subject to amortization under section 197, depreciation under section 168, or other cost recovery in the hands of the section 704(c)(1)(C) partner, the section 704(c)(1)(C) basis adjustment associated with the property is recovered in accordance with section 197(f)(2), section 168(i)(7), or another applicable Internal Revenue Code section. The amount of any section 704(c)(1)(C) basis adjustment that is recovered by the section 704(c)(1)(C) partner in any year is added to the section 704(c)(1)(C) partner's distributive share of the partnership's depreciation or amortization deductions for the year. The basis adjustment is adjusted under section 1016(a)(2) to reflect the recovery of the section 704(c)(1)(C) basis adjustment.

(2) Example.—A contributes Property, with an adjusted basis of $12,000 and a fair market value of $5,000 on January 1 of the year of contribution, and B contributes $5,000 to PRS, a partnership. Prior to the contribution, A depreciates Property under section 168 over 10 years using the straight-line method and the half-year convention. On the contribution date, Property has 7.5 years remaining in its recovery period. Property is section 704(c)(1)(C) property, and A's section 704(c)(1)(C) basis adjustment is $7,000. PRS's basis in Property is $5,000 (fair market value) and, in accordance with section 168(i)(7), the depreciation is $667 per year ($5,000 divided by 7.5 years), which is shared equally between A and B. A's $7,000 section 704(c)(1)(C) basis adjustment is subject to depreciation of $933 per year in accordance with section 168(i)(7) ($7,000 divided by 7.5 years), which is taken into account by A.

(iii) *Transfer of section 704(c)(1)(C) partner's partnership interest.*—(A) *General rule.*—Except as provided in paragraph (f)(3)(iii)(B) of this section, if a section 704(c)(1)(C) partner transfers its partnership interest, the portion of the section 704(c)(1)(C) basis adjustment attributable to the interest transferred is eliminated and the transferee is not treated as the section 704(c)(1)(C) partner with respect to the interest transferred. The transferor remains the section 704(c)(1)(C) partner with respect to any remaining section 704(c)(1)(C) basis adjustment.

(B) *Special rules.—(1) General rule for transfer of partnership interest in nonrecognition transaction.*—Except as provided in paragraph (f)(3)(iii)(B)*(2)* of this section, paragraph (f)(3)(iii)(A) of this section does not apply to the extent a section 704(c)(1)(C) partner transfers its partnership interest in a nonrecognition transaction. Instead, the transferee of all or a portion of a section 704(c)(1)(C) partner's partnership interest succeeds to the transferor's section 704(c)(1)(C) basis adjustments in an amount attributable to the interest transferred and the transferee will be treated as the section 704(c)(1)(C) partner with respect to the transferred interest. Regardless of whether a section 754 election is in effect or a substantial built in loss exists with respect to the transfer, the amount of any section 704(c)(1)(C) basis adjustment with respect to section 704(c)(1)(C) property to which the transferee succeeds shall be decreased by the amount of any negative section 743(b) adjustment that would be allocated to the section 704(c)(1)(C) property pursuant to the provisions of § 1.755-1 if the partnership had a section 754 election in effect upon the transfer. If the nonrecognition transaction is described in section 168(i)(7)(B), then the rules in section 168(i)(7)(A) apply with respect to transferor's cost recovery deductions under section 168. If gain or loss is recognized on the transaction, appropriate adjustments must be made to the section 704(c)(1)(C) basis adjustment.

(2) Exception for gifts.—Paragraph (f)(3)(iii)(B)*(1)* of this section does not apply to the transfer of all or a portion of a section 704(c)(1)(C) partner's partnership interest by gift.

* * *

(v) *Distributions.*—(A) *Current distribution of section 704(c)(1)(C) property to section 704(c)(1)(C) partner.*—If a partnership distributes property to a partner and the partner has a section 704(c)(1)(C) basis adjustment for the property, the section 704(c)(1)(C) basis adjustment is taken into account under section 732. *See* § 1.732-2(a). For certain adjustments to the basis of remaining partnership property after the distribution of section 704(c)(1)(C) property to the section 704(c)(1)(C) partner, see § 1.734-2(c).

(B) *Distribution of section 704(c)(1)(C) property to another partner.*—If a partner receives a distribution of property in which another partner has a section 704(c)(1)(C) basis adjustment, the distributee does not take the section 704(c)(1)(C) basis adjustment into account under section 732. If section 704(c)(1)(B) applies to treat the section 704(c)(1)(C) partner as recognizing loss on the sale of the distributed property, the section 704(c)(1)(C) basis adjustment is taken into account in determining the amount of the loss. A section 704(c)(1)(C) partner with a section 704(c)(1)(C) basis adjustment in the distributed property that is not taken into account as described in the prior sentence reallocates the section 704(c)(1)(C) basis adjustment among the remaining items of partnership property under § 1.755-1(c).

(C) *Distributions in complete liquidation of a section 704(c)(1)(C) partner's interest.*—If a section 704(c)(1)(C) partner receives a distribution of property (whether or not the partner has a section 704(c)(1)(C) basis adjustment in the property) in liquidation of its interest in the partnership, the adjusted basis to the partnership of the distributed property immediately before the distribution includes the section 704(c)(1)(C) partner's section 704(c)(1)(C) basis adjustment for the property in which the section 704(c)(1)(C) partner relinquished an interest. For purposes of determining the section 704(c)(1)(C) partner's basis in distributed property under section 732, the partnership reallocates any section 704(c)(1)(C) basis adjustment from section 704(c)(1)(C) property retained by the partnership to distributed properties of like character under the principles of § 1.755-1(c)(i), after applying sections 704(c)(1)(B) and 737. If section 704(c)(1)(C) property is retained by the partnership, and no property of like character is distributed, then that property's section 704(c)(1)(C) basis adjustment is not reallocated to the distributed property for purposes of applying section 732. *See* § 1.734-2(c)(2) for rules regarding the treatment of any section 704(c)(1)(C) adjustment that is not fully utilized by the section 704(c)(1)(C) partner.

* * *

[Prop. Reg. § 1.704-3.]

[Proposed 1-16-2014 (corrected 4-15-2014).]

Proposed Amendment to Regulation

§ 1.704-3. Contributed property.

(a) * * *

(9) * * * If a partnership (the upper-tier partnership) owns an interest in another partnership (the lower-tier partnership), and both the upper-tier partnership and the lower-tier partnership simultaneously revalue partnership property pursuant to § 1.704-1(b)(2)(iv)(f), the principles of this paragraph (a)(9) shall apply to any reverse section 704(c) allocations created upon the revaluation. * * *

* * *

[Prop. Reg. § 1.704-3.]

[Proposed 11-3-2014.]

§ 1.704-4. Distribution of contributed property.—(a) *Determination of gain and loss.*—(1) *In general.*—A partner that contributes section 704(c) property to a partnership must recognize gain or loss under section 704(c)(1)(B) and this section on the distribution of such property to another partner within five years of its contribution to the partnership in an amount equal to the gain or loss that would have been allocated to such partner under section 704(c)(1)(A) and § 1.704-3 if the distributed property had been sold by the partnership to the distributee partner for its fair market value at the time of the distribution. See § 1.704-3(a)(3)(i) for a definition of section 704(c) property.

(2) *Transactions to which section 704(c)(1)(B) applies.*—Section 704(c)(1)(B) and this section apply only to the extent that a distribution by a partnership is a distribution to a partner acting in the capacity of a partner within the meaning of section 731.

(3) *Fair market value of property.*—The fair market value of the distributed section 704(c) property is the price at which the property would change hands between a willing buyer and a willing seller at the time of the distribution, neither being under any compulsion to buy or sell and both having reasonable knowledge of the relevant facts. The fair market value that a partnership assigns to distributed section 704(c) property will be regarded as correct, provided that the value is reasonably agreed to among the partners in an arm's-length negotiation and the partners have sufficiently adverse interests.

(4) *Determination of five-year period.*—(i) *General rule.*—The five-year period specified in paragraph (a)(1) of this section begins on and includes the date of contribution.

(ii) *Section 708(b)(1)(B) terminations.*—A termination of the partnership under section 708(b)(1)(B) does not begin a new five-year period for each partner with respect to the built-in gain and built-in loss property that the terminated partnership is deemed to contribute to the new partnership under § 1.7081(b)(1)(iv). See § 1.704-3(a)(3)(ii) for the definitions of built-in gain and built-in loss on section 704(c) property. This paragraph (a)(4)(ii) applies to terminations of partnerships under section 708(b)(1)(B) occurring on or after May 9, 1997; however, this paragraph (a)(4)(ii) may be applied to terminations occurring on or after May 9, 1996, provided that the partnership and its partners apply this paragraph (a)(4)(ii) to the termination in a consistent manner.

(5) *Examples.*—The following examples illustrate the rules of this paragraph (a). Unless otherwise specified, partnership income equals partnership expenses (other than depreciation deductions for contributed property) for each year of the partnership, the fair market value of partnership property does not change, all distributions by the partnership are subject to section 704(c)(1)(B), and all partners are unrelated.

Example 1. Recognition of gain. (i) On January 1, 1995, A, B, and C form partnership ABC as equal partners. A contributes $10,000 cash and Property A, nondepreciable real property with a fair market value of $10,000 and an adjusted tax basis of $4,000. Thus, there is a built-in gain of $6,000 on Property A at the time of contribution. B contributes $10,000 cash and Property B, nondepreciable real property with a fair market value and adjusted tax basis of $10,000. C contributes $20,000 cash.

(ii) On December 31, 1998, Property A and Property B are distributed to C in complete liquidation of C's interest in the partnership.

(iii) A would have recognized $6,000 of gain under section 704(c)(1)(A) and § 1.704-3 on the sale of Property A at the time of the distribution ($10,000 fair market value less $4,000 adjusted tax basis). As a result, A must recognize $6,000 of gain on the distribution of Property A to C. B would not have recognized any gain or loss under section 704(c)(1)(A) and § 1.704-3 on the sale of Property B at the time of distribution because Property B was not section 704(c) property. As a result, B does not recognize any gain or loss on the distribution of Property B.

Example 2. Effect of post-contribution depreciation deductions. (i) On January 1, 1995, A, B, and C form partnership ABC as equal partners. A contributes Property A, depreciable property with a fair market value of $30,000 and an adjusted tax basis of $20,000. Therefore, there is a built-in gain of $10,000 on Property A. B and C each contribute $30,000 cash. ABC uses the traditional method of making section 704(c) allocations described in § 1.704-3(b) with respect to Property A.

(ii) Property A is depreciated using the straight-line method over its remaining 10-year recovery period. The partnership has book depreciation of $3,000 per year (10 percent of the $30,000 book basis), and each partner is allocated $1,000 of book depreciation per year (one-third of the total annual book depreciation of $3,000). The partnership has a tax depreciation deduction of $2,000 per year (10 percent of the $20,000 tax basis in Property A). This $2,000 tax depreciation deduction is allocated equally between B and C, the noncontributing partners with respect to Property A.

(iii) At the end of the third year, the book value of Property A is $21,000 ($30,000 initial book value less $9,000 aggregate book depreciation) and the adjusted tax basis is $14,000 ($20,000 initial tax basis less $6,000 aggregate tax depreciation). A's remaining section 704(c)(1)(A) built-in gain with respect to Property A is $7,000 ($21,000 book value less $14,000 adjusted tax basis).

(iv) On December 31, 1997, Property A is distributed to B in complete liquidation of B's interest in the partnership. If Property A had been sold for its fair market value at the time of the distribution, A would have recognized $7,000 of gain under section 704(c)(1)(A) and § 1.704-3(b). Therefore, A recognizes $7,000 of gain on the distribution of Property A to B.

Example 3. Effect of remedial method. (i) On January 1, 1995, A, B, and C form partnership ABC as equal partners. A contributes Property A1, nondepreciable real property with a fair market value of $10,000 and an adjusted tax basis of $5,000, and Property A2, nondepreciable real property with a fair market value and adjusted tax basis of $10,000. B and C each contribute $20,000 cash. ABC uses the remedial method of making section 704(c) allocations described in § 1.704-3(d) with respect to Property A1.

(ii) On December 31, 1998, when the fair market value of Property A1 has decreased to $7,000, Property A1 is distributed to C in a current distribution. If Property A1 had been sold by the partnership at the time of the distribution, ABC would have recognized the $2,000 of remaining built-in gain under section 704(c)(1)(A) on the sale (fair market value of $7,000 less $5,000 adjusted tax basis). All of this gain would have been allocated to A. ABC would also have recognized a book loss of $3,000 ($10,000 original book value less $7,000 current fair market value of the property). Book loss in the amount of $2,000 would have been allocated equally between B and C. Under the remedial method, $2,000 of tax loss would also have been allocated equally to B and C to match their share of the book loss. As a result, $2,000 of gain would also have been allocated to A as an offsetting remedial allocation. A would have recognized $4,000 of total gain under section 704(c)(1)(A) on the sale of Property A1 ($2,000 of section 704(c) recognized gain plus $2,000 remedial gain). Therefore, A recognizes $4,000 of gain on the distribution of Property A1 to C under this section.

(b) *Character of gain or loss.*—(1) *General rule.*—Gain or loss recognized by the contributing partner under section 704(c)(1)(B) and this section has the same character as the gain or loss that would have resulted if the distributed property had been sold by the partnership to the distributee partner at the time of the distribution.

(2) *Example.*—The following example illustrates the rule of this paragraph (b). Unless otherwise specified, partnership income equals partnership expenses (other than depreciation deductions for contributed property) for each year of the partnership, the fair market value of partnership property does not change, all distributions by the partnership are subject to section 704(c)(1)(B), and all partners are unrelated.

Example. Character of gain. (i) On January 1, 1995, A and B form partnership AB. A contributes $10,000 and Property A, nondepreciable real property with a fair market value of $10,000 and an adjusted tax basis of $4,000, in exchange for a 25 percent interest in partnership capital and profits. B contributes $60,000 cash for a 75 percent interest in partnership capital and profits.

(ii) On December 31, 1998, Property A is distributed to B in a current distribution. Property A is used in a trade or business of B.

(iii) A would have recognized $6,000 of gain under section 704(c)(1)(A) on a sale of Property A at the time of the distribution (the difference between the fair market value ($10,000) and the adjusted tax basis ($4,000) of the property at that time). Because Property A is not a capital asset in the hands of Partner B and B holds more than 50 percent of partnership capital and profits, the character of the gain on a sale of Property A to B would have been ordinary income under section 707(b)(2). Therefore, the character of the gain to A on the distribution of Property A to B is ordinary income.

* * *

(d) *Special rules.*—(1) *Nonrecognition transactions, installment obligations, contributed contracts, and capitalized costs.*—(i) *Nonrecognition transactions.*—Property received by the partnership in exchange for section 704(c) property in a nonrecognition transaction is treated as the section 704(c) property for purposes of section 704(c)(1)(B) and this section to the extent that the property received is treated as section 704(c) property under § 1.704-3(a)(8). See § 1.7372(d)(3) for a similar rule in the context of section 737.

(ii) [Reserved.]

(iii) [Reserved.]

(iv) *Capitalized costs.*—Property to which the cost of section 704(c) property is properly capitalized is treated as section 704(c) property for purposes of section 704(c)(1)(B) and this section to the extent that such property is treated as section 704(c) property under § 1.704-3(a)(8)(iv). See § 1.737-2(d)(3) for a similar rule in the context of section 737.

(2) *Transfers of a partnership interest.*—The transferee of all or a portion of the partnership interest of a contributing partner is treated as the contributing partner for purposes of section 704(c)(1)(B) and this section to the extent of the share of built-in gain or loss allocated to the transferee partner. See § 1.704-3(a)(7).

(3) *Distributions of like-kind property.*—If section 704(c) property is distributed to a partner other than the contributing partner and like-kind property (within the meaning of section 1031) is distributed to the contributing partner no later than the earlier of (i) 180 days following the date of the distribution to the noncontributing partner, or (ii) the due date (determined with regard to extensions) of the contributing partner's income tax return for the taxable year of the distribution to the noncontributing partner, the amount of gain or loss, if any, that the contributing partner would otherwise have recognized under section 704(c)(1)(B) and this section is reduced by the amount of built-in gain or loss in the distributed like-kind property in the hands of the contributing partner immediately after the distribution. The contributing partner's basis in the distributed like-kind property is determined as if the like-kind property were distributed in an unrelated distribution prior to the distribution of any other property distributed as part of the same distribution and is determined without regard to the increase in the contributing partner's adjusted tax basis in the partnership interest under section 704(c)(1)(B) and this section. See § 1.707-3 for provisions treating the distribution of the like-kind property to the contributing partner as a disguised sale in certain situations.

(4) *Example.*—The following example illustrates the rules of this paragraph (d). Unless otherwise specified, partnership income equals partnership expenses (other than depreciation deductions for contributed property) for each year of the partnership, the fair market value of partnership property does not change, all distributions by the partnership are subject to section 704(c)(1)(B), and all partners are unrelated.

Example. Distribution of like-kind property. (i) On January 1, 1995, A, B, and C form partnership ABC as equal partners. A contributes Property A, nondepreciable real property with a fair market value of $20,000 and an adjusted tax basis of $10,000. B and C each contribute $20,000 cash. The partnership subsequently buys Property X, nondepreciable real property of a like-kind to Property A with a fair market value and adjusted tax basis of $8,000. The fair market value of Property X subsequently increases to $10,000.

(ii) On December 31, 1998, Property A is distributed to B in a current distribution. At the same time, Property X is distributed to A in a current distribution. The distribution of Property X does not result in the contribution of Property A being properly characterized as a disguised sale to the partnership under § 1.707-3. A's basis in Property X is $8,000 under section 732(a)(1). A therefore has $2,000 of built-in gain in Property X ($10,000 fair market value less $8,000 adjusted tax basis).

(iii) A would generally recognize $10,000 of gain under section 704(c)(1)(B) on the distribution of Property A, the difference between the fair market value ($20,000) of the property and its adjusted tax basis ($10,000). This gain is reduced, however, by the amount of the built-in gain of Property X in the hands of A. As a result, A recognizes only $8,000 of gain on the distribution of Property A to B under section 704(c)(1)(B) and this section.

(e) *Basis adjustments.*—(1) *Contributing partner's basis in the partnership interest.*—The basis of the contributing partner's interest in the partnership is increased by the amount of the gain, or decreased by the amount of the loss, recognized by the partner under section 704(c)(1)(B) and this section. This increase or decrease is taken into account in determining (i) the contributing partner's adjusted tax basis under section 732 for any property distributed to the partner in a distribution that is part of the same distribution as the distribution of the contributed property, other than like-kind property described in paragraph (d)(3) of this section (pertaining to the special rule for distributions of like-kind property), and (ii) the amount of the gain recognized by the contributing partner under section 731 or section 737, if any, on a distribution of money or property to the contributing partner that is part of the same distribution as the distribution of the contributed property. For a determination of basis in a distribution subject to section 737, see § 1.737-3(a).

(2) *Partnership's basis in partnership property.*—The partnership's adjusted tax basis in the distributed section 704(c) property is increased or decreased immediately before the distribution by the amount of gain or loss recognized by the contributing partner under section 704(c)(1)(B) and this section. Any increase or decrease in basis is therefore taken into account in determining the distributee partner's adjusted tax basis in the distributed property under section 732. For a determination of basis in a distribution subject to section 737, see § 1.7373(b).

(3) *Section 754 adjustments.*—The basis adjustments to partnership property made pursuant to paragraph (e)(2) of this section are not elective and must be made regardless of whether the partnership has an election in effect under section 754. Any adjustments to the bases of partnership property (including the distributed section 704(c) property) under section 734(b) pursuant to a section 754 election must be made after (and must take into account) the adjustments to basis made under paragraph (e)(2) of this section. See § 1.737-3(c)(4) for a similar rule in the context of section 737.

(4) *Example.*—The following example illustrates the rules of this paragraph (e). Unless otherwise specified, partnership income equals partnership expenses (other than depreciation deductions for contributed property) for each year of the partnership, the fair market value of partnership property does not change, all distributions by the partnership are subject to section 704(c)(1)(B), and all partners are unrelated.

Example. Basis adjustment. (i) On January 1, 1995, A, B, and C form partnership ABC as equal partners. A contributes $10,000 cash and Property A, nondepreciable real property with a fair market value of $10,000 and an adjusted tax basis of $4,000. B and C each contribute $20,000 cash.

(ii) On December 31, 1998, Property A is distributed to B in a current distribution.

(iii) Under paragraph (a) of this section, A recognizes $6,000 of gain on the distribution of Property A because that is the amount of gain that would have been allocated to A under section 704(c)(1)(A) and § 1.704-3 on a sale of Property A for its fair market value at the time of the distribution (fair market value of Property A ($10,000) less its adjusted tax basis at the time of distribution ($4,000)). The adjusted tax basis of A's partnership interest is increased from $14,000 to $20,000 to reflect this gain. The partnership's adjusted tax basis in Property A is increased from $4,000 to $10,000 immediately prior to its distribution to B. B's adjusted tax basis in Property A is therefore $10,000 under section 732(a)(1).

(f) *Anti-abuse rule.*—(1) *In general.*—The rules of section 704(c)(1)(B) and this section must be applied in a manner consistent with the purpose of section 704(c)(1)(B). Accordingly, if a principal purpose of a transaction is to achieve a tax result that is inconsistent with the purpose of section 704(c)(1)(B), the Commissioner can recast the transaction for federal tax purposes as appropriate to achieve tax results that are consistent with the purpose of section 704(c)(1)(B) and this section. Whether a tax result is inconsistent with the purpose of section 704(c)(1)(B) and this section must be determined based on all the facts and circumstances. See § 1.7374 for an anti-abuse rule and examples in the context of section 737.

(2) *Examples.*—The following examples illustrate the anti-abuse rule of this paragraph (f). The examples set forth below do not delineate the boundaries of either permissible or impermissible types of transactions. Further, the addition of any facts or circumstances that are not specifically set forth in an example (or the deletion of any facts or circumstances) may alter the outcome of the transaction described in the example. Unless otherwise specified, partnership income equals partnership expenses (other than depreciation deductions for contributed property) for each year of the partnership, the fair market value of partnership property does not change, all distributions by the partnership are subject to section 704(c)(1)(B), and all partners are unrelated.

Example 1. Distribution in substance made within five-year period; results inconsistent with the purpose of section 704(c)(1)(B). (i) On January 1, 1995, A, B, and C form partnership ABC as equal partners. A contributes Property A, nondepreciable real property with a fair market value of $10,000 and an adjusted tax basis of $1,000. B and C each contributes $10,000 cash.

(ii) On December 31, 1998, the partners desire to distribute Property A to B in complete liquidation of B's interest in the partnership. If Property A were distributed at that time, however, A would recognize $9,000 of gain under section 704(c)(1)(B), the difference between the $10,000 fair market value and the $1,000 adjusted tax basis of Property A, because Property A was contributed to the partnership less than five years before December 31, 1998. On becoming aware of this potential gain recognition, and with a principal purpose of avoiding such gain, the partners amend the partnership agreement on December 31, 1998, and take any other steps necessary to provide that substantially all of the economic risks and benefits of Property A are borne by B as of December 31, 1998, and that substantially all of the economic risks and benefits of all other partnership property are borne by A and C. The partnership holds Property A until January 5, 2000, at which time it is distributed to B in complete liquidation of B's interest in the partnership.

(iii) The actual distribution of Property A occurred more than five years after the contribution of the property to the partnership. The steps taken by the partnership on December 31, 1998, however, are the functional equivalent of an actual distribution of Property A to B in complete liquidation of B's interest in the partnership as of that date. Section 704(c)(1)(B) requires recognition of gain when contributed section 704(c) property is in substance distributed to another partner within five years of its contribution to the partnership. Allowing a contributing partner to avoid section 704(c)(1)(B) through arrangements such as those in this *Example 1* that have the effect of a distribution of property within five years of the date of its contribution to the partnership would effectively undermine the purpose of section 704(c)(1)(B) and this section. As a result, the steps taken by the partnership on December 31, 1998, are treated as causing a distribution of Property A to B for purposes of section 704(c)(1)(B) on that date, and A recognizes gain of $9,000 under section 704(c)(1)(B) and this section at that time.

(iv) Alternatively, if on becoming aware of the potential gain recognition to A on a distribution of Property A on December 31, 1998, the partners had instead agreed that B would continue as a partner with no changes to the partnership agreement or to B's economic interest in partnership operations, the distribution of Property A to B on January 5, 2000, would not have been inconsistent with the purpose of section 704(c)(1)(B) and this section. In that situation, Property A would not have been distributed until after the expiration of the five-year period specified in section 704(c)(1)(B) and this section. Deferring the distribution of Property A until the end of the five-year period for a principal purpose of avoiding the recognition of gain under section 704(c)(1)(B) and this section is not inconsistent with the purpose of section 704(c)(1)(B). Therefore, A would not have recognized gain on the distribution of Property A in that case.

Example 2. Suspension of five-year period in manner consistent with the purpose of section 704(c)(1)(B). (i) A, B, and C form partnership ABC on January 1, 1995, to conduct bona fide business activities. A contributes Property A, nondepreciable real property with a fair market value of $10,000 and an adjusted tax basis of $1,000, in exchange for a 49.5 percent interest in partnership capital and profits. B contributes $10,000 in cash for a 49.5 percent interest in partnership capital and profits. C contributes cash for a 1 percent interest in partnership capital and profits. A and B are wholly owned subsidiaries of the same affiliated group and continue to control the management of Property A by virtue of their controlling interests in the partnership. The partnership is formed pursuant to a plan a principal purpose of which is to minimize the period of time that A would have to remain a partner with a potential acquiror of Property A.

(ii) On December 31, 1997, D is admitted as a partner to the partnership in exchange for $10,000 cash.

(iii) On January 5, 2000, Property A is distributed to D in complete liquidation of D's interest in the partnership.

(iv) The distribution of Property A to D occurred more than five years after the contribution of the property to the partnership. On these facts, however, a principal purpose of the transaction was to minimize the period of time that A would have to remain partners with a potential acquiror of Property A, and treating the five-year period of section 704(c)(1)(B) as running during a time when Property A was still effectively owned through the partnership by members of the contributing affiliated group of which A is a member is inconsistent with the purpose of section 704(c)(1)(B). Prior to the admission of D as a partner, the pooling of assets between A and B, on the one hand, and C, on the other hand, although sufficient to constitute ABC as a valid partnership for federal income tax purposes, is not a sufficient pooling of assets for purposes of running the five-year period with respect to the distribution of Property A to D. Allowing a contributing partner to avoid section 704(c)(1)(B) through arrangements such as those in this *Example 2* would have the effect of substantially nullifying the five-year requirement of section 704(c)(1)(B) and this section and elevating the form of the transaction over its substance. As a result, with respect to the distribution of Property A to D, the five-year period of section 704(c)(1)(B) is tolled until the admission of D as a partner on December 31, 1997. Therefore, the distribution of Property A occurred before the end of the five-year period of section 704(c)(1)(B), and A recognizes gain of $9,000 under section 704(c)(1)(B) on the distribution.

* * *

[Reg. § 1.704-4.]

☐ [*T.D.* 8642, 12-22-95. *Amended by T.D.* 8717, 5-8-97; *T.D.* 9193, 3-21-2005 *and T.D.* 9207, 5-23-2005.]

§ 1.705-1. Determination of basis of partner's interest.—(a) *General rule.*—(1) Section 705 and this section provide rules for determining the adjusted basis of a partner's interest in a partnership. A partner is required to determine the adjusted basis of his interest in a partnership only when necessary for the determination of his tax liability or that of any other person. The determination of the adjusted basis of a partnership interest is ordinarily made as of the end of a partnership taxable year. Thus, for example, such year-end determination is necessary in ascertaining the extent to which a partner's distributive share of partnership losses may be allowed. See section 704(d). However, where there has been a sale or exchange of all or a part of a partnership interest or a liquidation of a partner's entire interest in a partnership, the adjusted basis of the partner's interest should be determined as of the date of sale or exchange or liquidation. The adjusted basis of a partner's interest in a partnership is determined without regard to any amount shown in the partnership books as the partner's "capital", "equity", or similar account. For example, A contributes property with an adjusted basis to him of $400 (and a value of $1,000) to a partnership. B contributes $1,000 cash. While under their agreement each may have a "capital account" in the partnership of $1,000, the adjusted basis of A's interest is only $400 and B's interest $1,000.

(2) The original basis of a partner's interest in a partnership shall be determined under section 722 (relating to contributions to a partnership) or section 742 (relating to transfers of partnership interests). Such basis shall be increased under section 722 by any further contributions to the partnership and by the sum of the partner's distributive share for the taxable year and prior taxable years of—

(i) Taxable income of the partnership as determined under section 703(a),

(ii) Tax-exempt receipts of the partnership, and

(iii) The excess of the deductions for depletion over the basis of the depletable property, unless the property is an oil or gas property the basis of which has been allocated to partners under section 613A(c)(7)(D).

(3) The basis shall be decreased (but not below zero) by distributions from the partnership as provided in section 733 and by the sum of the partner's distributive share for the taxable year and prior taxable years of—

(i) Partnership losses (including capital losses), and

(ii) Partnership expenditures which are not deductible in computing partnership taxable income or loss and which are not capital expenditures.

(4) The basis shall be decreased (but not below zero) by the amount of the partner's deduction for depletion allowable under section 611 for any partnership oil and gas property to the extent the deduction does not exceed the proportionate share of the adjusted basis of the property allocated to the partner under section 613A(c)(7)(D).

(5) The basis shall be adjusted (but not below zero) to reflect any gain or loss to the partner resulting from a disposition by the partnership of a domestic oil or gas property after December 31, 1974.

(6) For the effect of liabilities in determining the amount of contributions made by a partner to a partnership or the amount of distributions made by a partnership to a partner, see section 752 and § 1.752-1, relating to the treat-

ment of certain liabilities. In determining the basis of a partnership interest on the effective date of subchapter K, chapter 1 of the Code, or any of the sections thereof, the partner's share of partnership liabilities on that date shall be included.

(7) For basis adjustments necessary to coordinate sections 705 and 1032 in certain situations in which a partnership disposes of stock or any position in stock to which section 1032 applies of a corporation that holds a direct or indirect interest in the partnership, see § 1.705-2.

(8) For basis adjustments necessary to coordinate sections 705 and 358(h), see § 1.358-7(b). For certain basis adjustments with respect to a § 1.752-7 liability assumed by a partnership from a partner, see § 1.752-7.

(9) For basis adjustments necessary to coordinate sections 705 and 362(e)(2), see § 1.362-4(e)(1).

(b) *Alternative rule.*—In certain cases, the adjusted basis of a partner's interest in a partnership may be determined by reference to the partner's share of the adjusted basis of partnership property which would be distributable upon termination of the partnership. The alternative rule may be used to determine the adjusted basis of a partner's interest where circumstances are such that the partner cannot practicably apply the general rule set forth in section 705(a) and paragraph (a) of this section, or where, from a consideration of all the facts, it is, in the opinion of the Commissioner, reasonable to conclude that the result produced will not vary substantially from the result obtainable under the general rule. Where the alternative rule is used, adjustments may be necessary in determining the adjusted basis of a partner's interest in a partnership. Adjustments would be required, for example, in order to reflect in a partner's share of the adjusted basis of partnership property any significant discrepancies arising as a result of contributed property, transfers of partnership interest, or distributions of property to the partners. The operation of the alternative rules may be illustrated by the following examples:

Example (1). The ABC partnership, in which A, B, and C are equal partners, owns various properties with a total adjusted basis of $1,500 and has earned and retained an additional $1,500. The total adjusted basis of partnership property is thus $3,000. Each partner's share in the adjusted basis of partnership property is one-third of this amount, or $1,000. Under the alternative rule, this amount represents each partner's adjusted basis for his partnership interest.

Example (2). Assume that partner A in example (1) of this paragraph sells his partnership interest to D for $1,250 at a time when the partnership property with an adjusted basis of $1,500 had appreciated in value to $3,000, and when the partnership also had $750 in cash. The total adjusted basis of all partnership property is $2,250 and the value of such property is $3,750. D's basis for his partnership interest is his cost, $1,250. However, his one-third share of the adjusted basis of partnership property is only $750. Therefore, for the purposes of the alternative rule, D has an adjustment of $500 in determining the basis of his interest. This amount represents the difference between the cost of his partnership interest and his share of partnership basis at the time of his purchase. If the partnership subsequently earns and retains an additional $1,500, its property will have an adjusted basis of $3,750. D's adjusted basis for his interest under the alternative rule is $1,750, determined by adding $500, his basis adjustment, to $1,250 (his one-third share of the $3,750 adjusted basis of partnership property). If the partnership distributes $250 to each partner in a current distribution, D's adjusted basis for his interest will be $1,500 ($1,000, his one-third share of the remaining basis of partnership property, $3,000, plus his basis adjustment of $500).

Example (3). Assume the BCD partnership in example (2) of this paragraph continues to operate. In 1960, D proposes to sell his partnership interest and wishes to evaluate the tax consequences of such sale. It is necessary, therefore, to determine the adjusted basis of his interest in the partnership. Assume further that D cannot determine the adjusted basis of his interest under the general rule. The balance sheet of the BCD partnership is as follows:

Assets	*Adjusted Basis per Books*	*Market Value*
Cash	$ 3,000	$ 3,000
Receivables	4,000	4,000
Depreciable Property	5,000	5,000
Land held for investment	18,000	30,000
Total	$30,000	$42,000

Liabilities and Capital	*Per Books*
Liabilities	$ 6,000
Capital Accounts: B	4,500
C	4,500
D	15,000
Total	$30,000

The $15,000 representing the amount of D's capital account does not reflect the $500 basis adjustment arising from D's purchase of his interest. See example (2) of this paragraph. The adjusted basis of D's partnership interest determined under the alternative rule is as follows:

D's share of the adjusted basis of partnership property (reduced by the amount of liabilities) at time of proposed sale	$15,000
D's share of partnership liabilities (under the partnership agreement liabilities are shared equally)	2,000
D's basis adjustment from example (2)	500
Adjusted basis of D's interest at the time of proposed sale, as determined under alternative rule	$17,500

[Reg. § 1.705-1.]

☐ [*T.D.* 6175, 5-23-56. *Amended by T.D.* 8437, 9-22-92; *T.D.* 8986, 3-28-2002; *T.D.* 9049, 3-17-2003; *T.D.* 9207, 5-23-2005, *T.D.* 9633, 8-30-2013 *and T.D.* 9759, 3-25-2016.]

§ 1.705-2. Basis adjustments coordinating sections 705 and 1032.—(a) *Purpose.*—This section coordinates the application of sections 705 and 1032 and is intended to prevent inappropriate increases or decreases in the adjusted basis of a corporate partner's interest in a partnership resulting from the partnership's disposition of the corporate partner's stock. The rules under section 705 generally are intended to preserve equality between the adjusted basis of a partner's interest in a partnership (outside basis) and such partner's share of the adjusted basis in partnership assets (inside basis). However, in situations where a section 754 election was not in effect for the year in which a partner acquired its interest, the partner's inside basis and outside basis may not be equal. Similarly, in situations where a section 754 election was not in effect for the year in which a partnership distributes money or other property to another partner and that partner recognizes gain or loss on the distribution or the basis of the property distributed to that partner is adjusted, the remaining partners' inside basis and outside basis may not be equal. In these situations, gain or loss allocated to the partner upon disposition of the partnership assets that is attributable to the difference between the adjusted basis of the partnership assets absent the section 754 election and the adjusted basis of the partnership assets had a section 754 election been in effect generally will result in an adjustment to the basis of the partner's interest in the partnership under section 705(a). Such gain (or loss) therefore generally will be offset by a corresponding decrease in the gain or increase in the loss (or increase in the gain or decrease in the loss) upon the subsequent disposition by the partner of its interest in the partnership. Where such a difference exists with respect to stock of a corporate partner that is held by the partnership, gain or loss from the disposition of corporate partner stock attributable to the difference is not recognized by the corporate partner under section 1032. To adjust the basis of the corporate partner's interest in the partnership for this unrecognized gain or loss would not be appropriate because it would create an opportunity for the recognition of taxable gain or loss on a subsequent disposition of the partnership interest where no economic gain or loss has been incurred by the corporate partner and no corresponding taxable gain or loss had previously been allocated to the corporate partner by the partnership.

(b) *Single partnership.*—(1) *Required adjustments relating to acquisitions of partnership interest.*—(i) This paragraph (b)(1) applies in situations where a corporation acquires an interest in a partnership that holds stock in that corporation (or the partnership subsequently acquires stock in that corporation in an exchanged basis transaction), the partnership does not have an election under section 754 in effect for the year in which the corporation acquires the interest, and the partnership later sells or exchanges the stock. In these situations, the increase (or decrease) in the corporation's adjusted basis in its partnership interest resulting from the sale or exchange of the stock equals the amount of gain (or loss) that the corporate partner would have recognized (absent the application of section 1032) if, for the year in which the corporation acquired the interest, a section 754 election had been in effect.

(ii) The provisions of this paragraph (b)(1) are illustrated by the following example:

Example. (i) A, B, and C form equal partnership PRS. Each partner contributes

$30,000 in exchange for its partnership interest. PRS has no liabilities. PRS purchases stock in corporation X for $30,000, which appreciates in value to $120,000. PRS also purchases inventory for $60,000, which appreciates in value to $150,000. A sells its interest in PRS to corporation X for $90,000 in a year for which an election under section 754 is not in effect. PRS later sells the X stock for $150,000. PRS realizes a gain of $120,000 on the sale of the X stock. X's share of the gain is $40,000. Under section 1032, X does not recognize its share of the gain.

(ii) Normally, X would be entitled to a $40,000 increase in the basis of its PRS interest for its allocable share of PRS's gain from the sale of the X stock, but a special rule applies in this situation. If a section 754 election had been in effect for the year in which X acquired its interest in PRS, X would have been entitled to a basis adjustment under section 743(b) of $60,000 (the excess of X's basis for the transferred partnership interest over X's share of the adjusted basis to PRS of PRS's property). See §1.743-1(b). Under §1.755-1(b), the basis adjustment under section 743(b) would have been allocated $30,000 to the X stock (the amount of the gain that would have been allocated to X from the hypothetical sale of the stock), and $30,000 to the inventory (the amount of the gain that would have been allocated to X from the hypothetical sale of the inventory).

(iii) If a section 754 election had been in effect for the year in which X acquired its interest in PRS, the amount of gain that X would have recognized upon PRS's disposition of X stock (absent the application of section 1032) would be $10,000 (X's share of PRS's gain from the stock sale, $40,000, minus the amount of X's basis adjustment under section 743(b), $30,000). See §1.743-1(j). Accordingly, the increase in the basis of X's interest in PRS is $10,000.

(2) *Required adjustments relating to distributions.*—(i) This paragraph (b)(2) applies in situations where a corporation owns a direct or indirect interest in a partnership that owns stock in that corporation, the partnership distributes money or other property to another partner and that partner recognizes gain or loss on the distribution or the basis of the property distributed to that partner is adjusted during a year in which the partnership does not have an election under section 754 in effect, and the partnership subsequently sells or exchanges the stock. In these situations, the increase (or decrease) in the corporation's adjusted basis in its partnership interest resulting from the sale or exchange of the stock equals the amount of gain (or loss) that the corporate partner would have recognized (absent the application of section 1032) if, for the year in which the partnership made the distribution, a section 754 election had been in effect.

(ii) The provisions of this paragraph (b)(2) are illustrated by the following example:

Example. (i) A, B, and corporation C form partnership PRS. A and B each contribute $10,000 and C contributes $20,000 in exchange for a partnership interest. PRS has no liabilities. PRS purchases stock in corporation C for $10,000, which appreciates in value to $70,000. PRS distributes $25,000 to A in complete liquidation of A's interest in PRS in a year for which an election under section 754 is not in effect. PRS later sells the C stock for $70,000. PRS realizes a gain of $60,000 on the sale of the C stock. C's share of the gain is $40,000. Under section 1032, C does not recognize its share of the gain.

(ii) Normally, C would be entitled to a $40,000 increase in the basis of its PRS interest for its allocable share of PRS's gain from the sale of the C stock, but a special rule applies in this situation. If a section 754 election had been in effect for the year in which PRS made the distribution to A, PRS would have been entitled to adjust the basis of partnership property under section 734(b)(1)(A) by $15,000 (the amount of gain recognized by A with respect to the distribution to A under section 731(a)(1)). See §1.734-1(b). Under §1.755-1(c)(1)(ii), the basis adjustment under section 734(b) would have been allocated to the C stock, increasing its basis to $25,000 (where there is a distribution resulting in an adjustment under section 734(b)(1)(A) to the basis of undistributed partnership property, the adjustment is allocated only to capital gain property).

(iii) If a section 754 election had been in effect for the year in which PRS made the distribution to A, the amount of gain that PRS would have recognized upon PRS's disposition of C stock would be $45,000 ($70,000 minus $25,000 basis in the C stock), and the amount of gain C would have recognized upon PRS's disposition of the C stock (absent the application of section 1032) would be $30,000 (C's share of PRS's gain of $45,000 from the stock sale). Accordingly, upon PRS's sale of the C stock, the increase in the basis of C's interest in PRS is $30,000.

* * *

(d) *Positions in stock.*—For purposes of this section, stock includes any position in stock to which section 1032 applies.

* * *

[Reg. §1.705-2.]

☐ [*T.D.* 8986, 3-28-2002. *Amended by T.D.* 9049, 3-17-2003.]

§ 1.706-1. Taxable years of partner and partnership.—(a) *Year in which partnership income is includible.*—(1) In computing taxable income for a taxable year, a partner is required to include the partner's distributive share of partnership items set forth in section 702 and the regulations thereunder for any partnership taxable year ending within or with the partner's taxable year. A partner must also include in taxable income for a taxable year guaranteed payments under section 707(c) that are deductible by the partnership under its method of accounting in the partnership taxable year ending within or with the partner's taxable year.

(2) The rules of paragraph (a)(1) of this section may be illustrated by the following example:

Example. Partner A reports income using a calendar year, while the partnership of which A is a member reports its income using a fiscal year ending May 31. The partnership reports its income and deductions under the cash method of accounting. During the partnership taxable year ending May 31, 2002, the partnership makes guaranteed payments of $120,000 to A for services and for the use of capital. Of this amount, $70,000 was paid to A between June 1 and December 31, 2001, and the remaining $50,000 was paid to A between January 1 and May 31, 2002. The entire $120,000 paid to A is includible in A's taxable income for the calendar year 2002 (together with A's distributive share of partnership items set forth in section 702 for the partnership taxable year ending May 31, 2002).

(3) If a partner receives distributions under section 731 or sells or exchanges all or part of a partnership interest, any gain or loss arising therefrom does not constitute partnership income.

(b) *Taxable year.*—(1) *Partnership treated as a taxpayer.*—The taxable year of a partnership must be determined as though the partnership were a taxpayer.

(2) *Partnership's taxable year.*—(i) *Required taxable year.*—Except as provided in paragraph (b)(2)(ii) of this section, the taxable year of a partnership must be—

(A) The majority interest taxable year, as defined in section 706(b)(4);

(B) If there is no majority interest taxable year, the taxable year of all of the principal partners of the partnership, as defined in 706(b)(3) (the principal partners' taxable year); or

(C) If there is no majority interest taxable year or principal partners' taxable year, the taxable year that produces the least aggregate deferral of income as determined under paragraph (b)(3) of this section.

(ii) *Exceptions.*—A partnership may have a taxable year other than its required taxable year if it makes an election under section 444, elects to use a 52-53-week taxable year that ends with reference to its required taxable year or a taxable year elected under section 444, or establishes a business purpose for such taxable year and obtains approval of the Commissioner under section 442.

(3) *Least aggregate deferral.*—(i) *Taxable year that results in the least aggregate deferral of income.*—The taxable year that results in the least aggregate deferral of income will be the taxable year of one or more of the partners in the partnership which will result in the least aggregate deferral of income to the partners. The aggregate deferral for a particular year is equal to the sum of the products determined by multiplying the month(s) of deferral for each partner that would be generated by that year and each partner's interest in partnership profits for that year. The partner's taxable year that produces the lowest sum when compared to the other partner's taxable years is the taxable year that results in the least aggregate deferral of income to the partners. If the calculation results in more than one taxable year qualifying as the taxable year with the least aggregate deferral, the partnership may select any one of those taxable years as its taxable year. However, if one of the qualifying taxable years is also the partnership's existing taxable year, the partnership must maintain its existing taxable year. The determination of the taxable year that results in the least aggregate deferral of income generally must be made as of the beginning of the partnership's current taxable year. The director, however, may determine that the first day of the current taxable year is not the appropriate testing day and require the use of some other day or period that will more accurately reflect the ownership of the partnership and thereby the actual aggregate deferral to the partners where the partners engage in a transaction that has as its principal purpose the avoidance of the principles of this section. Thus, for example the preceding sentence would apply where there is a transfer of an interest in the partnership that results in a temporary transfer of that interest principally for purposes of qualifying for a specific taxable year under the principles of this section. For purposes of this section, deferral to each partner is measured in terms of months from the end of the partnership's taxable year forward to the end of the partner's taxable year.

* * *

(4) *Measurement of partner's profits and capital interest.*—(i) *In general.*—The rules of this paragraph (b)(4) apply in determining the

majority interest taxable year, the principal partners' taxable year, and the least aggregate deferral taxable year.

(ii) *Profits interest.*—(A) *In general.*—For purposes of section 706(b), a partner's interest in partnership profits is generally the partner's percentage share of partnership profits for the current partnership taxable year. If the partnership does not expect to have net income for the current partnership taxable year, then a partner's interest in partnership profits instead must be the partner's percentage share of partnership net income for the first taxable year in which the partnership expects to have net income.

(B) *Percentage share of partnership net income.*—The partner's percentage share of partnership net income for a partnership taxable year is the ratio of: the partner's distributive share of partnership net income for the taxable year, to the partnership's net income for the year. If a partner's percentage share of partnership net income for the taxable year depends on the amount or nature of partnership income for that year (due to, for example, preferred returns or special allocations of specific partnership items), then the partnership must make a reasonable estimate of the amount and nature of its income for the taxable year. This estimate must be based on all facts and circumstances known to the partnership as of the first day of the current partnership taxable year. The partnership must then use this estimate in determining the partners' interests in partnership profits for the taxable year.

(C) *Distributive share.*—For purposes of this paragraph (b)(4)(ii), a partner's distributive share of partnership net income is determined by taking into account all rules and regulations affecting that determination, including, without limitation, sections 704(b), (c), and (e), 736, and 743.

(iii) *Capital interest.*—Generally, a partner's interest in partnership capital is determined by reference to the assets of the partnership that the partner would be entitled to upon withdrawal from the partnership or upon liquidation of the partnership. If the partnership maintains capital accounts in accordance with § 1.704-1(b)(2)(iv), then for purposes of section 706(b), the partnership may assume that a partner's interest in partnership capital is the ratio of the partner's capital account to all partners' capital accounts as of the first day of the partnership taxable year.

* * *

(c) *Closing of partnership year.*—(1) *General rule.*—Section 706(c) and this paragraph provide rules governing the closing of partnership years. The closing of a partnership taxable year or a termination of a partnership for Federal income tax purposes is not necessarily governed by the "dissolution", "liquidation", etc., of a partnership under State or local law. The taxable year of a partnership shall not close as the result of the death of a partner, the entry of a new partner, the liquidation of a partner's entire interest in the partnership (as defined in section 761(d)), or the sale or exchange of a partner's interest in the partnership, except in the case of a termination of a partnership and except as provided in subparagraph (2) of this paragraph. In the case of termination, the partnership taxable year closes for all partners as of the date of termination. See section 708(b) and paragraph (b) of § 1.708-1.

(2) *Disposition of entire interest.*—(i) *In general.*—A partnership taxable year shall close with respect to a partner who sells or exchanges his entire interest in the partnership, with respect to a partner whose entire interest in the partnership is liquidated, and with respect to a partner who dies. In the case of a death, liquidation, or sale or exchange of a partner's entire interest in the partnership, the partner shall include in his taxable income for his taxable year within or with which the partner's interest in the partnership ends the partner's distributive share of items described in section 702(a) and any guaranteed payments under section 707(c) for the partnership taxable year ending with the date of such termination. If the decedent partner's estate or other successor sells or exchanges its entire interest in the partnership, or if its entire interest is liquidated, the partnership taxable year with respect to the estate or other successor in interest shall close on the date of such sale or exchange, or the date of the completion of the liquidation. The sale or exchange of a partnership interest does not, for the purpose of this rule, include any transfer of a partnership interest which occurs at death as a result of inheritance or any testamentary disposition.

(ii) *Example.*—H is a partner of a partnership having a taxable year ending December 31. Both H and his wife W are on a calendar year and file joint returns. H dies on March 31, 2016. Administration of the estate is completed and the estate, including the partnership interest, is distributed to W as legatee on November 30, 2016. Such distribution by the estate is not a sale or exchange of H's partnership interest. The taxable year of the partnership will close with respect to H on March 31, 2016, and H will include in his final return for his final taxable year (January 1, 2016, through March 31, 2016) his distributive share of partnership items for that period under the rules of sections 706(d)(2), 706(d)(3), and § 1.706-4. W will include in her return for the taxable year ending December 31, 2016, her distributive share of partnership items for the period of April 1, 2016, through December 31, 2016, under the rules of sections 706(d)(2), 706(d)(3), and § 1.706-4.

(iii) *Deemed dispositions.*—A deemed disposition of the partner's interest pursuant to § 1.1502-76(b)(2)(vi) (relating to corporate partners that become or cease to be members of a consolidated group within the meaning of §§ 1.1502-1(h)), 1.1362-3(c)(1) (relating to the termination of the subchapter S election of an S corporation partner), or 1.1377-1(b)(3)(iv) (regarding an election to terminate the taxable year of an S corporation partner), shall be treated as a disposition of the partner's entire interest in the partnership solely for purposes of section 706.

(3) *Disposition of less than entire interest.*—If a partner sells or exchanges a part of his interest in a partnership, or if the interest of a partner is reduced, the partnership taxable year shall continue to its normal end.

(4) *Determination of distributive shares.*—See section 706(d)(2), 706(d)(3), and § 1.706-4 for rules regarding the methods to be used in determining the distributive shares of items described in section 702(a) for partners whose interests in the partnership vary during the partnership's taxable year as a result of a disposition of a partner's entire interest in a partnership as described in paragraph (c)(2) of this section or as a result of a disposition of less than a partner's entire interest as described in paragraph (c)(3) of this section.

(5) *Transfer of interest by gift.*—The transfer of a partnership interest by gift does not close the partnership taxable year with respect to the donor. However, the income up to the date of gift attributable to the donor's interest shall be allocated to him under section 704(e)(2).

* * *

[Reg. § 1.706-1.]

☐ [*T.D.* 6175, 5-23-56. *Amended by T.D.* 7286, 9-26-73; *T.D.* 8123, 2-4-87; *T.D.* 8996, 5-16-2002; *T.D.* 9009, 7-22-2002, *T.D.* 9576, 2-9-2012 *and T.D.* 9728, 7-31-2015 (*corrected* 11-3-2015).]

Proposed Regulation

§ 1.706-3. Items attributable to interest in lower-tier partnership.—(a) *General rule.*—Except as provided in paragraphs (b) and (c) of this section, if during any taxable year of the partnership—

(1) There is a change in any partner's interest in the partnership (the upper-tier partnership); and

(2) Such partnership is a partner in another partnership (the lower-tier partnership), then each partner's distributive share of any item of the upper-tier partnership attributable to the lower-tier partnership shall be determined by assigning the appropriate portion (determined by applying principles similar to the principles of § 1.706-2(a)(3) and (4)) of each such item to the appropriate days during which the upper-tier partnership is a partner in the lower-tier partnership and by allocating the portion assigned to any such day among the partners in proportion to their interests in the upper-tier partnership at the close of such day. An upper-tier partnership's distributive share of any items of income, gain, loss, deduction, or credit from a lower-tier partnership is considered to be realized or sustained by the upper-tier partnership at the same time and in the same manner as such items were realized or sustained by the lower-tier partnership. For an additional example of the application of the principles of this paragraph (a), see Revenue Ruling 77-311, 1977-2 CB 218. *See* section 601.601(d)(2)(ii)(b).

(b) *De minimis upper-tier partnership exception.*—A de minimis upper-tier partnership is not required to, but may, apply paragraph (a) of this section. For purposes of this paragraph, a de minimis upper-tier partnership is a partnership that directly owns an interest in less than 10 percent of the profits and capital of the lower-tier partnership. This paragraph (b) only applies if all de minimis upper-tier partnerships own an interest in, in the aggregate, less than 30 percent of the profits and capital of the lower-tier partnership, and if no partnership is created with a purpose of avoiding the application of this section.

(c) *Example 1*.—On January 1, 2015, A, B, and C are equal one-third partners in UTP, a calendar year partnership that uses the proration method and calendar day convention to account for variations during its taxable year. UTP is itself a partner in a lower-tier partnership, LTP, which is also a calendar year partnership. UTP owns a 15 percent interest in the profits and capital of LTP throughout 2015. On August 1, 2015, A sells her entire interest in UTP to D. During 2015, LTP incurred $100,000 of ordinary deductions, which were attributable to the period from January 1, 2015, to July 1, 2015. None of LTP's deductions were extraordinary items within the meaning of § 1.706-4(e). UTP's distributive share of LTP's deductions is $15,000. Under paragraph (a) of this section, UTP must assign the $15,000 equally among all days from January 1, 2015 to July 1, 2015, and allocate the assigned daily portions among its partners in accordance with their interests in UTP on those days. Accordingly, A, B, and C are each allocated $5,000 of the deduction, and D is not allocated any portion of the deduction.

Example 2. Assume the same facts as Example 1, except that UTP owned a 9 percent interest in the profits and capital of LTP throughout 2015, and that LTP had only one other partner, which owned the remaining 91 percent of LTP. UTP's distributive share of LTP's $100,000 ordinary deductions is $9,000. UTP qualifies as a de minimis upper-tier partnership under paragraph (b) of this section, and therefore UTP is not required to apply the rules of paragraph (a) of this section. Instead, UTP may apply the rules of § 1.706-4 to the $9,000 ordinary deduction. If UTP decides to apply the rules of § 1.706-4, UTP prorates the $9,000 deduction equally over its entire taxable year, and allocates it according to its partners' interests on each day. Because A was a partner in UTP for 213 days, and D was a partner in UTP for 152 days, UTP allocates the $9,000 deduction $3,000 to each of B and C, $1,750.68 to A, and $1,249.32 to D.

Example 3. Assume the same facts as Example 2, except that UTP uses the interim closing method rather than the proration method. UTP qualifies as a de minimis upper-tier partnership under paragraph (b) of this section, and therefore UTP is not required to apply the rules of paragraph (a) of this section. Instead, UTP may apply the rules of § 1.706-4 to the $9,000 ordinary deduction. UTP's distributive share of LTP items is considered to have been realized or sustained by UTP at the same time and in the same manner as such items were realized or sustained by LTP. Accordingly, even if UTP decides to apply the rules of § 1.706-4, UTP's application of the interim closing method of § 1.706-4 to the $9,000 deduction results in UTP allocating to each of A, B, and C $3,000 of the deduction, and not allocating any portion of the deduction to D. UTP would reach the same result if it had instead chosen to apply the rules of paragraph (a) of this section.

* * *

[Prop. Reg. § 1.706-3.]

[Proposed 8-3-2015 (corrected 10-29-2015).]

§ 1.706-4. Determination of distributive share when a partner's interest varies.—(a) *General rule.*—(1) *Variations subject to this section.*—Except as provided in paragraph (a)(2) of this section, this section provides rules for determining the partners' distributive shares of partnership items when a partner's interest in a partnership varies during the taxable year as a result of the disposition of a partial or entire interest in a partnership as described in § 1.706-1(c)(2) and (3), or with respect to a partner whose interest in a partnership is reduced as described in § 1.706-1(c)(3), including by the entry of a new partner (collectively, a "variation").

(2) Coordination with sections 706(d)(2) and 706(d)(3) and other Code sections. Items subject to allocation under other rules, including sections 108(e)(8) and 108(i) (which provide special allocation rules for certain items from the discharge or retirement of indebtedness section), section 704(c) (relating to allocations with respect to certain contributed property), § 1.704-3(a)(6) (relating to allocations with respect to revalued property), section 706(d)(2) (relating to the determination of partners' distributive shares of allocable cash basis items), and section 706(d)(3) (relating the determination of partners' distributive share of any item of an upper tier partnership attributable to a lower tier partnership), are not subject to the rules of this section. In addition, the rules of this section do not apply in making allocation of book items pursuant to § 1.704-1(b)(2)(iv)(e), (f), or (s). In all cases, all partnership items for each taxable year must be allocated among the partners, and no partnership items may be duplicated, regardless of the particular provision of section 706 (or other Code section) which applies, and regardless of the method or convention adopted by the partnership.

(3) *Allocation of items subject to this section.*—In determining the distributive share under section 702(a) of partnership items subject to this section, the partnership shall follow the steps described in this paragraph (a)(3)(i) through (x).

(i) First, determine whether either of the exceptions in paragraph (b) of this section (regarding certain changes among contemporaneous partners and partnerships for which capital is not a material income-producing factor) applies.

(ii) Second, determine which of its items are subject to allocation under the special rules for extraordinary items in paragraph (e) of this section, and allocate those items accordingly.

(iii) Third, determine with respect to each variation whether it will apply the interim closing method or the proration method. Absent an agreement of the partners (within the meaning of paragraph (f) of this section) to use the proration method, the partnership shall use the interim closing method. The partnership may use different methods (interim closing or proration) for different variations within each partnership taxable year; however, the Commissioner may place restrictions on the ability of partnerships to use different methods during the same taxable year in guidance published in the Internal Revenue Bulletin.

(iv) Fourth, determine when each variation is deemed to have occurred under the partnership's selected convention (as described in paragraph (c) of this section).

(v) Fifth, determine whether there is an agreement of the partners (within the meaning of paragraph (f) of this section) to perform regular monthly or semi-monthly interim closings (as described in paragraph (d) of this section). If so, then the partnership will perform an interim closing of its books at the end of each month (in the case of an agreement to perform monthly closings) or at the end and middle of each month (in the case of an agreement to perform semi-monthly closings), regardless of whether any variation occurs. Absent an agreement of the partners to perform regular monthly or semi-monthly interim closings, the only interim closings during the partnership's taxable year will be at the deemed time of the occurrence of variations for which the partnership uses the interim closing method.

(vi) Sixth, determine the partnership's segments, which are specific periods of the partnership's taxable year created by interim closings of the partnership's books. The first segment shall commence with the beginning of the taxable year of the partnership and shall end at the time of the first interim closing. Any additional segment shall commence immediately after the closing of the prior segment and shall end at the time of the next interim closing. However, the last segment of the partnership's taxable year shall end no later than the close of the last day of the partnership's taxable year. If there are no interim closings, the partnership has one segment, which corresponds to its entire taxable year.

(vii) Seventh, apportion the partnership's items for the year among its segments. The partnership shall determine the items of income, gain, loss, deduction, and credit of the partnership for each segment. In general, a partnership shall treat each segment as though the segment were a separate distributive share period. For example, a partnership may compute a capital loss for a segment of a taxable year even though the partnership has a net capital gain for the entire taxable year. For purposes of determining allocations to segments, any special limitation or requirement relating to the timing or amount of income, gain, loss, deduction, or credit applicable to the entire partnership taxable year will be applied based upon the partnership's satisfaction of the limitation or requirement as of the end of the partnership's taxable year. For example, the expenses related to the election to expense a section 179 asset must first be calculated (and limited if applicable) based on the partnership's full taxable year, and then the effect of any limitation must be apportioned among the segments in accordance with the interim closing method or the proration method using any reasonable method.

(viii) Eighth, determine the partnership's proration periods, which are specific portions of a segment created by a variation for which the partnership chooses to apply the proration method. The first proration period in each segment begins at the beginning of the segment, and ends at the first time of the first variation within the segment for which the partnership selects the proration method. The next proration period begins immediately after the close of the prior proration period and ends at the time of the next variation for which the partnership selects the proration method. However, each proration period shall end no later than the close of the segment.

(ix) Ninth, prorate the items of income, gain, loss, deduction, and credit in each segment among the proration periods within the segment.

(x) Tenth, determine the partners' distributive shares of partnership items under section 702(a) by taking into account the partners' interests in such items during each segment and proration period.

(4) *Example*.—At the beginning of 2017, PRS, a calendar year partnership, has three equal partners, A, B, and C. On April 16, 2017, A sells 50% of its interest in PRS to new partner D. On August 6, 2017, B sells 50% of its interest in PRS to new partner E. During 2015, PRS earned $75,000 of ordinary income, incurred $33,000 of ordinary deductions, earned $12,000 of capital gain in the ordinary course of its business, and sustained $9,000 of capital loss in the ordinary course of its business. Within that year, PRS earned $60,000 of ordinary income, incurred $24,000 of ordinary deductions, earned $12,000 of capital gain, and sustained $6,000 of capital loss between January 1, 2017, and July 31, 2017, and PRS earned $15,000 of gross ordinary income, incurred $9,000 of gross ordinary deductions, and sustained $3,000 of capital loss between August 1, 2017, and December 31, 2017. None of PRS's items are extraordinary items within the meaning of paragraph (e)(2) of this section. Capital is a material income-producing factor for PRS. For 2017, PRS determines the distributive shares of A, B, C, D, and E as follows:

(i) First, PRS determines that none of the exceptions in paragraph (b) of this section apply because capital is a material-income producing factor and no variation is the result of a change in allocations among contemporaneous partners.

(ii) Second, PRS determines that none of its items are extraordinary items subject to allocation under paragraph (e) of this section.

(iii) Third, the partners of PRS agree (within the meaning of paragraph (f) of this section) to apply the proration method to the April 16, 2017, variation, and PRS accepts the default application of the interim closing method to the August 6, 2017, variation.

(iv) Fourth, PRS determines the deemed date of the variations for purposes of this section based upon PRS's selected convention. Because PRS applied the proration method to the April 16, 2017, variation, PRS must use the calendar day convention with respect to the April 16, 2017, variation pursuant to paragraph (c) of this section. Therefore, the variation that resulted from A's sale to D on April 16, 2017, is deemed to occur for purposes of this section at the end of the day on April 16, 2017. Further, the partners of PRS agree (within the meaning of paragraph (f) of this section) to apply the semi-monthly convention to the August 6, 2017, variation. Therefore, the August 6, 2017, variation is deemed to occur at the end of the day on July 31, 2017.

(v) Fifth, the partners of PRS do not agree to perform regular semi-monthly or monthly closings as described in paragraph (d) of this section. Therefore, PRS will have only one interim closing for 2017, occurring at the end of the day on July 31.

(vi) Sixth, PRS determines that it has two segments for 2017. The first segment commences January 1, 2017, and ends at the close of the day on July 31, 2017. The second segment commences at the beginning of the day on August 1, 2017, and ends at the close of the day on December 31, 2017.

(vii) Seventh, PRS determines that during the first segment of its taxable year (beginning January 1, 2017, and ending July 31, 2017), it had $60,000 of ordinary income, $24,000 of ordinary deductions, $12,000 of capital gain, and $6,000 of capital loss. PRS determines that during the second segment of its taxable year (beginning August 1, 2017, and ending December 31, 2017), it had $15,000 of gross ordinary income, $9,000 of gross ordinary deductions, and $3,000 of capital loss.

(viii) Eighth, PRS determines that it has two proration periods. The first proration period begins January 1, 2017, and ends at the close of the day on April 16, 2017; the second proration period begins April 17, 2017, and ends at the close of the day on July 31, 2017.

(ix) Ninth, PRS prorates its income from the first segment of its taxable year among the two proration periods. Because each proration period has 106 days, PRS allocates 50% of its items from the first segment to each proration period. Thus, each proration period contains $30,000 gross ordinary income, $12,000 gross ordinary deductions, $6,000 capital gain, and $3,000 capital loss.

(x) Tenth, PRS calculates each partner's distributive share. Because A, B, and C were equal partners during the first proration period, each is allocated one-third of the partnership's items attributable to that proration period. Thus, A, B, and C are each allocated $10,000 gross ordinary income, $4,000 gross ordinary deductions, $2,000 capital gain, and $1,000 capital loss for the first proration period. For the second proration period, A and D each had a one-sixth interest in PRS and B and C each had a one-third interest in PRS. Thus, A and D are each allocated $5,000 gross ordinary income, $2,000 gross ordinary deductions, $1,000 capital gain, and $500 capital loss, and B and C are each allocated $10,000 gross ordinary income, $4,000 gross ordinary deductions, $2,000 capital gain, and $1,000 capital loss for the second proration period. For the second segment of PRS's taxable year, A, B, D, and E each had a one-sixth interest in PRS and C had a one-third interest in PRS. Thus, A, B, D, and E are each allocated $2,500 gross ordinary income, $1,500 gross ordinary deductions, and $500 capital loss, and C is allocated $5,000 gross ordinary income, $3,000 gross ordinary deductions, and $1,000 capital loss for the second segment.

(b) *Exceptions.*—(1) *Permissible changes among contemporaneous partners.*—The general rule of paragraph (a)(3) of this section, with respect to the varying interests of a partner described in § 1.706-1(c)(3), will not preclude changes in the allocations of the distributive share of items described in section 702(a) among contemporaneous partners for the entire partnership taxable year (or among contemporaneous partners for a segment if the item is entirely attributable to a segment), provided that—

(i) Any variation in a partner's interest is not attributable to a contribution of money or property by a partner to the partnership or a distribution of money or property by the partnership to a partner; and

(ii) The allocations resulting from the modification satisfy the provisions of section 704(b) and the regulations promulgated thereunder.

(2) *Safe harbor for partnerships for which capital is not a material income-producing factor.*—Notwithstanding paragraph (a)(3) of this section, with respect to any taxable year in which there is a change in any partner's interest in a partnership for which capital is not a material income-producing factor, the partner-

ship and such partner may choose to determine the partner's distributive share of partnership income, gain, loss, deduction, and credit using any reasonable method to account for the varying interests of the partners in the partnership during the taxable year provided that the allocations satisfy the provisions of section 704(b).

(c) *Conventions.*—(1) *In general.*—Conventions are rules of administrative convenience that determine when each variation is deemed to occur for purposes of this section. Because the timing of each variation is necessary to determine the partnership's segments and proration periods, which are used to determine the partners' distributive shares, the convention used by the partnership with respect to a variation will generally affect the allocation of partnership items. However, see paragraph (e) of this section for special rules regarding extraordinary items, which generally must be allocated without regard to the partnership's convention. Subject to the limitations set forth in paragraphs (c)(2) and (3) of this section, partnerships may generally choose from the following three conventions:

(i) *Calendar day convention.*—Under the calendar day convention, each variation is deemed to occur for purposes of this section at the end of the day on which the variation occurs.

(ii) *Semi-monthly convention.*—Under the semi-monthly convention, each variation is deemed to occur for purposes of this section either:

(A) In the case of a variation occurring on the 1st through the 15th day of a calendar month, at the end of the last day of the immediately preceding calendar month; or

(B) In the case of a variation occurring on the 16th through the last day of a calendar month, at the end of the 15th calendar day of that month.

(iii) *Monthly convention.*—Under the monthly convention, each variation is deemed to occur for purposes of this section either:

(A) In the case of a variation occurring on the 1st through the 15th day of a calendar month, at the end of the last day of the immediately preceding calendar month; or

(B) In the case of a variation occurring on the 16th through the last day of a calendar month, at the end of the last day of that calendar month.

(2) *Exceptions.*—(i) Notwithstanding paragraph (c)(1) of this section, all variations within a taxable year shall be deemed to occur no earlier than the first day of the partnership's taxable year, and no later than the close of the final day of the partnership's taxable year. Thus, in the case of a calendar year partnership applying either the semi-monthly or monthly convention to a variation occurring on January 1st through January 15th, the variation will be deemed to occur for purposes of this section at the beginning of the day on January 1st.

(ii) In the case of a partner who becomes a partner during the partnership's taxable year as a result of a variation, and ceases to be a partner as a result of another variation, if both such variations would be deemed to occur at the same time under the rules of paragraph (c)(1) of this section, then the variations with respect to that partner's interest will instead be treated as occurring on the dates each variation actually occurred. Thus, the partnership must treat such a partner as a partner for the entire portion of its taxable year during which the partner actually owned an interest. See *Example 2* of paragraph (c)(4) of this section. However, this paragraph (c)(2)(ii) does not apply to publicly traded partnerships (as defined in section 7704(b)) that are treated as partnerships with respect to holders of publicly traded units (as described in §1.7704-1(b) or 1.7704-1(c)(1)).

(iii) Notwithstanding paragraph (c)(1)(iii) of this section, a publicly traded partnership (as defined in section 7704(b)) that is treated as a partnership may consistently treat all variations occurring during each month as occurring at the end of the last day of that calendar month if the publicly traded partnership uses the monthly convention for those variations.

(3) *Permissible conventions for each variation.*—(i) *Rules applicable to all partnerships.*—A partnership generally shall use the calendar day convention for each variation; however, for all variations during a taxable year for which the partnership uses the interim closing method, the partnership may instead use the semi-monthly or monthly convention by agreement of the partners (within the meaning of paragraph (f) of this section). The partnership must use the same convention for all variations for which the partnership uses the interim closing method.

(ii) *Publicly traded partnerships.*—A publicly traded partnership (as defined in section 7704(b)) that is treated as a partnership may, by agreement of the partners (within the meaning of paragraph (f) of this section) use any of the calendar day, the semi-monthly, or the monthly conventions with respect to all variations during the taxable year relating to its publicly-traded units (as described in §1.7704-1(b) or (c)(1)), regardless of whether the publicly traded partnership uses the proration method with respect to those variations. A publicly traded partnership must use the same convention for all variations during the taxable year relating to its publicly traded units. A publicly traded partnership must use the calendar day convention with respect to all variations relating to its non-publicly traded units for which the publicly traded partnership uses the proration method.

(4) *Examples.*—The following examples illustrate the principles in this paragraph (c).

Example 1. PRS is a calendar year partnership with four equal partners A, B, C, and D. PRS is not a publicly traded partnership. PRS has the following three variations that occur during its 2016 taxable year: on March 11, A sells its entire interest in PRS to new partner E; on June 12, PRS partially redeems B's interest in PRS with a distribution comprising a partial return of B's capital; on October 21, C sells part of C's interest in PRS to new partner E. These transfers do not result in a termination of PRS under section 708. Pursuant to paragraph (a)(3)(iii) of this section, the partners of PRS agree (within the meaning of paragraph (f) of this section) to use the interim closing method with respect to the variations occurring on March 11 and October 21 and agree to use the proration method with respect to the variation occurring on June 12. Pursuant to paragraph (c)(3) of this section, the partners of PRS may agree (within the meaning of paragraph (f) of this section) to use any of the calendar day, semi-monthly, or monthly conventions with respect to the March 11 and October 21 variations, but must use the same convention for both variations. If the partners of PRS agree to use the calendar day convention, the March 11 and October 21 variations will be deemed to occur for purposes of this section at the end of the day on March 11, 2016, and October 21, 2016, respectively. If the partners of PRS agree to use the semi-monthly convention, the March 11 and October 21 variations will be deemed to occur for purposes of this section at the end of the day on February 29, 2016, and October 15, 2016, respectively. If the partners of PRS agree to use the monthly convention, the March 11 and October 21 variations will be deemed to occur for purposes of this section at the end of the day on February 29, 2016, and October 31, 2016, respectively. Pursuant to paragraph (c)(3) of this section PRS must use the calendar day convention with respect to the June 12 variation; thus, the June 12 variation is deemed to occur for purposes of this section at the end of the day on June 12, 2016.

Example 2. PRS is a calendar year partnership that uses the interim closing method and monthly convention to account for variations during its taxable year. PRS is not a publicly traded partnership. On January 20, 2016, new partner A purchases an interest in PRS from one of PRS's existing partners. On February 14, 2016, A sells its entire interest in PRS. These transfers do not result in a termination of PRS under section 708. Under the rules of paragraph (c)(1)(iii) of this section, the January 20, 2016, variation and the February 14, 2016, variation would both be deemed to occur at the same time: the end of the day on January 31, 2016. Therefore, under the exception in paragraph (c)(2)(ii) of this section, the rules of paragraph (c)(1) of this section do not apply, and instead the January 20, 2016, variation and the February 14 variation are considered to occur on January 20, 2016, and February 14, 2016, respectively. PRS must perform a closing of the books on both January 20, 2016, and February 14, 2016, and allocate A a share of PRS's items attributable to that segment.

(d)(1) *Optional regular monthly or semi-monthly interim closings.*—Under the rules of this section, a partnership is not required to perform an interim closing of its books except at the time of any variation for which the partnership uses the interim closing method (taking into account the applicable convention). However, a partnership may, by agreement of the partners (within the meaning of paragraph (f) of this section) perform regular monthly or semi-monthly interim closings of its books, regardless of whether any variation occurs. Regardless of whether the partners agree to perform these regular interim closings, the partnership must continue to apply the interim closing or proration method to its variations according to the rules of this section.

(2) *Example.*—The following example illustrates the principles in this paragraph (d).

Example. (i) PRS is a calendar year partnership with five equal partners A, B, C, D, and E. PRS has the following two variations that occur during its 2016 taxable year: on August 29, A sells its entire interest in PRS to new partner F; on December 27, PRS completely liquidates B's interest in PRS with a distribution. These variations do not result in a termination of PRS under section 708.

(ii) The partners of PRS agree (within the meaning of paragraph (f) of this section) to use the interim closing method and the semi-monthly convention with respect to the variation occurring on August 29. Thus, the August variation is deemed to occur for purposes of this section at the end of the day on August 15, 2016. The partners of PRS agree (within the meaning of paragraph (f) of this section) to use the proration method with respect to the December 27 variation. Therefore, PRS must use the calendar day convention with respect to the December variation pursuant to paragraph (c) of this section. Thus, the December variation is deemed to occur for purposes of this section at the end of the day on December 27, 2016.

(iii) Pursuant to paragraph (d)(1) of this section, the partners of PRS agree (within the meaning of paragraph (f) of this section) to perform regular monthly interim closings. Therefore, PRS will have twelve interim closings for its 2016 taxable year, one at the end of every month and one at the end of the day on August 15. Therefore, PRS will have thirteen segments for 2016, one corresponding to each month from January through July, one segment from August 1 through August 15, one segment from August 16 through August 31, and one corresponding to each month from September through December. PRS must apportion its items among these segments under the rules of paragraph (a)(3) of this section.

(iv) PRS will have two proration periods for 2016, one from December 1 through December 27, and one from December 28 through December 31. Pursuant to the rules of paragraph (a)(3) of this section, PRS will prorate the items in its December segment among these two proration periods. Therefore, PRS will apportion 27/31 of all items in its December segment to the proration period from December 1 through December 27, and 4/31 of all items in its December segment to the proration period from December 28 through December 31.

(v) Pursuant to the rules of paragraph (a)(3)(x) of this section, PRS determines the partners' distributive shares of partnership items under section 702(a) by taking into account the partners' interests in such items during each of the thirteen segments and two proration periods. Thus, A, B, C, D, and E will each be allocated one-fifth of all items in the following segments: January, February, March, April, May, June, July, and August 1 through August 15. B, C, D, E, and F will each be allocated one-fifth of all items in the following segments: August 16 through August 31, September, October, and November. B, C, D, E, and F will each be allocated one-fifth of all items in the proration period from December 1 through December 27. C, D, E, and F will each be allocated one-quarter of all items in the proration period from December 28 through December 31.

(e) *Extraordinary items.*—(1) *General principles.*—Extraordinary items may not be prorated. The partnership must allocate extraordinary items among the partners in proportion to their interests in the partnership item at the time of day on which the extraordinary item occurred, regardless of the method (interim closing or proration method) and convention (daily, semi-monthly, or monthly) otherwise used by the partnership. These rules require the allocation of extraordinary items as an exception to the proration method, which would otherwise ratably allocate the extraordinary items across the segment, and the conventions, which could otherwise inappropriately shift extraordinary items between a transferor and transferee. However, publicly traded partnerships (as defined in section 7704(b)) that are treated as partnerships may, but are not required to, apply their selected convention in determining who held publicly traded units (as described in § 1.7704-1(b) or (c)(1)) at the time of the occurrence of an extraordinary item. Extraordinary items continue to be subject to any special limitation or requirement relating to the timing or amount of income, gain, loss, deduction, or credit applicable to the entire partnership taxable year (for example, the limitation for section 179 expenses).

(2) *Definition.*—Except as provided in paragraph (e)(3) of this section, an extraordinary item is:

(i) Any item from the disposition or abandonment (other than in the ordinary course of business) of a capital asset as defined in section 1221 (determined without the application of any other rules of law);

(ii) Any item from the disposition or abandonment (other than in the ordinary course of business) of property used in a trade or business as defined in section 1231(b) (determined without the application of any holding period requirement);

(iii) Any item from the disposition or abandonment of an asset described in section 1221(a)(1), (a)(3), (a)(4), or (a)(5) if substantially all the assets in the same category from the same trade or business are disposed of or abandoned in one transaction (or series of related transactions);

(iv) Any item from assets disposed of in an applicable asset acquisition under section 1060(c);

(v) Any item resulting from any change in accounting method initiated by the filing of the appropriate form after a variation occurs;

(vi) Any item from the discharge or retirement of indebtedness (except items subject to section 108(e)(8) or 108(i), which are subject to special allocation rules provided in section 108(e)(8) and 108(i));

(vii) Any item from the settlement of a tort or similar third-party liability or payment of a judgment;

(viii) Any credit, to the extent it arises from activities or items that are not ratably allocated (for example, the rehabilitation credit under section 47, which is based on placement in service);

(ix) For all partnerships, any additional item if, the partners agree (within the meaning of paragraph (f) of this section) to consistently treat such item as an extraordinary item for that taxable year; however, this rule does not apply if treating that additional item as an extraordinary item would result in a substantial distortion of income in any partner's return; any additional extraordinary items continue to be subject to any special limitation or requirement relating to the timing or amount of income, gain, loss, deduction, or credit applicable to the entire partnership taxable year (for example, the limitation for section 179 expenses);

(x) Any item which, in the opinion of the Commissioner, would, if ratably allocated, result in a substantial distortion of income in any return in which the item is included;

(xi) Any item identified as an additional class of extraordinary item in guidance published in the Internal Revenue Bulletin.

(3) *Small item exception.*—A partnership may treat an item described in paragraph (e)(2) of this section as other than an extraordinary item for purposes of this paragraph (e) if, for the partnership's taxable year the total of all items in the particular class of extraordinary items (as enumerated in paragraphs (e)(2)(i) through (xi) of this section, for example, all tort or similar liabilities, but in no event counting an extraordinary item more than once) is less than five percent of the partnership's gross income, including tax-exempt income described in section 705(a)(1)(B), in the case of income or gain items, or gross expenses and losses, including section 705(a)(2)(B) expenditures, in the case of losses and expense items; and the total amount of the extraordinary items from all classes of extraordinary items amounting to less than five percent of the partnership's gross income, including tax-exempt income described in section 705(a)(1)(B), in the case of income or gain items, or gross expenses and losses, including section 705(a)(2)(B) expenditures, in the case of losses and expense items, does not exceed $10 million in the taxable year, determined by treating all such extraordinary items as positive amounts.

* * *

(f) *Agreement of the partners.*—For purposes of paragraphs (a)(3)(iii) (relating to selection of the proration method), (c)(3) (relating to selection of the semi-monthly or monthly convention), (d) (relating to performance of regular monthly or semi-monthly interim closings), and (e)(2)(ix) (relating to selection of additional extraordinary items) of this section, the term agreement of the partners means either an agreement of all the partners to select the method, convention, or extraordinary item in a dated, written statement maintained with the partnership's books and records, including, for example, a selection that is included in the partnership agreement, or a selection of the method, convention, or extraordinary item made by a person authorized to make that selection, including under a grant of general authority provided for by either state law or in the partnership agreement, if that person's selection is in a dated, written statement maintained with the partnership's books and records. In either case, the dated written agreement must be maintained with the partnership's books and records by the due date, including extension, of the partnership's tax return.

* * *

[Reg. § 1.706-4.]

☐ [*T.D.* 9728, 7-31-2015 (*corrected* 11-3-2015).]

⋙ Caution: Reg. § 1.707-1 does not reflect changes made by the Tax Reform Act of 1986 lowering the percentage in Section 707(b)(2) from 80% to 50%.

§ 1.707-1. Transactions between partner and partnership.—(a) *Partner not acting in capacity as partner.*—A partner who engages in a transaction with a partnership other than in his capacity as a partner shall be treated as if he were not a member of the partnership with respect to such transaction. Such transactions include, for example, loans of money or property by the partnership to the partner or by the partner to the partnership, the sale of property by the partner to the partnership, the purchase of property by the partner from the partnership, and the rendering of services by the partnership to the partner or by the partner to the partnership. Where a partner retains the ownership of property but allows the partnership to use such separately owned property for partnership purposes (for example, to obtain credit or to secure firm creditors by guaranty, pledge, or other agreement) the transaction is treated as one between a partnership and a partner not acting in his capacity as a partner. However, transfers of money or property by a partner to a partnership as contributions, or transfers of money or property by a partnership to a partner as distributions, are not transactions included within the provisions of this section. In all cases, the substance of the transaction will govern rather than its form. See paragraph (c)(3) of § 1.731-1.

(b) *Certain sales or exchanges of property with respect to controlled partnerships.*—(1) *Losses disallowed.*—(i) No deduction shall be allowed for a loss on a sale or exchange of property (other than an interest in the partnership), directly or indirectly, between a partnership and a partner who owns, directly or indirectly, more than 50 percent of the capital interest or profits interest in such partnership. A loss on a sale or exchange of property, directly or indirectly, between two partnerships in which the same persons own, directly or indirectly, more than 50 percent of the capital interest or profits interests in each partnership shall not be allowed.

(ii) If a gain is realized upon the subsequent sale or exchange by transferee of property with respect to which a loss was disallowed under the provisions of subdivision (i) of this subparagraph, section 267(d) (relating to amount of gain where loss previously disallowed) shall apply as though the loss were disallowed under section 267(a)(1).

(2) *Gains treated as ordinary income.*—Any gain recognized upon the sale or exchange, directly or indirectly, of property which, in the hands of the transferee immediately after the transfer, is property other than a capital asset, as defined in section 1221, shall be ordinary income if the transaction is between a partnership and a partner who owns, directly or indirectly, more than 80 percent of the capital interest or profits interest in the partnership. This rule also applies where such a transaction is between partnerships in which the same persons own, directly or indirectly, more than 80 percent of the capital interests or profits interests in each partnership. The term "property other than a capital asset" includes (but is not limited to) trade accounts receivable, inventory, stock in trade, and depreciable or real property used in the trade or business.

(3) *Ownership of a capital or profits interest.*—In determining the extent of the ownership by a partner, as defined in section 761(b), of his capital interest or profits interest in a partnership, the rules for constructive ownership of stock provided in section 267(c)(1), (2), (4), and (5) shall be applied for the purpose of section 707(b) and this paragraph. Under these rules, ownership of a capital or profits interest in a partnership may be attributed to a person who is not a partner as defined in section 761(b) in order that another partner may be considered the constructive owner of such interest under section 267(c). However, section 707(b)(1)(A) does not apply to a constructive owner of a partnership interest since he is not a partner as defined in section 761(b). For example, where trust T is a partner in the partnership ABT, and AW, A's wife, is the sole beneficiary of the trust, the ownership of a capital and profits interest in the partnership by T will be attributed to AW only for the purpose of further attributing the ownership of such interest to A. See section 267(c)(1) and (5). If A, B, and T are equal partners, then A will be considered as owning more than 50 percent of the capital and profits interest in the partnership, and losses on transactions between him and the partnership will be disallowed by section 707(b)(1)(A). However, a loss sustained by AW on a sale or exchange of property with the partnership would not be disallowed by section 707, but will be disallowed to the extent provided in paragraph (b) of § 1.267(b)-1. See section 267(a) and (b), and the regulations thereunder.

(c) *Guaranteed payments.*—Payments made by a partnership to a partner for services or for the use of capital are considered as made to a person who is not a partner, to the extent such payments are determined without regard to the income of the partnership. However, a partner must include such payments as ordinary income for his taxable year within or with which ends the partnership taxable year in which the partnership deducted such payments as paid or accrued under its method of accounting. See section 706(a) and paragraph (a) of § 1.706-1. Guaranteed payments are considered as made to one who is not a member of the partnership, only for the purposes of section 61(a) (relating to gross income) and section 162(a) (relating to trade or business expenses). For a guaranteed payment to be a partnership deduction, it must meet the same tests under section 162(a) as it would if the payment had been made to a person who is not a member of the partnership, and the rules of section 263 (relating to capital expenditures) must be taken into account. This rule does not affect the deductibility to the partnership of a payment described in section 736(a)(2) to a retiring partner or to a deceased partner's successor in interest. Guaranteed payments do not constitute an interest in partnership profits for purposes of sections 706(b)(3), 707(b), and 708(b). For the purposes of other provisions of the internal revenue laws, guaranteed payments are regarded as a partner's distributive share of ordinary income. Thus, a partner who receives guaranteed payments for a period during which he is absent from work because of personal injuries or sickness is not entitled to exclude such payments from his gross income under section 105(d). Similarly, a partner who receives guaranteed payments is not regarded as an employee of the partnership for the purposes of withholding of tax at source, deferred compensation plans, etc. The provisions of this paragraph may be illustrated by the following examples:

Example (1). Under the ABC partnership agreement, partner A is entitled to a fixed annual payment of $10,000 for services, without regard to the income of the partnership. His distributive share is 10 percent. After deducting the guaranteed payment, the partnership has $50,000 ordinary income. A must include $15,000 as ordinary income for his taxable year within or with which the partnership taxable year ends ($10,000 guaranteed payment plus $5,000 distributive share).

Example (2). Partner C in the CD partnership is to receive 30 percent of partnership income as determined before taking into account any guaranteed payments, but not less than $10,000. The income of the partnership is $60,000, and C is entitled to $18,000 (30 percent of $60,000) as his distributive share. No part of this amount is a guaranteed payment. However, if the partnership had income of $20,000 instead of $60,000, $6,000 (30 percent of $20,000) would be partner C's distributive share, and the remaining $4,000 payable to C would be a guaranteed payment.

Example (3). Partner X in the XY partnership is to receive a payment of $10,000 for services, plus 30 percent of the taxable income or loss of the partnership. After deducting the payment of $10,000 to partner X, the XY partnership has a loss of $9,000. Of this amount, $2,700 (30 percent of the loss) is X's distributive share of partnership loss and, subject to section 704(d), is to be taken into account by him in his return. In addition, he must report as ordinary income the guaranteed payment of $10,000 made to him by the partnership.

Example (4). Assume the same facts as in example (3) of this paragraph except that, instead of a $9,000 loss, the partnership has $30,000 in capital gains and no other items of income or deduction except the $10,000 paid X as a guaranteed payment. Since the items of partnership income or loss must be segregated under section 702(a), the partnership has a $10,000 ordinary loss and $30,000 in capital gains. X's 30 percent distributive shares of these amounts are $3,000 ordinary loss and $9,000 capital gain. In addition, X has received a $10,000 guaranteed payment which is ordinary income to him. [Reg. § 1.707-1.]

□ [*T.D.* 6175, 5-23-56. *Amended by T.D.* 6312, 9-10-58 *and T.D.* 7891, 5-3-83.]

Proposed Regulation

§ 1.707-2. Disguised payments for services.—(a) *In general*.—This section prescribes rules for characterizing arrangements as disguised payments for services. Paragraph (b) of this section outlines the elements necessary to characterize an arrangement as a payment for services, and it provides operational rules regarding application and timing of this section. Paragraph (c) of this section identifies the factors that weigh in the determination of whether an arrangement includes the elements described in paragraph (b) of this section that make it appropriate to characterize the arrangement as a payment for services. Paragraph (d) of this section provides examples applying these rules to determine whether an arrangement is a payment for services.

(b) *Elements necessary to characterize arrangements as disguised payments for services*.—(1) *In general*.—An arrangement will be treated as a disguised payment for services if—

(i) A person (service provider), either in a partner capacity or in anticipation of becoming a partner, performs services (directly or through its delegate) to or for the benefit of a partnership;

(ii) There is a related direct or indirect allocation and distribution to such service provider; and

(iii) The performance of such services and the allocation and distribution, when viewed together, are properly characterized as a transaction occurring between the partnership and a person acting other than in that person's capacity as a partner.

(2) *Application and timing*.—(i) *Timing and effect of the determination*.—Whether an arrangement is properly characterized as a payment for services is determined at the time the arrangement is entered into or modified and without regard to whether the terms of the arrangement require the allocation and distribution to occur in the same taxable year. An arrangement that is treated as a payment for services under this paragraph (b) is treated as a payment for services for all purposes of the Internal Revenue Code, including for example, sections 61, 409A, and 457A (as applicable). The amount paid to a person in consideration for services under this section is treated as a payment for services provided to the partnership, and, when appropriate, the partnership must capitalize these amounts (or otherwise treat such amounts in a manner consistent with their recharacterization). The partnership must also treat the arrangement as a payment to a non-partner in determining the remaining partners' shares of taxable income or loss.

(ii) *Timing of inclusion*.—The inclusion of income by the service provider and deduction (if applicable) by the partnership of amounts paid pursuant to an arrangement that is characterized as a payment for services under paragraph (b)(1) of this section is taken into account in the taxable year as required under applicable law by applying all relevant sections of the Internal Revenue Code, including for example, sections 409A and 457A (as applicable), to the allocation and distribution when they occur (or are deemed to occur under all other provisions of the Internal Revenue Code).

(3) *Application of disguised payment rules.*—If a person purports to provide services to a partnership in a capacity as a partner or in anticipation of becoming a partner, the rules of this section apply for purposes of determining whether the services were provided in exchange for a disguised payment, even if it is determined after applying the rules of this section that the service provider is not a partner. If after applying the rules of this section, no partnership exists as a result of the service provider failing to become a partner under the arrangement, then the service provider is treated as having provided services directly to the other purported partner.

(c) *Factors considered.*—Whether an arrangement constitutes a payment for services (in whole or in part) depends on all of the facts and circumstances. Paragraphs (c)(1) through (6) of this section provide a non-exclusive list of factors that may indicate that an arrangement constitutes (in whole or in part) a payment for services. The presence or absence of a factor is based on all of the facts and circumstances at the time the parties enter into the arrangement (or if the parties modify the arrangement, at the time of the modification). The most important factor is significant entrepreneurial risk as set forth in paragraph (c)(1) of this section. An arrangement that lacks significant entrepreneurial risk constitutes a payment for services. An arrangement that has significant entrepreneurial risk will generally not constitute a payment for services unless other factors establish otherwise. For purposes of making determinations under this paragraph (c), the weight to be given to any particular factor, other than entrepreneurial risk, depends on the particular case and the absence of a factor is not necessarily indicative of whether or not an arrangement is treated as a payment for services.

(1) The arrangement lacks significant entrepreneurial risk. Whether an arrangement lacks significant entrepreneurial risk is based on the service provider's entrepreneurial risk relative to the overall entrepreneurial risk of the partnership. Paragraphs (c)(1)(i) through (v) of this section provide facts and circumstances that create a presumption that an arrangement lacks significant entrepreneurial risk and will be treated as a disguised payment for services unless other facts and circumstances establish the presence of significant entrepreneurial risk by clear and convincing evidence:

(i) Capped allocations of partnership income if the cap is reasonably expected to apply in most years;

(ii) An allocation for one or more years under which the service provider's share of income is reasonably certain;

(iii) An allocation of gross income;

(iv) An allocation (under a formula or otherwise) that is predominantly fixed in amount, is reasonably determinable under all the facts and circumstances, or is designed to assure that sufficient net profits are highly likely to be available to make the allocation to the service provider (e.g. if the partnership agreement provides for an allocation of net profits from specific transactions or accounting periods and this allocation does not depend on the long-term future success of the enterprise); or

(v) An arrangement in which a service provider waives its right to receive payment for the future performance of services in a manner that is non-binding or fails to timely notify the partnership and its partners of the waiver and its terms.

(2) The service provider holds, or is expected to hold, a transitory partnership interest or a partnership interest for only a short duration.

(3) The service provider receives an allocation and distribution in a time frame comparable to the time frame that a non-partner service provider would typically receive payment.

(4) The service provider became a partner primarily to obtain tax benefits that would not have been available if the services were rendered to the partnership in a third party capacity.

(5) The value of the service provider's interest in general and continuing partnership profits is small in relation to the allocation and distribution.

(6) The arrangement provides for different allocations or distributions with respect to different services received, the services are provided either by one person or by persons that are related under sections 707(b) or 267(b), and the terms of the differing allocations or distributions are subject to levels of entrepreneurial risk that vary significantly.

(d) *Examples.*—The following examples illustrate the application of this section:

Example 1. Partnership ABC constructed a building that is projected to generate $100,000 of gross income annually. A, an architect, performs services for partnership ABC for which A's normal fee would be $40,000 and contributes cash in an amount equal to the value of a 25 percent interest in the partnership. In exchange, A will receive a 25 percent distributive share for the life of the partnership and a special allocation of $20,000 of partnership gross income for the first two years of the partnership's operations. The ABC partnership agreement satisfies the requirements for economic effect contained in § 1.704-1(b)(2)(ii), including requiring that liquidating distributions are made in accordance with the partners' positive capital account balances. Under paragraph (c) of this section, whether the arrangement is treated as a payment for services depends on the facts and circumstances. The special allocation to A is a capped amount and the cap is reasonably expected to apply. The special allocation is also made out of gross income. Under paragraphs (c)(1)(i) and (iii) of this section, the capped allocations of income and gross income allocations described are presumed to lack significant entrepreneurial risk. No additional facts and circumstances establish otherwise by clear and convincing evidence. Thus, the allocation lacks significant entrepreneurial risk. Accordingly, the arrangement provides for a disguised payment for services as of the date that A and ABC enter into the arrangement and, pursuant to paragraph (b)(2)(ii) of this section, should be included in income by A in the time and manner required under applicable law as determined by applying all relevant sections of the Internal Revenue Code to the arrangement.

Example 2. A, a stock broker, agrees to effect trades for Partnership ABC without the normal brokerage commission. A contributes 51 percent of partnership capital and in exchange, receives a 51 percent interest in residual partnership profits and losses. In addition, A receives a special allocation of gross income that is computed in a manner which approximates its foregone commissions. The special allocation to A is computed by means of a formula similar to a normal brokerage fee and varies with the value and amount of services rendered rather than with the income of the partnership. It is reasonably expected that Partnership ABC will have sufficient gross income to make this allocation. The ABC partnership agreement satisfies the requirements for economic effect contained in § 1.704-1(b)(2)(ii), including requiring that liquidating distributions are made in accordance with the partners' positive capital account balances. Under paragraph (c) of this section, whether the arrangement is treated as a payment for services depends on the facts and circumstances. Under paragraphs (c)(1)(iii) and (iv) of this section, because the allocation is an allocation of gross income and is reasonably determinable under the facts and circumstances, it is presumed to lack significant entrepreneurial risk. No additional facts and circumstances establish otherwise by clear and convincing evidence. Thus, the allocation lacks significant entrepreneurial risk. Accordingly, the arrangement provides for a disguised payment for services as of the date that A and ABC enter into the arrangement and, pursuant to paragraph (b)(2)(ii) of this section, should be included in income by A in the time and manner required under applicable law as determined by applying all relevant sections of the Internal Revenue Code to the arrangement.

Example 3. (i) M performs services for which a fee would normally be charged to new partnership ABC, an investment partnership that will acquire a portfolio of investment assets that are not readily tradable on an established securities market. M will also contribute $500,000 in exchange for a one percent interest in ABC's capital and profits. In addition to M's one percent interest, M is entitled to receive a priority allocation and distribution of net gain from the sale of any one or more assets during any 12-month accounting period in which the partnership has overall net gain in an amount intended to approximate the fee that would normally be charged for the services M performs. A, a company that controls M, is the general partner of ABC and directs all operations of the partnership consistent with the partnership agreement, including causing ABC to purchase or sell an asset during any accounting period. A also controls the timing of distributions to M including distributions arising from M's priority allocation. Given the nature of the assets in which ABC will invest and A's ability to control the timing of asset dispositions, the amount of partnership net income or gains that will be allocable to M under the ABC partnership agreement is highly likely to be available and reasonably determinable based on all facts and circumstances available upon formation of the partnership. A will be allocated 10 percent of any net profits or net losses of ABC earned over the life of the partnership. A undertakes an enforceable obligation to repay any amounts allocated and distributed pursuant to this interest (reduced by reasonable allowances for tax payments made on A's allocable shares of partnership income and gain) that exceed 10 percent of the overall net amount of partnership profits computed over the life of the partnership (a "clawback obligation"). It is reasonable to anticipate that A could and would comply fully with any repayment responsibilities that arise pursuant to this obligation. The ABC partnership agreement satisfies the requirements for economic effect contained in § 1.704-1(b)(2)(ii), including requiring that liquidating distributions are made in accordance with the partners' positive capital account balances.

(ii) Under paragraph (c) of this section, whether A's arrangement is treated as a payment for services in directing ABC's operations depends on the facts and circumstances. The most important factor in this facts and circumstances determination is the presence or absence of significant entrepreneurial risk. The arrangement with respect to A creates significant entrepreneurial risk under paragraph (c)(1) of this section because the allocation to A is of net profits earned over the life of the partnership, the allocation is subject to a clawback obligation and it is reasonable to anticipate that A could and would comply with this obligation, and the allocation is neither reasonably determinable nor highly likely to be available. Additionally, other relevant factors do not establish that the arrangement should be treated as a payment for services. Thus, the arrangement with respect to A does not constitute a payment for services for purposes of paragraph (b)(1) of this section.

(iii) Under paragraph (c) of this section, whether M's arrangement is treated as a payment for services depends on the facts and circumstances. The most important factor in this facts and circumstances determination is the presence or absence of entrepreneurial risk. The priority allocation to M is an allocation of net profit from any 12-month accounting period in which the partnership has net gain, and thus it does not depend on the overall success of the enterprise. Moreover, the sale of the assets by ABC, and hence the timing of recognition of gains and losses, is controlled by A, a company related to M. Taken in combination, the facts indicate that the allocation is reasonably determinable under all the facts and circumstances and that sufficient net profits are highly likely to be available to make the priority allocation to the service provider. As a result, the allocation presumptively lacks significant entrepreneurial risk. No additional facts and circumstances establish otherwise by clear and convincing evidence. Accordingly, the arrangement provides for a disguised payment for services as of the date M and ABC enter into the arrangement and, pursuant to paragraph (b)(2)(ii) of this section, should be included in income by M in the time and manner required under applicable law as determined by applying all relevant sections of the Internal Revenue Code to the arrangement.

(iv) Assume the facts are the same as paragraph (i) of this example, except that the partnership can also fund M's priority allocation and distribution of net gain from the revaluation of any partnership assets pursuant to § 1.704-1(b)(2)(iv)(f). As the general partner of ABC, A controls the timing of events that permit revaluation of partnership assets and assigns values to those assets for purposes of the revaluation. Under paragraph (c) of this section, whether M's arrangement is treated as a payment for services depends on the facts and circumstances. The most important factor in this facts and circumstances determination is the presence or absence of significant entrepreneurial risk. Under this arrangement, the valuation of the assets is controlled by A, a company related to M, and the assets of the company are difficult to value. This fact, taken in combination with the partnership's determination of M's profits by reference to a specified accounting period, causes the allocation to be reasonably determinable under all the facts and circumstances or to ensure that net profits are highly likely to be available to make the priority allocation to the service provider. No additional facts and circumstances establish otherwise by clear and convincing evidence. Accordingly, the arrangement provides for a disguised payment for services as of the date M and ABC enter into the arrangement and, pursuant to paragraph (b)(2)(ii) of this section, should be included in income by M in time and manner required under applicable law as determined by applying all relevant sections of the Internal Revenue Code to the arrangement.

Example 4. (i) The facts are the same as in *Example 3*, except that ABC's investment assets are securities that are readily tradable on an established securities market, and ABC is in the trade or business of trading in securities and has validly elected to mark-to-market under section 475(f)(1). In addition, M is entitled to receive a special allocation and distribution of partnership net gain attributable to a specified future 12-month taxable year. Although it is expected that one or more of the partnership's assets will be sold for a gain, it cannot reasonably be predicted whether the partnership will have net profits with respect to its entire portfolio in that 12-month taxable year.

(ii) Under paragraph (c) of this section, whether the arrangement is treated as a payment for services depends on the facts and circumstances. The most important factor in this facts and circumstances determination is the presence or absence of significant entrepreneurial risk. The special allocation to M is allocable out of net profits, the partnership assets have a readily ascertainable market value that is determined at the close of each taxable year, and it cannot reasonably be predicted whether the partnership will have net profits with respect to its entire portfolio for the year to which the special allocation would relate. Accordingly, the special allocation is neither reasonably determinable nor highly likely to be available because the partnership assets have a readily ascertainable fair market value that is determined at the beginning of the year and at the end of the year. Thus, the arrangement does not lack significant entrepreneurial risk under paragraph (c)(1) of this section. Additionally, the facts and circumstances do not establish the presence of other factors that would suggest that the arrangement is properly characterized as a payment for services. Accordingly, the arrangement does not constitute a payment for services under paragraph (b)(1) of this section.

Example 5. (i) A is a general partner in newly-formed partnership ABC, an investment fund. A is responsible for providing management services to ABC, but has delegated that management function to M, a company controlled by A. Funds that are comparable to ABC commonly require the general partner to contribute capital in an amount equal to one percent of the capital contributed by the limited partners, provide the general partner with an interest in 20 percent of future partnership net income and gains as measured over the life of the fund, and pay the fund manager annually an amount equal to two percent of capital committed by the partners.

(ii) Upon formation of ABC, the partners of ABC execute a partnership agreement with terms that differ from those commonly agreed upon by other comparable funds. The ABC partnership agreement provides that A will contribute nominal capital to ABC, that ABC will annually pay M an amount equal to one percent of capital committed by the partners, and that A will receive an interest in 20 percent of future partnership net income and gains as measured over the life of the fund. A will also receive an additional interest in future partnership net income and gains determined by a formula (the "Additional Interest"). The parties intend that the estimated present value of the Additional Interest approximately equals the present value of one percent of capital committed by the partners determined annually over the life of the fund. However, the amount of net profits that will be allocable to A under the Additional Interest is neither highly likely to be available nor reasonably determinable based on all facts and circumstances available upon formation of the partnership. A undertakes a clawback obligation, and it is reasonable to anticipate that A could and would comply fully with any repayment responsibilities that arise pursuant to this obligation. The ABC partnership agreement satisfies the requirements for economic effect contained in § 1.704-1(b)(2)(ii), including requiring that liquidating distributions are made in accordance with the partners' positive capital account balances.

(iii) Under paragraph (c) of this section, whether the arrangement relating to the Additional Interest is treated as a payment for services depends on the facts and circumstances. The most important factor in this facts and circumstances determination is the presence or absence of significant entrepreneurial risk. The arrangement with respect to A creates significant entrepreneurial risk under paragraph (c)(1) of this section because the allocation to A is of net profits, the allocation is subject to a clawback obligation over the life of the fund and it is reasonable to anticipate that A could and would comply with this obligation, and the allocation is neither reasonably determinable nor highly likely to be available. Additionally, the facts and circumstances do not establish the presence of other factors that would suggest that the arrangement is properly characterized as a payment for services. Accordingly, the arrangement does not constitute a payment for services under paragraph (b)(1) of this section.

Example 6. (i) A is a general partner in limited partnership ABC, an investment fund. A is responsible for providing management services to ABC, but has delegated that management function to M, a company controlled by A. The ABC partnership agreement provides that A must contribute capital in an amount equal to one percent of the capital contributed by the limited partners, that A is entitled to an interest in 20 percent of future partnership net income and gains as measured over the life of the fund, and that M is entitled to receive an annual fee in an amount equal to two percent of capital committed by the partners. The amount of partnership net income or gains that will be allocable to A under the ABC partnership agreement is neither highly likely to be available nor reasonably determinable based on all facts and circumstances available upon formation of the partnership. A also undertakes a clawback obligation, and it is reasonable to anticipate that A could and would comply fully with any repayment responsibilities that arise pursuant to this obligation.

(ii) ABC's partnership agreement also permits M (as A's appointed delegate) to waive all or a portion of its fee for any year if it provides written notice to the limited partners of ABC at least 60 days prior to the commencement of the partnership taxable year for which the fee is payable. If M elects to waive irrevocably its fee pursuant to this provision, the partnership will, immediately following the commencement of the partnership taxable year for which the fee would have been payable, issue to M an interest determined by a formula in subsequent partnership net income and gains (the "Additional Interest"). The parties intend that the estimated present value of the Additional Interest approximately equals the estimated present value of the fee that was waived. However, the amount of net income or gains that will be allocable to M is neither highly likely to be available nor reasonably determinable based on all facts and circumstances available at the time of the waiver of the fee. The ABC partnership agreement satisfies the requirements for economic effect contained in § 1.704-1(b)(2)(ii), including requiring that liquidating distributions are made in accordance with the partners' positive capital account balances. The partnership agreement also requires ABC to maintain capital accounts pursuant to § 1.704-1(b)(2)(iv) and to revalue partner capital accounts under § 1.704-1(b)(2)(iv)(f) immediately prior to the issuance of the partnership interest to M. M undertakes a clawback obligation, and it is reasonable to anticipate that M could and would comply fully with any repayment responsibilities that arise pursuant to this obligation.

(iii) Under paragraph (c) of this section, whether the arrangements relating to A's 20 percent interest in future partnership net income and gains and M's Additional Interest are treated as payment for services depends on the facts and circumstances. The most important factor in this facts and circumstances determination is the presence or absence of significant entrepreneurial risk. The allocations to A and M do not presumptively lack significant entrepreneurial risk under paragraph (c)(1) of this section because the allocations are based on net profits, the allocations are subject to a clawback obligation over the life of the fund and it is reasonable to anticipate that A and M could and would comply with this obligation, and the allocations are neither reasonably determinable nor highly likely to be available. Additionally, the facts and circumstances do not establish the presence of other factors that would suggest that the arrangement is properly characterized as a payment for services. Accordingly, the arrangements do not constitute payment for services under paragraph (b)(1) of this section. [Prop. Reg. § 1.707-2.]

[Proposed 7-23-2015 (corrected 8-19-2015).]

§ 1.707-3. Disguised sales of property to partnership; general rules.—(a) *Treatment of transfers as a sale.*—(1) *In general.*—Except as otherwise provided in this section, if a transfer of property by a partner to a partnership and one or more transfers of money or other consideration by the partnership to that partner are described in paragraph (b)(1) of this section, the transfers are treated as a sale of property, in whole or in part, to the partnership.

(2) *Definition and timing of sale.*—For purposes of §§ 1.707-3 through 1.707-5, the use of the term *sale* (or any variation of that word) to refer to a transfer of property by a partner to a partnership and a transfer of consideration by a partnership to a partner means a sale or exchange of that property, in whole or in part, to the partnership by the partner acting in a capacity other than as a member of the partnership, rather than a contribution and distribution to which sections 721 and 731, respectively, apply. A transfer that is treated as a sale under paragraph (a)(1) of this section is treated as a sale for all purposes of the Internal Revenue Code (*e.g.,* sections 453, 483, 1001, 1012, 1031 and 1274). The sale is considered to take place on the date that, under general principles of Federal tax law, the partnership is considered the owner of the property. If the transfer of money or other consideration from the partnership to the partner occurs after the transfer of property to the partnership, the partner and the partnership are treated as if, on the date of the sale, the partnership transferred to the partner an obligation to transfer to the partner money or other consideration.

(3) *Application of disguised sale rules.*—If a person purports to transfer property to a partnership in a capacity as a partner, the rules of this section apply for purposes of determining whether the property was transferred in a disguised sale, even if it is determined after the application of the rules of this section that such person is not a partner. If after the application of the rules of this section to a purported transfer of property to a partnership, it is determined that no partnership exists because the property was actually sold, or it is otherwise determined that the contributed property is not owned by the partnership for tax purposes, the transferor of the property is treated as having sold the property to the person (or persons) that acquired ownership of the property for tax purposes.

(4) *Deemed terminations under section 708.*—In applying the rules of this section, transfers resulting from a termination of a partnership under section 708(b)(1)(B) are disregarded.

(b) *Transfers treated as a sale.*—(1) *In general.*—A transfer of property (excluding money or an obligation to contribute money) by a partner to a partnership and a transfer of money or other consideration (including the assumption of or the taking subject to a liability) by the partnership to the partner constitute a sale of property, in whole or in part, by the partner to the partnership only if based on all the facts and circumstances—

(i) The transfer of money or other consideration would not have been made but for the transfer of property; and

(ii) In cases in which the transfers are not made simultaneously, the subsequent transfer is not dependent on the entrepreneurial risks of partnership operations.

(2) *Facts and circumstances.*—The determination of whether a transfer of property by a partner to the partnership and a transfer of money or other consideration by the partnership to the partner constitute a sale, in whole or

in part, under paragraph (b)(1) of this section is made based on all the facts and circumstances in each case. The weight to be given each of the facts and circumstances will depend on the particular case. Generally, the facts and circumstances existing on the date of the earliest of such transfers are the ones considered in determining whether a sale exists under paragraph (b)(1) of this section. Among the facts and circumstances that may tend to prove the existence of a sale under paragraph (b)(1) of this section are the following:

(i) That the timing and amount of a subsequent transfer are determinable with reasonable certainty at the time of an earlier transfer;

(ii) That the transferor has a legally enforceable right to the subsequent transfer;

(iii) That the partner's right to receive the transfer of money or other consideration is secured in any manner, taking into account the period during which it is secured;

(iv) That any person has made or is legally obligated to make contributions to the partnership in order to permit the partnership to make the transfer of money or other consideration;

(v) That any person has loaned or has agreed to loan the partnership the money or other consideration required to enable the partnership to make the transfer, taking into account whether any such lending obligation is subject to contingencies related to the results of partnership operations;

(vi) That the partnership has incurred or is obligated to incur debt to acquire the money or other consideration necessary to permit it to make the transfer, taking into account the likelihood that the partnership will be able to incur that debt (considering such factors as whether any person has agreed to guarantee or otherwise assume personal liability for that debt);

(vii) That the partnership holds money or other liquid assets, beyond the reasonable needs of the business, that are expected to be available to make the transfer (taking into account the income that will be earned from those assets);

(viii) That partnership distributions, allocations or control of partnership operations is designed to effect an exchange of the burdens and benefits of ownership of property;

(ix) That the transfer of money or other consideration by the partnership to the partner is disproportionately large in relationship to the partner's general and continuing interest in partnership profits; and

(x) That the partner has no obligation to return or repay the money or other consideration to the partnership, or has such an obligation but it is likely to become due at such a distant point in the future that the present value of that obligation is small in relation to the amount of money or other consideration transferred by the partnership to the partner.

(c) *Transfers made within two years presumed to be a sale—*.—(1) *In general.*—For purposes of this section, if within a two-year period a partner transfers property to a partnership and the partnership transfers money or other consideration to the partner (without regard to the order of the transfers), the transfers are presumed to be a sale of the property to the partnership unless the facts and circumstances clearly establish that the transfers do not constitute a sale.

(2) *Disclosure of transfers made within two years.*—Disclosure to the Internal Revenue Service in accordance with § 1.707-8 is required if—

(i) A partner transfers property to a partnership and the partnership transfers money or other consideration to the partner within a two-year period (without regard to the order of the transfers);

(ii) The partner treats the transfers other than as a sale for tax purposes; and

(iii) The transfer of money or other consideration to the partner is not presumed to be a guaranteed payment for capital under § 1.707-4(a)(1)(ii), is not a reasonable preferred return within the meaning of § 1.707-4(a)(3), and is not an operating cash flow distribution within the meaning of § 1.707-4(b)(2).

(d) *Transfers made more than two years apart presumed not to be a sale.*—For purposes of this section, if a transfer of money or other consideration to a partner by a partnership and the transfer of property to the partnership by that partner are more than two years apart, the transfers are presumed not to be a sale of the property to the partnership unless the facts and circumstances clearly establish that the transfers constitute a sale.

(e) *Scope.*—This section and §§ 1.707-4 through 1.707-9 apply to contributions and distributions of property described in section 707(a)(2)(A) and transfers described in section 707(a)(2)(B) of the Internal Revenue Code.

(f) *Examples.*—The following examples illustrate the application of this section.

Example 1. Treatment of simultaneous transfers as a sale. A transfers property X to partnership AB on April 9, 1992, in exchange for an interest in the partnership. At the time of the transfer, property X has a fair market value of $4,000,000 and an adjusted tax basis of $1,200,000. Immediately after the transfer, the partnership transfers $3,000,000 in cash to A.

Assume that, under this section, the partnership's transfer of cash to A is treated as part of a sale of property X to the partnership. Because the amount of cash A receives on April 9, 1992, does not equal the fair market value of the property, A is considered to have sold a portion of property X with a value of $3,000,000 to the partnership in exchange for the cash. Accordingly, A must recognize $2,100,000 of gain ($3,000,000 amount realized less $900,000 adjusted tax basis ($1,200,000 multiplied by $3,000,000/$4,000,000)). Assuming A receives no other transfers that are treated as consideration for the sale of the property under this section, A is considered to have contributed to the partnership, in A's capacity as a partner, $1,000,000 of the fair market value of the property with an adjusted tax basis of $300,000.

Example 2. Treatment of transfers at different times as a sale. (i) The facts are the same as in *Example 1*, except that the $3,000,000 is transferred to A one year after A's transfer of property X to the partnership. Assume that under this section the partnership's transfer of cash to A is treated as part of a sale of property X to the partnership. Assume also that the applicable Federal short-term rate for April, 1992, is 10 percent, compounded semiannually.

(ii) Under paragraph (a)(2) of this section, A and the partnership are treated as if, on April 9, 1992, A sold a portion of property X to the partnership in exchange for an obligation to transfer $3,000,000 to A one year later. Section 1274 applies to this obligation because it does not bear interest and is payable more than six months after the date of the sale. As a result, A's amount realized from the receipt of the partnership's obligation will be the imputed principal amount of the partnership's obligation to transfer $3,000,000 to A, which equals $2,721,088 (the present value on April 9, 1992, of a $3,000,000 payment due one year later, determined using a discount rate of 10 percent, compounded semiannually). Therefore, A's amount realized from the receipt of the partnership's obligation is $2,721,088 (without regard to whether the sale is reported under the installment method). A is therefore considered to have sold only $2,721,088 of the fair market value of property X. The remainder of the $3,000,000 payment ($278,912) is characterized in accordance with the provisions of section 1272. Accordingly, A must recognize $1,904,761 of gain ($2,721,088 amount realized less $816,327 adjusted tax basis ($1,200,000 multiplied by $2,721,088/$4,000,000)) on the sale of property X to the partnership. The gain is reportable under the installment method of section 453 if the sale is otherwise eligible. Assuming A receives no other transfers that are treated as consideration for the sale of property under this section, A is considered to have contributed to the partnership, in A's capacity as a partner, $1,278,912 of the fair market value of property X with an adjusted tax basis of $383,673.

Example 3. Operation of presumption for transfers within two years. (i) C transfers undeveloped land to the CD partnership in exchange for an interest in the partnership. The partnership intends to construct a building on the land. At the time the land is transferred to the partnership, it is unencumbered and has an adjusted tax basis of $500,000 and a fair market value of $1,000,000. The partnership agreement provides that upon completing construction of the building the partnership will distribute $900,000 to C.

(ii) If, within two years of C's transfer of land to the partnership, a transfer is made to C pursuant to the provision requiring a distribution upon completion of the building, the transfer is presumed to be, under paragraph (c) of this section, part of a sale of the land to the partnership. C may rebut the presumption that the transfer is part of a sale if the facts and circumstances clearly establish that—

(A) The transfer to C would have been made without regard to C's transfer of land to the partnership; or

(B) The partnership's obligation or ability to make this transfer to C depends, at the time of the transfer to the partnership, on the entrepreneurial risks of partnership operations.

(iii) For example, if the partnership will be able to fund the transfer of cash to C only to the extent that permanent loan proceeds exceed the cost of constructing the building, the fact that excess permanent loan proceeds will be available only if the cost to complete the building is significantly less than the amount projected by a reasonable budget would be evidence that the transfer to C is not part of a sale. Similarly, a condition that limits the amount of the permanent loan to the cost of constructing the building (and thereby limits the partnership's ability to make a transfer to C) unless all or a substantial portion of the building is leased would be evidence that the transfer to C is not part of a sale, if a significant risk exists that the partnership may not be able to lease the building to that extent. Another factor that may prove that the transfer of cash to C is not part of a sale would be that, at the time the land is transferred to the partnership, no lender has committed to make a permanent loan to fund the transfer of cash to C.

(iv) Facts indicating that the transfer of cash to C is not part of a sale, however, may be offset by other factors. An offsetting factor to restrictions on the permanent loan proceeds may be that the permanent loan is to be a recourse loan and certain conditions to the loan are likely to be waived by the lender because of the creditworthiness of the partners or the value of the partnership's other assets. Similarly, the factor that no lender has committed to fund the transfer of cash to C may be offset by facts establishing that the partnership is obligated to attempt to obtain such a loan and that its ability to obtain such a loan is not significantly dependent on the value that will be added by successful completion of the building, or that the partnership reasonably anticipates that it will have (and will utilize) an alternative source to fund the transfer of cash to C if the permanent loan proceeds are inadequate.

* * *

[Reg. § 1.707-3.]

☐ [*T.D.* 8439, 9-25-92.]

§ 1.707-4. Disguised sales of property to partnership; special rules applicable to guaranteed payments, preferred returns, operating cash flow distributions, and reimbursements of preformation expenditures.—(a) *Guaranteed payments and preferred returns.*—(1) *Guaranteed payment not treated as part of a sale.*—(i) *In general.*—A guaranteed payment for capital made to a partner is not treated as part of a sale of property under § 1.707-3(a) (relating to treatment of transfers as a sale). A party's characterization of a payment as a guaranteed payment for capital will not control in determining whether a payment is, in fact, a guaranteed payment for capital. The term *guaranteed payment for capital* means any payment to a partner by a partnership that is determined without regard to partnership income and is for the use of that partner's capital. *See* section 707(c). For this purpose, one or more payments are not made for the use of a partner's capital if the payments are designed to liquidate all or part of the partner's interest in property contributed to the partnership rather than to provide the partner with a return on an investment in the partnership.

(ii) *Reasonable guaranteed payments.*—Notwithstanding the presumption set forth in § 1.707-3(c) (relating) to transfers made within two years of each other), for purposes of section 707(a)(2) and the regulations thereunder a transfer of money to a partner that is characterized by the parties as a guaranteed payment for capital, is determined without regard to the income of the partnership and is reasonable (within the meaning of paragraph (a)(3) of this section) is presumed to be a guaranteed payment for capital unless the facts and circumstances clearly establish that the transfer is not a guaranteed payment for capital and is part of a sale.

(iii) *Unreasonable guaranteed payments.*—A transfer of money to a partner that is characterized by the parties as a guaranteed payment for capital but that is not reasonable (within the meaning of paragraph (a)(3) of this section) is presumed not to be a guaranteed payment for capital unless the facts and circumstances clearly establish that the transfer is a guaranteed payment for capital. A transfer that is not a guaranteed payment for capital is subject to the rules of § 1.707-3.

(2) *Presumption regarding reasonable preferred returns.*—Notwithstanding the presumption set forth in § 1.707-3(c) (relating to transfers made within two years of each other), a transfer of money to a partner that is characterized by the parties as a preferred return and that is reasonable (within the meaning of paragraph (a)(3) of this section) is presumed not to be part of a sale of property to the partnership unless the facts and circumstances (including the likelihood and expected timing of the subsequent allocation of income or gain to support the preferred return) clearly establish that the transfer is part of a sale. The term *preferred return* means a preferential distribution of partnership cash flow to a partner with respect to capital contributed to the partnership by the partner that will be matched, to the extent available, by an allocation of income or gain.

(3) *Definition of reasonable preferred returns and guaranteed payments.*—(i) *In general.*—A transfer of money to a partner that is characterized as a preferred return or guaranteed payment for capital is reasonable only to the extent that the transfer is made to the partner pursuant to a written provision of a partnership agreement that provides for payment for the use of capital in a reasonable amount, and only to the extent that the payment is made for the use of capital after the date on which that provision is added to the partnership agreement.

(ii) *Reasonable amount.*—A transfer of money that is made to a partner during any partnership taxable year and is characterized as a preferred return or guaranteed payment for capital is reasonable in amount if the sum of any preferred return and any guaranteed payment for capital that is payable for that year does not exceed the amount determined by multiplying either the partner's unreturned capital at the beginning of the year or, at the partner's option, the partner's weighted average capital balance for the year (with either amount appropriately adjusted, taking into account the relevant compounding periods, to reflect any unpaid preferred return or guaranteed payment for capital that is payable to the partner) by the safe harbor interest rate for that year. The safe harbor interest rate for a partnership's taxable year equals 150 percent of the highest applicable Federal rate, at the appropriate compounding period or periods, in effect at any time from the time that the right to the preferred return or guaranteed payment for capital is first established pursuant to a binding, written agreement among the partners through the end of the taxable year. A partner's unreturned capital equals the excess of the aggregate amount of money and the fair market value of other consideration (net of liabilities) contributed by the partner to the partnership over the aggregate amount of money and the fair market value of other consideration (net of liabilities) distributed by the partnership to the partner other than transfers of money that are presumed to be guaranteed payments for capital under paragraph (a) (1) (ii) of this section, transfers of money that are reasonable preferred returns within the meaning of this paragraph (a) (3), and operating cash flow distributions within the meaning of paragraph (b) (2) of this section.

(4) *Examples.*—The following examples illustrate the application of paragraph (a) of this section:

Example 1. Transfer presumed to be a guaranteed payment. (i) A transfers property with a fair market value of $100,000 to partnership AB. At the time of A's transfer, the partnership agreement is amended to provide that A is to receive a guaranteed payment for the use of A's capital of 10 percent (compounded annually) of the fair market value of the transferred property in each of the three years following the transfer. The partnership agreement provides that partnership net taxable income and loss will be allocated equally between partners A and B, and that partnership cash flow will be distributed in accordance with the allocation of partnership net taxable income and loss. The partnership would be allowed a deduction in the year paid if the transfers made to A are treated as guaranteed payments under section 707(c). Under the partnership agreement, that deduction would be allocated in the same manner as any other item of partnership deduction. The partnership agreement complies with the requirements of § 1.704-1(b) (2) (ii) (*b*). The partnership agreement does not provide for the payment of a preferred return and, other than the guaranteed payment to be paid to A, no transfer is expected to be made during the three year period following A's transfer that is not an operating cash flow distribution (within the meaning of paragraph (b) (2) of this section). Assume that the highest applicable Federal rate in effect at the time of A's transfer is eight percent compounded annually.

(ii) The transfer of money to be made to A under the partnership agreement is characterized by the parties as a guaranteed payment for capital and is determined without regard to the income of the partnership. The transfer is also reasonable within the meaning of § 1.707-4(a) (3). The transfer, therefore, is presumed to be a guaranteed payment for capital. The presumption set forth in § 1.707-3(c) (relating to transfers made within two years of each other) thus does not apply to this transfer. The transfer will not be treated as part of a sale of property to the partnership unless the facts and circumstances clearly establish that the transfer is not a guaranteed payment for capital but is part of a sale.

(iii) The presumption that the transfer is a guaranteed payment for capital is not rebutted, because there are no facts indicating that the transfer is not a guaranteed payment for the use of capital.

Example 2. Transfers characterized as guaranteed payments treated as part of a sale. (i) C and D form partnership CD. C transfers property with a fair market value of $100,000 and an adjusted tax basis of $20,000 in exchange for a partnership interest. D is responsible for managing the day-to-day operations of the partnership and makes no capital contribution to the partnership upon its formation. The partnership agreement provides that C is to receive payments characterized as guaranteed payments and determined without regard to partnership income of $8,333 per year for the first four years of partnership operations for the use of C's capital. In addition, the partnership agreement provides that—

(A) Partnership net taxable income and loss will be allocated 75 percent to C and 25 percent to D; and

(B) All partnership cash flow (determined prior to consideration of the guaranteed payment) will be distributed 75 percent to C and 25 percent to D except that guaranteed payments that the partnership is obligated to make to C are payable solely out of D's share of the partnership's cash flow.

(ii) If D's share of the partnership's cash flow is not sufficient to make the guaranteed payment to C, then D is obligated to contribute any shortfall to the partnership, even in the event the partnership is liquidated. Thus, the effect of the guaranteed payment arrangement is that the guaranteed payment to C is funded entirely by D. The partnership agreement complies with the requirements of § 1.704-1(b) (2) (ii) (*b*). Assume that, at the time the partnership is formed, the partnership or D could borrow $25,000 pursuant to a loan requiring equal payments of principal and interest over a four-year term at the current market interest rate of approximately 12 percent (compounded annually). Assume that the highest applicable Federal rate in effect at the time the partnership is formed is 10 percent compounded annually.

(iii) The transfer of money to be made to C under the partnership agreement is characterized by the parties as a guaranteed payment for capital and is determined without regard to the income of the partnership. The transfer is also reasonable within the meaning of § 1.707-4(a)(3). The transfer, therefore, is presumed to be a guaranteed payment for capital. The presumption set forth in § 1.707-3(c) (relating to transfers made within two years of each other) thus does not apply to this transfer. The transfer will not be treated as part of a sale of property to the partnership unless the facts and circumstances clearly establish that the transfer is not a guaranteed payment for capital and is part of a sale.

(iv) For the first four years of partnership operations, the total guaranteed payments made to C under the partnership agreement will equal $33,332. If the characterization of those payments as guaranteed payments for capital within the meaning of section 707(c) were respected, C would be allocated $24,999 of the deductions that would be claimed by the partnership for those payments, thereby leaving the balance in C's capital account approximately $25,000 less than it would have been if the guaranteed payments had not been made. The guaranteed payments thus have the effect of offsetting approximately $25,000 of the credit made to C's capital account for the property transferred to the partnership by C. C's resulting capital account is approximately equivalent to the capital account C would have had if C had only contributed 75 percent of the property to the partnership. Furthermore, the effect of D's funding the guaranteed payment to C (either through reduced distributions of cash flow to D or additional contributions) is that D's capital account is approximately equivalent to the capital account D would have had if D had contributed 25 percent of the property (or contributed cash so that the partnership could purchase the 25 percent). Moreover, a $25,000 loan requiring equal payments of principal and interest over a four-year term at the current market interest rate of 12 percent (compounded annually), would have resulted in annual payments of principal and interest of $8,230.86. Consequently, the guaranteed payments effectively place the partners in the same economic position that they would have been in had D purchased a one-quarter interest in the property from C financed at the current market rate of interest, and then C and D each contributed their share of the property to the partnership. In view of the burden the guaranteed payments place on D's right to transfers of partnership cash flow and D's legal obligation to make contributions to the partnership to the extent necessary to fund the guaranteed payments, D has effectively purchased through the partnership a one-quarter interest in the property from C.

(v) Under these facts, the presumption that the transfers to C are guaranteed payments for capital is rebutted, because the facts and circumstances clearly establish that the transfers are part of a sale and not guaranteed payments for capital. Under § 1.707-3(a), C and the partnership are treated as if C sold a one-quarter interest in the property to the partnership in exchange for a promissory note evidencing the partnership's obligation to make the guaranteed payments.

(b) *Presumption regarding operating cash flow distributions.*—(1) *In general.*—Notwithstanding the presumption set forth in § 1.707-3(c) (relating to transfers made within two years of each other), an operating cash flow distribution is presumed not to be part of a sale of property to the partnership unless the facts and circumstances clearly establish that the transfer is part of a sale.

(2) *Operating cash flow distributions.*—(i) *In general.*—One or more transfers of money by the partnership to a partner during a taxable year of the partnership are operating cash flow distributions for purposes of paragraph (b)(1) of this section to the extent that those transfers are not presumed to be guaranteed payments for capital under paragraph (a)(1)(ii) of this section, are not reasonable preferred returns within the meaning of paragraph (a)(3) of this section, are not characterized by the parties as distributions to the partner acting in a capacity other than as a partner, and to the extent they do not exceed the product of the net cash flow of the partnership from operations for the year multiplied by the lesser of the partner's percentage interest in overall partnership profits for that year or the partner's percentage interest in overall partnership profits for the life of the partnership. For purposes of the preceding sentence, the net cash flow of the partnership from operations for a taxable year is an amount equal to the taxable income or loss of the partnership arising in the ordinary course of the partnership's business and investment activities, increased by tax exempt interest, depreciation, amortization, cost recovery allowances and other noncash charges deducted in determining such taxable income and decreased by—

(A) Principal payments made on any partnership indebtedness;

(B) Property replacement or contingency reserves actually established by the partnership;

(C) Capital expenditures when made other than from reserves or from borrowings the proceeds of which are not included in operating cash flow; and

(D) Any other cash expenditures (including preferred returns) not deducted in determining such taxable income or loss.

(ii) *Operating cash flow safe harbor.*—For any taxable year, in determining a partner's operating cash flow distributions for the year, the partner may use the partner's smallest percentage interest under the terms of the partnership agreement in any material item of partnership income or gain that may be realized by the partnership in the three-year period beginning with such taxable year. This provision is merely intended to provide taxpayers with a safe harbor and is not intended to preclude a taxpayer from using a different percentage under the rules of paragraph (b)(2)(i) of this section.

(iii) *Tiered partnerships.*—In the case of tiered partnerships, the upper-tier partnership must take into account its share of the net cash flow from operations of the lower-tier partnership applying principles similar to those described in paragraph (b)(2)(i) of this section, so that the amount of the upper-tier partnership's operating cash flow distributions is neither overstated nor understated.

(c) *Accumulation of guaranteed payments, preferred returns, and operating cash flow distributions.*—Guaranteed payments for capital, preferred returns, and operating cash flow distributions presumed not to be part of a sale under the rules of paragraphs (a) and (b) of this section do not lose the benefit of the presumption by reason of being retained for distribution in a later year.

(d) *Exception for reimbursements of preformation expenditures.*—(1) *In general.*—A transfer of money or other consideration by the partnership to a partner is not treated as part of a sale of property by the partner to the partnership under § 1.707-3(a) (relating to treatment of transfers as a sale) to the extent that the transfer to the partner by the partnership is made to reimburse the partner for, and does not exceed the amount of, capital expenditures that—

(i) Are incurred during the two-year period preceding the transfer by the partner to the partnership; and

(ii) Are incurred by the partner with respect to—

(A) Partnership organization and syndication costs described in section 709; or

(B) Property transferred to the partnership by the partner, but only to the extent the reimbursed capital expenditures do not exceed 20 percent of the fair market value of such property at the time of the transfer (the 20-percent limitation). However, the 20-percent limitation of this paragraph (d)(1)(ii)(B) does not apply if the fair market value of the transferred property does not exceed 120 percent of the partner's adjusted basis in the transferred property at the time of the transfer (the 120-percent test). This paragraph (d)(1)(ii)(B) shall be applied on a property-by-property basis, except that a partner may aggregate any of the transferred property under this paragraph (d)(1) to the extent—

(1) The total fair market value of such aggregated property (of which no single property's fair market value exceeds 1 percent of the total fair market value of such aggregated property) is not greater than the lesser of 10 percent of the total fair market value of all property, excluding money and marketable securities (as defined under section 731(c)), transferred by the partner to the partnership, or $1,000,000;

(2) The partner uses a reasonable aggregation method that is consistently applied; and

(3) Such aggregation of property is not part of a plan a principal purpose of which is to avoid §§ 1.707-3 through 1.707-5.

(C) [Reserved].

(2) *Capital expenditures incurred by another person.*—For purposes of paragraph (d)(1) of this section, a partner steps in the shoes of a person (to the extent the person was not previously reimbursed under paragraph (d)(1) of this section) with respect to capital expenditures the person incurred with respect to property transferred to the partnership by the partner to the extent the partner acquired the property from the person in a nonrecognition transaction described in section 351, 381(a), 721, or 731.

(3) *Contribution of a partnership interest with capital expenditures property.*—If a person transfers property with respect to which the person incurred capital expenditures (capital expenditures property) to a partnership (lower-tier partnership) and, within the two-year period beginning on the date upon which the person incurred the capital expenditures, transfers an interest in the lower-tier partnership to another partnership (upper-tier partnership) in a nonrecognition transaction under section 721, the upper-tier partnership steps in the shoes of the person who transferred the capital expenditures property to the lower-tier partnership with respect to the capital expenditures that are not otherwise reimbursed to the person. The upper-tier partnership may be reimbursed by the lower-tier partnership under paragraph

(d)(1) of this section to the extent the person could have been reimbursed for the capital expenditures by the lower-tier partnership under paragraph (d)(1) of this section. In addition, for purposes of paragraph (d)(1) of this section, the person is deemed to have transferred the capital expenditures property to the upper-tier partnership and may be reimbursed by the upper-tier partnership under paragraph (d)(1) of this section to the extent the person could have been reimbursed for the capital expenditures by the lower-tier partnership under paragraph (d)(1) of this section and has not otherwise been previously reimbursed. The aggregate reimbursements for capital expenditures under this paragraph (d)(3) shall not exceed the amount that the person could have been reimbursed for such capital expenditures under paragraph (d)(1) of this section.

(4) *Special rule for qualified liabilities.*—(i) *In general.*—For purposes of paragraph (d)(1) of this section, if capital expenditures were funded by the proceeds of a qualified liability defined in § 1.707-5(a)(6)(i) that a partnership assumes or takes property subject to in connection with a transfer of property to the partnership by a partner, a transfer of money or other consideration by the partnership to the partner is not treated as made to reimburse the partner for such capital expenditures to the extent the transfer of money or other consideration by the partnership to the partner exceeds the partner's share of the qualified liability (as determined under § 1.707-5(a)(2), (3), and (4)). Capital expenditures are treated as funded by the proceeds of a qualified liability to the extent the proceeds are either traceable to the capital expenditures under § 1.163-8T or were actually used to fund the capital expenditures, irrespective of the tracing requirements under § 1.163-8T.

(ii) *Anti-abuse rule.*—If capital expenditures and a qualified liability are incurred under a plan a principal purpose of which is to avoid the requirements of paragraph (d)(4)(i) of this section, the capital expenditures are deemed funded by the qualified liability.

(5) *Scope of capital expenditures.*—For purposes of this section and § 1.707-5, the term *capital expenditures* has the same meaning as the term *capital expenditures* has under the Internal Revenue Code and applicable regulations, except that it includes capital expenditures taxpayers elect to deduct, and does not include deductible expenses taxpayers elect to treat as capital expenditures.

(6) *Example.*—The following example illustrates the application of paragraph (d) of this section:

Example. Intangible treated as separate property. (i) Z transfers to a partnership a business the material assets of which include a tangible asset and goodwill from the reputation of the business. At the time Z transfers the business to the partnership, the tangible asset has a fair market value of $550,000 and an adjusted basis of $450,000. The goodwill is a section 197 intangible with a fair market value of $100,000 and an adjusted basis of $0. Z incurred $130,000 of capital expenditures with respect to improvements to the tangible asset (which amount is reflected in its adjusted basis) one year preceding the transfer. Z would like to be reimbursed by the partnership for the capital expenditures with an amount that qualifies for the exception for reimbursement of preformation expenditures under paragraph (d)(1) of this section.

(ii) Under paragraph (d)(1)(ii)(B) of this section, the 20-percent limitation on reimbursed capital expenditures applies on a property-by-property basis. The 120-percent test also applies on a property-by-property basis. Accordingly, the tangible asset and the goodwill each constitutes a separate property. Z incurred the capital expenditures with respect to the tangible asset only. The $550,000 fair market value of the tangible asset exceeds 120 percent of Z's $450,000 adjusted basis in the asset at the time of the transfer (120 percent x $450,000 = $540,000). Thus, the 20-percent limitation applies so that the reimbursement of Z's $130,000 of capital expenditures is limited to 20 percent of the fair market value of the tangible asset, or $110,000 (20 percent x $550,000).

(e) *Other exceptions.*—The Commissioner may provide by guidance published in the Internal Revenue Bulletin that other payments or transfers to a partner are not treated as part of a sale for purposes of section 707(a)(2) and the regulations thereunder.

(f) *Ordering rule cross reference.*—For payments or transfers by a partnership to a partner to which the rules under this section and § 1.707-5(b) apply, see the ordering rule under § 1.707-5(b)(3). [Reg. § 1.707-4.]

☐ [*T.D.* 8439, 9-25-92. *Amended by T.D.* 9787, 10-4-2016.]

§ 1.707-5. Disguised sales of property to partnership; special rules relating to liabilities.—(a) *Liability assumed or taken subject to by partnership.*—(1) *In general.*—For purposes of this section and §§ 1.707-3 and 1.707-4, if a partnership assumes or takes property subject to a qualified liability (as defined in paragraph (a)(6) of this section) of a partner, the partnership is treated as transferring consideration to the partner only to the extent provided in paragraph (a)(5) of this section. By contrast, if the partnership assumes or takes property subject to a liability of the partner other than a qualified liability, the partnership is treated as transferring consideration to the partner to the extent that the amount of the liability exceeds the partner's share of that liability immediately after the partnership assumes or takes subject to the liability as provided in paragraphs (a)(2), (3) and (4) of this section.

(2) *Partner's share of liability.*—A partner's share of any liability of the partnership is determined under the following rules:

(i) *Recourse liability.*—A partner's share of a recourse liability of the partnership equals the partner's share of the liability under the rules of section 752 and the regulations in this part under section 752. A partnership liability is a recourse liability to the extent that the obligation is a recourse liability under § 1.752-1(a)(1) or would be treated as a recourse liability under that section if it were treated as a partnership liability for purposes of that section.

(ii) *Nonrecourse liability.*—A partner's share of a nonrecourse liability of the partnership is determined by applying the same percentage used to determine the partner's share of the excess nonrecourse liability under § 1.752-3(a)(3). A partnership liability is a nonrecourse liability of the partnership to the extent that the obligation is a nonrecourse liability under § 1.752-1(a)(2) or would be a nonrecourse liability of the partnership under § 1.752-1(a)(2) if it were treated as a partnership liability for purposes of that section.

(3) *Reduction of partner's share of liability.*—For purposes of this section, a partner's share of a liability, immediately after a partnership assumes or takes property subject to the liability, is determined by taking into account a subsequent reduction in the partner's share if—

(i) At the time that the partnership assumes or takes property subject to the liability, it is anticipated that the transferring partner's share of the liability will be subsequently reduced;

(ii) The anticipated reduction is not subject to the entrepreneurial risks of partnership operations; and

(iii) The reduction of the partner's share of the liability is part of a plan that has as one of its principal purposes minimizing the extent to which the assumption of or taking property subject to the liability is treated as part of a sale under § 1.707–3.

(4) *Special rule applicable to transfers of encumbered property to a partnership by more than one partner pursuant to a plan.*—For purposes of paragraph (a)(1) of this section, if the partnership assumes or takes property or properties subject to the liabilities of more than one partner pursuant to a plan, a partner's share of the liabilities assumed or taken subject to by the partnership pursuant to that plan immediately after the transfers equals the sum of that partner's shares of the liabilities (other than that partner's qualified liabilities, as defined in paragraph (a)(6) of this section) assumed or taken subject to by the partnership pursuant to the plan. This paragraph (a)(4) does not apply to any liability assumed or taken subject to by the partnership with a principal purpose of reducing the extent to which any other liability assumed or taken subject to by the partnership is treated as a transfer of consideration under paragraph (a)(1) of this section.

(5) *Special rule applicable to qualified liabilities.*—(i) If a transfer of property by a partner to a partnership is not otherwise treated as part of a sale, the partnership's assumption of or taking subject to a qualified liability in connection with a transfer of property is not treated as part of a sale. If a transfer of property by a partner to the partnership is treated as part of a sale without regard to the partnership's assumption of or taking subject to a qualified liability (as defined in paragraph (a)(6) of this section) in connection with the transfer of property, the partnership's assumption of or taking subject to that liability is treated as a transfer of consideration made pursuant to a sale of such property to the partnership only to the extent of the lesser of—

(A) The amount of consideration that the partnership would be treated as transferring to the partner under paragraph (a)(1) of this section if the liability were not a qualified liability; or

(B) The amount obtained by multiplying the amount of the qualified liability by the partner's net equity percentage with respect to that property.

(ii) A partner's net equity percentage with respect to an item of property equals the percentage determined by dividing—

(A) The aggregate transfers of money or other consideration to the partner by the partnership (other than any transfer described in this paragraph (a)(5)) that are treated as proceeds realized from the sale of the transferred property; by

(B) The excess of the fair market value of the property at the time it is transferred to the partnership over any qualified liability encumbering the property or, in the case of any qualified liability described in paragraph (a)(6)(i)(C) or (D) of this section, that is properly allocable to the property.

(iii) Notwithstanding paragraph (a)(5)(i) of this section, in connection with a transfer of property by a partner to a partnership that is treated as a sale due solely to the partnership's assumption of or taking property subject to a liability other than a qualified liability, the partnership's assumption of or taking property subject to a qualified liability is not treated as a transfer of consideration made pursuant to the sale if the total amount of all liabilities other than qualified liabilities that the partnership assumes or takes subject to is the lesser of 10 percent of the total amount of all qualified liabilities the partnership assumes or takes subject to, or $1,000,000.

(6) *Qualified liability of a partner defined.*—A liability assumed or taken subject to by a partnership in connection with a transfer of property to the partnership by a partner is a qualified liability of the partner only to the extent—

(i) The liability is—

(A) A liability that was incurred by the partner more than two years prior to the earlier of the date the partner agrees in writing to transfer the property or the date the partner transfers the property to the partnership and that has encumbered the transferred property throughout that two-year period;

(B) A liability that was not incurred in anticipation of the transfer of the property to a partnership, but that was incurred by the partner within the two-year period prior to the earlier of the date the partner agrees in writing to transfer the property or the date the partner transfers the property to the partnership and that has encumbered the transferred property since it was incurred (see paragraph (a)(7) of this section for further rules regarding a liability incurred within two years of a property transfer or of a written agreement to transfer);

(C) A liability that is allocable under the rules of §1.163-8T to capital expenditures (as described under §1.707-4(d)(5)) with respect to the property;

(D) A liability that was incurred in the ordinary course of the trade or business in which property transferred to the partnership was used or held but only if all the assets related to that trade or business are transferred other than assets that are not material to a continuation of the trade or business; or

(E) A liability that was not incurred in anticipation of the transfer of the property to a partnership, but that was incurred in connection with a trade or business in which property transferred to the partnership was used or held but only if all the assets related to that trade or business are transferred other than assets that are not material to a continuation of the trade or business (see paragraph (a)(7) of this section for further rules regarding a liability incurred within two years of a transfer presumed to be in anticipation of the transfer); and

(ii) If the liability is a recourse liability, the amount of the liability does not exceed the fair market value of the transferred property (less the amount of any other liabilities that are senior in priority and that either encumber such property or are liabilities described in paragraph (a)(6)(i)(C) or (D) of this section) at the time of the transfer.

(7) *Liability incurred within two years of transfer presumed to be in anticipation of the transfer.*—(i) *In general.*—For purposes of this section, if within a two-year period a partner incurs a liability (other than a liability described in paragraph (a)(6)(i)(C) or (D) of this section) and transfers property to a partnership or agrees in writing to transfer the property, and in connection with the transfer the partnership assumes or takes the property subject to the liability, the liability is presumed to be incurred in anticipation of the transfer unless the facts and circumstances clearly establish that the liability was not incurred in anticipation of the transfer.

(ii) *Disclosure of transfers of property subject to liabilities incurred within two years of the transfer.*—A partner that treats a liability assumed or taken subject to by a partnership in connection with a transfer of property as a qualified liability under paragraph (a)(6)(i)(B) of this section or under paragraph (a)(6)(i)(E) of this section (if the liability was incurred by the partner within the two-year period prior to the earlier of the date the partner agrees in writing to transfer the property or the date the partner transfers the property to the partnership) must disclose such treatment to the Internal Revenue Service in accordance with §1.707-8.

(8) *Liability incurred by another person.*—Except as provided in paragraph (e)(2) of this section, a partner steps in the shoes of a person for purposes of paragraph (a) of this section with respect to a liability the person incurred or assumed to the extent the partner assumed or took property subject to the liability from the person in a nonrecognition transaction described in section 351, 381(a), 721, or 731.

(b) *Treatment of debt-financed transfers of consideration by partnerships.*—(1) *In general.*—For purposes of §1.707-3, if a partner transfers property to a partnership, and the partnership incurs a liability and all or a portion of the proceeds of that liability are allocable under §1.163-8T to a transfer of money or other consideration to the partner made within 90 days of incurring the liability, the transfer of money or other consideration to the partner is taken into account only to the extent that the amount of money or the fair market value of the other consideration transferred exceeds that partner's allocable share of the partnership liability. For purposes of paragraph (b) of this section, an upper-tier partnership's share of the liability of a lower-tier partnership as described under § 1.707-5(a)(2) that is treated as a liability of the upper-tier partnership under § 1.752-4(a) shall be treated as a liability of the upper-tier partnership incurred on the same day the liability was incurred by the lower-tier partnership.

(2) *Partner's allocable share of liability.*—(i) *In general.*—A partner's allocable share of a partnership liability for purposes of paragraph (b)(1) of this section equals the amount obtained by multiplying the partner's share of the liability as described in paragraph (a)(2) of this section by the fraction determined by dividing—

(A) The portion of the liability that is allocable under § 1.163-8T to the money or other consideration transferred to the partner; by

(B) The total amount of the liability.

(ii) *Debt-financed transfers made pursuant to a plan.*

(A) *In general.*—Except as provided in paragraph (b)(2)(iii) of this section, if a partnership transfers to more than one partner pursuant to a plan all or a portion of the proceeds of one or more partnership liabilities, paragraph (b)(1) of this section is applied by treating all of the liabilities incurred pursuant to the plan as one liability, and each partner's allocable share of those liabilities equals the amount obtained by multiplying the sum of the partner's shares of each of the respective liabilities (as defined in paragraph (a)(2) of this section) by the fraction obtained by dividing—

(1) The portion of those liabilities that is allocable under § 1.163-8T to the money or other consideration transferred to the partners pursuant to the plan; by

(2) The total amount of those liabilities.

(B) *Special rule.*—Paragraph (b)(2)(ii)(A) of this section does not apply to any transfer of money or other property to a partner that is made with a principal purpose of reducing the extent to which any transfer is taken into account under paragraph (b)(1) of this section.

(iii) *Reduction of partner's share of liability.*—For purposes of paragraph (b)(2) of this section, a partner's share of a liability immediately after a partnership incurs the liability is determined by taking into account a subsequent reduction in the partner's share if—

(A) At the time that the partnership incurs the liability, it is anticipated that the partner's share of the liability that is allocable to a transfer of money or other consideration to the partner will be reduced subsequent to the transfer;

(B) The anticipated reduction is not subject to the entrepreneurial risks of partnership operations; and

(C) The reduction of the partner's share of the liability is part of a plan that has as one of its principal purposes minimizing the extent to which the partnership's distribution of the proceeds of the borrowing is treated as part of a sale.

(3) *Ordering rule.*—The treatment of a transfer of money or other consideration under paragraph (b) of this section is determined before applying the rules under § 1.707-4.

(c) *Refinancings.*—To the extent that the proceeds of a partner or partnership liability (the *refinancing debt*) are allocable under the rules of § 1.163-8T to payments discharging all or part of any other liability of that partner or of the partnership, as the case may be, the refinancing debt is treated as the other liability for purposes of applying the rules of this section.

(d) *Share of liability where assumption accompanied by transfer of money.*—For purposes of §§ 1.707-3 through 1.707-5, if pursuant to a plan a partner pays or contributes money to the partnership and the partnership assumes or takes subject to one or more liabilities (other than qualified liabilities) of the partner, the amount of those liabilities that the partnership is treated as assuming or taking subject to is reduced (but not below zero) by the money transferred.

(e) *Tiered partnerships and other related persons.*—(1) If a lower-tier partnership succeeds to a liability of an upper-tier partnership, the liability in the lower-tier partnership retains the characterization as qualified or nonqualified that it had under these rules in the upper-tier partnership. A similar rule applies to other related party transactions involving liabilities to the extent provided by guidance published in the Internal Revenue Bulletin.

(2) If an interest in a partnership that has one or more liabilities (the lower-tier partnership) is transferred to another partnership (the upper-tier partnership), the upper-tier partnership's share of any liability of the lower-tier partnership that is treated as a liability of the upper-tier partnership under § 1.752-4(a) is treated as a qualified liability under paragraph

(a)(6)(i) of this section to the extent the liability would be a qualified liability under paragraph (a)(6)(i) of this section had the liability been assumed or taken subject to by the upper-tier partnership in connection with a transfer of all of the lower-tier partnership's property to the upper-tier partnership by the lower-tier partnership. For purposes of determining whether the liability constitutes a qualified liability under paragraphs (a)(6)(i)(B) and (E) of this section, a determination that the liability was not incurred in anticipation of the transfer of property to the upper-tier partnership is based on whether the partner in the lower-tier partnership anticipated transferring its interest in the lower-tier partnership to the upper-tier partnership at the time the liability was incurred by the lower-tier partnership.

(f) *Examples.*—The following examples illustrate the application of this section.

(1) *Example 1. Partnership's assumption of nonrecourse liability encumbering transferred property.*—(i) A and B form partnership AB, which will engage in renting office space. A transfers $500,000 in cash to the partnership, and B transfers an office building to the partnership. At the time it is transferred to the partnership, the office building has a fair market value of $1,000,000, has an adjusted basis of $400,000, and is encumbered by a $500,000 nonrecourse liability, which B incurred 12 months earlier to finance the acquisition of other property and which the partnership assumed. No facts rebut the presumption that the liability was incurred in anticipation of the transfer of the property to the partnership. Assume that this liability is a nonrecourse liability of the partnership within the meaning of section 752 and the regulations thereunder. The partnership agreement provides that partnership items will be allocated equally between A and B, including excess nonrecourse liabilities under § 1.752-3(a)(3). The partnership agreement complies with the requirements of § 1.704-1(b)(2)(ii)(*b*).

(ii) The nonrecourse liability secured by the office building is not a qualified liability within the meaning of paragraph (a)(6) of this section. B would be allocated 50 percent of the excess nonrecourse liability under the partnership agreement. Accordingly, immediately after the partnership's assumption of that liability, B's share of the liability as determined under paragraph (a)(2) of this section is $250,000 (B's 50 percent share of the partnership's excess nonrecourse liability as determined in accordance with B's share of partnership profits under § 1.752-3(a)(3)).

(iii) The partnership's assumption of the liability encumbering the office building is treated as a transfer of $250,000 of consideration to B (the amount by which the liability ($500,000) exceeds B's share of that liability immediately after the partnership's assumption of the liability ($250,000)). B is treated as having sold $250,000 of the fair market value of the office building to the partnership in exchange for the partnership's assumption of a $250,000 liability. This results in a gain of $150,000 ($250,000 minus ($250,000/$1,000,000 multiplied by $400,000)).

(2) *Example 2. Partnership's assumption of recourse liability encumbering transferred property.*—(i) C transfers property Y to a partnership. At the time of its transfer to the partnership, property Y has a fair market value of $10,000,000 and is subject to an $8,000,000 liability that C incurred, immediately before transferring property Y to the partnership, in order to finance other expenditures. Upon the transfer of property Y to the partnership, the partnership assumed the liability encumbering that property. The partnership assumed this liability solely to acquire property Y. Under section 752 and the regulations in this part under section 752, immediately after the partnership's assumption of the liability encumbering property Y, the liability is a recourse liability of the partnership and C's share of that liability is $7,000,000.

(ii) Under the facts of paragraph (f)(2)(i) of this section (*Example 2*), the liability encumbering property Y is not a qualified liability. Accordingly, the partnership's assumption of the liability results in a transfer of consideration to C in connection with C's transfer of property Y to the partnership in the amount of $1,000,000 (the excess of the liability assumed by the partnership ($8,000,000) over C's share of the liability immediately after the assumption ($7,000,000)). See paragraphs (a)(1) and (2) of this section.

(3) *Example 3. Subsequent reduction of transferring partner's share of liability.*—(i) The facts are the same as in paragraph (f)(2) of this section (*Example 2*). In addition, property Y is a fully leased office building, the rental income from property Y is sufficient to meet debt service, and the remaining term of the liability is ten years. It is anticipated that, three years after the partnership's assumption of the liability, C's share of the liability under section 752 will be reduced to zero because of a shift in the allocation of partnership losses pursuant to the terms of the partnership agreement. Under the partnership agreement, this shift in the allocation of partnership losses is dependent solely on the passage of time.

(ii) Under paragraph (a)(3) of this section, if the reduction in C's share of the liability was anticipated at the time of C's transfer, was not subject to the entrepreneurial risks of partnership operations, and was part of a plan that has as one of its principal purposes minimizing the extent of sale treatment under § 1.707-3 (that is, a principal purpose of allocating a large percentage of losses to C in the first three years when losses were not likely to be realized was to minimize the extent to which C's transfer would be treated as part of a sale), C's share of the liability immediately after the assumption is treated as equal to C's reduced share.

(4) *Example 4. Trade payables as qualified liabilities.*—(i) D and E form partnership DE which will engage in a consulting business that requires no overhead and minimal cash on hand for daily operating expenses. Previously, D and E, as individual sole proprietors, operated separate consulting businesses. D and E each transfer to the partnership sufficient cash to cover daily operating expenses together with the goodwill and trade payables related to each sole proprietorship. Due to uncertainty over the collection rate on the trade receivables related to their sole proprietorships, D and E agree that none of the trade receivables will be transferred to the partnership.

(ii) Under the facts of this example, all the assets related to the consulting business (other than the trade receivables) together with the trade payables were transferred to partnership DE. The trade receivables retained by D and E are not material to a continuation of the trade or business by the partnership because D and E contributed sufficient cash to cover daily operating expenses. Accordingly, the trade payables transferred to the partnership constitute qualified liabilities under paragraph (a)(6) of this section.

(5) *Example 5. Partnership's assumption of a qualified liability as sole consideration.*—(i) F purchases property Z in 2012. In 2016, F transfers property Z to a partnership. At the time of its transfer to the partnership, property Z has a fair market value of $165,000 and an adjusted tax basis of $75,000. Also, at the time of the transfer, property Z is subject to a $75,000 nonrecourse liability that F incurred more than two years before transferring property Z to the partnership. The liability has been secured by property Z since it was incurred by F. Upon the transfer of property Z to the partnership, the partnership assumed the liability encumbering that property. The partnership made no other transfers to F in consideration for the transfer of property Z to the partnership. Assume that immediately after the partnership's assumption of the liability encumbering property Z, F's share of that liability for disguised sale purposes is $25,000 in accordance with § 1.707-5(a)(2).

(ii) The $75,000 liability secured by property Z is a qualified liability of F because F incurred the liability more than two years prior to the partnership's assumption of the liability and the liability has encumbered property Z for more than two years prior to F's transfer. See paragraph (a)(6) of this section. Therefore, since no other transfer to F was made as consideration for the transfer of property Z, under paragraph (a)(5) of this section, the partnership's assumption of the qualified liability of F encumbering property Z is not treated as part of a sale.

(6) *Example 6. Partnership's assumption of a qualified liability in addition to other consideration.*—(i) The facts are the same as in paragraph (f)(5) of this section (*Example 5*), except that the partnership makes a transfer to F of $30,000 in money that is consideration for F's transfer of property Z to the partnership under § 1.707-3.

(ii) As in paragraph (f)(5) of this section (*Example 5*), the $75,000 liability secured by property Z is a qualified liability of F. Since the partnership transferred $30,000 to F in addition to assuming the qualified liability under paragraph (a)(5) of this section, assuming no other exception to disguised sale treatment applies to the transfer of the $30,000, the partnership's assumption of this qualified liability is treated as a transfer of additional consideration to F to the extent of the lesser of—

(A) The amount that the partnership would be treated as transferring to F if the liability were not a qualified liability ($50,000 (that is, the excess of the $75,000 qualified liability over F's $25,000 share of that liability)); or

(B) The amount obtained by multiplying the qualified liability ($75,000) by F's net equity percentage with respect to property Z (one-third).

(iii) F's net equity percentage with respect to property Z equals the fraction determined by dividing—

(A) The aggregate amount of money or other consideration (other than the qualified liability) transferred to F and treated as part of a sale of property Z under § 1.707-3(a) ($30,000 transfer of money); by

(B) F's net equity in property Z ($90,000 (that is, the excess of the $165,000 fair market value over the $75,000 qualified liability)).

(iv) Accordingly, the partnership's assumption of the qualified liability of F encumbering property Z is treated as a transfer of $25,000 (one-third of $75,000) of consideration to F pursuant to a sale. Therefore, F is treated as having sold $55,000 of the fair market value of property Z to the partnership in exchange for

$30,000 in money and the partnership's assumption of $25,000 of the qualified liability. Accordingly, F must recognize $30,000 of gain on the sale (the excess of the $55,000 amount realized over $25,000 of F's adjusted basis for property Z (that is, one-third of F's adjusted basis for the property, because F is treated as having sold one-third of the property to the partnership)).

* * *

(8) *Example 8. Partnership's assumption of liability pursuant to a plan to avoid sale treatment of partnership assumption of another liability.*—(i) The facts are the same as in paragraph (f)(7) of this section (*Example 7*), except that—

(A) H transferred the proceeds of liability 2 to the partnership; and

(B) H incurred liability 2 in an attempt to reduce the extent to which the partnership's taking subject to liability 1 would be treated as a transfer of consideration to G (and thereby reduce the portion of G's transfer of property 1 to the partnership that would be treated as part of a sale).

(ii) Because the partnership assumed liability 2 with a principal purpose of reducing the extent to which the partnership's taking subject to liability 1 would be treated as a transfer of consideration to G, liability 2 is ignored in applying paragraph (a)(3) of this section. Accordingly, the partnership's taking subject to liability 1 is treated as a transfer of $4,000 of consideration to G (the amount by which liability 1 ($6,000) exceeds G's share of liability 1 ($2,000)). On the other hand, the partnership's assumption of liability 2 is not treated as a transfer of any consideration to H because H's share of that liability equals $7,000 as a result of H's transfer of $7,000 in money to the partnership.

(9) *Example 9. Partnership's assumptions of qualified liabilities encumbering properties transferred pursuant to a plan in addition to other consideration.*—(i) Pursuant to a plan, I transfers property 1 and J transfers property 2 plus $10,000 in cash to partnership IJ in exchange for equal interests in the partnership. At the time the properties are transferred to the partnership, property 1 has a fair market value of $100,000, an adjusted tax basis of $5,000, and is encumbered by a qualified liability of $50,000 (*liability 1*). Property 2 has a fair market value of $100,000, an adjusted tax basis of $5,000, and is encumbered by a qualified liability of $70,000 (*liability 2*). Pursuant to the plan, the partnership transferred to I $10,000 in cash. That amount is consideration for I's transfer of property 1 to the partnership under § 1.707-3. In accordance with § 1.707-5(a)(2), I and J are each allocated $25,000 of liability 1 and $35,000 of liability 2.

(ii) Because the partnership transferred $10,000 to I as consideration for the transfer of property, under § 1.707-5(a)(5), the partnership's assumption of liability 1 is treated as a transfer of additional consideration to I, even though liability 1 is a qualified liability, to the extent of the lesser of—

(A) The amount that the partnership would be treated as transferring to I if the liability were not a qualified liability; or

(B) The amount obtained by multiplying the qualified liability by I's net equity percentage with respect to property 1.

(iii) Because I and J transferred properties 1 and 2 to the partnership pursuant to a plan, treating I's qualified liability as a nonqualified liability under § 1.707-5(a)(5)(i)(A) enables I to apply the special rule applicable to transfers of encumbered property to a partnership by more than one partner pursuant to a plan under § 1.707-5(a)(4). Under this alternative test, the partnership's assumption of liability 1 encumbering property 1 is treated as a transfer of zero ($0) additional consideration to I pursuant to a sale. This is because the amount of liability 1 ($50,000) does not exceed the sum of I's share of liability 1 treated as a nonqualified liability ($25,000) and I's share of liability 2 ($35,000)).

(iv) The alternative under § 1.707-5(a)(5)(i)(B) is the amount obtained by multiplying the qualified liability ($50,000) by I's net equity percentage with respect to property 1. I's net equity percentage with respect to property 1 equals one-fifth, the fraction determined by dividing—

(A) The aggregate amount of money or other consideration (other than the qualified liability) transferred to I and treated as part of a sale of property 1 under § 1.707-3(a) (the $10,000 transfer of money); by

(B) I's net equity in property 1 ($50,000, *i.e.*, the excess of the $100,000 fair market value over the $50,000 qualified liability).

(v) Under this alternative test, the partnership's assumption of the qualified liability encumbering property 1 is treated as a transfer of $10,000 (one-fifth of the $50,000 qualified liability) of additional consideration to I pursuant to a sale.

(vi) Applying § 1.707-5(a)(5) to these facts, the partnership's assumption of liability 1 is treated as a transfer of additional consideration to I to the extent of the lesser of—

(A) zero; or

(B) $10,000.

(vii) Therefore, the partnership's assumption of I's qualified liability encumbering property 1 is not treated as a transfer of any additional consideration to I pursuant to a sale, and I is treated as having only received $10,000 of the fair market value of property 1 to the partnership in exchange for $10,000 in cash. Accordingly, I must recognize $9,500 of gain on the sale, that is, the excess of the $10,000 amount realized over $500 of I's adjusted tax basis for property 1 (one-tenth of I's adjusted tax basis for the property, because I is treated as having sold one-tenth of the property to the partnership). Since no other transfer to J was made as consideration for the transfer of property 2, the partnership's assumption of the qualified liability of J encumbering property 2 is not treated as part of a sale.

(10) *Example 10. Treatment of debt-financed transfers of consideration by partnership.*—(i) K transfers property Z to partnership KL in exchange for a 50 percent interest therein on April 9, 2016. On September 13, 2016, the partnership incurs a nonrecourse liability of $20,000. On November 17, 2016, the partnership transfers $20,000 to K, and $10,000 of this transfer is allocable under the rules of § 1.163-8T to proceeds of the partnership liability incurred on September 13, 2016. The remaining $10,000 is paid from other partnership funds. Assume that on November 17, 2016, for disguised sale purposes, K's share of the $20,000 liability incurred on September 13, 2016, is $10,000 in accordance with § 1.707-5(a)(2).

(ii) Because a portion of the transfer made to K on November 17, 2016, is allocable under § 1.163-8T to proceeds of a partnership liability that was incurred by the partnership within 90 days of that transfer, K is required to take the transfer into account in applying the rules of this section and § 1.707-3 only to the extent that the amount of the transfer exceeds K's allocable share of the liability used to fund the transfer. K's allocable share of the $20,000 liability used to fund $10,000 of the transfer to K is $5,000 (K's share of the liability ($10,000) multiplied by the fraction obtained by dividing—

(A) The amount of the liability that is allocable to the distribution to K ($10,000); by

(B) The total amount of such liability ($20,000)).

(iii) Therefore, K is required to take into account $15,000 of the $20,000 partnership transfer to K for purposes of this section and § 1.707-3. Under these facts, assuming no other exception applies and the within-two-year presumption is not rebutted, this $15,000 transfer will be treated under the rule in § 1.707-3 as part of a sale by K of property Z to the partnership.

(11) *Example 11. Treatment of debt-financed transfers of consideration and transfers characterized as guaranteed payments by a partnership.*—(i) The facts are the same as in paragraph (f)(10) of this section (*Example 10*), except that the entire $20,000 transfer to K is allocable under the rules of § 1.163-8T to proceeds of the partnership liability incurred on September 13, 2016. In addition, the partnership agreement provides that K is to receive a guaranteed payment for the use of K's capital in the amount of $10,000 in each of the three years following the transfer of property Z. Ten thousand dollars of the transfer made to K on November 17, 2016, is pursuant to this provision of the partnership agreement. Assume that the guaranteed payment to K constitutes a reasonable guaranteed payment within the meaning of § 1.707-4(a)(3).

(ii) Under these facts, the rules under both § 1.707-4(a) and § 1.707-5(b) apply to the November 17, 2016 transfer to K by the partnership. Thus, the ordering rule in § 1.707-5(b)(3) requires that the § 1.707-5(b) debt-financed distribution rules apply first to determine the treatment of the $20,000 transfer. Because the entire transfer made to K on November 17, 2016, is allocable under § 1.163-8T to proceeds of a partnership liability that was incurred by the partnership within 90 days of that transfer, K is required to take the transfer into account in applying the rules of this section and § 1.707-3 only to the extent that the amount of the transfer exceeds K's allocable share of the liability used to fund the transfer. K's allocable share of the $20,000 liability used to fund the transfer to K is $10,000 (K's share of the liability ($10,000) multiplied by the fraction obtained by dividing—

(A) The amount of the liability that is allocable to the distribution to K ($20,000); by

(B) The total amount of such liability ($20,000)).

(iii) The remaining $10,000 amount of the transfer to K that exceeds K's allocable share of the liability is tested to determine whether an exception under § 1.707-4 applies. Because $10,000 of the payment to K is a reasonable guaranteed payment for capital under § 1.707-4(a)(1)(ii), the $10,000 transfer will not be treated as part of a sale by K of property *Z* to the partnership under § 1.707-3.

(12) *Example 12. Treatment of debt-financed transfers of consideration by partnership made pursuant to plan.*—(i) O transfers property X, and P transfers property Y, to partnership OP in exchange for equal interests therein on June 1, 2016. On October 1, 2016, the partnership incurs two nonrecourse liabilities: Liability 1 of $8,000 and Liability 2 of $4,000. On December 15, 2016, the partnership transfers

$2,000 to each of O and P pursuant to a plan. The transfers made to O and P on December 15, 2016 are allocable under § 1.163-8T to the proceeds of either Liability 1 or Liability 2. Assume that under § 1.707-5(a)(2), O's and P's share of Liability 1 is $4,000 each and of Liability 2 is $2,000 each on December 15, 2016.

(ii) Because the partnership transferred pursuant to a plan a portion of the proceeds of the two liabilities to O and P, paragraph (b)(1) of this section is applied by treating Liability 1 and Liability 2 as a single $12,000 liability. Pursuant to paragraph (b)(2)(ii)(A) of this section, each partner's allocable share of the $12,000 liability equals the amount obtained by multiplying the sum of the partner's share of Liability 1 and Liability 2 ($6,000) ($4,000 for Liability 1 plus $2,000 for Liability 2) by the fraction obtained by dividing—

(A) The amount of the liability that is allocable to the distribution to O and P pursuant to the plan ($4,000); by

(B) The total amount of such liability ($12,000).

(iii) Therefore, O's and P's allocable share of the $12,000 liability is $2,000 each. Accordingly, because a portion of the proceeds of the $12,000 liability are allocable under § 1.163-8T to the $2,000 transfer made to each of O and P within 90 days of incurring the liability, and the $2,000 transfer does not exceed O's or P's $2,000 allocable share of that liability, each is required to take into account $0 of the $2,000 transfer for purposes of this section and § 1.707-3. Under these facts, no part of the transfers to O and P will be treated as part of a sale of property X by O or of property Y by P.

(13) *Example 13. Borrowing against pool of receivables.*—(i) M generates receivables which have an adjusted basis of zero in the ordinary course of its business. For M to use receivables as security for a loan, a commercial lender requires M to transfer the receivables to a partnership in which M has a 90 percent interest. In January, 1992, M transfers to the partnership receivables with a face value of $100,000. N (who is not related to M) transfers $10,000 cash to the partnership in exchange for a 10 percent interest. The partnership borrows $80,000, secured by the receivables, and makes a distribution of $72,000 of the proceeds to M and $8,000 of the proceeds to N within 90 days of incurring the liability. M's share of the liability under § 1.707-5(a)(2) is $72,000 (90 percent × $80,000).

(ii) Because the transfer of the loan proceeds to M is allocable under § 1.163-8T to proceeds of a partnership loan that was incurred by the partnership within 90 days of that transfer, M is required to take the transfer into account in applying the rules of this section and § 1.707-3 only to the extent that the amount of the transfer ($72,000) exceeds M's allocable share of the liability used to fund the transfer. Because the distribution was a debt-financed transfer pursuant to a plan, M's allocable share of the liability is $72,000 ($72,000 × $80,000/80,000) under § 1.707-5(b)(2)(ii). Therefore, M is not required to take into account any of the loan proceeds for purposes of this section and § 1.707-3.

(iii) When the receivables are collected, M must be allocated the gain on the contributed receivables under section 704(c). However, the lender permits the partnership to distribute cash to the partners only to the extent of the value of new receivables contributed to the partnership. In 1993, M contributes additional receivables and receives a distribution of cash. The taxable income recognized by the partnership on the receivables is taxable income of the partnership arising in the ordinary course of the partnership's activities. To the extent the distribution does not exceed 90 percent (M's percentage interest in overall partnership profits) of the partnership's operating cash flow under § 1.707-4(b), the distribution to M is presumed not to be a part of a sale of receivables by M to the partnership, and the presumption is not rebutted under these facts. [Reg. § 1.707-5.]

□ [*T.D.* 8439, 9-25-92. *Amended by T.D.* 9787, 10-4-2016; *T.D.* 9788, 10-4-2016 *and T.D.* 9876, 10-4-2019.]

§ 1.707-6. Disguised sales of property by partnership to partner; general rules.—(a) *In general.*—Rules similar to those provided in § 1.707-3 apply in determining whether a transfer of property by a partnership to a partner and one or more transfers of money or other consideration by that partner to the partnership are treated as a sale of property, in whole or in part, to the partner.

(b) *Special rules relating to liabilities.*—(1) *In general.*—Rules similar to those provided in § 1.707-5 apply to determine the extent to which an assumption of or taking subject to a liability by a partner, in connection with a transfer of property by a partnership, is considered part of a sale. Accordingly, if a partner assumes or takes property subject to a qualified liability (as defined in paragraph (b)(2) of this section) of a partnership, the partner is treated as transferring consideration to the partnership only to the extent provided in this paragraph (b). If the partner assumes or takes subject to a liability that is not a qualified liability, the amount treated as consideration transferred to the partnership is the amount that the liability assumed or taken subject to by the partner exceeds the partner's share of that liability (determined under the rules of § 1.707-5(a)(2)) immediately before the transfer. Similar to the rules provided in § 1.707-5(a)(4), if more than one partner assumes or takes subject to a liability pursuant to a plan, the amount that is treated as a transfer of consideration by each partner is the amount by which all of the liabilities (other than qualified liabilities) assumed or taken subject to by the partner pursuant to the plan exceed the partner's share of all of those liabilities immediately before the assumption or taking subject to. This paragraph (b)(1) does not apply to any liability assumed or taken subject to by a partner with a principal purpose of reducing the extent to which any other liability assumed or taken subject to by a partner is treated as a transfer of consideration under this paragraph (b).

(2) *Qualified liabilities.*—(i) If a transfer of property by a partnership to a partner is not otherwise treated as part of a sale, the partner's assumption of or taking subject to a qualified liability is not treated as part of a sale. If a transfer of property by a partnership to the partner is treated as part of a sale without regard to the partner's assumption of or taking subject to a qualified liability, the partner's assumption of or taking subject to that liability is treated as a transfer of consideration made pursuant to a sale of such property to the partner only to the extent of the lesser of—

(A) The amount of consideration that the partner would be treated as transferring to the partnership under paragraph (b) of this section if the liability were not a qualified liability; or

(B) The amount obtained by multiplying the amount of the liability at the time of its assumption or taking subject to by the partnership's net equity percentage with respect to that property.

(ii) A partnership's net equity percentage with respect to an item of property encumbered by a qualified liability equals the percentage determined by dividing—

(A) The aggregate transfers to the partnership from the partner (other than any transfer described in this paragraph (b)(2)) that are treated as the proceeds realized from the sale of the transferred property to the partner; by

(B) The excess of the fair market value of the property at the time it is transferred to the partner over any qualified liabilities of the partnership that are assumed or taken subject to by the partner at that time.

(iii) For purposes of this section, the definition of a qualified liability is that provided in § 1.707-5(a)(6) with the following exceptions—

(A) In applying the definition, the qualified liability is one that is originally an obligation of the partnership and is assumed or taken subject to by the partner in connection with a transfer of property to the partner; and

(B) If the liability was incurred by the partnership more than two years prior to the earlier of the date the partnership agrees in writing to transfer the property or the date the partnership transfers the property to the partner, that liability is a qualified liability whether or not it has encumbered the transferred property throughout the two-year period.

(c) *Disclosure rules.*—Similar to the rules provided in §§ 1.707-3(c)(2) and 1.707-5(a)(7)(ii), a partnership is to disclose to the Internal Revenue Service, in accordance with § 1.707-8, the facts in the following circumstances:

(1) When a partnership transfers property to a partner and the partner transfers money or other consideration to the partnership within a two-year period (without regard to the order of the transfers) and the partnership treats the transfers as other than a sale for tax purposes; and

(2) When a partner assumes or takes subject to a liability of a partnership in connection with a transfer of property by the partnership to the partner, and the partnership incurred the liability within the two-year period prior to the earlier of the date the partnership agrees in writing to the transfer of property or the date the partnership transfers the property, and the partnership treats the liability as a qualified liability under rules similar to § 1.707-5(a)(6)(i)(B).

(d) *Examples.*—The following examples illustrate the rules of this section.

Example 1. Sale of property by partnership to partner. (i) A is a member of a partnership. The partnership transfers property X to A. At the time of the transfer, property X has a fair market value of $1,000,000. One year after the transfer, A transfers $1,100,000 to the partnership. Assume that under the rules of section 1274 the imputed principal amount of an obligation to transfer $1,100,000 one year after the transfer of property X is $1,000,000 on the date of the transfer.

(ii) Since the transfer of $1,100,000 to the partnership by A is made within two years of the transfer of property X to A, under rules similar to those provided in § 1.707-3(c), the transfers are presumed to be a sale unless the facts and circumstances clearly establish otherwise. If no facts exist that would rebut this presumption, on the date that the partnership transfers property X to A, the partnership is treated as having sold property X to A in exchange for A's obligation to transfer $1,100,000 to the partnership one year later.

Example 2. Assumption of liability by partner. (i) B is a member of an existing partnership. The partnership transfers property Y to B. On the date of the transfer, property Y has a fair market value of $1,000,000 and is encumbered by a nonrecourse liability of $600,000. B takes the property subject to the liability. The partnership incurred the nonrecourse liability six months prior to the transfer of property Y to B and used the proceeds to purchase an unrelated asset. Assume that under § 1.707-5(a)(2), B's share of the nonrecourse liability immediately before the transfer of property Y was $100,000.

(ii) The liability is not allocable under the rules of § 1.163-8T to capital expenditures with respect to the property transferred to B and was not incurred in the ordinary course of the trade or business in which the property transferred to the partner was used or held. Since the partnership incurred the nonrecourse liability within two years of the transfer to B, under rules similar to those provided in § 1.707-5(a)(5), the liability is presumed to be incurred in anticipation of the transfer unless the facts and circumstances clearly establish the contrary. Assuming no facts exist to rebut this presumption, the liability taken subject to by B is not a qualified liability. The partnership is treated as having received, on the date of the transfer of property Y to B, $500,000 ($600,000 liability assumed by B less B's share of the $100,000 liability immediately prior to the transfer) as consideration for the sale of one-half ($500,000/$1,000,000) of property Y to B. The partnership is also treated as having distributed to B, in B's capacity as a partner, the other one-half of property Y. [Reg. § 1.707-6.]

☐ [*T.D.* 8439, 9-25-92. *Amended by T.D.* 9787, 10-4-2016.]

§ 1.708-1. Continuation of partnership.—(a) *General rule.*—For purposes of subchapter K, chapter 1 of the Code, an existing partnership shall be considered as continuing if it is not terminated.

(b) *Termination.*—(1) *General rule.*—A partnership shall terminate when the operations of the partnership are discontinued and no part of any business, financial operation, or venture of the partnership continues to be carried on by any of its partners in a partnership. For example, on November 20, 1956, A and B, each of whom is a 20-percent partner in partnership ABC, sell their interests to C, who is a 60-percent partner. Since the business is no longer carried on by any of its partners in a partnership, the ABC partnership is terminated as of November 20, 1956. However, where partners DEF agree on April 30, 1957, to dissolve their partnership, but carry on the business through a winding up period ending September 30, 1957, when all remaining assets, consisting only of cash, are distributed to the partners, the partnership does not terminate because of cessation of business until September 30, 1957.

(i) Upon the death of one partner in a 2-member partnership, the partnership shall not be considered as terminated if the estate or other successor in interest of the deceased partner continues to share in the profits or losses of the partnership business.

(ii) For the continuation of a partnership where payments are being made under section 736 (relating to payments to a retiring partner or a deceased partner's successor in interest), see paragraph (a)(6) of § 1.736-1.

(2) A partnership shall terminate when 50 percent or more of the total interest in partnership capital and profits is sold or exchanged within a period of 12 consecutive months. Such sale or exchange includes a sale or exchange to another member of the partnership. However, a disposition of a partnership interest by gift (including assignment to a successor in interest), bequest, or inheritance, or the liquidation of a partnership interest, is not a sale or exchange for purposes of this subparagraph. Moreover, if the sale or exchange of an interest in a partnership (upper-tier partnership) that holds an interest in another partnership (lower-tier partnership) results in a termination of the upper-tier partnership, the upper-tier partnership is treated as exchanging its entire interest in the capital and profits of the lower-tier partnership. If the sale or exchange of an interest in an upper-tier partnership does not terminate the upper-tier partnership, the sale or exchange of an interest in the upper-tier partnership is not treated as a sale or exchange of a proportionate share of the upper-tier partnership's interest in the capital and profits of the lower-tier partnership. The previous two sentences apply to terminations of partnerships under section 708(b)(1)(B) occurring on or after May 9, 1997; however, the sentences may be applied to terminations occurring on or after May 9, 1996, provided that the partnership and its partners apply the sentences to the termination in a consistent manner. Furthermore, the contribution of property to a partnership does not constitute such a sale or exchange. See, however, paragraph (c)(3) of § 1.731-1. Fifty percent or more of the total interest in partnership capital and profits means 50 percent or more of the total interest in partnership capital plus 50 percent or more of the total interest in partnership profits. Thus, the sale of a 30-percent interest in partnership capital and a 60-percent interest in partnership profits is not the sale or exchange of 50 percent or more of the total interest in

partnership capital and profits. If one or more partners sell or exchange interests aggregating 50 percent or more of the total interest in partnership capital and 50 percent or more of the total interest in partnership profits within a period of 12 consecutive months, such sale or exchange is considered as being within the provisions of this subparagraph. When interests are sold or exchanged on different dates, the percentages to be added are determined as of the date of each sale. For example, with respect to the ABC partnership, the sale by A on May 12, 1956, of a 30-percent interest in capital and profits to D, and the sale by B on March 27, 1957, of a 30-percent interest in capital and profits to E, is a sale of a 50-percent or more interest. Accordingly, the partnership is terminated as of March 27, 1957. However, if, on March 27, 1957, D, instead of B, sold his 30-percent interest in capital and profits to E, there would be no termination since only one 30-percent interest would have been sold or exchanged within a 12-month period.

(3) For purposes of subchapter K, chapter 1 of the Code, a partnership taxable year closes with respect to all partners on the date on which the partnership terminates. See section 706(c)(1) and paragraph (c)(1) of § 1.706-1. The date of termination is:

(i) For purposes of section 708(b)(1)(A), the date on which the winding up of the partnership affairs is completed.

(ii) For purposes of section 708(b)(1)(B), the date of the sale or exchange of a partnership interest which, of itself or together with sales or exchanges in the preceding 12 months, transfers an interest of 50 percent or more in both partnership capital and profits.

(4) If a partnership is terminated by a sale or exchange of an interest, the following is deemed to occur: The partnership contributes all of its assets and liabilities to a new partnership in exchange for an interest in the new partnership; and, immediately thereafter, the terminated partnership distributes interests in the new partnership to the purchasing partner and the other remaining partners in proportion to their respective interests in the terminated partnership in liquidation of the terminated partnership, either for the continuation of the business by the new partnership or for its dissolution and winding up. In the latter case, the new partnership terminates in accordance with (b)(1) of this section. This paragraph (b)(4) applies to terminations of partnerships under section 708(b)(1)(B) occurring on or after May 9, 1997; however, this paragraph (b)(4) may be applied to terminations occurring on or after May 9, 1996, provided that the partnership and its partners apply this paragraph (b)(4) to the termination in a consistent manner. The provisions of this paragraph (b)(4) are illustrated by the following example:

Example. (i) A and B each contribute $10,000 cash to form AB, a general partnership, as equal partners. AB purchases depreciable Property X for $20,000. Property X increases in value to $30,000, at which time A sells its entire 50 percent interest to C for $15,000 in a transfer that terminates the partnership under section 708(b)(1)(B). At the time of the sale, Property X had an adjusted tax basis of $16,000 and a book value of $16,000 (original $20,000 tax basis and book value reduced by $4,000 of depreciation). In addition, A and B each had a capital account balance of $8,000 (original $10,000 capital account reduced by $2,000 of depreciation allocations with respect to Property X).

(ii) Following the deemed contribution of assets and liabilities by the terminated AB partnership to a new partnership (new AB) and the liquidation of the terminated AB partnership, the adjusted tax basis of Property X in the hands of new AB is $16,000. See Section 723. The book value of Property X in the hands of new partnership AB is also $16,000 (the book value of Property X immediately before the termination) and B and C each have a capital account of $8,000 in new AB (the balance of their capital accounts in AB prior to the termination). See § 1.7041(b)(2)(iv)(l) (providing that the deemed contribution and liquidation with regard to the terminated partnership are disregarded in determining the capital accounts of the partners and the books of the new partnership). Additionally, under § 301.6109-1(d)(2)(iii) of this chapter, new AB retains the taxpayer identification number of the terminated AB partnership.

(iii) Property X was not section 704(c) property in the hands of terminated AB and is therefore not treated as section 704(c) property in the hands of new AB, even though Property X is deemed contributed to new AB at a time when the fair market value of Property X ($30,000) was different from its adjusted tax basis ($16,000). See § 1.704-3(a)(3)(i) (providing that property contributed to a new partnership under § 1.708-1(b)(4) is treated as section 704(c) property only to the extent that the property was section 704(c) property in the hands of the terminated partnership immediately prior to the termination).

(5) If a partnership is terminated by a sale or exchange of an interest in the partnership, a section 754 election (including a section 754 election made by the terminated partnership on its final return) that is in effect for the taxable year of the terminated partnership in which the sale occurs, applies with respect to the incoming partner. Therefore, the bases of partnership assets are adjusted pursuant to sections 743 and 755 prior to their deemed contribution to

the new partnership. This paragraph (b)(5) applies to terminations of partnerships under section 708(b)(1)(B) occurring on or after May 9, 1997; however, this paragraph (b)(5) may be applied to terminations occurring on or after May 9, 1996, provided that the partnership and its partners apply this paragraph (b)(5) to the termination in a consistent manner.

(6) *Treatment of certain start-up or organizational expenses following a technical termination.*—(i) *In general.*—If a partnership that has elected to amortize start-up expenditures under section 195(b) or organizational expenses under section 709(b)(1) terminates in a transaction (or a series of transactions) described in section 708(b)(1)(B) or paragraph (b)(2) of this section, the new partnership must continue to amortize those expenditures over the remaining portion of the amortization period adopted by the terminating partnership. See section 195 and § 1.195-1 for rules concerning the amortization of start-up expenditures and section 709 and § 1.709-1 for rules concerning the amortization of organizational expenses.

* * *

(d) *Division of a partnership.*—(1) *General rule.*—Upon the division of a partnership into two or more partnerships, any resulting partnership (as defined in paragraph (d)(4)(iv) of this section) or resulting partnerships shall be considered a continuation of the prior partnership (as defined in paragraph (d)(4)(ii) of this section) if the members of the resulting partnership or partnerships had an interest of more than 50 percent in the capital and profits of the prior partnership. Any other resulting partnership will not be considered a continuation of the prior partnership but will be considered a new partnership. If the members of none of the resulting partnerships owned an interest of more than 50 percent in the capital and profits of the prior partnership, none of the resulting partnerships will be considered a continuation of the prior partnership, and the prior partnership will be considered to have terminated. Where members of a partnership which has been divided into two or more partnerships do not become members of a resulting partnership which is considered a continuation of the prior partnership, such members' interests shall be considered liquidated as of the date of the division.

(2) *Tax consequences.*—(i) *Tax returns.*—The resulting partnership that is treated as the divided partnership (as defined in paragraph (d)(4)(i) of this section) shall file a return for the taxable year of the partnership that has been divided and retain the employer identification number (EIN) of the prior partnership. The return shall include the names, addresses, and EINs of all resulting partnerships that are regarded as continuing. The return shall also state that the partnership is a continuation of the prior partnership and shall set forth separately the respective distributive shares of the partners for the periods prior to and including the date of the division and subsequent to the date of division. All other resulting partnerships that are regarded as continuing and new partnerships shall file separate returns for the taxable year beginning on the day after the date of the division with new EINs for each partnership. The return for a resulting partnership that is regarded as continuing and that is not the divided partnership shall include the name, address, and EIN of the prior partnership.

(ii) *Elections.*—All resulting partnerships that are regarded as continuing are subject to preexisting elections that were made by the prior partnership. A subsequent election that is made by a resulting partnership does not affect the other resulting partnerships.

(3) *Form of a division.*—(i) *Assets-over form.*—When a partnership divides into two or more partnerships under applicable jurisdictional law without undertaking a form for the division, or undertakes a form that is not described in paragraph (d)(3)(ii) of this section, the transaction will be characterized under the assets-over form for Federal income tax purposes.

(A) *Assets-over form where at least one resulting partnership is a continuation of the prior partnership.*—In a division under the assets-over form where at least one resulting partnership is a continuation of the prior partnership, the divided partnership (as defined in paragraph (d)(4)(i) of this section) contributes certain assets and liabilities to a recipient partnership (as defined in paragraph (d)(4)(iii) of this section) or recipient partnerships in exchange for interests in such recipient partnership or partnerships; and, immediately thereafter, the divided partnership distributes the interests in such recipient partnership or partnerships to some or all of its partners in partial or complete liquidation of the partners' interests in the divided partnership.

(B) *Assets-over form where none of the resulting partnerships is a continuation of the prior partnership.*—In a division under the assets-over form where none of the resulting partnerships is a continuation of the prior partnership, the prior partnership will be treated as contributing all of its assets and liabilities to new resulting partnerships in exchange for interests in the resulting partnerships; and, immediately thereafter, the prior partnership will be treated as liquidating by distributing the interests in the new resulting partnerships to the prior partnership's partners.

(ii) *Assets-up form.*—(A) *Assets-up form where the partnership distributing assets is a continuation of the prior partnership.*—Despite the partners' transitory ownership of some of the prior partnership's assets, the form of a partnership division will be respected for Federal income tax purposes if the divided partnership (which, pursuant to § 1.708-1(d)(4)(i), must be a continuing partnership) distributes certain assets (in a manner that causes the partners to be treated, under the laws of the applicable jurisdiction, as the owners of such assets) to some or all of its partners in partial or complete liquidation of the partners' interests in the divided partnership, and immediately thereafter, such partners contribute the distributed assets to a recipient partnership or partnerships in exchange for interests in such recipient partnership or partnerships. In order for such form to be respected for transfers to a particular recipient partnership, all assets held by the prior partnership that are transferred to the recipient partnership must be distributed to, and then contributed by, the partners of the recipient partnership.

(B) *Assets-up form where none of the resulting partnerships are a continuation of the prior partnership.*—If none of the resulting partnerships are a continuation of the prior partnership, then despite the partners' transitory ownership of some or all of the prior partnership's assets, the form of a partnership division will be respected for Federal income tax purposes if the prior partnership distributes certain assets (in a manner that causes the partners to be treated, under the laws of the applicable jurisdiction, as the owners of such assets) to some or all of its partners in partial or complete liquidation of the partners' interests in the prior partnership, and immediately thereafter, such partners contribute the distributed assets to a resulting partnership or partnerships in exchange for interests in such resulting partnership or partnerships. In order for such form to be respected for transfers to a particular resulting partnership, all assets held by the prior partnership that are transferred to the resulting partnership must be distributed to, and then contributed by, the partners of the resulting partnership. If the prior partnership does not liquidate under the applicable jurisdictional law, then with respect to the assets and liabilities that, in form, are not transferred to a new resulting partnership, the prior partnership will be treated as transferring these assets and liabilities to a new resulting partnership under the assets-over form described in paragraph (d)(3)(i)(B) of this section.

(4) *Definitions.*—(i) *Divided partnership.*—For purposes of paragraph (d) of this section, the divided partnership is the continuing partnership which is treated, for Federal income tax purposes, as transferring the assets and liabilities to the recipient partnership or partnerships, either directly (under the assets-over form) or indirectly (under the assets-up form). If the resulting partnership that, in form, transferred the assets and liabilities in connection with the division is a continuation of the prior partnership, then such resulting partnership will be treated as the divided partnership. If a partnership divides into two or more partnerships and only one of the resulting partnerships is a continuation of the prior partnership, then the resulting partnership that is a continuation of the prior partnership will be treated as the divided partnership. If a partnership divides into two or more partnerships without undertaking a form for the division that is recognized under paragraph (d)(3) of this section, or if the resulting partnership that had, in form, transferred assets and liabilities is not considered a continuation of the prior partnership, and more than one resulting partnership is considered a continuation of the prior partnership, the continuing resulting partnership with the assets having the greatest fair market value (net of liabilities) will be treated as the divided partnership.

(ii) *Prior partnership.*—For purposes of paragraph (d) of this section, the prior partnership is the partnership subject to division that exists under applicable jurisdictional law before the division.

(iii) *Recipient partnership.*—For purposes of paragraph (d) of this section, a recipient partnership is a partnership that is treated as receiving, for Federal income tax purposes, assets and liabilities from a divided partnership, either directly (under the assets-over form) or indirectly (under the assets-up form).

(iv) *Resulting partnership.*—For purposes of paragraph (d) of this section, a resulting partnership is a partnership resulting from the division that exists under applicable jurisdictional law after the division and that has at least two partners who were partners in the prior partnership. For example, where a prior partnership divides into two partnerships, both partnerships existing after the division are resulting partnerships.

(5) *Examples.*—The following examples illustrate the rules in paragraphs (d)(1), (2), (3), and (4) of this section:

Example 1. Partnership ABCD is in the real estate and insurance businesses. A owns a 40-percent interest, and B, C, and D each owns a 20-percent interest, in the capital and profits of the partnership. The partnership and the partners report their income on a calendar year. On November 1, 1999, they separate the real estate and insurance businesses and form two partnerships. Partnership AB takes over the real estate business, and partnership CD takes over the insurance business. Because members of resulting partnership AB owned more than a 50-percent interest in the capital and profits of partnership ABCD (A, 40 percent, and B, 20 percent), partnership AB shall be considered a continuation of partnership ABCD. Partnership AB is required to file a return for the taxable year January 1 to December 31, 1999, indicating thereon that until November 1, 1999, it was partnership ABCD. Partnership CD is considered a new partnership formed at the beginning of the day on November 2, 1999, and is required to file a return for the taxable year it adopts pursuant to section 706(b) and the applicable regulations.

Example 2. (i) Partnership ABCD owns properties W, X, Y, and Z, and divides into partnership AB and partnership CD. Under paragraph (d)(1) of this section, partnership AB is considered a continuation of partnership ABCD and partnership CD is considered a new partnership. Partnership ABCD distributes property Y to C and titles property Y in C's name. Partnership ABCD distributes property Z to D and titles property Z in D's name. C and D then contribute properties Y and Z, respectively, to partnership CD in exchange for interests in partnership CD. Properties W and X remain in partnership AB.

(ii) Under paragraph (d)(3)(ii) of this section, partnership ABCD will be treated as following the assets-up form for Federal income tax purposes.

Example 3. (i) The facts are the same as in *Example 2*, except partnership ABCD distributes property Y to C and titles property Y in C's name. C then contributes property Y to partnership CD. Simultaneously, partnership ABCD contributes property Z to partnership CD in exchange for an interest in partnership CD. Immediately thereafter, partnership ABCD distributes the interest in partnership CD to D in liquidation of D's interest in partnership ABCD.

(ii) Under paragraph (d)(3)(i) of this section, because partnership ABCD did not undertake the assets-up form with respect to all of the assets transferred to partnership CD, partnership ABCD will be treated as undertaking the assets-over form in transferring the assets to partnership CD. Accordingly, for Federal income tax purposes, partnership ABCD is deemed to contribute property Y and property Z to partnership CD in exchange for interests in partnership CD, and immediately thereafter, partnership ABCD is deemed to distribute the interests in partnership CD to partner C and partner D in liquidation of their interests in partnership ABCD.

Example 4. (i) Partnership ABCD owns three parcels of property: property X, with a value of $500; property Y, with a value of $300; and property Z, with a value of $200. A and B each own a 40-percent interest in the capital and profits of partnership ABCD, and C and D each own a 10 percent interest in the capital and profits of partnership ABCD. On November 1, 1999, partnership ABCD divides into three partnerships (AB1, AB2, and CD) by contributing property X to a newly formed partnership (AB1) and distributing all interests in such partnership to A and B as equal partners, and by contributing property Z to a newly formed partnership (CD) and distributing all interests in such partnership to C and D as equal partners in exchange for all of their interests in partnership ABCD. While partnership ABCD does not transfer property Y, C and D cease to be partners in the partnership. Accordingly, after the division, the partnership holding property Y is referred to as partnership AB2.

(ii) Partnerships AB1 and AB2 both are considered a continuation of partnership ABCD, while partnership CD is considered a new partnership formed at the beginning of the day on November 2, 1999. Under paragraph (d)(3)(i)(A) of this section, partnership ABCD will be treated as following the assets-over form, with partnership ABCD contributing property X to partnership AB1 and property Z to partnership CD, and distributing the interests in such partnerships to the designated partners.

Example 5. (i) The facts are the same as in *Example 4*, except that partnership ABCD divides into three partnerships by operation of state law, without undertaking a form.

(ii) Under the last sentence of paragraph (d)(4)(i) of this section, partnership AB1 will be treated as the resulting partnership that is the divided partnership. Under paragraph (d)(3)(i)(A) of this section, partnership ABCD will be treated as following the assets-over form, with partnership ABCD contributing property Y to partnership AB2 and property Z to partnership CD, and distributing the interests in such partnerships to the designated partners.

Example 6. (i) The facts are the same as in *Example 4*, except that partnership ABCD divides into three partnerships by contributing property X to newly-formed partnership AB1 and property Y to newly-formed partnership AB2 and distributing all interests in each partnership to A and B in exchange for all of their interests in partnership ABCD.

(ii) Because resulting partnership CD is not a continuation of the prior partnership (partnership ABCD), partnership CD cannot be treated, for Federal income tax purposes, as the partnership that transferred assets (i.e., the divided partnership), but instead must be treated as a recipient partnership. Under the last sentence of paragraph (d)(4)(i) of this section, partnership AB1 will be treated as the resulting partnership that is the divided partnership. Under paragraph (d)(3)(i)(A) of this section, partnership ABCD will be treated as following the assets-over form, with partnership ABCD contributing property Y to partnership AB2 and property Z to partnership CD, and distributing the interests in such partnerships to the designated partners.

Example 7. (i) Partnership ABCDE owns Blackacre, Whiteacre, and Redacre, and divides into partnership AB, partnership CD, and partnership DE. Under paragraph (d)(1) of this section, partnership ABCDE is considered terminated (and, hence, none of the resulting partnerships are a continuation of the prior partnership) because none of the members of the new partnerships (partnership AB, partnership CD, and partnership DE) owned an interest of more than 50 percent in the capital and profits of partnership ABCDE.

(ii) Partnership ABCDE distributes Blackacre to A and B and titles Blackacre in the names of A and B. A and B then contribute Blackacre to partnership AB in exchange for interests in partnership AB. Partnership ABCDE will be treated as following the assets-up form described in paragraph (d)(3)(ii)(B) of this section for Federal income tax purposes.

(iii) Partnership ABCDE distributes Whiteacre to C and D and titles Whiteacre in the names of C and D. C and D then contribute Whiteacre to partnership CD in exchange for interests in partnership CD. Partnership ABCDE will be treated as following the assets-up form described in paragraph (d)(3)(ii)(B) of this section for Federal income tax purposes.

(iv) Partnership ABCDE does not liquidate under state law so that, in form, the assets in new partnership DE are not considered to have been transferred under state law. Partnership ABCDE will be treated as undertaking the assets-over form described in paragraph (d)(3)(i)(B) of this section for Federal income tax purposes with respect to the assets of partnership DE. Thus, partnership ABCDE will be treated as contributing Redacre to partnership DE in exchange for interests in partnership DE; and, immediately thereafter, partnership ABCDE will be treated as distributing interests in partnership DE to D and E in liquidation of their interests in partnership ABCDE. Partnership ABCDE then terminates.

(6) *Prescribed form not followed in certain circumstances.*—If any transactions described in paragraph (d)(3) of this section are part of a larger series of transactions, and the substance of the larger series of transactions is inconsistent with following the form prescribed in such paragraph, the Commissioner may disregard such form, and may recast the larger series of transactions in accordance with their substance.

* * *

[Reg. § 1.708-1.]

☐ [*T.D.* 6175, 5-23-56. *Amended by T.D.* 8717, 5-8-97; *T.D.* 8925, 1-3-2001 (*corrected* 9-9-2002) *and T.D.* 9681, 7-22-2014.]

§ 1.709-2. Definitions.—(a) *Organizational expenses.*—Section 709(b)(2) of the Internal Revenue Code defines organizational expenses as expenses which:

(1) Are incident to the creation of the partnership;

(2) Are chargeable to capital account; and

(3) Are of a character which, if expended incident to the creation of a partnership having an ascertainable life, would (but for section 709(a)) be amortized over such life.

An expenditure which fails to meet one or more of these three tests does not qualify as an organizational expense for purposes of section 709(b) and this section. To satisfy the statutory requirement described in paragraph (a)(1) of this section, the expense must be incurred during the period beginning at a point which is a reasonable time before the partnership begins business and ending with the date prescribed by law for filing the partnership return (determined without regard to any extensions of time) for the taxable year the partnership begins business. In addition, the expenses must be for creation of the partnership and not for operation or starting operation of the partnership trade or business. To satisfy the statutory requirement described in paragraph (a)(3) of this section, the expense must be for an item of a nature normally expected to benefit the partnership throughout the entire life of the partnership. The following are examples of organizational expenses within the meaning of section 709 and this section: Legal fees for services incident to the organization of the partnership, such as negotiation and preparation of a partnership agreement; accounting fees for services incident to the organization of the partnership; and filing fees. The following are examples of expenses that are not organizational expenses within the meaning of section 709 and this section (regardless of how the partnership characterizes them): Expenses connected with acquiring assets for the partnership or transferring assets to the partnership; expenses connected with the admission or removal of partners other than at the time the partnership is first organized; expenses connected with a contract relating to the operation of the partnership trade or business (even where the contract is between the partnership and one of its members); and syndication expenses.

(b) *Syndication expenses.*—Syndication expenses are expenses connected with the issuing and marketing of interests in the partnership. Examples of syndication expenses are brokerage fees; registration fees; legal fees of the underwriter or placement agent and the issuer (the general partner or the partnership) for securities advice and for advice pertaining to the adequacy of tax disclosures in the prospectus or placement memorandum for securities law purposes; accounting fees for preparation of representations to be included in the offering materials; and printing costs of the prospectus, placement memorandum, and other selling and promotional material. These expenses are not subject to the election under section 709(b) and must be capitalized.

(c) *Beginning business.*—The determination of the date a partnership begins business for purposes of section 709 presents a question of fact that must be determined in each case in light of all the circumstances of the particular case. Ordinarily, a partnership begins business when it starts the business operation for which it was organized. The mere signing of a partnership agreement is not alone sufficient to show the beginning of business. If the activities of the partnership have advanced to the extent necessary to establish the nature of its business operations, it will be deemed to have begun business. Accordingly, the acquisition of operating assets which are necessary to the type of business contemplated may constitute beginning business for these purposes. The term "operating assets", as used herein, means assets that are in a state of readiness to be placed in service within a reasonable period following their acquisition. [Reg. § 1.709-2.]

☐ [*T.D.* 7891, 5-3-83.]

Contributions, Distributions and Transfers

§ 1.721-1. Nonrecognition of gain or loss on contribution.—(a) No gain or loss shall be recognized either to the partnership or to any of its partners upon a contribution of property, including installment obligations, to the partnership in exchange for a partnership interest. This rule applies whether the contribution is made to a partnership in the process of formation or to a partnership which is already formed and operating. Section 721 shall not apply to a transaction between a partnership and a partner not acting in his capacity as a partner since such a transaction is governed by section 707. Rather than contributing property to a partnership, a partner may sell property to the partnership or may retain the ownership of property and allow the partnership to use it. In all cases, the substance of the transaction will govern, rather than its form. See paragraph (c)(3) of § 1.731-1. Thus, if the transfer of property by the partner to the partnership results in the receipt by the partner of money or other consideration, including a promissory obligation fixed in amount and time for payment, the transaction will be treated as a sale or exchange under section 707 rather than as a contribution under section 721. For the rules governing the treatment of liabilities to which contributed property is subject, see section 752 and § 1.752-1.

(b) (1) Normally, under local law, each partner is entitled to be repaid his contributions of money or other property to the partnership (at the value placed upon such property by the partnership at the time of the contribution) whether made at the formation of the partnership or subsequent thereto. To the extent that any of the partners gives up any part of his right to be repaid his contributions (as distinguished from a share in partnership profits) in favor of another partner as compensation for services (or in satisfaction of an obligation), section 721 does not apply. The value of an interest in such partnership capital so transferred to a partner as compensation for services constitutes income to the partner under section 61. The amount of such income is the fair market value of the interest in capital so transferred, either at the time the transfer is made for past services, or at the time the services have been rendered where the transfer is conditioned on the completion of the transferee's future services. The time when such income is realized depends on all the facts and circumstances, including any substantial restrictions or conditions on the compensated partner's right to withdraw or otherwise dispose of such interest. To the extent that an interest in capital representing compensation for services rendered by the decedent prior to his death is transferred after his death to the decedent's successor in interest, the fair market value of such interest is income in respect of a decedent under section 691.

(2) To the extent that the value of such interest is: (i) compensation for services rendered to the partnership, it is a guaranteed payment for services under section 707(c); (ii)

compensation for services rendered to a partner, it is not deductible by the partnership, but is deductible only by such partner to the extent allowable under this chapter.

(c) *Underwritings of partnership interests.*—(1) *In general.*—For the purpose of section 721, if a person acquires a partnership interest from an underwriter in exchange for cash in a qualified underwriting transaction, the person who acquires the partnership interest is treated as transferring cash directly to the partnership in exchange for the partnership interest and the underwriter is disregarded. A qualified underwriting transaction is a transaction in which a partnership issues partnership interests for cash in an underwriting in which either the underwriter is an agent of the partnership or the underwriter's ownership of the partnership interests is transitory.

(2) *Effective date.*—This paragraph (c) is effective for qualified underwriting transactions occurring on or after May 1, 1996.

(d) *Debt-for-equity exchange.*—(1) *In general.*—Except as otherwise provided in section 721 and the regulations under section 721, section 721 applies to a contribution of a partnership's indebtedness by a creditor to the debtor partnership in exchange for a capital or profits interest in the partnership (debt-for-equity exchange). See § 1.108-8(a) for rules in determining the debtor partnership's discharge of indebtedness income.

(2) *Exception.*—Section 721 does not apply to a debt-for-equity exchange to the extent the transfer of the partnership interest to the creditor is in exchange for the partnership's indebtedness for unpaid rent, royalties, or interest (including accrued original issue discount) that accrued on or after the beginning of the creditor's holding period for the indebtedness. The debtor partnership will not recognize gain or loss upon the transfer of a partnership interest to a creditor in a debt-for-equity exchange for unpaid rent, royalties, or interest (including accrued original issue discount).

(3) *Cross reference.*—For rules in determining whether a partnership interest transferred to a creditor in a debt-for-equity exchange is treated as payment of interest or accrued original issue discount, see § § 1.446-2 and 1.1275-2, respectively.

* * *

[Reg. § 1.721-1.]

☐ [*T.D.* 6175, 5-23-56. *Amended by T.D.* 8665, 4-30-96 *and T.D.* 9557, 11-15-2011.]

Proposed Amendment to Regulation

§ 1.721-1. Nonrecognition of gain or loss on contribution.

* * *

(b) (1) Except as otherwise provided in this section or § 1.721-2, section 721 does not apply to the transfer of a partnership interest in connection with the performance of services or in satisfaction of an obligation. The transfer of a partnership interest to a person in connection with the performance of services constitutes a transfer of property to which section 83 and the regulations thereunder apply. To the extent that a partnership interest transferred in connection with the performance of services rendered by a decedent prior to the decedent's death is transferred after the decedent's death to the decedent's successor in interest, the fair market value of such interest is an item of income in respect of a decedent under section 691.

(2) Except as provided in section 83(h) and 1.83-6(c), no gain or loss shall be recognized by a partnership upon—

(i) The transfer or substantial vesting of a compensatory partnership interest; or

(ii) The forfeiture of a compensatory partnership interest. See § 1.704-1(b)(4)(xii) for rules regarding forfeiture allocations of partnership items that may be required in the taxable year of a forfeiture.

(3) For purposes of this section, a compensatory partnership interest is an interest in the transferring partnership that is transferred in connection with the performance of services for that partnership (either before or after the formation of the partnership), including an interest that is transferred on the exercise of a compensatory partnership option. A compensatory partnership option is an option to acquire an interest in the issuing partnership that is granted in connection with the performance of services for that partnership (either before or after the formation of the partnership).

(4) To the extent that a partnership interest is—

(i) Transferred to a partner in connection with the performance of services rendered to the partnership, it is a guaranteed payment for services under section 707(c);

(ii) Transferred in connection with the performance of services rendered to a partner, it is not deductible by the partnership, but is deductible only by such partner to the extent allowable under Chapter 1 of the Code.

(5) This paragraph (b) applies to interests that are transferred on or after the date final regulations are published in the Federal Register.

* * *

[Prop. Reg. § 1.721-1.]
[Proposed 5-24-2005.]

Proposed Amendment to Regulation

§ 1.721-1. Nonrecognition of gain or loss on contribution.

(a) * * * For rules in determining a partner's gain or loss when an installment obligation of a partnership is contributed to the partnership, see section 453B and § 1.453B-1(c). The preceding sentence applies to satisfactions of installment obligations after the date these regulations are published as final regulations in the Federal Register.

* * *

[Prop. Reg. § 1.721-1.]
[Proposed 12-23-2014.]

§ 1.722-1. Basis of contributing partner's interest.—The basis to a partner of a partnership interest acquired by a contribution of property, including money, to the partnership shall be the amount of money contributed plus the adjusted basis at the time of contribution of any property contributed. If the acquisition of an interest in partnership capital results in taxable income to a partner, such income shall constitute an addition to the basis of the partner's interest. See paragraph (b) of § 1.721-1. If the contributed property is subject to indebtedness or if liabilities of the partner are assumed by the partnership, the basis of the contributing partner's interest shall be reduced by the portion of the indebtedness assumed by the other partners, since the partnership's assumption of his indebtedness is treated as a distribution of money to the partner. Conversely, the assumption by the other partners of a portion of the contributor's indebtedness is treated as a contribution of money by them. See section 752 and § 1.752-1. See § 1.460-4(k)(3)(iv)(A) for rules relating to basis adjustments required where a contract accounted for under a long-term contract method of accounting is transferred in a contribution to which section 721(a) applies. The provisions of this section may be illustrated by the following examples:

Example (1). A acquired a 20-percent interest in a partnership by contributing property. At the time of A's contribution, the property had a fair market value of $10,000, an adjusted basis to A of $4,000, and was subject to a mortgage of $2,000. Payment of the mortgage was assumed by the partnership. The basis of A's interest in the partnership is $2,400, computed as follows:

Adjusted basis to A of property contributed	$4,000
Less portion of mortgage assumed by other partners which must be treated as a distribution (80 percent of $2,000)	1,600
Basis of A's interest	2,400

Example (2). If, in example (1) of this section, the property contributed by A was subject to a mortgage of $6,000, the basis of A's interest would be zero, computed as follows:

Adjusted basis to A of property contributed	$4,000
Less portion of mortgage assumed by other partners which must be treated as a distribution (80 percent of $6,000)	4,800
	(800)

Since A's basis cannot be less than zero, the $800 in excess of basis, which is considered as a distribution of money under section 752(b), is treated as capital gain from the sale or exchange of a partnership interest. See section 731(a). [Reg. § 1.722-1.]

□ [*T.D.* 6175, 5-23-56. *Amended by T.D.* 9137, 7-15-2004.]

§ 1.723-1. Basis of property contributed to partnership.—The basis to the partnership of property contributed to it by a partner is the adjusted basis of such property to the contributing partner at the time of the contribution. Since such property has the same basis in the hands of the partnership as it had in the hands of the contributing partner, the holding period of such property for the partnership includes the period during which it was held by the partner. See section 1223(2). For elective adjustments to the basis of partnership property arising from distributions or transfers of partnership interests, see sections 732(d), 734(b), and 743(b). See § 1.460-4(k)(3)(iv)(B)(*2*) for rules relating to adjustments to the basis of contracts accounted for using a long-term contract method of accounting that are acquired in certain contributions to which section 721(a) applies. [Reg. § 1.723-1.]

□ [*T.D.* 6175, 5-23-56. *Amended by T.D.* 9137, 7-15-2004.]

§ 1.731-1. Extent of recognition of gain or loss on distribution.—(a) *Recognition of gain or loss to partner.*—(1) *Recognition of gain.*—(i) Where money is distributed by a partnership to a partner, no gain shall be recognized to the partner except to the extent that the amount of money distributed exceeds the adjusted basis of the partner's interest in the partnership immediately before the distribution. This rule is applicable both to current distributions (i. e., distributions other than in liquidation of an entire interest) and to distributions in liquidation of a partner's entire interest in a partnership. Thus, if a partner with a basis for his interest of $10,000 receives a distribution of cash of $8,000 and property with a fair market value of $3,000, no gain is recognized to him. If $11,000 cash were distributed, gain would be recognized to the extent of $1,000. No gain shall be recognized to a distributee partner with respect to a distribution of property (other than money) until he sells or otherwise disposes of such property, except to the extent otherwise provided by section 736 (relating to payments to a retiring partner or a deceased partner's successor in interest) and section 751 (relating to unrealized receivables and inventory items). See section 731(c) and paragraph (c) of this section.

(ii) For the purposes of sections 731 and 705, advances or drawings of money or property against a partner's distributive share of income shall be treated as current distributions made on the last day of the partnership taxable year with respect to such partner.

(2) *Recognition of loss.*—Loss is recognized to a partner only upon liquidation of his entire interest in the partnership, and only if the property distributed to him consists solely of money, unrealized receivables (as defined in section 751(c)), and inventory items (as defined in section 751(d)(2)). The term "liquidation of a partner's interest", as defined in section 761(d), is the termination of the partner's entire interest in the partnership by means of a distribution or a series of distributions. Loss is recognized to the distributee partner in such cases to the extent of the excess of the adjusted basis of such partner's interest in the partnership at the time of the distribution over the sum of—

(i) Any money distributed to him, and

(ii) The basis to the distributee, as determined under section 732, of any unrealized receivables and inventory items that are distributed to him. If the partner whose interest is liquidated receives any property other than money, unrealized receivables, or inventory items, then no loss will be recognized. Application of the provisions of this subparagraph may be illustrated by the following examples:

Example (1). Partner A has a partnership interest in partnership ABC with an adjusted basis to him of $10,000. He retires from the partnership and receives, as a distribution in liquidation of his entire interest, his share of partnership property. This share is $5,000 cash and inventory with a basis to him (under section 732) of $3,000. Partner A realizes a capital loss of $2,000, which is recognized under section 731(a)(2).

Example (2). Partner B has a partnership interest in partnership BCD with an adjusted basis to him of $10,000. He retires from the partnership and receives, as a distribution in liquidation of his entire interest, his share of partnership property. This share is $4,000 cash, real property (used in the trade or business) with an adjusted basis to the partnership of $2,000, and unrealized receivables having a basis to him (under section 732) of $3,000. No loss will be recognized to B on the transaction because he received property other than money, unrealized receivables, and inventory items. As determined under section 732, the basis to B for the real property received is $3,000.

(3) *Character of gain or loss.*—Gain or loss recognized under section 731(a) on a distribution is considered gain or loss from the sale or exchange of the partnership interest of the distributee partner, that is, capital gain or loss.

(b) *Gain or loss recognized by partnership.*—A distribution of property (including money) by a partnership to a partner does not result in recognized gain or loss to the partnership under section 731. However, recognized gain or loss may result to the partnership from certain distributions which, under section 751(b), must be treated as a sale or exchange of property between the distributee partner and the partnership.

(c) *Exceptions.*—(1) Section 731 does not apply to the extent otherwise provided by—

(i) Section 736 (relating to payments to a retiring partner or to a deceased partner's successor in interest), and

(ii) Section 751 (relating to unrealized receivables and inventory items). For example, payments under section 736(a), which are considered as a distributive share or guaranteed payment, are taxable as such under that section.

(2) The receipt by a partner from the partnership of money or property under an obligation to repay the amount of such money or to return such property does not constitute a distribution subject to section 731 but is a loan governed by section 707(a). To the extent that such an obligation is canceled, the obligor partner will be considered to have received a distribution of money or property at the time of cancellation.

(3) If there is a contribution of property to a partnership and within a short period:

(i) Before or after such contribution other property is distributed to the contributing partner and the contributed property is retained by the partnership, or

(ii) After such contribution the contributed property is distributed to another partner, such distribution may not fall within the scope of section 731. Section 731 does not apply to a distribution of property, if, in fact, the distribution was made in order to effect an exchange of property between two or more of the partners or between the partnership and a partner. Such a transaction shall be treated as an exchange of property. [Reg. § 1.731-1.]

☐ [*T.D.* 6175, 5-23-56.]

§ 1.731-2. Partnership distributions of marketable securities.—(a) *Marketable securities treated as money.*—Except as otherwise provided in section 731(c) and this section, for purposes of sections 731(a)(1) and 737, the term *money* includes marketable securities and such securities are taken into account at their fair market value as of the date of the distribution.

(b) *Reduction of amount treated as money.*—(1) *Aggregation of securities.*—For purposes of section 731(c)(3)(B) and this paragraph (b), all marketable securities held by a partnership are treated as marketable securities of the same class and issuer as the distributed security.

(2) *Amount of reduction.*—The amount of the distribution of marketable securities that is treated as a distribution of money under section 731(c) and paragraph (a) of this section is reduced (but not below zero) by the excess, if any, of—

(i) The distributee partner's distributive share of the net gain, if any, which would be recognized if all the marketable securities held by the partnership were sold (immediately before the transaction to which the distribution relates) by the partnership for fair market value; over

(ii) The distributee partner's distributive share of the net gain, if any, which is attributable to the marketable securities held by the partnership immediately after the transaction, determined by using the same fair market value as used under paragraph (b)(2)(i) of this section.

(3) *Distributee partner's share of net gain.*—For purposes of section 731(c)(3)(B) and paragraph (b)(2) of this section, a partner's distributive share of net gain is determined—

(i) By taking into account any basis adjustments under section 743(b) with respect to that partner;

(ii) Without taking into account any special allocations adopted with a principal purpose of avoiding the effect of section 731(c) and this section; and

(iii) Without taking into account any gain or loss attributable to a distributed security to which paragraph (d)(1) of this section applies.

(c) *Marketable securities.*—(1) *In general.*—For purposes of section 731(c) and this section, the term *marketable securities* is defined in section 731(c)(2).

(2) *Actively traded.*—For purposes of section 731(c) and this section, a financial instrument is actively traded (and thus is a marketable security) if it is of a type that is, as of the date of distribution, actively traded within the meaning of section 1092(d)(1). Thus, for example, if *XYZ* common stock is listed on a national securities exchange, particular shares of *XYZ* common stock that are distributed by a partnership are marketable securities even if those particular shares cannot be resold by the distributee partner for a designated period of time.

(3) *Interests in an entity.*—(i) *Substantially all.*—For purposes of section 731(c)(2)(B)(v) and this section, substantially all of the assets of an entity consist (directly or indirectly) of marketable securities, money, or both only if 90 percent or more of the assets of the entity (by value) at the time of the distribution of an interest in the entity consist (directly or indirectly) of marketable securities, money, or both.

(ii) *Less than substantially all.*—For purposes of section 731(c)(2)(B)(vi) and this section, an interest in an entity is a marketable security to the extent that the value of the interest is attributable (directly or indirectly) to marketable securities, money, or both, if less than 90 percent but 20 percent or more of the assets of the entity (by value) at the time of the distribution of an interest in the entity consist (directly or indirectly) of marketable securities, money, or both.

(4) *Value of assets.*—For purposes of section 731(c) and this section, the value of the assets of an entity is determined without regard to any debt that may encumber or otherwise be allocable to those assets, other than debt that is incurred to acquire an asset with a principal purpose of avoiding or reducing the effect of section 731(c) and this section.

(d) *Exceptions.*—(1) *In general.*—Except as otherwise provided in paragraph (d)(2) of this section, section 731(c) and this section do not apply to the distribution of a marketable security if—

(i) The security was contributed to the partnership by the distributee partner;

(ii) The security was acquired by the partnership in a nonrecognition transaction, and the following conditions are satisfied—

(A) The value of any marketable securities and money exchanged by the partnership in the nonrecognition transaction is less than 20 percent of the value of all the assets exchanged by the partnership in the nonrecognition transaction; and

(B) The partnership distributed the security within five years of either the date the security was acquired by the partnership or, if later, the date the security became marketable; or

(iii) The security was not a marketable security on the date acquired by the partnership, and the following conditions are satisfied—

(A) The entity that issued the security had no outstanding marketable securities at the time the security was acquired by the partnership;

(B) The security was held by the partnership for at least six months before the date the security became marketable; and

(C) The partnership distributed the security within five years of the date the security became marketable.

(2) *Anti-stuffing rule.*—Paragraph (d)(1) of this section does not apply to the extent that 20 percent or more of the value of the distributed security is attributable to marketable securities or money contributed (directly or indirectly) by the partnership to the entity to which the distributed security relates after the security was acquired by the partnership (other than marketable securities contributed by the partnership that were originally contributed to the partnership by the distributee partner). For purposes of this paragraph (d)(2), money contributed by the distributing partnership does not include any money deemed contributed by the partnership as a result of section 752.

(3) *Successor security.*—Section 731(c) and this section apply to the distribution of a marketable security acquired by the partnership in a nonrecognition transaction in exchange for a security the distribution of which immediately prior to the exchange would have been excepted under this paragraph (d) only to the extent that section 731(c) and this section otherwise would have applied to the exchanged security.

(e) *Investment partnerships.*—(1) *In general.*—Section 731(c) and this section do not apply to the distribution of marketable securities by an investment partnership (as defined in section 731(c)(3)(C)(i)) to an eligible partner (as defined in section 731(c)(3)(C)(iii)).

(2) *Eligible partner.*—(i) *Contributed services.*—For purposes of section 731(c)(3)(C)(iii) and this section, a partner is not treated as a partner other than an eligible partner solely because the partner contributed services to the partnership.

(ii) *Contributed partnership interests.*—For purposes of determining whether a partner is an eligible partner under section 731(c)(3)(C), if the partner has contributed to the investment partnership an interest in another partnership that meets the requirements of paragraph (e)(4)(i) of this section after the contribution, the contributed interest is treated as property specified in section 731(c)(3)(C)(i).ship is not treated as engaged in a trade or business by reason of—

(i) Any activity undertaken as an investor, trader, or dealer in any asset described in section 731(c)(3)(C)(i), including the receipt of commitment fees, break-up fees, guarantee fees, director's fees, or similar fees that are customary in and incidental to any activities of the partnership as an investor, trader, or dealer in such assets;

(ii) Reasonable and customary management services (including the receipt of reasonable and customary fees in exchange for such management services) provided to an investment partnership (within the meaning of section 731(c)(3)(C)(i)) in which the partnership holds a partnership interest; or

(iii) Reasonable and customary services provided by the partnership in assisting the formation, capitalization, expansion, or offering of interests in a corporation (or other entity) in which the partnership holds or acquires a significant equity interest (including the provision of advice or consulting services, bridge loans, guarantees of obligations, or service on a company's board of directors), provided that the anticipated receipt of compensation for the services, if any, does not represent a significant purpose for the partnership's investment in the entity and is incidental to the investment in the entity.

(4) *Partnership tiers.*—For purposes of section 731(c)(3)(C)(iv) and this section, a partnership (upper-tier partnership) is not treated as engaged in a trade or business engaged in by, or as holding (instead of a partnership interest) a proportionate share of the assets of, a partnership (lower-tier partnership) in which the partnership holds a partnership interest if—

(i) The upper-tier partnership does not actively and substantially participate in the management of the lower-tier partnership; and

(ii) The interest held by the upper-tier partnership is less than 20 percent of the total profits and capital interests in the lower-tier partnership.

(f) *Basis rules.*—(1) *Partner's basis.*—(i) *Partner's basis in distributed securities.*—The distributee partner's basis in distributed marketable securities with respect to which gain is recognized by reason of section 731(c) and this section is the basis of the security determined under section 732, increased by the amount of such gain. Any increase in the basis of the marketable securities attributable to gain recognized by reason of section 731(c) and this section is allocated to marketable securities in proportion to their respective amounts of unrealized appreciation in the hands of the partner before such increase.

(ii) *Partner's basis in partnership interest.*—The basis of the distributee partner's interest in the partnership is determined under section 733 as if no gain were recognized by the partner on the distribution by reason of section 731(c) and this section.

(2) *Basis of partnership property.*—No adjustment is made to the basis of partnership property under section 734 as a result of any gain recognized by a partner, or any step-up in the basis in the distributed marketable securities in the hands of the distributee partner, by reason of section 731(c) and this section.

(g) *Coordination with other sections.*—(1) *Sections 704(c)(1)(B) and 737.*—(i) *In general.*—If a distribution results in the application of sections 731(c) and one or both of sections 704(c)(1)(B) and 737, the effect of the distribution is determined by applying section 704(c)(1)(B) first, section 731(c) second, and finally section 737.

(ii) *Section 704(c)(1)(B).*—The basis of the distributee partner's interest in the partnership for purposes of determining the amount of gain, if any, recognized by reason of section 731(c) (and for determining the basis of the marketable securities in the hands of the distributee partner) includes the increase or decrease, if any, in the partner's basis that occurs under section 704(c)(1)(B)(iii) as a result of a distribution to another partner of property contributed by the distributee partner in a distribution that is part of the same distribution as the marketable securities.

(iii) *Section 737.*—(A) *Marketable securities as other property.*—A distribution of marketable securities is treated as a distribution of property other than money for purposes of section 737 to the extent that the marketable securities are not treated as money under section 731(c). In addition, marketable securities contributed to the partnership are treated as property other than money in determining the contributing partner's net precontribution gain under section 737(b).

(B) *Basis increase under section 737.*—The basis of the distributee partner's interest in the partnership for purposes of determining the amount of gain, if any, recognized by reason of section 731(c) (and for determining the basis of the marketable securities in the hands of the distributee partner) does not include the increase, if any, in the partner's basis that occurs under section 737(c)(1) as a result of a distribution of property to the distributee partner in a distribution that is part of the same distribution as the marketable securities.

(2) *Section 708(b)(1)(B).*—If a partnership termination occurs under section 708(b)(1)(B), the successor partnership will be treated as if there had been no termination for purposes of section 731(c) and this section. Accordingly, a section 708(b)(1)(B) termination will not affect whether a partnership qualifies for any of the exceptions in paragraphs (d) and (e) of this section. In addition, a deemed distribution that may occur as a result of a section 708(b)(1)(B) termination will not be subject to section 731(c) and this section.

(h) *Anti-abuse rule.*—The provisions of section 731(c) and this section must be applied in a manner consistent with the purpose of section 731(c) and the substance of the transaction. Accordingly, if a principal purpose of a transaction is to achieve a tax result that is inconsistent with the purpose of section 731(c) and this section, the Commissioner can recast the transaction for Federal tax purposes as appropriate to achieve tax results that are consistent with the purpose of section 731(c) and this section. Whether a tax result is inconsistent with the purpose of section 731(c) and this section must be determined based on all the facts and circumstances. For example, under the provisions of this paragraph (h)—

(1) A change in partnership allocations or distribution rights with respect to marketable securities may be treated as a distribution of the marketable securities subject to section 731(c) if the change in allocations or distribution rights is, in substance, a distribution of the securities;

(2) A distribution of substantially all of the assets of the partnership other than marketable securities and money to some partners may also be treated as a distribution of marketable securities to the remaining partners if the distribution of the other property and the withdrawal of the other partners is, in substance, equivalent to a distribution of the securities to the remaining partners; and

(3) The distribution of multiple properties to one or more partners at different times may also be treated as part of a single distribution if

the distributions are part of a single plan of distribution.

(i) [Reserved]

(j) *Examples.*—The following examples illustrate the rules of this section. Unless otherwise specified, all securities held by a partnership are marketable securities within the meaning of section 731(c); the partnership holds no marketable securities other than the securities described in the example; all distributions by the partnership are subject to section 731(a) and are not subject to sections 704(c)(1)(B), 707(a)(2)(B), 751(b), or 737; and no securities are eligible for an exception to section 731(c). The examples read as follows:

Example 1. Recognition of gain. (i) *A* and *B* form partnership *AB* as equal partners. *A* contributes property with a fair market value of $1,000 and an adjusted tax basis of $250. *B* contributes $1,000 cash. *AB* subsequently purchases Security *X* for $500 and immediately distributes the security to *A* in a current distribution. The basis in *A*'s interest in the partnership at the time of distribution is $250.

(ii) The distribution of Security *X* is treated as a distribution of money in an amount equal to the fair market value of Security *X* on the date of distribution ($500). (The amount of the distribution that is treated as money is not reduced under section 731(c)(3)(B) and paragraph (b) of this section because, if Security *X* had been sold immediately before the distribution, there would have been no gain recognized by *AB* and *A*'s distributive share of the gain would therefore have been zero.) As a result, *A* recognizes $250 of gain under section 731(a)(1) on the distribution ($500 distribution of money less $250 adjusted tax basis in *A*'s partnership interest).

Example 2. Reduction in amount treated as money—in general. (i) *A* and *B* form partnership *AB* as equal partners. *AB* subsequently distributes Security *X* to *A* in a current distribution. Immediately before the distribution, *AB* held securities with the following fair market values, adjusted tax bases, and unrecognized gain or loss:

	Value	Basis	Gain (Loss)
Security *X*	100	70	30
Security *Y*	100	80	20
Security *Z*	100	110	(10)

(ii) If *AB* had sold the securities for fair market value immediately before the distribution to *A*, the partnership would have recognized $40 of net gain ($30 gain on Security *X* plus $20 gain on Security *Y* minus $10 loss on Security *Z*). *A*'s distributive share of this gain would have been $20 (one-half of $40 net gain). If *AB* had sold the remaining securities immediately after the distribution of Security *X* to *A*, the partnership would have $10 of net gain ($20 of gain on Security *Y* minus $10 loss on Security *Z*). *A*'s distributive share of this gain would have been $5 (one-half of $10 net gain). As a result, the distribution resulted in a decrease of $15 in *A*'s distributive share of the net gain in *AB*'s securities ($20 net gain before distribution minus $5 net gain after distribution).

(iii) Under paragraph (b) of this section, the amount of the distribution of Security *X* that is treated as a distribution of money is reduced by $15. The distribution of Security *X* is therefore treated as a distribution of $85 of money to *A* ($100 fair market value of Security *X* minus $15 reduction).

* * *

[Reg. § 1.731-2.]

□ [*T.D.* 8707, 12-24-96.]

§ 1.732-1. Basis of distributed property other than money.—(a) *Distributions other than in liquidation of a partner's interest.*—The basis of property (other than money) received by a partner in a distribution from a partnership, other than in liquidation of his entire interest, shall be its adjusted basis to the partnership immediately before such distribution. However, the basis of the property to the partner shall not exceed the adjusted basis of the partner's interest in the partnership, reduced by the amount of any money distributed to him in the same transaction. The provisions of this paragraph may be illustrated by the following examples:

Example (1). Partner A, with an adjusted basis of $15,000 for his partnership interest, receives in a current distribution property having an adjusted basis of $10,000 to the partnership immediately before distribution, and $2,000 cash. The basis of the property in A's hands will be $10,000. Under sections 733 and 705, the basis of A's partnership interest will be reduced by the distribution to $3,000 ($15,000, less $2,000 cash, less $10,000, the basis of the distributed property to A).

Example (2). Partner R has an adjusted basis of $10,000 for his partnership interest. He receives a current distribution of $4,000 cash and property with an adjusted basis to the partnership of $8,000. The basis of the distributed property to partner R is limited to $6,000 ($10,000, the adjusted basis of his interest, reduced by $4,000, the cash distributed).

(b) *Distribution in liquidation.*—Where a partnership distributes property (other than money) in liquidation of a partner's entire interest in the partnership, the basis of such property to the partner shall be an amount equal to the adjusted basis of his interest in the partnership reduced by the amount of any money distributed to him in the same transaction. Application of this rule may be illustrated by the following example:

Example. Partner B, with a partnership interest having an adjusted basis to him of $12,000, retires from the partnership and receives cash of $2,000, and real property with an adjusted basis to the partnership of $6,000 and a fair market value of $14,000. The basis of the real property to B is $10,000 (B's basis for his partnership interest, $12,000, reduced by $2,000, the cash distributed).

(c) *Allocation of basis among properties distributed to a partner.*—(1) *General rule.*—(i) *Unrealized receivables and inventory items.*—Except as provided in paragraph (c)(1)(iii) of this section, the basis to be allocated to properties distributed to a partner under section 732(a)(2) or (b) is allocated first to any unrealized receivables (as defined in section 751(c)) and inventory items (as defined in section 751(d)(2)) in an amount equal to the adjusted basis of each such property to the partnership immediately before the distribution. If the basis to be allocated is less than the sum of the adjusted bases to the partnership of the distributed unrealized receivables and inventory items, the adjusted basis of the distributed property must be decreased in the manner provided in § 1.732-1(c)(2)(i). See § 1.460-4(k)(2)(iv)(D) for a rule determining the partnership's basis in long-term contract accounted for under a long-term contract method of accounting.

(ii) *Other distributed property.*—Any basis not allocated to unrealized receivables or inventory items under paragraph (c)(1)(i) of this section or to stock of persons that control the corporate partner or to the corporate partner's stock under paragraph (c)(1)(iii) of this section is allocated to any other property distributed to the partner in the same transaction by assigning to each distributed property an amount equal to the adjusted basis of the property to the partnership immediately before the distribution. However, if the sum of the adjusted bases to the partnership of such other distributed property does not equal the basis to be allocated among the distributed property, any increase or decrease required to make the amounts equal is allocated among the distributed property as provided in § 1.732-1(c)(2).

(iii) *Stock distributed to the corporate partner.*—If a partnership makes a distribution described in § 1.337(d)-3(e)(1), then for purposes of this section, the basis to be allocated to properties distributed under section 732(a)(2) or (b) is allocated first to the Stock of the Corporate Partner, as defined in § 1.337(d)-3(c)(2), before the distribution of any other property (other than cash). The amount allocated to the Stock of the Corporate Partner is as provided in § 1.337(d)-3(e)(2).

(2) *Adjustment to basis allocation.*—(i) *Decrease in basis.*—Any decrease to the basis of distributed property required under paragraph (c)(1) of this section is allocated first to distributed property with unrealized depreciation in proportion to each property's respective amount of unrealized depreciation before any decrease (but only to the extent of each property's unrealized depreciation). If the required decrease exceeds the amount of unrealized depreciation in the distributed property, the excess is allocated to the distributed property in proportion to the adjusted bases of the distributed property, as adjusted pursuant to the immediately preceding sentence.

(ii) *Increase in basis.*—Any increase to the basis of distributed property required under paragraph (c)(1)(ii) of this section is allocated first to distributed property (other than unrealized receivables and inventory items) with unrealized appreciation in proportion to each property's respective amount of unrealized appreciation before any increase (but only to the extent of each property's unrealized appreciation). If the required increase exceeds the amount of unrealized appreciation in the distributed property, the excess is allocated to the distributed property (other than unrealized receivables or inventory items) in proportion to the fair market value of the distributed property.

(3) *Unrealized receivables and inventory items.*—If the basis to be allocated upon a distribution in liquidation of the partner's entire interest in the partnership is greater than the adjusted basis to the partnership of the unrealized receivables and inventory items distributed to the partner, and if there is no other property distributed to which the excess can be allocated, the distributed partner sustains a capital loss under section 731(a)(2) to the extent of the unallocated basis of the partnership interest.

(4) *Examples.*—The provisions of this paragraph (c) are illustrated by the following examples:

Example 1. A is a one-fourth partner in partnership PRS and has an adjusted basis in its partnership interest of $650. PRS distributes inventory items and Assets X and Y to A in liquidation of A's entire partnership interest.

The distributed inventory items have a basis to the partnership of $100 and a fair market value of $200. Asset X has an adjusted basis to the partnership of $50 and a fair market value of $400. Asset Y has an adjusted basis to the partnership and a fair market value of $100. Neither Asset X nor Asset Y consists of inventory items or unrealized receivables. Under this paragraph (c), A's basis in its partnership interest is allocated first to the inventory items in an amount equal to their adjusted basis to the partnership. A, therefore, has an adjusted basis in the inventory items of $100. The remaining basis, $550, is allocated to the distributed property first in an amount equal to the property's adjusted basis to the partnership. Thus, Asset X is allocated $50 and Asset Y is allocated $100. Asset X is then allocated $350, the amount of unrealized appreciation in Asset X. Finally, the remaining basis, $50, is allocated to Assets X and Y in proportion to their fair market values: $40 to Asset X (400/500 × $50), and $10 to Asset Y (100/500 × $50). Therefore, after the distribution, A has an adjusted basis of $440 in Asset X and $110 in Asset Y.

Example 2. B is a one-fourth partner in partnership PRS and has an adjusted basis in its partnership interest of $200. PRS distributes Asset X and Asset Y to B in liquidation of its entire partnership interest. Asset X has an adjusted basis to the partnership and fair market value of $150. Asset Y has an adjusted basis to the partnership of $150 and a fair market value of $50. Neither of the assets consists of inventory items or unrealized receivables. Under this paragraph (c), B's basis is first assigned to the distributed property to the extent of the partnership's basis in each distributed property. Thus, Asset X and Asset Y are each assigned $150. Because the aggregate adjusted basis of the distributed property, $300, exceeds the basis to be allocated, $200, a decrease of $100 in the basis of the distributed property is required. Assets X and Y have unrealized depreciation of zero and $100, respectively. Thus, the entire decrease is allocated to Asset Y. After the distribution, B has an adjusted basis of $150 in Asset X and $50 in Asset Y.

Example 3. C, a partner in partnership PRS, receives a distribution in liquidation of its entire partnership interest of $6,000 cash, inventory items having an adjusted basis to the partnership of $6,000, and real property having an adjusted basis to the partnership of $4,000. C's basis in its partnership interest is $9,000. The cash distribution reduces C's basis to $3,000, which is allocated entirely to the inventory items. The real property has a zero basis in C's hands. The partnership bases not carried over to C for the distributed properties are lost unless an election under section 754 is in effect requiring the partnership to adjust the bases of remaining partnership properties under section 734(b).

Example 4. Assume the same facts as in *Example 3* of this paragraph except C receives a distribution in liquidation of its entire partnership interest of $1,000 cash and inventory items having a basis to the partnership of $6,000. The cash distribution reduces C's basis to $8,000, which can be allocated only to the extent of $6,000 to the inventory items. The remaining $2,000 basis, not allocable to the distributed property, constitutes a capital loss to partner C under section 731(a)(2). If the election under section 754 is in effect, see section 734(b) for adjustment of the basis of undistributed partnership property.

* * *

(d) *Special partnership basis to transferee under section 732(d).*—(1)(i) A transfer of a partnership interest occurs upon a sale or exchange of an interest or upon the death of a partner. Section 732(d) provides a special rule for the determination of the basis of property distributed to a transferee partner who acquired any part of his partnership interest in a transfer with respect to which the election under section 754 (relating to the optional adjustment to basis of partnership property) was not in effect.

(ii) Where an election under section 754 is in effect, see section 743(b) and §§1.743-1 and 1.732-2.

(iii) If a transferee partner receives a distribution of property (other than money) from the partnership within 2 years after he acquired his interest or part thereof in the partnership by a transfer with respect to which the election under section 754 was not in effect, he may elect to treat as the adjusted partnership basis of such property the adjusted basis such property would have if the adjustment provided in section 743(b) were in effect.

(iv) If an election under section 732(d) is made upon a distribution of property to a transferee partner, the amount of the adjustment with respect to the transferee partner is not diminished by any depletion or depreciation on that portion of the basis of partnership property which arises from the special basis adjustment under section 732(d), since depletion or depreciation on such portion for the period prior to distribution is allowed or allowable only if the optional adjustment under section 743(b) is in effect.

(v) If property is distributed to a transferee partner who elects under section 732(d), and if such property is not the same property which would have had a special basis adjustment, then such special basis adjustment shall apply to any like property received in the distribution, provided that the transferee, in exchange for the property distributed, has relinquished his interest in the property with respect to which he would have had a special basis adjustment. This rule applies whether the property in which the transferee has relinquished his interest is retained or disposed of by the partnership. (For a shift of transferee's basis adjustment under section 743(b) to like property, see § 1.743-1(g).)

(vi) The provisions of this paragraph (d)(1) may be illustrated by the following example:

Example. (i) Transferee partner, T, purchased a one-fourth interest in partnership PRS for $17,000. At the time T purchased the partnership interest, the election under section 754 was not in effect and the partnership inventory had a basis to the partnership of $14,000 and a fair market value of $16,000. T's purchase price reflected $500 of this difference. Thus, $4,000 of the $17,000 paid by T for the partnership interest was attributable to T's share of partnership inventory with a basis of $3,500. Within 2 years after T acquired the partnership interest, T retired from the partnership and received in liquidation of its entire partnership interest the following property:

Assets	*Adjusted Basis to PRS*	*Fair Market Value*
Cash	$1,500	$1,500
Inventory	$3,500	$4,000
Asset X	$2,000	$4,000
Asset Y	$4,000	$5,000

(ii) The fair market value of the inventory received by T was one-fourth of the fair market value of all partnership inventory and was T's share of such property. It is immaterial whether the inventory T received was on hand when T acquired the interest. In accordance with T's election under section 732(d), the amount of T's share of partnership basis that is attributable to partnership inventory is increased by $500 (one-fourth of the $2,000 difference between the fair market value of the property, $16,000, and its $14,000 basis to the partnership at the time T purchased its interest). This adjustment under section 732(d) applies only for purposes of distributions to T, and not for purposes of partnership depreciation, depletion, or gain or loss on disposition. Thus, the amount to be allocated among the properties received by T in the liquidating distribution is $15,500 ($17,000, T's basis for the partnership interest, reduced by the amount of cash received, $1,500). This amount is allocated as follows: The basis of the inventory items received is $4,000, consisting of the $3,500 common partnership basis, plus the basis adjustment of $500 which T would have had under section 743(b). The remaining basis of $11,500 ($15,500 minus $4,000) is allocated among the remaining property distributed to T by assigning to each property the adjusted basis to the partnership of such property and adjusting that basis by any required increase or decrease. Thus, the adjusted basis to T of Asset X is $5,111 ($2,000, the adjusted basis of Asset X to the partnership, plus $2,000, the amount of unrealized appreciation in Asset X, plus $1,111 ($4,000/$9,000 multiplied by $2,500)). Similarly, the adjusted basis of Asset Y to T is $6,389 ($4,000, the adjusted basis of Asset Y to the partnership, plus $1,000, the amount of unrealized appreciation in Asset Y, plus, $1,389 ($5,000/$9,000 multiplied by $2,500)).

(2) A transferee partner who wishes to elect under section 732(d) shall make the election with his tax return—

(i) For the year of the distribution, if the distribution includes any property subject to the allowance for depreciation, depletion, or amortization, or

(ii) For any taxable year no later than the first taxable year in which the basis of any of the distributed property is pertinent in determining his income tax, if the distribution does not include any such property subject to the allowance for depreciation, depletion or amortization.

(3) A taxpayer making an election under section 732(d) shall submit with the return in which the election is made a schedule setting forth the following:

(i) That under section 732(d) he elects to adjust the basis of property received in a distribution; and

(ii) The computation of the special basis adjustment for the property distributed and the properties to which the adjustment has been allocated. For rules of allocation, see section 755.

(4) A partner who acquired any part of his partnership interest in a transfer to which the election provided in section 754 was not in effect, is required to apply the special basis rule contained in section 732(d) to a distribution to him, whether or not made within 2 years after the transfer, if at the time of his acquisition of the transferred interest—

(i) The fair market value of all partnership property (other than money) exceeded 110 percent of its adjusted basis to the partnership,

(ii) An allocation of basis under section 732(c) upon a liquidation of his interest immediately after the transfer of the interest would have resulted in a shift of basis from property not subject to an allowance for depreciation, depletion, or amortization, to property subject to such an allowance, and

(iii) A basis adjustment under section 743(b) would change the basis to the transferee partner of the property actually distributed.

(5) *Required statements.*—If a transferee partner notifies a partnership that it plans to make the election under section 732(d) under paragraph (d)(3) of this section, or if a partnership makes a distribution to which paragraph (d)(4) of this section applies, the partnership must provide the transferee with such information as is necessary for the transferee properly to compute the transferee's basis adjustments under section 732(d).

(e) *Exception.*—When a partnership distributes unrealized receivables (as defined in section 751(c)) or substantially appreciated inventory items (as defined in section 751(d)) in exchange for any part of a partner's interest in other partnership property (including money), or, conversely, partnership property (including money) other than unrealized receivables or substantially appreciated inventory items in exchange for any part of a partner's interest in the partnership's unrealized receivables or substantially appreciated inventory items, the distribution will be treated as a sale or exchange of property under the provisions of section 751(b). In such case, section 732 (including subsection (d) thereof) applies in determining the partner's basis of the property which he is treated as having sold to or exchanged with the partnership (as constituted after the distribution). The partner is considered as having received such property in a current distribution and, immediately thereafter, as having sold or exchanged it. See section 751(b) and paragraph (b) of § 1.751-1. However, section 732 does not apply in determining the basis of that part of property actually distributed to a partner which is treated as received by him in a sale or exchange under section 751(b). Consequently, the basis of such property shall be its cost to the partner. [Reg. § 1.732-1.]

□ [*T.D.* 6175, 5-23-56. *Amended by T.D.* 8847, 12-14-99; *T.D.* 9137, 7-15-2004; *T.D.* 9722, 6-11-2015 *and T.D.* 9833, 6-7-2018.]

§ 1.732-2. Special partnership basis of distributed property.—(a) *Adjustments under section 734(b).*—In the case of a distribution of property to a partner, the partnership bases of the distributed properties shall reflect any increases or decreases to the basis of partnership property which have been made previously under section 734(b) (relating to the optional adjustment to basis of undistributed partnership property) in connection with previous distributions.

(b) *Adjustments under section 743(b).*—In the case of a distribution of property to a partner who acquired any part of his interest in a transfer as to which an election under section 754 was in effect, then, for the purposes of section 732 (other than subsection (d) thereof), the adjusted partnership bases of the distributed property shall take into account, in addition to any adjustments under section 734(b), the transferee's special basis adjustment for the distributed property under section 743(b). The application of this paragraph may be illustrated by the following example:

Example. Partner D acquired his interest in partnership ABD from a a previous partner. Since the partnership had made an election under section 754, a special basis adjustment with respect to D is applicable to the basis of partnership property in accordance with section 743(b). One of the assets of the partnership at the time D acquired his interest was property X, which is later distributed to D in a current distribution. Property X has an adjusted basis to the partnership of $1,000 and with respect to D it has a special basis adjustment of $500. Therefore, for purposes of section 732(a)(1), the adjusted basis of such property to the partnership with respect to D immediately before its distribution is $1,500. However, if property X is distributed to partner A, a nontransferee partner, its adjusted basis to the partnership for purposes of section 732(a)(1) is only $1,000. In such case, D's $500 special basis adjustment may shift over to other property. See § 1.743-1(g).

(c) *Adjustments to basis of distributed inventory and unrealized receivables.*—Under section 732, the basis to be allocated to distributed properties shall be allocated first to any unrealized receivables and inventory items. If the distributee partner is a transferee of a partnership interest and has a special basis adjustment for unrealized receivables or inventory items under either section 743(b) or section 732(d), then the partnership adjusted basis immediately prior to distribution of any unrealized receivables or inventory items distributed to such partner shall be determined as follows: If the distributee partner receives his entire share of the fair market value of the inventory items or unrealized receivables of the partnership, the adjusted basis of such distributed property to the partnership, for the purposes of section 732, shall take into account the entire amount of any special basis adjustment which the distributee partner may have for such assets. If the distributee partner receives less than his entire share of the fair market value of partnership inventory items or unrealized receivables, then, for purposes of section 732, the adjusted basis of such distributed property to the partnership shall take into account the same proportion of the distributee's special basis adjustment for unrealized receivables or inventory items as the value of such items distributed to him bears to his entire share of the total value of all such items of the partnership. The provisions of this paragraph may be illustrated by the following example:

Example. Partner C acquired his 40-percent interest in partnership AC from a previous partner. Since the partnership had made an election under section 754, C has a special basis adjustment to partnership property under section 743(b). C retires from the partnership when the adjusted basis of his partnership interest is $3,000. He receives from the partnership in liquidation of his entire interest, $1,000 cash, certain capital assets, depreciable property, and certain inventory items and unrealized receivables. C has a special basis adjustment of $800 with respect to partnership inventory items and of $200 with respect to unrealized receivables. The common partnership basis for the inventory items distributed to him is $500 and for the unrealized receivables is zero. If the value of inventory items and the unrealized receivables distributed to C in [is] his 40-percent share of the total value of all partnership inventory items and unrealized receivables, then, for purposes of section 732, the adjusted basis of such property in C's hands will be $1,300 for the inventory items ($500 plus $800) and $200 for the unrealized receivables (zero plus $200). The remaining basis of $500, which constitutes the basis of the capital assets and depreciable property distributed to C, is determined as follows: $3,000 (total basis) less $1,000 cash, or $2,000 (the amount to be allocated to the basis of all distributed property), less $1,500 ($800 and $200 special basis adjustments, plus $500 common partnership basis, the amount allocated to inventory items and unrealized receivables). However, if the value of the inventory items and unrealized receivables distributed to C consisted of only 20 percent of the total fair market value of such property (i.e., only one-half of C's 40-percent share), then only one-half of C's special basis adjustment of $800 for partnership inventory items and $200 for unrealized receivables would be taken into account. In that case, the basis of the inventory items in C's hands would be $650 ($250, the common partnership basis for inventory items distributed to him, plus $400, one-half of C's special basis adjustment for inventory items). The basis of the unrealized receivables in C's hands would be $100 (zero plus $100, one-half of C's special basis adjustment for unrealized receivables). [Reg. §1.732-2.]

☐ [*T.D.* 6175, 5-23-56. *Amended by T.D.* 8847, 12-14-99.]

Proposed Amendments to Regulation

§1.732-2. Special partnership basis of distributed property.

* * *

(b) *Adjustments under section 743(b).*—(1) *In general.*—In the case of a distribution of property to a partner who acquired any part of its interest in a transfer, if there was an election under section 754 in effect with respect to the transfer, or if the partnership had a substantial built-in loss (as defined in §1.743-1(a)(2)(i)) immediately after the transfer, then, for purposes of section 732 (other than subsection (d) thereof), the adjusted partnership basis of the distributed property shall take into account, in addition to any adjustments under section 734(b), the transferee's special basis adjustment for the distributed property under section 743(b). The application of this paragraph may be illustrated by the following example:

* * *

(2) *Effective/applicability date.*—Paragraph (b)(1) of this section relating to substantial built-in losses is applicable for partnership distributions occurring on or after the date of publication of the Treasury decision adopting these rules as final regulations in the Federal Register.

(c) *Adjustments under section 704(c)(1)(C).*—(1) *In general.*—In the case of a distribution of property to a section 704(c)(1)(C) partner (as defined in §1.704-3(f)(2)(ii)), for purposes of section 732 (other than subsection (d) thereof), the adjusted partnership basis of the distributed property shall take into account, in addition to any adjustments under section 734(b), the distributee's section 704(c)(1)(C) basis adjustment (if any) for the distributed property.

* * *

[Prop. Reg. §1.732-2.]

[Proposed 1-16-2014.]

§1.732-3. Corresponding adjustment to basis of assets of a distributed corporation controlled by a corporate partner.—(a) *Determination of control.*—The determination of whether a corporate partner that is a member of a consolidated group has control of a distributed corporation for purposes of section 732(f) shall be made by applying the special aggregate stock ownership rules of §1.1502-34.

(b) *Aggregation of basis within consolidated group.*—With respect to distributed stock of a corporation, if the following two conditions are met, then section 732(f) shall apply only to the extent that the partnership's adjusted basis in the distributed stock immediately before the distribution exceeds the aggregate basis of the distributed stock of the corporation in the hands of corporate partners that are members of the same consolidated group (as defined in § 1.1502-1(h)) immediately after the distribution:

(1) Two or more of the corporate partners receive a distribution of stock in another corporation; and

(2) The corporation, the stock of which was distributed by the partnership, is or becomes a member of the distributee partners' consolidated group following the distribution.

(c) *Application of section 732(f) to Gain Elimination Transactions.*—(1) *General rule.*— In the event of a Gain Elimination Transaction, section 732(f) shall apply as though the Corporate Partner acquired control (as defined in section 732(f)(5)) of the Distributed Corporation immediately before the Gain Elimination Transaction.

(2) *Definitions.*—The following definitions apply for purposes of this paragraph (c):

(i) *Corporate Partner.*—The term *Corporate Partner* means a person that is classified as a corporation for federal income tax purposes and that holds or acquires an interest in a partnership.

(ii) *Stock.*—The term *Stock* includes other equity interests, including options, warrants, and similar interests.

(iii) *Distributed Stock.*—The term *Distributed Stock* means Stock distributed by a partnership to a Corporate Partner, or Stock the basis of which is determined by reference to the basis of such Stock. *Distributed Stock* also includes Stock owned directly or indirectly by a Distributed Corporation if the basis of such Stock has been reduced pursuant to section 732(f).

(iv) *Distributed Corporation.*—The term *Distributed Corporation* means the issuer of Distributed Stock (or, in the case of an option, the issuer of the Stock into which the option is exercisable).

(v) *Gain Elimination Transaction.*— The term *Gain Elimination Transaction* means a transaction in which Distributed Stock is disposed of and less than all of the gain is recognized unless—

(A) The transferor of the Distributed Stock receives in exchange Stock or a partnership interest that is exchanged basis property (as defined in section 7701(a)(44)) with respect to the Distributed Stock; or

(B) A transferee corporation holds the Distributed Stock as transferred basis property (as defined in section 7701(a)(43)) with respect to the transferor corporation's gain. A Gain Elimination Transaction includes (without limitation) a reorganization under section 368(a) in which the Corporate Partner and the Distributed Corporation combine, and a distribution of the Distributed Stock by the Corporate Partner to which section 355(c)(1) or 361(c)(1) applies.

(d) *Tiered partnerships.*—The rules of this section shall apply to tiered partnerships in a manner that is consistent with the purposes of section 732(f).

(e) *Applicability date.*—This section applies to transactions occurring on or after June 8, 2018. [Reg. § 1.732-3.]

□ [*T.D.* 8949, 6-18-2001. *Amended by T.D.* 9833, 6-7-2018.]

§ 1.734-1. Optional adjustment to basis of undistributed partnership property.— (a) *General rule.*—A partnership shall not adjust the basis of partnership property as the result of a distribution of property to a partner, unless the election provided in section 754 (relating to optional adjustment to basis of partnership property) is in effect.

(b) *Method of adjustment.*—(1) *Increase in basis.*—Where an election under section 754 is in effect and a distribution of partnership property is made whether or not in liquidation of the partner's entire interest in the partnership, the adjusted basis of the remaining partnership assets shall be increased by—

(i) The amount of any gain recognized under section 731(a)(1) to the distributee partner, or [and]*

(ii) The excess of the adjusted basis to the partnership immediately before the distribution of any property distributed (including adjustments under section 743(b) or section 732(d) when applied) over the basis under section 732 (including such special basis adjustments) of such property to the distributee partner.

See § 1.460-4(k)(2)(iv)(D) for a rule determining the partnership's basis in a long-term contract accounted for under a long-term contract method of accounting. The provisions of this paragraph (b)(1) are illustrated by the following examples:

Example (1). Partner A has a basis of $10,000 for his one-third interest in partnership

* As it appears in Code Sec. 734(b)(1)(A).

ABC. The partnership has no liabilities and has assets consisting of cash of $11,000 and property with a partnership basis of $19,000 and a value of $22,000. A receives $11,000 in cash in liquidation of his entire interest in the partnership. He has a gain of $1,000 under section 731(a)(1). If the election under section 754 is in effect, the partnership basis for the property becomes $20,000 ($19,000 plus $1,000).

Example (2). Partner D has a basis of $10,000 for his one-third interest in partnership DEF. The partnership balance sheet before the distribution shows the following:

Assets	*Adjusted Basis*	*Value*
Cash	$4,000	$4,000
Property X	11,000	11,000
Property Y	15,000	18,000
Totals	30,000	33,000
Liabilities and Capital		
Liabilities	$0	$0
Capital: D	10,000	11,000
E	10,000	11,000
F	10,000	11,000
Totals	30,000	33,000

In liquidation of his entire interest in the partnership, D received property X with a partnership basis of $11,000. D's basis for property X is $10,000 under section 732(b). Where the election under section 754 is in effect, the excess of $1,000 (the partnership basis before the distribution less D's basis for property X after distribution) is added to the basis of property Y. The basis of property Y becomes $16,000 ($15,000 plus $1,000). If the distribution is made to a transferee partner who elects under section 732(d), see § 1.734-2.

(2) *Decrease in basis.*—Where the election provided in section 754 is in effect and a distribution is made in liquidation of a partner's entire interest, the partnership shall decrease the adjusted basis of the remaining partnership property by—

(i) The amount of loss, if any, recognized under section 731(a)(2) to the distributee partner, or [and]**

(ii) The excess of the basis of the distributed property to the distributee, as determined under section 732 (including adjustments under section 743(b) or section 732(d) when applied) over the adjusted basis of such property to the partnership (including such special basis adjustments) immediately before such distribution.

The provisions of this subparagraph may be illustrated by the following examples:

Example (1). Partner G has a basis of $11,000 for his one-third interest in partnership GHI. Partnership assets consist of cash of $10,000 and property with a basis of $23,000 and a value of $20,000. There are no partnership liabilities. In liquidation of his entire interest in the partnership, G receives $10,000 in cash. He has a loss of $1,000 under section 731(a)(2). If the election under section 754 is in effect, the partnership basis for the property becomes $22,000 ($23,000 less $1,000).

Example (2). Partner J has a basis of $11,000 for his one-third interest in partnership JKL. The partnership balance sheet before the distribution shows the following:

Assets	*Adjusted Basis*	*Value*
Cash	$5,000	$5,000
Property X	10,000	10,000
Property Y	18,000	15,000
Total	33,000	30,000
Liabilities and Capital		
Liabilities	$ 0	$ 0
Capital: J	11,000	10,000
K	11,000	10,000
L	11,000	10,000
Total	33,000	30,000

In liquidation of his entire interest in the partnership, J receives property X with a partnership basis of $10,000. J's basis for property X under section 732(b) is $11,000. Where the election under section 754 is in effect, the excess of $1,000 ($11,000 basis of property X to J, the distributee, less its $10,000 adjusted basis to the partnership immediately before the distribution) decreases the basis of property Y in the partnership. Thus, the basis of property Y becomes $17,000 ($18,000 less $1,000). If the distribution is made to a transferee partner who elects under section 732(d), see § 1.734-2.

(c) *Allocation of basis.*—For allocation among the partnership properties of basis adjustments under section 734(b) and paragraph (b) of this section, see section 755 and § 1.755-1.

(d) *Returns.*—A partnership which must adjust the bases of partnership properties under section 734 shall attach a statement to the partnership return for the year of the distribution setting forth the computation of the adjustment and the partnership properties to which the adjustment has been allocated.

(e) *Recovery of adjustments to basis of partnership property.*—(1) *Increases in basis.*—For purposes of section 168, if the basis of a part-

** As it appears in Code Sec. 734(b)(2)(A).

nership's recovery property is increased as a result of the distribution of property to a partner, then the increased portion of the basis must be taken into account as if it were newly-purchased recovery property placed in service when the distribution occurs. Consequently, any applicable recovery period and method may be used to determine the recovery allowance with respect to the increased portion of the basis. However, no change is made for purposes of determining the recovery allowance under section 168 for the portion of the basis for which there is no increase.

(2) *Decreases in basis.*—For purposes of section 168, if the basis of a partnership's recovery property is decreased as a result of the distribution of property to a partner, then the decrease in basis must be accounted for over the remaining recovery period of the property beginning with the recovery period in which the basis is decreased.

* * *

[Reg. § 1.734-1.]

☐ [*T.D.* 6175, 5-23-56. *Amended by T.D.* 8847, 12-14-99 *and T.D.* 9137, 7-15-2004.]

Proposed Amendments to Regulation

§ 1.734-1. Adjustment to basis of undistributed partnership property where partnership has a section 754 election or there is a substantial basis reduction with respect to a distribution.—(a) *General rule.*—(1) *Adjustments to basis.*—A partnership shall not adjust the basis of partnership property as the result of a distribution of property to a partner unless the election provided in section 754 (relating to optional adjustment to basis of partnership property) is in effect or there is a substantial basis reduction (within the meaning of paragraph (a)(2)(i) of this section) with respect to the distribution.

(2) *Substantial basis reduction.*—(i) *In general.*—For purposes of this section, there is a substantial basis reduction with respect to a distribution of property or properties to a partner if the sum of the amounts described in section 734(b)(2)(A) and (b)(2)(B) exceeds $250,000. If there is a substantial basis reduction under this section, the partnership is treated as having an election under section 754 in effect solely for the distribution to which the substantial basis reduction relates.

(ii) *Special rules for tiered partnerships.*—See paragraph (f) of this section for special rules regarding tiered partnerships.

(iii) *Special rules for securitization partnerships.*—See paragraph (g) of this section for special rules regarding securitization partnerships.

(b) * * *

(2) *Decrease in basis.*—(i) When a partnership with a section 754 election in effect makes a distribution in liquidation of a partner's entire interest in the partnership, or when there is a substantial basis reduction (within the meaning of paragraph (a)(2)(i) of this section), the partnership shall decrease the adjusted basis of the remaining partnership property by—

(ii) * * *

Example 3—(i) A, B, and C each contribute $2 million to PRS, a partnership. PRS purchases Property 1 and Property 2, both of which are capital assets, for $1 million and $5 million respectively. In Year 2, the fair market value of Property 1 increases to $3 million and the fair market value of Property 2 increases to $6 million. Also in Year 2, PRS distributes Property 1 to C in liquidation of C's interest in PRS at a time when C's basis in its PRS interest is still $2 million. PRS does not have an election under section 754 in effect.

(ii) Under section 732, the basis of Property 1 in the hands of C is $2 million. Because the excess of C's adjusted basis in Property 1 ($2 million) over PRS's adjusted basis in Property 1 ($1 million) is $1 million, the amount described in section 734(b)(2)(B) ($1 million) exceeds $250,000, and therefore, there is a substantial basis reduction with respect to the distribution. Accordingly, pursuant to paragraph (a)(2)(i) of this section, PRS is treated as having a section 754 election in effect in Year 2 and must reduce its basis in Property 2 in accordance with paragraph (b)(2)(i) of this section.

* * *

(d) * * * A partnership required to adjust the basis of partnership property following the distribution of property because there is a substantial basis reduction (within the meaning of paragraph (a)(2)(i) of this section) with respect to the distribution is subject to, and required to comply with, the provisions of this paragraph (d) solely with respect to the distribution to which the substantial basis reduction relates.

* * *

[Prop. Reg. § 1.734-1.]

[Proposed 1-16-2014 (corrected 4-15-2014).]

§ 1.734-2. Adjustment after distribution to transferee partner.—(a) In the case of a distribution of property by the partnership to a partner who has obtained all or part of his partnership interest by transfer, the adjustments to basis provided in section 743(b) and section 732(d) shall be taken into account in applying the rules under section 734(b). For determining the adjusted basis of distributed property to the partnership immediately before the distribution where there has been a prior transfer of a partnership interest with respect to which the election provided in section 754 or section 732(d) is in effect, see §§1.732-1 and 1.732-2.

(b)(1) If a transferee partner, in liquidation of his entire partnership interest, receives a distribution of property (including money) with respect to which he has no special basis adjustment, in exchange for his interest in property with respect to which he has a special basis adjustment, and does not utilize his entire special basis adjustment in determining the basis of the distributed property to him under section 732, the unused special basis adjustment of the distributee shall be applied as an adjustment to the partnership basis of the property retained by the partnership and as to which the distributee did not use his special basis adjustment. The provisions of this subparagraph may be illustrated by the following example:

Example. Upon the death of his father, partner S acquires by inheritance a half-interest in partnership ACS. Partners A and C each have a one-quarter interest. The assets of the partnership consist of $10,000 cash and land used in farming worth $10,000 with a basis of $1,000 to the partnership. Since the partnership had made the election under section 754 at the time of the transfer, partner S has a special basis adjustment of $4,500 under section 743(b) with respect to his undivided half-interest in the real estate. The basis of S's partnership interest, in accordance with section 742, is $10,000. S retires from the partnership and receives $10,000 in cash in exchange for his entire interest. Since S has received no part of the real estate, his special basis adjustment of $4,500 will be allocated to the real estate, the remaining partnership property, and will increase its basis to the partnership to $5,500.

(2) The provisions of this paragraph do not apply to the extent that certain distributions are treated as sales or exchanges under section 751(b) (relating to unrealized receivables and substantially appreciated inventory items). See section 751(b) and paragraph (b) of §1.751-1. [Reg. §1.734-2.]

☐ [*T.D.* 6175, 5-23-56.]

Proposed Amendment to Regulation

§1.734-2. Adjustment after distribution to transferee partner or section 704(c)(1)(C) partner.

* * *

(c)(1) Section 704(c)(1)(C) basis adjustments will be taken into account in determining the basis adjustment under section 734(b). However, section 704(c)(1)(C) basis adjustments, other than a section 704(c)(1)(C) basis adjustment applied as an adjustment to the basis of partnership property pursuant to paragraph (c)(2) of this section, will not be taken into account in making allocations under §1.755-1(c).

(2) *Liquidating distributions.*—If a section 704(c)(1)(C) partner receives a distribution of property (including money) in liquidation of its entire partnership interest, the section 704(c)(1)(C) partner's section 704(c)(1)(C) basis adjustments that are treated as basis in the distributed property pursuant to section 732 will be taken into account in determining the basis adjustment under section 734(b), regardless of whether the distributed property is section 704(c)(1)(C) property. If any section 704(c)(1)(C) basis adjustment cannot be reallocated to distributed property in connection with the distribution, then that remaining section 704(c)(1)(C) basis adjustment shall be treated as a positive section 734(b) adjustment. If the distribution also gives rise to a negative section 734(b) adjustment without regard to the section 704(c)(1)(C) basis adjustment reallocation, then the negative section 734(b) adjustment and the section 704(c)(1)(C) basis adjustment reallocation are netted together, and the net amount is allocated under §1.755-1(c). If the partnership does not have a section 754 election in effect at the time of the liquidating distribution, the partnership shall be treated as having made a section 754 election solely for purposes of computing any negative section 734(b) adjustment that would arise from the distribution.

* * *

[Prop. Reg. §1.734-2.]

[Proposed 1-16-2014 (corrected 4-15-2014).]

§1.735-1. Character of gain or loss on disposition of distributed property.—

(a) *Sale or exchange of distributed property.*—(1) *Unrealized receivables.*—Any gain realized or loss sustained by a partner on a sale or other disposition of unrealized receivables (as defined in paragraph (c)(1) of §1.751-1) received by him in a distribution from a partnership shall be considered gain or loss from the sale or exchange of property other than a capital asset.

(2) *Inventory items.*—Any gain realized or loss sustained by a partner on a sale or exchange of inventory items (as defined in section 751(d)(2)) received in a distribution from a partnership shall be considered gain or loss from the sale or exchange of property other than a capital asset if such inventory items are sold or exchanged within 5 years from the date of the distribution by the partnership. The character of any gain or loss from a sale or exchange by the distributee partner of such inventory items after 5 years from the date of distribution shall be determined as of the date

of such sale or exchange by reference to the character of the assets in his hands at that date (inventory items, capital assets, property used in a trade or business, etc.).

(b) *Holding period for distributed property.*—A partner's holding period for property distributed to him by a partnership shall include the period such property was held by the partnership. The provisions of this paragraph do not apply for the purpose of determining the 5-year period described in section 735(a)(2) and paragraph (a)(2) of this section. If the property has been contributed to the partnership by a partner, then the period that the property was held by such partner shall also be included. See section 1223(2). For a partnership's holding period for contributed property, see § 1.723-1.

* * *

[Reg. § 1.735-1.]

☐ [*T.D.* 6175, 5-23-56. *Amended by T.D.* 6832, 7-6-65.]

»»→ Caution: Reg. § 1.736-1 does not reflect changes made in Section 736(b) by the Revenue Reconciliation Act of 1993.

§ 1.736-1. Payments to a retiring partner or a deceased partner's successor in interest.—(a) *Payments considered as distributive share or guaranteed payment.*—(1)(i) Section 736 and this section apply only to payments made to a retiring partner or to a deceased partner's successor in interest in liquidation of such partner's entire interest in the partnership. See section 761(d). Section 736 and this section do not apply if the estate or other successor in interest of a deceased partner continues as a partner in its own right under local law. Section 736 and this section apply only to payments made by the partnership and not to transactions between the partners. Thus, a sale by partner A to partner B of his entire one-fourth interest in partnership ABCD would not come within the scope of section 736.

(ii) A partner retires when he ceases to be a partner under local law. However, for the purposes of subchapter K, chapter 1 of the Code, a retired partner or a deceased partner's successor will be treated as a partner until his interest in the partnership has been completely liquidated.

(2) When payments (including assumption of liabilities treated as a distribution of money under section 752) are made to a withdrawing partner, that is, a retiring partner or the estate or other successor in interest of a deceased partner, the amounts paid may represent several items. In part, they may represent the fair market value at the time of his death or retirement of the withdrawing partner's interest in all the assets of the partnership (including inventory) unreduced by partnership liabilities. Also, part of such payments may be attributable to his interest in unrealized receivables and part to an arrangement among the partners in the nature of mutual insurance. When a partnership makes such payments, whether or not related to partnership income, to retire the withdrawing partner's entire interest in the partnership, the payments must be allocated between (i) payments for the value of his interest in assets, except unrealized receivables and, under some circumstances, good will (section 736(b)), and (ii) other payments (section 736(a)). The amounts paid for his interest in assets are treated in the same manner as a distribution in complete liquidation under sections 731, 732, and where applicable, 751. See paragraph (b)(4)(ii) of § 1.751-1. The remaining partners are allowed no deduction for these payments since they represent either a distribution or a purchase of the withdrawing partner's capital interest by the partnership (composed of the remaining partners).

(3) Under section 736(a), the portion of the payments made to a withdrawing partner for his share of unrealized receivables, good will (in the absence of an agreement to the contrary), or otherwise not in exchange for his interest in assets under the rules contained in paragraph (b) of this section will be considered either—

(i) A distributive share of partnership income, if the amount of payment is determined with regard to income of the partnership; or

(ii) A guaranteed payment under section 707(c), if the amount of the payment is determined without regard to income of the partnership.

(4) Payments, to the extent considered as a distributive share of partnership income under section 736(a)(1), are taken into account under section 702 in the income of the withdrawing partner and thus reduce the amount of the distributive shares of the remaining partners. Payments, to the extent considered as guaranteed payments under section 736(a)(2), are deductible by the partnership under section 162(a) and are taxable as ordinary income to the recipient under section 61(a). See section 707(c).

(5) The amount of any payments under section 736(a) shall be included in the income of the recipient for his taxable year with or within which ends the partnership taxable year for which the payment is a distributive share, or in which the partnership is entitled to deduct such amount as a guaranteed payment. On the other hand, payments under section 736(b) shall be taken into account by the recipient for

his taxable year in which such payments are made. See paragraph (b)(4) of this section.

(6) A retiring partner or a deceased partner's successor in interest receiving payments under section 736 is regarded as a partner until the entire interest of the retiring or deceased partner is liquidated. Therefore, if one of the members of a 2-man partnership retires under a plan whereby he is to receive payments under section 736, the partnership will not be considered terminated, nor will the partnership year close with respect to either partner, until the retiring partner's entire interest is liquidated, since the retiring partner continues to hold a partnership interest in the partnership until that time. Similarly, if a partner in a 2-man partnership dies, and his estate or other successor in interest receives payments under section 736, the partnership shall not be considered to have terminated upon the death of the partner but shall terminate as to both partners only when the entire interest of the decedent is liquidated. See section 708(b).

(b) *Payments for interest in partnership.*—(1) Payments made in liquidation of the entire interest of a retiring partner or deceased partner shall, to the extent made in exchange for such partner's interest in partnership property (except for unrealized receivables and good will as provided in subparagraphs (2) and (3) of this paragraph), be considered as a distribution by the partnership (and not as a distributive share or guaranteed payment under section 736(a)). Generally, the valuation placed by the partners upon a partner's interest in partnership property in an arm's length agreement will be regarded as correct. If such valuation reflects only the partner's net interest in the property (i.e., total assets less liabilities), it must be adjusted so that both the value of the partner's interest in property and the basis for his interest take into account the partner's share of partnership liabilities. Gain or loss with respect to distributions under section 736(b) and this paragraph will be recognized to the distributee to the extent provided in section 731 and, where applicable, section 751.

(2) Payments made to a retiring partner or to the successor in interest of a deceased partner for his interest in unrealized receivables of the partnership in excess of their partnership basis, including any special basis adjustment for them to which such partner is entitled, shall not be considered as made in exchange for such partner's interest in partnership property. Such payments shall be treated as payments under section 736(a) and paragraph (a) of this section. For definition of unrealized receivables, see section 751(c).

(3) For the purposes of section 736(b) and this paragraph, payments made to a retiring partner or to a successor in interest of a deceased partner in exchange for the interest of such partner in partnership property shall not include any amount paid for the partner's share of good will of the partnership in excess of its partnership basis, including any special basis adjustments for it to which such partner is entitled, except to the extent that the partnership agreement provides for a reasonable payment with respect to such good will. Such payments shall be considered as payments under section 736(a). To the extent that the partnership agreement provides for a reasonable payment with respect to good will, such payments shall be treated under section 736(b) and this paragraph. Generally, the valuation placed upon good will be an arm's length agreement of the partners, whether specific in amount or determined by a formula, shall be regarded as correct.

(4) Payments made to a retiring partner or to a successor in interest of a deceased partner for his interest in inventory shall be considered as made in exchange for such partner's interest in partnership property for the purposes of section 736(b) and this paragraph. However, payments for an interest in substantially appreciated inventory items, as defined in section 751(d), are subject to the rules provided in section 751(b) and paragraph (b) of § 1.751-1. The partnership basis in inventory items as to a deceased partner's successor in interest does not change because of the death of the partner unless the partnership has elected the optional basis adjustment under section 754. But see paragraph (b)(3)(iii) of § 1.751-1.

(5) Where payments made under section 736 are received during the taxable year, the recipient must segregate that portion of each such payment which is determined to be in exchange for the partner's interest in partnership property and treated as a distribution under section 736(b) from that portion treated as a distributive share or guaranteed payment under section 736(a). Such allocation shall be made as follows—

(i) If a fixed amount (whether or not supplemented by any additional amounts) is to be received over a fixed number of years, the portion of each payment to be treated as a distribution under section 736(b) for the taxable year shall bear the same ratio to the total fixed agreed payments for such year (as distinguished from the amount actually received) as the total fixed agreed payments under section 736(b) bear to the total fixed agreed payments under sections 736(a) and (b). The balance, if any, of such amount received in the same taxable year shall be treated as a distributive share or a guaranteed payment under section 736(a)(1) or (2). However, if the total amount received in any one year is less than the amount considered as a distribution under section 736(b) for that year, then any unapplied portion shall be added to the portion of the payments for the following year or years which are to be treated as a distribution under section 736(b). For example, retiring partner W who is entitled to an annual payment of $6,000 for 10 years for his interest in partnership property, receives only $3,500 in 1955. In 1956, he receives $10,000. Of this amount, $8,500 ($6,000 plus $2,500 from 1955) is treated as a distribution under section 736(b) for 1956; $1,500, as a payment under section 736(a).

(ii) If the retiring partner or deceased partner's successor in interest receives payments which are not fixed in amount, such payments shall first be treated as payments in exchange for his interest in partnership property under section 736(b) to the extent of the value of that interest and, thereafter, as payments under section 736(a).

(iii) In lieu of the rules provided in subdivisions (i) and (ii) of this subparagraph, the allocation of each annual payment between section 736(a) and (b) may be made in any manner to which all the remaining partners and the withdrawing partner or his successor in interest agree, provided that the total amount allocated to property under section 736(b) does not exceed the fair market value of such property at the date of death or retirement.

(6) Except to the extent section 751(b) applies, the amount of any gain or loss with respect to payments under section 736(b) for a retiring or deceased partner's interest in property for each year of payment shall be determined under section 731. However, where the total of section 736(b) payments is a fixed sum, a retiring partner or a deceased partner's successor in interest may elect (in his tax return for the first taxable year for which he receives such payments), to report and to measure the amount of any gain or loss by the difference between—

(i) The amount treated as a distribution under section 736(b) in that year, and

(ii) The portion of the adjusted basis of the partner for his partnership interest attributable to such distribution (i.e., the amount which bears the same proportion to the partner's total adjusted basis for his partnership interest as the amount distributed under section 736(b) in that year bears to the total amount to be distributed under section 736(b)).

A recipient who elects under this subparagraph shall attach a statement to his tax return for the first taxable year for which he receives such payments, indicating his election and showing the computation of the gain included in gross income.

(7) The provisions of this paragraph may be illustrated by the following examples:

Example (1). Partnership ABC is a personal service partnership and its balance sheet is as follows:

Assets

	Adjusted basis per books	*Market value*
Cash	$13,000	$13,000
Unrealized receivables . . .	0	30,000
Capital and sec. 1231 assets	20,000	23,000
Total	$33,000	$66,000

Liabilities and Capital

	Per books	*Value*
Liabilities	$3,000	$3,000
Capital:		
A	10,000	21,000
B	10,000	21,000
C	10,000	21,000
Total	$33,000	$66,000

Partner A retires from the partnership in accordance with an agreement whereby his share of liabilities ($1,000) is assumed. In addition he is to receive $9,000 in the year of retirement plus $10,000 in each of the two succeeding years. Thus, the total that A receives for his partnership interest is $30,000 ($29,000 in cash and $1,000 in liabilities assumed). Under the agreement terminating A's interest, the value of A's interest in section 736(b) partnership property is $12,000 (one-third of $36,000, the sum of $13,000 cash and $23,000, the fair market value of capital and section 1231 assets). A's share in unrealized receivables is not included in his interest in partnership property described in section 736(b). Since the basis of A's interest is $11,000 ($10,000 plus $1,000, his share of partnership liabilities), he will realize a capital gain of $1,000 ($12,000 minus $11,000) from the disposition of his interest in partnership property. The remaining $18,000 ($30,000 minus $12,000) will constitute payments under section 736(a)(2) which are taxable to A as guaranteed payments under section 707(c). The payment for the first year is $10,000, consisting of $9,000 in cash, plus $1,000 in liability assumed (section 752(b)). Thus, unless the partners agree otherwise under subparagraph (5)(iii) of this paragraph, each annual payment of $10,000 will be allocated as follows: $6,000 (18,000/30,000 of $10,000) is a section 736(a)(2) payment and $4,000 (12,000/30,000 of $10,000) is a payment for an interest in section 736(b) partnership property. (The Partnership may deduct the $6,000 guaranteed payment made to A in each of the 3 years.) The gain on the payments for partnership property will be determined under section 731, as provided in subparagraph (6) of this paragraph. A will treat only $4,000 of each payment as a distribution in a series in liquidation of his entire interest and, under section 731, will have a capital gain of $1,000 when the last payment is made. However, if A so elects, as provided in subparagraph (6) of this paragraph, he may treat such gain as follows: Of each $4,000 payment attributable to A's interest in partnership property, $333 is capital gain (one-third of the total capital gain of $1,000), and $3,667 is a return of capital.

Example (2). Assume the same facts as in example (1) of this subparagraph except that the agreement between the partners provides for payments to A for 3 years of a percentage of annual income instead of a fixed amount. Unless the partners agree otherwise under subparagraph (5)(iii) of this paragraph, all payments received by A up to $12,000 shall be treated under section 736(b) as payments for A's interest in partnership property. His gain of $1,000 will be taxed only after he has received his full basis under section 731. Since the payments are not fixed in amount, the election provided in subparagraph (6) of this paragraph is not available. Any payments in excess of $12,000 shall be treated as a distributive share of partnership income to A under section 736(a)(1).

Example (3). Assume the same facts as in example (1) of this subparagraph except that the partnership agreement provides that the payment for A's interest in partnership property shall include payment for his interest in the good will of the partnership. At the time of A's retirement, the partners determine the value of partnership good will to be $9,000. The value of A's interest in partnership property described in section 736(b) is thus $15,000 (one-third of $45,000, the sum of $13,000 cash, plus $23,000, the value of capital and section 1231 assets, plus $9,000 good will). From the disposition of his interest in partnership property, A will realize a capital gain of $4,000 ($15,000, minus $11,000, the basis of his interest). The remaining $15,000 ($30,000 minus $15,000) will constitute payments under section 736(a)(2) which are taxable to A as guaranteed payments under section 707(c).

Example (4). Assume the same facts as in example (1) of this subparagraph except that the capital and section 1231 assets consist of an item of section 1245 property (as defined in section 1245(a)(3)). Assume further that under paragraph (c)(4) of § 1.751-1 the section 1245 property is an unrealized receivable to the extent of $2,000. Therefore, the value of A's interest in section 736(b) partnership property is only $11,333 (one-third of $34,000, the sum of $13,000 cash and $21,000, the fair market value of section 1245 property to the extent not an unrealized receivable). From the disposition of his interest in partnership property, A will realize a capital gain of $333 ($11,333 minus $11,000, the basis of his interest). The remaining $18,667 ($30,000 minus $11,333) will constitute payments under section 736(a)(2) which are taxable to A as guaranteed payments under section 707(c).

(c) *Cross reference.*—See section 753 for treatment of payments under section 736(a) as income in respect of a decedent under section 691. [Reg. § 1.736-1.]

☐ [*T.D.* 6175, 5-23-56. *Amended by T.D.* 6832, 7-6-65.]

§ 1.737-1. Recognition of precontribution gain.—(a) *Determination of gain.*—(1) *In general.*—A partner that receives a distribution of property (other than money) must recognize gain under section 737 and this section in an amount equal to the lesser of the excess distribution (as defined in paragraph (b) of this section) or the partner's net precontribution gain (as defined in paragraph (c) of this section). Gain recognized under section 737 and this section is in addition to any gain recognized under section 731.

(2) *Transactions to which section 737 applies.*—Section 737 and this section apply only to the extent that a distribution by a partnership is a distribution to a partner acting in the capacity of a partner within the meaning of section 731, except that section 737 and this section do not apply to the extent that section 751(b) applies to the distribution.

(b) *Excess distribution.*—(1) *Definition.*—The excess distribution is the amount (if any) by which the fair market value of the distributed property (other than money) exceeds the distributee partner's adjusted tax basis in the partner's partnership interest.

(2) *Fair market value of property.*—The fair market value of the distributed property is the price at which the property would change hands between a willing buyer and a willing seller at the time of the distribution, neither being under any compulsion to buy or sell and both having reasonable knowledge of the relevant facts. The fair market value that a partnership assigns to distributed property will be regarded as correct, provided that the value is reasonably agreed to among the partners in an arm's-length negotiation and the partners have sufficiently adverse interests.

(3) *Distributee partner's adjusted tax basis.*—(i) *General rule.*—In determining the amount of the excess distribution, the distributee partner's adjusted tax basis in the partnership interest includes any basis adjustment

resulting from the distribution that is subject to section 737 (for example, adjustments required under section 752) and from any other distribution or transaction that is part of the same distribution, except for—

(A) The increase required under section 737(c)(1) for the gain recognized by the partner under section 737; and

(B) The decrease required under section 733(2) for any property distributed to the partner other than property previously contributed to the partnership by the distributee partner. See § 1.704-4(e)(1) for a rule in the context of section 704(c)(1)(B). See also § 1.737-3(b)(2) for a special rule for determining a partner's adjusted tax basis in distributed property previously contributed by the partner to the partnership.

(ii) *Advances or drawings.*—The distributee partner's adjusted tax basis in the partnership interest is determined as of the last day of the partnership's taxable year if the distribution to which section 737 applies is properly characterized as an advance or drawing against the partner's distributive share of income. See § 1.731-1(a)(1)(ii).

(c) *Net precontribution gain.*—(1) *General rule.*—The distributee partner's net precontribution gain is the net gain (if any) that would have been recognized by the distributee partner under section 704(c)(1)(B) and § 1.704-4 if all property that had been contributed to the partnership by the distributee partner within five years of the distribution and is held by the partnership immediately before the distribution had been distributed by the partnership to another partner other than a partner who owns, directly or indirectly, more than 50 percent of the capital or profits interest in the partnership. See § 1.704-4 for provisions determining a contributing partner's gain or loss under section 704(c)(1)(B) on an actual distribution of contributed section 704(c) property to another partner.

(2) *Special rules.*—(i) *Property contributed on or before October 3, 1989.*—Property contributed to the partnership on or before October 3, 1989, is not taken into account in determining a partner's net precontribution gain. See § 1.704-4(c)(1) for a similar rule in the context of section 704(c)(1)(B).

(ii) *Section 734(b)(1)(A) adjustments.*—For distributions to a distributee partner of money by a partnership with a section 754 election in effect that are part of the same distribution as the distribution of property subject to section 737, for purposes of paragraph (a) and (c)(1) of this section the distributee partner's net precontribution gain is reduced by the basis adjustments (if any) made to section 704(c) property contributed by the distributee partner under section 734(b)(1)(A). See § 1.737-3(c)(4) for rules regarding basis adjustments for partnerships with a section 754 election in effect.

(iii) *Transfers of a partnership interest.*—The transferee of all or a portion of a contributing partner's partnership interest succeeds to the transferor's net precontribution gain, if any, in an amount proportionate to the interest transferred. See § 1.704-3(a)(7) and § 1.704-4(d)(2) for similar provisions in the context of section 704(c)(1)(A) and section 704(c)(1)(B).

(iv) *Section 704(c)(1)(B) gain recognized in related distribution.*—A distributee partner's net precontribution gain is determined after taking into account any gain or loss recognized by the partner under section 704(c)(1)(B) and § 1.704-4 (or that would have been recognized by the partner except for the like-kind exception in section 704(c)(2) and § 1.704-4(d)(3)) on an actual distribution to another partner of section 704(c) property contributed by the distributee partner that is part of the same distribution as the distribution to the distributee partner.

(v) *Section 704(c)(2) disregarded.*—A distributee partner's net precontribution gain is determined without regard to the provisions of section 704(c)(2) and § 1.704-4(d)(3) in situations in which the property contributed by the distributee partner is not actually distributed to another partner in a distribution related to the section 737 distribution.

(d) *Character of gain.*—The character of the gain recognized by the distributee partner under section 737 and this section is determined by, and is proportionate to, the character of the partner's net precontribution gain. For this purpose, all gains and losses on section 704(c) property taken into account in determining the partner's net precontribution gain are netted according to their character. Character is determined at the partnership level for this purpose, and any character with a net negative amount is disregarded. The character of the partner's gain under section 737 is the same as, and in proportion to, any character with a net positive amount. Character for this purpose is determined as if the section 704(c) property had been sold by the partnership to an unrelated third party at the time of the distribution and includes any item that would have been taken into account separately by the contributing partner under section 702(a) and § 1.702-1(a).

(e) *Examples.*—The following examples illustrate the provisions of this section. Unless otherwise specified, partnership income equals partnership expenses (other than depreciation deductions for contributed property) for each year of the partnership, the fair market value of partnership property does not change, all distributions by the partnership are subject to section 737, and all partners are unrelated.

Example 1. Calculation of excess distribution and net precontribution gain. (i) On January 1, 1995, A, B, and C form partnership ABC as equal partners. A contributes Property A, depreciable real property with a fair market value of $30,000 and an adjusted tax basis of $20,000. B contributes Property B, nondepreciable real property with a fair market value and adjusted tax basis of $30,000. C contributes $30,000 cash.

(ii) Property A has 10 years remaining on its cost recovery schedule and is depreciated using the straight-line method. The partnership uses the traditional method for allocating items under section 704(c) described in § 1.704-3(b)(1) for Property A. The partnership has book depreciation of $3,000 per year (10 percent of the $30,000 book basis in Property A) and each partner is allocated $1,000 of book depreciation per year (one-third of the total annual book depreciation of $3,000). The partnership also has tax depreciation of $2,000 per year (10 percent of the $20,000 adjusted tax basis in Property A). This $2,000 tax depreciation is allocated equally between B and C, the noncontributing partners with respect to Property A.

(iii) At the end of 1997, the book value of Property A is $21,000 ($30,000 initial book value less $9,000 aggregate book depreciation) and its adjusted tax basis is $14,000 ($20,000 initial tax basis less $6,000 aggregate tax depreciation).

(iv) On December 31, 1997, Property B is distributed to A in complete liquidation of A's partnership interest. The adjusted tax basis of A's partnership interest at that time is $20,000. The amount of the excess distribution is $10,000, the difference between the fair market value of the distributed Property B ($30,000) and A's adjusted tax basis in A's partnership interest ($20,000). A's net precontribution gain is $7,000, the difference between the book value of Property A ($21,000) and its adjusted tax basis at the time of the distribution ($14,000). A recognizes gain of $7,000 on the distribution, the lesser of the excess distribution and the net precontribution gain.

Example 2. Determination of distributee partner's basis. (i) On January 1, 1995, A, B, and C form general partnership ABC as equal partners. A contributes Property A, nondepreciable real property with a fair market value of $10,000 and an adjusted tax basis of $4,000. B and C each contributes $10,000 cash.

(ii) The partnership purchases Property B, nondepreciable real property with a fair market value of $9,000, subject to a $9,000 nonrecourse liability. This nonrecourse liability is allocated equally among the partners under section 752, increasing A's adjusted tax basis in A's partnership interest from $4,000 to $7,000.

(iii) On December 31, 1998, A receives $2,000 cash and Property B, subject to the $9,000 liability, in a current distribution.

(iv) In determining the amount of the excess distribution, the adjusted tax basis of A's partnership interest is adjusted to take into account the distribution of money and the shift in liabilities. A's adjusted tax basis is therefore increased to $11,000 for this purpose ($7,000 initial adjusted tax basis, less $2,000 distribution of money, less $3,000 (decrease in A's share of the $9,000 partnership liability), plus $9,000 (increase in A's individual liabilities)). As a result of this basis adjustment, the adjusted tax basis of A's partnership interest ($11,000) is greater than the fair market value of the distributed property ($9,000) and therefore, there is no excess distribution. A recognizes no gain under section 737.

Example 3. Net precontribution gain reduced for gain recognized under section 704(c)(1)(B). (i) On January 1, 1995, A, B, and C form partnership ABC as equal partners. A contributes Properties A1 and A2, nondepreciable real properties located in the United States each with a fair market value of $10,000 and an adjusted tax basis of $6,000. B contributes Property B, nondepreciable real property located outside the United States, with a fair market value and adjusted tax basis of $20,000. C contributes $20,000 cash.

(ii) On December 31, 1998, Property B is distributed to A in complete liquidation of A's interest and, as part of the same distribution, Property A1 is distributed to B in a current distribution.

(iii) A's net precontribution gain before the distribution is $8,000 ($20,000 fair market value of Properties A1 and A2 less $12,000 adjusted tax basis of such properties). A recognizes $4,000 of gain under section 704(c)(1)(B) and § 1.704-4 on the distribution of Property A1 to B ($10,000 fair market value of Property A1 less $6,000 adjusted tax basis of Property A1). This gain is taken into account in determining A's excess distribution and net precontribution gain. As a result, A's net precontribution gain is reduced from $8,000 to $4,000, and the adjusted tax basis in A's partnership interest is increased by $4,000 to $16,000.

(iv) A recognizes gain of $4,000 on the receipt of Property B under section 737, an amount equal to the lesser of the excess distribution of $4,000 ($20,000 fair market value of Property B less $16,000 adjusted tax basis of A's interest in the partnership) and A's remaining net precontribution gain of $4,000.

Example 4. Character of gain. (i) On January 1, 1995, A, B, and C form partnership ABC as equal partners. A contributes the following nondepreciable property to the partnership:

	Fair Market Value	*Adjusted Tax Basis*
Property A1	$30,000	$20,000
Property A2	30,000	38,000
Property A3	10,000	9,000

(ii) The character of gain or loss on Property A1 and Property A2 is long-term, U.S.-source capital gain or loss. The character of gain on Property A3 is long-term, foreign-source capital gain. B contributes Property B, nondepreciable real property with a fair market value and adjusted tax basis of $70,000. C contributes $70,000 cash.

(iii) On December 31, 1998, Property B is distributed to A in complete liquidation of A's interest in the partnership. A recognizes $3,000 of gain under section 737, an amount equal to the excess distribution of $3,000 ($70,000 fair market value of Property B less $67,000 adjusted tax basis in A's partnership interest) and A's net precontribution gain of $3,000 ($70,000 aggregate fair market value of properties contributed by A less $67,000 aggregate adjusted tax basis of such properties).

(iv) In determining the character of A's gain, all gains and losses on property taken into account in determining A's net precontribution gain are netted according to their character and allocated to A's recognized gain under section 737 based on the relative proportions of the net positive amounts. U.S.-source and foreign-source gains must be netted separately because A would have been required to take such gains into account separately under section 702. As a result, A's net precontribution gain of $3,000 consists of $2,000 of net long-term, U.S.-source capital gain ($10,000 gain on Property A1 and $8,000 loss on Property A2) and $1,000 of net long-term, foreign-source capital gain ($1,000 gain on Property A3).

(v) The character of A's gain under paragraph (d) of this section is therefore $2,000 long-term, U.S.-source capital gain ($3,000 gain recognized under section 737 × $2,000 net long-term, U.S.- source capital gain/$3,000 total net precontribution gain) and $1,000 long-term, foreign-source capital gain ($3,000 gain recognized under section 737 × $1,000 net long-term, foreign-source capital gain/$3,000 total net precontribution gain). [Reg. § 1.737-1.]

□ [*T.D.* 8642, 12-22-95.]

Proposed Amendment to Regulation

§ 1.737-1. Recognition of precontribution gain.

* * *

(c) *Net precontribution gain.*—(1) *General rule.*—The distributee partner's net precontribution gain is the net gain (if any) that would have been recognized by the distributee partner under section 704(c)(1)(B) and § 1.704-4 if all property that had been contributed to the partnership by the distributee partner within seven years of the distribution and is held by the partnership immediately before the distribution had been distributed by the partnership to another partner other than the partner who owns, directly or indirectly, more than 50 percent of the capital or profits interest in the partnership.

* * *

(3) *Determination of seven-year period.*—(i) *General rule.*—The seven-year period specified in paragraph (c)(1) of this section begins on, and includes, the date of contribution and ends on, and includes, the last date that is within seven years of the contribution. For example, if a partner contributes 704(c) property to a partnership on May 15, 2016, the seven-year period with respect to the section 704(c) property ends on, and includes, May 14, 2023.

(ii) *Section 708(b)(1)(B) terminations.*—A termination of the partnership under section 708(b)(1)(B) does not begin a new seven-year period for each partner with respect to built-in gain and built-in loss property that the terminated partnership is deemed to contribute to the new partnership under § 1.708-1(b)(4). *See* § 1.704-3(a)(3)(ii) for the definitions of built-in gain and built-in loss on section 704(c) property.

(4) *Effective/applicability date.*—The provisions of paragraph (c)(1) and (3) of this section relating to the seven-year period for determining the applicability of section 737(b) apply for partnership contributions occurring on or after the date of publication of the Treasury decision adopting these rules as final regulations in the Federal Register.

* * *

[Prop. Reg. § 1.737-1.]

[Proposed 1-16-2014.]

§ 1.737-2. Exceptions and special rules.—(a) *Section 708(b)(1)(B) terminations.*—Section 737 and this section do not apply to the deemed distribution of interests in a new partnership caused by the termination of a partnership under section 708(b)(1)(B). A subsequent distribution of property by the new partnership to a partner of the new partnership that was formerly a partner of the terminated partnership is subject to section 737 to the same extent that a distribution from the terminated partnership would have been subject to section 737. See also § 1.704-4(c)(3) for a similar rule in the context of section 704(c)(1)(B). This paragraph (a) applies to terminations of partnerships under section 708(b)(1)(B) occurring on or after May 9, 1997; however, this paragraph (a) may be applied to terminations occurring on or after May 9, 1996, provided that the partnership and its partners apply this paragraph (a) to the termination in a consistent manner.

(b) *Transfers to another partnership.*—(1) *Complete transfer.*—Section 737 and this section do not apply to a transfer by a partnership (transferor partnership) of all of its assets and liabilities to a second partnership (transferee partnership) in an exchange described in section 721, followed by a distribution of the interest in the transferee partnership in liquidation of the transferor partnership as part of the same plan or arrangement. See § 1.704-4(c)(4) for a similar rule in the context of section 704(c)(1)(B).

(2) *Certain divisive transactions.*—Section 737 and this section do not apply to a transfer by a partnership (transferor partnership) of all of the section 704(c) property contributed by a partner to a second partnership (transferee partnership) in an exchange described in section 721, followed by a distribution as part of the same plan or arrangement of an interest in the transferee partnership (and no other property) in complete liquidation of the interest of the partner that originally contributed the section 704(c) property to the transferor partnership.

(3) *Subsequent distributions.*—A subsequent distribution of property by the transferee partnership to a partner of the transferee partnership that was formerly a partner of the transferor partnership is subject to section 737 to the same extent that a distribution from the transferor partnership would have been subject to section 737.

(c) *Incorporation of a partnership.*—Section 737 and this section do not apply to an incorporation of a partnership by any method of incorporation (other than a method involving an actual distribution of partnership property to the partners followed by a contribution of that property to a corporation), provided that the partnership is liquidated as part of the incorporation transaction. See § 1.704-4(c)(5) for a similar rule in the context of section 704(c)(1)(B).

(d) *Distribution of previously contributed property.*—(1) *General rule.*—Any portion of the distributed property that consists of property previously contributed by the distributee partner (previously contributed property) is not taken into account in determining the amount of the excess distribution or the partner's net precontribution gain. The previous sentence applies on or after May 9, 1997. See § 1.737-3(b)(2) for a special rule for determining the basis of previously contributed property in the hands of a distributee partner who contributed the property to the partnership.

(2) *Limitation for distribution of previously contributed interest in an entity.*—An interest in an entity previously contributed to the partnership is not treated as previously contributed property to the extent that the value of the interest is attributable to property contributed to the entity after the interest was contributed to the partnership. The preceding sentence does not apply to the extent that the property contributed to the entity was contributed to the partnership by the partner that also contributed the interest in the entity to the partnership.

(3) *Nonrecognition transactions, installment sales, contributed contracts, and capitalized costs.*—(i) *Nonrecognition transactions.*—Property received by the partnership in exchange for contributed section 704(c) property in a nonrecognition transaction is treated as the contributed property with regard to the contributing partner for purposes of section 737 to the extent that the property received is treated as section 704(c) property under § 1.704-3(a)(8). See § 1.7044(d)(1) for a similar rule in the context of section 704(c)(1)(B).

(ii) *Installment sales.*—An installment obligation received by the partnership in an installment sale (as defined in section 453(b)) of section 704(c) property is treated as the contributed property with regard to the contributing partner for purposes of section 737 to the extent that the installment obligation received is treated as section 704(c) property under § 1.704-3(a)(8). See § 1.704-4(d)(1) for a similar rule in the context of section 704(c)(1)(B).

(iii) *Contributed contracts.*—Property acquired by a partnership pursuant to a contract that is section 704(c) property is treated as the contributed property with regard to the contributing partner for purposes of section 737 to the extent that the acquired property is treated as section 704(c) property under § 1.704-3(a)(8). See § 1.704-4(d)(1) for a similar rule in the context of section 704(c)(1)(B).

(iv) *Capitalized costs.*—Property to which the cost of section 704(c) property is properly capitalized is treated as section 704(c) property for purposes of section 737 to the extent that such property is treated as section 704(c) property under § 1.704-3(a)(8)(iv). See § 1.704-4(d)(1) for a similar rule in the context of section 704(c)(1)(B).

(4) *Undivided interests.*—The distribution of an undivided interest in property is treated as the distribution of previously contributed property to the extent that the undivided interest does not exceed the undivided interest, if any, contributed by the distributee partner in the same property. See § 1.704-4(c)(6) for the application of section 704(c)(1)(B) in a similar context. The portion of the undivided interest in property retained by the partnership after the distribution, if any, that is treated as contributed by the distributee partner, is reduced to the extent of the undivided interest distributed to the distributee partner.

(e) *Examples.*—The following examples illustrate the rules of this section. Unless otherwise specified, partnership income equals partnership expenses (other than depreciation deductions for contributed property) for each year of the partnership, the fair market value of partnership property does not change, all distributions by the partnership are subject to section 737, and all partners are unrelated.

Example 1. Distribution of previously contributed property. (i) On January 1, 1995, A, B, and C form partnership ABC as equal partners. A contributes the following nondepreciable real property to the partnership:

	Fair Market Value	*Adjusted Tax Basis*
Property A1	$20,000	$10,000
Property A2	10,000	6,000

(ii) A's total net precontribution gain on the contributed property is $14,000 ($10,000 on Property A1 plus $4,000 on Property A2). B contributes $10,000 cash and Property B, nondepreciable real property with a fair market value and adjusted tax basis of $20,000. C contributes $30,000 cash.

(iii) On December 31, 1998, Property A2 and Property B are distributed to A in complete liquidation of A's interest in the partnership. Property A2 was previously contributed by A and is therefore not taken into account in determining the amount of the excess distribution or A's net precontribution gain. The adjusted tax basis of Property A2 in the hands of A is also determined under section 732 as if that property were the only property distributed to A.

(iv) As a result of excluding Property A2 from these determinations, the amount of the excess distribution is $10,000 ($20,000 fair market value of distributed Property B less $10,000 adjusted tax basis in A's partnership interest). A's net precontribution gain is also $10,000 ($14,000 total net precontribution gain less $4,000 gain with respect to previously contributed Property A2). A therefore recognizes $10,000 of gain on the distribution, the lesser of the excess distribution and the net precontribution gain.

Example 2. Distribution of a previously contributed interest in an entity. (i) On January 1, 1995, A, B, and C form partnership ABC as equal partners. A contributes Property A, nondepreciable real property with a fair market value of $10,000 and an adjusted tax basis of $5,000, and all of the stock of Corporation X with a fair market value and adjusted tax basis of $500. B contributes $500 cash and Property B, nondepreciable real property with a fair market value and adjusted tax basis of $10,000. Partner C contributes $10,500 cash. On December 31, 1996, ABC contributes Property B to Corporation X in a nonrecognition transaction under section 351.

(ii) On December 31, 1998, all of the stock of Corporation X is distributed to A in complete liquidation of A's interest in the partnership. The stock is treated as previously contributed property with respect to A only to the extent of the $500 fair market value of the Corporation X stock contributed by A. The fair market value of the distributed stock for purposes of determining the amount of the excess distribution is therefore $10,000 ($10,500 total fair market value of Corporation X stock less $500 portion treated as previously contributed property). The $500 fair market value and adjusted tax basis of the Corporation X stock is also not taken into account in determining the amount of the excess distribution and the net precontribution gain.

(iii) A recognizes $5,000 of gain under section 737, the amount of the excess distribution ($10,000 fair market value of distributed property less $5,000 adjusted tax basis in A's partnership interest) and A's net precontribution gain ($10,000 fair market value of Property A less $5,000 adjusted tax basis in Property A).

Example 3. Distribution of undivided interest in property. (i) On January 1, 1995, A and B form partnership AB as equal partners. A contributes $500 cash and an undivided one-half interest in Property X. B contributes $500 cash and an undivided one-half interest in Property X.

(ii) On December 31, 1998, an undivided one-half interest in Property X is distributed to A in a current distribution. The distribution of the undivided one-half interest in Property X is treated as a distribution of previously contributed property because A contributed an undivided one-half interest in Property X. As a result, A does not recognize any gain under section 737 on the distribution. [Reg. § 1.737-2.]

□ [*T.D.* 8642, 12-22-95. *Amended by T.D.* 8717, 5-8-97; *T.D.* 9193, 3-21-2005 (*corrected* 8-5-2005) *and T.D.* 9207, 5-23-2005.]

§ 1.737-3. Basis adjustments; Recovery rules.—(a) *Distributee partner's adjusted tax basis in the partnership interest.*—The distributee partner's adjusted tax basis in the partnership interest is increased by the amount of gain recognized by the distributee partner under section 737 and this section. This increase is not taken into account in determining the amount of gain recognized by the partner under section 737(a)(1) and this section or in determining the amount of gain recognized by the partner under section 731(a) on the distribution of money in the same distribution or any related distribution. See § 1.704-4(e)(1) for a determination of the distributee partner's adjusted tax basis in a distribution subject to section 704(c)(1)(B).

(b) *Distributee partner's adjusted tax basis in distributed property.*—(1) *In general.*—The distributee partner's adjusted tax basis in the distributed property is determined under section 732(a) or (b) as applicable. The increase in the distributee partner's adjusted tax basis in the partnership interest under paragraph (a) of this section is taken into account in determining the distributee partner's adjusted tax basis in the distributed property other than property previously contributed by the partner. See § 1.704-4(e)(2) for a determination of basis in a distribution subject to section 704(c)(1)(B).

(2) *Previously contributed property.*—The distributee partner's adjusted tax basis in distributed property that the partner previously contributed to the partnership is determined as if it were distributed in a separate and independent distribution prior to the distribution that is subject to section 737 and § 1.737-1.

(c) *Partnership's adjusted tax basis in partnership property.*—(1) *Increase in basis.*—The partnership's adjusted tax basis in eligible property is increased by the amount of gain recognized by the distributee partner under section 737.

(2) *Eligible property.*—Eligible property is property that—

(i) Entered into the calculation of the distributee partner's net precontribution gain;

(ii) Has an adjusted tax basis to the partnership less than the property's fair market value at the time of the distribution;

(iii) Would have the same character of gain on a sale by the partnership to an unrelated party as the character of any of the gain recognized by the distributee partner under section 737; and

(iv) Was not distributed to another partner in a distribution subject to section 704(c)(1)(B) and § 1.704-4 that was part of the same distribution as the distribution subject to section 737.

(3) *Method of adjustment.*—For the purpose of allocating the basis increase under paragraph (c)(2) of this section among the eligible property, all eligible property of the same character is treated as a single group. Character for this purpose is determined in the same manner as the character of the recognized gain is determined under § 1.737-1(d). The basis increase is allocated among the separate groups of eligible property in proportion to the character of the gain recognized under section 737. The basis increase is then allocated among property within each group in the order in which the property was contributed to the partnership by the partner, starting with the property contributed first, in an amount equal to the difference between the property's fair market value and its adjusted tax basis to the partnership at the time of the distribution. For property that has the same character and was contributed in the same (or a related) transaction, the basis increase is allocated based on the respective amounts of unrealized appreciation in such properties at the time of the distribution.

(4) *Section 754 adjustments.*—The basis adjustments to partnership property made pursuant to paragraph (c)(1) of this section are not elective and must be made regardless of whether the partnership has an election in effect under section 754. Any adjustments to the bases of partnership property (including eligible property as defined in paragraph (c)(2) of this section) under section 734(b) pursuant to a section 754 election (other than basis adjustments under section 734(b)(1)(A) described in the following sentence) must be made after (and must take into account) the adjustments to basis made under paragraph (a) and paragraph (c)(1) of this section. Basis adjustments under section 734(b)(1)(A) that are attributable to distributions of money to the distributee partner that are part of the same distribution as the distribution of property subject to section

737 are made before the adjustments to basis under paragraph (a) and paragraph (c)(1) of this section. See §1.737-1(c)(2)(ii) for the effect, if any, of basis adjustments under section 734(b)(1)(A) on a partner's net precontribution gain. See also §1.704-4(e)(3) for a similar rule regarding basis adjustments pursuant to a section 754 election in the context of section 704(c)(1)(B).

(d) *Recovery of increase to adjusted tax basis.*—Any increase to the adjusted tax basis of partnership property under paragraph (c)(1) of this section is recovered using any applicable recovery period and depreciation (or other cost recovery) method (including first-year conventions) available to the partnership for newly purchased property (of the type adjusted) placed in service at the time of the distribution.

(e) *Examples.*—The following examples illustrate the rules of this section. Unless otherwise specified, partnership income equals partnership expenses (other than depreciation deductions for contributed property) for each year of the partnership, the fair market value of partnership property does not change, all distributions by the partnership are subject to section 737, and all partners are unrelated.

Example 1. Partner's basis in distributed property. (i) On January 1, 1995, A, B, and C form partnership ABC as equal partners. A contributes Property A, nondepreciable real property with a fair market value of $10,000 and an adjusted tax basis of $5,000. B contributes Property B, nondepreciable real property with a fair market value and adjusted tax basis of $10,000. C contributes $10,000 cash.

(ii) On December 31, 1998, Property B is distributed to A in complete liquidation of A's interest in the partnership. A recognizes $5,000 of gain under section 737, an amount equal to the excess distribution of $5,000 ($10,000 fair market value of Property B less $5,000 adjusted tax basis in A's partnership interest) and A's net precontribution gain of $5,000 ($10,000 fair market value of Property A less $5,000 adjusted tax basis of such property).

(iii) A's adjusted tax basis in A's partnership interest is increased by the $5,000 of gain recognized under section 737. This increase is taken into account in determining A's basis in the distributed property. Therefore, A's adjusted tax basis in distributed Property B is $10,000 under section 732(b).

Example 2. Partner's basis in distributed property in connection with gain recognized under section 704(c)(1)(B). (i) On January 1, 1995, A, B, and C form partnership ABC as equal partners. A contributes the following nondepreciable real property located in the United States to the partnership:

	Fair Market Value	*Adjusted Tax Basis*
Property A1	$10,000	$5,000
Property A2	10,000	2,000

(ii) B contributes $10,000 cash and Property B, nondepreciable real property located outside the United States, with a fair market value and adjusted tax basis of $10,000. C contributes $20,000 cash.

(iii) On December 31, 1998, Property B is distributed to A in a current distribution and Property A1 is distributed to B in a current distribution. A recognizes $5,000 of gain under section 704(c)(1)(B) and §1.704-4 on the distribution of Property A1 to B, the difference between the fair market value of such property ($10,000) and the adjusted tax basis in distributed Property A1 ($5,000). The adjusted tax basis of A's partnership interest is increased by this $5,000 of gain under section 704(c)(1)(B) and §1.704-4(e)(1).

(iv) The increase in the adjusted tax basis of A's partnership interest is taken into account in determining the amount of the excess distribution. As a result, there is no excess distribution because the fair market value of Property B ($10,000) is less than the adjusted tax basis of A's interest in the partnership at the time of distribution ($12,000). A therefore recognizes no gain under section 737 on the receipt of Property B. A's adjusted tax basis in Property B is $10,000 under section 732(a)(1). The adjusted tax basis of A's partnership interest is reduced from $12,000 to $2,000 under section 733. See *Example 3* of §1.737-1(e).

Example 3. Partnership's basis in partnership property after a distribution with section 737 gain. (i) On January 31, 1995, A, B, and C form partnership ABC as equal partners. A contributes the following nondepreciable property to the partnership:

	Fair Market Value	*Adjusted Tax Basis*
Property A1	$1,000	$ 500
Property A2	4,000	1,500
Property A3	4,000	6,000
Property A4	6,000	4,000

(ii) The character of gain or loss on Properties A1, A2, and A3 is long-term, U.S.-source capital gain or loss. The character of gain on Property A4 is long-term, foreign-source capital gain. B contributes Property B, nondepreciable real property with a fair market value and adjusted tax basis of $15,000. C contributes $15,000 cash.

(iii) On December 31, 1998, Property B is distributed to A in complete liquidation of A's interest in the partnership. A recognizes gain of $3,000 under section 737, an amount equal to the excess distribution of $3,000 ($15,000 fair market value of Property B less $12,000 adjusted tax basis in A's partnership interest) and A's net precontribution gain of $3,000 ($15,000 aggregate fair market value of the property contributed by A less $12,000 aggregate adjusted tax basis of such property).

(iv) $2,000 of A's gain is long-term, foreign-source capital gain ($3,000 total gain under section 737 × $2,000 net long-term, foreign-source capital gain/$3,000 total net precontribution gain). $1,000 of A's gain is long-term, U.S.-source capital gain ($3,000 total gain under section 737 × $1,000 net long-term, U.S.-source capital gain/ $3,000 total net precontribution gain).

(v) The partnership must increase the adjusted tax basis of the property contributed by A by $3,000. All property contributed by A is eligible property. Properties A1, A2, and A3 have the same character and are grouped into a single group for purposes of allocating this basis increase. Property A4 is in a separate character group.

(vi) $2,000 of the basis increase must be allocated to long-term, foreign-source capital assets because $2,000 of the gain recognized by A was long-term, foreign-source capital gain. The adjusted tax basis of Property A4 is therefore increased from $4,000 to $6,000. $1,000 of the increase must be allocated to Properties A1 and A2 because $1,000 of the gain recognized by A is long-term, U.S.-source capital gain. No basis increase is allocated to Property A3 because its fair market value is less than its adjusted tax basis. The $1,000 basis increase is allocated between Properties A1 and A2 based on the unrealized appreciation in each asset before such basis adjustment. As a result, the adjusted tax basis of Property A1 is increased by $167 ($1,000 × $500/$3,000) and the adjusted tax basis of Property A2 is increased by $833 ($1,000 × $2,500/3,000). [Reg. § 1.737-3.]

□ [*T.D.* 8642, 12-22-95.]

§ 1.737-4. Anti-abuse rule.—(a) *In general.*—The rules of section 737 and §§ 1.737-1, 1.737-2, and 1.737-3 must be applied in a manner consistent with the purpose of section 737. Accordingly, if a principal purpose of a transaction is to achieve a tax result that is inconsistent with the purpose of section 737, the Commissioner can recast the transaction for federal tax purposes as appropriate to achieve tax results that are consistent with the purpose of section 737. Whether a tax result is inconsistent with the purpose of section 737 must be determined based on all the facts and circumstances. See § 1.704-4(f) for an anti-abuse rule and examples in the context of section 704(c)(1)(B). The anti-abuse rule and examples under section 704(c)(1)(B) and § 1.704-4(f) are relevant to section 737 and §§ 1.737-1, 1.737-2, and 1.737-3 to the extent that the net precontribution gain for purposes of section 737 is determined by reference to section 704(c)(1)(B).

(b) *Examples.*—The following examples illustrate the rules of this section. The examples set forth below do not delineate the boundaries of either permissible or impermissible types of transactions. Further, the addition of any facts or circumstances that are not specifically set forth in an example (or the deletion of any facts or circumstances) may alter the outcome of the transaction described in the example. Unless otherwise specified, partnership income equals partnership expenses (other than depreciation deductions for contributed property) for each year of the partnership, the fair market value of partnership property does not change, all distributions by the partnership are subject to section 737, and all partners are unrelated.

Example 1. Increase in distributee partner's basis by temporary contribution; results inconsistent with the purpose of section 737. (i) On January 1, 1995, A, B, and C form partnership ABC as equal partners. A contributes Property A1, nondepreciable real property with a fair market value of $10,000 and an adjusted tax basis of $1,000. B contributes Property B, nondepreciable real property with a fair market value of $10,000 and an adjusted tax basis of $10,000. C contributes $10,000 cash.

(ii) On January 1, 1999, pursuant to a plan a principal purpose of which is to avoid gain under section 737, A transfers to the partnership Property A2, nondepreciable real property with a fair market value and adjusted tax basis of $9,000. A treats the transfer as a contribution to the partnership pursuant to section 721 and increases the adjusted tax basis of A's partnership interest from $1,000 to $10,000. On January 1, 1999, the partnership agreement is amended and all other necessary steps are taken so that substantially all of the economic risks and benefits of Property A2 are retained by A. On February 1, 1999, Property B is distributed to A in a current distribution. If the contribution of Property A2 is treated as a contribution to the partnership for purposes of section 737, there is no excess distribution because the fair market value of distributed Property B ($10,000) does not exceed the adjusted tax basis of A's interest in the partnership

($10,000), and therefore section 737 does not apply. A's adjusted tax basis in distributed Property B is $10,000 under section 732(a)(1) and the adjusted tax basis of A's partnership interest is reduced to zero under section 733.

(iii) On March 1, 2000, A receives Property A2 from the partnership in complete liquidation of A's interest in the partnership. A recognizes no gain on the distribution of Property A2 because the property was previously contributed property. See § 1.737-2(d).

(iv) Although A has treated the transfer of Property A2 as a contribution to the partnership that increased the adjusted tax basis of A's interest in the partnership, it would be inconsistent with the purpose of section 737 to recognize the transfer as a contribution to the partnership. Section 737 requires recognition of gain when the value of distributed property exceeds the distributee partner's adjusted tax basis in the partnership interest. Section 737 assumes that any contribution or other transaction that affects a partner's adjusted tax basis in the partnership interest is a contribution or transaction in substance and is not engaged in with a principal purpose of avoiding recognition of gain under section 737. Because the transfer of Property A2 to the partnership was not a contribution in substance and was made with a principal purpose of avoiding recognition of gain under section 737, the Commissioner can disregard the contribution of Property A2 for this purpose. As a result, A recognizes gain of $9,000 under section 737 on the receipt of Property B, an amount equal to the lesser of the excess distribution of $9,000 ($10,000 fair market value of distributed Property B less the $1,000 adjusted tax basis of A's partnership interest, determined without regard to the transitory contribution of Property A2) or A's net precontribution gain of $9,000 on Property A1.

Example 2. Increase in distributee partner's basis; section 752 liability shift; results consistent with the purpose of section 737. (i) On January 1, 1995, A and B form general partnership AB as equal partners. A contributes Property A, nondepreciable real property with a fair market value of $10,000 and an adjusted tax basis of $1,000. B contributes Property B, nondepreciable real property with a fair market value and adjusted tax basis of $10,000. The partnership also borrows $10,000 on a recourse basis and purchases Property C. The $10,000 liability is allocated equally between A and B under section 752, thereby increasing the adjusted tax basis in A's partnership interest to $6,000.

(ii) On December 31, 1998, the partners agree that A is to receive Property B in a current distribution. If A were to receive Property B at that time, A would recognize $4,000 of gain under section 737, an amount equal to the lesser of the excess distribution of $4,000 ($10,000 fair market value of Property B less $6,000 adjusted tax basis in A's partnership interest) or A's net precontribution gain of $9,000 ($10,000 fair market value of Property A less $1,000 adjusted tax basis of Property A).

(iii) With a principal purpose of avoiding such gain, A and B agree that A will be solely liable for the repayment of the $10,000 partnership liability and take the steps necessary so that the entire amount of the liability is allocated to A under section 752. The adjusted tax basis in A's partnership interest is thereby increased from $6,000 to $11,000 to reflect A's share of the $5,000 of liability previously allocated to B. As a result of this increase in A's adjusted tax basis, there is no excess distribution because the fair market value of distributed Property B ($10,000) is less than the adjusted tax basis of A's partnership interest. Recognizing A's increased adjusted tax basis as a result of the shift in liabilities is consistent with the purpose of section 737 and this section. Section 737 requires recognition of gain only when the value of the distributed property exceeds the distributee partner's adjusted tax basis in the partnership interest. The $10,000 recourse liability is a bona fide liability of the partnership that was undertaken for a substantial business purpose and A's and B's agreement that A will assume responsibility for repayment of that debt has substance. Therefore, the increase in A's adjusted tax basis in A's interest in the partnership due to the shift in partnership liabilities under section 752 is respected, and A recognizes no gain under section 737. [Reg. § 1.737-4.]

□ [*T.D.* 8642, 12-22-95.]

§ 1.741-1. Recognition and character of gain or loss on sale or exchange.—(a) The sale or exchange of an interest in a partnership shall, except to the extent section 751(a) applies, be treated as the sale or exchange of a capital asset, resulting in capital gain or loss measured by the difference between the amount realized and the adjusted basis of the partnership interest, as determined under section 705. For treatment of selling partner's distributive share up to date of sale, see section 706(c)(2). Where the provisions of section 751 require the recognition of ordinary income or loss with respect to a portion of the amount realized from such sale or exchange, the amount realized shall be reduced by the amount attributable under section 751 to unrealized receivables and substantially appreciated inventory items, and the adjusted basis of the transferor partner's interest in the partnership shall be reduced by the portion of such basis attributable to such unrealized receivables and substantially appreciated inventory items. See section 751 and § 1.751-1.

(b) Section 741 shall apply whether the partnership interest is sold to one or more members of the partnership or to one or more persons who are not members of the partnership. Section 741 shall also apply even though the sale of the partnership interest results in a termination of the partnership under section 708(b). Thus, the provisions of section 741 shall be applicable (1) to the transferor partner in a 2-man partnership when he sells his interest to the other partner, and (2) to all the members of a partnership when they sell their interest to one or more persons outside the partnership.

(c) See section 351 for nonrecognition of gain or loss upon transfer of a partnership interest to a corporation controlled by the transferor.

(d) For rules relating to the treatment of liabilities on the sale or exchange of interests in a partnership see § § 1.752-1 and 1.1001-2.

(e) For rules relating to the capital gain or loss recognized when a partner sells or exchanges an interest in a partnership that holds appreciated collectibles or section 1250 property with section 1250 capital gain, see § 1.1(h)-1. This paragraph (e) applies to transfers of interests in partnerships that occur on or after September 21, 2000.

(f) For rules relating to dividing the holding period of an interest in a partnership, see § 1.1223-3. This paragraph (f) applies to transfers of partnership interests and distributions of property from a partnership that occur on or after September 21, 2000. [Reg. § 1.741-1.]

☐ [*T.D.* 6175, 5-23-56. *Amended by T.D.* 7741, 12-11-80 *and T.D.* 8902, 9-20-2000.]

§ 1.742-1. Basis of transferee partner's interest.—(a) *In general.*—The basis to a transferee partner of an interest in a partnership shall be determined under the general basis rules for property provided by part II (section 1011 and following), Subchapter O, Chapter 1 of the Internal Revenue Code. Thus, the basis of a purchased interest will be its cost. Generally, the basis of a partnership interest acquired from a decedent is the fair market value of the interest at the date of his death or at the alternate valuation date, increased by his estate's or other successor's share of partnership liabilities, if any, on that date, and reduced to the extent that such value is attributable to items constituting income in respect of a decedent (see section 753 and § § 1.706-1(c)(3)(v) and 1.753-1(b)) under section 691. See section 1014(c). However, the basis of a partnership interest acquired from a decedent is determined under section 1022 if the decedent died in 2010 and the decedent's executor elected to have section 1022 apply to the decedent's estate. For basis of contributing partner's interest, see section 722. The basis so determined is then subject to the adjustments provided in section 705.

* * *

[Reg. § 1.742-1.]

☐ [*T.D.* 6175, 5-23-56. *Amended by T.D.* 9811, 1-18-2017.]

»→ Caution: Reg. § 1.743-1 does not reflect changes made in Section 743 by the American Jobs Creation Act of 2004.

§ 1.743-1. Optional adjustment to basis of partnership property.—(a) *Generally.*—The basis of partnership property is adjusted as a result of the transfer of an interest in a partnership by sale or exchange or on the death of a partner only if the election provided by section 754 (relating to optional adjustments to the basis of partnership property) is in effect with respect to the partnership. Whether or not the election provided in section 754 is in effect, the basis of partnership property is not adjusted as the result of a contribution of property, including money, to the partnership.

(b) *Determination of adjustment.*—In the case of the transfer of an interest in a partnership, either by sale or exchange or as a result of the death of a partner, a partnership that has an election under section 754 in effect—

(1) Increases the adjusted basis of partnership property by the excess of the transferee's basis for the transferred partnership interest over the transferee's share of the adjusted basis to the partnership of the partnership's property; or

(2) Decreases the adjusted basis of partnership property by the excess of the transferee's share of the adjusted basis to the partnership of the partnership's property over the transferee's basis for the transferred partnership interest.

(c) *Determination of transferee's basis in the transferred partnership interest.*—In the case of the transfer of a partnership interest by sale or exchange or as a result of the death of a partner, the transferee's basis in the transferred partnership interest is determined under section 742 and § 1.742-1. See also section 752 and § § 1.752-1 through 1.752-5.

(d) *Determination of transferee's share of the adjusted basis to the partnership of the partnership's property.*—(1) *Generally.*—A transferee's share of the adjusted basis to the partnership of partnership property is equal to the sum of the transferee's interest as a partner in the partnership's previously taxed capital, plus the transferee's share of partnership liabilities. Generally, a transferee's interest as a partner in the partnership's previously taxed capital is equal to—

(i) The amount of cash that the transferee would receive on a liquidation of the partnership following the hypothetical transaction, as defined in paragraph (d)(2) of this section (to the extent attributable to the acquired partnership interest); increased by

(ii) The amount of tax loss (including any remedial allocations under § 1.704-3(d)), that would be allocated to the transferee from the hypothetical transaction (to the extent attributable to the acquired partnership interest); and decreased by

(iii) The amount of tax gain (including any remedial allocations under § 1.704-3(d)), that would be allocated to the transferee from the hypothetical transaction (to the extent attributable to the acquired partnership interest).

(2) *Hypothetical transaction defined.*—For purposes of paragraph (d)(1) of this section, the hypothetical transaction means the disposition by the partnership of all of the partnership's assets, immediately after the transfer of the partnership interest, in a fully taxable transaction for cash equal to the fair market value of the assets. See § 1.460-4(k)(3)(v)(B) for a rule relating to the computation of income or loss that would be allocated to the transferee from a contract accounted for under a long-term contract method of accounting as a result of the hypothetical transaction.

(3) *Examples.*—The provisions of this paragraph (d) are illustrated by the following examples:

Example 1. (i) A is a member of partnership PRS in which the partners have equal interests in capital and profits. The partnership has made an election under section 754, relating to the optional adjustment to the basis of partnership property. A sells its interest to T for $22,000. The balance sheet of the partnership at the date of sale shows the following:

Assets

	Adjusted Basis	*Fair Market Value*
Cash	$ 5,000	$ 5,000
Accounts receivable	10,000	10,000
Inventory	20,000	21,000
Depreciable assets	20,000	40,000
Total	$55,000	$76,000

Liabilities and Capital

	Adjusted Per Books	*Fair Market Value*
Liabilities	$10,000	$10,000
Capital:		
A	15,000	22,000
B	15,000	22,000
C	15,000	22,000
Total	$55,000	$76,000

(ii) The amount of the basis adjustment under section 743(b) is the difference between the basis of T's interest in the partnership and T's share of the adjusted basis to the partnership of the partnership's property. Under section 742, the basis of T's interest is $25,333 (the cash paid for A's interest, $22,000, plus $3,333, T's share of partnership liabilities). T's interest in the partnership's previously taxed capital is $15,000 ($22,000, the amount of cash T would receive if PRS liquidated immediately after the hypothetical transaction, decreased by $7,000, the amount of tax gain allocated to T from the hypothetical transaction). T's share of the adjusted basis to the partnership of the partnership's property is $18,333 ($15,000 share of previously taxed capital, plus $3,333 share of the partnership's liabilities). The amount of the basis adjustment under section 743(b) to partnership property therefore, is $7,000, the difference between $25,333 and $18,333.

Example 2. A, B, and C form partnership PRS, to which A contributes land (Asset 1) with a fair market value of $1,000 and an adjusted basis to A of $400, and B and C each contribute $1,000 cash. Each partner has $1,000 credited to it on the books of the partnership as its capital contribution. The partners share in profits equally. During the partnership's first taxable year, Asset 1 appreciates in value to $1,300. A sells its one-third interest in the partnership to T for $1,100, when an election under section 754 is in effect. The amount of tax gain that would be allocated to T from the hypothetical transaction is $700 ($600 section 704(c) built-in gain, plus one-third of the additional gain). Thus, T's interest in the partnership's previously taxed capital is $400 ($1,100, the amount of cash T would receive if PRS liquidated immediately after the hypothetical transaction, decreased by $700, T's share of gain from the hypothetical transaction). The amount of T's basis adjustment under section 743(b) to partnership property is $700 (the excess of $1,100, T's cost basis for its interest, over $400, T's share of the adjusted basis to the partnership of partnership property).

(e) *Allocation of basis adjustment.*—For the allocation of the basis adjustment under this section among the individual items of partnership property, see section 755 and the regulations thereunder.

(f) *Subsequent transfers.*—Where there has been more than one transfer of a partnership interest, a transferee's basis adjustment is determined without regard to any prior transferee's basis adjustment. In the case of a gift of an interest in a partnership, the donor is treated as transferring, and the donee as receiving, that portion of the basis adjustment attributable to the gifted partnership interest. The provisions of this paragraph (f) are illustrated by the following example:

Example. (i) A, B, and C form partnership PRS. A and B each contribute $1,000 cash, and C contributes land with a basis and fair market value of $1,000. When the land has appreciated in value to $1,300, A sells its interest to T1 for $1,100 (one-third of $3,300, the fair market value of the partnership property). An election under section 754 is in effect; therefore, T1 has a basis adjustment under section 743(b) of $100.

(ii) After the land has further appreciated in value to $1,600, T1 sells its interest to T2 for $1,200 (one-third of $3,600, the fair market value of the partnership property). T2 has a basis adjustment under section 743(b) of $200. This amount is determined without regard to any basis adjustment under section 743(b) that T1 may have had in the partnership assets.

(iii) During the following year, T2 makes a gift to T3 of fifty percent of T2's interest in PRS. At the time of the transfer, T2 has a $200 basis adjustment under section 743(b). T2 is treated as transferring $100 of the basis adjustment to T3 with the gift of the partnership interest.

(g) *Distributions.*—(1) *Distribution of adjusted property to the transferee.*—(i) *Coordination with section 732.*—If a partnership distributes property to a transferee and the transferee has a basis adjustment for the property, the basis adjustment is taken into account under section 732. See § 1.732-2(b).

(ii) *Coordination with section 734.*—For certain adjustments to the common basis of remaining partnership property after the distribution of adjusted property to a transferee, see § 1.734-2(b).

(2) *Distribution of adjusted property to another partner.*—(i) *Coordination with section 732.*—If a partner receives a distribution of property with respect to which another partner has a basis adjustment, the distributee does not take the basis adjustment into account under section 732.

(ii) *Reallocation of basis.*—A transferee with a basis adjustment in property that is distributed to another partner reallocates the basis adjustment among the remaining items of partnership property under § 1.755-1(c).

(3) *Distributions in complete liquidation of a partner's interest.*—If a transferee receives a distribution of property (whether or not the transferee has a basis adjustment in such property) in liquidation of its interest in the partnership, the adjusted basis to the partnership of the distributed property immediately before the distribution includes the transferee's basis adjustment for the property in which the transferee relinquished an interest (either because it remained in the partnership or was distributed to another partner). Any basis adjustment for property in which the transferee is deemed to relinquish its interest is reallocated among the properties distributed to the transferee under § 1.755-1(c).

(4) *Coordination with other provisions.*—The rules of sections 704(c)(1)(B), 731, 737, and 751 apply before the rules of this paragraph (g).

(5) *Example.*—The provisions of this paragraph (g) are illustrated by the following example:

Example. (i) A, B, and C are equal partners in partnership PRS. Each partner originally contributed $10,000 in cash, and PRS used the contributions to purchase five nondepreciable capital assets. PRS has no liabilities. After five years, PRS's balance sheet appears as follows:

Assets

	Adjusted Basis	*Fair Market Value*
Asset 1	$10,000	$10,000
Asset 2	4,000	6,000
Asset 3	6,000	6,000
Asset 4	7,000	4,000
Asset 5	3,000	13,000
Total	$30,000	$39,000

Capital

	Adjusted Per Books	*Fair Market Value*
Partner A	$10,000	$13,000
Partner B	10,000	13,000
Partner C	10,000	13,000
Total	$30,000	$39,000

(ii) A sells its interest to T for $13,000 when PRS has an election in effect under section 754. T receives a basis adjustment under section 743(b) in the partnership property that is equal to $3,000 (the excess of T's basis in the partnership interest, $13,000, over T's share of the adjusted basis to the partnership of partnership property, $10,000). The basis adjustment is allocated under section 755, and the partnership's balance sheet appears as follows:

Assets

	Adjusted Basis	Fair Market Value	Basis Adjustment
Asset 1	$10,000	$10,000	$0.00
Asset 2	4,000	6,000	666.67
Asset 3	6,000	6,000	0.00
Asset 4	7,000	4,000	(1,000.00)
Asset 5	3,000	13,000	3,333.33
Total . . .	$30,000	$39,000	$3,000.00

Capital

	Adjusted Per Books	Fair Market Value	Special Basis
Partner T	$10,000	$13,000	$3,000
Partner B . . .	10,000	13,000	0
Partner C . . .	10,000	13,000	0
Total	$30,000	$39,000	$3,000

(iii) Assume that PRS distributes Asset 2 to T in partial liquidation of T's interest in the partnership. T has a basis adjustment under section 743(b) of $666.67 in Asset 2. Under paragraph (g)(1)(i) of this section, T takes the basis adjustment into account under section 732. Therefore, T will have a basis in Asset 2 of $4,666.67 following the distribution.

(iv) Assume instead that PRS distributes Asset 5 to C in complete liquidation of C's interest in PRS. T has a basis adjustment under section 743(b) of $3,333.33 in Asset 5. Under paragraph (g)(2)(i) of this section, C does not take T's basis adjustment into account under section 732. Therefore, the partnership's basis for purposes of sections 732 and 734 is $3,000. Under paragraph (g)(2)(ii) of this section, T's $3,333.33 basis adjustment is reallocated among the remaining partnership assets under §1.755-1(c).

(v) Assume instead that PRS distributes Asset 5 to T in complete liquidation of its interest in PRS. Under paragraph (g)(3) of this section, immediately prior to the distribution of Asset 5 to T, PRS must adjust the basis of Asset 5. Therefore, immediately prior to the distribution, PRS's basis in Asset 5 is equal to $6,000, which is the sum of (A) $3,000, PRS's common basis in Asset 5, plus (B) $3,333.33, T's basis adjustment to Asset 5, plus (C) ($333.33), the sum of T's basis adjustments in Assets 2 and 4. For purposes of sections 732 and 734, therefore, PRS will be treated as having a basis in Asset 5 equal to $6,000.

(h) *Contributions of adjusted property.*—(1) *Section 721(a) transactions.*—If, in a transaction described in section 721(a), a partnership (the upper tier) contributes to another partnership (the lower tier) property with respect to which a basis adjustment has been made, the basis adjustment is treated as contributed to the lower-tier partnership, regardless of whether the lower-tier partnership makes a section 754 election. The lower tier's basis in the contributed assets and the upper tier's basis in the partnership interest received in the transaction are determined with reference to the basis adjustment. However, that portion of the basis of the upper tier's interest in the lower tier attributable to the basis adjustment must be segregated and allocated solely to the transferee partner for whom the basis adjustment was made. Similarly, that portion of the lower tier's basis in its assets attributable to the basis adjustment must be segregated and allocated solely to the upper tier and the transferee. A partner with a basis adjustment in property held by a partnership that terminates under section 708(b)(1)(B) will continue to have the same basis adjustment with respect to property deemed contributed by the terminated partnership to the new partnership under §1.708-1(b)(1)(iv), regardless of whether the new partnership makes a section 754 election.

(2) *Section 351 transactions.*—(i) *Basis in transferred property.*—A corporation's adjusted tax basis in property transferred to the corporation by a partnership in a transaction described in section 351 is determined with reference to any basis adjustments to the property under section 743(b) (other than any basis adjustment that reduces a partner's gain under paragraph (h)(2)(ii) of this section).

(ii) *Partnership gain.*—The amount of gain, if any, recognized by the partnership on a transfer of property by the partnership to a corporation in a transfer described in section 351 is determined without reference to any basis adjustment to the transferred property under section 743(b). The amount of gain, if any, recognized by the partnership on the transfer that is allocated to a partner with a basis adjustment in the transferred property is adjusted to reflect the partner's basis adjustment in the transferred property.

(iii) *Basis in stock.*—The partnership's adjusted tax basis in stock received from a corporation in a transfer described in section 351 is determined without reference to the basis adjustment in property transferred to the corporation in the section 351 exchange. A partner with a basis adjustment in property transferred to the corporation, however, has a basis adjustment in the stock received by the partnership in the section 351 exchange in an amount equal to the partner's basis adjustment in the transferred property, reduced by any basis adjustment that reduced the partner's gain under paragraph (h)(2)(ii) of this section.

(iv) *Example.*—The following example illustrates the principles of this paragraph (h)(2):

Example. (i) A, B, and C are equal partners in partnership PRS. The partnership's only asset, Asset 1, has an adjusted tax basis of $60 and a fair market value of $120. Asset 1 is a nondepreciable capital asset and is not section 704(c) property. A has a basis in its partnership interest of $40, and a positive section 743(b) adjustment of $20 in Asset 1. In a transaction to which section 351 applies, PRS contributes Asset 1 to X, a corporation, in exchange for $15 in cash and X stock with a fair market value of $105.

(ii) Under paragraph (h)(2)(ii) of this section, PRS realizes $60 of gain on the transfer of Asset 1 to X ($120, its amount realized, minus $60, its adjusted basis), but recognizes only $15 of that gain under section 351(b)(1). Of this amount, $5 is allocated to each partner. A must use $5 of its basis adjustment in Asset 1 to offset A's share of PRS's gain. Under paragraph (h)(2)(iii) of this section, PRS's basis in the stock received from X is $60. However, A has a basis adjustment in the stock received by PRS equal to $15 (its basis adjustment in Asset 1, $20, reduced by the portion of the adjustment which reduced A's gain, $5). Under paragraph (h)(2)(i) of this section, X's basis in Asset 1 equals $90 (PRS's common basis in the asset, $60, plus the gain recognized by PRS under section 351(b)(1), $15, plus A's basis adjustment under section 743(b), $20, less the portion of the adjustment which reduced A's gain, $5).

(i) [Reserved].

(j) *Effect of basis adjustment.*—(1) *In general.*—The basis adjustment constitutes an adjustment to the basis of partnership property with respect to the transferee only. No adjustment is made to the common basis of partnership property. Thus, for purposes of calculating income, deduction, gain, and loss, the transferee will have a special basis for those partnership properties the bases of which are adjusted under section 743(b) and this section. The adjustment to the basis of partnership property under section 743(b) has no effect on the partnership's computation of any item under section 703.

(2) *Computation of partner's distributive share of partnership items.*—The partnership first computes its items of income, deduction, gain, or loss at the partnership level under section 703. The partnership then allocates the partnership items among the partners, including the transferee, in accordance with section 704, and adjusts the partners' capital accounts accordingly. The partnership then adjusts the transferee's distributive share of the items of partnership income, deduction, gain, or loss, in accordance with paragraphs (j)(3) and (4) of this section, to reflect the effects of the transferee's basis adjustment under section 743(b). These adjustments to the transferee's distributive shares must be reflected on Schedules K and K-1 of the partnership's return (Form 1065). These adjustments to the transferee's distributive shares do not affect the transferee's capital account. See § 1.460-4(k)(3)(v)(B) for rules relating to the effect of a basis adjustment under section 743(b) that is allocated to a contract accounted for under a long-term contract method of accounting in determining the transferee's distributive share of income or loss from the contract.

(3) *Effect of basis adjustment in determining items of income, gain, or loss.*—(i) *In general.*—The amount of a transferee's income, gain, or loss from the sale or exchange of a partnership asset in which the transferee has a basis adjustment is equal to the transferee's share of the partnership's gain or loss from the sale of the asset (including any remedial allocations under $1.704-3(d)), minus the amount of the transferee's positive basis adjustment for the partnership asset (determined by taking into account the recovery of the basis adjustment under paragraph (j)(4)(i)(B) of this section) or plus the amount of the transferee's negative basis adjustment for the partnership asset (determined by taking into the account the recovery of the basis adjustment under paragraph (j)(4)(ii)(B) of this section).

(ii) *Examples.*—The following examples illustrate the principles of this paragraph (j)(3):

Example 1. A and B form equal partnership PRS. A contributes nondepreciable property with a fair market value of $50 and an adjusted tax basis of $100. PRS will use the traditional allocation method under § 1.704-3(b). B contributes $50 cash. A sells its interest to T for $50. PRS has an election in effect to adjust the basis of partnership property under section 754. T receives a negative $50 basis adjustment under section 743(b) that, under section 755, is allocated to the nondepreciable property. PRS then sells the property for $60. PRS recognizes a book gain of $10 (allocated equally between T and B) and a tax loss of $40. T will receive an allocation of $40 of tax loss under the principles of section 704(c). However, because T has a negative $50 basis adjustment in the nondepreciable property, T recognizes a $10 gain from the partnership's sale of the property.

Example 2. A and B form equal partnership PRS. A contributes nondepreciable property with a fair market value of $100 and an adjusted tax basis of $50. B contributes $100 cash. PRS will use the traditional allocation method under §1.704-3(b). A sells its interest to T for $100. PRS has an election in effect to adjust the basis of partnership property under section 754. Therefore, T receives a $50 basis adjustment under section 743(b) that, under section 755, is allocated to the nondepreciable property. PRS then sells the nondepreciable property for $90. PRS recognizes a book loss of $10 (allocated equally between T and B) and a tax gain of $40. T will receive an allocation of the entire $40 of tax gain under the principles of section 704(c). However, because T has a $50 basis adjustment in the property, T recognizes a $10 loss from the partnership's sale of the property.

Example 3. A and B form equal partnership PRS. PRS will make allocations under section 704(c) using the remedial allocation method described in §1.704-3(d). A contributes nondepreciable property with a fair market value of $100 and an adjusted tax basis of $150. B contributes $100 cash. A sells its partnership interest to T for $100. PRS has an election in effect to adjust the basis of partnership property under section 754. T receives a negative $50 basis adjustment under section 743(b) that, under section 755, is allocated to the property. The partnership then sells the property for $120. The partnership recognizes a $20 book gain and a $30 tax loss. The book gain will be allocated equally between the partners. The entire $30 tax loss will be allocated to T under the principles of section 704(c). To match its $10 share of book gain, B will be allocated $10 of remedial gain, and T will be allocated an offsetting $10 of remedial loss. T was allocated a total of $40 of tax loss with respect to the property. However, because T has a negative $50 basis adjustment to the property, T recognizes a $10 gain from the partnership's sale of the property.

(4) *Effect of basis adjustment in determining items of deduction.*—(i) *Increases.*—(A) *Additional deduction.*—The amount of any positive basis adjustment that is recovered by the transferee in any year is added to the transferee's distributive share of the partnership's depreciation or amortization deductions for the year. The basis adjustment is adjusted under section 1016(a)(2) to reflect the recovery of the basis adjustment.

(B) *Recovery period.*—*(1) In general.*—Except as provided in paragraph (j)(4)(i)(B)(2) of this section, for purposes of section 168, if the basis of a partnership's recovery property is increased as a result of the transfer of a partnership interest, then the increased portion of the basis is taken into account as if it were newly-purchased recovery property placed in service when the transfer occurs. Consequently, any applicable recovery period and method may be used to determine the recovery allowance with respect to the increased portion of the basis. However, no change is made for purposes of determining the recovery allowance under section 168 for the portion of the basis for which there is no increase. The partnership is allowed to deduct the additional first year depreciation under section 168(k) and § 1.168(k)-2 for an increase in the basis of qualified property, as defined in section 168(k) and § 1.168(k)-2, under section 743(b) in a class of property, as defined in § 1.168(k)-2(f)(1)(ii)(A) through (F), even if the partnership made the election under section 168(k)(7) and § 1.168(k)-2(f)(1) not to deduct the additional first year depreciation for all other qualified property of the partnership in the same class of property, as defined in § 1.168(k)-2(f)(1)(ii)(A) through (F), and placed in service in the same taxable year, provided the section 743(b) basis adjustment meets all requirements of section 168(k) and § 1.168(k)-2. Further, the partnership may make an election under section 168(k)(7) and § 1.168(k)-2(f)(1) not to deduct the additional first year depreciation for an increase in the basis of qualified property, as defined in section 168(k) and § 1.168(k)-2, under section 743(b) in a class of property, as defined in § 1.168(k)-2(f)(1)(ii)(A) through (F), and placed in service in the same taxable year, even if the partnership does not make that election for all other qualified property of the partnership in the same class of property, as defined in § 1.168(k)-2(f)(1)(ii)(A) through (F), and placed in service in the same taxable year. In this case, the section 743(b) basis adjustment must be recovered under a reasonable method.

(2) Remedial allocation method.—If a partnership elects to use the remedial allocation method described in §1.704-3(d) with respect to an item of the partnership's recovery property, then the portion of any increase in the basis of the item of the partnership's recovery property under section 743(b) that is attributable to section 704(c) built-in gain is recovered over the remaining recovery period for the partnership's excess book basis in the property as determined in the final sentence of §1.704-3(d)(2). Any remaining portion of the basis increase is recovered under paragraph (j)(4)(i)(B)(*1*) of this section. The first sentence of this paragraph (j)(4)(i)(B)(*2*) does not apply to a partnership that is not a publicly traded partnership within the meaning of section 7704(b) with respect to any basis increase under section 743(b) that is recovered using the additional first year depreciation deduction under section 168(k).

(C) *Examples.*—The provisions of this paragraph (j)(4)(i) are illustrated by the following examples:

Example 1. (i) A, B, and C are equal partners in partnership PRS, which owns Asset 1, an item of depreciable property that has a fair market value in excess of its adjusted tax basis. C sells its interest in PRS to T while PRS has an election in effect under section 754. PRS, therefore, increases the basis of Asset 1 with respect to T.

(ii) Assume that in the year following the transfer of the partnership interest to T, T's distributive share of the partnership's common basis depreciation deductions from Asset 1 is $1,000. Also assume that, under paragraph (j)(4)(i)(B) of this section, the amount of the basis adjustment under section 743(b) that T recovers during the year is $500. The total amount of depreciation deductions from Asset 1 reported by T is equal to $1,500.

Example 2. (i) A and B form equal partnership PRS. A contributes property with an adjusted basis of $100,000 and a fair market value of $500,000. B contributes $500,000 cash. When PRS is formed, the property has five years remaining in its recovery period. The partnership's adjusted basis of $100,000 will, therefore, be recovered over the five years remaining in the property's recovery period. PRS elects to use the remedial allocation method under $1.704-3(d) with respect to the property. If PRS had purchased the property at the time of the partnership's formation, the basis of the property would have been recovered over a 10-year period. The $400,000 of section 704(c) built-in gain will, therefore, be amortized under $1.704-3(d) over a 10-year period beginning at the time of the partnership's formation.

(ii) (A) Except for the depreciation deductions, PRS's expenses equal its income in each year of the first two years commencing with the year the partnership is formed. After two years, A's share of the adjusted basis of partnership property is $120,000, while B's is $440,000:

Capital Accounts

	A		*B*	
	Book	*Tax*	*Book*	*Tax*
Initial Contribution	$500,000	$100,000	$500,000	$500,000
Depreciation Year 1	(30,000)		(30,000)	(20,000)
Remedial		10,000		(10,000)
	470,000	110,000	470,000	470,000
Depreciation Year 2	(30,000)		(30,000)	(20,000)
Remedial		10,000		(10,000)
	$440,000	$120,000	$440,000	$440,000

(B) A sells its interest in PRS to T for its fair market value of $440,000. A valid election under section 754 is in effect with respect to the sale of the partnership interest. Accordingly, PRS makes an adjustment, pursuant to section 743(b), to increase the basis of partnership property. Under section 743(b), the amount of the basis adjustment is equal to $320,000. Under section 755, the entire basis adjustment is allocated to the property.

(iii) At the time of the transfer, $320,000 of section 704(c) built-in gain from the property was still reflected on the partnership's books, and all of the basis adjustment is attributable to section 704(c) built-in gain. Therefore, the basis adjustment will be recovered over the remaining recovery period for the section 704(c) built-in gain under $1.704-3(d).

(ii) *Decreases.*—(A) *Reduced deduction.*—The amount of any negative basis adjustment allocated to an item of depreciable or amortizable property that is recovered in any year first decreases the transferee's distributive share of the partnership's depreciation or amortization deductions from that item of property for the year. If the amount of the basis adjustment recovered in any year exceeds the transferee's distributive share of the partnership's depreciation or amortization deductions from the item of property, then the transferee's distributive share of the partnership's depreciation or amortization deductions from other items of partnership property is decreased. The transferee then recognizes ordinary income to the extent of the excess, if any, of the amount of the basis adjustment recovered in any year over the transferee's distributive share of the partnership's depreciation or amortization deductions from all items of property.

(B) *Recovery period.*—For purposes of section 168, if the basis of an item of a partnership's recovery property is decreased as the result of the transfer of an interest in the partnership, then the decrease is recovered over the remaining useful life of the item of the partnership's recovery property. The portion of the decrease that is recovered in any year during the recovery period is equal to the product of—

(1) The amount of the decrease to the item's adjusted basis (determined as of the date of the transfer); multiplied by

(2) A fraction, the numerator of which is the portion of the adjusted basis of the item recovered by the partnership in that year, and the denominator of which is the adjusted basis of the item on the date of the transfer (determined prior to any basis adjustments).

(C) *Examples.*—The provisions of this paragraph (j) (4) (ii) are illustrated by the following examples:

Example 1. (i) A, B, and C are equal partners in partnership PRS, which owns Asset 2, an item of depreciable property that has a fair market value that is less than its adjusted tax basis. C sells its interest in PRS to T while PRS has an election in effect under section 754. PRS, therefore, decreases the basis of Asset 2 with respect to T.

(ii) Assume that in the year following the transfer of the partnership interest to T, T's distributive share of the partnership's common basis depreciation deductions from Asset 2 is $1,000. Also assume that, under paragraph (j) (4) (ii) (B) of this section, the amount of the basis adjustment under section 743(b) that T recovers during the year is $500. The total amount of depreciation deductions from Asset 2 reported by T is equal to $500.

Example 2. (i) A and B form equal partnership PRS. A contributes property with an adjusted basis of $100,000 and a fair market value of $50,000. B contributes $50,000 cash. When PRS is formed, the property has five years remaining in its recovery period. The partnership's adjusted basis of $100,000 will, therefore, be recovered over the five years remaining in the property's recovery period. PRS uses the traditional allocation method under § 1.704-3(b) with respect to the property. As a result, B will receive $5,000 of depreciation deductions from the property in each of years 1-5, and A, as the contributing partner, will receive $15,000 of depreciation deductions in each of these years.

(ii) Except for the depreciation deductions, PRS's expenses equal its income in each of the first two years commencing with the year the partnership is formed. After two years, A's share of the adjusted basis of partnership property is $70,000, while B's is $40,000. A sells its interest in PRS to T for its fair market value of $40,000. A valid election under section 754 is in effect with respect to the sale of the partnership interest. Accordingly, PRS makes an adjustment, pursuant to section 743(b), to decrease the basis of partnership property. Under section 743(b), the amount of the adjustment is equal to ($30,000). Under section 755, the entire adjustment is allocated to the property.

(iii) The basis of the property at the time of the transfer of the partnership interest was $60,000. In each of years 3 through 5, the partnership will realize depreciation deductions of $20,000 from the property. Thus, one third of the negative basis adjustment ($10,000) will be recovered in each of years 3 through 5. Consequently, T will be allocated, for tax purposes, depreciation of $15,000 each year from the partnership and will recover $10,000 of its negative basis adjustment. Thus, T's net depreciation deduction from the partnership in each year is $5,000.

Example 3. (i) A, B, and C are equal partners in partnership PRS, which owns Asset 2, an item of depreciable property that has a fair market value that is less than its adjusted tax basis. C sells its interest in PRS to T while PRS has an election in effect under section 754. PRS, therefore, decreases the basis of Asset 2 with respect to T.

(ii) Assume that in the year following the transfer of the partnership interest to T, T's distributive share of the partnership's common basis depreciation deductions from Asset 2 is $500. PRS allocates no other depreciation to T. Also assume that, under paragraph (j) (4) (ii) (B) of this section, the amount of the negative basis adjustment that T recovers during the year is $1,000. T will report $500 of ordinary income because the amount of the negative basis adjustment recovered during the year exceeds T's distributive share of the partnership's common basis depreciation deductions from Asset 2.

(5) *Depletion.*—Where an adjustment is made under section 743(b) to the basis of partnership property subject to depletion, any depletion allowance is determined separately for each partner, including the transferee partner, based on the partner's interest in such property. See § 1.702-1(a) (8). For partnerships that hold oil and gas properties that are depleted at the partner level under section 613A(c) (7) (D), the transferee partner (and not the partnership) must make the basis adjustments, if any, required under section 743(b) with respect to such properties. See § 1.613A-3(e) (6) (iv).

(6) *Example.*—The provisions of paragraph (j) (5) of this section are illustrated by the following example:

Example. A, B, and C each contributes $5,000 cash to form partnership PRS, which purchases a coal property for $15,000. A, B, and C have equal interests in capital and profits. C subsequently sells its partnership interest to T for $100,000 when the election under section 754 is in effect. T has a basis adjustment under section 743(b) for the coal property of $95,000 (the difference between T's basis, $100,000, and its share of the basis of partnership property, $5,000). Assume that the depletion allowance computed under the percentage method would be $21,000 for the taxable year so that each partner would be entitled to $7,000 as its share of the deduction for depletion. However, under the cost depletion method, at an assumed rate of 10 percent, the allowance with respect to T's one-third interest which has a basis to him of $100,000 ($5,000, plus its basis adjustment of $95,000) is $10,000, although the cost depletion allowance with respect to the one-third interest of A and B in the coal property, each of which has a basis of $5,000, is only $500. For partners A and B, the percentage depletion is greater than cost depletion and each will deduct $7,000 based on the percentage depletion method. However, as to T, the transferee partner, the cost depletion method results in a greater allowance and T will, therefore, deduct $10,000 based on cost depletion. See section 613(a).

* * *

[Reg. § 1.743-1.]

☐ [*T.D.* 6175, 5-23-56. *Amended by T.D.* 8717, 5-8-97; *T.D.* 8847, 12-14-99 (*corrected* 2-23-2000); *T.D.* 9137, 7-15-2004; *T.D.* 9811, 1-18-2017 *and T.D.* 9874, 9-17-2019.]

Proposed Amendments to Regulation

§ 1.743-1. Special rules where partnership has a section 754 election in effect or has a substantial built-in loss immediately after transfer of partnership interest.—(a) *Generally.*—(1) *Adjustment to basis.*—The basis of partnership property is adjusted as a result of the transfer of an interest in a partnership by sale or exchange or on the death of a partner if the election provided by section 754 (relating to optional adjustments to the basis of partnership property) is in effect with respect to the partnership, or if the partnership has a substantial built-in loss (within the meaning of paragraph (a)(2)(i) of this section) immediately after the transfer.

(2) *Substantial built-in loss.*—(i) *In general.*—A partnership has a substantial built-in loss with respect to a transfer of an interest in a partnership if the partnership's adjusted basis in partnership property exceeds the fair market value of the property (as determined in paragraph (a)(2)(iii) of this section) by more than $250,000 immediately after the transfer.

(ii) *Impact of section 743 basis adjustments and section 704(c)(1)(C) basis adjustments.*—For purposes of paragraph (a)(2)(i) of this section, any section 743 or section 704(c)(1)(C) basis adjustments (as defined in § 1.704-3(f)(2)(iii)) (other than the transferee's section 743(b) basis adjustments or section 704(c)(1)(C) basis adjustments) to partnership property are disregarded.

* * *

(b) *Determination of adjustment.*—In the case of the transfer of an interest in a partnership, either by sale or exchange or as a result of the death of a partner, a partnership that has an election under section 754 in effect or that has a substantial built-in loss (within the meaning of paragraph (a)(2)(i) of this section) —

* * *

(f) *Subsequent transfers.*—(1) *In general.*—Where there has been more than one transfer of a partnership interest, a transferee's basis adjustment is determined without regard to any prior transferee's basis adjustment. In the case of a gift of an interest in a partnership, the donor is treated as transferring, and the donee as receiving, that portion of the basis adjustment attributable to the gifted partnership interest. The following example illustrates the provisions of this paragraph (f)(1):

* * *

(m) *Anti-abuse rule for substantial built-in loss transactions.*—Provisions relating to substantial built-in loss transactions in paragraph (a) and paragraphs (k), (l), (n), and (o) of this section must be applied in a manner consistent with the purposes of these paragraphs and the substance of the transaction. Accordingly, if a principal purpose of a transaction is to achieve a tax result that is inconsistent with the purpose of one or more of these paragraphs, the Commissioner may recast the transaction for Federal income tax purposes, as appropriate, to achieve tax results that are consistent with the purpose of these paragraphs. Whether a tax result is inconsistent with the purposes of the provisions is determined based on all the facts and circumstances. For example, under the provisions of this paragraph (m)—

(1) Property held by related partnerships may be aggregated if the properties were transferred to the related partnerships with a principal purpose of avoiding the application of the substantial built-in loss provisions in section 743 and the regulations; and

(2) A contribution of property to a partnership may be disregarded if the transfer of the property was made with a principal purpose of avoiding the application of the substantial built-in loss provisions in section 743 and the regulations thereunder.

[Prop. Reg. § 1.743-1.]

[Proposed 1-16-2014.]

§ 1.751-1. Unrealized receivables and inventory items.—(a) *Sale or exchange of interest in a partnership.*—(1) *Character of amount realized.*—To the extent that money or property received by a partner in exchange for all or part of his partnership interest is attributable to his share of the value of partnership unrealized receivables or substantially appreciated inventory items, the money or fair market value of the property received shall be considered as an amount realized from the sale or exchange of property other than a capital asset. The remainder of the total amount realized on the sale or exchange of the partnership interest is realized from the sale or exchange of a capital asset under section 741. For definition of "unrealized receivables" and "inventory items which have appreciated substantially in value", see section 751(c) and (d). Unrealized receivables and substantially appreciated inventory items are hereafter in this section referred to as "section 751 property". See paragraph (e) of this section.

(2) *Determination of gain or loss.*—The income or loss realized by a partner upon the sale or exchange of its interest in section 751 property is the amount of income or loss from section 751 property (including any remedial allocations under § 1.704-3(d)) that would have been allocated to the partner (to the extent attributable to the partnership interest sold or exchanged) if the partnership had sold all of its property in a fully taxable transaction for cash in an amount equal to the fair market value of such property (taking into account section 7701(g)) immediately prior to the partner's transfer of the interest in the partnership. Any gain or loss recognized that is attributable to section 751 property will be ordinary gain or loss. The difference between the amount of capital gain or loss that the partner would realize in the absence of section 751 and the amount of ordinary income or loss determined under this paragraph (a)(2) is the transferor's capital gain or loss on the sale of its partnership interest. See § 1.460-4(k)(2)(iv)(E) for rules relating to the amount of ordinary income or loss attributable to a contract accounted for under a long-term contract method of accounting.

(3) *Statement required.*—A partner selling or exchanging any part of an interest in a partnership that has any section 751 property at the time of sale or exchange must submit with its income tax return for the taxable year in which the sale or exchange occurs a statement setting forth separately the following information—

(i) The date of the sale or exchange;

(ii) The amount of any gain or loss attributable to the section 751 property; and

(iii) The amount of any gain or loss attributable to capital gain or loss on the sale of the partnership interest.

(b) *Certain distributions treated as sales or exchanges.*—(1) *In general.*—(i) Certain distributions to which section 751(b) applies are treated in part as sales or exchanges of property between the partnership and the distributee partner, and not as distributions to which sections 731 through 736 apply. A distribution treated as a sale or exchange under section 751(b) is not subject to the provisions of section 707(b). Section 751(b) applies whether or not the distribution is in liquidation of the distributee partner's entire interest in the partnership. However, section 751(b) applies only to the extent that a partner either receives section 751 property in exchange for his relinquishing any part of his interest in other property, or receives other property in exchange for his relinquishing any part of his interest in section 751 property.

(ii) Section 751(b) does not apply to a distribution to a partner which is not in exchange for his interest in other partnership property. Thus, section 751(b) does not apply to the extent that a distribution consists of the distributee partner's share of section 751 property or his share of other property. Similarly, section 751(b) does not apply to current drawings or to advances against the partner's distributive share, or to a distribution which is, in fact, a gift or payment for services or for the use of capital. In determining whether a partner has received only his share of either section 751 property or of other property, his interest in such property remaining in the partnership immediately after a distribution must be taken into account. For example, the section 751 property in partnership ABC has a fair market value of $100,000 in which partner A has an interest of 30 percent, or $30,000. If A receives $20,000 of section 751 property in a distribution, and continues to have a 30-percent interest in the $80,000 of section 751 property remaining in the partnership after the distribution, only $6,000 ($30,000 minus $24,000 (30 percent of $80,000)) of the section 751 property received by him will be considered to be his share of such property. The remaining $14,000 ($20,000 minus $6,000) received is in excess of his share.

(iii) If a distribution is, in part, a distribution of the distributee partner's share of section 751 property, or of other property (including money) and, in part, a distribution in exchange of such properties, the distribution shall be divided for the purpose of applying section 751(b). The rules of section 751(b) shall first apply to the part of the distribution treated as a sale or exchange of such properties, and then the rules of sections 731 through 736 shall apply to the part of the distribution not treated as a sale or exchange. See paragraph (b)(4)(ii) of this section for treatment of payments under section 736(a).

(2) *Distribution of section 751 property (unrealized receivables or substantially appreciated inventory items)*.—(i) To the extent that a partner receives section 751 property in a distribution in exchange for any part of his interest in partnership property (including money) other than section 751 property, the transaction shall be treated as a sale or exchange of such properties between the distributee partner and the partnership (as constituted after the distribution).

(ii) At the time of the distribution, the partnership (as constituted after the distribution) realizes ordinary income or loss on the sale or exchange of the section 751 property. The amount of the income or loss to the partnership will be measured by the difference between the adjusted basis to the partnership of the section 751 property considered as sold to or exchanged with the partner, and the fair market value of the distributee partner's interest in other partnership property which he relinquished in the exchange. In computing the partners' distributive shares of such ordinary income or loss, the income or loss shall be allocated only to partners other than the distributee and separately taken into account under section 702(a)(8).

(iii) At the time of the distribution, the distributee partner realizes gain or loss measured by the difference between his adjusted basis for the property relinquished in the exchange (including any special basis adjustment which he may have) and the fair market value of the section 751 property received by him in exchange for his interest in other property which he has relinquished. The distributee's adjusted basis for the property relinquished is the basis such property would have had under section 732 (including subsection (d) thereof) if the distributee partner had received such property in a current distribution immediately before the actual distribution which is treated wholly or partly as a sale or exchange under section 751(b). The character of the gain or loss to the distributee partner shall be determined by the character of the property in which he relinquished his interest.

(3) *Distribution of partnership property other than section 751 property*.—(i) To the extent that a partner receives a distribution of partnership property (including money) other than section 751 property in exchange for any part of his interest in section 751 property of the partnership, the distribution shall be treated as a sale or exchange of such properties between the distributee partner and the partnership (as constituted after the distribution).

(ii) At the time of the distribution, the partnership (as constituted after the distribution) realizes gain or loss on the sale or exchange of the property other than section 751 property. The amount of the gain to the partnership will be measured by the difference between the adjusted basis to the partnership of the distributed property considered as sold to or exchanged with the partner, and the fair market value of the distributee partner's interest in section 751 property which he relinquished in the exchange. The character of the gain or loss to the partnership is determined by the character of the distributed property treated as sold or exchanged by the partnership. In computing the partners' distributive shares of such gain or loss, the gain or loss shall be allocated only to partners other than the distributee and separately taken into account under section 702(a)(8).

(iii) At the time of the distribution, the distributee partner realizes ordinary income or loss on the sale or exchange of the section 751 property. The amount of the distributee partner's income or loss shall be measured by the difference between his adjusted basis for the section 751 property relinquished in the exchange (including any special basis adjustment which he may have), and the fair market value of other property (including money) received by him in exchange for his interest in the section 751 property which he has relinquished. The distributee partner's adjusted basis for the section 751 property relinquished is the basis such property would have had under section 732 (including subsection (d) thereof) if the distributee partner had received such property in a current distribution immediately before the actual distribution which is treated wholly or partly as a sale or exchange under section 751(b).

(4) *Exceptions*.—(i) Section 751(b) does not apply to the distribution to a partner of property which the distributee partner contributed to the partnership. The distribution of such property is governed by the rules set forth in sections 731 through 736, relating to distributions by a partnership.

(ii) Section 751(b) does not apply to payments made to a retiring partner or to a deceased partner's successor in interest to the extent that, under section 736(a), such payments constitute a distributive share of partnership income or guaranteed payments. Payments to a retiring partner or to a deceased partner's successor in interest for his interest in unrealized receivables of the partnership in excess of their partnership basis, including any special basis adjustment for them to which such partner is entitled, constitute payments under section 736(a) and, therefore, are not subject to section 751(b). However, payments under section 736(b) which are considered as made in exchange for an interest in partnership property are subject to section 751(b) to the extent that they involve an exchange of substantially appreciated inventory items for other property. Thus, payments to a retiring partner or to a deceased partner's successor in interest under section 736 must first be divided between payments under section 736(a) and section 736(b).

The section 736(b) payments must then be divided, if there is an exchange of substantially appreciated inventory items for other property, between the payments treated as a sale or exchange under section 751(b) and payments treated as a distribution under sections 731 through 736. See subparagraph (1)(iii) of this paragraph, and section 736 and § 1.736-1.

(5) *Statement required.*—A partnership which distributes section 751 property to a partner in exchange for his interest in other partnership property, or which distributes other property in exchange for any part of the partner's interest in section 751 property, shall submit with its return for the year of the distribution a statement showing the computation of any income, gain, or loss to the partnership under the provisions of section 751(b) and this paragraph. The distributee partner shall submit with his return a statement showing the computation of any income, gain, or loss to him. Such statement shall contain information similar to that required under paragraph (a)(3) of this section.

(c) *Unrealized receivables.*—(1) The term "unrealized receivables", as used in subchapter K, chapter 1 of the Code, means any rights (contractual or otherwise) to payment for—

(i) Goods delivered or to be delivered (to the extent that such payment would be treated as received for property other than a capital asset), or

(ii) Services rendered or to be rendered, to the extent that income arising from such rights to payment was not previously includible in income under the method of accounting employed by the partnership. Such rights must have arisen under contracts or agreements in existence at the time of sale or distribution, although the partnership may not be able to enforce payment until a later time. For example, the term includes trade accounts receivable of a cash method taxpayer, and rights to payment for work or goods begun but incomplete at the time of the sale or distribution.

(2) The basis for such unrealized receivables shall include all costs or expenses attributable thereto paid or accrued but not previously taken into account under the partnership method of accounting.

(3) In determining the amount of the sale price attributable to such unrealized receivables, or their value in a distribution treated as a sale or exchange, full account shall be taken not only of the estimated cost of completing performance of the contract or agreement, but also of the time between the sale or distribution and the time of payment.

(4)(i) With respect to any taxable year of a partnership ending after September 12, 1966 (but only in respect of expenditures paid or incurred after that date), the term *unrealized receivables*, for purposes of this section and sections 731, 736, 741, and 751, also includes potential gain from mining property defined in section 617(f)(2). With respect to each item of partnership mining property so defined, the potential gain is the amount that would be treated as gain to which section 617(d)(1) would apply if (at the time of the transaction described in section 731, 736, 741, or 751, as the case may be) the item were sold by the partnership at its fair market value.

(ii) With respect to sales, exchanges, or other dispositions after December 31, 1975, in any taxable year of a partnership ending after that date, the term *unrealized receivables*, for purposes of this section and sections 731, 736, 741, and 751, also includes potential gain from stock in a DISC as described in section 992(a). With respect to stock in such a DISC, the potential gain is the amount that would be treated as gain to which section 995(c) would apply if (at the time of the transaction described in section 731, 736, 741, or 751, as the case may be) the stock were sold by the partnership at its fair market value.

(iii) With respect to any taxable year of a partnership beginning after December 31, 1962, the term *unrealized receivables*, for purposes of this section and sections 731, 736, 741, and 751, also includes potential gain from section 1245 property. With respect to each item of partnership section 1245 property (as defined in section 1245(a)(3)), potential gain from section 1245 property is the amount that would be treated as gain to which section 1245(a)(1) would apply if (at the time of the transaction described in section 731, 736, 741, or 751, as the case may be) the item of section 1245 property were sold by the partnership at its fair market value. See § 1.1245-1(e)(1). For example, if a partnership would recognize under section 1245(a)(1) gain of $600 upon a sale of one item of section 1245 property and gain of $300 upon a sale of its only other item of such property, the potential section 1245 income of the partnership would be $900.

(iv) With respect to transfers after October 9, 1975, and to sales, exchanges, and distributions taking place after that date, the term *unrealized receivables*, for purposes of this section and sections 731, 736, 741, and 751, also includes potential gain from stock in certain foreign corporations as described in section 1248. With respect to stock in such a foreign corporation, the potential gain is the amount that would be treated as gain to which section 1248(a) would apply if (at the time of the transaction described in section 731, 736, 741, or 751, as the case may be) the stock were sold by the partnership at its fair market value.

(v) With respect to any taxable year of a partnership ending after December 31, 1963, the term *unrealized receivables*, for purposes of this section and sections 731, 736, 741, and 751, also includes potential gain from section 1250 property. With respect to each item of partnership section 1250 property (as defined in section 1250(c)), potential gain from section 1250 property is the amount that would be treated as gain to which section 1250(a) would apply if (at the time of the transaction described in section 731, 736, 741, or 751, as the case may be) the item of section 1250 property were sold by the partnership at its fair market value. See § 1.1250-1(f)(1).

(vi) With respect to any taxable year of a partnership beginning after December 31, 1969, the term *unrealized receivables*, for purposes of this section and sections 731, 736, 741, and 751, also includes potential gain from farm recapture property as defined in section 1251(e)(1) (as in effect before enactment of the Tax Reform Act of 1984). With respect to each item of partnership farm recapture property so defined, the potential gain is the amount which would be treated as gain to which section 1251(c) (as in effect before enactment of the Tax Reform Act of 1984) would apply if (at the time of the transaction described in section 731, 736, 741, or 751, as the case may be) the item were sold by the partnership at its fair market value.

(vii) With respect to any taxable year of a partnership beginning after December 31, 1969, the term *unrealized receivables*, for purposes of this section and sections 731, 736, 741, and 751, also includes potential gain from farm land as defined in section 1252(a)(2). With respect to each item of partnership farm land so defined, the potential gain is the amount that would be treated as gain to which section 1252(a)(1) would apply if (at the time of the transaction described in section 731, 736, 741, or 751, as the case may be) the item were sold by the partnership at its fair market value.

(viii) With respect to transactions which occur after December 31, 1976, in any taxable year of a partnership ending after that date, the term *unrealized receivables*, for purposes of this section and sections 731, 736, 741, and 751, also includes potential gain from franchises, trademarks, or trade names referred to in section 1253(a). With respect to each such item so referred to in section 1253(a), the potential gain is the amount that would be treated as gain to which section 1253(a) would apply if (at the time of the transaction described in section 731, 736, 741, or 751, as the case may be) the items were sold by the partnership at its fair market value.

(ix) With respect to any taxable year of a partnership ending after December 31, 1975, the term *unrealized receivables*, for purposes of this section and sections 731, 736, 741, and 751, also includes potential gain under section 1254(a) from natural resource recapture property as defined in § 1.1254-1(b)(2). With respect to each separate partnership natural resource recapture property so described, the potential gain is the amount that would be treated as gain to which section 1254(a) would apply if (at the time of the transaction described in section 731, 736, 741, or 751, as the case may be) the property were sold by the partnership at its fair market value.

(5) For purposes of subtitle A of the Internal Revenue Code, the basis of any potential gain described in paragraph (c)(4) of this section is zero.

(6)(i) If (at the time of any transaction referred to in paragraph (c)(4) of this section) a partnership holds property described in paragraph (c)(4) of this section and if—

(A) A partner had a special basis adjustment under section 743(b) in respect of the property;

(B) The basis under section 732 of the property if distributed to the partner would reflect a special basis adjustment under section 732(d); or

(C) On the date a partner acquired a partnership interest by way of a sale or exchange (or upon the death of another partner) the partnership owned the property and an election under section 754 was in effect with respect to the partnership, the partner's share of any potential gain described in paragraph (c)(4) of this section is determined under paragraph (c)(6)(ii) of this section.

(ii) The partner's share of the potential gain described in paragraph (c)(4) of this section in respect of the property to which this paragraph (c)(6)(ii) applies is that amount of gain that the partner would recognize under section 617(d)(1), 995(c), 1245(a), 1248(a), 1250(a), 1251(c) (as in effect before the Tax

Reform Act of 1984), 1252(a), 1253(a), or 1254(a) (as the case may be) upon a sale of the property by the partnership, except that, for purposes of this paragraph (c)(6) the partner's share of such gain is determined in a manner that is consistent with the manner in which the partner's share of partnership property is determined; and the amount of a potential special basis adjustment under section 732(d) is treated as if it were the amount of a special basis adjustment under section 743(b). For example, in determining, for purposes of this paragraph (c)(6), the amount of gain that a partner would recognize under section 1245 upon a sale of partnership property, the items allocated under § 1.1245-1(e)(3)(ii) are allocated to the partner in the same manner as the partner's share of partnership property is determined. See § 1.1250-1(f) for rules similar to those contained in § 1.1245-1(e)(3)(ii).

(d) *Inventory items which have substantially appreciated in value.*—(1) *Substantial appreciation.*—Partnership inventory items shall be considered to have appreciated substantially in value if, at the time of the sale or distribution, the total fair market value of all the inventory items of the partnership exceeds 120 percent of the aggregate adjusted basis for such property in the hands of the partnership (without regard to any special basis adjustment of any partner) and, in addition, exceeds 10 percent of the fair market value of all partnership property other than money. The terms "inventory items which have appreciated substantially in value" or "substantially appreciated inventory items" refer to the aggregate of all partnership inventory items. These terms do not refer to specific partnership inventory items or to specific groups of such items. For example, any distribution of inventory items by a partnership the inventory items of which as a whole are substantially appreciated in value shall be a distribution of substantially appreciated inventory items for the purposes of section 751(b), even though the specific inventory items distributed may not be appreciated in value. Similarly, if the aggregate of partnership inventory items are not substantially appreciated in value, a distribution of specific inventory items, the value of which is more than 120 percent of their adjusted basis, will not constitute a distribution of substantially appreciated inventory items. For the purpose of this paragraph, the "fair market value" of inventory items has the same meaning as "market" value in the regulations under section 471, relating to general rule for inventories.

(2) *Inventory items.*—The term "inventory items" as used in subchapter K, chapter 1 of the Code, includes the following types of property:

(i) Stock in trade of the partnership, or other property of a kind which would properly be included in the inventory of the partnership if on hand at the close of the taxable year, or property held by the partnership primarily for sale to customers in the ordinary course of its trade or business. See section 1221(1).

(ii) Any other property of the partnership which, on sale or exchange by the partnership, would be considered property other than a capital asset and other than property described in section 1231. Thus, accounts receivable acquired in the ordinary course of business for services or from the sale of stock in trade constitute inventory items (see section 1221(4)), as do any unrealized receivables.

(iii) Any other property retained by the partnership which, if held by the partner selling his partnership interest or receiving a distribution described in section 751(b), would be considered property described in subdivisions (i) or (ii) of this subparagraph. Property actually distributed to the partner does not come within the provisions of section 751(d)(2)(C) and this subdivision.

(e) *Section 751 property and other property.*—For the purposes of this section, "section 751 property" means unrealized receivables or substantially appreciated inventory items, and "other property" means all property (including money) except section 751 property.

* * *

[Reg. § 1.751-1.]

☐ [*T.D.* 6175, 5-23-56. *Amended by T.D.* 6832, 7-6-65, *T.D.* 7084, 1-7-71; *T.D.* 8586, 1-9-95; *T.D.* 8847, 12-14-99 *and T.D.* 9137, 7-15-2004.]

Proposed Amendments to Regulation

§ 1.751-1. Unrealized receivables and inventory items.

(a) * * *

(1) *Character of amount realized.*—To the extent that money or property received by a partner in exchange for all or part of his partnership interest is attributable to his share of the value of partnership unrealized receivables or inventory items, the money or fair market value of the property received shall be considered as an amount realized from the sale or exchange of property other than a capital asset. The remainder of the total amount realized on the sale or exchange of the partnership interest is realized from the sale or exchange of a capital asset under section 741. For definition of "unrealized receivables" and "inventory items," see section 751(c) and (d). *See* paragraph (e) of this section for the definition of section 751 property.

(2) *Determination of gain or loss.*—The income or loss realized by a partner upon the sale or exchange of its interest in section 751 property is the amount of income or loss from section 751 property (taking into account allocations of tax items applying the principles of section 704(c), including any remedial allocations under § 1.704-3(d), and any section 743 basis adjustment pursuant to § 1.743-1(j)(3)) that would have been allocated to the partner (to the extent attributable to the partnership interest sold or exchanged) if the partnership had sold all of its property in a fully taxable transaction for cash in an amount equal to the fair market value of such property (taking into account section 7701(g)) immediately prior to the partner's transfer of the interest in the partnership. Any gain or loss recognized that is attributable to section 751 property will be ordinary gain or loss. The difference between the amount of capital gain or loss that the partner would realize in the absence of section 751 and the amount of ordinary income or loss determined under this paragraph (a)(2) is the transferor's capital gain or loss on the sale of its partnership interest. For purposes of section 751(a) and paragraph (a) of this section, the amount of money or the fair market value of property received by the partner in exchange for all or part of his partnership interest must take into account the partner's share of income or gain from section 751 property. *See Example 1* in paragraph (g) of this section. *See* § 1.460-4(k)(2)(iv)(E) for rules relating to the amount of ordinary income or loss attributable to a contract accounted for under a long-term contract method of accounting.

* * *

(b) *Certain distributions treated as sales or exchanges.*—(1) *In general.*—(i) Certain distributions to which section 751(b) applies are treated in whole or in part as sales or exchanges of property, and not as distributions to which sections 731 through 736 apply. * * * For purposes of section 751 and this section, a partner's interest in the partnership's section 751 property includes allocations of tax items applying the principles of section 704(c).

* * *

(iii) If a distribution is a section 751(b) distribution, as described in paragraph (b)(2)(i) of this section, the tax consequences of the section 751(b) distribution, as determined under paragraph (b)(3) of this section, shall first apply, and then the rules of sections 731 through 736 shall apply. *See* paragraph (b)(5)(vi) of this section for treatment of payments under section 736(a).

(2) *Distributions to which section 751(b) applies.*—(i) *Section 751(b) amount.*—A distribution is a section 751(b) distribution if it gives rise to a "section 751(b) amount" for any partner. A partner's section 751(b) amount (if any) associated with a distribution of partnership property (including money) equals the greatest of—

(A) The amount by which the partner's net section 751 unrealized gain immediately before the distribution exceeds the partner's net section 751 unrealized gain immediately after the distribution;

(B) The amount by which the partner's net section 751 unrealized loss immediately after the distribution exceeds the partner's net section 751 unrealized loss immediately before the distribution; and

(C) The amount of the partner's net section 751 unrealized gain immediately before the distribution, increased by the total amount of the partner's net section 751 unrealized loss immediately after the distribution (where neither of those numbers equals zero).

(ii) *Net section 751 unrealized gain or loss before a distribution.*—A partner's net section 751 unrealized gain or loss immediately before a distribution equals the amount of net income or loss, as the case may be, from section 751 property that would be allocated to the partner if the partnership disposed of all of the partnership's assets for cash in an amount equal to the fair market value of such property (taking into account section 7701(g)). For this purpose, a partner's net section 751 unrealized gain or loss includes any remedial allocations under § 1.704-3(d), and takes into account any section 743(b) basis adjustment pursuant to § 1.743-1(j)(3) and any carryover basis adjustment described in §§ 1.743-1(g)(2)(ii), 1.755-1(b)(5)(iii)(D), or 1.755-1(c)(4) as though the carryover basis adjustment was applied to the basis of new partnership section 751 property with fair market value of zero.

(iii) *Net section 751 unrealized gain or loss after a distribution.*—A partner's net section 751 unrealized gain or loss immediately after a distribution equals the sum of (to the extent applicable)—

(A) With respect to a partner remaining in the partnership immediately after the distribution (including a distributee partner remaining in the partnership), the amount of net income or loss, as the case may be (including any remedial allocations under § 1.704-3(d) and taking into account any section 743(b) basis adjustment pursuant to § 1.743-1(j)(3) and any carryover basis adjustment described in §§ 1.743-1(g)(2)(ii), 1.755-1(b)(5)(iii)(D), or 1.755-1(c)(4) as though the carryover basis adjustment was applied to the basis of new partnership section 751 property with fair market value of zero), from section 751 property that would be allocated to the partner if the partnership disposed of all of the partnership's assets for cash in an amount equal to the fair market value of such property (taking into account section 7701(g)); and

(B) With respect to a partner receiving a distribution, the amount of net income or loss, as the case may be, from section 751 property that would be recognized by the distributee if, immediately after the distribution, the distributee disposed of the distributed assets for cash in an amount equal to the fair market value of such property (taking into account section 7701(g)).

(iv) *Revaluation of assets.*—For a partnership that distributes money or property (other than a de minimis amount) to a partner as consideration for an interest in the partnership, and that owns section 751 property immediately after the distribution, if the partnership maintains capital accounts in accordance with § 1.704-1(b)(2)(iv), the partnership must revalue its assets immediately prior to the distribution in accordance with § 1.704-1(b)(2)(iv)(*f*). If a partnership does not maintain capital accounts in accordance with § 1.704-1(b)(2)(iv), the partnership must comply with this section by computing its partners' shares of partnership gain or loss immediately before the distribution as if the partnership assets were sold for cash in a fully taxable transaction (taking into account section 7701(g)), and by taking those computed shares of gain or loss into account under the principles of section 704(c) (making subsequent adjustments for cost recovery and other events that affect the basis of the property). In addition, if the partnership (upper-tier partnership) owns another partnership directly or indirectly through one or more partnerships (lower-tier partnership), and the same persons own, directly or indirectly (through one or more entities), more than 50 percent of the capital and profits interests in both the upper-tier partnership and the lower-tier partnership, the lower-tier partnership must also revalue its assets immediately prior to the distribution in accordance with § 1.704-1(b)(2)(iv)(f) if the lower-tier partnership owns section 751 property. If the same persons do not own, directly or indirectly, more than 50 percent of the capital and profits interests in both the upper-tier partnership and the lower-tier partnership, the upper-tier partnership must allocate its distributive share of the lower-tier partnership's items among its partners in a manner that reflects the allocations that would have been made had the lower-tier partnership revalued its property.

(3) *Tax consequences of a section 751(b) distribution.*—(i) *Reasonable approach.*—In the case of a section 751(b) distribution described in paragraph (b)(2) of this section, the partnership must choose a reasonable approach that is consistent with the purpose of section 751(b) under which each partner with a section 751(b) amount recognizes ordinary income (or takes it into account by eliminating a basis adjustment) equal to that section 751(b) amount immediately prior to the section 751(b) distribution. In certain circumstances described in paragraph (b)(3)(ii) of this section, a distributee partner may also be permitted or required to recognize capital gain. To be reasonable, an approach must conform to the general principles and anti-abuse rules described in paragraph (b)(4) of this section. An approach is not necessarily unreasonable merely because another approach would result in a higher aggregate tax liability. Once the partnership has adopted a reasonable approach, it must apply that approach consistently for all section 751(b) distributions, including for any distributions the partnership makes after a termination of the partnership under section 708(b)(1)(B). If the application of the adopted approach to a later section 751(b) distribution produces results inconsistent with the purpose of section 751, the partnership must adopt another reasonable approach that achieves the purposes of section 751 for that distribution only. *See Example 3* through *Example 8* in paragraph (g) of this section.

(ii) *Gain Recognition.*—(A) *Mandatory recognition.*—A partner's net section 751 unrealized gain or net section 751 unrealized loss for purposes of paragraph (b)(3)(i) of this section is determined before taking into account any basis adjustments required by paragraph (b)(3)(iii) of this section. In certain instances, the application of paragraph (b)(3)(iii) of this section may cause a partner to receive distributed property with a basis that differs from the basis of the property in the hands of the distributing partnership. If an adjustment to the basis of the distributed section 751 property results in a section 734(b) basis adjustment, and that basis adjustment would have altered the amount of net section 751 unrealized gain or loss computed under paragraph (b)(2) of this section if the section 734(b) adjustment had been included immediately prior to the distribution, then the distributee partner must recognize capital gain immediately prior to the distribution in an amount sufficient to eliminate that section 734(b) basis adjustment. *See Examples 5* and *6* in paragraph (g) of this section. If, however, the partnership makes an election under § 1.755-1(c)(2)(vi), then the partner must characterize all or a portion of the gain recognized under this paragraph as ordinary income or a dividend, as appropriate, to preserve the character of the gain in the adjusted asset. *See Example 9* in paragraph (g) of this section.

(B) *Elective recognition.*—A distributee partner may elect to recognize capital gain (in addition to amounts required to be recognized under this section) to eliminate section 732(a)(2) or (b) basis adjustments to the asset or assets received in distribution if, and to the extent that, the basis adjustments required by paragraph (b)(3)(iii) of this section would otherwise cause the distributee partner's net section 751 unrealized gain to be greater immediately after the distribution than it was immediately before the distribution or would cause the distributee partner's net section 751 unrealized loss to be less immediately after the distribution than it was immediately before the distribution. A distributee partner elects under this paragraph (b)(3)(ii)(B) by providing the partnership with written notification of its intent to make the election and reporting the capital gain on its return. An extension of time to make an election under this paragraph (b)(3)(ii)(B) will not be granted under § 301.9100-3 of this chapter. The requirement in paragraph (b)(1)(i) of this section that a partnership apply a chosen reasonable method consistently across all partnership distributions does not apply for purposes of this paragraph. *See Example 7* in paragraph (g) of this section.

(iii) *Adjustments to Basis.*—The partnership and its partners must make appropriate adjustments to the adjusted basis of the partners' interests in the partnership, and of section 751 property and other property held by the partnership or partners, in a manner consistent with the adopted approach to reflect any ordinary income or capital gain recognized upon application of paragraph (b)(3) of this section, and section 704(c) amounts must be adjusted accordingly.

(4) *General principles and anti-abuse rules.*—(i) The purpose of section 751 is to prevent a partner from converting its rights to ordinary income into capital gain, including by relying on the rules of section 704(c) to defer ordinary income while monetizing most of the value of the partnership interest. The partnership and all partners of the partnership must apply the rules of section 751 and § 1.751-1 in a manner consistent with the purpose of section 751. Accordingly, if a principal purpose of a transaction is to achieve a tax result that is inconsistent with the purpose of section 751, the Commissioner may recast the transaction for federal tax purposes as appropriate to achieve tax results that are consistent with the purpose of section 751. The Commissioner will determine whether a tax result is inconsistent with the purpose of section 751 based on all the facts and circumstances. The existence of one or more of the situations set forth below is presumed to establish that a transaction is inconsistent with the purpose of section 751 and disclosure to the Internal Revenue Service in accordance with § 1.751-1(b)(4)(ii) is required.

(A) Circumstances in which a partner received a distribution that would otherwise be subject to section 751(b), but for the application of the principles of section 704(c), and one or more of the following conditions exist (whether at the time of the distribution or, in the case of paragraph (b)(4)(i)(A)*(2)*, *(3)*, *(4)*, or *(5)* of this section, a later date):

(1) The partner's interest in net section 751 unrealized gain is at least four times greater than the partner's capital account immediately after the distribution, pursuant to § 1.704-1(b)(2)(iv) (or comparable amount for partnerships not maintaining capital accounts under § 1.704-1(b)(2)(iv));

(2) The partner is substantially protected from losses from the partnership's activities and has little or no participation in the profits from the partnership's activities other than a preferred return that is in the nature of a payment for the use of capital;

(3) The partner engages in a transaction that, at the time of the transaction, causes the net value of the partner (or its successor) to be less than the tax liability that the partner (or its successor) would incur with respect to its interest in the partnership's section 751 property upon a sale of its partnership interest for its fair market value at the time of the transaction. For this purpose, the net value of the partner (or its successor) equals—

(i) The fair market value of all assets owned by the partner (or its successor) that may be subject to creditor's claims under local law (including the partner's enforceable right to contributions from its owner or owners), less

(ii) All obligations of the partner (or its successor) other than the partner's obligation with respect to the tax liability for which the net value is being determined;

(4) The partner transfers a portion of its partnership interest within five years after the distribution in a manner that does not trigger ordinary income recognition, and ordinary income or gain with respect to the partnership interest is subject to Federal income tax in the hands of the transferor partner immediately before the transfer, but any ordinary income or gain with respect to the partnership interest is exempt from, or otherwise not subject to, Federal income tax in the hands of the transferee partner immediately after the transfer;

(5) The partnership transfers to a corporation in a nonrecognition transaction

section 751 property other than pursuant to a transfer of all property used in a trade or business (excluding assets that are not material to a continuation of the trade or business); or

(B) The partners agree to change (other than a de minimis change) the manner in which the partners share any item or class of items of income, gain, loss, deduction or credit of the partnership under the partnership agreement and that change reduces the partner's net section 751 unrealized gain.

(ii) If a partner participates in a transaction described in paragraph (b)(4)(i)(A) or (B) of this section and does not recognize and report its share of ordinary income from section 751 property on its tax return for the taxable year of the transaction, the partner must file Form 8275-R, Regulation Disclosure Statement, or any appropriate successor form, disclosing its participation in the transaction for the taxable year in which the transaction occurred.

* * *

(c) * * *

(4) * * *

(vi) With respect to any taxable year of a partnership beginning after July 18, 1984, amounts treated as ordinary income under section 467 are treated as ordinary income under this section in the same manner as amounts treated as ordinary income under section 1245 (*see* paragraph (c)(4)(iii) of this section) or section 1250 (*see* paragraph (c)(4)(v) of this section).

* * *

(x) With respect to any taxable year of a partnership beginning after July 18, 1984, the term *unrealized receivables,* for purposes of this section and sections 731, 732, and 741 (but not for purposes of section 736), includes any market discount bond (as defined in section 1278) and any short-term obligation (as defined in section 1283) but only to the extent of the amount that would be treated as ordinary income if (at the time of the transaction described in this section or section 731, 732, or 741, as the case may be) such property had been sold by the partnership.

* * *

(d) *Inventory items which have substantially appreciated in value.*—(1) *Substantial appreciation.*—Partnership inventory items shall be considered to have appreciated substantially in value if, at the time of the distribution, the total fair market value of all the inventory items of the partnership exceeds 120 percent of the aggregate adjusted basis for such property in the hands of the partnership (without regard to any special basis adjustment to the partner). The terms "inventory items which have appreciated substantially in value" or "substantially appreciated inventory items" refer to the aggregate of all partnership inventory items but do not include any unrealized receivables. * * *

* * *

(e) *Section 751 property and other property.*—For purposes of paragraph (a) of this section, *section 751 property* means unrealized receivables or inventory items. For purposes of paragraph (b) of this section, *section 751 property* means unrealized receivables or substantially appreciated inventory items. For purposes of all paragraphs of this section, *other property* means all property (including money) that is not section 751 property.

* * *

(g) *Examples.*—Application of the provisions of section 751 may be illustrated by the following examples. In each of *Examples 2* through *9* of this paragraph (g), none of the section 751 property qualifies as property that the distributee previously contributed as described in section 751(b)(2)(A), and no distribution to a retiring partner is a payment described in section 736(a):

Example 1. (i)(A) A and B are equal partners in personal service partnership PRS. A contributed nondepreciable capital assets (the "Capital Assets") to PRS with a basis and fair market value of $14,000. B contributed unrealized receivables described in paragraph (c) of this section (the "Unrealized Receivables") to PRS with a basis of zero and fair market value of $14,000. Later, when the fair market value of the Capital Assets had declined to $2,000, B transferred its interest in PRS to T for $9,000 when PRS's balance sheet (reflecting a cash receipts and disbursements method of accounting) was as follows:

Assets

	Adjusted Basis	Fair Market Value
Cash	$ 4,000	$ 4,000
Capital Assets	14,000	2,000
Unrealized Receivables	0	14,000
Total	18,000	20,000

Liabilities and Capital

	Adjusted Basis	Fair Market Value
Liabilities	$2,000	$2,000
Capital:		
A	15,000	9,000
B	1,000	9,000
Total	18,000	20,000

(B) The total amount realized by B is $10,000, consisting of the cash received, $9,000, plus $1,000, B's share of the partnership liabilities assumed by T. *See* section 752. B's interest in the partnership property includes an interest in the partnership's Unrealized Receivables. B's basis in its partnership interest is $2,000 ($1,000, plus $1,000, B's share of partnership liabilities). If section 751(a) did not apply to the sale, B would recognize $8,000 of capital gain from the sale of the interest in PRS. However, section 751(a) does apply to the sale.

(ii) For purposes of section 751(a), the amount of money or the fair market value of property received by the partner in exchange for all or part of his partnership interest must take into account the partner's share of income or gain from section 751 property. If PRS sold all of its section 751 property in a fully taxable transaction immediately prior to the transfer of B's partnership interest to T, B would have been allocated $14,000 of ordinary income from the sale of PRS's Unrealized Receivables under section 704(c). Therefore, B will recognize $14,000 of ordinary income with respect to the Unrealized Receivables. The difference between the amount of capital gain or loss that the partner would realize in the absence of section 751 ($8,000) and the amount of ordinary income or loss determined under paragraph (a)(2) of this section ($14,000) is the transferor's capital gain or loss on the sale of its partnership interest. In this case, B will recognize a $6,000 capital loss.

Example 2. (i) A, B, and C each contribute $120 to partnership ABC in exchange for a 1/3 interest. A, B, and C each share in the profits and losses of ABC in accordance with their 1/3 interest. ABC purchases land for $100 in Year 1. At the end of Year 3, when ABC holds $260 in cash and land with a value of $100 and has generated $90 in zero-basis unrealized receivables, ABC distributes $50 cash to C in a current distribution, reducing C's interest in ABC from 1/3 to 1/4. ABC has a section 754 election in effect. To determine if the distribution is a distribution to which section 751(b) applies, ABC must apply the test set forth in paragraph (b)(2) of this section.

(ii)(A) Pursuant to paragraph (b)(2)(iv) of this section, ABC revalues its assets and its partners' capital accounts are increased under § 1.704-1(b)(2)(iv)(f) to reflect each partner's share of the unrealized gain in the partnership's assets. Before the distribution, ABC's balance sheet is as follows:

	Tax	Book
Cash	$260	$260
Unrealized Receivable	0	90
Real Property	100	100
Totals	360	450

Capital	Tax	Book
A	$120	$150
B	120	150
C	120	150
	360	450

(B) If ABC disposed of all of its assets for cash in an amount equal to the fair market value of such property immediately before the distribution, A, B, and C would each be allocated $30 of net income from ABC's section 751 property. Accordingly, A, B, and C's net section 751 unrealized gain immediately before the distribution is $30 each under paragraph (b)(2)(ii) of this section.

(iii)(A) After the distribution (but before taking into account any consequences under this section), ABC's balance sheet would be as follows:

	Tax	Book
Cash	$210	$210
Unrealized Receivable	0	90
Real Property	100	100
Totals	310	400

Capital	Tax	Book
A	$120	$150
B	120	150
C	70	100
	310	400

(B) If ABC disposed of all of its assets in exchange for cash in amounts equal to the fair market values of those assets immediately after the distribution, A, B, and C would each still be allocated $30 of net income from ABC's section 751 property pursuant to § 1.704-3(a)(6). C did not receive any section 751 property in the distribution. Accordingly, A, B, and C's net section 751 unrealized gain immediately after the distribution is $30 each under paragraph (b)(2)(iii) of this section.

(iv) Because no partner's net section 751 unrealized gain is greater immediately before the distribution than immediately after the distribution, and because no partner's net section 751 unrealized loss is greater immediately after the distribution than immediately before the distribution, the distribution is not a section 751(b) distribution under paragraph (b)(2)(i) of this section. Accordingly, section 751(b) does not apply to the distribution.

Example 3. (i) Assume the same facts as in *Example 2* of this paragraph (g), but assume ABC distributes $150 cash to C in complete liquidation of C's interest. To determine if the distribution is a distribution to which section 751(b) applies, ABC must apply the test set forth in paragraph (b)(2) of this section.

(ii)(A) Pursuant to paragraph (b)(2)(iv) of this section, ABC revalues its assets and its partners' capital accounts are increased under § 1.704-1(b)(2)(iv)(f) to reflect each partner's share of the unrealized gain in the partnership's assets. Before the distribution, ABC's balance sheet is as follows:

	Tax	Book
Cash	$260	$260
Unrealized Receivable	0	90
Real Property	100	100
Totals	360	450

Capital	Tax	Book
A	$120	$150
B	120	150
C	120	150
	360	450

(B) If ABC disposed of all of its assets in exchange for cash in amounts equal to the fair market values of these assets immediately before the distribution, A, B, and C would each be allocated $30 of net income from ABC's section 751 property. Accordingly, A, B, and C's net section 751 unrealized gain immediately before the distribution is $30 each under paragraph (b)(2)(ii) of this section.

(iii)(A) Because ABC has elected under section 754, and because A recognizes $30 gain on the distribution of cash, the basis of the real property is increased to $130 under section 734(b). After the distribution (but before taking into account any consequences under this section), ABC's balance sheet would be as follows:

	Tax	Book
Cash	$110	$110
Unrealized Receivable	0	90
Real Property	130	100
Totals	240	300

Capital	Tax	Book
A	$120	$150
B	120	150
C	0	0
	240	300

(B) Because C is no longer a partner in ABC, C would not be allocated any net income from ABC's section 751 property immediately after the distribution. Also, C did not receive any section 751 property in the distribution. Accordingly, C's net section 751 unrealized gain immediately after the distribution is $0 under paragraph (b)(2)(iii) of this section.

(iv) Because C's net section 751 unrealized gain is greater immediately before the distribution than immediately after the distribution, section 751(b) applies to the distribution. Under paragraph (b)(2)(i) of this section, C has a section 751(b) amount equal to $30, the amount by which C's share of pre-distribution net section 751 unrealized gain ($30) exceeds C's share of post-distribution net section 751 unrealized gain ($0). Accordingly, paragraph (b)(3)(i) of this section requires C to recognize $30 of ordinary income using a reasonable approach consistent with the purpose of this section. ABC considers two approaches, the first of which is described in paragraphs (v) and (vi) of this example, and the second of which is described in paragraphs (vii) and (viii) of this example.

(v) Assume ABC adopts an approach under which, immediately before the section 751(b) distribution, C is deemed to recognize $30 of ordinary income. To reflect C's recognition of $30 of ordinary income, C increases its basis in its ABC partnership interest by $30, and the partnership increases its basis in the unrealized receivable by the $30 of income recognized by C, immediately before the distribution. Provided the partnership applies the approach consistently for all section 751(b) distributions, ABC's adopted approach is reasonable. After taking into account the tax consequences of the section 751(b) distribution immediately prior to the cash distribution, ABC's modified balance sheet is as follows:

	Tax	Book
Cash	$260	$260
Unrealized Receivable	30	90
Real Property	100	100
Totals	390	450

Capital	Tax	Book
A	$120	$150
B	120	150
C	150	150
	390	450

(vi) After determining the tax consequences of the section 751(b) distribution, the rules of sections 731 through 736 apply. Accordingly, C recognizes no gain or loss under section 731(a) upon the distribution. Because C recognizes no gain on the distribution, the basis of the partnership real property is not adjusted. After the distribution, ABC's balance sheet is as follows:

	Tax	Book
Cash	$110	$110
Unrealized Receivable	30	90
Real Property	100	100
Totals	240	300

Capital	Tax	Book
A	$120	$150
B	120	150
C	0	0
	240	300

(vii) Assume alternatively that ABC adopts an approach under which, immediately before the section 751(b) distribution, C is deemed to—

(A) Receive a distribution of ABC's unrealized receivables with a fair market value of $30 and a tax basis of $0;

(B) Sell the unrealized receivable to ABC in exchange for $30, recognizing $30 of ordinary income; and

(C) Contribute the $30 to ABC. Provided the partnership applies the approach consistently for all section 751(b) distributions, ABC's adopted approach is reasonable. After taking into account the tax consequences of the section 751(b) distribution immediately prior to the cash distribution, ABC's modified balance sheet is the same as the balance sheet shown in paragraph (v) of this example.

(viii) After determining the tax consequences of the section 751(b) distribution, the rules of sections 731 through 736 apply. The tax consequences under the rules of sections 731 through 736 are the same tax consequences described in paragraph (vi) of this example.

* * *

[Prop. Reg. § 1.751-1.]

[Proposed 11-3-2014 (corrected 1-26-2015).]

§ 1.752-1. Treatment of partnership liabilities.—(a) *Definitions.*—For purposes of section 752, the following definitions apply:

(1) *Recourse liability defined.*—A partnership liability is a recourse liability to the extent that any partner or related person bears the economic risk of loss for that liability under § 1.752-2.

(2) *Nonrecourse liability defined.*—A partnership liability is a nonrecourse liability to the extent that no partner or related person bears the economic risk of loss for that liability under § 1.752-2.

(3) *Related person.*—Related person means a person having a relationship to a partner that is described in § 1.752-4(b).

(4) *Liability defined.*—(i) *In general.*—An obligation is a liability for purposes of section 752 and the regulations thereunder (§ 1.752-1 liability), only if, when, and to the extent that incurring the obligation—

(A) Creates or increases the basis of any of the obligor's assets (including cash);

(B) Gives rise to an immediate deduction to the obligor; or

(C) Gives rise to an expense that is not deductible in computing the obligor's taxable income and is not properly chargeable to capital.

(ii) *Obligation.*—For purposes of this paragraph and § 1.752-7, an obligation is any fixed or contingent obligation to make payment without regard to whether the obligation is otherwise taken into account for purposes of the Internal Revenue Code. Obligations include, but are not limited to, debt obligations, environmental obligations, tort obligations, contract obligations, pension obligations, obligations under a short sale, and obligations under derivative financial instruments such as options, forward contracts, futures contracts, and swaps.

(iii) *Other liabilities.*—For obligations that are not § 1.752-1 liabilities, see §§ 1.752-6 and 1.752-7.

(iv) *Effective date.*—Except as otherwise provided in § 1.752-7(k), this paragraph (a)(4) applies to liabilities that are incurred or assumed by a partnership on or after June 24, 2003.

(b) *Increase in partner's share of liabilities.*—Any increase in a partner's share of partnership liabilities, or any increase in a partner's individual liabilities by reason of the partner's assumption of partnership liabilities, is treated as a contribution of money by that partner to the partnership.

(c) *Decrease in partner's share of liabilities.*—Any decrease in a partner's share of partnership liabilities, or any decrease in a partner's individual liabilities by reason of the partnership's assumption of the individual liabilities of the partner, is treated as a distribution of money by the partnership to that partner.

(d) *Assumption of liability.*—(1) *In general.*—Except as otherwise provided in paragraph (e) of this section, a person is considered to assume a liability only to the extent that:

(i) The assuming person is personally obligated to pay the liability; and

(ii) If a partner or related person assumes a partnership liability, the person to whom the liability is owed knows of the assumption and can directly enforce the partner's or related person's obligation for the liability, and no other partner or person that is a related person to another partner would bear the economic risk of loss for the liability under § 1.752-2 immediately after the assumption.

* * *

(e) *Property subject to a liability.*—If property is contributed by a partner to the partnership or distributed by the partnership to a partner and the property is subject to a liability of the transferor, the transferee is treated as having assumed the liability, to the extent that the amount of the liability does not exceed the fair market value of the property at the time of the contribution or distribution.

(f) *Netting of increases and decreases in liabilities resulting from same transaction.*—If, as a result of a single transaction, a partner incurs both an increase in the partner's share of the partnership liabilities (or the partner's individual liabilities) and a decrease in the partner's share of the partnership liabilities (or the partner's individual liabilities), only the net decrease is treated as a distribution from the partnership and only the net increase is treated as a contribution of money to the partnership. Generally, the contribution to or distribution from a partnership of property subject to a liability or the termination of the partnership under section 708(b) will require that increases and decreases in liabilities associated with the transaction be netted to determine if a partner will be deemed to have made a contribution or received a distribution as a result of the transaction. When two or more partnerships merge or consolidate under section 708(b)(2)(A), as described in § 1.708-1(c)(3)(i), increases and decreases in partnership liabilities associated with the merger or consolidation are netted by the partners in the terminating partnership and the resulting partnership to determine the effect of the merger under section 752.

(g) *Example.*—The following example illustrates the principles of paragraphs (b), (c), (e), and (f) of this section.

Example 1. Property contributed subject to a liability; netting of increase and decrease in partner's share of liability. B contributes property with an adjusted basis of $1,000 to a general partnership in exchange for a one-third interest in the partnership. At the time of the contribution, the partnership does not have any liabilities outstanding and the property is subject to a recourse debt of $150 and has a fair market value in excess of $150. After the contribution, B remains personally liable to the creditor and none of the other partners bears any of the economic risk of loss for the liability under state law or otherwise. Under paragraph (e) of this section, the partnership is treated as having assumed the $150 liability. As a result, B's individual liabilities decrease by $150. At the same time, however, B's share of liabilities of the partnership increases by $150. Only the net increase or decrease in B's share of the liabilities of the partnership and B's individual liabilities is taken into account in applying section 752. Because there is no net change, B is not treated as having contributed money to the partnership or as having received a distribution of money from the partnership under paragraph (b) or (c) of this section. Therefore B's basis for B's partnership interest is $1,000 (B's basis for the contributed property).

Example 2. Merger or consolidation of partnerships holding property encumbered by liabilities. (i) B owns a 70 percent interest in partnership T. Partnership T's sole asset is property X, which is encumbered by a $900 liability. Partnership T's adjusted basis in property X is $600, and the value of property X is $1,000. B's adjusted basis in its partnership T interest is $420. B also owns a 20 percent interest in partnership S. Partnership S's sole asset is property Y, which is encumbered by a $100 liability. Partnership S's adjusted basis in property Y is $200, the value of property Y is $1,000, and B's adjusted basis in its partnership S interest is $40.

(ii) Partnership T and partnership S merge under section 708(b)(2)(A). Under section 708(b)(2)(A) and § 1.708-1(c)(1), partnership T is considered terminated and the resulting partnership is considered a continuation of partnership S. Partnerships T and S undertake the form described in § 1.708-1(c)(3)(i) for the partnership merger. Under § 1.708-1(c)(3)(i), partnership T contributes property X and its $900 liability to partnership S in exchange for an interest in partnership S. Immediately thereafter, partnership T distributes the interests in partnership S to its partners in liquidation of their interests in partnership T. B owns a 25 percent interest in partnership S after partnership T distributes the interests in partnership S to B.

(iii) Under paragraph (f) of this section, B nets the increases and decreases in its share of partnership liabilities associated with the merger of partnership T and partnership S. Before the merger, B's share of partnership liabilities was $650 (B had a $630 share of partnership liabilities in partnership T and a $20 share of partnership liabilities in partnership S immediately before the merger). B's share of S's partnership liabilities after the merger is $250 (25 percent of S's total partnership liabilities of $1,000). Accordingly, B has a $400 net decrease in its share of S's partnership liabilities. Thus, B is treated as receiving a $400 distribution from partnership S under section 752(b). Because B's adjusted basis in its partnership S interest before the deemed distribution under section 752(b) is $460 ($420 + $40), B will not recognize gain under section 731. After the merger, B's adjusted basis in its partnership S interest is $60.

(h) *Sale or exchange of a partnership interest.*—If a partnership interest is sold or exchanged, the reduction in the transferor partner's share of partnership liabilities is treated as an amount realized under section 1001 and the regulations thereunder. For example, if a partner sells an interest in a partnership for $750 cash and transfers to the purchaser the partner's share of partnership liabilities in the amount of $250, the seller realizes $1,000 on the transaction.

(i) *Bifurcation of partnership liabilities.*—If one or more partners bears the economic risk of loss as to part, but not all, of a partnership liability represented by a single contractual obligation, that liability is treated as two or more separate liabilities for purposes of section 752. The portion of the liability as to which one or more partners bear the economic risk of loss is a recourse liability and the remainder of the liability, if any, is a nonrecourse liability. [Reg. § 1.752-1.]

☐ [*T.D.* 8380, 12-20-91. *Amended by T.D.* 8925, 1-3-2001; *T.D.* 9207, 5-23-2005 *and T.D.* 9877, 10-4-2019.]

§ 1.752-2. Partner's share of recourse liabilities.—(a) *In general.*—A partner's share of a recourse partnership liability equals the portion of that liability, if any, for which the partner or related person bears the economic risk of loss. The determination of the extent to which a partner bears the economic risk of loss for a partnership liability is made under the rules in paragraphs (b) through (k) of this section.

(b) *Obligation to make a payment.*—(1) *In general.*—Except as otherwise provided in this section, a partner bears the economic risk of loss for a partnership liability to the extent that, if the partnership constructively liquidated, the partner or related person would be obligated to make a payment to any person (or a contribution to the partnership) because that liability becomes due and payable and the partner or related person would not be entitled to reimbursement from another partner or person that is a related person to another partner. Upon a constructive liquidation, all of the following events are deemed to occur simultaneously:

(i) All of the partnership's liabilities become payable in full;

(ii) With the exception of property contributed to secure a partnership liability (see § 1.752-2(h)(2)), all of the partnership's assets, including cash, have a value of zero;

(iii) The partnership disposes of all of its property in a fully taxable transaction for no consideration (except relief from liabilities for which the creditor's right to repayment is limited solely to one or more assets of the partnership);

(iv) All items of income, gain, loss, or deduction are allocated among the partners; and

(v) The partnership liquidates.

(2) *Treatment upon deemed disposition.*—For purposes of paragraph (b)(1) of this section, gain or loss on the deemed disposition of the partnership's assets is computed in accordance with the following:

(i) If the creditor's right to repayment of a partnership liability is limited solely to one or more assets of the partnership, gain or loss is recognized in an amount equal to the difference between the amount of the liability that is extinguished by the deemed disposition and the tax basis (or book value to the extent section 704(c) or § 1.704-1(b)(4)(i) applies) in those assets.

(ii) A loss is recognized equal to the remaining tax basis (or book value to the extent section 704(c) or § 1.704-1(b)(4)(i) applies) of all of the partnership's assets not taken into account in paragraph (b)(2)(i) of this section.

(3) *Obligations recognized.*—(i) *In general.*—The determination of the extent to which a partner or related person has an obligation to make a payment under § 1.752-2(b)(1) is based on the facts and circumstances at the time of the determination. To the extent that the obligation of a partner or related person to make a payment with respect to a partnership liability is not recognized under this paragraph (b)(3), § 1.752-2(b) is applied as if the obligation did not exist. All statutory and contractual obligations relating to the partnership liability are taken into account for purposes of applying this section, including—

(A) Contractual obligations outside the partnership agreement such as guarantees, indemnifications, reimbursement agreements, and other obligations running directly to creditors, to other partners, or to the partnership;

(B) Obligations to the partnership that are imposed by the partnership agreement, including the obligation to make a capital contribution and to restore a deficit capital account upon liquidation of the partnership as described in § 1.704-1(b)(2)(ii)(*b*)(*3*) (taking into account § 1.704-1(b)(2)(ii)(*c*)); and

(C) Payment obligations (whether in the form of direct remittances to another partner or a contribution to the partnership) imposed by state or local law, including the governing state or local law partnership statute.

(ii) *Special rules for bottom dollar payment obligations.*—(A) *In general.*—For purposes of § 1.752-2, a bottom dollar payment obligation (as defined in paragraph (b)(3)(ii)(C) of this section) is not recognized under this paragraph (b)(3).

(B) *Exception.*—If a partner or related person has a payment obligation that would be recognized under this paragraph (b)(3) (initial payment obligation) but for the effect of an indemnity, a reimbursement agreement, or a similar arrangement, such bottom dollar payment obligation is recognized under this paragraph (b)(3) if, taking into account the indemnity, reimbursement agreement, or similar arrangement, the partner or related person is liable for at least 90 percent of the partner's or related person's initial payment obligation.

(C) *Definition of bottom dollar payment obligation.*—*(1) In general.*—Except as provided in paragraph (b)(3)(ii)(C)(*2*) of this section, a *bottom dollar payment obligation* is a payment obligation that is the same as or similar to a payment obligation or arrangement described in this paragraph (b)(3)(ii)(C)(*1*).

(i) With respect to a guarantee or similar arrangement, any payment obligation other than one in which the partner or related person is or would be liable up to the full amount of such partner's or related person's payment obligation if, and to the extent that, any amount of the partnership liability is not otherwise satisfied.

(ii) With respect to an indemnity or similar arrangement, any payment obligation other than one in which the partner or related person is or would be liable up to the full amount of such partner's or related person's payment obligation, if, and to the extent that, any amount of the indemnitee's or benefited party's payment obligation that is recognized under this paragraph (b)(3) is satisfied.

(iii) With respect to an obligation to make a capital contribution or to restore a deficit capital account upon liquidation of the partnership as described in § 1.704-1(b)(2)(ii)(*b*)(*3*) (taking into account § 1.704-1(b)(2)(ii)(c)), any payment obligation other than one in which the partner is or would be required to make the full amount of the partner's capital contribution or to restore the full amount of the partner's deficit capital account.

(iv) An arrangement with respect to a partnership liability that uses tiered partnerships, intermediaries, senior and subordinate liabilities, or similar arrangements to convert what would otherwise be a single liability into multiple liabilities if, based on the facts and circumstances, the liabilities were incurred pursuant to a common plan, as part of a single transaction or arrangement, or as part of a series of related transactions or arrangements, and with a principal purpose of avoiding having at least one of such liabilities or payment obligations with respect to such liabilities being treated as a bottom dollar payment obligation as described in paragraph (b)(3)(ii)(C)(*1*)(*i*), (*ii*), or (*iii*) of this section.

(2) Exceptions.—A payment obligation is not a bottom dollar payment obligation merely because a maximum amount is placed on the partner's or related person's payment obligation, a partner's or related person's payment obligation is stated as a fixed percentage of every dollar of the partnership liability to which such obligation relates, or there is a right of proportionate contribution running between partners or related persons who are co-obligors with respect to a payment obligation for which each of them is jointly and severally liable.

(3) Benefited party defined.—For purposes of § 1.752-2, a *benefited party* is the person to whom a partner or related person has the payment obligation.

(D) *Disclosure of bottom dollar payment obligations.*—A partnership must disclose to the Internal Revenue Service a bottom dollar payment obligation (including a bottom dollar payment obligation that is recognized under paragraph (b)(3)(ii)(B) of this section) with respect to a partnership liability on a completed Form 8275, Disclosure Statement, or successor form, attached to the return of the partnership for the taxable year in which the bottom dollar payment obligation is undertaken or modified, that includes all of the following information:

(1) A caption identifying the statement as a disclosure of a bottom dollar payment obligation under section 752.

(2) An identification of the payment obligation with respect to which disclosure is made (including whether the obligation is a guarantee, a reimbursement, an indemnity, or an obligation to restore a deficit balance in a partner's capital account).

(3) The amount of the payment obligation.

(4) The parties to the payment obligation.

(5) A statement of whether the payment obligation is treated as recognized for purposes of this paragraph (b)(3).

(6) If the payment obligation is recognized under paragraph (b)(3)(ii)(B) of this section, the facts and circumstances that clearly establish that a partner or related person is liable for up to 90 percent of the partner's or related person's initial payment obligation and, but for an indemnity, a reimbursement agreement, or a similar arrangement, the partner's or related person's initial payment obligation would have been recognized under this paragraph (b)(3).

(iii) *Special rule for indemnities and reimbursement agreements.*—An indemnity, a reimbursement agreement, or a similar arrangement will be recognized under this paragraph (b)(3) only if, before taking into account the indemnity, reimbursement agreement, or similar arrangement, the indemnitee's or other benefited party's payment obligation is recognized under this paragraph (b)(3), or would be recognized under this paragraph (b)(3) if such person were a partner or related person.

(4) *Contingent obligations.*—A payment obligation is disregarded if, taking into account all the facts and circumstances, the obligation is subject to contingencies that make it unlikely that the obligation will ever be discharged. If a payment obligation would arise at a future time after the occurrence of an event that is not determinable with reasonable certainty, the obligation is ignored until the event occurs.

(5) *Reimbursement rights.*—A partner's or related person's obligation to make a payment with respect to a partnership liability is reduced to the extent that the partner or related person is entitled to reimbursement from another partner or a person who is a related person to another partner.

(6) *Deemed satisfaction of obligation.*—For purposes of determining the extent to which a partner or related person has a payment obligation and the economic risk of loss, it is assumed that all partners and related persons who have obligations to make payments (a payment obligor) actually perform those obligations, irrespective of their actual net worth, unless the facts and circumstances indicate—

(i) A plan to circumvent or avoid the obligation under paragraph (j) of this section, or

(ii) That there is not a commercially reasonable expectation that the payment obligor will have the ability to make the required payments under the terms of the obligation if the obligation becomes due and payable as described in paragraph (k) of this section.

(c) *Partner or related person as lender.*—(1) *In general.*—A partner bears the economic risk of loss for a partnership liability to the extent that the partner or a related person makes (or acquires an interest in) a nonrecourse loan to the partnership and the economic risk of loss for the liability is not borne by another partner.

(2) *Wrapped debt.*—If a partnership liability is owed to a partner or related person and that liability includes (*i.e.,* is "wrapped" around) a nonrecourse obligation encumbering partnership property that is owed to another person, the partnership liability will be treated as two separate liabilities. The portion of the partnership liability corresponding to the wrapped debt is treated as a liability owed to another person.

(3) *[Reserved].*—For further guidance, see § 1.752-2T(c)(3).

(d) *De minimis exceptions.*—(1) *Partner as lender.*—The general rule contained in paragraph (c)(1) of this section does not apply if a partner or related person whose interest (directly or indirectly through one or more partnerships including the interest of any related person) in each item of partnership income, gain, loss, deduction, or credit for every taxable year that the partner is a partner in the partnership is 10 percent or less, makes a loan to the partnership which constitutes qualified nonrecourse financing within the meaning of section 465(b)(6) (determined without regard to the type of activity financed).

(2) *Partner as guarantor.*—The general rule contained in paragraph (b)(1) of this section does not apply if a partner or related person whose interest (directly or indirectly through one or more partnerships including the interest of any related person) in each item of partnership income, gain, loss, deduction, or credit for every taxable year that the partner is a partner in the partnership is 10 percent or less, guarantees a loan that would otherwise be a nonrecourse loan of the partnership and which would constitute qualified nonrecourse financing within the meaning of section 465(b)(6) (without regard to the type of activity financed) if the guarantor had made the loan to the partnership.

(e) *Special rule for nonrecourse liability with interest guaranteed by a partner.*—(1) *In general.*—For purposes of this section, if one or more partners or related persons have guaranteed the payment of more than 25 percent of the total interest that will accrue on a partnership nonrecourse liability over its remaining term, and it is reasonable to expect that the guarantor will be required to pay substantially all of the guaranteed future interest if the partnership fails to do so, then the liability is treated as two separate partnership liabilities. If this rule applies, the partner or related person that has guaranteed the payment of interest is treated as bearing the economic risk of loss for the partnership liability to the extent of the present value of the guaranteed future interest payments. The remainder of the stated principal amount of the partnership liability constitutes a nonrecourse liability. Generally, in applying this rule, it is reasonable to expect that the guarantor will be required to pay substantially all of the guaranteed future interest if, upon a default in payment by the partnership, the lender can enforce the interest guaranty without foreclosing on the property and thereby extinguishing the underlying debt. The guarantee of interest rule continues to apply even after the point at which the amount of guaranteed interest that will accrue is less than 25 percent of the total interest that will accrue on the liability.

(2) *Computation of present value.*—The present value of the guaranteed future interest payments is computed using a discount rate equal to either the interest rate stated in the loan documents, or if interest is imputed under either section 483 or section 1274, the applicable federal rate, compounded semi-annually. The computation takes into account any payment of interest that the partner or related person may be required to make only to the extent that the interest will accrue economically (determined in accordance with section 446 and the regulations thereunder) after the date of the interest guarantee. If the loan document contains a variable rate of interest that is an interest rate based on current values of an objective interest index, the present value is computed on the assumption that the interest determined under the objective interest index on the date of the computation will remain constant over the term of the loan. The term "objective interest index" has the meaning given to it in section 1275 and the regulations thereunder (relating to variable rate debt instruments). Examples of an objective interest index include the prime rate of a designated financial institution, LIBOR (London Interbank Offered Rate), and the applicable federal rate under section 1274(d).

(3) *Safe harbor.*—The general rule contained in paragraph (e)(1) of this section does not apply to a partnership nonrecourse liability if the guarantee of interest by the partner or related person is for a period not in excess of the lesser of five years or one-third of the term of the liability.

(4) *De minimis exception.*—The general rule contained in paragraph (e)(1) of this section does not apply if a partner or related person whose interest (directly or indirectly through one or more partnerships including the interest of any related person) in each item of partnership income, gain, loss, deduction, or credit for every taxable year that the partner is a partner in the partnership is 10 percent or less, guarantees the interest on a loan to that partnership which constitutes qualified nonrecourse financing within the meaning of section 465(b)(6) (determined without regard to the type of activity financed). An allocation of interest to the extent paid by the guarantor is not treated as a partnership item of deduction or loss subject to the 10 percent or less rule.

(f) *Examples.*—The following examples illustrate the principles of paragraphs (a) through (e) of this section. Unless otherwise provided, for purposes of paragraph (f)(1) through (9) of this section (*Examples 1* through *9*), assume that any obligation of a partner or related person to make a payment is recognized under paragraph (b)(3) of this section.

(1) *Example 1. Determining when a partner bears the economic risk of loss.*—A and B form a general partnership with each contributing $100 in cash. The partnership purchases an office building on leased land for $1,000 from an unrelated seller, paying $200 in cash and executing a note to the seller for the balance of $800. The note is a general obligation of the partnership, *i.e.,* no partner has been relieved from personal liability. The partnership agreement provides that all items are allocated equally except that tax losses are specially allocated 90% to A and 10% to B and that capital accounts will be maintained in accordance with the regulations under section 704(b), including a deficit capital account restoration obligation on liquidation. In a constructive liquidation, the $800 liability becomes due and payable. All of the partnership's assets, including the building, are deemed to be worthless. The building is deemed sold for a value of zero. Capital accounts are adjusted to reflect the loss on the hypothetical disposition, as follows:

	A	B
Initial contribution	$100	$100
Loss on hypothetical sale	(900)	(100)
	($800)	$-0-

Other than the partners' obligation to fund negative capital accounts on liquidation, there are no other contractual or statutory payment obligations existing between the partners, the partnership and the lender. Therefore, $800 of the partnership liability is classified as a recourse liability because one or more partners bears the economic risk of loss for non-payment. B has no share of the $800 liability since the constructive liquidation produces no payment obligation for B. A's share of the partnership liability is $800 because A would have an obligation in that amount to make a contribution to the partnership.

(2) *Example 2. Recourse liability; deficit restoration obligation.*—C and D each contribute $500 in cash to the capital of a new general partnership, CD. CD purchases property from an unrelated seller for $1,000 in cash and a $9,000 mortgage note. The note is a general obligation of the partnership, *i.e.*, no partner has been relieved from personal liability. The partnership agreement provides that profits and losses are to be divided 40% to C and 60% to D. C and D are required to make up any deficit in their capital accounts. In a constructive liquidation, all partnership assets are deemed to become worthless and all partnership liabilities become due and payable in full. The partnership is deemed to dispose of all its assets in a fully taxable transaction for no consideration. Capital accounts are adjusted to reflect the loss on the hypothetical disposition, as follows:

	C	*D*
Initial contribution	$ 500	$ 500
Loss on hypothetical sale	(4,000)	(6,000)
	($3,500)	($5,500)

C's capital account reflects a deficit that C would have to make up of $3,500 and D's capital account reflects a deficit that D would have to make up of $5,500. Therefore, the $9,000 mortgage note is a recourse liability because one or more partners bears the economic risk of loss for the liability. C's share of the recourse liability is $3,500 and D's share is $5,500.

(3) *Example 3. Guarantee by limited partner; partner deemed to satisfy obligation.*—E and F form a limited partnership. E, the general partner, contributes $2,000 and F, the limited partner, contributes $8,000 in cash to the partnership. The partnership agreement allocates losses 20% to E and 80% to F until F's capital account is reduced to zero, after which all losses are allocated to E. The partnership purchases depreciable property for $25,000 using its $10,000 cash and a $15,000 recourse loan from a bank. F guarantees payment of the $15,000 loan to the extent the loan remains unpaid after the bank has exhausted its remedies against the partnership. In a constructive liquidation, the $15,000 liability becomes due and payable. All of the partnership's assets, including the depreciable property, are deemed to be worthless. The depreciable property is deemed sold for a value of zero. Capital accounts are adjusted to reflect the loss on the hypothetical disposition, as follows:

	E	*F*
Initial contribution	$ 2,000	$ 8,000
Loss on hypothetical sale	(17,000)	(8,000)
	($15,000)	-0-

E, as a general partner, would be obligated by operation of law to make a net contribution to the partnership of $15,000. Because E is assumed to satisfy that obligation, it is also assumed that F would not have to satisfy F's guarantee. The $15,000 mortgage is treated as a recourse liability because one or more partners bear the economic risk of loss. E's share of the liability is $15,000, and F's share is zero. This would be so even if E's net worth at the time of the determination is less than $15,000, unless the facts and circumstances indicate a plan to circumvent or avoid E's obligation to contribute to the partnership.

(4) *Example 4. Partner guarantee with right of subrogation.*—G, a limited partner in the GH partnership, guarantees a portion of a partnership liability. The liability is a general obligation of the partnership, *i.e.*, no partner has been relieved from personal liability. If under state law G is subrogated to the rights of the lender, G would have the right to recover the amount G paid to the recourse lender from the general partner. Therefore, G does not bear the economic risk of loss for the partnership liability.

(5) *Example 5. Bifurcation of partnership liability; guarantee of part of nonrecourse liability.*—A partnership borrows $10,000, secured by a mortgage on real property. The mortgage note contains an exoneration clause which provides that in the event of default, the holder's only remedy is to foreclose on the property. The holder may not look to any other partnership asset or to any partner to pay the liability. However, to induce the lender to make the loan, a partner guarantees payment of $200 of the loan principal. The exoneration clause does not apply to the partner's guarantee. If the partner paid pursuant to the guarantee, the partner would be subrogated to the rights of the lender with respect to $200 of the mortgage debt, but the partner is not otherwise entitled to reimbursement from the partnership or any

partner. For purposes of section 752, $200 of the $10,000 mortgage liability is treated as a recourse liability of the partnership and $9,800 is treated as a nonrecourse liability of the partnership. The partner's share of the recourse liability of the partnership is $200.

(6) *Example 6. Wrapped debt.*—I, an individual, purchases real estate from an unrelated seller for $10,000, paying $1,000 in cash and giving a $9,000 purchase mortgage note on which I has no personal liability and as to which the seller can look only to the property for satisfaction. At a time when the property is worth $15,000, I sells the property to a partnership in which I is a general partner. The partnership pays for the property with a partnership purchase money mortgage note of $15,000 on which neither the partnership nor any partner (or person related to a partner) has personal liability. The $15,000 mortgage note is a wrapped debt that includes the $9,000 obligation to the original seller. The liability is a recourse liability to the extent of $6,000 because I is the creditor with respect to the loan and I bears the economic risk of loss for $6,000. I's share of the recourse liability is $6,000. The remaining $9,000 is treated as a partnership nonrecourse liability that is owed to the unrelated seller.

(7) *Example 7. Guarantee of interest by partner treated as part recourse and part nonrecourse.*—On January 1, 1992, a partnership obtains a $4,000,000 loan secured by a shopping center owned by the partnership. Neither the partnership nor any partner has any personal liability under the loan documents for repayment of the stated principal amount. Interest accrues at a 15 percent annual rate and is payable on December 31 of each year. The principal is payable in a lump sum on December 31, 2006. A partner guarantees payment of 50 percent of each interest payment required by the loan. The guarantee can be enforced without first foreclosing on the property. When the partnership obtains the loan, the present value (discounted at 15 percent, compounded annually) of the future interest payments is $3,508,422, and of the future principal payment is $491,578. If tested on that date, the loan would be treated as a partnership liability of $1,754,211 ($3,508,422 × .5) for which the guaranteeing partner bears the economic risk of loss and a partnership nonrecourse liability of $2,245,789 ($1,754,211 + $491,578).

(8) *Example 8. Contingent obligation not recognized.*—J and K form a general partnership with cash contributions of $2,500 each. J and K share partnership profits and losses equally. The partnership purchases an apartment building for its $5,000 of cash and a $20,000 nonrecourse loan from a commercial bank. The nonrecourse loan is secured by a mortgage on the building. The loan documents provide that the partnership will be liable for the outstanding balance of the loan on a recourse basis to the extent of any decrease in the value of the apartment building resulting from the partnership's failure properly to maintain the property. There are no facts that establish with reasonable certainty the existence of any liability on the part of the partnership (and its partners) for damages resulting from the partnership's failure properly to maintain the building. Therefore, no partner bears the economic risk of loss, and the liability constitutes a nonrecourse liability. Under § 1.752-3, J and K share this nonrecourse liability equally because they share all profits and losses equally.

(9) [Reserved].

(10) *Example 10. Guarantee of first and last dollars.*—(i) A, B, and C are equal members of a limited liability company, ABC, that is treated as a partnership for federal tax purposes. ABC borrows $1,000 from Bank. A guarantees payment of up to $300 of the ABC liability if any amount of the full $1,000 liability is not recovered by Bank. B guarantees payment of up to $200, but only if the Bank otherwise recovers less than $200. Both A and B waive their rights of contribution against each other.

(ii) Because A is obligated to pay up to $300 if, and to the extent that, any amount of the $1,000 partnership liability is not recovered by Bank, A's guarantee is not a bottom dollar payment obligation under paragraph (b)(3)(ii)(C) of this section. Therefore, A's payment obligation is recognized under paragraph (b)(3) of this section. The amount of A's economic risk of loss under § 1.752-2(b)(1) is $300.

(iii) Because B is obligated to pay up to $200 only if and to the extent that the Bank otherwise recovers less than $200 of the $1,000 partnership liability, B's guarantee is a bottom dollar payment obligation under paragraph (b)(3)(ii)(C) of this section and, therefore, is not recognized under paragraph (b)(3)(ii)(A) of this section. Accordingly, B bears no economic risk of loss under § 1.752-2(b)(1) for ABC's liability.

(iv) In sum, $300 of ABC's liability is allocated to A under § 1.752-2(a), and the remaining $700 liability is allocated to A, B, and C under § 1.752-3.

(11) *Example 11. Indemnification of guarantees.*—(i) The facts are the same as in paragraph (f)(10) of this section (*Example 10*), except that, in addition, C agrees to indemnify A up to $100 that A pays with respect to its

guarantee and agrees to indemnify B fully with respect to its guarantee.

(ii) The determination of whether C's indemnity is recognized under paragraph (b)(3) of this section is made without regard to whether C's indemnity itself causes A's guarantee not to be recognized. Because A's obligation would be recognized but for the effect of C's indemnity and C is obligated to pay A up to the full amount of C's indemnity if A pays any amount on its guarantee of ABC's liability, C's indemnity of A's guarantee is not a bottom dollar payment obligation under paragraph (b)(3)(ii)(C) of this section and, therefore, is recognized under paragraph (b)(3) of this section. The amount of C's economic risk of loss under § 1.752-2(b)(1) for its indemnity of A's guarantee is $100.

(iii) Because C's indemnity is recognized under paragraph (b)(3) of this section, A is treated as liable for $200 only to the extent any amount beyond $100 of the partnership liability is not satisfied. Thus, A is not liable if, and to the extent, any amount of the partnership liability is not otherwise satisfied, and the exception in paragraph (b)(3)(ii)(B) of this section does not apply. As a result, A's guarantee is a bottom dollar payment obligation under paragraph (b)(3)(ii)(C) of this section and is not recognized under paragraph (b)(3)(ii)(A) of this section. Therefore, A bears no economic risk of loss under § 1.752-2(b)(1) for ABC's liability.

(iv) Because B's obligation is not recognized under paragraph (b)(3)(ii) of this section independent of C's indemnity of B's guarantee, C's indemnity is not recognized under paragraph (b)(3)(iii) of this section. Therefore, C bears no economic risk of loss under § 1.752-2(b)(1) for its indemnity of B's guarantee.

(v) In sum, $100 of ABC's liability is allocated to C under § 1.752-2(a) and the remaining $900 liability is allocated to A, B, and C under § 1.752-3.

(g) *Time-value-of-money considerations.*—(1) *In general.*—The extent to which a partner or related person bears the economic risk of loss is determined by taking into account any delay in the time when a payment or contribution obligation with respect to a partnership liability is to be satisfied. If a payment obligation with respect to a partnership liability is not required to be satisfied within a reasonable time after the liability becomes due and payable, or if the obligation to make a contribution to the partnership is not required to be satisfied before the later of—

(i) The end of the year in which the partner's interest is liquidated, or

(ii) 90 days after the liquidation,

the obligation is recognized only to the extent of the value of the obligation.

(2) *Valuation of an obligation.*—The value of a payment or contribution obligation that is not required to be satisfied within the time period specified in paragraph (g)(1) of this section equals the entire principal balance of the obligation only if the obligation bears interest equal to or greater than the applicable federal rate under section 1274(d) at the time of valuation, commencing on—

(i) In the case of a payment obligation, the date that the partnership liability to a creditor or other person to whom the obligation relates becomes due and payable, or

(ii) In the case of a contribution obligation, the date of the liquidation of the partner's interest in the partnership.

If the obligation does not bear interest at a rate at least equal to the applicable federal rate at the time of valuation, the value of the obligation is discounted to the present value of all payments due from the partner or related person (*i.e.,* the imputed principal amount computed under section 1274(b)). For purposes of making this present value determination, the partnership is deemed to have constructively liquidated as of the date on which the payment obligation is valued and the payment obligation is assumed to be a debt instrument subject to the rules of section 1274 (*i.e.,* the debt instrument is treated as if it were issued for property at the time of the valuation).

(3) *Satisfaction of obligation with partner's promissory note.*—An obligation is not satisfied by the transfer to the obligee of a promissory note by a partner or related person unless the note is readily tradeable on an established securities market.

(4) *Example.*—The following example illustrates the principle of paragraph (g) of this section.

Example. Value of obligation not required to be satisfied within specified time period. A, the general partner, and B, the limited partner, each contributes $10,000 to partnership AB. AB purchases property from an unrelated seller for $20,000 in cash and a $70,000 recourse purchase money note. The partnership agreement provides that profits and losses are to be divided equally. A and B are required to make up any deficit in their capital accounts. While A is required to restore any deficit balance in A's capital account within 90 days after the date of liquidation of the partnership, B is not required to restore any deficit for two years following the date of liquidation. The deficit in B's capital account will not bear interest during that two-year period. In a constructive liquidation, all partnership assets are deemed to become worthless and all partnership liabilities become due and payable in full. The partnership is deemed to dispose of all its assets in a fully taxable transaction for no consideration. Capital accounts are adjusted to reflect the loss on the hypothetical disposition, as follows:

	A	*B*
Initial contribution	$10,000	$10,000
Loss on hypothetical sale	(45,000)	(45,000)
	($35,000)	($35,000)

A's and B's capital accounts each reflect deficits of $35,000. B's obligation to make a contribution pursuant to B's deficit restoration obligation is recognized only to the extent of the fair market value of that obligation at the time of the constructive liquidation because B is not required to satisfy that obligation by the later of the end of the partnership taxable year in which B's interest is liquidated or within 90 days after the date of the liquidation. Because B's obligation does not bear interest, the fair market value is deemed to equal the imputed principal amount under section 1274(b). Under section 1274(b), the imputed principal amount of a debt instrument equals the present value of all payments due under the debt instrument. Assume the applicable federal rate with respect to B's obligation is 10 percent compounded semiannually. Using this discount rate, the present value of the $35,000 payment that B would be required to make two years after the constructive liquidation to restore the deficit balance in B's capital account equals $28,795. To the extent that B's deficit restoration obligation is not recognized, it is assumed that B's obligation does not exist. Therefore, A, as the sole general partner, would be obligated by operation of law to contribute an additional $6,205 of capital to the partnership. Accordingly, under paragraph (g) of this section, B bears the economic risk of loss for $28,795 and A bears the economic risk of loss for $41,205 ($35,000 + $6,205).

(h) *Partner providing property as security for partnership liability.*—(1) *Direct pledge.*—A partner is considered to bear the economic risk of loss for a partnership liability to the extent of the value of any of the partner's or related person's separate property (other than a direct or indirect interest in the partnership) that is pledged as security for the partnership liability.

(2) *Indirect pledge.*—A partner is considered to bear the economic risk of loss for a partnership liability to the extent of the value of any property that the partner contributes to the partnership solely for the purpose of securing a partnership liability. Contributed property is not treated as contributed solely for the purpose of securing a partnership liability unless substantially all of the items of income, gain, loss, and deduction attributable to the contributed property are allocated to the contributing partner, and this allocation is generally greater than the partner's share of other significant items of partnership income, gain, loss, or deduction.

(3) *Valuation.*—The extent to which a partner bears the economic risk of loss for a partnership liability as a result of a direct pledge described in paragraph (h)(1) of this section or an indirect pledge described in paragraph (h)(2) of this section is limited to the net fair market value of the property (pledged property) at the time of the pledge or contribution. If a partner provides additional pledged property, the addition is treated as a new pledge and the net fair market value of the pledged property (including but not limited to the additional property) must be determined at that time. For purposes of this paragraph (h), if pledged property is subject to one or more other obligations, those obligations must be taken into account in determining the net fair market value of pledged property at the time of the pledge or contribution.

(4) *Partner's promissory note.*—For purposes of paragraph (h)(2) of this section, a promissory note of the partner or related person that is contributed to the partnership shall not be taken into account unless the note is readily tradeable on an established securities market.

(i) *Treatment of recourse liabilities in tiered partnerships.*—If a partnership (the "upper-tier partnership") owns (directly or indirectly through one or more partnerships) an interest in another partnership (the "lower-tier partnership"), the liabilities of the lower-tier partnership are allocated to the upper-tier partnership in an amount equal to the sum of the following—

(1) The amount of the economic risk of loss that the upper-tier partnership bears with respect to the liabilities; and

(2) Any other amount of the liabilities with respect to which partners of the upper-tier partnership bear the economic risk of loss.

(j) *Anti-abuse rules.*—(1) *In general.*—An obligation of a partner or related person to make a payment may be disregarded or treated as an obligation of another person for purposes of this section if facts and circumstances indicate that a principal purpose of the arrangement between the parties is to eliminate the partner's economic risk of loss with respect to that obligation or create the appearance of the partner or related person bearing the economic risk of loss when, in fact, the substance of the arrangement is otherwise. Circumstances with respect to which a payment obligation may be disregarded include, but are not limited to, the situations described in paragraphs (j)(2) and (j)(3) of this section.

(2) *Arrangements tantamount to a guarantee.*—(i) *In general.*—Irrespective of the form of a contractual obligation, a partner is considered to bear the economic risk of loss with respect to a partnership liability, or a portion thereof, to the extent that—

(A) The partner or related person undertakes one or more contractual obligations so that the partnership may obtain or retain a loan;

(B) The contractual obligations of the partner or related person significantly reduce the risk to the lender that the partnership will not satisfy its obligations under the loan, or a portion thereof; and

(C) With respect to the contractual obligations described in paragraphs (j)(2)(i)(A) and (B) of this section—

(1) One of the principal purposes of using the contractual obligations is to attempt to permit partners (other than those who are directly or indirectly liable for the obligation) to include a portion of the loan in the basis of their partnership interests; or

(2) Another partner, or a person related to another partner, enters into a payment obligation and a principal purpose of the arrangement is to cause the payment obligation described in paragraphs (j)(2)(i)(A) and (B) of this section to be disregarded under paragraph (b)(3) of this section.

(ii) *Economic risk of loss.*—For purposes of this paragraph (j)(2), partners are considered to bear the economic risk of loss for a liability in accordance with their relative economic burdens for the liability pursuant to the contractual obligations. For example, a lease between a partner and a partnership that is not on commercially reasonable terms may be tantamount to a guarantee by the partner of the partnership liability.

(3) *Plan to circumvent or avoid an obligation.*—(i) *General rule.*—An obligation of a partner or related person to make a payment is not recognized under paragraph (b) of this section if the facts and circumstances evidence a plan to circumvent or avoid the obligation.

(ii) *Factors indicating plan to circumvent or avoid an obligation.*—In the case of a payment obligation, other than an obligation to restore a deficit capital account upon liquidation of a partnership, paragraphs (j)(3)(ii)(A) through (G) of this section provide a non-exclusive list of factors that may indicate a plan to circumvent or avoid the payment obligation. The presence or absence of a factor is based on all of the facts and circumstances at the time the partner or related person makes the payment obligation or if the obligation is modified, at the time of the modification. For purposes of making determinations under this paragraph (j)(3), the weight to be given to any particular factor depends on the particular case and the presence or absence of a factor is not necessarily indicative of whether a payment obligation is or is not recognized under paragraph (b) of this section.

(A) The partner or related person is not subject to commercially reasonable contractual restrictions that protect the likelihood of payment, including, for example, restrictions on transfers for inadequate consideration or distributions by the partner or related person to equity owners in the partner or related person.

(B) The partner or related person is not required to provide (either at the time the payment obligation is made or periodically) commercially reasonable documentation regarding the partner's or related person's financial condition to the benefited party, including, for example, balance sheets and financial statements.

(C) The term of the payment obligation ends prior to the term of the partnership liability, or the partner or related person has a right to terminate its payment obligation, if the purpose of limiting the duration of the payment obligation is to terminate such payment obligation prior to the occurrence of an event or events that increase the risk of economic loss to the guarantor or benefited party (for example, termination prior to the due date of a balloon payment or a right to terminate that can be exercised because the value of loan collateral decreases). This factor typically will not be present if the termination of the obligation occurs by reason of an event or events that decrease the risk of economic loss to the guarantor or benefited party (for example, the payment obligation terminates upon the completion of a building construction project, upon the leasing of a building, or when certain income and asset coverage ratios are satisfied for a specified number of quarters).

(D) There exists a plan or arrangement in which the primary obligor or any other obligor (or a person related to the obligor) with respect to the partnership liability directly or indirectly holds money or other liquid assets in an amount that exceeds the reasonably foreseeable needs of such obligor (but not taking into account standard commercial insurance, for example, casualty insurance).

(E) The payment obligation does not permit the creditor to promptly pursue payment following a payment default on the partnership liability, or other arrangements with respect to the partnership liability or payment obligation otherwise indicate a plan to delay collection.

(F) In the case of a guarantee or similar arrangement, the terms of the partnership liability would be substantially the same had the partner or related person not agreed to provide the guarantee.

(G) The creditor or other party benefiting from the obligation did not receive executed documents with respect to the payment obligation from the partner or related person before, or within a commercially reasonable period of time after, the creation of the obligation.

(4) *Example.*—The following example illustrates the principles of paragraph (j) of this section.

(i) In 2020, A, B, and C form a domestic limited liability company (LLC) that is classified as a partnership for federal tax purposes. Also in 2020, LLC receives a loan from a bank. A, B, and C do not bear the economic risk of loss with respect to that partnership liability, and, as a result, the liability is treated as nonrecourse under § 1.752-1(a)(2) in 2020. In 2022, A guarantees the entire amount of the liability. The bank did not request the guarantee and the terms of the loan did not change as a result of the guarantee. A did not provide any executed documents with respect to A's guarantee to the bank. The bank also did not require any restrictions on asset transfers by A and no such restrictions exist.

(ii) Under paragraph (j)(3) of this section, A's 2022 guarantee (payment obligation) is not recognized under paragraph (b)(3) of this section if the facts and circumstances evidence a plan to circumvent or avoid the payment obligation. In this case, the following factors indicate a plan to circumvent or avoid A's payment obligation: the partner is not subject to commercially reasonable contractual restrictions that protect the likelihood of payment, such as restrictions on transfers for inadequate consideration or equity distributions; the partner is not required to provide (either at the time the payment obligation is made or periodically) commercially reasonable documentation regarding the partner's or related person's financial condition to the benefited party; in the case of a guarantee or similar arrangement, the terms of the liability are the same as they would have been without the guarantee; and the creditor did not receive executed documents with respect to the payment obligation from the partner or related person at the time the obligation was created. Absent the existence of other facts or circumstances that would weigh in favor of respecting A's guarantee, evidence of a plan to circumvent or avoid the obligation exists and, pursuant to paragraph (j)(3)(i) of this section, A's guarantee is not recognized under paragraph (b) of this section. As a result, LLC's liability continues to be treated as nonrecourse.

(k) *No reasonable expectation of payment.*—(1) *In general.*—An obligation of any partner or related person to make a payment is not recognized under paragraph (b) of this section if the facts and circumstances indicate that at the time the partnership must determine a partner's share of partnership liabilities under §§ 1.705-1(a) and 1.752-4(d) there is not a commercially reasonable expectation that the payment obligor will have the ability to make the required payments under the terms of the obligation if the obligation becomes due and payable. Facts and circumstances to consider in determining a commercially reasonable expectation of payment include factors a third party creditor would take into account when determining whether to grant a loan. For purposes of this section, a payment obligor includes an entity disregarded as an entity separate from its owner under section 856(i), section 1361(b)(3), or §§ 301.7701-1 through 301.7701-3 of this chapter (a disregarded entity), and a trust to which subpart E of part I of subchapter J of chapter 1 of the Code applies

(2) *Examples.*—The following examples illustrate the principles of paragraph (k) of this section.

(i) *Example 1. Undercapitalization.*—(A) In 2020, A forms a wholly owned domestic limited liability company, LLC, with a contribution of $100,000. A has no liability for LLC's debts, and LLC has no enforceable right to a contribution from A. Under § 301.7701-3(b)(1)(ii) of this chapter, LLC is treated for federal tax purposes as a disregarded entity. Also in 2020, LLC contributes $100,000 to LP, a limited partnership with a calendar year taxable year, in exchange for a general partnership interest in LP, and B and C each contributes $100,000 to LP in exchange for a limited partnership interest in LP. The partnership agreement provides that only LLC is required to restore any deficit in its capital account. On January 1, 2021, LP borrows $300,000 from a bank and uses $600,000 to purchase nondepreciable property. The $300,000 is secured by the property and is also a general obligation of LP. LP makes payments of only interest on its $300,000 debt during

2021. LP has a net taxable loss in 2021, and, under §§1.705-1(a) and 1.752-4(d), LP determines its partners' shares of the $300,000 debt at the end of its taxable year, December 31, 2021. As of that date, LLC holds no assets other than its interest in LP.

(B) Because LLC is a disregarded entity, A is treated as the partner in LP for federal income tax purposes. Only LLC has an obligation to make a payment on account of the $300,000 debt if LP were to constructively liquidate as described in paragraph (b)(1) of this section. Therefore, paragraph (k) of this section is applied to the LLC and not to A. LLC has no assets with which to pay if the payment obligation becomes due and payable. Because there is no commercially reasonable expectation that LLC will be able to satisfy its payment obligation, LLC's obligation to restore its deficit capital account is not recognized under paragraph (b) of this section. As a result, LP's $300,000 debt is characterized as nonrecourse under §1.752-1(a)(2) and is allocated among A, B, and C under §1.752-3.

(ii) *Example 2. Disregarded entity with ability to pay.*—(A) The facts are the same as in paragraph (k)(2)(i) of this section *(Example 1)*, except LLC also holds real property worth $475,000 subject to a $200,000 liability. Additionally, LLC reasonably projects to earn $20,000 of net rental income per year from such real property.

(B) Because LLC is a disregarded entity, A is treated as the partner in LP for federal income tax purposes. Only LLC has an obligation to make a payment on account of the $300,000 debt if LP were to constructively liquidate as described in paragraph (b)(1) of this section. Therefore, paragraph (k) of this section is applied to the LLC and not to A. Because there is a commercially reasonable expectation that LLC will be able to satisfy its payment obligation, LLC's obligation to restore its deficit capital account is recognized under paragraph (b) of this section. As a result, LP's $300,000 debt is characterized as recourse under §1.752-1(a)(1) and is allocated to A under §1.752-2.

* * *

[Reg. §1.752-2.]

☐ [*T.D.* 8380, 12-20-91. *Amended by T.D.* 9289, 10-10-2006; *T.D.* 9788, 10-4-2016; *T.D.* 9790, 10-13-2016 *and T.D.* 9877, 10-4-2019.]

Proposed Amendment to Regulation

§1.752-2. Partner's share of recourse liabilities.

* * *

(b) * * *

(1) * * * Except as otherwise provided in this section, a partner bears the economic risk of loss for a partnership liability to the extent that, if the partnership constructively liquidated, the partner or related person would be obligated to make a payment to any person (or a contribution to the partnership) because that liability becomes due and payable and the partner or related person would not be entitled to reimbursement from another person. * * *

* * *

(3) [The text of proposed §1.752-2(b)(3) is the same as the text of §1.752-2T(b)(3) as added by T.D. 9788].

* * *

[Prop. Reg. §1.752-2.]

[Proposed 1-30-2014 (corrected 10-5-2016 and 10-21-2016).]

§1.752-2T. Partner's share of recourse liabilities (temporary).—(a) [Reserved].

(b) [Reserved].

(c)(1) and (2) [Reserved].

(3) *Allocation of debt deemed transferred to a partner pursuant to regulations under section 385.*—For a special rule regarding the allocation of a partnership liability that is a debt instrument with respect to which there is one or more deemed transferred receivables within the meaning of §1.385-3T(g)(8), see §1.385-3T(f)(4)(vi).

(d) through (k) [Reserved].

* * *

[Temporary Reg. §1.752-2T.]

☐ *T.D.* 9788, 10-4-2016. *Amended by T.D.* 9790, 10-13-2016 (*corrected* 1-23-2017) *and T.D.* 9877, 10-4-2019.]

§1.752-3. Partner's share of nonrecourse liabilities.—(a) *In general.*—A partner's share of the nonrecourse liabilities of a partnership equals the sum of paragraphs (a)(1) through (a)(3) of this section as follows—

(1) The partner's share of partnership minimum gain determined in accordance with the rules of section 704(b) and the regulations thereunder;

(2) The amount of any taxable gain that would be allocated to the partner under section 704(c) (or in the same manner as section 704(c) in connection with a revaluation of partnership property) if the partnership disposed of (in a taxable transaction) all partnership property subject to one or more nonrecourse liabilities of the partnership in full satisfaction of the liabilities and for no other consideration; and

(3) The partner's share of the excess nonrecourse liabilities (those not allocated under paragraphs (a)(1) and (a)(2) of this section) of

the partnership as determined in accordance with the partner's share of partnership profits. The partner's interest in partnership profits is determined by taking into account all facts and circumstances relating to the economic arrangement of the partners. The partnership agreement may specify the partners' interests in partnership profits for purposes of allocating excess nonrecourse liabilities provided the interests so specified are reasonably consistent with allocations (that have substantial economic effect under the section 704(b) regulations) of some other significant item of partnership income or gain (significant item method). Alternatively, excess nonrecourse liabilities may be allocated among the partners in accordance with the manner in which it is reasonably expected that the deductions attributable to those nonrecourse liabilities will be allocated (alternative method). Additionally, the partnership may first allocate an excess nonrecourse liability to a partner up to the amount of built-in gain that is allocable to the partner on section 704(c) property (as defined under § 1.704-3(a)(3)(ii)) or property for which reverse section 704(c) allocations are applicable (as described in § 1.704-3(a)(6)(i)) where such property is subject to the nonrecourse liability to the extent that such built-in gain exceeds the gain described in paragraph (a)(2) of this section with respect to such property (additional method). The significant item method, alternative method, and additional method do not apply for purposes of § 1.707-5(a)(2). To the extent that a partnership uses this additional method and the entire amount of the excess nonrecourse liability is not allocated to the contributing partner, the partnership must allocate the remaining amount of the excess nonrecourse liability under one of the other methods in this paragraph (a)(3). Excess nonrecourse liabilities are not required to be allocated under the same method each year.

(b) *Allocation of a single nonrecourse liability among multiple properties.*—(1) *In general.*—For purposes of determining the amount of taxable gain under paragraph (a)(2) of this section, if a partnership holds multiple properties subject to a single nonrecourse liability, the partnership may allocate the liability among the multiple properties under any reasonable method. A method is not reasonable if it allocates to any item of property an amount of the liability that, when combined with any other liabilities allocated to the property, is in excess of the fair market value of the property at the time the liability is incurred. The portion of the nonrecourse liability allocated to each item of partnership property is then treated as a separate loan under paragraph (a)(2) of this section. In general, a partnership may not change the method of allocating a single nonrecourse liability under this paragraph (b) while any portion of the liability is outstanding. However, if one or more of the multiple properties subject to the liability is no longer subject to the liability, the portion of the liability allocated to that property must be reallocated among the properties still subject to the liability so that the amount of the liability allocated to any property does not exceed the fair market value of such property at the time of reallocation.

(2) *Reductions in principal.*—For purposes of this paragraph (b), when the outstanding principal of a partnership liability is reduced, the reduction of outstanding principal is allocated among the multiple properties in the same proportion that the partnership liability originally was allocated to the properties under paragraph (b)(1) of this section.

(c) *Examples.*—The following examples illustrate the principles of this section:

Example 1. Partner's share of nonrecourse liabilities. The AB partnership purchases depreciable property for a $1,000 purchase money note that is a nonrecourse liability under the rules of this section. Assume that this is the only nonrecourse liability of the partnership, and that no principal payments are due on the purchase money note for a year. The partnership agreement provides that all items of income, gain, loss, and deduction are allocated equally. Immediately after purchasing the depreciable property, the partners share the nonrecourse liability equally because they have equal interests in partnership profits. A and B are each treated as if they contributed $500 to the partnership to reflect each partner's increase in his or her share of partnership liabilities (from $0 to $500). The minimum gain with respect to an item of partnership property subject to a nonrecourse liability equals the amount of gain that would be recognized if the partnership disposed of the property in full satisfaction of the nonrecourse liability and for no other consideration. Therefore, if the partnership claims a depreciation deduction of $200 for the depreciable property for the year it acquires that property, partnership minimum gain for the year will increase by $200 (the excess of the $1,000 nonrecourse liability over the $800 adjusted tax basis of the property). See section 704(b) and the regulations thereunder. A and B each have a $100 share of partnership minimum gain at the end of that year because the depreciation deduction is treated as a nonrecourse deduction. See section 704(b) and the regulations thereunder. Accordingly, at the end of that year, A and B are allocated $100 each of the nonrecourse liability to match their shares of partnership minimum gain. The remaining $800 of the nonrecourse liability will be allocated equally between A and B ($400 each).

Example 2. Excess nonrecourse liabilities allocated consistently with reasonably expected deductions. The facts are the same as in *Example 1* except that the partnership agreement provides that depreciation deductions will be allocated to A. The partners agree to allocate excess nonrecourse liabilities in accordance with the manner in which it is reasonably expected that the deductions attributable to those nonrecourse liabilities will be allocated. Assuming that the allocation of all of the depreciation deductions to A is valid under section 704(b), immediately after purchasing the depreciable property, A's share of the nonrecourse liability is $1,000. Accordingly, A is treated as if A contributed $1,000 to the partnership.

Example 3. Allocation of liability among multiple properties. (i) A and B are equal partners in a partnership (PRS). A contributes $70 of cash in exchange for a 50-percent interest in PRS. B contributes two items of property, X and Y, in exchange for a 50-percent interest in PRS. Property X has a fair market value (and book value) of $70 and an adjusted basis of $40, and is subject to a nonrecourse liability of $50. Property Y has a fair market value (and book value) of $120, an adjusted basis of $40, and is subject to a nonrecourse liability of $70. Immediately after the initial contributions, PRS refinances the two separate liabilities with a single $120 nonrecourse liability. All of the built-in gain attributable to Property X ($30) and Property Y ($80) is section 704(c) gain allocable to B.

(ii) The amount of the nonrecourse liability ($120) is less than the total book value of all of the properties that are subject to such liability ($70+$120=$190), so there is no partnership minimum gain. § 1.704-2(d). Accordingly, no portion of the liability is allocated pursuant to paragraph (a)(1) of this section.

(iii) Pursuant to paragraph (b)(1) of this section, PRS decides to allocate the nonrecourse liability evenly between the Properties X and Y. Accordingly, each of Properties X and Y are treated as being subject to a separate $60 nonrecourse liability for purposes of applying paragraph (a)(2) of this section. Under paragraph (a)(2) of this section, B will be allocated $20 of the liability for each of Properties X and Y (in each case, $60 liability minus $40 adjusted basis). As a result, a portion of the liability is allocated pursuant to paragraph (a)(2) of this section as follows:

Partner	*Property*	*Tier 1*	*Tier 2*
A	X	$0	$0
	Y	$0	$0
B	X	$0	$20
	Y	$0	$20

(iv) PRS has $80 of excess nonrecourse liability that it may allocate in any manner consistent with paragraph (a)(3) of this section. PRS determines to allocate the $80 of excess nonrecourse liabilities to the partners up to their share of the remaining section 704(c) gain on the properties, with any remaining amount of liabilities being allocated equally to A and B consistent with their equal interests in partnership profits. B has $70 of remaining section 704(c) gain ($10 on Property X and $60 on Property Y), and thus will be allocated $70 of the liability in accordance with this gain. The remaining $10 is divided equally between A and B. Accordingly, the overall allocation of the $120 nonrecourse liability is as follows:

Partner	*Tier 1*	*Tier 2*	*Tier 3*	*Total*
A. . . .	$0	$0	$5	$5
B . . .	$0	$40	$75	$115

(d) *Effective/applicability dates.*—The third, fourth, fifth, and sixth sentences of paragraph (a)(3) of this section apply to liabilities that are incurred, taken subject to, or assumed by a partnership on or after October 5, 2016, other than liabilities incurred, taken subject to, or assumed by a partnership pursuant to a written binding contract in effect prior to October 5, 2016. For liabilities that are incurred, taken subject to, or assumed by a partnership before October 5, 2016, the third, fourth, fifth, and sixth sentences of paragraph (a)(3) of this section as contained in 26 CFR part 1 revised as of April 1, 2016, apply. [Reg. § 1.752-3.]

☐ [*T.D.* 8380, 12-20-91. *Amended by T.D.* 8906, 10-30-2000 *and T.D.* 9787, 10-4-2016.]

§ 1.752-4. Special rules.—(a) *Tiered partnerships.*—An upper-tier partnership's share of the liabilities of a lower-tier partnership (other than any liability of the lower-tier partnership that is owed to the upper-tier partnership) is treated as a liability of the upper-tier partnership for purposes of applying section 752 and the regulations thereunder to the partners of the upper-tier partnership.

(b) *Related person definition.*—(1) *In general.*—A person is related to a partner if the person and the partner bear a relationship to each other that is specified in sections 267(b) or 707(b)(1), subject to the following modifications:

(i) Substitute "80 percent or more" for "more than 50 percent" each place it appears in those sections;

(ii) A person's family is determined by excluding brothers and sisters; and

(iii) Disregard sections 267(e)(1) and 267(f)(1)(A).

(2) *Person related to more than one partner.*—(i) *In general.*—If, in applying the related person rules in paragraph (b)(1) of this section, a person is related to more than one partner, paragraph (b)(1) of this section is applied by treating the person as related only to the partner with whom there is the highest percentage of related ownership. If two or more partners have the same percentage of related ownership and no other partner has a greater percentage, the liability is allocated equally among the partners having the equal percentages of related ownership.

(ii) *Natural persons.*—For purposes of determining the percentage of related ownership between a person and a partner, natural persons who are related by virtue of being members of the same family are treated as having a percentage relationship of 100 percent with respect to each other.

(iii) *Related partner exception.*—Notwithstanding paragraph (b)(1) of this section (which defines related person), persons owning interests directly or indirectly in the same partnership are not treated as related persons for purposes of determining the economic risk of loss borne by each of them for the liabilities of the partnership. This paragraph (iii) does not apply when determining a partner's interest under the de minimis rules in § 1.752-2(d) and (e).

(iv) *Special rule where entity structured to avoid related person status.*—(A) *In general.*—If—

(1) A partnership liability is owed to or guaranteed by another entity that is a partnership, an S corporation, a C corporation, or a trust;

(2) A partner or related person owns (directly or indirectly) a 20 percent or more ownership interest in the other entity; and

(3) A principal purpose of having the other entity act as a lender or guarantor of the liability was to avoid the determination that the partner that owns the interest bears the economic risk of loss for federal income tax purposes for all or part of the liability;

then the partner is treated as holding the other entity's interest as a creditor or guarantor to the extent of the partner's or related person's ownership interest in the entity.

(B) *Ownership interest.*—For purposes of paragraph (b)(2)(iv)(A) of this section, a person's ownership interest in:

(1) A partnership equals the partner's highest percentage interest in any item of partnership loss or deduction for any taxable year;

(2) An S corporation equals the percentage of the outstanding stock in the S corporation owned by the shareholder;

(3) A C corporation equals the percentage of the fair market value of the issued and outstanding stock owned by the shareholder; and

(4) A trust equals the percentage of the actuarial interests owned by the beneficial owner of the trust.

(C) *Example. Entity structured to avoid related person status.*—A, B, and C form a general partnership, ABC. A, B, and C are equal partners, each contributing $1,000 to the partnership. A and B want to loan money to ABC and have the loan treated as nonrecourse for purposes of section 752. A and B form partnership AB to which each contributes $50,000. A and B share losses equally in partnership AB. Partnership AB loans partnership ABC $100,000 on a nonrecourse basis secured by the property ABC buys with the loan. Under these facts and circumstances, A and B bear the economic risk of loss with respect to the partnership liability equally based on their percentage interest in losses of partnership AB.

(c) *Limitation.*—The amount of an indebtedness is taken into account only once, even though a partner (in addition to the partner's liability for the indebtedness as a partner) may be separately liable therefor in a capacity other than as a partner.

(d) *Time of determination.*—A partner's share of partnership liabilities must be determined whenever the determination is necessary in order to determine the tax liability of the partner or any other person. See § 1.705-1(a) for rules regarding when the adjusted basis of a partner's interest in the partnership must be determined. [Reg. § 1.752-4.]

□ [*T.D.* 8380, 12-20-91.]

§ 1.753-1. Partner receiving income in respect of decedent.—(a) *Income in respect of a decedent under section 736(a).*—All payments coming within the provisions of section 736(a) made by a partnership to the estate or other successor in interest of a deceased partner are considered income in respect of the decedent under section 691. The estate or other successor in interest of a deceased partner shall be considered to have received income in respect of a decedent to the extent that amounts are paid by a third person in exchange for rights to future payments from the partnership under section 736(a). When a partner who is receiving payments under section 736(a) dies, section 753 applies to any remaining payments under section 736(a) made to his estate or other successor in interest.

(b) *Other income in respect of a decedent.*—When a partner dies, the entire portion of the distributive share which is attributable to the period ending with the date of his death and which is taxable to his estate or other successor constitutes income in respect of a decedent under section 691. This rule applies even though that part of the distributive share for the period before death which the decedent withdrew is not included in the value of the decedent's partnership interest for estate tax purposes. See paragraph (c)(3) of § 1.706-1.

* * *

[Reg. § 1.753-1.]

□ [*T.D.* 6175, 5-23-56.]

§ 1.754-1. Time and manner of making election to adjust basis of partnership property.—(a) *In general.*—A partnership may adjust the basis of partnership property under sections 734(b) and 743(b) if it files an election in accordance with the rules set forth in paragraph (b) of this section. An election may not be filed to make the adjustments provided in either section 734(b) or section 743(b) alone, but such an election must apply to both sections. An election made under the provisions of this section shall apply to all property distributions and transfers of partnership interests taking place in the partnership taxable year for which the election is made and in all subsequent partnership taxable years unless the election is revoked pursuant to paragraph (c) of this section.

(b) *Time and method of making election.*—(1) An election under section 754 and this section to adjust the basis of partnership property under sections 734(b) and 743(b), with respect to a distribution of property to a partner or a transfer of an interest in a partnership, shall be made in a written statement filed with the partnership return for the taxable year during which the distribution or transfer occurs. For the election to be valid, the return must be filed not later than the time prescribed by paragraph (e) of § 1.6031-1 (including extensions thereof) for filing the return for such taxable year (or before August 23, 1956, whichever is later). Notwithstanding the preceding two sentences, if a valid election has been made under section 754 and this section for a preceding taxable year and not revoked pursuant to paragraph (c) of this section, a new election is not required to be made. The statement required by this subparagraph shall (i) set forth the name and address of the partnership making the election, (ii) be signed by any one of the partners, and (iii) contain a declaration that the partnership elects under section 754 to apply the provisions of section 734(b) and section 743(b). For rules regarding extensions of time for filing elections, see § 1.9100-1.

(2) The principles of this paragraph may be illustrated by the following example:

Example. A, a U.S. citizen, is a member of partnership ABC, which has not previously made an election under section 754 to adjust the basis of partnership property. The partnership and the partners use the calendar year as the taxable year. A sells his interest in the partnership to D on January 1, 1971. The partnership may elect under section 754 and this section to adjust the basis of partnership property under sections 734(b) and 743(b). Unless an extension of time to make the election is obtained under the provisions of § 1.9100-1, the election must be made in a written statement filed with the partnership return for 1971 and must contain the information specified in subparagraph (1) of this paragraph. Such return must be filed by April 17, 1972 (unless an extension of time for filing the return is obtained). The election will apply to all distributions of property to a partner and transfers of an interest in the partnership occurring in 1971 and subsequent years, unless revoked pursuant to paragraph (c) of this section.

(c) *Revocation of election.*—(1) *In general.*—A partnership having an election in effect under this section may revoke such election with the approval of the district director for the internal revenue district in which the partnership return is required to be filed. A partnership which wishes to revoke such an election shall file with the district director for the internal revenue district in which the partnership return is required to be filed an application setting forth the grounds on which the revocation is desired. The application shall be filed not later than 30 days after the close of the partnership taxable year with respect to which revocation is intended to take effect and shall be signed by any one of the partners. Examples of situations which may be considered sufficient reason for approving an application for revocation include a change in the nature of the partnership business, a substantial increase in the assets of the partnership, a change in the character of partnership assets, or an increased frequency of retirements or shifts of partnership interests, so that an increased administrative burden would result to the partnership from the election. However, no application for revocation of an election shall be approved when the purpose of the revocation is primarily to avoid stepping down the basis of partnership assets upon a transfer or distribution.

* * *

[Reg. § 1.754-1.]

□ [*T.D.* 6175, 5-23-56. *Amended by T.D.* 7208, 10-2-72 *and T.D.* 8847, 12-14-99 (*corrected* 2-23-2000).]

§ 1.755-1. Rules for allocation of basis.—(a) *In general.*—(1) *Scope.*—This section provides rules for allocating basis adjustments under sections 743(b) and 734(b) among partnership property. If there is a basis adjustment to which this section applies, the basis adjustment is allocated among the partnership's assets as follows. First, the partnership must determine the value of each of its assets under paragraphs (a)(2) through (5) of this section. Second, the basis adjustment is allocated between the two classes of property described in section 755(b). These classes of property consist of capital assets and section 1231(b) property (capital gain property), and any other property of the partnership (ordinary income property). For purposes of this section, properties and potential gain treated as unrealized receivables under section 751(c) and the regulations thereunder shall be treated as separate assets that are ordinary income property. Third, the portion of the basis adjustment allocated to each class is allocated among the items within the class. Basis adjustments under section 743(b) are allocated among partnership assets under paragraph (b) of this section. Basis adjustments under section 734(b) are allocated among partnership assets under paragraph (c) of this section.

(2) *Coordination of sections 755 and 1060.*—If there is a basis adjustment to which this section applies, and the assets of the partnership constitute a trade or business (as described in § 1.1060-1(b)(2)), then the partnership is required to use the residual method to assign values to the partnership's section 197 intangibles. To do so, the partnership must, first, determine the value of partnership assets other than section 197 intangibles under paragraph (a)(3) of this section. The partnership then must determine partnership gross value under paragraph (a)(4) of this section. Last, the partnership must assign values to the partnership's section 197 intangibles under paragraph (a)(5) of this section. For purposes of this section, the term *section 197 intangibles* includes all section 197 intangibles (as defined in section 197), as well as any goodwill or going concern value that would not qualify as a section 197 intangible under section 197.

(3) *Values of properties other than section 197 intangibles.*—For purposes of this section, the fair market value of each item of partnership property other than section 197 intangibles shall be determined on the basis of all the facts and circumstances, taking into account section 7701(g).

(4) *Partnership gross value.*—(i) *Basis adjustments under section 743(b).*—(A) *In general.*—Except as provided in paragraph (a)(4)(ii) of this section, in the case of a basis adjustment under section 743(b), partnership gross value generally is equal to the amount that, if assigned to all partnership property, would result in a liquidating distribution to the partner equal to the transferee's basis in the transferred partnership interest immediately following the relevant transfer (reduced by the amount, if any, of such basis that is attributable to partnership liabilities).

(B) *Special situations.*—In certain circumstances, such as where income or loss with respect to particular section 197 intangibles are allocated differently among partners, partnership gross value may vary depending on the values of particular section 197 intangibles held by the partnership. In these special situations, the partnership must assign value, first, among section 197 intangibles (other than goodwill and going concern value) in a reasonable manner that is consistent with the ordering rule in paragraph (a)(5) of this section and would cause the appropriate liquidating distribution under paragraph (a)(4)(i)(A) of this section. If the actual fair market values, determined on the basis of all the facts and circumstances, of all section 197 intangibles (other than goodwill and going concern value) is not sufficient to cause the appropriate liquidating distribution, then the fair market value of goodwill and going concern value shall be presumed to equal an amount that if assigned to goodwill and going concern value would cause the appropriate liquidating distribution.

(C) *Income in respect of a decedent.*—Solely for the purpose of determining partnership gross value under this paragraph (a)(4)(i), where a partnership interest is transferred as a result of the death of a partner, the transferee's basis in its partnership interest is determined without regard to section 1014(c) or section 1022(f), and is deemed to be adjusted for that portion of the interest, if any, that is attributable to items representing income in respect of a decedent under section 691.

(ii) *Basis adjustments under section 743(b) resulting from substituted basis transactions.*—This paragraph (a)(4)(ii) applies to basis adjustments under section 743(b) that result from exchanges in which the transferee's basis in the partnership interest is determined in whole or in part by reference to the transferor's basis in the interest or to the basis of other property held at any time by the transferee (substituted basis transactions). In the case of a substituted basis transaction, partnership gross value equals the value of the entire partnership as a going concern, increased by the amount of partnership liabilities at the time of the exchange giving rise to the basis adjustment.

(iii) *Basis adjustments under section 734(b).*—In the case of a basis adjustment under section 734(b), partnership gross value equals the value of the entire partnership as a going concern immediately following the distribution causing the adjustment, increased by the amount of partnership liabilities immediately following the distribution.

(5) *Determining the values of section 197 intangibles.*—(i) *Two classes.*—If the aggregate value of partnership property other than section 197 intangibles (as determined in paragraph (a)(3) of this section) is equal to or greater than partnership gross value (as determined in paragraph (a)(4) of this section), then all section 197 intangibles are deemed to have a value of zero for purposes of this section. In all other cases, the aggregate value of the partnership's section 197 intangibles (the residual section 197 intangibles value) is deemed to equal the excess of partnership gross value over the aggregate value of partnership property other than section 197 intangibles. The residual section 197 intangibles value must be allocated between two asset classes in the following order—

(A) Among section 197 intangibles other than goodwill and going concern value; and

(B) To goodwill and going concern value.

(ii) *Values assigned to section 197 intangibles other than goodwill and going concern value.*—The fair market value assigned to a section 197 intangible (other than goodwill and going concern value) shall not exceed the actual fair market value (determined on the basis of all the facts and circumstances) of that asset on the date of the relevant transfer. If the residual section 197 intangibles value is less than the sum of the actual fair market values (determined on the basis of all the facts and circumstances) of all section 197 intangibles (other than goodwill and going concern value) held by the partnership, then the residual section 197 intangibles value must be allocated among the individual section 197 intangibles (other than goodwill and going concern value) as follows. The residual section 197 intangibles value is assigned first to any section 197 intangibles (other than goodwill and going concern value) having potential gain that would be treated as unrealized receivables under the flush language of section 751(c) (flush language receivables) to the extent of the basis of those section 197 intangibles and the amount of income arising from the flush language receivables that the partnership would recognize if the section 197 intangibles were sold for their actual fair market values (determined based on all the facts and circumstances) (collectively, the flush language receivables value). If the value assigned to section 197 intangibles (other than goodwill and going concern value) is less than the flush language receivables value, then the assigned value is allocated among the properties giving rise to the flush language receivables in proportion to the flush language receivables value in those properties. Any remaining residual section 197 intangibles value is allocated among the remaining portions of the section 197 intangibles (other than goodwill and going concern value) in proportion to the actual fair market values of such portions (determined based on all the facts and circumstances).

(iii) *Value assigned to goodwill and going concern value.*—The fair market value of goodwill and going concern value is the amount, if any, by which the residual section 197 intangibles value exceeds the aggregate value of the partnership's section 197 intangibles (other than goodwill and going concern value).

(6) *Examples.*—The provisions of paragraphs (a)(2) through (5) are illustrated by the following examples, which assume that the partnerships have an election in effect under section 754 at the time of the transfer and that the assets of each partnership constitute a trade or business (as described in § 1.1060-1(b)(2)). Except as provided, no partnership asset (other than inventory) is property described in section 751(a), and partnership liabilities are secured by all partnership assets. The examples are as follows:

Example 1. (i) A is the sole general partner in PRS, a limited partnership having three equal partners. PRS has goodwill and going concern value, two section 197 intangibles other than goodwill and going concern value (Intangible 1 and Intangible 2), and two other assets with fair market values (determined using all the facts and circumstances) as follows: inventory worth $1,000,000 and a building (a capital asset) worth $2,000,000. The fair market value of each of Intangible 1 and Intangible 2 is $50,000. PRS has one liability of $1,000,000, for which A bears the entire risk of loss under section 752 and the regulations thereunder. D purchases A's partnership interest for $650,000, resulting in a basis adjustment under section 743(b). After the purchase, D bears the entire risk of loss for PRS's liability under section 752 and the regulations thereunder. Therefore, D's basis in its interest in PRS is $1,650,000.

(ii) D's basis in the transferred partnership interest (reduced by the amount of such basis that is attributable to partnership liabilities) is $650,000 ($1,650,000 - $1,000,000). Under paragraph (a)(4)(i) of this section, partnership gross value is $2,950,000 (the amount that, if assigned to all partnership property, would result in a liquidating distribution to D equal to $650,000).

(iii) Under paragraph (a)(3) of this section, the inventory has a fair market value of $1,000,000, and the building has a fair market value of $2,000,000. Thus, the aggregate value of partnership property other than section 197 intangibles, $3,000,000, is equal to or greater than partnership gross value, $2,950,000, Accordingly, under paragraphs (a)(3) and (5) of this section, the value assigned to each of the partnership's assets is as follows: inventory, $1,000,000; building, $2,000,000; Intangibles 1 and 2, $0; and goodwill and going concern value, $0. D's section 743(b) adjustment must be allocated under paragraph (b) of this section using these assigned fair market values.

Example 2. (i) Assume the same facts as in *Example 1*, except that the fair market values of Intangible 1 and Intangible 2 are each $300,000, and that D purchases A's interest in PRS for $1,000,000. After the purchase, D's basis in its interest in PRS is $2,000,000.

(ii) D's basis in the transferred partnership interest (reduced by the amount of such basis that is attributable to partnership liabilities) is $1,000,000 ($2,000,000 - $1,000,000). Under paragraph (a)(4)(i) of this section, partnership gross value is $4,000,000 (the amount that, if assigned to all partnership property, would result in a liquidating distribution to D equal to $1,000,000).

(iii) Under paragraph (a)(5) of this section, the residual section 197 intangibles value is $1,000,000 (the excess of partnership gross value, $4,000,000, over the aggregate value of assets other than section 197 intangibles, $3,000,000 (the sum of the value of the inventory, $1,000,000, and the value of the building, $2,000,000)). The partnership must determine the values of section 197 assets by allocating the residual section 197 intangibles value among the partnership's assets. The residual section 197 intangibles value is assigned first to section 197 intangibles other than goodwill and going concern value, and then to goodwill and going concern value. Thus, $300,000 is assigned to each of Intangible 1 and Intangible 2, and $400,000 is assigned to goodwill and going concern value (the amount by which the residual section 197 intangibles value, $1,000,000, exceeds the fair market value of section 197 intangibles other than goodwill and going concern value, $600,000). D's section 743(b) adjustment must be allocated under paragraph (b) of this section using these assigned fair market values.

Example 3. (i) Assume the same facts as in *Example 1*, except that the fair market values of Intangible 1 and Intangible 2 are each $300,000, and that D purchases A's interest in PRS for $750,000. After the purchase, D's basis in its interest in PRS is $1,750,000. Also assume that Intangible 1 was originally purchased for $300,000, and that its adjusted basis has been decreased to $50,000 as a result of amortization. Assume that, if PRS were to sell Intangible 1 for $300,000, it would recognize $250,000 of gain that would be treated as an unrealized receivable under the flush language in section 751(c).

(ii) D's basis in the transferred partnership interest (reduced by the amount of such basis that is attributable to partnership liabilities) is $750,000 ($1,750,000 - $1,000,000). Under paragraph (a)(4)(i) of this section, partnership gross value is $3,250,000 (the amount that, if assigned to all partnership property, would result in a liquidating distribution to D equal to $750,000).

(iii) Under paragraph (a)(5) of this section, the residual section 197 intangibles value is $250,000 (the amount by which partnership gross value, $3,250,000, exceeds the aggregate value of partnership property other than section 197 intangibles, $3,000,000). Intangible 1 has potential gain that would be treated as unrealized receivables under the flush language of section 751(c). The flush language receivables value in Intangible 1 is $300,000 (the sum of PRS's basis in Intangible 1, $50,000, and the amount of ordinary income, $250,000, that the partnership would recognize if Intangible 1 were sold for its actual fair market value). Because the residual section 197 intangibles value, $250,000, is less than the flush language receivables value of Intangible 1, Intangible 1 is assigned a value of $250,000, and Intangible 2 and goodwill and going concern value are assigned a value of zero. D's section 743(b) adjustment must be allocated under paragraph (b) of this section using these assigned fair market values.

Example 4. Assume the same facts as in *Example 1*, except that the fair market values of Intangible 1 and Intangible 2 are each $300,000, and that A does not sell its interest in PRS. Instead, A contributes its interest in PRS to E, a newly formed corporation wholly-owned by A, in a transaction described in section 351. Assume that the contribution results in a basis adjustment under section 743(b) (other than zero). PRS determines that its value as a going concern immediately following the contribution is $3,000,000. Under paragraph (a)(4)(ii) of this section, partnership gross value is $4,000,000 (the value of PRS as a going concern, $3,000,000, increased by the partnership's liability, $1,000,000, immediately after the contribution). Under paragraph (a)(5) of this section, the residual section 197 intangibles value is $1,000,000 (the amount by which partnership gross value, $4,000,000, exceeds the aggregate value of partnership property other than section 197 intangibles, $3,000,000). Of the residual section 197 intangibles value, $300,000 is assigned to each of Intangible 1 and Intangible 2, and $400,000 is assigned to goodwill and going concern value (the amount by which the residual section 197 intangibles value, $1,000,000, exceeds the fair market value of section 197 intangibles other than goodwill and going concern value, $600,000). E's section 743(b) adjustment must be allocated under paragraph (b)(5) of this section using these assigned fair market values.

Example 5. G is the sole general partner in PRS, a limited partnership having three equal partners (G, H, and I). PRS has goodwill and going concern value, two section 197 intangibles other than goodwill and going concern value (Intangible 1 and Intangible 2), and two capital assets with fair market values (determined using all the facts and circumstances) as follows: vacant land worth $1,000,000, and a building worth $2,000,000. The fair market value of each of Intangible 1 and Intangible 2 is $300,000. PRS has one liability of $1,000,000, for which G bears the entire risk of loss under section 752 and the regulations thereunder. PRS distributes the land to H in liquidation of H's interest in PRS. Immediately prior to the distribution, PRS's basis in the land is $800,000, and H's basis in its interest in PRS is $750,000. The distribution causes the partnership to increase the basis of its remaining property by $50,000 under section 734(b)(1)(B). PRS determines that its value as a going concern immediately following the distribution is $2,000,000. Under paragraph (a)(4)(iii) of this section, partnership gross value is $3,000,000 (the value of PRS as a going concern, $2,000,000, increased by the partnership's liability, $1,000,000, immediately after the distribution). Under paragraph (a)(5) of this section, the residual section 197 intangibles value of PRS's section 197 intangibles is $1,000,000 (the amount by which partnership gross value, $3,000,000, exceeds the aggregate value of partnership property other than section 197 intangibles, $2,000,000). Of the residual section 197 intangibles value, $300,000 is assigned to each of Intangible 1 and Intangible 2, and $400,000 is assigned to goodwill and going concern value (the amount by which the residual section 197 intangibles value, $1,000,000, exceeds the fair market value of section 197 intangibles other than goodwill and going concern value, $600,000). PRS's section 734(b) adjustment must be allocated under paragraph (c) of this section using these assigned fair market values.

(b) *Adjustments under section 743(b).*—(1) *Generally.*—(i) *Application.*—For basis adjustments under section 743(b) resulting from substituted basis transactions, paragraph (b)(5) of this section shall apply. For basis adjustments under section 743(b) resulting from all other transfers, paragraphs (b)(2) through (4) of this section shall apply. For transfers subject to section 334(b)(1)(B), see § 1.334-1(b)(3)(iii)(C)(*1*) (treating a determination of basis under § 1.334-1(b)(3) as a determination not by reference to the transferor's basis solely for purposes of applying section 755); for transfers subject to section 362(e)(1), see § 1.362-3(b)(4)(i) (treating a determination of basis under § 1.362-3 as a determination not by reference to the transferor's basis solely for purposes of applying section 755); for transfers subject to section 362(e)(2), see § 1.362-4(c)(3)(i) (treating a determination of basis under § 1.362-4 as a determination by reference to the transferor's basis for all purposes). Except as provided in paragraph (b)(5) of this section, the portion of the basis adjustment allocated to one class of property may be an increase while the portion allocated to the other class is a decrease. This would be the case even though the total amount of the basis adjustment is zero. Except as provided in paragraph (b)(5) of this section, the portion of the basis adjustment allocated to one item of property within a class may be an increase while the portion allocated to another is a decrease. This would be the case even though the basis adjustment allocated to the class is zero.

(ii) *Hypothetical transaction.*—For purposes of paragraphs (b)(2) through (b)(4) of this section, the allocation of the basis adjustment under section 743(b) between the classes of property and among the items of property within each class are made based on the allocations of income, gain, or loss (including remedial allocations under § 1.704-3(d)) that the transferee partner would receive (to the extent attributable to the acquired partnership interest) if, immediately after the transfer of the partnership interest, all of the partnership's property were disposed of in a fully taxable transaction for cash in an amount equal to the fair market value of such property (the hypothetical transaction). See § 1.460-4(k)(3)(v)(B) for a rule relating to the computation of income or loss that would be allocated to the transferee from a contract accounted for under a long-term contract method of accounting as a result of the hypothetical transaction.

(2) *Allocations between classes of property*.—(i) *In general*.—The amount of the basis adjustment allocated to the class of ordinary income property is equal to the total amount of income, gain, or loss (including any remedial allocations under § 1.704-3(d)) that would be allocated to the transferee (to the extent attributable to the acquired partnership interest) from the sale of all ordinary income property in the hypothetical transaction. The amount of the basis adjustment to capital gain property is equal to—

(A) The total amount of the basis adjustment under section 743(b); less

(B) The amount of the basis adjustment allocated to ordinary income property under the preceding sentence; provided, however, that in no event may the amount of any decrease in basis allocated to capital gain property exceed the partnership's basis (or in the case of property subject to the remedial allocation method, the transferee's share of any remedial loss under § 1.704-3(d) from the hypothetical transaction) in capital gain property. In the event that a decrease in basis allocated to capital gain property would otherwise exceed the partnership's basis in capital gain property, the excess must be applied to reduce the basis of ordinary income property.

(ii) *Examples*.—The provisions of this paragraph (b)(2) are illustrated by the following examples:

Example 1. (i) A and B form equal partnership PRS. A contributes $50,000 and Asset 1, a nondepreciable capital asset with a fair market value of $50,000 and an adjusted tax basis of $25,000. B contributes $100,000. PRS uses the cash to purchase Assets 2, 3, and 4. After a year, A sells its interest in PRS to T for $120,000. At the time of the transfer, A's share of the partnership's basis in partnership assets is $75,000. Therefore, T receives a $45,000 basis adjustment.

(ii) Immediately after the transfer of the partnership interest to T, the adjusted basis and fair market value of PRS's assets are as follows:

Assets

	Adjusted Basis	*Fair Market Value*
Capital Gain Property:		
Asset 1	$25,000	$75,000
Asset 2	100,000	117,500
Ordinary Income Property:		
Asset 3	$40,000	$45,000
Asset 4	10,000	2,500
Total	$175,000	$240,000

(iii) If PRS sold all of its assets in a fully taxable transaction at fair market value immediately after the transfer of the partnership interest to T, the total amount of capital gain that would be allocated to T is equal to $46,250 ($25,000 section 704(c) built-in gain from Asset 1, plus fifty percent of the $42,500 appreciation in capital gain property). T would also be allocated a $1,250 ordinary loss from the sale of the ordinary income property.

(iv) The amount of the basis adjustment that is allocated to ordinary income property is equal to ($1,250) (the amount of the loss allocated to T from the hypothetical sale of the ordinary income property).

(v) The amount of the basis adjustment that is allocated to capital gain property is equal to $46,250 (the amount of the basis adjustment, $45,000, less ($1,250), the amount of loss allocated to T from the hypothetical sale of the ordinary income property).

Example 2. (i) A and B form equal partnership PRS. A and B each contribute $1,000 cash which the partnership uses to purchase Assets 1, 2, 3, and 4. After a year, A sells its partnership interest to T for $1,000. T's basis adjustment under section 743(b) is zero.

(ii) Immediately after the transfer of the partnership interest to T, the adjusted basis and fair market value of PRS's assets are as follows:

Assets

	Adjusted Basis	*Fair Market Value*
Capital Gain Property:		
Asset 1	$500	$750
Asset 2	500	500
Ordinary Income Property:		
Asset 3	$500	$250
Asset 4	500	500
Total	$2,000	$2,000

(iii) If, immediately after the transfer of the partnership interest to T, PRS sold all of its assets in a fully taxable transaction at fair market value, T would be allocated a loss of $125 from the sale of the ordinary income property. Thus, the amount of the basis adjustment to ordinary income property is ($125). The amount of the basis adjustment to capital gain property is $125 (zero, the amount of the basis adjustment under section 743(b), less ($125), the amount of the basis adjustment allocated to ordinary income property).

(3) *Allocation within the class*.—(i) *Ordinary income property*.—The amount of the basis adjustment to each item of property within the class of ordinary income property is equal to—

(A) The amount of income, gain, or loss (including any remedial allocations under § 1.704-3(d)) that would be allocated to the transferee (to the extent attributable to the acquired partnership interest) from the hypothetical sale of the item; reduced by

(B) The product of—

(1) Any decrease to the amount of the basis adjustment to ordinary income property required pursuant to the last sentence of paragraph (b)(2)(i) of this section; multiplied by

(2) A fraction, the numerator of which is the fair market value of the item of property to the partnership and the denominator of which is the total fair market value of all of the partnership's items of ordinary income property.

(ii) *Capital gain property.*—The amount of the basis adjustment to each item of property within the class of capital gain property is equal to—

(A) The amount of income, gain, or loss (including any remedial allocations under § 1.704-3(d)) that would be allocated to the transferee (to the extent attributable to the acquired partnership interest) from the hypothetical sale of the item; minus

(B) The product of—

(1) The total amount of gain or loss (including any remedial allocations under § 1.704-3(d)) that would be allocated to the transferee (to the extent attributable to the acquired partnership interest) from the hypothetical sale of all items of capital gain property, minus the amount of the positive basis adjustment to all items of capital gain property or plus the amount of the negative basis adjustment to capital gain property; multiplied by

(2) A fraction, the numerator of which is the fair market value of the item of property to the partnership, and the denominator of which is the fair market value of all of the partnership's items of capital gain property.

(iii) *Special rules.*—(A) *Assets in which partner has no interest.*—An asset with respect to which the transferee partner has no interest in income, gain, losses, or deductions shall not be taken into account in applying paragraph (b)(3)(ii)(B) of this section.

(B) *Limitation in decrease of basis.*—In no event may the amount of any decrease in basis allocated to an item of capital gain property under paragraph (b)(3)(ii)(B) of this section exceed the partnership's adjusted basis in that item (or in the case of property subject to the remedial allocation method, the transferee's share of any remedial loss under § 1.704-3(d) from the hypothetical transaction). In the event that a decrease in basis allocated under paragraph (b)(3)(ii)(B) of this section to an item of capital gain property would otherwise exceed the partnership's adjusted basis in that item, the excess must be applied to reduce the remaining basis, if any, of other capital gain assets pro rata in proportion to the bases of such assets (as adjusted under this paragraph (b)(3)).

(iv) *Examples.*—The provisions of this paragraph (b)(3) are illustrated by the following examples:

Example 1. (i) Assume the same facts as Example 1 in paragraph (b)(2)(ii) of this section. Of the $45,000 basis adjustment, $46,250 was allocated to capital gain property. The amount allocated to ordinary income property was ($1,250).

(ii) Asset 1 is a capital gain asset, and T would be allocated $37,500 from the sale of Asset 1 in the hypothetical transaction. Therefore, the amount of the adjustment to Asset 1 is $37,500.

(iii) Asset 2 is a capital gain asset, and T would be allocated $8,750 from the sale of Asset 2 in the hypothetical transaction. Therefore, the amount of the adjustment to Asset 2 is $8,750.

(iv) Asset 3 is ordinary income property, and T would be allocated $2,500 from the sale of Asset 3 in the hypothetical transaction. Therefore, the amount of the adjustment to Asset 3 is $2,500.

(v) Asset 4 is ordinary income property, and T would be allocated ($3,750) from the sale of Asset 4 in the hypothetical transaction. Therefore, the amount of the adjustment to Asset 4 is ($3,750).

Example 2. (i) Assume the same facts as Example 1 in paragraph (b)(2)(ii) of this section, except that A sold its interest in PRS to T for $110,000 rather than $120,000. T, therefore, receives a basis adjustment under section 743(b) of $35,000. Of the $35,000 basis adjustment, ($1,250) is allocated to ordinary income property, and $36,250 is allocated to capital gain property.

(ii) Asset 3 is ordinary income property, and T would be allocated $2,500 from the sale of Asset 3 in the hypothetical transaction. Therefore, the amount of the adjustment to Asset 3 is $2,500.

(iii) Asset 4 is ordinary income property, and T would be allocated ($3,750) from the sale of Asset 4 in the hypothetical transaction. Therefore, the amount of the adjustment to Asset 4 is ($3,750).

(iv) Asset 1 is a capital gain asset, and T would be allocated $37,500 from the sale of Asset 1 in the hypothetical transaction. Asset 2 is a capital gain asset, and T would be allocated $8,750 from the sale of Asset 2 in the hypothetical transaction. The total amount of gain that would be allocated to T from the sale of the capital gain assets in the hypothetical transaction is $46,250, which exceeds the amount of the basis adjustment allocated to capital gain property by $10,000. The amount of the adjustment to Asset 1 is $33,604 ($37,500 minus $3,896 ($10,000 × $75,000/192,500)). The amount of the basis adjustment to Asset 2 is $2,646 ($8,750 minus $6,104 ($10,000 × $117,500/192,500)).

(4) *Income in respect of a decedent.*—(i) *In general.*—Where a partnership interest is transferred as a result of the death of a partner, under section 1014(c) or section 1022(f), the transferee's basis in its partnership interest is not adjusted for that portion of the interest, if any, that is attributable to items representing income in respect of a decedent under section 691. See § 1.742-1. Accordingly, if a partnership interest is transferred as a result of the death of a partner, and the partnership holds assets representing income in respect of a decedent, no part of the basis adjustment under section 743(b) is allocated to these assets. See § 1.743-1(b).

(ii) The provisions of this paragraph (b)(4) are illustrated by the following example:

Example. (i) A and B are equal partners in personal service partnership PRS. In 2004, as a result of B's death, B's partnership interest is transferred to T when PRS's balance sheet (reflecting a cash receipts and disbursements method of accounting) is as follows (based on all the facts and circumstances):

Assets

	Adjusted Basis	*Fair Market Value*
Section 197 Intangible	$2,000	$5,000
Unrealized Receivables . . .	0	15,000
Total	$2,000	$20,000

Liabilities and Capital

	Adjusted Per Books	*Fair Market Value*
Capital:		
A	$1,000	$10,000
B	1,000	10,000
Total	$2,000	$20,000

(ii) None of the assets owned by PRS is section 704(c) property, and the section 197 intangible is not amortizable. The fair market value of T's partnership interest on the applicable date of valuation set forth in section 1014 is $10,000. Of this amount, $2,500 is attributable to T's 50% share of the partnership's section 197 intangible, and $7,500 is attributable to T's 50% share of the partnership's unrealized receivables. The partnership's unrealized receivables represent income in respect of a decedent. Accordingly, under section 1014(c), T's basis in its partnership interest is not adjusted for that portion of the interest which is attributable to the unrealized receivables. Therefore, T's basis in its partnership interest is $2,500.

(iii) Under paragraph (a)(4)(i)(C) of this section, solely for purposes of determining partnership gross value, T's basis in its partnership interest is deemed to be $10,000. Under paragraph (a)(4)(i) of this section, partnership gross value is $20,000 (the amount that, if assigned to all partnership property, would result in a liquidating distribution to T equal to $10,000).

(iv) Under paragraph (a)(5) of this section, the residual section 197 intangibles value is $5,000 (the excess of partnership gross value, $20,000, over the aggregate value of assets other than section 197 intangibles, $15,000). The residual section 197 intangibles value is assigned first to section 197 intangibles other than goodwill and going concern value, and then to goodwill and going concern value. Thus, $5,000 is assigned to the section 197 intangible, and $0 is assigned to goodwill and going concern value. T's section 743(b) adjustment must be allocated using these assigned fair market values.

(v) At the time of the transfer, B's share of the partnership's basis in partnership assets is $1,000. Accordingly, T receives a $1,500 basis adjustment under section 743(b). Under this paragraph (b)(4), the entire basis adjustment is allocated to the partnership's section 197 intangible.

(5) *Substituted basis transactions.*—(i) *In general.*—This paragraph (b)(5) applies to basis adjustments under section 743(b) that result from exchanges in which the transferee's basis in the partnership interest is determined in whole or in part by reference to the transferor's basis in that interest. For exchanges on or after June 9, 2003, this paragraph (b)(5) also applies to basis adjustments under section 743(b) that result from exchanges in which the transferee's basis in the partnership interest is determined by reference to other property held at any time by the transferee. For example, this paragraph (b)(5) applies if a partnership interest is contributed to a corporation in a transaction to which section 351 applies, if a partnership interest is contributed to a partnership in a transaction to which section 721(a) applies, or if a partnership interest is distrib-

uted by a partnership in a transaction to which section 731(a) applies.

(ii) *Allocations between classes of property.*—If the total amount of the basis adjustment under section 743(b) is zero, then no adjustment to the basis of partnership property will be made under this paragraph (b)(5). If there is an increase in basis to be allocated to partnership assets, such increase must be allocated to capital gain property or ordinary income property, respectively, only if the total amount of gain or loss (including any remedial allocations under § 1.704-3(d)) that would be allocated to the transferee (to the extent attributable to the acquired partnership interest) from the hypothetical sale of all such property would result in a net gain or net income, as the case may be, to the transferee. Where, under the preceding sentence, an increase in basis may be allocated to both capital gain assets and ordinary income assets, the increase shall be allocated to each class in proportion to the net gain or net income, respectively, which would be allocated to the transferee from the sale of all assets in each class. If there is a decrease in basis to be allocated to partnership assets, such decrease must be allocated to capital gain property or ordinary income property, respectively, only if the total amount of gain or loss (including any remedial allocations under § 1.704-3(d)) that would be allocated to the transferee (to the extent attributable to the acquired partnership interest) from the hypothetical sale of all such property would result in a net loss to the transferee. Where, under the preceding sentence, a decrease in basis may be allocated to both capital gain assets and ordinary income assets, the decrease shall be allocated to each class in proportion to the net loss which would be allocated to the transferee from the sale of all assets in each class.

(iii) *Allocations within the classes.*—(A) *Increases.*—If there is an increase in basis to be allocated within a class, the increase must be allocated first to properties with unrealized appreciation in proportion to the transferee's share of the respective amounts of unrealized appreciation before such increase (but only to the extent of the transferee's share of each property's unrealized appreciation). Any remaining increase must be allocated among the properties within the class in proportion to the transferee's share of the amount that would be realized by the partnership upon the hypothetical sale of each asset in the class.

(B) *Decreases.*—If there is a decrease in basis to be allocated within a class, the decrease must be allocated first to properties with unrealized depreciation in proportion to the transferee's shares of the respective amounts of unrealized depreciation before such decrease (but only to the extent of the transferee's share of each property's unrealized depreciation). Any remaining decrease must be allocated among the properties within the class in proportion to the transferee's shares of their adjusted bases (as adjusted under the preceding sentence).

(C) *Limitation in decrease of basis.*—Where, as the result of a transaction to which this paragraph (b)(5) applies, a decrease in basis must be allocated to capital gain assets, ordinary income assets, or both, and the amount of the decrease otherwise allocable to a particular class exceeds the transferee's share of the adjusted basis to the partnership of all depreciated assets in that class, the transferee's negative basis adjustment is limited to the transferee's share of the partnership's adjusted basis in all depreciated assets in that class.

(D) *Carryover adjustment.*—Where a transferee's negative basis adjustment under section 743(b) cannot be allocated to any asset, because the adjustment exceeds the transferee's share of the adjusted basis to the partnership of all depreciated assets in a particular class, the adjustment is made when the partnership subsequently acquires property of a like character to which an adjustment can be made.

(iv) *Examples.*—The provisions of this paragraph (b)(5) are illustrated by the following examples:

Example 1. A is a member of partnership LTP, which has made an election under section 754. The three partners in LTP have equal interests in capital and profits. Solely in exchange for a partnership interest in UTP, A contributes its interest in LTP to UTP in a transaction described in section 721. At the time of the transfer, A's basis in its partnership interest ($5,000) equals its share of inside basis (also $5,000). Under section 723, UTP's basis in its interest in LTP is $5,000. LTP's only two assets on the date of contribution are inventory with a basis of $5,000 and a fair market value of $7,500, and a nondepreciable capital asset with a basis of $10,000 and a fair market value of $7,500. The amount of the basis adjustment under section 743(b) to partnership property is $0 ($5,000, UTP's basis in its interest in LTP, minus $5,000, UTP's share of LTP's basis in partnership assets). Because UTP acquired its interest in LTP in a substituted basis transaction, and the total amount of the basis adjustment under section 743(b) is zero, UTP receives no special basis adjustments under section 743(b) with respect to the partnership property of LTP.

Example 2. (i) A purchases a partnership interest in LTP at a time when an election under section 754 is not in effect. The three partners in LTP have equal interests in capital and profits. During a later year for which LTP has an election under section 754 in effect, and in a transaction that is unrelated to A's purchase of the LTP interest, A contributes its interest in LTP to UTP in a transaction described in section 721 (solely in exchange for a partnership interest in UTP). At the time of the transfer, A's adjusted basis in its interest in LTP is $20,433. Under section 721, A recognizes no gain or loss as a result of the contribution of its partnership interest to UTP. Under section 723, UTP's basis in its partnership interest in LTP is $20,433. The balance sheet of LTP on the date of the contribution shows the following:

Assets

	Adjusted Basis	*Fair Market Value*
Cash	$5,000	$5,000
Accounts receivable	10,000	10,000
Inventory	20,000	21,000
Nondepreciable capital asset	20,000	40,000
Total	$55,000	$76,000

Liabilities and Capital

	Adjusted Per Books	*Fair Market Value*
Liabilities	$10,000	$10,000
Capital:		
A	15,000	22,000
B	15,000	22,000
C	15,000	22,000
Total	$55,000	$76,000

(ii) The amount of the basis adjustment under section 743(b) is the difference between the basis of UTP's interest in LTP and UTP's share of the adjusted basis to LTP of partnership property. UTP's interest in the previously taxed capital of LTP is $15,000 ($22,000, the amount of cash UTP would receive if LTP liquidated immediately after the hypothetical transaction, decreased by $7,000, the amount of tax gain allocated to UTP from the hypothetical transaction). UTP's share of the adjusted basis to LTP of partnership property is $18,333 ($15,000 share of previously taxed capital, plus $3,333 share of LTP's liabilities). The amount of the basis adjustment under section 743(b) to partnership property therefore, is $2,100 ($20,433 minus $18,333).

(iii) The total amount of gain that would be allocated to UTP from the hypothetical sale of capital gain property is $6,666.67 (one-third of the excess of the fair market value of LTP's nondepreciable capital asset, $40,000, over its basis, $20,000). The total amount of gain that would be allocated to UTP from the hypothetical sale of ordinary income property is $333.33 (one-third of the excess of the fair market value of LTP's inventory, $21,000, over its basis, $20,000). Under this paragraph (b)(5), LTP must allocate $2,000 ($6,666.67 divided by $7,000 times $2,100) of UTP's basis adjustment to the nondepreciable capital asset. LTP must allocate $100 ($333.33 divided by $7,000 times $2,100) of UTP's basis adjustment to the inventory.

(c) *Adjustments under section 734(b).*—(1) *Allocations between classes of property.*—(i) *General rule.*—Where there is a distribution of partnership property resulting in an adjustment to the basis of undistributed partnership property under section 734(b)(1)(B) or (b)(2)(B), the adjustment must be allocated to remaining partnership property of a character similar to that of the distributed property with respect to which the adjustment arose. Thus, when the partnership's adjusted basis of distributed capital gain property immediately prior to distribution exceeds the basis of the property to the distributee partner (as determined under section 732), the basis of the undistributed capital gain property remaining in the partnership is increased by an amount equal to the excess. Conversely, when the basis to the distributee partner (as determined under section 732) of distributed capital gain property exceeds the partnership's adjusted basis of such property immediately prior to the distribution, the basis of the undistributed capital gain property remaining in the partnership is decreased by an amount equal to such excess. Similarly, where there is a distribution of ordinary income property, and the basis of the property to the distributee partner (as determined under section 732) is not the same as the partnership's adjusted basis of the property immediately prior to distribution, the adjustment is made only to undistributed property of the same class remaining in the partnership.

(ii) *Special rule.*—Where there is a distribution resulting in an adjustment under section 734(b)(1)(A) or (b)(2)(A) to the basis of undistributed partnership property, the adjustment is allocated only to capital gain property.

(2) *Allocations within the classes.*—(i) *Increases.*—If there is an increase in basis to be allocated within a class, the increase must be allocated first to properties with unrealized appreciation in proportion to their respective amounts of unrealized appreciation before such increase (but only to the extent of each property's unrealized appreciation). Any remaining

increase must be allocated among the properties within the class in proportion to their fair market values.

(ii) *Decreases.*—If there is a decrease in basis to be allocated within a class, the decrease must be allocated first to properties with unrealized depreciation in proportion to their respective amounts of unrealized depreciation before such decrease (but only to the extent of each property's unrealized depreciation). Any remaining decrease must be allocated among the properties within the class in proportion to their adjusted bases (as adjusted under the preceding sentence).

(3) *Limitation in decrease of basis.*—Where a decrease in the basis of partnership assets is required under section 734(b)(2) and the amount of the decrease exceeds the adjusted basis to the partnership of property of the required character, the basis of such property is reduced to zero (but not below zero).

(4) *Carryover adjustment.*—Where, in the case of a distribution, an increase or a decrease in the basis of undistributed property cannot be made because the partnership owns no property of the character required to be adjusted, or because the basis of all the property of a like character has been reduced to zero, the adjustment is made when the partnership subsequently acquires property of a like character to which an adjustment can be made.

(5) *Cross reference.*—See § 1.460-4 (k)(3)(v)(B) for a rule relating to the computation of unrealized appreciation or depreciation in a contract accounted for under a long-term contract method of accounting.

(6) *Example.*—The following example illustrates this paragraph (c):

Example. (i) A, B, and C form equal partnership PRS. A contributes $50,000 and Asset 1, nondepreciable capital gain property with a fair market value of $50,000 and an adjusted tax basis of $25,000. B and C each contributes $100,000. PRS uses the cash to purchase Assets 2, 3, 4, 5, and 6. Assets 2 and 3 are nondepreciable capital assets, and Assets 4, 5, and 6 are inventory that has not appreciated substantially in value within the meaning of section 751(b)(3). Assets 4, 5, and 6 are the only assets held by the partnership that are subject to section 751. The partnership has an election in effect under section 754. After seven years, the adjusted basis and fair market value of PRS's assets are as follows:

Assets

	Adjusted Basis	*Fair Market Value*
Capital Gain Property:		
Asset 1	$25,000	$75,000
Asset 2	100,000	117,500
Asset 3	50,000	60,000
Ordinary Income Property:		
Asset 4	$40,000	$45,000
Asset 5	50,000	60,000
Asset 6	10,000	2,500
Total	$275,000	$360,000

(ii) *Allocation between classes.* Assume that PRS distributes Assets 3 and 5 to A in complete liquidation of A's interest in the partnership. A's basis in the partnership interest was $75,000. The partnership's basis in Assets 3 and 5 was $50,000 each. A's $75,000 basis in its partnership interest is allocated between Assets 3 and 5 under sections 732(b) and (c). A will, therefore, have a basis of $25,000 in Asset 3 (capital gain property), and a basis of $50,000 in Asset 5 (section 751 property). The distribution results in a $25,000 increase in the basis of capital gain property. There is no change in the basis of ordinary income property.

(iii) *Allocation within class.* The amount of the basis increase to capital gain property is $25,000 and must be allocated among the remaining capital gain assets in proportion to the difference between the fair market value and basis of each. The fair market value of Asset 1 exceeds its basis by $50,000. The fair market value of Asset 2 exceeds its basis by $17,500. Therefore, the basis of Asset 1 will be increased by $18,519 ($25,000, multiplied by $50,000, divided by $67,500), and the basis of Asset 2 will be increased by $6,481 ($25,000 multiplied by $17,500, divided by $67,500).

* * *

[Reg. § 1.755-1.]

☐ [*T.D.* 6175, 5-23-56. *Amended by T.D.* 8847, 12-14-99 (*corrected* 2-23-2000); *T.D.* 9059, 6-6-2003; *T.D.* 9137, 7-15-2004; *T.D.* 9759, 3-25-2016 *and T.D.* 9811, 1-18-2017.]

Proposed Amendment to Regulation

§ 1.755-1. Rules for allocation of basis.

* * *

(b) * * *

* * *

(5) *Substituted basis transactions.*—(i) *In general.*—This paragraph (b)(5) applies to basis adjustments under section 743(b) that result from exchanges in which the transferee's basis in the partnership interest is determined in whole or in part by reference to the trans-

feror's basis in that interest and from exchanges in which the transferee's basis in the partnership interest is determined by reference to other property held at any time by the transferee. For example, this paragraph (b)(5) applies if a partnership interest is contributed to a corporation in a transaction to which section 351 applies, if a partnership interest is contributed to a partnership in a transaction to which section 721(a) applies, or if a partnership interest is distributed by a partnership in a transaction to which section 731(a) applies.

(ii) *Allocations between classes of property.*—(A) *No adjustment.*—If the total amount of the basis adjustment under section 743(b) is zero, then no adjustment to the basis of partnership property will be made under this paragraph (b)(5).

(B) *Increases.*—If there is an increase in basis to be allocated to partnership assets, the increase must be allocated between capital gain property and ordinary income property in proportion to, and to the extent of, the gross gain or gross income (including any remedial allocations under § 1.704-3(d)) that would be allocated to the transferee (to the extent attributable to the acquired partnership interest) from the hypothetical sale of all property in each class. Any remaining increase must be allocated between the classes in proportion to the fair market value of all property in each class.

(C) *Decreases.*—If there is a decrease in basis to be allocated to partnership assets, the decrease must be allocated between capital gain property and ordinary income property in proportion to, and to the extent of, the gross loss (including any remedial allocations under § 1.704-3(d)) that would be allocated to the transferee (to the extent attributable to the acquired partnership interest) from the hypothetical sale of all property in each class. Any remaining decrease must be allocated between the classes in proportion to the transferee's shares of the adjusted bases of all property in each class (as adjusted under the preceding sentence).

(iii) *Allocations within the classes.*—(A) *Increases.*—If, under paragraph (b)(5)(ii) of this section, there is an increase in basis to be allocated within a class, the increase must be allocated first to properties with unrealized appreciation in proportion to the transferee's share of the respective amounts of unrealized appreciation (to the extent attributable to the acquired partnership interest) before the increase (but only to the extent of the transferee's share of each property's unrealized appreciation). Any remaining increase must be allocated among the properties within the class in proportion to their fair market values.

(B) *Decreases.*—If, under paragraph (b)(5)(ii) of this section, there is a decrease in basis to be allocated within a class, the decrease must be allocated first to properties with unrealized depreciation in proportion to the transferee's shares of the respective amounts of unrealized depreciation (to the extent attributable to the acquired partnership interest) before the decrease (but only to the extent of the transferee's share of each property's unrealized depreciation). Any remaining decrease must be allocated among the properties within the class in proportion to the transferee's shares of their adjusted bases (as adjusted under the preceding sentence).

(C) *Limitation in decrease of basis.*—Where, as a result of a transaction to which this paragraph (b)(5) applies, a decrease in basis must be allocated to capital gain assets, ordinary income assets, or both, and the amount of the decrease otherwise allocable to a particular class exceeds the transferee's share of the adjusted basis to the partnership of all assets in that class, the basis of the property is reduced to zero (but not below zero).

(D) *Carryover adjustment.*—Where a transferee's negative basis adjustment under section 743(b) cannot be allocated to any asset, the adjustment is made when the partnership subsequently acquires property of a like character to which an adjustment can be made.

(iv) *Examples.*—The provisions of this paragraph (b)(5) are illustrated by the following examples—

Example 1. * * *

Example 2. * * *

Example 3—(i) A is a one-third partner in UTP, a partnership, which has a valid election in effect under section 754. The three partners in UTP have equal interests in the capital and profits of UTP. UTP has three assets with the following adjusted bases and fair market values:

Assets	Adjusted basis	Fair market value
Intangible 1	$30	$200
Land	$200	$200
50% interest in LTP	$190	$200

LTP, a partnership, has a section 754 election in effect for the year of the distribution. LTP owns three assets with the following adjusted bases and fair market values:

Assets	Adjusted basis	Fair market value
Intangible 2	$340	$100
Intangible 3	$20	$280
Inventory	$20	$20

UTP distributes its interest in LTP in redemption of A's interest in UTP. At the time of the distribution, A's adjusted basis in its UTP interest is $140. A recognizes no gain or loss on the distribution. Under section 732(b), A's basis in the distributed LTP interest is $140. Under sections 734(b) and 755, UTP increases its adjusted basis in Intangible 1 by $50, the amount of the basis adjustment to the LTP interest in the hands of A.

(ii) The amount of the basis adjustment with respect to LTP under section 743(b) is the difference between A's basis in LTP of $140 and A's share of the adjusted basis to LTP of partnership property. A's share of the adjusted basis to LTP of partnership property is equal to the sum of A's share of LTP's liabilities of $0 plus A's interest in the previously taxed capital of LTP of $190 ($200, A's cash on liquidation, increased by $120, the amount of tax loss allocated to A from the sale of Intangible 2 in the hypothetical transaction, decreased by $130, the amount of tax gain allocated to A from the sale of Intangible 3 in the hypothetical transaction). Therefore, the amount of the negative basis adjustment under section 743(b) to partnership property is $50.

(iii) Under this paragraph (b)(5), LTP must allocate $50 of A's negative basis adjustment between capital gain property and ordinary income property in proportion to, and to the extent of, the gross loss (including any remedial allocations under § 1.704-3(d)) that would be allocated to A from the hypothetical sale of all property in each class. If LTP disposed of its assets in a hypothetical sale, A would be allocated $120 of gross loss from Intangible 2 only. Accordingly, the $50 negative adjustment must be allocated to capital assets. Under paragraph (b)(5)(iii)(B) of this section, the $50 negative adjustment must be allocated to the assets in the capital class first to properties with unrealized depreciation in proportion to the transferee's shares of the respective amounts of unrealized depreciation. Thus, the $50 negative adjustment must be allocated entirely to Intangible 2.

Example 4—(i) A is a one-third partner in LTP. The three partners in LTP have equal interests in the capital and profits of LTP. LTP has two assets: accounts receivable with an adjusted basis of $300 and a fair market value of $240 and a nondepreciable capital asset with an adjusted basis of $60 and a fair market value of $240. A contributes its interest in LTP to UTP in a transaction described in section 721. At the time of the transfer, A's basis in its LTP interest is $90. Under section 723, UTP's basis in its interest in LTP is $90. LTP makes an election under section 754 in connection with the transfer.

(ii) The amount of the basis adjustment under section 743(b) is the difference between UTP's $90 basis in its LTP interest and UTP's share of the adjusted basis to LTP of LTP's property. UTP's share of the adjusted basis to LTP of LTP's property is equal to the sum of UTP's share of LTP's liabilities of $0 plus UTP's interest in the previously taxed capital of LTP of $120 ($160, the amount of cash on liquidation, increased by $20, the amount of tax loss allocated to UTP from the hypothetical transaction, and decreased by $60, the amount of tax gain allocated to UTP from the hypothetical transaction). Therefore, the amount of the negative basis adjustment under section 743(b) to partnership property is $30.

(iii) The total amount of gross loss that would be allocated to UTP from the hypothetical sale of LTP's ordinary income property is $20 (one third of the excess of the basis of the accounts receivable ($300) over their fair market value ($240)). The hypothetical sale of LTP's capital gain property would result in a net gain. Therefore, under this paragraph (b)(5), $20 of the $30 basis adjustment must be allocated to ordinary income property. Because LTP holds only one ordinary income property, the $20 decrease must be allocated entirely to the accounts receivable. Pursuant to paragraph (b)(5)(ii)(C) of this section, the remaining $10 basis adjustment must be allocated between ordinary income property and capital gain property according to UTP's share of the adjusted bases of such properties. Therefore, $8 ($10 multiplied by $80 divided by $100) would be allocated to the accounts receivable and $2 ($10 multiplied by $20 divided by $100) would be allocated to the nondepreciable capital asset.* * *

* * *

[Prop. Reg. § 1.755-1.]

[Proposed 1-16-2014 (corrected 4-15-2014).]

Proposed Amendments to Regulation

§ 1.755-1. Rules for allocation of basis.

* * *

(c) * * *

(2) * * *

(iii) *Coordination with section 1245 and similar provisions.*—Any increase in basis allocated to capital gain property pursuant to the second sentence in paragraph (c)(2)(i) of this section is not taken into account in determining the recomputed or adjusted basis in the property for purposes of section 1245(a)(1). Notwithstanding the prior sentence, any depreciation or amortization of the increase in basis that is allowed or allowable is taken into account in computing the property's recomputed basis. In the case of property that is subject to section 617(d)(1), 1250(a)(1), 1252(a)(1), or 1254(a)(1), rules similar to the rule in this paragraph (c)(2)(iii) shall apply.

(iv) *Coordination with section 1231.*—Any increase in basis allocated to capital gain property pursuant to the second sentence in paragraph (c)(2)(i) of this section is not taken into account in determining section 1231 gain and loss, as defined in section 1231(a)(3). Any basis adjustment to an asset not taken into account pursuant to this paragraph (c)(2)(iv) shall be treated as gain from the sale or exchange of a capital asset with the same holding period as the underlying asset.

(v) *Coordination with sections 1248 and 995.*—Any increase in basis allocated to stock in a foreign corporation pursuant to the second sentence in paragraph (c)(2)(i) of this section, or any decrease in basis allocated to stock in a foreign corporation pursuant to the second sentence in paragraph (c)(2)(ii) of this section, is not taken into account in determining the amount of gain recognized on the sale or exchange of such stock for purposes of section 1248(a). In the case of property that is subject to section 995(c), rules similar to the rule set forth in this paragraph (c)(2)(v) shall apply.

(vi) *Election not to apply the provisions of paragraphs (c)(2)(iii), (iv), and (v).*—A partnership may elect not to apply paragraphs (c)(2)(iii), (iv), and (v) of this section, and § 1.732-1(c)(2)(iii), (iv), and (v). An election made under this paragraph (c)(2)(vi) shall apply to all property distributions taking place in the partnership taxable year for which the election is made and in all subsequent partnership taxable years (including after a termination of the partnership under section 708(b)(1)(B)). An election under this paragraph (c)(2)(vi) must be made in a written statement filed with the partnership return for the first taxable year in which any of paragraph (c)(2)(iii), (iv), or (v) of this section, or § 1.732-1(c)(2)(iii), (iv), or (v), would have applied if no election was made. An election under this paragraph (c)(2)(vi) is valid only if the required statement is included with a partnership return that is filed not later than the time prescribed by paragraph (e) of this section or § 1.6031(a)-1 (including extensions thereof) for filing the return for such taxable year. This election is a method of accounting under section 446, and once the election is made, it can be revoked only with the consent of the Commissioner. The revocation of the election, or the making of a late election, under this paragraph (c)(2)(vi) is a change in method of accounting to which the provisions of section 446(e) and the regulations under section 446(e) apply. *See* paragraph (c)(6), *Example 3*, of this section for the treatment of a section 734(b) adjustment if an election under this paragraph (c)(2)(vi) is made, and certain consequences of the election under section 751(b). The statement required by this paragraph (c)(2)(vi) shall—

(A) Set forth the name and address of the partnership making the election;

(B) Be signed by any officer, manager, or member of the partnership who is authorized (under local law or the partnership's organizational documents) to make the election and who represents to having such authorization under penalties of perjury; and

(C) Contain a declaration that the partnership elects not to apply paragraphs (c)(2)(iii), (iv), and (v) of this section and § 1.732-1(c)(2)(iii), (iv), and (v).

* * *

(6) *Examples.*—The following examples illustrate this paragraph (c):

* * *

Example 2. (i) A, B, and C are equal partners in ABC. Each partner has an outside basis in its partnership interest of $20. ABC owns depreciable equipment X with an adjusted basis of $30 and a fair market value of $150 and depreciable equipment Y with an adjusted basis of $30 and a fair market value of $30. ABC has made an election under section 754.

(ii) The depreciable equipment X has $120 of adjustments reflected in its adjusted basis within the meaning of § 1.1245-2(a)(2). Accordingly, the entire $120 of the gain with respect to depreciable equipment X would be treated as gain to which section 1245(a)(1) would apply if the partnership sold the depreciable equipment X for its fair market value. ABC, therefore, has a $120 unrealized receivable within the meaning of § 1.751-1(c)(4)(iii). Assume ABC makes a current distribution of the depreciable equipment Y to A. Because A's basis in his partnership interest is only $20, A's basis in the depreciable equipment Y will be limited to $20 under section 732(a). Under section 734(b), ABC will increase the basis in its capital gain property by $10 and will not adjust the basis of ordinary income property. Assume ABC has not made an election under § 1.755-1(c)(2)(vi).

(iii) *Allocation between classes.* Pursuant to § 1.755-1(a)(1), ABC's $120 unrealized receivable associated with the depreciable equipment

X is treated as a separate asset that is ordinary income property. Thus, ABC is treated as having two assets (each actually a component of the single asset, equipment X) after the distribution, one that is capital gain property with a basis of $30 and a fair market value of $30, and one that is ordinary income property with a basis of $0 and a fair market value of $120.

(iv) *Allocation within class.* ABC must allocate the $10 basis increase entirely to the capital gain portion of the depreciable equipment X, as it holds no other capital gain property after it distributes the depreciable equipment Y to A. Therefore, ABC increases the basis of the capital gain property to $40.

(v) *Treatment of section 734(b) adjustment.* Pursuant to paragraph (c)(2)(iii) of this section, if ABC sold its depreciable equipment X for $150 immediately after the distribution to A, ABC would not take into account the $10 section 734(b) adjustment in determining ABC's recomputed or adjusted basis in the depreciable equipment X for purposes of section 1245(a)(1) and, accordingly, would recognize $120 of ordinary income. Also pursuant to paragraph (c)(2)(iv) of this section, the $10 section 734(b) adjustment is not taken into account for purposes of determining section 1231 gain or loss. Thus, pursuant to paragraph (c)(2)(vi) of this section, ABC would recognize a $10 capital loss.

(vi) *Treatment of additional depreciation and appreciation.* (A) Assume, instead, that ABC continues to own the equipment and takes additional depreciation deductions of $16 ($15 with respect to the original remaining $30 basis and $1 with respect to the additional $10 basis resulting from the section 734(b) adjustment). At a time when the equipment has appreciated in value to $170, ABC sells the depreciable equipment X for $170 in a taxable transaction. In that same taxable year, ABC does not sell any other property used in its trade or business.

(B) Pursuant to section 1245(a)(1), ABC must recognize ordinary income in an amount by which the lesser of the following two amounts exceeds ABC's adjusted basis in the depreciable equipment X—

(*1*) ABC's recomputed basis in the depreciable equipment, or

(*2*) ABC's amount realized;

(C) Pursuant to section 1245(a)(2)(A), ABC's recomputed basis is an amount equal to the sum of—

(*1*) ABC's adjusted basis of the property, plus

(*2*) The amount of adjustments reflected in the adjusted basis on account of deductions allowed or allowable.

(D) Pursuant to (c)(2)(iii) of this section, the $9 remaining section 734(b) adjustment is not taken into account in determining ABC's recomputed or adjusted basis in the property for purposes of section 1245(a)(1). Thus, ABC's adjusted basis in the property is $15 (the remaining original basis). Also pursuant to (c)(2)(iii) of this section, however, any depreciation, or amortization of the section 734(b) adjustment that is allowed or allowable is taken into account in computing the property's recomputed basis. Thus, ABC's amount of adjustments reflected in the adjusted basis is $136 (the original $120 adjustment for depreciation deductions plus the additional $15 adjustment for depreciation deductions plus the additional $1 adjustment for depreciation deductions taken with respect to the section 734(b) adjustment). Accordingly, ABC's recomputed basis is $151 ($15 adjusted basis plus $136 of adjustments), which is lower than ABC's amount realized of $170. ABC, therefore, must recognize ordinary income in an amount by which ABC's recomputed basis of $151 exceeds ABC's adjusted basis in the depreciable equipment X. Pursuant to (c)(2)(iii) of this section, the $9 remaining section 734(b) adjustment is not taken into account in determining the adjusted basis in the property for purposes of section 1245(a)(1). Accordingly, ABC must recognize $136 of ordinary income (the excess of ABC's $151 recomputed basis in the depreciable equipment X over ABC's $15 adjusted basis in the depreciable equipment X).

(E) Pursuant to paragraph (c)(2)(iv) of this section, the section 734(b) adjustment is not taken into account in determining ABC's section 1231 gain or loss. Accordingly, pursuant to section 1231(a)(1), ABC recognizes $19 of capital gain (ABC's $170 amount realized on the disposition of the depreciable equipment X over ABC's adjusted basis of $15 in the depreciable equipment X, reduced by the $136 of ordinary income ABC recognized under section 1245(a)(1)). Pursuant to paragraph (c)(2)(vi) of this section, ABC also recognizes a capital loss equal to the remaining $9 section 734(b) adjustment.

Example 3. (i) Assume the same facts as *Example 2* of this paragraph (c), except ABC has made an election under paragraph (c)(2)(vi) of this section.

(ii) *Treatment of section 734(b) adjustment.* Because ABC has made an election under paragraph (c)(2)(vi) of this section, paragraph (c)(2)(iii) of this section does not apply. Thus, if ABC sold its depreciable equipment X immediately after the distribution to A, ABC would take into account the $10 section 734(b) adjustment in determining ABC's recomputed or adjusted basis in the depreciable equipment X for purposes of section 1245(a)(1) and, accordingly, would recognize $110 of ordinary income (including for purposes of applying section 751).

* * *

(e) * * *

(2) *Special rules.*—Paragraphs (a) and (b)(3)(iii) of this section apply to transfers of partnership interests and distributions of property from a partnership that occur on or after June 9, 2003, and paragraphs (c)(2)(iii), (iv), (v), (vi), and (c)(6) of this section and *Examples 2* and *3* of paragraph (c) of this section apply to distributions of property from a partnership that occur on or after the date of publication of a Treasury decision adopting these rules as final regulations in the Federal Register.

[Prop. Reg. § 1.755-1.]

[Proposed 11-3-2014 (corrected 1-26-2015).]

Definitions

§ 1.761-1. Terms defined.—(a) *Partnership.*—The term *partnership* means a partnership as determined under §§ 301.7701-1, 301.7701-2, and 301.7701-3 of this chapter.

(b) *Partner.*—The term "partner" means a member of a partnership.

(c) *Partnership agreement.*—For the purposes of subchapter K, a partnership agreement includes the original agreement and any modifications thereof agreed to by all the partners or adopted in any other manner provided by the partnership agreement. Such agreement or modifications can be oral or written. A partnership agreement may be modified with respect to a particular taxable year subsequent to the close of such taxable year, but not later than the date (not including any extension of time) prescribed by law for the filing of the partnership return. As to any matter on which the partnership agreement, or any modification thereof, is silent, the provisions of local law shall be considered to constitute a part of the agreement.

(d) *Liquidation of partner's interest.*—The term "liquidation of a partner's interest" means the termination of a partner's entire interest in a partnership by means of a distribution, or a series of distributions, to the partner by the partnership. A series of distributions will come within the meaning of this term whether they are made in one year or in more than one year. Where a partner's interest is to be liquidated by a series of distributions, the interest will not be considered as liquidated until the final distribution has been made. For the basis of property distributed in one liquidating distribution, or in a series of distributions in liquidation, see section 732(b). A distribution which is not in liquidation of a partner's entire interest, as defined in this paragraph, is a current distribution. Current distributions, therefore, include distributions in partial liquidation of a partner's interest, and distributions of the partner's distributive share. See paragraph (a)(1)(ii) of § 1.731-1.

(e) *Distribution of partnership interest.*—For purposes of section 708(b)(1)(B) and § 1.708-1(b)(1)(iv), the deemed distribution of an interest in a new partnership by a partnership that terminates under section 708(b)(1)(B) is not a sale or exchange of an interest in the new partnership. However, the deemed distribution of an interest in a new partnership by a partnership that terminates under section 708(b)(1)(B) is treated as an exchange of the interest in the new partnership for purposes of section 743. This paragraph (e) applies to terminations of partnerships under section 708(b)(1)(B) occurring on or after May 9, 1997; however, this paragraph (e) may be applied to terminations occurring on or after May 9, 1996, provided that the partnership and its partners apply this paragraph (e) to the termination in a consistent manner. [Reg. § 1.761-1.]

□ [*T.D.* 6175, 5-23-56. *Amended by T.D.* 6198, 8-15-56; *T.D.* 7012, 5-14-69; *T.D.* 7208, 10-2-72; *T.D.* 8697, 12-17-96 *and T.D.* 8717, 5-8-97.]

Proposed Amendment to Regulation

§ 1.761-1. Terms defined.

* * *

(b) * * * If a partnership interest is transferred in connection with the performance of services, and that partnership interest is substantially nonvested (within the meaning of § 1.83-3(b)), then the holder of the partnership interest is not treated as a partner solely by reason of holding the interest, unless the holder makes an election with respect to the interest under section 83(b). The previous sentence applies to partnership interests that are transferred on or after the date final regulations are published in the Federal Register.

* * *

[Prop. Reg. § 1.761-1.]

[Proposed 5-24-2005.]

§ 1.761-2. Exclusion of certain unincorporated organizations from the application of all or part of subchapter K of chapter 1 of the Internal Revenue Code.—(a) *Exclusion* *of eligible unincorporated organizations.*—(1) *In general.*—Under conditions set forth in this section, an unincorporated organization described in subparagraph (2) or (3) of this paragraph may be excluded from the application of all or a part of the provisions of subchapter K of chapter 1 of the Code. Such organization must be availed of (i) for investment purposes only and not for the active conduct of a business, or (ii) for the joint production, extraction or use of property, but not for the purpose of selling services or property produced or extracted. The members of such organization must be able to compute their income without the necessity of computing partnership taxable income. Any syndicate, group, pool, or joint venture which is classifiable as an association, or any group operating under an agreement which creates an organization classifiable as an association, does not fall within these provisions.

(2) *Investing partnership.*—Where the participants in the joint purchase, retention, sale, or exchange of investment property—

(i) Own the property as coowners,

(ii) Reserve the right separately to take or dispose of their shares of any property acquired or retained, and

(iii) Do not actively conduct business or irrevocably authorize some person or persons acting in a representative capacity to purchase, sell, or exchange such investment property, although each separate participant may delegate authority to purchase, sell, or exchange his share of any such investment property for the time being for his account, but not for a period of more than a year, then

such group may be excluded from the application of the provisions of subchapter K under the rules set forth in paragraph (b) of this section.

(3) *Operating agreements.*—Where the participants in the joint production, extraction, or use of property—

(i) Own the property as coowners, either in fee or under lease or other form of contract granting exclusive operating rights, and

(ii) Reserve the right separately to take in kind or dispose of their shares of any property produced, extracted, or used, and

(iii) Do not jointly sell services or the property produced or extracted, although each separate participant may delegate authority to sell his share of the property produced or extracted for the time being for his account, but not for a period of time in excess of the minimum needs of the industry, and in no event for more than one year, then

such group may be excluded from the application of the provisions of subchapter K under the rules set forth in paragraph (b) of this section. However, the preceding sentence does not apply to any unincorporated organization one of whose principal purposes is cycling, manufacturing, or processing for persons who are not members of the organization. * * *

* * *

(c) *Partial exclusion from subchapter K.*—An unincorporated organization which wishes to be excluded from only certain sections of subchapter K must submit to the Commissioner, no later than 90 days after the beginning of the first taxable year for which partial exclusion is desired, a request for permission to be excluded from certain provisions of subchapter K. The request shall set forth the sections of subchapter K from which exclusion is sought and shall state that such organization qualifies under subparagraphs (1) and either (2) or (3) of paragraph (a) of this section, and that the members of the organization elect to be excluded to the extent indicated. Such exclusion shall be effective only upon approval of the election by the Commissioner and subject to the conditions he may impose.

* * *

(e) *Cross reference.*—For requirements with respect to the filing of a return on Form 1065 by a partnership, see §1.6031-1. [Reg. §1.761-2.]

☐ [*T.D.* 7208, 10-2-72. *Amended by T.D.* 8578, 12-22-94.]

Determination and Recognition of Gain or Loss

§1.1001-1. Computation of gain or loss.—(a) *General Rule.*—Except as otherwise provided in subtitle A of the Code, the gain or loss realized from the conversion of property into cash, or from the exchange of property for other property differing materially either in kind or in extent, is treated as income or as loss sustained. The amount realized from a sale or other disposition of property is the sum of any money received plus the fair market value of any property (other than money) received. The fair market value of property is a question of fact, but only in rare and extraordinary cases will property be considered to have no fair market value. The general method of computing such gain or loss is prescribed by section 1001(a) through (d) which contemplates that from the amount realized upon the sale or exchange there shall be withdrawn a sum sufficient to restore the adjusted basis prescribed by section 1011 and the regulations thereunder (i.e., the cost or other basis adjusted for receipts, expenditures, losses, allowances, and other items chargeable against and applicable to such cost or other basis). The amount which remains after the adjusted basis has been restored to the taxpayer constitutes the realized gain. If the amount realized upon the sale or exchange is insufficient to restore to the taxpayer the adjusted basis of the property, a loss is sustained to the extent of the difference between such adjusted basis and the amount realized. The basis may be different depending upon whether gain or loss is being computed. For example, see section 1015(a) and the regulations thereunder. Section 1001(e) and paragraph (f) of this section prescribe the method of computing gain or loss upon the sale or other disposition of a term interest in property the adjusted basis (or a portion) of which is determined pursuant, or by reference, to section 1014 (relating to the basis of property acquired from a decedent), section 1015 (relating to the basis of property acquired by gift or by a transfer in trust), or section 1022 (relating to the basis of property acquired from certain decedents who died in 2010).

(b) *Real estate taxes as amounts received.*—(1) Section 1001(b) and section 1012 state rules applicable in making an adjustment upon a sale of real property with respect to the real property taxes apportioned between seller and purchaser under section 164(d). Thus, if the seller pays (or agrees to pay) real property taxes attributable to the real property tax year in which the sale occurs, he shall not take into account, in determining the amount realized from the sale under section 1001(b), any amount received as reimbursement for taxes which are treated under section 164(d) as imposed upon the purchaser. Similarly, in computing the cost of the property under section 1012, the purchaser shall not take into account any amount paid to the seller as reimbursement for real property taxes which are treated under section 164(d) as imposed upon the purchaser. These rules apply whether or not the contract of sale calls for the purchaser to reimburse the seller for such real property taxes paid or to be paid by the seller.

(2) On the other hand, if the purchaser pays (or is to pay) an amount representing real property taxes which are treated under section 164(d) as imposed upon the seller, that amount shall be taken into account both in determining the amount realized from the sale under section 1001(b) and in computing the cost of the property under section 1012. It is immaterial whether or not the contract of sale specifies that the sale price has been reduced by, or is in any way intended to reflect, the taxes allocable to the seller. See also paragraph (b) of § 1.1012-1.

(3) Subparagraph (1) of this paragraph shall not apply to a seller who, in a taxable year prior to the taxable year of sale, pays an amount representing real property taxes which are treated under section 164(d) as imposed on the purchaser, if such seller has elected to capitalize such amount in accordance with section 266 and the regulations thereunder (relating to election to capitalize certain carrying charges and taxes).

(4) The application of this paragraph may be illustrated by the following examples:

Example (1). Assume that the contract price on the sale of a parcel of real estate is $50,000 and that real property taxes thereon in the amount of $1,000 for the real property tax year in which occurred the date of sale were previously paid by the seller. Assume further that $750 of the taxes are treated under section 164(d) as imposed upon the purchaser and that he reimburses the seller in that amount in addition to the contract price. The amount realized by the seller is $50,000. Similarly, $50,000 is the purchaser's cost. If, in this example, the purchaser made no payment other than the contract price of $50,000, the amount realized by the seller would be $49,250, since the sales price would be deemed to include $750 paid to the seller in reimbursement for real property taxes imposed upon the purchaser. Similarly, $49,250 would be the purchaser's cost.

Example (2). Assume that the purchaser in example (1) above, paid all of the real property taxes. Assume further that $250 of the taxes are treated under section 164(d) as imposed upon the seller. The amount realized by the seller is $50,250. Similarly, $50,250 is the purchaser's cost, regardless of the taxable year in which the purchaser makes actual payment of the taxes.

Example (3). Assume that the seller described in the first part of example (1), above, paid the real property taxes of $1,000 in the taxable year prior to the taxable year of sale and elected under section 266 to capitalize the $1,000 of taxes. In such a case, the amount realized is $50,750. Moreover, regardless of whether the seller elected to capitalize the real property taxes, the purchaser in that case could elect under section 266 to capitalize the $750 of taxes treated under section 164(d) as imposed upon him, in which case his adjusted basis would be $50,750 (cost of $50,000 plus capitalized taxes of $570 [$750]).

(c) *Other rules.*—(1) Even though property is not sold or otherwise disposed of, gain is realized if the sum of all the amounts received which are required by section 1016 and other applicable provisions of subtitle A of the Code to be applied against the basis of the property exceeds such basis. Except as otherwise provided in section 301(c)(3)(B) with respect to distributions out of increase in value of property accrued prior to March 1, 1913, such gain is includible in gross income under section 61 as "income from whatever source derived". On the other hand, a loss is not ordinarily sustained prior to the sale or other disposition of the property, for the reason that until such sale or other disposition occurs there remains the possibility that the taxpayer may recover or recoup the adjusted basis of the property. Until some identifiable event fixes the actual sustaining of a loss and the amount thereof, it is not taken into account.

(2) The provisions of subparagraph (1) of this paragraph may be illustrated by the following example:

Example. A, an individual on a calendar year basis, purchased certain shares of stock subsequent to February 28, 1913, for $10,000. On January 1, 1954, A's adjusted basis for the stock had been reduced to $1,000 by reason of receipts and distributions described in sections 1016(a)(1) and 1016(a)(4). He received in 1954 a further distribution of $5,000, being a distribution covered by section 1016(a)(4), other than a distribution out of increase of value of property accrued prior to March 1, 1913. This distribution applied against the adjusted basis as required by section 1016(a)(4) exceeds that basis by $4,000. The $4,000 excess is a gain realized by A in 1954 and is includible in gross income in his return for that calendar year. In computing gain from the stock, as in adjusting basis, no distinction is made between items of receipts or distributions described in section 1016. If A sells the stock in 1955 for $5,000, he realizes in 1955 a gain of $5,000, since the adjusted basis of the stock for the purpose of computing gain or loss from the sale is zero.

(d) *Installment sales.*—In the case of property sold on the installment plan, special rules for the taxation of the gain are prescribed in section 453.

(e) *Transfers in part a sale and in part a gift.*—(1) Where a transfer of property is in part a sale and in part a gift, the transferor has a gain to the extent that the amount realized by him exceeds his adjusted basis in the property. However, no loss is sustained on such a transfer if the amount realized is less than the adjusted basis. For determination of basis of the property in the hands of the transferee, see § 1.1015-4. For the allocation of the adjusted basis of property in the case of a bargain sale to a charitable organization, see § 1.1011-2.

(2) *Examples.*—The provisions of subparagraph (1) may be illustrated by the following examples:

Example (1). A transfers property to his son for $60,000. Such property in the hands of A has an adjusted basis of $30,000 (and a fair market value of $90,000). A's gain is $30,000, the excess of $60,000, the amount realized, over the adjusted basis, $30,000. He has made a gift of $30,000, the excess of $90,000, the fair market value, over the amount realized, $60,000.

Example (2). A transfers property to his son for $30,000. Such property in the hands of A has an adjusted basis of $60,000 (and a fair market value of $90,000). A has no gain or loss, and has made a gift of $60,000, the excess of $90,000, the fair market value, over the amount realized, $30,000.

Example (3). A transfers property to his son for $30,000. Such property in A's hands has an adjusted basis of $30,000 (and a fair market value of $60,000). A has no gain and has made a gift of $30,000, the excess of $60,000, the fair market value, over the amount realized, $30,000.

Example (4). A transfers property to his son for $30,000. Such property in A's hands has an adjusted basis of $90,000 (and a fair market value of $60,000). A has sustained no loss, and has made a gift of $30,000, the excess of $60,000, the fair market value, over the amount realized, $30,000.

(f) *Sale or other disposition of a term interest in property.*—(1) *General rule.*—Except as otherwise provided in paragraph (f)(3) of this section, for purposes of determining gain or loss from the sale or other disposition after October 9, 1969, of a term interest in property (as defined in paragraph (f)(2) of this section), a taxpayer shall not take into account that portion of the adjusted basis of such interest that is determined pursuant, or by reference, to section 1014 (relating to the basis of property acquired from a decedent), section 1015 (relating to the basis of property acquired by gift or by a transfer in trust), or section 1022 (relating to the basis of property acquired from certain decedents who died in 2010) to the extent that such adjusted basis is a portion of the adjusted uniform basis of the entire property (as defined in § 1.1014-5). Where a term interest in property is transferred to a corporation in connection with a transaction to which section 351 applies and the adjusted basis of the term interest:

(i) Is determined pursuant to sections 1014, 1015, or 1022; and

(ii) Is also a portion of the adjusted uniform basis of the entire property, a subsequent sale or other disposition of such term interest by the corporation will be subject to the provisions of section 1001(e) and this paragraph (f) to the extent that the basis of the term interest so sold or otherwise disposed of is determined by reference to its basis in the hands of the transferor as provided by section 362(a). See paragraph (f)(2) of this section for rules relating to the characterization of stock received by the transferor of a term interest in property in connection with a transaction to which section 351 applies. That portion of the adjusted uniform basis of the entire property that is assignable to such interest at the time of its sale or other disposition shall be determined under the rules provided in § 1.1014-5. Thus, gain or loss realized from a sale or other disposition of a term interest in property shall be determined by comparing the amount of the proceeds of such sale with that part of the adjusted basis of such interest that is not a portion of the adjusted uniform basis of the entire property.

(2) *Term interest defined.*—For purposes of section 1001(e) and this paragraph, a "term interest in property" means—

(i) A life interest in property,

(ii) An interest in property for a term of years, or

(iii) An income interest in a trust.

Generally subdivisions (i), (ii), and (iii) refer to an interest, present or future, in the income from property or the right to use property which will terminate or fail on the lapse of time, on the occurrence of an event or contingency, or on the failure of an event or contingency to occur. Such divisions do not refer to remainder or reversionary interests in the property itself or other interests in the property which will ripen into ownership of the entire property upon termination or failure of a preceding term interest. A "term interest in property" also includes any property received upon a sale or other disposition of a life interest in property, an interest in property for a term of years, or an income interest in a trust by the original holder of such interest, but only to the extent that the adjusted basis of the property received is determined by reference to the adjusted basis of the term interest so transferred.

(3) *Exception.*—Paragraph (1) of section 1001(e) and subparagraph (1) of this paragraph shall not apply to a sale or other disposition of a term interest in property as a part of a single transaction in which the entire interest in the property is transferred to a third person or to two or more other persons, including persons who acquire such entire interest as joint tenants, tenants by the entirety, or tenants in common. See § 1.1014-5 for computation of gain or loss upon such a sale or other disposition where the property has been acquired from a decedent or by gift or transfer in trust.

(4) *Illustrations.*—For examples illustrating the application of this paragraph, see paragraph (d) of § 1.1014-5.

(g) *Debt instruments issued in exchange for property.*—(1) *In general.*—If a debt instrument is issued in exchange for property, the amount realized attributable to the debt instrument is the issue price of the debt instrument as determined under § 1.1273-2 or § 1.1274-2; whichever is applicable. If, however, the issue price of the debt instrument is determined under section 1273(b)(4), the amount realized attributable to the debt instrument is its stated principal amount reduced by any unstated interest (as determined under section 483).

* * *

[Reg. § 1.1001-1.]

☐ [*T.D.* 6265, 11-6-57. *Amended by T.D.* 7142, 9-23-71; *T.D.* 7207, 10-3-72; *T.D.* 7213, 10-17-72; *T.D.* 8517, 1-27-94; *T.D.* 8674, 6-11-96; *T.D.* 9348, 8-1-2007; *T.D.* 9729, 8-11-2015 *and T.D.* 9811, 1-18-2017.]

§ 1.1001-2. Discharge of liabilities.—

(a) *Inclusion in amount realized.*—(1) *In general.*—Except as provided in paragraph (a)(2) and (3) of this section, the amount realized from a sale or other disposition of property includes the amount of liabilities from which the transferor is discharged as a result of the sale or disposition.

(2) *Discharge of indebtedness.*—The amount realized on a sale or other disposition of property that secures a recourse liability does not include amounts that are (or would be if realized and recognized) income from the discharge of indebtedness under section 61(a)(12). For situations where amounts arising from the discharge of indebtedness are not realized and recognized, see section 108 and § 1.61-12(b)(1).

(3) *Liability incurred on acquisition.*—In the case of a liability incurred by reason of the acquisition of the property, this section does not apply to the extent that such liability was not taken into account in determining the transferor's basis for such property.

(4) *Special rules.*—For purposes of this section—

(i) The sale or other disposition of property that secures a nonrecourse liability discharges the transferor from the liability;

(ii) The sale or other disposition of property that secures a recourse liability discharges the transferor from the liability if another person agrees to pay the liability (whether or not the transferor is in fact released from liability);

(iii) A disposition of property includes a gift of the property or a transfer of the property in satisfaction of liabilities to which it is subject;

(iv) Contributions and distributions of property between a partner and a partnership are not sales or other dispositions of property; and

(v) The liabilities from which a transferor is discharged as a result of the sale or disposition of a partnership interest include the transferor's share of the liabilities of the partnership.

(b) *Effect of fair market value of security.*—The fair market value of the security at the time of sale or disposition is not relevant for purposes of determining under paragraph (a) of this section the amount of liabilities from which the taxpayer is discharged or treated as discharged. Thus, the fact that the fair market value of the property is less than the amount of the liabilities it secures does not prevent the full amount of those liabilities from being treated as money received from the sale or other disposition of the property. However, see paragraph (a)(2) of this section for a rule relating to certain income from discharge of indebtedness.

(c) *Examples.*—The provisions of this section may be illustrated by the following examples. In each example assume the taxpayer uses the cash receipts and disbursements method of accounting, makes a return on the basis of the calendar year, and sells or disposes of all property which is security for a given liability.

Example (1). In 1976 A purchases an asset for $10,000. A pays the seller $1,000 in cash and signs a note payable to the seller for $9,000. A is personally liable for repayment with the seller having full recourse in the event of default. In addition, the asset which was purchased is pledged as security. During the years 1976 and 1977, A takes depreciation deductions on the asset in the amount of $3,100. During this same time period A reduces the outstanding principal on the note to $7,600. At the beginning of 1978 A sells the asset. The buyer pays A $1,600 in cash and assumes personal liability for the $7,600 outstanding liability. A becomes secondarily liable for repayment of the liability. A's amount realized is $9,200 ($1,600 + $7,600). Since A's adjusted basis in the asset is $6,900 ($10,000 – $3,100) A realizes a gain of $2,300 ($9,200 – $6,900).

Example (2). Assume the same facts as in example (1) except that A is not personally liable on the $9,000 note given to the seller and in the event of default the seller's only recourse is to the asset. In addition, on the sale of the asset by A, the purchaser takes the asset subject to the liability. Nevertheless, A's amount realized is $9,200 and A's gain realized is $2,300 on the sale.

Example (3). In 1975 L becomes a limited partner in partnership GL. L contributes $10,000 in cash to GL and L's distributive share of partnership income and loss is 10 percent. L is not entitled to receive any guaranteed payments. In 1978 M purchases L's entire interest in partnership GL. At the time of the sale L's adjusted basis in the partnership interest is $20,000. At that time L's proportionate share of liabilities, of which no partner has assumed personal liability, is $15,000. M pays $10,000 in cash for L's interest in the partnership. Under section 752(d) and this section, L's share of partnership liabilities, $15,000, is treated as money received. Accordingly, L's amount realized on the sale of the partnership interest is $25,000 ($10,000 + $15,000). L's gain realized on the sale is $5,000 ($25,000 – $20,000).

Example (4). In 1976 B becomes a limited partner in partnership BG. In 1978 B contributes B's entire interest in BG to a charitable organization described in section 170(c). At the time of the contribution all of the partnership liabilities are liabilities for which neither B nor G has assumed any personal liability and B's proportionate share of which is $9,000. The charitable organization does not pay any cash or other property to B, but takes the partnership interest subject to the $9,000 of liabilities. Assume that the contribution is treated as a bargain sale to a charitable organization and that under section 1011 (b) $3,000 is determined to be the portion of B's basis in the partnership interest allocable to the sale. Under section 752(d) and this section, the $9,000 of liabilities is treated by B as money received, thereby making B's amount realized $9,000. B's gain realized is $6,000 ($9,000 – $3,000).

Example (5). In 1975 C, an individual, creates T, an irrevocable trust. Due to certain powers expressly retained by C, T is a "grantor trust" for purposes of subpart E of part 1 of subchapter J of the Code and therefore C is treated as the owner of the entire trust. T purchases an interest in P, a partnership. C, as owner of T, deducts the distributive share of partnership losses attributable to the partnership interest held by T. In 1978, when the adjusted basis of the partnership interest held by T is $1,200, C renounces the powers previously and expressly retained that initially resulted in T being classified as a grantor trust. Consequently, T ceases to be a grantor trust and C is no longer considered to be the owner of the trust. At the time of the renunciation all of J's liabilities are liabilities on which none of the partners have assumed any personal liability and the proportionate share of which of the interest held by T is $11,000. Since prior to the renunciation C was the owner of the entire trust, C was considered the owner of all the trust property for Federal income tax purposes, including the partnership interest. Since C was considered to be the owner of the partnership interest, C not T, was considered to be the partner in P during the time T was a "grantor trust." However, at the time C renounced the powers that gave rise to T's classification as a grantor trust, T no longer qualified as a grantor trust with the result that C was no longer considered to be the owner of the trust and trust property for Federal income tax purposes. Consequently, at that time, C is considered to have transferred ownership of the interest in P to T, now a separate taxable entity, independent of its grantor C. On the transfer, C's share of partnership liabilities ($11,000) is treated as money received. Accordingly, C's amount realized is $11,000 and C's gain realized is $9,800 ($11,000 - $1,200).

Example (6). In 1977 D purchases an asset for $7,500. D pays the seller $1,500 in cash and signs a note payable to the seller for $6,000. D is not personally liable for repayment but pledges as security the newly purchased asset. In the event of default, the seller's only recourse is to the asset. During the years 1977 and 1978 D takes depreciation deductions on the asset totaling $4,200 thereby reducing D's basis in the asset to $3,300 ($7,500 - $4,200). In 1979 D transfers the asset to a trust which is not a "grantor trust" for purposes of subpart E of part 1 of subchapter J of the Code. Therefore D is not treated as the owner of the trust. The trust takes the asset subject to the liability and in addition pays D $750 in cash. Prior to the transfer D had reduced the amount outstanding on the liability to $4,700. D's amount realized on the transfer is $5,450 ($4,700 + $750). Since D's adjusted basis is $3,300, D's gain realized is $2,150 ($5,450 - $3,300).

Example (7). In 1974 E purchases a herd of cattle for breeding purposes. The purchase price is $20,000 consisting of $1,000 cash and a $19,000 note. E is not personally liable for repayment of the liability and the seller's only recourse in the event of default is to the herd of cattle. In 1977 E transfers the herd back to the original seller thereby satisfying the indebtedness pursuant to a provision in the original sales agreement. At the time of the transfer the fair market value of the herd is $15,000 and the remaining principal balance on the note is $19,000. At the time E's adjusted basis in the herd is $16,500 due to a deductible loss incurred when a portion of the herd died as a result of a disease. As a result of the indebtedness being satisfied, E's amount realized is $19,000 notwithstanding the fact that the fair market value of the herd was less than $19,000. E's realized gain is $2,500 ($19,000 - $16,500).

Example (8). In 1980, F transfers to a creditor an asset with a fair market value of $6,000 and the creditor discharges $7,500 of indebtedness for which F is personally liable. The amount realized on the disposition of the asset is its fair market value ($6,000). In addition, F has income from the discharge of indebtedness of $1,500 ($7,500 - $6,000). [Reg. § 1.1001-2.]

☐ [*T.D.* 7741, 12-11-80.]

§ 1.1002-1. Sales or exchanges.—(a) *General rule.*—The general rule with respect to gain or loss realized upon the sale or exchange of property as determined under section 1001 is that the entire amount of such gain or loss is recognized except in cases where specific provisions of subtitle A of the Code provide otherwise.

(b) *Strict construction of exceptions from general rule.*—The exceptions from the general rule requiring the recognition of all gains and losses, like other exceptions from a rule of taxation of general and uniform application, are strictly construed and do not extend either beyond the words or the underlying assumptions and purposes of the exception. Nonrecognition is accorded by the Code only if the exchange is one which satisfies both (1) the specific description in the Code of an excepted exchange, and (2) the underlying purpose for which such exchange is excepted from the general rule. The exchange must be germane to, and a necessary incident of, the investment or enterprise in hand. The relationship of the exchange to the venture or enterprise is always material, and the surrounding facts and circumstances must be shown. As elsewhere, the taxpayer claiming the benefit of the exception must show himself within the exception.

(c) *Certain exceptions to general rule.*—Exceptions to the general rule are made, for example, by sections 351(a), 354, 361(a), 371(a)(1), 371(b)(1), 721, 1031, 1035 and 1036. These sections describe certain specific exchanges of property in which at the time of the exchange particular differences exist between the property parted with and the property acquired, but such differences are more formal than substantial. As to these, the Code provides that such differences shall not be deemed controlling, and that gain or loss shall not be recognized at the time of the exchange. The underlying assumption of these exceptions is that the new property is substantially a continuation of the old investment still unliquidated; and, in the case of reorganizations, that the new enterprise, the new corporate structure, and the new property are substantially continuations of the old still unliquidated.

(d) *Exchange.*—Ordinarily, to constitute an exchange, the transaction must be a reciprocal transfer of property, as distinguished from a transfer of property for a money consideration only. [Reg. § 1.1002-1.]

☐ [*T.D.* 6265, 11-6-57.]

Basis Rules of General Application

§ 1.1011-1. Adjusted basis.—The adjusted basis for determining the gain or loss from the sale or other disposition of property is the cost or other basis prescribed in section 1012 or other applicable provisions of subtitle A of the Code, adjusted to the extent provided in sections 1016, 1017, and 1018 or as otherwise specifically provided for under applicable provisions of internal revenue laws. [Reg. § 1.1011-1.]

☐ [*T.D.* 6265, 11-6-57.]

§ 1.1011-2. Bargain sale to a charitable organization.—(a) *In general.*—(1) If for the taxable year a charitable contributions deduction is allowable under section 170 by reason of a sale or exchange of property, the taxpayer's adjusted basis of such property for purposes of determining gain from such sale or exchange must be computed as provided in section 1011(b) and paragraph (b) of this section. If after applying the provisions of section 170 for the taxable year, including the percentage limitations of section 170(b), no deduction is allowable under that section by reason of the sale or exchange of the property, section 1011(b) does not apply and the adjusted basis of the property is not required to be apportioned pursuant to paragraph (b) of this section. In such case the entire adjusted basis of the property is to be taken into account in determining gain from the sale or exchange, as provided in § 1.1011-1(e). In ascertaining whether or not a charitable contributions deduction is allowable under section 170 for the taxable year for such purposes, that section is to be applied without regard to this section and the amount by which the contributed portion of the property must be reduced under section 170(e)(1) is the amount determined by taking into account the amount of gain which would have been ordinary income or long-term capital gain if the contributed portion of the property had been sold by the donor at its fair market value at the time of the sale or exchange.

(2) If in the taxable year there is a sale or exchange of property which gives rise to a charitable contribution which is carried over under section 170(b)(1)(D)(ii) or section 170(d) to a subsequent taxable year or is postponed under section 170(a)(3) to a subsequent taxable year, section 1011(b) and paragraph (b) of this section must be applied for purposes of apportioning the adjusted basis of the property for the year of the sale or exchange, whether or not such contribution is allowable as a deduction under section 170 in such subsequent year.

(3) If property is transferred subject to an indebtedness, the amount of the indebtedness must be treated as an amount realized for purposes of determining whether there is a sale or exchange to which section 1011(b) and this section apply, even though the transferee does not agree to assume or pay the indebtedness.

(4)(i) Section 1011(b) and this section apply where property is sold or exchanged in return for an obligation to pay an annuity and a charitable contributions deduction is allowable under section 170 by reason of such sale or exchange.

(ii) If in such case the annuity received in exchange for the property is nonassignable, or is assignable but only to the charitable organization to which the property is sold or exchanged, and if the transferor is the only annuitant or the transferor and a designated survivor annuitant or annuitants are the only annuitants, any gain on such exchange is to be reported as provided in example (8) in paragraph (c) of this section. In determining the period over which gain may be reported as provided in such example, the life expectancy of the survivor annuitant may not be taken into account. The fact that the transferor may retain the right to revoke the survivor's annuity or relinquish his own right to the annuity will not be considered, for purposes of this subdivision, to make the annuity assignable to someone other than the charitable organization. Gain on an exchange of the type described in this subdivision pursuant to an agreement which is entered into after December 19, 1969, and before May 3, 1971, may be reported as provided in example (8) in paragraph (c) of this section, even though the annuity is assignable.

(iii) In the case of an annuity to which subdivision (ii) of this subparagraph applies, the gain unreported by the transferor with respect to annuity payments not yet due when the following events occur is not required to be included in gross income of any person where—

(a) The transferor dies before the entire amount of gain has been reported and there is no surviving annuitant, or

(b) The transferor relinquishes the annuity to the charitable organization. If the transferor dies before the entire amount of gain on a two-life annuity has been reported, the unreported gain is required to be reported by

the surviving annuitant or annuitants with respect to the annuity payments received by them.

(b) *Apportionment of adjusted basis.*—For purposes of determining gain on a sale or exchange to which this paragraph applies, the adjusted basis of the property which is sold or exchanged shall be that portion of the adjusted basis of the entire property which bears the same ratio to the adjusted basis as the amount realized bears to the fair market value of the entire property. The amount of such gain which shall be treated as ordinary income (or long-term capital gain) shall be that amount which bears the same ratio to the ordinary income (or long-term capital gain) which would have been recognized if the entire property had been sold by the donor at its fair market value at the time of the sale or exchange as the amount realized on the sale or exchange bears to the fair market value of the entire property at such time. The terms "ordinary income" and "long-term capital gain", as used in this section, have the same meaning as they have in paragraph (a) of § 1.170A-4. For determining the portion of the adjusted basis, ordinary income, and long-term capital gain allocated to the contributed portion of the property for purposes of applying section 170(e)(1) and paragraph (a) of § 1.170A-4 to the contributed portion of the property, and for determining the donee's basis in such contributed portion, see paragraph (c)(2) and (4) of § 1.170A-4. For determining the holding period of such contributed portion, see section 1223(2) and the regulations thereunder.

(c) *Illustrations.*—The application of this section may be illustrated by the following examples, which are supplemented by other examples in paragraph (d) of § 1.170A-4:

Example (1). In 1970, a calendar-year individual taxpayer, sells to a church for $4,000 stock held for more than 6 months which has an adjusted basis of $4,000 and a fair market value of $10,000. A's contribution base for 1970, as defined in section 170(b)(1)(F), is $100,000, and during that year he makes no other charitable contributions. Thus, A makes a charitable contribution to the church of $6,000 ($10,000 value − $4,000 amount realized). Without regard to this section, A is allowed a deduction under section 170 of $6,000 for his charitable contribution to the church, since there is no reduction under section 170(e)(1) with respect to the long-term capital gain. Accordingly, under paragraph (b) of this section the adjusted basis for determining gain on the bargain sale is $1,600 ($4,000 adjusted basis × $4,000 amount realized/$10,000 value of property). A has recognized long-term capital gain of $2,400 ($4,000 amount realized − $1,600 adjusted basis) on the bargain sale.

Example (2). The facts are the same as in Example (1) except that A also makes a charitable contribution in 1970 of $50,000 cash to the church. By reason of section 170(b)(1)(A), the deduction allowed under section 170 for 1970 is $50,000 for the amount of cash contributed to the church; however, the $6,000 contribution of property is carried over to 1971 under section 170(d). Under paragraphs (a)(2) and (b) of this section the adjusted basis for determining gain for 1970 on the bargain sale in that year is $1,600 ($4,000 × $4,000/$10,000). A has a recognized long-term capital gain for 1970 of $2,400 ($4,000 − $1,600) on the sale.

* * *

[Reg. § 1.1011-2.]

☐ [*T.D.* 7207, 10-3-72. *Amended by T.D.* 7741, 12-11-80, *T.D.* 8176, 2-24-88 *and T.D.* 8540, 6-9-94.]

§ 1.1012-1. Basis of property.—(a) *General rule.*—In general, the basis of property is the cost thereof. The cost is the amount paid for such property in cash or other property. This general rule is subject to exceptions stated in subchapter O (relating to gain or loss on the disposition of property), subchapter C (relating to corporate distributions and adjustments), subchapter K (relating to partners and partnerships), and subchapter P (relating to capital gains and losses), chapter 1 of the Code.

(b) *Real estate taxes as part of cost.*—In computing the cost of real property, the purchaser shall not take into account any amount paid to the seller as reimbursement for real property taxes which are treated under section 164(d) as imposed upon the purchaser. This rule applies whether or not the contract of sale calls for the purchaser to reimburse the seller for such real estate taxes paid or to be paid by the seller. On the other hand, where the purchaser pays (or assumes liability for) real estate taxes which are treated under section 164(d) as imposed upon the seller, such taxes shall be considered part of the cost of the property. It is immaterial whether or not the contract of sale specifies that the sale price has been reduced by, or is in any way intended to reflect, real estate taxes allocable to the seller under section 164(d). For illustrations of the application of the paragraph, see paragraph (b) of § 1.1001-1.

(c) *Sale of stock.*—(1) *In general.*—(i) Except as provided in paragraph (e)(2) of this section (dealing with stock for which the average basis method is permitted), if a taxpayer sells or transfers shares of stock in a corporation that the taxpayer purchased or acquired on different dates or at different prices and the taxpayer does not adequately identify the lot from which the stock is sold or transferred, the stock sold or transferred is charged against the earliest lot the taxpayer purchased or acquired to determine the basis and holding period of the stock. If the earliest lot purchased or acquired is held in a stock certificate that represents multiple lots of stock, and the taxpayer does not adequately identify the lot from which the stock is sold or transferred, the stock sold or transferred is charged against the earliest lot included in the certificate. See paragraphs (c)(2), (c)(3), and (c)(4) of this section for rules on what constitutes an adequate identification.

(ii) A taxpayer must determine the basis of identical stock (within the meaning of paragraph (e)(4) of this section) by averaging the cost of each share if the stock is purchased at separate times on the same calendar day in executing a single trade order and the broker executing the trade provides a single confirmation that reports an aggregate total cost or an average cost per share. However, the taxpayer may determine the basis of the stock by the actual cost per share if the taxpayer notifies the broker in writing of this intent. The taxpayer must notify the broker by the earlier of the date of the sale of any of the stock for which the taxpayer received the confirmation or one year after the date of the confirmation. A broker may extend the one-year period but the taxpayer must notify the broker no later than the date of sale of any of the stock.

(2) *Identification of stock.*—An adequate identification is made if it is shown that certificates representing shares of stock from a lot which was purchased or acquired on a certain date or for a certain price were delivered to the taxpayer's transferee. Except as otherwise provided in subparagraph (3) or (4) of this paragraph, such stock certificates delivered to the transferee constitute the stock sold or transferred by the taxpayer. Thus, unless the requirements of subparagraph (3) or (4) of this paragraph are met, the stock sold or transferred is charged to the lot to which the certificates delivered to the transferee belong, whether or not the taxpayer intends, or instructs his broker or other agent, to sell or transfer stock from a lot purchased or acquired on a different date or for a different price.

(3) *Identification on confirmation document.*—(i) Where the stock is left in the custody of a broker or other agent, an adequate identification is made if—

(a) At the time of the sale or transfer, the taxpayer specifies to such broker or other agent having custody of the stock the particular stock to be sold or transferred, and

(b) Within a reasonable time thereafter, confirmation of such specification is set forth in a written document from such broker or other agent.

Stock identified pursuant to this subdivision is the stock sold or transferred by the taxpayer, even though stock certificates from a different lot are delivered to the taxpayer's transferee.

(ii) Where a single stock certificate represents stock from different lots, where such certificate is held by the taxpayer rather than his broker or other agent, and where the taxpayer sells a part of the stock represented by such certificate through a broker or other agent, an adequate identification is made if—

(a) At the time of the delivery of the certificate to the broker or other agent, the taxpayer specifies to such broker or other agent the particular stock to be sold or transferred, and

(b) Within a reasonable time thereafter, confirmation of such specification is set forth in a written document from such broker or agent.

Where part of stock represented by a single certificate is sold or transferred directly by the taxpayer to the purchaser or transferee instead of through a broker or other agent, an adequate identification is made if the taxpayer maintains a written record of the particular stock which he intended to sell or transfer.

(4) *Stock held by a trustee, executor, or administrator.*—(i) A trustee or executor or administrator of an estate holding stock (not left in the custody of a broker) makes an adequate identification if the trustee, executor, or administrator—

(a) Specifies in writing in the books and records of the trust or estate the particular stock to be sold, transferred, or distributed;

(b) In the case of a distribution, furnishes the distributee with a written document identifying the particular stock distributed; and

(c) In the case of a sale or transfer through a broker or other agent, specifies to the broker or agent the particular stock to be sold or transferred, and within a reasonable time thereafter the broker or agent confirms the specification in a written document.

(ii) The stock the trust or estate identifies under paragraph (c)(4)(i) of this section is the stock treated as sold, transferred, or distributed, even if the trustee, executor, or administrator delivers stock certificates from a different lot.

(5) *Subsequent sales.*—If stock identified under subparagraph (3) or (4) of this paragraph as belonging to a particular lot is sold,

transferred, or distributed, the stock so identified shall be deemed to have been sold, transferred, or distributed, and such sale, transfer, or distribution will be taken into consideration in identifying the taxpayer's remaining stock for purposes of subsequent sales, transfers, or distributions.

(6) *Bonds.*—Paragraphs (1) through (5), (8), and (9) of this section apply to the sale or transfer of bonds.

* * *

(e) *Election to use average basis method.*—(1) *In general.*—Notwithstanding paragraph (c) of this section, and except as provided in paragraph (e)(8) of this section, a taxpayer may use the average basis method described in paragraph (e)(7) of this section to determine the cost or other basis of identical shares of stock if—

(i) The taxpayer leaves shares of stock in a regulated investment company (as defined in paragraph (e)(5) of this section) or shares of stock acquired after December 31, 2010, in connection with a dividend reinvestment plan (as defined in paragraph (e)(6) of this section) with a custodian or agent in an account maintained for the acquisition or redemption, sale, or other disposition of shares of the stock; and

(ii) The taxpayer acquires identical shares of stock at different prices or bases in the account.

(2) *Determination of method.*—(i) If a taxpayer places shares of stock described in paragraph (e)(1)(i) of this section acquired on or after January 1, 2012, in the custody of a broker (as defined by section 6045(c)(1)), including by transfer from an account with another broker, the basis of the shares is determined in accordance with the broker's default method, unless the taxpayer notifies the broker that the taxpayer elects another permitted method. The taxpayer must report gain or loss using the method the taxpayer elects or, if the taxpayer fails to make an election, the broker's default method. *See* paragraphs (e)(9)(i) and (e)(9)(v), *Example 2,* of this section.

(ii) The provisions of this paragraph (e)(2) are illustrated by the following example:

Example. (i) In connection with a dividend reinvestment plan, Taxpayer B acquires 100 shares of G Company in 2012 and 100 shares of G Company in 2013, in an account B maintains with R Broker. B notifies R in writing that B elects to use the average basis method to compute the basis of the shares of G Company. In 2014, B transfers the shares of G Company to an account with S Broker. B does not notify S of the basis determination method B chooses to use for the shares of G Company, and S's default method is first-in, first-out. In 2015, B purchases 200 shares of G Company in the account with S. In 2016, B instructs S to sell 150 shares of G Company.

(ii) Because B does not notify S of a basis determination method for the shares of G Company, under paragraph (e)(2)(i) of this section, the basis of the 150 shares of G Company S sells for B in 2016 must be determined under S's default method, first-in, first-out.

(3) *Shares of stock.*—For purposes of this paragraph (e), securities issued by unit investment trusts described in paragraph (e)(5) of this section are treated as shares of stock and the term *share* or *shares* includes fractions of a share.

(4) *Identical stock.*—For purposes of this paragraph (e), *identical shares of stock* means stock with the same Committee on Uniform Security Identification Procedures (CUSIP) number or other security identifier number as permitted in published guidance of general applicability, *see* § 601.601(d)(2) of this chapter.

(5) *Regulated investment company.*—(i) For purposes of this paragraph, a "regulated investment company" means any domestic corporation (other than a personal holding company as defined in section 542) which meets the limitations of section 851(b) and § 1.851-2, and which is registered at all times during the taxable year under the Investment Company Act of 1940, as amended (15 U.S.C. 80a-1 to 80b-2), either as a management company, or as a unit investment trust.

(ii) Notwithstanding subdivision (i), this paragraph shall not apply in the case of a unit investment trust unless it is one—

(a) Substantially all of the assets of which consist *(1)* of securities issued by a single management company (as defined in such Act) and securities acquired pursuant to subdivision *(b)* of this subdivision (ii), or *(2)* securities issued by a single other corporation, and

(b) Which has no power to invest in any other securities except securities issued by a single other management company, when permitted by such Act or the rules and regulations of the Securities and Exchange Commission.

(6) *Dividend reinvestment plan.*—(i) *In general.*—For purposes of this paragraph (e), the term *dividend reinvestment plan* means any written plan, arrangement, or program under which at least 10 percent of every dividend (within the meaning of section 316) on any share of stock is reinvested in stock identical to the stock on which the dividend is paid. A plan is a dividend reinvestment plan if the plan docu-

ments require that at least 10 percent of any dividend paid is reinvested in identical stock even if the plan includes stock on which no dividends have ever been declared or paid or on which an issuer ceases paying dividends. A plan that holds one or more different stocks may permit a taxpayer to reinvest a different percentage of dividends in the stocks held. A dividend reinvestment plan may reinvest other distributions on stock, such as capital gain distributions, non-taxable returns of capital, and cash in lieu of fractional shares. The term dividend reinvestment plan includes both issuer administered dividend reinvestment plans and non-issuer administered dividend reinvestment plans.

(ii) *Acquisition of stock.*—Stock is acquired in connection with a dividend reinvestment plan if the stock is acquired under that plan, arrangement, or program, or if the dividends and other distributions paid on the stock are subject to that plan, arrangement, or program. Shares of stock acquired in connection with a dividend reinvestment plan include the initial purchase of stock in the dividend reinvestment plan, transfers of identical stock into the dividend reinvestment plan, additional periodic purchases of identical stock in the dividend reinvestment plan, and identical stock acquired through reinvestment of the dividends or other distributions paid on the stock held in the plan.

* * *

(7) *Computation of average basis.*—(i) *In general.*—Average basis is determined by averaging the basis of all shares of identical stock in an account regardless of holding period. However, for this purpose, shares of stock in a dividend reinvestment plan are not identical to shares of stock with the same CUSIP number that are not in a dividend reinvestment plan. The basis of each share of identical stock in the account is the aggregate basis of all shares of that stock in the account divided by the aggregate number of shares. Unless a single-account election is in effect, see paragraph (e)(11) of this section, a taxpayer may not average together the basis of identical stock held in separate accounts that the taxpayer sells, exchanges, or otherwise disposes of on or after January 1, 2012.

(ii) *Order of disposition of shares sold or transferred.*—In the case of the sale or transfer of shares of stock to which the average basis method election applies, shares sold or transferred are deemed to be the shares first acquired. Thus, the first shares sold or transferred are those with a holding period of more than 1 year (long-term shares) to the extent that the account contains long-term shares. If the number of shares sold or transferred exceeds the number of long-term shares in the account, the excess shares sold or transferred are deemed to be shares with a holding period of 1 year or less (short-term shares). Any gain or loss attributable to shares held for more than 1 year constitutes long-term gain or loss, and any gain or loss attributable to shares held for 1 year or less constitutes short-term gain or loss. For example, if a taxpayer sells 50 shares from an account containing 100 long-term shares and 100 short-term shares, the shares sold or transferred are all long-term shares. If, however, the account contains 40 long-term shares and 100 short-term shares, the taxpayer has sold 40 long-term shares and 10 short-term shares.

* * *

(g) *Debt instruments issued in exchange for property.*—(1) *In general.*—For purposes of paragraph (a) of this section, if a debt instrument is issued in exchange for property, the cost of the property that is attributable to the debt instrument is the issue price of the debt instrument as determined under § 1.1273-2 or § 1.1274-2, whichever is applicable. If, however, the issue price of the debt instrument is determined under section 1273(b)(4), the cost of the property attributable to the debt instrument is its stated principal amount reduced by any unstated interest (as determined under section 483).

* * *

[Reg. § 1.1012-1.]

☐ [*T.D.* 6265, 11-6-57. *Amended by T.D.* 6311, 9-10-58; *T.D.* 6837, 7-12-65; *T.D.* 6887, 6-23-66; *T.D.* 6934, 11-13-67; *T.D.* 6984, 12-23-68; *T.D.* 7015, 6-19-69; *T.D.* 7081, 12-30-70; *T.D.* 7129, 7-6-71; *T.D.* 7154, 12-27-71; *T.D.* 7213, 10-17-72; *T.D.* 7568, 10-11-78; *T.D.* 7728, 10-31-80; *T.D.* 8517, 1-27-94; *T.D.* 8674, 6-11-96 *and T.D.* 9504, 10-12-2010.]

Proposed Amendments to Regulation

§ 1.1012-2. Certain sales or exchanges between related parties.—(a) *In general.*—In the case of a sale or exchange of property in which the relationship between the seller and the buyer is such that the sale or exchange is not necessarily an arm's-length transaction, the transaction shall be examined to determine whether the value of the consideration provided by the buyer is greater than or less than the value of the property. If the value of the consideration exceeds the value of the property, this excess shall not be treated as relating to the sale or exchange and will be recharacterized according to the relationship between the parties. If the value of the property exceeds the value of the consideration, this excess generally shall be treated as transferred from the seller to the buyer based on the relationship between the parties and not as transferred in exchange for the debt instrument. The preceding sentence shall not apply to any transaction that would be characterized as in part a gift and in part a sale under § 1.170A-4(c)(2) and § 1.1011-2(b) or under § 1.1015-4.

(b) *Value.*—In applying this section to any sale or exchange where all or a part of the consideration furnished by the buyer consists of one or more debt instruments issued by the buyer to the seller, then, for purposes of this section—

(1) The value of any such debt instrument to which section 1274 applies or which has adequate stated interest within the meaning of section 1274(c)(2) or § 1.483-2 shall be its issue price;

(2) The value of any such debt instrument issued under a contract to which section 483 applies shall be the amount described in § 1.483-3(a)(2)(i); and

(3) In determining whether the value of the consideration furnished by the buyer exceeds the value of the property, the value of the property shall be determined by reference to the price that an unrelated buyer (having the same creditworthiness as the actual buyer) would be willing to pay for the property in an arm's-length transaction if seller financing (taken into account at its issue price) were offered on the same terms as those offered to the actual buyer.

(c) *Examples.*—The provisions of this section may be illustrated by the following examples:

Example (1). (i) On January 1, 1986, Corporation X sells nonpublicly traded property to A, the sole shareholder of X. In consideration for the sale, A makes a down payment of $200,000 and issues a debt instrument calling for a single payment of $1,000,000 due in five years. No interest is provided for in the debt instrument. Because A is the sole shareholder of X, the transaction must be examined to determine whether the value of the property exceeds the value of the consideration furnished by A. For this purpose, the value of the property is its fair market value (determined without regard to any seller financing).

(ii) Assume that the fair market value of the property is $900,000 and that the issue price of the debt instrument under § 1.1274-4 is $643,928. Thus, the value of the consideration furnished by A is $843,928 (the sum of $200,000 (the portion of the consideration attributable to the down payment) and $643,928 (the portion of the consideration attributable to the debt instrument)). Since the value of the property ($900,000) exceeds the value of the consideration ($843,928), X Corporation is treated as having made a distribution to shareholder A to which section 301 applies. The amount of the distribution is $56,072 (the difference between $900,000 and $843,928). The basis of the property in the hands of A is $900,000 ($843,928 (consideration actually furnished by A) increased by $56,072 (the amount of the section 301 distribution)).

Example (2). The facts are the same as in Example (1) except that the fair market value of the property is $800,000. X is not treated as having made a section 301 distribution to A and A's basis in the property is $800,000. The transaction need not be examined for excessive consideration since a sale from a corporation to a shareholder ordinarily would not be used to disguise a contribution to capital from the shareholder to the corporation.

Example (3). (i) C sells nonpublicly traded property to his employer D for $300,000 in cash and D's debt instrument having a face amount of $1,000,000, payable in 5 years with interest payable semiannually at a rate of 9 percent. Because D is C's employer, the transaction must be examined to determine if a portion of the amount designated as consideration for the property is in fact disguised compensation.

(ii) Assume that the fair market value of the property (assuming no seller financing), is $1,000,000 and that the issue price of D's debt instrument is $1,000,000. Assume further that a buyer unrelated to D and having the same creditworthiness as C would be willing to pay $1,200,000 for the property if allowed to pay $300,000 in cash and $900,000 in the form of a 5-year debt instrument calling for semiannual payments of interest at a rate of 9 percent. The value of the consideration furnished by D is $1,300,000 (cash of $300,000 plus a debt instrument having an issue price of $1,000,000). Since this amount exceeds the value of the property by $100,000, only $200,000 of the $300,000 transferred from D to C is treated as consideration furnished for the property. The remaining $100,000 is treated as compensation. D's basis in the property is $1,200,000 (cash consideration of $200,000 plus a debt instrument with an issue price of $1,000,000).

Example (4). The facts are the same as in Example (3) except that the property could be sold to the unrelated buyer for $1,400,000 (assuming a down payment of $300,000 and 5-year seller financing at 9 percent for the balance of the purchase price). Because the value of the consideration furnished by D ($1,300,000) does not exceed the value of the property ($1,400,000), D is not treated as having paid compensation to C. D's basis in the property is $1,300,000. The transaction need not be examined for insufficient consideration since employees ordinarily do not make bargain sales to their employers. [Prop. Reg. § 1.1012-2.]

[Proposed 4-8-86.]

§ 1.1014-1. Basis of property acquired from a decedent.—(a) *General rule.*—The purpose of section 1014 is, in general, to provide a basis for property acquired from a decedent that is equal to the value placed upon such property for purposes of the federal estate tax. Accordingly, the general rule is that the basis of property acquired from a decedent is the fair market value of such property at the date of the decedent's death, or, if the decedent's executor so elects, at the alternate valuation date prescribed in section 2032, or in section 811(j) of the Internal Revenue Code (Code) of 1939. However, the basis of property acquired from certain decedents who died in 2010 is determined under section 1022, if the decedent's executor made an election under section 301(c) of the Tax Relief, Unemployment Insurance Reauthorization, and Job Creation Act of 2010, Public Law 111-312 (124 Stat. 3296, 3300 (2010)). See section 1022. Property acquired from a decedent includes, principally, property acquired by bequest, devise, or inheritance, and, in the case of decedents dying after December 31, 1953, property required to be included in determining the value of the decedent's gross estate under any provision of the Code of 1954 or the Code of 1939. The general rule governing basis of property acquired from a decedent, as well as other rules prescribed elsewhere in this section, shall have no application if the property is sold, exchanged, or otherwise disposed of before the decedent's death by the person who acquired the property from the decedent. For general rules on the applicable valuation date where the executor of a decedent's estate elects under section 2032, or under section 811(j) of the Code of 1939, to value the decedent's gross estate at the alternate valuation date prescribed in such sections, see § 1.1014-3(e).

(c) *Property to which section 1014 does not apply.*—Section 1014 shall have no application to the following classes of property:

(1) Property which constitutes a right to receive an item of income in respect of a decedent under section 691; and

(2) Restricted stock options described in section 421 which the employee has not exercised at death if the employee died before January 1, 1957. In the case of employees dying after December 31, 1956, see paragraph (d)(4) of § 1.421-5. In the case of employees dying in a taxable year ending after December 31, 1963, see paragraph (c)(4) of § 1.421-9 with respect to an option described in part II of subchapter D.

* * *

[Reg. § 1.1014-1.]

□ [*T.D.* 6265, 11-6-57. *Amended by T.D.* 6527, 1-18-61; *T.D.* 6887, 6-23-66; *T.D.* 7283, 8-2-73 *and T.D.* 9811, 1-18-2017.]

§ 1.1014-2. Property acquired from a decedent.—(a) *In general.*—The following property, except where otherwise indicated, is considered to have been acquired from a decedent and the basis thereof is determined in accordance with the general rule in § 1.1014-1:

(1) Without regard to the date of the decedent's death, property acquired by bequest, devise, or inheritance, or by the decedent's estate from the decedent, whether the property was acquired under the decedent's will or under the law governing the descent and distribution of the property of decedents. However, see paragraph (c)(1) of this section if the property was acquired by bequest or inheritance from a decedent dying after August 26, 1937, and if such property consists of stock or securities of a foreign personal holding company.

(2) Without regard to the date of the decedent's death, property transferred by the decedent during his lifetime in trust to pay the income for life to or on the order or direction of the decedent, with the right reserved to the decedent at all times before his death to revoke the trust.

(3) In the case of decedents dying after December 31, 1951, property transferred by the decedent during his lifetime in trust to pay the income for life to or on the order or direction of the decedent with the right reserved to the decedent at all times before his death to make any change in the enjoyment thereof through the exercise of a power to alter, amend, or terminate the trust.

(4) Without regard to the date of the decedent's death, property passing without full and adequate consideration under a general power of appointment exercised by the decedent by will. (See section 2041(b) for definition of general power of appointment.)

(5) In the case of decedents dying after December 31, 1947, property which represents the surviving spouse's one-half share of community property held by the decedent and the surviving spouse under the community property laws of any State, Territory, or possession of the United States or any foreign country, if at least one-half of the whole of the community interest in that property was includible in determining the value of the decedent's gross estate under part III, chapter 11 of the Internal Revenue Code of 1954 (relating to the estate tax) or section 811 of the Internal Revenue Code of 1939. It is not necessary for the application of this subparagraph that an estate tax return be

required to be filed for the estate of the decedent or that an estate tax be payable.

* * *

(b) *Property acquired from a decedent dying after December 31, 1953.*—(1) *In general.*—In addition to the property described in paragraph (a) of this section, and except as otherwise provided in subparagraph (3) of this paragraph, in the case of a decedent dying after December 31, 1953, property shall also be considered to have been acquired from the decedent to the extent that both of the following conditions are met: (i) the property was acquired from the decedent by reason of death, form of ownership, or other conditions (including property acquired through the exercise or non-exercise of a power of appointment), and (ii) the property is includible in the decedent's gross estate under the provisions of the Internal Revenue Code of 1954, or the Internal Revenue Code of 1939, because of such acquisition. The basis of such property in the hands of the person who acquired it from the decedent shall be determined in accordance with the general rule in § 1.1014-1. See, however, § 1.1014-6 for special adjustments if such property is acquired before the death of the decedent. See also subparagraph (3) of this paragraph for a description of property not within the scope of this paragraph.

(2) *Rules for the application of subparagraph (1) of this paragraph.*—Except as provided in subparagraph (3) of this paragraph, this paragraph generally includes all property acquired from a decedent, which is includible in the gross estate of the decedent if the decedent died after December 31, 1953. It is not necessary for the application of this paragraph that an estate tax return be required to be filed for the estate of the decedent or that an estate tax be payable. Property acquired prior to the death of a decedent which is includible in the decedent's gross estate, such as property transferred by a decedent in contemplation of death, and property held by a taxpayer and the decedent as joint tenants or as tenants by the entireties is within the scope of this paragraph. Also, this paragraph includes property acquired through the exercise or non-exercise of a power of appointment where such property is includible in the decedent's gross estate. It does not include property not includible in the decedent's gross estate such as property not situated in the United States acquired from a nonresident who is not a citizen of the United States.

(3) *Exceptions to application of this paragraph.*—The rules of this paragraph are not applicable to the following property:

(i) Annuities described in section 72;

(ii) Stock or securities of a foreign personal holding company as described in section 1014(b)(5) (see paragraph (c)(1) of this section);

(iii) Property described in any paragraph other than paragraph (9) of section 1014(b). See paragraphs (a) and (c) of this section.

In illustration of subdivision (ii), assume that A acquired by gift stock of a character described in paragraph (c)(1) of this section from a donor and upon the death of the donor the stock was includible in the donor's estate as being a gift in contemplation of death. A's basis in the stock would not be determined by reference to its fair market value at the donor's death under the general rule in section 1014(a). Furthermore, the special basis rules prescribed in paragraph (c)(1) are not applicable to such property acquired by gift in contemplation of death. It will be necessary to refer to the rules in section 1015(a) to determine the basis.

* * *

[Reg. § 1.1014-2.]

☐ [*T.D.* 6265, 11-6-57.]

§ 1.1014-4. Uniformity of basis; adjustment to basis.—(a) *In general.*—(1) The basis of property acquired from a decedent, as determined under section 1014(a) or section 1022, is uniform in the hands of every person having possession or enjoyment of the property at any time under the will or other instrument or under the laws of descent and distribution. The principle of uniform basis means that the basis of the property (to which proper adjustments must, of course, be made) will be the same, or uniform, whether the property is possessed or enjoyed by the executor or administrator, the heir, the legatee or devisee, or the trustee or beneficiary of a trust created by a will or an inter vivos trust. In determining the amount allowed or allowable to a taxpayer in computing taxable income as deductions for depreciation or depletion under section 1016(a)(2), the uniform basis of the property shall at all times be used and adjusted. The sale, exchange, or other disposition by a life tenant or remainderman of his interest in property will, for purposes of this section, have no effect upon the uniform basis of the property in the hands of those who acquired it from the decedent. Thus, gain or loss on sale of trust assets by the trustee will be determined without regard to the prior sale of any interest in the property. Moreover, any adjustment for depreciation shall be made to the uniform basis of the property without regard to such prior sale, exchange, or other disposition.

(2) Under the law governing wills and the distribution of the property of decedents, all titles to property acquired by bequest, devise,

or inheritance relate back to the death of the decedent, even though the interest of the person taking the title was, at the date of death of the decedent, legal, equitable, vested, contingent, general, specific, residual, conditional, executory, or otherwise. Accordingly, there is a common acquisition date for all titles to property acquired from a decedent within the meaning of section 1014 or section 1022, and, for this reason, a common or uniform basis for all such interests. For example, if distribution of personal property left by a decedent is not made until one year after his death, the basis of such property in the hands of the legatee is its fair market value at the time when the decedent died, and not when the legatee actually received the property. If the bequest is of the residue to trustees in trust, and the executors do not distribute the residue to such trustees until five years after the death of the decedent, the basis of each piece of property left by the decedent and thus received, in the hands of the trustees, is its fair market value at the time when the decedent dies. If the bequest is to trustees in trust to pay to A during his lifetime the income of the property bequeathed, and after his death to distribute such property to the survivors of a class, and upon A's death the property is distributed to the taxpayer as the sole survivor, the basis of such property, in the hands of the taxpayer, is its fair market value at the time when the decedent died. The purpose of the Code in prescribing a general uniform basis rule for property acquired from a decedent is, on the one hand, to tax the gain, in respect of such property, to him who realizes it (without regard to the circumstance that at the death of the decedent it may have been quite uncertain whether the taxpayer would take or gain anything); and, on the other hand, not to recognize as gain any element of value resulting solely from the circumstance that the possession or enjoyment of the taxpayer was postponed. Such postponement may be, for example, until the administration of the decedent's estate is completed, until the period of the possession or enjoyment of another has terminated, or until an uncertain event has happened. It is the increase or decrease in the value of property reflected in a sale or other disposition which is recognized as the measure of gain or loss.

(3) The principles stated in subparagraphs (1) and (2) of this paragraph do not apply to property transferred by an executor, administrator or trustee, to an heir, legatee, devisee or beneficiary under circumstances such that the transfer constitutes a sale or exchange. In such a case, gain or loss must be recognized by the transferor to the extent required by the revenue laws, and the transferee acquires a basis equal to the fair market value of the property on the date of the transfer. Thus, for example, if the trustee of a trust created by will transfers to a beneficiary, in satisfaction of a specific bequest of $10,000, securities which had a fair market value of $9,000 on the date of the decedent's death (the applicable valuation date) and $10,000 on the date of the transfer, the trust realizes a taxable gain of $1,000 and the basis of the securities in the hands of the beneficiary would be $10,000. As a further example, if the executor of an estate transfers to a trust property worth $200,000, which had a fair market value of $175,000 on the date of the decedent's death (the applicable valuation date), in satisfaction of the decedent's bequest in trust for the benefit of his wife of cash or securities to be selected by the executor in an amount sufficient to utilize the marital deduction to the maximum extent authorized by law (after taking into consideration any other property qualifying for the marital deduction), capital gain in the amount of $25,000 would be realized by the estate and the basis of the property in the hands of the trustees would be $200,000. If, on the other hand, the decedent bequeathed a fraction of his residuary estate to a trust for the benefit of his wife, which fraction will not change regardless of any fluctuations in value of property in the decedent's estate after his death, no gain or loss would be realized by the estate upon transfer of property to the trust, and the basis of the property in the hands of the trustee would be its fair market value on the date of the decedent's death or on the alternate valuation date.

(b) *Multiple interests.*—Where more than one person has an interest in property acquired from a decedent, the basis of such property shall be determined and adjusted without regard to the multiple interests. The basis for computing gain or loss on the sale of any one of such multiple interests shall be determined under § 1.1014-5. Thus, the deductions for depreciation and for depletion allowed or allowable, under sections 167 and 611, to a legal life tenant as if the life tenant were the absolute owner of the property, constitute an adjustment to the basis of the property not only in the hands of the life tenant, but also in the hands of the remainderman and every other person to whom the same uniform basis is applicable. Similarly, the deductions allowed or allowable under sections 167 and 611, both to the trustee and to the trust beneficiaries, constitute an adjustment to the basis of the property not only in the hands of the trustee, but also in the hands of the trust beneficiaries and every other person to whom the uniform basis is applicable. See, however, section 262. Similarly, adjustments in respect of capital expenditures or losses, tax-free distributions, or other distributions applicable in reduction of basis, or other items for which the basis is adjustable are made without regard to which one of the persons to whom the same uniform basis is applicable makes the capital expenditures or sustains the capital losses, or to whom the tax-free or other distributions are made, or to whom the deductions are allowed or allowable. See § 1.1014-6 for adjustments in respect of property acquired from a decedent prior to his death.

(c) *Records.*—The executor or other legal representative of the decedent, the fiduciary of a trust under a will, the life tenant and every other person to whom a uniform basis under this section is applicable, shall maintain records showing in detail all deductions, distributions, or other items for which adjustment to basis is required to be made by sections 1016 and 1017, and shall furnish to the district director such information with respect to those adjustments as he may require.

(d) *Effective/applicability date.*—This section applies on and after January 19, 2017. For rules before January 19, 2017, see § 1.1014-4 as contained in 26 CFR part 1 revised as of April 1, 2016. [Reg. § 1.1014-4.]

□ [*T.D.* 6265, 11-6-57. *Amended by T.D.* 9811, 1-18-2017.]

§ 1.1014-5. Gain or loss.—(a) *Sale or other disposition of a life interest, remainder interest, or other interest in property acquired from a decedent.*—(1) Except as provided in paragraph (b) or (c) of this section with respect to the sale or other disposition after October 9, 1969, of a term interest in property, gain or loss from a sale or other disposition of a life interest, remainder interest, or other interest in property acquired from a decedent is determined by comparing the amount of the proceeds with the amount of that part of the adjusted uniform basis which is assignable to the interest so transferred. The adjusted uniform basis is the uniform basis of the entire property adjusted to the date of sale or other disposition of any such interest as required by sections 1016 and 1017. The uniform basis is the unadjusted basis of the entire property determined immediately after the decedent's death under the applicable sections of part II of subchapter O of chapter 1 of the Code.

(2) Except as provided in paragraph (b) of this section, the proper measure of gain or loss resulting from a sale or other disposition of an interest in property acquired from a decedent is so much of the increase or decrease in the value of the entire property as is reflected in such sale or other disposition. Hence, in ascertaining the basis of a life interest, remainder interest, or other interest which has been so transferred, the uniform basis rule contemplates that proper adjustments will be made to reflect the change in relative value of the interests on account of the passage of time.

(3) The factors set forth in the tables contained in § 20.2031-7 or, for certain prior periods, § 20.2031-7A of Part 20 of this chapter (Estate Tax Regulations) shall be used in the manner provided therein in determining the basis of the life interest, the remainder interest, or the term certain interest in the property on the date such interest is sold. The basis of the life interest, the remainder interest, or the term certain interest is computed by multiplying the uniform basis (adjusted to the time of the sale) by the appropriate factor. In the case of the sale of a life interest or a remainder interest, the factor used is the factor (adjusted where appropriate) which appears in the life interest or the remainder interest column of the table opposite the age (on the date of the sale) of the person at whose death the life interest will terminate. In the case of the sale of a term certain interest, the factor used is the factor (adjusted where appropriate) which appears in the term certain column of the table opposite the number of years remaining (on the date of sale) before the term certain interest will terminate.

(b) *Sale or other disposition of certain term interests.*—(1) *In general.*—In determining gain or loss from the sale or other disposition after October 9, 1969, of a term interest in property (as defined in § 1.1001-1(f)(2)) the adjusted basis of which is determined pursuant, or by reference, to section 1014 (relating to the basis of property acquired from a decedent), section 1015 (relating to the basis of property acquired by gift or by a transfer in trust), or section 1022 (relating to the basis of property acquired from certain decedents who died in 2010), that part of the adjusted uniform basis assignable under the rules of paragraph (a) of this section to the interest sold or otherwise disposed of shall be disregarded to the extent and in the manner provided by section 1001(e) and § 1.1001-1(f).

* * *

(c) *Sale or other disposition of a term interest in a tax-exempt trust.*—(1) *In general.*—In the case of any sale or other disposition by a taxable beneficiary of a term interest (as defined in § 1.1001-1(f)(2)) in a tax-exempt trust (as defined in paragraph (c)(2) of this section) to which section 1001(e)(3) applies, the taxable beneficiary's share of adjusted uniform basis, determined as of (and immediately before) the sale or disposition of that interest, is—

(i) That part of the adjusted uniform basis assignable to the term interest of the taxable beneficiary under the rules of paragraph (a) of this section reduced, but not below zero, by

(ii) An amount determined by applying the same actuarial share applied in paragraph (c)(1)(i) of this section to the sum of—

(A) The trust's undistributed net ordinary income within the meaning of section 664(b)(1) and § 1.664-1(d)(1)(ii)(*a*)(*1*) for the current and prior taxable years of the trust, if any; and

(B) The trust's undistributed net capital gains within the meaning of section 664(b)(2) and § 1.664-1(d)(1)(ii)(*a*)(*1*) for the current and prior taxable years of the trust, if any.

(2) *Tax-exempt trust defined.*—For purposes of this section, the term *tax-exempt trust* means a charitable remainder annuity trust or a charitable remainder unitrust as defined in section 664.

(3) *Taxable beneficiary defined.*—For purposes of this section, the term *taxable beneficiary* means any person other than an organization described in section 170(c) or exempt from taxation under section 501(a).

* * *

[Reg. § 1.1014-5.]

☐ [*T.D.* 6265, 11-6-57. *Amended by T.D.* 7142, 9-23-71, *T.D.* 8540, 6-9-94, *T.D.* 9729, 8-11-2015 *and T.D.* 9811, 1-18-2017.]

§ 1.1015-1. Basis of property acquired by gift after December 31, 1920.—(a) *General rule.*—(1) In the case of property acquired by gift after December 31, 1920 (whether by a transfer in trust or otherwise), the basis of the property for the purpose of determining gain is the same as it would be in the hands of the donor or the last preceding owner by whom it was not acquired by gift. The same rule applies in determining loss unless the basis (adjusted for the period prior to the date of gift in accordance with sections 1016 and 1017) is greater than the fair market value of the property at the time of the gift. In such case, the basis for determining loss is the fair market value at the time of the gift.

(2) The provisions of subparagraph (1) of this paragraph may be illustrated by the following example.

Example. A acquires by gift income-producing property which has an adjusted basis of $100,000 at the date of gift. The fair market value of the property at the date of gift is $90,000. A later sells the property for $95,000. In such case there is neither gain nor loss. The basis for determining loss is $90,000; therefore, there is no loss. Furthermore, there is no gain, since the basis for determining gain is $100,000.

(3) If the facts necessary to determine the basis of property in the hands of the donor or the last preceding owner by whom it was not acquired by gift are unknown to the donee, the district director shall, if possible, obtain such facts from such donor or last preceding owner, or any other person cognizant thereof. If the district director finds it impossible to obtain such facts, the basis in the hands of such donor or last preceding owner shall be the fair market value of such property as found by the district director as of the date or approximate date at which, according to the best information the district director is able to obtain, such property was acquired by such donor or last preceding owner. See paragraph (e) of this section for rules relating to fair market value.

(b) *Uniform basis; proportionate parts of.*—Property acquired by gift has a single or uniform basis although more than one person may acquire an interest in such property. The uniform basis of the property remains fixed subject to proper adjustment for items under sections 1016 and 1017. However, the value of the proportionate parts of the uniform basis represented, for instance, by the respective interests of the life tenant and remainderman are adjustable to reflect the change in the relative values of such interest on account of the lapse of time. The portion of the basis attributable to an interest at the time of its sale or other disposition shall be determined under the rule provided in § 1.1014-5. In determining gain or loss from the sale or other disposition after October 9, 1969, of a term interest in property (as defined in § 1.1001-1(f)(2)) the adjusted basis of which is determined pursuant, or by reference, to section 1015, that part of the adjusted uniform basis assignable under the rules of § 1.1014-5(a) to the interest sold or otherwise disposed of shall be disregarded to the extent and in the manner provided by section 1001(e) and § 1.1001-1(f).

(c) *Time of acquisition.*—The date that the donee acquires an interest in property by gift is when the donor relinquishes dominion over the property and not necessarily when title to the property is acquired by the donee. Thus, the date that the donee acquires an interest in property by gift where he is a successor in interest, such as in the case of a remainderman of a life estate or a beneficiary of the distribution of the corpus of a trust, is the date such interests are created by the donor and not the date the property is actually acquired.

(d) *Property acquired by gift from a decedent dying after December 31, 1953.*—If an interest in property was acquired by the taxpayer by gift from a donor dying after December 31, 1953, under conditions which require the inclusion of the property in the donor's gross estate for estate tax purposes, and the property had not been sold, exchanged, or otherwise disposed of by the taxpayer before the donor's death, see the rules prescribed in section 1014 and the regulations thereunder.

(e) *Fair market value.*—For the purposes of this section, the value of property as appraised for the purpose of the Federal gift tax, or, if the gift is not subject to such tax, its value as appraised for the purpose of a State gift tax, shall be deemed to be the fair market value of the property at the time of the gift.

(f) *Reinvestments by fiduciary.*—If the property is an investment by the fiduciary under the terms of the gift (as, for example, in the case of a sale by the fiduciary of property transferred under the terms of the gift, and the reinvestment of the proceeds), the cost or other basis to the fiduciary is taken in lieu of the basis specified in paragraph (a) of this section.

* * *

[Reg. § 1.1015-1.]

☐ [*T.D.* 6265, 11-6-57. *Amended by T.D.* 6693, 12-2-63 *and T.D.* 7142, 9-23-71.]

§ 1.1015-2. Transfer of property in trust after December 31, 1920.—(a) *General rule.*—(1) In the case of property acquired after December 31, 1920, by transfer in trust (other than by a transfer in trust by a gift, bequest, or devise) the basis of property so acquired is the same as it would be in the hands of the grantor increased in the amount of gain or decreased in the amount of loss recognized to the grantor upon such transfer under the law applicable to the year in which the transfer was made. If the taxpayer acquired the property by a transfer in trust, this basis applies whether the property be in the hands of the trustee, or the beneficiary, and whether acquired prior to the termination of the trust and distribution of the property, or thereafter.

(2) The principles stated in paragraph (b) of § 1.1015-1 concerning the uniform basis are applicable in determining the basis of property where more than one person acquires an interest in property by transfer in trust after December 31, 1920.

(b) *Reinvestment by fiduciary.*—If the property is an investment made by the fiduciary (as, for example, in the case of a sale by the fiduciary of property transferred by the grantor, and the reinvestment of the proceeds), the cost or other basis to the fiduciary is taken in lieu of the basis specified in paragraph (a) of this section. [Reg. § 1.1015-2.]

☐ [*T.D.* 6265, 11-6-57.]

§ 1.1015-4. Transfers in part a gift and in part a sale.—(a) *General rule.*—Where a transfer of property is in part a sale and in part a gift, the unadjusted basis of the property in the hands of the transferee is the sum of—

(1) Whichever of the following is the greater:

(i) The amount paid by the transferee for the property, or

(ii) The transferor's adjusted basis for the property at the time of the transfer, and

(2) The amount of increase, if any, in basis authorized by section 1015(d) for gift tax paid (see § 1.1015-5).

For determining loss, the unadjusted basis of the property in the hands of the transferee shall not be greater than the fair market value of the property at the time of such transfer. For determination of gain or loss of the transferor, see § 1.1001-1(e) and § 1.1011-2. For special rule where there has been a charitable contribution of less than a taxpayer's entire interest in property, see section 170(e)(2) and § 1.170A-4(c).

(b) *Examples.*—The rule of paragraph (a) of this section is illustrated by the following examples:

Example (1). If A transfers property to his son for $30,000, and such property at the time of the transfer has an adjusted basis of $30,000 in A's hands (and a fair market value of $60,000), the unadjusted basis of the property in the hands of the son is $30,000.

Example (2). If A transfers property to his son for $60,000, and such property at the time of transfer had an adjusted basis of $30,000 in A's hands (and a fair market value of $90,000), the unadjusted basis of such property in the hands of the son is $60,000.

Example (3). If A transfers property to his son for $30,000, and such property at the time of transfer has an adjusted basis in A's hands of $60,000 (and a fair market value of $90,000), the unadjusted basis of such property in the hands of the son is $60,000.

Example (4). If A transfers property to his son for $30,000 and such property at the time of transfer has an adjusted basis of $90,000 in A's hands (and a fair market value of $60,000), the unadjusted basis of the property in the hands of the son is $90,000. However, since the adjusted basis of the property in A's hands at the time of the transfer was greater than the fair market value at that time, for the purpose of determining any loss on a later sale or other disposition of the property by the son its unadjusted basis in his hands is $60,000. [Reg. § 1.1015-4.]

☐ [*T.D.* 6265, 11-6-57. *Amended by T.D.* 6693, 12-2-63, *and T.D.* 7207, 10-3-72.]

§1.1016-2. Items properly chargeable to capital account.—(a) The cost or other basis shall be properly adjusted for any expenditure, receipt, loss, or other item, properly chargeable to capital account, including the cost of improvements and betterments made to the property. No adjustment shall be made in respect of any item which, under any applicable provision of law or regulation, is treated as an item not properly chargeable to capital account but is allowable as a deduction in computing net or taxable income for the taxable year. For example, in the case of oil and gas wells no adjustment may be made in respect of any intangible drilling and development expense allowable as a deduction in computing net or taxable income. See the regulations under section 263(c).

(b) The application of the foregoing provisions may be illustrated by the following example:

Example. A, who makes his returns on the calendar year basis, purchased property in 1941 for $10,000. He subsequently expended $6,000 for improvements. Disregarding, for the purpose of this example, the adjustments required for depreciation, the adjusted basis of the property is $16,000. If A sells the property in 1954 for $20,000, the amount of his gain will be $4,000.

(c) Adjustment to basis shall be made for carrying charges such as taxes and interest, with respect to property (whether real or personal, improved or unimproved, and whether productive or unproductive), which the taxpayer elects to treat as chargeable to capital account under section 266, rather than as an allowable deduction. The term "taxes" for this purpose includes duties and excise taxes but does not include income taxes.

(d) Expenditures described in section 173 to establish, maintain, or increase the circulation of a newspaper, magazine, or other periodical are chargeable to capital account only in accordance with and in the manner provided in the regulations under section 173. [Reg. §1.1016-2.]

□ [*T.D.* 6265, 11-6-57.]

§1.1016-3. Exhaustion, wear and tear, obsolescence, amortization, and depletion for periods since February 28, 1913.—(a) *In general.*—(1) *Adjustment where deduction is claimed.*—(i) For taxable periods beginning on or after January 1, 1952, the cost or other basis of property shall be decreased for exhaustion, wear and tear, obsolescence, amortization, and depletion by the greater of the following two amounts: (*a*) the amount allowed as deductions in computing taxable income, to the extent resulting in a reduction of the taxpayer's income taxes, or (*b*) the amount allowable for the years involved. See paragraph (b) of this section. Where the taxpayer makes an appropriate election the above rule is applicable for periods since February 28, 1913, and before January 1, 1952. See paragraph (d) of this section. For rule for such periods where no election is made, see paragraph (c) of this section.

(ii) The determination of the amount properly allowable for exhaustion, wear and tear, obsolescence, amortization, and depletion must be made on the basis of facts reasonably known to exist at the end of the taxable year. A taxpayer is not permitted to take advantage in a later year of the taxpayer's prior failure to take any such allowance or the taxpayer's taking an allowance plainly inadequate under the known facts in prior years. In the case of depreciation, if in prior years the taxpayer has consistently taken proper deductions under one method, the amount allowable for such prior years may not be increased, even though a greater amount would have been allowable under another proper method. For rules governing losses on retirement or disposition of depreciable property, including rules for determining basis, see §1.167(a)-8, 1.168(i)-1(e), or 1.168(i)-8, as applicable. The application of this paragraph is illustrated by the following example (for purposes of this example, assume section 167(f)(1) as in effect on September 19, 2013, applies to taxable years beginning on or after January 1, 2014):

Example. On July 1, 2014, A, a calendar-year taxpayer, purchased and placed in service "off-the-shelf" computer software at a cost of $36,000. This computer software is not an amortizable section 197 intangible. Pursuant to section 167(f)(1), the useful life of the computer software is 36 months. It has no salvage value. Computer software placed in service in 2014 is not eligible for the additional first year depreciation deduction provided by section 168(k). A did not deduct any depreciation for the computer software for 2014 and deducted depreciation of $12,000 for the computer software for 2015. As a result, the total amount of depreciation allowed for the computer software as of December 31, 2015, was $12,000. However, the total amount of depreciation allowable for the computer software as of December 31, 2015, is $18,000 ($6,000 for 2014 + $12,000 for 2015). As a result, the unrecovered cost of the computer software as of December 31, 2015, is $18,000 (cost of $36,000 less the depreciation allowable of $18,000 as of December 31, 2015). Accordingly, depreciation for 2016 for the computer software is $12,000 (unrecovered cost of $18,000 divided by the remaining useful life of 18 months as of January 1, 2016, multiplied by 12 full months in 2016).

(2) *Adjustment for amount allowable where no depreciation deduction claimed.*—(i) If the taxpayer has not taken a depreciation deduction either in the taxable year or for any prior taxable year, adjustments to basis of the property for depreciation allowable shall be determined by using the straight-line method of depreciation. (See § 1.1016-4 for adjustments in the case of persons exempt from income taxation.)

(ii) For taxable years beginning after December 31, 1953, and ending after August 16, 1954, if the taxpayer with respect to any property has taken a deduction for depreciation properly under one of the methods provided in section 167(b) for one or more years but has omitted the deduction in other years, the adjustment to basis for the depreciation allowable in such a case will be the deduction under the method which was used by the taxpayer with respect to that property. Thus, if A acquired property in 1954 on which he properly computed his depreciation deduction under the method described in section 167(b)(2) (the declining-balance method) for the first year of its useful life but did not take a deduction in the second and third year of the asset's life, the adjustment to basis for depreciation allowable for the second and third year will be likewise computed under the declining-balance method.

* * *

[Reg. § 1.1016-3.]

☐ [*T.D.* 6265, 11-6-57. *Amended by T.D.* 9105, 12-30-2003; *T.D.* 9307, 12-22-2006; *T.D.* 9564, 12-23-2011; *T.D.* 9636, 9-13-2013 *and T.D.* 9689, 8-14-2014.]

§ 1.1016-10. Substituted basis.—(a) When-ever it appears that the basis of property in the hands of the taxpayer is a substituted basis, as defined in section 1016(b), the adjustments indicated in §§ 1.1016-1 to 1.1016-6, inclusive, shall be made after first making in respect of such substituted basis proper adjustments of a similar nature in respect of the period during which the property was held by the transferor, donor, or grantor, or during which the other property was held by the person for whom the basis is to be determined. In addition, whenever it appears that the basis of property in the hands of the taxpayer is a substituted basis, as defined in section 1016(b)(1), the adjustments indicated in §§ 1.1016-7 to 1.1016-9, inclusive, and in section 1017 shall also be made, whenever necessary, after first making in respect of such substituted basis a proper adjustment of a similar nature in respect of the period during which the property was held by the transferor, donor, or grantor. Similar rules shall also be applied in the case of a series of substituted bases.

(b) The application of this section may be illustrated by the following example:

Example. A, who makes his returns upon the calendar year basis, in 1935 purchased the X Building and subsequently gave it to his son B. B exchanged the X Building for the Y Building in a tax-free exchange, and then gave the Y Building to his wife C. C, in determining the gain from the sale or disposition of the Y Building in 1954, is required to reduce the basis of the building by deductions for depreciation which were successively allowed (but not less than the amount allowable) to A and B upon the X Building and to B upon the Y Building, in addition to the deductions for depreciation allowed (but not less than the amount allowable) to herself during her ownership of the Y Building. [Reg. § 1.1016-10.]

☐ [*T.D.* 6265, 11-6-57.]

§ 1.1017-1. Basis reductions following a discharge of indebtedness.—(a) *General rule for section 108(b)(2)(E).*—This paragraph (a) applies to basis reductions under section 108(b)(2)(E) that are required by section 108(a)(1)(A) or (B) because the taxpayer excluded discharge of indebtedness (COD income) from gross income. A taxpayer must reduce in the following order, to the extent of the excluded COD income (but not below zero), the adjusted bases of property held on the first day of the taxable year following the taxable year that the taxpayer excluded COD income from gross income (in proportion to adjusted basis)—

(1) Real property used in a trade or business or held for investment, other than real property described in section 1221(1), that secured the discharged indebtedness immediately before the discharge;

(2) Personal property used in a trade or business or held for investment, other than inventory, accounts receivable, and notes receivable, that secured the discharged indebtedness immediately before the discharge;

(3) Remaining property used in a trade or business or held for investment, other than inventory, accounts receivable, notes receivable, and real property described in section 1221(1);

(4) Inventory, accounts receivable, notes receivable, and real property described in section 1221(1); and

(5) Property not used in a trade or business nor held for investment.

(b) *Operating rules.*—(1) *Prior tax-attribute reduction.*—The amount of excluded COD income applied to reduce basis does not include any COD income applied to reduce tax attributes under sections 108(b)(2)(A) through (D) and, if applicable, section 108(b)(5). For example, if a taxpayer excludes $100 of COD income from gross income under section 108(a) and reduces tax attributes by $40 under sections 108(b)(2)(A) through (D), the taxpayer is required to reduce the adjusted bases of property by $60 ($100 - $40) under section 108(b)(2)(E).

(2) *Multiple discharged indebtednesses.*—If a taxpayer has COD income attributable to more than one discharged indebtedness resulting in the reduction of tax attributes under sections 108(b)(2)(A) through (D) and, if applicable, section 108(b)(5), paragraph (b)(1) of this section must be applied by allocating the tax-attribute reductions among the indebtednesses in proportion to the amount of COD income attributable to each discharged indebtedness. For example, if a taxpayer excludes $20 of COD income attributable to secured indebtedness A and excludes $80 of COD income attributable to unsecured indebtedness B (a total exclusion of $100), and if the taxpayer reduces tax attributes by $40 under sections 108(b)(2)(A) through (D), the taxpayer must reduce the amount of COD income attributable to secured indebtedness A to $12 ($20 - ($20 / $100 × $40)) and must reduce the amount of COD income attributable to unsecured indebtedness B to $48 ($80 - ($80 / $100 × $40)).

(3) *Limitation on basis reductions under section 108(b)(2)(E) in bankruptcy or insolvency.*—If COD income arises from a discharge of indebtedness in a title 11 case or while the taxpayer is insolvent, the amount of any basis reduction under section 108(b)(2)(E) shall not exceed the excess of—

(i) The aggregate of the adjusted bases of property and the amount of money held by the taxpayer immediately after the discharge; over

(ii) The aggregate of the liabilities of the taxpayer immediately after the discharge.

(4) *Transactions to which section 381 applies.*—If a taxpayer realizes COD income that is excluded from gross income under section 108(a) either during or after a taxable year in which the taxpayer is the distributor or transferor of assets in a transaction described in section 381(a), the basis of property acquired by the acquiring corporation in the transaction must reflect the reductions required by section 1017 and this section. For this purpose, the basis of property of the distributor or transferor corporation immediately prior to the transaction described in section 381(a), but after the determination of tax for the year of the distribution or transfer of assets, will be available for reduction under section 108(b)(2). However, the basis of stock or securities of the acquiring corporation, if any, received by the taxpayer in exchange for the transferred assets shall not be available for reduction under section 108(b)(2). See § 1.108-7. This paragraph (b)(4) applies to discharges of indebtedness occurring on or after May 10, 2004.

(c) *Modification of ordering rules for basis reductions under sections 108(b)(5) and 108(c).*—(1) *In general.*—The ordering rules prescribed in paragraph (a) of this section apply, with appropriate modifications, to basis reductions under sections 108(b)(5) and (c). Thus, a taxpayer that elects to reduce basis under section 108(b)(5) may, to the extent that the election applies, reduce only the adjusted basis of property described in paragraphs (a)(1), (2), and (3) of this section and, if an election is made under paragraph (f) of this section, paragraph (a)(4) of this section. Within paragraphs (a)(1),(2), (3) and (4) of this section, such a taxpayer may reduce only the adjusted bases of depreciable property. A taxpayer that elects to apply section 108(c) may reduce only the adjusted basis of property described in paragraphs (a)(1) and (3) of this section and, within paragraphs (a)(1) and (3) of this section, may reduce only the adjusted bases of depreciable real property. Furthermore, for basis reductions under section 108(c), a taxpayer must reduce the adjusted basis of the qualifying real property to the extent of the discharged qualified real property business indebtedness before reducing the adjusted bases of other depreciable real property. The term *qualifying real property* means real property with respect to which the indebtedness is qualified real property business indebtedness within the meaning of section 108(c)(3). See paragraphs (f) and (g) of this section for elections relating to section 1221(1) property and partnership interests.

(2) *Partial basis reductions under section 108(b)(5).*—If the amount of basis reductions under section 108(b)(5) is less than the amount of the COD income excluded from gross income under section 108(a), the taxpayer must reduce the balance of its tax attributes, including any remaining adjusted bases of depreciable and other property, by following the ordering rules under section 108(b)(2). For example, if a taxpayer excludes $100 of COD income from gross income under section 108(a) and elects to reduce the adjusted bases of depreciable property by $10 under section 108(b)(5), the taxpayer must reduce its remaining tax attributes by $90, starting with net operating losses under section 108(b)(2).

(3) *Modification of fresh start rule for prior basis reductions under section 108(b)(5).*—After reducing the adjusted bases of depreciable property under section 108(b)(5), a taxpayer

must compute the limitation on basis reductions under section 1017(b)(2) using the aggregate of the remaining adjusted bases of property. For example, if, immediately after the discharge of indebtedness in a title 11 case, a taxpayer's adjusted bases of property is $100 and its undischarged indebtedness is $70, and if the taxpayer elects to reduce the adjusted bases of depreciable property by $10 under section 108(b)(5), section 1017(b)(2) limits any further basis reductions under section 108(b)(2)(E) to $20 (($100 - $10) - $70).

(d) *Changes in security.*—If any property is added or eliminated as security for an indebtedness during the one-year period preceding the discharge of that indebtedness, such addition or elimination shall be disregarded where a principal purpose of the change is to affect the taxpayer's basis reductions under section 1017.

(e) *Depreciable property.*—For purposes of this section, the term *depreciable property* means any property of a character subject to the allowance for depreciation or amortization, but only if the basis reduction would reduce the amount of depreciation or amortization which otherwise would be allowable for the period immediately following such reduction. Thus, for example, a lessor cannot reduce the basis of leased property where the lessee's obligation in respect of the property will restore to the lessor the loss due to depreciation during the term of the lease, since the lessor cannot take depreciation in respect of such property.

* * *

[Reg. § 1.1017-1.]

☐ [*T.D.* 6158, 1-6-56. *Amended by T.D.* 8787, 10-21-98; *T.D.* 8847, 12-14-99; *T.D.* 9080, 7-17-2003; *T.D.* 9100, 12-18-2003 (*corrected* 2-2-2004); *T.D.* 9127, 5-10-2004 *and T.D.* 9300, 12-7-2006.]

§ 1.1019-1. Property on which lessee had made improvements.—In any case in which a lessee of real property has erected buildings or made other improvements upon the leased property and the lease is terminated by forfeiture or otherwise resulting in the realization by such lessor of income which, were it not for the provisions of section 109, would be includible in gross income of the lessor, the amount so excluded from gross income shall not be taken into account in determining the basis or the adjusted basis of such property or any portion thereof in the hands of the lessor. If, however, in any taxable year beginning before January 1, 1942, there has been included in the gross income of the lessor an amount representing any part of the value of such property attributable to such buildings or improvements, the basis of each portion of such property shall be properly adjusted for the amount so included in gross income. For example, A leased in 1930 to B for a period of 25 years unimproved real property and in accordance with the terms of the lease B erected a building on the property. It was estimated that upon expiration of the lease the building would have a depreciated value of $50,000, which value the lessor elected to report (beginning in 1931) as income over the term of the lease. This method of reporting was used until 1942. In 1952 B forfeits the lease. The amount of $22,000 reported as income by A during the years 1931 to 1941, inclusive, shall be added to the basis of the property represented by the improvements in the hands of A. If in such case A did not report during the period of the lease any income attributable to the value of the building erected by the lessee and the lease was forfeited in 1940 when the building was worth $75,000, such amount, having been included in gross income under the law applicable to that year, is added to the basis of the property represented by the improvements in the hands of A. As to treatment of such property for the purposes of capital gains and losses, see subchapter P (sections 1201 and following), chapter 1 of the Code. [Reg. § 1.1019-1.]

☐ [*T.D.* 6265, 11-6-57.]

Common Nontaxable Exchanges

»»→ Caution: Reg. § 1.1031(a)-1 does not reflect changes made by the Tax Cuts and Jobs Act of 2017, which repealed the application of Section 1031 to personal property.

§ 1.1031(a)-1. Property held for productive use in trade or business or for investment.—(a) *In general.*—(1) *Exchanges of property solely for property of a like kind.*—Section 1031(a)(1) provides an exception from the general rule requiring the recognition of gain or loss upon the sale or exchange of property. Under section 1031(a)(1), no gain or loss is recognized if property held for productive use in a trade or business or for investment is exchanged solely for property of a like kind to be held either for productive use in a trade or business or for investment. Under section 1031(a)(1), property held for productive use in trade or business may be exchanged for property held for investment. Similarly, under section 1031(a)(1), property held for investment may be exchanged for property held for productive use in a trade or business. However, section 1031(a)(2) provides that section 1031(a)(1) does not apply to any exchange of—

(i) Stock in trade or other property held primarily for sale;

(ii) Stocks, bonds, or notes;

(iii) Other securities or evidences of indebtedness or interest;

(iv) Interests in a partnership;

(v) Certificates of trust or beneficial interests; or

(vi) Choses in action.

Section 1031(a)(1) does not apply to any exchange of interests in a partnership regardless of whether the interests exchanged are general or limited partnership interests or are interests in the same partnership or in different partnerships. An interest in a partnership that has in effect a valid election under section 761(a) to be excluded from the application of all of subchapter K is treated as an interest in each of the assets of the partnership and not as an interest in a partnership for purposes of section 1031(a)(2)(D) and paragraph (a)(1)(iv) of this section. An exchange of an interest in such a partnership does not qualify for nonrecognition of gain or loss under section 1031 with respect to any asset of the partnership that is described in section 1031(a)(2) or to the extent the exchange of assets of the partnership does not otherwise satisfy the requirements of section 1031(a).

(2) *Exchanges of property not solely for property of a like kind.*—A transfer is not within the provisions of section 1031(a) if, as part of the consideration, the taxpayer receives money or property which does not meet the requirements of section 1031(a), but the transfer, if otherwise qualified, will be within the provisions of either section 1031(b) or (c). Similarly, a transfer is not within the provisions of section 1031(a) if, as part of the consideration, the other party to the exchange assumes a liability of the taxpayer (or acquires property from the taxpayer that is subject to a liability), but the transfer, if otherwise qualified, will be within the provisions of either section 1031(b) or (c). A transfer of property meeting the requirements of section 1031(a) may be within the provisions of section 1031(a) even though the taxpayer transfers in addition property not meeting the requirements of section 1031(a) or money. However, the nonrecognition treatment provided by section 1031(a) does not apply to the property transferred which does not meet the requirements of section 1031(a).

(b) *Definition of "like kind."* .—As used in section 1031(a), the words "like kind" have reference to the nature or character of the property and not to its grade or quality. One kind or class of property may not, under that section, be exchanged for property of a different kind or class. The fact that any real estate involved is improved or unimproved is not material, for that fact relates only to the grade or quality of the property and not to its kind or class. Unproductive real estate held by one other than a dealer for future use or future realization of the increment in value is held for investment and not primarily for sale. For additional rules for exchanges of personal property, see § 1.1031(a)-2.

(c) *Examples of exchanges of property of a "like kind."* .—No gain or loss is recognized if (1) a taxpayer exchanges property held for productive use in his trade or business, together with cash, for other property of like kind for the same use, such as a truck for a new truck or a passenger automobile for a new passenger automobile to be used for a like purpose; or (2) a taxpayer who is not a dealer in real estate exchanges city real estate for a ranch or farm, or exchanges a leasehold of a fee with 30 years or more to run for real estate, or exchanges improved real estate for unimproved real estate; or (3) a taxpayer exchanges investment property and cash for investment property of a like kind.

(d) *Examples of exchanges not solely in kind.*—Gain or loss is recognized if, for instance, a taxpayer exchanges (1) Treasury bonds maturing March 15, 1958, for Treasury bonds maturing December 15, 1968, unless section 1037(a) (or so much of section 1031 as relates to section 1037(a)) applies to such exchange, or (2) a real estate mortgage for consolidated farm loan bonds.

* * *

[Reg. § 1.1031(a)-1.]

□ [*T.D.* 6210, 11-6-56. *Amended by T.D.* 6935, 11-16-67; *T.D.* 8343, 4-11-91 *and T.D.* 8346, 4-25-91.]

§ 1.1031(b)-1. Receipt of other property or money in tax-free exchange.—(a) If the taxpayer receives other property (in addition to property permitted to be received without recognition of gain) or money—

(1) In an exchange described in section 1031(a) of property held for investment or productive use in trade or business for property of like kind to be held either for productive use or for investment,

(2) In an exchange described in section 1035(a) of insurance policies or annuity contracts,

(3) In an exchange described in section 1036(a) of common stock for common stock, or preferred stock for preferred stock, in the same corporation and not in connection with a corporate reorganization, or

(4) In an exchange described in section 1037(a) of obligations of the United States, issued under the Second Liberty Bond Act (31 U.S.C. 774(2)), solely for other obligations issued under such Act,

the gain, if any, to the taxpayer will be recognized under section 1031(b) in an amount not in excess of the sum of the money and the fair market value of the other property, but the loss, if any, to the taxpayer from such an exchange will not be recognized under section 1031(c) to any extent.

(b) The application of this section may be illustrated by the following examples:

Example (1). A, who is not a dealer in real estate, in 1954 exchanges real estate held for investment, which he purchased in 1940 for $5,000, for other real estate (to be held for productive use in trade or business) which has a fair market value of $6,000, and $2,000 in cash. The gain from the transaction is $3,000, but is recognized only to the extent of the cash received of $2,000.

Example (2). (a) B, who uses the cash receipts and disbursements method of accounting and the calendar year as his taxable year, has never elected under section 454(a) to include in gross income currently the annual increase in the redemption price of non-interest-bearing obligations issued at a discount. In 1943, for $750 each, B purchased four $1,000 series E United States savings bonds bearing an issue date of March 1, 1943.

(b) On October 1, 1963, the redemption value of each such bond was $1,396, and the total redemption value of the four bonds was $5,584. On that date B submitted the four $1,000 series E bonds to the United States in a transaction in which one of such $1,000 bonds was reissued by issuing four $100 series E United States savings bonds bearing an issue date of March 1, 1943, and by considering six $100 series E bonds bearing an issue date of March 1, 1943, to have been issued. The redemption value of each such $100 series E bond was $139.60 on October 1, 1963. Then, as part of the transaction, the six $100 series E bonds so considered to have been issued and the three $1,000 series E bonds were exchanged, in an exchange qualifying under section 1037(a), for five $1,000 series H United States savings bonds plus $25.60 in cash.

(c) The gain realized on the exchange qualifying under section 1037(a) is $2,325.60, determined as follows:

Amount realized:		
Par value of five series H bonds		$5,000.00
Cash received		25.60
Total realized		5,025.60
Less: Adjusted basis of series E bonds surrendered in the exchange:		
Three $1,000 series E bonds	$2,250	
Six $100 series E bonds at $75 each	450	2,700.00
Gain realized		$2,325.60

(d) Pursuant to section 1031(b), only $25.60 (the money received) of the total gain of $2,325.60 realized on the exchange is recognized at the time of exchange and must be included in B's gross income for 1963. The $2,300 balance of the gain ($2,325.60 less $25.60) must be included in B's gross income for the taxable year in which the series H bonds are redeemed or disposed of, or reach final maturity, whichever is earlier, as provided in paragraph (c) of § 1.454-1.

(e) The gain on the four $100 series E bonds, determined by using $75 as a basis for each such bond, must be included in B's gross income for the taxable year in which such bonds are redeemed or disposed of, or reach final maturity, whichever is earlier.

Example (3). (a) The facts are the same as in example (2), except that, as part of the transaction, the $1,000 series E bond is reissued by considering ten $100 series E bonds bearing an issue date of March 1, 1943, to have been issued. Six of the $100 series E bonds so considered to have been issued are surrendered to the United States as part of the exchange qualifying under section 1037(a) and the other four are immediately redeemed.

(b) Pursuant to section 1031(b), only $25.60 (the money received) of the total gain of $2,325.60 realized on the exchange qualifying under section 1037(a) is recognized at the time of the exchange and must be included in B's gross income for 1963. The $2,300 balance of the gain ($2,325.60 less $25.60) realized on such exchange must be included in B's gross income for the taxable year in which the series H bonds are redeemed or disposed of, or reach final maturity, whichever is earlier, as provided in paragraph (c) of § 1.454-1.

(c) The redemption on October 1, 1963, of the four $100 series E bonds considered to have been issued at such time results in gain of $258.40, which is then recognized and must be included in B's gross income for 1963. This gain of $258.40 is the difference between the $558.40 redemption value of such bonds on the date of the exchange and the $300 (4 × $75) paid for such series E bonds in 1943.

Example (4). On November 1, 1963, C purchased for $91 a marketable United States bond which was originally issued at its par value of $100 under the Second Liberty Bond Act. On February 1, 1964, in an exchange qualifying under section 1037(a), C surrendered the bond to the United States for another marketable United States bond, which then had a fair market value of $92, and $1.85 in cash, $0.85 of which was interest. The $0.85 interest received is includible in gross income for the taxable year of the exchange, but the $2 gain ($93 less $91) realized on the exchange is recognized for such year under section 1031(b) to the extent of $1 (the money received). Under section 1031(d), C's basis in the bond received in exchange is $91 (his basis of $91 in the bond surrendered, reduced by the $1 money received and increased by the $1 gain recognized).

(c) Consideration received in the form of an assumption of liabilities (or a transfer subject to a liability) is to be treated as "other property or money" for the purposes of section 1031(b). Where, on an exchange described in section 1031(b), each party to the exchange either assumes a liability of the other party or acquires property subject to a liability, then, in determining the amount of "other property or money" for purposes of section 1031(b), consideration given in the form of an assumption of liabilities (or a receipt of property subject to a liability) shall be offset against consideration received in the form of an assumption of liabilities (or a transfer subject to a liability). See § 1.1031(d)-2, examples (1) and (2). [Reg. § 1.1031(b)-1.]

□ [*T.D.* 6210, 11-6-56. *Amended by T.D.* 6935, 11-16-67.]

§ 1.1031(b)-2. Safe harbor for qualified intermediaries.—(a) In the case of simultaneous transfers of like-kind properties involving a qualified intermediary (as defined in § 1.1031(k)-1(g)(4)(iii)), the qualified intermediary is not considered the agent of the taxpayer for purposes of section 1031(a). In such a case, the transfer and receipt of property by the taxpayer is treated as an exchange.

(b) In the case of simultaneous exchanges of like-kind properties involving a qualified intermediary (as defined in § 1.1031(k)-1(g)(4)(iii)), the receipt by the taxpayer of an evidence of indebtedness of the transferee of the qualified intermediary is treated as the receipt of an evidence of indebtedness of the person acquiring property from the taxpayer for purposes of section 453 and § 15a.453-1(b)(3)(i) of this chapter.

(c) Paragraph (a) of this section applies to transfers of property made by taxpayers on or after June 10, 1991.

(d) Paragraph (b) of this section applies to transfers of property made by taxpayers on or after April 20, 1994. A taxpayer may choose to apply paragraph (b) of this section to transfers of property made on or after June 10, 1991. [Reg. § 1.1031(b)-2.]

□ [*T.D.* 8346, 4-25-91. *Amended by T.D.* 8535, 4-19-94.]

§ 1.1031(d)-1. Property acquired upon a tax-free exchange.—(a) If, in an exchange of property solely of the type described in section 1031, section 1035(a), section 1036(a), or section 1037(a), no part of the gain or loss was recognized under the law applicable to the year in which the exchange was made, the basis of the property acquired is the same as the basis of the property transferred by the taxpayer with proper adjustments to the date of the exchange. If additional consideration is given by the taxpayer in the exchange, the basis of the property acquired shall be the same as the property transferred increased by the amount of additional consideration given (see section 1016 and the regulations thereunder).

(b) If, in an exchange of properties of the type indicated in section 1031, section 1035(a), section 1036(a), or section 1037(a), gain to the taxpayer was recognized under the provisions of section 1031(b) or a similar provision of a prior revenue law, on account of the receipt of money in the transaction, the basis of the property acquired is the basis of the property transferred (adjusted to the date of the exchange), decreased by the amount of money received and increased by the amount of gain recognized on the exchange. The application of this paragraph may be illustrated by the following example:

Example. A, an individual in the moving and storage business, in 1954 transfers one of his moving trucks with an adjusted basis in his hands of $2,500 to B in exchange for a truck (to be used in A's business) with a fair market value of $2,400 and $200 in cash. A realizes a gain of $100 upon the exchange, all of which is recognized under section 1031(b). The basis of the truck acquired by A is determined as follows:

Adjusted basis of A's former truck	$2,500
Less: Amount of money received	200
Difference	2,300
Plus: Amount of gain recognized	100
Basis of truck acquired by A	$2,400

(c) If, upon an exchange of properties of the type described in section 1031, section 1035(a), section 1036(a), or section 1037(a), the taxpayer received other property (not permitted to be received without the recognition of gain) and gain from the transaction was recognized as required under section 1031(b), or a similar provision of a prior revenue law, the basis (adjusted to the date of the exchange) of the property transferred by the taxpayer, decreased by the amount of any money received and increased by the amount of gain recognized, must be allocated to and is the basis of the properties (other than money) received on the exchange. For the purpose of the allocation of the basis of the properties received, there must be assigned to such other property an amount equivalent to its fair market value at the date of the exchange. The application of this paragraph may be illustrated by the following example:

Example. A, who is not a dealer in real estate, in 1954 transfers real estate held for investment which he purchased in 1940 for $10,000 in exchange for other real estate (to be held for investment) which has a fair market value of $9,000, an automobile which has a fair market value of $2,000, and $1,500 in cash. A realizes a gain of $2,500, all of which is recognized under section 1031(b). The basis of the property received in exchange is the basis of the real estate A transfers ($10,000) decreased by the amount of money received ($1,500) and increased in the amount of gain that was recognized ($2,500), which results in a basis for the property received of $11,000. This basis of $11,000 is allocated between the automobile and the real estate received by A, the basis of the automobile being its fair market value at the date of the exchange, $2,000, and the basis of the real estate received being the remainder, $9,000.

(d) Section 1031(c) and, with respect to section 1031 and section 1036(a), similar provisions of prior revenue laws provide that no loss may be recognized on an exchange of properties of a type described in section 1031, section 1035(a), section 1036(a), or section 1037(a), although the taxpayer receives other property or money from the transaction. However, the basis of the property or properties (other than money) received by the taxpayer is the basis (adjusted to the date of the exchange) of the property transferred, decreased by the amount of money received. This basis must be allocated to the properties received, and for this purpose there must be allocated to such other property an amount of such basis equivalent to its fair market value at the date of the exchange.

(e) If, upon an exchange of properties of the type described in section 1031, section 1035(a), section 1036(a), or section 1037(a), the taxpayer also exchanged other property (not permitted to be transferred without the recognition of gain or loss) and gain or loss from the transaction is recognized under section 1002 or a similar provision of a prior revenue law, the basis of the property acquired is the total basis of the properties transferred (adjusted to the date of the exchange) increased by the amount of gain and decreased by the amount of loss recognized on the other property. For purposes of this rule, the taxpayer is deemed to have received in exchange for such other property an amount equal to its fair market value on the date of the exchange. The application of this paragraph may be illustrated by the following example:

Example. A exchanges real estate held for investment plus stock for real estate to be held for investment. The real estate transferred has an adjusted basis of $10,000 and a fair market value of $11,000. The stock transferred has an adjusted basis of $4,000 and a fair market value of $2,000. The real estate acquired has a fair market value of $13,000. A is deemed to have received a $2,000 portion of the acquired real estate in exchange for the stock, since $2,000 is the fair market value of the stock at the time of the exchange. A $2,000 loss is recognized under section 1002 on the exchange of the stock for real estate. No gain or loss is recognized on the exchange of the real estate since the property received is of the type permitted to be received without recognition of gain or loss. The basis of the real estate acquired by A is determined as follows:

Adjusted basis of real estate transferred	$10,000
Adjusted basis of stock transferred	4,000
	14,000
Less:	
Loss recognized on transfer of stock	2,000
Basis of real estate acquired upon the exchange	12,000

[Reg. § 1.1031(d)-1.]

□ [*T.D.* 6210, 11-6-56. *Amended by T.D.* 6453, 2-16-60 *and T.D.* 6935, 11-16-67.]

§ 1.1031(d)-2. Treatment of assumption of liabilities.—For the purposes of section 1031(d), the amount of any liabilities of the taxpayer assumed by the other party to the exchange (or of any liabilities to which the property exchanged by the taxpayer is subject) is to be treated as money received by the taxpayer upon the exchange, whether or not the assumption resulted in a recognition of gain or loss to the taxpayer under the law applicable to the year in which the exchange was made. The application of this section may be illustrated by the following examples:

Example (1). B, an individual, owns an apartment house which has an adjusted basis in his hands of $500,000, but which is subject to a mortgage of $150,000. On September 1, 1954, he transfers the apartment house to C, receiving in exchange therefor $50,000 in cash and another apartment house with a fair market value on that date of $600,000. The transfer to C is made subject to the $150,000 mortgage. B realizes a gain of $300,000 on the exchange, computed as follows:

Value of property received	$600,000
Cash	50,000
Liabilities subject to which old property was transferred	150,000
Total consideration received	800,000
Less: Adjusted basis of property transferred	500,000
Gain realized	300,000

Under section 1031(b), $200,000 of the $300,000 gain is recognized. The basis of the apartment house acquired by B upon the exchange is $500,000, computed as follows:

Adjusted basis of property transferred		$500,000
Less: Amount of money received:		
Cash	$50,000	
Amount of liabilities subject to which property was transferred	150,000	
		200,000
Difference		300,000
Plus: Amount of gain recognized upon the exchange		200,000
Basis of property acquired upon the exchange		$500,000

Example (2). (a) D, an individual, owns an apartment house. On December 1, 1955, the apartment house owned by D has an adjusted basis in his hands of $100,000, a fair market value of $220,000, but is subject to a mortgage of $80,000. E, an individual, also owns an apartment house. On December 1, 1955, the apartment house owned by E has an adjusted basis of $175,000, a fair market value of $250,000, but is subject to a mortgage of $150,000. On December 1, 1955, D transfers his apartment house to E, receiving in exchange therefor $40,000 in cash and the apartment house owned by E. Each apartment house is transferred subject to the mortgage on it.

(b) D realizes a gain of $120,000 on the exchange, computed as follows:

Value of property received		$250,000
Cash		40,000
Liabilities subject to which old property was transferred		80,000
Total consideration received		370,000
Less: Adjusted basis of property transferred	$100,000	
Liabilities to which new property is subject	150,000	$250,000
Gain realized		$120,000

For purposes of section 1031(b), the amount of "other property or money" received by D is $40,000. (Consideration received by D in the form of a transfer subject to a liability of $80,000 is offset by consideration given in the form of a receipt of property subject to a $150,000 liability. Thus, only the consideration received in the form of cash, $40,000, is treated as "other property or money" for purposes of section 1031(b).) Accordingly, under section 1031(b), $40,000 of the $120,000 gain is recognized. The basis of the apartment house acquired by D is $170,000, computed as follows:

Adjusted basis of property transferred		$100,000
Liabilities to which new property is subject		150,000
Total		$250,000
Less: Amount of money received:		
Cash	$40,000	
Amount of liabilities subject to which property was transferred	80,000	
		$120,000
Difference		$130,000
Plus: Amount of gain recognized upon the exchange		40,000
Basis of property acquired upon the exchange		$170,000

(c) E realizes a gain of $75,000 on the exchange, computed as follows:

Value of property received		$220,000
Liabilities subject to which old property was transferred		$150,000
Total consideration received		370,000
Less: Adjusted basis of property transferred	$175,000	
Cash	40,000	
Liabilities to which new property is subject	80,000	
		$295,000
Gain realized		$ 75,000

For purposes of section 1031(b), the amount of "other property or money" received by E is $30,000. (Consideration received by E in the form of a transfer subject to a liability of $150,000 is offset by consideration given in the form of a receipt of property subject to an $80,000 liability and by the $40,000 cash paid by E. Although consideration received in the form of cash or other property is not offset by consideration given in the form of an assumption of liabilities or a receipt of property subject to a liability, consideration given in the form of cash or other property is offset against consideration received in the form of an assumption of liabilities or a transfer of property subject to a liability.) Accordingly, under section 1031(b), $30,000 of the $75,000 gain is recognized. The basis of the apartment house acquired by E is $175,000, computed as follows:

Adjusted basis of property transferred	$175,000
Cash	40,000
Liabilities to which new property is subject	80,000
Total	295,000

Less: Amount of money received:	
Amount of liabilities subject to which property was transferred	$150,000
	150,000
Difference	$145,000
Plus: Amount of gain recognized upon the exchange	30,000
Basis of property acquired upon the exchange	$175,000

[Reg. § 1.1031(d)-2.]

□ [*T.D.* 6210, 11-6-56.]

§ 1.1031(k)-1. Treatment of deferred exchanges.—(a) *Overview.*—This section provides rules for the application of section 1031 and the regulations thereunder in the case of a "deferred exchange." For purposes of section 1031 and this section, a deferred exchange is defined as an exchange in which, pursuant to an agreement, the taxpayer transfers property held for productive use in a trade or business or for investment (the "relinquished property") and subsequently receives property to be held either for productive use in a trade or business or for investment (the "replacement property"). In the case of a deferred exchange, if the requirements set forth in paragraphs (b), (c), and (d) of this section (relating to identification and receipt of replacement property) are not satisfied, the replacement property received by the taxpayer will be treated as property which is not of a like kind to the relinquished property. In order to constitute a deferred exchange, the transaction must be an exchange (i.e., a transfer of property for property, as distinguished from a transfer of property for money). For example, a sale of property followed by a purchase of property of a like kind does not qualify for nonrecognition of gain or loss under section 1031 regardless of whether the identification and receipt requirements of section 1031(a)(3) and paragraphs (b), (c), and (d) of this section are satisfied. The transfer of relinquished property in a deferred exchange is not within the provisions of section 1031(a) if, as part of the consideration, the taxpayer receives money or property which does not meet the requirements of section 1031(a), but the transfer, if otherwise qualified, will be within the provisions of either section 1031(b) or (c). See § 1.1031(a)-1(a)(2). In addition, in the case of a transfer of relinquished property in a deferred exchange, gain or loss may be recognized if the taxpayer actually or constructively receives money or property which does not meet the requirements of section 1031(a) before the taxpayer actually receives like-kind replacement property. If the taxpayer actually or constructively receives money or property which does not meet the requirements of section 1031(a) in the full amount of the consideration for the relinquished property, the transaction will constitute a sale, and not a deferred exchange, even though the taxpayer may ultimately receive like-kind replacement property. For purposes of this section, property which does not meet the requirements of section 1031(a) (whether by being described in section 1031(a)(2) or otherwise) is referred to as "other property." For rules regarding actual and constructive receipt, and safe harbors therefrom, see paragraphs (f) and (g), respectively, of this section. For rules regarding the determination of gain or loss recognized and the basis of property received in a deferred exchange, see paragraph (j) of this section.

(b) *Identification and receipt requirements.*—(1) *In general.*—In the case of a deferred exchange, any replacement property received by the taxpayer will be treated as property which is not of a like kind to the relinquished property if—

(i) The replacement property is not "identified" before the end of the "identification period," or

(ii) The identified replacement property is not received before the end of the "exchange period."

(2) *Identification period and exchange period.*—(i) The identification period begins on the date the taxpayer transfers the relinquished property and ends at midnight on the 45th day thereafter.

(ii) The exchange period begins on the date the taxpayer transfers the relinquished property and ends at midnight on the earlier of the 180th day thereafter or the due date (including extensions) for the taxpayer's return of the tax imposed by chapter 1 of subtitle A of the Code for the taxable year in which the transfer of the relinquished property occurs.

(iii) If, as part of the same deferred exchange, the taxpayer transfers more than one relinquished property and the relinquished properties are transferred on different dates, the identification period and the exchange period are determined by reference to the earliest date on which any of the properties are transferred.

(iv) For purposes of this paragraph (b)(2), property is transferred when the property is disposed of within the meaning of section 1001(a).

(3) *Example.*—This paragraph (b) may be illustrated by the following example.

Example. (i) M is a corporation that files its Federal income tax return on a calendar year basis. M and C enter into an agreement for an exchange of property that requires M to transfer property X to C. Under the agreement, M is to identify like-kind replacement property which C is required to purchase and to transfer to M. M transfers property X to C on November 16, 1992.

(ii) The identification period ends at midnight on December 31, 1992, the day which is 45 days after the date of transfer of property X. The exchange period ends at midnight on March 15, 1993, the due date for M's Federal income tax return for the taxable year in which M transferred property X. However, if M is allowed the automatic six-month extension for filing its tax return, the exchange period ends at midnight on May 15, 1993, the day which is 180 days after the date of transfer of property X.

(c) *Identification of replacement property before the end of the identification period.*—(1) *In general.*—For purposes of paragraph (b) (1) (i) of this section (relating to the identification requirement), replacement property is identified before the end of the identification period only if the requirements of this paragraph (c) are satisfied with respect to the replacement property. However, any replacement property that is received by the taxpayer before the end of the identification period will in all events be treated as identified before the end of the identification period.

(2) *Manner of identifying replacement property.*—Replacement property is identified only if it is designated as replacement property in a written document signed by the taxpayer and hand delivered, mailed, telecopied, or otherwise sent before the end of the identification period to either—

(i) The person obligated to transfer the replacement property to the taxpayer (regardless of whether that person is a disqualified person as defined in paragraph (k) of this section); or

(ii) Any other person involved in the exchange other than the taxpayer or a disqualified person (as defined in paragraph (k) of this section).

Examples of persons involved in the exchange include any of the parties to the exchange, an intermediary, an escrow agent, and a title company. An identification of replacement property made in a written agreement for the exchange of properties signed by all parties thereto before the end of the identification period will be treated as satisfying the requirements of this paragraph (c) (2).

(3) *Description of replacement property.*—Replacement property is identified only if it is unambiguously described in the written document or agreement. Real property generally is unambiguously described if it is described by a legal description, street address, or distinguishable name (e.g., the Mayfair Apartment Building). Personal property generally is unambiguously described if it is described by a specific description of the particular type of property. For example, a truck generally is unambiguously described if it is described by a specific make, model, and year.

(4) *Alternative and multiple properties.*—(i) The taxpayer may identify more than one replacement property. Regardless of the number of relinquished properties transferred by the taxpayer as part of the same deferred exchange, the maximum number of replacement properties that the taxpayer may identify is—

(A) Three properties without regard to the fair market values of the properties (the "3-property rule"), or

(B) Any number of properties as long as their aggregate fair market value as of the end of the identification period does not exceed 200 percent of the aggregate fair market value of all the relinquished properties as of the date the relinquished properties were transferred by the taxpayer (the "200-percent rule").

(ii) If, as of the end of the identification period, the taxpayer has identified more properties as replacement properties than permitted by paragraph (c) (4) (i) of this section, the taxpayer is treated as if no replacement property had been identified. The preceding sentence will not apply, however, and an identification satisfying the requirements of paragraph (c) (4) (i) of this section will be considered made, with respect to—

(A) Any replacement property received by the taxpayer before the end of the identification period, and

(B) Any replacement property identified before the end of the identification period and received before the end of the exchange period, but only if the taxpayer receives before the end of the exchange period identified replacement property the fair market value of which is at least 95 percent of the aggregate fair market value of all identified replacement properties (the "95-percent rule").

For this purpose, the fair market value of each identified replacement property is determined as of the earlier of the date the property is received by the taxpayer or the last day of the exchange period.

(iii) For purposes of applying the 3-property rule, the 200-percent rule, and the 95-percent rule, all identifications of replacement property, other than identifications of replacement property that have been revoked in the manner provided in paragraph (c) (6) of this section, are taken into account. For example, if, in a deferred exchange, B transfers property X with a fair market value of $100,000 to C and B receives like-kind property Y with a fair market value of $50,000 before the end of the identification period, under paragraph (c) (1) of this section, property Y is treated as identified by reason of being received before the end of the identification period. Thus, under paragraph (c)(4)(i) of this section, B may identify either two additional replacement properties of any fair market value or any number of additional replacement properties as long as the aggregate fair market value of the additional replacement properties does not exceed $150,000.

(5) *Incidental property disregarded.*—(i) Solely for purposes of applying this paragraph (c), property that is incidental to a larger item of property is not treated as property that is separate from the larger item of property. Property is incidental to a larger item of property if—

(A) In standard commercial transactions, the property is typically transferred together with the larger item of property, and

(B) The aggregate fair market value of all of the incidental property does not exceed 15 percent of the aggregate fair market value of the larger item of property.

(ii) This paragraph (c)(5) may be illustrated by the following examples.

Example 1. For purposes of paragraph (c) of this section, a spare tire and tool kit will not be treated as separate property from a truck with a fair market value of $10,000, if the aggregate fair market value of the spare tire and tool kit does not exceed $1,500. For purposes of the 3-property rule, the truck, spare tire, and tool kit are treated as 1 property. Moreover, for purposes of paragraph (c)(3) of this section (relating to the description of replacement property), the truck, spare tire, and tool kit are all considered to be unambiguously described if the make, model, and year of the truck are specified, even if no reference is made to the spare tire and tool kit.

Example 2. For purposes of paragraph (c) of this section, furniture, laundry machines, and other miscellaneous items of personal property will not be treated as separate property from an apartment building with a fair market value of $1,000,000 if the aggregate fair market value of the furniture, laundry machines, and other personal property does not exceed $150,000. For purposes of the 3-property rule, the apartment building, furniture, laundry machines, and other personal property are treated as 1 property. Moreover, for purposes of paragraph (c)(3) of this section (relating to the description of replacement property), the apartment building, furniture, laundry machines, and other personal property are all considered to be unambiguously described if the legal description, street address, or distinguishable name of the apartment building is specified, even if no reference is made to the furniture, laundry machines, and other personal property.

(6) *Revocation of identification.*—An identification of replacement property may be revoked at any time before the end of the identification period. An identification of replacement property is revoked only if the revocation is made in a written document signed by the taxpayer and hand delivered, mailed, telecopied, or otherwise sent before the end of the identification period to the person to whom the identification of the replacement property was sent. An identification of replacement property that is made in a written agreement for the exchange of properties is treated as revoked only if the revocation is made in a written amendment to the agreement or in a written document signed by the taxpayer and hand delivered, mailed, telecopied, or otherwise sent before the end of the identification period to all of the parties to the agreement.

(7) *Examples.*—This paragraph (c) may be illustrated by the following examples. Unless otherwise provided in an example, the following facts are assumed: B, a calendar year taxpayer, and C agree to enter into a deferred exchange. Pursuant to their agreement, B transfers real property X to C on May 17, 1991. Real property X, which has been held by B for investment, is unencumbered and has a fair market value on May 17, 1991, of $100,000. On or before July 1, 1991 (the end of the identification period), B is to identify replacement property that is of a like kind to real property X. On or before November 13, 1991 (the end of the exchange period), C is required to purchase the property identified by B and to transfer that property to B. To the extent the fair market value of the replacement property transferred to B is greater or less than the fair market value of real property X, either B or C, as applicable, will make up the difference by paying cash to the other party after the date the replacement property is received by B. No replacement property is identified in the agreement. When subsequently identified, the replacement property is described by legal description and is of a like kind to real property X (determined without regard to section 1031(a)(3) and this section). B intends to hold the replacement property received for investment.

Example 1. (i) On July 2, 1991, B identifies real property E as replacement property by designating real property E as replacement property in a written document signed by B and personally delivered to C.

(ii) Because the identification was made after the end of the identification period, pursuant to paragraph (b)(1)(i) of this section (relating to the identification requirement), real property E is treated as property which is not of a like kind to real property X.

Example 2. (i) C is a corporation of which 20 percent of the outstanding stock is owned by B. On July 1, 1991, B identifies real property F as replacement property by designating real property F as replacement property in a written document signed by B and mailed to C.

(ii) Because C is the person obligated to transfer the replacement property to B, real property F is identified before the end of the identification period. The fact that C is a "disqualified person" as defined in paragraph (k) of this section does not change this result.

(iii) Real property F would also have been treated as identified before the end of the identification period if, instead of sending the identification to C, B had designated real property F as replacement property in a written agreement for the exchange of properties signed by all parties thereto on or before July 1, 1991.

Example 3. (i) On June 3, 1991, B identifies the replacement property as "unimproved land located in Hood County with a fair market value not to exceed $100,000." The designation is made in a written document signed by B and personally delivered to C. On July 8, 1991, B and C agree that real property G is the property described in the June 3, 1991 document.

(ii) Because real property G was not unambiguously described before the end of the identification period, no replacement property is identified before the end of the identification period.

Example 4. (i) On June 28, 1991, B identifies real properties H, J, and K as replacement properties by designating these properties as replacement properties in a written document signed by B and personally delivered to C. The written document provides that by August 1, 1991, B will orally inform C which of the identified properties C is to transfer to B. As of July 1, 1991, the fair market values of real properties H, J, and K are $75,000, $100,000, and $125,000, respectively.

(ii) Because B did not identify more than three properties as replacement properties, the requirements of the 3-property rule are satisfied, and real properties H, J, and K are all identified before the end of the identification period.

Example 5. (i) On May 17, 1991, B identifies real properties L, M, N, and P as replacement properties by designating these properties as replacement properties in a written document signed by B and personally delivered to C. The written document provides that by July 2, 1991, B will orally inform C which of the identified properties C is to transfer to B. As of July 1, 1991, the fair market values of real properties L, M, N, and P are $30,000, $40,000, $50,000, and $60,000, respectively.

(ii) Although B identified more than three properties as replacement properties, the aggregate fair market value of the identified properties as of the end of the identification period ($180,000) did not exceed 200 percent of the aggregate fair market value of real property X (200% × $100,000 = $200,000). Therefore, the requirements of the 200-percent rule are satisfied, and real properties L, M, N, and P are all identified before the end of the identification period.

Example 6. (i) On June 21, 1991, B identifies real properties Q, R, and S as replacement properties by designating these properties as replacement properties in a written document signed by B and mailed to C. On June 24, 1991, B identifies real properties T and U as replacement properties in a written document signed by B and mailed to C. On June 28, 1991, B revokes the identification of real properties Q and R in a written document signed by B and personally delivered to C.

(ii) B has revoked the identification of real properties Q and R in the manner provided by paragraph (c)(6) of this section. Identifications of replacement property that have been revoked in the manner provided by paragraph (c)(6) of this section are not taken into account for purposes of applying the 3-property rule. Thus, as of June 28, 1991, B has identified only replacement properties S, T, and U for purposes of the 3-property rule. Because B did not identify more than three properties as replacement properties for purposes of the 3-property rule, the requirements of that rule are satisfied, and real properties S, T, and U are all identified before the end of the identification period.

Example 7. (i) On May 20, 1991, B identifies real properties V and W as replacement properties by designating these properties as replacement properties in a written document signed by B and personally delivered to C. On June 4, 1991, B identifies real properties Y and Z as replacement properties in the same manner. On June 5, 1991, B telephones C and orally revokes the identification of real properties V and W. As of July 1, 1991, the fair market values of real properties V, W, Y, and Z are $50,000, $70,000, $90,000, and $100,000, respectively. On July 31, 1991, C purchases real property Y and Z and transfers them to B.

(ii) Pursuant to paragraph (c)(6) of this section (relating to revocation of identification), the oral revocation of the identification of real properties V and W is invalid. Thus, the identification of real properties V and W is taken into account for purposes of determining whether the requirements of paragraph (c)(4) of this section (relating to the identification of alternative and multiple properties) are satisfied. Because B identified more than three properties and the aggregate fair market value of the identified properties as of the end of the identification period ($310,000) exceeds 200 percent of the fair market value of real property X (200% × $100,000 = $200,000), the requirements of paragraph (c)(4) of this section are not satisfied, and B is treated as if B did not identify any replacement property.

(d) *Receipt of identified replacement property.*—(1) *In general.*—For purposes of paragraph (b)(1)(ii) of this section (relating to the receipt requirement), the identified replacement property is received before the end of the exchange period only if the requirements of this paragraph (d) are satisfied with respect to the replacement property. In the case of a deferred exchange, the identified replacement property is received before the end of the exchange period if—

(i) The taxpayer receives the replacement property before the end of the exchange period, and

(ii) The replacement property received is substantially the same property as identified.

If the taxpayer has identified more than one replacement property, section 1031(a)(3)(B) and this paragraph (d) are applied separately to each replacement property.

(2) *Examples.*—This paragraph (d) may be illustrated by the following examples. The following facts are assumed: B, a calendar year taxpayer, and C agree to enter into a deferred exchange. Pursuant to their agreement, B transfers real property X to C on May 17, 1991. Real property X, which has been held by B for investment, is unencumbered and has a fair market value on May 17, 1991, of $100,000. On or before July 1, 1991 (the end of the identification period), B is to identify replacement property that is of a like kind to real property X. On or before November 13, 1991 (the end of the exchange period), C is required to purchase the property identified by B and to transfer that property to B. To the extent the fair market value of the replacement property transferred to B is greater or less than the fair market value of real property X, either B or C, as applicable, will make up the difference by paying cash to the other party after the date the replacement property is received by B. The replacement property is identified in a manner that satisfies paragraph (c) of this section (relating to identification of replacement property) and is of a like kind to real property X (determined without regard to section 1031(a)(3) and this section). B intends to hold any replacement property received for investment.

Example 1. (i) In the agreement, B identifies real properties J, K, and L as replacement properties. The agreement provides that by July 26, 1991, B will orally inform C which of the properties C is to transfer to B.

(ii) As of July 1, 1991, the fair market values of real properties J, K, and L are $75,000, $100,000, and $125,000, respectively. On July 26, 1991, B instructs C to acquire real property K. On October 31, 1991, C purchases real property K for $100,000 and transfers the property to B.

(iii) Because real property K was identified before the end of the identification period and was received before the end of the exchange period, the identification and receipt requirements of section 1031(a)(3) and this section are satisfied with respect to real property K.

Example 2. (i) In the agreement, B identifies real property P as replacement property. Real property P consists of two acres of unimproved land. On October 15, 1991, the owner of real property P erects a fence on the property. On November 1, 1991, C purchases real property P and transfers it to B.

(ii) The erection of the fence on real property P subsequent to its identification did not alter the basic nature or character of real property P as unimproved land. B is considered to have received substantially the same property as identified.

Example 3. (i) In the agreement, B identifies real property Q as replacement property. Real property Q consists of a barn on two acres of land and has a fair market value of $250,000 ($187,500 for the barn and underlying land and $87,500 for the remaining land). As of July 26, 1991, real property Q remains unchanged and has a fair market value of $250,000. On that date, at B's direction, C purchases the barn and underlying land for $187,500 and transfers it to B, and B pays $87,500 to C.

(ii) The barn and underlying land differ in basic nature or character from real property Q as a whole. B is not considered to have received substantially the same property as identified.

Example 4. (i) In the agreement, B identifies real property R as replacement property. Real property R consists of two acres of unimproved land and has a fair market value of $250,000. As of October 3, 1991, real property R remains unimproved and has a fair market value of $250,000. On that date, at B's direction, C purchases 1½ acres of real property R for $187,500 and transfers it to B, and B pays $87,500 to C.

(ii) The portion of real property R that B received does not differ from the basic nature or character of real property R as a whole. Moreover, the fair market value of the portion of real property R that B received ($187,500) is 75 percent of the fair market value of real property R as of the date of receipt. Accordingly, B is considered to have received substantially the same property as identified.

(e) *Special rules for identification and receipt of replacement property to be produced.*—(1) *In general.*—A transfer of relinquished property in a deferred exchange will not fail to qualify for nonrecognition of gain or loss under section 1031 merely because the replacement property is not in existence or is being produced at the time the property is identified as replacement property. For purposes of this paragraph (e), the terms "produced" and "production" have the same meanings as provided in section 263A(g)(1) and the regulations thereunder.

(2) *Identification of replacement property to be produced.*—(i) In the case of replacement property that is to be produced, the replacement property must be identified as provided in paragraph (c) of this section (relating to identification of replacement property). For example, if the identified replacement property consists of improved real property where the improvements are to be constructed, the description of the replacement property satisfies the requirements of paragraph (c)(3) of this section (relating to description of replacement property) if a legal description is provided for the underlying land and as much detail is provided regarding construction of the improvements as is practicable at the time the identification is made.

(ii) For purposes of paragraphs (c)(4)(i)(B) and (c)(5) of this section (relating to the 200-percent rule and incidental property), the fair market value of replacement property that is to be produced is its estimated fair market value as of the date it is expected to be received by the taxpayer.

(3) *Receipt of replacement property to be produced.*—(i) For purposes of paragraph (d)(1)(ii) of this section (relating to receipt of the identified replacement property), in determining whether the replacement property received by the taxpayer is substantially the same property as identified where the identified replacement property is property to be produced, variations due to usual or typical production changes are not taken into account. However, if substantial changes are made in the property to be produced, the replacement property received will not be considered to be substantially the same property as identified.

(ii) If the identified replacement property is personal property to be produced, the replacement property received will not be considered to be substantially the same property as identified unless production of the replacement property received is completed on or before the date the property is received by the taxpayer.

(iii) If the identified replacement property is real property to be produced and the production of the property is not completed on or before the date the taxpayer receives the property, the property received will be considered to be substantially the same property as identified only if, had production been completed on or before the date the taxpayer receives the replacement property, the property received would have been considered to be substantially the same property as identified. Even so, the property received is considered to be substantially the same property as identified only to the extent the property received constitutes real property under local law.

(4) *Additional rules.*—The transfer of relinquished property is not within the provisions of section 1031(a) if the relinquished property is transferred in exchange for services (including production services). Thus, any additional production occurring with respect to the replacement property after the property is received by the taxpayer will not be treated as the receipt of property of a like kind.

(5) *Example.*—This paragraph (e) may be illustrated by the following example.

Example. (i) B, a calendar year taxpayer, and C agree to enter into a deferred exchange. Pursuant to their agreement, B transfers improved real property X and personal property Y to C on May 17, 1991. On or before November 13, 1991 (the end of the exchange period), C is required to transfer to B real property M, on which C is constructing improvements, and personal property N, which C is producing. C is obligated to complete the improvements and production regardless of when properties M and N are transferred to B. Properties M and N are identified in a manner that satisfies paragraphs (c) (relating to identification of replacement property) and (e)(2) of this section. In addition, properties M and N are of a like kind, respectively, to real property X and personal property Y (determined without regard to section 1031(a)(3) and this section). On November 13, 1991, when construction of the improvements to property M is 20 percent completed and the production of property N is 90 percent completed, C transfers to B property M and property N. If construction of the improvements had been completed, property M would have been considered to be substantially the same property as identified. Under local law, property M constitutes real property to the extent of the underlying land and the 20 percent of the construction that is completed

(ii) Because property N is personal property to be produced and production of property N is not completed before the date the property is received by B, property N is not considered to be substantially the same property as identified and is treated as property which is not of a like kind to property Y.

(iii) Property M is considered to be substantially the same property as identified to the extent of the underlying land and the 20 percent of the construction that is completed when property M is received by B. However, any additional construction performed by C with respect to property M after November 13, 1991, is not treated as the receipt of property of a like kind.

(f) *Receipt of money or other property.*—(1) *In general.*—A transfer of relinquished property in a deferred exchange is not within the provisions of section 1031(a) if, as part of the consideration, the taxpayer receives money or other property. However, such a transfer, if otherwise qualified, will be within the provisions of either section 1031(b) or (c). See § 1.1031(a)-1(a)(2). In addition, in the case of a transfer of relinquished property in a deferred exchange, gain or loss may be recognized if the taxpayer actually or constructively receives money or other property before the taxpayer actually receives like-kind replacement property. If the taxpayer actually or constructively receives money or other property in the full amount of the consideration for the relinquished property before the taxpayer actually receives like-kind replacement property, the transaction will constitute a sale and not a deferred exchange, even though the taxpayer may ultimately receive like-kind replacement property.

(2) *Actual and constructive receipt.*—Except as provided in paragraph (g) of this section (relating to safe harbors), for purposes of section 1031 and this section, the determination of whether (or the extent to which) the taxpayer is in actual or constructive receipt of money or other property before the taxpayer actually receives like-kind replacement property is made under the general rules concerning actual and constructive receipt and without regard to the taxpayer's method of accounting. The taxpayer is in actual receipt of money or property at the time the taxpayer actually receives the money or property or receives the economic benefit of the money or property. The taxpayer is in constructive receipt of money or property at the time the money or property is credited to the taxpayer's account, set apart for the taxpayer, or otherwise made available so that the taxpayer may draw upon it at any time or so that the taxpayer can draw upon it if notice of intention to draw is given. Although the taxpayer is not in constructive receipt of money or property if the taxpayer's control of its receipt is subject to substantial limitations or restrictions, the taxpayer is in constructive receipt of the money or property at the time the limitations or restrictions lapse, expire, or are waived. In addition, actual or constructive receipt of money or property by an agent of the taxpayer (determined without regard to paragraph (k) of this section) is actual or constructive receipt by the taxpayer.

(3) *Example.*—This paragraph (f) may be illustrated by the following example.

Example. (i) B, a calendar year taxpayer, and C agree to enter into a deferred exchange. Pursuant to the agreement, on May 17, 1991, B transfers real property X to C. Real property X, which has been held by B for investment, is unencumbered and has a fair market value on May 17, 1991, of $100,000. On or before July 1, 1991 (the end of the identification period), B is to identify replacement property that is of a like kind to real property X. On or before November 13, 1991 (the end of the exchange period), C is required to purchase the property identified by B and to transfer that property to B. At any time after May 17, 1991, and before C has purchased the replacement property, B has the right, upon notice, to demand that C pay $100,000 in lieu of acquiring and transferring the replacement property. Pursuant to the agreement, B identifies replacement property, and C purchases the replacement property and transfers it to B.

(ii) Under the agreement, B has the unrestricted right to demand the payment of $100,000 as of May 17, 1991. B is therefore in constructive receipt of $100,000 on that date. Because B is in constructive receipt of money in the full amount of the consideration for the relinquished property before B actually receives the like-kind replacement property, the transaction constitutes a sale, and the transfer of real property X does not qualify for nonrecognition of gain or loss under section 1031. B is treated as if B received the $100,000 in consideration for the sale of real property X and then purchased the like-kind replacement property.

(iii) If B's right to demand payment of the $100,000 were subject to a substantial limitation or restriction (e.g., the agreement provided that B had no right to demand payment before November 14, 1991 (the end of the exchange period)), then, for purposes of this section, B would not be in actual or constructive receipt of the money unless (or until) the limitation or restriction lapsed, expired, or was waived.

(g) *Safe harbors.*—(1) *In general.*—Paragraphs (g)(2) through (g)(5) of this section set forth four safe harbors the use of which will result in a determination that the taxpayer is not in actual or constructive receipt of money or other property for purposes of section 1031 and this section. More than one safe harbor can be used in the same deferred exchange, but the terms and conditions of each must be separately satisfied. For purposes of the safe harbor rules, the term "taxpayer" does not include a person or entity utilized in a safe harbor (e.g., a qualified intermediary). See paragraph (g)(8), *Example 3(v)*, of this section.

(2) *Security or guarantee arrangements.*—(i) In the case of a deferred exchange, the determination of whether the taxpayer is in actual or constructive receipt of money or other property before the taxpayer actually receives like-kind replacement property will be made without regard to the fact that the obligation of the taxpayer's transferee to transfer the replacement property to the taxpayer is or may be secured or guaranteed by one or more of the following—

(A) A mortgage, deed of trust, or other security interest in property (other than cash or a cash equivalent),

(B) A standby letter of credit which satisfies all of the requirements of § 15A.453-1(b)(3)(iii) and which may not be drawn upon in the absence of a default of the transferee's obligation to transfer like-kind replacement property to the taxpayer, or

(C) A guarantee of a third party.

(ii) Paragraph (g)(2)(i) of this section ceases to apply at the time the taxpayer has an immediate ability or unrestricted right to receive money or other property pursuant to the security or guarantee arrangement.

(3) *Qualified escrow accounts and qualified trusts.*—(i) In the case of a deferred exchange, the determination of whether the taxpayer is in actual or constructive receipt of money or other property before the taxpayer actually receives like-kind replacement property will be made without regard to the fact that the obligation of the taxpayer's transferee to transfer the replacement property to the taxpayer is or may be secured by cash or a cash equivalent if the cash or cash equivalent is held in a qualified escrow account or in a qualified trust.

(ii) A qualified escrow account is an escrow account wherein—

(A) The escrow holder is not the taxpayer or a disqualified person (as defined in paragraph (k) of this section), and

(B) The escrow agreement expressly limits the taxpayer's rights to receive, pledge, borrow, or otherwise obtain the benefits of the cash or cash equivalent held in the escrow account as provided in paragraph (g)(6) of this section.

(iii) A qualified trust is a trust wherein—

(A) The trustee is not the taxpayer or a disqualified person (as defined in paragraph (k) of this section, except that for this purpose the relationship between the taxpayer and the trustee created by the qualified trust will not be considered a relationship under section 267(b)), and

(B) The trust agreement expressly limits the taxpayer's rights to receive, pledge, borrow, or otherwise obtain the benefits of the cash or cash equivalent held by the trustee as provided in paragraph (g)(6) of this section.

(iv) Paragraph (g)(3)(i) of this section ceases to apply at the time the taxpayer has an immediate ability or unrestricted right to receive, pledge, borrow, or otherwise obtain the benefits of the cash or cash equivalent held in the qualified escrow account or qualified trust. Rights conferred upon the taxpayer under state law to terminate or dismiss the escrow holder of a qualified escrow account or the trustee of a qualified trust are disregarded for this purpose.

(v) A taxpayer may receive money or other property directly from a party to the exchange, but not from a qualified escrow account or a qualified trust, without affecting the application of paragraph (g)(3)(i) of this section.

(4) *Qualified intermediaries.*—(i) In the case of a taxpayer's transfer of relinquished property involving a qualified intermediary, the qualified intermediary is not considered the agent of the taxpayer for purposes of section 1031(a). In such a case, the taxpayer's transfer of relinquished property and subsequent receipt of like-kind replacement property is treated as an exchange, and the determination of whether the taxpayer is in actual or constructive receipt of money or other property before the taxpayer actually receives like-kind replacement property is made as if the qualified intermediary is not the agent of the taxpayer.

(ii) Paragraph (g)(4)(i) of this section applies only if the agreement between the taxpayer and the qualified intermediary expressly limits the taxpayer's rights to receive, pledge, borrow, or otherwise obtain the benefits of money or other property held by the qualified intermediary as provided in paragraph (g)(6) of this section.

(iii) A qualified intermediary is a person who—

(A) Is not the taxpayer or a disqualified person (as defined in paragraph (k) of this section), and

(B) Enters into a written agreement with the taxpayer (the "exchange agreement") and, as required by the exchange agreement, acquires the relinquished property from the taxpayer, transfers the relinquished property, acquires the replacement property, and transfers the replacement property to the taxpayer.

(iv) Regardless of whether an intermediary acquires and transfers property under general tax principals [principles], solely for purposes of paragraph (g) (4) (iii) (B) of this section—

(A) An intermediary is treated as acquiring and transferring property if the intermediary acquires and transfers legal title to that property,

(B) An intermediary is treated as acquiring and transferring the relinquished property if the intermediary (either on its own behalf or as the agent of any party to the transaction) enters into an agreement with a person other than the taxpayer for the transfer of the relinquished property to that person and, pursuant to that agreement, the relinquised property is transferred to that person, and

(C) An intermediary is treated as acquiring and transferring replacement property if the intermediary (either on its own behalf or as the agent of any party to the transaction) enters into an agreement with the owner of the replacement property for the transfer of that property and, pursuant to that agreement, the replacement property is transferred to the taxpayer.

(v) Solely for purposes of paragraphs (g) (4) (iii) and (g) (4) (iv) of this section, an intermediary is treated as entering into an agreement if the rights of a party to the agreement are assigned to the intermediary and all parties to that agreement are notified in writing of the assignment on or before the date of the relevant transfer of property. For example, if a taxpayer enters into an agreement for the transfer of relinquished property and thereafter assigns its rights in that agreement to an intermediary and all parties to that agreement are notified in writing of the assignment on or before the date of the transfer of the relinquished property, the intermediary is treated as entering into that agreement. If the relinquished property is transferred pursuant to that agreement, the intermediary is treated as having acquired and transferred the relinquished property.

(vi) Paragraph (g) (4) (i) of this section ceases to apply at the time the taxpayer has an immediate ability or unrestricted right to receive, pledge, borrow, or otherwise obtain the benefits of money or other property held by the qualified intermediary. Rights conferred upon the taxpayer under state law to terminate or dismiss the qualified intermediary are disregarded for this purpose.

(vii) A taxpayer may receive money or other property directly from a party to the transaction other than the qualified intermediary without affecting the application of paragraph (g) (4) (i) of this section.

(5) *Interest and growth factors.*—In the case of a deferred exchange, the determination of whether the taxpayer is in actual or constructive receipt of money or other property before the taxpayer actually receives the like-kind replacement property will be made without regard to the fact that the taxpayer is or may be entitled to receive any interest or growth factor with respect to the deferred exchange. The preceding sentence applies only if the agreement pursuant to which the taxpayer is or may be entitled to the interest or growth factor expressly limits the taxpayer's rights to receive the interest or growth factor as provided in paragraph (g) (6) of this section. For additional rules concerning interest or growth factors, see paragraph (h) of this section.

(6) *Additional restrictions on safe harbors under paragraphs (g) (3) through (g) (5).*—(i) An agreement limits a taxpayer's rights as provided in this paragraph (g) (6) only if the agreement provides that the taxpayer has no rights, except as provided in paragraphs (g) (6) (ii) and (g) (6) (iii) of this section, to receive, pledge, borrow, or otherwise obtain the benefits of money or other property before the end of the exchange period.

(ii) The agreement may provide that if the taxpayer has not identified replacement property by the end of the identification period, the taxpayer may have rights to receive, pledge, borrow, or otherwise obtain the benefits of money or other property at any time after the end of the identification period.

(iii) The agreement may provide that if the taxpayer has identified replacement property, the taxpayer may have rights to receive, pledge, borrow, or otherwise obtain the benefits of money or other property upon or after—

(A) The receipt by the taxpayer of all of the replacement property to which the taxpayer is entitled under the exchange agreement, or

(B) The occurrence after the end of the identification period of a material and substantial contingency that—

(1) Relates to the deferred exchange,

(2) Is provided for in writing, and

(3) Is beyond the control of the taxpayer and of any disqualified person (as defined in paragraph (k) of this section), other than the person obligated to transfer the replacement property to the taxpayer.

(7) *Items disregarded in applying safe harbors under paragraphs (g) (3) through (g) (5).*—In determining whether a safe harbor under paragraphs (g) (3) through (g) (5) of this section ceases to apply and whether the taxpayer's rights to receive, pledge, borrow, or

otherwise obtain the benefits of money or other property are expressly limited as provided in paragraph (g)(6) of this section, the taxpayer's receipt of or right to receive any of the following items will be disregarded—

(i) Items that a seller may receive as a consequence of the disposition of property and that are not included in the amount realized from the disposition of property (e.g., prorated rents), and

(ii) Transactional items that relate to the disposition of the relinquished property or to the acquisition of the replacement property and appear under local standards in the typical closing statement as the responsibility of a buyer or seller (e.g., commissions, prorated taxes, recording or transfer taxes, and title company fees).

* * *

(m) *Definition of fair market value.*—For purposes of this section, the fair market value of property means the fair market value of the property without regard to any liabilities secured by the property.

(n) *No inference with respect to actual or constructive receipt rules outside of section 1031.*—The rules provided in this section relating to actual or constructive receipt are intended to be rules for determining whether there is actual or constructive receipt in the case of a deferred exchange. No inference is intended regarding the application of these rules for purposes of determining whether actual or constructive receipt exists for any other purpose.

* * *

[Reg. § 1.1031(k)-1.]

☐ [*T.D.* 8346, 4-25-91. *Amended by T.D.* 8535, 4-19-94; *T.D.* 8982, 1-31-2002 *and T.D.* 9413, 7-9-2008.]

§ 1.1032-1. Disposition by a corporation of its own capital stock.—(a) The disposition by a corporation of shares of its own stock (including treasury stock) for money or other property does not give rise to taxable gain or deductible loss to the corporation regardless of the nature of the transaction or the facts and circumstances involved. For example, the receipt by a corporation of the subscription price of shares of its stock upon their original issuance gives rise to neither taxable gain nor deductible loss, whether the subscription or issue price be equal to, in excess of, or less than, the par or stated value of such stock. Also, the exchange or sale by a corporation of its own shares for money or other property does not result in taxable gain or deductible loss, even though the corporation deals in such shares as it might in the shares of another corporation. A transfer by a corporation of shares of its own stock (including treasury stock) as compensation for services is considered, for purposes of section 1032(a), as a disposition by the corporation of such shares for money or other property.

(b) Section 1032(a) does not apply to the acquisition by a corporation of shares of its own stock except where the corporation acquires such shares in exchange for shares of its own stock (including treasury stock). See paragraph (e) of § 1.311-1, relating to treatment of acquisition of a corporation's own stock. Section 1032(a) also does not relate to the tax treatment of the recipient of a corporation's stock.

(c) Where a corporation acquires shares of its own stock in exchange for shares of its own stock (including treasury stock) the transaction may qualify not only under section 1032(a), but also under section 368(a)(1)(E) (recapitalization) or section 305(a) (distribution of stock and stock rights).

(d) For basis of property acquired by a corporation in connection with a transaction to which section 351 applies or in connection with a reorganization, see section 362. For basis of property acquired by a corporation in a transaction to which section 1032 applies but which does not qualify under any other nonrecognition provision, see section 1012. [Reg. § 1.1032-1.]

☐ [*T.D.* 6210, 11-6-56.]

§ 1.1032-2. Disposition by a corporation of stock of a controlling corporation in certain triangular reorganizations.—(a) *Scope.*—This section provides rules for certain triangular reorganizations described in § 1.358-6(b) when the acquiring corporation (*S*) acquires property or stock of another corporation (*T*) in exchange for stock of the corporation (*P*) in control of S.

(b) *General nonrecognition of gain or loss.*—For purposes of § 1.1032-1(a), in the case of a forward triangular merger, a triangular C reorganization, or a triangular B reorganization (as described in § 1.358-6(b)), *P* stock provided by *P* to *S*, or directly to *T* or *T*'s shareholders on behalf of *S*, pursuant to the plan of reorganization is treated as a disposition by *P* of shares of its own stock for *T*'s assets or stock, as applicable. For rules governing the use of *P* stock in a reverse triangular merger, see section 361.

(c) *Treatment of S.*—*S* must recognize gain or loss on its exchange of *P* stock as consideration in a forward triangular merger, a triangular C reorganization, or a triangular B reorganization (as described in § 1.358-6(b)), if *S* did not receive the *P* stock from *P* pursuant to the plan of reorganization. See § 1.358-6(d) for the effect on *P*'s basis in its *S* or *T* stock, as applicable.

For rules governing S's use of P stock in a reverse triangular merger, see section 361.

(d) *Examples.*—The rules of this section are illustrated by the following examples. For purposes of these examples, P, S, and T are domestic corporations, P and S do not file consolidated returns P owns all of the only class of S stock, the P stock exchanged in the transaction satisfies the requirements of the applicable reorganization provisions, and the facts set forth the only corporate activity.

Example 1. Forward triangular merger solely for P stock. (a) *Facts.* T has assets with an aggregate basis of $60 and fair market value of $100 and no liabilities. Pursuant to a plan, P forms S by transferring $100 of P stock to S and T merges into S. In the merger, the T shareholders receive, in exchange for their T stock, the P stock that P transferred to S. The transaction is a reorganization to which sections 368(a)(1)(A) and (a)(2)(D) apply.

(b) *No gain or loss recognized on the use of P stock.* Under paragraph (b) of this section, the P stock provided by P pursuant to the plan of reorganization is treated for purposes of § 1.1032-1 (a) as disposed of by P for the T assets acquired by S in the merger. Consequently, neither P nor S has taxable gain or deductible loss on the exchange.

Example 2. Forward triangular merger solely for P stock provided in part by S. (a) *Facts.* T has assets with an aggregate basis of $60 and fair market value of $100 and no liabilities. S is an operating company with substantial assets that has been in existence for several years. S also owns P stock with a $20 adjusted basis and $30 fair market value. S acquired the P stock in an unrelated transaction several years before the reorganization. Pursuant to a plan, P transfers additional P stock worth $70 to S and T merges into S. In the merger, the T shareholders receive $100 of P stock ($70 of P stock provided by P to S as part of the plan and $30 of P stock held by S previously). The transaction is a reorganization to which sections 368(a)(1)(A) and (a)(2)(D) apply.

(b) *Gain or loss recognized by S on the use of its P stock.* Under paragraph (b) of this section, the $70 of P stock provided by P pursuant to the plan of reorganization is treated as disposed of by P for the T assets acquired by S in the merger. Consequently, neither P nor S has taxable gain or deductible loss on the exchange of those shares. Under paragraph (c) of this section, however, S recognizes $10 of gain on the exchange of its P stock in the reorganization because S did not receive the P stock from P pursuant to the plan of reorganization. See § 1.358-6(d) for the effect on P's basis in its S stock.

* * *

[Reg. § 1.1032-2.]

☐ [*T.D.* 8648, 12-20-95. *Amended by T.D.* 8883, 5-11-2000.]

§ 1.1032-3. Disposition of stock or stock options in certain transactions not qualifying under any other nonrecognition provision.—(a) *Scope.*—This section provides rules for certain transactions in which a corporation or a partnership (the acquiring entity) acquires money or other property (as defined in § 1.1032-1) in exchange, in whole or in part, for stock of a corporation (the issuing corporation).

(b) *Nonrecognition of gain or loss.*—(1) *General rule.*—In a transaction to which this section applies; no gain or loss is recognized on the disposition of the issuing corporation's stock by the acquiring entity. The transaction is treated as if, immediately before the acquiring entity disposes of the stock of the issuing corporation, the acquiring entity purchased the issuing corporation's stock from the issuing corporation for fair market value with cash contributed to the acquiring entity by the issuing corporation (or, if necessary, through intermediate corporations or partnerships). For rules that may apply in determining the issuing corporation's adjustment to basis in the acquiring entity (or, if necessary, in determining the adjustment to basis in intermediate entities), see sections 358, 722, and the regulations thereunder.

(2) *Special rule for actual payment for stock of the issuing corporation.*—If the issuing corporation receives money or other property in payment for its stock, the amount of cash deemed contributed under paragraph (b)(1) of this section is the difference between the fair market value of the issuing corporation stock and the amount of money or the fair market value of other property that the issuing corporation receives as payment.

(c) *Applicability.*—The rules of this section apply only if, pursuant to a plan to acquire money or other property—

(1) The acquiring entity acquires stock of the issuing corporation directly or indirectly from the issuing corporation in a transaction in which, but for this section, the basis of the stock of the issuing corporation in the hands of the acquiring entity would be determined, in whole or in part, with respect to the issuing corporation's basis in the issuing corporation's stock under section 362(a) or 723 (provided that, in the case of an indirect acquisition by the acquiring entity, the transfers of issuing corporation stock through intermediate entities occur immediately after one another);

(2) The acquiring entity immediately transfers the stock of the issuing corporation to acquire money or other property (from a person other than an entity from which the stock was directly or indirectly acquired);

(3) The party receiving stock of the issuing corporation in the exchange specified in paragraph (c)(2) of this section from the acquiring entity does not receive a substituted basis in the stock of the issuing corporation within the meaning of section 7701(a)(42); and

(4) The issuing corporation stock is not exchanged for stock of the issuing corporation.

(d) *Stock options.*—The rules of this section shall apply to an option issued by a corporation to buy or sell its own stock in the same manner as the rules of this section apply to the stock of an issuing corporation.

(e) *Examples.*—The following examples illustrate the application of this section:

Example 1. (i) *X*, a corporation, owns all of the stock of *Y* corporation. *Y* reaches an agreement with *C*, an individual, to acquire a truck from *C* in exchange for 10 shares of *X* stock with a fair market value of $100. To effectuate *Y*'s agreement with *C*, *X* transfers to *Y* the *X* stock in a transaction in which, but for this section, the basis of the *X* stock in the hands of *Y* would be determined with respect to *X*'s basis in the *X* stock under section 362(a). *Y* immediately transfers the *X* stock to *C* to acquire the truck.

(ii) In this *Example 1*, no gain or loss is recognized on the disposition of the *X* stock by *Y*. Immediately before *Y*'s disposition of the *X* stock, *Y* is treated as purchasing the *X* stock from *X* for $100 of cash contributed to *Y* by *X*. Under section 358, *X*'s basis in its *Y* stock is increased by $100.

Example 2. (i) Assume the same facts as *Example 1*, except that, rather than *X* stock, *X* transfers an option with a fair market value of $100 to purchase *X* stock.

(ii) In this *Example 2*, no gain or loss is recognized on the disposition of the *X* stock option by *Y*. Immediately before *Y*'s disposition of the *X* stock option, *Y* is treated as purchasing the *X* stock option from *X* for $100 of cash contributed to *Y* by *X*. Under section 358, *X*'s basis in its *Y* stock is increased by $100.

Example 3. (i) *X*, a corporation, owns all of the outstanding stock of *Y* corporation. *Y* is a partner in partnership *Z*. *Z* reaches an agreement with *C*, an individual, to acquire a truck from *C* in exchange for 10 shares of *X* stock with a fair market value of $100. To effectuate *Z*'s agreement with *C*, *X* transfers to *Y* the *X* stock in a transaction in which, but for this section, the basis of the *X* stock in the hands of *Y* would be determined with respect to *X*'s basis in the *X* stock under section 362(a). *Y* immediately transfers the *X* stock to *Z* in a transaction in which, but for this section, the basis of the *X* stock in the hands of *Z* would be determined under section 723. *Z* immediately transfers the *X* stock to *C* to acquire the truck.

(ii) In this *Example 3*, no gain or loss is recognized on the disposition of the *X* stock by *Z*. Immediately before *Z*'s disposition of the *X* stock, *Z* is treated as purchasing the *X* stock from *X* for $100 of cash indirectly contributed to *Z* by *X* through an intermediate corporation, *Y*. Under section 722, *Y*'s basis in its *Z* partnership interest is increased by $100, and, under section 358, *X*'s basis in its *Y* stock is increased by $100.

Example 4. (i) *X*, a corporation, owns all of the outstanding stock of *Y* corporation. *B*, an individual, is an employee of *Y*. Pursuant to an agreement between *X* and *Y* to compensate *B* for services provided to *Y*, *X* transfers to *B* 10 shares of *X* stock with a fair market value of $100. Under § 1.83-6(d), but for this section, the transfer of *X* stock by *X* to the would be treated as a contribution of the *X* stock by *X* to the capital of *Y*, and immediately thereafter, a transfer of the *X* stock by *Y* to *B*. But for this section, the basis of the *X* stock in the hands of *Y* would be determined with respect to *X*'s basis in the *X* stock under section 362(a).

(ii) In this *Example 4*, no gain or loss is recognized on the deemed disposition of the *X* stock by *Y*. Immediately before *Y*'s deemed disposition of the *X* stock, *Y* is treated as purchasing the *X* stock from *X* for $100 of cash contributed to *Y* by *X*. Under section 358, *X*'s basis in its *Y* stock is increased by $100.

Example 5. (i) *X*, a corporation, owns all of the outstanding stock of *Y* corporation. *B*, an individual, is an employee of *Y*. To compensate *B* for services provided to *Y*, *B* is offered the opportunity to purchase 10 shares of *X* stock with a fair market value of $100 at a reduced price of $80. *B* transfers $80 and *Y* transfers $10 to *X* as partial payment for the *X* stock.

(ii) In this *Example 5*, no gain or loss is recognized on the deemed disposition of the *X* stock by *Y*. Immediately before *Y*'s deemed disposition of the *X* stock, *Y* is treated as purchasing the *X* stock from *X* for $100, $80 of which *Y* is deemed to have received from *B*, $10 of which originated with *Y*, and $10 of which is deemed to have been contributed to *Y* by *X*. Under section 358, *X*'s basis in its *Y* stock is increased by $10.

* * *

[Reg. § 1.1032-3.]

☐ [*T.D.* 8883, 5-11-2000 (*corrected* 6-14-2000).]

§1.1033(a)-1. Involuntary conversion; nonrecognition of gain.—(a) *In general.*—Section 1033 applies to cases where property is compulsorily or involuntarily converted. An "involuntary conversion" may be the result of the destruction of property in whole or in part, the theft of property, the seizure of property, the requisition or condemnation of property, or the threat or imminence of requisition or condemnation of property. An "involuntary conversion" may be a conversion into similar property or into money or into dissimilar property. Section 1033 provides that, under certain specified circumstances, any gain which is realized from an involuntary conversion shall not be recognized. In cases where property is converted into other property similar or related in service or use to the converted property, no gain shall be recognized regardless of when the disposition of the converted property occurred and regardless of whether or not the taxpayer elects to have the gain not recognized. In other types of involuntary conversion cases, however, the proceeds arising from the disposition of the converted property must (within the time limits specified) be reinvested in similar property in order to avoid recognition of any gain realized. Section 1033 applies only with respect to gains; losses from involuntary conversions are recognized or not recognized without regard to this section.

(b) *Special rules.*—For rules relating to the application of section 1033 to involuntary conversions of a principal residence with respect to which an election has been made under section 121 (relating to gain from sale or exchange of residence of individual who has attained age 65), see paragraph (g) of §1.121-5. For rules applicable to involuntary conversions of a principal residence occurring before January 1, 1951, see §1.1033(a)-3. For rules applicable to involuntary conversions of a principal residence occurring after December 31, 1950, and before January 1, 1954, see paragraph (h)(1) of §1.1034-1. For rules applicable to involuntary conversions of a personal residence occurring after December 31, 1953, see §1.1033(a)-3. For special rules relating to the election to have section 1034 apply to certain involuntary conversions of a principal residence occurring after December 31, 1957, see paragraph (h) (2) of §1.1034-1. For special rules relating to certain involuntary conversions of real property held either for productive use in trade or business or for investment and occurring after December 31, 1957, see §1.1033(g)-1. See also special rules applicable to involuntary conversions of property sold pursuant to reclamation laws, livestock destroyed by disease, and livestock sold on account of drought provided in §§1.1033(c)-1, 1.1033(d)-1, and 1.1033(e)-1, respectively. For rules relating to basis of property acquired through involuntary conversions, see §1.1033(b)-1. For determination of the period for which the taxpayer has held property acquired as a result of certain involuntary conversions, see section 1223 and regulations issued thereunder. For treatment of gains from involuntary conversions as capital gains in certain cases, see section 1231(a) and regulations issued thereunder. For portion of war loss recoveries treated as gain on involuntary conversion, see section 1332(b)(3) and regulations issued thereunder. [Reg. §1.1033(a)-1.]

☐ [*T.D.* 6222, 1-9-57. *Amended by T.D.* 6338, 12-11-58, *T.D.* 6453, 2-6-60, *T.D.* 6856, 10-19-65, *T.D.* 7625, 5-29-79 *and T.D.* 7758, 1-16-81.]

§1.1033(a)-2. Involuntary conversion into similar property, into money or into dissimilar property.—(a) *In general.*—The term "disposition of the converted property" means the destruction, theft, seizure, requisition, or condemnation of the converted property, or the sale or exchange of such property under threat or imminence of requisition or condemnation.

(b) *Conversion into similar property.*—If property (as a result of its destruction in whole or in part, theft, seizure, or requisition or condemnation or threat or imminence thereof) is compulsorily or involuntarily converted only into property similar or related in service or use to the property so converted, no gain shall be recognized. Such nonrecognition of gain is mandatory.

(c) *Conversion into money or into dissimilar property.*—(1) If property (as a result of its destruction in whole or in part, theft, seizure, or requisition or condemnation or threat or imminence thereof) is compulsorily or involuntarily converted into money or into property not similar or related in service or use to the converted property, the gain, if any, shall be recognized, at the election of the taxpayer, only to the extent that the amount realized upon such conversion exceeds the cost of other property purchased by the taxpayer which is similar or related in service or use to the property so converted, or the cost of stock of a corporation owning such other property which is purchased by the taxpayer in the acquisition of control of such corporation, if the taxpayer purchased such other property, or such stock, for the purpose of replacing the property so converted and during the period specified in subparagraph (3) of this paragraph. For the purposes of section 1033 the term "control" means the ownership of stock possessing at least 80 percent of the total combined voting power of all classes of stock entitled to vote and at least 80 percent of the total number of shares of all other classes of stock of the corporation.

(2) All of the details in connection with an involuntary conversion of property at a gain (including those relating to the replacement of the converted property, or a decision not to replace, or the expiration of the period for replacement) shall be reported in the return for the taxable year or years in which any of such gain is realized. An election to have such gain recognized only to the extent provided in subparagraph (1) of this paragraph shall be made by including such gain in gross income for such year or years only to such extent. If, at the time of filing such a return, the period within which the converted property must be replaced has expired, or if such an election is not desired, the gain should be included in gross income for such year or years in the regular manner. A failure to so include such gain in gross income in the regular manner shall be deemed to be an election by the taxpayer to have such gain recognized only to the extent provided in subparagraph (1) of this paragraph even though the details in connection with the conversion are not reported in such return. If, after having made an election under section 1033(a)(2), the converted property is not replaced within the required period of time, or replacement is made at a cost lower than was anticipated at the time of the election, or a decision is made not to replace, the tax liability for the year or years for which the election was made shall be recomputed. Such recomputation should be in the form of an "amended return". If a decision is made to make an election under section 1033(a)(2) after the filing of the return and the payment of the tax for the year or years in which any of the gain on an involuntary conversion is realized and before the expiration of the period within which the converted property must be replaced, a claim for credit or refund for such year or years should be filed. If the replacement of the converted property occurs in a year or years in which none of the gain on the conversion is realized, all of the details in connection with such replacement shall be reported in the return for such year or years.

(3) The period referred to in subparagraphs (1) and (2) of this paragraph is the period of time commencing with the date of the disposition of the converted property, or the date of the beginning of the threat or imminence of requisition or condemnation of the converted property, whichever is earlier, and ending two years (or, in the case of a disposition occurring before December 31, 1969, one year) after the close of the first taxable year in which any part of the gain upon the conversion is realized, or at the close of such later date as may be designated pursuant to an application of the taxpayer. Such application shall be made prior to the expiration of two years (or, in the case of a disposition occurring before December 31, 1969, one year) after the close of the first taxable year in which any part of the gain from the conversion is realized, unless the taxpayer can show to the satisfaction of the district director—

(i) reasonable cause for not having filed the application within the required period of time, and

(ii) the filing of such application was made within a reasonable time after the expiration of the required period of time.

See section 1033(g)(4) and § 1.1033(g)-1 for the circumstances under which, in the case of the conversion of real property held either for productive use in trade or business or for investment, the 2-year period referred to in this paragraph (c)(3) shall be extended to 3 years. The application shall contain all of the details in connection with the involuntary conversion. Such application shall be made to the district director for the internal revenue district in which the return is filed for the first taxable year in which any of the gain from the involuntary conversion is realized. No extension of time shall be granted pursuant to such application unless the taxpayer can show reasonable cause for not being able to replace the converted property within the required period of time.

(4) Property or stock purchased before the disposition of the converted property shall be considered to have been purchased for the purpose of replacing the converted property only if such property or stock is held by the taxpayer on the date of the disposition of the converted property. Property or stock shall be considered to have been purchased only if, but for the provisions of section 1033(b), the unadjusted basis of such property or stock would be its cost to the taxpayer within the meaning of section 1012. If the taxpayer's unadjusted basis of the replacement property would be determined, in the absence of section 1033(b), under any of the exceptions referred to in section 1012, the unadjusted basis of the property would not be its cost within the meaning of section 1012. For example, if property similar or related in service or use to the converted property is acquired by gift and its basis is determined under section 1015, such property will not qualify as a replacement for the converted property.

(5) If a taxpayer makes an election under section 1033(a)(2), any deficiency, for any taxable year in which any part of the gain upon the conversion is realized, which is attributable to such gain may be assessed at any time before the expiration of three years from the date the district director with whom the return for such year has been filed is notified by the taxpayer

of the replacement of the converted property or of an intention not to replace, or of a failure to replace, within the required period, notwithstanding the provisions of section 6212(c) or the provisions of any other law or rule of law which would otherwise prevent such assessment. If replacement has been made, such notification shall contain all of the details in connection with such replacement. Such notification should be made in the return for the taxable year or years in which the replacement occurs, or the intention not to replace is formed, or the period for replacement expires, if this return is filed with such district director. If this return is not filed with such district director, then such notification shall be made to such district director at the time of filing this return. If the taxpayer so desires, he may, in either event, also notify such district director before the filing of such return.

(6) If a taxpayer makes an election under section 1033(a)(2) and the replacement property or stock was purchased before the beginning of the last taxable year in which any part of the gain upon the conversion is realized, any deficiency, for any taxable year ending before such last taxable year, which is attributable to such election may be assessed at any time before the expiration of the period within which a deficiency for such last taxable year may be assessed, notwithstanding the provisions of section 6212(c) or 6501 or the provisions of any law or rule of law which would otherwise prevent such assessment.

(7) If the taxpayer makes an election under section 1033(a)(2), the gain upon the conversion shall be recognized to the extent that the amount realized upon such conversion exceeds the cost of the replacement property or stock, regardless of whether such amount is realized in one or more taxable years.

(8) The proceeds of a use and occupancy insurance contract, which by its terms insured against actual loss sustained of net profits in the business, are not proceeds of an involuntary conversion but are income in the same manner that the profits for which they are substituted would have been.

(9) There is no investment in property similar in character and devoted to a similar use if—

(i) The proceeds of unimproved real estate, taken upon condemnation proceedings, are invested in improved real estate.

(ii) The proceeds of conversion of real property are applied in reduction of indebtedness previously incurred in the purchase of a leasehold.

(iii) The owner of a requisitioned tug uses the proceeds to buy barges.

(10) If, in a condemnation proceeding, the Government retains out of the award sufficient funds to satisfy special assessments levied against the remaining portion of the plot or parcel of real estate affected for benefits accruing in connection with the condemnation, the amount so retained shall be deducted from the gross award in determining the amount of the net award.

(11) If, in a condemnation proceeding, the Government retains out of the award sufficient funds to satisfy liens (other than liens due to special assessments levied against the remaining portion of the plot or parcel of real estate affected for benefits accruing in connection with the condemnation) and mortgages against the property, and itself pays the same, the amount so retained shall not be deducted from the gross award in determining the amount of the net award. If, in a condemnation proceeding, the Government makes an award to a mortgagee to satisfy a mortgage on the condemned property, the amount of such award shall be considered as a part of the "amount realized" upon the conversion regardless of whether or not the taxpayer was personally liable for the mortgage debt. Thus, if a taxpayer has acquired property worth $100,000 subject to a $50,000 mortgage (regardless of whether or not he was personally liable for the mortgage debt) and, in a condemnation proceeding, the Government awards the taxpayer $60,000 and awards the mortgagee $50,000 in satisfaction of the mortgage, the entire $110,000 is considered to be the "amount realized" by the taxpayer.

(12) An amount expended for replacement of an asset, in excess of the recovery for loss, represents a capital expenditure and is not a deductible loss for income tax purposes. [Reg. § 1.1033(a)-2.]

☐ [*T.D.* 6222, 1-9-57. *Amended by T.D.* 6679, 9-30-63, *T.D.* 7075, 11-23-70, *T.D.* 7625, 5-29-79 *and T.D.* 7758, 1-16-81.]

§ 1.1033(b)-1. Basis of property acquired as a result of an involuntary conversion.—(a) The provisions of the first sentence of section 1033(b) may be illustrated by the following example:

Example. A's vessel which has an adjusted basis of $100,000 is destroyed in 1950 and A receives in 1951 insurance in the amount of $200,000. If A invests $150,000 in a new vessel, taxable gain to the extent of $50,000 would be recognized. The basis of the new vessel is $100,000; that is, the adjusted basis of the old vessel ($100,000) minus the money received by the taxpayer which was not expended in the acquisition of the new vessel ($50,000) plus the amount of gain recognized upon the conversion ($50,000). If any amount in excess of the proceeds of the conversion is expended in the acquisition of the new property, such amount may be added to the basis otherwise determined.

(b) The provisions of the last sentence of section 1033(b) may be illustrated by the following example:

Example. A taxpayer realizes $22,000 from the involuntary conversion of his barn in 1955; the adjusted basis of the barn to him was $10,000, and he spent in the same year $20,000 for a new barn which resulted in the nonrecognition of $10,000 of the $12,000 gain on the conversion. The basis of the new barn to the taxpayer would be $10,000—the cost of the new barn ($20,000) less the amount of the gain not recognized on the conversion ($10,000). The basis of the new barn would not be a substituted basis in the hands of the taxpayer within the meaning of section 1016(b)(2). If the replacement of the converted barn had been made by the purchase of two smaller barns which, together, were similar or related in service or use to the converted barn and which cost $8,000 and $12,000, respectively, then the basis of the two barns would be $4,000 and $6,000, respectively, the total basis of the purchased property ($10,000) allocated in proportion to their respective costs (8,000/20,000 of $10,000 or $4,000; and 12,000/20,000 of $10,000, or $6,000). [Reg. § 1.1033(b)-1.]

☐ [*T.D.* 6222, 1-9-57. *Amended by T.D.* 7625, 5-29-79.]

§ 1.1036-1. Stock for stock of the same corporation.—(a) Section 1036 permits the exchange, without the recognition of gain or loss, of common stock for common stock, or of preferred stock for preferred stock, in the same corporation. Section 1036 applies even though voting stock is exchanged for nonvoting stock or nonvoting stock is exchanged for voting stock. It is not limited to an exchange between two individual stockholders; it includes a transaction between a stockholder and the corporation. However, a transaction between a stockholder and the corporation may qualify not only under section 1036(a), but also under section 368(a)(1)(E) (recapitalization) or section 305(a) (distribution of stock and stock rights). The provisions of section 1036(a) do not apply if stock is exchanged for bonds, or preferred stock is exchanged for common stock, or common stock is exchanged for preferred stock, or common stock in one corporation is exchanged for common stock in another corporation. See paragraph (1) of § 1.301-1 for certain transactions treated as distributions under section 301. See paragraph (e)(5) of § 1.368-2 for certain transactions which result in deemed distributions under section 305(c) to which sections 305(b)(4) and 301 apply.

(b) For rules relating to recognition of gain or loss where an exchange is not wholly in kind, see subsections (b) and (c) of section 1031. For rules relating to the basis of property acquired in an exchange described in paragraph (a) of this section, see subsection (d) of section 1031.

(c) A transfer is not within the provisions of section 1036(a) if as part of the consideration the other party to the exchange assumes a liability of the taxpayer (or if the property transferred is subject to a liability), but the transfer, if otherwise qualified, will be within the provisions of section 1031(b).

* * *

[Reg. § 1.1036-1.]

☐ [*T.D.* 6210, 11-6-56. *Amended by T.D.* 7281, 7-11-73 *and T.D.* 8904, 9-29-2000.]

§ 1.1041-1T. Treatment of transfer of property between spouses or incident to divorce (temporary).—

Q-1. How is the transfer of property between spouses treated under section 1041?

A-1. Generally, no gain or loss is recognized on a transfer of property from an individual to (or in trust for the benefit of) a spouse or, if the transfer is incident to a divorce, a former spouse. The following questions and answers describe more fully the scope, tax consequences and other rules which apply to transfers of property under section 1041.

(a) *Scope of section 1041 in general.*

Q-2. Does section 1041 apply only to transfers of property incident to divorce?

A-2. No. Section 1041 is not limited to transfers of property incident to divorce. Section 1041 applies to any transfer of property between spouses regardless of whether the transfer is a gift or is a sale or exchange between spouses acting at arm's length (including a transfer in exchange for the relinquishment of property or marital rights or an exchange otherwise governed by another nonrecognition provision of the Code). A divorce or legal separation need not be contemplated between the spouses at the time of the transfer nor must a divorce or legal separation ever occur.

Example (1). A and B are married and file a joint return. A is the sole owner of a condominium unit. A sale or gift of the condominium from A to B is a transfer which is subject to the rules of section 1041.

Example (2). A and B are married and file separate returns. A is the owner of an independent sole proprietorship, X Company. In the ordinary course of business, X Company makes a sale of property to B. This sale is a transfer of property between spouses and is subject to the rules of section 1041.

Example (3). Assume the same facts as in example (2), except that X Company is a corporation wholly owned by A. This sale is not a sale between spouses subject to the rules of section 1041. However, in appropriate circumstances, general tax principles, including the step-transaction doctrine, may be applicable in recharacterizing the transaction.

Q-3. Do the rules of section 1041 apply to a transfer between spouses if the transferee spouse is a nonresident alien?

A-3. No. Gain or loss (if any) is recognized (assuming no other nonrecognition provision applies) at the time of a transfer of property if the property is transferred to a spouse who is a nonresident alien.

Q-4. What kinds of transfers are governed by section 1041?

A-4. Only transfers of property (whether real or personal, tangible or intangible) are governed by section 1041. Transfers of services are not subject to the rules of section 1041.

Q-5. Must the property transferred to a former spouse have been owned by the transferor spouse during the marriage?

A-5. No. A transfer of property acquired after the marriage ceases may be governed by section 1041.

(b) *Transfer incident to the divorce.*

Q-6. What is a transfer of property "incident to the divorce"?

A-6. A transfer of property is "incident to the divorce" in either of the following 2 circumstances—

(1) the transfer occurs not more than one year after the date on which the marriage ceases, or

(2) the transfer is related to the cessation of the marriage.

Thus, a transfer of property occurring not more than one year after the date on which the marriage ceases need not be related to the cessation of the marriage to qualify for section 1041 treatment. (See A-7 for transfers occurring more than one year after the cessation of the marriage.)

Q-7. When is a transfer of property "related to the cessation of the marriage"?

A-7. A transfer of property is treated as related to the cessation of the marriage if the transfer is pursuant to a divorce or separation instrument, as defined in section 71(b)(2), and the transfer occurs not more than 6 years after the date on which the marriage ceases. A divorce or separation instrument includes a modification or amendment to such decree or instrument. Any transfer not pursuant to a divorce or separation instrument and any transfer occurring more than 6 years after the cessation of the marriage is presumed to be not related to the cessation of the marriage. This presumption may be rebutted only by showing that the transfer was made to effect the division of property owned by the former spouses at the time of the cessation of the marriage. For example, the presumption may be rebutted by showing that (a) the transfer was not made within the one- and six-year periods described above because of factors which hampered an earlier transfer of the property, such as legal or business impediments to transfer or disputes concerning the value of the property owned at the time of the cessation of the marriage, and (b) the transfer is effected promptly after the impediment to transfer is removed.

Q-8. Do annulments and the cessations of marriages that are void *ab initio* due to violations of state law constitute divorces for purposes of section 1041?

A-8. Yes.

(c) *Transfers on behalf of a spouse.*

Q-9. May transfers of property to third parties on behalf of a spouse (or former spouse) qualify under section 1041?

A-9. Yes. There are three situations in which a transfer of property to a third party on behalf of a spouse (or former spouse) will qualify under section 1041, provided all other requirements of the section are satisfied. The first situation is where the transfer to the third party is required by a divorce or separation instrument. The second situation is where the transfer to the third party is pursuant to the written request of the other spouse (or former spouse). The third situation is where the transferor receives from the other spouse (or former spouse) a written consent or ratification of the transfer to the third party. Such consent or ratification must state that the parties intend the transfer to be treated as a transfer to the nontransferring spouse (or former spouse) subject to the rules of section 1041 and must be received by the transferor prior to the date of filing of the transferor's first return of tax for the taxable year in which the transfer was made. In the three situations described above, the transfer of property will be treated as made directly to the nontransferring spouse (or former spouse) and the nontransferring spouse will be treated as immediately transferring the property to the third party. The deemed transfer from the nontransferring spouse (or former spouse) to the third party is not a transaction that qualifies for nonrecognition of gain under section 1041. This A-9 shall not apply to transfers to which § 1.1041-2 applies.

(d) *Tax consequences of transfers subject to section 1041.*

Q-10. How is the transferor of property under section 1041 treated for income tax purposes?

A-10. The transferor of property under section 1041 recognizes no gain or loss on the transfer even if the transfer was in exchange for the release of marital rights or other consideration. This rule applies regardless of whether the transfer is of property separately owned by the transferor or is a division (equal or unequal) of community property. Thus, the result under section 1041 differs from the result in *United States v. Davis,* 370 U.S. 65 (1962).

Q-11. How is the transferee of property under section 1041 treated for income tax purposes?

A-11. The transferee of property under section 1041 recognizes no gain or loss upon receipt of the transferred property. In all cases, the basis of the transferred property in the hands of the transferee is the adjusted basis of such property in the hands of the transferor immediately before the transfer. Even if the transfer is a bona fide sale, the transferee does not acquire a basis in the transferred property equal to the transferee's cost (the fair market value). This carryover basis rule applies whether the adjusted basis of the transferred property is less than, equal to, or greater than its fair market value at the time of transfer (or the value of any consideration provided by the transferee) and applies for purposes of determining loss as well as gain upon the subsequent disposition of the property by the transferee. Thus, this rule is different from the rule applied in section 1015(a) for determining the basis of property acquired by gift.

Q-12. Do the rules described in A-10 and A-11 apply even if the transferred property is subject to liabilities which exceed the adjusted basis of the property?

A-12. Yes. For example, assume A owns property having a fair market value of $10,000 and an adjusted basis of $1,000. In contemplation of making a transfer of this property incident to a divorce from B, A borrows $5,000 from a bank, using the property as security for the borrowing. A then transfers the property to B and B assumes, or takes the property subject to, the liability to pay the $5,000 debt. Under section 1041, A recognizes no gain or loss upon the transfer of the property, and the adjusted basis of the property in the hands of B is $1,000.

* * *

[Temporary Reg. § 1.1041-1T.]

☐ [*T.D.* 7973, 8-30-84. *Amended by T.D.* 9035, 1-10-2003.]

Special Rules

§ 1.1059(e)-1. Non-pro rata redemptions.—(a) *In general.*—Section 1059(d)(6) (exception where stock held during entire existence of corporation) and section 1059(e)(2) (qualifying dividends) do not apply to any distribution treated as an extraordinary dividend under section 1059(e)(1). For example, if a redemption of stock is not pro rata as to all shareholders, any amount treated as a dividend under section 301 is treated as an extraordinary dividend regardless of whether the dividend is a qualifying dividend.

(b) *Reorganizations.*—For purposes of section 1059(e)(1), any exchange under section 356 is treated as a redemption and, to the extent any amount is treated as a dividend under section 356(a)(2), it is treated as a dividend under section 301.

* * *

[Reg. § 1.1059(e)-1.]

☐ [*T.D.* 8724, 7-15-97.]

§ 1.1060-1. Special allocation rules for certain asset acquisitions.—(a) *Scope.*—(1) *In general.*—This section prescribes rules relating to the requirements of section 1060, which, in the case of an applicable asset acquisition, requires the transferor (the seller) and the transferee (the purchaser) each to allocate the consideration paid or received in the transaction among the assets transferred in the same manner as amounts are allocated under section 338(b)(5) (relating to the allocation of adjusted grossed-up basis among the assets of the target corporation when a section 338 election is made). In the case of an applicable asset acquisition described in paragraph (b)(1) of this section, sellers and purchasers must allocate the consideration under the residual method as described in §§ 1.338-6 and 1.338-7 in order to determine, respectively, the amount realized from, and the basis in, each of the transferred assets. For rules relating to distributions of partnership property or transfers of partnership interests which are subject to section 1060(d), see § 1.755-2T.

* * *

(b) *Applicable asset acquisition.*—(1) *In general.*—An applicable asset acquisition is any transfer, whether direct or indirect, of a group of assets if the assets transferred constitute a trade or business in the hands of either the seller or the purchaser and, except as provided in paragraph (b)(8) of this section, the purchaser's basis in the transferred assets is determined wholly by reference to the purchaser's consideration.

(2) *Assets constituting a trade or business.*—(i) *In general.*—For purposes of this

section, a group of assets constitutes a trade or business if—

(A) The use of such assets would constitute an active trade or business under section 355; or

(B) Its character is such that goodwill or going concern value could under any circumstances attach to such group.

(ii) *Goodwill or going concern value.*—Goodwill is the value of a trade or business attributable to the expectancy of continued customer patronage. This expectancy may be due to the name or reputation of a trade or business or any other factor. Going concern value is the additional value that attaches to property because of its existence as an integral part of an ongoing business activity. Going concern value includes the value attributable to the ability of a trade or business (or a part of a trade or business) to continue functioning or generating income without interruption notwithstanding a change in ownership. It also includes the value that is attributable to the immediate use or availability of an acquired trade or business, such as, for example, the use of the revenues or net earnings that otherwise would not be received during any period if the acquired trade or business were not available or operational.

(iii) *Factors indicating goodwill or going concern value.*—In making the determination in this paragraph (b)(2), all the facts and circumstances surrounding the transaction are taken into account. Whether sufficient consideration is available to allocate to goodwill or going concern value after the residual method is applied is not relevant in determining whether goodwill or going concern value could attach to a group of assets. Factors to be considered include—

(A) The presence of any intangible assets (whether or not those assets are section 197 intangibles), provided, however, that the transfer of such an asset in the absence of other assets will not be a trade or business for purposes of section 1060;

(B) The existence of an excess of the total consideration over the aggregate book value of the tangible and intangible assets purchased (other than goodwill and going concern value) as shown in the financial accounting books and records of the purchaser; and

(C) Related transactions, including lease agreements, licenses, or other similar agreements between the purchaser and seller (or managers, directors, owners, or employees of the seller) in connection with the transfer.

(3) *Examples.*—The following examples illustrate paragraphs (b)(1) and (2) of this section:

Example 1. S is a high grade machine shop that manufactures microwave connectors in limited quantities. It is a successful company with a reputation within the industry and among its customers for manufacturing unique, high quality products. Its tangible assets consist primarily of ordinary machinery for working metal and plating. It has no secret formulas or patented drawings of value. P is a company that designs, manufactures, and markets electronic components. It wants to establish an immediate presence in the microwave industry, an area in which it previously has not been engaged. P is acquiring assets of a number of smaller companies and hopes that these assets will collectively allow it to offer a broad product mix. P acquires the assets of S in order to augment its product mix and to promote its presence in the microwave industry. P will not use the assets acquired from S to manufacture microwave connectors. The assets transferred are assets that constitute a trade or business in the hands of the seller. Thus, P's purchase of S's assets is an applicable asset acquisition. The fact that P will not use the assets acquired from S to continue the business of S does not affect this conclusion.

Example 2. S, a sole proprietor who operates a car wash, both leases the building housing the car wash and sells all of the car wash equipment to P. S's use of the building and the car wash equipment constitute a trade or business. P begins operating a car wash in the building it leases from S. Because the assets transferred together with the asset leased are assets which constitute a trade or business, P's purchase of S's assets is an applicable asset acquisition.

Example 3. S, a corporation, owns a retail store business in State X and conducts activities in connection with that business enterprise that meet the active trade or business requirement of section 355. P is a minority shareholder of S. S distributes to P all the assets of S used in S's retail business in State X in complete redemption of P's stock in S held by P. The distribution of S's assets in redemption of P's stock is treated as a sale or exchange under sections 302(a) and 302(b)(3), and P's basis in the assets distributed to it is determined wholly by reference to the consideration paid, the S stock. Thus, S's distribution of assets constituting a trade or business to P is an applicable asset acquisition.

Example 4. S is a manufacturing company with an internal financial bookkeeping department. P is in the business of providing a financial bookkeeping service on a contract basis. As part of an agreement for P to begin providing financial bookkeeping services to S, P agrees to buy all of the assets associated with S's internal bookkeeping operations and provide employment to any of S's bookkeeping department employees who choose to accept a position with P. In addition to selling P the assets associated with its bookkeeping operation, S will enter into a long term contract with P for bookkeeping services. Because assets transferred from S to P, along with the related contract for bookkeeping services, are a trade or business in the hands of P, the sale of the bookkeeping assets from S to P is an applicable asset acquisition.

(4) *Asymmetrical transfers of assets.*—A purchaser is subject to section 1060 if—

(i) Under general principles of tax law, the seller is not treated as transferring the same assets as the purchaser is treated as acquiring;

(ii) The assets acquired by the purchaser constitute a trade or business; and

(iii) Except as provided in paragraph (b)(8) of this section, the purchaser's basis in the transferred assets is determined wholly by reference to the purchaser's consideration.

(5) *Related transactions.*—Whether the assets transferred constitute a trade or business is determined by aggregating all transfers from the seller to the purchaser in a series of related transactions. Except as provided in paragraph (b)(8) of this section, all assets transferred from the seller to the purchaser in a series of related transactions are included in the group of assets among which the consideration paid or received in such series is allocated under the residual method. The principles of §1.338-1(c) are also applied in determining which assets are included in the group of assets among which the consideration paid or received is allocated under the residual method.

(6) *More than a single trade or business.*—If the assets transferred from a seller to a purchaser include more than one trade or business, then, in applying this section, all of the assets transferred (whether or not transferred in one transaction or a series of related transactions and whether or not part of a trade or business) are treated as a single trade or business.

(7) *Covenant entered into by the seller.*—If, in connection with an applicable asset acquisition, the seller enters into a covenant (e.g., a covenant not to compete) with the purchaser, that covenant is treated as an asset transferred as part of a trade or business.

(8) *Partial non-recognition exchanges.*—A transfer may constitute an applicable asset acquisition notwithstanding the fact that no gain or loss is recognized with respect to a portion of the group of assets transferred. All of the assets transferred, including the non-recognition assets, are taken into account in determining whether the group of assets constitutes a trade or business. The allocation of consideration under paragraph (c) of this section is done without taking into account either the non-recognition assets or the amount of money or other property that is treated as transferred in exchange for the non-recognition assets (together, the non-recognition exchange property). The basis in and gain or loss recognized with respect to the non-recognition exchange property are determined under such rules as would otherwise apply to an exchange of such property. The amount of the money and other property treated as exchanged for non-recognition assets is the amount by which the fair market value of the non-recognition assets transferred by one party exceeds the fair market value of the non-recognition assets transferred by the other (to the extent of the money and the fair market value of property transferred in the exchange). The money and other property that are treated as transferred in exchange for the non-recognition assets (and which are not included among the assets to which section 1060 applies) are considered to come from the following assets in the following order: first from Class I assets, then from Class II assets, then from Class III assets, then from Class IV assets, then from Class V assets, then from Class VI assets, and then from Class VII assets. For this purpose, liabilities assumed (or to which a non-recognition exchange property is subject) are treated as Class I assets. See *Example 1* in paragraph (d) of this section for an example of the application of section 1060 to a single transaction which is, in part, a non-recognition exchange.

* * *

(c) *Allocation of consideration among assets under the residual method.*—(1) *Consideration.*—The seller's consideration is the amount, in the aggregate, realized from selling the assets in the applicable asset acquisition under section 1001(b). The purchaser's consideration is the amount, in the aggregate, of its cost of purchasing the assets in the applicable asset acquisition that is properly taken into account in basis.

(2) *Allocation of consideration among assets.*—For purposes of determining the seller's amount realized for each of the assets sold in an applicable asset acquisition, the seller allocates consideration to all the assets sold by

using the residual method under §§1.338-6 and 1.338-7, substituting consideration for ADSP. For purposes of determining the purchaser's basis in each of the assets purchased in an applicable asset acquisition, the purchaser allocates consideration to all the assets purchased by using the residual method under §§1.338-6 and 1.338-7, substituting consideration for AGUB. In allocating consideration, the rules set forth in paragraphs (c)(3) and (4) of this section apply in addition to the rules in §§1.338-6 and 1.338-7.

(3) *Certain costs.*—The seller and purchaser each adjusts the amount allocated to an individual asset to take into account the specific identifiable costs incurred in transferring that asset in connection with the applicable asset acquisition (e.g., real estate transfer costs or security interest perfection costs). Costs so allocated increase, or decrease, as appropriate, the total consideration that is allocated under the residual method. No adjustment is made to the amount allocated to an individual asset for general costs associated with the applicable asset acquisition as a whole or with groups of assets included therein (e.g., non-specific appraisal fees or accounting fees). These latter amounts are taken into account only indirectly through their effect on the total consideration to be allocated. If an election described in §1.338-6(c)(5) is made with respect to an applicable asset acquisition, any allocation of costs pursuant to this paragraph (c)(3) shall be made as if such election had not been made. The preceding sentence applies to applicable asset acquisitions occurring on or after September 11, 2007. For applicable asset acquisitions occurring before September 11, 2007 and on or after September 15, 2004, see §1.1060-1T as contained in 26 CFR Part 1 in effect on April 1, 2007. For applicable asset acquisitions occurring before September 15, 2004, see §§1.338-6 and 1.1060-1 as contained in 26 CFR Part 1 in effect on April 1, 2004.

(4) *Effect of agreement between parties.*—If, in connection with an applicable asset acquisition, the seller and purchaser agree in writing as to the allocation of any amount of consideration to, or as to the fair market value of, any of the assets, such agreement is binding on them to the extent provided in this paragraph (c)(4). Nothing in this paragraph (c)(4) restricts the Commissioner's authority to challenge the allocations or values arrived at in an allocation agreement. This paragraph (c)(4) does not apply if the parties are able to refute the allocation or valuation under the standards set forth in *Commissioner v. Danielson*, 378 F.2d 771 (3d Cir.), *cert. denied*, 389 U.S. 858 (1967) (a party wishing to challenge the tax consequences of an agreement as construed by the Commissioner must offer proof that, in an action between the parties to the agreement, would be admissible to alter that construction or show its unenforceability because of mistake, undue influence, fraud, duress, etc.).

* * *

(d) *Examples.*—The following examples illustrate this section:

Example 1. (i) On January 1, 2001, A transfers assets X, Y, and Z to B in exchange for assets D, E, and F plus $1,000 cash.

(ii) Assume the exchange of assets constitutes an exchange of like-kind property to which section 1031 applies. Assume also that goodwill or going concern value could under any circumstances attach to each of the DEF and XYZ groups of assets and, therefore, each group constitutes a trade or business under section 1060.

(iii) Assume the fair market values of the assets and the amount of money transferred are as follows:

By A

Asset	*Fair Market Value*
X	$400
Y	400
Z	200
Total	$1,000

By B

Asset	*Fair Market Value*
D	$40
E	30
F	30
Cash (amount)	1,000
Total	$1,100

(iv) Under paragraph (b)(8) of this section, for purposes of allocating consideration under paragraph (c) of this section, the like-kind assets exchanged and any money or other property that are treated as transferred in exchange for the like-kind property are excluded from the application of section 1060.

(v) Since assets X, Y, and Z are like-kind property, they are excluded from the application of the section 1060 allocation rules.

(vi) Since assets D, E, and F are like-kind property, they are excluded from the application of the section 1060 allocation rules. Thus, the allocation rules of section 1060 do not apply in determining B's gain or loss with respect to the disposition of assets D, E, and F, and the allocation rules of section 1060 and paragraph (c) of this section are not applied to determine A's bases of assets D, E, and F. In addition, $900 of the $1,000 cash B gave to A for A's like-kind assets (X, Y, and Z) is treated as transferred in exchange for the like-kind property in order to equalize the fair market values of the like-kind assets. Therefore, $900 of the cash is excluded from the application of the section 1060 allocation rules.

(vii) $100 of the cash is allocated under section 1060 and paragraph (c) of this section.

(viii) A received $100 that must be allocated under section 1060 and paragraph (c) of this section. Since A transferred no Class I, II, III, IV, V, or VI assets to which section 1060 applies, in determining its amount realized for the part of the exchange to which section 1031 does not apply, the $100 is allocated to Class VII assets (goodwill and going concern value).

(ix) B gave A $100 that must be allocated under section 1060 and paragraph (c) of this section. Since B received from A no Class I, II, III, IV, V, or VI assets to which section 1060 applies, the $100 consideration is allocated by B to Class VII assets (goodwill and going concern value).

Example 2. (i) On January 1, 2001, S, a sole proprietor, sells to P, a corporation, a group of assets that constitutes a trade or business under paragraph (b)(2) of this section. S, who plans to retire immediately, also executes in P's favor a covenant not to compete. P pays S $3,000 in cash and assumes $1,000 in liabilities. Thus, the total consideration is $4,000.

(ii) On the purchase date, P and S also execute a separate agreement that states that the fair market values of the Class II, Class III, Class V, and Class VI assets S sold to P are as follows:

Asset Class	*Asset*	*Fair Market Value*
II	Actively traded securities	$500
	Total Class II	500
III	Accounts receivable	200
	Total Class III	200
V	Furniture and fixtures	800
	Building	800
	Land	200
	Equipment	400
	Total Class V	2,200
VI	Covenant not to compete	900
	Total Class VI	900

(iii) P and S each allocate the consideration in the transaction among the assets transferred under paragraph (c) of this section in accordance with the agreed upon fair market values of the assets, so that $500 is allocated to Class II assets, $200 is allocated to the Class III asset, $2,200 is allocated to Class V assets, $900 is allocated to Class VI assets, and $200 ($4,000 total consideration less $3,800 allocated to assets in Classes II, III, V, and VI) is allocated to the Class VII assets (goodwill and going concern value).

(iv) In connection with the examination of P's return, the Commissioner, in determining the fair market values of the assets transferred, may disregard the parties' agreement. Assume that the Commissioner correctly determines that the fair market value of the covenant not to compete was $500. Since the allocation of consideration among Class II, III, V, and VI assets results in allocation up to the fair market value limitation, the $600 of unallocated consideration resulting from the Commissioner's redetermination of the value of the covenant not to compete is allocated to Class VII assets (goodwill and going concern value).

* * *

[Reg. § 1.1060-1.]

☐ [*T.D.* 8940, 2-12-2001. *Amended by T.D.* 9059, 6-6-2003; *T.D.* 9158, 9-15-2004; *T.D.* 9257, 4-7-2006; *T.D.* 9358, 9-10-2007 *and T.D.* 9377, 1-22-2008 (*corrected* 3-17-2008).]

Wash Sales; Straddles

§ 1.1091-1. Losses from wash sales of stock or securities.—(a) A taxpayer cannot deduct any loss claimed to have been sustained from the sale or other disposition of stock or securities if, within a period beginning 30 days before the date of such sale or disposition and ending 30 days after such date (referred to in this section as the 61-day period), he has acquired (by purchase or by an exchange upon which the entire amount of gain or loss was recognized by law), or has entered into a contract or option so to acquire, substantially identical stock or securities. However, this prohibition does not apply (1) in the case of a taxpayer, not a corporation, if the sale or other disposition of stock or securities is made in connection with the taxpayer's trade or business, or (2) in the case of a corporation, a dealer in stock or securities, if the sale or other disposition of stock or securities is made in the ordinary course of its business as such dealer.

(b) Where more than one loss is claimed to have been sustained within the taxable year from the sale or other disposition of stock or securities, the provisions of this section shall be applied to the losses in the order in which the stock or securities the disposition of which resulted in the respective losses were disposed of (beginning with the earliest disposition). If the order of disposition of stock or securities disposed of at a loss on the same day cannot be determined, the stock or securities will be considered to have been disposed of in the order in which they were originally acquired (beginning with the earliest acquisition).

(c) Where the amount of stock or securities acquired within the 61-day period is less than the amount of stock or securities sold or otherwise disposed of, then the particular shares of stock or securities the loss from the sale or other disposition of which is not deductible shall be those with which the stock or securities acquired are matched in accordance with the following rule: The stock or securities acquired will be matched in accordance with the order of their acquisition (beginning with the earliest acquisition) with an equal number of the shares of stock or securities sold or otherwise disposed of.

(d) Where the amount of stock or securities acquired within the 61-day period is not less than the amount of stock or securities sold or otherwise disposed of, then the particular shares of stock or securities the acquisition of which resulted in the nondeductibility of the loss shall be those with which the stock or securities disposed of are matched in accordance with the following rule: The stock or securities sold or otherwise disposed of will be matched with an equal number of the shares of stock or securities acquired in accordance with the order of acquisition (beginning with the earliest acquisition) of the stock or securities acquired.

(e) The acquisition of any share of stock or any security which results in the nondeductibility of a loss under the provisions of this section shall be disregarded in determining the deductibility of any other loss.

(f) The word "acquired" as used in this section means acquired by purchase or by an exchange upon which the entire amount of gain or loss was recognized by law, and comprehends cases where the taxpayer has entered into a contract or option within the 61-day period to acquire by purchase or by such an exchange.

(g) For purposes of determining under this section the 61-day period applicable to a short sale of stock or securities, the principles of paragraph (a) of § 1.1233-1 for determining the consummation of a short sale shall generally apply except that the date of entering into the short sale shall be deemed to be the date of sale if, on the date of entering into the short sale, the taxpayer owns (or on or before such date has entered into a contract or option to acquire) stock or securities identical to those sold short and subsequently delivers such stock or securities to close the short sale.

(h) The following examples illustrate the application of this section:

Example (1). A, whose taxable year is the calendar year, on December 1, 1954, purchased 100 shares of common stock in the M Company for $10,000 and on December 15, 1954, purchased 100 additional shares for $9,000. On January 3, 1955, he sold the 100 shares purchased on December 1, 1954, for $9,000. Because of the provisions of section 1091, no loss from the sale is allowable as a deduction.

Example (2). A, whose taxable year is the calendar year, on September 21, 1954, purchased 100 shares of the common stock of the M Company for $5,000. On December 21, 1954, he purchased 50 shares of substantially identical stock for $2,750, and on December 27, 1954, he purchased 25 additional shares of such stock for $1,125. On January 3, 1955, he sold for $4,000 the 100 shares purchased on September 21, 1954. There is an indicated loss of $1,000 on the sale of the 100 shares. Since, within the 61-day period, A purchased 75 shares of substantially identical stock, the loss on the sale of 75 of the shares ($3,750 – $3,000, or $750) is not allowable as a deduction because of the provisions of section 1091. The loss on the sale of the remaining 25 shares ($1,250 – $1,000, or $250) is deductible subject to the limitations provided in sections 267 and 1211. The basis of the 50 shares purchased December 21, 1954, the acquisition of which resulted in the nondeductibility of the loss ($500) sustained on 50 of the 100 shares sold on January 3, 1955, is $2,500 (the cost of 50 of the shares sold on January 3, 1955) + $750 (the difference between the purchase price ($2,750) of 50 of the shares acquired on December 21, 1954, and the selling price ($2,000) of the 50 shares sold on January 3, 1955, or $3,250). Similarly, the basis of the 25 shares purchased on December 27, 1954, the acquisition of which resulted in the nondeductibility of the loss ($250) sustained on 25 of the shares sold on January 3, 1955, is $1,250 + $125, or $1,375. See § 1.1091-2.

Example (3). A, whose taxable year is the calendar year, on September 15, 1954, purchased 100 shares of the stock of the M Company for $5,000. He sold these shares on February 1, 1956, for $4,000. On each of the four days from February 15, 1956, to February 18, 1956, inclusive, he purchased 50 shares of substantially identical stock for $2,000. There is an indicated loss of $1,000 from the sale of the 100 shares on February 1, 1956, but, since within the 61-day period A purchased not less than 100 shares of substantially identical stock, the loss is not deductible. The particular shares of stock the purchase of which resulted in the nondeductibility of the loss are the first 100 shares purchased within such period, that is, the 50 shares purchased on February 15, 1956, and the 50 shares purchased on February 16, 1956. In determining the period for which the 50 shares purchased on February 15, 1956, and the 50 shares purchased on February 16, 1956, were held, there is to be included the period for which the 100 shares purchased on September 15, 1954, and sold on February 1, 1956, were held. [Reg. § 1.1091-1.]

□ [*T.D.* 6178, 6-1-56. *Amended by T.D.* 6926, 8-8-67.]

§ 1.1091-2. Basis of stock or securities acquired in "wash sales".—(a) *In general.*—The application of section 1091(d) may be illustrated by the following examples:

Example (1). A purchased a share of common stock of the X Corporation for $100 in 1935, which he sold January 15, 1955, for $80. On February 1, 1955, he purchased a share of common stock of the same corporation for $90. No loss from the sale is recognized under section 1091. The basis of the new share is $110; that is, the basis of the old share ($100) increased by $10, the excess of the price at which the new share was acquired ($90) over the price at which the old share was sold ($80).

Example (2). A purchased a share of common stock of the Y Corporation for $100 in 1935, which he sold January 15, 1955, for $80. On February 1, 1955, he purchased a share of common stock of the same corporation for $70. No loss from the sale is recognized under section 1091. The basis of the new share is $90; that is, the basis of the old share ($100) decreased by $10, the excess of the price at which the old share was sold ($80) over the price at which the new share was acquired ($70).

(b) *Special rule.*—For a special rule as to the adjustment to basis required under section 1091(d) in the case of wash sales involving certain regulated investment company stock for which there is an average basis, see paragraph (e)(3)(iii)(*c*) and (*d*) of § 1.1012-1. [Reg. § 1.1091-2.]

□ [*T.D.* 6178, 6-1-56. *Amended by T.D.* 7129, 7-6-71.]

General Rules for Determining Capital Gains and Losses

»»→ Caution: Reg. § 1.1221-1 does not reflect Section 1221(b)(3), relating to musical works, added by the Tax Increase Prevention and Reconciliation Act of 2005.

§ 1.1221-1. Meaning of terms.—(a) The term "capital assets" includes all classes of property not specifically excluded by section 1221. In determining whether property is a "capital asset", the period for which held is immaterial.

(b) Property used in the trade or business of a taxpayer of a character which is subject to the allowance for depreciation provided in section 167 and real property used in the trade or business of a taxpayer is excluded from the term "capital assets". Gains and losses from the sale or exchange of such property are not treated as gains and losses from the sale or exchange of capital assets, except to the extent provided in section 1231. See § 1.1231-1. Property held for the production of income, but not used in a trade or business of the taxpayer, is not excluded from the term "capital assets" even though depreciation may have been allowed with respect to such property under section 23(1) of the Internal Revenue Code of 1939 before its amendment by section 121(c) of the Revenue Act of 1942 (56 Stat. 819). However, gain or loss upon the sale or exchange of land held by a taxpayer primarily for sale to customers in the ordinary course of his business, as in the case of a dealer in real estate, is not subject to the provisions of subchapter P (section 1201 and following), chapter 1 of the Code.

(c)(1) A copyright, a literary, musical, or artistic composition, and similar property are excluded from the term "capital assets" if held by a taxpayer whose personal efforts created such property, or if held by a taxpayer in whose hands the basis of such property is determined, for purposes of determining gain from a sale or exchange, in whole or in part by reference to the basis of such property in the hands of a taxpayer whose personal efforts created such property. For purposes of this subparagraph, the phrase "similar property" includes, for example, such property as a theatrical production, a radio program, a newspaper cartoon strip, or any other property eligible for copyright protection (whether under statute or common law), but does not include a patent or an invention, or a design which may be protected only under the patent law and not under the copyright law.

(2) In the case of sales and other dispositions occurring after July 25, 1969, a letter, a memorandum, or similar property is excluded from the term "capital asset" if held by (i) a

taxpayer whose personal efforts created such property, (ii) a taxpayer for whom such property was prepared or produced, or (iii) a taxpayer in whose hands the basis of such property is determined, for purposes of determining gain from a sale or exchange, in whole or in part by reference to the basis of such property in the hands of a taxpayer described in subdivision (i) or (ii) of this subparagraph. In the case of a collection of letters, memorandums, or similar property held by a person who is a taxpayer described in subdivision (i), (ii), or (iii) of this subparagraph as to some of such letters, memorandums, or similar property but not as to others, this subparagraph shall apply only to those letters, memorandums, or similar property as to which such person is a taxpayer described in such subdivision. For purposes of this subparagraph, the phrase "similar property" includes, for example, such property as a draft of a speech, a manuscript, a research paper, an oral recording of any type, a transcript of an oral recording, a transcript of an oral interview or of dictation, a personal or business diary, a log or journal, a corporate archive, including a corporate charter, office correspondence, a financial record, a drawing, a photograph, or a dispatch. A letter, memorandum, or property similar to a letter or memorandum, addressed to a taxpayer shall be considered as prepared or produced for him. This subparagraph does not apply to property, such as a corporate archive, office correspondence, or a financial record, sold or disposed of as part of a going business if such property has no significant value separate and apart from its relation to and use in such business; it also does not apply to any property to which subparagraph (1) of this paragraph applies (i.e., property to which section 1221(3) applied before its amendment by section 514(a) of the Tax Reform Act of 1969 (83 Stat. 643).

(3) For purposes of this paragraph, in general property is created in whole or in part by the personal efforts of a taxpayer if such taxpayer performs literary, theatrical, musical, artistic, or other creative or productive work which affirmatively contributes to the creation of the property, or if such taxpayer directs and guides others in the performance of such work. A taxpayer, such as corporate executive, who merely has administrative control of writers, actors, artists, or personnel and who does not substantially engage in the direction and guidance of such persons in the performance of their work, does not create property by his personal efforts. However, for purposes of subparagraph (2) of this paragraph, a letter or memorandum, or property similar to a letter or memorandum, which is prepared by personnel who are under the administrative control of a taxpayer, such as a corporate executive, shall be deemed to have been prepared or produced for him whether or not such letter, memorandum, or similar property is reviewed by him.

(4) For the application of section 1231 to the sale or exchange of property to which this paragraph applies, see § 1.1231-1. For the application of section 170 to the charitable contribution of property to which this paragraph applies, see section 170(e) and the regulations thereunder.

(d) Section 1221(4) excludes from the definition of "capital asset" accounts or notes receivable acquired in the ordinary course of trade or business for services rendered or from the sale of stock in trade or inventory or property held for sale to customers in the ordinary course of trade or business. Thus, if a taxpayer acquires a note receivable for services rendered, reports the fair market value of the note as income, and later sells the note for less than the amount previously reported, the loss is an ordinary loss. On the other hand, if the taxpayer later sells the note for more than the amount originally reported, the excess is treated as ordinary income.

(e) Obligations of the United States or any of its possessions, or of a State or Territory, or any political subdivision thereof, or of the District of Columbia, issued on or after March 1, 1941, on a discount basis and payable without interest at a fixed maturity date not exceeding one year from the date of issue, are excluded from the term "capital assets." An obligation may be issued on a discount basis even though the price paid exceeds the face amount. Thus, although the Second Liberty Bond Act (31 U.S.C. 754) provides that United States Treasury bills shall be issued on a discount basis, the issuing price paid for a particular bill may, by reason of competitive bidding, actually exceed the face amount of the bill. Since the obligations of the type described in this paragraph are excluded from the term "capital assets", gains or losses from the sale or exchange of such obligations are not subject to the limitations provided in such subchapter P. It is, therefore, not necessary for a taxpayer (other than a life insurance company taxable under part I (section 801 and following), subchapter L, chapter 1 of the Code, as amended by the Life Insurance Company Tax Act of 1955 (70 Stat. 36), and, in the case of taxable years beginning before January 1, 1955, subject to taxation only on interest, dividends, and rents) to segregate the original discount accrued and the gain or loss realized upon the sale or other disposition of any such obligation. See section 454(b) with respect to the original discount accrued. The provisions of this paragraph may be illustrated by the following examples:

Example (1). A (not a life insurance company) buys a $100,000, 90-day Treasury bill upon issuance for $99,998. As of the close of the forty-fifth day of the life of such bill, he sells it to B (not a life insurance company) for $99,999.50. The entire net gain to A of $1.50 may be taken into account as a single item of income, without allocating $1 to interest and $0.50 to gain. If B holds the bill until maturity his net gain of $0.50 may similarly be taken into account as a single item of income, without allocating $1 to interest and $0.50 to loss.

Example (2). The facts in this example are the same as in example (1) except that the selling price to B is $99,998.50. The net gain to A of $0.50 may be taken into account without allocating $1 to interest and $0.50 to loss, and, similarly, if B holds the bill until maturity his entire net gain of $1.50 may be taken into account as a single item of income without allocating $1 to interest and $0.50 to gain. [Reg. § 1.1221-1.]

□ [*T.D.* 6243, 7-23-57. *Amended by T.D.* 7369, 7-15-75.]

§ 1.1221-2. Hedging transactions.—(a) *Treatment of hedging transactions.*—(1) *In general.*—This section governs the treatment of hedging transactions under section 1221(a)(7). Except as provided in paragraph (g)(2) of this section, the term capital asset does not include property that is part of a hedging transaction (as defined in paragraph (b) of this section).

(2) *Short sales and options.*—This section also governs the character of gain or loss from a short sale or option that is part of a hedging transaction. Except as provided in paragraph (g)(2) of this section, gain or loss on a short sale or option that is part of a hedging transaction (as defined in paragraph (b) of this section) is ordinary income or loss.

(3) *Exclusivity.*—If a transaction is not a hedging transaction as defined in paragraph (b) of this section, gain or loss from the transaction is not made ordinary on the grounds that property involved in the transaction is a surrogate for a noncapital asset, that the transaction serves as insurance against a business risk, that the transaction serves a hedging function, or that the transaction serves a similar function or purpose.

(4) *Coordination with section 988.*—This section does not apply to determine the character of gain or loss realized on a section 988 transaction as defined in section 988(c)(1) or realized with respect to any qualified fund as defined in section 988(c)(1)(E)(iii).

(b) *Hedging transaction defined.*—Section 1221(b)(2)(A) provides that a hedging transaction is any transaction that a taxpayer enters into in the normal course of the taxpayer's trade or business primarily—

(1) To manage risk of price changes or currency fluctuations with respect to ordinary property (as defined in paragraph (c)(2) of this section) that is held or to be held by the taxpayer;

(2) To manage risk of interest rate or price changes or currency fluctuations with respect to borrowings made or to be made, or ordinary obligations incurred or to be incurred, by the taxpayer; or

(3) To manage such other risks as the Secretary may prescribe in regulations (see paragraph (d)(6) of this section).

(c) *General rules.*—(1) *Normal course.*—Solely for purposes of paragraph (b) of this section, if a transaction is entered into in furtherance of a taxpayer's trade or business, the transaction is entered into in the normal course of the taxpayer's trade or business. This rule includes managing risks relating to the expansion of an existing business or the acquisition of a new trade or business.

(2) *Ordinary property and obligations.*—Property is ordinary property to a taxpayer only if a sale or exchange of the property by the taxpayer could not produce capital gain or loss under any circumstances. Thus, for example, property used in a trade or business within the meaning of section 1231(b) (determined without regard to the holding period specified in that section) is not ordinary property. An obligation is an ordinary obligation if performance or termination of the obligation by the taxpayer could not produce capital gain or loss. For purposes of this paragraph (c)(2), the term termination has the same meaning as it does in section 1234A.

(3) *Hedging an aggregate risk.*—The term hedging transaction includes a transaction that manages an aggregate risk of interest rate changes, price changes, and/or currency fluctuations only if all of the risk, or all but a de minimis amount of the risk, is with respect to ordinary property, ordinary obligations, or borrowings.

(4) *Managing risk.*—(i) *In general.*—Whether a transaction manages a taxpayer's risk is determined based on all of the facts and circumstances surrounding the taxpayer's business and the transaction. Whether a transaction manages a taxpayer's risk may be determined on a business unit by business unit basis (for example by treating particular groups of activities, including the assets and liabilities attributable to those activities, as separate business units), provided that the business unit is within a single entity or consolidated return

group that adopts the single-entity approach. A taxpayer's hedging strategies and policies as reflected in the taxpayer's minutes or other records are evidence of whether particular transactions were entered into primarily to manage the taxpayer's risk.

(ii) *Limitation of risk management transactions to those specifically described.*—Except as otherwise determined by published guidance or by private letter ruling, a transaction that is not treated as a hedging transaction under paragraph (d) does not manage risk. Moreover, a transaction undertaken for speculative purposes will not be treated as a hedging transaction.

* * *

[Reg. § 1.1221-2.]

☐ [*T.D.* 8555, 7-13-94. *Amended by T.D.* 8653, 1-5-96; *T.D.* 8985, 3-15-2002; *T.D.* 9264, 5-26-2006 *and T.D.* 9329, 6-13-2007.]

§ 1.1222-1. Other terms relating to capital gains and losses.—(a) The phrase "short-term" applies to the category of gains and losses arising from the sale or exchange of capital assets held for 1 year (6 months for taxable years beginning before 1977; 9 months for taxable years beginning in 1977) or less; the phrase "long-term" to the category of gains and losses arising from the sale or exchange of capital assets held for more than 1 year (6 months for taxable years beginning before 1977; 9 months for taxable years beginning in 1977). The fact that some part of a loss from the sale or exchange of a capital asset may be finally disallowed because of the operation of section 1211 does not mean that such loss is not "taken into account in computing taxable income" within the meaning of that phrase as used in sections 1222(2) and 1222(4).

(b) (1) In the definition of "net short-term capital gain", as provided in section 1222(5), the amounts brought forward to the taxable year under section 1212 (other than section 1212 (b) (1) (B)) are short-term capital losses for such taxable year.

(2) In the definition of "net long-term capital gain", as provided in section 1222(7), the amounts brought forward to the taxable year under section 1212(b) (1) (B) are long-term capital losses for such taxable year.

(c) Gains and losses from the sale or exchange of capital assets held for not more than 1 year (6 months for taxable years beginning before 1977; 9 months for taxable years beginning in 1977) (described as short-term capital gains and short-term capital losses) shall be segregated from gains and losses arising from the sale or exchange of such assets held for more than 1 year (6 months for taxable years beginning before 1977; 9 months for taxable years beginning in 1977) (described as long-term capital gains and long-term capital losses).

(d) (1) The term "capital gain net income" (net capital gain for taxable years beginning before January 1, 1977) means the excess of the gains from sales or exchanges of capital assets over the losses from sales or exchanges of capital assets, which losses include any amounts carried to the taxable year pursuant to section 1212(a) or section 1212(b).

* * *

(e) The term "net capital loss" means the excess of the losses from sales or exchanges of capital assets over the sum allowed under section 1211. However, in the case of a corporation, amounts which are short-term capital losses under § 1.1212-1(a) are excluded in determining such "net capital loss".

(f) See section 165(g) and section 166(e), under which losses from worthless stocks, bonds, and other securities (if they constitute capital assets) are required to be treated as losses under subchapter P (section 1201 and following), chapter 1 of the Code, from the sale or exchange of capital assets, even though such securities are not actually sold or exchanged. See also section 1231 and § 1.1231-1 for the determination of whether or not gains and losses from the involuntary conversion of capital assets and from the sale, exchange, or involuntary conversion of certain property used in the trade or business shall be treated as gains and losses from the sale or exchange of capital assets. See also section 1236 and § 1.1236-1 for the determination of whether or not gains from the sale or exchange of securities by a dealer in securities shall be treated as capital gains, or whether losses from such sales or exchanges shall be treated as ordinary losses.

(g) In the case of nonresident alien individuals not engaged in trade or business within the United States, see section 871 and the regulations thereunder for the determination of the net amount of capital gains subject to tax.

(h) The term "net capital gain" ("net section 1201 gain" for taxable years beginning before January 1, 1977) means the excess of the net long-term capital gain for the taxable year over the net short-term capital loss for such year. [Reg. § 1.1222-1.]

☐ [*T.D.* 6243, 7-23-57. *Amended by T.D.* 6828, 6-16-65; *T.D.* 6867, 12-6-65; *T.D.* 7301, 1-3-74; *T.D.* 7337, 12-26-74 *and T.D.* 7728, 10-31-80.]

§ 1.1223-1. Determination of period for which capital assets are held.—(a) The holding period of property received in an exchange by a taxpayer includes the period for which the property which he exchanged was held by him, if the property received has the same basis in whole or in part for determining gain or loss in the hands of the taxpayer as the property exchanged. However, this rule shall apply, in the case of exchanges after March 1, 1954, only if the property exchanged was at the time of the exchange a capital asset in the hands of the taxpayer or property used in his trade or business as defined in section 1231(b). For the purposes of this paragraph the term "exchange" includes the following transactions: (1) An involuntary conversion described in section 1033, and (2) a distribution to which section 355 (or so much of section 356 as relates to section 355) applies. Thus, if property acquired as the result of a compulsory or involuntary conversion of other property of the taxpayer has under section 1033(c) the same basis in whole or in part in the hands of the taxpayer as the property so converted, its acquisition is treated as an exchange and the holding period of the newly acquired property shall include the period during which the converted property was held by the taxpayer. Thus, also, where stock of a controlled corporation is received by a taxpayer pursuant to a distribution to which section 355 (or so much of section 356 as relates to section 355) applies, the distribution is treated as an exchange and the period for which the taxpayer has held the stock of the controlled corporation shall include the period for which he held the stock of the distributing corporation with respect to which such distribution was made.

(b) The holding period of property in the hands of a taxpayer shall include the period during which the property was held by any other person, if such property has the same basis in whole or in part in the hands of the taxpayer for determining gain or loss from a sale or exchange as it would have in the hands of such other person. For example, the period for which property acquired by gift after December 31, 1920, was held by the donor must be included in determining the period for which the property was held by the taxpayer if, under the provisions of section 1015, such property has, for the purpose of determining gain or loss from the sale or exchange, the same basis in the hands of the taxpayer as it would have in the hands of the donor. Similarly, the period for which property acquired from a decedent who died in 2010 was held by the decedent must be included in determining the period during which the property was held by the recipient, if the recipient's basis in the property is determined under section 1022.

* * *

(d) If the acquisition of stock or securities resulted in the nondeductibility (under section 1091, relating to wash sales) of the loss from the sale or other disposition of substantially identical stock or securities, the holding period of the newly acquired securities shall include the period for which the taxpayer held the securities with respect to which the loss was not allowable.

(e) The period for which the taxpayer has held stock, or stock subscription rights, received on a distribution shall be determined as though the stock dividend, or stock right, as the case may be, were the stock in respect of which the dividend was issued if the basis for determining gain or loss upon the sale or other disposition of such stock dividend or stock right is determined under section 307. If the basis of stock received by a taxpayer pursuant to a spin-off is determined under so much of section 1052(c) as refers to section 113(a)(23) of the Internal Revenue Code of 1939, and such stock is sold or otherwise disposed of in a taxable year which is subject to the Internal Revenue Code of 1954, the period for which the taxpayer has held the stock received in such spin-off shall include the period for which he held the stock of the distributing corporation with respect to which such distribution was made.

(f) The period for which the taxpayer has held stock or securities issued to him by a corporation pursuant to the exercise by him of rights to acquire such stock or securities from the corporation will, in every case and whether or not the receipt of taxable gain was recognized in connection with the distribution of the rights, begin with and include the day upon which the rights to acquire such stock or securities were exercised. A taxpayer will be deemed to have exercised rights received from a corporation to acquire stock or securities therein where there is an expression of assent to the terms of such rights made by the taxpayer in the manner requested or authorized by the corporation.

* * *

(h) If a taxpayer accepts delivery of a commodity in satisfaction of a commodity futures contracts, the holding period of the commodity shall include the period for which the taxpayer held the commodity futures contract, if such futures contract was a capital asset in his hands.

(i) If shares of stock in a corporation are sold from lots purchased at different dates or at different prices and the identity of the lots cannot be determined, the rules prescribed by the regulations under section 1012 for determining the cost or other basis of such stocks so sold or transferred shall also apply for the purpose of determining the holding period of such stock.

(j) In the case of a person acquiring property, or to whom property passed, from a decedent (within the meaning of section 1014(b)) dying after December 31, 1970, such person shall be considered to have held the property for more than 6 months if the property—

(1) Has a basis in the hands of such person which is determined in whole or in part under section 1014, and

(2) Is sold or otherwise disposed of by such person within 6 months after the decedent's death.

The provisions of this paragraph apply to sales of such property included in the decedent's gross estate for the purposes of the estate tax by the executor or administrator of the estate and to sales of such property by other persons who have acquired property from the decedent. The provisions of this paragraph may also be applicable to cases involving joint tenancies, community property, and properties transferred in contemplation of death. Thus, if a surviving joint tenant, who acquired property by right of survivorship, sells or otherwise disposes of such property within 1 year (6 months for taxable years beginning before 1977; 9 months for taxable years beginning in 1977) after the date of the decedent's death, and the basis of the property in his hands is determined in whole or in part under section 1014, the property shall be considered to have been held by the surviving joint tenant for more than 1 year (6 months for taxable years beginning before 1977; 9 months for taxable years beginning in 1977). Similarly, a surviving spouse's share of community property shall be considered to have been held by her for more than 1 year (6 months for taxable years beginning before 1977; 9 months for taxable years beginning in 1977) if it is sold or otherwise disposed of within 1 year (6 months for taxable years beginning before 1977; 9 months for taxable years beginning in 1977) after the date of the decedent's death, regardless of when the property was actually acquired by the marital community. For the purposes of this paragraph, it is immaterial that the sale or other disposition produces gain or loss. If property is considered to have been held for more than 1 year (6 months for taxable years beginning before 1977; 9 months for taxable years beginning in 1977) by reason of this paragraph, it also is considered to have been held for that period for purposes of section 1231 (if that section is otherwise applicable).

* * *

[Reg. § 1.1223-1.]

☐ [*T.D.* 6243, 7-23-57. *Amended by T.D.* 7238, 12-28-72; *T.D.* 7728, 10-31-80; *T.D.* 9811, 1-18-2017 *and T.D.* 9849, 3-11-2019.]

§ 1.1223-3. Rules relating to the holding periods of partnership interests.—(a) *In general.*—A partner shall not have a divided holding period in an interest in a partnership unless—

(1) The partner acquired portions of an interest at different times; or

(2) The partner acquired portions of the partnership interest in exchange for property transferred at the same time but resulting in different holding periods (e.g., section 1223).

(b) *Accounting for holding periods of an interest in a partnership.*—(1) *General rule.*—The portion of a partnership interest to which a holding period relates shall be determined by reference to a fraction, the numerator of which is the fair market value of the portion of the partnership interest received in the transaction to which the holding period relates, and the denominator of which is the fair market value of the entire partnership interest (determined immediately after the transaction).

(2) *Special rule.*—For purposes of applying paragraph (b)(1) of this section to determine the holding period of a partnership interest (or portion thereof) that is sold or exchanged (or with respect to which gain or loss is recognized upon a distribution under section 731), if a partner makes one or more contributions of cash to the partnership and receives one or more distributions of cash from the partnership during the one-year period ending on the date of the sale or exchange (or distribution with respect to which gain or loss is recognized under section 731), the partner may reduce the cash contributions made during the year by cash distributions received on a last-in-first-out basis, treating all cash distributions as if they were received immediately before the sale or exchange (or at the time of the distribution with respect to which gain or loss is recognized under section 731).

(3) *Deemed contributions and distributions.*—For purposes of paragraphs (b)(1) and (2) of this section, deemed contributions of cash under section 752(a) and deemed distributions of cash under section 752(b) shall be disregarded to the same extent that such amounts are disregarded under § 1.704-1(b)(2)(iv)(c).

(4) *Adjustment with respect to contributed section 751 assets.*—For purposes of applying paragraph (b)(1) of this section to determine the holding period of a partnership interest (or portion thereof) that is sold or exchanged, if a partner receives a portion of the partnership interest in exchange for property described in section 751(c) or (d) (section 751 assets) within the one-year period ending on the date of the sale or exchange of all or a portion of the partner's interest in the partnership, and the partner recognizes ordinary income or loss on account of such a section 751 asset in a fully taxable transaction (either as a result of the

sale of all or part of the partner's interest in the partnership or the sale by the partnership of the section 751 asset), the contribution of the section 751 asset during the one-year period shall be disregarded. However, if, in the absence of this paragraph, a partner would not be treated as having held any portion of the interest for more than one year (e.g., because the partner's only contributions to the partnership are contributions of section 751 assets or section 751 assets and cash within the prior one-year period), this adjustment is not available.

(5) *Exception.*—The Commissioner may prescribe by guidance published in the Internal Revenue Bulletin (see § 601.601(d)(2) of this chapter) a rule disregarding certain cash contributions (including contributions of a de minimis amount of cash) in applying paragraph (b)(1) of this section to determine the holding period of a partnership interest (or portion thereof) that is sold or exchanged.

(c) *Sale or exchange of all or a portion of an interest in a partnership.*—(1) *Sale or exchange of entire interest in a partnership.*—If a partner sells or exchanges the partner's entire interest in a partnership, any capital gain or loss recognized shall be divided between long-term and short-term capital gain or loss in the same proportions as the holding period of the interest in the partnership is divided between the portion of the interest held for more than one year and the portion of the interest held for one year or less.

(2) *Sale or exchange of a portion of an interest in a partnership.*—(i) *Certain publicly traded partnerships.*—A selling partner in a publicly traded partnership (as defined under section 7704(b)) may use the actual holding period of the portion of a partnership interest transferred if—

(A) The ownership interest is divided into identifiable units with ascertainable holding periods;

(B) The selling partner can identify the portion of the partnership interest transferred; and

(C) The selling partner elects to use the identification method for all sales or exchanges of interests in the partnership after September 21, 2000. The selling partner makes the election referred to in this paragraph (c)(2)(i)(C) by using the actual holding period of the portion of the partner's interest in the partnership first transferred after September 21, 2000 in reporting the transaction for federal income tax purposes.

(ii) *Other partnerships.*—If a partner has a divided holding period in a partnership interest, and paragraph (c)(2)(i) of this section does not apply, then the holding period of the transferred interest shall be divided between long-term and short-term capital gain or loss in the same proportions as the long-term and short-term capital gain or loss that the transferor partner would realize if the entire interest in the partnership were transferred in a fully taxable transaction immediately before the actual transfer.

(d) *Distributions.*—(1) *In general.*—Except as provided in paragraph (b)(2) of this section, a partner's holding period in a partnership interest is not affected by distributions from the partnership.

(2) *Character of capital gain or loss recognized as a result of a distribution from a partnership.*—If a partner is required to recognize capital gain or loss as a result of a distribution from a partnership, then the capital gain or loss recognized shall be divided between long-term and short-term capital gain or loss in the same proportions as the long-term and short-term capital gain or loss that the distributee partner would realize if such partner's entire interest in the partnership were transferred in a fully taxable transaction immediately before the distribution.

(e) *Section 751(c) assets.*—For purposes of this section, properties and potential gain treated as unrealized receivables under section 751(c) shall be treated as separate assets that are not capital assets as defined in section 1221 or property described in section 1231.

(f) *Examples.*—The provisions of this section are illustrated by the following examples:

Example 1. Division of holding period—contribution of money and a capital asset. (i) *A* contributes $5,000 of cash and a nondepreciable capital asset *A* has held for two years to a partnership (*PRS*) for a 50 percent interest in *PRS*. *A*'s basis in the capital asset is $5,000, and the fair market value of the asset is $10,000. After the exchange, *A*'s basis in *A*'s interest in *PRS* is $10,000, and the fair market value of the interest is $15,000. *A* received one-third of the interest in *PRS* for a cash payment of $5,000 ($5,000/$15,000). Therefore, *A*'s holding period in one-third of the interest received (attributable to the contribution of money to the partnership) begins on the day after the contribution. *A* received two-thirds of the interest in *PRS* in exchange for the capital asset ($10,000/$15,000). Accordingly, pursuant to section 1223(1), *A* has a two-year holding period in two-thirds of the interest received in *PRS*.

(ii) Six months later, when *A*'s basis in *PRS* is $12,000 (due to a $2,000 allocation of partnership income to *A*), *A* sells the interest in *PRS* for $17,000. Assuming *PRS* holds no inventory or unrealized receivables (as defined under section 751(c)) and no collectibles or section 1250 property, *A* will realize $5,000 of capital gain. As determined above, one-third of *A*'s interest in *PRS* has a holding period of one year or less, and two-thirds of *A*'s interest in *PRS* has a holding period equal to two years and six months. Therefore, one-third of the capital gain will be short-term capital gain, and two-thirds of the capital gain will be long-term capital gain.

Example 2. Division of holding period—contribution of section 751 asset and a capital asset. A contributes inventory with a basis of $2,000 and a fair market value of $6,000 and a capital asset which *A* has held for more than one year with a basis of $4,000 and a fair market value of $6,000, and *B* contributes cash of $12,000 to form a partnership (*AB*). As a result of the contribution, one-half of *A*'s interest in *AB* is treated as having been held for more than one year under section 1223(1). Six months later. *A* transfers one-half of *A*'s interest in *AB* to *C* for $6,000, realizing a gain of $3,000. If *AB* were to sell all of its section 751 property in a fully taxable transaction immediately before *A*'s transfer of the partnership interest, *A* would be allocated $4,000 of ordinary income on account of the inventory. Accordingly, *A* will recognize $2,000 of ordinary income and $1,000 of capital gain ($3,000 – $2,000) on account of the transfer to *C*. Because *A* recognizes ordinary income on account of the inventory that was contributed to *AB* within the one year period ending on the date of the sale, the inventory will be disregarded in determining the holding period of *A*'s interest in *AB*. All of the capital gain will be long-term.

Example 3. Netting of cash contributions and distributions. (i) On January 1, 2000,*A* holds a 50 percent interest in the capital and profits of a partnership (*PS*). The value of *A*'s *PS* interest is $900, and *A*'s holding period in the entire interest is long-term. On January 2, 2000, when the value of *A*'s *PS* interest is still $900, *A* contributes $100 to *PS*. On June 1, 2000, *A* receives a distribution of $40 cash from the partnership. On September 1, 2000, when the value of *A*'s interest in *PS* is $1,350, *A* contributes an additional $230 cash to *PS*, and on October 1, 2000, *A* receives another $40 cash distribution from *PS*. *A* sells *A*'s entire partnership interest on November 1, 2000, for $1,600. *A*'s adjusted basis in the *PS* interest at the time of the sale is $1,000.

(ii) For purposes of netting cash contributions and distributions in determining the holding period of *A*'s interest in *PS*, *A* is treated as having received a distribution of $80 on November 1, 2000. Applying that distribution on a last-in-first-out basis to reduce prior contributions during the year, the contribution made on September 1, 2000, is reduced to $150 ($230 – $80). The holding period then is determined as follows: Immediately after the contribution of $100 on January 2, 2000, *A*'s holding period in *A*'s *PS* interest is 90 percent long-term ($900 ÷ ($900 + $100)) and 10 percent short-term ($100 ÷ ($900 + $100)). The contribution of $150 on September 1, 2000, causes 10 percent of *A*'s partnership interest ($150 ÷ ($1,350 + $150)) to have a short-term holding period. Accordingly, immediately after the contribution on September 1, 2000, *A*'s holding period in *A*'s *PS* interest is 81 percent long-term (.90 × .90) and 19 percent short-term ((.10 × .90) + .10). Accordingly, $486 ($600 × .81) of the gain from *A*'s sale of the *PS* interest is long-term capital gain, and $114 ($600 × .19) is short-term capital gain.

Example 4. Division of holding period when capital account is increased by contribution. A, B, C, and *D* are equal partners in a partnership (*PRS*), and the fair market value of a 25 percent interest in *PRS* is $100. *A, B, C*, and *D* each contribute an additional $100 to partnership capital, thereby increasing the fair market value of each partner's interest to $200. As a result of the contribution, each partner has a new holding period in the portion of the partner's interest in *PRS* that is attributable to the contribution. That portion equals 50 percent ($100 ÷ $200) of each partners interest in *PRS*.

Example 5. Sale or exchange of a portion of an interest in a partnership. (i) *A, B*, and *C* form an equal partnership (*PRS*). In connection with the formation, *A* contributes $5,000 in cash and a capital asset (capital asset 1) with a fair market value of $5,000 and a basis of $2,000; *B* contributes $7,000 in cash and a capital asset (capital asset 2) with a fair market value of $3,000 and a basis of $3,000; and *C* contributes $10,000 in cash. At the time of the contribution, *A* had held the contributed property for two years. Six months later, when *A*'s basis in *PRS* is $7,000, *A* transfers one-half of *A*'s interest in *PRS* to *T* for $7,000 at a time when *PRS*'s balance sheet (reflecting a cash receipts and disbursements method of accounting) is as follows:

	ASSETS	
	Adjusted Basis	*Market Value*
Cash	$22,000	$22,000
Unrealized Receivables	0	6,000
Capital Asset 1	2,000	5,000
Capital Asset 2	3,000	9,000
Capital Assets	5,000	14,000
Total	$27,000	$42,000

(ii) Although at the time of the transfer *A* has not held *A*'s interest in *PRS* for more than one year, 50 percent of the fair market value of *A*'s interest in *PRS* was received in exchange for a capital asset with a long-term holding period. Therefore, 50 percent of *A*'s interest in *PRS* has a long-term holding period.

(iii) If *PRS* were to sell all of its section 751 property in a fully taxable transaction immediately before *A*'s transfer of the partnership interest, *A* would be allocated $2,000 of ordinary income. One-half of that amount ($1,000) is attributable to the portion of *A*'s interest in *PRS* transferred to *T*. Accordingly, *A* will recognize $1,000 ordinary income and $2,500 ($3,500 – $1,000) of capital gain on account of the transfer to *T* of one-half of *A*'s interest in *PRS*. Fifty percent ($1,250) of that gain is long-term capital gain and 50 percent ($1,250) is short-term capital gain.

Example 6. Sale of units of interests in a partnership. A publicly traded partnership (*PRS*) has ownership interests that are segregated into identifiable units of interest. *A* owns 10 limited partnership units in *PRS* for which *A* paid $10,000 on January 1, 1999. On August 1, 2000, *A* purchases five additional units for $10,000. At the time of purchase, the fair market value of each unit has increased to $2,000. *A*'s holding period for one-third ($10,000/$30,000) of the interest in *PRS* begins on the day after the purchase of the five additional units. Less than one year later, *A* sells five units of ownership in *PRS* for $11,000. At the time, *A*'s basis in the 15 units *PRS* is $20,000, and *A*'s capital gain on the sale of 5 units is $4,333 (amount realized of $11,000 – one-third of the adjusted basis or $6,667). For purposes of determining the holding period, *A* can designate the specific units of *PRS* sold. If *A* properly identifies the five units sold as five of the ten units for which A has a long-term holding period and elects to use the identification method for all subsequent sales or exchanges of interests in the partnership by using the actual holding period in reporting the transaction on *A*'s federal income tax return, the capital gain realized will be long-term capital gain.

Example 7. Disproportionate distribution. In 1997, *A* and *B* each contribute cash of $50,000 to form and become equal partners in a partnership (*PRS*). More than one year later, *A* receives a distribution worth $22,000 from *PRS*, which reduces *A*'s interest in *PRS* to 36 percent. After the distribution, *B* owns 64 percent of *PRS*. The holding periods of *A* and *B* in their interests in *PRS* are not affected by the distribution.

Example 8. Gain or loss as a result of a distribution—(i) On January 1, 1996, *A* contributes property with a basis of $10 and a fair market value of $10,000 in exchange for an interest in a partnership (*ABC*). On September 30, 2000, when *A*'s interest in *ABC* is worth $12,000 (and the basis of *A*'s partnership interest is still $10), *A* contributes $12,000 cash in exchange for an additional interest in *ABC*. *A* is allocated a loss equal to $10,000 by *ABC* for the taxable year ending December 31, 2000, thereby reducing the basis of *A*'s partnership interest to $2,010. On February 1, 2001, *ABC* makes a cash distribution to *A* of $10,000. *ABC* holds no inventory or unrealized receivables. (Assume that *A* is allocated no gain or loss for the taxable year ending December 31, 2001, so that the basis of *A*'s partnership interest does not increase or decrease as a result of such allocations.)

(ii) The netting rule contained in paragraph (b)(2) of this section provides that, in determining the holding period of *A*'s interest in *ABC*, the cash contribution made on September 30, 2000, must be reduced by the distribution made on February 1, 2001. Accordingly, for purposes of determining the holding period of *A*'s interest in *ABC*, *A* is treated as having made a cash contribution of $2,000 ($12,000 – $10,000) to *ABC* on September 30, 2000. *A*'s holding period in one-seventh of *A*'s interest in *ABC* ($2,000 cash contributed over the $14,000 value of the entire interest (determined as if only $2,000 were contributed rather than $12,000)) begins on the day after the cash contribution. *A* recognizes $7,990 of capital gain as a result of the distribution. See section 731(a)(1). One-seventh of the capital gain recognized as a result of the distribution is short-term capital gain, and six-sevenths of the capital gain is long-term capital gain. After the distribution, *A*'s basis in the interest in *PRS* is $0, and the holding period for the interest in *PRS* continues to be divided in the same proportions as before the distribution.

* * *

[Reg. § 1.1223-3.]

☐ [*T.D.* 8902, 9-20-2000.]

Special Rules for Determining Capital Gains and Losses

§1.1231-1. Gains and losses from the sale or exchange of certain property used in the trade or business.—(a) *In general.*—Section 1231 provides that, subject to the provisions of paragraph (e) of this section, a taxpayer's gains and losses from the disposition (including involuntary conversion) of assets described in that section as "property used in the trade or business" and from the involuntary conversion of capital assets held for more than 1 year (6 months for taxable years beginning before 1977; 9 months for taxable years beginning in 1977) shall be treated as long-term capital gains and losses if the total gains exceed the total losses. If the total gains do not exceed the total losses, all such gains and losses are treated as ordinary gains and losses. Therefore, if the taxpayer has no gains subject to section 1231, a recognized loss from the condemnation (or from a sale or exchange under threat of condemnation) of even a capital asset held for more than 1 year (6 months for taxable years beginning before 1977; 9 months for taxable years beginning in 1977) is an ordinary loss. Capital assets subject to section 1231 treatment include only capital assets involuntarily converted. The noncapital assets subject to section 1231 treatment are (1) depreciable business property and business real property held for more than 1 year (6 months for taxable years beginning before 1977; 9 months for taxable years beginning in 1977), other than stock in trade and certain copyrights and artistic property and, in the case of sales and other dispositions occurring after July 25, 1969, other than a letter, memorandum, or property similar to a letter or memorandum; (2) timber, coal, and iron ore which do not otherwise meet the requirements of section 1231 but with respect to which section 631 applies; and (3) certain livestock and unharvested crops. See paragraph (c) of this section.

(b) *Treatment of gains and losses.*—For the purpose of applying section 1231, a taxpayer must aggregate his recognized gains and losses from—

(1) The sale, exchange, or involuntary conversion of property used in the trade or business (as defined in section 1231(b)), and

(2) The involuntary conversion (but not sale or exchange) of capital assets held for more than 1 year (6 months for taxable years beginning before 1977; 9 months for taxable years beginning in 1977).

If the gains to which section 1231 applies exceed the losses to which the section applies, the gains and losses are treated as long-term capital gains and losses and are subject to the provisions of parts I and II (section 1201 and following), subchapter P, chapter 1, of the Code, relating to capital gains and losses. If the gains to which section 1231 applies do not exceed the losses to which the section applies, the gains and losses are treated as ordinary gains and losses. Therefore, in the latter case, a loss from the involuntary conversion of a capital asset held for more than 1 year (6 months for taxable years beginning before 1977; 9 months for taxable years beginning in 1977) is treated as an ordinary loss and is not subject to the limitation on capital losses in section 1211. The phrase "involuntary conversion" is defined in paragraph (e) of this section.

(c) *Transactions to which section applies.*—Section 1231 applies to recognized gains and losses from the following:

(1) The sale, exchange, or involuntary conversion of property held for more than 1 year (6 months for taxable years beginning before 1977; 9 months for taxable years beginning in 1977) and used in the taxpayer's trade or business, which is either real property or is of a character subject to the allowance for depreciation under section 167 (even though fully depreciated), and which is not—

(i) Property of a kind which would properly be includible in the inventory of the taxpayer if on hand at the close of the taxable year, or property held by the taxpayer primarily for sale to customers in the ordinary course of business;

(ii) A copyright, a literary, musical, or artistic composition, or similar property, or (in the case of sales and other dispositions occurring after July 25, 1969) a letter, memorandum, or property similar to a letter or memorandum, held by a taxpayer described in section 1221(3); or

(iii) Livestock held for draft, breeding, dairy, or sporting purposes, except to the extent included under subparagraph (4) of this paragraph, or poultry.

(2) The involuntary conversion of capital assets held for more than 1 year (6 months for taxable years beginning before 1977; 9 months for taxable years beginning in 1977).

(3) The cutting or disposal of timber, or the disposal of coal or iron ore, to the extent considered arising from a sale or exchange by reason of the provisions of section 631 and the regulations thereunder.

(4) The sale, exchange, or involuntary conversion of livestock if the requirements of §1.1231-2 are met.

(5) The sale, exchange, or involuntary conversion of unharvested crops on land which is (i) used in the taxpayer's trade or business and held for more than 1 year (6 months for taxable years beginning before 1977; 9 months for taxable years beginning in 1977), and (ii) sold or exchanged at the same time and to the

same person. See paragraph (f) of this section. For purposes of section 1231, the phrase "property used in the trade or business" means property described in this paragraph (other than property described in subparagraph (2) of this paragraph). Notwithstanding any of the provisions of this paragraph, section 1231(a) does not apply to gains and losses under the circumstances described in paragraph (e)(2) or (3) of this section.

(d) *Extent to which gains and losses are taken into account.*—All gains and losses to which section 1231 applies must be taken into account in determining whether and to what extent the gains exceed the losses. For the purpose of this computation, the provisions of section 1211 limiting the deduction of capital losses do not apply, and no losses are excluded by that section. With that exception, gains are included in the computations under section 1231 only to the extent that they are taken into account in computing gross income, and losses are included only to the extent that they are taken into account in computing taxable income. The following are examples of gains and losses not included in the computations under section 1231:

(1) Losses of a personal nature which are not deductible by reason of section 165(c) or (d), such as losses from the sale of property held for personal use;

(2) Losses which are not deductible under section 267 (relating to losses with respect to transactions between related taxpayers) or section 1091 (relating to losses from wash sales);

(3) Gain on the sale of property (to which section 1231 applies) reported for any taxable year on the installment method under section 453, except to the extent the gain is to be reported under section 453 for the taxable year; and

(4) Gains and losses which are not recognized under section 1002, such as those to which sections 1031 through 1036, relating to common nontaxable exchanges, apply.

(e) *Involuntary conversion.*—(1) *General rule.*—For purposes of section 1231, the terms "compulsory or involuntary conversion" and "involuntary conversion" of property mean the conversion of property into money or other property as a result of complete or partial destruction, theft or seizure, or an exercise of the power of requisition or condemnation, or the threat of imminence thereof. Losses upon the complete or partial destruction, theft, seizure, requisition, or condemnation of property are treated as losses upon an involuntary conversion whether or not there is a conversion of the property into other property or money and whether or not the property is uninsured, partially insured, or totally insured. For example, if a capital asset held for more than 1 year (6 months for taxable years beginning before 1977; 9 months for taxable years beginning in 1977), with an adjusted basis of $400, but not held for the production of income, is stolen, and the loss which is sustained in the taxable year 1956 is not compensated for by insurance or otherwise, section 1231 applies to the $400 loss. For certain exceptions to this subparagraph, see subparagraphs (2) and (3) of this paragraph.

(2) *Certain uninsured losses.*—Notwithstanding the provisions of subparagraph (1) of this paragraph, losses sustained during a taxable year beginning after December 31, 1957, and before January 1, 1970, with respect to both property used in the trade or business and any capital asset held for more than 6 months and held for the production of income, which losses arise from fire, storm, shipwreck, or other casualty, or from theft, and which are not compensated for by insurance in any amount, are not losses to which section 1231(a) applies. Such losses shall not be taken into account in applying the provisions of this section.

(3) *Exclusion of gains and losses from certain involuntary conversions.*—Notwithstanding the provisions of subparagraph (1) of this paragraph, if for any taxable year beginning after December 31, 1969, the recognized losses from the involuntary conversion as a result of fire, storm, shipwreck, or other casualty, or from theft, of any property used in the trade or business or of any capital asset held for more than 1 year (6 months for taxable years beginning before 1977; 9 months for taxable years beginning in 1977) exceed the recognized gains from the involuntary conversion of any such property as a result of fire, storm, shipwreck, or other casualty, or from theft, such gains and losses are not gains and losses to which section 1231 applies and shall not be taken into account in applying the provisions of this section. The net loss, in effect, will be treated as an ordinary loss. This subparagraph shall apply whether such property is uninsured, partially insured, or totally insured and, in the case of a capital asset held for more than 1 year (6 months for taxable years beginning before 1977; 9 months for taxable years beginning in 1977), whether the property is property used in the trade or business, property held for the production of income, or a personal asset.

(f) *Unharvested crops.*—Section 1231 does not apply to a sale, exchange or involuntary conversion of an unharvested crop if the taxpayer retains any right or option to reacquire the land the crop is on, directly or indirectly (other than a right customarily incident to a mortgage or other security transaction). The length of time for which the crop, as distinguished from the land, is held is immaterial. A leasehold or estate for years is not "land" for the purpose of section 1231.

(g) *Examples.*—The provisions of this section may be illustrated by the following examples:

Example (1). A, an individual, makes his income tax return on the calendar year basis. A's recognized gains and losses for 1957 of the kind described in section 1231 are as follows:

		Gains	Losses
1.	Gain on sale of machinery, used in the business and subject to an allowance for depreciation, held for more than 6 months	$4,000	
2.	Gain reported in 1957 (under sec. 453) on installment sale in 1956 of factory premises used in the business (including building and land, each held for more than 6 months)	6,000	
3.	Gain reported in 1957 (under sec. 453) on installment sale in 1957 of land held for more than 6 months, used in the business as a storage lot for trucks	2,000	
4.	Gain on proceeds from requisition by Government of boat, held for more than 6 months, used in the business and subject to an allowance for depreciation	500	
5.	Loss upon the destruction by fire of warehouse, held for more than 6 months and used in the business (excess of adjusted basis of warehouse over compensation by insurance, etc.)		$3,000
6.	Loss upon theft of unregistered bearer bonds, held for more than 6 months		5,000
7.	Loss in storm of pleasure yacht, purchased in 1950 for $1,800 and having a fair market value of $1,000 at the time of the storm		1,000
8.	Total gains	$12,500	
9.	Total losses		$9,000
10.	Excess of gains over losses	$3,500	

Since the aggregate of the recognized gains ($12,500) exceeds the aggregate of the recognized losses ($9,000), such gains and losses are treated under section 1231 as gains and losses from the sale or exchange of capital assets held for more than six months. For any taxable year ending after December 31, 1957, and before January 1, 1970, the $5,000 loss upon theft of bonds (item 6) would not be taken into account under section 1231. See paragraph (e)(2) of this section.

Example (2). If in example (1), A also had a loss of $4,000 from the sale under threat of condemnation of a capital asset acquired for profit and held for more than six months, then the gains ($12,500) would not exceed the losses ($9,000 plus $4,000 or $13,000). Neither the loss on that sale nor any of the other items set forth in example (1) would then be treated as gains and losses from the sale or exchange of capital assets, but all of such items would be treated as ordinary gains and losses. Likewise, if A had no other gain or loss, the $4,000 loss would be treated as an ordinary loss.

Example (3). A's yacht, used for pleasure and acquired for that use in 1945 at a cost of $25,000, was requisitioned by the Government in 1957 for $15,000. A sustained no loss deductible under section 165(c) and since no loss with respect to the requisition is recognizable, the loss will not be included in the computations under section 1231.

Example (4). A, an individual, makes his income tax return on a calendar year basis. During 1970 trees on A's residential property which were planted in 1950 after the purchase of such property were destroyed by fire. The loss, which was in the amount of $2,000 after applying section 165(c)(3), was not compensated for by insurance or otherwise. During the same year A also recognized a $1,500 gain from insurance proceeds compensating him for the theft sustained in 1970 of a diamond brooch purchased in 1960 for personal use. A has no other gains or losses for 1970 from the involuntary conversion of property. Since the recognized losses exceed the recognized gains from the involuntary conversion for 1970 as a result of fire, storm, shipwreck, or other casualty, or from theft, of any property used in the trade or business or of any capital asset held for more than 6 months, neither the gain nor loss is included in making the computations under section 1231.

Example (5). The facts are the same as in example (4), except that A also recognized a gain of $1,000 from insurance proceeds compensating him for the total destruction by fire of a truck, held for more than 6 months, used in A's business and subject to an allowance for depreciation. A has no other gains or losses for 1970 from the involuntary conversion of property. Since the recognized losses ($2,000) do not exceed the recognized gains ($2,500) from the involuntary conversion for 1970 as a result of fire, storm, shipwreck, or other casualty, or from theft, of any property used in the trade or business or of any capital asset held for more than 6 months, such gains and losses are included in making the computations under section 1231. Thus, if A has no other gains or losses for 1970 to which section 1231 applies, the gains and losses from these involuntary conversions are treated under section 1231 as gains and losses from the sale or exchange of capital assets held for more than 6 months.

Example (6). The facts are the same as in example (5) except that A also has the following recognized gains and losses for 1970 to which section 1231 applies:

	Gains	*Losses*
Gain on sale of machinery, used in the business and subject to an allowance for depreciation, held for more than 6 months	$ 4,000	
Gain reported in 1970 (under sec. 453) on installment sale in 1969 of factory premises used in the business (including building and land, each held for more than 6 months)	6,000	
Gain reported in 1970 (under sec. 453) on installment sale in 1970 of land held for more than 6 months, used in the business as a storage lot for trucks	2,000	
Loss upon the sale in 1970 of warehouse, used in the business and subject to an allowance for depreciation, held for more than 6 months		$5,000
Total gains	12,000	
Total losses		5,000

Since the aggregate of the recognized gains ($14,500) exceeds the aggregate of the recognized losses ($7,000), such gains and losses are treated under section 1231 as gains and losses from the sale or exchange of capital assets held for more than 6 months.

Example (7). B, an individual, makes his income tax return on the calendar year basis. During 1970 furniture used in his business and held for more than 6 months was destroyed by fire. The recognized loss, after compensation by insurance, was $2,000. During the same year B recognized a $1,000 gain upon the sale of a parcel of real estate used in his business and held for more than 6 months, and a $6,000 loss upon the sale of stock held for more than 6 months. B has no other gains or losses for 1970 from the involuntary conversion, or the sale or exchange of, property. The $6,000 loss upon the sale of stock is not a loss to which section 1231 applies since the stock is not property used in the trade or business, as defined in section 1231(b). The $2,000 loss upon the destruction of the furniture is not a loss to which section 1231 applies since the recognized losses ($2,000) exceed the recognized gains ($0) from the involuntary conversion for 1970 as a result of fire, storm, shipwreck, or other casualty, or from theft, of any property used in the trade or business or of any capital asset held for more than 6 months. Accordingly, the $1,000 gain upon the sale of real estate is considered to be gain from the sale or exchange of a capital asset held for more than 6 months since the gains ($1,000) to which section 1231 applies exceed the losses ($0) to which such section applies.

Example (8). The facts are the same as in example (7) except that B also recognized a gain of $4,000 from insurance proceeds compensating him for the total destruction by fire of a freighter, held for more than 6 months, used in B's business and subject to an allowance for depreciation. Since the recognized losses ($2,000) do not exceed the recognized gains ($4,000) from the involuntary conversion for 1970 as a result of fire, storm, shipwreck, or other casualty, or from theft, of any property used in the trade or business or of any capital asset held for more than 6 months, such gains and losses are included in making the computations under section 1231. Since the aggregate of the recognized gains to which section 1231 applies ($5,000) exceeds the aggregate of the recognized losses to which such section applies ($2,000), such gains and losses are treated under section 1231 as gains and losses from the sale or exchange of capital assets held for more than 6 months. The $6,000 loss upon the sale of stock is not taken into account in making such computation since it is not a loss to which section 1231 applies. [Reg. § 1.1231-1.]

□ [*T.D.* 6253, 9-25-57. *Amended by T.D.* 6394, 7-1-59; *T.D.* 6841, 7-26-65; *T.D.* 7141, 9-21-71; *T.D.* 7369, 7-15-75; *T.D.* 7728, 10-31-80 *and T.D.* 7829, 8-31-82.]

§ 1.1231-2. Livestock held for draft, breeding, dairy, or sporting purposes.—(a)(1) In the case of cattle, horses, or other livestock acquired by the taxpayer after December 31, 1969, section 1231 applies to the sale, exchange, or involuntary conversion of such cattle, horses, or other livestock, regardless of age, held by the taxpayer for draft, breeding, dairy, or sporting purposes, and held by him—

(i) For 24 months or more from the date of acquisition in the case of cattle or horses, or

(ii) For 12 months or more from the date of acquisition in the case of such other livestock.

(2) In the case of livestock (including cattle or horses) acquired by the taxpayer on or before December 31, 1969, section 1231 applies to the sale, exchange, or involuntary conversion of such livestock, regardless of age, held by the taxpayer for draft, breeding, or dairy purposes, and held by him for 12 months or more from the date of acquisition.

(3) For the purposes of section 1231, the term "livestock" is given a broad, rather than a narrow, interpretation and includes cattle, hogs, horses, mules, donkeys, sheep, goats, fur-bearing animals, and other mammals. However, it does not include poultry, chickens, turkeys, pigeons, geese, other birds, fish, frogs, reptiles, etc.

(b)(1) Whether or not livestock is held by the taxpayer for draft, breeding, dairy, or sporting purposes depends upon all of the facts and circumstances in each case. The purpose for which the animal is held is ordinarily shown by the taxpayer's actual use of the animal. However, a draft, breeding, dairy, or sporting purpose may be present if an animal is disposed of within a reasonable time after its intended use for such purpose is prevented or made undesirable by reason of accident, disease, drought, unfitness of the animal for such purpose, or a similar factual circumstance. Under certain circumstances, an animal held for ultimate sale to customers in the ordinary course of the taxpayer's trade or business may be considered as held for draft, breeding, dairy, or sporting purposes. However, an animal is not held by the taxpayer for draft, breeding, dairy, or sporting purposes merely because it is suitable for such purposes or merely because it is held by the taxpayer for sale to other persons for use by them for such purposes. Furthermore, an animal held by the taxpayer for other purposes is not considered as held for draft, breeding, dairy, or sporting purposes merely because of a negligible use of the animal for such purposes or merely because of the use of the animal for such purposes as an ordinary or necessary incident to the other purposes for which the animal is held. See paragraph (c) of this section for the rules to be used in determining when horses are held for racing purposes and, therefore, are considered as held for sporting purposes.

(2) The application of this paragraph is illustrated by the following examples:

Example (1). An animal intended by the taxpayer for use by him for breeding purposes is discovered to be sterile or unfit for the breeding purposes for which it was held, and is disposed of within a reasonable time thereafter. This animal is considered as held for breeding purposes.

Example (2). The taxpayer retires from the breeding or dairy business and sells his entire herd, including young animals which would have been used by him for breeding or dairy purposes if he had remained in business. These young animals are considered as held for breeding or dairy purposes. The same would be true with respect to young animals which would have been used by the taxpayer for breeding or dairy purposes but which are sold by him in reduction of his breeding or dairy herd, because of, for example, drought.

Example (3). A taxpayer in the business of raising hogs for slaughter customarily breeds sows to obtain a single litter to be raised by him for sale, and sells these brood sows after obtaining the litter. Even though these brood sows are held for ultimate sale to customers in the ordinary course of the taxpayer's trade or business, they are considered as held for breeding purposes.

Example (4). A taxpayer in the business of raising horses for sale to others for use by them as draft horses uses them for draft purposes on his own farm in order to train them. This use is an ordinary or necessary incident to the purpose of selling the animals, and, accordingly, these horses are not considered as held for draft purposes.

Example (5). The taxpayer is in the business of raising registered cattle for sale to others for use by them as breeding cattle. It is the business practice of this particular taxpayer to breed the offspring of his herd which he is holding for sale to others prior to sale in order to establish their fitness for sale as registered breeding cattle. In such case, the taxpayer's breeding of such offspring is an ordinary and necessary incident to his holding them for the purpose of selling them as bred heifers or proven bulls and does not demonstrate that the taxpayer is holding them for breeding purposes. However, those cattle held by the taxpayer as additions or replacements to his own breeding herd to produce calves are considered to be held for breeding purposes, even though they may not actually have produced calves.

Example (6). A taxpayer, engaged in the business of buying cattle and fattening them for slaughter, purchased cows with calf. The calves were born while the cows were held by the taxpayer. These cows are not considered as held for breeding purposes.

(c)(1) For purposes of paragraph (b) of this section, a horse held for racing purposes shall be considered as held for sporting purposes. Whether a horse is held for racing purposes shall be determined in accordance with the following rules:

(i) A horse which has actually been raced at a public race track shall, except in rare and unusual circumstances, be considered as held for racing purposes.

(ii) A horse which has not been raced at a public track shall be considered as held for racing purposes if it has been trained to race and other facts and circumstances in the particular case also indicate that the horse was held for this purpose. For example, assume that the taxpayer maintains a written training record on all horses he keeps in training status, which shows that a particular horse does not meet objective standards (including, but not limited to, such considerations as failure to achieve predetermined standards of performance during training, or the existence of a physical or other defect) established by the taxpayer for determining the fitness and quality of horses to be retained in his racing stable. Under such circumstances, if the taxpayer disposes of the horse within a reasonable time after he determined that it did not meet his objective standards for retention, the horse shall be considered as held for racing purposes.

(iii) A horse which has neither been raced at a public track nor trained for racing shall not, except in rare and unusual circumstances, be considered as held for racing purposes.

(2) This paragraph may be illustrated by the following examples:

Example (1). The taxpayer breeds, raises, and trains horses for the purpose of racing. Every year he culls some horses from his racing stable. In 1971, the taxpayer decided that in order to prevent his racing stable from getting too large to be effectively operated he must cull six horses from it. All six of the horses culled by the taxpayer had been raced at public tracks in 1970. Under subparagraph (1)(i) of this paragraph, all these horses are considered as held for racing purposes.

Example (2). Assume the same facts as in example (1). Assume further that the taxpayer decided to cull four more horses from his racing stable in 1971. All these horses had been trained to race but had not been raced at public tracks. The taxpayer culled these four horses because the training log which the taxpayer maintains on all the horses he trains showed these horses to be unfit to remain in his racing stable. Horse A was culled because it developed shin splints during training. Horses B and C were culled because of poor temperament. B bolted every time a rider tried to mount it, and C became extremely nervous when it was placed in the starting gate. Horse D was culled because it did not qualify for retention under one of the objective standards the taxpayer had established for determining which horses to retain since it was unable to run a specified distance in a minimum time. These four horses were disposed of within a reasonable time after the taxpayer determined that they were unfit to remain in his stable. Under subparagraph (1)(ii) of this paragraph, all these horses are considered as held for racing purposes. [Reg. § 1.1231-2.]

□ [*T.D.* 6253, 9-25-57. *Amended by T.D.* 7141, 9-21-71.]

§ 1.1245-1. General rule for treatment of gain from dispositions of certain depreciable property.—(a) *General.*—(1) In general, section 1245(a)(1) provides that, upon a disposition of an item of section 1245 property, the amount by which the lower of (i) the "recomputed basis" of the property, or (ii) the amount realized on a sale, exchange, or involuntary conversion (or the fair market value of the property on any other disposition), exceeds the adjusted basis of the property shall be treated as gain from the sale or exchange of property which is neither a capital asset nor property described in section 1231 (that is, shall be recognized as ordinary income). The amount of such gain shall be determined separately for each item of section 1245 property. In general, the term "recomputed basis" means the adjusted basis of property plus all adjustments reflected in such adjusted basis on account of depreciation allowed or allowable for all periods after December 31, 1961. See section 1245(a)(2) and § 1.1245-2. Generally, the ordinary income treatment applies even though in the absence of section 1245 no gain would be recognized under the Code. For example, if a corporation distributes section 1245 property as a dividend, gain may be recognized as ordinary income to the corporation even though, in the absence of section 1245, section 311(a) would preclude any recognition of gain to the corporation. For the definition of "section 1245 property," see section 1245(a)(3) and § 1.1245-3. For exceptions and limitations to the application of section 1245(a)(1), see section 1245(b) and § 1.1245-4.

(2) Section 1245(a)(1) applies to dispositions of section 1245 property in taxable years beginning after December 31, 1962, except that—

(i) In respect of section 1245 property which is an elevator or escalator, section 1245(a)(1) applies to dispositions after December 31, 1963, and

(ii) In respect of section 1245 property which is livestock (described in subparagraph (4) of § 1.1245-3(a)), section 1245(a)(1) applies to dispositions made in taxable years beginning after December 31, 1969, and

(iii) [reserved].

(3) For purposes of this section and §§1.1245-2 through 1.1245-6, the term "disposition" includes a sale in a sale-and-leaseback transaction and a transfer upon the foreclosure of a security interest, but such term does not include a mere transfer of title to a creditor upon creation of a security interest or to a debtor upon termination of a security interest. Thus, for example, a disposition occurs upon a sale of property pursuant to a conditional sales contract even though the seller retains legal title to the property for purposes of security but a disposition does not occur when the seller ulitmately gives up his security interest following payment by the purchaser.

(4) For purposes of applying section 1245, the facts and circumstances of each disposition shall be considered in determining what is the appropriate item of section 1245 property. A taxpayer may treat any number of units of section 1245 property in any particular depreciation account (as defined in §1.167(a)-7) as one time of section 1245 property as long as it is reasonably clear, from the best estimates obtainable on the basis of all the facts and circumstances, that the amount of gain to which section 1245(a)(1) applies is not less than the total of the gain under section 1245(a)(1) which would be computed separately for each unit. Thus, for example, if 50 units of section 1245 property X, 25 units of section 1245 property Y, and other property are accounted for in one depreciation account, and if each such unit is sold at a gain in one transaction in which the total gain realized on the sale exceeds the sum of the adjustments reflected in the adjusted basis (as defined in paragraph (a)(2) of §1.1245-2) of each such unit on account of depreciation allowed or allowable for periods after December 31, 1961, all 75 units may be treated as one item of section 1245 property. If, however, 5 such units of section 1245 property Y were sold at a loss, then only 70 of such units (50 of X plus the 20 of Y sold at a gain) may be treated as one item of section 1245 property.

(5) In case of a sale, exchange, or involuntary conversion of section 1245 and nonsection 1245 property in one transaction, the total amount realized upon the disposition shall be allocated between the section 1245 property and the nonsection 1245 property in proportion to their respective fair market values. In general, if a buyer and seller have adverse interests as to the allocation of the amount realized between the section 1245 property and the nonsection 1245 property, any arm's length agreement between the buyer and the seller will establish the allocation. In the absence of such an agreement, the allocation shall be made by taking into account the appropriate facts and circumstances. Some of the facts and circumstances which shall be taken into account to the extent appropriate include, but are not limited to, a comparison between the section 1245 property and all the property disposed of in such transaction of (i) the original cost and reproduction cost of construction, erection, or production, (ii) the remaining economic useful life, (iii) state of obsolescence, and (iv) anticipated expenditures to maintain, renovate, or to modernize.

(b) *Sale, exchange, or involuntary conversion.*—(1) In the case of a sale, exchange, or involuntary conversion of section 1245 property, the gain to which section 1245(a)(1) applies is the amount by which (i) the lower of the amount realized upon the disposition of the property or the recomputed basis of the property, exceeds (ii) the adjusted basis of the property.

(2) The provisions of this paragraph may be illustrated by the following examples:

Example (1). On January 1, 1964, Brown purchases section 1245 property for use in his manufacturing business. The property has a basis for depreciation of $3,300. After taking depreciation deductions of $1,300 (the amount allowable), Brown realizes after selling expenses the amount of $2,900 upon sale of the property on January 1, 1969. Brown's gain is $900 ($2,900 amount realized minus $2,000 adjusted basis). Since the amount realized upon disposition of the property ($2,900) is lower than its recomputed basis ($3,300, i.e., $2,000 adjusted basis plus $1,300 in depreciation deductions), the entire gain is treated as ordinary income under section 1245(a)(1) and not as gain from the sale or exchange of property described in section 1231.

Example (2). Assume the same facts as in example (1) except that Brown exchanges the section 1245 property for land which has a fair market value of $3,700, thereby realizing a gain of $1,700 ($3,700 amount realized minus $2,000 adjusted basis). Since the recomputed basis of the property ($3,300) is lower than the amount realized upon its disposition ($3,700), the excess of recomputed basis over adjusted basis, or $1,300, is treated as ordinary income under section 1245(a)(1). The remaining $400 of the gain may be treated as gain from the sale or exchange of property described in section 1231.

(c) *Other dispositions.*—(1) In the case of a disposition of section 1245 property other than by way of a sale, exchange, or involuntary conversion, the gain to which section 1245(a)(1) applies is the amount by which (i) the lower of the fair market value of the property on the date of disposition or the recomputed basis of the property, exceeds (ii) the adjusted basis of the property. If property is transferred by a corporation to a shareholder for an amount less than its fair market value in a sale or exchange, for purposes of applying section 1245 such transfer shall be treated as a disposition other than by way of a sale, exchange, or involuntary conversion.

(2) The provisions of this paragraph may be illustrated by the following examples:

Example (1). X Corporation distributes section 1245 property to its shareholders as a dividend. The property has an adjusted basis of $2,000 to the corporation, a recomputed basis of $3,300, and a fair market value of $3,100. Since the fair market value of the property ($3,100) is lower than its recomputed basis ($3,300), the excess of fair market value over adjusted basis, or $1,100, is treated under section 1245(a)(1) as ordinary income to the corporation even though, in the absence of section 1245, section 311(a) would preclude recognition of gain to the corporation.

Example (2). Assume the same facts as in example (1) except that X Corporation distributes the section 1245 property to its shareholders in complete liquidation of the corporation. Assume further that section 1245(b)(3) does not apply and that the fair market value of the property is $3,800 at the time of the distribution. Since the recomputed basis of the property ($3,300) is lower than its fair market value ($3,800), the excess of recomputed basis over adjusted basis, or $1,300, is treated under section 1245(a)(1) as ordinary income to the corporation even though, in the absence of section 1245, section 336 would preclude recognition of gain to the corporation.

(d) *Losses.*—Section 1245(a)(1) does not apply to losses. Thus, section 1245(a)(1) does not apply if a loss is realized upon a sale, exchange, or involuntary conversion of property, all of which is considered section 1245 property, nor does the section apply to a disposition of such property other than by way of sale, exchange, or involuntary conversion if at the time of the disposition the fair market value of such property is not greater than its adjusted basis.

* * *

[Reg. § 1.1245-1.]

☐ [*T.D.* 6832, 7-6-65. *Amended by T.D.* 7084, 1-7-71; *T.D.* 7141, 9-21-71 *and T.D.* 8730, 8-19-97.]

§ 1.1245-2. Definition of recomputed basis.—(a) *General rule.*—(1) *Recomputed basis defined.*—The term "recomputed basis" means, with respect to any property, an amount equal to the sum of—

(i) The adjusted basis of the property, as defined in section 1011, plus

(ii) The amount of the adjustments reflected in the adjusted basis.

(2) *Definition of adjustments reflected in adjusted basis.*—The term "adjustments reflected in the adjusted basis" means—

(i) with respect to any property other than property described in subdivision (ii), (iii), or (iv) of this subparagraph, the amount of the adjustments attributable to periods after December 31, 1961,

(ii) with respect to an elevator or escalator, the amount of the adjustments attributable to periods after June 30, 1963,

(iii) with respect to livestock (described in subparagraph (4) of § 1.1245-3(a)), the amount of the adjustments attributable to periods after December 31, 1969, or

(iv) [reserved]

which are reflected in the adjusted basis of such property on account of deductions allowed or allowable for depreciation or amortization (within the meaning of subparagraph (3) of this paragraph). For cases where the taxpayer can establish that the amount allowed for any period was less than the amount allowable, see subparagraph (7) of this paragraph. For determination of adjusted basis of property in a multiple asset account, see paragraph (c)(3) of § 1.167(a)-8.

(3) *Meaning of "depreciation or amortization."* .—(i) For purposes of subparagraph (2) of this paragraph, the term "depreciation or amortization" includes allowances (and amounts treated as allowances) for depreciation (or amortization in lieu thereof), and deductions for amortization of emergency facilities under section 168. Thus, for example, such term includes a reasonable allowance for exhaustion, wear and tear (including a reasonable allowance for obsolescence) under section 167, an expense allowance (additional first-year depreciation allowance for property placed in service before January 1, 1981) under section 179, an expenditure treated as an amount allowed under section 167 by reason of the application of section 182(d)(2)(B) (relating to expenditures by farmers for clearing land), and a deduction for depreciation of improvements under section 611 (relating to depletion). For further examples, the term "depreciation or amortization" includes periodic deductions referred to in § 1.162-11 in respect of a specified sum paid for the acquisition of a leasehold and in respect of the cost to a lessee of improvements on property of which he is the lessee. However, such term does not include deductions for the periodic payment of rent.

(ii) The provisions of this subparagraph may be illustrated by the following example:

Example. On January 1, 1966, Smith purchases for $1,000, and places in service, an item of property described in section 1245(a)(3)(A). Smith deducts an additional first-year allowance for depreciation under section 179 of $200. Accordingly, the basis of the property for purposes of depreciation is $800 on January 1, 1966. Between that date and January 1, 1974, Smith deducts $640 in depreciation (the amount allowable) with respect to the property, thereby reducing its adjusted basis to $160. Since this adjusted basis reflects deductions for depreciation and amortization (within the meaning of this subparagraph) amounting to $840 ($200 plus $640), the recomputed basis of the property is $1,000 ($160 plus $840).

(4) *Adjustments of other taxpayers or in respect of other property.*—(i) For purposes of subparagraph (2) of this paragraph, the adjustments reflected in adjusted basis on account of depreciation or amortization which must be taken into account in determining recomputed basis are not limited to those adjustments on account of depreciation or amortization with respect to the property disposed of, nor are such adjustments limited to those on account of depreciation or amortization allowed or allowable to the taxpayer disposing of such property. Except as provided in subparagraph (7) of this paragraph, all such adjustments are taken into account, whether the deductions were allowed or allowable in respect of the same or other property and whether to the taxpayer or to any other person. For manner of determining the amount of adjustments reflected in the adjusted basis of property immediately after certain dispositions, see paragraph (c) of this section.

(ii) The provisions of this subparagraph may be illustrated by the following example:

Example. On January 1, 1966, Jones purchases machine X for use in his trade or business. The machine, which is section 1245 property, has a basis for depreciation of $10,000. After taking depreciation deductions of $2,000 (the amount allowable), Jones transfers the machine to his son as a gift on January 1, 1968. Since the exception for gifts in section 1245(b)(1) applies, Jones does not recognize gain under section 1245(a)(1). The son's adjusted basis for the machine is $8,000. On January 1, 1969, after taking a depreciation deduction of $1,000 (the amount allowable), the son exchanges machine X for machine Y in a like kind exchange described in section 1031. Since the exception for like kind exchanges in section 1245(b)(4) applies, the son does not recognize gain under section 1245(a)(1). The son's adjusted basis for machine Y is $7,000. In 1969, the son takes a depreciation deduction of $1,000 (the amount allowable) in respect of machine Y. The son sells machine Y on June 30, 1970. No depreciation was allowed or allowable for 1970, the year of the sale. The recomputed basis of machine Y on June 30, 1970, is determined in the following manner:

Adjusted basis		$6,000
Adjustments reflected in the adjusted basis:		
Depreciation deducted by Jones for 1966 and 1967 on machine X	$2,000	
Depreciation deducted by son for 1968 on machine X	$1,000	
Depreciation deducted by son for 1969 on machine Y	$1,000	
Total adjustments reflected in the adjusted basis		$4,000
Recomputed basis		$10,000

(5) *Adjustments reflected in adjusted basis of property described in section 1245(a)(3)(B).*—For purposes of subparagraph (2) of this paragraph, the adjustments reflected in the adjusted basis of property described in section 1245(a)(3)(B), on account of depreciation or amortization which must be taken into account in determining recomputed basis, may include deductions attributable to periods during which the property is not used as an integral part of an activity, or does not constitute a facility, specified in section 1245(a)(3)(B)(i) or (ii). Thus, for example, if depreciation deductions taken with respect to such property after December 31, 1961, amount to $10,000 (the amount allowable), of which $6,000 is attributable to periods during which the property is used as an integral part of a specified activity or constitutes a specified facility, then the entire $10,000 of depreciation deductions are adjustments reflected in the adjusted basis for purposes of determining recomputed basis. Moreover, if the property was never so used but was acquired in a transaction to which section 1245(b)(4) (relating to like kind exchanges and involuntaray conversions) applies, and if by reason of the application of paragraph (d)(3) of § 1.1245-4 the property is considered as section 1245 property described in section 1245(a)(3)(B), then the entire $10,000 of depreciation deductions would also be adjustments reflected in the adjusted basis for purposes of determining recomputed basis.

* * *

(7) *Depreciation or amortization allowed or allowable.*—For purposes of determining recomputed basis, generally all adjustments (for periods after Dec. 31, 1961, or, in the case of property described in subparagraph (2)(ii),

(iii), or (iv) of this paragraph, for periods after the applicable date, 1969, as the case may be) attributable to allowed or allowable depreciation or amortization must be taken into account. See section 1016(a)(2) and the regulations thereunder for the meaning of "allowed" and "allowable". However, if a taxpayer can establish by adequate records or other sufficient evidence that the amount allowed for depreciation or amortization for any period was less than the amount allowable for such period, the amount to be taken into account for such period shall be the amount allowed. No adjustment is to be made on account of the tax imposed by section 56 (relating to the minimum tax for tax preferences). See paragraph (b) of this section (relating to records to be kept and information to be filed). For example, assume that in the year 1967 it becomes necessary to determine the recomputed basis of property, the $500 adjusted basis of which reflects adjustments of $1,000 with respect to depreciation deductions allowable for periods after December 31, 1961. If the taxpayer can establish by adequate records or other sufficient evidence that he had been allowed deductions amounting to $800 for the period, then in determining recomputed basis the amount added to adjusted basis with respect to the $1,000 adjustments to basis for the period will be only $800.

* * *

[Reg. § 1.1245-2.]

☐ [*T.D.* 6832, 7-6-65. *Amended by T.D.* 7084, 1-7-71; *T.D.* 7141, 9-21-71; *T.D.* 7564, 9-11-78; *T.D.* 8121, 1-5-87 *and T.D.* 9811, 1-18-2017.]

§ 1.1245-3. Definition of section 1245 property.—(a) *In general.*—(1) The term "section 1245 property" means any property (other than livestock excluded by the effective date limitation in subparagraph (4) of this paragraph) which is or has been property of a character subject to the allowance for depreciation provided in section 167 and which is either—

(i) Personal property (within the meaning of paragraph (b) of this section),

(ii) Property described in section 1245(a)(3)(B) (see paragraph (c) of this section), or

(iii) An elevator or an escalator within the meaning of subparagraph (C) of section 48(a)(1) (relating to the definition of "section 38 property" for purposes of the investment credit), but without regard to the limitations in such subparagraph (C).

(2) If property is section 1245 property under a subdivision of subparagraph (1) of this paragraph, a leasehold of such property is also section 1245 property under such subdivision. Thus, for example, if A owns personal property which is section 1245 property under subparagraph (1)(i) of this paragraph, and if A leases the personal property to B, B's leasehold is also section 1245 property under such provision. For a further example, if C owns and leases to D for a single lump-sum payment of $100,000 property consisting of land and a fully equipped factory building thereon, and if 40 percent of the fair market value of such property is properly allocable to section 1245 property, then 40 percent of D's leasehold is also section 1245 property. A leasehold of land is not section 1245 property.

(3) Even though property may not be of a character subject to the allowance for depreciation in the hands of the taxpayer, such property may nevertheless be section 1245 property if the taxpayer's basis for the property is determined by reference to its basis in the hands of a prior owner of the property and such property was of a character subject to the allowance for depreciation in the hands of such prior owner, or if the taxpayer's basis for the property is determined by reference to the basis of other property that in the hands of the taxpayer was property of a character subject to the allowance for depreciation, or if the taxpayer's basis for the property is determined under section 1022 and such property was of a character subject to the allowance for depreciation in the hands of the decedent. Thus, for example, if a father uses an automobile in his trade or business during a period after December 31, 1961, and then gives the automobile to his son as a gift for the son's personal use, the automobile is section 1245 property in the hands of the son.

(4) Section 1245 property includes livestock, but only with respect to taxable years beginning after December 31, 1969. For purposes of section 1245, the term "livestock" includes horses, cattle, hogs, sheep, goats, and mink and other furbearing animals, irrespective of the use to which they are put or the purpose for which they are held.

(b) *Personal property defined.*—The term "personal property" means—

(1) Tangible personal property (as defined in paragraph (c) of § 1.48-1, relating to the definition of "section 38 property" for purposes of the investment credit), and

(2) Intangible personal property.

(c) *Property described in section 1245(a)(3)(B).*—(1) The term "property described in section 1245(a)(3)(B)" means tangible property of the requisite depreciable character other than personal property (and other than a building and its structural components), but only if there are adjustments reflected in the adjusted basis of the property (within the meaning of paragraph (a)(2) of §1.1245-2) for a period during which such property (or other property)—

(i) Was used as an integral part of manufacturing, production, or extraction, or as an integral part of furnishing transportation, communications, electrical energy, gas, water, or sewage disposal services by a person engaged in a trade or business of furnishing any such service, or

(ii) Constituted a research or storage facility used in connection with any of the foregoing activities.

Thus, even though during the period immediately preceding its disposition the property is not used as an integral part of an activity specified in subdivision (i) of this subparagraph and does not constitute a facility specified in subdivision (ii) of this subparagraph, such property is nevertheless property described in section 1245(a)(3)(B) if, for example, there are no adjustments reflected in the adjusted basis of the property for a period during which the property was used as an integral part of manufacturing by the taxpayer or another taxpayer, or for a period during which other property (which was involuntarily converted into, or exchanged in a like kind exchange for, the property) was so used by the taxpayer or another taxpayer. For rules applicable to involuntary conversions and like kind exchanges, see paragraph (d)(3) of §1.1245-4.

(2) The language used in subparagraph (1)(i) and (ii) of this paragraph shall have the same meaning as when used in paragraph (a) of §1.48-1, and the terms "building" and "structural components" shall have the meanings assigned to those terms in paragraph (e) of §1.48-1.

* * *

[Reg. §1.1245-3.]

☐ [*T.D.* 6832, 7-6-65. *Amended by T.D.* 7141, 9-21-71 *and T.D.* 9811, 1-18-2017.]

§1.1245-4. Exceptions and limitations.—(a) *Exception for gifts.*—(1) *General rule.*—Section 1245(b)(1) provides that no gain shall be recognized under section 1245(a)(1) upon a disposition by gift. For purposes of this paragraph (a), the term *gift* means, except to the extent that paragraph (a)(3) of this section applies, a transfer of property that, in the hands of the transferee, has a basis determined under the provisions of section 1015(a) or 1015(d) (relating to basis of property acquired by gifts) or section 1022 (relating to basis of property acquired from certain decedents who died in 2010). For reduction in amount of charitable contribution in case of a gift of section 1245 property, see section 170(e) and the regulations thereunder.

(b) *Exception for transfers at death.*—(1) *General rule.*—Section 1245(b)(2) provides that, except as provided in section 691 (relating to income in respect of a decedent), no gain shall be recognized under section 1245(a)(1) upon a transfer at death. For purposes of this paragraph, the term "transfer at death" means a transfer of property which, in the hands of the transferee, has a basis determined under the provisions of section 1014(a) (relating to basis of property acquired from a decedent) because of the death of the transferor. For recomputed basis of property acquired in a transfer at death, see paragraph (c)(1)(iv) of §1.1245-2.

* * *

(c) *Limitation for certain tax-free transactions.*—(1) *Limitation on amount of gain.*—Section 1245(b)(3) provides that upon a transfer of property described in subparagraph (2) of this paragraph, the amount of gain taken into account by the transferor under section 1245(a)(1) shall not exceed the amount of gain recognized to the transferor on the transfer (determined without regard to section 1245). For purposes of this subparagraph, in case of a transfer of both section 1245 property and non-section 1245 property in one transaction, the amount realized from the disposition of the section 1245 property (as determined under paragraph (a)(5) of §1.1245-1) shall be deemed to consist of that portion of the fair market value of each property acquired which bears the same ratio to the fair market value of such acquired property as the amount realized from the disposition of the section 1245 property bears to the total amount realized. The preceding sentence shall be applied solely for purposes of computing the portion of the total gain (determined without regard to section 1245) which shall be recognized as ordinary income under section 1245(a)(1). For determination of the recomputed basis of the section 1245 property in the hands of the transferee, see paragraph (c)(2) of §1.1245-2. Section 1245(b)(3) does not apply to a disposition of property to an organization (other than a cooperative described in section 521) which is exempt from the tax imposed by chapter 1 of the Code.

(2) *Transfers covered.*—The transfers referred to in subparagraph (1) of this paragraph are transfers of property which the basis of the property in the hands of the transferee is determined by reference to its basis in the hands of the transferor by reason of the application of any of the following provisions:

(i) Section 332 (relating to distributions in complete liquidation of an 80-percent-or-more controlled subsidiary corporation). See subparagraph (3) of this paragraph.

(ii) Section 351 (relating to transfer to a corporation controlled by transferor).

(iii) Section 361 (relating to exchanges pursuant to certain corporate reorganizations).

(iv) Section 371(a) (relating to exchanges pursuant to certain receivership and bankruptcy proceedings).

(v) Section 374(a) (relating to exchanges pursuant to certain railroad reorganizations).

(vi) Section 721 (relating to transfers to a partnership in exchange for a partnership interest).

(vii) Section 731 (relating to distributions by a partnership to a partner). For special carryover basis rule, see section 1245(b)(6)(A) and paragraph (f)(1) of this section.

* * *

(d) *Limitation for like kind exchanges and involuntary conversions.*—(1) *General rule.*—Section 1245(b)(4) provides that if property is disposed of and gain (determined without regard to section 1245) is not recognized in whole or in part under section 1031 (relating to like kind exchanges) or section 1033 (relating to involuntary conversions), then the amount of gain taken into account by the transferor under section 1245(a)(1) shall not exceed the sum of—

(i) The amount of gain recognized on such disposition (determined without regard to section 1245), plus

(ii) The fair market value of property acquired which is not section 1245 property and which is not taken into account under subdivision (i) of this subparagraph (that is, the fair market value of non-section 1245 property acquired which is qualifying property under section 1031 or 1033, as the case may be).

* * *

[Reg. § 1.1245-4.]

□ [*T.D.* 6832, 7-6-65. *Amended by T.D.* 7084, 1-7-71, *T.D.* 7207, 10-3-72, *T.D.* 7728, 10-31-80, *T.D.* 7927, 12-15-83 *and T.D.* 9811, 1-18-2017.]

§ 1.1245-5. Adjustments to basis.—In order to reflect gain recognized under section 1245(a)(1), the following adjustments to the basis of property shall be made:

(a) *Property acquired in like kind exchange or involuntary conversion.*—(1) If property is acquired in a transaction to which section 1245(b)(4) applies, its basis shall be determined under the rules of section 1031(d) or 1033(c).

(2) The provisions of this paragraph may be illustrated by the following example:

Example. Jones exchanges property A, which is section 1245 property with an adjusted basis of $10,000, for property B, which has a fair market value of $9,000, and property C, which has a fair market value of $3,500, in a like kind exchange as to which no gain would be recognized under section 1031(a). Upon the exchange $2,500 gain is recognized under section 1245(a)(1), since property C is not section 1245 property. See section 1245(b)(4). Under the rules of section 1031(d), the basis of the properties received in the exchange is $12,500 (i.e., the basis of property transferred, $10,000, plus the amount of gain recognized, $2,500), of which the amount allocated to property C is $3,500 (the fair market value thereof), and the residue, $9,000, is allocated to property B.

* * *

[Reg. § 1.1245-5.]

□ [*T.D.* 6832, 7-6-65.]

§ 1.1245-6. Relation of section 1245 to other sections.—(a) *General.*—The provisions of section 1245 apply notwithstanding any other provision of subtitle A of the Code. Thus, unless an exception or limitation under section 1245 (b) applies, gain under section 1245(a)(1) is recognized notwithstanding any contrary nonrecognition provision or income characterizing provision. For example, since section 1245 overrides section 1231 (relating to property used in the trade or business), the gain recognized under section 1245(a)(1) upon a disposition will be treated as ordinary income and only the remaining gain, if any, from the disposition may be considered as gain from the sale or exchange of a capital asset if section 1231 is applicable. See example (2) of paragraph (b)(2) of § 1.1245-1. For effect of section 1245 on basis provisions of the Code, see § 1.1245-5.

(b) *Nonrecognition sections overridden.*—The nonrecognition provisions of subtitle A of the Code which section 1245 overrides include, but are not limited to, sections 267(d), 311(a), 336, 337, 501(a), 512(b)(5), and 1039. See section 1245(b) for the extent to which section 1245(a)(1) overrides sections 332, 351, 361, 371(a), 374(a), 721, 731, 1031, 1033, 1071, and 1081(b)(1) and (d)(1)(A). For limitation on amount of adjustments reflected in adjusted basis of property disposed of by an organization exempt from income taxes (within the meaning of section 501(a)), see paragraph (a)(8) of § 1.1245-2.

(c) *Normal retirement of asset in multiple asset account.*—Section 1245(a)(1) does not require recognition of gain upon normal retirements of section 1245 property in a multiple asset account as long as the taxpayer's method of accounting, as described in paragraph (e)(2) of § 1.167(a)-8 (relating to accounting treatment of asset retirements), does not require recognition of such gain.

(d) *Installment method.*—(1) Gain from a disposition to which section 1245(a)(1) applies may be reported under the installment method if such method is otherwise available under section 453 of the Code. In such case, the income (other than interest) on each installment payment shall be deemed to consist of gain to which section 1245(a)(1) applies until all such gain has been reported, and the remaining portion (if any) of such income shall be deemed to consist of gain to which section 1245(a)(1) does not apply. For treatment of amounts as interest on certain deferred payments, see section 483.

(2) The provisions of this paragraph may be illustrated by the following example:

Example. Jones contracts to sell an item of section 1245 property for $10,000 to be paid in 10 equal payments of $1,000 each, plus a sufficient amount of interest so that section 483 does not apply. He properly elects under section 453 to report under the installment method gain of $2,000 to which section 1245(a)(1) applies and gain of $1,000 to which section 1231 applies. Accordingly, $300 of each of the first 6 installment payments and $200 of the seventh installment payment is ordinary income under section 1245(a)(1), and $100 of the seventh installment payment and $300 of each of the last 3 installment payments is gain under section 1231.

(e) *Exempt income.*—The fact that section 1245 provides for recognition of gain as ordinary income does not change into taxable income any income which is exempt under section 115 (relating to income of states, etc.), 892 (relating to income of foreign governments), or 894 (relating to income exempt under treaties).

(f) *Treatment of gain not recognized under section 1245.*—Section 1245 does not prevent gain which is not recognized under section 1245 from being considered as gain under another provision of the Code, such as, for example, section 311(c) (relating to liability in excess of basis), section 341(f) (relating to collapsible corporations), section 357(c) (relating to liabilities in excess of basis), section 1238 (relating to amortization in excess of depreciation), or section 1239 (relating to gain from sale of depreciable property between certain related persons). Thus, for example, if section 1245 property, which has an adjusted basis of $1,000 and a recomputed basis of $1,500, is sold for $1,750 in a transaction to which section 1239 applies, $500 of the gain would be recognized under section 1245(a)(1) and the remaining $250 of the gain would be treated as ordinary income under section 1239. [Reg. § 1.1245-6.]

☐ [*T.D.* 6832, 7-6-65. *Amended by T.D.* 7084, 1-7-71 *and T.D.* 7400, 2-3-76.]

Special Rules for Bonds & Other Debt Instruments

§ 1.1272-1. Current inclusion of OID in income.—(a) *Overview.*—(1) *In general.*—Under section 1272(a)(1), a holder of a debt instrument includes accrued OID in gross income (as interest), regardless of the holder's regular method of accounting. A holder includes qualified stated interest (as defined in § 1.1273-1(c)) in income under the holder's regular method of accounting. See §§ 1.446-2 and 1.451-1.

(2) *Debt instruments not subject to OID inclusion rules.*—Sections 1272(a)(2) and 1272(c) list exceptions to the general inclusion rule of section 1272(a)(1). For purposes of section 1272(a)(2)(E) (relating to certain loans between natural persons), a loan does not include a stripped bond or stripped coupon within the meaning of section 1286(e), and the rule in section 1272(a)(2)(E)(iii), which treats a husband and wife as 1 person, does not apply to loans made between a husband and wife.

(b) *Accrual of OID.*—(1) *Constant yield method.*—Except as provided in paragraphs (b)(2) and (b)(3) of this section, the amount of OID includible in the income of a holder of a debt instrument for any taxable year is determined using the constant yield method as described under this paragraph (b)(1).

(i) *Step one: Determine the debt instrument's yield to maturity.*—The yield to maturity or yield of a debt instrument is the discount rate that, when used in computing the present value of all principal and interest payments to be made under the debt instrument, produces an amount equal to the issue price of the debt instrument. The yield must be constant over the term of the debt instrument and, when expressed as a percentage, must be calculated to at least two decimal places. See paragraph (c) of this section for rules relating to the yield of certain debt instruments subject to contingencies.

(ii) *Step two: Determine the accrual periods.*—An accrual period is an interval of time over which the accrual of OID is measured. Accrual periods may be of any length and may vary in length over the term of the debt instrument, provided that each accrual period is no longer than 1 year and each scheduled payment of principal or interest occurs either on the final day of an accrual period or on the first day of an accrual period. In general, the computation of OID is simplest if accrual periods correspond to the intervals between payment dates provided by the terms of the debt instrument. In computing the length of accrual periods, any reasonable counting convention may be used (e.g., 30 days per month/360 days per year).

(iii) *Step three: Determine the OID allocable to each accrual period.*—Except as provided in paragraph (b)(4) of this section, the OID allocable to an accrual period equals the product of the adjusted issue price of the debt instrument (as defined in § 1.1275-1(b)) at the beginning of the accrual period and the yield of the debt instrument, less the amount of any qualified stated interest allocable to the accrual period. In performing this calculation, the yield must be stated appropriately taking into account the length of the particular accrual period. *Example 1* in paragraph (j) of this section provides a formula for converting a yield based upon an accrual period of one length to an equivalent yield based upon an accrual period of a different length.

(iv) *Step four: Determine the daily portions of OID.*—The daily portions of OID are determined by allocating to each day in an accrual period the ratable portion of the OID allocable to the accrual period. The holder of the debt instrument includes in income the daily portions of OID for each day during the taxable year on which the holder held the debt instrument.

(2) *Exceptions.*—Paragraph (b)(1) of this section does not apply to—

(i) A debt instrument to which section 1272(a)(6) applies (certain interests in or mortgages held by a REMIC, and certain other debt instruments with payments subject to acceleration);

(ii) A debt instrument that provides for contingent payments, other than a debt instrument described in paragraph (c) or (d) of this section or except as provided in § 1.1275-4; or

(iii) A variable rate debt instrument to which § 1.1275-5 applies, except as provided in § 1.1275-5.

(3) *Modifications.*—The amount of OID includible in income by a holder under paragraph (b)(1) of this section is adjusted if—

(i) The holder purchased the debt instrument at a premium or an acquisition premium (within the meaning of § 1.1272-2); or

(ii) The holder made an election for the debt instrument under § 1.1272-3 to treat all interest as OID.

(4) *Special rules for determining the OID allocable to an accrual period.*—The following rules apply to determine the OID allocable to an accrual period under paragraph (b)(1)(iii) of this section.

(i) *Unpaid qualified stated interest allocable to an accrual period.*—In determining the OID allocable to an accrual period, if an interval between payments of qualified stated interest contains more than 1 accrual period—

(A) The amount of qualified stated interest payable at the end of the interval (including any qualified stated interest that is payable on the first day of the accrual period immediately following the interval) is allocated on a pro rata basis to each accrual period in the interval; and

(B) The adjusted issue price at the beginning of each accrual period in the interval must be increased by the amount of any qualified stated interest that has accrued prior to the first day of the accrual period but that is not payable until the end of the interval. See *Example 2* of paragraph (j) of this section for an example illustrating the rules in this paragraph (b)(4)(i).

(ii) *Final accrual period.*—The OID allocable to the final accrual period is the difference between the amount payable at maturity (other than a payment of qualified stated interest) and the adjusted issue price at the beginning of the final accrual period.

(iii) *Initial short accrual period.*—If all accrual periods are of equal length, except for either an initial shorter accrual period or an initial and a final shorter accrual period, the amount of OID allocable to the initial accrual period may be computed using any reasonable method. See *Example 3* in paragraph (j) of this section.

(iv) *Payment on first day of an accrual period.*—The adjusted issue price at the beginning of an accrual period is reduced by the amount of any payment (other than a payment of qualified stated interest) that is made on the first day of the accrual period.

* * *

(g) *Basis adjustment.*—The basis of a debt instrument in the hands of the holder is increased by the amount of OID included in the holder's gross income and decreased by the amount of any payment from the issuer to the holder under the debt instrument other than a payment of qualified stated interest. See, however, § 1.1275-2(f) for rules regarding basis adjustments on a pro rata prepayment.

* * *

[Reg. § 1.1272-1.]

□ [*T.D.* 8517, 1-27-94. *Amended by T.D.* 8674, 6-11-96 *and T.D.* 9612, 2-4-2013.]

§ 1.1272-2. Treatment of debt instruments purchased at a premium.—(a) *In general.*—Under section 1272(c)(1), if a holder purchases a debt instrument at a premium, the holder does not include any OID in gross income. Under section 1272(a)(7), if a holder purchases a debt instrument at an acquisition premium, the holder reduces the amount of OID includible in gross income by the fraction determined under paragraph (b)(4) of this section.

(b) *Definitions and special rules.*—(1) *Purchase.*—For purposes of section 1272 and this section, purchase means any acquisition of a debt instrument, including the acquisition of a newly issued debt instrument in a debt-for-debt exchange or the acquisition of a debt instrument from a donor.

(2) *Premium.*—A debt instrument is purchased at a premium if its adjusted basis, immediately after its purchase by the holder (including a purchase at original issue), exceeds the sum of all amounts payable on the instrument after the purchase date other than payments of qualified stated interest (as defined in § 1.1273-1(c)).

(3) *Acquisition premium.*—A debt instrument is purchased at an acquisition premium if its adjusted basis, immediately after its purchase (including a purchase at original issue), is—

(i) Less than or equal to the sum of all amounts payable on the instrument after the purchase date other than payments of qualified stated interest (as defined in § 1.1273-1(c)); and

(ii) Greater than the instrument's adjusted issue price (as defined in § 1.1275-1(b)).

(4) *Acquisition premium fraction.*—In applying section 1272(a)(7), the cost of a debt instrument is its adjusted basis immediately after its acquisition by the purchaser. Thus, the numerator of the fraction determined under section 1272(a)(7)(B) is the excess of the adjusted basis of the debt instrument immediately after its acquisition by the purchaser over the adjusted issue price of the debt instrument. The denominator of the fraction determined under section 1272(a)(7)(B) is the excess of the sum of all amounts payable on the debt instrument after the purchase date, other than payments of qualified stated interest, over the instrument's adjusted issue price.

(5) *Election to accrue discount on a constant yield basis.*—Rather than applying the acquisition premium fraction, a holder of a debt instrument purchased at an acquisition premium may elect under § 1.1272-3 to compute OID accruals by treating the purchase as a purchase at original issuance and applying the mechanics of the constant yield method.

* * *

[Reg. § 1.1272-2.]

□ [*T.D.* 8517, 1-27-94.]

§ 1.1273-1. Definition of OID.—(a) *In general.*—Section 1273(a)(1) defines OID as the excess of a debt instrument's stated redemption price at maturity over its issue price. Section 1.1273-2 defines issue price, and paragraph (b) of this section defines stated redemption price at maturity. Paragraph (d) of this section provides rules for de minimis amounts of OID. Although the total amount of OID for a debt instrument may be indeterminate, § 1.1272-1(d) provides a rule to determine OID accruals on certain debt instruments that provide for a fixed yield. See *Example 10* in § 1.1272-1(j).

(b) *Stated redemption price at maturity.*—A debt instrument's stated redemption price at maturity is the sum of all payments provided by the debt instrument other than qualified stated interest payments. If the payment schedule of a debt instrument is determined under § 1.1272-1(c) (relating to certain debt instruments subject to contingencies), that payment schedule is used to determine the instrument's stated redemption price at maturity.

(c) *Qualified stated interest.*—(1) *Definition.*—(i) *In general.*—Qualified stated interest is stated interest that is unconditionally payable in cash or in property (other than debt instruments of the issuer), or that will be constructively received under section 451, at least annually at a single fixed rate (within the meaning of paragraph (c)(1)(iii) of this section).

(ii) *Unconditionally payable.*—Interest is unconditionally payable only if reasonable legal remedies exist to compel timely payment or the debt instrument otherwise provides terms and conditions that make the likelihood of late payment (other than a late payment that occurs within a reasonable grace period) or nonpayment a remote contingency (within the meaning of § 1.1275-2(h)). For purposes of the preceding sentence, remedies or other terms and conditions are not taken into account if the lending transaction does not reflect arm's length dealing and the holder does not intend to enforce the remedies or other terms and conditions. For purposes of determining whether interest is unconditionally payable, the possibility of nonpayment due to default, insolvency, or similar circumstances, or due to the exercise of a conversion option described in § 1.1272-1(e) is ignored. This paragraph (c)(1)(ii) applies to debt instruments issued on or after August 13, 1996.

(iii) *Single fixed rate.*—(A) *In general.*—Interest is payable at a single fixed rate only if the rate appropriately takes into account the length of the interval between payments. Thus, if the interval between payments varies during the term of the debt instrument, the value of the fixed rate on which a payment is based generally must be adjusted to reflect a compounding assumption that is consistent with the length of the interval preceding the payment. See *Example 1* in paragraph (f) of this section.

(B) *Special rule for certain first and final payment intervals.*—Notwithstanding paragraph (c)(1)(iii)(A) of this section, if a debt instrument provides for payment intervals that are equal in length throughout the term of the instrument, except that the first or final payment interval differs in length from the other payment intervals, the first or final interest payment is considered to be made at a fixed rate if the value of the rate on which the payment is based is adjusted in any reasonable manner to take into account the length of the interval. See *Example 2* of paragraph (f) of this section. The rule in this paragraph (c)(1)(iii)(B) also applies if the lengths of both the first and final payment intervals differ from the length of the other payment intervals.

(2) *Debt instruments subject to contingencies.*—The determination of whether a debt instrument described in § 1.1272-1(c) (a debt instrument providing for an alternative payment schedule (or schedules) upon the occurrence of one or more contingencies) provides for qualified stated interest is made by analyzing each alternative payment schedule (including the stated payment schedule) as if it were the debt instrument's sole payment schedule. Under this analysis, the debt instrument provides for qualified stated interest to the extent of the lowest fixed rate at which qualified stated interest would be payable under any payment schedule. See *Example 4* of paragraph (f) of this section.

(3) *Variable rate debt instrument.*—In the case of a variable rate debt instrument, qualified stated interest is determined under § 1.1275-5(e).

(4) *Stated interest in excess of qualified stated interest.*—To the extent that stated interest payable under a debt instrument exceeds qualified stated interest, the excess is included in the debt instrument's stated redemption price at maturity.

(5) *Short-term obligations.*—In the case of a debt instrument with a term that is not more than 1 year from the date of issue, no payments of interest are treated as qualified stated interest payments.

(6) *Business day convention.*—(i) *Rule.*—For purposes of this paragraph (c), if a scheduled payment date for stated interest falls on a Saturday, Sunday, or Federal holiday (within the meaning of 5 U.S.C. 6103) but, under the terms of the debt instrument, the stated interest is payable on the first business day that immediately follows the scheduled payment date, the stated interest is treated as payable on the scheduled payment date, provided no additional interest is payable as a result of the deferral.

(ii) *Effective/applicability date.*—Paragraph (c)(6)(i) of this section applies to a debt instrument issued on or after September 13, 2012. A taxpayer, however, may rely on paragraph (c)(6)(i) of this section for a debt instrument issued before that date.

(d) *De minimis OID.*—(1) *In general.*—If the amount of OID with respect to a debt instrument is less than the de minimis amount, the amount of OID is treated as zero, and all stated interest (including stated interest that would otherwise be characterized as OID) is treated as qualified stated interest.

(2) *De minimis amount.*—The de minimis amount is an amount equal to 0.0025 multiplied by the product of the stated redemption price at maturity and the number of complete years to maturity from the issue date.

(3) *Installment obligations.*—In the case of an installment obligation (as defined in paragraph (e)(1) of this section), paragraph (d)(2) of this section is applied by substituting for the number of complete years to maturity the weighted average maturity (as defined in paragraph (e)(3) of this section). Alternatively, in the case of a debt instrument that provides for payments of principal no more rapidly than self-amortizing installment obligation (as defined in paragraph (e)(2) of this section), the de minimis amount defined in paragraph (d)(2) of this section may be calculated by substituting 0.00167 for 0.0025.

(4) *Special rule for interest holidays, teaser rates, and other interest shortfalls.*—(i) *In general.*—This paragraph (d)(4) provides a special rule to determine whether a debt instrument with a teaser rate (or rates), an interest holiday,

or any other interest shortfall has de minimis OID. This rule applies if—

(A) The amount of OID on the debt instrument is more than the de minimis amount as otherwise determined under paragraph (d) of this section; and

(B) All stated interest provided for in the debt instrument would be qualified stated interest under paragraph (c) of this section except that for 1 or more accrual periods the interest rate is below the rate applicable for the remainder of the instrument's term (e.g., if as a result of an interest holiday, none of the stated interest is qualified stated interest).

(ii) *Redetermination of OID for purposes of the de minimis test.*—For purposes of determining whether a debt instrument described in paragraph (d)(4)(i) of this section has de minimis OID, the instrument's stated redemption price at maturity is treated as equal to the instrument's issue price plus the greater of the amount of foregone interest or the excess (if any) of the instrument's stated principal amount over its issue price. The amount of foregone interest is the amount of additional stated interest that would be required to be payable on the debt instrument during the period of the teaser rate, holiday, or shortfall so that all stated interest would be qualified stated interest under paragraph (c) of this section. See *Example 5* and *Example 6* of paragraph (f) of this section. In addition, for purposes of computing the de minimis amount of OID the weighted average maturity of the debt instrument is determined by treating all stated interest payments as qualified stated interest payments.

(5) *Treatment of de minimis OID by holders.*—(i) *Allocation of de minimis OID to principal payments.*—The holder of a debt instrument includes any de minimis OID (other than de minimis OID treated as qualified stated interest under paragraph (d)(1) of this section, such as de minimis OID attributable to a teaser rate or interest holiday) in income as stated principal payments are made. The amount includible in income with respect to each principal payment equals the product of the total amount of de minimis OID on the debt instrument and a fraction, the numerator of which is the amount of the principal payment made, and the denominator of which is the stated principal amount of the instrument.

(ii) *Character of de minimis OID.*—(A) *De minimis OID treated as gain recognized on retirement.*—Any amount of de minimis OID includible in income under this paragraph (d)(5) is treated as gain recognized on retirement of the debt instrument. See section 1271 to determine whether a retirement is treated as an exchange of the debt instrument.

(B) *Treatment of de minimis OID on sale or exchange.*—Any gain attributable to de minimis OID that is recognized on the sale or exchange of a debt instrument is capital gain if the debt instrument is a capital asset in the hands of the seller.

(iii) *Treatment of subsequent holders.*—If a subsequent holder purchases a debt instrument issued with de minimis OID at a premium (as defined in § 1.1272-2(b)(2)), the subsequent holder does not include the de minimis OID in income. Otherwise, a subsequent holder includes any discount in income under the market discount rules (sections 1276 through 1278) rather than under the rules of this paragraph (d)(5).

(iv) *Cross-reference.*—See § 1.1272-3 for an election by a holder to treat de minimis OID as OID.

(e) *Definitions.*—(1) *Installment obligation.*—An installment obligation is a debt instrument that provides for the payment of any amount other than qualified stated interest before maturity.

(2) *Self-amortizing installment obligation.*—A self-amortizing installment obligation is an obligation that provides for equal payments composed of principal and qualified stated interest that are unconditionally payable at least annually during the entire term of the debt instrument with no additional payment required at maturity.

(3) *Weighted average maturity.*—The weighted average maturity of a debt instrument is the sum of the following amounts determined for each payment under the instrument (other than a payment of qualified stated interest)—

(i) The number of complete years from the issue date until the payment is made, multiplied by

(ii) A fraction, the numerator of which is the amount of the payment and the denominator of which is the debt instrument's stated redemption price at maturity.

(f) *Examples.*—The following examples illustrate the rules of this section.

Example 1. Qualified stated interest—(i) *Facts.* On January 1, 1995, A purchases at original issue for $100,000, a debt instrument that matures on January 1, 1999, and has a stated principal amount of $100,000, payable at maturity. The debt instrument provides for interest payments of $8,000 on January 1, 1996, and

January 1, 1997, and quarterly interest payments of $1,942.65, beginning on April 1, 1997.

(ii) *Amount of qualified stated interest.* The annual payments of $8,000 and the quarterly payments of $1,942.65 are payable at a single fixed rate because 8 percent, compounded annually, is equivalent to 7.77 percent, compounded quarterly. Consequently, all stated interest payments under the debt instrument are qualified stated interest payments.

Example 2. Qualified stated interest with short initial payment interval. On October 1, 1994, A purchases at original issue, for $100,000, a debt instrument that matures on January 1, 1998, and has a stated principal amount of $100,000, payable at maturity. The debt instrument provides for an interest payment of $2,000 on January 1, 1995, and interest payments of $8,000 on January 1, 1996, January 1, 1997, and January 1, 1998. Under paragraph (c)(1)(iii)(B) of this section, all stated interest payments on the debt instrument are computed at a single fixed rate and are qualified stated interest payments.

Example 3. Stated interest in excess of qualified stated interest—(i) *Facts.* On January 1, 1995, B purchases at original issue, for $100,000, C corporation's 5-year debt instrument. The debt instrument provides for a principal payment of $100,000, payable at maturity, and calls for annual interest payments of $10,000 for the first 3 years and annual interest payments of $10,600 for the last 2 years.

(ii) *Payments in excess of qualified stated interest.* All of the first three interest payments and $10,000 of each of the last two interest payments are qualified stated interest payments within the meaning of paragraph (c)(1) of this section. Under paragraph (c)(4) of this section, the remaining $600 of each of the last two interest payments is included in the stated redemption price at maturity, so that the stated redemption price at maturity is $101,200. Pursuant to paragraph (e)(3) of this section, the weighted average maturity of the debt instrument is 4.994 years [(4 years × $600/$101,200) + (5 years × $100,600/$101,200)]. The de minimis amount, or one-fourth of 1 percent of the stated redemption price at maturity multiplied by the weighted average maturity, is $1,263.50. Because the actual amount of discount, $1,200, is less than the de minimis amount, the instrument is treated as having no OID, and, under paragraph (d)(1) of this section, all of the interest payments are treated as qualified stated interest payments.

* * *

[Reg. § 1.1273-1.]

□ [*T.D.* 8517, 1-27-94. *Amended by T.D.* 8674, 6-11-96 *and T.D.* 9599, 9-12-2012.]

§ 1.1273-2. Determination of issue price and issue date.—(a) *Debt instruments issued for money.*—(1) *Issue price.*—If a substantial amount of the debt instruments in an issue is issued for money, the issue price of each debt instrument in the issue is the first price at which a substantial amount of the debt instruments is sold for money. Thus, if an issue consists of a single debt instrument that is issued for money, the issue price of the debt instrument is the amount paid for the instrument. For example, in the case of a debt instrument evidencing a loan to a natural person, the issue price of the instrument is the amount loaned. See § 1.1275-2(d) for rules regarding Treasury securities. For purposes of this paragraph (a), money includes functional currency and, in certain circumstances, nonfunctional currency. See § 1.988-2(b)(2) for circumstances when nonfunctional currency is treated as money rather than as property.

(2) *Issue date.*—The issue date of an issue described in paragraph (a)(1) of this section is the first settlement date or closing date, whichever is applicable, on which a substantial amount of the debt instruments in the issue is sold for money.

(b) *Publicly traded debt instruments issued for property.*—(1) *Issue price.*—If a substantial amount of the debt instruments in an issue is traded on an established market (within the meaning of paragraph (f) of this section) and the issue is not described in paragraph (a)(1) of this section, the issue price of each debt instrument in the issue is the fair market value of the debt instrument, determined as of the issue date (as defined in paragraph (b)(2) of this section). See paragraph (f) of this section for rules to determine the fair market value of a debt instrument for purposes of this section.

(2) *Issue date.*—The issue date of an issue described in paragraph (b)(1) of this section is the first date on which a substantial amount of the traded debt instruments in the issue is issued.

(c) *Debt instruments issued for publicly traded property.*—(1) *Issue price.*—If a substantial amount of the debt instrument in an issue is issued for property that is traded on an established market (within the meaning of paragraph (f) of this section) and the issue is not described in paragraph (a)(1) or (b)(1) of this section, the issue price of each debt instrument in the issue is the fair market value of the property, determined as of the issue date (as defined in paragraph (c)(2) of this section). For purposes of the preceding sentence, property means a debt instrument, stock, security, contract, commodity, or nonfunctional currency.

But see § 1.988-2(b)(2) for circumstances when nonfunctional currency is treated as money rather than as property. See paragraph (f) of this section for rules to determine the fair market value of property for purposes of this section.

(2) *Issue date.*—The issue date of an issue described in paragraph (c)(1) of this section is the first date on which a substantial amount of the debt instruments in the issue is issued for traded property.

(d) *Other debt instruments.*—(1) *Issue price.*—If an issue of debt instruments is not described in paragraph (a)(1), (b)(1), or (c)(1) of this section, the issue price of each debt instrument in the issue is determined as if the debt instrument were a separate issue. If the issue price of a debt instrument that is treated as a separate issue under the preceding sentence is not determined under paragraph (a)(1), (b)(1), or (c)(1) of this section, and if section 1274 applies to the debt instrument, the issue price of the instrument is determined under section 1274. Otherwise, the issue price of the debt instrument is its stated redemption price at maturity under section 1273(b)(4). See section 1274(c) and § 1.1274-1 to determine if section 1274 applies to a debt instrument.

(2) *Issue date.*—The issue date of an issue described in paragraph (d)(1) of this section is the date on which the debt instrument is issued for money or in a sale or exchange.

(e) *Special rule for certain sales to bond houses, brokers, or similar persons.*—For purposes of determining the issue price and issue date of a debt instrument under this section, sales to bond houses, brokers, or similar persons or organizations acting in the capacity of underwriters, placement agents, or wholesalers are ignored.

(f) *Traded on an established market (publicly traded).*—(1) *In general.*—Except as provided in paragraph (f)(6) of this section, property (including a debt instrument described in paragraph (b)(1) of this section) is traded on an established market for purposes of this section if, at any time during the 31-day period ending 15 days after the issue date—

(i) There is a sales price for the property as described in paragraph (f)(2) of this section;

(ii) There are one or more firm quotes for the property as described in paragraph (f)(3) of this section; or

(iii) There are one or more indicative quotes for the property as described in paragraph (f)(4) of this section.

(2) *Sales price.*—(i) *In general.*—A sales price exists if the price for an executed purchase or sale of the property within the 31-day period described in paragraph (f)(1) of this section is reasonably available within a reasonable period of time after the sale.

(ii) *Pricing information for a debt instrument.*—For purposes of paragraph (f)(2)(i) of this section, the price of a debt instrument is considered reasonably available if the sales price (or information sufficient to calculate the sales price) appears in a medium that is made available to issuers of debt instruments, persons that regularly purchase or sell debt instruments (including a price provided only to certain customers or to subscribers), or persons that broker purchases or sales of debt instruments.

(3) *Firm quote.*—A firm quote is considered to exist when a price quote is available from at least one broker, dealer, or pricing service (including a price provided only to certain customers or to subscribers) for property and the quoted price is substantially the same as the price for which the person receiving the quoted price could purchase or sell the property. A price quote is considered to be available whether the quote is initiated by a person providing the quote or provided at the request of the person receiving the quote. The identity of the person providing the quote must be reasonably ascertainable for a quote to be considered a firm quote for purposes of this paragraph (f)(3). A quote will be considered a firm quote if the quote is designated as a firm quote by the person providing the quote or if market participants typically purchase or sell, as the case may be, at the quoted price, even if the party providing the quote is not legally obligated to purchase or sell at that price.

(4) *Indicative quote.*—An indicative quote is considered to exist when a price quote is available from at least one broker, dealer, or pricing service (including a price provided only to certain customers or to subscribers) for property and the price quote is not a firm quote described in paragraph (f)(3) of this section.

(5) *Presumption that price or quote is equal to fair market value.*—(i) *In general.*—For purposes of this section, the fair market value of property will be presumed to be equal to its sales price or quoted price determined under paragraphs (f)(2) through (f)(4) of this section. If there is more than one sales price under paragraph (f)(2) of this section, more than one quoted price under paragraph (f)(3) or (f)(4) of this section, or both one or more sales prices under paragraph (f)(2) of this section and quoted prices under paragraph (f)(3) or (f)(4)

of this section, a taxpayer may use any reasonable method, consistently applied to the same or substantially similar facts, to determine the fair market value. For example, to determine the fair market value under a reasonable method, a taxpayer may consider factors such as (but not necessarily limited to) the timing of each relevant sale or quote in relation to the issue date; whether the price is derived from a sale, a firm quote, or an indicative quote; the size of each relevant sale or quote; or whether the sales price or quote corresponds to pricing information provided by an independent bond or loan pricing service.

(ii) *Special rule for property for which there is only an indicative quote.*—If property is described only in paragraph (f)(4) of this section, and the taxpayer determines that the quote (or an average of the quotes) materially misrepresents the fair market value of the property, the taxpayer can use any method that provides a reasonable basis to determine the fair market value of the property. A taxpayer must establish that the method chosen more accurately reflects the value of the property than the quote or quotes for the property to use the method provided in this paragraph (f)(5)(ii). For an equity or debt instrument, a volume discount or control premium will not be considered to create a material misrepresentation of value for purposes of this paragraph (f)(5)(ii).

(6) *Exception for small debt issues.*—Notwithstanding any other provision in paragraph (f) of this section, a debt instrument will not be treated as traded on an established market if at the time the determination is made the outstanding stated principal amount of the issue that includes the debt instrument does not exceed US$100 million (or, for a debt instrument denominated in a currency other than the U.S. dollar, the equivalent amount in the currency in which the debt instrument is denominated).

(7) *Anti-abuse rules.*—(i) *Effect of certain temporary restrictions on trading.*—If there is any temporary restriction on trading a purpose of which is to avoid the characterization of the property as one that is traded on an established market for Federal income tax purposes, then the property is treated as traded on an established market. For purposes of the preceding sentence, a temporary restriction on trading need not be imposed by the issuer.

(ii) *Artificial pricing information.*—If a principal purpose for the existence of any sale or price quotation is to cause the property to be traded on an established market or to materially misrepresent the value of property, that sale or price quotation is disregarded.

(8) *Convertible debt instruments.*—A debt instrument is not treated as traded on an established market solely because the debt instrument is convertible into property that is so traded.

(9) *Issuer-holder consistency requirement.*—(i) *General rule.*—For purposes of this section, an issuer must determine whether property is traded on an established market and, if so, the fair market value of the property. An issuer is required to exercise reasonable diligence to determine whether purchases or sales have taken place, the quantity of purchases and sales, the price at which purchases or sales occurred, the existence of firm or indicative quotes, and any other relevant information using the rules provided in paragraph (f) of this section to determine the fair market value of the property. If an issuer determines that property is traded on an established market, the issuer is required to make that determination as well as the fair market value of the property (which can be stated as the issue price of the debt instrument) available to holders in a commercially reasonable fashion, including by electronic publication, within 90 days of the date that the debt instrument is issued. Each determination by an issuer is binding on a holder of the debt instrument unless the holder explicitly discloses that its determination is different from the issuer's determination (for example, the holder determines a different fair market value for the property or determines that the property is not traded on an established market). A holder must describe in the disclosure the reasons for its different determination and, if applicable, how the holder determined the fair market value. A holder's disclosure must be filed on a timely filed Federal income tax return for the taxable year that includes the acquisition date of the debt instrument. If an issuer for any reason does not make the fair market value or issue price of a debt instrument reasonably available to a holder, the holder must determine the fair market value of the property and issue price of the debt instrument using the rules provided in paragraph (f) of this section.

(ii) *Co-obligors.*—If a debt instrument has more than one obligor, the obligors must designate one obligor (issuer) to determine whether property is traded on an established market and, if so, the fair market value of the property and issue price of the debt instrument and make the price available to holders using the rules provided in paragraph (f)(9)(i) of this section.

* * *

(k) *Below-market loans subject to section 7872(b).*—The issue price of a below-market loan subject to section 7872(b) (a term loan other than a gift loan) is the issue price determined under this section, reduced by the excess amount determined under section 7872(b)(1).

(l) [Reserved]

* * *

[Reg. § 1.1273-2.]

☐ [*T.D.* 8517, 1-27-94. *Amended by T.D.* 9599, 9-12-2012 *and T.D.* 9612, 2-4-2013.]

§ 1.1274-1. Debt instruments to which section 1274 applies.—(a) *In general.*—Subject to the exceptions and limitations in paragraph (b) of this section, section 1274 and this section apply to any debt instrument issued in consideration for the sale or exchange of property. For purposes of section 1274, property includes debt instruments and investment units, but does not include money, services, or the right to use property. For the treatment of certain obligations given in exchange for services or the use of property, see sections 404 and 467. For purposes of this paragraph (a), money includes functional currency and, in certain circumstances, nonfunctional currency. See § 1.988-2(b)(2) for circumstances when nonfunctional currency is treated as money rather than as property.

(b) *Exceptions.*—(1) *Debt instrument with adequate stated interest and no OID.*—Section 1274 does not apply to a debt instrument if—

(i) All interest payable on the instrument is qualified stated interest;

(ii) The stated rate of interest is at least equal to the test rate of interest (as defined in § 1.1274-4);

(iii) The debt instrument is not issued in a potentially abusive situation (as defined in § 1.1274-3); and

(iv) No payment from the buyer-borrower to the seller-lender designated as points or interest is made at the time of issuance of the debt instrument.

(2) *Exceptions under sections 1274(c)(1)(B), 1274(c)(3), 1274A(c), and 1275(b)(1).*—(i) *In general.*—Sections 1274(c)(1)(B), 1274(c)(3), 1274A(c), and 1275(b)(1) describe certain transactions to which section 1274 does not apply. This paragraph (b)(2) provides certain rules to be used in applying those exceptions.

(ii) *Special rules for certain exceptions under section 1274(c)(3).*—(A) *Determination of sales price for certain sales of farms.*—For purposes of section 1274(c)(3)(A), the determination as to whether the sales price cannot exceed $1,000,000 is made without regard to any other exception to, or limitation on, the applicability of section 1274 (e.g., without regard to the special rules regarding sales of principal residences and land transfers between related persons). In addition, the sales price is determined without regard to section 1274 and without regard to any stated interest. The sales price includes the amount of any liability included in the amount realized from the sale or exchange. See § 1.1001-2.

(B) *Sales involving total payments of $250,000 or less.*—Under section 1274(c)(3)(C), the determination of the amount of payments due under all debt instruments and the amount of other consideration to be received is made as of the date of the sale or exchange or, if earlier, the contract date. If the precise amount due under any debt instrument or the precise amount of any other consideration to be received cannot be determined as of that date, section 1274(c)(3)(C) applies only if it can be determined that the maximum of the aggregate amount of payments due under the debt instruments and other consideration to be received cannot exceed $250,000. For purposes of section 1274(c)(3)(C), if a liability is assumed or property is taken subject to a liability, the aggregate amount of payments due includes the outstanding principal balance or adjusted issue price (in the case of an obligation originally issued at a discount) of the obligation.

(C) *Coordination with section 1273 and § 1.1273-2.*—In accordance with section 1274(c)(3)(D), section 1274 and this section do not apply if the issue price of a debt instrument issued in consideration for the sale or exchange of property is determined under paragraph (a)(1), (b)(1), or (c)(1) of § 1.1273-2.

(3) *Other exceptions to section 1274.*—(i) *Holders of certain below-market instruments.*—Section 1274 does not apply to any holder of a debt instrument that is issued in consideration for the sale or exchange of personal use property (within the meaning of section 1275(b)(3)) in the hands of the issuer and that evidences a below-market loan described in section 7872(c)(1).

(ii) *Transactions involving certain demand loans.*—Section 1274 does not apply to any debt instrument that evidences a demand loan that is a below-market loan described in section 7872(c)(1).

(iii) *Certain transfers subject to section 1041.*—Section 1274 does not apply to any debt instrument issued in consideration for a transfer of property subject to section 1041 (relating to transfers of property between spouses or incident to divorce).

(c) *Examples.*—The following examples illustrate the rules of this section.

Example 1. Single stated rate paid semiannually. A debt instrument issued in consideration for the sale of nonpublicly traded property in a transaction that is not a potentially abusive situation calls for the payment of a principal amount of $1,000,000 at the end of a 10-year term and 20 semiannual interest payments of $60,000. Assume that the test rate of interest is 12 percent, compounded semiannually. The debt instrument is not subject to section 1274 because it provides for interest equal to the test rate and all interest payable on the instrument is qualified stated interest.

Example 2. Sale of farm for debt instrument with contingent interest—(i) *Facts.* On July 1, 1995, A, an individual, sells to B land used as a farm within the meaning of section 6420(c)(2). As partial consideration for the sale, B issues a debt instrument calling for a single $500,000 payment due in 10 years unless profits from the land in each of the 10 years preceding maturity of the debt instrument exceed a specified amount, in which case B is to make a payment of $1,200,000. The debt instrument does not provide for interest.

(ii) *Total payments may exceed $1,000,000.* Even though the total payments ultimately payable under the contract may be less than $1,000,000, at the time of the sale or exchange it cannot be determined that the sales price cannot exceed $1,000,000. Thus, the sale of the land used as a farm is not an excepted transaction described in section 1274(c)(3)(A).

Example 3. Sale between related parties subject to section 483(e)—(i) *Facts.* On July 1, 1995, A, an individual, sells land (not used as a farm within the meaning of section 6420(c)(2)) to A's child B for $650,000. In consideration for the sale, B issues a 10-year debt instrument to A that calls for a payment of $650,000. No other consideration is given. The debt instrument does not provide for interest.

(ii) *Treatment of debt instrument.* For purposes of section 483(e), the $650,000 debt instrument is treated as two separate debt instruments: a $500,000 debt instrument and a $150,000 debt instrument. The $500,000 debt instrument is subject to section 483(e), and accordingly is covered by the exception from section 1274 described in section 1274(c)(3)(F). Because the amount of the payments due as consideration for the sale exceeds $250,000, however, the $150,000 debt instrument is subject to section 1274.

[Reg. § 1.1274-1.]

□ [*T.D.* 8517, 1-27-94.]

§ 1.1274-2. Issue price of debt instruments to which section 1274 applies.—(a) *In general.*—If section 1274 applies to a debt instrument, section 1274 and this section determine the issue price of the debt instrument. For rules relating to the determination of the amount and timing of OID to be included in income, see section 1272 and the regulations thereunder.

(b) *Issue price.*—(1) *Debt instruments that provide for adequate stated interest; stated principal amount.*—The issue price of a debt instrument that provides for adequate stated interest is the stated principal amount of the debt instrument. For purposes of section 1274, the stated principal amount of a debt instrument is the aggregate amount of all payments due under the debt instrument, excluding any amount of stated interest. Under § 1.1273-2(g)(2)(ii), however, the stated principal amount of a debt instrument is reduced by any payment from the buyer-borrower to the seller-lender that is designated as interest or points. See *Example 2* of § 1.1273-2(g)(5).

(2) *Debt instruments that do not provide for adequate stated interest; imputed principal amount.*—The issue price of a debt instrument that does not provide for adequate stated interest is the imputed principal amount of the debt instrument.

(3) *Debt instruments issued in a potentially abusive situation; fair market value.*—Notwithstanding paragraphs (b)(1) and (b)(2) of this section, in the case of a debt instrument issued in a potentially abusive situation (as defined in § 1.1274-3), the issue price of the debt instrument is the fair market value of the property received in exchange for the debt instrument, reduced by the fair market value of any consideration other than the debt instrument issued in consideration for the sale or exchange.

(c) *Determination of whether a debt instrument provides for adequate stated interest.*—(1) *In general.*—A debt instrument provides for adequate stated interest if its stated principal amount is less than or equal to its imputed principal amount. Imputed principal amount means the sum of the present values, as of the issue date, of all payments, including payments of stated interest, due under the debt instrument (determined by using a discount rate equal to the test rate of interest as determined under § 1.1274-4). If a debt instrument has a single fixed rate of interest that is paid or compounded at least annually, and that rate is equal to or greater than the test rate, the debt instrument has adequate stated interest.

(2) *Determination of present value.*—The present value of a payment is determined by discounting the payment from the date it becomes due to the date of the sale or exchange at the test rate of interest. To determine pre-

sent value, a compounding period must be selected, and the test rate must be based on the same compounding period.

* * *

[Reg. § 1.1274-2.]

☐ [*T.D.* 8517, 1-27-94. *Amended by T.D.* 8674, 6-11-96.]

§ 1.1274-4. Test rate.—(a) *Determination of test rate of interest.*—(1) *In general.*—(i) *Test rate is the 3-month rate.*—Except as provided in paragraph (a)(2) of this section, the test rate of interest for a debt instrument issued in consideration for the sale or exchange of property is the 3-month rate.

(ii) *The 3-month rate.*—Except as provided in paragraph (a)(1)(iii) of this section, the 3-month rate is the lower of—

(A) The lowest applicable Federal rate (based on the appropriate compounding period) in effect during the 3-month period ending with the first month in which there is a binding written contract that substantially sets forth the terms under which the sale or exchange is ultimately consummated; or

(B) The lowest applicable Federal rate (based on the appropriate compounding period) in effect during the 3-month period ending with the month in which the sale or exchange occurs.

(iii) *Special rule if there is no binding written contract.*—If there is no binding written contract that substantially sets forth the terms under which the sale or exchange is ultimately consummated, the 3-month rate is the lowest applicable Federal rate (based on the appropriate compounding period) in effect during the 3-month period ending with the month in which the sale or exchange occurs.

(2) *Test rate for certain debt instruments.*—(i) *Sale-leaseback transactions.*—Under section 1274(e) (relating to certain sale-leaseback transactions), the test rate is 110 percent of the 3-month rate determined under paragraph (a)(1) of this section. For purposes of section 1274(e)(3), related party means a person related to the transferor within the meaning of section 267(b) or 707(b)(1).

(ii) *Qualified debt instrument.*—Under section 1274A(a), the test rate for a qualified debt instrument is no greater than 9 percent, compounded semiannually, or an equivalent rate based on an appropriate compounding period.

(iii) *Alternative test rate for short-term obligations.*—(A) *Requirements.*—This paragraph (a)(2)(iii)(A) provides an alternative test rate under section 1274(d)(1)(D) for a debt instrument with a maturity of 1 year or less. This alternative test rate applies, however, only if the debt instrument provides for adequate stated interest using the alternative test rate, the issuer provides on the face of the debt instrument that the instrument qualifies as having adequate stated interest under section 1274(d)(1)(D), and the issuer and holder treat or agree to treat the instrument as having adequate stated interest.

(B) *Alternative test rate.*—For purposes of paragraph (a)(2)(iii)(A), the alternative test rate is the market yield on U.S. Treasury bills with the same maturity date as the debt instrument. If the same maturity date is not available, the market yield on U.S. Treasury bills that mature in the same week or month as the debt instrument is used. The alternative test rate is determined as of the date on which there is a binding written contract that substantially sets forth the terms under which the sale or exchange is ultimately consummated or as of the date of the sale or exchange, whichever date results in a lower rate. If there is no binding written contract, however, the alternative test rate is determined as of the date of the sale or exchange.

(b) *Applicable Federal rate.*—Except as otherwise provided in this section, the applicable Federal rate for a debt instrument is based on the term of the instrument (i.e., short-term, mid-term, or long-term). See section 1274(d)(1). The Internal Revenue Service publishes the applicable Federal rates for each month in the Internal Revenue Bulletin (see § 601.601(d)(2)(ii) of this chapter). The applicable Federal rates are based on the yield to maturity of outstanding marketable obligations of the United States of similar maturities during the one month period ending on the 14th day of the month preceding the month for which the rates are applicable.

(c) *Special rules to determine the term of a debt instrument for purposes of determining the applicable Federal rate.*—(1) *Installment obligation.*—If a debt instrument is an installment obligation (as defined in § 1.1273-1(e)(1)), the term of the instrument is the instrument's weighted average maturity (as defined in § 1.1273-1(e)(3)).

(2) *Certain variable rate debt instruments.*—(i) *In general.*—Except as otherwise provided in paragraph (c)(2)(ii) of this section, if a variable rate debt instrument (as defined in § 1.1275-5(a)) provides for stated interest at a qualified floating rate (or rates), the term of the instrument is determined by reference to the longest interval between interest adjustment dates, or, if the variable rate debt instrument

provides for a fixed rate, the interval between the issue date and the last day on which the fixed rate applies, if this interval is longer.

(ii) *Restrictions on adjustments.*—If, due to significant restrictions on variations in a qualified floating rate or the use of certain formulae pursuant to § 1.1275-5(b) (2) (e.g., 15 percent of 1-year LIBOR, plus 800 basis points), the rate in substance resembles a fixed rate, the applicable Federal rate is determined by reference to the term of the debt instrument.

(3) *Counting of either the issue date or the maturity date.*—The term of a debt instrument includes either the issue date or the maturity date, but not both dates.

(4) *Certain debt instruments that provide for principal payments uncertain as to time.*—If a debt instrument provides for principal payments that are fixed in total amount but uncertain as to time, the term of the instrument is determined by reference to the latest possible date on which a principal payment can be made or, in the case of an installment obligation, by reference to the longest weighted average maturity under any possible payment schedule.

(e) *Examples.*—The following examples illustrate the rules of this section.

Example 1. Variable rate debt instrument that limits the amount of increase and decrease in the rate—(i) *Facts.* On July 1, 1996, A sells nonpublicly traded property to B in return for a 5-year debt instrument that provides for interest to be paid on July 1 of each year, beginning on July 1, 1997, based on the prime rate of a local bank on that date. However, the interest rate cannot increase or decrease from one year to the next by more than .25 percentage points (25 basis points).

(ii) *Significant restriction.* The debt instrument is a variable rate debt instrument (as defined in § 1.1275-5) that provides for stated interest at a qualified floating rate. Assume that based on all the facts and circumstances, the restriction is a significant restriction on the variations in the rate of interest. Under paragraph (c) (2) (ii) of this section, the applicable Federal rate is determined by reference to the term of the debt instrument, and the applicable Federal rate is the Federal mid-term rate.

Example 2. Installment obligation—(i) *Facts.* On January 1, 1996, A sells nonpublicly traded property to B in exchange for a debt instrument that calls for a payment of $500,000 on January 1, 2001, and a payment of $1,000,000 on January 1, 2006. The debt instrument does not provide for any stated interest.

(ii) *Determination of term.* The debt instrument is an installment obligation. Under paragraph (c) (1) of this section, the term of the debt instrument is its weighted average maturity (as defined in § 1.1273-1(e) (3)). The debt instrument's weighted average maturity is 8.33 years, which is the sum of (A) the ratio of the first payment to total payments (500,000/1,500,000), multiplied by the number of complete years from the issue date until the payment is due (5 years), and (b) the ratio of the second payment to total payments (1,000,000/1,500,000), multiplied by the number of complete years from the issue date until the second payment is due (10 years).

(iii) *Applicable Federal rate.* Based on the calculation in paragraph (ii) of this example, the term of the debt instrument is treated as 8.33 years. Consequently, the applicable Federal rate is the Federal mid-term rate.

[Reg. § 1.1274-4.]

□ [*T.D.* 8517, 1-27-94.]

§ 1.1274A-1. Special rules for certain transactions where stated principal amount does not exceed $2,800,000.—(a) *In general.*—Section 1274A allows the use of a lower test rate for purposes of sections 483 and 1274 in the case of a qualified debt instrument (as defined in section 1274A(b)) and, if elected by the borrower and the lender, the use of the cash receipts and disbursements method of accounting for interest on a cash method debt instrument (as defined in section 1274A(c) (2)). This section provides special rules for qualified debt instruments and cash method debt instruments.

(b) *Rules for both qualified and cash method debt instruments.*—(1) *Sale-leaseback transactions.*—A debt instrument issued in a sale-leaseback transaction (within the meaning of section 1274(e)) cannot be either a qualified debt instrument or a cash method debt instrument.

(2) *Debt instruments calling for contingent payments.*—A debt instrument that provides for contingent payments cannot be a qualified debt instrument unless it can be determined at the time of the sale or exchange that the maximum stated principal amount due under the debt instrument cannot exceed the amount specified in section 1274A(b). Similarly, a debt instrument that provides for contingent payments cannot be a cash method debt instrument unless it can be determined at the time of the sale or exchange that the maximum stated principal amount due under the debt instrument cannot exceed the amount specified in section 1274A(c) (2) (A).

(3) *Aggregation of transactions.*—(i) *General rule.*—The aggregation rules of section 1274A(d) (1) are applied using a facts and circumstances test.

(ii) *Examples.*—The following examples illustrate the application of section 1274A(d)(1) and paragraph (b)(3)(i) of this section.

Example 1. Aggregation of two sales to a single person. In two transactions evidenced by separate sales agreements, A sells undivided half interests in Blackacre to B. The sales are pursuant to a plan for the sale of a 100 percent interest in Blackacre to B. These sales or exchanges are part of a series of related transactions and, thus, are treated as a single sale for purposes of section 1274A.

Example 2. Aggregation of two purchases by unrelated individuals. Pursuant to a plan, unrelated individuals X and Y purchase undivided half interests in Blackacre from A and subsequently contribute these interests to a partnership in exchange for equal interests in the partnership. These purchases are treated as part of the same transaction and, thus, are treated as a single sale for purposes of section 1274A.

Example 3. Aggregation of sales made pursuant to a tender offer. Fifteen unrelated individuals own all of the stock of X Corporation. Y Corporation makes a tender offer to these 15 shareholders. The terms offered to each shareholder are identical. Shareholders holding a majority of the shares of X Corporation elect to tender their shares pursuant to Y Corporation's offer. These sales are part of the same transaction and, thus, are treated as a single sale for purposes of section 1274A.

Example 4. No aggregation for separate sales of similar property to unrelated persons. Pursuant to a newspaper advertisement, X Corporation offers for sale similar condominiums in a single building. The prices of the units vary due to a variety of factors, but the financing terms offered by X Corporation to all buyers are identical. The units are purchased by unrelated buyers who decided whether to purchase units in the building at the price and on the terms offered by X Corporation, without regard to the actions of other buyers. Because each buyer acts individually, the sales are not part of the same transaction or a series of related transactions and, thus, are treated as separate sales.

(4) *Inflation adjustment of dollar amounts.*—Under section 1274A(d)(2), the dollar amounts specified in sections 1274A(b) and 1274A(c)(2)(A) are adjusted for inflation. The dollar amounts, adjusted for inflation, are published in the Internal Revenue Bulletin (see § 601.601(d)(2)(ii) of this chapter).

(c) *Rules for cash method debt instruments.*—(1) *Time and manner of making cash method election.*—The borrower and lender make the election described in section 1274A(c)(2)(D) by jointly signing a statement that includes the names, addresses, and taxpayer identification numbers of the borrower and lender, a clear indication that an election is being made under section 1274A(c)(2), and a declaration that debt instrument with respect to which the election is being made fulfills the requirements of a cash method debt instrument. Both the borrower and the lender must sign this statement not later than the earlier of the last day (including extensions) for filing the Federal income tax return of the borrower or lender for the taxable year in which the debt instrument is issued. The borrower and lender should attach this signed statement (or a copy thereof) to their timely filed Federal income tax returns.

(2) *Successors of electing parties.*—Except as othewise provided in this paragraph (c)(2), the cash method election under section 1274A(c) applies to any successor of the electing lender or borrower. Thus, for any period after the transfer of a cash method debt instrument, the successor takes into account the interest (including unstated interest) on the instrument under the cash receipts and disbursements method of accounting. Nevertheless, if the lender (or any successor thereof) transfers the cash method debt instrument to a taxpayer who uses an accrual method of accounting, section 1272 rather than section 1274A(c) applies to the successor of the lender with respect to the debt instrument for any period after the date of the transfer. The borrower (or any successor thereof), however, remains on the cash receipts and disbursements method of accounting with respect to the cash method debt instrument.

(3) *Modified debt instrument.*—In the case of a debt instrument issued in a debt-for-debt exchange that qualifies as an exchange under section 1001, the debt instrument is eligible for the election to be a cash method debt instrument if the other prerequisites to making the election in section 1274A(c) are met. However, if a principal purpose of the modification is to defer interest income or deductions through the use of the election, then the debt instrument is not eligible for the election.

(4) *Debt incurred or continued to purchase or carry a cash method debt instrument.*—If a debt instrument is incurred or continued to purchase or carry a cash method debt instrument, rules similar to those under section 1277 apply to determine the timing of the interest deductions for the debt instrument. For purposes of the preceding sentence, rules similar to those under section 265(a)(2) apply to determine whether a debt instrument is incurred or continued to purchase or carry a cash method debt instrument. [Reg. § 1.1274A-1.]

☐ [*T.D.* 8517, 1-27-94.]

§ 1.1275-1. Definitions.—(a) *Applicability.*—The definitions contained in this section apply for purposes of sections 163(e) and 1271 through 1275 and the regulations thereunder.

(b) *Adjusted issue price.*—(1) *In general.*—The adjusted issue price of a debt instrument at the beginning of the first accrual period is the issue price. Thereafter, the adjusted issue price of the debt instrument is the issue price of the debt instrument—

(i) Increased by the amount of OID previously includible in the gross income of any holder (determined without regard to section 1272(a)(7) and section 1272(c)(1)); and

(ii) Decreased by the amount of any payment previously made on the debt instrument other than a payment of qualified stated interest. See § 1.1275-2(f) for rules regarding adjustments to adjusted issue price on a pro rata prepayment.

(2) *Bond issuance premium.*—If a debt instrument is issued with bond issuance premium (as defined in § 1.163-13(c)), for purposes of determining the issuer's adjusted issue price, the adjusted issue price determined under paragraph (b)(1) of this section is also decreased by the amount of bond issuance premium previously allocable under § 1.163-13(d)(3).

(3) *Adjusted issue price for subsequent holders.*—for purposes of calculating OID accruals, acquisition premium, or market discount, a holder (other than a purchaser at original issuance) determines adjusted issue price in any manner consistent with the regulations under sections 1271 through 1275.

(c) *OID.*—OID means original issue discount (as defined in section 1273(a) and § 1.1273-1).

(d) *Debt instrument.*—Except as provided in section 1275(a)(1)(B) (relating to certain annuity contracts; see paragraph (j) of this section), debt instrument means any instrument or contractual arrangement that constitutes indebtedness under general principles of Federal income tax law (including, for example, a certificate of deposit or a loan). Nothing in the regulations under sections 163(e), 483, and 1271 through 1275, however, shall influence whether an instrument constitutes indebtedness for Federal income tax purposes. See § 1.385–3 for rules that treat certain instruments that otherwise would be treated as indebtedness as stock for Federal tax purposes.

(e) *Tax-exempt obligations.*—For purposes of section 1275(a)(3)(B), exempt from tax means exempt from Federal income tax.

(f) *Issue.*—(1) *Debt instruments issued on or after March 13, 2001.*—Except as provided in paragraph (f)(3) of this section, two or more debt instruments are part of the same issue if the debt instruments—

(i) Have the same credit and payment terms;

(ii) Are issued either pursuant to a common plan or as part of a single transaction or a series of related transactions;

(iii) Are issued within a period of thirteen days beginning with the date on which the first debt instrument that would be part of the issue is issued to a person other than a bond house, broker, or similar person or organization acting in the capacity of an underwriter, placement agent, or wholesaler; and

(iv) Are issued on or after March 13, 2001.

* * *

(g) *Debt instruments issued by a natural person.*—If an entity is a primary obligor under a debt instrument, the debt instrument is considered to be issued by the entity and not by a natural person even if a natural person is a comaker and is jointly liable for the debt instrument's repayment. A debt instrument issued by a partnership is considered to be issued by the partnership as an entity even if the partnership is composed entirely of natural persons.

(h) *Publicly offered debt instrument.*—A debt instrument is publicly offered if it is part of an issue of debt instruments the initial offering of which—

(1) Is registered with the Securities and Exchange Commission; or

(2) Would be required to be registered under the Securities Act of 1933 (15 U.S.C. 77a et seq.) but for an exemption from registration—

(i) Under section 3 of the Securities Act of 1933 (relating to exempted securities);

(ii) Under any law (other than the Securities Act of 1933) because of the identity of the issuer or the nature of the security; or

(iii) Because the issue is intended for distribution to persons who are not United States persons.

(i) [Reserved]

* * *

[Reg. § 1.1275-1.]

☐ [*T.D.* 8517, 1-27-94. *Amended by T.D.* 8746, 12-30-97; *T.D.* 8754, 1-7-98; *T.D.* 8934, 1-11-2001; *T.D.* 8993, 5-6-2002; *T.D.* 9790, 10-13-2016 *and T.D.* 9880, 10-31-2019.]

S Corporations and Their Shareholders

§ 1.1361-1. S corporation defined.—(a) *In general.*—For purposes of this title, with respect to any taxable year—

(1) The term *S corporation* means a small business corporation (as defined in paragraph (b) of this section) for which an election under section 1362(a) is in effect for that taxable year.

(2) The term *C corporation* means a corporation that is not an S corporation for that taxable year.

(b) *Small business corporation defined.*—(1) *In general.*—For purposes of subchapter S, chapter 1 of the Code and the regulations thereunder, the term *small business corporation* means a domestic corporation that is not an ineligible corporation (as defined in section 1361(b)(2)) and that does not have—

(i) More than the number of shareholders provided in section 1361(b)(1)(A);

(ii) As a shareholder, a person (other than an estate, a trust described in section 1361(c)(2), or, for taxable years beginning after December 31, 1997, an organization described in section 1361(c)(6)) who is not an individual;

(iii) A nonresident alien as a shareholder; or

(iv) More than one class of stock.

(2) *Estate in bankruptcy.*—The term *estate*, for purposes of this paragraph, includes the estate of an individual in a case under title 11 of the United States Code.

(3) *Treatment of restricted stock.*—For purposes of subchapter S, stock that is issued in connection with the performance of services (within the meaning of § 1.83-3(f)) and that is substantially nonvested (within the meaning of § 1.83-3(b)) is not treated as outstanding stock of the corporation, and the holder of that stock is not treated as a shareholder solely by reason of holding the stock, unless the holder makes an election with respect to the stock under section 83(b). In the event of such an election, the stock is treated as outstanding stock of the corporation, and the holder of the stock is treated as a shareholder for purposes of subchapter S. See paragraphs (l)(1) and (3) of this section for rules for determining whether substantially nonvested stock with respect to which an election under section 83(b) has been made is treated as a second class of stock.

(4) *Treatment of deferred compensation plans.*—For purposes of subchapter S, an instrument, obligation, or arrangement is not outstanding stock if it—

(i) Does not convey the right to vote;

(ii) Is an unfunded and unsecured promise to pay money or property in the future;

(iii) Is issued to an individual who is an employee in connection with the performance of services for the corporation or to an individual who is an independent contractor in connection with the performance of services for the corporation (and is not excessive by reference to the services performed); and

(iv) Is issued pursuant to a plan with respect to which the employee or independent contractor is not taxed currently on income.

A deferred compensation plan that has a current payment feature (*e.g.*, payment of dividend equivalent amounts that are taxed currently as compensation) is not for that reason excluded from this paragraph (b)(4).

(5) *Treatment of straight debt.*—For purposes of subchapter S, an instrument or obligation that satisfies the definition of straight debt in paragraph (l)(5) of this section is not treated as outstanding stock.

* * *

(c) *Domestic corporation.*—For purposes of paragraph (b) of this section, the term *domestic corporation* means a domestic corporation as defined in § 301.7701-5 of this chapter, and the term *corporation* includes an entity that is classified as an association taxable as a corporation under § 301.7701-2 of this chapter.

(d) *Ineligible corporation.*—(1) *General rule.*—Except as otherwise provided in this paragraph (d), the term *ineligible corporation* means a corporation that is—

(i) For taxable years beginning on or after January 1, 1997, a financial institution that uses the reserve method of accounting for bad debts described in section 585 (for taxable years beginning prior to January 1, 1997, a financial institution to which section 585 applies (or would apply but for section 585(c)) or to which section 593 applies);

(ii) An insurance company subject to tax under subchapter

(iii) A corporation to which an election under section 936 applies; or

(iv) A DISC or former DISC.

(2) *Exceptions.*—See the special rules and exceptions provided in sections 6(c)(2), (3) and (4) of Pub. L. 97-354 that are applicable for certain casualty insurance companies and qualified oil corporations.

(e) *Number of shareholders.*—(1) *General rule.*—A corporation does not qualify as a small business corporation if it has more than the number of shareholders provided in section

1361(b)(1)(A). Ordinarily, the person who would have to include in gross income dividends distributed with respect to the stock of the corporation (if the corporation were a C corporation) is considered to be the shareholder of the corporation. For example, if stock (owned other than by a husband and wife or members of a family described in section 1361(c)(1)) is owned by tenants in common or joint tenants, each tenant in common or joint tenant is generally considered to be a shareholder of the corporation. (For special rules relating to stock owned by husband and wife or members of a family, see paragraphs (e)(2) and (3) of this section, respectively; for special rules relating to restricted stock, see paragraphs (b)(3) and (6) of this section.) The person for whom stock of a corporation is held by a nominee, guardian, custodian, or an agent is considered to be the shareholder of the corporation for purposes of this paragraph (e) and paragraphs (f) and (g) of this section. For example, a partnership may be a nominee of S corporation stock for a person who qualifies as a shareholder of an S corporation. However, if the partnership is the beneficial owner of the stock, then the partnership is the shareholder, and the corporation does not qualify as a small business corporation. In addition, in the case of stock held for a minor under a uniform transfers to minors act or similar statute, the minor and not the custodian is the shareholder. Except as otherwise provided in paragraphs (h) and (j) of this section, and for purposes of this paragraph (e) and paragraphs (f) and (g) of this section, if stock is held by a decedent's estate or a trust described in section 1361(c)(2)(A)(ii) or (iii), the estate or trust (and not the beneficiaries of the estate or trust) is considered to be the shareholder; however, if stock is held by a subpart E trust (which includes a voting trust) or an electing QSST described in section 1361(d)(1), the deemed owner of the trust is considered to be the shareholder. If stock is held by an ESBT described in section 1361(c)(2)(A)(v), each potential current beneficiary of the trust shall be treated as a shareholder, except that the trust shall be treated as the shareholder during any period in which there is no potential current beneficiary of the trust. If stock is held by a trust described in section 1361(c)(2)(A)(vi), the individual for whose benefit the trust was created shall be treated as the shareholder. See paragraph (h) of this section for special rules relating to trusts.

(2) *Special rules relating to stock owned by husband and wife.*—For purposes of paragraph (e)(1) of this section, stock owned by a husband and wife (or by either or both of their estates) is treated as if owned by one shareholder, regardless of the form in which they own the stock. For example, if husband and wife are owners of a subpart E trust, they will be treated as one individual. Both husband and wife must be U.S. citizens or residents, and a decedent spouse's estate must not be a foreign estate as defined in section 7701(a)(31). The treatment described in this paragraph (e)(2) will cease upon dissolution of the marriage for any reason other than death.

(3) *Special rules relating to stock owned by members of a family.*—(i) *In general.*—For purposes of paragraph (e)(1) of this section, stock owned by members of a family is treated as owned by one shareholder. Members of a family include a common ancestor, any lineal descendant of the common ancestor (without any generational limit), and any spouse (or former spouse) of the common ancestor or of any lineal descendants of the common ancestor. An individual shall not be considered to be a common ancestor if, on the applicable date, the individual is more than six generations removed from the youngest generation of shareholders who would be members of the family determined by deeming that individual as the common ancestor. For purposes of this six-generation test, a spouse (or former spouse) is treated as being of the same generation as the individual to whom the spouse is or was married. This test is applied on the latest of the date the election under section 1362(a) is made for the corporation, the earliest date that a member of the family (determined by deeming that individual as the common ancestor) holds stock in the corporation, or October 22, 2004. For this purpose, the date the election under section 1362(a) is made for the corporation is the effective date of the election, not the date it is signed or received by any person. The test is only applied as of the applicable date, and lineal descendants (and spouses) more than six generations removed from the common ancestor will be treated as members of the family even if they acquire stock in the corporation after that date. The members of a family are treated as one shareholder under this paragraph (e)(3) solely for purposes of section 1361(b)(1)(A), and not for any other purpose, whether under section 1361 or any other provision. Specifically, each member of the family who owns or is deemed to own stock must meet the requirements of sections 1361(b)(1)(B) and (C) (regarding permissible shareholders) and section 1362(a)(2) (regarding shareholder consents to an S corporation election). Although a person may be a member of more than one family under this paragraph (e)(3), each family (not all of whose members are also members of the other family) will be treated as one shareholder. For purposes of this paragraph (e)(3),

any legally adopted child of an individual, any child who is lawfully placed with an individual for legal adoption by that individual, and any eligible foster child of an individual (within the meaning of section 152(f)(1)(C)), shall be treated as a child of such individual by blood.

(ii) *Certain entities treated as members of a family.*—For purposes of this paragraph (e)(3), the estate or trust (described in section 1361(c)(2)(A)(ii) or (iii)) of a deceased member of the family will be considered to be a member of the family during the period in which the estate or such trust (if the trust is described in section 1361(c)(2)(A)(ii) or (iii)), holds stock in the S corporation. The members of the family also will include—

(A) In the case of an ESBT, each potential current beneficiary who is a member of the family;

(B) In the case of a QSST, the income beneficiary who makes the QSST election, if that income beneficiary is a member of the family;

(C) In the case of a trust created primarily to exercise the voting power of stock transferred to it, each beneficiary who is a member of the family;

(D) The individual for whose benefit a trust described in section 1361(c)(2)(A)(vi) was created, if that individual is a member of the family;

(E) The deemed owner of a trust described in section 1361(c)(2)(A)(i) if that deemed owner is a member of the family; and

(F) The owner of an entity disregarded as an entity separate from its owner under § 301.7701-3 of this chapter, if that owner is a member of the family.

(f) *Shareholder must be an individual or estate.*—Except as otherwise provided in paragraph (e)(1) of this section (relating to nominees), paragraph (h) of this section (relating to certain trusts), and, for taxable years beginning after December 31, 1997, section 1361(c)(6) (relating to certain exempt organizations), a corporation in which any shareholder is a corporation, partnership, or trust does not qualify as a small business corporation.

(g) *Nonresident alien shareholder.*—(1) *General rule.*—(i) A corporation having a shareholder who is a nonresident alien as defined in section 7701(b)(1)(B) does not qualify as a small business corporation. If a U.S. shareholder's spouse is a nonresident alien who has a current ownership interest (as opposed, for example, to a survivorship interest) in the stock of the corporation by reason of any applicable law, such as a state community property law or a foreign country's law, the corporation does not qualify as a small business corporation from the time the nonresident alien spouse acquires the interest in the stock. If a corporation's S election is inadvertently terminated as a result of a nonresident alien spouse being considered a shareholder, the corporation may request relief under section 1362(f).

(ii) The following examples illustrate this paragraph (g)(1)(i):

Example 1. In 1990, W, a U.S. citizen, married H, a citizen of a foreign country. At all times H is a nonresident alien under section 7701(b)(1)(B). Under the foreign country's law, all property acquired by a husband and wife during the existence of the marriage is community property and owned jointly by the husband and wife. In 1996 while residing in the foreign country, W formed X, a U.S. corporation, and X simultaneously filed an election to be an S corporation. X issued all of its outstanding stock in W's name. Under the foreign country's law, X's stock became the community property of and jointly owned by H and W. Thus, X does not meet the definition of a small business corporation and therefore could not file a valid S election because H, a nonresident alien, has a current interest in the stock.

Example 2. Assume the same facts as *Example 1,* except that in 1991, W and H filed a section 6013(g) election allowing them to file a joint U.S. tax return and causing H to be treated as a U.S. resident for purposes of chapters 1, 5, and 24 of the Internal Revenue Code. The section 6013(g) election applies to the taxable year for which made and to all subsequent taxable years until terminated. Because H is treated as a U.S. resident under section 6013(g), X does meet the definition of a small business corporation. Thus, the election filed by X to be an S corporation is valid.

(2) *Special rule for dual residents.*—[Reserved]

(h) *Special rules relating to trusts.*—(1) *General rule.*—In general, a trust is not a permitted small business corporation shareholder. However, except as provided in paragraph (h)(2) of this section, the following trusts are permitted shareholders:

(i) *Qualified subpart E trust.*—A trust all of which is treated (under subpart E, part I, subchapter J, chapter 1) as owned by an individual (whether or not the grantor) who is a citizen or resident of the United States (a qualified subpart E trust). This requirement applies only during the period that the trust holds S corporation stock.

(ii) *Subpart E trust ceasing to be a qualified subpart E trust after the death of deemed owner.*—A trust that was a qualified subpart E trust immediately before the death of the deemed owner and that continues in existence after the death of the deemed owner, but only for the 2-year period beginning on the day of the deemed owner's death. A trust is considered to continue in existence if the trust continues to hold the stock pursuant to the terms of the will or the trust agreement, or if the trust continues to hold the stock during a period reasonably necessary to wind up the affairs of the trust. See § 1.641(b)-3 for rules concerning the termination of trusts for federal income tax purposes.

(iii) *Electing qualified subchapter S trusts.*—A qualified subchapter S trust (QSST) that has a section 1361(d)(2) election in effect (an electing QSST). See paragraph (j) of this section for rules concerning QSSTs including the manner for making the section 1361(d)(2) election.

(iv) *Testamentary trusts.*—A trust (other than a qualified subpart E trust, an electing QSST, or an electing small business trust) to which S corporation stock is—

(A) Transferred pursuant to the terms of a will, but only for the 2-year period beginning on the day the stock is transferred to the trust except as otherwise provided in paragraph (h)(3)(i)(D) of this section; or

(B) Transferred pursuant to the terms of an electing trust as defined in § 1.645-1(b)(2) during the election period as defined in § 1.645-1(b)(6), or deemed to be distributed at the close of the last day of the election period pursuant to § 1.645-1(h)(1), but in each case only for the 2-year period beginning on the day the stock is transferred or deemed distributed to the trust except as otherwise provided in paragraph (h)(3)(i)(D) of this section.

(v) *Qualified voting trusts.*—A trust created primarily to exercise the voting power of S corporation stock transferred to it. To qualify as a voting trust for purposes of this section (a qualified voting trust), the beneficial owners must be treated as the owners of their respective portions of the trust under subpart E and the trust must have been created pursuant to a written trust agreement entered into by the shareholders, that—

(A) Delegates to one or more trustees the right to vote;

(B) Requires all distributions with respect to the stock of the corporation held by the trust to be paid to, or on behalf of, the beneficial owners of that stock;

(C) Requires title and possession of that stock to be delivered to those beneficial owners upon termination of the trust; and

(D) Terminates, under its terms or by state law, on or before a specific date or event.

(vi) *Electing small business trusts.*—An electing small business trust (ESBT) under section 1361(e). See paragraph (m) of this section for rules concerning ESBTs including the manner of making the election to be an ESBT under section 1361(e)(3).

(vii) *Individual retirement accounts.*—In the case of a corporation which is a bank (as defined in section 581) or a depository institution holding company (as defined in section 3(w)(1) of the Federal Deposit Insurance Act (12 U.S.C. 1813(w)(1)), a trust which constitutes an individual retirement account under section 408(a), including one designated as a Roth IRA under section 408A, but only to the extent of the stock held by such trust in such bank or company as of October 22, 2004. Individual retirement accounts (including Roth IRAs) are not otherwise eligible S corporation shareholders.

(2) *Foreign trust.*—For purposes of paragraph (h)(1) of this section, in any case where stock is held by a foreign trust as defined in section 7701(a)(31), the trust is considered to be the shareholder and is an ineligible shareholder. Thus, even if a foreign trust qualifies as a subpart E trust (e.g., a qualified voting trust), any corporation in which the trust holds stock does not qualify as a small business corporation.

(3) *Determination of shareholders.*—(i) *General rule.*—For purposes of paragraph (b) of this section (qualification as a small business corporation), and, except as provided in paragraph (h)(3)(ii) of this section, for purposes of sections 1366 (relating to the passthrough of items of income, loss, deduction, or credit), 1367 (relating to adjustments to basis of shareholder's stock), and 1368 (relating to distributions), the shareholder of S corporation stock held by a trust that is a permitted shareholder under paragraph (h)(1) of this section is determined as follows:

(A) If stock is held by a qualified subpart E trust, the deemed owner of the trust is treated as the shareholder.

(B) If stock is held by a trust defined in paragraph (h)(1)(ii) of this section, the estate of the deemed owner is generally treated as the shareholder as of the day of the deemed owner's death. However, if stock is held by such a trust in a community property state, the decedent's estate is the shareholder only of the portion of the trust included in the decedent's gross estate (and the surviving spouse continues to be the shareholder of the portion of the trust owned by that spouse under the applicable state's community property law). The estate ordinarily will cease to be treated as the shareholder upon the eariler of the transfer of the stock by the trust or the expiration of the 2-year period beginning on the day of the deemed owner's death. If the trust qualifies and becomes an electing QSST, the beneficiary and not the estate is treated as the shareholder as of the effective date of the QSST election, and the rules provided in paragraph (j)(7) of this section apply. If the trust qualifies and becomes an ESBT, the shareholders are determined under paragraphs (h)(3)(i)(F) and (h)(3)(ii) of this section as of the effective date of the ESBT election, and the rules provided in paragraph (m) of this section apply.

(C) If stock is held by an electing QSST, see paragraph (j)(7) of this section for the rules on who is treated as the shareholder.

(D) If stock is transferred or deemed distributed to a testamentary trust described in paragraph (h)(1)(iv) of this section (other than a qualified subpart E trust, an electing QSST, or an ESBT), the estate of the testator is treated as the shareholder until the earlier of the transfer of that stock by the trust of the expiration of the 2-year period beginning on the day that the stock is transferred or deemed distributed to the trust. If the trust qualifies and becomes an electing QSST, the beneficiary and not the estate is treated as the shareholder as of the effective date of the QSST election, and the rules provided in paragraph (j)(7) of this section apply. If the trust qualifies and becomes an ESBT, the shareholders are determined under paragraphs (h)(3)(i)(F) and (h)(3)(ii) of this section as of the effective date of the ESBT election, and the rules provided in paragraph (m) of this section apply.

(E) If stock is held by a qualified voting trust, each beneficial owner of the stock, as determined under subpart E, is treated as a shareholder with respect to the owner's proportionate share of the stock held by the trust.

(F) If S corporation stock is held by an ESBT, each potential current beneficiary is treated as a shareholder. However, if for any period there is no potential current beneficiary of the ESBT, the ESBT is treated as the shareholder during such period. See paragraph (m)(4) of this section for the definition of potential current beneficiary.

(G) If stock in an S corporation bank or depository institution holding company is held by an individual retirement account (including a Roth IRA) described in paragraph (h)(1)(vii) of this section, the individual for whose benefit the trust was created shall be treated as the shareholder.

(ii) *Exceptions.*—See § 1.641(c)-1 for the rules for the taxation of an ESBT. Solely for purposes of section 1366, 1367, and 1368 the shareholder of S corporation stock held by a trust is determined as follows—

(A) If stock is held by a trust as defined in paragraph (h)(1)(ii) of this section (other than an electing QSST or an ESBT), the trust is treated as the shareholder. If the trust continues to own the stock after the expiration of the 2-year period, the corporation's S election will terminate unless the trust is otherwise a permitted shareholder.

(B) If stock is transferred or deemed distributed to a testamentary trust described in paragraph (h)(1)(iv) of this section (other than a qualified subpart E trust, an electing QSST, or an ESBT), the trust is treated as the shareholder. If the trust continues to own the stock after the expiration of the 2-year period, the corporation's S election will terminate unless the trust otherwise qualifies as a permitted shareholder.

(i) [Reserved]

(j) *Qualified subchapter S trust.*—(1) *Definition.*—A qualified subchapter S trust (QSST) is a trust (whether intervivos or testamentary), other than a foreign trust described in section 7701(a)(31), that satisfies the following requirements:

(i) All of the income (within the meaning of § 1.643(b)-1) of the trust is distributed (or is required to be distributed) currently to one individual who is a citizen or resident of the United States. For purposes of the preceding sentence, unless otherwise provided under local law (including pertinent provisions of the governing instrument that are effective under local law), income of the trust includes distributions to the trust from the S corporation for the taxable year in question, but does not include the trust's pro rata share of the S corporation's items of income, loss, deduction, or credit determined under section 1366. See §§ 1.651(a)-2(a) and 1.663(b)-1(a) for rules relating to the determination of whether all of the income of a trust is distributed (or is required to be distributed) currently. If under the terms of the trust income is not required to be distributed currently, the trustee may elect under section 663(b) to consider a distribution made in the first 65 days of a taxable year as made on the last day of the preceding taxable year. See section 663(b) and § 1.663(b)-2 for rules on the time and manner for making the election. The income distribution requirement must be satisfied for the taxable year of the trust or for that part of the trust's taxable year during which it holds S corporation stock.

(ii) The terms of the trust must require that—

(A) During the life of the current income beneficiary, there will be only one income beneficiary of the trust;

(B) Any corpus distributed during the life of the current income beneficiary may be distributed only to that income beneficiary;

(C) The current income beneficiary's income interest in the trust will terminate on the earlier of that income beneficiary's death or the termination of the trust; and

(D) Upon termination of the trust during the life of the current income beneficiary, the trust will distribute all of its assets to that income beneficiary.

(iii) The terms of the trust must satisfy the requirements of paragraph (j)(1)(ii) of this section from the date the QSST election is made or from the effective date of the QSST election, whichever is earlier, throughout the entire period that the current income beneficiary and any successor income beneficiary is the income beneficiary of the trust. If the terms of the trust do not preclude the possibility that any of the requirements stated in paragraph (j)(1)(ii) of this section will not be met, the trust will not qualify as a QSST. For example, if the terms of the trust are silent with respect to corpus distributions, and distributions of corpus to a person other than the current income beneficiary are permitted under local law during the life of the current income beneficiary, then the terms of the trust do not preclude the possibility that corpus may be distributed to a person other than the current income beneficiary and, therefore, the trust is not a QSST.

(2) *Special rules.*—(i) If a husband and wife are income beneficiaries of the same trust, the husband and wife file a joint return, and each is a U.S. citizen or resident, the husband and wife are treated as one beneficiary for purposes of paragraph (j) of this section. If a husband and wife are treated by the preceding sentence as one beneficiary, any action required by this section to be taken by an income beneficiary requires joinder of both of them. For example, each spouse must sign the QSST election, continue to be a U.S. citizen or resident, and continue to file joint returns for the entire period that the QSST election is in effect.

(ii)(A) *Terms of the trust and applicable local law.*—The determination of whether the terms of a trust meet all of the requirements under paragraph (j)(1)(ii) of this section depends upon the terms of the trust instrument and the applicable local law. For example, a trust whose governing instrument provides that A is the sole income beneficiary of the trust is, nevertheless, considered to have two income beneficiaries if, under the applicable local law, A and B are considered to be the income beneficiaries of the trust.

(B) *Legal obligation to support.*—If under local law a distribution to the income beneficiary is in satisfaction of the grantor's legal obligation of support to that income beneficiary, the trust will not qualify as a QSST as of the date of distribution because, under section 677(b), if income is distributed, the grantor will be treated as the owner of the ordinary income portion of the trust or, if trust corpus is distributed, the grantor will be treated as a beneficiary under section 662. See § 1.677(b)-1 for rules on the treatment of trusts for support and § 1.662(a)-4 for rules concerning amounts used in discharge of a legal obligation.

(C) *Example.*—The following example illustrates the rules of paragraph (j)(2)(ii)(B) of this section:

Example. F creates a trust for the benefit of F's minor child, G. Under the terms of the trust, all income is payable to G until the trust terminates on the earlier of G's attaining age 35 or G's death. Upon the termination of the trust, all corpus must be distributed to G or G's estate. The trust includes all of the provisions prescribed by section 1361(d)(3)(A) and paragraph (j)(1)(ii) of this section, but does not preclude the trustee from making income distributions to G that will be in satisfaction of F's legal obligation to support G. Under the applicable local law, distributions of trust income to G will satisfy F's legal obligation to support G. If the trustee distributes income to G in satisfaction of F's legal obligation to support G, the trust will not qualify as a QSST because F will be treated as the owner of the ordinary income portion of the trust. Further, the trust will not be a qualified subpart E trust because the trust will be subject to tax on the income allocable to corpus.

(iii) If, under the terms of the trust, a person (including the income beneficiary) has a special power to appoint, during the life of the income beneficiary, trust income or corpus to any person other than the current income beneficiary, the trust will not qualify as a QSST. However, if the power of appointment results in the grantor being treated as the owner of the entire trust under the rules of subpart E, the trust may be a permitted shareholder under section 1361(c)(2)(A)(i) and paragraph (h)(1)(i) of this section.

(iv) If the terms of a trust or local law do not preclude the current income beneficiary from transferring the beneficiary's interest in the trust or do not preclude a person other than the current income beneficiary named in the trust instrument from being treated as a beneficiary of the trust under § 1.643(c)-1, the trust will still qualify as a QSST. However, if the income beneficiary transfers or assigns the income interest or a portion of the income interest to another, the trust may no longer qualify as a QSST, depending on the facts and circumstances, because any transferee of the current income beneficiary's income interest and any person treated as a beneficiary under § 1.643(c)-1 will be treated as a current income beneficiary for purposes of paragraph (j)(1)(ii) of this section and the trust may no longer meet the QSST requirements.

(v) If the terms of the trust do not preclude a person other than the current income beneficiary named in the trust instrument from being awarded an interest in the trust by the order of a court, the trust will qualify as a QSST assuming the trust meets the requirements of paragraphs (j)(1)(i) and (ii) of this section. However, if as a result of such court order, the trust no longer meets the QSST requirements, the trust no longer qualifies as a QSST and the corporation's S election will terminate.

(vi) A trust may qualify as a QSST even though a person other than the current income beneficiary is treated under subpart E as the owner of a part or all of that portion of a trust which does not consist of the S corporation stock, provided the entire trust meets the QSST requirements stated in paragraphs (j)(1)(i) and (ii) of this section.

(3) *Separate and independent shares of a trust.*—For purposes of sections 1361(c) and (d), a substantially separate and independent share of a trust, within the meaning of section 663(c) and the regulations thereunder, is treated as a separate trust. For a separate share which holds S corporation stock to qualify as a QSST, the terms of the trust applicable to that separate share must meet the QSST requirements stated in paragraphs (j)(1)(i) and (ii) of this section.

(4) *Qualified terminable interest property trust.*—If property, including S corporation stock, or stock of a corporation that intends to make an S election, is transferred to a trust and an election is made to treat all or a portion of the transferred property as qualified terminable interest property (QTIP) under section 2056(b)(7), the income beneficiary may make the QSST election if the trust meets the requirements set out in paragraphs (j)(1)(i) and (ii) of this section. However, if property is transferred to a QTIP trust under section 2523(f), the income beneficiary may not make a QSST election even if the trust meets the requirements set forth in paragraph (j)(1)(ii) of this section because the grantor would be treated as the owner of the income portion of the trust under section 677. In addition, if property is transferred to a QTIP trust under section 2523(f), the trust does not qualify as a permitted shareholder under section 1361(c)(2)(A)(i) and paragraph (h)(1)(i) of this section (a qualified subpart E trust), unless under the terms of the QTIP trust, the grantor is treated as the owner of the entire trust under sections 671 to 677. If the grantor ceases to be the income beneficiary's spouse, the trust may qualify as a QSST if it otherwise satisfies the requirements under paragraphs (j)(1)(i) and (ii) of this section.

(5) *Ceasing to meet the QSST requirements.*—If a QSST for which an election under section 1361(d)(2) has been made (as described in paragraph (j)(6) of this section) ceases to meet any of the requirements specified in paragraph (j)(1)(ii) of this section, the provisions of this paragraph (j) will cease to apply as of the first day on which that requirement ceases to be met. If such a trust ceases to meet the income distribution requirement specified in paragraph (j)(1)(i) of this section, but continues to meet all of the requirements in paragraph (j)(1)(ii) of this section, the provisions of this paragraph (j) will cease to apply as of the first day of the first taxable year beginning after the first taxable year for which the trust ceased to meet the income distribution requirement of paragraph (j)(1)(i) of this section. If a corporation's S election is inadvertently terminated as a result of a trust ceasing to meet the QSST requirements, the corporation may request relief under section 1362(f).

(6) *Qualified subchapter S trust election.*—(i) *In general.*—This paragraph (j)(6) applies to the election provided in section 1361(d)(2) (the QSST election) to treat a QSST (as defined in paragraph (j)(1) of this section) as a trust described in section 1361(c)(2)(A)(i), and thus a permitted shareholder. This election must be made separately with respect to each corporation whose stock is held by the trust. The QSST election does not itself constitute an election as to the status of the corporation; the corporation must make the election provided by section 1362(a) to be an S corporation. Until the effective date of a corporation's S election, the beneficiary is not treated as the owner of the stock of the corporation for purposes of section 678. Any action required by this paragraph (j) to be taken by a person who is under a legal disability by reason of age may be taken by that person's guardian or other legal representative, or if there be none, by that person's natural or adoptive parent.

* * *

(7) *Treatment as shareholder.*—(i) The income beneficiary who makes the QSST election and is treated (for purposes of section

678(a)) as the owner of that portion of the trust that consists of S corporation stock is treated as the shareholder for purposes of sections 1361(b)(1), 1366, 1367, and 1368.

(ii) If, upon the death of an income beneficiary, the trust continues in existence, continues to hold S corporation stock but no longer satisfies the QSST requirements, is not a qualified subpart E trust, and does not qualify as an ESBT, then, solely for purposes of section 1361(b)(1), as of the date of the income beneficiary's death, the estate of that income beneficiary is treated as the shareholder of the S corporation with respect to which the income beneficiary made the QSST election. The estate ordinarily will cease to be treated as the shareholder for purposes of section 1361(b)(1) upon the earlier of the transfer of that stock by the trust or the expiration of the 2-year period beginning on the day of the income beneficiary's death. During the period that the estate is treated as the shareholder for purposes of section 1361(b)(1), the trust is treated as the shareholder for purposes of sections 1366, 1367, and 1368. If, after the 2-year period, the trust continues to hold S corporation stock and does not otherwise qualify as a permitted shareholder, the corporation's S election terminates. If the termination is inadvertent, the corporation may request relief under section 1362(f).

(8) *Coordination with grantor trust rules.*—If a valid QSST election is made, the income beneficiary is treated as the owner, for purposes of section 678(a), of that portion of the trust that consists of the stock of the S corporation for which the QSST election was made. However, solely for purposes of applying the preceding sentence to a QSST, an income beneficiary who is a deemed section 678 owner only by reason of section 1361(d)(1) will not be treated as the owner of the S corporation stock in determining and attributing the federal income tax consequences of a disposition of the stock by the QSST. For example, if the disposition is a sale, the QSST election terminates as to the stock sold and any gain or loss recognized on the sale will be that of the trust, not the income beneficiary. Similarly, if a QSST distributes its S corporation stock to the income beneficiary, the QSST election terminates as to the distributed stock and the consequences of the distribution are determined by reference to the status of the trust apart from the income beneficiary's terminating ownership status under sections 678 and 1361(d)(1). The portions of the trust other than the portion consisting of S corporation stock are subject to subparts A through D of subchapter J of chapter 1, except as otherwise required by subpart E of the Internal Revenue Code. However, solely for purposes of applying sections 465 and 469 to the income beneficiary, a disposition of S corporation stock by a QSST shall be treated as a disposition by the income beneficiary.

(9) *Successive income beneficiary.*—(i) If the income beneficiary of a QSST who made a QSST election dies, each successive income beneficiary of that trust is treated as consenting to the election unless a successive income beneficiary affirmatively refuses to consent to the election. For this purpose, the term *successive income beneficiary* includes a beneficiary of a trust whose interest is a separate share within the meaning of section 663(c), but does not include any beneficiary of a trust that is created upon the death of the income beneficiary of the QSST and which is a new trust under local law.

(ii) The application of this paragraph (j)(9) is illustrated by the following examples:

Example 1. Shares of stock in Corporation X, an S corporation, are held by Trust A, a QSST for which a QSST election was made. B is the sole income beneficiary of Trust A. On B's death, under the terms of Trust A, J and K become the current income beneficiaries of Trust A. J and K each hold a separate and independent share of Trust A within the meaning of section 663(c). J and K are successive income beneficiaries of Trust A, and they are treated as consenting to B's QSST election.

Example 2. Assume the same facts as in *Example 1,* except that on B's death, under the terms of Trust A and local law, Trust A terminates and the principal is to be divided equally and held in newly created Trust B and Trust C. The sole income beneficiaries of Trust B and Trust C are J and K, respectively. Because Trust A terminated, J and K are not successive income beneficiaries of Trust A. J and K must make QSST elections for their respective trusts to qualify as QSSTs, if they qualify. The result is the same whether or not the trustee of Trusts B and C is the same as the trustee of trust A.

* * *

(k)(1) *Examples.*—The provisions of paragraphs (h) and (j) of this section are illustrated by the following examples in which it is assumed that all noncorporate persons are citizens or residents of the United States:

Example 1. (i) *Terms of the trust.* In 1996, A and A's spouse, B, created an intervivos trust and each funded the trust with separately owned stock of an S corporation. Under the terms of the trust, A and B designated themselves as the income beneficiaries and each, individually, retained the power to amend or revoke the trust with respect to the trust assets attributable to their respective trust contributions. Upon A's death, the trust is to be divided into two separate parts; one part attributable to the assets A contributed to the trust and one part attributable to B's contributions. Before the trust is divided, and during the administration of A's estate, all trust income is payable to B. The part of the trust attributable to B's contributions is to continue in trust under the terms of which B is designated as the sole income beneficiary and retains the power to amend or revoke the trust. The part attributable to A's contributions is to be divided into two separate trusts both of which have B as the sole income beneficiary for life. One trust, the *Credit Shelter Trust,* is to be funded with an amount that can pass free of estate tax by reason of A's available estate tax unified credit. The terms of the Credit Shelter Trust meet the requirements of section 1361(d)(3) as a QSST. The balance of the property passes to a Marital Trust, the terms of which satisfy the requirements of section 1361(d)(3) as a QSST and section 2056(b)(7) as QTIP. The appropriate fiduciary under § 20.2056(b)-7(b)(3) is directed to make an election under section 2056(b)(7).

(ii) *Results after deemed owner's death.* On February 3, 1997, A dies and the portion of the trust assets attributable to A's contributions including the S stock contributed by A, is includible in A's gross estate under sections 2036 and 2038. During the administration of A's estate, the trust holds the S corporation stock. Under section 1361(c)(2)(B)(ii), A's estate is treated as the shareholder of the S corporation stock that was included in A's gross estate for purposes of section 1361(b)(1); however, for purposes of sections 1366, 1367, and 1368, the trust is treated as the shareholder. B's part of the trust continues to be a qualified subpart E trust of which B is the owner under sections 676 and 677. B, therefore, continues to be treated as the shareholder of the S corporation stock in that portion of the trust. On May 13, 1997, during the continuing administration of A's estate, the trust is divided into separate trusts in accordance with the terms of the trust instrument. The S corporation stock that was included in A's gross estate is distributed to the Marital Trust and to the Credit Shelter Trust. A's estate will cease to be treated as the shareholder of the S corporation under section 1361(c)(2)(B)(ii) on May 13, 1997 (the date on which the S corporation stock was transferred to the trusts). B, as the income beneficiary of the Marital Trust and the Credit Shelter Trust, must make the QSST election for each trust by July 28, 1997 (the end of the 16-day-and-2-month period beginning on the date the estate ceases to be treated as a shareholder) to have the trusts become permitted shareholders of the S corporation.

Example 2. (i) *Qualified subpart E trust as shareholder.* In 1997, A, an individual established a trust and transferred to the trust A's shares of stock of Corporation M, an S corporation. A has the power to revoke the entire trust. The terms of the trust require that all income be paid to B and otherwise meet the requirements of a QSST under section 1361(d)(3). The trust will continue in existence after A's death. The trust is a qualified subpart E trust described in section 1361(c)(2)(A)(i) during A's life, and A (not the trust) is treated as the shareholder for purposes of sections 1361(b)(1), 1366, 1367, and 1368.

(ii) *Trust ceasing to be a qualified subpart E trust on deemed owner's death.* Assume the same facts as paragraph (i) of this *Example 2,* except that A dies without having exercised A's power to revoke. Upon A's death, the trust ceases to be a qualified subpart E trust described in section 1361(c)(2)(A)(i). A's estate (and not the trust) is treated as the shareholder for purposes of section 1361(b)(1). A's estate will cease to be treated as the shareholder for purposes of section 1361(b)(1) upon the earlier of the transfer of the Corporation M stock by the trust (other than to A's estate), the expiration of the 2-year period beginning on the day of A's death, or the effective date of a QSST or ESBT election if the trust qualifies as a QSST or ESBT. However, until that time, because the trust continues in existence after A's death and will receive any distributions with respect to the stock it holds, the trust is treated as the shareholder for purposes of sections 1366, 1367, and 1368. If no QSST or ESBT election is made effective upon the expiration of the 2-year period, the corporation ceases to be an S corporation, but the trust continues as the shareholder of a C corporation.

(iii) *Trust continuing to be a qualified subpart E trust on deemed owner's death.* Assume the same facts as paragraph (ii) of this *Example 2,* except that the terms of the trust also provide that if A does not exercise the power to revoke before A's death, B will have the sole power to withdraw all trust property at any time after A's death. The trust continues to qualify as a qualified subpart E trust after A's death because, upon A's death, B is deemed to be the owner of the entire trust under section 678. Because the trust does not cease to be a qualified subpart E trust upon A's death, B (and not A's estate) is treated as the shareholder for purposes of sections 1361(b)(1), 1366, 1367, and 1368. Since the trust qualifies as a QSST, B may make a protective QSST election under paragraph (j)(6)(iv) of this section.

Example 3. (i) *2-year rule under section 1361(c)(2)(A)(ii) and (iii).* F owns stock of Corporation P, an S corporation. In addition, F is the deemed owner of a qualified subpart E trust that holds stock in Corporation O, an S corporation. F dies on July 1, 2003. The trust continues in existence after F's death but is no longer a qualified subpart E trust. On August 1, 2003, F's shares of stock in Corporation P are transferred to the trust pursuant to the terms of F's will. Because the stock of Corporation P was not held by the trust when F died, section 1361(c)(2)(A)(ii) does not apply with respect to that stock. Under section 1361(c)(2)(A)(iii), the last day on which the trust could be treated as a permitted shareholder of Corporation P is July 31, 2005 (that is, the last day of the 2-year period that begins on the date of the transfer from the estate to the trust). With respect to the shares of stock in Corporation O held by the trust at the time of F's death, section 1361(c)(2)(A)(ii) applies and the last day on which the trust could be treated as a permitted shareholder of Corporation O is June 30, 2005 (that is, the last day of the 2-year period that begins on the date of F's death).

(ii) *Section 645 electing trust and successor trust.* Assume the same facts as in paragraph (i) of this *Example 3,* except that F's trust is a qualified revocable trust for which a valid section 645 election is made on October 1, 2003 (electing trust). Because under section 645 the electing trust is treated and taxed for purposes of subtitle A of the Code as part of F's estate, the trust may continue to hold the O stock pursuant to §1361(b)(1)(B), without causing the termination of Corporation O's S election, for the duration of the section 645 election period. However, on January 1, 2004, during the election period, the shares of stock in Corporation O are transferred pursuant to the terms of the electing trust to a successor trust. Because the successor trust satisfies the definition of a testamentary trust under paragraph (h)(1)(iv) of this section, the successor trust is a permitted shareholder until the earlier of the expiration of the 2-year period beginning on January 1, 2004, or the effective date of a QSST or ESBT election for the successor trust.

* * *

(l) *Classes of stock.*—(1) *General rule.*—A corporation that has more than one class of stock does not qualify as a small business corporation. Except as provided in paragraph (l)(4) of this section (relating to instruments, obligations, or arrangements treated as a second class of stock), a corporation is treated as having only one class of stock if all outstanding shares of stock of the corporation confer identical rights to distribution and liquidation proceeds. Differences in voting rights among shares of stock of a corporation are disregarded in determining whether a corporation has more than one class of stock. Thus, if all shares of stock of an S corporation have identical rights to distribution and liquidation proceeds, the corporation may have voting and nonvoting common stock, a class of stock that may vote only on certain issues, irrevocable proxy agreements, or groups of shares that differ with respect to rights to elect members of the board of directors.

(2) *Determination of whether stock confers identical rights to distribution and liquidation proceeds.*—(i) *In general.*—The determination of whether all outstanding shares of stock confer identical rights to distribution and liquidation proceeds is made based on the corporate charter, articles of incorporation, bylaws, applicable state law, and binding agreements relating to distribution and liquidation proceeds (collectively, the governing provisions). A commercial contractual agreement, such as a lease, employment agreement, or loan agreement, is not a binding agreement relating to distribution and liquidation proceeds and thus is not a governing provision unless a principal purpose of the agreement is to circumvent the one class of stock requirement of section 1361(b)(1)(D) and this paragraph (l). Although a corporation is not treated as having more than one class of stock so long as the governing provisions provide for identical distribution and liquidation rights, any distributions (including actual, constructive, or deemed distributions) that differ in timing or amount are to be given appropriate tax effect in accordance with the facts and circumstances.

(ii) *State law requirements for payment and withholding of income tax.*—State laws may require a corporation to pay or withhold state income taxes on behalf of some or all of the corporation's shareholders. Such laws are disregarded in determining whether all outstanding shares of stock of the corporation confer identical rights to distribution and liquidation proceeds, within the meaning of paragraph (l)(1) of this section, provided that, when the constructive distributions resulting from the payment or withholding of taxes by the corporation are taken into account, the outstanding shares confer identical rights to distribution and liquidation proceeds. A difference in timing between the constructive distributions and the actual distributions to the other shareholders does not cause the corporation to be treated as having more than one class of stock.

(iii) *Buy-sell and redemption agreements.*—(A) *In general.*—Buy-sell agreements among shareholders, agreements restricting the transferability of stock, and redemption agreements are disregarded in determining whether a corporation's outstanding shares of stock confer identical distribution and liquidation rights unless—

(1) A principal purpose of the agreement is to circumvent the one class of stock requirement of section 1361(b)(1)(D) and this paragraph (l), and

(2) The agreement establishes a purchase price that, at the time the agreement is entered into, is significantly in excess of or below the fair market value of the stock.

Agreements that provide for the purchase or redemption of stock at book value or at a price between fair market value and book value are not considered to establish a price that is significantly in excess of or below the fair market value of the stock and, thus, are disregarded in determining whether the outstanding shares of stock confer identical rights. For purposes of this paragraph (l)(2)(iii)(A), a good faith determination of fair market value will be respected unless it can be shown that the value was substantially in error and the determination of the value was not performed with reasonable diligence. Although an agreement may be disregarded in determining whether shares of stock confer identical distribution and liquidation rights, payments pursuant to the agreement may have income or transfer tax consequences.

(B) *Exception for certain agreements.*—Bona fide agreements to redeem or purchase stock at the time of death, divorce, disability, or termination of employment are disregarded in determining whether a corporation's shares of stock confer identical rights. In addition, if stock that is substantially nonvested (within the meaning of § 1.83-3(b)) is treated as outstanding under these regulations, the forfeiture provisions that cause the stock to be substantially nonvested are disregarded. Furthermore, the Commissioner may provide by Revenue Ruling or other published guidance that other types of bona fide agreements to redeem or purchase stock are disregarded.

(C) *Safe harbors for determinations of book value.*—A determination of book value will be respected if—

(1) The book value is determined in accordance with Generally Accepted Accounting Principles (including permitted optional adjustments); or

(2) The book value is used for any substantial nontax purpose.

(iv) *Distributions that take into account varying interests in stock during a taxable year.*—A governing provision does not, within the meaning of paragraph (l)(2)(i) of this section, alter the rights to liquidation and distribution proceeds conferred by an S corporation's stock merely because the governing provision provides that, as a result of a change in stock ownership, distributions in a taxable year are to be made on the basis of the shareholders' varying interests in the S corporation's income in the current or immediately preceding taxable year. If distributions pursuant to the provision are not made within a reasonable time after the close of the taxable year in which the varying interests occur, the distributions may be recharacterized depending on the facts and circumstances, but will not result in a second class of stock.

(v) *Special rule for section 338(h)(10) elections.*—If the shareholders of an S corporation sell their stock in a transaction for which an election is made under section 338(h)(10) and § 1.338(h)(10)-1, the receipt of varying amounts per share by the shareholders will not cause the S corporation to have more than one class of stock, provided that the varying amounts are determined in arm's length negotiations with the purchaser.

(vi) *Examples.*—The application of paragraph (l)(2) of this section may be illustrated by the following examples. In each of the examples, the S corporation requirements of section 1361 are satisfied except as otherwise stated, the corporation has in effect an S election under section 1362, and the corporation has only the shareholders described.

Example 1. Determination of whether stock confers identical rights to distribution and liquidation proceeds. (i) The law of State A requires that permission be obtained from the State Commissioner of Corporations before stock may be issued by a corporation. The Commissioner grants permission to S, a corporation, to issue its stock subject to the restriction that any person who is issued stock in exchange for property, and not cash, must waive all rights to receive distributions until the shareholders who contributed cash for stock have received distributions in the amount of their cash contributions.

(ii) The condition imposed by the Commissioner pursuant to state law alters the rights to distribution and liquidation proceeds conferred by the outstanding stock of S so that those rights are not identical. Accordingly, under paragraph (l)(2)(i) of this section, S is treated as having more than one class of stock and does not qualify as a small business corporation.

Example 2. Distributions that differ in timing. (i) S, a corporation, has two equal shareholders, A and B. Under S's bylaws, A and B are entitled to equal distributions. S distributes $50,000 to A in the current year, but does not distribute $50,000 to B until one year later. The circumstances indicate that the difference in timing did not occur by reason of a binding agreement relating to distribution or liquidation proceeds.

(ii) Under paragraph (l) (2) (i) of this section, the difference in timing of the distributions to A and B does not cause S to be treated as having more than one class of stock. However, section 7872 or other recharacterization principles may apply to determine the appropriate tax consequences.

Example 3. Treatment of excessive compensation. (i) S, a corporation, has two equal shareholders, C and D, who are each employed by S and have binding employment agreements with S. The compensation paid by S to C under C's employment agreement is reasonable. The compensation paid by S to D under D's employment agreement, however, is found to be excessive. The facts and circumstances do not reflect that a principal purpose of D's employment agreement is to circumvent the one class of stock requirement of section 1361 (b) (1) (D) and this paragraph (l).

(ii) Under paragraph (l) (2) (i) of this section, the employment agreements are not governing provisions. Accordingly, S is not treated as having more than one class of stock by reason of the employment agreements, even though S is not allowed a deduction for the excessive compensation paid to D.

Example 4. Agreement to pay fringe benefits. (i) S, a corporation, is required under binding agreements to pay accident and health insurance premiums on behalf of certain of its employees who are also shareholders. Different premium amounts are paid by S for each employee-shareholder. The facts and circumstances do not reflect that a principal purpose of the agreements is to circumvent the one class of stock requirement of section 1361 (b) (1) (D) and this paragraph (1).

(ii) Under paragraph (l) (2) (i) of this section, the agreements are not governing provisions. Accordingly, S is not treated as having more than one class of stock by reason of the agreements. In addition, S is not treated as having more than one class of stock by reason of the payment of fringe benefits.

* * *

Example 8. Redemption agreements. (i) F, G, and H are shareholders of S, a corporation. F is also an employee of S. By agreement, S is to redeem F's shares on the termination of F's employment.

(ii) On these facts, under paragraph (l) (2) (iii) (B) of this section, the agreement is disregarded in determining whether all outstanding shares of S's stock confer identical rights to distribution and liquidation proceeds.

Example 9. Analysis of redemption agreements. (i) J, K, and L are shareholders of S, a corporation. L is also an employee of S. L's shares were not issued to L in connection with the performance of services. By agreement, S is to redeem L's shares for an amount significantly below their fair market value on the termination of L's employment or if S's sales fall below certain levels.

(ii) Under paragraph (l) (2) (iii) (B) of this section, the portion of the agreement providing for redemption of L's stock on termination of employment is disregarded. Under paragraph (l) (2) (iii) (A), the portion of the agreement providing for redemption of L's stock if S's sales fall below certain levels is disregarded unless a principal purpose of that portion of the agreement is to circumvent the one class of stock requirement of section 1361 (b) (1) (D) and this paragraph (l).

(3) *Stock taken into account.*—Except as provided in paragraphs (b) (3), (4), and (5) of this section (relating to restricted stock, deferred compensation plans, and straight debt), in determining whether all outstanding shares of stock confer identical rights to distribution and liquidation proceeds, all outstanding shares of stock of a corporation are taken into account. For example, substantially nonvested stock with respect to which an election under section 83 (b) has been made is taken into account in determining whether a corporation has a second class of stock, and such stock is not treated as a second class of stock if the stock confers rights to distribution and liquidation proceeds that are identical, within the meaning of paragraph (l) (1) of this section, to the rights conferred by the other outstanding shares of stock.

(4) *Other instruments, obligations, or arrangements treated as a second class of stock.*—(i) *In general.*—Instruments, obligations, or arrangements are not treated as a second class of stock for purposes of this paragraph (l) unless they are described in paragraphs (l) (4) (ii) or (iii) of this section. However, in no event are instruments, obligations, or arrangements described in paragraph (b) (4) of this section (relating to deferred compensation plans), paragraphs (l) (4) (iii) (B) and (C) of this section (relating to the exceptions and safe harbor for options), paragraph (l) (4) (ii) (B) of this section (relating to the safe harbors for certain short-term unwritten advances and proportionally-held debt), or paragraph (l) (5) of this section (relating to the safe harbor for straight debt), treated as a second class of stock for purposes of this paragraph (l).

(ii) *Instruments, obligations, or arrangements treated as equity under general principles.—(A) In general.*—Except as provided in paragraph (l) (4) (i) of this section, any instrument, obligation, or arrangement issued by a corporation (other than outstanding shares of stock described in paragraph (l) (3) of this section), regardless of whether designated as debt, is treated as a second class of stock of the corporation—

(1) If the instrument, obligation, or arrangement constitutes equity or otherwise results in the holder being treated as the owner of stock under general principles of Federal tax law; and

(2) A principal purpose of issuing or entering into the instrument, obligation, or arrangement is to circumvent the rights to distribution or liquidation proceeds conferred by the outstanding shares of stock or to circumvent the limitation on eligible shareholders contained in paragraph (b)(1) of this section.

(B) *Safe harbor for certain short-term unwritten advances and proportionately held obligations.—(1) Short-term unwritten advances.*—Unwritten advances from a shareholder that do not exceed $10,000 in the aggregate at any time during the taxable year of the corporation, are treated as debt by the parties, and are expected to be repaid within a reasonable time are not treated as a second class of stock for that taxable year, even if the advances are considered equity under general principles of Federal tax law. The failure of an unwritten advance to meet this safe harbor will not result in a second class of stock unless the advance is considered equity under paragraph (l)(4)(ii)(A)(*1*) of this section and a principal purpose of the advance is to circumvent the rights of the outstanding shares of stock or the limitation on eligible shareholders under paragraph (l)(4)(ii)(A)(*2*) of this section.

(2) Proportionately-held obligations.—Obligations of the same class that are considered equity under general principles of Federal tax law, but are owned solely by the owners of, and in the same proportion as, the outstanding stock of the corporation, are not treated as a second class of stock. Furthermore, an obligation or obligations owned by the sole shareholder of a corporation are always held proportionately to the corporation's outstanding stock. The obligations that are considered equity that do not meet this safe harbor will not result in a second class of stock unless a principal purpose of the obligations is to circumvent the rights of the outstanding shares of stock or the limitation on eligible shareholders under paragraph (l)(4)(ii)(A)(*2*) of this section.

(iii) *Certain call options, warrants or similar instruments.*—(A) *In general.*—Except as otherwise provided in this paragraph (l)(4)(iii), a call option, warrant, or similar instrument (collectively, call option) issued by a corporation is treated as a second class of stock of the corporation if, taking into account all the facts and circumstances, the call option is substantially certain to be exercised (by the holder or a potential transferee) and has a strike price substantially below the fair market value of the underlying stock on the date that the call option is issued, transferred by a person who is an eligible shareholder under paragraph (b)(1) of this section to a person who is not an eligible shareholder under paragraph (b)(1) of this section, or materially modified. For purposes of this paragraph (l)(4)(iii), if an option is issued in connection with a loan and the time period in which the option can be exercised is extended in connection with (and consistent with) a modification of the terms of the loan, the extension of the time period in which the option may be exercised is not considered a material modification. In addition, a call option does not have a strike price substantially below fair market value if the price at the time of exercise cannot, pursuant to the terms of the instrument, be substantially below the fair market value of the underlying stock at the time of exercise.

(B) *Certain exceptions.—(1)* A call option is not treated as a second class of stock for purposes of this paragraph (l) if it is issued to a person that is actively and regularly engaged in the business of lending and issued in connection with a commercially reasonable loan to the corporation. This paragraph (l)(4)(iii)(B)(*1*) continues to apply if the call option is transferred with the loan (or if a portion of the call option is transferred with a corresponding portion of the loan). However, if the call option is transferred without a corresponding portion of the loan, this paragraph (l)(4)(iii)(B)(*1*) ceases to apply. Upon that transfer, the call option is tested under paragraph (l)(4)(iii)(A) (notwithstanding anything in that paragraph to the contrary) if, but for this paragraph, the call option would have been treated as a second class of stock on the date it was issued.

(2) A call option that is issued to an individual who is either an employee or an independent contractor in connection with the performance of services for the corporation or a related corporation (and that is not excessive by reference to the services performed) is not treated as a second class of stock for purposes of this paragraph (l) if—

(i) The call option is nontransferable within the meaning of § 1.83-3(d); and

(ii) The call option does not have a readily ascertainable fair market value as defined in § 1.83-7(b) at the time the option is issued.

If the call option becomes transferable, this paragraph (l)(4)(iii)(B)(*2*) ceases to apply. Solely for purposes of this paragraph (l)(4)(iii)(B)(*2*), a corporation is related to the issuing corporation if more than 50 percent of the total voting power and total value of its stock is owned by the issuing corporation.

(3) The Commissioner may provide other exceptions by Revenue Ruling or other published guidance.

(C) *Safe harbor for certain options.*—A call option is not treated as a second class of stock if, on the date the call option is issued, transferred by a person who is an eligible shareholder under paragraph (b) (1) of this section to a person who is not an eligible shareholder under paragraph (b) (1) of this section, or materially modified, the strike price of the call option is at least 90 percent of the fair market value of the underlying stock on that date. For purposes of this paragraph (l) (4) (iii) (C), a good faith determination of fair market value by the corporation will be respected unless it can be shown that the value was substantially in error and the determination of the value was not performed with reasonable diligence to obtain a fair value. Failure of an option to meet this safe harbor will not necessarily result in the option being treated as a second class of stock.

(iv) *Convertible debt.*—A convertible debt instrument is considered a second class of stock if—

(A) It would be treated as a second class of stock under paragraph (l) (4) (ii) of this section (relating to instruments, obligations, or arrangements treated as equity under general principles); or

(B) It embodies rights equivalent to those of a call option that would be treated as a second class of stock under paragraph (l) (4) (iii) of this section (relating to certain call options, warrants, and similar instruments).

* * *

(5) *Straight debt safe harbor.*—(i) *In general.*—Notwithstanding paragraph (l) (4) of this section, straight debt is not treated as a second class of stock. For purposes of section 1361 (c) (5) and this section, the term straight debt means a written unconditional obligation, regardless of whether embodied in a formal note, to pay a sum certain on demand, or on a specified due date, which—

(A) Does not provide for an interest rate or payment dates that are contingent on profits, the borrower's discretion, the payment of dividends with respect to common stock, or similar factors;

(B) Is not convertible (directly or indirectly) into stock or any other equity interest of the S corporation; and

(C) Is held by an individual (other than a nonresident alien), an estate, or a trust described in section 1361 (c) (2).

(ii) *Subordination.*—The fact that an obligation is subordinated to other debt of the corporation does not prevent the obligation from qualifying as straight debt.

(iii) *Modification or transfer.*—An obligation that originally qualifies as straight debt ceases to so qualify if the obligation—

(A) Is materially modified so that it no longer satisfies the definition of straight debt; or

(B) Is transferred to a third party who is not an eligible shareholder under paragraph (b) (1) of this section.

(iv) *Treatment of straight debt for other purposes.*—An obligation of an S corporation that satisfies the definition of straight debt in paragraph (l) (5) (i) of this section is not treated as a second class of stock even if it is considered equity under general principles of Federal tax law. Such an obligation is generally treated as debt and when so treated is subject to the applicable rules governing indebtedness for other purposes of the Code. Accordingly, interest paid or accrued with respect to a straight debt obligation is generally treated as interest by the corporation and the recipient and does not constitute a distribution to which section 1368 applies. However, if a straight debt obligation bears a rate of interest that is unreasonably high, an appropriate portion of the interest may be recharacterized and treated as a payment that is not interest. Such a recharacterization does not result in a second class of stock.

(v) *Treatment of C corporation debt upon conversion to S status.*—If a C corporation has outstanding an obligation that satisfies the definition of straight debt in paragraph (l) (5) (i) of this section, but that is considered equity under general principles of Federal tax law, the obligation is not treated as a second class of stock for purposes of this section if the C corporation converts to S status. In addition, the conversion from C corporation status to S corporation status is not treated as an exchange of debt for stock with respect to such an instrument.

(6) *Inadvertent terminations.*—See section 1362 (f) and the regulations thereunder for rules relating to inadvertent terminations in cases where the one class of stock requirement has been inadvertently breached.

* * *

(m) *Electing small business trust (ESBT).*—(1) *Definition.*—(i) *General rule.*—An electing small business trust (ESBT) means any trust if it meets the following requirements: the trust does not have as a beneficiary any person other than an individual, an estate, an organization described in section 170 (c) (2) through (5), or an organization described in section 170(c)(1) that holds a contingent interest in such trust and is not a potential current beneficiary; no interest in the trust has been acquired by purchase; and the trustee of the trust makes a timely ESBT election for the trust.

(ii) *Qualified beneficiaries.*—(A) *In general.*—For purposes of this section, a beneficiary includes a person who has a present, remainder, or reversionary interest in the trust.

(B) *Distributee trusts.*—A distributee trust is the beneficiary of the ESBT only if the distributee trust is an organization described in section 170(c)(2) or (3). In all other situations, any person who has a beneficial interest in a distributee trust is a beneficiary of the ESBT. A distributee trust is a trust that receives or may receive a distribution from an ESBT, whether the rights to receive the distribution are fixed or contingent, or immediate or deferred.

(C) *Powers of appointment.*—A person in whose favor a power of appointment could be exercised is not a beneficiary of an ESBT until the holder of the power of appointment actually exercises the power in favor of such person.

(D) *Nonresident aliens.*—A nonresident alien (NRA), as defined in section 7701(b)(1)(B), is an eligible beneficiary of an ESBT and an eligible potential current beneficiary.

(iii) *Interests acquired by purchase.*—A trust does not qualify as an ESBT if any interest in the trust has been acquired by purchase. Generally, if a person acquires an interest in the trust and thereby becomes a beneficiary of the trust as defined in paragraph (m)(1)(ii)(A), and any portion of the basis in the acquired interest in the trust is determined under section 1012, such interest has been acquired by purchase. This includes a net gift of a beneficial interest in the trust, in which the person acquiring the beneficial interest pays the gift tax. The trust itself may acquire S corporation stock or other property by purchase or in a part-gift, part-sale transaction.

(iv) *Ineligible trusts.*—An ESBT does not include—

(A) Any qualified subchapter S trust (as defined in section 1361(d)(3)) if an election under section 1361(d)(2) applies with respect to any corporation the stock of which is held by the trust;

(B) Any trust exempt from tax or not subject to tax under subtitle A; or

(C) Any charitable remainder annuity trust or charitable remainder unitrust (as defined in section 664(d)).

(2) *ESBT election.*—(i) *In general.*—The trustee of the trust must make the ESBT election by signing and filing, with the service center where the S corporation files its income tax return, a statement that meets the requirements of paragraph (m)(2)(ii) of this section. If there is more than one trustee, the trustee or trustees with authority to legally bind the trust must sign the election statement. If any one of several trustees can legally bind the trust, only one trustee needs to sign the election statement. Generally, only one ESBT election is made for the trust, regardless of the number of S corporations whose stock is held by the ESBT. However, if the ESBT holds stock in multiple S corporations that file in different service centers, the ESBT election must be filed with all the relevant service centers where the corporations file their income tax returns. This requirement applies only at the time of the initial ESBT election; if the ESBT later acquires stock in an S corporation which files its income tax return at a different service center, a new ESBT election is not required.

* * *

(3) *Effect of ESBT election.*—(i) *General rule.*—If a trust makes a valid ESBT election, the trust will be treated as an ESBT for purposes of chapter 1 of the Internal Revenue Code as of the effective date of the ESBT election.

(ii) *Employer Identification Number.*—An ESBT has only one employer identification number (EIN). If an existing trust makes an ESBT election, the trust continues to use the EIN it currently uses.

(iii) *Taxable year.*—If an ESBT election is effective on a day other than the first day of the trust's taxable year, the ESBT election does not cause the trust's taxable year to close. The termination of the ESBT election (including a termination caused by a conversion of the ESBT to a QSST) other than on the last day of the trust's taxable year also does not cause the trust's taxable year to close. In either case, the trust files one tax return for the taxable year.

(iv) *Allocation of S corporation items.*—If, during the taxable year of an S corporation, a trust is an ESBT for part of the year and an eligible shareholder under section 1361(c)(2)(A)(i) through (iv) for the rest of the year, the S corporation items are allocated between the two types of trusts under section 1377(a). See § 1.1377-1(a)(2)(iii).

(v) *Estimated taxes.*—If an ESBT election is effective on a day other than the first day of the trust's taxable year, the trust is considered one trust for purposes of estimated taxes under section 6654.

(4) *Potential current beneficiaries.*—(i) *In general.*—For purposes of determining whether a corporation is a small business corporation within the meaning of section 1361(b)(1), each potential current beneficiary of an ESBT generally is treated as a shareholder of the corporation. Subject to the provisions of this paragraph (m)(4), a potential current beneficiary generally is, with respect to any period, any person who at any time during such period is entitled to, or in the discretion of any person may receive, a distribution from the principal or income of the trust. A person is treated as a shareholder of the S corporation at any moment in time when that person is entitled to, or in the discretion of any person may, receive a distribution of principal or income of the trust. No person is treated as a potential current beneficiary solely because that person holds any future interest in the trust. An NRA potential current beneficiary of an ESBT is treated as a shareholder for purposes of the 100-shareholder limit under section 1361(b)(1)(A). However, an NRA potential current beneficiary of an ESBT is not treated as a shareholder in determining whether a corporation is a small business corporation for purposes of the NRA-shareholder prohibition under section 1361(b)(1)(C).

(ii) *Grantor trusts.*—If all or a portion of an ESBT is treated as owned by a person under subpart E, part I, subchapter J, chapter 1 of the Internal Revenue Code, such owner is a potential current beneficiary in addition to persons described in paragraph (m)(4)(i) of this section.

(iii) *Special rule for dispositions of stock.*—Notwithstanding the provisions of paragraph (m)(4)(i) of this section, if a trust disposes of all of the stock which it holds in an S corporation, then, with respect to that corporation, any person who first met the definition of a potential current beneficiary during the 1-year period ending on the date of such disposition is not a potential current beneficiary and thus is not a shareholder of that corporation.

(iv) *Distributee trusts.*—(A) *In general.*—This paragraph (m)(4)(iv) contains the rules for determining who are the potential current beneficiaries of an ESBT if a distributee trust becomes entitled to, or at the discretion of any person, may receive a distribution from principal or income of an ESBT. A distributee trust does not include a trust that is not currently in existence. For this purpose, a trust is not currently in existence if the trust has no assets and no items of income, loss, deduction, or credit. Thus, if a trust instrument provides for a trust to be funded at some future time, the future trust is not currently a distributee trust.

(B) If the distributee trust is not a trust described in section 1361(c)(2)(A), then the distributee trust is the potential current beneficiary of the ESBT and the corporation's S corporation election terminates.

(C) If the distributee trust is a trust described in section 1361(c)(2)(A), the persons who would be its potential current beneficiaries (as defined in paragraphs (m)(4)(i) and (ii) of this section) if the distributee trust were an ESBT are treated as the potential current beneficiaries of the ESBT. Notwithstanding the preceding sentence, however, if the distributee trust is a trust described in section 1361(c)(2)(A)(ii) or (iii), the estate described in section 1361(c)(2)(B)(ii) or (iii) is treated as the potential current beneficiary of the ESBT for the 2-year period during which such trust would be permitted as a shareholder.

(D) For the purposes of paragraph (m)(4)(iv)(C) of this section, a trust will be deemed to be described in section 1361(c)(2)(A) if such trust would qualify for a QSST election under section 1361(d) or an ESBT election under section 1361(e) if it owned S corporation stock.

(v) *Contingent distributions.*—A person who is entitled to receive a distribution only after a specified time or upon the occurrence of a specified event (such as the death of the holder of a power of appointment) is not a potential current beneficiary until such time or the occurrence of such event.

(vi) *Currently exercisable powers of appointment and other powers.*—(A) *Powers of appointment.*—A person to whom a distribution may be made during any period pursuant to a power of appointment (as described for transfer tax purposes in section 2041 and §20.2041-1(b) of this chapter and section 2514 and §25.2514-1(b) of this chapter) is not a potential current beneficiary unless the power is exercised in favor of that person during the period. It is immaterial for purposes of this paragraph (m)(4)(vi)(A) whether such power of appointment is a "general power of appointment" for transfer tax purposes as described in §§20.2041-1(c) and 25.2514-1(c) of this chapter. The mere existence of one or more powers of appointment during the lifetime of a power holder that would permit current distributions from the trust to be made to more than the number of persons described in section 1361(b)(1)(A) or to a person described in section 1361(b)(1)(B) or (C) will not cause the S corporation election to terminate unless one or more of such powers are exercised, collectively, in favor of an excessive number of persons or in favor of a person who is ineligible to be an S corporation shareholder. For purposes of this paragraph (m)(4)(vi)(A), a "power of appointment" includes a power, regardless of by whom held, to add a beneficiary or class of beneficiaries to the class of potential current beneficiaries, but generally does not include a power held by a fiduciary who is not also a beneficiary of the trust to spray or sprinkle trust distributions among beneficiaries. Nothing in this paragraph (m)(4)(vi)(A) alters the definition of "power of appointment" for purposes of any provision of the Internal Revenue Code or the regulations.

(B) *Powers to distribute to certain organizations not pursuant to powers of appointment.*—If a trustee or other fiduciary has a power (that does not constitute a power of appointment for transfer tax purposes as described in §§20.2041-1(b) and 25.2514-1(b) of this chapter) to make distributions from the trust to one or more members of a class of organizations described in section 1361(c)(6), such organizations will be counted collectively as only one potential current beneficiary for purposes of this paragraph (m), except that each organization receiving a distribution also will be counted as a potential current beneficiary. This paragraph (m)(4)(vi)(B) shall not apply to a power to currently distribute to one or more particular charitable organizations described in section 1361(c)(6). Each of such organizations is a potential current beneficiary of the trust.

(vii) *Number of shareholders.*—Each potential current beneficiary of the ESBT, as defined in paragraphs (m)(4)(i) through (vi) of this section, is counted as a shareholder of any S corporation whose stock is owned by the ESBT. During any period in which the ESBT has no potential current beneficiaries, the ESBT is counted as the shareholder. A person is counted as only one shareholder of an S corporation even though that person may be treated as a shareholder of the S corporation by direct ownership and through one or more eligible trusts described in section 1361(c)(2)(A). Thus, for example, if a person owns stock in an S corporation and is a potential current beneficiary of an ESBT that owns stock in the same S corporation, that person is counted as one shareholder of the S corporation. Similarly, if a husband owns stock in an S corporation and his wife is a potential current beneficiary of an ESBT that owns stock in the same S corporation, the husband and wife will be counted as one shareholder of the S corporation.

(viii) *Miscellaneous.*—Payments made by an ESBT to a third party on behalf of a beneficiary are considered to be payments made directly to the beneficiary. The right of a beneficiary to assign the beneficiary's interest to a third party does not result in the third party being a potential current beneficiary until that interest is actually assigned.

(5) *ESBT terminations.*—(i) *Ceasing to meet ESBT requirements.*—A trust ceases to be an ESBT on the first day the trust fails to meet the definition of an ESBT under section 1361(e). The last day the trust is treated as an ESBT is the day before the date on which the trust fails to meet the definition of an ESBT.

(ii) *Disposition of S stock.*—In general, a trust ceases to be an ESBT on the first day following the day the trust disposes of all S corporation stock. However, if the trust is using the installment method to report income from the sale or disposition of its stock in an S corporation, the trust ceases to be an ESBT on the day following the earlier of the day the last installment payment is received by the trust or the day the trust disposes of the installment obligation.

(iii) *Potential current beneficiaries that are ineligible shareholders.*—If a potential current beneficiary of an ESBT is not an eligible shareholder of a small business corporation within the meaning of section 1361(b)(1), the S corporation election terminates. For example, the S corporation election will terminate if a charitable remainder trust becomes a potential current beneficiary of an ESBT. Such a potential current beneficiary is treated as an ineligible shareholder beginning on the day such person becomes a potential current beneficiary, and the S corporation election terminates on that date. However, see the special rule of paragraph (m)(4)(iii) of this section. If the S corporation election terminates, relief may be available under section 1362(f).

(6) *Revocation of ESBT election.*—An ESBT election may be revoked only with the consent of the Commissioner. The application for consent to revoke the election must be submitted to the Internal Revenue Service in the form of a letter ruling request under the appropriate revenue procedure.

* * *

[Reg. § 1.1361-1.]

☐ [*T.D.* 8419, 5-28-92. *Amended by T.D.* 8600, 7-20-95; *T.D.* 8869, 1-20-2000; *T.D.* 8940, 2-12-2001; *T.D.* 8994, 5-13-2002; *T.D.* 9078, 7-16-2003; *T.D.* 9422, 8-13-2008 *and T.D.* 9868, 6-13-2019.]

§1.1361-2. Definitions relating to S corporation subsidiaries.—(a) *In general.*—The term *qualified subchapter S subsidiary* (QSub) means any domestic corporation that is not an ineligible corporation (as defined in section 1361(b)(2) and the regulations thereunder), if—

(1) 100 percent of the stock of such corporation is held by an S corporation; and

(2) The S corporation properly elects to treat the subsidiary as a QSub under § 1.1361-3.

(b) *Stock treated as held by S corporation.*—For purposes of satisfying the 100 percent stock ownership requirement in section 1361(b)(3)(B)(i) and paragraph (a)(1) of this section—

(1) Stock of a corporation is treated as held by an S corporation if the S corporation is the owner of that stock for Federal income tax purposes; and

(2) Any outstanding instruments, obligations, or arrangements of the corporation which would not be considered stock for purposes of section 1361(b)(1)(D) if the corporation were an S corporation are not treated as outstanding stock of the QSub.

(c) *Straight debt safe harbor.*—Section 1.1361-1(l)(5)(iv) and (v) apply to an obligation of a corporation for which a QSub election is made if that obligation would satisfy the definition of straight debt in § 1.1361-1(l)(5) if issued by the S corporation.

(d) *Examples.*—The following examples illustrate the application of this section:

Example 1. X, an S corporation, owns 100 percent of Y, a corporation for which a valid QSub election is in effect for the taxable year. Y owns 100 percent of Z, a corporation otherwise eligible for QSub status. X may elect to treat Z as a QSub under section 1361(b)(3)(B)(ii).

Example 2. Assume the same facts as in *Example 1,* except that Y is a business entity that is disregarded as an entity separate from its owner under § 301.7701-2(c)(2) of this chapter. X may elect to treat Z as a QSub.

Example 3. Assume the same facts as in *Example 1,* except that Y owns 50 percent of Z, and X owns the other 50 percent. X may elect to treat Z as a QSub.

Example 4. Assume the same facts as in *Example 1,* except that Y is a C corporation. Although Y is a domestic corporation that is otherwise eligible to be a QSub, no QSub election has been made for Y. Thus, X is not treated as holding the stock of Z. Consequently, X may not elect to treat Z as a QSub.

Example 5. Individuals A and B own 100 percent of the stock of corporation X, an S corporation, and, except for C's interest (described below), X owns 100 percent of corporation Y, a C corporation. Individual C holds an instrument issued by Y that is considered to be equity under general principles of tax law but would satisfy the definition of straight debt under § 1.1361-1(l)(5) if Y were an S corporation. In determining whether X owns 100 percent of Y for purposes of making the QSub election, the instrument held by C is not considered outstanding stock. In addition, under § 1.1361-1(l)(5)(v), the QSub election is not treated as an exchange of debt for stock with respect to such instrument, and § 1.1361-1(l)(5)(iv) applies to determine the tax treatment of payments on the instrument while Y's QSub election is in effect.

[Reg. § 1.1361-2.]

□ [*T.D.* 8869, 1-20-2000.]

§ 1.1361-4. Effect of QSub election.—(a) *Separate existence ignored.*—(1) *In general.*—Except as otherwise provided in paragraphs (a)(3), (a)(6), (a)(7), (a)(8), and (a)(9) of this section, for Federal tax purposes—

(i) A corporation that is a QSub shall not be treated as a separate corporation; and

(ii) All assets, liabilities, and items of income, deduction, and credit of a QSub shall be treated as assets, liabilities, and items of income, deduction, and credit of the S corporation.

(2) *Liquidation of subsidiary.*—(i) *In general.*—If an S corporation makes a valid QSub election with respect to a subsidiary, the subsidiary is deemed to have liquidated into the S corporation. Except as provided in paragraph (a)(5) of this section, the tax treatment of the liquidation or of a larger transaction that includes the liquidation will be determined under the Internal Revenue Code and general principles of tax law, including the step transaction doctrine. Thus, for example, if an S corporation forms a subsidiary and makes a valid QSub election (effective upon the date of the subsidiary's formation) for the subsidiary, the transfer of assets to the subsidiary and the deemed liquidation are disregarded, and the corporation will be deemed to be a QSub from its inception.

(ii) *Examples.*—The following examples illustrate the application of this paragraph (a)(2)(i) of this section:

Example 1. Corporation X acquires all of the outstanding stock of solvent corporation Y from an unrelated individual for cash and short-term notes. Thereafter, as part of the same plan, X immediately makes an S election and a QSub election for Y. Because X acquired all of the stock of Y in a qualified stock purchase within the meaning of section 338(d)(3), the liquidation described in paragraph (a)(2) of this section is respected as an independent step separate from the stock acquisition, and the tax consequences of the liquidation are determined under sections 332 and 337.

Example 2. Corporation X, pursuant to a plan, acquires all of the outstanding stock of corporation Y from the shareholders of Y solely in exchange for 10 percent of the voting stock of X. Prior to the transaction, Y and its shareholders are unrelated to X. Thereafter, as part of the same plan, X immediately makes an S election and a QSub election for Y. The transaction is a reorganization described in section 368(a)(1)(C), assuming the other conditions for reorganization treatment (e.g., continuity of business enterprise) are satisfied.

Example 3. After the expiration of the transition period provided in paragraph (a)(5)(i) of this section, individual A, pursuant to a plan, contributes all of the outstanding stock of Y to his wholly owned S corporation, X, and immediately causes X to make a QSub election for Y. The transaction is a reorganization under section 368(a)(1)(D), assuming the other conditions for reorganization treatment (e.g., continuity of business enterprise) are satisfied. If the sum of the amount of liabilities of Y treated as assumed by X exceeds the total of the adjusted basis of the property of Y, then section 357(c) applies and such excess is considered as gain from the sale or exchange of a capital asset or of property which is not a capital asset, as the case may be.

(iii) *Adoption of plan of liquidation.*—For purposes of satisfying the requirement of adoption of a plan of liquidation under section 332, unless a formal plan of liquidation that contemplates the QSub election is adopted on an earlier date, the making of the QSub election is considered to be the adoption of a plan of liquidation immediately before the deemed liquidation described in paragraph (a)(2)(i) of this section.

(iv) *Example.*—The following example illustrates the application of paragraph (a)(2)(iii) of this section:

Example. Corporation X owns 75 percent of a solvent corporation Y, and individual A owns the remaining 25 percent of Y. As part of a plan to make a QSub election for Y, X causes Y to redeem A's 25 percent interest on June 1 for cash and makes a QSub election for Y effective on June 3. The making of the QSub election is considered to be the adoption of a plan of liquidation immediately before the deemed liquidation. The deemed liquidation satisfies the requirements of section 332.

(v) *Stock ownership requirements of section 332.*—The deemed exercise of an option under § 1.1504-4 and any instruments, obligations, or arrangements that are not considered stock under § 1.1361-2(b)(2) are disregarded in determining if the stock ownership requirements of section 332(b) are met with respect to the deemed liquidation provided in paragraph (a)(2)(i) of this section.

* * *

(4) *Treatment of stock of QSub.*—Except for purposes of section 1361(b)(3)(B)(i) and § 1.1361-2(a)(1), the stock of a QSub shall be disregarded for all Federal tax purposes.

* * *

(6) *Treatment of certain QSubs.*—(i) *In general.*—A QSub, even though it is generally not treated as a corporation separate from the S corporation, is treated as a separate corporation for purposes of:

(A) Federal tax liabilities of the QSub with respect to any taxable period for which the QSub was treated as a separate corporation.

(B) Federal tax liabilities of any other entity for which the QSub is liable.

(C) Refunds or credits of Federal tax.

(ii) *Examples.*—The following examples illustrate the application of paragraph (a)(6)(i) of this section:

Example 1. X has owned all of the outstanding stock of Y, a domestic corporation that reports its taxes on a calendar year basis, since 2001. X and Y do not report their taxes on a consolidated basis. For 2003, X makes a timely S election and simultaneously makes a QSub election for Y. In 2004, the Internal Revenue Service (IRS) seeks to extend the period of limitations on assessment for Y's 2001 taxable year. Because Y was treated as a separate corporation for its 2001 taxable year, Y is the proper party to sign the consent to extend the period of limitations.

Example 2. The facts are the same as in *Example 1*, except that in 2004, the IRS determines that Y miscalculated and underreported its income tax liability for 2001. Because Y was treated as a separate corporation for its 2001 taxable year, the deficiency for Y's 2001 taxable year may be assessed against Y and, in the event that Y fails to pay the liability after notice and demand, a general tax lien will arise against all of Y's property and rights to property.

Example 3. X is a QSub of Y. In 2001, Z, a domestic corporation that reports its taxes on a calendar year basis, merges into X in a state law merger. Z was not a member of a consolidated group at any time during its taxable year ending in December 2000. Under the applicable state law, X is the successor to Z and is liable for all of Z's debts. In 2003, the IRS seeks to extend the period of limitations on assessment for Z's 2000 taxable year. Because X is the successor to Z and is liable for Z's 2000 taxes that remain unpaid, X is the proper party to execute the consent to extend the period of limitations on assessment.

* * *

(7) *Treatment of QSubs for purposes of employment taxes.*—(i) *In general.*—A QSub is treated as a separate corporation for purposes of Subtitle C—Employment Taxes and Collection of Income Tax (Chapters 21, 22, 23, 23A, 24, and 25 of the Internal Revenue Code).

* * *

(8) *Treatment of QSubs for purposes of certain excise taxes.*—(i) *In general.*—A QSub is treated as a separate corporation for purposes of—

(A) Federal tax liabilities imposed by Chapters 31, 32 (other than section 4181), 33, 34, 35, 36 (other than section 4461), 38, and 49 of the Internal Revenue Code, or any floor stocks tax imposed on articles subject to any of these taxes;

(B) Collection of tax imposed by Chapters 33 and 49 of the Internal Revenue Code;

(C) Registration under sections 4101, 4222, and 4412;

(D) Claims of a credit (other than a credit under section 34), refund, or payment related to a tax described in paragraph (a)(8)(i)(A) of this section or under section 6426 or 6427; and

(E) Assessment and collection of an assessable payment imposed by section 4980H and reporting required by section 6056.

* * *

(9) *Information returns.*—(i) *In general.*—Except to the extent provided by the Secretary or Commissioner in guidance (including forms or instructions), paragraph (a)(1) of this section shall not apply to part III of subchapter A of chapter 61, relating to information returns.

(ii) *Effective/applicability date.*—This paragraph (a)(9) is effective on August 14, 2008.

(b) *Timing of the liquidation.*—(1) *In general.*—Except as otherwise provided in paragraph (b)(3) or (4) of this section, the liquidation described in paragraph (a)(2) of this section occurs at the close of the day before the Qsub election is effective. Thus, for example, if a C corporation elects to be treated as an S corporation and makes a QSub election (effective the same date as the S election) with respect to a subsidiary, the liquidation occurs immediately before the S election becomes effective, while the S electing parent is still a C corporation.

(2) *Application to elections in tiered situations.*—When QSub elections for a tiered group of subsidiaries are effective on the same date, the S corporation may specify the order of the liquidations. If no order is specified, the liquidations that are deemed to occur as a result of the QSub elections will be treated as occurring first for the lowest tier entity and proceed successively upward until all of the liquidations under paragraph (a)(2) of this section have occurred. For example, S, an S corporation, owns 100 percent of C, the common parent of an affiliated group of corporations that includes X and Y. C owns all of the stock of X and X owns all of the stock of Y. S elects under § 1.1361-3 to treat C, X and Y as QSubs effective on the same date. If no order is specified for the elections, the following liquidations are deemed to occur as a result of the elections, with each successive liquidation occuring on the same day immediately after the preceding liquidation: Y is treated as liquidating into X, then X is treated as liquidating into C, and finally C is treated as liquidating into S.

(3) *Acquisitions.*—(i) *In general.*—If an S corporation does not own 100 percent of the stock of the subsidiary on the day before the QSub election is effective, the liquidation described in paragraph (a)(2) of this section occurs immediately after the time at which the S corporation first owns 100 percent of the stock.

(ii) *Special rules for acquired S corporations.*—Except as provided in paragraph (b)(4) of this section, if a corporation (Y) for which an election under section 1362(a) was in effect is acquired, and a QSub election is made effective on the day Y is acquired, Y is deemed to liquidate into the S corporation at the beginning of the day the termination of its S election is effective. As a result, if corporation X acquires Y, an S corporation, and makes an S election for itself and a QSub election for Y effective on the day of acquisition, Y liquidates into X at the beginning of the day when X's S election is effective, and there is no period between the termination of Y's S election and the deemed liquidation of Y during which Y is a C corporation. Y's taxable year ends for all Federal income tax purposes at the close of the preceding day. Furthermore, if Y owns Z, a corporation for which a QSub election was in effect prior to the acquisition of Y by X, and X makes QSub elections for Y and Z, effective on the day of acquisition, the transfer of assets to Z and the deemed liquidation of Z are disregarded. See §§ 1.1361-4(a)(2) and 1.1361-5(b)(1)(i).

(4) *Coordination with section 338 election.*—An S corporation that makes a qualified stock purchase of a target may make an election under section 338 with respect to the acquisition if it meets the requirements for the election, and may make a QSub election with respect to the target. If an S corporation makes an election under section 338 with respect to a subsidiary acquired in a qualified stock purchase, a QSub election made with respect to that subsidiary is not effective before the day after the acquisition date (within the meaning of section 338(h)(2)). If the QSub election is effective on the day after the acquisition date, the liquidation under paragraph (a)(2) of this section occurs immediately after the deemed asset purchase by the new target corporation under section 338. If an S corporation makes an election under section 338 (without a section 338(h)(10) election) with respect to a target, the target must file a final return as a C corporation reflecting the deemed sale. See § 1.338-10(a). If the target was an S corporation on the day before the acquisition date, the final return as a C corporation must reflect the activities of the target for the acquisition date, including the deemed sale. See § 1.338-10(a)(3).

(c) *Carryover of disallowed losses and deductions.*—If an S corporation (S1) acquires the stock of another S corporation (S2), and S1 makes a QSub election with respect to S2 effective on the day of the acquisition, see § 1.1366-2(c)(1) for provisions relating to the carryover of losses and deductions with respect to a former shareholder of S2 that may be available to that shareholder as a shareholder of S1.

* * *

[Reg. § 1.1361-4.]

□ [*T.D.* 8869, 1-20-2000 (*corrected* 3-27-2000). *Amended by T.D.* 8940, 2-12-2001; *T.D.* 9183, 2-24-2005; *T.D.* 9356, 8-15-2007; *T.D.* 9422, 8-13-2008; *T.D.* 9596, 6-22-2012; *T.D.* 9655, 2-10-2014 *and T.D.* 9670, 6-25-2014.]

§ 1.1361-5. Termination of QSub election.—(a) *In general.*—(1) *Effective date.*—The termination of a QSub election is effective—

(i) On the effective date contained in the revocation statement if a QSub election is revoked under § 91.1361-3(b);

(ii) At the close of the last day of the parent's last taxable year as an S corporation if the parent's S election terminates under § 1.1362-2; or

(iii) At the close of the day on which an event (other than an event described in paragraph (a)(1)(ii) of this section) occurs that renders the subsidiary ineligible for QSub status under section 1361(b)(3)(B).

(2) *Information to be provided upon termination of QSub election by failure to qualify as a Qsub.*—If a QSub election terminates because an event renders the subsidiary ineligible for QSub status, the S corporation must attach to its return for the taxable year in which the termination occurs a notification that a QSub election has terminated, the date of the termination, and the names, addresses, and employer identification numbers of both the parent corporation and the QSub.

(3) *QSub joins a consolidated group.*—If a QSub election terminates because the S corporation becomes a member of a consolidated group (and no election under section 338(g) is made) the principles of § 1.1502-76(b)(1)(ii)(A)(2) (relating to a special rule for S corporations that join a consolidated group) apply to any QSub of the S corporation that also becomes a member of the consolidated group at the same time as the S corporation. See *Example 4* of paragraph (a)(4) of this section.

* * *

(b) *Effect of termination of QSub election.*—(1) *Formation of new corporation.*—(i) *In general.*—If a QSub election terminates under paragraph (a) of this section, the former QSub is treated as a new corporation acquiring all of its assets (and assuming all of its liabilities) immediately before the termination from the S corporation parent in exchange for stock of the new corporation. The tax treatment of this transaction or of a larger transaction that includes this transaction will be determined under the Internal Revenue Code and general principles of tax law, including the step transaction doctrine. For purposes of determining the application of section 351 with respect to this transaction, instruments, obligations, or other arrangements that are not treated as stock of the QSub under § 1.1361-2(b) are disregarded in determining control for purposes of section 368(c) even if they are equity under general principles of tax law.

(ii) *Termination for tiered QSubs.*—If QSub elections terminate for tiered QSubs on the same day, the formation of any higher tier subsidiary precedes the formation of its lower tier subsidiary. See *Example 6* in paragraph (b)(3) of this section.

(2) *Carryover of disallowed losses and deductions.*—If a QSub terminates because the S corporation distributes the QSub stock to some or all of the S corporation's shareholders in a transaction to which section 368(a)(1)(D) applies by reason of section 355 (or so much of section 356 as relates to section 355), see § 1.1366-2(c)(2) for provisions relating to the

carryover of disallowed losses and deductions that may be available.

* * *

(c) *Election after QSub termination.*—(1) *In general.*—Absent the Commissioner's consent, and except as provided in paragraph (c)(2) of this section, a corporation whose QSub election has terminated under paragraph (a) of this section (or a successor corporation as defined in paragraph (b) of this section) may not make an S election under section 1362 or have a QSub election under section 1361(b)(3)(B)(ii) made with respect to it for five taxable years (as described in section 1361(b)(3)(D)). The Commissioner may permit an S election by the corporation or a new QSub election with respect to the corporation before the five-year period expires. The corporation requesting consent to make the election has the burden of establishing that, under the relevant facts and circumstances, the Commissioner should consent to a new election.

(2) *Exception.*—In the case of S and QSub elections effective after December 31, 1996, if a corporation,'s QSub election terminates, the corporation may, without requesting the Commissioner's consent, make an S election or have a QSub election made with respect to it before the expiration of the five-year period described in section 1361(b)(3)(D) and paragraph (c)(1) of this section, provided that—

(i) Immediately following the termination, the corporation (or its successor corporation) is otherwise eligible to make an S election or have a QSub election made for it; and

(ii) The relevant election is made effective immediately following the termination of the QSub election.

(3) *Examples.*—The following examples illustrate the application of this paragraph (c):

Example 1. Termination upon distribution of QSub stock to shareholders of parent. X, an S corporation, owns Y, a QSub. X distributes all of its Y stock to X's shareholders. The distribution terminates the QSub election because Y no longer satisfies the requirements of a QSub. Assuming Y is otherwise eligible to be treated as an S corporation, Y's shareholders may elect to treat Y as an S corporation effective on the date of the stock distribution without requesting the Commissioner's consent.

Example 2. Sale of 100 percent of QSub stock. X, an S corporation, owns Y, a QSub. X sells 100 percent of the stock of Y to Z, an unrelated S corporation. Z may elect to treat Y as a QSub effective on the date of purchase without requesting the Commissioner's consent.

[Reg. § 1.1361-5.]

□ [*T.D.* 8869, 1-20-2000 (*corrected* 10-23-2002).]

§ 1.1362-1. Election to be an S corporation.—(a) *In general.*—Except as provided in § 1.1362-5, a small business corporation as defined in section 1361 may elect to be an S corporation under section 1362(a). An election may be made only with the consent of all of the shareholders of the corporation at the time of the election. See § 1.1362-6(a) for rules concerning the time and manner of making this election.

(b) *Years for which election is effective.*—An election under section 1362(a) is effective for the entire taxable year of the corporation for which it is made and for all succeeding taxable years of the corporation, until the election is terminated. [Reg. § 1.1362-1.]

□ [*T.D.* 8449, 11-24-92.]

§ 1.1362-2. Termination of election.—(a) *Termination by revocation.*—(1) *In general.*—An election made under section 1362(a) is terminated if the corporation revokes the election for any taxable year of the corporation for which the election is effective, including the first taxable year. A revocation may be made only with the consent of shareholders who, at the time the revocation is made, hold more than one-half of the number of issued and outstanding shares of stock (including non-voting stock) of the corporation. See § 1.1362-6(a) for rules concerning the time and manner of revoking an election made under section 1362(a).

(2) *When effective.*—(i) *In general.*—Except as provided in paragraph (a)(2)(ii) of this section, a revocation made during the taxable year and before the 16th day of the third month of the taxable year is effective on the first day of the taxable year and a revocation made after the 15th day of the third month of the taxable year is effective for the following taxable year. If a corporation makes an election to be an S corporation that is to be effective beginning with the next taxable year and revokes its election on or before the first day of the next taxable year, the corporation is deemed to have revoked its election on the first day of the next taxable year.

(ii) *Revocations specifying a prospective revocation date.*—If a corporation specifies a date for revocation and the date is expressed in terms of a stated day, month, and year that is on or after the date the revocation is filed, the revocation is effective on and after the date so specified.

(3) *Effect on taxable year of corporation.*—In the case of a corporation that revokes its election to be an S corporation effective on the

first day of the first taxable year for which its election is to be effective, any statement made with the election regarding a change in the corporation's taxable year has no effect.

(4) *Rescission of a revocation.*—A corporation may rescind a revocation made under paragraph (a)(2) of this section at any time before the revocation becomes effective. A rescission may be made only with the consent of each person who consented to the revocation and by each person who became a shareholder of the corporation within the period beginning on the first day after the date the revocation was made and ending on the date on which the rescission is made. See § 1.1362-6(a) for rules concerning the time and manner of rescinding a revocation.

(b) *Termination by reason of corporation ceasing to be a small business corporation.*—(1) *In general.*—If a corporation ceases to be a small business corporation, as defined in section 1361(b), at any time on or after the first day of the first taxable year for which its election under section 1362(a) is effective, the election terminates. In the event of a termination under this paragraph (b)(1), the corporation should attach to its return for the taxable year in which the termination occurs a notification that a termination has occurred and the date of the termination.

(2) *When effective.*—If an election terminates because of a specific event that causes the corporation to fail to meet the definition of a small business corporation, the termination is effective as of the date on which the event occurs. If a corporation makes an election to be an S corporation that is effective beginning with the following taxable year and is not a small business corporation on the first day of that following taxable year, the election is treated as having terminated on that first day. If a corporation is a small business corporation on the first day of the taxable year for which its election is effective, its election does not terminate even if the corporation was not a small business corporation during all or part of the period beginning after the date the election was made and ending before the first day of the taxable year for which the election is effective.

(3) *Effect on taxable year of corporation.*—In the case of a corporation that fails to meet the definition of a small business corporation on the first day of the first taxable year for which its election to be an S corporation is to be effective, any statement made with the election regarding a change in the corporation's taxable year has no effect.

(c) *Termination by reason of excess passive investment income.*—(1) *In general.*—A corporation's election under section 1362(a) terminates if the corporation has subchapter C earnings and profits at the close of each of three consecutive taxable years and, for each of those taxable years, has passive investment income in excess of 25 percent of gross receipts. See section 1375 for the tax imposed on excess passive investment income.

(2) *When effective.*—A termination under this paragraph (c) is effective on the first day of the first taxable year beginning after the third consecutive year in which the S corporation had excess passive investment income.

(3) *Subchapter C earnings and profits.*—For purposes of this paragraph (c), *subchapter C earnings and profits* of a corporation are the earnings and profits of any corporation, including the S corporation or an acquired or predecessor corporation, for any period with respect to which an election under section 1362(a) (or under section 1372 of prior law) was not in effect. The subchapter C earnings and profits of an S corporation are modified as required by section 1371(c).

(4) *Gross receipts.*—(i) *In general.*—For purposes of this paragraph (c), *gross receipts* generally means the total amount received or accrued under the method of accounting used by the corporation in computing its taxable income and is not reduced by returns and allowances, cost of goods sold, or deductions.

(ii) *Special rules for sales of capital assets, stock and securities.*—(A) *Sales of capital assets.*—For purposes of this paragraph (c), gross receipts from the sales or exchanges of capital assets (as defined in section 1221), other than stock and securities, are taken into account only to the extent of capital gain net income (as defined in section 1222).

(B) *Sales of stock or securities.*—*(1) In general.*—For purposes of this paragraph (c), gross receipts from the sales or exchanges of stock or securities are taken into account only to the extent of gains therefrom. In addition, for purposes of computing gross receipts from sales or exchanges of stock or securities, losses do not offset gains.

(2) Treatment of certain liquidations.—Gross receipts from the sales or exchanges of stock or securities do not include amounts described in section 1362(d)(3)(D)(iv), relating to the treatment of certain liquidations. For purposes of section 1362(d)(3)(D)(iv), stock of the liquidating corporation owned by an S corporation shareholder is not treated as owned by the S corporation.

(3) Definition of stock or securities.—For purposes of this paragraph (c), *stock or securities* includes shares or certificates of stock, stock rights or warrants, or an interest in any corporation (including any joint stock company, insurance company, association, or other organization classified as a corporation under section 7701); an interest as a limited partner in a partnership; certificates of interest or participation in any profit-sharing agreement, or in any oil, gas, or other mineral property, or lease; collateral trust certificates; voting trust certificates; bonds; debentures; certificates of indebtedness; notes; car trust certificates; bills of exchange; or obligations issued by or on behalf of a State, Territory, or political subdivision thereof.

(4) General partner interests.—*(i) In general.*—Except as provided in paragraph (c)(4)(ii)(B)(*4*)(*ii*) of this section, if an S corporation disposes of a general partner interest, the gain on the disposition is treated as gain from the sale of stock or securities to the extent of the amount the S corporation would have received as a distributive share of gain from the sale of stock or securities held by the partnership if all of the stock and securities held by the partnership had been sold by the partnership at fair market value at the time the S corporation disposes of the general partner interest. In applying this rule, the S corporation's distributive share of gain from the sale of stock or securities held by the partnership is not reduced to reflect any loss that would be recognized from the sale of stock or securities held by the partnership. In the case of tiered partnerships, the rules of this section apply by looking through each tier.

(ii) Exception.—An S corporation that disposes of a general partner interest may treat the disposition, for purposes of this paragraph (c), in the same manner as the disposition of an interest as a limited partner.

(iii) *Other exclusions from gross receipts.*—For purposes of this paragraph (c), gross receipts do not include—

(A) Amounts received in nontaxable sales or exchanges except to the extent that gain is recognized by the corporation on the sale or exchange; or

(B) Amounts received as a loan, as a repayment of a loan, as a contribution to capital, or on the issuance by the corporation of its own stock.

(5) *Passive investment income.*—(i) *In general.*—In general, *passive investment income* means gross receipts (as defined in paragraph (c)(4) of this section) derived from royalties, rents, dividends, interest, annuities, and gains from the sales or exchanges of stock or securities.

(ii) *Definitions.*—For purposes of this paragraph (c)(5), the following definitions apply:

(A) *Royalties.*—*(1) In general.*—*Royalties* means all royalties, including mineral, oil, and gas royalties, and amounts received for the privilege of using patents, copyrights, secret processes and formulas, good will, trademarks, tradebrands, franchises, and other like property. The gross amount of royalties is not reduced by any part of the cost of the rights under which the royalties are received or by any amount allowable as a deduction in computing taxable income.

(2) Royalties derived in the ordinary course of a trade or business.—*Royalties* does not include royalties derived in the ordinary course of a trade or business of franchising or licensing property. Royalties received by a corporation are derived in the ordinary course of a trade or business of franchising or licensing property only if, based on all the facts and circumstances, the corporation—

(i) Created the property; or

(ii) Performed significant services or incurred substantial costs with respect to the development or marketing of the property.

(3) Copyright, mineral, oil and gas, and active business computer software royalties.—*Royalties* does not include copyright royalties, nor mineral, oil and gas royalties if the income from those royalties would not be treated as personal holding company income under sections 543(a)(3) and (a)(4) if the corporation were a C corporation; amounts received upon disposal of timber, coal, or domestic iron ore with respect to which the special rules of sections 631(b) and (c) apply; and active business computer software royalties as defined under section 543(d) (without regard to paragraph (d)(5) of section 543).

(B) *Rents.*—*(1) In general.*—*Rents* means amounts received for the use of, or right to use, property (whether real or personal) of the corporation.

(2) Rents derived in the active trade or business of renting property.—*Rents* does not include rents derived in the active trade or business of renting property. Rents received by a corporation are derived in an active trade or business of renting property only if, based on all the facts and circumstances, the corporation provides significant services or incurs substantial costs in the rental business. Generally, significant services are not rendered and

substantial costs are not incurred in connection with net leases. Whether significant services are performed or substantial costs are incurred in the rental business is determined based upon all the facts and circumstances including, but not limited to, the number of persons employed to provide the services and the types and amounts of costs and expenses incurred (other than depreciation).

(3) Produced film rents.—Rents does not include produced film rents as defined under section 543(a)(5).

(4) Income from leasing self-produced tangible property.—Rents does not include compensation, however designated, for the use of, or right to use, any real or tangible personal property developed, manufactured, or produced by the taxpayer, if during the taxable year the taxpayer is engaged in substantial development, manufacturing, or production of real or tangible personal property of the same type.

(C) *Dividends.—Dividends* includes dividends as defined in section 316, amounts to be included in gross income under section 551 (relating to foreign personal holding company income taxed to U.S. shareholders), and consent dividends as provided in section 565. See paragraphs (c)(5)(iii)(B) and (C) of this section for special rules for the treatment of certain dividends and certain payments to a patron of a cooperative. See § 1.1362-8 for special rules regarding the treatment of dividends received by an S corporation from a C corporation in which the S corporation holds stock meeting the requirements of section 1504(a)(2).

(D) *Interest.—(1) In general.—Interest* means any amount received for the use of money (including tax-exempt interest and amounts treated as interest under section 483, 1272, 1274, or 7872). See paragraph (c)(5)(iii)(B) of this section for a special rule for the treatment of interest derived in certain businesses.

(2) Interest on obligations acquired in the ordinary course of a trade or business.—Interest does not include interest on any obligation acquired from the sale of property described in section 1221(1) or the performance of services in the ordinary course of a trade or business of selling the property or performing the services.

(E) *Annuities.—Annuities* means the entire amount received as an annuity under an annuity, endowment, or life insurance contract, if any part of the amount would be includible in gross income under section 72.

(F) *Gross receipts from the sale of stock or securities.*—Gross receipts from the sales or exchanges of stock or securities, as described in paragraph (c)(4)(ii)(B) of this section, are passive investment income to the extent of gains therefrom. See paragraph (c)(5)(iii)(B) of this section for a special rule for the treatment of gains derived in certain businesses.

(G) *Identified income.—Passive investment income* does not include income identified by the Commissioner by regulations, revenue ruling, or revenue procedure as income derived in the ordinary course of a trade or business for purposes of this section.

(iii) *Special rules.*—For purposes of this paragraph (c)(5), the following special rules apply:

(A) *Options or commodities dealers.*—In the case of an options dealer or commodities dealer, *passive investment income* does not include any gain or loss (in the normal course of the taxpayer's activity of dealing in or trading section 1256 contracts) from any section 1256 contract or property related to the contract. *Options dealer, commodities dealer,* and *section 1256 contract* have the same meaning as in section 1362(d)(3)(E)(ii).

(B) *Treatment of certain lending, financing and other businesses.—(1) In general.—Passive investment income* does not include gross receipts that are directly derived in the ordinary course of a trade or business of—

(i) Lending or financing;

(ii) Dealing in property;

(iii) Purchasing or discounting accounts receivable, notes, or installment obligations; or

(iv) Servicing mortgages.

(2) Directly derived.—For purposes of this paragraph (c)(5)(iii)(B), gross receipts directly derived in the ordinary course of business includes gain (as well as interest income) with respect to loans originated in a lending business, or interest income (as well as gain) from debt obligations of a dealer in such obligations. However, interest earned from the investment of idle funds in short-term securities does not constitute gross receipts directly derived in the ordinary course of business. Similarly, a dealer's income or gain from an item of property is not directly derived in the ordinary course of its trade or business if the dealer held the property for investment at any time before the income or gain is recognized.

(C) *Payment to a patron of a cooperative. Passive investment income* does not include amounts included in the gross income of a patron of a cooperative (within the meaning of section 1381(a), without regard to paragraph (2)(A) or (C) of section 1381(a)) by reason of any payment or allocation to the patron based on patronage occurring in the case of a trade or business of the patron.

* * *

[Reg. § 1.1362-2.]

☐ [*T.D.* 8449, 11-24-92. *Amended by T.D.* 8869, 1-20-2000 *and T.D.* 8995, 5-14-2002.]

§ 1.1362-3. Treatment of S termination year.—(a) *In general.*—If an S election terminates under section 1362(d) on a date other than the first day of a taxable year of the corporation, the corporation's taxable year in which the termination occurs is an S termination year. The portion of the S termination year ending at the close of the day prior to the termination is treated as a short taxable year for which the corporation is an S corporation (the *S short year*). The portion of the S termination year beginning on the day the termination is effective is treated as a short taxable year for which the corporation is a C corporation (the *C short year*). Except as provided in paragraphs (b) and (c)(1) of this section, the corporation allocates income or loss for the entire year on a pro rata basis as described in section 1362(e)(2). To the extent that income or loss is not allocated on a pro rata basis under this section, items of income, gain, loss, deduction, and credit are assigned to each short taxable year on the basis of the corporation's normal method of accounting as determined under section 446. See, however, § 1.1502-76(b)(1)(ii)(A)(*2*) for special rules for an S election that terminates under section 1362(d) immediately before the S corporation becomes a member of a consolidated group (within the meaning of § 1.1502-1(h)). See § 1.460-4(k)(3)(iv)(D) for rules relating to the computation of the S corporation's income or loss from a contract accounted for under a long-term contract method of accounting in the S termination year.

(b) *Allocations other than pro rata.*—(1) *Elections under section 1362(e)(3).*—The pro rata allocation rules of section 1362(e)(2) do not apply if the corporation elects to allocate its S termination year income on the basis of its normal tax accounting method. This election may be made only with the consent of each person who is a shareholder in the corporation at any time during the S short year and of each person who is a shareholder in the corporation on the first day of the C short year. See § 1.1362-6(a) for rules concerning the time and manner of making this election.

(2) *Purchase of stock treated as an asset purchase.*—The pro rata allocation rules of section 1362(e)(2) do not apply with respect to any item resulting from the application of section 338.

(3) *50 percent change in ownership during S termination year.*—The pro rata allocation rules of section 1362(e)(2) do not apply if at any time during the S termination year, as a result of sales or exchanges of stock in the corporation during that year, there is a change in ownership of 50 percent or more of the issued and outstanding shares of stock of the corporation. If stock has already been sold or exchanged during the S termination year, subsequent sales or exchanges of that stock are not taken into account for purposes of this paragraph (b)(3).

* * *

(d) *Examples.*—The provisions of this section are illustrated by the following examples:

Example 1. S termination year not created. (i) On January 1, 1993, the first day of its taxable year, a subchapter C corporation had three eligible shareholders. During 1993, the corporation properly elected to be treated as an S corporation effective January 1, 1994, the first day of the succeeding taxable year. Subsequently, a transfer of some of the stock in the corporation was made to an ineligible shareholder. The ineligible shareholder still holds the stock on January 1, 1994.

(ii) The corporation fails to meet the definition of a small business corporation on January 1, 1994, and its election is treated as having terminated on that date. See § 1.1362-2(b)(2) for the termination rules. Because the corporation ceases to be a small business corporation on the first day of a taxable year, an S termination year is not created. In addition, if the corporation in the future meets the definition of a small business corporation and desires to elect to be treated as an S corporation, the corporation is automatically granted consent to reelect before the expiration of the 5-year waiting period. See § 1.1362-5 for special rules concerning automatic consent to reelect.

Example 2. More than 50 percent change in ownership during S short year. A, an individual, owns all 100 outstanding shares of stock of *S*, a calendar year S corporation. On January 31, 1993, *A* sells 60 shares of *S* stock to *B*, an individual. On June 1, 1993, *A* sells 5 shares of *S* stock to *PRS*, a partnership. *S* ceases to be a small business corporation on June 1, 1993, and pursuant to section 1362(d)(2), its election terminates on that date. Because there was a more than 50 percent change in ownership of the issued and outstanding shares of *S* stock, *S* must assign the items of income, loss, deduction, or credit for the S termination year to the two short taxable years on the basis of *S*'s normal method of accounting under the rules of paragraph (b)(3) of this section.

Example 3. More than 50 percent change in ownership during C short year. A, an individual, owns all 100 outstanding shares of stock of *S*, a calendar year S corporation. On June 1, 1993, *A* sells 5 shares of *S* stock to *PRS*, a partnership. *S* ceases to be a small business corporation on that date and pursuant to section 1362(d)(3), its election terminates on that date. On July 1, 1993, *A* sells 60 shares of *S* stock to *B*, an individual. Since there was a more than 50 percent change in ownership of the issued and outstanding shares of *S* stock during the S termination year, *S* must assign the items of income, loss, deduction, or credit for the S termination year to the two short taxable years on the basis of *S*'s normal method of accounting under the rules of paragraph (b)(3) of this section.

Example 4. Stock acquired other than by sale or exchange. C and *D* are shareholders in *S*, a calendar year S corporation. Each owns 50 percent of the issued and outstanding shares of the corporation on December 31, 1993. On March 1, 1994, *C* makes a gift of his entire shareholder interest to *T*, a trust not permitted as a shareholder under section 1361(c)(2). *S* ceases to be a small business corporation on March 1, 1994, and pursuant to section 1362(d)(2), its S corporation election terminates effective on that date. As a result of the gift, *T* owns 50 percent of S's issued and outstanding stock. However, because *T* acquired the stock by gift from *C* rather than by sale or exchange, there has not been a more than 50 percent change in ownership by sale or exchange of *S* that would cause the rules of paragraph (b)(3) of this section to apply. [Reg. § 1.1362-3.]

□ [*T.D.* 8449, 11-24-92. *Amended by T.D.* 8842, 11-9-99 *and T.D.* 9137, 7-15-2004.]

§ 1.1362-4. Inadvertent terminations and inadvertently invalid elections.—(a) *In general.*—A corporation is treated as continuing to be an S corporation or a QSub (or, an invalid election to be either an S corporation or a QSub is treated as valid) during the period specified by the Commissioner if—

(1) The corporation made a valid election under section 1362(a) or section 1361(b)(3) and the election terminated or the corporation made an election under section 1362(a) or section 1361(b)(3) that was invalid;

(2) The Commissioner determines that the termination or invalidity was inadvertent;

(3) Within a reasonable period of time after discovery of the terminating event or invalid election, steps were taken so that the corporation for which the election was made or the termination occurred is a small business corporation or a QSub, as the case may be, or to acquire the required shareholder consents; and

(4) The corporation and shareholders agree to adjustments that the Commissioner may require for the period.

(b) *Inadvertent termination or inadvertently invalid election.*—For purposes of paragraph (a) of this section, the determination of whether a termination or invalid election was inadvertent is made by the Commissioner. The corporation has the burden of establishing that under the relevant facts and circumstances the Commissioner should determine that the termination or invalid election was inadvertent. The fact that the terminating event or invalidity of the election was not reasonably within the control of the corporation and, in the case of a termination, was not part of a plan to terminate the election, or the fact that the terminating event or circumstance took place without the knowledge of the corporation, notwithstanding its due diligence to safeguard itself against such an event or circumstance, tends to establish that the termination or invalidity of the election was inadvertent.

* * *

(f) *Status of corporation.*—The status of the corporation after the terminating event or invalid election and before the determination of inadvertence is determined by the Commissioner. Inadvertent termination or inadvertent invalid election relief may be granted retroactively for all years for which the terminating event or circumstance giving rise to invalidity is effective, in which case the corporation is treated as if its election was valid or had not terminated. Alternatively, relief may be granted only for the period in which the corporation became eligible for subchapter S or QSub treatment, in which case the corporation is treated as a C corporation or, in the case of a QSub with an inadvertently terminated or invalid election, as a separate C corporation, during the period for which the corporation was not eligible for its intended status.

(g) *Effective/applicability date.*—Paragraphs (a), (b), (c), (d), and (f) of this section are effective on August 14, 2008. [Reg. § 1.1362-4.]

□ [*T.D.* 8449, 11-24-92. *Amended by T.D.* 9422, 8-13-2008.]

§ 1.1362-5. Election after termination.—(a) *In general.*—Absent the Commissioner's consent, an S corporation whose election has terminated (or a successor corporation) may not make a new election under section 1362(a) for five taxable years as described in section 1362(g). However, the Commissioner may permit the corporation to make a new election before the 5-year period expires.

The corporation has the burden of establishing that under the relevant facts and circumstances, the Commissioner should consent to a new election. The fact that more than 50 percent of the stock in the corporation is owned by persons who did not own any stock in the corporation on the date of the termination tends to establish that consent should be granted. In the absence of this fact, consent ordinarily is denied unless the corporation shows that the event causing termination was not reasonably within the control of the corporation or shareholders having a substantial interest in the corporation and was not part of a plan on the part of the corporation or of such shareholders to terminate the election.

(b) *Successor corporation.*—A corporation is a *successor corporation* to a corporation whose election under section 1362 has been terminated if—

(1) 50 percent or more of the stock of the corporation (the new corporation) is owned, directly or indirectly, by the same persons who, on the date of the termination, owned 50 percent or more of the stock of the corporation whose election terminated (the old corporation); and

(2) Either the new corporation acquires a substantial portion of the assets of the old corporation, or a substantial portion of the assets of the new corporation were assets of the old corporation.

(c) *Automatic consent after certain terminations.*—A corporation may, without requesting the Commissioner's consent, make a new election under section 1362(a) before the 5-year period described in section 1362(g) expires if the termination occurred because the corporation—

(1) Revoked its election effective on the first day of the first taxable year for which its election was to be effective (see § 1.1362-2(a)(2)); or

(2) Failed to meet the definition of a small business corporation on the first day of the first taxable year for which its election was to be effective (see § 1.1362-2(b)(2)). [Reg. § 1.1362-5.]

☐ [*T.D.* 8449, 11-24-92.]

§ 1.1362-6. Elections and consents.—(a) *Time and manner of making elections.*—(1) *In general.*—An election statement made under this section must identify the election being made, set forth the name, address, and taxpayer identification number of the corporation, and be signed by a person authorized to sign the return required to be filed under section 6037.

(2) *Election to be an S corporation.*—(i) *Manner of making election.*—A small business corporation makes an election under section 1362(a) to be an S corporation by filing a completed Form 2553. The election form must be filed with the service center designated in the instructions applicable to Form 2553. The election is not valid unless all shareholders of the corporation at the time of the election consent to the election in the manner provided in paragraph (b) of this section. However, once a valid election is made, new shareholders need not consent to that election.

(ii) *Time of making election.*—(A) *In general.*—The election described in paragraph (a)(2)(i) of this section may be made by a small business corporation at any time during the taxable year that immediately precedes the taxable year for which the election is to be effective, or during the taxable year for which the election is to be effective provided that the election is made before the 16th day of the third month of the year. If a corporation makes an election for a taxable year, and the election meets all the requirements of this section but is made during the period beginning after the 15th day of the third month of the taxable year, the election is treated as being made for the following taxable year provided that the corporation meets all the requirements of section 1361(b) at the time the election is made. For taxable years of 2½ months or less, an election made before the 16th day of the third month after the first day of the taxable year is treated as made during that year.

(B) *Elections made during the first 2½ months treated as made for the following taxable year.*—A timely election made by a small business corporation during the taxable year for which it is intended to be effective is nonetheless treated as made for the following taxable year if—

(1) The corporation is not a small business corporation during the entire portion of the taxable year which occurs before the date the election is made; or

(2) Any person who held stock in the corporation at any time during the portion of the taxable year which occurs before the time the election is made, and who does not hold stock at the time the election is made, does not consent to the election.

(C) *Definition of month and beginning of the taxable year.*—*Month* means a period commencing on the same numerical day of any calendar month as the day of the calendar month on which the taxable year began and ending with the close of the day preceding the numerically corresponding day of the succeeding calendar month or, if there is no corresponding day, with the close of the last day of the succeeding calendar month. In addition, the taxable year of a new corporation begins on the date that the corporation has shareholders, acquires assets, or begins doing business, whichever is the first to occur. The existence of incorporators does not necessarily begin the taxable year of a new corporation.

(iii) *Examples.*—The provisions of this section are illustrated by the following examples:

Example 1. Effective election; no prior taxable year. A calendar year small business corporation begins its first taxable year on January 7, 1993. To be an S corporation beginning with its first taxable year, the corporation must make the election set forth in this section during the period that begins January 7, 1993, and ends before March 22, 1993. Because the corporation had no taxable year immediately preceding the taxable year for which the election is to be effective, an election made earlier than January 7, 1993, will not be valid.

Example 2. Effective election; taxable year less than 2½ months. A calendar year small business corporation begins its first taxable year on November 8, 1993. To be an S corporation beginning with its first taxable year, the corporation must make the election set forth in this section during the period that begins November 8, 1993, and ends before January 23, 1994.

Example 3. Election effective for the following taxable year; ineligible shareholder. On January 1, 1993, two individuals and a partnership own all of the stock of a calendar year subchapter C corporation. On January 31, 1993, the partnership dissolved and distributed its shares in the corporation to its five partners, all individuals. On February 28, 1993, the seven shareholders of the corporation consented to the corporation's election of subchapter S status. The corporation files a properly completed Form 2553 on March 2, 1993. The corporation is not eligible to be a subchapter S corporation for the 1993 taxable year because during the period of the taxable year prior to the election it had an ineligible shareholder. However, under paragraph (a)(2)(ii)(B) of this section, the election is treated as made for the corporation's 1994 taxable year.

(3) *Revocation of S election.*—(i) *Manner of revoking election.*—To revoke an election, the corporation files a statement that the corporation revokes the election made under section 1362(a). The statement must be filed with the service center where the election was properly filed. The revocation statement must include the number of shares of stock (including non-voting stock) issued and outstanding at the time the revocation is made. A revocation may be made only with the consent of shareholders who, at the time the revocation is made, hold more than one-half of the number of issued and outstanding shares of stock (including non-voting stock) of the corporation. Each shareholder who consents to the revocation must consent in the manner required under paragraph (b) of this section. In addition, each consent should indicate the number of issued and outstanding shares of stock (including non-voting stock) held by each shareholder at the time of the revocation.

(ii) *Time of revoking election.*—For rules concerning when a revocation is effective, see §1.1362-2(a)(2).

(iii) *Examples.*—The principles of this paragraph (a)(3) are illustrated by the following examples:

Example 1. Revocation; consent of shareholders owning more than one-half of issued and outstanding shares. A calendar year S corporation has issued and outstanding 40,000 shares of class A voting common stock and 20,000 shares of class B non-voting common stock. The corporation wishes to revoke its election of subchapter S status. Shareholders owning 11,000 shares of class A stock sign revocation consents. Shareholders owning 20,000 shares of class B stock sign revocation consents. The corporation has obtained the required shareholder consent to revoke its subchapter S election because shareholders owning more than one-half of the total number of issued and outstanding shares of stock of the corporation consented to the revocation.

Example 2. Effective prospective revocation. In June 1993, a calendar year S corporation determines that it will revoke its subchapter S election effective August 1, 1993. To do so it must file its revocation statement with consents attached on or before August 1, 1993, and the statement must indicate that the revocation is intended to be effective August 1, 1993.

(4) *Rescission of a revocation.*—(i) *Manner of rescinding a revocation.*—To rescind a revocation, the corporation files a statement that the corporation rescinds the revocation made under section 1362(d)(1). The statement must be filed with the service center where the revocation was properly filed. A rescission may be made only with the consent (in the manner required under paragraph (b)(1) of this section) of each person who consented to the revocation and of each person who became a shareholder of the corporation within the period beginning on the first day after the date the revocation was made and ending on the date on which the rescission is made.

(ii) *Time of rescinding a revocation.*—If the rescission statement is filed before the revocation becomes effective and is filed with proper service center, the rescission is effective on the date it is so filed.

(5) *Election not to apply pro rata allocation.*—To elect not to apply the pro rata allocation rules to an S termination year, a corporation files a statement that it elects under section 1362(e)(3) not to apply the rules provided in section 1362(e)(2). In addition to meeting the requirements of paragraph (a)(1) of this section, the statement must set forth the cause of the termination and the date thereof. The statement must be filed with the corporation's return for the C short year. This election may be made only with the consent of all persons who are shareholders of the corporation at any time during the S short year and all persons who are shareholders of the corporation on the first day of the C short year (in the manner required under paragraph (b)(1) of this section).

(b) *Shareholders' consents.*—(1) *Manner of consents in general.*—A shareholder's consent required under paragraph (a) of this section must be in the form of a written statement that sets forth the name, address, and taxpayer identification number of the shareholder, the number of shares of stock owned by the shareholder, the date (or dates) on which the stock was acquired, the date on which the shareholder's taxable year ends, the name of the S corporation, the corporation's taxpayer identification number, and the election to which the shareholder consents. The statement must be signed by the shareholder under penalties of perjury. Except as provided in paragraph (b)(3)(iii) of this section, the election of the corporation is not valid if any required consent is not filed in accordance with the rules contained in this paragraph (b). The consent statement should be attached to the corporation's election statement.

(2) *Persons required to consent.*—The following rules apply in determining persons required to consent:

(i) *Community interest in stock.*—When stock of the corporation is owned by husband and wife as community property (or the income from the stock is community property), or is owned by tenants in common, joint tenants, or tenants by the entirety, each person having a community interest in the stock or income therefrom and each tenant in common, joint tenant and tenant by the entirety must consent to the election.

(ii) *Minor.*—The consent of a minor must be made by the minor or by the legal representative of the minor (or by a natural or an adoptive parent of the minor if no legal representative has been appointed).

(iii) *Estate.*—The consent of an estate must be made by an executor or administrator thereof, or by any other fiduciary appointed by testamentary instrument or appointed by the court having jurisdiction over the administration of the estate.

(iv) *Trusts.*—In the case of a trust described in section 1361(c)(2)(A) (including a trust treated under section 1361(d)(1)(A) as a trust described in section 1361(c)(2)(A)(i) and excepting an electing small business trust described in section 1361(c)(2)(A)(v) (ESBT)), only the person treated as the shareholder for purposes of section 1361(b)(1) must consent to the election. When stock of the corporation is held by a trust, both husband and wife must consent to any election if the husband and wife have a community interest in the trust property. See paragraph (b)(2)(i) of this section for rules concerning community interests in S corporation stock. In the case of an ESBT, the trustee and the owner of any portion of the trust that consists of the stock in one or more S corporations under subpart E, part I, subchapter J, chapter 1 of the Internal Revenue Code must consent to the S corporation election. If there is more than one trustee, the trustee or trustees with authority to legally bind the trust must consent to the S corporation election.

(3) *Special rules for consent of shareholder to election to be an S corporation.*—(i) *In general.*—The consent of a shareholder to an election by a small business corporation under section 1362(a) may be made on Form 2553 or on a separate statement in the manner described in paragraph (b)(1) of this section. In addition, the separate statement must set forth the name, address, and taxpayer identification number of the corporation. A shareholder's consent is binding and may not be withdrawn after a valid election is made by the corporation. Each person who is a shareholder (including any person who is treated as a shareholder under section 1361(c)(2)(B)) at the time the election is made) must consent to the election. If the election is made before the 16th day of the third month of the taxable year and is intended to be effective for that year, each person who was a shareholder (including any person who was treated as a shareholder under section 1361(c)(2)(B)) at any time during the portion of that year which occurs before the time the election is made, and who is not a shareholder at the time the election is made, must also consent to the election. If the election is to be effective for the following taxable

year, no consent need be filed by any shareholder who is not a shareholder on the date of the election. Any person who is considered to be a shareholder under applicable state law solely by virtue of his or her status as an incorporator is not treated as a shareholder for purposes of this paragraph (b)(3)(i).

(ii) *Examples.*—The principles of this section are illustrated by the following examples:

Example 1. Effective election; shareholder consents. On January 1, 1993, the first day of its taxable year, a subchapter C corporation had 15 shareholders. On January 30, 1993, two of the C corporation's shareholders, *A* and *B,* both individuals, sold their shares in the corporation to *P, Q,* and *R,* all individuals. On March 1, 1993, the corporation filed its election to be an S corporation for the 1993 taxable year. The election will be effective (assuming the other requirements of section 1361(b) are met) provided that all of the shareholders as of March 1, 1993, as well as former shareholders *A* and *B,* consent to the election.

Example 2. Consent of new shareholder unnecessary. On January 1, 1993, three individuals own all of the stock of a calendar year subchapter C corporation. On April 15, 1993, the corporation, in accordance with paragraph (a)(2) of this section, files a properly completed Form 2553. The corporation anticipates that the election will be effective beginning January 1, 1994, the first day of the succeeding taxable year. On October 1, 1993, the three shareholders collectively sell 75% of their shares in the corporation to another individual. On January 1, 1994, the corporation's shareholders are the three original individuals and the new shareholder. Because the election was valid and binding when made, it is not necessary for the new shareholder to consent to the election. The corporation's subchapter S election is effective on January 1, 1994 (assuming the other requirements of section 1361(b) are met).

* * *

[Reg. § 1.1362-6.]

☐ [*T.D.* 8449, 11-24-92. *Amended by T.D.* 8994, 5-13-2002.]

§ 1.1362-8. Dividends received from affiliated subsidiaries.—(a) *In general.*—For purposes of section 1362(d)(3), if an S corporation holds stock in a C corporation meeting the requirements of section 1504(a)(2), the term *passive investment income* does not include dividends from the C corporation to the extent those dividends are attributable to the earnings and profits of the C corporation derived from the active conduct of a trade or business (active earnings and profits). For purposes of applying section 1362(d)(3), earnings and profits of a C corporation are active earnings and profits to the extent that the earnings and profits are derived from activities that would not produce passive investment income (as defined in section 1362(d)(3)) if the C corporation were an S corporation.

* * *

[Reg. § 1.1362-8.]

☐ [*T.D.* 8869, 1-20-2000 (*corrected* 3-27-2000).]

§ 1.1363-1. Effect of election on corporation.—(a) *Exemption of corporation from income tax.*—(1) *In general.*—Except as provided in this paragraph (a), a small business corporation that makes a valid election under section 1362(a) is exempt from the taxes imposed by chapter 1 of the Internal Revenue Code with respect to taxable years of the corporation for which the election is in effect.

(2) *Corporate level taxes.*—An S corporation is not exempt from the tax imposed by section 1374 (relating to the tax imposed on certain built-in gains), or section 1375 (relating to the tax on excess passive investment income). See also section 1363(d) (relating to the recapture of LIFO benefits) for the rules regarding the payment by an S corporation of LIFO recapture amounts.

(b) *Computation of corporate taxable income.*—The taxable income of an S corporation is computed as described in section 1363(b).

(c) *Elections of the S corporation.*—(1) *In general.*—Any elections (other than those described in paragraph (c)(2) of this section) affecting the computation of items derived from an S corporation are made by the corporation. For example, elections of methods of accounting, of computing depreciation, of treating soil and water conservation expenditures, and the option to deduct as expenses intangible drilling and development costs, are made by the corporation and not by the shareholders separately. All corporate elections are applicable to all shareholders.

(2) *Exceptions.*—(i) Each shareholder's pro rata share of expenses described in section 617 paid or accrued by the S corporation is treated according to the shareholder's method of treating those expenses, notwithstanding the treatment of the expenses by the corporation.

(ii) Each shareholder may elect to amortize that shareholder's pro rata share of any qualified expenditure described in section 59(e) paid or accrued by the S corporation.

(iii) Each shareholder's pro rata share of taxes described in section 901 paid or accrued by the S corporation to foreign countries or possessions of the United States (according to its method of treating those taxes) is treated according to the shareholder's method of treating those taxes, and each shareholder may elect to use the total amount either as a credit against tax or as a deduction from income.

* * *

[Reg. § 1.1363-1.]

□ [*T.D.* 8449, 11-24-92.]

§ 1.1366-1. Shareholder's share of items of an S corporation.—(a) *Determination of shareholder's tax liability.*—(1) *In general.*—An S corporation must report, and a shareholder is required to take into account in the shareholder's return, the shareholder's pro rata share, whether or not distributed, of the S corporation's items of income, loss, deduction, or credit described in paragraphs (a)(2), (3), and (4) of this section. A shareholder's pro rata share is determined in accordance with the provisions of section 1377(a) and the regulations thereunder. The shareholder takes these items into account in determining the shareholder's taxable income and tax liability for the shareholder's taxable year with or within which the taxable year of the corporation ends. If the shareholder dies (or if the shareholder is an estate or trust and the estate or trust terminates) before the end of the taxable year of the corporation, the shareholder's pro rata share of these items is taken into account on the shareholder's final return. For the limitation on allowance of a shareholder's pro rata share of S corporation losses or deductions, see section 1366(d) and § 1.1366-2.

(2) *Separately stated items of income, loss, deduction, or credit.*—Each shareholder must take into account separately the shareholder's pro rata share of any item of income (including tax-exempt income), loss, deduction, or credit of the S corporation that if separately taken into account by any shareholder could affect the shareholder's tax liability for that taxable year differently than if the shareholder did not take the item into account separately. The separately stated items of the S corporation include, but are not limited to, the following items—

(i) The corporation's combined net amount of gains and losses from sales or exchanges of capital assets grouped by applicable holding periods, by applicable rate of tax under section 1(h), and by any other classification that may be relevant in determining the shareholder's tax liability;

(ii) The corporation's combined net amount of gains and losses from sales or exchanges of property described in section 1231 (relating to property used in the trade or business and involuntary conversions), grouped by applicable holding periods, by applicable rate of tax under section 1(h), and by any other classification that may be relevant in determining the shareholder's tax liability;

(iii) Charitable contributions, grouped by the percentage limitations of section 170(b), paid by the corporation within the taxable year of the corporation;

(iv) The taxes described in section 901 that have been paid (or accrued) by the corporation to foreign countries or to possessions of the United States;

(v) Each of the corporation's separate items involved in the determination of credits against tax allowable under part IV of subchapter A (section 21 and following) of the Internal Revenue Code, except for any credit allowed under section 34 (relating to certain uses of gasoline and special fuels);

(vi) Each of the corporation's separate items of gains and losses from wagering transactions (section 165(d)); soil and water conservation expenditures (section 175); deduction under an election to expense certain depreciable business expenses (section 179); medical, dental, etc., expenses (section 213); the additional itemized deductions for individuals provided in part VII of subchapter B (section 212 and following) of the Internal Revenue Code; and any other itemized deductions for which the limitations on itemized deductions under sections 67 or 68 applies;

(vii) Any of the corporation's items of portfolio income or loss, and expenses related thereto, as defined in the regulations under section 469;

(viii) The corporation's tax-exempt income. For purposes of subchapter S, tax-exempt income is income that is permanently excludible from gross income in all circumstances in which the applicable provision of the Internal Revenue Code applies. For example, income that is excludible from gross income under section 101 (certain death benefits) or section 103 (interest on state and local bonds) is tax-exempt income, while income that is excludible from gross income under section 108 (income from discharge of indebtedness) or section 109 (improvements by lessee on lessor's property) is not tax-exempt income;

(ix) The corporation's adjustments described in sections 56 and 58, and items of tax preference described in section 57; and

(x) Any item identified in guidance (including forms and instructions) issued by the Commissioner as an item required to be separately stated under this paragraph (a)(2).

(3) *Nonseparately computed income or loss.*—Each shareholder must take into account separately the shareholder's pro rata share of the nonseparately computed income or loss of

the S corporation. For this purpose, nonseparately computed income or loss means the corporation's gross income less the deductions allowed to the corporation under chapter 1 of the Internal Revenue Code, determined by excluding any item requiring separate computation under paragraph (a)(2) of this section.

(4) *Separate activities requirement.*—An S corporation must report, and each shareholder must take into account in the shareholder's return, the shareholder's pro rata share of an S corporation's items of income, loss, deduction, or credit described in paragraphs (a)(2) and (3) of this section for each of the corporation's activities as defined in section 469 and the regulations thereunder.

(5) *Aggregation of deductions or exclusions for purposes of limitations.*—(i) *In general.*—A shareholder aggregates the shareholder's separate deductions or exclusions with the shareholder's pro rata share of the S corporation's separately stated deductions or exclusions in determining the amount of any deduction or exclusion allowable to the shareholder under subtitle A of the Internal Revenue Code as to which a limitation is imposed.

(ii) *Example.*—The provisions of paragraph (a)(5)(i) of this section are illustrated by the following example:

Example. In 1999, Corporation M, a calendar year S corporation, purchases and places in service section 179 property costing $10,000. Corporation M elects to expense the entire cost of the property. Shareholder A owns 50 percent of the stock of Corporation M. Shareholder A's pro rata share of this item after Corporation M applies the section 179(b) limitations is $5,000. Because the aggregate amount of Shareholder A's pro rata share and separately acquired section 179 expense may not exceed $19,000 (the aggregate maximum cost that may be taken into account under section 179(a) for the applicable taxable year), Shareholder A may elect to expense up to $14,000 of separately acquired section 179 property that is purchased and placed in service in 1999, subject to the limitations of section 179(b).

(b) *Character of items constituting pro rata share.*—(1) *In general.*—Except as provided in paragraph (b)(2) or (3) of this section, the character of any item of income, loss, deduction, or credit described in section 1366(a)(1)(A) or (B) and paragraph (a) of this section is determined for the S corporation and retains that character in the hands of the shareholder. For example, if an S corporation has capital gain on the sale or exchange of a capital asset, a shareholder's pro rata share of that gain will also be characterized as a capital gain regardless of whether the shareholder is otherwise a dealer in that type of property. Similarly, if an S corporation engages in an activity that is not for profit (as defined in section 183), a shareholder's pro rata share of the S corporation's deductions will be characterized as not for profit. Also, if an S corporation makes a charitable contribution to an organization qualifying under section 170(b)(1)(A), a shareholder's pro rata share of the S corporation's charitable contribution will be characterized as made to an organization qualifying under section 170(b)(1)(A).

(2) *Exception for contribution of noncapital gain property.*—If an S corporation is formed or availed of by any shareholder or group of shareholders for a principal purpose of selling or exchanging contributed property that in the hands of the shareholder or shareholders would not have produced capital gain if sold or exchanged by the shareholder or shareholders, then the gain on the sale or exchange of the property recognized by the corporation is not treated as a capital gain.

(3) *Exception for contribution of capital loss property.*—If an S corporation is formed or availed of by any shareholder or group of shareholders for a principal purpose of selling or exchanging contributed property that in the hands of the shareholder or shareholders would have produced capital loss if sold or exchanged by the shareholder or shareholders, then the loss on the sale or exchange of the property recognized by the corporation is treated as a capital loss to the extent that, immediately before the contribution, the adjusted basis of the property in the hands of the shareholder or shareholders exceeded the fair market value of the property.

(c) *Gross income of a shareholder.*—(1) *In general.*—Where it is necessary to determine the amount or character of the gross income of a shareholder, the shareholder's gross income includes the shareholder's pro rata share of the gross income of the S corporation. The shareholder's pro rata share of the gross income of the S corporation is the amount of gross income of the corporation used in deriving the shareholder's pro rata share of S corporation taxable income or loss (including items described in section 1366(a)(1)(A) or (B) and paragraph (a) of this section). For example, a shareholder is required to include the shareholder's pro rata share of S corporation gross income in computing the shareholder's gross income for the purposes of determining the necessity of filing a return (section 6012(a)) and the shareholder's gross income derived from farming (sections 175 and 6654(i)).

(2) *Gross income for substantial omission of items.*—(i) *In general.*—For purposes of determining the applicability of the 6-year period of limitation on assessment and collection provided in section 6501(e) (relating to omission of more than 25 percent of gross income), a shareholder's gross income includes the shareholder's pro rata share of S corporation gross income (as described in section 6501(e)(1)(A)(i)). In this respect, the amount of S corporation gross income used in deriving the shareholder's pro rata share of any item of S corporation income, loss, deduction, or credit (as included or disclosed in the shareholder's return) is considered as an amount of gross income stated in the shareholder's return for purposes of section 6501(e).

(ii) *Example.*—The following example illustrates the provisions of paragraph (c)(2)(i) of this section:

Example. Shareholder A, an individual, owns 25 percent of the stock of Corporation N, an S corporation that has $10,000 gross income and $2,000 taxable income. A reports only $300 as A's pro rata share of N's taxable income. A should have reported $500 as A's pro rata share of taxable income, derived from A's pro rata share, $2,500, of N's gross income. Because A's return included only $300 without a disclosure meeting the requirements of section 6501(e)(1)(A)(ii) describing the difference of $200, A is regarded as having reported on the return only $1,500 ($300/$500 of $2,500) as gross income from N.

(d) *Shareholders holding stock subject to community property laws.*—If a shareholder holds S corporation stock that is community property, then the shareholder's pro rata share of any item or items listed in paragraphs (a)(2), (3), and (4) of this section with respect to that stock is reported by the husband and wife in accordance with community property rules.

(e) *Net operating loss deduction of shareholder of S corporation.*—For purposes of determining a net operating loss deduction under section 172, a shareholder of an S corporation must take into account the shareholder's pro rata share of items of income, loss, deduction, or credit of the corporation. See section 1366(b) and paragraph (b) of this section for rules on determining the character of the items. In determining under section 172(d)(4) the nonbusiness deductions allowable to a shareholder of an S corporation (arising from both corporation sources and any other sources), the shareholder separately takes into account the shareholder's pro rata share of the deductions of the corporation that are not attributable to a trade or business and combines this amount with the shareholder's nonbusiness deductions from any other sources. The shareholder also separately takes into account the shareholder's pro rata share of the gross income of the corporation not derived from a trade or business and combines this amount with the shareholder's nonbusiness income from all other sources. See section 172 and the regulations thereunder.

(f) *Cross-reference.*—For rules relating to the consistent tax treatment of subchapter S items, see section 6037(c). [Reg. § 1.1366-1.]

☐ [*T.D.* 8852, 12-21-99.]

§ 1.1366-2. Limitations on deduction of passthrough items of an S corporation to its shareholders.—(a) *In general.*—(1) *Limitation on losses and deductions.*—The aggregate amount of losses and deductions taken into account by a shareholder under § 1.1366-1(a)(2), (3), and (4) for any taxable year of an S corporation cannot exceed the sum of—

(i) The adjusted basis of the shareholder's stock in the corporation (as determined under paragraph (a)(4)(i) of this section); and

(ii) The adjusted basis of any indebtedness of the corporation to the shareholder (as determined under paragraphs (a)(2) and (a)(4)(ii) of this section).

(2) *Basis of indebtedness.*—(i) *In general.*—The term *basis of any indebtedness of the S corporation to the shareholder* means the shareholder's adjusted basis (as defined in § 1.1011-1 and as specifically provided in section 1367(b)(2)) in any bona fide indebtedness of the S corporation that runs directly to the shareholder. Whether indebtedness is bona fide indebtedness to a shareholder is determined under general Federal tax principles and depends upon all of the facts and circumstances.

(ii) *Special rule for guarantees.*—A shareholder does not obtain basis of indebtedness in the S corporation merely by guaranteeing a loan or acting as a surety, accommodation party, or in any similar capacity relating to a loan. When a shareholder makes a payment on bona fide indebtedness of the S corporation for which the shareholder has acted as guarantor or in a similar capacity, then the shareholder may increase the shareholder's basis of indebtedness to the extent of that payment.

(iii) *Examples.*—The following examples illustrate the provisions of paragraph (a)(2)(i) and (ii) of this section:

Example 1. Shareholder loan transaction. A is the sole shareholder of S, an S corporation. S received a loan from A. Whether the loan from A to S constitutes bona fide indebtedness from S to A is determined under general Federal tax principles and depends upon all of the facts and circumstances. See paragraph (a)(2)(i) of this section. If the loan constitutes bona fide indebtedness from S to A, A's loan to S increases A's basis of indebtedness under paragraph (a)(2)(i) of this section. The result is the same if A made the loan to S through an entity that is disregarded as an entity separate from A under § 301.7701-3 of this chapter.

Example 2. Back-to-back loan transaction. A is the sole shareholder of two S corporations, S1 and S2. S1 loaned $200,000 to A. A then loaned $200,000 to S2. Whether the loan from A to S2 constitutes bona fide indebtedness from S2 to A is determined under general Federal tax principles and depends upon all of the facts and circumstances. See paragraph (a)(2)(i) of this section. If A's loan to S2 constitutes bona fide indebtedness from S2 to A, A's back-to-back loan increases A's basis of indebtedness in S2 under paragraph (a)(2)(i) of this section.

Example 3. Loan restructuring through distributions. A is the sole shareholder of two S corporations, S1 and S2. In May 2014, S1 made a loan to S2. In December 2014, S1 assigned its creditor position in the note to A by making a distribution to A of the note. Under local law, after S1 distributed the note to A, S2 was relieved of its liability to S1 and was directly liable to A. Whether S2 is indebted to A rather than S1 is determined under general Federal tax principles and depends upon all of the facts and circumstances. See paragraph (a)(2)(i) of this section. If the note constitutes bona fide indebtedness from S2 to A, the note increases A's basis of indebtedness in S2 under paragraph (a)(2)(i) of this section.

Example 4. Guarantee. A is a shareholder of S, an S corporation. In 2014, S received a loan from Bank. Bank required A's guarantee as a condition of making the loan to S. Beginning in 2015, S could no longer make payments on the loan and A made payments directly to Bank from A's personal funds until the loan obligation was satisfied. For each payment A made on the note, A obtains basis of indebtedness under paragraph (a)(2)(ii) of this section. Thus, A's basis of indebtedness is increased during 2015 under paragraph (a)(2)(ii) of this section to the extent of A's payments to Bank pursuant to the guarantee agreement.

(3) *Carryover of disallowance.*—A shareholder's aggregate amount of losses and deductions for a taxable year in excess of the sum of the adjusted basis of the shareholder's stock in an S corporation and of any indebtedness of the S corporation to the shareholder is not allowed for the taxable year. However, any disallowed loss or deduction retains its character and is treated as incurred by the corporation in the corporation's first succeeding taxable year, and subsequent taxable years, with respect to the shareholder. For rules on determining the adjusted bases of stock of an S corporation and indebtedness of the corporation to the shareholder, see paragraphs (a)(4)(i) and (ii) of this section.

(4) *Basis limitation amount.*—(i) *Stock portion.*—A shareholder generally determines the adjusted basis of stock for purposes of paragraphs (a)(1)(i) and (3) of this section (limiting losses and deductions) by taking into account only increases in basis under section 1367(a)(1) for the taxable year and decreases in basis under section 1367(a)(2)(A), (D) and (E) (relating to distributions, noncapital, nondeductible expenses, and certain oil and gas depletion deductions) for the taxable year. In so determining this loss limitation amount, the shareholder disregards decreases in basis under section 1367(a)(2)(B) and (C) (for losses and deductions, including losses and deductions previously disallowed) for the taxable year., However, if the shareholder has in effect for the taxable year an election under § 1.1367-1(g) to decrease basis by items of loss and deduction prior to decreasing basis by noncapital, nondeductible expenses and certain oil and gas depletion deductions, the shareholder also disregards decreases in basis under section 1367(a)(2)(D) and (E). This basis limitation amount for stock is determined at the time prescribed under § 1.1367-1(d)(1) for adjustments to the basis of stock.

(ii) *Indebtedness portion.*—A shareholder determines the shareholder's adjusted basis in indebtedness of the corporation for purposes of paragraphs (a)(1)(ii) and (3) of this section (limiting losses and deductions) without regard to any adjustment under section 1367(b)(2)(A) for the taxable year. This basis limitation amount for indebtedness is determined at the time prescribed under § 1.1367-2(d)(1) for adjustments to the basis of indebtedness.

(5) *Limitation on losses and deductions allocated to each item.*—If a shareholder's pro rata share of the aggregate amount of losses and deductions specified in § 1.1366-1(a)(2), (3), and (4) exceeds the sum of the adjusted basis of the shareholder's stock in the corporation (determined in accordance with paragraph (a)(4)(i) of this section) and the adjusted basis of any indebtedness of the corporation to the shareholder (determined in accordance with paragraph (a)(4)(ii) of this section), then the limitation on losses and deductions under section 1366(d)(1) must be allocated among the

shareholder's pro rata share of each loss or deduction. The amount of the limitation allocated to any loss or deduction is an amount that bears the same ratio to the amount of the limitation as the loss or deduction bears to the total of the losses and deductions. For this purpose, the total of losses and deductions for the taxable year is the sum of the shareholder's pro rata share of losses and deductions for the taxable year, and the losses and deductions disallowed and carried forward from prior years pursuant to section 1366(d)(2).

(6) *Nontransferability of losses and deductions.*—(i) *In general.*—Except as provided in paragraph (a)(6)(ii) of this section, any loss or deduction disallowed under paragraph (a)(1) of this section is personal to the shareholder and cannot in any manner be transferred to another person. If a shareholder transfers some but not all of the shareholder's stock in the corporation, the amount of any disallowed loss or deduction under this section is not reduced and the transferee does not acquire any portion of the disallowed loss or deduction. If a shareholder transfers all of the shareholder's stock in the corporation, any disallowed loss or deduction is permanently disallowed.

(ii) *Exceptions for transfers of stock under section 1041(a).*—If a shareholder transfers stock of an S corporation after December 31, 2004, in a transfer described in section 1041(a), any loss or deduction with respect to the transferred stock that is disallowed to the transferring shareholder under paragraph (a)(1) of this section shall be treated as incurred by the corporation in the following taxable year with respect to the transferee spouse or former spouse. The amount of any loss or deduction with respect to the stock transferred shall be determined by prorating any losses or deductions disallowed under paragraph (a)(1) of this section for the year of the transfer between the transferor and the spouse or former spouse based on the stock ownership at the beginning of the following taxable year. If a transferor claims a deduction for losses in the taxable year of transfer, then under paragraph (a)(5) of this section, if the transferor's pro rata share of the losses and deductions in the year of transfer exceeds the transferor's basis in stock and the indebtedness of the corporation to the transferor, then the limitation must be allocated among the transferor spouse's pro rata share of each loss or deduction, including disallowed losses and deductions carried over from the prior year.

(iii) *Examples.*—The following examples illustrates the provisions of paragraph (a)(6)(ii) of this section:

Example 1. *A* owns all 100 shares in *X*, a calendar year S corporation. For *X*'s taxable year ending December 31, 2006, *A* has zero basis in the shares and *X* does not have any indebtedness to *A*. For the 2006 taxable year, *X* had $100 in losses that *A* cannot use because of the basis limitation in section 1366(d)(1) and that are treated as incurred by the corporation with respect to *A* in the following taxable year. Halfway through the 2007 taxable year, *A* transfers 50 shares to *B*, *A*'s former spouse in a transfer to which section 1041(a) applies. In the 2007 taxable year, *X* has $80 in losses. On *A*'s 2007 individual income tax return, *A* may use the entire $100 carryover loss from 2006, as well as *A*'s share of the $80 2007 loss determined under section 1377(a) ($60), assuming *A* acquires sufficient basis in the *X* stock. On *B*'s 2007 individual income tax return, *B* may use *B*'s share of the $80 2007 loss determined under section 1377(a) ($20), assuming *B* has sufficient basis in the *X* stock. If any disallowed 2006 loss is disallowed to *A* under section 1366(d)(1) in 2007, that loss is prorated between *A* and *B* based on their stock ownership at the beginning of 2008. On *B*'s 2008 individual income tax return, *B* may use that loss, assuming *B* acquires sufficient basis in the *X* stock. If neither *A* nor *B* acquires any basis during the 2007 taxable year, then as of the beginning of 2008, the corporation will be treated as incurring $50 of loss with respect to A and $50 of loss with respect to B for the $100 of disallowed 2006 loss, and the corporation will be treated as incurring $60 of loss with respect to *A* and $20 with respect to *B* for the $80 of disallowed 2007 loss.

Example 2. Assume the same facts as *Example 1*, except that during the 2007 taxable year, *A* acquires $10 of basis in *A*'s shares in *X*. For the 2007 taxable year, *A* may claim a $10 loss deduction, which represents $6.25 of the disallowed 2006 loss of $100 and $3.75 of *A*'s 2007 loss of $60. The disallowed 2006 loss is reduced to $93.75. As of the beginning of 2008, the corporation will be treated as incurring half of the remaining $93.75 of loss with respect to *A* and half of that loss with respect to *B* for the remaining $93.75 of disallowed 2006 loss, and if *B* does not acquire any basis during 2007, the corporation will be treated as incurring $56.25 of loss with respect to *A* and $20 with respect to *B* for the remaining disallowed 2007 loss.

(7) *Basis of stock acquired by gift.*—For purposes of section 1366(d)(1)(A) and paragraphs (a)(1)(i) and (3) of this section, the basis of stock in a corporation acquired by gift is the basis of the stock that is used for purposes of determining loss under section 1015(a).

(b) *Special rules for carryover of disallowed losses and deductions to post-termination transition period described in section 1377(b).*—(1) *In general.*—If, for the last taxable year of a corporation for which it was an S corporation, a loss or deduction was disallowed to a shareholder by reason of the limitation in paragraph (a) of this section, the loss or deduction is treated under section 1366(d)(3) as incurred by that shareholder on the last day of any post-termination transition period (within the meaning of section 1377(b)).

(2) *Limitation on losses and deductions.*—The aggregate amount of losses and deductions taken into account by a shareholder under paragraph (b)(1) of this section cannot exceed the adjusted basis of the shareholder's stock in the corporation determined at the close of the last day of the post-termination transition period. For this purpose, the adjusted basis of a shareholder's stock in the corporation is determined at the close of the last day of the post-termination transition period without regard to any reduction required under paragraph (b)(4) of this section. If a shareholder disposes of a share of stock prior to the close of the last day of the post-termination transition period, the adjusted basis of that share is its basis as of the close of the day of disposition. Any losses and deductions in excess of a shareholder's adjusted stock basis are permanently disallowed. For purposes of section 1366(d)(3)(B) and this paragraph (b)(2), the basis of stock in a corporation acquired by gift is the basis of the stock that is used for purposes of determining loss under section 1015(a).

(3) *Limitation on losses and deductions allocated to each item.*—If the aggregate amount of losses and deductions treated as incurred by the shareholder under paragraph (b)(1) of this section exceeds the adjusted basis of the shareholder's stock determined under paragraph (b)(2) of this section, the limitation on losses and deductions under section 1366(d)(3)(B) must be allocated among each loss or deduction. The amount of the limitation allocated to each loss or deduction is an amount that bears the same ratio to the amount of the limitation as the amount of each loss or deduction bears to the total of all the losses and deductions.

(4) *Adjustment to the basis of stock.*—The shareholder's basis in the stock of the corporation is reduced by the amount allowed as a deduction by reason of this paragraph (b). For rules regarding adjustments to the basis of a shareholder's stock in an S corporation, see § 1.1367-1.

(c) *Carryover of disallowed losses and deductions in the case of liquidations, reorganizations, and divisions.*—(1) *Liquidations and reorganizations.*—If a corporation acquires the assets of an S corporation in a transaction to which section 381(a) applies, any loss or deduction disallowed under paragraph (a) of this section with respect to a shareholder of the distributor or transferor S corporation is available to that shareholder as a shareholder of the acquiring corporation. Thus, where the acquiring corporation is an S corporation, a loss or deduction of a shareholder of the distributor or transferor S corporation disallowed prior to or during the taxable year of the transaction is treated as incurred by the acquiring S corporation with respect to that shareholder if the shareholder is a shareholder of the acquiring S corporation after the transaction. Where the acquiring corporation is a C corporation, a post-termination transition period arises the day after the last day that an S corporation was in existence and the rules provided in paragraph (b) of this section apply with respect to any shareholder of the acquired S corporation that is also a shareholder of the acquiring C corporation after the transaction. See the special rules under section 1377 for the availability of the post-termination transition period if the acquiring corporation is a C corporation.

(2) *Corporate separations to which section 368(a)(1)(D) applies.*—If an S corporation transfers a portion of its assets constituting an active trade or business to another corporation in a transaction to which section 368(a)(1)(D) applies, and immediately thereafter the stock and securities of the controlled corporation are distributed in a distribution or exchange to which section 355 (or so much of section 356 as relates to section 355) applies, any loss or deduction disallowed under paragraph (a) of this section with respect to a shareholder of the distributing S corporation immediately before the transaction is allocated between the distributing corporation and the controlled corporation with respect to the shareholder. Such allocation shall be made according to any reasonable method, including a method based on the relative fair market value of the shareholder's stock in the distributing and controlled corporations immediately after the distribution, a method based on the relative adjusted basis of the assets in the distributing and controlled corporations immediately after the distribution, or, in the case of losses and deductions clearly attributable to either the distributing or controlled corporation, any method that allocates such losses and deductions accordingly. [Reg. § 1.1366-2.]

☐ [*T.D.* 8247, 4-4-89. *Amended by T.D.* 8852, 12-21-99; *T.D.* 9422, 8-13-2008 *and T.D.* 9682, 7-22-2014.]

§1.1366-3. Treatment of family groups.—(a) *In general.*—Under section 1366(e), if an individual, who is a member of the family of one or more shareholders of an S corporation, renders services for, or furnishes capital to, the corporation without receiving reasonable compensation, the Commissioner shall prescribe adjustments to those items taken into account by the individual and the shareholders as may be necessary to reflect the value of the services rendered or capital furnished. For these purposes, in determining the reasonable value for services rendered, or capital furnished, to the corporation, consideration will be given to all the facts and circumstances, including the amount that ordinarily would be paid in order to obtain comparable services or capital from a person (other than a member of the family) who is not a shareholder in the corporation. In addition, for purposes of section 1366(e), if a member of the family of one or more shareholders of the S corporation holds an interest in a passthrough entity (e.g., a partnership, S corporation, trust, or estate), that performs services for, or furnishes capital to, the S corporation without receiving reasonable compensation, the Commissioner shall prescribe adjustments to the passthrough entity and the corporation as may be necessary to reflect the value of the services rendered or capital furnished. For purposes of section 1366(e), the term *family* of any shareholder includes only the shareholder's spouse, ancestors, lineal descendants, and any trust for the primary benefit of any of these persons.

(b) *Examples.*—The provisions of this section may be illustrated by the following examples:

Example 1. The stock of an S corporation is owned 50 percent by F and 50 percent by T, the minor son of F. For the taxable year, the corporation has items of taxable income equal to $70,000. Compensation of $10,000 is paid by the corporation to F for services rendered during the taxable year, and no compensation is paid to T, who rendered no services. Based on all the relevant facts and circumstances, reasonable compensation for the services rendered by F would be $30,000. In the discretion of the Internal Revenue Service, up to an additional $20,000 of the $70,000 of the corporation's taxable income, for tax purposes, may be allocated to F as compensation for services rendered. If the Internal Revenue Service allocates $20,000 of the corporation's taxable income to F as compensation for services, taxable income of the corporation would be reduced by $20,000 to $50,000, of which F and T each would be allocated $25,000. F would have $30,000 of total compensation paid by the corporation for services rendered.

Example 2. The stock of an S corporation is owned by A and B. For the taxable year, the corporation has paid compensation to a partnership that rendered services to the corporation during the taxable year. The spouse of A is a partner in that partnership. Consequently, if based on all the relevant facts and circumstances the partnership did not receive reasonable compensation for the services rendered to the corporation, the Internal Revenue Service, in its discretion, may make adjustments to those items taken into account by the partnership and the corporation as may be necessary to reflect the value of the services rendered. [Reg. §1.1366-3.]

☐ [*T.D.* 8852, 12-21-99.]

§1.1366-4. Special rules limiting the passthrough of certain items of an S corporation to its shareholders.—(a) *Passthrough inapplicable to section 34 credit.*—Section 1.1366-1(a) does not apply to any credit allowable under section 34 (relating to certain uses of gasoline and special fuels).

(b) *Reduction in passthrough for tax imposed on built-in gains.*—For purposes of §1.1366-1(a), if for any taxable year of the S corporation a tax is imposed on the corporation under section 1374, the amount of the tax imposed is treated as a loss sustained by the S corporation during the taxable year. The character of the deemed loss is determined by allocating the loss proportionately among the net recognized built-in gains giving rise to the tax and attributing the character of each net recognized built-in gain to the allocable portion of the loss.

(c) *Reduction in passthrough for tax imposed on excess net passive income.*—For purposes of §1.1366-1(a), if for any taxable year of the S corporation a tax is imposed on the corporation under section 1375, each item of passive investment income shall be reduced by an amount that bears the same ratio to the amount of the tax as the net amount of the item bears to the total net passive investment income for that taxable year. [Reg. §1.1366-4.]

☐ [*T.D.* 8852, 12-21-99 (*corrected* 3-8-2000).]

§1.1367-1. Adjustments to basis of shareholder's stock in an S corporation.—(a) *In general.*—(1) *Adjustments under section 1367.*—This section provides rules relating to adjustments required by section 1367 to the basis of a shareholder's stock in an S corporation. Paragraph (b) of this section provides rules concerning increases in the basis of a shareholder's stock, and paragraph (c) of this section provides rules concerning decreases in the basis of a shareholder's stock.

(2) *Applicability of other Internal Revenue Code provisions.*—In addition to the adjustments required by section 1367 and this section, the basis of stock is determined or adjusted under other applicable provisions of the Internal Revenue Code.

(b) *Increase in basis of stock.*—(1) *In general.*—Except as provided in § 1.1367-2(c) (relating to restoration of basis of indebtedness to the shareholder), the basis of a shareholder's stock in an S corporation is increased by the sum of the items described in section 1367(a)(1). The increase in basis described in section 1367(a)(1)(C) for the excess of the deduction for depletion over the basis of the property subject to depletion does not include the depletion deduction attributable to oil or gas property. See section 613(A)(c)(11).

(2) *Amount of increase in basis of individual shares.*—The basis of a shareholder's share of stock is increased by an amount equal to the shareholder's pro rata portion of the items described in section 1367(a)(1) that is attributable to that share, determined on a per share, per day basis in accordance with section 1377(a).

(c) *Decrease in basis of stock.*—(1) *In general.*—The basis of a shareholder's stock in an S corporation is decreased (but not below zero) by the sum of the items described in section 1367(a)(2).

(2) *Noncapital, nondeductible expenses.*—For purposes of section 1367(a)(2)(D), expenses of the corporation not deductible in computing its taxable income and not properly chargeable to a capital account (*noncapital, nondeductible expenses*) are only those items for which no loss or deduction is allowable and do not include items the deduction for which is deferred to a later taxable year. Examples of noncapital, nondeductible expenses include (but are not limited to) the following: illegal bribes, kickbacks, and other payments not deductible under section 162(c); fines and penalties not deductible under section 162(f); expenses and interest relating to tax-exempt income under section 265; losses for which the deduction is disallowed under section 267(a)(1); the portion of meals and entertainment expenses disallowed under section 274; and the two-thirds portion of treble damages paid for violating antitrust laws not deductible under section 162. For basis adjustments necessary to coordinate sections 1367 and 362(e)(2), see § 1.362-4(e)(2).

(3) *Amount of decrease in basis of individual shares.*—The basis of a shareholder's share of stock is decreased by an amount equal to the shareholder's pro rata portion of the passthrough items and distributions described in section 1367(a)(2) attributable to that share, determined on a per share, per day basis in accordance with section 1377(a). If the amount attributable to a share exceeds its basis, the excess is applied to reduce (but not below zero) the remaining bases of all other shares of stock in the corporation owned by the shareholder in proportion to the remaining basis of each of those shares.

(d) *Time at which adjustments to basis of stock are effective.*—(1) *In general.*—The adjustments described in section 1367(a) to the basis of a shareholder's stock are determined as of the close of the corporation's taxable year, and the adjustments generally are effective as of that date. However, if a shareholder disposes of stock during the corporation's taxable year, the adjustments with respect to that stock are effective immediately prior to the disposition.

(2) *Adjustment for nontaxable item.*—An adjustment for a nontaxable item is determined for the taxable year in which the item would have been includible or deductible under the corporation's method of accounting for federal income tax purposes if the item had been subject to federal income taxation.

(3) *Effect of election under section 1377(a)(2) or § 1.1368-1(g)(2).*—If an election under section 1377(a)(2) (to terminate the year in the case of the termination of a shareholder's interest) or under § 1.1368-1(g)(2) (to terminate the year in the case of a qualifying disposition) is made with respect to the taxable year of a corporation, this paragraph (d) applies as if the taxable year consisted of separate taxable years, the first of which ends at the close of the day on which either the shareholder's interest is terminated or a qualifying disposition occurs, whichever the case may be.

* * *

(f) *Ordering rules for taxable years beginning on or after August 18, 1998.*—For any taxable year of a corporation beginning on or after August 18, 1998, except as provided in paragraph (g) of this section, the adjustments required by section 1367(a) are made in the following order—

(1) Any increase in basis attributable to the income items described in section 1367(a)(1)(A) and (B), and the excess of the deductions for depletion described in section 1367(a)(1)(C);

(2) Any decrease in basis attributable to a distribution by the corporation described in section 1367(a)(2)(A);

(3) Any decrease in basis attributable to noncapital, nondeductible expenses described in section 1367(a)(2)(D), and the oil and gas depletion deduction described in section 1367(a)(2)(E); and

(4) Any decrease in basis attributable to items of loss or deduction described in section 1367(a)(2)(B) and (C).

(g) *Elective ordering rule.*—A shareholder may elect to decrease basis under paragraph (e)(3) or (f)(4) of this section, whichever applies, prior to decreasing basis under paragraph (e)(2) or (f)(3) of this section, whichever applies. If a shareholder makes this election, any amount described in paragraph (e)(2) or (f)(3) of this section, whichever applies, that is in excess of the shareholder's basis in stock and indebtedness is treated, solely for purposes of this section, as an amount described in paragraph (e)(2) or (f)(3) of this section, whichever applies, in the succeeding taxable year. A shareholder makes the election under this paragraph by attaching a statement to the shareholder's timely filed original or amended return that states that the shareholder agrees to the carryover rule of the preceding sentence. Once a shareholder makes an election under this paragraph with respect to an S corporation, the shareholder must continue to use the rules of this paragraph for that S corporation in future taxable years unless the shareholder receives the permission of the Commissioner.

(h) *Examples.*—The following examples illustrate the principles of §1.1367-1. In each example, the corporation is a calendar year S corporation:

* * *

Example 2. Adjustments to basis of stock for taxable years beginning on or after August 18, 1998. (i) On December 31, 2001, A owns a block of 50 shares of stock with an adjusted basis per share of $6 in Corporation S. On December 31, 2001, A purchases for $400 an additional block of 50 shares of stock with an adjusted basis of $8 per share. Thus, A holds 100 shares of stock for each day of the 2002 taxable year. For S's 2002 taxable year, A's pro rata share of the amount of items described in section 1367(a)(1)(A) (relating to increases in basis of stock) is $300, A's pro rata share of the amount of the items described in section 1367(a)(2)(B) (relating to decreases in basis of stock attributable to items of loss and deduction) is $300, and A's pro rata share of the amount of the items described in section 1367(a)(2)(D) (relating to decreases in basis of stock attributable to noncapital, nondeductible expenses) is $200. S makes a distribution to A in the amount of $100 during 2002.

(ii) Pursuant to the ordering rules of paragraph (f) of this section, A first increases the basis of each share of stock by $3 ($300/100 shares) and then decreases the basis of each share by $1 ($100/100 shares) for the distribution. A next decreases the basis of each share by $2 ($200/100 shares) for the noncapital, nondeductible expenses and then decreases the basis of each share by $3 ($300/100 shares) for the items of loss. Thus, on January 1, 2003, A has a basis of $3 per share in the original block of 50 shares ($6 + $3 – $1 – $2 – $3) and a basis of $5 per share in the second block of 100 shares ($8 + $3 – $1 – $2 – $3).

Example 3. Adjustments attributable to basis of individual shares of stock. (i) On December 31, 1993, B owns one share of S corporation's 10 outstanding shares of stock. The basis of B's share is $30. On July 2, 1994, B purchases from another shareholder two shares for $25 each. During 1994, S corporation has no income or deductions but incurs a loss of $365. Under section 1377(a)(1)(A) and paragraph (c)(3) of this section, the amount of the loss assigned to each day of S's taxable year is $1.00 ($365/365 days). For each day, $.10 is allocated to each outstanding share ($1.00 amount of loss assigned to each day/10 shares).

(ii) B owned one share for 365 days and, therefore, reduces the basis of that share by the amount of loss attributable to it, *i.e.*, $36.50 ($.10 × 365 days). B owned two shares for 182 days and, therefore, reduces the basis of each of those shares by the amount of the loss attributable to each, *i.e.*, $18.20 ($.10 × 182 days).

(iii) The bases of the shares are decreased as follows:

Share	*Original Basis*	*Decrease*	*Adjusted Basis*	*Excess Basis Reduction*
No. 1	$30.00	$36.50	$0	$6.50
No. 2	25.00	18.20	6.80	0
No. 3	25.00	18.20	6.80	0
Total remaining basis			13.60	

(iv) Because the decrease in basis attributable to share No. 1 exceeds the basis of share No. 1 by $6.50 ($36.50 – $30.00), the excess is applied to reduce the bases of shares No. 2 and No. 3 in proportion to their remaining bases. Therefore, the bases of share No. 2 and share No. 3 are each decreased by an additional $3.25 ($6.50 × $6.80/$13.60). After this decrease, Share No. 1 has a basis of zero, Share No. 2 has a basis of $3.55, and Share No. 3 has a basis of $3.55.

* * *

Example 5. Effects of section 1377(a)(2) election and distribution on basis of stock for taxable years beginning on or after August 18, 1998. (i) The facts are the same as in *Example 4*, except that all of the events occur in 2001 rather than in 1994 and except as follows: On June 30, 2001, B sells 25 shares of her stock for $5,000 to D and 25 shares back to Corporation S for $5,000. Under section 1377(a)(2)(B) and §1.1377-1(b)(2), B, C, and D are affected shareholders because B has transferred shares to Corporations S and D. Pursuant to section 1377(a)(2)(A) and §1.1377-1(b)(1), B, C, and D, the affected shareholders, and Corporation S agree to treat the taxable year 2001 as if it consisted of two separate taxable years for all affected shareholders for the purposes set forth in §1.1377-1(b)(3)(i).

(ii) On June 30, 2001, B and C, pursuant to the ordering rules of paragraph (f)(1) of this section, increase the basis of each share by $60 ($6,000/100 shares) for the nonseparately computed income. Then B and C reduce the basis of each share by $120 ($12,000/100 shares) for the distribution. Finally, B and C decrease the basis of each share by $40 ($4,000/100 shares) for the separately stated deduction item.

(iii) The basis of the stock of B is reduced from $120 to $20 per share ($120 + $60 – $120 – $40). Prior to accounting for the separately stated deduction item, the basis of the stock of C is reduced from $80 to $20 ($80 + $60 – $120). Finally, because the period from January 1 through June 30, 2001 is treated under §1.1377-1(b)(3)(i) as a separate taxable year for purposes of making adjustments to the basis of stock, under section 1366(d) and §1.1366-2(a)(3), C may deduct only $20 per share of the remaining $40 of the separately stated deduction item, and the basis of the stock of C is reduced from $20 per share to $0 per share. Under section 1366 and §1.1366-2(a)(3), C's remaining separately stated deduction item of $20 per share is treated as having been incurred in the first succeeding taxable year of Corporation S, which, for this purpose, begins on July 1, 2001.

(i) [Reserved]

(j) *Adjustments for items of income in respect of a decedent.*—The basis determined under section 1014 of any stock in an S corporation is reduced by the portion of the value of the stock that is attributable to items constituting income in respect of a decedent. For the determination of items realized by an S corporation constituting income in respect of a decedent, see sections 1367(b)(4)(A) and 691 and applicable regulations thereunder. For the determination of the allowance of a deduction for the amount of estate tax attributable to income in respect of a decedent, see section 691(c) and applicable regulations thereunder. [Reg. §1.1367-1.]

□ [*T.D.* 8508, 12-30-93. *Amended by T.D.* 8852, 12-21-99 (*corrected* 3-8-2000); *T.D.* 9633, 8-30-2013, *T.D.* 9682, 7-22-2014 *and T.D.* 9759, 3-25-2016.]

§1.1367-2. Adjustments to basis of indebtedness to shareholder.—(a) *In general.*—(1) *Adjustments under section 1367.*—This section provides rules relating to adjustments required by subchapter S to the basis of indebtedness (including open account debt as described in paragraph (a)(2) of this section) of an S corporation to a shareholder. The basis of indebtedness of the S corporation to a shareholder is reduced as provided in paragraph (b) of this section and restored as provided in paragraph (c) of this section in accordance with the timing rules in paragraph (d) of this section.

(2) *Open account debt.*—(i) *General rule.*—The term *open account debt* means shareholder advances not evidenced by separate written instruments and repayments on the advances, the aggregate outstanding principal of which does not exceed $25,000 of indebtedness of the S corporation to the shareholder at the close of the S corporation's taxable year. Advances and repayments on open account debt are treated as a single indebtedness.

(ii) *Exception.*—If the shareholder advances not evidenced by a separate written instrument, net of repayments, exceeds an aggregate outstanding principal amount of $25,000 at the close of the S corporation's taxable year, for any subsequent taxable year the aggregate principal amount of that indebtedness is treated in the same manner as indebtedness evidenced by a separate written instrument for purposes of this section. For any subsequent taxable year, that indebtedness is not open account debt and is subject to all basis adjustment rules applicable to basis of indebtedness of an S corporation to a shareholder in this section.

(b) *Reduction in basis of indebtedness.*—(1) *General rule.*—If, after making the adjustments required by section 1367(a)(1) for any taxable year of the S corporation, the amounts specified in section 1367(a)(2)(B), (C), (D), and (E) (relating to losses, deductions, noncapital, nondeductible expenses, and certain oil and gas depletion deductions) exceed the basis of a shareholder's stock in the corporation, the excess is applied to reduce (but not below zero) the basis of any indebtedness of the S corporation to the shareholder held by the shareholder at the close of the corporation's taxable year. Any such indebtedness that has been satisfied by the corporation, or disposed of or forgiven by the shareholder, during the taxable year, is not held by the shareholder at the close of that year and is not subject to basis reduction.

(2) *Termination of shareholder's interest in corporation during taxable year.*—If a shareholder terminates his or her interest in the corporation during the taxable year, the rules of this paragraph (b) are applied with respect to any indebtedness of the S corporation held by the shareholder immediately prior to the termination of the shareholder's interest in the corporation.

(3) *Multiple indebtedness.*—If a shareholder holds more than one indebtedness at the close of the corporation's taxable year or, if applicable, immediately prior to the termination of the shareholder's interest in the corporation, the reduction in basis is applied to each indebtedness in the same proportion that the basis of each indebtedness bears to the aggregate bases of the indebtedness to the shareholder.

(c) *Restoration of basis.*—(1) *General rule.*—If, for any taxable year of an S corporation beginning after December 31, 1982, there has been a reduction in the basis of an indebtedness of the S corporation to a shareholder under section 1367(b)(2)(A), any *net increase* in any subsequent taxable year of the corporation is applied to restore that reduction. For purposes of this section, *net increase* with respect to a shareholder means the amount by which the shareholder's pro rata share of the items described in section 1367(a)(1) (relating to income items and excess deduction for depletion) exceed the items described in section 1367(a)(2) (relating to losses, deductions, noncapital, nondeductible expenses, certain oil and gas depletion deductions, and certain distributions) for the taxable year. These restoration rules apply only to indebtedness held by a shareholder as of the beginning of the taxable year in which the net increase arises. The reduction in basis of indebtedness must be restored before any net increase is applied to restore the basis of a shareholder's stock in an S corporation. In no event may the shareholder's basis of indebtedness be restored above the adjusted basis of the indebtedness under section 1016(a), excluding any adjustments under section 1016(a)(17) for prior taxable years, determined as of the beginning of the taxable year in which the net increase arises.

(2) *Multiple indebtedness.*—If a shareholder holds more than one indebtedness (including any open account debt and any debt treated as a single indebtedness under paragraph (a)(2)(ii) of this section) as of the beginning of an S corporation's taxable year, any net increase is applied first to restore the reduction of basis in any indebtedness repaid (in whole or in part) in that taxable year to the extent necessary to offset any gain that would otherwise be realized on the repayment. Any remaining net increase is applied to restore each outstanding indebtedness (including any open account debt and any debt treated as a single indebtedness under paragraph (a)(2)(ii) of this section) in proportion to the amount that the basis of each outstanding indebtedness has been reduced under section 1367(b)(2)(A) and paragraph (b) of this section and not restored under section 1367(b)(2)(B) and this paragraph (c).

(d) *Time at which adjustments to basis of indebtedness are effective.*—(1) *In general.*—The amounts of the adjustments to basis of indebtedness (including open account debt) provided in section 1367(b)(2) and this section are determined as of the close of the S corporation's taxable year, and the adjustments are generally effective as of the close of the S corporation's taxable year. However, if the shareholder is not a shareholder in the S corporation at that time, these adjustments are effective immediately before the shareholder terminates his or her interest in the S corporation. Except as provided in paragraph (d)(2) of this section, if a debt is disposed of or repaid in whole or in part before the close of the taxable year, the basis of that indebtedness is restored under paragraph (c) of this section, effective immediately before the disposition or the first repayment on the debt during the taxable year. To the extent any indebtedness of the S corporation to the shareholder is disposed of or repaid (in whole or in part) during the taxable year and the shareholder's basis in that indebtedness has been reduced under paragraph (b) of this section and is not restored completely under paragraph (c) of this section, the disposition or repayment is a recognition event effective immediately before the indebtedness is disposed of or repaid (in whole or in part).

(2) *Open account debt.*—(i) *In general.*—All advances and repayments on open account debt (as described in paragraph (a)(2)(i) of this section) during the S corporation's taxable year are netted at the close of the S corporation's taxable year to determine the amount of any net advance or net repayment. The net advance or net repayment is combined with the outstanding aggregate principal balance of the existing open account debt and that amount is carried forward to the beginning of the subsequent taxable year as the outstanding aggregate principal amount of the open account debt (unless the aggregate principal amount meets the exception defined in paragraph (a)(2)(ii) of

this section at the close of the taxable year). However, if the shareholder in the S corporation is not a shareholder of the S corporation at the close of the S corporation's taxable year, such advances and repayments on open account debt are netted, and the basis of that indebtedness is restored under paragraph (c) of this section, effective immediately before the shareholder terminates his or her interest in the S corporation. If any open account debt is disposed of before or upon the close of the taxable year, the disposition is effective at the close of the S corporation's taxable year, and all advances and repayments are netted immediately prior to the disposition and the basis of that indebtedness is restored under paragraph (c) of this section, effective at the close of the S corporation's taxable year.

(ii) *Exception.*—Shareholder indebtedness that is open account debt at the beginning of the taxable year but meets the exception defined in paragraph (a)(2)(ii) of this section at the close of the taxable year, adjustments to the basis of the indebtedness for that taxable year follow the provisions for open account debt. The resulting aggregate principal amount of indebtedness is treated as the principal amount of a debt evidenced by a separate written instrument for any subsequent taxable year, and is no longer subject to the open account debt provisions of this section.

(3) *Effect of election under section 1377(a)(2) or §1.1368-1(g)(2)* .—If an election is made under section 1377(a)(2) (to terminate the year in the case of the termination of a shareholder's interest) or under §1.1368-1(g)(2) (to terminate the year in the case of a qualifying disposition), this paragraph (d) applies as if the taxable year consisted of separate taxable years, the first of which ends at the close of the day on which the shareholder either terminates his or her interest in the corporation or disposes of a substantial amount of stock, whichever the case may be.

(e) *Examples.*—The following examples illustrate the principles of §1.1367-2. In each example, the corporation is a calendar year S corporation. The lending transactions described in the examples do not result in foregone interest (within the meaning of section 7872(e)(2)), original issue discount (within the meaning of section 1273), or total unstated interest (within the meaning of section 483(b)).

Example 1. Reduction in basis of indebtedness. (i) A has been the sole shareholder in Corporation S since 1992. In 1993, A loans S $1,000 (Debt No. 1), which is evidenced by a ten-year promissory note in the face amount of $1,000. In 1996, A loans S $5,000 (Debt No. 2), which is evidenced by a demand promissory note. On December 31, 1996, the basis of A's stock is zero; the basis of Debt No. 1 has been reduced under paragraph (b) of this section to $0; and the basis of Debt No. 2 has been reduced to $1,000. On January 1, 1997, A loans S $4,000 (Debt No. 3), which is evidenced by a demand promissory note. For S's 1997 taxable year, the sum of the amounts specified in section 1367(a)(1) (in this case, nonseparately computed income and the excess deduction for depletion) is $6,000, and the sum of the amounts specified in section 1367(a)(2)(B), (D) and (E) (in this case, items of separately stated deductions and losses, noncapital, nondeductible expenses, and certain oil and gas depletion deductions— there is no nonseparately computed loss) is $10,000. Corporation S makes no payments to A on any of the loans during 1997.

(ii) The $4,000 excess of loss and deduction items is applied to reduce the basis of each indebtedness in proportion to the basis of that indebtedness over the aggregate bases of the indebtedness to the shareholder (determined immediately before any adjustment under section 1367(b)(2)(A) and paragraph (b) of this section is effective for the taxable year). Thus, the basis of Debt No. 2 is reduced in an amount equal to $800 ($4,000 (excess) × $1,000 (basis of Debt No. 2)/ $5,000 (total basis of all debt)). Similarly, the basis in Debt No. 3 is reduced in an amount equal to $3,200 ($4,000 × $4,000/$5,000). Accordingly, on December 31, 1997, A's basis in his stock is zero and his bases in the three debts are as follows:

Debt	*1/1/96 Basis*	*12/31/96 Reduction*	*1/1/97 Basis*	*12/31/97 Reduction*	*1/1/98 Basis*
No. 1	$1,000	$1,000	$0	$0	$0
No. 2	5,000	4,000	1,000	800	200
No. 3			4,000	3,200	800

Example 2. Restoration of basis of indebtedness. (i) The facts are the same as in *Example 1.* On July 1, 1998, S completely repays Debt No. 3, and, for S's 1998 taxable year, the net increase (within the meaning of paragraph (c) of this section) with respect to A equals $4,500.

(ii) The net increase is applied first to restore the bases in the debts held on January 1, 1998, before any of the net increase is applied to increase A's basis in his shares of S stock. The net increase is applied to restore first the reduction of basis in indebtedness repaid in 1998. Any remaining net increase is applied to restore the bases of the outstanding debts in proportion to the amount that each of these outstanding debts have been reduced previously under paragraph (b) of this section and have not been restored. As of December 31, 1998, the total reduction in A's debts held on January 1, 1998 equals $9,000. Thus, the basis of Debt No. 3 is restored by $3,200 (the amount of the previous reduction) to $4,000. A's basis in Debt No. 3 is treated as restored immediately before that debt is repaid. Accordingly, A does not realize any gain on the repayment. The remaining net increase of $1,300 ($4,500 – $3,200) is applied to restore the bases of Debt No. 1 and Debt No. 2. As of December 31, 1998, the total reduction in these outstanding debts is $5,800 ($9,000 – $3,200). The basis of Debt No. 1 is restored in an amount equal to $224 ($1,300 × $1,000/$5,800). Similarly, the basis in Debt No. 2 is restored in an amount equal to $1,076 ($1,300 × $4,800/$5,800). On December 31, 1998, A's basis in his S stock is zero and his bases in the two remaining debts are as follows:

Original Basis	*Amount Reduced*	*1/1/98 Basis*	*Amount Restored*	*12/31/98 Basis*
$1,000	$1,000	$0	$224	$224
5,000	4,800	200	1,076	1,276

Example 3. Full restoration of basis in indebtedness when debt is repaid in part during the taxable year. (i) C has been a shareholder in Corporation S since 1992. In 1997, C loans S $1,000. S issues its note to C in the amount of $1,000, of which $950 is payable on March 1, 1998, and $50 is payable on March 1, 1999. On December 31, 1997, C's basis in all her shares of S stock is zero and her basis in the note has been reduced under paragraph (b) of this section to $900. For 1998, the net increase (within the meaning of paragraph (c) of this section) with respect to C is $300.

(ii) Because C's basis of indebtedness was reduced in a prior taxable year under § 1.1367-2(b), the net increase for 1998 is applied to restore this reduction. The restored basis cannot exceed the adjusted basis of the debt as of the beginning of the first day of 1998, excluding prior adjustments under section 1367, or $1,000. Therefore, $100 of the $300 net increase is applied to restore the basis of the debt from $900 to $1,000 effective immediately before the repayment on March 1, 1998. The remaining net increase of $200 increases C's basis in her stock.

Example 4. Determination of net increase—distribution in excess of increase in basis. (i) D has been the sole shareholder in Corporation S since 1990. On January 1, 1996, D loans S $10,000 in return for a note from S in the amount of $10,000 of which $5,000 is payable on each of January 1, 2000, and January 1, 2001. On December 31, 1997, the basis of D's shares of S stock is zero, and his basis in the note has been reduced under paragraph (b) of this section to $8,000. During 1998, the sum of the items under section 1367(a)(1) (relating to increases in basis of stock) with respect to D equals $10,000 (in this case, nonseparately computed income), and the sum of the items under section 1367(a)(2)(B), (C), (D), and (E) (relating to decreases in basis of stock) with respect to D equals $0. During 1998, S also makes distributions to D totaling $11,000. This distribution is an item that reduces basis of stock under section 1367(a)(2)(A) and must be taken into account for purposes of determining whether there is a net increase for the taxable year. Thus, for 1998, there is no net increase with respect to D because the amount of the items provided in section 1367(a)(1) do not exceed the amount of the items provided in section 1367(a)(2).

(ii) Because there is no net increase with respect to D for 1998, none of the 1997 reduction in D's basis in the indebtedness is restored. The $10,000 increase in basis under section 1367(a)(1) is applied to increase D's basis in his S stock. Under section 1367(a)(2)(A), the $11,000 distribution with respect to D's stock reduces D's basis in his shares of S stock to $0. See section 1368 and § 1.1368-1(c) and (d) for the tax treatment of the $1,000 distribution in excess of D's basis.

Example 5. Distributions less than increase in basis. (i) The facts are the same as in *Example 4*, except that in 1998 S makes distributions to D totaling $8,000. On these facts, for 1998, there is a net increase with respect to D of $2,000 (the amount by which the items provided in section 1367(a)(1) exceed the amount of the items provided in section 1367(a)(2)).

(ii) Because there is a net increase of $2,000 with respect to D for 1998, $2,000 of the $10,000 increase in basis under section 1367(a)(1) is first applied to restore D's basis in the indebtedness to $10,000 ($8,000 + $2,000). Accordingly, on December 31, 1998, D has a basis in his shares of S stock of $0 ($0 + $8,000 (increase in basis remaining after restoring basis in indebtedness) – $8,000 (distribution)) and a basis in the note of $10,000.

Example 6. The $25,000 aggregate principal amount applies to each shareholder. (i) A and B have been the two shareholders in Corporation S since 2000. As of the end of the 2008 taxable year, the bases of A's and B's stock are both zero. On June 1, 2009, A advances S $16,000, which is not evidenced by a written instrument.

On August 1, 2009, B advances S $22,000, which is not evidenced by a written instrument. Both the $16,000 advance and the $22,000 advance are open account debt and remain outstanding at those amounts during 2009. There is no net increase under paragraph (c) of this section in year 2009.

(ii) At the close of the 2009 taxable year, A's open account debt does not exceed $25,000. A therefore carries forward to the beginning of the 2010 taxable year the $16,000 as open account debt.

(iii) At the close of the 2009 taxable year, B's open account debt does not exceed $25,000. B therefore carries forward to the beginning of the 2010 taxable year the $22,000 as open account debt.

Example 7. Treatment of open account debt. (i) The facts are the same as in *Example 6*, in addition to which, on December 31, 2009, A's basis in the open account debt is reduced under paragraph (b) of this section to $8,000. On April 1, 2010, S repays A $4,000 of the open account indebtedness. On September 1, 2010, A advances S an additional $1,000, which is not evidenced by a written instrument. There is no net increase under paragraph (c) of this section in year 2010.

(ii) The $4,000 April repayment S makes to A and A's $1,000 September advance are netted to result in a net repayment of $3,000 for the taxable year on A's $16,000 open account debt carried forward from 2009. Because there is no net increase in 2010, no basis of indebtedness is restored for the 2010 taxable year, and A realizes $1,500 of income on the $3,000 net repayment at the close of the 2010 taxable year.

(iii) At close of the 2010 taxable year, A's open account debt does not exceed $25,000. The net repayment of $3,000 for the taxable year on A's $16,000 open account debt carried forward from 2009, leaves A with an open account debt of $13,000 to carry forward as open account debt to the beginning of the 2011 taxable year.

Example 8. Treatment of shareholder indebtedness not evidenced by a written instrument which exceeds $25,000. (i) The facts are the same as in *Example 7*, in addition to which, on February 1, 2011, S repays $5,000 of the open account debt and on March 1, 2011, A advances S $20,000, which is not evidenced by a written instrument.

(ii) At the close of the 2010 taxable year, A has an open account debt of $13,000 to carry forward as open account debt to the beginning of the 2011 taxable year.

(iii) The 2011 advances and repayments are netted to result in a net advance of $15,000 on A's $13,000 open account debt carried forward from 2010, increasing A's open account debt to $28,000 as of the close of the 2011 taxable year. Because A's open account debt exceeds $25,000, for any subsequent taxable year the $28,000 indebtedness will be treated in the same manner as indebtedness evidenced by a separate written instrument for the purposes of this section. Because there is no net increase in 2011, no basis of indebtedness is restored for the 2011 taxable year. [Reg. § 1.1367-2.]

□ [*T.D.* 8508, 12-30-93. *Amended by T.D.* 9428, 10-17-2008 (*corrected* 11-13-2008).]

§ 1.1368-1. Distributions by S corporations.—(a) *In general.*—This section provides rules for distributions made by an S corporation with respect to its stock which, but for section 1368(a) and this section, would be subject to section 301(c) and other rules of the Internal Revenue Code that characterize a distribution as a dividend.

(b) *Date distribution made.*—For purposes of section 1368, a distribution is taken into account on the date the corporation makes the distribution, regardless of when the distribution is treated as received by the shareholder.

(c) *S corporation with no earnings and profits.*—A distribution made by an S corporation that has no accumulated earnings and profits as of the end of the taxable year of the S corporation in which the distribution is made is treated in the manner provided in section 1368(b).

(d) *S corporation with earnings and profits.*—(1) *General treatment of distribution.*—Except as provided in paragraph (d)(2) of this section, a distribution made with respect to its stock by an S corporation that has accumulated earnings and profits as of the end of the taxable year of the S corporation in which the distribution is made is treated in the manner provided in section 1368(c). See section 316 and § 1.316-2 for provisions relating to the allocation of earnings and profits among distributions.

(2) *Previously taxed income.*—This paragraph (d)(2) applies to distributions by a corporation that has both accumulated earnings and profits and previously taxed income (within the meaning of section 1375(d)(2), as in effect prior to its amendment by the Subchapter S Revision Act of 1982, and the regulations thereunder) with respect to one or more shareholders. In the case of such a distribution, that portion remaining after the application of section 1368(c)(1) (relating to distributions from the accumulated adjustments account (AAA) as defined in § 1.1368-2(a)) is treated in the manner provided in section 1368(b) (relating to S corporations without earnings and profits) to the extent that portion is a distribution of money and does not exceed the shareholder's net share immediately before the distribution of

the corporation's previously taxed income. The AAA and the earnings and profits of the corporation are not decreased by that portion of the distribution. Any distribution remaining after the application of this paragraph (d)(2) is treated in the manner provided in section 1368(c)(2) and (3).

(e) *Certain adjustments taken into account.*—

* * *

(2) *Taxable years beginning on or after August 18, 1998.*—For any taxable year of the corporation beginning on or after August 18, 1998, paragraphs (c) and (d) of this section are applied only after taking into account—

(i) The adjustments to the basis of the shares of a shareholder's stock described in section 1367(a)(1) (relating to increases in basis of stock) for the S corporation's taxable year; and

(ii) The adjustments to the AAA required by section 1368(e)(1)(A) (but without regard to the adjustments for distributions under § 1.1368-2(a)(3)(iii)) for the S corporation's taxable year. Any net negative adjustment (as defined in section 1368(e)(1)(C)(ii)) for the taxable year shall not be taken into account.

(f) *Elections relating to source of distributions.*—(1) *In general.*—An S corporation may modify the application of paragraphs (c) and (d) of this section by electing (pursuant to paragraph (f)(5) of this section)—

(i) To distribute earnings and profits first as described in paragraph (f)(2) of this section;

(ii) To make a deemed dividend as described in paragraph (f)(3) of this section; or

(iii) To forego previously taxed income as described in paragraph (f)(4) of this section.

(2) *Election to distribute earnings and profits first.*—(i) *In general.*—An S corporation with accumulated earnings and profits may elect under this paragraph (f)(2) for any taxable year to distribute earnings and profits first as provided in section 1368(e)(3). Except as provided in paragraph (f)(2)(ii) of this section, distributions made by an S corporation making this election are treated as made first from earnings and profits under section 1368(c)(2) and second from the AAA under section 1368(c)(1). Any remaining portion of the distribution is treated in the manner provided in section 1368(b). This election is effective for all distributions made during the year for which the election is made.

(ii) *Previously taxed income.*—If a corporation to which paragraph (d)(2) of this section (relating to corporations with previously taxed income) applies makes the election provided in this paragraph (f)(2) for the taxable year, and does not make the election to forego previously taxed income under paragraph (f)(4) of this section, distributions by the S corporation during the taxable year are treated as made first, from previously taxed income under paragraph (d)(2) of this section; second, from earnings and profits under section 1368(c)(2); and third, from the AAA under section 1368(c)(1). Any portion of a distribution remaining after the previously taxed income, earnings and profits, and the AAA are exhausted is treated in the manner provided in section 1368(b).

(iii) *Corporation with subchapter C and subchapter S earnings and profits.*—If an S corporation that makes the election provided in this paragraph (f)(2) has both subchapter C earnings and profits (as defined in section 1362(d)(3)(B)) and subchapter S earnings and profits in a taxable year of the corporation in which the distribution is made, the distribution is treated as made first from subchapter C earnings and profits, and second from subchapter S earnings and profits. *Subchapter S earnings and profits* are earnings and profits accumulated in a taxable year beginning before January 1, 1983 (or in the case of a qualified casualty insurance electing small business corporation or a qualified oil corporation, earnings and profits accumulated in any taxable year), for which an election under subchapter S of chapter 1 of the Internal Revenue Code was in effect.

(3) *Election to make a deemed dividend.*—An S corporation may elect under this paragraph (f)(3) to distribute all or part of its subchapter C earnings and profits through a deemed dividend. If an S corporation makes the election provided in this paragraph (f)(3), the S corporation will be considered to have made the election provided in paragraph (f)(2) of this section (relating to the election to distribute earnings and profits first). The amount of the deemed dividend may not exceed the subchapter C earnings and profits of the corporation on the last day of the taxable year, reduced by any actual distributions of subchapter C earnings and profits made during the taxable year. The amount of the deemed dividend is considered, for all purposes of the Internal Revenue Code, as if it were distributed in money to the shareholders in proportion to their stock ownership, received by the shareholders, and immediately contributed by the shareholders to the corporation, all on the last day of the corporation's taxable year.

(4) *Election to forego previously taxed income.*—An S corporation may elect to forego

distributions of previously taxed income. If such an election is made, paragraph (d)(2) of this section (relating to corporations with previously taxed income) does not apply to any distribution made during the taxable year. Thus, distributions by a corporation that makes the election to forego previously taxed income for a taxable year under this paragraph (f)(4) and does not make the election to distribute earnings and profits first under paragraph (f)(2) of this section are treated in the manner provided in section 1368(c) (relating to distributions by corporations with earnings and profits). Distributions by a corporation that makes both the election to distribute earnings and profits first under paragraph (f)(2) of this section and the election to forego previously taxed income under this paragraph (f)(4), are treated in the manner provided in paragraph (f)(2)(i) of this section.

(5) *Time and manner of making elections.*—(i) *For earnings and profits.*—If an election is made under paragraph (f)(2) of this section to distribute earnings and profits first, see section 1368(e)(3) regarding the consent required by shareholders.

(ii) *For previously taxed income and deemed dividends.*—If an election is made to forego previously taxed income under paragraph (f)(4) of this section or to make a deemed dividend under paragraph (f)(3) of this section, consent by each "affected shareholder," as defined in section 1368(e)(3)(B), is required.

* * *

(iv) *Irrevocable elections.*—The elections under this paragraph (f) are irrevocable and are effective only for the taxable year for which they are made. In applying the preceding sentence to elections under this paragraph (f), an election to terminate the taxable year under section 1377(a)(2) or § 1.1368-1(g)(2) is disregarded.

(g) *Special rule.*—(1) *Election to terminate year under § 1.1368-1(g)(2).*—If an election is made under paragraph (g)(2) of this section to terminate the year when there is a qualifying disposition, this section applies as if the taxable year consisted of separate taxable years, the first of which ends at the close of the day on which there is a qualifying disposition of stock.

(2) *Election in case of a qualifying disposition.*—(i) *In general.*—In the case of a qualifying disposition, a corporation may elect under this paragraph (g)(2)(i) to treat the year as if it consisted of separate taxable years, the first of which ends at the close of the day on which the qualifying disposition occurs. A *qualifying disposition* is—

(A) A disposition by a shareholder of 20 percent or more of the outstanding stock of the corporation in one or more transactions during any thirty-day period during the corporation's taxable year;

(B) A redemption treated as an exchange under section 302(a) or section 303(a) of 20 percent or more of the outstanding stock of the corporation from a shareholder in one or more transactions during any thirty-day period during the corporation's taxable year; or

(C) An issuance of an amount of stock equal to or greater than 25 percent of the previously outstanding stock to one or more new shareholders during any thirty-day period during the corporation's taxable year.

(ii) *Effect of the election.*—A corporation making an election under paragraph (g)(2)(i) of this section must treat the taxable year as separate taxable years for purposes of allocating items of income and loss; making adjustments to the AAA, earnings and profits, and basis; and determining the tax effect of distributions under section 1368(b) and (c). An election made under paragraph (g)(2)(i) of this section may be made upon the occurrence of any qualifying disposition. Dispositions of stock that are taken into account as part of a qualifying disposition are not taken into account in determining whether a subsequent qualifying disposition has been made.

* * *

(iv) *Coordination with election under section 1377(a)(2).*—If the event resulting in a qualifying disposition also results in a termination of a shareholder's entire interest as described in § 1.1377-1(b)(4), the election under this paragraph (g)(2) cannot be made. Rather, the election under section 1377(a)(2) and § 1.1377-1(b) may be made. See § 1.1377-1(b) (concerning the election under section 1377(a)(2)). [Reg. § 1.1368-1.]

□ [*T.D.* 8508, 12-30-93. *Amended by T.D.* 8696, 12-20-96; *T.D.* 8852, 12-21-99 *T.D.* 9100, 12-18-2003 *and T.D.* 9300, 12-7-2006.]

§ 1.1368-2. Accumulated adjustments account (AAA).—(a) *Accumulated adjustments account.*—(1) *In general.*—The accumulated adjustments account is an account of the S corporation and is not apportioned among shareholders. The AAA is relevant for all taxable years beginning on or after January 1, 1983, for which the corporation is an S corporation. On the first day of the first year for which the corporation is an S corporation, the balance of the AAA is zero. The AAA is increased in the manner provided in paragraph (a)(2) of this section and is decreased in the manner provided in paragraph (a)(3) of this section. For the adjustments to the AAA in the case of redemptions, liquidations, reorganizations, and corporate separations, see paragraph (d) of this section.

(2) *Increases to the AAA.*—The AAA is increased for the taxable year of the corporation by the sum of the following items with respect to the corporation for the taxable year:

(i) The items of income described in section 1366(a)(1)(A) other than income that is exempt from tax;

(ii) Any nonseparately computed income determined under section 1366(a)(1)(B); and

(iii) The excess of the deductions for depletion over the basis of property subject to depletion unless the property is an oil or gas property the basis of which has been allocated to shareholders under section 613A(c)(11).

(3) *Decreases to the AAA.*—(i) *In general.*—The AAA is decreased for the taxable year of the corporation by the sum of the following items with respect to the corporation for the taxable year—

(A) The items of loss or deduction described in section 1366(a)(1)(A);

(B) Any nonseparately computed loss determined under section 1366(a)(1)(B);

(C) Any expense of the corporation not deductible in computing its taxable income and not properly chargeable to a capital account, other than—

(1) Federal taxes attributable to any taxable year in which the corporation was a C corporation; and

(2) Expenses related to income that is exempt from tax; and

(D) The sum of the shareholders' deductions for depletion for any oil or gas property held by the corporation described in section 1367(a)(2)(E).

(ii) *Extent of allowable reduction.*—The AAA may be decreased under paragraph (a)(3)(i) of this section below zero. The AAA is decreased by noncapital, nondeductible expenses under paragraph (a)(3)(i)(C) of this section even though a portion of the noncapital, nondeductible expenses is not taken into account by a shareholder under § 1.1367-1(g) (relating to the elective ordering rule). The AAA is also decreased by the entire amount of any loss or deduction even though a portion of the loss or deduction is not taken into account by a shareholder under section 1366(d)(1) or is otherwise not currently deductible under the Internal Revenue Code. However, in any subsequent taxable year in which the loss, deduction, or noncapital, nondeductible expense is treated as incurred by the corporation with respect to the shareholder under section 1366(d)(2) or § 1.1367-1(g) (or in which the loss or deduction is otherwise allowed to the shareholder), no further adjustment is made to the AAA.

(iii) *Decrease to the AAA for distributions.*—The AAA is decreased (but not below zero) by any portion of a distribution to which section 1368(b) or (c)(1) applies.

* * *

(5) *Ordering rules for the AAA for taxable years beginning on or after August 18, 1998.*—For any taxable year of the S corporation beginning on or after August 18, 1998, the adjustments to the AAA are made in the following order—

(i) The AAA is increased under paragraph (a)(2) of this section before it is decreased under paragraph (a)(3)(i) of this section for the taxable year;

(ii) The AAA is decreased under paragraph (a)(3)(i) of this section (without taking into account any net negative adjustment (as defined in section 1368(e)(1)(C)(ii)) before it is decreased under paragraph (a)(3)(iii) of this section;

(iii) The AAA is decreased (but not below zero) by any portion of an ordinary distribution to which section 1368(b) or (c)(1) applies;

(iv) The AAA is decreased by any net negative adjustment (as defined in section 1368(e)(1)(C)(ii)); and

(v) The AAA is adjusted (whether negative or positive) for redemption distributions under paragraph (d)(1) of this section.

(b) *Distributions in excess of the AAA.*—(1) *In general.*—A portion of the AAA (determined under paragraph (b)(2) of this section) is allocated to each of the distributions made for the taxable year if—

(i) An S corporation makes more than one distribution of property with respect to its stock during the taxable year of the corporation (including an S short year as defined under section 1362(e)(1)(A));

(ii) The AAA has a positive balance at the close of the year; and

(iii) The sum of the distributions made during the corporation's taxable year exceeds the balance of the AAA at the close of the year.

(2) *Amount of the AAA allocated to each distribution.*—The amount of the AAA allocated to each distribution is determined by multiplying the balance of the AAA at the close of the current taxable year by a fraction, the numerator of which is the amount of the distribution

and the denominator of which is the amount of all distributions made during the taxable year. For purposes of this paragraph (b)(2), the term *all distributions made during the taxable year* does not include any distribution treated as from earnings and profits or previously taxed income pursuant to an election made under section 1368(e)(3) and § 1.1368-1(f)(2). See paragraph (d)(1) of this section for rules relating to the adjustments to the AAA for redemptions and distributions in the year of a redemption.

(c) *Distribution of money and loss property.*—(1) *In general.*—The amount of the AAA allocated to a distribution under this section must be further allocated (under paragraph (c)(2) of this section) if the distribution—

(i) Consists of property the adjusted basis of which exceeds its fair market value on the date of the distribution and money;

(ii) Is a distribution to which § 1.1368-1(d)(1) applies; and

(iii) Exceeds the amount of the corporation's AAA properly allocable to that distribution.

(2) *Allocating the AAA to loss property.*—The amount of the AAA allocated to the property other than money is equal to the amount of the AAA allocated to the distribution multiplied by a fraction, the numerator of which is the fair market value of the property other than money on the date of distribution and the denominator of which is the amount of the distribution. The amount of the AAA allocated to the money is equal to the amount of the AAA allocated to the distribution reduced by the amount of the AAA allocated to the property other than money.

(d) *Adjustment in the case of redemptions, liquidations, reorganizations, and divisions.*—(1) *Redemptions.*—(i) *General Rule.*—In the case of a redemption distribution by an S corporation that is treated as an exchange under section 302(a) or section 303(a) (a *redemption distribution*), the AAA of the corporation is adjusted in an amount equal to the ratable share of the corporation's AAA (whether negative or positive) attributable to the redeemed stock as of the date of the redemption.

(ii) *Special rule for years in which a corporation makes both ordinary and redemption distributions.*—In any year in which a corporation makes one or more distributions to which section 1368(a) applies (*ordinary distributions*) and makes one or more redemption distributions, the AAA of the corporation is adjusted first for any ordinary distributions and then for any redemption distributions.

(iii) *Adjustments to earnings and profits.*—Earnings and profits are adjusted under section 312 independently of any adjustments made to the AAA.

(2) *Liquidations and reorganizations.*—An S corporation acquiring the assets of another S corporation in a transaction to which section 381(a) applies will succeed to and merge its AAA (whether positive or negative) with the AAA (whether positive or negative) of the distributor or transferor S corporation as of the close of the date of distribution or transfer. Thus, the AAA of the acquiring corporation after the transaction is the sum of the AAAs of the corporations prior to the transaction.

(3) *Corporate separations to which section 368(a)(1)(D) applies.*—If an S corporation with accumulated earnings and profits transfers a part of its assets constituting an active trade or business to another corporation in a transaction to which section 368(a)(1)(D) applies, and immediately thereafter the stock and securities of the controlled corporation are distributed in a distribution or exchange to which section 355 (or so much of section 356 as relates to section 355) applies, the AAA of the distributing corporation immediately before the transaction is allocated between the distributing corporation and the controlled corporation in a manner similar to the manner in which the earnings and profits of the distributing corporation are allocated under section 312(h). See § 1.312-10(a).

(e) *Election to terminate year under section 1377(a)(2) or § 1.1368-1(g)(2).*—If an election is made under section 1377(a)(2) (to terminate the year in the case of termination of a shareholder's interest) or § 1.1368-1(g)(2) (to terminate the year in the case of a qualifying disposition), this section applies as if the taxable year consisted of separate taxable years, the first of which ends at the close of the day on which the shareholder terminated his or her interest in the corporation or makes a substantial disposition of stock, whichever the case may be. [Reg. § 1.1368-2.]

☐ [*T.D.* 8508, 12-30-93. *Amended by T.D.* 8852, 12-21-99 *and T.D.* 8869, 1-20-2000.]

§ 1.1368-3. Examples.—The principles of §§ 1.1368-1 and 1.1368-2 are illustrated by the examples below. In each example Corporation S is a calendar year corporation:

* * *

Example 2. Distributions by S corporations without earnings and profits for taxable years beginning on or after August 18, 1998. (i) Corporation S, an S corporation, has no earnings and profits as of January 1, 2001, the first day of its 2001 taxable year. S's sole shareholder, A, holds 10 shares of S stock with a basis of $1 per share as of that date. On March 1, 2001, S makes a distribution of $38 to A. The balance in Corporation S's AAA is $100. For S's 2001 taxable year, A's pro rata share of the amount of the items described in section 1367(a)(1) (relating to increases in basis of stock) is $50. A's pro rata share of the amount of the items described in sections 1367(a)(2)(B) through (D) (relating to decreases in basis of stock for items other than distributions) is $26, $20 of which is attributable to items described in section 1367(a)(2)(B) and (C) and $6 of which is attributable to items described in section 1367(a)(2)(D) (relating to decreases in basis attributable to noncapital, nondeductible expenses).

(ii) Under section 1368(d)(1) and § 1.1368-1(e)(1) and (2), the adjustments to the basis of A's stock in S described in sections 1367(a)(1) are made before the distribution rules of section 1368 are applied. Thus, A's basis per share in the stock is $6.00 ($1 + [$50/10]) before taking into account the distribution. Under section 1367(a)(2)(A), the basis of A's stock is decreased by distributions to A that are not includible in A's income. Under § 1.1367-1(c)(3), the amount of the distribution that is attributable to each share of A's stock is $3.80 ($38 distribution/10 shares). Thus, A's basis per share in the stock is $2.20 ($6.00 – $3.80), after taking into account the distribution. Under section 1367(a)(2)(D), the basis of each share of A's stock in S after taking into account the distribution, $2.20, is decreased by $.60 ($6 noncapital, nondeductible expenses/10). Thus, A's basis per share after taking into account the nondeductible, noncapital expenses is $1.60. Under section 1367(a)(2)(B) and (C), A's basis per share is further decreased by $2 ($20 items described in section 1367(a)(2)(B) and (C) /10 shares). However, basis may not be reduced below zero. Therefore, the basis of each share of A's stock is reduced to zero. As of January 1, 2002, A has a basis of $0 in his shares of S stock. Pursuant to section 1366(d)(2), the $.40 of loss in excess of A's basis in each of his shares of S stock is treated as incurred by the corporation in the succeeding taxable year with respect to A.

* * *

Example 4. Distributions by S corporations with earnings and profits and no net negative adjustment for taxable years beginning on or after August 18, 1998. (i) Corporation S, an S corporation, has accumulated earnings and profits of $1,000 and a balance in the AAA of $2,000 on January 1, 2001. S's sole shareholder B holds 100 shares of stock with a basis of $20 per share as of January 1, 2001. On April 1, 2001, S makes a distribution of $1,500 to B. B's pro rata share of the income earned by S during 2001 is $2,000 and B's pro rata share of S's losses is $1,500. For the taxable year ending December 31, 2001, S does not have a net negative adjustment as defined in section 1368(e)(1)(C). S does not make the election under section 1368(e)(3) and § 1.1368-1(f)(2) to distribute its earnings and profits before its AAA.

(ii) The AAA is increased from $2,000 to $4,000 for the $2,000 of income earned during the 2001 taxable year. The AAA is decreased from $4,000 to $2,500 for the $1,500 of losses. The AAA is decreased from $2,500 to $1,000 for the portion of the distribution ($1,500) to B that does not exceed the AAA.

(iii) As of December 31, 2001, B's basis in his stock is $10 ($20 + $20 ($2,000 income/100 shares) – $15 ($1,500 distribution/100 shares) – $15 ($1,500 loss/100 shares).

Example 5. Distributions by S corporations with earnings and profits and net negative adjustment for taxable years beginning on or after August 18, 1998. (i) Corporation S, an S corporation, has accumulated earnings and profits of $1,000 and a balance in the AAA of $2,000 on January 1, 2001. S's sole shareholder B holds 100 shares of stock with a basis of $20 per share as of January 1, 2001. On April 1, 2001, S makes a distribution of $2,000 to B. B's pro rata share of the income earned by S during 2001 is $2,000 and B's pro rata share of S's losses is $3,500. For the taxable year ending December 31, 2001, S has a net negative adjustment as defined in section 1368(e)(1)(C). S does not make the election under section 1368(e)(3) and § 1.1368-1(f)(2) to distribute its earnings and profits before its AAA.

(ii) The AAA is increased from $2,000 to $4,000 for the $2,000 of income earned during the 2001 taxable year. Because under section 1368(e)(1)(C)(ii) and § 1.1368-2(a)(ii), the net negative adjustment is not taken into account, the AAA is decreased from $4,000 to $2,000 for the portion of the losses ($2,000) that does not exceed the income earned during the 2001 taxable year. The AAA is reduced from $2,000 to zero for the portion of the distribution to B ($2,000) that does not exceed the AAA. The AAA is decreased from zero to a negative $1,500 for the portion of the $3,500 of loss that exceeds the $2,000 of income earned during the 2001 taxable year.

(iii) Under § 1.1367-1(c)(1), the basis of a shareholder's share in an S corporation stock may not be reduced below zero. Accordingly, as of December 31, 2001, B's basis per share in his stock is zero ($20 + $20 income – $20 distribution – $35 loss). Pursuant to section 1366(d)(2), the $15 of loss in excess of B's basis in each of his shares of S stock is treated as incurred by the corporation in the succeeding taxable year with respect to B.

Example 6. Election in case of disposition of substantial amount of stock. (i) Corporation S, an S corporation, has earnings and profits of $3,000 and a balance in the AAA of $1,000 on January 1, 1997. C, an individual and the sole shareholder of Corporation S, has 100 shares of S stock with a basis of $10 per share. On July 3, 1997, C sells 50 shares of his S stock to D, an individual, for $250. For 1997, S has taxable income of $1,000, of which $500 was earned on or before July 3, 1997, and $500 earned after July 3, 1997. During its 1997 taxable year, S distributes $1,000 to C on February 1 and $1,000 to each of C and D on August 1. S does not make the election under section 1368(e)(3) and § 1.1368-1(f)(2) to distribute its earnings and profits before its AAA. S makes the election under § 1.1368-1(g)(2) to treat its taxable year as if it consisted of separate taxable years, the first of which ends at the close of July 3, 1997, the date of the qualifying disposition.

(ii) Under section § 1.1368-1(g)(2), for the period ending on July 3, 1997, S's AAA is $500 ($1,000 (AAA as of January 1, 1997) + $500 (income earned from January 1, 1997 through July 3, 1997) – $1,000 (distribution made on February 1, 1997)). C's bases in his shares of stock is decreased to $5 per share ($10 (original basis) + $5 (increase per share for income) – $10 (decrease per share for distribution)).

(iii) The AAA is adjusted at the end of the taxable year for the period July 4 through December 31, 1997. It is increased from $500 (AAA as of the close of July 3, 1997) to $1,000 for the income earned during this period and is decreased by $1,000, the portion of the distribution ($2,000 in total) made to C and D on August 1 that does not exceed the AAA. The $1,000 portion of the distribution that remains after the AAA is reduced to zero is attributable to earnings and profits. Therefore C and D each have a dividend of $500, which does not affect their basis or S's AAA. The earnings and profits account is reduced from $3,000 to $2,000.

(iv) As of December 31, 1997, C and D have bases in their shares of stock of zero ($5 (basis as of July 4) + $5 ($500 income/100 shares) – $10 ($1,000 distribution/100 shares)). C and D each will report $500 as dividend income, which does not affect their basis or S's AAA.

Example 7. Election to distribute earnings and profits first. (i) Corporation S has been a calendar year C corporation since 1975. For 1982, S elects for the first time to be taxed under subchapter S, and during 1982 has $60 of earnings and profits. As of December 31, 1995, S has an AAA of $10 and earnings and profits of $160, consisting of $100 of subchapter C earnings and profits and $60 of subchapter S earnings and profits. For 1996, S has $200 of taxable income and the AAA is increased to $210 (before taking distributions into account). During 1996, S distributes $240 to its shareholders. With its 1996 tax return, S properly elects under section 1368(e)(3) and § 1.1368-1(f)(2) to distribute its earnings and profits before its AAA.

(ii) Because S elected to distribute its earnings and profits before its AAA, the first $100 of the distribution is characterized as a distribution from subchapter C earnings and profits; the next $60 of the distribution is characterized as a distribution from subchapter S earnings and profits. Because $160 of the distribution is from earnings and profits, the shareholders of S have a $160 dividend. The remaining $80 of the distribution is a distribution from S's AAA and is treated by the shareholders as a return of capital or gain from the sale or exchange of property, as appropriate, under § 1.1368-1(d)(1). S's AAA, as of December 31, 1996, equals $130 ($210 – $80).

Example 8. Distributions in excess of the AAA. (i) On January 1, 1995, Corporation S has $40 of earnings and profits and a balance in the AAA of $100. S has two shareholders, E and F, each of whom own 50 shares of S's stock. For 1995, S has taxable income of $50, which increases the AAA to $150 as of December 31, 1995 (before taking into account distributions made during 1995). On February 1, 1995, S distributes $60 to each shareholder. On September 1, 1995, S distributes $30 to each shareholder. S does not make the election under section 1368(e)(3) and § 1.1368-1(f)(2) to distribute its earnings and profits before its AAA.

(ii) The sum of the distributions exceed S's AAA. Therefore, under § 1.1368-2(b), a portion of S's $150 balance in the AAA as of December 31, 1995, is allocated to each of the February 1 and September 1 distributions based on the respective sizes of the distributions. Accordingly, S must allocate $100 ($150 (AAA) × ($120 (February 1 distribution) / $180 (the sum of the distributions))) of the AAA to the February 1 distribution, and $50 ($150 × ($60 / $180)) to the September 1 distribution. The portions of the distributions to which the AAA is allocated are treated by the shareholder as a return of capital or gain from the sale or exchange of property, as appropriate. The remainder of the two distributions is treated as a dividend to the extent that it does not exceed S's earnings and profits. E and F must each report $10 of dividend income for the February 1 distribution. For the September 1 distribution, E and F must each report $5 of dividend income.

* * *

[Reg. § 1.1368-3.]

☐ [*T.D.* 8508, 12-30-93. *Amended by T.D.* 8852, 12-21-99.]

§ 1.1374-1. General rules and definitions.—(a) *Computation of tax.*—The tax imposed on the income of an S corporation by section 1374(a) for any taxable year during the recognition period is computed as follows—

(1) Step One: Determine the net recognized built-in gain of the corporation for the taxable year under section 1374(d)(2) and § 1.1374-2;

(2) Step Two: Reduce the net recognized built-in gain (but not below zero) by any net operating loss and capital loss carryforward allowed under section 1374(b)(2) and § 1.1374-5;

(3) Step Three: Compute a tentative tax by applying the rate of tax determined under section 1374(b)(1) for the taxable year to the amount determined under paragraph (a)(2) of this section;

(4) Step Four: Compute the final tax by reducing the tentative tax (but not below zero) by any credit allowed under section 1374(b)(3) and § 1.1374-6.

(b) *Anti-trafficking rules.*—If section 382, 383, or 384 would have applied to limit the use of a corporation's recognized built-in loss or section 1374 attributes at the beginning of the first day of the recognition period if the corporation had remained a C corporation, these sections apply to limit their use in determining the S corporation's pre-limitation amount, taxable income limitation, net unrealized built-in gain limitation, deductions against net recognized built-in gain, and credits against the section 1374 tax.

(c) *Section 1374 attributes.*—Section 1374 attributes are the loss carryforwards allowed under section 1374(b)(2) as a deduction against net recognized built-in gain and the credit and credit carryforwards allowed under section 1374(b)(3) as a credit against the section 1374 tax.

(d) *Recognition period.*—The recognition period is the 10-year (120-month) period beginning on the first day the corporation is an S corporation or the day an S corporation acquires assets in a section 1374(d)(8) transaction. For example, if the first day of the recognition period is July 14, 1996, the last day of the recognition period is July 13, 2006. If the recognition period for certain assets ends during an S corporation's taxable year (for example, because the corporation was on a fiscal year as a C corporation and changed to a calendar year as an S corporation or because an S corporation acquired assets in a section 1374(d)(8) transaction during a taxable year), the S corporation must determine its pre-limitation amount (as defined in § 1.1374-2(a)(1)) for the year as if the corporation's books were closed at the end of the recognition period.

(e) *Predecessor corporation.*—For purposes of section 1374(c)(1), if the basis of an asset of the S corporation is determined (in whole or in part) by reference to the basis of the asset (or any other property) in the hands of another corporation, the other corporation is a predecessor corporation of the S corporation. [Reg. § 1.1374-1.]

☐ [*T.D.* 8579, 12-23-94.]

§ 1.1374-2. Net recognized built-in gain.—(a) *In general.*—An S corporation's net recognized built-in gain for any taxable year is the least of—

(1) Its taxable income determined by using all rules applying to C corporations and considering only its recognized built-in gain, recognized built-in loss, and recognized built-in gain carryover (pre-limitation amount);

(2) Its taxable income determined by using all rules applying to C corporations as modified by section 1375(b)(1)(B) (taxable income limitation); and

(3) The amount by which its net unrealized built-in gain exceeds its net recognized built-in gain for all prior taxable years (net unrealized built-in gain limitation).

(b) *Allocation rule.*—If an S corporation's pre-limitation amount for any taxable year exceeds its net recognized built-in gain for that year, the S corporation's net recognized built-in gain consists of a ratable portion of each item of income, gain, loss, and deduction included in the pre-limitation amount.

(c) *Recognized built-in gain carryover.*—If an S corporation's net recognized built-in gain for any taxable year is equal to its taxable income limitation, the amount by which its pre-limitation amount exceeds its taxable income limitation is a recognized built-in gain carryover included in its pre-limitation amount for the succeeding taxable year. The recognized built-in gain carryover consists of that portion of each item of income, gain, loss, and deduction not included in the S corporation's net recognized built-in gain for the year the carryover arose, as determined under paragraph (b) of this section.

(d) *Accounting methods.*—In determining its taxable income for pre-limitation amount and taxable income limitation purposes, a corporation must use the accounting method(s) it uses for tax purposes as an S corporation.

(e) *Example.*—The rules of this section are illustrated by the following example.

Example. Net recognized built-in gain. X is a calendar year C corporation that elects to become an S corporation on January 1, 1996. X has a net unrealized built-in gain of $50,000 and no net operating loss or capital loss carryforwards. In 1996, X has a pre-limitation amount of $20,000, consisting of ordinary income of $15,000 and capital gain of $5,000, a taxable income limitation of $9,600, and a net unrealized built-in gain limitation of $50,000. Therefore, X's net recognized built-in gain for 1996 is $9,600, because that is the least of the three amounts described in paragraph (a) of this section. Under paragraph (b) of this section, X's net recognized built-in gain consists of recognized built-in ordinary income of $7,200 [$15,000 × ($9,600/$20,000) = $7,200] and recognized built-in capital gain of $2,400 [$5,000 × ($9,600/$20,000) = $2,400]. Under paragraph (c) of this section, X has a recognized built-in gain carryover to 1997 of $10,400 ($20,000 - $9,600 = $10,400), consisting of $7,800 ($15,000 - $7,200 = $7,800) of recognized built-in ordinary income and $2,600 ($5,000 - $2,400 = $2,600) of recognized built-in capital gain.

[Reg. § 1.1374-2.]

[*T.D.* 8579, 12-23-94.]

§ 1.1374-3. Net unrealized built-in gain.—(a) *In general.*—An S corporation's net unrealized built-in gain is the total of the following—

(1) The amount that would be the amount realized if, at the beginning of the first day of the recognition period, the corporation had remained a C corporation and had sold all its assets at fair market value to an unrelated party that assumed all its liabilities; decreased by

(2) Any liability of the corporation that would be included in the amount realized on the sale referred to in paragraph (a)(1) of this section, but only if the corporation would be allowed a deduction on payment of the liability; decreased by

(3) The aggregate adjusted bases of the corporation's assets at the time of the sale referred to in paragraph (a)(1) of this section; increased or decreased by

(4) The corporation's section 481 adjustments that would be taken into account on the sale referred to in paragraph (a)(1) of this section; and increased by

(5) Any recognized built-in loss that would not be allowed as a deduction under section 382, 383, or 384 on the sale referred to in paragraph (a)(1) of this section.

(b) *Adjustment to net unrealized built-in gain.*—(1) *In general.*—If section 1374(d)(8) applies to an S corporation's acquisition of assets, some or all of the stock of the corporation from which such assets were acquired was taken into account in the computation of the net unrealized built-in gain for a pool of assets of the S corporation, and some or all of such stock is redeemed or canceled in such transaction, then, subject to the limitations of paragraph (b)(2) of this section, such net unrealized built-in gain is adjusted to eliminate any effect that any built-in gain or built-in loss in the redeemed or canceled stock (other than stock with respect to which a loss under section 165 is claimed) had on the initial computation of net unrealized built-in gain for that pool of assets. For purposes of this paragraph, stock described in section 1374(d)(6) shall be treated as taken into account in the computation of the net unrealized built-in gain for a pool of assets of the S corporation.

(2) *Limitations on adjustment.*—(i) *Recognized built-in gain or loss.*—Net unrealized built-in gain for a pool of assets of the S corporation is only adjusted under paragraph (b)(1) of this section to reflect built-in gain or built-in loss in the redeemed or canceled stock that has not resulted in recognized built-in gain or recognized built-in loss during the recognition period.

(ii) *Anti-duplication rule.*—Paragraph (b)(1) of this section shall not be applied to duplicate an adjustment to the net unrealized built-in gain for a pool of assets made pursuant to paragraph (b)(1) of this section.

(3) *Effect of adjustment.*—Any adjustment to the net unrealized built-in gain made pursuant to this paragraph (b) only affects computations of the amount subject to tax under section 1374 for taxable years that end on or after the date of the acquisition to which section 1374(d)(8) applies.

(4) *Pool of assets.*—For purposes of this section, a pool of assets means—

(i) The assets held by the corporation on the first day it became an S corporation, if the corporation was previously a C corporation; or

(ii) The assets the S corporation acquired from a C corporation in a section 1374(d)(8) transaction.

(c) *Examples.*—The following examples illustrate the rules of this section:

Example 1. Computation of net unrealized built-in gain. (i)(A) X, a calendar year C corporation using the cash method, elects to become an S corporation on January 1, 1996. On December 31, 1995, X has assets and liabilities as follows:

Assets	*FMV*	*Basis*
Factory	$500,000	$900,000
Accounts Receivable . . .	300,000	0
Goodwill	250,000	0
Total	1,050,000	900,000

Liabilities	*Amount*
Mortgage	$200,000
Accounts Payable	100,000
Total	300,000

(B) Further, X must include a total of $60,000 in taxable income in 1996, 1997, and 1998 under section 481(a).

(ii) If, on December 31, 1995, X sold all its assets to a third party that assumed all its liabilities, X's amount realized would be $1,050,000 ($750,000 cash received + $300,000 liabilities assumed = $1,050,000). Thus, X's net unrealized built-in gain is determined as follows:

Amount realized	$1,050,000
Deduction allowed (A/P)	(100,000)
Basis of X's assets	(900,000)
Section 481 adjustments	60,000
Net unrealized built-in gain	110,000

Example 2. Adjustment to net unrealized built-in gain for built-in gain in eliminated C corporation stock. (i) X, a calendar year C corporation, elects to become an S corporation effective January 1, 2005. On that date, X's assets (the first pool of assets) have a net unrealized built-in gain of $15,000. Among the assets in the first pool of assets is all of the outstanding stock of Y, a C corporation, with a fair market value of $33,000 and an adjusted basis of $18,000. On March 1, 2009, X sells an asset that it owned on January 1, 2005, and as a result has $10,000 of recognized built-in gain. X has had no other recognized built-in gain or built-in loss. X's taxable income limitation for 2009 is $50,000. Effective June 1, 2009, X elects under section 1361 to treat Y as a qualified subchapter S subsidiary (QSub). The election is treated as a transfer of Y's assets to X in a liquidation to which sections 332 and 337(a) apply.

(ii) Under paragraph (b) of this section, the net unrealized built in-gain of the first pool of assets is adjusted to account for the elimination of the Y stock in the liquidation. The net unrealized built-in gain of the first pool of assets, therefore, is decreased by $15,000, the amount by which the fair market value of the Y stock exceeded its adjusted basis as of January 1, 2005. Accordingly, for taxable years ending after June 1, 2009, the net unrealized built-in gain of the first pool of assets is $0.

(iii) Under §1.1374-2(a), X's net recognized built-in gain for any taxable year equals the least of X's pre-limitation amount, taxable income limitation, and net unrealized built-in gain limitation. In 2009, X's pre-limitation amount is $10,000, X's taxable income limitation is $50,000, and X's net unrealized built-in gain limitation is $0. Because the net umealized built-in gain of the first pool of assets has been adjusted to $0, despite the $10,000 of recognized built-in gain in 2009, X has $0 net recognized built-in gain for the taxable year ending on December 31, 2009.

Example 3. Adjustment to net unrealized built-in gain for built-in loss in eliminated C corporation stock. (i) X, a calendar year C corporation, elects to become an S corporation effective January 1, 2005. On that date, X's assets (the first pool of assets) have a net unrealized built-in gain of negative $5,000. Among the assets in the first pool of assets is 10 percent of the outstanding stock of Y, a C corporation, with a fair market value of $18,000 and an adjusted basis of $33,000. On March 1, 2009, X sells an asset that it owned on January 1, 2005, resulting in $8,000 of recognized built-in gain. X has had no other recognized built-in gains or built-in losses. X's taxable income limitation for 2009 is $50,000. On June 1, 2009, Y transfers its assets to X in a reorganization under section 368(a)(1)(C).

(ii) Under paragraph (b) of this section, the net unrealized built in-gain of the first pool of assets is adjusted to account for the elimination of the Y stock in the reorganization. The net unrealized built-in gain of the first pool of assets, therefore, is increased by $15,000, the amount by which the adjusted basis of the Y stock exceeded its fair market value as of January 1, 2005. Accordingly, for taxable years ending after June 1, 2009, the net unrealized built-in gain of the first pool of assets is $10,000.

(iii) Under §1.1374-2(a), X's net recognized built-in gain for any taxable year equals the least of X's pre-limitation amount, taxable income limitation, and net unrealized built-in gain limitation. In 2009, X's pre-limitation amount is $8,000 and X's taxable income limitation is $50,000. The net unrealized built-in gain of the first pool of assets has been adjusted to $10,000, so X's net unrealized built-in gain limitation is $10,000. X, therefore, has $8,000 net recognized built-in gain for the taxable year ending on December 31, 2009. X's net unrealized built-in gain limitation for 2010 is $2,000.

Example 4. Adjustment to net unrealized built-in gain in case of prior gain recognition. (i) X, a calendar year C corporation, elects to become an S corporation effective January 1, 2005. On that date, X's assets (the first pool of assets) have a net unrealized built-in gain of $30,000. Among the assets in the first pool of assets is all of the outstanding stock of Y, a C corporation, with a fair market value of $45,000 and an adjusted basis of $10,000. Y has no current or accumulated earnings and profits. On April 1, 2007, Y distributes $18,000 to X, $8,000 of which is treated as gain to X from the sale or exchange of property under section 301(c)(3). That $8,000 is recognized built-in gain to X under section 1374(d)(3), and results in $8,000 of net recognized built-in gain to X for 2007. X's net unrealized built-in gain limitation for 2008 is $22,000. On June 1, 2009, Y transfers its assets to X in a liquidation to which sections 332 and 337(a) apply.

(ii) Under paragraph (b) of this section, the net unrealized built in-gain of the first pool of assets is adjusted to account for the elimination of the Y stock in the liquidation. The net unrealized built-in gain of that pool of assets, however, can only be adjusted to reflect the amount of built-in gain that was inherent in the Y stock on January 1, 2005 that has not resulted in recognized built-in gain during the recognition period. In this case, therefore, the net unrealized built-in gain of the first pool of assets cannot be reduced by more than $27,000 ($35,000, the amount by which the fair market value of the Y stock exceeded its adjusted basis as of January 1, 2005, minus $8,000, the recognized built-in gain with respect to the stock during the recognition period). Accordingly, for taxable years ending after June 1, 2009, the net unrealized built-in gain of the first pool of assets is $3,000. The net unrealized built-in gain limitation for 2009 is $0.

[Reg. § 1.1374-3.]

□ [*T.D.* 8579, 12-23-94. *Amended by T.D.* 9180, 2-22-2005.]

§ 1.1374-4. Recognized built-in gain or loss.—(a) *Sales and exchanges.*—(1) *In general.*—Section 1374(d)(3) or 1374(d)(4) applies to any gain or loss recognized during the recognition period in a transaction treated as a sale or exchange for federal income tax purposes.

* * *

[Reg. § 1.1374-4.]

□ [*T.D.* 8579, 12-23-94. *Amended by T.D.* 8995, 5-14-2002.]

§ 1.1374-7. Inventory.—(a) *Valuation.*—The fair market value of the inventory of an S corporation on the first day of the recognition period equals the amount that a willing buyer would pay a willing seller for the inventory in a purchase of all the S corporation's assets by a buyer that expects to continue to operate the S corporation's business. For purposes of the preceding sentence, the buyer and seller are presumed not to be under any compulsion to buy or sell and to have reasonable knowledge of all relevant facts.

(b) *Identity of dispositions.*—The inventory method used by an S corporation for tax purposes must be used to identify whether the inventory it disposes of during the recognition period is inventory it held on the first day of that period. Thus, a corporation using the LIFO method does not dispose of inventory it held on the first day of the recognition period unless the carrying value of its inventory for a taxable year during that period is less than the carrying value of its inventory on the first day of the recognition period (determined using the LIFO method as described in section 472). However, if a corporation changes its method of accounting for inventory (for example, from the FIFO method to the LIFO method or from the LIFO method to the FIFO method) with a principal purpose of avoiding the tax imposed under section 1374, it must use its former method to identify its dispositions of inventory. [Reg. § 1.1374-7.]

□ [*T.D.* 8579, 12-23-94.]

§ 1.1374-8. Section 1374(d)(8) transactions.—(a) *In general.*—If any S corporation acquires any asset in a transaction in which the S corporation's basis in the asset is determined (in whole or in part) by reference to a C corporation's basis in the assets (or any other property) (a section 1374(d)(8) transaction), section 1374 applies to the net recognized built-in gain attributable to the assets acquired in any section 1374(d)(8) transaction.

* * *

(c) *Separate determination of tax.*—For purposes of the tax imposed under section 1374(d)(8), a separate determination of tax is made with respect to the assets the S corporation acquires in one section 1374(d)(8) transaction from the assets the S corporation acquires in another section 1374(d)(8) transaction and from the assets the corporation held when it became an S corporation. Thus, an S corporation's section 1374 attributes when it became an S corporation may only be used to reduce the section 1374 tax imposed on dispositions of assets the S corporation held at that time. Similarly, an S corporation's section 1374 attributes acquired in a section 1374(d)(8) transaction may only be used to reduce a section 1374 tax imposed on dispositions of assets the S corporation acquired in the same transaction. If an S corporation makes QSub elections under section 1361(b)(3) for a tiered group of subsidiaries effective on the same day, see § 1.1361-4(b)(2).

(d) *Taxable income limitation.*—For purposes of paragraph (a) of this section, an S corporation's taxable income limitation under § 1.1374-2(a)(2) for any taxable year is allocated between or among each of the S corporation's separate determinations of net recognized built-in gain for that year (determined without regard to the taxable income limitation) based on the ratio of each of those determinations to the sum of all of those determinations.

(e) *Examples.*—The rules of this section are illustrated by the following examples.

Example 1. Separate determination of tax. (i) X is a C corporation that elected to become an S corporation effective January 1, 1986 (before section 1374 was amended in the Tax Reform Act of 1986). X has a net operating loss carryforward of $20,000 arising in 1985 when X was a C corporation. On January 1, 1996, Y (an unrelated C corporation) merges into X in a transaction to which section 368(a)(1)(A) applies. Y has no loss carryforwards, credits, or credit carryforwards. The assets X acquired from Y are subject to tax under section 1374 and have a net unrealized built-in gain of $150,000.

(ii) In 1996, X has a pre-limitation amount of $50,000 on dispositions of assets acquired from Y and a taxable income limitation of $100,000 (because only one group of assets is subject to section 1374, there is no allocation of the taxable income limitation). As a result, X has a net recognized built-in gain on those assets of $50,000. X's $20,000 net operating loss carryforward may not be used as a deduction against its $50,000 net recognized built-in gain on the assets X acquired from Y. Therefore, X has a section 1374 tax of $17,500 ($50,000 × .35 = $17,500, assuming a 35 percent tax rate) for its 1996 taxable year.

Example 2. Allocation of taxable income limitation. (i) Y is a C corporation that elects to become an S corporation effective January 1, 1996. The assets Y holds when it becomes an S corporation have a net unrealized built-in gain of $5,000. Y has no loss carryforwards, credits, or credit carryforwards. On January 1, 1997, Z (an unrelated C corporation) merges into Y in a transaction to which section 368(a)(1)(A) applies. Z has no loss carryforwards, credits, or credit carryforwards. The assets Y acquired from Z are subject to tax under section 1374 and have a net unrealized built-in gain of $80,000.

(ii) In 1997, Y has a pre-limitation amount on the assets it held when it became an S corporation of $15,000, a pre-limitation amount on the assets Y acquired from Z of $15,000, and a taxable income limitation of $10,000. However, because the assets Y held on becoming an S corporation have a net unrealized built-in gain of $5,000, its net recognized built-in gain on those assets is limited to $5,000 before taking into account the taxable income limitation. Y's taxable income limitation of $10,000 is allocated between the assets Y held on becoming an S corporation and the assets Y acquired from Z for purposes of determining the net recognized built-in gain from each pool of assets. Thus, Y's net recognized built-in gain on the assets Y held on becoming an S corporation is $2,500 [$10,000 × ($5,000/$20,000) = $2,500]. Y's net recognized built-in gain on the assets Y acquired from Z is $7,500 [$10,000 × ($15,000/$20,000) = $7,500]. Therefore, Y has a section 1374 tax of $3,500 [($2,500 + $7,500) × .35 = $3,500, assuming a 35 percent tax rate] for its 1997 taxable year.

[Reg. § 1.1374-8.]

□ [*T.D.* 8579, 12-23-94. *Amended by T.D.* 8869, 1-20-2000; *T.D.* 9170, 12-21-2004 *and T.D.* 9236, 12-20-2005.]

§ 1.1377-1. Pro rata share.—(a) *Computation of pro rata shares.*—(1) *In general.*—For purposes of subchapter S of chapter 1 of the Internal Revenue Code and this section, each shareholder's pro rata share of any S corporation item described in section 1366(a) for any taxable year is the sum of the amounts determined with respect to the shareholder by assigning an equal portion of the item to each day of the S corporation's taxable year, and then dividing that portion pro rata among the shares outstanding on that day. See paragraph (b) of this section for rules pertaining to the computation of each shareholder's pro rata share when an election is made under section 1377(a)(2) to treat the taxable year of an S corporation as if it consisted of two taxable years in the case of a termination of a shareholder's entire interest in the corporation. See § 1.460-4(k)(3)(iv)(D) for rules relating to the computation of the shareholders' pro rata share of S corporation's income or loss from a contract accounted for under a long-term contract method of accounting.

(2) *Special rules.*—(i) *Days on which stock has not been issued.*—Solely for purposes of determining a shareholder's pro rata share of an item for a taxable year under section 1377(a) and this section, the beneficial owners of the corporation are treated as the shareholders of the corporation for any day on which the corporation has not issued any stock.

(ii) *Determining shareholder for day of stock disposition.*—A shareholder who disposes of stock in an S corporation is treated as the shareholder for the day of the disposition. A shareholder who dies is treated as the shareholder for the day of the shareholder's death.

(iii) *Shareholder trust conversions.*—If, during the taxable year of an S corporation, a trust that is an eligible shareholder of the S corporation converts from a trust described in section 1361(c)(2)(A)(i), (ii), (iii), or (v) for the first part of the year to a trust described in a different subpart of section 1361(c)(2)(A)(i), (ii), or (v) for the remainder of the year, the trust's share of the S corporation items is allocated between the two types of trusts. The first day that a qualified subchapter S trust (QSST) or an electing small business trust (ESBT) is treated as an S corporation shareholder is the effective date of the QSST or ESBT election. Upon the conversion, the trust is not treated as terminating its entire interest in the S corporation for purposes of paragraph (b) of this section, unless the trust was a trust described in section 1361(c)(2)(A)(ii) or (iii) before the conversion.

(b) *Election to terminate year.*—(1) *In general.*—If a shareholder's entire interest in an S corporation is terminated during the S corporation's taxable year and the corporation and all affected shareholders agree, the S corporation may elect under section 1377(a)(2) and this paragraph (b) (terminating election) to apply paragraph (a) of this section to the affected shareholders as if the corporation's taxable year consisted of two separate taxable years, the first of which ends at the close of the day on which the shareholder's entire interest in the S corporation is terminated. If the event resulting in the termination of the shareholder's entire interest also constitutes a qualifying disposition as described in § 1.1368-1(g)(2)(i), the election under § 1.1368-1(g)(2) cannot be made. An S corporation may not make a terminating election if the cessation of a shareholder's interest occurs in a transaction that results in a termination under section 1362(d)(2) of the corporation's election to be an S corporation. (See section 1362(e)(3) for an election to have items assigned to each short taxable year under normal tax accounting rules in the case of a termination of a corporation's election to be an S corporation.) A terminating election is irrevocable and is effective only for the terminating event for which it is made.

(2) *Affected shareholders.*—For purposes of the terminating election under section 1377(a)(2) and paragraph (b) of this section, the term *affected shareholders* means the shareholder whose interest is terminated and all shareholders to whom such shareholder has transferred shares during the taxable year. If such shareholder has transferred shares to the corporation, the term *affected shareholders* includes all persons who are shareholders during the taxable year.

(3) *Effect of the terminating election.*—(i) *In general.*—An S corporation that makes a terminating election for a taxable year must treat the taxable year as separate taxable years for all affected shareholders for purposes of allocating items of income (including tax-exempt income), loss, deduction, and credit; making adjustments to the accumulated adjustments account, earnings and profits, and basis; and determining the tax effect of a distribution. An S corporation that makes a terminating election must assign items of income (including tax-exempt income), loss, deduction, and credit to each deemed separate taxable year using its normal method of accounting as determined under section 446(a).

(ii) *Due date of S corporation return.*—A terminating election does not affect the due date of the S corporation's return required to be filed under section 6037(a) for a taxable year (determined without regard to a terminating election).

(iii) *Taxable year of inclusion by shareholder.*—A terminating election does not affect the taxable year in which an affected shareholder must take into account the affected shareholder's pro rata share of the S corporation's items of income, loss, deduction, and credit.

(iv) *S corporation that is a partner in a partnership.*—A terminating election by an S corporation that is a partner in a partnership is treated as a sale or exchange of the corporation's entire interest in the partnership for purposes of section 706(c) (relating to closing the partnership taxable year), if the taxable year of the partnership ends after the shareholder's interest is terminated and within the taxable year of the S corporation (determined without regard to any terminating election) for which the terminating election is made.

(4) *Determination of whether an S shareholder's entire interest has terminated.*—For purposes of the terminating election under section 1377(a)(2) and paragraph (b) of this section, a shareholder's entire interest in an S corporation is terminated on the occurrence of any event through which a shareholder's entire stock ownership in the S corporation ceases, including a sale, exchange, or other disposition of all of the stock held by the shareholder; a gift under section 102(a) of all the shareholder's stock; a spousal transfer under section 1041(a) of all the shareholder's stock; a redemption, as defined in section 317(b), of all the shareholder's stock, regardless of the tax treatment of the redemption under section 302; and the death of the shareholder. A shareholder's entire interest in an S corporation is not terminated if the shareholder retains ownership of any stock (including an interest treated as stock under § 1.1361-1(l)) that would result in the shareholder continuing to be considered a shareholder of the corporation for purposes of section 1362(a)(2). Thus, in determining whether a shareholder's entire interest in an S corporation has been terminated, any interest held by the shareholder as a creditor,

employee, director, or in any other non-shareholder capacity is disregarded.

(5) *Time and manner of making a terminating election.*—(i) *In general.*—An S corporation makes a terminating election by attaching a statement to its timely filed original or amended return required to be filed under section 6037(a) (that is, a Form 1120S) for the taxable year during which a shareholder's entire interest is terminated. A single election statement may be filed by the S corporation for all terminating elections for the taxable year. The election statement must include—

(A) A declaration by the S corporation that it is electing under section 1377(a)(2) and this paragraph to treat the taxable year as if it consisted of two separate taxable years;

(B) Information setting forth when and how the shareholder's entire interest was terminated (for example, a sale or gift);

(C) The signature on behalf of the S corporation of an authorized officer of the corporation under penalties of perjury, except that for taxable years beginning after December 31, 2002, the election statement described in § 1.1377-1(b)(5)(i) of this section shall be verified, and the requirement of this paragraph (b)(5)(i)(C) is satisfied, by the signature on the Form 1120S filed by the S corporation.

(D) A statement by the corporation that the corporation and each affected shareholder consent to the S corporation making the terminating election.

(ii) *Affected shareholders required to consent.*—For purposes of paragraph (b)(5)(i)(D) of this section, a shareholder of the S corporation for the taxable year is a shareholder as described in section 1362(a)(2). For example, the person who under § 1.1362-6(b)(2) must consent to a corporation's S election in certain special cases is the person who must consent to the terminating election. In addition, an executor or administrator of the estate of a deceased affected shareholder may consent to the terminating election on behalf of the deceased affected shareholder.

(iii) *More than one terminating election.*—A shareholder whose entire interest in an S corporation is terminated in an event for which a terminating election was made is not required to consent to a terminating election made with respect to a subsequent termination within the same taxable year unless the shareholder is an affected shareholder with respect to the subsequent termination.

(c) *Examples.*—The following examples illustrate the provisions of this section:

Example 1. Shareholder's pro rata share in the case of a partial disposition of stock. (i) On January 6, 1997, X incorporates as a calendar year corporation, issues 100 shares of common stock to each of A and B, and files an election to be an S corporation for its 1997 taxable year. On July 24, 1997, B sells 50 shares of X stock to C. Thus, in 1997, A owned 50 percent of the outstanding shares of X on each day of X's 1997 taxable year, B owned 50 percent on each day from January 6, 1997, to July 24, 1997 (200 days), and 25 percent from July 25, 1997, to December 31, 1997 (160 days), and C owned 25 percent from July 25, 1997, to December 31, 1997 (160 days).

(ii) Because B's entire interest in X is not terminated when B sells 50 shares to C on July 24, 1997, X cannot make a terminating election under section 1377(a)(2) and paragraph (b) of this section for B's sale of 50 shares to C. Although B's sale of 50 shares to C is a qualifying disposition under § 1.1368-1(g)(2)(i), X does not make an election to terminate its taxable year under § 1.1368-1(g)(2). During its 1997 taxable year, X has nonseparately computed income of $720,000.

(iii) For each day in X's 1997 taxable year, A's daily pro rata share of X's nonseparately computed income is $1,000 ($720,000/360 days × 50%). Thus, A's pro rata share of X's nonseparately computed income for 1997 is $360,000 ($1,000 × 360 days). B's daily pro rata share of X's nonseparately computed income is $1,000 ($720,000/360 × 50%) for the first 200 days of X's 1997 taxable year, and $500 ($720,000/360 × 25%) for the following 160 days in 1997. Thus, B's pro rata share of X's nonseparately computed income for 1997 is $280,000 (($1,000 × 200 days) + ($500 × 160 days)). C's daily pro rata share of X's nonseparately computed income is $500 ($720,000/360 × 25%) for 160 days in 1997. Thus, C's pro rata share of X's nonseparately computed income for 1997 is $80,000 ($500 × 160 days).

Example 2. Shareholder's pro rata share when an S corporation makes a terminating election under section 1377(a)(2). (i) On January 6, 1997, X incorporates as a calendar year corporation, issues 100 shares of common stock to each of A and B, and files an election to be an S corporation for its 1997 taxable year. On July 24, 1997, B sells B's entire 100 shares of X stock to C. With the consent of B and C, X makes an election under section 1377(a)(2) and paragraph (b) of this section for the termination of B's entire interest arising from B's sale of 100 shares to C. As a result of the election, the pro rata shares of B and C are determined as if X's taxable year consisted of two separate taxable years, the first of which ends on July 24, 1997, the date B's entire interest in X terminates. Because A is not an affected shareholder as defined by section

1377(a)(2)(B) and paragraph (b)(2) of this section, the treatment as separate taxable years does not apply to A.

(ii) During its 1997 taxable year, X has nonseparately computed income of $720,000. Under X's normal method of accounting, $200,000 of the $720,000 of nonseparately computed income is allocable to the period of January 6, 1997, through July 24, 1997 (the first deemed taxable year), and the remaining $520,000 is allocable to the period of July 25, 1997, through December 31, 1997 (the second deemed taxable year).

(iii) B's pro rata share of the $200,000 of nonseparately computed income for the first deemed taxable year is determined by assigning the $200,000 of nonseparately computed income to each day of the first deemed taxable year ($200,000/200 days = $1,000 per day). Because B held 50% of X's authorized and issued shares on each day of the first deemed taxable year, B's daily pro rata share for each day of the first deemed taxable year is $500 ($1,000 per day × 50%). Thus, B's pro rata share of the $200,000 of nonseparately computed income for the first deemed taxable year is $100,000 ($500 per day x 200 days). B must report this amount for B's taxable year with or within which X's full taxable year ends (December 31, 1997).

(iv) C's pro rata share of the $520,000 of nonseparately computed income for the second deemed taxable year is determined by assigning the $520,000 of nonseparately computed income to each day of the second deemed taxable year ($520,000/160 days = $3,250 per day). Because C held 50% of X's authorized and issued shares on each day of the second deemed taxable year, C's daily pro rata shares for each day of the second deemed taxable year is $1,625 ($3,250 per day × 50%). Therefore, C's pro rata share of the $520,000 of nonseparately computed income is $260,000 ($1,625 per day × 160 days). C must report this amount for C's taxable year with or within which X's full taxable year ends (December 31, 1997).

* * *

[Reg. § 1.1377-1.]

□ [*T.D.* 8696, 12-20-96. *Amended by T.D.* 8994, 5-13-2002; *T.D.* 9100, 12-18-2003; *T.D.* 9137, 7-15-2004 *and T.D.* 9300, 12-7-2006.]

§ 1.1377-2. Post-termination transition period.—(a) *In general.*—For purposes of subchapter S of chapter 1 of the Internal Revenue Code (Code) and this section, the term *post-termination transition period* means—

(1) The period beginning on the day after the last day of the corporation's last taxable year as an S corporation and ending on the later of—

(i) The day which is 1 year after such last day; or

(ii) The due date for filing the return for the last taxable year as an S corporation (including extensions);

(2) The 120-day period beginning on the date of any determination pursuant to an audit of the taxpayer which follows the termination of the corporation's election and which adjusts a subchapter S item of income, loss, or deduction of the corporation arising during the S period (as defined in section 1368(e)(2)); and

(3) The 120-day period beginning on the date of a determination that the corporation's election under section 1362(a) had terminated for a previous taxable year.

(b) *Special rules for post-termination transition period.*—Pursuant to section 1377(b)(1) and paragraph (a)(1) of this section, a post-termination transition period arises the day after the last day that an S corporation was in existence if a C corporation acquires the assets of the S corporation in a transaction to which section 381(a)(2) applies. However, if an S corporation acquires the assets of another S corporation in a transaction to which section 381(a)(2) applies, a post-termination transition period does not arise. (See § 1.1368-2(d)(2) for the treatment of the acquisition of the assets of an S corporation by another S corporation in a transaction to which section 381(a)(2) applies.) The special treatment under section 1371(e)(1) of distributions of money by a corporation with respect to its stock during the post-termination transition period is available only to those shareholders who were shareholders in the S corporation at the time of the termination.

(c) *Determination defined.*—For purposes of section 1377(b)(1) and paragraph (a) of this section, the term *determination* means—

(1) A determination as defined in section 1313(a);

(2) A written agreement between the corporation and the Commissioner (including a statement acknowledging that the corporation's election to be an S corporation terminated under section 1362(d)) that the corporation failed to qualify as an S corporation;

(3) For a corporation subject to the audit and assessment provisions of subchapter C of chapter 63 of subtitle A of the Code, the expiration of the period specified in section 6226 for filing a petition for readjustment of a final S corporation administrative adjustment finding that the corporation failed to qualify as an S corporation, provided that no petition was timely filed before the expiration of the period; and

(4) For a corporation not subject to the audit and assessment provisions of subchapter C of chapter 63 of subtitle A of the Code, the expiration of the period for filing a petition under section 6213 for the shareholder's taxable year for which the Commissioner has made a finding that the corporation failed to qualify as an S corporation, provided that no petition was timely filed before the expiration of the period.

(d) *Date a determination becomes effective.*—(1) *Determination under section 1313(a).*—A determination under paragraph (c)(1) of this section becomes effective on the date prescribed in section 1313 and the regulations thereunder.

(2) *Written agreement.*—A determination under paragraph (c)(2) of this section becomes effective when it is signed by the district director having jurisdiction over the corporation (or by another Service official to whom authority to sign the agreement is delegated) and by an officer of the corporation authorized to sign on its behalf. Neither the request for a written agreement nor the terms of the written agreement suspend the running of any statute of limitations.

(3) *Implied agreement.*—A determination under paragraph (c)(3) or (4) of this section becomes effective on the day after the date of expiration of the period specified under section 6226 or 6213, respectively. [Reg. § 1.1377-2.]

□ [*T.D.* 8696, 12-20-96.]

§ 1.1378-1. Taxable year of S corporation.—(a) *In general.*—The taxable year of an S corporation must be a permitted year. A permitted year is the required taxable year (i.e., a taxable year ending on December 31), a taxable year elected under section 444, a 52-53-week taxable year ending with reference to the required taxable year or a taxable year elected under section 444, or any other taxable year for which the corporation establishes a business purpose to the satisfaction of the Commissioner under section 442.

(b) *Adoption of taxable year.*—An electing S corporation may adopt, in accordance with § 1.441-1(c), its required taxable year, a taxable year elected under section 444, or a 52-53-week taxable year ending with reference to its required taxable year or a taxable year elected under section 444 without the approval of the Commissioner. See § 1.441-1. An electing S corporation that wants to adopt any other taxable year, must establish a business purpose and obtain the approval of the Commissioner under section 442.

(c) *Change in taxable year.*—(1) *Approval required.*—An S corporation or electing S corporation that wants to change its taxable year must obtain the approval of the Commissioner under section 442 or make an election under section 444. However, an S corporation or electing S corporation may obtain automatic approval for certain changes, including a change to its required taxable year, pursuant to administrative procedures published by the Commissioner.

(2) *Short period tax return.*—An S corporation or electing S corporation that changes its taxable year must make its return for a short period in accordance with section 443, but must not annualize the corporation's taxable income.

(d) *Retention of taxable year.*—In certain cases, an S corporation or electing S corporation will be required to change its taxable year unless it obtains the approval of the Commissioner under section 442, or makes an election under section 444, to retain its current taxable year. For example, a corporation using a June 30 fiscal year that elects to be an S corporation and, as a result, is required to use the calendar year must obtain the approval of the Commissioner to retain its current fiscal year.

* * *

[Reg. § 1.1378-1.]

□ [*T.D.* 8996, 5-16-2002.]

Net Investment Income Tax

§ 1.1411-1. General rules.—(a) *General rule.*—Except as otherwise provided, all Internal Revenue Code (Code) provisions that apply for chapter 1 purposes in determining taxable income (as defined in section 63(a)) of a taxpayer also apply in determining the tax imposed by section 1411.

(b) *Adjusted gross income.*—All references to an individual's adjusted gross income are treated as references to adjusted gross income as defined in section 62, and all references to an estate's or trust's adjusted gross income are treated as references to adjusted gross income as defined in section 67(e). However, there may be additional adjustments to adjusted gross income because of investments in controlled foreign corporations (CFCs) or passive foreign investment companies (PFICs). See § 1.1411-10(e).

(c) *Effect of section 1411 and the regulations thereunder for other purposes.*—The inclusion or exclusion of items of income, gain, loss, or deduction in determining net investment income for purposes of section 1411, and the assignment of items of income, gain, loss, or deduction to a particular category of net investment income under section 1411(c)(1)(A), does not affect the treatment of any item of income, gain, loss, or deduction under any provision of the Code other than section 1411.

(d) *Definitions.*—The following definitions apply for purposes of calculating net investment income under section 1411 and the regulations thereunder—

(1) The term *gross income from annuities* under section 1411(c)(1)(A) includes the amount received as an annuity under an annuity, endowment, or life insurance contract that is includible in gross income as a result of the application of section 72(a) and section 72(b), and an amount not received as an annuity under an annuity contract that is includible in gross income under section 72(e). In the case of a sale of an annuity, to the extent the sales price of the annuity does not exceed its surrender value, the gain recognized would be treated as gross income from an annuity within the meaning of section 1411(c)(1)(A)(i) and § 1.1411-4(a)(1)(i). However, if the sales price of the annuity exceeds its surrender value, the seller would treat the gain equal to the difference between the basis in the annuity and the surrender value as gross income from an annuity described in section 1411(c)(1)(A)(i) and § 1.1411-4(a)(1)(i) and the excess of the sales price over the surrender value as gain from the disposition of property included in section 1411(c)(1)(A)(iii) and § 1.1411-4(a)(1)(iii). The term *gross income from annuities* does not include amounts paid in consideration for services rendered. For example, distributions from a foreign retirement plan that are paid in the form of an annuity and include investment income that was earned by the retirement plan does not constitute income from an annuity within the meaning of section 1411(c)(1)(A)(i).

(2) The term *controlled foreign corporation (CFC)* is as defined in section 953(c)(1)(B) or 957(a).

(3) The term *gross income from dividends* includes any item treated as a dividend for purposes of chapter 1. See also § 1.1411-10 for additional amounts that constitute gross income from dividends. The term *gross income from dividends* includes, but is not limited to, amounts treated as dividends—

(i) Pursuant to subchapter C that are included in gross income (including constructive dividends);

(ii) Pursuant to section 1248(a), other than as provided in § 1.1411-10;

(iii) Pursuant to § 1.367(b)-2(e)(2);

(iv) Pursuant to section 1368(c)(2); and

(v) Substitute dividends that represent payments made to the transferor of a security in a securities lending transaction or a sale-repurchase transaction.

(4) The term *excluded income* means:

(i) Items of income excluded from gross income in chapter 1. For example, interest on state and local bonds excluded from gross income under section 103 and gain from the sale of a principal residence excluded from gross income under section 121.

(ii) Items of income not included in net investment income, as determined under §§ 1.1411-4 and 1.1411-10. For example, wages, unemployment compensation, Alaska Permanent Fund Dividends, alimony, and Social Security Benefits.

(iii) Items of gross income and net gain specifically excluded by section 1411, the regulations thereunder, or other guidance published in the Internal Revenue Bulletin. For example, gains from the disposition of property used in a trade of business not described in section 1411(c)(2) under § 1.1411-4(d)(4)(i), distributions from certain Qualified Plans described in section 1411(c)(5) and § 1.1411-8, income taken into account in determining self-employment income that is subject to tax under section 1401(b) described in section 1411(c)(6) and § 1.1411-9, and section 951(a) inclusions from a CFC for which a § 1.1411-10(g) election is not in effect.

(5) The term *individual* means any natural person.

(6) The term *gross income from interest* includes any item treated as interest income for purposes of chapter 1 and substitute interest that represents payments made to the transferor of a security in a securities lending transaction or a sale-repurchase transaction.

(7) The term *married* and *married taxpayer* has the same meaning as in section 7703.

(8) The term *net investment income (NII)* means net investment income as defined in section 1411(c) and § 1.1411-4, as adjusted pursuant to the rules described in § 1.1411-10(c).

(9) The term *passive foreign investment company (PFIC)* is as defined in section 1297(a).

(10) The term *gross income from rents* includes amounts paid or to be paid principally for the use of (or the right to use) tangible property.

(11) The term *gross income from royalties* includes amounts received from mineral, oil, and gas royalties, and amounts received for the privilege of using patents, copyrights, secret processes and formulas, goodwill, trademarks, tradebrands, franchises, and other like property.

(12) The term *trade or business* refers to a trade or business within the meaning of section 162.

(13) The term *United States person* is as defined in section 7701(a)(30).

(14) The term *United States shareholder* is as defined in section 951(b).

(e) *Disallowance of certain credits against the section 1411 tax.*—Amounts that may be credited against only the tax imposed by chapter 1 of the Code may not be credited against the section 1411 tax imposed by chapter 2A of the Code unless specifically provided in the Code. For example, the foreign income, war profits, and excess profits taxes that are allowed as a foreign tax credit by section 27(a), section 642(a), and section 901, respectively, are not allowed as a credit against the section 1411 tax.

* * *

[Reg. §1.1411-1.]

☐ [*T.D.* 9644, 11-26-2013.]

§1.1411-4. Definition of net investment income.—(a) *In general.*—For purposes of section 1411 and the regulations thereunder, net investment income means the excess (if any) of—

(1) The sum of—

(i) Gross income from interest, dividends, annuities, royalties, and rents, except to the extent excluded by the ordinary course of a trade or business exception described in paragraph (b) of this section;

(ii) Other gross income derived from a trade or business described in §1.1411-5; and

(iii) Net gain (to the extent taken into account in computing taxable income) attributable to the disposition of property, except to the extent excluded by the exception described in paragraph (d)(4)(i)(A) of this section for gain or loss attributable to property held in a trade or business not described in §1.1411-5; over

(2) The deductions allowed by subtitle A that are properly allocable to such gross income or net gain (as determined in paragraph (f) of this section).

(b) *Ordinary course of a trade or business exception.*—Gross income described in paragraph (a)(1)(i) of this section is excluded from net investment income if it is derived in the ordinary course of a trade or business not described in §1.1411-5. See §1.1411-6 for rules regarding working capital. To determine whether gross income described in paragraph (a)(1)(i) of this section is derived in a trade or business, the following rules apply.

(1) In the case of an individual, estate, or trust that owns or engages in a trade or business directly (or indirectly through ownership of an interest in an entity that is disregarded as an entity separate from its owner under §301.7701-3), the determination of whether gross income described in paragraph (a)(1)(i) of this section is derived in a trade or business is made at the individual, estate, or trust level.

(2) In the case of an individual, estate, or trust that owns an interest in a passthrough entity (for example, a partnership or S corporation), and that entity is engaged in a trade or business, the determination of whether gross income described in paragraph (a)(1)(i) of this section is—

(i) Derived in a trade or business described in §1.1411-5(a)(1) is made at the owner level; and

(ii) Derived in a trade or business described in §1.1411-5(a)(2) is made at the entity level.

(3) The following examples illustrate the provisions of this paragraph (b). For purposes of these examples, assume that the taxpayer is a United States citizen, uses a calendar taxable year, and Year 1 and all subsequent years are taxable years in which section 1411 is in effect:

Example 1. Multiple passthrough entities. A, an individual, owns an interest in UTP, a partnership, which is engaged in a trade or business. UTP owns an interest in LTP, also a partnership, which is not engaged in a trade or business. LTP receives $10,000 in dividends, $5,000 of which is allocated to A through UTP. The $5,000 of dividends is not derived in a trade or business because LTP is not engaged in a trade or business. This is true even though UTP is engaged in a trade or business. Accordingly, the ordinary course of a trade or business exception described in paragraph (b) of this section does not apply, and A's $5,000 of dividends is net investment income under paragraph (a)(1)(i) of this section.

Example 2. Multiple passthrough entities. B, an individual, owns an interest in UTP2, a partnership, which is not engaged in a trade or business. UTP2 owns an interest in LTP2, also a partnership, which is engaged in a commercial lending trade or business. LTP2 is not engaged in a trade or business described in §1.1411-5(a)(2). LTP2's trade or business is not a passive activity (within the meaning of section 469) with respect to B. LTP2 earns $10,000 of interest income from its trade or business which is allocated to B through UTP2. Although UTP2 is not engaged in a trade or business, the $10,000 of interest income is derived in the ordinary course of LTP2's lending trade or business. Because LTP2 is not engaged in a trade or business described in §1.1411-5(a)(2) and because LTP2's trade or business is not a passive activity with respect to

B (as described in § 1.1411-5(a)(1)), the ordinary course of a trade or business exception described in paragraph (b) of this section applies, and B's $10,000 of interest is not included as net investment income under paragraph (a)(1)(i) of this section.

Example 3. Entity engaged in trading in financial instruments. C, an individual, owns an interest in PRS, a partnership, which is engaged in a trade or business of trading in financial instruments (as defined in § 1.1411-5(a)(2)). PRS' trade or business is not a passive activity (within the meaning of section 469) with respect to C. In addition, C is not directly engaged in a trade or business of trading in financial instruments or commodities. PRS earns interest of $50,000, and C's distributive share of the interest is $25,000. Because PRS is engaged in a trade or business described in § 1.1411-5(a)(2), the ordinary course of a trade or business exception described in paragraph (b) of this section does not apply, and C's $25,000 distributive share of the interest is net investment income under paragraph (a)(1)(i) of this section.

Example 4. Application of ordinary course of a trade or business exception. D, an individual, owns stock in S corporation, S. S is engaged in a banking trade or business (that is not a trade or business of trading in financial instruments or commodities), and S's trade or business is not a passive activity (within the meaning of section 469) with respect to D because D materially participates in the activity. S earns $100,000 of interest in the ordinary course of its trade or business, of which $5,000 is D's pro rata share. For purposes of paragraph (b) of this section, the interest income is derived in the ordinary course of S's banking business because it is not working capital under section 1411(c)(3) and § 1.1411-6(a) (because it is considered to be derived in the ordinary course of a trade or business under the principles of § 1.469-2T(c)(3)(ii)(A)). Because S is not engaged in a trade or business described in § 1.1411-5(a)(2) and because S's trade or business is not a passive activity with respect to D (as described in § 1.1411-5(a)(1)), the ordinary course of a trade or business exception described in paragraph (b) of this section applies, and D's $5,000 of interest is not included under paragraph (a)(1)(i) of this section.

(c) *Other gross income from a trade or business described in § 1.1411-5.*—For a trade or business described in § 1.1411-5, paragraph (a)(1)(ii) of this section includes all other gross income (within the meaning of section 61) that is not gross income described in paragraph (a)(1)(i) of this section or net gain described in paragraph (a)(1)(iii) of this section.

(d) *Net gain.*—This paragraph (d) describes special rules for purposes of paragraph (a)(1)(iii) of this section.

(1) *Definition of disposition.*—For purposes of section 1411 and the regulations thereunder, the term *disposition* means a sale, exchange, transfer, conversion, cash settlement, cancellation, termination, lapse, expiration, or other disposition (including a deemed disposition, for example, under section 877A).

(2) *Limitation.*—The calculation of net gain may not be less than zero. Losses allowable under section 1211(b) are permitted to offset gain from the disposition of assets other than capital assets that are subject to section 1411.

(3) *Net gain attributable to the disposition of property.*—(i) *General rule.*—Net gain attributable to the disposition of property is the gain described in section 61(a)(3) recognized from the disposition of property reduced, but not below zero, by losses deductible under section 165, including losses attributable to casualty, theft, and abandonment or other worthlessness. The rules in subchapter O of chapter 1 and the regulations thereunder apply. See, for example, § 1.61-6(b). For purposes of this paragraph, net gain includes, but is not limited to, gain or loss attributable to the disposition of property from the investment of working capital (as defined in § 1.1411-6); gain or loss attributable to the disposition of a life insurance contract; and gain attributable to the disposition of an annuity contract to the extent the sales price of the annuity exceeds the annuity's surrender value.

(ii) *Examples.*—The following examples illustrate the provisions of this paragraph (d)(3). For purposes of these examples, assume that the taxpayer is a United States citizen, uses a calendar taxable year, and Year 1 and all subsequent years are taxable years in which section 1411 is in effect:

Example 1. Calculation of net gain. (i) In Year 1, A, an unmarried individual, realizes a capital loss of $40,000 on the sale of P stock and realizes a capital gain of $10,000 on the sale of Q stock, resulting in a net capital loss of $30,000. Both P and Q are C corporations. A has no other capital gain or capital loss in Year 1. In addition, A receives wages of $300,000 and earns $5,000 of gross income from interest. For income tax purposes, under section 1211(b), A may use $3,000 of the net capital loss against other income. Under section 1212(b)(1), the remaining $27,000 is a capital loss carryover. For purposes of determining A's Year 1 net gain under paragraph (a)(1)(iii) of this section, A's gain of $10,000 on the sale of the Q stock is reduced by A's loss of $40,000 on the sale of the P stock. In addition, A may reduce net investment income by the $3,000 of the excess of capital losses over capital gains allowed for income tax purposes under section 1211(b).

(ii) In Year 2, A has a capital gain of $30,000 on the sale of Y stock. Y is a C corporation. A has no other capital gain or capital loss in Year 2. For income tax purposes, A may reduce the $30,000 gain by the Year 1 section 1212(b) $27,000 capital loss carryover. For purposes of determining A's Year 2 net gain under paragraph (a)(1)(iii) of this section, A's $30,000 gain may also be reduced by the $27,000 capital loss carryover from Year 1. Therefore, in Year 2, A has $3,000 of net gain for purposes of paragraph (a)(1)(iii) of this section.

Example 2. Calculation of net gain. The facts are the same as in *Example 1*, except that in Year 1, A also realizes a gain of $20,000 on the sale of Rental Property D, all of which is treated as ordinary income under section 1250. For income tax purposes, under section 1211(b), A may use $3,000 of the net capital loss against other income. Under section 1212(b)(1) the remaining $27,000 is a capital loss carryover. For purposes of determining A's net gain under paragraph (a)(1)(iii) of this section, A's gain of $10,000 on the sale of the Q stock is reduced by A's loss of $40,000 on the sale of the P stock. A's $20,000 gain on the sale of Rental Property D is reduced to the extent of the $3,000 loss allowed under section 1211(b). Therefore, A's net gain for Year 1 is $17,000 ($20,000 gain treated as ordinary income on the sale of Rental Property D reduced by $3,000 loss allowed under section 1211).

Example 3. Section 121(a) exclusion. (i) In Year 1, A, an unmarried individual, sells a house that A has owned and used as A's principal residence for the five years preceding the sale and realizes $200,000 in gain. In addition to the gain realized from the sale of A's principal residence, A also realizes $7,000 in long-term capital gain. A has a $5,000 short-term capital loss carryover from a year preceding the effective date of section 1411.

(ii) For income tax purposes, under section 121(a), A excludes the $200,000 gain realized from the sale of A's principal residence from A's Year 1 gross income. In determining A's Year 1 adjusted gross income, A also reduces the $7,000 capital gain by the $5,000 capital loss carryover allowed under section 1211(b).

(iii) For section 1411 purposes, under section 121(a), A excludes the $200,000 gain realized from the sale of A's principal residence from A's Year 1 gross income and, consequently, from A's net investment income. In determining A's Year 1 net gain under paragraph (a)(1)(iii) of this section, A reduces the $7,000 capital gain by the $5,000 capital loss carryover allowed under section 1211(b).

Example 4. Section 1031 like-kind exchange. (i) In Year 1, A, an unmarried individual who is not a dealer in real estate, purchases Greenacre, a piece of undeveloped land, for $10,000. A intends to hold Greenacre for investment.

(ii) In Year 3, A enters into an exchange in which A transfers Greenacre, now valued at $20,000, and $5,000 cash for Blackacre, another piece of undeveloped land, which has a fair market value of $25,000. The exchange is a transaction for which no gain or loss is recognized under section 1031.

(iii) In Year 3, for income tax purposes, A does not recognize any gain from the exchange of Greenacre for Blackacre. A's basis in Blackacre is $15,000 ($10,000 substituted basis in Greenacre plus $5,000 additional cost of acquisition). For purposes of section 1411, A's net investment income for Year 3 does not include any realized gain from the exchange of Greenacre for Blackacre.

(iv) In Year 5, A sells Blackacre to an unrelated party for $35,000 in cash.

(v) In Year 5, for income tax purposes, A recognizes capital gain of $20,000 ($35,000 sale price minus $15,000 basis). For purposes of section 1411, A's net investment income includes the $20,000 gain recognized from the sale of Blackacre.

(4) *Gains and losses excluded from net investment income.*—(i) *Exception for gain or loss attributable to property held in a trade or business not described in § 1.1411-5.*—(A) *General rule.*—Net gain does not include gain or loss attributable to property (other than property from the investment of working capital (as described in § 1.1411-6)) held in a trade or business not described in § 1.1411-5.

(B) *Special rules for determining whether property is held in a trade or business.*—To determine whether net gain described in paragraph (a)(1)(iii) of this section is from property held in a trade or business—

(1) A partnership interest or S corporation stock generally is not property held in a trade or business. Therefore, gain from the sale of a partnership interest or S corporation stock is generally gain described in paragraph (a)(1)(iii) of this section. However, net gain does not include certain gain or loss attributable to the disposition of certain interests in partnerships and S corporations as provided in § 1.1411-7.

(2) In the case of an individual, estate, or trust that owns or engages in a trade or business directly (or indirectly through owner-

ship of an interest in an entity that is disregarded as an entity separate from its owner under § 301.7701-3), the determination of whether net gain described in paragraph (a) (1) (iii) of this section is attributable to property held in a trade or business is made at the individual, estate, or trust level.

(3) In the case of an individual, estate, or trust that owns an interest in a passthrough entity (for example, a partnership or S corporation), and that entity is engaged in a trade or business, the determination of whether net gain described in paragraph (a) (1) (iii) of this section from such entity is attributable to—

(i) Property held in a trade or business described in § 1.1411-5 (a) (1) is made at the owner level; and

(ii) Property held in a trade or business described in § 1.1411-5 (a) (2) is made at the entity level.

(C) *Examples.*—The following examples illustrate the provisions of this paragraph (d) (4) (i). For purposes of these examples, assume the taxpayer is a United States citizen, uses a calendar taxable year, and Year 1 and all subsequent years are taxable years in which section 1411 is in effect:

Example 1. Gain from rental activity. A, an unmarried individual, rents a boat to B for $100,000 in Year 1. A's rental activity does not involve the conduct of a section 162 trade or business, and under section 469 (c) (2), A's rental activity is a passive activity. In Year 2, A sells the boat to B, and A realizes and recognizes taxable gain attributable to the disposition of the boat of $500,000. Because the exception provided in paragraph (d) (4) (i) (A) of this section requires a trade or business, this exception is inapplicable, and therefore, A's $500,000 gain will be taken into account under § 1.1411-4 (a) (1) (iii).

Example 2. Installment sale. (i) PRS, a partnership for Federal income tax purposes, operates an automobile dealership. B and C, unmarried individuals, each own a 40% interest in PRS and both materially participate in the activities of PRS for all relevant years. Therefore, with respect to B and C, PRS is not a trade or business described in section 1411 (c) (2) and § 1.1411-5. D owns the remaining 20% of PRS. Assume, for purposes of this example, that PRS is a passive activity with respect to D, and therefore is a trade or business described in section 1411 (c) (2) (A) and § 1.1411-5 (a) (1).

(ii) (A) In Year 0, a year preceding the effective date of section 1411, PRS relocates its dealership to a larger location. As a result of the relocation, PRS sells its old dealership facility to a real estate developer in exchange for $1,000,000 cash and a $4,500,000 promissory note, fully amortizing over the subsequent 15 years, and bearing adequate stated interest. PRS reports the sale transaction under section 453. PRS's adjusted tax basis in the old dealership facility is $1,075,000. Assume for purposes of this example that PRS has $300,000 of recapture income (within the meaning of section 453 (i)); the buyer is not related to PRS, B, C, or D; and the buyer is not assuming any liabilities of PRS in the transaction.

(B) For chapter 1 purposes, PRS has realized gain on the transaction of $4,425,000 ($5,500,000 less $1,075,000). Pursuant to section 453 (i), PRS will take into account $300,000 of the recapture income in Year 0, and the gain in excess of the recapture income ($4,125,000) will be taken into account under the installment method. For purposes of section 453, PRS's profit percentage is 75% ($4,125,000 gain divided by $5,500,000 gross selling price). In Year 0, PRS will take into account $750,000 of capital gain attributable to the $1,000,000 cash payment. In the subsequent 15 years, PRS will receive annual payments of $300,000 (plus interest). Each payment will result in PRS recognizing $225,000 of capital gain (75% of $300,000).

(iii) (A) In Year 1, PRS receives a payment of $300,000 plus the applicable amount of interest. For purposes of chapter 1, PRS recognizes $225,000 of capital gain. B and C's distributive share of the gain is $90,000 each and D's distributive share of the gain is $45,000.

(B) The old dealership facility constituted property held in PRS's trade or business. In the case of section 453 installment sales, section 453 governs the timing of the gain recognition, but does not alter the character of the gain. See § 1.1411-1 (a). The determination of whether the gain is attributable to the disposition of property used in a trade or business described in paragraph (d) (4) (i) of this section constitutes an element of the gain's character for Federal tax purposes. As a result, the applicability of paragraph (d) (4) (i) of this section is determined in Year 0 and applies to all gain received on the promissory note during the 15 year payment period. This result is consistent with the section 469 determination of the passive or nonpassive classification of the gain under § 1.469-2T (c) (2) (i) (A).

(C) In the case of D, PRS's trade or business is described in section 1411 (c) (2) (A) and § 1.1411-5 (a) (1). Therefore, the exclusion in paragraph (d) (4) (i) of this section does not apply, and D must include the $45,000 of gain in D's net investment income.

(D) In the case of B and C, PRS's trade or business is not described in section 1411 (c) (2) or § 1.1411-5. Therefore, B and C exclude the $90,000 gain from net investment income pursuant to paragraph (d) (4) (i) of this section.

(iv) In Year 2, C dies and C's 40% interest in PRS passes to Estate.

(v) (A) In Year 3, PRS receives a payment of $300,000 plus the applicable amount of interest. For purposes of chapter 1, PRS recognizes $225,000 of capital gain. B and Estate each have a distributive share of the gain equal to $90,000 and D's distributive share of the gain is $45,000.

(B) The calculation of net investment income for B and D in Year 3 is the same as in (iii) for Year 1.

(C) In the case of Estate, the distributive share of the $90,000 gain constitutes income in respect of a decedent (IRD) under section 691(a)(4) and subchapter K. See § 1.1411-1(a). Assume that Estate paid estate taxes of $5,000 that were attributable to the $90,000 of IRD. Pursuant to section 691(c)(4), the amount of gain taken into account in computing Estate's taxable income in Year 3 is $85,000 ($90,000 reduced by the $5,000 of allocable estate taxes). Pursuant to section 691(a)(3) and § 1.691(a)-3(a), the character of the gain to the Estate is the same character as the gain would have been if C had survived to receive it. Although the amount of taxable gain for chapter 1 has been reduced, the remaining $85,000 retains its character attributable to the disposition of property used in a trade or business described in paragraph (d)(4)(i) of this section. Therefore, Estate may exclude the $85,000 gain from net investment income pursuant to paragraph (d)(4)(i) of this section.

(ii) *Other gains and losses excluded from net investment income.*—Net gain, as determined under paragraph (d) of this section, does not include gains and losses excluded from net investment income by any other provision in §§ 1.1411-1 through 1.1411-10. For example, see § 1.1411-7 (certain gain or loss attributable to the disposition of certain interests in partnerships and S corporations) and § 1.1411-8(b)(4)(ii) (net unrealized appreciation attributable to employer securities realized on a disposition of those employer securities).

(iii) *Adjustment for capital loss carryforwards for previously excluded income.*—[Reserved]

* * *

(f) *Properly allocable deductions.*—(1) *General rule.*—(i) *In general.*—Unless provided elsewhere in §§ 1.1411-1 through 1.1411-10, only properly allocable deductions described in this paragraph (f) may be taken into account in determining net investment income.

(ii) *Limitations.*—Any deductions described in this paragraph (f) in excess of gross income and net gain described in section 1411(c)(1)(A) are not taken into account in determining net investment income in any other taxable year, except as allowed under chapter 1.

(2) *Properly allocable deductions described in section 62.*—(i) *Deductions allocable to gross income from rents and royalties.*—Deductions described in section 62(a)(4) allocable to rents and royalties described in paragraph (a)(1)(i) of this section are taken into account in determining net investment income.

(ii) *Deductions allocable to gross income from trades or businesses described in § 1.1411-5.*—Deductions described in section 62(a)(1) allocable to income from a trade or business described in § 1.1411-5 are taken into account in determining net investment income to the extent the deductions have not been taken into account in determining self-employment income within the meaning of § 1.1411-9.

(iii) *Penalty on early withdrawal of savings.*—Deductions described in section 62(a)(9) are taken into account in determining net investment income.

(iv) *Net operating loss.*—The total section 1411 NOL amount of a net operating loss deduction allowed under section 172 is allowed as a properly allocable deduction in determining net investment income for any taxable year. See paragraph (h) of this section for the calculation of the total section 1411 NOL amount of a net operating loss deduction.

(v) *Examples.*—The following examples illustrate the provisions of this paragraph (f)(2). For purposes of these examples, assume the taxpayer is a United States citizen, uses a calendar taxable year, and Year 1 and all subsequent years are taxable years in which section 1411 is in effect:

Example 1. (i) A, an individual, is a 40% shareholder in SCo, an S corporation. SCo is engaged in a trade or business described in section 1411(c)(2)(A). SCo is the only passive activity owned by A. In Year 1, SCo reported a loss of $11,000 to A which was comprised of gross operating income of $29,000 and operating deductions of $40,000. A's at risk amount at the beginning of Year 1 is $7,000. There were no other events that affected A's at risk amount in Year 1.

(ii) For purposes of calculating A's net investment income, A's $29,000 distributive share of SCo's gross operating income is income within the meaning of section 1411(c)(1)(A)(ii).

(iii) As a result of A's at risk limitation, for chapter 1 purposes, A may only deduct $7,000 of the operating deductions in excess of the gross operating income. The remaining $4,000 deductions are suspended because A's amount at risk at the end of Year 1 is zero.

(iv) For purposes of section 469, A has passive activity gross income of $29,000 and passive activity deductions of $36,000 ($40,000 of operating deductions allocable to A less $4,000 suspended under section 465). Because A has no other passive activity income from any other source, section 469 limits A's passive activity deductions to A's passive activity gross income. As a result, section 469 allows A to deduct $29,000 of SCo's operating deductions and suspends the remaining $7,000.

(v) For purposes of calculating A's net investment income, A has $29,000 of properly allocable deductions allowed by section 1411(c)(1)(B) and paragraph (f)(2)(ii) of this section.

Example 2. (i) Same facts as *Example 1.* In Year 2, SCo reported net income of $13,000 to A, which was comprised of gross operating income of $43,000 and operating deductions of $30,000. There were no other events that affected A's at risk amount in Year 2.

(ii) For purposes of calculating A's net investment income, A's $43,000 distributive share of gross operating income is income within the meaning of section 1411(c)(1)(A)(ii).

(iii) Pursuant to section 465(a)(2), A's deductions attributable to the gross income of SCo include the $30,000 deduction allocable to A in Year 2 plus the $4,000 loss that was suspended and carried over to Year 2 from Year 1 pursuant to section 465(a)(2). Under section 465(a)(2), the $4,000 of losses from Year 1 are treated as deductions from the activity in Year 2. As a result, A's net operating income from SCo in Year 2 is $9,000 ($43,000 -$30,000 -$4,000) in Year 2. A's amount at risk at the end of Year 2 is $9,000.

(iv) For purposes of section 469, A has passive activity gross income of $43,000. A's passive activity deductions attributable to SCo are the sum of the Year 2 operating deductions allocable to A from S ($30,000), deductions formerly suspended by section 465 ($4,000), and passive activity losses suspended by section 469 ($7,000). Therefore, in Year 2, A has passive activity deductions of $41,000. Because A's passive activity gross income exceeds A's passive activity deductions, section 469 does not limit any of the deductions in Year 2. At the end of Year 2, A has no suspended passive activity losses.

(v) Although A's distributive share of Year 2 deductions allocable to SCo's operating income was $30,000; the operative provisions of sections 465 and 469 do not change the character of the deductions when such amounts are suspended under either section. Furthermore, section 465(a)(2) and §§1.469-1(f)(4) and 1.469-2T(d)(1) treat amounts suspended from prior years as deductions in the current year. See §1.1411-1(a). Therefore, for purposes of calculating A's net investment income, A has $41,000 of properly allocable deductions allowed by section 1411(c)(1)(B) and paragraph (f)(2)(ii) of this section.

(3) *Properly allocable deductions described in section 63(d).*—In determining net investment income, the following itemized deductions are taken into account:

(i) *Investment interest expense.*—Investment interest (as defined in section 163(d)(3)) to the extent allowed under section 163(d)(1). Any investment interest not allowed under section 163(d)(1) is treated as investment interest paid or accrued by the taxpayer in the succeeding taxable year. The following example illustrates the provisions of this paragraph. For purposes of this example, assume that the taxpayer uses a calendar taxable year, and Year 1 and all subsequent years are taxable years in which section 1411 is in effect:

(A) In Year 1, A, an unmarried individual, pays interest of $4,000 on debt incurred to purchase stock. Under §1.163-8T, this interest is allocable to the stock and is investment interest within the meaning of section 163(d)(3). A has no investment income as defined by section 163(d)(4). A has $10,000 of income from a trade or business that is a passive activity (as defined in §1.1411-5(a)(1)) with respect to A. For income tax purposes, under section 163(d)(1), A may not deduct the $4,000 investment interest in Year 1 because A does not have any section 163(d)(4) net investment income. Under section 163(d)(2), the $4,000 investment interest is a carryforward of disallowed interest that is treated as investment interest paid by A in the succeeding taxable year. Similarly, for purposes of determining A's Year 1 net investment income, A may not deduct the $4,000 investment interest.

(B) In Year 2, A has $5,000 of section 163(d)(4) net investment income. For both income tax purposes and for determining section 1411 net investment income, A's $4,000 carryforward of interest expense disallowed in Year 1 may be deducted in Year 2.

(ii) *Investment expenses.*—Investment expenses (as defined in section 163(d)(4)(C)).

(iii) *Taxes described in section 164(a)(3).*—State, local, and foreign income, war profits, and excess profit taxes described in section 164(a)(3) that are allocable to net investment income pursuant to paragraph (g)(1) of this section. Except to the extent specifically expected from section 275(a)(4), foreign income, war profits, and excess profit taxes are not allowed as deductions under section 164(a)(3) in determining net investment income if the taxpayer claims the benefit of the foreign tax credit under section 901 with respect to the same taxable year. For rules applicable to refunds of taxes described in this paragraph, see paragraph (g)(2) of this section.

(iv) *Items described in section 72(b)(3).*—In the case of an amount allowed as a deduction to the annuitant for the annuitant's last taxable year under section 72(b)(3), such amount is allowed as a properly allocable deduction in the same taxable year if the income from the annuity (had the annuitant lived to receive such income) would have been included in net investment income under paragraph (a)(1)(i) of this section (and not excluded from net investment income by reason of § 1.1411-8).

(v) *Items described in section 691(c).*—Deductions for estate and generation-skipping taxes allowed by section 691(c) that are allocable to net investment income; provided, however, that any portion of the section 691(c) deduction described in section 691(c)(4) is taken into account instead in computing net gain under paragraph (d) and not under this paragraph (f)(3)(v).

(vi) *Items described in section 212(3).*—Amounts described in section 212(3) and § 1.212-1(l) to the extent they are allocable to net investment income pursuant to paragraph (g)(1) of this section.

(vii) *Amortizable bond premium.*—A deduction allowed under section 171(a)(1) for the amortizable bond premium on a taxable bond (for example, see § 1.171-2(a)(4)(i)(C) for the treatment of a bond premium carryforward as a deduction under section 171(a)(1)).

(viii) *Fiduciary expenses.*—In the case of an estate or trust, amounts described in § 1.212-1(i) to the extent they are allocable to net investment income pursuant to paragraph (g)(1) of this section.

(4) *Loss deductions.*—(i) *General rule.*—Losses described in section 165, whether described in section 62 or section 63(d), are allowed as properly allocable deductions to the extent such losses exceed the amount of gain described in section 61(a)(3) and are not taken into account in computing net gain by reason of paragraph (d) of this section.

(ii) *Examples.*—The following examples illustrate the provisions of this paragraph (f)(4). For purposes of these examples, assume the taxpayer is a United States citizen, uses a calendar taxable year, and Year 1 and all subsequent years are taxable years in which section 1411 is in effect:

Example 1. (i) A, an unmarried individual, owns an interest in PRS, a partnership for Federal income tax purposes. PRS is engaged in a trading business described in section 1411(c)(2)(B) and § 1.1411-5(a)(2) and has made a valid and timely election under section 475(f)(2). A's distributive share from PRS in Year 1 consists of $125,000 of interest and dividends and $60,000 of ordinary losses from the trading business. In addition to A's investment in PRS, A sold undeveloped land in Year 1 for a long-term capital gain of $50,000. A has no capital losses carried over from a preceding year.

(ii) For purposes of chapter 1, A includes the $125,000 of interest and dividends, $60,000 of ordinary loss, and $50,000 of long-term capital gain in the computation of A's adjusted gross income.

(iii) For purposes of calculating net investment income, A includes the $125,000 of interest and dividends. Pursuant to paragraph (d) of this section, A takes into account the $60,000 at ordinary loss from PRS and the $50,000 of long term capital gain in the computation of A's net gain. A's losses ($60,000) exceed A's gains ($50,000). Therefore, A's net gain under paragraph (d) of this section is zero. Additionally, A is allowed a deduction under paragraph (f)(4)(i) of this section for $10,000 (the amount of ordinary losses that were allowable under chapter 1 in excess of the amounts taken into account in computing net gain). A's net investment income in Year 1 is $115,000.

Example 2. (i) In Year 1, T, a nongrantor trust, incurs a capital loss of $5,000 on the sale of publicly traded stocks. In addition, T receives $17,000 of interest and dividend income. T has no capital losses carried over from a preceding year.

(ii) For purposes of chapter 1, T includes the $17,000 of interest and dividends and only $3,000 of the capital loss in the computation of adjusted gross income. The remaining $2,000 capital loss is carried over to Year 2.

(iii) For purposes of calculating net investment income, T includes the $17,000 of interest and dividends in net investment income. Pursuant to paragraph (d) of this section, T takes into account the $3,000 capital loss allowed by chapter 1. T's losses ($3,000) exceed T's gains ($0). Therefore, T's net gain under paragraph (d) of this section is zero. However, T is allowed a deduction under paragraph (f)(4)(i) of this section for $3,000 (the amount of losses that were allowable under chapter 1 in excess of the amounts taken into account in computing net gain). T's net investment income in Year 1 is $14,000.

Example 3. (i) In Year 1, B, an unmarried individual, incurs a short-term capital loss of $15,000 on the sale of publicly traded stocks. B also receives annuity income of $50,000. In addition, B disposes of property used in his sole proprietorship (which is not a trade or business described in section 1411(c)(2) or § 1.1411-5(a) for a gain of $21,000. Pursuant to section 1231, the gain of $21,000 is treated as a long-term capital gain for purposes of chapter 1. B has no capital losses carried over from a preceding year.

(ii) For purposes of chapter 1, B includes the $50,000 of annuity income in the computation of adjusted gross income. The $21,000 long-term capital gain is offset by the $15,000 short-term capital loss, so B includes $6,000 of net long-term capital gain in the computation of adjusted gross income.

(iii) For purposes of calculating net investment income, B includes the $50,000 of annuity income in net investment income. Pursuant to paragraph (d)(4)(i) of this section, B's net gain does not include the $21,000 long-term capital gain because it is attributable to property held in B's sole proprietorship (a nonpassive activity). Pursuant to paragraph (d) of this section, T takes into account the $15,000 capital loss allowed by chapter 1. B's losses ($15,000) exceed B's gains ($0). Therefore, A's net gain under paragraph (d) of this section is zero. However, B is allowed a deduction under paragraph (f)(4)(i) of this section for $15,000 (the amount of losses that were allowable under chapter 1 in excess of the amounts taken into account in computing net gain). B's net investment income in Year 1 is $35,000.

* * *

[Reg. § 1.1411-4.]

☐ [*T.D.* 9644, 11-26-2013 (*corrected* 3-31-2014).]

§ 1.1411-6. Income on investment of working capital subject to tax.—(a) *General rule.*—For purposes of section 1411, any item of gross income from the investment of working capital will be treated as not derived in the ordinary course of a trade or business, and any net gain that is attributable to the investment of working capital will be treated as not derived in the ordinary course of a trade or business. In determining whether any item is gross income from or net gain attributable to an investment of working capital, principles similar to those described in § 1.469-2T(c)(3)(ii) apply. See § 1.1411-4(f) for rules regarding properly allocable deductions with respect to an investment of working capital and § 1.1411-7 for rules relating to the adjustment to net gain on the disposition of interests in a partnership or S corporation.

(b) *Example.*—The following example illustrates the principles of this section. Assume for purposes of the example that the taxpayer uses a calendar taxable year, the taxpayer is a United States citizen, and Year 1 and all subsequent years are taxable years in which section 1411 is in effect:

Example. (i) A, an unmarried individual, operates a restaurant, which is a section 162 trade or business but is not a trade or business described in § 1.1411-5(a)(1) with respect to A. A owns and conducts the restaurant business through S, an S corporation wholly-owned by A. S is able to pay all of the restaurant's current obligations with cash flow generated by the restaurant. S utilizes an interest-bearing checking account at a local bank to make daily deposits of cash receipts generated by the restaurant, and also to pay the recurring ordinary and necessary business expenses of the restaurant. The average daily balance of the checking account is approximately $2,500, but at any given time the balance may be significantly more or less than this amount depending on the short-term cash flow needs of the business. In addition, S has set aside $20,000 for the potential future needs of the business in case the daily cash flow into and from the checking account becomes insufficient to pay the restaurant's recurring business expenses. S does not currently need to spend or use the $20,000 capital to conduct the restaurant business, and S deposits and maintains the $20,000 in an interest-bearing savings account at a local bank.

(ii) Both the $2,500 average daily balance of the checking account and the $20,000 savings account balance constitute working capital under § 1.469-2T(c)(3)(ii) and, pursuant to paragraph (a) of this section, the interest generated by this working capital will not be treated as derived in the ordinary course of S's restaurant business. Accordingly, the interest income derived by S from its checking and savings accounts and allocated to A under section 1366 constitutes gross income from interest under § 1.1411-4(a)(1)(i).

* * *

[Reg. § 1.1411-6.]

☐ [*T.D.* 9644, 11-26-2013.]

§ 1.1411-8. Exception for distributions from qualified plans.—(a) *General rule.*—Net investment income does not include any distribution from a qualified plan or arrangement. For this purpose, the term qualified plan or arrangement means any plan or arrangement described in section 401(a), 403(a), 403(b), 408, 408A, or 457(b).

(b) *Rules relating to distributions.*—This paragraph (b) provides rules for purposes of paragraph (a) of this section. For purposes of section 1411(c)(5) and this section, a distribution means the following:

(1) *Actual distributions.*—Any amount actually distributed from a qualified plan or arrangement, as defined in paragraph (a) of this section, is a distribution within the meaning of section 1411(c)(5), and thus is not included in net investment income. Examples include a rollover to an eligible retirement plan within the meaning of section 402(c)(8)(B), a distribution of a plan loan offset amount within the meaning of Q&A-13(b) of § 1.72(p)-1, and certain corrective distributions under the Internal Revenue Code (Code).

(2) *Amounts treated as distributed.*—Any amount that is treated as distributed from a qualified plan or arrangement under the Code for purposes of income tax is a distribution within the meaning of section 1411(c)(5), and thus is not included in net investment income. Examples include a conversion to a Roth IRA described in section 408A and a deemed distribution under section 72(p).

(3) *Amounts includible in gross income.*—Any amount that is not treated as a distribution but is otherwise includible in gross income pursuant to a rule relating to amounts held in a qualified plan or arrangement described in paragraph (a) of this section is a distribution within the meaning of section 1411(c)(5), and thus is not included in net investment income. For example, any income of the trust of a qualified plan or arrangement that is applied to purchase a participant's life insurance coverage (the P.S. 58 costs) is a distribution within the meaning of section 1411(c)(5), and thus is not included in net investment income.

(4) *Amounts related to employer securities.*—(i) *Dividends related to employer securities.*—Any dividend that is deductible under section 404(k) and is paid in cash directly to plan participants or beneficiaries is a distribution within the meaning of section 1411(c)(5), and thus is not included in net investment income. However, any amount paid as a dividend after the employer securities have been distributed from a qualified plan is not a distribution within the meaning of section 1411(c)(5), and thus is included in net investment income.

(ii) *Amounts related to the net unrealized appreciation in employer securities.*—The amount of any net unrealized appreciation attributable to employer securities (within the meaning of section 402(e)(4)) realized on a disposition of those employer securities is a distribution within the meaning of section 1411(c)(5), and thus is not included in net investment income. However, any appreciation in value of the employer securities after the distribution from the qualified plan is not a distribution within the meaning of section 1411(c)(5), and is included in net investment income.

* * *

[Reg. § 1.1411-8.]

□ [*T.D.* 9644, 11-26-2013.]

Consolidated Returns

§ 1.1502-34. Special aggregate stock ownership rules.—For purposes of §§ 1.1502-1 through 1.1502-80, in determining the stock ownership of a member of the group in another corporation (the "issuing corporation") for purposes of determining the application of section 165(g)(3)(A), 332(b)(1), 333(b), 351(a), 732(f), or 904(f), in a consolidated return year, there shall be included stock owned by all other members of the group in the issuing corporation. Thus, assume that members A, B, and C each own 33⅓ percent of the stock issued by D. In such case, A, B, and C shall each be treated as meeting the 80-percent stock ownership requirement for purposes of section 332, and no member can elect to have section 333 apply. Furthermore, the special rule for minority shareholders in section 337(d) cannot apply with respect to amounts received by A, B, or C in liquidation of D. [Reg. § 1.1502-34.]

□ [*T.D.* 6894, 9-7-66. *Amended by T.D.* 8949, 6-18-2001.]

Certain Controlled Corporations

§ 1.1563-1. Definition of controlled group of corporations and component members and related concepts.—(a) *Controlled group of corporations.*—(1) *In general.*—(i) *Types of controlled groups.*—For purposes of sections 1561 through 1563, the term *controlled group of corporations* means any group of corporations which is—

(A) A *parent-subsidiary controlled group* (as defined in paragraph (a)(2) of this section);

(B) A *brother-sister controlled group* (as defined in paragraph (a)(3)(i) of this section);

(C) A *combined group* (as defined in paragraph (a)(4) of this section); or

(D) A *life insurance controlled group* (as defined in paragraph (a)(5) of this section).

(ii) *Special rules.*—In determining whether a corporation is included in a controlled group of corporations, section 1563(b) and paragraph (b) of this section shall not be taken into account. For rules defining a component member of a controlled group of corporations, including rules defining an excluded member and an additional member, see section 1563(b) and paragraph (b) of this section.

(iii) *Cross reference.*—For the exclusion of certain stock for purposes of applying the definitions contained in this paragraph, see section 1563(c) and § 1.1563-2.

(2) *Parent-subsidiary controlled group.*—(i) *Definition.*—The term *parent-subsidiary controlled group* means one or more chains of corporations connected through stock ownership with a common parent corporation if—

(A) Stock possessing at least 80 percent of the total combined voting power of all classes of stock entitled to vote or at least 80 percent of the total value of shares of all classes of stock of each of the corporations, except the common parent corporation, is owned (directly and with the application of § 1.1563-3(b)(1), relating to options) by one or more of the other corporations; and

(B) The common parent corporation owns (directly and with the application of § 1.1563-3(b)(1), relating to options) stock possessing at least 80 percent of the total combined voting power of all classes of stock entitled to vote or at least 80 percent of the total value of shares of all classes of stock of at least one of the other corporations, excluding, in computing such voting power or value, stock owned directly by such other corporations.

(ii) *Examples.*—The definition of a parent-subsidiary controlled group of corporations may be illustrated by the following examples:

Example 1. P Corporation owns stock possessing 80 percent of the total combined voting power of all classes of stock entitled to vote of S Corporation. P is the common parent of a parent-subsidiary controlled group consisting of member corporations P and S.

Example 2. Assume the same facts as in *Example 1.* Assume further that S owns stock possessing 80 percent of the total value of shares of all classes of stock of X Corporation. P is the common parent of a parent-subsidiary controlled group consisting of member corporations P, S, and X. The result would be the same if P, rather than S, owned the X stock.

Example 3. P Corporation owns 80 percent of the only class of stock of S Corporation and S, in turn, owns 40 percent of the only class of stock of X Corporation. P also owns 80 percent of the only class of stock of Y Corporation and Y, in turn, owns 40 percent of the only class of stock of X. P is the common parent of a parent-subsidiary controlled group consisting of member corporations P, S, X, and Y.

Example 4. P Corporation owns 75 percent of the only class of stock of Y and Z Corporations; Y owns all the remaining stock of Z; and Z owns all the remaining stock of Y. Since intercompany stockholdings are excluded (that is, are not treated as outstanding) for purposes of determining whether P owns stock possessing at least 80 percent of the voting power or value of at least one of the other corporations, P is treated as the owner of stock possessing 100 percent of the voting power and value of Y and of Z for purposes of paragraph (a)(2)(i)(B) of this section. Also, stock possessing 100 percent of the voting power and value of Y and Z is owned by the other corporations in the group within the meaning of paragraph (a)(2)(i)(A) of this section. (P and Y together own stock possessing 100 percent of the voting power and value of Z, and P and Z together own stock possessing 100 percent of the voting power and value of Y.) Therefore, P is the common parent of a parent-subsidiary controlled group of corporations consisting of member corporations P, Y, and Z.

(3) *Brother-sister controlled group.*—(i) *Definition.*—The term *brother-sister controlled group* means two or more corporations if the same five or fewer persons who are individuals, estates, or trusts own (directly and with the application of the rules contained in § 1.1563-3(b)) stock possessing more than 50 percent of the total combined voting power of all classes of stock entitled to vote or more than 50 percent of the total value of shares of all classes of stock of each corporation, taking into account the stock ownership of each such person only to the extent such stock ownership is identical with respect to each such corporation.

(ii) *Additional stock ownership requirement for purposes of certain other provisions of law.*—For purposes of any provision of law (other than sections 1561 through 1563) that incorporates the section 1563(a) definition of a controlled group, the term *brother-sister controlled group* means two or more corporations if the same five or fewer persons who are individuals, estates, or trusts own (directly and with the application of the rules contained in § 1.1563-3(b)) stock possessing—

(A) At least 80 percent of the total combined voting power of all classes of stock entitled to vote or at least 80 percent of the total value of shares of all classes of stock of each corporation (the 80 percent requirement);

(B) More than 50 percent of the total combined voting power of all classes of stock entitled to vote or more than 50 percent of the total value of shares of all classes of stock of each corporation, taking into account the stock ownership of each such person only to the extent such stock ownership is identical with respect to each such corporation (the more-than-50 percent identical ownership requirement); and

(C) The five or fewer persons whose stock ownership is considered for purposes of the 80 percent requirement must be the same persons whose stock ownership is considered for purposes of the more-than-50 percent identical ownership requirement.

(iii) *Examples.*—The principles of paragraph (a)(3)(ii) of this section may be illustrated by the following examples:

Example 1. (i) The outstanding stock of corporations P, W, X, Y, and Z, which have only one class of stock outstanding, is owned by the following unrelated individuals:

Individuals	P (%)	W (%)	X (%)	Y (%)	Z (%)	Identical Ownership
A	55	51	55	55	55	51
B	45	49				(45% in P and W)
C			45			
D				45		
E					45	
Total	100	100	100	100	100	

(ii) Corporations P and W are members of a brother-sister controlled group of corporations. Although the more-than-50 percent identical ownership requirement is met for all 5 corporations, corporations X, Y, and Z are not members because at least 80 percent of the stock of each of those corporations is not owned by the same 5 or fewer persons whose stock ownership is considered for purposes of the more-than-50 percent identical ownership requirement.

Example 2. (i) The outstanding stock of corporations X and Y, which have only one class of stock outstanding, is owned by the following unrelated individuals:

Individuals	Corporations	
	X (%)	Y (%)
A	12	12
B	12	12
C	12	12
D	12	12
E	13	13
F	13	13
G	13	13
H	13	13
Total	100	100

(ii) Any group of five of the shareholders will own more than 50 percent of the stock in each corporation, in identical holdings. However, X and Y are not members of a brother-sister controlled group because at least 80 percent of the stock of each corporation is not owned by the same five or fewer persons.

Example 3. (i) Corporation X and Y each have two classes of stock outstanding, voting common and non-voting common. (None of this stock is excluded from the definition of stock under section 1563(c).) Unrelated individuals A and B own the following percentages of the class of stock entitled to vote (voting) and of the total value of shares of all classes of stock (value) in each of corporations X and Y:

Individuals	Corporations	
	X	Y
A	100% voting; 60% value	75% voting; 60% value
B	0% voting; 10% value	25% voting; 10% value

(ii) No other shareholder of X owns (or is considered to own) any stock in Y. X and Y are a brother-sister controlled group of corporations. The group meets the more-than-50 percent identical ownership requirement because A and B own more than 50 percent of the total value of shares of all classes of stock of X and Y in identical holdings. (The group also meets the more-than-50 percent identical ownership requirement because of A's voting stock ownership.) The group meets the 80 percent requirement because A and B own at least 80 percent of the total combined voting power of all classes of stock entitled to vote.

Example 4. Assume the same facts as in *Example 3* except that the value of the stock owned by A and B is not more than 50 percent of the total value of shares of all classes of stock of each corporation in identical holdings. X and Y are not a brother-sister controlled group of corporations. The group meets the more-than-50 percent identical ownership requirement because A owns more than 50 percent of the total combined voting power of the voting stock of each corporation. For purposes of the 80 percent requirement, B's voting stock in Y cannot be combined with A's voting stock in Y since B, who does not own any voting stock in X, is not a person whose ownership is considered for purposes of the more-than-50 percent identical ownership requirement. Because no other shareholder owns stock in both X and Y, these other shareholders' stock ownership is not counted towards meeting either the more-than-50 percent identical ownership requirement or the 80 percent ownership requirement.

(iv) *Special rule if prior law applies.*—Paragraph (a)(3)(ii) of this section, as amended by TD 8179, applies to taxable years ending on or after December 31, 1970. See, however, the transitional rule in paragraph (d) of this section.

(4) *Combined group.*—(i) *Definition.*—The term *combined group* means any group of three or more corporations if—

(A) Each such corporation is a member of either a parent-subsidiary controlled group of corporations or a brother-sister controlled group of corporations; and

(B) At least one of such corporations is the common parent of a parent-subsidiary controlled group and also is a member of a brother-sister controlled group.

(ii) *Examples.*—The definition of a combined group of corporations may be illustrated by the following examples:

Example 1. A, an individual, owns stock possessing 80 percent of the total combined voting power of all classes of the stock of corporations X and Y. Y, in turn, owns stock possessing 80 percent of the total combined voting power of all classes of the stock of corporation Z. X, Y, and Z are members of the same combined group since—

(i) X, Y, and Z are each members of either a parent-subsidiary or brother-sister controlled group of corporations; and

(ii) Y is the common parent of a parent-subsidiary controlled group of corporations consisting of Y and Z, and also is a member of a brother-sister controlled group of corporations consisting of X and Y.

Example 2. Assume the same facts as in *Example 1*, and further assume that corporation X owns 80 percent of the total value of shares of all classes of stock of corporation S. X, Y, Z, and S are members of the same combined group.

* * *

(6) *Voting power of stock.*—For purposes of this section, and § § 1.1563-2 and 1.1563-3, in determining whether the stock owned by a person (or persons) possesses a certain percentage of the total combined voting power of all classes of stock entitled to vote of a corporation, consideration will be given to all the facts and circumstances of each case. A share of stock will generally be considered as possessing the voting power accorded to such share by the corporate charter, by-laws, or share certificate. On the other hand, if there is any agreement, whether express or implied, that a shareholder will not vote his stock in a corporation, the formal voting rights possessed by his stock may be disregarded in determining the percentage of the total combined voting power possessed by the stock owned by other shareholders in the corporation, if the result is that the corporation becomes a component member of a controlled group of corporations. Moreover, if a shareholder agrees to vote his stock in a corporation in the manner specified by another shareholder in the corporation, the voting rights possessed by the stock owned by the first shareholder may be considered to be possessed by the stock owned by such other shareholder if the result is that the corporation becomes a component member of a controlled group of corporations.

(b) *Component members.*—(1) *In general.*—(i) *Definition.*—For purposes of sections 1561 through 1563, a corporation is with respect to its taxable year a component member of a controlled group of corporations for the group's testing date if such corporation—

(A) Is a member of such controlled group on such testing date and is not treated as an excluded member under paragraph (b)(2) of this section; or

(B) Is not a member of such controlled group on such testing date but is treated as an additional member under paragraph (b)(3) of this section.

(ii) *Member of a controlled group of corporations.*—For purposes of sections 1561 through 1563, a member of a controlled group is a corporation connected with other member(s) of a controlled group under the stock ownership rules and the stock qualification rules set forth in section 1563. Under these rules, for a corporation to qualify as a component member of the group with respect to a group's December 31st testing date (or the short-year testing date for a short-year member), that corporation does not have to be a member of that group on that group's testing date. In addition, a corporation that is a member of a controlled group on the group's testing date does not necessarily qualify as a component member of that group with respect to that testing date.

(iii) *Additional concepts used in applying the controlled group rules.*

(A) The term *testing date* means the date used for determining the status of controlled group members as either component members or excluded members. That testing date is then also used to determine which taxable years of those component members are to be subjected to the controlled group rules. Generally, a member's testing date is the December 31st date included within that member's taxable year, whether such member is on a calendar or fiscal taxable year. However, if a component member of a controlled group has a short taxable year that does not include a December 31st date, then the last day of that short taxable year becomes that member's testing date.

(B) The term *testing period* means the time period used for determining the status of controlled group members as either component members or excluded members. The testing period begins on the first day of a member's taxable year and ends on the day before its testing date. (Generally, the testing date is December 31st, but for a component member having a short taxable year not ending on December 31st, the testing date for the short taxable year of that member (and only that member) becomes the last day of that member's short taxable year.) Thus, for a member on a fiscal taxable year, the portion of its taxable year beginning on December 31st and ending on the last day of its taxable year is not taken into account for determining its status as a component member or an excluded member.

(2) *Excluded members.*—(i) *Temporal test.*—A corporation, which is a member of a controlled group of corporations on the group's testing date, a date included within that member's taxable year, but who was a member of such group for less than one-half of the number of days of its testing period, shall be treated as an excluded member of such group for that group's testing date.

(ii) *Qualification test.*—A corporation which is a member of a controlled group of corporations on a testing date shall be treated as an excluded member of such group on such date if, for its taxable year including such date, such corporation is—

(A) Exempt from taxation under section 501(a) (except a corporation which is subject to tax on its unrelated business taxable income under section 511) or 521 for such taxable year;

(B) A foreign corporation not subject to taxation under section 882(a) for the taxable year;

(C) An S corporation (as defined in section 1361) for purposes of any tax benefit item described in section 1561(a) to which it is not subject;

(D) A franchised corporation (as defined in section 1563(f)(4) and § 1.1563-4); or

(E) An insurance company subject to taxation under section 801, unless such insurance company (without regard to this paragraph (b)(2)(ii)(E)) is a component member of a life insurance controlled group described in paragraph (a)(5)(i) of this section or unless § 1.1502-47(f)(6) applies (which treats a life insurance company, for which a section 1504(c)(2) election is effective, as a member (whether eligible or ineligible) of a life-nonlife affiliated group).

(3) *Additional members.*—A corporation shall be treated as an additional member of a controlled group of corporations, that is, an additional component member, on the group's testing date if it—

(i) Is not a member of such group on such date;

(ii) Is not described, with respect to such taxable year, in paragraph (b)(2)(ii)(A), (b)(2)(ii)(B), (b)(2)(ii)(C), (b)(2)(ii)(D), or (b)(2)(ii)(E) of this section; and

(iii) Was a member of such group for one-half (or more) of the number of days in its testing period.

(4) *Examples.*—The provisions of this paragraph (b) may be illustrated by the following examples:

Example 1. B, an individual, owns all of the stock of corporations W and X on each day of 1964. W and X each use the calendar year as their taxable year. On January 1, 1964, B also owns all the stock of corporation Y (a fiscal year corporation with a taxable year beginning on July 1, 1964, and ending on June 30, 1965), which stock he sells on October 15, 1964. On December 1, 1964, B purchases all the stock of corporation Z (a fiscal year corporation with a taxable year beginning on September 1, 1964, and ending on August 31, 1965). On December 31, 1964, W, X, and Z are members of the same controlled group. However, the component members of the group on such December 31st are W, X, and Y. Under paragraph (b) (2) (i) of this section, Z is treated as an excluded member of the group on December 31, 1964, since Z was a member of the group for less than one-half of the number of days (29 out of 121 days) during the period beginning on September 1, 1964 (the first day of its taxable year) and ending on December 30, 1964. Under paragraph (b) (3) of this section, Y is treated as an additional member of the group on December 31, 1964, since Y was a member of the group for at least one-half of the number of days (107 out of 183 days) during the period beginning on July 1, 1964 (the first day of its taxable year) and ending on December 30, 1964.

Example 2. On January 1, 1964, corporation P owns all the stock of corporation S, which in turn owns all the stock of corporation S-1. On November 1, 1964, P purchases all of the stock of corporation X from the public and sells all of the stock of S to the public. Corporation X owns all the stock of corporation Y during 1964. P, S, S-1, X, and Y file their returns on the basis of the calendar year. On December 31, 1964, P, X, and Y are members of a parent-subsidiary controlled group of corporations; also, corporations S and S-1 are members of a different parent-subsidiary controlled group on such date. However, since X and Y have been members of the parent-subsidiary controlled group of which P is the common parent for less than one-half the number of days during the period January 1 through December 30, 1964, they are not component members of such group on such date. On the other hand, X and Y have been members of a parent-subsidiary controlled group of which X is the common parent for at least one-half the number of days during the period January 1 through December 30, 1964, and therefore they are component members of such group on December 31, 1964. Also since S and S-1 were members of the parent-subsidiary controlled group of which P is the common parent for at least one-half the number of days in the taxable years of each such corporation during the period January 1 through December 30, 1964, P, S, and S-1 are component members of such group on December 31, 1964.

* * *

Example 4. Individual A owns all of the stock of corporations X, Y and Z. Each of these corporations is an S corporation. X, Y, and Z are each members of a brother-sister controlled group, even though each such corporation is treated as an excluded member of such group. See § 1.1563-1 (b) (2) (ii) (C).

(5) *Application of constructive ownership rules.*—For purposes of paragraphs (b) (2) (i) and (b) (3) (iii) of this section, it is necessary to determine whether a corporation was a member of a controlled group of corporations for one-half (or more) of the number of days in its taxable year which precede the December 31st falling within such taxable year. Therefore, the constructive ownership rules contained in § 1.1563-3 (b) (to the extent applicable in making such determination) must be applied on a day-by-day basis. For example, if P Corporation owns all the stock of X Corporation on each day of 1964, and on December 30, 1964, acquires an option to purchase all the stock of Y Corporation (a calendar-year taxpayer which has been in existence on each day of 1964), the application of § 1.1563-3 (b) (1) on a day-by-day basis results in Y being a member of the brother-sister controlled group on only one day of Y's 1964 year which precedes December 31, 1964. Accordingly, since Y is not a member of such group for one-half or more of the number of days in its 1964 year preceding December 31, 1964, Y is treated as an excluded member of such group on December 31, 1964.

* * *

[Reg. § 1.1563-1.]

☐ [*T.D.* 9451, 5-26-2009. *Amended by T.D.* 9522, 4-8-2011.]

§ 1.1563-3. Rules for determining stock ownership.—(a) *In general.*—In determining stock ownership for purposes of §§ 1.1562-5, 1.1563-1, 1.1563-2, and this section, the constructive ownership rules of paragraph (b) of this section apply to the extent such rules are referred to in such sections. The application of such rules shall be subject to the operating rules and special rules contained in paragraphs (c) and (d) of this section.

(b) *Constructive ownership.*—(1) *Options.*—If a person has an option to acquire any outstanding stock of a corporation, such stock shall be considered as owned by such person. For purposes of this subparagraph, an option to acquire such an option, and each one of a series of such options, shall be considered as an option to acquire such stock. For example, assume Smith owns an option to purchase 100 shares of the outstanding stock of M Corporation. Under this subparagraph, Smith is considered to own such 100 shares. The result would be the same if Smith owned an option to acquire the option (or one of a series of options) to purchase 100 shares of M stock.

(2) *Attribution from partnerships.*—(i) Stock owned, directly or indirectly, by or for a partnership shall be considered as owned by any partner having an interest of 5 percent or more in either the capital or profits of the partnership in proportion to his interest in capital or profits, whichever such proportion is the greater.

(ii) The provisions of this subparagraph may be illustrated by the following example:

Example. Green, Jones, and White, unrelated individuals, are partners in the GJW partnership. The partners' interests in the capital and profits of the partnership are as follows:

Partner	*Capital*	*Profits*
Green	36 %	25 %
Jones	60	71
White	4	4

The GJW partnership owns the entire outstanding stock (100 shares) of X Corporation. Under this subparagraph, Green is considered to own the X stock owned by the partnership in proportion to his interest in capital (36 percent) or profits (25 percent), whichever such proportion is the greater. Therefore, Green is considered to own 36 shares of the X stock. However, since Jones has a greater interest in the profits of the partnership, he is considered to own the X stock in proportion to his interest in such profits. Therefore, Jones is considered to own 71 shares of the X stock. Since White does not have an interest of 5 percent or more in either the capital or profits of the partnership, he is not considered to own any shares of the X stock.

(3) *Attribution from estates or trusts.*—(i) Stock owned, directly or indirectly, by or for an estate or trust shall be considered as owned by any beneficiary who has an actuarial interest of 5 percent or more in such stock, to the extent of such actuarial interest. For purposes of this subparagraph, the actuarial interest of each beneficiary shall be determined by assuming the maximum exercise of discretion by the fiduciary in favor of such beneficiary and the maximum use of such stock to satisfy his rights as a beneficiary. A beneficiary of an estate or trust who cannot under any circumstances receive any interest in stock held by the estate or trust, including the proceeds from the disposition thereof, or the income therefrom, does not have an actuarial interest in such stock. Thus, where stock owned by a decedent's estate has been specifically bequeathed to certain beneficiaries and the remainder of the estate is bequeathed to other beneficiaries, the stock is attributable only to the beneficiaries to whom it is specifically bequeathed. Similarly, a remainderman of a trust who cannot under any circumstances receive any interest in the stock of a corporation which is a part of the corpus of the trust (including any accumulated income therefrom or the proceeds from a disposition thereof) does not have an actuarial interest in such stock. However, an income beneficiary of a trust does have an actuarial interest in stock if he has any right to the income from such stock even though under the terms of the trust instrument such stock can never be distributed to him. The factors and methods prescribed in § 20.2031-7 of this chapter (Estate Tax Regulations) [Reg. § 20.2031-7 of this chapter is reproduced at ¶ 2391.05.—CCH.] for use in ascertaining the value of an interest in property for estate tax purposes shall be used for purposes of this subdivision in determining a beneficiary's actuarial interest in stock owned directly or indirectly by or for a trust.

(ii) For the purposes of this subparagraph, property of a decedent shall be considered as owned by his estate if such property is subject to administration by the executor or administrator for the purposes of paying claims against the estate and expenses of administration notwithstanding that, under local law, legal title to such property vests in the decedent's heirs, legatees or devisees immediately upon death. With respect to an estate, the term "beneficiary" includes any person entitled to receive property of the decedent pursuant to a will or pursuant to laws of descent and distribution. A person shall no longer be considered a beneficiary of an estate when all the property to which he is entitled has been received by him, when he no longer has a claim against the estate arising out of having been a beneficiary, and when there is only a remote possibility that it will be necessary for the estate to seek the return of property or to seek payment from him by contribution or otherwise to satisfy claims against the estate or expenses of administration. When pursuant to the preceding sentence, a person ceases to be a beneficiary, stock owned by the estate shall not thereafter be considered owned by him.

(iii) Stock owned, directly or indirectly, by or for any portion of a trust of which a person is considered the owner under subpart E, part I, subchapter J of the Code (relating to grantors and others treated as substantial owners) is considered as owned by such person.

(iv) This subparagraph does not apply to stock owned by any employees' trust described in section 401(a) which is exempt from tax under section 501(a).

(4) *Attribution from corporations.*—(i) Stock owned, directly or indirectly, by or for a corporation shall be considered as owned

by any person who owns (within the meaning of section 1563(d)) 5 percent or more in value of its stock in that proportion which the value of the stock which such person so owns bears to the value of all the stock in such corporation.

(ii) The provisions of this subparagraph may be illustrated by the following example:

Example. Brown, an individual, owns 60 shares of the 100 shares of the only class of outstanding stock of corporation P. Smith, an individual, owns 4 shares of the P stock, and corporation X owns 36 shares of the P stock. Corporation P owns, directly and indirectly, 50 shares of the stock of corporation S. Under this subparagraph, Brown is considered to own 30 shares of the S stock (60/100 × 50), and X is considered to own 18 shares of the S stock (36/100 × 50). Since Smith does not own 5 percent or more in value of the P stock, he is not considered as owning any of the S stock owned by P. If, in this example, Smith's wife had owned directly 1 share of the P stock, Smith (and his wife) would each own 5 shares of the P stock, and therefore Smith (and his wife) would be considered as owning 2.5 shares of the S stock (5/100 × 50).

(5) *Spouse.*—(i) Except as provided in subdivision (ii) of this subparagraph, an individual shall be considered to own the stock owned, directly or indirectly, by or for his spouse, other than a spouse who is legally separated from the individual under a decree of divorce, whether interlocutory or final, or a decree of separate maintenance.

(ii) An individual shall not be considered to own stock in a corporation owned, directly or indirectly, by or for his spouse on any day of a taxable year of such corporation, provided that each of the following conditions are satisfied with respect to such taxable year:

(a) Such individual does not, at any time during such taxable year, own directly any stock in such corporation.

(b) Such individual is not a member of the board of directors or an employee of such corporation and does not participate in the management of such corporation at any time during such taxable year.

(c) Not more than 50 percent of such corporation's gross income for such taxable year was derived from royalties, rents, dividends, interest, and annuities.

(d) Such stock in such corporation is not, at any time during such taxable year, subject to conditions which substantially restrict or limit the spouse's right to dispose of such stock and which run in favor of the individual or his children who have not attained the age of 21 years. The principles of paragraph (b)(2)(iii) of § 1.1563-2 shall apply in determining whether a condition is a condition described in the preceding sentence.

(iii) For purposes of subdivision (ii)*(c)* of this subparagraph, the gross income of a corporation for a taxable year shall be determined under section 61 and the regulations thereunder. The terms "royalties", "rents", "dividends", "interest", and "annuities" shall have the same meanings such terms are given for purposes of section 1244(c). See paragraph (e)(1)(ii), (iii), (iv), (v), and (vi) of § 1.1244(c)-1.

(6) *Children, grandchildren, parents, and grandparents.*—(i) An individual shall be considered to own the stock owned, directly or indirectly, by or for his children who have not attained the age of 21 years, and, if the individual has not attained the age of 21 years, the stock owned, directly or indirectly, by or for his parents.

(ii) If an individual owns (directly, and with the application of the rules of this paragraph but without regard to this subdivision) stock possessing more than 50 percent of the total combined voting power of all classes of stock entitled to vote or more than 50 percent of the total value of shares of all classes of stock in a corporation, then such individual shall be considered to own the stock in such corporation owned, directly or indirectly, by or for his parents, grandparents, grandchildren, and children who have attained the age of 21 years. In determining whether the stock owned by an individual possesses the requisite percentage of the total combined voting power of all classes of stock entitled to vote of a corporation, see paragraph (a)(6) of § 1.1563-1.

(iii) For purposes of section 1563, and §§ 1.1563-1 through 1.1563-4, a legally adopted child of an individual shall be treated as a child of such individual by blood.

(iv) The provisions of this subparagraph may be illustrated by the following example:

Example—*(a) Facts.* Individual F owns directly 40 shares of the 100 shares of the only class of stock of Z Corporation. His son, M (20 years of age), owns directly 30 shares of such stock, and his son, A (30 years of age), owns directly 20 shares of such stock. The remaining 10 shares of the Z stock are owned by an unrelated person.

(b) F's ownership. Individual F owns 40 shares of the Z stock directly and is considered to own the 30 shares of Z stock owned directly by M. Since, for purposes of the more-than-50-percent stock ownership test contained in subdivision (ii) of this subparagraph, F is treated as owning 70 shares or 70 percent of the total voting power and value of the Z stock, he is also considered as owning the 20 shares

owned by his adult son, A. Accordingly, F is considered as owning a total of 90 shares of the Z stock.

(*c*) *M's ownership.* Minor son, M, owns 30 shares of the Z stock directly, and is considered to own the 40 shares of Z stock owned directly by his father, F. However, M is not considered to own the 20 shares of Z stock owned directly by his brother, A, and constructively by F, because stock constructively owned by F by reason of family attribution is not considered as owned by him for purposes of making another member of his family the constructive owner of such stock. See paragraph (c)(2) of this section. Accordingly, M owns and is considered as owning a total of 70 shares of the Z stock.

(*d*) *A's ownership.* Adult son, A, owns 20 shares of the Z stock directly. Since, for purposes of the more-than-50-percent stock ownership test contained in subdivision (ii) of this subparagraph, A is treated as owning only the Z stock which he owns directly, he does not satisfy the condition precedent for the attribution of Z stock from his father. Accordingly, A is treated as owning only the 20 shares of Z stock which he owns directly.

(c) *Operating rules and special rules.*—(1) *In general.*—Except as provided in subparagraph (2) of this paragraph, stock constructively owned by a person by reason of the application of subparagraph (1), (2), (3), (4), (5), or (6) of paragraph (b) of this section shall, for purposes of applying such subparagraphs, be treated as actually owned by such person.

(2) *Members of family.*—Stock constructively owned by an individual by reason of the application of subparagraph (5) or (6) of paragraph (b) of this section shall not be treated as owned by him for purposes of again applying such subparagraphs in order to make another the constructive owner of such stock.

(3) *Precedence of option attribution.*—For purposes of this section, if stock may be considered as owned by a person under subparagraph (1) of paragraph (b) of this section (relating to option attribution) and under any other subparagraph of such paragraph, such stock shall be considered as owned by such person under subparagraph (1) of such paragraph.

(4) *Examples.*—The provisions of this paragraph may be illustrated by the following examples:

Example (1). A, 30 years of age, has a 90 percent interest in the capital and profits of a partnership. The partnership owns all the outstanding stock of corporation X and X owns 60 shares of the 100 outstanding shares of corporation Y. Under subparagraph (1) of this paragraph, the 60 shares of Y constructively owned by the partnership by reason of subparagraph (4) of paragraph (b) of this section is treated as actually owned by the partnership for purposes of applying subparagraph (2) of paragraph (b) of this section. Therefore, A is considered as owning 54 shares of the Y stock (90 percent of 60 shares).

Example (2). Assume the same facts as in example (1). Assume further that B, who is 20 years of age and the brother of A, directly owns 40 shares of Y stock. Although the stock of Y owned by B is considered as owned by C (the father of A and B) under paragraph (b)(6)(i) of this section, under subparagraph (2) of this paragraph such stock may not be treated as owned by C for purposes of applying paragraph (b)(6)(ii) of this section in order to make A the constructive owner of such stock.

Example (3). Assume the same facts assumed for purposes of example (2), and further assume that C has an option to acquire the 40 shares of Y stock owned by his son, B. The rule contained in subparagraph (2) of this paragraph does not prevent the reattribution of such 40 shares to A because, under subparagraph (3) of this paragraph, C is considered as owning the 40 shares by reason of option attribution and not by reason of family attribution. Therefore, since A satisfies the more-than-50-percent stock ownership test contained in paragraph (b)(6)(ii) of this section with respect to Y, the 40 shares of Y stock constructively owned by C are reattributed to A, and A is considered as owning a total of 94 shares of Y stock.

* * *

[Reg. § 1.1563-3.]

☐ [*T.D.* 6845, 8-4-65. *Amended by T.D.* 7181, 4-24-72; *T.D.* 7779, 6-1-81; *T.D.* 8179, 3-1-88 *T.D.* 9264, 5-26-2006; *T.D.* 9304, 12-21-2006; *T.D.* 9329, 6-13-2007 *and T.D.* 9451, 5-26-2009.]

Tax Returns or Statements

§ 1.6015-1. Relief from joint and several liability on a joint return.—(a) *In general.*—(1) An individual who qualifies and elects under section 6013 to file a joint Federal income tax return with another individual is jointly and severally liable for the joint Federal income tax liabilities for that year. A spouse or former spouse may be relieved of joint and several liability for Federal income tax for that year under the following three relief provisions:

(i) Innocent spouse relief under § 1.6015-2.

(ii) Allocation of deficiency under § 1.6015-3.

(iii) Equitable relief under § 1.6015-4.

* * *

[Reg. § 1.6015-1.]

☐ [*T.D.* 9003, 7-17-2002.]

§ 1.6015-2. Relief from liability applicable to all qualifying joint filers.—(a) *In general.*—A requesting spouse may be relieved of joint and several liability for tax (including additions to tax, penalties, and interest) from an understatement for a taxable year under this section if the requesting spouse elects the application of this section in accordance with §§ 1.6015-1(h)(5) and 1.6015-5, and—

(1) A joint return was filed for the taxable year;

(2) On the return there is an understatement attributable to erroneous items of the nonrequesting spouse;

(3) The requesting spouse establishes that in signing the return he or she did not know and had no reason to know of the understatement; and

(4) It is inequitable to hold the requesting spouse liable for the deficiency attributable to the understatement.

(b) *Understatement.*—The term *understatement* has the meaning given to such term by section 6662(d)(2)(A) and the regulations thereunder.

(c) *Knowledge or reason to know.*—A requesting spouse has knowledge or reason to know of an understatement if he or she actually knew of the understatement, or if a reasonable person in similar circumstances would have known of the understatement. For rules relating to a requesting spouse's actual knowledge, see § 1.6015-3(c)(2). All of the facts and circumstances are considered in determining whether a requesting spouse had reason to know of an understatement. The facts and circumstances that are considered include, but are not limited to, the nature of the erroneous item and the amount of the erroneous item relative to other items; the couple's financial situation; the requesting spouse's educational background and business experience; the extent of the requesting spouse's participation in the activity that resulted in the erroneous item; whether the requesting spouse failed to inquire, at or before the time the return was signed, about items on the return or omitted from the return that a reasonable person would question; and whether the erroneous item represented a departure from a recurring pattern reflected in prior years' returns (e.g., omitted income from an investment regularly reported on prior years' returns).

(d) *Inequity.*—All of the facts and circumstances are considered in determining whether it is inequitable to hold a requesting spouse jointly and severally liable for an understatement. One relevant factor for this purpose is whether the requesting spouse significantly benefitted, directly or indirectly, from the understatement. A significant benefit is any benefit in excess of normal support. Evidence of direct or indirect benefit may consist of transfers of property or rights to property, including transfers that may be received several years after the year of the understatement. Thus, for example, if a requesting spouse receives property (including life insurance proceeds) from the nonrequesting spouse that is beyond normal support and traceable to items omitted from gross income that are attributable to the nonrequesting spouse, the requesting spouse will be considered to have received significant benefit from those items. Other factors that may also be taken into account, if the situation warrants, include the fact that the requesting spouse has been deserted by the nonrequesting spouse, the fact that the spouses have been divorced or separated, or that the requesting spouse received benefit on the return from the understatement. For guidance concerning the criteria to be used in determining whether it is inequitable to hold a requesting spouse jointly and severally liable under this section, see Rev. Proc. 2000-15 (2000-1 C.B. 447), or other guidance published by the Treasury and IRS (see § 601.601(d)(2) of this chapter).

* * *

[Reg. § 1.6015-2.]

☐ [*T.D.* 9003, 7-17-2002.]

§ 1.6015-3. Allocation of deficiency for individuals who are no longer married, are legally separated, or are not members of the same household.—(a) *Election to allocate deficiency.*—A requesting spouse may elect to allocate a deficiency if, as defined in paragraph (b) of this section, the requesting spouse is divorced, widowed, or legally separated, or has not been a member of the same household as the nonrequesting spouse at any time during the 12-month period ending on the date an election for relief is filed. For purposes of this section, the marital status of a deceased requesting spouse will be determined on the earlier of the date of the election or the date of death in accordance with section 7703(a)(1). Subject to the restrictions of paragraph (c) of this section, an eligible requesting spouse who elects the application of this section in accordance with §§ 1.6015-1(h)(5) and 1.6015-5 generally may be relieved of joint and several liability for the portion of any deficiency that is allocated to the nonrequesting spouse pursuant to the allocation methods set forth in paragraph

(d) of this section. Relief may be available to both spouses filing the joint return if each spouse is eligible for and elects the application of this section.

(b) *Definitions.*—(1) *Divorced.*—A determination of whether a requesting spouse is divorced for purposes of this section will be made in accordance with section 7703 and the regulations thereunder. Such determination will be made as of the date the election is filed.

(2) *Legally separated.*—A determination of whether a requesting spouse is legally separated for purposes of this section will be made in accordance with section 7703 and the regulations thereunder. Such determination will be made as of the date the election is filed.

(3) *Members of the same household.*—(i) *Temporary absences.*—A requesting spouse and a nonrequesting spouse are considered members of the same household during either spouse's temporary absences from the household if it is reasonable to assume that the absent spouse will return to the household, and the household or a substantially equivalent household is maintained in anticipation of such return. Examples of temporary absences may include, but are not limited to, absence due to incarceration, illness, business, vacation, military service, or education.

(ii) *Separate dwellings.*—A husband and wife who reside in the same dwelling are considered members of the same household. In addition, a husband and wife who reside in two separate dwellings are considered members of the same household if the spouses are not estranged or one spouse is temporarily absent from the other's household within the meaning of paragraph (b)(3)(i) of this section.

* * *

[Reg. § 1.6015-3.]

☐ [*T.D.* 9003, 7-17-2002.]

§ 1.6015-4. Equitable relief.—(a) A requesting spouse who files a joint return for which a liability remains unpaid and who does not qualify for full relief under § 1.6015-2 or 1.6015-3 may request equitable relief under this section. The Internal Revenue Service has the discretion to grant equitable relief from joint and several liability to a requesting spouse when, considering all of the facts and circumstances, it would be inequitable to hold the requesting spouse jointly and severally liable.

(b) This section may not be used to circumvent the limitation of § 1.6015-3(c)(1) (i.e., no refunds under § 1.6015-3). Therefore, relief is not available under this section to obtain a refund of liabilities already paid, for which the requesting spouse would otherwise qualify for relief under § 1.6015-3.

(c) For guidance concerning the criteria to be used in determining whether it is inequitable to hold a requesting spouse jointly and severally liable under this section, see Rev. Proc. 2000-15 (2000-1 C.B. 447), or other guidance published by the Treasury and IRS (see § 601.601(d)(2) of this chapter). [Reg. § 1.6015-4.]

☐ [*T.D.* 9003, 7-17-2002.]

Accuracy-Related and Fraud Penalties

§ 1.6662-1. Overview of the accuracy-related penalty.—Section 6662 imposes an accuracy-related penalty on any portion of an underpayment of tax required to be shown on a return that is attributable to one or more of the following:

(a) Negligence or disregard of rules or regulations;

(b) Any substantial understatement of income tax;

(c) Any substantial valuation misstatement under chapter 1;

(d) Any substantial overstatement of pension liabilities; or

(e) Any substantial estate or gift tax valuation understatement.

Sections 1.6662-1 through 1.6662-5 address only the first three components of the accuracy-related penalty, *i.e.*, the penalties for negligence or disregard of rules or regulations, substantial understatements of income tax, and substantial (or gross) valuation misstatements under chapter 1. The penalties for disregard of rules or regulations and for a substantial understatement of income tax may be avoided by adequately disclosing certain information as provided in § 1.6662-3(c) and §§ 1.6662-4(e) and (f), respectively. The penalties for negligence and for a substantial (or gross) valuation misstatement under chapter 1 may not be avoided by disclosure. No accuracy-related penalty may be imposed on any portion of an underpayment if there was reasonable cause for, and the taxpayer acted in good faith with respect to, such portion. The reasonable cause and good faith exception to the accuracy-related penalty is set forth in § 1.6664-4. [Reg. § 1.6662-1.]

☐ [*T.D.* 8381, 12-30-91. *Amended by T.D.* 8617, 8-31-95.]

§ 1.6662-2. Accuracy-related penalty.—(a) *In general.*—Section 6662(a) imposes an accuracy-related penalty on any portion of an underpayment of tax (as defined in section

6664(a) and § 1.6664-2) required to be shown on a return if such portion is attributable to one or more of the following types of misconduct:

(1) Negligence or disregard of rules or regulations (see § 1.6662-3);

(2) Any substantial understatement of income tax (see § 1.6662-4); or

(3) Any substantial (or gross) valuation misstatement under chapter 1 ("substantial valuation misstatement" or "gross valuation misstatement"), provided the applicable dollar limitation set forth in section 6662(e)(2) is satisfied (see § 1.6662-5).

The accuracy-related penalty applies only in cases in which a return of tax is filed, except that the penalty does not apply in the case of a return prepared by the Secretary under the authority of section 6020(b). The accuracy-related penalty under section 6662 and the penalty under section 6651 for failure to timely file a return of tax may both be imposed on the same portion of an underpayment if a return is filed, but is filed late. The fact that a return is filed late, however, is not taken into account in determining whether an accuracy-related penalty should be imposed. No accuracy-related penalty may be imposed on any portion of an underpayment of tax on which the fraud penalty set forth in section 6663 is imposed.

(b) *Amount of penalty.*—(1) *In general.*—The amount of the accuracy-related penalty is 20 percent of the portion of an underpayment of tax required to be shown on a return that is attributable to any of the types of misconduct listed in paragraphs (a)(1) through (a)(3) of this section, except as provided in paragraph (b)(2) of this section.

(2) *Increase in penalty for gross valuation misstatement.*—In the case of a gross valuation misstatement, as defined in section 6662(h)(2) and § 1.6662-5(e)(2), the amount of the accuracy-related penalty is 40 percent of the portion of an underpayment of tax required to be shown on a return that is attributable to the gross valuation misstatement, provided the applicable dollar limitation set forth in section 6662(e)(2) is satisfied.

(c) *No stacking of accuracy-related penalty components.*—The maximum accuracy-related penalty imposed on a portion of an underpayment may not exceed 20 percent of such portion (40 percent of the portion attributable to a gross valuation misstatement), notwithstanding that such portion is attributable to more than one of the types of misconduct described in paragraph (a) of this section. For example, if a portion of an underpayment of tax required to be shown on a return is attributable both to negligence and a substantial understatement of income tax, the maximum accuracy-related penalty is 20 percent of such portion. Similarly, the maximum accuracy-related penalty imposed on any portion of an underpayment that is attributable both to negligence and a gross valuation misstatement is 40 percent of such portion.

* * *

[Reg. § 1.6662-2.]

□ [*T.D.* 8381, 12-30-91. *Amended by T.D.* 8617, 8-31-95; *T.D.* 8790, 12-1-98 *and T.D.* 9109, 12-29-2003.]

§ 1.6662-3. Negligence or disregard of rules or regulations.—(a) *In general.*—If any portion of an underpayment, as defined in section 6664(a) and § 1.6664-2, of any income tax imposed under subtitle A of the Internal Revenue Code that is required to be shown on a return is attributable to negligence or disregard of rules or regulations, there is added to the tax an amount equal to 20 percent of such portion. The penalty for disregarding rules or regulations does not apply, however, if the requirements of paragraph (c)(1) of this section are satisfied and the position in question is adequately disclosed as provided in paragraph (c)(2) of this section (and, if the position relates to a reportable transaction as defined in § 1.6011-4(b) (or § 1.6011-4T(b), as applicable), the transaction is disclosed in accordance with § 1.6011-4 (or § 1.6011-4T, as applicable)), or to the extent that the reasonable cause and good faith exception to this penalty set forth in § 1.6664-4 applies. In addition, if a position with respect to an item (other than with respect to a reportable transaction, as defined in § 1.6011-4(b) or § 1.6011-4T(b), as applicable) is contrary to a revenue ruling or notice (other than a notice of proposed rulemaking) issued by the Internal Revenue Service and published in the Internal Revenue Bulletin (see § 601.601(d)(2) of this chapter), this penalty does not apply if the position has a realistic possibility of being sustained on its merits. See § 1.6694-2(b) of the income tax return preparer penalty regulations for a description of the realistic possibility standard.

(b) *Definitions and rules.*—(1) *Negligence.*—The term "negligence" includes any failure to make a reasonable attempt to comply with the provisions of the internal revenue laws or to exercise ordinary and reasonable care in the preparation of a tax return. "Negligence" also includes any failure by the taxpayer to keep adequate books and records or to substantiate items properly. A return position that has a reasonable basis as defined in paragraph (b)(3) of this section is not attributable to negligence. Negligence is strongly indicated where—

(i) A taxpayer fails to include on an income tax return an amount of income shown on an information return, as defined in section 6724(d)(1);

(ii) A taxpayer fails to make a reasonable attempt to ascertain the correctness of a deduction, credit or exclusion on a return which would seem to a reasonable and prudent person to be "too good to be true" under the circumstances;

(iii) A partner fails to comply with the requirements of section 6222, which requires that a partner treat partnership items on its return in a manner that is consistent with the treatment of such items on the partnership return (or notify the Secretary of the inconsistency); or

(iv) A shareholder fails to comply with the requirements of section 6242, which requires that an S corporation shareholder treat subchapter S items on its return in a manner that is consistent with the treatment of such items on the corporation's return (or notify the Secretary of the inconsistency).

(2) *Disregard of rules or regulations.*—The term "disregard" includes any careless, reckless or intentional disregard of rules or regulations. The term "rules or regulations" includes the provisions of the Internal Revenue Code, temporary or final Treasury regulations issued under the Code, and revenue rulings or notices (other than notices of proposed rulemaking) issued by the Internal Revenue Service and published in the Internal Revenue Bulletin. A disregard of rules or regulations is "careless" if the taxpayer does not exercise reasonable diligence to determine the correctness of a return position that is contrary to the rule or regulation. A disregard is "reckless" if the taxpayer makes little or no effort to determine whether a rule or regulation exists, under circumstances which demonstrate a substantial deviation from the standard of conduct that a reasonable person would observe. A disregard is "intentional" if the taxpayer knows of the rule or regulation that is disregarded. Nevertheless, a taxpayer who takes a position (other than with respect to a reportable transaction, as defined in § 1.6011-4(b) or § 1.6011-4T(b), as applicable) contrary to a revenue ruling or notice has not disregarded the ruling or notice if the contrary position has a realistic possibility of being sustained on its merits.

(3) *Reasonable basis.*—Reasonable basis is a relatively high standard of tax reporting, that is, significantly higher than not frivolous or not patently improper. The reasonable basis standard is not satisfied by a return position that is merely arguable or that is merely a colorable claim. If a return position is reasonably based on one or more of the authorities set forth in § 1.6662-4(d)(3)(iii) (taking into account the relevance and persuasiveness of the authorities, and subsequent developments), the return position will generally satisfy the reasonable basis standard even though it may not satisfy the substantial authority standard as defined in § 1.6662-4(d)(2). (See § 1.6662-4(d)(3)(ii) for rules with respect to relevance, persuasiveness, subsequent developments, and use of a well-reasoned construction of an applicable statutory provision for purposes of the substantial understatement penalty.) In addition, the reasonable cause and good faith exception in § 1.6664-4 may provide relief from the penalty for negligence or disregard of rules or regulations, even if a return position does not satisfy the reasonable basis standard.

(c) *Exception for adequate disclosure.*—(1) *In general.*—No penalty under section 6662(b)(1) may be imposed on any portion of an underpayment that is attributable to a position contrary to a rule or regulation if the position is disclosed in accordance with the rules of paragraph (c)(2) of this section (and, if the position relates to a reportable transaction as defined in § 1.6011-4(b) (or § 1.6011-4T(b), as applicable), the transaction is disclosed in accordance with § 1.6011-4 (or § 1.6011-4T, as applicable)) and, in case of a position contrary to a regulation, the position represents a good faith challenge to the validity of the regulation. This disclosure exception does not apply, however, in the case of a position that does not have a reasonable basis or where the taxpayer fails to keep adequate books and records or to substantiate items properly.

(2) *Method of disclosure.*—Disclosure is adequate for purposes of the penalty for disregarding rules or regulations if made in accordance with the provisions of §§ 1.6662-4(f)(1), (3), (4) and (5), which permit disclosure on a properly completed and filed Form 8275 or 8275-R, as appropriate. In addition, the statutory or regulatory provision or ruling in question must be adequately identified on the Form 8275 or 8275-R, as appropriate. The provisions of § 1.6662-4(f)(2), which permit disclosure in accordance with an annual revenue procedure for purposes of the substantial understatement penalty, do not apply for purposes of this section.

* * *

[Reg. § 1.6662-3.]

☐ [*T.D.* 8381, 12-30-91. *Amended by T.D.* 8617, 8-31-95; *T.D.* 8790, 12-1-98 *and T.D.* 9109, 12-29-2003.]

§ 1.6662-4. Substantial understatement of income tax.—(a) *In general.*—If any portion of an underpayment, as defined in section 6664(a) and § 1.6664-2, of any income tax imposed under subtitle A of the Code that is required to be shown on a return is attributable to a substantial understatement of such income tax, there is added to the tax an amount equal to 20 percent of such portion. Except in the case of any item attributable to a tax shelter (as defined in paragraph (g)(2) of this section), an understatement is reduced by the portion of the understatement that is attributable to the tax treatment of an item for which there is substantial authority, or with respect to which there is adequate disclosure. General rules for determining the amount of an understatement are set forth in paragraph (b) of this section and more specific rules in the case of carrybacks and carryovers are set forth in paragraph (c) of this section. The rules for determining when substantial authority exists are set forth in § 1.6662-4(d). The rules for determining when there is adequate disclosure are set forth in § 1.6662-4(e) and (f). This penalty does not apply to the extent that the reasonable cause and good faith exception to this penalty set forth in § 1.6664-4 applies.

(b) *Definitions and computational rules*—.—(1) *Substantial.*—An understatement (as defined in paragraph (b)(2) of this section) is "substantial" if it exceeds the greater of—

(i) 10 percent of the tax required to be shown on the return for the taxable year (as defined in paragraph (b)(3) of this section); or

(ii) $5,000 ($10,000 in the case of a corporation other than an S corporation (as defined in section 1361(a)(1)) or a personal holding company (as defined in section 542)).

(2) *Understatement.*—Except as provided in paragraph (c)(2) of this section (relating to special rules for carrybacks), the term "understatement" means the excess of—

(i) The amount of the tax required to be shown on the return for the taxable year (as defined in paragraph (b)(3) of this section), over

(ii) The amount of the tax imposed which is shown on the return for the taxable year (as defined in paragraph (b)(4) of this section), reduced by any rebate (as defined in paragraph (b)(5) of this section).

The definition of understatement also may be expressed as—

$$Understatement = X - (Y - Z)$$

where X = the amount of the tax required to be shown on the return; Y = the amount of the tax imposed which is shown on the return; and Z = any rebate.

(3) *Amount of the tax required to be shown on the return.*—The "amount of the tax required to be shown on the return" for the taxable year has the same meaning as the "amount of income tax imposed" as defined in § 1.6664-2(b).

(4) *Amount of the tax imposed which is shown on the return.*—The "amount of the tax imposed which is shown on the return" for the taxable year has the same meaning as the "amount shown as the tax by the taxpayer on his return," as defined in § 1.6664-2(c), except that—

(i) There is no reduction for the excess of the amount described in § 1.6664-2(c)(1)(i) over the amount described in § 1.6664-2(c)(1)(ii), and

(ii) The tax liability shown by the taxpayer on his return is recomputed as if the following items had been reported properly:

(A) Items (other than tax shelter items as defined in § 1.6662-4(g)(3)) for which there is substantial authority for the treatment claimed (as provided in § 1.6662-4(d)).

(B) Items (other than tax shelter items as defined in § 1.6662-4(g)(3)) with respect to which there is adequate disclosure (as provided in § 1.6662-4(e) and (f)).

(C) Tax shelter items (as defined in § 1.6662-4(g)(3)) for which there is substantial authority for the treatment claimed (as provided in § 1.6662-4(d)), and with respect to which the taxpayer reasonably believed that the tax treatment of the items was more likely than not the proper tax treatment (as provided in § 1.6662-4(g)(4)).

(5) *Rebate.*—The term "rebate" has the meaning set forth in § 1.6664-2(e), except that—

(i) "Amounts not so shown previously assessed (or collected without assessment)" includes only amounts not so shown previously assessed (or collected without assessment) as a deficiency, and

(ii) The amount of the rebate is determined as if any items to which the rebate is attributable that are described in paragraph (b)(4) of this section had received the proper tax treatment.

(6) *Examples.*—The following examples illustrate the provisions of paragraph (b) of this section. These examples do not take into account the reasonable cause exception under § 1.6664-4:

Example 1. In 1990, Individual A, a calendar year taxpayer, files a return for 1989, which shows taxable income of $18,200 and tax liability of $2,734. Subsequent adjustments on audit for 1989 increase taxable income to $51,500 and tax liability to $12,339. There was substantial authority for an item resulting in an adjustment that increases taxable income by $5,300. The item is not a tax shelter item. In computing the amount of the understatement, the amount of tax shown on A's return is determined as if the item for which there was substantial authority had been given the proper tax treatment. Thus, the amount of tax that is treated as shown on A's return is $4,176, i.e., the tax on $23,500 ($18,200 taxable income actually shown on A's return plus $5,300, the amount of the adjustment for which there was substantial authority). The amount of the understatement is $8,163, i.e., $12,339 (the amount of tax required to be shown) less $4,176 (the amount of tax treated as shown on A's return after adjustment for the item for which there was substantial authority). Because the $8,163 understatement exceeds the greater of 10 percent of the tax required to be shown on the return for the year, i.e., $1,234 ($12,339 × .10) or $5,000, A has a substantial understatement of income tax for the year.

Example 2. Individual B, a calendar year taxpayer, files a return for 1990 that fails to include income reported on an information return, Form 1099, that was furnished to B. The Service detects this omission through its document matching program and assesses $3,000 in unreported tax liability. B's return is later examined and as a result of the examination the Service makes an adjustment to B's return of $4,000 in additional tax liability. Assuming there was neither substantial authority nor adequate disclosure with respect to the items adjusted, there is an understatement of $7,000 with respect to B's return. There is also an underpayment of $7,000. (See § 1.6664-2.) The amount of the understatement is not reduced by imposition of a negligence penalty on the $3,000 portion of the underpayment that is attributable to the unreported income. However, if the Service does impose the negligence penalty on this $3,000 portion, the Service may only impose the substantial understatement penalty on the remaining $4,000 portion of the underpayment. (See § 1.6662-2(c), which prohibits stacking of accuracy-related penalty components.)

* * *

(d) *Substantial authority—.*—(1) *Effect of having substantial authority.*—If there is substantial authority for the tax treatment of an item, the item is treated as if it were shown properly on the return for the taxable year in computing the amount of the tax shown on the return. Thus, for purposes of section 6662(d), the tax attributable to the item is not included in the understatement for that year. (For special rules relating to tax shelter items see § 1.6662-4(g).)

(2) *Substantial authority standard.*—The substantial authority standard is an objective standard involving an analysis of the law and application of the law to relevant facts. The substantial authority standard is less stringent than the more likely than not standard (the standard that is met when there is a greater than 50-percent likelihood of the position being upheld), but more stringent than the reasonable basis standard as defined in § 1.6662-3(b)(3). The possibility that a return will not be audited or, if audited, that an item will not be raised on audit, is not relevant in determining whether the substantial authority standard (or the reasonable basis standard) is satisfied.

(3) *Determination of whether substantial authority is present.*—(i) *Evaluation of authorities.*—There is substantial authority for the tax treatment of an item only if the weight of the authorities supporting the treatment is substantial in relation to the weight of authorities supporting contrary treatment. All authorities relevant to the tax treatment of an item, including the authorities contrary to the treatment, are taken into account in determining whether substantial authority exists. The weight of authorities is determined in light of the pertinent facts and circumstances in the manner prescribed by paragraph (d)(3)(ii) of this section. There may be substantial authority for more than one position with respect to the same item. Because the substantial authority standard is an objective standard, the taxpayer's belief that there is substantial authority for the tax treatment of an item is not relevant in determining whether there is substantial authority for that treatment.

(ii) *Nature of analysis.*—The weight accorded an authority depends on its relevance and persuasiveness, and the type of document providing the authority. For example, a case or revenue ruling having some facts in common with the tax treatment at issue is not particularly relevant if the authority is materially distinguishable on its facts, or is otherwise inapplicable to the tax treatment at issue. An authority that merely states a conclusion ordinarily is less persuasive than one that reaches its conclusion by cogently relating the applicable law to pertinent facts. The weight of an authority from which information has been deleted, such as a private letter ruling, is diminished to the extent that the deleted information may have affected the authority's conclusions. The type of document also must be considered. For example, a revenue ruling is accorded greater weight than a private letter ruling addressing the same issue. An older private letter ruling, technical advice memorandum, general counsel memorandum or action on decision generally must be accorded less weight than a more recent one. Any document described in the preceding sentence that is more than 10 years old generally is accorded very little weight. However, the persuasiveness and relevance of a document, viewed in light of subsequent developments, should be taken into account along with the age of the document. There may be substantial authority for the tax treatment of an item despite the absence of certain types of authority. Thus, a taxpayer may have substantial authority for a position that is supported only by a well-reasoned construction of the applicable statutory provision.

(iii) *Types of authority.*—Except in cases described in paragraph (d)(3)(iv) of this section concerning written determinations, only the following are authority for purposes of determining whether there is substantial authority for the tax treatment of an item: applicable provisions of the Internal Revenue Code and other statutory provisions; proposed, temporary and final regulations construing such statutes; revenue rulings and revenue procedures; tax treaties and regulations thereunder, and Treasury Department and other official explanations of such treaties; court cases; congressional intent as reflected in committee reports, joint explanatory statements of managers included in conference committee reports, and floor statements made prior to enactment by one of a bill's managers; General Explanations of tax legislation prepared by the Joint Committee on Taxation (the Blue Book); private letter rulings and technical advice memoranda issued after October 31, 1976; actions on decisions and general counsel memoranda issued after March 12, 1981 (as well as general counsel memoranda published in pre-1955 volumes of the Cumulative Bulletin); Internal Revenue Service information or press releases; and notices, announcements and other administrative pronouncements published by the Service in the Internal Revenue Bulletin. Conclusions reached in treatises, legal periodicals, legal opinions or opinions rendered by tax professionals are not authority. The authorities underlying such expressions of opinion where applicable to the facts of a particular case, however, may give rise to substantial authority for the tax treatment of an item. Notwithstanding the preceding list of authorities, an authority does not continue to be an authority to the extent it is overruled or modified, implicitly or explicitly, by a body with the power to overrule or modify the earlier authority. In the case of court decisions, for example, a district court opinion on an issue is not an authority if overruled or reversed by the United States Court of Appeals for such district. However, a Tax Court opinion is not considered to be overruled or modified by a court of appeals to which a taxpayer does not have a right of appeal, unless the Tax Court adopts the holding of the court of appeals. Similarly, a private letter ruling is not authority if revoked or if inconsistent with a subsequent proposed regulation, revenue ruling or other administrative pronouncement published in the Internal Revenue Bulletin.

(iv) *Special rules.*—(A) *Written determinations.*—There is substantial authority for the tax treatment of an item by a taxpayer if the treatment is supported by the conclusion of a ruling or a determination letter (as defined in § 301.6110-2(d) and (e)) issued to the taxpayer, by the conclusion of a technical advice memorandum in which the taxpayer is named, or by an affirmative statement in a revenue agent's report with respect to a prior taxable year of the taxpayer ("written determinations"). The preceding sentence does not apply, however, if—

(1) There was a misstatement or omission of a material fact or the facts that subsequently develop are materially different from the facts on which the written determination was based, or

(2) The written determination was modified or revoked after the date of issuance by—

(i) A notice to the taxpayer to whom the written determination was issued,

(ii) The enactment of legislation or ratification of a tax treaty,

(iii) A decision of the United States Supreme Court,

(iv) The issuance of temporary or final regulations, or

(v) The issuance of a revenue ruling, revenue procedure, or other statement published in the Internal Revenue Bulletin.

Except in the case of a written determination that is modified or revoked on account of § 1.6662-4(d)(3)(iv)(A)(*1*), a written determination that is modified or revoked as described in § 1.6662-4(d)(3)(iv)(A)(*2*) ceases to be authority on the date, and to the extent, it is so modified or revoked. See section 6404(f) for rules which require the Secretary to abate a penalty that is attributable to erroneous written advice furnished to a taxpayer by an officer or employee of the Internal Revenue Service.

(B) *Taxpayer's jurisdiction.*—The applicability of court cases to the taxpayer by reason of the taxpayer's residence in a particular jurisdiction is not taken into account in determining whether there is substantial authority for the tax treatment of an item. Notwithstanding the preceding sentence, there is substantial authority for the tax treatment of an item if the treatment is supported by controlling precedent of a United States Court of Appeals to which the taxpayer has a right of appeal with respect to the item.

(C) *When substantial authority determined.*—There is substantial authority for the tax treatment of an item if there is substantial authority at the time the return containing the item is filed or there was substantial authority on the last day of the taxable year to which the return relates.

* * *

(e) *Disclosure of certain information.*—(1) *Effect of adequate disclosure.*—Items for which there is adequate disclosure as provided in this paragraph (e) and in paragraph (f) of this section are treated as if such items were shown properly on the return for the taxable year in computing the amount of the tax shown on the return. Thus, for purposes of section 6662(d), the tax attributable to such items is not included in the understatement for that year.

(2) *Circumstances where disclosure will not have an effect.*—The rules of paragraph (e)(1) of this section do not apply where the item or position on the return —

(i) Does not have a reasonable basis (as defined in § 1.6662-3(b)(3));

(ii) Is attributable to a tax shelter (as defined in section 6662(d)(2)(C)(iii) and paragraph (g)(2) of this section); or

(iii) Is not properly substantiated, or the taxpayer failed to keep adequate books and records with respect to the item or position.

(3) *Restriction for corporations.*—For purposes of paragraph (e)(2)(i) of this section, a corporation will not be treated as having a reasonable basis for its tax treatment of an item attributable to a multi-party financing transaction entered into after August 5, 1997, if the treatment does not clearly reflect the income of the corporation.

(f) *Method of making adequate disclosure.*—(1) *Disclosure statement.*—Disclosure is adequate with respect to an item (or group of similar items, such as amounts paid or incurred for supplies by a taxpayer engaged in business) or a position on a return if the disclosure is made on a properly completed form attached to the return or to a qualified amended return (as defined in § 1.6664-2(c)(3)) for the taxable year. In the case of an item or position other than one that is contrary to a regulation, disclosure must be made on Form 8275 (Disclosure Statement); in the case of a position contrary to a regulation, disclosure must be made on Form 8275-R (Regulation Disclosure Statement).

(2) *Disclosure on return.*—The Commissioner may by annual revenue procedure (or otherwise) prescribe the circumstances under which disclosure of information on a return (or qualified amended return) in accordance with applicable forms and instructions is adequate. If the revenue procedure does not include an item, disclosure is adequate with respect to that item only if made on a properly completed Form 8275 or 8275-R, as appropriate, attached to the return for the year or to a qualified amended return.

(3) *Recurring item.*—Disclosure with respect to a recurring item, such as the basis of recovery property, must be made for each taxable year in which the item is taken into account.

(4) *Carrybacks and carryovers.*—Disclosure is adequate with respect to an item which is included in any loss, deduction or credit that is carried to another year only if made in connection with the return (or qualified amended return) for the taxable year in which the carryback or carryover arises (the "loss or credit year"). Disclosure is not also required in connection with the return for the taxable year in which the carryback or carryover is taken into account.

(5) *Pass-through entities.*—Disclosure in the case of items attributable to a pass-through entity (pass-through items) is made with respect to the return of the entity, except as provided in this paragraph (f)(5). Thus, disclosure in the case of pass-through items must be made on a Form 8275 or 8275-R, as appropriate, attached to the return (or qualified amended return) of the entity, or on the entity's return in accordance with the revenue procedure described in paragraph (f)(2) of this section, if applicable. A taxpayer (i.e., partner, shareholder, beneficiary, or holder of a residual interest in a REMIC) also may make adequate disclosure with respect to a pass-through item, however, if the taxpayer files a properly completed Form 8275 or 8275-R, as appropriate, in duplicate, one copy attached to the taxpayer's return (or qualified amended return) and the other copy filed with the Internal Revenue Service Center with which the return of the entity is required to be filed. Each Form 8275 or 8275-R, as appropriate, filed by the taxpayer should relate to the pass-through items of only one entity. For purposes of this paragraph (f)(5), a pass-through entity is a partnership, S corporation (as defined in section 1361(a)(1)), estate, trust, regulated investment company (as defined in section 851(a)), real estate investment trust (as defined in section 856(a)), or real estate mortgage investment conduit ("REMIC") (as defined in section 860D(a)).

* * *

[Reg. § 1.6662-4.]

☐ [*T.D.* 8381, 12-30-91. *Amended by T.D.* 8617, 8-31-95; *T.D.* 8790, 12-1-98 *and T.D.* 9109, 12-29-2003.]

»»→ Caution: Reg. § 1.6662-5 does not reflect changes made in Sections 6662(e) and (h) in 2006.

§ 1.6662-5. Substantial and gross valuation misstatements under chapter 1.—(a) *In general.*—If any portion of an underpayment, as defined in section 6664(a) and § 1.6664-2, of any income tax imposed under chapter 1 of subtitle A of the Code that is required to be shown on a return is attributable to a substantial valuation misstatement under chapter 1 ("substantial valuation misstatement"), there is added to the tax an amount equal to 20 percent of such portion. Section 6662(h) increases the penalty to 40 percent in the case of a gross valuation misstatement under chapter 1 ("gross valuation misstatement"). No penalty under section 6662(b)(3) is imposed, however, on a portion of an underpayment that is attributable to a substantial or gross valuation misstatement unless the aggregate of all portions of the underpayment attributable to substantial or gross valuation misstatements exceeds the applicable dollar limitation ($5,000 or $10,000), as provided in section 6662(e)(2) and paragraphs (b) and (f)(2) of this section. This penalty also does not apply to the extent that the reasonable cause and good faith exception to this penalty set forth in § 1.6664-4 applies. There is no disclosure exception to this penalty.

(b) *Dollar limitation.*—No penalty may be imposed under section 6662(b)(3) for a taxable year unless the portion of the underpayment for that year that is attributable to substantial or gross valuation misstatements exceeds $5,000 ($10,000 in the case of a corporation other than an S corporation (as defined in section 1361(a)(1)) or a personal holding company (as defined in section 542)). This limitation is applied separately to each taxable year for which there is a substantial or gross valuation misstatement.

* * *

(e) *Definitions.*—(1) *Substantial valuation misstatement.*—There is a substantial valuation misstatement if the value or adjusted basis of any property claimed on a return of tax imposed under chapter 1 is 200 percent or more of the correct amount.

(2) *Gross valuation misstatement.*—There is a gross valuation misstatement if the value or adjusted basis of any property claimed on a return of tax imposed under chapter 1 is 400 percent or more of the correct amount.

(3) *Property.*—For purposes of this section, the term "property" refers to both tangible and intangible property. Tangible property includes property such as land, buildings, fixtures and inventory. Intangible property includes property such as goodwill, covenants not to compete, leaseholds, patents, contract rights, debts and choses in action.

(f) *Multiple valuation misstatements on a return.*—(1) *Determination of whether valuation misstatements are substantial or gross.*—The determination of whether there is a substantial or gross valuation misstatement on a return is made on a property-by-property basis. Assume, for example, that property A has a value of 60 but a taxpayer claims a value of 110, and that property B has a value of 40 but the taxpayer claims a value of 100. Because the claimed and correct values are compared on a property-by-property basis, there is a substantial valuation misstatement with respect to property B, but not with respect to property A, even though the claimed values (210) are 200 percent or more of the correct values (100) when compared on an aggregate basis.

(2) *Application of dollar limitation.*—For purposes of applying the dollar limitation set forth in section 6662(e)(2), the determination of the portion of an underpayment that is attributable to a substantial or gross valuation misstatement is made by aggregating all portions of the underpayment attributable to substantial or gross valuation misstatements. Assume, for example, that the value claimed for property C on a return is 250 percent of the correct value, and that the value claimed for property D on the return is 400 percent of the correct value. Because the portions of an underpayment that are attributable to a substantial or gross valuation misstatement on a return are aggregated in applying the dollar limitation, the dollar limitation is satisfied if the portion of the underpayment that is attributable to the misstatement of the value of property C, when aggregated with the portion of the underpayment that is attributable to the misstatement of the value of property D, exceeds $5,000 ($10,000 in the case of most corporations).

(g) *Property with a value or adjusted basis of zero.*—The value or adjusted basis claimed on a return of any property with a correct value or adjusted basis of zero is considered to be 400 percent or more of the correct amount. There is a gross valuation misstatement with respect to such property, therefore, and the applicable penalty rate is 40 percent.

(h) *Pass-through entities.*—(1) *In general.*—The determination of whether there is a substantial or gross valuation misstatement in the case of a return of a pass-through entity (as defined in § 1.6662-4(f)(5)) is made at the entity level. However, the dollar limitation ($5,000 or $10,000, as the case may be) is applied at the taxpayer level (*i.e.,* with respect to the return of the shareholder, partner, beneficiary, or holder of a residual interest in a REMIC).

* * *

[Reg. § 1.6662-5.]

☐ [*T.D.* 8381, 12-30-91.]

§ 1.6664-4. Reasonable cause and good faith exception to section 6662 penalties.—(a) *In general.*—No penalty may be imposed under section 6662 with respect to any portion of an underpayment upon a showing by the taxpayer that there was reasonable cause for, and the taxpayer acted in good faith with respect to, such portion. Rules for determining whether the reasonable cause and good faith exception applies are set forth in paragraphs (b) through (h) of this section.

(b) *Facts and circumstances taken into account.*—(1) *In general.*—The determination of whether a taxpayer acted with reasonable cause and in good faith is made on a case-by-case basis, taking into account all pertinent facts and circumstances. (See paragraph (e) of this section for certain rules relating to a substantial understatement penalty attributable to tax shelter items of corporations.) Generally, the most important factor is the extent of the taxpayer's effort to assess the taxpayer's proper tax liability. Circumstances that may indicate reasonable cause and good faith include an honest misunderstanding of fact or law that is reasonable in light of all of the facts and circumstances, including the experience, knowledge, and education of the taxpayer. An isolated computational or transcriptional error generally is not inconsistent with reasonable cause and good faith. Reliance on an information return or on the advice of a professional tax advisor or an appraiser does not necessarily demonstrate reasonable cause and good faith. Similarly, reasonable cause and good faith is not necessarily indicated by reliance on facts that, unknown to the taxpayer, are incorrect. Reliance on an information return, professional advice, or other facts, however, constitutes reasonable cause and good faith if, under all the circumstances, such reliance was reasonable and the taxpayer acted in good faith. (See paragraph (c) of this section for certain rules relating to reliance on the advice of others.) For example, reliance on erroneous information (such as an error relating to the cost or adjusted basis of property, the date property was placed in service, or the amount of opening or closing inventory) inadvertently included in data compiled by the various divisions of a multidivisional corporation or in financial books and records prepared by those divisions generally indicates reasonable cause and good faith, provided the corporation employed internal controls and procedures, reasonable under the circumstances, that were designed to identify such factual errors. Reasonable cause and good faith ordinarily is not indicated by the mere fact that there is an appraisal of the value of property. Other factors to consider include the methodology and assumptions underlying the appraisal, the appraised value, the relationship between appraised value and purchase price, the circumstances under which the appraisal was obtained, and the appraiser's relationship to the taxpayer or to the activity in which the property is used. (See paragraph (g) of this section for certain rules relating to appraisals for charitable deduction property.) A taxpayer's reliance on erroneous information reported on a Form W-2, Form 1099, or other information return indicates reasonable cause and good faith, provided the taxpayer did not know or have reason to know that the information was incorrect. Generally, a taxpayer knows, or has reason to know, that the information on an information return is incorrect if such information is inconsistent with other information reported or otherwise furnished to the taxpayer, or with the taxpayer's knowledge of the transaction. This knowledge includes, for example, the taxpayer's knowledge of the terms of his employment relationship or of the rate of return on a payor's obligation.

(2) *Examples.*—The following examples illustrate this paragraph (b). They do not involve tax shelter items. (See paragraph (e) of this section for certain rules relating to the substantial understatement penalty attributable to the tax shelter items of corporations.)

Example 1. A, an individual calendar year taxpayer, engages B, a professional tax advisor, to give A advice concerning the deductibility of certain state and local taxes. A provides B with full details concerning the taxes at issue. B advises A that the taxes are fully deductible. A, in preparing his own tax return, claims a deduction for the taxes. Absent other facts, and assuming the facts and circumstances surrounding B's advice and A's reliance on such advice satisfy the requirements of paragraph (c) of this section, A is considered to have demonstrated good faith by seeking the advice of a professional tax advisor, and to have shown reasonable cause for any underpayment attributable to the deduction claimed for the taxes. However, if A had sought advice from someone that A knew, or should have known, lacked knowledge in the relevant aspects of Federal tax law, or if other facts demonstrate that A failed to act reasonably or in good faith, A would not be considered to have shown reasonable cause or to have acted in good faith.

* * *

(c) *Reliance on opinion or advice.*—(1) *Facts and circumstances; minimum requirements.*—All facts and circumstances must be taken into account in determining whether a taxpayer has reasonably relied in good faith on advice (including the opinion of a professional tax advisor) as to the treatment of the taxpayer (or any entity, plan, or arrangement) under Federal tax law. For example, the taxpayer's education, sophistication and business experience will be relevant in determining whether the taxpayer's reliance on tax advice was reasonable and made in good faith. In no event will a taxpayer be considered to have reasonably relied in good faith on advice (including an opinion) unless the requirements of this paragraph (c)(1) are satisfied. The fact that these requirements are satisfied, however, will not necessarily establish that the taxpayer reasonably relied on the advice (including the opinion of a tax advisor) in good faith. For example, reliance may not be reasonable or in good faith if the taxpayer knew, or reasonably should have known, that the advisor lacked knowledge in the relevant aspects of Federal tax law.

(i) *All facts and circumstances considered.*—The advice must be based upon all pertinent facts and circumstances and the law as it relates to those facts and circumstances. For example, the advice must take into account the taxpayer's purposes (and the relative weight of such purposes) for entering into a transaction and for structuring a transaction in a particular manner. In addition, the requirements of this paragraph (c)(1) are not satisfied if the taxpayer fails to disclose a fact that it knows, or reasonably should know, to be relevant to the proper tax treatment of an item.

(ii) *No unreasonable assumptions.*—The advice must not be based on unreasonable factual or legal assumptions (including assumptions as to future events) and must not unreasonably rely on the representations, statements, findings, or agreements of the taxpayer or any other person. For example, the advice must not be based upon a representation or assumption which the taxpayer knows, or has reason to know, is unlikely to be true, such as an inaccurate representation or assumption as to the taxpayer's purposes for entering into a transaction or for structuring a transaction in a particular manner.

(iii) *Reliance on the invalidity of a regulation.*—A taxpayer may not rely on an opinion or advice that a regulation is invalid to establish that the taxpayer acted with reasonable cause and good faith unless the taxpayer adequately disclosed, in accordance with § 1.6662-3(c)(2), the position that the regulation in question is invalid.

(2) *Advice defined.*—Advice is any communication, including the opinion of a professional tax advisor, setting forth the analysis or conclusion of a person, other than the taxpayer, provided to (or for the benefit of) the taxpayer and on which the taxpayer relies, directly or indirectly, with respect to the imposition of the section 6662 accuracy-related penalty. Advice does not have to be in any particular form.

(3) *Cross-reference.*—For rules applicable to advisors, see e.g., §§ 1.6694-1 through 1.6694-3 (regarding preparer penalties), 31 CFR 10.22 (regarding diligence as to accuracy), 31 CFR 10.33 (regarding tax shelter opinions), and 31 CFR 10.34 (regarding standards for advising with respect to tax return positions and for preparing or signing returns).

(d) *Underpayments attributable to reportable transactions.*—If any portion of an underpayment is attributable to a reportable transaction, as defined in § 1.6011-4(b) (or § 1.6011-4T(b), as applicable), then failure by the taxpayer to disclose the transaction in accordance with § 1.6011-4 (or § 1.6011-4T, as applicable) is a strong indication that the taxpayer did not act in good faith with respect to the portion of the underpayment attributable to the reportable transaction.

(e) *Pass-through items.*—The determination of whether a taxpayer acted with reasonable cause and in good faith with respect to an underpayment that is related to an item reflected on the return of a pass-through entity is made on the basis of all pertinent facts and circumstances, including the taxpayer's own actions, as well as the actions of the pass-through entity.

(f) *Special rules for substantial understatement penalty attributable to tax shelter items of corporations.*—(1) *In general; facts and circumstances.*—The determination of whether a corporation acted with reasonable cause and in good faith in its treatment of a tax shelter item (as defined in § 1.6662-4(g)(3)) is based on all pertinent facts and circumstances. Paragraphs (f)(2), (3), and (4) of this section set forth rules that apply, in the case of a penalty attributable to a substantial understatement of income tax (within the meaning of section 6662(d)), in determining whether a corporation acted with reasonable cause and in good faith with respect to a tax shelter item.

(2) *Reasonable cause based on legal justification.*—(i) *Minimum requirements.*—A corporation's legal justification (as defined in paragraph (f)(2)(ii) of this section) may be taken into account, as appropriate, in establishing that the corporation acted with reasonable cause and in good faith in its treatment of a tax shelter item only if the authority requirement of paragraph (f)(2)(i)(A) of this section and the belief requirement of paragraph (f)(2)(i)(B) of this section are satisfied (the minimum requirements). Thus, a failure to satisfy the minimum requirements will preclude a finding of reasonable cause and good faith based (in whole or in part) on the corporation's legal justification.

(A) *Authority requirement.*—The authority requirement is satisfied only if there is substantial authority (within the meaning of § 1.6662-4(d)) for the tax treatment of the item.

(B) *Belief requirement.*—The belief requirement is satisfied only if, based on all facts and circumstances, the corporation reasonably believed, at the time the return was filed, that the tax treatment of the item was more likely than not the proper treatment. For purposes of the preceding sentence, a corporation is considered reasonably to believe that the tax treatment of an item is more likely than not the proper-tax treatment if (without taking into account the possibility that a return will not be audited, that an issue will not be raised on audit, or that an issue will be settled)—

(1) The corporation analyzes the pertinent facts and authorities in the manner described in § 1.6662-4(d)(3)(ii), and in reliance upon that analysis, reasonably concludes in good faith that there is a greater than 50-percent likelihood that the tax treatment of the item will be upheld if challenged by the Internal Revenue Service; or

(2) The corporation reasonably relies in good faith on the opinion of a professional tax advisor, if the opinion is based on the tax advisor's analysis of the pertinent facts and authorities in the manner described in § 1.6662-4(d)(3)(ii) and unambiguously states that the tax advisor concludes that there is a greater than 50-percent likelihood that the tax treatment of the item will be upheld if challenged by the Internal Revenue Service. (For this purpose, the requirements of paragraph (c) of this section must be met with respect to the opinion of a professional tax advisor.)

(ii) *Legal justification defined.*—For purposes of this paragraph (f), *legal justification* includes any justification relating to the treatment or characterization under the Federal tax law of the tax shelter item or of the entity, plan, or arrangement that gave rise to the item. Thus, a taxpayer's belief (whether independently formed or based on the advice of others) as to the merits of the taxpayer's underlying position is a legal justification.

(3) *Minimum requirements not dispositive.*—Satisfaction of the minimum requirements of paragraph (f)(2) of this section is an important factor to be considered in determining whether a corporate taxpayer acted with reasonable cause and in good faith, but is not necessarily dispositive. For example, depending on the circumstances, satisfaction of the minimum requirements may not be dispositive if the taxpayer's participation in the tax shelter lacked significant business purpose, if the taxpayer claimed tax benefits that are unreasonable in comparison to the taxpayer's investment in the tax shelter, or if the taxpayer agreed with the organizer or promoter of the tax shelter that the taxpayer would protect the confidentiality of the tax aspects of the structure of the tax shelter.

(4) *Other factors.*—Facts and circumstances other than a corporation's legal justification may be taken into account, as appropriate, in determining whether the corporation acted with reasonable cause and in good faith with respect to a tax shelter item regardless of whether the minimum requirements of paragraph (f)(2) of this section are satisfied.

(g) *Transactions between persons described in section 482 and net section 482 transfer price adjustments.*—[Reserved]

(h) *Valuation misstatements of charitable deduction property.*—(1) *In general.*—There may be reasonable cause and good faith with respect to a portion of an underpayment that is attributable to a substantial (or gross) valuation misstatement of charitable deduction property (as defined in paragraph (h)(2) of this section) only if—

(i) The claimed value of the property was based on a qualified appraisal (as defined in paragraph (h)(2) of this section) by a qualified appraiser (as defined in paragraph (h)(2) of this section); and

(ii) In addition to obtaining a qualified appraisal, the taxpayer made a good faith investigation of the value of the contributed property.

(2) *Definitions.*—For purposes of this paragraph (h):

Charitable deduction property means any property (other than money or publicly traded securities, as defined in § 1.170A-13(c)(7)(xi)) contributed by the taxpayer in a contribution for which a deduction was claimed under section 170.

Qualified appraisal means a qualified appraisal as defined in § 1.170A-13(c)(3).

Qualified appraiser means a qualified appraiser as defined in § 1.170A-13(c)(5).

(3) *Special rules.*—The rules of this paragraph (h) apply regardless of whether § 1.170A-13 permits a taxpayer to claim a charitable contribution deduction for the property without obtaining a qualified appraisal. The rules of this paragraph (h) apply in addition to the generally applicable rules concerning reasonable cause and good faith. [Reg. § 1.6664-4.]

□ [*T.D.* 8381, 12-30-91. *Amended by T.D.* 8617, 8-31-95; *T.D.* 8790, 12-1-98 *and T.D.* 9109, 12-29-2003.]

Assessable Penalties

§ 1.6694-2. Penalty for understatement due to an unreasonable position.—(a) *In general.*—(1) *Proscribed conduct.*—Except as otherwise provided in this section, a tax return preparer is liable for a penalty under section 6694(a) equal to the greater of $1,000 or 50 percent of the income derived (or to be derived) by the tax return preparer for any return or claim for refund that it prepares that results in an understatement of liability due to a position if the tax return preparer knew (or reasonably should have known) of the position and either—

(i) The position is with respect to a tax shelter (as defined in section 6662(d)(2)(C)(ii)) or a reportable transaction to which section 6662A applies, and it was not reasonable to believe that the position would more likely than not be sustained on its merits;

(ii) The position was not disclosed as provided in this section, the position is not with respect to a tax shelter (as defined in section 6662(d)(2)(C)(ii)) or a reportable transaction to which section 6662A applies, and there was not substantial authority for the position; or

(iii) The position (other than a position with respect to a tax shelter or a reportable transaction to which section 6662A applies) was disclosed as provided in this section but there was no reasonable basis for the position.

(2) *Special rule for corporations, partnerships, and other firms.*—A firm that employs a tax return preparer subject to a penalty under section 6694(a) (or a firm of which the individual tax return preparer is a partner, member, shareholder or other equity holder) is also subject to penalty if, and only if—

(i) One or more members of the principal management (or principal officers) of the firm or a branch office participated in or knew of the conduct proscribed by section 6694(a);

(ii) The corporation, partnership, or other firm entity failed to provide reasonable and appropriate procedures for review of the position for which the penalty is imposed; or

(iii) The corporation, partnership, or other firm entity disregarded its reasonable and appropriate review procedures through willfulness, recklessness, or gross indifference (including ignoring facts that would lead a person of reasonable prudence and competence to investigate or ascertain) in the formulation of the advice, or the preparation of the return or claim for refund, that included the position for which the penalty is imposed.

(b) *Reasonable to believe that the position would more likely than not be sustained on its merits.*—(1) *In general.*—If a position is with respect to a tax shelter (as defined in section 6662(d)(2)(C)(ii)) or a reportable transaction to which section 6662A applies, it is "reasonable to believe that a position would more likely than not be sustained on its merits" if the tax return preparer analyzes the pertinent facts and authorities and, in reliance upon that analysis, reasonably concludes in good faith that the position has a greater than 50 percent likelihood of being sustained on its merits. In reaching this conclusion, the possibility that the position will not be challenged by the Internal Revenue Service (IRS) (for example, because the taxpayer's return may not be audited or because the issue may not be raised on audit) is not to be taken into account. The analysis prescribed by § 1.6662-4(d)(3)(ii) (or any successor provision) for purposes of determining whether substantial authority is present applies for purposes of determining whether the more likely than not standard is satisfied. Whether a tax return preparer meets this standard will be determined based upon all facts and circumstances, including the tax return preparer's diligence. In determining the level of diligence in a particular situation, the tax return preparer's experience with the area of Federal tax law and familiarity with the taxpayer's affairs, as well as the complexity of the issues and facts, will be taken into account. A tax return preparer may reasonably believe that a position more likely than not would be sustained on its merits despite the absence of other types of authority if the position is supported by a well-reasoned construction of the applicable statutory provision. For purposes of determining whether it is reasonable to believe that the position would more likely than not be sustained on the merits, a tax return preparer may rely in good faith without verification upon information furnished by the taxpayer and information and advice furnished by another advisor, another tax return preparer, or other party (including another advisor or tax return preparer at the tax return preparer's firm), as provided in § § 1.6694-1(e) and 1.6694-2(e)(5).

(2) *Authorities.*—The authorities considered in determining whether a position satisfies the more likely than not standard are those authorities provided in § 1.6662-4(d)(3)(iii) (or any successor provision).

(3) *Written determinations.*—The tax return preparer may avoid the section 6694(a) penalty by taking the position that the tax return preparer reasonably believed that the taxpayer's position satisfies the "more likely than not" standard if the taxpayer is the subject of a "written determination" as provided in § 1.6662-4(d)(3)(iv)(A).

(4) *Taxpayer's jurisdiction.*—The applicability of court cases to the taxpayer by reason of the taxpayer's residence in a particular jurisdiction is not taken into account in determining whether it is reasonable to believe that the position would more likely than not be sustained on the merits. Notwithstanding the preceding sentence, the tax return preparer may reasonably believe that the position would more likely than not be sustained on the merits if the position is supported by controlling precedent of a United States Court of Appeals to which the taxpayer has a right of appeal with respect to the item.

(5) *When "more likely than not" standard must be satisfied.*—For purposes of this section, the requirement that a position satisfies the "more likely than not" standard must be satisfied on the date the return is deemed prepared, as prescribed by § 1.6694-1(a)(2).

* * *

(d) *Exception for adequate disclosure of positions with a reasonable basis.*—(1) *In general.*—The section 6694(a) penalty will not be imposed on a tax return preparer if the position taken (other than a position with respect to a tax shelter or a reportable transaction to which section 6662A applies) has a reasonable basis and is adequately disclosed within the meaning of paragraph (c)(3) of this section. For an exception to the section 6694(a) penalty for reasonable cause and good faith, see paragraph (e) of this section.

(2) *Reasonable basis.*—For purposes of this section, "reasonable basis" has the same meaning as in § 1.6662-3(b)(3) or any successor provision of the accuracy-related penalty regulations. For purposes of determining whether the tax return preparer has a reasonable basis for a position, a tax return preparer may rely in good faith without verification upon information furnished by the taxpayer and information and advice furnished by another advisor, another tax return preparer, or other party (including another advisor or tax return preparer at the tax return preparer's firm), as provided in § § 1.6694-1(e) and 1.6694-2(e)(5).

(3) *Adequate disclosure.*—(i) *Signing tax return preparers.*—In the case of a signing tax return preparer within the meaning of § 301.7701-15(b)(1) of this chapter, disclosure of a position (other than a position with respect to a tax shelter or a reportable transaction to which section 6662A applies) for which there is a reasonable basis but for which there is not substantial authority is adequate if the tax return preparer meets any of the following standards:

(A) The position is disclosed in accordance with § 1.6662-4(f) (which permits disclosure on a properly completed and filed Form 8275, "Disclosure Statement," or Form 8275-R, "Regulation Disclosure Statement," as appropriate, or on the tax return in accordance with the annual revenue procedure described in § 1.6662-4(f)(2));

(B) The tax return preparer provides the taxpayer with the prepared tax return that includes the disclosure in accordance with § 1.6662-4(f); or

(C) For returns or claims for refund that are subject to penalties pursuant to section 6662 other than the accuracy-related penalty attributable to a substantial understatement of income tax under section 6662(b)(2) and (d), the tax return preparer advises the taxpayer of the penalty standards applicable to the taxpayer under section 6662. The tax return preparer must also contemporaneously document the advice in the tax return preparer's files.

(ii) *Nonsigning tax return preparers.*—In the case of a nonsigning tax return preparer within the meaning of § 301.7701-15(b)(2) of this chapter, disclosure of a position (other than a position with respect to a tax shelter or a reportable transaction to which section 6662A applies) that satisfies the reasonable basis standard but does not satisfy the substantial authority standard is adequate if the position is disclosed in accordance with § 1.6662-4(f) (which permits disclosure on a properly completed and filed Form 8275 or Form 8275-R, as applicable, or on the return in accordance with an annual revenue procedure described in § 1.6662-4(f)(2)). In addition, disclosure of a position is adequate in the case of a nonsigning tax return preparer if, with respect to that position, the tax return preparer complies with the provisions of paragraph (d)(3)(ii)(A) or (B) of this section, whichever is applicable.

(A) *Advice to taxpayers.*—If a nonsigning tax return preparer provides advice to the taxpayer with respect to a position (other than a position with respect to a tax shelter or a reportable transaction to which section 6662A applies) for which there is a reasonable basis but for which there is not substantial authority, disclosure of that position is adequate if the tax return preparer advises the taxpayer of any opportunity to avoid penalties under section 6662 that could apply to the position, if relevant, and of the standards for disclosure to the extent applicable. The tax return preparer must also contemporaneously document the advice in the tax return preparer's files. The contemporaneous documentation should reflect that the affected taxpayer has been advised by a tax return preparer in the firm of the potential penalties and the opportunity to avoid penalty through disclosure.

(B) *Advice to another tax return preparer.*—If a nonsigning tax return preparer provides advice to another tax return preparer with respect to a position (other than a position with respect to a tax shelter or a reportable transaction to which section 6662A applies) for which there is a reasonable basis but for which there is not substantial authority, disclosure of that position is adequate if the tax return preparer advises the other tax return preparer that disclosure under section 6694(a) may be required. The tax return preparer must also contemporaneously document the advice in the tax return preparer's files. The contemporaneous documentation should reflect that the tax return preparer outside the firm has been advised that disclosure under section 6694(a) may be required. If the advice is to another nonsigning tax return preparer within the same firm, contemporaneous documentation is satisfied if there is a single instance of contemporaneous documentation within the firm.

* * *

(e) *Exception for reasonable cause and good faith.*—The penalty under section 6694(a) will not be imposed if, considering all the facts and circumstances, it is determined that the understatement was due to reasonable cause and that the tax return preparer acted in good faith. Factors to consider include:

(1) *Nature of the error causing the understatement.*—The error resulted from a provision that was complex, uncommon, or highly technical, and a competent tax return preparer of tax returns or claims for refund of the type at issue reasonably could have made the error. The reasonable cause and good faith exception, however, does not apply to an error that would have been apparent from a general review of the return or claim for refund by the tax return preparer.

(2) *Frequency of errors.*—The understatement was the result of an isolated error (such as an inadvertent mathematical or clerical error) rather than a number of errors. Although the reasonable cause and good faith exception generally applies to an isolated error, it does not apply if the isolated error is so obvious, flagrant, or material that it should have been discovered during a review of the return or claim for refund. Furthermore, the reasonable cause and good faith exception does not apply if there is a pattern of errors on a return or claim for refund even though any one error, in isolation, would have qualified for the reasonable cause and good faith exception.

(3) *Materiality of errors.*—The understatement was not material in relation to the correct tax liability. The reasonable cause and good faith exception generally applies if the understatement is of a relatively immaterial amount. Nevertheless, even an immaterial understatement may not qualify for the reasonable cause and good faith exception if the error or errors creating the understatement are sufficiently obvious or numerous.

(4) *Tax return preparer's normal office practice.*—The tax return preparer's normal office practice, when considered together with other facts and circumstances, such as the knowledge of the tax return preparer, indicates that the error in question would occur rarely and the normal office practice was followed in preparing the return or claim for refund in question. Such a normal office practice must be a system for promoting accuracy and consistency in the preparation of returns or claims for refund and generally would include, in the case of a signing tax return preparer, checklists, methods for obtaining necessary information from the taxpayer, a review of the prior year's return, and review procedures. Notwithstanding these rules, the reasonable cause and good faith exception does not apply if there is a flagrant error on a return or claim for refund, a pattern of errors on a return or claim for refund, or a repetition of the same or similar errors on numerous returns or claims for refund.

(5) *Reliance on advice of others.*—For purposes of demonstrating reasonable cause and good faith, a tax return preparer may rely without verification upon advice and information furnished by the taxpayer and information and advice furnished by another advisor, another tax return preparer or other party, as provided

in § 1.6694-1(e). The tax return preparer may rely in good faith on the advice of, or schedules or other documents prepared by, the taxpayer, another advisor, another tax return preparer, or other party (including another advisor or tax return preparer at the tax return preparer's firm), who the tax return preparer had reason to believe was competent to render the advice or other information. The advice or information may be written or oral, but in either case the burden of establishing that the advice or information was received is on the tax return preparer. A tax return preparer is not considered to have relied in good faith if—

(i) The advice or information is unreasonable on its face;

(ii) The tax return preparer knew or should have known that the other party providing the advice or information was not aware of all relevant facts; or

(iii) The tax return preparer knew or should have known (given the nature of the tax return preparer's practice), at the time the return or claim for refund was prepared, that the advice or information was no longer reliable due to developments in the law since the time the advice was given.

(6) *Reliance on generally accepted administrative or industry practice.*—The tax return preparer reasonably relied in good faith on generally accepted administrative or industry practice in taking the position that resulted in the understatement. A tax return preparer is not considered to have relied in good faith if the tax return preparer knew or should have known (given the nature of the tax return preparer's practice), at the time the return or claim for refund was prepared, that the administrative or industry practice was no longer reliable due to developments in the law or IRS administrative practice since the time the practice was developed.

* * *

[Reg. § 1.6694-2.]

☐ [*T.D.* 7519, 11-17-77. *Amended by T.D.* 8382, 12-30-91 *and T.D.* 9436, 12-15-2008 (*corrected* 1-28-2009).]

§ 1.6694-3. Penalty for understatement due to willful, reckless, or intentional conduct.—(a) *In general.*—(1) *Proscribed conduct.*—A tax return preparer is liable for a penalty under section 6694(b) equal to the greater of $5,000 or 50 percent of the income derived (or to be derived) by the tax return preparer if any part of an understatement of liability for a return or claim for refund that is prepared is due to—

(i) A willful attempt by a tax return preparer to understate in any manner the liability for tax on the return or claim for refund; or

(ii) Any reckless or intentional disregard of rules or regulations by a tax return preparer.

(2) *Special rule for corporations, partnerships, and other firms.*—A firm that employs a tax return preparer subject to a penalty under section 6694(b) (or a firm of which the individual tax return preparer is a partner, member, shareholder or other equity holder) is also subject to penalty if, and only if—

(i) One or more members of the principal management (or principal officers) of the firm or a branch office participated in or knew of the conduct proscribed by section 6694(b);

(ii) The corporation, partnership, or other firm entity failed to provide reasonable and appropriate procedures for review of the position for which the penalty is imposed; or

(iii) The corporation, partnership, or other firm entity disregarded its reasonable and appropriate review procedures through willfulness, recklessness, or gross indifference (including ignoring facts that would lead a person of reasonable prudence and competence to investigate or ascertain) in the formulation of the advice, or the preparation of the return or claim for refund, that included the position for which the penalty is imposed.

(b) *Willful attempt to understate liability.*—A preparer is considered to have willfully attempted to understate liability if the preparer disregards, in an attempt wrongfully to reduce the tax liability of the taxpayer, information furnished by the taxpayer or other persons. For example, if a preparer disregards information concerning certain items of taxable income furnished by the taxpayer or other persons, the preparer is subject to the penalty. Similarly, if a taxpayer states to a preparer that the taxpayer has only two dependents, and the preparer reports six dependents on the return, the preparer is subject to the penalty.

(c) *Reckless or intentional disregard.*—(1) Except as provided in paragraphs (c)(2) and (c)(3) of this section, a preparer is considered to have recklessly or intentionally disregarded a rule or regulation if the preparer takes a position on the return or claim for refund that is contrary to a rule or regulation (as defined in paragraph (f) of this section) and the preparer knows of, or is reckless in not knowing of, the rule or regulation in question. A preparer is reckless in not knowing of a rule or regulation if the preparer makes little or no effort to determine whether a rule or regulation exists, under circumstances which demonstrate a substantial deviation from the standard of conduct that a reasonable preparer would observe in the situation.

(2) A tax return preparer is not considered to have recklessly or intentionally disregarded a rule or regulation if the position contrary to the rule or regulation has a reasonable basis as defined in § 1.6694-2(d)(2) and is adequately disclosed in accordance with §§ 1.6694-2(d)(3)(i)(A) or (C) or 1.6694-2(d)(3)(ii). In the case of a position contrary to a regulation, the position must represent a good faith challenge to the validity of the regulation and, when disclosed in accordance with §§ 1.6694-2(d)(3)(i)(A) or (C) or 1.6694-2(d)(3)(ii), the tax return preparer must identify the regulation being challenged. For purposes of this section, disclosure on the return in accordance with an annual revenue procedure under § 1.6662-4(f)(2) is not applicable.

(3) In the case of a position contrary to a revenue ruling or notice (other than a notice of proposed rulemaking) published by the Internal Revenue Service in the Internal Revenue Bulletin, a tax return preparer also is not considered to have recklessly or intentionally disregarded the ruling or notice if the position meets the substantial authority standard described in § 1.6662-4(d) and is not with respect to a reportable transaction to which section 6662A applies.

* * *

[Reg. § 1.6694-3.]

☐ [*T.D.* 8382, 12-30-91. *Amended by T.D.* 9436, 12-15-2008 (*corrected* 1-28-2009).]

Definitions

§ 301.7701-1. Classification of organizations for federal tax purposes.—(a) *Organizations for federal tax purposes.*—(1) *In general.*—The Internal Revenue Code prescribes the classification of various organizations for federal tax purposes. Whether an organization is an entity separate from its owners for federal tax purposes is a matter of federal tax law and does not depend on whether the organization is recognized as an entity under local law.

(2) *Certain joint undertakings give rise to entities for federal tax purposes.*—A joint venture or other contractual arrangement may create a separate entity for federal tax purposes if the participants carry on a trade, business, financial operation, or venture and divide the profits therefrom. For example, a separate entity exists for federal tax purposes if co-owners of an apartment building lease space and in addition provide services to the occupants either directly or through an agent. Nevertheless, a joint undertaking merely to share expenses does not create a separate entity for federal tax purposes. For example, if two or more persons jointly construct a ditch merely to drain surface water from their properties, they have not created a separate entity for federal tax purposes. Similarly, mere co-ownership of property that is maintained, kept in repair, and rented or leased does not constitute a separate entity for federal tax purposes. For example, if an individual owner, or tenants in common, of farm property lease it to a farmer for a cash rental or a share of the crops, they do not necessarily create a separate entity for federal tax purposes.

(3) *Certain local law entities not recognized.*—An entity formed under local law is not always recognized as a separate entity for federal tax purposes. For example, an organization wholly owned by a State is not recognized as a separate entity for federal tax purposes if it is an integral part of the State. Similarly, tribes incorporated under section 17 of the Indian Reorganization Act of 1934, as amended, 25 U.S.C. 477, or under section 3 of the Oklahoma Indian Welfare Act, as amended, 25 U.S.C. 503, are not recognized as separate entities for federal tax purposes.

(4) *Single owner organizations.*—Under §§ 301.7701-2 and 301.7701-3, certain organizations that have a single owner can choose to be recognized or disregarded as entities separate from their owners.

(b) *Classification of organizations.*—The classification of organizations that are recognized as separate entities is determined under §§ 301.7701-2, 301.7701-3, and 301.7701-4 unless a provision of the Internal Revenue Code (such as section 860A addressing Real Estate Mortgage Investment Conduits (REMICs)) provides for special treatment of that organization. For the classification of organizations as trusts, see § 301.7701-4. That section provides that trusts generally do not have associates or an objective to carry on business for profit. Sections 301.7701-2 and 301.7701-3 provide rules for classifying organizations that are not classified as trusts.

(c) *Cost sharing arrangements.*—A cost sharing arrangement that is described in § 1.482-7 of this chapter, including any arrangement that the Commissioner treats as a CSA under § 1.482-7(b)(5) of this chapter, is not recognized as a separate entity for purposes of the Internal Revenue Code. See § 1.482-7 of this chapter for the rules regarding CSAs.

(d) *Domestic and foreign business entities.*—See § 301.7701-5 for the rules that determine whether a business entity is domestic or foreign.

(e) *State.*—For purposes of this section and §301.7701-2, the term *State* includes the District of Columbia.

* * *

[Reg. §301.7701-1.]

☐ [*T.D.* 6503, 11-15-80. *Amended by T.D.* 6797, 2-2-65; *T.D.* 7515, 10-17-77; *T.D.* 8697, 12-17-96; *T.D.* 9153, 8-11-2004; *T.D.* 9246, 1-27-2006; *T.D.* 9441, 12-31-2008 *and T.D.* 9568, 12-16-2011.]

Proposed Amendment to Regulation

§301.7701-1. Classification of organizations for Federal tax purposes.—(a) * * *

(5) *Series and series organizations.*—(i) *Entity status of a domestic series.*—For Federal tax purposes, except as provided in paragraph (a)(5)(ix) of this section, a series (as defined in paragraph (a)(5)(viii)(C) of this section) organized or established under the laws of the United States or of any State, whether or not a juridical person for local law purposes, is treated as an entity formed under local law.

* * *

(iii) *Recognition of entity status.*—Whether a series that is treated as a local law entity under paragraph (a)(5)(i) or (ii) of this section is recognized as a separate entity for Federal tax purposes is determined under this section and general tax principles.

(iv) *Classification of series.*—The classification of a series that is recognized as a separate entity for Federal tax purposes is determined under paragraph (b) of this section.

(v) *Jurisdiction in which series is organized or established.*—A series is treated as created or organized under the laws of a State or foreign jurisdiction if the series is established under the laws of such jurisdiction. See §301.7701-5 for rules that determine whether a business entity is domestic or foreign.

(vi) *Ownership of series and the assets of series.*—For Federal tax purposes, the ownership of interests in a series and of the assets associated with a series is determined under general tax principles. A series organization is not treated as the owner for Federal tax purposes of a series or of the assets associated with a series merely because the series organization holds legal title to the assets associated with the series.

* * *

(viii) *Definitions.*—(A) *Series organization.*—A *series organization* is a juridical entity that establishes and maintains, or under which is established and maintained, a series (as defined in paragraph (a)(5)(viii)(C) of this section). A series organization includes a series limited liability company, series partnership, series trust, protected cell company, segregated cell company, segregated portfolio company, or segregated account company.

(B) *Series statute.*—A *series statute* is a statute of a State or foreign jurisdiction that explicitly provides for the organization or establishment of a series of a juridical person and explicitly permits—

(1) Members or participants of a series organization to have rights, powers, or duties with respect to the series;

(2) A series to have separate rights, powers, or duties with respect to specified property or obligations; and

(3) The segregation of assets and liabilities such that none of the debts and liabilities of the series organization (other than liabilities to the State or foreign jurisdiction related to the organization or operation of the series organization, such as franchise fees or administrative costs) or of any other series of the series organization are enforceable against the assets of a particular series of the series organization.

(C) *Series.*—A *series* is a segregated group of assets and liabilities that is established pursuant to a series statute (as defined in paragraph (a)(5)(viii)(B) of this section) by agreement of a series organization (as defined in paragraph (a)(5)(viii)(A) of this section). A series includes a series, cell, segregated account, or segregated portfolio, including a cell, segregated account, or segregated portfolio that is formed under the insurance code of a jurisdiction or is engaged in an insurance business. However, the term *series* does not include a segregated asset account of a life insurance company. See section 817(d)(1); §1.817-5(e). An election, agreement, or other arrangement that permits debts and liabilities of other series or the series organization to be enforceable against the assets of a particular series, or a failure to comply with the record keeping requirements for the limitation on liability available under the relevant series statute, will be disregarded for purposes of this paragraph (a)(5)(viii)(C).

* * *

(x) *Examples.*—The following examples illustrate the principles of this paragraph (a)(5):

Example 1. Domestic Series LLC. (i) *Facts.* Series LLC is a series organization (within the meaning of paragraph (a)(5)(viii)(A) of this section). Series LLC has three members (1, 2, and 3). Series LLC establishes two series (A and B) pursuant to the LLC statute of state Y, a series statute within the meaning of paragraph (a)(5)(viii)(B) of this section. Under general tax principles, Members 1 and 2 are the owners of Series A, and Member 3 is the owner of Series B. Series A and B are not described in §301.7701-2(b) or paragraph (a)(3) of this section and are not trusts within the meaning of §301.7701-4.

(ii) *Analysis*. Under paragraph (a)(5)(i) of this section, Series A and Series B are each treated as an entity formed under local law. The classification of Series A and Series B is determined under paragraph (b) of this section. The default classification under §301.7701-3 of Series A is a partnership and of Series B is a disregarded entity.

* * *

[Prop. Reg. §301.7701-1.]

[Proposed 9-14-2010.]

§301.7701-2. Business entities; definitions.—(a) *Business entities.*—For purposes of this section and §301.7701-3, a *business entity* is any entity recognized for federal tax purposes (including an entity with a single owner that may be disregarded as an entity separate from its owner under §301.7701-3) that is not properly classified as a trust under §301.7701-4 or otherwise subject to special treatment under the Internal Revenue Code. A business entity with two or more members is classified for federal tax purposes as either a corporation or a partnership. A business entity with only one owner is classified as a corporation or is disregarded; if the entity is disregarded, its activities are treated in the same manner as a sole proprietorship, branch, or division of the owner. But see paragraphs (c)(2)(iii) through (vi) of this section for special rules that apply to an eligible entity that is otherwise disregarded as an entity separate from its owner.

(b) *Corporations.*—For federal tax purposes, the term *corporation* means—

(1) A business entity organized under a Federal or State statute, or under a statute of a federally recognized Indian tribe, if the statute describes or refers to the entity as incorporated or as a corporation, body corporate, or body politic;

(2) An association (as determined under §301.7701-3);

(3) A business entity organized under a State statute, if the statute describes or refers to the entity as a joint-stock company or joint-stock association;

(4) An insurance company;

(5) A State-chartered business entity conducting banking activities, if any of its deposits are insured under the Federal Deposit Insurance Act, as amended, 12 U.S.C. 1811 et seq., or a similar federal statute;

(6) A business entity wholly owned by a State or any political subdivision thereof, or a business entity wholly owned by a foreign government or any other entity described in §1.892-2T;

(7) A business entity that is taxable as a corporation under a provision of the Internal Revenue Code other than section 7701(a)(3); and

* * *

(c) *Other business entities.*—For federal tax purposes—

(1) The term ***partnership*** means a business entity that is not a corporation under paragraph (b) of this section and that has at least two members.

(2) *Wholly owned entities.*—(i) *In general.*—Except as otherwise provided in this paragraph (c), a business entity that has a single owner and is not a corporation under paragraph (b) of this section is disregarded as an entity separate from its owner.

(ii) *Special rule for certain business entities.*—If the single owner of a business entity is a bank (as defined in section 581, or, in the case of a foreign bank, as defined in section 585(a)(2)(B) without regard to the second sentence thereof), then the special rules applicable to banks under the Internal Revenue Code will continue to apply to the single owner as if the wholly owned entity were a separate entity. For this purpose, the special rules applicable to banks under the Internal Revenue Code do not include the rules under sections 864(c), 882(c), and 884.

(iii) *Tax liabilities of certain disregarded entities.*—(A) *In general.*—An entity that is disregarded as separate from its owner for any purpose under this section is treated as an entity separate from its owner for purposes of—

(1) Federal tax liabilities of the entity with respect to any taxable period for which the entity was not disregarded;

(2) Federal tax liabilities of any other entity for which the entity is liable; and

(3) Refunds or credits of Federal tax.

(B) *Examples.*—The following examples illustrate the application of paragraph (c)(2)(iii)(A) of this section:

Example 1. In 2006, X, a domestic corporation that reports its taxes on a calendar year basis, merges into Z, a domestic LLC wholly owned by Y that is disregarded as an entity separate from Y, in a state law merger. X was not a member of a consolidated group at any time during its taxable year ending in December 2005. Under the applicable state law, Z is the successor to X and is liable for all of X's debts. In 2009, the Internal Revenue Service (IRS) seeks to extend the period of limitations on assessment for X's 2005 taxable year. Because Z is the successor to X and is liable for X's 2005 taxes that remain unpaid, Z is the proper party to sign the consent to extend the period of limitations.

Example 2. The facts are the same as in *Example 1*, except that in 2007, the IRS determines that X miscalculated and underreported its income tax liability for 2005. Because Z is the successor to X and is liable for X's 2005 taxes that remain unpaid, the deficiency may be assessed against Z and, in the event that Z fails to pay the liability after notice and demand, a general tax lien will arise against all of Z's property and rights to property.

(iv) *Special rule for employment tax purposes.*—(A) *In general.*—Except as provided in paragraph (c)(2)(iv)(C) of this section, paragraph (c)(2)(i) of this section (relating to certain wholly owned entities) does not apply to taxes imposed under Subtitle C—Employment Taxes and Collection of Income Tax (Chapters 21, 22, 23, 23A, 24, and 25 of the Internal Revenue Code).

(B) *Treatment of entity.*—Except as provided in paragraph (c)(2)(iv)(C) of this section, an entity that is disregarded as an entity separate from its owner for any purpose under this section is treated as a corporation with respect to taxes imposed under Subtitle C—Employment Taxes and Collection of Income Tax (Chapters 21, 22, 23, 23A, 24, and 25 of the Internal Revenue Code). For special rules regarding the application of certain employment tax exceptions, see §§31.3121(b)(3)-1(d), 31.3127-1(b), and 31.3306(c)(5)-1(d) of this chapter.

(C) *Special rules.*—*(1)* Paragraphs (c)(2)(iv)(A) and (B) of this section do not apply to withholding requirements imposed by section 3406 (backup withholding). Thus, in the case of an entity that is disregarded as an entity separate from its owner for any purpose under this section, the owner is subject to the withholding requirements imposed by section 3406 (backup withholding).

(2) Paragraph (c)(2)(i) of this section applies to taxes imposed under subtitle A of the Code, including Chapter 2—Tax on Self-Employment Income. Thus, an entity that is treated in the same manner as a sole proprietorship under paragraph (a) of this section is not treated as a corporation for purposes of employing its owner; instead, the entity is disregarded as an entity separate from its owner for this purpose and is not the employer of its owner. The owner will be subject to self-employment tax on self-employment income with respect to the entity's activities. Also, if a partnership is the owner of an entity that is disregarded as an entity separate from its owner for any purpose under this section, the entity is not treated as a corporation for purposes of employing a partner of the partnership that owns the entity; instead, the entity is disregarded as an entity separate from the partnership for this purpose and is not the employer of any partner of the partnership that owns the entity. A partner of a partnership that owns an entity that is disregarded as an entity separate from its owner for any purpose under this section is subject to the same self-employment tax rules as a partner of a partnership that does not own an entity that is disregarded as an entity separate from its owner for any purpose under this section.

(D) *Example.*—The following example illustrates the application of paragraph (c)(2)(iv) of this section:

Example. (i) LLCA is an eligible entity owned by individual A and is generally disregarded as an entity separate from its owner for Federal tax purposes. However, LLCA is treated as an entity separate from its owner for purposes of subtitle C of the Internal Revenue Code. LLCA has employees and pays wages as defined in sections 3121(a), 3306(b), and 3401(a).

(ii) LLCA is subject to the provisions of subtitle C of the Internal Revenue Code and related provisions under 26 CFR subchapter C, Employment Taxes and Collection of Income Tax at Source, parts 31 through 39. Accordingly, LLCA is required to perform such acts as are required of an employer under those provisions of the Internal Revenue Code and regulations thereunder that apply. All provisions of law (including penalties) and the regulations prescribed in pursuance of law applicable to employers in respect of such acts are applicable to LLCA. Thus, for example, LLCA is liable for income tax withholding, Federal Insurance Contributions Act (FICA) taxes, and Federal Unemployment Tax Act (FUTA) taxes. See sections 3402 and 3403 (relating to income tax withholding); 3102(b) and 3111 (relating to FICA taxes), and 3301 (relating to FUTA taxes). In addition, LLCA must file under its name and EIN the applicable Forms in the 94X series, for example, Form 941, "Employer's Quarterly Employment Tax Return," Form 940, "Employer's Annual Federal Unemployment Tax Return;" file with the Social Security Administration and furnish to LLCA's employees statements on Forms W-2, "Wage and Tax Statement;" and make timely employment tax deposits. See §§31.6011(a)-1, 31.6011(a)-3, 31.6051-1, 31.6051-2, and 31.6302-1 of this chapter.

(iii) A is self-employed for purposes of subtitle A, chapter 2, Tax on Self-Employment Income, of the Internal Revenue Code. Thus, A is subject to tax under section 1401 on A's net earnings from self-employment with respect to LLCA's activities. A is not an employee of LLCA for purposes of subtitle C of the Internal Revenue Code. Because LLCA is treated as a sole proprietorship of A for income tax purposes, A is entitled to deduct trade or business expenses paid or incurred with respect to activities carried on through LLCA, including the employer's share of employment taxes imposed under sections 3111 and 3301, on A's Form 1040, Schedule C, "Profit or Loss for Business (Sole Proprietorship)."

* * *

[Reg. § 301.7701-2.]

□ [*T.D.* 6503, 11-15-60. *Amended by T.D.* 6797, 2-2-65; *T.D.* 7515, 10-17-77; *T.D.* 7889, 4-25-83; *T.D.* 8475, 5-13-93; *T.D.* 8697, 12-17-96 (*corrected* 4-3-2008); *T.D.* 8844, 11-26-99; *T.D.* 9012, 7-31-2002; *T.D.* 9093, 10-21-2003; *T.D.* 9153, 8-11-2004; *T.D.* 9183, 2-24-2005 *T.D.* 9197, 4-13-2005; *T.D.* 9235, 12-15-2005; *T.D.* 9246, 1-27-2006; *T.D.* 9356, 8-15-2007; *T.D.* 9388, 3-20-2008; *T.D.* 9433, 11-26-2008; *T.D.* 9462, 9-11-2009; *T.D.* 9553, 10-25-2011; *T.D.* 9554, 10-31-2011; *T.D.* 9596, 6-22-2012; *T.D.* 9655, 2-10-2014; *T.D.* 9670, 6-25-2014; *T.D.* 9766, 5-3-2016; *T.D.* 9796, 12-12-2016 *and T.D.* 9869, 6-28-2019.]

§ 301.7701-3. Classification of certain business entities.—(a) *In general.*—A business entity that is not classified as a corporation under § 301.7701-2(b)(1), (3), (4), (5), (6), (7), or (8) (an *eligible entity*) can elect its classification for federal tax purposes as provided in this section. An eligible entity with at least two members can elect to be classified as either an association (and thus a corporation under § 301.7701-2(b)(2)) or a partnership, and an eligible entity with a single owner can elect to be classified as an association or to be disregarded as an entity separate from its owner. Paragraph (b) of this section provides a default classification for an eligible entity that does not make an election. Thus, elections are necessary only when an eligible entity chooses to be classified initially as other than the default classification or when an eligible entity chooses to change its classification. An entity whose classification is determined under the default classification retains that classification (regardless of any changes in the members' liability that occurs at any time during the time that the entity's classification is relevant as defined in paragraph (d) of this section) until the entity makes an election to change that classification under paragraph (c)(1) of this section. Paragraph (c) of this section provides rules for making express elections, including a rule under which a domestic eligible entity that elects to be classified as an association consents to be subject to the dual consolidated loss rules of section 1503(d). Paragraph (e) of this section provides special rules for classifying entities resulting from partnership terminations and divisions under section 708(b). Paragraph (f) of this section sets forth the effective date of this section and a special rule relating to prior periods.

(b) *Classification of eligible entities that do not file an election.*—(1) *Domestic eligible entities.*—Except as provided in paragraph (b)(3) of this section, unless the entity elects otherwise, a domestic eligible entity is—

(i) A partnership if it has two or more members; or

(ii) Disregarded as an entity separate from its owner if it has a single owner.

* * *

(3) *Existing eligible entities.*—(i) *In general.*—Unless the entity elects otherwise, an eligible entity in existence prior to the effective date of this section will have the same classification that the entity claimed under §§ 301.7701-1 through 301.7701-3 as in effect on the date prior to the effective date of this section; except that if an eligible entity with a single owner claimed to be a partnership under those regulations, the entity will be disregarded as an entity separate from its owner under this paragraph (b)(3)(i). For special rules regarding the classification of such entities for periods prior to the effective date of this section, see paragraph (f)(2) of this section.

(ii) *Special rules.*—For purposes of paragraph (b)(3)(i) of this section, a foreign eligible entity is treated as being in existence prior to the effective date of this section only if the entity's classification was relevant (as defined in paragraph (d) of this section) at any time during the sixty months prior to the effective date of this section. If an entity claimed different classifications prior to the effective date of this section, the entity's classification for purposes of paragraph (b)(3)(i) of this section is the last classification claimed by the entity. If a foreign eligible entity's classification is relevant prior to the effective date of this section, but no federal tax or information return is filed or the federal tax or information return does not indicate the classification of the entity, the entity's classification for the period prior to the effective date of this section is determined under the regulations in effect on the date prior to the effective date of this section.

(c) *Elections.*—(1) *Time and place for filing.*—(i) *In general.*—Except as provided in paragraphs (c)(1)(iv) and (v) of this section, an eligible entity may elect to be classified other than as provided under paragraph (b) of this section, or to change its classification, by filing Form 8832, Entity Classification Election, with the service center designated on Form 8832. An election will not be accepted unless all of the information required by the form and instructions, including the taxpayer identifying number of the entity, is provided on Form 8832. See § 301.6109-1 for rules on applying for and displaying Employer Identification Numbers.

(ii) *Further notification of elections.*—An eligible entity required to file a Federal tax or information return for the taxable year for which an election is made under § 301.7701-3(c)(1)(i) must attach a copy of its Form 8832 to its Federal tax or information return for that year. If the entity is not required to file a return for that year, a copy of its Form 8832 ("Entity Classification Election") must be attached to the Federal income tax or information return of any direct or indirect owner of the entity for the taxable year of the owner that includes the date on which the election was effective. An indirect owner of the entity does not have to attach a copy of the Form 8832 to its return if an entity in which it has an interest is already filing a copy of the Form 8832 with its return. If an entity, or one of its direct or indirect owners, fails to attach a copy of a Form 8832 to its return as directed in this section, an otherwise valid election under § 301.7701-3(c)(1)(i) will not be invalidated, but the non-filing party may be subject to penalties, including any applicable penalties if the Federal tax or information returns are inconsistent with the entity's election under § 301.7701-3(c)(1)(i). In the case of returns for taxable years beginning after December 31, 2002, the copy of Form 8832 attached to a return pursuant to this paragraph (c)(1)(ii) is not required to be a signed copy.

(iii) *Effective date of election.*—An election made under paragraph (c)(1)(i) of this section will be effective on the date specified by the entity on Form 8832 or on the date filed if no such date is specified on the election form. The effective date specified on Form 8832 can not be more than 75 days prior to the date on which the election is filed and can not be more than 12 months after the date on which the election is filed. If an election specifies an effective date more than 75 days prior to the date on which the election is filed, it will be effective 75 days prior to the date it was filed. If an election specifies an effective date more than 12 months from the date on which the election is filed, it will be effective 12 months after the date it was filed. If an election specifies an effective date before January 1, 1997, it will be effective as of January 1, 1997. If a purchasing corporation makes an election under section 338 regarding an acquired subsidiary, an election under paragraph (c)(1)(i) of this section for the acquired subsidiary can be effective no earlier than the day after the acquisition date (within the meaning of section 338(h)(2)).

(iv) *Limitation.*—If an eligible entity makes an election under paragraph (c)(1)(i) of this section to change its classification (other than an election made by an existing entity to change its classification as of the effective date of this section), the entity cannot change its classification by election again during the sixty months succeeding the effective date of the election. However, the Commissioner may permit the entity to change its classification by election within the sixty months if more than fifty percent of the ownership interests in the entity as of the effective date of the subsequent election are owned by persons that did not own any interests in the entity on the filing date or on the effective date of the entity's prior election. An election by a newly formed eligible entity that is effective on the date of formation is not considered a change for purposes of this paragraph (c)(1)(iv).

(v) *Deemed elections.*—(A) *Exempt organizations.*—An eligible entity that has been determined to be, or claims to be, exempt from taxation under section 501(a) is treated as having made an election under this section to be classified as an association. Such election will be effective as of the first day for which exemption is claimed or determined to apply, regardless of when the claim or determination is made, and will remain in effect unless an election is made under paragraph (c)(1)(i) of this section after the date the claim for exempt status is withdrawn or rejected or the date the determination of exempt status is revoked.

(B) *Real estate investment trusts.*—An eligible entity that files an election under section 856(c)(1) to be treated as a real estate investment trust is treated as having made an election under this section to be classified as an association. Such election will be effective as of the first day the entity is treated as a real estate investment trust.

(C) *S corporations.*—An eligible entity that timely elects to be an S corporation under section 1362(a)(1) is treated as having made an election under this section to be classified as an association, provided that (as of the effective date of the election under section 1362(a)(1)) the entity meets all other requirements to qualify as a small business corporation under section 1361(b). Subject to §301.7701-3(c)(1)(iv), the deemed election to be classified as an association will apply as of the effective date of the S corporation election and will remain in effect until the entity makes a valid election, under §301.7701-3(c)(1)(i), to be classified as other than an association.

(vi) *Examples.*—The following examples illustrate the rules of this paragraph (c)(1):

Example 1. On July 1, 1998, X, a domestic corporation, purchases a 10% interest in Y, an eligible entity formed under Country A law in 1990. The entity's classification was not relevant to any person for federal tax or information purposes prior to X's acquisition of an interest in Y. Thus, Y is not considered to be in existence on the effective date of this section for purposes of paragraph (b)(3) of this section. Under the applicable Country A statute, all members of Y have limited liability as defined in paragraph (b)(2)(ii) of this section. Accordingly, Y is classified as an association under paragraph (b)(2)(i)(B) of this section unless it elects under this paragraph (c) to be classified as a partnership. To be classified as a partnership as of July 1, 1998, Y must file a Form 8832 by September 14, 1998. See paragraph (c)(1)(i) of this section. Because an election cannot be effective more than 75 days prior to the date on which it is filed, if Y files its Form 8832 after September 14, 1998, it will be classified as an association from July 1, 1998, until the effective date of the election. In that case, it could not change its classification by election under this paragraph (c) during the sixty months succeeding the effective date of the election.

Example 2. (i) Z is an eligible entity formed under Country B law and is in existence on the effective date of this section within the meaning of paragraph (b)(3) of this section. Prior to the effective date of this section, Z claimed to be classified as an association. Unless Z files an election under this paragraph (c), it will continue to be classified as an association under paragraph (b)(3) of this section.

(ii) Z files a Form 8832 pursuant to this paragraph (c) to be classified as a partnership, effective as of the effective date of this section. Z can file an election to be classified as an association at any time thereafter, but then would not be permitted to change its classification by election during the sixty months succeeding the effective date of that subsequent election.

(2) *Authorized signatures.*—(i) *In general.*—An election made under paragraph (c)(1)(i) of this section must be signed by—

(A) Each member of the electing entity who is an owner at the time the election is filed; or

(B) Any officer, manager, or member of the electing entity who is authorized (under local law or the entity's organizational documents) to make the election and who represents to having such authorization under penalties of perjury.

(ii) *Retroactive elections.*—For purposes of paragraph (c)(2)(i) of this section, if an election under paragraph (c)(1)(i) of this section is to be effective for any period prior to the time that it is filed, each person who was an owner between the date the election is to be effective and the date the election is filed, and who is not an owner at the time the election is filed, must also sign the election.

(iii) *Changes in classification.*—For paragraph (c)(2)(i) of this section, if an election under paragraph (c)(1)(i) of this section is made to change the classification of an entity, each person who was an owner on the date that any transactions under paragraph (g) of this section are deemed to occur, and who is not an owner at the time the election is filed, must also sign the election. This paragraph (c)(2)(iii) applies to elections filed on or after November 29, 1999.

(3) *Consent to be subject to section 1503(d).*—(i) *Rule.*—A domestic eligible entity that elects to be classified as an association consents to be treated as a dual resident corporation for purposes of section 1503(d) (such an entity, a *domestic consenting corporation*), for any taxable year for which it is classified as an association and the condition set forth in §1.1503(d)-1(c)(1) of this chapter is satisfied.

(ii) *Transition rule — deemed consent.*—If, as a result of the applicability date (see paragraph (c)(3)(iii) of this section) relating to paragraph (c)(3)(i) of this section, a domestic eligible entity that is classified as an association has not consented to be treated as a domestic consenting corporation pursuant to paragraph (c)(3)(i) of this section, then the domestic eligible entity is deemed to consent to be so treated as of its first taxable year beginning on or after December 20, 2019. The first sentence of this paragraph (c)(3)(ii) does not apply if the domestic eligible entity elects, on or after December 20, 2018 and effective before its first taxable year beginning on or after December 20, 2019, to be classified as a partnership or disregarded entity such that it ceases to be a domestic eligible entity that is classified as an association. For purposes of the election described in the second sentence of this paragraph

(c) (3) (ii), the sixty month limitation under paragraph (c) (1) (iv) of this section is waived.

(iii) *Applicability date.*—The sixth sentence of paragraph (a) of this section and paragraph (c) (3) (i) of this section apply to a domestic eligible entity that on or after December 20, 2018 files an election to be classified as an association (regardless of whether the election is effective before December 20, 2018). Paragraph (c) (3) (ii) of this section applies as of December 20, 2018.

* * *

(f) *Changes in number of members of an entity.*—(1) *Associations.*—The classification of an eligible entity as an association is not affected by any change in the number of members of the entity.

(2) *Partnerships and single member entities.*—An eligible entity classified as a partnership becomes disregarded as an entity separate from its owner when the entity's membership is reduced to one member. A single member entity disregarded as an entity separate from its owner is classified as a partnership when the entity has more than one member. If an elective classification change under paragraph (c) of this section is effective at the same time as a membership change described in this paragraph (f) (2), the deemed transactions in paragraph (g) of this section resulting from the elective change preempt the transactions that would result from the change in membership.

(3) *Effect on sixty month limitation.*—A change in the number of members of an entity does not result in the creation of a new entity for purposes of the sixty month limitation on elections under paragraph (c) (1) (iv) of this section.

* * *

(g) *Elective changes in classification.*—(1) *Deemed treatment of elective change.*—(i) *Partnership to association.*—If an eligible entity classified as a partnership elects under paragraph (c) (1) (i) of this section to be classified as an association, the following is deemed to occur: The partnership contributes all of its assets and liabilities to the association in exchange for stock in the association, and immediately thereafter, the partnership liquidates by distributing the stock of the association to its partners.

(ii) *Association to partnership.*—If an eligible entity classified as an association elects under paragraph (c) (1) (i) of this section to be classified as a partnership, the following is deemed to occur: The association distributes all of its assets and liabilities to its shareholders in liquidation of the association, and immediately thereafter, the shareholders contribute all of the distributed assets and liabilities to a newly formed partnership.

(iii) *Association to disregarded entity.*—If an eligible entity classified as an association elects under paragraph (c) (1) (i) of this section to be disregarded as an entity separate from its owner, the following is deemed to occur: The association distributes all of its assets and liabilities to its single owner in liquidation of the association.

(iv) *Disregarded entity to an association.*—If an eligible entity that is disregarded as an entity separate from its owner elects under paragraph (c) (1) (i) of this section to be classified as an association, the following is deemed to occur: The owner of the eligible entity contributes all of the assets and liabilities of the entity to the association in exchange for stock of the association.

(2) *Effect of elective chanqes.*—(i) *In general.*—The tax treatment of a change in the classification of an entity for federal tax purposes by election under paragraph (c) (1) (i) of this section is determined under all relevant provisions of the Internal Revenue Code and general principles of tax law, including the step transaction doctrine.

(ii) *Adoption of plan of liquidation.*—For purposes of satisfying the requirement of adoption of a plan of liquidation under section 332, unless a formal plan of liquidation that contemplates the election to be classified as a partnership or to be disregarded as an entity separate from its owner is adopted on an earlier date, the making, by an association, of an election under paragraph (c) (1) (i) of this section to be classified as a partnership or to be disregarded as an entity separate from its owner is considered to be the adoption of a plan of liquidation immediately before the deemed liquidation described in paragraph (g) (1) (ii) or (iii) of this section. This paragraph (g) (2) (ii) applies to elections filed on or after December 17, 2001. Taxpayers may apply this paragraph (g) (2) (ii) retroactively to elections filed before December 17, 2001, if the corporate owner claiming treatment under section 332 and its subsidiary making the election take consistent positions with respect to the federal tax consequences of the election.

(3) *Timing of election.*—(i) *In general.*—An election under paragraph (c) (1) (i) of this section that changes the classification of an eligible entity for federal tax purposes is treated as occurring at the start of the day for which the election is effective. Any transactions that are deemed to occur under this paragraph (g) as a result of a change in classification are

treated as occurring immediately before the close of the day before the election is effective. For example, if an election is made to change the classification of an entity from an association to a partnership effective on January 1, the deemed transactions specified in paragraph (g) (1) (ii) of this section (including the liquidation of the association) are treated as occurring immediately before the close of December 31 and must be reported by the owners of the entity on December 31. Thus, the last day of the association's taxable year will be December 31 and the first day of the partnership's taxable year will be January 1.

(ii) *Coordination with section 338 election.*—A purchasing corporation that makes a qualified stock purchase of an eligible entity taxed as a corporation may make an election under section 338 regarding the acquisition if it satisfies the requirements for the election, and may also make an election to change the classification of the target corporation. If a taxpayer makes an election under section 338 regarding its acquisition of another entity taxable as a corporation and makes an election under paragraph (c) of this section for the acquired corporation (effective at the earliest possible date as provided by paragraph (c) (1) (iii) of this section), the transactions under paragraph (g) of this section are deemed to occur immediately after the deemed asset purchase by the new target corporation under section 338.

(iii) *Application to successive elections in tiered situations.*—When elections under paragraph (c) (1) (i) of this section for a series of tiered entities are effective on the same date, the eligible entities may specify the order of the elections on Form 8832. If no order is specified for the elections, any transactions that are deemed to occur in this paragraph (g) as a result of the classification change will be treated as occurring first for the highest tier entity's classification change, then for the next highest tier entity's classification change, and so forth down the chain of entities until all the transactions under this paragraph (g) have occurred. For example, Parent, a corporation, wholly owns all of the interest of an eligible entity classified as an association (S1), which wholly owns another eligible entity classified as an association (S2), which wholly owns another eligible entity classified as an association (S3). Elections under paragraph (c) (1) (i) of this section are filed to classify S1, S2, and S3 each as disregarded as an entity separate from its owner effective on the same day. If no order is specified for the elections, the following transactions are deemed to occur under this paragraph (g) as a result of the elections, with each successive transaction occurring on the same day immediately after the preceding transaction: S1 is treated as liquidating into Parent, then S2 is treated as liquidating into Parent, and finally S3 is treated as liquidating into Parent.

* * *

[Reg. § 301.7701-3.]

☐ [*T.D.* 6503, 11-15-60. *Amended by T.D.* 8632, 12-19-95; *T.D.* 8697, 12-17-96; *T.D.* 8767, 3-23-98; *T.D.* 8827, 7-12-99 (*corrected* 10-29-99); *T.D.* 8844, 11-26-99; *T.D.* 8970, 12-14-2001; *T.D.* 9093, 10-21-2003; *T.D.* 9100, 12-18-2003; *T.D.* 9139, 7-19-2004; *T.D.* 9153, 8-11-2004; *T.D.* 9203, 5-20-2005; *T.D.* 9300, 12-7-2006 *and T.D.* 9896, 4-7-2020.]

§ 301.7701-4. Trusts.—(a) *Ordinary trusts.*—In general, the term "trust" as used in the Internal Revenue Code refers to an arrangement created either by a will or by an inter vivos declaration whereby trustees take title to property for the purpose of protecting or conserving it for the beneficiaries under the ordinary rules applied in chancery or probate courts. Usually the beneficiaries of such a trust do no more than accept the benefits thereof and are not the voluntary planners or creators of the trust arrangement. However, the beneficiaries of such a trust may be the persons who create it and it will be recognized as a trust under the Internal Revenue Code if it was created for the purpose of protecting or conserving the trust property for beneficiaries who stand in the same relation to the trust as they would if the trust had been created by others for them. Generally speaking, an arrangement will be treated as a trust under the Internal Revenue Code if it can be shown that the purpose of the arrangement is to vest in trustees responsibility for the protection and conservation of property for beneficiaries who cannot share in the discharge of this responsibility and, therefore, are not associates in a joint enterprise for the conduct of business for profit.

(b) *Business trusts.*—There are other arrangements which are known as trusts because the legal title to property is conveyed to trustees for the benefit of beneficiaries, but which are not classified as trusts for purposes of the Internal Revenue Code because they are not simply arrangements to protect or conserve the property for the beneficiaries. These trusts, which are often known as business or commercial trusts, generally are created by the beneficiaries simply as a device to carry on a profit-making business which normally would have been carried on through business organizations that are classified as corporations or partnerships under the Internal Revenue Code. However, the fact that the corpus of the trust is not supplied by the beneficiaries is not sufficient reason in itself for classifying the arrangement as an ordinary trust rather than as an association or partnership. The fact that any organization is technically cast in the trust form, by conveying title to property to trustees for the benefit of persons designated as beneficiaries, will not change the real character of the organization if the organization is more properly classified as a business entity under § 301.7701-2.

(c) *Certain investment trusts.*—(1) An "investment" trust will not be classified as a trust if there is a power under the trust agreement to vary the investment of the certificate holders. *See Commissioner v. North American Bond Trust,* 122 F. 2d 545 [41-2 USTC ¶ 9644] (2d Cir. 1941), *cert. denied,* 314 U.S. 701 (1942). An investment trust with a single class of ownership interests, representing undivided beneficial interests in the assets of the trust, will be classified as a trust if there is no power under the trust agreement to vary the investment of the certificate holders. An investment trust with multiple classes of ownership interests ordinarily will be classified as a business entity under § 301.7701-2; however, an investment trust with multiple classes of ownership interests, in which there is no power under the trust agreement to vary the investment of the certificate holders, will be classified as a trust if the trust is formed to facilitate direct investment in the assets of the trust and the existence of multiple classes of ownership interests is incidental to that purpose.

* * *

(d) *Liquidating trusts.*—Certain organizations which are commonly known as liquidating trusts are treated as trusts for purposes of the Internal Revenue Code. An organization will be considered a liquidating trust if it is organized for the primary purpose of liquidating and distributing the assets transferred to it, and if its activities are all reasonably necessary to, and consistent with, the accomplishment of that purpose. A liquidating trust is treated as a trust for purposes of the Internal Revenue Code because it is formed with the objective of liquidating particular assets and not as an organization having as its purpose the carrying on of a profit-making business which normally would be conducted through business organizations classified as corporations or partnerships. However, if the liquidation is unreasonably prolonged or if the liquidation purpose becomes so obscured by business activities that the declared purpose of liquidation can be said to be lost or abandoned, the status of the organization will no longer be that of a liquidating trust. Bondholders' protective committees, voting trusts, and other agencies formed to protect the interests of security holders during insolvency, bankruptcy, or corporate reorganization proceedings are analogous to liquidating trusts but if subsequently utilized to further the control or profitable operation of a going business on a permanent continuing basis, they will lose their classification as trusts for purposes of the Internal Revenue Code.

* * *

[Reg. § 301.7701-4.]

☐ [*T.D.* 6503, 11-15-60. *Amended by T.D.* 8080, 3-21-86; *T.D.* 8668, 4-30-96 *and T.D.* 8697, 12-17-96.]

§ 301.7701-6. Definitions; person, fiduciary.—(a) *Person.*—The term *person* includes an individual, a corporation, a partnership, a trust or estate, a joint-stock company, an association, or a syndicate, group, pool, joint venture, or other unincorporated organization or group. The term also includes a guardian, committee, trustee, executor, administrator, trustee in bankruptcy, receiver, assignee for the benefit of creditors, conservator, or any person acting in a fiduciary capacity.

(b) *Fiduciary.*—(1) *In general.*—Fiduciary is a term that applies to persons who occupy positions of peculiar confidence toward others, such as trustees, executors, and administrators. A fiduciary is a person who holds in trust an estate to which another has a beneficial interest, or receives and controls income of another, as in the case of receivers. A committee or guardian of the property of an incompetent person is a fiduciary.

(2) *Fiduciary distinguished from agent.*—There may be a fiduciary relationship between an agent and a principal, but the word agent does not denote a fiduciary. An agent having entire charge of property, with authority to effect and execute leases with tenants entirely on his own responsibility and without consulting his principal, merely turning over the net profits from the property periodically to his principal by virtue of authority conferred upon him by a power of attorney, is not a fiduciary within the meaning of the Internal Revenue Code. In cases when no legal trust has been created in the estate controlled by the agent and attorney, the liability to make a return rests with the principal.

(c) *Effective date.*—The rules of this section are effective as of January 1, 1997. [Reg. § 301.7701-6.]

☐ [*T.D.* 6503, 11-15-60. *Amended by T.D.* 8697, 12-17-96.]

§ 301.7701-15. Tax return preparer.—(a) *In general.*—A *tax return preparer* is any person who prepares for compensation, or who employs one or more persons to prepare for compensation, all or a substantial portion of any return of tax or any claim for refund of tax under the Internal Revenue Code (Code).

(b) *Definitions.*—(1) *Signing tax return preparer.*—A *signing tax return preparer* is the individual tax return preparer who has the primary responsibility for the overall substantive accuracy of the preparation of such return or claim for refund.

(2) *Nonsigning tax return preparer.*—(i) *In general.*—A *nonsigning tax return preparer* is any tax return preparer who is not a signing tax return preparer but who prepares all or a substantial portion of a return or claim for refund within the meaning of paragraph (b)(3) of this section with respect to events that have occurred at the time the advice is rendered. In determining whether an individual is a nonsigning tax return preparer, time spent on advice that is given after events have occurred that represents less than 5 percent of the aggregate time incurred by such individual with respect to the position(s) giving rise to the understatement shall not be taken into account. Notwithstanding the preceding sentence, time spent on advice before the events have occurred will be taken into account if all facts and circumstances show that the position(s) giving rise to the understatement is primarily attributable to the advice, the advice was substantially given before events occurred primarily to avoid treating the person giving the advice as a tax return preparer, and the advice given before events occurred was confirmed after events had occurred for purposes of preparing a tax return. Examples of nonsigning tax return preparers are tax return preparers who provide advice (written or oral) to a taxpayer (or to another tax return preparer) when that advice leads to a position or entry that constitutes a substantial portion of the return within the meaning of paragraph (b)(3) of this section.

* * *

[Reg. § 301.7701-15.]

□ [*T.D.* 7519, 11-17-77. *Amended by T.D.* 7675, 2-20-80; *T.D.* 9026, 12-17-2002 *and T.D.* 9436, 12-15-2008 (*corrected* 1-28-2009).]

§ 301.7701-18. Definitions; spouse, husband and wife, husband, wife, marriage.—(a) *In general.*—For federal tax purposes, the terms *spouse, husband,* and *wife* mean an individual lawfully married to another individual. The term *husband and wife* means two individuals lawfully married to each other.

(b) *Persons who are lawfully married for federal tax purposes.*—(1) *In general.*—Except as provided in paragraph (b)(2) of this section regarding marriages entered into under the laws of a foreign jurisdiction, a marriage of two individuals is recognized for federal tax purposes if the marriage is recognized by the state, possession, or territory of the United States in which the marriage is entered into, regardless of domicile.

(2) *Foreign marriages.*—Two individuals who enter into a relationship denominated as marriage under the laws of a foreign jurisdiction are recognized as married for federal tax purposes if the relationship would be recognized as marriage under the laws of at least one state, possession, or territory of the United States, regardless of domicile.

(c) *Persons who are not lawfully married for federal tax purposes.*—The terms *spouse, husband,* and *wife* do not include individuals who have entered into a registered domestic partnership, civil union, or other similar formal relationship not denominated as a marriage under the law of the state, possession, or territory of the United States where such relationship was entered into, regardless of domicile. The term *husband and wife* does not include couples who have entered into such a formal relationship, and the term *marriage* does not include such formal relationships.

(d) *Applicability date.*—The rules of this section apply to taxable years ending on or after September 2, 2016. [Reg. § 301.7701-18.]

□ [*T.D.* 9785, 8-31-2016.]

§ 1.7704-4. Qualifying income – mineral and natural resources.—(a) *In general.*—For purposes of section 7704(d)(1)(E), qualifying income is income and gains from qualifying activities with respect to minerals or natural resources as defined in paragraph (b) of this section. Qualifying activities are section 7704(d)(1)(E) activities (as described in paragraph (c) of this section) and intrinsic activities (as described in paragraph (d) of this section).

(b) *Mineral or natural resource.*—The term mineral or natural resource (including fertilizer, geothermal energy, and timber) means any product of a character with respect to which a deduction for depletion is allowable under section 611, except that such term does not include any product described in section 613(b)(7)(A) or (B) (soil, sod, dirt, turf, water, mosses, or minerals from sea water, the air, or other similar inexhaustible sources). For purposes of this section, the term mineral or natural resource does not include industrial source carbon dioxide, fuels described in section 6426(b) through (e), any alcohol fuel defined in section 6426(b)(4)(A), or any biodiesel fuel as defined in section 40A(d)(1).

(c) *Section 7704(d)(1)(E) activities.*—(1) *Definition.*—Section 7704(d)(1)(E) activities include the exploration, development, mining or production, processing, refining, transportation, or marketing of any mineral or natural resource. Solely for purposes of section 7704(d), such terms are defined as provided in this paragraph (c).

(2) *Exploration.*—An activity constitutes exploration if it is performed to ascertain the existence, location, extent, or quality of any deposit of mineral or natural resource before the beginning of the development stage of the natural deposit including by—

(i) Drilling an exploratory or stratigraphic type test well;

(ii) Conducting drill stem and production flow tests to verify commerciality of the deposit;

(iii) Conducting geological or geophysical surveys;

(iv) Interpreting data obtained from geological or geophysical surveys; or

(v) For minerals, testpitting, trenching, drilling, driving of exploration tunnels and adits, and similar types of activities described in Rev. Rul. 70-287 (1970-1 CB 146), (see §601.601(d)(2)(ii)(*b*) of this chapter) if conducted prior to development activities with respect to the minerals.

(3) *Development.*—An activity constitutes development if it is performed to make accessible minerals or natural resources, including by—

(i) Drilling wells to access deposits of minerals or natural resources;

(ii) Constructing and installing drilling, production, or dual purpose platforms in marine locations, or any similar supporting structures necessary for extraordinary non-marine terrain (such as swamps or tundra);

(iii) Completing wells, including by installing lease and well equipment, such as pumps, flow lines, separators, and storage tanks, so that wells are capable of producing oil and gas, and the production can be removed from the premises;

(iv) Performing a development technique such as, for minerals other than oil and natural gas, stripping, benching and terracing, dredging by dragline, stoping, and caving or room-and-pillar excavation, and for oil and natural gas, fracturing; or

(v) Constructing and installing gathering systems and custody transfer stations.

(4) *Mining or production.*—An activity constitutes mining or production if it is performed to extract minerals or natural resources from the ground including by operating equipment to extract minerals or natural resources from mines and wells, or to extract minerals or natural resources from the waste or residue of prior mining or production allowable under this section. The recycling of scrap or salvaged metals or minerals from previously manufactured products or manufacturing processes is not considered to be the extraction of ores or minerals from waste or residue.

(5) *Processing.*—An activity constitutes processing if it is performed to convert raw mined or harvested products or raw well effluent to substances that can be readily transported or stored, as described in this paragraph (c)(5).

(i) *Natural gas.*—An activity constitutes processing of natural gas if it is performed to—

(A) Purify natural gas, including by removal of oil or condensate, water, or non-hydrocarbon gases (such as carbon dioxide, hydrogen sulfide, nitrogen, and helium); and

(B) Separate natural gas into its constituents which are normally recovered in a gaseous phase (methane and ethane) and those which are normally recovered in a liquid phase (propane, butane, pentane, and heavier streams).

(ii) *Crude oil.*—An activity constitutes processing of crude oil if it is performed to separate produced fluids by passing crude oil through mechanical separators to remove gas, placing crude oil in settling tanks to recover basic sediment and water, dehydrating crude oil, and operating heater-treaters that separate raw oil well effluent into crude oil, natural gas, and salt water.

(iii) *Ores and minerals other than natural gas or crude oil.*—An activity constitutes processing of ores and minerals other than natural gas or crude oil if it meets the definition of mining processes under §1.613-4(f)(1)(ii), without regard to §1.613-4(f)(2)(iv).

(iv) *Timber.*—An activity constitutes processing of timber if it is performed to modify the physical form of timber, including by the application of heat or pressure to timber, without adding any foreign substances. Processing of timber does not include activities that add chemicals or other foreign substances to timber to manipulate its physical or chemical properties, such as using a digester to produce pulp. Products that result from timber processing include wood chips, sawdust, rough lumber, kiln-dried lumber, veneers, wood pellets, wood bark, and rough poles. Products that are not the result of timber processing include pulp, paper, paper products, treated lumber, oriented strand board/plywood, and treated poles.

(6) *Refining.*—An activity constitutes refining if the activity is set forth in this paragraph (c)(6).

(i) *Natural gas and crude oil.*—(A) The refining of natural gas and crude oil includes the further physical or chemical conversion or separation processes of products resulting from activities listed in paragraph (c)(5)(i) and (ii) of this section, and the blending of petroleum hydrocarbons, to the extent they give rise to a product listed in paragraph (c)(5)(i) or (ii) of this section or to the products of a type produced in a petroleum refinery or natural gas processing plant listed in this paragraph (c)(6)(i)(A). Refining of natural gas and crude oil also includes the further physical or chemical conversion or separation processes and blending of the products listed in this paragraph (c)(6)(i)(A), to the extent that the resulting product is also listed in this paragraph (c)(6)(i)(A). The following products are of a type produced in a petroleum refinery or natural gas processing plant:

(1) Ethane.

(2) Ethylene.

(3) Propane.

(4) Propylene.

(5) Normal butane.

(6) Butylene.

(7) Isobutane.

(8) Isobutene.

(9) Isobutylene.

(10) Pentanes plus.

(11) Unfinished naphtha.

(12) Unfinished kerosene and light gas oils.

(13) Unfinished heavy gas oils.

(14) Unfinished residuum.

(15) Reformulated gasoline with fuel ethanol.

(16) Reformulated other motor gasoline.

(17) Conventional gasoline with fuel ethanol – Ed55 and lower gasoline.

(18) Conventional gasoline with fuel ethanol – greater than Ed55 gasoline.

(19) Conventional gasoline with fuel ethanol – other conventional finished gasoline.

(20) Reformulated blendstock for oxygenate (RBOB).

(21) Conventional blendstock for oxygenate (CBOB).

(22) Gasoline treated as blendstock (GTAB).

(23) Other motor gasoline blending components defined as gasoline blendstocks as provided in §48.4081-1(c)(3) of this chapter.

(24) Finished aviation gasoline and blending components.

(25) Special naphthas (solvents).

(26) Kerosene-type jet fuel.

(27) Kerosene.

(28) Distillate fuel oil (heating oils, diesel fuel, and ultra-low sulfur diesel fuel).

(29) Residual fuel oil.

(30) Lubricants (lubricating base oils).

(31) Asphalt and road oil (atmospheric or vacuum tower bottom).

(32) Waxes.

(33) Petroleum coke.

(34) Still gas.

(35) Naphtha less than 401°F endpoint.

(36) Other products of a refinery that the Commissioner may identify through published guidance.

* * *

(7) *Transportation.*—(i) *General rule.*—An activity constitutes transportation if it is performed to move minerals or natural resources, and products under paragraph (c)(4), (5), or (6) of this section, including by pipeline, marine vessel, rail, or truck. Except as provided in paragraph (c)(7)(ii) of this section, transportation does not include the movement of minerals or natural resources, and products produced under paragraph (c)(4), (5), or (6) of this section, directly to retail customers or to a place that sells or dispenses to retail customers. Retail customers do not include a person who acquires oil or gas for refining or processing, or a utility. Transportation includes the following activities:

(A) Providing storage services.

(B) Providing terminalling services, including the following: receiving products from pipelines, marine vessels, railcars, or trucks; storing products; loading products to pipelines, marine vessels, railcars, or trucks for distribution; testing and treating, as well as blending and additization, if income from such activities would be qualifying income pursuant to paragraph (c)(10)(iv) and (v) of this section; and separating and selling excess renewable identification numbers acquired as part of additization services to comply with environmental regulations.

(C) Moving or carrying (whether by owner or operator) products via pipelines, gathering systems, and custody transfer stations.

(D) Operating marine vessels (including time charters), railcars, or trucks.

(E) Providing compression services to a pipeline.

(F) Liquefying or regasifying natural gas.

(ii) *Transportation to retail customers or to a place that sells to retail customers.*—Transportation includes the movement of minerals or natural resources, and products under paragraph (c)(4), (5), or (6) of this section, via pipeline to a place that sells to retail customers. Transportation also includes the movement of liquefied petroleum gas via trucks, rail cars, or pipeline to a place that sells to retail customers or directly to retail customers.

(8) *Marketing.*—(i) *General rule.*—An activity constitutes marketing if it is the bulk sale of minerals or natural resources, and products under paragraph (c)(4), (5), or (6) of this section. Except as provided in paragraph (c)(8)(ii) of this section, marketing does not include retail sales (sales made in small quantities directly to end users), which includes the operation of gasoline service stations, home heating oil delivery services, and local natural gas delivery services.

(ii) *Retail sales of liquefied petroleum gas.*—Retail sales of liquefied petroleum gas are included in marketing.

(iii) *Certain activities that facilitate sale.*—Marketing also includes certain activities that facilitate sales that constitute marketing under paragraphs (c)(8)(i) and (ii) of this section, including packaging, as well as and blending and additization, if income from blending and additization would be qualifying income pursuant to paragraph (c)(10)(iv) and (v) of this section.

* * *

(d) *Intrinsic activities.*—(1) *General requirements.*—An activity is an intrinsic activity only if the activity is specialized to support a section 7704(d)(1)(E) activity, is essential to the completion of the section 7704(d)(1)(E) activity, and requires the provision of significant services to support the section 7704(d)(1)(E) activity. Whether an activity is an intrinsic activity is determined on an activity-by-activity basis.

* * *

[Reg. § 1.7704-4.]

☐ [*T.D.* 9817, 1-19-2017.]

Provisions Affecting More Than One Subtitle

Proposed Regulation

§ 1.7872-1. Introduction.—(a) *Statement of purpose.*—Section 7872 generally treats certain loans in which the interest rate charged is less than the applicable Federal rate as economically equivalent to loans bearing interest at the applicable Federal rate, coupled with a payment by the lender to the borrower sufficient to fund all or part of the payment of interest by the borrower. Such loans are referred to as "below-market loans." See § 1.7872-3 for detailed definitions of below-market loans and the determination of the applicable Federal rate.

Accordingly, section 7872 recharacterizes a below-market loan as two transactions:

(1) An arm's-length transaction in which the lender makes a loan to the borrower in exchange for a note requiring the payment of interest at the applicable Federal rate; and

(2) A transfer of funds by the lender to the borrower ("imputed transfer").

The timing and the characterization of the amount of the imputed transfer by the lender to the borrower are determined in accordance with the substance of the transaction. The timing and the amount of the imputed interest payment (the excess of the amount of interest required to be paid using the applicable Federal rate, *over* the amount of interest required to be paid according to the loan agreement) by the borrower to the lender depend on the character of the imputed transfer by the lender to the borrower and whether the loan is a term loan or a demand loan. If the imputed transfer by the lender is characterized as a gift, the provisions of chapter 12 of the Internal Revenue Code, relating to gift tax, also apply. All imputed transfers under section 7872 (*e.g.,* interest, compensation, gift) are characterized in accordance with the substance of the transaction, and, except as otherwise provided in the regulations under section 7872, are treated as so characterized for all purposes of the Code. For example, for purposes of section 170, an interest-free loan to a charity referred to in section 170 for which interest is imputed under section 7872, is treated as an interest bearing loan coupled with periodic gifts to the charity in the amount of the imputed transfer, for purposes of section 170. In addition, all applicable information and reporting requirements (*e.g.,* reporting on W-2 and Form 1099) must be satisfied.

* * *

[Prop. Reg. § 1.7872-1.]

[Proposed 8-20-85.]

Proposed Regulation

§ 1.7872-2. Definition of loan.—(a) *In general.*—(1) *"Loan" interpreted broadly.*—For purposes of section 7872, the term "loan" includes generally any extension of credit (including, for example, a purchase money mortgage) and any transaction under which the owner of money permits another person to use the money for a period of time after which the money is to be transferred to the owner or applied according to an express or implied agreement with the onwer. The term "loan" is interpreted broadly to implement the anti-abuse intent of the statute. An integrated series of transactions which is the equivalent of a loan is treated as a loan. A payment for property, goods, or services under a contract, however, is not a loan merely because one of the payor's remedies for breach of the contract is recovery of the payment. Similarly, a bona fide prepayment made in a manner consistent with normal commercial practices for services, property, or the use of property, generally, is not a loan; see section 461 and the regulations thereunder for the treatment of certain prepaid expenses and for the special rules of sections 461(h) and (i). However, a taxpayer's characterization of a transaction as a prepayment or as a loan is not conclusive. Transactions will be characterized for tax purposes according to their economic substance, rather than the terms used to describe them. Thus, for example, receipt by a partner from a partnership of money is treated as a loan if it is so characterized under § 1.731-1(c)(2).

* * *

(b) *Examples of transactions treated as loans.*—(1) *Refundable deposits.*—(i) *In general.*—If an amount is treated for Federal tax purposes as a deposit rather than as a prepayment or an advance payment, the amount is treated as a loan for purposes of section 7872.

(ii) *Partially refundable deposits.*—If an amount is treated for Federal tax purposes as a deposit rather than as a prepayment or an advance payment and the amount is refundable only for a certain period of time or is only partially refundable, then the deposit is treated as a loan only to the extent that it is refundable and only for the period of time that it is refundable.

(iii) *Exception.*—Paragraph (b)(1)(i) does not apply if the deposit is custodial in nature or is held in trust for the benefit of the transferor. The deposit is treated as custodial in nature if the transferee is not entitled to the beneficial enjoyment of the amount deposited including interest thereon (except as security for an obligation of the transferor). Thus, if an amount is placed in escrow to secure a contractual obligation of the transferor, and the escrow agreement provides that all interest earned is paid to the transferor and that the transferee has no rights to or interest in the escrowed amount unless and until the transferor defaults on the obligation, then, in the absence of any facts which indicate that the transaction was entered into for tax avoidance purposes, the deposit is not a loan.

* * *

[Prop. Reg. § 1.7872-2.]

[Proposed 8-20-85.]

Proposed Regulation

§ 1.7872-4. Types of below-market loans.—(a) *In general.*—Section 7872 applies only to certain categories of below-market loans. These categories are gift loans, compensation-related loans, corporation-shareholder loans, tax avoidance loans, and certain other loans classified in the regulations under section 7872 as significant tax effect loans (*i.e.,* loans whose interest arrangements have a significant effect on any Federal tax liability of the lender or the borrower).

(b) *Gift loans.*—(1) *In general.*—The term "gift loan" means any below-market loan in which the foregoing of interest is in the nature of a gift within the meaning of Chapter 12 of the Internal Revenue Code (whether or not the lender is a natural person).

(2) *Cross reference.*—See § 1.7872-8 for special rules limiting the application of section 7872 to gift loans. See paragraph (g) of this section for rules with respect to below-market loans which are indirectly gift loans.

(c) *Compensation-related loans.*—(1) *In general.*—A compensation-related loan is a below-market loan that is made in connection with the performance of services, directly or indirectly, between—

(i) An employer and an employee,

(ii) An independent contractor and a person for whom such independent contractor provides services, or

(iii) A partnership and a partner if the loan is made in consideration for services performed by the partner acting other than in his capacity as a member of the partnership.

The imputed transfer (amount of money treated as transferred) by the lender to the borrower is compensation. For purposes of this section, the term "in connection with the performance of services" has the same meaning as the term has for purposes of section 83. A loan from a qualified pension, profit-sharing, or stock bonus plan to a participant of the plan is not, directly or indirectly, a compensation-related loan.

(2) *Loan in part in exchange for services.*—Except as provided in paragraph (d)(2) of this section (relating to a loan from a corporation to an employee who is also a shareholder of the corporation), a loan which is made in part in exchange for services and in part for other reasons is treated as a compensation-related loan for purposes of section 7872(c)(3) only if more than 25 percent of the amount loaned is attributable to the performance of services. If 25 percent or less of the amount loaned is attributable to the performance of services, the loan is not subject to section 7872 by reason of being a compensation-related loan. The loan may, however, be subject to section 7872 by reason of being a below-market loan characterized other than as a compensation-related loan (*e.g.*, corporation-shareholder loan or tax avoidance loan). If—

(i) a loan is characterized as a "compensation-related" loan under this paragraph (c),

(ii) less than 100 percent of the amount loaned is attributable to the performance of services, and

(iii) the portion of the amount loaned that is not attributable to the performance of services is not subject to section 7872,

then the amounts of imputed transfer (as defined in § 1.7872-1(a)(2)) and imputed interest (as defined in § 1.7872-1(a)) are determined only with respect to that part of the loan which is attributable to services. All of the facts and circumstances surrounding the loan agreement and the relationship between the lender and the borrower are taken into account in determining the portion of the loan made in exchange for services.

(3) *Third-party lender as agent.*—A below-market loan by an unrelated third-party lender to an employee is treated as attributable to the performance of services if, taking into account all the facts and circumstances, the transaction is in substance a loan by the employer made with the aid of a third-party lender acting as an agent of the employer. Among the facts and circumstances which indicate whether such a loan has been made is whether the employer bears the risk of default at and immediately after the time the loan is made. The principles of this paragraph (c)(3) also apply with respect to a below-market loan by an unrelated third-party lender to an independent contractor.

(4) *Special rule for continuing care facilities.*—Any loan to a continuing care facility will not be treated, in whole or in part, as a compensation-related loan.

(5) *Cross-references.*—For a special rule in the case of a below-market loan that could be characterized as both a compensation-related loan and a corporation-shareholder loan, see paragraph (d)(2) of this section. See paragraph (g) of this section for rules with respect to below-market loans which are indirectly compensation-related loans.

(d) *Corporation-shareholder loans.*—(1) *In general.*—A below-market loan is a corporation-shareholder loan if the loan is made directly or indirectly between a corporation and any shareholder of the corporation. The amount of money treated as transferred by the lender to the borrower is a distribution of money (characterized according to section 301 or, in the case of an S corporation, section 1368) if the corporation is the lender, or a contribution to capital if the shareholder is the lender.

(2) *Special rule.*—A below-market loan—

(i) from a publicly held corporation to an employee of the corporation who is also a shareholder owning directly or indirectly more than 0.5 percent of the total voting power of all classes of stock entitled to vote or more than 0.5 percent of the total value of shares of all other classes of stock or 0.5 percent of the total value of shares of all other classes of stock or 5 percent of the total value of shares of all classes of stock (including voting stock) of the corporation; or

(ii) from a corporation that is not a publicly held corporation to an employee of the corporation who is also a shareholder owning directly or indirectly more than 5 percent of the total voting power of all classes of stock entitled to vote or more than 5 percent of the total number of shares of all other classes of stock or 5 percent of the total value of shares of all classes of stock (including voting stock) of the corporation;

will be presumed to be a corporation-shareholder loan, in the absence of clear and convincing evidence that the loan is made solely in connection with the performance of services. For purposes of determining the percentage of direct and indirect stock ownership, the constructive ownership rules of section 267(c) apply.

(3) *Cross-reference.*—See paragraph (g) of this section for rules with respect to below-market loans which are indirectly corporation-shareholder loans.

(e) *Tax avoidance loans.*—(1) *In general.*—A tax avoidance loan is any below-market loan one of the principal purposes for the interest arrangements of which is the avoidance of Federal tax with respect to either the borrower or the lender, or both. For purposes of this rule, tax avoidance is a principal purpose of the interest arrangements if a principal factor in the decision to structure the transaction as a below-market loan (rather than, for example, as a market interest rate loan and a payment by the lender to the borrower) is to reduce the Federal tax liability of the borrower or the lender or both. The purpose for entering into the transaction (for example, to make a gift or to pay compensation) is irrelevant in determining whether a principal purpose of the interest arrangements of the loan is the avoidance of Federal tax.

(2) *Certain loans incident to sales or exchanges.*—If, pursuant to a plan that is incident to a sale or exchange of property, a party who is related (within the meaning of section 168(e)(4)(D)) to the seller—

(i) Makes a below-market loan to the buyer of the property, or

(ii) Makes a below-market loan to the seller that is assumed by the buyer in connection with the sale or exchange,

then the loan shall be treated as a tax avoidance loan within the meaning of paragraph (e)(1) of this section. There shall be an irrebuttable presumption that such a plan exists if such a loan is made within one year of the sale or exchange.

(3) *Examples.*—The provisions of paragraph (e) of this section may be illustrated by the following examples:

Example (1). (i) S and T are each wholly-owned subsidiaries of P. S sells property to an individual, A, for cash of $3,000,000. Three months after the sale, T loans to A $2,000,000 for 10 years at an interest rate of 6%, payable semiannually. On the date the loan is made, the Federal long-term rate is 12%, compounded semiannually.

(ii) The loan from T to A is a tax avoidance loan pursuant to paragraph (e)(2) of this section. The issue price of the debt instrument given in exchange for the loan is $1,311,805, and the total amount of foregone interest is $688,195. On the date the loan is made, A is treated as having received a refund of $688,195 of the purchase price of the property from S, thereby reducing A's basis in the property by this amount. T is treated as having paid a dividend of $688,195 to P, and P is treated as having made a contribution to the capital of S in the same amount.

Example (2). The facts are the same as in example (1), except that T loans the $2,000,000 to S immediately before the sale. A purchases the property for cash of $1,000,000 and assumes S's debt to T. On the date of the sale, the Federal long-term rate is 12%, compounded semiannually. The loan from T to S is a tax-avoidance loan. The issue price of the debt instrument and the amount of foregone interest are the same as in example (1). A's basis in the property is limited to $2,311,805 (see § 1.1274-7(d)). T is treated as having paid a dividend of $688,195 to P, and P is treated as having made a contribution to the capital of S in the same amount.

(f) *Certain below-market loans with significant effect on tax liability ("significant-effect" loans).*—[Reserved].

(g) *Indirect loans.*—(1) *In general.*—If a below-market loan is made between two persons and, based on all the facts and circumstances, the effect of the loan is to make a gift or a capital contribution or a distribution of money (under section 301 or in the case of an S corporation, section 1368), or to pay compensation to a third person ("indirect participant"), or is otherwise attributable to the relationship of the lender or borrower to the indirect participant, the loan is restructured as two or more successive below-market loans ("deemed loans") for purposes of section 7872, as follows:

(i) A deemed below-market loan made by the named lender to the indirect participant; and

(ii) A deemed below-market loan made by the indirect participant to the borrower.

Section 7872 is applied separately to each deemed loan, and each deemed loan is treated as having the same provisions as the original loan between the lender and the borrower. Thus, for example, if a father makes an interest-free loan to his daughter's corporation, the loan is restructured as a below-market loan from father to daughter (deemed gift loan) and a second below-market loan from daughter to corporation (deemed corporation-shareholder loan). Similarly, if a corporation makes an interest-free loan to another commonly controlled corporation, the loan is restructured as a below-market loan from the lending corporation to the common parent corporation and a second below-market loan from the parent corporation to the borrowing corporation.

(2) *Special rule for intermediaries.*—If a lender and a borrower use another person, such as an individual, a trust, a partnership, or a corporation, as an intermediary or middleman in a loan transaction and a purpose for such use is to avoid the application of section 7872(c)(1)(A), (B), or (C), the intermediary will be ignored and the loan will be treated as made directly between the lender and the borrower. Thus, for example, if a father and a son arrange their below-market loan transaction by having the father make a below-market loan to the father's partnership, followed by a second below-market loan (with substantially identical

terms and conditions as the first loan) made by the partnership to the son, the two below-market loans will be restructured as one below-market loan from the father to the son. [Prop. Reg. § 1.7872-4.]

[Proposed 8-20-85 and 4-8-86.]

§ 1.7872-5T. Exempted loans (temporary).—(a) *In general.*—(1) *General rule.*—Except as provided in paragraph (a) (2) of this section, notwithstanding any other provision of section 7872 and the regulations thereunder, section 7872 does not apply to the loans listed in paragraph (b) of this section because the interest arrangements do not have a significant effect on the Federal tax liability of the borrower or the lender.

(2) *No exemption for tax avoidance loans.*—If a taxpayer structures a transaction to be a loan described in paragraph (b) of this section and one of the principal purposes of so structuring the transaction is the avoidance of Federal tax, then the transaction will be recharacterized as a tax avoidance loan as defined in section 7872(c) (1) (D).

(b) *List of exemptions.*—Except as provided in paragraph (a) of this section, the following transactions are exempt from section 7872:

(1) Loans which are made available by the lender to the general public on the same terms and conditions and which are consistent with the lender's customary business practice;

(2) Accounts or withdrawable shares with a bank (as defined in section 581), or an institution to which section 591 applies, or a credit union, made in the ordinary course of its business;

(3) Acquisitions of publicly traded debt obligations for an amount equal to the public trading price at the time of acquisition;

(4) Loans made by a life insurance company (as defined in section 816(a)), in the ordinary course of its business, to an insured, under a loan right contained in a life insurance policy and in which the cash surrender values are used as collateral for the loans;

(5) Loans subsidized by the Federal, State (including the District of Columbia), or Municipal government (or any agency or instrumentality thereof), and which are made available under a program of general application to the public;

(6) Employee-relocation loans that meet the requirements of paragraph (c) (1) of this section;

(7) Obligations the interest on which is excluded from gross income under section 103;

(8) Obligations of the United States government;

(9) Gift loans to a charitable organization (described in section 170(c)), but only if at no time during the taxable year will the aggregate outstanding amount of loans by the lender to that organization exceed $250,000. Charitable organizations which are effectively controlled, within the meaning of section 1.482-1(a) (1), by the same person or persons shall be considered one charitable organization for purposes of this limitation.

(10) Loans made to or from a foreign person that meet the requirements of paragraph (c) (2) of this section;

(11) Loans made by a private foundation or other organization described in section 170(c), the primary purpose of which is to accomplish one or more of the purposes described in section 170(c) (2) (B);

(12) Indebtedness subject to section 482, but such indebtedness is exempt from the application of section 7872 only during the interest-free period, if any, determined under § 1.482-2(a) (1) (iii) with respect to intercompany trade receivables described in § 1.482-2(a) (1) (ii) (A) (*ii*). See also § 1.482-2(a) (3);

(13) All money, securities, and property—

(i) Received by a futures commission merchant or registered broker/dealer or by a clearing organization (A) to margin, guarantee or secure contracts for future delivery on or subject to the rules of a qualified board or exchange (as defined in section 1256(g) (7)), or (B) to purchase, margin, guarantee or secure options contracts traded on or subject to the rules of a qualified board or exchange, so long as the amounts so received to purchase, margin, guarantee or secure such contracts for future delivery or such options contracts are reasonably necessary for such purposes and so long as any commissions received by the futures commission merchant, registered broker/dealer, or clearing organization are not reduced for those making deposits of money, and all money accruing to account holders as the result of such futures and options contracts or

(ii) Received by a clearing organization from a member thereof as a required deposit to a clearing fund, guaranty fund, or similar fund maintained by the clearing organization to protect it against defaults by members.

(14) Loans the interest arrangements of which the taxpayer is able to show have no significant effect of any Federal tax liability of the lender or the borrower, as described in paragraph (c) (3) of this section; and

(15) Loans, described in revenue rulings or revenue procedures issued under section 7872(g) (1) (C), if the Commissioner finds that the factors justifying an exemption for such

loans are sufficiently similar to the factors justifying the exemptions contained in this section.

(c) *Special rules.*—(1) *Employee-relocation loans.*—(i) *Mortgage loans.*—In the case of a compensation-related loan to an employee, where such loan is secured by a mortgage on the new principal residence (within the meaning of section 217 and the regulations thereunder) of the employee, acquired in connection with the transfer of that employee to a new principal place of work (which meets the requirements in section 217(c) and the regulations thereunder), the loan will be exempt from section 7872 if the following conditions are satisfied:

(A) The loan is a demand loan or is a term loan the benefits of the interest arrangements of which are not transferable by the employee and are conditioned on the future performance of substantial services by the employee;

(B) The employee certifies to the employer that the employee reasonably expects to be entitled to and will itemize deductions for each year the loan is outstanding; and

(C) The loan agreement requires that the loan proceeds be used only to purchase the new principal residence of the employee.

(ii) *Bridge loans.*—In the case of a compensation-related loan to an employee which is not described in paragraph (c)(1)(i) of this section, and which is used to purchase a new principal residence (within the meaning of section 217 and the regulations thereunder) of the employee acquired in connection with the transfer of that employee to a new principal place of work (which meets the requirements in section 217(c) and the regulations thereunder), the loan will be exempt from section 7872 if the following conditions are satisfied:

(A) The conditions contained in paragraphs (c)(1)(i)(A), (B), and (C) of this section;

(B) The loan agreement provides that the loan is payable in full within 15 days after the date of the sale of the employee's immediately former principal residence;

(C) The aggregate principal amount of all outstanding loans described in this paragraph (c)(1)(ii) to an employee is no greater than the employer's reasonable estimate of the amount of the equity of the employee and the employee's spouse in the employee's immediately former principal residence; and

(D) The employee's immediately former principal residence is not converted to business or investment use.

* * *

(3) *Loans without significant tax effect.*—Whether a loan will be considered to be a loan the interest arrangements of which have a significant effect on any Federal tax liability of the lender or the borrower will be determined according to all of the facts and circumstances. Among the factors to be considered are—

(i) whether items of income and deduction generated by the loan offset each other;

(ii) the amount of such items;

(iii) the cost to the taxpayer of complying with the provisions of section 7872 if such section were applied; and

(iv) any non-tax reasons for deciding to structure the transaction as a below-market loan rather than a loan with interest at a rate equal to or greater than the applicable Federal rate and a payment by the lender to the borrower. [Temp Reg. § 1.7872-5T.]

☐ [*T.D.* 8045, 8-15-85. *Amended by T.D.* 8093, 7-9-86 *and T.D.* 8204, 5-20-88.]

INDEX TO CODE

References are to Code Section numbers.

A

Index to Code

References are to Code Section numbers.

References are to Code Section numbers.

Index to Code

References are to Code Section numbers.

Index to Code

References are to Code Section numbers.

Index to Code

References are to Code Section numbers.

Index to Code

References are to Code Section numbers.

U